The Sporting News

BASEBALL GUIDE

1 9 9 7   E D I T I O N

Editors/Baseball Guide

CRAIG CARTER
DAVE SLOAN

PUBLISHING CO.

Efrem Zimbalist III, President and Chief Executive Officer, Times Mirror Magazines; **James H. Nuckols,** President, The Sporting News; **Francis X. Farrell,** Senior Vice President, Publisher; **John D. Rawlings,** Senior Vice President, Editorial Director; **John Kastberg,** Vice President, General Manager; **Kathy Kinkeade,** Vice President, Operations; **Mike Nahrstedt,** Managing Editor; **Joe Hoppel,** Senior Editor; **Craig Carter,** Statistical Editor; **Sean Stewart,** Assistant Editor; **Fred Barnes,** Director of Graphics; **Marilyn Kasal,** Production Director; **Chris Placzek,** Database Analyst; **Michael Behrens and Christen Webster,** Macintosh Production Artists.

A Times Mirror
Company

EXPLANATION OF STATISTICAL ABBREVIATIONS

A: assists. **AB:** at-bats. **Avg.:** batting average (hits divided by at-bats). **BB:** bases on balls. **Bk.:** balks. **CG:** complete games. **CS:** caught stealing. **E:** errors. **ER:** earned runs. **ERA:** earned-run average (earned runs times nine divided by innings pitched). **G:** games **GB:** games behind. **GF:** games finished. **GDP:** grounding into double plays. **GS:** games started. **H:** hits. **HB:** hit batsmen. **HP:** hit by pitches. **HR:** home runs. **IBB:** intentional bases on balls. **IP:** innings pitched. **L:** losses. **OBP:** on-base percentage (hits plus bases on balls plus hit by pitches divided by at-bats plus bases on balls plus hit by pitches plus sacrifice flies). **Pct.:** winning percentage. **PO** putouts. **Pos.:** position. **R:** runs. **RBI:** runs batted in. **SB:** stolen bases. **SF:** sacrifice flies (run-scoring flyouts). **SH:** sacrifice hits (bunts that advance one or more runners but result in the batter being retired at first base or reaching first on an error). **ShO:** shutouts. **Slg.:** slugging percentage (total bases divided by at-bats). **SO:** strikeouts. **Sv.:** saves. **TB:** total bases (hits plus doubles plus two times the number of triples plus three times the number of home runs). **TBF:** total batters faced. **TC:** total chances (putout plus assists plus errors). **TPA:** total plate appearances (at-bats plus bases on balls plus sacrifice hits plus sacrifice flies plus hit by pitches plus times reaching base on catcher's interference). **W:** wins. **WP:** wild pitches. **2B:** doubles. **3B:** triples.

World Series, A.L. Championship Series, N.L. Championship Series, A.L. Division Series, N.L. Division Series and Al Star Game highlights written by Mark Bonavita, Tom Dienhart, Joe Hoppel, Mike Huguenin, Anna Jones, Leslie Gibsc McCarthy, Mark Shimabukuro and Dave Sloan of THE SPORTING NEWS.

Major league statistics compiled by STATS, Inc., Lincolnwood, Ill.

Minor league statistics compiled by Howe Sportsdata International Inc., Boston.

ISBN: 0-89204-569-8

10 9 8 7 6 5 4 3 2 1

CONTENTS

ON THE COVER: Atlanta's John Smoltz led the major leagues with 24 victories and 276 strikeouts and won the National League Cy Young Award in 1996. (Photo by Robert Seale/The Sporting News)

Spine photo of Mike Piazza by Albert Dickson/The Sporting News.

1997 SEASON

Major League Baseball directories

Team by team

MAJOR LEAGUE BASEBALL

Address
350 Park Avenue
New York, NY 10022
Telephone
212-339-7800
FAX
212-355-0007
Executive director, market development
Kathleen Francis
Director, special events
Carolyn Taylor

Exec. dir., security/facility management
Kevin Hallinan
Executive director, public relations
Richard Levin
Executive director, baseball operations
William Murray
General counsel
Thomas J. Ostertag
Exec. director, minor league relations
Jimmie Lee Solomon

Chief financial officer
Jeffrey White
President, MLB Enterprises
Gregory Murphy
V.p., broadcasting and new media dev.
Leslie Sullivan
COO, MLB International
Timothy Brosnan

AMERICAN LEAGUE

Address
350 Park Avenue
New York, NY 10022
Telephone
212-339-7600
President
Gene A. Budig
Vice president
Gene Autry
Executive director of umpiring
Martin J. Springstead
Coordinator of umpire operations
Artesia Basta-Marino
V.p., administration and media affairs
Phyllis Merhige
Director of finance
Derek Irwin
Director, waivers and player records
Kimberly J. Ng

Media relations aide
James Kim
Administrator of umpires/travel
Tess Basta-Marino
Administrative assistant
Carolyn Coen
Umpires
Larry Barnett
Joseph Brinkman
Gary Cederstrom
Alan Clark
Drew Coble
Derryl Cousins
Terry Craft
Donald Denkinger
James Evans
Dale Ford
Richard Garcia
Ted Hendry
John Hirschbeck
Mark Johnson

Jim Joyce
Kenneth Kaiser
Greg Kosc
Tim McClelland
Larry McCoy
James McKean
Chuck Meriwether
Durwood Merrill
Dan Morrison
David Phillips
Rick Reed
Michael Reilly
John (Rocky) Roe
Dale Scott
John Shulock
Tim Tschida
Tim Welke
Larry Young

NATIONAL LEAGUE

Address
350 Park Avenue
New York, NY 10022
Telephone
212-339-7700
President and treasurer
Leonard S. Coleman Jr.
Senior vice president and secretary
Katy Feeney
Executive director, public relations
Ricky Clemons
Director of umpire supervision
Ed Vargo
Assistant secretary and executive director, player records
Nancy Crofts
Executive secretary
Rita Aughavin

Administrative assistant, umpires
Cathy Davis
Public relations assistant
Glenn Wilburn
Umpires
Wally Bell
Greg Bonin
Jerry Crawford
Gary Darling
Bob Davidson
Gerry Davis
Dana DeMuth
Bruce Froemming
Brian Gorman
Eric Gregg
Tom Hallion
Angel Hernandez
Mark Hirschbeck
Bill Hohn
Jeff Kellogg

Jerry Layne
Randy Marsh
Ed Montague
Larry Poncino
Frank Pulli
Jim Quick
Ed Rapuano Jr.
Charlie Reliford
Rich Rieker
Steve Rippley
Paul Runge
Terry Tata
Larry Vanover
Harry Wendelstedt
Joe West
Charlie Williams
Mike Winters

OTHER ORGANIZATIONS

PLAYER RELATIONS COMMITTEE

Address
350 Park Avenue
New York, NY 10022
Telephone
212-339-7400
212-371-2242 (FAX)

Chief labor negotiator and general counsel
Randy L. Levine
Associate counsels
Louis Melendez
John Westhoff

Contract administrator
John Ricco
Director, public relations
Richard Levin

NATIONAL BASEBALL HALL OF FAME AND MUSEUM

Address
P.O. Box 590
Cooperstown, NY 13326
Telephone
607-547-7200
607-547-2044 (FAX)
Chairman of Hall of Fame
Edward W. Stack
President
Donald C. Marr Jr.
Vice president
Frank Simio
Curator
William T. Spencer Jr.
Registrar
Peter P. Clark
Director of merchandising
Barbara Shinn
Controller
Frances L. Althiser
Librarian
James L. Gates
Dir. of public relations and promotions
Jeff Idelson

NATIONAL ASSOCIATION OF PROFESSIONAL BASEBALL LEAGUES

Address
P.O. Box A
St. Petersburg, FL 33731
Telephone
813-822-6937
813-821-5819 (FAX)
President
Mike Moore
Vice president/administration
Pat O'Conner
Chief operating officer
Rob Dlugozima
General counsel
Ben Hayes
Director/licensing
Misann Ellmaker
Director/media relations
Jim Ferguson
Director of operations
Tim Brunswick
Director of business/finance
Eric Krupa
Director of professional baseball employment opportunities
Ann Perkins

HOWE SPORTSDATA INTERNATIONAL INC.

Address
Boston Fish Pier
West Building No. 2, Suite 306
Boston, MA 02210
Telephone
617-951-0070
617-951-1379 (stats request)
617-737-9960 (FAX)
President
Jay Virshbo
Historical consultant
William Weiss

MAJOR LEAGUE BASEBALL MAJOR LEAGUE SCOUTING BUREAU

Address
23712 Birtcher Dr., Suite A
Lake Forest, CA 92630
Telephone
714-458-7600
714-458-9454 (FAX)
Director
Donald F. Pries

BASEBALL WRITERS' ASSOCIATION OF AMERICA

President
Hal McCoy, Dayton Daily News
Vice president
Jim Street, Seattle Post-Intelligencer
Secretary/treasurer
Jack O'Connell, Hartford Courant

MAJOR LEAGUE BASEBALL PLAYERS ASSOCIATION

Address
12 E. 49th St., 24th Floor
New York, NY 10017
Telephone
212-826-0808
212-752-3649 (FAX)
Executive director and general counsel
Donald M. Fehr
Special assistants
Tony Bernazard
Mark Belanger
Associate general counsel
Eugene D. Orza
Assistant general counsel
Doyle R. Pryor
Lauren Rich
Michael Weiner
Counsel
Arthur Schack
Robert Leneghan
Director of licensing
Judy Heeter
Director of couumications
Richard A. Weiss

MAJOR LEAGUE BASEBALL PLAYERS ALUMNI ASSOC.

Address
3637 4th St., North, Suite 480
St. Petersburg, FL 33704
Telephone
813-822-3399
813-822-6300 (FAX)
President
Brooks Robinson
Vice presidents
Bobby Bonds
Bob Boone
George Brett
Mike Hegan
Chuck Hinton
Al Kaline
Carl Erskine
Rusty Staub
Robin Yount
Secretary/treasurer
Fred Valentine

ELIAS SPORTS BUREAU

Address
500 Fifth Ave.
New York, NY 10110
Telephone
212-869-1530
212-354-0980 (FAX)
General manager
Seymour Siwoff

UMPIRE DEVELOPMENT

Address
P.O. Box A
St. Petersburg, FL 33731
Telephone
813-823-1286
813-823-7212 (FAX)
Executive director
Edwin W. Lawrence
Director of field supervision
Mike Fitzpatrick

MAJOR LEAGUE UMPIRES ASSOCIATION

Address
1735 Market St., Suite 3420
Philadelphia, PA 19103
Telephone
215-979-3220
215-979-3201 (FAX)
General counsel
Richard G. Phillips

BASEBALL ASSISTANCE TEAM INC.

Address
350 Park Avenue
New York, NY 10022
Telephone
212-339-7884
Chairman
Ralph Branca
President
Joe Garagiola
Vice presidents
Joe Black
Earl Wilson
Executive director
Frank Slocum
Secretary/treasurer
Tom Ostertag

ASSOCIATION OF PROFESSIONAL BASEBALL PLAYERS OF AMERICA

Address
12062 Valley View, Suite 211
Garden Grove, CA 92645
Telephone
714-892-9900
714-897-0233 (FAX)
President
John J. McHale
Secretary/treasurer
Chuck Stevens

ANAHEIM ANGELS
AMERICAN LEAGUE WEST DIVISION

1997 ANGELS SCHEDULE

Home games shaded.
* — All-Star Game at Jacobs Field (Cleveland)
D — Day game (any game starting before 5 p.m.)

APRIL

SUN	MON	TUE	WED	THU	FRI	SAT
		1	2 BOS	3 BOS	4 CLE	5 CLE
6 CLE	7 CLE	8 NYY	9 NYY	10	11 D CLE	12 D CLE
13 D CLE	14 NYY	15 NYY	16 MIN	17 D MIN	18 MIN	19 D KC
20 D KC	21 KC	22 TBR	23 TOR	24	25 DET	26 DET
27 D DET	28	29 BOS	30 BOS			

MAY

SUN	MON	TUE	WED	THU	FRI	SAT
				1 BOS	2 CWS	3 CWS
4 D CWS	5 BAL	6 BAL	7 BAL	8	9 MIL	10 D MIL
11 D MIL	12 CWS	13 CWS	14 BAL	15 BAL	16 MIL	17 MIL
18 D MIL	19 SEA	20 SEA	21 SEA	22	23 TOR	24 D TOR
25 D TOR	26 DET	27 DET	28 OAK	29 OAK	30 D MIN	31 MIN

JUNE

SUN	MON	TUE	WED	THU	FRI	SAT
1 D MIN	2 KC	3 KC	4	5 MIN	6 MIN	7 MIN
8 D MIN	9 KC	10 KC	11 D KC	12 MIN	13 SF	14 SF
15 D SF	16	17 LA	18 LA	19 OAK	20 OAK	21 OAK
22 D OAK	23 TEX	24 TEX	25 D SEA	26 SEA	27 SEA	28 SEA
29 SEA	30 COL					

JULY

SUN	MON	TUE	WED	THU	FRI	SAT
		1 D COL	2 COL	3 LA	4 SEA	5 SEA
6 SEA	7	8	*9	10 OAK	11 D OAK	12 D OAK
13 D OAK	14 TEX	15 TEX	16 DET	17 DET	18 TOR	19 TOR
20 D TOR	21	22 NYY	23 NYY	24 D NYY	25 BOS	26 BOS
27 D BOS	28 CLE	29 CLE	30 CLE	31 CWS		

AUGUST

SUN	MON	TUE	WED	THU	FRI	SAT
					1 CWS	2 CWS
3 CWS	4 MIL	5 MIL	6 D MIL	7	8 BAL	9 BAL
10 D BAL	11	12 CWS	13 CWS	14 D MIL	15 MIL	16 BAL
17 BAL	18 BAL	19 NYY	20 NYY	21 NYY	22 BOS	23 BOS
24 D BOS	25	26 CLE	27 CLE	28 D SD	29 SD	30 SF
31 D SF						

SEPTEMBER

SUN	MON	TUE	WED	THU	FRI	SAT
	1 COL	2 COL	3	4 DET	5 DET	6 D DET
7 D DET	8 TOR	9 TOR	10	11 KC	12 KC	13 D KC
14 KC	15 MIN	16 MIN	17 OAK	18 D OAK	19 TEX	20 TEX
21 TEX	22	23 SEA	24 SEA	25 TEX	26 TEX	27 TEX
28 B TEX						

1997 SEASON

CLUB DIRECTORY

Owner
Gene Autry
Chairman and CEO, The Walt Disney Co.
Michael Eisner
President
Tony Tavares
Vice president and general manager
Bill Bavasi
Vice president of finance and admin.
Andy Roundtree
Vice president of business affairs
Kevin Gilmore
Director of communications
Bill Robertson
Director of finance
Marty Greenspan
Director of marketing
Bill Holford
Director of entertainment
Charlie Messerly
Director of stadium operations
Kevin Uhlich
Dir. of advertising and broadcast sales
Bob Wagner
Assistant general manager
Tim Mead
Special assistants to general manager
Preston Gomez
Bob Harrison
Secretary to general manager
Cathy Carey
Director of player development
Ken Forsch
Manager, baseball operations
Jeff Parker
Equipment manager
Kevin Higdon
Video coordinator
Diego Lopez

Manager, media services
Larry Babcock
Media relations coordinator
Marc Simon
Secretary, media relations
Carolyn LaPierre
Club photographers
V.J. Lovero
John Cordes
Manager, publications
Doug Ward
Manager, civic affairs
Tory Whittingham
Medical director
Dr. Lewis Yocum
Trainers
Ned Bergert
Rick Smith
Director of international operations
Ta Honda
Scouts
John Burden, Tom Burns, Pete Coachman, Marco Davalillo, Pompey Davalillo, Tom Davis, Red Gaskill, Steve Gruwell, Ta Honda, Rick Ingalls, Hal Keller, Tim Kelly, Kris Kline, Tom Kotchman, Tony LaCava, Ron Marigny, Jim McLaughlin, Darrell Miller, Jon Neiderer, Tom Osowski, Eusebio Perez, Paul Robinson, Rick Schlenker, Jerry Streeter, Rip Tutor, Jack Uhey, Dick Wilson
Major league scouts
Dave Garcia, Jay Hankins, Bob Harrison, Nick Kamzic, Matt Keough, Joe McDonald, Tom Romenesko, Moose Stubing, Dale Sutherland

MINOR LEAGUE AFFILIATES

Class	Team	League	Manager
AAA	Vancouver	Pacific Coast	Don Long
AA	Midland	Texas	Mario Mendoza
A	Lake Elsinore	California	To be announced
A	Cedar Rapids	Midwest	To be announced
A	Boise	Northwest	To be announced
Rookie	Butte	Pioneer	To be announced

BROADCAST INFORMATION

Radio: KMPC-AM (710).
TV: KCAL-TV (Channel 9).
Cable TV: Fox Sports West.

SPRING TRAINING

Ballpark (city): Diablo Stadium (Tempe, Ariz.).
Ticket information: 602-678-4444 (Ticketmaster); 714-634-2000 (Anaheim Stadium).

SPRING TRAINING ROSTER

Manager—Terry Collins (1).
Coaches—Larry Bowa (2), Rod Carew (29), Joe Coleman (47), Marcel Lachemann (53), Joe Maddon (70), Dave Parker (39).

No.	PITCHERS	B/T	Ht./Wt.	Born	1996 clubs
52	Abbott, Jim	L/L	6-3/210	9-19-67	California, Vancouver
19	Dickson, Jason	L/R	6-0/190	3-30-73	Midland, Vancouver, California
	Edsell, Geoff	R/R	6-3/190	12-12-71	Midland, Vancouver
55	Ellis, Robert	R/R	6-5/220	12-15-70	Nashville, Birmingham, Vancouver, California
31	Finley, Chuck	L/L	6-6/214	11-26-62	California
	Freehill, Mike	R/R	6-3/185	6-1-71	Midland, Vancouver
36	Gohr, Greg	R/R	6-3/205	10-29-67	Detroit, Toledo, California
	Gubicza, Mark	R/R	6-5/230	8-14-62	Kansas City
48	Harris, Pep	R/R	6-2/185	9-23-72	Midland, Vancouver, California
65	Holtz, Mike	L/L	5-9/175	10-10-72	Midland, California
46	James, Mike	R/R	6-4/216	8-15-67	California
37	Janicki, Pete	R/R	6-4/190	1-26-71	Vancouver, Midland
12	Langston, Mark	R/L	6-2/184	8-20-60	California, Lake Elsinore
64	Macey, Fausto	R/R	6-4/185	9-10-75	Shreveport
21	May, Darrell	L/L	6-2/170	6-13-72	Calgary, Pittsburgh, California
17	McElroy, Chuck	L/L	6-0/195	10-1-67	Indianapolis, Cincinnati, California
40	Percival, Troy	R/R	6-3/200	8-9-69	California
	Perisho, Matt	L/L	6-0/175	6-8-75	Lake Elsinore, Midland
37	Schmidt, Jeff	R/R	6-5/190	2-21-71	Vancouver, California
35	Springer, Dennis	R/R	5-10/190	2-12-65	California, Vancouver
	Van Poppel, Todd	R/R	6-2/210	12-9-71	Oakland, Detroit
34	Watson, Allen	L/L	6-3/190	11-18-70	San Francisco, San Jose
59	Williams, Shad	R/R	6-0/185	3-10-71	Vancouver, California

No.	CATCHERS	B/T	Ht./Wt.	Born	1996 clubs
14	Fabregas, Jorge	L/R	6-3/205	3-13-70	California, Vancouver
8	Greene, Todd	R/R	5-9/195	5-8-71	Vancouver, California
63	Hemphill, Bret	B/R	6-3/200	12-17-71	Lake Elsinore
13	Leyritz, Jim	R/R	6-0/195	12-27-63	New York A.L.
20	Turner, Chris	R/R	6-1/190	3-23-69	Vancouver, California

No.	INFIELDERS	B/T	Ht./Wt.	Born	1996 clubs
7	Arias, George	R/R	5-11/190	3-12-72	California, Vancouver
9	DiSarcina, Gary	R/R	6-1/178	11-19-67	California
11	Eenhorn, Robert	R/R	6-3/185	2-9-68	Columbus, New York A.L., California
	Grebeck, Craig	R/R	5-7/148	12-29-64	Florida
10	Hollins, Dave	B/R	6-1/210	5-25-66	Minnesota, Seattle
33	Murray, Eddie	B/R	6-2/220	2-24-56	Cleveland, Baltimore
28	Pritchett, Chris	L/R	6-4/185	1-31-70	Vancouver, California
18	Velarde, Randy	R/R	6-0/192	11-24-62	California

No.	OUTFIELDERS	B/T	Ht./Wt.	Born	1996 clubs
16	Anderson, Garret	L/L	6-3/190	6-30-72	California
25	Edmonds, Jim	L/L	6-1/190	6-27-70	California, Lake Elsinore
27	Erstad, Darin	L/L	6-2/210	6-4-74	Vancouver, California
3	Palmeiro, Orlando	L/R	5-11/155	1-19-69	Vancouver, California
15	Salmon, Tim	R/R	6-3/220	8-24-68	California

BALLPARK INFORMATION

Ballpark (capacity, surface)
Anaheim Stadium (To be announced, grass)

Address
2000 Gene Autry Way
Anaheim, CA 92806

Business phones
714-937-7200
213-625-1123

Ticket information
714-634-2000

Ticket prices
$14.50 (field & club level, MVP)
$12 (field & club level, box)
$11 (terrace level, MVP)
$9 (terrace level, box)
$8 (view level, lower box)
$7 (view level, upper box)
$5 (pavillion, reserved)

Field dimensions (from home plate)
To left field at foul line, 333 feet
To center field, 404 feet
To right field at foul line, 333 feet

First game played
April 19, 1966 (White Sox 3, Angels 1)

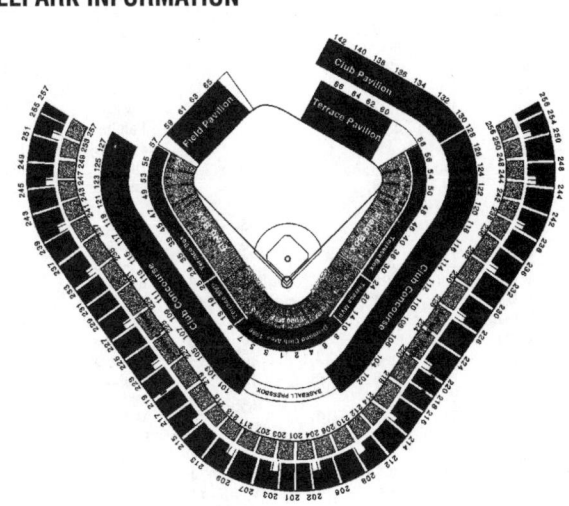

DAY BY DAY

Date	Opp.	Res.	Score	(inn.*)	Hits	Opp. hits	Winning pitcher	Losing pitcher	Save	Record	Pos.	GB
4-2	Mil.	L	9-15		15	22	Wickander	Finley		0-1	T3rd	1 1/2
4-3	Mil.	W	3-2	(11)	8	7	James	Lloyd		1-1	3rd	1
4-5	Chi.	W	7-6	(11)	14	12	James	McCaskill		2-1	2nd	1
4-6	Chi.	L	4-8		7	13	Fernandez	J. Abbott		2-2	3rd	2
4-7	Chi.	W	6-5		10	9	Finley	Alvarez	Percival	3-2	3rd	2 1/2
4-9	At Tor.	L	0-5		5	11	Hentgen	Langston		3-3	3rd	3 1/2
4-10	At Tor.	W	2-1		6	6	Holzemer	Guzman	Percival	4-3	2nd	3
4-11	At Tor.	L	4-7		9	12	Hanson	J. Abbott	Timlin	4-4	3rd	3
4-12	At Det.	W	5-4		6	9	Finley	Lira	Percival	5-4	3rd	2
4-13	At Det.	L	5-9		11	13	Keagle	Sanderson		5-5	3rd	3
4-14	At Det.	L	4-5		7	7	R. Lewis	James		5-6	T3rd	3
4-15	At Sea.	L	10-11		17	11	Charlton	Eichhorn		5-7	4th	3 1/2
4-16	At Sea.	L	3-5		7	7	Johnson	J. Abbott		5-8	4th	4 1/2
4-17	Tor.	W	5-1		9	3	Finley	Quantrill		6-8	T3rd	4 1/2
4-18	Tor.	W	9-6		13	9	James	Ware	Percival	7-8	3rd	4 1/2
4-19	Det.	W	4-3		7	7	Langston	Myers		8-8	3rd	3 1/2
4-20	Det.	W	2-1		7	7	Grimsley	Keagle		9-8	3rd	3 1/2
4-21	Det.	W	6-5		8	7	Eichhorn	R. Lewis	Percival	10-8	3rd	3 1/2
4-22	Det.	W	6-5		12	10	James	Christopher	Percival	11-8	3rd	2 1/2
4-24	At Mil.	W	4-3		9	11	Boskie	McDonald	Percival	12-8	3rd	1
4-25	At Mil.	L	5-6		9	11	Fetters	James		12-9	3rd	1
4-27	At Chi.	L	1-2		5	5	Fernandez	J. Abbott	Hernandez	12-10	3rd	2 1/2
4-28	At Chi.	L	1-10		9	11	Baldwin	Finley		12-11	4th	3 1/2
4-29	At Chi.	L	3-4		11	8	Alvarez	Grimsley	Hernandez	12-12	4th	3 1/2
4-30	At Oak.	W	7-3		11	11	Langston	Prieto		13-12	T3rd	2 1/2
5-1	At Oak.	W	6-4		12	7	Boskie	Van Poppel	Percival	14-12	3rd	2 1/2
5-2	At Oak.	W	3-1		7	6	J. Abbott	Johns	Percival	15-12	3rd	1 1/2
5-3	Min.	W	4-1		8	6	Finley	Robertson	Percival	16-12	2nd	1 1/2
5-4	Min.	W	5-2		7	3	Grimsley	Rodriguez		17-12	2nd	1 1/2
5-5	Min.	W	5-1		12	6	Boskie	Hawkins		18-12	2nd	1 1/2
5-6	K.C.	L	4-9		12	16	Belcher	Leftwich	Pichardo	18-13	2nd	2
5-7	K.C.	L	3-5		8	8	Valera	J. Abbott	Montgomery	18-14	2nd	3
5-8	K.C.	L	1-3	(14)	10	10	Pichardo	Eichhorn		18-15	2nd	4
5-9	K.C.	L	2-8		7	9	Gubicza	Grimsley		18-16	T2nd	4
5-10	Cle.	W	13-8		12	11	Boskie	Lopez		19-16	2nd	4
5-11	Cle.	L	5-6		7	14	McDowell	Sanderson	Mesa	19-17	T2nd	5
5-12	Cle.	L	1-4		6	9	Poole	Percival	Mesa	19-18	4th	5
5-14	At Bos.	L	3-4	(12)	11	9	Belinda	Boskie		19-19	T3rd	6 1/2
5-15	At Bos.	L	6-17		9	17	Moyer	Grimsley		19-20	4th	6 1/2
5-17	At N.Y.	L	5-8		9	10	Pettitte	J. Abbott	M. Rivera	19-21	4th	6 1/2
5-18	At N.Y.	L	3-7		11	6	Rogers	Williams	M. Rivera	19-22	4th	7 1/2
5-19	At N.Y.	W	10-1		15	6	Finley	Kamieniecki		20-22	4th	6 1/2
5-20	At Bal.	L	1-13		5	17	Wells	Grimsley		20-23	4th	7
5-21	At Bal.	W	5-2		7	8	Boskie	Krivda	Percival	21-23	3rd	6
5-22	At Bal.	L	5-10		8	14	Haynes	J. Abbott	McDowell	21-24	4th	7
5-24	Bos.	W	3-1		7	4	Finley	Sele	Percival	22-24	3rd	5 1/2
5-25	Bos.	L	3-10		10	12	Gordon	Williams		22-25	T3rd	6 1/2
5-26	Bos.	W	12-2		14	7	Boskie	Eshelman		23-25	3rd	6 1/2
5-27	N.Y.	L	5-16		9	15	Pettitte	J. Abbott		23-26	3rd	7 1/2
5-28	N.Y.	W	1-0		2	5	Grimsley	Rogers		24-26	3rd	7 1/2
5-29	N.Y.	W	4-0		8	8	Finley	Mendoza		25-26	3rd	7 1/2
5-31	Bal.	W	10-3		12	9	Langston	Wells		26-26	3rd	7 1/2
6-1	Bal.	W	8-3		13	7	Boskie	Haynes		27-26	3rd	6 1/2
6-2	Bal.	L	1-14		6	17	Erickson	J. Abbott		27-27	3rd	6 1/2
6-3	At Min.	L	3-9		8	15	Trombley	Finley		27-28	3rd	7 1/2
6-4	At Min.	L	3-5		8	8	Rodriguez	Grimsley	Guardado	27-29	3rd	7 1/2
6-5	At Min.	L	3-14		9	17	Aldred	Langston	Hansell	27-30	3rd	7 1/2
6-7	At Cle.	L	3-4		4	6	McDowell	Boskie	Mesa	27-31	T3rd	6
6-8	At Cle.	L	0-5		6	10	Hershiser	Finley		27-32	4th	9 1/2
6-9	At Cle.	W	8-6	(13)	15	13	Hancock	Tavarez		28-32	3rd	9 1/2
6-10	At K.C.	W	7-5	(10)	15	10	McElroy	Pugh	Percival	29-32	3rd	9 1/2
6-11	At K.C.	W	11-9		18	8	McElroy	Valera	Percival	30-32	3rd	8 1/2
6-12	At K.C.	W	4-3	(10)	7	10	McElroy	Montgomery	Percival	31-32	3rd	8 1/2
6-13	Tor.	W	6-4		11	9	Finley	Guzman	James	32-32	3rd	7 1/2
6-14	Tor.	W	7-4		10	8	Grimsley	Hanson	Percival	33-32	3rd	6 1/2
6-15	Tor.	W	7-5		11	4	Langston	Crabtree	Percival	34-32	3rd	6 1/2
6-16	Tor.	L	4-6		10	11	Quantrill	J. Abbott	Timlin	34-33	3rd	6 1/2
6-17	Chi.	W	9-8	(13)	18	13	Hancock	McCaskill		35-33	3rd	6
6-18	Chi.	W	5-4		14	9	Finley	Simas	Percival	36-33	3rd	6
6-19	Chi.	W	14-2		12	6	McElroy	Alvarez		37-33	T2nd	6
6-20	At Mil.	W	10-3		15	6	Langston	Givens		38-33	T2nd	5
6-21	At Mil.	L	5-10		11	11	McDonald	J. Abbott		38-34	3rd	6

Date	Opp.	Res.	Score	(inn.*)	Hits	Opp. hits	Winning pitcher	Losing pitcher	Save	Record	Pos.	GB
6-22	At Mil.	W	6-4		7	11	Boskie	Miranda	Percival	39-34	3rd	6
6-23	At Mil.	L	4-8		12	12	Garcia	Finley		39-35	3rd	6
6-24†	At Chi.	L	2-4		10	6	Alvarez	James	Hernandez	39-36		
6-24‡	At Chi.	W	6-4		9	8	Hancock	Sirotka	Percival	40-36	3rd	5 1/2
6-25	At Chi.	L	2-3		5	9	Tapani	Langston	Hernandez	40-37	3rd	6 1/2
6-27	Oak.	L	2-18		8	17	Johns	Boskie		40-38	3rd	7 1/2
6-28	Oak.	L	3-6		5	8	Chouinard	Finley		40-39	3rd	7 1/2
6-29	Oak.	L	9-11		16	13	Groom	Monteleone		40-40	3rd	8 1/2
6-30	Oak.	W	1-0		4	5	Hancock	Wasdin	Percival	41-40	3rd	7 1/2
7-1	Tex.	L	6-8		13	12	Gross	Langston	Henneman	41-41	3rd	8 1/2
7-2	Tex.	W	6-5		11	7	James	Henneman		42-41	3rd	7 1/2
7-3	Tex.	L	1-8		12	15	Pavlik	Finley		42-42	3rd	8 1/2
7-4	At Oak.	L	7-8	(11)	14	13	Taylor	Monteleone		42-43	3rd	8 1/2
7-5	At Oak.	L	8-16		13	13	Wasdin	Hancock		42-44	T3rd	8 1/2
7-6	At Oak.	L	5-6	(10)	12	7	Taylor	James		42-45	4th	8 1/2
7-7	At Oak.	W	9-4		16	11	Boskie	Johns		43-45	T3rd	8 1/2
7-11	At Sea.	L	4-5	(12)	16	9	Carmona	Monteleone		43-46	4th	8 1/2
7-12	At Sea.	L	6-7	(10)	11	9	Ayala	McElroy		43-47	4th	9 1/2
7-13	At Sea.	W	6-4		14	9	Boskie	Ayala	Percival	44-47	T3rd	9 1/2
7-14	At Sea.	L	0-8		4	13	Wells	Grimsley		44-48	4th	9 1/2
7-15	At Tex.	W	10-7		11	11	Schmidt	Brandenburg	Percival	45-48	T3rd	8 1/2
7-16	At Tex.	L	2-6		5	7	Oliver	J. Abbott	Russell	45-49	4th	9 1/2
7-17	At Tex.	L	3-7		11	8	Hill	Finley		45-50	4th	10 1/2
7-18	Sea.	L	3-15		11	21	Meacham	Boskie		45-51	4th	10 1/2
7-19	Sea.	W	9-4		18	8	Grimsley	Wells		46-51	4th	9 1/2
7-20	Sea.	W	5-4		12	6	Schmidt	Charlton	Percival	47-51	4th	9 1/2
7-21	Sea.	L	2-6		11	12	Hitchcock	J. Abbott		47-52	4th	9 1/2
7-22	Det.	W	1-0		4	6	Finley	Olivares	Percival	48-52	4th	9 1/2
7-23	Det.	L	3-8		10	11	Lima	James		48-53	4th	9 1/2
7-25	Mil.	W	5-4		10	5	Holtz	Lloyd		49-53	4th	9
7-26	Mil.	W	6-5		8	6	Springer	D'Amico	Percival	50-53	4th	8
7-27	Mil.	W	7-0		9	6	Finley	McDonald		51-53	4th	8
7-28	Mil.	L	3-4	(13)	13	12	Miranda	Holtz	Garcia	51-54	4th	8
7-30	At Det.	L	9-12		9	9	Nitkowski	Grimsley		51-55	4th	9
7-31	At Det.	L	5-10		9	12	Lima	Holtz		51-56	4th	10
8-1	At Det.	L	5-13		10	16	B. Williams	Boskie		51-57	4th	10
8-2	At Tor.	L	2-9		10	12	Hentgen	Finley		51-58	4th	10
8-3	At Tor.	W	11-6		18	9	Langston	Castillo		52-58	4th	9
8-4	At Tor.	L	1-7		9	9	Flener	J. Abbott		52-59	4th	10
8-6	Min.	L	1-4		5	8	Radke	Springer	Guardado	52-60	4th	10 1/2
8-7	Min.	L	0-4		4	12	Robertson	Finley		52-61	4th	10 1/2
8-8	Min.	L	5-13		6	17	Aguilera	Boskie		52-62	4th	10 1/2
8-9	K.C.	L	3-5		9	7	Rosado	Langston	Montgomery	52-63	4th	11 1/2
8-10	K.C.	L	3-18		8	15	Haney	J. Abbott		52-64	4th	12 1/2
8-11	K.C.	W	6-5		14	6	Springer	Belcher		53-64	4th	12 1/2
8-12	Cle.	L	4-5		6	9	Hershiser	Finley	Mesa	53-65	4th	13 1/2
8-13	Cle.	W	4-2		11	11	Boskie	Ogea	Percival	54-65	4th	13 1/2
8-14	Cle.	W	8-7		13	12	Gohr	McDowell	Percival	55-65	4th	13 1/2
8-16	At Bos.	W	6-3		10	4	Springer	Wakefield	Percival	56-65	4th	13 1/2
8-17	At Bos.	L	0-6		7	7	Clemens	Finley		56-66	4th	13 1/2
8-18	At Bos.	W	4-3		12	9	Holtz	Brandenburg	Percival	57-66	4th	13 1/2
8-19	At Bos.	L	9-10		15	16	Lacy	Gohr	Slocumb	57-67	4th	14 1/2
8-20	At N.Y.	L	6-17		8	16	Boehringer	Springer		57-68	4th	14 1/2
8-21	At N.Y.	W	7-1		9	13	Dickson	Key	Percival	58-68	4th	14 1/2
8-22	At N.Y.	W	12-3		14	6	Finley	Rogers		59-68	4th	14 1/2
8-23	At Bal.	W	2-0		5	5	Boskie	Wells	Percival	60-68	4th	13 1/2
8-24	At Bal.	L	4-5		11	11	Mussina	K. Abbott	R. Myers	60-69	4th	13 1/2
8-25	At Bal.	W	13-0		18	5	Springer	Erickson		61-69	4th	13 1/2
8-26	Bos.	L	1-4		6	9	Wakefield	Dickson		61-70	4th	14
8-27	Bos.	L	1-2		5	9	Clemens	Finley	Slocumb	61-71	4th	14
8-28	Bos.	L	4-7		5	9	Gordon	Boskie		61-72	4th	14
8-29	N.Y.	W	14-3		15	6	Holtz	Whitehurst		62-72	4th	13 1/2
8-30	N.Y.	L	2-6		8	7	Pettitte	Springer		62-73	4th	14 1/2
8-31	N.Y.	L	3-14		7	16	Key	Dickson		62-74	4th	15 1/2
9-1	N.Y.	W	4-0		6	4	Finley	Rogers		63-74	4th	14 1/2
9-2	Bal.	L	8-12		10	13	Mussina	Boskie		63-75	4th	14 1/2
9-3	Bal.	W	10-2		17	7	Harris	Coppinger		64-75	4th	14 1/2
9-4	Bal.	L	2-4		6	9	Erickson	Springer	R. Myers	64-76	4th	14 1/2
9-6	At Min.	L	2-6		5	13	Radke	Finley		64-77	4th	15 1/2
9-7	At Min.	L	3-6		6	11	Stevens	Boskie	Trombley	64-78	4th	16 1/2
9-8	At Min.	W	4-2		8	10	J. Abbott	Rodriguez	Percival	65-78	4th	16 1/2
9-9	At Cle.	L	3-4		11	7	Shuey	Holtz	Mesa	65-79	4th	17 1/2
9-10	At Cle.	L	5-7		10	11	Assenmacher	Percival		65-80	4th	18 1/2
9-11	At Cle.	L	0-2		6	5	McDowell	Finley	Mesa	65-81	4th	18 1/2
9-12	At Cle.	L	2-11		9	9	Anderson	Boskie		65-82	4th	18 1/2

Date	Opp.	Res.	Score	(inn.*)	Hits	Opp. hits	Winning pitcher	Losing pitcher	Save	Record	Pos.	GB
9-13	At K.C.	L	2-8		10	11	Belcher	J. Abbott		65-83	4th	18 1/
9-14	At K.C.	L	5-8		11	10	Appier	Dickson		65-84	4th	18 1/
9-17	Oak.	L	1-5		8	5	Prieto	Springer		65-85	4th	18 1/
9-18	Oak.	W	3-1		8	6	Finley	Adams	Percival	66-85	4th	17 1/
9-20	Tex.	W	6-5	(10)	12	8	McElroy	Stanton		67-85	4th	16
9-21	Tex.	L	1-7		7	10	Burkett	J. Abbott		67-86	4th	17
9-22	Tex.	L	1-4		8	12	Hill	Dickson		67-87	4th	18
9-23	Sea.	W	4-3		9	5	Finley	Hitchcock	Percival	68-87	4th	17
9-24	Sea.	W	11-6		16	14	Springer	Wells		69-87	4th	17
9-25	Sea.	L	2-11		10	10	Torres	Boskie		69-88	4th	17 1/
9-26	At Tex.	L	5-6		8	8	Burkett	J. Abbott	Henneman	69-89	4th	18 1/
9-27	At Tex.	W	4-3	(15)	14	9	Harris	Whiteside	Gohr	70-89	4th	17 1/
9-28	At Tex.	L	3-4		10	7	Oliver	Finley	Heredia	70-90	4th	18 1/
9-29	At Tex.	L	3-4		7	5	Witt	Springer		70-91	4th	19 1/

Monthly records: April (13-12), May (13-14), June (15-14), July (10-16), August (11-18), September (8-17).
*Innings, if other than nine. †First game of doubleheader. ‡Second game of doubleheader.

HIGHLIGHTS

High point: On May 5, Mark Langston was a late scratch from his scheduled start because of a sore left knee. Shawn Boskie stepped in and beat Minnesota, 5-1, to give the Angels their sixth consecutive victory, leaving them 1½ games out of first place. They didn't get that close to the top again.

Low point: In a season filled with low points, the worst came August 20, when the Angels built a 5-0 lead in New York, only to lose 17-6. The next morning, interim manager John McNamara was hospitalized with potentially life-threatening blood clots in his right leg.

Turning point: Manager Marcel Lachemann stunned the team by resigning on August 6. His announcement came during a stretch in which the Angels lost 11 of 12 games. The Angels drifted like a ship without a rudder after that.

Most valuable player: Outfielder Tim Salmon. Even without the protection of dangerous hitters around him in the line-up, Salmon managed to produce yet another impressive season. He ended up with 30 home runs, 98 RBIs and a .286 batting average.

Most valuable pitcher: Closer Troy Percival. He didn't take over as the closer until Lee Smith was traded May 27, but he finished with 36 saves, the third-highest single-season total in Angels history. Percival struck out 100 batters in 74 innings and had a 2.31 ERA.

Most improved player: Reliever Mike James. During his first eight years as a pro, James didn't distinguish himself as a bona fide major-leaguer, but he suddenly emerged as a big-time setup man in '96. James got into staff-high 69 games, compiling a 2.67 ERA and setting up most of Troy Percival's 36 saves.

Most pleasant surprise: Utilityman Rex Hudler. At age 35, Hudler was expected to play his customary role of cheerleader and utilityman, contributing what little he had left. As it turned out, Hudler—nicknamed "Wonder Dog"—had plenty left, batting .311 with a career-high 16 home runs in 92 games.

Biggest disappointment: Pitcher Jim Abbott. He inexplicably lost his ability to win in the big leagues. He moved in and out of the rotation and up and down from the minors, eventually finishing 2-18 with a 7.48 ERA.

Key injuries: Starting pitcher Mark Langston went on the disabled list three times with knee problems, and center fielder Jim Edmonds missed 46 games because of a strained thumb and a pulled abdominal muscle.

Notable: The Angels executed the fifth triple play in club history on September 8, going around the horn from Jack Howell to Rex Hudler to J.T. Snow. . . . Bullpen coach Mick Billmeyer, who hadn't swung a bat in three years, pinch hit in the Angels' Hall of Fame exhibition game against Montreal in August—and hit a home run. . . . The Angels set club records for most runs allowed (943), highest ERA (5.30), most wild pitches (80) and most hit batsmen (84). They also grounded into a club-record 148 double plays and put more players on the disabled list (21) than ever before.

—DAVE CUNNINGHAM

RECORDS

1996 regular-season record: 70-91 (4th in A.L. West); 43-38 at home; 27-53 on road; 30-31 vs. East; 25-36 vs. Central; 15-24 vs. West; 22-29 vs. lefthanded starters; 48-62 vs. righthanded starters; 66-77 on grass; 4-14 on turf; 17-25 in daytime; 53-66 at night; 26-22 in one-run games; 8-7 in extra-inning games; 0-0-1 in doubleheaders.

Team record past five years: 338-407 (.454, ranks 13th in league in that span).

TEAM LEADERS

Batting average: Chili Davis (.292).
At-bats: Garret Anderson (607).
Runs: Tim Salmon (90).
Hits: Garret Anderson (173).
Total bases: Tim Salmon (291).
Doubles: Garret Anderson (33).
Triples: Gary DiSarcina, Tim Salmon (4).
Home runs: Tim Salmon (30).
Runs batted in: Tim Salmon (98).
Stolen bases: Rex Hudler (14).
Slugging percentage: Tim Salmon (.501).

On-base percentage: Chili Davis (.387).
Wins: Chuck Finley (15).
Earned-run average: Chuck Finley (4.16).
Complete games: Chuck Finley (4).
Shutouts: Chuck Finley, Jason Grimsley, Dennis Springer (1).
Saves: Troy Percival (36).
Innings pitched: Chuck Finley (238.0).
Strikeouts: Chuck Finley (215).

GAMES BY POSITION

Catcher: Jorge Fabregas 89, Don Slaught 59, Todd Greene 26, Pat Borders 19, Chris Turner 3.
First base: J.T. Snow 154, Rex Hudler 7, Chris Pritchett 5, Tim Wallach 3, Jack Howell 2, Mike Aldrete 1.
Second base: Randy Velarde 114, Rex Hudler 53, Damion Easley 9, Robert Eenhoorn 2, Dick Schofield 2, Jack Howell 1.
Third base: George Arias 83, Tim Wallach 46, Jack Howell 43, Randy Velarde 28, Damion Easley 3, Dick Schofield 1.
Shortstop: Gary DiSarcina 150, Damion Easley 13, Dick Schofield 7, Randy Velarde 7, Robert Eenhoorn 4.
Outfield: Tim Salmon 153, Garret Anderson 146, Jim Edmonds 111, Darin Erstad 48, Orlando Palmeiro 31, Rex Hudler 21, Mike Aldrete 6, Damion Easley 2, Chris Turner 1.
Designated hitter: Chili Davis 143, Tim Wallach 8, Rex Hudler 7, Mike Aldrete 6, Jack Howell 4, Orlando Palmeiro 4, Tim Salmon 3, Damion Easley 2, Garret Anderson 1, George Arias 1, Shawn Boskie 1, Jim Edmonds 1, Jorge Fabregas 1, Todd Greene 1, Don Slaught 1.

TOP DRAFT CHOICES

1. None.
2. **Chuck Abbott**, SS, Austin Peay State.
3. **Scott Schoeneweis**, LHP, Duke.
4. **Brandon Steele**, RHP, Hunting Beach (Calif.) H.S.
5. **Bobby Hill**, SS, Leland H.S., San Jose, Calif.
6. **Jason Verdugo**, RHP, Arizona State.
7. **Marcus Knight**, OF, Miramar H.S., Pembroke Pines, Fla.
8. **Jerrod Riggan**, RHP, San Diego State.
9. **Jason Stephens**, RHP, U. of Arkansas.
10. **Eric Gillespie**, 3B, Cal State Northridge.

BALTIMORE ORIOLES
AMERICAN LEAGUE EAST DIVISION

1997 ORIOLES SCHEDULE

Home games shaded.
* — All-Star Game at Jacobs Field (Cleveland)
D — Day game (any game starting before 5 p.m.)

APRIL

SUN	MON	TUE	WED	THU	FRI	SAT
		1 D	2	3 KC	4 TEX	5 TEX
6 D TEX	7 D KC	8	9 KC	10 KC	11 TEX	12 D TEX
13 D TEX	14 MIN	15 MIN	16 CWS	17 CWS	18 BOS	19 D BOS
20 D BOS	21 D BOS	22 CWS	23 CWS	24 BOS	25 BOS	26 BOS
27 D BOS	28	29 MIN	30 MIN			

MAY

SUN	MON	TUE	WED	THU	FRI	SAT
				1 MIN	2 OAK	3 OAK
4 D OAK	5 ANA	6 ANA	7 ANA	8 SEA	9 SEA	10 D SEA
11 SEA	12 OAK	13 D OAK	14 ANA	15 ANA	16 SEA	17 SEA
18 D SEA	19 DET	20 DET	21 D DET	22	23 CLE	24 D CLE
25 CLE	26 D NYY	27 NYY	28 DET	29 DET	30 CLE	31 D CLE

JUNE

SUN	MON	TUE	WED	THU	FRI	SAT
1 CLE	2 CLE	3 NYY	4 NYY	5	6 CWS	7 D CWS
8 D CWS	9 CWS	10 BOS	11 BOS	12	13 ATL	14 D ATL
15 D TOR	16 MON	17 MON	18 D MON	19	20 TOR	21 D TOR
22 D TOR	23 MIL	24 MIL	25 D MIL	26 TOR	27 TOR	28 TOR
29 D TOR	30 PHI					

JULY

SUN	MON	TUE	WED	THU	FRI	SAT
		1 PHI	2 PHI	3 D DET	4 DET	5 DET
6 D DET	7	8	9 D	10	11 MIL	12 MIL
13 D MIL	14 TOR	15 TOR	16 BOS	17 BOS	18 CWS	19 D CWS
20 D CWS	21 TEX	22 TEX	23 TEX	24	25 MIN	26 MIN
27 D MIN	28	29 TEX	30 D TEX	31 OAK		

AUGUST

SUN	MON	TUE	WED	THU	FRI	SAT
					1 OAK	2 D OAK
3 D OAK	4	5 SEA	6 SEA	7	8 ANA	9 ANA
10 ANA	11	12 OAK	13 OAK	14 SEA	15 SEA	16 ANA
17 D ANA	18 D ANA	19 KC	20 KC	21 KC	22 MIN	23 D MIN
24 D MIN	25	26 KC	27 KC	28 D KC	29 NYM	30 NYM
31 D NYM						

SEPTEMBER

SUN	MON	TUE	WED	THU	FRI	SAT
	1 D FLA	2 FLA	3 FLA	4	5 NYY	6 D NYY
7 D NYY	8 D CLE	9 CLE	10	11 NYY	12 NYY	13 D NYY
14 D NYY	15 CLE	16 CLE	17 MIL	18 MIL	19 DET	20 D DET
21 D DET	22 DET	23 TOR	24 TOR	25 TOR	26 MIL	27 MIL
28 D MIL						

1997 SEASON

CLUB DIRECTORY

Managing general partner
Peter Angelos
Vice chairman, business & finance
Joe Foss
General manager
Pat Gillick
Assistant general manager
Kevin Malone
Exec. dir., marketing & broadcasting
Mike Lehr
Director of player development
Syd Thrift
Asst. director of player development
Don Buford
Scouting director
Gary Nickels
Special assistant to the g.m.
Fred Uhlman Sr.
Scouting administrator
Matt Slater
Assistant, player development
Mike Wong
Director of business affairs
Walter Gutowski
Director of finance
Robert Ames
Traveling secretary
Philip Itzoe
Director of public relations
John Maroon
Asst. director of public relations
Bill Stetka
Director of marketing and advertising
Scott Nickle
Director of stadium operations
Walter Gutowski
Director of community relations
Julie Wagner
Asst. director of community relations
Stacey Beckwith

Coordinator of events
Spiro Alafassos
Publishing coordinator
Stephanie Parrillo
Director of computer services
James Kline
Director of ticket operations
Audrey Brown
Trainers
Richard Bancells
Brian Ebel
Strength and conditioning
Tim Bishop
Scouts
Rick Arnold
Carlos Bernhardt
Dean Decillis
Lane Decker
Manny Estrada
John Green
Patrick Guerrero
Jesus Halabi
Ubaldo Heredia
Jim Howard
Deacon Jones
Gil Kubski
Mike Ledna
Curt Motton
Lamar North
Fred Petersen
Arturo Sanchez
Harry Shelton
Ed Sprague
John Stoke
Marc Tramuta
Mike Tullier
Brett Ward
Don Welke
Logan White
Earl Winn
Mario Ziegler
Jerry Zimmerman

MINOR LEAGUE AFFILIATES

Class	Team	League	Manager
AAA	Rochester	International	Marv Foley
AA	Bowie	Eastern	Joe Ferguson
A	Frederick	Carolina	Dave Hilton
A	Delmarva	South Atlantic	Tomy Shields
Rookie	Bluefield	Appalachian	Bobby Dickerson
Rookie	Gulf Coast Orioles	Gulf Coast	Butch Davis

BROADCAST INFORMATION

Radio: WBAL-AM (1090).
TV: WJZ (Channel 13), WNUV
(Channel 54), WFTY (Channel 50,
Washington, D.C.).
Cable TV: Home Team Sports.

SPRING TRAINING

Ballpark (city): Ft. Lauderdale Stadium
(Ft. Lauderdale, Fla.).
Ticket information: 954-776-1921,
1-800-236-8908.

1997 SEASON *Baltimore Orioles*

SPRING TRAINING ROSTER

Manager—Davey Johnson (15).
Coaches—Rick Down (48), Andy Etchebarren (13), Elrod Hendricks (44), Ray Miller, Sam Perlozzo (2), John Stearns (18).

No.	PITCHERS	B/T	Ht./Wt.	Born	1996 clubs
49	Benitez, Armando	R/R	6-4/225	11-3-72	Baltimore, Gulf Coast Orioles, Bowie, Rochester
	Boskie, Shawn	R/R	6-3/200	3-28-67	California
27	Coppinger, Rocky	R/R	6-5/225	3-19-74	Rochester, Baltimore
41	Corbin, Archie	R/R	6-4/187	12-30-67	Reynoso, Rochester, Baltimore
	Davey, Tom	R/R	6-7/215	9-11-73	Hagerstown
19	Erickson, Scott	R/R	6-4/230	2-2-68	Baltimore
50	Haynes, Jimmy	R/R	6-4/185	9-5-72	Baltimore, Rochester
22	Key, Jimmy	R/L	6-1/185	4-22-61	New York A.L., Tampa, Gulf Coast Yankees
51	Mathews, Terry	L/R	6-2/225	10-5-64	Florida, Baltimore
75	Mills, Alan	B/R	6-1/195	10-18-66	Baltimore
	Moreno, Julio	R/R	6-1/145	10-23-75	Frederick
35	Mussina, Mike	R/R	6-1/180	12-8-68	Baltimore
28	Myers, Randy	L/L	6-1/225	9-19-62	Baltimore
47	Orosco, Jesse	R/L	6-2/205	4-21-57	Baltimore
	Percibal, Billy	R/R	6-1/156	2-2-74	DID NOT PLAY
53	Rhodes, Arthur	L/L	6-2/205	10-24-69	Baltimore
39	Rodriguez, Nerio	R/R	6-1/195	3-22-73	Frederick, Baltimore, Rochester
	Saneaux, Francisco	R/R	6-4/178	2-16-74	Frederick, High Desert
	Yan, Esteban	R/R	6-4/230	6-22-74	Bowie, Rochester, Baltimore

No.	CATCHERS	B/T	Ht./Wt.	Born	1996 clubs
29	Devarez, Cesar	R/R	5-10/175	9-22-69	Rochester, Baltimore
23	Hoiles, Chris	R/R	6-0/215	3-20-65	Baltimore
	Waszgis, B.J.	R/R	6-2/210	8-24-70	Rochester
	Webster, Lenny	R/R	5-9/202	2-10-65	Montreal

No.	INFIELDERS	B/T	Ht./Wt.	Born	1996 clubs
6	Alexander, Manny	R/R	5-10/160	3-20-71	Baltimore
12	Alomar, Roberto	B/R	6-0/185	2-5-68	Baltimore
	Bautista, Juan	R/R	6-0/165	6-24-75	Bowie
14	Bordick, Mike	R/R	5-11/175	7-21-65	Oakland
	Magee, Danny	R/R	6-2/175	11-25-74	Durham
	McClain, Scott	R/R	6-4/210	5-19-72	Rochester
	Otanez, Willis	R/R	5-11/150	4-19-73	Bowie
25	Palmeiro, Rafael	L/L	6-0/190	9-24-64	Baltimore
8	Ripken, Cal	R/R	6-4/220	8-24-60	Baltimore
17	Surhoff, B.J.	L/R	6-1/200	8-4-64	Baltimore

No.	OUTFIELDERS	B/T	Ht./Wt.	Born	1996 clubs
	Almonte, Wady	R/R	6-0/180	4-20-75	Frederick, Gulf Coast Orioles
9	Anderson, Brady	L/L	6-1/190	1-18-64	Baltimore
	Clyburn, Danny	R/R	6-3/220	4-6-74	Bowie
	Davis, Eric	R/R	6-3/185	5-29-62	Cincinnati
11	Hammonds, Jeffrey	R/R	6-0/195	3-5-71	Baltimore, Rochester
	Incaviglia, Pete	R/R	6-1/230	4-2-64	Philadelphia, Baltimore
40	Kingsale, Gene	B/R	6-3/170	8-20-76	Frederick, Baltimore
	Tarasco, Tony	L/R	6-1/205	12-9-70	Baltimore, Rochester, Frederick, Gulf Coast Orioles
	Walton, Jerome	R/R	6-1/185	7-8-65	Atlanta, Greenville, Richmond

BALLPARK INFORMATION

Ballpark (capacity, surface)
Oriole Park at Camden Yards (48,876, grass)
Address
333 W. Camden St.
Baltimore, MD 21201
Business phone
410-685-9800
Ticket information
410-481-SEAT
Ticket prices
$30 (club box)
$25 (field box)
$20 (left field club, lower box)
$18 (terrace box)
$16 (left field lower box, upper box)
$14 (left field upper box)
$11 (upper reserve, lower reserve)
$9 (left field upper reserve)
$7 (bleacher)
$5 (standing room)
Field dimensions (from home plate)
To left field at foul line, 333 feet
To center field, 400 feet
To right field at foul line, 318
First game played
April 6, 1992 (Orioles 2, Indians 0)

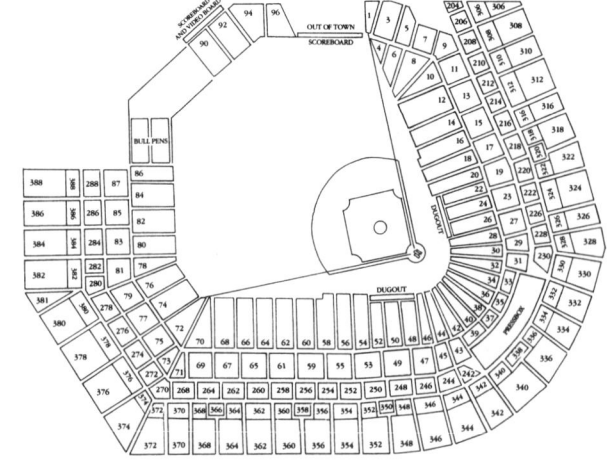

DAY BY DAY

Date	Opp.	Res.	Score	(inn.*)	Hits	Opp. hits	Winning pitcher	Losing pitcher	Save	Record	Pos.	GB
4-2	K.C.	W	4-2		9	5	Mussina	Appier	R. Myers	1-0	T1st	...
4-3	K.C.	W	7-1		14	6	Wells	Gubicza		2-0	T1st	...
4-4	K.C.	W	5-3		10	10	Rhodes	Pichardo	R. Myers	3-0	1st	+ $1/2$
4-5	At Min.	W	2-1		7	7	Mercker	Guardado	R. Myers	4-0	1st	+ $1/2$
4-6	At Min.	L	3-8		8	13	Radke	Haynes		4-1	1st	+ $1/2$
4-7	At Min.	W	4-2		7	7	Mussina	Robertson	R. Myers	5-1	1st	+1 $1/2$
4-10	Cle.	W	3-2	(10)	7	6	Orosco	Tavarez		6-1	1st	+2
4-11	Cle.	W	14-4		13	7	Erickson	Hershiser	Rhodes	7-1	1st	+2
4-12	Min.	W	3-2		7	2	Mussina	Robertson		8-1	1st	+2 $1/2$
4-13	Min.	W	7-6		13	11	Benitez	Mahomes		9-1	1st	+3 $1/2$
4-14	Min.	L	1-4		3	8	Rodriguez	Haynes	Stevens	9-2	1st	+2 $1/2$
4-16	Bos.	W	6-1		7	7	Wells	Clemens		10-2	1st	+3 $1/2$
4-17	Bos.	W	6-5	(12)	11	10	Rhodes	Maddux		11-2	1st	+4 $1/2$
4-18	Bos.	L	7-10		17	14	Moyer	Mussina	Slocumb	11-3	1st	+4
4-19	At Tex.	L	7-26		10	19	Cook	Mercker	Vosberg	11-4	1st	+4
4-20	At Tex.	L	3-8		7	10	Gross	Haynes		11-5	1st	+3
4-21	At Tex.	L	6-9		11	11	Oliver	Wells		11-6	1st	+2
4-22	At Cle.	L	3-6		10	12	Nagy	Erickson	Mesa	11-7	1st	+1
4-23	At Cle.	L	8-9		13	10	Ogea	Mussina	Mesa	11-8	1st	+1
4-24	At K.C.	W	11-8		18	10	Mercker	Haney		12-8	1st	+1
4-25	At K.C.	W	3-2		6	10	Rhodes	Valera	R. Myers	13-8	1st	+2
4-26	Tex.	L	4-5		5	12	Brandenburg	Wells	Henneman	13-9	1st	+1
4-27	Tex.	L	2-4		4	9	Witt	Erickson	Vosberg	13-10	1st	+1
4-28	Tex.	L	4-5	(10)	8	10	Heredia	McDowell	Henneman	13-11	T1st	...
4-29	Tex.	W	8-7		10	9	Haynes	Helling	R. Myers	14-11	1st	+ $1/2$
4-30	N.Y.	L	10-13		11	17	Nelson	Shepherd	Wetteland	14-12	2nd	$1/2$
5-1	N.Y.	L	6-11	(15)	13	20	Pettitte	Mercker		14-13	2nd	1 $1/2$
5-3	Mil.	W	8-2		9	4	Erickson	Bones		15-13	2nd	2
5-4	Mil.	W	10-5		9	13	Mussina	Sparks		16-13	2nd	1
5-5	Mil.	L	1-13		4	13	McDonald	Haynes		16-14	2nd	2
5-7	At Chi.	L	2-3		6	7	Fernandez	Wells	Hernandez	16-15	2nd	3 $1/2$
5-8	At Chi.	L	2-11		6	12	Baldwin	Erickson		16-16	2nd	4 $1/2$
5-9	At Chi.	W	6-4		10	7	Mussina	Alvarez	R. Myers	17-16	2nd	3 $1/2$
5-10	At Mil.	W	10-7	(12)	18	6	Orosco	Garcia	McDowell	18-16	2nd	2 $1/2$
5-11	At Mil.	W	5-3	(10)	4	3	Rhodes	Potts	R. Myers	19-16	2nd	1 $1/2$
5-12	At Mil.	L	4-6		7	11	Miranda	Erickson	Fetters	19-17	2nd	2 $1/2$
5-13	At Oak.	W	4-3		9	11	Krivda	Johns	R. Myers	20-17	2nd	2
5-14	At Oak.	W	9-1		8	7	Mussina	Reyes		21-17	2nd	2
5-17	Sea.	W	14-13		21	21	Mills	Charlton		22-17	2nd	1 $1/2$
5-18	Sea.	L	3-7		8	11	Milacki	Mercker		22-18	2nd	2 $1/2$
5-19	Sea.	W	8-7		10	15	Mussina	Hurtado	R. Myers	23-18	2nd	1 $1/2$
5-20	Cal.	W	13-1		17	5	Wells	Grimsley		24-18	2nd	1
5-21	Cal.	L	2-5		8	7	Boskie	Krivda	Percival	24-19	2nd	2
5-22	Cal.	W	10-5		14	8	Haynes	J. Abbott	McDowell	25-19	2nd	1
5-24	Oak.	W	5-4	(10)	10	9	McDowell	Reyes		26-19	2nd	$1/2$
5-25	Oak.	L	3-6		8	9	Johns	Wells	Groom	26-20	2nd	1 $1/2$
5-26	Oak.	W	6-1		9	3	Mercker	Chouinard	McDowell	27-20	2nd	$1/2$
5-28	At Sea.	W	12-8		11	13	Rhodes	Guetterman	Haynes	28-20	T1st	...
5-29	At Sea.	L	8-9		10	15	Charlton	R. Myers		28-21	T1st	...
5-31	At Cal.	L	3-10		9	12	Langston	Wells		28-22	2nd	1
6-1	At Cal.	L	3-8		7	13	Boskie	Haynes		28-23	2nd	2
6-2	At Cal.	W	14-1		17	6	Erickson	J. Abbott		29-23	2nd	2
6-4	Det.	W	10-7		12	14	Mussina	Gohr	R. Myers	30-23	2nd	2
6-5	Det.	W	6-4		12	6	Rhodes	Myers	R. Myers	31-23	2nd	1
6-6	Det.	W	13-6		12	14	Krivda	Lira		32-23	2nd	1
6-7	Chi.	L	2-8		11	14	Fernandez	Erickson		32-24	2nd	1
6-8	Chi.	L	1-2		9	11	Baldwin	Mercker	Hernandez	32-25	2nd	1
6-9	Chi.	L	9-12		13	18	Karchner	Mussina	Hernandez	32-26	2nd	2
6-10	At Det.	L	3-8		7	14	Olivares	Wells		32-27	2nd	3
6-11	At Det.	W	12-9		15	10	Coppinger	Lira		33-27	2nd	3
6-12	At Det.	W	10-7		11	10	Rhodes	R. Lewis	R. Myers	34-27	2nd	2
6-13	At K.C.	L	2-10		3	14	Linton	Mercker		34-28	2nd	2
6-14	At K.C.	W	6-1		8	7	Mussina	Gubicza		35-28	2nd	2
6-15	At K.C.	L	6-7	(16)	18	17	Magnante	Krivda		35-29	2nd	2
6-16	At K.C.	W	13-5		18	9	Coppinger	Jacome	Mills	36-29	2nd	2
6-17	Tex.	T	1-1	(6)	2	5	......	......		36-29	2nd	1 $1/2$
6-18	Tex.	L	0-7		5	9	Oliver	Mercker		36-30	2nd	2 $1/2$
6-19	Tex.	L	2-3		7	8	Witt	Mussina	Russell	36-31	2nd	3
6-20	Tex.	W	3-2		8	6	Wells	Gross	R. Myers	37-31	2nd	2 $1/2$
6-21	K.C.	W	9-3		13	8	Rhodes	Haney		38-31	2nd	3
6-22	K.C.	W	5-3		6	8	Erickson	Montgomery		39-31	2nd	3

1997 SEASON *Baltimore Orioles*

Date	Opp.	Res.	Score	(inn.*)	Hits	Opp. hits	Winning pitcher	Losing pitcher	Save	Record	Pos.	GB
6-23	K.C.	L	0-4		2	9	Appier	Krivda		39-32	2nd	4
6-24	At Tex.	W	8-3		13	8	Mussina	Witt		40-32	2nd	3
6-25	At Tex.	L	2-5		7	8	Gross	Wells	Henneman	40-33	2nd	3 1/2
6-26	At Tex.	L	5-6		6	9	Cook	Orosco	Henneman	40-34	2nd	4 1/2
6-27	At N.Y.	L	2-3		7	8	Rogers	Erickson	Wetteland	40-35	2nd	5 1/2
6-28	At N.Y.	W	7-4		14	10	Rhodes	M. Rivera	R. Myers	41-35	2nd	4 1/2
6-29	At N.Y.	L	3-4		6	9	Pettitte	Mussina	Wetteland	41-36	2nd	5 1/2
6-30	At N.Y.	W	9-1		11	4	Wells	Mendoza		42-36	2nd	4 1/2
7-1	At Tor.	W	7-4		10	8	Coppinger	Hentgen	R. Myers	43-36	2nd	4 1/2
7-2	At Tor.	W	8-2		14	9	Erickson	Quantrill		44-36	2nd	4 1/2
7-3	At Tor.	L	2-5		9	8	Guzman	Krivda	Timlin	44-37	2nd	5
7-4	Bos.	W	8-6		10	9	Mussina	Wakefield	R. Myers	45-37	2nd	5
7-5	Bos.	L	3-7		4	11	Sele	Wells		45-38	2nd	6
7-6	Bos.	W	4-3		8	7	Coppinger	Clemens	R. Myers	46-38	2nd	6
7-7	Bos.	L	5-7		8	10	Hudson	R. Myers	Slocumb	46-39	2nd	6
7-11	N.Y.	L	2-4		6	7	Key	Mussina	Wetteland	46-40	2nd	7
7-13†	N.Y.	L	2-3		10	6	Nelson	Wells	Wetteland	46-41		
7-13‡	N.Y.	L	5-7		9	10	Gooden	Rhodes	Wetteland	46-42	2nd	9
7-14	N.Y.	L	1-4		8	6	Pettitte	Erickson	Wetteland	46-43	2nd	10
7-15	Tor.	W	8-6		7	9	Haynes	Timlin		47-43	2nd	9
7-16	Tor.	L	0-6		5	14	Guzman	Mussina		47-44	2nd	10
7-17	Tor.	W	11-10		11	15	Coppinger	Timlin		48-44	2nd	9
7-18	At Bos.	W	6-3		10	8	Wells	Sele	R. Myers	49-44	2nd	8
7-19	At Bos.	L	2-13		8	17	Moyer	Erickson		49-45	2nd	8
7-20	At Bos.	L	0-2		6	8	Wakefield	Coppinger	Slocumb	49-46	2nd	9
7-21	At Bos.	W	10-6	(10)	12	9	R. Myers	Stanton		50-46	2nd	8
7-22	Min.	L	5-9		10	10	Robertson	Haynes	Trombley	50-47	2nd	8
7-23	Min.	L	2-3		5	9	Aguilera	Wells	Naulty	50-48	2nd	9
7-24	Min.	L	4-11		8	15	Rodriguez	Erickson		50-49	2nd	10
7-25	Cle.	L	7-10		12	16	Nagy	Coppinger		50-50	2nd	10
7-26	Cle.	L	9-14		13	20	Assenmacher	Mussina		50-51	2nd	11
7-27	Cle.	W	14-2		14	9	Wells	Hershiser		51-51	2nd	11
7-28	Cle.	L	3-6	(13)	8	15	Mesa	Stephenson		51-52	2nd	12
7-30	At Min.	W	16-4		17	7	Coppinger	Rodriguez		52-52	2nd	11
7-31	At Min.	W	9-3		11	9	Mussina	Trombley		53-52	2nd	10
8-1	At Min.	W	4-2		6	4	Wells	Robertson	R. Myers	54-52	2nd	10
8-2	At Cle.	L	1-11		2	16	Hershiser	Erickson		54-53	2nd	10
8-3	At Cle.	W	9-4		14	11	Orosco	Ogea		55-53	2nd	9
8-4	At Cle.	L	2-14		11	11	Anderson	Coppinger		55-54	2nd	10
8-5	At Cle.	W	13-10		21	19	Wells	Assenmacher		56-54	2nd	10
8-6	At Mil.	W	13-3		15	4	Mussina	McDonald		57-54	2nd	10
8-7	At Mil.	W	12-2		14	10	Erickson	Karl		58-54	2nd	9
8-8	At Mil.	W	6-4		7	13	Coppinger	D'Amico	R. Myers	59-54	2nd	9
8-9	At Chi.	L	3-4	(10)	6	9	Simas	R. Myers		59-55	2nd	9
8-10	At Chi.	W	13-4		14	7	Mussina	Alvarez	McDowell	60-55	2nd	8
8-11	At Chi.	L	5-8		8	19	Tapani	Mills	Hernandez	60-56	2nd	9
8-13	Mil.	W	4-3		2	6	Corbin	Lloyd	R. Myers	61-56	2nd	7 1/2
8-14	Mil.	W	8-5		9	7	Milchin	Bones	R. Myers	62-56	2nd	7 1/2
8-15	At Oak.	W	18-5		19	12	Mussina	Adams		63-56	2nd	7
8-16†	At Oak.	W	14-3		19	7	Erickson	Wasdin		64-56		
8-16‡	At Oak.	W	5-4	(10)	12	9	R. Myers	Mohler		65-56	2nd	5 1/2
8-17	At Oak.	L	1-3		5	3	Prieto	Coppinger	Acre	65-57	2nd	5 1/2
8-18	At Oak.	L	6-9		10	15	Wengert	Wells		65-58	2nd	5 1/2
8-20	Sea.	W	4-1		9	3	Mussina	Wagner	R. Myers	66-58	2nd	6
8-21	Sea.	W	10-5		12	8	Erickson	Hitchcock		67-58	2nd	5
8-22	Sea.	L	3-10		6	15	Moyer	Coppinger		67-59	2nd	5
8-23	Cal.	L	0-2		5	5	Boskie	Wells	Percival	67-60	2nd	6
8-24	Cal.	W	5-4		11	11	Mussina	K. Abbott	R. Myers	68-60	2nd	6
8-25	Cal.	L	0-13		5	18	Springer	Erickson		68-61	2nd	6
8-26	Oak.	W	12-11	(10)	13	13	R. Myers	Acre		69-61	2nd	5
8-27	Oak.	W	3-1		6	6	Wells	Prieto	R. Myers	70-61	2nd	4
8-28	Oak.	L	0-3		9	11	Wengert	Mussina		70-62	2nd	4
8-29	At Sea.	L	6-9		10	11	Charlton	R. Myers		70-63	2nd	4
8-30	At Sea.	W	5-2		12	10	Coppinger	Hitchcock	Mills	71-63	2nd	4
8-31	At Sea.	W	7-6		12	9	Erickson	Bosio	Benitez	72-63	2nd	4
9-1	At Sea.	L	1-5		7	9	Mulholland	Wells		72-64	2nd	4
9-2	At Cal.	W	12-8		13	10	Mussina	Boskie		73-64	2nd	4
9-3	At Cal.	L	2-10		7	17	Harris	Coppinger		73-65	2nd	4
9-4	At Cal.	W	4-2		9	6	Erickson	Springer	R. Myers	74-65	2nd	4
9-6	Det.	L	4-5	(12)	10	10	Cummings	Mathews		74-66	2nd	5
9-7	Det.	W	6-0		10	6	Mussina	Thompson		75-66	2nd	4
9-8	Det.	W	6-2		12	4	Mills	Eischen		76-66	2nd	3
9-9	Det.	W	5-4		7	7	Erickson	Olivares	R. Myers	77-66	2nd	2 1/2
9-10	Chi.	W	5-1		8	8	Wells	Tapani		78-66	2nd	2 1/2

ate	Opp.	Res.	Score	(inn.*)	Hits	Opp. hits	Winning pitcher	Losing pitcher	Save	Record	Pos.	GB
-11	Chi.	W	7-6	(10)	11	10	Mills	Hernandez		79-66	2nd	2 1/2
-12	Chi.	L	3-11		3	16	Fernandez	Mussina		79-67	2nd	3 1/2
-13	At Det.	W	7-4		9	11	Erickson	Miller	Mills	80-67	2nd	3 1/2
-14	At Det.	W	7-6		14	8	Mathews	Cummings	R. Myers	81-67	2nd	3 1/2
-15	At Det.	W	16-6		13	7	Corbin	Van Poppel		82-67	2nd	2 1/2
-18	At N.Y.	L	2-3	(10)	5	10	M. Rivera	Mills		82-68	2nd	4
-19†	At N.Y.	L	3-9		6	14	Rogers	Mussina		82-69		
-19‡	At N.Y.	W	10-9		14	11	Mathews	M. Rivera	R. Myers	83-69	2nd	4
-20	Tor.	L	1-5		8	11	Hentgen	Krivda	Spoljaric	83-70	2nd	4
-21	Tor.	W	6-3		2	7	Coppinger	Williams	R. Myers	84-70	2nd	4
-22	Tor.	W	5-4		7	8	Erickson	Flener	Benitez	85-70	2nd	4
-23	Mil.	L	7-8	(10)	13	11	Jones	Mathews	Fetters	85-71	2nd	4
-24	At Bos.	L	8-13		12	12	Gordon	Wells	Mahomes	85-72	2nd	4 1/2
-25	At Bos.	W	6-2		5	7	Krivda	Wakefield	Benitez	86-72	2nd	5
-26	At Tor.	W	4-1		8	5	Coppinger	Williams	Benitez	87-72	2nd	4
-27	At Tor.	L	2-3		7	7	Flener	Erickson	Timlin	87-73	2nd	4
-28	At Tor.	W	3-2	(10)	8	5	R. Myers	Spoljaric		88-73	2nd	4
-29	At Tor.	L	1-4		8	4	Hentgen	Rodriguez	Timlin	88-74	2nd	4

Monthly records: April (14-12), May (14-10), June (14-14), July (11-16), August (19-11), September (16-11).
*Innings, if other than nine. †First game of doubleheader. ‡Second game of doubleheader.

HIGHLIGHTS

High point: The Orioles won 11 of their first 13 games, which stood as the high point in the season until they upset the defending league champion Cleveland Indians in the Divisional Series.

Low point: The division favorite fell 12 games out of first place on July 28 before rallying in August and September to press the division-leading Yankees. It was in July that general manager Pat Gillick and manager Davey Johnson considered breaking up the club to build for 1997, but were dissuaded by owner Peter Angelos.

Turning point: Owner Peter Angelos vetoed a couple of prospective trades and insisted that the club remain intact because of the negative effect that rebuilding might have on the club's following. The Orioles also re-acquired Eddie Murray at about the same time, and the club began its long march back into contention.

Most valuable player: First baseman Rafael Palmeiro. He broke Jim Gentile's club record for RBIs in a season and was the steadiest hitter in a star-studded lineup. Palmeiro is a durable player whose power and run-production numbers have been right there with the best hitters in the game in each of the past four seasons.

Most valuable pitcher: Righthander Mike Mussina. He struggled through a difficult year in which his ERA at one point was two full runs above his career mark, but he finished as the Orioles' winningest pitcher, just missing his first 20-win season.

Most improved player: Center fielder Brady Anderson. He eclipsed his personal home run high two months into the season and went on to break Frank Robinson's club record for homers in a season. He ended up with 50, then hit three more in the postseason.

Most pleasant surprise: Rookie starter Rocky Coppinger. He wasn't expected to pitch regularly in the majors last year but was recalled out of necessity when No. 4 starter Kent Mercker flopped and rookie Jimmy Haynes could not hold down the No. 5 job. Coppinger won 10 games in a little more than half a season.

Biggest disappointment: Rookie starter Jimmy Haynes. He opened the season as the club's No. 5 starter but ended it with an 8.29 ERA and an ego so bruised that club officials wondered if they had rushed him into the rotation too soon.

Key injuries: Lefthander Arthur Rhodes was bothered by shoulder soreness. Righthander Roger McDowell had shoulder surgery. Reliever Armando Benitez had elbow soreness. Outfielder Jeffrey Hammonds was bothered by a strained knee.

Notable: Eddie Murray became the third player in major league history with 500 homers and 3,000 hits when he hit home run No. 500 on September 6. . . . The Orioles broke the major league record for home runs with 257, easily eclipsing the record of 241 by the 1961 Yankees. . . . The Orioles were the first team to field a starting lineup entirely made up of players with 20 homers. . . . Cal Ripken played in every game for the 14th consecutive season.

—PETER SCHMUCK

RECORDS

1996 regular-season record: 88-74 (2nd in A.L. East); 43-38 at home; 45-36 on road; 29-23 vs. East; 34-26 vs. Central; 25-25 vs. West; 24-25 vs. lefthanded starters; 64-49 vs. righthanded starters; 76-67 on grass; 12-7 on turf; 29-24 in daytime; 59-50 at night; 25-18 in one-run games; 10-8 in extra-inning games; 1-1-1 in doubleheaders.
Team record past five years: 396-346 (.534, ranks 4th in league in that span).

TEAM LEADERS

Batting average: Roberto Alomar (.328).
At-bats: Cal Ripken (640).
Runs: Roberto Alomar (132).
Hits: Roberto Alomar (193).
Total bases: Brady Anderson (369).
Doubles: Roberto Alomar (43).
Triples: B.J. Surhoff (6).
Home runs: Brady Anderson (50).
Runs batted in: Rafael Palmeiro (142).
Stolen bases: Brady Anderson (21).
Slugging percentage: Brady Anderson (.637).
On-base percentage: Roberto Alomar (.411).

Wins: Mike Mussina (19).
Earned-run average: Mike Mussina (4.81).
Complete games: Scott Erickson (6).
Shutouts: Mike Mussina (1).
Saves: Randy Myers (31).
Innings pitched: Mike Mussina (243.1).
Strikeouts: Mike Mussina (204).

GAMES BY POSITION

Catcher: Chris Hoiles 126, Greg Zaun 49, Mark Parent 18, Cesar Devarez 10.
First base: Rafael Palmeiro 159, Bobby Bonilla 9, B.J. Surhoff 2, Chris Hoiles 1, Billy Ripken 1.
Second base: Roberto Alomar 141, Billy Ripken 30, Jeff Huson 12, Manny Alexander 7.
Third base: B.J. Surhoff 106, Todd Zeile 29, Billy Ripken 25, Manny Alexander 7, Cal Ripken 6, Bobby Bonilla 4, Jeff Huson 3.
Shortstop: Cal Ripken 158, Manny Alexander 21.
Outfield: Brady Anderson 143, Mike Devereaux 112, Bobby Bonilla 108, Jeffrey Hammonds 70, Luis Polonia 34, B.J. Surhoff 27, Tony Tarasco 23, Brent Bowers 21, Mark Smith 20, Pete Incaviglia 7, Manny Alexander 3, Gene Kingsale 2, Jeff Huson 1.
Designated hitter: Eddie Murray 62, Bobby Bonilla 44, Luis Polonia 18, Roberto Alomar 10, Mike Devereaux 10, B.J. Surhoff 10, Mark Smith 6, Tony Tarasco 5, Pete Incaviglia 4, Rafael Palmeiro 3, Brady Anderson 2, Manny Alexander 1, Jeffrey Hammonds 1.

TOP DRAFT CHOICES

1. None.
2. **Brian Falkenborg**, RHP, Redmond (Wash.) H.S.
3. **Darren Hooper**, OF, U. of Arizona.
4. **Mark Seaver**, RHP, Wake Forest U.
5. **Frank Figueroa**, 1B-OF, Florida Bible H.S., Hialeah, Fla.
6. **Josh McNatt**, LHP, Motlow State (Tenn.) C.C.
7. **Brent Schoening**, RHP, Columbus (Ga.) H.S.
8. **Chad Paronto**, RHP, U. of Massachusetts.
9. **Luis Ramirez**, 1B, Arroyo, P.R.
10. **Luis Matos**, OF, Bayamon, P.R.

BOSTON RED SOX
AMERICAN LEAGUE EAST DIVISION

1997 RED SOX SCHEDULE

Home games shaded.
* — All-Star Game at Jacobs Field (Cleveland)
D — Day game (any game starting before 5 p.m.)

APRIL

SUN	MON	TUE	WED	THU	FRI	SAT
		1	2 ANA	3 D ANA	4 SEA	5 SEA
6 D SEA	7 D OAK	8 OAK	9 D OAK	10	11 D SEA	12 SEA
13 D SEA	14 D OAK	15 OAK	16 CLE	17 CLE	18 BAL	19 D BAL
20 BAL	21 D BAL	22 CLE	23 D CLE	24 BAL	25 BAL	26 D BAL
27 D BAL	28	29 ANA	30 ANA			

MAY

SUN	MON	TUE	WED	THU	FRI	SAT
				1 ANA	2 TEX	3 TEX
4 D TEX	5 KC	6	7 MIN	8 MIN	9 TEX	10 D TEX
11 D TEX	12	13 KC	14 KC	15	16 MIN	17 MIN
18 D MIN	19	20 CWS	21 CWS	22 NYY	23 NYY	24 D NYY
25 NYY	26 D MIL	27 MIL	28 CWS	29 CWS	30 NYY	31 B NYY

JUNE

SUN	MON	TUE	WED	THU	FRI	SAT
1 NYY	2	3 MIL	4 MIL	5 D MIL	6 CLE	7 CLE
8 CLE	9	10 BAL	11 BAL	12	13 NYM	14 D NYM
15 NYM	16 PHI	17 PHI	18 PHI	19	20 DET	21 DET
22 D DET	23 TOR	24 TOR	25 DET	26 DET	27 DET	28 DET
29 D DET	30 FLA					

JULY

SUN	MON	TUE	WED	THU	FRI	SAT
		1 FLA	2 FLA	3 CWS	4 CWS	5 CWS
6 D CWS	7	8 ◇	9	10 TOR	11 TOR	12 TOR
13 D TOR	14 DET	15 DET	16 BAL	17 BAL	18 CLE	19 D CLE
20 D CLE	21 CLE	22 OAK	23 OAK	24 OAK	25 ANA	26 ANA
27 D ANA	28	29 SEA	30 SEA	31 KC		

AUGUST

SUN	MON	TUE	WED	THU	FRI	SAT
					1 KC	2 D KC
3 KC	4 TEX	5 TEX	6 MIN	7 MIN	8 KC	9 KC
10 KC	11 TEX	12 TEX	13 TEX	14 MIN	15 MIN	16 MIN
17 MIN	18	19 OAK	20 OAK	21 OAK	22 ANA	23 ANA
24 D ANA	25 SEA	26 SEA	27 D SEA	28	29 ATL	30 D ATL
31 ATL						

SEPTEMBER

SUN	MON	TUE	WED	THU	FRI	SAT
	1 MON	2 MON	3 MON	4	5 MIL	6 D MIL
7 MIL	8	9 NYY	10 NYY	11 MIL	12 MIL	13 MIL
14 MIL	15 NYY	16 NYY	17 TOR	18 TOR	19 CWS	20 CWS
21 D CWS	22	23 DET	24 DET	25 DET	26 TOR	27 D TOR
28 D TOR						

1997 SEASON
CLUB DIRECTORY

Chief executive officer
John L. Harrington
Exec. v.p. and general manager
Daniel F. Duquette
Exec. v.p. for administration
John S. Buckley
V.p. and chief financial officer
Robert C. Furbush
V.p. broadcasting
James P. Healey
Vice president public relations
Richard L. Bresciani
Vice president sales and marketing
Lawrence C. Cancro
Vice president stadium operations
Joseph F. McDermott
Assistant general manager
Michael D. Port
Assistant g.m. and legal counsel
Elaine W. Steward
Director of baseball operations
Steven W. August
Director of field operations
Robert W. Schaefer
Director of Florida operations
William A. MacKay
Dir. of player dev. and administration
Edward P. Kenney
Director of scouting
W. Wayne Britton
Exec. dir. of int'l baseball operations
R. Ray Poitevint
Assistant scouting director
Erwin L. Bryant
Coordinator of baseball operations
Kent A. Qualls
Traveling secretary
John F. McCormick
Special asst. for player development
John M. Pesky
Major league scout
Frank J. Malzone
Major league special assignment scout
G. Edwin Haas
Medical director
Arthur M. Pappas, M.D.
Trainer
James W. Rowe Jr.
Physical therapist
Richard M. Zawacki
Strength and conditioning coordinator
Thomas L. Moore

Instructors
Theodore S. Williams
Carl M. Yastrzemski
Executive administrative assistant
Lorraine Leong
Equip. manager and clubhouse operations
J. Joseph Cochran
Controller
Stanley H. Tran
Director of facilities management
Thomas L. Queenan Jr.
Director of food services
Patricia T. Flanagan
Director of sales
Robert G. Capilli
Director of ticket operations
Joseph P. Helyar
Superintendent of grounds and maint.
Joseph Mooney
Box office manager
Richard J. Beaton Jr.
Broadcasting manager
James E. Shannahan
Community relations manager
Ronald E. Burton Jr.
Corporate communications manager
Fred Seymour Jr.
Customer relations manager
Ann Marie C. Starzyk
Ground crew manager
Casey Erven
Group sales manager
Timothy J. Dalton
Promotions and special events mgr.
Susan P. Salerno
Property maintenance manager
John M. Caron
Publications manager
Debra A. Matson
Season ticket manager
Joseph L. Matthews
600 Club and suites manager
Daniel E. Lyons
Scouts
Ray Blanco, Charles (Buzz) Bowers, Wayne Britton, Martin Crespo, Ray Crone, Luis Delgado, Ray Fagnant, Eddie Haas, Frank Malzone, Steve McAllister, Howard McCullouch, Danny Monzon, Mike Rizzo, Phillip Rossi, Gary Rajsich, Alex Scott, Matt Sczesny, Jerry Stephenson, Fay Thompson, Luke Wrenn, Jeffrey Zona

MINOR LEAGUE AFFILIATES

Class	Team	League	Manager
AAA	Pawtucket	International	Ken Macha
AA	Trenton	Eastern	DeMarlo Hale
A	Sarasota	Florida State	Rob Derksen
A	Battle Creek	Midwest	Billy Gardner Jr.
A	Lowell	New York-Pennsylvania	Dick Berardino
Rookie	Gulf Coast Red Sox	Gulf Coast	Luis Aguayo

BROADCAST INFORMATION
Radio: WEEI-AM (680).
TV: WBAU-TV (Channel 68).
Cable TV: New England Sports Network.

SPRING TRAINING
Ballpark (city): City of Palms Park (Ft. Myers, Fla.).
Ticket information: 941-334-4700.

SPRING TRAINING ROSTER

Manager—Jimy Williams (22).
Coaches—Dave Jauss, Joe Kerrigan, Wendell Kim, Grady Little, Jim Rice (14), Herm Starrette.

No.	PITCHERS	B/T	Ht./Wt.	Born	1996 clubs
	Avery, Steve	L/L	6-4/205	4-14-70	Atlanta, Greenville
50	Brandenburg, Mark	R/R	6-0/180	7-14-70	Texas, Boston
	Checo, Robinson	/R	6-1/185	9-9-71	Hiroshima Toyo Carp
52	Eshelman, Vaughn	L/L	6-3/215	5-22-69	Pawtucket, Boston
34	Garces, Richard	R/R	6-0/215	5-18-71	Pawtucket, Boston
36	Gordon, Tom	R/R	5-9/180	11-18-67	Boston
11	Hammond, Chris	L/L	6-1/195	1-21-66	Florida, Brevard County, Charlotte
27	Henry, Butch	L/L	6-1/205	10-7-68	DID NOT PLAY
54	Hudson, Joe	R/R	6-1/180	9-29-70	Pawtucket, Boston
53	Lacy, Kerry	R/R	6-2/215	8-7-72	Tulsa, Oklahoma City, Pawtucket, Boston
19	Maddux, Mike	L/R	6-2/185	8-27-61	Boston, Pawtucket
	Mahay, Ron	L/L	6-2/190	6-28-71	Sarasota, Trenton
59	Mahomes, Pat	R/R	6-4/212	8-9-70	Minnesota, Salt Lake, Boston
	Orellano, Rafael	L/L	6-2/160	4-28-73	Pawtucket
	Ruffin, Johnny	R/R	6-3/170	7-29-71	Cincinnati
	Saberhagen, Bret	R/R	6-1/200	4-11-64	Colorado
26	Sele, Aaron	R/R	6-5/215	6-25-70	Boston, Pawtucket
51	Slocumb, Heathcliff	R/R	6-3/220	6-7-66	Boston
55	Suppan, Jeff	R/R	6-2/210	1-2-75	Boston, Pawtucket
49	Wakefield, Tim	R/R	6-2/206	8-2-66	Boston

No.	CATCHERS	B/T	Ht./Wt.	Born	1996 clubs
37	Haselman, Bill	R/R	6-3/223	5-25-66	Boston
47	Hatteberg, Scott	L/R	6-1/195	12-14-69	Pawtucket, Boston
45	McKeel, Walt	R/R	6-0/200	1-17-72	Trenton, Boston
20	Stanley, Mike	R/R	6-0/190	6-25-63	Boston

No.	INFIELDERS	B/T	Ht./Wt.	Born	1996 clubs
12	Cordero, Wil	R/R	6-2/195	10-3-71	Boston, Gulf Coast Red Sox, Pawtucket
	Dodson, Bo	L/L	6-2/195	12-7-70	Pawtucket
	Donnels, Chris	L/R	6-0/185	4-21-66	Kintetsu
3	Frye, Jeff	R/R	5-9/165	8-31-66	Oklahoma City, Boston
5	Garciaparra, Nomar	R/R	6-0/167	7-23-73	Pawtucket, Gulf Coast Red Sox, Boston
18	Jefferson, Reggie	L/L	6-4/215	9-25-68	Boston
	Mejia, Roberto	R/R	5-11/165	4-14-72	Indianapolis, Pawtucket
11	Naehring, Tim	R/R	6-2/203	2-1-67	Boston, Trenton
48	Pozo, Arquimedez	R/R	5-10/160	8-24-73	Tacoma, Boston, Pawtucket
13	Valentin, John	R/R	6-0/180	2-18-67	Boston
42	Vaughn, Mo	L/R	6-1/240	12-15-67	Boston

No.	OUTFIELDERS	B/T	Ht./Wt.	Born	1996 clubs
56	Bragg, Darren	L/R	5-9/180	9-7-69	Seattle, Tacoma, Boston
33	Canseco, Jose	R/R	6-4/240	7-2-64	Pawtucket, Boston
	Hyzdu, Adam	R/R	6-2/210	12-6-71	Trenton
	Mack, Shane	R/R	6-0/190	12-7-63	Yomiuri Giants
	Malave, Jose	R/R	6-2/212	5-31-71	Pawtucket, Boston
7	Nixon, Trot	L/L	6-2/196	4-11-74	Trenton, Boston
25	O'Leary, Troy	L/L	6-0/198	8-4-69	Boston
	Padilla, Roy	L/L	6-5/225	8-4-75	Sarasota, Michigan
57	Pemberton, Rudy	R/R	6-1/185	12-17-69	Oklahoma City, Pawtucket, Boston
	Tavarez, Jesus	B/R	6-0/170	3-26-71	Florida

BALLPARK INFORMATION

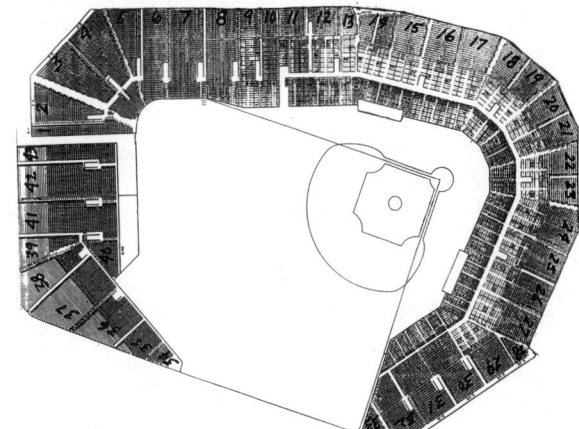

Ballpark (capacity, surface)
Fenway Park (33,871, grass)

Address
4 Yawkey Way
Boston, MA 02215

Business phone
617-267-9440

Ticket information
617-267-8661

Ticket prices
$26 (field box)
$21 (upper box, right field roof box)
$16 (reserved grandstand)
$10 (bleachers, standing room)

Field dimensions (from home plate)
To left field at foul line, 310 feet
To center field, 420 feet
To right field at foul line, 302 feet

First game played
April 20, 1912
(Red Sox 7, New York Highlanders 6)

DAY BY DAY

Boston Red Sox — 1997 SEASON

Date	Opp.	Res.	Score	(inn.*)	Hits	Opp. hits	Winning pitcher	Losing pitcher	Save	Record	Pos.	GB
4-1	At Tex.	L	3-5		8	5	Hill	Clemens	Vosberg	0-1	T4th	1
4-3	At Tex.	L	2-7		4	11	Pavlik	Gordon		0-2	5th	2
4-4	At Tex.	L	2-13		6	16	Gross	Wakefield		0-3	5th	3
4-5	At K.C.	L	4-5	(12)	8	13	Clark	Pennington		0-4	5th	4
4-6	At K.C.	L	3-7		6	11	Pichardo	Belinda		0-5	5th	4
4-7	At K.C.	W	3-1		9	5	Moyer	Gubicza	Slocumb	1-5	5th	4
4-9	Min.	W	9-1		9	7	Gordon	Rodriguez		2-5	5th	3 1/2
4-11	Min.	L	5-6		7	8	Radke	Clemens	Stevens	2-6	5th	5
4-12	Cle.	L	1-3		5	9	Nagy	Sele	Mesa	2-7	5th	6
4-13	Cle.	L	2-14		9	14	Martinez	Moyer		2-8	5th	7
4-14	Cle.	L	6-7	(11)	13	9	Tavarez	Stanton	Mesa	2-9	5th	7
4-15	Cle.	L	0-8		9	11	McDowell	Wakefield		2-10	5th	7 1/2
4-16	At Bal.	L	1-6		7	7	Wells	Clemens		2-11	5th	8 1/2
4-17	At Bal.	L	5-6	(12)	10	11	Rhodes	Maddux		2-12	5th	9 1/2
4-18	At Bal.	W	10-7		14	17	Moyer	Mussina	Slocumb	3-12	5th	8 1/2
4-19	At Cle.	L	4-9		9	13	Martinez	Gordon		3-13	5th	8 1/2
4-20	At Cle.	L	1-2		6	5	McDowell	Wakefield	Mesa	3-14	5th	8 1/2
4-21	At Cle.	L	7-11		14	11	Ogea	Pennington		3-15	5th	8 1/2
4-22	At Min.	W	4-1		9	5	Sele	Robertson	Slocumb	4-15	5th	7 1/2
4-23	At Min.	L	6-8		7	14	Naulty	Hudson	Stevens	4-16	5th	7 1/2
4-24	Tex.	W	11-9		15	13	Stanton	Heredia	Slocumb	5-16	5th	7 1/2
4-25	Tex.	W	8-3		9	9	Wakefield	Gross		6-16	5th	7 1/2
4-26	K.C.	L	3-4		10	7	Belcher	Clemens	Montgomery	6-17	5th	7 1/2
4-27	K.C.	L	0-10		5	12	Appier	Sele		6-18	5th	7 1/2
4-28	K.C.	L	7-9		16	13	Robinson	Slocumb	Montgomery	6-19	5th	7 1/2
4-30	Det.	W	13-4		16	10	Wakefield	Lima		7-19	5th	7 1/2
5-1	Det.	W	5-1		11	6	Clemens	Aldred		8-19	5th	7 1/2
5-3	Tor.	W	8-7		12	9	Moyer	Quantrill	Slocumb	9-19	T4th	8
5-4	Tor.	W	8-4		12	12	Gordon	Viola	Slocumb	10-19	4th	7
5-5	Tor.	L	4-11		10	11	Hentgen	Wakefield		10-20	4th	8
5-7	At Mil.	W	4-2		7	5	Clemens	Miranda	Slocumb	11-20	4th	8 1/2
5-9	At Mil.	L	2-17		6	17	Bones	Sele		11-21	4th	9
5-10	At Tor.	W	6-5	(11)	9	9	Slocumb	Carrara		12-21	4th	8
5-11	At Tor.	L	8-9	(11)	10	11	Quantrill	Knackert		12-22	4th	8
5-12	At Tor.	L	7-8	(10)	15	11	Janzen	Slocumb		12-23	4th	9
5-14	Cal.	W	4-3	(12)	9	11	Belinda	Boskie		13-23	4th	8
5-15	Cal.	W	17-6		17	9	Moyer	Grimsley		14-23	4th	8
5-17	Oak.	W	5-3	(11)	12	6	Stanton	Van Poppel		15-23	4th	8
5-18	Oak.	L	5-6	(10)	10	9	Groom	Garces	Taylor	15-24	4th	8
5-19	Oak.	W	12-2		15	9	Sele	Wengert		16-24	4th	8
5-20	Oak.	W	16-4		21	8	Gordon	Johns		17-24	4th	7 1/2
5-21	Sea.	L	7-13		13	19	Wells	Eshelman		17-25	4th	8 1/2
5-22	Sea.	L	1-6		6	10	Wolcott	Wakefield		17-26	4th	8 1/2
5-23	Sea.	W	11-4		14	9	Clemens	Milacki		18-26	4th	8 1/2
5-24	At Cal.	L	1-3		4	7	Finley	Sele	Percival	18-27	4th	8 1/2
5-25	At Cal.	W	10-3		12	10	Gordon	Williams		19-27	4th	8 1/2
5-26	At Cal.	L	2-12		7	14	Boskie	Eshelman		19-28	4th	8 1/2
5-27	At Oak.	W	10-3		16	8	Wakefield	Wojciechowski		20-28	4th	8 1/2
5-28	At Oak.	L	2-6		11	8	Wasdin	Clemens		20-29	4th	8 1/2
5-29	At Oak.	L	6-7	(10)	10	7	Mohler	Slocumb		20-30	4th	8 1/2
5-30	At Sea.	W	10-1		11	2	Gordon	Torres		21-30	4th	8
5-31	At Sea.	L	6-9		12	8	Wells	Garces		21-31	4th	9
6-1	At Sea.	W	6-5		9	8	Wakefield	Milacki	Slocumb	22-31	4th	9
6-2	At Sea.	L	1-3		6	11	Wolcott	Clemens	Jackson	22-32	4th	10
6-4	Chi.	L	4-6		9	12	Alvarez	Gunderson	Hernandez	22-33	4th	11
6-5	Chi.	L	6-8	(12)	17	11	Keyser	Slocumb		22-34	4th	11
6-6	Chi.	W	7-4		12	12	Eshelman	Magrane	Stanton	23-34	4th	11
6-7	Mil.	W	10-7		10	16	Garces	Garcia	Slocumb	24-34	4th	10
6-8	Mil.	L	2-3	(10)	9	6	Lloyd	Hudson	Fetters	24-35	4th	10
6-9	Mil.	L	8-11	(10)	9	18	Burrows	Slocumb	Fetters	24-36	4th	11
6-10	At Chi.	L	2-8		6	16	Tapani	Wakefield		24-37	4th	12
6-11	At Chi.	W	9-2		11	7	Eshelman	Magrane		25-37	4th	12
6-12	At Chi.	W	3-2	(12)	5	11	Hudson	Karchner		26-37	4th	11
6-13	Tex.	W	8-7	(10)	15	14	Slocumb	Henneman		27-37	3rd	10
6-14	Tex.	W	4-3		6	8	Stanton	Witt		28-37	3rd	10
6-15	Tex.	L	3-13		9	18	Gross	Wakefield		28-38	3rd	10
6-16	Tex.	W	10-9		13	13	Hudson	Henneman		29-38	3rd	10
6-18	At Cle.	L	7-9		14	13	Swindell	Sele	Mesa	29-39	3rd	10 1/2
6-19	At Cle.	L	4-11		14	13	Hershiser	Gordon		29-40	4th	11
6-20	At Cle.	L	4-5		10	10	Shuey	Stanton		29-41	4th	11 1/2
6-21	At Tex.	L	4-14		12	17	Hill	Minchey		29-42	4th	13
6-22	At Tex.	L	2-8		6	10	Pavlik	Wakefield		29-43	4th	14

Date	Opp.	Res.	Score	(inn.*)	Hits	Opp. hits	Winning pitcher	Losing pitcher	Save	Record	Pos.	GB
6-23	At Tex.	W	6-4		12	12	Stanton	Cook	Slocumb	30-43	4th	14
6-25	Cle.	L	0-4		7	9	Hershiser	Gordon		30-44	4th	14
6-26	Cle.	W	6-4	(15)	15	10	Garces	Embree		31-44	4th	14
6-27	Det.	L	6-9		9	14	Lira	Minchey		31-45	4th	15
6-28	Det.	W	8-5		14	11	Wakefield	B. Williams		32-45	4th	14
6-29	Det.	W	13-6		16	11	Eshelman	Keagle		33-45	4th	14
6-30	Det.	W	9-4		10	8	Gordon	Sodowsky		34-45	4th	13
7-1	At N.Y.	L	0-2		6	5	Key	Clemens	Wetteland	34-46	4th	14
7-2	At N.Y.	L	5-7		9	15	Nelson	Hudson	Wetteland	34-47	4th	15
7-4	At Bal.	L	6-8		9	10	Mussina	Wakefield	R. Myers	34-48	4th	16
7-5	At Bal.	W	7-3		11	4	Sele	Wells		35-48	4th	16
7-6	At Bal.	L	3-4		7	8	Coppinger	Clemens	R. Myers	35-49	4th	17
7-7	At Bal.	W	7-5		10	8	Hudson	R. Myers	Slocumb	36-49	4th	16
7-11	At Det.	W	11-4		10	7	Clemens	B. Williams		37-49	4th	16
7-12	At Det.	W	11-3		12	6	Gordon	Olivares		38-49	T3rd	15 1/2
7-13	At Det.	W	10-5		13	6	Sele	Nitkowski		39-49	T3rd	16
7-14	At Det.	W	6-4		10	9	Moyer	Lira	Slocumb	40-49	T3rd	16
7-15	N.Y.	W	8-6		13	14	Wakefield	Hutton	Slocumb	41-49	3rd	15
7-16	N.Y.	L	5-9		7	11	Key	Clemens		41-50	T3rd	16
7-17	N.Y.	W	12-11		12	19	Eshelman	Wetteland		42-50	3rd	15
7-18	Bal.	L	3-6		8	10	Wells	Sele	R. Myers	42-51	T3rd	15
7-19	Bal.	W	13-2		17	8	Moyer	Erickson		43-51	3rd	14
7-20	Bal.	W	2-0		8	6	Wakefield	Coppinger	Slocumb	44-51	3rd	14
7-21	Bal.	L	6-10	(10)	9	12	R. Myers	Stanton		44-52	3rd	14
7-22	K.C.	L	2-5		6	12	Belcher	Gordon		44-53	3rd	14
7-23	K.C.	L	5-7		10	13	Appier	Sele		44-54	T3rd	15
7-24	K.C.	W	12-2		14	7	Moyer	Linton		45-54	3rd	15
7-25	At Min.	L	6-16		12	19	Parra	Wakefield		45-55	T3rd	15
7-26	At Min.	L	1-5		5	9	Radke	Clemens		45-56	T3rd	16
7-27	At Min.	W	9-5		14	9	Gordon	Naulty		46-56	T3rd	16
7-28	At Min.	L	8-9		11	14	Aguilera	Sele	Naulty	46-57	4th	17
7-30	At K.C.	L	0-7		3	10	Rosado	Eshelman		46-58	4th	17
7-31	At K.C.	W	5-3		10	5	Wakefield	Haney	Slocumb	47-58	4th	16
8-1	At K.C.	L	4-9		8	14	Belcher	Clemens		47-59	4th	17
8-2	Min.	W	11-10		15	13	Brandenburg	Naulty		48-59	4th	16
8-3†	Min.	W	6-3		10	8	Sele	Rodriguez	Hudson	49-59		
8-3‡	Min.	L	0-6		7	9	Aldred	Suppan		49-60	4th	15 1/2
8-4	Min.	W	13-6		12	13	Eshelman	Klingenbeck		50-60	4th	15 1/2
8-5	Tor.	W	3-1		7	6	Wakefield	Guzman		51-60	4th	15 1/2
8-6	Tor.	W	3-2		4	9	Maddux	Hanson	Slocumb	52-60	3rd	15 1/2
8-7	Tor.	W	8-0		9	3	Gordon	Hentgen		53-60	3rd	14 1/2
8-8	Tor.	L	6-9		10	17	Williams	Sele	Timlin	53-61	3rd	15 1/2
8-9†	At Mil.	W	9-7		9	12	Suppan	Vanegmond	Slocumb	54-61		
8-9‡	At Mil.	W	4-1		9	6	Eshelman	Bones	Belinda	55-61	3rd	14
8-10	At Mil.	W	3-2		5	8	Wakefield	Eldred		56-61	3rd	13
8-11	At Mil.	W	2-0		6	6	Clemens	McDonald	Belinda	57-61	3rd	13
8-12	At Tor.	L	1-5		9	9	Hentgen	Gordon		57-62	3rd	13
8-13	At Tor.	W	7-5		15	5	Brandenburg	Williams	Slocumb	58-62	3rd	12
8-14	At Tor.	W	8-6		9	9	Belinda	Crabtree	Slocumb	59-62	3rd	12
8-16	Cal.	L	3-6		4	10	Springer	Wakefield	Percival	59-63	3rd	12
8-17	Cal.	W	6-0		7	7	Clemens	Finley		60-63	3rd	11
8-18	Cal.	L	3-4		9	12	Holtz	Brandenburg	Percival	60-64	3rd	11
8-19	Cal.	W	10-9		16	15	Lacy	Gohr	Slocumb	61-64	3rd	11
8-20	Oak.	W	4-3		10	7	Garces	Mohler	Slocumb	62-64	3rd	11
8-21	Oak.	W	6-4		11	7	Brandenburg	Johns	Slocumb	63-64	3rd	10
8-22	Oak.	W	2-1		8	8	Clemens	Acre		64-64	3rd	9
8-23	Sea.	L	4-6		8	7	Bosio	Brandenburg	Ayala	64-65	3rd	10
8-24	Sea.	W	9-5		9	11	Lacy	Wells		65-65	3rd	10
8-25	Sea.	W	8-5		14	9	Maddux	Wagner	Slocumb	66-65	3rd	9
8-26	At Cal.	W	4-1		9	6	Wakefield	Dickson		67-65	3rd	8
8-27	At Cal.	W	2-1		9	5	Clemens	Finley	Slocumb	68-65	3rd	7
8-28	At Cal.	W	7-4		9	5	Gordon	Boskie		69-65	3rd	6
8-30	At Oak.	L	0-7		7	9	Telgheder	Maddux		69-66	3rd	6 1/2
8-31	At Oak.	L	0-8		5	8	Adams	Wakefield		69-67	3rd	7 1/2
9-1	At Oak.	W	8-3		12	6	Sele	Wasdin		70-67	3rd	6 1/2
9-2	At Sea.	W	9-8	(10)	7	10	Slocumb	Carmona		71-67	3rd	6 1/2
9-3	At Sea.	L	9-11		13	11	Torres	Gordon	Charlton	71-68	3rd	6 1/2
9-4	At Sea.	W	7-5		10	8	Mahomes	Hitchcock	Slocumb	72-68	3rd	6 1/2
9-6	At Chi.	W	10-3		15	9	Wakefield	Alvarez		73-68	3rd	6 1/2
9-7	At Chi.	L	3-4		9	7	Fernandez	Clemens	Hernandez	73-69	3rd	6 1/2
9-8	At Chi.	L	4-7		10	10	Baldwin	Sele	Hernandez	73-70	3rd	6 1/2
9-9	Mil.	L	0-6		6	10	Karl	Gordon		73-71	3rd	7
9-10	Mil.	L	10-11		14	14	Garcia	Hudson	Fetters	73-72	3rd	8
9-11	Mil.	W	4-1		10	5	Wakefield	Eldred	Slocumb	74-72	3rd	8
9-13	Chi.	W	9-5		14	9	Clemens	Baldwin	Slocumb	75-72	3rd	8 1/2

Date	Opp.	Res.	Score	(inn.*)	Hits	Opp. hits	Winning pitcher	Losing pitcher	Save	Record	Pos.	GB
9-14	Chi.	L	5-13		10	15	Castillo	Gordon	Simas	75-73	3rd	9 1/
9-15	Chi.	W	9-8		11	9	Slocumb	Hernandez		76-73	3rd	8 1/
9-17	At Det.	W	4-2		9	8	Brandenburg	Lira	Slocumb	77-73	3rd	8 1/
9-18	At Det.	W	4-0		11	5	Clemens	Thompson		78-73	3rd	8 1/
9-19	At Det.	W	8-3		12	11	Gordon	Miller		79-73	3rd	8
9-20	At N.Y.	W	4-2		10	6	Wakefield	Polley	Slocumb	80-73	3rd	7
9-21	At N.Y.	L	11-12	(10)	14	20	Wetteland	Hudson		80-74	3rd	8
9-22	At N.Y.	L	3-4		9	10	M. Rivera	Sele	Wetteland	80-75	3rd	9
9-23	At N.Y.	W	4-3	(11)	12	11	Slocumb	Boehringer	Mahomes	81-75	3rd	8
9-24	Bal.	W	13-8		12	12	Gordon	Wells	Mahomes	82-75	3rd	7 1/
9-25	Bal.	L	2-6		7	5	Krivda	Wakefield	Benitez	82-76	3rd	9
9-26	N.Y.	W	5-3		8	10	Maddux	Key	Slocumb	83-76	3rd	8
9-27	N.Y.	W	7-5		11	10	Sele	Gooden	Slocumb	84-76	3rd	7
9-28	N.Y.	L	2-4		9	5	Mendoza	Clemens	Wetteland	84-77	3rd	8
9-29	N.Y.	W	6-5		14	11	Mahomes	Polley		85-77	3rd	7

Monthly records: April (7-19), May (14-12), June (13-14), July (13-13), August (22-9), September (16-10).
*Innings, if other than nine. †First game of doubleheader. ‡Second game of doubleheader.

HIGHLIGHTS

High point: The Red Sox went on a 26-10 run starting August 1 to close within 2 1/2 games of the wild card spot on September 7 and were 38-18 through the end of the season.

Low point: The Red Sox got off to the worst start (2-12) in the history of the franchise and continued on to lose 19 of the first 25.

Turning point: The Sox were staggering along at 35-49 and were a season-high 17 games out of first when a Mo Vaughn swing saved the season. During the final game of the first half of the season July 7, the Red Sox were trailing the Orioles by two runs in the ninth. Vaughn stepped to the plate against closer Randy Myers and hit a titanic, three-run homer to center field.

Most valuable player: First baseman Mo Vaughn. He put up better numbers in 1996 than during his league MVP season of 1995, hitting .326 with 44 homers and 143 RBIs.

Most valuable pitcher: Starter Roger Clemens. Despite his 10-13 record and 3.63 ERA, Clemens was a steady performer all season. He led the league in strikeouts for the third time in his career with 257 and had a 20-strikeout game in Detroit, tying his major league record set in 1986.

Most improved player: Third baseman Tim Naehring. He tailed off offensively from an all-star first half, when he hit .324 with 12 home runs and 42 RBIs, to finish an injury-plagued season with a .288 mark, 17 homers and 65 RBIs.

Most pleasant surprise: Reggie Jefferson. Once the lefthanded hitter got the chance, he provided plenty of offense. His average was well over the .300 mark all season and he finished at .347 with 19 homers and 74 RBIs.

Biggest disappointment: Righthanders Tom Gordon and Aaron Sele. Gordon came in as a free agent; while he had a winning record (12-9), he had a disgraceful 5.59 ERA. Sele had the worst record among the starters (7-11).

Key injuries: The losses of reliever Stan Belinda with elbow, shoulder and groin problems and power man Jose Canseco, who didn't play from July 25 until September 17 because of a back problem. Belinda appeared in 31 games. Canseco had 29 homers and 77 RBIs in 85 games before having back surgery August 1. He returned for the final two weeks but was no factor.

Notable: Roger Clemens tied his major league strikeout mark by fanning 20 Tigers in September, 10 years after he fanned 20 Mariners on April 29, 1986.

—JOE GIULIOTTI

RECORDS

1996 regular-season record: 85-77 (3rd in A.L. East); 47-34 at home; 38-43 on road; 33-19 vs. East; 23-37 vs. Central; 29-21 vs. West; 28-17 vs. lefthanded starters; 57-60 vs. righthanded starters; 76-67 on grass; 9-10 on turf; 22-30 in daytime; 63-47 at night; 20-19 in one-run games; 8-12 in extra-inning games; 1-0-1 in doubleheaders.

Team record past five years: 378-367 (.507, ranks 6th in league in that span).

TEAM LEADERS

Batting average: Mo Vaughn (.326).
At-bats: Mo Vaughn (635).
Runs: Mo Vaughn (118).
Hits: Mo Vaughn (207).
Total bases: Mo Vaughn (370).
Doubles: Reggie Jefferson (30).
Triples: Troy O'Leary (5).
Home runs: Mo Vaughn (44).
Runs batted in: Mo Vaughn (143).
Stolen bases: Jeff Frye (18).
Slugging percentage: Mo Vaughn (.583).
On-base percentage: Mo Vaughn (.420).
Wins: Tim Wakefield (14).
Earned-run average: Roger Clemens (3.63).
Complete games: Roger Clemens, Tim Wakefield (6).
Shutouts: Roger Clemens (2).
Saves: Heathcliff Slocumb (31).
Innings pitched: Roger Clemens (242.2).
Strikeouts: Roger Clemens (257).

GAMES BY POSITION

Catcher: Mike Stanley 105, Bill Haselman 69, Alex Delgado 14, Scott Hatteberg 10, Walt McKeel 1.

First base: Mo Vaughn 146, Reggie Jefferson 16, Bill Haselman 2, Phil Clark 1, Wil Cordero 1, Alex Delgado 1, Jeff Manto 1.

Second base: Jeff Frye 100, Wil Cordero 37, Bill Selby 14, Arquimedez Pozo 10, Esteban Beltre 8, Jeff Manto 4, Alex Delgado 1, Nomar Garciaparra 1, Tim Naehring 1.

Third base: Tim Naehring 116, Bill Selby 14, Esteban Beltre 13, John Valentin 12, Jeff Manto 10, Arquimedez Pozo 10, Tony Rodriguez 5, Alex Delgado 4, Jimmy Tatum 2, Phil Clark 1.

Shortstop: John Valentin 118, Nomar Garciaparra 22, Tony Rodriguez 21, Esteban Beltre 6, Jeff Manto 4, Jeff Frye 3.

Outfield: Troy O'Leary 146, Lee Tinsley 83, Mike Greenwell 76, Darren Bragg 58, Milt Cuyler 45, Reggie Jefferson 45, Jose Malave 38, Dwayne Hosey 26, Alex Cole 24, Kevin Mitchell 21, Rudy Pemberton 13, Jose Canseco 11, Alex Delgado 6, Bill Selby 6, Jeff Frye 5, Trot Nixon 2.

Designated hitter: Jose Canseco 84, Reggie Jefferson 49, Mo Vaughn 15, Wil Cordero 10, Mike Stanley 10, Kevin Mitchell 4, Bill Haselman 2, Esteban Beltre 1, Phil Clark 1, Milt Cuyler 2, Jeff Frye 1, Nomar Garciaparra 1, Dwayne Hosey 1, Arquimedez Pozo 1, Bill Selby 1, John Valentin 1.

TOP DRAFT CHOICES

1a. **Josh Garrett**, RHP, South Spencer H.S. Richland, Ind.

1b. **Chris Reitsma**, RHP, Calgary (Alta.) Christian H.S.

2a. **Gary LoCurto**, 1B, University H.S., San Diego.

2b. **Jason Sekany**, RHP, U. of Virginia.

3. **Dernell Stenson**, OF, LaGrange H.S., (Ga.).

4. **John Barnes**, OF, Grossmont (Calif.) C.C.

5. **Bobby Brito**, C, Cypress (Calif.) H.S.

6. **Mike Perini**, OF, Carlsbad (N.M.) H.S.

7. **Rob Ramsay**, LHP, Washington State U.

8. **Justin Duchscherer**, RHP, Coronado H.S., Lubbock, Tex.

9. **Marcus Martinez**, LHP, Monterey H.S., Lubbock, Tex.

10. **Shea Hillenbrand**, SS, Mesa (Ariz.) C.C.

CHICAGO WHITE SOX
AMERICAN LEAGUE CENTRAL DIVISION

1997 WHITE SOX SCHEDULE

Home games shaded.
* — All-Star Game at Jacobs Field (Cleveland)
D — Day game (any game starting before 5 p.m.)

APRIL

SUN	MON	TUE	WED	THU	FRI	SAT
		1 D TOR	2 TOR	3	4 D DET	5 D DET
6 D NET	D 7	8 TOR	9 TOR	10 D TOR	11 D DET	12 D DET
13 D NET	14 TEX	15 TEX	16 BAL	17 BAL	18 NYY	19 D NYY
20 D NYY	D 21 NYY	22 BAL	23 BAL	24	25 NYY	26 D NYY
27 D NYY	D 28	29 TEX	30 TEX			

MAY

SUN	MON	TUE	WED	THU	FRI	SAT
				1	2 ANA	3 ANA
D 5	6 SEA	7 SEA	8 OAK	9 OAK	10 OAK	
11 D OAK	12 ANA	13 ANA	14 SEA	15 D SEA	16 OAK	17 D OAK
18 D OAK	D 19	20 BOS	21 BOS	22	23 MIL	24 MIL
25 D MIL	26 D CLE	27 CLE	28 BOS	29 BOS	30 MIL	31 MIL

JUNE

SUN	MON	TUE	WED	THU	FRI	SAT
D 2 MIL	2	3 CLE	4 CLE	5 CLE	6 BAL	7 D BAL
RAL	D 9 BAL	10 NYY	11 NYY	12	13 CIN	14 D CIN
5 IN	16 D CUB	D 17 CUB	18 CUB	19	20 MIN	21 MIN
AIN	22 KC	23 KC	24 KC	D 25	26 MIN	27 MIN	28 MIN
29 MIN	30 PIT					

JULY

SUN	MON	TUE	WED	THU	FRI	SAT
		1 PIT	2 PIT	3 BOS	4 BOS	5 BOS
D 7	8	* 9	10 KC	11 KC	12 KC	
0 14 MIN	15 MIN	16 NYY	17 NYY	18 D BAL	19 D BAL	
D 21 DET	22 DET	23 DET	D 24 TEX	25 TEX	26 D TEX	
28	29 DET	30 DET	D 31 ANA			

AUGUST

SUN	MON	TUE	WED	THU	FRI	SAT
					1 ANA	2 D ANA
NA	4	5 D OAK	6 OAK	7 SEA	8 SEA	9 SEA
D	11	12 ANA	13 ANA	14 OAK	15 D OAK	16 D SEA
A	18 SEA	19 TOR	20 TOR	21 D TEX	22 TEX	23 TEX
4	25	26 TOR	27 TOR	28 D TOR	29 HOU	30 HOU
D						

SEPTEMBER

SUN	MON	TUE	WED	THU	FRI	SAT
	1 STL	D 2 STL	3 STL	4	5 CLE	6 D CLE
LE	8 MIL	9 MIL	10 MIL	11 CLE	12 CLE	13 CLE
LE	15 MIL	16 MIL	17 KC	18 KC	19 BOS	20 BOS
0S	22	23 MIN	24 MIN	25 MIN	26 KC	27 KC
c	D					

1997 SEASON

CLUB DIRECTORY

Chairman
Jerry Reinsdorf

Vice chairman
Eddie Einhorn

Executive vice president
Howard Pizer

Senior v.p., major league operations
Ron Schueler

Sr. v.p., marketing and broadcasting
Rob Gallas

Senior vice president, baseball
Jack Gould

Vice president, finance
Tim Buzard

Vice president, stadium operations
Terry Savarise

V.p., free agent and major league scouting
Larry Monroe

Director of baseball operations
Dan Evans

Special assistants to Ron Schueler
Ed Brinkman
Dave Yoakum

Director of scouting
Duane Shaffer

Director of player development
Steve Noworyta

Director of minor league instruction
Jim Snyder

Traveling secretary
Glen Rosenbaum

Assistant to the director of scouting
Grace Guerrero Zwit

Director of marketing and broadcasting
Bob Grim

Director of communications
Eric Webb

Director of community relations
Christine Makowski

Director of ticket sales
Jim Muno

Director of ticket operations
Bob Devoy

Dir. of management information services
Don Brown

Director of human resources
Moira Foy

Controller
Bill Waters

Assistant director of communications
Scott Reifert

Trainers
Herm Schneider
Mark Anderson

Director of conditioning
Steve Odgers

Team physicians
Dr. James Boscardin
Dr. Hugo Cuadros
Dr. Bernard Feldman
Dr. David Orth
Dr. Scott Price
Dr. Lowell Scott Weil

Scouting national cross-checker
George Bradley

Scouting supervisors
Doug Laumann
Ed Pebley

Full-time scouts
Juan Ramon Bernhardt, Joseph Butler, Scott Cerny, Hernan Cortes, Alex Cosmidis, Ed Crosby, Roberto Espinoza, Larry Grefer, Warren Hughes, Miguel Ibarra, Joe Karp, John Kazanas, Reginald Lewis, Jose Ortega, David Owen, Gary Pellant, Paul Provas, Hector Rincones, Michael Sgobba, Ken Stauffer, Jun Teramotto, John Tumminia, Mark Weidemaier

Part-time scouts
Jose Bernhardt, Javier Ceteno, John Doldeorian, Joe Ingalls, Jack Jolly, George Kachigian, Dario Lodigiani, Donald Metzger, Al Otto, Michael Paris, Joe Thurman

MINOR LEAGUE AFFILIATES

Class	Team	League	Manager
AAA	Nashville	American Assoc.	Tom Spencer
AA	Birmingham	Southern	Dave Huppert
A	Hickory	South Atlantic	Chris Cron
A	Winston-Salem	Carolina	Mike Heath
Rookie	Bristol	Appalachian	Nick Capra
Rookie	Gulf Coast White Sox	Gulf Coast	Roly de Armas

BROADCAST INFORMATION

Radio: WMVP-AM (1000).
TV: WGN-TV (Channel 9).
Cable TV: SportsChannel.

SPRING TRAINING

Ballpark (city): Ed Smith Stadium (Sarasota, Fla.).
Ticket information: 813-287-8844.

1997 SEASON   Chicago White Sox

SPRING TRAINING ROSTER

Manager—Terry Bevington (18).
Coaches—Bill Buckner (22), Ron Jackson (52), Art Kusyner, Joe Nossek (21), Mike Pazik (25), Doug Rader, Mark Salas (58).

No.	PITCHERS	B/T	Ht./Wt.	Born	1996 clubs
40	Alvarez, Wilson	L/L	6-1/235	3-24-70	Chicago A.L.
37	Baldwin, James	R/R	6-3/210	7-15-71	Nashville, Chicago A.L.
46	Bere, Jason	R/R	6-3/215	5-26-71	Chicago A.L., Nashville, Gulf Coast White Sox-Cardinals, Hickory, Birmingham
51	Bertotti, Mike	L/L	6-1/185	1-18-70	Nashville, Chicago A.L.
	Castillo, Carlos	R/R	6-2/240	4-21-75	South Bend, Prince William
44	Castillo, Tony	L/L	5-10/190	3-1-63	Toronto, Chicago A.L.
	Clemons, Chris	R/R	6-4/215	10-31-72	Prince William, Birmingham
	Cruz, Nelson	R/R	6-1/175	9-13-72	Birmingham
48	Darwin, Jeff	R/R	6-3/180	7-6-69	Nashville, Chicago A.L.
	Drabek, Doug	R/R	6-1/185	7-25-62	Houston
	Durocher, Jayson	R/R	6-2/185	8-18-74	West Palm Beach
	Eyre, Scott	L/L	6-1/160	5-30-72	Birmingham
	Fordham, Tom	L/L	6-2/210	2-20-74	Birmingham, Nashville
39	Hernandez, Roberto	R/R	6-4/235	11-11-64	Chicago A.L.
47	Karchner, Matt	R/R	6-4/210	6-28-67	Chicago A.L., Nashville
54	Levine, Alan	L/R	6-3/180	5-22-68	Nashville, Chicago A.L.
	McDowell, Roger	R/R	6-1/197	12-21-60	Baltimore
	Navarro, Jaime	R/R	6-5/235	3-27-68	Chicago N.L.
42	Ruffcorn, Scott	R/R	6-4/210	12-29-69	Nashville, Chicago A.L.
41	Simas, Bill	L/R	6-3/220	11-28-71	Chicago A.L.
38	Sirotka, Mike	L/L	6-1/200	5-13-71	Nashville, Chicago A.L.
50	Thomas, Larry	R/L	6-1/195	10-25-69	Chicago A.L.
	Woods, Brian	R/R	6-6/212	6-7-71	Birmingham

No.	CATCHERS	B/T	Ht./Wt.	Born	1996 clubs
20	Karkovice, Ron	R/R	6-1/219	8-8-63	Chicago A.L.
55	Machado, Robert	R/R	6-1/205	6-3-73	Birmingham, Chicago A.L.
	Pena, Tony	R/R	6-0/185	6-4-57	Cleveland

No.	INFIELDERS	B/T	Ht./Wt.	Born	1996 clubs
5	Durham, Ray	B/R	5-8/170	11-30-71	Chicago A.L.
13	Guillen, Ozzie	L/R	5-11/164	1-20-64	Chicago A.L.
7	Martin, Norberto	R/R	5-10/164	12-10-66	Chicago A.L., Nashville
31	Norton, Greg	B/R	6-1/190	7-6-72	Birmingham, Nashville, Chicago A.L.
	Saenz, Olmedo	R/R	6-0/185	10-8-70	Nashville
27	Snopek, Chris	R/R	6-1/185	9-20-70	Chicago A.L., Nashville
35	Thomas, Frank	R/R	6-5/257	5-27-68	Chicago A.L.
23	Ventura, Robin	L/R	6-1/198	7-14-67	Chicago A.L.

No.	OUTFIELDERS	B/T	Ht./Wt.	Born	1996 clubs
	Abbott, Jeff	R/L	6-2/190	8-17-72	Nashville
3	Baines, Harold	L/L	6-2/195	3-15-59	Chicago A.L.
	Belle, Albert	R/R	6-2/225	8-25-66	Cleveland
24	Cameron, Mike	R/R	6-2/190	1-8-73	Birmingham, Chicago A.L.
29	Hurst, Jimmy	R/R	6-6/225	3-1-72	Birmingham, Nashville
10	Lewis, Darren	R/R	6-0/189	8-28-67	Chicago A.L.
14	Martinez, Dave	L/L	5-10/175	9-26-64	Chicago A.L.
28	Mouton, Lyle	R/R	6-4/240	5-13-69	Chicago A.L.
8	Phillips, Tony	B/R	5-10/175	4-25-59	Chicago A.L.

BALLPARK INFORMATION

Ballpark (capacity, surface)
Comiskey Park (44,321, grass)

Address
333 W. 35th St.
Chicago, IL 60616

Business phone
312-674-1000

Ticket information
312-674-1000

Ticket prices
$20 (club level)
$20 (lower deck box)
$15 (lower deck reserved)
$13 (upper deck box)
$12 (bleacher reserved)
$8 (upper deck reserved)

Field dimensions (from home plate)
To left field at foul line, 347 feet
To center field, 400 feet
To right field at foul line, 347 feet

First game played
April 18, 1991 (Tigers 16, White Sox 0)

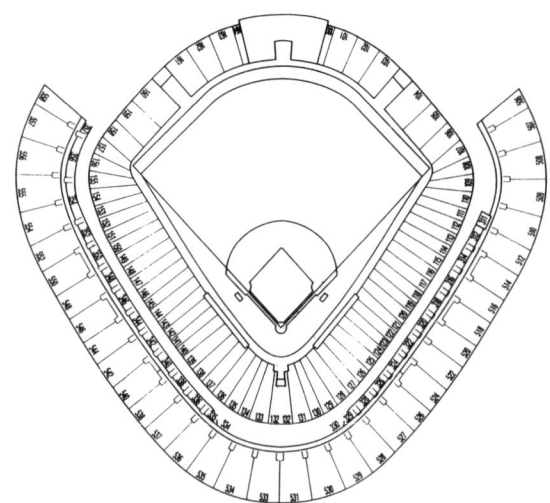

DAY BY DAY

Date	Opp.	Res.	Score	(inn.*)	Hits	Opp. hits	Winning pitcher	Losing pitcher	Save	Record	Pos.	GB
-31	At Sea.	L	2-3	(12)	5	9	Hurtado	Simas		0-1	5th	1/2
-2	At Sea.	L	2-3		5	4	Hitchcock	Alvarez	Charlton	0-2	5th	1 1/2
-3	At Sea.	W	4-2		9	6	Magrane	Wolcott	Hernandez	1-2	3rd	1
-5	At Cal.	L	6-7	(11)	12	14	James	McCaskill		1-3	T3rd	1 1/2
-6	At Cal.	W	8-4		13	7	Fernandez	J. Abbott		2-3	T3rd	1
-7	At Cal.	L	5-6		9	10	Finley	Alvarez	Percival	2-4	T4th	1
-9	Tex.	L	2-3		9	6	Gross	L. Thomas	Henneman	2-5	T4th	1 1/2
-11	Tex.	W	8-5	(11)	13	10	L. Thomas	Henneman		3-5	3rd	1
-12	Oak.	L	2-7		6	15	Reyes	Fernandez		3-6	T4th	1
-13	Oak.	W	6-5	(12)	10	9	Karchner	Wengert		4-6	T2nd	1/2
-14	Oak.	L	5-10		11	13	Groom	Simas		4-7	T4th	1 1/2
-15	At K.C.	W	11-10		14	11	Karchner	Pichardo	Hernandez	5-7	T3rd	1 1/2
-16	At K.C.	L	5-6		10	8	Belcher	Bere	Montgomery	5-8	T4th	2 1/2
-17	At K.C.	W	3-1		8	9	Fernandez	Appier	Hernandez	6-8	4th	1 1/2
-19	At Oak.	W	4-3		7	7	Karchner	Briscoe	Hernandez	7-8	4th	1 1/2
-20	At Oak.	W	8-3		8	9	Tapani	Van Poppel		8-8	3rd	1 1/2
-21	At Oak.	L	5-6		9	9	Corsi	Simas	Mohler	8-9	3rd	2 1/2
-22	At Tex.	W	12-4		16	12	Fernandez	Witt	Karchner	9-9	3rd	2 1/2
-23	At Tex.	W	6-5		11	9	Baldwin	Hill	Hernandez	10-9	3rd	2 1/2
-24	Sea.	W	2-1		7	3	Alvarez	Bosio	Hernandez	11-9	2nd	1 1/2
-25	Sea.	W	4-3		10	7	Tapani	Wolcott	Hernandez	12-9	2nd	1 1/2
-27	Cal.	W	2-1		5	5	Fernandez	J. Abbott	Hernandez	13-9	2nd	1
-28	Cal.	W	10-1		11	9	Baldwin	Finley		14-9	2nd	1
-29	Cal.	W	4-3		8	11	Alvarez	Grimsley	Hernandez	15-9	2nd	1/2
-30	At Cle.	L	3-5		4	12	Martinez	Tapani	Mesa	15-10	2nd	1 1/2
-1	At Cle.	L	5-9		11	12	McDowell	McCaskill	Plunk	15-11	2nd	2 1/2
-2	At N.Y.	L	1-5		5	7	Cone	Fernandez		15-12	2nd	3 1/2
-3	At N.Y.	L	0-2		3	8	M. Rivera	L. Thomas	Wetteland	15-13	2nd	4 1/2
-4	At N.Y.	W	11-5		11	10	Karchner	Nelson		16-13	2nd	3 1/2
-5	At N.Y.	L	1-7		4	9	Pettitte	Tapani		16-14	2nd	4 1/2
-7	Bal.	W	3-2		7	6	Fernandez	Wells	Hernandez	17-14	2nd	3
-8	Bal.	W	11-2		12	6	Baldwin	Erickson		18-14	2nd	3
-9	Bal.	L	4-6		7	10	Mussina	Alvarez	R. Myers	18-15	2nd	3 1/2
-10	N.Y.	W	5-2		5	3	Tapani	Pettitte	Hernandez	19-15	2nd	2 1/2
-11	N.Y.	W	7-5		10	8	McCaskill	Wetteland		20-15	2nd	2 1/2
-12	N.Y.	L	8-9		10	13	Wickman	L. Thomas	Wetteland	20-16	2nd	3 1/2
-13	At Mil.	L	2-6		8	11	Sparks	Baldwin	Boze	20-17	2nd	4
-15	At Mil.	W	20-8		21	12	Alvarez	Bones	Keyser	21-17	2nd	4 1/2
-16	At Mil.	L	2-3		6	11	Lloyd	Tapani	Fetters	21-18	2nd	5 1/2
-17	At Det.	W	11-6	(10)	12	12	Hernandez	R. Lewis		22-18	2nd	5 1/2
-18	At Det.	W	16-4		21	10	McCaskill	Farrell	Simas	23-18	2nd	4 1/2
-19	At Det.	W	14-3		17	7	Alvarez	Gohr		24-18	2nd	4 1/2
21	Tor.	W	2-1		2	5	Tapani	Ware	Hernandez	25-18	2nd	4 1/2
22	Tor.	W	2-1	(11)	9	8	McCaskill	Timlin		26-18	2nd	3 1/2
24	Mil.	W	4-3		10	7	L. Thomas	Sparks	Hernandez	27-18	2nd	4
25	Mil.	W	9-7		11	12	Alvarez	Bones	Hernandez	28-18	2nd	4
26	Mil.	W	12-1		17	7	Tapani	McDonald		29-18	2nd	4
27	At Tor.	L	4-5		9	8	Janzen	Fernandez	Timlin	29-19	2nd	4
28	At Tor.	W	8-5		10	12	Baldwin	Viola	Hernandez	30-19	2nd	3
29	At Tor.	L	5-6		9	11	Hanson	Magrane	Timlin	30-20	2nd	3
30	Det.	W	8-2		10	6	Alvarez	Olivares		31-20	2nd	3
31	Det.	W	9-0		15	8	Tapani	Lira		32-20	2nd	3
2†	Det.	W	4-2		8	4	Baldwin	Thompson	Hernandez	33-20		
2‡	Det.	W	13-5		11	12	McCaskill	Keagle		34-20	2nd	2
4	At Bos.	W	6-4		12	9	Alvarez	Gunderson	Hernandez	35-20	2nd	1
5	At Bos.	W	8-6	(12)	11	17	Keyser	Slocumb		36-20	2nd	1
6	At Bos.	L	4-7		12	12	Eshelman	Magrane	Stanton	36-21	2nd	1
7	At Bal.	W	8-2		14	11	Fernandez	Erickson		37-21	2nd	1
8	At Bal.	W	2-1		11	9	Baldwin	Mercker	Hernandez	38-21	2nd	1
9	At Bal.	W	12-9		18	13	Karchner	Mussina	Hernandez	39-21	T1st	...
10	Bos.	W	8-2		16	6	Tapani	Wakefield		40-21	T1st	...
11	Bos.	L	2-9		7	11	Eshelman	Magrane		40-22	2nd	1
12	Bos.	L	2-3	(12)	11	5	Hudson	Karchner		40-23	2nd	1
14	At Sea.	W	4-1		7	5	Alvarez	Hitchcock	Hernandez	41-23	2nd	1/2
15	At Sea.	L	6-8	(12)	12	16	Carmona	McCaskill		41-24	2nd	1 1/2
16	At Sea.	L	6-7		12	12	Wells	Magrane	Jackson	41-25	2nd	1 1/2
17	At Cal.	L	8-9	(13)	13	18	Hancock	McCaskill		41-26	2nd	2
18	At Cal.	L	4-5		9	14	Finley	Simas	Percival	41-27	2nd	3
19	At Cal.	L	2-14		6	12	McElroy	Alvarez		41-28	2nd	4
20	Sea.	L	5-8		12	15	Hitchcock	Tapani	Charlton	41-29	2nd	5
21	Sea.	L	2-12		7	11	Wagner	Magrane		41-30	2nd	4 1/2

Date	Opp.	Res.	Score	(inn.*)	Hits	Opp. hits	Winning pitcher	Losing pitcher	Save	Record	Pos.	G
6-22	Sea.	L	2-4		6	11	Wells	Fernandez	Charlton	41-31	2nd	4
6-23	Sea.	W	7-6	(10)	12	9	McCaskill	Guetterman		42-31	2nd	3
6-24†	Cal.	W	4-2		6	10	Alvarez	James	Hernandez	43-31		
6-24‡	Cal.	L	4-6		8	9	Hancock	Sirotka	Percival	43-32	2nd	3
6-25	Cal.	W	3-2		9	5	Tapani	Langston	Hernandez	44-32	2nd	3
6-27	Cle.	W	15-10		17	16	Fernandez	Swindell		45-32	2nd	2
6-28	Cle.	W	4-2		6	6	Baldwin	Tavarez	Hernandez	46-32	2nd	1
6-29	Cle.	L	2-3	(10)	8	7	Shuey	Karchner		46-33	2nd	2
6-30	Cle.	L	2-4		7	10	Hershiser	Tapani	Mesa	46-34	2nd	3
7-1	Min.	L	7-10		13	15	Aguilera	Sirotka		46-35	2nd	3
7-2	Min.	W	7-4		12	8	Fernandez	Aldred	Hernandez	47-35	2nd	3
7-3	Min.	L	5-6		9	14	Radke	Andujar	Stevens	47-36	2nd	4
7-4	At Cle.	W	6-5	(10)	12	13	Karchner	Mesa	Hernandez	48-36	2nd	3
7-5	At Cle.	W	7-0		14	6	Alvarez	Hershiser		49-36	2nd	2
7-6	At Cle.	W	3-2		7	7	Karchner	Shuey	Hernandez	50-36	2nd	1
7-7	At Cle.	L	1-6		6	12	Ogea	Fernandez	Assenmacher	50-37	2nd	2
7-11	At K.C.	L	2-3		8	10	Haney	Alvarez		50-38	2nd	3
7-12	At K.C.	W	7-6		11	9	Tapani	Belcher	Hernandez	51-38	2nd	3
7-13	At K.C.	W	3-1		8	4	Fernandez	Rosado		52-38	2nd	3
7-14	At K.C.	W	3-2		8	3	Baldwin	Linton	Hernandez	53-38	2nd	2
7-15	At Min.	L	5-16		7	16	Aldred	McCaskill		53-39	2nd	2
7-16	At Min.	W	11-2		11	8	Alvarez	Radke		54-39	2nd	2
7-17	At Min.	L	3-4		4	10	Trombley	Simas		54-40	2nd	2
7-18	K.C.	L	1-7		3	11	Appier	Fernandez	Pichardo	54-41	2nd	3
7-19	K.C.	L	4-7	(10)	9	13	Montgomery	Hernandez		54-42	2nd	3
7-20	K.C.	L	5-7		10	11	Linton	Keyser	Montgomery	54-43	2nd	4
7-21	K.C.	W	6-3		8	8	Alvarez	Haney	Hernandez	55-43	2nd	4
7-22	Oak.	L	5-6		8	12	Taylor	Karchner		55-44	2nd	5
7-23	Oak.	L	4-8		8	10	Wengert	Fernandez	Corsi	55-45	2nd	5
7-24	Oak.	L	5-6		13	7	Corsi	Simas	Taylor	55-46	2nd	6
7-25	Tex.	L	3-4	(12)	13	10	Russell	Keyser	Henneman	55-47	2nd	7
7-26	Tex.	W	6-2		8	5	Alvarez	Oliver		56-47	2nd	7
7-27	Tex.	L	4-6	(10)	7	8	Heredia	Simas	Vosberg	56-48	2nd	7
7-28	Tex.	W	5-1		9	5	Fernandez	Pavlik		57-48	2nd	7
7-30	At Oak.	W	2-1		9	3	Baldwin	Telgheder	Hernandez	58-48	2nd	6
7-31	At Oak.	L	4-5		8	8	Witasick	Karchner	Taylor	58-49	2nd	7
8-1	At Oak.	W	8-3		8	9	Tapani	Wasdin	Hernandez	59-49	2nd	6
8-2	At Tex.	W	9-0		14	3	Fernandez	Pavlik		60-49	2nd	6
8-3	At Tex.	W	11-9		16	13	Hernandez	Russell		61-49	2nd	5
8-4	At Tex.	L	5-9		10	12	Witt	Baldwin		61-50	2nd	6
8-5	At Tex.	W	15-5		19	10	Alvarez	Oliver		62-50	2nd	5
8-6	At N.Y.	L	2-9		7	13	Rogers	Tapani		62-51	2nd	6
8-7	At N.Y.	W	8-4	(10)	10	7	Hernandez	Nelson		63-51	2nd	6
8-8	At N.Y.	L	4-8		8	11	Wickman	Andujar	M. Rivera	63-52	2nd	7
8-9	Bal.	W	4-3	(10)	9	6	Simas	R. Myers		64-52	2nd	7
8-10	Bal.	L	4-13		7	14	Mussina	Alvarez	McDowell	64-53	2nd	7
8-11	Bal.	W	8-5		19	8	Tapani	Mills	Hernandez	65-53	2nd	6
8-12	N.Y.	W	3-2	(10)	6	5	Hernandez	Wetteland		66-53	2nd	6
8-13	N.Y.	W	8-4		11	9	Bertotti	Weathers		67-53	2nd	5
8-14	N.Y.	L	1-3		8	9	Pettitte	Baldwin	M. Rivera	67-54	2nd	5
8-16†	At Mil.	L	7-9		11	11	Miranda	Levine	Villone	67-55		
8-16‡	At Mil.	L	2-3		8	5	Vanegmond	Tapani	Fetters	67-56	2nd	6
8-17	At Mil.	W	6-2		12	10	Fernandez	McDonald	Hernandez	68-56	2nd	6
8-18	At Mil.	L	7-8		9	11	Miranda	Darwin	Fetters	68-57	2nd	7
8-19	At Det.	W	12-7		13	10	Simas	Lima		69-57	2nd	6
8-20	At Det.	L	11-16		11	15	R. Lewis	Tapani		69-58	2nd	7
8-21	At Det.	L	4-7		8	11	Lima	Simas	Olson	69-59	2nd	7
8-22	Tor.	L	0-1	(7)	3	4	Hanson	Fernandez		69-60	2nd	8
8-23	Tor.	L	2-4		6	10	Hentgen	Ruffcorn		69-61	2nd	8
8-24	Tor.	L	2-9		11	12	Williams	Baldwin		69-62	2nd	8
8-25	Tor.	W	10-9	(10)	16	16	Hernandez	Timlin		70-62	2nd	8
8-26	Mil.	L	2-3		9	9	Eldred	Alvarez	Jones	70-63	2nd	9
8-27	Mil.	L	2-4		7	11	Vanegmond	Fernandez	Fetters	70-64	2nd	10
8-28	Mil.	W	2-0		7	6	Baldwin	McDonald	Hernandez	71-64	2nd	10
8-30	At Tor.	W	11-2		18	7	Tapani	Williams		72-64	2nd	9
8-31	At Tor.	W	5-1		12	7	Alvarez	Flener		73-64	2nd	8
9-1	At Tor.	W	4-2	(11)	5	6	Hernandez	Spoljaric		74-64	2nd	8
9-2	Det.	L	6-8		11	11	Myers	Hernandez	Lima	74-65	2nd	8
9-3	Det.	W	6-4		12	9	Bertotti	Olivares	Hernandez	75-65	2nd	7
9-4	Det.	W	11-6		13	8	Castillo	Miller		76-65	2nd	3
9-6	Bos.	L	3-10		9	15	Wakefield	Alvarez		76-66	2nd	3
9-7	Bos.	W	4-3		7	9	Fernandez	Clemens	Hernandez	77-66	2nd	7
9-8	Bos.	W	7-4		10	10	Baldwin	Sele	Hernandez	78-66	2nd	6
9-10	At Bal.	L	1-5		8	8	Wells	Tapani		78-67	2nd	7
9-11	At Bal.	L	6-7	(10)	10	11	Mills	Hernandez		78-68	2nd	

ate	Opp.	Res.	Score	(inn.*)	Hits	Opp. hits	Winning pitcher	Losing pitcher	Save	Record	Pos.	GB
12	At Bal.	W	11-3		16	3	Fernandez	Mussina		79-68	2nd	9
13	At Bos.	L	5-9		9	14	Clemens	Baldwin	Slocumb	79-69	2nd	9 1/2
14	At Bos.	W	13-5		15	10	Castillo	Gordon	Simas	80-69	2nd	10
15	At Bos.	L	8-9		9	11	Slocumb	Hernandez		80-70	2nd	10
16	Cle.	L	3-4		9	9	McDowell	Alvarez		80-71	2nd	11
17	Cle.	L	4-9		9	15	Anderson	Fernandez	Plunk	80-72	2nd	12
18	Cle.	L	3-4		9	7	Lopez	Baldwin	Mesa	80-73	2nd	13
19	Min.	W	8-3		9	9	Sirotka	Rodriguez	Castillo	81-73	2nd	13
20	Min.	W	7-3		8	11	Tapani	Robertson		82-73	2nd	12
21	Min.	L	3-4		8	11	Radke	Alvarez	Trombley	82-74	2nd	13
22	Min.	W	5-1		7	5	Fernandez	Aldred		83-74	2nd	13
24	K.C.	W	3-2		8	6	Castillo	Belcher		84-74	2nd	13 1/2
25	K.C.	L	2-8		9	12	Appier	Tapani		84-75	2nd	14 1/2
27	At Min.	W	4-2		9	10	Fernandez	Radke	Hernandez	85-75	2nd	13 1/2
28	At Min.	L	6-7		13	15	Trombley	Castillo		85-76	2nd	14 1/2
29	At Min.	L	4-5	(10)	8	6	Guardado	Hernandez		85-77	2nd	14 1/2

onthly records: March (0-1), April (15-9), May (17-10), June (14-14), July (12-15), August (15-15), September (12-13).
innings, if other than nine. †First game of doubleheader. ‡Second game of doubleheader.

HIGHLIGHTS

gh point: Harold Baines hit two homers lift the White Sox to a 3-2 victory over e Indians on July 6. The victory was the ox's third in a row in Cleveland and oved them one game behind the Indians the A.L. Central. But that was as close as e Sox would get to the Indians for the st of the season.

ow point: For the first time in his career, ank Thomas was placed on the disabled t. Thomas went down with a stress frac-re in his left foot and missed 18 games, ll them White Sox losses. The injury also rced Thomas to miss the All-Star Game.

rning point: In a supposed easy stretch at started with Milwaukee on August 16 d ended with Boston on September 8, e White Sox flopped, going 11-12 and riously damaging their wild-card hopes.

ost valuable player: First baseman Frank omas. Even though he missed 18 games th a stress fracture in his left foot, omas carried the offense again, hitting 49 with 40 home runs and 134 RBIs.

ost valuable pitcher: Closer Roberto rnandez. One year after going 3-7 with a 92 ERA and blowing 10 save opportuni-s, Hernandez re-established himself as e of the top closers in the game. He tied s career-high with 38 saves, the third-ost in the A.L. Hernandez also had the st ERA (1.91) of any reliever in the league.

ost improved player: Third baseman bin Ventura. He is one of the best third semen in either league, but his success 1996 was quite a surprise. Ventura estab-hed career-highs in home runs (34), Is (105), games (158), runs (96), total ses (305), extra-base hits (67) and bles (two). He also won his fourth Gold ove Award.

ost pleasant surprise: Righthanded arter James Baldwin. He lived up to his an't-miss" tag last season, going 11-6 th a 4.42 ERA. Baldwin, who throws a teran-like curveball, finished second to nkees shortstop Derek Jeter in A.L. okie of the Year voting.

ggest disappointments: Starter Jason re and center fielder Darren Lewis. Bere as shelled at the start of the season, then sted his ailing right elbow for two

months before trying another comeback. It failed. He pitched against the Tigers on September 3 and lasted three innings. Bere has elbow surgery 10 days later and may not be ready to pitch again until July. Lewis was great defensively, but his .228 batting average kept him on the bench for most of the stretch run.

Key injuries: Frank Thomas suffered a stress fracture in his left foot at Cleveland on July 4 and wound up missing 18 games. The White Sox insisted they weren't a one-man team, but they badly missed their best hitter. Backup catcher Chad Kreuter was lost for the season on July 19 after shattering his left shoulder in a colli-sion at the plate with the Royals' Johnny Damon. For the fifth time, starting catcher Ron Karkovice had surgery on his right knee, which ended his season in September.

Notable: The White Sox set team records in three offensive categories: homers (195), slugging percentage (.447) and at-bats (5,644). . . . For the first time in club history, the Sox had three players with 100 or more RBIs: Frank Thomas (134), Robin Ventura (105) and Danny Tartabull (101).

—SCOT GREGOR

RECORDS

1996 regular-season record: 85-77 (2nd in A.L. Central); 44-37 at home; 41-40 on road; 37-25 vs. East; 24-28 vs. Central; 24-24 vs. West; 24-21 vs. left-handed starters; 61-56 vs. righthanded starters; 77-67 on grass; 8-10 on turf; 29-21 in daytime; 56-52 at night; 25-34 in one-run games; 12-11 in extra-inning games; 1-1-1 in doubleheaders.
Team record past five years: 400-343 (.538, ranks 3rd in league in that span).

TEAM LEADERS

Batting average: Frank Thomas (.349).
At-bats: Robin Ventura (586).
Runs: Tony Phillips (119).
Hits: Frank Thomas (184).
Total bases: Frank Thomas (330).
Doubles: Ray Durham (33).
Triples: Ozzie Guillen, Dave Martinez (8).
Home runs: Frank Thomas (40).
Runs batted in: Frank Thomas (134).

Stolen bases: Ray Durham (30).
Slugging percentage: Frank Thomas (.626).
On-base percentage: Frank Thomas (.459).
Wins: Alex Fernandez (16).
Earned-run average: Alex Fernandez (3.45).
Complete games: Alex Fernandez (6).
Shutouts: Alex Fernandez (1).
Saves: Roberto Hernandez (38).
Innings pitched: Alex Fernandez (258.0).
Strikeouts: Alex Fernandez (200).

GAMES BY POSITION

Catcher: Ron Karkovice 111, Chad Kreuter 38, Pat Borders 30, Don Slaught 12, Robert Machado 4.
First base: Frank Thomas 139, Dave Martinez 23, Robin Ventura 14, Chad Kreuter 2, Mike Robertson 2, Tony Phillips 1.
Second base: Ray Durham 150, Norberto Martin 10, Jose Munoz 7, Domingo Cedeno 2, Tony Phillips 2.
Third base: Robin Ventura 150, Chris Snopek 27, Norberto Martin 3, Greg Norton 2, Jose Munoz 1.
Shortstop: Ozzie Guillen 146, Norberto Martin 24, Chris Snopek 12, Greg Norton 6, Domingo Cedeno 2, Jose Munoz 2.
Outfield: Tony Phillips 146, Darren Lewis 138, Danny Tartabull 122, Dave Martinez 121, Lyle Mouton 47, Mike Cameron 8, Ozzie Guillen 2, Jose Munoz 1.
Designated hitter: Harold Baines 141, Lyle Mouton 28, Norberto Martin 19, Danny Tartabull 10, Ray Durham 3, Chris Snopek 3, Jose Munoz 2, Pat Borders 1, Mike Cameron 1, Domingo Cedeno 1, Chad Kreuter 1, Greg Norton 1, Mike Robertson 1, Don Slaught 1.

TOP DRAFT CHOICES

1. **Bobby Seay**, LHP, Sarasota (Fla.) H.S.
2. **Josh Paul**, OF, Vanderbilt University.
3. **Jimmy Terrell**, SS, Tri-City Christian H.S., Blue Springs, Mo.
4. **Mark Roberts**, RHP, U. of South Florida.
5. **Joe Crede**, 3B, Fatima H.S., Westphalia, Mo.
6. **Dan Olson**, OF, Indiana State University.
7. **Kevin Knorst**, RHP, Lake Howell H.S., Winter Park, Fla.
8. **Marcus Jones**, RHP, Long Beach State U.
9. **Edwin Cochran**, 2B, Arroyo, P.R.
10. **Gene Forti**, LHP, Del Valle H.S., El Paso,

1997 SEASON Chicago White Sox

CLEVELAND INDIANS
AMERICAN LEAGUE CENTRAL DIVISION

1997 INDIANS SCHEDULE

Home games shaded.
* — All-Star Game at Jacobs Field (Cleveland)
D — Day game (any game starting before 5 p.m.)

APRIL

SUN	MON	TUE	WED	THU	FRI	SAT
		1	2 OAK	3 D OAK	4 ANA	5 ANA
6 ANA	7 SEA	8 SEA	9 D SEA	10	11 D ANA	12 D ANA
13 ANA	14 SEA	15 SEA	16 BOS	17 BOS	18 MIL	19 MIL
20 MIL	21	22 BOS	23 BOS	24 MIL	25 MIL	26 MIL
27 MIL	28	29 OAK	30 OAK			

MAY

SUN	MON	TUE	WED	THU	FRI	SAT
				1 OAK	2 DET	3 D DET
4 D DET	5 TEX	6 TEX	7 TOR	8 TOR	9 DET	10 D DET
11 D DET	12 TEX	13 TEX	14 TEX	15	16 TOR	17 D TOR
18 D TOR	19	20 KC	21 KC	22 D KC	23 BAL	24 D BAL
25 D BAL	26 D CWS	27 CWS	28 KC	29 KC	30 BAL	31 D BAL

JUNE

SUN	MON	TUE	WED	THU	FRI	SAT
1 BAL	2 BAL	3 CWS	4 CWS	5 CWS	6 BOS	7 BOS
8 BOS	9	10 MIL	11 MIL	12 MIL	13 STL	14 D STL
15 STL	16 CIN	17 CIN	18 CIN	19	20 NYY	21 NYY
22 NYY	23 MIN	24 MIN	25 MIN	26	27 NYY	28 D NYY
29 NYY	30 HOU					

JULY

SUN	MON	TUE	WED	THU	FRI	SAT
		1 HOU	2 HOU	3	4 KC	5 D KC
6 D KC	7	8	9	10 MIN	11 MIN	12 MIN
13 MIN	14 NYY	15 D NYY	16 NYY	17 MIL	18 BOS	19 D BOS
20 D BOS	21 SEA	22 SEA	23 SEA	24 SEA	25 OAK	26 D OAK
27 D OAK	28 ANA	29 ANA	30 ANA	31		

AUGUST

SUN	MON	TUE	WED	THU	FRI	SAT
					1 TEX	2 TEX
3 TEX	4 DET	5 DET	6 D TOR	7 TOR	8 TEX	9 D TEX
10 D TEX	11	12 DET	13 DET	14 DET	15 TOR	16 D TOR
17 D TOR	18 TOR	19 SEA	20 SEA	21 SEA	22 OAK	23 OAK
24 OAK	25	26 ANA	27 ANA	28	29 CUB	30 D CUB
31 D CUB						

SEPTEMBER

SUN	MON	TUE	WED	THU	FRI	SAT
	1 D PIT	2 PIT	3 PIT	4	5 CWS	6 CWS
7 CWS	8 BAL	9 BAL	10	11 CWS	12 CWS	13 CWS
14 CWS	15 BAL	16 BAL	17 MIN	18 MIN	19 KC	20 KC
21 D KC	22 KC	23 NYY	24 NYY	25 NYY	26 MIN	27 D MIN
28 D MIN						

1997 SEASON
CLUB DIRECTORY

Board of directors
Richard E. Jacobs
Martin J. Cleary
Gary L. Bryenton

Chairman of the board and CEO
Richard E. Jacobs

Executive vice president, general manager
John Hart

Executive vice president, business
Dennis Lehman

V.p., marketing and communications
Jeff Overton

Vice president
Martin J. Cleary

Vice president, public relations
Bob DiBiasio

Vice president, finance
Ken Stefanov

Dir. of baseball operations/asst. g.m.
Dan O'Dowd

Director, scouting
Lee MacPhail

Director, team travel
Mike Seghi

Director, minor league operations
Mark Shapiro

Administrator, player personnel
Wendy Hoppel

Administrator, scouting
Brad Grant

Manager, media relations
Bart Swain

Assistant director, media relations
Susie Gharrity

Director, community relations
Allen Davis

Manager, community relations
Melissa Zapanta

Manager, promotions
Chris Previte

Director, broadcasting
To be announced

Manager, advertising/publications
Kim Jarrell

Controller
Ron McQuate

Director, ticket services
John Schulze

Director, ticket sales
Scott Sterneckert

Coordinator, season/group sales
Diane Stack

Director, ballpark operations
Jim Folk

Director, merchandising/licensing
Jayne Churchmack

Home clubhouse mgr./equipment mgr.
Ted Walsh

Equipment manager
Jeff Sipos

Visiting clubhouse manager
Cy Buynak

Medical director
William T. Wilder, M.D.

Head trainer
Paul Spicuzza

Assistant trainer
Jim Warfield

Strength and conditioning coach
Fernando Montes

Team physicians
Ronald Golovan M.D.
Godofredo Domingo, M.D.
K.V. Gopal, M.D.
Zenos Vangelos, M.D.

Major league/spec. assignment scouts
Dan Carnevale, Tom Giordano, Ted
Simmons, Bill Werle

Full-time scouts
Luis Aponte, Steve Avila, Brad
Cameron, Tom Couston, Rene Gay,
Mark Germann, Winston Llenas,
Guy Mader, Bob Mayer, Kasey
McKeon, Jim Richardson, Max
Semler, Jim Stevenson, Gene
Thompson, Gary Tuck, Craig
Wallenbrock, Mark Weidemaier

MINOR LEAGUE AFFILIATES

Class	Team	League	Manager
AAA	Buffalo	American Association	Brian Graham
AA	Akron	Eastern	Jeff Datz
A	Kinston	Carolina	Joel Skinner
A	Columbus	South Atlantic	Jack Mull
A	Watertown	New York-Pennsylvania	Ted Kubiak
Rookie	Burlington	Appalachian	Harry Spilman

BROADCAST INFORMATION

Radio: WKNR-AM (1220).
TV: WUAB-TV (Channel 43).
Cable TV: SportsChannel.

SPRING TRAINING

Ballpark (city): Chain O'Lakes (Winter
Haven, Fla.).
Ticket information: 813-293-3900.

SPRING TRAINING ROSTER

Manager—Mike Hargrove (21).
Coaches—Johnny Goryl, Luis Isaac (6), Charlie Manuel (42), Dave Nelson (1), Jeff Newman (16), Mark Wiley (28), Dan Williams (43).

No.	PITCHERS	B/T	Ht./Wt.	Born	1996 clubs
34	Anderson, Brian	B/L	6-1/190	4-26-72	Buffalo, Cleveland
45	Assenmacher, Paul	L/L	6-3/210	12-10-60	Cleveland
	Clark, Terry	R/R	6-2/195	10-10-60	Kansas City, Omaha, Houston
40	Colon, Bartolo	R/R	6-0/185	5-24-75	Canton/Akron, Buffalo
	De La Rosa, Maximo	R/R	5-11/170	7-12-71	Canton/Akron
	Driskill, Travis	R/R	6-0/185	8-1-71	Canton/Akron
56	Embree, Alan	L/L	6-2/190	1-23-70	Cleveland, Buffalo
	Gordon, Mike	L/R	6-3/210	11-30-72	Dunedin
35	Graves, Danny	R/R	5-11/200	8-7-73	Buffalo, Cleveland
55	Hershiser, Orel	R/R	6-3/195	9-16-58	Cleveland
48	Jackson, Mike	R/R	6-2/225	12-22-64	Seattle
44	Kline, Steve	B/L	6-2/200	8-22-72	Canton/Akron
59	Lopez, Albie	R/R	6-2/235	8-18-71	Buffalo, Cleveland
	Matthews, Mike	L/L	6-2/175	10-24-73	Canton/Akron
29	McDowell, Jack	R/R	6-5/190	1-16-66	Cleveland
49	Mesa, Jose	R/R	6-3/230	5-22-66	Cleveland
41	Nagy, Charles	L/R	6-3/200	5-5-67	Cleveland
37	Ogea, Chad	L/R	6-2/220	11-9-70	Cleveland, Buffalo
38	Plunk, Eric	R/R	6-6/220	9-3-63	Cleveland
53	Shuey, Paul	R/R	6-3/215	9-16-70	Buffalo, Cleveland
	Warrecker, Teddy	L/R	6-6/215	10-1-72	Kinston
63	Whitten, Casey	L/L	6-0/175	5-23-72	Canton/Akron, Buffalo
	Wright, Jaret	R/R	6-2/220	12-29-75	Kinston

No.	CATCHERS	B/T	Ht./Wt.	Born	1996 clubs
15	Alomar, Sandy	R/R	6-5/220	6-18-66	Cleveland
10	Borders, Pat	R/R	6-2/200	5-14-63	St. Louis, California, Chicago A.L.
2	Diaz, Einar	R/R	5-10/165	12-28-72	Canton/Akron, Cleveland

No.	INFIELDERS	B/T	Ht./Wt.	Born	1996 clubs
25	Busch, Mike	R/R	6-5/220	7-7-68	Los Angeles, Albuquerque
2	Fernandez, Tony	B/R	6-2/175	6-30-62	New York A.L.
23	Franco, Julio	R/R	6-1/200	8-23-61	Cleveland
	Jackson, Damian	R/R	5-10/160	8-16-73	Buffalo, Cleveland
36	Perry, Herbert	R/R	6-2/215	9-15-69	Buffalo, Cleveland
20	Seitzer, Kevin	R/R	5-11/190	3-26-62	Milwaukee, Cleveland
	Sexson, Richie	R/R	6-6/205	12-29-74	Canton/Akron
25	Thome, Jim	L/R	6-4/225	8-27-70	Cleveland
13	Vizquel, Omar	B/R	5-9/170	4-24-67	Cleveland
9	Williams, Matt	R/R	6-2/216	11-28-65	San Francisco
66	Wilson, Enrique	B/R	5-11/160	7-27-75	Canton/Akron, Buffalo

No.	OUTFIELDERS	B/T	Ht./Wt.	Born	1996 clubs
	Aven, Bruce	R/R	5-9/180	3-4-72	Canton/Akron, Buffalo
9	Curtis, Chad	R/R	5-10/185	11-6-68	Detroit, Los Angeles
22	Giles, Brian	L/L	5-11/200	1-21-71	Buffalo, Cleveland
	Hubbard, Trenidad	R/R	5-8/183	5-11-66	Colorado, Colorado Springs, San Francisco
7	Lofton, Kenny	L/L	6-0/190	5-31-67	Cleveland
	Mitchell, Kevin	R/R	5-11/244	1-13-62	Boston, Pawtucket, Cincinnati
	Ramirez, Alex	R/R	5-11/180	10-3-74	Canton/Akron
24	Ramirez, Manny	R/R	6-0/200	5-30-72	Cleveland

BALLPARK INFORMATION

Ballpark (capacity, surface)
Jacobs Field (42,865, grass)

Address
2401 Ontario St.
Cleveland, OH 44115

Business phone
216-420-4200

Ticket information
216-241-8888

Ticket prices
$21 (field box)
$18 (lower box & view box)
$15 (lower reserved, upper box
& mezzanine seating)
$10 (upper reserved, bleachers)
$6 (reserved g.a.)
$6 (Standing room only)

Field dimensions (from home plate)
To left field at foul line, 325 feet
To center field, 405 feet
To right field at foul line, 325 feet

First game played
April 4, 1994
(Indians 4, Mariners 3, 11 innings)

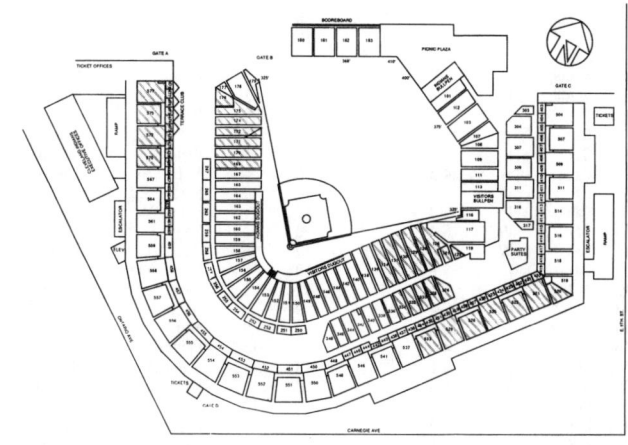

DAY BY DAY

Date	Opp.	Res.	Score	(inn.*)	Hits	Opp. hits	Winning pitcher	Losing pitcher	Save	Record	Pos.	GB
4-2	N.Y.	L	1-7		4	10	Cone	Martinez		0-1	T3rd	1
4-3	N.Y.	L	1-5		9	8	Pettitte	McDowell	Nelson	0-2	T4th	1
4-5	Tor.	L	1-7		6	10	Guzman	Hershiser		0-3	5th	2
4-6	Tor.	W	5-3		7	7	Nagy	Hanson	Mesa	1-3	5th	1
4-7	Tor.	W	8-3		10	8	Martinez	Quantrill		2-3	T2nd	1
4-10	At Bal.	L	2-3	(10)	6	7	Orosco	Tavarez		2-4	3rd	1
4-11	At Bal.	L	4-14		7	13	Erickson	Hershiser	Rhodes	2-5	4th	1
4-12	At Bos.	W	3-1		9	5	Nagy	Sele	Mesa	3-5	T2nd	
4-13	At Bos.	W	14-2		14	9	Martinez	Moyer		4-5	1st	+
4-14	At Bos.	W	7-6	(11)	9	13	Tavarez	Stanton	Mesa	5-5	1st	+
4-15	At Bos.	W	8-0		11	9	McDowell	Wakefield		6-5	1st	+1
4-16	At Min.	W	7-2		13	8	Hershiser	Radke		7-5	1st	+1
4-17	At Min.	L	8-9		15	8	Hansell	Shuey	Stevens	7-6	1st	+
4-19	Bos.	W	9-4		13	9	Martinez	Gordon		8-6	T1st	...
4-20	Bos.	W	2-1		5	6	McDowell	Wakefield	Mesa	9-6	T1st	...
4-21	Bos.	W	11-7		11	14	Ogea	Pennington		10-6	T1st	...
4-22	Bal.	W	6-3		12	10	Nagy	Erickson	Mesa	11-6	1st	+1
4-23	Bal.	W	9-8		10	13	Ogea	Mussina	Mesa	12-6	1st	+2
4-24	At N.Y.	L	8-10		11	13	Kamieniecki	Martinez		12-7	1st	+1
4-25	At N.Y.	W	4-3		12	9	Poole	Pettitte	Mesa	13-7	1st	+1
4-26	At Tor.	W	6-3		10	8	Hershiser	Hanson	Mesa	14-7	1st	+2
4-27	At Tor.	L	6-11		9	16	Castillo	Nagy		14-8	1st	+1
4-28	At Tor.	W	17-3		20	10	Lopez	Viola		15-8	1st	+1
4-30	Chi.	W	5-3		12	4	Martinez	Tapani	Mesa	16-8	1st	+1
5-1	Chi.	W	9-5		12	11	McDowell	McCaskill	Plunk	17-8	1st	+2
5-2	At Sea.	W	6-4		11	7	Hershiser	Wolcott	Mesa	18-8	1st	+3
5-3	At Sea.	W	5-2		10	7	Nagy	Hitchcock	Mesa	19-8	1st	+4
5-4	At Sea.	L	1-5		8	8	Menhart	Lopez		19-9	1st	+3
5-5	At Sea.	W	2-0		9	6	Martinez	Bosio	Mesa	20-9	1st	+4
5-6	At Oak.	L	3-5		9	11	Taylor	Assenmacher	Mohler	20-10	1st	+4
5-7	At Oak.	L	4-8		7	16	Johns	Hershiser		20-11	1st	+3
5-8	At Oak.	W	7-3		9	10	Nagy	Reyes		21-11	1st	+3
5-10	At Cal.	L	8-13		11	12	Boskie	Lopez		21-12	1st	+2
5-11	At Cal.	W	6-5		14	7	McDowell	Sanderson	Mesa	22-12	1st	+2
5-12	At Cal.	W	4-1		9	6	Poole	Percival	Mesa	23-12	1st	+3
5-14	Det.	W	5-1		7	7	Nagy	Gohr		24-12	1st	+4
5-15	Det.	W	5-2		11	6	Martinez	Lima	Mesa	25-12	1st	+4
5-16	Det.	W	8-3		5	7	McDowell	B. Williams	Mesa	26-12	1st	+5
5-17	Tex.	W	12-10		17	14	Embree	Heredia	Mesa	27-12	1st	+5
5-18	Tex.	L	3-6		7	10	Oliver	Anderson	Henneman	27-13	1st	+4
5-19	Tex.	W	8-5		11	9	Nagy	Witt	Mesa	28-13	1st	+4
5-21	Mil.	W	6-5		9	13	Tavarez	Boze		29-13	1st	+4
5-22	Mil.	L	8-10		12	13	Karl	McDowell	Fetters	29-14	1st	+3
5-23	Mil.	W	5-1		10	8	Hershiser	Miranda		30-14	1st	+4
5-24	At Det.	W	6-3		11	6	Plunk	Veres	Mesa	31-14	1st	+4
5-25	At Det.	W	7-6		11	10	Nagy	R. Lewis	Mesa	32-14	1st	+4
5-26	At Det.	W	5-0		3	8	Martinez	B. Williams		33-14	1st	+4
5-27	At Tex.	L	2-3		6	8	Pavlik	McDowell		33-15	1st	+4
5-28	At Tex.	L	3-11		9	13	Oliver	Hershiser		33-16	1st	+3
5-29	At Tex.	L	4-5		9	10	Cook	Tavarez	Henneman	33-17	1st	+3
5-30	At Mil.	W	2-0		6	7	Nagy	Bones	Mesa	34-17	1st	+3
5-31	At Mil.	W	10-4		18	10	Martinez	McDonald		35-17	1st	+3
6-1	At Mil.	L	1-2		7	6	Garcia	McDowell	Fetters	35-18	1st	+2
6-2	At Mil.	W	11-6		15	12	Poole	Karl		36-18	1st	+2
6-4	Sea.	L	7-10		12	12	Carmona	Mesa	Charlton	36-19	1st	+1
6-5	Sea.	W	13-5		13	11	Plunk	Milacki		37-19	1st	+1
6-6	Sea.	L	2-5		6	12	Wells	Martinez	Charlton	37-20	1st	+1
6-7	Cal.	W	4-3		6	4	McDowell	Boskie	Mesa	38-20	1st	+1
6-8	Cal.	W	5-0		10	6	Hershiser	Finley		39-20	1st	+1
6-9	Cal.	L	6-8	(13)	13	15	Hancock	Tavarez		39-21	T1st	...
6-10	Oak.	W	5-4		9	9	Nagy	Johns	Mesa	40-21	T1st	...
6-11	Oak.	W	6-5	(13)	10	15	Ogea	Reyes		41-21	1st	+1
6-12	Oak.	L	6-9		10	9	Montgomery	McDowell	Mohler	41-22	1st	+1
6-13	At N.Y.	W	6-2		12	5	Hershiser	Rogers	Shuey	42-22	1st	+1
6-14	At N.Y.	L	3-4		9	6	Gooden	Ogea	Wetteland	42-23	1st	+
6-15	At N.Y.	W	10-3		14	9	Nagy	Boehringer		43-23	1st	+1
6-16	At N.Y.	L	4-5		11	13	Pettitte	Martinez	Wetteland	43-24	1st	+1
6-18	Bos.	W	9-7		13	14	Swindell	Sele	Mesa	44-24	1st	+3
6-19	Bos.	W	11-4		13	14	Hershiser	Gordon		45-24	1st	+4
6-20	Bos.	W	5-4		10	10	Shuey	Stanton		46-24	1st	+5
6-21†	N.Y.	L	7-8	(10)	14	12	Nelson	Mesa	Wetteland	46-25		
6-21‡	N.Y.	L	3-9		7	17	Mendoza	Tavarez		46-26	1st	+4

Cleveland Indians 1997 SEASON

te	Opp.	Res.	Score	(inn.*)	Hits	Opp. hits	Winning pitcher	Losing pitcher	Save	Record	Pos.	GB
2	N.Y.	L	9-11		12	15	Brewer	Martinez	Wetteland	46-27	1st	+4 1/2
3	N.Y.	L	5-6		9	7	Gooden	McDowell	Wetteland	46-28	1st	+3 1/2
5	At Bos.	W	4-0		9	7	Hershiser	Gordon		47-28	1st	+3 1/2
6	At Bos.	L	4-6	(15)	10	15	Garces	Embree		47-29	1st	+3
7	At Chi.	L	10-15		16	17	Fernandez	Swindell		47-30	1st	+2
8	At Chi.	L	2-4		6	6	Baldwin	Tavarez	Hernandez	47-31	1st	+1
9	At Chi.	W	3-2	(10)	7	8	Shuey	Karchner		48-31	1st	+2
0	At Chi.	W	4-2		10	7	Hershiser	Tapani	Mesa	49-31	1st	+3
	K.C.	L	2-4		7	10	Haney	Nagy		49-32	1st	+3
	K.C.	W	3-2		8	10	Poole	Belcher		50-32	1st	+3
	K.C.	W	6-4		9	10	Tavarez	Magnante	Shuey	51-32	1st	+4
	Chi.	L	5-6	(10)	13	12	Karchner	Mesa	Hernandez	51-33	1st	+3
	Chi.	L	0-7		6	14	Alvarez	Hershiser		51-34	1st	+2
	Chi.	L	2-3		7	7	Karchner	Shuey	Hernandez	51-35	1st	+1
	Chi.	W	6-1		12	6	Ogea	Fernandez	Assenmacher	52-35	1st	+2
1	At Min.	W	11-7		13	13	McDowell	Radke		53-35	1st	+3
2	At Min.	W	7-5		10	9	Mesa	Stevens	Shuey	54-35	1st	+3
3	At Min.	W	19-11		22	15	Ogea	Aguilera		55-35	1st	+3
4	At Min.	L	4-5		11	13	Guardado	Plunk		55-36	1st	+2
5	At K.C.	L	3-6		5	11	Magnante	Tavarez	Montgomery	55-37	1st	+2
6	At K.C.	W	10-4		17	8	McDowell	Haney		56-37	1st	+2
7	At K.C.	L	2-3		11	7	Belcher	Hershiser	Montgomery	56-38	1st	+2
8	Min.	W	5-4		9	6	Graves	Guardado		57-38	1st	+3
9	Min.	L	2-3		6	3	Rodriguez	Nagy	Naulty	57-39	1st	+3
0	Min.	W	6-5	(11)	16	11	Shuey	Stevens		58-39	1st	+4
1	Min.	W	7-5		12	10	McDowell	Radke	Shuey	59-39	1st	+4
2	At Tor.	W	4-2		8	4	Hershiser	Hanson	Mesa	60-39	1st	+5
3	At Tor.	L	1-3		5	5	Hentgen	Ogea	Timlin	60-40	1st	+5
4	At Tor.	W	10-0		11	3	Martinez	Janzen		61-40	1st	+6
5	At Bal.	W	10-7		16	12	Nagy	Coppinger		62-40	1st	+7
6	At Bal.	W	14-9		20	13	Assenmacher	Mussina		63-40	1st	+7
7	At Bal.	L	2-14		9	14	Wells	Hershiser		63-41	1st	+7
8	At Bal.	W	6-3	(13)	15	8	Mesa	Stephenson		64-41	1st	+7
0	Tor.	L	1-3		4	8	Flener	Martinez	Timlin	64-42	1st	+6
1	Tor.	W	4-2		9	8	Assenmacher	Timlin		65-42	1st	+7
	Tor.	L	3-5		12	9	Hanson	Lopez	Timlin	65-43	1st	+6
	Bal.	W	11-1		16	2	Hershiser	Erickson		66-43	1st	+6
	Bal.	L	4-9		11	14	Orosco	Ogea		66-44	1st	+5
	Bal.	W	14-2		11	11	Anderson	Coppinger		67-44	1st	+6
	Bal.	L	10-13		19	21	Wells	Assenmacher		67-45	1st	+5
	At Sea.	W	4-3		12	7	Lopez	Wells	Mesa	68-45	1st	+6
	At Sea.	W	5-4		7	10	Tavarez	Charlton	Mesa	69-45	1st	+6
	At Sea.	W	2-1		5	3	Ogea	Mulholland	Mesa	70-45	1st	+7
	At Oak.	W	10-4		15	9	McDowell	Telgheder		71-45	1st	+7
0	At Oak.	L	1-5		8	7	Adams	Nagy		71-46	1st	+7
1	At Oak.	L	3-9		7	13	Wasdin	Lopez		71-47	1st	+6
2	At Cal.	W	5-4		9	6	Hershiser	Finley	Mesa	72-47	1st	+6
3	At Cal.	L	2-4		11	11	Boskie	Ogea	Percival	72-48	1st	+5
4	At Cal.	L	7-8		12	13	Gohr	McDowell	Percival	72-49	1st	+5
6	Det.	W	3-1	(12)	7	7	Assenmacher	R. Lewis		73-49	1st	+6 1/2
7	Det.	W	6-3		7	8	Hershiser	Thompson	Mesa	74-49	1st	+6 1/2
8	Det.	W	11-3		13	6	Ogea	B. Williams		75-49	1st	+7 1/2
9	Tex.	L	3-10		4	12	Pavlik	McDowell		75-50	1st	+6 1/2
0	Tex.	W	10-4		12	11	Lopez	Witt		76-50	1st	+7 1/2
1	Tex.	L	8-10	(10)	17	17	Vosberg	Tavarez		76-51	1st	+7 1/2
3	Mil.	L	5-6	(11)	10	12	Jones	Mesa	Fetters	76-52	1st	+8
4	Mil.	L	3-4	(10)	10	9	Wickman	Plunk	Fetters	76-53	1st	+8
5	Mil.	W	8-5		11	7	Shuey	Miranda	Mesa	77-53	1st	+8
6	At Det.	W	2-1		4	3	Nagy	Lira		78-53	1st	+9
7	At Det.	W	12-2		14	7	Lopez	Thompson		79-53	1st	+10
8	At Det.	W	9-3		12	11	Hershiser	Sager		80-53	1st	+10
0	At Tex.	L	3-5		7	9	Pavlik	Ogea	Russell	80-54	1st	+9
1	At Tex.	L	3-6		9	8	Oliver	McDowell	Vosberg	80-55	1st	+8
	At Tex.	W	8-2		16	8	Nagy	Burkett		81-55	1st	+8
	At Mil.	L	6-7		8	9	Jones	Mesa		81-56	1st	+8
	At Mil.	L	2-8		10	12	Karl	Hershiser		81-57	1st	+7
	At Mil.	W	7-0		14	4	Ogea	D'Amico		82-57	1st	+7
†	Sea.	W	2-1		8	6	Nagy	Mulholland		83-57		
‡	Sea.	L	5-6		8	10	Charlton	Mesa		83-58	1st	+6 1/2
	Cal.	W	4-3		7	11	Shuey	Holtz	Mesa	84-58	1st	+7
0	Cal.	W	7-5		11	10	Assenmacher	Percival		85-58	1st	+8
1	Cal.	W	2-0		5	6	McDowell	Finley	Mesa	86-58	1st	+9
2	Cal.	W	11-2		9	9	Anderson	Boskie		87-58	1st	+9
4†	Oak.	W	9-2		15	8	Nagy	Wengert		88-58		
4‡	Oak.	W	9-8		10	12	Plunk	Small	Mesa	89-58	1st	+10

1997 SEASON Cleveland Indians

Date	Opp.	Res.	Score	(inn.*)	Hits	Opp. hits	Winning pitcher	Losing pitcher	Save	Record	Pos.	
9-15	Oak.	L	9-10	(10)	15	14	Reyes	Mesa		89-59	1st	+1
9-16	At Chi.	W	4-3		9	9	McDowell	Alvarez		90-59	1st	+1
9-17	At Chi.	W	9-4		15	9	Anderson	Fernandez	Plunk	91-59	1st	+1
9-18	At Chi.	W	4-3		7	9	Lopez	Baldwin	Mesa	92-59	1st	+1
9-19	K.C.	W	9-1		9	3	Ogea	Appier		93-59	1st	+1
9-20	K.C.	L	4-6		6	14	Bevil	Nagy	Bluma	93-60	1st	+1
9-21	K.C.	W	13-4		16	8	Hershiser	Rosado		94-60	1st	+1
9-22	K.C.	W	6-5		10	8	McDowell	Jacome	Mesa	95-60	1st	+1
9-23	Min.	W	7-6		15	8	Graves	Parra	Mesa	96-60	1st	+1
9-24	Min.	W	7-5		12	10	Ogea	Rodriguez	Mesa	97-60	1st	+1
9-25	Min.	W	6-3		9	5	Nagy	Robertson		98-60	1st	+1
9-27	At K.C.	L	6-11		12	13	Rosado	Hershiser		98-61	1st	+1
9-28	At K.C.	W	5-4		9	11	Mercker	Scanlan	Mesa	99-61	1st	+1
9-29	At K.C.	L	1-4		8	11	Belcher	Ogea	Pichardo	99-62	1st	+1

Monthly records: April (16-8), May (19-9), June (14-14), July (16-11), August (15-13), September (19-7).
*Innings, if other than nine. †First game of doubleheader. ‡Second game of doubleheader.

HIGHLIGHTS

High point: The Indians moved into sole possession of first place in the A.L. Central on April 13. Except for sharing it briefly on two occasions (April 19-21 and June 9-10), they held the top spot for the rest of the season.

Low point: After losing the first two games of the A.L. Division Series in Baltimore, the Indians won Game 3 and took a 3-2 lead into the ninth inning of Game 4. They were one strike away from forcing Game 5 when closer Jose Mesa gave up a game-tying single to Roberto Alomar. Alomar hit the game- and series-winning homer off Mesa in the 12th.

Turning point: The Indians led the White Sox by two games at the All-Star break, but they began the second half by making two controversial trades: sending Carlos Baerga to the Mets and Eddie Murray to the Orioles. The Indians wound up winning the A.L. Central by 14½ games, but they folded in the playoffs.

Most valuable player: Outfielder Albert Belle. He turned in another outstanding season, batting .311 with 48 home runs and a league-leading 148 RBIs. He signed a huge free-agent deal with the White Sox after the season.

Most valuable pitcher: Righthander Charles Nagy. He went 17-5 with a 3.41 ERA and emerged as the staff ace. After Cleveland losses, Nagy was 8-0 with a 2.53 ERA.

Most improved player: Third baseman Jim Thome. Moved up in the order because of off-years and subsequent trades of Baerga and Murray, Thome responded by hitting .311 with 38 homers and 116 RBIs.

Most pleasant surprise: Righthander Chad Ogea. Moved into the rotation after injuries to others, he went 10-6 with a 4.79 ERA.

Biggest disappointment: Righthander Jack McDowell. After signing a two-year contract as a free agent, he went 13-9 with a 5.11 ERA and spent time on the disabled list for the first time in his career.

Key injuries: Righthander Dennis Martinez strained a tendon in his right elbow on June 28 and made only three more starts the rest of the season. Jack McDowell missed three weeks with a strained right forearm. First baseman Julio Franco had only 40 at-bats in a two-month stretch because of a pulled hamstring muscle. First baseman Mark Carreon, acquired from the Giants on July 9, didn't play after fouling a ball off his left shin on August 23. Shortstop Omar Vizquel was bothered by a sore right shoulder all season and made a career-high 20 errors.

Notable: Cleveland finished with the best record in baseball for the second consecutive season (99-62). The team also had baseball's best road record (48-33). . . . The Indians spent 170 days in first place, the most in club history. . . . The Indians set franchise records for home (3,318,174) and road (2,337,869) attendance. . . . Mike Hargrove became the only manager in club history to guide the team to consecutive postseason apperances. . . . The Indians led the league in batting for the second consecutive season, the first time the club has done so since 1905-06. The Indians' team mark of .293 was the club's best since 1936. . . . The Indians led the league in ERA for the second consecutive season. As such, Cleveland became the first major league team to lead its league in batting average and ERA in consecutive seasons since the 1957-58 Yankees.

—STEVE HERRICK

RECORDS

1996 regular-season record: 99-62 (1st in A.L. Central); 51-29 at home; 48-33 on road; 40-20 vs. East; 32-20 vs. Central; 27-22 vs. West; 28-22 vs. lefthanded starters; 71-40 vs. righthanded starters; 85-57 on grass; 14-5 on turf; 31-21 in daytime; 68-41 at night; 28-20 in one-run games; 6-9 in extra-inning games; 1-1 in doubleheaders.

Team record past five years: 417-325 (.562, ranks 1st in league in that span).

TEAM LEADERS

Batting average: Kenny Lofton (.317).
At-bats: Kenny Lofton (662).
Runs: Kenny Lofton (132).
Hits: Kenny Lofton (210).
Total bases: Albert Belle (375).
Doubles: Manny Ramirez (45).
Triples: Jim Thome (5).
Home runs: Albert Belle (48).
Runs batted in: Albert Belle (148).
Stolen bases: Kenny Lofton (75).
Slugging percentage: Albert Belle (.623).

On-base percentage: Jim Thome (.4█).
Wins: Charles Nagy (17).
Earned-run average: Charles Nagy (3.█).
Complete games: Jack McDowell, Charles Nagy (5).
Shutouts: Dennis Martinez, Jack McDo█ Chad Ogea (1).
Saves: Jose Mesa (39).
Innings pitched: Charles Nagy (222.0█).
Strikeouts: Charles Nagy (167).

GAMES BY POSITION

Catcher: Sandy Alomar Jr 124, Tony Pena 67, Einar Diaz 4.
First base: Julio Franco 97, Mark Carreon 34, Jeff Kent 20, Alvaro Espinoza 18, Scott Leius 7, Herbert P█ 5, Kevin Seitzer 5, Sandy Alomar Jr 1█ Eddie Murray 1.
Second base: Carlos Baerga 100, Jos█ Vizcaino 45, Casey Candaele 11, Jeff Kent 9, Scott Leius 6, Alvaro Espinoz█ Geronimo Pena 1.
Third base: Jim Thome 150, Alvaro Espinoza 20, Scott Leius 8, Jeff Kent █ Casey Candaele 3, Geronimo Pena 3, Herbert Perry 1.
Shortstop: Omar Vizquel 150, Alvaro Espinoza 16, Damian Jackson 5, Jose█ Vizcaino 4, Casey Candaele 1.
Outfield: Albert Belle 152, Kenny Loft█ 152, Manny Ramirez 149, Jeromy Burnitz 30, Wayne Kirby 18, Brian S.█ Giles 16, Ryan Thompson 8, Mark Carreon 5, Nigel Wilson 1.
Designated hitter: Eddie Murray 87, Brian S. Giles 21, Kevin Seitzer 17, Jeromy Burnitz 15, Julio Franco 13, Albert Belle 6, Jeff Kent 5, Wayne Kir█ 3, Manny Ramirez 3, Nigel Wilson 3, Mark Carreon 2, Alvaro Espinoza 1, S█ Leius 1, Jim Thome 1, Jose Vizcaino█

TOP DRAFT CHOICES

1. **Danny Peoples**, 1B, University of Tex█
2. **Ryan McDermott**, RHP, Alamogordo (N.M.) H.S.
3. **Jarrod Mays**, RHP, Southwest Misso█ State University.
4. **J.D. Brammer**, RHP, Stanford Univer█
5. **Grant Sharpe**, 1B, Watkins H.S., Lau█ Miss.
6. **Paul Rigdon**, RHP, University of Flor█
7. **Jim Hamilton**, LHP, Ferrum (Va.) Colle█
8. **Rob Stanton**, OF, Rollins (Fla.) College█
9. **Sean DePaula**, RHP, Wake Forest Uni█
10. **William Jackson**, OF, Collin County (Tex..) C.C.

DETROIT TIGERS
AMERICAN LEAGUE EAST DIVISION

1997 TIGERS SCHEDULE

▨ Home games shaded.
* — All-Star Game at Jacobs Field (Cleveland)
D — Day game (any game starting before 5 p.m.)

APRIL
SUN	MON	TUE	WED	THU	FRI	SAT
		1 MIN	2 MIN	3 MIN	4 CWS	5 D CWS
6 CWS	7 D MIN	8	9 D MIN	10 MIN	11 D CWS	12 D CWS
13 D CWS	14 MIL	15 D MIL	16 SEA	17 D SEA	18 D OAK	19 D OAK
20 OAK	21 TEX	22	23 TEX	24 TEX	25 ANA	26 ANA
27 D ANA	28	29 MIL	30 D MIL			

MAY
SUN	MON	TUE	WED	THU	FRI	SAT
			1	2 CLE	3 D CLE	
4 D CLE	5 TOR	6 TOR	7 KC	8 KC	9 D CLE	10 D CLE
11 D CLE	12	13 TOR	14 D TOR	15 KC	16 KC	17 KC
18 D KC	19	20 BAL	21 D BAL	22	23 TEX	24 TEX
25 D KC	26 D ANA	27 ANA	28 BAL	29 D BAL	30 SEA	31 SEA
25 D TEX						

JUNE
SUN	MON	TUE	WED	THU	FRI	SAT
1 D SEA	2 D OAK	3 OAK	4	5 SEA	6 SEA	7 D SEA
8 D SEA	9 OAK	10 OAK	11 OAK	12 MON	13 MON	14 MON
15 D MON	16 FLA	17 FLA	18 FLA	19	20 BOS	21 BOS
22 BOS	23 NYY	24 NYY	25 NYY	26 BOS	27 BOS	28 BOS
29 D BOS	30 NYM					

JULY
SUN	MON	TUE	WED	THU	FRI	SAT
		1 NYM	2 NYM	3 BAL	4 BAL	5 BAL
6 D BAL	7	8	* 9	10 NYY	11 NYY	12 D NYY
13 D NYY	14 BOS	15 BOS	16 ANA	17 ANA	18 TEX	19 TEX
20 TEX	21 CWS	22 CWS	23 D CWS	24	25 MIL	26 MIL
27 D MIL	28	29 CWS	30 D CWS	31 TOR		

AUGUST
SUN	MON	TUE	WED	THU	FRI	SAT
				1 TOR	2 TOR	
3 D TOR	4 CLE	5 CLE	6 KC	7 D KC	8 TOR	9 D TOR
10 D TOR	11 CLE	12 CLE	13 CLE	14 CLE	15 KC	16 KC
17 D KC	18 MIN	19 MIN	20 MIN	21 MIL	22 MIL	23 MIL
24 D MIL	25 MIN	26 MIN	27 MIN	28	29 PHI	30 PHI
31 D PHI						

SEPTEMBER
SUN	MON	TUE	WED	THU	FRI	SAT
	1 ATL	2 ATL	3 D ATL	4 ANA	5 ANA	6 D ANA
7 ANA	8 D TEX	9 TEX	10 SEA	11 SEA	12 OAK	13 D OAK
14 D ANA	15 OAK	16 NYY	17 NYY	18 NYY	19 BAL	20 D BAL
21 D BAL	22 BAL	23 BOS	24 BOS	25 BOS	26 NYY	27 D NYY
28 D NYY						

1997 SEASON
CLUB DIRECTORY

Owners
Michael Ilitch
Marian Ilitch

Board of directors
Michael Ilitch, Chairman; Marian Ilitch;
Charles P. Jones; Jay Bielfield;
Denise Ilitch Lites; Ronald Ilitch;
Michael Ilitch Jr.; Lisa Ilitch Murray;
Atanas Ilitch; Christopher Ilitch;
Carole Ilitch Trepeck

President, chief executive officer
John McHale Jr.

Vice president, baseball operations/g.m.
Randy Smith

Vice president, business operations
David H. Glazier

Assistant general manager
Steve Lubratich

Director of baseball administration
Darrell "Doc" Rodgers

Special assistants to the g.m.
Al Hargesheimer
Randy Johnson

Director of scouting
Jeff Scott

Director minor league operations
Dave Miller

Advance scout
Tom Runnells

Special assignment scout
Larry Bearnarth

Traveling secretary
Bill Brown

Director of public relations
Tyler Barnes

Assistant director of public relations
David Matheson

Manager, community relations
Celia Bobrowsky

Manager, public relations
Jill Ulle

Coordinator, public relations
Giovanni Loria

Admin. Assistant, public relations
Connie Bell

Coordinator, community relations
Christina Branham

Sr. director, marketing and operations
Michael Dietz

Director of stadium operations
Tom Folk

Head groundskeeper
Frank Feneck

Senior director, corporate sales
Gary Vitto

Director of corporate sales
Martin Pawlusiak

Director of broadcasting
Amy Goan

Controller
Scott Fisher

Director of ticket services
Ken Marchetti

Group sales manager
Bob Palmisano

Season ticket manager
Kevin Marcy

Director of merchandise
Kayla French

Head trainer
Russ Miller

Assistant trainer
Steve Carter

Strength and conditioning coach
Brad Andress

Manager, home clubhouse
Jim Schmakel

Assistant manager, visiting clubhouse
John Nelson

Team physicians
Clarence Livingood, M.D.
David Collon, M.D.
Terry Lock, M.D.
Louis Saco, M.D. (Florida)

Scouts
Larry Bearnarth, Ricky Bennett, Tom
Chandler, Nathan Durst, Rob Guzik,
Jack Hays, Ray Hayward, Mike
Humphreys, Lou Laslo, Dennis
Lieberthal, Jeff Malinoff, John
Mirabelli, Mark Monahan, Glenn
Murdock, David Owen, Ramon
Pena, Dave Roberts, Tom Runnells,
Mike Stafford, Chuck Stone, Clyde
Weir, Jeff Wetherby, Rob Wilfong

MINOR LEAGUE AFFILIATES
Class	Team	League	Manager
AAA	Toledo	International	Glenn Ezell
AA	Jacksonville	Southern	Dave Anderson
A	Lakeland	Florida State	Mark Meleski
A	West Michigan	Midwest	Bruce Fields
A	Jamestown	New York-Pennsylvania	Dwight Lowry
Rookie	Gulf Coast Tigers	Gulf Coast	Kevin Bradshaw

BROADCAST INFORMATION
Radio: WJR-AM (760).
TV: WKBD-TV (Channel 50).
Cable TV: Pro Am Sports Systems.

SPRING TRAINING
Ballpark (city): Marchant Stadium
(Lakeland, Fla.).
Ticket information: 813-499-8229.

SPRING TRAINING ROSTER

Manager—Buddy Bell (25).
Coaches—Rick Adair (56), Larry Herndon (31), Perry Hill, Fred Kendall (18), Larry Parrish, Jerry White.

No.	PITCHERS	B/T	Ht./Wt.	Born	1996 clubs
	Blair, Willie	R/R	6-1/185	12-18-65	San Diego
46	Brocail, Doug	L/R	6-5/235	5-16-67	Houston, Jackson, Tucson
	Corey, Bryan	R/R	6-0/160	10-21-73	Fayetteville
34	Cummings, John	L/L	6-3/200	5-10-69	Los Angeles, Albuquerque, Detroit
35	Dishman, Glenn	R/L	6-1/195	11-5-70	Las Vegas, San Diego, Philadelphia
	Duran, Roberto	L/L	6-0/167	3-6-73	Knoxville, Dunedin
53	Fermin, Ramon	R/R	6-3/180	11-25-72	Jacksonville
	Hernandez, Fernando	R/R	6-2/185	6-16-71	Memphis
	Jones, Todd	L/R	6-3/200	4-24-68	Houston, Tucson
57	Keagle, Greg	R/R	6-1/185	6-20-71	Detroit, Toledo
40	Lira, Felipe	R/R	6-0/170	4-26-72	Detroit
	Miceli, Dan	R/R	6-0/216	9-9-70	Pittsburgh, Carolina
38	Moehler, Brian	R/R	6-3/195	12-31-71	Detroit, Jacksonville
27	Myers, Mike	L/L	6-3/197	6-26-69	Detroit
28	Olivares, Omar	R/R	6-1/193	7-6-67	Detroit, Toledo
	Roberts, Willie	R/R	6-3/175	6-19-75	Lakeland
	Rosengren, John	L/L	6-4/190	8-10-72	Jacksonville
22	Thompson, Justin	L/L	6-3/175	3-8-73	Toledo, Detroit, Fayetteville, Visalia
	Whiteman, Greg	L/L	6-2/180	6-12-73	Lakeland

No.	CATCHERS	B/T	Ht./Wt.	Born	1996 clubs
33	Casanova, Raul	B/R	5-11/200	8-23-72	Toledo, Detroit, Jacksonville
	Johnson, Brian	R/R	6-2/210	1-8-68	San Diego
	Walbeck, Matt	B/R	5-11/191	10-2-69	Fort Myers, New Britain, Minnesota

No.	INFIELDERS	B/T	Ht./Wt.	Born	1996 clubs
	Almanzar, Richard	R/R	5-10/155	4-3-76	Lakeland
17	Clark, Tony	B/R	6-8/250	6-15-72	Toledo, Detroit
	Cruz, Deivi	R/R	5-11/160	11-6-75	Burlington
9	Easley, Damion	R/R	5-11/185	11-11-69	Vancouver, Midland, California, Detroit
24	Fryman, Travis	R/R	6-1/194	3-25-69	Detroit
	Garcia, Luis	R/R	6-0/175	5-20-75	Jacksonville
	Hajek, Dave	R/R	5-10/165	10-14-67	Tucson, Houston
	Hyers, Tim	L/L	6-1/195	10-3-71	Toledo, Detroit
	Miller, Orlando	R/R	6-1/180	1-13-69	Houston
12	Nevin, Phil	R/R	6-2/180	1-19-71	Jacksonville, Detroit

No.	OUTFIELDERS	B/T	Ht./Wt.	Born	1996 clubs
39	Bartee, Kim	B/R	6-0/175	7-21-72	Detroit
	Conner, Decomba	R/R	5-10/185	7-17-73	Winston-Salem
	Encarnacion, Juan	R/R	6-2/160	3-8-76	Lakeland
4	Higginson, Bobby	L/R	5-11/180	8-18-70	Detroit, Toledo
	Hunter, Brian L.	R/R	6-4/180	3-5-71	Houston, Tucson
30	Nieves, Melvin	B/R	6-2/210	12-28-71	Detroit
36	Pride, Curtis	L/R	6-0/200	12-17-68	Detroit, Toledo
	Trammell, Bubba	R/R	6-3/205	11-6-71	Jacksonville, Toledo

1997 SEASON Detroit Tigers

BALLPARK INFORMATION

Ballpark (capacity, surface)
Tiger Stadium (46,945, grass)

Address
Tiger Stadium
Detroit, MI 48216

Business phone
313-962-4000

Ticket information
313-963-2050

Ticket prices
$15 and $10 (box seats)
$12 and $8 (reserved seats)
$8 (grandstand reserved seats)
$4 (bleacher seats)

Field dimensions (from home plate)
To left field at foul line, 340 feet
To center field, 440 feet
To right field at foul line, 325 feet

First game played
April 20, 1912
(Tigers 6, Cleveland Naps 5, 11 innings)

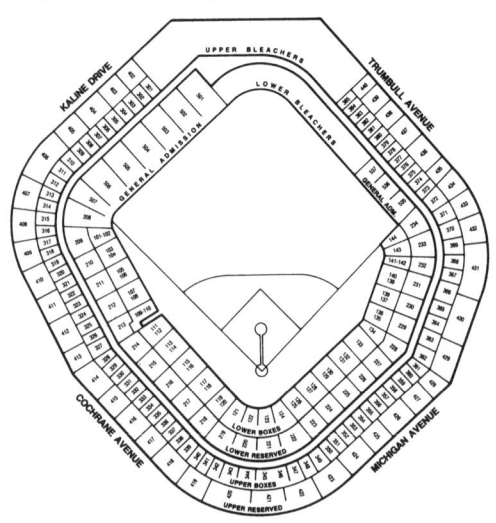

DAY BY DAY

Date	Opp.	Res.	Score	(inn.*)	Hits	Opp. hits	Winning pitcher	Losing pitcher	Save	Record	Pos.	GB
1	At Min.	L	6-8		10	12	Radke	Lira	Stevens	0-1	T4th	1
2	At Min.	W	10-6		14	14	Sodowsky	Robertson		1-1	4th	1/2
3	At Min.	L	7-16		8	14	Mahomes	Aldred		1-2	4th	1 1/2
4	At Oak.§	W	10-9	(15)	13	13	Keagle	Small		2-2	4th	1 1/2
5	At Oak.§	L	2-13		4	16	Johns	Gohr		2-3	4th	2 1/2
6	At Oak.§	W	6-1		12	5	Lira	Reyes		3-3	4th	1 1/2
7	At Oak.§	L	6-7		11	11	Corsi	B. Williams		3-4	T3rd	2 1/2
9	Sea.	W	10-9		4	12	Keagle	Menhart	B. Williams	4-4	T3rd	2
10	Sea.	W	7-3		9	5	Olivares	Hurtado		5-4	T2nd	2
11	Sea.	L	1-9		3	14	Johnson	Gohr		5-5	4th	3
12	Cal.	L	4-5		9	6	Finley	Lira	Percival	5-6	4th	4
13	Cal.	W	9-5		13	11	Keagle	Sanderson		6-6	T3rd	4
14	Cal.	W	5-4		7	7	R. Lewis	James		7-6	3rd	3
15	At Tor.	L	2-8		6	9	Guzman	Olivares		7-7	T3rd	3 1/2
16	At Tor.	W	13-8		18	11	Gohr	Hanson	R. Lewis	8-7	T2nd	3 1/2
17	At Sea.	L	3-8		12	10	Jackson	Veres		8-8	T2nd	4 1/2
18	At Sea.	L	3-11		12	12	Bosio	Sodowsky	Hurtado	8-9	3rd	4 1/2
19	At Cal.	L	3-4		7	7	Langston	Myers		8-10	T3rd	4 1/2
20	At Cal.	L	1-2		7	7	Grimsley	Keagle	Percival	8-11	4th	4 1/2
21	At Cal.	L	5-6		7	8	Eichhorn	R. Lewis	Percival	8-12	4th	4 1/2
22	At Cal.	L	5-6		10	12	James	Christopher	Percival	8-13	4th	4 1/2
24	Min.	L	11-24		14	19	Bennett	Veres		8-14	4th	5
25	Min.	L	1-11		3	15	Hawkins	Aldred	Hansell	8-15	4th	6
26	Oak.	W	14-5		11	8	Christopher	Johns		9-15	4th	5
27	Oak.	L	1-4		6	8	Reyes	Lira	Taylor	9-16	4th	5
28	Oak.	L	3-6		8	9	Wojciechowski	Gohr	Taylor	9-17	4th	5
30	At Bos.	L	4-13		10	16	Wakefield	Lima		9-18	4th	6
1	At Bos.	L	1-5		6	11	Clemens	Aldred		9-19	4th	7
2	Tex.	W	5-2		6	4	Lira	Witt	B. Williams	10-19	4th	7
3	Tex.	L	0-11		1	14	Hill	Keagle		10-20	T4th	8
4	Tex.	L	1-3		1	11	Pavlik	Gohr		10-21	5th	8
5	Tex.	L	2-3		5	9	Gross	Lima	Henneman	10-22	5th	9
6	At N.Y.	L	5-10		10	14	Wickman	Myers		10-23	5th	10
7	At N.Y.	L	5-12		11	13	Mecir	R. Lewis	Nelson	10-24	5th	11
8	At N.Y.	L	3-10		2	13	Gooden	Keagle		10-25	5th	12
9	At N.Y.	W	4-2		8	12	Gohr	Key	Myers	11-25	5th	11
10	At Tex.	L	2-6		9	8	Pavlik	Lima	Henneman	11-26	5th	11
11	At Tex.	L	7-11		14	18	Gross	Aldred		11-27	5th	11
12	At Tex.	W	5-3		7	5	Lira	Oliver	Myers	12-27	5th	11
14	At Cle.	L	1-5		7	7	Nagy	Gohr		12-28	5th	12
15	At Cle.	L	2-5		6	11	Martinez	Lima	Mesa	12-29	5th	12
16	At Cle.	L	3-8		7	5	McDowell	B. Williams		12-30	5th	12 1/2
17	Chi.	L	6-11	(10)	12	12	Hernandez	R. Lewis		12-31	5th	13 1/2
18	Chi.	L	4-16		10	21	McCaskill	Farrell	Simas	12-32	5th	14 1/2
19	Chi.	L	3-14		7	17	Alvarez	Gohr		12-33	5th	14 1/2
21	K.C.	L	1-7		4	12	Linton	B. Williams	Valera	12-34	5th	15 1/2
22	K.C.	L	4-6		10	10	Belcher	Farrell	Montgomery	12-35	5th	15 1/2
24	Cle.	L	3-6		6	11	Plunk	Veres	Mesa	12-36	5th	16
25	Cle.	L	6-7		10	11	Nagy	R. Lewis	Mesa	12-37	5th	17
26	Cle.	L	0-5		8	3	Martinez	B. Williams		12-38	5th	17
27	At K.C.	L	4-5	(13)	9	10	Montgomery	Veres		12-39	5th	18
29	At K.C.	W	5-4		9	7	Gohr	Appier	Walker	13-39	5th	16 1/2
30	At Chi.	L	2-8		6	10	Alvarez	Olivares		13-40	5th	17
31	At Chi.	L	0-9		8	15	Tapani	Lira		13-41	5th	18
2†	At Chi.	L	2-4		4	8	Baldwin	Thompson	Hernandez	13-42		
2‡	At Chi.	L	5-13		12	11	McCaskill	Keagle		13-43	5th	20
4	At Bal.	L	7-10		14	12	Mussina	Gohr	R. Myers	13-44	5th	21
5	At Bal.	L	4-6		6	12	Rhodes	Myers	R. Myers	13-45	5th	21
6	At Bal.	L	6-13		14	12	Krivda	Lira		13-46	5th	22
7	N.Y.	W	6-5		13	10	R. Lewis	Nelson		14-46	5th	21
8	N.Y.	W	9-7		13	12	Olson	Rogers	R. Lewis	15-46	5th	20
9	N.Y.	L	2-3		6	13	Gooden	Gohr	Wetteland	15-47	5th	21
10	Bal.	W	8-3		14	7	Olivares	Wells		16-47	5th	21
11	Bal.	L	9-12		10	15	Coppinger	Lira		16-48	5th	22
12	Bal.	L	7-10		10	11	Rhodes	R. Lewis	R. Myers	16-49	5th	22
14	At Min.	W	5-4		9	9	Gohr	Robertson	Olson	17-49	5th	21 1/2
15	At Min.	W	6-4		12	9	Olivares	Rodriguez	Olson	18-49	5th	20 1/2
16	At Min.	L	1-4		4	8	Aguilera	Lira	Hansell	18-50	5th	21 1/2
17	Oak.	L	4-8	(10)	11	8	Corsi	Myers		18-51	5th	21 1/2
18	Oak.	L	5-8		10	11	Van Poppel	Urbani	Taylor	18-52	5th	22 1/2
19	Oak.	L	3-10		6	15	Wasdin	Keagle		18-53	5th	23
20	Min.	L	3-7		10	12	Rodriguez	Olivares		18-54	5th	23 1/2

1997 SEASON *Detroit Tigers*

Date	Opp.	Res.	Score	(inn.*)	Hits	Opp. hits	Winning pitcher	Losing pitcher	Save	Record	Pos.	GB
6-21	Min.	W	2-0		6	4	Lira	Aguilera		19-54	5th	24
6-22	Min.	W	6-0		12	4	B. Williams	Aldred		20-54	5th	24
6-23	Min.	W	10-8		9	14	Urbani	Radke		21-54	5th	24
6-24	At Oak.	L	2-4		4	8	Wasdin	Sodowsky	Taylor	21-55	5th	24
6-25	At Oak.	W	10-8		16	13	Olivares	Wengert	Olson	22-55	5th	23
6-27	At Bos.	W	9-6		14	9	Lira	Minchey		23-55	5th	24
6-28	At Bos.	L	5-8		11	14	Wakefield	B. Williams		23-56	5th	24
6-29	At Bos.	L	6-13		11	16	Eshelman	Keagle		23-57	5th	25
6-30	At Bos.	L	4-9		8	10	Gordon	Sodowsky		23-58	5th	25
7-1	Mil.	L	0-2		7	9	Sparks	Olivares	Fetters	23-59	5th	26
7-2	Mil.	L	1-2	(11)	6	10	Garcia	Sager	Fetters	23-60	5th	27
7-3	Mil.	W	8-5		11	13	B. Williams	D'Amico		24-60	5th	26
7-4	Tor.	W	6-1		9	7	Nitkowski	Janzen	Myers	25-60	5th	26
7-5	Tor.	W	4-3		6	9	Sager	Hanson	Olson	26-60	5th	26
7-6	Tor.	L	0-15		3	19	Hentgen	Olivares		26-61	5th	27
7-7	Tor.	W	9-0		8	6	Lira	Ware		27-61	5th	26
7-11	Bos.	L	4-11		7	10	Clemens	B. Williams		27-62	5th	27
7-12	Bos.	L	3-11		6	12	Gordon	Olivares		27-63	5th	28
7-13	Bos.	L	5-10		6	13	Sele	Nitkowski		27-64	5th	29
7-14	Bos.	L	4-6		9	10	Moyer	Lira	Slocumb	27-65	5th	30
7-15	At Mil.	W	10-9		17	16	Sager	Bones	Olson	28-65	5th	29
7-16	At Mil.	L	7-20		10	18	D'Amico	B. Williams		28-66	5th	30
7-17	At Mil.	L	2-3	(10)	6	5	Fetters	Urbani		28-67	5th	30
7-18	At Tor.	L	4-8		4	13	Hentgen	Nitkowski		28-68	5th	30
7-19	At Tor.	W	8-6		8	13	Urbani	Janzen	Olson	29-68	5th	29
7-20	At Tor.	W	5-4	(10)	7	9	Olson	Quantrill	Lima	30-68	5th	29
7-21	At Tor.	L	4-5	(12)	10	13	Spoljaric	Lima		30-69	5th	29
7-22	At Cal.	L	0-1		6	4	Finley	Olivares	Percival	30-70	5th	29
7-23	At Cal.	W	8-3		11	10	Lima	James		31-70	5th	29
7-25	At Sea.	W	7-4	(10)	11	9	Lima	Ayala		32-70	5th	29
7-26	At Sea.	L	4-6		10	8	Hitchcock	Sager	Jackson	32-71	5th	30
7-27	At Sea.	L	7-13		10	17	T. Davis	B. Williams		32-72	5th	31
7-28	At Sea.	W	14-6		15	10	Olivares	Bosio		33-72	5th	31
7-30	Cal.	W	12-9		9	9	Nitkowski	Grimsley		34-72	5th	30
7-31	Cal.	W	10-5		12	9	Lima	Holtz		35-72	5th	29
8-1	Cal.	W	13-5		16	10	B. Williams	Boskie		36-72	5th	29
8-2	Sea.	W	8-2		10	3	Olivares	Wagner		37-72	5th	28
8-3	Sea.	W	6-3		10	5	Olson	Charlton		38-72	5th	27
8-4	Sea.	L	3-9		9	12	Wolcott	Nitkowski		38-73	5th	28
8-6	Tex.	L	2-4		8	9	Hill	Lira	Henneman	38-74	5th	29
8-7	Tex.	W	4-2		9	8	Cummings	Pavlik	Myers	39-74	5th	28
8-8	Tex.	W	3-2		6	9	Olivares	Heredia		40-74	5th	28
8-9	At N.Y.	W	5-3		7	9	Cummings	Pettitte	Myers	41-74	5th	27
8-10	At N.Y.	W	13-7		13	12	R. Lewis	Key		42-74	5th	26
8-11	At N.Y.	L	0-12		6	15	Rogers	Lira		42-75	5th	27
8-12	At Tex.	L	0-7		5	10	Hill	B. Williams		42-76	5th	27
8-13	At Tex.	L	2-6		5	9	Pavlik	Olivares		42-77	5th	27
8-14	At Tex.	L	4-5		9	6	Witt	Van Poppel	Henneman	42-78	5th	28
8-16	At Cle.	L	1-3	(12)	7	7	Assenmacher	R. Lewis		42-79	5th	28
8-17	At Cle.	L	3-6		8	7	Hershiser	Thompson	Mesa	42-80	5th	28
8-18	At Cle.	L	3-11		6	13	Ogea	B. Williams		42-81	5th	28
8-19	Chi.	L	7-12		10	13	Simas	Lima		42-82	5th	29
8-20	Chi.	W	16-11		15	11	R. Lewis	Tapani		43-82	5th	29
8-21	Chi.	W	7-4		11	8	Lima	Simas	Olson	44-82	5th	28
8-22	At K.C.	W	10-3		14	8	Thompson	Belcher		45-82	5th	27
8-23	At K.C.	W	3-2		6	8	Sager	Appier	Olson	46-82	5th	27
8-24	At K.C.	L	2-9		7	11	Rosado	Olivares		46-83	5th	28
8-25	At K.C.	W	7-4		12	11	Van Poppel	Linton	Myers	47-83	5th	27
8-26	Cle.	L	1-2		3	4	Nagy	Lira		47-84	5th	27
8-27	Cle.	L	2-12		7	14	Lopez	Thompson		47-85	5th	27
8-28	Cle.	L	3-9		11	12	Hershiser	Sager		47-86	5th	27
8-29	K.C.	W	4-1		9	12	Eischen	Appier	Lima	48-86	5th	26
8-30	K.C.	W	4-0		6	5	Van Poppel	Rosado		49-86	5th	26
8-31	K.C.	L	1-3		6	5	Linton	Lira	Montgomery	49-87	5th	27
9-1	K.C.	L	2-3	(13)	7	7	Huisman	Myers	Jacome	49-88	5th	27
9-2	At Chi.	W	8-6		11	11	Myers	Hernandez	Lima	50-88	5th	27
9-3	At Chi.	L	4-6		9	12	Bertotti	Olivares	Hernandez	50-89	5th	27
9-4	At Chi.	L	6-11		8	13	Castillo	Miller		50-90	5th	28
9-6	At Bal.	W	5-4	(12)	10	10	Cummings	Mathews		51-90	5th	28
9-7	At Bal.	L	0-6		6	10	Mussina	Thompson		51-91	5th	28
9-8	At Bal.	L	2-6		4	12	Mills	Eischen		51-92	5th	28
9-9	At Bal.	L	4-5		7	7	Erickson	Olivares	R. Myers	51-93	5th	29
9-10	N.Y.	L	8-9		12	15	M. Rivera	Sager	Wetteland	51-94	5th	30
9-11	N.Y.	L	3-7		8	6	Key	Lira		51-95	5th	31
9-12	N.Y.	L	3-12		8	13	Cone	Thompson		51-96	5th	32

te	Opp.	Res.	Score	(inn.*)	Hits	Opp. hits	Winning pitcher	Losing pitcher	Save	Record	Pos.	GB
13	Bal.	L	4-7		11	9	Erickson	Miller	Mills	51-97	5th	33
14	Bal.	L	6-7		8	14	Mathews	Cummings	R. Myers	51-98	5th	34
15	Bal.	L	6-16		7	13	Corbin	Van Poppel		51-99	5th	34
17	Bos.	L	2-4		8	9	Brandenburg	Lira	Slocumb	51-100	5th	35
18	Bos.	L	0-4		5	11	Clemens	Thompson		51-101	5th	36
19	Bos.	L	3-8		11	12	Gordon	Miller		51-102	5th	36 1/2
20	At Mil.	W	10-1		10	7	Sager	Karl		52-102	5th	35 1/2
21	At Mil.	L	6-13		9	13	D'Amico	Van Poppel	Villone	52-103	5th	36 1/2
22	At Mil.	W	7-5		12	11	Lima	Fetters		53-103	5th	36 1/2
23	Tor.	L	4-6		8	10	Hanson	Sager	Timlin	53-104	5th	36 1/2
24	Tor.	L	1-4		7	9	Hentgen	Miller	Timlin	53-105	5th	37
25	Tor.	L	11-13		14	18	Brow	Cummings	Timlin	53-106	5th	38 1/2
27	Mil.	L	6-7	(6)	6	8	Wickman	Van Poppel		53-107	5th	38
28	Mil.	L	2-7		6	8	Eldred	Moehler		53-108	5th	39
29	Mil.	L	5-7	(10)	10	15	Reyes	Cummings	Fetters	53-109	5th	39

onthly records: April (9-18), May (4-23), June (10-17), July (12-14), August (14-15), September (4-22). **nnings**, if other than nine. †First game of doubleheader. ‡Second game of doubleheader. §At Las Vegas.

HIGHLIGHTS

gh point: After winning behind three cil Fielder home runs at the SkyDome, e Tigers were a surprising 8-7 on April . Rookie manager Buddy Bell had rea-n to think his club might be better than pected, especially after a strong spring aining.

w point: That night, the team left for attle to open one of the longest retches of futility in club history. The gers bottomed out on June 6, the end a 5-39 dive that left them 13-46.

rning point: On June 7, the team pro-oted slugging first baseman Tony Clark om Class AAA Toledo and activated out-lder Bobby Higginson from the dis-led list. The two spurred a respectable -29 run through August 10 that includ-a six-game winning streak and culmi-ted with 10 wins in 12 games. But the am won only 12 of its last 46 games.

ost valuable player: Outfielder Bobby gginson. He came to spring training a estion mark after an awful second half 1995 left him with a .224 rookie sea-n. But better contact hitting and proved discipline at the plate resulted a team-leading .320 average with 26 me runs and 81 RBIs in '96—despite ssing a month with a foot injury.

ost valuable pitcher: Righthander nar Olivares. The first acquisition by neral manager Randy Smith, Olivares as the most consistent starter on a ebegone staff (7-11, 4.89, 169 hits in 0 innings). The club's 5-39 debacle incided almost exactly with the six eeks he missed with a hamstring injury.

ost improved player: Fisrt baseman ny Clark. After a so-so September '95 his first stint with the club, he banged homers after being promoted June 7 d led the team in that category for the ason. Clark also showed improved fense and instincts at first base in eryday duty after the Cecil Fielder trade ly 31.

ost pleasant surprise: Third baseman il Nevin. He hit .292 with eight homers a little over a month as an experiment third base.

ggest disappointment: Righthander eg Gohr. A former No. 1 pick, he ened the season in the rotation but as clobbered (4-8, 7.17 ERA, 24

homers in 91 2/3 innings) before being traded to the Angels on July 31.

Key injuries: Three short stints on the D.L. interrupted outfielder Melvin Nieves' 24-homer season. . . . Higginson was out from May 10 to June 7 with a sprained right arch. . . . Omar Olivares was out from mid-April to the end of May with a hamstring injury. . . . Prized pitching prospect Justin Thompson was idle June 7 to August 17 with shoulder stiffness.

Notable: The team's 109 losses were a franchise record, and its 6.38 ERA was worst in A.L. history. . . . The club allowed a major league-record 241 homers and struck out a record 1,268 times. . . . The season ended with a 17-game home losing streak. . . . Longtime shortstop Alan Trammell retired after a 20-year career with the club. . . . Cecil Fielder, a mainstay since his 51-homer season in 1990, got his wish to be traded when sent to the Yankees on July 31 for Ruben Sierra and minor league pitcher Matt Drews, a former first-round pick.
—**REID CREAGER**

RECORDS

1996 regular-season record: 53-109 (5th in A.L. East); 27-54 at home; 26-55 on road; 14-38 vs. East; 19-42 vs. Central; 20-29 vs. West; 17-22 vs. left-handed starters; 36-87 vs. righthanded starters; 45-99 on grass; 8-10 on turf; 21-38 in daytime; 32-71 at night; 12-21 in one-run games; 4-9 in extra-inning games; 0-1-0 in doubleheaders.
Team record past five years: 326-419 (.438, ranks 14th in league in that span).

TEAM LEADERS

Batting average: Bob Higginson (.320).
At-bats: Travis Fryman (616).
Runs: Travis Fryman (90).
Hits: Travis Fryman (165).
Total bases: Travis Fryman (269).
Doubles: Bob Higginson (35).
Triples: Curtis Pride (5).
Home runs: Tony Clark (27).
Runs batted in: Travis Fryman (100).
Stolen bases: Kimera Bartee (20).
Slugging percentage: Bob Higginson (.577).
On-base percentage: Bob Higginson (.404).

Wins: Omar Olivares (7).
Earned-run average: Felipe Lira (5.22).
Complete games: Omar Olivares (4).
Shutouts: Felipe Lira (2).
Saves: Gregg Olson (8).
Innings pitched: Felipe Lira (194.2).
Strikeouts: Felipe Lira (113).

GAMES BY POSITION

Catcher: Brad Ausmus 73, John Flaherty 46, Mark Parent 33, Raul Casanova 22, Phil Nevin 4.
First base: Tony Clark 86, Cecil Fielder 71, Tim Hyers 9, Eddie Williams 7, Mark Parent 1.
Second base: Mark Lewis 144, Alan Trammell 11, Fausto Cruz 8, Damion Easley 8.
Third base: Travis Fryman 128, Phil Nevin 24, Alan Trammell 8, Phil Hiatt 3, Eddie Williams 3, Damion Easley 2, Andujar Cedeno 1.
Shortstop: Andujar Cedeno 51, Chris Gomez 47, Alan Trammell 43, Travis Fryman 29, Damion Easley 8, Fausto Cruz 4.
Outfield: Bob Higginson 123, Melvin Nieves 105, Chad Curtis 104, Kimera Bartee 99, Curtis Pride 48, Ruben Sierra 23, Danny Bautista 22, Duane Singleton 15, Phil Nevin 9, Phil Hiatt 2, Eddie Williams 2, Tim Hyers 1, Shannon Penn 1, Alan Trammell 1.
Designated hitter: Eddie Williams 52, Cecil Fielder 36, Curtis Pride 31, Ruben Sierra 20, Tony Clark 12, Melvin Nieves 11, Bob Higginson 5, Shannon Penn 4, Raul Casanova 3, Kimera Bartee 2, Tim Hyers 2, Danny Bautista 1, Fausto Cruz 1, Damion Easley 1, Phil Hiatt 1, Mark Lewis 1, Phil Nevin 1.

TOP DRAFT CHOICES

1. **Seth Greisinger**, RHP, Univ. of Virginia.
2. **Matt Miller**, LHP, Texas Tech.
3. **Antonio McKinney**, OF, Jefferson H.S., Portland, Ore.
4. **Kris Keller**, RHP, Fletcher H.S., Neptune Beach, Fla.
5. **Robert Fick**, C, Cal State Northridge.
6. **Chris Bauer**, RHP, Wichita State Univ.
7. **Scott Sollmann**, OF, U. of Notre Dame.
8. **Craig Quintal**, RHP, Southern University.
9. **Keith Whitner**, OF, Los Angeles C.C.
10. **Justin Hazleton**, OF, Philipsburg-Osceola H.S., Philipsburg, Pa.

1997 SEASON *Detroit Tigers*

– 37 –

KANSAS CITY ROYALS
AMERICAN LEAGUE CENTRAL DIVISION

1997 ROYALS SCHEDULE

Home games shaded.
* — All-Star Game at Jacobs Field (Cleveland)
D — Day game (any game starting before 5 p.m.)

APRIL

SUN	MON	TUE	WED	THU	FRI	SAT
		1 D BAL	2	3 BAL	4 MIN	5 MIN
6 D MIN	7 D BAL	8	9 BAL	10 BAL	11 MIN	12 D MIN
13 D MIN	14 TOR	15 TOR	16 TEX	17 TEX	18	19 D ANA
20 D ANA	21 SEA	22 SEA	23 SEA	24	25 OAK	26 D OAK
27 OAK	28	29 TOR	30 TOR			

MAY

SUN	MON	TUE	WED	THU	FRI	SAT
				1 TOR	2 NYY	3 NYY
4 D NYY	5 BOS	6 BOS	7 DET	8 D DET	9 NYY	10 D NYY
11 D NYY	12	13 BOS	14 BOS	15 BOS	16 DET	17 DET
18 D DET	19	20 CLE	21 CLE	22 D CLE	23 SEA	24 SEA
25 SEA	26 D OAK	27 OAK	28 CLE	29 CLE	30 TEX	31 TEX

JUNE

SUN	MON	TUE	WED	THU	FRI	SAT
1 TEX	2 D ANA	3 ANA	4	5 TEX	6 TEX	7 TEX
8 TEX	9 ANA	10 ANA	11 ANA	12	13 PIT	14 PIT
15 PIT	16 D HOU	17 HOU	18 HOU	19	20 MIL	21 MIL
22 D MIL	23 CWS	24 CWS	25 CWS	26 D MIL	27 MIL	28 MIL
29 D MIL	30 D CUB					

JULY

SUN	MON	TUE	WED	THU	FRI	SAT
		1 D CUB	2 D CUB	3 D	4 CLE	5 D CLE
6 D CLE	7	8 *	9	10 CWS	11 CWS	12 CWS
13 D CWS	14 MIL	15 MIL	16 OAK	17 D OAK	18 SEA	19 SEA
20 D SEA	21 MIN	22 MIN	23 MIN	24 TOR	25 D TOR	26 TOR
27 TOR	28 MIN	29 MIN	30 MIN	31 BOS		

AUGUST

SUN	MON	TUE	WED	THU	FRI	SAT
					1 BOS	2 D BOS
3 D BOS	4 NYY	5 NYY	6 DET	7 D DET	8 D BOS	9 BOS
10 D BOS	11	12 NYY	13 NYY	14 D NYY	15 DET	16 DET
17 D DET	18	19 BAL	20 BAL	21 BAL	22 TOR	23 TOR
24 D TOR	25	26 BAL	27 BAL	28 D BAL	29 STL	30 STL
31 D STL						

SEPTEMBER

SUN	MON	TUE	WED	THU	FRI	SAT
	1 CIN	2 D CIN	3 CIN	4 OAK	5 OAK	6 OAK
7 D OAK	8 SEA	9 SEA	10	11 ANA	12 ANA	13 D ANA
14 ANA	15 TEX	16 TEX	17 CWS	18 CWS	19 CLE	20 CLE
21 CLE	22 D CLE	23 MIL	24 MIL	25 D MIL	26 CWS	27 CWS
28 D CWS						

1997 SEASON
CLUB DIRECTORY

Board of directors
David D. Glass
Mike Herman
Larry Kauffman
Janice C. Kreamer
Louis Smith
Joseph T. McGuff

Chairman of the board & CEO
David D. Glass

President
Mike Herman

Exec. v.p. and general manager
Spencer (Herk) Robinson

V.p., finance/corporate secretary
Dale Rohr

Vice president, baseball operations
George Brett

V.p., administration and development
Dennis Cryder

V.p., marketing and communications
Mike Levy

Director, media relations
Steve Fink

Director, community relations
Jim Lachimia

Director, administration
John Johnson

Director, human resources
Lauris P. Hawthorne

Director, scouting
Art Stewart

Assistant general manager
Jay Hinrichs

Director, minor league operations
Bob Hegman

Director, marketing and sales
Mike Behymer

Director, stadium operations
Rodney Lewallen

Director, season ticket sales
Joe Grigoli

Director, information systems
Jim Edwards

Controller
Patrick Fleischmann

Director, team travel
Dave Witty

Director, player personnel
Larry Doughty

Assistant director, player personnel
Dan Glass

Director, ticket operations
John Walker

Manager, community relations
Barry Holmes

Stadium engineer
Wes Earring

Equipment manager
Mike Burkhalter

Team physician
Dr. Steve Joyce

Trainer
Nick Swartz

Assistant trainer
Steve Morrow

Scouts
Frank Baez, Allard Baird, Bob Bishop, Carl Blando, Bob Carter, Balos Davis, Steve Flores, álbert Gonzale, Dave Herrera, Ray Jackson, Gary Johnson, Tony Levato, Tom McDevitt, Jeff McKay, Cliff Pastornicky, Bill Price, Wil Rutenschroer, Bill Schudlich, Luis Silverio, Jerry Stephens, Terry Wetzel, Dick Wiencek, Dennis Woody

MINOR LEAGUE AFFILIATES

Class	Team	League	Manager
AAA	Omaha	American Assoc.	Mike Jirschle
AA	Wichita	Texas	Ron Johnson
A	Wilmington	Carolina	John Mizerock
A	Lansing	Midwest	Bob Herold
A	Spokane	Northwest	Jeff Garber
Rookie	Gulf Coast Royals	Gulf Coast	Al Pedrique

BROADCAST INFORMATION

Radio: WIBW-AM (580).
TV: KMBC (Channel 9), KCWB (Channel 29).
Cable TV: Fox Sports Rocky Mountain.

SPRING TRAINING

Ballpark (city): Baseball City Stadium (Haines City, Fla.).
Ticket information: 941-424-2500.

SPRING TRAINING ROSTER

Manager—Bob Boone (8).
Coaches—Rich Dauer (56), Guy Hansen (55), Bruce Kison (54), Greg Luzinski (19), Mitchell Page (39), Jamie Quirk (9).

No.	PITCHERS	B/T	Ht./Wt.	Born	1996 clubs
17	Appier, Kevin	R/R	6-2/195	12-6-67	Kansas City
41	Belcher, Tim	R/R	6-3/225	10-19-61	Kansas City
47	Bevil, Brian	R/R	6-4/225	9-5-71	Wichita, Omaha, Kansas City
25	Bluma, Jamie	R/R	5-11/195	5-18-72	Omaha, Kansas City
46	Brewington, Jamie	R/R	6-4/190	9-28-71	Phoenix
36	Bunch, Melvin	R/R	6-1/185	11-4-71	Omaha
33	Haney, Chris	L/L	6-3/205	11-16-68	Kansas City
37	Huisman, Rick	R/R	6-3/210	5-17-69	Omaha, Kansas City
45	Jacome, Jason	L/L	6-1/185	11-24-70	Kansas City
40	Linton, Doug	R/R	6-1/190	9-2-65	Omaha, Kansas City
21	Montgomery, Jeff	R/R	5-11/180	1-7-62	Kansas City
35	Pichardo, Hipolito	R/R	6-1/185	8-22-69	Kansas City
34	Pittsley, Jim	R/R	6-7/215	4-3-74	Wilmington, Wichita, Omaha
61	Ray, Ken	R/R	6-2/180	1-27-74	Wichita
50	Rosado, Jose	L/L	6-0/175	11-9-74	Wichita, Omaha, Kansas City
53	Rusch, Glendon	L/L	6-2/170	11-7-74	Omaha
24	Scanlan, Bob	R/R	6-4/220	8-9-66	Lakeland, Toledo, Detroit, Omaha, Kansas City

No.	CATCHERS	B/T	Ht./Wt.	Born	1996 clubs
	Fasano, Sal	R/R	6-2/220	8-10-71	Kansas City, Omaha
15	Macfarlane, Mike	R/R	6-1/210	4-12-64	Kansas City
29	Sweeney, Mike	R/R	6-2/215	7-22-73	Wichita, Omaha, Kansas City

No.	INFIELDERS	B/T	Ht./Wt.	Born	1996 clubs
3	Bell, Jay	R/R	6-0/185	12-11-65	Pittsburgh
34	Cooper, Scott	L/R	6-3/205	10-13-67	Seibu (Japan)
3	Hamelin, Bob	L/L	6-0/235	11-29-67	Kansas City, Omaha
65	Hansen, Jed	R/R	6-1/180	8-19-72	Wichita, Omaha
6	Howard, David	B/R	6-0/175	2-26-67	Kansas City
7	King, Jeff	R/R	6-1/188	12-26-64	Pittsburgh
4	Lockhart, Keith	L/R	5-10/170	11-10-64	Kansas City
62	Lopez, Mendy	R/R	6-2/165	10-15-74	Wichita
68	Martinez, Felix	B/R	6-0/170	5-18-74	Omaha
66	Nunez, Sergio	R/R	5-11/155	1-3-75	Wilmington
30	Offerman, Jose	B/R	6-0/190	11-8-68	Kansas City
12	Paquette, Craig	R/R	6-0/190	3-28-69	Omaha, Kansas City
1	Roberts, Bip	B/R	5-7/165	10-27-63	Kansas City
14	Stynes, Chris	R/R	5-9/175	1-19-73	Omaha, Kansas City
32	Vitiello, Joe	R/R	6-3/230	4-11-70	Kansas City, Omaha

No.	OUTFIELDERS	B/T	Ht./Wt.	Born	1996 clubs
18	Damon, Johnny	L/L	6-2/190	11-5-73	Kansas City
	Davis, Chili	B/R	6-3/217	1-17-60	California
42	Goodwin, Tom	L/R	6-1/175	7-27-68	Kansas City
58	Myers, Rod	L/L	6-1/190	1-14-73	Omaha, Kansas City
22	Nunnally, Jon	L/R	5-10/190	11-9-71	Kansas City, Omaha
31	Tucker, Michael	L/R	6-2/185	6-25-71	Kansas City, Wichita

BALLPARK INFORMATION

Ballpark (capacity, surface)
Kauffman Stadium (40,625, grass)

Address
P.O. Box 419969
Kansas City, MO 64141-6969

Business phone
816-921-2200

Ticket information
816-921-8000

Ticket prices
$14 (club box)
$13 (field box)
$11 (plaza reserved)
$10 (view upper box)
$9 (view upper reserved)
$4.50 (Royal nights)
$5 (general admission)

Field dimensions (from home plate)
To left field at foul line, 330 feet
To center field, 400 feet
To right field at foul line, 330 feet

First game played
April 10, 1973 (Royals 12, Rangers 1)

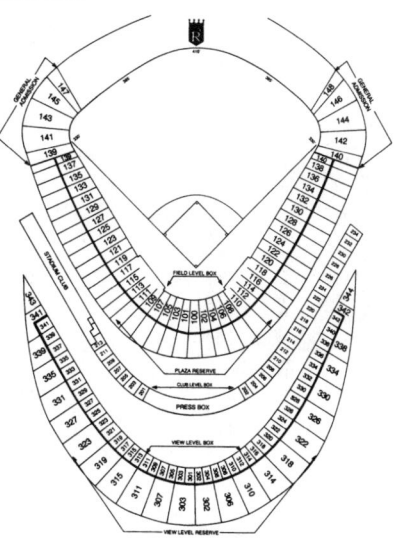

DAY BY DAY

Date	Opp.	Res.	Score	(inn.*)	Hits	Opp. hits	Winning pitcher	Losing pitcher	Save	Record	Pos.	GB
4-2	At Bal.	L	2-4		5	9	Mussina	Appier	R. Myers	0-1	T3rd	1
4-3	At Bal.	L	1-7		6	14	Wells	Gubicza		0-2	T4th	1
4-4	At Bal.	L	3-5		10	10	Rhodes	Pichardo	R. Myers	0-3	5th	2
4-5	Bos.	W	5-4	(12)	13	8	Clark	Pennington		1-3	T3rd	1
4-6	Bos.	W	7-3		11	6	Pichardo	Belinda		2-3	T3rd	1
4-7	Bos.	L	1-3		5	9	Moyer	Gubicza	Slocumb	2-4	T4th	1
4-9	At N.Y.	L	3-7		7	10	Pettitte	Haney		2-5	T4th	1
4-11	At N.Y.	L	3-5		9	8	Key	Belcher	Howe	2-6	5th	2
4-12	At Mil.	W	4-1		8	3	Appier	Bones	Montgomery	3-6	T4th	1
4-13	At Mil.	W	3-2		1	7	Gubicza	Sparks	Montgomery	4-6	T2nd	
4-14	At Mil.	L	2-5		6	9	McDonald	Haney	Miranda	4-7	T4th	1
4-15	Chi.	L	10-11		11	14	Karchner	Pichardo	Hernandez	4-8	5th	2
4-16	Chi.	W	6-5		8	10	Belcher	Bere	Montgomery	5-8	5th	2
4-17	Chi.	L	1-3		9	8	Fernandez	Appier	Hernandez	5-9	5th	2
4-18	Mil.	L	2-8		9	8	Sparks	Gubicza		5-10	5th	3
4-19	Mil.	L	2-8		8	12	McDonald	Haney		5-11	5th	4
4-20	Mil.	L	4-12		6	20	Miranda	Jacome		5-12	5th	5
4-21	Mil.	L	4-5		9	10	Wickander	Pichardo	Fetters	5-13	5th	6
4-22	N.Y.	L	2-6		6	14	Cone	Appier		5-14	5th	7
4-23	N.Y.	W	5-2		7	7	Gubicza	Key	Montgomery	6-14	5th	7
4-24	Bal.	L	8-11		10	18	Mercker	Haney		6-15	5th	7
4-25	Bal.	L	2-3		10	6	Rhodes	Valera	R. Myers	6-16	5th	8
4-26	At Bos.	W	4-3		7	10	Belcher	Clemens	Montgomery	7-16	5th	8
4-27	At Bos.	W	10-0		12	5	Appier	Sele		8-16	5th	7
4-28	At Bos.	W	9-7		13	16	Robinson	Slocumb	Montgomery	9-16	5th	7
4-29	At Min.	L	6-11		9	15	Hansell	Clark	Bennett	9-17	5th	7
4-30	At Min.	L	7-16		13	16	Naulty	Magnante		9-18	5th	8
5-1	At Min.	L	5-6	(10)	7	9	Stevens	Montgomery		9-19	5th	9
5-3	Oak.	W	3-1		7	6	Appier	Reyes	Montgomery	10-19	5th	10
5-4	Oak.	L	2-5		10	6	Wojciechowski	Gubicza	Groom	10-20	5th	10
5-5	Oak.	W	2-0		7	3	Haney	Prieto		11-20	5th	10
5-6	At Cal.	W	9-4		16	12	Belcher	Leftwich	Pichardo	12-20	5th	9
5-7	At Cal.	W	5-3		8	8	Valera	J. Abbott	Montgomery	13-20	5th	8
5-8	At Cal.	W	3-1	(14)	10	10	Pichardo	Eichhorn		14-20	5th	8
5-9	At Cal.	W	8-2		9	7	Gubicza	Grimsley		15-20	5th	7
5-10	At Sea.	W	14-10		14	11	Valera	T. Davis		16-20	T4th	6
5-11	At Sea.	L	1-11		6	17	Wolcott	Belcher	Carmona	16-21	T4th	7
5-12	At Sea.	L	5-8		8	12	Johnson	Linton	Charlton	16-22	5th	8
5-13	At Tex.	L	6-7		10	15	Cook	Montgomery	Henneman	16-23	5th	9
5-14	At Tex.	L	0-10		4	15	Hill	Gubicza		16-24	5th	10
5-15	At Tex.	W	3-1		8	10	Haney	Pavlik	Montgomery	17-24	5th	10
5-17	Tor.	W	4-2		8	7	Belcher	Guzman	Montgomery	18-24	5th	10
5-18	Tor.	L	2-6		8	10	Viola	Appier		18-25	5th	10
5-19	Tor.	L	2-3		8	10	Hanson	Gubicza	Timlin	18-26	5th	11
5-20	Tor.	W	5-4		8	7	Haney	Hentgen	Montgomery	19-26	5th	11
5-21	At Det.	W	7-1		12	4	Linton	B. Williams	Valera	20-26	5th	11
5-22	At Det.	W	6-4		10	10	Belcher	Farrell	Montgomery	21-26	4th	10
5-23	Tex.	W	4-2		8	10	Appier	Oliver	Montgomery	22-26	4th	10
5-24	Tex.	W	8-0		11	4	Gubicza	Witt		23-26	4th	10
5-25	Tex.	L	1-2		3	8	Helling	Haney	Henneman	23-27	4th	11
5-26	Tex.	L	4-6		11	10	Hill	Linton	Henneman	23-28	5th	12
5-27	Det.	W	5-4	(13)	10	9	Montgomery	Veres		24-28	T4th	11
5-29	Det.	L	4-5		7	9	Gohr	Appier	Walker	24-29	5th	10
5-31	At Tor.	L	2-4		7	9	Hentgen	Gubicza	Timlin	24-30	5th	12
6-1	At Tor.	L	3-5	(10)	11	10	Crabtree	Montgomery		24-31	5th	12
6-2	At Tor.	W	7-5		15	5	Belcher	Janzen	Montgomery	25-31	5th	12
6-3	At Oak.	L	1-2		7	7	Wasdin	Appier	Taylor	25-32	5th	12
6-4	At Oak.	L	3-8		10	16	Wengert	Gubicza		25-33	3rd	12
6-5	At Oak.	W	5-2		12	7	Haney	Johns	Montgomery	26-33	5th	12
6-7	Sea.	W	9-5		13	8	Valera	Wolcott		27-33	5th	12
6-8	Sea.	W	12-8		15	17	Appier	Milacki	Montgomery	28-33	5th	12
6-9	Sea.	L	2-3		11	11	Hitchcock	Gubicza	Charlton	28-34	5th	12
6-10	Cal.	L	5-7	(10)	10	15	McElroy	Pugh	Percival	28-35	5th	13
6-11	Cal.	L	9-11		8	18	McElroy	Valera	Percival	28-36	5th	14
6-12	Cal.	L	3-4	(10)	10	7	McElroy	Montgomery	Percival	28-37	5th	14
6-13	Bal.	W	10-2		14	3	Linton	Mercker		29-37	5th	14
6-14	Bal.	L	1-6		7	8	Mussina	Gubicza		29-38	5th	14
6-15	Bal.	W	7-6	(16)	17	18	Magnante	Krivda		30-38	5th	14
6-16	Bal.	L	5-13		9	18	Coppinger	Jacome	Mills	30-39	5th	14
6-17	At Mil.	L	4-9		10	14	Burrows	Appier		30-40	5th	14
6-18	At Mil.	L	1-9		8	9	Karl	Linton	Potts	30-41	5th	15
6-19	At Mil.	W	8-4	(10)	16	6	Pichardo	Mercedes		31-41	5th	15

ate	Opp.	Res.	Score	(inn.*)	Hits	Opp. hits	Winning pitcher	Losing pitcher	Save	Record	Pos.	GB
-21	At Bal.	L	3-9		8	13	Rhodes	Haney		31-42	5th	15 1/2
-22	At Bal.	L	3-5		8	6	Erickson	Montgomery		31-43	5th	15 1/2
-23	At Bal.	W	4-0		9	2	Appier	Krivda		32-43	5th	14 1/2
-25	Mil.	L	3-5		8	11	Bones	Gubicza	Fetters	32-44	5th	15 1/2
-26	Mil.	W	7-3		10	8	Haney	Givens		33-44	5th	14 1/2
-27	Mil.	L	2-6		6	10	McDonald	Belcher		33-45	5th	14 1/2
-28	Min.	W	6-2		10	5	Appier	Radke		34-45	5th	13 1/2
-29	Min.	L	7-12		9	16	Trombley	Linton		34-46	5th	14 1/2
-30	Min.	L	2-5		7	6	Rodriguez	Gubicza	Stevens	34-47	5th	15 1/2
-1	At Cle.	W	4-2		10	7	Haney	Nagy		35-47	5th	14 1/2
-2	At Cle.	L	2-3		10	8	Poole	Belcher		35-48	5th	15 1/2
-3	At Cle.	L	4-6		10	9	Tavarez	Magnante	Shuey	35-49	5th	16 1/2
-4	At Min.	W	5-3		7	10	Linton	Robertson	Montgomery	36-49	5th	15 1/2
-5	At Min.	L	8-9		9	13	Guardado	Montgomery		36-50	5th	15 1/2
-6	At Min.	W	8-5		10	7	Haney	Aguilera	Montgomery	37-50	5th	14 1/2
-7	At Min.	W	8-2		9	10	Belcher	Aldred		38-50	5th	14 1/2
-11	Chi.	W	3-2		10	8	Haney	Alvarez		39-50	5th	14 1/2
-12	Chi.	L	6-7		9	11	Tapani	Belcher	Hernandez	39-51	5th	15 1/2
-13	Chi.	L	1-3		4	8	Fernandez	Rosado		39-52	5th	16 1/2
-14	Chi.	L	2-3		3	8	Baldwin	Linton	Hernandez	39-53	5th	16 1/2
-15	Cle.	W	6-3		11	5	Magnante	Tavarez	Montgomery	40-53	5th	15 1/2
-16	Cle.	L	4-10		8	17	McDowell	Haney		40-54	5th	16 1/2
-17	Cle.	W	3-2		7	11	Belcher	Hershiser	Montgomery	41-54	5th	15 1/2
-18	At Chi.	W	7-1		11	3	Appier	Fernandez	Pichardo	42-54	5th	15 1/2
-19	At Chi.	W	7-4	(10)	13	9	Montgomery	Hernandez		43-54	5th	14 1/2
-20	At Chi.	W	7-5		11	10	Linton	Keyser	Montgomery	44-54	5th	14 1/2
-21	At Chi.	L	3-6		8	8	Alvarez	Haney	Hernandez	44-55	5th	15 1/2
-22	At Bos.	W	5-2		12	6	Belcher	Gordon		45-55	5th	15 1/2
-23	At Bos.	W	7-5		13	10	Appier	Sele		46-55	5th	14 1/2
-24	At Bos.	L	2-12		7	14	Moyer	Linton		46-56	5th	15 1/2
-25	At N.Y.	W	7-0		13	8	Rosado	Hutton		47-56	5th	15 1/2
-26	At N.Y.	L	1-15		6	21	Key	Haney		47-57	5th	16 1/2
-27	At N.Y.	L	4-5		9	10	Rogers	Belcher	Wetteland	47-58	5th	16 1/2
-28	At N.Y.	L	2-3		7	5	Wetteland	Jacome		47-59	5th	17 1/2
-30	Bos.	W	7-0		10	3	Rosado	Eshelman		48-59	5th	16 1/2
-31	Bos.	L	3-5		5	10	Wakefield	Haney	Slocumb	48-60	5th	17 1/2
-1	Bos.	W	9-4		14	8	Belcher	Clemens		49-60	5th	16 1/2
-2	N.Y.	W	4-3	(10)	8	8	Montgomery	M. Rivera		50-60	5th	16 1/2
-3	N.Y.	W	11-4		12	6	Linton	Weathers		51-60	5th	15 1/2
-4	N.Y.	L	3-5		8	12	Pettitte	Rosado		51-61	5th	16 1/2
-5	N.Y.	L	2-5		5	12	Key	Pichardo	Wetteland	51-62	5th	16 1/2
-6	Oak.	W	9-2		12	13	Belcher	Wasdin		52-62	5th	16 1/2
-7	Oak.	W	7-0		8	2	Appier	Prieto		53-62	5th	16 1/2
-8	Oak.	L	1-2		5	4	Wengert	Linton	Taylor	53-63	5th	17 1/2
-9	At Cal.	W	5-3		7	9	Rosado	Langston	Montgomery	54-63	5th	17 1/2
-10	At Cal.	W	18-3		15	8	Haney	J. Abbott		55-63	5th	16 1/2
-11	At Cal.	L	5-6		6	14	Springer	Belcher		55-64	T4th	16 1/2
-12	At Sea.	W	10-4		15	12	Appier	Moyer	Huisman	56-64	4th	16 1/2
-13	At Sea.	L	5-9		6	13	Mulholland	Linton	Johnson	56-65	4th	16 1/2
-14	At Sea.	W	3-1		10	10	Rosado	Wolcott	Montgomery	57-65	4th	15 1/2
-16	At Tex.	L	3-5		7	10	Burkett	Haney	Henneman	57-66	T4th	16 1/2
-17	At Tex.	W	4-1		15	6	Belcher	Hill		58-66	4th	16 1/2
-18	At Tex.	L	3-10		10	17	Gross	Appier		58-67	T4th	17 1/2
-19	Tor.	L	1-2		6	6	Spoljaric	Rosado	Timlin	58-68	5th	17 1/2
-20	Tor.	L	5-6	(14)	15	15	Timlin	Huisman		58-69	5th	18 1/2
-21	Tor.	L	2-6		6	10	Guzman	Haney		58-70	5th	18 1/2
-22	Det.	L	3-10		8	14	Thompson	Belcher		58-71	5th	19
-23	Det.	L	2-3		8	6	Sager	Appier	Olson	58-72	5th	19
-24	Det.	W	9-2		11	7	Rosado	Olivares		59-72	5th	18
-25	Det.	L	4-7		11	12	Van Poppel	Linton	Myers	59-73	5th	19
-27	Tex.	W	4-3	(10)	9	10	Montgomery	Russell		60-73	5th	19 1/2
-28	Tex.	W	4-3	(12)	13	6	Huisman	Gross		61-73	5th	19 1/2
-29	At Det.	L	1-4		12	9	Eischen	Appier	Lima	61-74	5th	20
-30	At Det.	L	0-4		5	6	Van Poppel	Rosado		61-75	5th	20
-31	At Det.	W	3-1		5	6	Linton	Lira	Montgomery	62-75	5th	19
-1	At Det.	W	3-2	(13)	7	7	Huisman	Myers	Jacome	63-75	5th	19
-2	At Tor.	W	2-0		6	4	Belcher	Hanson		64-75	5th	18
-3	At Tor.	W	5-2		12	7	Appier	Hentgen		65-75	5th	17
-4	At Tor.	L	0-6		6	9	Williams	Rosado		65-76	5th	18
-6	At Oak.	L	1-7		9	11	Adams	Haney		65-77	5th	18 1/2
-7	At Oak.	L	6-13		10	19	Prieto	Belcher		65-78	5th	19
-8	At Oak.	L	7-8	(10)	13	13	Corsi	Pichardo		65-79	5th	19 1/2
-10	Sea.	W	4-2		7	6	Rosado	Torres	Bluma	66-79	5th	20
-11	Sea.	W	4-2		8	7	Linton	Moyer	Bluma	67-79	5th	20
-12	Sea.	L	5-8		8	15	Mulholland	Haney	Charlton	67-80	5th	21

Date	Opp.	Res.	Score	(inn.*)	Hits	Opp. hits	Winning pitcher	Losing pitcher	Save	Record	Pos.	GB
9-13	Cal.	W	8-2		11	10	Belcher	J. Abbott		68-80	5th	20½
9-14	Cal.	W	8-5		10	11	Appier	Dickson		69-80	5th	21
9-16	Min.	W	6-5		11	12	Rosado	Radke	Bluma	70-80	5th	20½
9-17	Min.	W	4-2		11	10	Haney	Aldred	Bluma	71-80	5th	20½
9-18	Min.	L	4-7		7	11	Miller	Belcher		71-81	5th	21½
9-19	At Cle.	L	1-9		3	9	Ogea	Appier		71-82	5th	22½
9-20	At Cle.	W	6-4		14	6	Bevil	Nagy	Bluma	72-82	5th	21½
9-21	At Cle.	L	4-13		8	16	Hershiser	Rosado		72-83	5th	22½
9-22	At Cle.	L	5-6		8	10	McDowell	Jacome	Mesa	72-84	5th	23½
9-24	At Chi.	L	2-3		6	8	Castillo	Belcher		72-85	5th	25
9-25	At Chi.	W	8-2		12	9	Appier	Tapani		73-85	5th	25
9-27	Cle.	W	11-6		13	12	Rosado	Hershiser		74-85	5th	24
9-28	Cle.	L	4-5		11	9	Mercker	Scanlan	Mesa	74-86	5th	25
9-29	Cle.	W	4-1		11	8	Belcher	Ogea	Pichardo	75-86	5th	24

Monthly records: April (9-18), May (15-12), June (10-17), July (14-13), August (14-15), September (13-11).
*Innings, if other than nine.

HIGHLIGHTS

High point: After a sluggish start, the Royals went 37-36 following the All-Star break. That record ranked second in the A.L. Central only to Cleveland. Their longest winning streak—six games—was from May 5-10, which included a four-game sweep in Anaheim.

Low point: A 6-16 getaway effectively doomed any chance the Royals had of competing, even though they played nearly .500 (69-70) ball thereafter. The Royals finished last for the first time since the franchise began in 1969.

Turning point: Oddly enough, it came on August 11, 1995, when general manager Herk Robinson committed the Royals to a youth and rebuilding movement for 1996 with a slew of minor-league callups. Once that decision was made, any realistic chance of a title disappeared.

Most valuable player: Center fielder Tom Goodwin. He always could be counted on to ignite a generally powerless offense with infield hits, by trying to take an extra base or by attempting to steal. He hit .282 and stole 66 bases before injuries sidelined him in late September.

Most valuable pitcher: Righthander Tim Belcher. Belcher, signed as a free agent, paced the staff with a 15-11 record and 238⅔ innings pitched. He had a 3.92 ERA, second on the club to Kevin Appier's 3.62.

Most improved player: Third baseman Craig Paquette. Paquette, released by Oakland, was called up in late April and led the Royals with 22 homers and 67 RBIs, both career highs.

Most pleasant surprise: Rookie left-hander Jose Rosado. Rosado, just 21, made 16 starts and showed great poise in posting an 8-6 record and 3.21 ERA.

Biggest disappointment: Designated hitter/first baseman Bob Hamelin. The 1994 Rookie of the Year struggled so much he was sent to the minors. He returned but finished with nine homers, 40 RBIs and a .255 average.

Key injuries: Righthander Mark Gubicza had his right leg broken by a Paul Molitor line drive and was finished after 19 starts. Second baseman Bip Roberts was limited to 90 games by a hamstring pull

and rib-cage strain. Outfielder Michael Tucker's season was ended in August by a dislocated finger. Closer Jeff Montgomery had shoulder surgery in early September. Outfielder Tom Goodwin, nagged by a few late-season injuries, had shoulder surgery after the season.

Notable: After failing defensively at shortstop, Jose Offerman was switched to first base and later to second base. He tied third baseman Joe Randa as the club's leading hitter at .303 and led in runs (85), hits (170) and walks (74). . . . After a poor season with Boston, catcher Mike Macfarlane rebounded to hit .274 with 19 homers. . . . Manager Bob Boone used 151 batting orders in 161 games. . . . With closer Jeff Montgomery out, rookie Jaime Bluma recorded five saves.

—DICK KAEGEL

RECORDS

1996 regular-season record: 75-86 (5th in A.L. Central); 37-43 at home; 38-43 on road; 27-34 vs. East; 22-30 vs. Central; 26-22 vs. West; 23-29 vs. lefthanded starters; 52-57 vs. righthanded starters; 66-76 on grass; 9-10 on turf; 15-29 in daytime; 60-57 at night; 14-26 in one-run games; 10-6 in extra-inning games; 0-0-0 in doubleheaders.

Team record past five years: 365-379 (.491), ranks 8th in league in that span).

TEAM LEADERS

Batting average: Jose Offerman (.303).
At-bats: Jose Offerman (561).
Runs: Jose Offerman (85).
Hits: Jose Offerman (170).
Total bases: Jose Offerman (234).
Doubles: Keith Lockhart, Jose Offerman (33).
Triples: Jose Offerman (8).
Home runs: Craig Paquette (22).
Runs batted in: Craig Paquette (67).
Stolen bases: Tom Goodwin (66).
Slugging percentage: Jose Offerman (.417).
On-base percentage: Jose Offerman (.384).
Wins: Tim Belcher (15).
Earned-run average: Kevin Appier (3.62).

Complete games: Kevin Appier (5).
Shutouts: Kevin Appier, Tim Belcher, Mark Gubicza, Chris Haney, Jose Rosado (1).
Saves: Jeff Montgomery (24).
Innings pitched: Tim Belcher (238.2).
Strikeouts: Kevin Appier (207).

GAMES BY POSITION

Catcher: Mike Macfarlane 99, Sal Fasano 51, Mike Sweeney 26, Henry Mercedes 4.
First base: Jose Offerman 96, Bob Hamelin 33, Kevin Young 27, Craig Paquette 19, Michael Tucker 9, Joe Vitiello 9, Joe Randa 7, Dave Howard 2.
Second base: Keith Lockhart 84, Bip Roberts 63, Jose Offerman 38, Joe Randa 15, Chris Stynes 5, Dave Howard 3.
Third base: Joe Randa 92, Keith Lockhart 55, Craig Paquette 51, Kevin Young 7, Chris Stynes 2.
Shortstop: Dave Howard 135, Jose Offerman 36, Craig Paquette 11.
Outfield: Johnny Damon 144, Tom Goodwin 136, Michael Tucker 98, Craig Paquette 47, Les Norman 38, Jon Nunnally 29, Rod Myers 19, Chris Stynes 19, Kevin Young 17, Patrick Lennon 11, Bip Roberts 11, Dave Howard 1, Jose Offerman 1, Joe Vitiello 1.
Designated hitter: Joe Vitiello 70, Bob Hamelin 47, Mike Sweeney 22, Bip Roberts 16, Mike Macfarlane 9, Les Norman 7, Craig Paquette 6, Tom Goodwin 5, Jon Nunnally 4, Michael Tucker 4, Chris Stynes 3, Kevin Young 2, Johnny Damon 1, Dave Howard 1, Patrick Lennon 1, Keith Lockhart 1, Joe Randa 1.

TOP DRAFT CHOICES

1. **Dermal Brown**, OF, Marlboro (N.Y.) Central H.S.
2. **Taylor Myers**, RHP, Green Valley H.S., Henderson, Nev.
3. **Chad Durbin**, SS-RHP, Woodlawn H.S., Baton Rouge, La.
4. **Corey Thurman**, RHP, Texas H.S., Wake Village, Tex.
5. **Jeremy Hill**, C, W.T. White H.S., Dallas.
6. **Jeremy Giambi**, OF, Cal State Fullerton.
7. **Scott Mullen**, LHP, Dallas Baptist Univ.
8. **Javier Flores**, C, Univ. of Oklahoma.
9. **Jeremy Morris**, OF, Florida State Univ.
10. **Steve Hueston**, RHP, Long Beach State U.

MILWAUKEE BREWERS
AMERICAN LEAGUE CENTRAL DIVISION

1997 BREWERS SCHEDULE

Home games shaded.
* — All-Star Game at Jacobs Field (Cleveland)
D — Day game (any game starting before 5 p.m.)

APRIL

SUN	MON	TUE	WED	THU	FRI	SAT
		1 D	2	3 TEX	4 TOR	5 D TOR
6 D TOR	7 D TEX	8 D	9 TEX	10 D TEX	11 TOR	12 D TOR
13 D TOR	14 TEX	15 D DET	16 NYY	17 D NYY	18 CLE	19 D CLE
20 D CLE	21	22 NYY	23 D NYY	24 CLE	25 CLE	26 CLE
27 D CLE	28	29 DET	30 D DET			

MAY

SUN	MON	TUE	WED	THU	FRI	SAT
				1	2 SEA	3 SEA
4 D SEA	5 OAK	6 OAK	7 D OAK	8 ANA	9 ANA	10 ANA
11 ANA	12 SEA	13 D SEA	14 OAK	15 OAK	16 ANA	17 ANA
18 ANA	19	20 MIN	21 D MIN	22	23 CWS	24 CWS
25 D CWS	26 D BOS	27 BOS	28 MIN	29 D MIN	30 CWS	31 CWS

JUNE

SUN	MON	TUE	WED	THU	FRI	SAT
CWS	2 D CWS	3 BOS	4 BOS	5 D BOS	6 NYY	7 D NYY
8 D NYY	9	10 CLE	11 CLE	12 CLE	13 D CUB	14 D CUB
15 D CUB	16 STL	17 STL	18 STL	19	20 KC	21 KC
22 KC	23 BAL	24 BAL	25 D BAL	26 KC	27 KC	28 KC
29 D KC	30 CIN					

JULY

SUN	MON	TUE	WED	THU	FRI	SAT
		1 CIN	2 CIN	3 D MIN	4 D MIN	5 MIN
6 D MIN	7	8 *	9 *	10	11 BAL	12 BAL
13 D BAL	14 KC	15 KC	16 CLE	17 CLE	18 NYY	19 NYY
20 NYY	21 NYY	22 TOR	23 TOR	24 TOR	25 DET	26 DET
27 D DET	28 TOR	29 D TOR	30	31 SEA		

AUGUST

SUN	MON	TUE	WED	THU	FRI	SAT
					1 SEA	2 SEA
3 D SEA	4 ANA	5 ANA	6 ANA	7 D OAK	8 OAK	9 D OAK
10 D SEA	11 SEA	12 ANA	13	14 D ANA	15 OAK	16 OAK
17 D OAK	18 TEX	19 TEX	20 TEX	21 DET	22 DET	23 DET
24 D TEX	25 TEX	26 TEX	27 D TEX	28	29 PIT	30 PIT
31 D PIT						

SEPTEMBER

SUN	MON	TUE	WED	THU	FRI	SAT
	1 D HOU	2 HOU	3 HOU	4	5 BOS	6 D BOS
7 D BOS	8 CWS	9 CWS	10 CWS	11	12 BOS	13 BOS
14 D BOS	15 CWS	16 CWS	17 BAL	18 BAL	19 MIN	20 MIN
21 D MIN	22 MIN	23 KC	24 KC	25 KC	26 BAL	27 BAL
28 D BAL						

1997 SEASON

CLUB DIRECTORY

President, chief executive officer
Allan H. (Bud) Selig

Sr. vice president, baseball operations
Sal Bando

Vice president & general counsel
Wendy Selig-Prieb

Vice president, broadcast operations
Bill Haig

Vice president, broadcast sales
Mitch Nye

V.p., new ballpark development
Michael Bucek

Vice president, stadium operations
Gabe Paul Jr.

Vice president of corporate affairs
Laurel Prieb

Director, finance
Paul Baniel

Director of Brewers Gold Club
Geoff Campion

Scouting director
Ken Califano

Senior consultant, baseball operations
Dee Fondy

Special assistants, baseball operations
Larry Haney
Chuck Tanner

Assistant general counsel
Eugene (Pepi) Randolph

Director of community relations
Michael Downs

Director of stadium administration
Terry Ann Peterson

Director of grounds
Gary Vandenberg

Director of media relations
Jon Greenberg

Director of player development
Cecil Cooper

V.p., admin. & human resources
Tom Gausden

Director of publications
Mario Ziino

Director of ticket operations
John Barnes

Vice president of ticket sales
Bob Voight

Traveling secretary
Steve Ethier

Trainers
John Adam
Al Price

Strength and conditioning coach
John Rewolinski

Team physicians
Dr. Dennis Sullivan
Dr. Drew Palin

Western crosschecker
Lou Snipp

Eastern crosschecker
Ron Rizzi

Midwest supervisor
Fred Beene

West Coast supervisor
Kevin Christman

East Coast supervisor
Russ Bove

International scouting supervisor
Epy Guerrero

Special assignment scouts
Felix Delgado
Paul Tretiak
Walter Youse

Scouts
Walter Boggen, Jeff Brookens, Domingo Carrasquel, Rich Chiles, Ramon Conde, Dick Fanning, Bill Foley, Dick Foster, Danny Garcia, Mike Gibbons, Manolo Hernandez, Ken Houp, Elvio Jiminez, Harvey Kuenn Jr., John Logan, Demie Mainieri, Alex Morales, Mike Powers, Doug Reynolds, Corey Rodriguez, Bob Sloan, Jonathan Story, Tom Tanous, John Viney, Red Whitsett, Ric Wilson, David Young

MINOR LEAGUE AFFILIATES

Class	Team	League	Manager
AAA	Tucson	Pacific Coast	Tim Ireland
AA	El Paso	Texas	Dave Machemer
A	Stockton	California	Greg Mahlberg
A	Beloit	Midwest	Luis Salazar
Rookie	Helena	Pioneer	Alex Morales
Rookie	Ogden	Pioneer	Bernie Moncallo

BROADCAST INFORMATION
Radio: WTMJ-AM (620).
TV: WVTV-TV (Channel 24).
Cable TV: Wisconsin Sports Network.

SPRING TRAINING
Ballpark (city): Compadre Stadium (Chandler, Ariz.).
Ticket information: 602-895-1200.

1997 SEASON Milwaukee Brewers

SPRING TRAINING ROSTER

Manager—Phil Garner (3).
Coaches—Chris Bando (12), Bill Castro (35), Jim Gantner (17), Lamar Johnson (23), Don Rowe (45).

No.	PITCHERS	B/T	Ht./Wt.	Born	1996 clubs
38	Adamson, Joel	L/L	6-4/185	7-2-71	Charlotte, Florida
59	Benny, Peter	R/R	6-3/195	11-9-75	Beloit
13	D'Amico, Jeff	R/R	6-7/245	12-27-75	El Paso, Milwaukee
58	De Los Santos, Valerio	L/L	6-2/180	9-6-75	Beloit
21	Eldred, Cal	R/R	6-4/235	11-24-67	New Orleans, Milwaukee
36	Fetters, Mike	R/R	6-4/224	12-19-64	Milwaukee
39	Florie, Bryce	R/R	5-11/190	5-21-70	San Diego, Milwaukee
42	Karl, Scott	L/L	6-2/195	8-9-71	Milwaukee
	Maloney, Sean	R/R	6-7/210	5-25-71	El Paso
40	McDonald, Ben	R/R	6-7/214	11-24-67	Milwaukee
41	Mercedes, Jose	R/R	6-1/199	3-5-71	New Orleans, Milwaukee
25	Miranda, Angel	L/L	6-1/195	11-9-69	Milwaukee
	Potts, Michael	L/L	5-9/170	9-5-70	Milwaukee, New Orleans
47	Reyes, Al	R/R	6-1/193	4-10-71	Beloit, Milwaukee
53	Santos, Henry	L/L	6-1/175	1-17-73	El Paso
50	Sparks, Steve	R/R	6-0/187	7-2-65	Milwaukee, New Orleans
31	Vanegmond, Tim	R/R	6-2/180	5-31-69	Pawtucket, New Orleans, Milwaukee
49	Villone, Ron	L/L	6-3/235	1-16-70	Las Vegas, San Diego, Milwaukee
43	Ware, Jeff	R/R	6-3/190	11-11-70	Syracuse, Toronto
27	Wickman, Bob	R/R	6-1/212	2-6-69	New York A.L., Milwaukee

No.	CATCHERS	B/T	Ht./Wt.	Born	1996 clubs
15	Hughes, Bobby	R/R	6-4/237	3-10-71	New Orleans, El Paso
16	Levis, Jesse	L/R	5-9/180	4-14-68	Milwaukee
22	Matheny, Mike	R/R	6-3/205	9-22-70	Milwaukee, New Orleans
11	Stinnett, Kelly	R/R	5-11/195	2-14-70	Milwaukee, New Orleans

No.	INFIELDERS	B/T	Ht./Wt.	Born	1996 clubs
52	Belliard, Ronnie	R/R	5-8/180	7-4-76	El Paso
26	Cirillo, Jeff	R/R	6-2/188	9-23-69	Milwaukee
32	Jaha, John	R/R	6-1/222	5-27-66	Milwaukee
	Landry, Todd	R/L	6-4/215	9-21-72	New Orleans
8	Loretta, Mark	R/R	6-0/175	8-14-71	New Orleans, Milwaukee
14	Nilsson, Dave	L/R	6-3/231	12-14-69	New Orleans, Milwaukee
9	Unroe, Tim	R/R	6-3/200	10-7-70	New Orleans, Milwaukee
2	Valentin, Jose	L/R	5-10/166	10-12-69	Milwaukee
1	Vina, Fernando	L/R	5-9/170	4-16-69	Milwaukee
5	Williamson, Antone	L/R	6-1/195	7-18-73	New Orleans

No.	OUTFIELDERS	B/T	Ht./Wt.	Born	1996 clubs
7	Banks, Brian	B/R	6-3/200	9-28-70	New Orleans, Milwaukee
20	Burnitz, Jeromy	L/R	6-0/180	4-15-69	Cleveland, Milwaukee
24	Carr, Chuck	B/R	5-10/165	8-10-68	New Orleans, Milwaukee
18	Dunn, Todd	R/R	6-5/220	7-29-70	El Paso, Milwaukee
28	Felder, Ken	R/R	6-3/220	2-9-71	New Orleans
30	Mieske, Matt	R/R	6-0/192	2-13-68	Milwaukee
10	Newfield, Marc	R/R	6-4/205	10-19-72	San Diego, Milwaukee
29	Williams, Gerald	R/R	6-2/190	8-10-66	New York A.L., Milwaukee

BALLPARK INFORMATION

Ballpark (capacity, surface)
County Stadium (53,192, grass)

Address
County Stadium
P.O. Box 3099 Milwaukee, WI
53201-3099

Business phone
414-933-4114

Ticket information
414-933-9000

Ticket prices
$20 (diamond box)
$17 (mezzanine, lower box)
$13 (upper box, lower grandstand)
$8 (upper grandstand)
$7 (general admission)
$4 (bleachers)

Field dimensions (from home plate)
To left field at foul line, 315 feet
To center field, 402 feet
To right field at foul line, 315 feet

First game played
April 7, 1970 (Angels 12, Brewers 0)

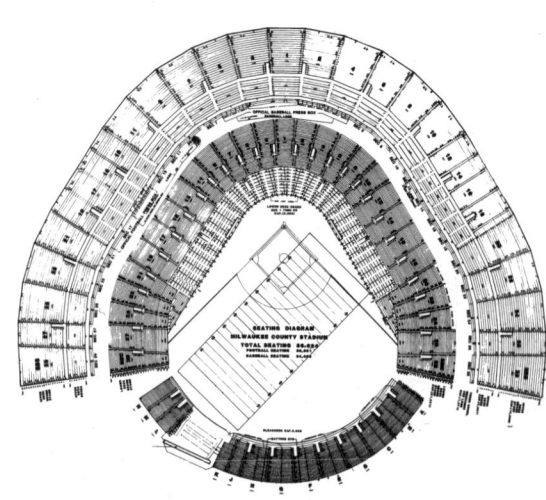

DAY BY DAY

Date	Opp.	Res.	Score	(inn.*)	Hits	Opp. hits	Winning pitcher	Losing pitcher	Save	Record	Pos.	GB
4-2	At Cal.	W	15-9		22	15	Wickander	Finley		1-0	1st	+1/2
4-3	At Cal.	L	2-3	(11)	7	8	James	Lloyd		1-1	2nd	1/2
4-5	At Sea.	W	10-6		11	6	Karl	Hurtado		2-1	1st	+1/2
4-6	At Sea.	L	5-8		6	8	Johnson	Sparks		2-2	2nd	1/2
4-7	At Sea.	L	1-3		3	7	Hitchcock	Bones	Jackson	2-3	T2nd	1/2
4-9	Oak.	W	10-4		12	7	McDonald	Van Poppel		3-3	1st	+1/2
4-11	Oak.	L	0-11		6	13	Johns	Karl		3-4	2nd	1/2
4-12	K.C.	L	1-4		3	8	Appier	Bones	Montgomery	3-5	T2nd	1/2
4-13	K.C.	L	2-3		7	1	Gubicza	Sparks	Montgomery	3-6	5th	1
4-14	K.C.	W	5-2		9	6	McDonald	Haney	Miranda	4-6	3rd	1
4-16	N.Y.	W	6-3		12	10	Karl	Key		5-6	2nd	1 1/2
4-17	N.Y.	W	8-4		12	9	Bones	Cone		6-6	2nd	1/2
4-18	At K.C.	W	8-2		8	9	Sparks	Gubicza		7-6	T1st	...
4-19	At K.C.	W	8-2		12	8	McDonald	Haney		8-6	T1st	...
4-20	At K.C.	W	12-4		20	6	Miranda	Jacome		9-6	T1st	...
4-21	At K.C.	W	5-4		10	9	Wickander	Pichardo	Fetters	10-6	T1st	...
4-22	At Oak.	L	2-6		5	7	Reyes	Bones	Briscoe	10-7	2nd	1
4-23	At Oak.	L	6-9		8	10	Wojciechowski	Sparks	Mohler	10-8	2nd	2
4-24	Cal.	L	3-4		11	9	Boskie	McDonald	Percival	10-9	3rd	2
4-25	Cal.	W	6-5		11	9	Fetters	James		11-9	3rd	2
4-26	Sea.	L	5-6		6	11	Carmona	Potts	Charlton	11-10	3rd	3
4-27	Sea.	L	5-6		12	11	Wells	Bones	Charlton	11-11	T3rd	3
4-28	Sea.	W	16-9		16	8	Potts	T. Davis		12-11	3rd	3
4-30	At Tor.	L	8-9		12	15	Crabtree	Boze		12-12	4th	4
5-1	At Tor.	L	3-9		4	10	Guzman	Miranda		12-13	4th	5
5-2	At Tor.	L	5-7		6	10	Hanson	Karl	Timlin	12-14	4th	6
5-3	At Bal.	L	2-8		4	9	Erickson	Bones		12-15	4th	7
5-4	At Bal.	L	5-10		13	9	Mussina	Sparks		12-16	4th	7
5-5	At Bal.	W	13-1		13	4	McDonald	Haynes		13-16	4th	7
5-7	Bos.	L	2-4		5	7	Clemens	Miranda	Slocumb	13-17	4th	6 1/2
5-9	Bos.	W	17-2		17	6	Bones	Sele		14-17	4th	6 1/2
5-10	Bal.	L	7-10	(12)	6	18	Orosco	Garcia	McDowell	14-18	T4th	6 1/2
5-11	Bal.	L	3-5	(10)	3	4	Rhodes	Potts	R. Myers	14-19	T4th	7 1/2
5-12	Bal.	W	6-4		11	7	Miranda	Erickson	Fetters	15-19	4th	7 1/2
5-13	Chi.	W	6-2		11	8	Sparks	Baldwin	Boze	16-19	T3rd	7
5-15	Chi.	L	8-20		12	21	Alvarez	Bones	Keyser	16-20	4th	8 1/2
5-16	Chi.	W	3-2		11	6	Lloyd	Tapani	Fetters	17-20	4th	8 1/2
5-17	At Min.	W	12-1		15	5	Karl	Parra		18-20	3rd	8 1/2
5-18	At Min.	W	7-3		13	8	Miranda	Mahomes	Fetters	19-20	3rd	7 1/2
5-19	At Min.	W	4-2		9	9	Sparks	Robertson	Fetters	20-20	3rd	7 1/2
5-20	At Min.	W	3-2		10	8	Bones	Rodriguez	Fetters	21-20	3rd	7
5-21	At Cle.	L	5-6		13	9	Tavarez	Boze		21-21	3rd	8
5-22	At Cle.	W	10-8		13	12	Karl	McDowell	Fetters	22-21	3rd	7
5-23	At Cle.	L	1-5		8	10	Hershiser	Miranda		22-22	3rd	8
5-24	At Chi.	L	3-4		7	10	L. Thomas	Sparks	Hernandez	22-23	3rd	9
5-25	At Chi.	L	7-9		12	11	Alvarez	Bones	Hernandez	22-24	3rd	10
5-26	At Chi.	L	1-12		7	17	Tapani	McDonald		22-25	3rd	11
5-28	Min.	W	7-3		10	8	Karl	Mahomes	Garcia	23-25	3rd	9 1/2
5-29	Min.	L	7-8	(12)	14	12	Hansell	Lloyd		23-26	3rd	9 1/2
5-30	Cle.	L	0-2		7	6	Nagy	Bones	Mesa	23-27	T3rd	10 1/2
5-31	Cle.	L	4-10		10	18	Martinez	McDonald		23-28	T3rd	11 1/2
6-1	Cle.	W	2-1		6	7	Garcia	McDowell	Fetters	24-28	T3rd	10 1/2
6-2	Cle.	L	6-11		12	15	Poole	Karl		24-29	4th	11 1/2
6-3	Tex.	L	6-9		10	12	Witt	Sparks	Henneman	24-30	4th	12
6-4	Tex.	W	6-2		7	8	Bones	Gross		25-30	4th	11
6-5	Tex.	W	6-4		12	9	McDonald	Hill	Fetters	26-30	4th	11
6-7	At Bos.	L	7-10		16	10	Garces	Garcia	Slocumb	26-31	4th	11 1/2
6-8	At Bos.	W	3-2	(10)	6	9	Lloyd	Hudson	Fetters	27-31	4th	11 1/2
6-9	At Bos.	W	11-8	(10)	18	9	Burrows	Slocumb	Fetters	28-31	4th	10 1/2
6-10	At Tex.	L	3-8		8	14	Gross	Givens		28-32	4th	11 1/2
6-11	At Tex.	W	14-4		20	14	McDonald	Hill	Garcia	29-32	4th	11 1/2
6-12	At Tex.	L	6-13		9	12	Pavlik	Miranda		29-33	4th	11 1/2
6-13	Oak.	W	16-3		19	12	Karl	Wojciechowski		30-33	4th	11 1/2
6-14	Oak.	W	6-2		10	6	Bones	Wasdin		31-33	T3rd	10 1/2
6-15	Oak.	W	12-9		15	12	Givens	Wengert	Garcia	32-33	3rd	10 1/2
6-16	Oak.	L	9-10		12	13	Taylor	Fetters	Mohler	32-34	T3rd	10 1/2
6-17	K.C.	W	9-4		14	10	Burrows	Appier		33-34	T3rd	10
6-18	K.C.	W	9-1		9	8	Karl	Linton	Potts	34-34	3rd	10
6-19	K.C.	L	4-8	(10)	6	16	Pichardo	Mercedes		34-35	3rd	11
6-20	Cal.	L	3-10		6	15	Langston	Givens		34-36	4th	12
6-21	Cal.	W	10-5		11	11	McDonald	J. Abbott		35-36	3rd	10 1/2
6-22	Cal.	L	4-6		11	7	Boskie	Miranda	Percival	35-37	3rd	10 1/2

1997 SEASON **Milwaukee Brewers**

Date	Opp.	Res.	Score	(inn.*)	Hits	Opp. hits	Winning pitcher	Losing pitcher	Save	Record	Pos.	GB
6-23	Cal.	W	8-4		12	12	Garcia	Finley		36-37	3rd	9¹
6-25	At K.C.	W	5-3		11	8	Bones	Gubicza	Fetters	37-37	3rd	9¹
6-26	At K.C.	L	3-7		8	10	Haney	Givens		37-38	3rd	9¹
6-27	At K.C.	W	6-2		10	6	McDonald	Belcher		38-38	3rd	8¹
6-28	At Tor.	W	5-1		11	4	D'Amico	Guzman	Fetters	39-38	3rd	7¹
6-29	At Tor.	W	7-4		9	10	Karl	Janzen		40-38	3rd	7¹
6-30	At Tor.	L	2-15		7	17	Hanson	Bones		40-39	3rd	8¹
7-1	At Det.	W	2-0		9	7	Sparks	Olivares	Fetters	41-39	3rd	7¹
7-2	At Det.	W	2-1	(11)	10	6	Garcia	Sager	Fetters	42-39	3rd	7¹
7-3	At Det.	L	5-8		13	11	B. Williams	D'Amico		42-40	3rd	8¹
7-4	At N.Y.	L	1-4		8	7	Pettitte	Karl	Wetteland	42-41	3rd	8¹
7-5	At N.Y.	L	3-12		10	15	Gooden	Bones		42-42	3rd	8¹
7-6	At N.Y.	L	0-2		8	11	Key	Sparks	Wetteland	42-43	3rd	8¹
7-7	At N.Y.	W	4-1		7	9	McDonald	Rogers	Fetters	43-43	3rd	8¹
7-11	Tor.	L	3-6		4	8	Guzman	D'Amico	Castillo	43-44	3rd	9¹
7-12	Tor.	W	12-5		15	10	McDonald	Hanson		44-44	3rd	9¹
7-13	Tor.	L	7-15		13	18	Hentgen	Karl		44-45	3rd	10¹
7-14	Tor.	L	5-7	(10)	9	9	Crabtree	Garcia	Timlin	44-46	3rd	10¹
7-15	Det.	L	9-10		16	17	Sager	Bones	Olson	44-47	3rd	10¹
7-16	Det.	W	20-7		18	10	D'Amico	B. Williams		45-47	3rd	10¹
7-17	Det.	W	3-2	(10)	5	6	Fetters	Urbani		46-47	3rd	9¹
7-18	N.Y.	W	16-4		13	10	Karl	Gooden		47-47	3rd	9¹
7-19	N.Y.	W	7-5		10	12	Eldred	Pettitte	Fetters	48-47	3rd	8¹
7-20	N.Y.	L	2-4		6	9	M. Rivera	Vanegmond	Wetteland	48-48	3rd	9¹
7-21	N.Y.	W	3-2		7	6	D'Amico	Key	Fetters	49-48	3rd	9¹
7-22	At Sea.	L	3-8		5	13	Wagner	Mercedes		49-49	3rd	10¹
7-23	At Sea.	W	7-3		12	9	Karl	Carmona		50-49	3rd	9¹
7-24	At Sea.	L	7-8		11	15	Ayala	Fetters		50-50	3rd	10¹
7-25	At Cal.	L	4-5		5	10	Holtz	Lloyd		50-51	3rd	11¹
7-26	At Cal.	L	5-6		6	8	Springer	D'Amico	Percival	50-52	T3rd	12¹
7-27	At Cal.	L	0-7		6	9	Finley	McDonald		50-53	T3rd	12¹
7-28	At Cal.	W	4-3	(13)	12	13	Miranda	Holtz	Garcia	51-53	T3rd	12¹
7-30†	Sea.	L	5-6		11	12	Wells	Eldred	Ayala	51-54	4th	12¹
7-30‡	Sea.	W	4-3		8	7	Vanegmond	Wolcott	Fetters	52-54	3rd	12
7-31	Sea.	L	3-9		10	11	Hitchcock	D'Amico		52-55	3rd	13
8-1	Sea.	L	2-9		6	16	Moyer	McDonald		52-56	3rd	13
8-2	At Oak.	W	4-3	(10)	10	9	Miranda	Taylor	Fetters	53-56	3rd	13
8-3	At Oak.	W	7-0		7	4	Bones	Johns		54-56	3rd	12
8-4	At Oak.	L	2-4		8	8	Telgheder	Vanegmond	Taylor	54-57	3rd	13
8-5	At Oak.	W	13-3		12	6	Eldred	Adams		55-57	3rd	12
8-6	Bal.	L	3-13		4	15	Mussina	McDonald		55-58	3rd	13
8-7	Bal.	L	2-12		10	14	Erickson	Karl		55-59	3rd	14
8-8	Bal.	L	4-6		13	7	Coppinger	D'Amico	R. Myers	55-60	4th	15
8-9†	Bos.	L	7-9		12	9	Suppan	Vanegmond	Slocumb	55-61		
8-9‡	Bos.	L	1-4		6	9	Eshelman	Bones	Belinda	55-62	4th	16¹
8-10	Bos.	L	2-3		8	5	Wakefield	Eldred		55-63	T4th	16¹
8-11	Bos.	L	0-2		6	6	Clemens	McDonald	Belinda	55-64	T4th	16¹
8-13	At Bal.	L	3-4		6	2	Corbin	Lloyd	R. Myers	55-65	5th	17
8-14	At Bal.	L	5-8		7	9	Milchin	Bones	R. Myers	55-66	5th	17
8-16†	Chi.	W	9-7		11	11	Miranda	Levine	Villone	56-66		
8-16‡	Chi.	W	3-2		5	8	Vanegmond	Tapani	Fetters	57-66	T4th	16¹
8-17	Chi.	L	2-6		10	12	Fernandez	McDonald	Hernandez	57-67	5th	17¹
8-18	Chi.	W	8-7		11	9	Miranda	Darwin	Fetters	58-67	T4th	17¹
8-19	At Min.	W	6-1		10	4	D'Amico	Rodriguez		59-67	4th	16¹
8-20	At Min.	L	7-12		15	20	Parra	Bones		59-68	4th	17¹
8-21	At Min.	W	10-7		12	12	Jones	Stevens	Fetters	60-68	4th	16¹
8-23	At Cle.	W	6-5	(11)	12	10	Jones	Mesa	Fetters	61-68	4th	15¹
8-24	At Cle.	W	4-3	(10)	9	10	Wickman	Plunk	Fetters	62-68	4th	14¹
8-25	At Cle.	L	5-8		7	11	Shuey	Miranda	Mesa	62-69	4th	15¹
8-26	At Chi.	W	3-2		9	9	Eldred	Alvarez	Jones	63-69	4th	15¹
8-27	At Chi.	W	4-2		11	7	Vanegmond	Fernandez	Fetters	64-69	4th	15¹
8-28	At Chi.	L	0-2		6	7	Baldwin	McDonald	Hernandez	64-70	4th	16¹
8-29	Min.	L	1-6		9	11	Rodriguez	Karl		64-71	4th	17
8-30	Min.	W	5-4	(12)	13	12	Wickman	Parra		65-71	4th	16
8-31	Min.	W	3-2		9	6	Jones	Robertson	Fetters	66-71	4th	15
9-1	Min.	L	2-6		10	11	Aldred	Vanegmond		66-72	4th	16
9-2	Cle.	W	7-6		9	8	Jones	Mesa		67-72	4th	15
9-3	Cle.	W	8-2		12	10	Karl	Hershiser		68-72	4th	14
9-4	Cle.	L	0-7		4	14	Ogea	D'Amico		68-73	4th	15
9-6	Tex.	L	3-7		7	8	Burkett	Eldred		68-74	4th	15¹
9-7	Tex.	L	1-2		4	7	Hill	McDonald	Henneman	68-75	4th	16
9-8	Tex.	L	1-7		5	11	Witt	Florie		68-76	4th	16¹
9-9	At Bos.	W	6-0		10	6	Karl	Gordon		69-76	4th	16¹
9-10	At Bos.	W	11-10		14	14	Garcia	Hudson	Fetters	70-76	4th	16¹
9-11	At Bos.	L	1-4		5	10	Wakefield	Eldred	Slocumb	70-77	4th	17¹

Date	Opp.	Res.	Score	(inn.*)	Hits	Opp. hits	Winning pitcher	Losing pitcher	Save	Record	Pos.	GB
9-12	At Tex.	W	15-4		18	9	McDonald	Hill		71-77	4th	17 1/2
9-13	At Tex.	W	6-3		11	7	D'Amico	Witt	Fetters	72-77	4th	17
9-14	At Tex.	W	8-6		11	9	Karl	Pavlik	Fetters	73-77	4th	17 1/2
9-15	At Tex.	L	2-6		10	11	Oliver	Garcia	Vosberg	73-78	4th	17 1/2
9-17	Tor.	W	4-0		5	3	McDonald	Andujar		74-78	4th	18
9-18	Tor.	W	2-1		7	4	Fetters	Timlin		75-78	4th	18
9-20	Det.	L	1-10		7	10	Sager	Karl		75-79	T3rd	18 1/2
9-21	Det.	W	13-6		13	9	D'Amico	Van Poppel	Villone	76-79	T3rd	18 1/2
9-22	Det.	L	5-7		11	12	Lima	Fetters		76-80	T3rd	19 1/2
9-23	At Bal.	W	8-7	(10)	11	13	Jones	Mathews	Fetters	77-80	3rd	19 1/2
9-25†	At N.Y.	L	2-19		5	20	Cone	Vanegmond		77-81		
9-25‡	At N.Y.	L	2-6		7	8	Rogers	Karl		77-82	3rd	21 1/2
9-27	At Det.	W	7-6	(6)	8	6	Wickman	Van Poppel		78-82	3rd	20 1/2
9-28	At Det.	W	7-2		8	6	Eldred	Moehler		79-82	3rd	20 1/2
9-29	At Det.	W	7-5	(10)	15	10	Reyes	Cummings	Fetters	80-82	3rd	19 1/2

Monthly records: April (12-12), May (11-16), June (17-11), July (12-16), August (14-16), September (14-11).
*Innings, if other than nine. †First game of doubleheader. ‡Second game of doubleheader.

HIGHLIGHTS

High point: The Brewers won a season-high seven consecutive games from April 14-21, the last time they would hold or share first place all season. The winning streak included the club's first four-game sweep over the Royals in Kansas City.
Low point: A nine-game losing streak from August 6-14 dropped the club's record to 11 games under .500 (55-66) and sabotaged any hopes it had of a wild-card berth.
Turning point: Two weeks before the nine-game losing streak, the Brewers lost eight of 11 games against Seattle and California, several of the demoralizing, late-inning variety.
Most valuable player: First baseman John Jaha. He stayed off the D.L. for the first time in two years and led the club in homers (34), runs (108) and RBIs (118). He also hit an even .300 and played solid defense.
Most valuable pitcher: Closer Mike Fetters. Not only did he save 32 games in 37 opportunities, he held the bullpen together through some tough times in the first half of the season.
Most improved player: Second baseman Fernando Vina. He won a starting job in spring training and proved to be a durable, dependable performer. Though somewhat miscast as a leadoff hitter, Vina hit .283 and was outstanding at turning double plays.
Most pleasant surprise: Righthander Cal Eldred. His comeback from reconstructive elbow surgery in June 1995 was a resounding success. Eldred, who made just four starts in '95, joined the club after the All-Star break and pitched better than his 4-4 record and 4.46 ERA would indicate.
Biggest disappointment: Shortstop Jose Valentin. He had a breakthrough year offensively but committed a whopping 37 errors. Valentin has excellent range and a strong arm, but the distressing thing was that most of his errors came on routine plays.
Key injuries: Flamboyant center fielder Chuckie Carr was on the verge of becoming a fan favorite when his season ended on May 30 because of a knee injury. A shoulder injury kept outfielder Turner

Ward on the disabled list for most of the season.
Notable: The Brewers set an Opening Day record by pounding out 22 hits and 37 total bases in a 15-9 victory over California on April 2. . . . Jaha became the first Brewer to hit .300 with at least 30 homers and 100 RBIs since Cecil Cooper in 1983. . . . On May 17 at Minnesota, Dave Nilsson became the 12th player in A.L. history to hit two home runs in the same inning (the sixth). . . . The Brewers homered in 19 consecutive games from June 11-30. . . . Vina, with 10, became only the third Brewer to reach double-digits in triples (Robin Yount and Paul Molitor). . . . Righthander Ben McDonald suffered through an 11-game winless streak that lasted two months but still finished 12-10 with a 3.90 ERA. . . . In a one-month span beginning July 31, G.M. Sal Bando revamped the roster by trading veterans Greg Vaughn, Pat Listach, Ricky Bones and Kevin Seitzer in deals that brought young players such as Marc Newfield, Bryce Florie, Ron Villone, Bob Wickman, Gerald Williams and Jeromy Burnitz to Milwaukee. The changes energized the clubhouse and improved the club's outlook for '97. . . . The Brewers have not played in a postseason game since the 1982 World Series, the longest drought in the American League.

—DREW OLSON

RECORDS

1996 regular-season record: 80-82 (3rd in A.L. Central); 38-43 at home; 42-39 on road; 27-33 vs. East; 31-21 vs. Central; 22-28 vs. West; 20-25 vs. lefthanded starters; 60-57 vs. righthanded starters; 70-73 on grass; 10-9 on turf; 30-30 in daytime; 50-52 at night; 24-18 in one-run games; 11-6 in extra-inning games; 1-2-1 in doubleheaders.
Team record past five years: 359-386 (.482, ranks 11th in league in that span).

TEAM LEADERS

Batting average: Dave Nilsson (.331).
At-bats: Jeff Cirillo (566).
Runs: John Jaha (108).
Hits: Jeff Cirillo (184).
Total bases: John Jaha (295).

Doubles: Jeff Cirillo (46).
Triples: Fernando Vina (10).
Home runs: John Jaha (34).
Runs batted in: John Jaha (118).
Stolen bases: Pat Listach (25).
Slugging percentage: John Jaha (.543).
On-base percentage: Dave Nilsson (.407).
Wins: Scott Karl (13).
Earned-run average: Ben McDonald (3.90).
Complete games: Scott Karl (3).
Shutouts: Scott Karl (1).
Saves: Mike Fetters (32).
Innings pitched: Ben McDonald (221.1).
Strikeouts: Ben McDonald (146).

GAMES BY POSITION

Catcher: Mike Matheny 104, Jesse Levis 90, Kelly Stinnett 14, Dave Nilsson 2.
First base: John Jaha 85, Kevin Seitzer 65, Dave Nilsson 24, Tim Unroe 11, Jeff Cirillo 2, Brian Banks 1.
Second base: Fernando Vina 137, Mark Loretta 28, Pat Listach 12, Jeff Cirillo 1.
Third base: Jeff Cirillo 154, Mark Loretta 23, Kevin Seitzer 12, Tim Unroe 3.
Shortstop: Jose Valentin 151, Mark Loretta 21, Pat Listach 7.
Outfield: Matt Mieske 122, Greg Vaughn 100, David Hulse 68, Pat Listach 68, Dave Nilsson 61, Marc Newfield 49, Turner Ward 32, Chuck Carr 27, Gerald Williams 26, Jeromy Burnitz 22, Kevin Koslofski 22, Todd Dunn 6, Brian Banks 3, Danny Perez 3, Tim Unroe 1.
Designated hitter: John Jaha 63, Kevin Seitzer 56, Dave Nilsson 3, Jesse Levis 6, Jeff Cirillo 3, David Hulse 3, Kevin Koslofski 1, Pat Listach 1, Mike Matheny 1, Danny Perez 1, Kelly Stinnett 1, Tim Unroe 1, Greg Vaughn 1, Turner Ward 1.

TOP DRAFT CHOICES

1. **Chad Green,** OF, University of Kentucky.
2. **Jose Garcia,** RHP, Baldwin Park (Calif.) H.S.
3. **Kevin Barker,** OF, Virginia Tech.
4. **Josh Hancock,** RHP, Vestavia Hills (Ala.) H.S.
5. **Philip Kendall,** C, Jasper (Ind.) H.S.
6. **Paul Stewart,** RHP, Garner (N.C.) H.S.
7. **Mike Wetmore,** SS, Washington State U.
8. **Brian Passini,** LHP, Miami (O.) University.
9. **Doug Johnston,** RHP, Millard South H.S., Omaha, Neb.
10. **Josh Klimek,** SS, University of Illinois.

MINNESOTA TWINS
AMERICAN LEAGUE CENTRAL DIVISION

1997 TWINS SCHEDULE

Home games shaded.
* — All-Star Game at Jacobs Field (Cleveland)
D — Day game (any game starting before 5 p.m.)

APRIL

SUN	MON	TUE	WED	THU	FRI	SAT
		1 DET	2 DET	3 DET	4 KC	5 KC
6 D 7 D KC DET	8	9 D DET	10 D DET	11 KC	12 D KC	
13 D 14 KC BAL	15 BAL	16 ANA	17 D ANA	18 SEA	19 SEA	
20 D 21 SEA	22 D OAK	23 OAK	24 D OAK	25 D TEX	26 TEX	
27 D 28 TEX	29 BAL	30 BAL				

MAY

SUN	MON	TUE	WED	THU	FRI	SAT
				1 BAL	2 TOR	3 D TOR
4 D 5 TOR NYY	6 NYY	7 NYY	8 BOS	9 TOR	10 TOR	
11 D 12 TOR TOR	13 NYY	14 D NYY	15	16 BOS	17 BOS	
18 D 19 BOS	20 MIL	21 D MIL	22	23 OAK	24 OAK	
25 D 26 D OAK SEA	27 SEA	28 MIL	29 D MIL	30 ANA	31 ANA	

JUNE

SUN	MON	TUE	WED	THU	FRI	SAT
1 D 2 ANA TEX	3 TEX	4		5 ANA	6 ANA	7 ANA
8 D 9 ANA	10 TEX	11 TEX	12	13 HOU	14 HOU	
15 D 16 HOU PIT	17 PIT	18 D PIT	19	20 CWS	21 CWS	
22 D 23 CWS CLE	24 CLE	25 CLE	26 CWS	27 CWS	28 CWS	
29 D 30 CWS STL						

JULY

SUN	MON	TUE	WED	THU	FRI	SAT
		1 STL	2 STL	3 D MIL	4 D MIL	5 MIL
6 D 7 MIL	8 * 9	10 CLE	11 CLE	12 CLE		
13 D 14 CLE	15 CWS	16 TOR	17 SEA	18 OAK	19 D OAK	
20 D 21 OAK	22 KC	23 KC	24 D KC	25 D BAL	26 BAL	
27 D 28 BAL KC	29 KC	30 KC	31			

AUGUST

SUN	MON	TUE	WED	THU	FRI	SAT
					1 NYY	2 D NYY
3 D 4 NYY TOR	5 D 6 TOR BOS	7 BOS	8 NYY	9 NYY		
10 D 11 NYY NYY	12 TOR	13 TOR	14 D BOS	15 BOS	16 BOS	
17 D 18 BOS	19 DET	20 DET	21	22 BAL	23 BAL	
24 D 25 BAL DET	26 DET	27 DET	28	29 CIN	30 CIN	
31 D CIN						

SEPTEMBER

SUN	MON	TUE	WED	THU	FRI	SAT
	1 D 2 CUB CUB	3 D CUB	4	5 SEA	6 SEA	
7 D 8 SEA OAK	9 D OAK	10	11 TEX	12 TEX	13 TEX	
14 D 15 TEX ANA	16 ANA	17 CLE	18 CLE	19 MIL	20 MIL	
21 D 22 MIL MIL	23 CWS	24 CWS	25 CWS	26 CLE	27 D CLE	
28 D CLE						

1997 SEASON

CLUB DIRECTORY

Owner
Carl R. Pohlad
President
Jerry Bell
Chairman of executive committee
Howard Fox
Directors
Donald E. Benson
Paul R. Christen
James O. Pohlad
Robert C. Pohlad
William M. Pohlad
Kirby Puckett
Vice president, general manager
Terry Ryan
Vice president, asst. general manager
Bill Smith
Executive vice president, baseball
Kirby Puckett
Vice president, operations
Matt Hoy
Director of minor leagues
Jim Rantz
Director of scouting
Mike Radcliff
Director of baseball operations
Rob Antony
Traveling secretary
Remzi Kiratli
Manager, media relations
Sean Harlin

Club physicians
Dr. Leonard J. Michienzi
Dr. John Steubs
Scouts
Ellsworth Brown
Ray Coley
Gene DeBoer
Cal Ermer
Marty Esposito
Vern Followell
Earl Frishman
Scott Groot
Bill Harford
Deron Johnson
Wayne Krivsky
John Leavitt
Joel Lepel
Bill Lohr
Bill Milos
Kevin Murphy
Tim O'Neil
Mark Quimuyog
Clair Rierson
Eddie Robinson
Mike Ruth
Ricky Taylor
Brad Weitzel
John Wilson
International scouts
Enrique Brito
Howard Norsetter
Johnny Sierra

MINOR LEAGUE AFFILIATES

Class	Team	League	Manager
AAA	Salt Lake	Pacific Coast	Phil Roof
AA	New Britain	Eastern	Al Newman
A	Fort Myers	Florida State	John Russell
A	Fort Wayne	Midwest	Mike Boulanger
Rookie	Elizabethton	Appalachian	Jose Maizon
Rookie	Gulf Coast Twins	Gulf Coast	Steve Liddle

BROADCAST INFORMATION
Radio: WCCO-AM (830).
TV: WCCO-TV (Channel 4).
Cable TV: Midwest SportsChannel.

SPRING TRAINING
Ballpark (city): Lee County Sports Complex (Fort Myers, Fla.).
Ticket information: 800-33-TWINS.

SPRING TRAINING ROSTER

Manager—Tom Kelly (10).
Coaches—Terry Crowley (46), Ron Gardenhire (35), Rick Stelmaszek (43), Dick Such (42), Scott Ullger (45).

No.	PITCHERS	B/T	Ht./Wt.	Born	1996 clubs
38	Aguilera, Rick	R/R	6-5/204	12-31-61	Fort Myers, Minnesota
57	Aldred, Scott	L/L	6-4/228	6-12-68	Detroit, Minnesota
18	Guardado, Eddie	R/L	6-0/195	10-2-70	Minnesota
32	Hawkins, LaTroy	R/R	6-5/201	12-21-72	Minnesota, Salt Lake
52	Klingenbeck, Scott	R/R	6-2/218	2-3-71	Salt Lake, Minnesota
20	Miller, Travis	R/L	6-3/204	11-2-72	Minnesota, Salt Lake
31	Naulty, Dan	R/R	6-6/223	1-6-70	Minnesota
56	Parra, Jose	R/R	5-11/169	11-28-72	Salt Lake, Minnesota
49	Perkins, Dan	R/R	6-2/185	3-15-75	Fort Myers
22	Radke, Brad	R/R	6-2/185	10-27-72	Minnesota
30	Ritchie, Todd	R/R	6-3/190	11-7-71	New Britain, Salt Lake
47	Robertson, Rich	L/L	6-4/180	9-15-68	Minnesota
33	Rodriguez, Frank	R/R	6-0/197	12-11-72	Minnesota
16	Serafini, Dan	B/L	6-1/180	1-25-74	Salt Lake, Minnesota
41	Stevens, Dave	R/R	6-3/195	3-4-70	Minnesota
19	Tewksbury, Bob	R/R	6-4/205	11-30-60	San Diego
21	Trombley, Mike	R/R	6-2/203	4-14-67	Salt Lake, Minnesota

No.	CATCHERS	B/T	Ht./Wt.	Born	1996 clubs
24	Myers, Greg	L/R	6-2/208	4-14-66	Minnesota
36	Steinbach, Terry	R/R	6-1/195	3-2-62	Oakland
26	Valentin, Javier	B/R	5-10/191	9-19-75	Fort Myers, New Britain

No.	INFIELDERS	B/T	Ht./Wt.	Born	1996 clubs
60	Arias, David	L/L	6-4/190	2-18-75	Wisconsin Rapids
8	Coomer, Ron	R/R	5-11/225	11-18-66	Minnesota
7	Hocking, Denny	B/R	5-10/180	4-2-70	Minnesota, Salt Lake
11	Knoblauch, Chuck	R/R	5-9/169	7-7-68	Minnesota
15	Koskie, Corey	L/R	6-3/215	6-28-73	Fort Myers
	Lane, Ryan	R/R	6-1/185	7-6-74	Fort Myers, New Britain
2	Meares, Pat	R/R	6-0/187	9-6-68	Minnesota
4	Molitor, Paul	R/R	6-0/193	8-22-56	Minnesota
37	Stahoviak, Scott	L/R	6-5/230	3-6-70	Minnesota
12	Walker, Todd	L/R	6-0/177	5-25-73	Salt Lake, Minnesota

No.	OUTFIELDERS	B/T	Ht./Wt.	Born	1996 clubs
9	Anthony, Eric	L/L	6-2/195	11-8-67	Indianapolis, Cincinnati, Colorado
25	Becker, Rich	L/L	5-10/192	2-1-72	Minnesota
51	Brede, Brent	L/L	6-4/198	9-13-71	Salt Lake, Minnesota
40	Cordova, Marty	R/R	6-0/201	7-10-69	Minnesota
	Hunter, Torii	R/R	6-2/200	7-18-75	New Britain, Fort Myers
44	Johnson, J.J.	R/R	6-0/195	8-31-73	New Britain, Salt Lake
5	Kelly, Roberto	R/R	6-2/198	10-1-64	Minnesota
59	Latham, Chris	B/R	6-0/195	5-26-73	Salt Lake
50	Lawton, Matt	L/R	5-10/190	11-3-71	Minnesota, Salt Lake
55	Ogden, Jamie	L/L	6-5/233	1-19-72	Salt Lake
23	Radmanovich, Ryan	L/R	6-2/190	8-9-71	New Britain

BALLPARK INFORMATION

Ballpark (capacity, surface)
Hubert H. Humphrey Metrodome (48,678, artificial)

Address
34 Kirby Puckett Place
Minneapolis, MN 55415

Business phone
612-375-1366

Ticket information
1-800-33-TWINS

Ticket prices
$19 (VIP level, lower deck club level)
$13 (lower deck reserved)
$11 (upper deck club level)
$7 (g.a., lower left field)
$4 (g.a., upper deck)

Field dimensions (from home plate)
To left field at foul line, 343 feet
To center field, 408 feet
To right field at foul line, 327 feet

First game played
April 6, 1982 (Mariners 11, Twins 7)

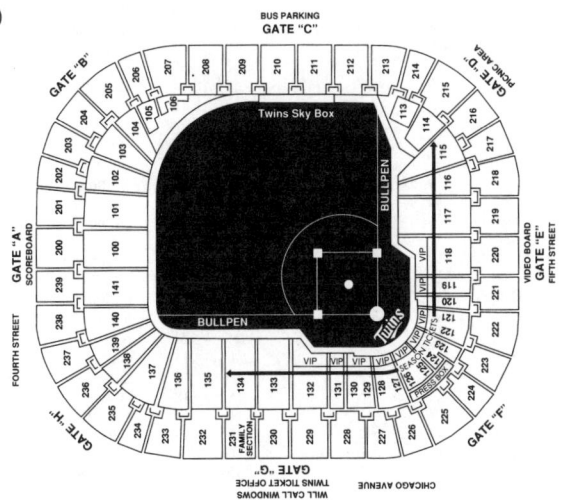

DAY BY DAY

Date	Opp.	Res.	Score	(inn.*)	Hits	Opp. hits	Winning pitcher	Losing pitcher	Save	Record	Pos.	GB
4-1	Det.	W	8-6		12	10	Radke	Lira	Stevens	1-0	1st	+
4-2	Det.	L	6-10		14	14	Sodowsky	Robertson		1-1	2nd	
4-3	Det.	W	16-7		14	8	Mahomes	Aldred		2-1	1st	+
4-5	Bal.	L	1-2		7	7	Mercker	Guardado	R. Myers	2-2	2nd	
4-6	Bal.	W	8-3		13	8	Radke	Haynes		3-2	1st	+
4-7	Bal.	L	2-4		7	7	Mussina	Robertson	R. Myers	3-3	1st	+
4-9	At Bos.	L	1-9		7	9	Gordon	Rodriguez		3-4	T2nd	
4-11	At Bos.	W	6-5		8	7	Radke	Clemens	Stevens	4-4	1st	+
4-12	At Bal.	L	2-3		2	7	Mussina	Robertson		4-5	1st	+
4-13	At Bal.	L	6-7		11	13	Benitez	Mahomes		4-6	T2nd	
4-14	At Bal.	W	4-1		8	3	Rodriguez	Haynes	Stevens	5-6	2nd	
4-16	Cle.	L	2-7		8	13	Hershiser	Radke		5-7	3rd	2
4-17	Cle.	W	9-8		8	15	Hansell	Shuey	Stevens	6-7	3rd	1
4-19	N.Y.	W	7-1		12	8	Rodriguez	Gooden		7-7	3rd	1
4-20	N.Y.	L	6-7		10	16	Wickman	Guardado	Wetteland	7-8	4th	3
4-21	N.Y.	L	5-9		5	11	Rogers	Radke		7-9	4th	3
4-22	Bos.	L	1-4		5	9	Sele	Robertson	Slocumb	7-10	4th	4
4-23	Bos.	W	8-6		14	7	Naulty	Hudson	Stevens	8-10	4th	4
4-24	At Det.	W	24-11		19	14	Bennett	Veres		9-10	4th	3
4-25	At Det.	W	11-1		15	3	Hawkins	Aldred	Hansell	10-10	4th	3
4-26	At N.Y.	L	4-5		11	8	M. Rivera	Radke	Wetteland	10-11	4th	4
4-27	At N.Y.	W	8-6	(10)	14	14	Bennett	Wickman		11-11	T3rd	3
4-28	At N.Y.	L	3-6		8	11	M. Rivera	Rodriguez	Wetteland	11-12	4th	4
4-29	K.C.	W	11-6		15	9	Hansell	Clark	Bennett	12-12	4th	3
4-30	K.C.	W	16-7		16	13	Naulty	Magnante		13-12	3rd	3
5-1	K.C.	W	6-5	(10)	9	7	Stevens	Montgomery		14-12	3rd	3
5-3	At Cal.	L	1-4		6	8	Finley	Robertson	Percival	14-13	3rd	5
5-4	At Cal.	L	2-5		3	7	Grimsley	Rodriguez		14-14	3rd	5
5-5	At Cal.	L	1-5		6	12	Boskie	Hawkins		14-15	3rd	6
5-6	At Sea.	L	4-5		8	7	Wells	Radke	Charlton	14-16	3rd	6
5-7	At Sea.	W	2-0		8	6	Parra	Wolcott	Stevens	15-16	3rd	5
5-8	At Sea.	W	7-5	(10)	13	9	Guardado	Wells	Stevens	16-16	3rd	5
5-10	At Oak.	L	5-15		10	18	Wojciechowski	Rodriguez		16-17	3rd	5
5-11	At Oak.	L	5-12		10	13	Prieto	Radke		16-18	3rd	6
5-12	At Oak.	L	3-8		5	14	Wengert	Parra		16-19	3rd	7
5-14	Tor.	L	2-4		9	7	Hanson	Robertson	Timlin	16-20	4th	8
5-15	Tor.	W	2-1		7	6	Rodriguez	Hentgen		17-20	3rd	8
5-16	Tor.	W	4-1		8	6	Radke	Quantrill	Stevens	18-20	3rd	8
5-17	Mil.	L	1-12		5	15	Karl	Parra		18-21	4th	9
5-18	Mil.	L	3-7		8	13	Miranda	Mahomes	Fetters	18-22	4th	9
5-19	Mil.	L	2-4		9	9	Sparks	Robertson	Fetters	18-23	4th	10
5-20	Mil.	L	2-3		8	10	Bones	Rodriguez	Fetters	18-24	4th	10*
5-21	Tex.	W	4-3		9	8	Milchin	Henneman		19-24	4th	10*
5-22	Tex.	L	5-6		12	13	Pavlik	Parra	Henneman	19-25	5th	10*
5-23	At Tor.	L	4-5	(10)	9	14	Janzen	Milchin		19-26	5th	11*
5-24	At Tor.	W	4-0		11	4	Robertson	Hanson		20-26	5th	11*
5-25	At Tor.	W	6-4	(10)	11	7	Guardado	Castillo	Stevens	21-26	5th	11*
5-26	At Tor.	W	9-3		16	7	Naulty	Bohanon		22-26	4th	11*
5-28	At Mil.	L	3-7		8	10	Karl	Mahomes	Garcia	22-27	5th	11
5-29	At Mil.	W	8-7	(12)	12	14	Hansell	Lloyd		23-27	4th	10
5-31	At Tex.	L	2-7		7	10	Hill	Rodriguez		23-28	T3rd	11*
6-1	At Tex.	W	9-5		15	13	Milchin	Henneman		24-28	T3rd	10*
6-2	At Tex.	W	6-5		13	8	Guardado	Russell		25-28	3rd	10*
6-3	Cal.	W	9-3		15	8	Trombley	Finley		26-28	3rd	10
6-4	Cal.	W	5-3		8	8	Rodriguez	Grimsley	Guardado	27-28	3rd	9
6-5	Cal.	W	14-3		17	9	Aldred	Langston	Hansell	28-28	3rd	9
6-7	Oak.	L	4-6		12	9	Reyes	Radke	Corsi	28-29	3rd	9*
6-8†	Oak.	W	4-2		10	7	Robertson	Wojciechowski	Guardado	29-29		
6-8‡	Oak.	L	7-13		14	14	Wasdin	Mahomes		29-30	3rd	10
6-9	Oak.	W	5-3		10	8	Rodriguez	Wengert		30-30	3rd	9
6-10	Sea.	W	13-6		16	9	Aldred	Wagner	Trombley	31-30	3rd	9
6-11	Sea.	L	8-18		11	24	Wells	Aguilera	Hurtado	31-31	3rd	10
6-12	Sea.	L	3-5		10	11	Wolcott	Radke	Charlton	31-32	3rd	10
6-14	Det.	L	4-5		9	9	Gohr	Robertson	Olson	31-33	T3rd	10*
6-15	Det.	L	4-6		9	12	Olivares	Rodriguez	Olson	31-34	4th	11*
6-16	Det.	W	4-1		8	4	Aguilera	Lira	Hansell	32-34	T3rd	10*
6-17	At N.Y.	W	6-3		12	10	Aldred	Mendoza	Naulty	33-34	T3rd	10
6-18	At N.Y.	L	0-2		6	3	Rogers	Radke	Wetteland	33-35	4th	11
6-20	At Det.	W	7-3		12	10	Rodriguez	Olivares		34-35	3rd	11*
6-21	At Det.	L	0-2		4	6	Lira	Aguilera		34-36	4th	11
6-22	At Det.	L	0-6		4	12	B. Williams	Aldred		34-37	4th	11
6-23	At Det.	L	8-10		14	9	Urbani	Radke		34-38	4th	11

Date	Opp.	Res.	Score	(inn.*)	Hits	Opp. hits	Winning pitcher	Losing pitcher	Save	Record	Pos.	GB
6-24	N.Y.	W	3-0		6	8	Robertson	Pettitte		35-38	4th	10 1/2
6-25†	N.Y.	W	6-1		12	5	Rodriguez	Boehringer		36-38		
6-25‡	N.Y.	L	2-6		8	12	Mendoza	Serafini		36-39	4th	11
6-26	N.Y.	L	1-2		10	5	Polley	Guardado	Wetteland	36-40	4th	11
6-28	At K.C.	L	2-6		5	10	Appier	Radke		36-41	4th	10 1/2
6-29	At K.C.	W	12-7		16	9	Trombley	Linton		37-41	4th	10 1/2
6-30	At K.C.	W	5-2		6	7	Rodriguez	Gubicza	Stevens	38-41	4th	10 1/2
7-1	At Chi.	W	10-7		15	13	Aguilera	Sirotka		39-41	4th	9 1/2
7-2	At Chi.	L	4-7		8	12	Fernandez	Aldred	Hernandez	39-42	4th	10 1/2
7-3	At Chi.	W	6-5		14	9	Radke	Andujar	Stevens	40-42	4th	10 1/2
7-4	K.C.	L	3-5		10	7	Linton	Robertson	Montgomery	40-43	4th	10 1/2
7-5	K.C.	W	9-8		13	9	Guardado	Montgomery		41-43	4th	9 1/2
7-6	K.C.	L	5-8		7	10	Haney	Aguilera	Montgomery	41-44	4th	9 1/2
7-7	K.C.	L	2-8		10	9	Belcher	Aldred		41-45	4th	10 1/2
7-11	Cle.	L	7-11		13	13	McDowell	Radke		41-46	4th	11 1/2
7-12	Cle.	L	5-7		9	10	Mesa	Stevens	Shuey	41-47	4th	12 1/2
7-13	Cle.	L	11-19		15	22	Ogea	Aguilera		41-48	4th	13 1/2
7-14	Cle.	W	5-4		13	11	Guardado	Plunk		42-48	4th	12 1/2
7-15	Chi.	W	16-5		16	7	Aldred	McCaskill		43-48	4th	11 1/2
7-16	Chi.	L	2-11		8	11	Alvarez	Radke		43-49	4th	12 1/2
7-17	Chi.	W	4-3		10	4	Trombley	Simas		44-49	4th	11 1/2
7-18	At Cle.	L	4-5		6	9	Graves	Guardado		44-50	4th	12 1/2
7-19	At Cle.	W	3-2		3	6	Rodriguez	Nagy	Naulty	45-50	4th	11 1/2
7-20	At Cle.	L	5-6	(11)	11	16	Shuey	Stevens		45-51	4th	12 1/2
7-21	At Cle.	L	5-7		10	12	McDowell	Radke	Shuey	45-52	4th	13 1/2
7-22	At Bal.	W	9-5		10	10	Robertson	Haynes	Trombley	46-52	4th	13 1/2
7-23	At Bal.	W	3-2		9	5	Aguilera	Wells	Naulty	47-52	4th	12 1/2
7-24	At Bal.	W	11-4		15	8	Rodriguez	Erickson		48-52	4th	12 1/2
7-25	Bos.	W	16-6		19	12	Parra	Wakefield		49-52	4th	12 1/2
7-26	Bos.	W	5-1		9	5	Radke	Clemens		50-52	T3rd	12 1/2
7-27	Bos.	L	5-9		9	14	Gordon	Naulty		50-53	T3rd	12 1/2
7-28	Bos.	W	9-8		14	11	Aguilera	Sele	Naulty	51-53	T3rd	12 1/2
7-30	Bal.	L	4-16		7	17	Coppinger	Rodriguez		51-54	4th	12 1/2
7-31	Bal.	L	3-9		9	11	Mussina	Trombley		51-55	4th	13 1/2
8-1	Bal.	L	2-4		4	6	Wells	Robertson	R. Myers	51-56	4th	13 1/2
8-2	At Bos.	L	10-11		13	15	Brandenburg	Naulty		51-57	4th	14 1/2
8-3†	At Bos.	L	3-6		8	10	Sele	Rodriguez	Hudson	51-58		
8-3‡	At Bos.	W	6-0		9	7	Aldred	Suppan		52-58	4th	14
8-4	At Bos.	L	6-13		13	12	Eshelman	Klingenbeck		52-59	4th	15
8-6	At Cal.	W	4-1		8	5	Radke	Springer	Guardado	53-59	4th	14 1/2
8-7	At Cal.	W	4-0		12	4	Robertson	Finley		54-59	4th	14 1/2
8-8	At Cal.	W	13-5		17	6	Aguilera	Boskie		55-59	3rd	14 1/2
8-9	At Sea.	W	6-5		10	9	Parra	Wolcott	Rodriguez	56-59	3rd	14 1/2
8-10	At Sea.	W	10-4		18	9	Klingenbeck	Hitchcock		57-59	3rd	13 1/2
8-11	At Sea.	W	6-3		7	9	Radke	Wells	Rodriguez	58-59	3rd	12 1/2
8-12	At Oak.	L	1-11		5	13	Prieto	Robertson		58-60	3rd	13 1/2
8-13	At Oak.	W	6-2		11	6	Aguilera	Wengert		59-60	3rd	12 1/2
8-14	At Oak.	W	13-7		14	7	Rodriguez	Telgheder		60-60	3rd	11 1/2
8-16	Tor.	W	5-4	(10)	9	10	Parra	Quantrill		61-60	3rd	11 1/2
8-17	Tor.	W	11-1		13	4	Robertson	Hanson		62-60	3rd	11 1/2
8-18	Tor.	L	2-6		6	12	Hentgen	Aguilera		62-61	3rd	12 1/2
8-19	Mil.	L	1-6		4	10	D'Amico	Rodriguez		62-62	3rd	12 1/2
8-20	Mil.	W	12-7		20	15	Parra	Bones		63-62	3rd	12 1/2
8-21	Mil.	L	7-10		12	12	Jones	Stevens	Fetters	63-63	3rd	12 1/2
8-22	Tex.	L	2-11		10	10	Hill	Robertson		63-64	3rd	13
8-23	Tex.	W	9-2		15	8	Aguilera	Oliver		64-64	3rd	12
8-24	Tex.	W	6-5		10	9	Rodriguez	Pavlik	Trombley	65-64	3rd	11
8-25	Tex.	L	2-13		7	14	Witt	Miller		65-65	3rd	12
8-26	At Tor.	L	3-5		9	14	Guzman	Radke	Timlin	65-66	3rd	13
8-27	At Tor.	W	6-4	(11)	12	9	Trombley	Quantrill		66-66	3rd	13
8-28	At Tor.	L	1-6		5	12	Hentgen	Aguilera		66-67	3rd	14
8-29	At Mil.	W	6-1		11	9	Rodriguez	Karl		67-67	3rd	13 1/2
8-30	At Mil.	L	4-5	(12)	12	13	Wickman	Parra		67-68	3rd	13 1/2
8-31	At Mil.	L	2-3		6	9	Jones	Robertson	Fetters	67-69	3rd	13 1/2
9-1	At Mil.	W	6-2		11	10	Aldred	Vanegmond		68-69	3rd	13 1/2
9-2	At Tex.	W	6-4		11	11	Aguilera	Hill	Guardado	69-69	3rd	12 1/2
9-3	At Tex.	L	7-9		12	9	Witt	Rodriguez	Henneman	69-70	3rd	12 1/2
9-4	At Tex.	W	7-6		11	9	Robertson	Heredia	Trombley	70-70	3rd	12 1/2
9-6	Cal.	W	6-2		13	5	Radke	Finley		71-70	3rd	12
9-7	Cal.	W	6-3		11	6	Stevens	Boskie	Trombley	72-70	3rd	11 1/2
9-8	Cal.	L	2-4		10	8	J. Abbott	Rodriguez	Percival	72-71	3rd	12
9-10	Oak.	L	0-7		3	11	Telgheder	Robertson		72-72	3rd	13 1/2
9-11	Oak.	W	7-2		11	5	Radke	Adams		73-72	3rd	13 1/2
9-12	Oak.	W	4-3	(12)	10	5	Stevens	Mohler		74-72	3rd	13 1/2
9-13	Sea.	L	7-13		14	12	Wells	Miller		74-73	3rd	14

Date	Opp.	Res.	Score	(inn.*)	Hits	Opp. hits	Winning pitcher	Losing pitcher	Save	Record	Pos.	GB
9-14	Sea.	L	3-5	(10)	7	5	Ayala	Guardado	Charlton	74-74	3rd	15[1]
9-15	Sea.	L	0-7		2	10	Torres	Robertson		74-75	3rd	15[1]
9-16	At K.C.	L	5-6		12	11	Rosado	Radke	Bluma	74-76	3rd	16[1]
9-17	At K.C.	L	2-4		10	11	Haney	Aldred	Bluma	74-77	3rd	17[1]
9-18	At K.C.	W	7-4		11	7	Miller	Belcher		75-77	3rd	17[1]
9-19	At Chi.	L	3-8		9	9	Sirotka	Rodriguez	Castillo	75-78	T3rd	18[1]
9-20	At Chi.	L	3-7		11	8	Tapani	Robertson		75-79	T3rd	18[1]
9-21	At Chi.	W	4-3		11	8	Radke	Alvarez	Trombley	76-79	T3rd	18[1]
9-22	At Chi.	L	1-5		5	7	Fernandez	Aldred		76-80	T3rd	19[1]
9-23	At Cle.	L	6-7		8	15	Graves	Parra	Mesa	76-81	4th	20[1]
9-24	At Cle.	L	5-7		10	12	Ogea	Rodriguez	Mesa	76-82	4th	21[1]
9-25	At Cle.	L	3-6		5	9	Nagy	Robertson		76-83	4th	22[1]
9-27	Chi.	L	2-4		10	9	Fernandez	Radke	Hernandez	76-84	4th	22[1]
9-28	Chi.	W	7-6		15	13	Trombley	Castillo		77-84	4th	22[1]
9-29	Chi.	W	5-4	(10)	6	8	Guardado	Hernandez		78-84	4th	21[1]

Monthly records: April (13-12), May (10-16), June (15-13), July (13-14), August (16-14), September (11-15).
*Innings, if other than nine. †First game of doubleheader. ‡Second game of doubleheader.

HIGHLIGHTS

High point: On a cool Monday night in mid-September, St. Paul native Paul Molitor became the 21st player in major league history to collect his 3,000th hit. Signed by the Twins as a free agent, Molitor's big moment was the highlight of a spectacular season in which he turned 40. He finished with a career-high 225 hits and batted .341.

Low point: Despite what happened on the field, 1996 always will be remembered by the Twins as the year glaucoma robbed Kirby Puckett of the sight in his right eye and forced him to retire. Puckett woke up one late-March morning in Fort Myers, Fla., with blurred vision in his right eye and never played again. Several laser surgeries couldn't correct the problem.

Turning point: The late-season stretch in which the Twins simply ran out of gas. Brad Radke, Frankie Rodriguez and Rich Robertson worked more innings than in any of their previous pro seasons. Scott Stahoviak and Rich Becker, among others, compiled more at-bats than ever.

Most valuable player: Second baseman Chuck Knoblauch. He played in his third All-Star Game and finished with career highs in batting average (.341), home runs (13), triples (14), RBIs (72) and runs (140).

Most valuable pitcher: Starter Brad Radke. Finding a top pitcher on the Twins' staff is usually like looking for a Porsche at the junkyard, but second-year man Radke overcame a severe midseason slump to finish 11-16 with a 4.46 ERA. His best statistic, however, was the fact that he threw 232 innings.

Most improved player: Center fielder Rich Becker. Few players have turned around a season like Becker. Hitting .070 a month into the season, Becker found his groove and batted nearly .300 the rest of the way to finish with a .291 average. He also hit 12 homers.

Most pleasant surprise: Two relievers stood out. Mike Trombley, after being removed from the 40-man roster and shipped to the minors at the end of spring training, questioned how much longer he would play baseball. But he discovered a forkball at Class AAA Salt Lake, was recalled two months into the season and compiled a 5-1 record and 3.01 ERA in 43 games. Rookie Dan Naulty also pitched well out of the pen, going 3-2 with a 3.79 ERA before circulatory problems forced surgery and a premature end to his season in August.

Biggest disappointment: Pitcher Pat Mahomes. Once a highly touted prospect, Mahomes finally completed his fall in the Twins' organization when he was traded to Boston in late August.

Key injuries: In addition to Kirby Puckett's eye problem, the team was dealt a blow when starter-turned-closer Rick Aguilera developed a tendinitis problem in his right wrist when he picked up his wife's suitcase to load it on a moving truck during spring training. He was able to make only one start in the season's first two months. When Aguilera was healthy, the Twins' big experiment seemed to work. But Aguilera was bothered by other nagging injuries and, in just 19 starts, went 8-6 with a 5.42 ERA.

Notable: The Twins were severely lacking in power, finishing last in the major leagues with 118 home runs. Marty Cordova led the way with 16. . . . Cordova also set a club record with 46 doubles. . . . The Twins hit into 170 double plays, just four short of Boston's major league record of 174, set in 1990.

—SCOTT MILLER

RECORDS

1996 regular-season record: 78-84 (4th in A.L. Central); 39-43 at home; 39-41 on road; 30-31 vs. East; 21-31 vs. Central; 27-22 vs. West; 20-23 vs. lefthanded starters; 58-61 vs. righthanded starters; 30-37 on grass; 48-47 on turf; 26-26 in daytime; 52-58 at night; 22-18 in one-run games; 9-4 in extra-inning games; 0-2 in doubleheaders.

Team record past five years: 348-395 (.468, ranks 12th in league in that span).

TEAM LEADERS

Batting average: Paul Molitor, Chuck Knoblauch (.341).
At-bats: Paul Molitor (660).
Runs: Chuck Knoblauch (140).
Hits: Paul Molitor (225).
Total bases: Paul Molitor (309).
Doubles: Marty Cordova (46).
Triples: Chuck Knoblauch (14).
Home runs: Marty Cordova (16).
Runs batted in: Paul Molitor (113).
Stolen bases: Chuck Knoblauch (45).
Slugging percentage: Chuck Knoblauch (.517).
On-base percentage: Chuck Knoblauch (.448).
Wins: Frankie Rodriguez (13).
Earned-run average: Brad Radke (4.46).
Complete games: Rich Robertson (5).
Shutouts: Rich Robertson (3).
Saves: Dave Stevens (11).
Innings pitched: Brad Radke (232.0).
Strikeouts: Brad Radke (148).

GAMES BY POSITION

Catcher: Greg Myers 90, Matt Walbeck 61, Mike Durant 37.
First base: Scott Stahoviak 114, Ron Coomer 57, Paul Molitor 17, Jeff Reboulet 13, Chip Hale 6, Denny Hocking 1.
Second base: Chuck Knoblauch 151, Jeff Reboulet 22, Chip Hale 14, Todd Walker 4, Denny Hocking 2, Brian Raabe 1.
Third base: Dave Hollins 116, Jeff Reboulet 36, Todd Walker 20, Ron Coomer 9, Brian Raabe 6, Tom Quinlan 4, Chip Hale 3.
Shortstop: Pat Meares 150, Jeff Reboulet 37, Denny Hocking 6, Dave Hollins 1.
Outfield: Rich Becker 146, Marty Cordova 145, Roberto Kelly 93, Matt Lawton 75, Denny Hocking 33, Ron Coomer 23, Brent Brede 7, Jeff Reboulet 7, Chip Hale 3, Pat Meares 1.
Designated hitter: Paul Molitor 143, Chip Hale 10, Scott Stahoviak 9, Ron Coomer 3, Dave Hollins 3, Jeff Reboulet 3, Roberto Kelly 2, Chuck Knoblauch 2, Denny Hocking 1, Matt Lawton 1, Todd Walker 1.

TOP DRAFT CHOICES

1. **Travis Lee,** 1B, San Diego State U.
2. **Jacque Jones,** OF, U. of Southern California.
3. **Dan Cey,** SS, University of California.
4. **Chad Allen,** OF, Texas A&M University.
5. **Michael Ryan,** SS, Indiana (Pa.) H.S.
6. **Tommy LaRosa,** RHP, U. of Nevada-Las Vegas.
7. **Chad Moeller,** C, U. of Southern California.
8. **Corey Spiers,** LHP, Univ. of Alabama.
9. **Nate Yeskie,** RHP, U. of Nevada-Las Vegas.
10. **Joey Cranford,** 2B, University of Georgia.

NEW YORK YANKEES
AMERICAN LEAGUE EAST DIVISION

1997 YANKEES SCHEDULE

Home games shaded.
* — All-Star Game at Jacobs Field (Cleveland)
D — Day game (any game starting before 5 p.m.)

APRIL
SUN	MON	TUE	WED	THU	FRI	SAT
	1	2	3	4 D OAK	5 D OAK	
		SEA	SEA			
6 D OAK	D 7 ANA	8 ANA	9 ANA	10	11 D OAK	12 D OAK
13 D OAK	14 ANA	15 ANA	16 MIL	17 D MIL	18 CWS	19 D CWS
20 CWS	D 21 CWS	22 MIL	23 D MIL	24	25 CWS	26 D CWS
27 CWS	D 28 SEA	29 SEA	30 SEA			

MAY
SUN	MON	TUE	WED	THU	FRI	SAT
				1	2 KC	3 KC
4 D KC	D 5 MIN	6 MIN	7 TEX	8 D TEX	9 KC	10 D KC
11 D KC	12	13 MIN	14 D MIN	15 TEX	16 TEX	17 TEX
18 D TEX	19	20 TOR	21 TOR	22 D TOR	23 BOS	24 D BOS
25 BOS	26 D BAL	27 D BAL	28 TOR	29 TOR	30 D BOS	31 BOS

JUNE
SUN	MON	TUE	WED	THU	FRI	SAT
1 D BOS	D 2 BOS	3 BAL	4 BAL	5	6 MIL	7 D MIL
8 D MIL	9	10 CWS	11 CWS	12	13 FLA	14 FLA
15 FLA	16 D NYM	17 NYM	18 NYM	19	20 CLE	21 D CLE
22 CLE	23 DET	24 DET	25 D DET	26	27 CLE	28 D CLE
29 CLE	30 ATL					

JULY
SUN	MON	TUE	WED	THU	FRI	SAT
		1 ATL	2 ATL	D 3 TOR	4 TOR	5 D TOR
6 D TOR	D 7	8	* 9	10 DET	11 D DET	12 D DET
13 DET	14 CLE	15 D CLE	16 CWS	17 CWS	18 MIL	19 MIL
20 MIL	21 MIL	22 D ANA	23 ANA	D 24 ANA	25 SEA	26 D SEA
27 SEA	D 28 OAK	29 OAK	30 D OAK	31		

AUGUST
SUN	MON	TUE	WED	THU	FRI	SAT
					1 MIN	2 D MIN
3 D MIN	4 KC	5 KC	6 TEX	7 TEX	8 MIN	9 MIN
10 D MIN	D 11 MIN	12 KC	13 KC	D 14 KC	15 TEX	16 D TEX
17 D TEX	18	19 ANA	20 ANA	21	22 SEA	23 D SEA
24 D SEA	D 25	26 D OAK	D 27 OAK	28	29 D MON	30 MON
31 D MON						

SEPTEMBER
SUN	MON	TUE	WED	THU	FRI	SAT
	1 2 PHI	2 PHI	3 PHI	4 BAL	5 BAL	6 D BAL
7 D BAL	8	9 BOS	10 BOS	11 BAL	12 BAL	13 D BAL
14 BAL	15 BOS	16 BOS	17 DET	18 DET	19 TOR	20 D TOR
21 D TOR	22 TBR	23 CLE	24 CLE	25 CLE	26 DET	27 DET
28 D DET						

1997 SEASON
CLUB DIRECTORY

Principal owner
George M. Steinbrenner III
General partners
Harold Steinbrenner
Joseph A. Molloy
Executive vice president, general counsel
David W. Sussman
Vice president, chief financial officer
Barry Pincus
V.p., marketing and promotions
Derek Schiller
Vice president, ticket operations
Frank Swaine
Vice president
Ed Weaver
Associate general counsel
John J. Agliano
Special advisory group
Reggie Jackson, Clyde King, Dick Williams
Vice president and general manager
Robert Watson
V.p., player development and scouting
Mark Newman
Director of scouting
Lin Garrett
Assistant general manager
Brian Cashman
Major League administrator
Thomas May
Assistant, baseball operations
Gene Keohane
Traveling secretary
David Szen
Director of stadium operations
Sonny Hight
Manager, stadium operations
Kirk Randazzo
Asst. dir., video & broadcast operations
Mayra L. Jimenez
Executive director of ticket operations
Jeff Kline
Ticket director
Ken Skrypek
Director of media relations and publicity
Richard Cerrone
Asst. dir. of media relations and publicity
John Thursby

Asst. dir., pub. rel./special programs
Annette Guardabascio
Dir. of TV and video production
Joe Violone
Assistant director of scouting
Joe Caro
Coord. of Latin American player dev.
Ken Dominguez
Team physician
Dr. Stuart Hershon
Head trainer
Gene Monahan
Assistant trainer
Steve Donohue
Strength & conditioning coach
Paul Mastropasqua
Clubhouse coord./equipment manager
David Hays
Clubhouse manager
Eric Sims
Video coordinator
Mark Ferrar
Cross-checkers
John Cox, Damon Oppenheimer, Donnie Rowland
Special assignment scouts
Ket Barber, Bobby Dejardin, Bill Emslie
Scouts
Rich Arena, Joe Arnold, Mike Baker, Mark Batchko, Lee Elder, Tim Kelly, Greg Orr, Scott Pleis, Cesar Presbott, Joe Robison, Reggie Waller, Steve Webber, Roy White, J. Leon Wurth, Bill Young
Coordinator of international scouting
Gordon Blakeley
Coordinator of Canadian scouting
Dick Groch
Foreign scouts
Karl Heron, Ricardo Heron, Ruddy Jabalera, Francisco Lugo, Victor Mata, Manuel Medina, Roberto Morillo, Jorge Oquendo, Raul Ortega, Jim Patterson, Marc Picard, Jose Quintero, Luis Ramos, Arquimedes Rojas, Dale Tilleman, Modesto Ulloa

MINOR LEAGUE AFFILIATES

Class	Team	League	Manager
AAA	Columbus	International	Stump Merrill
AA	Norwich	Eastern	Jim Essian
A	Tampa	Florida State	Trey Hillman
A	Greensboro	South Atlantic	Ricky Patterson
A	Oneonta	New York-Pennsylvania	Rob Thompson
Rookie	Gulf Coast Yankees	Gulf Coast	Ken Dominguez

BROADCAST INFORMATION
Radio: To be announced.
TV: To be announced.
Cable TV: Madison Square Garden Network.

SPRING TRAINING
Ballpark (city): Legends Field (Tampa, Fla.).
Ticket information: 305-776-1921.

1997 SEASON New York Yankees

– 53 –

SPRING TRAINING ROSTER

Manager—Joe Torre (6).
Coaches—Jose Cardenal (53), Chris Chambliss (50), Tony Cloninger (40), Willie Randolph (30), Mel Stottlemyre (34), Don Zimmer (48).

No.	PITCHERS	B/T	Ht./Wt.	Born	1996 clubs
41	Boehringer, Brian	B/R	6-2/190	1-8-70	Columbus, New York A.L.
36	Cone, David	L/R	6-1/190	1-2-63	New York A.L., Norwich
	Cumberland, Chris	R/L	6-1/190	1-15-73	Columbus, Norwich
11	Gooden, Dwight	R/R	6-3/210	11-16-64	New York A.L.
27	Lloyd, Graeme	L/L	6-7/234	4-9-67	Milwaukee, New York A.L.
54	Mecir, Jim	B/R	6-1/195	5-16-70	Columbus, New York A.L.
	Medina, Rafael	R/R	6-3/195	2-15-75	Norwich
57	Mendoza, Ramiro	R/R	6-2/154	6-15-72	Columbus, New York A.L.
43	Nelson, Jeff	R/R	6-8/235	11-17-66	New York A.L.
46	Pettitte, Andy	L/L	6-5/235	6-15-72	New York A.L.
	Rios, Dan	R/R	6-2/190	11-11-72	Norwich, Columbus
42	Rivera, Mariano	R/R	6-2/168	11-29-69	New York A.L.
17	Rogers, Kenny	L/L	6-1/205	11-10-64	New York A.L.
45	Rumer, Tim	L/L	6-3/205	8-8-69	Norwich, Columbus, Gulf Coast Yankees
	Stanton, Mike	L/L	6-1/215	6-2-67	Boston, Texas
52	Weathers, Dave	R/R	6-3/220	9-25-69	Florida, Charlotte, New York A.L., Columbus
	Wells, David	L/L	6-4/225	5-20-63	Baltimore

No.	CATCHERS	B/T	Ht./Wt.	Born	1996 clubs
	Figga, Mike	R/R	6-0/200	7-31-70	Columbus
25	Girardi, Joe	R/R	5-11/195	10-14-64	New York A.L.
55	Posada, Jorge	B/R	6-2/205	8-17-71	Columbus, New York A.L.

No.	INFIELDERS	B/T	Ht./Wt.	Born	1996 clubs
12	Boggs, Wade	L/R	6-2/197	6-15-58	New York A.L.
18	Duncan, Mariano	R/R	6-0/185	3-13-63	New York A.L., Columbus
	Fielder, Cecil	R/R	6-3/250	9-21-63	Detroit, New York A.L.
26	Fox, Andy	L/R	6-4/205	1-12-71	New York A.L.
33	Hayes, Charlie	R/R	6-0/215	5-29-65	Pittsburgh, New York A.L.
2	Jeter, Derek	R/R	6-3/185	6-26-74	New York A.L.
14	Kelly, Pat	R/R	6-0/182	10-14-67	Gulf Coast Yankees, Tampa, Columbus, New York A.L., Norwich
	Martinez, Gabby	B/R	6-2/170	1-7-74	El Paso
24	Martinez, Tino	L/R	6-2/210	12-7-67	New York A.L.
	Sojo, Luis	R/R	5-11/175	1-3-66	Seattle, New York A.L.

No.	OUTFIELDERS	B/T	Ht./Wt.	Born	1996 clubs
	Ledee, Ricky	L/L	6-1/160	11-22-73	Norwich, Columbus
	Luke, Matt	L/L	6-5/220	2-26-71	New York A.L., Columbus, Tampa
21	O'Neill, Paul	L/L	6-4/215	2-25-63	New York A.L.
31	Raines, Tim	B/R	5-8/186	9-16-59	Tampa, Columbus, New York A.L., Gulf Coast Yankees, Norwich
28	Rivera, Ruben	R/R	6-3/200	11-14-73	Columbus, New York A.L.
	Spencer, Shane	R/R	5-11/210	2-20-72	Norwich, Columbus
39	Strawberry, Darryl	L/L	6-6/215	3-12-62	Columbus, New York A.L.
	Whiten, Mark	R/R	6-3/235	11-25-66	Philadelphia, Atlanta, Seattle
51	Williams, Bernie	B/R	6-2/205	9-13-68	New York A.L.

BALLPARK INFORMATION

Ballpark (capacity, surface)
Yankee Stadium (57,545, grass)

Address
Yankee Stadium
E. 161 St. and River Ave.
Bronx, NY 10451

Business phone
718-293-4300

Ticket information
718-293-6000

Ticket prices
$23 (field, main and loge boxes)
$21 (main and loge boxes)
$20 (main reserved-infield)
$18 (tier boxes, main reserved-outfield)
$12 (tier reserved)
$6 (bleachers)
$2 (senior citizens)

Field dimensions (from home plate)
To left field at foul line, 318 feet
To center field, 408 feet
To right field at foul line, 314 feet

First game played
April 18, 1923 (Yankees 4, Red Sox 1)

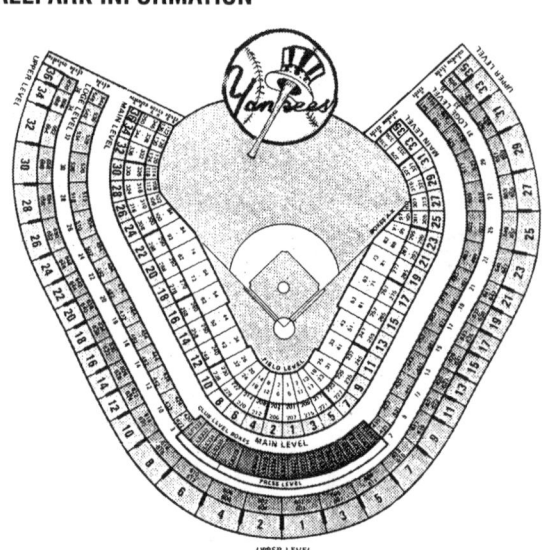

DAY BY DAY

ate	Opp.	Res.	Score	(inn.*)	Hits	Opp. hits	Winning pitcher	Losing pitcher	Save	Record	Pos.	GB
2	At Cle.	W	7-1		10	4	Cone	Martinez		1-0	T1st	...
3	At Cle.	W	5-1		8	9	Pettitte	McDowell	Nelson	2-0	T1st	...
6	At Tex.	L	2-4		7	9	Witt	Key	Henneman	2-1	3rd	1
7†	At Tex.	L	2-7		8	8	Hill	Gooden		2-2		
7‡	At Tex.	L	1-4		6	8	Pavlik	Howe	Vosberg	2-3	T3rd	2½
9	K.C.	W	7-3		10	7	Pettitte	Haney		3-3	T3rd	2
11	K.C.	W	5-3		8	9	Key	Belcher	Howe	4-3	3rd	2½
12	Tex.	W	4-3		6	5	Cone	Hill	Wetteland	5-3	2nd	2½
13	Tex.	L	6-10		11	14	Pavlik	Gooden	Vosberg	5-4	2nd	3½
14	Tex.	W	12-3		15	10	Pettitte	Gross		6-4	2nd	2½
16	At Mil.	L	3-6		10	12	Karl	Key		6-5	3rd	3½
17	At Mil.	L	4-8		9	12	Bones	Cone		6-6	T2nd	4½
19	At Min.	L	1-7		8	12	Rodriguez	Gooden		6-7	2nd	4
20	At Min.	W	7-6		16	10	Wickman	Guardado	Wetteland	7-7	2nd	3
21	At Min.	W	9-5		11	5	Rogers	Radke		8-7	2nd	2
22	At K.C.	W	6-2		14	6	Cone	Appier		9-7	2nd	1
23	At K.C.	L	2-5		7	7	Gubicza	Key	Montgomery	9-8	2nd	1
24	Cle.	W	10-8		13	11	Kamieniecki	Martinez		10-8	2nd	1
25	Cle.	L	3-4		9	12	Poole	Pettitte	Mesa	10-9	2nd	2
26	Min.	W	5-4		8	11	M. Rivera	Radke	Wetteland	11-9	2nd	1
27	Min.	L	6-8	(10)	14	14	Bennett	Wickman		11-10	2nd	1
28	Min.	W	6-3		11	8	M. Rivera	Rodriguez	Wetteland	12-10	T1st	...
30	At Bal.	W	13-10		17	11	Nelson	Shepherd	Wetteland	13-10	1st	+½
1	At Bal.	W	11-6	(15)	20	13	Pettitte	Mercker		14-10	1st	+1½
2	Chi.	W	5-1		7	5	Cone	Fernandez		15-10	1st	+2
3	Chi.	W	2-0		8	3	M. Rivera	L. Thomas	Wetteland	16-10	1st	+2
4	Chi.	L	5-11		10	11	Karchner	Nelson		16-11	1st	+1
5	Chi.	W	7-1		9	4	Pettitte	Tapani		17-11	1st	+2
6	Det.	W	10-5		14	10	Wickman	Myers		18-11	1st	+2½
7	Det.	W	12-5		13	11	Mecir	R. Lewis	Nelson	19-11	1st	+3½
8	Det.	W	10-3		13	2	Gooden	Keagle		20-11	1st	+4½
9	Det.	L	2-4		12	8	Gohr	Key	Myers	20-12	1st	+3½
10	At Chi.	L	2-5		3	5	Tapani	Pettitte	Hernandez	20-13	1st	+2½
11	At Chi.	L	5-7		8	10	McCaskill	Wetteland		20-14	1st	+1½
12	At Chi.	W	9-8		13	10	Wickman	L. Thomas	Wetteland	21-14	1st	+2½
14	Sea.	W	2-0		7	0	Gooden	Hitchcock		22-14	1st	+2
15	Sea.	L	5-10		8	19	Hurtado	Key		22-15	1st	+1½
17	Cal.	W	8-5		10	9	Pettitte	J. Abbott	M. Rivera	23-15	1st	+1½
18	Cal.	W	7-3		6	11	Rogers	Williams	M. Rivera	24-15	1st	+2½
19	Cal.	L	1-10		6	15	Finley	Kamieniecki		24-16	1st	+1½
21	Oak.	W	7-3		17	7	Gooden	Reyes		25-16	1st	+2
22	Oak.	L	1-5		5	9	Wojciechowski	Pettitte	Mohler	25-17	1st	+1
23	Oak.	W	4-3		13	6	Rogers	Taylor	Wetteland	26-17	1st	+1½
24	At Sea.	L	4-10		9	14	Hitchcock	Kamieniecki		26-18	1st	+½
25	At Sea.	W	5-4		8	9	Mendoza	Hurtado	Wetteland	27-18	1st	+1½
26	At Sea.	L	3-4		7	8	Menhart	Gooden	Charlton	27-19	1st	+½
27	At Cal.	W	16-5		15	9	Pettitte	J. Abbott		28-19	1st	+1
28	At Cal.	L	0-1		5	2	Grimsley	Rogers		28-20	T1st	...
29	At Cal.	L	0-4		8	8	Finley	Mendoza		28-21	T1st	...
31	At Oak.	W	4-1		9	3	Key	Johns	Wetteland	29-21	1st	+1
1	At Oak.	W	6-3		10	10	Pettitte	Chouinard	Wetteland	30-21	1st	+2
2	At Oak.	W	11-4		12	11	Rogers	Wojciechowski	Wetteland	31-21	1st	+2
4	Tor.	W	5-4		8	10	Gooden	Hanson	Wetteland	32-21	1st	+2
5	Tor.	L	7-12		10	14	Hentgen	Key		32-22	1st	+1
6	Tor.	W	8-1		14	6	Pettitte	Quantrill		33-22	1st	+1
7	At Det.	L	5-6		10	13	R. Lewis	Nelson		33-23	1st	+1
8	At Det.	L	7-9		12	13	Olson	Rogers	R. Lewis	33-24	1st	+1
9	At Det.	W	3-2		13	6	Gooden	Gohr	Wetteland	34-24	1st	+2
10	At Tor.	W	5-3		13	8	Key	Hentgen	Wetteland	35-24	1st	+3
11	At Tor.	W	6-4		11	9	Pettitte	Quantrill	Wetteland	36-24	1st	+3
12	At Tor.	L	4-7		9	12	Janzen	Mendoza		36-25	1st	+2
13	Cle.	L	2-6		5	12	Hershiser	Rogers	Shuey	36-26	1st	+2
14	Cle.	W	4-3		6	9	Gooden	Ogea	Wetteland	37-26	1st	+2
15	Cle.	L	3-10		9	14	Nagy	Boehringer		37-27	1st	+2
16	Cle.	W	5-4		13	11	Pettitte	Martinez	Wetteland	38-27	1st	+2
17	Min.	L	3-6		10	12	Aldred	Mendoza	Naulty	38-28	1st	+1½
18	Min.	W	2-0		3	6	Rogers	Radke	Wetteland	39-28	1st	+2½
21†	At Cle.	W	8-7	(10)	12	14	Nelson	Mesa	Wetteland	40-28		
21‡	At Cle.	W	9-3		17	7	Mendoza	Tavarez		41-28	1st	+3
22	At Cle.	W	11-9		15	12	Brewer	Martinez	Wetteland	42-28	1st	+3
23	At Cle.	W	6-5		7	9	Gooden	McDowell	Wetteland	43-28	1st	+4
24	At Min.	L	0-3		8	6	Robertson	Pettitte		43-29	1st	+3

1997 SEASON *New York Yankees*

Date	Opp.	Res.	Score	(inn.*)	Hits	Opp. hits	Winning pitcher	Losing pitcher	Save	Record	Pos.	GB
6-25†	At Min.	L	1-6		5	12	Rodriguez	Boehringer		43-30		
6-25‡	At Min.	W	6-2		12	8	Mendoza	Serafini		44-30	1st	+3
6-26	At Min.	W	2-1		5	10	Polley	Guardado	Wetteland	45-30	1st	+4
6-27	Bal.	W	3-2		8	7	Rogers	Erickson	Wetteland	46-30	1st	+5
6-28	Bal.	L	4-7		10	14	Rhodes	M. Rivera	R. Myers	46-31	1st	+4
6-29	Bal.	W	4-3		9	6	Pettitte	Mussina	Wetteland	47-31	1st	+5
6-30	Bal.	L	1-9		4	11	Wells	Mendoza		47-32	1st	+4
7-1	Bos.	W	2-0		5	6	Key	Clemens	Wetteland	48-32	1st	+4
7-2	Bos.	W	7-5		15	9	Nelson	Hudson	Wetteland	49-32	1st	+4
7-4	Mil.	W	4-1		7	8	Pettitte	Karl	Wetteland	50-32	1st	+5
7-5	Mil.	W	12-3		15	10	Gooden	Bones		51-32	1st	+6
7-6	Mil.	W	2-0		11	8	Key	Sparks	Wetteland	52-32	1st	+6
7-7	Mil.	L	1-4		9	7	McDonald	Rogers	Fetters	52-33	1st	+6
7-11	At Bal.	W	4-2		7	6	Key	Mussina	Wetteland	53-33	1st	+7
7-13†	At Bal.	W	3-2		6	10	Nelson	Wells	Wetteland	54-33		
7-13‡	At Bal.	W	7-5		10	9	Gooden	Rhodes	Wetteland	55-33	1st	+9
7-14	At Bal.	W	4-1		6	8	Pettitte	Erickson	Wetteland	56-33	1st	+10
7-15	At Bos.	L	6-8		14	13	Wakefield	Hutton	Slocumb	56-34	1st	+9
7-16	At Bos.	W	9-5		11	7	Key	Clemens		57-34	1st	+10
7-17	At Bos.	L	11-12		19	12	Eshelman	Wetteland		57-35	1st	+9
7-18	At Mil.	L	4-16		10	13	Karl	Gooden		57-36	1st	+8
7-19	At Mil.	L	5-7		12	10	Eldred	Pettitte	Fetters	57-37	1st	+8
7-20	At Mil.	W	4-2		9	6	M. Rivera	Vanegmond	Wetteland	58-37	1st	+9
7-21	At Mil.	L	2-3		6	7	D'Amico	Key	Fetters	58-38	1st	+8
7-22	Tex.	L	1-6		6	11	Hill	Rogers		58-39	1st	+8
7-23	Tex.	W	6-0		11	2	Gooden	Pavlik		59-39	1st	+9
7-24	Tex.	W	4-2		9	9	Pettitte	Alberro	Wetteland	60-39	1st	+10
7-25	K.C.	L	0-7		8	13	Rosado	Hutton		60-40	1st	+10
7-26	K.C.	W	15-1		21	6	Key	Haney		61-40	1st	+11
7-27	K.C.	W	5-4		10	9	Rogers	Belcher	Wetteland	62-40	1st	+11
7-28	K.C.	W	3-2		5	7	Wetteland	Jacome		63-40	1st	+12
7-30	At Tex.	L	2-15		5	21	Witt	Pettitte		63-41	1st	+11
7-31	At Tex.	L	2-9		11	9	Oliver	Key		63-42	1st	+10
8-1	At Tex.	W	6-5		11	9	Rogers	Hill	Wetteland	64-42	1st	+10
8-2	At K.C.	L	3-4	(10)	8	8	Montgomery	M. Rivera		64-43	1st	+10
8-3	At K.C.	L	4-11		6	12	Linton	Weathers		64-44	1st	+9
8-4	At K.C.	W	5-3		12	8	Pettitte	Rosado		65-44	1st	+10
8-5	At K.C.	W	5-2		12	5	Key	Pichardo	Wetteland	66-44	1st	+10
8-6	Chi.	W	9-2		13	7	Rogers	Tapani		67-44	1st	+10
8-7	Chi.	L	4-8	(10)	7	10	Hernandez	Nelson		67-45	1st	+9
8-8	Chi.	W	8-4		11	8	Wickman	Andujar	M. Rivera	68-45	1st	+9
8-9	Det.	L	3-5		9	7	Cummings	Pettitte	Myers	68-46	1st	+9
8-10	Det.	L	7-13		12	13	R. Lewis	Key		68-47	1st	+8
8-11	Det.	W	12-0		15	6	Rogers	Lira		69-47	1st	+9
8-12	At Chi.	L	2-3	(10)	5	6	Hernandez	Wetteland		69-48	1st	+8
8-13	At Chi.	L	4-8		9	11	Bertotti	Weathers		69-49	1st	+7
8-14	At Chi.	W	3-1		9	8	Pettitte	Baldwin	M. Rivera	70-49	1st	+7
8-16	Sea.	L	5-6		10	11	Hitchcock	Polley	Jackson	70-50	1st	+5
8-17	Sea.	L	3-10		8	12	Moyer	Rogers		70-51	1st	+5
8-18	Sea.	L	12-13	(12)	19	19	Ayala	Mecir	Jackson	70-52	1st	+5
8-19	Sea.	W	10-4		16	3	Pettitte	Carmona		71-52	1st	+6
8-20	Cal.	W	17-6		16	8	Boehringer	Springer		72-52	1st	+6
8-21	Cal.	L	1-7		13	9	Dickson	Key	Percival	72-53	1st	+5
8-22	Cal.	L	3-12		6	14	Finley	Rogers		72-54	1st	+5
8-23	Oak.	W	5-3		7	11	Gooden	Wengert	M. Rivera	73-54	1st	+6
8-24	Oak.	W	5-4		8	13	Whitehurst	Telgheder	Pavlas	74-54	1st	+6
8-25	Oak.	L	4-6		10	10	Mohler	Nelson	Acre	74-55	1st	+6
8-26	At Sea.	L	1-2		5	9	Ayala	Lloyd	Charlton	74-56	1st	+5
8-27	At Sea.	L	4-7		7	6	Moyer	Lloyd		74-57	1st	+4
8-28	At Sea.	L	2-10		9	10	Mulholland	Gooden		74-58	1st	+4
8-29	At Cal.	L	3-14		6	15	Holtz	Whitehurst		74-59	1st	+4
8-30	At Cal.	W	6-2		7	8	Pettitte	Springer		75-59	1st	+4
8-31	At Cal.	W	14-3		16	7	Key	Dickson		76-59	1st	+4
9-1	At Cal.	L	0-4		4	6	Finley	Rogers		76-60	1st	+4
9-2	At Oak.	W	5-0		10	1	Cone	Prieto		77-60	1st	+4
9-3	At Oak.	L	9-10		12	13	Acre	Boehringer	Johns	77-61	1st	+4
9-4	At Oak.	W	10-3		16	8	Pettitte	Telgheder		78-61	1st	+4
9-6	Tor.	W	4-3		5	9	M. Rivera	Risley		79-61	1st	+5
9-7	Tor.	L	2-3		7	5	Quantrill	Cone	Timlin	79-62	1st	+4
9-8	Tor.	L	2-4		9	6	Hanson	Pettitte	Timlin	79-63	1st	+3
9-10	At Det.	W	9-8		15	12	M. Rivera	Sager	Wetteland	80-63	1st	+2
9-11	At Det.	W	7-3		6	8	Key	Lira		81-63	1st	+2¹
9-12	At Det.	W	12-3		13	8	Cone	Thompson		82-63	1st	+3¹
9-13	At Tor.	W	4-1		10	7	Pettitte	Hanson	Wetteland	83-63	1st	+3¹
9-14	At Tor.	W	3-1		11	5	Boehringer	Hentgen	Wetteland	84-63	1st	+3¹

te	Opp.	Res.	Score	(inn.*)	Hits	Opp. hits	Winning pitcher	Losing pitcher	Save	Record	Pos.	GB
15	At Tor.	L	1-3		6	9	Williams	Mendoza	Timlin	84-64	1st	+2 1/2
16	At Tor.	W	10-0		12	2	Key	Quantrill		85-64	1st	+3
18	Bal.	W	3-2	(10)	10	5	M. Rivera	Mills		86-64	1st	+4
19†	Bal.	W	9-3		14	6	Rogers	Mussina		87-64		
19‡	Bal.	L	9-10		11	14	Mathews	M. Rivera	R. Myers	87-65	1st	+4
20	Bos.	L	2-4		6	10	Wakefield	Polley	Slocumb	87-66	1st	+4
21	Bos.	W	12-11	(10)	20	14	Wetteland	Hudson		88-66	1st	+4
22	Bos.	W	4-3		10	9	M. Rivera	Sele	Wetteland	89-66	1st	+4
23	Bos.	L	3-4	(11)	11	12	Slocumb	Boehringer	Mahomes	89-67	1st	+4
25†	Mil.	W	19-2		20	5	Cone	Vanegmond		90-67		
25‡	Mil.	W	6-2		8	7	Rogers	Karl		91-67	1st	+5
26	At Bos.	L	3-5		10	8	Maddux	Key	Slocumb	91-68	1st	+4
27	At Bos.	L	5-7		10	11	Sele	Gooden	Slocumb	91-69	1st	+4
28	At Bos.	W	4-2		5	9	Mendoza	Clemens	Wetteland	92-69	1st	+4
29	At Bos.	L	5-6		11	14	Mahomes	Polley		92-70	1st	+4

onthly records: April (13-10), May (16-11), June (18-11), July (16-10), August (13-17), September (16-11).
nnings, if other than nine. †First game of doubleheader. ‡Second game of doubleheader.

HIGHLIGHTS

gh point: The Yankees clinched their first orld Series title in 18 years on October with a 3-2 victory over the Braves in ame 6. World Series MVP John etteland saved all four Series victories. w point: In a season with few low ints, the lowest came early, on April , when Dwight Gooden was rocked in s second start. The Yankees fell below 00 (at 6-7) for the second and final ne all season. rning point: Already in a strong posi-n, the Yankees put a stranglehold on st place with a four-game sweep at cond-place Baltimore in the first series er the All-Star break. ost valuable players: There are four: chers Mariano Rivera and Andy ttitte, center fielder Bernie Williams d shortstop Derek Jeter. Jeter, who s the A.L. Rookie of the Year, hit .350 ter the All-Star break and .314 overall, d showed no signs of wilting under the ual New York pressures. ost valuable pitcher: Setup man ariano Rivera. He was arguably the ost dominant pitcher in the league, riking out 130 in 107⅔ innings. st improved player: Setup man ariano Rivera. Rivera went 8-3 with a 09 ERA after going 5-3 with a 5.51 ERA a rookie in 1995. ost pleasant surprises: Again, there ere more than one—shortstop Derek ter, second baseman Mariano Duncan, cher Dwight Gooden and outfielder arryl Strawberry. In addition, new man-er Joe Torre was magnificent, and M. Bob Watson and owner George einbrenner coexisted the entire season. ggest disappointments: Pitchers David ne and Scott Kamienicki and second seman Pat Kelly. All three were both-ed by injuries and had wasted seasons. y injuries: Pitcher David Cone missed ur months with an aneurysm in his ght shoulder. Outfielder Tim Raines ssed 75 days with nagging hamstring uries. Second baseman Pat Kelly was

limited to 13 games because of shoulder problems. Pitcher Melido Perez missed the season with arm trouble. Infielder Tony Fernandez missed the season after breaking his elbow during spring train-ing. Pitcher Scott Kamienicki missed most of the season with arm trouble. Notables: Third baseman Wade Boggs became one of only four players ever to appear in 12 consecutive All-Star Games (the others are Brooks Robinson, Yogi Berra and Cal Ripken). . . . Dwight Gooden pitched his first career no-hitter, beating Seattle, 2-0, on May 14. . . . Andy Pettitte became the first Yankee to win 20 games since Ron Guidry in 1985.
—JON HEYMAN

RECORDS

1996 regular-season record: 92-70 (1st in A.L. East); 49-31 at home; 43-39 on road; 32-20 vs. East; 37-24 vs. Central; 23-26 vs. West; 20-27 vs. lefthanded starters; 72-43 vs. righthanded starters; 82-60 on grass; 10-10 on turf; 35-22 in daytime; 57-48 at night; 25-16 in one-run games; 4-6 in extra-inning games; 3-1-2 in doubleheaders.
Team record past five years: 405-338 (.545, ranks 2nd in league in that span).

TEAM LEADERS

Batting average: Derek Jeter (.314).
At-bats: Tino Martinez (595).
Runs: Bernie Williams (108).
Hits: Derek Jeter (183).
Total bases: Bernie Williams (295).
Doubles: Paul O'Neill (35).
Triples: Bernie Williams (7).
Home runs: Bernie Williams (29).
Runs batted in: Tino Martinez (117).
Stolen bases: Bernie Williams (17).
Slugging percentage: Bernie Williams (.535).
On-base percentage: Paul O'Neill (.411).
Wins: Andy Pettitte (21).
Earned-run average: Andy Pettitte (3.87).
Complete games: Andy Pettitte, Kenny Rogers (2).
Shutouts: Dwight Gooden, Kenny Rogers (1).

Saves: John Wetteland (43).
Innings pitched: Andy Pettitte (221.0).
Strikeouts: Andy Pettitte (162).

GAMES BY POSITION

Catcher: Joe Girardi 120, Jim Leyritz 55, Jorge Posada 4, Tim McIntosh 1.
First base: Tino Martinez 151, Cecil Fielder 9, Mike Aldrete 8, Jim Leyritz 5, Tim McIntosh 1, Paul O'Neill 1.
Second base: Mariano Duncan 104, Andy Fox 72, Matt Howard 30, Luis Sojo 14, Robert Eenhoorn 10, Pat Kelly 10, Jim Leyritz 2.
Third base: Wade Boggs 123, Andy Fox 31, Charlie Hayes 19, Jim Leyritz 13, Matt Howard 6, Mariano Duncan 3, Robert Eenhoorn 2, Tim McIntosh 1, Luis Sojo 1.
Shortstop: Derek Jeter 157, Andy Fox 9, Luis Sojo 4.
Outfield: Paul O'Neill 146, Bernie Williams 140, Gerald Williams 92, Tim Raines 50, Ruben Rivera 45, Darryl Strawberry 33, Mike Aldrete 9, Dion James 4, Mariano Duncan 3, Jim Leyritz 3, Andy Fox 1.
Designated hitter: Ruben Sierra 61, Cecil Fielder 43, Darryl Strawberry 26, Jim Leyritz 13, Mike Aldrete 9, Wade Boggs 4, Andy Fox 3, Pat Kelly 3, Tino Martinez 3, Paul O'Neill 3, Jorge Posada 3, Mariano Duncan 2, Joe Girardi 2, Tim Raines 2, Bernie Williams 2, Gerald Williams 2, Dion James 1, Matt Luke 1.

TOP DRAFT CHOICES

1. **Eric Milton**, LHP, Univ. of Maryland.
2. **Jason Coble**, LHP, Lincoln County H.S., Fayetteville, Tenn.
3. **Nick Johnson**, 1B, McClatchy H.S., Sacramento, Calif.
4. **Vidal Candelaria**, C, Manati, P.R.
5. **Zach Day**, RHP, LaSalle H.S., Cincinnati.
6. **Brian Reith**, RHP, Concordia Lutheran H.S., Fort Wayne, Ind.
7. **Brian Aylor**, OF, Oklahoma State Univ.
8. **Allen Butler**, 3B, Lincoln Memorial (Tenn.) University.
9. **Chris Fulbright**, RHP, Libertyville (Ill.) H.S.
10. **Rudy Gomez**, 2B, University of Miami.

OAKLAND ATHLETICS
AMERICAN LEAGUE WEST DIVISION

1997 ATHLETICS SCHEDULE

Home games shaded.
* — All-Star Game at Jacobs Field (Cleveland)
D — Day game (any game starting before 5 p.m.)

APRIL

SUN	MON	TUE	WED	THU	FRI	SAT
		1	2 CLE	3 D CLE	4 NYY	5 D NYY
6 D NYY	7 BOS	8 BOS	9 D BOS	10	11 D NYY	12 D NYY
13 NYY	14 BOS	15 BOS	16 TOR	17 D TOR	18 DET	19 D DET
20 D DET	21	22 D MIN	23 MIN	24 MIN	25 KC	26 D KC
27 KC	28	29 CLE	30 CLE			

MAY

SUN	MON	TUE	WED	THU	FRI	SAT
				1 CLE	2 BAL	3 D BAL
4 BAL	5 D MIL	6 MIL	7 D MIL	8 CWS	9 CWS	10 CWS
11 CWS	12 D BAL	13 D MIL	14 MIL	15 MIL	16 CWS	17 D CWS
18 D CWS	19	20 TEX	21 TEX	22 D TEX	23 MIN	24 MIN
25 MIN	26 D KC	27 KC	28 ANA	29 ANA	30 TOR	31 D TOR

JUNE

SUN	MON	TUE	WED	THU	FRI	SAT
1 TOR	2 D DET	3 D DET	4	5 TOR	6 TOR	7 D TOR
8 D TOR	9 D	10 DET	11 D DET	12 LA	13 LA	14 D COL
15 COL	16	17 SD	18 SD	19 ANA	20 ANA	21 ANA
22 D ANA	23 SEA	24 SEA	25 SEA	26 TEX	27 TEX	28 TEX
29 TEX	30 SD					

JULY

SUN	MON	TUE	WED	THU	FRI	SAT
		1 SD	2 D SF	3 D SF	4 TEX	5 TEX
6 TEX	7	8 °	9	10 D ANA	11 ANA	12 D ANA
13 ANA	14 D SEA	15 D SEA	16 KC	17 D KC	18 MIN	19 D MIN
20 D MIN	21 BOS	22 BOS	23 BOS	24 CLE	25 D CLE	26 D CLE
27 CLE	28 NYY	29 NYY	30 D NYY	31 BAL		

AUGUST

SUN	MON	TUE	WED	THU	FRI	SAT
					1 BAL	2 D BAL
3 BAL	4	5 D CWS	6 CWS	7 D MIL	8 MIL	9 D MIL
10 MIL	11	12 BAL	13 BAL	14 CWS	15 CWS	16 MIL
17 MIL	18	19 BOS	20 BOS	21 D BOS	22 CLE	23 CLE
24 CLE	25	26 D NYY	27 NYY	28 LA	29 LA	30 COL
31 COL						

SEPTEMBER

SUN	MON	TUE	WED	THU	FRI	SAT
	1 D SF	2	3 SF	4 KC	5 D KC	6 KC
7 D KC	8 MIN	9 MIN	10 D TOR	11 D TOR	12 D DET	13 D DET
14 DET	15 DET	16	17 ANA	18 D ANA	19 D SEA	20 D SEA
21 D SEA	22 D SEA	23 TEX	24 D TEX	25	26 SEA	27 SEA
28 D SEA						

1997 SEASON

CLUB DIRECTORY

Owners
Stephen C. Schott
Ken Hofmann

President and general manager
Sandy Alderson

Vice president, finance
Goy Fuller

Special assistant to the g.m.
Bill Rigney

Assistant general manager
Billy Beane

Director of player development
Keith Lieppman

Director of scouting
Grady Fuson

Assistant director of scouting
Dave Seifert

Director of baseball administration
Pam Pitts

Traveling secretary
Mickey Morabito

Baseball information manager
Mike Selleck

Admin. asst., baseball operations
Betty Shinoda

Director of broadcasting
Ken Pries

Broadcasting and pub. rel. coordinator
Robert Buan

Director of stadium operations
David Rinetti

Director of corporate sales
Mark Sowinski

Director of purchasing & merchandis
David Alioto

Director of events and promotions
Susan Bress

Dir. of tickets, skybox sales and op.
Paul Solby

Admin. assistant, executive office
Erin Buckert

Director of information resources
David Lozow

Team physician
Dr. Allan Pont

Team orthopedist
Dr. Jerrald Goldman

Trainers
Barry Weinberg
Larry Davis

Equipment manager
Steve Vucinich

Visiting clubhouse manager
Mike Thalblum

Scouts
Tony Arias, Dick Bogard, Steve
Bowden, Tom Clark, Ed Crosby, R
Elam, Ruben Escalera, Grady Fuse
Ubaldo Heredia, Tim Holt, Ron
Hopkins, Eric Kubota, John Kuehl
Miguel Machado, Rick Magnante,
Gary McGraw, Billy Merkel, Marty
Miller, Steve Nichols, Chris Pittard
John Poloni, J.P. Ricciardi, Joe
Robinson, Will Schock, Mike Sop
Rich Sparks, Ron Vaughn, Santia
Villalona

MINOR LEAGUE AFFILIATES

Class	Team	League	Manager
AAA	Edmonton	Pacific Coast	Gary Jones
AA	Huntsville	Southern	Mike Quade
A	Modesto	California	Jeffrey Leonard
A	Visalia	California	Tony DeFrancesco
A	Southern Oregon	Northwest	John Kuehl
Rookie	Scotttsdale A's	Arizona	Juan Navarrete

BROADCAST INFORMATION

Radio: KFRC-AM (610); KNTA-AM
(1430, Spanish language).
TV: KRON-TV (Channel 4).
Cable TV: SportsChannel.

SPRING TRAINING

Ballpark (city): Phoenix Stadium
(Phoenix, Ariz.).
Ticket information: 602-392-0074.

SPRING TRAINING ROSTER

Manager—Art Howe (18).
Coaches—Bob Alejo (46), Bob Cluck (3), Duffy Dyer (9), Brad Fischer (35), Denny Walling (15), Ron Washington (38).

No.	PITCHERS	B/T	Ht./Wt.	Born	1996 clubs
55	Acre, Mark	R/R	6-8/240	9-16-68	Edmonton, Oakland
40	Adams, Willie	R/R	6-7/215	10-8-72	Edmonton, Oakland
62	Baker, Scott	L/L	6-2/175	5-18-70	DID NOT PLAY
54	Chouinard, Bobby	R/R	6-1/172	5-1-72	Edmonton, Oakland
58	Dale, Carl	R/R	6-2/215	12-7-72	Modesto
27	Dunbar, Matt	L/L	6-0/175	10-15-68	Norwich, Columbus, Greensboro
42	Groom, Buddy	L/L	6-2/200	7-10-65	Oakland
51	Johns, Doug	R/L	6-2/185	12-19-67	Oakland
59	Johnson, Dane	R/R	6-5/205	2-10-63	Syracuse, Toronto
20	Karsay, Steve	R/R	6-3/205	3-24-72	Modesto
32	Mohler, Mike	R/L	6-2/195	7-26-68	Oakland
	Montoya, Wilmer	R/R	5-10/165	3-15-74	Kinston, Canton/Akron
48	Prieto, Ariel	R/R	6-3/225	10-22-69	Oakland, Modesto, Edmonton
57	Rigby, Brad	R/R	6-6/195	5-14-73	Huntsville
30	Small, Aaron	R/R	6-5/208	11-23-71	Oakland, Edmonton
22	Taylor, Bill	R/R	6-8/200	10-16-61	Edmonton, Oakland
50	Telgheder, David	R/R	6-3/212	11-11-66	Edmonton, Modesto, Oakland
53	Wagner, Bret	L/L	6-0/205	4-18-73	Huntsville
31	Wasdin, John	R/R	6-2/190	8-5-72	Edmonton, Oakland
56	Wengert, Don	R/R	6-2/205	11-6-69	Oakland
52	Witasick, Jay	R/R	6-4/205	8-28-72	Huntsville, Oakland, Edmonton

No.	CATCHERS	B/T	Ht./Wt.	Born	1996 clubs
13	Molina, Izzy	R/R	6-1/200	6-3-71	Edmonton, Oakland
19	Williams, George	B/R	5-10/190	4-22-69	Oakland, Edmonton

No.	INFIELDERS	B/T	Ht./Wt.	Born	1996 clubs
28	Batista, Tony	R/R	6-0/165	12-9-73	Edmonton, Oakland
26	Bournigal, Rafael	R/R	5-11/165	5-12-66	Oakland
7	Brosius, Scott	R/R	6-1/185	8-15-66	Oakland, Edmonton
6	Catalanotto, Frank	L/R	6-0/170	4-27-74	Jacksonville
47	Cox, Steve	L/L	6-4/200	10-31-74	Huntsville
8	Gates, Brent	B/R	6-1/180	3-14-70	Oakland
2	McDonald, Jason	B/R	5-8/175	3-20-72	Edmonton
25	McGwire, Mark	R/R	6-5/250	10-1-63	Oakland
21	Spiezio, Scott	B/R	6-2/195	9-21-72	Edmonton, Oakland

No.	OUTFIELDERS	B/T	Ht./Wt.	Born	1996 clubs
23	Battle, Allen	R/R	6-0/170	11-29-68	Oakland, Edmonton
29	Berroa, Geronimo	R/R	6-0/195	3-18-65	Oakland
16	Giambi, Jason	L/R	6-2/200	1-8-71	Oakland
	Grieve, Ben	L/R	6-4/200	5-4-76	Modesto, Huntsville
44	Herrera, Jose	L/L	6-0/165	8-30-72	Huntsville, Oakland
24	Lesher, Brian	R/L	6-5/205	3-5-71	Edmonton, Oakland
12	Stairs, Matt	L/R	5-9/200	2-27-69	Oakland, Edmonton
11	Young, Ernie	R/R	6-1/190	7-8-69	Oakland

BALLPARK INFORMATION

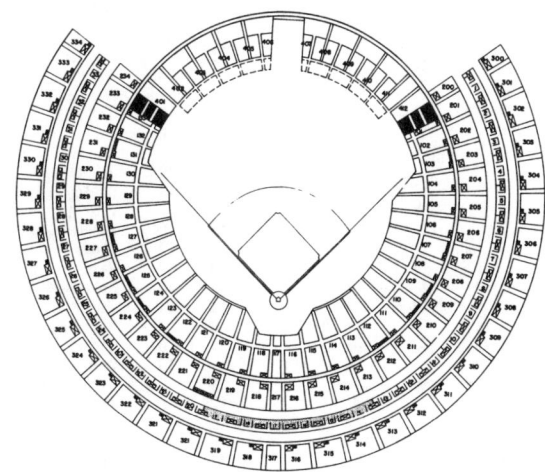

Ballpark (capacity, surface)
Oakland-Alameda County Coliseum (45,000, grass)

Address
Oakland Athletics
7677 Oakport St., Suite 200
Oakland, CA 94621

Business phone
510-638-4900

Ticket information
510-638-4627

Ticket prices
$20 (club MVP)
$17.50 (MVP)
$14 (field level-infield)
$13 (field level, plaza-infield)
$11 (plaza)
$5 (upper reserved)
$4 (bleachers)

Field dimensions (from home plate)
To left field at foul line, 330 feet
To center field, 400 feet
To right field at foul line, 330 feet

First game played
April 17, 1968 (Orioles 4, Athletics 1)

DAY BY DAY

Date	Opp.	Res.	Score	(inn.*)	Hits	Opp. hits	Winning pitcher	Losing pitcher	Save	Record	Pos.	GB
4-1	Tor.§	L	6-9		5	13	Hanson	Reyes	Timlin	0-1	4th	1
4-3	Tor.§	L	4-10		7	11	Hentgen	Prieto		0-2	4th	2
4-4	Det.§	L	9-10	(15)	13	13	Keagle	Small		0-3	4th	3
4-5	Det.§	W	13-2		16	4	Johns	Gohr		1-3	4th	2
4-6	Det.§	L	1-6		5	12	Lira	Reyes		1-4	4th	3
4-7	Det.§	W	7-6		11	11	Corsi	B. Williams		2-4	4th	4
4-9	At Mil.	L	4-10		7	12	McDonald	Van Poppel		2-5	4th	5
4-11	At Mil.	W	11-0		13	6	Johns	Karl		3-5	4th	4
4-12	At Chi.	W	7-2		15	6	Reyes	Fernandez		4-5	4th	3
4-13	At Chi.	L	5-6	(12)	9	10	Karchner	Wengert		4-6	4th	4
4-14	At Chi.	W	10-5		13	11	Groom	Simas		5-6	T3rd	3
4-15	At Tex.	W	8-3		12	6	Mohler	Heredia		6-6	3rd	2
4-16	At Tex.	L	3-5		6	12	Witt	Johns	Henneman	6-7	3rd	3
4-17	At Tex.	L	1-12		4	13	Hill	Reyes		6-8	T3rd	4
4-19	Chi.	L	3-4		7	7	Karchner	Briscoe	Hernandez	6-9	4th	5
4-20	Chi.	L	3-8		9	8	Tapani	Van Poppel		6-10	4th	6
4-21	Chi.	W	6-5		9	9	Corsi	Simas	Mohler	7-10	4th	6
4-22	Mil.	W	6-2		7	5	Reyes	Bones	Briscoe	8-10	4th	5
4-23	Mil.	W	9-6		10	8	Wojciechowski	Sparks	Mohler	9-10	4th	4
4-24	At Tor.	W	7-6		11	11	Prieto	Hentgen	Corsi	10-10	4th	3
4-25	At Tor.	W	4-3	(11)	9	8	Mohler	Crabtree		11-10	4th	2
4-26	At Det.	L	5-14		8	11	Christopher	Johns		11-11	4th	3
4-27	At Det.	W	4-1		8	6	Reyes	Lira	Taylor	12-11	4th	3
4-28	At Det.	W	6-3		9	8	Wojciechowski	Gohr	Taylor	13-11	3rd	3
4-30	Cal.	L	3-7		11	11	Langston	Prieto		13-12	T3rd	2
5-1	Cal.	L	4-6		7	12	Boskie	Van Poppel	Percival	13-13	4th	3
5-2	Cal.	L	1-3		6	7	J. Abbott	Johns	Percival	13-14	4th	3
5-3	At K.C.	L	1-3		6	7	Appier	Reyes	Montgomery	13-15	4th	4
5-4	At K.C.	W	5-2		6	10	Wojciechowski	Gubicza	Groom	14-15	4th	4
5-5	At K.C.	L	0-2		3	7	Haney	Prieto		14-16	4th	5
5-6	Cle.	W	5-3		11	9	Taylor	Assenmacher	Mohler	15-16	4th	5
5-7	Cle.	W	8-4		16	7	Johns	Hershiser		16-16	4th	5
5-8	Cle.	L	3-7		10	9	Nagy	Reyes		16-17	4th	6
5-10	Min.	W	15-5		18	10	Wojciechowski	Rodriguez		17-17	4th	5
5-11	Min.	W	12-5		13	10	Prieto	Radke		18-17	4th	5
5-12	Min.	W	8-3		14	5	Wengert	Parra		19-17	3rd	4
5-13	Bal.	L	3-4		11	9	Krivda	Johns	R. Myers	19-18	T3rd	5
5-14	Bal.	L	1-9		7	8	Mussina	Reyes		19-19	T3rd	6
5-17	At Bos.	L	3-5	(11)	6	12	Stanton	Van Poppel		19-20	3rd	6
5-18	At Bos.	W	6-5	(10)	9	10	Groom	Garces	Taylor	20-20	3rd	6
5-19	At Bos.	L	2-12		9	15	Sele	Wengert		20-21	3rd	6
5-20	At Bos.	L	4-16		8	21	Gordon	Johns		20-22	3rd	6
5-21	At N.Y.	L	3-7		7	17	Gooden	Reyes		20-23	4th	6
5-22	At N.Y.	W	5-1		9	5	Wojciechowski	Pettitte	Mohler	21-23	3rd	6
5-23	At N.Y.	L	3-4		6	13	Rogers	Taylor	Wetteland	21-24	T3rd	6
5-24	At Bal.	L	4-5	(10)	9	10	McDowell	Reyes		21-25	4th	6
5-25	At Bal.	W	6-3		9	8	Johns	Wells	Groom	22-25	T3rd	6
5-26	At Bal.	L	1-6		3	9	Mercker	Chouinard	McDowell	22-26	4th	7
5-27	Bos.	L	3-10		8	16	Wakefield	Wojciechowski		22-27	4th	8
5-28	Bos.	W	6-2		8	11	Wasdin	Clemens		23-27	4th	8
5-29	Bos.	W	7-6	(10)	7	10	Mohler	Slocumb		24-27	4th	8
5-31	N.Y.	L	1-4		3	9	Key	Johns	Wetteland	24-28	4th	9
6-1	N.Y.	L	3-6		10	10	Pettitte	Chouinard	Wetteland	24-29	4th	9
6-2	N.Y.	L	4-11		11	12	Rogers	Wojciechowski	Wetteland	24-30	4th	9
6-3	K.C.	W	2-1		7	7	Wasdin	Appier	Taylor	25-30	4th	9
6-4	K.C.	W	8-3		16	10	Wengert	Gubicza		26-30	4th	8
6-5	K.C.	L	2-5		7	12	Haney	Johns	Montgomery	26-31	4th	8
6-7	At Min.	W	6-4		9	12	Reyes	Radke	Corsi	27-31	T3rd	8
6-8†	At Min.	L	2-4		7	10	Robertson	Wojciechowski	Guardado	27-32	4th	9
6-8‡	At Min.	W	13-7		14	14	Wasdin	Mahomes		28-32	3rd	9
6-9	At Min.	L	3-5		8	10	Rodriguez	Wengert		28-33	4th	10
6-10	At Cle.	L	4-5		9	9	Nagy	Johns	Mesa	28-34	4th	11
6-11	At Cle.	L	5-6	(13)	15	10	Ogea	Reyes		28-35	4th	11
6-12	At Cle.	W	9-6		9	8	Montgomery	McDowell	Mohler	29-35	4th	11
6-13	At Mil.	L	3-16		12	19	Karl	Wojciechowski		29-36	4th	11
6-14	At Mil.	L	2-6		6	10	Bones	Wasdin		29-37	4th	11
6-15	At Mil.	L	9-12		12	15	Givens	Wengert	Garcia	29-38	4th	12
6-16	At Mil.	W	10-9		13	12	Taylor	Fetters	Mohler	30-38	4th	11
6-17	At Det.	W	8-4	(10)	8	11	Corsi	Myers		31-38	4th	10
6-18	At Det.	W	8-5		11	10	Van Poppel	Urbani	Taylor	32-38	4th	10
6-19	At Det.	W	10-3		15	6	Wasdin	Keagle		33-38	4th	10
6-20	Tor.	L	0-1		2	9	Hentgen	Wengert	Timlin	33-39	4th	10

ate	Opp.	Res.	Score	(inn.*)	Hits	Opp. hits	Winning pitcher	Losing pitcher	Save	Record	Pos.	GB
21	Tor.	L	5-7		10	9	Quantrill	Johns	Timlin	33-40	4th	11 1/2
22	Tor.	W	8-4		12	7	Chouinard	Ware		34-40	4th	11 1/2
23	Tor.	L	4-5		7	9	Guzman	Wojciechowski	Timlin	34-41	4th	11 1/2
24	Det.	W	4-2		8	4	Wasdin	Sodowsky	Taylor	35-41	4th	10 1/2
25	Det.	L	8-10		13	16	Olivares	Wengert	Olson	35-42	4th	11 1/2
27	At Cal.	W	18-2		17	8	Johns	Boskie		36-42	4th	11 1/2
28	At Cal.	W	6-3		8	5	Chouinard	Finley		37-42	4th	10 1/2
29	At Cal.	W	11-9		13	16	Groom	Monteleone		38-42	4th	10 1/2
30	At Cal.	L	0-1		5	4	Hancock	Wasdin	Percival	38-43	4th	10 1/2
1	At Sea.	W	6-4		9	11	Wengert	Wagner	Taylor	39-43	4th	10 1/2
2	At Sea.	W	11-6		16	13	Mohler	Charlton		40-43	4th	9 1/2
3	At Sea.	L	3-4		6	9	Ayala	Reyes		40-44	4th	10 1/2
4	Cal.	W	8-7	(11)	13	14	Taylor	Monteleone		41-44	4th	9 1/2
5	Cal.	W	16-8		13	13	Wasdin	Hancock		42-44	T3rd	8 1/2
6	Cal.	W	6-5	(10)	7	12	Taylor	James		43-44	3rd	7 1/2
7	Cal.	L	4-9		11	16	Boskie	Johns		43-45	T3rd	8 1/2
11	Tex.	W	8-3		13	11	Chouinard	Oliver		44-45	3rd	7 1/2
12	Tex.	L	4-8	(10)	10	16	Russell	Taylor		44-46	3rd	8 1/2
13	Tex.	L	1-8		3	12	Pavlik	Wengert		44-47	T3rd	9 1/2
14	Tex.	W	9-1		14	11	Johns	Gross		45-47	3rd	8 1/2
15	Sea.	L	1-5		5	8	Wolcott	Telgheder		45-48	T3rd	8 1/2
16	Sea.	W	12-5		16	11	Chouinard	Hitchcock		46-48	3rd	8 1/2
17	Sea.	W	7-6		9	9	Corsi	Minor	Taylor	47-48	3rd	8 1/2
18	At Tex.	W	5-4	(11)	12	10	Reyes	Brandenburg	Van Poppel	48-48	3rd	7 1/2
19	At Tex.	W	9-6		11	11	Reyes	Helling	Taylor	49-48	3rd	6 1/2
20	At Tex.	L	4-8		13	15	Witt	Van Poppel		49-49	3rd	7 1/2
21	At Tex.	W	11-8		16	16	Groom	Brandenburg	Mohler	50-49	3rd	6 1/2
22	At Chi.	W	6-5		12	8	Taylor	Karchner		51-49	3rd	6 1/2
23	At Chi.	W	8-4		10	8	Wengert	Fernandez	Corsi	52-49	3rd	5 1/2
24	At Chi.	W	6-5		7	13	Corsi	Simas	Taylor	53-49	3rd	4 1/2
25	At Tor.	L	3-4		7	12	Crabtree	Witasick		53-50	3rd	5 1/2
26	At Tor.	W	5-3		9	4	Groom	Castillo	Taylor	54-50	3rd	4 1/2
27	At Tor.	L	4-6		9	6	Hanson	Wasdin	Timlin	54-51	3rd	5 1/2
28	At Tor.	L	0-1		3	4	Hentgen	Prieto		54-52	3rd	5 1/2
30	Chi.	L	1-2		3	9	Baldwin	Telgheder	Hernandez	54-53	3rd	6 1/2
31	Chi.	W	5-4		8	8	Witasick	Karchner	Taylor	55-53	3rd	6 1/2
1	Chi.	L	3-8		9	8	Tapani	Wasdin	Hernandez	55-54	3rd	6 1/2
2	Mil.	L	3-4	(10)	9	10	Miranda	Taylor	Fetters	55-55	3rd	6 1/2
3	Mil.	L	0-7		4	7	Bones	Johns		55-56	3rd	6 1/2
4	Mil.	W	4-2		8	8	Telgheder	Vanegmond	Taylor	56-56	3rd	6 1/2
5	Mil.	L	3-13		6	12	Eldred	Adams		56-57	3rd	6 1/2
6	At K.C.	L	2-9		13	12	Belcher	Wasdin		56-58	3rd	7 1/2
7	At K.C.	L	0-7		2	8	Appier	Prieto		56-59	3rd	7 1/2
8	At K.C.	W	2-1		4	5	Wengert	Linton	Taylor	57-59	3rd	6 1/2
9	Cle.	L	4-10		9	15	McDowell	Telgheder		57-60	3rd	7 1/2
10	Cle.	W	5-1		7	8	Adams	Nagy		58-60	3rd	7 1/2
11	Cle.	W	9-3		13	7	Wasdin	Lopez		59-60	3rd	7 1/2
12	Min.	W	11-1		13	5	Prieto	Robertson		60-60	3rd	7 1/2
13	Min.	L	2-6		6	11	Aguilera	Wengert		60-61	3rd	8 1/2
14	Min.	L	7-13		7	14	Rodriguez	Telgheder		60-62	3rd	8 1/2
15	Bal.	L	5-18		12	19	Mussina	Adams		60-63	3rd	10
16†	Bal.	L	3-14		7	19	Erickson	Wasdin		60-64		
16‡	Bal.	L	4-5	(10)	9	12	R. Myers	Mohler		60-65	3rd	11 1/2
17	Bal.	W	3-1		3	5	Prieto	Coppinger	Acre	61-65	3rd	10 1/2
18	Bal.	W	9-6		15	10	Wengert	Wells		62-65	3rd	10 1/2
20	At Bos.	L	3-4		7	10	Garces	Mohler	Slocumb	62-66	3rd	11
21	At Bos.	L	4-6		9	11	Brandenburg	Johns	Slocumb	62-67	3rd	13
22	At Bos.	L	1-2		8	8	Clemens	Acre		62-68	3rd	13
23	At N.Y.	L	3-5		11	7	Gooden	Wengert	M. Rivera	62-69	3rd	13
24	At N.Y.	L	4-5		13	8	Whitehurst	Telgheder	Pavlas	62-70	3rd	13
25	At N.Y.	W	6-4		10	10	Mohler	Nelson	Acre	63-70	3rd	13
26	At Bal.	L	11-12	(10)	13	13	R. Myers	Acre		63-71	3rd	13 1/2
27	At Bal.	L	1-3		6	6	Wells	Prieto	R. Myers	63-72	3rd	13 1/2
28	At Bal.	W	3-0		11	9	Wengert	Mussina		64-72	3rd	12 1/2
30	Bos.	W	7-0		9	7	Telgheder	Maddux		65-72	3rd	12 1/2
31	Bos.	W	8-0		8	5	Adams	Wakefield		66-72	3rd	12 1/2
1	Bos.	L	3-8		6	12	Sele	Wasdin		66-73	3rd	12 1/2
2	N.Y.	L	0-5		1	10	Cone	Prieto		66-74	3rd	12 1/2
3	N.Y.	W	10-9		13	12	Acre	Boehringer	Johns	67-74	3rd	12 1/2
4	N.Y.	L	3-10		8	16	Pettitte	Telgheder		67-75	3rd	12 1/2
6	K.C.	W	7-1		11	9	Adams	Haney		68-75	3rd	12 1/2
7	K.C.	W	13-6		19	10	Prieto	Belcher		69-75	3rd	12 1/2
8	K.C.	W	8-7	(10)	13	13	Corsi	Pichardo		70-75	3rd	12 1/2
10	At Min.	W	7-0		11	3	Telgheder	Robertson		71-75	3rd	13
11	At Min.	L	2-7		5	11	Radke	Adams		71-76	3rd	13

Date	Opp.	Res.	Score	(inn.*)	Hits	Opp. hits	Winning pitcher	Losing pitcher	Save	Record	Pos.	GB
9-12	At Min.	L	3-4	(12)	5	10	Stevens	Mohler		71-77	3rd	13
9-14†	At Cle.	L	2-9		8	15	Nagy	Wengert		71-78		
9-14‡	At Cle.	L	8-9		12	10	Plunk	Small	Mesa	71-79	3rd	13
9-15	At Cle.	W	10-9	(10)	14	15	Reyes	Mesa		72-79	3rd	13
9-17	At Cal.	W	5-1		5	8	Prieto	Springer		73-79	3rd	11
9-18	At Cal.	L	1-3		6	8	Finley	Adams	Percival	73-80	3rd	11
9-20	At Sea.	L	2-12		4	14	Carmona	Wengert	Meacham	73-81	3rd	11
9-21	At Sea.	L	2-9		8	12	Moyer	Telgheder		73-82	3rd	12
9-22	At Sea.	W	13-11		13	11	Mohler	Mulholland	Taylor	74-82	3rd	12
9-23	Tex.	W	5-3		11	12	Wasdin	Witt	Taylor	75-82	3rd	11
9-24	Tex.	L	3-7		4	11	Cook	Small		75-83	3rd	12
9-26	Sea.	W	7-5		9	12	Taylor	Charlton		76-83	3rd	12
9-27	Sea.	W	8-1		12	7	Telgheder	Mulholland		77-83	3rd	11
9-28	Sea.	L	3-5	(10)	8	8	Carmona	Acre	Charlton	77-84	3rd	12
9-29	Sea.	W	3-1		5	6	Small	Torres	Taylor	78-84	3rd	12

Monthly records: April (13-12), May (11-16), June (14-15), July (17-10), August (11-19), September (12-12).
*Innings, if other than nine. †First game of doubleheader. ‡Second game of doubleheader. §At Las Vegas.

HIGHLIGHTS

High point: After the A's concluded a three-game sweep in Chicago on July 24, they were 53-49 (a season-high five games over .500) and just 4½ games behind first-place Texas. To that point, the A's had posted a 15-6 record in July—and, for a few days, anyway, it felt as if Oakland was in a playoff race.

Low point: The night after the sweep in Chicago, the A's lost in Toronto when Joe Carter slammed a game-winning, two-run home run with two outs in the ninth. The A's never recovered, losing 25 of 38 games and dropping out of the A.L. West chase.

Turning point: After losing second baseman Brent Gates because of a leg fracture on June 15, the A's found themselves a season-worst nine games below .500 (29-38). Oakland then went on a binge, winning 24 of its next 35 games before Joe Carter jolted the A's at SkyDome.

Most valuable player: First baseman Mark McGwire. As McGwire goes, so go the A's. The big bopper returned to relatively good health, missing only 32 games because of injury, and belted a majors-leading 52 home runs. He also batted .312, 60 points higher than his career average entering the season. He anchored the A's potent lineup, which was thin when he was sidelined.

Most valuable pitcher: Billy Taylor. He waited 14 years before making his big-league debut in 1994. In '96, Taylor showed what he had learned in the minors by going 17-for-19 in save opportunities and ranking among the best closers in the A.L.

Most improved player: Third baseman Scott Brosius. He finally emerged from the long and intimidating shadow cast by former manager Tony La Russa. Brosius finished with 22 home runs and 71 RBIs despite missing seven weeks because of an arm fracture.

Most pleasant surprise: Rookie starter Willie Adams. Adams came up for good in July and apparently earned a spot in Oakland's 1997 rotation.

Biggest disappointment: Jason Giambi. He was forced to move from first base to left field once Mark McGwire returned

from the D.L. Giambi showed flashes of brilliance in the first half (.323 average, 16 homers and 60 RBIs) before plummeting in the second half (.245, four homers, 19 RBIs).

Key injuries: Right fielder/DH Pedro Munoz was supposed to lend even more offense to a club that smacked 243 home runs, the third-best total in big-league history. Munoz went down with a knee injury on June 2 and never returned. Brent Gates broke his left leg 13 days later. On May 18, Ariel Prieto was lost for two months because of a strained tendon in his right elbow. And Scott Brosius, who was having an All-Star-type first six weeks, was lost on May 4 when a Mark Gubicza fastball clipped him on the right elbow.

Notable: The A's won more games, 78, than any Oakland club since 1992, which was the last time the A's were in the postseason.

—PEDRO GOMEZ

RECORDS

1996 regular-season record: 78-84 (3rd in A.L. West); 40-41 at home; 38-43 on road; 24-38 vs. East; 32-29 vs. Central; 22-17 vs. West; 19-25 vs. lefthanded starters; 59-59 vs. righthanded starters; 69-74 on grass; 9-10 on turf; 39-32 in daytime; 39-52 at night; 19-23 in one-run games; 9-11 in extra-inning games; 0-2-1 in doubleheaders.

Team record past five years: 360-384 (.484, ranks 9th in league in that span).

TEAM LEADERS

Batting average: Mark McGwire (.312).
At-bats: Geronimo Berroa (586).
Runs: Mark McGwire (104).
Hits: Geronimo Berroa (170).
Total bases: Geronimo Berroa (312).
Doubles: Jason Giambi (40).
Triples: Mike Bordick, Ernie Young (4).
Home runs: Mark McGwire (52).
Runs batted in: Mark McGwire (113).
Stolen bases: Allen Battle (10).
Slugging percentage: Mark McGwire (.730).
On-base percentage: Mark McGwire (.467).
Wins: John Wasdin (8).

Earned-run average: None.
Complete games: Ariel Prieto (2).
Shutouts: Willie Adams, Dave Telgheder, Don Wengert (1).
Saves: Billy Taylor (17).
Innings pitched: Don Wengert (161.1).
Strikeouts: Carlos Reyes (78).

GAMES BY POSITION

Catcher: Terry Steinbach 137, George Williams 43, Izzy Molina 12.
First base: Mark McGwire 109, Jason Giambi 45, Torey Lovullo 42, Scott Brosius 10, Webster Garrison 1, Brian Lesher 1, Matt Stairs 1, Terry Steinbach 1.
Second base: Rafael Bournigal 64, Brent Gates 63, Tony Batista 52, Webster Garrison 3, Torey Lovullo 2.
Third base: Scott Brosius 109, Jason Giambi 39, Tony Batista 18, Torey Lovullo 11, Scott Spiezio 5.
Shortstop: Mike Bordick 155, Rafael Bournigal 23, Tony Batista 4, Torey Lovullo 1.
Outfield: Ernie Young 140, Jose Herrera 101, Phil Plantier 68, Geronimo Berroa 6, Damon Mashore 48, Allen Battle 47, Jason Giambi 45, Matt Stairs 44, Brian Lesher 25, Kerwin Moore 18, Pedro Munoz 14, Scott Brosius 4, Torey Lovullo 1.
Designated hitter: Geronimo Berroa 91, Mark McGwire 18, Pedro Munoz 18, Jason Giambi 12, George Williams 11, Matt Stairs 5, Tony Batista 4, Torey Lovullo 4, Scott Spiezio 4, Terry Steinbach 4, Jose Herrera 1, Izzy Molina 1, Kerwin Moore 1, Phil Plantier 1, Steve Wojciechowski 1.

TOP DRAFT CHOICES

1. **Eric Chavez**, 3B, Mount Carmel H.S., San Diego.
2. **Josue Espada**, SS, U. of Mobile (Ala.).
3. **A.J. Hinch**, C, Stanford University.
4. **Tom Graham**, RHP, Beyer H.S., Modesto, Calif.
5. **Julian Leyva**, RHP, Arlington H.S., Riverside, Calif.
6. **Nick Sosa**, 1B, Lake Mary (Fla.) H.S.
7. **Mike Paradis**, RHP, Auburn Hills (Mass.) H.S.
8. **Brad Blumenstock**, RHP, Southern Illinois University.
9. **Cody McKay**, C-3B, Arizona State University.
10. **Eric Lee**, OF, Clear Lake H.S., Houston.

SEATTLE MARINERS
AMERICAN LEAGUE WEST DIVISION

997 MARINERS SCHEDULE

☐ Home games shaded.
— All-Star Game at Jacobs Field (Cleveland)
— Day game (any game starting before 5 p.m.)

APRIL
UN	MON	TUE	WED	THU	FRI	SAT
		1 NYY	2 NYY	3	4 BOS	5 BOS
6 7 NYY	8 CLE	9 CLE	10 CLE		11 D BOS	12 BOS
D 14 CLE	15 CLE	16 DET	17 D DET	18 MIN	19 MIN	
D 21 KE	22 KC	23 KC	24	25 TOR	26 D TOR	
D 28 NYY	29 NYY	30 NYY				

MAY
UN	MON	TUE	WED	THU	FRI	SAT
				1	2 MIL	3 MIL
5 5	6 CWS	7 CWS	8 BAL	9 BAL	10 D BAL	
D 12 MIL	13 D MIL	14 CWS	15 CWS	16 BAL	17 BAL	
D 19 ANA	20 ANA	21 ANA	22	23 KC	24 KC	
D 26 MIN	27 MIN	28 TEX	29 TEX	30 DET	31 DET	

JUNE
UN	MON	TUE	WED	THU	FRI	SAT
D 2 TOR	3 TOR	D 4	5 DET	6 DET	7 D DET	
D 9	10 TOR	11 TOR	D 12 COL	13 COL	14 LA	
D 16	17 SF	18 D SF	19 TEX	20 TEX	21 TEX	
23 OAK	24 OAK	25 OAK	26 ANA	27 ANA	28 ANA	
D 30 SF						

JULY
UN	MON	TUE	WED	THU	FRI	SAT
		1 SD	D 2 SD	3 SD	4 ANA	5 ANA
7	8 ° 9	9	10 TEX	11 TEX	12 D TEX	
D 14 OAK	15 D OAK	16 MIN	17 MIN	18 KC	19 KC	
21	22 CLE	23 CLE	24 CLE	25 NYY	26 D NYY	
D 28	29 BOS	30 D BOS	31 MIL			

AUGUST
UN	MON	TUE	WED	THU	FRI	SAT
					1 MIL	2 MIL
D 4	5 BAL	6 BAL	CWS	8 CWS	9 D CWS	
11 MIL	12 D MIL	13	14 BAL	15 BAL	16 CWS	
D 18 CWS	19 CLE	20 CLE	21 CLE	22 NYY	23 D NYY	
D 25 BOS	26 BOS	27 D BOS	28 COL	29 COL	30 D LA	
D						

SEPTEMBER
UN	MON	TUE	WED	THU	FRI	SAT
	1 SD	2	3 SD	4 MIN	5 MIN	6 MIN
D 8	9 KC	10 DET	11 DET	12 TOR	13 TOR	
D 15 TOR	16	17 TEX	18 TEX	19 OAK	20 OAK	
D 22 OAK	23 ANA	24 ANA	25	26 OAK	27 OAK	
28						

Seattle Mariners

1997 SEASON
CLUB DIRECTORY

Board of directors
John Ellis, chairman; Minoru Arakawe;
Chris Larson; Howard Lincoln; John
McCaw; Frank Shrontz; Craig Watjen

Chairman and chief executive officer
John Ellis

President and chief operating officer
Chuck Armstrong

Vice president, baseball operations
Woody Woodward

Vice president, communications
Randy Adamack

V.p., finance and administration
Kevin Mather

Vice president, business development
Paul Isaki

V.p., scouting and player development
Roger Jongewaard

V.p., ballpark planning and development
John Palmer

Controller
Denise Podosek

Sr. director of baseball administration
Lee Pelekoudas

Assistant to v.p., baseball operations
George Zuraw

Director, player development
Larry Beinfest

Coordinator of minor league instruction
Mike Guff

Director, team travel
Craig Detwiler

Director, community relations
Joe Chard

Director, sales
Beth Wojick

Director, merchandising
Todd Vecchio

Director, public relations
Dave Aust

Director, stadium operations
Tony Pereira

Assistant director, public relations
Tim Hevly

Exec. asst., ownership/business dev.
Janet O'Brien

Manager, payroll and benefits admin.
Shirley Shreve

Trainers
Rick Griffin, Tom Newberg

Video coordinator
Carl Hamilton

Home clubhouse manager
Henry Genzale

Visiting clubhouse manager
Scott Gilbert

Strength and conditioning coach
Allen Wirtale

Club physicians
Dr. Larry Pedegana
Dr. Mitchel Storey

Club dentist
Dr. Richard Leshgold

Public address announcer
Tom Hutyler

Major lg. and special assignment scouts
Bill Kearns
Ken Compton

Nat. supervisor and assignment scout
Benny Looper

Scouting supervisors
Ken Madeja, Frank Mattox, Steve Pope,
Carroll Sembera

Area scouts
Dave Alexander, Maximo Alvarez,
Fernando Arguelles, Brian Ballentine,
Jeff Brissom, Mark Brown, Darrin
Chamberlain, Rodney Davis, Ramon
de los Santos, Curtis Dishman,
Orlando Gomez, Ron Hafner ,Larry
Harper, Guadalupe Jabalara, Steve
Jungewaard, Stan Lewis, Wilmer
Mardera, John McMichen, Tom
McNamara, Mauro Mazzotti, Billy
Merkel, Julio Molina, Omer Munoz,
Myron Pines, Don Poplin, Phil Pote,
Alex Smith, Chris Smith, Jim
Stewart, Roberto Valdez, Ray Vince,
Curtis Wallace, Ken Wandzel, Craig
Weissmann, Darren Wittcke, Selwyn
Young

1997 SEASON Seattle Mariners

MINOR LEAGUE AFFILIATES

Class	Team	League	Manager
AAA	Tacoma	Pacific Coast League	Dave Myers
AA	Memphis	Southern	Dave Brundage
A	Lancaster	California	Rick Burleson
A	Wisconsin	Midwest	Gary Varsho
A	Everett	Northwest	Orlando Gomez
Rookie	Peoria Mariners	Arizona	Darrin Garner

BROADCAST INFORMATION
Radio: KIRO-AM (710).
TV: KIRO-TV (Channel 7).
Cable TV: Fox Sports Northwest.

SPRING TRAINING
Ballpark: Peoria Stadium (Peoria,
Ariz.).
Ticket information: 602-784-4444.

SPRING TRAINING ROSTER

Manager—Lou Piniella (14).
Coaches—Nardi Contreras, Lee Elia (4), John McLaren (7), Sam Mejias (49), Steve Smith (2), Matt Sinatro (15).

No.	PITCHERS	B/T	Ht./Wt.	Born	1996 clubs
13	Ayala, Bobby	R/R	6-3/200	7-8-69	Seattle, Port City, Tacoma
22	Carmona, Rafael	L/R	6-2/185	10-2-72	Tacoma, Seattle
37	Charlton, Norm	B/L	6-3/205	1-6-63	Seattle
	Crow, Dean	L/R	6-4/215	8-21-72	Port City
47	Davis, Tim	L/L	5-11/165	7-14-70	Tacoma, Seattle, Everett
	Fassero, Jeff	L/L	6-1/195	1-5-63	Montreal
	Harikkala, Tim	R/R	6-2/185	7-15-71	Tacoma, Seattle
	Hurtado, Edwin	R/R	6-3/215	2-1-70	Seattle, Tacoma
51	Johnson, Randy	R/L	6-10/225	9-10-63	Seattle, Everett
	Lowe, Derek	R/R	6-6/170	6-1-73	Port City, Tacoma
	Manzanillo, Josias	R/R	6-0/190	10-16-67	DID NOT PLAY
	Marte, Damasco	L/L	6-0/170	2-14-75	Wisconsin Rapids
40	McCarthy, Greg	L/L	6-2/215	10-30-68	Tacoma, Seattle
	Menhart, Paul	R/R	6-2/190	3-25-69	Seattle, Tacoma
	Montane, Ivan	R/R	6-2/195	6-3-73	Lancaster, Port City
	Moyer, Jamie	L/L	6-0/170	11-18-62	Boston, Seattle
	Pacheco, Alex	R/R	6-3/200	7-19-73	Ottawa, Montreal, Harrisburg
	Sanders, Scott	R/R	6-4/220	3-25-69	San Diego
	Suzuki, Makoto	R/R	6-3/195	5-31-75	Tacoma, Port City, Seattle
38	Torres, Salomon	R/R	5-11/165	3-11-72	Tacoma, Seattle
46	Wells, Bob	R/R	6-0/180	11-1-66	Seattle
33	Wolcott, Bob	R/R	6-0/195	9-8-73	Seattle, Lancaster, Tacoma

No.	CATCHERS	B/T	Ht./Wt.	Born	1996 clubs
	Ibanez, Raul	L/R	6-2/200	6-2-72	Tacoma, Port City, Seattle
17	Marzano, John	R/R	5-11/195	2-14-63	Seattle
	Mayne, Brent	L/R	6-1/190		New York N.L.
6	Wilson, Dan	R/R	6-3/190	3-25-69	Seattle

No.	INFIELDERS	B/T	Ht./Wt.	Born	1996 clubs
28	Cora, Joey	B/R	5-8/155	5-14-65	Seattle
18	Davis, Russ	R/R	6-0/195	9-13-69	Seattle
	Guevara, Giomar	B/R	5-8/150	10-23-72	Port City
11	Martinez, Edgar	R/R	5-11/190	1-2-63	Seattle
	Patterson, John	B/R	5-9/168	2-11-67	DID NOT PLAY
3	Rodriguez, Alex	R/R	6-3/190	7-27-75	Seattle, Tacoma
30	Sheets, Andy	R/R	6-2/180	11-19-70	Tacoma, Seattle
9	Silvestri, Dave	R/R	6-0/196	9-29-67	Montreal
44	Sorrento, Paul	L/R	6-2/220	11-17-65	Seattle

No.	OUTFIELDERS	B/T	Ht./Wt.	Born	1996 clubs
8	Amaral, Rich	R/R	6-0/175	4-1-62	Seattle
19	Buhner, Jay	R/R	6-3/210	8-13-64	Seattle
	Cruz, Jose	B/R	6-0/190	4-19-74	Lancaster, Port City, Tacoma
	Frazier, Lou	B/R	6-2/175	1-26-65	Texas, Oklahoma City
24	Griffey Jr., Ken	L/L	6-3/205	11-21-69	Seattle
	Sturdivant, Marcus	L/L	5-10/150	10-29-73	Lancaster, Port City
	Tinsley, Lee	B/R	5-10/198	3-4-69	Philadelphia, Clearwater, Boston

BALLPARK INFORMATION

Ballpark (capacity, surface)
The Kingdome (59,856, artificial)
Address
P.O. Box 4100
83 King St.
Seattle, WA 98104
Business phone
206-628-3555
Ticket information
206-628-3555
Ticket prices
$22 (box)
$20 (field)
$18 (club)
$12 (view box)
$11 (view)
$9 (view, children 14 and under)
$8 (outfield reserved, family)
$6 (family, children 14 and under)
$6 (of reserved, children 14 and under)
$5 (Southwest Airlines Cloud Crowd)
Field dimensions (from home plate)
To left field at foul line, 331 feet
To center field, 405 feet
To right field at foul line, 312 feet
First game played
April 6, 1977 (Angels 7, Mariners 0)

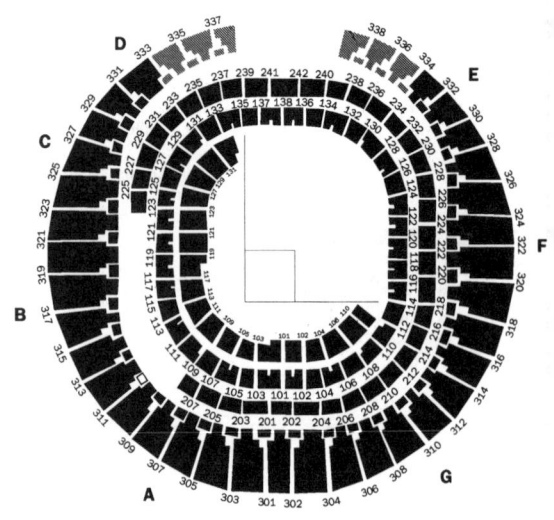

DAY BY DAY

Date	Opp.	Res.	Score	(inn.*)	Hits	Opp. hits	Winning pitcher	Losing pitcher	Save	Record	Pos.	GB
-31	Chi.	W	3-2	(12)	9	5	Hurtado	Simas		1-0	1st	+1/2
4-2	Chi.	W	3-2		4	5	Hitchcock	Alvarez	Charlton	2-0	1st	+1/2
4-3	Chi.	L	2-4		6	9	Magrane	Wolcott	Hernandez	2-1	2nd	1/2
4-5	Mil.	L	6-10		6	11	Karl	Hurtado		2-2	3rd	1 1/2
4-6	Mil.	W	8-5		8	6	Johnson	Sparks		3-2	2nd	1 1/2
4-7	Mil.	W	3-1		7	3	Hitchcock	Bones	Jackson	4-2	2nd	2
4-9	At Det.	W	9-10		12	4	Keagle	Menhart	B. Williams	4-3	2nd	3
4-10	At Det.	L	3-7		5	9	Olivares	Hurtado		4-4	3rd	3 1/2
4-11	At Det.	W	9-1		11	3	Johnson	Gohr		5-4	2nd	2 1/2
4-12	At Tor.	W	9-6		13	11	Hitchcock	Quantrill		6-4	2nd	1 1/2
4-13	At Tor.	W	14-3		12	4	Bosio	Ware		7-4	2nd	1 1/2
4-14	At Tor.	W	9-4		10	7	Wolcott	Hentgen		8-4	2nd	1/2
4-15	Cal.	W	11-10		11	17	Charlton	Eichhorn		9-4	1st	+1/2
4-16	Cal.	L	5-3		7	7	Johnson	J. Abbott		10-4	1st	+1/2
4-17	Det.	W	8-3		10	12	Jackson	Veres		11-4	1st	+1/2
4-18	Det.	W	11-3		12	12	Bosio	Sodowsky	Hurtado	12-4	1st	+1
4-19	Tor.	L	4-10		9	12	Hentgen	Wolcott	Bohanon	12-5	T1st	...
4-20	Tor.	L	1-3		5	9	Guzman	Menhart	Timlin	12-6	2nd	1
4-21	Tor.	W	9-5		13	9	Johnson	Hanson		13-6	2nd	1
4-22	Tor.	L	7-16		11	17	Castillo	Hurtado		13-7	2nd	1
4-24	At Chi.	L	1-2		3	7	Alvarez	Bosio	Hernandez	13-8	2nd	1/2
4-25	At Chi.	L	3-4		7	10	Tapani	Wolcott	Hernandez	13-9	2nd	1/2
4-26	At Mil.	W	6-5		11	6	Carmona	Potts	Charlton	14-9	2nd	1/2
4-27	At Mil.	W	6-5		11	12	Wells	Bones	Charlton	15-9	2nd	1/2
4-28	At Mil.	L	9-16		8	16	Potts	T. Davis		15-10	2nd	1 1/2
4-30	At Tex.	W	8-0		19	4	Bosio	Gross		16-10	T1st	...
5-1	At Tex.	L	4-5		8	10	Russell	Jackson	Henneman	16-11	2nd	1
5-2	Cle.	L	4-6		7	11	Hershiser	Wolcott	Mesa	16-12	2nd	1
5-3	Cle.	L	2-5		7	10	Nagy	Hitchcock	Mesa	16-13	3rd	2
5-4	Cle.	W	5-1		8	8	Menhart	Lopez		17-13	3rd	2
5-5	Cle.	L	0-2		6	9	Martinez	Bosio	Mesa	17-14	3rd	3
5-6	Min.	W	5-4		7	8	Wells	Radke	Charlton	18-14	3rd	2 1/2
5-7	Min.	L	0-2		6	8	Parra	Wolcott	Stevens	18-15	3rd	3 1/2
5-8	Min.	L	5-7	(10)	9	13	Guardado	Wells	Stevens	18-16	3rd	4 1/2
5-10	K.C.	L	10-14		11	14	Valera	T. Davis		18-17	3rd	5
5-11	K.C.	W	11-1		17	6	Wolcott	Belcher	Carmona	19-17	T2nd	5
5-12	K.C.	W	8-5		12	8	Johnson	Linton	Charlton	20-17	2nd	4
5-14	At N.Y.	L	0-2		0	7	Gooden	Hitchcock		20-18	2nd	5 1/2
5-15	At N.Y.	W	10-5		19	8	Hurtado	Key		21-18	2nd	4 1/2
5-17	At Bal.	L	13-14		21	21	Mills	Charlton		21-19	2nd	4 1/2
5-18	At Bal.	W	7-3		11	8	Milacki	Mercker		22-19	2nd	4 1/2
5-19	At Bal.	L	7-8		15	10	Mussina	Hurtado	R. Myers	22-20	2nd	4 1/2
5-21	At Bos.	W	13-7		19	13	Wells	Eshelman		23-20	2nd	3 1/2
5-22	At Bos.	W	6-1		10	6	Wolcott	Wakefield		24-20	2nd	3 1/2
5-23	At Bos.	L	4-11		9	14	Clemens	Milacki		24-21	2nd	3 1/2
5-24	N.Y.	W	10-4		14	9	Hitchcock	Kamieniecki		25-21	2nd	2 1/2
5-25	N.Y.	L	4-5		9	8	Mendoza	Hurtado	Wetteland	25-22	2nd	3 1/2
5-26	N.Y.	W	4-3		8	7	Menhart	Gooden	Charlton	26-22	2nd	3 1/2
5-28	Bal.	L	8-12		13	11	Rhodes	Guetterman	Haynes	26-23	2nd	5
5-29	Bal.	W	9-8		15	10	Charlton	R. Myers		27-23	2nd	5
5-30	Bos.	L	1-10		2	11	Gordon	Torres		27-24	2nd	5 1/2
5-31	Bos.	W	9-6		8	12	Wells	Garces		28-24	2nd	5 1/2
6-1	Bos.	L	5-6		8	9	Wakefield	Milacki	Slocumb	28-25	2nd	5 1/2
6-2	Bos.	W	3-1		11	6	Wolcott	Clemens	Jackson	29-25	2nd	4 1/2
6-4	At Cle.	W	10-7		12	12	Carmona	Mesa	Charlton	30-25	2nd	4
6-5	At Cle.	L	5-13		11	13	Plunk	Milacki		30-26	2nd	4
6-6	At Cle.	W	5-2		12	6	Wells	Martinez	Charlton	31-26	2nd	3 1/2
6-7	At K.C.	L	5-9		8	13	Valera	Wolcott		31-27	2nd	4 1/2
6-8	At K.C.	L	8-12		17	15	Appier	Milacki	Montgomery	31-28	2nd	5 1/2
6-9	At K.C.	W	3-2		11	11	Hitchcock	Gubicza	Charlton	32-28	2nd	5 1/2
6-10	At Min.	L	6-13		9	16	Aldred	Wagner	Trombley	32-29	2nd	6 1/2
6-11	At Min.	W	18-8		24	11	Wells	Aguilera	Hurtado	33-29	2nd	5 1/2
6-12	At Min.	W	5-3		11	10	Wolcott	Radke	Charlton	34-29	2nd	5 1/2
6-14	Chi.	L	1-4		5	7	Alvarez	Hitchcock	Hernandez	34-30	2nd	5
6-15	Chi.	W	8-6	(12)	16	12	Carmona	McCaskill		35-30	2nd	5
6-16	Chi.	W	7-6		12	12	Wells	Magrane	Jackson	36-30	2nd	4
6-18	Tor.	L	3-11		4	14	Guzman	Wolcott		36-31	2nd	5
6-19	Tor.	L	2-9		7	10	Hanson	Harikkala		36-32	T2nd	6
6-20	At Chi.	W	8-5		15	12	Hitchcock	Tapani	Charlton	37-32	T2nd	5
6-21	At Chi.	W	12-2		11	7	Wagner	Magrane		38-32	2nd	5
6-22	At Chi.	W	4-2		11	6	Wells	Fernandez	Charlton	39-32	2nd	5

1997 SEASON *Seattle Mariners*

Date	Opp.	Res.	Score	(inn.*)	Hits	Opp. hits	Winning pitcher	Losing pitcher	Save	Record	Pos.	GB
6-23	At Chi.	L	6-7	(10)	9	12	McCaskill	Guetterman		39-33	2nd	5
6-25	At Tor.	L	7-8		10	6	Crabtree	Charlton		39-34	2nd	5¹/₂
6-26	At Tor.	L	5-6		4	8	Ware	Ayala	Crabtree	39-35	2nd	6¹/₂
6-27	At Tor.	W	9-1		13	10	Wells	Quantrill		40-35	2nd	6
6-28	Tex.	W	19-8		22	16	Carmona	Pavlik		41-35	2nd	5
6-29	Tex.	L	5-9		6	13	Oliver	Meacham		41-36	2nd	6
6-30	Tex.	W	4-3		12	7	Hitchcock	Witt	Charlton	42-36	2nd	5
7-1	Oak.	L	4-6		11	9	Wengert	Wagner	Taylor	42-37	2nd	6
7-2	Oak.	L	6-11		13	16	Mohler	Charlton		42-38	2nd	6
7-3	Oak.	W	4-3		9	6	Ayala	Reyes		43-38	2nd	6
7-4	At Tex.	W	9-5		13	9	Carmona	Henneman		44-38	2nd	5
7-5	At Tex.	W	6-3		15	6	Hitchcock	Witt		45-38	2nd	4
7-6	At Tex.	W	9-5		8	9	Wagner	Gross		46-38	2nd	3
7-7	At Tex.	L	3-8		8	9	Hill	Wells		46-39	2nd	4
7-11	Cal.	W	5-4	(12)	9	16	Carmona	Monteleone		47-39	2nd	3
7-12	Cal.	W	7-6	(10)	9	11	Ayala	McElroy		48-39	2nd	3
7-13	Cal.	L	4-6		9	14	Boskie	Ayala	Percival	48-40	2nd	4
7-14	Cal.	W	8-0		13	4	Wells	Grimsley		49-40	2nd	3
7-15	At Oak.	W	5-1		8	5	Wolcott	Telgheder		50-40	2nd	2
7-16	At Oak.	L	5-12		11	16	Chouinard	Hitchcock		50-41	2nd	3
7-17	At Oak.	L	6-7		9	9	Corsi	Minor	Taylor	50-42	2nd	4
7-18	At Cal.	W	15-3		21	11	Meacham	Boskie		51-42	2nd	3
7-19	At Cal.	L	4-9		8	18	Grimsley	Wells		51-43	2nd	3
7-20	At Cal.	L	4-5		6	12	Schmidt	Charlton	Percival	51-44	2nd	4
7-21	At Cal.	W	6-2		12	11	Hitchcock	J. Abbott		52-44	2nd	3
7-22	Mil.	W	8-3		13	5	Wagner	Mercedes		53-44	2nd	3
7-23	Mil.	L	3-7		9	12	Karl	Carmona		53-45	2nd	3
7-24	Mil.	W	8-7		15	11	Ayala	Fetters		54-45	2nd	2
7-25	Det.	L	4-7	(10)	9	11	Lima	Ayala		54-46	2nd	3
7-26	Det.	W	6-4		8	10	Hitchcock	Sager	Jackson	55-46	2nd	2
7-27	Det.	W	13-7		17	10	T. Davis	B. Williams		56-46	2nd	2
7-28	Det.	L	6-14		10	15	Olivares	Bosio		56-47	2nd	2
7-30†	At Mil.	W	6-5		12	11	Wells	Eldred	Ayala	57-47		
7-30‡	At Mil.	L	3-4		7	8	Vanegmond	Wolcott	Fetters	57-48	2nd	2¹/₂
7-31	At Mil.	W	9-3		11	10	Hitchcock	D'Amico		58-48	2nd	2¹/₂
8-1	At Mil.	W	9-2		16	6	Moyer	McDonald		59-48	2nd	1¹/₂
8-2	At Det.	L	2-8		3	10	Olivares	Wagner		59-49	2nd	1¹/₂
8-3	At Det.	L	3-6		5	10	Olson	Charlton		59-50	2nd	1¹/₂
8-4	At Det.	W	9-3		12	9	Wolcott	Nitkowski		60-50	2nd	1¹/₂
8-6	Cle.	L	3-4		7	12	Lopez	Wells	Mesa	60-51	2nd	2
8-7	Cle.	L	4-5		10	7	Tavarez	Charlton	Mesa	60-52	2nd	2
8-8	Cle.	L	1-2		3	5	Ogea	Mulholland	Mesa	60-53	2nd	2
8-9	Min.	L	5-6		9	10	Parra	Wolcott	Rodriguez	60-54	2nd	3
8-10	Min.	L	4-10		9	18	Klingenbeck	Hitchcock		60-55	2nd	4
8-11	Min.	L	3-6		9	7	Radke	Wells	Rodriguez	60-56	2nd	5
8-12	K.C.	L	4-10		12	15	Appier	Moyer	Huisman	60-57	2nd	6
8-13	K.C.	W	9-5		13	6	Mulholland	Linton	Johnson	61-57	2nd	6
8-14	K.C.	L	1-3		10	10	Rosado	Wolcott	Montgomery	61-58	2nd	7
8-16	At N.Y.	W	6-5		11	10	Hitchcock	Polley	Jackson	62-58	2nd	7
8-17	At N.Y.	W	10-3		12	8	Moyer	Rogers		63-58	2nd	6
8-18	At N.Y.	W	13-12	(12)	19	19	Ayala	Mecir	Jackson	64-58	2nd	6
8-19	At N.Y.	L	4-10		3	16	Pettitte	Carmona		64-59	2nd	7
8-20	At Bal.	L	1-4		3	9	Mussina	Wagner	R. Myers	64-60	2nd	7
8-21	At Bal.	L	5-10		8	12	Erickson	Hitchcock		64-61	2nd	8
8-22	At Bal.	W	10-3		15	6	Moyer	Coppinger		65-61	2nd	7
8-23	At Bos.	W	6-4		7	8	Bosio	Brandenburg	Ayala	66-61	2nd	7
8-24	At Bos.	L	5-9		11	9	Lacy	Wells		66-62	2nd	7
8-25	At Bos.	L	5-8		9	14	Maddux	Wagner	Slocumb	66-63	2nd	8
8-26	N.Y.	W	2-1		9	5	Ayala	Lloyd	Charlton	67-63	2nd	7¹/₂
8-27	N.Y.	W	7-4		6	7	Moyer	Lloyd		68-63	2nd	6¹/₂
8-28	N.Y.	W	10-2		10	9	Mulholland	Gooden		69-63	2nd	5¹/₂
8-29	Bal.	W	9-6		11	10	Charlton	R. Myers		70-63	2nd	5
8-30	Bal.	L	2-5		10	12	Coppinger	Hitchcock	Mills	70-64	2nd	6
8-31	Bal.	L	6-7		9	12	Erickson	Bosio	Benitez	70-65	2nd	7
9-1	Bal.	W	5-1		9	7	Mulholland	Wells		71-65	2nd	6
9-2	Bos.	L	8-9	(10)	10	7	Slocumb	Carmona		71-66	2nd	6
9-3	Bos.	W	11-9		11	13	Torres	Gordon	Charlton	72-66	2nd	6
9-4	Bos.	L	5-7		8	10	Mahomes	Hitchcock	Slocumb	72-67	2nd	6
9-8†	At Cle.	L	1-2		6	8	Nagy	Mulholland		72-68		
9-8‡	At Cle.	W	6-5		10	8	Charlton	Mesa		73-68	2nd	7¹/₂
9-10	At K.C.	L	2-4		6	7	Rosado	Torres	Bluma	73-69	2nd	9
9-11	At K.C.	L	2-4		7	8	Linton	Moyer	Bluma	73-70	2nd	9
9-12	At K.C.	W	8-5		15	8	Mulholland	Haney	Charlton	74-70	2nd	8
9-13	At Min.	W	13-7		12	14	Wells	Miller		75-70	2nd	7
9-14	At Min.	W	5-3	(10)	5	7	Ayala	Guardado	Charlton	76-70	2nd	6

ate	Opp.	Res.	Score	(inn.*)	Hits	Opp. hits	Winning pitcher	Losing pitcher	Save	Record	Pos.	GB
15	At Min.	W	7-0		10	2	Torres	Robertson		77-70	2nd	6
16	Tex.	W	6-0		13	4	Moyer	Burkett		78-70	2nd	5
17	Tex.	W	5-2		7	6	Mulholland	Hill	Ayala	79-70	2nd	4
18	Tex.	W	5-2		9	4	Hitchcock	Witt	Charlton	80-70	2nd	3
19	Tex.	W	7-6		12	9	T. Davis	Cook	Charlton	81-70	2nd	2
20	Oak.	W	12-2		14	4	Carmona	Wengert	Meacham	82-70	2nd	1
21	Oak.	W	9-2		12	8	Moyer	Telgheder		83-70	2nd	1
22	Oak.	L	11-13		11	13	Mohler	Mulholland	Taylor	83-71	2nd	2
23	At Cal.	L	3-4		5	9	Finley	Hitchcock	Percival	83-72	2nd	2
24	At Cal.	L	6-11		14	16	Springer	Wells		83-73	2nd	3
25	At Cal.	W	11-2		10	10	Torres	Boskie		84-73	2nd	2 1/2
26	At Oak.	L	5-7		12	9	Taylor	Charlton		84-74	2nd	3 1/2
27	At Oak.	L	1-8		7	12	Telgheder	Mulholland		84-75	2nd	3 1/2
28	At Oak.	L	5-3	(10)	8	8	Carmona	Acre	Charlton	85-75	2nd	3 1/2
29	At Oak.	L	1-3		6	5	Small	Torres	Taylor	85-76	2nd	4 1/2

Monthly records: March (1-0), April (15-10), May (12-14), June (14-12), July (16-12), August (12-17), September (15-11).
*Innings, if other than nine.†First game of doubleheader. ‡Second game of doubleheader.

HIGHLIGHTS

High point: The Mariners ran off a club-record 10 consecutive victories September 12-21 to cut their deficit to the Rangers in the A.L. West from nine games to one. It rekindled memories of 1995's September dash that resulted in Seattle's first division title.

Low point: On August 1, the Mariners were a season-high 11 games over .500 (59-48), in second place and only 1 1/2 games behind Texas. But they returned to the Kingdome and promptly lost three consecutive one-run games to the Indians, leading to a 1-8 homestand. By the time they hit the road again, the Mariners were six games behind.

Turning point: Going into the fourth inning in the series finale against the A's on September 22, the Mariners led, 3-0, and seemingly were en route to their 11th consecutive win. But Mark McGwire hit two home runs in one inning, including a grand slam, as Oakland built a 13-3 lead. A furious comeback wasn't enough and the Mariners lost, 13-11. They went 2-5 the rest of the way.

Most valuable player: Shortstop Alex Rodriguez. The youngster batted .358, hit 36 homers and had 123 RBIs. Center fielder Ken Griffey Jr. also deserves mention. Besides his usual Gold Glove-caliber defense, Griffey established personal highs in home runs (49) and RBIs (140) despite missing 20 games with a broken bone in his right wrist.

Most valuable pitcher: Spring-training invitee Bob Wells. The righthander was superb in long relief (4-1, 1.79 ERA in 16 appearances) before being promoted to the rotation because of injuries to Randy Johnson (back) and Chris Bosio (knee). He responded and finished with a 12-7 record.

Most improved player: Shortstop Alex Rodriguez. Everyone expected Rodriguez to be the everyday shortstop at age 20, but no one expected him to have the kind of season he did. He became Cal Ripken and Ernie Banks all in one.

Most pleasant surprise: Catcher Dan Wilson. He has gotten better in each of his three seasons with the Mariners. He became the franchise's first All-Star catcher and improved his numbers to 18 homers (up from nine) and 83 RBIs (up from 51).

Biggest disappointment: Righthander Bob Wolcott. After the way he pitched late in '95, including an ALCS win over the Indians, Wolcott was expected to be a rotation mainstay. Instead, he was 7-10 with a 5.73 ERA.

Key injuries: Where to start? Reliever Tim Davis suffered a broken leg and missed 37 games. Third baseman Russ Davis suffered a broken leg and injured ankle on June 7 and never returned. Defending Cy Young Award winner Randy Johnson went 5-0, suffered from a bulging disk and didn't start a game after May 12. Designated hitter Edgar Martinez broke four ribs on July 20 and missed 21 games. Shortstop Alex Rodriguez missed 13 games because of a pulled hamstring.

Notable: The Mariners established club records by using 25 pitchers, including 15 who started games.

—JIM STREET

RECORDS

1996 regular-season record: 85-76 (2nd in A.L. West); 43-38 at home; 42-38 on road; 31-30 vs. East; 31-30 vs. Central; 23-16 vs. West; 24-17 vs. lefthanded starters; 61-59 vs. righthanded starters; 33-35 on grass; 52-41 on turf; 25-23 in daytime; 60-53 at night; 21-22 in one-run games; 7-4 in extra-inning games; 0-0-2 in doubleheaders.

Team record past five years: 359-383 (.484), ranks 10th in league in that span).

TEAM LEADERS

Batting average: Alex Rodriguez (.358).
At-bats: Alex Rodriguez (601).
Runs: Alex Rodriguez (141).
Hits: Alex Rodriguez (215).
Total bases: Alex Rodriguez (379).
Doubles: Alex Rodriguez (54).
Triples: Joey Cora (6).
Home runs: Ken Griffey Jr (49).
Runs batted in: Ken Griffey Jr (140).
Stolen bases: Rich Amaral (25).
Slugging percentage: Alex Rodriguez (.631).
On-base percentage: Edgar Martinez (.464).

Wins: Sterling Hitchcock (13).
Earned-run average: Sterling Hitchcock (5.35).
Complete games: Salomon Torres, Matt Wagner, Bob Wells, Bob Wolcott (1).
Shutouts: Salomon Torres, Bob Wells (1).
Saves: Norm Charlton (20).
Innings pitched: Sterling Hitchcock (196.2).
Strikeouts: Sterling Hitchcock (132).

GAMES BY POSITION

Catcher: Dan Wilson 135, John Marzano 39, Chris Widger 7.
First base: Paul Sorrento 138, Brian Hunter 41, Rich Amaral 10, Edgar Martinez 4, Doug Strange 3, Greg Pirkl 2, Dave Hollins 1.
Second base: Joey Cora 140, Luis Sojo 27, Andy Sheets 18, Rich Amaral 15, Doug Strange 3.
Third base: Russ Davis 51, Doug Strange 39, Luis Sojo 33, Dave Hollins 28, Jeff Manto 16, Edgar Martinez 2, Rich Amaral 1, Joey Cora 1.
Shortstop: Alex Rodriguez 146, Luis Sojo 19, Andy Sheets 7.
Outfield: Jay Buhner 142, Ken Griffey 137, Rich Amaral 91, Darren Bragg 63, Mark Whiten 39, Brian Hunter 29, Alex Diaz 28, Doug Strange 11, Manny Martinez 8, Jeff Manto 1.
Designated hitter: Edgar Martinez 134, Doug Strange 10, Jay Buhner 8, Ken Griffey 5, Rich Amaral 4, Greg Pirkl 3, Brian Hunter 2, Raul Ibanez 2, Ricky Jordan 2, Jeff Manto 2, Alex Diaz 1.

TOP DRAFT CHOICES

1. **Gil Meche**, RHP, Acadiana H.S., Lafayette, Ind.
2. **Jeff Farnsworth**, RHP, Okaloosa-Walton (Fla.) C.C.
3. **Tony DeJesus,** LHP, Havelock (N.C.) H.S.
4. **Denny Stark**, RHP, University of Toledo.
5. **Chris Mears**, RHP, Lord Byng H.S., Vancouver, B.C.
6. **Pat D. Williams,** C, Nacogdoches (Tex.) H.S.
7. **Danny Garey**, RHP, St. Joseph (Mich.) H.S.
8. **Willie Bloomquist**, SS, South Kitsap H.S., Port Orchard, Wash.
9. **Rob Luce**, RHP, U. of Nevada-Las Vegas.
10. **Matthew Noe**, LHP, Riverside (Calif.) C.C.

1997 SEASON *Seattle Mariners*

TEXAS RANGERS
AMERICAN LEAGUE WEST DIVISION

1997 RANGERS SCHEDULE

☐ Home games shaded.
* — All-Star Game at Jacobs Field (Cleveland)
D — Day game (any game starting before 5 p.m.)

APRIL
SUN	MON	TUE	WED	THU	FRI	SAT
		1 D MIL	2	3 MIL	4 D BAL	5 BAL
6 D BAL	7 D MIL	8	9 MIL	10 D MIL	11 D BAL	12 D BAL
13 D BAL	14 CWS	15 CWS	16 KC	17 KC	18 TOR	19 TOR
20 TOR	21 DET	22	23 DET	24 D DET	25 MIN	26 MIN
27 MIN	28	29 CWS	30 CWS			

MAY
SUN	MON	TUE	WED	THU	FRI	SAT
				1	2 BOS	3 BOS
4 D BOS	5 CLE	6 CLE	7 NYY	8 NYY	9 BOS	10 D BOS
11 D BOS	12 CLE	13 CLE	14 CLE	15 NYY	16 NYY	17 NYY
18 D NYY	19	20 OAK	21 OAK	22 D OAK	23 DET	24 DET
25 D DET	26 TOR	27 TOR	28 SEA	29 SEA	30 D KC	31 KC

JUNE
SUN	MON	TUE	WED	THU	FRI	SAT
1 D KC	2 MIN	3 MIN	4	5 KC	6 KC	7 D KC
8 D KC	9	10 MIN	11 MIN	12 SF	13 SF	14 SF
15 D SD	16	17 COL	18 D COL	19 SEA	20 SEA	21 SEA
22 SEA	23 ANA	24 ANA	25 D ANA	26 OAK	27 OAK	28 OAK
29 OAK	30 LA					

JULY
SUN	MON	TUE	WED	THU	FRI	SAT
		1 LA	2 COL	3 COL	4 OAK	5 OAK
6 D OAK	7	8 *	9	10 SEA	11 SEA	12 D SEA
13 D SEA	14 ANA	15 ANA	16 TOR	17 TOR	18 DET	19 DET
20 D DET	21 BAL	22 BAL	23 BAL	24 CWS	25 D CWS	26 CWS
27 CWS	28	29 BAL	30 D BAL	31		

AUGUST
SUN	MON	TUE	WED	THU	FRI	SAT
					1 CLE	2 CLE
3 CLE	4 BOS	5 BOS	6 NYY	7 NYY	8 CLE	9 D CLE
10 D CLE	11 D BOS	12 BOS	13 BOS	14	15 NYY	16 D NYY
17 D NYY	18 MIL	19 MIL	20 MIL	21	22 CWS	23 CWS
24 CWS	25 MIL	26 MIL	27 MIL	28 SF	29 SF	30 SD
31 D SD						

SEPTEMBER
SUN	MON	TUE	WED	THU	FRI	SAT
	1	2 LA	3 LA	4 TOR	5 TOR	6 D TOR
7 D TOR	8 DET	9 DET	10	11 MIN	12 MIN	13 MIN
14 D MIN	15 KC	16 KC	17 SEA	18 SEA	19 ANA	20 ANA
21 ANA	22	23 OAK	24 OAK	25 ANA	26 ANA	27 ANA
28 D ANA						

1997 SEASON
CLUB DIRECTORY

General partners
Edward W. (Rusty) Rose
J. Thomas Schieffer
President
J. Thomas Schieffer
Exec. v.p., general manager
R. Douglas Melvin
Exec. v.p., bus. operations/treasurer
John F. McMichael
Vice president, marketing
Charles Searphin
Vice president, public relations
John C. Blake
Vice president, community development
Norman B. Lyons
Vice president, legal affairs
William D. Miller
V.p. and chief information officer
Steve McNeill
Vice president, human resources
Kimberly A. Smith
General counsel
Gerald W. Haddock
Assistant v.p., controller
Chip Sawicki
Assistant v.p., facilities
Billy Ray Johnson
Assistant v.p., customer service
Tim Murphy
Director of grounds
Tim Burns
Assistant general manager
Dan O'Brien III
Dir., professional and int'l scouting
Omar Minaya
Director of amateur scouting
Chuck McMichael
Director, player development
Reid Nichols
Traveling secretary
Dan Schimek
Dir. of major league scouting
Judy Johns

Dir. of player development admin.
Monty Clegg
Director of medical services
Dr. Mike Mycoskie
Visiting clubhouse manager
Joe Macko
Equipment and home clubhouse manag
Zack Minasian
Director, corporate sales
Mike Phillips
Director, client services
Dave Fendrick
Director, in-park entertainment
Chuck Morgan
Director, merchandising
Nancy Hill
Director, ticket operations
Cathy Beatty
Director, sales
Ross Scott
Director, player relations
Taunee Taylor
Dir., Spanish broadcasting and Latin American liasion
Luis R. Mayoral
Director, publications
Eric Kolb
Assistant director, public relations
Charley Green
Assistant, special projects
Bobby Bragan
Admin. asst., public relations
Michelle Baugh
National crosscheckers
Tim Hallgren
David Klipstein
Jeff Taylor
Scouts
Manuel Batista, Joe Branzell, Mike Cadahia, Mike Daughtry, Dave Direc, Kip Fagg, Jim Fairey, Mark Giegler, Joel Grampietro, Mike Grouse, Todd Guggiana, Doug Harris, Bob Heck, Larry Izzo, Jim Lentine, Pat Rigby, Randy Taylor, Greg Whitworth

MINOR LEAGUE AFFILIATES

Class	Team	League	Manager
AAA	Oklahoma City	American Association	Greg Biagini
AA	Tulsa	Texas	Bobby Jones
A	Charlotte	Florida State	Butch Wynegar
Rookie	Pulaski	Appalachian	To be announced
Rookie	Gulf Coast Rangers	Gulf Coast	James Byrd

BROADCAST INFORMATION

Radio: KRLD-AM (1080); KXEB-AM (910, Spanish language).
TV: KXAS-TV (Channel 5); KXTX-TV (Channel 39).
Cable TV: Fox Sports Southwest.

SPRING TRAINING

Ballpark (city): Charlotte County Stadium (Port Charlotte, Fla.).
Ticket information: 941-625-9500.

1997 SEASON *Texas Rangers*

SPRING TRAINING ROSTER

Manager—Johnny Oates (26).
Coaches—Dick Bosman (17), Bucky Dent (20), Larry Hardy (25), Rudy Jaramillo (8), Ed Napoleon (12), Jerry Narron (5).

#	PITCHERS	B/T	Ht./Wt.	Born	1996 clubs
8	Alberro, Jose	R/R	6-2/190	6-29-69	Oklahoma City, Texas
	Bailey, Cory	R/R	6-1/208	1-24-71	St. Louis, Louisville
3	Burkett, John	R/R	6-3/215	11-28-64	Florida, Texas
	Heredia, Wilson	R/R	6-0/175	3-30-72	DID NOT PLAY
1	Hernandez, Xavier	L/R	6-2/195	8-16-65	Cincinnati, Houston
4	Hill, Ken	R/R	6-2/205	12-14-65	Texas
	Moody, Eric	R/R	6-6/185	1-6-71	Tulsa
8	Oliver, Darren	R/L	6-2/200	10-6-70	Charlotte, Texas
6	Patterson, Danny	R/R	6-0/185	2-17-71	Oklahoma City, Texas
9	Pavlik, Roger	R/R	6-2/220	10-4-67	Texas
0	Santana, Julio	R/R	6-0/175	1-20-74	Oklahoma City
	Sturtze, Tanyon	R/R	6-5/205	10-12-70	Iowa, Chicago N.L.
2	Vosberg, Ed	L/L	6-1/190	9-28-61	Texas
5	Wetteland, John	R/R	6-2/215	8-21-66	New York A.L.
7	Whiteside, Matt	R/R	6-0/205	8-8-67	Texas, Oklahoma City
6	Witt, Bobby	R/R	6-2/205	5-11-64	Texas

#	CATCHERS	B/T	Ht./Wt.	Born	1996 clubs
6	Brown, Kevin	R/R	6-2/200	4-21-73	Tulsa, Texas
	Mercedes, Henry	R/R	6-1/210	7-23-69	Omaha, Kansas City
7	Rodriguez, Ivan	R/R	5-9/205	11-30-71	Texas

#	INFIELDERS	B/T	Ht./Wt.	Born	1996 clubs
	Bell, Mike	R/R	6-2/185	12-7-74	Tulsa
	Browne, Jerry	B/R	5-10/170	2-3-66	DID NOT PLAY
2	Clark, Will	L/L	6-1/200	3-13-64	Texas, Tulsa
	Diaz, Edwin	R/R	5-11/170	1-15-75	Tulsa
	Frias, Hanley	B/R	6-0/160	12-5-73	Tulsa
3	Gil, Benji	R/R	6-2/182	10-6-72	Charlotte, Oklahoma City, Texas
3	McLemore, Mark	B/R	5-11/207	10-4-64	Texas
6	Palmer, Dean	R/R	6-1/210	12-27-68	Texas
2	Ripken, Billy	R/R	6-1/190	12-16-64	Baltimore
1	Stevens, Lee	L/L	6-4/219	7-10-67	Oklahoma City, Texas
	Tatis, Fernando	L/R	6-1/175	1-1-75	Charlotte, Oklahoma City

#	OUTFIELDERS	B/T	Ht./Wt.	Born	1996 clubs
2	Buford, Damon	R/R	5-10/170	6-12-70	Texas
9	Gonzalez, Juan	R/R	6-3/220	10-16-69	Texas
9	Greer, Rusty	L/L	6-0/190	1-21-69	Texas
	Little, Mark	R/R	6-0/200	7-11-72	Tulsa
1	Newson, Warren	L/L	5-7/202	7-3-64	Texas
	Roberts, Lonell	B/R	6-0/180	6-7-71	Knoxville
	Sagmoen, Marc	L/L	5-11/185	4-16-71	Tulsa, Oklahoma City
5	Tettleton, Mickey	B/R	6-2/212	9-16-60	Texas
	Vessel, Andrew	R/R	6-3/210	3-11-75	Charlotte

BALLPARK INFORMATION

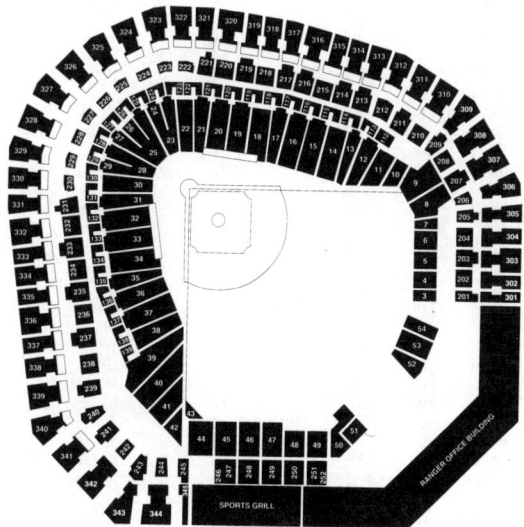

Ballpark (capacity, surface)
The Ballpark in Arlington (49,178, grass)

Address
1000 Ballpark Way
Arlington, TX 76011

Business phone
817-273-5222

Ticket information
817-273-5100

Ticket prices
$20 (lower box, club box)
$18 (corner box)
$16 (club box)
$12 (terrace club box, upper box)
$10 (upper reserved, left field reserved,
    lower home run porch)
$9 (upper box, upper reserved)
$8 (upper home run porch)
$6 (grandstand reserved and bleachers, adults)
$3 (grandstand reserved and bleachers,
    children 13 and under)
$4 (grandstand, adults)
$2 (grandstand, children 13 and under)

Field dimensions (from home plate)
To left field at foul line, 332 feet
To center field, 400 feet
To right field at foul line, 325 feet

First game played
April 11, 1994 (Brewers 4, Rangers 3)

DAY BY DAY

Date	Opp.	Res.	Score	(inn.*)	Hits	Opp. hits	Winning pitcher	Losing pitcher	Save	Record	Pos.	GB
4-1	Bos.	W	5-3		5	8	Hill	Clemens	Vosberg	1-0	T1st	...
4-3	Bos.	W	7-2		11	4	Pavlik	Gordon		2-0	1st	+
4-4	Bos.	W	13-2		16	6	Gross	Wakefield		3-0	1st	+1
4-6	N.Y.	W	4-2		9	7	Witt	Key	Henneman	4-0	1st	+1
4-7†	N.Y.	W	7-2		8	8	Hill	Gooden		5-0		
4-7‡	N.Y.	W	4-1		8	6	Pavlik	Howe	Vosberg	6-0	1st	+2
4-9	At Chi.	W	3-2		6	9	Gross	L. Thomas	Henneman	7-0	1st	+3
4-11	At Chi.	L	5-8	(11)	10	13	L. Thomas	Henneman		7-1	1st	+2
4-12	At N.Y.	L	3-4		5	6	Cone	Hill	Wetteland	7-2	1st	+1
4-13	At N.Y.	W	10-6		14	11	Pavlik	Gooden	Vosberg	8-2	1st	+1
4-14	At N.Y.	L	3-12		10	15	Pettitte	Gross		8-3	1st	+1
4-15	Oak.	L	3-8		6	12	Mohler	Heredia		8-4	2nd	*
4-16	Oak.	W	5-3		12	6	Witt	Johns	Henneman	9-4	2nd	*
4-17	Oak.	W	12-1		13	4	Hill	Reyes		10-4	2nd	*
4-19	Bal.	W	26-7		19	10	Cook	Mercker	Vosberg	11-4	T1st	...
4-20	Bal.	W	8-3		10	7	Gross	Haynes		12-4	1st	+1
4-21	Bal.	W	9-6		11	11	Oliver	Wells		13-4	1st	+1
4-22	Chi.	L	4-12		12	16	Fernandez	Witt	Karchner	13-5	1st	+1
4-23	Chi.	L	5-6		9	11	Baldwin	Hill	Hernandez	13-6	1st	+1
4-24	At Bos.	L	9-11		13	15	Stanton	Heredia	Slocumb	13-7	1st	+1
4-25	At Bos.	L	3-8		9	9	Wakefield	Gross		13-8	1st	+1
4-26	At Bal.	W	5-4		12	5	Brandenburg	Wells	Henneman	14-8	1st	+1
4-27	At Bal.	W	4-2		9	4	Witt	Erickson	Vosberg	15-8	1st	+1
4-28	At Bal.	W	5-4	(10)	10	8	Heredia	McDowell	Henneman	16-8	1st	+1
4-29	At Bal.	L	7-8		9	10	Haynes	Helling	R. Myers	16-9	1st	+1
4-30	Sea.	L	0-8		4	19	Bosio	Gross		16-10	T1st	...
5-1	Sea.	W	5-4		10	8	Russell	Jackson	Henneman	17-10	1st	+1
5-2	At Det.	L	2-5		4	6	Lira	Witt	B. Williams	17-11	1st	+1
5-3	At Det.	W	11-0		14	1	Hill	Keagle		18-11	1st	+1
5-4	At Det.	W	3-1		11	1	Pavlik	Gohr		19-11	1st	+1
5-5	At Det.	W	3-2		9	5	Gross	Lima	Henneman	20-11	1st	+1
5-7	Tor.	W	5-1		8	5	Oliver	Guzman		21-11	1st	+3
5-8	Tor.	W	4-2		8	9	Witt	Hanson	Henneman	22-11	1st	+4
5-9	Tor.	L	2-5		7	10	Quantrill	Hill	Timlin	22-12	1st	+4
5-10	Det.	W	6-2		8	9	Pavlik	Lima	Henneman	23-12	1st	+4
5-11	Det.	W	11-7		18	14	Gross	Aldred		24-12	1st	+5
5-12	Det.	L	3-5		5	7	Lira	Oliver	Myers	24-13	1st	+4
5-13	K.C.	W	7-6		15	10	Cook	Montgomery	Henneman	25-13	1st	+4
5-14	K.C.	W	10-0		15	4	Hill	Gubicza		26-13	1st	+5
5-15	K.C.	L	1-3		10	8	Haney	Pavlik	Montgomery	26-14	1st	+4
5-17	At Cle.	L	10-12		14	17	Embree	Heredia	Mesa	26-15	1st	+4
5-18	At Cle.	W	6-3		10	7	Oliver	Anderson	Henneman	27-15	1st	+4
5-19	At Cle.	L	5-8		9	11	Nagy	Witt	Mesa	27-16	1st	+4
5-21	At Min.	L	3-4		8	9	Milchin	Henneman		27-17	1st	+3
5-22	At Min.	W	6-5		13	12	Pavlik	Parra	Henneman	28-17	1st	+3
5-23	At K.C.	L	2-4		10	8	Appier	Oliver	Montgomery	28-18	1st	+3
5-24	At K.C.	L	0-8		4	11	Gubicza	Witt		28-19	1st	+2
5-25	At K.C.	W	2-1		8	3	Helling	Haney	Henneman	29-19	1st	+3
5-26	At K.C.	W	6-4		10	11	Hill	Linton	Henneman	30-19	1st	+3
5-27	Cle.	W	3-2		8	6	Pavlik	McDowell		31-19	1st	+4
5-28	Cle.	W	11-3		13	9	Oliver	Hershiser		32-19	1st	+5
5-29	Cle.	W	5-4		10	9	Cook	Tavarez	Henneman	33-19	1st	+5
5-31	Min.	W	7-2		10	7	Hill	Rodriguez		34-19	1st	+5
6-1	Min.	L	5-9		13	15	Milchin	Henneman		34-20	1st	+5
6-2	Min.	L	5-6		8	13	Guardado	Russell		34-21	1st	+4
6-3	At Mil.	W	9-6		12	10	Witt	Sparks	Henneman	35-21	1st	+5
6-4	At Mil.	L	2-6		8	7	Bones	Gross		35-22	1st	+4
6-5	At Mil.	L	4-6		9	12	McDonald	Hill	Fetters	35-23	1st	+4
6-7	Tor.	W	10-7		13	11	Pavlik	Janzen	Henneman	36-23	1st	+4
6-8	Tor.	W	2-0		5	5	Oliver	Guzman		37-23	1st	+5
6-9	Tor.	W	8-6		14	6	Witt	Hanson	Henneman	38-23	1st	+5
6-10	Mil.	W	8-3		14	8	Gross	Givens		39-23	1st	+6
6-11	Mil.	L	4-14		14	20	McDonald	Hill	Garcia	39-24	1st	+5
6-12	Mil.	W	13-6		12	9	Pavlik	Miranda		40-24	1st	+5
6-13	At Bos.	L	7-8	(10)	14	15	Slocumb	Henneman		40-25	1st	+5
6-14	At Bos.	L	3-4		8	6	Stanton	Witt		40-26	1st	+5
6-15	At Bos.	W	13-3		18	9	Gross	Wakefield		41-26	1st	+5
6-16	At Bos.	L	9-10		13	13	Hudson	Henneman		41-27	1st	+4
6-17	At Bal.	T	1-1	(6)	5	2	......	......		41-27	1st	+4
6-18	At Bal.	W	7-0		9	5	Oliver	Mercker		42-27	1st	+5
6-19	At Bal.	W	3-2		8	7	Witt	Mussina	Russell	43-27	1st	+6
6-20	At Bal.	L	2-3		6	8	Wells	Gross	R. Myers	43-28	1st	+5

te	Opp.	Res.	Score	(inn.*)	Hits	Opp. hits	Winning pitcher	Losing pitcher	Save	Record	Pos.	GB
21	Bos.	W	14-4		17	12	Hill	Minchey		44-28	1st	+5
22	Bos.	W	8-2		10	6	Pavlik	Wakefield		45-28	1st	+5
23	Bos.	L	4-6		12	12	Stanton	Cook	Slocumb	45-29	1st	+5
24	Bal.	L	3-8		8	13	Mussina	Witt		45-30	1st	+4¹/₂
25	Bal.	W	5-2		8	7	Gross	Wells	Henneman	46-30	1st	+5¹/₂
26	Bal.	W	6-5		9	6	Cook	Orosco	Henneman	47-30	1st	+6¹/₂
28	At Sea.	L	8-19		16	22	Carmona	Pavlik		47-31	1st	+5
29	At Sea.	W	9-5		13	6	Oliver	Meacham		48-31	1st	+6
30	At Sea.	L	3-4		7	12	Hitchcock	Witt	Charlton	48-32	1st	+5
1	At Cal.	W	8-6		12	13	Gross	Langston	Henneman	49-32	1st	+6
2	At Cal.	L	5-6		7	11	James	Henneman		49-33	1st	+6
3	At Cal.	W	8-1		15	12	Pavlik	Finley		50-33	1st	+6
4	Sea.	L	5-9		9	13	Carmona	Henneman		50-34	1st	+5
5	Sea.	L	3-6		6	15	Hitchcock	Witt		50-35	1st	+4
6	Sea.	L	5-9		9	8	Wagner	Gross		50-36	1st	+3
7	Sea.	W	8-3		9	8	Hill	Wells		51-36	1st	+4
11	At Oak.	L	3-8		11	13	Chouinard	Oliver		51-37	1st	+3
12	At Oak.	W	8-4	(10)	16	10	Russell	Taylor		52-37	1st	+3
13	At Oak.	W	8-1		12	3	Pavlik	Wengert		53-37	1st	+4
14	At Oak.	L	1-9		11	14	Johns	Gross		53-38	1st	+3
15	Cal.	L	7-10		11	11	Schmidt	Brandenburg	Percival	53-39	1st	+2
16	Cal.	W	6-2		7	5	Oliver	J. Abbott	Russell	54-39	1st	+3
17	Cal.	W	7-3		8	11	Hill	Finley		55-39	1st	+4
18	Oak.	L	4-5	(11)	10	12	Reyes	Brandenburg	Van Poppel	55-40	1st	+3
19	Oak.	L	6-9		11	11	Reyes	Helling	Taylor	55-41	1st	+3
20	Oak.	W	8-4		15	13	Witt	Van Poppel		56-41	1st	+4
21	Oak.	L	8-11		16	16	Groom	Brandenburg	Mohler	56-42	1st	+3
22	At N.Y.	W	6-1		11	6	Hill	Rogers		57-42	1st	+3
23	At N.Y.	L	0-6		2	11	Gooden	Pavlik		57-43	1st	+3
24	At N.Y.	L	2-4		9	9	Pettitte	Alberro	Wetteland	57-44	1st	+2
25	At Chi.	W	4-3	(12)	10	13	Russell	Keyser	Henneman	58-44	1st	+3
26	At Chi.	L	2-6		5	8	Alvarez	Oliver		58-45	1st	+2
27	At Chi.	W	6-4	(10)	8	7	Heredia	Simas	Vosberg	59-45	1st	+2
28	At Chi.	L	1-5		5	9	Fernandez	Pavlik		59-46	1st	+2
30	N.Y.	W	15-2		21	5	Witt	Pettitte		60-46	1st	+2¹/₂
31	N.Y.	W	9-2		9	11	Oliver	Key		61-46	1st	+2¹/₂
1	N.Y.	L	5-6		9	11	Rogers	Hill	Wetteland	61-47	1st	+1¹/₂
2	Chi.	L	0-9		3	14	Fernandez	Pavlik		61-48	1st	+1¹/₂
3	Chi.	L	9-11		13	16	Hernandez	Russell		61-49	1st	+1¹/₂
4	Chi.	W	9-5		12	10	Witt	Baldwin		62-49	1st	+1¹/₂
5	Chi.	L	5-15		10	19	Alvarez	Oliver		62-50	1st	+1
6	At Det.	W	4-2		9	8	Hill	Lira	Henneman	63-50	1st	+2
7	At Det.	L	2-4		8	9	Cummings	Pavlik	Myers	63-51	1st	+2
8	At Det.	L	2-3		9	6	Olivares	Heredia		63-52	1st	+2
9	At Tor.	W	5-4		12	12	Witt	Quantrill	Henneman	64-52	1st	+3
10	At Tor.	W	12-1		17	7	Oliver	Guzman		65-52	1st	+4
11	At Tor.	W	6-0		7	6	Burkett	Hanson		66-52	1st	+5
12	Det.	W	7-0		10	5	Hill	B. Williams		67-52	1st	+6
13	Det.	W	6-2		9	5	Pavlik	Olivares		68-52	1st	+6
14	Det.	W	5-4		6	9	Witt	Van Poppel	Henneman	69-52	1st	+7
16	K.C.	W	5-3		10	7	Burkett	Haney	Henneman	70-52	1st	+7
17	K.C.	L	1-4		6	15	Belcher	Hill		70-53	1st	+6
18	K.C.	W	10-3		17	10	Gross	Appier		71-53	1st	+6
19	At Cle.	W	10-3		12	4	Pavlik	McDowell		72-53	1st	+7
20	At Cle.	L	4-10		11	12	Lopez	Witt		72-54	1st	+7
21	At Cle.	W	10-8	(10)	17	17	Vosberg	Tavarez		73-54	1st	+8
22	At Min.	W	11-2		10	10	Hill	Robertson		74-54	1st	+8
23	At Min.	L	2-9		8	15	Aguilera	Oliver		74-55	1st	+7
24	At Min.	L	5-6		9	10	Rodriguez	Pavlik	Trombley	74-56	1st	+7
25	At Min.	W	13-2		14	7	Witt	Miller		75-56	1st	+8
27	At K.C.	L	3-4	(10)	10	9	Montgomery	Russell		75-57	1st	+6¹/₂
28	At K.C.	L	3-4	(12)	6	13	Huisman	Gross		75-58	1st	+5¹/₂
30	Cle.	W	5-3		9	7	Pavlik	Ogea	Russell	76-58	1st	+6
31	Cle.	W	6-3		8	9	Oliver	McDowell	Vosberg	77-58	1st	+7
1	Cle.	L	2-8		8	16	Nagy	Burkett		77-59	1st	+6
2	Min.	L	4-6		11	11	Aguilera	Hill	Guardado	77-60	1st	+6
3	Min.	W	9-7		9	12	Witt	Rodriguez	Henneman	78-60	1st	+6
4	Min.	L	6-7		9	11	Robertson	Heredia	Trombley	78-61	1st	+6
6	At Mil.	W	7-3		8	7	Burkett	Eldred		79-61	1st	+6¹/₂
7	At Mil.	W	2-1		7	4	Hill	McDonald	Henneman	80-61	1st	+7
8	At Mil.	W	7-1		11	5	Witt	Florie		81-61	1st	+7¹/₂
9	At Tor.	W	4-3		7	10	Gross	Hentgen	Henneman	82-61	1st	+8
10	At Tor.	W	11-8		14	14	Oliver	Williams	Henneman	83-61	1st	+9
11	At Tor.	L	3-8		9	13	Andujar	Vosberg		83-62	1st	+9
12	Mil.	L	4-15		9	18	McDonald	Hill		83-63	1st	+8

– 71 –

Date	Opp.	Res.	Score	(inn.*)	Hits	Opp. hits	Winning pitcher	Losing pitcher	Save	Record	Pos.	GB
9-13	Mil.	L	3-6		7	11	D'Amico	Witt	Fetters	83-64	1st	+7
9-14	Mil.	L	6-8		9	11	Karl	Pavlik	Fetters	83-65	1st	+6
9-15	Mil.	W	6-2		11	10	Oliver	Garcia	Vosberg	84-65	1st	+6
9-16	At Sea.	L	0-6		4	13	Moyer	Burkett		84-66	1st	+5
9-17	At Sea.	L	2-5		6	7	Mulholland	Hill	Ayala	84-67	1st	+4
9-18	At Sea.	L	2-5		4	9	Hitchcock	Witt	Charlton	84-68	1st	+3
9-19	At Sea.	L	6-7		9	12	T. Davis	Cook	Charlton	84-69	1st	+2
9-20	At Cal.	L	5-6	(10)	8	12	McElroy	Stanton		84-70	1st	+1
9-21	At Cal.	W	7-1		10	7	Burkett	J. Abbott		85-70	1st	+1
9-22	At Cal.	W	4-1		12	8	Hill	Dickson		86-70	1st	+2
9-23	At Oak.	L	3-5		12	11	Wasdin	Witt	Taylor	86-71	1st	+2
9-24	At Oak.	W	7-3		11	4	Cook	Small		87-71	1st	+3
9-26	Cal.	W	6-5		8	8	Burkett	J. Abbott	Henneman	88-71	1st	+3¹/
9-27	Cal.	L	3-4	(15)	9	14	Harris	Whiteside	Gohr	88-72	1st	+3¹/
9-28	Cal.	W	4-3		7	10	Oliver	Finley	Heredia	89-72	1st	+3¹/
9-29	Cal.	W	4-3		5	7	Witt	Springer		90-72	1st	+4¹/

Monthly records: April (16-10), May (18-9), June (14-13), July (13-14), August (16-12), September (13-14).
*Innings, if other than nine. †First game of doubleheader. ‡Second game of doubleheader.

HIGHLIGHTS

High point: On May 27, the Rangers trailed the Indians, 2-1, in the bottom of the eighth. But Dean Palmer homered in the eighth and Darryl Hamilton doubled home Kevin Elster from first with two out in the ninth. The Rangers won, 3-2, then stunned the Indians with a three-game sweep at The Ballpark that left them 34-19 at the end of May and 5½ games in front of the American League West.

Low point: The Rangers nearly suffered one of the biggest collapses in baseball history. They had a nine-game lead with 17 to play, then lost their next 10. That included four in a row to the Mariners, which left them with a one-game lead with nine to play.

Turning point: The Rangers started August by losing six of eight, cutting their lead to two games. But G.M. Doug Melvin acquired pitcher John Burkett from Florida and he won his first start, beating Toronto with a shutout. That started a seven-game winning streak and the Rangers built their lead back to seven.

Most valuable player: Outfielder Juan Gonzalez. Despite missing 28 games, he had the best season of his career, hitting a personal-best .310 while setting club records with 47 home runs and 144 RBIs. He averaged 1.07 RBIs per game, the best ratio since Jimmie Foxx drove in 1.17 in 1938.

Most valuable pitcher: Ken Hill. He lived up to the responsibility of being the staff ace, going 16-10 with a 3.63 ERA. He also led the team with 250⅔ innings, seven complete games, three shutouts and 170 strikeouts.

Most improved player: Outfielder Rusty Greer. He went from being solid and steady to a borderline star. Despite missing 26 games because of injuries, Greer hit .332 with 96 runs and 100 RBIs.

Most pleasant surprise: Shortstop Kevin Elster. After playing 49 total games over the previous four seasons, Elster became a starter with the Rangers and hit .252 with 24 homers and 99 RBIs.

Key injuries: First baseman Will Clark missed 45 games because of three stays on the disabled list and set career lows with 69 runs, 13 homers and 72 RBIs. Shortstop Benji Gil lost his job to Kevin Elster because of a bad back. Kevin Gross put his career in doubt with a bad back. He pitched in just 129 innings, the second-lowest total of his career.

Notable: The Rangers won their first division title. They held or shared first place for all but four of 182 days. . . . Catcher Ivan Rodriguez hit 44 doubles, the most by a catcher in major league history. His 116 runs were the most by a catcher since Yogi Berra scored 116 in 1950. . . . The Rangers led the A.L. in fielding for the first time since 1983 and set a league record with 15 consecutive errorless games.

—T.R. SULLIVAN

RECORDS

1996 regular-season record: 90-72 (1st in A.L. West); 50-31 at home; 40-41 on road; 42-20 vs. East; 30-31 vs. Central; 18-21 vs. West; 28-20 vs. lefthanded starters; 62-52 vs. righthanded starters; 81-62 on grass; 9-10 on turf; 28-16 in daytime; 62-56 at night; 20-21 in one-run games; 5-7 in extra-inning games; 1-0-0 in doubleheaders.

Team record past five years: 379-365 (.509, ranks 5th in league in that span).

TEAM LEADERS

Batting average: Rusty Greer (.332).
At-bats: Ivan Rodriguez (639).
Runs: Ivan Rodriguez (116).
Hits: Ivan Rodriguez (192).
Total bases: Juan Gonzalez (348).
Doubles: Ivan Rodriguez (47).
Triples: Rusty Greer (6).
Home runs: Juan Gonzalez (47).
Runs batted in: Juan Gonzalez (144).
Stolen bases: Mark McLemore (27).
Slugging percentage: Juan Gonzalez (.643).
On-base percentage: Rusty Greer (.397).
Wins: Ken Hill, Bobby Witt (16).

Earned-run average: Ken Hill (3.63).
Complete games: Ken Hill, Roger Pavli (7).
Shutouts: Ken Hill (3).
Saves: Mike Henneman (31).
Innings pitched: Ken Hill (250.2).
Strikeouts: Ken Hill (170).

GAMES BY POSITION

Catcher: Ivan Rodriguez 146, Dave Vall 35, Kevin L. Brown 2.
First base: Will Clark 117, Rene Gonzal 23, Mickey Tettleton 23, Lee Stevens 18 Craig Worthington 6, Dave Valle 5, Rust Greer 1, Kurt Stillwell 1.
Second base: Mark McLemore 147, Kurt Stillwell 21, Rene Gonzales 5, Lou Frazier 1.
Third base: Dean Palmer 154, Rene Gonzales 15, Craig Worthington 7, Kurt Stillwell 6, Jack Voigt 1.
Shortstop: Kevin Elster 157, Rene Gonzales 10, Kurt Stillwell 9, Benji Gil 1.
Outfield: Darryl Hamilton 147, Rusty Greer 137, Juan Gonzalez 102, Damon Buford 80, Warren Newson 66, Lou Frazier 15, Rikkert Faneyte 6, Lee Stevens 5, Jack Voigt 3, Rene Gonzales 1, Mark McLemore 1.
Designated hitter: Mickey Tettleton 115, Juan Gonzalez 32, Lou Frazier 11, Warren Newson 8, Lou Frazier 11, Damon Buford 3, Rikkert Faneyte 2, Kevin L. Brown 1, Rusty Greer 1, Luis Ortiz 1, Dean Palmer 1, Kurt Stillwell 1, Dave Valle 1.

TOP DRAFT CHOICES

1a. **R.A. Dickey,** RHP, Univ. of Tennessee.
1b. **Sam Marsonek,** RHP, Jesuit H.S., Tampa.
1c. **Corey Lee,** LHP, North Carolina State U.
2. **Derrick Cook,** RHP, James Madison Univ.
3. **Derek Baker,** 3B, Rancho Santiago (Calif) J.C.
4. **Kelly Dransfeldt,** SS, Univ. of Michigan.
5. **Warren Morris,** 2B, Louisiana State Univ.
6. **Tony Fisher,** OF, U. of St. Thomas (Minn.)
7. **Juan Pinella,** OF, North Stafford (Va.) H.S.
8. **Luis Acevedo,** SS, Isabella, P.R.
9. **Randy Rodriguez,** LHP, Florida Air Academy H.S., Melbourne, Fla.
10. **Doug Davis,** LHP, C.C. of San Francisco.

TORONTO BLUE JAYS
AMERICAN LEAGUE EAST DIVISION

1997 BLUE JAYS SCHEDULE

Home games shaded.
* — All-Star Game at Jacobs Field (Cleveland)
D — Day game (any game starting before 5 p.m.)

APRIL
SUN	MON	TUE	WED	THU	FRI	SAT
		1 D CWS	2 CWS	3	4 MIL	5 D MIL
6 MIL	7 D	8 CWS	9 CWS	10 D CWS	11 D MIL	12 D MIL
13 D MIL	14 KC	15 KC	16 KC	17 D OAK	18 TEX	19 TEX
20 TEX	21 ANA	22 ANA	23 ANA	24	25 SEA	26 D SEA
27 SEA	28 D	29 KC	30 KC			

MAY
SUN	MON	TUE	WED	THU	FRI	SAT
				1 KC	2 MIN	3 D MIN
4 MIN	5 DET	6 DET	7 CLE	8 CLE	9 MIN	10 MIN
11 MIN	12 DET	13 DET	14 D DET	15	16 CLE	17 D CLE
18 CLE	19 D NYY	20 NYY	21 NYY	22	23 ANA	24 D ANA
25 D ANA	26 TEX	27 TEX	28 NYY	29 D NYY	30 OAK	31 D OAK

JUNE
SUN	MON	TUE	WED	THU	FRI	SAT
1 D OAK	2 SEA	3 D SEA	4	5 OAK	6 OAK	7 D OAK
8 OAK	9	10 SEA	11 D SEA	12	13 PHI	14 PHI
15 D PHI	16 ATL	17 ATL	18 ATL	19	20 BAL	21 D BAL
22 BAL	23 BOS	24 BOS	25 BOS	26 BAL	27 BAL	28 BAL
29 BAL	30 MON					

JULY
SUN	MON	TUE	WED	THU	FRI	SAT
		1 D MON	2 MON	3 NYY	4 NYY	5 NYY
6 NYY	7 D	8 D	9 BOS	10 BOS	11 BOS	12 BOS
13 D BOS	14 BAL	15 BAL	16 TEX	17 TEX	18 ANA	19 ANA
20 D ANA	21 D	22 MIL	23 MIL	24 MIL	25 KC	26 D KC
27 KC	28 MIL	29 MIL	30 D DET	31 DET		

AUGUST
SUN	MON	TUE	WED	THU	FRI	SAT
					1 DET	2 DET
3 DET	4 D MIN	5 MIN	6 D MIN	7 CLE	8 CLE	9 D DET
10 D DET	11 DET	12 MIN	13 MIN	14	15 CLE	16 D CLE
17 CLE	18 D CWS	19 CWS	20 CWS	21 D CWS	22 KC	23 KC
24 D KC	25	26 CWS	27 CWS	28 CWS	29 FLA	30 D FLA
31 D FLA						

SEPTEMBER
SUN	MON	TUE	WED	THU	FRI	SAT
	1 NYM	2 NYM	3 NYM	4 TEX	5 TEX	6 D TEX
7 TEX	8 ANA	9 ANA	10 OAK	11 OAK	12 SEA	13 SEA
14 D SEA	15 SEA	16	17 BOS	18 BOS	19 NYY	20 D NYY
21 D NYY	22 NYY	23 BAL	24 BAL	25 BOS	26 BOS	27 D BOS
28 D BOS						

1997 SEASON

CLUB DIRECTORY

President and chief executive officer
Paul Beeston
Vice president, business
Bob Nicholson
Vice president, development
Christine Legein
Vice president, general manager
Gord Ash
Vice president, baseball
Bob Mattick
Special asst. to v.p., baseball, g.m.
Al Widmar
Gordon Lakey
Moose Johnson
Assistant general managers
Bob Engle
Tim McCleary
Director, public relations
Howard Starkman
Director, stadium and ticket operations
George Holm
Director, marketing
Paul Markle
Director, finance
Susan Quigley
Director, scouting
Tim Wilken
Director, international scouting
Wayne Morgan
Director, player development
Karl Kuehl
Director, Canadian scouting
Bill Byckowski
Director, minor league business
Ken Carson
Director, baseball administration
Bob Nelson
Asst. dir., tickets and box office manager
Randy Low
Director, Latin America operations
Herb Raybourn

Manager, group sales
Maureen Haffey
Manager, team travel
John Brioux
Manager, promotions and advertising
Rick Amos
Manager, accounting
Cathy McNamara
Manager, employee compensation
Perry Nicoletta
Manager, information systems
Bart MacNeil
Manager, game operations
Mario Coutinho
Supervisor, office service
Mick Bazinet
Trainers
Tommy Craig
Brent Andrews
Strength and conditioning coordinator
Geoffrey Horne
Team physician
Dr. Ron Taylor
Special assignment scouts
Moose Johnson
Gordon Lakey
Advance scout
Sal Butera
Scouts
Tony Arias, David Blume, Chris Bourjos, Chris Buckley, Bus Campbell, John Cole, Ellis Dungan, Joe Ford, Tim Hewes, Tom Hinkle, Jim Hughes, Duane Larson, Ted Lekas, Ben McLure, Marty Miller, Bill Moore, Andy Pienovi, Alvin Rittman, Jorge Rivera, Mike Russell, Joe Siers, Mark Snipp, Jerry Sobeck, Ron Tostenson, Steve Williams

MINOR LEAGUE AFFILIATES

Class	Team	League	Manager
AAA	Syracuse	International	Garth Iorg
AA	Knoxville	Southern	Omar Malave
A	Dunedin	Florida State	Dennis Holmberg
A	Hagerstown	South Atlantic	J.J. Cannon
A	St. Catharines	New York-Penn.	Rocket Wheeler
Rookie	Medicine Hat	Pioneer	Marty Pevey

BROADCAST INFORMATION
Radio: THE-FAN (590).
TV: To be announced.
Cable TV: To be announced.

SPRING TRAINING
Ballpark (city): Dunedin Stadium at Grant Field (Dunedin, Fla.).
Ticket information: 800-707-8269; 813-733-0429

1997 SEASON *Toronto Blue Jays*

SPRING TRAINING ROSTER

Manager—Cito Gaston (43).
Coaches—Alfredo Griffin (4), Jim Lett (10), Nick Leyva (16), Mel Queen (34), Gene Tenace (18), Willie Upshaw (28).

No.	PITCHERS	B/T	Ht./Wt.	Born	1996 clubs
49	Andujar, Luis	R/R	6-2/210	11-22-72	Nashville, Gulf Coast White Sox-Cardinals, Chicago A.L., Syracuse, Toronto
21	Clemens, Roger	R/R	6-4/230	8-4-62	Boston
	Cornett, Brad	R/R	6-3/190	2-4-69	Dunedin
37	Crabtree, Tim	R/R	6-4/200	10-13-69	Toronto
45	Escobar, Kelvim	R/R	6-1/205	4-11-76	Dunedin, Knoxville
38	Flener, Huck	B/L	5-11/190	2-25-69	Syracuse, Toronto
57	Guzman, Juan	R/R	5-11/195	10-28-66	Toronto
32	Halladay, Roy	R/R	6-6/200	5-14-77	Dunedin
39	Hanson, Erik	R/R	6-6/215	5-18-65	Toronto
41	Hentgen, Pat	R/R	6-2/200	11-13-68	Toronto
36	Janzen, Marty	R/R	6-3/200	5-31-73	Syracuse, Toronto
	Person, Robert	R/R	6-0/185	10-6-69	New York N.L., Norfolk
19	Plesac, Dan	L/L	6-5/220	2-4-62	Pittsburgh
48	Quantrill, Paul	L/R	6-1/185	11-3-68	Toronto
55	Risley, Bill	R/R	6-2/220	5-29-67	Toronto, Syracuse, St. Catharines
42	Sievert, Mark	L/R	6-4/195	2-16-73	Syracuse, Knoxville
24	Spoljaric, Paul	R/L	6-3/210	9-24-70	Syracuse, Toronto, St. Catharines
40	Timlin, Mike	R/R	6-4/210	3-10-66	Toronto
54	Williams, Woody	R/R	6-0/190	8-19-66	Dunedin, Syracuse, Toronto, St. Catharines
47	Young, Joe	R/R	6-4/205	4-28-75	Hagerstown, Dunedin

No.	CATCHERS	B/T	Ht./Wt.	Born	1996 clubs
35	Martinez, Sandy	L/R	6-2/205	10-3-72	Toronto, Knoxville
46	Mosquera, Julio	R/R	6-0/190	1-29-72	Knoxville, Syracuse, Toronto
22	O'Brien, Charlie	R/R	6-2/205	5-1-61	Toronto
14	Santiago, Benito	R/R	6-1/185	3-9-65	Philadelphia

No.	INFIELDERS	B/T	Ht./Wt.	Born	1996 clubs
14	Brito, Tilson	R/R	6-0/180	5-28-72	Toronto, Syracuse
6	Crespo, Felipe	B/R	5-11/200	3-5-73	Dunedin, Toronto, Syracuse
21	Delgado, Carlos	L/R	6-3/225	6-25-72	Toronto
26	Evans, Tom	R/R	6-1/208	7-9-74	Knoxville
13	Garcia, Carlos	R/R	6-1/197	10-15-67	Pittsburgh, Calgary
8	Gonzalez, Alex	R/R	6-0/190	4-8-73	Toronto
	Jones, Ryan	R/R	6-3/225	11-5-74	Knoxville
23	Patzke, Jeff	B/R	6-0/185	11-18-73	Knoxville
1	Perez, Tomas	B/R	5-11/172	12-29-73	Syracuse, Toronto
11	Samuel, Juan	R/R	5-11/185	12-9-60	Toronto
33	Sprague, Ed	R/R	6-2/205	7-25-67	Toronto

No.	OUTFIELDERS	B/T	Ht./Wt.	Born	1996 clubs
5	Brumfield, Jacob	R/R	6-0/186	5-27-65	Pittsburgh, Toronto
29	Carter, Joe	R/R	6-3/215	3-7-60	Toronto
15	Green, Shawn	L/L	6-4/195	11-10-72	Toronto
6	Merced, Orlando	L/R	5-11/190	11-2-66	Pittsburgh
2	Nixon, Otis	B/R	6-2/180	1-9-59	Toronto
17	Perez, Robert	R/R	6-3/220	6-4-69	Toronto
27	Sanders, Anthony	R/R	6-2/190	3-2-74	Dunedin, Knoxville
7	Stewart, Shannon	R/R	6-1/194	2-25-74	Syracuse, Toronto

BALLPARK INFORMATION

Ballpark (capacity, surface)
SkyDome (50,516, artificial)

Address
One Blue Jays Way
Suite 3200
Toronto, Ontario M5V 1J1

Business phone
416-341-1000

Ticket information
416-341-1111

Ticket prices
$25 (esplanade IF, club level OF)
$20 (skydeck IF, esplanade OF)
$13 (skydeck)
$4 (skydeck outfield)

Field dimensions (from home plate)
To left field at foul line, 330 feet
To center field, 400 feet
To right field at foul line, 330 feet

First game played
June 5, 1989 (Brewers 5, Blue Jays 3)

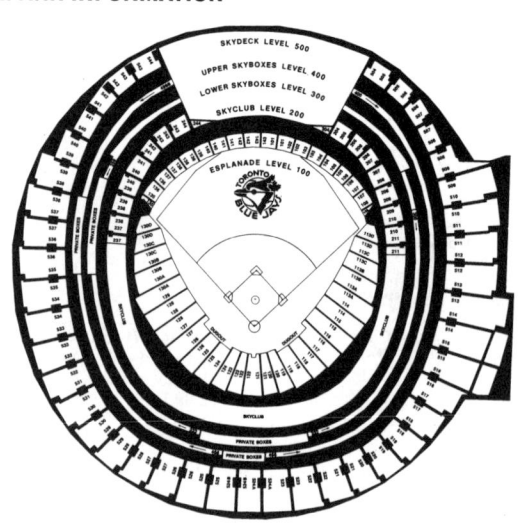

DAY BY DAY

te	Opp.	Res.	Score	(inn.*)	Hits	Opp. hits	Winning pitcher	Losing pitcher	Save	Record	Pos.	GB
	At Oak.§	W	9-6		13	5	Hanson	Reyes	Timlin	1-0	1st	+1/2
	At Oak.§	W	10-4		11	7	Hentgen	Prieto		2-0	T1st	...
	At Cle.	W	7-1		10	6	Guzman	Hershiser		3-0	2nd	1/2
	At Cle.	L	3-5		7	7	Nagy	Hanson	Mesa	3-1	2nd	1/2
	At Cle.	L	3-8		8	10	Martinez	Quantrill		3-2	2nd	11/2
	Cal.	W	5-0		11	5	Hentgen	Langston		4-2	2nd	1
0	Cal.	L	1-2		6	6	Holzemer	Guzman	Percival	4-3	T2nd	2
1	Cal.	W	7-4		12	9	Hanson	J. Abbott	Timlin	5-3	2nd	2
2	Sea.	L	6-9		11	13	Hitchcock	Quantrill		5-4	3rd	3
3	Sea.	L	3-14		4	12	Bosio	Ware		5-5	T3rd	4
4	Sea.	L	4-9		7	10	Wolcott	Hentgen		5-6	4th	4
5	Det.	W	8-2		9	6	Guzman	Olivares		6-6	T3rd	31/2
6	Det.	L	8-13		11	18	Gohr	Hanson	R. Lewis	6-7	4th	41/2
7	At Cal.	L	1-5		3	9	Finley	Quantrill		6-8	4th	51/2
8	At Cal.	L	6-9		9	13	James	Ware	Percival	6-9	4th	51/2
9	At Sea.	W	10-4		12	9	Hentgen	Wolcott	Bohanon	7-9	T3rd	41/2
0	At Sea.	W	3-1		9	5	Guzman	Menhart	Timlin	8-9	3rd	31/2
1	At Sea.	L	5-9		9	13	Johnson	Hanson		8-10	3rd	31/2
2	At Sea.	W	16-7		17	11	Castillo	Hurtado		9-10	3rd	21/2
4	Oak.	L	6-7		11	11	Prieto	Hentgen	Corsi	9-11	3rd	3
5	Oak.	L	3-4	(11)	8	9	Mohler	Crabtree		9-12	3rd	4
6	Cle.	L	3-6		8	10	Hershiser	Hanson	Mesa	9-13	3rd	4
7	Cle.	W	11-6		16	9	Castillo	Nagy		10-13	3rd	3
8	Cle.	L	3-17		10	20	Lopez	Viola		10-14	3rd	3
0	Mil.	W	9-8		15	12	Crabtree	Boze		11-14	3rd	3
	Mil.	W	9-3		10	4	Guzman	Miranda		12-14	3rd	3
2	Mil.	W	7-5		10	6	Hanson	Karl	Timlin	13-14	3rd	3
3	At Bos.	L	7-8		9	12	Moyer	Quantrill	Slocumb	13-15	3rd	4
4	At Bos.	L	4-8		12	12	Gordon	Viola	Slocumb	13-16	3rd	4
5	At Bos.	W	11-4		11	10	Hentgen	Wakefield		14-16	3rd	4
7	At Tex.	L	1-5		5	8	Oliver	Guzman		14-17	3rd	51/2
8	At Tex.	L	2-4		9	8	Witt	Hanson	Henneman	14-18	3rd	61/2
9	At Tex.	W	5-2		10	7	Quantrill	Hill	Timlin	15-18	3rd	51/2
10	Bos.	L	5-6	(11)	9	9	Slocumb	Carrara		15-19	3rd	51/2
11	Bos.	W	9-8	(11)	11	10	Quantrill	Knackert		16-19	3rd	41/2
12	Bos.	W	8-7	(10)	11	15	Janzen	Slocumb		17-19	3rd	41/2
14	At Min.	W	4-2		7	9	Hanson	Robertson	Timlin	18-19	3rd	41/2
15	At Min.	L	1-2		6	7	Rodriguez	Hentgen		18-20	3rd	41/2
16	At Min.	L	1-4		6	8	Radke	Quantrill	Stevens	18-21	3rd	5
17	At K.C.	L	2-4		7	8	Belcher	Guzman	Montgomery	18-22	3rd	6
18	At K.C.	W	6-2		10	8	Viola	Appier		19-22	3rd	6
19	At K.C.	W	3-2		10	8	Hanson	Gubicza	Timlin	20-22	3rd	5
20	At K.C.	L	4-5		7	8	Haney	Hentgen	Montgomery	20-23	3rd	51/2
21	At Chi.	L	1-2		5	2	Tapani	Ware	Hernandez	20-24	3rd	61/2
22	At Chi.	L	1-2	(11)	8	9	McCaskill	Timlin		20-25	3rd	61/2
23	Min.	W	5-4	(10)	14	9	Janzen	Milchin		21-25	3rd	61/2
24	Min.	L	0-4		4	11	Robertson	Hanson		21-26	3rd	61/2
25	Min.	L	4-6	(10)	7	11	Guardado	Castillo	Stevens	21-27	3rd	71/2
26	Min.	L	3-9		7	16	Naulty	Bohanon		21-28	3rd	71/2
27	Chi.	W	5-4		8	9	Janzen	Fernandez	Timlin	22-28	3rd	71/2
28	Chi.	L	5-8		12	10	Baldwin	Viola	Hernandez	22-29	3rd	71/2
29	Chi.	W	6-5		11	9	Hanson	Magrane	Timlin	23-29	3rd	61/2
31	K.C.	W	4-2		9	7	Hentgen	Gubicza	Timlin	24-29	3rd	61/2
1	K.C.	W	5-3	(10)	10	11	Crabtree	Montgomery		25-29	3rd	61/2
2	K.C.	L	5-7		5	15	Belcher	Janzen	Montgomery	25-30	3rd	71/2
4	At N.Y.	L	4-5		10	8	Gooden	Hanson	Wetteland	25-31	3rd	81/2
5	At N.Y.	W	12-7		14	10	Hentgen	Key		26-31	3rd	71/2
6	At N.Y.	L	1-8		6	14	Pettitte	Quantrill		26-32	3rd	81/2
7	At Tex.	L	7-10		11	13	Pavlik	Janzen	Henneman	26-33	3rd	81/2
8	At Tex.	L	0-2		5	5	Oliver	Guzman		26-34	3rd	81/2
9	At Tex.	L	6-8		6	14	Witt	Hanson	Henneman	26-35	3rd	91/2
10	N.Y.	L	3-5		8	13	Key	Hentgen	Wetteland	26-36	3rd	101/2
11	N.Y.	L	4-6		9	11	Pettitte	Quantrill	Wetteland	26-37	3rd	111/2
12	N.Y.	W	7-4		12	9	Janzen	Mendoza		27-37	3rd	101/2
13	At Cal.	L	4-6		9	11	Finley	Guzman	James	27-38	4th	101/2
14	At Cal.	L	4-7		8	10	Grimsley	Hanson	Percival	27-39	4th	111/2
15	At Cal.	L	5-7		4	11	Langston	Crabtree	Percival	27-40	4th	111/2
16	At Cal.	W	6-4		11	10	Quantrill	J. Abbott	Timlin	28-40	4th	111/2
18	At Sea.	W	11-3		14	4	Guzman	Wolcott		29-40	4th	11
19	At Sea.	W	9-2		10	7	Hanson	Harikkala		30-40	3rd	101/2
20	At Oak.	W	1-0		9	2	Hentgen	Wengert	Timlin	31-40	3rd	10
21	At Oak.	W	7-5		9	10	Quantrill	Johns	Timlin	32-40	3rd	101/2

Date	Opp.	Res.	Score	(inn.*)	Hits	Opp. hits	Winning pitcher	Losing pitcher	Save	Record	Pos.	GB
6-22	At Oak.	L	4-8		7	12	Chouinard	Ware		32-41	3rd	11¹/
6-23	At Oak.	W	5-4		9	7	Guzman	Wojciechowski	Timlin	33-41	3rd	11¹/
6-25	Sea.	W	8-7		6	10	Crabtree	Charlton		34-41	3rd	10¹/
6-26	Sea.	W	6-5		8	4	Ware	Ayala	Crabtree	35-41	3rd	10¹/
6-27	Sea.	L	1-9		10	13	Wells	Quantrill		35-42	3rd	11¹/
6-28	Mil.	L	1-5		4	11	D'Amico	Guzman	Fetters	35-43	3rd	11¹/
6-29	Mil.	L	4-7		10	9	Karl	Janzen		35-44	3rd	12¹/₂
6-30	Mil.	W	15-2		17	7	Hanson	Bones		36-44	3rd	11¹/₂
7-1	Bal.	L	4-7		8	10	Coppinger	Hentgen	R. Myers	36-45	3rd	12¹/₂
7-2	Bal.	L	2-8		9	14	Erickson	Quantrill		36-46	3rd	13¹/₂
7-3	Bal.	W	5-2		8	9	Guzman	Krivda	Timlin	37-46	3rd	13
7-4	At Det.	L	1-6		7	9	Nitkowski	Janzen	Myers	37-47	3rd	14
7-5	At Det.	L	3-4		9	6	Sager	Hanson	Olson	37-48	3rd	15
7-6	At Det.	W	15-0		19	3	Hentgen	Olivares		38-48	3rd	15
7-7	At Det.	L	0-9		6	8	Lira	Ware		38-49	3rd	15
7-11	At Mil.	W	6-3		8	4	Guzman	D'Amico	Castillo	39-49	3rd	15
7-12	At Mil.	L	5-12		10	15	McDonald	Hanson		39-50	T3rd	15¹/₂
7-13	At Mil.	W	15-7		18	13	Hentgen	Karl		40-50	T3rd	16
7-14	At Mil.	W	7-5	(10)	9	9	Crabtree	Garcia	Timlin	41-50	T3rd	16
7-15	At Bal.	L	6-8		9	7	Haynes	Timlin		41-51	4th	16
7-16	At Bal.	W	6-0		14	5	Guzman	Mussina		42-51	T3rd	16
7-17	At Bal.	L	10-11		15	11	Coppinger	Timlin		42-52	4th	16
7-18	Det.	W	8-4		13	4	Hentgen	Nitkowski		43-52	T3rd	15
7-19	Det.	L	6-8		13	8	Urbani	Janzen	Olson	43-53	4th	15
7-20	Det.	L	4-5	(10)	9	7	Olson	Quantrill	Lima	43-54	4th	16
7-21	Det.	W	5-4	(12)	13	10	Spoljaric	Lima		44-54	4th	15
7-22	Cle.	L	2-4		4	8	Hershiser	Hanson	Mesa	44-55	4th	15
7-23	Cle.	W	3-1		5	5	Hentgen	Ogea	Timlin	45-55	T3rd	15
7-24	Cle.	L	0-10		3	11	Martinez	Janzen		45-56	4th	16
7-25	Oak.	W	4-3		12	7	Crabtree	Witasick		46-56	T3rd	15
7-26	Oak.	L	3-5		4	9	Groom	Castillo	Taylor	46-57	T3rd	16
7-27	Oak.	W	6-4		6	9	Hanson	Wasdin	Timlin	47-57	T3rd	16
7-28	Oak.	W	1-0		4	3	Hentgen	Prieto		48-57	3rd	16
7-30	At Cle.	W	3-1		8	4	Flener	Martinez	Timlin	49-57	3rd	15
7-31	At Cle.	L	2-4		8	9	Assenmacher	Timlin		49-58	3rd	15
8-1	At Cle.	W	5-3		9	12	Hanson	Lopez	Timlin	50-58	3rd	15
8-2	Cal.	W	9-2		12	10	Hentgen	Finley		51-58	3rd	14
8-3	Cal.	L	6-11		9	18	Langston	Castillo		51-59	3rd	14
8-4	Cal.	W	7-1		9	9	Flener	J. Abbott		52-59	3rd	14
8-5	At Bos.	L	1-3		6	7	Wakefield	Guzman		52-60	4th	15
8-6	At Bos.	L	2-3		9	4	Maddux	Hanson	Slocumb	52-61	4th	16
8-7	At Bos.	L	0-8		3	9	Gordon	Hentgen		52-62	4th	16
8-8	At Bos.	W	9-6		17	10	Williams	Sele	Timlin	53-62	4th	16
8-9	Tex.	L	4-5		12	12	Witt	Quantrill	Henneman	53-63	4th	16
8-10	Tex.	L	1-12		7	17	Oliver	Guzman		53-64	4th	16
8-11	Tex.	L	0-6		6	7	Burkett	Hanson		53-65	4th	17
8-12	Bos.	W	5-1		9	9	Hentgen	Gordon		54-65	4th	16
8-13	Bos.	L	5-7		5	15	Brandenburg	Williams	Slocumb	54-66	4th	16
8-14	Bos.	L	6-8		9	9	Belinda	Crabtree	Slocumb	54-67	4th	17
8-16	At Min.	L	4-5	(10)	10	9	Parra	Quantrill		54-68	4th	17
8-17	At Min.	L	1-11		4	13	Robertson	Hanson		54-69	4th	17
8-18	At Min.	W	6-2		12	6	Hentgen	Aguilera		55-69	4th	16
8-19	At K.C.	W	2-1		6	6	Spoljaric	Rosado	Timlin	56-69	4th	16
8-20	At K.C.	W	6-5	(14)	15	15	Timlin	Huisman		57-69	4th	16
8-21	At K.C.	W	6-2		10	6	Guzman	Haney		58-69	4th	15
8-22	At Chi.	W	1-0	(7)	4	3	Hanson	Fernandez		59-69	4th	14
8-23	At Chi.	W	4-2		10	6	Hentgen	Ruffcorn		60-69	4th	14
8-24	At Chi.	W	9-2		12	11	Williams	Baldwin		61-69	4th	14
8-25	At Chi.	L	9-10	(10)	16	16	Hernandez	Timlin		61-70	4th	14
8-26	Min.	W	5-3		14	9	Guzman	Radke	Timlin	62-70	4th	13
8-27	Min.	L	4-6	(11)	9	12	Trombley	Quantrill		62-71	4th	13
8-28	Min.	W	6-1		12	5	Hentgen	Aguilera		63-71	4th	12
8-30	Chi.	L	2-11		7	18	Tapani	Williams		63-72	4th	12¹/₂
8-31	Chi.	L	1-5		7	12	Alvarez	Flener		63-73	4th	13¹/₂
9-1	Chi.	L	2-4	(11)	6	5	Hernandez	Spoljaric		63-74	4th	13¹/₂
9-2	K.C.	L	0-2		4	6	Belcher	Hanson		63-75	4th	14¹/₂
9-3	K.C.	L	2-5		7	12	Appier	Hentgen		63-76	4th	14¹/₂
9-4	K.C.	W	6-0		9	6	Williams	Rosado		64-76	4th	14¹/₂
9-6	At N.Y.	L	3-4		9	5	M. Rivera	Risley		64-77	4th	15¹/₂
9-7	At N.Y.	W	3-2		5	7	Quantrill	Cone	Timlin	65-77	4th	14¹/₂
9-8	At N.Y.	W	4-2		6	9	Hanson	Pettitte	Timlin	66-77	4th	13¹/₂
9-9	Tex.	L	3-4		10	7	Gross	Hentgen	Henneman	66-78	4th	14
9-10	Tex.	L	8-11		14	14	Oliver	Williams	Henneman	66-79	4th	15
9-11	Tex.	W	8-3		13	9	Andujar	Vosberg		67-79	4th	15
9-13	N.Y.	L	1-4		7	10	Pettitte	Hanson	Wetteland	67-80	4th	16¹/₂

ate	Opp.	Res.	Score	(inn.*)	Hits	Opp. hits	Winning pitcher	Losing pitcher	Save	Record	Pos.	GB
·14	N.Y.	L	1-3		5	11	Boehringer	Hentgen	Wetteland	67-81	4th	17$^1/_2$
·15	N.Y.	W	3-1		9	6	Williams	Mendoza	Timlin	68-81	4th	16$^1/_2$
·16	N.Y.	L	0-10		2	12	Key	Quantrill		68-82	4th	17$^1/_2$
·17	At Mil.	L	0-4		3	5	McDonald	Andujar		68-83	4th	18
·18	At Mil.	L	1-2		4	7	Fetters	Timlin		68-84	4th	19
·20	At Bal.	W	5-1		11	8	Hentgen	Krivda	Spoljaric	69-84	4th	18
·21	At Bal.	L	3-6		7	2	Coppinger	Williams	R. Myers	69-85	4th	19
·22	At Bal.	L	4-5		8	7	Erickson	Flener	Benitez	69-86	4th	20
·23	At Det.	W	6-4		10	8	Hanson	Sager	Timlin	70-86	4th	19
·24	At Det.	W	4-1		9	7	Hentgen	Miller	Timlin	71-86	4th	18$^1/_2$
·25	At Det.	W	13-11		18	14	Brow	Cummings	Timlin	72-86	4th	19
·26	Bal.	L	1-4		5	8	Coppinger	Williams	Benitez	72-87	4th	19
·27	Bal.	W	3-2		7	7	Flener	Erickson	Timlin	73-87	4th	18
·28	Bal.	L	2-3	(10)	5	8	R. Myers	Spoljaric		73-88	4th	19
·29	Bal.	W	4-1		4	8	Hentgen	Rodriguez	Timlin	74-88	4th	18

Monthly records: April (11-14), May (13-15), June (12-15), July (13-14), August (14-15), September (11-15).
*Innings, if other than nine. §At Las Vegas.

HIGHLIGHTS

High point: The Blue Jays set a club record with 42 April home runs. And they homered in 14 consecutive games (April 19-May 3), hitting 27 in that stretch.

Low point: After a road swing that included seven straight victories, the club returned to SkyDome on August 26 with a 61-70 record and renewed hopes of reaching G.M. Gord Ash's goal of a .500 season. But the team produced just three wins on a nine-game homestand. At that point, a break-even finish would have required a 17-5 run.

Turning point: On a trip to Minnesota, Kansas City and Chicago in May, the Blue Jays spoiled some decent pitching with poor run production, striking a theme for the rest of the season. They went 3-6 on the trip, scoring only 23 runs.

Most valuable player: Third baseman Ed Sprague. He reached the century mark in RBIs for the first time and played solidly, if unspectacularly, in the field. He endured constant knee pain but hit 36 home runs and drove in 101 runs.

Most valuable pitcher: Starter Pat Hentgen. The Cy Young Award winner went 20-10 and led the league in innings pitched (265$^2/_3$) and complete games (10), tied for the lead in shutouts (three) and was second in ERA (3.22).

Most improved player: Starting pitcher Juan Guzman. After going 4-14 with a 6.32 ERA in 1995, Guzman rediscovered his dominating fastball and won the American League ERA crown (2.93). He won 11 games.

Biggest disappointment: First baseman John Olerud. Three years after hitting .363 with 107 RBIs and 80 extra-base hits, the first baseman saw his average drop for the third consecutive season to .274. Used primarily in a platoon role, Olerud had 61 RBIs and 43 extra-base hits. Of his 18 homers, 14 came with the bases empty.

Key injuries: After earning the starting job at second base, Felipe Crespo pulled a hamstring the day before camp broke, lost his position and was optioned to Class AAA Syracuse in late May.

Recovering from rotator-cuff surgery, starter Woody Williams was transferred to the 60-day disabled list and didn't break into the rotation until August.

Reliever Bill Risley, regarded as a setup man or closer, was disabled twice for a total of nine weeks because of shoulder strains. And Juan Guzman missed two starts in May with a right pectoral strain and all but one start in September because of an appendectomy.

Notable: The Jays delighted a Canada Day (July 1) holiday crowd of 43,377 by wearing red jerseys with "Canada" printed on the back instead of their names. . . . Team policy against midseason negotiations ended when the Jays decided to re-up outfielder Joe Carter through 1997. Manager Cito Gaston's contract also was extended through '97.

—TOM MALONEY

RECORDS

1996 regular-season record: 74-88 (4th in A.L. East); 35-46 at home; 39-42 on road; 22-30 vs. East; 30-32 vs. Central; 22-26 vs. West; 26-26 vs. lefthanded starters; 48-62 vs. righthanded starters; 32-37 on grass; 42-51 on turf; 25-31 in daytime; 49-57 at night; 19-22 in one-run games; 7-10 in extra-inning games; 0-0-0 in doubleheaders.

Team record past five years: 376-369 (.505, ranks 7th in league in that span).

TEAM LEADERS

Batting average: Otis Nixon (.286).
At-bats: Joe Carter (625).
Runs: Ed Sprague (88).
Hits: Joe Carter (158).
Total bases: Joe Carter (297).
Doubles: Joe Carter, Ed Sprague (35).
Triples: Joe Carter (7).
Home runs: Ed Sprague (36).
Runs batted in: Joe Carter (107).
Stolen bases: Otis Nixon (54).
Slugging percentage: Ed Sprague (.496).
On-base percentage: Otis Nixon (.377).
Wins: Pat Hentgen (20).
Earned-run average: Juan Guzman (2.93).
Complete games: Pat Hentgen (10).

Shutouts: Pat Hentgen (3).
Saves: Mike Timlin (31).
Innings pitched: Pat Hentgen (265.2).
Strikeouts: Pat Hentgen (177).

GAMES BY POSITION

Catcher: Charlie O'Brien 105, Sandy Martinez 75, Julio Mosquera 8.
First base: John Olerud 101, Joe Carter 41, Carlos Delgado 27, Juan Samuel 17, Felipe Crespo 2.
Second base: Tomas Perez 75, Domingo Cedeno 62, Tilson Brito 18, Felipe Crespo 10, Miguel Cairo 9.
Third base: Ed Sprague 148, Tomas Perez 11, Domingo Cedeno 6, Felipe Crespo 4, Michael Huff 3.
Shortstop: Alex Gonzalez 147, Tilson Brito 5, Domingo Cedeno 5, Tomas Perez 5.
Outfield: Shawn Green 127, Otis Nixon 125, Joe Carter 115, Jacob Brumfield 83, Robert Perez 79, Juan Samuel 24, Michael Huff 9, Shannon Stewart 6.
Designated hitter: Carlos Delgado 108, Juan Samuel 24, Joe Carter 15, John Olerud 15, Ed Sprague 10, Jacob Brumfield 5, Tilson Brito 2, Robert Perez 2, Shawn Green 1.

TOP DRAFT CHOICES

1a. **Billy Koch,** RHP, Clemson University.
1b. **Joe Lawrence,** SS, Barbe H.S., Lake Charles, La.
1c. **Pete Tucci,** 1B-OF, Providence College.
2. **Brent Abernathy,** SS, The Lovett School, Atlanta.
3a. **Yan Lachapelle,** RHP, Montreal.
3b. **Clayton Andrews,** LHP, Seminole H.S., Largo, Fla.
4. **Ryan Stromsborg,** 2B, University of Southern California.
5. **John Bale,** LHP, University of Southern Missippippi.
6. **Mike Rodriguez,** C, Tarleton State University, Tex.
7. **Casey Blake,** 3B, Wichita State Univ.
8. **Davan Keathley,** LHP, Johansen H.S., Turlock, Calif.
9. **Sam Goure,** LHP, County H.S., Pueblo, Colo.
10. **Josh Phelps,** C, Lakeland H.S., Rathdrum, Idaho.

Toronto Blue Jays — **1997 SEASON**

ATLANTA BRAVES
NATIONAL LEAGUE EAST DIVISION

1997 BRAVES SCHEDULE

Home games shaded.
* — All-Star Game at Jacobs Field (Cleveland)
D — Day game (any game starting before 5 p.m.)

APRIL

SUN	MON	TUE	WED	THU	FRI	SAT
		1 HOU	2 HOU	3 HOU	4 CUB	5 CUB
6 CUB	D 7	8 HOU	9 HOU	10 HOU	11 D CUB	12 D CUB
13 D CUB	14 CIN	15 CIN	16 D CIN	17	18 COL	19 D COL
20 D COL	21	22 SF	23 D SF	24	25 SD	26 SD
27 D SD	28 LA	29 LA	30 CIN			

MAY

SUN	MON	TUE	WED	THU	FRI	SAT
				1 D CIN	2 PIT	3 PIT
4 D PIT	5 STL	6 STL	7 FLA	8 FLA	9 PIT	10 PIT
11 D PIT	12 PIT	13 FLA	14 FLA	15	16 STL	17 STL
18 STL	19 MON	20 MON	21 D MON	22	23 LA	24 LA
25 D LA	26 SD	27 SD	28	29 SF	30 SF	31 SF

JUNE

SUN	MON	TUE	WED	THU	FRI	SAT
1 SF	D 2 SD	3 SD	4 MON	5 D MON	6 SF	7 D SF
8 SF	D 9 COL	10 COL	11 D COL	12	13 D BAL	14 D BAL
15 D BAL	16 TOR	17 TOR	18 TOR	19	20 PHI	21 PHI
22 PHI	23 NYM	24 NYM	25 D NYM	26 PHI	27 PHI	28 PHI
29 PHI	30 NYY					

JULY

SUN	MON	TUE	WED	THU	FRI	SAT
		1 NYY	2 D NYY	3 MON	4 MON	5 MON
6 MON	D 7	8 © 9	10 NYM	11 NYM	12 D NYM	
13 NYM	14 PHI	15 PHI	16 COL	17 COL	18 LA	19 LA
20 D LA	21 LA	22 D CUB	23 CUB	24 D	25 CIN	26 D CIN
27 CIN	28 CUB	29 CUB	30 CUB	31 FLA		

AUGUST

SUN	MON	TUE	WED	THU	FRI	SAT
					1 FLA	2 FLA
3 D FLA	4 FLA	5 FLA	6 PIT	7 STL	8 STL	9 D STL
10 D FLA	11 FLA	12 PIT	13 PIT	14	15 STL	16 D STL
17 STL	18 HOU	19 HOU	20 HOU	21	22 CIN	23 D CIN
24 D CIN	25	26 HOU	27 HOU	28 HOU	29 BOS	30 D BOS
31 BOS						

SEPTEMBER

SUN	MON	TUE	WED	THU	FRI	SAT
	1 DET	2 DET	3 DET	4 D SD	5 D SD	6 SD
7 SD	D 8	9 LA	10 LA	11	12 COL	13 COL
14 D COL	15 SF	16 D SF	17 NYM	18 NYM	19 MON	20 MON
21 MON	22 MON	23 PHI	24 PHI	25 PHI	26 NYM	27 D NYM
28 D NYM	29	30				

1997 SEASON
CLUB DIRECTORY

Owner
R.E. Turner III
Chairman of the board of directors
William C. Bartholomay
President
Stanley H. Kasten
Exec. v.p. and general manager
John Schuerholz
Sr. v.p. and asst. to the president
Henry L. Aaron
Senior v.p., administration
Bob Wolfe
V.p., dir. of marketing and broadcasting
Wayne Long
Vice president
Lee Douglas
Vice president of development
Janet Marie Smith
Assistant general manager
Dean Taylor
Dir. of scouting and player development
Paul Snyder
Director of minor league operations
Deric Ladnier
Assistant director of scouting
Dayton Moore
Baseball operations assistant
Tyrone Brooks
Special assistants to general manager
Bill Lajoie, Brian Murphy
Special assistants to g.m./player dev.
Willie Stargell, Jose Martinez
Dir. of team travel and equipment manager
Bill Acree
Executive assistant
June Cornillaud
Sr. dir. of promotions and civic affairs
Miles McRea
Controller
Chip Moore
Director of ticket sales
Paul Adams
Dir. of minor league business operations
Bruce Baldwin
Dir. of stadium operations and security
Larry Bowman
Director of Braves Foundation
Danny Goodwin
Field director
Ed Mangan
Director of ticket operations
Ed Newman

Team counsel
David Payne
Dir. of advertising
Amy Richter
Dir. of community rel. and fan dev.
Dexter Santos
Director of sports human resources
Lisa Stricklin
Director of public relations
Jim Schultz
Media relations managers
Glen Serra, Thurman Brooks
Trainer
Dave Pursley
Assistant trainer
Jeff Porter
Club physician
Dr. David T. Watson
Associate physicians
Dr. John Cantwell, Dr. Robert Crow, Dr. Norman Elliott
Club orthopedists
Dr. Joe Chandler, Dr. Marvin Royster
Major league scouts
Scott Nethery, Fred Shaffer, Bill Wight, Bobby Wine
National supervisors
Roy Clark, Bob Wadsworth
Regional supervisors
Butch Baccala, Harold Cronin, John Flannery
International supervisor
Bill Clark
Area supervisors
Matt Anderson, Stu Cann, Sherard Clinkscales, Phil Dale, Tom Ealy, Rene Francisco, Rod Gilbreath, John Hagemann, J. Harrison, Brian Kohlscheen, Scott Littlefield, Jim Martz, Marco Paddy, Julian Perez, Rolando Petit, John Ramey, Alan Regier, Malcolm Seibert, John Stewart, Reyes Vizcaino
Scouts
Mike Baker, Ray Belanger, Steve Bishop, Jim Buchert, Jorge Calvo, Joe Caputo, Bob Dunning, Rob English, Edgar Fernandez, Pedro Flores, Felix Francisco, Bill Froberg, Ruben Garcia, Ralph Garr, Gil Garrido, Luis Herrera, Bob Irwin, Bob Isabelle, Al Kubski, Jose Leon, William Marcot, Giorgio Moretti, Dario Paulino, Ernie Pedersen, Charlie Smith, Marvin Throneberry, Carlos Torres, Bob Turzilli, Giovanni Viceisza

MINOR LEAGUE AFFILIATES

Class	Team	League	Manager
AAA	Richmond	International	Bill Dancy
AA	Greenville	Southern	Randy Ingle
A	Durham	Carolina	Paul Runge
A	Macon	South Atlantic	Brian Snitker
A	Eugene	Northwest	Jim Saul
Rookie	Danville	Appalachian	To be announced
Rookie	Gulf Coast Braves	Gulf Coast	Frank Howard

BROADCAST INFORMATION
Radio: WSB-AM (750).
TV: TBS-TV (Channel 17).
Cable TV: SportsSouth.

SPRING TRAINING
Ballpark (city): Municipal Stadium (West Palm Beach, Fla.).
Ticket information: 407-683-6100.

SPRING TRAINING ROSTER

Manager—Bobby Cox (6).
Coaches—Jim Beauchamp (37), Pat Corrales (39), Bobby Dews, Clarence Jones (28), Leo Mazzone (54), Jimy Williams (22), Ned Yost (42).

No.	PITCHERS	B/T	Ht./Wt.	Born	1996 clubs
26	Bielecki, Mike	R/R	6-3/200	7-31-59	Atlanta
51	Borbon, Pedro	L/L	6-1/205	11-15-67	Atlanta, Greenville
50	Borowski, Joe	R/R	6-2/225	5-4-71	Richmond, Atlanta
	Brow, Scott	R/R	6-3/200	3-17-69	Syracuse, Toronto
	Byrd, Paul	R/R	6-1/185	12-3-70	New York N.L., Norfolk
52	Clontz, Brad	R/R	6-1/180	4-25-71	Atlanta
47	Glavine, Tom	L/L	6-1/185	3-25-66	Atlanta
34	Hartgraves, Dean	R/L	6-0/185	8-12-66	Tucson, Houston, Richmond, Atlanta
34	Harvey, Bryan	R/R	6-2/212	6-2-63	California
	LeRoy, John	R/R	6-3/175	4-19-75	Durham, Greenville
31	Maddux, Greg	R/R	6-0/175	4-14-66	Atlanta
	Millwood, Kevin	R/R	6-4/205	12-24-74	Durham
15	Neagle, Denny	L/L	6-2/225	9-13-68	Pittsburgh, Atlanta
	Perez, Yorkis	L/L	6-0/180	9-30-67	Florida, Charlotte
29	Smoltz, John	R/R	6-3/185	5-15-67	Atlanta
36	Wade, Terrell	L/L	6-3/205	1-25-73	Atlanta
	Walker, Jamie	L/L	6-2/190	7-1-71	Jackson
43	Wohlers, Mark	R/R	6-4/207	1-23-70	Atlanta

No.	CATCHERS	B/T	Ht./Wt.	Born	1996 clubs
8	Lopez, Javy	R/R	6-3/200	11-5-70	Atlanta
12	Perez, Eddie	R/R	6-1/175	5-4-68	Atlanta

No.	INFIELDERS	B/T	Ht./Wt.	Born	1996 clubs
2	Belliard, Rafael	R/R	5-6/160	10-24-61	Atlanta
4	Blauser, Jeff	R/R	6-1/180	11-8-65	Atlanta
11	Giovanola, Ed	L/R	5-10/170	3-4-69	Richmond, Atlanta
14	Graffanino, Tony	R/R	6-1/175	6-6-72	Richmond, Atlanta
10	Jones, Chipper	B/R	6-3/195	4-24-72	Atlanta
20	Lemke, Mark	B/R	5-9/167	8-13-65	Atlanta
	Malloy, Marty	L/R	5-10/160	4-6-72	Greenville, Richmond
27	McGriff, Fred	L/L	6-3/215	10-31-63	Atlanta
16	Mordecai, Mike	R/R	5-11/175	12-13-67	Atlanta, Richmond
	Simon, Randall	L/L	6-0/180	5-26-75	Greenville
61	Smith, Bobby	R/R	6-3/190	5-10-74	Richmond

No.	OUTFIELDERS	B/T	Ht./Wt.	Born	1996 clubs
	Bautista, Danny	R/R	5-11/170	5-24-72	Detroit, Atlanta
24	Dye, Jermaine	R/R	6-4/210	1-28-74	Richmond, Atlanta
9	Grissom, Marquis	R/R	5-11/190	4-17-67	Atlanta
66	Hollins, Damon	R/L	5-11/180	6-12-74	Richmond
25	Jones, Andruw	R/R	6-1/185	4-23-77	Durham, Greenville, Richmond, Atlanta
23	Justice, David	L/L	6-3/200	4-14-66	Atlanta
18	Klesko, Ryan	L/L	6-3/220	6-12-71	Atlanta
	Lewis, Marc	R/R	6-2/175	5-20-75	Macon, Durham
	Monds, Wonderful	R/R	6-3/190	1-11-73	Greenville, Bradenton Braves

BALLPARK INFORMATION

Ballpark (capacity, surface)
Turner Field (50,528, grass)

Address
P.O. Box 4064
Atlanta, GA 30302

Business phone
404-522-7630

Ticket information
404-522-7630

Ticket prices
$30 (dugout level)
$25 (club level)
$20 (field level, terrace level)
$15 (field pavilion, terrace pavilion)
$10 (upper level)
$5 (upper pavilion)
$1 (skyline)

Field dimensions (from home plate)
To left field at foul line, 335 feet
To center field, 401 feet
To right field at foul line, 330 feet

First game played
Scheduled for April 4, 1997

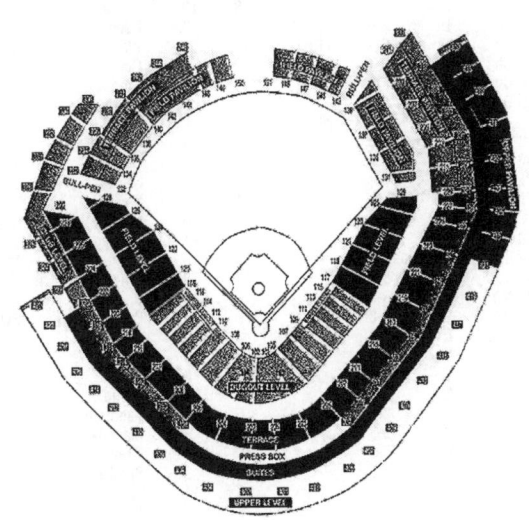

1997 SEASON Atlanta Braves

DAY BY DAY

Date	Opp.	Res.	Score	(inn.*)	Hits	Opp. hits	Winning pitcher	Losing pitcher	Save	Record	Pos.	GB
4-1	S.F.	W	10-8		9	12	Maddux	Leiter	Borbon	1-0	T1st	...
4-3	S.F.	W	15-2		16	6	Glavine	VanLandingham		2-0	1st	+1
4-4	S.F.	L	1-7		7	9	Watson	Smoltz		2-1	T1st	...
4-5	St.L.	L	4-5	(14)	11	10	Bailey	Bielecki	Eckersley	2-2	T2nd	1
4-6	St.L.	L	2-3	(12)	7	7	Parrett	Clontz		2-3	T2nd	1
4-7	St.L.	W	13-3		10	6	Schmidt	Busby		3-3	2nd	1
4-8	At L.A.	L	0-1		3	5	Nomo	Glavine		3-4	3rd	2
4-9	At L.A.	W	3-1		7	5	Smoltz	Astacio	Wohlers	4-4	T2nd	1¹/₂
4-10	At L.A.	L	2-9		8	12	Candiotti	Avery		4-5	3rd	1¹/₂
4-11	At S.D.	L	1-2		4	5	Ashby	Maddux	Hoffman	4-6	3rd	2¹/₂
4-12	At S.D.	W	5-3		9	9	Schmidt	Bergman	Wohlers	5-6	T2nd	2¹/₂
4-13	At S.D.	L	2-6		8	11	Hamilton	Glavine	Bochtler	5-7	3rd	2¹/₂
4-14	At S.D.	W	4-0		11	2	Smoltz	Valenzuela		6-7	T2nd	1¹/₂
4-16	Fla.	W	5-2		13	6	Avery	Brown	Wohlers	7-7	2nd	1¹/₂
4-17	Fla.	W	4-2		9	6	Maddux	Burkett	Wohlers	8-7	2nd	¹/₂
4-18	Fla.	L	3-5		8	9	Hammond	Glavine	Nen	8-8	T2nd	¹/₂
4-19	S.D.	W	7-1		8	3	Smoltz	Hamilton		9-8	2nd	¹/₂
4-20	S.D.	W	6-5		10	12	McMichael	Bochtler	Wohlers	10-8	2nd	¹/₂
4-21	S.D.	L	1-2	(15)	6	14	Worrell	Thobe	Bochtler	10-9	2nd	1¹/₂
4-22	L.A.	W	4-1		8	8	Maddux	Candiotti		11-9	2nd	1¹/₂
4-23	L.A.	L	2-3		6	6	Osuna	Clontz	Worrell	11-10	2nd	2¹/₂
4-24	At S.F.	W	8-3		14	7	Smoltz	Watson		12-10	2nd	2¹/₂
4-25	At S.F.	L	0-8		4	6	Gardner	Schmidt		12-11	T2nd	3¹/₂
4-26	At St.L.	W	6-1		10	8	Avery	An. Benes		13-11	T2nd	3¹/₂
4-27	At St.L.	W	7-2		11	9	Maddux	Osborne		14-11	T2nd	2¹/₂
4-29	At St.L.	W	4-1		5	7	Glavine	Stottlemyre	Wohlers	15-11	2nd	2
4-30	At Hou.	W	7-5		16	8	Smoltz	Jones	McMichael	16-11	2nd	1¹/₂
5-1	At Hou.	L	0-3		3	10	Hampton	Avery		16-12	2nd	2
5-3	Phi.	L	3-6		11	8	Mulholland	Maddux	Bottalico	16-13	3rd	2
5-4	Phi.	W	6-3		12	8	McMichael	Ryan	Clontz	17-13	T2nd	2
5-5	Phi.	W	11-8		18	8	Smoltz	Williams		18-13	2nd	2
5-6	Col.	W	4-1		12	6	Avery	M. Thompson		19-13	2nd	2
5-7	Col.	W	6-5	(10)	8	8	Clontz	Leskanic		20-13	2nd	2
5-8	Col.	W	5-1		9	6	Glavine	Reynoso		21-13	2nd	2
5-10	At Phi.	W	11-0		18	4	Smoltz	Mulholland		22-13	2nd	1¹/₂
5-11	At Phi.	W	11-3		19	10	Avery	Mimbs		23-13	2nd	1¹/₂
5-12	At Phi.	L	0-6		4	6	Grace	Maddux		23-14	2nd	2¹/₂
5-13	Pit.	W	9-3		14	7	Glavine	Darwin		24-14	2nd	2¹/₂
5-14	Pit.	W	7-3		14	9	Smoltz	Wagner		25-14	2nd	1¹/₂
5-15	Pit.	L	0-3		5	5	Neagle	Avery		25-15	2nd	1¹/₂
5-17	Cin.	W	8-2		10	10	Maddux	Smiley		26-15	2nd	¹/₂
5-18	Cin.	W	2-1		4	8	Clontz	Ruffin	Wohlers	27-15	2nd	¹/₂
5-19	Cin.	W	9-5		16	7	Smoltz	Schourek	Wohlers	28-15	1st	+¹/₂
5-20	Chi.	W	18-1		17	7	Avery	Castillo		29-15	1st	+1¹/₂
5-21	Chi.	L	2-4		7	10	Telemaco	Wohlers	Patterson	29-16	1st	+1¹/₂
5-22	Chi.	W	9-4		9	8	Glavine	Bullinger		30-16	1st	+1¹/₂
5-24	At Pit.	W	5-3		13	10	Smoltz	Darwin	Wohlers	31-16	1st	+2¹/₂
5-25	At Pit.	L	2-6		8	8	Neagle	Avery		31-17	1st	+2¹/₂
5-26	At Pit.	W	6-3	(13)	11	12	Wade	Miceli	Bielecki	32-17	1st	+3¹/₂
5-27	At Chi.	W	9-1		9	6	Glavine	Telemaco		33-17	1st	+4¹/₂
5-29	At Chi.	W	2-0		5	4	Smoltz	Trachsel		34-17	1st	+5
5-31	At Cin.	W	9-1		15	5	Avery	Schourek		35-17	1st	+5
6-1	At Cin.	L	2-3		6	8	Portugal	Maddux	Brantley	35-18	1st	+4
6-2	At Cin.	W	6-2		7	11	Glavine	Smiley		36-18	1st	+5
6-3	N.Y.	W	5-4		6	9	Clontz	MacDonald	Wohlers	37-18	1st	+5¹/₂
6-4	N.Y.	L	6-12		11	16	Wilson	Schmidt		37-19	1st	+5¹/₂
6-5	N.Y.	W	8-6		9	10	McMichael	Mlicki	Wohlers	38-19	1st	+5¹/₂
6-7	At Col.	L	8-19		12	21	Painter	Bielecki		38-20	1st	+4¹/₂
6-8	At Col.	L	12-13		18	16	Holmes	McMichael	Ruffin	38-21	1st	+4¹/₂
6-9	At Col.	W	8-3		12	8	Smoltz	M. Thompson		39-21	1st	+5¹/₂
6-10	At N.Y.	L	3-8		16	14	B. Jones	Avery		39-22	1st	+5¹/₂
6-11	At N.Y.	W	4-3	(13)	9	14	Borbon	Byrd	Wade	40-22	1st	+5¹/₂
6-12	At N.Y.	L	2-3		8	9	Clark	Maddux	J. Franco	40-23	1st	+4¹/₂
6-13	L.A.	L	3-6		9	10	Valdes	Glavine	Worrell	40-24	1st	+4
6-14	L.A.	W	3-1		8	6	Smoltz	Astacio	Wohlers	41-24	1st	+4
6-15	L.A.	L	2-6		9	6	Nomo	Avery	Worrell	41-25	1st	+3
6-16	L.A.	L	2-3		6	5	Candiotti	Schmidt	Worrell	41-26	1st	+3
6-17	S.D.	W	9-3		10	5	Maddux	Bergman		42-26	1st	+3
6-18	S.D.	W	5-3		10	10	Clontz	Hamilton	Wohlers	43-26	1st	+3
6-19	S.D.	W	5-1		11	2	Smoltz	Tewksbury		44-26	1st	+4
6-21	S.F.	W	8-7	(11)	9	14	Wade	Beck		45-26	1st	+3¹/₂
6-22	S.F.	W	6-0		8	4	Maddux	Gardner		46-26	1st	+4¹/₂

Date	Opp.	Res.	Score	(inn.*)	Hits	Opp. hits	Winning pitcher	Losing pitcher	Save	Record	Pos.	GB
23	S.F.	W	1-0		6	3	Glavine	Fernandez	Wohlers	47-26	1st	+4½
24	St.L.	L	2-9		9	12	An. Benes	Smoltz		47-27	1st	+3½
25	St.L.	W	4-3		5	9	Schmidt	Stottlemyre	Wohlers	48-27	1st	+3½
26	St.L.	L	7-11		8	17	Al. Benes	Avery		48-28	1st	+3½
27	St.L.	W	3-0		8	3	Maddux	Morgan	Wohlers	49-28	1st	+4
28	At Fla.	L	0-2		9	5	Leiter	Glavine	Nen	49-29	1st	+4
29	At Fla.	L	3-5		8	11	Rapp	Smoltz		49-30	1st	+3
30	At Fla.	W	5-4		10	8	Clontz	Burkett	Wohlers	50-30	1st	+3
1	At Mon.	W	7-2		8	6	Avery	Rueter		51-30	1st	+4
2	At Mon.	L	1-5		3	11	Cormier	Maddux		51-31	1st	+3
3	At Mon.	W	3-1		8	3	Glavine	Scott	Wohlers	52-31	1st	+4
4	Hou.	L	2-5		9	13	Reynolds	Smoltz	Hernandez	52-32	1st	+4
5	Hou.	L	1-7		9	8	Kile	Schmidt		52-33	1st	+4
6	Hou.	W	4-2		9	7	Bielecki	Hampton		53-33	1st	+5
7	Hou.	W	9-1		10	10	Maddux	Wall		54-33	1st	+5
11	Fla.	L	8-9		14	16	Burkett	Avery	Nen	54-34	1st	+5
12	Fla.	W	6-3		8	8	Glavine	Leiter	Wohlers	55-34	1st	+6
13	Fla.	W	3-0		6	2	Smoltz	Brown		56-34	1st	+7
14	Fla.	W	15-10		14	13	McMichael	Perez		57-34	1st	+7
15	Mon.	W	5-4		11	5	Maddux	Manuel	Wohlers	58-34	1st	+8
16	Mon.	W	3-2		10	10	Wohlers	Scott		59-34	1st	+9
18	At Hou.	W	3-2		12	7	Smoltz	Jones	Wohlers	60-34	1st	+9
19	At Hou.	L	6-7		9	10	Kile	Woodall	Wagner	60-35	1st	+8
20	At Hou.	L	1-2		7	4	Wagner	Maddux		60-36	1st	+8
21	At Hou.	L	3-4	(10)	8	9	Hernandez	McMichael		60-37	1st	+7
22	At St.L.	W	8-6		11	11	McMichael	Mathews	Wohlers	61-37	1st	+7½
23	At St.L.	W	3-2		8	5	Smoltz	Stottlemyre	Wohlers	62-37	1st	+8½
24	At St.L.	W	4-1		7	2	Wade	Al. Benes	McMichael	63-37	1st	+9½
25	At S.F.	L	3-4		3	9	Watson	Maddux	Beck	63-38	1st	+8½
26	At S.F.	W	2-1		6	8	Glavine	Leiter	Wohlers	64-38	1st	+8½
27	At S.F.	L	5-7		7	9	Gardner	Woodall	Beck	64-39	1st	+8½
28	At S.F.	L	3-10		7	11	Estes	Smoltz	Beck	64-40	1st	+8½
30	At S.D.	L	1-2		7	8	Valenzuela	Maddux	Hoffman	64-41	1st	+7
31	At S.D.	W	7-4		11	10	Glavine	Tewksbury	Wohlers	65-41	1st	+7
1	At S.D.	W	3-2		11	6	Bielecki	Worrell	Wohlers	66-41	1st	+8
2	At L.A.	L	1-2		7	9	Radinsky	Smoltz	Guthrie	66-42	1st	+7
3	At L.A.	W	5-3	(18)	12	11	Woodall	Martinez		67-42	1st	+7
4	At L.A.	W	6-4		14	9	Borbon	Guthrie	Wohlers	68-42	1st	+7
6	Phi.	W	10-4		16	3	Bielecki	Springer		69-42	1st	+7
7	Phi.	W	14-1	(8)	18	6	Smoltz	Munoz		70-42	1st	+7
8	Phi.	L	1-4		4	12	Beech	Maddux	Bottalico	70-43	1st	+7
9	Col.	L	4-6		8	9	Wright	Glavine	Ruffin	70-44	1st	+7
10	Col.	L	7-9	(10)	8	9	S. Reed	Wohlers	Ruffin	70-45	1st	+7
11	Col.	W	4-1		6	5	Smoltz	Freeman	Wohlers	71-45	1st	+7
13†	At Phi.	W	2-0		5	8	Maddux	Hunter		72-45		
13‡	At Phi.	W	5-2		8	4	Hartgraves	Beech	Wohlers	73-45	1st	+7
14	At Phi.	L	1-4		9	8	West	Glavine	Bottalico	73-46	1st	+7
15	At Phi.	W	8-5		14	13	Wade	Schilling		74-46	1st	+7½
16	Pit.	W	5-4		12	8	Smoltz	Neagle	Wohlers	75-46	1st	+8½
17	Pit.	W	7-1		7	5	Bielecki	Ruebel		76-46	1st	+9½
18	Pit.	W	2-1	(14)	12	9	Borowski	Cordova		77-46	1st	+9½
20	Cin.	W	4-1		10	5	Glavine	Burba	Wohlers	78-46	1st	+11
21	Cin.	W	4-3		10	10	Borbon	Brantley		79-46	1st	+12
22	Cin.	L	2-3	(13)	6	11	Carrasco	Borowski	Brantley	79-47	1st	+11
23	Chi.	W	4-3		10	5	Maddux	Trachsel	Wohlers	80-47	1st	+11
24	Chi.	W	6-5		11	8	Clontz	Casian		81-47	1st	+11
25	Chi.	L	2-3		7	11	Foster	Wohlers	Wendell	81-48	1st	+11
27	At Pit.	L	2-3		6	7	Neagle	Smoltz	Plesac	81-49	1st	+11
28	At Pit.	W	9-4		13	6	Wade	Loaiza		82-49	1st	+11
29	At Pit.	W	5-1		9	7	Maddux	Lieber	Wohlers	83-49	1st	+12
30†	At Chi.	L	2-3		3	6	Foster	Glavine	Patterson	83-50		
30‡	At Chi.	W	6-5		12	10	Borowski	Bottenfield	Wohlers	84-50	1st	+12½
31	At Chi.	L	0-12		3	12	Castillo	Neagle	Adams	84-51	1st	+11½
1	At Chi.	L	1-2	(12)	8	6	Campbell	Borowski		84-52	1st	+10½
2	At Cin.	L	6-7		14	9	Shaw	McMichael	Brantley	84-53	1st	+9½
3	At Cin.	L	1-5		1	9	Burba	Bielecki	Shaw	84-54	1st	+8½
4	At Cin.	L	6-12		8	15	Salkeld	Glavine		84-55	1st	+7½
6	N.Y.	W	8-7		14	12	Wohlers	Henry		85-55	1st	+8
7	N.Y.	W	6-1		9	7	Smoltz	B. Jones		86-55	1st	+8
8	N.Y.	L	2-6		5	10	Clark	Maddux		86-56	1st	+8
10	At Col.	L	8-9		15	13	Holmes	Clontz	Ruffin	86-57	1st	+8½
11	At Col.	L	5-6		10	8	Wright	Neagle	Swift	86-58	1st	+7½
12	At Col.	L	8-16		12	17	Burke	Smoltz		86-59	1st	+6½
13	At N.Y.	L	4-6		11	12	DiPoto	Borowski	Wallace	86-60	1st	+5½
14	At N.Y.	L	5-6	(12)	13	11	Wallace	Borowski		86-61	1st	+4½

Date	Opp.	Res.	Score	(inn.*)	Hits	Opp. hits	Winning pitcher	Losing pitcher	Save	Record	Pos.	GB
9-15	At N.Y.	W	3-2		8	10	Glavine	Wilson	Wohlers	87-61	1st	+5½
9-16	At N.Y.	W	5-2		8	7	Neagle	Harnisch		88-61	1st	+6
9-17	Hou.	W	5-4		8	11	Smoltz	Kile	Wohlers	89-61	1st	+6
9-18	Hou.	W	6-2		13	6	Maddux	Hampton		90-61	1st	+6
9-19	Mon.	L	1-5		6	10	Urbina	Wohlers		90-62	1st	+5
9-20	Mon.	W	3-2		10	6	Glavine	Leiper	Wohlers	91-62	1st	+6
9-21	Mon.	W	5-4		8	11	Neagle	Daal	Wohlers	92-62	1st	+7
9-22	Mon.	W	8-2		15	8	Smoltz	Fassero		93-62	1st	+8
9-23	Mon.	W	3-1		8	5	Maddux	Leiter	Bielecki	94-62	1st	+9
9-24	At Fla.	L	1-12		10	21	Rapp	Avery		94-63	1st	+8
9-25	At Fla.	L	0-3		7	5	Brown	Glavine	Nen	94-64	1st	+8
9-26	At Fla.	L	1-7		6	11	Leiter	Neagle		94-65	1st	+7
9-27	At Mon.	W	6-4		13	7	Smoltz	Fassero	Wohlers	95-65	1st	+8
9-28	At Mon.	W	4-0		6	6	Woodall	Leiter		96-65	1st	+9
9-29	At Mon.	L	3-6		9	8	Alvarez	Avery	Rojas	96-66	1st	+8

Monthly records: April (16-11), May (19-6), June (15-13), July (15-11), August (19-10), September (12-15).
*Innings, if other than nine. †First game of doubleheader. ‡Second game of doubleheader.

HIGHLIGHTS

High point: The Braves got off to an uncharacteristically fast start, playing their best ball in the first half of the season. Hitting .302 in May, they set an Atlanta record with 19 victories and had a five-game lead in the N.L. East at the end of the month.

Low point: The Braves started September by losing 10 of their first 12 games and wound up with their first losing month (12-15) since April 1993. Among the losses were three-game sweeps by the Reds, Rockies and Marlins, the only times Atlanta was swept all season.

Turning point: The Braves played eight of their last 11 games against the second-place Expos and won six of them. They clinched the division by beating Montreal, 8-2, on September 22.

Most valuable player: Outfielder Marquis Grissom. He finished among the league's top 10 in five offensive categories and set personal highs with 23 homers and 207 hits. His hit total was the club's best since 1974. Grissom also set a franchise record with 671 at-bats.

Most valuable pitcher: Starter John Smoltz. He won the Cy Young after leading the majors in wins and strikeouts and the league in innings pitched and winning percentage. His 24 victories set an Atlanta record and his 276 strikeouts set a modern-era franchise record.

Most improved player: Outfielder Ryan Klesko. Given an opportunity to be an everyday player for the first time, he responded with a club-leading 34 homers and drove in 93 runs. Klesko hit an Atlanta-record 10 homers in April.

Most pleasant surprise: Outfielder Jermaine Dye. With only 36 games of experience in Class AAA, the 22-year-old Dye replaced the injured David Justice in right field in May and started with a bang, hitting a home run on his first major league swing. In 98 games, he hit .281 with 12 homers and 37 RBIs.

Biggest disappointment: Reliever Brad Clontz. After fashioning a solid rookie season in 1995, the side-arming Clontz was inconsistent and his ERA jumped by more than two runs. Perhaps he was overworked; he led the league with 81 appearances.

Key injuries: Outfielder David Justice was off to a solid start before being lost for the season with a shoulder injury in May. Shortstop Jeff Blauser missed nine weeks after suffering a broken left hand on July 15. Lefthander Steve Avery missed most of the second half with a strained side muscle.

Notable: Glavine (106) and Maddux (105) have the most wins of any major league pitchers since 1991. . . . Wohlers saved 39 games to break Gene Garber's single-season team record. . . . On May 17 against Cincinnati, Dye became the first Brave since Chuck Tanner in 1955 to homer in his first major league at-bat. . . . Chipper Jones tied an Atlanta franchise record by reaching base safely in 34 consecutive games. . . . On May 11 at Philadelphia, Jeff Blauser became the first Brave since Orlando Cepeda in 1970 to drive in seven runs in one game. . . . On August 22 against Cincinnati, Andruw Jones (19 years, 3 months, 30 days) became the youngest major leaguer in 35 years to hit two homers in one game.
—BILL ZACK

RECORDS

1996 regular-season record: 96-66 (1st in N.L. East); 56-25 at home; 40-41 on road; 32-20 vs. East; 38-23 vs. Central; 26-23 vs. West; 27-20 vs. lefthanded starters; 69-46 vs. righthanded starters; 79-52 on grass; 17-14 on turf; 30-22 in daytime; 66-44 at night; 26-26 in one-run games; 6-8 in extra-inning games; 1-0-1 in doubleheaders.

Team record past five years: 456-288 (.613, ranks 1st in league in that span).

TEAM LEADERS

Batting average: Chipper Jones (.309).
At-bats: Marquis Grissom (671).
Runs: Chipper Jones (114).
Hits: Marquis Grissom (207).
Total bases: Marquis Grissom (328).
Doubles: Fred McGriff (37).
Triples: Marquis Grissom (10).
Home runs: Ryan Klesko (34).
Runs batted in: Chipper Jones (110).
Stolen bases: Marquis Grissom (28).

Slugging percentage: Ryan Klesko (.530).
On-base percentage: Chipper Jones (.393).
Wins: John Smoltz (24).
Earned-run average: Greg Maddux (2.72).
Complete games: John Smoltz (6).
Shutouts: John Smoltz (2).
Saves: Mark Wohlers (39).
Innings pitched: John Smoltz (253.2).
Strikeouts: John Smoltz (276).

GAMES BY POSITION

Catcher: Javy Lopez 135, Eddie Perez 5, Joe Ayrault 7.
First base: Fred McGriff 158, Tyler Houston 11, Eddie Perez 7, Ryan Klesko 2, Mike Mordecai 1.
Second base: Mark Lemke 133, Mike Mordecai 20, Tony Graffanino 18, Rafael Belliard 15, Ed Giovanola 5.
Third base: Chipper Jones 118, Terry Pendleton 41, Mike Mordecai 10, Ed Giovanola 6, Tyler Houston 0.
Shortstop: Jeff Blauser 79, Rafael Belliard 63, Chipper Jones 38, Ed Giovanola 25, Mike Mordecai 6, Pablo Martinez 1.
Outfield: Marquis Grissom 158, Ryan Klesko 144, Jermaine Dye 92, Dave Justice 40, Andruw Jones 29, Dwight Smith 29, Mark Whiten 29, Jerome Walton 28, Danny Bautista 14, Luis Polonia 7, Tyler Houston 1, Chipper Jones 1.

TOP DRAFT CHOICES

1a. **A.J. Zapp,** 1B, Center Grove H.S., Greenwood, Ind.
1b. **Jason Marquis,** RHP, Tottenville H.S., Staten Island, N.Y.
2. **Eric Munson,** C, Mount Carmel H.S., San Diego.
3. **Junior Brignac,** OF, Cleveland H.S., Reseda, Calif.
4. **Joe Nelson,** RHP, U. of San Francisco.
5. **Josh Pugh,** C, Henry Clay H.S., Lexington, Ky.
6. **Shawn Onley,** RHP, Rice University.
7. **Mark DeRosa,** 3B, U. of Pennsylvania.
8. **A.D. Thorpe,** SS, Southern H.S., Durham, N.C.
9. **Nathan Harden,** RHP, Dripping Springs (Tex.) H.S.
10. **Winston Lee,** RHP, Glendale (Ariz.) C.C.

CHICAGO CUBS
NATIONAL LEAGUE CENTRAL DIVISION

1997 CUBS SCHEDULE

Home games shaded.
* — All-Star Game at Jacobs Field (Cleveland)
D — Day game (any game starting before 5 p.m.)

APRIL
SUN	MON	TUE	WED	THU	FRI	SAT
		1 D FLA	2 FLA	3 FLA	4 ATL	5 ATL
6 D ATL	7	8 FLA	9 FLA	10 D FLA	11 D ATL	12 D ATL
13 D ATL	14	15 D COL	16 D COL	17	18 NYM	19 D NYM
20 D NYM	21 NYM	22 MON	23 MON	24 PIT	25 PIT	26 D PIT
27 D PIT	28 MON	29 MON	30 COL			

MAY
SUN	MON	TUE	WED	THU	FRI	SAT
				1 D COL	2 LA	3 LA
4 D LA	5	6 SD	7 SD	8 D SF	9 D SF	10 D SF
11 D SF	12	13 D LA	14 D LA	15 D SD	16 D SD	17 SF
18 D SF	19 SF	20 D PHI	21 D PHI	22	23 CIN	24 D CIN
25 CIN	26 D PIT	27 D PIT	28 PIT	29 CIN	30 D CIN	31 D CIN

JUNE
SUN	MON	TUE	WED	THU	FRI	SAT
1 D CIN	2 PIT	3 PIT	4 PHI	5 PHI	6 MON	7 MON
8 D MON	9 MON	10 NYM	11 D NYM	12	13 D MIL	14 D MIL
15 MIL	16 D CWS	17 CWS	18 CWS	19	20 D HOU	21 D HOU
22 D HOU	23 STL	24 STL	25 STL	26 HOU	27 D HOU	28 D HOU
29 HOU	30 D KC					

JULY
SUN	MON	TUE	WED	THU	FRI	SAT
		1 D KC	2 D KC	3 PHI	4 PHI	5 PHI
6 D PHI	7	8 ° 9	10 D STL	11 STL	12 D STL
13 D STL	14 HOU	15 D HOU	16 NYM	17 D NYM	18 COL	19 D COL
20 D COL	21	22 ATL	23 D ATL	24 COL	25 COL	26 COL
27 D COL	28 ATL	29 ATL	30 ATL	31 LA		

AUGUST
SUN	MON	TUE	WED	THU	FRI	SAT
					1 D LA	2 D LA
3	4	5 SF	6 D SF	7 D SF	8 SD	9 SD
10 D SD	11 LA	12 LA	13 D SF	14 D SF	15 SD	16 SD
17 D SD	18	19 FLA	20 FLA	21	22 D MON	23 D MON
24 D MON	25 FLA	26 FLA	27 D FLA	28 D FLA	29 CLE	30 CLE
31 D CLE						

SEPTEMBER
SUN	MON	TUE	WED	THU	FRI	SAT
	1 D MIN	2 MIN	3 D MIN	4	5 NYM	6 D NYM
7 D NYM	8 CIN	9 CIN	10	11	12 PIT	13 PIT
14 D PIT	15 D CIN	16 CIN	17 D STL	18 STL	19 PHI	20 D PHI
21 D PHI	22	HOU	HOU	25 STL	26 STL	27 D STL
28 D STL						

1997 SEASON
CLUB DIRECTORY

Board of directors
James Dowdle
Andrew B. MacPhail
Andrew McKenna
President and chief executive officer
Andrew B. MacPhail
General manager
Ed Lynch
Director, baseball administration
Scott Nelson
Special assistants to the g.m.
Larry Himes
Ken Kravec
Special player consultant
Hugh Alexander
Major league advance scout
Keith Champion
Traveling secretary
Jimmy Bank
Director, minor leagues
David Wilder
Field coordinator
Tom Gamboa
Hitting coordinator
Gary Matthews
Pitching coordinator
Lester Strode
Roving infield instructor
Sandy Alomar
Roving outfield instructor
Jimmy Piersall
Equipment manager
Michael Burkhart
Director, scouting
Jim Hendry
Regional scouting supervisors
John Stockstill
Tony DeMacio
Larry Maxie
Latin American coordinator
Oneri Fleita
Director, media relations
Sharon Pannozzo
Media information coordinator
Chuck Wasserstrom
Media relations assistant
Wanda Taylor
Team physicians
John Marquardt, M.D.
Michael Schafer, M.D.

Head trainer
David Tumbas
Assistant trainer
Brian McCann
Strength coordinator
Bruce Hammel
Equipment manager
Yosh Kawano
Assistant equipment manager
Dana Noeltner
Visiting clubhouse manager
Tom Hellmann
Exec. v.p., business operations
Mark McGuire
Dir., minor league business operations
Connie Kowal
V.p., marketing and broadcasting
John McDonough
Director, promotions and advertising
Jay Blunk
Manager, broadcasting/special events
Phil Bedella
Mgr., Cubs Care/community relations
Rebecca Polihronis
Director, publications/special projects
Ernie Roth
Manager, publications
Lena McDonagh
Photographer
Stephen Green
Director, stadium operations
Tom Cooper
Assistant director, stadium operations
Paul Rathje
Director, ticket operations
Frank Maloney
Scouts
Mark Adair, Billy Blitzer, Tom Bourque, Moi Camacho, Bill Capps, Jim Crawford, Frank Demoss, Oneri Fleita, Steve Fuller, Al Geddes, John Gracio, Gene Handley, Joe Housey, Spider Jorgensen, Buzzy Keller, Brad Kelley, Jose Lugo, Scott May, Brian Milner, Tad Powers, Alberto Rondon, Marc Russo, Jose Sera, Mark Servais, Billy Swoope

MINOR LEAGUE AFFILIATES
Class	Team	League	Manager
AAA	Iowa	American Association	Tim Johnson
AA	Orlando	Southern	Dave Trembley
A	Daytona	Florida State	Steve Roadcap
A	Rockford	Midwest	Ruben Amaro
A	Williamsport	New York-Pennsylvania	To be announced
Rookie	Mesa Cubs	Arizona	Terry Kennedy

BROADCAST INFORMATION
Radio: WGN-AM (720).
TV: WGN-TV (Channel 9).
Cable TV: CLTV.

SPRING TRAINING
Ballpark (city): HoHoKam Park (Mesa, Ariz.).
Ticket information: 800-638-4253.

1997 SEASON Chicago Cubs

SPRING TRAINING ROSTER

Manager—Jim Riggleman (5).
Coaches—Dave Bialas (43), Tony Muser (40), Mako Oliveras (2), Dan Radison (42) Phil Regan (27), Billy Williams (26).

No.	PITCHERS	B/T	Ht./Wt.	Born	1996 clubs
51	Adams, Terry	R/R	6-3/205	3-6-73	Chicago N.L.
	Batista, Miguel	R/R	6-0/180	2-19-71	Charlotte, Florida
45	Bottenfield, Kent	B/R	6-3/245	11-14-68	Iowa, Chicago N.L.
55	Casian, Larry	R/L	6-0/175	10-28-65	Chicago N.L., Iowa
49	Castillo, Frank	R/R	6-1/200	4-1-69	Chicago N.L.
32	Foster, Kevin	R/R	6-1/165	1-13-69	Chicago N.L., Iowa
	Gonzalez, Jeremi	R/R	6-1/180	1-8-75	Orlando
	Moten, Scott	R/R	6-1/195	4-12-72	Iowa, Orlando
	Mulholland, Terry	R/L	6-3/212	3-9-63	Philadelphia, Seattle
59	Myers, Rod	R/R	6-1/210	6-26-69	Chicago N.L.
35	Patterson, Bob	R/L	6-1/195	5-16-59	Chicago N.L.
33	Pisciotta, Marc	R/R	6-5/227	8-7-70	Calgary
31	Rain, Steve	R/R	6-6/245	6-2-75	Orlando, Iowa
41	Rojas, Mel	R/R	5-11/195	12-10-66	Montreal
	Stephenson, Brian	R/R	6-3/205	7-17-73	Orlando
36	Swartzbaugh, Dave	R/R	6-2/205	2-11-68	Iowa, Chicago N.L.
	Tapani, Kevin	R/R	6-0/189	2-18-64	Chicago A.L.
	Tatis, Ramon	L/L	6-2/185	1-5-73	St. Lucie
44	Telemaco, Amaury	R/R	6-3/215	1-19-74	Iowa, Chicago N.L.
46	Trachsel, Steve	R/R	6-4/200	10-31-70	Orlando, Chicago N.L.
13	Wendell, Turk	L/R	6-2/205	5-19-67	Chicago N.L.

No.	CATCHERS	B/T	Ht./Wt.	Born	1996 clubs
4	Cline, Pat	R/R	6-3/225	10-9-74	Daytona
7	Houston, Tyler	L/R	6-1/205	1-17-71	Atlanta, Chicago N.L.
6	Hubbard, Mike	R/R	6-1/200	2-16-71	Iowa, Chicago N.L.
9	Servais, Scott	R/R	6-2/205	6-4-67	Chicago N.L.

No.	INFIELDERS	B/T	Ht./Wt.	Born	1996 clubs
37	Brown, Brant	L/L	6-3/205	6-22-71	Iowa, Chicago N.L.
20	Cairo, Miguel	R/R	6-0/192	5-4-74	Syracuse, Toronto
12	Dunston, Shawon	R/R	6-1/180	3-21-63	San Francisco
17	Grace, Mark	L/L	6-2/195	6-28-64	Chicago N.L.
18	Hernandez, Jose	R/R	6-1/180	7-14-69	Chicago N.L.
50	Maxwell, Jason	R/R	6-1/175	3-21-72	Orlando
15	Orie, Kevin	R/R	6-4/210	9-1-72	Orlando, Iowa
11	Sanchez, Rey	R/R	5-9/170	10-5-67	Chicago N.L., Iowa
23	Sandberg, Ryne	R/R	6-2/190	9-18-59	Chicago N.L.

No.	OUTFIELDERS	B/T	Ht./Wt.	Born	1996 clubs
1	Glanville, Doug	R/R	6-2/175	8-25-70	Iowa, Chicago N.L.
39	Jennings, Robin	L/L	6-2/210	4-11-72	Iowa, Chicago N.L.
19	Kieschnick, Brooks	L/R	6-4/230	6-6-72	Chicago N.L., Iowa
56	McRae, Brian	B/R	6-0/195	8-27-67	Chicago N.L.
21	Sosa, Sammy	R/R	6-0/200	11-12-68	Chicago N.L.
30	Timmons, Ozzie	R/R	6-2/225	9-18-70	Chicago N.L., Iowa
28	Valdes, Pedro	L/L	6-1/180	6-29-73	Iowa, Chicago N.L.

BALLPARK INFORMATION

Ballpark (capacity, surface)
Wrigley Field (38,765, grass)

Address
1060 W. Addison St.
Chicago, IL 60613-4397

Business phone
312-404-2827

Ticket information
312-404-2827

Ticket prices
$21 (club box, field box)
$17 (terrace box, upper deck box, family section)
$14 (terrace reserved)
$12 (bleachers)
$9 (adult upper deck reserved)
$6 (under 14 upper deck reserved)
All weekday afternoon games in April, May and September are less.

Field dimensions (from home plate)
To left field at foul line, 355 feet
To center field, 400 feet
To right field at foul line, 353 feet

First game played
April 20, 1916 (Cubs 7, Reds 6)

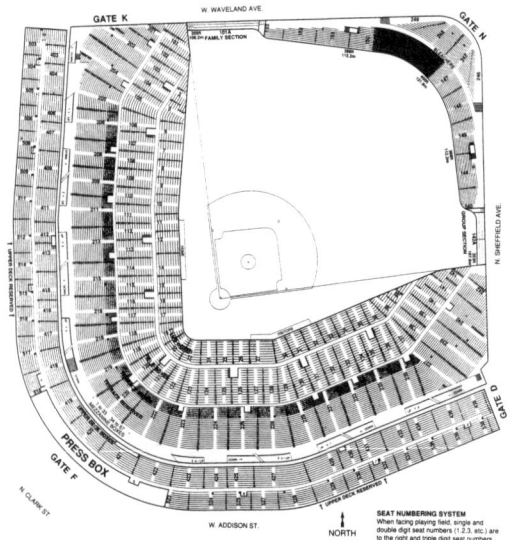

DAY BY DAY

Date	Opp.	Res.	Score	(inn.*)	Hits	Opp. hits	Winning pitcher	Losing pitcher	Save	Record	Pos.	GB
-1	S.D.	W	5-4	(10)	8	6	Patterson	Hoffman		1-0	T1st	...
-3	S.D.	L	5-7		8	12	Hamilton	Castillo	Hoffman	1-1	T3rd	1
-4	L.A.	W	9-4		14	8	Foster	Astacio		2-1	T1st	...
-5	L.A.	W	11-1		16	7	Bullinger	Candiotti		3-1	T1st	...
-6	L.A.	L	1-3		9	5	Park	Navarro	Worrell	3-2	T2nd	1
-7	L.A.	W	5-4		8	8	Jones	Osuna		4-2	2nd	1/2
-8	At Col.	W	9-6		12	12	Adams	Ritz	Jones	5-2	1st	+1/2
-10	At Col.	L	9-10		12	11	Leskanic	Jones		5-3	T1st	...
-12	At S.F.	L	1-4		10	6	Leiter	Navarro	Beck	5-4	2nd	1/2
-13	At S.F.	L	2-3	(10)	3	10	Juden	Myers		5-5	T2nd	1/2
-14	At S.F.	W	6-2		8	6	Foster	Watson	Wendell	6-5	T3rd	1/2
-15	Cin.	L	2-3	(10)	5	9	Moore	Patterson	Brantley	6-6	T3rd	11/2
-16	Cin.	W	6-3		11	6	Trachsel	Portugal		7-6	T3rd	1/2
-17	Cin.	W	8-6	(10)	9	10	Wendell	Ruffin		8-6	2nd	1/2
-18	S.F.	W	7-6		14	12	Perez	VanLandingham	Wendell	9-6	1st	+1/2
-19	S.F.	W	10-6		15	10	Foster	Watson		10-6	1st	+1/2
-20	S.F.	L	4-8		9	14	Gardner	Bullinger		10-7	2nd	1/2
-21	S.F.	L	6-7		11	6	Fernandez	Trachsel	Beck	10-8	2nd	1/2
-22	Col.	L	2-4		4	7	Freeman	Navarro	Leskanic	10-9	T2nd	1/2
-23	Col.	L	3-4		8	11	Rekar	Castillo	Leskanic	10-10	3rd	1
-24	At S.D.	L	4-5		8	10	Hamilton	Foster	Hoffman	10-11	T3rd	11/2
-25	At S.D.	L	3-8		5	11	Tewksbury	Bullinger		10-12	T3rd	11/2
-26	At L.A.	L	0-1		5	6	Astacio	Trachsel	Worrell	10-13	4th	11/2
-27	At L.A.	W	4-3	(10)	7	9	Navarro	Osuna	Jones	11-13	4th	1
-28	At L.A.	W	3-0		5	6	Castillo	Park		12-13	T2nd	1
-29	At L.A.	L	4-10		6	12	Valdes	Foster		12-14	T2nd	1
-30	St.L.	W	7-6		12	11	Wendell	Eckersley		13-14	T1st	...
5-1	St.L.	W	9-3		12	9	Trachsel	An. Benes		14-14	T1st	...
5-3	N.Y.	W	4-2		4	7	Navarro	Wilson		15-14	T1st	...
5-4	N.Y.	L	3-7		6	11	B. Jones	Castillo	Henry	15-15	T1st	...
5-5	N.Y.	W	5-4		8	10	Wendell	DiPoto		16-15	1st	+1/2
5-6	At Mon.	L	2-6		6	6	Martinez	Bullinger		16-16	T1st	...
5-7	At Mon.	L	3-8		7	11	Veres	Adams		16-17	T2nd	1
5-8	At Mon.	L	2-4		8	10	Cormier	Navarro	Rojas	16-18	3rd	1
5-10	At N.Y.	L	0-2		4	5	B. Jones	Castillo	J. Franco	16-19	T3rd	11/2
5-11	At N.Y.	L	6-7		11	10	Henry	Jones		16-20	T3rd	11/2
5-12	At N.Y.	W	3-0		7	2	Bullinger	Clark		17-20	3rd	1/2
5-13	Hou.	W	6-0		11	1	Trachsel	Reynolds		18-20	T1st	...
5-14	Hou.	L	3-6		6	10	Kile	Navarro	Jones	18-21	T2nd	1/2
5-15	Hou.	L	5-7		12	15	Wall	Castillo	Jones	18-22	3rd	11/2
5-16	Hou.	W	13-1		13	3	Telemaco	Drabek		19-22	T2nd	1/2
5-17	Fla.	W	3-1		4	5	Bullinger	Leiter	Wendell	20-22	2nd	1/2
5-18	Fla.	L	2-3		3	13	Burkett	Trachsel	Nen	20-23	2nd	1/2
5-19	Fla.	L	7-8	(11)	9	14	Mantei	Wendell	Nen	20-24	2nd	11/2
5-20	At Atl.	L	1-18		7	17	Avery	Castillo		20-25	2nd	11/2
5-21	At Atl.	W	4-2		10	7	Telemaco	Wohlers	Patterson	21-25	2nd	1/2
5-22	At Atl.	L	4-9		8	9	Glavine	Bullinger		21-26	2nd	1/2
5-24	At Hou.	L	7-8	(10)	9	12	Jones	Patterson		21-27	4th	11/2
5-25	At Hou.	L	2-5		6	11	Drabek	Navarro	Jones	21-28	4th	21/2
5-26	At Hou.	L	2-7		5	8	Reynolds	Castillo		21-29	4th	31/2
5-27	Atl.	L	1-9		6	9	Glavine	Telemaco		21-30	4th	41/2
5-29	Atl.	L	0-2		4	5	Smoltz	Trachsel		21-31	4th	5
5-31	At Fla.	W	2-1		4	7	Navarro	Rapp		22-31	T3rd	4
6-1	At Fla.	W	5-4	(10)	7	11	Wendell	Mathews		23-31	T3rd	3
6-2	At Fla.	L	2-3		7	7	Brown	Telemaco	Nen	23-32	T3rd	3
6-3	Phi.	W	4-3		7	11	Patterson	Ryan		24-32	3rd	3
6-4	Phi.	L	3-12		8	14	Williams	Bullinger		24-33	T3rd	4
6-5	Phi.	W	9-6		11	13	Adams	Borland	Wendell	25-33	T3rd	31/2
6-7	Mon.	L	3-9		6	13	Fassero	Castillo		25-34	T4th	4
6-8	Mon.	W	6-4		11	10	Telemaco	Martinez	Wendell	26-34	4th	4
6-9	Mon.	W	4-2		6	4	Trachsel	Rueter	Wendell	27-34	4th	4
6-10	At Phi.	W	2-1		6	3	Navarro	Mulholland		28-34	4th	4
6-11	At Phi.	W	9-2		13	5	Campbell	Munoz		29-34	4th	3
6-12	At Phi.	L	3-4		5	9	Fernandez	Castillo	Bottalico	29-35	4th	3
6-13	S.D.	W	6-3	(14)	9	12	Jones	Blair		30-35	T3rd	2
6-14	S.D.	W	5-1		5	5	Trachsel	Tewksbury		31-35	T3rd	2
6-15	S.D.	L	1-2		5	4	Worrell	Navarro	Hoffman	31-36	4th	3
6-16	S.D.	W	8-4		9	4	Castillo	Valenzuela	Bullinger	32-36	T3rd	2
6-18†	L.A.	L	6-9		9	15	Martinez	Telemaco	Worrell	32-37	4th	21/2
6-18‡	L.A.	W	7-4		10	6	Campbell	Valdes		33-37	3rd	2
6-19	L.A.	L	3-4	(13)	9	10	Park	Adams	Worrell	33-38	T3rd	3
6-20	At S.D.	W	3-2		7	5	Navarro	Worrell	Wendell	34-38	3rd	2

Date	Opp.	Res.	Score	(inn.*)	Hits	Opp. hits	Winning pitcher	Losing pitcher	Save	Record	Pos.	GB
6-21	At S.D.	L	1-2	(10)	5	9	Hoffman	Wendell		34-39	3rd	3
6-22	At S.D.	W	9-6	(16)	21	11	Myers	Blair		35-39	3rd	2
6-23	At S.D.	L	4-5		7	9	Hamilton	Telemaco	Hoffman	35-40	4th	2
6-25	At L.A.	W	2-0		6	6	Trachsel	Nomo		36-40	3rd	2
6-26	At L.A.	W	6-4		11	8	Navarro	Candiotti	Adams	37-40	3rd	2
6-28	At Cin.	L	4-7		9	9	Smiley	Castillo	Smith	37-41	4th	2
6-29	At Cin.	L	5-9		7	11	Portugal	Bullinger		37-42	4th	3
6-30	At Cin.	W	6-0		11	4	Trachsel	Burba		38-42	4th	3
7-1	At Pit.	L	1-4		8	11	Darwin	Navarro	Plesac	38-43	4th	4
7-2	At Pit.	W	15-7		22	14	Telemaco	Wagner		39-43	4th	4
7-3	At Pit.	L	2-3		8	7	Neagle	Castillo	Plesac	39-44	4th	5
7-4	Cin.	L	1-2		7	6	Portugal	Bullinger	Brantley	39-45	4th	6
7-5	Cin.	L	0-3		4	4	Burba	Trachsel	Brantley	39-46	4th	7
7-6	Cin.	W	6-2		11	9	Patterson	Carrasco		40-46	4th	6
7-7	Cin.	W	7-6	(13)	15	14	Sturtze	Ruffin		41-46	4th	5
7-11	St.L.	W	6-0		8	5	Navarro	Osborne		42-46	3rd	4
7-12	St.L.	L	3-13		9	18	An. Benes	Trachsel		42-47	4th	5
7-13	St.L.	L	5-10		9	13	Stottlemyre	Bullinger	Eckersley	42-48	4th	6
7-14	St.L.	L	6-7		7	13	Al. Benes	Adams	Eckersley	42-49	4th	7
7-15	Pit.	W	12-2		16	8	Castillo	Miceli		43-49	4th	7
7-16	Pit.	L	5-10		6	13	Neagle	Navarro		43-50	4th	8
7-18	At St.L.	W	6-5		10	9	Bottenfield	Petkovsek	Wendell	44-50	T3rd	7½
7-19	At St.L.	L	1-9		3	13	Al. Benes	Castillo		44-51	4th	8½
7-20	At St.L.	W	3-0		7	5	Trachsel	Morgan	Wendell	45-51	4th	7½
7-21	At St.L.	L	5-6	(10)	13	12	Petkovsek	Wendell		45-52	4th	8½
7-22	At S.F.	L	2-3		6	5	Bautista	Bottenfield		45-53	4th	8½
7-23	At S.F.	W	9-6		14	9	Myers	DeLucia	Patterson	46-53	4th	7½
7-24	At S.F.	W	7-1		11	5	Castillo	VanLandingham		47-53	4th	6½
7-25	At Col.	W	10-8		17	15	Bottenfield	Ruffin	Patterson	48-53	4th	5½
7-26	At Col.	W	17-4		17	10	Navarro	Freeman	Adams	49-53	4th	5
7-27	At Col.	L	6-10		10	12	M. Thompson	Telemaco		49-54	4th	5½
7-28	At Col.	W	7-5		13	9	Bullinger	Ritz	Bottenfield	50-54	4th	5½
7-30	S.F.	W	4-0		4	10	Castillo	VanLandingham	Adams	51-54	4th	4½
7-31	S.F.	W	4-1		5	5	Trachsel	Watson	Wendell	52-54	4th	4
8-1	Col.	W	4-1		8	7	Navarro	M. Thompson	Patterson	53-54	4th	3½
8-2	Col.	L	2-7		7	5	Ritz	Telemaco		53-55	4th	4½
8-3	Col.	L	2-8		5	8	Wright	Bullinger		53-56	4th	5
8-4	Col.	L	1-6		4	10	Reynoso	Castillo		53-57	4th	6
8-5	N.Y.	W	7-3		11	5	Trachsel	Wilson		54-57	4th	5½
8-6	N.Y.	W	3-0		7	7	Navarro	Clark	Patterson	55-57	4th	4½
8-7	N.Y.	L	7-11		10	17	DiPoto	Adams		55-58	4th	5½
8-9	At Mon.	W	11-9		9	14	Bullinger	Cormier	Patterson	56-58	4th	5
8-10	At Mon.	W	3-2		7	10	Casian	Dyer	Wendell	57-58	4th	5
8-11	At Mon.	L	3-4	(10)	8	5	Rojas	Bottenfield		57-59	4th	6
8-12	At N.Y.	W	11-1		12	5	Navarro	Isringhausen		58-59	3rd	5
8-13	At N.Y.	W	3-2		8	6	Telemaco	Harnisch	Wendell	59-59	3rd	4
8-14	At N.Y.	L	5-8		11	9	B. Jones	Bullinger	J. Franco	59-60	4th	5
8-16	Hou.	L	3-8		12	15	Hampton	Castillo		59-61	4th	5
8-17	Hou.	W	12-3		13	7	Trachsel	Kile		60-61	4th	5
8-18	Hou.	W	10-8		17	9	Navarro	Brocail	Wendell	61-61	4th	5
8-19	Fla.	L	3-4		6	7	Brown	Telemaco	Nen	61-62	4th	5½
8-20	Fla.	W	8-1		11	2	Foster	Hutton		62-62	4th	5
8-21	Fla.	W	8-3		8	9	Castillo	Rapp		63-62	3rd	4
8-23	At Atl.	L	3-4		5	10	Maddux	Trachsel	Wohlers	63-63	4th	4
8-24	At Atl.	L	5-6		8	11	Clontz	Casian		63-64	4th	4½
8-25	At Atl.	W	3-2		11	7	Foster	Wohlers	Wendell	64-64	3rd	4½
8-27	At Hou.	L	5-6		6	8	Morman	Adams	Hernandez	64-65	T3rd	5
8-28	At Hou.	L	4-5		9	10	Olson	Bottenfield		64-66	T3rd	5
8-29	At Hou.	W	4-3		8	9	Navarro	Reynolds	Wendell	65-66	T3rd	5
8-30†	Atl.	W	3-2		6	3	Foster	Glavine	Patterson	66-66			
8-30‡	Atl.	L	5-6		10	12	Borowski	Bottenfield	Wohlers	66-67	3rd	5½
8-31	Atl.	W	12-0		12	3	Castillo	Neagle	Adams	67-67	3rd	5½
9-1	Atl.	W	2-1	(12)	6	8	Campbell	Borowski		68-67	3rd	4½
9-2	At Fla.	L	3-4		7	10	Valdes	Trachsel	Nen	68-68	3rd	4½
9-3	At Fla.	W	11-3		9	9	Navarro	Leiter		69-68	3rd	4
9-4	At Fla.	L	2-9		5	10	Brown	Foster		69-69	4th	5
9-5	At Phi.	L	1-6		6	12	Schilling	Castillo		69-70	4th	5½
9-6	At Phi.	W	6-4		6	9	Bullinger	Ryan	Wendell	70-70	4th	5½
9-7	At Phi.	L	2-4		7	9	Hunter	Bottenfield	Bottalico	70-71	4th	6½
9-8	At Phi.	W	5-3		8	11	Navarro	Mimbs	Wendell	71-71	4th	5½
9-9	Mon.	W	3-1		6	6	Foster	Paniagua		72-71	4th	5½
9-10	Mon.	W	10-3		12	13	Bottenfield	Daal		73-71	3rd	5½
9-11	Mon.	L	1-2		4	7	Urbina	Adams	Rojas	73-72	3rd	5½
9-13	Phi.	W	4-2		5	8	Trachsel	Hunter	Wendell	74-72	3rd	5
9-14	Phi.	L	2-6		6	11	Mimbs	Navarro	Ryan	74-73	3rd	5

ate	Opp.	Res.	Score	(inn.*)	Hits	Opp. hits	Winning pitcher	Losing pitcher	Save	Record	Pos.	GB
-15	Phi.	L	1-6		6	9	Schilling	Foster		74-74	3rd	5
-17	At St.L.	L	3-5		9	10	Osborne	Patterson	Mathews	74-75	3rd	6
-18	At St.L.	L	3-5		6	10	Stottlemyre	Trachsel	Eckersley	74-76	3rd	7
-19	At St.L.	L	4-5	(13)	11	9	Bailey	Campbell		74-77	3rd	8
-20	At Pit.	L	4-6		7	11	Lieber	Foster	Ericks	74-78	4th	8
-21	At Pit.	L	3-8		10	8	Loiselle	Swartzbaugh		74-79	4th	8½
-22	At Pit.	L	3-11		9	14	Cordova	Castillo		74-80	4th	8
-23	At Pit.	W	4-3		9	5	Trachsel	Schmidt	Patterson	75-80	4th	8
-24	At Cin.	L	3-6		8	10	Lyons	Navarro	Brantley	75-81	4th	9
-25	At Cin.	L	3-4		9	6	Burba	Foster	Brantley	75-82	4th	10
-26	At Cin.	L	4-12		6	9	Jarvis	Swartzbaugh		75-83	4th	10½
-27†	Pit.	L	4-7	(10)	11	8	Plesac	Wendell		75-84		
-27‡	Pit.	W	10-9		11	15	Adams	Boever		76-84	4th	11
-28	Pit.	L	7-8	(10)	12	12	Plesac	Wendell		76-85	4th	12
-29	Pit.	L	3-8		9	8	Loaiza	Navarro		76-86	4th	12

onthly records: April (13-14), May (9-17), June (16-11), July (14-12), August (15-13), September (9-19).
nnings, if other than nine. †First game of doubleheader. ‡Second game of doubleheader.

HIGHLIGHTS

igh point: After sinking to a 21-31 ecord on May 29, the Cubs went 53-41 o improve to 74-72 on September 13. hey went into St. Louis on September 7 only five games out of first place with 4 games to play and three against the ardinals.

ow point: After a late Ryne Sandberg ome run gave the Cubs the lead in the pener of that mid-September series in t. Louis, the Cubs lost the game, were wept in the series and went on to lose 2 of their last 14 games to finish 10 ames under .500.

urning point: The Cubs were 45-53 and bout to fall nine games below .500 on uly 23 when Sammy Sosa hit two ome runs to help rally Chicago from a -0 deficit to a 9-6 triumph in San rancisco. That victory sent the Cubs on n 8-1 roll and they went 29-19 to climb ack into the N.L. Central race.

ost valuable player: Outfielder Sammy osa. He hit 40 homers and drove in 100 uns in 124 games before his season nded August 20 because of a hand frac- ure. The Cubs' offense overcame his bsence for about a month before hitting late skid.

ost valuable pitcher: Starter Steve rachsel. He bounced back from a tough 995 to make the All-Star team and fin- sh with a 13-9 record, 3.03 ERA (sixth- est in the N.L.) and 205 innings pitched.

ost improved player: Reliever Turk Vendell. He went from being placed on waivers on August 31,1995, to winning he Cubs' closer job in 1996. He finished 8-for-21 in save opportunities and was -5 with a 2.84 ERA in 70 appearances.

ost pleasant surprise: Second base- man Ryne Sandberg. No one could xpect Sandberg to return to his All-Star orm after nearly two years away from he game, but he almost did. Sandberg's efense and speed on the bases were ust as good as in the past, and he wal- oped 25 homers and knocked in 92 runs he third-highest RBI total of his career). Only his .244 batting average was below ar.

iggest disappointment: The starting otation, which saw Frank Castillo, Kevin Foster and Jim Bullinger struggle after

big 1995 seasons.

Key injuries: Third baseman Dave Magadan (hand) went down in spring training and didn't play until May 31. Shortstop Rey Sanchez (hand) was on the D.L. twice and missed 60 games. And Sammy Sosa missed the final six weeks.

Notable: During the last week of the sea- son, manager Jim Riggleman and G.M. Ed Lynch received contract extensions through 1998 with club options for 1999. Pitching coach Fergie Jenkins was fired. . . . The Cubs led the National League in fielding percentage (.983) and fewest errors committed (104). They played a club-record 90 errorless games. . . . On May 16 vs. Houston, Sosa became the first Cub ever to hit two homers in one inning (7th). . . . Sandberg ended the season one homer shy of tying Joe Morgan (266) for most homers hit as a second baseman. . . . The Cubs did not start a lefthanded pitcher for the third straight season. The last lefty to start for the team was Greg Hibbard on September 29, 1993.

—BARRY ROZNER

RECORDS

1996 regular-season record: 76-86 (4th in N.L. Central); 43-38 at home; 33-48 on road; 31-30 vs. East; 19-33 vs. Central; 26-23 vs. West; 18-16 vs. lefthanded starters; 58-70 vs. righthanded starters; 66-64 on grass; 10-22 on turf; 43-53 in daytime; 33-33 at night; 21-34 in one- run games; 8-11 in extra-inning games; 0-0-3 in doubleheaders.

Team record past five years: 360-383 (.485, ranks 8th in league in that span).

TEAM LEADERS

Batting average: Mark Grace (.331).
At-bats: Brian McRae (624).
Runs: Brian McRae (111).
Hits: Mark Grace (181).
Total bases: Sammy Sosa (281).
Doubles: Mark Grace (39).
Triples: Brian McRae (5).
Home runs: Sammy Sosa (40).
Runs batted in: Sammy Sosa (100).

Stolen bases: Brian McRae (37).
Slugging percentage: Sammy Sosa (.564).
On-base percentage: Mark Grace (.396).
Wins: Jaime Navarro (15).
Earned-run average: Steve Trachsel (3.03).
Complete games: Jaime Navarro (4).
Shutouts: Steve Trachsel (2).
Saves: Turk Wendell (18).
Innings pitched: Jaime Navarro (236.2).
Strikeouts: Jaime Navarro (158).

GAMES BY POSITION

Catcher: Scott Servais 128, Tyler Houston 27, Brian Dorsett 15, Mike Hubbard 14.
First base: Mark Grace 141, Brant Brown 18, Dave Magadan 10, Leo Gomez 8, Luis Gonzalez 2, Tyler Houston 1, Scott Servais 1.
Second base: Ryne Sandberg 146, Todd Haney 23, Bret Barberie 6, Felix Fermin 6, Terry Shumpert 4, Tyler Houston 2, Jose Hernandez 1.
Third base: Leo Gomez 124, Dave Magadan 51, Jose Hernandez 43, Terry Shumpert 10, Tyler Houston 9, Todd Haney 4, Bret Barberie 2.
Shortstop: Rey Sanchez 92, Jose Hernandez 87, Todd Haney 3, Felix Fermin 2, Bret Barberie 1, Leo Gomez 1, Terry Shumpert 1.
Outfield: Brian McRae 155, Luis Gonzalez 139, Sammy Sosa 124, Scott Bullett 58, Ozzie Timmons 47, Doug Glanville 35, Robin Jennings 11, Brooks Kieschnick 8, Pedro Valdes 2, Jose Hernandez 1.

TOP DRAFT CHOICES

1. **Todd Noel,** RHP, North Vermillion H.S., Maurice, La.
2. **Quincy Carter,** OF, Southwest DeKalb H.S., Ellenwood, Ga.
3. **Skip Ames,** RHP, University of Alabama.
4. **Chris Gissell,** RHP, Hudson's Bay H.S., Vancouver, Wash.
5. **Chad Meyers,** 2B-OF, Creighton University.
6. **Doug Hall,** OF, University of Alabama.
7. **Jon Cannon,** LHP, Canada (Calif.) J.C.
8. **Brian Connell,** LHP, Dunedin (Fla.) H.S.
9. **Nate Manning,** 3B, Austin Peay State U.
10. **Phillip Norton,** LHP, Texarkana (Tex.) J.C.

CINCINNATI REDS
NATIONAL LEAGUE CENTRAL DIVISION

1997 REDS SCHEDULE

▪ Home games shaded.
* — All-Star Game at Jacobs Field (Cleveland)
D — Day game (any game starting before 5 p.m.)

APRIL

SUN	MON	TUE	WED	THU	FRI	SAT
		1 D	2 COL	3 D COL	4 FLA	5 FLA
6 FLA	7 D COL	8 D	9 COL	10 D COL	11 D FLA	12 D FLA
13 FLA	14 ATL	15 ATL	16 ATL	17 PIT	18 PIT	19 D PIT
20 D PIT	21	22 D NYM	23 D NYM	24	25 PHI	26 D PHI
27 D PHI	28 NYM	29 NYM	30 ATL			

MAY

SUN	MON	TUE	WED	THU	FRI	SAT
				1 ATL	2 D SF	3 D SF
4 D SF	5 LA	6 LA	7 LA	8	9 SD	10 SD
11 SD	12	13 LA	14 SF	15 LA	16 LA	17 D SD
18 D SD	19 D SD	20 HOU	21 HOU	22	23 CUB	24 D CUB
25 D CUB	26 PHI	27 PHI	28 PHI	29 CUB	30 D CUB	31 D CUB

JUNE

SUN	MON	TUE	WED	THU	FRI	SAT
1 CUB	2	3 D PHI	4 HOU	5 D HOU	6 D NYM	7 D NYM
8 NYM	9	10 PIT	11 PIT	12	13 D CWS	14 D CWS
15 D CWS	16 CLE	17 CLE	18 CLE	19	20 STL	21 STL
22 STL	23 MON	24 MON	25 MON	26 STL	27 D STL	28 D STL
29 STL	30 MIL					

JULY

SUN	MON	TUE	WED	THU	FRI	SAT
		1 MIL	2 MIL	3 D HOU	4 HOU	5 HOU
6 D HOU	7 D	8	9 *	10	11 D MON	12 MON
13 D MON	14 STL	15 STL	16 PIT	17 PIT	18 NYM	19 D NYM
20 D NYM	21 D FLA	22 FLA	23 FLA	24	25 ATL	26 D ATL
27 D ATL	28 FLA	29 FLA	30 FLA	31		

AUGUST

SUN	MON	TUE	WED	THU	FRI	SAT
					1 SF	2 SF
3 D SF	4 SD	5 SD	6 SD	7 LA	8 D LA	9 LA
10 D LA	11 SF	12 D SD	13 D SD	14 SD	15 D LA	16 LA
17 D LA	18	19 COL	20 D COL	21	22 ATL	23 D ATL
24 D ATL	25 COL	26 COL	27 COL	28 D	29 MIN	30 MIN
31 D MIN						

SEPTEMBER

SUN	MON	TUE	WED	THU	FRI	SAT
	1 D KC	2 KC	3 KC	4 PIT	5 D PIT	6 D PIT
7 D PIT	8 D CUB	9 CUB	10 CUB	11	12 D PHI	13 D PHI
14 D PHI	15 CUB	16 CUB	17 MON	18 D MON	19 D HOU	20 D HOU
21 HOU	22 HOU	23 STL	24 STL	25 STL	26 MON	27 MON
28 D MON						

1997 SEASON

CLUB DIRECTORY

General partner
Marge Schott

President and chief executive officer
Marge Schott

Managing executive
John Allen

General manager
Jim Bowden

Director, scouting
Julian Mock

Assistant/baseball operations
Brad Kullman

Special assistant to the general manager
Gene Bennett

Senior advisor/baseball operations
Larry Barton Jr.

Controller
Anthony Ward

Director, stadium operations
Jody Pettyjohn

Director, ticket department
John O'Brien

Director, season ticket sales
Pat McCaffrey

Director, group sales
Barb McManus

Director, marketing
Chip Baker

Dir., public relations and publications
Mike Ringering

Director, media relations
Rob Butcher

Publicity assistant
Charles Henderson

Administrative assistant/publicity
Kelly Lippincott

Director, player development
Sheldon "Chief" Bender

Senior advisor/player personnel
Jack McKeon

Sr. dir./scouting and player development
Al Goldis

Sr. advisor/baseball operations
Bob Zuk

Traveling secretary
Gary Wahoff

Assistant ticket director
Ken Ayer

Chief administrative assistant
Joyce Pfarr

Administrative assistant, business
Ginny Kamp

Administrative assistant, scouting
Wilma Mann

Admin. assistant, player development
Lois Schneider

Scouting secretary
Lois Hudson

Head trainer
Greg Lynn

Assistant trainer
Mark Mann

Field superintendent
Howard Alford

Equipment manager
Bernie Stowe

Cross-checkers
Jeff Barton, Hank Sargent, Tom Wilson

Scouting supervisors
Johnny Almaraz, Ray Bellino, George Brill, Bobby Filotei, Jerry Flowers, Chris Gill, Jimmy Gonzales, Robbie Guzik, Les Houser, David Jennings, Robert Koontz, Steve Kring, Mike LaCoss, Mike Mangan, Tom Severtson, Bob Szymkowski, Marion "Bo" Trumbo, Mike Wallace

Scouts
Fred Blair, Jim Grief, Don Hill, Don Gust, Fred Hayes, Thomas Herrera, Fred Leone, Anthony Dion Lowe, Armando Morales, Jose Moreno, Denny Nagel, Jerry Raddatz, R. Douglas Stuart, Marlon Styles, Lee Toole, John Walsh, Fate Young, Murray Zuk

MINOR LEAGUE AFFILIATES

Class	Team	League	Manager
AAA	Indianapolis	American Association	Dave Miley
AA	Chattanooga	Southern	Mark Berry
A	Burlington	Midwest	Phillip Wellman
A	Charleston (WV)	South Atlantic	Barry Lyons
Rookie	Billings	Pioneer	To be announced

BROADCAST INFORMATION

Radio: WLW-AM (700).
TV: WSTR-TV (Channel 64).
Cable TV: SportsChannel Cincinnati.

SPRING TRAINING

Ballpark (city): Plant City Stadium (Plant City, Fla.).
Ticket information: 813-752-7337.

SPRING TRAINING ROSTER

Manager—Ray Knight (25).
Coaches—Ken Griffey Sr., Donald Gullett (35), Denis Menke, Ron Oester, Joel Youngblood (2).

No.	PITCHERS	B/T	Ht./Wt.	Born	1996 clubs
40	Bones, Ricky	R/R	6-0/193	4-7-69	Milwaukee, New York A.L.
45	Brantley, Jeff	R/R	5-10/180	9-5-63	Cincinnati
34	Burba, Dave	R/R	6-4/240	7-7-66	Cincinnati
58	Carrasco, Hector	R/R	6-2/180	10-22-69	Cincinnati, Indianapolis
32	Jarvis, Kevin	L/R	6-2/200	8-1-69	Indianapolis, Cincinnati
59	Lyons, Curt	R/R	6-5/240	10-17-74	Chattanooga, Cincinnati
38	Mercker, Kent	L/L	6-2/195	2-1-68	Baltimore, Buffalo, Cleveland
31	Morgan, Mike	R/R	6-2/220	10-8-59	St. Petersburg, Louisville, St. Louis, Cincinnati
50	Najera, Noe	L/L	6-2/190	12-9-70	Kinston
43	Remlinger, Mike	L/L	6-0/195	3-26-66	Indianapolis, Cincinnati
27	Rijo, Jose	R/R	6-3/215	5-13-65	Cincinnati
42	Salkeld, Roger	R/R	6-5/215	3-6-71	Cincinnati
46	Schourek, Pete	L/L	6-5/205	5-10-69	Cincinnati
36	Service, Scott	R/R	6-6/225	2-26-67	Indianapolis, Cincinnati
41	Shaw, Jeff	R/R	6-2/200	7-7-66	Cincinnati
57	Smiley, John	L/L	6-4/210	3-17-65	Cincinnati
56	Sullivan, Scott	R/R	6-4/210	3-13-71	Indianapolis, Cincinnati
48	White, Gabe	L/L	6-2/200	11-20-71	Indianapolis

No.	CATCHERS	B/T	Ht./Wt.	Born	1996 clubs
60	Bako, Paul	L/R	6-2/195	6-20-72	Chattanooga
6	Fordyce, Brook	R/R	6-1/185	5-7-70	Indianapolis, Cincinnati
10	Taubensee, Eddie	L/R	6-4/205	10-31-68	Cincinnati
67	Towle, Justin	R/R	6-2/210	2-21-74	Winston-Salem

No.	INFIELDERS	B/T	Ht./Wt.	Born	1996 clubs
55	Boone, Aaron	R/R	6-2/190	3-9-73	Chattanooga
29	Boone, Bret	R/R	5-10/180	4-6-69	Cincinnati
20	Branson, Jeff	L/R	6-0/180	1-26-67	Cincinnati
12	Greene, Willie	L/R	5-11/185	9-23-71	Cincinnati
28	Harris, Lenny	L/R	5-10/210	10-28-64	Cincinnati
11	Larkin, Barry	R/R	6-0/195	4-28-64	Cincinnati
23	Morris, Hal	L/L	6-4/210	4-9-65	Cincinnati, Indianapolis
18	Owens, Eric	R/R	6-1/185	2-3-71	Indianapolis, Cincinnati
39	Perez, Eduardo	R/R	6-4/215	9-11-69	Indianapolis, Cincinnati
3	Reese, Pokey	R/R	5-11/180	6-10-73	Indianapolis

No.	OUTFIELDERS	B/T	Ht./Wt.	Born	1996 clubs
33	Gibralter, Steve	R/R	6-0/190	10-9-72	Indianapolis, Cincinnati
00	Goodwin, Curtis	L/L	5-11/180	9-30-72	Indianapolis, Cincinnati
54	Kelly, Mike	R/R	6-4/195	6-2-70	Cincinnati, Indianapolis
15	Mottola, Chad	R/R	6-3/220	10-15-71	Indianapolis, Cincinnati
26	Murray, Glenn	R/R	6-2/225	11-23-70	Scranton/Wilkes-Barre, Philadelphia
16	Sanders, Reggie	R/R	6-1/185	12-1-67	Cincinnati, Indianapolis
22	Sierra, Ruben	B/R	6-1/200	10-6-65	New York A.L., Detroit
68	Watkins, Pat	R/R	6-2/185	9-2-72	Chattanooga

BALLPARK INFORMATION

Ballpark (capacity, surface)
Cinergy Field (52,952, artificial)

Address
100 Cinergy Field
Cincinnati, OH 45202

Business phone
513-421-4510

Ticket information
513-421-7337, 1-800-829-5353

Ticket prices
$14 (blue level box seats)
$11 (green level box seats)
$11 (yellow level box seats)
$9 (red level box seats)
$8 (green level reserved seats)
$6 (red level reserved seats)
$3 ("top six" reserved seats)

Field dimensions (from home plate)
To left field at foul line, 330 feet
To center field, 404 feet
To right field at foul line, 330 feet

First game played
June 30, 1970 (Braves 8, Reds 2)

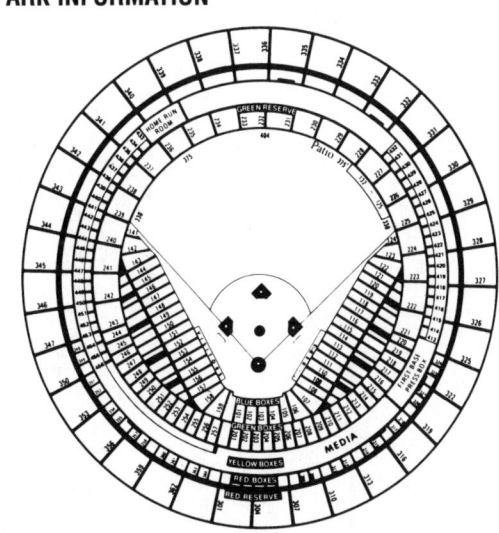

DAY BY DAY

Date	Opp.	Res.	Score	(inn.*)	Hits	Opp. hits	Winning pitcher	Losing pitcher	Save	Record	Pos.	GB
4-2	Mon.	W	4-1		7	7	Schourek	Fassero	Moore	1-0	T2nd	1/2
4-3	Mon.	L	4-8		6	15	Veres	Shaw		1-1	T3rd	1
4-4	Mon.	L	2-10		8	14	Paniagua	Burba		1-2	T4th	1
4-5	At Phi.	W	6-5	(10)	9	10	Shaw	Borland	Moore	2-2	T3rd	1
4-6	At Phi.	W	8-4		11	8	Salkeld	Hunter		3-2	T2nd	1
4-8	N.Y.	W	7-6		8	12	Schourek	B. Jones	Brantley	4-2	T2nd	1/2
4-9	N.Y.	L	5-12		9	12	Isringhausen	Smiley	J. Franco	4-3	3rd	1
4-10	N.Y.	W	9-7		12	11	Pugh	MacDonald	Brantley	5-3	T1st	...
4-11	Hou.	L	4-9		7	18	Reynolds	Portugal		5-4	T2nd	1/2
4-12	Hou.	L	8-10	(10)	12	12	Jones	Moore	Tabaka	5-5	3rd	1
4-14†	Hou.	W	5-3		8	8	Schourek	Hampton	Brantley	6-5	T3rd	1/2
4-14‡	Hou.	W	9-8		11	14	Shaw	Young	Brantley	7-5	T1st	...
4-15	At Chi.	W	3-2	(10)	9	5	Moore	Patterson	Brantley	8-5	T1st	...
4-16	At Chi.	L	3-6		6	11	Trachsel	Portugal		8-6	T1st	...
4-17	At Chi.	L	6-8	(10)	10	9	Wendell	Ruffin		8-7	3rd	1
4-19	At Hou.	L	5-13		7	18	Brocail	Schourek		8-8	T3rd	2
4-20	At Hou.	W	6-1		14	8	Smiley	Drabek		9-8	3rd	1 1/2
4-21	At Hou.	L	5-7		14	11	Jones	Brantley		9-9	3rd	1 1/2
4-22	At N.Y.	L	1-5		5	11	Wilson	Portugal		9-10	T4th	1 1/2
4-23	At N.Y.	L	6-8	(10)	9	13	Henry	Shaw		9-11	T4th	2
4-24	At Mon.	L	6-7	(10)	10	14	Dyer	Moore		9-12	5th	2 1/2
4-25	At Mon.	L	4-8		7	9	Martinez	Smiley		9-13	5th	2 1/2
4-26	Phi.	L	0-2		3	5	Grace	Burba	Bottalico	9-14	5th	2 1/2
4-27	Phi.	L	2-3		6	5	Leiper	Portugal	Bottalico	9-15	5th	3
4-30	Pit.	L	7-10		15	12	Neagle	Smiley	Cordova	9-16	5th	3
5-1	Pit.	L	3-4		5	7	Hope	Burba	Plesac	9-17	5th	4
5-3	At S.F.	W	5-3		6	8	McElroy	Creek	Brantley	10-17	5th	4
5-4	At S.F.	W	9-7		10	9	Moore	Leiter	Brantley	11-17	5th	3
5-5	At S.F.	W	12-6		9	9	Smiley	VanLandingham		12-17	5th	3
5-7	L.A.	W	3-2	(12)	6	7	Moore	Worrell		13-17	T4th	2 1/2
5-8	L.A.	W	5-0		8	3	Schourek	Park	Shaw	14-17	4th	1 1/2
5-10	S.D.	W	8-6		8	14	McElroy	Florie	Brantley	15-17	2nd	1
5-11	S.D.	W	1-0		3	6	Smiley	Hamilton	Brantley	16-17	T1st	...
5-12	S.D.	L	0-5		7	9	Tewksbury	Burba		16-18	T1st	...
5-14	Col.	L	3-5		6	7	S. Reed	Schourek	Ruffin	16-19	T2nd	1/2
5-17	At Atl.	L	2-8		10	10	Maddux	Smiley		16-20	3rd	1 1/2
5-18	At Atl.	L	1-2		8	4	Clontz	Ruffin	Wohlers	16-21	3rd	1 1/2
5-19	At Atl.	L	5-9		7	16	Smoltz	Schourek	Wohlers	16-22	3rd	2 1/2
5-20	Fla.	L	3-5		7	9	Rapp	Burba	Nen	16-23	3rd	2 1/2
5-21	Fla.	L	2-3		7	6	Weathers	Salkeld	Mathews	16-24	4th	2 1/2
5-22	Fla.	W	4-1		4	6	Smiley	Leiter	Brantley	17-24	4th	1 1/2
5-23	At Col.	W	7-5		8	4	Carrasco	Ruffin	Brantley	18-24	T3rd	1
5-24	At Col.	W	11-9		13	11	Ruffin	M. Thompson		19-24	T2nd	1
5-25	At Col.	L	5-7		9	7	Leskanic	Moore		19-25	3rd	2
5-27	At Fla.	L	2-6		4	8	Leiter	Smiley		19-26	3rd	3 1/2
5-28	At Fla.	L	2-6		5	8	Brown	Burba	Mathews	19-27	3rd	3 1/2
5-31	Atl.	L	1-9		5	15	Avery	Schourek		19-28	T3rd	4
6-1	Atl.	W	3-2		8	6	Portugal	Maddux	Brantley	20-28	T3rd	3
6-2	Atl.	L	2-6		11	7	Glavine	Smiley		20-29	T3rd	3
6-3	S.F.	L	3-6		8	9	VanLandingham	Burba		20-30	T4th	4
6-4	S.F.	W	4-1		9	5	Salkeld	Watson	Brantley	21-30	T3rd	4
6-5	S.F.	L	4-15		14	17	Gardner	Jarvis		21-31	5th	4 1/2
6-7	At L.A.	W	2-1		7	7	Smiley	Valdes	Brantley	22-31	T4th	4
6-8	At L.A.	L	4-5	(10)	13	8	Worrell	Carrasco		22-32	5th	5
6-9	At L.A.	L	2-3		6	8	Nomo	Smith	Worrell	22-33	5th	6
6-10	At S.D.	W	6-3		10	9	Smith	Bochtler	Brantley	23-33	5th	6
6-11	At S.D.	W	4-1		9	11	Jarvis	Valenzuela	Brantley	24-33	5th	5
6-12	At S.D.	W	9-4		14	6	Smiley	Florie		25-33	5th	4
6-14	Mon.	L	1-6		4	9	Martinez	Portugal		25-34	5th	4 1/2
6-15	Mon.	L	5-6		12	9	Rueter	Burba	Rojas	25-35	5th	5 1/2
6-16	Mon.	W	7-0		12	4	Salkeld	Cormier		26-35	5th	4 1/2
6-17	At Hou.	L	4-5		8	10	Young	Shaw	Jones	26-36	5th	5 1/2
6-18	At Hou.	W	6-4	(10)	11	7	Brantley	Hernandez		27-36	5th	4 1/2
6-19	At Hou.	W	10-7		11	10	Portugal	Hampton	Brantley	28-36	5th	4 1/2
6-20	At N.Y.	W	5-3		9	6	Burba	B. Jones	Shaw	29-36	5th	3 1/2
6-21	At N.Y.	L	4-9		10	14	DiPoto	Salkeld	Mlicki	29-37	5th	4 1/2
6-22	At N.Y.	L	2-5		4	11	Clark	Schourek	J. Franco	29-38	5th	4 1/2
6-23	At N.Y.	W	2-1		9	6	Smiley	Person	Brantley	30-38	5th	3 1/2
6-24	Phi.	W	7-0		12	4	Portugal	Schilling		31-38	5th	3 1/2
6-25†	Phi.	W	9-1		7	4	Burba	Quirico		32-38	5th	3
6-25‡	Phi.	W	3-1		7	8	Jarvis	Mimbs	Smith	33-38	4th	2 1/2
6-26	Phi.	W	4-2		7	7	Salkeld	Williams	Brantley	34-38	4th	2 1/2

ate	Opp.	Res.	Score	(inn.*)	Hits	Opp. hits	Winning pitcher	Losing pitcher	Save	Record	Pos.	GB
-28	Chi.	W	7-4		9	9	Smiley	Castillo	Smith	35-38	3rd	1¹/₂
-29	Chi.	W	9-5		11	7	Portugal	Bullinger		36-38	3rd	1¹/₂
-30	Chi.	L	0-6		4	11	Trachsel	Burba		36-39	3rd	2¹/₂
-1	At St.L.	W	8-5		8	8	Carrasco	Al. Benes	Brantley	37-39	3rd	2¹/₂
-2	At St.L.	L	3-4		10	6	Honeycutt	Smith	Eckersley	37-40	3rd	3¹/₂
-3	At St.L.	L	0-4		4	9	Osborne	Smiley		37-41	3rd	4¹/₂
-4	At Chi.	W	2-1		6	7	Portugal	Bullinger	Brantley	38-41	3rd	4¹/₂
-5	At Chi.	W	3-0		4	4	Burba	Trachsel	Brantley	39-41	3rd	4¹/₂
-6	At Chi.	L	2-6		9	11	Patterson	Carrasco		39-42	3rd	4¹/₂
-7	At Chi.	L	6-7	(13)	14	15	Sturtze	Ruffin		39-43	3rd	4¹/₂
-11	Pit.	L	3-5		8	12	Neagle	Smiley	Plesac	39-44	4th	4¹/₂
-12	Pit.	W	5-2		9	6	Portugal	Darwin	Brantley	40-44	3rd	4¹/₂
-13	Pit.	W	3-0		6	3	Jarvis	Lieber		41-44	3rd	4¹/₂
-14	Pit.	W	7-6		9	9	Burba	Wagner	Brantley	42-44	3rd	4¹/₂
-15	St.L.	L	3-8		8	8	Morgan	Salkeld		42-45	3rd	5¹/₂
-16	St.L.	L	4-5		8	13	Osborne	Shaw	Eckersley	42-46	3rd	6¹/₂
-17	St.L.	L	4-6		8	8	An. Benes	Portugal	Eckersley	42-47	3rd	7¹/₂
-18	At Pit.	L	3-8		7	11	Lieber	Jarvis		42-48	T3rd	7¹/₂
-19	At Pit.	W	11-3		15	8	Burba	Wagner		43-48	3rd	7¹/₂
-20	At Pit.	W	9-3		12	10	Salkeld	Miceli		44-48	3rd	6¹/₂
-21	At Pit.	L	4-6		9	8	Neagle	Smiley	Plesac	44-49	3rd	7¹/₂
-22†	At Phi.	W	5-2		9	9	Portugal	Mulholland	Brantley	45-49		
-22‡	At Phi.	W	5-3		12	10	Smith	Ryan	Brantley	46-49	3rd	6
-23	At Phi.	W	5-3		10	9	Jarvis	Mimbs		47-49	3rd	5
-24	At Phi.	W	3-1		9	6	Burba	Williams	Brantley	48-49	3rd	4
-26	N.Y.	W	7-4		11	9	Smiley	Wilson		49-49	3rd	3
-27	N.Y.	W	7-5		13	8	Service	Clark	Brantley	50-49	3rd	2¹/₂
-28	N.Y.	L	1-7		3	11	B. Jones	Jarvis		50-50	3rd	3¹/₂
-29	Hou.	L	1-2		4	8	Hampton	Portugal	Wagner	50-51	3rd	4
-30	Hou.	W	5-4	(10)	8	8	Shaw	Clark		51-51	3rd	3
-31	Hou.	W	10-0		13	4	Smiley	Wall		52-51	3rd	2¹/₂
-1	At Mon.	W	9-7		10	8	Shaw	Dyer	Brantley	53-51	3rd	2
-2	At Mon.	L	1-11		4	14	Martinez	Jarvis		53-52	3rd	3
-3	At Mon.	L	2-6		4	11	Cormier	Portugal	Rojas	53-53	3rd	3¹/₂
-4	At Mon.	L	3-7		9	11	Urbina	Burba	Rojas	53-54	3rd	4¹/₂
-5	At S.F.	W	4-3		9	6	Salkeld	VanLandingham	Brantley	54-54	3rd	4
-6	At S.F.	W	3-2		5	6	Carrasco	Beck	Brantley	55-54	3rd	3
-7	At S.F.	L	2-9		7	10	Gardner	Jarvis		55-55	3rd	4
-9	L.A.	W	9-4		12	5	Portugal	Valdes		56-55	3rd	3¹/₂
-10	L.A.	L	5-7		6	9	Nomo	Burba	Worrell	56-56	3rd	4¹/₂
-11	L.A.	L	5-10		11	9	Osuna	Carrasco		56-57	3rd	5¹/₂
-12	L.A.	L	5-6		9	9	Martinez	Smiley	Worrell	56-58	4th	5¹/₂
-13	S.D.	W	10-4		12	8	Jarvis	Hamilton		57-58	4th	4¹/₂
-14	S.D.	W	2-1	(13)	7	8	Smith	Bergman		58-58	3rd	4¹/₂
-15	S.D.	W	3-2		9	6	Burba	Tewksbury	Brantley	59-58	3rd	4
-16	Col.	L	4-8		12	17	Reynoso	Salkeld		59-59	3rd	5
-17†	Col.	W	5-3		9	6	Smiley	Munoz	Brantley	60-59		
-17‡	Col.	W	9-5		14	13	Shaw	S. Reed		61-59	3rd	3¹/₂
-18	Col.	W	9-4		7	8	Jarvis	Ritz	Shaw	62-59	3rd	3¹/₂
-19	Col.	L	3-6		9	10	M. Thompson	Portugal		62-60	3rd	4
-20	At Atl.	L	1-4		5	10	Glavine	Burba	Wohlers	62-61	3rd	4¹/₂
-21	At Atl.	L	3-4		10	10	Borbon	Brantley		62-62	4th	4¹/₂
-22	At Atl.	W	3-2	(13)	11	6	Carrasco	Borowski	Brantley	63-62	T3rd	3¹/₂
-23†	At Fla.	W	6-5		12	11	Carrara	Valdes	Brantley	64-62		
-23‡	At Fla.	L	3-8		8	10	Leiter	Jarvis		64-63	3rd	3¹/₂
-24	At Fla.	L	3-5		7	9	Brown	Burba	Nen	64-64	3rd	4
-25	At Fla.	L	5-6		12	7	Nen	Smith		64-65	4th	5
-26	At Col.	L	5-9	(7)	6	13	Swift	Jarvis	Bailey	64-66	4th	5
-27	At Col.	W	4-3		8	9	Smiley	Reynoso	Brantley	65-66	T3rd	5
-28	At Col.	L	9-10		12	11	Ruffin	Shaw		65-67	T3rd	6
-29	At Col.	W	18-7		17	12	Burba	M. Thompson		66-67	T3rd	5
-30	Fla.	L	1-3		8	8	Brown	Remlinger		66-68	4th	6
-31	Fla.	W	22-8		18	12	Jarvis	Miller		67-68	4th	6
-1	Fla.	L	1-6		8	12	Hutton	Smiley		67-69	4th	6
-2	Atl.	W	7-6		9	14	Shaw	McMichael	Brantley	68-69	4th	5
-3	Atl.	W	5-1		9	1	Burba	Bielecki	Shaw	69-69	4th	4¹/₂
-4	Atl.	W	12-6		15	8	Salkeld	Glavine		70-69	3rd	4¹/₂
-6†	S.F.	L	0-2		5	5	Fernandez	Smiley	Beck	70-70	3rd	5¹/₂
-6‡	S.F.	W	14-1		15	6	Morgan	Bourgeois		71-70	3rd	5
-7	S.F.	W	7-5		13	11	Salkeld	Scott	Brantley	72-70	3rd	5
-8	S.F.	W	8-3		12	4	Shaw	Bautista		73-70	3rd	4
-9	At L.A.	L	2-7		7	11	Martinez	Jarvis		73-71	3rd	5
-10	At L.A.	L	4-5		7	11	Candiotti	Salkeld	Worrell	73-72	4th	6
-11	At L.A.	L	2-3		6	5	Valdes	Smiley	Worrell	73-73	4th	6
-13	At S.D.	W	3-1		6	6	Morgan	Ashby	Brantley	74-73	4th	5¹/₂

Date	Opp.	Res.	Score	(inn.*)	Hits	Opp. hits	Winning pitcher	Losing pitcher	Save	Record	Pos.	GB
9-14	At S.D.	L	2-3	(12)	6	9	Veras	Smith		74-74	4th	5$\frac{1}{2}$
9-15	At S.D.	L	0-8		8	15	Hamilton	Jarvis	Blair	74-75	4th	5$\frac{1}{2}$
9-17	At Pit.	L	3-5		10	10	Cordova	Smiley	Ericks	74-76	4th	6$\frac{1}{2}$
9-18	At Pit.	L	3-5		5	11	Schmidt	Morgan	Plesac	74-77	4th	7$\frac{1}{2}$
9-19	At Pit.	L	4-6		9	9	Peters	Pugh	Ericks	74-78	4th	8$\frac{1}{2}$
9-20	St.L.	W	4-2		5	7	Burba	Al. Benes	Brantley	75-78	3rd	7$\frac{1}{2}$
9-22†	St.L.	W	6-3		10	5	Shaw	Mathews	Brantley	76-78		
9-22‡	St.L.	W	6-0		3	1	Smiley	Jackson		77-78	3rd	5$\frac{1}{2}$
9-23	St.L.	L	2-3		6	10	Stottlemyre	Morgan	Eckersley	77-79	3rd	6$\frac{1}{2}$
9-24	Chi.	W	6-3		10	8	Lyons	Navarro	Brantley	78-79	T2nd	6$\frac{1}{2}$
9-25	Chi.	W	4-3		6	9	Burba	Foster	Brantley	79-79	T2nd	6$\frac{1}{2}$
9-26	Chi.	W	12-4		9	6	Jarvis	Swartzbaugh		80-79	T2nd	6
9-27	At St.L.	L	1-2	(11)	6	9	Batchelor	Shaw		80-80	T2nd	7
9-28	At St.L.	L	2-5		3	11	Jackson	Morgan	Honeycutt	80-81	3rd	8
9-29	At St.L.	W	6-3		11	8	Lyons	Ludwick	Brantley	81-81	3rd	7

Monthly records: April (9-16), May (10-12), June (17-11), July (16-12), August (15-17), September (14-13).
*Innings, if other than nine. †First game of doubleheader. ‡Second game of doubleheader.

HIGHLIGHTS

High point: On August 8, the Reds defeated San Francisco, 8-3, to move four games out of first place. It was their third consecutive win and sixth in their past seven games. At 73-70, Cincinnati tied its season-high for games over .500.

Low point: The Reds followed their high point by heading on a nine-game trip to Los Angeles, San Diego and Pittsburgh that turned into a disaster. Cincinnati went 1-8 on the trip, scoring only 23 runs (2.6 per game).

Turning point: On the West Coast trip that essentially eliminated the run-starved Reds, outfielder Kevin Mitchell became so ill that he was allowed to stay in San Diego (his home) later than the team. But then he didn't show up in Pittsburgh for the ensuing series, and he was suspended for the remainder of the season.

Most valuable player: Shortstop Barry Larkin. The 1995 N.L. MVP was even better in '96, becoming the first short-stop in major league history to join the 30-30 club in home runs (a career-high 33) and stolen bases (36) in one season. He also hit .298, drove in a career-high 89 runs and captured his third consecutive Gold Glove Award.

Most improved player: Reliever Jeff Shaw. He had been essentially a journey-man middleman playing for four major league teams. But in 1996, Shaw developed into a standout setup man for Jeff Brantley, going 8-6 with a 2.49 ERA and four saves in 78 games, setting career-highs in victories, ERA, saves and appearances.

Most pleasant surprise: Outfielder Eric Davis. Trying to return from a one-year retirement caused by a herniated disk in his neck, Davis was given an outside chance just to be an extra outfielder for the team that once counted him as its franchise player. All Davis did was hit .287 with 26 homers, 83 RBIs and 23 stolen bases in 129 games as the regular center fielder.

Biggest disappointment: Outfielder Reggie Sanders. He had a breakout year in 1995 (.306, 28 homers, 99 RBIs, 36 steals) and was expected to help carry the club in '96, what with left fielder Ron Gant gone to St. Louis via free agency.

Instead, Sanders struggled with injuries (he played in only 81 games) and with production (.251, 14 homers, 33 RBIs), especially in the clutch (.177 with run-ners in scoring position).

Key injuries: Cincinnati was ravaged by injuries early in the season to closer Jeff Brantley, second baseman Bret Boone and outfielder Reggie Sanders, which is one reason manager Ray Knight was shuffling lineups on a daily basis. But the biggest losses came in the starting rota-tion. Jose Rijo never pitched in 1996 because of his elbow problems. That wasn't totally unexpected, but defending Cy Young Award runnerup Pete Schourek ended up missing much of the season because of elbow surgery after the injury had caused him to struggle with a 4-5 record and 6.01 ERA in 12 games.

Notable: Boone failed to win a Gold Glove despite leading N.L. second basemen in fielding percentage. The Reds finished out of first place for the first time since they were assigned to the Central Division. . . . Owner Marge Schott was suspended through the 1998 season for her contin-ued insensitive remarks, and controller John Allen was named the managing executive to replace her until she returns. . . . Hal Morris finished the season with a 29-game hitting streak, the highest in the majors for the season and the second-highest in franchise history behind Pete Rose's 44-game streak in 1978.

—MIKE BASS

RECORDS

1996 regular-season record: 81-81 (3rd in N.L. Central); 46-35 at home; 35-46 on road; 27-33 vs. East; 25-27 vs. Central; 29-21 vs. West; 18-21 vs. lefthanded starters; 63-60 vs. righthanded starters; 23-33 on grass; 58-48 on turf; 25-26 in daytime; 56-55 at night; 21-22 in one-run games; 7-8 in extra-inning games; 5-0-2 in doubleheaders.

Team record past five years: 395-349 (.531, ranks 3rd in league in that span).

TEAM LEADERS

Batting average: Hal Morris (.313).
At-bats: Hal Morris (528).
Runs: Barry Larkin (117).
Hits: Hal Morris (165).
Total bases: Barry Larkin (293).

Doubles: Barry Larkin, Hal Morris (32).
Triples: Thomas Howard (10).
Home runs: Barry Larkin (33).
Runs batted in: Barry Larkin (89).
Stolen bases: Barry Larkin (36).
Slugging percentage: Barry Larkin (.567).
On-base percentage: Barry Larkin (.410).
Wins: John Smiley (13).
Earned-run average: John Smiley (3.64).
Complete games: Kevin Jarvis, John Smiley (2).
Shutouts: John Smiley (2).
Saves: Jeff Brantley (44).
Innings pitched: John Smiley (217.1).
Strikeouts: John Smiley (171).

GAMES BY POSITION

Catcher: Joe Oliver 97, Eddie Taubensee 94, Brook Fordyce 4.
First base: Hal Morris 140, Lenny Harris 16, Eduardo Perez 8, Tim Belk 6, Kevin Mitchell 3, Joe Oliver 3, Willie Greene 2, Eric Davis 1.
Second base: Bret Boone 141, Jeff Branson 9, Lenny Harris 8, Eric Owens 6, Willie Greene 1.
Third base: Willie Greene 74, Jeff Branson 64, Chris Sabo 43, Lenny Harris 24, Eric Owens 5, Eduardo Perez 3.
Shortstop: Barry Larkin 151, Jeff Branson 38, Willie Greene 1.
Outfield: Eric Davis 126, Thomas Howard 103, Reggie Sanders 80, Eric Owens 52, Curtis Goodwin 42, Eric Anthony 37, Lenny Harris 37, Kevin Mitchell 31, Chad Mottola 31, Vince Coleman 20, Mike Kelly 17, Willie Greene 10, Keith Mitchell 5, Joe Oliver 3, Steve Gibralter 2.

TOP DRAFT CHOICES

1a. **John Oliver,** OF, Lake-Lehman H.S., Lehman, Pa.
1b. **Matt McClendon,** RHP, Dr. Phillips H.S., Orlando, Fla.
2a. **Buddy Carlyle,** LHP, Bellevue (Neb.) East H.S.
2b. **Randi Mallard,** RHP, Hillsborough (Fla.) C.C.
3. **David Shepard,** RHP, Clemson University
4. **Phillip Merrell,** RHP, Nampa (Idaho) H.S.
5. **Nick Presto,** SS, Florida Atlantic Univ.
6. **Carl Caddell,** LHP, Northwood (Tex.) Univ.
7. **Wylie Campbell,** 2B, University of Texas.
8. **Kevin Marn,** OF, Kent University.
9. **Desi Herrera,** RHP, San Diego State Univ.
10. **Michael Vento,** OF, Cibola H.S., Albuquerque, N.M.

1997 SEASON Cincinnati Reds

COLORADO ROCKIES
NATIONAL LEAGUE WEST DIVISION

1997 ROCKIES SCHEDULE

Home games shaded.
* — All-Star Game at Jacobs Field (Cleveland)
D — Day game (any game starting before 5 p.m.)

APRIL

SUN	MON	TUE	WED	THU	FRI	SAT
		1 D CIN	2 CIN	3 D CIN	4 D MON	5 D MON
6 D MON	7 CIN	8	9 D CIN	10 D CIN	11 D MON	12 D MON
13 D MON	14	15 D CUB	16 D CUB	17	18 ATL	19 D ATL
20 ATL	21	22 FLA	23 D FLA	24	25 STL	26 D STL
27 D STL	28 HOU	29 D HOU	30 CUB			

MAY

SUN	MON	TUE	WED	THU	FRI	SAT
				1 D CUB	2 PHI	3 D PHI
4 D PHI	5 NYM	6 D NYM	7 PIT	8 D PIT	9 PHI	10 PHI
11 D PHI	12 PHI	13	14 PIT	15 PIT	16 D NYM	17 D NYM
18 D NYM	19 D SF	20 SF	21 D SF	22 D SF	23 HOU	24 D HOU
25 HOU	26 STL	27 D STL	28	29 FLA	30 FLA	31 D FLA

JUNE

SUN	MON	TUE	WED	THU	FRI	SAT
1 FLA	2 D STL	3 STL	4 D SD	5 D SD	6 FLA	7 D FLA
8 FLA	9 ATL	10 ATL	11 D ATL	12 SEA	13 SEA	14 D OAK
15 D OAK	16	17 TEX	18 TEX	19 D SD	20 SD	21 SD
22 D OAK	23 LA	24 LA	25 LA	26 SF	27 SF	28 SF
29 SF	30 ANA					

JULY

SUN	MON	TUE	WED	THU	FRI	SAT
		1 D ANA	2 TEX	3 TEX	4 SF	5 SF
6	7	8	* 9	10 D SD	11 SD	12 D SD
13 SD	14 TEX	15 D TEX	16 ATL	17 ATL	18 CUB	19 D CUB
20 LA	21 LA	22 MON	23 MON	24 CUB	25 CUB	26 CUB
27 MON	28 D MON	29 MON	30 D MON	31 PIT		

AUGUST

SUN	MON	TUE	WED	THU	FRI	SAT
					1 PIT	2 PIT
3 D PHI	4 PHI	5 NYM	6 NYM	7 D PIT	8 PIT	9 PIT
10 PHI	11 PHI	12 PHI	13 PHI	14 NYM	15 NYM	16 NYM
17 D YM	18 CIN	19 CIN	20 D HOU	21 HOU	22 HOU	23 D HOU
24 CIN	25 CIN	26 CIN	27 CIN	28 SEA	29 SEA	30 OAK
31 OAK						

SEPTEMBER

SUN	MON	TUE	WED	THU	FRI	SAT
	1 ANA	2 ANA	3	4 STL	5 STL	6 D STL
7 STL	8	9 HOU	10 HOU	11	12 HOU	13 HOU
14 FLA	15 D FLA	16 SD	17 SD	18 D LA	19 LA	20 LA
21 FLA	22	23 SF	24 SF	25 LA	26 LA	27 LA
28 SF						

1997 SEASON

CLUB DIRECTORY

Chairman, president and CEO
Jerry McMorris

Exec. vice president/general manager
Bob Gebhard

Sr. v.p./secretary and corporate counsel
Clark Weaver

Sr. vice president/chief financial officer
Hal Roth

Sr. vice president/business operations
Keli McGregor

Assistant general manager
Tony Siegle

Vice president/finance
Michael Kent

Vice president/player personnel
Dick Balderson

Vice president/sales and marketing
Greg Feasel

Vice president/scouting
Pat Daugherty

Vice president/ticket operations
Sue Ann McClaren

Director, broadcasting
Eric Brummond

Dir., management information systems
Mary Burns

Dir., promotions and special events
Alan Bossart

Director, public relations
Mike Swanson

Director, publications
Jimmy Oldham

Director, stadium services
Kevin Kahn

Director, team travel
Peter Durso

Director, ticket operations
Chuck Javernick

Dir., charitable and community affairs
Roger Kinney

Assistant director, player personnel
Paul Egins

Assistant director, scouting
Jay Darnell

Head groundskeeper
Mark Razum

Coordinator of instruction
Rick Mathews

National cross-checkers
Dave Holliday
Jeff Schugel

Regional cross-checkers
Bruce Andrew
Bill Gayton
Robyn Lynch

Major league scouts
Jack Bloomfield, Jim Fanning, Bill Harford, Larry High, Bill Wood

Scouts
Ty Coslow, Dar Cox, Mike Ericson, Abe Flores, Mike Garlatti, Bert Holt, Greg Hopkins, Bill Hughes, Damon Iannelli, Pat Jones, Bill Mackenzie, Danny Montgomery, Lance Nichols, Steve Payne, Art Pontarelli, Ed Santa, Nick Venuto, Tom Wheeler

International scouts
Phil Allen, Dario Arias, Roland de Lima Gamez, Cristobal A. Giron, Jim Hovorka, Brian McRobie, Amilcar Medina, Enrique Melendez, Atanacio Mendez, Jimmy Moreno, Jorge Posada, Rodolfo Rosario, Reed Spencer, Ron Steele, Herminio Toribio

MINOR LEAGUE AFFILIATES

Class	Team	League	Manager
AAA	Colorado Springs	Pacific Coast	Paul Zuvella
AA	New Haven	Eastern	Bill Hayes
A	Salem	Carolina	Bill McGuire
A	Asheville	South Atlantic	Ron Gideon
A	Portland	Northwest	Jim Eppard
Rookie	Mesa Rockies	Arizona	Tim Blackwell

BROADCAST INFORMATION

Radio: KOA-AM (850).
TV: KWGN-TV (Channel 2).
Cable TV: None.

SPRING TRAINING

Ballpark (city): Hi Corbett Field (Tucson, Ariz.).
Ticket information: 1-800-388-ROCK.

1997 SEASON Colorado Rockies

SPRING TRAINING ROSTER

Manager—Don Baylor (25).
Coaches—Paul Carey, Frank Funk (45), Gene Glynn (2), Jackie Moore (47), Clint Hurdle.

No.	PITCHERS	B/T	Ht./Wt.	Born	1996 clubs
50	Alston, Garvin	R/R	6-1/185	12-8-71	Colorado Springs, Colorado
31	Bailey, Roger	R/R	6-1/180	10-3-70	Colorado, Colorado Springs
41	Beckett, Robbie	R/L	6-5/225	7-16-72	Portland, New Haven, Colorado Springs, Colorado
37	Burke, John	B/R	6-4/215	2-9-70	Colorado Springs, Salem, Colorado
44	DeJean, Mike	R/R	6-2/205	9-28-70	Colorado Springs, New Haven
47	DiPoto, Jerry	R/R	6-2/200	5-24-68	New York N.L.
49	Hackman, Luther	R/R	6-4/195	10-6-74	Salem
40	Holmes, Darren	R/R	6-0/202	4-25-66	Colorado
38	Jones, Bobby	R/L	6-0/175	4-11-72	Colorado Springs
16	Leskanic, Curtis	R/R	6-0/180	4-2-68	Colorado, Colorado Springs
43	Munoz, Mike	L/L	6-2/192	7-12-65	Colorado, Colorado Springs
39	Reed, Steve	R/R	6-2/212	3-11-66	Colorado
23	Rekar, Bryan	R/R	6-3/210	6-3-72	Colorado Springs, Colorado
30	Ritz, Kevin	R/R	6-4/222	6-8-65	Colorado
18	Ruffin, Bruce	B/L	6-2/215	10-4-63	Colorado
20	Swift, Bill	R/R	6-0/197	10-27-61	Salem, Colorado
32	Thompson, Mark	R/R	6-2/205	4-7-71	Colorado
48	Thomson, John	R/R	6-3/175	10-1-73	New Haven, Colorado Springs
19	Wright, Jamey	R/R	6-5/203	12-24-74	New Haven, Colorado Springs, Colorado

No.	CATCHERS	B/T	Ht./Wt.	Born	1996 clubs
27	Decker, Steve	R/R	6-3/220	10-25-65	San Francisco, Colorado Springs, Colorado
8	Manwaring, Kirt	R/R	5-11/203	7-15-65	San Francisco, Phoenix, Houston
34	Owens, Jayhawk	R/R	6-1/213	2-10-69	Colorado Springs, Colorado
15	Reed, Jeff	L/R	6-2/190	11-12-62	Colorado

No.	INFIELDERS	B/T	Ht./Wt.	Born	1996 clubs
6	Bates, Jason	B/R	5-10/185	1-5-71	Colorado
9	Castilla, Vinny	R/R	6-1/200	7-4-67	Colorado
4	Counsell, Craig	L/R	6-0/170	8-21-70	Colorado Springs
14	Galarraga, Andres	R/R	6-3/235	6-18-61	Colorado
12	Huson, Jeff	L/R	6-3/180	8-15-64	Baltimore, Rochester, Frederick, Bowie, Colorado Springs
5	Perez, Neifi	L/R	6-0/173	2-2-75	Colorado Springs, Colorado
35	Vander Wal, John	L/L	6-2/198	4-29-66	Colorado
22	Weiss, Walt	B/R	6-0/175	11-28-63	Colorado
21	Young, Eric	R/R	5-9/170	5-18-67	New Haven, Salem, Colorado Springs, Colorado

No.	OUTFIELDERS	B/T	Ht./Wt.	Born	1996 clubs
10	Bichette, Dante	R/R	6-3/230	11-18-63	Colorado
26	Burks, Ellis	R/R	6-2/198	9-11-64	Colorado
11	Echevarria, Angel	R/R	6-3/219	5-25-71	Colorado Springs, Colorado
28	Gibson, Derrick	R/R	6-2/230	2-5-75	New Haven
1	Jones, Terry	B/R	5-10/165	2-15-71	Colorado Springs, Colorado
3	McCracken, Quinton	B/R	5-7/173	3-16-70	Colorado
29	Velazquez, Edgard	R/R	5-11/170	12-15-75	New Haven
33	Walker, Larry	L/R	6-3/225	12-1-66	Colorado, Salem, Colorado Springs

BALLPARK INFORMATION

Ballpark (capacity, surface)
Coors Field (50,200, grass)

Address
2001 Blake St.
Denver, CO 80205-2000

Business phone
303-292-0200

Ticket information
303-762-5437

Ticket prices
$28 (club level)
$22 (infield box)
$18 (outfield box)
$13 (lower reserved)
$11 (upper reserved, RF box)
$9 (RF mezzanine)
$7 (lower pavilion)
$6 (lower RF reserved)
$5 (upper RF reserved)
$4 (rockpile)
$1 (rockpile)

Field dimensions (from home plate)
To left field at foul line, 347 feet
To center field, 415 feet
To right field at foul line, 350

First game played
April 26, 1995 (Rockies 11, Mets 9, 14 innings)

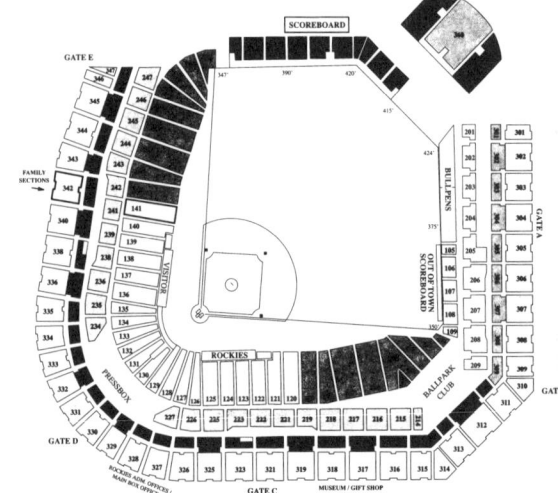

DAY BY DAY

Opp.	Res.	Score	(inn.*)	Hits	Opp. hits	Winning pitcher	Losing pitcher	Save	Record	Pos.	GB
At Phi.	W	5-3		5	4	Ritz	Fernandez		1-0	1st	+1/2
At Phi.	L	1-3		6	4	Grace	Freeman	Bottalico	1-1	T1st	...
At Phi.	L	4-7		8	10	Mulholland	Rekar	Bottalico	1-2	T2nd	1/2
At Mon.	L	4-6		9	10	Dyer	Munoz	Rojas	1-3	3rd	11/2
At Mon.	W	5-4		8	8	M. Thompson	Rueter	Leskanic	2-3	T2nd	11/2
At Mon.	L	1-9		3	9	Fassero	Painter		2-4	3rd	21/2
Chi.	L	6-9		12	12	Adams	Ritz	Jones	2-5	4th	31/2
Chi.	W	10-9		11	12	Leskanic	Jones		3-5	T3rd	3
N.Y.	W	7-3		13	7	Reynoso	Mlicki		4-5	T3rd	3
N.Y.	W	6-5		11	9	Freeman	Clark	Leskanic	5-5	3rd	2
N.Y.	L	4-10		12	16	Harnisch	Ritz	Henry	5-6	4th	21/2
S.D.	W	11-9		16	12	Ruffin	Blair	Leskanic	6-6	T3rd	11/2
S.D.	L	6-10		10	19	Ashby	Reynoso		6-7	T3rd	21/2
S.D.	L	6-11		13	17	Florie	Freeman		6-8	4th	31/2
At N.Y.	W	5-3		9	9	Ritz	Harnisch	Leskanic	7-8	T3rd	21/2
At N.Y.	L	3-4	(10)	10	9	J. Franco	Habyan		7-9	T3rd	21/2
At N.Y.	W	6-4		6	7	Leskanic	J. Franco		8-9	3rd	21/2
At Chi.	W	4-2		7	4	Freeman	Navarro	Leskanic	9-9	3rd	21/2
At Chi.	W	4-3		11	8	Rekar	Castillo	Leskanic	10-9	2nd	21/2
Phi.	L	8-10		13	8	Borland	S. Reed	Bottalico	10-10	2nd	31/2
Phi.	L	1-7		6	11	Fernandez	M. Thompson	Ryan	10-11	T3rd	41/2
Mon.	L	2-6		8	12	Alvarez	Reynoso		10-12	4th	51/2
Mon.	W	6-5	(13)	15	14	Painter	Daal		11-12	T3rd	41/2
Mon.	L	9-21		13	20	Rueter	Rekar		11-13	T3rd	41/2
At L.A.	L	4-7		7	10	Nomo	Ritz	Worrell	11-14	4th	5
At L.A.	W	4-1		5	6	M. Thompson	Astacio	Ruffin	12-14	4th	5
Fla.	W	9-5		11	12	Reynoso	Burkett		13-14	4th	4
Fla.	W	17-5		21	7	Freeman	Hammond		14-14	2nd	3
Fla.	W	5-4		11	7	Ritz	Perez		15-14	2nd	3
At Atl.	L	1-4		6	12	Avery	M. Thompson		15-15	2nd	31/2
At Atl.	L	5-6	(10)	8	8	Clontz	Leskanic		15-16	T2nd	4
At Atl.	L	1-5		6	9	Glavine	Reynoso		15-17	3rd	41/2
At Fla.	L	2-6		7	10	Miller	Freeman		15-18	T3rd	51/2
At Fla.	L	2-4		8	7	Rapp	Ritz	Nen	15-19	4th	51/2
At Fla.	L	0-11		0	11	Leiter	M. Thompson		15-20	4th	51/2
At Fla.	L	5-7		8	10	Nen	Leskanic		15-21	4th	61/2
At Cin.	W	5-3		7	6	S. Reed	Schourek	Ruffin	16-21	4th	7
St.L.	W	12-11		14	10	Leskanic	Bailey	Ruffin	17-21	4th	7
St.L.	W	9-8		14	11	Habyan	Eckersley		18-21	4th	6
St.L.	W	10-3		13	7	M. Thompson	An. Benes		19-21	4th	6
Pit.	W	10-7		14	12	Reynoso	Neagle		20-21	4th	51/2
Pit.	W	12-10		20	11	Holmes	Christiansen	Ruffin	21-21	4th	41/2
Pit.	W	6-3		11	10	Ritz	Smith	Ruffin	22-21	3rd	41/2
Cin.	L	5-7		4	8	Carrasco	Ruffin	Brantley	22-22	T3rd	51/2
Cin.	L	9-11		11	13	Ruffin	M. Thompson		22-23	4th	61/2
Cin.	W	7-5		7	9	Leskanic	Moore		23-23	4th	61/2
At St.L.	W	5-2		8	5	Ritz	Stottlemyre	Ruffin	24-23	4th	6
At St.L.	W	6-5		9	10	Painter	Mathews	Holmes	25-23	T2nd	6
At St.L.	L	5-6		7	9	Petkovsek	Leskanic	An. Benes	25-24	4th	6
At Pit.	L	4-8		6	13	Neagle	Reynoso	Cordova	25-25	T3rd	7
At Pit.	W	2-0		3	9	Ritz	Wagner	Ruffin	26-25	3rd	7
At Pit.	L	2-5		8	6	Smith	Holmes	Cordova	26-26	T3rd	7
At Pit.	L	2-7		7	12	Ruebel	Farmer		26-27	4th	7
At Hou.	L	8-16		9	13	Hampton	M. Thompson		26-28	4th	7
At Hou.	L	1-4		5	8	Wall	Reynoso		26-29	4th	8
At Hou.	W	14-7		18	9	Ritz	Drabek		27-29	4th	71/2
Atl.	W	19-8		21	12	Painter	Bielecki		28-29	4th	61/2
Atl.	W	13-12		16	18	Holmes	McMichael	Ruffin	29-29	1st	51/2
Atl.	L	3-8		8	12	Smoltz	M. Thompson		29-30	4th	51/2
Hou.	L	9-10		11	13	Wall	Reynoso		29-31	4th	51/2
Hou.	W	7-5		12	5	Alston	Young	Ruffin	30-31	4th	41/2
Hou.	W	8-0		13	8	Freeman	Reynolds		31-31	T3rd	31/2
Phi.	W	4-1		9	4	Rekar	Schilling	Ruffin	32-31	T3rd	21/2
Phi.	W	10-6		11	9	Painter	Springer		33-31	3rd	11/2
Phi.	W	4-2		12	5	Reynoso	Mulholland	Ruffin	34-31	3rd	11/2
Phi.	W	11-3		14	9	Ritz	Munoz		35-31	3rd	1/2
Mon.	L	3-5		8	9	Urbina	Freeman	Rojas	35-32	3rd	1
Mon.	L	8-12		12	15	Dyer	Holmes		35-33	T3rd	11/2
Mon.	W	7-6	(10)	13	15	Ruffin	Scott		36-33	T2nd	11/2
At Phi.	L	3-4	(10)	9	7	Borland	Ruffin		36-34	T2nd	1
At Phi.	L	4-5		7	11	Blazier	Hawblitzel	Bottalico	36-35	T2nd	2
At Phi.	W	7-4		7	9	Freeman	Fernandez	Ruffin	37-35	T2nd	2

Date	Opp.	Res.	Score	(inn.*)	Hits	Opp. hits	Winning pitcher	Losing pitcher	Save	Record	Pos.	GB
6-24	At N.Y.	L	1-2		9	8	Isringhausen	Holmes	J. Franco	37-36	3rd	
6-25	At N.Y.	L	2-3		7	7	B. Jones	M. Thompson	J. Franco	37-37	3rd	
6-26	At N.Y.	L	5-9		10	9	Mlicki	S. Reed		37-38	3rd	
6-27	L.A.	W	13-1		17	6	Ritz	Astacio		38-38	3rd	
6-28	L.A.	W	13-4		16	9	Freeman	Martinez		39-38	3rd	
6-29	L.A.	L	10-13		16	20	Valdes	Rekar		39-39	3rd	
6-30	L.A.	W	16-15		20	18	Ruffin	Worrell		40-39	3rd	
7-1	At S.F.	L	6-9		9	15	Juden	Painter	Beck	40-40	3rd	
7-2	At S.F.	L	1-5		5	7	Gardner	Ritz		40-41	3rd	
7-3	At S.F.	W	3-2		12	5	Leskanic	Beck	Ruffin	41-41	3rd	
7-4	At L.A.	L	4-9		9	9	Valdes	Freeman		41-42	3rd	
7-5	At L.A.	L	1-8		6	12	Nomo	Bailey		41-43	3rd	
7-6	At L.A.	L	2-3		5	6	Osuna	Ruffin	Worrell	41-44	3rd	
7-7	At L.A.	W	3-0		5	5	Ritz	Astacio		42-44	3rd	
7-11	S.D.	W	8-5	(10)	13	12	Ruffin	Hoffman		43-44	3rd	
7-12	S.D.	W	13-12		12	14	Holmes	Blair		44-44	3rd	
7-13	S.D.	W	11-6		11	11	Ritz	Sanders		45-44	3rd	
7-14	S.D.	W	8-4		13	8	Reynoso	Valenzuela		46-44	3rd	
7-15	S.F.	W	7-3		13	5	Bailey	Bourgeois		47-44	2nd	
7-16	S.F.	W	5-3		6	7	Freeman	Leiter	Ruffin	48-44	2nd	
7-17	S.F.	W	4-3		12	7	Wright	Fernandez	Ruffin	49-44	1st	
7-18	At S.D.	L	2-9		7	12	Sanders	Ritz		49-45	3rd	
7-19	At S.D.	L	3-4		7	7	Valenzuela	Reynoso	Hoffman	49-46	3rd	
7-20	At S.D.	W	5-4		8	11	Leskanic	Bochtler	Ruffin	50-46	2nd	
7-21	At S.D.	L	0-2		5	6	Tewksbury	Freeman	Hoffman	50-47	3rd	
7-23†	N.Y.	W	10-7		19	9	Ruffin	Henry		51-47		
7-23‡	N.Y.	W	11-10		16	15	S. Reed	Henry		52-47	T2nd	
7-24	N.Y.	W	7-6	(10)	17	11	Leskanic	Byrd		53-47	1st	
7-25	Chi.	L	8-10		15	17	Bottenfield	Ruffin	Patterson	53-48	T1st	
7-26	Chi.	L	4-17		10	17	Navarro	Freeman	Adams	53-49	T2nd	
7-27	Chi.	W	10-6		12	10	M. Thompson	Telemaco		54-49	T2nd	
7-28	Chi.	L	5-7		9	13	Bullinger	Ritz	Bottenfield	54-50	T2nd	
7-29	At Mon.	L	1-4		8	9	Cormier	Wright	Rojas	54-51	3rd	
7-30	At Mon.	L	1-3		3	4	Urbina	Reynoso	Rojas	54-52	3rd	
7-31	At Mon.	L	2-6		6	8	Fassero	Bailey		54-53	3rd	
8-1	At Chi.	L	1-4		7	8	Navarro	M. Thompson	Patterson	54-54	3rd	
8-2	At Chi.	W	7-2		5	7	Ritz	Telemaco		55-54	3rd	
8-3	At Chi.	W	8-2		8	5	Wright	Bullinger		56-54	3rd	
8-4	At Chi.	W	6-1		10	4	Reynoso	Castillo		57-54	3rd	
8-5	Fla.	L	9-16		11	22	Hutton	Freeman		57-55	3rd	
8-6	Fla.	W	11-0		17	7	M. Thompson	Burkett		58-55	3rd	
8-7	Fla.	W	12-5		16	10	Ritz	Leiter		59-55	T2nd	
8-9	At Atl.	W	6-4		9	8	Wright	Glavine	Ruffin	60-55	2nd	
8-10	At Atl.	W	9-7	(10)	9	8	S. Reed	Wohlers	Ruffin	61-55	2nd	
8-11	At Atl.	L	1-4		5	6	Smoltz	Freeman	Wohlers	61-56	T2nd	
8-13	At Fla.	L	0-5		2	10	Leiter	Ritz		61-57	3rd	
8-14	At Fla.	L	1-2		3	5	Brown	Leskanic	Nen	61-58	3rd	
8-15	At Fla.	L	6-7		11	11	Powell	Ruffin	Nen	61-59	3rd	
8-16	At Cin.	W	8-4		17	12	Reynoso	Salkeld		62-59	3rd	
8-17†	At Cin.	L	3-5		6	9	Smiley	Munoz	Brantley	62-60		
8-17‡	At Cin.	L	5-9		13	14	Shaw	S. Reed		62-61	3rd	
8-18	At Cin.	L	4-9		8	7	Jarvis	Ritz	Shaw	62-62	3rd	
8-19	At Cin.	W	6-3		10	9	M. Thompson	Portugal		63-62	3rd	
8-20	St.L.	W	5-4	(13)	10	11	Munoz	Mathews		64-62	3rd	
8-21	St.L.	W	10-2		18	15	Reynoso	An. Benes		65-62	3rd	
8-22	St.L.	W	10-5		16	8	Bailey	Morgan		66-62	3rd	
8-23	Pit.	L	3-5		7	11	Lieber	Ritz	Cordova	66-63	3rd	
8-24	Pit.	W	9-3		12	8	M. Thompson	Peters		67-63	3rd	
8-25	Pit.	W	13-9		13	15	Munoz	Wilkins		68-63	3rd	
8-26	Cin.	W	9-5	(7)	13	6	Swift	Jarvis	Bailey	69-63	3rd	
8-27	Cin.	L	3-4		9	8	Smiley	Reynoso	Brantley	69-64	3rd	
8-28	Cin.	W	10-9		11	12	Ruffin	Shaw		70-64	3rd	
8-29	Cin.	L	7-18		12	17	Burba	M. Thompson		70-65	3rd	
8-30	At St.L.	L	4-7		8	13	Al. Benes	Wright	Eckersley	70-66	3rd	
8-31	At St.L.	L	1-2		4	5	An. Benes	Bailey	Eckersley	70-67	3rd	
9-1	At St.L.	L	6-15		9	18	Petkovsek	Rekar		70-68	3rd	
9-2	At Pit.	W	8-3		8	6	Ritz	Loaiza		71-68	3rd	
9-4	At Pit.	L	2-5		9	6	Lieber	M. Thompson	Plesac	71-69	3rd	
9-6	At Hou.	L	1-2		2	10	Hernandez	Leskanic		71-70	3rd	
9-7	At Hou.	L	4-5		10	6	Kile	Holmes	Hudek	71-71	3rd	
9-8	At Hou.	W	5-2		7	6	S. Reed	Reynolds	Ruffin	72-71	3rd	
9-9	At Hou.	W	4-2		12	10	Ritz	Wall	Ruffin	73-71	3rd	
9-10	Atl.	W	9-8		13	15	Holmes	Clontz	Ruffin	74-71	3rd	
9-11	Atl.	W	6-5		8	10	Wright	Neagle	Swift	75-71	3rd	
9-12	Atl.	W	16-8		17	12	Burke	Smoltz		76-71	3rd	

ate	Opp.	Res.	Score	(inn.*)	Hits	Opp. hits	Winning pitcher	Losing pitcher	Save	Record	Pos.	GB
-13	Hou.	W	6-3		9	6	Holmes	Hernandez	Ruffin	77-71	3rd	5¹/₂
-14	Hou.	W	7-3		12	12	Ritz	Wall		78-71	3rd	5¹/₂
-15	Hou.	W	11-4		14	6	M. Thompson	Drabek		79-71	3rd	5¹/₂
-16	L.A.	L	4-6		9	11	Valdes	Wright		79-72	3rd	6¹/₂
-17	L.A.	L	0-9		0	14	Nomo	Swift		79-73	3rd	7¹/₂
-18	L.A.	W	6-4		8	6	Burke	Astacio	Ruffin	80-73	3rd	6¹/₂
-19	At S.F.	L	4-11		9	11	VanLandingham	Ritz		80-74	3rd	7¹/₂
-20	At S.F.	L	2-6		9	6	Gardner	M. Thompson		80-75	3rd	7¹/₂
-21	At S.F.	L	2-6		8	9	Rueter	Wright		80-76	3rd	8¹/₂
-22	At S.F.	L	3-7		7	9	Soderstrom	Nied		80-77	3rd	8¹/₂
-24	At S.D.	W	5-4	(11)	8	15	Ruffin	Hoffman	Swift	81-77	3rd	8¹/₂
-25	At S.D.	W	5-3		9	9	M. Thompson	Hamilton	Ruffin	82-77	3rd	8¹/₂
-27	S.F.	L	3-9		7	12	Soderstrom	Nied		82-78	3rd	8
-28	S.F.	L	5-8		11	12	Carlson	Burke	Beck	82-79	3rd	8
-29	S.F.	W	12-3		13	8	Ritz	Watson		83-79	3rd	8

Monthly records: April (11-14), May (14-11), June (15-14), July (14-14), August (16-14), September (13-12).
*Innings, if other than nine. †First game of doubleheader. ‡Second game of doubleheader.

HIGHLIGHTS

High point: The Rockies stayed in the race on the strength of their astounding 55-26 home record. They were never hotter than during an eight-game winning streak (the latter six victories coming at Coors Field) that pushed them eight games over .500 on September 15.
Low point: As good as the Rockies were at home, they were just as bad on the road, where they finished 28-53. A seven-game road losing streak May 6-12 included getting no-hit by the Marlins' Al Leiter on May 11.
Turning point: The Dodgers' Hideo Nomo did the unthinkable on September 17, throwing a no-hitter at Coors Field. That was the beginning of the end for the Rockies, who lost eight of their final 12 games.
Most valuable player: Center fielder Ellis Burks. He did what only Hank Aaron had done before—hit 40 homers, steal 30 bases and collect 200 hits in a season. And if that wasn't enough, he led the league with 142 runs, drove in 128 and batted .344.
Most valuable pitcher: Starter Kevin Ritz. If the Rockies' offensive accomplishments are going to be labeled as altitude-aided, then it only stands to reason that Ritz's 5.28 ERA be downplayed in comparison to his 17 wins, 213 innings and 35 starts.
Most improved player: Second baseman Eric Young. He started the season on the disabled list with a broken bone in his hand. But he made up for lost time by playing in the All-Star game and hitting .324 with 113 runs and a league-leading 3 steals.
Most pleasant surprise: Outfielder Quinton McCracken. He spent the first two months of his rookie season on the bench. But when his opportunity came after right fielder Larry Walker fractured his collarbone, McCracken established himself by hitting .290, scoring 50 runs and driving in 40 in 283 at-bats.
Biggest disappointment: The bullpen dropped off precipitously from 1995,

headlined by righthander Curtis Leskanic's fall. After six saves in April, he spent a month on the disabled list, then struggled to a 6.23 ERA, serving up 12 homers in 73²/₃ innings.
Key injuries: Nobody had more money on the disabled list than the Rockies, who lost righthander Bret Saberhagen ($4.3 million) for the season, got only 18¹/₃ innings out of righthander Bill Swift ($4.2 million) and lost Larry Walker ($4.2 million) for almost three months.
Notable: Take your pick of offensive accomplishments: three players with 40 homers, four players with 30 homers, five .300 hitters, the first team to hit 200 homers and steal 200 bases. . . . Burks and Bichette achieved the 30-30 club on consecutive days—Burks on September 12 (vs. Atlanta) and Bichette on September 13 (vs. Houston). . . . The Rockies led the major leagues in attendance with 3,891,014, a per-game average of 48,037. . . . At 280-305 (.479) the Rockies have the highest winning percentage of any expansion team in its first four years.

—TONY DeMARCO

RECORDS

1996 regular-season record: 83-79 (3rd in N.L. West); 55-26 at home; 28-53 on road; 28-33 vs. East; 36-26 vs. Central; 19-20 vs. West; 20-24 vs. lefthanded starters; 63-55 vs. righthanded starters; 72-59 on grass; 11-20 on turf; 36-27 in daytime; 47-52 at night; 23-16 in one-run games; 7-3 in extra-inning games; 1-1-0 in doubleheaders.
Team record past five years: 280-305 in four years (.479, ranks 10th in league in that span).

TEAM LEADERS

Batting average: Ellis Burks (.344).
At-bats: Dante Bichette (633).
Runs: Ellis Burks (142).
Hits: Ellis Burks (211).
Total bases: Ellis Burks (392).
Doubles: Ellis Burks (45).

Triples: Ellis Burks (8).
Home runs: Andres Galarraga (47).
Runs batted in: Andres Galarraga (150).
Stolen bases: Eric Young (53).
Slugging percentage: Ellis Burks (.639).
On-base percentage: Ellis Burks (.408).
Wins: Kevin Ritz (17).
Earned-run average: Armando Reynoso (4.96).
Complete games: Mark Thompson (3).
Shutouts: Mark Thompson (1).
Saves: Bruce Ruffin (24).
Innings pitched: Kevin Ritz (213.0).
Strikeouts: Kevin Ritz (105).

GAMES BY POSITION

Catcher: Jeff Reed 111, Jayhawk Owens 68, Steve Decker 10, Jorge Brito 8.
First base: Andres Galarraga 159, John Vander Wal 10.
Second base: Eric Young 139, Jason Bates 37, Neifi Perez 4, Pedro Castellano 3.
Third base: Vinny Castilla 160, Jason Bates 12, Pedro Castellano 1, Andres Galarraga 1.
Shortstop: Walt Weiss 155, Jason Bates 18, Neifi Perez 14.
Outfield: Dante Bichette 156, Ellis Burks 152, Quinton McCracken 93, Larry Walker 83, John Vander Wal 26, Eric Anthony 19, Trent Hubbard 19, Angel Echevarria 11, Terry Jones 4, Harvey Pulliam 3, Pedro Castellano 1, Alan Cockrell 1, Milt Thompson 1.

TOP DRAFT CHOICES

1. **Jake Westbrook,** RHP, Madison County H.S., Danielsville, Ga.
2. **John Nicholson,** RHP, Episcopal H.S., Houston.
3. **Shawn Chacon,** RHP, Greeley (Colo.) Central H.S.
4. **Steve Matcuk,** RHP, Indian River (Fla.) C.C.
5. **Jeff Sebring,** LHP, Iowa State University.
6. **Dean Brueggeman,** LHP, Belleville Area (Ill.) C.C.
7. **Clint Bryant,** 3B, Texas Tech.
8. **Alvin Rivera,** RHP, Yabucoa, P.R.
9. **Chris Kennedy,** RHP, Jones County (Miss.) J.C.
10. **Tom Stepka,** RHP, Le Moyne College.

1997 SEASON Colorado Rockies

FLORIDA MARLINS
NATIONAL LEAGUE EAST DIVISION

1997 MARLINS SCHEDULE

☐ Home games shaded.
* — All-Star Game at Jacobs Field (Cleveland)
D — Day game (any game starting before 5 p.m.)

APRIL

SUN	MON	TUE	WED	THU	FRI	SAT
		1 D CUB	2 CUB	3 D CUB	4 CIN	5 CIN
6 D CIN	D 7	CUB	D 9	10 D CUB	11 CIN	12 D CIN
13 D CIN	14	15 STL	16 STL	17 D STL	18 SF	19 D SF
20 D SF	21	22 COL	23 D COL	24	25 LA	26 LA
27 LA	28 SD	29 SD	30 STL			

MAY

SUN	MON	TUE	WED	THU	FRI	SAT
				1 STL	D 2 HOU	3 HOU
4 D HOU	D 5 PIT	6 PIT	7 ATL	8 ATL	9 HOU	10 HOU
11 D HOU	D 12 HOU	13 ATL	14 ATL	15	16 PIT	17 PIT
18 D PIT	D 19	20 NYM	21 NYM	22	23 SD	24 SD
25 D SD	26 LA	27 LA	28	29 COL	30 COL	31 D COL

JUNE

SUN	MON	TUE	WED	THU	FRI	SAT
1 D COL	2 SF	3 D SF	D 4 NYM	5 NYM	D 6 COL	7 D COL
8 D COL	9 SF	10 D SF	11 D SF	12	13 NYY	14 NYY
15 D NYY	16 DET	17 DET	18 DET	D 19	20 MON	21 D MON
22 D MON	23 PHI	24 PHI	25 D PHI	26 MON	27 MON	28 MON
29 D MON	30 BOS					

JULY

SUN	MON	TUE	WED	THU	FRI	SAT
		1 BOS	2 BOS	3 NYM	4 NYM	5 D NYM
6 D NYM	D 7	8 *	9	10 PHI	11 PHI	12 PHI
13 D PHI	14 MON	15 MON	16 LA	17 LA	18 D SD	19 SD
20 D SD	21 D SD	22 CIN	23 CIN	24	25 STL	26 D STL
27 D STL	28 CIN	29 CIN	30 CIN	31 ATL		

AUGUST

SUN	MON	TUE	WED	THU	FRI	SAT
					1 ATL	2 ATL
3 D ATL	D 4 HOU	5 HOU	6 PIT	D 7 PIT	D 8 ATL	9 D ATL
10 D ATL	D 11 ATL	12 HOU	13 HOU	14	15 PIT	16 PIT
17 D PIT	D 18 PIT	19 CUB	20 CUB	21	22 STL	23 STL
24 D STL	D 25 CUB	26 CUB	27 D CUB	28 CUB	29 TOR	30 D TOR
31 D TOR						

SEPTEMBER

SUN	MON	TUE	WED	THU	FRI	SAT
	1 BAL	D 2 BAL	3 BAL	4	5 LA	6 D LA
7 D LA	D 8 LA	9 SD	10 SD	11	12 SF	13 D SF
14 D SF	15 COL	16 COL	17 PHI	D 18 PHI	D 19 NYM	20 NYM
21 D NYM	D 22 NYM	23 MON	24 MON	25 MON	26 PHI	27 PHI
28 D PHI						

(sidebar) **1997 SEASON** *Florida Marlins*

1997 SEASON

CLUB DIRECTORY

Chairman
H. Wayne Huizenga
President
Donald A. Smiley
Exec. vice president and general manager
David Dombrowski
Vice president of broadcasting
Dean Jordan
Vice president of finance & administration
Jonathan Mariner
Vice president of sales and marketing
Jim Ross
Special counsel
James J. Blosser
Special consultant
Richard C. Rochon
V.p. and assistant general manager
Frank Wren
Vice president of player personnel
Gary Hughes
Vice president of player development
John Boles
Senior adviser, player personnel
Whitey Lockman
Dir. of Latin American operations
Al Avila
Director of minor league administration
Dan Lunetta
Director of scouting
Orrin Freeman
Assistant, baseball operations
DeJon Watson
Director of team travel
Bill Beck
Director of international relations
Tony Perez
Director of season & group sales
Lou De Paoli
Director of communications
Mark Geddis
Director of marketing partnerships
Ben Creed
Dir. of baseball information and publicity
Ron Colangelo

Asst. dir. of baseball info. and publicit
Julio C. Sarmiento
Director of Brevard County operations
Ken Lehner
Equipment manager
Mike Wallace
Team physician
Dr. Dan Kanell
Head trainer
Larry Starr
Major league scout
Scott Reid
International crosschecker
Tim Schmidt
National crosschecker
Jax Robertson
Regional crosscheckers
Dick Egan, Murray Cook, Greg Zunino
Scouts
Kelvin Bowles, Ty Brown, Joe Campise,
John Castleberry, Jon Deeble, Brad
Del Barba, Louis Eljaua, David Finley,
Lou Fitzgerald, William George, Stan
Saleski, Stan Zielinski, Ed Bockman,
Richard Bordi, David Chadd, Matthew
King, Robert Laurie, Steve McFarland
Deni Pacini, Mike Russell, Charlie
Silvera, Keith Snider, Steve Minor,
Cucho Rodriguez, Bill Singer, Wally
Walker, DeJon Watson, Jeff Wren
Director Dominican Republic operation
Jesus Alou
Dominican Republic scouts
Julian Camilo, Carlos de la Cruz, Pabl
Lantigua
Puerto Rico scouts
Cucho Rodriguez, Pedro Cintron
Venezuela scout
Miguel-Angel Garcia
Colombia scout
Hobert Cabrera
Panama scout
Ramon Webster

MINOR LEAGUE AFFILIATES

Class	Team	League	Manager
AAA	Charlotte	International	Carlos Tosca
AA	Portland	Eastern	Fredi Gonzalez
A	Brevard County	Florida State	Lorenzo Bundy
A	Kane County	Midwest	Lynn Jones
A	Utica	New York-Pennsylvania	Juan Bustabad
Rookie	Gulf Coast Marlins	Gulf Coast	Jon Deeble

BROADCAST INFORMATION
Radio: WQAM-AM (560); WCMQ-AM (1210, Spanish language).
TV: WBFS-TV (Channel 33).
Cable TV: SportsChannel, Sunshine Network.

SPRING TRAINING
Ballpark (city): Space Coast Stadium (Viera, Fla.).
Ticket information: 407-633-9200.

SPRING TRAINING ROSTER

Manager—Jim Leyland (11).
Coaches—Rich Donnelly (45), Bruce Kimm (12), Jerry Manuel (17), Milt May (29),Larry Rothschild (47), Tommy Sandt (37).

o.	PITCHERS	B/T	Ht./Wt.	Born	1996 clubs
57	Alfonseca, Antonio	R/R	6-4/180	4-16-72	Charlotte
27	Brown, Kevin	R/R	6-4/195	3-14-65	Florida
42	Cook, Dennis	L/L	6-3/190	10-4-62	Texas
20	Darensbourg, Vic	L/L	5-10/165	11-13-70	Brevard County, Charlotte
32	Fernandez, Alex	R/R	6-1/215	8-13-69	Chicago A.L.
33	Helling, Rick	R/R	6-3/215	12-15-70	Oklahoma City, Texas, Florida
49	Heredia, Felix	L/L	6-0/185	6-18-76	Portland, Florida
46	Hermanson, Dustin	R/R	6-2/195	12-21-72	Las Vegas, San Diego
51	Hernandez, Livan	R/R	6-2/220	2-20-75	Charlotte, Portland, Florida
50	Hurst, Bill	R/R	6-7/215	4-28-70	Portland, Florida
52	Hutton, Mark	R/R	6-6/240	2-6-70	New York A.L., Tampa, Columbus, Florida
25	Larkin, Andy	R/R	6-4/175	6-27-74	Brevard County, Portland, Florida
25	Leiter, Al	L/L	6-3/215	10-23-65	Florida
48	Mantei, Matt	R/R	6-1/181	7-7-73	Florida, Charlotte
35	Miller, Kurt	R/R	6-5/205	8-24-72	Charlotte, Florida
31	Nen, Robb	R/R	6-4/200	11-28-69	Florida
39	Powell, Jay	R/R	6-4/225	1-19-72	Florida, Brevard County
48	Rapp, Pat	R/R	6-3/215	7-13-67	Florida, Charlotte
41	Saunders, Tony	L/L	6-2/205	4-29-74	Portland
38	Stanifer, Rob	R/R	6-3/205	3-10-72	Brevard County, Portland
42	Ward, Bryan	L/L	6-2/210	1-28-72	Portland
30	Whisenant, Matt	B/L	6-3/215	6-8-71	Charlotte

o.	CATCHERS	B/T	Ht./Wt.	Born	1996 clubs
23	Johnson, Charles	R/R	6-2/215	7-20-71	Florida
9	Zaun, Greg	B/R	5-10/170	4-14-71	Baltimore, Rochester, Florida

o.	INFIELDERS	B/T	Ht./Wt.	Born	1996 clubs
7	Abbott, Kurt	R/R	6-0/185	6-2-69	Florida, Charlotte
26	Arias, Alex	R/R	6-3/185	11-20-67	Florida
24	Bonilla, Bobby	B/R	6-4/240	2-23-63	Baltimore
2	Booty, Josh	R/R	6-3/210	4-29-75	Kane County, Florida
1	Castillo, Luis	B/R	5-11/155	9-12-75	Portland, Florida
19	Conine, Jeff	R/R	6-1/220	6-27-66	Florida
21	Milliard, Ralph	R/R	5-11/170	12-30-73	Portland, Charlotte, Florida
3	Renteria, Edgar	R/R	6-1/172	8-7-75	Charlotte, Florida

o.	OUTFIELDERS	B/T	Ht./Wt.	Born	1996 clubs
18	Alou, Moises	R/R	6-3/195	7-3-66	Montreal
28	Cangelosi, John	B/L	5-8/160	3-10-63	Houston
15	Dunwoody, Todd	L/L	6-1/190	4-11-75	Portland
8	Eisenreich, Jim	L/L	5-11/195	4-18-59	Philadelphia
40	McMillon, Billy	L/L	5-11/172	11-17-71	Charlotte, Florida
6	Orsulak, Joe	L/L	6-1/205	5-31-62	Florida
	Riley, Marquis	R/R	5-11/170	12-27-70	Vancouver, Charlotte
10	Sheffield, Gary	R/R	5-11/190	11-18-68	Florida
22	White, Devon	B/R	6-2/190	12-29-62	Florida

BALLPARK INFORMATION

allpark (capacity, surface)
Pro Player Stadium (40,585, grass)

ddress
2267 N.W. 199th St.
Miami, Fla. 33056

usiness phone
305-626-7400

cket information
305-930-HITS

cket prices
$18 (club level section B)
$13 (club level section C)
$11 (terrace box, mezzanine box)
$8 (outfield reserved, adult)
$6 (mezzanine reserved)
$1.50 (outfield res., 12 and under)
$2 (fish tank-adults)
$1.50 (fish tank, 12 and under)

eld dimensions (from home plate)
To left field at foul line, 335 feet
To center field, 410 feet
To right field at foul line, 345 feet

st game played
April 5, 1993 (Marlins 6, Dodgers 3)

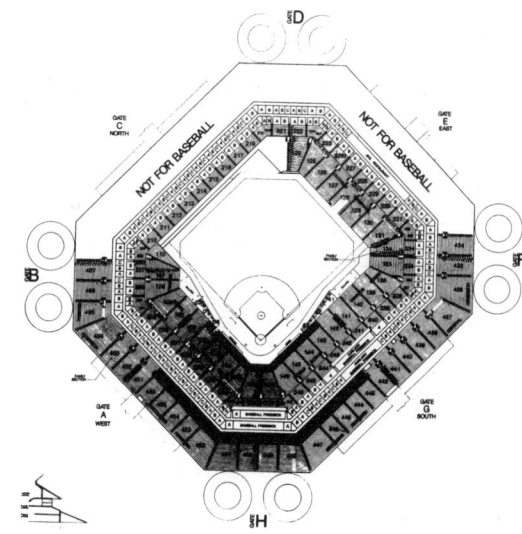

DAY BY DAY

Date	Opp.	Res.	Score	(inn.*)	Hits	Opp. hits	Winning pitcher	Losing pitcher	Save	Record	Pos.	GB
4-1	Pit.	L	0-4		3	9	Wagner	Brown		0-1	5th	1
4-2	Pit.	L	1-4		7	7	Christiansen	Pena	Miceli	0-2	5th	1¹/₂
4-4	Pit.	W	6-2		11	5	Leiter	Ericks		1-2	5th	1
4-5	S.F.	L	1-7		5	8	Fernandez	Rapp		1-3	5th	2
4-6	S.F.	W	1-0	(10)	5	7	Nen	Dewey		2-3	T2nd	1
4-7	S.F.	L	7-14		15	14	Bourgeois	Burkett		2-4	5th	2
4-8	At S.D.	L	2-9		6	10	Hamilton	Hammond		2-5	5th	3
4-9	At S.D.	W	5-2	(10)	7	8	Leiter	Blair		3-5	5th	2¹/₂
4-10	At S.D.	L	0-3		5	11	Tewksbury	Rapp	Hoffman	3-6	5th	2¹/₂
4-11	At L.A.	L	0-5		4	7	Park	Brown	Worrell	3-7	5th	3¹/₂
4-12	At L.A.	W	3-1		9	2	Burkett	Valdes		4-7	4th	3¹/₂
4-13	At L.A.	L	1-3		3	3	Nomo	Hammond		4-8	T4th	3¹/₂
4-14	At L.A.	L	1-6		8	8	Astacio	Leiter		4-9	5th	3¹/₂
4-16	At Atl.	L	2-5		6	13	Avery	Brown	Wohlers	4-10	5th	4¹/₂
4-17	At Atl.	L	2-4		6	9	Maddux	Burkett	Wohlers	4-11	5th	4¹/₂
4-18	At Atl.	W	5-3		9	8	Hammond	Glavine	Nen	5-11	5th	3¹/₂
4-19	L.A.	W	5-0		10	3	Powell	Hall		6-11	4th	3¹/₂
4-20	L.A.	W	7-4		10	11	Leiter	Nomo	Nen	7-11	4th	3¹/₂
4-21	L.A.	W	5-4		6	10	Brown	Hall	Mathews	8-11	4th	3¹/₂
4-22	S.D.	L	3-5		7	10	Ashby	Burkett		8-12	5th	4¹/₂
4-23	S.D.	L	2-7		5	11	Bergman	Hammond		8-13	5th	5¹/₂
4-24	At Pit.	L	3-6		9	11	Neagle	Rapp		8-14	5th	6¹/₂
4-25	At Pit.	W	4-1		6	6	Leiter	Hope	Nen	9-14	5th	6¹/₂
4-26	At S.F.	W	3-0		8	7	Brown	Fernandez		10-14	4th	6¹/₂
4-27	At S.F.	L	3-6		6	13	Leiter	Burkett	Beck	10-15	5th	6¹/₂
4-28	At S.F.	L	4-10		6	15	VanLandingham	Hammond		10-16	5th	7¹/₂
4-30	Phi.	W	7-2		7	8	Rapp	Williams	Nen	11-16	5th	6¹/₂
5-1	Phi.	L	5-6		13	9	Ryan	Leiter	Bottalico	11-17	5th	7
5-2	Phi.	L	0-2		5	5	Grace	Brown	Bottalico	11-18	5th	7¹/₂
5-3	At Col.	L	5-9		12	11	Reynoso	Burkett		11-19	5th	7¹/₂
5-4	At Col.	L	5-17		7	21	Freeman	Hammond		11-20	5th	8¹/₂
5-5	At Col.	L	4-5		7	11	Ritz	Perez		11-21	5th	9¹/₂
5-6	N.Y.	W	4-1		10	9	Leiter	Clark	Nen	12-21	5th	9¹/₂
5-7	N.Y.	W	3-2		13	9	Hammond	Isringhausen	Nen	13-21	5th	9¹/₂
5-8	N.Y.	W	6-3		9	5	Perez	Henry	Nen	14-21	5th	9¹/₂
5-9	Col.	W	6-2		10	7	Miller	Freeman		15-21	T4th	8¹/₂
5-10	Col.	W	4-2		7	8	Rapp	Ritz	Nen	16-21	T4th	8¹/₂
5-11	Col.	W	11-0		11	0	Leiter	M. Thompson		17-21	T4th	8¹/₂
5-12	Col.	W	7-5		10	8	Nen	Leskanic		18-21	4th	8¹/₂
5-13	St.L.	W	5-2		6	7	Burkett	An. Benes	Powell	19-21	4th	8¹/₂
5-14	St.L.	W	11-5		13	8	Mathews	Parrett		20-21	4th	7¹/₂
5-15	St.L.	L	0-6		4	8	Stottlemyre	Rapp		20-22	4th	7¹/₂
5-17	At Chi.	L	1-3		5	4	Bullinger	Leiter	Wendell	20-23	4th	7¹/₂
5-18	At Chi.	W	3-2		13	3	Burkett	Trachsel	Nen	21-23	4th	7¹/₂
5-19	At Chi.	W	8-7	(11)	14	9	Mantei	Wendell	Nen	22-23	4th	7
5-20	At Cin.	W	5-3		9	7	Rapp	Burba	Nen	23-23	T3rd	7
5-21	At Cin.	W	3-2		6	7	Weathers	Salkeld	Mathews	24-23	T3rd	6
5-22	At Cin.	L	1-4		6	4	Smiley	Leiter	Brantley	24-24	T3rd	7
5-24	St.L.	L	2-4		3	7	Morgan	Burkett	Mathews	24-25	4th	8
5-25	St.L.	L	0-5		5	12	An. Benes	Rapp		24-26	4th	8
5-26	St.L.	W	8-2	(8)	10	8	Weathers	Osborne		25-26	4th	8
5-27	Cin.	W	6-2		8	4	Leiter	Smiley		26-26	T3rd	8
5-28	Cin.	W	6-2		8	5	Brown	Burba	Mathews	27-26	T3rd	7¹/₂
5-31	Chi.	L	1-2		7	4	Navarro	Rapp		27-27	T3rd	9
6-1	Chi.	L	4-5	(10)	11	7	Wendell	Mathews		27-28	T3rd	9
6-2	Chi.	W	3-2		7	7	Brown	Telemaco	Nen	28-28	T3rd	9
6-4	Mon.	W	5-0		9	5	Burkett	Rueter		29-28	3rd	8¹/₂
6-5	Mon.	L	1-2		8	6	Cormier	Rapp	Veres	29-29	3rd	9¹/₂
6-7	At N.Y.	W	12-2		19	10	Leiter	Harnisch		30-29	3rd	8¹/₂
6-8	At N.Y.	L	6-7		13	12	Clark	Weathers	J. Franco	30-30	3rd	8¹/₂
6-9	At N.Y.	L	0-3		6	6	Isringhausen	Burkett		30-31	3rd	9¹/₂
6-10	At Mon.	W	5-2		12	8	Nen	Dyer		31-31	3rd	8¹/₂
6-11	At Mon.	L	2-3		8	8	Scott	Brown	Veres	31-32	3rd	9¹/₂
6-12	At Mon.	L	0-8		5	8	Fassero	Leiter		31-33	3rd	9¹/₂
6-13	At Pit.	W	4-3		11	7	Perez	Cordova	Nen	32-33	3rd	8¹/₂
6-14	At Pit.	L	4-5		9	10	Plesac	Nen		32-34	3rd	9¹/₂
6-15	At Pit.	L	8-12		14	15	Darwin	Rapp		32-35	3rd	9¹/₂
6-16	At Pit.	W	4-2		12	11	Brown	Neagle	Nen	33-35	3rd	8¹/₂
6-17	At S.F.	L	0-1		3	4	Fernandez	Leiter	Beck	33-36	3rd	9¹/₂
6-18	At S.F.	L	8-9	(15)	18	16	Juden	Rapp		33-37	3rd	10¹/₂
6-19	At S.F.	L	4-7	(15)	9	13	Bautista	Mathews		33-38	3rd	11¹/₂
6-21	Pit.	W	4-0		9	5	Brown	Darwin		34-38	3rd	11¹/₂

e	Opp.	Res.	Score	(inn.*)	Hits	Opp. hits	Winning pitcher	Losing pitcher	Save	Record	Pos.	GB
2	Pit.	L	1-4	(10)	5	7	Plesac	Perez		34-39	3rd	12½
3	Pit.	L	3-5		8	11	Lieber	Rapp	Cordova	34-40	3rd	13½
4	S.F.	W	2-1		3	4	Burkett	Leiter	Nen	35-40	3rd	12½
5	S.F.	W	5-4	(10)	9	7	Powell	Beck		36-40	3rd	12½
6	S.F.	W	3-2		11	7	Brown	Watson		37-40	3rd	11½
8	Atl.	W	2-0		5	9	Leiter	Glavine	Nen	38-40	3rd	11
9	Atl.	W	5-3		11	8	Rapp	Smoltz		39-40	3rd	10
0	Atl.	L	4-5		8	10	Clontz	Burkett	Wohlers	39-41	3rd	11
	At Hou.	L	2-6		5	7	Hampton	Brown		39-42	3rd	12
	At Hou.	L	3-4	(12)	10	11	Johnstone	Mathews		39-43	3rd	12
	At Hou.	L	3-4		10	9	Drabek	Leiter	Jones	39-44	3rd	13
	At Phi.	L	5-8		11	14	Blazier	Rapp	Bottalico	39-45	T3rd	13
	At Phi.	L	4-7		14	14	Borland	Miller	Bottalico	39-46	4th	13
	At Phi.	L	1-2		5	5	Williams	Brown	Bottalico	39-47	4th	14
	At Phi.	W	7-4	(10)	8	8	Mathews	R. Jordan	Nen	40-47	4th	14
1	At Atl.	W	9-8		16	14	Burkett	Avery	Nen	41-47	4th	13
2	At Atl.	L	3-6		8	8	Glavine	Leiter	Wohlers	41-48	4th	14
3	At Atl.	L	0-3		2	6	Smoltz	Brown		41-49	4th	15
4	At Atl.	L	10-15		13	14	McMichael	Perez		41-50	4th	16
5	Hou.	W	15-5		24	7	Pall	Wall		42-50	4th	16
6	Hou.	W	3-2		4	5	Perez	Jones		43-50	4th	16
7	Hou.	W	11-2		14	2	Leiter	Reynolds		44-50	4th	15½
8	Phi.	W	7-0		6	3	Brown	Mimbs		45-50	4th	15½
9	Phi.	W	11-2		13	11	Hammond	Williams		46-50	T3rd	14½
0	Phi.	W	7-4		11	12	Rapp	Springer	Nen	47-50	T3rd	13½
1	Phi.	L	3-12		8	13	Schilling	Burkett	Bottalico	47-51	T3rd	13½
	L.A.	L	1-7		7	4	Valdes	Leiter		47-52	3rd	15
4	L.A.	W	3-0		5	6	Brown	Nomo	Nen	48-52	3rd	15
5	L.A.	L	3-6		9	11	Astacio	Hammond	Worrell	48-53	3rd	15
6	S.D.	L	0-3	(11)	4	8	Hoffman	Pall		48-54	3rd	16
7	S.D.	L	12-20		17	19	Villone	Mathews		48-55	3rd	16
8	S.D.	W	8-2		15	2	Leiter	Hamilton		49-55	3rd	15
9	S.D.	L	3-5		5	7	Sanders	Brown	Hoffman	49-56	T3rd	15½
0	At L.A.	L	4-5	(10)	6	13	Osuna	Weathers		49-57	4th	15½
1	At L.A.	L	0-3		4	6	Martinez	Rapp	Worrell	49-58	4th	16½
	At L.A.	W	7-6	(14)	15	10	Hammond	Dreifort	Mathews	50-58	4th	16½
	At S.D.	L	1-2		7	6	Hoffman	Perez		50-59	4th	16½
	At S.D.	W	5-2		9	3	Brown	Sanders	Nen	51-59	4th	16½
	At S.D.	L	4-6		11	8	Valenzuela	Hammond	Hoffman	51-60	4th	17½
	At Col.	W	16-9		22	11	Hutton	Freeman		52-60	4th	17
	At Col.	L	0-11		7	17	M. Thompson	Burkett		52-61	4th	18
	At Col.	L	5-12		10	16	Ritz	Leiter		52-62	4th	19
	N.Y.	L	0-3		4	7	Harnisch	Brown	J. Franco	52-63	4th	19
	N.Y.	W	2-1	(10)	5	8	Nen	Henry		53-63	4th	18
0	N.Y.	W	9-6		15	16	Rapp	Wilson	Nen	54-63	4th	17
1	N.Y.	L	3-5		6	10	Clark	Valdes	J. Franco	54-64	4th	18
3	Col.	W	5-0		10	2	Leiter	Ritz		55-64	T3rd	18½
4	Col.	W	2-1		5	3	Brown	Leskanic	Nen	56-64	T3rd	17½
5	Col.	W	7-6		11	11	Powell	Ruffin	Nen	57-64	3rd	17½
6	At St.L.	L	2-6		7	10	An. Benes	Rapp		57-65	3rd	18½
7	At St.L.	L	3-4		6	10	Mathews	Powell	Eckersley	57-66	4th	19½
8	At St.L.	L	3-5		7	10	Stottlemyre	Leiter	Eckersley	57-67	4th	20½
9	At Chi.	W	4-3		7	6	Brown	Telemaco	Nen	58-67	3rd	20
0	At Chi.	L	1-8		2	11	Foster	Hutton		58-68	3rd	21
1	At Chi.	L	3-8		9	8	Castillo	Rapp		58-69	4th	22
3†	Cin.	L	5-6		11	12	Carrara	Valdes	Brantley	58-70		
3‡	Cin.	W	8-3		10	8	Leiter	Jarvis		59-70	T3rd	22
4	Cin.	W	5-3		9	7	Brown	Burba	Nen	60-70	3rd	22
5	Cin.	W	6-5		7	12	Nen	Smith		61-70	3rd	21
7	At St.L.	W	6-3		8	6	Hutton	Morgan	Nen	62-70	3rd	20
8	At St.L.	W	3-2	(10)	9	10	Hammond	Bailey	Nen	63-70	3rd	20
9	At St.L.	W	10-9		13	14	Leiter	Stottlemyre	Nen	64-70	3rd	20
0	At Cin.	W	3-1		8	8	Brown	Remlinger	Nen	65-70	3rd	19½
1	At Cin.	L	8-22		12	18	Jarvis	Miller		65-71	3rd	19½
	At Cin.	W	6-1		12	8	Hutton	Smiley		66-71	3rd	18½
	Chi.	W	4-3		10	7	Valdes	Trachsel	Nen	67-71	3rd	17½
	Chi.	L	3-11		9	9	Navarro	Leiter		67-72	3rd	17½
	Chi.	W	9-2		10	5	Brown	Foster		68-72	3rd	16½
	Mon.	L	2-6		7	14	Manuel	Rapp		68-73	3rd	17
	Mon.	W	4-0		11	7	Hutton	Fassero	Powell	69-73	3rd	17
	Mon.	L	1-2		5	7	Leiter	Valdes	Rojas	69-74	3rd	18
	Mon.	W	2-1		6	4	Helling	Martinez	Nen	70-74	3rd	17
	At N.Y.	L	1-6		7	12	Mlicki	Brown		70-75	3rd	17½
0	At N.Y.	W	9-3	(12)	14	12	Powell	Henry		71-75	3rd	16½
1	At N.Y.	L	1-3		6	10	Isringhausen	Rapp	Wallace	71-76	3rd	16½

Date	Opp.	Res.	Score	(inn.*)	Hits	Opp. hits	Winning pitcher	Losing pitcher	Save	Record	Pos.	GB
9-12	At Mon.	L	4-5		8	6	Veres	Powell	Rojas	71-77	3rd	16¹
9-13	At Mon.	L	2-3		6	4	Martinez	Helling	Rojas	71-78	3rd	16¹
9-14	At Mon.	L	2-3		9	10	Veres	Powell	Rojas	71-79	3rd	16¹
9-15	At Mon.	W	4-3		10	6	Leiter	Daal	Nen	72-79	3rd	16¹
9-17	At Phi.	W	11-5		14	12	Rapp	Beech		73-79	3rd	17
9-18	At Phi.	L	6-8		7	17	Borland	Miller	Bottalico	73-80	3rd	18
9-20	Hou.	W	3-1		5	7	Brown	Reynolds	Nen	74-80	3rd	17¹
9-21	Hou.	W	2-1		7	5	Heredia	Wagner		75-80	3rd	17¹
9-22	Hou.	W	6-0		7	2	Helling	Kile		76-80	3rd	17¹
9-24	Atl.	W	12-1		21	10	Rapp	Avery		77-80	3rd	17
9-25	Atl.	W	3-0		5	7	Brown	Glavine	Nen	78-80	3rd	16
9-26	Atl.	W	7-1		11	6	Leiter	Neagle		79-80	3rd	15
9-27	At Hou.	W	3-2		11	6	Hutton	Kile	Nen	80-80	3rd	15
9-28	At Hou.	L	1-5		7	10	Darwin	Heredia		80-81	3rd	16
9-29	At Hou.	L	4-5	(10)	9	11	Hudek	Hammond		80-82	3rd	16

Monthly records: April (11-16), May (16-11), June (12-14), July (10-17), August (16-13), September (15-11).
*Innings, if other than nine. †First game of doubleheader. ‡Second game of doubleheader.

HIGHLIGHTS

High points: When the team signed Al Leiter last winter, the organization endured a blitz of criticism because a career .500 pitcher was getting $8.6 million over three years. But Leiter emerged as a bargain, and on May 11 he threw the first no-hitter in Marlins history, blanking the Rockies, 11-0. It was victory No. 6 in a club-record nine-game win streak.

Low point: A team that came into 1996 preceded by high expectations found itself losers of seven straight on July 6. Not only did that match a club record, the 39-47 record cost Rene Lachemann, the first and only manager in Marlins history, his job on July 7.

Turning point: The Marlins made a bold move by naming player development director John Boles as the interim manager. Boles came to the job with no major league managing or playing experience. With a lineup shuffle, some late-season roster moves and a touch of discipline, Boles went 40-35 in the second half, including a 22-12 finish.

Most valuable player: Right fielder Gary Sheffield. He answered the questions about what he could do if he stayed healthy an entire season. He played in a career-high 161 games, while setting club records with a .314 average, 42 homers and 120 RBIs.

Most valuable pitcher: Kevin Brown would have been a lock for the Cy Young Award were it not for John Smoltz. Brown's 1.89 ERA was the lowest in the majors, and he set a club record with 17 wins. In his 11 losses, the Marlins scored a combined 11 runs.

Most improved player: Reliever Robb Nen. He became one of the game's most dominating closers. After battling confidence problems the previous year, Nen saved 35 games and converted 20 of his last 21 save chances of 1996. He also nearly cut his 1995 ERA in half, finishing with a mark of 1.95.

Most pleasant surprise: Rookie shortstop Edgar Renteria. He made the jump from Class AAA to the big leagues in mid-May because of his glove. Yet after hitting .248 before the All-Star break, Renteria hit .334 the rest of the way. He had a club-record 22-game hitting streak and stole 16 bases in 18 attempts—all in the second half.

Biggest disappointment: Righthander Pat Rapp. He went from a team-leading 14 wins in '95 to a league-leading 16 losses in '96. In addition, his ERA ballooned from 3.44 to 5.10 and he walked a career-high 91.

Key injuries: Veteran reliever Alejandro Pena went on the disabled list two weeks into the season with a slight tear of the rotator cuff and was later forced to have surgery. That left the Marlins without a proven setup man, and it turned out to be a glaring weakness throughout the season. Gold Glove catcher Charles Johnson was sidelined the entire month of August with a sprained ligament in the middle finger of his throwing hand. The pitching staff's ERA was almost a run higher when Johnson didn't catch. Hard-throwing middle reliever Matt Mantei, one of the team's brightest pitching prospects, was shelved June 18 with shoulder problems and missed the rest of the season.

Notable: The Marlins finished a franchise-best 80-82. Their 80-80 record with two games remaining was the latest point in the season in team history the Marlins have been at .500. . . . Until the Braves' Andruw Jones was called up, the Marlins had the majors' three youngest players in reliever Felix Heredia (who turned 20 on June 18), second baseman Luis Castillo (21 on Sept. 12) and shortstop Edgar Renteria (21 on August 7). . . . Outfielder Andre Dawson retired after 21 seasons in the majors.
—SCOTT TOLLEY

RECORDS

1996 regular-season record: 80-82 (3rd in N.L. East); 52-29 at home; 28-53 on road; 25-27 vs. East; 33-27 vs. Central; 22-28 vs. West; 24-14 vs. lefthanded starters; 56-68 vs. righthanded starters; 68-63 on grass; 12-19 on turf; 18-31 in daytime; 62-51 at night; 26-23 in one-run games; 9-8 in extra-inning games; 0-0-1 in doubleheaders.

Team record past five years: 262-320 in four years (.450, ranks 13th in league in that span).

TEAM LEADERS

Batting average: Gary Sheffield (.314).
At-bats: Jeff Conine (597).
Runs: Gary Sheffield (118).
Hits: Jeff Conine (175).
Total bases: Gary Sheffield (324).
Doubles: Devon White (37).
Triples: Kurt Abbott (7).
Home runs: Gary Sheffield (42).
Runs batted in: Gary Sheffield (120).
Stolen bases: Devon White (22).
Slugging percentage: Gary Sheffield (.624).
On-base percentage: Gary Sheffield (.46*).
Wins: Kevin Brown (17).
Earned-run average: Kevin Brown (1.89).
Complete games: Kevin Brown (5).
Shutouts: Kevin Brown (3).
Saves: Robb Nen (35).
Innings pitched: Kevin Brown (233.0).
Strikeouts: Al Leiter (200).

GAMES BY POSITION

Catcher: Charles Johnson 120, Bob Na* 43, Joe Siddall 18, Greg Zaun 10.
First base: Greg Colbrunn 134, Jeff Conine 48, Russ Morman 2, Joe Orsula* 2, Alex Arias 1, Jerry Brooks 1.
Second base: Quilvio Veras 67, Luis Castillo 41, Craig Grebeck 29, Ralph Milliard 2, Kurt Abbott 20, Alex Arias 1.
Third base: Terry Pendleton 108, Alex Arias 59, Kurt Abbott 33, Josh Booty 1, Craig Grebeck 1.
Shortstop: Edgar Renteria 106, Kurt Abbott 44, Alex Arias 20, Craig Grebeck 1.
Outfield: Gary Sheffield 161, Devon White 139, Jeff Conine 128, Jesus Tavarez 65, Joe Orsulak 59, Billy McMillon 38, Andre Dawson 6, Jerry Brooks 2.

TOP DRAFT CHOICES

1. **Mark Kotsay,** OF, Cal State Fullerton.
2. None.
3. None.
4. **Blaine Neal,** RHP, Bishop Eustace H.S. Pennsauken, N.J.
5. **Brent Billingsley,** LHP, Cal State Fullerto*
6. **David Townsend,** RHP, Delta State (Miss.) U.
7. **Chris Moore,** RHP, Harlan Community H.S., Chicago.
8. **Quantaa Jackson,** Jackson, OF, Wharto* (Tex.) H.S.
9. **Vaughn Schill,** SS, Audubon (N.J.) H.S*
10. **Cory Washington,** OF, Westover H.S., Fayetteville, N.C.

HOUSTON ASTROS
NATIONAL LEAGUE CENTRAL DIVISION

1997 ASTROS SCHEDULE

Home games shaded.
* — All-Star Game at Jacobs Field (Cleveland)
D — Day game (any game starting before 5 p.m.)

APRIL

SUN	MON	TUE	WED	THU	FRI	SAT
		1 ATL	2 ATL	3 ATL	4 STL	5 STL
6 D STL	7	8 ATL	9 ATL	10 ATL	11 STL	12 D STL
13 STL	14 D STL	15 MON	16 MON	17	18 LA	19 LA
20 D LA	21	22 SD	23 SD	24	25 SF	26 SF
27 SF	28 COL	29 D COL	30 MON			

MAY

SUN	MON	TUE	WED	THU	FRI	SAT
				1 D MON	2 FLA	3 FLA
4 D LA	5 PHI	6 PHI	7 NYM	8 NYM	9 FLA	10 FLA
11 D LA	12 FLA	13 NYM	14 NYM	15	16 PHI	17 PHI
18 D PHI	19 PHI	20 CIN	21 CIN	22	23 COL	24 D COL
25 D COL	26 D SF	27 D SF	28	29 SD	30 SD	31 SD

JUNE

SUN	MON	TUE	WED	THU	FRI	SAT
1 D SD	2 LA	3 D LA	4 CIN	5 D CIN	6 SD	7 SD
8 D SD	9 LA	10 LA	11 LA	12	13 MIN	14 MIN
15 D MIN	16 KC	17 KC	18 KC	19	20 CUB	21 D CUB
22 D CUB	23 PIT	24 PIT	25 D PIT	26 CUB	27 D CUB	28 D CUB
29 D CUB	30 CLE					

JULY

SUN	MON	TUE	WED	THU	FRI	SAT
		1 CLE	2 CLE	3 CIN	4 CIN	5 CIN
6 D CIN	7	8 *	9 PIT	10 PIT	11 PIT	12 PIT
13 D PIT	14 CUB	15 CUB	16 SF	17 SF	18 D MON	19 MON
20 D MON	21	22 STL	23 STL	24 MON	25 MON	26 MON
27 MON	28 STL	29 STL	30 STL	31		

AUGUST

SUN	MON	TUE	WED	THU	FRI	SAT
					1 NYM	2 D NYM
3 NYM	4 FLA	5 FLA	6 PHI	7 PHI	8 D NYM	9 NYM
10 D NYM	11 NYM	12 FLA	13 FLA	14	15 PHI	16 D PHI
17 D PHI	18	19 ATL	20 ATL	21 COL	22 COL	23 D COL
24 COL	25	26 ATL	27 ATL	28 ATL	29 CWS	30 CWS
31 D CWS						

SEPTEMBER

SUN	MON	TUE	WED	THU	FRI	SAT
	1 D MIL	2 MIL	3 D MIL	4 SF	5 SF	6 D SF
7 D SF	8	9 COL	10 D COL	11	12 LA	13 LA
14 D LA	15 D SD	16 SD	17 PIT	18 PIT	19 CIN	20 D CIN
21 D CIN	22 D CUB	23 D CUB	24 CUB	25 CUB	26 PIT	27 PIT
28 D PIT						

1997 SEASON

CLUB DIRECTORY

Chairman and CEO
Drayton McLane Jr.
President
Tal Smith
Sr. vice president, business operations
Bob McClaren
General manager
Gerry Hunsicker
Assistant general manager
Tim Purpura
Special assistant to the general manager
Matt Galante
Director of player development
Jim Duquette
Director of scouting
David Lakey
Director of baseball administration
Barry Waters
Asst. dir. of scouting & dir. of int'l dev.
David Rawnsley
Vice president of marketing
Pam Gardner
Director of media relations
Rob Matwick
Assistant director of media relations
Darrell Simon
Director of broadcasting & promotions
Jamie Hildreth
Director of community development
Gene Pemberton
Director of ticket sales & services
John Sorrentino
Controller
Robert McBurnett

Scouts
Stan Benjamin
Bob Blair
Stan Boroski
Ralph Bratton
Gerry Craft
Doug Deutsch
James Farrar
Brian Granger
Dan Huston
Marc Johnson
Brian Keegan
Bill Kelso
Bob King
Julio Linares
Mike Maggart
Walt Matthews
Domingo Mercedes
Tom Mooney
Fred Nelson
Joe Pittman
Jim Pransky
Andres Reiner
Anibal Reluz
Adriano Rodriguez
Deron Rombach
Rich Schroeder
Bob Skinner
Tad Slowik
Larry Slusser
Steve Smith
Scipio Spinks
Lynwood Stallings
Kevin Stein
Frankie Thon
Tim Tolman
Paul Weaver
Grant Weir
Gene Wellman
Tom Wiedenbauer

MINOR LEAGUE AFFILIATES

Class	Team	League	Manager
AAA	New Orleans	American Association	Steve Swisher
AA	Jackson	Texas	Gary Allenson
A	Kissimmee	Florida State	John Tamargo
A	Quad City	Midwest	Manny Acta
A	Auburn	New York-Pennsylvania	To be announced
Rookie	Gulf Coast Astros	Gulf Coast	Julio Linares

BROADCAST INFORMATION
Radio: KILT-AM (610); KXYZ-AM (1320, Spanish language).
TV: KTXH-TV (Channel 20).
Cable TV: Fox Sports Southwest.

SPRING TRAINING
Ballpark (city): Osceola County Stadium (Kissimmee, Fla.).
Ticket information: 407-933-2520.

1997 SEASON *Houston Astros*

SPRING TRAINING ROSTER

Manager—Larry Dierker (49).
Coaches—Alan Ashby, Jose Cruz (25), Mike Cubbage (4), Tom McCraw, Vern Ruhle (48), Bill Virdon (18).

No.	PITCHERS	B/T	Ht./Wt.	Born	1996 clubs
38	Creek, Ryan	R/R	6-1/180	9-24-72	Jackson
50	Fernandez, Sid	L/L	6-1/230	10-12-62	Philadelphia, Clearwater
	Garcia, Ramon	R/R	6-2/200	12-9-69	New Orleans, Milwaukee
43	Grzanich, Mike	R/R	6-1/180	8-24-72	Jackson
10	Hampton, Mike	R/L	5-10/180	9-9-72	Houston
53	Henriquez, Oscar	R/R	6-6/220	1-28-74	Kissimmee
45	Holt, Chris	R/R	6-4/205	9-18-71	Tucson, Houston
35	Hudek, John	B/R	6-1/200	8-8-66	Kissimmee, Tucson, Houston
57	Kile, Darryl	R/R	6-5/185	12-2-68	Houston
	Lima, Jose	R/R	6-2/170	9-30-72	Toledo, Detroit
	Martin, Tom	L/L	6-1/185	5-21-70	Tucson, Jackson
	Miller, Trever	R/L	6-3/175	5-29-73	Toledo, Detroit
50	Mlicki, Doug	R/R	6-3/175	4-12-71	Tucson
51	Morman, Alvin	L/L	6-3/210	1-6-69	Houston
	Nitkowski, C.J.	L/L	6-3/190	3-3-73	Toledo, Detroit
37	Reynolds, Shane	R/R	6-3/210	3-26-68	Houston
36	Small, Mark	R/R	6-3/205	11-12-67	Tucson, Houston
33	Springer, Russ	R/R	6-4/205	11-7-68	Philadelphia
13	Wagner, Billy	L/L	5-11/180	6-25-71	Tucson, Houston
56	Wall, Donne	R/R	6-1/180	7-11-67	Tucson, Houston
	Walter, Mike	R/R	6-1/190	10-23-74	Quad City

No.	CATCHERS	B/T	Ht./Wt.	Born	1996 clubs
7	Ausmus, Brad	R/R	5-11/190	4-14-69	San Diego, Detroit
20	Eusebio, Tony	R/R	6-2/210	4-27-67	Houston, Tucson
9	Knorr, Randy	R/R	6-2/215	11-12-68	Syracuse, Houston

No.	INFIELDERS	B/T	Ht./Wt.	Born	1996 clubs
5	Bagwell, Jeff	R/R	6-0/195	5-27-68	Houston
17	Berry, Sean	R/R	5-11/200	3-22-66	Houston
7	Biggio, Craig	R/R	5-11/180	12-14-65	Houston
22	Cedeno, Andujar	R/R	6-1/170	8-21-69	San Diego, Detroit, Houston
12	Gutierrez, Ricky	R/R	6-1/175	5-23-70	Houston
	Listach, Pat	B/R	5-9/180	9-12-67	Milwaukee, Beloit
	Spiers, Bill	L/R	6-2/190	6-5-66	Houston

No.	OUTFIELDERS	B/T	Ht./Wt.	Born	1996 clubs
21	Abreu, Bob	L/R	6-0/160	3-11-74	Tucson, Houston
14	Bell, Derek	R/R	6-2/215	12-11-68	Houston
	Gonzalez, Luis	L/R	6-2/185	9-3-67	Chicago N.L.
60	Hidalgo, Richard	R/R	6-3/190	7-2-75	Jackson
22	Howard, Thomas	B/R	6-2/205	12-11-64	Cincinnati, Chattanooga, Indianapolis
39	Montgomery, Ray	R/R	6-3/195	8-8-69	Tucson, Houston
6	Mouton, James	R/R	5-9/175	12-29-68	Houston, Tucson

BALLPARK INFORMATION

Ballpark (capacity, surface)
The Astrodome (54,370, artificial)

Address
P.O. Box 288
Houston, TX 77001-0288

Business phone
713-799-9500

Ticket information
713-799-9555

Ticket prices
$21 (star deck)
$17 (field level)
$15 (mezzanine)
$12 (outfield mezzanine, sky box)
$11 (loge)
$7 (upper box)
$5 (upper reserved)
$4 (adult pavilion)
$1 (youth pavilion)

Field dimensions (from home plate)
To left field at foul line, 325 feet
To center field, 400 feet
To right field at foul line, 325 feet

First game played
April 12, 1965 (Phillies 2, Astros 0)

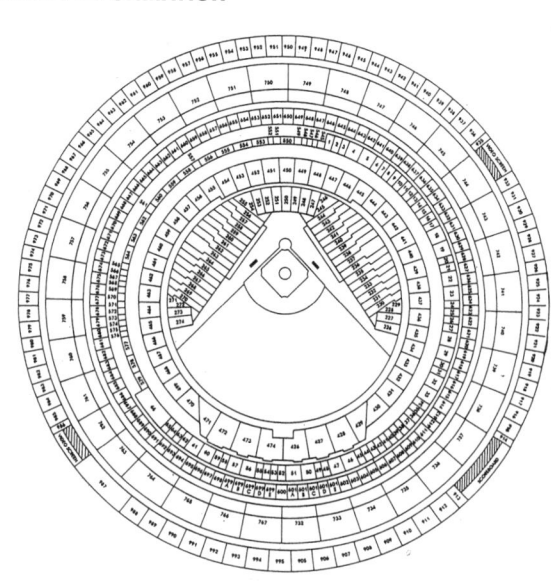

DAY BY DAY

ate	Opp.	Res.	Score	(inn.*)	Hits	Opp. hits	Winning pitcher	Losing pitcher	Save	Record	Pos.	GB
1	L.A.	L	3-4		6	11	Martinez	Reynolds	Worrell	0-1	T4th	1
2	L.A.	W	5-4		14	11	Jones	Cummings		1-1	4th	1
3	L.A.	W	5-2		10	11	Hampton	Nomo	Jones	2-1	2nd	1/2
5	S.D.	L	4-10		9	15	Tewksbury	Kile		2-2	T3rd	1
6	S.D.	L	4-8	(13)	10	15	Hoffman	Small		2-3	5th	2
7	S.D.	L	2-17		4	17	Bergman	Swindell		2-4	5th	2¹/₂
8	S.F.	W	6-2		5	4	Hampton	VanLandingham		3-4	T4th	2
9	S.F.	L	1-3	(10)	6	8	Juden	Tabaka	Beck	3-5	5th	2¹/₂
10	S.F.	L	5-11		13	11	Fernandez	Kile		3-6	5th	2¹/₂
11	At Cin.	W	9-4		18	7	Reynolds	Portugal		4-6	5th	2
12	At Cin.	W	10-8	(10)	12	12	Jones	Moore	Tabaka	5-6	T4th	1¹/₂
14†	At Cin.	L	3-5		8	8	Schourek	Hampton	Brantley	5-7		
14‡	At Cin.	L	8-9		14	11	Shaw	Young	Brantley	5-8	5th	2¹/₂
16	At N.Y.	W	9-6		12	9	Reynolds	Isringhausen	Jones	6-8	5th	2
17	At N.Y.	W	7-5		11	12	Kile	Wilson	Jones	7-8	5th	2
19	Cin.	W	13-5		18	7	Brocail	Schourek		8-8	T3rd	2
20	Cin.	L	1-6		8	14	Smiley	Drabek		8-9	T4th	2¹/₂
21	Cin.	W	7-5		11	14	Jones	Brantley		9-9	T3rd	1¹/₂
22	At S.F.	W	11-8		15	14	Reynolds	Leiter		10-9	2nd	1/2
23	At S.F.	W	8-4		11	8	Kile	VanLandingham		11-9	1st	+1/2
24	At L.A.	L	2-5		6	8	Valdes	Brocail		11-10	2nd	1/2
25	At L.A.	L	4-6		7	9	Nomo	Drabek	Worrell	11-11	2nd	1/2
26	At S.D.	L	2-3		7	6	Worrell	Hampton	Hoffman	11-12	T2nd	1/2
27	At S.D.	W	6-0		12	4	Reynolds	Ashby		12-12	1st	+1/2
28	At S.D.	W	3-2		9	5	Kile	Bergman	Jones	13-12	1st	+1
29	At S.D.	L	0-2		4	6	Hamilton	Brocail		13-13	1st	+1
30	Atl.	L	5-7		8	16	Smoltz	Jones	McMichael	13-14	T1st	...
1	Atl.	W	3-0		10	3	Hampton	Avery		14-14	T1st	...
3	Mon.	W	4-1		9	4	Reynolds	Cormier	Jones	15-14	T1st	...
4	Mon.	L	1-2		6	6	Veres	Hernandez	Rojas	15-15	T1st	...
5	Mon.	L	0-5		7	7	Fassero	Brocail		15-16	3rd	1
6	At Phi.	W	11-5		10	7	Drabek	Hunter		16-16	1st	...
7	At Phi.	W	7-5		13	9	Young	Springer	Jones	17-16	1st	+1
8	At Phi.	L	1-2	(10)	3	6	Ryan	Tabaka		17-17	1st	+1/2
9	At Mon.	W	11-4		18	10	Kile	Rueter		18-17	1st	+1¹/₂
10	At Mon.	L	2-5		7	8	Fassero	Dougherty	Rojas	18-18	1st	+1
11	At Mon.	L	9-10	(13)	12	15	Dyer	Dougherty		18-19	T1st	...
12	At Mon.	L	6-7		10	13	Urbina	Hampton	Rojas	18-20	T1st	...
13	At Chi.	L	0-6		1	11	Trachsel	Reynolds		18-21	3rd	1/2
14	At Chi.	W	6-3		10	6	Kile	Navarro	Jones	19-21	1st	+1/2
15	At Chi.	W	7-5		15	12	Wall	Castillo	Jones	20-21	1st	+1
16	At Chi.	L	1-13		3	13	Telemaco	Drabek		20-22	1st	+1/2
17	Pit.	W	4-2		7	4	Reynolds	Lieber	Jones	21-22	1st	+1/2
18	Pit.	L	1-2	(11)	3	6	Cordova	Young	Plesac	21-23	1st	+1/2
19	Pit.	W	4-3		10	4	Jones	Lieber		22-23	1st	+1¹/₂
20	St.L.	L	3-5		8	14	Osborne	Drabek		22-24	1st	+1¹/₂
21	St.L.	L	2-8		11	13	Stottlemyre	Reynolds		22-25	1st	+1/2
22	St.L.	L	2-5		5	11	Al. Benes	Kile	Mathews	22-26	1st	+1/2
24	Chi.	W	8-7	(10)	12	9	Jones	Patterson		23-26	1st	+1
25	Chi.	W	5-2		11	6	Drabek	Navarro	Jones	24-26	1st	+1
26	Chi.	W	7-2		8	5	Reynolds	Castillo		25-26	1st	+2
27	At Pit.	W	5-3		7	6	Kile	Smith		26-26	1st	+3
28	At Pit.	L	5-6		11	8	Miceli	Swindell	Cordova	26-27	1st	+3
29	At Pit.	W	7-4		15	14	Morman	Darwin	Jones	27-27	1st	+3
31	At St.L.	L	4-6		8	9	Osborne	Swindell	Fossas	27-28	1st	+2
1	At St.L.	L	4-5	(10)	11	12	Bailey	Hernandez		27-29	1st	+1
2	At St.L.	L	0-2		7	7	Stottlemyre	Kile		27-30	T1st	...
4	Col.	W	16-8		13	9	Hampton	M. Thompson		28-30	2nd	1/2
5	Col.	W	4-1		8	5	Wall	Reynoso		29-30	1st	+1/2
6	Col.	L	7-14		9	18	Ritz	Drabek		29-31	T1st	...
7	Phi.	W	11-5		13	8	Reynolds	Crawford		30-31	T1st	...
8	Phi.	W	7-3		7	10	Wagner	Springer		31-31	1st	+1
9	Phi.	W	2-1		5	9	Young	Williams	Jones	32-31	1st	+2
10	At Col.	W	10-9		13	11	Wall	Reynoso		33-31	1st	+3
11	At Col.	L	5-7		5	12	Alston	Young	Ruffin	33-32	1st	+2
12	At Col.	L	0-8		8	13	Freeman	Reynolds		33-33	1st	+1¹/₂
13	At S.F.	L	8-12		9	16	Leiter	Kile		33-34	1st	+1¹/₂
14	At S.F.	W	9-1		11	6	Hampton	VanLandingham	Wagner	34-34	1st	+1¹/₂
15	At S.F.	W	4-3		7	9	Wall	Watson	Jones	35-34	1st	+1¹/₂
16	At S.F.	L	7-8		12	13	DeLucia	Morman		35-35	1st	+1/2
17	Cin.	W	5-4		10	8	Young	Shaw	Jones	36-35	1st	+1
18	Cin.	L	4-6	(10)	7	11	Brantley	Hernandez		36-36	T1st	...

Date	Opp.	Res.	Score	(inn.*)	Hits	Opp. hits	Winning pitcher	Losing pitcher	Save	Record	Pos.	GB
6-19	Cin.	L	7-10		10	11	Portugal	Hampton	Brantley	36-37	2nd	1
6-20	At L.A.	W	4-2		6	8	Wall	Nomo	Jones	37-37	T1st	...
6-21	At L.A.	W	11-3		14	10	Drabek	Candiotti		38-37	1st	+1
6-22	At L.A.	L	0-3		7	9	Martinez	Reynolds		38-38	T1st	...
6-23	At L.A.	L	3-4		3	10	Worrell	Hernandez		38-39	T1st	...
6-25	At S.D.	W	9-4		6	11	Jones	Sanders		39-39	1st	+1/2
6-26	At S.D.	W	4-3		8	10	Wall	Worrell	Wagner	40-39	1st	+1/2
6-28	N.Y.	L	2-7		7	12	Clark	Drabek	Henry	40-40	T1st	...
6-29	N.Y.	W	9-1		14	8	Reynolds	Person		41-40	1st	...
6-30	N.Y.	W	9-3		14	6	Kile	Isringhausen		42-40	T1st	...
7-1	Fla.	W	6-2		7	5	Hampton	Brown		43-40	1st	+1
7-2	Fla.	W	4-3	(12)	11	10	Johnstone	Mathews		44-40	1st	+1
7-3	Fla.	W	4-3		9	10	Drabek	Leiter	Jones	45-40	1st	+1
7-4	At Atl.	W	5-2		13	9	Reynolds	Smoltz	Hernandez	46-40	1st	+1
7-5	At Atl.	W	7-1		8	9	Kile	Schmidt		47-40	1st	+1
7-6	At Atl.	L	2-4		7	9	Bielecki	Hampton		47-41	T1st	...
7-7	At Atl.	L	1-9		10	10	Maddux	Wall		47-42	T1st	...
7-11	At N.Y.	L	2-8		7	14	Clark	Drabek		47-43	T1st	...
7-12	At N.Y.	W	3-1		6	7	Reynolds	B. Jones	Wagner	48-43	T1st	...
7-14†	At N.Y.	W	7-5	(11)	15	12	Hernandez	Mlicki	Jones	49-43		
7-14‡	At N.Y.	L	3-10		8	13	Harnisch	Hampton		49-44	2nd	1
7-15	At Fla.	L	5-15		7	24	Pall	Wall		49-45	2nd	2
7-16	At Fla.	L	2-3		5	4	Perez	Jones		49-46	2nd	3
7-17	At Fla.	L	2-11		2	14	Leiter	Reynolds		49-47	2nd	4
7-18	Atl.	L	2-3		7	12	Smoltz	Jones	Wohlers	49-48	2nd	4
7-19	Atl.	W	7-6		10	9	Kile	Woodall	Wagner	50-48	2nd	4
7-20	Atl.	W	2-1		4	7	Wagner	Maddux		51-48	2nd	3
7-21	Atl.	W	4-3	(10)	9	8	Hernandez	McMichael		52-48	2nd	3
7-22	S.D.	W	1-0		3	4	Reynolds	Hamilton	Wagner	53-48	2nd	2
7-23	S.D.	L	4-7		7	11	Sanders	Hampton	Hoffman	53-49	2nd	2
7-24	S.D.	W	6-4	(10)	10	9	Hernandez	Villone		54-49	2nd	1
7-26	L.A.	W	4-3		10	9	Darwin	Guthrie	Wagner	55-49	1st	+1/2
7-27	L.A.	L	5-6	(11)	8	11	Osuna	Clark	Worrell	55-50	2nd	1/2
7-28	L.A.	W	3-2		10	11	Darwin	Eischen		56-50	2nd	1/2
7-29	At Cin.	W	2-1		8	4	Hampton	Portugal	Wagner	57-50	T1st	...
7-30	At Cin.	L	4-5	(10)	8	8	Shaw	Clark		57-51	T1st	...
7-31	At Cin.	L	0-10		4	13	Smiley	Wall		57-52	2nd	1/2
8-2	S.F.	W	5-1		10	8	Drabek	Gardner	Hernandez	58-52	2nd	1/2
8-3	S.F.	W	4-1		6	3	Reynolds	Estes		59-52	1st	+1/2
8-4	S.F.	W	7-6		7	9	Hampton	Fernandez	Wagner	60-52	1st	+1/2
8-6	Mon.	L	5-7		12	12	Fassero	Kile	Rojas	60-53	T1st	...
8-7	Mon.	L	5-13		13	16	Leiter	Wall		60-54	2nd	1
8-8	Mon.	W	6-2		9	6	Drabek	Martinez		61-54	T1st	...
8-9	At Phi.	W	5-1		11	4	Reynolds	West		62-54	1st	+1
8-10	At Phi.	W	3-1		9	8	Hampton	Schilling	Wagner	63-54	1st	+1
8-11	At Phi.	W	10-5		13	11	Kile	Williams		64-54	1st	+1
8-12	At Mon.	L	1-8		3	10	Leiter	Darwin		64-55	1st	+1/2
8-13	At Mon.	L	4-7		5	10	Martinez	Drabek	Rojas	64-56	1st	+1/2
8-14	At Mon.	W	8-3		14	9	Reynolds	Cormier		65-56	1st	+1/2
8-16	At Chi.	W	8-3		15	12	Hampton	Castillo		66-56	1st	+1
8-17	At Chi.	L	3-12		7	13	Trachsel	Kile		66-57	T1st	...
8-18	At Chi.	L	8-10		9	17	Navarro	Brocail	Wendell	66-58	2nd	1
8-19	Pit.	W	2-1	(13)	10	7	Morman	Morel		67-58	2nd	1/2
8-20	Pit.	W	9-4		13	10	Wall	Miceli	Hernandez	68-58	1st	1/2
8-21	Pit.	L	2-5		10	14	Neagle	Hampton	Ericks	68-59	1st	1/2
8-22	Pit.	L	6-8		13	11	Wilkins	Wagner	Ericks	68-60	1st	1/2
8-23	St.L.	L	0-1		7	7	Osborne	Kile	Eckersley	68-61	2nd	1/2
8-24	St.L.	W	3-1		7	5	Reynolds	Stottlemyre		69-61	1st	+1/2
8-25	St.L.	W	4-1		8	3	Wall	Al. Benes	Hernandez	70-61	1st	+11/2
8-26	St.L.	L	2-3		6	8	An. Benes	Hampton	Eckersley	70-62	1st	+1/2
8-27	Chi.	W	6-5		8	6	Morman	Adams	Hernandez	71-62	1st	+11/2
8-28	Chi.	W	5-4		10	9	Olson	Bottenfield		72-62	1st	+21/2
8-29	Chi.	L	3-4		9	8	Navarro	Reynolds	Wendell	72-63	1st	+21/2
8-30	At Pit.	W	10-0		17	7	Wall	Peters		73-63	1st	+21/2
8-31	At Pit.	W	5-4		9	11	Hernandez	Ericks	Hudek	74-63	1st	+21/2
9-1	At Pit.	L	5-9		5	8	Wainhouse	Darwin		74-64	1st	+11/2
9-2	At St.L.	L	7-8	(10)	13	17	Al. Benes	Brocail		74-65	1st	+1/2
9-3	At St.L.	L	3-12		6	15	Stottlemyre	Reynolds		74-66	2nd	1/2
9-4	At St.L.	L	4-6		8	9	An. Benes	Wall	Eckersley	74-67	2nd	11/2
9-6	Col.	W	2-1		10	2	Hernandez	Leskanic		75-67	2nd	11/2
9-7	Col.	W	5-4		6	10	Kile	Holmes	Hudek	76-67	2nd	11/2
9-8	Col.	L	2-5		6	7	S. Reed	Reynolds	Ruffin	76-68	2nd	11/2
9-9	Col.	L	2-4		10	12	Ritz	Wall	Ruffin	76-69	2nd	21/2
9-10	Phi.	W	4-3		10	6	Morman	Schilling	Hernandez	77-69	2nd	21/2
9-11	Phi.	L	8-10		15	14	Parrett	Holt	Bottalico	77-70	2nd	21/2

te	Opp.	Res.	Score	(inn.*)	Hits	Opp. hits	Winning pitcher	Losing pitcher	Save	Record	Pos.	GB
12	Phi.	W	4-1		6	7	Kile	Williams		78-70	2nd	1½
13	At Col.	L	3-6		6	9	Holmes	Hernandez	Ruffin	78-71	2nd	2½
14	At Col.	L	3-7		12	12	Ritz	Wall		78-72	2nd	2½
15	At Col.	L	4-11		6	14	M. Thompson	Drabek		78-73	2nd	2½
17	At Atl.	L	4-5		11	8	Smoltz	Kile	Wohlers	78-74	2nd	3½
18	At Atl.	L	2-6		6	13	Maddux	Hampton		78-75	2nd	4½
20	At Fla.	L	1-3		7	5	Brown	Reynolds	Nen	78-76	2nd	5
21	At Fla.	L	1-2		5	7	Heredia	Wagner		78-77	2nd	5½
22	At Fla.	L	0-6		2	7	Helling	Kile		78-78	2nd	5
24	N.Y.	L	0-4		4	9	B. Jones	Wall		78-79	T2nd	6½
25	N.Y.	W	5-4	(10)	10	10	Hudek	Wallace		79-79	T2nd	6½
26	N.Y.	W	6-2		9	9	Drabek	Trlicek		80-79	T2nd	6
27	Fla.	L	2-3		6	11	Hutton	Kile	Nen	80-80	T2nd	7
28	Fla.	W	5-1		10	7	Darwin	Heredia		81-80	2nd	7
29	Fla.	W	5-4	(10)	11	9	Hudek	Hammond		82-80	2nd	6

onthly records: April (13-14), May (14-14), June (15-12), July (15-12), August (17-11), September (8-17).
nnings, if other than nine. †First game of doubleheader. ‡Second game of doubleheader.

HIGHLIGHTS

gh point: When the Astros won in ttsburgh on August 31, they were 11 mes over .500 for the first time in the ason. They led the Cardinals by 2½ mes.

w point: The Astros opened ptember with four consecutive losses, cluding three in St. Louis, and went on lose 12 road games in a row.

rning point: By getting swept by the rdinals (September 2-4), the Astros rned a 1½-game lead into a 1½-game ficit. They steadily lost ground after at.

ost valuable player: First baseman Jeff gwell. He finished in the league's Top in batting (.315) and RBIs (120). He as the only player in the league to start 162 games, and he set club records r RBIs and doubles (48).

ost valuable pitcher: Shane Reynolds. e had a breakthrough year, with 16 ns, though he failed seven times to get s 17th. He pitched 239 innings, had 4 strikeouts and averaged only 1.6 alks per nine innings.

ost improved player: Pitcher Darryl le. He came back from a 4-12 disap- intment in 1995 to go 12-11, striking ut 219 batters in 219 innings.

ost pleasant surprise: Billy Wagner. e rookie lefthander established himself a closer, blowing batters away with s 95-mph fastball. He struck out 67 tters in 51⅔ and opponents hit just 65 (28-for-170) against him.

ggest disappointment: Todd Jones. He cked the mental toughness to be a oser and he broke down physically, ith shoulder instability and tendinitis.

ey injuries: Wagner missed 15 days ith a pulled groin during a critical retch (August 23-September 6). John dek, who pitched in the '94 All-Star ame, missed most of the season with roken ribs. Third baseman Sean Berry ffered a torn rotator cuff in the first eek of the season. He bravely played on nd had a career-high 95 RBIs, but his defensive work was impaired. Catcher Tony Eusebio suffered a broken bone in his wrist in June and never recovered all his bat speed.

Notable: The Astros established a club record for runs scored with 753, six more than in '95. Despite that offense, Houston finished last in the league in pinch-hitting (.192) and on-base percent- age (.269). . . . The Astros also allowed more runs, 792, than any Houston team ever. The Astros (84) were hit by pitches more times than any N.L. team this cen- tury. . . . Bagwell and Craig Biggio played in every game, the only major leaguers besides Baltimore's Cal Ripken to do so. . . . The pitching staff set all-time highs for ERA (4.37), hits (1,541), runs (792), and home runs (154). . . .The Astros went 2- 11 against the Cardinals and finished second in the Central Division for the third consecutive year. . . . Derek Bell had 113 RBIs but, oddly, none against the Cardinals. . . . When the season ended, manager Terry Collins was replaced by broadcaster Larry Dierker, an Astros pitching star in the 1960s and '70s.

—ALAN TRUEX

RECORDS

1996 regular-season record: 82-80 (2nd in N.L. Central); 48-33 at home; 34-47 on road; 33-28 vs. East; 24-28 vs. Central; 25-24 vs. West; 16-22 vs. lefthanded starters; 66-58 vs. righthanded starters; 20-35 on grass; 62-45 on turf; 29-28 in daytime; 53-52 at night; 28-23 in one- run games; 9-10 in extra-inning games; 0-1-1 in doubleheaders.

Team record past five years: 390-355 (.523, ranks 4th in league in that span).

TEAM LEADERS

Batting average: Jeff Bagwell (.315).
At-bats: Derek Bell (627).
Runs: Craig Biggio (113).
Hits: Jeff Bagwell (179).
Total bases: Jeff Bagwell (324).
Doubles: Jeff Bagwell (48).
Triples: Craig Biggio, John Cangelosi (4).

Home runs: Jeff Bagwell (31).
Runs batted in: Jeff Bagwell (120).
Stolen bases: Brian L. Hunter (35).
Slugging percentage: Jeff Bagwell (.570).
On-base percentage: Jeff Bagwell (.451).
Wins: Shane Reynolds (16).
Earned-run average: Shane Reynolds (3.65).
Complete games: Darryl Kile, Shane Reynolds (4).
Shutouts: Mike Hampton, Shane Reynolds, Donne Wall (1).
Saves: Todd Jones (17).
Innings pitched: Shane Reynolds (239.0).
Strikeouts: Darryl Kile (219).

GAMES BY POSITION

Catcher: Rick Wilkins 82, Tony Eusebio 47, Kirt Manwaring 37, Randy Knorr 33, Jerry Goff 1.
First base: Jeff Bagwell 162, Mike Simms 5, Bill Spiers 4.
Second base: Craig Biggio 162, Bill Spiers 7, Ricky Gutierrez 5, Dave Hajek 2.
Third base: Sean Berry 110, Bill Spiers 77, Orlando Miller 29, Ricky Gutierrez 6, Dave Hajek 3, Andujar Cedeno 1.
Shortstop: Orlando Miller 117, Ricky Gutierrez 74, Bill Spiers 5, Andujar Cedeno 2.
Outfield: Derek Bell 157, Brian L. Hunter 127, James Mouton 108, John Cangelosi 78, Derrick May 71, Mike Simms 12, Bob Abreu 7, Ray Montgomery 6, Bill Spiers 2.

TOP DRAFT CHOICES

1. Mark Johnson, RHP, Univ. of Hawaii.
2. John Huber, RHP, Lakota H.S., Cincinnati.
3. Brandon Byrd, 3B, Trinity Presbyterian H.S., Montgomery, Ala.
4. Bryan Braswell, LHP, University of Toledo.
5. Tucker Barr, C, Georgia Tech.
6. Michael Wheeler, SS, Oak Hills H.S., Cincinnati.
7. Esteban Maldonado, RHP, Lambuth (Tenn.) University.
8. Jason Hill, C, Mount San Antonio (Calif.) J.C.
9. Brian Dallimore, 2B, Stanford University.
10. John Blackmore, RHP, Plainville (Conn.) H.S.

1997 SEASON   Houston Astros

LOS ANGELES DODGERS
NATIONAL LEAGUE WEST DIVISION

1997 DODGERS SCHEDULE

Home games shaded.
* — All-Star Game at Jacobs Field (Cleveland)
D — Day game (any game starting before 5 p.m.)

APRIL
SUN	MON	TUE	WED	THU	FRI	SAT
		1 PHI	2 PHI	3 PHI	4 PIT	5 PIT
6 PIT	7 NYM	8 NYM	9 NYM	10	11 PIT	12 D PIT
13 PIT	14	15 NYM	16 D NYM	17	18 HOU	19 HOU
20 HOU	21	22 STL	23 STL	24	25 FLA	26 FLA
27 FLA	28 ATL	29 ATL	30 PHI			

MAY
SUN	MON	TUE	WED	THU	FRI	SAT
				1 D PHI	2 CUB	3 CUB
4 CUB	5 CIN	6 CIN	7 D CIN	8	9 MON	10 MON
11 MON	12	13 CIN	14 D CUB	15 CIN	16 CIN	17 MON
18 D MON	19 D SD	20 SD	21 SD	22 SD	23 ATL	24 ATL
25 D ATL	26 D FLA	27 FLA	28	29 STL	30 STL	31 D STL

JUNE
SUN	MON	TUE	WED	THU	FRI	SAT
1 D STL	2 HOU	3 HOU	4 D SF	5 SF	6 STL	7 STL
8 STL	9 HOU	10 HOU	11 HOU	12 OAK	13 OAK	14 D SEA
15 SEA	16 ANA	17 ANA	18 SF	19 SF	20 SD	21 D SF
22 SF	23 COL	24 COL	25 COL	26 SD	27 SD	28 D SD
29 SD	30 TEX					

JULY
SUN	MON	TUE	WED	THU	FRI	SAT
		1 TEX	2 ANA	3 ANA	4 D SD	5 D SD
6 D SD	7	8 *	9 SF	10 SF	11 ATL	12 ATL
13 D SF	14 COL	15 D COL	16 FLA	17 FLA	18 ATL	19 ATL
20 ATL	21 ATL	22 NYM	23 NYM	24 NYM	25 PHI	26 PHI
27 PHI	28 PIT	29 D PIT	30	31 CUB		

AUGUST
SUN	MON	TUE	WED	THU	FRI	SAT
					1 D CUB	2 D CUB
3 CUB	4	5 MON	6 MON	7 MON	8 CIN	9 D CIN
10 D CIN	11 D CUB	12 CUB	13 MON	14 D MON	15 CIN	16 CIN
17 D CIN	18	19 NYM	20 NYM	21 NYM	22 PHI	23 PHI
24 D PHI	25 PIT	26 PIT	27 D OAK	28 OAK	29 SEA	30 D SEA
31 D SEA						

SEPTEMBER
SUN	MON	TUE	WED	THU	FRI	SAT
	1	2 TEX	3 TEX	4	5 FLA	6 FLA
7 FLA	8	9 ATL	10 ATL	11	12 HOU	13 HOU
14 HOU	15 STL	16 STL	17 SF	18 D SF	19 COL	20 COL
21 COL	22	23 SD	24 SD	25	26 COL	27 COL
28 D COL						

1997 SEASON

CLUB DIRECTORY

Board of directors
Peter O'Malley
Roland Seidler
Mrs. Roland (Terry) Seidler

President
Peter O'Malley

Executive vice president
Fred Claire

Vice president, communications
Tom Hawkins

Vice president, finance
Bob Graziano

Vice president, marketing
Barry Stockhamer

Director, stadium operations
Doug Duennes

Vice president, treasurer
Roland Seidler

Vice president, Campo Las Palmas
Ralph Avila

Assistant secretary and general counsel
Santiago Fernandez

Director, accounting and finance
Bill Foltz

Director, advertising and special events
Paul Kalil

Director, broadcasting and publications
Brent Shyer

Director, community relations
Don Newcombe

Director, community affairs
Monique Brandon

Director, human resources and admin.
Irene Tanji

Dir., management information services
Mike Mularky

Vice president, minor league operation
Charlie Blaney

Director, scouting
Terry Reynolds

Director, publicity
Derrick Hall

Assistant director, publicity
Shaun Rachau

Traveling secretary
Bill DeLury

Director, ticket operations
Debra Duncan

Club physicians
Dr. Frank W. Jobe
Dr. Michael F. Mellman

Scouts
Eleodoro Arias, Eddie Bane, Bill Barkley, Rick Birmingham, Gib Bodet, Flores Bolivar, Mike Brito, Joe Campbell, Jim Chapman, Bob Darwin, Eddie Fajardo Rodriguez, Joe Ferrone, Rafael Gonzalez, Carl Greene, Michael Hankins, Dick, Hanlon, Dennis Haren, Hank Jones, Lon Joyce, John Keenan, Gary LaRocque, Don LeJohn, Carl Lowenstine, Teodoro Mata, Ed Mathes, Dale McReynolds, Tommy Mixon, Alberto Osorio, Deni Pacini, Camilo Pasqual, Pablo Peguero, Claude Pelletier, Bill Pleis, Silvano Quesada, Ross Sapp, Mark Sheehy, Jim Stoeckel, Tom Thomas, Glen Van Proyen

Coordinator of professional scouting
Gary Sutherland

MINOR LEAGUE AFFILIATES

Class	Team	League	Manager
AAA	Albuquerque	Pacific Coast	Glenn Hoffman
AA	San Antonio	Texas	Ron Roenicke
A	San Bernardino	California	Del Crandall
A	Vero Beach	Florida State	John Shoemaker
A	Yakima	Northwest	Joe Vavra
A	Savannah	South Atlantic	John Shelby
Rookie	Great Falls	Pioneer	Mickey Hatcher

BROADCAST INFORMATION

Radio: KABC-AM (790); KWKW-AM (1330, Spanish language).
TV: KTLA-TV (Channel 5); Fox Sports West (Channel 2).

SPRING TRAINING

Ballpark (city): Holman Stadium (Vero Beach, Fla.).
Ticket information: 561-569-6858.

SPRING TRAINING ROSTER

Manager—Bill Russell (18).
Coaches—Joe Amalfitano (8), Mark Cresse (58), Manny Mota (11), Reggie Smith (9), David Wallace (17).

No.	PITCHERS	B/T	Ht./Wt.	Born	1996 clubs
56	Astacio, Pedro	R/R	6-2/195	11-28-69	Los Angeles
	Brown, Alvin	R/R	6-1/200	9-2-70	San Bernardino
49	Candiotti, Tom	R/R	6-2/221	8-31-57	Los Angeles, San Bernardino
37	Dreifort, Darren	R/R	6-2/205	5-18-72	Albuquerque, Los Angeles
	Gorecki, Rick	R/R	6-3/167	8-27-73	DID NOT PLAY
44	Guthrie, Mark	R/L	6-4/207	9-22-65	Los Angeles
52	Hall, Darren	R/R	6-3/205	7-14-64	Los Angeles, Yakima
	Herges, Matt	L/R	6-0/200	4-1-70	San Antonio, Albuquerque
47	Martinez, Jesus	L/L	6-2/145	3-13-74	San Antonio
48	Martinez, Ramon J.	B/R	6-4/186	3-22-68	San Antonio, Vero Beach, Los Angeles
16	Nomo, Hideo	R/R	6-2/210	8-31-68	Los Angeles
13	Osuna, Antonio	R/R	5-11/160	4-12-73	Albuquerque, Los Angeles
61	Park, Chan Ho	R/R	6-2/195	6-30-73	Los Angeles
36	Radinsky, Scott	L/L	6-3/204	3-3-68	San Bernardino, Los Angeles
	Rath, Gary	L/L	6-2/185	1-10-73	Albuquerque
	Spykstra, Dave	R/R	6-2/200	8-26-73	Savannah
59	Valdes, Ismael	R/R	6-3/207	8-21-73	Los Angeles
38	Worrell, Todd	R/R	6-5/227	9-28-59	Los Angeles

No.	CATCHERS	B/T	Ht./Wt.	Born	1996 clubs
	Blanco, Henry	R/R	5-11/168	8-29-71	San Antonio, Albuquerque
41	Huckaby, Kenneth	R/R	6-1/205	1-27-71	Albuquerque
31	Piazza, Mike	R/R	6-3/215	9-4-68	Los Angeles
15	Prince, Tom	R/R	5-11/202	8-13-64	Albuquerque, Los Angeles

No.	INFIELDERS	B/T	Ht./Wt.	Born	1996 clubs
	Berblinger, Jeff	R/R	6-0/190	11-19-70	Arkansas
60	Castro, Juan	R/R	5-10/163	6-20-72	Albuquerque, Los Angeles
3	Fonville, Chad	B/R	5-6/155	3-5-71	Los Angeles, Albuquerque
7	Gagne, Greg	R/R	5-11/180	11-12-61	Los Angeles, Albuquerque
30	Guerrero, Wilton	R/R	5-11/145	10-24-74	Albuquerque, Los Angeles
	Hale, Chip	L/R	5-11/193	12-2-64	Minnesota
23	Karros, Eric	R/R	6-4/222	11-4-67	Los Angeles
	Lirlano, Nelson	B/R	5-10/185	6-3-64	Pittsburgh
	Riggs, Adam	R/R	6-0/194	10-4-72	San Antonio
12	Wehner, John	R/R	6-3/206	6-29-67	Pittsburgh
	Zeile, Todd	R/R	6-1/200	9-9-65	Philadelphia, Baltimore

No.	OUTFIELDERS	B/T	Ht./Wt.	Born	1996 clubs
21	Ashley, Billy	R/R	6-7/235	7-11-70	Los Angeles, Albuquerque
22	Butler, Brett	L/L	5-10/161	6-15-57	Los Angeles
27	Cedeno, Roger	B/R	6-1/165	8-16-74	Los Angeles, Albuquerque
12	Garcia, Karim	L/L	6-0/172	10-29-75	Albuquerque, San Antonio, Los Angeles
28	Hollandsworth, Todd	L/L	6-2/193	4-20-73	Los Angeles
55	Kirby, Wayne	L/R	5-10/190	1-22-64	Cleveland, Los Angeles
43	Mondesi, Raul	R/R	5-11/212	3-12-71	Los Angeles

BALLPARK INFORMATION

Ballpark (capacity, surface)
Dodger Stadium (56,000, grass)

Address
1000 Elysian Park Ave.
Los Angeles, CA 90012

Business phone
213-224-1500

Ticket information
213-224-1400

Ticket prices
$17 (preferred box-not available)
$14 (middle box-not available)
$12 (box seats)
$11 (preferred reserved)
$8 (reserved)
$6 (top deck and pavilion)
$3 (g.a., youth 12 and under)

Field dimensions (from home plate)
To left field at foul line, 330 feet
To center field, 395 feet
To right field at foul line, 330 feet

First game played
April 10, 1962 (Reds 6, Dodgers 3)

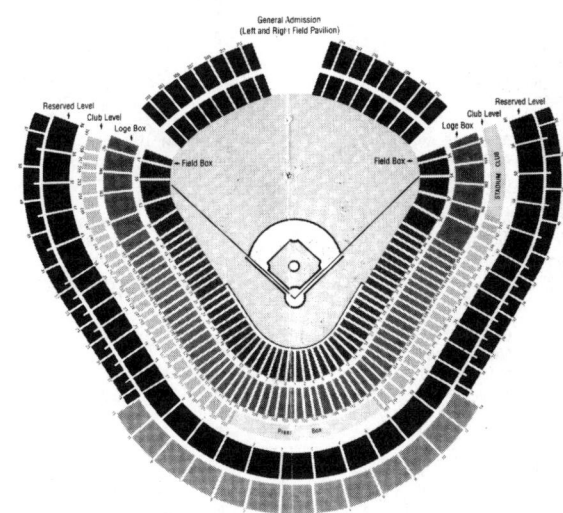

DAY BY DAY

Date	Opp.	Res.	Score	(inn.*)	Hits	Opp. hits	Winning pitcher	Losing pitcher	Save	Record	Pos.	GB
4-1	At Hou.	W	4-3		11	6	Martinez	Reynolds	Worrell	1-0	1st	+1/2
4-2	At Hou.	L	4-5		11	14	Jones	Cummings		1-1	2nd	1/2
4-3	At Hou.	L	2-5		11	10	Hampton	Nomo	Jones	1-2	3rd	1/2
4-4	At Chi.	L	4-9		8	14	Foster	Astacio		1-3	4th	1
4-5	At Chi.	L	1-11		7	16	Bullinger	Candiotti		1-4	4th	2
4-6	At Chi.	W	3-1		5	9	Park	Navarro	Worrell	2-4	4th	2
4-7	At Chi.	L	4-5		8	8	Jones	Osuna		2-5	4th	3
4-8	Atl.	W	1-0		5	3	Nomo	Glavine		3-5	3rd	3
4-9	Atl.	L	1-3		5	7	Smoltz	Astacio	Wohlers	3-6	T3rd	3
4-10	Atl.	W	9-2		12	8	Candiotti	Avery		4-6	T3rd	3
4-11	Fla.	W	5-0		7	4	Park	Brown	Worrell	5-6	T3rd	3
4-12	Fla.	L	1-3		2	9	Burkett	Valdes		5-7	4th	3
4-13	Fla.	W	3-1		3	3	Nomo	Hammond		6-7	4th	3
4-14	Fla.	W	6-1		8	8	Astacio	Leiter		7-7	3rd	2
4-16	At S.F.	L	3-5		9	9	Dewey	Osuna	Beck	7-8	T3rd	2 1/2
4-17	At S.F.	W	11-2		13	3	Osuna	Leiter		8-8	3rd	2 1/2
4-19	At Fla.	L	0-5		3	10	Powell	Hall		8-9	T3rd	2 1/2
4-20	At Fla.	L	4-7		11	10	Leiter	Nomo	Nen	8-10	T3rd	2 1/2
4-21	At Fla.	L	4-5		10	6	Brown	Hall	Mathews	8-11	4th	3 1/2
4-22	At Atl.	L	1-4		8	8	Maddux	Candiotti		8-12	4th	4 1/2
4-23	At Atl.	W	3-2		6	6	Osuna	Clontz	Worrell	9-12	4th	4 1/2
4-24	Hou.	W	5-2		8	6	Valdes	Brocail		10-12	4th	4 1/2
4-25	Hou.	W	6-4		9	7	Nomo	Drabek	Worrell	11-12	T3rd	4 1/2
4-26	Chi.	W	1-0		6	5	Astacio	Trachsel	Worrell	12-12	2nd	4 1/2
4-27	Chi.	L	3-4	(10)	9	7	Navarro	Osuna	Jones	12-13	T3rd	4 1/2
4-28	Chi.	L	0-3		6	5	Castillo	Park		12-14	T3rd	4 1/2
4-29	Chi.	W	10-4		12	6	Valdes	Foster		13-14	3rd	4 1/2
4-30	Col.	W	7-4		10	7	Nomo	Ritz	Worrell	14-14	3rd	3 1/2
5-1	Col.	L	1-4		6	5	M. Thompson	Astacio	Ruffin	14-15	3rd	4 1/2
5-3	At Pit.	W	10-1		11	9	Park	Darwin		15-15	T2nd	3 1/2
5-4	At Pit.	L	2-7		5	13	Wagner	Candiotti		15-16	T3rd	3 1/2
5-5	At Pit.	L	2-4		9	7	Neagle	Valdes	Plesac	15-17	T3rd	4 1/2
5-6	At Pit.	W	8-4		8	11	Nomo	Hope	Radinsky	16-17	3rd	4
5-7	At Cin.	L	2-3	(12)	7	6	Moore	Worrell		16-18	4th	4 1/2
5-8	At Cin.	L	0-5		3	8	Schourek	Park	Shaw	16-19	4th	5
5-10	At St.L.	W	3-2	(12)	9	12	Worrell	Eckersley		17-19	3rd	4 1/2
5-11	At St.L.	W	4-2		6	6	Valdes	Al. Benes	Worrell	18-19	3rd	3 1/2
5-12	At St.L.	L	5-6		10	13	Petkovsek	Nomo	Eckersley	18-20	3rd	4 1/2
5-13	Mon.	L	2-3		8	8	Manuel	Worrell	Rojas	18-21	3rd	5 1/2
5-14	Mon.	W	2-1		7	8	Martinez	Veres	Worrell	19-21	3rd	5 1/2
5-15	Mon.	W	7-2		10	4	Candiotti	Fassero		20-21	3rd	5 1/2
5-16	Phi.	W	8-2		8	6	Valdes	Mimbs		21-21	3rd	4 1/2
5-17	Phi.	W	6-3		9	9	Nomo	Grace	Worrell	22-21	T2nd	4 1/2
5-18	Phi.	W	7-2		9	8	Astacio	Fernandez	Osuna	23-21	2nd	3 1/2
5-19	Phi.	L	4-5		11	11	Leiper	Radinsky	Bottalico	23-22	3rd	4 1/2
5-20	N.Y.	L	1-7		9	16	B. Jones	Candiotti		23-23	3rd	5
5-21	N.Y.	W	6-4		12	7	Valdes	Harnisch	Worrell	24-23	3rd	4
5-22	N.Y.	L	2-3		5	7	Clark	Nomo	J. Franco	24-24	4th	5
5-24	At Mon.	W	5-4	(11)	11	9	Osuna	Daal	Worrell	25-24	3rd	5 1/2
5-25	At Mon.	W	5-3		8	9	Martinez	Cormier	Worrell	26-24	3rd	5 1/2
5-26	At Mon.	W	4-3		8	5	Candiotti	Rojas	Worrell	27-24	2nd	4 1/2
5-28	At Phi.	L	3-9		11	15	Grace	Valdes		27-25	T2nd	6
5-29	At Phi.	W	3-2	(11)	8	8	Guthrie	Bottalico	Worrell	28-25	2nd	5
5-30	At Phi.	L	2-3		9	13	Borland	Worrell		28-26	2nd	5 1/2
5-31	At N.Y.	W	10-3		16	7	Martinez	B. Jones		29-26	2nd	5 1/2
6-1	At N.Y.	L	3-4		5	7	Harnisch	Candiotti	J. Franco	29-27	2nd	6 1/2
6-2	At N.Y.	W	1-0		3	6	Valdes	Clark	Worrell	30-27	2nd	5 1/2
6-4	Pit.	L	0-3		5	8	Darwin	Nomo	Cordova	30-28	2nd	5
6-5	Pit.	L	3-7		8	11	Wilkins	Astacio	Cordova	30-29	T2nd	6
6-6	Pit.	W	8-3		12	5	Candiotti	Miceli		31-29	2nd	5 1/2
6-7	Cin.	L	1-2		7	7	Smiley	Valdes	Brantley	31-30	2nd	5 1/2
6-8	Cin.	W	5-4	(10)	8	13	Worrell	Carrasco		32-30	2nd	4 1/2
6-9	Cin.	W	3-2		8	6	Nomo	Smith	Worrell	33-30	2nd	3 1/2
6-10	St.L.	W	2-1		5	3	Park	Morgan	Osuna	34-30	2nd	2 1/2
6-11	St.L.	L	3-6		12	13	Osborne	Martinez	Honeycutt	34-31	2nd	2 1/2
6-13	At Atl.	W	6-3		10	9	Valdes	Glavine	Worrell	35-31	2nd	1
6-14	At Atl.	L	1-3		6	8	Smoltz	Astacio	Wohlers	35-32	2nd	1
6-15	At Atl.	W	6-2		6	9	Nomo	Avery	Worrell	36-32	2nd	1
6-16	At Atl.	W	3-2		5	6	Candiotti	Schmidt	Worrell	37-32	T1st	...
6-18†	At Chi.	W	9-6		15	9	Martinez	Telemaco	Worrell	38-32		
6-18‡	At Chi.	L	4-7		6	10	Campbell	Valdes		38-33	1st	+1
6-19	At Chi.	W	4-3	(13)	10	9	Park	Adams	Worrell	39-33	1st	+1 1/2

Date	Opp.	Res.	Score	(inn.*)	Hits	Opp. hits	Winning pitcher	Losing pitcher	Save	Record	Pos.	GB
6-20	Hou.	L	2-4		8	6	Wall	Nomo	Jones	39-34	1st	+1
6-21	Hou.	L	3-11		10	14	Drabek	Candiotti		39-35	1st	+1
6-22	Hou.	W	3-0		9	7	Martinez	Reynolds		40-35	1st	+2
6-23	Hou.	W	4-3		10	3	Worrell	Hernandez		41-35	1st	+2
6-25	Chi.	L	0-2		6	6	Trachsel	Nomo		41-36	1st	+2
6-26	Chi.	L	4-6		8	11	Navarro	Candiotti	Adams	41-37	1st	+2
6-27	At Col.	L	1-13		6	17	Ritz	Astacio		41-38	1st	+1
6-28	At Col.	L	4-13		9	16	Freeman	Martinez		41-39	T1st	...
6-29	At Col.	W	13-10		20	16	Valdes	Rekar		42-39	T1st	...
6-30	At Col.	L	15-16		18	20	Ruffin	Worrell		42-40	2nd	1
7-1	At S.D.	W	10-2		17	11	Candiotti	Worrell		43-40	T1st	...
7-2	At S.D.	W	7-3		11	9	Astacio	Valenzuela		44-40	1st	+1
7-3	At S.D.	L	2-3		8	6	Hamilton	Martinez	Hoffman	44-41	T1st	...
7-4	Col.	W	9-4		9	9	Valdes	Freeman		45-41	T1st	...
7-5	Col.	W	8-1		12	6	Nomo	Bailey		46-41	T1st	...
7-6	Col.	W	3-2		6	5	Osuna	Ruffin	Worrell	47-41	T1st	...
7-7	Col.	L	0-3		5	5	Ritz	Astacio		47-42	2nd	1
7-11	S.F.	W	8-3		15	4	Martinez	Leiter		48-42	T1st	...
7-12	S.F.	W	6-1		8	5	Valdes	Fernandez		49-42	1st	+1
7-13	S.F.	L	0-7		4	13	Estes	Nomo		49-43	1st	+1
7-14	S.F.	L	0-6		2	8	VanLandingham	Park		49-44	1st	+1
7-15	S.D.	W	1-0	(10)	7	5	Guthrie	Hoffman		50-44	1st	+1½
7-16	S.D.	L	1-10		7	11	Tewksbury	Martinez	Worrell	50-45	1st	+½
7-17	S.D.	L	4-5		7	11	Florie	Osuna	Hoffman	50-46	T2nd	½
7-18	At S.F.	W	8-3		11	4	Nomo	Estes		51-46	T1st	...
7-19	At S.F.	L	4-5		10	11	VanLandingham	Candiotti	Beck	51-47	2nd	1
7-20	At S.F.	L	6-7		13	12	Bautista	Worrell		51-48	3rd	1
7-21	At S.F.	W	7-6		12	10	Osuna	DeLucia	Worrell	52-48	2nd	1
7-23	At Fla.	W	7-1		4	7	Valdes	Leiter		53-48	T2nd	½
7-24	At Fla.	L	0-3		6	5	Brown	Nomo	Nen	53-49	3rd	1
7-25	At Fla.	W	6-3		11	9	Astacio	Hammond	Worrell	54-49	T1st	...
7-26	At Hou.	L	3-4		9	10	Darwin	Guthrie	Wagner	54-50	T2nd	1
7-27	At Hou.	W	6-5	(11)	11	8	Osuna	Clark	Worrell	55-50	T2nd	1
7-28	At Hou.	L	2-3		11	10	Darwin	Eischen		55-51	T2nd	1
7-30	Fla.	W	5-4	(10)	13	6	Osuna	Weathers		56-51	2nd	1½
7-31	Fla.	W	3-0		6	4	Martinez	Rapp	Worrell	57-51	2nd	½
8-1	Fla.	L	6-7	(14)	10	15	Hammond	Dreifort	Mathews	57-52	2nd	½
8-2	Atl.	W	2-1		9	7	Radinsky	Smoltz	Guthrie	58-52	2nd	½
8-3	Atl.	L	3-5	(18)	11	12	Woodall	Martinez		58-53	2nd	½
8-4	Atl.	L	4-6		9	14	Borbon	Guthrie	Wohlers	58-54	2nd	1½
8-6	At Pit.	W	3-1		8	10	Astacio	Parris	Worrell	59-54	2nd	1
8-7	At Pit.	L	2-12		10	15	Lieber	Martinez	Wilkins	59-55	T2nd	1
8-9	At Cin.	L	4-9		5	12	Portugal	Valdes		59-56	3rd	2½
8-10	At Cin.	W	7-5		9	6	Nomo	Burba	Worrell	60-56	3rd	2½
8-11	At Cin.	W	10-5		9	11	Osuna	Carrasco		61-56	T2nd	2½
8-12	At Cin.	W	6-5		9	9	Martinez	Smiley	Worrell	62-56	2nd	2
8-13	At St.L.	W	8-4		12	7	Candiotti	Stottlemyre		63-56	2nd	1
8-14	At St.L.	L	1-6		5	11	Al. Benes	Valdes		63-57	2nd	1
8-15	At St.L.	W	5-2		11	4	Nomo	Morgan	Worrell	64-57	T1st	...
8-16	Mon.	W	8-2		10	9	Astacio	Urbina		65-57	T1st	...
8-17	Mon.	W	7-6		10	8	Worrell	Veres		66-57	1st	+1
8-18	Mon.	L	3-7		7	10	Leiter	Candiotti		66-58	T1st	...
8-20	Phi.	L	1-3		5	12	R. Jordan	Osuna	Bottalico	66-59	2nd	1½
8-21	Phi.	L	0-6		2	9	Schilling	Nomo		66-60	2nd	2½
8-22	Phi.	W	8-5		11	14	Astacio	Williams	Worrell	67-60	2nd	2
8-23	N.Y.	W	7-5		12	8	Martinez	Clark	Worrell	68-60	2nd	1
8-24	N.Y.	W	7-5		8	8	Candiotti	Wilson	Worrell	69-60	2nd	1
8-25	N.Y.	W	6-5		8	6	Radinsky	J. Franco	Worrell	70-60	2nd	1
8-27	At Mon.	W	5-1		7	10	Nomo	Fassero		71-60	2nd	1
8-28	At Mon.	L	5-6		11	11	Rojas	Park		71-61	2nd	2
8-29	At Mon.	W	2-1		6	3	Martinez	Martinez	Worrell	72-61	2nd	2
8-30	At Phi.	W	7-6	(12)	9	12	Dreifort	Parrett	Worrell	73-61	2nd	2
8-31	At Phi.	W	11-7		18	10	Valdes	Schilling	Osuna	74-61	2nd	1
9-1	At Phi.	L	3-6		4	8	Williams	Worrell	Bottalico	74-62	2nd	1
9-2	At N.Y.	W	8-5		12	9	Astacio	Clark	Worrell	75-62	2nd	1
9-3	At N.Y.	W	7-6		12	11	Radinsky	Henry		76-62	T1st	...
9-4	At N.Y.	L	2-3	(12)	10	11	Wallace	Dreifort		76-63	2nd	1
9-6	Pit.	W	2-1		7	7	Osuna	Wilkins	Worrell	77-63	T1st	...
9-7	Pit.	W	4-3		7	6	Nomo	Schmidt	Worrell	78-63	1st	+1
9-8	Pit.	L	1-4		8	7	Plesac	Dreifort	Ericks	78-64	T1st	...
9-9	Cin.	W	7-2		11	7	Martinez	Jarvis		79-64	T1st	...
9-10	Cin.	W	5-4		11	7	Candiotti	Salkeld	Worrell	80-64	T1st	...
9-11	Cin.	W	3-2		5	6	Valdes	Smiley	Worrell	81-64	T1st	...
9-12	St.L.	W	4-1		6	2	Nomo	Osborne	Osuna	82-64	1st	+½
9-13	St.L.	L	0-2		5	8	Batchelor	Guthrie	Eckersley	82-65	1st	+½

Date	Opp.	Res.	Score	(inn.*)	Hits	Opp. hits	Winning pitcher	Losing pitcher	Save	Record	Pos.	GB
9-14	St.L.	W	9-5		10	11	Martinez	An. Benes		83-65	1st	+1/2
9-15	St.L.	W	6-5		14	7	Radinsky	Eckersley	Worrell	84-65	1st	+1/2
9-16	At Col.	W	6-4		11	9	Valdes	Wright		85-65	1st	+1/2
9-17	At Col.	W	9-0		14	0	Nomo	Swift		86-65	1st	+1¹/2
9-18	At Col.	L	4-6		6	8	Burke	Astacio	Ruffin	86-66	1st	+1/2
9-19	At S.D.	W	7-0		8	6	Martinez	Valenzuela		87-66	1st	+1¹/2
9-20	At S.D.	L	2-4		3	9	Hamilton	Candiotti	Hoffman	87-67	1st	+1/2
9-21	At S.D.	W	9-2		16	4	Valdes	Sanders		88-67	1st	+1¹/2
9-22	At S.D.	L	2-3		8	10	Ashby	Nomo	Hoffman	88-68	1st	+1/2
9-24	S.F.	W	6-2		8	2	Martinez	Watson		89-68	1st	+1/2
9-25	S.F.	W	7-5		9	8	Radinsky	DeLucia	Worrell	90-68	1st	+2¹/2
9-26	S.F.	L	1-6		7	11	Gardner	Candiotti		90-69	1st	+2
9-27	S.D.	L	2-5	(10)	8	11	Worrell	Osuna	Hoffman	90-70	1st	+1
9-28	S.D.	L	2-4		5	10	Worrell	Dreifort	Hoffman	90-71	T1st	...
9-29	S.D.	L	0-2	(11)	4	7	Veras	Park	Hoffman	90-72	2nd	1

Monthly records: April (14-14), May (15-12), June (13-14), July (15-11), August (17-10), September (16-11).
*Innings, if other than nine. †First game of doubleheader. ‡Second game of doubleheader.

HIGHLIGHTS

High point: On September 17, Hideo Nomo pitched a no-hitter at Coors Field, the first no-hitter pitched there. More important, it came during the Dodgers' longest hold on first place in the N.L. West all season—16 days, from September 12-27.

Low point: There were a few. On May 6, center fielder/leadoff man Brett Butler was found to have throat cancer; then, in late June, manager Tommy Lasorda suffered a heart attack that ultimately led to his retirement a month later. The Dodgers were swept by San Diego in their final three games of the regular season, costing them the division title, a collapse that foreshadowed their second successive three-and-out showing the National League playoffs.

Turning point: Two games ahead of the Padres with four games to play, the Dodgers lost all four to finish one game behind San Diego in the N.L. West.

Most valuable player: Catcher Mike Piazza. He slugged an L.A. Dodger-record 36 homers, drove in 105 runs and batted .336. More importantly, he carried the club pretty much singlehandedly early in the year, when other Dodgers bats were cool.

Most valuable pitcher: Starter Ramon Martinez. The righthander finished the year with a seven-game winning streak, was 9-1 in starts after a Dodgers loss and won nine of 12 decisions after the All-Star break.

Most improved player: Outfielder Billy Ashley. He nearly qualified for "biggest disappointment" after losing his starting job in left field, but he became a feared hitter off the bench. He hit .345 (10-for-29) as a pinch-hitter, drove in 12 runs—nearly half the 29 driven in by L.A. pinch hitters—and hit five pinch homers to tie an L.A. Dodgers record.

Most pleasant surprise: Outfielder Todd Hollandsworth. He wasn't a complete surprise; it's just that injuries restricted him to only 41 games in 1995. Healthy, he batted .291 with 12 homers and 59 RBIs en route to winning N.L. Rookie of the Year honors.

Biggest disappointment: Second baseman Delino DeShields. Laboring through the poorest season of his career, he hit just .224 and committed 17 errors, only one fewer than he had in his first two years in Los Angeles combined. He signed with St. Louis after the season.

Key injuries: Brett Butler's throat cancer limited him to 34 games. Third baseman Mike Blowers was lost for the season after suffering a knee injury on July 17. Ramon Martinez missed five weeks after sustaining a groin injury in his second start of the season (April 6).

Notable: Todd Worrell broke his team record and tied for the major league lead with 44 saves. . . . After finishing last in the N.L. in fielding in 1995, the Dodgers tied for fifth in '96, their best performance in seven years and only the second time in 15 years they've finished that high. . . . The Dodgers completed their fourth successive season without having at least one game started by a lefthanded pitcher. Righthanders have started 591 consecutive games (a major league record) since Bobby Ojeda made a start on September 24, 1992. . . . The Dodgers pulled off their first triple play in 47 years on June 15 at Atlanta. The last previous one came on April 26, 1949, and the names were Gene Hermanski, Jackie Robinson and Gil Hodges. This time, the players were Juan Castro, Delino DeShields and Eric Karros. . . . Karros became the first Dodger first baseman with 30 or more homers and 100 or more RBIs in two consecutive seasons since Hodges in 1953-54.

—GORDON VERRELL

RECORDS

1996 regular-season record: 90-72 (2nd in N.L. West); 47-34 at home; 43-38 on road; 38-24 vs. East; 33-28 vs. Central; 19-20 vs. West; 24-11 vs. lefthanded starters; 66-61 vs. righthanded starters; 74-58 on grass; 16-14 on turf; 26-21 in daytime; 64-51 at night; 33-23 in one-run games; 9-7 in extra-inning games; 0-1 in doubleheaders.

Team record past five years: 370-374 (.497, ranks 6th in league in that span).

TEAM LEADERS

Batting average: Mike Piazza (.336).
At-bats: Raul Mondesi (634).
Runs: Raul Mondesi (98).
Hits: Raul Mondesi (188).
Total bases: Raul Mondesi (314).
Doubles: Raul Mondesi (40).
Triples: Delino DeShields (8).
Home runs: Mike Piazza (36).
Runs batted in: Eric Karros (111).
Stolen bases: Delino DeShields (48).
Slugging percentage: Mike Piazza (.563).
On-base percentage: Mike Piazza (.422).
Wins: Hideo Nomo (16).
Earned-run average: Hideo Nomo (3.19).
Complete games: Hideo Nomo (3).
Shutouts: Ramon Martinez, Hideo Nomo (2).
Saves: Todd Worrell (44).
Innings pitched: Hideo Nomo (228.1).
Strikeouts: Hideo Nomo (234).

GAMES BY POSITION

Catcher: Mike Piazza 146, Tom Prince 35, Carlos Hernandez 9.
First base: Eric Karros 154, Dave Hansen 8, Mike Blowers 6, Mike Busch 1, Oreste Marrero 1.
Second base: Delino DeShields 154, Chad Fonville 23, Juan Castro 9.
Third base: Mike Blowers 90, Tim Wallach 45, Mike Busch 23, Juan Castro 23, Dave Hansen 19, Chad Fonville 2.
Shortstop: Greg Gagne 127, Juan Castro 30, Chad Fonville 20, Mike Blowers 1.
Outfield: Raul Mondesi 157, Todd Hollandsworth 142, Roger Cedeno 71, Wayne Kirby 53, Chad Curtis 40, Billy Ashley 38, Chad Fonville 35, Brett Butler 34, Milt Thompson 17, Rick Parker 4, Juan Castro 1, Dave Clark 1.

TOP DRAFT CHOICES

1. **Damian Rolls**, 3B, Schlagel H.S., Kansas City, Kan.
2. **Josh Glassey**, C, Mission Bay H.S., San Diego.
3. **Alex Cora**, SS, University of Miami.
4. **Peter Bergeron**, OF, Greenfield (Mass.) H.S.
5. **Nick Leach**, 1B, Madera (Calif.) H.S.
6. **Jack Jones**, SS, Cal State Fullerton.
7. **Ben Simon**, RHP, Eastern Michigan Univ.
8. **Chris Karabinus**, LHP, Towson State U.
9. **David Falcon**, C, Bayamon, P.R.
10. **Jeff Auterson**, OF, Norte Vista H.S., Riverside, Calif.

MONTREAL EXPOS
NATIONAL LEAGUE EAST DIVISION

1997 EXPOS SCHEDULE

Home games shaded.
* — All-Star Game at Jacobs Field (Cleveland)
D — Day game (any game starting before 5 p.m.)

APRIL

SUN	MON	TUE	WED	THU	FRI	SAT
		1 D STL	2 STL	3 STL	4 COL	5 D COL
6 L	7 STL	8 STL	9	10 D COL	11 D COL	12 D COL
13 OL	14	15 HOU	16 HOU	17 PHI	18 PHI	19 PHI
20 HI	21	22 CUB	23 CUB	24	25 NYM	26 D NYM
27 YM	28 CUB	29 CUB	30 HOU			

MAY

SUN	MON	TUE	WED	THU	FRI	SAT
				1 HOU	2 D SD	3 SD
4 D	5 SF	6 SF	7 SF	8 D LA	9 LA	10 LA
11 A	12	13 SD	14 D SD	15 SD	16 SF	17 LA
18 A	19 D ATL	20 ATL	21 D PIT	22 PIT	23 PIT	24 PIT
25 T	26 NYM	27 NYM	28	29	30 PIT	31 PIT

JUNE

SUN	MON	TUE	WED	THU	FRI	SAT
1 IT	2 NYM	3 NYM	4 ATL	5 D ATL	6 CUB	7 CUB
8 UB	9 D CUB	10 PHI	11 PHI	12	13 DET	14 DET
15 ET	16 BAL	17 BAL	18 D BAL	19	20 FLA	21 D FLA
22 LA	23 CIN	24 CIN	25 CIN	26 FLA	27 FLA	28 FLA
29 A	30 TOR					

JULY

SUN	MON	TUE	WED	THU	FRI	SAT
		1 TOR	2 TOR	3 ATL	4 ATL	5 ATL
6 L	7	8 D	9	10	11 CIN	12 CIN
13 IN	14 FLA	15 FLA	16 PHI	17 PHI	18 HOU	19 HOU
20 U	21 D COL	22 COL	23	24 HOU	25 HOU	26 HOU
27 U	28 COL	29 COL	30 D COL	31 SD		

AUGUST

SUN	MON	TUE	WED	THU	FRI	SAT
					1 SD	2 SD
3	4 D	5 LA	6 LA	7 LA	8 SF	9 SF
10	11 SD	12 SD	13 LA	14 D LA	15 SF	16 D SF
17	18 D	19 STL	20 STL	21 STL	22 CUB	23 CUB
24 B	25	26 STL	27 STL	28 STL	29 NYY	30 D NYY
31 Y						

SEPTEMBER

SUN	MON	TUE	WED	THU	FRI	SAT
UN	1 BOS	2 BOS	3 BOS	4 PHI	5 PHI	6 PHI
7 I	8	9 PIT	10 PIT	11 NYM	12 NYM	13 D NYM
14 YM	15 PIT	16 PIT	17 CIN	18 CIN	19 ATL	20 ATL
21 L	22 ATL	23 FLA	24 FLA	25 FLA	26 CIN	27 CIN
28 N						

1997 SEASON

CLUB DIRECTORY

President and general partner
Claude R. Brochu

Chairman of the partnership committee
Jacques Menard

Vice chairmen of the partnership comm.
Claude Blanchet
Jocelyn Proteau
Louis A. Tanguay

Vice president, baseball operations
Bill Stoneman

Vice president and general manager
Jim Beattie

Vice president, finance
Laurier M. Carpentier

Director, financial planning & admin.
Michel Bussiere

Manager, accounting services
Francois Lalonde

Dir., int'l op. & special asst. to the g.m.
Fred Ferreira

Director, scouting
Ed Creech

Assistant director, scouting
Gregg Leonard

Director, player development
Dave Littlefield

Asst. dir., player development, scouting
Neal Huntington

V.p., marketing and communications
Richard Morency

Vice president, stadium operations
Claude Delorme

Vice president, sales
Lucien Baril

Directors, advertising sales
Luigi Carolo, John D. Terlizzi, Danielle
La Roche

Director, ticket office
Chantal Dalpe

Director, media services
Monique Giroux

Director, media relations
P.J. Loyello

Director, advertising
Johanne Heroux

Director, operations
Pierre Touzin

Director, merchandising and licensing
Susan LeBlanc

Director, group sales
Jean Cyr

Director, season ticket sales
Gilles Beauregard

Club physician
Dr. Mike Thomassin

Club orthopedist
Dr. Larry Coughlin

Scouts
Alex Agostino, Mark Baca, Mike
Berger, Dennis Cardoza, Doug
Carpenter, Robby Corsaro, Marc Del
Piano, Joel Escobar, Phil Favia, Jim
Fleming, Dan Freed, Scott Goldby,
John Hughes, Jimmy Lester, Dave
Malpass, Roy McMillan, Dennis
Meeks, Bob Oldis, B.D. Parker,
Barry Petrachenko, Jerry Scavarda,
Scott Stanley, Bob Vostry

MINOR LEAGUE AFFILIATES

Class	Team	League	Manager
AAA	Ottawa	International	Pat Kelly
AA	Harrisburg	Eastern	Rick Sofield
A	West Palm Beach	Florida State	Doug Sisson
A	Cape Fear	South Atlantic	To be announced
A	Vermont	New York-Pennsylvania	Kevin Higgins
Rookie	Gulf Coast Expos	Gulf Coast	Luis Dorante

BROADCAST INFORMATION

Radio: CIQC-AM (600); CKAC-AM (73,
French language).
TV: CBFT (2, French language).
Cable TV: The Sports Network; RDS
(French language).

SPRING TRAINING

Ballpark (city): Municipal Stadium
(West Palm Beach, Fla.).
Ticket information: 407-684-6801.

1997 SEASON Montreal Expos

SPRING TRAINING ROSTER

Manager—Felipe Alou (17).
Coaches—Pierre Arsenault (67), Bobby Cuellar, Tommy Harper (21), Pete Mackanin, Luis Pujols (55), Jim Tracy (23).

No.	PITCHERS	B/T	Ht./Wt.	Born	1996 clubs
48	Alvarez, Tavo	R/R	6-3/235	11-25-71	Ottawa, Montreal
66	Aucoin, Derek	R/R	6-7/235	3-27-70	Ottawa, Montreal
	Baker, Jason	R/R	6-4/195	11-21-74	Delmarva
37	Cormier, Rheal	L/L	5-10/187	4-23-67	Montreal
47	Daal, Omar	L/L	6-3/185	3-1-72	Montreal
53	Falteisek, Steve	R/R	6-2/200	1-28-72	Ottawa, Harrisburg
14	Juden, Jeff	R/R	6-8/265	1-19-71	San Francisco, Montreal
44	Manuel, Barry	R/R	5-11/185	8-12-65	Montreal
45	Martinez, Pedro J.	R/R	5-11/175	7-25-71	Montreal
36	Paniagua, Jose	R/R	6-2/185	8-20-73	Ottawa, Montreal, Harrisburg
33	Perez, Carlos	L/L	6-3/195	1-14-71	Montreal
	Phelps, Tommy	L/L	6-4/205	3-4-74	West Palm Beach, Harrisburg
64	Stull, Everett	R/R	6-3/200	8-24-71	Harrisburg, Ottawa
	Thurman, Mike	R/R	6-5/190	7-22-73	West Palm Beach, Harrisburg
41	Urbina, Ugueth	R/R	6-2/185	2-15-74	West Palm Beach, Ottawa, Montreal
	Valdes, Marc	R/R	6-0/187	12-20-71	Charlotte, Portland, Florida
43	Veres, Dave	R/R	6-2/195	10-19-66	Montreal
	Wagner, Matt	R/R	6-5/215	4-4-72	Tacoma, Seattle
57	Weber, Neil	L/L	6-5/215	12-6-72	Harrisburg

No.	CATCHERS	B/T	Ht./Wt.	Born	1996 clubs
12	Chavez, Raul	R/R	5-11/175	3-18-73	Ottawa, Montreal
24	Fletcher, Darrin	L/R	6-1/200	10-3-66	Montreal
	Henley, Bob	R/R	6-2/190	1-30-73	Harrisburg
19	Laker, Tim	R/R	6-3/200	11-27-69	Montreal
	Widger, Chris	R/R	6-3/195	5-21-71	Tacoma, Seattle

No.	INFIELDERS	B/T	Ht./Wt.	Born	1996 clubs
56	Alcantara, Israel	R/R	6-2/180	5-6-73	Harrisburg, Gulf Coast Expos, West Palm Beach
11	Andrews, Shane	R/R	6-1/215	8-28-71	Montreal
	Cabrera, Orlando	R/R	5-9/150	11-2-74	Delmarva
4	Grudzielanek, Mark	R/R	6-1/185	6-30-70	Montreal
3	Lansing, Mike	R/R	6-0/185	4-3-68	Montreal
52	McGuire, Ryan	L/L	6-2/210	11-23-71	Ottawa
25	Segui, David	B/L	6-1/202	7-19-66	Montreal

No.	OUTFIELDERS	B/T	Ht./Wt.	Born	1996 clubs
15	Benitez, Yamil	R/R	6-2/195	5-10-72	Ottawa, Montreal
30	Floyd, Cliff	L/R	6-4/235	12-5-72	Ottawa, Montreal
27	Guerrero, Vladimir	R/R	6-2/165	2-9-76	West Palm Beach, Harrisburg, Montreal
29	Obando, Sherman	R/R	6-4/220	1-23-70	Montreal
40	Rodriguez, Henry	L/L	6-1/205	11-8-67	Montreal
7	Santangelo, F.P.	B/R	5-10/170	10-24-67	Montreal
50	Stovall, DaRond	B/L	6-1/185	1-3-73	Harrisburg, Bradenton Expos, West Palm Beach
22	White, Rondell	R/R	6-1/205	2-23-72	Montreal, West Palm Beach, Bradenton Expos, Harrisbur

BALLPARK INFORMATION

Ballpark (capacity, surface)
Olympic Stadium (46,500, artificial)
Address
4549 Pierre-de-Coubertin Ave.
Montreal, QC H1V 3N7
Business phone
514-253-3434
Ticket information
800-GO-EXPOS
Ticket prices
$30 (VIP box seats)
$20 (box seats)
$10 (terrace)
$5 (general admission)
Field dimensions (from home plate)
To left field at foul line, 325 feet
To center field, 404 feet
To right field at foul line, 325 feet
First game played
April 15, 1977 (Phillies 7, Expos 2)

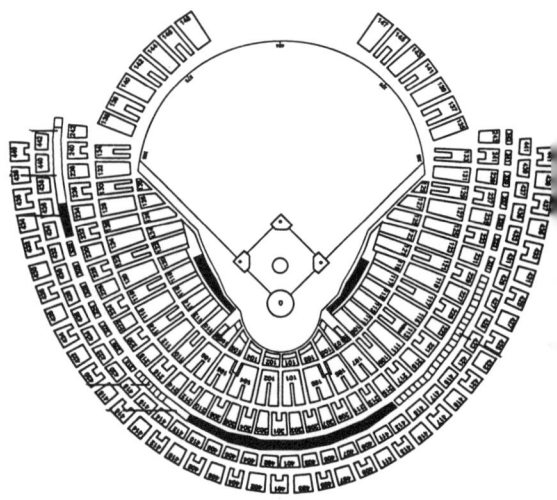

DAY BY DAY

Date	Opp.	Res.	Score	(inn.*)	Hits	Opp. hits	Winning pitcher	Losing pitcher	Save	Record	Pos.	GB
-2	At Cin.	L	1-4		7	7	Schourek	Fassero	Moore	0-1	T3rd	1
-3	At Cin.	W	8-4		15	6	Veres	Shaw		1-1	T2nd	1
-4	At Cin.	W	10-2		14	8	Paniagua	Burba		2-1	T1st	...
-5	Col.	W	6-4		10	9	Dyer	Munoz		3-1	1st	+1
-6	Col.	L	4-5		8	8	M. Thompson	Rueter	Leskanic	3-2	1st	+1
-7	Col.	W	9-1		9	3	Fassero	Painter		4-2	1st	+1
-8	At St.L.	W	4-3	(10)	9	11	Rojas	Parrett		5-2	1st	+1¹/₂
-10	At St.L.	L	1-4		4	9	Al. Benes	Paniagua		5-3	1st	+¹/₂
-11	At Pit.	W	6-5	(11)	11	10	Rojas	Cordova	Veres	6-3	1st	+1¹/₂
-12	At Pit.	W	13-3		14	6	Rueter	Darwin		7-3	1st	+2¹/₂
-13	At Pit.	L	3-9		10	12	Wagner	Fassero		7-4	1st	+1¹/₂
-14	At Pit.	L	2-5		10	8	Neagle	Martinez		7-5	1st	+1¹/₂
-16	Phi.	W	7-6		10	11	Rojas	Springer		8-5	1st	+1¹/₂
-17	Phi.	L	3-9		10	13	Mulholland	Cormier		8-6	1st	+¹/₂
-18	Phi.	L	8-9		12	11	Bottalico	Rojas		8-7	1st	+¹/₂
-19	Pit.	W	2-1		9	8	Manuel	Plesac		9-7	1st	+¹/₂
-20	Pit.	W	11-2		11	3	Martinez	Ericks		10-7	1st	+¹/₂
-21	Pit.	W	9-4		16	7	Veres	Christiansen		11-7	1st	+1¹/₂
-22	St.L.	W	8-0		10	3	Cormier	Osborne		12-7	1st	+1¹/₂
-23	St.L.	W	12-11		14	14	Scott	Mathews		13-7	1st	+2¹/₂
-24	Cin.	W	7-6	(10)	14	10	Dyer	Moore		14-7	1st	+2¹/₂
-25	Cin.	W	8-4		9	7	Martinez	Smiley		15-7	1st	+3¹/₂
-26	At Col.	W	6-2		12	8	Alvarez	Reynoso		16-7	1st	+3¹/₂
-27	At Col.	L	5-6	(13)	14	15	Painter	Daal		16-8	1st	+2¹/₂
-28	At Col.	W	21-9		20	13	Rueter	Rekar		17-8	1st	+3
-29	At N.Y.	L	2-3		7	7	Harnisch	Fassero	J. Franco	17-9	1st	+2
-1†	At N.Y.	W	4-0		8	2	Martinez	Clark		18-9		
-1‡	At N.Y.	L	0-6		4	10	Isringhausen	Alvarez		18-10	1st	+2
-3	At Hou.	L	1-4		4	9	Reynolds	Cormier	Jones	18-11	1st	+1
-4	At Hou.	W	2-1		6	6	Veres	Hernandez	Rojas	19-11	1st	+2
-5	At Hou.	W	5-0		7	7	Fassero	Brocail		20-11	1st	+2
-6	Chi.	W	6-2		6	6	Martinez	Bullinger		21-11	1st	+2
-7	Chi.	W	8-3		11	7	Veres	Adams		22-11	1st	+2
-8	Chi.	W	4-2		10	8	Cormier	Navarro	Rojas	23-11	1st	+2
-9	Hou.	L	4-11		10	18	Kile	Rueter		23-12	1st	+1¹/₂
-10	Hou.	W	5-2		8	7	Fassero	Dougherty	Rojas	24-12	1st	+1¹/₂
-11	Hou.	W	10-9	(13)	15	12	Dyer	Dougherty		25-12	1st	+1¹/₂
-12	Hou.	W	7-6		13	10	Urbina	Hampton	Rojas	26-12	1st	+2¹/₂
-13	At L.A.	W	3-2		8	8	Manuel	Worrell	Rojas	27-12	1st	+2¹/₂
-14	At L.A.	L	1-2		8	7	Martinez	Veres	Worrell	27-13	1st	+1¹/₂
-15	At L.A.	L	2-7		4	10	Candiotti	Fassero		27-14	1st	+1¹/₂
-17	At S.D.	L	1-2	(12)	7	5	Hoffman	Rojas		27-15	1st	+¹/₂
-18	At S.D.	W	3-2		9	6	Urbina	Valenzuela	Rojas	28-15	1st	+¹/₂
-19	At S.D.	L	3-4		11	7	Worrell	Veres	Hoffman	28-16	2nd	¹/₂
-20	At S.F.	L	6-9		12	7	Dewey	Dyer	Beck	28-17	2nd	1¹/₂
-21	At S.F.	L	5-8		6	13	Dewey	Aucoin	Beck	28-18	2nd	1¹/₂
-22	At S.F.	W	4-3		7	9	Martinez	VanLandingham	Rojas	29-18	2nd	1¹/₂
-24	L.A.	L	4-5	(11)	9	11	Osuna	Daal	Worrell	29-19	2nd	2¹/₂
-25	L.A.	L	3-5		9	8	Martinez	Cormier	Worrell	29-20	2nd	2¹/₂
-26	L.A.	L	3-4		5	8	Candiotti	Rojas	Worrell	29-21	2nd	3¹/₂
-27	S.D.	L	3-4		7	6	Hamilton	Fassero	Hoffman	29-22	2nd	4¹/₂
-28	S.D.	L	2-3	(10)	5	7	Hoffman	Scott	Bochtler	29-23	2nd	5
-29	S.D.	W	9-4		13	10	Urbina	Valenzuela		30-23	2nd	5
-31	S.F.	W	7-4		13	13	Daal	DeLucia	Veres	31-23	2nd	5
-1	S.F.	W	5-1		7	5	Fassero	Fernandez	Dyer	32-23	2nd	4
-2	S.F.	L	1-8		5	13	Leiter	Martinez		32-24	2nd	5
-4	At Fla.	L	0-5		5	9	Burkett	Rueter		32-25	2nd	5¹/₂
-5	At Fla.	W	2-1		6	8	Cormier	Rapp	Veres	33-25	2nd	5¹/₂
-7	At Chi.	W	9-3		13	6	Fassero	Castillo		34-25	2nd	4¹/₂
-8	At Chi.	L	4-6		10	11	Telemaco	Martinez	Wendell	34-26	2nd	4¹/₂
-9	At Chi.	L	2-4		4	6	Trachsel	Rueter	Wendell	34-27	2nd	5¹/₂
-10	Fla.	L	2-5		8	12	Nen	Dyer		34-28	2nd	5¹/₂
-11	Fla.	W	3-2		8	8	Scott	Brown	Veres	35-28	2nd	5¹/₂
-12	Fla.	W	8-0		8	5	Fassero	Leiter		36-28	2nd	4¹/₂
-14	At Cin.	W	6-1		9	4	Martinez	Portugal		37-28	2nd	4
-15	At Cin.	W	6-5		9	12	Rueter	Burba	Rojas	38-28	2nd	3
-16	At Cin.	L	0-7		4	12	Salkeld	Cormier		38-29	2nd	3
-17	At Col.	W	5-3		9	8	Urbina	Freeman	Rojas	39-29	2nd	3
-18	At Col.	W	12-8		15	12	Dyer	Holmes		40-29	2nd	3
-19	At Col.	L	6-7	(10)	15	13	Ruffin	Scott		40-30	2nd	4
-20	St.L.	W	8-3		11	8	Rueter	Stottlemyre		41-30	2nd	3¹/₂
-21	St.L.	W	4-3	(12)	12	9	Rojas	Eckersley		42-30	2nd	3¹/₂

Date	Opp.	Res.	Score	(inn.*)	Hits	Opp. hits	Winning pitcher	Losing pitcher	Save	Record	Pos.	GB
6-22	St.L.	L	4-9		9	9	Morgan	Urbina		42-31	2nd	4$^{1}/_{2}$
6-23	St.L.	W	3-2		7	3	Fassero	Osborne	Rojas	43-31	2nd	4$^{1}/_{2}$
6-24	Pit.	W	11-3		14	8	Martinez	Dessens		44-31	2nd	3$^{1}/_{2}$
6-25	Pit.	W	8-2		13	6	Rueter	Smith	Scott	45-31	2nd	3$^{1}/_{2}$
6-26	Pit.	L	1-3		8	7	Darwin	Cormier	Cordova	45-32	2nd	3$^{1}/_{2}$
6-28	At Phi.	L	3-7		8	16	Mulholland	Urbina	Ryan	45-33	2nd	4
6-29	At Phi.	W	1-0		5	2	Fassero	Schilling		46-33	2nd	3
6-30	At Phi.	W	6-5		6	9	Rojas	Bottalico	Dyer	47-33	2nd	3
7-1	Atl.	L	2-7		6	8	Avery	Rueter		47-34	2nd	4
7-2	Atl.	W	5-1		11	3	Cormier	Maddux		48-34	2nd	3
7-3	Atl.	L	1-3		3	8	Glavine	Scott	Wohlers	48-35	2nd	4
7-4	N.Y.	L	0-4		6	6	Person	Fassero		48-36	2nd	4
7-5	N.Y.	L	6-9		12	14	DiPoto	Scott	J. Franco	48-37	2nd	4
7-6	N.Y.	L	3-11		10	19	B. Jones	Rueter		48-38	2nd	5
7-7	N.Y.	W	4-3		8	8	Cormier	Harnisch	Rojas	49-38	2nd	5
7-11	Phi.	L	2-3		5	5	Schilling	Fassero	Bottalico	49-39	2nd	5
7-12	Phi.	L	3-5		9	8	Mulholland	Martinez		49-40	2nd	6
7-13	Phi.	L	2-6		10	8	Mimbs	Cormier		49-41	2nd	7
7-14	Phi.	W	5-2		8	5	Scott	Williams	Rojas	50-41	2nd	7
7-15	At Atl.	L	4-5		5	11	Maddux	Manuel	Wohlers	50-42	2nd	8
7-16	At Atl.	L	2-3		10	10	Wohlers	Scott		50-43	2nd	9
7-18	At N.Y.	W	7-3		13	8	Martinez	Harnisch		51-43	2nd	9
7-19	At N.Y.	W	5-4		9	9	Dyer	Isringhausen	Rojas	52-43	2nd	8
7-20	At N.Y.	L	1-4		3	9	Wilson	Urbina	J. Franco	52-44	2nd	8
7-21	At N.Y.	W	4-3		10	9	Fassero	Clark	Rojas	53-44	2nd	7
7-23	At Pit.	L	1-5		7	7	Lieber	Martinez		53-45	2nd	8$^{1}/_{2}$
7-24	At Pit.	L	4-5		7	11	Ericks	Rojas		53-46	2nd	9$^{1}/_{2}$
7-25	At St.L.	W	4-2		11	3	Urbina	Petkovsek	Rojas	54-46	2nd	8$^{1}/_{2}$
7-26	At St.L.	W	5-1		13	3	Fassero	Osborne		55-46	2nd	8$^{1}/_{2}$
7-27	At St.L.	L	3-6		4	7	An. Benes	Dyer	Eckersley	55-47	2nd	8$^{1}/_{2}$
7-28	At St.L.	L	4-6		11	7	Petkovsek	Martinez	Mathews	55-48	2nd	8$^{1}/_{2}$
7-29	Col.	W	4-1		9	8	Cormier	Wright	Rojas	56-48	2nd	8
7-30	Col.	W	3-1		4	3	Urbina	Reynoso	Rojas	57-48	2nd	7
7-31	Col.	W	6-2		8	6	Fassero	Bailey		58-48	2nd	7
8-1	Cin.	L	7-9		8	10	Shaw	Dyer	Brantley	58-49	2nd	8
8-2	Cin.	W	11-1		14	4	Martinez	Jarvis		59-49	2nd	7
8-3	Cin.	W	6-2		11	4	Cormier	Portugal	Rojas	60-49	2nd	7
8-4	Cin.	W	7-3		11	9	Urbina	Burba	Rojas	61-49	2nd	7
8-6	At Hou.	W	7-5		12	12	Fassero	Kile	Rojas	62-49	2nd	7
8-7	At Hou.	W	13-5		16	13	Leiter	Wall		63-49	2nd	7
8-8	At Hou.	L	2-6		6	9	Drabek	Martinez		63-50	2nd	7
8-9	Chi.	L	9-11		14	9	Bullinger	Cormier	Patterson	63-51	2nd	7
8-10	Chi.	L	2-3		10	7	Casian	Dyer	Wendell	63-52	2nd	7
8-11	Chi.	W	4-3	(10)	5	8	Rojas	Bottenfield		64-52	2nd	7
8-12	Hou.	W	8-1		10	3	Leiter	Darwin		65-52	2nd	6$^{1}/_{2}$
8-13	Hou.	W	7-4		10	5	Martinez	Drabek	Rojas	66-52	2nd	7
8-14	Hou.	L	3-8		9	14	Reynolds	Cormier		66-53	2nd	7
8-16	At L.A.	L	2-8		9	10	Astacio	Urbina		66-54	2nd	8$^{1}/_{2}$
8-17	At L.A.	L	6-7		8	10	Worrell	Veres		66-55	2nd	9$^{1}/_{2}$
8-18	At L.A.	W	7-3		10	7	Leiter	Candiotti		67-55	2nd	9$^{1}/_{2}$
8-19	At S.D.	L	3-7		6	12	Sanders	Martinez	Hoffman	67-56	2nd	10
8-20	At S.D.	L	0-3		3	8	Tewksbury	Cormier	Hoffman	67-57	2nd	11
8-21	At S.D.	L	2-7		5	11	Valenzuela	Urbina		67-58	2nd	12
8-22	At S.F.	W	5-4		8	10	Fassero	Bautista	Rojas	68-58	2nd	11
8-23	At S.F.	W	10-8		12	12	Daal	Creek	Rojas	69-58	2nd	11
8-24	At S.F.	W	3-0		9	2	Martinez	Estes	Rojas	70-58	2nd	11
8-25	At S.F.	L	2-7		7	8	Fernandez	Cormier		70-59	2nd	11
8-27	L.A.	L	1-5		10	7	Nomo	Fassero		70-60	2nd	11
8-28	L.A.	W	6-5		11	11	Rojas	Park		71-60	2nd	11
8-29	L.A.	L	1-2		3	6	Martinez	Martinez	Worrell	71-61	2nd	12
8-30	S.D.	L	0-6		2	13	Sanders	Paniagua		71-62	2nd	12$^{1}/_{2}$
8-31	S.D.	W	4-2		8	4	Daal	Tewksbury	Rojas	72-62	2nd	11$^{1}/_{2}$
9-1	S.D.	W	7-6		12	10	Fassero	Ashby	Rojas	73-62	2nd	10$^{1}/_{2}$
9-2	S.F.	W	4-3	(11)	12	7	Manuel	Beck		74-62	2nd	9$^{1}/_{2}$
9-3	S.F.	W	9-2		14	9	Martinez	Gardner		75-62	2nd	8$^{1}/_{2}$
9-4	S.F.	W	6-0		8	3	Paniagua	Estes		76-62	2nd	7$^{1}/_{2}$
9-5	At Fla.	W	6-2		14	7	Manuel	Rapp		77-62	2nd	7
9-6	At Fla.	L	0-4		7	11	Hutton	Fassero	Powell	77-63	2nd	8
9-7	At Fla.	W	2-1		7	5	Leiter	Valdes	Rojas	78-63	2nd	8
9-8	At Fla.	L	1-2		4	6	Helling	Martinez	Nen	78-64	2nd	8
9-9	At Chi.	L	1-3		6	6	Foster	Paniagua		78-65	2nd	8$^{1}/_{2}$
9-10	At Chi.	L	3-10		13	12	Bottenfield	Daal		78-66	2nd	8$^{1}/_{2}$
9-11	At Chi.	W	2-1		7	4	Urbina	Adams	Rojas	79-66	2nd	7$^{1}/_{2}$
9-12	Fla.	W	5-4		6	8	Veres	Powell	Rojas	80-66	2nd	6$^{1}/_{2}$
9-13	Fla.	W	3-2		4	6	Martinez	Helling	Rojas	81-66	2nd	5$^{1}/_{2}$

Date	Opp.	Res.	Score	(inn.*)	Hits	Opp. hits	Winning pitcher	Losing pitcher	Save	Record	Pos.	GB
-14	Fla.	W	3-2		10	9	Veres	Powell	Rojas	82-66	2nd	4¹/₂
-15	Fla.	L	3-4		6	10	Leiter	Daal	Nen	82-67	2nd	5¹/₂
-17	N.Y.	W	7-1		10	6	Fassero	Isringhausen		83-67	2nd	6
-18	N.Y.	W	4-3		8	8	Urbina	Mlicki	Rojas	84-67	2nd	6
-19	At Atl.	W	5-1		10	6	Urbina	Wohlers		85-67	2nd	5
-20	At Atl.	L	2-3		6	10	Glavine	Leiper	Wohlers	85-68	2nd	6
-21	At Atl.	L	4-5		11	8	Neagle	Daal	Wohlers	85-69	2nd	7
-22	At Atl.	L	2-8		8	15	Smoltz	Fassero		85-70	2nd	8
-23	At Atl.	L	1-3		5	8	Maddux	Leiter	Bielecki	85-71	2nd	9
-24	At Phi.	W	6-2		11	10	Juden	Williams	Rojas	86-71	2nd	8
-25	At Phi.	L	1-3		4	7	West	Paniagua	Bottalico	86-72	2nd	8
-26	At Phi.	W	5-2		6	8	Daal	Schilling	Rojas	87-72	2nd	7
-27	Atl.	L	4-6		7	13	Smoltz	Fassero	Wohlers	87-73	2nd	8
-28	Atl.	L	0-4		6	6	Woodall	Leiter		87-74	2nd	9
-29	Atl.	W	6-3		8	9	Alvarez	Avery	Rojas	88-74	2nd	8

Monthly records: April (17-9), May (14-14), June (16-10), July (11-15), August (14-14), September (16-12).
Innings, if other than nine. †First game of doubleheader. ‡Second game of doubleheader.

HIGHLIGHTS

High point: Picked by many to finish in last place, the Expos went 17-9 in April and were 3¹/₂ games ahead of the Braves in the National League East on April 26. The Expos were either in first or leading the wild-card race from April to August 27.

Low point: The Expos officially were eliminated from the wild-card hunt on September 28, the next-to-last day of the regular season. But the low point of the year actually came three days earlier, when they lost, 3-1, to the Phillies. The Padres lost, 3-1, to the Rockies that night; an Expos win over the Phils would have left them just a half-game back in the wild-card race.

Turning point: The Expos played a five-game series against the Braves from September 19-23, losing the last four games. The series was necessitated because the Expos only played two games on their previous trip to Atlanta, three days before the start of the Olympics.

Most valuable player: F.P. Santangelo. He played every position but catcher, pitcher and first base and hit everywhere in the lineup but third, fourth and ninth. When Rondell White was out for 68 games with a bruised kidney and spleen, Santangelo filled in admirably, hitting .269 with 30 RBIs. He also filled in for Shane Andrews and Moises Alou before the season was over.

Most valuable pitcher: Closer Mel Rojas. In a year when numerous club records fell, Rojas closed out the year by converting his last 23 save opportunities, bettering by two the franchise mark set by John Wetteland in 1993.

Most improved player: Shortstop Mark Grudzielanek. He was overmatched in 1995, then showed up in spring training with a new, taller stance and proceeded to become only the second Expos to break the 200-hit barrier with 201, three behind Al Oliver's club record set in 1982. He finished with 99 runs, one away from becoming the first player in franchise history with 200 hits and 100 runs.

Most pleasant surprise: Outfielder/first baseman Henry Rodriguez. He faded down the stretch and spent a great deal of time on the bench but still set a club

record with 36 home runs and had the fifth-highest RBI total in club history with 103. He entered the season with 21 homers and 101 RBIs in his previous 278 major league games.

Biggest disappointment: Starting pitcher Pedro Martinez. He has yet to turn into the big winner everyone thinks he'll be. Martinez was 13-10 with a 3.70 ERA and had 222 strikeouts. But he still suffered from lapses in concentration and showed up late for a start against the Padres in San Diego, rushing through his warmup and coming into the game directly from the bullpen. He didn't make it out of the second inning.

Key injuries: Rondell White suffered a bruised kidney and spleen on April 28 and missed 68 games. David Segui missed 36 with a fractured right thumb and five more with tendinitis in his left wrist. Moises Alou was on the 15-day disabled list with a strained right hamstring suffered while running in the outfield before the club's first game of the second half. Shane Andrews missed six games with a lacerated right thumb after being hit by a pitch from the Dodgers' Ramon Martinez on August 17.

Notable: The Expos hit a major league record six grand slams in April, surpassing both the 1983 Orioles (who hit five in September) and the 1995 Mariners (five in August). The Expos tied an N.L. record with nine grand slams, tying the mark set by Chicago (1929) and San Diego (1995).

—JEFF BLAIR

RECORDS

1996 regular-season record: 88-74 (2nd in N.L. East); 50-31 at home; 38-43 on road; 24-28 vs. East; 39-22 vs. Central; 25-24 vs. West; 21-15 vs. lefthanded starters; 67-59 vs. righthanded starters; 24-33 on grass; 64-41 on turf; 25-22 in daytime; 63-52 at night; 33-23 in one-run games; 7-5 in extra-inning games; 0-1 in doubleheaders.
Team record past five years: 409-335 (.550, ranks 2nd in league in that span).

TEAM LEADERS

Batting average: Mark Grudzielanek (.306).
At-bats: Mark Grudzielanek (657).

Runs: Mark Grudzielanek, Mike Lansing (99).
Hits: Mark Grudzielanek (201).
Total bases: Henry Rodriguez (299).
Doubles: Henry Rodriguez (42).
Triples: F.P. Santangelo (5).
Home runs: Henry Rodriguez (36).
Runs batted in: Henry Rodriguez (103).
Stolen bases: Mark Grudzielanek (33).
Slugging percentage: Henry Rodriguez (.562).
On-base percentage: Mike Lansing (.341).
Wins: Jeff Fassero (15).
Earned-run average: Jeff Fassero (3.30).
Complete games: Jeff Fassero (5).
Shutouts: Rheal Cormier, Jeff Fassero, Pedro Martinez (1).
Saves: Mel Rojas (36).
Innings pitched: Jeff Fassero (231.2).
Strikeouts: Jeff Fassero, Pedro Martinez (222).

GAMES BY POSITION

Catcher: Darrin Fletcher 112, Lenny Webster 63, Tim Spehr 58, Raul Chavez 3.
First base: David Segui 113, Henry Rodriguez 51, Cliff Floyd 2, Dave Silvestri 1.
Second base: Mike Lansing 159, Andy Stankiewicz 19, F.P. Santangelo 5, Dave Silvestri 1.
Third base: Shane Andrews 123, Dave Silvestri 47, F.P. Santangelo 23, Rick Schu 1, Andy Stankiewicz 1.
Shortstop: Mark Grudzielanek 153, Andy Stankiewicz 13, Dave Silvestri 10, Mike Lansing 2, F.P. Santangelo 1.
Outfield: Moises Alou 142, F.P. Santangelo 124, Henry Rodriguez 89, Rondell White 86, Cliff Floyd 85, Sherman Obando 47, Vladimir Guerrero 8, Yamil Benitez 4, Dave Silvestri 2, Tim Spehr 1.

TOP DRAFT CHOICES

1. **John Patterson,** RHP, West Orange (Tex.) Stark H.S.
2. **Milton Bradley,** OF, Poly H.S., Long Beach, Calif.
3. **Joe Fraser,** RHP, Katella H.S., Anaheim.
4. **Christian Parker,** RHP, U. of Notre Dame.
5. **Tony Lawrence,** OF, Louisiana Tech.
6. **Karl Chatman,** OF, Dallas Baptist Univ.
7. **Luis Rivera,** C, Bayamon, P.R.
8. **Keith Evans,** RHP, Univ. of California.
9. **Brian Matz,** LHP, Clemson University.
10. **Paul Blandford,** 2B, Univ. of Kentucky.

1997 SEASON *Montreal Expos*

NEW YORK METS
NATIONAL LEAGUE EAST DIVISION

1997 METS SCHEDULE

Home games shaded.
* — All-Star Game at Jacobs Field (Cleveland)
D — Day game (any game starting before 5 p.m.)

APRIL

SUN	MON	TUE	WED	THU	FRI	SAT
		1 D SD	2 SD	3 D SD	4 SF	5 SF
6 D SF	7 LA	8 LA	9 LA	10	11	12 D SF
13 D SF	14 SF	15 LA	16 D LA	17	18 CUB	19 D CUB
20 D CUB	21 CUB	22 D CIN	23 CIN	24	25 MON	26 D MON
27 D MON	28 CIN	29 CIN	30 SD			

MAY

SUN	MON	TUE	WED	THU	FRI	SAT
				1 D SD	2 STL	3 D STL
4 STL	5 COL	6 D COL	7 HOU	8 D HOU	9 STL	10 STL
11 D STL	12	13 HOU	14 HOU	15	16 CBL	17 D COL
18 D COL	19 COL	20 FLA	21 FLA	22 PHI	23 PHI	24 PHI
25 PHI	26 MON	27 MON	28 MON	29	30 PHI	31 PHI

JUNE

SUN	MON	TUE	WED	THU	FRI	SAT
1 PHI	2 MON	3 MON	4 FLA	5 FLA	6 CIN	7 D CIN
8 CIN	9 CUB	10 CUB	11 D CUB	12	13 BOS	14 D BOS
15 BOS	16 NYY	17 NYY	18 D NYY	19 PIT	20 PIT	21 D PIT
22 PIT	23 ATL	24 ATL	25 D ATL	26	27 PIT	28 PIT
29 PIT	30 DET					

JULY

SUN	MON	TUE	WED	THU	FRI	SAT
		1 DET	2 DET	3 FLA	4 FLA	5 D FLA
6 D FLA	7	8 °	9	10 ATL	11 ATL	12 D ATL
13 ATL	14 PIT	15 PIT	16 CUB	17 CUB	18 CIN	19 CIN
20 CIN	21 D CIN	22 LA	23 LA	24 SD	25 SD	26 SD
27 SD	28	29 SF	30 D SF	31		

AUGUST

SUN	MON	TUE	WED	THU	FRI	SAT
					1 HOU	2 D HOU
3 D HOU	4 STL	5 COL	6 COL	7 D COL	8 HOU	9 HOU
10 D HOU	11 STL	12 STL	13 STL	14 STL	15 COL	16 COL
17 D COL	18	19 LA	20 LA	21 LA	22 SD	23 SD
24 D SD	25 SF	26 SF	27 SF	28	29 BAL	30 D BAL
31 D BAL						

SEPTEMBER

SUN	MON	TUE	WED	THU	FRI	SAT
	1 TBR	2 TOR	3 TOR	4	5 D CUB	6 D CUB
7 CUB	8 PHI	9 PHI	10 PHI	11 MON	12 MON	13 MON
14 MON	15 PHI	16 PHI	17 ATL	18 ATL	19 FLA	20 FLA
21 FLA	22 PIT	23 PIT	24	25 ATL	26 ATL	27 D ATL
28 ATL						

1997 SEASON

CLUB DIRECTORY

Chairman of the board
Nelson Doubleday
President and chief executive officer
Fred Wilpon
Directors
Nelson Doubleday
Fred Wilpon
Saul B. Katz
Joe McIlvaine
Marvin B. Tepper
Special advisor to the board of directors
Richard Cummins
Executive v.p., baseball operations
Joe McIlvaine
Assistant general manager
Steve Phillips
Director of scouting
John Barr
Director of minor league operations
Jack Zduriencik
Baseball administrator
Maureen Cooke
Admin. asst., minor leagues
Thomas Hutchison
Senior v.p. and treasurer
Harold W. O'Shaughnessy
V.p. bus. aff., gen. counsel & secretary
David Howard
Vice president, marketing
Mark Bingham
Vice president, stadium operations
Bob Mandt
Vice president, ticket sales and services
Bill Ianniciello
Senior v.p. and consultant
J. Frank Cashen
Vice president, broadcasting
Mark Bingham
Dir., admin. and data processing
Russ Richardson
Director, community outreach
Jill Knee
Director of promotions
James Plummer
Director of media relations
Jay Horwitz
Director, ticket operations
Dan DeMato

Manager, customer relations
Joann Galardy
Club physicians
Dr. David Altchek
Club psychologist/E.A.P.
Dr. Allan Lans
Team trainers
Fred Hina
Scott Lawrenson
Special assistants to the g.m.
Carmen Fusco
Harry Minor
Special assignment scouts
Buddy Kerr
Darrell Johnson
Major league scouts
Dick Gernert
Roland Johnson
Bill Latham
National cross-checkers
Paul Fryer
Paul Ricciarini
Regional scouting supervisors
Joe Mason
Bob Minor
Scouting supervisors
Tom Allison, Paul Baretta, Kevin Blankenship, Larry Chase, Clark Crist, Joe DelliCarri, Chuck Hensley Jr., Dave Lottsfeldt, Lee May Jr., Marlin McPhail, Randy Milligan, Joe Nigro, Carlos Pascual, Jim Reeves, Junior Roman, Bob Rossi, Eddy Toledo, Terry Tripp, Greg Tubbs
Part-time scouts
Chet Atkins, Wilfredo Blanco, Joe Bogar, Marcos Briceno, Bill Buck, Carl Cassell, David De La Cruz, James Ford, Steve Free, Ollie Goulston, Michael Herbert, Rich Hinell, Joe Hodges, Andy Lawrence, Gregorio Machado, Cookie Mitchell, Charlie Ready, Tim Rock, Felix Rodriguez, Doug Sisk, James Waddell, George Walden, Joe Willingham
Associate scouts
Vincent Bochicchio, Warren Garrett, Mark Harris, Bruce Homis, Jack Johnston, Red Kephardt, Ron Malcom, Tom McKenna, Bob Nichols, Joe Salermo, Walter Sharp, Vernon Thomas, Duke Ziegler

MINOR LEAGUE AFFILIATES

Class	Team	League	Manager
AAA	Norfolk	International	Rick Dempsey
AA	Binghamton	Eastern	Rick Sweet
A	St. Lucie	Florida State	John Gibbons
A	Capital City	South Atlantic	Doug Mansolino
A	Pittsfield	New York-Pennsylvania	Doug Davis
Rookie	Kingsport	Appalachian	Ken Berry
Rookie	Gulf Coast Mets	Gulf Coast	John Stephenson

BROADCAST INFORMATION
Radio: WFAN-AM (660).
TV: WWOR-TV (Channel 9).
Cable TV: SportsChannel.

SPRING TRAINING
Ballpark (city): St. Lucie County Stadium (Port St. Lucie, Fla.).
Ticket information: 561-871-2115.

SPRING TRAINING ROSTER

Manager—Bobby Valentine (2).
Coaches—Bob Apodaca (34), Bruce Benedict (20), Randy Niemann (52), Tom Robson (53), Cookie Rojas (4), Mookie Wilson (51).

No.	PITCHERS	B/T	Ht./Wt.	Born	1996 clubs
39	Acevedo, Juan	R/R	6-2/218	5-5-70	Norfolk
45	Baron, Jim	L/L	6-3/230	2-22-74	Rancho Cucamonga
43	Borland, Toby	R/R	6-6/193	5-29-69	Philadelphia
54	Clark, Mark	R/R	6-5/225	5-12-68	New York N.L.
49	Crawford, Joe	L/L	6-3/225	5-2-70	Norfolk, Binghamton
52	Dotel, Octavio	R/R	6-5/160	11-25-75	Columbia
31	Franco, John	L/L	5-10/185	9-17-60	New York N.L.
27	Harnisch, Pete	R/R	6-0/207	9-23-66	St. Lucie, New York N.L.
44	Isringhausen, Jason	R/R	6-3/196	9-7-72	New York N.L.
28	Jones, Bobby	R/R	6-4/225	2-10-70	New York N.L.
48	Jordan, Ricardo	L/L	6-0/180	6-27-70	Scranton//Wilkes-Barre-Richmond, Philadelphia
56	Lidle, Cory	R/R	5-11/175	3-22-72	Binghamton
36	McMichael, Greg	R/R	6-3/215	12-1-66	Atlanta
38	Mlicki, Dave	R/R	6-4/205	6-8-68	New York N.L.
21	Pulsipher, Bill	L/L	6-3/200	10-9-73	New York N.L.
55	Ramirez, Hector	R/R	6-3/218	12-15-71	Binghamton, Norfolk
40	Reynoso, Armando	R/R	6-0/204	5-1-66	Colorado
53	Sanchez, Jesus	L/L	5-10/155	10-11-74	St. Lucie
47	Wallace, Derek	R/R	6-3/185	9-1-71	Norfolk, New York N.L.
54	Welch, Mike	L/R	6-2/205	8-25-72	Binghamton, Norfolk
32	Wilson, Paul	R/R	6-5/235	3-28-73	New York N.L., St. Lucie, Binghamton

No.	CATCHERS	B/T	Ht./Wt.	Born	1996 clubs
30	Castillo, Alberto	R/R	6-0/184	2-10-70	New York N.L., Norfolk
7	Greene, Charlie	R/R	6-1/177	1-23-71	Binghamton, New York N.L.
9	Hundley, Todd	B/R	5-11/185	5-27-69	New York N.L.
	Pratt, Todd	R/R	6-3/224	2-9-67	DID NOT PLAY

No.	INFIELDERS	B/T	Ht./Wt.	Born	1996 clubs
13	Alfonzo, Ed	R/R	5-11/187	8-11-73	New York N.L.
6	Baerga, Carlos	B/R	5-11/200	11-4-68	Cleveland, New York N.L.
11	Bogar, Tim	R/R	6-2/198	10-28-66	New York N.L.
12	Espinoza, Alvaro	R/R	6-0/190	2-19-62	Cleveland, New York N.L.
42	Huskey, Butch	R/R	6-3/244	11-10-71	New York N.L.
5	Olerud, John	L/L	6-5/220	8-5-68	Toronto
0	Ordonez, Rey	R/R	5-9/159	1-11-72	New York N.L.
10	Petagine, Roberto	L/L	6-1/170	6-7-71	Norfolk, New York N.L.

No.	OUTFIELDERS	B/T	Ht./Wt.	Born	1996 clubs
3	Everett, Carl	B/R	6-0/190	6-3-71	New York N.L.
23	Gilkey, Bernard	R/R	6-0/200	9-24-66	New York N.L.
1	Johnson, Lance	L/L	5-11/160	7-6-63	New York N.L.
51	Mendoza, Carlos	L/L	5-11/160	11-4-74	Columbia
22	Ochoa, Alex	R/R	6-0/185	3-29-72	Norfolk, New York N.L.
25	Payton, Jay	R/R	5-10/185	11-22-72	Norfolk, Binghamton, Gulf Coast Mets
18	Wilson, Preston	R/R	6-2/195	7-19-74	Kingsport, St. Lucie

1997 SEASON New York Mets

BALLPARK INFORMATION

Ballpark (capacity, surface)
Shea Stadium (55,777, grass)

Address
123-10 Roosevelt Ave.
Flushing, NY 11368

Business phone
718-507-6387

Ticket information
718-507-8499

Ticket prices
$25 (Metropolitan Club seating)
$19 (inner field box, inner loge box)
$18 (outer field box, outer loge box,
    mezzanine box)
$14 (loge reserved)
$13 (mezzanine box, upper box)
$7 (upper reserved, back rows loge and mezzanine)

Field dimensions (from home plate)
To left field at foul line, 338 feet
To center field, 410 feet
To right field at foul line, 338 feet

First game played
April 17, 1964 (Pirates 4, Mets 3)

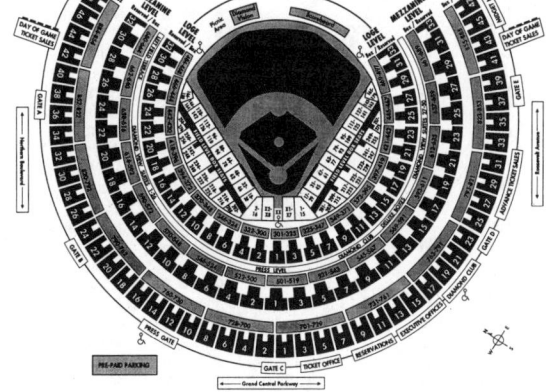

DAY BY DAY

Date	Opp.	Res.	Score	(inn.*)	Hits	Opp. hits	Winning pitcher	Losing pitcher	Save	Record	Pos.	GB
4-1	St.L.	W	7-6		10	13	DiPoto	Fossas	J. Franco	1-0	T1st	...
4-3	St.L.	L	3-5		7	11	Stottlemyre	Person	Eckersley	1-1	T2nd	1
4-4	St.L.	W	10-9		11	12	J. Franco	Eckersley		2-1	T1st	...
4-5	Pit.	L	5-7		11	10	Smith	Mlicki		2-2	T2nd	1
4-6	Pit.	L	0-5		6	11	Darwin	Clark		2-3	T2nd	1
4-8	At Cin.	L	6-7		12	8	Schourek	B. Jones	Brantley	2-4	4th	2½
4-9	At Cin.	W	12-5		12	9	Isringhausen	Smiley	J. Franco	3-4	4th	2
4-10	At Cin.	L	7-9		11	12	Pugh	MacDonald	Brantley	3-5	4th	2
4-11	At Col.	L	3-7		7	13	Reynoso	Mlicki		3-6	4th	3
4-12	At Col.	L	5-6		9	11	Freeman	Clark	Leskanic	3-7	5th	4
4-14	At Col.	W	10-4		16	12	Harnisch	Ritz	Henry	4-7	4th	2½
4-16	Hou.	L	6-9		9	12	Reynolds	Isringhausen	Jones	4-8	5th	3½
4-17	Hou.	L	5-7		12	11	Kile	Wilson	Jones	4-9	5th	3½
4-19	Col.	L	3-5		9	9	Ritz	Harnisch	Leskanic	4-10	5th	4
4-20	Col.	W	4-3	(10)	9	10	J. Franco	Habyan		5-10	5th	4
4-21	Col.	L	4-6		7	6	Leskanic	J. Franco		5-11	5th	5
4-22	Cin.	W	5-1		11	5	Wilson	Portugal		6-11	5th	5
4-23	Cin.	W	8-6	(10)	13	9	Henry	Shaw		7-11	4th	5
4-24	At St.L.	L	4-9		11	12	Petkovsek	Harnisch		7-12	4th	6
4-25	At St.L.	W	9-3		12	7	Clark	Al. Benes		8-12	4th	6
4-26	At Pit.	L	6-10		9	11	Christiansen	Isringhausen		8-13	5th	7
4-27	At Pit.	W	7-4		13	8	Mlicki	Miceli	J. Franco	9-13	4th	6
4-28	At Pit.	W	7-5		12	8	B. Jones	Wagner	J. Franco	10-13	4th	6
4-29	Mon.	W	3-2		7	7	Harnisch	Fassero	J. Franco	11-13	4th	5
5-1†	Mon.	L	0-4		2	8	Martinez	Clark		11-14		
5-1‡	Mon.	W	6-0		10	4	Isringhausen	Alvarez		12-14	4th	5
5-3	At Chi.	L	2-4		7	4	Navarro	Wilson		12-15	5th	5
5-4	At Chi.	W	7-3		11	6	B. Jones	Castillo	Henry	13-15	5th	5
5-5	At Chi.	L	4-5		10	8	Wendell	DiPoto		13-16	5th	6
5-6	At Fla.	L	1-4		9	10	Leiter	Clark	Nen	13-17	4th	7
5-7	At Fla.	L	2-3		9	13	Hammond	Isringhausen	Nen	13-18	4th	8
5-8	At Fla.	L	3-6		5	9	Perez	Henry	Nen	13-19	4th	9
5-10	Chi.	W	2-0		5	4	B. Jones	Castillo	J. Franco	14-19	T4th	8½
5-11	Chi.	W	7-6		10	11	Henry	Jones		15-19	T4th	8½
5-12	Chi.	L	0-3		2	7	Bullinger	Clark		15-20	5th	9½
5-13	At S.D.	L	2-5		7	10	Valenzuela	Isringhausen		15-21	5th	10½
5-14	At S.D.	L	4-9		10	10	Ashby	Wilson		15-22	5th	10½
5-15	At S.D.	L	3-4	(10)	5	9	Worrell	J. Franco		15-23	5th	10½
5-16	At S.D.	W	6-3		12	5	Harnisch	Hamilton	J. Franco	16-23	5th	10
5-18	At S.F.	W	14-5		15	8	Clark	VanLandingham		17-23	5th	9½
5-19†	At S.F.	L	0-1		4	5	Watson	Isringhausen	Beck	17-24		
5-19‡	At S.F.	L	2-6		6	9	Gardner	Wilson		17-25	5th	10½
5-20	At L.A.	W	7-1		16	9	B. Jones	Candiotti		18-25	5th	10½
5-21	At L.A.	L	4-6		7	12	Valdes	Harnisch	Worrell	18-26	5th	10½
5-22	At L.A.	W	3-2		7	5	Clark	Nomo	J. Franco	19-26	5th	10½
5-24	S.D.	L	1-13		6	16	Valenzuela	Isringhausen		19-27	5th	11½
5-25	S.D.	L	2-7		10	10	Ashby	Wilson		19-28	5th	11½
5-26	S.D.	W	1-0		6	6	B. Jones	Bergman	J. Franco	20-28	5th	11½
5-28	S.F.	W	4-0		8	5	Clark	Leiter	Henry	21-28	5th	11½
5-29	S.F.	L	2-4		6	6	VanLandingham	Isringhausen	Beck	21-29	5th	12½
5-30	S.F.	W	1-0		6	4	Wilson	Watson	J. Franco	22-29	5th	12
5-31	L.A.	L	3-10		7	16	Martinez	B. Jones		22-30	5th	13
6-1	L.A.	W	4-3		7	5	Harnisch	Candiotti	J. Franco	23-30	5th	12
6-2	L.A.	L	0-1		6	3	Valdes	Clark	Worrell	23-31	5th	13
6-3	At Atl.	L	4-5		9	6	Clontz	MacDonald	Wohlers	23-32	5th	14
6-4	At Atl.	W	12-6		16	11	Wilson	Schmidt		24-32	5th	13
6-5	At Atl.	L	6-8		10	9	McMichael	Mlicki	Wohlers	24-33	5th	14
6-7	Fla.	L	2-12		10	19	Leiter	Harnisch		24-34	5th	14
6-8	Fla.	W	7-6		12	13	Clark	Weathers	J. Franco	25-34	5th	13
6-9	Fla.	W	3-0		6	6	Isringhausen	Burkett		26-34	5th	13
6-10	Atl.	W	8-3		14	16	B. Jones	Avery		27-34	5th	13
6-11	Atl.	L	3-4	(13)	14	9	Borbon	Byrd	Wade	27-35	5th	13
6-12	Atl.	W	3-2		9	8	Clark	Maddux	J. Franco	28-35	5th	12
6-13	At St.L.	W	2-1		8	6	Person	An. Benes	Henry	29-35	T4th	11
6-14	At St.L.	L	4-13		6	16	Stottlemyre	Isringhausen		29-36	T4th	12
6-15	At St.L.	L	2-4		6	9	Al. Benes	B. Jones	Eckersley	29-37	T4th	12
6-16	At St.L.	L	4-5		7	10	Petkovsek	Henry	Eckersley	29-38	T4th	12
6-17	At Pit.	W	7-6	(10)	14	12	Mlicki	Cordova	J. Franco	30-38	4th	12
6-19†	At Pit.	L	5-6		6	10	Plesac	Isringhausen		30-39		
6-19‡	At Pit.	W	5-3		12	8	Mlicki	Cordova	J. Franco	31-39	4th	13
6-20	Cin.	L	3-5		6	9	Burba	B. Jones	Shaw	31-40	4th	13½
6-21	Cin.	W	9-4		14	10	DiPoto	Salkeld	Mlicki	32-40	4th	13½

te	Opp.	Res.	Score	(inn.*)	Hits	Opp. hits	Winning pitcher	Losing pitcher	Save	Record	Pos.	GB
22	Cin.	W	5-2		11	4	Clark	Schourek	J. Franco	33-40	4th	13½
23	Cin.	L	1-2		6	9	Smiley	Person	Brantley	33-41	4th	14½
24	Col.	W	2-1		8	9	Isringhausen	Holmes	J. Franco	34-41	4th	13½
25	Col.	W	3-2		7	7	B. Jones	M. Thompson	J. Franco	35-41	4th	13½
26	Col.	W	9-5		9	10	Mlicki	S. Reed		36-41	4th	12½
28	At Hou.	W	7-2		12	7	Clark	Drabek	Henry	37-41	4th	12
29	At Hou.	L	1-9		8	14	Reynolds	Person		37-42	4th	12
30	At Hou.	L	3-9		6	14	Kile	Isringhausen		37-43	4th	13
1	At Phi.	L	4-6		10	12	Williams	B. Jones	Ryan	37-44	4th	14
2	At Phi.	L	2-3		7	8	Springer	Harnisch	Bottalico	37-45	4th	14
3	At Phi.	W	10-6		16	13	Byrd	Ryan	Henry	38-45	4th	14
4	At Mon.	W	4-0		6	6	Person	Fassero		39-45	T3rd	13
5	At Mon.	W	9-6		14	12	DiPoto	Scott	J. Franco	40-45	3rd	12
6	At Mon.	W	11-3		19	10	B. Jones	Rueter		41-45	3rd	12
7	At Mon.	L	3-4		8	8	Cormier	Harnisch	Rojas	41-46	3rd	13
11	Hou.	W	8-2		14	7	Clark	Drabek		42-46	3rd	12
12	Hou.	L	1-3		7	6	Reynolds	B. Jones	Wagner	42-47	3rd	13
14†	Hou.	L	5-7	(11)	12	15	Hernandez	Mlicki	Jones	42-48		
14‡	Hou.	W	10-3		13	8	Harnisch	Hampton		43-48	3rd	14
15	Phi.	W	7-5		16	11	DiPoto	Springer	Henry	44-48	3rd	14
16	Phi.	W	6-3		5	11	Clark	Schilling	J. Franco	45-48	3rd	14
17	Phi.	W	3-2		9	10	Mlicki	Frey		46-48	3rd	13½
18	Mon.	L	3-7		8	13	Martinez	Harnisch		46-49	3rd	14½
19	Mon.	L	4-5		9	9	Dyer	Isringhausen	Rojas	46-50	T3rd	14½
20	Mon.	W	4-1		9	3	Wilson	Urbina	J. Franco	47-50	T3rd	13½
21	Mon.	L	3-4		9	10	Fassero	Clark	Rojas	47-51	T3rd	13½
23†	At Col.	L	7-10		9	19	Ruffin	Henry		47-52	3rd	15
23‡	At Col.	L	10-11		15	16	S. Reed	Henry		47-53	4th	15½
24	At Col.	L	6-7	(10)	11	17	Leskanic	Byrd		47-54	4th	16½
26	At Cin.	L	4-7		9	11	Smiley	Wilson		47-55	4th	17
27	At Cin.	L	5-7		8	13	Service	Clark	Brantley	47-56	4th	17
28	At Cin.	W	7-1		11	3	B. Jones	Jarvis		48-56	4th	16
29	Pit.	W	5-0		7	4	Harnisch	Peters		49-56	T3rd	15½
30†	Pit.	W	5-4		12	10	Isringhausen	Cordova	J. Franco	50-56		
30‡	Pit.	W	4-3	(12)	12	11	J. Franco	Lieber		51-56	3rd	14
31	Pit.	W	3-2	(10)	7	5	DiPoto	Plesac		52-56	3rd	14
	Pit.	L	9-13		16	16	Morel	Mlicki	Ericks	52-57	3rd	15
	St.L.	L	3-4		9	7	Stottlemyre	B. Jones	Honeycutt	52-58	3rd	15
	St.L.	W	5-4		6	6	Harnisch	Al. Benes	J. Franco	53-58	3rd	15
	St.L.	L	2-4		5	6	Morgan	Isringhausen	Eckersley	53-59	3rd	16
	At Chi.	L	3-7		5	11	Trachsel	Wilson		53-60	3rd	16½
	At Chi.	L	0-3		7	7	Navarro	Clark	Patterson	53-61	3rd	17½
	At Chi.	W	11-7		17	10	DiPoto	Adams		54-61	3rd	16½
	At Fla.	W	3-0		7	4	Harnisch	Brown	J. Franco	55-61	3rd	16½
	At Fla.	L	1-2	(10)	8	5	Nen	Henry		55-62	3rd	16½
0	At Fla.	L	6-9		16	15	Rapp	Wilson	Nen	55-63	3rd	16½
1	At Fla.	W	5-3		10	6	Clark	Valdes	J. Franco	56-63	3rd	16½
2	Chi.	L	1-11		5	12	Navarro	Isringhausen		56-64	3rd	17
3	Chi.	L	2-3		6	8	Telemaco	Harnisch	Wendell	56-65	T3rd	18½
4	Chi.	W	8-5		9	11	B. Jones	Bullinger	J. Franco	57-65	T3rd	17½
6	At S.D.§	L	10-15		13	14	Valenzuela	Person		57-66	4th	19
7	At S.D.§	W	7-3		12	12	Clark	Worrell	Henry	58-66	3rd	19
8	At S.D.§	L	0-8		7	12	Hamilton	Wilson		58-67	3rd	20
9	At S.F.	L	4-5		12	8	Scott	Harnisch	Beck	58-68	4th	20½
0	At S.F.	W	7-3		12	4	B. Jones	Fernandez	J. Franco	59-68	3rd	20½
1	At S.F.	L	11-12		17	10	Dewey	Person	Beck	59-69	3rd	21½
3	At L.A.	L	5-7		8	12	Martinez	Clark	Worrell	59-70	T3rd	22
4	At L.A.	L	5-7		8	8	Candiotti	Wilson	Worrell	59-71	4th	23
5	At L.A.	L	5-6		6	8	Radinsky	J. Franco	Worrell	59-72	4th	23
7	S.D.	L	3-4		7	8	Blair	Mlicki	Hoffman	59-73	4th	23
8	S.D.	L	2-3	(12)	8	13	Bergman	Wallace	Hoffman	59-74	4th	24
9	S.D.	L	2-3		6	11	Hamilton	Wilson	Hoffman	59-75	4th	23
0	S.F.	L	4-6		5	10	Estes	Harnisch	Beck	59-76	4th	25½
1	S.F.	W	7-2		13	6	Person	Scott	Henry	60-76	4th	24½
	S.F.	W	6-5	(10)	11	12	J. Franco	Beck		61-76	4th	23½
	L.A.	L	5-8		9	12	Astacio	Clark	Worrell	61-77	4th	23½
	L.A.	L	6-7		11	12	Radinsky	Henry		61-78	4th	23½
	L.A.	W	3-2	(12)	11	10	Wallace	Dreifort		62-78	4th	22½
	At Atl.	L	7-8		12	14	Wohlers	Henry		62-79	4th	23½
	At Atl.	L	1-6		7	9	Smoltz	B. Jones		62-80	4th	24½
	At Atl.	W	6-2		10	5	Clark	Maddux		63-80	4th	23½
	Fla.	W	6-1		12	7	Mlicki	Brown		64-80	4th	23
0	Fla.	L	3-9	(12)	12	14	Powell	Henry		64-81	4th	23
1	Fla.	W	3-1		10	6	Isringhausen	Rapp	Wallace	65-81	4th	22
3	Atl.	W	6-4		12	11	DiPoto	Borowski	Wallace	66-81	4th	20½

Date	Opp.	Res.	Score	(inn.*)	Hits	Opp. hits	Winning pitcher	Losing pitcher	Save	Record	Pos.	GB
9-14	Atl.	W	6-5	(12)	11	13	Wallace	Borowski		67-81	4th	19 1/2
9-15	Atl.	L	2-3		10	8	Glavine	Wilson	Wohlers	67-82	4th	20 1/2
9-16	Atl.	L	2-5		7	8	Neagle	Harnisch		67-83	4th	21 1/2
9-17	At Mon.	L	1-7		6	10	Fassero	Isringhausen		67-84	4th	22 1/2
9-18	At Mon.	L	3-4		8	8	Urbina	Mlicki	Rojas	67-85	4th	23 1/2
9-19	At Phi.	W	7-2		10	9	Clark	Hunter		68-85	4th	22 1/2
9-20	At Phi.	W	5-2		7	6	Wilson	Mimbs	J. Franco	69-85	4th	22 1/2
9-21	At Phi.	L	1-2		5	6	Schilling	Harnisch		69-86	4th	23 1/2
9-22	At Phi.	L	3-4		8	7	Bottalico	Wallace		69-87	4th	24 1/2
9-24	At Hou.	W	4-0		9	4	B. Jones	Wall		70-87	4th	24
9-25	At Hou.	L	4-5	(10)	10	10	Hudek	Wallace		70-88	4th	24
9-26	At Hou.	L	2-6		9	9	Drabek	Trlicek		70-89	4th	24
9-27	Phi.	L	5-6		8	13	R. Jordan	DiPoto	Bottalico	70-90	4th	25
9-28	Phi.	W	4-2		5	5	Person	Maduro	Wallace	71-90	4th	25
9-29	Phi.	L	5-9		10	13	Blazier	Fyhrie		71-91	4th	25

Monthly records: April (11-13), May (11-17), June (15-13), July (15-13), August (8-20), September (11-15).
*Innings, if other than nine. †First game of doubleheader. ‡Second game of doubleheader. §At Monterrey, Mexico.

HIGHLIGHTS

High point: The Mets thought they were ready to assert themselves after sweeping the Phillies July 15-17. They had won four in a row and nine of 12, were two games short of .500 (46-48) and were 4 1/2 games behind the second-place Expos. The team was hoping for a second-half surge similar to what it produced in 1995.

Low point: By August 26, the Mets were out of contention, losers of 24 of 37 games subsequent to the sweep of the Phillies, and Dallas Green was out of a job. It didn't get much better thereafter, either: The Mets' record under Bobby Valentine was 12-19.

Turning point: "They don't belong in the big leagues. That may sound harsh and negative. But what have they done to get here?" Green spoke those words about pitchers Paul Wilson and Jason Isringhausen in San Francisco on August 20, 5 1/2 months after he had predicted success for the two as well as for lefthander Bill Pulsipher. General manager Joe McIlvaine later acknowledged Green's August remark forced him to make a move he hadn't planned to make. Green's dismissal marked a new start for a franchise that currently has gone longer than any other without a winning record—six seasons.

Most valuable player: Outfielder Bernard Gilkey. In his first year with the Mets, Gilkey batted .317, with 108 runs, 30 homers and a .406 average with runners in scoring position. He led the team with 117 RBIs, tying a club record, and hit 44 doubles. He also ranked second in the league in go-ahead RBIs (34) and first in outfield assists (18).

Most valuable pitcher: Starter Mark Clark. On a team that finished 20 games below .500, any pitcher with a winning record might qualify. With the Mets, Clark qualified by default and merit. He led the team in victories (14) and innings (212 1/3) and led Mets in ERA (3.43).

Most improved player: Catcher Todd Hundley. He hit 41 home runs, as many as any New York player since Roger Maris hit 61 for the Yankees in 1961, and broke the major league record for most homers by a catcher. He also drove in a career-high 112 runs.

Most pleasant surprise: The July 29 trade that brought Carlos Baerga to the team was an unexpected positive, but it was followed by a negative—a abdominal muscle pull that kept him in the dugout through most of the final two months.

Biggest disappointment: Take your pick—outfielder Carl Everett (16 RBIs), righthander Paul Byrd (48 hits allowed and 21 walks in 46 2/3 innings), righthander Paul Wilson (5-12 record, 5.38 ERA), righthander Jason Isringhausen (6-14, 4.77), or shortstop Rey Ordonez (27 errors). One last thing: a fourth-place finish, nine games out of third.

Key injuries: When the medial collateral ligament in Bill Pulsipher's left elbow blew out in spring training, it denied the Mets their only lefthanded starter and a clubhouse presence some believed had been critical to the team's 1995 second-half surge. Losing Rico Brogna (right shoulder injury) damaged the offense and the infield defense. Injuries to Jason Isringhausen (elbow and shoulder), Paul Wilson (right shoulder) and Butch Huskey (left knee) undermined seasons of learning.

Notable: John Franco earned his 300th save and finished the season with 323 career saves. . . . Alex Ochoa became the sixth Met to hit for the cycle (July 3). . . . Lance Johnson had 21 triples and 227 hits to lead the league, and also finished with 31 doubles, nine home runs, 117 runs, 50 steals and 69 RBIs.

—MARTY NOBLE

RECORDS

1996 regular-season record: 71-91 (4th in N.L. East); 42-39 at home; 29-52 on road; 25-27 vs. East; 28-33 vs. Central; 18-31 vs. West; 17-26 vs. lefthanded starters; 54-65 vs. righthanded starters; 57-74 on grass; 14-17 on turf; 27-31 in daytime; 44-60 at night; 23-35 in one-run games; 8-8 in extra-inning games; 1-2 in doubleheaders.

Team record past five years: 326-417 (.439, ranks 14th in league in that span).

TEAM LEADERS

Batting average: Lance Johnson (.333).
At-bats: Lance Johnson (682).
Runs: Lance Johnson (117).
Hits: Lance Johnson (227).
Total bases: Lance Johnson (327).
Doubles: Bernard Gilkey (44).
Triples: Lance Johnson (21).
Home runs: Todd Hundley (41).
Runs batted in: Bernard Gilkey (117).
Stolen bases: Lance Johnson (50).
Slugging percentage: Bernard Gilkey (.562).
On-base percentage: Bernard Gilkey (.39?
Wins: Mark Clark (14).
Earned-run average: Mark Clark (3.43).
Complete games: Bobby Jones (3).
Shutouts: Pete Harnisch, Jason Isringhausen, Bobby Jones (1).
Saves: John Franco (28).
Innings pitched: Mark Clark (212.1).
Strikeouts: Mark Clark (142).

GAMES BY POSITION

Catcher: Todd Hundley 150, Brent May 21, Alberto Castillo 6, Charlie Greene 1.
First base: Butch Huskey 75, Rico Brogna 52, Roberto Petagine 40, Tim Bogar 32, Carlos Baerga 16, Chris Jone 5, Matt Franco 2, Alvaro Espinoza 1, Andy Tomberlin 1.
Second base: Jose Vizcaino 93, Edgard Alfonzo 66, Jason Hardtke 18, Tim Bog 8, Alvaro Espinoza 2, Carlos Baerga 1.
Third base: Jeff Kent 89, Alvaro Espino 38, Edgardo Alfonzo 36, Tim Bogar 25, Matt Franco 8, Carlos Baerga 6, Butch Huskey 6.
Shortstop: Rey Ordonez 150, Tim Bogar 19, Edgardo Alfonzo 15, Alvaro Espinoza
Outfield: Lance Johnson 157, Bernard Gilkey 151, Alex Ochoa 76, Chris Jones 66, Carl Everett 55, Butch Huskey 40, Andy Tomberlin 17, Kevin Roberson 10

TOP DRAFT CHOICES

1. **Robert Stratton**, OF, San Marcos H.S., Santa Barbara, Calif.
2. **Brendan Behn**, LHP, Merced (Calif.) J.C
3. **Eddie Yarnall**, LHP, Louisiana State U.
4. **Jeromie Lovingood**, LHP, McMinn County H.S., Riceville, Tenn.
5. **Patrick Burns**, OF, Ryan H.S., Denton, Te
6. **Tom Johnson**, OF, Brookdale (N.J.) H.S.
7. **Tony Milo**, LHP, Laguna Hills (Calif.) H.S.
8. **Pee Wee Lopez**, C, Miami-Dade C.C. Sout
9. **Willie Suggs**, RHP, Mount Vernon (Ill.) H.S
10. **Scott Comer**, LHP, Mazama H.S., Klamath Falls, Ore.

PHILADELPHIA PHILLIES
NATIONAL LEAGUE EAST DIVISION

1997 PHILLIES SCHEDULE

▨ Home games shaded.
* — All-Star Game at Jacobs Field (Cleveland)
D — Day game (any game starting before 5 p.m.)

APRIL

SUN	MON	TUE	WED	THU	FRI	SAT
		1 D LA	2 LA	3 LA	4 D SD	5 SD
6 D SD	7 SF	8 D SF	9 SF	10 D	11 D SD	12 SD
13 D SD	14	15 SF	16 SF	17 MON	18 MON	19 MON
20 D MON	21 PIT	22	23 PIT	24	25 CIN	26 D CIN
27 CIN	28 PIT	29 PIT	30 LA			

MAY

SUN	MON	TUE	WED	THU	FRI	SAT
				1 D COL	2 COL	3 D COL
4 D COL	5 HOU	6 HOU	7 STL	8 D CBL	9 COL	10 COL
11 D COL	12 STL	13 STL	14 STL	15	16 D HOU	17 HOU
18 D HOU	19 CUB	20 CUB	21 D CUB	22 NYM	23 NYM	24 NYM
25 D NYM	26 CIN	27 CIN	28 CIN	29	30 NYM	31 NYM

JUNE

SUN	MON	TUE	WED	THU	FRI	SAT
1 D NYM	2 CIN	3 CUB	4 CUB	5 D CUB	6 PIT	7 PIT
8 D PIT	9	10 MON	11 MON	12	13 TOR	14 TOR
15 TOR	16 BOS	17 BOS	18 BOS	19	20 ATL	21 ATL
22 ATL	23 FLA	24 FLA	25 D FLA	26 ATL	27 ATL	28 ATL
29 ATL	30 BAL					

JULY

SUN	MON	TUE	WED	THU	FRI	SAT
		1 BAL	2 D BAL	3 D CUB	4 CUB	5 D CUB
6 D CUB	7	8 ° 9		10 FLA	11 FLA	12 FLA
13 D FLA	14 ATL	15 ATL	16 MON	17 MON	18 PIT	19 D PIT
20 D PIT	21 D PIT	22 SF	23 D SF	24 D SF	25 LA	26 LA
27 D LA	28 SD	29 SD	30	31 STL		

AUGUST

SUN	MON	TUE	WED	THU	FRI	SAT
					1 STL	2 D STL
3 D STL	4 COL	5 COL	6 HOU	7 D HOU	8 STL	9 STL
10 D STL	11 COL	12 COL	13 D COL	14	15 HOU	16 D HOU
17 D HOU	18	19 SF	20 D SF	21 SF	22 LA	23 LA
24 D LA	25 SD	26 SD	27 D SD	28	29 DET	30 DET
31 D DET						

SEPTEMBER

SUN	MON	TUE	WED	THU	FRI	SAT
	1 D NYY	2 NYY	3 NYY	4 MON	5 MON	6 MON
7 D MON	8 NYM	9 NYM	10 NYM	11	12 CIN	13 D CIN
14 D CIN	15 NYM	16 NYM	17 FLA	18 FLA	19 D CUB	20 D CUB
21 D CUB	22	23 ATL	24 ATL	25 FLA	26 FLA	27 FLA
28 D FLA						

1997 SEASON — Philadelphia Phillies

1997 SEASON

CLUB DIRECTORY

President/CEO/general partner
Bill Giles

Partners
Claire S. Betz
Tri-Play Associates (Alexander K. Buck, J. Mahlon Buck Jr., William C. Buck)
Double Play, Inc. (Herbert H. Middleton Jr.)
Fitz Eugene Dixon Jr.

Executive v.p., COO/co-general partner
David Montgomery

Senior vice president, finance and planning
Jerry Clothier

Executive secretary
Nancy Nolan

Secretary and general counsel
William Y. Webb

Director, business development
Joseph W. Giles

Sr. vice president, general manager
Lee Thomas

Assistant general manager
Ed Wade

Director, player development
Del Unser

Director, scouting
Mike Arbuckle

Assistant to the president
Paul Owens

Traveling secretary
Eddie Ferenz

Vice president, public relations
Larry Shenk

Broadcaster/director speakers' bureau
Chris Wheeler

Director, community relations
Regina Castellani

Administrator, public relations
Karen Nocella

Manager, media relations
Gene Dias

Manager, publicity
Leigh Tobin

Vice president, marketing
Dennis Mannion

Manager, advertising and broadcasting
Jo-Ann Levy-Lamoreaux

V.p., ticket sales and operations
Richard Deats

Director, ticket department
Dan Goroff

Director, group sales
Kathy Killian

Director, stadium operations
Mike DiMuzio

Club physician
Dr. Phillip Marone

Club trainers
Jeff Cooper
Mark Anderson

National supervisor
Mark Wolever

Regional supervisor, scouts
Dick Lawlor

Spec. assignment, major league scout
Jimmy Stewart

Advance scout, major leagues
Hank King

Special assignment scouts
Bing Devine
Larry Rojas

Regular supervisor, scouts
Sonny Bowers
Dean Jongewood

Minor league and scouting
Maryann Skedzielewski

Regular scouts
Sal Agostinelli, Emil Belich, Tom Ferguson, Jim Fregosi Jr., Jose Gomez, Eli Grba, Bill Harper, Ken Hultzapple, John Kennedy, Jerry Lafferty, George Lauzerique, Jose Leiva, Terry Logan, Fred Mazuca, Lloyd Merritt, Willie Montanez, Arthur Parrack, Bob Poole, David Sirak, Mitch Sokel, Roy Tanner, Scott Trcka

MINOR LEAGUE AFFILIATES

Class	Team	League	Manager
AAA	Scranton/Wilkes-Barre	International	Marc Bombard
AA	Reading	Eastern	Al LeBoeuf
A	Clearwater	Florida State	Roy Majtyka
A	Piedmont	South Atlantic	Ken Oberkfell
A	Batavia	New York-Pennsylvania	Greg Legg
Rookie	Martinsville	Appalachian	Kelly Heath

BROADCAST INFORMATION

Radio: Talk Radio 1210.
TV: WPHL-TV (Channel 17).
Cable TV: PRISM, SportsChannel.

SPRING TRAINING

Ballpark (city): Jack Russell Stadium (Clearwater, Fla.).
Ticket information: 215-463-1000, 813-442-8496.

SPRING TRAINING ROSTER

Manager—Terry Francona (7).
Coaches—Galen Cisco (42), Chuck Cottier (3), Hal McRae (56), Brad Mills (9), Joe Rigoli (59), John Vukovich (18).

No.	PITCHERS	B/T	Ht./Wt.	Born	1996 clubs
55	Beech, Matt	L/L	6-2/205	1-20-72	Reading, Scranton/Wilkes-Barre, Philadelphia
22	Blazier, Ron	R/R	6-5/205	7-30-71	Scranton/Wilkes-Barre, Philadelphia
52	Bottalico, Ricky	L/R	6-1/208	8-26-69	Philadelphia
62	Boyd, Jason	R/R	6-2/165	2-23-73	Clearwater
61	Gomes, Wayne	R/R	6-2/205	1-15-73	Reading
44	Grace, Mike	R/R	6-4/220	6-20-70	Philadelphia
28	Green, Tyler	R/R	6-5/211	2-18-70	Philadelphia
39	Hunter, Rich	R/R	6-1/185	9-25-74	Philadelphia, Scranton/Wilkes-Barre, Reading
31	Leiter, Mark	R/R	6-3/210	4-13-63	San Francisco, Montreal
50	Maduro, Calvin	R/R	6-0/175	9-5-74	Bowie, Rochester, Philadelphia
45	Mimbs, Michael	L/L	6-2/190	2-13-69	Philadelphia, Scranton/Wilkes-Barre
35	Munoz, Bobby	R/R	6-8/259	3-3-68	Clearwater, Scranton/Wilkes-Barre, Philadelphia, Reading
65	Nye, Ryan	R/R	6-2/195	6-24-73	Reading, Scranton/Wilkes-Barre
21	Portugal, Mark	R/R	6-0/190	10-30-62	Cincinnati
49	Ramos, Edgar	R/R	6-5/190	3-6-75	Kissimmee, Jackson
51	Ryan, Ken	R/R	6-3/230	10-24-68	Philadelphia
38	Schilling, Curt	R/R	6-4/226	11-14-66	Clearwater, Scranton/Wilkes-Barre, Philadelphia
48	Spradlin, Jerry	B/R	6-7/240	6-14-67	Indianapolis, Cincinnati

No.	CATCHERS	B/T	Ht./Wt.	Born	1996 clubs
27	Estalella, Robert	R/R	6-1/195	8-23-74	Reading, Scranton/Wilkes-Barre, Philadelphia
24	Lieberthal, Mike	R/R	6-0/178	1-18-72	Philadelphia
8	Parent, Mark	R/R	6-5/245	9-16-61	Detroit, Baltimore

No.	INFIELDERS	B/T	Ht./Wt.	Born	1996 clubs
2	Brogna, Rico	L/L	6-2/205	4-18-70	New York N.L.
26	Doster, Dave	R/R	5-10/185	10-8-70	Scranton/Wilkes-Barre, Philadelphia
	Hudler, Rex	R/R	6-0/195	9-2-60	California
23	Jordan, Kevin	R/R	6-1/193	10-9-69	Philadelphia
12	Morandini, Mickey	L/R	5-11/176	4-22-66	Philadelphia
30	Relaford, Desi	B/R	5-8/155	9-16-73	Tacoma, Scranton/Wilkes-Barre, Philadelphia
6	Rolen, Scott	R/R	6-4/195	4-4-75	Reading, Scranton/Wilkes-Barre, Philadelphia
6	Schall, Gene	R/R	6-3/206	6-5-70	Scranton/Wilkes-Barre, Philadelphia
31	Sefcik, Kevin	R/R	5-10/175	2-10-71	Philadelphia, Scranton/Wilkes-Barre
19	Stocker, Kevin	B/R	6-1/175	2-13-70	Philadelphia, Scranton/Wilkes-Barre, Philadelphia
	Zuber, Jon	L/L	6-0/190	12-10-69	Scranton/Wilkes-Barre, Philadelphia

No.	OUTFIELDERS	B/T	Ht./Wt.	Born	1996 clubs
37	Amaro, Ruben	B/R	5-10/175	2-12-65	Syracuse, Philadelphia, Scranton/Wilkes-Barre
	Bowers, Brent	L/R	6-3/190	5-2-71	Bowie, Rochester, Baltimore
4	Dykstra, Lenny	L/L	5-10/188	2-10-63	Philadelphia
25	Jefferies, Gregg	B/R	5-10/184	8-1-67	Philadelphia, Scranton/Wilkes-Barre
16	Longmire, Tony	L/R	6-1/218	8-12-68	Philadelphia
29	Magee, Wendell	R/R	6-0/220	8-3-72	Reading, Scranton/Wilkes-Barre, Philadelphia
15	Otero, Ricky	B/R	5-5/150	4-15-72	Scranton/Wilkes-Barre, Philadelphia

BALLPARK INFORMATION

Ballpark (capacity, surface)
Veterans Stadium (62,363, artificial)

Address
P.O. Box 7575
Philadelphia, PA 19101

Business phone
215-463-6000

Ticket information
215-463-1000

Ticket prices
$16 (field box)
$14 (sections 258-274)
$14 (terrace box)
$14 (loge box)
$10 (reserved, 600 level)
$5 (reserved, 700 level)

Field dimensions (from home plate)
To left field at foul line, 330 feet
To center field, 408 feet
To right field at foul line, 330 feet

First game played
April 10, 1971 (Phillies 4, Expos 1)

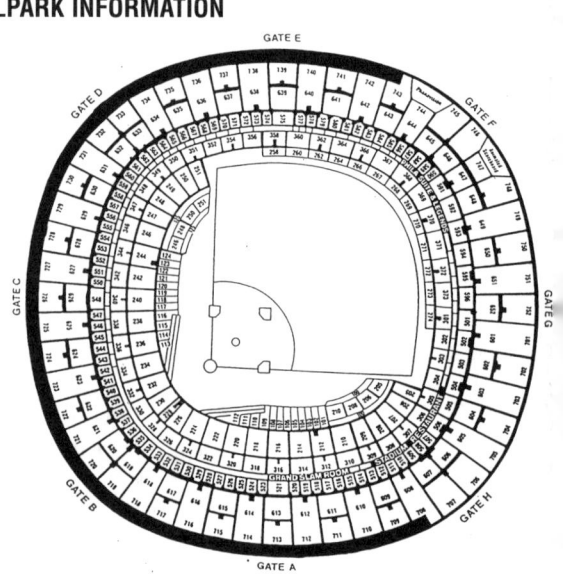

DAY BY DAY

te	Opp.	Res.	Score	(inn.*)	Hits	Opp. hits	Winning pitcher	Losing pitcher	Save	Record	Pos.	GB
2	Col.	L	3-5		4	5	Ritz	Fernandez		0-1	T3rd	1
3	Col.	L	3-1		4	6	Grace	Freeman	Bottalico	1-1	T2nd	1
4	Col.	W	7-4		10	8	Mulholland	Rekar	Bottalico	2-1	T1st	...
5	Cin.	L	5-6	(10)	10	9	Shaw	Borland	Moore	2-2	T2nd	1
6	Cin.	L	4-8		8	11	Salkeld	Hunter		2-3	T2nd	1
8	At Pit.	W	6-3		10	9	Fernandez	Neagle		3-3	2nd	1½
10	At Pit.	W	7-6		10	10	Grace	Christiansen	Bottalico	4-3	2nd	½
11	At St.L.	L	1-2		4	8	An. Benes	Mulholland	Mathews	4-4	2nd	1½
12	At St.L.	L	1-6		4	12	Urbani	Williams		4-5	T2nd	2½
13	At St.L.	W	4-2		8	11	Hunter	Fossas	Bottalico	5-5	2nd	1½
14	At St.L.	L	5-6		6	8	Mathews	Fernandez	Eckersley	5-6	T2nd	1½
16	At Mon.	L	6-7		11	10	Rojas	Springer		5-7	3rd	2½
17	At Mon.	W	9-3		13	10	Mulholland	Cormier		6-7	3rd	1½
18	At Mon.	W	9-8		11	12	Bottalico	Rojas		7-7	T2nd	½
19	St.L.	L	0-1		6	8	Bailey	Springer	Eckersley	7-8	3rd	1½
20	St.L.	L	0-1		2	4	Al. Benes	Bottalico	Eckersley	7-9	3rd	2½
21	St.L.	W	4-2		7	9	Grace	An. Benes	Bottalico	8-9	3rd	2½
22	Pit.	L	3-9		6	16	Darwin	Mulholland		8-10	3rd	3½
23	Pit.	W	6-2		10	9	Springer	Wagner	Ryan	9-10	3rd	3½
24	At Col.	W	10-8		8	13	Borland	S. Reed	Bottalico	10-10	3rd	3½
25	At Col.	W	7-1		11	6	Fernandez	M. Thompson	Ryan	11-10	T2nd	3½
26	At Cin.	W	2-0		5	3	Grace	Burba	Bottalico	12-10	T2nd	3½
27	At Cin.	W	3-2		5	6	Leiper	Portugal	Bottalico	13-10	T2nd	2½
30	At Fla.	L	2-7		8	7	Rapp	Williams	Nen	13-11	3rd	3
1	At Fla.	W	6-5		9	13	Ryan	Leiter	Bottalico	14-11	3rd	2½
2	At Fla.	W	2-0		5	5	Grace	Brown	Bottalico	15-11	T2nd	2
3	At Atl.	W	6-3		8	11	Mulholland	Maddux	Bottalico	16-11	2nd	1
4	At Atl.	L	3-6		8	12	McMichael	Ryan	Clontz	16-12	T2nd	2
5	At Atl.	L	8-11		8	18	Smoltz	Williams		16-13	3rd	3
6	Hou.	L	5-11		7	10	Drabek	Hunter		16-14	3rd	4
7	Hou.	L	5-7		9	13	Young	Springer	Jones	16-15	3rd	5
8	Hou.	W	2-1	(10)	6	3	Ryan	Tabaka		17-15	3rd	5
10	Atl.	L	0-11		4	18	Smoltz	Mulholland		17-16	3rd	5½
11	Atl.	L	3-11		10	19	Avery	Mimbs		17-17	3rd	6½
12	Atl.	W	6-0		6	4	Grace	Maddux		18-17	3rd	6½
13	S.F.	L	1-2		6	11	Gardner	Fernandez	Beck	18-18	3rd	7½
14	S.F.	W	7-0		11	6	Schilling	Fernandez		19-18	3rd	6½
15	S.F.	W	7-6	(10)	14	8	Bottalico	Beck		20-18	3rd	5½
16	At L.A.	L	2-8		6	8	Valdes	Mimbs		20-19	3rd	6
17	At L.A.	L	3-6		9	9	Nomo	Grace	Worrell	20-20	3rd	6
18	At L.A.	L	2-7		8	9	Astacio	Fernandez	Osuna	20-21	3rd	7
19	At L.A.	W	5-4		11	11	Leiper	Radinsky	Bottalico	21-21	3rd	6½
21	At S.D.	W	5-4		9	9	Mulholland	Bergman	Bottalico	22-21	T3rd	6
22	At S.D.	L	2-5		6	7	Hamilton	Grace	Hoffman	22-22	T3rd	7
23	At S.D.	L	5-7		11	14	Sanders	Springer	Hoffman	22-23	4th	7½
24	At S.F.	W	5-1		10	3	Schilling	Watson		23-23	3rd	7½
25	At S.F.	L	2-3		4	8	Gardner	Williams	Beck	23-24	3rd	7½
26	At S.F.	W	10-1		14	6	Mulholland	Fernandez	Bottalico	24-24	3rd	7½
27	L.A.	W	9-3		15	11	Grace	Valdes		25-24	3rd	7½
29	L.A.	L	2-3	(11)	8	8	Guthrie	Bottalico	Worrell	25-25	4th	8½
30	L.A.	W	3-2		13	9	Borland	Worrell		26-25	T3rd	8
31	S.D.	L	2-4		3	7	Ashby	Mulholland	Hoffman	26-26	T3rd	9
	S.D.	L	3-8		9	10	Bergman	Mimbs		26-27	T3rd	9
2	S.D.	W	9-8	(12)	16	8	Borland	Hoffman		27-27	T3rd	9
3	At Chi.	L	3-4		11	7	Patterson	Ryan		27-28	4th	10
4	At Chi.	W	12-3		14	8	Williams	Bullinger		28-28	4th	9
5	At Chi.	L	6-9		13	11	Adams	Borland	Wendell	28-29	4th	10
6	At Hou.	L	5-11		8	13	Reynolds	Crawford		28-30	4th	10
7	At Hou.	L	3-7		10	7	Wagner	Springer		28-31	4th	10
8	At Hou.	L	1-2		9	5	Young	Williams	Jones	28-32	4th	11
10	Chi.	L	1-2		3	6	Navarro	Mulholland		28-33	4th	11
11	Chi.	L	2-9		5	13	Campbell	Munoz		28-34	4th	12
12	Chi.	W	4-3		9	5	Fernandez	Castillo	Bottalico	29-34	4th	11
13	At Col.	L	1-4		4	9	Rekar	Schilling	Ruffin	29-35	T4th	11
14	At Col.	L	6-10		9	11	Painter	Springer		29-36	T4th	12
15	At Col.	L	2-4		5	12	Reynoso	Mulholland	Ruffin	29-37	T4th	12
16	At Col.	L	3-11		9	14	Ritz	Munoz		29-38	T4th	12
18	At St.L.	L	2-3		5	5	Osborne	Fernandez	Eckersley	29-39	5th	13½
19	At St.L.	L	2-3		5	5	An. Benes	Bottalico		29-40	5th	14½
21	Col.	W	4-3	(10)	7	9	Borland	Ruffin		30-40	5th	14½
22	Col.	W	5-4		11	7	Blazier	Hawblitzel	Bottalico	31-40	5th	14½
23	Col.	L	4-7		9	7	Freeman	Fernandez	Ruffin	31-41	5th	15½

Date	Opp.	Res.	Score	(inn.*)	Hits	Opp. hits	Winning pitcher	Losing pitcher	Save	Record	Pos.	GB
6-24	At Cin.	L	0-7		4	12	Portugal	Schilling		31-42	5th	15¹/
6-25†	At Cin.	L	1-9		4	7	Burba	Quirico		31-43		
6-25‡	At Cin.	L	1-3		8	7	Jarvis	Mimbs	Smith	31-44	5th	17
6-26	At Cin.	L	2-4		7	7	Salkeld	Williams	Brantley	31-45	5th	17
6-28	Mon.	W	7-3		16	8	Mulholland	Urbina	Ryan	32-45	5th	16¹/
6-29	Mon.	L	0-1		2	5	Fassero	Schilling		32-46	5th	16¹/
6-30	Mon.	L	5-6		9	6	Rojas	Bottalico	Dyer	32-47	5th	17¹/
7-1	N.Y.	W	6-4		12	10	Williams	B. Jones	Ryan	33-47	5th	17¹/
7-2	N.Y.	W	3-2		8	7	Springer	Harnisch	Bottalico	34-47	5th	16¹/
7-3	N.Y.	L	6-10		13	16	Byrd	Ryan	Henry	34-48	5th	17¹/
7-4	Fla.	W	8-5		14	11	Blazier	Rapp	Bottalico	35-48	5th	16¹/
7-5	Fla.	W	7-4		14	14	Borland	Miller	Bottalico	36-48	5th	15¹/
7-6	Fla.	W	2-1		5	5	Williams	Brown	Bottalico	37-48	5th	15¹/
7-7	Fla.	L	4-7	(10)	8	8	Mathews	R. Jordan	Nen	37-49	5th	16¹/
7-11	At Mon.	W	3-2		5	5	Schilling	Fassero	Bottalico	38-49	5th	15¹/
7-12	At Mon.	W	5-3		8	9	Mulholland	Martinez		39-49	5th	15¹/
7-13	At Mon.	W	6-2		8	10	Mimbs	Cormier		40-49	5th	15¹/
7-14	At Mon.	L	2-5		5	8	Scott	Williams	Rojas	40-50	5th	16¹/
7-15	At N.Y.	L	5-7		11	16	DiPoto	Springer	Henry	40-51	5th	17¹/
7-16	At N.Y.	L	3-6		11	5	Clark	Schilling	J. Franco	40-52	5th	18¹/
7-17	At N.Y.	L	2-3		10	9	Mlicki	Frey		40-53	5th	19
7-18	At Fla.	L	0-7		3	6	Brown	Mimbs		40-54	5th	20
7-19	At Fla.	L	2-11		11	13	Hammond	Williams		40-55	5th	20
7-20	At Fla.	L	4-7		12	11	Rapp	Springer	Nen	40-56	5th	20
7-21	At Fla.	W	12-3		13	8	Schilling	Burkett	Bottalico	41-56	5th	19
7-22†	Cin.	L	2-5		9	9	Portugal	Mulholland	Brantley	41-57		
7-22‡	Cin.	L	3-5		10	12	Smith	Ryan	Brantley	41-58	5th	20¹/
7-23	Cin.	L	3-5		9	10	Jarvis	Mimbs		41-59	5th	21¹/
7-24	Cin.	L	1-3		6	9	Burba	Williams	Brantley	41-60	5th	22¹/
7-25	At Pit.	L	4-6		5	11	Miceli	Springer	Cordova	41-61	5th	22¹/
7-26	At Pit.	L	4-7		13	7	Ericks	Bottalico	Plesac	41-62	5th	23¹/
7-27	At Pit.	W	2-1		9	5	Mulholland	Parris		42-62	5th	22¹/
7-28	At Pit.	L	8-12		10	17	Ericks	Borland		42-63	5th	22¹/
7-30	St.L.	W	8-7		22	9	Ryan	Mathews		43-63	5th	21¹/
8-1†	St.L.	W	2-1		10	7	Springer	Osborne	Ryan	44-63		
8-1‡	St.L.	L	1-7		4	13	An. Benes	Mimbs		44-64	5th	22¹/
8-2	Pit.	L	3-8		8	15	Wilkins	Blazier		44-65	5th	22¹/
8-3	Pit.	W	7-6		10	10	Bottalico	Plesac		45-65	5th	22¹/
8-4	Pit.	W	4-2		7	7	Williams	Miceli	Ryan	46-65	5th	22¹/
8-5	Pit.	W	3-0		10	4	Schilling	Neagle		47-65	5th	22
8-6	At Atl.	L	4-10		3	16	Bielecki	Springer		47-66	5th	23
8-7	At Atl.	L	1-14	(8)	6	18	Smoltz	Munoz		47-67	5th	24
8-8	At Atl.	W	4-1		12	4	Beech	Maddux	Bottalico	48-67	5th	23
8-9	Hou.	L	1-5		4	11	Reynolds	West		48-68	5th	23
8-10	Hou.	L	1-3		8	9	Hampton	Schilling	Wagner	48-69	5th	23
8-11	Hou.	L	5-10		11	13	Kile	Williams		48-70	5th	24
8-13†	Atl.	L	0-2		8	5	Maddux	Hunter		48-71		
8-13‡	Atl.	L	2-5		4	8	Hartgraves	Beech	Wohlers	48-72	5th	26
8-14	Atl.	W	4-1		8	9	West	Glavine	Bottalico	49-72	5th	25
8-15	Atl.	L	5-8		13	14	Wade	Schilling		49-73	5th	26
8-16	S.F.	L	4-6		8	10	VanLandingham	Williams	Beck	49-74	5th	27
8-17	S.F.	L	4-8		11	11	Watson	Hunter	Beck	49-75	5th	28
8-18	S.F.	W	7-6		12	10	Borland	Gardner	Bottalico	50-75	5th	28
8-20	At L.A.	W	3-1		12	5	R. Jordan	Osuna	Bottalico	51-75	5th	28
8-21	At L.A.	W	6-0		9	2	Schilling	Nomo		52-75	5th	28
8-22	At L.A.	L	5-8		14	11	Astacio	Williams	Worrell	52-76	5th	28
8-23	At S.D.	W	7-4		10	7	Hunter	Worrell	Bottalico	53-76	5th	28
8-24	At S.D.	L	1-7		3	13	Hamilton	Beech		53-77	5th	29
8-25	At S.D.	L	2-11		12	17	Sanders	West		53-78	5th	29
8-26	At S.F.	L	0-1		3	6	VanLandingham	Schilling	Beck	53-79	5th	29¹/
8-27	At S.F.	W	3-2		7	8	Williams	Bautista	Bottalico	54-79	5th	28¹/
8-28	At S.F.	L	6-7		10	11	Dewey	R. Jordan	Beck	54-80	5th	29¹/
8-30	L.A.	L	6-7	(12)	12	9	Dreifort	Parrett	Worrell	54-81	5th	30¹/
8-31	L.A.	L	7-11		10	18	Valdes	Schilling	Osuna	54-82	5th	30¹.
9-1	L.A.	W	6-3		8	4	Williams	Worrell	Bottalico	55-82	5th	29¹/
9-2	S.D.	L	1-5		8	10	Valenzuela	Hunter		55-83	5th	29¹/
9-3	S.D.	W	8-2		13	5	Mimbs	Hamilton	Ryan	56-83	5th	28¹/
9-4	S.D.	L	1-2		4	9	Sanders	Beech	Hoffman	56-84	5th	28¹,
9-5	Chi.	W	6-1		12	6	Schilling	Castillo		57-84	5th	28
9-6	Chi.	L	4-6		9	6	Bullinger	Ryan	Wendell	57-85	5th	29
9-7	Chi.	W	4-2		9	7	Hunter	Bottenfield	Bottalico	58-85	5th	29
9-8	Chi.	L	3-5		11	8	Navarro	Mimbs	Wendell	58-86	5th	29
9-10	At Hou.	L	3-4		6	10	Morman	Schilling	Hernandez	58-87	5th	28
9-11	At Hou.	W	10-8		14	15	Parrett	Holt	Bottalico	59-87	5th	28
9-12	At Hou.	L	1-4		7	6	Kile	Williams		59-88	5th	28

	Opp.	Res.	Score	(inn.*)	Hits	Opp. hits	Winning pitcher	Losing pitcher	Save	Record	Pos.	GB
	At Chi.	L	2-4		8	5	Trachsel	Hunter	Wendell	59-89	5th	28
	At Chi.	W	6-2		11	6	Mimbs	Navarro	Ryan	60-89	5th	27
	At Chi.	W	6-1		9	6	Schilling	Foster		61-89	5th	27
	Fla.	L	5-11		12	14	Rapp	Beech		61-90	5th	28½
	Fla.	W	8-6		17	7	Borland	Miller	Bottalico	62-90	5th	28½
	N.Y.	L	2-7		9	10	Clark	Hunter		62-91	5th	28½
	N.Y.	L	2-5		6	7	Wilson	Mimbs	J. Franco	62-92	5th	29½
	N.Y.	W	2-1		6	5	Schilling	Harnisch		63-92	5th	29½
	N.Y.	W	4-3		7	8	Bottalico	Wallace		64-92	5th	29½
	Mon.	L	2-6		10	11	Juden	Williams	Rojas	64-93	5th	30
	Mon.	W	3-1		7	4	West	Paniagua	Bottalico	65-93	5th	29
	Mon.	L	2-5		8	6	Daal	Schilling	Rojas	65-94	5th	29
	At N.Y.	W	6-5		13	8	R. Jordan	DiPoto	Bottalico	66-94	5th	29
	At N.Y.	L	2-4		5	5	Person	Maduro	Wallace	66-95	5th	30
	At N.Y.	W	9-5		13	10	Blazier	Fyhrie		67-95	5th	29

Monthly records: April (13-11), May (13-15), June (6-21), July (11-16), August (11-19), September (13-13). *Innings, if other than nine. †First game of doubleheader. ‡Second game of doubleheader.

HIGHLIGHTS

High point: Looking at the final record of 67-95 and all the injuries suffered by the Phillies, the first two months of the season weren't all that hard to handle. A 13-11 April was followed by a 13-15 May, which sent the Phillies into June at 26-26 despite the loss of Darren Daulton and Lenny Dykstra for the season and Gregg Jefferies for the first two months. They were nine games behind first-place Atlanta when June began, but it was also the last time the Phillies hit the break-even mark. They lost 21 of the next 27 games.

Low point: June was cruel in more ways than one. Not only did the Phillies suffer through a 6-21 record despite the return of Gregg Jefferies from thumb surgery, rookie righthander Mike Grace was shut down for the rest of the season with a shoulder ailment.

Turning point: The season began slipping away in early June and went completely south during a six-game road trip that started in Colorado and ended in St. Louis. The Phillies dropped four to the Rockies and two to the Cardinals. Not even winning eight of the first 10 games really could right the ship.

Most valuable player: Catcher Benito Santiago. He hit a career-high 30 home runs, led the club in RBIs with 85, hit .264 and was outstanding behind the plate. He did much to enhance a reputation that he won't play hard on a bad team.

Most valuable pitcher: Closer Ricky Bottalico. Pitching as well as Curt Schilling did after tricky shoulder surgery was impressive, but Bottalico saving 34 games for a team that won 67 was more valuable. Bottalico was an All-Star and blew just two save chances.

Most improved player: Shortstop Kevin Stocker. After a slow start, Stocker hit during the last six weeks of the season and raised his average from .222 to .254 by the end of the year.

Most pleasant surprise: Pitcher Curt Schilling. Having watched so many of its pitchers not make it back from surgery in recent years, the Phillies didn't let themselves become too excited about the progress Schilling made in spring training. But Schilling made 26 starts, posted a 9-10 record and led the NL in complete games with eight.

Biggest disappointment: Outfielder Mark Whiten. Because Darren Daulton and Lenny Dykstra were question marks going into the season, their seasons couldn't be listed as major disappointments. That label goes to Whiten. Expected to provide run-production from the middle of the order, Whiten hit .236 with seven home runs and 21 RBIs before he was released June 17.

Key injuries: Darren Daulton's knees and Lenny Dykstra's back have put their careers in jeopardy. Pitcher Mike Grace was 7-2 and on his way to a stellar rookie season when he was lost for the year in early June. Third baseman Scott Rolen broke a bone in his right wrist the first week of September. Sid Fernandez worked in only 11 games because of shoulder and elbow problems. Second baseman Mickey Morandini found his way onto the D.L. for the first time in his career with a separated shoulder. Gregg Jefferies missed two months after surgery on his left thumb. Mike Lieberthal had knee surgery in late August.

Notable: The Phillies tied an N.L. record by using 54 players—29 position players and 25 pitchers.

—GEORGE A. KING III

RECORDS

1996 regular-season record: 67-95 (5th in N.L. East); 35-46 at home; 32-49 on road; 24-28 vs. East; 21-40 vs. Central; 22-27 vs. West; 11-15 vs. lefthanded starters; 56-80 vs. righthanded starters; 21-35 on grass; 46-60 on turf; 24-24 in daytime; 43-71 at night; 25-22 in one-run games; 4-4 in extra-inning games; 0-3-1 in doubleheaders.

Team record past five years: 357-388 (.479, ranks 9th in league in that span).

TEAM LEADERS

Batting average: Todd Zeile (.268).
At-bats: Mickey Morandini (539).
Runs: Benito Santiago (71).
Hits: Mickey Morandini (135).
Total bases: Benito Santiago (242).
Doubles: Jim Eisenreich, Mickey Morandini, Todd Zeile (24).

Triples: Ricky Otero (7).
Home runs: Benito Santiago (30).
Runs batted in: Benito Santiago (85).
Stolen bases: Mickey Morandini (26).
Slugging percentage: Benito Santiago (.503).
On-base percentage: Todd Zeile (.353).
Wins: Curt Schilling (9).
Earned-run average: Curt Schilling (3.19).
Complete games: Curt Schilling (8).
Shutouts: Curt Schilling (2).
Saves: Ricky Bottalico (34).
Innings pitched: Curt Schilling (183.1).
Strikeouts: Curt Schilling (182).

GAMES BY POSITION

Catcher: Benito Santiago 114, Mike Lieberthal 43, Gary Bennett 5, Bobby Estalella 4.
First base: Gregg Jefferies 53, Kevin Jordan 30, Todd Zeile 28, Jon Zuber 22, Gene Schall 19, Benito Santiago 14, J.R. Phillips 11, Ruben Amaro 1.
Second base: Mickey Morandini 137, David Doster 24, Kevin Jordan 7, Desi Relaford 4, Mike Benjamin 1, Kevin Sefcik 1.
Third base: Todd Zeile 106, Scott Rolen 37, Kevin Sefcik 20, Howard Battle 1, David Doster 1, Kevin Jordan 1.
Shortstop: Kevin Stocker 119, Mike Benjamin 31, Kevin Sefcik 21, Desi Relaford 9.
Outfield: Ricky Otero 100, Jim Eisenreich 91, Pete Incaviglia 71, Gregg Jefferies 51, Mark Whiten 51, Lenny Dykstra 39, Wendell Magee 37, Ruben Amaro 35, Glenn Murray 27, Lee Tinsley 22, J.R. Phillips 15, Manny Martinez 11, Darren Daulton 5.

TOP DRAFT CHOICES

1. **Adam Eaton**, RHP, Snohomish (Wash.) H.S.
2. **Jimmy Rollins**, SS, Encinal H.S., Alameda, Calif.
3. **Kris Stevens**, LHP, Fontana (Calif.) H.S.
4. **Ryan Brannan**, RHP, Long Beach State U.
5. **Ira Tilton**, RHP, Siena College.
6. **Kevin Burford**, OF, Fountain Valley (Calif.) H.S.
7. **B.J. Schlicker**, C-1B, North Montgomery H.S., Crawfordsville, Ind.
8. **David Francia**, OF, U. of South Alabama.
9. **Brandon Marsters**, C, Oral Roberts Univ.
10. **Evan Thomas**, RHP, Fla. International U.

PITTSBURGH PIRATES
NATIONAL LEAGUE CENTRAL DIVISION

1997 PIRATES SCHEDULE

Home games shaded.
* — All-Star Game at Jacobs Field (Cleveland)
D — Day game (any game starting before 5 p.m.)

APRIL

SUN	MON	TUE	WED	THU	FRI	SAT
		1 D SF	2 SF	3 SF	4 LA	5 LA
6 D LA	7 SD	8 SD	9 SD	10	11 LA	12 D LA
13 D LA	14	15 SD	16 SD	17 CIN	18 CIN	19 D CIN
20 D CIN	21 D PHI	22	23 PHI	24 CUB	25 D CUB	26 D CUB
27 CUB	28 PHI	29 PHI	30 SF			

MAY

SUN	MON	TUE	WED	THU	FRI	SAT
				1 D SF	2 ATL	3 ATL
4 D ATL	5 FLA	6 FLA	7 COL	8 COL	9 D ATL	10 ATL
11 D ATL	12 FLA	13	14 COL	15 COL	16 FLA	17 FLA
18 D FLA	19	20 STL	21 STL	22 D MON	23 MON	24 MON
25 MON	26 D CUB	27 CUB	28 CUB	29	30 MON	31 MON

JUNE

SUN	MON	TUE	WED	THU	FRI	SAT
1 D MON	2 CUB	3 D CUB	4 STL	5 D STL	6 PHI	7 PHI
8 D PHI	9	10 CIN	11 CIN	12	13 KC	14 KC
15 D KC	16 MIN	17 MIN	18 D MIN	19 NYM	20 NYM	21 D NYM
22 NYM	23 HOU	24 HOU	25 D HOU	26	27 NYM	28 NYM
29 NYM	30 CWS					

JULY

SUN	MON	TUE	WED	THU	FRI	SAT
		1 CWS	2 CWS	3 STL	4 STL	5 D STL
6 D STL	7	8 ° 9	10 HOU	11 HOU	12 D HOU
13 D HOU	14 NYM	15 NYM	16 CIN	17 CIN	18 D PHI	19 D PHI
20 PHI	21 D PHI	22 SD	23 SD	24 D SD	25 SF	26 D SF
27 D SF	28 LA	29 D LA	30	31 COL		

AUGUST

SUN	MON	TUE	WED	THU	FRI	SAT
					1 COL	2 COL
3 COL	4 D ATL	5 ATL	6 FLA	7 FLA	8 D COL	9 COL
10 COL	11	12 ATL	13 ATL	14	15 FLA	16 FLA
17 D FLA	18 D FLA	19 SD	20 SD	21 SD	22 SF	23 SF
24 D SF	25 LA	26 LA	27 D LA	28	29 MIL	30 MIL
31 D MIL						

SEPTEMBER

SUN	MON	TUE	WED	THU	FRI	SAT
	1 CLE	2 D CLE	3 CLE	4 CIN	5 CIN	6 D CIN
7 CIN	8 D MON	9 MON	10 MON	11	12 CUB	13 CUB
14 D CUB	15 MON	16 MON	17 HOU	18 HOU	19 STL	20 STL
21 STL	22 STL	23 NYM	24 NYM	25	26 HOU	27 HOU
28 D HOU						

1997 SEASON

CLUB DIRECTORY

General partner
Kevin S. McClatchy

Board of directors
Donald Beaver
Frank Brenner
Floyd R. (Chip) Ganassi Jr.
Kevin S. McClatchy
Mayor Tom Murphy
G. Ogden Nutting
Kenneth L. Pollock
William E. Springer

Chief operating officer
Dick Freeman

Sr. v.p. and general manager
Cam Bonifay

Asst. general manager
John Sirignano

Special assistants to the g.m.
Chet Montgomery
Ken Parker
Lenny Yochim

V.p., finance and administration
Jim Plake

V.p., broadcasting and advertising sales
Mark Driscoll

V.p., marketing and public relations
Steven N. Greenberg

Director of finance
Patti Mistick

Traveling secretary
Greg Johnson

Sales mgr., broadcasting and promotions
Mark Ferraco

Director of Bradenton baseball operations
Jeff Podobnik

Director of community services
Al Gordon

Director of corporate relations
Nellie Briles

Director of information systems
Dale Dressler

Director of in-game entertainment
Eric Wolff

Director of marketing communicatio
Mike Gordon

Director of media relations
Jim Trdinich

Director of merchandising
Joe Billetdeaux

Director of operations
Dennis DaPra

Director of player development
Paul Tinnell

Director of player relations
Kathy Guy

Asst. director of player development
Bill Bryk

Director of scouting
Leland Maddox

Club physician
Dr. Joseph Coroso

Team orthopedist
Dr. Jack Failla

Head trainer
Kent Biggerstaff

Equipment manager
Roger Wilson

Scouting coordinators
Tom Barnard, Ron King, Fred Wrigh

Special assignment scouts
Angel Figueroa, Jim Guinn, Boyd
Odom, Roy Smith

Latin America coordinators
Pablo Cruz, Jose Luna

Scouting supervisors
Grant Brittain, Dana Brown, Steve
Fleming, Duane Gustavson, Jame
House, Craig Kornfeld, Jose Luna
Greg McClain, Steve Riha, Ed
Roebuck, Delvy Santiago, Bruce
Seid, Robert Sidwell, George Swa
Douglas Takaragawa, Michael
Williams

MINOR LEAGUE AFFILIATES

Class	Team	League	Manager
AAA	Calgary	Pacific Coast	Trent Jewett
AA	Carolina	Southern	Marc Hill
A	Lynchburg	Carolina	Jeff Banister
A	Augusta	South Atlantic	Jeff Richardson
A	Erie	New York-Pennsylvania	Marty Brown
Rookie	Gulf Coast Pirates	Gulf Coast	Woody Huyke

BROADCAST INFORMATION

Radio: KDKA-AM (1020).
TV: To be announced.
Cable TV: To be announced.

SPRING TRAINING

Ballpark (city): McKechnie Field
(Bradenton, Fla.).
Ticket information: 941-748-4610.

SPRING TRAINING ROSTER

Manager—Gene Lamont (32).
Coaches—Joe Jones, Jack Lind, Lloyd McClendon, Pete Vuckovich, Spin Williams (54).

No.	PITCHERS	B/T	Ht./Wt.	Born	1996 clubs
	Christiansen, Jason	R/L	6-5/230	9-21-69	Calgary, Pittsburgh
36	Cooke, Steve	R/L	6-6/230	1-14-70	Carolina, Pittsburgh
67	Cordova, Francisco	R/R	6-1/171	4-26-72	Pittsburgh
	Davis, Kane	R/R	6-3/170	6-25-75	Lynchburg
71	Dessens, Elmer	R/R	6-0/185	1-13-72	Calgary, Mexico City Red Devils, Pittsburgh, Carolina
31	Dillinger, John	R/R	6-6/205	8-28-73	Lynchburg
57	Ericks, John	R/R	6-7/250	9-16-67	Pittsburgh, Calgary
	Granger, Jeff	R/L	6-4/200	12-16-71	Omaha, Kansas City
	Kelly, Jeff	L/L	6-6/215	1-11-75	Augusta, Lynchburg
47	Lieber, Jon	L/R	6-2/220	4-2-70	Pittsburgh
34	Loaiza, Esteban	R/R	6-2/195	12-31-71	Calgary, Pittsburgh
51	Loiselle, Rich	R/R	6-5/240	1-12-72	Jackson, Tucson, Calgary, Pittsburgh
55	Morel, Ramon	R/R	6-2/200	8-15-74	Carolina, Pittsburgh
38	Peters, Chris	L/L	6-1/169	1-28-72	Carolina, Calgary, Pittsburgh
	Pett, Jose	R/R	6-6/210	1-8-76	Knoxville, Syracuse
49	Ruebel, Matt	L/L	6-2/180	10-16-69	Calgary, Pittsburgh
42	Schmidt, Jason	R/R	6-5/207	1-29-73	Atlanta, Richmond, Greenville, Pittsburgh
	Silva, Jose	R/R	6-5/210	12-19-73	Knoxville, Toronto
	Sodowsky, Clint	L/R	6-4/200	7-13-72	Detroit, Toledo
43	Wagner, Paul	R/R	6-1/210	11-14-67	Pittsburgh, Gulf Coast Pirates
62	Wilkins, Marc	R/R	5-10/210	10-21-70	Carolina, Pittsburgh

No.	CATCHERS	B/T	Ht./Wt.	Born	1996 clubs
2	Encarnacion, Angelo	R/R	5-8/180	4-18-73	Calgary, Pittsburgh
18	Kendall, Jason	R/R	6-0/190	6-26-74	Pittsburgh
15	Osik, Keith	R/R	6-0/190	10-22-68	Pittsburgh, Erie

No.	INFIELDERS	B/T	Ht./Wt.	Born	1996 clubs
	Collier, Lou	R/R	5-10/176	8-21-73	Carolina
	Cromer, Brandon	L/R	6-2/175	1-25-74	Knoxville
19	Elster, Kevin	R/R	6-2/200	8-3-64	Texas
22	Garcia, Freddy	R/R	6-2/205	8-1-72	Lynchburg
36	Johnson, Mark	L/L	6-4/230	10-17-67	Pittsburgh
16	Randa, Joe	R/R	5-11/185	12-18-69	Kansas City, Omaha
51	Womack, Tony	L/R	5-9/155	9-25-69	Calgary, Pittsburgh

No.	OUTFIELDERS	B/T	Ht./Wt.	Born	1996 clubs
46	Allensworth, Jermaine	R/R	6-0/190	1-11-72	Calgary, Pittsburgh
25	Beamon, Trey	L/R	6-0/192	2-11-74	Calgary, Pittsburgh
	Brown, Adrian	R/R	6-0/175	2-7-74	Lynchburg, Carolina
	Brown, Emil	R/R	6-2/195	12-29-74	Modesto, Arizona Athletics
30	Cummings, Midre	L/R	6-0/195	10-14-71	Calgary, Pittsburgh
	Guillen, Jose	R/R	5-11/165	5-17-76	Lynchburg
11	Kingery, Mike	L/L	6-0/185	3-29-61	Pittsburgh
28	Martin, Al	L/L	6-2/210	11-24-67	Pittsburgh
56	Peterson, Charles	R/R	6-3/203	5-8-74	Carolina
	Staton, T.J.	L/L	5-10/175	2-17-75	Carolina

BALLPARK INFORMATION

Ballpark (capacity, surface)
Three Rivers Stadium (48,044, artificial)

Address
600 Stadium Circle
Pittsburgh, PA 15212

Business phone
412-323-5000

Ticket information
800-BUY-BUCS

Ticket prices
$15 (club boxes)
$10 (terrace boxes)
$10 (family boxes)
$8 (reserved seats)
$5 (general admission)
$1 (g.a., children 14 and under)

Field dimensions (from home plate)
To left field at foul line, 335 feet
To center field, 400 feet
To right field at foul line, 335 feet

First game played
July 16, 1970 (Reds 3, Pirates 2)

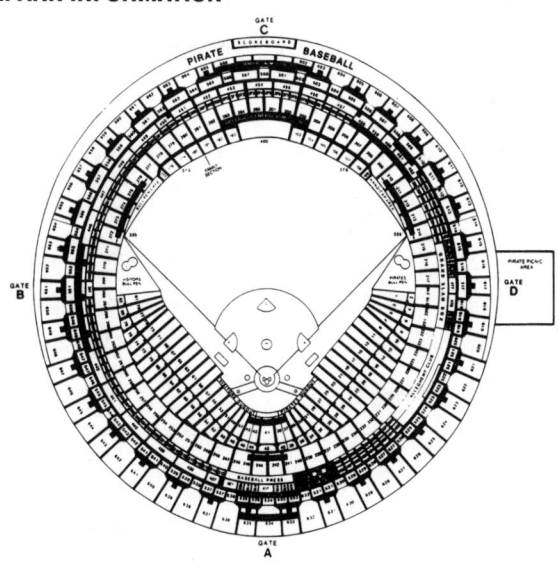

DAY BY DAY

Date	Opp.	Res.	Score	(inn.*)	Hits	Opp. hits	Winning pitcher	Losing pitcher	Save	Record	Pos.	GB
4-1	At Fla.	W	4-0		9	3	Wagner	Brown		1-0	T1st	...
4-2	At Fla.	W	4-1		7	7	Christiansen	Pena	Miceli	2-0	1st	+1/2
4-4	At Fla.	L	2-6		5	11	Leiter	Ericks		2-1	T1st	...
4-5	At N.Y.	W	7-5		10	11	Smith	Mlicki		3-1	T1st	...
4-6	At N.Y.	W	5-0		11	6	Darwin	Clark		4-1	1st	+1
4-8	Phi.	L	3-6		9	10	Fernandez	Neagle		4-2	T2nd	1/2
4-10	Phi.	L	6-7		10	10	Grace	Christiansen	Bottalico	4-3	3rd	1/2
4-11	Mon.	L	5-6	(11)	10	11	Rojas	Cordova	Veres	4-4	4th	1
4-12	Mon.	L	3-13		6	14	Rueter	Darwin		4-5	T4th	11/2
4-13	Mon.	W	9-3		12	10	Wagner	Fassero		5-5	T2nd	1/2
4-14	Mon.	W	5-2		8	10	Neagle	Martinez		6-5	T3rd	1/2
4-15	At St.L.	L	4-6		8	10	Al. Benes	Ericks	Honeycutt	6-6	T3rd	11/2
4-16	At St.L.	W	13-3		20	11	Smith	An. Benes	Lieber	7-6	T3rd	1/2
4-17	At St.L.	L	1-6		3	7	Osborne	Darwin		7-7	4th	11/2
4-18	At St.L.	W	6-2		13	5	Wagner	Stottlemyre		8-7	T3rd	1
4-19	At Mon.	L	1-2		8	9	Manuel	Plesac		8-8	3rd	2
4-20	At Mon.	L	2-11		3	11	Martinez	Ericks		8-9	T4th	21/2
4-21	At Mon.	L	4-9		7	16	Veres	Christiansen		8-10	5th	21/2
4-22	At Phi.	W	9-3		16	6	Darwin	Mulholland		9-10	T4th	11/2
4-23	At Phi.	L	2-6		9	10	Springer	Wagner	Ryan	9-11	T4th	2
4-24	Fla.	W	6-3		11	9	Neagle	Rapp		10-11	T3rd	11/2
4-25	Fla.	L	1-4		6	6	Leiter	Hope	Nen	10-12	T3rd	11/2
4-26	N.Y.	W	10-6		11	9	Christiansen	Isringhausen		11-12	T2nd	1/2
4-27	N.Y.	L	4-7		8	13	Mlicki	Miceli	J. Franco	11-13	T3rd	1
4-28	N.Y.	L	5-7		8	12	B. Jones	Wagner	J. Franco	11-14	4th	2
4-30	At Cin.	W	10-7		12	15	Neagle	Smiley	Cordova	12-14	3rd	1/2
5-1	At Cin.	W	4-3		7	5	Hope	Burba	Plesac	13-14	3rd	1/2
5-3	L.A.	L	1-10		9	11	Park	Darwin		13-15	3rd	11/2
5-4	L.A.	W	7-2		13	5	Wagner	Candiotti		14-15	3rd	1/2
5-5	L.A.	W	4-2		7	9	Neagle	Valdes	Plesac	15-15	2nd	1/2
5-6	L.A.	L	4-8		11	8	Nomo	Hope	Radinsky	15-16	3rd	1/2
5-8†	S.D.	L	4-5		8	6	Tewksbury	May	Hoffman	15-17	3rd	1
5-8‡	S.D.	W	4-3		8	6	Christiansen	Sanders	Cordova	16-17	2nd	1/2
5-9	S.D.	L	1-7		9	11	Ashby	Wagner		16-18	T2nd	11/2
5-10	S.F.	L	4-5	(10)	7	11	DeLucia	Cordova	Beck	16-19	T3rd	11/2
5-11	S.F.	L	7-12		10	13	VanLandingham	Hope		16-20	T3rd	11/2
5-12	S.F.	L	2-7		7	15	Watson	Smith		16-21	T4th	11/2
5-13	At Atl.	L	3-9		7	14	Glavine	Darwin		16-22	T4th	2
5-14	At Atl.	L	3-7		9	14	Smoltz	Wagner		16-23	T4th	21/2
5-15	At Atl.	W	3-0		5	5	Neagle	Avery		17-23	T4th	21/2
5-17	At Hou.	L	2-4		4	7	Reynolds	Lieber	Jones	17-24	T4th	3
5-18	At Hou.	W	2-1	(11)	6	3	Cordova	Young	Plesac	18-24	4th	2
5-19	At Hou.	L	3-4		4	10	Jones	Lieber		18-25	4th	3
5-20	At Col.	L	7-10		12	14	Reynoso	Neagle		18-26	T4th	3
5-21	At Col.	L	10-12		11	20	Holmes	Christiansen	Ruffin	18-27	5th	3
5-22	At Col.	L	3-6		10	11	Ritz	Smith	Ruffin	18-28	5th	3
5-24	Atl.	L	3-5		10	13	Smoltz	Darwin	Wohlers	18-29	5th	4
5-25	Atl.	W	6-2		8	8	Neagle	Avery		19-29	5th	4
5-26	Atl.	L	3-6	(13)	12	11	Wade	Miceli	Bielecki	19-30	5th	5
5-27	Hou.	L	3-5		6	7	Kile	Smith		19-31	5th	6
5-28	Hou.	W	6-5		8	11	Miceli	Swindell	Cordova	20-31	5th	5
5-29	Hou.	L	4-7		14	15	Morman	Darwin	Jones	20-32	5th	6
5-31	Col.	W	8-4		13	6	Neagle	Reynoso	Cordova	21-32	5th	5
6-1	Col.	L	0-2		9	3	Ritz	Wagner	Ruffin	21-33	5th	5
6-2	Col.	W	5-2		6	8	Smith	Holmes	Cordova	22-33	5th	4
6-3	Col.	W	7-2		12	7	Ruebel	Farmer		23-33	T4th	4
6-4	At L.A.	W	3-0		8	5	Darwin	Nomo	Cordova	24-33	T3rd	4
6-5	At L.A.	W	7-3		11	8	Wilkins	Astacio	Cordova	25-33	T3rd	31/2
6-6	At L.A.	L	3-8		5	12	Candiotti	Miceli		25-34	4th	31/2
6-7	At S.D.	W	10-0		13	6	Smith	Bergman		26-34	3rd	31/2
6-8	At S.D.	W	9-8	(14)	17	13	Cordova	Blair		27-34	3rd	31/2
6-9	At S.D.	W	6-0		12	6	Darwin	Tewksbury		28-34	3rd	31/2
6-10	At S.F.	W	5-4		8	12	Morel	DeLucia	Cordova	29-34	3rd	31/2
6-11	At S.F.	W	7-2		11	10	Neagle	Fernandez		30-34	3rd	21/2
6-13	Fla.	L	3-4		7	11	Perez	Cordova	Nen	30-35	T3rd	2
6-14	Fla.	W	5-4		10	9	Plesac	Nen		31-35	T3rd	2
6-15	Fla.	W	12-8		15	14	Darwin	Rapp		32-35	3rd	2
6-16	Fla.	L	2-4		11	12	Brown	Neagle	Nen	32-36	T3rd	2
6-17	N.Y.	L	6-7	(10)	12	14	Mlicki	Cordova	J. Franco	32-37	4th	3
6-19†	N.Y.	W	6-5		10	6	Plesac	Isringhausen		33-37		
6-19‡	N.Y.	L	3-5		8	12	Mlicki	Cordova	J. Franco	33-38	T3rd	3
6-21	At Fla.	L	0-4		5	9	Brown	Darwin		33-39	4th	31/2

te	Opp.	Res.	Score	(inn.*)	Hits	Opp. hits	Winning pitcher	Losing pitcher	Save	Record	Pos.	GB
22	At Fla.	W	4-1	(10)	7	5	Plesac	Perez		34-39	4th	2¹/₂
23	At Fla.	W	5-3		11	8	Lieber	Rapp	Cordova	35-39	3rd	1¹/₂
24	At Mon.	L	3-11		8	14	Martinez	Dessens		35-40	T3rd	2¹/₂
25	At Mon.	L	2-8		6	13	Rueter	Smith	Scott	35-41	5th	3
26	At Mon.	W	3-1		7	8	Darwin	Cormier	Cordova	36-41	5th	3
28	At St.L.	L	1-6		6	8	Osborne	Neagle		36-42	5th	3
29	At St.L.	L	5-6		11	15	Honeycutt	Miceli		36-43	5th	4
30	At St.L.	L	3-10		8	15	Stottlemyre	Smith		36-44	5th	5
1	Chi.	W	4-1		11	8	Darwin	Navarro	Plesac	37-44	5th	5
2	Chi.	L	7-15		14	22	Telemaco	Wagner		37-45	5th	6
3	Chi.	W	3-2		7	8	Neagle	Castillo	Plesac	38-45	5th	6
4	St.L.	L	1-7		8	11	An. Benes	Dessens		38-46	5th	7
5	St.L.	L	4-7		9	11	Stottlemyre	Smith	Fossas	38-47	5th	8
6	St.L.	L	5-9		9	17	Al. Benes	Darwin		38-48	5th	8
7	St.L.	W	8-2		14	4	Lieber	Morgan		39-48	5th	7
11	At Cin.	W	5-3		12	8	Neagle	Smiley	Plesac	40-48	5th	6
12	At Cin.	L	2-5		6	9	Portugal	Darwin	Brantley	40-49	5th	7
13	At Cin.	L	0-3		3	6	Jarvis	Lieber		40-50	5th	8
14	At Cin.	L	6-7		9	9	Burba	Wagner	Brantley	40-51	5th	9
15	At Chi.	L	2-12		8	16	Castillo	Miceli		40-52	5th	10
16	At Chi.	W	10-5		13	6	Neagle	Navarro		41-52	5th	10
18	Cin.	W	8-3		11	7	Lieber	Jarvis		42-52	5th	9¹/₂
19	Cin.	L	3-11		8	15	Burba	Wagner		42-53	5th	10¹/₂
20	Cin.	L	3-9		10	12	Salkeld	Miceli		42-54	5th	10¹/₂
21	Cin.	W	6-4		8	9	Neagle	Smiley	Plesac	43-54	5th	10¹/₂
23	Mon.	W	5-1		7	7	Lieber	Martinez		44-54	5th	9
24	Mon.	W	5-4		11	7	Ericks	Rojas		45-54	5th	8
25	Phi.	W	6-4		11	5	Miceli	Springer	Cordova	46-54	5th	7
26	Phi.	W	7-4		7	13	Ericks	Bottalico	Plesac	47-54	5th	6¹/₂
27	Phi.	L	1-2		5	9	Mulholland	Parris		47-55	5th	7
28	Phi.	W	12-8		17	10	Ericks	Borland		48-55	5th	7
29	At N.Y.	L	0-5		4	7	Harnisch	Peters		48-56	5th	7¹/₂
30†	At N.Y.	L	4-5		10	12	Isringhausen	Cordova	J. Franco	48-57		
30‡	At N.Y.	L	3-4	(12)	11	12	J. Franco	Lieber		48-58	5th	8
31	At N.Y.	L	2-3	(10)	5	7	DiPoto	Plesac		48-59	5th	8¹/₂
1	At N.Y.	W	13-9		16	16	Morel	Mlicki	Ericks	49-59	5th	8
2	At Phi.	W	8-3		15	8	Wilkins	Blazier		50-59	5th	8
3	At Phi.	L	6-7		10	10	Bottalico	Plesac		50-60	5th	8¹/₂
4	At Phi.	L	2-4		7	7	Williams	Miceli	Ryan	50-61	5th	9¹/₂
5	At Phi.	L	0-3		4	10	Schilling	Neagle		50-62	5th	10
6	L.A.	L	1-3		10	8	Astacio	Parris	Worrell	50-63	5th	10
7	L.A.	W	12-2		15	10	Lieber	Martinez	Wilkins	51-63	5th	10
8	S.D.	L	3-12		6	19	Sanders	Peters		51-64	5th	10
9	S.D.	L	1-4		3	9	Valenzuela	Miceli	Hoffman	51-65	5th	11
10	S.D.	L	2-6		9	12	Veras	Plesac		51-66	5th	12
11	S.D.	L	5-7		14	10	Bergman	Parris	Hoffman	51-67	5th	13
13	S.F.	L	10-12		10	16	Dewey	Plesac	Beck	51-68	5th	12¹/₂
14	S.F.	W	4-3		10	6	Peters	Estes	Ericks	52-68	5th	12¹/₂
16	At Atl.	L	4-5		8	12	Smoltz	Neagle	Wohlers	52-69	5th	13¹/₂
17	At Atl.	L	1-7		5	7	Bielecki	Ruebel		52-70	5th	13¹/₂
18	At Atl.	L	1-2	(14)	9	12	Borowski	Cordova		52-71	5th	14¹/₂
19	At Hou.	L	1-2	(13)	7	10	Morman	Morel		52-72	5th	15
20	At Hou.	L	4-9		10	13	Wall	Miceli	Hernandez	52-73	5th	15¹/₂
21	At Hou.	W	5-2		14	10	Neagle	Hampton	Ericks	53-73	5th	14¹/₂
22	At Hou.	W	8-6		11	13	Wilkins	Wagner	Ericks	54-73	5th	13¹/₂
23	At Col.	W	5-3		11	7	Lieber	Ritz	Cordova	55-73	5th	13
24	At Col.	L	3-9		8	12	M. Thompson	Peters		55-74	5th	13¹/₂
25	At Col.	L	9-13		15	13	Munoz	Wilkins		55-75	5th	14¹/₂
27	Atl.	W	3-2		7	6	Neagle	Smoltz	Plesac	56-75	5th	14
28	Atl.	L	4-9		6	13	Wade	Loaiza		56-76	5th	15
29	Atl.	L	1-5		7	9	Maddux	Lieber	Wohlers	56-77	5th	15
30	Hou.	L	0-10		7	17	Wall	Peters		56-78	5th	16
31	Hou.	L	4-5		11	9	Hernandez	Ericks	Hudek	56-79	5th	17
1	Hou.	W	9-5		8	5	Wainhouse	Darwin		57-79	5th	16
2	Col.	L	3-8		6	8	Ritz	Loaiza		57-80	5th	16
4	Col.	W	5-2		6	9	Lieber	M. Thompson	Plesac	58-80	5th	16
5	At L.A.	L	1-2		7	7	Osuna	Wilkins	Worrell	58-81	5th	17
7	At L.A.	L	3-4		6	7	Nomo	Schmidt	Worrell	58-82	5th	18
8	At L.A.	W	4-1		7	8	Plesac	Dreifort	Ericks	59-82	5th	17
9	At S.D.	L	5-6		11	7	Hermanson	Wilkins	Hoffman	59-83	5th	18
10	At S.D.	L	5-6		11	12	Hoffman	Boever		59-84	5th	19
11	At S.D.	L	7-8		12	15	Bochtler	Ericks		59-85	5th	19
12	At S.F.	W	10-4		13	9	Schmidt	Dewey	Boever	60-85	5th	18
13	At S.F.	W	9-0		13	6	Loaiza	VanLandingham		61-85	5th	18
14	At S.F.	W	7-5	(12)	14	7	Ericks	Hook	Boever	62-85	5th	17

Date	Opp.	Res.	Score	(inn.*)	Hits	Opp. hits	Winning pitcher	Losing pitcher	Save	Record	Pos.	GB
9-15†	At S.F.	W	4-1		11	10	Lieber	Rueter	Ruebel	63-85		
9-15‡	At S.F.	W	11-9	(10)	16	12	Wilkins	Poole		64-85	5th	15¹
9-17	Cin.	W	5-3		10	10	Cordova	Smiley	Ericks	65-85	5th	15¹
9-18	Cin.	W	5-3		11	5	Schmidt	Morgan	Plesac	66-85	5th	15¹
9-19	Cin.	W	6-4		9	9	Peters	Pugh	Ericks	67-85	5th	15¹
9-20	Chi.	W	6-4		11	7	Lieber	Foster	Ericks	68-85	5th	14¹
9-21	Chi.	W	8-3		8	10	Loiselle	Swartzbaugh		69-85	5th	14
9-22	Chi.	W	11-3		14	9	Cordova	Castillo		70-85	5th	12¹
9-23	Chi.	L	3-4		5	9	Trachsel	Schmidt	Patterson	70-86	5th	13¹
9-24	St.L.	L	1-7		8	12	An. Benes	Loaiza		70-87	5th	14¹
9-25	St.L.	L	7-8	(11)	7	11	Bailey	Miceli	Mathews	70-88	5th	15¹
9-27†	At Chi.	W	7-4	(10)	8	11	Plesac	Wendell		71-88		
9-27‡	At Chi.	L	9-10		15	11	Adams	Boever		71-89	5th	16
9-28	At Chi.	W	8-7	(10)	12	12	Plesac	Wendell		72-89	5th	16
9-29	At Chi.	W	8-3		8	9	Loaiza	Navarro		73-89	5th	15

Monthly records: April (12-14), May (9-18), June (15-12), July (12-15), August (8-20), September (17-10).
*Innings, if other than nine. †First game of doubleheader. ‡Second game of doubleheader.

HIGHLIGHTS

High point: The Pirates ignored considerable off-field turmoil to put together an 11-game winning streak from September 12-22. It was the longest winning streak in the major leagues in 1996. Their best pitcher, Denny Neagle, had been traded and manager Jim Leyland announced during the streak he was bailing out at season's end. The streak was the club's longest since 1992, when it won 11 in a row en route to a division title.

Low point: The team lost three consecutive games in the opponent's last at-bat at San Diego on September 9-11. The tough losses probably helped influence Leyland's decision to leave.

Turning point: In mid-August, general manager Cam Bonifay and Leyland went to a meeting armed with a list of 1997 free agents they'd like to pursue. Instead, owner Kevin McClatchy told them the payroll would be cut. The fallout from that meeting included Leyland's resignation and the trading of Neagle and other veterans.

Most valuable player: Infielder Jeff King. He was a solid run producer and became the first righthanded batter to hit 30 home runs for the Pirates in more than 30 years. As a sign of the times in Pittsburgh, King was traded (to the Kansas City Royals) two months after the season ended.

Most valuable pitcher: Lefthander Denny Neagle. Before he was traded to Atlanta on August 28, Neagle consistently gave the Pirates quality work, going 14-6 with a 3.05 ERA.

Most improved player: Righthander Jon Lieber. He bounced back from an awful 1995 and embraced the challenge of replacing Neagle as the anchor in the rotation. He finished 9-5.

Most pleasant surprise: Rookie catchers Jason Kendall and Keith Osik. Neither had any major league experience. Both held their own against major league pitching, with Kendall hitting .300 and Osik reaching .293.

Biggest disappointment: Shortstop Jay Bell. He wound up with a respectable .250 average thanks to a hot September

but was terrible offensively through four months of the season. He was traded along with King to the Royals in December.

Key injuries: Carlos Garcia missed a third of the season with nagging leg injuries, and Orlando Merced spent two stretches on the disabled list with leg problems. Pitcher Paul Wagner needed Tommy John surgery on his right elbow.

Notable: Pirate hurlers yielded a club-record 183 homers, smashing the previous record of 168 in 1953. . . . The Pirates hit seven grand slams, to tie a team record. . . . Eighteen different pitchers started at least one game for Pittsburgh, the most for any N.L. team since the 1967 Mets (20). . . . The club had 11 pinch homers, breaking the 1944 team record of eight. . . . Mark Johnson pinch hit four homers, also a club record. . . . Gene Lamont became the Pirates' third manager in the past 21 years on October 3. . . . The Pirates used 25 pitchers, breaking the team record of 23 set in 1990 and matched in 1993. . . . The club's 319 doubles beat a team high of 316 that had stood since 1925. . . . Jason Kendall was hit by 15 pitches, a team record and most ever by a National League catcher.

—JOHN MEHNO

RECORDS

1996 regular-season record: 73-89 (5th in N.L. Central); 36-44 at home; 37-45 on road; 25-36 vs. East; 25-27 vs. Central; 23-26 vs. West; 17-17 vs. lefthanded starters; 56-72 vs. righthanded starters; 28-29 on grass; 45-60 on turf; 24-29 in daytime; 49-60 at night; 13-27 in one-run games; 7-9 in extra-inning games; 1-1-3 in doubleheaders.

Team record past five years: 355-389 (.477, ranks 11th in league in that span).

TEAM LEADERS

Batting average: Al Martin (.300).
At-bats: Al Martin (630).
Runs: Al Martin (101).
Hits: Al Martin (189).
Total bases: Jeff King (294).
Doubles: Al Martin (40).

Triples: Jason Kendall (5).
Home runs: Jeff King (30).
Runs batted in: Jeff King (111).
Stolen bases: Al Martin (38).
Slugging percentage: Jeff King (.497).
On-base percentage: Orlando Merced (.357).
Wins: Denny Neagle (14).
Earned-run average: Denny Neagle (3.0
Complete games: Esteban Loaiza, Den Neagle, Jason Schmidt, Zane Smith, P. Wagner (1).
Shutouts: Esteban Loaiza, Zane Smith (
Saves: Francisco Cordova (12).
Innings pitched: Denny Neagle (182.2
Strikeouts: Denny Neagle (131).

GAMES BY POSITION

Catcher: Jason Kendall 129, Keith Osik Angelo Encarnacion 7, John Wehner 1.
First base: Mark Johnson 100, Jeff Kin 92, Rich Aude 4, Orlando Merced 1.
Second base: Carlos Garcia 77, Jeff K 71, Nelson Liriano 36, John Wehner 1 Tony Womack 4.
Third base: Charlie Hayes 124, John Wehner 24, Jeff King 17, Carlos Garcia 14, Dale Sveum 10, Nelson Liriano 9, Keith Osik 2.
Shortstop: Jay Bell 151, Carlos Garcia 19, Nelson Liriano 5.
Outfield: Al Martin 152, Orlando Merced 115, Mike Kingery 83, Jermaine Allensworth 61, Dave Clark 61, John Wehner 29, Jacob Brumfield 22, Midre Cummings 21, Trey Beamon 15, Tony Womack 6, Keith Osik 2, Mark Johnson

TOP DRAFT CHOICES

1. **Kris Benson,** RHP, Clemson University
2. **Andy Prater,** RHP, McCluer North H.S. Florissant, Mo.
3. **Luis Lorenzana,** SS, Montgomery H.S. San Diego.
4. **Lee Evans,** C, Tuscaloosa County H.S. Northport, Ala.
5. **Julian Redman,** OF, Tuscaloosa (Ala.) Academy.
6. **Yustin Jordan,** SS, Monticello (Ark.) H.
7. **Andrew Hohenstein,** RHP, Norte Vista H.S., Riverside, Calif.
8. **Bobby Vogt,** LHP, Armwood H.S., Tamp
9. **Jess Siciliano,** RHP, Rockland (N.Y.) C.
10. **Carlos Rivera,** 1B, Rio Grande, P.R.

ST. LOUIS CARDINALS
NATIONAL LEAGUE CENTRAL DIVISION

1997 CARDINALS SCHEDULE

- ▦ Home games shaded.
- * — All-Star Game at Jacobs Field (Cleveland)
- D — Day game (any game starting before 5 p.m.)

APRIL
SUN	MON	TUE	WED	THU	FRI	SAT
		1 D MON	2 MON	3 MON	4 HOU	5 HOU
6 D HOU	7	8	9	10 D MON	11 D HOU	12 D HOU
13 HOU	14 D HOU	15 FLA	16 FLA	17 D FLA	18 SD	19 SD
20 SD	21	22	23	24	25 COL	26 D COL
27 D COL	28 SF	29 SF	30 FLA			

MAY
SUN	MON	TUE	WED	THU	FRI	SAT
				1 FLA	2 NYM	3 D NYM
4 NYM	5 ATL	6 ATL	7 D PHI	8 PHI	9 NYM	10 NYM
11 D NYM	12	13 PHI	14 PHI	15 PHI	16 ATL	17 ATL
18 ATL	19 PIT	20 PIT	21 D PIT	22	23 SF	24 D SF
25 SF	26 COL	27 D COL	28	29 LA	30 LA	31 D LA

JUNE
SUN	MON	TUE	WED	THU	FRI	SAT
1 D LA	2 COL	3 D COL	4 PIT	5 D PIT	6 LA	7 LA
8 D LA	9 SD	10 SD	11 SD	12	13 CLE	14 D CLE
15 D CLE	16 MIL	17 MIL	18 MIL	19	20 CIN	21 CIN
22 CIN	23 CUB	24 CUB	25 CUB	26 CIN	27 CIN	28 D CIN
29 D CIN	30 MIN					

JULY
SUN	MON	TUE	WED	THU	FRI	SAT
		1 MIN	2 MIN	3 PIT	4 D PIT	5 D PIT
6 D PIT	7	8	* 9	10 D CUB	11 D CUB	12 D CUB
13 D CUB	14 CIN	15 CIN	16 SD	17 SD	18 SF	19 SF
20 D SF	21 SF	22 HOU	23 HOU	24	25 D FLA	26 D FLA
27 FLA	28 HOU	29 HOU	30 HOU	31 PHI		

AUGUST
SUN	MON	TUE	WED	THU	FRI	SAT
					1 PHI	2 D PHI
3 PHI	4 D NYM	5 NYM	6 NYM	7 ATL	8 PHI	9 PHI
10 D PHI	11	12 NYM	13 NYM	14 NYM	15 ATL	16 D ATL
17 ATL	18	19 MON	20 MON	21 D MON	22 FLA	23 FLA
24 D FLA	25	26 MON	27 MON	28 MON	29 KC	30 KC
31 KC						

SEPTEMBER
SUN	MON	TUE	WED	THU	FRI	SAT
	1	2 CWS	3 CWS	4 CWS	5 COL	6 D COL
7 D COL	8	9 SF	10 D SF	11	12 COL	13 D COL
14 D COL	15 LA	16 LA	17 CUB	18 CUB	19 PIT	20 PIT
21 D SD	22 LA	23 LA	24 CUB	25 CUB	26 CUB	27 D CUB
28 D CUB						

1997 SEASON

CLUB DIRECTORY

Chairman of the board/general partner
William O. DeWitt Jr.

Chairman
Frederick O. Hanser

President
Mark C. Lamping

Vice president, general manager
Walt Jocketty

Admin. asst. to the president and CEO
Elaine Milo

Sr. exec. asst. to v.p., general manager
Judy Carpenter-Barada

Secretary-treasurer
Andrew N. Baur

Executive officer, business operations
Bill DeWitt III

Director, ticket operations
Josie Arnold

Group director, sales
Kevin Wade

Manager, season sales
Chris Scherting

Director, group sales
Joe Strohm

Vice president, corporate sales
Dan Farrell

Vice president, community relations
Marty Hendin

Admin. asst. to the v.p., com. relations
Mary Ellen Edmiston

Director, promotions
Thane van Breusegen

Controller
Brad Wood

Director, media relations
Brian Bartow

Media relations assistants
Shawn Bertani
Mary Ford

Dir., major league player personnel
Jerry Walker

Executive, baseball operations
Tim Hanser

Director, scouting
Marty Maier

Major league trainer
Gene Gieselmann

Assistant major league trainer
Brad Henderson

Equipment manager
Buddy Bates

Assistant equipment manager
Rip Rowan

Traveling secretary
C.J. Cherre

Scouting supervisors
Jorge Aranzamendi, Jim Bayens, Jim Belz, Randy Benson, Tim Conroy, Roberto Diaz, John DiPuglia, Charles Fick, Manuel Guerra, Mike Harris, Marty Keough, Tom McCormack, Joe Morlan, Scott Nichols, Jay North, Joe Rigoli, Mike Roberts, Hal Smith, Roger Smith

Special assignment scouts
Fred McAlister, Mike Squires

National cross checker
Marty Keough

East region cross checker
Michael Roberts

Scouting assistant
John Mozeliak

Major league scout
Mike Squires

Major league advance scout
Art Kusnyer

Special assignment scout
Fred McAlister

Director, player development
Mike Jorgensen

Player development assistants
Scott Smulczenski
John Vuch

Scouts
Jorge Aranzamendi, Jim Belz, Randy Benson, Tim Conroy, Roberto Diaz, John Dipuglia, Chuck Fick, Ben Galante, Manny Guerra, Dave Karaff, Tom McCormack, Joe Morlan, Scott Nichols, Jay North, Hal Smith, Roger Smith

MINOR LEAGUE AFFILIATES

Class	Team	League	Manager
AAA	Louisville	American Association	Gaylen Pitts
AA	Arkansas	Texas	Rick Mahler
A	Prince William	Carolina	Roy Silver
A	Peoria	Midwest	Joe Cunningham
A	New Jersey	New York-Pennsylvania	Jeff Shireman
Rookie	Johnson City	Appalachian	Steve Turco

BROADCAST INFORMATION
Radio: KMOX-AM (1120).
TV: KPLR-TV (Channel 11).
Cable TV: Fox Sports Midwest.

SPRING TRAINING
Ballpark (city): Al Lang Stadium (St. Petersburg, Fla.).
Ticket information: 813-896-4641.

SPRING TRAINING ROSTER

Manager—Tony La Russa (10).
Coaches—Mark Dejohn (9), Dave Duncan (18), George Hendrick (25), Dave McKay (39), Tommie Reynolds (15).

No.	PITCHERS	B/T	Ht./Wt.	Born	1996 clubs
65	Aybar, Manuel	R/R	6-1/165	10-5-74	Arkansas, Louisville
52	Barber, Brian	R/R	6-1/175	3-4-73	Louisville, St. Louis
44	Batchelor, Richard	R/R	6-1/195	4-8-67	Louisville, St. Louis
41	Benes, Alan	R/R	6-5/215	1-21-72	St. Louis
40	Benes, Andy	R/R	6-6/245	8-20-67	St. Louis
43	Eckersley, Dennis	R/R	6-2/195	10-3-54	St. Louis
48	Fossas, Tony	L/L	6-0/198	9-23-57	St. Louis
50	Frascatore, John	R/R	6-1/200	2-4-70	Louisville
32	Honeycutt, Rick	L/L	6-1/191	6-29-54	St. Louis
29	Jackson, Danny	R/L	6-0/220	1-5-62	St. Petersburg, Louisville, St. Louis
	King, Curtis	R/R	6-5/200	10-25-70	Arkansas, St. Petersburg
54	Ludwick, Eric	R/R	6-5/220	12-14-71	Louisville, St. Louis
33	Mathews, T.J.	R/R	6-2/200	1-19-70	St. Louis
31	Osborne, Donovan	L/L	6-2/195	6-21-69	St. Petersburg, Louisville, St. Louis
	Painter, Lance	L/L	6-1/197	7-21-67	Colorado
46	Petkovsek, Mark	R/R	6-0/185	11-18-65	St. Petersburg, Louisville, St. Louis
	Raggio, Brady	R/R	6-4/210	9-17-72	Arkansas
	Stein, Blake	R/R	6-7/210	8-3-73	St. Petersburg
30	Stottlemyre, Todd	L/R	6-3/200	5-20-65	St. Louis

No.	CATCHERS	B/T	Ht./Wt.	Born	1996 clubs
49	Difelice, Mike	R/R	6-2/205	5-28-69	Louisville, St. Louis
	Lampkin, Tom	L/R	5-11/185	3-4-64	San Jose, San Francisco
71	Marrero, Eli	R/R	6-1/180	11-17-73	Arkansas
19	Pagnozzi, Tom	R/R	6-1/190	7-30-62	Louisville, St. Louis
4	Sheaffer, Danny	R/R	6-0/195	8-2-61	St. Louis

No.	INFIELDERS	B/T	Ht./Wt.	Born	1996 clubs
27	Bell, David	R/R	5-10/170	9-14-72	St. Louis, Louisville
12	Clayton, Royce	R/R	6-0/183	1-2-70	St. Louis
	DeShields, Delino	L/R	6-1/175	1-15-69	Los Angeles
8	Gaetti, Gary	R/R	6-0/205	8-19-58	St. Louis
53	Gulan, Mike	R/R	6-1/192	12-18-70	Louisville
13	Holbert, Aaron	R/R	6-0/160	1-9-73	Louisville, St. Louis
47	Mabry, John	L/R	6-4/195	10-17-70	St. Louis
	Ordaz, Luis	R/R	5-11/170	8-12-75	St. Petersburg
24	Young, Dmitri	B/R	6-2/240	10-11-73	Louisville, St. Louis

No.	OUTFIELDERS	B/T	Ht./Wt.	Born	1996 clubs
55	Bradshaw, Terry	L/R	6-0/180	2-3-69	Louisville, St. Louis
5	Gant, Ron	R/R	6-0/200	3-2-65	St. Louis
3	Jordan, Brian	R/R	6-1/205	3-29-67	St. Louis
16	Lankford, Ray	L/L	5-11/198	6-5-67	St. Louis
51	McGee, Willie	B/R	6-1/185	11-2-58	St. Louis
35	Mejia, Miguel	R/R	6-1/155	3-25-75	St. Louis, St. Petersburg
23	Sweeney, Mark	L/L	6-1/195	10-26-69	St. Louis

BALLPARK INFORMATION

Ballpark (capacity, surface)
Busch Stadium (49,676, grass)
Address
250 Stadium Plaza
St. Louis, MO 63102
Business phone
314-421-3060
Ticket information
314-421-2400
Ticket prices
$19 (field boxes-infield)
$18 (loge boxes-infield)
$16 (field boxes-outfield, loge boxes-outfield)
$14 (terrace boxes)
$13 (loge reserved-infield)
$12 (loge reserved-outfield, terrace boxes-outfield)
$11 (terrace reserved-infield)
$10 (terrace reserved-outfield)
$6 (upper terrace reserved-outfield, bleachers)
$2 (upper terrace reserved-children)
Field dimensions (from home plate)
To left field at foul line, 330 feet
To center field, 402 feet
To right field at foul line, 330 feet
First game played
May 12, 1966 (Cardinals 4, Braves 3)

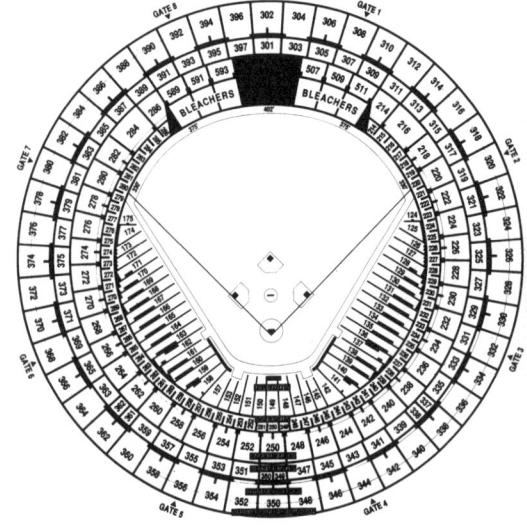

DAY BY DAY

te	Opp.	Res.	Score	(inn.*)	Hits	Opp. hits	Winning pitcher	Losing pitcher	Save	Record	Pos.	GB
	At N.Y.	L	6-7		13	10	DiPoto	Fossas	J. Franco	0-1	T4th	1
	At N.Y.	W	5-3		11	7	Stottlemyre	Person	Eckersley	1-1	T3rd	1
	At N.Y.	L	9-10		12	11	J. Franco	Eckersley		1-2	T4th	1
	At Atl.	W	5-4	(14)	10	11	Bailey	Bielecki	Eckersley	2-2	T3rd	1
	At Atl.	W	3-2	(12)	7	7	Parrett	Clontz		3-2	T2nd	1
	At Atl.	L	3-13		6	10	Schmidt	Busby		3-3	4th	1½
	Mon.	L	3-4	(10)	11	9	Rojas	Parrett		3-4	T4th	2
0	Mon.	W	4-1		9	4	Al. Benes	Paniagua		4-4	4th	1
1	Phi.	W	2-1		8	4	An. Benes	Mulholland	Mathews	5-4	T2nd	½
2	Phi.	W	6-1		12	4	Urbani	Williams		6-4	1st	+½
3	Phi.	L	2-4		11	8	Hunter	Fossas	Bottalico	6-5	1st	+½
4	Phi.	W	6-5		8	6	Mathews	Fernandez	Eckersley	7-5	T1st	...
5	Pit.	W	6-4		10	8	Al. Benes	Ericks	Honeycutt	8-5	T1st	...
6	Pit.	L	3-13		11	20	Smith	An. Benes	Lieber	8-6	T1st	...
7	Pit.	W	6-1		7	3	Osborne	Darwin		9-6	1st	+½
8	Pit.	L	2-6		5	13	Wagner	Stottlemyre		9-7	2nd	½
9	At Phi.	W	1-0		8	6	Bailey	Springer	Eckersley	10-7	2nd	½
?0	At Phi.	W	1-0		4	2	Al. Benes	Bottalico	Eckersley	11-7	1st	+½
?1	At Phi.	L	2-4		9	7	Grace	An. Benes	Bottalico	11-8	1st	+½
?2	At Mon.	L	0-8		3	10	Cormier	Osborne		11-9	1st	+½
?3	At Mon.	L	11-12		14	14	Scott	Mathews		11-10	2nd	½
?4	N.Y.	W	9-4		12	11	Petkovsek	Harnisch		12-10	1st	+½
?5	N.Y.	L	3-9		7	12	Clark	Al. Benes		12-11	1st	+½
?6	Atl.	L	1-6		8	10	Avery	An. Benes		12-12	1st	+½
?7	Atl.	L	2-7		9	11	Maddux	Osborne		12-13	2nd	½
?9	Atl.	L	1-4		7	5	Glavine	Stottlemyre	Wohlers	12-14	T2nd	1
?0	At Chi.	L	6-7		11	12	Wendell	Eckersley		12-15	4th	1
	At Chi.	L	3-9		9	12	Trachsel	An. Benes		12-16	4th	2
?	At S.D.	W	3-1		8	7	Osborne	Ashby	Eckersley	13-16	4th	2
?	At S.D.	W	4-3		5	9	Stottlemyre	Bergman	Eckersley	14-16	4th	1
?	At S.D.	L	4-10		7	15	Hamilton	Al. Benes		14-17	4th	2
?	S.F.	L	2-4		9	8	Watson	Fossas	Beck	14-18	T4th	2½
?	S.F.	L	7-10		7	15	Gardner	An. Benes	Beck	14-19	5th	2½
?	S.F.	W	16-8		16	6	Parrett	Dewey		15-19	5th	2½
?0	L.A.	L	2-3	(12)	12	9	Worrell	Eckersley		15-20	5th	2½
?1	L.A.	L	2-4		6	6	Valdes	Al. Benes	Worrell	15-21	5th	2½
?2	L.A.	W	6-5		13	10	Petkovsek	Nomo	Eckersley	16-21	T4th	1½
?3	At Fla.	L	2-5		7	6	Burkett	An. Benes	Powell	16-22	T4th	2
?4	At Fla.	L	5-11		8	13	Mathews	Parrett		16-23	T4th	2½
?5	At Fla.	W	6-0		8	4	Stottlemyre	Rapp		17-23	T4th	2½
?7	At Col.	L	11-12		10	14	Leskanic	Bailey	Ruffin	17-24	T4th	3
?8	At Col.	L	8-9		11	14	Habyan	Eckersley		17-25	5th	3
?9	At Col.	L	3-10		7	13	M. Thompson	An. Benes		17-26	5th	4
?0	At Hou.	W	5-3		14	8	Osborne	Drabek		18-26	T4th	3
?1	At Hou.	W	8-2		13	11	Stottlemyre	Reynolds		19-26	3rd	2
?2	At Hou.	W	5-2		11	5	Al. Benes	Kile	Mathews	20-26	3rd	1
?4	At Fla.	W	4-2		7	3	Morgan	Burkett	Mathews	21-26	T2nd	1
?5	At Fla.	W	5-0		12	5	An. Benes	Rapp		22-26	2nd	1
?6	At Fla.	L	2-8	(8)	8	10	Weathers	Osborne		22-27	2nd	2
?7	Col.	L	2-5		5	8	Ritz	Stottlemyre	Ruffin	22-28	2nd	3
?8	Col.	L	5-6		10	9	Painter	Mathews	Holmes	22-29	2nd	3
?9	Col.	W	6-5		9	7	Petkovsek	Leskanic	An. Benes	23-29	2nd	3
?1	Hou.	W	6-4		9	8	Osborne	Swindell	Fossas	24-29	2nd	2
1	Hou.	W	5-4	(10)	12	11	Bailey	Hernandez		25-29	2nd	1
2	Hou.	W	2-0		7	7	Stottlemyre	Kile		26-29	T1st	...
3	At S.D.	W	3-0		5	6	Al. Benes	Tewksbury		27-29	1st	+½
4	At S.D.	W	11-5		15	10	Petkovsek	Worrell		28-29	1st	+½
5	At S.D.	L	4-6		10	10	Hoffman	Fossas		28-30	2nd	½
7	At S.F.	W	9-4		13	8	An. Benes	Fernandez		29-30	T1st	...
8	At S.F.	L	1-4		5	5	DeLucia	Stottlemyre	Beck	29-31	2nd	1
9	At S.F.	L	0-9		8	16	Watson	Al. Benes		29-32	2nd	2
10	At L.A.	L	1-2		3	5	Park	Morgan	Osuna	29-33	2nd	3
11	At L.A.	W	6-3		13	12	Osborne	Martinez	Honeycutt	30-33	2nd	2
13	N.Y.	L	1-2		6	8	Person	An. Benes	Henry	30-34	2nd	1½
14	N.Y.	W	13-4		16	6	Stottlemyre	Isringhausen		31-34	2nd	1½
15	N.Y.	W	4-2		9	6	Al. Benes	B. Jones	Eckersley	32-34	2nd	1½
16	N.Y.	W	5-4		10	7	Petkovsek	Henry	Eckersley	33-34	2nd	½
18	Phi.	W	3-2		5	5	Osborne	Fernandez	Eckersley	34-34	T1st	...
19	Phi.	W	3-2		5	5	An. Benes	Bottalico		35-34	1st	+1
20	At Mon.	L	3-8		8	11	Rueter	Stottlemyre		35-35	1st	...
21	At Mon.	L	3-4	(12)	9	12	Rojas	Eckersley		35-36	2nd	1
22	At Mon.	W	9-4		9	9	Morgan	Urbina		36-36	T1st	...

1997 SEASON St. Louis Cardinals

Date	Opp.	Res.	Score	(inn.*)	Hits	Opp. hits	Winning pitcher	Losing pitcher	Save	Record	Pos.	GB
6-23	At Mon.	L	2-3		3	7	Fassero	Osborne	Rojas	36-37	T1st	...
6-24	At Atl.	W	9-2		12	9	An. Benes	Smoltz		37-37	1st	+1/
6-25	At Atl.	L	3-4		9	5	Schmidt	Stottlemyre	Wohlers	37-38	2nd	1/
6-26	At Atl.	W	11-7		17	8	Al. Benes	Avery		38-38	2nd	1/
6-27	At Atl.	L	0-3		3	8	Maddux	Morgan	Wohlers	38-39	2nd	1
6-28	Pit.	W	6-1		8	6	Osborne	Neagle		39-39	T1st	...
6-29	Pit.	W	6-5		15	11	Honeycutt	Miceli		40-39	T1st	...
6-30	Pit.	W	10-3		15	8	Stottlemyre	Smith		41-39	T1st	...
7-1	Cin.	L	5-8		8	8	Carrasco	Al. Benes	Brantley	41-40	2nd	1
7-2	Cin.	W	4-3		6	10	Honeycutt	Smith	Eckersley	42-40	2nd	1
7-3	Cin.	W	4-0		9	4	Osborne	Smiley		43-40	2nd	1
7-4	At Pit.	W	7-1		11	8	An. Benes	Dessens		44-40	2nd	1
7-5	At Pit.	W	7-4		11	9	Stottlemyre	Smith	Fossas	45-40	2nd	1
7-6	At Pit.	W	9-5		17	9	Al. Benes	Darwin		46-40	T1st	...
7-7	At Pit.	L	2-8		4	14	Lieber	Morgan		46-41	T1st	...
7-11	At Chi.	L	0-6		5	8	Navarro	Osborne		46-42	T1st	...
7-12	At Chi.	W	13-3		18	9	An. Benes	Trachsel		47-42	T1st	...
7-13	At Chi.	W	10-5		13	9	Stottlemyre	Bullinger	Eckersley	48-42	1st	+1/
7-14	At Chi.	W	7-6		13	7	Al. Benes	Adams	Eckersley	49-42	1st	+1
7-15	At Cin.	W	8-3		9	8	Morgan	Salkeld		50-42	1st	+2
7-16	At Cin.	W	5-4		13	8	Osborne	Shaw	Eckersley	51-42	1st	+3
7-17	At Cin.	W	6-4		8	8	An. Benes	Portugal	Eckersley	52-42	1st	+4
7-18	Chi.	L	5-6		9	10	Bottenfield	Petkovsek	Wendell	52-43	1st	+4
7-19	Chi.	W	9-1		13	3	Al. Benes	Castillo		53-43	1st	+4
7-20	Chi.	L	0-3		5	7	Trachsel	Morgan	Wendell	53-44	1st	+3
7-21	Chi.	W	6-5	(10)	12	13	Petkovsek	Wendell		54-44	1st	+3
7-22	Atl.	L	6-8		11	11	McMichael	Mathews	Wohlers	54-45	1st	+2
7-23	Atl.	L	2-3		5	8	Smoltz	Stottlemyre	Wohlers	54-46	1st	+2
7-24	Atl.	L	1-4		2	7	Wade	Al. Benes	McMichael	54-47	1st	+1
7-25	Mon.	L	2-4		3	11	Urbina	Petkovsek	Rojas	54-48	1st	+1/
7-26	Mon.	L	1-5		3	13	Fassero	Osborne		54-49	2nd	1/
7-27	Mon.	W	6-3		7	4	An. Benes	Dyer	Eckersley	55-49	1st	+1/
7-28	Mon.	W	6-4		7	11	Petkovsek	Martinez	Mathews	56-49	1st	+1/
7-30	At Phi.	L	7-8		9	22	Ryan	Mathews		56-50	T1st	...
8-1†	At Phi.	L	1-2		7	10	Springer	Osborne	Ryan†	56-51	2nd	1/
8-1‡	At Phi.	W	7-1		13	4	An. Benes	Mimbs		57-51	1st	+1/
8-2	At N.Y.	W	4-3		7	9	Stottlemyre	B. Jones	Honeycutt	58-51	1st	+1/
8-3	At N.Y.	L	4-5		6	6	Harnisch	Al. Benes	J. Franco	58-52	2nd	1/
8-4	At N.Y.	W	4-2		6	5	Morgan	Isringhausen	Eckersley	59-52	2nd	1/
8-5	S.D.	W	8-2		13	5	An. Benes	Tewksbury		60-52	T1st	...
8-6	S.D.	L	0-1		5	4	Worrell	Osborne	Hoffman	60-53	T1st	...
8-7	S.D.	W	1-0		5	4	Petkovsek	Bochtler		61-53	1st	+1
8-8	S.F.	L	3-5	(10)	9	12	Poole	Honeycutt	Beck	61-54	T1st	...
8-9	S.F.	L	6-8		13	16	Fernandez	Morgan	Beck	61-55	2nd	1
8-10	S.F.	W	7-1		10	7	An. Benes	VanLandingham		62-55	2nd	1
8-11	S.F.	W	5-3		8	6	Osborne	Watson	Eckersley	63-55	2nd	1
8-13	L.A.	L	4-8		7	12	Candiotti	Stottlemyre		63-56	2nd	1/
8-14	L.A.	W	6-1		11	5	Al. Benes	Valdes		64-56	2nd	1/
8-15	L.A.	L	2-5		4	11	Nomo	Morgan	Worrell	64-57	2nd	1
8-16	Fla.	W	6-2		10	7	An. Benes	Rapp		65-57	2nd	1
8-17	Fla.	W	4-3		10	6	Mathews	Powell	Eckersley	66-57	T1st	...
8-18	Fla.	W	5-3		10	7	Stottlemyre	Leiter	Eckersley	67-57	1st	+1
8-20	At Col.	L	4-5	(13)	11	10	Munoz	Mathews		67-58	2nd	1/
8-21	At Col.	L	2-10		15	18	Reynoso	An. Benes		67-59	2nd	1/
8-22	At Col.	L	5-10		8	16	Bailey	Morgan		67-60	2nd	1/
8-23	At Hou.	W	1-0		7	7	Osborne	Kile	Eckersley	68-60	1st	+1/
8-24	At Hou.	L	1-3		5	7	Reynolds	Stottlemyre		68-61	2nd	1/
8-25	At Hou.	L	1-4		3	8	Wall	Al. Benes	Hernandez	68-62	2nd	11/2
8-26	At Hou.	W	3-2		8	6	An. Benes	Hampton	Eckersley	69-62	2nd	1/
8-27	Fla.	L	3-6		6	8	Hutton	Morgan	Nen	69-63	2nd	11/2
8-28	Fla.	L	2-3	(10)	10	9	Hammond	Bailey	Nen	69-64	2nd	21/2
8-29	Fla.	L	9-10		14	13	Leiter	Stottlemyre	Nen	69-65	2nd	21/2
8-30	Col.	W	7-4		13	8	Al. Benes	Wright	Eckersley	70-65	2nd	21/2
8-31	Col.	W	2-1		5	4	An. Benes	Bailey	Eckersley	71-65	2nd	21/2
9-1	Col.	W	15-6		18	9	Petkovsek	Rekar		72-65	2nd	11/2
9-2	Hou.	W	8-7	(10)	17	13	Al. Benes	Brocail		73-65	2nd	1/
9-3	Hou.	W	12-3		15	6	Stottlemyre	Reynolds		74-65	1st	+1/
9-4	Hou.	W	6-4		9	8	An. Benes	Wall	Eckersley	75-65	1st	+11/2
9-6	S.D.	W	8-3		11	10	Petkovsek	Tewksbury		76-65	1st	+11/2
9-7	S.D.	W	8-3		10	5	Osborne	Ashby		77-65	1st	+11/2
9-8	S.D.	L	4-5		7	9	Valenzuela	Stottlemyre	Hoffman	77-66	1st	+11/2
9-9	At S.F.	W	6-2		10	6	An. Benes	Gardner		78-66	1st	+21/2
9-10	At S.F.	W	1-0		6	5	Petkovsek	Rueter	Eckersley	79-66	1st	+21/2
9-11	At S.F.	L	2-4		10	9	Scott	Al. Benes	Beck	79-67	1st	+21/2
9-12	At L.A.	L	1-4		2	6	Nomo	Osborne	Osuna	79-68	1st	+11/2

te	Opp.	Res.	Score	(inn.*)	Hits	Opp. hits	Winning pitcher	Losing pitcher	Save	Record	Pos.	GB
13	At L.A.	W	2-0		8	5	Batchelor	Guthrie	Eckersley	80-68	1st	+2½
14	At L.A.	L	5-9		11	10	Martinez	An. Benes		80-69	1st	+2½
15	At L.A.	L	5-6		7	14	Radinsky	Eckersley	Worrell	80-70	1st	+2½
17	Chi.	W	5-3		10	9	Osborne	Patterson	Mathews	81-70	1st	+3½
18	Chi.	W	5-3		10	6	Stottlemyre	Trachsel	Eckersley	82-70	1st	+4½
19	Chi.	W	5-4	(13)	9	11	Bailey	Campbell		83-70	1st	+5
20	At Cin.	L	2-4		7	5	Burba	Al. Benes	Brantley	83-71	1st	+5
22†	At Cin.	L	3-6		5	10	Shaw	Mathews	Brantley	83-72		
22‡	At Cin.	L	0-6		1	3	Smiley	Jackson		83-73	1st	+5
23	At Cin.	W	3-2		10	6	Stottlemyre	Morgan	Eckersley	84-73	1st	+5½
24	At Pit.	W	7-1		12	8	An. Benes	Loaiza		85-73	1st	+6½
25	At Pit.	W	8-7	(11)	11	7	Bailey	Miceli	Mathews	86-73	1st	+6½
27	Cin.	W	2-1	(11)	9	6	Batchelor	Shaw		87-73	1st	+7
28	Cin.	W	5-2		11	3	Jackson	Morgan	Honeycutt	88-73	1st	+7
29	Cin.	L	3-6		8	11	Lyons	Ludwick	Brantley	88-74	1st	+6

onthly records: April (12-15), May (12-14), June (17-10), July (15-11), August (15-15), September (17-9).
nnings, if other than nine. †First game of doubleheader. ‡Second game of doubleheader.

HIGHLIGHTS

gh point: The Cardinals won their first tional League Central Division title after nning just 62 games the year before.

ey then dispatched the San Diego Padres three games in the divisional playoffs d had Atlanta down 3-1 in the league ampionship series.

w point: The Cardinals were 17-26 on ay 19 after being swept in Denver. A sec-d low point was their 15-0 shellacking in me 7 of the NLCS. The Cardinals were tscored, 32-1, in their final three games the series.

rning point: After slipping nine games der .500, the Cardinals went to Houston May 20-22 and swept the Astros. A sec-t turning point came September 2 when e Cardinals erased a four-run lead to beat ouston. They went on to sweep the series d go past the Astros for good in the ntral Division race.

ost valuable player: Outfielder Brian rdan. He drove in 104 runs and batted a ague-high .422 with men in scoring posi-n. Two years ago, he batted just .042 in ose situations. Jordan also sacrificed his dy time and time again while making tches in the outfield.

ost valuable pitcher: Righthander Andy nes. From a 1-7 start, he reeled off 17 ns in his last 20 decisions (including 10 raight at one point) and pitched three rong games in postseason play. He came the pitcher everyone thought he ways should have been.

ost improved player: Shortstop Ozzie nith. He made the most strides from one ar to the next, even at age 41. Smith hit 99 in 1995 and was plagued by shoulder roblems. Last season, he batted .282 and splayed a stronger throwing arm than he d in years.

ost pleasant surprise: Third baseman ry Gaetti. He had 23 homers and 80 BIs at age 38. But it was his defense that ew the most notice. He showed better nge than expected and displayed a rong, accurate arm.

iggest disappointment: Pitcher Danny ckson. The lefthander didn't really get ntracked after missing half the season fol-

lowing ankle surgery. He was a $3.6 million investment—and a bad one, so far.

Key injuries: The torn rotator cuff suffered by center fielder Ray Lankford at the end of the regular season was costly in the play-offs. Lankford tried to play but couldn't throw or hit. Left fielder Ron Gant finished with 30 home runs but missed five early weeks because of a hamstring strain. Reliever Dennis Eckersley went on the dis-abled list for just the second time with elbow problems but bounced back strongly in the second half of the season.

Notable: The Cardinals failed to win a play-off series for the first time in their history when they lost to Atlanta. They had won five previous pre-World Series playoffs. . . . Eckersley failed to win a game for the first time in his 22-year career. . . . Gant's 30 homers were the most by a Cardinals left fielder since Stan Musial hit 32 in 1951. . . . Lankford hit a 468-foot homer into the upper deck in right field on April 17 vs. Pittsburgh, the longest ever by a Cardinal at Busch Stadium. . . . John Mabry hit for the cycle on May 18 at Colorado, the first Cardinal since Ken Boyer in 1964 to do it in order (single, double, triple, homer). . . . Three players hit 20 homers—Lankford, Gaetti and Gant. Three players stole 20 bases—Lankford, Jordan and Royce Clayton. . . . Tony La Russa ended the sea-son ranked first among active managers in career wins (1,408).

—RICK HUMMEL

RECORDS

1996 regular-season record: 88-74 (1st in N.L. Central); 48-33 at home; 40-41 on road; 29-32 vs. East; 37-15 vs. Central; 22-27 vs. West; 18-18 vs. lefthanded starters; 70-56 vs. righthanded starters; 70-60 on grass; 18-14 on turf; 27-27 in daytime; 61-47 at night; 30-25 in one-run games; 8-6 in extra-inning games; 0-1 in doubleheaders.

Team record past five years: 373-370 (.502, ranks 5th in league in that span).

TEAM LEADERS

Batting average: Brian Jordan (.310).
At-bats: Ray Lankford (545).

Runs: Ray Lankford (100).
Hits: John Mabry (161).
Total bases: Ray Lankford (265).
Doubles: Brian Jordan, Ray Lankford (36).
Triples: Ray Lankford (8).
Home runs: Ron Gant (30).
Runs batted in: Brian Jordan (104).
Stolen bases: Ray Lankford (35).
Slugging percentage: Ron Gant (.504).
On-base percentage: Ray Lankford (.366).
Wins: Andy Benes (18).
Earned-run average: Donovan Osborne (3.53).
Complete games: Todd Stottlemyre (5).
Shutouts: Todd Stottlemyre (2).
Saves: Dennis Eckersley (30).
Innings pitched: Andy Benes (230.1).
Strikeouts: Todd Stottlemyre (194).

GAMES BY POSITION

Catcher: Tom Pagnozzi 116, Danny Sheaffer 47, Pat Borders 17, Mike Difelice 4.
First base: John Mabry 146, Mark Sweeney 15, Gary Gaetti 14, Dmitri Young 10, Willie McGee 6, Danny Sheaffer 6, Pat Borders 1, Brian Jordan 1, Tom Pagnozzi 1.
Second base: Luis Alicea 125, Mike Gallego 43, David Bell 20, Aaron Holbert 1.
Third base: Gary Gaetti 133, David Bell 45, Danny Sheaffer 17, Mike Gallego 7.
Shortstop: Royce Clayton 113, Ozzie Smith 52, David Bell 1, Mike Gallego 1.
Outfield: Ray Lankford 144, Brian Jordan 136, Ron Gant 116, Willie McGee 83, Mark Sweeney 43, Miguel Mejia 21, John Mabry 14, Terry Bradshaw 7, Danny Sheaffer 3.

TOP DRAFT CHOICES

1. Braden Looper, RHP, Wichita State Univ.
2. None.
3. Brent Butler, SS, Scotland County H.S., Laurinburg, N.C.
4. Bryan Britt, OF, UNC Wilmington.
5. Jeff Rizzo, 3B, La Jolla (Calif.) H.S.
6. Jim Gargiulo, C, University of Miami.
7. Kevin Sheredy, RHP, UCLA.
8. Dave Schmidt, C, Oregon State Univ.
9. Shawn Hogge, RHP, Western H.S., Las Vegas.
10. Cordell Farley, OF, Va. Commonwealth U.

1997 SEASON St. Louis Cardinals

SAN DIEGO PADRES
NATIONAL LEAGUE WEST DIVISION

1997 PADRES SCHEDULE

Home games shaded.
* — All-Star Game at Jacobs Field (Cleveland)
D — Day game (any game starting before 5 p.m.)

APRIL
SUN	MON	TUE	WED	THU	FRI	SAT
		1 D NYM	2 NYM	3 D NYM	4 D PHI	5 PHI
6 D PHI	7 PIT	8 PIT	9 PIT	10	11 D PHI	12 PHI
13 D PHI	14	15 PIT	16 PIT	17	18 STL	19 STL
20 STL	21	22 HOU	23 HOU	24	25 ATL	26 ATL
27 ATL	28 FLA	29 FLA	30 NYM			

MAY
SUN	MON	TUE	WED	THU	FRI	SAT
				1 NYM	2 MON	3 MON
4 D MON	5	6 CUB	7 CUB	8 CUB	9 CIN	10 CIN
11 D CIN	12	13 MON	14 D MON	15 CUB	16 D CUB	17 D CUB
18 D CIN	19 D CIN	20 LA	21 LA	22 LA	23 FLA	24 FLA
25 D FLA	26 ATL	27 ATL	28	29 HOU	30 HOU	31 HOU

JUNE
SUN	MON	TUE	WED	THU	FRI	SAT
1 D HOU	2 ATL	3 ATL	4 COL	5 COL	6 D HOU	7 HOU
8 D HOU	9 STL	10 STL	11 STL	12 ANA	13 ANA	14 TEX
15 TEX	16	17 OAK	18 OAK	19 D COL	20 COL	21 COL
22 COL	23 SF	24 D SF	25 D SF	26 LA	27 LA	28 D LA
29 LA	30 OAK					

JULY
SUN	MON	TUE	WED	THU	FRI	SAT
		1 D OAK	2 D SEA	3 SEA	4 LA	5 D LA
6 D LA	7	8 ° D	9 COL	10 COL	11 COL	12 D COL
13 D COL	14 SF	15 SF	16 STL	17 STL	18 FLA	19 FLA
20 D FLA	21 D PIT	22 PIT	23 PIT	24 D PIT	25 NYM	26 NYM
27 D NYM	28 PHI	29 PHI	30	31 MON		

AUGUST
SUN	MON	TUE	WED	THU	FRI	SAT
					1 MON	2 MON
3 D MON	4	5 CIN	6 CIN	7 CIN	8 D CUB	9 D CUB
10 D CUB	11 MON	12 MON	13 CIN	14 CIN	15 D CUB	16 CUB
17 D CUB	18	19 PIT	20 PIT	21 PIT	22 NYM	23 NYM
24 D NYM	25 PHI	26 PHI	27 PHI	28 D ANA	29 ANA	30 TEX
31 D TEX						

SEPTEMBER
SUN	MON	TUE	WED	THU	FRI	SAT
	1 SEA	2	3 SEA	4 D ATL	5 ATL	6 ATL
7 D ATL	8	9 FLA	10 FLA	11	12 D STL	13 STL
14 D STL	15 HOU	16 HOU	17 D COL	18 COL	19 SF	20 SF
21 D SF	22 SF	23 LA	24 LA	25	26 SF	27 D SF
28 D SF						

1997 SEASON

CLUB DIRECTORY

Chairman
John Moores
President & chief executive officer
Larry Lucchino
Executive vice president
Bill Adams
V.p./baseball operations and g.m.
Kevin Towers
Vice president/marketing
Don Johnson
Vice president/public affairs
Charles Steinberg
Vice president/finance
Bob Wells
Assistant general manager
Fred Uhlman Jr.
Director/community relations
Michele Anderson
Director/merchandising
Michael Babida
Director/corporate development
Michael Dee
Controller
Steve Fitch
Director/administrative services
Lucy Freeman
Director/ticket operations & services
Dave Gilmore
Director/stadium operations
Mark Guglielmo
Director/Hispanic marketing
Enrique Morones
Director/Padres Foundation
Jennifer Moores
Director/player development
Jim Skaalen
Director/minor league administration
Priscilla Oppenheimer
Club counsel
Alan Ostfield
Dir./major league admin. and team travel
Roger Riley

Director/media relations
Ken Nigro
Director/fan services
Tim Katzman
Director/sales
Louis Ruvane
Director/scouting
Brad Sloan
Trainer
Larry Duensing
Assistant trainer
Todd Hutcheson
Strength and conditioning coach
Sam Gannelli
Club physicians
Cliff Colwell
Jan Fronek
Paul Hirshman
Blaine Phillips
Major league scouts
Ken Bracey
Ray Crone Sr.
Advance scout
Jeff Gardner
Supervisor
Bob Cummings, Andy Hancock, Jim Woodward
Area scouts
Chas Bolton, Howard Bowens, Eddie Dixon, Jimmy Dreyer, Denny Galehouse, Ronquito Garcia, Rich Hacker, Gary Kendall, Don Lyle, Tim McWilliam, Bill Mele, Juan Melo, Rene Mons, Pat Murtaugh, Steve Nichols, Gary Roenicke, Van Smith, Mark Wasinger, Gene Watson
Part-time scouts
Cesar Berroteran, Bob Buob, Julio Coronado, Leroy Dreyer, Robert Gutierrez, Timothy Harkness, William Killian, Steve Leavitt, Darry Milne, Chuck Pierce, Gene Thompson

MINOR LEAGUE AFFILIATES

Class	Team	League	Manager
AAA	Las Vegas	Pacific Coast	Jerry Royster
AA	Mobile	Southern	Mike Ramsey
A	Rancho Cucamonga	California	Mike Basso
A	Clinton	Midwest	Tom Le Vasseur
Rookie	Idaho Falls	Pioneer	Don Werner
Rookie	Peoria Padres	Arizona	Randy Whisler

BROADCAST INFORMATION
Radio: KFMB-AM (760).
TV: To be announced.
Cable TV: Channel 4 Padres.

SPRING TRAINING
Ballpark (city): Peoria Stadium (Peoria, Ariz.).
Ticket information: 602-878-4337.

SPRING TRAINING ROSTER

Manager—Bruce Bochy (15).
Coaches—Greg Booker (38), Tim Flannery (11), Davey Lopes (42), Rob Picciolo (5), Merv Rettenmund (16), Dan Warthen (37).

No.	PITCHERS	B/T	Ht./Wt.	Born	1996 clubs
53	Ashby, Andy	R/R	6-5/190	7-11-67	San Diego
44	Bergman, Sean	R/R	6-4/225	4-11-70	San Diego
45	Berumen, Andres	R/R	6-2/205	4-5-71	Las Vegas, San Diego
45	Bochtler, Doug	R/R	6-3/200	7-5-70	San Diego
49	Cunnane, Will	R/R	6-2/175	4-24-74	Portland
	Dennis, Shane	R/L	6-2/200	7-3-71	Rancho Cucamonga, Memphis
40	Eischen, Joey	L/L	6-1/190	5-25-70	Los Angeles, Detroit
50	Erdos, Todd	R/R	6-1/190	11-21-73	Rancho Cucamonga
40	Hamilton, Joey	R/R	6-4/230	9-9-70	San Diego
41	Hitchcock, Sterling	L/L	6-1/192	4-29-71	Seattle
51	Hoffman, Trevor	R/R	6-0/205	10-13-67	San Diego
56	Kaufman, Brad	R/R	6-2/210	4-26-72	Memphis
54	Kroon, Marc	R/R	6-2/195	4-2-73	Memphis
42	Long, Joey	R/L	6-2/220	7-15-70	Memphis, Las Vegas
46	Murphy, Rob	L/L	6-2/215	5-26-60	DID NOT PLAY
18	Murray, Heath	L/L	6-4/205	4-19-73	Memphis
46	Smith, Cam	R/R	6-3/185	9-20-73	Lakeland
	Valenzuela, Fernando	L/L	5-11/202	11-1-60	San Diego
53	Veras, Dario	R/R	6-1/155	3-13-73	Memphis, Las Vegas, San Diego
36	Worrell, Tim	R/R	6-1/190	7-5-67	San Diego

No.	CATCHERS	B/T	Ht./Wt.	Born	1996 clubs
23	Flaherty, John	R/R	6-1/205	10-21-67	Detroit, San Diego
59	Mulligan, Sean	R/R	6-2/210	4-25-70	Las Vegas, San Diego
11	Slaught, Don	R/R	6-1/185	9-11-58	California, Chicago A.L.

No.	INFIELDERS	B/T	Ht./Wt.	Born	1996 clubs
7	Bush, Homer	R/R	5-10/175	11-12-72	Las Vegas
21	Caminiti, Ken	B/R	6-0/200	4-21-63	San Diego
29	Cianfrocco, Archi	R/R	6-5/215	10-6-66	San Diego
10	Gomez, Chris	R/R	6-1/195	6-16-71	Detroit, San Diego
22	Joyner, Wally	L/L	6-2/200	6-16-62	San Diego, Rancho Cucamonga
52	Lee, Derrek	R/R	6-5/205	9-6-75	Memphis
8	Livingstone, Scott	L/R	6-0/190	7-15-65	San Diego
1	Lopez, Luis	B/R	5-11/175	9-4-70	Las Vegas, San Diego
63	Melo, Juan	B/R	6-1/160	5-11-76	Rancho Cucamonga
3	Reed, Jody	R/R	5-9/165	7-26-62	San Diego
48	Shipley, Craig	R/R	6-1/190	1-7-63	San Diego, Las Vegas, Arizona Padres
35	Thompson, Jason	L/L	6-4/205	6-13-71	San Diego, Las Vegas
57	Velandia, Jorge	R/R	5-9/160	1-12-75	Memphis
4	Veras, Quilvio	B/R	5-9/166	4-3-71	Florida, Charlotte

No.	OUTFIELDERS	B/T	Ht./Wt.	Born	1996 clubs
12	Finley, Steve	L/L	6-2/180	3-12-65	San Diego
19	Gwynn, Tony	L/L	5-11/220	5-9-60	San Diego
24	Henderson, Rickey	R/L	5-10/190	12-25-58	San Diego
58	Johnson, Earl	B/R	5-10/165	10-3-71	Memphis
20	Jones, Chris	R/R	6-2/205	12-16-65	New York N.L.
23	Vaughn, Greg	R/R	6-0/202	7-3-65	Milwaukee, San Diego

BALLPARK INFORMATION

Ballpark (capacity, surface)
San Diego/Jack Murphy Stadium (46,510, grass)

Address
P.O. Box 2000
San Diego, CA 92112-2000

Business phone
619-283-4494

Ticket information
619-283-4494, 888-723-7379

Ticket prices
$16 (sky boxes, field level, IF)
$14.50 (field level/OF, plaza level/IF)
$13 (plaza level/OF)
$12.50 (loge level)
$11 (press level)
$8 (left field grandstand)
$6 (view)
$5 (bleachers)

Field dimensions (from home plate)
To left field at foul line, 327 feet
To center field, 405 feet
To right field at foul line, 327 feet

First game played
April 8, 1969 (Padres 2, Astros 1)

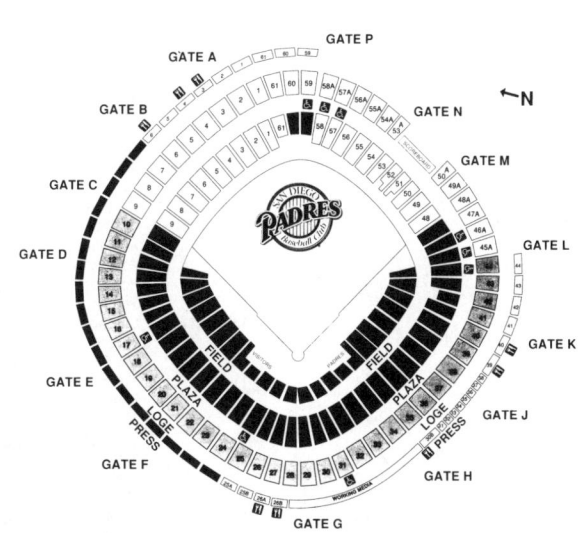

DAY BY DAY

Date	Opp.	Res.	Score	(inn.*)	Hits	Opp. hits	Winning pitcher	Losing pitcher	Save	Record	Pos.	GB
4-1	At Chi.	L	4-5	(10)	6	8	Patterson	Hoffman		0-1	T3rd	1
4-3	At Chi.	W	7-5		12	8	Hamilton	Castillo	Hoffman	1-1	T1st	...
4-5	At Hou.	W	10-4		15	9	Tewksbury	Kile		2-1	1st	+1/2
4-6	At Hou.	W	8-4	(13)	15	10	Hoffman	Small		3-1	1st	+1 1/2
4-7	At Hou.	W	17-2		17	4	Bergman	Swindell		4-1	1st	+1 1/2
4-8	Fla.	W	9-2		10	6	Hamilton	Hammond		5-1	1st	+2 1/2
4-9	Fla.	L	2-5	(10)	8	7	Leiter	Blair		5-2	1st	+1 1/2
4-10	Fla.	W	3-0		11	5	Tewksbury	Rapp	Hoffman	6-2	1st	+1 1/2
4-11	Atl.	W	2-1		5	4	Ashby	Maddux	Hoffman	7-2	1st	+2
4-12	Atl.	L	3-5		9	9	Schmidt	Bergman	Wohlers	7-3	1st	+1
4-13	Atl.	W	6-2		11	8	Hamilton	Glavine	Bochtler	8-3	1st	+1
4-14	Atl.	L	0-4		2	11	Smoltz	Valenzuela		8-4	1st	+1
4-15	At Col.	L	9-11		12	16	Ruffin	Blair	Leskanic	8-5	1st	+1/2
4-16	At Col.	W	10-6		19	10	Ashby	Reynoso		9-5	1st	+1/2
4-17	At Col.	W	11-6		17	13	Florie	Freeman		10-5	1st	+1 1/2
4-19	At Atl.	L	1-7		3	8	Smoltz	Hamilton		10-6	1st	+2
4-20	At Atl.	L	5-6		12	10	McMichael	Bochtler	Wohlers	10-7	1st	+1
4-21	At Atl.	W	2-1	(15)	14	6	Worrell	Thobe	Bochtler	11-7	1st	+1
4-22	At Fla.	W	5-3		10	7	Ashby	Burkett		12-7	1st	+2
4-23	At Fla.	W	7-2		11	5	Bergman	Hammond		13-7	1st	+2 1/2
4-24	Chi.	W	5-4		10	8	Hamilton	Foster	Hoffman	14-7	1st	+3 1/2
4-25	Chi.	W	8-3		11	5	Tewksbury	Bullinger		15-7	1st	+4
4-26	Hou.	W	3-2		6	7	Worrell	Hampton	Hoffman	16-7	1st	+4 1/2
4-27	Hou.	L	0-6		4	12	Reynolds	Ashby		16-8	1st	+4
4-28	Hou.	L	2-3		5	9	Kile	Bergman	Jones	16-9	1st	+3
4-29	Hou.	W	2-0		6	4	Hamilton	Brocail		17-9	1st	+3 1/2
4-30	S.F.	L	4-9		8	11	Watson	Tewksbury		17-10	1st	+2 1/2
5-1	S.F.	W	9-4		11	10	Valenzuela	Gardner		18-10	1st	+3 1/2
5-3	St.L.	L	1-3		7	8	Osborne	Ashby	Eckersley	18-11	1st	+3 1/2
5-4	St.L.	L	3-4		9	5	Stottlemyre	Bergman	Eckersley	18-12	1st	+3
5-5	St.L.	W	10-4		15	7	Hamilton	Al. Benes		19-12	1st	+3
5-8†	At Pit.	W	5-4		6	8	Tewksbury	May	Hoffman	20-12		
5-8‡	At Pit.	L	3-4		6	8	Christiansen	Sanders	Cordova	20-13	1st	+3 1/2
5-9	At Pit.	W	7-1		11	9	Ashby	Wagner		21-13	1st	+4 1/2
5-10	At Cin.	L	6-8		14	8	McElroy	Florie	Brantley	21-14	1st	+3 1/2
5-11	At Cin.	L	0-1		6	3	Smiley	Hamilton	Brantley	21-15	1st	+2 1/2
5-12	At Cin.	W	5-0		9	7	Tewksbury	Burba		22-15	1st	+2 1/2
5-13	N.Y.	W	5-2		10	7	Valenzuela	Isringhausen		23-15	1st	+2 1/2
5-14	N.Y.	W	9-4		10	10	Ashby	Wilson		24-15	1st	+3 1/2
5-15	N.Y.	W	4-3	(10)	9	5	Worrell	J. Franco		25-15	1st	+4 1/2
5-16	N.Y.	L	3-6		5	12	Harnisch	Hamilton	J. Franco	25-16	1st	+4
5-17	Mon.	W	2-1	(12)	5	7	Hoffman	Rojas		26-16	1st	+4 1/2
5-18	Mon.	L	2-3		6	9	Urbina	Valenzuela	Rojas	26-17	1st	+3 1/2
5-19	Mon.	W	4-3		7	11	Worrell	Veres	Hoffman	27-17	1st	+4
5-21	Phi.	L	4-5		9	9	Mulholland	Bergman	Bottalico	27-18	1st	+2 1/2
5-22	Phi.	W	5-2		7	6	Hamilton	Grace	Hoffman	28-18	1st	+3 1/2
5-23	Phi.	W	7-5		14	11	Sanders	Springer	Hoffman	29-18	1st	+4
5-24	At N.Y.	W	13-1		16	6	Valenzuela	Isringhausen		30-18	1st	+5
5-25	At N.Y.	W	7-2		10	10	Ashby	Wilson		31-18	1st	+5
5-26	At N.Y.	L	0-1		6	6	B. Jones	Bergman	J. Franco	31-19	1st	+4 1/2
5-27	At Mon.	W	4-3		6	7	Hamilton	Fassero	Hoffman	32-19	1st	+5
5-28	At Mon.	W	3-2	(10)	7	5	Hoffman	Scott	Bochtler	33-19	1st	+6
5-29	At Mon.	L	4-9		10	13	Urbina	Valenzuela		33-20	1st	+5
5-31	At Phi.	W	4-2		7	3	Ashby	Mulholland	Hoffman	34-20	1st	+5 1/2
6-1	At Phi.	W	8-3		10	9	Bergman	Mimbs		35-20	1st	+6 1/2
6-2	At Phi.	L	8-9	(12)	8	16	Borland	Hoffman		35-21	1st	+5 1/2
6-3	St.L.	L	0-3		6	5	Al. Benes	Tewksbury		35-22	1st	+5
6-4	St.L.	L	5-11		10	15	Petkovsek	Worrell		35-23	1st	+5
6-5	St.L.	W	6-4		10	10	Hoffman	Fossas		36-23	T1st	+6
6-7	Pit.	L	0-10		6	13	Smith	Bergman		36-24	1st	+5 1/2
6-8	Pit.	L	8-9	(14)	13	17	Cordova	Blair		36-25	1st	+4 1/2
6-9	Pit.	L	0-6		6	12	Darwin	Tewksbury		36-26	1st	+3 1/2
6-10	Cin.	L	3-6		9	10	Smith	Bochtler	Brantley	36-27	1st	+2 1/2
6-11	Cin.	L	1-4		11	9	Jarvis	Valenzuela	Brantley	36-28	1st	+2 1/2
6-12	Cin.	L	4-9		6	14	Smiley	Florie		36-29	1st	+2
6-13	At Chi.	L	3-6	(14)	12	9	Jones	Blair		36-30	1st	+1
6-14	At Chi.	L	1-5		5	5	Trachsel	Tewksbury		36-31	1st	+1
6-15	At Chi.	W	2-1		4	5	Worrell	Navarro	Hoffman	37-31	1st	+1
6-16	At Chi.	L	4-8		4	9	Castillo	Valenzuela	Bullinger	37-32	T1st	...
6-17	At Atl.	L	3-9		5	10	Maddux	Bergman		37-33	2nd	1/2
6-18	At Atl.	L	3-5		10	10	Clontz	Hamilton	Wohlers	37-34	2nd	1
6-19	At Atl.	L	1-5		2	11	Smoltz	Tewksbury		37-35	4th	2

Date	Opp.	Res.	Score	(inn.*)	Hits	Opp. hits	Winning pitcher	Losing pitcher	Save	Record	Pos.	GB
0	Chi.	L	2-3		5	7	Navarro	Worrell	Wendell	37-36	4th	2
1	Chi.	W	2-1	(10)	9	5	Hoffman	Wendell		38-36	T2nd	1
2	Chi.	L	6-9	(16)	11	21	Myers	Blair		38-37	T2nd	2
3	Chi.	W	5-4		9	7	Hamilton	Telemaco	Hoffman	39-37	2nd	2
5	Hou.	L	4-9		11	6	Jones	Sanders		39-38	2nd	2
6	Hou.	L	3-4		10	8	Wall	Worrell	Wagner	39-39	2nd	2
7	At S.F.	W	11-1		12	7	Valenzuela	Gardner		40-39	2nd	1
8	At S.F.	W	6-1		9	6	Ashby	Fernandez	Hoffman	41-39	T1st	...
9	At S.F.	W	7-6		12	8	Blair	Beck	Hoffman	42-39	T1st	...
30	At S.F.	W	7-4		16	14	Tewksbury	VanLandingham	Hoffman	43-39	1st	+1
1	L.A.	L	2-10		11	17	Candiotti	Worrell		43-40	T1st	...
2	L.A.	L	3-7		9	11	Astacio	Valenzuela		43-41	2nd	1
3	L.A.	W	3-2		6	8	Hamilton	Martinez	Hoffman	44-41	T1st	...
4	S.F.	W	8-4		11	12	Tewksbury	Leiter		45-41	T1st	...
5	S.F.	W	7-6	(11)	13	7	Bergman	Bautista		46-41	T1st	...
6	S.F.	W	7-3		12	8	Worrell	Bourgeois	Hoffman	47-41	T1st	...
7	S.F.	W	10-3		10	7	Valenzuela	Fernandez		48-41	1st	+1
11	At Col.	L	5-8	(10)	12	13	Ruffin	Hoffman		48-42	T1st	...
12	At Col.	L	12-13		14	12	Holmes	Blair		48-43	2nd	1
13	At Col.	L	6-11		11	11	Ritz	Sanders		48-44	2nd	1
14	At Col.	L	4-8		8	13	Reynoso	Valenzuela		48-45	2nd	1
15	At L.A.	L	0-1	(10)	5	7	Guthrie	Hoffman		48-46	3rd	2
16	At L.A.	W	10-1		11	7	Tewksbury	Martinez	Worrell	49-46	3rd	1
17	At L.A.	W	5-4		11	7	Florie	Osuna	Hoffman	50-46	T2nd	1/2
18	Col.	W	9-2		12	7	Sanders	Ritz		51-46	T1st	...
19	Col.	W	4-3		7	7	Valenzuela	Reynoso	Hoffman	52-46	1st	+1
20	Col.	L	4-5		11	8	Leskanic	Bochtler	Ruffin	52-47	1st	+1/2
21	Col.	W	2-0		6	5	Tewksbury	Freeman	Hoffman	53-47	1st	+1
22	At Hou.	L	0-1		4	3	Reynolds	Hamilton	Wagner	53-48	1st	+1/2
23	At Hou.	W	7-4		11	7	Sanders	Hampton	Hoffman	54-48	1st	+1/2
24	At Hou.	L	4-6	(10)	9	10	Hernandez	Villone		54-49	2nd	1/2
26	At Fla.	W	3-0	(11)	8	4	Hoffman	Pall		55-49	1st	+1
27	At Fla.	W	20-12		19	17	Villone	Mathews		56-49	1st	+1
28	At Fla.	L	2-8		2	15	Leiter	Hamilton		56-50	1st	+1
29	At Fla.	W	5-3		7	5	Sanders	Brown	Hoffman	57-50	1st	+1 1/2
30	Atl.	W	2-1		8	7	Valenzuela	Maddux	Hoffman	58-50	1st	+1 1/2
31	Atl.	L	4-7		10	11	Glavine	Tewksbury	Wohlers	58-51	1st	+1/2
1	Atl.	L	2-3		6	11	Bielecki	Worrell	Wohlers	58-52	1st	+1/2
2	Fla.	W	2-1		6	7	Hoffman	Perez		59-52	1st	+1/2
3	Fla.	L	2-5		3	9	Brown	Sanders	Nen	59-53	1st	+1/2
4	Fla.	W	6-4		8	11	Valenzuela	Hammond	Hoffman	60-53	1st	+1 1/2
5	At St.L.	L	2-8		5	13	An. Benes	Tewksbury		60-54	1st	+1
6	At St.L.	W	1-0		4	5	Worrell	Osborne	Hoffman	61-54	1st	+1
7	At St.L.	L	0-1		4	5	Petkovsek	Bochtler		61-55	1st	+1
8	At Pit.	W	12-3		19	6	Sanders	Peters		62-55	1st	+1 1/2
9	At Pit.	W	4-1		9	3	Valenzuela	Miceli	Hoffman	63-55	1st	+1 1/2
10	At Pit.	W	6-2		12	9	Veras	Plesac		64-55	1st	+1 1/2
11	At Pit.	W	7-5		10	14	Bergman	Parris	Hoffman	65-55	1st	+2 1/2
13	At Cin.	L	4-10		8	12	Jarvis	Hamilton		65-56	1st	+1
14	At Cin.	L	1-2	(13)	8	7	Smith	Bergman		65-57	1st	+1
15	At Cin.	L	2-3		6	9	Burba	Tewksbury	Brantley	65-58	T1st	...
16	N.Y.§	W	15-10		14	13	Valenzuela	Person		66-58	T1st	...
17	N.Y.§	L	3-7		12	12	Clark	Worrell	Henry	66-59	2nd	1
18	N.Y.§	W	8-0		12	7	Hamilton	Wilson		67-59	T1st	...
19	Mon.	W	7-3		12	6	Sanders	Martinez	Hoffman	68-59	1st	+1/2
20	Mon.	W	3-0		8	3	Tewksbury	Cormier	Hoffman	69-59	1st	+1 1/2
21	Mon.	W	7-2		11	5	Valenzuela	Urbina		70-59	1st	+2 1/2
23	Phi.	L	4-7		7	10	Hunter	Worrell	Bottalico	70-60	1st	+1
24	Phi.	W	7-1		13	3	Hamilton	Beech		71-60	1st	+1
25	Phi.	W	11-2		17	12	Sanders	West		72-60	1st	+1
27	At N.Y.	W	4-3		8	7	Blair	Mlicki	Hoffman	73-60	1st	+1
28	At N.Y.	W	3-2	(12)	13	8	Bergman	Wallace	Hoffman	74-60	1st	+2
29	At N.Y.	W	3-2		11	6	Hamilton	Wilson	Hoffman	75-60	1st	+2
30	At Mon.	W	6-0		13	2	Sanders	Paniagua		76-60	1st	+2
31	At Mon.	L	2-4		4	8	Daal	Tewksbury	Rojas	76-61	1st	+1
1	At Mon.	L	6-7		10	12	Fassero	Ashby	Rojas	76-62	1st	+1
2	At Phi.	W	5-1		10	8	Valenzuela	Hunter		77-62	1st	+1
3	At Phi.	L	2-8		5	13	Mimbs	Hamilton	Ryan	77-63	T1st	...
4	At Phi.	W	2-1		9	4	Sanders	Beech	Hoffman	78-63	1st	+1
6	At St.L.	L	3-8		10	11	Petkovsek	Tewksbury		78-64	T1st	...
7	At St.L.	L	3-8		5	10	Osborne	Ashby		78-65	2nd	1
8	At St.L.	W	5-4		9	7	Valenzuela	Stottlemyre	Hoffman	79-65	T1st	...
9	Pit.	W	6-5		7	11	Hermanson	Wilkins	Hoffman	80-65	T1st	...
10	Pit.	W	6-5		12	11	Hoffman	Boever		81-65	T1st	...
11	Pit.	W	8-7		15	12	Bochtler	Ericks		82-65	T1st	...

Date	Opp.	Res.	Score	(inn.*)	Hits	Opp. hits	Winning pitcher	Losing pitcher	Save	Record	Pos.	GB
9-13	Cin.	L	1-3		6	6	Morgan	Ashby	Brantley	82-66	2nd	1/2
9-14	Cin.	W	3-2	(12)	9	6	Veras	Smith		83-66	2nd	1/2
9-15	Cin.	W	8-0		15	8	Hamilton	Jarvis	Blair	84-66	2nd	1/2
9-16	At S.F.	W	2-1	(11)	8	8	Hoffman	Beck		85-66	2nd	1/2
9-17	At S.F.	L	7-9		8	11	Poole	Veras	Beck	85-67	2nd	1 1/2
9-18	At S.F.	W	8-5		11	11	Bochtler	DeLucia	Hoffman	86-67	2nd	1/2
9-19	L.A.	L	0-7		6	8	Martinez	Valenzuela		86-68	2nd	1 1/2
9-20	L.A.	W	4-2		9	3	Hamilton	Candiotti	Hoffman	87-68	2nd	1/2
9-21	L.A.	L	2-9		4	16	Valdes	Sanders		87-69	2nd	1 1/2
9-22	L.A.	W	3-2		10	8	Ashby	Nomo	Hoffman	88-69	2nd	1/2
9-24	Col.	L	4-5	(11)	15	8	Ruffin	Hoffman	Swift	88-70	2nd	1 1/2
9-25	Col.	L	3-5		9	9	M. Thompson	Hamilton	Ruffin	88-71	2nd	2 1/2
9-27	At L.A.	W	5-2	(10)	11	8	Worrell	Osuna	Hoffman	89-71	2nd	1
9-28	At L.A.	W	4-2		10	5	Worrell	Dreifort	Hoffman	90-71	T1st	...
9-29	At L.A.	W	2-0	(11)	7	4	Veras	Park	Hoffman	91-71	1st	+1

Monthly records: April (17-10), May (17-10), June (9-19), July (15-12), August (18-10), September (15-10).
*Innings, if other than nine. †First game of doubleheader. ‡Second game of doubleheader. §At Monterrey, Mexico.

HIGHLIGHTS

High point: In the season's final three days, the Padres swept a three-game series at Dodger Stadium to finish atop the N.L. West by one game over Los Angeles. By sweeping, the club set a franchise record for road wins (46) and finished with 91 victories overall, the second-highest total in team history ('84 Padres are first with 92).

Low point: After moving to 35-20 June 1 (the best 55-game start in franchise history), the Padres lost the next game in Philadelphia and lost first baseman Wally Joyner, who broke his left thumb, until after the All-Star break. The team went on to lose 19 of its next 23.

Turning point: On June 27, the Padres hit five home runs in San Francisco to win, 11-1, and went on to sweep the four-game series. A week later, they won four more from the Giants to assume first place entering the All-Star break.

Most valuable player: Third baseman Ken Caminiti. He was the first Padre to win league MVP honors. He overcame several injuries to hit 40 home runs, drive in 130 runs and bat .326. His teammates said he was an inspiration to them.

Most improved player: Center fielder Steve Finley. For the second consecutive year, he reached career-highs in batting average (.298), runs (126) and hits (195), but this time he also produced a power explosion: 30 home runs, which was 19 more than his career-best total.

Most pleasant surprise: Pitcher Fernando Valenzuela. Thought to be washed up by many scouts, he posted his best numbers in 10 years, going 13-8 with an ERA of 3.62. He was 8-2 with a 3.39 ERA after the All-Star break.

Biggest disappointment: Outfielder Greg Vaughn. Acquired August 1 from Milwaukee, the All-Star slugger batted .206 and .125 with men in scoring position.

Key injuries: Ken Caminiti suffered a left rotator cuff tear that required surgery in October. Wally Joyner's thumb injury sidelined him for six weeks, after which he hit only .161 against lefthanders. Tony Gwynn was sidelined five weeks with an Achilles' tendon injury. Torn shoulder cartilage sent pitcher Andy Ashby to the disabled list three times. Scott Livingstone, the team's top pinch-hitter, was sidelined in June with back pain.

Notable: From July 22 through September 8, the Padres played 44 games in 10 different cities and three different countries, going 26-18. . . . Gwynn is the only Padre to play on both the '84 and '96 division title-winning teams. He played 1,648 regular-season games between postseason appearances. . . . Gwynn won his seventh N.L. batting title, moving him to within one of Honus Wagner's league record eight between 1900 and 1911. . . . Caminiti and Finley combined for more home runs (70) and RBIs (225) than any tandem in club history. . . . On July 9 at Philadelphia, Caminiti hit the first Padres homer in All-Star Game history. . . . The Padres set club records for most extra-inning games (24) and wins (13). . . . The Padres never were more than 2 1/2 games out of first place and held the top spot for 142 days. . . . The Padres set club record for sellouts (nine), crowds of 40,000 or more (17) and crowds of 50,000 or more (seven).

—TOM KRASOVIC

RECORDS

1996 regular-season record: 91-71 (1st in N.L. West); 45-36 at home; 46-35 on road; 39-23 vs. East; 28-33 vs. Central; 24-15 vs. West; 24-17 vs. lefthanded starters; 67-54 vs. righthanded starters; 73-58 on grass; 18-13 on turf; 35-19 in daytime; 56-52 at night; 32-23 in one-run games; 13-11 in extra-inning games; 0-0-1 in doubleheaders.

Team record past five years: 351-396 (.470, ranks 12th in league in that span).

TEAM LEADERS

Batting average: Tony Gwynn (.353).
At-bats: Steve Finley (655).
Runs: Steve Finley (126).
Hits: Steve Finley (195).
Total bases: Steve Finley (348).
Doubles: Steve Finley (45).
Triples: Steve Finley (9).
Home runs: Ken Caminiti (40).
Runs batted in: Ken Caminiti (130).
Stolen bases: Rickey Henderson (37).
Slugging percentage: Ken Caminiti (.621).
On-base percentage: Rickey Henderson (.410).
Wins: Joey Hamilton (15).
Earned-run average: Fernando Valenzuela (3.62).
Complete games: Joey Hamilton (3).
Shutouts: Joey Hamilton (1).
Saves: Trevor Hoffman (42).
Innings pitched: Joey Hamilton (211.2).
Strikeouts: Joey Hamilton (184).

GAMES BY POSITION

Catcher: John Flaherty 72, Brian Johnson 66, Brad Ausmus 46, Archi Cianfrocco 1.
First base: Wally Joyner 119, Archi Cianfrocco 33, Scott Livingstone 22, Jason Thompson 13, Marc Newfield 2, Chris Gwynn 1, Brian Johnson 1.
Second base: Jody Reed 145, Luis Lopez 22, Craig Shipley 17, Archi Cianfrocco 6.
Third base: Ken Caminiti 145, Scott Livingstone 16, Archi Cianfrocco 11, Craig Shipley 4, Andujar Cedeno 2, Luis Lopez 2, Brian Johnson 1, Jimmy Tatum 1.
Shortstop: Chris Gomez 89, Andujar Cedeno 47, Luis Lopez 35, Archi Cianfrocco 10, Craig Shipley 7.
Outfield: Steve Finley 160, Rickey Henderson 134, Tony Gwynn 111, Marc Newfield 51, Greg Vaughn 39, Chris Gwynn 29, Rob Deer 18, Doug Dascenzo 10, Archi Cianfrocco 8, Craig Shipley 3.

TOP DRAFT CHOICES

1. **Matt Holoran**, SS, Chancellor H.S., Fredericksburg, Va.
2. **Vernon Maxwell**, OF, Midwest City (Okla.) H.S.
3. **Widd Workman**, RHP, Arizona State U.
4. **Nathan Dunn**, 3B, Louisiana State Univ.
5. **Brian Loyd**, C, Cal State Fullerton.
6. **Tom Szymborski**, LHP, U. of Ill.-Chicago.
7. **Brian Carmody**, LHP, Santa Clara Univ.
8. **Chance Capel**, RHP, Carroll H.S., Southlake, Tex.
9. **Jason Middlebrook**, RHP, Stanford Univ.
10. **Tim Lanier**, C, Louisiana State Univ.

SAN FRANCISCO GIANTS
NATIONAL LEAGUE WEST DIVISION

1997 GIANTS SCHEDULE

Home games shaded.
* — All-Star Game at Jacobs Field (Cleveland)
D — Day game (any game starting before 5 p.m.)

APRIL
SUN	MON	TUE	WED	THU	FRI	SAT
		1 PIT D	2 PIT D	3 PIT D	4 NYM	5 NYM D
6 NYM	7 PHI D	8 PHI D	9 PHI D	10	11	12 NYM D
13 NYM D	14 NYM	15 PHI	16 PHI	17	18 FLA	19 FLA D
20 NYM D	21	22 ATL	23 ATL D	24	25 HOU	26 HOU
27 HOU D	28 STL D	29 STL	30 PIT			

MAY
SUN	MON	TUE	WED	THU	FRI	SAT
			1 PIT D	2 CIN	3 CIN D	
4 CIN	5 MON D	6 MON	7 MON D	8	9 CUB	10 CUB D
11 CUB D	12	13 CIN	14 CIN	15 MON	16 MON	17 CUB
18 CUB D	19 COL	20 COL	21 COL	22 STL D	23 STL	24 STL D
25 STL D	26 HOU D	27 HOU D	28	29 ATL	30 ATL	31 ATL

JUNE
SUN	MON	TUE	WED	THU	FRI	SAT
1 ATL D	2 FLA	3 FLA	4 LA	5 LA	6 LA	7 ATL D
8 D	9 FLA	10 FLA D	11 FLA D	12 TEX	13 TEX	14 ANA
15 ANA D	16 SD	17 SEA	18 SEA	19 SEA D	20 LA	21 LA D
22 LA	23 SD	24 SD	25 SD D	26 COL	27 COL	28 COL
29 COL D	30 SEA					

JULY
SUN	MON	TUE	WED	THU	FRI	SAT
		1 SEA D	2 OAK D	3 OAK	4 COL	5 COL D
6 COL D	7	8	9 D	10 LA	11 LA	12 LA
13 LA D	14 SD	15 SD	16 HOU	17 HOU D	18 STL	19 STL
20 STL D	21 STL	22 PHI	23 PHI D	24 PHI D	25 PIT	26 PIT D
27 PIT D	28	29 NYM	30 NYM D	31		

AUGUST
SUN	MON	TUE	WED	THU	FRI	SAT
					1 CIN	2 CIN D
3 CIN D	4 CIN	5 CUB	6 CUB D	7 CUB	8 MON	9 MON
10 MON D	11 CIN	12 CIN	13 CUB D	14 CUB	15 MON D	16 MON D
17 MON D	18	19 PHI	20 PHI	21 PHI	22 PIT	23 PIT
24 PIT D	25 NYM	26 NYM	27 NYM D	28 TEX	29 TEX	30 ANA
31 ANA						

SEPTEMBER
SUN	MON	TUE	WED	THU	FRI	SAT
	1 OAK D	2	3 OAK	4 HOU D	5 HOU	6 HOU D
7 HOU D	8	9 STL	10 STL	11	12 FLA	13 FLA D
14 FLA D	15 ATL	16 ATL	17 LA D	18 LA	19 SD	20 SD
21 SD D	22 SD	23 COL	24 COL D	25	26 SD	27 SD D
28 SD D						

1997 SEASON

CLUB DIRECTORY

President and managing general partner
Peter A. Magowan

Executive vice president/COO
Larry Baer

Senior v.p. and general manager
Brian Sabean

Senior vice president, business operations
Pat Gallagher

Senior advisor, baseball operations
Bob Quinn

Special assistant to the general manager
Dick Tidrow

Director of major league administration
Ned Colletti

Sr. v.p. and chief financial officer
John Yee

V.p., stadium operations/security
Jorge Costa

Vice president, communications
Bob Rose

Vice president, marketing
Mario Alioto

General manager, retail/Internet
Connie Kullberg

Director of stadium operations
Gene Telucci

Vice president, ticket sales
Mark Norrelli

Vice president, ticket services
Russ Stanley

Director of travel
Reggie Younger Jr.

V.p., legal and governmental affairs
Jack Bair

Media relations manager
Jim Moorehead

Coordinator of scouting
Bob Hartsfield

National cross-checker
Randy Waddill

Western cross-checker
Doug Mapson

Southern cross-checker
Larry Osborne

Northern cross-checker
Jack Bowen

Major league advance scout
Cal Emery

Coordinator of Latin American operations
Luis Rosa

Scouts
Claudio Brito, Jose Cassino, Richard Cole, Pablo Delgado, Joe DiCarlo, Bob Gardner, Carlos Hernandez, Diego Herrera, Andres James, Mike Keenan, Tom Korenek, Jose Marcano, Alan Marr, Abraham Martinez, Doug McMillan, Tony Michalak, Bob Myrick, Rick Ragazzo, Hector Rivera, Milton Rosario, John Shafer, Joe Strain, Todd Thomas, Dick Tidrow, Paul Turco, Elanis Westbrooks, Tom Zimmer

MINOR LEAGUE AFFILIATES

Class	Team	League	Manager
AAA	Phoenix	Pacific Coast	Ron Wotus
AA	Shreveport	Texas	Carlos Lezcano
A	San Jose	California	Frank Cacciatore
A	Bakersfield	California	Glenn Tufts
Rookie	Salem-Keizer	Northwest	Shane Turner

BROADCAST INFORMATION

Radio: KNBR-AM (680); KIQI-AM (1010, Spanish language).
TV: KTVU-TV (Channel 2).
Cable TV: SportsChannel Pacific.

SPRING TRAINING

Ballpark (city): Scottsdale Stadium (Scottsdale, Ariz.).
Ticket information: 602-990-7972.

1997 SEASON San Francisco Giants

SPRING TRAINING ROSTER

Manager— Dusty Baker (12).
Coaches—Carlos Alfonso (17), Gene Clines, Sonny Jackson (15), Ron Perranoski (16), Dick Pole (48).

No.	PITCHERS	B/T	Ht./Wt.	Born	1996 clubs
47	Beck, Rod	R/R	6-1/236	8-3-68	San Francisco
33	Bourgeois, Steve	R/R	6-1/220	8-4-72	San Francisco, Phoenix
29	Carlson, Dan	R/R	6-1/185	1-26-70	Phoenix, San Francisco
51	Creek, Doug	L/L	5-10/205	3-1-69	San Francisco
41	DeLucia, Rich	R/R	6-0/185	10-7-64	San Jose, San Francisco
55	Estes, Shawn	B/L	6-2/185	2-18-73	Phoenix, San Francisco
22	Fernandez, Osvaldo	R/R	6-2/190	11-4-68	San Francisco
53	Foulke, Keith	R/R	6-0/195	10-19-72	Shreveport
54	Frontera, Chad	R/R	6-2/200	11-22-72	Shreveport
26	Gardner, Mark	R/R	6-1/205	3-1-62	San Francisco, San Jose
	Henry, Doug	R/R	6-4/205	12-10-63	New York N.L.
19	Poole, Jim	L/L	6-2/203	4-28-66	Cleveland, San Francisco
	Roa, Joe	R/R	6-1/195	10-11-71	Buffalo, Cleveland
42	Rueter, Kirk	L/L	6-3/195	12-1-70	Ottawa, Montreal, San Francisco, Phoenix
65	Soderstrom, Steve	R/R	6-3/205	4-3-72	Phoenix, San Francisco
52	Tavarez, Julian	R/R	6-2/190	5-22-73	Cleveland, Buffalo
31	Valdez, Carlos	R/R	5-11/175	12-26-71	Phoenix
50	VanLandingham, William	R/R	6-2/210	7-16-70	San Francisco
63	Villano, Mike	R/R	6-0/200	8-10-71	San Jose, Shreveport

No.	CATCHERS	B/T	Ht./Wt.	Born	1996 clubs
30	Jensen, Marcus	B/R	6-4/195	12-14-72	Phoenix, San Francisco
66	Mirabelli, Doug	R/R	6-0/210	10-18-70	Shreveport, Phoenix, San Francisco
2	Wilkins, Rick	L/R	6-2/215	6-4-67	Houston, San Francisco

No.	INFIELDERS	B/T	Ht./Wt.	Born	1996 clubs
35	Aurilia, Rich	R/R	6-1/170	9-2-71	Phoenix, San Francisco
36	Canizaro, Jay	R/R	5-9/170	7-4-73	Phoenix, San Francisco
60	Delgado, Wilson	L/R	5-11/165	7-15-75	San Jose, Phoenix, San Francisco
21	Kent, Jeff	R/R	6-1/190	3-7-68	New York N.L., Cleveland
14	Lewis, Mark	R/R	6-1/190	11-30-69	Detroit
32	Mueller, Bill	B/R	5-11/175	3-17-71	Phoenix, San Francisco
6	Snow, J.T.	B/L	6-2/202	2-26-68	California
10	Vizcaino, Jose	B/R	6-1/180	3-26-68	New York N.L., Cleveland
8	Wilson, Desi	L/L	6-7/230	5-9-69	Phoenix, San Francisco

No.	OUTFIELDERS	B/T	Ht./Wt.	Born	1996 clubs
7	Benard, Marvin	L/L	5-9/180	1-20-70	Phoenix, San Francisco
25	Bonds, Barry	L/L	6-1/185	7-24-64	San Francisco
62	Cruz, Jacob	L/L	6-0/175	1-28-73	Phoenix, San Francisco
	Hamilton, Darryl	L/R	6-1/180	12-3-64	Texas
1	Hill, Glenallen	R/R	6-2/220	3-22-65	San Francisco, Phoenix
28	Javier, Stan	B/R	6-0/185	1-9-64	San Francisco, San Jose
23	Powell, Dante	R/R	6-2/185	8-25-73	Shreveport, Phoenix
56	Rios, Armando	L/L	5-9/185	9-13-71	Shreveport
61	Singleton, Chris	L/L	6-2/195	8-15-72	Shreveport, Phoenix

BALLPARK INFORMATION

Ballpark (capacity, surface)
3Com Park at Candlestick Point (63,000, grass)

Address
Candlestick Park
San Francisco, CA 94124

Business phone
415-468-3700

Ticket information
415-467-8000

Ticket prices
$15 (lower box)
$12 (upper box)
$12 (lower reserved)
$7 (upper reserved)
$6 (pavilion)
$5 (bleachers)

Field dimensions (from home plate)
To left field at foul line, 335 feet
To center field, 400 feet
To right field at foul line, 328 feet

First game played
April 12, 1960 (Giants 3, Cardinals 1)

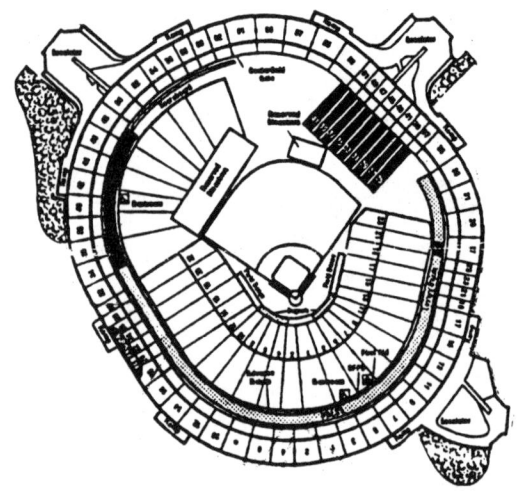

DAY BY DAY

	Opp.	Res.	Score	(inn.*)	Hits	Opp. hits	Winning pitcher	Losing pitcher	Save	Record	Pos.	GB
	At Atl.	L	8-10		12	9	Maddux	Leiter	Borbon	0-1	T3rd	1
	At Atl.	L	2-15		6	16	Glavine	VanLandingham		0-2	4th	1
	At Atl.	W	7-1		9	7	Watson	Smoltz		1-2	T2nd	½
	At Fla.	W	7-1		8	5	Fernandez	Rapp		2-2	2nd	½
	At Fla.	L	0-1	(10)	7	5	Nen	Dewey		2-3	T2nd	1½
	At Fla.	W	14-7		14	15	Bourgeois	Burkett		3-3	2nd	1½
	At Hou.	L	2-6		4	5	Hampton	VanLandingham		3-4	2nd	2½
	At Hou.	W	3-1	(10)	8	6	Juden	Tabaka	Beck	4-4	2nd	1½
	At Hou.	W	11-5		11	13	Fernandez	Kile		5-4	2nd	1½
0	Chi.	W	4-1		6	10	Leiter	Navarro	Beck	6-4	2nd	1
3	Chi.	W	3-2	(10)	10	3	Juden	Myers		7-4	2nd	1
4	Chi.	L	2-6		6	8	Foster	Watson	Wendell	7-5	2nd	1
6	L.A.	W	5-3		9	9	Dewey	Osuna	Beck	8-5	2nd	½
7	L.A.	L	2-11		3	13	Osuna	Leiter		8-6	2nd	1½
8	At Chi.	L	6-7		12	14	Perez	VanLandingham	Wendell	8-7	2nd	2
9	At Chi.	L	6-10		10	15	Foster	Watson		8-8	2nd	2
0	At Chi.	W	8-4		14	9	Gardner	Bullinger		9-8	2nd	1
1	At Chi.	W	7-6		6	11	Fernandez	Trachsel	Beck	10-8	2nd	1
2	Hou.	L	8-11		14	15	Reynolds	Leiter		10-9	2nd	2
3	Hou.	L	4-8		8	11	Kile	VanLandingham		10-10	3rd	3
4	Atl.	L	3-8		7	14	Smoltz	Watson		10-11	3rd	4
5	Atl.	W	8-0		6	4	Gardner	Schmidt		11-11	2nd	4
6	Fla.	L	0-3		7	8	Brown	Fernandez		11-12	3rd	5
7	Fla.	W	6-3		13	6	Leiter	Burkett	Beck	12-12	2nd	4
8	Fla.	W	10-4		15	6	VanLandingham	Hammond		13-12	2nd	3
0	At S.D.	W	9-4		11	8	Watson	Tewksbury		14-12	2nd	2½
	At S.D.	L	4-9		10	11	Valenzuela	Gardner		14-13	2nd	3½
	Cin.	L	3-5		8	6	McElroy	Creek	Brantley	14-14	T2nd	3½
	Cin.	L	7-9		9	10	Moore	Leiter	Brantley	14-15	T3rd	3½
	Cin.	L	6-12		9	9	Smiley	VanLandingham		14-16	T3rd	4½
	At St.L.	W	4-2		8	9	Watson	Fossas	Beck	15-16	T2nd	4
	At St.L.	W	10-7		15	7	Gardner	An. Benes	Beck	16-16	2nd	3½
	At St.L.	L	8-16		6	16	Parrett	Dewey		16-17	2nd	4½
0	At Pit.	W	5-4	(10)	11	7	DeLucia	Cordova	Beck	17-17	2nd	3½
1	At Pit.	W	12-7		13	10	VanLandingham	Hope		18-17	2nd	2½
2	At Pit.	W	7-2		15	7	Watson	Smith		19-17	2nd	2½
3	At Phi.	W	2-1		11	6	Gardner	Fernandez	Beck	20-17	2nd	2½
4	At Phi.	L	0-7		6	11	Schilling	Fernandez		20-18	2nd	3½
5	At Phi.	L	6-7	(10)	8	14	Bottalico	Beck		20-19	2nd	4½
8	N.Y.	L	5-14		8	15	Clark	VanLandingham		20-20	3rd	4½
9†	N.Y.	W	1-0		5	4	Watson	Isringhausen	Beck	21-20	3rd	4½
9‡	N.Y.	W	6-2		9	6	Gardner	Wilson		22-20	2nd	4
0	Mon.	W	9-6		7	12	Dewey	Dyer	Beck	23-20	2nd	3½
1	Mon.	W	8-5		13	6	Dewey	Aucoin	Beck	24-20	2nd	2½
2	Mon.	L	3-4		9	7	Martinez	VanLandingham	Rojas	24-21	2nd	3½
4	Phi.	L	1-5		3	10	Schilling	Watson		24-22	2nd	5
5	Phi.	W	3-2		8	4	Gardner	Williams	Beck	25-22	2nd	5
6	Phi.	L	1-10		6	14	Mulholland	Fernandez	Bottalico	25-23	3rd	5
8	At N.Y.	L	0-4		5	8	Clark	Leiter	Henry	25-24	4th	6½
9	At N.Y.	W	4-2		6	6	VanLandingham	Isringhausen	Beck	26-24	2nd	5½
0	At N.Y.	L	0-1		4	6	Wilson	Watson	J. Franco	26-25	T3rd	6
1	At Mon.	L	4-7		13	13	Daal	DeLucia	Veres	26-26	T3rd	7
	At Mon.	L	1-5		5	7	Fassero	Fernandez	Dyer	26-27	4th	8
2	At Mon.	W	8-1		13	5	Leiter	Martinez		27-27	T3rd	7
3	At Cin.	W	6-3		9	8	VanLandingham	Burba		28-27	3rd	6
4	At Cin.	L	1-4		5	9	Salkeld	Watson	Brantley	28-28	3rd	6
5	At Cin.	W	15-4		17	14	Gardner	Jarvis		29-28	T2nd	6
7	St.L.	L	4-9		8	13	An. Benes	Fernandez		29-29	3rd	6
8	St.L.	W	4-1		5	5	DeLucia	Stottlemyre	Beck	30-29	3rd	5
9	St.L.	W	9-0		16	8	Watson	Al. Benes		31-29	3rd	4
0	Pit.	L	4-5		12	8	Morel	DeLucia	Cordova	31-30	3rd	4
1	Pit.	L	2-7		10	11	Neagle	Fernandez		31-31	3rd	4
3	Hou.	W	12-8		16	9	Leiter	Kile		32-31	T3rd	2½
4	Hou.	L	1-9		6	11	Hampton	VanLandingham	Wagner	32-32	4th	2½
5	Hou.	L	3-4		9	7	Wall	Watson	Jones	32-33	4th	3½
6	Hou.	W	8-7		13	12	DeLucia	Morman		33-33	4th	2½
7	Fla.	W	1-0		4	3	Fernandez	Leiter	Beck	34-33	4th	2
8	Fla.	W	9-8	(15)	16	18	Juden	Rapp		35-33	T3rd	1½
9	Fla.	W	7-4	(15)	13	9	Bautista	Mathews		36-33	T2nd	1½
1	At Atl.	L	7-8	(11)	14	9	Wade	Beck		36-34	T2nd	1
2	At Atl.	L	0-6		4	8	Maddux	Gardner		36-35	T2nd	2
3	At Atl.	L	0-1		3	6	Glavine	Fernandez	Wohlers	36-36	4th	3

Date	Opp.	Res.	Score	(inn.*)	Hits	Opp. hits	Winning pitcher	Losing pitcher	Save	Record	Pos.	GB
6-24	At Fla.	L	1-2		4	3	Burkett	Leiter	Nen	36-37	4th	3¹
6-25	At Fla.	L	4-5	(10)	7	9	Powell	Beck		36-38	4th	3¹
6-26	At Fla.	L	2-3		7	11	Brown	Watson		36-39	4th	3¹
6-27	S.D.	L	1-11		7	12	Valenzuela	Gardner		36-40	4th	3¹
6-28	S.D.	L	1-6		6	9	Ashby	Fernandez	Hoffman	36-41	4th	3¹
6-29	S.D.	L	6-7		8	12	Blair	Beck	Hoffman	36-42	4th	4¹
6-30	S.D.	L	4-7		14	16	Tewksbury	VanLandingham	Hoffman	36-43	4th	5¹
7-1	Col.	W	9-6		15	9	Juden	Painter	Beck	37-43	4th	4¹
7-2	Col.	W	5-1		7	5	Gardner	Ritz		38-43	4th	4¹
7-3	Col.	L	2-3		5	12	Leskanic	Beck	Ruffin	38-44	4th	4¹
7-4	At S.D.	L	4-8		12	11	Tewksbury	Leiter		38-45	4th	5¹
7-5	At S.D.	L	6-7	(11)	7	13	Bergman	Bautista		38-46	4th	6¹
7-6	At S.D.	L	3-7		8	12	Worrell	Bourgeois	Hoffman	38-47	4th	7¹
7-7	At S.D.	L	3-10		7	10	Valenzuela	Fernandez		38-48	4th	8¹
7-11	At L.A.	L	3-8		4	15	Martinez	Leiter		38-49	4th	8¹
7-12	At L.A.	L	1-6		5	8	Valdes	Fernandez		38-50	4th	9¹
7-13	At L.A.	W	7-0		13	4	Estes	Nomo		39-50	4th	8¹
7-14	At L.A.	W	6-0		8	2	VanLandingham	Park		40-50	4th	7¹
7-15	At Col.	L	3-7		5	13	Bailey	Bourgeois		40-51	4th	8¹
7-16	At Col.	L	3-5		7	6	Freeman	Leiter	Ruffin	40-52	4th	8¹
7-17	At Col.	L	3-4		7	12	Wright	Fernandez	Ruffin	40-53	4th	9
7-18	L.A.	L	3-8		4	11	Nomo	Estes		40-54	4th	9¹
7-19	L.A.	W	5-4		11	10	VanLandingham	Candiotti	Beck	41-54	4th	9¹
7-20	L.A.	W	7-6		12	13	Bautista	Worrell		42-54	4th	8¹
7-21	L.A.	L	6-7		10	12	Osuna	DeLucia	Worrell	42-55	4th	9¹
7-22	Chi.	W	3-2		5	6	Bautista	Bottenfield		43-55	4th	8¹
7-23	Chi.	L	6-9		9	14	Myers	DeLucia	Patterson	43-56	4th	9¹
7-24	Chi.	L	1-7		5	11	Castillo	VanLandingham		43-57	4th	10
7-25	Atl.	W	4-3		9	3	Watson	Maddux	Beck	44-57	4th	9
7-26	Atl.	L	1-2		8	6	Glavine	Leiter	Wohlers	44-58	4th	10
7-27	Atl.	W	7-5		9	7	Gardner	Woodall	Beck	45-58	4th	10
7-28	Atl.	W	10-3		11	7	Estes	Smoltz	Beck	46-58	4th	9
7-30	At Chi.	L	0-4		10	4	Castillo	VanLandingham	Adams	46-59	4th	10¹
7-31	At Chi.	L	1-4		5	5	Trachsel	Watson	Wendell	46-60	4th	10¹
8-2	At Hou.	L	1-5		8	10	Drabek	Gardner	Hernandez	46-61	4th	11
8-3	At Hou.	L	1-4		3	6	Reynolds	Estes		46-62	4th	11
8-4	At Hou.	L	6-7		9	7	Hampton	Fernandez	Wagner	46-63	4th	12
8-5	Cin.	L	3-4		6	9	Salkeld	VanLandingham	Brantley	46-64	4th	12
8-6	Cin.	L	2-3		6	5	Carrasco	Beck	Brantley	46-65	4th	13
8-7	Cin.	W	9-2		10	7	Gardner	Jarvis		47-65	4th	12
8-8	At St.L.	W	5-3	(10)	12	9	Poole	Honeycutt	Beck	48-65	4th	12
8-9	At St.L.	W	8-6		16	13	Fernandez	Morgan	Beck	49-65	4th	12
8-10	At St.L.	L	1-7		7	10	An. Benes	VanLandingham		49-66	4th	13
8-11	At St.L.	L	3-5		6	8	Osborne	Watson	Eckersley	49-67	4th	14
8-13	At Pit.	W	12-10		16	10	Dewey	Plesac	Beck	50-67	4th	13
8-14	At Pit.	L	3-4		6	10	Peters	Estes	Ericks	50-68	4th	13
8-16	At Phi.	W	6-4		10	8	VanLandingham	Williams	Beck	51-68	4th	12¹
8-17	At Phi.	W	8-4		11	11	Watson	Hunter	Beck	52-68	4th	12¹
8-18	At Phi.	L	6-7		10	12	Borland	Gardner	Bottalico	52-69	4th	12¹
8-19	N.Y.	W	5-4		8	12	Scott	Harnisch	Beck	53-69	4th	12¹
8-20	N.Y.	L	3-7		4	12	B. Jones	Fernandez	J. Franco	53-70	4th	13¹
8-21	N.Y.	W	12-11		10	17	Dewey	Person	Beck	54-70	4th	13¹
8-22	Mon.	L	4-5		10	8	Fassero	Bautista	Rojas	54-71	4th	14
8-23	Mon.	L	8-10		12	12	Daal	Creek	Rojas	54-72	4th	14
8-24	Mon.	L	0-3		2	9	Martinez	Estes	Rojas	54-73	4th	15
8-25	Mon.	W	7-2		8	7	Fernandez	Cormier		55-73	4th	15
8-26	Phi.	W	1-0		6	3	VanLandingham	Schilling	Beck	56-73	4th	14¹
8-27	Phi.	L	2-3		8	7	Williams	Bautista	Bottalico	56-74	4th	15¹
8-28	Phi.	W	7-6		11	10	Dewey	R. Jordan	Beck	57-74	4th	15¹
8-30	At N.Y.	W	6-4		10	5	Estes	Harnisch	Beck	58-74	4th	16
8-31	At N.Y.	L	2-7		6	13	Person	Scott	Henry	58-75	4th	16
9-1	At N.Y.	L	5-6	(10)	12	11	J. Franco	Beck		58-76	4th	16
9-2	At Mon.	L	3-4	(11)	7	12	Manuel	Beck		58-77	4th	17
9-3	At Mon.	L	2-9		9	14	Martinez	Gardner		58-78	4th	17
9-4	At Mon.	L	0-6		3	8	Paniagua	Estes		58-79	4th	18
9-6†	At Cin.	W	2-0		5	5	Fernandez	Smiley	Beck	59-79		
9-6‡	At Cin.	L	1-14		6	15	Morgan	Bourgeois		59-80	4th	17¹⁄₂
9-7	At Cin.	L	5-7		11	13	Salkeld	Scott	Brantley	59-81	4th	18¹⁄
9-8	At Cin.	L	3-8		4	12	Shaw	Bautista		59-82	4th	18¹⁄
9-9	St.L.	L	2-6		6	10	An. Benes	Gardner		59-83	4th	19¹⁄
9-10	St.L.	L	0-1		5	6	Petkovsek	Rueter	Eckersley	59-84	4th	20¹⁄
9-11	St.L.	W	4-2		9	10	Scott	Al. Benes	Beck	60-84	4th	20¹⁄
9-12	Pit.	L	4-10		9	13	Schmidt	Dewey	Boever	60-85	4th	21¹⁄
9-13	Pit.	L	0-9		6	13	Loaiza	VanLandingham		60-86	4th	21¹⁄
9-14	Pit.	L	5-7	(12)	7	14	Ericks	Hook	Boever	60-87	4th	22¹⁄

– 146 –

ate	Opp.	Res.	Score	(inn.*)	Hits	Opp. hits	Winning pitcher	Losing pitcher	Save	Record	Pos.	GB
15†	Pit.	L	1-4		10	11	Lieber	Rueter	Ruebel	60-88		
15‡	Pit.	L	9-11	(10)	12	16	Wilkins	Poole		60-89	4th	24
16	S.D.	L	1-2	(11)	8	8	Hoffman	Beck		60-90	4th	25
17	S.D.	W	9-7		11	8	Poole	Veras	Beck	61-90	4th	25
18	S.D.	L	5-8		11	11	Bochtler	DeLucia	Hoffman	61-91	4th	25
19	Col.	W	11-4		11	9	VanLandingham	Ritz		62-91	4th	25
20	Col.	W	6-2		6	9	Gardner	M. Thompson		63-91	4th	24
21	Col.	W	6-2		9	8	Rueter	Wright		64-91	4th	24
22	Col.	W	7-3		9	7	Soderstrom	Nied		65-91	4th	23
24	At L.A.	L	2-6		2	8	Martinez	Watson		65-92	4th	24
25	At L.A.	L	5-7		8	9	Radinsky	DeLucia	Worrell	65-93	4th	25
26	At L.A.	W	6-1		11	7	Gardner	Candiotti		66-93	4th	24
27	At Col.	W	9-3		12	7	Soderstrom	Nied		67-93	4th	23
28	At Col.	W	8-5		12	11	Carlson	Burke	Beck	68-93	4th	22
29	At Col.	L	3-12		8	13	Ritz	Watson		68-94	4th	23

onthly records: April (14-12), May (12-14), June (10-17), July (10-17), August (12-15), September (10-19).
nnings, if other than nine. †First game of doubleheader. ‡Second game of doubleheader.

HIGHLIGHTS

igh point: Thanks to a potent offense led ▼ 3-4-5-6 hitters Mark Carreon, Barry ɔnds, Matt Williams and Glenallen Hill, the iants were three games above .500 (36-3) after winning their second consecutive 5-inning game against the Marlins on June 5. Confounding the experts who predicted last-place finish, the Giants were one ame out of first in the N.L. West.

ɔw point: By September, a crippling series ⸱ injuries forced the Giants to field lineups ɔnsisting largely of players rushed up ɔm the minors. Toward the end of the eason, the Giants were losing consistently, ɩd while the N.L. West race raged around ɪem, the Giants' most significant goal as not losing 100 games.

ɪrning point: Immediately after the two 5-inning victories over the Marlins, the iants began a 10-game losing streak ɡainst Atlanta, Florida and division rival an Diego. Hill's loss to a broken left wrist ι May 26, a cool-down by Carreon and ɪtching failures began to take their toll.

ɪost valuable player: Left fielder Barry ɔnds. With no supporting cast to speak of, ɔnds managed to hit .308 with 42 homers ɪd a career-high 129 RBIs. He became ɑseball's second 40/40 man despite being ⸱alked an N.L.-record 151 times. Bonds ɪso hit his 300th career homer in May, ⸱ecoming the fourth major-leaguer to hit ɪat many and steal 300 bases.

ɪost valuable pitcher: Starter Mark ɑrdner. Gardner, a 34-year-old journey-ɪan who wasn't signed until the weekend ⸱efore the season began, became the ace f the rotation. His 12 victories (against ⸱even losses) were the most by a Giants ⸱tarter since Bill Swift and John Burkett ɑch won 20 in 1993.

ɪost improved player: Reliever Jose ⸱autista. In 1995, troubled by a serious ill-⸱ess in his family, Bautista allowed 24 ɔme runs and went 3-8 with a 6.44 ERA. ⸱ven though he had a two-year contract, ⸱autista didn't win a major league job after ⸱pring training 1996. But after clearing his ⸱ead in the minors, he came up and ⸱ecame one of Dusty Baker's most valued ⸱itchers, working long and middle relief ɪd finishing 3-4 with a 3.36 ERA and just 0 homers allowed.

ɪost pleasant surprise: Infielder Bill ɪueller. Mueller, a rookie called up August 5 to replace injured third baseman Matt Williams, did a splendid job filling in for the All-Star and finished at .330, all but secur-ing a job for this season.

Biggest disappointment: Starter William VanLandingham. VanLandingham, who was considered a possible future ace of the staff, went 9-14 with a 5.40 ERA.

Key injuries: You name it, the Giants suf-fered it. Second baseman Robby Thompson was limited to 63 games by muscle injuries in his ribcage, neck and hip. Williams missed the final two months because of a shoulder injury that required surgery. Shortstop Shawon Dunston also missed the last two months with a frac-tured skull he suffered in a collision at sec-ond base. Hill missed 61 games with his fractured wrist. Center fielder Stan Javier didn't play the final 2¹/₂ months because of a pulled hamstring. Catchers Kirt Manwaring and Tom Lampkin missed time with broken hands. On the other hand, no starting pitcher missed significant time because of injuries, although Gardner was out two weeks after an emergency appen-dectomy.

Notable: The Giants' 68-94 finish was their second-worst since the franchise moved West in 1958. . . . Coaches Bobby Bonds, Wendell Kim and Jimmy Davenport were fired after the season by Brian Sabean, who replaced Bob Quinn as general manager, and an unhappy Barry Bonds asked for a trade.

—HENRY SCHULMAN

RECORDS

1996 regular-season record: 68-94 (4th in N.L. West); 38-44 at home; 30-50 on road; 28-33 vs. East; 24-38 vs. Central; 16-23 vs. West; 10-23 vs. lefthanded starters; 58-71 vs. righthanded starters; 55-77 on grass; 13-17 on turf; 35-43 in daytime; 33-51 at night; 17-29 in one-run games; 6-10 in extra-inning games; 1-1-1 in doubleheaders.
Team record past five years: 365-380 (.490, ranks 7th in league in that span).

TEAM LEADERS

Batting average: Barry Bonds (.308).
At-bats: Barry Bonds (517).
Runs: Barry Bonds (122).
Hits: Barry Bonds (159).

Total bases: Barry Bonds (318).
Doubles: Barry Bonds (27).
Triples: Marvin Benard (4).
Home runs: Barry Bonds (42).
Runs batted in: Barry Bonds (129).
Stolen bases: Barry Bonds (40).
Slugging percentage: Barry Bonds (.615).
On-base percentage: Barry Bonds (.461).
Wins: Mark Gardner (12).
Earned-run average: Mark Gardner (4.42).
Complete games: Mark Gardner (4).
Shutouts: Mark Gardner (1).
Saves: Rod Beck (35).
Innings pitched: Allen Watson (185.2).
Strikeouts: Mark Gardner (145).

GAMES BY POSITION

Catcher: Tom Lampkin 53, Kirt Manwaring 49, Rick Wilkins 42, Steve Decker 30, Doug Mirabelli 8, Marcus Jensen 7.
First base: Mark Carreon 73, Dave McCarty 51, Desi Wilson 33, Dan Peltier 13, Matt Williams 13, J.R. Phillips 10, Rick Wilkins 7, Steve Decker 3, Steve Scarsone 1.
Second base: Steve Scarsone 74, Robby Thompson 62, Jay Canizaro 35, Rich Aurilia 11, Bill Mueller 8.
Third base: Matt Williams 92, Bill Mueller 45, Kim Batiste 25, Steve Scarsone 14, Steve Decker 2.
Shortstop: Rich Aurilia 93, Shawon Dunston 78, Kim Batiste 7, Jay Canizaro 7, Wilson Delgado 6, Steve Scarsone 1, Matt Williams 1.
Outfield: Barry Bonds 152, Marvin Benard 132, Glenallen Hill 98, Stan Javier 71, Dax Jones 33, Jacob Cruz 23, Dave McCarty 20, Trent Hubbard 9, Mark Carreon 5, Mel Hall 4, Keith Williams 4, Dan Peltier 1.

TOP DRAFT CHOICES

1. **Matt White,** RHP, Waynesboro (Pa.) Area H.S.
2. **Mike Caruso,** SS, Stoneman Douglas H.S., Parkland, Fla.
3. **David Kenna,** C, N. Fort Myers (Fla.) H.S.
4. **Ken Vining,** LHP, Clemson University.
5. **Matt Wells,** LHP, University of Nevada.
6. **Bill Malloy,** RHP, Rutgers University.
7. **Brandon Leese,** RHP, Butler University.
8. **Ryan Jensen,** RHP, Southern Utah Univ.
9. **Brian Manning,** OF, Allentown (Pa.) College.
10. **Mike Glendenning,** 3B, Los Angeles Pierce J.C.

1997 SEASON San Francisco Giants

1996 REVIEW

YEAR IN REVIEW
THE TOP STORIES OF THE PAST YEAR

By STEVE GIETSCHIER
TSN Archivist

Baseball endured its fourth straight year of labor-management turmoil in 1996 although, for a change, most of the negotiations aimed at reaching a new collective bargaining agreement transpired away from the steady glare of media attention. For the first time since 1993, American and National League teams played complete 162-game schedules. Power hitters entertained fans, if not purists, with record displays of their prowess, but attendance, which traditionally responds to increases in offense, did not rebound to pre-strike levels. After 1995's dismal experiment, when Division Series and League Championship Series games were televised on a regional, simultaneous basis, all postseason games were shown on national television. But even the nostalgic feelings engendered by the upset victory of the New York Yankees in the World Series could not hide the sport's critical need for labor peace, which came, unexpectedly, just a few weeks later.

The season began as it never had before, with the Seattle Mariners defeating the Chicago White Sox, 3-2, in 12 innings on March 31, the earliest regular-season game in the sport's long history. The Official Playing Rules Committee lowered the bottom of the strike zone, but this change failed to achieve its goals, neither reducing the average time it took to play a game nor providing beleaguered pitchers some significant relief in their battle against superior hitters. The season could, in fact, rightly be dubbed "The Year of the Home Run" for the enormous number of records broken.

LABOR AGREEMENT FINALLY REACHED

The world of baseball received a Thanksgiving present two days early when, on Tuesday, November 26, owners voted, 26-4, to accept a contract with the Major League Baseball Players Association. Only the White Sox, Cleveland Indians, Kansas City Royals and Oakland Athletics voted no. Coming three weeks after a previous vote had rejected the same contract, the news brought a collective sigh of relief from fans who had long before grown tired of baseball's labor wars.

The agreement will run through October 31, 2000, with the union having an option to extend it for an additional year. Among its terms are provisions for:

■ Revenue sharing among the clubs, to commence in 1997 according to a plan approved on March 21;

■ A luxury tax system on the portion of team payrolls that exceeds set thresholds: 1997—35 percent on payroll amounts above $51 million; 1998—35 percent on payroll amounts above $55 million; 1999—34 percent on payroll amounts above $58.9 million; 2000-2001—no tax;

■ Interleague play, approved for 1997 only, with each team playing 15 or 16 games against teams in the corresponding division of the other league and the desig-

nated hitter to be used in A.L. home games;

■ Increases in the minimum salary for players from $109,000 in 1996 to $150,000 in 1997, $170,000 in 1998 and $200,000 in 1999, with cost-of-living adjustment for 2000 and 2001 if the Players Association does not exercise its option;

■ Credit for major-league service for regular-season days cancelled by the strike begun in August, 1994.

Why 14 owners voted to approve this contract after previously voting to reject it remained a cause for speculation. Some observers credited Allan H. (Bud) Selig, president of the Milwaukee Brewers and chairman of the Executive Council, with persuading several teams to change their votes. Others suggested that Jerry Reinsdorf, Chairman of the White Sox and a proponent of fiscal restraint, had angered several of his colleagues November 19 by signing Albert Belle to a five-year contract worth more than $50 million. Whatever the cause for the reversal, the Players Association approved the agreement on December 5, and the two sides signed papers implementing it on December 9.

(For details, see CHRONOLOGY OF KEY EVENTS IN BASEBALL, 1996 LABOR NEGOTIATIONS.)

UMPIRE McSHERRY DIES

Opening Day in Cincinnati, Monday, April 1, was marred by the death of home plate umpire John McSherry, who collapsed seven pitches into the game between the Reds and the Montreal Expos and died about an hour later. The game was postponed until April 2 when, ironically, McSherry had been scheduled to see a doctor for an irregular heartbeat. A coroner's autopsy revealed that McSherry suffered "sudden cardiac death" brought on by severe heart disease, an enlarged heart and blocked arteries.

McSherry's death prompted his colleague Eric Gregg to seek help in addressing his weight problem at Duke University. Gregg went on leave April 8 and returned to work on July 13. A.L. umpire Rocky Roe took similar leave on May 6 and returned July 22.

YANKEES WIN WORLD SERIES

The season came to a dramatic conclusion on Saturday night, October 26, when New York Yankees third baseman Charlie Hayes drifted into foul territory to catch a pop fly hit by Mark Lemke, second baseman for the Atlanta Braves. Lemke's out gave the Yankees a 3-2 victory in Game 6 of the World Series and clinched New York's 23rd championship, more than any other team.

The Yankees had returned to the Series after a 15-year absence. Their triumph, as do most World Series, had a noticeably salutary effect on their home town fans, and was made additionally poignant by Joe and Frank Torre's excellent adventure. Manager Joe, hired in November 1995, to replace Buck Showalter, made it to the Series for the first time in his career, after playing 18 seasons in the majors and previously managing e New York Mets, the Braves and the St. Louis ardinals. His brother Frank, also a former major ague player, was suffering from heart disease and onfined to a New York hospital bed as the Series egan. Early on the day before the sixth game, he nderwent successful heart transplant surgery. The ankees became the first team since the 1986 Mets to in the Series after dropping the first two games.

ATLANTA WINS N.L. EAST AGAIN

The Braves, champions of the N.L. East for the fifth ear in a row (not counting the interrupted 1994 sea- n), extended their own league record for consecutive vision titles. The Braves spotted the Montreal Expos early lead in the division race, but took over first ace for good on May 19. They led the Expos by three ames at the end of June, 11 1/2 at the end of August d clinched the division on September 22.

Atlanta hit .270 as a team, .020 higher than in 1995 nd second in the league, but did not lead the N.L. in ny of the key offensive categories. The Braves fin- hed second in home runs, fourth in runs scored and ird in hits. Only Chipper Jones with 114 runs (ninth the league) and Marquis Grissom with 207 hits hird) and 10 triples (tied for second) finished among e league's offensive leaders. Jones and Grissom were lso the only Braves regulars to hit over .300. Ryan lesko led the team in home runs with 34, and Jones d in RBIs with 110. Right fielder David Justice was st for the season when he dislocated his right shoul- er on May 15.

The Braves' pitching was once again outstanding, but is time John Smoltz, not Greg Maddux, stood out. he team finished first in complete games, strikeouts nd fewest walks allowed and second in earned runs, west hits allowed and fewest home runs allowed. moltz lost his first start and then won 14 games in a ow. He led the majors with 24 wins and 276 strikeouts nd led the N.L. in innings pitched (253.2) and winning ercentage (.750). Smoltz won The Sporting News' .L. Pitcher of the Year award.

CARDINALS SNARE N.L. CENTRAL CROWN

The Cardinals won the N.L. Central Division by six ames over the Houston Astros, clinching the title on eptember 24 with a win over the Pittsburgh Pirates. he Cardinals relied on balanced pitching and hitting nd the intense leadership of first-year manager Tony a Russa, hired in October 1995. Rightfielder Brian ordan batted .310, hit 17 home runs and drove in 104 uns and played superb defense. Ron Gant hit 30 omers and drove in 82 runs. Five pitchers won 11 or nore games, including Alan Benes (13-10, 4.90 ERA), he Sporting News' N.L. Rookie Pitcher of the Year. Jennis Eckersley, acquired in a trade with Oakland in ebruary, tallied 30 saves. The Astros were in first lace as late as September 2 but faded badly in the tretch, losing 17 of their last 25 games.

PADRES SQUEAK BY DODGERS

The San Diego Padres swept three games from the Jodgers on the season's final weekend to win the N.L. West by one game. The Padres spent 142 days in or tied for first place and never trailed by more than 2 1/2 games. But they dropped behind Los Angeles after los- ing on September 13 and did not regain the lead until shutting out the Dodgers, 2-0, in the last game. San Diego was led offensively by third baseman Ken Caminiti, who finished fifth in the league in hitting (.326) and home runs (40, tied) and third in RBIs (130), fifth in total bases (339) and third in slugging percent- age (.621). Joey Hamilton led Padres pitchers with 15 wins, and Trevor Hoffman racked up 42 saves, earning The Sporting News' N.L. Fireman of the Year award.

The Dodgers were in first place on June 24 when Manager Tommy Lasorda drove himself to a hospital complaining of abdominal pains. Later diagnosed as having suffered a heart attack, Lasorda underwent coronary catheterization to open the distal right coro- nary artery. Cleared a month later to resume manag- ing, Lasorda nevertheless opted to retire on July 29 and accept a Dodgers vice-presidency.

Bench coach Bill Russell served as acting manager during Lasorda's leave of absence during which the Dodgers compiled a 14-16 record. Upon Lasorda's retirement, Russell was named manager and guided the team to a 35-21 finish. A game-and-a-half behind San Diego when Russell got promoted, Los Angeles battled for first place the rest of the way, never falling more than 2 1/2 games out of the lead but never build- ing a margin of more than 2 1/2 games.

The Dodgers' pitching staff finished with an ERA of 3.46, best in the majors. Hideo Nomo won 16 games, and Ramon Martinez and Ismael Valdes won 15 each. Todd Worrell tied for the league lead with 44 saves. Catcher Mike Piazza hit .336 (second in the league), drove in 105 runs and hit 36 home runs, a personal high and Los Angeles Dodgers record.

LASORDA'S RECORD

Lasorda retired in his 20th season as Dodgers man- ager and his 47th in the team's organization. He joined Connie Mack, John McGraw and Walter Alston, Lasorda's predecessor, as the only four managers to be with the same team for at least 20 seasons. Lasorda's overall record, 1,599-1,439, puts him 12th in games managed, 13th on the all-time win list and 23rd in win- ning percentage. His teams won eight division titles, four N.L. pennants and two World Series.

YANKEES TRIUMPH IN A.L. EAST

When the Yankees beat the Baltimore Orioles, 13-10, on April 30, the game, certainly no testimonial to base- ball's desire to speed up play, consumed a major-league record four hours and 21 minutes. But for New York, last winners of a division title in 1981 (not including the shortened 1994 season), the wait was worth it. They moved into first place in the A.L. East and were never again headed. New York built a steady lead over the Orioles and clinched the division on September 25 with a doubleheader sweep of the Milwaukee Brewers.

For the surprising Yankees, youngsters Derek Jeter and Andy Pettitte complemented the work of several veterans. Shortstop Jeter hit .314 with 78 runs batted in and played marvelous defense to earn The Sporting News' A.L. Rookie Player of the Year award. Lefthander Pettitte led the A.L. in wins with 21. Bernie Williams hit 29 homers and drove in 102 runs, Tino Martinez added 25 HRs and 117 RBIs and Cecil Fielder, acquired from the Detroit Tigers on July 31, hit 13 home runs in 53 games. Pitchers Jimmy Key and Kenny Rogers won 12 games each, and reliever Mariano Rivera (8-3, 2.09 ERA) excelled as a setup man for closer John Wetteland (43 saves), who was named TSN's A.L. Fireman of the Year.

The Orioles started fast, but then fell into a prolonged slump, losing 50 of their next 90 games. They challenged the Yankees again in September but could not get closer than $2^1/2$ games. They held off the Chicago White Sox and the Seattle Mariners to take the wild card spot in the playoffs. Cal Ripken played in all of the Orioles' games to extend his record streak of consecutive games played to 2,316.

INDIANS REPEAT IN A.L. CENTRAL

The Indians won their second straight division title in 1996. They held first place from April 13 on, a total of 170 days, but in contrast to 1995, they did not break the race wide open until after the All-Star break. By the end of July, their lead had increased to seven games, and thereafter it never dropped below five. The Indians clinched the pennant on September 17 by defeating Chicago, 9-4.

Cleveland batters led the assault on A.L. pitching, finishing first in batting average (.293), hits and fewest strikeouts, and second in runs scored (952, a club record), total bases and slugging percentage. The Indians hit 218 home runs, 11 better than the team's previous high, but still finished fifth in the league. Cleveland became the third team in A.L. history to have three players with 30 or more home runs and 100 or more runs batted in. Albert Belle led the offensive barrage with 48 home runs, 148 RBIs (first in the A.L.) and a .311 batting average. Jim Thome also hit .311 with 38 homers and 116 RBIs, and Manny Ramirez added 33 homers and 112 runs batted in. Kenny Lofton led the A.L. in stolen bases for the fifth consecutive year with 75. Indians pitchers led the A.L. in ERA (4.34) for the second year in a row. Charles Nagy led the team in wins with 17. Orel Hershiser added 15, and Jack McDowell had 13. Jose Mesa recorded 39 saves, second best in the league.

RANGERS WIN FIRST DIVISION TITLE

The Texas Rangers overcame years of futility to win the A.L. West championship, the first division title in the franchise's history. The Rangers won 90 games to finish $4^1/2$ games ahead of the Mariners, whose loss on September 29 handed the pennant to Texas. Except for three days in mid-April, the Rangers were in first place the entire season.

The Rangers' offense was led by Juan Gonzalez (.314, 47 HRs, 144 RBIs), Dean Palmer (38 HRs, 107 RBIs), Rusty Greer (18 HRs, 100 RBIs) and Mickey Tettleton (24 HRs, 83 RBIs). Texas set single-season club records in several offensive categories and came within one RBI

(by Kevin Elster) of becoming the 18th team in major league history to have four players with 100 or more runs batted in.

The Texas pitching staff was led by Bobby Witt and Ken Hill, each with 16 wins. Mike Henneman recorded 31 saves.

R. ALOMAR SUSPENDED FOR SPITTING

The last weekend of the regular season was marred by one of the ugliest incidents in baseball history. In the first inning of the Baltimore-Toronto game on Friday, September 27, home plate umpire John Hirschbeck called Orioles second baseman Roberto Alomar out on strikes and then ejected him following an argument. Alomar followed manager Dave Johnson back onto the field and, as the argument continued, spat into the umpire's face. After the game Alomar said that Hirschbeck had sworn at him, behavior Alomar attributed to a personality change pursuant to the death of the umpire's son in 1993.

On September 29, A.L. President Gene A. Budig suspended Alomar for five regular-season games. When reporters told Hirschbeck about the suspension, generally viewed as quite lenient, and informed him of Alomar's comments the night before, the umpire charged into the Orioles' clubhouse looking to confront the player. Other umpires restrained him, and Hirschbeck did not work that day's game. Alomar, having appealed the suspension immediately, was permitted to play. He hit a game-winning, 10th-inning home run that propelled Baltimore into the playoffs.

Alomar issued a written apology, but when it became clear that his appeal would not be heard until after the World Series, the Major League Umpires Association, arguing for a more severe suspension to commence during the postseason, threatened to boycott the opening of the Division Series. The first game between the Orioles and the Indians on Tuesday, October 2, began 30 minutes late, only after Budig agreed to move the appeal up to October 4.

Still, the possibility remained that the umpires would strike if the suspension were not served during the postseason. Alomar dropped his appeal on October 3 and Major League Baseball successfully sought an injunction in U.S. District Court to prevent an umpires' strike. Alomar played the entire Orioles' postseason and will sit out the first five games in 1997.

DIVISION SERIES END QUICKLY

Both N.L. Division (or Wild Card) Series ended in three-game sweeps. The Braves, playing the first two games on the road, eliminated the Dodgers, and the Cardinals, opening at home, defeated the Padres. Both A.L. series went to four games. The Orioles shocked the Indians, taking the first two games at home, dropping the third and then winning the fourth on a 12th-inning home run by Roberto Alomar. The Yankees dropped the first game at home before taking the next three from Texas, despite the heroics of Juan Gonzalez who batted .438 and hit five home runs.

Baseball pundits continued to debate whether the wild-card system enhances the regular season or tracts from it, but opinion seemed more uniform that e present playoff arrangement, in its second year, is ot entirely satisfactory. Critics contend that the division champion with the best regular-season record iould oppose the playoff qualifier with the worse cord regardless of division, and that home field ivantage, at least in the first round of the playoffs, iould be determined by record and not by rotation. irther, they argue that requiring a team with the ome field advantage to play the first two games of a est-of-five series on the road opens the door too wide- to the possibility of upsets.

BRAVES POUND CARDINALS

Atlanta and St. Louis played a stunning N.L. hampionship Series with the Braves, teetering on the ink of elimination, storming back to slam the ardinals in the final three games by the collective ore of 32-1. After John Smoltz pitched Atlanta to a 4- victory in Game 1, the Cards came back to win ames 2, 3 and 4. Gary Gaetti's grand slam defeated reg Maddux in Game 2, Donovan Osborne out- tched Tom Glavine in Game 3, 3-2, and Dmitri Young id Brian Jordan engineered a four-run comeback to in Game 4.

Held to 31 hits in the first four games, the Braves xploded for 22 hits in Game 5, winning, 14-0. Maddux iut down the Cards in Game 6, 3-1, and then Atlanta ompleted its comeback with a 15-0 romp, setting ecords for most runs in a single LCS game and in a

seven-game series (44). The Braves became the first N.L. team to trail three games to one in an LCS and rebound to win and the eighth team to do so in any post-season series.

YANKS OUST ORIOLES IN FIVE

The A.L. Championship Series saw the Yankees make relatively quick work of their division rivals, the Orioles. After a rainout on October 8 which eliminated a scheduled travel day, New York won the series open- er, 5-4. Bernie Williams' 11th-inning home run won the game, but a controversial homer was hit by Derek Jeter to tie the score in the eighth inning. A 12-year-old fan, Jeffrey Maier, reached over the right field wall to deflect a ball that Baltimore outfielder Tony Tarasco probably would have caught. Umpire Richie Garcia chose not to invoke Rule 3.16, covering fan interfer- ence, and ruled the ball a home run. Later, having reviewed a videotape of the play, Garcia did not agree with Tarasco, but admitted he had erred and should have ruled the play a double.

The Orioles rebounded to win Game 2, 5-3, but when the series shifted to Baltimore, the Yankees won three straight games, powered by eight home runs. Jimmy Key beat Mike Mussina in Game 3, and the Yankees bullpen—David Weathers, Graeme Lloyd, Rivera and Wetteland—shut down the Orioles in Game 4. New York scored six times in the third inning of Game 5, with homers by Jim Leyritz, Cecil Fielder and Darryl Strawberry, to put the series away.

CHRONOLOGY OF KEY EVENTS IN BASEBALL'S 1996 LABOR NEGOTIATIONS

January 18—Owners approve a plan for interleague play dur- g the 1997 season. Teams in the N.L. East and N.L. Central ill play a three-game series against each team in the A.L. East id A.L. Central, respectively. Teams in the N.L. West will play four-game series against each team in the A.L. West.

February 8—Union responds to owners' proposal of ovember 15, 1995, with a new proposal of its own calling for a 5 percent tax on all player salaries for three years and a luxu- r tax on team payrolls to take effect in 1999.

February 21—Owners accept union's plan for a 2.5 percent x on all player salaries, but only for 1996. Owners offer two ternatives for 1997: A 5 percent tax on all salaries or a 25 per- ent luxury tax on team payroll amounts above $44 million.

March 21—Meeting in Phoenix, owners approve a revenue aring plan by a vote of 26-1-1, contingent upon approval by e union. Under this plan, a percentage of each team's reve- iue (60 percent in 1996 and 1997, 80 percent in 1998, 85 per- ent in 1999 and 100 percent in 2000 and 2001) would be taxed 15 percent. The resulting pool would be split with 85 percent vided equally among all 28 clubs and 15 percent distributed the low-revenue clubs.

Owners also submit to the union a new six-year proposal, opping the luxury tax rate and increasing the threshold. fter two years of a straight tax on all player salaries, the lux- ry tax would start in 1998 with payroll amounts over $46 mil- on being taxed at 40 percent. The threshold would rise 7 per- ent per year until it reaches $56.3 million in 2001.

April 30—Union makes an informal proposal for a 30 percent x on portions of payrolls over $64 million in the middle two ears of a six-year agreement.

May 23—Owners modify their proposal, reducing the luxury x rate to 39.5 percent and raising the threshold at which the

tax would take effect to $46.5 million. Management negotiator Randy Levine offers the union two options: a 53-month agree- ment with the luxury tax in the second, third and fourth years or a six-year agreement with the tax in the third, fourth and fifth years.

August 7—The Executive Council authorizes Levine to make a "last and final" offer to the union if talks do not progress in the next few days. This strategy would set the stage for the owners to ask U.S. District Court Judge Sonia Sotomayor to lift the injunction of March 31, 1995, so that the owners could impose new rules upon the players unilaterally.

August 9-11—Parties meet 13 times over three days amidst reports that service time for days on strike is the key issue holding up an agreement.

October 24—After meeting regularly during the postseason, Donald Fehr, Executive Director of the Players Association, and Levine complete an agreement.

November 6—Owners meet and reject the Fehr-Levine accord by a vote of 12 votes for and 18 against. The owners then vote, 30-0, to empower the Executive Council to seek "cer- tain clarifications and modifications to finalize the agreement without further approval by the clubs."

November 11—Union rejects two major proposed changes in the agreement.

November 19—Albert Belle signs a five-year, $52.5 million contract with the White Sox.

November 26—Owners approve Fehr-Levine accord by a vote of 26-4.

December 4—Union postpones vote on the proposed contract.

December 5—Acting through each team's player represen- tative, union votes to approve the contract.

December 9—Parties sign formal agreement.

YANKEES STUN BRAVES

The World Series opened in New York, and after a rainout, Atlanta won the first two games. Rookie Andruw Jones hit two home runs in his first two Series at-bats (the second player to do so), and Maddux scattered six hits over eight innings to silence the Yankees in Game 2, 4-0.

After the Series moved to Atlanta, New York won the third game, 5-2, scoring three runs in the eighth inning off reliever Greg McMichael. The following night, the Braves took a 6-0 lead after five innings, but the Yankees got three runs in the sixth, three in the eighth and two in the 10th to win, 8-6. New York won Game 5, 1-0, on a unearned run made possible by a muffed fly ball as outfielders Marquis Grissom and Jermaine Dye came close to colliding. The game was the final one played in Atlanta-Fulton County Stadium as the Braves will move next door to the refurbished stadium used for the 1996 Summer Olympics.

Back in New York, the Yankees closed out the Series with a 3-2 win as all three New York runs came off Maddux. The Braves outhit the Yankees overall, .254 to .216, and outscored them, 26-18. But time and again in key situations, New York's relievers kept Atlanta's hitters, especially the Braves' reserves, at bay. Each member of the Yankees voted a full World Series share received $216,870.08. Atlanta's full shares came to $143,524.36.

NEW STRIKE ZONE

When the Official Playing Rules Committee met in January, it altered the size of the strike zone, lowering the bottom of the zone from "a line at the top of the knees" to "a line at the hollow beneath the kneecap." For several years, critics had complained that the strike zone had become too small, too low and too far outside. Simultaneously, it was argued, this evolving strike zone was not only handicapping pitchers but also contributing to longer games.

The new definition, whether or not it was observed by umpires long accustomed to the old rule, had little effect on the time of games. The average time for a 9-inning game in the American League dropped three minutes (from 2:56 to 2:53), but in the National League average game time increased two minutes (from 2:45 to 2:47). Moreover, although pitchers struck out 15 percent more batters in 1996 than they had in 1995, walks increased at nearly the same rate. League batting averages moved in opposite directions, up .007 in the A.L. and down .001 in the N.L.

THE YEAR OF THE HOME RUN

Both leagues set records for total home runs in 1996. A.L. batters hit 2,742 homers, breaking the mark of 2,634 set in 1987. N.L. batters hit 2,220, breaking their 1993 mark of 1,956. The two-league total, 4,962, smashed the previous record of 4,458 (set in 1987 when the A.L. had 14 teams and the N.L. only 12) and the mark for two 14-team leagues, 4,030, set in 1993.

Three players, the Baltimore Orioles' Brady Anderson, Barry Bonds of the San Francisco Giants, and Gary Sheffield of the Florida Marlins, tied the major league record for most homers in April with 11.

Bonds finished the year with 42 homers and 40 stolen bases, becoming the second member of the 40-40 club. Henry Rodriguez, one of the year's surprising new sluggers, hit 20 homers in the season's first two months for the Montreal Expos, setting an N.L. record. Eddie Murray of the Orioles became the 15th player in major league history to hit 500 home runs when he connected off Felipe Lira of the Detroit Tigers in the seventh inning of a game on September 6. Murray thus joined Willie Mays and Henry Aaron as the only players to hit 500 home runs with 3,000 hits.

Seventeen players hit 40 or more home runs, a record. Mark McGwire of the Oakland Athletics led the A.L. with 52, despite playing in only 130 games. Andres Galarraga of the Colorado Rockies led the N.L. with 47. Nine players, including the league leaders, set single-season records for their teams, and 10 teams set new marks for their franchises. Baltimore set a major league record for home runs by a team, 257, with Brady Anderson's 50 homers leading the way. The Orioles hit five homers on September 15 to shatter the old mark, 240 by the 1961 New York Yankees. Two days before, Baltimore's Rafael Palmeiro and Bobby Bonilla had homered on consecutive pitches against the Tigers to give Detroit 228 homers allowed, breaking the major league mark of 227, set in 1987 by the Orioles. The Tigers wound up with 241 homers allowed. McGwire and Anderson became the 13th and 14th players to hit 50 or more homers in a season, a feat that has now been acccomplished 21 times. The 1996 season marked the fourth time two players hit 50 or more in the same season.

OTHER OFFENSIVE FEATS

Paul Molitor of the Minnesota Twins got the 3,000th hit of his career on September 16 when he tripled in the fifth inning off the Kansas City Royals' Jose Rosado. Molitor became the 21st player to reach 3,000 hits (not including Adrian "Cap" Anson, whose hit total is disputed) and the first to do so by hitting a triple.

Tony Gwynn of the San Diego Padres hit .353 and won his seventh N.L. batting title, despite falling four plate appearances short of the required 502. Gwynn won the title under the exception to Rule 10.23(a), which allows a player with fewer than the required number of plate appearances to be credited with enough mythical at-bats to reach the minimum. Adding an extra 0-for-4 to Gwynn's totals left him with a mythical average of .349, still better than Colorado's Ellis Burks at .344.

Alex Rodriguez of the Seattle Mariners hit .358 to win the A.L. batting title. Rodriguez hit 36 home runs and drove in 123 runs and was named Major League Player of the Year by The Sporting News.

THREE NO-HITTERS

Despite all these batting pyrotechnics, three pitchers still managed to throw no-hitters. On May 11, Al Leiter pitched the first no-hitter in Marlins' history, defeating the Rockies, 11-0, in Joe Robbie Stadium. Leiter struck out six and walked two and was aided by six Marlins runs in the first inning.

Dwight Gooden, out of baseball most of 1994 and all 1995 but re-signed by the Yankees, no-hit the ariners, 2-0, on May 14 in New York. It was only ooden's second win since June 19, 1994, when he was spended from baseball for violations of his addiction tercare program.

The Dodgers' Hideo Nomo no-hit the Rockies at oors Field, the major league park most friendly to hit-rs, on September 17. The Dodgers won, 9-0. Nomo ruck out eight and walked five. He pitched from the retch from the fourth inning on because of control oblems.

Roger Clemens of the Boston Red Sox tied his own ajor league record for most strikeouts in a nine-ning game when he struck out 20 Tigers on ptember 18. Pat Hentgen of the Toronto Blue Jays on 20 games and led the A.L. in innings pitched 65.2), complete games (10) and shutouts (3) and was med TSN's A.L. Pitcher of the Year.

AN EARTHQUAKE AND OTHER EVENTS

The May 2 game between the Cleveland Indians and eattle Mariners was postponed after a 4.8 earthquake ook the Kingdome at 9:04 pm PDT. Cleveland was ading, 6-3, with Seattle at bat in the seventh inning. he game was suspended for a few minutes and then ostponed to the next day when the Indians won it, 6-4.

Ongoing renovations to Oakland Coliseum forced the thletics to play their first six "home" games at ashman Field, the 9,353-seat home of the Las Vegas ars, Oakland's Class AAA affiliate. Oakland finished is special homestand with a record of 2-4 and com-eted a triple play in their final Las Vegas game.

In order to avoid possible conflicts with the Repub-can National Convention, scheduled for San Diego, e Padres and the Mets played a three-game series in Ionterrey, Mexico, August 16, 17 and 18. In the first gular-season major league game played outside the nited States and Canada, Fernando Valenzuela, a ative Mexican, threw out the ceremonial first pitch d then pitched San Diego to a 15-10 victory.

ALBERT BELLE DISCIPLINED

On May 16, A.L. President Gene Budig ordered leveland's Albert Belle, who had thrown a ball at a nagazine photographer, to perform community ser-ice and to seek counseling immediately. Less than two eeks later, Belle cursed a fan who wanted to trade a all Belle had hit for a home run. Three nights after nat, on May 31, Belle threw a forearm at Fernando ina of the Milwaukee Brewers in attempt to break up double play. Some observers called his action legiti-nate; others saw it as vicious. It led to a bench-clearing rawl and to five-game suspensions for Belle, Indians itcher Julian Tavarez and Milwaukee pitcher Mike Matheny. Belle's suspension, his fifth in six years, was ut to three games after an appeal hearing and then to ne game and a $25,000 fine after threat of a suit by the layers Association.

ATTENDANCE OFF FROM 1993

Major league attendance for 1996 totalled 60,097,381, 14.5 percent dropoff from 1993, baseball's last full

season. N.L. clubs outdrew A.L. clubs slightly, 30,379,288 to 29,718,093. Two teams in each league drew more than 3 million fans: The Rockies (who led both leagues with 3,891,014) and Dodgers in the N.L. and the Orioles and Indians in the A.L. Nine other teams drew more than 2 million, and all clubs exceed-ed the one million mark.

MANAGERIAL CHANGES

Besides the Dodgers, three teams changed man-agers during the season, and four others made changes after the season. The Marlins fired Rene Lachemann, the first manager in their four-year histo-ry, on July 7, with the Marlins in fourth place in the N.L. East with a record of 40-47. Third base coach Cookie Rojas handled the team for one game, after which John Boles, Florida's director of player develop-ment and a former minor league manager, took the job. He guided the Marlins to a 40-35 mark, good for third place in the division.

On August 6, Marcel Lachemann, Rene's brother, resigned as manager of the California Angels with the team in last place in the A.L. West. California named John McNamara, who had managed the Angels in 1983-84, to replace Lachemann for the balance of the season. But McNamara had to be hospitalized on August 21 because of a blood clot in his right calf. Third base coach Joe Maddon took over the team for 10 days.

The Mets fired Dallas Green on August 26 and replaced him with Bobby Valentine, manager of their Class AAA team in Norfolk, Va. The Mets were 59-72 at the time of the change and in fourth place in the divi-sion. Valentine's record for the balance of the season was 12-19.

On September 17, Jim Leyland, manager of the Pittsburgh Pirates for 11 seasons, announced that he would not return for 1997. Despite having given assur-ances three weeks before that he would honor his con-tract that extended through 2000, Leyland felt compelled to change his mind, citing the club's desire to reduce its player payroll drastically. The Pirates hired their third base coach, Gene Lamont, former manager of the Chicago White Sox, to replace Leyland on October 3.

The Phillies, after finishing last in the N.L. East with a 67-95 record, fired Jim Fregosi on September 30. They hired Detroit third base coach Terry Francona as his replacement on October 30. The Red Sox, third in the A.L. East, fired Kevin Kennedy, also on September 30. They hired Atlanta Braves third base coach Jimy Williams, former manager of the Blue Jays, as his replacement on November 19.

On October 4 the Astros fired Terry Collins, replac-ing him with broadcaster and former pitcher Larry Dierker. On the same date, John Boles relinquished the manager's job in Florida, returning to his previous position, and the Marlins hired Leyland. Collins, in turn, was hired by the Angels on November 4.

SCHOTT SUSPENDED

Cincinnati General Partner Marge Schott, long a con-troversial figure for things said and done, agreed on

June 12 to surrender day-to-day control of the Reds through the 1998 season for disciplinary reasons. Under terms of the agreement, Schott retained ownership of her share (6½ of 15 units) of the Reds, but she was no longer able to be the spokesperson for the team. She had the right to help select her successor and to make major financial decisions.

In 1993 the Executive Council had suspended Schott for a year, fined her $25,000 and forced her to attend multicultural sensitivity sessions for her repeated use of racial and ethnic slurs. Her 1996 troubles began on Opening Day when she bemoaned postponement of the Reds' first game after the collapse of umpire John McSherry. In the following weeks, other news media took advantage of Schott's proclivity for saying things bound to embroil her in further difficulties. On May 5, for example, she appeared on ESPN's "Sunday Conversation," part of "Sports Center," and talked about Adolf Hitler. "Everything you read, when he came in, he was good," she said. "But then he went too far."

Schott was replaced as chief executive officer on an interim basis by Reds controller John Allen, but Schott could not abide several fan-friendly gestures he made soon after assuming control of the team. Her continued interference in the club's operation and her effort to prevent Allen from attending the All-Star Game caused N.L. President Leonard Coleman to ban her from Riverfront Stadium on July 17. The ban was lifted July 28.

Schott's preference for a long-term successor was not Allen but Reds General Manager Jim Bowden. When Coleman refused to approve Bowden, saying that the team's business affairs and baseball affairs should be directed by two people, she agreed to Allen's appointment as Managing Executive.

OWNERSHIP CHANGES

Owners approved the sale of the Pirates on February 13 and the sale of the St. Louis Cardinals on March 21. Newspaper executive Kevin McClatchy headed a group that took control of the Pirates. The Cardinals, along with Busch Stadium and related properties, were sold by Anheuser-Busch to a group led by Frederick Hanser, William DeWitt Jr. and Andrew Baur.

After prolonged negotiations, the Walt Disney Company signed an agreement on May 15 giving it a 25 percent stake in the Angels, immediate control of daily operations and the right to acquire the whole team upon the death of Owner Gene Autry. The sale proceeded after Disney and the City of Anaheim agreed on a plan to renovate Anaheim Stadium with Disney contributing $70 million and the city $30 million. On November 19 Disney Baseball Enterprises announced that the team's name would be changed to the Anaheim Angels.

PLAYERS SCORE IN SALARY ARBITRATION

Seventy-six players filed for salary arbitration, but only 10 cases proceeded all the way through the hearing and decision stage. Players won more cases than they lost for the first time since 1990, but the average raise for all players who filed was the lowest in several years. Seven players (Steve Avery, Jeff Fassero, Chuck

Knoblauch, Mike Stanton, Mark Lewis, Rick Wilk and Bernie Williams) won their cases and got rais averaging 55 percent. The three who lost (Willie Ban Arthur Rhodes and Ivan Rodriguez) got an average percent raise. Those who settled prior to an arbitrato decision received an average 67 percent raise.

SALARIES RISE SLIGHTLY

Figures released near the end of the year showe slight increase in the average player salary from 1995 1996. According to the Player Relations Committee, t average salary in 1996 was $1,099,875, up 0.5 perc from 1995's $1,094,440. The Players Association, whi calculates salaries slightly differently, reported increase of 0.8 percent from $1,110,766 to $1,119,981.

Fifteen teams paid an average salary over $1 milli but no team exceeded the $2 million mark. T Yankees had the largest payroll, and the Brewers h the smallest, paying an average salary of $420,3 according to the association.

BELLE SIGNS RECORD CONTRACT

Whether or not Jerry Reinsdorf's decision to si Albert Belle to a contract valued at over $50 million p suaded several other owners to change their votes the proposed collective bargaining agreement, Bell deal still stands as baseball's richest, both as ann compensation and as a total package. According to p lished reports, Belle signed a five-year contract th will pay him $10 million for each of the next five ye plus an option for a sixth year with a $5 million buyo The contract eclipsed both Barry Bonds' six-year c tract for $43.75 million, signed in December, 1992, a the four-year, $34 million contract extension signed Ken Griffey in January.

In the postseason market for free agents, Toror and Florida also made big headlines. The Blue Ja signed Roger Clemens (three years, $24.75 millio and the Marlins signed Bobby Bonilla (four yea $23.3 million), pitcher Alex Fernandez (five years, $ million) and Moises Alou (five years, $25 millio Other players who signed large, long-term contra included pitcher Jaime Navarro with the White S (four years, $20 million), John Smoltz with the Brav (four years, $31 million) and John Wetteland with t Rangers (four years, $23 million).

RETIREMENTS

Twins outfielder Kirby Puckett went on the disabl list March 28 complaining of blurred vision, later di nosed as glaucoma. He had laser surgery April 17 a took batting practice May 28, but his vision problen persisted. A second laser procedure showed irn versible damage to his retina and forced his retireme after a 12-year career in which he hit .318 with 2 home runs and 1,085 runs batted in.

Dave Winfield, who last played for Cleveland in 199 announced his retirement on February 8. He spent years in the majors (plus one year on the disabled li with six different teams. Winfield batted .283 and f ished in the top 20 on several all-time lists: 2,973 gam (7th), 3,110 hits (14th), 465 home runs (19th) a 1,833 runs batted in (11th).

Outfielder Andre Dawson announced in August that he would retire at the end of the season after a career spanning 21 years. Dawson hit 438 home runs, good for 22nd place on the all-time list, drove in 1,591 runs (24th place) and had 2,774 hits (37th place).

Tigers shortstop Alan Trammell announced his retirement after his team's final game. Trammell played 20 major league seasons, won the A.L. Most Valuable Player Award in 1984 and teamed with second baseman Lou Whitaker for 19 years to form one of the game's best and most durable double play combinations.

Perhaps the most celebrated retirement of the year was that of Ozzie Smith, generally recognized as the greatest defensive shortstop of all time. Smith's continued productivity caused some distress in the St. Louis clubhouse after manager Tony La Russa picked Royce Clayton as the Cardinals' everyday shortstop, but Smith left the game in style to the plaudits of fans around the league.

CONCLUSION

When former pitcher Jim Bunning was inducted into the Hall of Fame on August 4, he complained that "for over four years baseball has been rudderless. Get a rudder," he urged all those in positions of power. Whether the agreement forged over four years of difficult negotiations will provide the basis for building that rudder remains to be seen. But on the field, here's how the game in 1996 ended up:

FINAL STANDINGS

AMERICAN LEAGUE

EAST DIVISION

Team	N.Y.	Bal.	Bos.	Tor.	Det.	Cle.	Chi.	Min.	K.C.	Tex.	Sea.	Oak.	Cal.	W	L	Pct.	GB
New York	.....	10	6	8	8	9	7	6	7	8	5	3	9	6	92	70	.568	.....
Baltimore	3	....	7	8	11	5	4	9	7	9	3	7	9	6	88	74	.543	4
Boston	7	6	....	8	12	1	6	7	6	3	6	7	8	8	85	77	.525	7
Toronto	5	5	5	....	7	5	5	7	5	8	2	7	8	5	74	88	.457	18
Detroit	5	2	1	6	....	0	3	4	6	6	4	6	4	6	53	109	.327	39

CENTRAL DIVISION

Team	Cle.	Chi.	Mil.	Min.	K.C.	N.Y.	Bal.	Bos.	Tor.	Det.	Tex.	Sea.	Oak.	Cal.	W	L	Pct.	GB
Cleveland	...	8	7	10	7	3	7	11	7	12	4	8	6	9	99	62	.615	.....
Chicago	5	....	6	6	7	6	8	6	7	10	8	5	5	6	85	77	.525	14 1/2
Milwaukee	6	7	....	9	9	6	3	5	5	8	6	4	7	5	80	82	.494	19 1/2
Minnesota	3	7	4	....	7	5	5	6	8	6	7	6	6	8	78	84	.481	21 1/2
Kansas City	6	6	4	6	....	4	3	9	5	6	6	7	5	8	75	86	.466	24

WEST DIVISION

Team	Tex.	Sea.	Oak.	Cal.	N.Y.	Bal.	Bos.	Tor.	Det.	Cle.	Chi.	Mil.	Min.	K.C.	W	L	Pct.	GB
Texas	....	3	6	9	7	10	6	10	9	8	4	7	5	6	90	72	.556	.....
Seattle	10	....	5	8	9	5	6	5	6	4	7	9	6	5	85	76	.528	4 1/2
Oakland	7	8	....	7	3	4	5	4	8	6	7	5	7	7	78	84	.481	12
California	4	5	6	....	7	6	4	7	6	4	6	7	4	7	70	91	.435	19 1/2

Tie game—Texas at Baltimore, June 17 (6 innings).
NOTE: Read across for wins, down for losses.
Clinching dates: New York (East)—September 25, first game; Cleveland (Central)—September 17; Texas (West)—September 27; Baltimore (wild card)—September 28.

NATIONAL LEAGUE

EAST DIVISION

Team	Atl.	Mon.	Fla.	N.Y.	Phi.	St.L.	Hou.	Cin.	Chi.	Pit.	S.D.	L.A.	Col.	S.F.	W	L	Pct.	GB
Atlanta	....	10	6	7	9	9	6	7	7	9	9	5	5	7	96	66	.593	.....
Montreal	3	....	8	7	6	8	9	9	6	7	4	3	9	9	88	74	.543	8
Florida	7	5	....	7	6	6	7	9	6	5	3	6	8	5	80	82	.494	16
New York	6	6	6	....	7	5	4	6	5	8	3	4	5	6	71	91	.438	25
Philadelphia	4	7	7	6	....	4	2	2	6	7	4	6	6	6	67	95	.414	29

CENTRAL DIVISION

Team	St.L.	Hou.	Cin.	Chi.	Pit.	Atl.	Mon.	Fla.	N.Y.	Phi.	S.D.	L.A.	Col.	S.F.	W	L	Pct.	GB
St. Louis	....	11	8	8	10	4	4	6	7	8	8	4	4	6	88	74	.543	.....
Houston	2	....	6	8	8	6	4	5	8	10	6	6	5	8	82	80	.506	6
Cincinnati	5	7	....	8	5	5	3	3	6	10	9	4	7	9	81	81	.500	7
Chicago	5	5	5	....	4	5	6	6	7	7	6	8	5	7	76	86	.469	12
Pittsburgh	3	5	8	9	....	3	5	7	5	5	4	6	5	8	73	89	.451	15

WEST DIVISION

Team	S.D.	L.A.	Col.	S.F.	Atl.	Mon.	Fla.	N.Y.	Phi.	St.L.	Hou.	Cin.	Chi.	Pit.	W	L	Pct.	GB
San Diego	....	8	5	11	4	8	9	10	8	4	6	3	6	9	91	71	.562	.....
Los Angeles	5	....	7	7	7	9	7	8	7	8	6	8	5	6	90	72	.556	1
Colorado	8	6	....	5	7	3	5	7	6	8	8	6	7	7	83	79	.512	8
San Francisco	2	6	8	....	5	4	7	6	6	7	4	4	5	4	68	94	.420	23

NOTE: Read across for wins, down for losses.
Clinching dates: Atlanta (East)—September 22; St. Louis (Central)—September 24; San Diego (West)—September 29; Los Angeles (wild card)—September 29.

1996 REVIEW Year in review

A.L. DIVISION SERIES

BALTIMORE VS. CLEVELAND

GAME 1

HIGHLIGHTS

BALTIMORE 10, CLEVELAND 4

Why the Orioles won: As they had all season, the Orioles used their big bats to subdue Cleveland. Baltimore clubbed four homers, including two by B.J. Surhoff, and Cleveland starter Charles Nagy lasted just $5^1/_3$ innings.

Why the Indians lost: Nagy had gone 17-5 with a 3.41 ERA during the season, but he yielded nine hits—including two homers—and seven earned runs. Power hitter Albert Belle went 0-for-4 and left two of the Indians' five runners in scoring position.

The turning point: The Orioles led, 4-3, entering their half of the sixth, and they exploded for five runs to put the game out of reach. The key shot in the inning was a grand slam by Bobby Bonilla that gave Baltimore a 9-3 lead.

Notable: Brady Anderson hit Nagy's fourth pitch of the game out of the park. It was Anderson's 51st homer of the year and his 13th leadoff shot. Entering the season, Anderson had hit 72 career homers. . . . The Orioles never went down one-two-three in an inning. . . . Bonilla's slam was the first by an Orioles non-pitcher in postseason play. Mike Cuellar hit one in the 1970 ALCS and Dave McNally cranked one in the 1970 World Series.

Quotable: Baltimore's Anderson, on his knack for hitting home runs: "Maybe if somebody else was doing it, it would seem more amazing. But when you're the one doing it, it's not that mind-boggling." . . . Baltimore's Bonilla, on the slugfests between the Orioles and Indians: "It seems like we play games like this all the time with Cleveland. No matter how many runs you score, it seems like it ain't enough."

BOX SCORE

TUESDAY, OCTOBER 1, AT BALTIMORE

Cleveland	AB	R	H	RBI	PO	A
Lofton, cf	5	0	1	1	3	0
Seitzer, dh	5	0	1	0	0	0
Thome, 3b	4	0	1	0	0	0
Belle, lf	4	0	0	0	4	0
Franco, 1b	4	0	1	0	10	0
Ramirez, rf	4	2	3	1	1	0
Kent, 2b	4	1	1	0	2	2
S. Alomar, c	3	0	1	1	3	1
Giles, ph	1	0	0	0	0	0
Pena, c	0	0	0	0	1	0
Vizquel, ss	2	1	1	1	0	3
Nagy, p	0	0	0	0	0	4
Embree, p	0	0	0	0	0	0
Shuey, p	0	0	0	0	0	0
Tavarez, p	0	0	0	0	0	0
Totals	36	4	10	4	24	10

Baltimore	AB	R	H	RBI	PO	A
Anderson, cf	5	2	2	1	0	0
Zeile, 3b	4	2	2	0	3	3
R. Alomar, 2b	4	0	1	1	1	1

Baltimore	AB	R	H	RBI	PO
Palmeiro, 1b	4	2	1	1	8
Bonilla, rf	3	1	1	4	3
Devereaux, pr-rf	0	0	0	0	2
Ripken, ss	5	0	3	1	2
Murray, dh	4	0	0	0	0
Surhoff, lf	4	2	2	2	4
Hoiles, c	2	1	0	0	3
Parent, c	0	0	0	0	3
Wells, p	0	0	0	0	0
Orosco, p	0	0	0	0	0
Mathews, p	0	0	0	0	0
Rhodes, p	0	0	0	0	0
Myers, p	0	0	0	0	0
Totals	35	10	12	10	27

Cleveland	0	1	0	2	0	0	1	0	0—
Baltimore	1	1	2	0	0	5	1	0	x—

Cleveland	IP	H	R	ER	BB
Nagy (L)	$5^1/_3$	9	7	7	3
Embree	$^1/_3$	0	1	1	0
Shuey	$1^1/_3$	3	2	2	0
Tavarez	1	0	0	0	1

Baltimore	IP	H	R	ER	BB
Wells (W)	$6^2/_3$	8	4	4	1
Orosco	*0	0	0	0	0
Mathews	$^2/_3$	2	0	0	0
Rhodes	$^2/_3$	0	0	0	0
Myers	1	0	0	0	0

*Pitched to one batter in seventh.

E—Zeile. LOB—Cleveland 8, Baltimore 8. 2B—Kent, Vizquel, Palme Ripken. HR—Ramirez, Anderson, Bonilla, Surhoff 2. SF—Vizquel, R.Alor SB—Vizquel. CS—Vizquel. HBP—By Orosco (Thome), by Emb (Palmeiro), by Nagy (Hoiles). WP—Mathews. T—3:25. A—47,644. Coble, plate; Kosc, first; Tschida, second; Welke, third; Shulock, left fi Hendry, right field.

GAME 2

HIGHLIGHTS

BALTIMORE 7, CLEVELAND 4

Why the Orioles won: For the second consecuti game, Baltimore got effective starting pitchin Scott Erickson worked $6^2/_3$ innings and allowed s hits and just three earned runs. He fanned six a walked just two. The Orioles' relief pitching also w effective, as three hurlers yielded one earned run $2^1/_3$ innings.

Why the Indians lost: Starter Orel Hershis pitched well for five innings, but reliever Eric Plu got ripped for three runs in two innings. In additio the final five hitters in Cleveland's batting ord went a combined 1-for-17 with two walks and fi strikeouts.

Turning points:

1. With no outs in the Orioles' eighth and the sco tied at 4, B.J. Surhoff hit a chopper to reliever Pa Assenmacher, who tossed the ball to catcher San Alomar for a forceout at home. But with Surhoff ru ning just inside the first-base line, Alomar uncork a wild throw that skipped past first baseman J Kent. Cal Ripken raced home from second with t go-ahead run and Eddie Murray moved from first third. The Orioles scored twice more in the inni

7-4 lead.

Orioles reliever Armando Benitez got the three ?est outs of the game after the Indians loaded the ?s with nobody out in the eighth. He got Kenny ?on on a sacrifice fly, struck out Manny Ramirez ? sinker and retired Alomar on a pop-up to second. ?Brady Anderson highlighted the Orioles' three-fifth by clubbing his second homer of the series, one a solo shot.

able: The Indians were playing so tight, they ?an impromptu meeting in the dugout. . . . With ?on and one out in the third, the Indians' Kevin ?zer hit a wicked shot up the middle. It deflected ?Erickson's glove to Roberto Alomar, who turned ?to an inning-ending double play.

table: Sandy Alomar, on his bad throw in the ?th inning that led to a Baltimore rally: "(Surhoff) ?itely was blocking my view. I tried to aim the ?w. Maybe I should have held the ball, but I made ?decision to throw it. Usually when you hit the ?you get the interference call, but I wasn't going ?ike the chance." . . . Umpire Tim Tschida, on ?ly Alomar's throw to first: "In our judgment, it ?simply an errant throw." . . . Cleveland manager ?e Hargrove, on his team's ability to win three ?es in a row: "You bet."

BOX SCORE
WEDNESDAY, OCTOBER 2, AT BALTIMORE

?land	AB	R	H	RBI	PO	A
?, cf	5	1	2	0	1	0
?, 1b	4	0	2	1	7	1
pr-1b	0	1	0	0	0	0
?e, 3b	4	1	2	0	0	1
?lf	3	1	1	2	2	1
?, dh	3	0	0	1	0	0
?ez, rf	4	0	0	0	2	1
?mar, c	4	0	0	0	7	1
?l, ss	3	0	0	0	2	6
?no, 2b	3	0	1	0	2	2
?ser, p	0	0	0	0	1	1
?p	0	0	0	0	0	0
?macher, p	0	0	0	0	0	1
?z, p	0	0	0	0	0	0
?als	33	4	8	4	24	15

?ore	AB	R	H	RBI	PO	A
?son, cf	4	1	2	2	2	0
?3b	4	0	0	0	0	0
?mar, 2b	4	1	1	1	2	3
?iro, 1b	3	1	1	0	10	0
?a, rf	2	1	0	0	1	0
?eaux, pr-rf	0	0	0	0	1	0
?, ss	3	1	2	1	1	4
?y, dh	3	0	2	1	0	0
?nder, pr-dh	0	1	0	0	0	0
?ff, lf	4	0	0	0	1	0
?glia, pr-lf	0	1	0	0	0	0
?, c	3	0	1	0	8	0
?, ph-c	0	0	0	0	0	0
?on, p	0	0	0	0	1	3
?o, p	0	0	0	0	0	0
?z, p	0	0	0	0	0	0
?, p	0	0	0	0	0	0
?als	30	7	9	5	27	10

?and	0	0	0		0	0	3		0	1	0—4
?ore	1	0	0		0	3	0		0	3	x—7

?land	IP	H	R	ER	BB	SO
?ser	5	7	4	3	3	3
?(L)	*2	1	3	3	2	2
?macher	2/3	0	0	0	1	0
?z	1/3	1	0	0	1	0

Baltimore	IP	H	R	ER	BB	SO
Erickson	6 2/3	6	3	3	2	6
Orosco	†1/3	2	1	1	0	1
Benitez (W)	1	0	0	0	1	1
Myers (S)	1	0	0	0	0	0

*Pitched to three batters in eighth. †Pitched to two batters in eighth.
E—Seitzer, S. Alomar. DP—Cleveland 1, Baltimore 1. LOB—Cleveland 6, Baltimore 8. 2B—Seitzer, Ripken, Murray. HR—Belle, Anderson. SF—Franco, Anderson. SB—Lofton 2, Vizquel. HBP—By Hershiser (Ripken). T—3:27. A—48,970. U—Kosc, plate; Tschida, first; Welke, second; Shulock, third; Hendry, left field; Coble, right field.

GAME 3

HIGHLIGHTS
CLEVELAND 9, BALTIMORE 4

Why the Indians won: Returning to Jacobs Field, where they had lost just two games since September 8, the Indians remained alive thanks to a near-flawless performance by their bullpen. Alan Embree, Paul Shuey, Paul Assenmacher, Eric Plunk and Jose Mesa combined to pitch 3 1/3 innings of two-hit ball. Jack McDowell set the trend for good pitching by starting and working 5 2/3 effective innings.

Why the Orioles lost: Jesse Orosco got bombed. After coming in for Mike Mussina, who was pitching well, to face some lefthanders in the seventh, Orosco faced three batters and allowed three runs and three walks. He left the game without retiring a batter.

Turning point: With the game tied at 4, Orioles starter Mike Mussina—after struggling mightily early—had just thrown back-to-back hitless innings. But manager Davey Johnson hooked him anyway. Mussina wasn't pleased. Orosco came on because two of the next three hitters—Kenny Lofton and Jim Thome—were lefthanders. But Orosco walked Lofton on four pitches. With Kevin Seitzer up next, Lofton stole second. The Orioles pitched out, but catcher Mark Parent's throw sailed wide and short-hopped into the runner. Seitzer eventually walked, putting runners on first and second. Thome was lifted for pinch hitter Casey Candaele, who was inserted to bunt but ended up drawing a walk. Johnson then brought in righthander Armando Benitez. "If (Candaele) bunts them over," Johnson says, "we walk Albert (Belle). Instead, he walked Candaele. That's what wasn't in our game plan." Belle responded by belting a grand slam.

Notable: Belle got two of his three hits in the series in this game. . . . When pitching to Belle in the seventh, Benitez jumped to an 0-2 count on Belle. But Belle crushed the third pitch for his grand slam.

Quotable: Cleveland shortstop Omar Vizquel, on Belle's game-winning grand slam: "One swing can change the whole thing. And, hopefully, that one will." . . . Seitzer, on his team's precarious situation: "If things didn't change, I knew we could go home tomorrow. And I didn't want to go home."

BOX SCORE
FRIDAY, OCTOBER 4, AT CLEVELAND

Baltimore	AB	R	H	RBI	PO	A
Anderson, cf	3	0	0	1	1	0
Zeile, 3b	5	0	1	0	0	0

Baltimore	AB	R	H	RBI	PO	A
R. Alomar, 2b	3	0	0	0	2	1
Palmeiro, 1b	4	0	0	0	9	1
Bonilla, rf	4	1	1	0	1	0
Ripken, ss	4	1	1	0	1	7
Murray, dh	4	1	2	0	0	0
Surhoff, lf	4	1	2	3	1	0
Devereaux, pr	0	0	0	0	0	0
Hoiles, c	2	0	1	0	7	0
Alexander, pr	0	0	0	0	0	0
Parent, c	1	0	0	0	2	0
Mussina, p	0	0	0	0	0	0
Orosco, p	0	0	0	0	0	0
Benitez, p	0	0	0	0	0	1
Rhodes, p	0	0	0	0	0	0
Mathews, p	0	0	0	0	0	0
Totals	34	4	8	4	24	10

Cleveland	AB	R	H	RBI	PO	A
Lofton, cf	3	2	0	0	3	0
Seitzer, dh	4	1	2	3	0	0
Thome, 3b	2	0	0	0	1	0
Candaele, ph	0	1	0	0	0	0
Kent, 3b	1	0	0	0	0	0
Belle, lf	4	1	2	4	4	0
Franco, 1b	4	0	0	0	5	1
Ramirez, rf	4	1	1	1	2	0
S. Alomar, c	4	0	0	0	8	0
Vizquel, ss	4	3	3	0	1	1
Vizcaino, 2b	4	0	2	1	2	1
McDowell, p	0	0	0	0	1	2
Embree, p	0	0	0	0	0	0
Shuey, p	0	0	0	0	0	0
Assenmacher, p	0	0	0	0	0	0
Plunk, p	0	0	0	0	0	0
Mesa, p	0	0	0	0	0	0
Totals	34	9	10	9	27	5

Baltimore	0	1	0	3	0	0	0	0	0—4
Cleveland	1	2	0	1	0	0	4	1	x—9

Baltimore	IP	H	R	ER	BB	SO
Mussina	6	7	4	3	2	6
Orosco (L)	*0	0	3	3	3	0
Benitez	1	1	1	1	0	1
Rhodes	1/3	1	1	1	1	0
Mathews	2/3	1	0	0	0	1

Cleveland	IP	H	R	ER	BB	SO
McDowell	5 2/3	6	4	4	1	5
Embree	1/3	0	0	0	0	0
Shuey	2/3	1	0	0	2	0
Assenmacher (W)	1/3	0	0	0	0	0
Plunk	1	0	0	0	0	0
Mesa	1	1	0	0	0	1

*Pitched to four batters in seventh.
E—Zeile, Bonilla. DP—Baltimore 1, Cleveland 1. LOB—Baltimore 7, Cleveland 7. 2B—Vizcaino 2. HR—Surhoff, Belle, Ramirez. SB—Murray, Lofton 3, Belle, Vizquel. HBP—By McDowell (Anderson). T—3:44. A—44,250. U—Merrill, plate; Young, first; Clark, second; Johnson, third; Evans, left field; Kaiser, right field.

GAME 4

HIGHLIGHTS

BALTIMORE 4, CLEVELAND 3 (12 INNINGS)

Why the Orioles won: Starter David Wells set the tone by working seven strong innings and allowing three runs and seven hits. Four relievers combined to allow just one walk and no hits with seven strikeouts over the final five innings.

Why the Indians lost: The bats were silent. Kenny Lofton and Albert Belle went hitless. In the series, Lofton hit .167 and Belle batted .200. Other Indians who flopped at the plate were Sandy Alomar (.125) and Julio Franco (.133).

Turning point: Roberto Alomar, who many felt shouldn't have been playing after spitting in the face of umpire John Hirschbeck during the final regular-

season series, hit a game-winning home run in 12th to give Baltimore the victory. Booed throu out the game by Cleveland fans, Alomar tied game with a single in the ninth inning.

Notable: The Orioles returned to the ALCS for first time since 1983. . . . Seven Indians pitchers c bined to strike out a playoff-record 23 batters. Sta Charles Nagy set the pace by fanning 12 and reli Jose Mesa recorded six. . . . The umpires threate to strike because Roberto Alomar's suspension spitting in the face of an umpire was to be serve the start of the 1997 season and not in the post son. But a federal judge ordered them to work.

Quotable: Baltimore manager Davey Johnson, Roberto Alomar: "He's a great player. But he is v sensitive. The thing in Toronto really hurt him a g deal. When we needed a big hit, he hit the home to win it. The same thing here. He got the hit to ti and then you almost knew the script was already v ten that when he had a chance to win it, he was g to win it." . . . Cleveland manager Mike Hargrove his staff's knack for fanning Orioles in Game 4 wish we would have gotten one more strike Either that or score one more run. We didn't get big hits. All of our pitchers were outstanding. B doesn't matter how many strikeouts you get."

BOX SCORE

SATURDAY, OCTOBER 5, AT CLEVELAND

Baltimore	AB	R	H	RBI	PO
Anderson, cf	5	0	1	0	4
Zeile, 3b	6	0	2	0	1
R. Alomar, 2b	6	1	3	2	5
Palmeiro, 1b	6	1	1	1	8
Bonilla, rf	6	1	1	1	4
Ripken, ss	6	0	2	0	3
Murray, dh	4	0	2	0	0
Incaviglia, lf	5	0	1	0	0
Devereaux, lf	1	0	0	0	1
Hoiles, c	3	0	0	0	4
Surhoff, ph	1	0	1	0	0
Alexander, pr	0	1	0	0	0
Parent, c	1	0	0	0	6
Wells, p	0	0	0	0	0
Mathews, p	0	0	0	0	0
Orosco, p	0	0	0	0	0
Benitez, p	0	0	0	0	0
Myers, p	0	0	0	0	0
Totals	50	4	14	4	36

Cleveland	AB	R	H	RBI	PO
Lofton, cf	5	0	0	0	3
Vizquel, ss	5	0	2	1	3
Seitzer, dh	4	0	0	0	0
Candaele, pr-dh	0	0	0	0	0
Belle, lf	4	0	0	0	1
Franco, 1b	4	1	1	0	3
Ramirez, rf	4	1	2	0	3
Kent, 3b	3	0	0	0	1
Wilson, ph	1	0	0	0	0
Thome, 3b	0	0	0	0	0
S. Alomar, c	5	0	1	2	22
Vizcaino, 2b	5	1	1	0	0
Nagy, p	0	0	0	0	0
Embree, p	0	0	0	0	0
Shuey, p	0	0	0	0	0
Assenmacher, p	0	0	0	0	0
Plunk, p	0	0	0	0	0
Mesa, p	0	0	0	0	0
Ogea, p	0	0	0	0	0
Totals	40	3	7	3	36

Baltimore..	0	2	0	0	0	0	0	0	1	0	0	1
Cleveland..	0	0	0	2	1	0	0	0	0	0	0	0

timore	IP	H	R	ER	BB	SO
ls	7	7	3	3	3	3
hews	1 1/3	0	0	0	1	1
sco	2/3	0	0	0	0	1
itez (W)	2	0	0	0	1	4
rs (S)	1	0	0	0	0	1

veland	IP	H	R	ER	BB	SO
y	6	6	2	2	2	12
oree	1/3	0	0	0	0	1
ey	*0	1	0	0	0	0
enmacher	2/3	0	0	0	0	2

Cleveland	IP	H	R	ER	BB	SO
Plunk	1	0	0	0	0	2
Mesa (L)	3 2/3	7	2	2	0	6
Ogea	1/3	0	0	0	1	0

*Pitched to one batter in seventh.

E—R.Palmeiro, Vizcaino. LOB—Baltimore 13, Cleveland 8. 2B—Zeile, Ripken, Ramirez 2. HR—R. Alomar, Palmeiro, Bonilla. SH—Lofton, Kent. SB—Vizquel, Seitzer. CS—Anderson, Vizquel, S. Alomar. T—4:41. A—44,280. U—Young, plate; Clark, first; Johnson, second; Evans, third; Kaiser, left field; Merrill, right field.

STATISTICS

BALTIMORE ORIOLES' BATTING AND FIELDING AVERAGES

yer, position	G	AB	R	H	TB	2B	3B	HR	RBI	BB	IBB	SO	Avg.	PO	A	E	Avg.
ken, ss	4	18	2	8	11	3	0	0	2	0	0	3	.444	7	15	0	1.000
rray, dh	4	15	1	6	7	1	0	0	1	3	2	4	.400	0	0	0	.000
hoff, lf-ph	4	13	3	5	14	0	0	3	5	0	0	1	.385	6	0	0	1.000
mar, 2b	4	17	2	5	8	0	0	1	4	2	0	3	.294	10	6	0	1.000
derson, cf	4	17	3	5	11	0	0	2	4	2	0	3	.294	7	0	0	1.000
le, 3b	4	19	2	5	6	1	0	0	0	2	0	5	.263	4	9	2	.867
illa, rf	4	15	4	3	9	0	0	2	5	4	0	6	.200	9	0	1	.900
aviglia, lf-pr	2	5	1	1	1	0	0	0	0	0	0	4	.200	0	0	0	.000
ent, c	4	5	0	1	1	0	0	0	0	0	0	2	.200	19	0	0	1.000
meiro, 1b	4	17	4	3	7	1	0	1	2	1	0	6	.176	35	1	1	.973
les, c-ph	4	7	1	1	1	0	0	0	0	3	1	3	.143	14	3	0	1.000
xander, dh-pr	3	0	2	0	0	0	0	0	0	0	0	0	.000	0	0	0	.000
itez, p	3	0	0	0	0	0	0	0	0	0	0	0	.000	0	2	0	1.000
ckson, p	1	0	0	0	0	0	0	0	0	0	0	0	.000	1	3	0	1.000
thews, p	3	0	0	0	0	0	0	0	0	0	0	0	.000	0	1	0	1.000
ssina, p	1	0	0	0	0	0	0	0	0	0	0	0	.000	0	0	0	.000
rs, p	3	0	0	0	0	0	0	0	0	0	0	0	.000	0	0	0	.000
sco, p	4	0	0	0	0	0	0	0	0	0	0	0	.000	0	0	0	.000
des, p	2	0	0	0	0	0	0	0	0	0	0	0	.000	0	0	0	.000
ls, p	2	0	0	0	0	0	0	0	0	0	0	0	.000	0	3	0	1.000
vereaux, rf-pr-lf	4	1	0	0	0	0	0	0	0	0	0	0	.000	2	0	0	1.000
otals	4	149	25	43	76	6	0	9	23	17	3	40	.289	114	43	4	.975

CLEVELAND INDIANS' BATTING AND FIELDING AVERAGES

yer, position	G	AB	R	H	TB	2B	3B	HR	RBI	BB	IBB	SO	Avg.	PO	A	E	Avg.
quel, ss	4	14	4	6	7	1	0	0	2	3	0	4	.429	6	10	0	1.000
mirez, rf	4	16	4	6	14	2	0	2	2	1	0	4	.375	8	2	0	1.000
caino, 2b	3	12	1	4	6	2	0	0	1	1	0	1	.333	4	3	1	.875
me, 3b	4	10	1	3	3	0	0	0	0	1	0	5	.300	1	1	0	1.000
tzer, dh-1b	4	17	1	5	6	1	0	0	4	2	0	4	.294	7	1	1	.889
e, lf	4	15	2	3	9	0	0	2	6	3	1	2	.200	11	1	0	1.000
ton, cf	4	18	3	3	3	0	0	0	1	2	0	3	.167	10	0	0	1.000
nco, 1b-dh	4	15	1	2	2	0	0	0	1	1	0	6	.133	18	1	0	1.000
mar, c	4	16	0	2	2	0	0	0	3	0	0	2	.125	40	4	1	.978
t, 2b-1b-pr-3b	4	8	2	1	2	1	0	0	0	0	0	0	.125	3	3	0	1.000
enmacher, p	3	0	0	0	0	0	0	0	0	0	0	0	.000	0	1	0	1.000
daele, ph-dh-pr	2	0	1	0	0	0	0	0	0	1	0	0	.000	0	0	0	.000
oree, p	3	0	0	0	0	0	0	0	0	0	0	0	.000	0	0	0	.000
shiser, p	1	0	0	0	0	0	0	0	0	0	0	0	.000	1	1	0	1.000
Dowell, p	1	0	0	0	0	0	0	0	0	0	0	0	.000	1	2	0	1.000
sa, p	2	0	0	0	0	0	0	0	0	0	0	0	.000	0	0	0	.000
jy, p	2	0	0	0	0	0	0	0	0	0	0	0	.000	0	4	0	1.000
ea, p	1	0	0	0	0	0	0	0	0	0	0	0	.000	0	0	0	.000
a, c	1	0	0	0	0	0	0	0	0	0	0	0	.000	1	0	0	1.000
nk, p	3	0	0	0	0	0	0	0	0	0	0	0	.000	0	0	0	.000
ey, p	3	0	0	0	0	0	0	0	0	0	0	0	.000	0	0	0	.000
arez, p	2	0	0	0	0	0	0	0	0	0	0	0	.000	0	0	0	.000
s, ph	1	1	0	0	0	0	0	0	0	0	0	1	.000	0	0	0	.000
son, ph	1	1	0	0	0	0	0	0	0	0	0	0	.000	0	0	0	.000
otals	4	143	20	35	54	7	0	4	20	15	1	32	.245	111	34	3	.980

BALTIMORE ORIOLES' PITCHING RECORDS

cher	G	GS	CG	IP	H	R	ER	HR	BB	IBB	SO	HB	WP	W	L	Pct.	ERA
ers	3	0	0	3	0	0	0	0	0	0	3	0	0	0	0	.000	0.00
thews	3	0	0	2 2/3	3	0	0	0	1	0	2	0	1	0	0	.000	0.00

Pitcher	G	GS	CG	IP	H	R	ER	HR	BB	IBB	SO	HB	WP	W	L	Pct.	E
Benitez	3	0	0	4	1	1	1	1	2	0	6	0	0	2	0	1.000	2.
Erickson	1	1	0	6 2/3	6	3	3	1	2	0	6	0	0	0	0	.000	4.
Mussina	1	1	0	6	7	4	3	1	2	0	6	0	0	0	0	.000	4.
Wells	2	2	0	13 2/3	15	7	7	1	4	1	6	0	0	1	0	1.000	4.
Rhodes	2	0	0	1	1	1	1	0	1	0	1	0	0	0	0	.000	9.
Orosco	4	0	0	1	2	4	4	0	3	0	2	1	0	0	1	.000	36.
Totals	4	4	0	38	35	20	19	4	15	1	32	1	1	3	1	.750	4.

No shutouts. Saves—Myers 2.

CLEVELAND INDIANS' PITCHING RECORDS

Pitcher	G	GS	CG	IP	H	R	ER	HR	BB	IBB	SO	HB	WP	W	L	Pct.	E
Assenmacher	3	0	0	1 2/3	1	0	0	0	1	1	2	0	0	1	0	1.000	0.
Tavarez	2	0	0	1 1/3	1	0	0	0	2	0	1	0	0	0	0	.000	0.
Ogea	1	0	0	1/3	0	0	0	0	1	1	0	0	0	0	0	.000	0.
Mesa	2	0	0	4 2/3	8	2	2	1	0	0	7	0	0	0	1	.000	3.
Hershiser	1	1	0	5	7	4	3	1	3	0	3	1	0	0	0	.000	5.
McDowell	1	1	0	5 2/3	6	4	4	1	1	0	5	1	0	0	0	.000	6.
Plunk	3	0	0	4	1	3	3	0	2	1	6	0	0	0	1	.000	6.
Nagy	2	2	0	11 1/3	15	9	9	4	5	0	13	1	0	0	1	.000	7.
Shuey	3	0	0	2	5	2	2	2	2	0	2	0	0	0	0	.000	9.
Embree	3	0	0	1	0	1	1	0	0	0	1	1	0	0	0	.000	9.
Totals	4	4	0	37	43	25	24	9	17	3	40	4	0	1	3	.250	5.

No shutouts or saves.

SCORE BY INNINGS

Baltimore	2	4	2		3	3	5		1	3	1	0 0	1—
Cleveland	1	3	0		5	1	3		5	2	0	0 0	0—

MISCELLANEOUS STATISTICS

Sacrifice hits—Kent, Lofton.
Sacrifice flies—R. Alomar, Anderson, Franco, Vizquel.
Stolen bases—Lofton 5, Vizquel 4, Belle, Murray, Seitzer.
Caught stealing—Vizquel 2, R. Alomar, Anderson.
Double plays—R. Alomar, Ripken and Palmeiro; Erickson, R. Alomar and Palmeiro; Hershiser, Vizquel and Seitzer; Vizquel, Vizca
and Franco.
Left on bases—Baltimore 8, 8, 7, 13—36; Cleveland 8, 6, 7, 8—29.
Hit by pitcher—By Orosco (Thome), by Hershiser (Ripken), by McDowell (Anderson), by Nagy (Hoiles), by Embree (Palmeiro).
Passed balls—None.
Balks— None.
Time of games— First game, 3:25; second game, 3:27; third game, 3:44; fourth game, 4:41.
Attendance— First game, 47,644; second game, 48,970; third game, 44,250; fourth game, 44,280.
Umpires—Clark, Coble, Evans, Hendry, Johnson, Kaiser, Kosc, Merrill, Shulock, Tschida, Welke and Young.
Official scorers—Hank Kozloski, Jim Oremland.

NEW YORK VS. TEXAS

GAME 1

HIGHLIGHTS

TEXAS 6, NEW YORK 2

Why the Rangers won: Newly acquired John Burkett pitched the game of his life. Pitching in his first postseason game, Burkett consistently dodged Yankees threats, stranding nine baserunners. This was most evident in the sixth. With runners on first and third and no outs, Burkett struck out Darryl Strawberry and Mariano Duncan. After a walk to Joe Girardi, Derek Jeter popped to first to end the threat.

Why the Yankees lost: David Cone was roughed up, and the offense failed to get hits when they were needed. In six innings, Cone surrendered six runs on eight hits. On top of that, New York hitters were only 1-for-12 with runners in scoring position. Manager Joe Torre's decision to start Darryl Strawberry instead of Cecil Fielder at DH backfired. Strawberry went 0-for-4 with two strikeouts and stranded three runners.

The turning points:

1. Dean Palmer's outstanding play on Paul O'Neil line drive in the first inning stopped a potential b inning by New York. The Yankees started stron with Tim Raines leading off with a single and Wa Boggs following with a double to left. With runne on first and third, O'Neill lined a one-hopper towa the corner in left. Palmer then made a backhande diving play and threw O'Neill out at first, forcin Raines to stay at third. Bernie Williams follow with a run-scoring groundout, the only run of t inning.

2. After David Cone dominated the first three nings, Texas' Juan Gonzalez lined his first homer the series, a three-run shot with no outs, giving t Rangers a 3-1 lead. Three batters later, Palmer f lowed with a two-run homer to left. The home gave Texas a 5-1 lead.

Notable: Texas was making its first postseas appearance in the franchise's 36-year history; t nkees were appearing in the 36th postseason of eir 94-year history. . . . The game was delayed for out 10 minutes because of a umpires' protest of e Roberto Alomar ruling. . . . Jeter and Strawberry ere a combined 1-for-8, with three strikeouts and ne runners left on base. . . . Gonzalez batted .541 th five homers and 16 RBIs in 10 games against e Yankees in the regular season.

uotable: Yankees owner George Steinbrenner, on s team's performance: "I think we got our fannies ipped." . . . Rangers first baseman Will Clark, on e atmosphere at Yankee Stadium: "We've got a few ys in here with postseason experience. But you n't prepare people for what Yankee Stadium is all out. All those people, screaming nonstop."

BOX SCORE

TUESDAY, OCTOBER 1, AT NEW YORK

kas	AB	R	H	RBI	PO	A
milton, cf	4	0	0	0	2	0
driguez, c	4	1	1	0	7	0
er, lf	3	1	1	0	2	0
nzalez, rf	4	1	1	3	3	0
rk, 1b	4	1	1	0	8	1
tleton, dh	3	1	0	0	0	0
mer, 3b	4	1	2	2	1	2
Lemore, 2b	4	0	1	1	1	4
ter, ss	4	0	1	0	2	1
rkett, p	0	0	0	0	1	0
Totals	**34**	**6**	**8**	**6**	**27**	**8**

w York	AB	R	H	RBI	PO	A
ines, lf	5	1	1	0	0	0
ggs, 3b	5	0	1	0	1	0
Neill, rf	4	0	0	0	2	0
lliams, cf	4	0	1	1	4	0
rtinez, 1b	4	1	3	0	6	2
awberry, dh	4	0	0	0	0	0
ncan, 2b	4	0	2	1	1	4
ardi, c	3	0	1	0	10	1
ter, ss	4	0	1	0	1	1
ne, p	0	0	0	0	1	0
yd, p	0	0	0	0	1	0
athers, p	0	0	0	0	0	0
Totals	**37**	**2**	**10**	**2**	**27**	**8**

kas	0	0	0	5	0	1	0	0	0—6
w York	1	0	0	1	0	0	0	0	0—2

kas	IP	H	R	ER	BB	SO
rkett (W)	9	10	2	2	1	7

w York	IP	H	R	ER	BB	SO
ne (L)	6	8	6	6	2	8
yd	1	0	0	0	0	0
athers	2	0	0	0	0	2

DP—New York 1. LOB—Texas 3, New York 9. 2B—Elster, Boggs, rtinez 2. HR—Gonzalez, Palmer. CS—McLemore. T—2:50. A—57,205. —Evans, plate; Kaiser, first; Merrill, second; Young, third; Clark, left field; hnson, right field.

GAME 2

HIGHLIGHTS

NEW YORK 5, TEXAS 4 (12 INNINGS)

hy the Yankees won: Relief pitching and good eaks. Andy Pettitte started the game and gave the am 6⅓ innings of respectable pitching, but the llpen keyed the win. Six relievers combined to shut t the Rangers over the final 5⅔ innings, with Brian oehringer getting the victory. The club continued to ruggle with runners in scoring position. While they ally received a few timely hits, the victory was ulti-

mately decided because of a mistake by Texas.

Why the Rangers lost: Bad defense. After ranking as the major's best defensive team during the regular season, the Rangers lost on an error. Derek Jeter led off the bottom of the 12th with a single. Tim Raines then walked, moving Jeter to second base. With no one out, Charlie Hayes dropped down a perfect sacrifice bunt. In an attempt to throw Hayes out at first, third baseman Dean Palmer bounced his throw past Mark McLemore at first, allowing the winning run to score.

The turning points:

1. The biggest decision was made before the game started—New York manager Joe Torre decided to start Cecil Fielder over Darryl Strawberry at DH. The decision resulted in two crucial runs. With the score 4-1 in the Rangers' favor, Fielder lined a solo homer to left, helping to get the New York crowd back into the game. Then in the ninth, Fielder tied it at 4 with a single to right.

2. The deciding 12th inning. The Yankees escaped the top of the inning without allowing a run, then scored the game-winner. Torre was able to maneuver his pitchers to create favorable matchups for New York. After a leadoff single, Jeff Nelson relieved Graeme Lloyd. Nelson struck out the next two batters before allowing a single to Juan Gonzalez. Nelson then was replaced by Kenny Rogers, who walked Will Clark on four pitches to load the bases. Boehringer then came on and got Palmer to fly out to deep right-center.

Notable: Before Fielder's RBI single in the eighth, the Yankees had been 2-for-22 with runners in scoring position. . . . The teams left a combined 32 runners on base. . . . Through two games, Gonzalez had driven in seven of the Rangers' 10 runs and hit three homers. . . . Hayes had two sacrifices: a sacrifice fly in the seventh inning and the sacrifice bunt in the 12th.

Quotable: Torre, on the Yankees' comeback: "Tonight was a real charge for us. That was a better victory than if we had won it from the first inning because of how emotional it was for us." . . . Palmer, on his 12th-inning error: "It was a little bit wet. Still, it's a routine play." . . . Rangers manager Johnny Oates: "We came here trying to win two. We tried to make all the moves, but then we ran out of players. The pitching was getting thin at the end."

BOX SCORE

WEDNESDAY, OCTOBER 2, AT NEW YORK

Texas	AB	R	H	RBI	PO	A
Hamilton, cf	6	0	2	0	6	1
Rodriguez, c	4	0	0	0	2	2
Greer, lf	5	1	0	0	4	0
Gonzalez, rf	5	2	3	4	1	0
Clark, 1b	4	0	1	0	12	1
Palmer, 3b	6	0	1	0	1	3
Tettleton, dh	3	0	0	0	0	0
McLemore, 2b	4	0	0	0	5	5
Elster, ss	4	1	1	0	1	1
Hill, p	0	0	0	0	1	2
Cook, p	0	0	0	0	0	0
Russell, p	0	0	0	0	0	0
Stanton, p	0	0	0	0	0	1
Henneman, p	0	0	0	0	0	0
Totals	**41**	**4**	**8**	**4**	**33**	**16**

New York	AB	R	H	RBI	PO	A
Raines, lf	4	0	1	0	0	0
Boggs, 3b	3	0	0	0	1	1
Hayes, ph-3b	1	0	0	1	1	0
O'Neill, rf	5	0	1	0	6	0
Williams, cf	3	1	1	0	1	0
Martinez, 1b	4	1	0	0	12	1
Fielder, dh	3	1	2	2	0	0
Fox, pr-dh	0	0	0	0	0	0
Strawberry, ph-dh	1	0	0	0	0	0
Duncan, 2b	5	0	0	0	2	5
Leyritz, c	2	0	1	0	4	0
Girardi, pr-c	1	1	0	0	5	0
Jeter, ss	5	1	3	0	3	4
Pettitte, p	0	0	0	0	0	2
M. Rivera, p	0	0	0	0	0	0
Wetteland, p	0	0	0	0	1	1
Lloyd, p	0	0	0	0	0	0
Nelson, p	0	0	0	0	0	0
Rogers, p	0	0	0	0	0	0
Gooden, p	0	0	0	0	0	0
Totals	37	5	8	4	36	14

Texas	0	1	3	0	0	0	0	0	0	0	0	0—4
New York	0	1	0	1	0	0	1	1	0	0	0	1—5

Texas	IP	H	R	ER	BB	SO
Hill	*6	5	3	3	3	1
Cook	1	0	0	0	0	0
Russell	2 1/3	2	1	1	0	0
Stanton (L)	†1 2/3	1	1	0	3	1
Henneman	‡0	0	0	0	0	0

New York	IP	H	R	ER	BB	SO
Pettitte	6 1/3	4	4	4	6	3
M. Rivera	2 2/3	0	0	0	0	1
Wetteland	2	2	0	0	1	2
Lloyd	‡0	1	0	0	0	0
Nelson	2/3	1	0	0	0	2
Rogers	‡0	0	0	0	1	0
Boehringer (W)	1/3	0	0	0	0	0

*Pitched to two batters in seventh. †Pitched to two batters in 12th. ‡Pitched to one batter in 12th.

E—Palmer. DP—Texas 1, New York 1. LOB—Texas 11, New York 9. 2B—Elster, Jeter. HR—Gonzalez 2, Fielder. SH—Rodriguez, McLemore, Raines, Hayes. SF—Hayes. HBP—By Hill (Leyritz). WP—Pettitte. T—4:25. A—57,156. U—Kaiser, plate; Merrill, first; Young, second; Clark, third; Johnson, left field; Evans, right field.

GAME 3

HIGHLIGHTS

NEW YORK 3, TEXAS 2

Why the Yankees won: The Yankees were able to fend off Juan Gonzalez just enough to keep themselves in the game. And it paid off. With two outs in the ninth, unlikely hero Mariano Duncan singled home the winning run. Jimmy Key pitched five solid innings, and once again the Yankees' relievers held Texas scoreless. Jeff Nelson got the win and John Wetteland picked up another save.

Why the Rangers lost: Texas went into hibernation after the fifth inning. After Gonzalez hit a solo shot in the fourth and Ivan Rodriguez's RBI double in the fifth, the Rangers had only two hits in the final four innings.

The turning points:

1. Bernie Williams homered in the top of the first to put the Yankees up, 1-0, but his major contribution came with the Rangers at the plate. With two outs in the first, Rusty Greer stepped to the plate and drove the ball to deep center. Williams raced to the fence, leaped and pulled the ball back from over the fence. Thus, the score remained 1-0.

2. The Yankees had runners on first and third w one out and were headed for a big fourth inning w their leading regular-season RBI man—Tino M tinez—at the plate. But Texas met the challenge, ev if it was in an unconventional manner. With Ber Williams on first, Darren Oliver threw over a caught Williams in a rundown. Williams eventua was tagged out by Will Clark, who then threw hor to catch Tim Raines to complete the double play.

3. With a one-run lead and one out in the nin Yankees closer Wetteland made a spectacular p throwing out Warren Newson on a bouncer behi the mound. Because of the play, Texas had a runr on third with two outs, instead of runners on fi and third with one out. Wetteland then struck the next batter to end the game.

Notable: Derek Jeter batted leadoff for the fi time in the series, collecting three hits.... Throu $12 1/3$ innings, the Yankees' bullpen had allowed runs on five hits, while collecting both wins. . After Game 3, only Gonzalez (.462) was hitti above .300 for the Rangers in the series.

Quotable: Duncan, on Texas intentionally walki Martinez to pitch to him in the ninth: "If I was t manager, I would have done the same thing. Wh if they pitched to Tino and he hit a two-run home They'd be all over (Oates). He did the right thin ... Yankees manager Joe Torre, on the comeba "After the Rangers took the lead, the guys start yelling and screaming and they came to li Everybody rallied around. That's been our club year."

BOX SCORE

FRIDAY, OCTOBER 4, AT TEXAS

New York	AB	R	H	RBI	PO
Jeter, ss	4	1	2	0	1
Raines, lf	3	1	1	0	1
Williams, cf	3	1	2	2	2
Fielder, dh	4	0	0	0	0
Martinez, 1b	3	0	0	0	11
Duncan, 2b	3	0	2	1	2
Sojo, 2b	0	0	0	0	1
O'Neill, rf	3	0	0	0	2
R. Rivera, ph-rf	1	0	0	0	0
Hayes, 3b	3	0	0	0	0
Girardi, c	2	0	0	0	7
Key, p	0	0	0	0	0
Nelson, p	0	0	0	0	0
Wetteland, p	0	0	0	0	0
Totals	29	3	7	3	27

Texas	AB	R	H	RBI	PO
Hamilton, cf	5	0	1	0	2
Rodriguez, c	4	0	2	1	5
Greer, lf	4	0	1	0	3
Gonzalez, rf	4	1	2	1	3
Clark, 1b	3	0	0	0	9
Palmer, 3b	4	0	0	0	1
Tettleton, dh	3	0	0	0	0
Buford, pr	0	0	0	0	0
McLemore, 2b	3	0	0	0	2
Elster, ss	1	1	0	0	2
Newson, ph	1	0	0	0	0
Oliver, p	0	0	0	0	0
Henneman, p	0	0	0	0	0
Stanton, p	0	0	0	0	0
Totals	32	2	6	2	27

New York	1	0	0	0	0	0	0	0	2—
Texas	0	0	0	1	1	0	0	0	0—

York	IP	H	R	ER	BB	SO
....	5	5	2	2	1	3
son (W)..........................	3	1	0	0	2	3
teland (S).......................	1	0	0	0	1	1

as	IP	H	R	ER	BB	SO
er (L).............................	*8	6	3	3	2	3
neman..............................	2/3	1	0	0	1	0
nton..............................	1/3	0	0	0	0	1

Pitched to two batters in ninth.
—Girardi, Elster. DP—Texas 2. LOB—New York 4, Texas 8. 2B—
riguez. HR—Williams, Gonzalez. SH—McLemore. SF—Williams. SB—
er. CS—Williams, Hayes. HBP—By Oliver (Duncan). T—3:09. A—
)60. U—Tschida, plate; Welke, first; Shulock, second; Hendry, third;
le, left field; Kosc, right field.

GAME 4

HIGHLIGHTS

NEW YORK 6, TEXAS 4

hy the Yankees won: For the third consecutive me, the Yankees came from behind to win. They rted their comeback after Texas extended its lead 4-0 in the third inning. All nine players hit for the nkees in the fourth inning, as they scored three ns on four hits to cut it to 4-3. Bernie Williams was countable for two of the next three runs, slamng two solo shots.

hy the Rangers lost: The Rangers' pitching uldn't hold a lead. On top of that, the offense was nexistent in the late innings against the New York llpen—they didn't score in the last six innings. d the last three Yankees pitchers (six innings of rk) combined to hold the Rangers to one hit.

e turning points:
. With the Yankees trailing, 4-3, in the fourth, vid Weathers came on with two on, no outs, and an Gonzalez at the plate. Earlier in the game, nzalez hit his fifth homer of the series. But athers struck out Gonzalez with a slider in the t on a 3-2 pitch, then forced Will Clark to bounce o a 6-4-3 double play to end the inning.
. In the seventh, Cecil Fielder rewarded manager e Torre's confidence by driving in the winning run h a single to left against Roger Pavlik. Before the me, Fielder had been 2-for-23 in his career against vlik. Torre still had lefty Darryl Strawberry availle to hit on the bench. After the Yankees took the d, 5-4, Mariano Rivera and John Wetteland shut e door on the Rangers for good, pitching the final ee innings.

table: In 19²/3 innings, the New York bullpen owed only nine hits and two runs—only one rned.... Williams homered from both sides of the te in the playoffs for the second time in his reer. Last year, he became the first player to do so d is the only player to accomplish the feat.... th Derek Jeter (.412) and Williams (.467) hit safen every game of the series.... In the three loss-the Rangers were 5-for-28 with runners in scor-position. And Rusty Greer, Will Clark and Dean mer were a combined 0-for-12.... Gonzalez finied the series with five homers and nine RBIs, ile hitting .438.

Quotable: Wetteland, on Weathers' performance: "(It was) probably the single most impressive outing from the bullpen this series." . . . Gonzalez, on his fourth-inning strikeout: "I was trying too hard. It was an emotional series. I hit five home runs. But we lost. I'm disappointed." . . . Clark, on losing: "It's no fun to lose. We had a lot of success this season. Now we have to pick up the pieces and come back next year."

BOX SCORE

SATURDAY, OCTOBER 5, AT TEXAS

New York	AB	R	H	RBI	PO	A
Raines, lf	4	1	1	0	4	0
Boggs, 3b	4	0	0	0	0	0
Williams, cf	5	3	3	2	3	0
Martinez, 1b	4	1	1	0	4	0
Fielder, dh	4	1	2	2	0	0
Fox, pr-dh	0	0	0	0	0	0
Leyritz, ph-dh	1	0	0	0	0	0
O'Neill, rf	3	0	1	0	3	0
Hayes, ph	1	0	1	0	0	0
R. Rivera, rf	0	0	0	0	0	0
Duncan, 2b	4	0	1	1	4	2
Sojo, 2b	0	0	0	0	0	1
Girardi, c	3	0	1	0	6	0
Jeter, ss	4	0	1	1	3	3
Rogers, p	0	0	0	0	0	0
Boehringer, p	0	0	0	0	0	0
Weathers, p	0	0	0	0	0	1
M. Rivera, p	0	0	0	0	0	0
Wetteland, p	0	0	0	0	0	0
Totals	37	6	12	6	27	7

Texas	AB	R	H	RBI	PO	A
Hamilton, cf	4	0	0	0	5	0
Rodriguez, c	4	0	3	1	7	0
Greer, lf	4	0	0	0	3	0
Gonzalez, rf	3	1	1	1	2	0
Clark, 1b	5	0	0	0	6	1
Palmer, 3b	5	2	1	0	0	3
Tettleton, dh	3	0	1	1	0	0
McLemore, 2b	4	1	1	1	2	3
Elster, ss	3	0	2	0	1	2
Newson, ph	0	0	0	0	0	0
Buford, pr	0	0	0	0	0	0
Gonzales, ss	0	0	0	0	0	0
Witt, p	0	0	0	0	0	0
Patterson, p	0	0	0	0	0	0
Cook, p	0	0	0	0	0	0
Pavlik, p	0	0	0	0	1	0
Vosberg, p	0	0	0	0	0	0
Russell, p	0	0	0	0	0	0
Stanton, p	0	0	0	0	0	0
Henneman, p	0	0	0	0	0	0
Totals	35	4	9	4	27	9

New York	0	0	0	3	1	0	1	0	1—6
Texas	0	2	2	0	0	0	0	0	0—4

New York	IP	H	R	ER	BB	SO
Rogers	2	5	2	2	1	1
Boehringer	*1	3	2	1	2	0
Weathers (W)	3	1	0	0	0	3
M. Rivera	2	0	0	0	1	0
Wetteland (S)	1	0	0	0	2	1

Texas	IP	H	R	ER	BB	SO
Witt	3 1/3	4	3	3	2	3
Patterson	1/3	1	0	0	0	0
Cook	1/3	0	0	0	1	0
Pavlik (L)	2 2/3	4	2	2	0	1
Vosberg	†0	1	0	0	0	0
Russell	2/3	1	0	0	0	1
Stanton	1 1/3	1	1	1	0	1
Henneman	1/3	0	0	0	0	1

*Pitched to two battters in fourth. †Pitched to one batter in seventh.
E—Jeter. DP—New York 1, Texas 1. LOB—New York 8, Texas 11. 2B—Palmer. HR—Williams 2, Gonzalez. SH—Boggs, Hamilton. SB—Williams. WP—Witt. T—3:57. A—50,066. U—Welke, plate; Shulock, first; Hendry, second; Coble, third; Kosc, left field; Tschida, right field.

NEW YORK YANKEES' BATTING AND FIELDING AVERAGES

Player, position	G	AB	R	H	TB	2B	3B	HR	RBI	BB	IBB	SO	Avg.	PO	A	E	A
Williams, cf	4	15	5	7	16	0	0	3	5	2	0	1	.467	10	0	0	1.
Jeter, ss	4	17	2	7	8	1	0	0	1	0	0	2	.412	8	10	1	.
Fielder, dh	3	11	2	4	7	0	0	1	4	1	0	2	.364	0	0	0	.
Duncan, 2b	4	16	0	5	5	0	0	0	3	0	0	4	.313	9	13	0	1.
Martinez, 1b	4	15	3	4	6	2	0	0	0	3	1	1	.267	33	3	0	1.
Raines, lf	4	16	3	4	4	0	0	0	0	3	0	1	.250	5	0	0	1.
Girardi, c-pr	4	9	1	2	2	0	0	0	0	4	0	1	.222	28	1	1	.
Hayes, 3b-ph	3	5	0	1	1	0	0	0	1	0	0	0	.200	1	3	0	1.
O'Neill, rf	4	15	0	2	2	0	0	0	0	0	0	2	.133	13	0	0	1.
Boggs, 3b	3	12	0	1	2	1	0	0	0	0	0	2	.083	2	1	0	1.
Boehringer, p	2	0	0	0	0	0	0	0	0	0	0	0	.000	0	0	0	.
Cone, p	1	0	0	0	0	0	0	0	0	0	0	0	.000	1	0	0	1.
Fox, dh-pr	2	0	0	0	0	0	0	0	0	0	0	0	.000	0	0	0	.
Key, p	1	0	0	0	0	0	0	0	0	0	0	0	.000	0	0	0	.
Lloyd, p	2	0	0	0	0	0	0	0	0	0	0	0	.000	1	0	0	1.
Nelson, p	2	0	0	0	0	0	0	0	0	0	0	0	.000	0	1	0	1.
Pettitte, p	1	0	0	0	0	0	0	0	0	0	0	0	.000	0	2	0	1.
M. Rivera, p	2	0	0	0	0	0	0	0	0	0	0	0	.000	0	0	0	.
Rogers, p	2	0	0	0	0	0	0	0	0	0	0	0	.000	0	0	0	.
Sojo, 2b	2	0	0	0	0	0	0	0	0	0	0	0	.000	1	1	0	1.
Weathers, p	2	0	0	0	0	0	0	0	0	0	0	0	.000	0	1	0	1.
Wetteland, p	3	0	0	0	0	0	0	0	0	0	0	0	.000	1	2	0	1.
R. Rivera, rf-ph	2	1	0	0	0	0	0	0	0	0	0	1	.000	0	0	0	.
Leyritz, c-dh	2	3	0	0	0	0	0	0	1	0	0	1	.000	4	0	0	1.
Strawberry, dh	2	5	0	0	0	0	0	0	0	0	0	2	.000	0	0	0	.
Totals	4	140	16	37	53	4	0	4	15	13	1	20	.264	117	38	2	.

TEXAS RANGERS' BATTING AND FIELDING AVERAGES

Player, position	G	AB	R	H	TB	2B	3B	HR	RBI	BB	IBB	SO	Avg.	PO	A	E	A
Gonzalez, rf	4	16	5	7	22	0	0	5	9	3	1	2	.438	9	0	0	1.
Rodriguez, c	4	16	1	6	7	1	0	0	2	2	0	3	.375	21	3	0	1.
Elster, ss	4	12	2	4	6	2	0	0	0	3	0	2	.333	6	7	1	.
Palmer, 3b	4	19	3	4	8	1	0	1	2	0	0	5	.211	3	10	1	.
Hamilton, cf	4	19	0	3	3	0	0	0	0	0	0	2	.158	15	1	0	1.
McLemore, 2b	4	15	1	2	2	0	0	0	2	0	0	4	.133	10	16	0	1.
Clark, 1b	4	16	1	2	2	0	0	0	3	1	0	2	.125	35	4	0	1.
Greer, lf	4	16	2	2	2	0	0	0	3	0	0	3	.125	12	0	0	1.
Tettleton, dh	4	12	1	1	1	0	0	0	1	5	0	7	.083	0	0	0	.
Buford, pr	2	0	0	0	0	0	0	0	0	0	0	0	.000	0	0	0	.
Burkett, p	1	0	0	0	0	0	0	0	0	0	0	0	.000	1	0	0	1.
Cook, p	2	0	0	0	0	0	0	0	0	0	0	0	.000	0	0	0	.
Gonzales, ss	1	0	0	0	0	0	0	0	0	0	0	0	.000	0	0	0	.
Henneman, p	3	0	0	0	0	0	0	0	0	0	0	0	.000	0	0	0	.
Hill, p	1	0	0	0	0	0	0	0	0	0	0	0	.000	1	2	0	1.
Oliver, p	1	0	0	0	0	0	0	0	0	0	0	0	.000	0	3	0	1.
Patterson, p	1	0	0	0	0	0	0	0	0	0	0	0	.000	0	0	0	.
Pavlik, p	1	0	0	0	0	0	0	0	0	0	0	0	.000	1	0	0	1.
Russell, p	2	0	0	0	0	0	0	0	0	0	0	0	.000	0	0	0	.
Stanton, p	3	0	0	0	0	0	0	0	0	0	0	0	.000	0	1	0	1.
Vosberg, p	1	0	0	0	0	0	0	0	0	0	0	0	.000	0	0	0	.
Witt, p	1	0	0	0	0	0	0	0	0	0	0	0	.000	0	0	0	.
Newson, ph	2	1	0	0	0	0	0	0	0	1	0	0	.000	0	0	0	.
Totals	4	142	16	31	53	4	0	6	16	20	2	30	.218	114	47	2	.

NEW YORK YANKEES' PITCHING RECORDS

Pitcher	G	GS	CG	IP	H	R	ER	HR	BB	IBB	SO	HB	WP	W	L	Pct.	E
Weathers	2	0	0	5	1	0	0	0	0	0	5	0	0	1	0	1.000	0
M. Rivera	2	0	0	4²/₃	0	0	0	0	1	0	1	0	0	0	0	.000	0
Wetteland	3	0	0	4	2	0	0	0	4	1	4	0	0	0	0	.000	0
Nelson	2	0	0	3²/₃	2	0	0	0	2	1	5	0	0	1	0	1.000	0
Lloyd	2	0	0	1	1	0	0	0	0	0	0	0	0	0	0	.000	0
Key	1	1	0	5	5	2	2	1	1	0	3	0	0	0	0	.000	3
Pettitte	1	1	0	6¹/₃	4	4	4	2	6	0	3	0	1	0	0	.000	5
Boehringer	2	0	0	1¹/₃	3	2	1	1	2	0	0	0	1	0	1	1.000	6

tcher	G	GS	CG	IP	H	R	ER	HR	BB	IBB	SO	HB	WP	W	L	Pct.	ERA
ne	1	1	0	6	8	6	6	2	2	0	8	0	0	0	1	.000	9.00
gers	2	1	0	2	5	2	2	0	2	0	1	0	0	0	0	.000	9.00
Totals	4	4	0	39	31	16	15	6	20	2	30	0	1	3	1	.750	3.46

No shutouts. Saves—Wetteland 2.

TEXAS RANGERS' PITCHING RECORDS

tcher	G	GS	CG	IP	H	R	ER	HR	BB	IBB	SO	HB	WP	W	L	Pct.	ERA
ok	2	0	0	1 1/3	0	0	0	0	1	0	0	0	0	0	0	.000	0.00
nneman	3	0	0	1	1	0	0	0	1	1	1	0	0	0	0	.000	0.00
tterson	1	0	0	1/3	1	0	0	0	0	0	0	0	0	0	0	.000	0.00
rkett	1	1	1	9	10	2	2	0	1	0	7	0	0	1	0	1.000	2.00
anton	3	0	0	3 1/3	2	1	1	3	0	3	0	0	0	1	.000	2.70
ssell	2	0	0	3	3	1	1	0	0	0	1	0	0	0	0	.000	3.00
ver	1	1	0	8	6	3	3	1	2	0	3	1	0	0	1	.000	3.38
ll	1	1	0	6	5	3	3	1	3	0	1	1	0	0	0	.000	4.50
vlik	1	0	0	2 2/3	4	2	2	1	0	0	1	0	0	0	1	.000	6.75
tt	1	1	0	3 1/3	4	3	3	0	2	0	3	0	1	0	0	.000	8.10
sberg	1	0	0	0	1	0	0	0	0	0	0	0	0	0	0	.000	-
Totals	4	4	1	38	37	16	15	4	13	1	20	2	1	1	3	.250	3.55

No shutouts or saves.

SCORE BY INNINGS

ew York	2	1	0	5	1	0	2	1	3	0	0	1—16
xas	0	3	5	6	1	1	0	0	0	0	0	0—16

MISCELLANEOUS STATISTICS

crifice hits—McLemore 2, Boggs, Hamilton, Hayes, Raines, Rodriguez.
crifice flies—Hayes, Williams.
olen bases—Elster, Williams.
ught stealing—Hayes, McLemore, Williams.
ouble plays—Elster, McLemore and Clark 2; Hamilton and Clark; Jeter, Duncan and Martinez; Oliver, Elster and Clark; Pettitte, Jeter and Martinez.
ft on bases—New York 9, 9, 4, 8—30; Texas 3, 11, 8, 11—33.
t by pitcher—By Hill (Leyritz), by Oliver (Duncan).
ssed balls—None.
lks—None.
ne of games—First game, 2:50; second game, 4:25; third game, 3:09; fourth game, 3:57.
tendance—First game, 57,205; second game, 57,156; third game, 50,860; fourth game, 50,066.
npires—Clark, Coble, Evans, Hendry, Johnson, Kaiser, Kosc, Merrill, Shulock, Tschida, Welke and Young.
ficial scorers—Red Foley, Kurt Iverson.

1996 REVIEW A.L. Division Series

N.L. DIVISION SERIES
ST. LOUIS VS. SAN DIEGO

GAME 1

HIGHLIGHTS
ST. LOUIS 3, SAN DIEGO 1

Why the Cardinals won: Playoff experience paid off. Pitchers Todd Stottlemyre, Rick Honeycutt and Dennis Eckersley, third baseman Gary Gaetti and manager Tony La Russa had a combined 105 games of postseason experience, and each drew on that experience to defeat the Padres in the first game at Busch Stadium. Stottlemyre shook off a history of postseason flops and pitched 6 2/3 innings while giving up only one run and striking out seven; Honeycutt and Eckersley excelled in relief; and Gaetti's first-inning homer proved the difference in the game.

Why the Padres lost: The inability to capitalize on late-inning scoring opportunities doomed them in Game 1 and likely set the tone for the series. In the eighth inning, the Padres had a man on second with nobody out and failed to score, and in the ninth had men on first and second and couldn't get the two-out hit.

The turning points:

1. Gaetti took advantage of the late-afternoon start and got the key hit before the shadows started creeping across the Busch Stadium infield. With Ron Gant on second and Brian Jordan on first, Gaetti hit a 1-1 pitch from Padres starter Joey Hamilton into the bleachers in right-center field and the Cardinals led, 3-0.

2. Twice in the ninth inning, Eckersley was one strike away from victory, but twice he surrendered singles. So with two outs and men on first and second, Eckersley, a future Hall of Famer, battled another future Hall of Famer, N.L. batting champ Tony Gwynn. True to form, Gwynn made contact but it was hit right at the pitcher. Eckersley snared it on the short hop, tossed to first for the final out, then jammed his fist into the air.

Notable: Former A's pitcher Dave Stewart left a message of support on Stottlemyre's answering machine the night before the game. Whatever he said worked. . . . Gaetti continued his regular-season success against San Diego. In nine regular-season games, he hit five homers and had 12 RBIs. The first-inning homer also was Gaetti's fourth postseason homer. . . . N.L. MVP Ken Caminiti was 0-for-3 with one walk, striking out three times. . . . A rarity occurred at Busch Stadium: empty seats at a playoff game. Paid attendance was announced at 54,193, but actual attendance was 51,328. . . . The Cardinals' relief tandem of Honeycutt and Eckersley had 11 league championship series and five World Series appearances between them. . . . Rickey Henderson, who scored the Padres' only run with a sixth-inning

homer, put on a show of his own by exchanging taunts and barbs with the fans in left field.

Quotable: Stottlemyre, on exorcising his playoff demons: "I had a lot of failure in the postseason and I think, based on that failure, I had a lot of motivation when I was traded to this ballclub. I drew on a those past experiences. A lot of my disappointment in the past was that I got too intense, too emotional." . . . Padres manager Bruce Bochy, on Gaetti regular-season and postseason performance: "We haven't done a very good job of pitching to him He's hurt us." . . . Gaetti in response: "I can describe it really. Certainly I've had some bad a bats against those people, too." . . . Eckersley, on getting Gwynn to ground out for the game's last out: "He hit it right at me. I really got lucky. You've got no time to react. It just sort of went in my glove thank God." . . . La Russa, on the matchup between Gwynn and Eckersley: " I thought it was kind of magical moment."

BOX SCORE

San Diego	AB	R	H	RBI	PO	A
Henderson, lf	4	1	2	1	1	0
T. Gwynn, rf	5	0	2	0	0	0
Finley, cf	3	0	1	0	2	0
Caminiti, 3b	3	0	0	0	0	0
Joyner, 1b	3	0	1	0	4	0
Vaughn, lf	1	0	0	0	0	0
Cianfrocco, 1b	0	0	0	0	0	0
Gomez, ss	4	0	0	0	5	3
Johnson, c	4	0	0	0	9	1
Reed, 2b	4	0	1	0	2	2
Hamilton, p	2	0	0	0	1	0
Livingstone, ph	1	0	0	0	0	0
Blair, p	0	0	0	0	0	0
C. Gwynn, ph	1	0	1	0	0	0
Totals	35	1	8	1	24	9

St. Louis	AB	R	H	RBI	PO	A
Clayton, ss	3	0	1	0	3	2
McGee, cf	4	0	0	0	6	0
Gant, lf	2	1	1	0	0	0
Jordan, rf	4	1	1	0	1	0
Gaetti, 3b	3	1	1	3	1	0
Mabry, 1b	3	0	0	0	7	0
Pagnozzi, c	3	0	0	0	9	0
Alicea, 2b	3	0	2	0	0	3
Stottlemyre, p	2	0	0	0	0	0
Honeycutt, p	1	0	0	0	0	0
Eckersley, p	0	0	0	0	0	1
Totals	28	3	6	3	27	6

San Diego	0	0	0		0	0	1		0	0	0—1
St. Louis	3	0	0		0	0	0		0	0	x—3

San Diego	IP	H	R	ER	BB	SO
Hamilton (L)	6	5	3	3	0	6
Blair	2	1	0	0	2	3

St. Louis	IP	H	R	ER	BB	SO
Stottlemyre (W)	6 2/3	5	1	1	2	7
Honeycutt	2/3	1	0	0	0	0
Eckersley (S)	1 2/3	2	0	0	0	1

E—Caminiti. DP—San Diego 2. LOB—San Diego 10, St. Louis 4. 2B—Gwynn, Alicea 2. HR—Henderson, Gaetti. SB—T. Gwynn, Finley, Gant 2. CS—Clayton, Alicea. HBP—By Stottlemyre (Finley), by Hamilton (Gant). T—2:39. A—54,193. U—Quick, plate; Davis, first; DeMuth, second; Pulli, third; Wendelstedt, left field; Bonin, right field.

GAME 2

HIGHLIGHTS

ST. LOUIS 5, SAN DIEGO 4

Why the Cardinals won: Solid pitching from 18-game winner Andy Benes, who didn't allow a baserunner until the fifth inning, and the bullpen combination of Rick Honeycutt and Dennis Eckersley. The Cardinals' offense refused to let the Padres gain momentum, answering the bell in the bottom half of the inning each time San Diego tied the score.

Why the Padres lost: The pitching staff did nothing to help San Diego's cause. Five Padres pitchers gave up eight walks, three of which resulted in runs, and pitcher Doug Botchler, who walked Brian Jordan to lead off the inning, threw a wild pitch in the eighth inning, which advanced runners to second and third, negated an intentional walk, and set the stage for Tom Pagnozzi's game-winning RBI.

The turning points:
1. With the Cardinals leading, 4-3, in the top of the eighth, the Padres had Tony Gwynn at the plate with runners on first and second and nobody out. Rick Honeycutt was brought in to pitch to Gwynn. Instead of starting his runners and having Gwynn, the N.L. batting champion with a .353 batting average, try for the hit and run, Padres manager Bruch Bochy had Gwynn bunt the runners over. Steve Finley followed with a grounder to first and the tying run scored, but the Padres blew their chance for a big inning.
2. With men on second and third and one out in the eighth, Tom Pagnozzi hit a soft infield nubber to pitcher Trevor Hoffman, which scored a charging Brian Jordan with the game-winning run. If the ball had been hit any harder, it likely would have been caught by Hoffman and resulted in an inning-ending double play.

Notable: Dennis Eckersley, giving himself a birthday present, retired all three Padres in the ninth to earn his record 12th career playoff save. Eckersley turned 42 that day, joining teammate Rick Honeycutt, also 42, as the oldest relief tandem in baseball. . . . The crowd of 56,752 was the largest paid crowd to watch a baseball game in Missouri.

Quotable: Cardinals first baseman John Mabry, on why he thought the Padres opted to intentionally walk him: "I guess they thought I was due. I don't know what anyone's been saying, but I've been rubbish the last two days." . . . Gwynn, on convincing manager Bruce Bochy to let him bunt in the eighth inning off Honeycutt: "He asked me if I wanted to play hit-and-run, and to be honest I wasn't sure I could put the ball on the ground against Honeycutt. The way he was pitching me with that breaking ball, I thought I would have a hard time doing that." . . . Pagnozzi, on his game-winning RBI: "That's probably the softest game-winning RBI I've ever had. I think I've heard some suicide squeeze bunts harder than that." . . . Hoffman, on fielding Pagnozzi's ball:

"I probably looked like a Little Leaguer going after that. I'm used to them being hit on the ground, not right back at you in the air like that. I just couldn't judge the velocity of the ball and it fooled me."

BOX SCORE

THURSDAY, OCTOBER 3, AT ST. LOUIS

San Diego	AB	R	H	RBI	PO	A
Henderson, lf	3	1	1	0	2	0
T. Gwynn, rf	3	0	1	1	1	0
Finley, cf	4	0	0	1	5	0
Caminiti, 3b	3	1	1	1	0	1
Joyner, 1b	4	0	0	0	6	0
Hoffman, p	0	0	0	0	0	1
Flaherty, c	4	0	0	0	7	0
Gomez, ss	4	0	1	0	0	0
Reed, 2b	3	0	0	0	2	1
Vaughn, ph	1	0	0	0	0	0
Sanders, p	1	0	0	0	0	1
Veras, p	0	0	0	0	0	1
C. Gwynn, ph	1	1	1	0	0	0
Worrell, p	0	0	0	0	0	1
Livingstone, ph	1	1	1	0	0	0
Bochtler, p	0	0	0	0	0	0
Cianfrocco, 1b	0	0	0	0	1	0
Totals	**32**	**4**	**6**	**3**	**24**	**6**

St. Louis	AB	R	H	RBI	PO	A
Smith, ss	2	1	1	0	2	1
McGee, cf	3	1	1	1	1	0
Gant, lf	4	0	1	3	3	0
Jordan, rf	3	1	0	0	2	0
Gaetti, 3b	4	0	0	0	0	2
Mabry, 1b	3	0	0	0	8	1
Pagnozzi, c	4	0	1	1	10	0
Alicea, 2b	3	1	0	0	0	1
Eckersley, p	0	0	0	0	0	0
An. Benes, p	2	1	1	0	1	0
Honeycutt, p	0	0	0	0	0	1
Gallego, 2b	0	0	0	0	0	0
Totals	**28**	**5**	**5**	**5**	**27**	**6**

San Diego	0	0	0		0	1	2		0	1	0—4
St. Louis	0	0	1		0	3	0		0	1	x—5

San Diego	IP	H	R	ER	BB	SO
Sanders	4 1/3	3	4	4	4	4
Veras	2/3	1	0	0	0	1
Worrell	2	1	0	0	0	2
Bochtler (L)	1/3	0	1	1	2	0
Hoffman	2/3	0	0	0	0	0

St. Louis	IP	H	R	ER	BB	SO
An. Benes	*7	6	4	4	1	9
Honeycutt (W)	1	0	0	0	1	0
Eckersley (S)	1	0	0	0	0	1

*Pitched to two batters in eighth.

E—McGee. LOB—San Diego 4, St. Louis 6. 2B—Gant. HR—Caminiti. SH—T. Gwynn, An. Benes. WP—Bochtler. T—2:55. A—56,752. U—Davis, plate; DeMuth, first; Pulli, second; Wendelstedt, third; Bonin, left field; Quick, right field.

GAME 3

HIGHLIGHTS

ST. LOUIS 7, SAN DIEGO 5

Why the Cardinals won: Brian Jordan used this game and the national TV audience as his coming out party. He singlehandedly took over and won it, first with his glove, then with his bat. With the score tied in the bottom of the eighth, two out and a man on second, Jordan made a diving catch of a Jody Reed liner, saving the go-ahead run. Then in the ninth with one out, he hit a two-run homer to seal the victory.

1996 REVIEW N.L. Division Series

– 169 –

1996 REVIEW *N.L. Division Series*

Why the Padres lost: Trevor Hoffman, The Sporting News Fireman of the Year with 42 saves in the regular season, couldn't get it done when it counted and served up the full-count hanging slider to Jordan.

The turning points:

1. In the bottom of the eighth, Padres third baseman Ken Caminiti hit his second home run of the night, tying the game at 5. That was after Caminiti, in the top half of that inning, made a brilliant stab of Royce Clayton's grounder to his left with the bases loaded and the Cardinals ahead by a run.

2. After falling behind, 4-1, the Cardinals tied it with three runs in the sixth on a home run by Ron Gant, a single by Brian Jordan, a triple by John Mabry and a bloop single by Tom Pagnozzi.

Notable: Ken Caminiti, the N.L. MVP with 40 home runs and 130 RBIs, homered in what turned out to be his last at-bat of the season. . . . Cardinals starter Donovan Osborne had been dominant against the Padres in the regular season, with a 2.22 ERA and a 2-1 record in four starts. But in four innings, he gave up four runs on seven hits. . . . Cardinals reliever Mark Petkovsek pitched two perfect innings of relief in the fifth and sixth innings, keeping the Cardinals in the game. . . . Cardinals second baseman Luis Alicea was introduced twice before the game, first with the reserves, then he ran back into the dugout and came out when the starting lineup was announced.

Quotable: Jordan on his game-winning homer, which came on a full-count, hanging slider: "I've always wanted to play in pressure situations. I've always wanted to step up to the challenge. I just want to win so bad. To see that ball come down, over the fence, it was satisfying. This is what I've worked for." . . . Mabry on his triple, a grounder into the right-field corner: "I always said the only way I would get a triple is for the ball to roll into the bullpen and then into the catcher's equipment bag. I'll be darned if it didn't happen that way." . . . Gant, on his performance in the playoffs: "In the past playoffs, I tried to do too much. I tried to be the guy who everyone could expect something from, and that didn't work. I just worked on being patient this time, doing what I was capable of doing and nothing else whenever I got up there to bat."

BOX SCORE

SATURDAY, OCTOBER 5, AT SAN DIEGO

St. Louis	AB	R	H	RBI	PO
Clayton, ss	3	1	1	0	1
McGee, cf	3	0	0	0	2
Petkovsek, p	0	0	0	0	0
Sweeney, ph	1	0	1	0	0
Honeycutt, p	0	0	0	0	0
Mathews, p	0	0	0	0	0
Smith, ph	1	0	0	0	0
Eckersley, p	0	0	0	0	0
Gant, lf	4	2	2	1	2
Jordan, rf	5	2	3	3	2
Gaetti, 3b	4	0	0	0	0
Mejia, pr	0	0	0	0	0
Gallego, 3b	1	0	0	0	0
Mabry, 1b	4	1	3	1	5
Pagnozzi, c	4	0	2	1	9
Alicea, 2b	5	0	0	0	2
Osborne, p	1	0	0	0	0
Lankford, ph-cf	2	1	1	0	4
Totals	38	7	13	6	27

San Diego	AB	R	H	RBI	PO
Henderson, lf	5	0	1	0	1
T. Gwynn, rf	5	0	1	0	1
Finley, cf	5	0	0	0	3
Caminiti, 3b	4	2	2	2	0
Cianfrocco, 1b	3	1	1	0	7
Worrell, p	0	0	0	0	0
Valenzuela, p	0	0	0	0	0
Veras, p	0	0	0	0	0
Vaughn, ph	1	0	0	0	0
Flaherty, c	0	0	0	0	2
Johnson, c	4	2	3	0	6
Lopez, 2b	0	0	0	0	0
Hoffman, p	0	0	0	0	0
Gomez, ss	4	0	1	1	3
Reed, 2b	4	0	2	2	2
Ashby, p	1	0	0	0	0
Joyner, 1b	2	0	0	0	1
Totals	38	5	11	5	27

St. Louis	1 0 0	0 0 3	1 0	2—7
San Diego	0 2 1	1 0 0	0 1	0—5

St. Louis	IP	H	R	ER	BB	SO
Osborne	4	7	4	4	0	5
Petkovsek	2	0	0	0	0	1
Honeycutt	*1	2	1	1	0	1
Mathews (W)	1	1	0	0	0	2
Eckersley (S)	1	1	0	0	0	0

San Diego	IP	H	R	ER	BB	SO
Ashby	5 1/3	7	4	4	1	5
Worrell	*1 2/3	3	1	1	1	0
Valenzuela	2/3	0	0	0	2	0
Veras	1/3	0	0	0	0	0
Hoffman (L)	1	3	2	2	1	2

*Pitched to one batter in eighth.

E—Alicea, Caminiti 2. DP—San Diego 2. LOB—St. Louis 10, San Diego 7. 2B—Johnson, Reed. 3B—Mabry. HR—Gant, Jordan, Caminiti 2. SH—Mabry, Ashby. SB—Jordan. CS—Alicea. WP—Ashby. T—3:32. A—53,899. U—Hallion, plate; Tata, first; Froemming, second; Hohn, third; Rippley, left field; Gregg, right field.

STATISTICS

ST. LOUIS CARDINALS' BATTING AND FIELDING AVERAGES

Player, position	G	AB	R	H	TB	2B	3B	HR	RBI	BB	IBB	SO	Avg.	PO	A	E	Avg.
Sweeney, ph	1	1	0	1	1	0	0	0	0	0	0	0	1.000	0	0	0	.000
An. Benes, p	1	2	1	1	1	0	0	0	0	0	0	1	.500	1	0	0	1.000
Lankford, cf-ph	1	2	1	1	1	0	0	0	0	1	0	0	.500	4	0	0	1.000
Gant, lf	3	10	3	4	8	1	0	1	4	2	0	3	.400	5	0	0	1.000
Jordan, rf	3	12	4	4	7	0	0	1	3	1	0	3	.333	5	0	0	1.000
Clayton, ss	2	6	1	2	2	0	0	0	0	3	0	1	.333	4	5	0	1.000
Smith, ss-ph	2	3	1	1	1	0	0	0	0	2	0	0	.333	2	1	0	1.000
Mabry, 1b	3	10	1	3	5	0	1	0	1	1	1	1	.300	20	1	0	1.000
Pagnozzi, c	3	11	0	3	3	0	0	0	2	1	1	3	.273	28	0	0	1.000
Alicea, 2b	3	11	1	2	4	2	0	0	0	1	0	4	.182	2	5	1	.875

er, position	G	AB	R	H	TB	2B	3B	HR	RBI	BB	IBB	SO	Avg.	PO	A	E	Avg.
;ee, cf	3	10	1	1	1	0	0	0	1	1	0	3	.100	9	0	1	.900
tti, 3b	3	11	1	1	4	0	0	1	3	0	0	3	.091	1	3	0	1.000
ersley, p	3	0	0	0	0	0	0	0	0	0	0	0	.000	0	1	0	1.000
hews, p	1	0	0	0	0	0	0	0	0	0	0	0	.000	0	0	0	.000
ia, pr	1	0	0	0	0	0	0	0	0	0	0	0	.000	0	0	0	.000
covsek, p	1	0	0	0	0	0	0	0	0	0	0	0	.000	0	0	0	.000
ego, 2b-3b	2	1	0	0	0	0	0	0	0	0	0	1	.000	0	0	0	.000
eycutt, p	3	1	0	0	0	0	0	0	0	0	0	1	.000	0	1	0	1.000
orne, p	1	1	0	0	0	0	0	0	0	0	0	0	.000	0	1	0	1.000
tlemyre, p	1	2	0	0	0	0	0	0	0	0	0	2	.000	0	0	0	.000
otals	3	94	15	24	38	3	1	3	14	13	2	23	.255	81	18	2	.980

SAN DIEGO PADRES' BATTING AND FIELDING AVERAGES

er, position	G	AB	R	H	TB	2B	3B	HR	RBI	BB	IBB	SO	Avg.	PO	A	E	Avg.
;wynn, ph	2	2	1	2	2	0	0	0	0	0	0	0	1.000	0	0	0	.000
ngstone, ph	2	2	1	1	1	0	0	0	0	0	0	0	.500	0	0	0	.000
nson, c	2	8	2	3	4	1	0	0	0	0	0	1	.375	15	3	0	1.000
derson, lf	3	12	2	4	7	0	0	1	1	2	0	3	.333	4	0	0	1.000
frocco, 1b	3	3	1	1	1	0	0	0	0	0	0	1	.333	8	2	0	1.000
wynn, rf	3	13	0	4	5	1	0	0	1	0	0	2	.308	2	0	0	1.000
niti, 3b	3	10	3	3	12	0	0	3	3	2	1	5	.300	0	5	3	.625
d, 2b	3	11	0	3	4	1	0	0	2	0	0	1	.273	6	6	0	1.000
nez, ss	3	12	0	2	2	0	0	0	1	0	0	4	.167	8	5	0	1.000
ner, 1b	3	9	0	1	1	0	0	0	0	0	0	2	.111	12	2	0	1.000
ey, cf	3	12	0	1	1	0	0	0	1	0	0	4	.083	10	0	0	1.000
r, p	1	0	0	0	0	0	0	0	0	0	0	0	.000	0	0	0	.000
htler, p	1	0	0	0	0	0	0	0	0	0	0	0	.000	0	0	0	.000
fman, p	2	0	0	0	0	0	0	0	0	0	0	0	.000	0	1	0	1.000
ez, pr	1	0	0	0	0	0	0	0	0	0	0	0	.000	0	0	0	.000
enzuela, p	1	0	0	0	0	0	0	0	0	0	0	0	.000	0	1	0	1.000
as, p	2	0	0	0	0	0	0	0	0	0	0	0	.000	0	1	0	1.000
rrell, p	2	0	0	0	0	0	0	0	0	0	0	0	.000	0	1	0	1.000
by, p	1	1	0	0	0	0	0	0	0	0	0	1	.000	0	0	0	.000
ders, p	1	1	0	0	0	0	0	0	0	0	0	0	.000	0	1	0	1.000
nilton, p	1	2	0	0	0	0	0	0	0	0	0	2	.000	1	0	0	1.000
ghn, ph	3	3	0	0	0	0	0	0	0	0	0	1	.000	0	0	0	.000
erty, c	2	4	0	0	0	0	0	0	0	0	0	1	.000	9	0	0	1.000
otals	3	105	10	25	40	3	0	4	9	4	1	28	.238	75	28	3	.972

ST. LOUIS CARDINALS' PITCHING RECORDS

cher	G	GS	CG	IP	H	R	ER	HR	BB	IBB	SO	HB	WP	W	L	Pct.	ERA
ersley	3	0	0	$3^2/_3$	3	0	0	0	0	0	2	0	0	0	0	.000	0.00
kovsek	1	0	0	2	0	0	0	0	0	0	1	0	0	0	0	.000	0.00
thews	1	0	0	1	1	0	0	0	0	0	2	0	0	1	0	1.000	0.00
tlemyre	1	1	0	$6^2/_3$	5	1	1	1	2	0	7	1	0	1	0	1.000	1.35
eycutt	3	0	0	$2^2/_3$	3	1	1	1	1	1	2	0	0	1	0	1.000	3.38
Benes	1	1	0	7	6	4	4	1	1	0	9	0	0	0	0	.000	5.14
orne	1	1	0	4	7	4	4	1	0	0	5	0	0	0	0	.000	9.00
otals	3	3	0	27	25	10	10	4	4	1	28	1	0	3	0	1.000	3.33

lo shutouts. Saves—Eckersley 3.

SAN DIEGO PADRES' PITCHING RECORDS

cher	G	GS	CG	IP	H	R	ER	HR	BB	IBB	SO	HB	WP	W	L	Pct.	ERA
ir	1	0	0	2	1	0	0	0	2	0	3	0	0	0	0	.000	0.00
as	2	0	0	1	0	0	0	0	0	0	1	0	0	0	0	.000	0.00
enzuela	1	0	0	$^2/_3$	0	0	0	0	2	1	0	0	0	0	0	.000	0.00
rrell	2	0	0	$3^2/_3$	4	1	1	0	1	0	2	0	0	0	0	.000	2.45
nilton	1	1	0	6	5	3	3	1	0	0	6	1	0	0	1	.000	4.50
by	1	1	0	$5^1/_3$	7	4	4	1	1	0	5	0	1	0	0	.000	6.75
ders	1	1	0	$4^1/_3$	3	4	4	0	4	0	4	0	0	0	0	.000	8.31
ffman	2	0	0	$1^2/_3$	3	2	2	1	1	0	2	0	0	0	1	.000	10.80
htler	1	0	0	$^1/_3$	0	1	1	0	2	1	0	0	1	0	1	.000	27.00
otals	3	3	0	25	24	15	15	3	13	2	23	1	2	0	3	.000	5.40

Jo shutouts or saves.

SCORE BY INNINGS

Louis	4	0	1	0	3	3	1	1	2	—15
Diego	0	2	1	1	1	3	0	2	0	—10

Sacrifice hits—Ashby, An. Benes, T. Gwynn, Mabry.
Sacrifice flies—None.
Stolen bases—Gant 2, Finley, T. Gwynn, Jordan.
Caught stealing—Alicea 2, Clayton.
Double plays—Gomez, Reed and Joyner; Reed, Gomez and Joyner.
Left on bases—St. Louis 4, 6, 10—20; San Diego 10, 4, 7—21.
Hit by pitcher—By Stottlemyre (Finley), by Hamilton (Gant).
Passed balls—None.
Balks—None.
Time of games—First game, 2:39; second game, 2:55; third game, 3:32.
Attendance—First game, 54,193; second game, 56,752; third game, 53,899.
Umpires—Bonin, Davis, DeMuth, Froemming, Gregg, Hallion, Hohn, Pulli, Quick, Rippley, Tata and Wendelstedt.
Official scorers—Jack Herman, Bill Zavestoski.

ATLANTA VS. LOS ANGELES

GAME 1

HIGHLIGHTS

ATLANTA 2, LOS ANGELES 1 (10 INNINGS)

Why the Braves won: Catcher Javier Lopez turned Antonio Osuna's full-count fastball into an opposite-field home run in the top of the 10th. John Smoltz, the '96 Cy Young winner, allowed one run in nine innings.

Why the Dodgers lost: Lack of offense. Starter Ramon Martinez allowed one run and three hits through the first eight innings, but the Dodgers stranded six runners—three in scoring position. The bullpen then blew its fourth consecutive game (dating to the regular season).

The turning points:

1. In the second and third innings, the Dodgers put runners on the corners. But Greg Gagne struck out to end the second and Eric Karros fouled out to end the third.

2. After Gagne doubled and scored on Todd Hollandsworth's double in the fifth, Smoltz collected 13 consecutive outs and threw 17 consecutive strikes. Amid Smoltz's stretch, with two outs in the bottom of the eighth, Mike Piazza hit a long fly to right that would've given the Dodgers a 2-1 lead had it not died at the warning track. . . . Three other Dodger at-bats ended in long flies that fell short, including two in the ninth, by Tim Wallach and Karros.

3. Through eight innings, Martinez struck out six and allowed just three singles, but manager Bill Russell pulled him anyway. Osuna came in with one out in the ninth and struck out Terry Pendleton to end the inning. With no outs in the 10th, Osuna had an 0-2 count on Lopez. But Lopez battled back to 3-2, fought off three more pitches, then connected on a fastball over the plate for the winning home run.

Notable: The loss was the Dodgers' fifth in a row, dating to the end of the regular season. The Dodgers produced just six runs and a .173 average without a home run in those five losses (49 innings). . . . Lopez also hit a game-winning homer in Game 2 of the '95 World Series and a three-run shot in the 10th of Game 2 of the '95 NLCS. . . . In 14 postseason starts, Smoltz climbed to 6-1 with a 2.59 ERA. He was the only N.L. pitcher with a better winning percentage than Martinez in '96. . . . The crowd of 47,428 was about 9,000 less than the listed capacity of Dodger Stadium.

Quotable: Smoltz, on Piazza's long shot in the eighth: "I feel I got lucky against Piazza (in the eighth). I had one of the worst sliders I'd thrown all season, and I got away with it." . . . Lopez, on his home run: "Everyone expects Chipper (Jones) (Fred) McGriff or (Ryan) Klesko to have the big hit. No one thinks about me." . . . Karros: "When you're facing a staff like Atlanta's, you're going to get two or three pitches to hit all day, and you've got to hit them. If you don't, you're going to be in trouble." . . . Martinez, on being removed: "I was actually feeling stronger as the game was going on. But they wanted me to throw a certain amount of pitches, and so I come out. I'm not mad. I didn't complain. But I wish I could have kept pitching."

BOX SCORE

WEDNESDAY, OCTOBER 2, AT LOS ANGELES

Atlanta	AB	R	H	RBI	PO	
Grissom, cf	4	1	1	0	2	
Lemke, 2b	4	0	0	0	2	
C. Jones, 3b	2	0	0	0	1	
McGriff, 1b	3	0	1	1	7	
Klesko, lf	1	0	0	0	1	
Pendleton, ph	1	0	0	0	0	
A. Jones, lf	0	0	0	0	0	
Lopez, c	4	1	1	1	10	
Dye, rf	4	0	0	0	5	
Blauser, ss	3	0	1	0	0	
Wohlers, p	0	0	0	0	0	
Smoltz, p	2	0	0	0	2	
Polonia, ph	1	0	0	0	0	
Belliard, ss	0	0	0	0	0	
Totals	29	2	4	2	30	
Los Angeles	**AB**	**R**	**H**	**RBI**	**PO**	
Kirby, cf	4	0	1	0	1	
Hollandsworth, lf	4	0	1	1	1	
Piazza, c	4	0	1	0	10	
Karros, 1b	3	0	0	0	10	
Mondesi, rf	4	0	0	0	1	
Wallach, 3b	4	0	0	0	2	
DeShields, 2b	4	0	0	0	3	
Gagne, ss	4	1	2	0	2	
Martinez, p	3	0	0	0	0	
Radinsky, p	0	0	0	0	0	
Osuna, p	0	0	0	0	0	
Clark, ph	1	0	0	0	0	
Totals	35	1	5	1	30	11

Atlanta	0	0	0	1	0	0	0	0	0	1—2
Los Angeles	0	0	0	0	1	0	0	0	0	0—1

nta	IP	H	R	ER	BB	SO
oltz (W)	9	4	1	1	2	7
lers (S)	1	1	0	0	0	2

Angeles	IP	H	R	ER	BB	SO
tinez	8	3	1	1	3	6
linsky	1/3	0	0	0	1	0
na (L)	1 2/3	1	1	1	0	3

—Lopez. DP—Los Angeles 2. LOB—Atlanta 4, Los Angeles 6. 2B—
landsworth, Gagne. HR—Lopez. SH—Smoltz. SF—McGriff. SB—
ssom, Klesko. CS—C. Jones, McGriff, Blauser, Kirby. HBP—By Osuna
user). T—3:08. A—47,428. U—Rippley, plate; Gregg, first; Hallion, sec-
; Tata, third; Froemming, left field; Hohn, right field.

GAME 2

HIGHLIGHTS

ATLANTA 3, LOS ANGELES 2

hy the Braves won: Three solo homers off odgers starter Ismael Valdes, the last two in the venth by Fred McGriff and Jermaine Dye. The aves had five hits, but that was two more than eg Maddux, Greg McMichael and Mark Wohlers mbined to allow the Dodgers.

hy the Dodgers lost: The pitch to Dye, and, once ain, a lack of offense. Like the previous day, the odgers scored on an RBI double (this time, Raul ondesi's in the fourth), but were shut out after at—the final 16 Dodgers batters were retired. nly three of those 16 got the ball out of the infield. either Dodger run was earned.

rning points:

. Both Dodger runs developed from Atlanta errors d gave L.A. an early 2-1 lead. Braves left fielder an Klesko, who homered in the second, bobbled dd Hollandsworth's single in the first and allowed m to reach second; Hollandsworth later scored on ike Piazza's groundout. The second error came in e fourth, when centerfielder Marquis Grissom obbled Mike Piazza's single, allowing Piazza to ke second. Piazza scored on Mondesi's double.

. McGriff's homer in the seventh put the Dodgers their heels, but it didn't do the damage that Dye's d. McGriff's homer just missed centerfielder ayne Kirby's glove on the way out, and Valdes ounced right back and struck out Ryan Klesko. hen, after throwing 54 strikes in 74 pitches, Valdes tempted to throw a curveball that Dye hit into the ats in left field.

otable: Dodgers manager Bill Russell made two neup changes, substituting rookie Juan Castro for umping second baseman Delino DeShields eShields returned in the ninth) and flip-flopping irby and Hollandsworth in the batting order from 2 to 2-1. . . . In nine previous postseason games, addux had a 4-3 mark and 4.66 ERA. In this start, e threw 58 strikes in 72 pitches, allowed three hits, ruck out seven (four looking) and walked none. e left after seven innings after aggravating a right amstring injury. . . . The game lasted just two hours, ght minutes. . . . The Dodgers' losing streak, all at ome, climbed to six, their longest of the season. . . . our of the Braves' five postseason runs and nine

postseason hits (in 60 at-bats) came on solo home runs.

Quotable: Dye: "Tonight was a dream." . . . Maddux, on the dominance of the Braves' starters: "I think because we respect their hitters so much, our focus is better and our concentration is better." . . . Piazza: "It's pretty bad right now, when they just have to win one out of three games. Maybe they'll let up a little bit. That's what we're hoping." . . . Braves Game 3 pitcher Tom Glavine: "Coming into the series, it was slated to be a pitchers' duel. I don't think anybody has been disappointed. That's the essence of playoff baseball." . . . Valdes, amid growing team bickering in which hitters were blaming the pitching and vice versa: "I feel like a failure. I was pitching good, then boom! I made one mistake (to Dye). It's all my fault. Two runs is enough to win the ballgame." . . . Braves third baseman Chipper Jones: "I think you're seeing how much postseason experience means. Nobody panics. Being able to perform in a game when you've got your heart in your throat, believe me, takes some getting used to."

BOX SCORE

THURSDAY, OCTOBER 3, AT LOS ANGELES

Atlanta	AB	R	H	RBI	PO	A
Grissom, cf	4	0	0	0	1	0
Lemke, 2b	4	0	1	0	0	5
C. Jones, 3b	4	0	0	0	0	1
McGriff, 1b	4	1	1	1	11	1
Klesko, lf	3	1	1	1	0	0
A. Jones, pr-lf	0	0	0	0	0	0
Dye, rf	3	1	1	1	3	0
Perez, c	3	0	1	0	10	0
Blauser, ss	3	0	0	0	0	1
Belliard, ss	0	0	0	0	0	0
Maddux, p	2	0	0	0	2	2
Polonia, ph	1	0	0	0	0	0
McMichael, p	0	0	0	0	0	0
Wohlers, p	0	0	0	0	0	0
Totals	31	3	5	3	27	10

Los Angeles	AB	R	H	RBI	PO	A
Hollandsworth, lf	4	1	1	0	2	0
Kirby, cf	4	0	0	0	3	0
Piazza, c	4	1	1	1	7	1
Karros, 1b	3	0	0	0	11	1
Mondesi, rf	3	0	1	1	1	0
Wallach, 3b	3	0	0	0	0	2
Gagne, ss	3	0	0	0	1	2
Castro, 2b	2	0	0	0	1	2
Hansen, ph	1	0	0	0	0	0
DeShields, 2b	0	0	0	0	0	0
Valdes, p	2	0	0	0	1	2
Astacio, p	0	0	0	0	0	1
Ashley, ph	1	0	0	0	0	0
Worrell, p	0	0	0	0	0	0
Totals	30	2	3	2	27	11

Atlanta									
Atlanta	0	1	0	0	0	0	2	0	0—3
Los Angeles	1	0	0	1	0	0	0	0	0—2

Atlanta	IP	H	R	ER	BB	SO
Maddux (W)	7	3	2	0	0	7
McMichael	1	0	0	0	0	2
Wohlers (S)	1	0	0	0	0	1

Los Angeles	IP	H	R	ER	BB	SO
Valdes (L)	6 1/3	5	3	3	0	5
Astacio	1 2/3	0	0	0	0	1
Worrell	1	0	0	0	1	1

E—Klesko, Grissom. LOB—Atlanta 2, Los Angeles 1. 2B—Mondesi. HR—McGriff, Klesko, Dye. T—2:08. A—51,916. U—Gregg, plate; Hallion, first; Tata, second; Froemming, third; Hohn, left field; Rippley, right field.

HIGHLIGHTS

ATLANTA 5, LOS ANGELES 2

Why the Braves won: A two-run double by Mark Lemke, followed by a two-run homer from Chipper Jones, knocked Dodger starter Hideo Nomo out in the fourth inning.

Why the Dodgers lost: The Dodgers' pitching staff, which had the league's best ERA entering the postseason, gave up five runs in the first four innings. For the series, they had a 3.33 ERA to the Braves' 0.96 while the offense batted just .147 to the Braves .180. . . . For the series, the Dodgers had 14 hits and no homers. The heart of the batting order—Mike Piazza, Eric Karros and Raul Mondesi—was 5-for 30.

Turning points:

1. Nomo struggled early, walking four while taking nine of 15 batters to three-ball counts. Despite his struggles, he trailed just 1-0 with two outs in the fourth. But it fell apart when Braves pitcher Tom Glavine doubled, Marquis Grissom walked and Lemke doubled in two runs. Jones, who had been 0-for-12 against Nomo entering the game, homered on the next pitch, giving the Braves a 5-0 lead. It was Nomo's earliest exit since August 1995 and his first loss in five career starts against the Braves.

2. The Dodgers put up a few small fights before succumbing. In the first, Hollandsworth doubled and Piazza hit a bloop single. But Piazza was caught between first and second and Hollandsworth, who tried to score on the play, was caught at the plate. The Dodgers collected runs in the seventh and eighth but also stranded two runners in each inning. The biggest threat came in the eighth, when Wayne Kirby led off with a walk and Hollandsworth doubled. Mike Bielecki entered and allowed a sacrifice fly to Piazza, walked Karros and struck out Raul Mondesi with runners on first and third. Mark Wohlers ended the threat when he struck out Tim Wallach.

Notable: The Braves advancement to the NLCS made them the second team to play in five consecutive Championship Series (Oakland was the first, 1971-75). . . . The postseason sweep was the second in two years for the Dodgers. . . . The 52,529 in attendance marked a Braves postseason franchise record. . . . The victory was the Braves' 14th in their last 17 postseason games. . . . For the series, the Dodgers had more strikeouts (29) than total bases (21).

Quotable: Lemke, on getting Hollandsworth at the plate in the first: "If we don't make that play, they have a runner at second with one out, and you don't know what can happen. Right after that, Tommy (Glavine) settled down. Once he settled down, we knew we were in business." . . . Wohlers, on the Braves' lack of celebration: "I guess it's unfortunate.

When you expect to win and you win, you don't celebrate as much." . . . Glavine: "I've never been a believer that you can just turn on the switch and play better in the postseason. But if there's a team that can do it, we're the one." . . . Piazza, on the sweep: "Is it hard to put into words? No. We lost. We got to the playoffs, so we must have done something right. But then we just fizzled." . . . Dodgers closer Todd Worrell: "It's too bad it had to end this way because I think it takes away a lot of things this team had to overcome and accomplished. But this game showed no mercy."

BOX SCORE

SATURDAY, OCTOBER 5, AT ATLANTA

Los Angeles	AB	R	H	RBI	PO
Curtis, cf	2	0	0	0	2
Kirby, ph-cf	0	1	0	0	0
Hollandsworth, lf	4	0	2	0	1
Piazza, c	2	0	1	1	8
Karros, 1b	3	0	0	0	7
Mondesi, rf	4	0	1	0	0
Wallach, 3b	4	0	0	0	0
Osuna, p	0	0	0	0	0
Dreifort, p	0	0	0	0	1
Gagne, ss	4	1	1	0	0
Castro, 2b	3	0	1	1	3
Nomo, p	1	0	0	0	1
Guthrie, p	0	0	0	0	0
Clark, ph	1	0	0	0	0
Candiotti, p	0	0	0	0	0
Ashley, ph	1	0	0	0	0
Radinsky, p	0	0	0	0	0
Hansen, 3b	1	0	0	0	1
Totals	30	2	6	2	24

Atlanta	AB	R	H	RBI	PO
Grissom, cf	4	1	0	0	1
Lemke, 2b	4	1	1	2	2
C. Jones, 3b	3	2	2	2	0
McGriff, 1b	2	0	1	1	7
Klesko, lf	4	0	0	0	1
Wohlers, p	0	0	0	0	0
Lopez, c	3	0	1	0	11
Dye, rf	4	0	1	0	3
Blauser, ss	3	0	0	0	0
Belliard, ss	0	0	0	0	0
Glavine, p	2	1	1	0	0
McMichael, p	0	0	0	0	0
Bielecki, p	0	0	0	0	0
A. Jones, lf	0	0	0	0	2
Totals	29	5	7	5	27

Los Angeles	0	0	0	0	0	0	1	1	0—2
Atlanta	1	0	0	4	0	0	0	0	x—5

Los Angeles	IP	H	R	ER	BB	SO
Nomo (L)	3 2/3	5	5	5	5	
Guthrie	1/3	0	0	0	1	
Candiotti	2	0	0	0	0	
Radinsky	1	0	0	0	0	
Osuna	1/3	2	0	0	1	
Dreifort	2/3	0	0	0	0	

Atlanta	IP	H	R	ER	BB	SO
Glavine (W)	6 2/3	5	1	1	3	
McMichael	*1/3	1	1	1	1	
Bielecki	2/3	0	0	0	1	
Wohlers (S)	1 1/3	0	0	0	1	

*Pitched to two batters in the eighth.

E—Wallach. DP—Los Angeles 2, Atlanta 1. LOB—Los Angeles 7, Atlanta 8. 2B—Hollandsworth 2, Mondesi, Castro, Lemke, McGriff, Glavine. HR—C. Jones. SH—Glavine. SF—Piazza. SB—C. Jones, Lopez, Dye. T—3:19. A—52,529. U—DeMuth, plate; Pulli, first; Wendelstedt, second; Bonin, third; Quick, left field; Davis, right field.

STATISTICS

ATLANTA BRAVES' BATTING AND FIELDING AVERAGES

ayer, position	G	AB	R	H	TB	2B	3B	HR	RBI	BB	IBB	SO	Avg.	PO	A	E	Avg.
avine, p	1	2	1	1	2	1	0	0	0	0	0	0	.500	0	1	0	1.000
cGriff, 1b	3	9	1	3	7	1	0	1	3	2	0	1	.333	25	3	0	1.000
rez, c	1	3	0	1	1	0	0	0	0	0	0	0	.333	10	0	0	1.000
pez, c	2	7	1	2	5	0	0	1	1	1	0	0	.286	21	2	1	.958
Jones, 3b	3	9	2	2	5	0	0	1	2	3	0	4	.222	1	2	0	1.000
e, rf	3	11	1	2	5	0	0	1	1	0	0	6	.182	11	1	0	1.000
mke, 2b	3	12	1	2	3	1	0	0	2	0	0	1	.167	4	9	0	1.000
esko, lf	3	8	1	1	4	0	0	1	1	3	0	4	.125	2	0	1	.667
auser, ss	3	9	0	1	1	0	0	0	0	1	0	3	.111	0	7	0	1.000
issom, cf	3	12	2	1	1	0	0	0	0	1	0	2	.083	4	0	1	.800
lliard, ss	3	0	0	0	0	0	0	0	0	0	0	0	.000	0	0	0	.000
elecki, p	1	0	0	0	0	0	0	0	0	0	0	0	.000	0	0	0	.000
Jones, lf-pr	3	0	0	0	0	0	0	0	1	0	0	0	.000	0	1	0	1.000
cMichael ,p	2	0	0	0	0	0	0	0	0	0	0	0	.000	0	0	0	.000
ohlers, p	3	0	0	0	0	0	0	0	0	0	0	0	.000	0	0	0	.000
ndleton, ph	1	1	0	0	0	0	0	0	0	0	0	1	.000	0	0	0	.000
addux, p	1	2	0	0	0	0	0	0	0	0	0	1	.000	2	2	0	1.000
lonia, ph	2	2	0	0	0	0	0	0	0	0	0	1	.000	0	0	0	.000
noltz, p	1	2	0	0	0	0	0	0	0	0	0	0	.000	2	1	0	1.000
Totals	3	89	10	16	34	3	0	5	10	12	0	24	.180	84	28	3	.974

LOS ANGELES DODGERS' BATTING AND FIELDING AVERAGES

ayer, position	G	AB	R	H	TB	2B	3B	HR	RBI	BB	IBB	SO	Avg.	PO	A	E	Avg.
ollandsworth, lf	3	12	1	4	7	3	0	0	1	0	0	3	.333	4	0	0	1.000
azza, c	3	10	1	3	3	0	0	0	2	1	0	2	.300	25	4	0	1.000
gne, ss	3	11	2	3	4	1	0	0	0	0	0	5	.273	3	9	0	1.000
stro, 2b	2	5	0	1	2	1	0	0	1	1	0	1	.200	4	3	0	1.000
ondesi, rf	3	11	0	2	4	2	0	0	1	0	0	4	.182	2	0	0	1.000
rby, cf-ph	3	8	1	1	1	0	0	0	0	2	0	1	.125	4	0	0	1.000
tacio, p	1	0	0	0	0	0	0	0	0	0	0	0	.000	0	1	0	1.000
ndiotti, p	1	0	0	0	0	0	0	0	0	0	0	0	.000	0	0	0	.000
eifort, p	1	0	0	0	0	0	0	0	0	0	0	0	.000	1	1	0	1.000
thrie, p	1	0	0	0	0	0	0	0	0	0	0	0	.000	0	0	0	.000
suna, p	2	0	0	0	0	0	0	0	0	0	0	0	.000	0	0	0	.000
adinsky, p	2	0	0	0	0	0	0	0	0	0	0	0	.000	0	0	0	.000
orrell, p	1	0	0	0	0	0	0	0	0	0	0	0	.000	0	1	0	1.000
omo, p	1	1	0	0	0	0	0	0	0	0	0	1	.000	1	0	0	1.000
shley, ph	2	2	0	0	0	0	0	0	0	0	0	2	.000	0	0	0	.000
ark, ph	2	2	0	0	0	0	0	0	0	0	0	2	.000	0	0	0	.000
rtis, cf	1	2	0	0	0	0	0	0	0	1	0	1	.000	2	0	0	1.000
ansen, ph-3b	2	2	0	0	0	0	0	0	0	0	0	0	.000	1	0	0	1.000
aldes, p	1	2	0	0	0	0	0	0	0	0	0	0	.000	1	2	0	1.000
artinez, p	1	3	0	0	0	0	0	0	0	0	0	2	.000	0	0	0	.000
eShields, 2b	2	4	0	0	0	0	0	0	0	0	0	1	.000	3	2	0	1.000
arros, 1b	3	9	0	0	0	0	0	0	0	2	0	3	.000	28	2	0	1.000
allach, 3b	3	11	0	0	0	0	0	0	0	0	0	1	.000	2	8	1	.909
Totals	3	95	5	14	21	7	0	0	5	7	0	29	.147	81	32	1	.991

ATLANTA BRAVES' PITCHING RECORDS

tcher	G	GS	CG	IP	H	R	ER	HR	BB	IBB	SO	HB	WP	W	L	Pct.	ERA
addux	1	1	0	7	3	2	0	0	0	0	7	0	0	1	0	1.000	0.00
ohlers	3	0	0	3 1/3	1	0	0	0	0	0	4	0	0	0	0	.000	0.00
elecki	1	0	0	2/3	0	0	0	0	1	0	1	0	0	0	0	.000	0.00
moltz	1	1	0	9	4	1	1	0	2	0	7	0	0	1	0	1.000	1.00
avine	1	1	0	6 2/3	5	1	1	0	3	0	7	0	0	1	0	1.000	1.35
cMichael	2	0	0	1 1/3	1	1	1	0	1	0	3	0	0	0	0	.000	6.75
Totals	3	3	0	28	14	5	3	0	7	0	29	0	0	3	0	1.000	0.96

No shutouts. Saves—Wohlers 3.

LOS ANGELES DODGERS' PITCHING RECORDS

tcher	G	GS	CG	IP	H	R	ER	HR	BB	IBB	SO	HB	WP	W	L	Pct.	ERA
andiotti	1	0	0	2	0	0	0	0	0	0	1	0	0	0	0	.000	0.00
stacio	1	0	0	1 2/3	0	0	0	0	0	0	1	0	0	0	0	.000	0.00
adinsky	2	0	0	1 1/3	0	0	0	0	1	0	2	0	0	0	0	.000	0.00

Pitcher	G	GS	CG	IP	H	R	ER	HR	BB	IBB	SO	HB	WP	W	L	Pct.	ER
Worrell	1	0	0	1	0	0	0	0	1	0	1	0	0	0	0	.000	0.0
Dreifort	1	0	0	$2/3$	0	0	0	0	0	0	0	0	0	0	0	.000	0.0
Guthrie	1	0	0	$1/3$	0	0	0	0	1	0	1	0	0	0	0	.000	0.0
Martinez	1	1	0	8	3	1	1	0	3	0	6	0	0	0	0	.000	1.1
Valdes	1	1	0	$6 1/3$	5	3	3	3	0	0	5	0	0	0	1	.000	4.2
Osuna	2	0	0	2	3	1	1	1	1	0	4	1	0	0	1	.000	4.5
Nomo	1	1	0	$3 2/3$	5	5	5	1	5	0	3	0	0	0	1	.000	12.2
Totals	3	3	0	27	16	10	10	5	12	0	24	1	0	0	3	.000	3.3

No shutouts or saves.

SCORE BY INNINGS

Atlanta	1	1	0		5	0	0		2	0	0		1—1
Los Angeles	1	0	0		1	1	0		1	1	0		0—

MISCELLANEOUS STATISTICS

Sacrifice hits—Glavine, Smoltz.
Sacrifice flies—McGriff, Piazza.
Stolen bases—Dye, Grissom, C. Jones, Klesko, Lopez.
Caught stealing—Blauser, C. Jones, Kirby, McGriff.
Double plays—Blauser, Lemke and McGriff; Dreifort and Hansen; Wallach, Castro and Karros.
Left on bases—Atlanta 4, 2, 8—14; Los Angeles 6, 1, 7—14.
Hit by pitcher—By Osuna (Blauser).
Passed balls—None.
Balks—None.
Time of games—First game, 3:08; second game, 2:08; third game, 3:19.
Attendance—First game, 47,428; second game, 51,916; third game, 52,529.
Umpires—Bonin, Davis, DeMuth, Froemming, Gregg, Hallion, Hohn, Pulli, Quick, Rippley, Tata and Wendelstedt.
Official scorers—Terry Bales, Larry Kahn, Scott McGregor.

A.L. CHAMPIONSHIP SERIES

GAME 1

HIGHLIGHTS

NEW YORK 5, BALTIMORE 4 (11 INNINGS)

ʜy the Yankees won: Aided by the bullpen and a ʌtroversial call, the team used late-inning power rally from a deficit for the fourth consecutive ʍe. With the bases empty and the Yankees trail-ʇ, 4-3, in the eighth, shortstop Derek Jeter hit a ep fly to right that appeared to be playable. But a ung fan reached over the wall, pulling it into the ʌnds, and right-field umpire Rich Garcia ruled it a ʍe run. In the 11th, center fielder Bernie ɪlliams hit a lead-off homer against Randy Myers ˙ the win. The Yankees were in a position to come ck because, after starter Andy Pettitte allowed ʌr runs in seven innings, relievers Jeff Nelson, ʌn Wetteland and Mariano Rivera shut out the ʀioles the rest of the way.

ʜy the Orioles lost: Defensive mistakes and a ːk of timely hitting prevented the team from tak-ɟ a larger lead into the late innings. In the first, left ɪder B.J. Surhoff lost a Tim Raines popup in the ˎ, allowing the ball to drop in front of him for a dou-ℓ. Raines later scored on a groundout by Williams. the second, an error by second baseman Roberto ʍar, an errant throw by shortstop Cal Ripken on double-play attempt and a fumbled grounder by ɪrd baseman Todd Zeile that ruined another dou-ℓe-play chance ended up costing Baltimore another ℷn. The Orioles left 11 runners on base.

ʌrning points:
ʌ. Ahead, 3-2, in the sixth, the Orioles loaded the ˌses with one out. But they scored only one run, on sacrifice fly by Surhoff. Starter Scott Erickson had ʇched well enough to take a shutout into the sev-ʌth, but he took the mound that inning with only a ˌ2 lead.
ˌ. With one out in the eighth and reliever Armando ʌnitez pitching, Jeter's fly backed up right fielder ʌny Tarasco to the wall, raising his glove as the ball ˌscended. But a 12-year-old boy, Jeff Maier, ʌached over the wall with his glove and deflected ʌe ball up into the stands. Garcia, standing only a ˌw feet away on the warning track, signaled home ʌn. Tarasco argued vehemently and was joined by ʌnitez and manager Davey Johnson. But Garcia ˌayed with his call. Instead of the Orioles being four ʌts away from a win, the game was tied, Johnson ˌas ejected and the team's momentum had van-ʌhed. After Garcia saw a replay after the game, he ˌid he would have ruled the play a double.
ˌ. In the ninth, the Orioles still had a chance to pre-ˌil despite the controversy. With one out, Brady ˌnderson hit a shallow fly to left that Raines and ˌter allowed to drop between them for a double. ˌut Wetteland retired Zeile on a fly out and struck ˌut Alomar, stranding Anderson at second.

Notable: The game was played a day later than orig-inally scheduled because of rain. . . . Besides his error, which led to a run, Alomar made the last out in five innings—the first, third, fifth, ninth and 11th. . . . Pettitte allowed two home runs to lefthanded hit-ters, one more than his regular-season total against lefthanders. . . . The length of the game—4 hours, 24 minutes—wasn't surprising. In the regular season, the games between the teams averaged 3:28. On April 30, they played the longest nine-inning game in history (4:21) and played a 15-inning game the next night that lasted 5:34. . . . The Yankees stranded nine runners from the fifth through eighth innings.

Quotable: Garcia, on his call: "Obviously, once I saw the replay, it was not a home run." . . . Johnson, on the impact of the call: "I always say one play doesn't beat you, but this is as close as it comes." . . . Tarasco, on his view at the wall: "To me, it was a routine fly ball. It was like a magic trick because the ball just dis-appeared in midair." . . . Rivera, on the Yankees' relievers: "I think when our bullpen comes into the games, it's like our team's confidence grows. They feel strong, they don't give up and they know we'll keep them in the game." . . . First baseman Rafael Palmeiro, on the Orioles' defensive problems: "We probably should have had a 4-1 lead in the eighth. So the home run would not have been that big a deal."

BOX SCORE
WEDNESDAY, OCTOBER 9, AT NEW YORK

Baltimore	AB	R	H	RBI	PO	A
Anderson, cf	5	1	2	1	2	0
Zeile, 3b	6	0	1	0	1	3
Alomar, 2b	6	0	1	0	4	4
Palmeiro, 1b	3	3	3	1	11	1
Bonilla, rf	4	0	0	0	1	0
Tarasco, rf	1	0	0	0	1	0
Ripken, ss	5	0	2	0	2	6
Murray, dh	4	0	1	1	0	0
Surhoff, lf	3	0	0	1	2	0
Devereaux, lf	1	0	0	0	0	0
Parent, c	5	0	1	0	6	0
Erickson, p	0	0	0	0	0	2
Orosco, p	0	0	0	0	0	0
Benitez, p	0	0	0	0	0	0
Rhodes, p	0	0	0	0	0	0
Mathews, p	0	0	0	0	0	0
Myers, p	0	0	0	0	0	0
Totals	43	4	11	4	30	16

New York	AB	R	H	RBI	PO	A
Raines, lf	6	1	2	0	3	0
Boggs, 3b	5	1	0	0	1	2
Williams, cf	4	1	2	2	4	0
Martinez, 1b	5	0	1	0	10	0
Fielder, dh	2	1	0	0	0	0
Fox, pr-dh	0	0	0	0	0	0
O'Neill, rf	3	0	0	0	2	0
Hayes, ph	0	0	0	0	0	0
Strawberry, ph-rf	1	0	0	1	0	0
Duncan, 2b	4	0	1	0	2	2
Leyritz, c	4	0	1	1	8	1
Aldrete, ph	0	0	0	0	0	0
Girardi, ph-c	1	0	0	0	3	0
Jeter, ss	5	1	4	1	0	3
Pettitte, p	0	0	0	0	0	0
Nelson, p	0	0	0	0	0	0
Wetteland, p	0	0	0	0	0	0
M. Rivera, p	0	0	0	0	0	0
Totals	40	5	11	5	33	8

Baltimore	0 1 1	1 0 1	0 0 0	0 0—4
New York	1 1 0	0 0 0	1 1 0	0 1—5

Baltimore	IP	H	R	ER	BB	SO
Erickson	6⅓	7	3	2	3	3
Orosco	⅓	0	0	0	1	1
Benitez	1	2	1	1	2	2
Rhodes	⅓	0	0	0	0	0
Mathews	⅓	0	0	0	1	0
Myers (L)	*1⅔	2	1	1	0	0

New York	IP	H	R	ER	BB	SO
Pettitte	7	7	4	4	4	4
Nelson	1	0	0	0	0	1
Wetteland	1	1	0	0	0	2
M. Rivera (W)	2	3	0	0	0	3

*Pitched to one batter in 11th.

E—Alomar. DP—Baltimore 2. LOB—Baltimore 11, New York 13. 2B—Anderson, Ripken, Raines, Williams. HR—Anderson, Palmeiro, Williams, Jeter. SF—Surhoff. SB—Jeter. HBP—By Mathews (Duncan). Balk—Pettitte. T—4:23. A—56,495. U—Barnett, plate; Scott, first; Reilly, second; Morrison, third; Roe, left field; Garcia, right field.

GAME 2

HIGHLIGHTS

BALTIMORE 5, NEW YORK 3

Why the Orioles won: They did what they do best—hit home runs—and they received a gritty outing from starter David Wells, whose elusiveness gave the team a lift in the wake of the demoralizing Game 1 loss. The Orioles, who set a major league record with 257 homers during the regular season, connected for a pair of two-run shots. Todd Zeile hit one in the third to tie the game at 2, and Rafael Palmeiro hit one in the seventh for a 4-2 lead. Wells, who had been dangled as trade bait two months earlier when the Orioles were in danger of dropping out of playoff contention, gave up two runs in the first, but he pitched out of several jams after that and allowed only one more run in his 6⅔ innings.

Why the Yankees lost: The team couldn't use premier setup man Mariano Rivera when it needed him, and received little offense besides that of Derek Jeter and Bernie Williams. Manager Joe Torre needed to rest Rivera after he threw 44 pitches and two innings the night before. His replacement, Jeff Nelson, allowed the winning homer in the seventh—only the second and third earned runs the bullpen had surrendered in the postseason—and gave up another run in the eighth.

Turning points:

1. The Yankees squandered a chance at a big inning in the first. Jeter, Tim Raines and Williams singled off Wells, with Jeter scoring. But Cecil Fielder grounded into a 4-6-3 double play (scoring Raines), and Tino Martinez flied out to left. Wells allowed only one hit over the next three innings.

2. With the score tied at 2 in the fifth, Joe Girardi led off with a triple, but Wells escaped again. He struck out Jeter, and after a walk to Raines, struck out Williams and got Fielder to ground out to second.

3. A bold move by Davey Johnson staved off another Yankees comeback. Jeter singled off Randy Myers leading off the ninth, and after a Raines strikeout, Williams walked. Johnson then pulled Myers, bringing in Armando Benitez. He retired Fielder on a popup to first and got Martinez to flyout to right get the save.

Notable: Orioles right fielder Bobby Bonilla, wh started despite a sore left shoulder that he hurt cha ing a double to the wall in Game 1, struck out fo times, tying the LCS record by the Phillies' Jol Kruk in 1993. . . . Wells won despite failing to reco a 1-2-3 inning, and he improved his career record Yankee Stadium to 10-1. . . . Jeter singled twice a Williams reached base four times (two singles a two walks). Excluding those two players, th Yankees went 12-for-59 (.203) in the first two game

Quotable: Wells, on the effect of the Game 1 co troversy on the team: "We put it behind us. We ha to. You can't worry about your last game, and that what we did." . . . Johnson, on winning by the lor ball: "That's what we do. Everybody in the lineu can hit the ball out of the ballpark. We don't do a l of bunting or stealing. We don't hit-and-run and w don't hit behind the runner." . . . Yankees secon baseman Mariano Duncan, on the team relying sol ly on Jeter and Williams: "We don't want to put pre sure on those two guys and say they have to carr us. We just haven't hit the way we're supposed to hi Sooner or later, we have to score some runs." . . Rafael Palmeiro, on beating the Yankees' bullpe: "Without a doubt, they have the best bullpen i baseball. But we have good hitters on this team an if you give us time, eventually we'll get them."

BOX SCORE

THURSDAY, OCTOBER 10, AT NEW YORK

Baltimore	AB	R	H	RBI	PO	
Anderson, cf	4	2	1	0	1	
Zeile, 3b	4	1	2	2	0	
Alomar, 2b	4	1	2	1	1	
Palmeiro, 1b	4	1	1	2	8	
Bonilla, rf	4	0	0	0	3	
Tarasco, rf	0	0	0	0	1	
Ripken, ss	5	0	2	0	2	
Murray, dh	4	0	1	0	0	
Surhoff, lf	4	0	1	0	3	
Devereaux, lf	0	0	0	0	0	
Hoiles, c	3	0	0	0	7	
Wells, p	0	0	0	0	1	
Mills, p	0	0	0	0	0	
Orosco, p	0	0	0	0	0	
Myers, p	0	0	0	0	0	
Benitez, p	0	0	0	0	0	
Totals	36	5	10	5	27	1

New York	AB	R	H	RBI	PO	
Jeter, ss	5	1	2	0	1	2
Raines, lf	4	1	1	0	1	
Williams, cf	3	0	2	1	3	
Fielder, dh	5	0	1	1	0	0
Martinez, 1b	4	0	0	0	9	
Duncan, 2b	4	0	1	0	1	2
O'Neill, rf	2	0	1	0	5	
Leyritz, ph-rf	1	0	0	0	0	0
Hayes, 3b	4	0	1	0	0	
Girardi, c	4	1	2	0	7	0
Cone, p	0	0	0	0	0	1
Nelson, p	0	0	0	0	0	
Lloyd, p	0	0	0	0	0	0
Weathers, p	0	0	0	0	0	0
Totals	36	3	11	2	27	

Baltimore	0 0 2	0 0 0	2 1 0—5
New York	2 0 0	0 0 0	1 0 0—3

timore	IP	H	R	ER	BB	SO
lls (W)	6 2/3	8	3	3	3	6
s	*0	1	0	0	0	0
sco	1 1/3	1	0	0	0	1
ers	1/3	1	0	0	1	0
itez (S)	2/3	0	0	0	0	0

w York	IP	H	R	ER	BB	SO
ne	6	5	2	2	5	5
son (L)	1 1/3	5	3	3	0	1
yd	1 1/3	0	0	0	0	1
athers	1/3	0	0	0	0	0

*Pitched to one batter in seventh.

:—Duncan. DP—Baltimore 2, New York 1. LOB—Baltimore 10, New York 2B—R. Alomar, Duncan. 3B—Girardi. HR—Zeile, Palmeiro. SF—mar. HBP—By Wells (Martinez). WP—Cone. T—4:13. A—56,432. U—tt, plate; Reilly, first; Morrison, second; Roe, third; Garcia, left field; nett, right field.

GAME 3

HIGHLIGHTS

NEW YORK 5, BALTIMORE 2

hy the Yankees won: Starter Jimmy Key kept the nkees' struggling offense in the game by allowing ree hits and only two runs in eight innings, and erek Jeter and Bernie Williams ignited a dramatic ghth-inning comeback that included another zarre play.

hy the Orioles lost: Third baseman Todd Zeile ent from hero to goat in the span of eight innings. e hit a two-run homer in the first to give the team 2-0 lead, but after the Yankees tied it in the eighth, s error allowed New York to score the go-ahead n. The bungle also rattled starter Mike Mussina, ho gave up a two-run homer to the next hitter, ecil Fielder.

urning points:

. The game tightened on two throws in the fourth. n a 3-2 pitch to Bernie Williams with one out, ussina threw what he thought was strike three. ut umpire Mike Reilly called it a ball. After illiams advanced to third on a single by Tino artinez, Fielder hit a roller to third for what looked be an inning-ending double play. But second base-an Roberto Alomar appeared to be thrown off by artinez coming into second and threw a weak ouncer to first, allowing Fielder to beat the throw d Williams to score the Yankees' first run. If the rioles had turned the double play, Mussina might ot have faced Jeter and Williams in the pivotal ghth inning.

2. Another freakish play, another heart-breaking ghth inning for the Orioles. After Joe Girardi flied ut and Tim Raines grounded out to start the inning, ussina had retired 10 in a row and stood four outs om a 2-1 victory, and a 2-1 series lead. But Jeter oubled to right, and Williams singled to left, scor-g Jeter. Martinez then doubled into the left-field orner, advancing Williams to third. That's where e play should have ended. But third baseman Zeile oked to throw to second to catch Martinez off the ag, and when he saw he didn't have a chance to get m, he decided to pump-fake the throw in an tempt to catch Williams napping off the third-base ag. The ball slipped out of Zeile's hand and drib-

bled toward shortstop. And with half the Yankees not paying attention, Williams dashed for home and barely slid in ahead of Cal Ripken's throw for a 3-2 lead. "It was a reaction play," Williams said. "I saw the ball on the ground and figured by the time Cal got it, he'd have to make a perfect throw to get me." The play flustered Mussina, and two pitches later, Fielder capped the scoring with a two-run blast into the seats in left.

Notable: Before Williams' single in the eighth, the Yankees had been 2-for-29 in the series with runners in scoring position. . . . Yankees manager Joe Torre, looking for more offense, replaced slumping and ail-ing regulars Wade Boggs and Paul O'Neill with Charlie Hayes at third and Darryl Strawberry in right, respectively. . . . After Zeile's homer in the first, Key allowed only a two-out single to B.J. Surhoff in the second and a leadoff walk to Eddie Murray in the fifth. Key became the first Yankees starter in this postseason to be credited with a win. . . . The Orioles fell to 0-7 against the Yankees this season at Camden Yards. . . . Cal Ripken's 14-game hitting streak that began in the regular-season came to an end.

Quotable: Mussina, on the effect of Zeile's error: "I think it probably did bother me a little. I shouldn't have let it, but I did. I really wasn't concentrating on what I was doing." . . . John Wetteland, on yet anoth-er comeback: "It's funny. Every time it seems like it's the most grim, we find a way." . . . Torre, on his club playing so many tight games: "We've played a ton of one-run and two-run games, and I think we've gotten used to doing it. Close games don't bother us." . . . Zeile, on his error: "It was a bizarre play. It all seemed like slow motion." . . . Boggs, on how his missing games in September because of a bad back affected his swing: "When you have some time off, your swing can go south. And it's in the Carribean right now." . . . Torre, on Williams' run: "I saw Bernie stop and figured it was second and third. I was starting to look ahead to what might happen next, and all off a sudden I look up and he's halfway home."

BOX SCORE

FRIDAY, OCTOBER 11, AT BALTIMORE

New York	AB	R	H	RBI	PO	A
Raines, lf	5	0	1	0	1	0
Jeter, ss	4	1	1	0	0	2
Williams, cf	3	2	1	1	5	0
Martinez, 1b	4	1	2	0	9	1
Fielder, 1b	4	1	1	3	0	0
Strawberry, rf	4	0	1	0	3	0
Duncan, 2b	4	0	0	0	2	1
Sojo, 2b	0	0	0	0	0	1
Hayes, 3b	2	0	0	0	0	2
Girardi, c	4	0	1	0	6	0
Key, p	0	0	0	0	1	0
Wetteland, p	0	0	0	0	0	0
Totals	34	5	8	4	27	7
Baltimore	AB	R	H	RBI	PO	A
Anderson, cf	4	1	1	0	2	0
Zeile, 3b	4	1	1	2	0	1
Alomar, 2b	4	0	0	0	5	6
Palmeiro, 1b	3	0	0	0	9	0
Bonilla, rf	3	0	0	0	3	0
Ripken, ss	3	0	0	0	0	3
Murray, dh	2	0	0	0	0	0

Baltimore	AB	R	H	RBI	PO	A
Surhoff, lf	3	0	1	0	2	0
Hoiles, c	3	0	0	0	6	1
Mussina, p	0	0	0	0	0	0
Orosco, p	0	0	0	0	0	0
Mathews, p	0	0	0	0	0	1
Totals	29	2	3	2	27	12

New York	0	0 0	1 0 0	0 4	0—5
Baltimore	2	0 0	0 0 0	0 0	0—2

New York	IP	H	R	ER	BB	SO
Key (W)	8	3	2	2	1	5
Wetteland (S)	1	0	0	0	0	1

Baltimore	IP	H	R	ER	BB	SO
Mussina (L)	$7^2/3$	8	5	5	2	6
Orosco	$^1/3$	0	0	0	0	0
Mathews	1	0	0	0	1	1

E—Zeile, Ripken. DP—New York 1, Baltimore 2. LOB—New York 5, Baltimore 1. 2B—Jeter, Martinez. HR—Fielder, Zeile. T—2:50. A—48,635. U—Reilly, plate; Morrison, first; Roe, second; Garcia, third; Barnett, left field; Scott, right field.

GAME 4

HIGHLIGHTS

NEW YORK 8, BALTIMORE 4

Why the Yankees won: They jumped on the Orioles early for a change, behind home runs from Bernie Williams, Darryl Strawberry and Paul O'Neill. Williams hit a two-run shot in the first to make it 2-0, Strawberry hit a solo homer in the second to make it 3-1, and O'Neill hit a two-run shot in the fourth to make it 5-2. The early runs gave a much-needed cushion to starter Kenny Rogers and reliever David Weathers, who, combined, managed to survive $5^2/3$ sometimes shaky innings.

Why the Orioles lost: Rookie Rocky Coppinger, who was 10-6 with a 5.18 ERA in the regular season after being called up in June, was overmatched in his playoff debut. Although he lasted into the sixth inning, Coppinger allowed three of the Yankees' four homers. In his defense, he didn't receive enough support from the hitters, who went 2-for-15 with runners in scoring position, allowing Rogers and Weathers to squirm out of several jams with minimal damage.

The turning points:

1. Having already given up a run in the first, Rogers stood on the brink of disaster in the third. He gave up a leadoff homer to Chris Hoiles, retired Brady Anderson on a flyout to the warning track, then allowed singles to Zeile and Alomar. With runners on first and second, Rogers ran the count on Palmeiro to 3-2, prompting a visit from Girardi. Whatever it was Rogers worked, as he struck out Palmeiro on a pitch low and away, then got Bonilla to hit into an inning-ending forceout.

2. Torre gambled in the fourth by pulling Rogers with a 5-2 lead. But it worked. When Torre went to the mound for the change, Rogers had walked Cal Ripken, thrown a wild pitch and allowed a single to Pete Incaviglia, advancing Ripken to third. Weathers entered the game and allowed a run-scoring single to pinch-hitter B.J. Surhoff. But he got Hoiles to ground out to third (scoring Incaviglia), and retired

Anderson on a grounder to second. Baltimore ha scored twice to cut the lead to 5-4, but for th Yankees, it could have been much worse.

3. In the eighth, the Orioles threatened to turn th tables and stage a dramatic comeback when the started the inning with three singles off Rivera. Bu he struck out Hoiles and Anderson and retired Zeil on a pop to shortstop. End of inning, end of hope.

Notables: Bonilla struck out four times for the sec ond time in the series. . . . Torre started Strawberr in left field instead of Raines on "a hunch," an Strawberry responded with a single, two homer and three RBIs. . . . The Yankees and Orioles hit fiv home runs combined, tying an ALCS record. . . . Williams tied the postseason record with his fift home run.

Quotable: Johnson, on his team's lack of clutch hi ting: "We're setting the table, but certain guys in th lineup are cold." . . . Torre, on sticking with O'Nei despite a 3-for-21 postseason slump (all singles) an a sore left hamstring: "As long as he can physicall put a swing on the ball, he'll be out there. O'Neill ha played all year, and the loyalty factor is a big part o this game."

BOX SCORE

SATURDAY, OCTOBER 12, AT BALTIMORE

New York	AB	R	H	RBI	PO	A
Jeter, ss	5	1	1	0	4	4
Boggs, 3b	5	0	0	0	1	3
Williams, cf	4	2	2	2	4	0
Martinez, 1b	4	1	1	0	9	0
Fielder, dh	4	0	0	1	0	0
Strawberry, lf	4	3	3	3	1	0
Raines, lf	0	0	0	0	0	0
O'Neill, rf	3	1	1	2	1	0
Duncan, 2b	3	0	1	0	1	1
Sojo, 2b	1	0	0	0	0	0
Girardi, c	3	0	0	0	6	0
Rogers, p	0	0	0	0	0	0
Weathers, p	0	0	0	0	0	0
Lloyd, p	0	0	0	0	0	0
M. Rivera, p	0	0	0	0	0	0
Wetteland, p	0	0	0	0	0	0
Totals	36	8	9	8	27	8

Baltimore	AB	R	H	RBI	PO	A
Anderson, cf	4	1	0	0	2	0
Zeile, 3b	5	0	2	0	2	1
Alomar, 2b	5	0	2	0	0	5
Palmeiro, 1b	3	0	0	1	8	0
Bonilla, rf	5	0	0	0	3	0
Ripken, ss	3	1	1	0	0	1
Incaviglia, dh	2	1	1	0	0	0
Murray, ph-dh	2	0	1	0	0	0
Devereaux, lf	1	0	0	0	1	0
Surhoff, ph-lf	3	0	2	1	2	0
Hoiles, c	4	1	2	2	8	0
Coppinger, p	0	0	0	0	1	1
Rhodes, p	0	0	0	0	0	0
Mills, p	0	0	0	0	0	0
Orosco, p	0	0	0	0	0	0
Benitez, p	0	0	0	0	0	0
Mathews, p	0	0	0	0	0	0
Totals	37	4	11	4	27	9

New York	2	1 0	2 0 0	0 3	0—8
Baltimore	1	0 1	2 0 0	0 0	0—4

New York	IP	H	R	ER	BB	SO
Rogers	*3	5	4	4	2	3
Weathers (W)	$2^2/3$	3	0	0	0	0
Lloyd	$^1/3$	0	0	0	0	0
M. Rivera	2	3	0	0	1	2
Wetteland	1	0	0	0	0	1

timore	IP	H	R	ER	BB	SO
ppinger (L)......................	5 1/3	6	5	5	1	3
des..................................	2/3	0	0	0	0	1
s..................................	1 1/3	1	1	1	0	2
sco................................	†0	1	1	1	0	0
aitez..............................	2/3	1	1	1	1	0
thews............................	1	0	0	0	0	2

*Pitched to three batters in fourth. †Pitched to one batter in eighth.
.OB—New York 3, Baltimore 10. 2B—Jeter, Williams, Duncan, Alomar. —Williams, Strawberry 2, O'Neill, Hoiles. SF—Palmeiro. WP—Rogers. -3:45. A—48,974. U—Morrison, plate; Roe, first; Garcia, second; nett, third; Scott, left field; Reilly, right field.

GAME 5

HIGHLIGHTS
NEW YORK 6, BALTIMORE 4

hy the Yankees won: Andy Pettitte controlled e Orioles for eight innings, walking one and allow- g only three hits (two of them solo home runs), d the offense, powered by Cecil Fielder, proved portunistic once again by pouncing on an Orioles istake.

hy the Orioles lost: Roberto Alomar failed to ep a ground ball in front of him, and starter Scott rickson failed to keep the ball in the park. Five of e six runs Erickson allowed were unearned cause of Alomar's third-inning error. But five of e six also came from home runs—off the bats of m Leyritz, Cecil Fielder and Darryl Strawberry. "I ould have made better pitches," Erickson said. "I t a couple of fastballs up, that's what hurt me."

urning point:
. Alomar's error paved the way for the Yankees' in e decisive third. Jim Leyritz led off with a home n to make it 1-0. After Luis Sojo grounded out to cond, Jeter singled to center and Boggs reached an infield hit to shortstop. That's when Bernie illiams hit an ordinary grounder to Alomar for hat should have been an inning-ending double ay. Instead, the ball rolled under Alomar's glove d into right field, scoring Jeter and sending Boggs third. After Tino Martinez grounded into a field- 's choice in which Alomar threw Boggs out at ome, Fielder hit a three-run homer to left center, ith Williams and Martinez scoring ahead of him. ve pitches later, Strawberry homered to center. he Orioles didn't come close to threatening the ad until the ninth, when Bobby Bonilla hit a two- ut, two-run homer off John Wetteland. But Ripken en grounded out to shortstop, ending the series.

otable: The Orioles finished the year 0-9 against e Yankees in Camden Yards. . . . After getting a hit each of the four first-round playoff games, illiams hit safely in all five ALCS games and was amed Most Valuable Player. . . . The teams set a cord for home runs in a league championship ries with 19; the Yankees outhomered the Orioles,

10-9. . . . The Yankees' bullpen allowed three runs—all by Jeff Nelson—in 14 innings.

Quotable: Torre, on the feeling of reaching the World Series for the first time after a 17-year career as a player and a 15-year career as a manager: "This is easily the best moment of my life in this game. Nothing else is even close." . . . Baltimore's Brady Anderson, on the Yankees' late-inning dominance: "When they get to the seventh inning with a lead, you don't beat them. In that situation, they're proba- bly the best team in baseball." . . . Alomar, on his error: "I can't remember that ever happening in a big game. The ball tricked me. I thought it was going to take a bounce, but kind of skidded and I missed it. But I don't think that play lost the game. They were just better than us."

BOX SCORE
SUNDAY, OCTOBER 13, AT BALTIMORE

New York	AB	R	H	RBI	PO	A
Jeter, ss	5	1	2	0	1	2
Boggs, 3b	5	0	2	0	0	6
Williams, cf	5	1	2	0	4	0
Martinez, 1b	5	1	0	0	11	1
Fielder, dh	3	1	1	3	0	0
Fox, pr-dh	0	0	0	0	0	0
Hayes, ph-dh....................	1	0	0	0	0	0
Strawberry, lf	3	1	1	1	1	0
Raines, lf.........................	0	0	0	0	0	0
O'Neill, rf........................	3	0	1	0	1	0
Leyritz, c	3	1	1	1	3	1
Sojo, 2b	4	0	1	0	4	3
Pettitte, p	0	0	0	0	2	0
Wetteland, p.....................	0	0	0	0	0	0
Totals	37	6	11	5	27	13

Baltimore	AB	R	H	RBI	PO	A
Anderson, cf	4	0	0	0	1	0
Zeile, 3b	3	1	2	1	0	1
Alomar, 2b	4	1	0	0	5	5
Palmeiro, 1b	4	0	0	0	8	0
Bonilla, rf	4	1	1	2	1	0
Ripken, ss	4	0	0	0	0	3
Murray, dh	3	1	1	1	0	0
Surhoff, lf........................	2	0	0	0	2	1
Parent, c	1	0	0	0	8	0
Hoiles, ph-c......................	2	0	0	0	2	0
Erickson, p	0	0	0	0	0	0
Rhodes, p	0	0	0	0	0	0
Mills, p	0	0	0	0	0	0
Myers, p	0	0	0	0	0	0
Totals	31	4	4	4	27	10

New York..................	0	0	6	0	0	0	0	0	0—6
Baltimore..................	0	0	0	0	0	1	0	1	2—4

New York	IP	H	R	ER	BB	SO
Pettitte (W)	8	3	2	2	1	3
Wetteland	1	1	2	2	1	1

Baltimore	IP	H	R	ER	BB	SO
Erickson (L)	5	7	6	1	1	5
Rhodes.............................	1	2	0	0	0	1
Mills	*1	1	0	0	1	1
Myers	2	1	0	0	2	1

*Pitched to one batter in eighth.
E—Alomar. DP—Baltimore 1. LOB—New York 8, Baltimore 2. 2B—Williams. HR—Fielder, Strawberry, Leyritz, Zeile, Bonilla, Murray. SB—Jeter, Williams. WP—Rhodes. T—2:57. A—48,718. U—Roe, plate; Garcia, first; Barnett, second; Scott, third; Reilly, left field; Morrison, right field.

NEW YORK YANKEES' BATTING AND FIELDING AVERAGES

Player, position	G	AB	R	H	TB	2B	3B	HR	RBI	BB	IBB	SO	Avg.	PO	A	E	Avg
Williams, cf	5	19	6	9	18	3	0	2	6	5	1	4	.474	20	0	0	1.000
Jeter, ss	5	24	5	10	15	2	0	1	1	0	0	5	.417	6	13	0	1.000
Strawberry, rf-ph-lf	4	12	4	5	14	0	0	3	5	2	0	2	.417	5	0	0	1.000
O'Neill, rf	4	11	1	3	6	0	0	1	2	3	0	2	.273	9	1	0	1.000
Raines, lf	5	15	2	4	5	1	0	0	0	1	0	1	.267	5	0	0	1.000
Girardi, c-ph	4	12	1	3	5	0	1	0	0	1	0	3	.250	22	0	0	1.000
Leyritz, c-rf-ph	3	8	1	2	5	0	0	1	2	1	0	4	.250	11	2	0	1.000
Duncan, 2b	4	15	0	3	5	2	0	0	0	0	0	3	.200	6	6	1	.923
Sojo, 2b	3	5	0	1	1	0	0	0	0	0	0	1	.200	4	4	0	1.000
Martinez, 1b	5	22	3	4	5	1	0	0	0	0	0	2	.182	48	2	0	1.000
Fielder, dh	5	18	3	3	9	0	0	2	8	4	1	5	.167	0	0	0	.000
Hayes, ph-3b-dh	4	7	0	1	1	0	0	0	0	2	0	2	.143	0	3	0	1.000
Boggs, 3b	3	15	1	2	2	0	0	0	0	1	0	3	.133	2	11	0	1.000
Aldrete, ph	1	0	0	0	0	0	0	0	0	0	0	0	.000	0	0	0	.000
Cone, p	1	0	0	0	0	0	0	0	0	0	0	0	.000	0	1	0	1.000
Fox, dh-pr	2	0	0	0	0	0	0	0	0	0	0	0	.000	0	0	0	.000
Key, p	1	0	0	0	0	0	0	0	0	0	0	0	.000	1	0	0	1.000
Lloyd, p	2	0	0	0	0	0	0	0	0	0	0	0	.000	0	0	0	.000
Nelson, p	2	0	0	0	0	0	0	0	0	0	0	0	.000	0	0	0	.000
Pettitte, p	2	0	0	0	0	0	0	0	0	0	0	0	.000	2	0	0	1.000
M. Rivera, p	2	0	0	0	0	0	0	0	0	0	0	0	.000	0	0	0	.000
Rogers, p	1	0	0	0	0	0	0	0	0	0	0	0	.000	0	0	0	.000
Weathers, p	2	0	0	0	0	0	0	0	0	0	0	0	.000	0	0	0	.000
Wetteland, p	4	0	0	0	0	0	0	0	0	0	0	0	.000	0	0	0	.000
Totals	5	183	27	50	91	9	1	10	24	20	2	37	.273	141	43	1	.995

BALTIMORE ORIOLES' BATTING AND FIELDING AVERAGES

Player, position	G	AB	R	H	TB	2B	3B	HR	RBI	BB	IBB	SO	Avg.	PO	A	E	Avg
Incaviglia, dh	1	2	1	1	1	0	0	0	0	0	0	0	.500	0	0	0	.000
Zeile, 3b	5	22	3	8	17	0	0	3	5	2	0	1	.364	3	7	1	.909
Murray, dh	5	15	1	4	7	0	0	1	2	2	0	2	.267	0	0	0	.000
Surhoff, lf-ph	5	15	0	4	4	0	0	0	2	1	0	2	.267	11	1	0	1.000
Ripken, ss	5	20	1	5	6	1	0	0	0	1	0	4	.250	4	15	1	.947
Palmeiro, 1b	5	17	4	4	10	0	0	2	4	4	0	4	.235	44	3	0	1.000
Alomar, 2b	5	23	2	5	7	2	0	0	1	0	0	4	.217	15	25	2	.953
Anderson, cf	5	21	5	4	8	1	0	1	1	3	0	5	.190	8	0	0	1.000
Hoiles, c-ph	4	12	1	2	5	0	0	1	2	1	0	3	.167	23	2	0	1.000
Parent, c	2	6	0	1	1	0	0	0	0	0	0	2	.167	14	0	0	1.000
Bonilla, rf	5	20	1	1	4	0	0	1	2	1	0	4	.050	11	0	0	1.000
Benitez, p	3	0	0	0	0	0	0	0	0	0	0	0	.000	0	0	0	.000
Coppinger, p	1	0	0	0	0	0	0	0	0	0	0	0	.000	1	1	0	1.000
Erickson, p	2	0	0	0	0	0	0	0	0	0	0	0	.000	0	2	0	1.000
Mathews, p	3	0	0	0	0	0	0	0	0	0	0	0	.000	0	1	0	1.000
Mills, p	3	0	0	0	0	0	0	0	0	0	0	0	.000	0	0	0	.000
Mussina, p	1	0	0	0	0	0	0	0	0	0	0	0	.000	0	0	0	.000
Myers, p	3	0	0	0	0	0	0	0	0	0	0	0	.000	0	0	0	.000
Orosco, p	4	0	0	0	0	0	0	0	0	0	0	0	.000	0	1	0	1.000
Rhodes, p	3	0	0	0	0	0	0	0	0	0	0	0	.000	0	0	0	.000
Wells, p	1	0	0	0	0	0	0	0	0	0	0	0	.000	1	0	0	1.000
Tarasco, rf	2	1	0	0	0	0	0	0	0	0	0	1	.000	2	0	0	1.000
Devereaux, lf	3	2	0	0	0	0	0	0	0	0	0	1	.000	1	0	0	1.000
Totals	5	176	19	39	70	4	0	9	19	15	0	33	.222	138	58	4	.980

NEW YORK YANKEES' PITCHING RECORDS

Pitcher	G	GS	CG	IP	H	R	ER	HR	BB	IBB	SO	HB	WP	W	L	Pct.	ERA
M. Rivera	2	0	0	4	6	0	0	0	1	0	5	0	0	1	0	1.000	0.00
Weathers	2	0	0	3	3	0	0	0	0	0	0	0	0	1	0	1.000	0.00
Lloyd	2	0	0	1 2/3	0	0	0	0	0	0	1	0	0	0	0	.000	0.00
Key	1	1	0	8	3	2	2	1	1	0	5	0	0	1	0	1.000	2.25
Cone	1	1	0	6	5	2	2	1	5	0	5	0	1	0	0	.000	3.00
Pettitte	2	2	0	15	10	6	6	4	5	0	7	0	1	1	0	1.000	3.60
Wetteland	4	0	0	4	2	2	2	1	1	0	5	0	0	0	0	.000	4.50
Nelson	2	0	0	2 1/3	5	3	3	1	0	0	2	0	0	0	1	.000	11.57
Rogers	1	1	0	3	5	4	4	1	2	0	3	0	1	0	0	.000	12.00
Totals	5	5	0	47	39	19	19	9	15	0	33	0	2	4	1	.800	3.64

No shutouts. Save—Wetteland.

BALTIMORE ORIOLES' PITCHING RECORDS

her	G	GS	CG	IP	H	R	ER	HR	BB	IBB	SO	HB	WP	W	L	Pct.	ERA
hews	3	0	0	2$\frac{1}{3}$	0	0	0	0	2	0	3	1	0	0	0	.000	0.00
des	3	0	0	2	2	0	0	0	0	0	2	0	1	0	0	.000	0.00
rs	3	0	0	4	4	1	1	1	3	0	2	0	0	0	1	.000	2.25
kson	2	2	0	11$\frac{1}{3}$	14	9	3	3	4	0	8	0	0	0	1	.000	2.38
s	3	0	0	2$\frac{1}{3}$	3	1	1	0	1	0	3	0	0	0	0	.000	3.86
ls	1	1	0	6$\frac{2}{3}$	8	3	3	0	3	0	6	1	0	1	0	1.000	4.05
sco	4	0	0	2	2	1	1	0	1	1	2	0	0	0	0	.000	4.50
ssina	1	1	0	7$\frac{2}{3}$	8	5	5	1	2	0	6	0	0	0	1	.000	5.87
itez	3	0	0	2$\frac{1}{3}$	2	2	2	0	3	1	2	0	0	0	0	.000	7.71
pinger	1	1	0	5$\frac{1}{3}$	6	5	5	3	1	0	3	0	0	0	1	.000	8.44
tals	5	5	0	46	50	27	21	10	20	2	37	2	1	1	4	.200	4.11

o shutouts. Save—Benitez.

SCORE BY INNINGS

York	5	2	6	3	0	0	2	8	0	0	1—27
imore	3	1	4	3	0	2	2	2	2	0	0—19

MISCELLANEOUS STATISTICS

rifice hits—None.
rifice flies—Alomar, Palmeiro, Surhoff.
en bases—Jeter 2, Williams.
ght stealing—None.
ble plays—Ripken, Alomar and Palmeiro 3; Zeile, Alomar and Palmeiro 2; Alomar, Ripken and Palmeiro; Ripken and Alomar;
Martinez (unassisted).
on bases—New York 13, 11, 5, 3, 8—40; Baltimore 11, 10, 1, 10, 2—34.
by pitcher—By Wells (Martinez), by Mathews (Duncan).
sed balls—None.
—Pettitte.
e of games—First game, 4:23; second game, 4:13; third game, 2:50; fourth game, 3:45; fifth game, 2:57.
ndance—First game, 56,495; second game, 56,432; third game, 48,635; fourth game, 48,974; fifth game, 48,718.
pires—Barnett, Garcia, Morrison, Roe, Reilly and Scott.
cial scorers—Mark Jacobson, Bill Shannon.

N.L. CHAMPIONSHIP SERIES

GAME 1

HIGHLIGHTS

ATLANTA 4, ST. LOUIS 2

Why the Braves won: N.L. Cy Young Award winner John Smoltz was terrific, limiting St. Louis to two runs and five hits in eight innings of work. The first three batters in the Cardinals' lineup combined to go 0-for-12 against him.

Why the Cardinals lost: They wasted the few opportunities they had against Smoltz and played poor fundamentally, making the kind of mental mistakes that often don't show up in box scores.

The turning points:

1. Trailing, 2-1, in the seventh, the Cardinals pushed a run across against Smoltz to tie the game and had runners on first and second with no outs. The next batter, light-hitting Luis Alicea, swung away instead of bunting. He hit a soft liner to left. The next two batters, Willie McGee and Ozzie Smith, made outs, as well, and the inning ended in a 2-2 tie.

2. With the score still tied in the Atlanta eighth, Cardinals reliever Mark Petkovsek walked leadoff batter Mark Lemke, who then was replaced by pinch-runner Andruw Jones. The next batter, Chipper Jones, bunted the ball off the plate, and it shot toward Petkovsek. The pitcher slipped and lost his balance, but was able to field the ball nonetheless. Second baseman Alicea had broken toward first to cover on the play, but slowed when it appeared the ball would get by Petkovsek. Once he sped up again, he was too late, and he took the throw behind the bag. Alicea then tried to tag Chipper Jones—who was already two steps past the bag—and dropped the ball, allowing Andruw Jones to move to third. Later, with the bases loaded, Javy Lopez singled home two runs on an 0-2 count to give Atlanta its winning margin.

Notable: Chipper Jones (30 homers and 110 RBIs) had attempted just one sacrifice in the regular season. . . . Lopez got his game-winning hit off reliever T.J. Mathews, who yielded two hits in two at-bats against the Atlanta catcher during the regular season. . . . The paid crowd of 48,686 was some 3,000 short of capacity and ended a streak of 27 consecutive postseason sellouts for the Braves.

Quotable: St. Louis manager Tony La Russa, on his decision to have Mathews pitch to Lopez despite his lack of success: "If you have 20 or 30 at-bats, then you pay more attention." . . . La Russa, on his decision not to have Alicea bunt: "You had a couple of guys on the bases where speed wasn't their greatest asset. They're playing the bunt, which makes it real tough to execute. Plus, (Alicea) is a real good fastball hitter." . . . Petkovsek, on the pivotal eighth inning: "When you commit two blunders in an inning against a team like the Braves, you're not giving your defense much of a chance."

BOX SCORE

WEDNESDAY, OCTOBER 9, AT ATLANTA

St. Louis	AB	R	H	RBI	PO
Smith, ss	4	0	0	0	3
Lankford, cf	4	0	0	0	2
Gant, lf	4	0	0	0	2
Jordan, rf	4	1	1	0	3
Gaetti, 3b	3	0	1	0	0
Mejia, pr	0	1	0	0	0
Gallego, 3b	0	0	0	0	0
Sweeney, ph	1	0	0	0	0
Mabry, 1b	4	0	1	0	2
Pagnozzi, c	4	0	1	1	11
Alicea, 2b	2	0	0	0	1
An. Benes, p	1	0	1	0	0
McGee, ph	1	0	0	0	0
Petkovsek, p	0	0	0	0	0
Fossas, p	0	0	0	0	0
Mathews, p	0	0	0	0	0
Totals	32	2	5	1	24

Atlanta	AB	R	H	RBI	PO
Grissom, cf	4	1	1	0	4
Lemke, 2b	3	0	1	2	2
A. Jones, pr-lf	0	1	0	0	0
C. Jones, 3b	4	1	4	0	0
McGriff, 1b	4	0	0	0	7
Klesko, lf	3	0	1	0	4
Pendleton, ph	0	0	0	0	0
Belliard, 2b	0	0	0	0	0
Lopez, c	4	0	1	2	7
Dye, rf	4	0	0	0	3
Blauser, ss	4	1	1	0	0
Smoltz, p	3	0	0	0	0
Wohlers, p	0	0	0	0	0
Totals	33	4	9	4	27

St. Louis	0	1	0	0	0	0	1	0	0—
Atlanta	0	0	0	0	2	0	0	2	x—

St. Louis	IP	H	R	ER	BB	S
An. Benes	6	7	2	2	0	
Petkovsek (L)	*1	2	2	1	1	
Fossas	1/3	0	0	0	0	
Mathews	2/3	1	0	0	1	

Atlanta	IP	H	R	ER	BB	
Smoltz (W)	8	5	2	2	2	
Wohlers (S)	1	0	0	0	0	

*Pitched to three batters in eighth.

E—Alicea. LOB—St. Louis 5, Atlanta 7. 2B—An. Benes, Grissom. 3B Jordan. SB—C. Jones. WP—Smoltz 2. T—2:35. A—48,686. U—Rur plate; Hirschbeck, first; Davidson, second; West, third; Crawford, left fi Montague, right field.

GAME 2

HIGHLIGHTS

ST. LOUIS 8, ATLANTA 3

Why the Cardinals won: They kept the game clo against Atlanta ace Greg Maddux until they we able to blow it open by scoring five runs in the se enth inning, four of them coming on third basem Gary Gaetti's grand slam.

Why the Braves lost: Like St. Louis in Game 1, th made a lot of mistakes. In addition to Maddux's i pitch to Gaetti, Marquis Grissom, a Gold Glove cent fielder, misplayed a single in the first inning that set the Cardinals' first run. Third baseman Chipper Jon later threw wildly to first after fielding a bunt.

The turning points:

1. The Cardinals' Royce Clayton led off the gan

a single to right. One out later, Ron Gant sin-
to center, sending Clayton to third. Grissom
mishandled the ball, allowing Clayton to score
Gant to take second. The fact the Cardinals
e able to score early against Maddux was big; he
dominated them (2-0, 0.78 ERA) during the reg-
season.

With the score tied at 3 in the seventh and a run-
on first, St. Louis pinch-hitter Mark Sweeney
ped a bunt attempt down the third-base line.
es dove for the ball but missed. He got up firing,
his poor throw eluded second baseman Mark
ake, who was covering first on the play. Jones'
or left runners on second and third with none
Later in the inning, with the bases loaded,
etti homered to left.

table: Maddux gave up eight runs for the first
e since joining the Braves in 1993. Five were
arned. . . . The victory was Cardinals starter
ld Stottlemyre's first in League Championship
ies play. He went 0-3 with Toronto from 1989-93.

Maddux became the first pitcher to yield two
nd slams in N.L. Championship Series history.
other was hit by the Giants' Will Clark in 1989.
two slams were hit in a total of 34⅔ NLCS
ings. Maddux had given up just one slam in
55⅔ regular-season innings in his 11-year career.

After going 0-for-9 against Maddux during the
ular season, Gant was 3-for-5, with one RBI. . . .
slam was the ninth of Gaetti's career, but his
t in postseason play.

otable: Gaetti, on the Cardinals' 4-10 record
inst Atlanta before this game: "We felt we could
t these guys, but doing it is another thing." . . .
etti, who homered on the first pitch Maddux
ew him: "You can't take too many pitches with
t guy. You get deep in the count, he can make you
k silly." . . . Maddux, on Jones' decision to field
eeney's bunt: "It goes foul if he lets it go, there's
question about that. But the next 10 times they
that, he'll probably catch it." . . . Stottlemyre: "I
s fortunate tonight. We scored eight runs off a
at pitcher."

BOX SCORE

THURSDAY, OCTOBER 10, AT ATLANTA

ouis	AB	R	H	RBI	PO	A
on, ss	4	2	2	0	0	2
ford, cf	3	1	0	1	4	0
, lf	5	1	3	1	2	0
an, rf	4	1	2	1	2	0
ti, 3b	5	1	1	4	1	0
y, 1b	4	0	1	0	6	0
ozzi, c	4	0	1	0	11	0
go, 2b	4	1	1	0	2	2
lemyre, p	2	0	0	0	0	0
eney, p	0	1	0	0	0	0
ovsek, p	0	0	0	0	0	1
g, ph	1	0	0	0	0	0
eycutt, p	0	0	0	0	0	0
rsley, p	0	0	0	0	0	1
tals	36	8	11	7	27	6

nta	AB	R	H	RBI	PO	A
som, cf	5	2	2	2	4	0
ke, 2b	3	0	1	0	1	5
nes, 3b	4	0	0	0	2	1

Atlanta	AB	R	H	RBI	PO	A
Avery, p	0	0	0	0	0	0
McGriff, 1b	3	0	0	0	9	1
Klesko, lf	4	0	1	1	1	0
Dye, rf	4	0	0	0	0	0
Perez, c	1	0	0	0	2	0
Pendleton, ph	1	0	0	0	0	0
Lopez, c	1	0	1	0	5	0
Blauser, ss	4	1	0	0	2	3
Maddux, p	2	0	0	0	1	1
McMichael, p	0	0	0	0	0	0
Polonia, ph	1	0	0	0	0	0
Neagle, p	0	0	0	0	0	0
Mordecai, 3b	1	0	0	0	0	0
Totals	34	3	5	3	27	11

St. Louis	1	0	2	0	0	0	5	0	0—8
Atlanta	0	0	2	0	0	1	0	0	0—3

St. Louis	IP	H	R	ER	BB	SO
Stottlemyre (W)	6	4	3	3	3	8
Petkovsek	1	0	0	0	0	0
Honeycutt	⅔	0	0	0	0	0
Eckersley	1⅓	1	0	0	0	1

Atlanta	IP	H	R	ER	BB	SO
Maddux (L)	6⅔	9	8	3	2	3
McMichael	⅓	1	0	0	0	1
Neagle	1	0	0	0	0	2
Avery	1	1	0	0	1	1

E—Gallego, Clayton, C. Jones, Grissom. DP—Atlanta 1. LOB—St. Louis 6, Atlanta 7. 2B—Gant, Jordan, Pagnozzi. HR—Gaetti, Grissom. SH—Sweeney. SF—Lankford. SB—Clayton, Grissom. WP—Maddux. T—2:53. A—52,067. U—Hirschbeck, plate; Davidson, first; West, second; Crawford, third; Montague, left field; Runge, right field.

GAME 3

HIGHLIGHTS

ST. LOUIS 3, ATLANTA 2

Why the Cardinals won: Left fielder Ron Gant swung a hot bat, driving in all three St. Louis runs with two home runs—a two-run blast in the first inning and a solo shot in the sixth.

Why the Braves lost: Besides their inability to handle Gant, the Braves could do little against Cardinals lefthander Donovan Osborne, who held Atlanta to two runs over seven innings in winning the first postseason game of his career.

The turning points:

1. In the top of the first inning, the Braves took a 1-0 lead on an infield single, a groundout, a wild pitch and a sacrifice fly. But with runners on second and third and two out, St. Louis shortstop Royce Clayton kept Atlanta from scoring twice more by leaping to backhand a liner off the bat of rookie Jermaine Dye.

2. In the bottom of the first, Clayton led off with a single to center. After Ray Lankford was retired, Gant hit a two-run homer off Tom Glavine, giving St. Louis a lead it never relinquished.

Notable: The victory was the Cardinals' eighth in a row at home in postseason play, but their first at home in 1996 against the Braves, who swept six previous games. . . . Gant, who came up through the Atlanta organization, was released by the Braves in March 1994 after breaking his lower right leg in a motorcycle accident. . . . Gant became the first player to hit two homers in an NLCS game since the Braves' David Justice in 1992. ... As a member of the Cincinnati Reds in 1995, Gant hit just .188 (3-for-16) against the Braves in the N.L. Championship Series.

Quotable: Atlanta second baseman Mark Lemke, on former teammate Gant: "I don't think I've ever seen a guy more ready to play." . . . Glavine, on Gant's second homer: "I had him set up for a fastball in. I wanted to go one more fastball away and he made me pay for that. That was a case of me out-thinking myself. It wasn't a bad pitch, just up more than I'd like." . . . Clayton, on catching Dye's first-inning liner: "Actually, it was knuckling and the ball kind of had a sink to it. It's tough to pick up rotation." . . . Justice, on Gant: "He did an awful lot for this organization. But when he got hurt, it was, 'See you later.' Now he's taking his vengeance out on us."

BOX SCORE

SATURDAY, OCTOBER 12, AT ST. LOUIS

Atlanta	AB	R	H	RBI	PO	A
Grissom, cf	5	1	2	0	1	0
Lemke, 2b	4	0	1	0	1	3
C. Jones, 3b	3	1	1	1	0	1
McGriff, 1b	3	0	1	0	8	0
Lopez, c	4	0	3	0	8	0
Dye, rf	3	0	0	1	3	0
A. Jones, lf	2	0	0	0	1	0
Pendleton, ph	1	0	0	0	0	0
McMichael, p	0	0	0	0	0	0
Blauser, ss	4	0	0	0	2	1
Glavine, p	2	0	0	0	0	2
Mordecai, ph	1	0	0	0	0	0
Bielecki, p	0	0	0	0	0	0
Klesko, lf	1	0	0	0	0	0
Totals	33	2	8	2	24	7

St. Louis	AB	R	H	RBI	PO	A
Clayton, ss	4	1	2	0	2	3
Lankford, cf	4	0	0	0	1	0
Honeycutt, p	0	0	0	0	0	0
Eckersley, p	0	0	0	0	0	0
Gant, lf	4	2	2	3	1	0
Jordan, rf	4	0	0	0	3	0
Gaetti, 3b	3	0	2	0	0	3
Mabry, 1b	2	0	1	0	10	0
Pagnozzi, c	3	0	0	0	8	0
Gallego, 2b	3	0	0	0	1	2
Osborne, p	3	0	0	0	0	1
Petkovsek, p	0	0	0	0	0	0
McGee, cf	0	0	0	0	1	0
Totals	30	3	7	3	27	9

Atlanta	1	0	0	0	0	0	0	1	0	—2
St. Louis	2	0	0	0	0	1	0	0	x	—3

Atlanta	IP	H	R	ER	BB	SO
Glavine (L)	6	7	3	3	0	5
Bielecki	1	0	0	0	0	1
McMichael	1	0	0	0	0	2

St. Louis	IP	H	R	ER	BB	SO
Osborne (W)	*7	7	2	2	3	6
Petkovsek	1	1	0	0	0	1
Honeycutt	1/3	0	0	0	0	0
Eckersley (S)	2/3	0	0	0	0	1

*Pitched to two batters in the 8th.
E—Blauser. DP—Atlanta 1. LOB—Atlanta 9, St. Louis 4. 2B—Lopez. HR—Gant 2. SF—C. Jones, Dye. HBP—By Glavine (Mabry). WP—Osborne. T—2:46. A—56,769. U—Davidson, plate; West, first; Crawford, second; Montague, third; Runge, left field; Hirschbeck, right field.

GAME 4

HIGHLIGHTS

ST. LOUIS 4, ATLANTA 3

Why the Cardinals won: They were able to rally from a 3-0 deficit by scoring three runs in the seventh inning and one in the eighth, the final coming on a solo home run by Brian Jordan.

Why the Braves lost: Their bullpen failed the Starter Denny Neagle pitched 6⅔ strong innin, but when he faltered at the 100-pitch mark, he g no relief. Greg McMichael yielded a two-run tri to the first batter he faced and later gave up t game-tying and game-winning runs.

The turning points:
1. With two outs in the bottom of the seventh a Atlanta leading, 3-0, John Mabry singled for t Cardinals' second hit of the game. The next batt Tom Pagnozzi, drew a walk after a lengthy at-b Braves manager Bobby Cox then replaced Nea with McMichael, who promptly yielded a two-r triple to rookie Dmitri Young. After pinch-hitter L Alicea walked, Royce Clayton beat out a tapper to t right of McMichael as Young scored the tying ru
2. With the game tied at 3 in the eighth—anc shaky McMichael still on the mound—Jord homered to left on a 2-1 pitch, giving the Cards th eventual winning margin.

Notable: The victory improved the Cardinals' reco to 18-4 in home playoff games since 1982. . . . Nea became the first pitcher other than Greg Madd John Smoltz, Tom Glavine or Steve Avery to star postseason game for Atlanta since Charlie Leibrar started Game 1 of the 1991 World Series. . . . Youn triple was the first extra-base hit of his career. . Cardinals reliever Dennis Eckersley, who did not v a game in 63 regular-season appearances, won t one. It was the first postseason win of his 22-ye career. . . . Atlanta second baseman Mark Lemke h not homered in 191 postseason at-bats before hitti one in the sixth inning.

Quotable: Young, who turned 23 two days earlier, the second postseason at-bat of his career: "Anybo in that situation would be nervous unless they're zombie. But I'm still confident. I go up to the pl thinking I can hit anyone." . . . Cox, on McMicha "He got beat on tonight, and that was really the sto of the game. 'Mac' has been our ace, but tonight was not good. But if he doesn't give up that chop to Clayton, we win the ballgame." . . . Cox, on l decision to lift Neagle: "He was done. He had come out." . . . Cox, on his team trailing three gam to one in the series: "We feel very confident we c reel off three in a row, but it ticks you off that v didn't get tonight's game."

BOX SCORE

SUNDAY, OCTOBER 13, AT ST. LOUIS

Atlanta	AB	R	H	RBI	PO
Grissom, cf	5	0	0	0	1
Lemke, 2b	4	1	1	1	2
C. Jones, 3b	3	1	2	0	2
McGriff, 1b	3	0	0	0	5
Klesko, lf	3	1	1	1	4
Lopez, c	3	0	0	0	6
Wohlers, p	0	0	0	0	0
Dye, rf	4	0	3	1	1
Blauser, ss	3	0	1	0	0
Polonia, ph	1	0	0	0	0
Neagle, p	2	0	1	0	0
McMichael, p	0	0	0	0	1

anta	AB	R	H	RBI	PO	A
ez, c	0	0	0	0	2	0
dleton, ph	1	0	0	0	0	0
otals	32	3	9	3	24	7

Louis	AB	R	H	RBI	PO	A
ton, ss	4	0	1	1	3	5
Gee, cf	4	0	1	0	1	0
t, lf	2	0	0	0	1	0
dan, rf	4	1	1	1	2	0
tti, 3b	4	0	0	3	1	3
ory, 1b	4	1	1	0	11	1
nozzi, c	2	1	0	0	3	1
ego, 2b	2	0	0	0	3	3
ng, ph	1	1	1	2	0	0
neycutt, p	0	0	0	0	0	0
ersley, p	0	0	0	0	0	0
Benes, p	2	0	0	0	1	1
sas, p	0	0	0	0	0	0
thews, p	0	0	0	0	0	0
Benes, p	0	0	0	0	0	0
ea, ph-2b	0	0	0	0	1	1
otals	29	4	5	4	27	15

anta	0	1	0	0	0	2	0	0	0—3
Louis	0	0	0	0	0	0	3	1	x—4

anta	IP	H	R	ER	BB	SO
agle	6 2/3	2	2	2	3	6
Michael (L)	2/3	3	2	2	1	0
hlers	2/3	0	0	0	0	2

Louis	IP	H	R	ER	BB	SO
Benes	*5	7	3	3	1	0
sas	2/3	0	0	0	2	0
thews	†0	1	0	0	0	0
Benes	1 1/3	0	0	0	0	1
neycutt	2/3	0	0	0	1	0
ersley (W)	1 1/3	1	0	0	0	2

*Pitched to two batters in sixth. †Pitched to one batter in sixth.
E—McGriff. DP—Atlanta 1, St. Louis 2. LOB—Atlanta 7, St. Louis 5.
—C. Jones, Dye. 3B—Young. HR—Lemke, Klesko, Jordan. SH—Neagle.
—Dye. T—3:17. A—56,764. U—West, plate; Crawford, first; Montague,
ond; Runge, third; Hirschbeck, left field; Davidson, right field.

GAME 5

HIGHLIGHTS

ATLANTA 14, ST. LOUIS 0

hy the Braves won: They jumped on the Cardinals
rly, scoring five runs in the first inning and two in
e second. It was a shocking offensive display by a
aves team that had scored just 12 runs in the first
ur games of the series and had hit an anemic .213 in
first seven postseason games of 1996.

hy the Cardinals lost: Righthander Todd Stottle-
yre did not remotely resemble the 14-game winner
had been in the regular season. Starting for the
st time all season on three days' rest, he was ham-
ered for seven runs and nine hits in one inning of
ork.

e turning points:
. With the Braves leading, 3-0, in the first and run-
rs on first and second and two outs, Jeff Blauser
lted a drive into the gap in right-center. Center
lder Willie McGee and right fielder Brian Jordan
nverged on the ball, but each thought the other
uld catch it; alas, neither did. The ball fell in for a
o-run triple to increase the Braves' lead to 5-0.
2. In the bottom of the first, the Cardinals loaded
e bases against Braves righthander John Smoltz
ith two outs. The next batter, John Mabry, hit a
ive deep and over the head of center fielder

Marquis Grissom, but Grissom caught the ball to
preserve the five-run lead.

Notable: The Braves' 22 hits set a new League
Championship Series record. ... Of the first 14 batters Atlanta sent to the plate, 10 got hits and seven
scored. ... Braves second baseman Mark Lemke, a
.255 hitter in the regular season, was 4-for-4 by the
fourth inning. ... The loss snapped a nine-game winning streak in home playoff games for the Cardinals.
... The game was the most lopsided in the history
of League Championship Series play, surpassing a
13-0 win by the Cubs over the Padres in 1984. ...
With the win, Smoltz increased his career postseason record to 8-1.

Quotable: Lemke: "Taking the crowd here out early
was big for us. They really had an effect those first
two games." ... Cardinals third baseman Gary
Gaetti: "It was a joke. They set the table—and they
cleaned the dishes, too." ... St. Louis catcher Tom
Pagnozzi: "You'd like to be in the game and have a
chance, but we weren't. Hopefully, with the day off,
they'll cool off." ... Braves manager Bobby Cox,
whose team staved off playoff elimination: "It's nothing new to us to win three games in a row." ...
Braves third baseman Chipper Jones: "We swing the
bat like this the rest of the way, and I'm pretty confident we'll be two-time World Series champions."

BOX SCORE

MONDAY, OCTOBER 14, AT ST. LOUIS

Atlanta	AB	R	H	RBI	PO	A
Grissom, cf	6	2	3	1	2	0
Lemke, 2b	5	2	4	1	1	3
Mordecai, 2b	1	1	1	0	0	0
C. Jones, 3b	3	1	2	3	1	0
Pendleton, ph-3b	2	0	0	0	0	0
McGriff, 1b	6	1	2	3	8	0
Klesko, lf	4	0	1	1	3	0
A. Jones, ph-lf	1	0	0	0	1	0
Lopez, c	5	4	4	1	8	1
Wade, p	0	0	0	0	0	0
Clontz, p	0	0	0	0	0	0
Dye, rf	6	1	1	0	0	0
Blauser, ss	2	1	1	2	1	1
Belliard, pr-ss	1	0	1	1	1	2
Smoltz, p	4	1	2	1	0	0
Polonia, ph	1	0	0	0	0	0
Bielecki, p	0	0	0	0	0	0
Perez, c	0	0	0	0	1	0
Totals	47	14	22	14	27	7

St. Louis	AB	R	H	RBI	PO	A
Smith, ss	4	0	0	0	4	1
McGee, cf	3	0	1	0	0	0
Mejia, cf	1	0	0	0	1	0
Gant, lf	3	0	1	0	1	0
Gallego, 3b	0	0	0	0	0	0
Jordan, rf	2	0	1	0	0	0
Fossas, p	0	0	0	0	0	0
Young, 3b-1b	2	0	1	0	1	1
Gaetti, 3b	2	0	2	0	0	1
Petkovsek, p	0	0	0	0	1	0
Lankford, ph	1	0	0	0	0	0
Honeycutt, p	0	0	0	0	0	0
Mabry, 1b-rf	4	0	1	0	7	0
Pagnozzi, c	1	0	0	0	4	0
Sheaffer, ph-c	3	0	0	0	3	0
Alicea, 2b	4	0	0	0	3	5
Stottlemyre, p	0	0	0	0	0	0
Jackson, p	1	0	0	0	0	0
Sweeney, rf-lf	2	0	0	0	2	0
Totals	33	0	7	0	27	8

Atlanta	5 2 0		3 1 0		0 1 2—14
St. Louis	0 0 0		0 0 0		0 0 0—0

Atlanta	IP	H	R	ER	BB	SO
Smoltz (W)	7	7	0	0	1	6
Bielecki	1	0	0	0	1	2
Wade	1/3	0	0	0	0	1
Clontz	2/3	0	0	0	0	0

St. Louis	IP	H	R	ER	BB	SO
Stottlemyre (L)	*1	9	7	7	0	1
Jackson	3	7	3	3	3	3
Fossas	2	1	1	1	1	1
Petkovsek	2	2	1	1	0	1
Honeycutt	1	3	2	2	1	1

*Pitched to three batters in second.
DP—Atlanta 1, St. Louis 2. LOB—Atlanta 11, St. Louis 8. 2B—Lemke, C. Jones, Lopez 2. 3B—Blauser. HR—McGriff, Lopez. SB—Grissom. T—2:57. A—56,782. U—Crawford, plate; Montague, first; Runge, second; Hirschbeck, third; Davidson, left field; West, right field.

GAME 6

HIGHLIGHTS

ATLANTA 3, ST. LOUIS 1

Why the Braves won: Greg Maddux was masterful. The Atlanta righthander walked none and struck out seven in 7²/₃ innings. All six hits he allowed were singles, and he had just one three-ball count. The only run the Cardinals scored came when Maddux's successor, Mark Wohlers, threw a wild pitch.

Why the Cardinals lost: For the second straight game, they did not hit, falling victim to four-time Cy Young Award winner Maddux just two days after John Smoltz, the 1996 Cy Young winner, had silenced their bats.

The turning points:

1. With the tying run on second base and two outs in the eighth, Wohlers induced Cardinals slugger Ron Gant to hit a fly to left to preserve a 2-1 Braves lead.

2. In the bottom of the eighth, Cardinals reliever Todd Stottlemyre hit Javier Lopez with a pitch. The next batter, Jermaine Dye, singled to center, with Lopez moving to third. St. Louis manager Tony La Russa elected to pitch to the eighth-place hitter, Rafael Belliard, instead of walking him to get to the pitcher, Wohlers. Belliard hit a soft liner that shortstop Royce Clayton was able to knock down but couldn't make a play on, enabling Lopez to score an insurance run.

Notable: St. Louis righthander Alan Benes was the first rookie to start a League Championship Series game since 1992, when Tim Wakefield started two games for the Pittsburgh Pirates. . . . Benes and his older brother, Andy, became only the second brothers to pitch in the same postseason for the same team. Dizzy and Dazzy Dean did it for the Cardinals in 1934. . . . Before this game, Maddux had been 5-4 with a 4.14 ERA in 11 career postseason starts, including an 8-3 loss in Game 2 of this series.

Quotable: Maddux, on his struggles in Game 2 against his success in Game 6: "I think the adrenaline was a little bit higher tonight. Maybe that came from the crowd. Maybe it came because if you lose, you pack." . . . La Russa, on Maddux: "Everything about his pitching was a little crisper, his stuff a little better, his location a little better. This was a tough

game to be a hitter." . . . Cardinals catcher To Pagnozzi, whose team was in the process of blowi a 3-1 series lead: "A three-game-to-one lead is no down to a zero-game lead." . . . Atlanta third ba man Chipper Jones, on Game 7 starter Tom Glavi "Glavine is a big-game pitcher. We'll see if he's up the challenge. I think I know the answer."

BOX SCORE

WEDNESDAY, OCTOBER 16, AT ATLANTA

St. Louis	AB	R	H	RBI	PO
Clayton, ss	4	1	1	0	0
McGee, rf	4	0	2	0	2
Gant, lf	4	0	0	0	2
Jordan, cf	4	0	1	0	2
Gaetti, 3b	4	0	1	0	1
Mabry, 1b	4	0	1	0	9
Pagnozzi, c	3	0	0	0	8
Gallego, 2b	2	0	0	0	0
Sweeney, ph	1	0	0	0	0
Stottlemyre, p	0	0	0	0	0
Al. Benes, p	1	0	0	0	0
Lankford, ph	1	0	0	0	0
Fossas, p	0	0	0	0	0
Petkovsek, p	0	0	0	0	0
Alicea, ph-2b	1	0	0	0	0
Totals	33	1	6	0	24

Atlanta	AB	R	H	RBI	PO
Grissom, cf	4	0	0	0	1
Lemke, 2b	4	0	2	1	1
C. Jones, 3b	4	0	0	0	0
McGriff, 1b	4	1	1	0	12
Klesko, lf	1	0	0	0	1
A. Jones, ph-lf	2	0	0	0	1
Lopez, c	3	1	2	0	8
Dye, rf	2	0	1	1	3
Blauser, ss	0	1	0	0	0
Belliard, ss	1	0	1	1	0
Maddux, p	2	0	0	0	0
Wohlers, p	1	0	0	0	0
Totals	28	3	7	3	27

St. Louis	0 0 0		0 0 0		0 1 0—
Atlanta	0 1 0		0 1 0		0 1 x—

St. Louis	IP	H	R	ER	BB	S
Al. Benes (L)	5	3	2	2	2	
Fossas	1/3	0	0	0	0	
Petkovsek	1 2/3	2	0	0	2	
Stottlemyre	1	2	1	1	0	

Atlanta	IP	H	R	ER	BB	S
Maddux (W)	7²/₃	6	1	1	0	
Wohlers (S)	1¹/₃	0	0	0	0	

E—Petkovsek. DP—St. Louis 1. LOB—St. Louis 5, Atlanta 9. 2B—Lop SH—G.Maddux. SF—Dye. SB—Lopez. HBP—By Al. Benes (Blauser), Stottlemyre (Lopez). WP—Petkovsek, Wohlers. T—2:41. A—52,067. L Montague, plate; Runge, first; Hirschbeck, second; Davidson, third; We left field; Crawford, right field.

GAME 7

HIGHLIGHTS

ATLANTA 15, ST. LOUIS 0

Why the Braves won: For the second time in thre games, they hammered St. Louis pitching, scori 15 runs on 17 hits. Lefthander Tom Glavine backe up the offensive assault by holding the Cardinals three singles and no runs in seven innings.

Why the Cardinals lost: Their starting pitche lefthander Donovan Osborne, clearly had big-gam jitters. His first two pitches resulted in hits, givi the Braves runners on second and third wi nobody out. Osborne allowed six earned runs ly two-thirds of an inning.

e turning points:

In a 15-0 game, there aren't many, but left fielder n Gant's inability to at least block a liner off avine's bat with two outs and the bases loaded in e first was pivotal. The Braves already were lead-g 3-0, and Glavine's hit cleared the bases, increas-g the lead to 6-0. The hit, which should have been ingle, became a triple when Gant missed on a div-g attempt to catch it. Giving up a three-run triple to e opposing pitcher was a crushing blow.

Six-run leads after one inning aren't insurmount-e, but 10-0 leads after four innings usually are. at's what the score was after the Braves scored r runs against Osborne's successor, Andy Benes.

table: Atlanta's 15 runs set a League ampionship Series record, and the margin of eat was the largest ever in postseason history, passing the Braves' 14-0 win in Game 5 three hts earlier and an 18-4 win by the New York kees over the New York Giants in Game 2 of the 6 World Series. . . . The Cardinals became the t team to lose three postseason series after lead-three games to one. They also did so in the 1968 1985 World Series. . . . Atlanta outscored St. is, 32-1, and outhit the Cardinals, 46-17, in the l three games. All 17 St. Louis hits were singles, the only run scored on a wild pitch. . . . Every yer in the Braves' starting lineup had a hit except rtstop Jeff Blauser, who left in the second with a injury. His replacement, Rafael Belliard, had two s. . . . Braves rookie Andruw Jones hit a two-run ner in the sixth to become the youngest player) to homer in a postseason game. Mickey Mantle s 20 when he homered in Game 6 of the 1952 rld Series for the Yankees. . . . Lopez, who drove six runs, scored eight times and hit .542 in the ies, was named MVP. . . . This was the first Game r Cardinals manager Tony La Russa, the former ite Sox and A's skipper who was managing in the h postseason series in six different years.

otable: Osborne, on what he was thinking after Braves ripped his first two pitches for hits: "Oh, e we go again." . . . La Russa, on why he didn't nove Osborne sooner: "I second-guess myself as ch as anybody. But there's no way I'd get borne out with the bottom of the lineup up." . . . vine, a .289 hitter in the regular season, on his ting: "No one wants to feel like he's an automatic ." . . . St. Louis shortstop Royce Clayton: "It was-over after the first inning. The Braves obviously n't think so, or they would have sat back on their runs. But they kept pouring it on." . . . Cardinals fielder Willie McGee, who also played on the St.

Louis team that blew a three-games-to-one lead to Kansas City in the 1985 World Series: "That series was different. That one we should have won. This one, we just got beat. You can live with that. It's hard to swallow, but you just got beat." . . . Lopez, on the Braves' comeback: "Once we got three games behind, everybody said to themselves we can win because we've done it before. We never die. We fight back."

BOX SCORE

THURSDAY, OCTOBER 17, AT ATLANTA

St. Louis	AB	R	H	RBI	PO	A
Clayton, ss	4	0	1	0	0	3
McGee, rf	3	0	1	0	1	0
Sweeney, lf	0	0	0	0	0	0
Gant, lf	3	0	0	0	3	0
Sheaffer, c	0	0	0	0	0	0
Jordan, cf	3	0	0	0	1	0
Mejia, cf	0	0	0	0	1	0
Gaetti, 3b	3	0	0	0	2	6
Young, 1b	3	0	0	0	10	0
Pagnozzi, c	2	0	1	0	4	0
Mabry, rf	1	0	0	0	0	0
Gallego, 2b	3	0	1	0	2	2
Osborne, p	0	0	0	0	0	0
An. Benes, p	1	0	0	0	0	2
Smith, ph	1	0	0	0	0	0
Petkovsek, p	0	0	0	0	0	0
Honeycutt, p	0	0	0	0	0	0
Fossas, p	0	0	0	0	0	0
Alicea, ph	1	0	0	0	0	0
Totals	**28**	**0**	**4**	**0**	**24**	**13**

Atlanta	AB	R	H	RBI	PO	A
Grissom, cf	6	1	2	0	4	0
Lemke, 2b	4	1	2	0	2	1
Mordecai, ph-2b	1	0	0	0	1	1
C. Jones, 3b	4	2	2	0	0	2
Perez, 1b	0	0	0	0	2	0
McGriff, 1b	5	4	3	4	5	0
Bielecki, p	0	0	0	0	0	0
Avery, p	0	0	0	0	0	0
Lopez, c	4	3	2	3	6	1
Dye, rf	5	1	1	1	4	0
A. Jones, lf	4	2	2	3	2	0
Blauser, ss	0	1	0	0	0	0
Belliard, ss	4	0	2	0	1	1
Glavine, p	4	0	1	3	0	1
Pendleton, 3b	1	0	0	0	0	1
Totals	**42**	**15**	**17**	**14**	**27**	**8**

St. Louis	0	0	0	0	0	0	0	0	0—	0
Atlanta	6	0	0	4	0	3	2	0	x—	15

St. Louis	IP	H	R	ER	BB	SO
Osborne (L)	2/3	5	6	6	1	0
An. Benes	4 1/3	5	4	4	2	2
Petkovsek	2/3	5	3	3	0	1
Honeycutt	1 1/3	2	2	2	1	1
Fossas	1	0	0	0	0	0

Atlanta	IP	H	R	ER	BB	SO
Glavine (W)	7	3	0	0	0	4
Bielecki	1	0	0	0	0	2
Avery	1	1	0	0	0	0

E—McGee, Clayton. DP—Atlanta 2. LOB—St. Louis 1, Atlanta 8. 2B—Lemke, Lopez. 3B—McGriff, Glavine. HR—McGriff, Lopez, A. Jones. CS—Clayton. HBP—St. Louis 0. Atlanta 1, Blauser by Osborne. T—2:25. A—52,067. U—Runge, plate; Hirschbeck, first; Davidson, second; West, third; Crawford, left field; Montague, right field.

STATISTICS

ATLANTA BRAVES' BATTING AND FIELDING AVERAGES

				BATTING										FIELDING			
er, position	G	AB	R	H	TB	2B	3B	HR	RBI	BB	IBB	SO	Avg.	PO	A	E	Avg.
ard, 2b-ss-pr	4	6	0	4	4	0	0	0	2	0	0	0	.667	2	5	0	1.000
ez, c	7	24	8	13	24	5	0	2	6	3	1	1	.542	48	3	0	1.000
gle, p	2	2	0	1	1	0	0	0	0	0	0	0	.500	0	1	0	1.000

Player, position	G	AB	R	H	TB	2B	3B	HR	RBI	BB	IBB	SO	Avg.	PO	A	E	A
Lemke, 2b	7	27	4	12	17	2	0	1	5	4	0	2	.444	10	18	0	1.0
C. Jones, 3b	7	25	6	11	13	2	0	0	4	3	0	1	.440	5	7	1	.9
Grissom, cf	7	35	7	10	14	1	0	1	3	0	0	8	.286	17	0	1	.9
Smoltz, p	2	7	1	2	2	0	0	0	1	0	0	3	.286	0	1	0	1.0
McGriff, 1b	7	28	6	7	15	0	1	2	7	3	0	5	.250	54	2	1	.9
Klesko, lf	6	16	1	4	7	0	0	1	3	2	0	6	.250	13	0	0	1.0
Mordecai, 3b-ph-2b	4	4	1	1	1	0	0	0	0	0	0	1	.250	1	1	0	1.0
A. Jones, lf-pr-ph	5	9	3	2	5	0	0	1	3	3	0	2	.222	5	0	0	1.0
Dye, rf	7	28	2	6	7	1	0	0	4	1	0	7	.214	14	0	0	1.0
Blauser, ss	7	17	5	3	5	0	1	0	2	4	2	6	.176	5	9	1	.9
Glavine, p	2	6	0	1	3	0	1	0	3	0	0	3	.167	0	3	0	1.0
Avery, p	2	0	0	0	0	0	0	0	0	0	0	0	.000	0	0	0	.C
Bielecki, p	3	0	0	0	0	0	0	0	0	0	0	0	.000	0	0	0	.C
Clontz, p	1	0	0	0	0	0	0	0	0	0	0	0	.000	0	0	0	.C
McMichael, p	3	0	0	0	0	0	0	0	0	0	0	0	.000	1	0	0	1.0
Wade, p	1	0	0	0	0	0	0	0	0	0	0	0	.000	0	0	0	.0
Perez, c-1b	4	1	0	0	0	0	0	0	0	0	1	0	.000	7	0	0	1.0
Wohlers, p	3	1	0	0	0	0	0	0	0	0	0	1	.000	0	0	0	.C
Polonia, ph	3	3	0	0	0	0	0	0	0	0	0	2	.000	0	0	0	.0
Maddux, p	2	4	0	0	0	0	0	0	0	0	0	2	.000	1	4	0	1.0
Pendleton, ph-3b	6	6	0	0	0	0	0	0	0	1	1	3	.000	0	1	0	1.0
Totals	7	249	44	77	118	11	3	8	43	25	4	51	.309	183	55	4	.9

ST. LOUIS CARDINALS' BATTING AND FIELDING AVERAGES

Player, position	G	AB	R	H	TB	2B	3B	HR	RBI	BB	IBB	SO	Avg.	PO	A	E	A
Clayton, ss	5	20	4	7	7	0	0	0	1	1	0	4	.350	5	16	2	.9
McGee, ph-cf-rf	6	15	0	5	5	0	0	0	0	0	0	3	.333	5	0	1	.8
Gaetti, 3b	7	24	1	7	10	0	0	1	4	1	0	5	.292	4	13	0	1.0
Young, ph-1b	4	7	1	2	4	0	1	0	2	0	0	2	.286	11	1	0	1.0
Mabry, 1b-rf	7	23	1	6	6	0	0	0	0	0	0	6	.261	45	1	0	1.0
An. Benes, p	3	4	0	1	2	1	0	0	0	1	0	2	.250	1	4	0	1.0
Gant, lf	7	25	3	6	13	1	0	2	4	2	0	6	.240	12	0	0	1.0
Jordan, rf-cf	7	25	3	6	12	1	1	1	2	1	1	3	.240	13	0	0	1.0
Pagnozzi, c	7	19	1	3	4	1	0	0	1	1	0	4	.158	49	1	0	1.0
Gallego, 3b-2b	7	14	1	2	2	0	0	0	0	1	0	3	.143	8	12	1	.9
Eckersley, p	3	0	0	0	0	0	0	0	0	0	0	0	.000	0	1	0	1.0
Fossas, p	5	0	0	0	0	0	0	0	0	0	0	0	.000	0	0	0	.0
Honeycutt, p	5	0	0	0	0	0	0	0	0	0	0	0	.000	0	0	0	.0
Mathews, p	2	0	0	0	0	0	0	0	0	0	0	0	.000	0	0	0	.0
Petkovsek, p	6	0	0	0	0	0	0	0	0	0	0	0	.000	1	2	1	.7
Al. Benes, p	2	1	0	0	0	0	0	0	0	0	0	1	.000	0	1	0	1.0
Jackson, p	1	1	0	0	0	0	0	0	0	0	0	1	.000	0	0	0	.C
Mejia, pr-cf	3	1	1	0	0	0	0	0	0	0	0	1	.000	2	0	0	1.0
Stottlemyre, p	3	2	0	0	0	0	0	0	0	0	0	0	.000	0	0	0	.0
Osborne, p	2	3	0	0	0	0	0	0	0	0	0	3	.000	0	1	0	1.0
Sheaffer, c-ph	2	3	0	0	0	0	0	0	0	0	0	1	.000	3	0	0	1.0
Sweeney, ph-lf-rf	5	4	1	0	0	0	0	0	0	0	0	2	.000	2	0	0	1.0
Alicea, 2b-ph	5	8	0	0	0	0	0	0	0	2	0	1	.000	5	7	1	.9
Smith, ss-ph	3	9	0	0	0	0	0	0	0	0	0	1	.000	7	2	0	1.0
Lankford, cf-ph	5	13	1	0	0	0	0	0	1	1	0	4	.000	7	0	0	1.0
Totals	7	221	18	45	65	4	2	4	15	11	1	53	.204	180	62	6	.9

ATLANTA BRAVES' PITCHING RECORDS

Pitcher	G	GS	CG	IP	H	R	ER	HR	BB	IBB	SO	HB	WP	W	L	Pct.	E
Bielecki	3	0	0	3	0	0	0	0	1	0	5	0	0	0	0	.000	0.
Wohlers	3	0	0	3	0	0	0	0	0	0	4	0	1	0	0	.000	0.
Avery	2	0	0	2	2	0	0	1	0	1	0	0	0	0	.000	0.
Clontz	1	0	0	2/3	0	0	0	0	0	0	0	0	0	0	0	.000	0.
Wade	1	0	0	1/3	0	0	0	0	0	1	0	0	0	0	0	.000	0.
Smoltz	2	2	0	15	12	2	2	0	3	0	12	0	2	2	0	1.000	1.
Glavine	2	2	0	13	10	3	3	2	0	0	9	1	0	1	1	.500	2.
Neagle	2	1	0	7 2/3	2	2	2	0	3	0	8	0	0	0	0	.000	2.
Maddux	2	2	0	14 1/3	15	9	4	1	2	1	10	0	1	1	1	.500	2.
McMichael	3	0	0	2	4	2	2	1	0	3	0	0	0	0	1	.000	9.
Totals	7	7	0	61	45	18	13	4	11	1	53	1	4	4	3	.571	1.

Shutouts—Smoltz, Bielecki, Wade and Clontz (combined); Glavine, Bielecki and Avery (combined). Saves—Wohlers 2.

ST. LOUIS CARDINALS' PITCHING RECORDS

er	G	GS	CG	IP	H	R	ER	HR	BB	IBB	SO	HB	WP	W	L	Pct.	ERA
rsley	3	0	0	3$\frac{1}{3}$	2	0	0	0	0	0	4	0	0	1	0	1.000	0.00
1ews	2	0	0	$\frac{2}{3}$	2	0	0	0	1	1	2	0	0	0	0	.000	0.00
as	5	0	0	4$\frac{1}{3}$	1	1	1	1	3	1	1	0	0	0	0	.000	2.08
enes	2	1	0	6$\frac{1}{3}$	3	2	2	0	2	1	5	1	0	0	1	.000	2.84
3enes	3	2	0	15$\frac{1}{3}$	19	9	9	3	3	0	9	0	0	0	0	.000	5.28
ovsek	6	0	0	7$\frac{1}{3}$	11	6	6	1	3	1	7	0	1	0	1	.000	7.36
eycutt	5	0	0	4	5	4	4	2	3	0	3	0	0	0	0	.000	9.00
son	1	0	0	3	7	3	3	0	3	0	3	0	0	0	0	.000	9.00
rne	2	2	0	7$\frac{2}{3}$	12	8	8	0	4	0	6	1	1	1	1	.500	9.39
lemyre	3	2	0	8	15	11	11	1	3	0	11	1	0	1	1	.500	12.38
tals	7	7	0	60	77	44	44	8	25	4	51	3	2	3	4	.429	6.60

shutouts. Save—Eckersley.

SCORE BY INNINGS

ta	12	4	2		7	4	6		2	5	2—44
ouis	3	1	2		0	0	1		9	2	0—18

MISCELLANEOUS STATISTICS

ifice hits—Maddux, Neagle, Sweeney.

ifice flies—Dye 2, C. Jones, Lankford.

en bases—Grissom 2, Clayton, C. Jones, Lopez.

ht stealing—Clayton, Dye.

ole plays—C. Jones, Lemke and McGriff 2; Gallego, Clayton and Mabry 2; Blauser and McGriff; Glavine, Blauser and McGriff; emke and McGriff; Mabry (unassisted); Pendleton, Mordecai and Perez; Smith, Alicea and Mabry.

on bases—Atlanta 7, 7, 9, 7, 11, 9, 8—58; St. Louis 5, 6, 4, 5, 8, 5, 1—34.

y pitcher—By Glavine (Mabry), by Stottlemyre (Lopez), by Osborne (Blauser), by Al. Benes (Blauser).

ed balls—None.

s—None.

of games—First game, 2:35; second game, 2:53; third game, 2:46; fourth game, 3:17; fifth game, 2:57; sixth game, 2:41; venth game, 2:25.

idance—First game, 48,686; second game, 52,067; third game, 56,769; fourth game, 56,764; fifth game, 56,782; sixth game, :,067; seventh game, 52,067.

ires—Crawford, Davidson, Hirschbeck, Montague, Runge and West.

al scorers—Mark Frederickson, Jack Herman, Rob Rains.

WORLD SERIES

GAME 1

HIGHLIGHTS

ATLANTA 12, NEW YORK 1

Why the Braves won: They were able to maintain their momentum from the N.L. Championship Series—Atlanta won that playoff when it outscored the Cardinals, 32-1, in the final three games—by bolting to an 8-0 lead in the third inning and getting typical Braves-style pitching throughout. John Smoltz, the N.L. Cy Young Award winner, and four relievers limited the Yankees to four hits.

Why the Yankees lost: Although Andy Pettitte, a 21-game winner and second-place finisher in the A.L. Cy Young balloting, pitched a 1-2-3 first inning, he was then Bronx-bombed for six hits and seven runs in the next $1\frac{1}{3}$ innings.

The turning points:

1. Amid the pressure of playing in his first World Series at storied Yankee Stadium, Andruw Jones drilled a two-run homer off Pettitte in his first Series at-bat. The second-inning smash erased any jitters the Braves may have felt playing in the historic House That Ruth Built—and it was delivered by a 19-year-old player who had begun the season with Class A Durham.

2. After Atlanta extended its lead to 5-0 in third on Chipper Jones' two-run single and Fred McGriff's RBI single, the irrepressible Andruw Jones rocketed a three-run homer into the seats in left field later in the inning. The blow off reliever Brian Boehringer removed any doubt about the outcome. Called upon to keep the Yankees at least within hailing distance, Boehringer surrendered five runs (three earned) and five hits in a three-inning stint.

Notable: Andruw Jones' slugging earned him two prominent places in the record book. He became the youngest player to hit a Series homer, supplanting Mickey Mantle, who at 20 connected twice in the 1952 World Series. And with his second smash, Jones became only the second player in history to hit home runs in his first two Series at-bats (Oakland's Gene Tenace was the other, in 1972). . . . Smoltz held the Yankees hitless until Wade Boggs stroked a double with two outs in the fifth. . . . Game 1 was to have been played a night earlier but drenching rains pounded the New York area on Saturday. . . . The game marked the Yankees' 34th appearance in Series play but their first since 1981. . . . The 11-run pummeling was the worst Series defeat for the Yanks, who suffered eight-run losses to the Giants in 1921, the Cardinals in 1926 and the Braves in 1958.

Quotable: Although Andruw Jones didn't appear outwardly overwhelmed by the Yankee Stadium setting or the magnitude of the goings-on, he did gaze around baseball's most noted edifice and, simply but eloquently, said: "Some place." . . . Teammate Chipper Jones, on Andruw: "He's gotten a little the hot-dog taken out of him (after getting a .2 comeuppance in the majors in the regular seas after dominating in three minor league stops ear in '96). That's not only made him a better player more of an intriguing player to watch." . . . Brav general manager John Schuerholz, on the teenag from the island of Curacao (off the coast Venezuela) and his opening-night exploits in N York: "It's Broadway, and that's where stars a born." . . . A little concerned over Yankee fans' gro ing reputation as being a bit too raucous, Brav manager Bobby Cox, a Yankees infielder in the la 1960s, wound up praising the game atmosphe "This crowd was great. It's not really that bad he It's what baseball is all about."

BOX SCORE

SUNDAY, OCTOBER 20, AT NEW YORK

Atlanta	AB	R	H	RBI	PO
Grissom, cf	5	2	2	1	4
Lemke, 2b	4	0	2	1	3
C. Jones, 3b	4	1	1	3	2
McGriff, 1b	5	2	2	2	6
Lopez, c	4	2	1	0	6
Perez, c	0	0	0	0	0
Dye, rf	5	0	1	0	4
A. Jones, lf	4	3	3	5	1
Klesko, lf	4	1	0	0	0
Blauser, ss	3	1	1	0	1
*Polonia, ph	1	0	0	0	0
Belliard, ss	0	0	0	0	0
Smoltz, p	0	0	0	0	0
McMichael, p	0	0	0	0	0
Neagle, p	0	0	0	0	0
Wade, p	0	0	0	0	0
Clontz, p	0	0	0	0	0
Totals	39	12	13	12	27

New York	AB	R	H	RBI	PO
Jeter, ss	3	1	0	0	1
Boggs, 3b	4	0	2	1	0
Williams, cf	3	0	0	0	5
Martinez, 1b	3	0	1	0	3
Fielder, dh	4	0	0	0	0
Strawberry, lf	3	0	0	0	7
Raines, lf	1	0	0	0	1
O'Neill, rf	2	0	0	0	1
Aldrete, rf	0	0	0	0	0
†Hayes, ph	1	0	0	0	0
Duncan, 2b	3	0	0	0	1
Fox, 2b	0	0	0	0	1
‡Sojo, ph	1	0	0	0	0
Leyritz, c	3	0	1	0	7
Pettitte, p	0	0	0	0	0
Boehringer, p	0	0	0	0	0
Weathers, p	0	0	0	0	0
Nelson, p	0	0	0	0	0
Wetteland, p	0	0	0	0	0
Totals	31	1	4	1	27

Atlanta	0	2	6	0	1	3	0	0	0—
New York	0	0	0	0	1	0	0	0	0—

Atlanta	IP	H	R	ER	BB
Smoltz (W)	6	2	1	1	5
McMichael	1	2	0	0	0
Neagle	1	0	0	0	0
Wade	$2/3$	0	0	0	0
Clontz	$1/3$	0	0	0	0

New York	IP	H	R	ER	BB
Pettitte (L)	$2\,1/3$	6	7	7	1
Boehringer	3	5	5	3	0

Bases on balls—Off Smoltz 5 (O'Neill, Leyritz, Martinez, Williams, Jeter), Pettitte 1 (Lopez). Strikeouts—By Smoltz 4 (Fielder, Leyritz, Martinez, Williams), by Michael 1 (Jeter), by Wetteland 2 (McGriff, Dye), by Boehringer 2 (esko, Lopez), by Nelson 1 (Polonia), by Pettitte 1 (McGriff). *Struck out for Blauser in eighth. †Flied out for Aldrete in ninth. rounded out for Fox in ninth. E—Duncan. LOB—Atlanta 3, New York 8. —Boggs. HR—McGriff, A. Jones 2. SH—Lemke. SF—C. Jones. SB—C. nes. T—3:02. A—56,365. U—Evans (A.L.), plate; Tata (N.L.), first; Welke L.), second; Rippley (N.L.), third; Young (A.L.), left field; Davis (N.L.), nt field.

PLAY BY PLAY

FIRST INNING

Atlanta—Grissom flied to left. Lemke fouled to the catcher. C. nes lined to right.

New York—Jeter popped to second. Boggs grounded to short. lliams and Martinez walked. Fielder flied to right.

SECOND INNING

Atlanta—McGriff struck out. Lopez singled to center. Dye flied left. A. Jones homered to left, scoring Lopez. Klesko grounded the pitcher.

New York—Strawberry flied to left. O'Neill walked. Duncan uled to second. Leyritz walked. Jeter forced Leyritz at second, cond baseman to shortstop.

THIRD INNING

Atlanta—Blauser singled to left. Grissom singled to center, auser went to second. Lemke sacrificed Blauser to third and issom to second, first baseman unassisted. C. Jones singled to t, scoring Blauser and Grissom. C. Jones went to second on e throw home. C. Jones stole third. McGriff singled to left, scor- g C. Jones. Lopez walked. Boehringer now pitching. Dye flied to t. A. Jones homered to left, scoring McGriff and Lopez. Klesko uck out.

New York—Boggs grounded to short. Williams and Martinez uck out.

FOURTH INNING

Atlanta—Blauser flied to center. Grissom flied to left. Lemke ounded to first.

New York—Fielder struck out. Strawberry grounded to first. Neill lined to center.

FIFTH INNING

Atlanta—C. Jones flied to left. McGriff homered to right. Lopez uck out. Dye flied to center.

New York—Duncan flied to right. Leyritz struck out. Jeter alked. Boggs doubled to center, scoring Jeter. Williams flied to nter.

SIXTH INNING

Atlanta—A. Jones singled to third. Klesko reached base on an or by the second baseman, A. Jones went to second. Blauser ed to left, A. Jones went to third. Grissom singled to left, scor- A. Jones as Klesko went to second. Lemke singled to right, oring Klesko as Grissom went to third. Weathers now pitching. Jones hit a sacrifice fly to left, scoring Grissom. McGriff flied center.

New York—Martinez singled to right. Fielder flied to center. awberry forced Martinez at third, second baseman to third seman. O'Neill popped to third.

SEVENTH INNING

Atlanta—Raines now in left field. Lopez flied to center. Dye sin- d to center. A. Jones forced Dye at second, shortstop to second seman. Klesko forced A. Jones at second, shortstop unassisted.

New York—McMichael now pitching. Duncan grounded to ort. Leyritz singled to center. Jeter struck out. Boggs singled to nter, Leyritz went to second. Williams lined to second.

EIGHTH INNING

Atlanta—Nelson now pitching, Fox at second. Polonia, pinch-

hitting for Blauser, struck out. Grissom flied to center. Lemke sin-gled to center. C. Jones lined to second.

New York—Neagle now pitching, Belliard at shortstop. Martinez grounded to second. Fielder flied to center. Raines fouled to the catcher.

NINTH INNING

Atlanta—Wetteland now pitching, Aldrete in right field. McGriff struck out. Lopez flied to left. Dye struck out.

New York—Wade now pitching, Perez catching. Hayes, pinch-hitting for Aldrete, flied to right. Sojo, pinch-hitting for Fox, grounded to short. Clontz now pitching. Leyritz flied to right.

GAME 2

HIGHLIGHTS

ATLANTA 4, NEW YORK 0

Why the Braves won: Coming off a disappointing (for him) season after winning four consecutive Cy Young Awards, Greg Maddux pitched like, well, Cy Young. He allowed six hits over eight innings and didn't issue a walk. Keeping the ball low in his trade-mark style and forcing batters to nibble at his pitch-es, Maddux had Yankees hitters beating the ball into the ground; in fact, five bouncers were hit back to the mound.

Why the Yankees lost: The axiom that good (make that great) pitching stops good hitting proved true once again. The Yankees, who had a .288 team bat-ting average in 1996, were hitting .175 after the first two games of the Series. They managed only six sin-gles and a double in Game 2 after getting just three singles and a double in Game 1.

The turning points:

1. A 1-0 deficit—in the first inning, no less—is hard-ly insurmountable, but the fact the Yankees trailed almost immediately and were going against Maddux didn't bode well for the A.L. champions. The Braves scored that run when Mark Lemke doubled and Fred McGriff singled him home. McGriff wound up with three RBIs in a 2-for-3 night that included a sac-rifice fly.

2. Behind 4-0, the Yankees got singles from Derek Jeter and Tim Raines to start the sixth inning and, with Wade Boggs and Bernie Williams coming up, were in a position to get back into the game. But Maddux induced Boggs to hit into a double play and Williams to ground out.

Notable: The victory was Atlanta's fifth in a row in '96 postseason play. In those five games, the Braves had outscored their opponents—the Cardinals and Yankees—by 48-2. . . . A review of Series history indicated the Yankees' chances of rebounding were slim. From the first-ever Series in 1903 through the 1984 fall classic, no team had lost the first two games at home and gone on to win the Series. The 1985 Royals and 1986 Mets then became the only teams to accomplish the feat.

Quotable: After two games, a highly impressed Joe Torre had just about seen enough of the Braves' pitching staff in general and Greg Maddux in partic-ular. "He's something. He really is. He has his way with you. He was a master tonight. You don't see pitching like this every day. Unfortunately, we are seeing it every day." . . . Torre, on Maddux, first-game starter John Smoltz and lefthander Tom Glavine: "You have pitchers like this in our league, but they're not all on the same team." . . . Although talk of a Braves sweep was rampant, Maddux was having none of it: "We understand it takes four (victories) to win. We know it's not over. We know it's not even close to being over." . . . Boggs was effusive in his praise of Maddux, who compiled a 15-11 record in '96 after going 75-29 in the previous four seasons: "It's incredible he has so much movement on his pitches. It's like playing wiffleball in your backyard." . . . McGriff, on his run production in Game 2: "Coming into the game, I wasn't thinking about RBIs. I was thinking about getting us another win and another ring."

BOX SCORE

MONDAY, OCTOBER 21, AT NEW YORK

Atlanta	AB	R	H	RBI	PO	A
Grissom, cf	5	1	2	1	0	0
Lemke, 2b	4	2	2	0	1	5
C. Jones, 3b	3	0	1	0	0	0
McGriff, 1b	3	0	2	3	15	2
Lopez, c	4	0	1	0	5	1
Dye, rf	4	0	1	0	0	0
A. Jones, lf	3	0	0	0	1	0
Pendleton, dh	4	1	1	0	0	0
Blauser, ss	2	0	0	0	3	4
*Polonia, ph	1	0	0	0	0	0
Belliard, ss	0	0	0	0	0	0
Maddux, p	0	0	0	0	2	6
Wohlers, p	0	0	0	0	0	0
Totals	33	4	10	4	27	18

New York	AB	R	H	RBI	PO	A
Raines, lf	4	0	2	0	1	0
Boggs, 3b	4	0	1	0	0	0
Williams, cf	4	0	0	0	1	0
Martinez, 1b	4	0	0	0	13	0
Fielder, dh	4	0	2	0	0	0
†Fox, pr	0	0	0	0	0	0
O'Neill, rf	4	0	1	0	4	0
Duncan, 2b	3	0	0	0	2	7
Girardi, c	3	0	0	0	5	0
Jeter, ss	2	0	1	0	1	5
Key, p	0	0	0	0	0	2
Lloyd, p	0	0	0	0	0	0
Nelson, p	0	0	0	0	0	0
M. Rivera, p	0	0	0	0	0	0
Totals	32	0	7	0	27	14

Atlanta	1	0	1		0	1	1	0	0	0—4
New York	0	0	0		0	0	0	0	0	0—0

Atlanta	IP	H	R	ER	BB	SO
Maddux (W)	8	6	0	0	0	2
Wohlers	1	1	0	0	0	3

New York	IP	H	R	ER	BB	SO
Key (L)	6	10	4	4	2	0
Lloyd	2/3	0	0	0	0	2
Nelson	1 1/3	0	0	0	0	2
M. Rivera	1	0	0	0	0	1

Bases on balls—Off Key 2 (Blauser, C. Jones).
Strikeouts—By Wohlers 3 (O'Neill, Martinez, Williams), by Maddux 2 (Martinez, Duncan), by Nelson 2 (Pendleton, A. Jones), by Lloyd 2 (McGriff, C. Jones), by M. Rivera 1 (Grissom).
*Grounded out for Blauser in ninth. †Ran for Fielder in ninth. E—Raines. DP—Atlanta 1, New York 1. LOB—Atlanta 7, New York 6. 2B—Grissom, Lemke, C. Jones, Pendleton, O'Neill. SH—Lemke. SF—McGriff. CS—Raines. HBP—By Key (A. Jones), by Maddux (Jeter). T—2:44. A—56,340. U—Tata (N.L.), plate; Welke (A.L.), first; Rippley (N.L.), second; Young (A.L.), third; Davis (N.L.), left field; Evans (A.L.), right field.

PLAY BY PLAY

FIRST INNING
Atlanta—Grissom flied to left. Lemke doubled to left. C. Jones grounded to first. McGriff, singled to left-center, scoring Lemke. Lopez singled to right, McGriff went to second. Dye flied to right.
New York—Raines grounded to the first baseman, who tossed to the pitcher covering first. Boggs singled to center. Williams flied to left. Martinez grounded to first.

SECOND INNING
Atlanta—A. Jones hit by a pitch. Pendleton popped to first. Blauser grounded into a double play, second baseman to shortstop to first baseman.
New York—Fielder grounded to the pitcher. O'Neill doubled to right. Duncan grounded to the first baseman, who tossed to the pitcher covering first as O'Neill went to third. Girardi grounded to the pitcher.

THIRD INNING
Atlanta—Grissom doubled to right. Lemke sacrificed Grissom to third, pitcher to second baseman. C. Jones walked. McGriff singled to center, scoring Grissom as C. Jones went to second. Lopez grounded into a double play, pitcher to second baseman to first baseman.
New York—Jeter hit by a pitch. Raines forced Jeter at second, pitcher to shortstop. Raines was caught stealing, catcher to second baseman. Boggs grounded to the pitcher.

FOURTH INNING
Atlanta—Dye singled to left and went to second on the left fielder's error fielding the grounder. A. Jones grounded to short. Pendleton grounded to second, Dye went to third. Blauser walked. Grissom grounded to second.
New York—Williams lined to first. Martinez grounded to the pitcher. Fielder grounded to short.

FIFTH INNING
Atlanta—Lemke singled to center. C. Jones doubled to right, Lemke went to third. McGriff hit a sacrifice to right, scoring Lemke as C. Jones went to third. Lopez grounded to short. Dye flied to right.
New York—O'Neill grounded to first. Duncan grounded to second. Girardi grounded to short.

SIXTH INNING
Atlanta—A. Jones flied to center. Pendleton doubled to short. Blauser grounded to short, Pendleton went to third. Grissom singled to center, scoring Pendleton. Lemke flied to right.
New York—Jeter singled to second. Raines singled to center, Jeter went to second. Boggs grounded into a double play, second baseman to shortstop to first baseman, as Jeter went to third. Williams grounded to second.

SEVENTH INNING
Atlanta—Lloyd now pitching. C. Jones and McGriff struck out. Nelson now pitching. Lopez grounded to second.
New York—Martinez struck out. Fielder singled to first. O'Neill forced Fielder at second, pitcher to shortstop. Duncan struck out.

EIGHTH INNING
Atlanta—Dye grounded to second. A. Jones and Pendleton struck out.
New York—Girardi grounded to second. Jeter grounded to short. Raines singled to center. Boggs grounded to second.

NINTH INNING
Atlanta—M. Rivera now pitching. Polonia, pinch-hitting for Blauser, grounded to second. Grissom struck out. Lemke grounded to short.
New York—Wohlers now pitching, Belliard at shortstop. Williams and Martinez struck out. Fielder singled to center. Fox, pinch-running for Fielder, went to second on defensive indifference. O'Neill struck out.

1996 REVIEW World Series

HIGHLIGHTS

NEW YORK 5, ATLANTA 2

Why the Yankees won: David Cone, sidelined for [fou]r months during the season because of surgery [to r]emove an aneurysm in his right shoulder, turned [in a] gutty performance by pitching four-hit, one-run [ball] over six innings. The performance was crucial [for] the Yanks, who needed a king-sized lift after los-[ing] Games 1 and 2 in their home park and facing the [blea]k prospect of trying to rebound at Atlanta-Fulton [Cou]nty Stadium (where the Braves compiled the [maj]ors' best home record in 1996).

Why the Braves lost: Although starter Tom Glavine [was] his usual stingy self (one earned run and four [hits] in seven innings) and kept Atlanta in the game, [reli]ever Greg McMichael was torched upon taking [ove]r in the eighth. With the Yankees leading, 2-1, [Mc]Michael yielded a leadoff single to Derek Jeter, a [hom]e run to Bernie Williams and a double to Cecil [Fie]lder before exiting. By the time Brad Clontz got [thin]gs under control, New York had scored another [run] and seized a comfortable 5-1 lead. Meanwhile, [th]e Yankees relievers held Atlanta at bay.

The turning points:
Yankees manager Joe Torre wasn't burned by [stic]king with righthander Cone in a bases-loaded, [two]-out jam in the sixth inning. With New York [gua]rding a 2-0 lead and lefthanded sluggers Fred [Mc]Griff and Ryan Klesko coming up, Torre could [hav]e played the percentages and summoned left-[han]der Graeme Lloyd or called upon bullpen sensa-[tion] Mariano Rivera; instead, he let Cone continue [and] the veteran got McGriff on a popup before walk-[ing] Klesko to force in a run. Cone then ended the [inn]ing by getting Javier Lopez to foul out.

Mark Lemke failed to get a bunt down for Atlanta [earl]ier in the sixth. With two on, no one out and the [Bra]ves down by two runs, a sacrifice would have put [two] runners in scoring position, with Chipper Jones [and] McGriff the next two batters. Lemke popped out [on] his bunt attempt, though, and the chemistry of [the] inning seemed to change.

Notable: Catcher Joe Girardi quelled two Braves [thr]eats, throwing out potential basestealers in the [first] (Andruw Jones) and seventh inning (Luis [Pol]onia). . . . A first-inning sacrifice is rare, but that [did]n't deter Torre. After Tim Raines led off the game [with] a walk, Jeter bunted him to second and Williams [foll]owed with a run-scoring single. Torre explained [tha]t the Yankees had never had a lead in this Series [and] that it was crucial to get one.

Quotable: So what did Cone really say when Torre [tr]udged to the mound with the bases full in the [sixt]h? Torre's version: "His pitch count was low, but [I w]anted him to level with me. I trust him. I needed [for] him to be truthful with me. I said, 'It's very [imp]ortant here. I have to know if you're OK.' He [sai]d, 'I'm fine. I'm just losing my splitter.' I looked into his eyes and believed him." . . . Cone's take: "Joe got face-to-face, and implored me to be honest with him. I did my best to lie and tell him I still had some-thing left and would get him through this inning. Apparently, he believed me." . . . More from Cone: "I got us in that jam, and there's no worse feeling than coming out with the bases loaded." . . . Torre: "Sometimes playing at home in the postseason isn't an advantage because you get yourself so charged up you lose sight of what you have to do."

BOX SCORE

TUESDAY, OCTOBER 22, AT ATLANTA

New York	AB	R	H	RBI	PO	A
Raines, lf	4	1	1	0	1	0
Jeter, ss	3	1	1	0	4	2
Williams, cf	5	2	2	3	2	0
Fielder, 1b	3	0	1	0	6	3
§Fox, pr	0	1	0	0	0	0
Martinez, 1b	0	0	0	0	1	0
Hayes, 3b	5	0	0	0	0	0
Strawberry, rf	3	0	1	1	0	0
Duncan, 2b	3	0	1	0	1	1
Sojo, 2b	1	0	1	1	2	1
Girardi, c	2	0	0	0	8	2
Cone, p	2	0	0	0	2	1
†Leyritz, ph	1	0	0	0	0	0
Rivera, p	1	0	0	0	0	0
Lloyd, p	0	0	0	0	0	0
Wetteland, p	0	0	0	0	0	0
Totals	33	5	8	5	27	10

Atlanta	AB	R	H	RBI	PO	A
Grissom, cf	4	1	3	0	0	0
Lemke, 2b	4	0	1	1	2	3
C. Jones, 3b	3	0	1	0	1	1
McGriff, 1b	3	0	0	0	9	1
Klesko, lf	3	0	0	1	0	0
Lopez, c	4	0	1	0	11	1
A. Jones, rf	4	0	0	0	3	1
Blauser, ss	4	0	0	0	0	3
Glavine, p	1	1	0	0	0	2
‡Polonia, ph	0	0	0	0	0	0
McMichael, p	0	0	0	0	0	0
Clontz, p	0	0	0	0	0	0
Bielecki, p	0	0	0	0	1	0
∞Pendleton, ph	1	0	0	0	0	0
Totals	31	2	6	2	27	12

New York	1	0	0	1	0	0	0	3	0—5
Atlanta	0	0	0	0	0	1	0	1	0—2

New York	IP	H	R	ER	BB	SO
Cone (W)	6	4	1	1	4	3
M. Rivera	1 1/3	2	1	1	1	1
Lloyd	2/3	0	0	0	0	1
Wetteland (S)	1	0	0	0	0	2

Atlanta	IP	H	R	ER	BB	SO
Glavine (L)	7	4	2	1	3	8
McMichael	*0	3	3	3	0	0
Clontz	1	1	0	0	1	1
Bielecki	1	0	0	0	2	2

*Pitched to three batters in eighth.

Bases on balls—Off Cone 4 (McGriff, Glavine, Klesko, C. Jones), off M. Rivera (Polonia), off Glavine 3 (Raines, Fielder, Girardi), off Bielecki 2 (Martinez, Jeter), off Clontz 1 (Strawberry).

Strikeouts—By Cone 3 (Blauser, Klesko, A. Jones), by Wetteland 2 (Blauser, A. Jones), by Lloyd 1 (Klesko), by M. Rivera 1 (C. Jones), by Glavine 8 (Strawberry 2, Hayes 2, Duncan, Cone, Girardi, Jeter), by Bielecki 2 (Hayes, Williams), by Clontz 1 (Girardi).

†Grounded out for Cone in seventh. ‡Walked for Glavine in seventh. §Ran for Fielder in eighth. ∞Grounded out for Bielecki in ninth. E—Jeter, Blauser. DP—New York 1, Atlanta 1. LOB—New York 9, Atlanta 7. 2B—Fielder. 3B—Grissom. HR—Williams. SH—Jeter, Girardi. CS—A. Jones, Polonia. T—3:22. A—51,843. U—Welke (A.L.), plate; Rippley (N.L.), first; Young (A.L.), second; Davis (N.L.), third; Evans (A.L.), left field; Tata (N.L.), right field.

PLAY BY PLAY

FIRST INNING
New York—Raines walked. Jeter sacrificed Raines to second, catcher to second baseman covering first. Williams singled to center, scoring Raines. Fielder grounded to second, Williams went to second. Hayes struck out.

Atlanta—Grissom singled to left. Lemke grounded into a double play, first baseman to shortstop to first baseman. C. Jones singled to right. McGriff grounded to first.

SECOND INNING
New York—Strawberry struck out. Duncan grounded to the pitcher. Girardi struck out.

Atlanta—Klesko grounded to the first baseman, who tossed to the pitcher covering first. Lopez grounded to short. A. Jones struck out.

THIRD INNING
New York—Cone struck out. Raines grounded to short. Jeter flied to right.

Atlanta—Blauser fouled to first. Glavine grounded to the pitcher. Grissom popped to second.

FOURTH INNING
New York—Williams reached first on an error by the shortstop. Fielder walked. Hayes flied to right, Williams went to third. Strawberry singled to left, scoring Williams as Fielder went to second. Duncan struck out. Girardi walked. Cone forced Strawberry at third, third baseman unassisted.

Atlanta—Lemke flied to left. C. Jones grounded to the first baseman, who tossed to the pitcher covering first. McGriff walked. Klesko struck out.

FIFTH INNING
New York—Raines singled to left. Jeter struck out. Williams flied into a double play, right fielder to first baseman.

Atlanta—Lopez singled to center. A. Jones forced Lopez at second, second baseman to shortstop. A. Jones caught stealing, catcher to shortstop. Blauser struck out.

SIXTH INNING
New York—Fielder grounded to third. Hayes and Strawberry struck out.

Atlanta—Glavine walked. Grissom singled to left, Glavine went to second. Lemke popped to first. C. Jones walked. McGriff popped to short. Klesko walked, scoring Glavine. Lopez fouled to the catcher.

SEVENTH INNING
New York—Duncan singled to right-center. Girardi sacrificed Duncan to second, pitcher to second baseman covering first. Leyritz, pinch-hitting for Cone, grounded to short, Duncan went to third. Raines grounded to second.

Atlanta—M. Rivera now pitching, Sojo at second base. A. Jones popped to second. Blauser flied to center. Polonia, pinch-hitting for Glavine, walked. Polonia caught stealing, catcher to second baseman.

EIGHTH INNING
New York—McMichael now pitching. Jeter singled to short. Williams homered to right, scoring Jeter. Fielder doubled to center. Clontz now pitching. Fox pinch ran for Fielder. Hayes grounded to shortstop, Fox went to third. Strawberry was intentionally walked. Sojo singled to right, scoring Fox as Strawberry went to second. Girardi struck out. M. Rivera grounded to second.

Atlanta—Martinez now at first base. Grissom tripled to center. Lemke singled to right, scoring Grissom. C. Jones struck out. Lloyd now pitching. McGriff flied to center. Klesko struck out.

NINTH INNING
New York—Bielecki now pitching. Raines grounded to the first baseman, who tossed to the pitcher covering first. Jeter walked. Williams struck out. Martinez walked. Hayes struck out.

Atlanta—Wetteland now pitching. Lopez reached first on an error by the shortstop. A. Jones and Blauser struck out. Pendleton, pinch-hitting for Bielecki, grounded to second.

HIGHLIGHTS
NEW YORK 8, ATLANTA 6 (10 INNINGS)

Why the Yankees won: They showed remarka[ble] stick-to-itiveness after seeing their starting pitc[h] driven from the game after two-plus innings a[nd] watching their deficit grow to 6-0 after five innin[gs]. In the sixth, the Yanks got to Braves lefthand[er] Denny Neagle for three runs (two earned), o[n] three hits, a walk and an Atlanta error doing t[he] damage. Then, in the eighth, Jim Leyritz, inser[ted] into the game two innings earlier as a defensi[ve] replacement, rocked Braves bullpen stalwart Ma[rk] Wohlers for a three-run homer that tied the game [at] 6 and meant Atlanta no doubt would have to go dee[p]-er into its bullpen before the night was over.

Why the Braves lost: After Wohlers was roughed [up] for six hits in two innings, Atlanta was forced to tu[rn] to Steve Avery when the game went into ex[tra] innings. Avery had made only two relief appearanc[es] in 203 regular-season games when thrust into acti[on] to open the Yankees' 10th. He quickly got two Yan[ks] to ground out but walked Tim Raines and yielde[d a] single to Derek Jeter. He then was ordered to w[alk] Bernie Williams intentionally. With two out and t[he] bases loaded, the Yankees sent up Wade Boggs [to] pinch hit for rookie Andy Fox and Boggs, after falli[ng] behind in the count 1-2, coaxed a walk to force in t[he] tie-breaking run. Charlie Hayes followed with a loo[p] off Brad Clontz that first baseman Ryan Klesko lost [in] the lights, sending an insurance run across the pla[te.]

The turning points:
1. Atlanta manager Bobby Cox's decision to bring [in] closer Wohlers an inning earlier than usual. He we[nt] to the big guy in the eighth inning—the Braves we[re] leading 6-3—with the hope of assuring a victory a[nd] putting the Yankees on the brink of elimination.

2. A sixth-inning foul ball that Cox considere[d] crucial. With Atlanta ahead, 6-0, Jeter's inning-ope[n]-ing foul drive down the right-field line seemed catc[h]-able but outfielder Jermaine Dye couldn't maneuv[er] around umpire Tim Welke and the ball dropp[ed.] Cox was steamed. Jeter followed with a single th[at] started a three-run New York outburst.

Notable: The game was the longest in Series his[to]-ry, lasting 4 hours, 17 minutes. . . . Dye made a tu[m]-bling catch with the bases loaded and two out in t[he] Yankees' ninth, keeping the game tied. . . . In t[he] Braves' half of the ninth, New York reliever Grae[me] Lloyd—facing a two-on, one-out situation—got Fr[ed] McGriff to hit into a double play.

Quotable: Cox, on why he gave Williams the inte[n]-tional walk with runners on first and second and tw[o] out in the 10th: "Because it was the smart thing [to] do. He's their best hitter. He's carried them [ ] through the postseason and has kicked the livi[ng] hell out of us." . . . Boggs, on his walk that followe[d:] "Probably the biggest base on balls I ever got in m[y] career. Surprisingly, I was relaxed. I cleared ever[y]

ng out of my mind as I walked to the plate. I was
rtunate enough to lay off some pretty nasty sliders
d work the count to 3-and-2." ... Cox, on whey he
ought on Wohlers in the eighth: "It's very simple.
ain, it was the smart thing to do. Why wouldn't
u want to bring in Wohlers? He's well-rested. He's
rfectly capable of going two innings and then
ching again the next day." ... Cox, on umpire
lke's inability to get out of Dye's way in the sixth:
hat was the turning point right there as far as I
s concerned. (Dye) could have made the catch,
t he had to run around the damn umpire."

BOX SCORE

WEDNESDAY, OCTOBER 23, AT ATLANTA

York	AB	R	H	RBI	PO	A
nes, lf	5	1	0	0	2	0
r, ss	4	2	2	0	2	5
iams, cf	4	1	0	0	2	0
der, 1b	4	1	2	1	8	1
ox, pr-3b	0	0	0	0	0	0
oggs, ph-3b	0	0	0	1	0	0
es, 3b-1b	5	1	3	1	1	2
wberry, rf	5	0	2	0	1	0
can, 2b	5	1	0	0	3	3
rdi, c	2	0	0	0	5	0
Neill, ph	1	0	0	0	0	0
ritz, c	2	1	1	3	4	0
ers, p	1	0	1	0	0	0
hringer, p	0	0	0	0	0	0
io, ph	1	0	1	0	0	0
athers, p	0	0	0	0	0	0
lartinez, ph	1	0	0	0	0	0
son, p	0	0	0	0	2	0
drete, ph	1	0	0	0	0	0
Rivera, p	0	0	0	0	0	2
d, p	1	0	0	0	0	0
teland, p	0	0	0	0	0	0
otals	42	8	12	6	30	13

nta	AB	R	H	RBI	PO	A
som, cf	5	0	1	2	1	0
ke, 2b	5	0	1	0	2	4
ones, 3b-ss	3	2	1	0	0	3
riff, 1b	3	1	2	1	12	0
tz, p	0	0	0	0	0	0
ez, c	2	1	0	1	7	0
lers, c	0	0	0	0	0	0
y, p	0	0	0	0	0	0
ko, 1b	1	0	0	0	0	0
ones, lf	4	1	3	1	1	0
rf	4	0	0	0	5	0
ser, ss	3	1	1	1	0	2
ard, ss	0	0	0	0	0	2
lonia, ph	1	0	0	0	0	0
dleton, 3b	1	0	0	0	0	2
gle, p	1	0	0	0	0	1
e, p	0	0	0	0	0	0
ecki, p	1	0	0	0	0	0
z, p	1	0	0	0	2	0
otals	35	6	9	6	30	14

York			0	0	0	0	0	3	0	3	0	2—8
nta			0	4	1	0	1	0	0	0	0	0—6

York	IP	H	R	ER	BB	SO
ers	*2	5	5	5	2	0
hringer	2	0	0	0	0	3
thers	1	1	1	1	2	2
on	2	0	0	0	1	2
Rivera	1 1/3	2	0	0	1	1
d (W)	1	0	0	0	0	1
teland (S)	2/3	1	0	0	0	0

nta	IP	H	R	ER	BB	SO
gle	†5	5	3	2	4	3
e	‡0	0	0	0	1	0
ecki	2	0	0	0	1	4
lers	2	6	3	3	0	1

Atlanta	IP	H	R	ER	BB	SO
Avery (L)	2/3	1	2	1	3	0
Clontz	1/3	0	0	0	0	1

*Pitched to two batters in third. †Pitched to four batters in sixth. ‡Pitched to one batter in sixth.

Bases on balls—Off Rogers 2 (Lopez, A. Jones), off Weathers 2 (McGriff, C. Jones), off Nelson 1 (McGriff), off M. Rivera 1 (C. Jones), off Neagle 4 (Fielder, Hayes, Williams, Jeter), off Avery 3 (Williams, Raines, Boggs), off Bielecki 1 (Jeter), off Wade 1 (Strawberry).

Strikeouts—By Boehringer 3 (Blauser, Neagle, A. Jones), by Weathers 2 (Lemke, Lopez), by Nelson 2 (Blauser, Bielecki), by Lloyd 1 (Klesko), by M. Rivera 1 (Polonia), by Bielecki 4 (Duncan, O'Neill, Martinez, Williams), by Neagle 3 (Raines, Strawberry, Jeter), by Wohlers 1 (Jeter), by Clontz 1 (Strawberry).

§Singled for Boehringer in fifth. ∞Struck out for Girardi in sixth. ▲Struck out for Weathers in sixth. ◆Grounded out for Nelson in eighth. ■Struck out for Belliard in eighth. ▼Ran for Fielder in ninth. @Walked for Fox in 10th. E—Klesko, Dye. DP—New York 1, Atlanta 1. LOB—New York 13, Atlanta 8. 2B—Grissom, A. Jones. HR—Leyritz, McGriff. SH—Dye, Neagle. SF—Lopez. Balk—Weathers. T—4:17. A—51,881. U—Rippley (N.L.), plate; Young (A.L.), first; Davis (N.L.), second; Evans (A.L.), third; Tata (N.L.), left field; Welke (A.L.), right field.

PLAY BY PLAY

FIRST INNING
New York—Raines and Jeter struck out. Williams flied to right.
Atlanta—Grissom grounded to second. Lemke grounded to third. C. Jones grounded to short.

SECOND INNING
New York—Fielder grounded to second. Hayes flied to right. Strawberry grounded to short.
Atlanta—McGriff homered to center. Lopez and A. Jones walked. Dye flied to right, Lopez went to third. Blauser singled in front of the plate on a squeeze play, scoring Lopez as A. Jones went to second. Neagle sacrificed A. Jones to third and Blauser to second, third baseman to second baseman covering first. Grissom doubled to center, scoring A. Jones and Blauser. Lemke grounded to short.

THIRD INNING
New York—Duncan grounded to second. Girardi grounded to third. Rogers singled to third. Raines flied to right.
Atlanta—C. Jones singled to right-center. McGriff singled to center, C. Jones went to third. Boehringer now pitching. Lopez hit a sacrifice fly to center, scoring C. Jones as McGriff went to second. A. Jones struck out. Dye popped to short.

FOURTH INNING
New York—Jeter walked. Williams grounded into a double play, shortstop to second baseman to first baseman. Fielder and Hayes walked. Strawberry struck out.
Atlanta—Blauser and Neagle struck out. Grissom grounded to short.

FIFTH INNING
New York—Duncan grounded to third. Girardi grounded to the pitcher. Sojo, pinch-hitting for Boehringer, singled to center. Raines flied to center.
Atlanta—Weathers now pitching. Lemke struck out. C. Jones walked. C. Jones went to second on a balk. McGriff was intentionally walked. Lopez struck out. A. Jones doubled off third baseman's glove, scoring C. Jones as McGriff went to third. Dye grounded to short.

SIXTH INNING
New York—Jeter singled to right. Williams walked. Fielder singled to right and went to second on the right fielder's error in fielding the grounder. Jeter scored, Williams went to third and scored on the error. Hayes singled to right, scoring Fielder. Wade now pitching. Strawberry walked. Bielecki now pitching. Duncan struck out. O'Neill, pinch-hitting for Girardi, struck out. Martinez, pinch-hitting for Weathers, struck out.
Atlanta—Nelson now pitching, Leyritz catching. Blauser and Bielecki struck out. Grissom flied to center.

SEVENTH INNING
New York—Belliard now at shortstop. Raines flied to right.

Jeter walked. Williams struck out. Fielder flied to left.

Atlanta—Lemke grounded to the first baseman, who tossed to the pitcher covering first. C. Jones grounded to second. McGriff walked. Lopez grounded to the pitcher, unassisted.

EIGHTH INNING

New York—Wohlers now pitching, Perez catching. Hayes singled to third. Strawberry singled to left, Hayes went to second. Duncan forced Strawberry at second, shortstop to the second baseman, as Hayes went to third. Leyritz homered to left, scoring Hayes and Duncan. Aldrete, pinch-hitting for Nelson, grounded to short. Raines grounded to second.

Atlanta—M. Rivera now pitching. A. Jones singled to right. Dye sacrificed A. Jones to second, pitcher to second baseman covering first. Polonia, pinch-hitting for Belliard, struck out. Perez grounded to the pitcher.

NINTH INNING

New York—Pendleton now at third, C. Jones moved to shortstop. Jeter struck out. Williams grounded to third. Fielder singled to right. Hayes singled to left. Fox now pinch-running for Fielder. Strawberry singled to third, Fox went to third and Hayes to second. Duncan flied to right.

Atlanta—Fox now at third and Hayes moved to first. Grissom popped to shortstop. Lemke singled to center. C. Jones walked. Lloyd now pitching. McGriff grounded into double play, shortstop to second baseman to first baseman.

10TH INNING

New York—Avery now pitching. Leyritz grounded to third. Lloyd grounded to shortstop. Raines walked. Jeter singled to left, Raines went to second. Williams was intentionally walked. Boggs, pinch-hitting for Fox, walked, scoring Raines. Clontz now pitching, Klesko at first base. Hayes reached base on an error by the first baseman, scoring Jeter as Williams went to third and Boggs went to second. Strawberry struck out.

Atlanta—Boggs now at third base. Klesko struck out. Wetteland now pitching. A. Jones singled to left. Dye and Pendleton flied to left.

GAME 5

HIGHLIGHTS

NEW YORK 1, ATLANTA 0

Why the Yankees won: Lefthander Andy Pettitte did what had been common for him in 1996—pitch with consummate skill. And slugger Cecil Fielder continued to do in this Series what he had really never done in his career—hit for an impressive average. Pettitte hurled five-hit, shutout ball over 8⅓ innings and Fielder collected three hits—including the game-winner in the fourth inning—to boost his Series batting average to .421.

Why the Braves lost: Gold Glove center field Marquis Grissom and right fielder Jermaine Dye couldn't get together on Charlie Hayes' leadoff drive to right-center in the fourth. Dye cut in front of Grissom, blocking his view, and the ball kicked off Grissom's glove. Hayes, who reached second on the play, moved to third on Bernie Williams' grounder, then scored the only run when Fielder rammed a double to left. Although the misplay (Grissom was charged with a two-base error) was crucial, the Braves' failure to mount any semblance of an offense was a key factor, too.

The turning points:

1. Pettitte's fielding prowess in the sixth inning, which foiled a big opportunity for Atlanta. After pitch-er John Smoltz led off the Braves' at-bat with a sing and Grissom followed with another hit, Pettitte bar headed Mark Lemke's bunt and threw out Smoltz third. On the next pitch, Pettitte induced Chipp Jones to hit a grounder to the mound, which tri gered an inning-ending double play.

2. The efforts of relief ace John Wetteland and rig fielder Paul O'Neill, who rescued the Yankees in th ninth. Wetteland, who led the American League wi 43 saves but always seemed to make a sticky situ tion a little stickier before closing out the oppositio was his usual self. After Chipper Jones started th Atlanta ninth with a double off Pettitte and moved third on Fred McGriff's groundout, Wetteland cam on to face Javier Lopez. The Braves' catcher hit sharp grounder to third baseman Hayes, who he Jones at third and threw to first base for out No. Ryan Klesko, pinch-hitting for Andruw Jones, wa walked intentionally, putting the go-ahead run c base in the 1-0 thriller. Then Luis Polonia, batting fe Dye, fouled off six consecutive pitches before ta ging a Wetteland offering into deep right-cente O'Neill, on the run and his glove extended, made marvelous game-ending catch by pulling the ball over his shoulder.

Notable: The game was the last to be played Atlanta-Fulton County Stadium, home of the Brave since the club moved from Milwaukee to Atlan after the 1965 season. In 1997, the team will mo into the next-door stadium that housed the 199 Summer Olympics. . . . Smoltz, going for his 30th vi tory of the year (24 regular-season wins, an All-St Game triumph and four postseason victories pitched well enough to get it. He struck out 10 ba ters in eight innings, allowing only four hits and on unearned run.

Quotable: Polonia, on his two-on, two-out drive the ninth: "I wanted to be the hero. I thought th was a gapper for sure. As soon as I hit it, I said, 'Th game is over.' It was, but for the wrong team." . . O'Neill, on Polonia's smash: "When the ball was h I thought I had it all the way. But then it sailed o me, and it kept carrying and carrying." . . . Yanke second baseman Mariano Duncan, on the hype su rounding the Braves' quick start in this Series an their overall success in recent years: "People wer saying that they were the greatest team ever, th there was no way we could beat them. But they fo got that this is a best-of-seven series."

BOX SCORE

THURSDAY, OCTOBER 24, AT ATLANTA

New York	AB	R	H	RBI	PO
Jeter, ss	4	0	0	0	2
Hayes, 3b	4	1	0	0	1
Williams, cf	4	0	0	0	1
Fielder, 1b	4	0	3	1	7
Martinez, 1b	0	0	0	0	4
Strawberry, lf	3	0	0	0	1
O'Neill, rf	2	0	0	0	5
Duncan, 2b	4	0	0	0	2
Sojo, 2b	0	0	0	0	0
Leyritz, c	2	0	1	0	4

w York	AB	R	H	RBI	PO	A
ʳitte, p	4	0	0	0	0	4
ᵗteland, p	0	0	0	0	0	0
Totals	31	1	4	1	27	15

ᵃnta	AB	R	H	RBI	PO	A
ssom, cf	3	0	2	0	1	0
ᵑke, 2b	4	0	0	0	1	5
ᴶones, 3b	4	0	1	0	2	1
Griff, 1b	3	0	0	0	7	0
ᵉz, c	4	0	0	0	9	1
ᴶones, lf	2	0	1	0	1	0
ᵉsko, ph	0	0	0	0	0	0
ᵉ, rf	3	0	0	0	3	0
ᵒlonia, ph	1	0	0	0	0	0
ᵘser, ss	3	0	0	0	3	1
ᵒltz, p	2	0	1	0	0	1
ᵒrdecai, ph	1	0	0	0	0	0
ᵸlers, p	0	0	0	0	0	1
Totals	30	0	5	0	27	10

w York				0	0	0	1	0	0	0	0	0—1
ᵃnta				0	0	0	0	0	0	0	0	0—0

w York	IP	H	R	ER	BB	SO
ᵗitte (W)	8 1/3	5	0	0	3	4
ᵗteland (S)	2/3	0	0	0	1	0

ᵃnta	IP	H	R	ER	BB	SO
ᵒltz (L)	8	4	1	0	3	10
ᵸlers	1	0	0	0	2	0

ᴮases on balls—Off Pettitte 3 (McGriff, Grissom, A. Jones), off Wetteland ᴷlesko), off Smoltz 3 (Strawberry, O'Neill, Leyritz), off Wohlers 2 (O'Neill, ᵣitz).
ᵗrikeouts—By Pettitte 4 (Lemke 2, McGriff, Grissom), by Smoltz 10 ᵃyes 2, Williams 2, Strawberry, Fielder, Duncan, Leyritz, Pettitte, Jeter). *Grounded out for Smoltz in eighth. †Was intentionally walked for A. ᵉs in ninth. ‡Flied out for Dye in ninth. E—Jeter, Grissom. DP—New ᵏ 2, Atlanta 1. LOB—New York 8, Atlanta 7. 2B—Fielder, C. Jones. SB— ᵸcan, Leyritz, Grissom, A. Jones. CS—A. Jones. WP—Wohlers. T—2:54. ᵸ51,881. U—Young (A.L.), plate; Davis (N.L.), first; Evans (A.L.), second; ᵃ (N.L.), third; Welke (A.L.), left field; Rippley (N.L.), right field.

PLAY BY PLAY

FIRST INNING
ᴺew York—Jeter, Hayes and Williams struck out.
ᴬtlanta—Grissom and Lemke struck out. C. Jones flied to ᵸt.

SECOND INNING
ᴺew York—Fielder singled to left. Strawberry struck out. ᴺeill forced Fielder at second, shortstop to second baseman. ᵸncan forced O'Neill at second, shortstop to second baseman.
ᴬtlanta—McGriff struck out. Lopez grounded to second. A. ᵸes walked. Dye grounded to short.

THIRD INNING
ᴺew York—Leyritz and Pettitte struck out. Jeter lined to third.
ᴬtlanta—Blauser and Smoltz flied to right. Grissom walked. ᵖssom stole second. Lemke struck out.

FOURTH INNING
ᴺew York—Hayes reached second on an error by the center ᵸder. Williams grounded to second, Hayes went to third. Fielder ᵘbled to left, scoring Hayes. Strawberry flied to center. O'Neill ᵸlked. Duncan grounded to second.
ᴬtlanta—C. Jones grounded to third. McGriff walked. Lopez ᵖunded into a double play, second baseman to shortstop to ᵗ baseman.

FIFTH INNING
ᴺew York—Leyritz singled to left. Pettitte fouled to third. Jeter ᵈ to right. Hayes struck out.
ᴬtlanta—A. Jones singled to left. A. Jones caught stealing, ᵖcher to first baseman to shortstop. Dye flied to right. Blauser ᵖunded to third.

SIXTH INNING
ᴺew York—Williams struck out and was out on the dropped ᵈrd strike, catcher to first baseman. Fielder singled to center. ᵃwberry walked. O'Neill grounded to second, Fielder went to

third and Strawberry went to second. Duncan struck out.
Atlanta—Smoltz singled to left. Grissom singled to left, Smoltz went to second. Lemke forced Smoltz at third, pitcher to third baseman, Grissom went to second. C. Jones grounded into a double play, pitcher to second baseman to first baseman.

SEVENTH INNING
New York—Leyritz walked. Leyritz stole second. Pettitte reached first on a fielder's choice, Leyritz was tagged out, pitcher to third baseman to shortstop. Jeter lined into a double play, first baseman, unassisted.
Atlanta—McGriff reached first on an error by the shortstop. Lopez forced McGriff at second, second baseman, unassisted. A. Jones flied to center. Dye grounded to the pitcher.

EIGHTH INNING
New York—Hayes and Williams flied to right. Fielder struck out.
Atlanta—Martinez now at first base. Blauser flied to left. Mordecai, pinch-hitting for Smoltz, grounded to short. Grissom singled to center. Lemke grounded to third.

NINTH INNING
New York—Wohlers now pitching. Strawberry grounded to the pitcher. O'Neill walked. Duncan forced O'Neill at second, second baseman to shortstop. Duncan stole second. Leyritz was intentionally walked. Duncan went to third on a wild pitch during the intentional walk. Pettitte flied to left.
Atlanta—Sojo now at second base. C. Jones doubled to left. McGriff grounded to first, C. Jones went to third. Wetteland now pitching. Lopez grounded to third. Klesko, pinch-hitting for A. Jones, was intentionally walked. Polonia, pinch-hitting for Dye, flied to right.

GAME 6

HIGHLIGHTS
NEW YORK 3, ATLANTA 2

Why the Yankees won: Unsung catcher Joe Girardi contributed offensively and defensively. After Paul O'Neill doubled and went to third on a groundout in the third inning, Girardi slammed a triple off the wall in center field. Derek Jeter followed with a run-scoring single. Before Braves starter Greg Maddux could close out the inning, the Yanks had netted a third run on Jeter's stolen base and Bernie Williams' RBI single. Defensively, Girardi made a critical play in the fifth when, after a pitch in the dirt got away, he recovered to throw out Marquis Grissom at second base as the Atlanta center fielder tried to advance from first. New York led, 3-1, at the time.

Why the Braves lost: Their middle relief wasn't as deep as the Yankees'. Not exactly household names, righthander David Weathers and lefthander Graeme Lloyd turned in stellar work in Atlanta's sixth. After Chipper Jones doubled off New York starter Jimmy Key and moved to third on a groundout, Weathers entered and struck out Javier Lopez. Andruw Jones then drew a walk. When Ryan Klesko was sent up to hit for Jermaine Dye, Lloyd came on and got Klesko to pop up. Mariano Rivera then pitched two scoreless innings for the Yankees.

The turning points:

1. The Braves nicked Yankees closer John Wetteland for three hits and one run in the ninth—whittling their deficit to 3-2—but then let the righthander off the hook. Wetteland struck out Andruw Jones to

open the ninth, then yielded singles to Klesko and Terry Pendleton. After striking out pinch hitter Luis Polonia, Wetteland allowed a single to Grissom—making it a one-run game with two on, two out and Mark Lemke heading to the plate. Ever the escape artist, Wetteland ran the count to 3-2, then got Lemke to foul out to third baseman Charlie Hayes—and the Yankees were World Series champions for the first time since 1978.

2. When Maddux, who induced 19 groundouts in Game 2, showed early (the third inning) that he was a bit off his form in this outing. And considering the way the Yankees' pitching had been coming around, there was little margin for error.

Notable: It was a particularly emotional time for Yankees manager Joe Torre, whose brother Frank had undergone a heart transplant the day before Game 6. Plus, Torre was caught up in the most memorable experience of his baseball career—he had never even reached the World Series in 18 years as a major league player or in 14 previous seasons as a big-league manager. . . . Atlanta manager Bobby Cox, unhappy with the umpiring earlier in the Series, was ejected after arguing that Grissom had made it safely to second on that key fifth-inning play. Replays indicated Grissom was safe. . . . Wetteland, with saves in all four of the Yankees' victories, was voted the Series MVP.

Quotable: Torre: "This is the best feeling, between yesterday (his brother's life-saving operation) and today, the best feeling of my life." . . . As for Wetteland's knack for getting into and out of trouble, Torre viewed it as business as usual: "Once they got a couple of men on (in the ninth), I said, 'This is the way it's gone all year long.' " . . . Girardi, on his third-inning triple that broke a scoreless tie and fired up his team as well as the Yankee Stadium throng: "When I got on third base, I almost started crying."

BOX SCORE

SATURDAY, OCTOBER 26, AT NEW YORK

Atlanta	AB	R	H	RBI	PO	A
Grissom, cf	5	0	2	1	1	0
Lemke, 2b	5	0	0	0	3	5
C. Jones, 3b	4	0	1	0	0	1
McGriff, 1b	3	1	0	0	13	1
Lopez, c	3	0	1	0	3	1
A. Jones, lf-rf	3	0	1	0	0	0
Dye, rf	1	0	0	1	3	0
*Klesko, ph-lf	2	1	1	0	1	0
Pendleton, dh	3	0	1	0	0	0
†Belliard, pr	0	0	0	0	0	0
Blauser, ss	3	0	1	0	0	2
‡Polonia, ph	1	0	0	0	0	0
Maddux, p	0	0	0	0	0	2
Wohlers, p	0	0	0	0	0	0
Totals	33	2	8	2	24	12

New York	AB	R	H	RBI	PO	A
Jeter, ss	4	1	1	1	4	6
Boggs, 3b	3	0	0	0	0	0
Hayes, 3b	1	0	0	0	1	0
Williams, cf	4	0	2	1	4	0
Fielder, dh	4	0	1	0	0	0
Martinez, 1b	3	0	0	0	6	0
Strawberry, lf	2	0	0	0	2	0
O'Neill, rf	3	1	1	0	2	0
Duncan, 2b	1	0	0	0	0	0
Sojo, 2b	2	0	1	0	3	1

New York	AB	R	H	RBI	PO
Girardi, c	3	1	2	1	5
Key, p	0	0	0	0	0
Weathers, p	0	0	0	0	0
Lloyd, p	0	0	0	0	0
M. Rivera, p	0	0	0	0	0
Wetteland, p	0	0	0	0	0
Totals	30	3	8	3	27

Atlanta	0	0	0	1	0	0	0	0	1—
New York	0	0	3	0	0	0	0	0	x—

Atlanta	IP	H	R	ER	BB	S
Maddux (L)	7²/₃	8	3	3	1	
Wohlers	¹/₃	0	0	0	0	

New York	IP	H	R	ER	BB	S
Key (W)	5¹/₃	5	1	1	3	
Weathers	¹/₃	0	0	0	1	
Lloyd	¹/₃	0	0	0	1	
M. Rivera	2	0	0	0	1	
Wetteland (S)	1	3	1	1	0	

Bases on balls—Off Maddux 1 (Strawberry), off Key 3 (McGriff, Lop Dye), off Weathers 1 (A. Jones), off M. Rivera 1 (Pendleton). Strikeouts—By Maddux 3 (Strawberry, Martinez, Jeter), by Wetteland (Polonia, A. Jones), by Key 1 (A. Jones), by Weathers 1 (Lopez), by Rivera 1 (Lopez).
*Popped out for Dye in sixth. †Ran for Pendleton in ninth. ‡Struck out Blauser in ninth. E—Duncan. DP—Atlanta 2, New York 1. LOB—Atlanta New York 4. 2B—C. Jones, Blauser, O'Neill, Sojo. 3B—Girardi. SB—Jet Williams. CS—Pendleton. T—2:53. A—56,375. U—Davis (N.L.), pla Evans (A.L.), first; Tata (N.L.), second: Welke (A.L.), third; Rippley (N.L.), l field; Young (A.L.), right field.

PLAY BY PLAY

FIRST INNING

Atlanta—Grissom flied to left. Lemke grounded to short. Jones flied to right.

New York—Jeter grounded to the pitcher. Boggs flied to rig Williams grounded to first.

SECOND INNING

Atlanta—McGriff grounded to short. Lopez walked. A. Jon struck out. Dye flied to right.

New York—Fielder grounded to first. Martinez struck o Strawberry grounded to first.

THIRD INNING

Atlanta—Pendleton reached base on an error by the seco baseman. Pendleton caught stealing, catcher to shortstc Blauser doubled to center. Grissom grounded to short. Lem flied to center.

New York—O'Neill doubled ro right. Duncan grounded to se ond, O'Neill went to third. Girardi tripled to center, scoring O'Ne Jeter singled to center, scoring Girardi. Jeter stole second. Bog flied to right. Williams singled to center, scoring Jeter as Willian advanced to second on the throw home. Fielder grounded to t catcher.

FOURTH INNING

Atlanta—Sojo now at second base. C. Jones flied to le McGriff walked. Lopez singled to right, McGriff went to secor A. Jones singled to right, McGriff went to third, Lopez went second. Dye walked, scoring McGriff. Pendleton grounded intc double play, shortstop to first baseman.

New York—Martinez flied to center. Strawberry struck o O'Neill grounded to second.

FIFTH INNING

Atlanta—Blauser lined to short. Grissom singled to cent Grissom out attempting to advance to second on a ball that ter porarily got away from the catcher, catcher to shortstop. Lem flied to center.

New York—Sojo flied to right. Girardi single to left-center. Jet grounded into a double play, third baseman to second basem to first baseman.

SIXTH INNING

Atlanta—C. Jones doubled to right. McGriff grounded to se ond, C. Jones went to third. Weathers now pitching. Lopez stru

. A. Jones walked. Klesko pinch hit for Dye. Lloyd now pitch-
, Klesko popped to second.

ew York—Klesko now in left field, A. Jones moved to right
d. Boggs grounded to second. Williams flied to left. Fielder
gled to left. Martinez lined to second.

SEVENTH INNING

tlanta—M. Rivera now pitching, Hayes at third base.
ndleton walked. Blauser popped to second. Grissom forced
ndleton at second, shortstop to second baseman. Lemke flied
:enter fielder.

lew York—Strawberry walked. O'Neill grounded into a double
y, first baseman to second baseman to first baseman. Sojo
ibled to left. Girardi grounded to short.

EIGHTH INNING

Atlanta—C. Jones flied to center. McGriff grounded to short.
Lopez struck out.

New York—Jeter struck out. Hayes grounded to the pitcher.
Williams singled to center. Wohlers now pitching. Williams stole
second. Fielder grounded to short.

NINTH INNING

Atlanta—Wetteland now pitching. A. Jones struck out. Klesko
singled to short. Pendleton singled to right, Klesko went to third.
Polonia, pinch-hitting for Blauser, struck out. Belliard pinch ran
for Pendleton. Grissom singled to center, scoring Klesko as
Belliard went to second. Lemke fouled to third.

STATISTICS

NEW YORK YANKEES' BATTING AND FIELDING AVERAGES

yer, position	G	AB	R	H	TB	2B	3B	HR	RBI	BB	IBB	SO	Avg.	PO	A	E	Avg.
gers, p	1	1	0	1	1	0	0	0	0	0	0	0	1.000	0	0	0	.000
o, ph-2b	5	5	0	3	4	1	0	0	1	0	0	0	.600	5	2	0	1.000
lder, dh-1b	6	23	1	9	11	2	0	0	2	2	0	2	.391	21	5	0	1.000
ritz, c-ph	4	8	1	3	6	0	0	1	3	3	1	2	.375	15	0	0	1.000
ggs, 3b-ph	4	11	0	3	4	1	0	0	2	1	0	0	.273	0	0	0	.000
er, ss	6	20	5	5	5	0	0	0	1	4	0	6	.250	14	22	2	.947
nes, lf	4	14	2	3	3	0	0	0	0	2	0	1	.214	5	0	1	.833
ardi, c	4	10	1	2	4	0	1	0	1	1	0	2	.200	23	4	0	1.000
yes, ph-3b-1b	5	16	2	3	3	0	0	0	1	1	0	5	.188	3	6	0	1.000
awberry, lf-rf	5	16	0	3	3	0	0	0	1	4	1	6	.188	11	0	0	1.000
Williams, cf	6	24	3	4	7	0	0	1	4	3	1	6	.167	15	0	0	1.000
leill, rf-ph	5	12	1	2	4	2	0	0	0	3	0	2	.167	12	0	0	1.000
rtinez, 1b-ph	6	11	0	1	1	0	0	0	0	2	0	5	.091	27	0	0	1.000
ncan, 2b	6	19	1	1	1	0	0	0	0	0	0	4	.053	9	14	2	.920
ehringer, p	2	0	0	0	0	0	0	0	0	0	0	0	.000	0	0	0	.000
<, 2b-pr-3b	4	0	1	0	0	0	0	0	0	0	0	0	.000	1	0	0	1.000
y, p	2	0	0	0	0	0	0	0	0	0	0	0	.000	0	2	0	1.000
son, p	3	0	0	0	0	0	0	0	0	0	0	0	.000	2	0	0	1.000
athers, p	3	0	0	0	0	0	0	0	0	0	0	0	.000	0	0	0	.000
tteland, p	5	0	0	0	0	0	0	0	0	0	0	0	.000	0	0	0	.000
rete, rf-ph	2	1	0	0	0	0	0	0	0	0	0	0	.000	0	0	0	.000
yd, p	4	1	0	0	0	0	0	0	0	0	0	0	.000	0	2	0	1.000
Rivera, p	4	1	0	0	0	0	0	0	0	0	0	0	.000	0	0	0	.000
ne, p	1	2	0	0	0	0	0	0	0	0	0	1	.000	2	1	0	1.000
ttitte, p	2	4	0	0	0	0	0	0	0	0	0	1	.000	0	5	0	1.000
Totals	6	199	18	43	57	6	1	2	16	26	3	43	.216	165	63	5	.979

ATLANTA BRAVES' BATTING AND FIELDING AVERAGES

ayer, position	G	AB	R	H	TB	2B	3B	HR	RBI	BB	IBB	SO	Avg.	PO	A	E	Avg.
noltz, p	2	2	0	1	1	0	0	0	0	0	0	0	.500	0	1	0	1.000
ssom, cf	6	27	4	12	16	2	1	0	5	1	0	2	.444	7	0	1	.875
Jones, lf-rf	6	20	4	8	15	1	0	2	6	3	0	6	.400	7	1	0	1.000
:Griff, 1b	6	20	4	6	12	0	0	2	6	5	1	4	.300	62	4	0	1.000
Jones, 3b-ss	6	21	3	6	9	3	0	0	3	4	0	2	.286	5	6	0	1.000
mke, 2b	6	26	2	6	7	1	0	0	2	0	0	3	.231	12	25	0	1.000
ndleton, dh-ph-3b	4	9	1	2	3	1	0	0	0	1	0	1	.222	0	2	0	1.000
pez, c	6	21	3	4	4	0	0	0	1	3	0	4	.190	41	4	0	1.000
auser, ss	6	18	2	3	4	1	0	0	1	1	0	4	.167	7	15	1	.957
re, rf	5	17	0	2	2	0	0	0	1	1	0	1	.118	15	0	1	.938
esko, dh-lf-1b-ph	5	10	2	1	1	0	0	0	1	2	1	4	.100	1	0	1	.500
ery, p	1	0	0	0	0	0	0	0	0	0	0	0	.000	0	0	0	.000
lliard, ss-pr	4	0	0	0	0	0	0	0	0	0	0	0	.000	0	3	0	1.000
ontz, p	3	0	0	0	0	0	0	0	0	0	0	0	.000	0	0	0	.000
addux, p	2	0	0	0	0	0	0	0	0	0	0	0	.000	2	8	0	1.000
:Michael, p	2	0	0	0	0	0	0	0	0	0	0	0	.000	0	0	0	.000
ade, p	2	0	0	0	0	0	0	0	0	0	0	0	.000	0	0	0	.000
ohlers, p	4	0	0	0	0	0	0	0	0	0	0	0	.000	0	1	0	1.000
elecki, p	2	1	0	0	0	0	0	0	0	0	0	1	.000	1	0	0	1.000
avine, p	1	1	1	0	0	0	0	0	0	0	0	0	.000	0	2	0	1.000
ordecai, ph	1	1	0	0	0	0	0	0	0	0	0	0	.000	0	0	0	.000
agle, p	2	1	0	0	0	0	0	0	0	0	0	1	.000	0	1	0	1.000
rez, c	2	1	0	0	0	0	0	0	0	0	0	0	.000	2	0	0	1.000
Ionia, ph	6	5	0	0	0	0	0	0	0	1	0	3	.000	0	0	0	.000
Totals	6	201	26	51	74	9	1	4	26	23	2	36	.254	162	73	4	.983

1996 REVIEW *World Series*

NEW YORK YANKEES' PITCHING RECORDS

Pitcher	G	GS	CG	IP	H	R	ER	HR	BB	IBB	SO	HB	WP	W	L	Pct.	ERA
Nelson	3	0	0	4⅓	1	0	0	0	1	0	5	0	0	0	0	.000	0.0
Lloyd	4	0	0	2⅔	0	0	0	0	0	0	4	0	0	1	0	1.000	0.0
Cone	1	1	0	6	4	1	1	0	4	0	3	0	0	1	0	1.000	1.5
M. Rivera	4	0	0	5⅔	4	1	1	0	3	0	4	0	0	0	0	.000	1.5
Wetteland	5	0	0	4⅓	4	1	1	0	1	1	6	0	0	0	0	.000	2.0
Weathers	3	0	0	3	2	1	1	0	3	1	3	0	0	0	0	.000	3.0
Key	2	2	0	11⅓	15	5	5	0	5	0	1	1	0	1	1	.500	3.9
Boehringer	2	0	0	5	5	5	3	2	0	0	5	0	0	0	0	.000	5.4
Pettitte	2	2	0	10⅔	11	7	7	1	4	0	5	0	0	1	1	.500	5.9
Rogers	1	1	0	2	5	5	5	1	2	0	0	0	0	0	0	.000	22.5
Totals	6	6	0	55	51	26	24	4	23	2	36	1	0	4	2	.667	3.9

Shutout—Pettitte and Wetteland (combined). Saves—Wetteland 4.

ATLANTA BRAVES' PITCHING RECORDS

Pitcher	G	GS	CG	IP	H	R	ER	HR	BB	IBB	SO	HB	WP	W	L	Pct.	ERA
Bielecki	2	0	0	3	0	0	0	0	3	0	6	0	0	0	0	.000	0.0
Clontz	3	0	0	1⅔	1	0	0	0	1	1	2	0	0	0	0	.000	0.0
Wade	2	0	0	⅔	0	0	0	0	1	0	0	0	0	0	0	.000	0.0
Smoltz	2	2	0	14	6	2	1	0	8	0	14	0	0	1	1	.500	0.6
Glavine	1	1	0	7	4	2	1	0	3	0	8	0	0	0	1	.000	1.2
Maddux	2	2	0	15⅔	14	3	3	0	1	0	5	1	0	1	1	.500	1.7
Neagle	2	1	0	6	5	3	2	0	4	0	3	0	0	0	0	.000	3.0
Wohlers	4	0	0	4⅓	7	3	3	1	2	1	4	0	1	0	0	.000	6.2
Avery	1	0	0	⅔	1	2	1	0	3	1	0	0	0	0	1	.000	13.5
McMichael	2	0	0	1	5	3	3	1	0	0	1	0	0	0	0	.000	27.0
Totals	6	6	0	54	43	18	14	2	26	3	43	1	1	2	4	.333	2.3

Shutout—Maddux and Wohlers (combined). No saves.

SCORE BY INNINGS

New York	1	0	3	2	1	3	0	6	0	2—18
Atlanta	1	6	8	1	3	5	0	1	1	0—26

MISCELLANEOUS STATISTICS

Sacrifice hits—Lemke 2, Dye, Girardi, Jeter, Neagle.
Sacrifice flies—C. Jones, Lopez, McGriff.
Stolen bases—Duncan, Grissom, Jeter, A. Jones, C. Jones, Leyritz, B. Williams.
Caught stealing—A. Jones 2, Pendleton, Polonia, Raines.
Double plays—A. Jones and McGriff; Blauser, Lemke and McGriff; C. Jones, Lemke and McGriff; Duncan, Jeter and Fielder; Duncan, Jeter and Martinez; Fielder, Jeter and Fielder; Jeter and Martinez; Jeter, Duncan and Hayes; Key, Duncan and Martinez; Lemke, Blauser and McGriff; McGriff (unassisted); McGriff, Blauser and McGriff; Pettitte, Duncan and Fielder.
Left on bases—New York 8, 6, 9, 13, 8, 4—48; Atlanta 3, 7, 7, 8, 7, 9—41.
Hit by pitcher—By Key (A. Jones), by Maddux (Jeter).
Passed balls—None.
Balks—Weathers.
Time of games—First game, 3:02; second game, 2:44; third game, 3:22; fourth game, 4:17; fifth game, 2:54; sixth game, 2:53.
Attendance—First game, 56,365; second game, 56,340; third game, 51,843; fourth game, 51,881; fifth game, 51,881; sixth game, 56,375.
Umpires—Davis, Evans, Rippley, Tata, Welke and Young.
Official scorers—Red Foley, Jerome Holtzman, Scott McGregor.

ALL-STAR GAME

HIGHLIGHTS

NATIONAL LEAGUE 6, AMERICAN LEAGUE 0

Why the National League won: Dodger catcher Mike Piazza swung a hot bat, driving in two runs with a homer and a double to win MVP honors.

Why the American League lost: Their big bats were silenced. In a season marked by offensive fireworks, the A.L. managed just seven hits against nine N.L. pitchers, only one of which (a double by Boston's Mo Vaughn) went for extra bases.

The turning points:

1. In the bottom of the first, N.L. leadoff man Lance Johnson of the Mets hit the first pitch from Cleveland's Charles Nagy to left field. Indians outfielder Albert Belle slid in trying to block the one-hop liner, but the ball rolled far enough away to allow Johnson to take second base. He later scored the game's first run after consecutive groundouts by the Reds' Barry Larkin and the Giants' Barry Bonds.

2. After the American League failed to score for the second consecutive inning after putting its leadoff man on second base with no out, Piazza increased the N.L. advantage to 2-0 by hammering a Nagy pitch 445 feet for a home run to lead off the bottom of the second. The blast seemed to take a lot of fight out of an A.L. squad that already had blown two good scoring opportunities.

Notable: The victory was the third in a row for the National League, which extended its series lead to 40-36-1. . . . Piazza, who was born in nearby Norristown, Pa., once was a visiting team batboy at Veterans Stadium. . . . For the first time in All-Star history, neither team issued a walk. . . . Baltimore's Cal Ripken suffered a broken nose when White Sox pitcher Roberto Hernandez accidentally struck him with a forearm as American League players descended from a platform after the team picture was taken. . . . Piazza became the first player to homer in consecutive All-Star Games since Fred Lynn in 1979-80. Combined with his homer in his last at-bat in the 1995 game, Piazza became the first player to homer in consecutive All-Star at-bats since Gary Carter in 1981. . . . Belle became the first player to strike out three times in a nine-inning All-Star game since Willie McCovey in 1968 and the first American Leaguer since Mickey Mantle in 1956. . . . The shutout was the seventh in All-Star Game history, the fifth by the National League. . . . John Smoltz became the first Braves pitcher to win an All-Star Game since Gene Conley (Milwaukee) in 1955. . . . A number of prominent players missed the game because of injury or illness, including Ken Griffey, Tony Gwynn, Frank Thomas and Matt Williams.

Quotable: N.L. manager Bobby Cox, on the American League: "Believe me, these guys can bomb the ball out of the ballpark. We just made some exceptional pitches." . . . Nagy: "I was very nervous before the game. (Piazza's homer) was a fastball, belt high, and he hit it

a long way." . . . Piazza, on his big night: "I could remember so many games as a kid watching the Phillies play. I just didn't want to embarrass myself tonight. I didn't think of any heroics."

BOX SCORE

American League	AB	R	H	RBI	PO	A
Lofton, cf (Indians)	3	0	2	0	0	0
Carter, cf (Blue Jays)	1	0	1	0	1	0
Boggs, 3b (Yankees)	3	0	0	0	1	2
◆Fryman, ph-3b (Tigers)	1	0	0	0	0	1
R. Alomar, 2b (Orioles)	3	0	1	0	0	3
Knoblauch, 2b (Twins)	1	0	1	0	3	1
Belle, lf (Indians)	4	0	0	0	1	0
M. Vaughn, 1b (Red Sox)	3	0	1	0	5	1
McGwire, 1b (Athletics)	1	0	1	0	2	1
I. Rodriguez, c (Rangers)	2	0	0	0	6	2
∞S. Alomar, ph-c (Indians)	2	0	0	0	1	0
Ripken, ss (Orioles)	3	0	0	0	1	1
Percival, p (Angels)	0	0	0	0	0	0
Hernandez, p (White Sox)	0	0	0	0	1	0
■Wilson, ph (Mariners)	1	0	0	0	0	0
Anderson, rf (Orioles)	2	0	0	0	0	0
Pavlik, p (Rangers)	0	0	0	0	0	0
▲A. Rodriguez, ph-ss (M's)	1	0	0	0	0	0
Nagy, p (Indians)	0	0	0	0	1	0
†E. Martinez, ph (Mariners)	1	0	0	0	0	0
Finley, p (Angels)	0	0	0	0	0	0
‡Buhner, ph-rf (Mariners)	2	0	0	0	1	0
Totals	34	0	7	0	24	12

Nationl League	AB	R	H	RBI	PO	A
Johnson, cf (Mets)	4	1	3	0	5	0
Larkin, ss (Reds)	3	1	1	0	0	2
Smith, ss (Cardinals)	1	0	0	0	0	3
Bonds, lf (Giants)	3	0	1	1	2	0
P. Martinez, p (Expos)	0	0	0	0	0	0
Sheffield, rf (Marlins)	1	0	0	0	2	0
McGriff, 1b (Braves)	2	0	0	0	2	1
Glavine, p (Braves)	0	0	0	0	0	0
Caminiti, 3b (Padres)	2	1	1	1	0	0
Worrell, p (Dodgers)	0	0	0	0	0	0
Kendall, c (Pirates)	0	0	0	0	0	0
Piazza, c (Dodgers)	3	1	2	2	4	0
Hundley, c (Mets)	1	0	0	0	1	0
Wohlers, p (Braves)	0	0	0	0	0	0
Leiter, p (Marlins)	0	0	0	0	0	0
Bichette, rf (Rockies)	3	1	1	0	0	0
Trachsel, p (Cubs)	0	0	0	0	0	0
Grudzielanek, 3b (Expos)	1	0	0	0	0	0
Jones, 3b (Braves)	2	1	1	0	1	1
Bottalico, p (Phillies)	0	0	0	0	0	0
Burks, lf (Rockies)	2	0	1	0	1	0
Biggio, 2b (Astros)	3	0	0	1	1	1
§Young, pr-2b (Rockies)	1	0	0	0	2	1
Smoltz, p (Braves)	0	0	0	0	1	0
*H. Rodriguez, ph (Expos)	1	0	1	1	0	0
Brown, p (Marlins)	0	0	0	0	0	0
Bagwell, 1b (Astros)	2	0	0	0	5	0
Totals	35	6	12	6	27	9

American League	0	0	0	0 0 0	0 0	0—0
National League	1	2	1	0 0 2	0 0	x—6

American League	IP	H	R	ER	BB	SO
Nagy (Indians)	2	4	3	3	0	1
Finley (Angels)	2	3	1	1	0	4
Pavlik (Rangers)	2	3	2	2	0	2
Percival (Angels)	1	1	0	0	0	1
Hernandez (White Sox)	1	1	0	0	0	0

National League	IP	H	R	ER	BB	SO
Smoltz (Braves)	2	2	0	0	0	1
Brown (Marlins)	1	0	0	0	0	0
Glavine (Braves)	1	0	0	0	0	1
Bottalico (Phillies)	1	0	0	0	0	1

1996 REVIEW *All-Star Game*

National League	IP	H	R	ER	BB	SO
P. Martinez (Expos)	1	2	0	0	0	1
Trachsel (Cubs)	1	0	0	0	0	3
Worrell (Dodgers)	1	2	0	0	0	1
Wohlers (Braves)	2/3	1	0	0	0	0
Leiter (Marlins)	1/3	0	0	0	0	0

Winning pitcher—Smoltz. Losing pitcher—Nagy.
*Singled for Smoltz in second. †Grounded out for Nagy in third. ‡Lined out for Finley in fifth. §Ran for Biggio in sixth. ∞Flied out for I. Rodriguez in seventh. ▲Flied out for Pavlik in seventh. ◆Struck out for Boggs in eighth. ■Flied out for Hernandez in ninth. E—Caminiti. DP—A.L. 1, N.L. 1. LOB—A.L. 7, N.L. 5. 2B—Vaughn, Johnson, Piazza, Bichette. 3B—Burks. HR—Piazza, Caminiti. SB—Lofton 2, Johnson 1. CS—Bonds, Johnson. WP—Pavlik. BB—None. SO—By Nagy 1 (McGriff), by Finley 4 (McGriff, Bichette, Biggio, Bagwell), by Pavlik 2 (Piazza, Burks), by Percival 1 (Caminiti), by Smoltz 1 (Belle), by Glavine 1 (Belle), by Bottalico 1 (I. Rodriguez), by P. Martinez 1 (Belle), by Worrell 1 (Fryman). T—2:35. A—62,670. U—Marsh (N.L.), plate; McCoy (A.L.), first; Reliford (N.L.), second; Brinkman (A.L.), third; Poncino (N.L.), left field; Meriwether (A.L.), right field. Official scorers—Jay Dunn, Jerome Holtzman, Bob Kenney.
Players listed on rosters but not used: A.L.—Mesa (Indians), Montgomery (Royals), Pettitte (Yankees), Thomas (White Sox), G. Vaughn (Brewers), Wetteland (Yankees); N.L.—Maddux (Braves).

PLAY BY PLAY

FIRST INNING

A.L.—Lofton singled to center. Lofton stole second. Boggs popped to third. R. Alomar flied to center, Lofton went to third. Belle struck out.

N.L.—Johnson doubled to left-center. Larkin grounded out to second, Johnson went to third. Bonds grounded out to the first baseman, who tossed to the pitcher covering first as Johnson scored. McGriff struck out.

SECOND INNING

A.L.—M. Vaughn doubled to right. I. Rodriguez popped to second. Ripken flied to left. Anderson grounded out to first baseman, who tossed to pitcher covering first.

N.L.—Piazza homered to left. Bichette grounded to second. Jones singled to center. Biggio grounded to third as Jones went to second. H. Rodriguez, pinch-hitting for Smoltz, singled to right, scoring Jones. Johnson grounded to second.

THIRD INNING

A.L.—Brown now pitching. E. Martinez, pinch-hitting for Nagy, grounded to short. Lofton flied to center. Boggs grounded to short.

N.L.—Finley now pitching. Larkin singled to center. Bonds singled to right, Larkin went to second. McGriff struck out into a double play as Bonds was caught stealing, catcher to shortstop. Piazza doubled to right-center, scoring Larkin. Bichette struck out.

FOURTH INNING

A.L.—Glavine now pitching, Bagwell at first. R. Alomar grounded to third. Belle struck out. Vaughn grounded to second.

N.L.—Jones lined to left. Biggio and Bagwell struck out.

FIFTH INNING

A.L.—Bottalico now pitching, Caminiti at third. I. Rodriguez struck out. Ripken flied to left. Anderson reached first on an error by the third baseman. Buhner, pinch-hitting for Finley, lined center.

N.L.—Pavlik now pitching, Buhner in right. Johnson singled to right-center. Johnson stole second. Larkin lined to right. Johnson caught stealing, catcher to third baseman. Bonds grounded to first.

SIXTH INNING

A.L.—P. Martinez now pitching, Smith at shortstop, Burks left field. Lofton singled to right. Boggs flied to left. Lofton stole second. R. Alomar singled to short, Lofton went to third. Belle struck out. M. Vaughn grounded to short.

N.L.—McGwire now at first, Knoblauch at second. Caminiti homered to right. Piazza struck out. Bichette doubled to right. Burks struck out but reached first base on a third-strike wild pitch as Bichette went to third. Biggio forced Burks at second, short to second baseman, as Bichette scored. Young pinch-ran for Biggio. Bagwell forced Young at second, third baseman to second baseman.

SEVENTH INNING

A.L.—Trachsel now pitching, Young at second, Sheffield right field and Hundley catching. S. Alomar, pinch-hitting for Rodriguez, flied to center. Ripken grounded to short. Rodriguez, pinch-hitting for Pavlik, flied to right.

N.L.—Percival now pitching, S. Alomar catching, A. Rodriguez at shortstop, Carter in center field. Johnson singled to center. Smith grounded to second, Johnson went to second. Sheffield popped to second. Caminiti struck out.

EIGHTH INNING

A.L.—Worrell now pitching, Grudzielanek at third. Buhner popped to second. Carter singled to left. Fryman, pinch-hitting for Boggs, struck out. Knoblauch singled to left, Carter went to second. Belle lined to center.

N.L.—Hernandez now pitching, Fryman at third. Hundley flied to center. Grudzielanek grounded to third. Burks tripled to right-center. Young grounded to first baseman, who tossed to pitcher covering first.

NINTH INNING

A.L.—Wohlers now pitching, Kendall catching. McGwire singled to center. S. Alomar grounded into a double play, shortstop to second baseman to first baseman. Wilson, pinch-hitting for Hernandez. Leiter now pitching. Wilson flied to right.

NOTABLE PERFORMANCES

BOX SCORES OF NO-HIT GAMES

AL LEITER

MAY 11

Florida 11, Colorado 0 (N)

COLORADO	AB	R	H	RBI	FLORIDA	AB	R	H	RBI
ung, 2b	4	0	0	0	White, cf	5	0	0	0
iss, ss	3	0	0	0	Arias, ss	5	1	1	0
hette, rf	3	0	0	0	Colbrunn, 1b	5	3	3	0
arraga, 1b	2	0	0	0	Sheffield, rf	1	3	0	0
rks, lf	2	0	0	0	Conine, lf	2	1	1	3
stilla, 3b	3	0	0	0	Pendleton, 3b	4	2	3	5
bbard, cf	2	0	0	0	Johnson, c	4	1	1	3
noz, p	0	0	0	0	Grebeck, 2b	4	0	2	0
es, ph	1	0	0	0	Leiter, p	3	0	0	0
nter, p	0	0	0	0					
wens, c	2	0	0	0					
ompson, p	0	0	0	0					
byan, p	1	0	0	0					
Cracken, ph-cf	2	0	0	0					
TALS	25	0	0	0	TOTALS	33	11	11	11

lorado	0 0 0	0 0 0	0 0 0—0
rida	6 2 0	0 1 2	0 0 x—11

DP—Colorado 1, Florida 2. LOB—Colorado 1, Florida 5. 2B—Conine. —Johnson, Pendleton. S—Leiter.

COLORADO	IP	H	R	ER	BB	SO
ompson (L, 2-3)	1 1/3	7	8	8	3	1
byan	3 2/3	2	1	1	0	5
unoz	2	2	2	2	2	1
inter	1	0	0	0	0	0

FLORIDA	IP	H	R	ER	BB	SO
ter (W, 6-2)	9	0	0	0	2	6

HBP—By Leiter (Burks), by Habyan (Sheffield). WP—Habyan. T—2:22. A—,549. Umpires—HP, Rippley; 1B, Hirschbeck; 2B, Nauert; 3B, Reiker.

DWIGHT GOODEN

MAY 14

New York 2, Seattle 0 (N)

SEATTLE	AB	R	H	RBI	NEW YORK	AB	R	H	RBI
agg, lf	3	0	0	0	Boggs, 3b	4	1	2	0
driguez, ss	2	0	0	0	Girardi, c	3	1	1	0
iffey, cf	3	0	0	0	O'Neill, rf	4	0	1	0
Martinez, dh	3	0	0	0	Sierra, lf	3	0	0	0
naral, pr	0	0	0	0	T. Martinez, 1b	3	0	0	1
hner, rf	4	0	0	0	Leyritz, dh	4	0	2	1
rrento, 1b	3	0	0	0	G. Williams, cf	1	0	0	0
lson, c	3	0	0	0	Eenhoorn, 2b	1	0	0	0
ra, 2b	3	0	0	0	Fox, ph-2b	1	0	0	0
vis, 3b	3	0	0	0	Jeter, ss	3	0	1	0
range, ph-3b	1	0	0	0					
TALS	27	0	0	0	TOTALS	27	2	7	2

Seattle	0 0 0	0 0 0	0 0 0—0
New York	0 0 0	0 0 2	0 0 x—2

E—Wilson, T. Martinez. DP—Seattle 1, New York 1. LOB—Seattle 6, New York 7. SF—T. Martinez. SB—Leyritz. CS—G. Williams 2.

SEATTLE	IP	H	R	ER	BB	SO
Hitchcock (L, 3-2)	5 2/3	6	2	2	4	3
Jackson	1	1	0	0	1	0
Davis	1	0	0	0	0	0
Hurtado	1/3	0	0	0	0	1

NEW YORK	IP	H	R	ER	BB	SO
Gooden (W, 2-3)	9	0	0	0	6	5

WP—Gooden. T—2:43. A—20,786. Umpires—HP, Morrison; 1B, Barnett; 2B, Kosc; 3B, Clark.

HIDEO NOMO

SEPTEMBER 17

Los Angeles 9, Colorado 0 (N)

LOS ANGELES	AB	R	H	RBI	COLORADO	AB	R	H	RBI
Hollandsworth, lf	4	1	0	0	Young, 2b	3	0	0	0
Kirby, cf	4	1	3	0	McCracken, cf	3	0	0	0
Curtis, cf	1	1	0	0	Burks, lf	3	0	0	0
Piazza, c	4	1	0	0	Bichette, rf	3	0	0	0
Karros, 1b	4	0	1	1	Galarraga, 1b	2	0	0	0
Mondesi, rf	5	3	3	2	Castilla, 3b	3	0	0	0
Wallach, 3b	4	2	2	2	Decker, c	2	0	0	0
DeShields, 2b	5	0	1	0	Jones, ph	1	0	0	0
Gagne, ss	4	0	2	1	Reed, c	0	0	0	0
Nomo, p	5	0	1	1	Perez, ss	3	0	0	0
					Swift, p	2	0	0	0
					Reed, p	0	0	0	0
					Rekar, p	0	0	0	0
					Vander Wal, ph	1	0	0	0
					Beckett, p	0	0	0	0
TOTALS	40	9	14	7	TOTALS	26	0	0	0

Los Angeles	0 2 1	0 0 2	0 1 3—9
Colorado	0 0 0	0 0 0	0 0 0—0

E—Burks. DP—Colorado 1. LOB—Los Angeles 9, Colorado 3. 2B—Kirby, Mondesi. HR—Wallach. SB—McCracken, Galarraga. CS—Young.

LOS ANGELES	IP	H	R	ER	BB	SO
Nomo (W, 16-10)	9	0	0	0	4	8

FLORIDA	IP	H	R	ER	BB	SO
Swift (L, 1-1)	*5	7	5	5	2	2
Reed	2	1	0	0	1	3
Rekar	1	3	1	1	0	1
Beckett	1	3	3	3	2	1

*Pitched to four batters in sixth.

WP—Beckett. T— 2:52. A—48,048. U—HP, Hohn; 1B, Rapuano; 2B, Davis; 3B, Tata.

LOW-HIT GAMES

AMERICAN LEAGUE

ONE-HIT GAMES

Date Pitcher(s), Team, Opponent, Result—Player with hit

-13 Steve Sparks (8 innings) and Graeme Lloyd (1 inning), Milwaukee vs. Kansas City, L 2-3—Michael Tucker (home run in fifth)

-3 Ken Hill, Texas at Detroit, W 11-0—Bob Higginson (single in first)

-4 Roger Pavlik, Texas at Detroit, W 3-1—Mark Lewis (home run in fifth)

-2 David Cone (7 innings) and Mariano Rivera (2 innings), New York at Oakland, W 5-0—Jose Herrera (single in ninth)

TWO-HIT GAMES

Date Pitcher(s), Team, Opponent, Result—Player(s) with hit(s)

-12 Mike Mussina, Baltimore vs. Minnesota, W 3-2—Chuck Knoblauch (home run in fourth), Scott Stahoviak (home run in ninth)

-8 Dwight Gooden (8 innings) and Bob Wickman (1 inning), New York vs. Detroit, W 10-3—Alan Trammell (single in first), Chris Gomez (single in first)

-21 Jeff Ware (6 1/3 innings) and Tony Castillo (1 2/3 innings), Toronto at Chicago, L 1-2—Darren Lewis (double in third), Frank Thomas (double in first)

Date	Pitcher(s), Team, Opponent, Result—Player(s) with hit(s)
5-28	Kenny Rogers, New York at California, L 0-1—Randy Velarde (double in ninth), Garret Anderson (single in eighth)
5-30	Tom Gordon, Boston at Seattle, W 10-1—Paul Sorrento (home run in fifth and single in eighth)
6-17	Roger Pavlik, Texas at Baltimore, T 1-1—Rafael Palmeiro (single in sixth), Greg Zaun (single in fifth)
6-20	Pat Hentgen (8 innings) and Mike Timlin (1 inning), Toronto at Oakland, W 1-0—Geronimo Berroa (single in seventh), Ernie Young (double in sixth)
6-23	Kevin Appier (8 innings) and Mike Magnante (1 inning), Kansas City at Baltimore, W 4-0—Roberto Alomar (single in first), Greg Zaun (single in third)
7-23	Dwight Gooden (7 innings), Mariano Rivera (1 inning) and Dale Polley (1 inning), New York vs. Texas, W 6-0—Mark McLemore (double in third), Kevin Elster (double in sixth)
8-2	Orel Hershiser (7 innings) and Danny Graves (2 innings), Cleveland vs. Baltimore, W 11-1—Bobby Bonilla (single in fifth), Greg Zaun (single in third)
8-7	Kevin Appier, Kansas City vs. Oakland, W 7-0—Geronimo Berroa (single in eighth), Tony Batista (single in third)
8-13	Scott Karl (7 innings), Doug Jones (0 innings), Graeme Lloyd ($\frac{1}{3}$ inning) and Bryce Florie ($\frac{2}{3}$ inning), Milwaukee at Baltimore, L 3-4—Rafael Palmeiro (single in first), Chris Hoiles (single in fourth)
9-15	Salomon Torres, Seattle at Minnesota, W 7-0—Chuck Knoblauch (single in third), Marty Cordova (single in second)
9-16	Jimmy Key (8 innings) and Dave Weathers (1 inning), New York at Toronto, W 10-0—Charlie O'Brien (single in eighth), Tomas Perez (single in sixth)
9-21	Woody Williams ($5\frac{2}{3}$ innings) and Scott Brow ($2\frac{1}{3}$ innings), Toronto at Baltimore, L 3-6—Eddie Murray (home run in sixth), Chris Hoiles (single in sixth)

NATIONAL LEAGUE
ONE-HIT GAMES

Date	Pitcher(s), Team, Opponent, Result—Player with hit
5-13	Steve Trachsel, Chicago vs. Houston, W 6-0—Brian L. Hunter (double in first)
9-3	Dave Burba (6 innings) and Jeff Shaw (3 innings), Cincinnati vs. Atlanta, W 5-1—Marquis Grissom (home run in first)
9-22	John Smiley, Cincinnati vs. St. Louis, W 6-0—Royce Clayton (single in fourth)

TWO-HIT GAMES

Date	Pitcher(s), Team, Opponent, Result—Player(s) with hit(s)
4-12	John Burkett, Florida at Los Angeles, W 3-1—Brett Butler (single in seventh), Raul Mondesi (home run in eighth)
4-14	John Smoltz (8 innings) and Mark Wohlers (1 inning), Atlanta at San Diego, W 4-0—Steve Finley (single in ninth), Tony Gwynn (double in seventh)
4-20	Alan Benes (8 innings) and Dennis Eckersley (1 inning), St. Louis at Philadelphia, W 1-0—Mickey Morandini (single in eighth) Mark Whiten (single in fifth)
5-1	Pedro Martinez, Montreal at New York, W 4-0—Kevin Roberson (single in seventh), Butch Huskey (single in seventh)
5-12	Jim Bullinger, Chicago at New York, W 3-0—Jeff Kent (single in fifth and single in eighth)
6-19	John Smoltz, Atlanta vs. San Diego, W 5-1—Chris Gomez (double in seventh), Tony Gwynn (double in seventh)
6-29	Jeff Fassero, Montreal at Philadelphia, W 1-0—Gregg Jefferies (double in seventh), Curt Schilling (single in sixth)
7-13	John Smoltz, Atlanta vs. Florida, W 3-0—Kurt Abbott (single in first), Joe Orsulak (single in eighth)
7-14	William VanLandingham ($7\frac{2}{3}$ innings), Jim Poole ($\frac{1}{3}$ inning), Doug Creek ($\frac{1}{3}$ inning) and Mark Dewey ($\frac{2}{3}$ inning), San Francisco at Los Angeles, W 6-0—Raul Mondesi (single in eighth), Mike Blowers (single in eighth)
7-17	Al Leiter (6 innings), Donn Pall (1 inning), Jay Powell (1 inning) and Robb Nen (1 inning), Florida vs. Houston, W 11-2—Derek Bell (home run in third), Randy Knorr (double in fourth)
7-24	Terrell Wade (5 innings), Brad Clontz (2 innings) and Greg McMichael (2 innings), Atlanta at St. Louis, W 4-1—Royce Clayton (single in first), Gary Gaetti (single in third)
7-28	Al Leiter ($6\frac{2}{3}$ innings), Jay Powell ($1\frac{1}{3}$ innings) and Robb Nen (1 inning), Florida vs. San Diego, W 8-2—Steve Finley (double in fourth), Ken Caminiti (single in fourth)
8-13	Al Leiter (7 innings), Jay Powell (1 inning) and Robb Nen (1 inning), Florida vs. Colorado, W 5-0—Andres Galarraga (double in seventh), Dante Bichette (single in fifth)
8-20	Kevin Foster (5 innings), Terry Adams (3 innings) and Turk Wendell (1 inning), Chicago vs. Florida, W 8-1—Luis Castillo (single in third), Craig Grebeck (single in fifth)
8-21	Curt Schilling, Philadelphia at Los Angeles, W 6-0—Wayne Kirby (single in first), Raul Mondesi (single in fifth)
8-24	Pedro Martinez (8 innings) and Mel Rojas (1 inning), Montreal at San Francisco, W 3-0—Rick Wilkins (single in second and single in seventh)
8-30	Scott Sanders (8 innings) and Mike Oquist (1 inning), San Diego at Montreal, W 6-0—F.P. Santangelo (single in ninth), David Segui (double in second)
9-6	Danny Darwin (7 innings) and Xavier Hernandez (2 innings), Houston vs. Colorado, W 2-1—Ellis Burks (double in third), Walt Weiss (single in fifth)
9-12	Hideo Nomo (8 innings) and Antonio Osuna (1 inning), Los Angeles vs. St. Louis, W 4-1—Ron Gant (home run in sixth), Dmitri Young (single in eighth)
9-22	Rick Helling (8 innings) and Chris Hammond (1 inning), Florida vs. Houston, W 6-0—Craig Biggio (single in seventh), Jeff Bagwell (single in ninth)
9-24	Ramon Martinez (7 innings), Antonio Osuna (1 inning) and Todd Worrell (1 inning), Los Angeles vs. San Francisco, W 6-2—Desi Wilson (single in fifth), Allen Watson (single in fifth)

15-STRIKEOUT GAMES

Date	Pitcher, Team, Opponent	IP	H	R	ER	BB	SO	Result
4-13	Hideo Nomo, Los Angeles vs. Florida..................	9	3	1	1	3	17	W 3-1
9-18	Roger Clemens, Boston at Detroit	9	5	0	0	0	20	W 4-0

10-STRIKEOUT GAMES

AMERICAN LEAGUE

Team	No.	Pitchers
Boston	12	Roger Clemens 8, Tom Gordon 3, Tim Wakefield 1.
Chicago	7	Alex Fernandez 4, Wilson Alvarez 3.
California	6	Chuck Finley 5, Shawn Boskie 1.
Kansas City	5	Kevin Appier 5.
Minnesota	4	Rick Aguilera 1, Rich Robertson 1, LaTroy Hawkins 1, Brad Radke 1.
Toronto	4	Juan Guzman 2, Pat Hentgen 2.
Baltimore	3	David Wells 1, Mike Mussina 1, Rocky Coppinger 1.
Oakland	2	Willie Adams 2.
Seattle	2	Randy Johnson 2.
Cleveland	1	Charles Nagy 1.
Milwaukee	1	Ben McDonald 1.
New York	1	Andy Pettitte 1.
Texas	1	Roger Pavlik 1.
Detroit	0	None.

NATIONAL LEAGUE

Team	No.	Pitchers
Atlanta	13	John Smoltz 12, Tom Glavine 1.
Montreal	10	Pedro Martinez 6, Jeff Fassero 4.
Philadelphia	10	Curt Schilling 8, Sid Fernandez 2.
Houston	7	Darryl Kile 4, Shane Reynolds 2, Doug Drabek 1.
Pittsburgh	7	Denny Neagle 3, Paul Wagner 3, Jason Schmidt 1.
St. Louis	6	Todd Stottlemyre 2, Andy Benes 2, Alan Benes 2.
Los Angeles	5	Hideo Nomo 3, Ramon Martinez 1, Ismael Valdes 1.
San Diego	5	Joey Hamilton 3, Scott Sanders 2.
San Francisco	5	Mark Gardner 2, Mark Leiter 1, Shawn Estes 1, Osvaldo Fernandez 1.
Cincinnati	4	Mark Portugal 1, John Smiley 1, Dave Burba 1, Pete Schourek 1.
New York	3	Bobby Jones 1, Jason Isringhausen 1, Paul Wilson 1.
Florida	2	Kevin Brown 1, Al Leiter 1.
Chicago	0	None.
Colorado	0	None.

1-0 GAMES

AMERICAN LEAGUE

Date	Winner	Loser	Inn.*	Site
5-28	Jason Grimsley, California	Kenny Rogers, New York	9	California
6-20	†Pat Hentgen, Toronto	†Don Wengert, Oakland	3	Oakland
6-30	†Ryan Hancock, California	John Wasdin, Oakland	1	California
7-22	†Chuck Finley, California	Omar Olivares, Detroit	3	California
7-28	Pat Hentgen, Toronto	†Ariel Prieto, Oakland	6	Toronto
8-22	Erik Hanson, Toronto	Alex Fernandez, Chicago	6	Chicago

PLAYERS HITTING HOME RUNS IN 1-0 GAMES: 7-22—Jim Edmonds, California; 7-28—Carlos Delgado, Toronto.
*Inning in which run scored. †Did not pitch complete game.

NATIONAL LEAGUE

Date	Winner	Loser	Inn.*	Site
4-6	†Robb Nen, Florida	†Mark Dewey, San Francisco	10	Florida
4-8	Hideo Nomo, Los Angeles	†Tom Glavine, Atlanta	3	Los Angeles
4-19	†Cory Bailey, St. Louis	†Russ Springer, Philadelphia	9	Philadelphia
4-20	†Alan Benes, St. Louis	†Ricky Bottalico, Philadelphia	9	Philadelphia
4-26	†Pedro Astacio, Los Angeles	†Steve Trachsel, Chicago	5	Los Angeles
5-11	†John Smiley, Cincinnati	Joey Hamilton, San Diego	1	Cincinnati
5-19‡	†Allen Watson, San Francisco	†Jason Isringhausen, New York	6	San Francisco
5-26	†Bobby Jones, New York	†Sean Bergman, San Diego	1	New York
5-30	†Paul Wilson, New York	Allen Watson, San Francisco	8	New York
6-2	†Ismael Valdes, Los Angeles	†Mark Clark, New York	6	New York
6-17	†Osvaldo Fernandez, San Francisco	†Al Leiter, Florida	4	San Francisco
6-23	†Tom Glavine, Atlanta	†Osvaldo Fernandez, San Francisco	4	Atlanta
6-29	Jeff Fassero, Montreal	†Curt Schilling, Philadelphia	8	Philadelphia
7-15	†Mark Guthrie, Los Angeles	†Trevor Hoffman, San Diego	10	Los Angeles
7-22	†Shane Reynolds, Houston	Joey Hamilton, San Diego	1	Houston
8-6	†Tim Worrell, San Diego	†Donovan Osborne, St. Louis	4	St. Louis
8-7	†Mark Petkovsek, St. Louis	†Doug Bochtler, San Diego	9	St. Louis
8-23	†Donovan Osborne, St. Louis	†Darryl Kile, Houston	3	Houston
8-26	†William VanLandingham, San Francisco	†Curt Schilling, Philadelphia	1	San Francisco
9-10	†Mark Petkovsek, St. Louis	†Kirk Rueter, San Francisco	6	San Francisco

PLAYERS HITTING HOME RUNS IN 1-0 GAMES: 4-6—Terry Pendleton, Florida; 4-26—Delino DeShields, Los Angeles; 5-26—Bernard Gilkey, New York; 6-17—Barry Bonds, San Francisco; 6-23—Chipper Jones, Atlanta; 8-6—Ken Caminiti, San Diego; 8-7—Gary Gaetti, St. Louis; 8-23—Ray Lankford, St. Louis.
*Inning in which run scored. †Did not pitch complete game. ‡First game of doubleheader.

FOUR OR MORE HITS IN ONE GAME

AMERICAN LEAGUE

Team	No.	Hitters
Minnesota	20	Paul Molitor 4, Rich Becker 3, Marty Cordova 3, Matt Lawton 3, Greg Myers 2, Chuck Knoblauch 2, Roberto Kelly 1, Pat Meares 1, Ron Coomer 1.
Baltimore	18	Roberto Alomar 6, Cal Ripken 3, Rafael Palmeiro 2, Brady Anderson 2, B.J. Surhoff 1, Luis Polonia 1, Mike Devereaux 1, Chris Hoiles 1, Jeffrey Hammonds 1.

Team	No.	Hitters
California	18	Chili Davis 3, Tim Salmon 3, Garret Anderson 3, Rex Hudler 2, Randy Velarde 2, Jim Edmonds 2, Jack Howell 1, Gary DiSarcina 1, J.T. Snow 1.
Seattle	18	Joey Cora 4, Alex Rodriguez 4, Edgar Martinez 2, Brian Hunter 2, Dan Wilson 2, Jay Buhner 1, Ken Griffey 1, Luis Sojo 1, Dave Hollins 1.
Texas	17	Rusty Greer 5, Kevin Elster 2, Darryl Hamilton 2, Dean Palmer 2, Ivan Rodriguez 2, Mark McLemore 1, Kurt Stillwell 1, Juan Gonzalez 1, Warren Newson 1.
Chicago	16	Harold Baines 3, Dave Martinez 3, Ozzie Guillen 2, Robin Ventura 2, Ray Durham 2, Danny Tartabull 1, Ron Karkovice 1, Darren Lewis 1, Norberto Martin 1.
Cleveland	16	Kevin Seitzer 2, Omar Vizquel 2, Albert Belle 2, Jim Thome 2, Kenny Lofton 2, Manny Ramirez 2, Tony Pena 1, Julio Franco 1, Eddie Murray 1, Jeromy Burnitz 1.
New York	15	Bernie Williams 3, Wade Boggs 2, Paul O'Neill 2, Tino Martinez 2, Derek Jeter 2, Cecil Fielder 1, Mariano Duncan 1, Joe Girardi 1, Gerald Williams 1.
Oakland	14	Jason Giambi 2, Geronimo Berroa 2, Mike Bordick 2, Scott Brosius 2, Tony Batista 2, Pedro Munoz 2, Ernie Young 1, Damon Mashore 1.
Boston	13	Mo Vaughn 5, John Valentin 2, Mike Greenwell 1, Jose Canseco 1, Bill Haselman 1, Reggie Jefferson 1, Jeff Frye 1, Wil Cordero 1.
Toronto	12	Carlos Delgado 3, John Olerud 2, Joe Carter 1, Charlie O'Brien 1, Ed Sprague 1, Domingo Cedeno 1, Alex Gonzalez 1, Robert Perez 1, Julio Mosquera 1.
Detroit	8	Bob Higginson 3, Mark Lewis 2, Chad Curtis 1, Melvin Nieves 1, Curtis Pride 1.
Milwaukee	8	Jose Valentin 2, Jeff Cirillo 2, Kevin Seitzer 1, Chuck Carr 1, John Jaha 1, Fernando Vina 1.
Kansas City	5	Jose Offerman 2, Tom Goodwin 2, Craig Paquette 1.

NATIONAL LEAGUE

Team	No.	Hitters
Atlanta	26	Fred McGriff 8, Marquis Grissom 4, Chipper Jones 4, Javy Lopez 3, Jeff Blauser 2, Terry Pendleton 1, Luis Polonia 1, Mark Lemke 1, Ryan Klesko 1, Andruw Jones 1.
Colorado	17	Eric Young 6, Dante Bichette 4, Ellis Burks 3, Larry Walker 2, Vinny Castilla 1, Quinton Mccracken 1.
Houston	15	Jeff Bagwell 4, Derek Bell 3, Craig Biggio 2, John Cangelosi 1, Sean Berry 1, Rick Wilkins 1, James Mouton 1, Brian L. Hunter 1, Orlando Miller 1.
Los Angeles	15	Raul Mondesi 6, Todd Hollandsworth 3, Mike Piazza 2, Roger Cedeno 2, Brett Butler 1, Eric Karros 1.
New York	14	Lance Johnson 3, Rey Ordonez 2, Jose Vizcaino 2, Bernard Gilkey 2, Todd Hundley 1, Rico Brogna 1, Edgardo Alfonzo 1, Alex Ochoa 1.
Pittsburgh	14	Jeff King 6, Carlos Garcia 2, Jermaine Allensworth 2, Nelson Liriano 1, Orlando Merced 1, Al Martin 1, Mark Johnson 1.
St. Louis	14	John Mabry 6, Willie McGee 2, Brian Jordan 2, Gary Gaetti 1, Ray Lankford 1, Royce Clayton 1, Terry Bradshaw 1.
Florida	14	Edgar Renteria 4, Terry Pendleton 2, Devon White 2, Gary Sheffield 2, Jeff Conine 2, Andre Dawson 1, Alex Arias 1.
San Diego	13	Tony Gwynn 3, Steve Finley 3, Chris Gomez 2, Rickey Henderson 1, Craig Shipley 1, Ken Caminiti 1, Andy Ashby 1, Marc Newfield 1.
Montreal	12	Mark Grudzielanek 6, David Segui 3, Darrin Fletcher 1, Shane Andrews 1, F.P. Santangelo 1.
Chicago	9	Brian McRae 2, Ryne Sandberg 1, Mark Grace 1, Sammy Sosa 1, Jose Hernandez 1, Scott Bullett 1, Tyler Houston 1, Brant Brown 1.
Cincinnati	8	Eric Davis 1, Barry Larkin 1, Hal Morris 1, Lenny Harris 1, Thomas Howard 1, Reggie Sanders 1, Bret Boone 1, Willie Greene 1.
Philadelphia	8	Mickey Morandini 2, Jim Eisenreich 1, Lenny Dykstra 1, Gregg Jefferies 1, Ruben Amaro 1, Kevin Stocker 1, Ricky Otero 1.
San Francisco	7	Barry Bonds 2, Marvin Benard 2, Glenallen Hill 1, Mark Carreon 1, Rick Wilkins 1.

FIVE- AND SIX-HIT GAMES

Date	Player, Team, Opponent	AB	R	H	2B	3B	HR	RBI	Result
4-7	Craig Shipley, San Diego at Houston	5	4	5	2	0	1	1	W 17-2
4-24	Greg Myers, Minnesota at Detroit	6	3	5	2	0	0	5	W24-11
4-27	Eric Young, Colorado vs. Montreal	6	2	5	1	0	0	0	W 6-5
4-28	Mark Grudzielanek, Montreal at Colorado	7	2	5	1	0	0	2	W 21-9
4-30	Fred McGriff, Atlanta at Houston	5	2	5	0	0	1	2	W 7-5
5-1	Bernie Williams, New York at Baltimore	8	2	5	2	0	1	1	W 11-6
5-1	Gerald Williams, New York at Baltimore	8	1	6	0	0	1	3	W 11-6
5-12	Mark Grudzielanek, Montreal vs. Houston	5	3	5	0	0	0	0	W 7-6
5-17	Rafael Palmeiro, Baltimore vs. Seattle	6	1	5	1	0	1	6	W14-13
5-23	Steve Finley, San Diego vs. Philadelphia	5	2	5	1	0	1	2	W 7-5
5-26	Rex Hudler, California vs. Boston	5	3	5	0	0	1	2	W 12-2
5-27	Bernie Williams, New York at California	7	3	5	0	0	0	3	W 16-5
5-31	Roger Cedeno, Los Angeles at New York	5	1	5	0	0	0	1	W 10-3
6-1	Chuck Knoblauch, Minnesota at Texas	5	3	5	0	0	0	0	W 9-5
6-5	Mo Vaughn, Boston vs. Chicago	6	1	5	1	0	0	0	L 6-8
6-10	Jeff Blauser, Atlanta at New York	5	0	5	0	0	0	0	L 3-8
6-11	Dan Wilson, Seattle at Minnesota	6	2	5	1	0	0	3	W 18-8
6-11	Scott Bullett, Chicago at Philadelphia	5	2	5	0	0	1	4	W 9-2
6-22	Brant Brown, Chicago at San Diego	9	1	5	1	0	1	2	W 9-6

Player, Team, Opponent	AB	R	H	2B	3B	HR	RBI	Result
Luis Sojo, Seattle vs. Texas	6	2	5	0	0	0	2	W 19-8
Dante Bichette, Colorado vs. Los Angeles	6	2	5	1	0	1	4	W16-15
Todd Hollandsworth, Los Angeles at San Diego	5	1	5	0	1	1	3	W 10-2
Jason Giambi, Oakland at Seattle	5	2	5	2	0	0	1	W 11-6
Alex Ochoa, New York at Philadelphia	5	3	5	2	1	1	3	W 10-6
John Mabry, St. Louis at Pittsburgh	5	2	5	0	0	0	2	W 9-5
Kenny Lofton, Cleveland vs. Minnesota	6	2	5	1	0	0	0	W 6-5
Rusty Greer, Texas vs. Oakland	5	2	5	1	0	1	2	L 8-11
Juan Gonzalez, Texas vs. New York	5	3	5	1	0	2	2	W 15-2
Fred McGriff, Atlanta vs. Chicago	5	2	5	1	0	4	6	W 6-5
Jeff King, Pittsburgh at Colorado	5	2	5	1	0	1	3	L 9-13
Paul Molitor, Minnesota at Toronto	5	0	5	0	0	0	1	W 6-4
Alex Rodriguez, Seattle vs. Baltimore	5	3	5	2	0	0	2	W 9-6
Fernando Vina, Milwaukee at Texas	6	4	5	0	1	2	3	W 15-4
Terry Pendleton, Atlanta at New York	5	3	5	1	0	0	0	L 5-6
Garret Anderson, California at Texas	7	0	6	0	0	0	3	W 4-3

HITTING STREAKS OF 15 OR MORE GAMES

AMERICAN LEAGUE

Player, Team	Span of streak
Marty Cordova, Minnesota	June 5-June 29
Roberto Alomar, Baltimore	May 12-June 8
Albert Belle, Cleveland	Apr. 27-May 21
Randy Velarde, California	June 9-July 4
Juan Gonzalez, Texas	June 25-July 19
Juan Gonzalez, Texas	Aug. 8-Aug. 31
Alex Rodriguez, Seattle	Aug. 16-Sept. 4
Jason Giambi, Oakland	Apr. 7-Apr. 30
Ivan Rodriguez, Texas	May 28-June 19
Tim Naehring, Boston	May 9-May 28
Joey Cora, Seattle	July 12-July 30
Reggie Jefferson, Boston	Aug. 22-Sept. 20
Sandy Alomar, Cleveland	Apr. 11-May 4
Derek Jeter, New York	Sep. 7-Sept. 25
Mo Vaughn, Boston	June 12-June 29
Frank Thomas, Chicago	Mar. 31-Apr. 19
Rafael Palmeiro, Baltimore	June 2-June 17
Greg Vaughn, Milwaukee	June 14-June 29
Robin Ventura, Chicago	June 23-July 7
Manny Ramirez, Cleveland	June 29-July 16

NATIONAL LEAGUE

G	Player, Team	Span of streak
29	Hal Morris, Cincinnati	Aug. 27-Sept. 29
28	Marquis Grissom, Atlanta	July 25-Aug. 24
27	John Flaherty, San Diego	June 21-July 27
22	Edgar Renteria, Florida	July 25-Aug. 16
21	Greg Colbrunn, Florida	May 31-June 23
	Steve Finley, San Diego	June 20-July 14
19	Mike Blowers, Los Angeles	June 18-July 6
	Mike Piazza, Los Angeles	Aug. 22-Sept. 12
18	Chipper Jones, Atlanta	Aug. 6-Aug. 24
17	Mark Grudzielanek, Montreal	Apr. 7-Apr. 25
	Eric Young, Colorado	June 3-June 21
	Lance Johnson, New York	Aug. 31-Sept. 18
16	Mike Piazza, Los Angeles	Apr. 16-May 3
	Mark Grace, Chicago	Aug. 5-Aug. 23

MULTI-HOMER GAMES

AMERICAN LEAGUE

Team	No.	Hitters
Seattle	23	Ken Griffey 7, Jay Buhner 5, Edgar Martinez 4, Alex Rodriguez 3, Paul Sorrento 2, Dan Wilson 2.
Baltimore	21	Brady Anderson 7, Cal Ripken 3, Rafael Palmeiro 2, B.J. Surhoff 2, Roberto Alomar 2, Chris Hoiles 2, Bobby Bonilla 1, Eddie Murray 1, Todd Zeile 1.
Oakland	20	Mark McGwire 5, Geronimo Berroa 4, Scott Brosius 4, Terry Steinbach 3, Ernie Young 1, Jason Giambi 1, Jose Herrera 1, Tony Batista 1.
Texas	17	Juan Gonzalez 5, Mickey Tettleton 4, Dean Palmer 3, Kevin Elster 2, Ivan Rodriguez 2, Warren Newson 1.
Boston	16	Mo Vaughn 6, Reggie Jefferson 3, Jose Canseco 2, John Valentin 2, Mike Greenwell 1, Tim Naehring 1, Milt Cuyler 1.
Detroit	14	Cecil Fielder 4, Melvin Nieves 2, Tony Clark 2, Travis Fryman 1, Mark Lewis 1, John Flaherty 1, Bob Higginson 1, Phil Nevin 1, Raul Casanova 1.
Milwaukee	13	Dave Nilsson 4, Greg Vaughn 3, John Jaha 2, Kevin Seitzer 1, Fernando Vina 1, Matt Mieske 1, Jeff Cirillo 1.
New York	13	Darryl Strawberry 3, Ruben Sierra 3, Bernie Williams 3, Tim Raines 2, Cecil Fielder 2.
Cleveland	11	Albert Belle 4, Jim Thome 3, Manny Ramirez 2, Julio Franco 1, Jeromy Burnitz 1.
Toronto	10	Ed Sprague 3, Joe Carter 2, Charlie O'Brien 1, John Olerud 1, Jacob Brumfield 1, Carlos Delgado 1, Robert Perez 1.
California	7	Chili Davis 2, Tim Wallach 1, Pat Borders 1, Tim Salmon 1, J.T. Snow 1, Jim Edmonds 1.
Chicago	6	Robin Ventura 3, Harold Baines 1, Frank Thomas 1, Chris Snopek 1.
Minnesota	5	Greg Myers 1, Chuck Knoblauch 1, Rich Becker 1, Ron Coomer 1, Marty Cordova 1.
Kansas City	4	Mike Macfarlane 2, Bob Hamelin 1, Joe Vitiello 1.

NATIONAL LEAGUE

Team	No.	Hitters
Colorado	20	Andres Galarraga 8, Vinny Castilla 4, Ellis Burks 3, Dante Bichette 2, Larry Walker 2, Eric Anthony 1.
Atlanta	16	Fred McGriff 3, Javy Lopez 3, Chipper Jones 3, Ryan Klesko 2, Jeff Blauser 1, Mark Lemke 1, Dave Justice 1, Eddie Perez 1, Andruw Jones 1.

Notable performances

Team	No.	Hitters
Montreal	12	Henry Rodriguez 5, Shane Andrews 2, Darrin Fletcher 1, David Segui 1, Moises Alou 1, Sherman Obando 1, M Lansing 1.
Philadelphia	12	Pete Incaviglia 3, Benito Santiago 2, Todd Zeile 2, Jim Eisenreich 1, Mark Whiten 1, Kevin Stocker 1, J.R. Phil 1, Scott Rolen 1.
Chicago	11	Sammy Sosa 5, Ryne Sandberg 3, Brian McRae 1, Leo Gomez 1, Brant Brown 1.
San Diego	11	Ken Caminiti 7, Steve Finley 3, Wally Joyner 1.
New York	10	Todd Hundley 3, Bernard Gilkey 3, Lance Johnson 1, Rico Brogna 1, Butch Huskey 1, Edgardo Alfonzo 1.
St. Louis	10	Tom Pagnozzi 3, Ray Lankford 3, Gary Gaetti 2, Ron Gant 1, Brian Jordan 1.
Cincinnati	9	Barry Larkin 3, Eric Davis 2, Reggie Sanders 2, Eric Anthony 1, Willie Greene 1.
Pittsburgh	6	Jeff King 2, Orlando Merced 1, Al Martin 1, Mark Johnson 1, Jermaine Allensworth 1.
Houston	5	Jeff Bagwell 2, Craig Biggio 1, Derrick May 1, Derek Bell 1.
Los Angeles	5	Mike Piazza 2, Eric Karros 1, Raul Mondesi 1, Todd Hollandsworth 1.
San Francisco	5	Barry Bonds 3, Glenallen Hill 1, Mark Carreon 1.
Florida	5	Gary Sheffield 3, Jeff Conine 2.

THREE-HOMER GAMES

Date	Player, Team, Opponent	AB	R	H	2B	3B	HR	RBI	Res
4-11	Dan Wilson, Seattle at Detroit	4	3	3	0	0	3	4	W 9
4-16	Cecil Fielder, Detroit at Toronto	4	3	3	0	0	3	5	W 13
5-10	Ernie Young, Oakland vs. Minnesota	5	4	4	0	0	3	6	W 15
5-22	Geronimo Berroa, Oakland at New York	4	3	4	0	0	3	3	W 5
5-24	Ken Griffey, Seattle vs. New York	4	5	4	0	0	3	6	W 10
5-28	Cal Ripken, Baltimore at Seattle	5	3	3	0	0	3	8	W 12
6-5	Sammy Sosa, Chicago vs. Philadelphia	4	3	3	0	0	3	5	W 9
6-29	Mike Piazza, Los Angeles at Colorado	5	3	3	0	0	3	6	W 13-
7-6	Edgar Martinez, Seattle at Texas	3	3	3	0	0	3	3	W 9
8-6	Darryl Strawberry, New York vs. Chicago	4	3	3	0	0	3	4	W 9
8-12	Geronimo Berroa, Oakland vs. Minnesota	5	3	4	0	0	3	5	W 11
9-15	Frank Thomas, Chicago at Boston	4	4	3	0	0	3	3	L 8
9-15	Benito Santiago, Philadelphia at Chicago	3	3	3	0	0	3	6	W 6
9-24	Mo Vaughn, Boston vs. Baltimore	5	3	4	0	0	3	5	W 13
9-24	Willie Greene, Cincinnati vs. Chicago	4	3	4	0	0	3	5	W 6

GRAND SLAMS

AMERICAN LEAGUE

Date	Batter, Team	Pitcher, Team	Inn.*	Site
4-2	Jim Edmonds, California	Ricky Bones, Milwaukee	5	California
4-6	Paul Sorrento, Seattle	Steve Sparks, Milwaukee	1	Seattle
4-9	Cecil Fielder, Detroit	Bob Wells, Seattle	4	Detroit
4-15	Mike Aldrete, California	Edwin Hurtado, Seattle	4	Seattle
4-16	Dan Wilson, Seattle	Jim Abbott, California	7	Seattle
4-18	Alex Rodriguez, Seattle	Clint Sodowsky, Detroit	2	Seattle
4-19	Kevin Elster, Texas	Manny Alexander, Baltimore	8	Texas
4-21	Dean Palmer, Texas	David Wells, Baltimore	3	Texas
4-22	Joe Carter, Toronto	Tim Davis, Seattle	5	Seattle
4-26	Bernie Williams, New York	Brad Radke, Minnesota	6	New York
4-28	Jay Buhner, Seattle	Steve Sparks, Milwaukee	5	Milwaukee
5-1	Tino Martinez, New York	Jimmy Myers, Baltimore	15	Baltimore
5-1	Mark McGwire, Oakland	Phil Leftwich, California	4	Oakland
5-4	Roberto Alomar, Baltimore	Kevin Wickander, Milwaukee	6	Baltimore
5-4	Harold Baines, Chicago	Jim Mecir, New York	9	New York
5-11	Rusty Greer, Texas	Scott Aldred, Detroit	1	Texas
5-14	B.J. Surhoff, Baltimore	Carlos Reyes, Oakland	6	Oakland
5-17	Alex Rodriguez, Seattle	Alan Mills, Baltimore	8	Baltimore
5-17	Chris Hoiles, Baltimore	Norm Charlton, Seattle	9	Baltimore
5-17	Manny Ramirez, Cleveland	Gil Heredia, Texas	7	Cleveland
5-18	Ray Durham, Chicago	Greg Keagle, Detroit	4	Detroit
5-19	Robin Ventura, Chicago	Greg Gohr, Detroit	3	Detroit
5-19	Darren Lewis, Chicago	Gregg Olson, Detroit	9	Detroit
5-27	John Olerud, Toronto	Alex Fernandez, Chicago	3	Toronto
5-28	Cal Ripken, Baltimore	Mike Jackson, Seattle	7	Seattle
5-30	Jose Canseco, Boston	Salomon Torres, Seattle	5	Seattle
6-5	Chuck Knoblauch, Minnesota	Mark Eichhorn, California	4	Minnesota
6-6	B.J. Surhoff, Baltimore	Felipe Lira, Detroit	1	Baltimore
6-8†	George Williams, Oakland	Greg Hansell, Minnesota	5	Minnesota
6-9	Tim Naehring, Boston	Ricky Bones, Milwaukee	1	Boston
6-12	Damon Buford, Texas	Kevin Wickander, Milwaukee	5	Texas
6-16	John Jaha, Milwaukee	Doug Johns, Oakland	3	Milwaukee
6-17	Terry Steinbach, Oakland	Gregg Olson, Detroit	10	Detroit

ate	Batter, Team	Pitcher, Team	Inn.*	Site
18	Omar Vizquel, Cleveland	Aaron Sele, Boston	2	Cleveland
18	Jose Valentin, Milwaukee	Julio Valera, Kansas City	7	Milwaukee
27	Geronimo Berroa, Oakland	Shad Williams, California	4	California
30	Matt Lawton, Minnesota	Mark Gubicza, Kansas City	3	Kansas City
3	Ed Sprague, Toronto	Rick Krivda, Baltimore	5	Toronto
4	Paul Sorrento, Seattle	Dennis Cook, Texas	9	Texas
5	Matt Stairs, Oakland	Ryan Hancock, California	1	Oakland
6	Alex Rodriguez, Seattle	Kevin Gross, Texas	4	Texas
7	Cecil Fielder, Detroit	Jeff Ware, Toronto	1	Detroit
11	Manny Ramirez, Cleveland	Brad Radke, Minnesota	2	Minnesota
12	Mo Vaughn, Boston	Omar Olivares, Detroit	2	Detroit
16	Greg Vaughn, Milwaukee	Jeff Mccurry, Detroit	4	Milwaukee
22	Doug Strange, Seattle	Jose Mercedes, Milwaukee	8	Seattle
23	Terry Steinbach, Oakland	Alex Fernandez, Chicago	6	Chicago
27	Rafael Palmeiro, Baltimore	Orel Hershiser, Cleveland	6	Baltimore
27	J.T. Snow, California	Ben McDonald, Milwaukee	2	California
28	Arquimedez Pozo, Boston	Eddie Guardado, Minnesota	9	Minnesota
30	Rusty Greer, Texas	Jim Mecir, New York	5	Texas
31	Albert Belle, Cleveland	Bill Risley, Toronto	9	Cleveland
1	Tony Clark, Detroit	Greg Gohr, California	6	Detroit
2	Travis Fryman, Detroit	Rafael Carmona, Seattle	7	Detroit
4	Harold Baines, Chicago	Ed Vosberg, Texas	8	Texas
5	Mike Matheny, Milwaukee	Willie Adams, Oakland	2	Oakland
5	Kevin Elster, Texas	Wilson Alvarez, Chicago	4	Texas
10	Johnny Damon, Kansas City	Jim Abbott, California	1	California
10	Eddie Murray, Baltimore	Jeff Darwin, Chicago	9	Chicago
13	Robin Ventura, Chicago	Dave Weathers, New York	5	Chicago
18	Jim Thome, Cleveland	Gregg Olson, Detroit	8	Cleveland
20	Manny Ramirez, Cleveland	Jeff Russell, Texas	6	Cleveland
22	Paul Sorrento, Seattle	Rocky Coppinger, Baltimore	5	Baltimore
24	Darren Bragg, Boston	Randy Johnson, Seattle	6	Boston
25	Randy Velarde, California	Scott Erickson, Baltimore	4	Baltimore
26	Chris Hoiles, Baltimore	Carlos Reyes, Oakland	3	Baltimore
28	Albert Belle, Cleveland	A.J. Sager, Detroit	6	Detroit
29	Garret Anderson, California	Wally Whitehurst, New York	1	California
29	Mark Whiten, Seattle	Randy Myers, Baltimore	9	Seattle
30	Pete Incaviglia, Baltimore	Sterling Hitchcock, Seattle	6	Seattle
1	Julio Franco, Cleveland	John Burkett, Texas	5	Texas
2	Mike Greenwell, Boston	Bobby Ayala, Seattle	7	Seattle
12	Bernie Williams, New York	Jose Lima, Detroit	9	Detroit
13	Mark Whiten, Seattle	Jose Parra, Minnesota	7	Minnesota
14	Danny Tartabull, Chicago	Mark Brandenburg, Boston	8	Boston
15	Bobby Bonilla, Baltimore	Brian Williams, Detroit	8	Detroit
17	Kevin Seitzer, Cleveland	Alex Fernandez, Chicago	2	Chicago
20	Frank Thomas, Chicago	Rich Robertson, Minnesota	2	Chicago
21	Eddie Murray, Baltimore	Scott Brow, Toronto	6	Baltimore
21	Jeromy Burnitz, Milwaukee	Todd Van Poppel, Detroit	2	Milwaukee
22	Mark McGwire, Oakland	Matt Wagner, Seattle	5	Seattle

*Inning in which grand slam was hit. †Second game of doubleheader

NATIONAL LEAGUE

ate	Batter, Team	Pitcher, Team	Inn.*	Site
6	Ken Caminiti, San Diego	Alvin Morman, Houston	13	Houston
6	Vinny Castilla, Colorado	Kirk Rueter, Montreal	1	Montreal
7	Marquis Grissom, Atlanta	Mike Busby, St. Louis	2	Atlanta
10	Glenallen Hill, San Francisco	Darryl Kile, Houston	4	Houston
16	Shane Andrews, Montreal	Mike Grace, Philadelphia	6	Montreal
16	Orlando Merced, Pittsburgh	Andy Benes, St. Louis	1	St. Louis
16	Jay Bell, Pittsburgh	Tom Urbani, St. Louis	6	St. Louis
19	Brian McRae, Chicago	Allen Watson, San Francisco	6	Chicago
20	Darrin Fletcher, Montreal	Lee Hancock, Pittsburgh	3	Montreal
21	David Segui, Montreal	Jason Christiansen, Pittsburgh	6	Montreal
25	Shane Andrews, Montreal	Tim Pugh, Cincinnati	7	Montreal
28	David Segui, Montreal	Mike Munoz, Colorado	8	Colorado
28	Darrin Fletcher, Montreal	Bryan Rekar, Colorado	1	Colorado
30	Jeff King, Pittsburgh	Tim Pugh, Cincinnati	4	Cincinnati
30	Barry Bonds, San Francisco	Bob Tewksbury, San Diego	5	San Diego
3	Benito Santiago, Philadelphia	Greg Maddux, Atlanta	9	Atlanta
4	Eric Davis, Cincinnati	Mark Dewey, San Francisco	7	San Francisco
5	Eric Davis, Cincinnati	Jeff Juden, San Francisco	7	San Francisco
8	Ron Gant, St. Louis	Mark Gardner, San Francisco	6	St. Louis
9	Willie McGee, St. Louis	Doug Creek, San Francisco	8	St. Louis

Date	Batter, Team	Pitcher, Team	Inn.*	Site
5-11	Jeff Blauser, Atlanta	Michael Mimbs, Philadelphia	1	Philadelphia
5-13	Terry Pendleton, Florida	T.J. Mathews, St. Louis	6	Florida
5-24	Ryne Sandberg, Chicago	Greg Swindell, Houston	7	Houston
5-24	Brian Johnson, San Diego	Blas Minor, New York	7	New York
5-26	Todd Zeile, Philadelphia	Jose Bautista, San Francisco	9	San Francisco
5-27	Ryan Klesko, Atlanta	Amaury Telemaco, Chicago	4	Chicago
6-1	Steve Finley, San Diego	Dave Leiper, Philadelphia	6	Philadelphia
6-7	Devon White, Florida	Bob MacDonald, New York	7	New York
6-13	Sean Berry, Houston	Mark Leiter, San Francisco	5	San Francisco
6-14	Gary Gaetti, St. Louis	Paul Byrd, New York	8	St. Louis
6-18	Mike Lansing, Montreal	Darren Holmes, Colorado	8	Colorado
6-25	Sean Berry, Houston	Doug Bochtler, San Diego	8	San Diego
6-26	Willie Greene, Cincinnati	Mike Williams, Philadelphia	1	Cincinnati
6-29	Mike Piazza, Los Angeles	Bryan Rekar, Colorado	5	Colorado
7-12	Vinny Castilla, Colorado	Willie Blair, San Diego	7	Colorado
7-13	Brian Jordan, St. Louis	Tanyon Sturtze, Chicago	6	Chicago
7-18	Mike Busch, Los Angeles	Mark Dewey, San Francisco	7	San Francisco
7-19	Devon White, Florida	Steve Frey, Philadelphia	8	Florida
7-21	Benito Santiago, Philadelphia	Jay Powell, Florida	9	Florida
7-23	Mike Kingery, Pittsburgh	Pedro Martinez, Montreal	6	Pittsburgh
7-27	Ryan Klesko, Atlanta	Mark Gardner, San Francisco	6	San Francisco
7-27	John Flaherty, San Diego	Terry Mathews, Florida	8	Florida
7-28	Gregg Jefferies, Philadelphia	Darrell May, Pittsburgh	4	Pittsburgh
8-2	Ron Gant, St. Louis	Bobby Jones, New York	5	New York
8-7	Barry Bonds, San Francisco	Scott Service, Cincinnati	6	San Francisco
8-9	Ryne Sandberg, Chicago	Barry Manuel, Montreal	5	Montreal
8-11	Tim Wallach, Los Angeles	Hector Carrasco, Cincinnati	9	Cincinnati
8-13	Jermaine Allensworth, Pittsburgh	Mark Gardner, San Francisco	4	Pittsburgh
8-13	Rick Wilkins, San Francisco	Francisco Cordova, Pittsburgh	8	Pittsburgh
8-16	Greg Vaughn, San Diego	Derek Wallace, New York	6	San Diego
8-18	Rondell White, Montreal	Tom Candiotti, Los Angeles	1	Los Angeles
8-19	Ken Caminiti, San Diego	Pedro Martinez, Montreal	1	San Diego
8-21	Jay Canizaro, San Francisco	Robert Person, New York	1	San Francisco
8-22	Jeff King, Pittsburgh	Xavier Hernandez, Houston	9	Houston
8-25	Willie Greene, Cincinnati	Kurt Miller, Florida	3	Florida
8-29	Joe Oliver, Cincinnati	John Burke, Colorado	6	Colorado
8-31	Lenny Harris, Cincinnati	Chris Hammond, Florida	5	Cincinnati
9-7	Donovan Osborne, St. Louis	Andy Ashby, San Diego	5	St. Louis
9-13	Jeff King, Pittsburgh	Tim Scott, San Francisco	7	San Francisco
9-26	Henry Rodriguez, Montreal	Curt Schilling, Philadelphia	6	Philadelphia

*Inning in which grand slam was hit.

TRANSACTIONS

JANUARY 2
gers signed 1B Eddie Williams.
eds organization signed OF Eric Davis, C Brook Fordyce, C Don
aught, P Bryan Hickerson, P Rich Rodriguez, P Jeff Shaw and
Roberto Mejia.

JANUARY 3
ariners signed 1B Paul Sorrento.
aves signed OF Jerome Walton.

JANUARY 4
ngels re-signed P Chuck Finley.
rates organization signed C Lance Parrish.

JANUARY 5
ngels organization signed P Dennis Springer.
arlins organization re-signed OF Andre Dawson.
stros organization signed P Anthony Young.
adres signed IF Craig Shipley.

JANUARY 8
ariners organization signed P Bob Milacki.
aves signed OF Dwight Smith.

JANUARY 9
ngels re-signed P Jim Abbott.
iants signed SS Shawon Dunston.
angers organization re-signed 3B Mike Pagliarulo and signed
B Rene Gonzales.
eds traded P Chad Fox and a player to be named to Braves for
F Mike Kelly.
hillies organization signed P Dave Leiper.
ardinals traded OF Allen Battle, P Bret Wagner, P Jay Witasick
nd P Carl Dale to A's for P Todd Stottlemyre.

JANUARY 10
igers signed P Brian Williams.
stros organization signed IF Bill Spiers.
xpos traded SS Wil Cordero and P Bryan Eversgerd to Red Sox
or P Rheal Cormier, 1B Ryan McGuire and P Shayne Bennett.
ardinals signed C Pat Borders.

JANUARY 11
rioles signed OF Mike Devereaux.
ardinals signed IF Mike Gallego.

JANUARY 12
eds organization signed P Trevor Wilson and P Gene Harris.
ockies organization signed P John Habyan.
odgers organization signed OF Milt Thompson.

JANUARY 13
arlins signed P Livan Hernandez.
adres organization signed OF Chris Gwynn.

JANUARY 16
angers organization signed IF Kevin Elster.
lue Jays organization signed IF Juan Samuel.
ubs signed P Bob Patterson.
odgers organization signed P Scott Radinsky.
iants signed P Osvaldo Fernandez.

JANUARY 17
rioles signed IF Jeff Huson and P Alan Mills.
ets traded C Kelly Stinnett to Brewers for P Cory Lidle.

JANUARY 18
ets traded IF Aaron Ledesma to Angels for OF Kevin Flora.

JANUARY 19
Yankees organization re-signed P Dave Pavlas.

JANUARY 20
White Sox signed OF Tony Phillips.

JANUARY 22
Red Sox signed OF Alex Cole, IF Esteban Beltre and P Jeremy
Hernandez.
A's traded OF/DH Danny Tartabull to White Sox for P Andrew
Lorraine and OF Charles Poe.
Mets traded P Eric Ludwick, P Erik Hiljus and OF Yudith Ozorio
to Cardinals for OF Bernard Gilkey.
Phillies signed 2B Mickey Morandini.

JANUARY 23
Brewers traded OF Duane Singleton to Tigers for P Henry
Santos.
Brewers signed P Ben McDonald.
Mariners claimed P Aaron Small on waivers from Marlins.
Cardinals organization signed P Gregg Olson.

JANUARY 24
Tigers re-signed IF Alan Trammell.
Blue Jays organization signed OF Ruben Amaro.
Cubs organization signed IF Leo Gomez and IF Bret Barberie.

JANUARY 25
Mets traded OF Damon Buford to Rangers for OF Terrell Lowery.

JANUARY 29
Red Sox traded OF Lee Tinsley, OF Glenn Murray and P Ken
Ryan to Phillies for P Heathcliff Slocumb, P Larry Wimberly and
OF Rick Holyfield.
Angels organization re-signed P Shawn Boskie.
Twins organization signed OF Roberto Kelly.

JANUARY 30
Reds organization signed OF Vince Coleman.
Phillies signed C Benito Santiago.

JANUARY 31
Royals signed P Tim Belcher.

FEBRUARY 1
Mariners organization signed OF Luis Polonia.

FEBRUARY 3
White Sox signed P Kevin Tapani.

FEBRUARY 4
Pirates organization signed P Danny Darwin.

FEBRUARY 6
White Sox organization signed P Joe Magrane.

FEBRUARY 13
Yankees organization signed P Steve Howe.
A's traded P Dennis Eckersley to Cardinals for P Steve
Montgomery.

FEBRUARY 16
Cubs organization signed P Duane Ward.

FEBRUARY 17
Phillies organization signed P Terry Mulholland.
Pirates organization signed P Zane Smith.

1996 REVIEW *Transactions*

FEBRUARY 21

Mets organization signed OF Gary Varsho.

FEBRUARY 26

Reds signed C Joe Oliver.
Giants organization signed OF Mel Hall.

FEBRUARY 29

Reds sold contract of C Don Slaught to Angels for an undisclosed amount.

MARCH 5

White Sox organization signed P Bobby Thigpen.

MARCH 8

Red Sox signed OF Kevin Mitchell.

MARCH 13

Orioles traded OF Sherman Obando to Expos for OF Tony Tarasco.

MARCH 15

Yankees released 1B/OF Gerald Perry.

MARCH 19

Cardinals claimed IF Luis Alicea on waivers from Red Sox.

MARCH 22

A's traded IF Fausto Cruz and P Ramon Fermin to Tigers for OF Phil Plantier.
Rangers organization signed P Jeff Russell.

MARCH 25

Royals announced retirement of P Tom Browning.
Blue Jays released P Danny Cox.

MARCH 26

Cardinals released P Gregg Olson.
A's released 3B Craig Paquette.

MARCH 27

Phillies announced retirement of IF Jose Oquendo.
Padres released OF Rob Deer

MARCH 28

Brewers released C Matt Nokes.

MARCH 31

Indians traded P Mark Clark to Mets for OF Ryan Thompson and P Reid Cornelius.

APRIL 1

Expos claimed P Mike Dyer on waivers from Pirates.

APRIL 2

Rangers organization signed IF Spike Owen

APRIL 4

Indians traded C Jesse Levis to Brewers for P Scott Nate and a player to be named; Brewers sent P Jared Camp to Indians to complete deal (June 9).
Pirates claimed P Darrell May on waivers from Braves.

APRIL 5

Angels traded IF Eduardo Perez to Reds for OF Will Pennyfeather.

APRIL 10

Rangers organization released IF Spike Owen.

APRIL 18

Red Sox traded P Bryan Eversgerd to Rangers for a player to be named; Rangers sent OF Rudy Pemberton to Red Sox to complete deal (April 24).

APRIL 19

Orioles organization signed OF Luis Polonia.

APRIL 24

Astros signed P Xavier Hernandez.

APRIL 25

Marlins claimed OF Marquis Riley on waivers from Angels.

APRIL 26

Reds traded P Gregg Olson to Tigers for IF Yuri Sanchez.

MAY 1

Yankees released OF Dion James.

MAY 2

Giants traded 1B J.R. Phillips to Phillies for a player to be named or cash; Phillies sent Giants an undisclosed amount of cash to complete deal (June 14).

MAY 7

Blue Jays claimed P Ken Robinson on waivers from Royals.

MAY 10

Royals claimed P Tim Pugh on waivers from Reds.

MAY 15

Pirates traded OF Jacob Brumfield to Blue Jays for 1B D.J. Boston.

MAY 16

Angels released P Scott Sanderson.

MAY 17

Angels claimed P Brad Pennington on waivers from Red Sox.
Blue Jays traded C Randy Knorr to Astros for cash.

MAY 22

Blue Jays sold contract of OF Wes Chamberlain to Chiba Lotte Marines of the Japanese Pacific League.

MAY 24

Blue Jays organization signed OF Felix Jose.

MAY 27

Angels traded P Lee Smith to Reds for P Chuck McElroy.

MAY 28

Twins claimed P Scott Aldred on waivers from Tigers.

MAY 31

Braves traded OF Anton French to Tigers for OF Danny Bautista

JUNE 3

Astros released P Greg Swindell.

JUNE 5

Red Sox signed IF Jeff Frye.
Blue Jays released P Frank Viola.

JUNE 7

Tigers traded P Brian Maxcy and OF Micah Franklin to Cardinals for P Tom Urbani and IF Miguel Inzunza.

JUNE 9

Mets traded P Blas Minor to Mariners for IF Randy Vickers.
Phillies traded OF Lee Tinsley to Red Sox for P Scott Bakkum.

JUNE 10

Indians traded P Bill Wertz to Mariners for P Mike Butcher.

JUNE 12

Yankees traded P Rich Monteleone to Angels for OF Mike Aldrete.

JUNE 15

lians signed P Greg Swindell.

bs released P Doug Jones.

rdinals traded C Pat Borders to Angels for P Ben VanRyn.

JUNE 17

gels traded P Ken Edenfield to Yankees for a player to be
med.

illies released OF Mark Whiten and P Dave Leiper.

JUNE 18

dres traded C Brad Ausmus, SS Andujar Cedeno and P Russ
ear to Tigers for C John Flaherty and SS Chris Gomez.

ds released OF Vince Coleman.

JUNE 22

nkees traded P Mike Judd to Dodgers for P Billy Brewer.

JUNE 24

nkees released P Steve Howe.

aves signed OF Mark Whiten.

dgers claimed OF Wayne Kirby on waivers from Indians.

JUNE 25

pos organization signed P John Habyan.

JUNE 27

aves traded IF Tyler Houston to Cubs for P Ismael Villegas.

gels organization signed OF Vince Coleman.

ckies claimed OF Milt Thompson on waivers from Dodgers.

JULY 3

ds claimed P Giovanni Carrara on waivers from Blue Jays.

JULY 8

ds claimed P Tim Pugh on waivers from Royals.

JULY 9

ants traded 1B/OF Mark Carreon to Indians for P Jim Poole
d a player to be named or cash.

JULY 11

ariners organization signed P Jose Guzman.

pos claimed P Jeff Juden on waivers from Giants.

illies claimed OF Manny Martinez on waivers from Mariners.

JULY 12

ins announced retirement of OF Kirby Puckett.

JULY 19

gels released IF Tim Wallach.

JULY 21

dians traded 1B Eddie Murray to Orioles for P Kent Mercker.

JULY 23

d Sox trade IF Jeff Manto to Mariners for IF Arquimedez
zo.

tros signed P Terry Clark.

rates traded P Danny Darwin to Astros for P Rich Loiselle.

JULY 24

hite Sox released P Kirk McCaskill.

rdinals released P Jeff Parrett.

JULY 25

aves claimed P Dean Hartgraves on waivers from Astros.

dgers organization signed 3B Tim Wallach.

JULY 27

gels traded C Pat Borders to White Sox for P Robert Ellis.

ants traded C Kirt Manwaring to Astros for C Rick Wilkins and
sh.

JULY 29

Indians traded 2B Carlos Baerga and IF Alvaro Espinoza to Mets
for IF Jose Vizcaino and IF Jeff Kent.

JULY 30

Mariners traded OF Darren Bragg to Red Sox for P Jamie Moyer.

Red Sox traded OF Kevin Mitchell to Reds for IF Roberto Mejia
and P Brad Tweedlie.

Giants traded P Mark Leiter to Expos for P Tim Scott and P Kirk
Rueter.

JULY 31

Tigers traded OF Chad Curtis to Dodgers for P Joey Eischen and
P John Cummings.

Tigers traded P Greg Gohr to Angels for IF Damion Easley.

Brewers traded OF Greg Vaughn and a player to be named to
Padres for P Bryce Florie, P Ron Villone and OF Marc Newfield;
Brewers sent OF Gerald Parent to Padres to complete deal
(September 16).

Yankees traded OF Ruben Sierra and P Matt Drews to Tigers for
1B/DH Cecil Fielder.

Phillies traded P Terry Mulholland to Mariners for IF Desi
Relaford.

Red Sox traded P Mike Stanton and a player to be named to
Rangers for P Mark Brandenburg and P Kerry Lacy; Red Sox sent
OF Dwayne Hosey to Rangers to complete deal (November 4).

Marlins traded P David Weathers to Yankees for P Mark Hutton.

AUGUST 1

Red Sox claimed 1B Greg Pirkl on waivers from Mariners.

Padres organization signed P Al Osuna.

AUGUST 6

Orioles claimed P Mike Milchin on waivers from Twins.

Orioles signed IF Domingo Martinez.

Tigers claimed P Todd Van Poppel on waivers from A's.

Mariners released P Jose Guzman.

AUGUST 8

Marlins traded P John Burkett to Rangers for P Ryan Dempster
and a player to be named; Rangers sent P Rick Helling to
Marlins to complete deal (September 3).

Phillies signed P Jeff Parrett.

AUGUST 12

Brewers released P Kevin Wickander.

AUGUST 13

Marlins traded 3B Terry Pendleton to Braves for OF Roosevelt
Brown.

AUGUST 14

Braves traded OF Mark Whiten to Mariners for P Roger Blanco.

AUGUST 15

Reds organization claimed P Tim Pugh on waivers from Royals.

AUGUST 16

Braves signed OF Luis Polonia.

AUGUST 19

Phillies released P Mitch Williams.

AUGUST 21

Marlins traded P Terry Mathews to Orioles for a player to be
named; Orioles sent C Gregg Zaun to Marlins to complete deal
(August 23).

Giants claimed OF Trenidad Hubbard on waivers from Rockies.

Tigers released C Mark Parent.

AUGUST 22

White Sox traded P Luis Andujar and P Allen Halley to Blue Jays
for P Tony Castillo and IF Domingo Cedeno.

Yankees claimed IF Luis Sojo on waivers from Mariners.

AUGUST 23

Brewers traded P Graeme Lloyd and OF Pat Listach to Yankees for OF Gerald Williams and P Bob Wickman.
Rockies released P Marvin Freeman.

AUGUST 26

Twins traded P Pat Mahomes to Red Sox for a player to be named; Red Sox sent P Brian Looney to Twins to complete deal (December 17).

AUGUST 28

Pirates traded P Denny Neagle to Braves for 1B Ron Wright and a player to be named; Braves sent P Jason Schmidt to Pirates to complete deal (August 30).
Cardinals released P Mike Morgan.

AUGUST 29

Phillies traded 3B Todd Zeile and OF Pete Incaviglia to Orioles for two players to be named; Orioles sent P Calvin Maduro and P Garrett Stephenson to Phillies to complete deal (September 4).
Red Sox claimed 3B Jeff Manto on waivers from Mariners.
Brewers traded P Ricky Bones and a player to be named to Yankees as compensation for the injured status of OF/IF Pat Listach.
Twins traded 3B Dave Hollins to Mariners for a player to be named; Mariners sent 1B Dave Arias to Twins to complete deal (September 13).

AUGUST 30

Pirates traded 3B Charlie Hayes to Yankees for a player to be named; Yankees sent P Chris Corn to Pirates to complete deal. (August 31).

AUGUST 31

Angels traded C Don Slaught to White Sox for a player to be named; White Sox sent C Scott Vollmer to Angels to complete deal. (November 14).
Brewers traded 3B Kevin Seitzer to Indians for OF Jeromy Burnitz.
Pirates traded OF Dave Clark to Dodgers for P Carl South.

SEPTEMBER 2

Angels released P Rich Monteleone.

SEPTEMBER 3

Reds signed P Mike Morgan.

SEPTEMBER 6

Angels claimed IF Robert Eenhorn on waivers from Yankees.
Angels claimed P Darrell May on waivers from Pirates.

SEPTEMBER 11

Tigers traded IF Andujar Cedeno to Astros for a player to be named.

SEPTEMBER 13

Reds claimed P Pedro Martinez on waivers from Mets.
Reds released P Derek Lilliquist.

SEPTEMBER 30

Dodgers claimed 3B Howard Battle on waivers from Phillies.

OCTOBER 1

Braves claimed P Scott Brow on waivers from Blue Jays.

OCTOBER 2

Yankees returned IF/OF Pat Listach to Brewers as part of a compensation agreement.

OCTOBER 3

Tigers claimed P Glenn Dishman on waivers from Phillies.
Rangers claimed P Wilson Heredia on waivers from Marlins.

OCTOBER 4

Royals released P Mike Magnante.
A's claimed P Dane Johnson on waivers from Blue Jays.
Reds claimed OF Glenn Murray on waivers from Phillies.

OCTOBER 9

Red Sox claimed P Mike Campbell on waivers from Cubs.
Red Sox claimed P Bob Milacki on waivers from Mariners.

OCTOBER 10

Dodgers claimed IF Tripp Cromer on waivers from Cardinals.

OCTOBER 11

Red Sox claimed P Greg Hansell on waivers from Twins.
Dodgers announced retirement of 3B Tim Wallach.

OCTOBER 14

Tigers signed IF Damion Easley.
Tigers claimed IF Dave Hajek on waivers from Astros.
Reds claimed P Tim Scott on waivers from Giants.

OCTOBER 15

Dodgers claimed IF John Wehner on waivers from Pirates.

OCTOBER 16

Expos organization signed IF Andy Stankiewicz.

OCTOBER 28

Royals traded P Mark Gubicza and P Mike Bovee to Angels for DH Chili Davis.
Tigers traded OF Ruben Sierra to Reds for OF Decomba Conner and P Ben Bailey.

OCTOBER 29

Mariners traded C Chris Widger, P Trey Moore and P Matt Wagner to Expos for P Jeff Fassero and P Alex Pacheco.

OCTOBER 30

Reds released P Jerry Spradlin.

OCTOBER 31

Yankees released P Dave Pavlas and P Dale Polley.

NOVEMBER 1

Tigers traded P Clint Sodowsky to Pirates for P Dan Miceli.

NOVEMBER 11

Phillies organization signed OF Brent Bowers.

NOVEMBER 12

Angels claimed P Todd Van Poppel on waivers from Tigers.

NOVEMBER 13

Rangers released P Gil Heredia.
Giants traded 3B Matt Williams and a player to be named to Indians for IF Jeff Kent, IF Jose Vizcaino, P Julian Tavarez and player to be named; Giants sent OF Trenidad Hubbard to Indians for P Joe Roa to complete deal (December 16).
Reds re-signed IF Lenny Harris.

NOVEMBER 14

Reds signed P David Nied.
Pirates traded OF Orlando Merced, IF Carlos Garcia and P Dan Plesac to Blue Jays for P Jose Silva, P Jose Pett, IF Brandon Cromer and three players to be named; Blue Jays sent P Mike Halperin, IF Abraham Nunez and C/OF Craig Wilson to Pirates to complete deal (December 11).
Mets re-signed IF Alvaro Espinoza.

NOVEMBER 15

Mariners claimed IF Dave Silvestri on waivers from Expos.

NOVEMBER 18

Reds released OF Thomas Howard.

NOVEMBER 19

hite Sox signed OF Albert Belle.
ngers released IF Luis Ortiz and OF Dwayne Hosey.

NOVEMBER 20

gels signed 3B Dave Hollins.
jers released P Richie Lewis, OF Duane Singleton, IF Fausto
uz and IF Shannon Penn.
ariners re-signed P Jamie Moyer.
ue Jays traded OF Lonell Roberts to Rangers for a player to be
med.
aves re-signed P John Smoltz.
ue Jays traded IF Miguel Cairo to Cubs for P Jason Stevenson.
bs claimed P Marc Pisciotta on waivers from Pirates.
arlins re-signed P Pat Rapp.
dgers claimed IF Nelson Liriano on waivers from Pirates.
rdinals signed 2B Delino DeShields.

NOVEMBER 21

ngers re-signed P Matt Whiteside.
dres traded P Dustin Hermanson to Marlins for IF Quilvio Veras.
illies signed IF Rex Hudler.
rates re-signed P Steve Cooke.

NOVEMBER 22

ckies re-signed IF/OF John Vander Wal.
arlins signed OF Bobby Bonilla.

NOVEMBER 25

aves traded P Greg McMichael to Mets for P Paul Byrd and a
ayer to be named.
arlins traded OF Jesus Tavarez to Red Sox for a player to be
med; Red Sox sent P Robert Rodgers to Marlins to complete
al (December 10).
arlins traded P Joel Adamson to Brewers for a player to be
med; Brewers sent P Ed Collins to Marlins to complete deal
ecember 10).
ewers re-signed 2B Fernando Vina.
ets organization signed P John Habyan.
d Sox traded OF Lee Tinsley to Mariners for a player to be named.

NOVEMBER 26

arlins signed OF John Cangelosi.
ets organization signed 3B Jose Oliva.
gels traded 1B J.T. Snow to Giants for P Allen Watson and P
usto Macey.

NOVEMBER 27

bs re-signed 2B Ryne Sandberg.
ants traded P Jamie Brewington to Royals for a player to be
med.
ewers claimed P Jeff Ware on waivers from Blue Jays.
ckies traded P Armando Reynoso to Mets for P Jerry DiPoto.
ets traded 1B Rico Brogna to Phillies for P Ricardo Jordan
d P Toby Borland.

DECEMBER 2

bs signed SS Shawon Dunston.
tros re-signed IF Bill Spiers.
tros signed IF Pat Listach and P Sid Fernandez.
rdinals claimed P Lance Painter on waivers from Rockies.
dres organization signed IF Rene Gonzales, C Carlos
rnandez and P Bryan Eversgerd.

DECEMBER 3

dians claimed P Mike Gordon on waivers from Blue Jays.
nkees re-signed C Joe Girardi.
arlins signed OF Jim Eisenreich.

DECEMBER 4

dians sold contract of OF Nigel Wilson to Chiba Lotte Marines
the Japanese Pacific League.
tros signed OF Thomas Howard.
rdinals re-signed OF Willie McGee.

DECEMBER 5

Twins signed C Terry Steinbach.
Yankees traded C/IF Jim Leyritz to Angels for two players to be
named; Angels sent 3B Ryan Kane and P Jeremy Blevins to
Yankees to complete deal (December 9).
Rangers released IF Lou Frazier.
Phillies signed P Jerry Spradlin.

DECEMBER 6

Angels signed IF Craig Grebeck.
Mariners organization re-signed P Greg Hibbard.
Braves re-signed SS Rafael Belliard.
Cardinals re-signed C Tom Pagnozzi.
Mariners traded P Sterling Hitchcock to Padres for P Scott
Sanders.

DECEMBER 7

Red Sox re-signed P Mike Maddux.
Brewers re-signed P Doug Jones.

DECEMBER 8

Orioles signed P Jimmy Key.

DECEMBER 9

Red Sox organization signed P Bret Saberhagen.
Blue Jays signed C Benito Santiago.
Cubs signed P Terry Mulholland.
Rockies signed C Kirt Manwaring.
Marlins signed P Alex Fernandez.
Dodgers signed 3B Todd Zeile.
Tigers traded 2B Jeff Berblinger to Dodgers for SS Deivi Cruz
and OF Juan Hernaiz.

DECEMBER 10

Indians re-signed P Eric Plunk.
Mariners claimed OF Lou Frazier on waivers from Rangers.
Rangers signed IF Bill Ripken.
Reds signed P Kent Mercker.
Reds organization signed P Rodney Bolton, P Ricky Bones and
P David Nied.
Cubs signed P Mel Rojas.
Rockies signed P Mike Munoz.
Marlins signed P Dennis Cook.
Astros traded OF Brian Hunter, IF Orlando Miller, P Doug
Brocail, P Todd Jones and a player to be named to Tigers for C
Brad Ausmus, P Jose Lima, P C.J. Nitkowski, P Trever Miller
and IF Daryle Ward.

DECEMBER 11

White Sox signed P Jaime Navarro.
White Sox re-signed P Tony Castillo.
Tigers traded P Brent Stentz to Twins for C Matt Walbeck.
Yankees signed P Mike Stanton.
Rangers re-signed 2B Mark McLemore.
Blue Jays traded P Roberto Duran to Tigers for OF Anton French.
Phillies signed P Mark Leiter, P Mark Portugal and P Mark Parent.

DECEMBER 12

Orioles signed SS Mike Bordick.
Red Sox re-signed 3B Tim Naehring.
Twins signed P Bob Tewksbury.
Marlins signed OF Moises Alou.
Expos claimed P Marc Valdes on waivers from Marlins.

DECEMBER 13

Indians signed P Mike Jackson.
Indians organization signed OF Kevin Mitchell and C Pat Borders.
Rangers signed P Xavier Hernandez.
Blue Jays signed P Roger Clemens.
Marlins traded P Yorkis Perez to Braves for P Martin Sanchez.
Cubs signed P Kevin Tapani.
Pirates traded SS Jay Bell and 1B Jeff King to Royals for 3B Joe
Randa, P Jeff Granger, P Jeff Martin and P Jeff Wallace.

DECEMBER 14

Red Sox signed OF Shane Mack.

DECEMBER 16

Orioles signed P Shawn Boskie.
Royals organization signed 3B Scott Cooper.
Rangers signed P John Wetteland.
Cardinals traded P Cory Bailey to Rangers for P David Chavarria and a player to be named.
Tigers traded IF Mark Lewis to Giants for 1B Jesus Ibarra.

DECEMBER 17

Red Sox signed P Chris Hammond.
Royals organization signed P Juan Agosto.
Yankees signed P David Wells.
Cubs released IF Leo Gomez
Cubs claimed P Miguel Batista on waivers from Marlins.
Padres traded C Brian Johnson and P Willie Blair to Tigers for P Joey Eischen and P Cam Smith.

DECEMBER 18

Angels signed 1B Eddie Murray.
Orioles organization signed OF Jerome Walton and C Lenny Webster.
Indians signed OF Chad Curtis.
Twins organization signed P Greg Swindell.
Mariners organization signed 2B Brian Raabe.
Blue Jays organization signed IF Juan Samuel.
Braves re-signed 2B Mark Lemke.
Mets organization signed P Brian Bohanon.

DECEMBER 19

Orioles signed OF Eric Davis and OF Pete Incaviglia.
Orioles organization signed 3B Kelly Gruber.
Indians organization signed OF Les Norman and P Terry Clark.
Twins organization signed OF Eric Anthony.
Rangers organization signed P Tom Urbani and OF Mike Simms.

Braves re-signed P Mike Bielecki and released P Ben VanRyn.
Astros signed OF Luis Gonzalez.
Astros organization signed P Mike Magnante.
Pirates signed SS Kevin Elster.
Padres re-signed OF Greg Vaughn.
Giants traded C Tom Lampkin to Cardinals for a player to be named or cash.

DECEMBER 20

Angels organization re-signed IF Jack Howell.
Brewers traded IF Wes Weger to Expos for P Scott Pisciotta.
Twins organization signed P Gregg Olson.
Reds claimed P Felix Rodriguez on waivers from Dodgers.
Mets traded P Robert Person to Blue Jays for 1B John Olerud and cash.
Giants organization signed OF Darrin Jackson.

DECEMBER 21

Reds organization signed P Stan Belinda and P Billy Brewer.

DECEMBER 23

Rangers traded OF Rikkert Faneyte to Reds for a player to be named.
Astros organization re-signed C Randy Knorr.
Padres re-signed IF Craig Shipley.
Padres organization signed C Don Slaught.

DECEMBER 26

Indians signed SS Tony Fernandez.
Rockies organization signed P Mike Dyer.

DECEMBER 27

Red Sox organization signed P Johnny Ruffin.

DECEMBER 30

Cubs organization signed P Julio Valera.
Astros signed P Russ Springer.

AWARD WINNERS

THE SPORTING NEWS

AMERICAN LEAGUE
Pitcher of the Year: Pat Hentgen, Toronto
Rookie Player of the Year: Derek Jeter, New York, SS
Rookie Pitcher of the Year: James Baldwin, Chicago
Fireman of the Year: John Wetteland, New York
Comeback Player of the Year: Kevin Elster, Texas, SS
Manager of the Year: Johnny Oates, Texas

MAJOR LEAGUE
Player of the Year: Alex Rodriguez, Seattle
Executive of the Year: Doug Melvin, Texas

NATIONAL LEAGUE
Pitcher of the Year: John Smoltz, Atlanta
Rookie Player of the Year: Jason Kendall, Pittsburgh, C
Rookie Pitcher of the Year: Alan Benes, St. Louis
Fireman of the Year: Trevor Hoffman, San Diego
Comeback Player of the Year: Eric Davis, Cincinnati, OF
Manager of the Year: Bruce Bochy, San Diego

MINOR LEAGUE
Player of the Year: Vladimir Guerrero, West Palm Beach, Florida State; Harrisburg, Eastern
Manager of the Year: John Mizerock, Wilmington, Carolina
Executive of the Year: Wayne Hodes, Trenton

BASEBALL WRITERS' ASSOCIATION OF AMERICA

AMERICAN LEAGUE
MOST VALUABLE PLAYER

Player, Team	1	2	3	4	5	6	7	8	9	10	Pts.
Juan Gonzalez, Texas	11	7	5	3	2	-	-	-	-	-	290
Alex Rodriguez, Seattle	10	10	4	3	-	-	1	-	-	-	287
Albert Belle, Cleveland	2	8	10	4	2	1	-	1	-	-	228
Ken Griffey Jr., Seattle	4	1	2	5	6	3	1	5	1	-	188
Mo Vaughn, Boston	-	1	3	2	5	5	4	4	1	2	134
Rafael Palmeiro, Baltimore	-	-	2	5	4	2	3	-	3	1	104
Mark McGwire, Oakland	-	-	2	4	1	4	2	3	5	3	100
Frank Thomas, Chicago	-	-	-	-	4	5	7	2	2	1	88
Brady Anderson, Baltimore	-	-	-	-	-	3	3	2	9	2	53
Ivan Rodriguez, Texas	1	-	-	-	1	2	3	1	2	3	52
Kenny Lofton, Cleveland	-	-	-	1	2	2	-	1	1	-	34
Mariano Rivera, New York	-	1	-	-	1	1	1	1	-	-	27
Paul Molitor, Minnesota	-	-	-	1	-	-	-	1	2	5	19
Andy Pettitte, New York	-	-	-	-	-	-	1	2	-	1	11
Jim Thome, Cleveland	-	-	-	-	-	-	1	1	-	2	9
Chuck Knoblauch, Minnesota	-	-	-	-	-	-	-	-	2	4	8
Jay Buhner, Seattle	-	-	-	-	-	-	-	2	-	-	6
Bernie Williams, New York	-	-	-	-	-	-	-	2	-	-	6
John Wetteland, New York	-	-	-	-	-	-	1	-	-	-	4
Roberto Alomar, Baltimore	-	-	-	-	-	-	-	-	-	3	3
Terry Steinbach, Oakland	-	-	-	-	-	-	-	-	-	1	1

Fourteen points awarded for a first-place vote, nine for second and down to one for 10th.

CY YOUNG AWARD

Pitcher, Team	1	2	3	Pts.
Pat Hentgen, Toronto	16	9	3	110
Andy Pettitte, New York	11	16	1	104
Mariano Rivera, New York	1	1	10	18
Charles Nagy, Cleveland	-	1	9	12
Mike Mussina, Baltimore	-	1	2	5
Alex Fernandez, Chicago	-	-	1	1
Roberto Hernandez, Chicago	-	-	1	1
Ken Hill, Texas	-	-	1	1

Five points awarded for a first-place vote, three for second and one for third.

ROOKIE OF THE YEAR

Player, Team	1	2	3	Pts.
Derek Jeter, New York	28	-	-	140
James Baldwin, Chicago	-	19	7	64
Tony Clark, Detroit	-	6	12	30
Rocky Coppinger, Baltimore	-	1	3	6
Jose Rosado, Kansas City	-	1	3	6
Darin Erstad, California	-	1	-	3
Jose Batista, Oakland	-	-	1	1
Tim Crabtree, Toronto	-	-	1	1
Jeff D'Amico, Milwaukee	-	-	1	1

Five points awarded for a first-place vote, three for second and one third.

MANAGER OF THE YEAR

Manager, Team	1	2	3	Pts.
Johnny Oates, Texas*	12	8	5	89
Joe Torre, New York*	10	12	3	89
Lou Piniella, Seattle	3	4	8	35
Mike Hargrove, Cleveland	2	3	3	22
Buddy Bell, Detroit	1	-	-	5
Davey Johnson, Baltimore	-	-	4	4
Tom Kelly, Minnesota	-	-	4	4
Art Howe, Oakland	-	1	-	3
Kevin Kennedy, Boston	-	-	1	1

*Co-winner.
Five points awarded for a first-place vote, three for second and one for third.

1996 REVIEW *Award winners*

NATIONAL LEAGUE

MOST VALUABLE PLAYER

Player, Team	1	2	3	4	5	6	7	8	9	10	P*
Ken Caminiti, San Diego	28	-	-	-	-	-	-	-	-	-	3*
Mike Piazza, Los Angeles	-	18	7	2	-	1	-	-	-	-	2*
Ellis Burks, Colorado	-	5	4	9	3	4	1	1	-	1	1*
Chipper Jones, Atlanta	-	2	7	5	4	2	2	2	-	1	1*
Barry Bonds, San Francisco	-	-	4	5	3	4	4	2	2	1	1*
Andres Galarraga, Colorado	-	1	2	2	4	2	4	5	4	-	1*
Gary Sheffield, Florida	-	1	2	3	2	4	3	3	5	3	1*
Brian Jordan, St. Louis	-	1	1	1	4	1	1	3	1	1	*
Jeff Bagwell, Houston	-	-	-	-	2	3	4	1	4	5	*
Steve Finley, San Diego	-	-	-	-	2	2	1	2	2	2	*
John Smoltz, Atlanta	-	-	1	1	1	1	1	1	-	-	*
Barry Larkin, Cincinnati	-	-	-	-	-	2	1	3	2	2	*
Marquis Grissom, Atlanta	-	-	-	-	1	1	1	2	1	-	*
Bernard Gilkey, New York	-	-	-	-	-	-	2	1	-	2	*
Sammy Sosa, Chicago	-	-	-	-	-	1	1	-	1	1	*
Eric Karros, Los Angeles	-	-	-	-	1	-	1	-	-	-	
Henry Rodriguez, Montreal	-	-	-	-	1	-	-	1	-	-	
Todd Hundley, New York	-	-	-	-	-	-	-	-	2	3	
Lance Johnson, New York	-	-	-	-	-	-	1	-	-	3	
Dante Bichette, Colorado	-	-	-	-	-	-	-	-	2	2	
Todd Worrell, Los Angeles	-	-	-	-	-	-	-	1	-	-	
Kevin Brown, Florida	-	-	-	-	-	-	-	-	1	-	
Trevor Hoffman, San Diego	-	-	-	-	-	-	-	-	1	-	
Moises Alou, Montreal	-	-	-	-	-	-	-	-	-	1	

Fourteen points awarded for a first-place vote, nine for second and down to one for 10th.

MANAGER OF THE YEAR

Manager, Team	1	2	3	Pts.
Bruce Bochy, San Diego	10	7	5	76
Felipe Alou, Montreal	8	9	7	74
Tony La Russa, St. Louis	7	8	10	69
Bobby Cox, Atlanta	3	2	3	24
Bill Russell, Los Angeles	-	1	3	6
Terry Collins, Houston	-	1	-	3

Five points awarded for a first-place vote, three for second and one for third.

ROOKIE OF THE YEAR

Player, Team	1	2	3	Pts.
Todd Hollandsworth, Los Angeles	15	9	3	105
Edgar Renteria, Florida	10	10	4	84
Jason Kendall, Pittsburgh	1	5	10	30
F.P. Santangelo, Montreal	1	2	4	15
Rey Ordonez, New York	1	-	2	7
Jermaine Dye, Atlanta	-	2	-	6
Alan Benes, St. Louis	-	-	5	5

Five points awarded for a first-place vote, three for second and one for third.

CY YOUNG AWARD

Pitcher, Team	1	2	3	Pts
John Smoltz, Atlanta	26	2	-	13*
Kevin Brown, Florida	2	26	-	8*
Andy Benes, St. Louis	-	-	9	*
Hideo Nomo, Los Angeles	-	-	5	*
Trevor Hoffman, San Diego	-	-	3	*
Greg Maddux, Atlanta	-	-	3	*
Todd Worrell, Los Angeles	-	-	3	*
Denny Neagle, Pit.-Atl.	-	-	2	*
Jeff Fassero, Montreal	-	-	1	*
Al Leiter, Florida	-	-	1	*
Shane Reynolds, Houston	-	-	1	*

Five points awarded for a first-place vote, three for second and o* for third.

MISCELLANEOUS

ATTENDANCE

AMERICAN LEAGUE

	Home	Road
ltimore	3,646,950	2,168,279
ston	2,315,231	2,113,889
lifornia	1,820,521	2,105,769
icago	1,676,403	2,158,712
eveland	3,318,174	2,337,869
troit	1,168,610	2,074,472
nsas City	1,435,997	2,084,205
lwaukee	1,327,155	2,074,013
nnesota	1,437,352	2,013,348
w York	2,250,877	2,226,768
kland	1,148,380	2,091,337
attle	2,723,850	2,221,455
xas	2,889,020	2,067,580
ronto	2,559,573	1,980,397
Totals	29,718,093	29,718,093

NATIONAL LEAGUE

	Home	Road
Atlanta	2,901,242	2,417,089
Chicago	2,219,110	2,258,054
Cincinnati	1,861,428	2,126,259
Colorado	3,891,014	2,130,129
Florida	1,746,767	2,187,246
Houston	1,975,888	2,030,978
Los Angeles	3,188,454	2,370,728
Montreal	1,616,709	2,227,074
New York	1,588,323	2,056,551
Philadelphia	1,801,677	2,027,076
Pittsburgh	1,332,150	2,003,854
St. Louis	2,654,718	2,115,594
San Diego	2,187,886	2,186,114
San Francisco	1,413,922	2,242,542
Totals	30,379,288	30,379,288

DEBUTS

ayer	Pos.	Team	Birth date	Birthplace	Debut
reu, Bob Kelly	PH	Houston	3-11-74	Aragua, Venezuela	9-1
ams, William Edward	P	Oakland	10-8-72	Gallup, N.M.	6-11
amson, Joel Lee	P	Florida	7-2-71	Lakewood, Calif.	4-10
ensworth, Jermaine LaMont	OF	Pittsburgh	1-11-72	Anderson, Ind.	7-23
ston, Garvin James	P	Colorado	12-8-71	Mt. Vernon, N.Y.	6-6
as, George Albert	3B	California	3-12-72	Tucson, Ariz.	4-2
coin, Derek Alfred	P	Montreal	3-27-70	Lachine, Quebec	5-21
rault, Joseph Allen	C	Atlanta	10-8-71	Rochester, Mich.	9-1
nks, Brian Glen	PH	Milwaukee	9-28-70	Mesa, Ariz.	9-9
rron, Anthony D.	PH	Montreal	8-17-66	Portland, Ore.	6-2
rtee, Kimera Anotchi	OF	Detroit	7-21-72	Omaha, Neb.	4-3
tista, Leocadio Francisco	3B	Oakland	12-9-73	Puerto Plata, D.R.	6-3
amon, Trey Clifford	OF	Pittsburgh	2-11-74	Dallas	8-4
ckett, Robert Joseph	P	Colorado	7-16-72	Austin, Texas	9-12
ech, Lucas Matthew	P	Philadelphia	1-20-72	Oakland	8-8
lk, Timothy William	1B	Cincinnati	4-6-70	Cincinnati	6-25
vil, Brian Scott	P	Kansas City	9-5-71	Houston	6-17
azier, Ronald Patrick	P	Philadelphia	7-30-71	Altoona, Pa.	5-31
uma, James Andrew	P	Kansas City	5-18-72	Beaufort, S.C.	8-9
oty, Joshua Gibson	PH	Florida	4-29-75	Starkville, Miss.	9-24
urgeois, Steven James	P	San Francisco	8-4-72	Lutcher, La.	4-3
wers, Brent	OF	Baltimore	5-2-71	Bridgeview, Ill.	8-16
ze, Marshall Wayne	P	Milwaukee	5-23-71	San Manuel, Ariz.	4-28
ede, Brent David	PH	Minnesota	9-13-71	Belleville, Ill.	9-8
to, Tilson Manuel	PH	Toronto	5-28-72	Santo Domingo, D.R.	4-1
own, Brant Michael	1B	Chicago N.L.	6-22-71	Porterville, Calif.	6-15
own, Kevin Lee	PH	Texas	4-21-73	Valparaiso, Ind.	9-12
rke, John C.	P	Colorado	2-9-70	Durango, Colo.	8-13
sby, Michael J.	P	St. Louis	12-27-72	Lomita, Calif.	4-7
iro, Miguel Jesus	2B	Toronto	5-4-74	Anaco, Venezuela	4-17
nizaro, Jason Kyle	PH	San Francisco	7-4-73	Beaumont, Tex.	4-28
rlson, Daniel Steven	P	San Francisco	1-26-70	Portland, Ore.	9-13
sanova, Raul	DH	Detroit	8-23-72	Humacao, P.R.	5-24
stillo, Luis	2B	Florida	9-12-75	San Pedro de Macoris, D.R.	8-8
avez, Raul Alexander	PH	Montreal	3-18-73	Valencia, Venezuela	9-2
ouinard, Robert William	P	Oakland	5-1-72	Manila, Philippines	5-26
ckrell, Alan	PH	Colorado	12-5-62	Kansas City, Kan.	9-7
ppinger, John Thomas	P	Baltimore	3-19-74	El Paso, Texas	6-11
rdova, Francisco	P	Pittsburgh	4-26-72	Veracruz, Mexico	4-2
awford, Carlos Lamonte	P	Philadelphia	10-4-71	Charlotte, N.C.	6-7
espo, Felipe Javier Clauso	3B	Toronto	3-5-73	Rio Piedras, P.R.	4-28
uz, Jacob	OF	San Francisco	1-28-73	Oxnard, Calif.	7-18
Amico, Jeffrey Charles	P	Milwaukee	12-27-75	St. Petersburg, Fla.	6-28
lgado, Alexander	C	Boston	1-11-71	Palmerejo, Venezuela	4-4
lgado, Wilson Duran	SS	San Francisco	7-15-75	San Cristobal, D.R.	9-24
ssens, Elmer	P	Pittsburgh	1-13-72	Hermosillo, Mexico	6-24
az, Einar Antonio	C	Cleveland	12-28-72	Chiriqui, Panama	9-9

Player	Pos.	Team	Birth date	Birthplace	Deb
Dickson, Jason	P	California	3-30-73	Ontario, Canada	8-
Difelice, Michael William	C	St. Louis	5-28-69	Philadelphia	9
Doster, David Eric	2B	Philadelphia	10-8-70	Fort Wayne, Ind.	6-
Dunn, Todd Kent	OF	Milwaukee	7-29-70	Tulsa, Okla.	9
Durant, Michael Joseph	C	Minnesota	9-14-69	Columbus, Ohio	4
Dye, Jermaine Terrell	OF	Atlanta	1-28-74	Oakland	5-
Echevarria, Angel Santos	PH	Colorado	5-25-71	Bridgeport, Conn.	7-
Ellis, Robert Randolph	P	California	12-15-70	Baton Rouge, La.	9-
Erstad, Darin Charles	OF	California	6-4-74	Jamestown, N.D.	6-
Estalella, Robert M.	PH	Philadelphia	8-23-74	Hialeah, Fla.	9-
Farmer, Michael Anthony	P	Colorado	7-3-68	Gary, Ind.	5
Fasano, Salvatore Frank	C	Kansas City	8-10-71	Chicago	4
Fernandez, Osvaldo	P	San Francisco	11-4-68	Holguin, Cuba	4
Fox, Andrew Junipero	2B	New York A.L.	1-12-71	Sacramento, Calif.	4
Fyhrie, Michael Edwin	P	New York N.L.	12-9-69	Long Beach, Calif.	9-
Garciaparra, Anthony Nomar	2B	Boston	7-23-73	Whittier, Calif.	8-
Garrison, Webster L.	2B	Oakland	8-24-65	Marrero, La.	8
Glanville, Douglas Metunwa	OF	Chicago N.L.	8-25-70	Hackensack, N.J.	6
Graffanino, Anthony Joseph	2B	Atlanta	6-6-72	Amityville, N.Y.	4-
Graves, Daniel Peter	P	Cleveland	8-7-73	Saigon, Vietnam	7-
Greene, Charles P.	C	New York N.L.	1-23-71	Miami	9-
Greene, Todd Anthony	PH	California	5-8-71	Augusta, Ga.	7-
Grundt, Kenneth A.	P	Boston	8-26-69	Melrose Park, Ill.	8
Guerrero, Vladimir	OF	Montreal	2-9-76	Nizao Bani, D.R.	9-
Guerrero, Wilton	PR	Los Angeles	10-24-74	Don Gregorio, D.R.	9
Hancock, Ryan Lee	P	California	11-11-71	Santa Clara, Calif.	6
Hardtke, Jason Robert	2B	New York N.L.	9-15-71	Milwaukee, Wis.	9
Harris, Hernando Petrocelli	P	California	9-23-72	Lancaster, S.C.	8-
Hawblitzel, Ryan	P	Colorado	4-30-71	West Palm Beach, Fla.	6
Heflin, Bronson Wayne	P	Philadelphia	8-29-71	Clarksville, Tenn.	8
Heredia, Felix	P	Florida	6-18-76	Barahona, D.R.	8
Hernandez, Eisler Livan	P	Florida	2-20-75	Villa Clara, Cuba	9-
Holbert, Aaron Keith	2B	St. Louis	1-9-73	Torrance, Calif.	4-
Holt, Christopher Michael	P	Houston	9-18-71	Dallas	9
Holtz, Michael James	P	California	10-10-72	Arlington, Va.	7-
Houston, Tyler Sam	PH	Atlanta	1-17-71	Las Vegas, Nev.	4
Howard, Matthew Christopher	2B	New York A.L.	9-22-67	Fall River, Mass.	5-1
Hunter, Richard Thomas	P	Philadelphia	9-25-74	Pasadena, Calif.	4
Hurst, William Hansel	P	Florida	4-28-70	Miami Beach, Fla.	9-
Ibanez, Raul Javier	PH	Seattle	6-2-72	New York City	8
Jackson, Damian Jacques	SS	Cleveland	8-16-73	Los Angeles	9-1
Janzen, Martin Thomas	P	Toronto	5-31-73	Homestead, Fla.	5-
Jennings, Robin Christopher	PH	Chicago N.L.	4-11-72	Singapore	4-
Jensen, Marcus C.	C	San Francisco	12-14-72	Oakland	4-
Jones, Andruw Rudolf	OF	Atlanta	4-23-77	Wellemstad, Curacao	8-1
Jones, Dax Xenos	PH	San Francisco	8-4-70	Pittsburgh	7-1
Jones, Terry Lee	PR	Colorado	2-15-71	Birmingham, Ala.	9
Keagle, Gregory Charles	P	Detroit	6-28-71	Corning, N.Y.	4
Kendall, Jason Daniel	C	Pittsburgh	6-26-74	San Diego	4
Kieschnick, Michael Brooks	PH	Chicago N.L.	6-6-72	Robstown, Texas	4
Kingsale, Eugene Humphrey	OF	Baltimore	8-20-76	Aruba, Aruba	9
Lacy, Kerry Ardeen	P	Boston	8-7-72	Chattanooga, Tenn.	8-
Larkin, Andrew Dane	P	Florida	6-27-74	Chelan, Wash.	9-2
Lesher, Brian Herbert	OF	Oakland	3-5-71	Antwerp, Belgium	8-2
Levine, Alan Brian	P	Chicago A.L.	5-22-68	Park Ridge, Ill.	6-2
Loiselle, Richard Frank	P	Pittsburgh	1-12-72	Neenah, Wis.	9-
Ludwick, Eric David	P	St. Louis	12-14-71	Whiteman AFB, Mo.	9
Lukachyk, Robert James	PH	Montreal	7-24-68	Jersey City, N.J.	7
Luke, Matthew Cliff	PR	New York A.L.	2-26-71	Long Beach, Calif.	4-
Lyons, Curt Russell	P	Cincinnati	10-17-74	Greencastle, Ind.	9-
Machado, Robert	C	Chicago A.L.	6-3-73	Caracas, Venezuela	7-2
Maduro, Calvin Gregory	P	Philadelphia	9-5-74	Santa Cruz, Aruba	9
Magee, Wendell Errol	PH	Philadelphia	8-3-72	Hattiesburg, Miss.	8-1
Malave, Jose Francisco	PR	Boston	5-31-71	Cumana, Venezuela	5-2
Martinez, Manuel DeJesus	OF	Seattle	10-3-70	San Pedro de Macoris, D.R.	6-1
Martinez, Pablo	PR	Atlanta	6-29-69	Sabana Grande, D.R.	7-2
Mashore, Damon Wayne	OF	Oakland	10-31-69	Ponce, P.R.	6-
McCarthy, Gregory O'Neil	P	Seattle	10-30-68	Norwalk, Conn.	8-2
McKeel, Walt	C	Boston	1-17-72	Stantonsburg, N.C.	9-1
McMillon, William Edward	OF	Florida	11-17-71	Otero, N.M.	7-2
Mejia, Miguel	PR	St. Louis	3-25-75	San Pedro de Macoris, D.R.	4
Mendoza, Ramiro	P	New York A.L.	6-15-72	Los Santos, Panama	5-2
Milchin, Michael	P	Minnesota	2-28-68	Knoxville, Tenn.	5-1

er	Pos.	Team	Birth date	Birthplace	Debut
er, Travis Eugene	P	Minnesota	11-2-72	Dayton, Ohio	8-25
er, Trever Douglas	P	Detroit	5-29-73	Louisville, Ky.	9-4
ard, Ralph Gregory	2B	Florida	12-30-73	Wilhelmstad, Curacao	5-12
abelli, Douglas Anthony	C	San Francisco	10-18-70	Kingman, Ariz.	8-27
chell, Larry Paul II	P	Philadelphia	10-16-71	Flint, Mich.	8-11
hler, Brian Merritt	P	Detroit	12-31-71	Rockingham, N.C.	9-22
ina, Islay	PH	Oakland	6-3-71	New York, N.Y.	8-15
tgomery, Raymond James	PR	Houston	8-8-69	Bronxville, N.Y.	7-3
tgomery, Steven Lewis	P	Oakland	12-25-70	Westminster, Calif.	4-3
re, Kerwin Lamar	OF	Oakland	10-29-70	Detroit	8-30
man, Alvin	P	Houston	1-6-69	Rockingham, N.C.	4-2
squera, Julio Alberto	C	Toronto	1-29-72	Panama City, Panama	8-17
tola, Charles Edward	OF	Cincinnati	10-15-71	Augusta, Ga.	4-23
ller, William Richard	PR	San Francisco	3-17-71	Maryland Heights, Mo.	4-18
ligan, Sean Patrick	PH	San Diego	4-25-70	Lynwood, Calif.	9-1
noz, Jose Luis	SS	Chicago A.L.	11-11-67	Chicago	4-7
ray, Glenn Everett	OF	Philadelphia	11-23-70	Manning, S.C.	5-10
rs, James Xavier	P	Baltimore	4-28-69	Oklahoma City, Okla.	4-6
rs, Roderick Demond	PH	Kansas City	1-14-73	Conroe, Texas	6-21
rs, Rodney Luther	P	Chicago N.L.	6-26-69	Rockford, Ill.	4-3
lty, Daniel Donovan	P	Minnesota	1-6-70	Los Angeles	4-2
on, Christopher Trotman	PR	Boston	4-11-74	Durham, N.C.	9-21
ton, Gregory Blakemo	PR	Chicago A.L.	7-6-72	San Leandro, Calif.	8-18
onez, Reynaldo	SS	New York N.L.	11-11-72	Havana, Cuba	4-1
x, Keith Richard	C	Pittsburgh	10-22-68	Port Jefferson, N.Y.	4-5
heco, Alexander Melchor	P	Montreal	7-19-73	Caracas, Venezuela	4-17
agua, Jose Luis Sanchez	P	Montreal	8-20-73	San Jose de Ocoa, D.R.	4-4
erson, Danny Shane	P	Texas	2-17-71	San Gabriel, Calif.	7-26
z, Daniel	OF	Milwaukee	2-26-71	El Paso, Texas	6-30
z, Neifi Neftali	2B	Colorado	2-2-75	Villa Mella, D.R.	8-31
rs, Christopher Michael	P	Pittsburgh	1-28-72	Fort Thomas, Ky.	7-19
ey, Ezra Dale	P	New York A.L.	8-9-64	Georgetown, Ky.	6-23
s, Michael Larry	P	Milwaukee	9-5-70	Langdale, Ala.	4-6
hett, Christopher Davis	1B	California	1-31-70	Merced, Calif.	9-6
ico, Rafael Octavio	P	Philadelphia	9-7-69	Santo Domingo, D.R.	6-25
ford, Desmond Lamont	SS	Philadelphia	9-16-73	Valdosta, Ga.	8-1
teria, Edgar Enrique	SS	Florida	8-7-75	Barranquilla, Colombia	5-10
ertson, Michael	PH	Chicago A.L.	10-9-70	Norwich, Conn.	9-6
riguez, Luis Antonio	PR	Boston	8-15-70	Rio Piedras, P.R.	7-6
riguez, Nerio	P	Baltimore	3-22-73	Bani, D.R.	8-16
in, Scott Bruce	3B	Philadelphia	4-4-75	Evansville, Ind.	8-1
ado, Jose Antonio	P	Kansas City	11-9-74	Jersey City, N.J.	6-12
bel, Matthew Alexander	P	Pittsburgh	10-16-69	Cincinnati	5-21
kinsky, Brian Walter	P	Baltimore	6-22-71	Pittsburgh	4-20
midt, Jeffrey Thomas	P	California	2-21-71	Northfield, Minn.	5-17
utz, Carl James	P	Atlanta	8-22-71	Hammond, La.	9-3
y, William Frank	PH	Boston	6-11-70	Monroeville, Ala.	4-19
fini, Daniel Joseph	P	Minnesota	1-25-74	San Francisco	6-25
ets, Andrew Mark	PH	Seattle	11-19-71	Baton Rouge, La.	4-22
a, Jose Leonel	P	Toronto	12-19-73	Tijuana, Mexico	9-10
ll, Mark Allen	P	Houston	11-12-67	Portland, Ore.	4-5
erstrom, Steve	P	San Francisco	4-3-72	Turlock, Calif.	9-17
zio, Scott Edward	3B	Oakland	9-21-72	Joliet, Ill.	9-14
henson, Garrett Charles	P	Baltimore	1-2-72	Takoma Park, Md.	7-25
ki, Makoto	P	Seattle	5-31-75	Kobe, Japan	7-7
maco, Amaury Regalado	P	Chicago N.L.	1-19-74	Higuey, D.R.	5-16
mpson, Jason Michael	1B	San Diego	6-13-71	Orlando, Fla.	6-9
mpson, Justin Willard	P	Detroit	3-8-73	San Antonio, Texas	5-27
es, Pedro Jose Manzo	PH	Chicago N.L.	6-29-73	Fajardo, P.R.	5-15
Ryn, Benjamin Ashley	P	California	8-9-71	Fort Wayne, Ind.	5-9
s, Dario Antonio	P	San Diego	3-13-73	Santiago, D.R.	7-31
ner, Matthew William	P	Seattle	4-4-72	Cedar Falls, Iowa	6-5
er, Todd Arthur	3B	Minnesota	5-25-73	Bakersfield, Calif.	8-30
ace, Derek Robert	P	New York N.L.	9-1-71	Van Nuys, Calif.	8-13
ins, Marc Allen	P	Pittsburgh	10-21-70	Mansfield, Ohio	5-11
ams, David Keith	PH	San Francisco	4-21-72	Bedford, Pa.	6-7
ams, Shad Clayton	P	California	3-10-71	Fresno, Calif.	5-18
on, Desi Benard	1B	San Francisco	5-9-69	Glen Cove, N.Y.	8-7
on, Paul Anthony	P	New York N.L.	3-28-73	Orlando, Fla.	4-4
sick, Gerald Alfonse	P	Oakland	8-28-72	Baltimore	7-7
ht, Jamey Alan	P	Colorado	12-24-74	Oklahoma City, Okla.	7-3
Esteban	P	Baltimore	6-22-74	Campina Del Seibo, D.R.	5-20
g, Dmitri Dell	1B	St. Louis	10-11-73	Vicksburg, Miss.	8-29
r, Jon Edward	PH	Philadelphia	12-10-69	Encino, Calif.	4-19

SALARY ARBITRATION RESULTS

WINNERS

Player, Team	Salary awarded	Team's offer
Steve Avery, Atlanta	$4,200,000	$3,600,000
Jeff Fassero, Montreal	$2,800,000	$2,000,000
Chuck Knoblauch, Minnesota	$4,670,000	$4,000,000
Mark Lewis, Detroit	$670,000	$450,000
Mike Stanton, Boston	$1,750,000	$1,200,000
Rick Wilkins, Houston	$1,550,000	$1,250,000
Bernie Williams, N.Y. Yankees	$3,000,000	$2,555,000

LOSERS

Player, Team	Salary awarded	Playe reque
Willie Banks, Philadelphia	$240,000	$590
Arthur Rhodes, Baltimore	$300,000	$675
Ivan Rodriguez, Texas	$4,000,000	$4,950

1996 FREE-AGENT FILINGS

AMERICAN LEAGUE

Baltimore: Bobby Bonilla, Mike Devereaux, Pete Incaviglia, Roger McDowell, Eddie Murray, Jesse Orosco, Mark Parent, Bill Ripken, David Wells, Todd Zeile.
Boston: Roger Clemens, Mike Maddux, Tim Naehring*, Mike Stanley.
California: Shawn Boskie, Jack Howell, Rex Hudler.
Chicago: Harold Baines, Pat Borders, Tony Castillo*, Alex Fernandez*, Marvin Freeman, Don Slaught, Kevin Tapani, Danny Tartabull.
Cleveland: Albert Belle, Mark Carreon, Dennis Martinez, Kent Mecker, Tony Pena, Eric Plunk.
Milwaukee: Doug Jones.
New York: Mike Aldrete, Tony Fernandez, Joe Girardi, Jimmy Key*, Melido Perez, John Wetteland.
Oakland: Mike Bordick*, Jim Corsi, Terry Steinbach.
Seattle: Chris Bosio, Greg Hibbard, Dave Hollins, Mike Jackson, Terry Mulholland, Mark Whiten*.
Texas: Dennis Cook, Kevin Elster, Rene Gonzales, Kevin Gross, Darryl Hamilton, Mike Henneman, Mark McLemore*, Jeff Russell, Mike Stanton, Dave Valle, Kurt Stillwell.
Toronto: Juan Samuel.

NATIONAL LEAGUE

Atlanta: Steve Avery, Rafael Belliard, Mike Bielecki, Mark Le... Terry Pendleton, Luis Polonia, Dwight Smith, John Sm... Jerome Walton.
Chicago: Luis Gonzalez*, Dave Magadan, Jaime Navarro, ... Patterson, Ryne Sandberg.
Cincinnati: Eric Davis, Thomas Howard, Kevin Mitchell, ... Oliver, Mark Portugal, Chris Sabo, Lee Smith.
Colorado: Eric Anthony, Bret Saberhagen.
Florida: Andre Dawson, Craig Grebeck, Alejandro Pena.
Houston: John Cangelosi, Danny Darwin, Doug Drabek, X... Hernandez, Kirt Manwaring, Gregg Olson, Bill Spiers.
Los Angeles: Brett Butler, Dave Clark, Delino DeShields.
Montreal: Moises Alou*, Mark Leiter, Mel Rojas*.
New York: Brent Mayne*.
Philadelphia: Jim Eisenreich, Sid Fernandez, Jeff Parrett, B... Santiago, David West.
St. Louis: Luis Alicea, Mike Gallego, Willie McGee, Tom Pagn... Ozzie Smith.
San Diego: Chris Gwynn, Craig Shipley*, Bob Tewks... Fernando Valenzuela, Greg Vaughn.
San Francisco: Shawon Dunston, Robby Thompson.

*Granted free agency December 5, 1996 upon ratificatio new labor agreement, which credited players with service during 1994 strike.

MAJOR LEAGUE DRAFT

(Listed in order of selection)

Player	Pos.	Drafted by	Drafted from (major league organization)
Edgar Ramos	P	Philadelphia	Tucson, Pacific Coast League (Astros)
Jeff Berblinger	2B	Detroit	Louisville, American Association (Cardinals)
Mike Johnson	P	San Francisco	Syracuse, International League (Blue Jays)
Jim Baron	P	New York N.L.	Las Vegas, Pacific Coast League (Padres)
Emil Brown	OF	Pittsburgh	Edmonton, Pacific Coast League (Athletics)
Ramon Tatis	P	Chicago N.L.	Norfolk, International League (Mets)
Wilmer Montoya	P	Oakland	Buffalo, American Association (Indians)
Noe Najera	P	Cincinnati	Buffalo, American Association (Indians)
Ramon Garcia	P	Houston	New Orleans, American Association (Brewers)
Jayson Durocher	P	Chicago A.L.	Ottawa, International League (Expos)
Thomas Davey	P	Baltimore	Syracuse, International League (Blue Jays)
Deivi Cruz	SS	Los Angeles	Phoenix, Pacific Coast League (Giants)
William Cunnane	P	San Diego	Charlotte, International League (Marlins)
Jamie Walker	P	Atlanta	Tucson, Pacific Coast League (Astros)
Frank Catalanotto	2B	Oakland	Toledo, International League (Tigers)
James Magee	3B	Baltimore	Richmond, International League (Braves)

NECROLOGY

Mel Allen, 83, at Greenwich, Conn., on June 16. One of baseball's great broadcasters, Allen was the radio voice of the New York Yankees for a quarter of a century (1940-64) and had a presence much like that of some of the franchise's great stars. He later was the host of the highly popular This Week in Baseball program, which was aired on TV and at ballparks throughout the nation.

John Bateman, 54, at Sand Springs, Okla., on December 3. Bateman was a big-league catcher from 1963-72. His best season was 1966 when, playing for the Astros, he hit 17 home runs and batted .279.

Jim Baumer, 65, at Paoli, Pa., on July 8. Baumer was general manager of the Brewers in the 1970s and farm and scouting director for the Phillies in the 1980s. The former infielder had two stints in the majors more than a decade apart, playing briefly for the White Sox in 1949 and sparingly for the Reds in 1961.

Jim Baxes, 68, at Garden Grove, Calif., on November 14. Infielder Baxes hit 17 home runs in his only big-league season, 1959. He homered twice in 33 at-bats for the Dodgers and then connected 15 times in 247 at-bats after going to the Indians.

John Berardino, 79, at Los Angeles on May 19. Infielder Berardino, who spent 11 years in the majors, was a regular for the Browns in his first three big-league seasons (1939-41) and was a member of the World Series-champion Indians in 1948. Later, he was a daytime-TV star for more than three decades on General Hospital.

Hank Biasatti, 74, at Dearborn, Mich., on April 20. Biasatti, a first baseman, played 21 games for the 1949 A's.

Ewell Blackwell, 74, at Hendersonville, N.C., on October 29. Blackwell, whose sidearming style made him one of the most feared pitchers of his time, pitched in six consecutive All-Star games (1946-51) as a representative of the Reds and was a 22-game winner in 1947. His performance in '47 was memorable—he led the N.L. in victories, complete games and strikeouts, won 16 consecutive decisions and threw a no-hitter. In his first start after the mid-June no-hitter, he worked 8⅓ innings before allowing a hit. He finished with an 82-78 record over 10 major league seasons.

Lou "Buddy" Blair, 85, at Monroe, La., on June 7. In his lone big-league season, 1942, Blair was the Athletics' regular third baseman. He batted .279 and drove in 66 runs.

Don Bollweg, 75, at Wheaton, Ill., on March 26. He hit .297 as a backup first baseman/pinch hitter for the 1953 World Series champion Yankees and also played for the Cardinals and Athletics.

Gene Brabender, 55, at Madison, Wis., on December 27. Brabender, a reliever for the World Series-winning Orioles in '66, was used primarily as a starter for the first-year Seattle Pilots in 1969 and led the staff in victories with 13. He was 35-43 in his five-year career in the majors.

Bob Brady, 73, at Manchester, Conn., on April 22. Catcher Brady played in a total of four games for the Braves in 1946-47.

Willard Brown, 81, at Houston on August 8. He became the fourth black player in modern major league history when he made his debut with the St. Louis Browns on July 19, 1947. Although he got only 67 at-bats in the majors, outfielder Brown was the first black to hit a home run in the American League.

Johnny Bucha, 71, at Bethlehem, Pa., on April 28. Catcher Bucha played in 84 big-league games—60 with the 1953 Tigers.

Jim Busby, 69, at Augusta, Ga., on July 8. An outfielder who spent 13 seasons in the majors, he was a superb defensive player who posted a .262 lifetime batting average. Busby wasn't known for his power—he had 48 career homers—but hit grand slams in two consecutive games for Cleveland in 1956.

Hank Camelli, 81, at Wellesley, Mass., on July 14. Catcher Camelli played a total of 159 games for the Pirates and Braves from 1943-47.

Chuck Coles, 64, at Myrtle Beach, S.C., on January 25. Outfielder Coles' big-league career consisted of 11 at-bats with the 1958 Reds. He got two hits.

Walker "Foots" Cress, 79, at Baton Rouge, La., on April 21. Righthander Cress was 0-1 in a total of 33 appearances for the Reds in 1948 and 1949.

Babe Dahlgren, 84, at Arcadia, Calif., on September 4. He is the man who played first base for the Yankees on May 2, 1939, the day Lou Gehrig's consecutive-games streak ended at 2,130. Dahlgren spent 12 years in the majors, batting .261 with 82 homers. He drove in 101 runs for the 1944 Pirates.

Charles "Red" Embree, 79, at Eugene, Ore., on September 24. Embree won 31 games and lost 48 while pitching in the American League for most of the decade of the '40s.

Gil English, 87, at Trinity, N.C., on August 31. Infielder English was a reserve for the Giants, Tigers, Braves and Dodgers in a six-season major league career that ended in 1944.

Del Ennis, 70, at Huntingdon Valley, Pa., on February 8. Ennis had 100 RBIs seven times and twice finished with 95 RBIs in a 14-year major league career spent primarily with the Phillies. His best season was 1950, when he helped the Phils to the N.L. pennant by slugging 31 homers, knocking in 126 runs and hitting .311. Overall, he collected 2,063 hits and batted .284.

Nanny Fernandez, 77, at Harbor City, Calif., on September 19. Fernandez, who played four big-league seasons (three with the Braves, one with the Pirates), had a career batting average of .248. The infielder/outfielder saw extensive duty with the Braves in 1942 and again in 1946, hitting .255 both seasons.

Tom Ferrick, 81, at Lima, Pa., on October 15. Ferrick, later a big-league coach and scout, was primarily a reliever over nine big-league seasons and compiled a 40-40 record while pitching for the Athletics, Indians, Browns, Senators and Yankees. Acquired by the Yanks in June 1950, he won eight games for New York the remainder of that season and was the winning pitcher in Game 3 of the '50 Series.

Charles O. Finley, 77, at Chicago on February 19. Longtime owner of the A's beginning when the team was still based in Kansas City, Finley was a colorful, innovative and controversial executive who lured fans to the ballpark with myriad promotions and wasn't afraid to challenge the game's establishment or the sport's traditions. Although he once had sheep grazing beyond the outfield fence, a mechanical rabbit delivering balls to the umpire and his team dressing in green and gold uniforms when home whites and road grays were still the rule, Finley also could be deadly serious—as evidenced by his rebuffed attempt in 1976 to sell off some of his top stars before they left the A's through free agency. Overall, though, Finley might be best remembered for putting together a baseball juggernaut—his Oakland A's won three consecutive World Series in the early 1970s.

Roger Freed, 49, at Chino, Calif., on January 9. A feared minor league slugger, outfielder/first baseman Freed played sparingly in the majors over eight seasons in the 1970s. He hit only 22 homers in the big leagues—but one made him a cult hero of sorts to St. Louis fans. After Houston had taken a 6-3 lead in the top of the 11th inning of a May 1, 1979, game, Freed hit a pinch grand slam with two out in the bottom half of the inning for a 7-6 Cardinals victory.

Milt Gaston, 100, at Hyannis, Mass., on April 26. Gaston, who broke into the majors with the Yankees in 1924 and then pitched for the Browns, Senators, Red Sox and White Sox, fashioned a 97-164 record over 11 big-league seasons. He once pitched a 14-hit shutout, yielded four of Babe Ruth's 60 home runs in 1927 and twice led the A.L. in defeats.

Gary Geiger, 59, at Murphysboro, Ill., on April 24. Outfielder Geiger, a 12-year major leaguer, saw regular duty with the Red Sox in 1961 and 1962, seasons in which he hit 18 and 16 home runs.

Jimmy Gleeson, 84, at Kansas City on May 1. Outfielder Gleeson enjoyed his best big-league season in 1940, when his .313 average ranked sixth in the N.L. batting race. Gleeson made his major league debut with the Indians in 1936, played for the Cubs in 1939 and '40 and was with the Reds in '41 and '42.

Gordon Goldsberry, 68, at Lake Forest, Calif., on February 23. A scouting and player-development official for the Cubs, Brewers, Phillies and Orioles over the past three decades, Goldsberry was a reserve first baseman for the White Sox and Browns in a four-year (1949-52) big-league career.

Hank Gornicki, 85, at Riviera Beach, Fla., on February 16. Gornicki, who threw a shutout in his first big-league start (for the Cardinals, in 1941) but then saw extensive duty as a relief pitcher, was 15-19 in four big-league seasons. In 25 appearances for the Pirates in 1942, he had a 2.57 ERA.

Howie Goss, 61, at Reno, Nev., on July 31. Goss played two seasons in the majors, the first as a part-time outfielder for Pittsburgh in 1962 and the second as regular for Houston in 1963. He hit .216 overall.

Fred Green, 63, at Titusville, N.J., on December 22. Lefthanded reliever Green made 45 appearances for the 1960 World Series champion Pirates and finished with an 8-4 record and a 3.21 ERA. He spent five years in the big leagues.

Bob Grim, 66, at Shawnee, Kan., on October 23. Grim, who had a 61-41 record in eight big-league seasons and pitched in two World Series, was the A.L. Rookie of the Year in 1954 when he went 20-6 for the Yankees with a 3.26 ERA.

Tom Hafey, 83, at El Cerrito, Calif., on October 2. Third baseman/outfielder Hafey played in 78 big-league games—70 for the Giants in 1939 and eight for the Browns in 1944.

Harry Hanebrink, 68, at St. Louis on September 9. Hanebrink was a utility player for the 1958 N.L. champion Milwaukee Braves and made two pinch-hitting appearances in the World Series that fall.

Luman Harris, 81, at Pell City, Ala., on November 11. Harris, who went 35-63 as a big-league pitcher in the 1940s, was Atlanta's manager in 1969 when the Braves won their first divisional championship.

Joe Hoerner, 59, in a farming accident at Hermann, Mo., on October 4. Reliever Hoerner pitched 14 years in the majors, compiling a 39-34 record and a 2.99 ERA in 493 games. He had a sub-2.00 ERA three times in his career and, coming out of the Cardinals' bullpen, made two appearances in the 1967 World Series and three in the '68 Series.

Joe Holden, 82, at St. Clair, Pa., on May 10. Catcher Holden played in a total of 17 games for the Phillies from 1934-36.

Al Hollingsworth, 88, at Austin, Texas, on April 28. Lefthander Hollingsworth pitched 11 seasons in the majors, saving his best effort for his next-to-last year, 1945. He went 12-9 for the Browns in '45 and was among the A.L.'s ERA leaders with a figure of 2.70.

Bill Jackowski, 81, at Springfield, Vt., on July 29. He umpired in the National League for 17 years, beginning in 1952.

Vic Janowicz, 66, at Columbus, Ohio, on February 27. A Heisman Trophy-winning football player at Ohio State, Janowicz was a catcher/third baseman for the Pirates in 1953-54. In '54, he played for the Pirates and the NFL's Washington Redskins.

Alex Kellner, 71, at Tucson, Ariz., on May 3. Kellner was a 20-game winner for the Athletics in 1949 and a 20-game loser for the A's in 1950, his first two full seasons in the majors. The lefthander wound up pitching 12 years in the big leagues and compiled a 101-112 record.

Gus Keriazakos, 64, at Hilton Head Island, S.C., on May 4. Righthander Keriazakos appeared in 28 big-league games—22 of them for the 1954 Senators, for whom he went 2-3 with a 3.77 ERA.

Bruno Konopka, 77, at Denver on September 27. First baseman Konopka played a total of 45 games for the Athletics in 1942, 1943 and 1946.

Andy Lapihuska, 73, at Millville, N.J., on February 17. He pitched in a total of four games for the Phillies in 1942 and 1943 and was 0-2.

Dan Lewandowski, 68, at Hamilton, Ont., on July 19. Lewandowski made two relief appearances for the Cardinals in 1951.

Wes Livengood, 86, at Winston-Salem, N.C., on September Livengood pitched in five games for the 1939 Reds.

Cliff Mapes, 74, at Pryor, Okla., on December 5. Mapes, an ou fielder, spent 3½ seasons with the Yankees—he played in t 1949 and 1950 World Series with the New York club—before fi ishing his five-season major league career with the Browns a Tigers. Overall, he batted .242.

Jerry May, 52, in a farm accident at Harrisonburg, Va., on June 3 May, a catcher, played 10 big-league seasons, seven of them with t Pirates. He was Pittsburgh's primary catcher in 1967 and 1968.

Dutch McCall, 75, at Little Rock, Ark., on January 7. In his lo major league season, 1948, lefthander McCall was 4-13 for t Cubs.

Barney McCosky, 78, at Venice, Fla., on September 6. A .3 hitter over his first seven big-league seasons, McCosky then s out the 1949 season because of back problems before finishi his career with four subpar years. The outfielder wound up with .312 career average while playing mostly for the Tigers a Athletics. In 1940, he batted .340 for Detroit in the regular seas and .304 in the World Series.

John McSherry, 51, at Cincinnati on April 1. A National Leag umpire since 1971, McSherry collapsed and died of a heart atta in the early moments of the Expos-Reds season opener.

John Michaels, 89, at Sebring, Fla., on November 18. Le hander Michaels went 1-6 for the Red Sox in 1932, his only maj league season.

Willy Miranda, 70, at Baltimore on September 7. A slick-fie ing shortstop, Miranda played 824 big-league games in the 195 and was a regular for the Orioles in 1955 and 1956.

Danny Monzon, 49, in a car accident at Santo Doming Dominican Republic, on January 21. Monzon, a reserve infield for the Twins in 1972 and 1973, was director of internatio scouting for the Red Sox at the time of his death.

Walt Moryn, 70, at Winfield, Ill., on July 21. Moryn was a me ber of the N.L. All-Star team in 1958, a year in which he hit home runs for the Cubs. The outfielder played eight years in t majors and hit 101 homers.

Bob Muncrief, 80, at Dallas on February 7. Muncrief was member of the rotation for the Browns' only pennant-winni team in 1944 and was a reliever/starter for the Indians' 19 World Series champions. He was a 13-game winner four times one five-year stretch.

George "Red" Munger, 77, at Houston on July 23. Mung went 11-3 with a 1.34 ERA for the 1944 Cardinals, compiled a 1 5 record for the Cards in 1947 and won 15 games for the S Louis club in 1949. In 1946, he notched a complete-game vict ry against the Red Sox in the World Series.

Sam Narron, 83, at Middlesex, N.C., on December 31. Narron catcher, had only 28 at-bats over three big-league seasons—all w the Cardinals—but managed to play briefly in a World Series, agair the Yankees in 1943. He was a coach for the 1960 World Ser champion Pirates.

Charlie Neal, 65, at Los Angeles on November 18. An eig year major leaguer, Neal enjoyed his best season in 1959 when hit .287 and scored 103 runs for the Dodgers and then batt .370 with two homers in the '59 World Series. In 1962, he w the Mets' starting second baseman in the club's first-ever gam

Bill Nicholson, 81, at Chestertown, Md., on March 8. Playi for the Cubs, outfielder Nicholson led the N.L. in homers a RBIs in 1943 and 1944 and finished a 16-year career in t majors with 235 homers. In a doubleheader against the Giants '44, he hit four consecutive home runs—three of them in Gar 1—and, in a stunning move, was walked intentionally with t bases loaded in Game 2.

Jim Pendleton, 72, at Houston on March 20. As a rook Pendleton slugged three of the eight home runs the Braves hit a 1953 game but finished his eight-year career with only homers. He was Houston's left fielder in that team's first N game in 1962.

Ray Pepper, 90, at Belle Mina, Ala., on March 24. Outfield Pepper played his five-season major league career with St. Lou ms, spending two years with the Cardinals and three with the owns. He batted .298 and drove in 101 runs for the Browns in 34.

ed Petosky, 85, at Elkin, N.C. on November 30. Petosky, an outder, played a total of 10 games for the Reds in 1934 and 1935.

Al Piechota, 82, at Chicago on June 13. Piechota won two of en N.L. decisions while pitching for Boston in 1940-41.

Andy Pilney, 83, at Kenner, La., on September 15. Pilney, a ndout Notre Dame football player, made two pinch-hitting pearances for the Braves in 1936.

John Pramesa, 71, at Los Angeles on September 9. Catcher amesa batted .307 in 228 at-bats for the Reds in 1950, his best ort in four big-league seasons.

Dick Rand, 64, at Moreno Valley, Calif., on January 22. Catcher nd played 72 games over three big-league seasons. He saw his eatest playing time in 1957, when he appeared in 60 games for Pirates.

Jerry Robertson, 52, at Burlington, Kan., on March 24 of uries suffered in a car accident. He pitched in relief in the os' first-ever game in 1969 and, inserted into the rotation, nt on to post a 5-16 record for Montreal that year. He pitched only 11 other big-league games, all for the Tigers in 1970.

Don Ross, 81, at Arcadia., Calif., on April 4. Third baseman/out-der Ross played for the Tigers, Dodgers and Indians in a seven-ar major league career that ended in 1946. Ross was an effective ch hitter for Detroit from 1942-44, batting .300 in 70 at-bats in t capacity

Ralph Rowe, 71, at Newberry, S.C., on February 29. A longtime nor league outfielder and manager, Rowe was a coach for the 83 World Series champion Orioles.

Connie Ryan, 75, at Metairie, La., on January 3. Ryan, who had ef managerial stints with the Braves in 1975 and the Rangers 1977, was a major league infielder for 12 seasons. He appeared he 1948 World Series for the Boston Braves.

Joe Ryan, 80, at Miami on August 10. Ryan, a longtime minor gue executive, was business manager of the Class AAA Miami m in 1956 when, with Satchel Paige pitching for the home b, it drew a crowd of 57,713 to the Orange Bowl.

oe Schultz, 77, at St. Louis on January 10. A backup catcher nine big-league seasons and twice the A.L. leader in pinch Schultz managed the Seattle Pilots in their one season of stence, 1969, before the franchise moved to Milwaukee and ame the Brewers.

ill Serena, 71, at Hayward, Calif., on April 17. Serena was the os' regular third baseman in 1950, a year in which he hit 17 ne runs, and spent six seasons with the Chicago club. In 1947, le playing for Lubbock in the low minors, he hit 70 homers— in the regular season and 13 in the playoffs.

Mike Sharperson, 34, in a car accident at Las Vegas on May Apparently on the verge of being called up from the minors by

the Padres when he was killed, infielder Sharperson batted .280 in eight big-league seasons while playing for the Blue Jays, Dodgers and Braves.

Ray Shore, 75, at St. Louis, on August 13. Shore, used mainly as a reliever in three seasons with the Browns in the late 1940s, was a major league scout for the Phillies at the time of his death.

Harry Shuman, 80, at Philadelphia on October 25. Pennsylvania native Shuman made a total of 30 relief appearances for his home-state Pirates and Phillies from 1942-44.

Elmer Singleton, 77, at Ogden, Utah, on January 5. Singleton posted an 11-17 lifetime record, finishing his eight-season major league career in 1959. After pitching in the majors from 1945-48 and again in 1950, he found himself back in the minors in 1951 and didn't resurface in the majors until 1957—when he was 39 years old.

C. Arnholt Smith, 97, at Del Mar, Calif., on June 8. Smith was the original owner of the Padres, bringing the expansion franchise to San Diego in 1969.

Gene Snyder, 65, at York, Pa., on June 2. Lefthander Snyder's big-league career consisted of 11 games with the 1959 Dodgers. He went 1-1.

Bob Thorpe, 69, at Waveland, Miss., on October 30. Thorpe, an outfielder, batted .260 in 81 games for the Braves in 1952, their last season in Boston, and also played briefly for the club in 1951 and again in 1953 after it moved to Milwaukee.

Les Tietje, 85, at Rochester, Minn., on October 2. A big-league pitcher from 1933-38, Tietje was 22-41 for the White Sox and Browns.

Overton Tremper, 89, at Clearwater, Fla., on January 9. Outfielder Tremper saw brief service with Brooklyn in 1927 and 1928.

Sam "Red" Webb, 71, at Hyattsville, Md., on February 7. Webb made a total of 25 appearances for the Giants in 1948 and 1949, going 3-2.

Dick West, 80, at Fort Wayne, Ind., on March 13. West was a reserve catcher for the Reds from 1938-43.

Pete Whisenant, 66, at Port Charlotte, Fla., on March 22. Reserve outfielder Whisenant played with different clubs (Braves, Cardinals, Cubs and Reds) in his first four big-league seasons and wound up playing eight years (1952, 1955-61) in the majors.

Ed Wineapple, 89, at Delray Beach, Fla., on July 23. Wineapple pitched in one big-league game—in 1929, for the Senators.

Burnis "Wild Bill" Wright, 82, at Aguascalientes, Mexico, on August 3. Wright was a slugging outfielder in the Negro leagues and in the Mexico League in the 1930s and 1940s.

Al Zarilla, 77, at Honolulu on August 28. Outfielder Zarilla was among the American League's leading hitters in 1948 and 1950. In '48, he batted .329 for the Browns, the fourth-best figure in the league; in '50, his .325 mark for the Red Sox ranked fifth in the A.L. He hit .276 over 10 big-league seasons and was a member of the Browns' only pennant-winning team in 1944.

1996 A.L. STATISTICS

atting

esignated hitting

inch-hitting

itching

elding

liscellaneous

BATTING

TEAM

Team	Avg.	G	TPA	AB	R	H	TB	2B	3B	HR	RBI	SH	SF	HP	BB	IBB	SO	SB	CS	GDP	LOB	ShO	Slg.	OB
Cleveland	.293	161	6486	5681	952	1665	2700	335	23	218	904	34	57	43	671	44	844	160	50	164	1224	1	.475	.36
New York	.288	162	6414	5628	871	1621	2456	293	28	162	830	41	72	41	632	56	909	96	46	153	1258	5	.436	.36
Minnesota	.288	162	6403	5673	877	1633	2413	332	47	118	812	20	63	65	576	42	958	143	53	172	1194	5	.425	.35
Seattle	.287	161	6518	5668	993	1625	2741	343	19	245	954	46	58	75	670	57	1052	90	39	121	1238	3	.484	.36
Texas	.284	163	6494	5702	928	1622	2672	323	32	221	890	32	69	31	660	51	1041	83	26	128	1253	5	.469	.35
Boston	.283	162	6545	5756	928	1631	2628	308	31	209	882	33	47	67	642	50	1020	91	44	148	1251	9	.457	.35
Chicago	.281	162	6497	5644	898	1586	2521	284	33	195	860	56	62	34	701	68	927	105	41	139	1231	2	.447	.36
Milwaukee	.279	162	6434	5662	894	1578	2496	304	40	178	845	45	50	53	624	35	986	101	48	115	1198	7	.441	.35
California	.276	161	6320	5686	762	1571	2451	256	24	192	727	45	33	29	527	40	974	53	39	148	1209	6	.431	.35
Baltimore	.274	163	6494	5689	949	1557	2685	299	29	257	914	31	67	61	645	49	915	76	40	134	1154	7	.472	.35
Kansas City	.267	161	6229	5542	746	1477	2208	286	38	123	689	66	49	43	529	36	943	195	85	102	1117	3	.398	.33
Oakland	.265	162	6402	5630	861	1492	2546	283	21	243	823	35	39	58	640	36	1114	58	35	134	1175	7	.452	.34
Toronto	.259	162	6295	5599	766	1451	2354	302	35	177	712	38	37	92	529	19	1105	116	38	120	1169	9	.420	.33
Detroit	.256	162	6203	5530	783	1413	2324	257	21	204	741	48	49	29	546	26	1268	87	50	132	1040	10	.420	.32
Totals	.277	1133	89734	79090	12208	21922	35195	4205	421	2742	11583	570	752	721	8592	609	14056	1454	634	1910	16711	79	.445	.35

INDIVIDUAL

TOP QUALIFIERS FOR BATTING CHAMPIONSHIP

Minimum 502 plate appearances. *Lefthanded batter. †Switch-hitter.

Player, Team	Avg.	G	TPA	AB	R	H	TB	2B	3B	HR	RBI	SH	SF	HP	BB	IBB	SO	SB	CS	GDP	Slg.	O
Rodriguez, Alex, Seattle	.358	146	677	601	141	215	379	54	1	36	123	6	7	4	59	1	104	15	4	15	.631	.4
Thomas, Frank, Chicago	.349	141	649	527	110	184	330	26	0	40	134	0	8	5	109	26	70	1	1	25	.626	.4
Molitor, Paul, Minnesota	.341	161	729	660	99	225	309	41	8	9	113	0	9	3	56	10	72	18	6	21	.468	.3
Knoblauch, Chuck, Minnesota	.341	153	701	578	140	197	299	35	14	13	72	0	6	19	98	6	74	45	14	9	.517	.4
Greer, Rusty, Texas*	.332	139	617	542	96	180	287	41	6	18	100	0	10	3	62	4	86	9	0	9	.530	.4
Nilsson, Dave, Milwaukee*	.331	123	516	453	81	150	238	33	2	17	84	0	3	3	57	6	68	2	3	4	.525	.4
Alomar, Roberto, Baltimore†	.328	153	699	588	132	193	310	43	4	22	94	8	12	1	90	10	65	17	6	14	.527	.4
Martinez, Edgar, Seattle	.327	139	634	499	121	163	297	52	2	26	103	0	4	8	123	12	84	3	3	15	.595	.4
Seitzer, Kevin, Mil.-Cle	.326	154	675	573	85	187	267	35	3	13	78	5	5	5	87	7	79	6	1	13	.466	.4
Vaughn, Mo, Boston*	.326	161	752	635	118	207	370	29	1	44	143	0	8	14	95	19	154	2	0	17	.583	.4
Cirillo, Jeff, Milwaukee	.325	158	643	566	101	184	285	46	5	15	83	6	6	7	58	0	69	4	9	14	.504	.3
Higginson, Bob, Detroit*	.320	130	515	440	75	141	254	35	0	26	81	3	6	1	65	7	66	6	3	7	.577	.4
Lofton, Kenny, Cleveland*	.317	154	736	662	132	210	295	35	4	14	67	7	6	0	61	3	82	75	17	7	.446	.3
Jeter, Derek, New York	.314	157	654	582	104	183	250	25	6	10	78	6	9	9	48	1	102	14	7	13	.430	.3
Gonzalez, Juan, Texas	.314	134	592	541	89	170	348	33	2	47	144	0	3	4	45	12	82	2	0	10	.643	.3

DEPARTMENTAL LEADERS: G—C. Ripken, Bal., 163; AB—Lofton, Cle., 662; R—Rodriguez, Sea., 141; H—Molitor, Min., 225; TB—Rodriguez, Sea., 379; 1B—Molitor, Min., 167; 2B—Rodriguez, Sea., 54; 3B—Knoblauch, Min., 14; HR—McGwire, Oak., 52; RBI—Belle, Cle., 148; SH—Goodwin, K.C., 21; SF—Bonilla, Bal., 17; HP—Anderson, Bal., 22; BB—Phillips, Chi., 125; IBB—F. Thomas, Chi., 26; SO—Buhner, Sea., 159; SB—Lofton, Cle., 75; CS—Goodwin, K.C., 22; GIDP—C. Ripken, Bal., ; Slg. Pct.—McGwire, Oak., .730; OB. Pct.—McGwire, Oak., .467.

ALL PLAYERS

*Lefthanded batter. †Switch-hitter.

Player, Team	Avg.	G	TPA	AB	R	H	TB	2B	3B	HR	RBI	SH	SF	HP	BB	IBB	SO	SB	CS	GDP	Slg.	O
Aldrete, Mike, Cal.-N.Y.*	.213	63	123	108	16	23	47	6	0	6	20	0	1	0	14	0	19	0	1	4	.435	.3
Alexander, Manny, Baltimore	.103	54	73	68	6	7	7	0	0	0	4	2	0	0	3	0	27	3	3	2	.103	.1
Alomar, Roberto, Baltimore†	.328	153	699	588	132	193	310	43	4	22	94	8	12	1	90	10	65	17	6	14	.527	.4
Alomar, Sandy, Cleveland	.263	127	444	418	53	110	166	23	0	11	50	2	2	3	19	0	42	1	0	20	.397	.3
Amaral, Rich, Seattle	.292	118	369	312	69	91	111	11	3	1	29	4	1	5	47	0	55	25	6	6	.356	.3
Anderson, Brady, Baltimore*	.297	149	687	579	117	172	369	37	5	50	110	6	4	22	76	1	106	21	8	11	.637	.3
Anderson, Garret, California*	.285	150	642	607	79	173	246	33	2	12	72	5	3	0	27	5	84	7	9	22	.405	.3
Arias, George, California	.238	84	274	252	19	60	88	8	1	6	28	6	0	0	16	2	50	2	0	6	.349	.2
Ausmus, Brad, Detroit	.248	75	261	226	30	56	80	12	0	4	22	5	2	2	26	1	45	3	4	4	.354	.3
Baerga, Carlos, Cleveland†	.267	100	453	424	54	113	168	25	0	10	55	2	4	7	16	0	25	1	1	15	.396	.3
Baines, Harold, Chicago*	.311	143	572	495	80	154	249	29	0	22	95	0	3	1	73	7	62	3	1	20	.503	.3
Banks, Brian, Milwaukee*	.571	4	8	7	2	4	9	2	0	1	2	0	0	0	1	0	2	0	0	0	1.286	.6
Bartee, Kimera, Detroit	.253	110	247	217	32	55	66	6	1	1	14	13	0	0	17	0	77	20	10	1	.304	.3
Batista, Tony, Oakland	.298	74	260	238	38	71	103	10	2	6	25	0	2	1	19	0	49	7	3	2	.433	.3
Battle, Allen, Oakland	.192	47	151	130	20	25	31	3	0	1	5	1	1	2	17	1	26	10	2	3	.238	.2
Bautista, Danny, Detroit	.250	25	73	64	12	16	24	2	0	2	8	0	0	0	9	0	15	1	2	1	.375	.3
Becker, Rich, Minnesota*	.291	148	606	525	92	153	228	31	4	12	71	5	4	2	68	1	118	19	5	14	.434	.3
Belle, Albert, Cleveland	.311	158	715	602	124	187	375	38	3	48	148	0	7	7	99	15	87	11	0	20	.623	.4
Beltre, Esteban, Boston	.258	27	68	62	6	16	18	2	0	0	6	1	0	0	4	0	14	1	0	1	.290	.2
Berroa, Geronimo, Oakland	.290	153	643	586	101	170	312	32	1	36	106	0	6	4	47	0	122	0	3	16	.532	.3
Boggs, Wade, New York*	.311	132	574	501	80	156	195	29	2	2	41	1	5	0	67	7	32	1	2	10	.389	.3
Bonilla, Bobby, Baltimore†	.287	159	693	595	107	171	292	27	5	28	116	0	17	5	75	7	85	1	3	13	.491	.3
Borders, Pat, Cal.-Chi.	.258	50	163	151	12	39	58	4	0	5	14	4	0	0	8	0	29	0	1	3	.384	.2
Bordick, Mike, Oakland	.240	155	587	525	46	126	176	18	4	5	54	4	5	1	52	0	59	5	6	8	.318	.3
Bournigal, Rafael, Oakland	.242	88	277	252	33	61	79	14	2	0	18	8	0	1	16	0	19	4	3	6	.313	.2
Bowers, Brent, Baltimore*	.308	21	39	39	6	12	14	2	0	0	3	0	0	0	0	0	7	0	0	1	.359	.3
Bragg, Darren, Sea.-Bos.*	.261	127	499	417	74	109	169	26	2	10	47	2	7	4	69	6	74	14	9	5	.405	.3
Brede, Brent, Minnesota*	.300	10	21	20	2	6	8	0	1	0	2	0	0	0	1	0	5	0	0	1	.400	.3
Brito, Tilson, Toronto	.238	26	95	80	10	19	29	7	0	1	7	2	0	3	10	0	18	1	1	0	.363	.3

1996 A.L. STATISTICS — Batting

ayer, Team	Avg.	G	TPA	AB	R	H	TB	2B	3B	HR	RBI	SH	SF	HP	BB	IBB	SO	SB	CS	GDP	Slg.	OBP
osius, Scott, Oakland	.304	114	500	428	73	130	221	25	0	22	71	1	5	7	59	4	85	7	2	11	.516	.393
own, Kevin L., Texas	.000	3	8	4	1	0	0	0	0	0	0	1	0	1	1	2	0	2	0	0	.000	.375
umfield, Jacob, Toronto	.256	90	340	308	52	79	138	19	2	12	52	1	3	4	24	1	58	12	3	10	.448	.316
ford, Damon, Texas	.283	90	162	145	30	41	68	9	0	6	20	1	1	0	15	0	34	8	5	3	.469	.348
hner, Jay, Seattle	.271	150	667	564	107	153	314	29	0	44	138	0	10	9	84	5	159	0	1	11	.557	.369
rnitz, Jeromy, Cle.-Mil.*	.265	94	239	200	38	53	94	14	0	9	40	0	2	4	33	2	47	4	1	4	.470	.377
iro, Miguel, Toronto	.222	9	30	27	5	6	8	2	0	0	1	0	0	1	2	0	9	0	0	1	.296	.300
meron, Mike, Chicago	.091	11	12	11	1	1	1	0	0	0	0	0	0	0	1	0	3	0	1	0	.091	.167
ndaele, Casey, Cleveland†	.250	24	45	44	8	11	16	2	0	1	4	0	0	1	0		9	0	0	1	.364	.267
nseco, Jose, Boston	.289	96	432	360	68	104	212	22	1	28	82	0	3	6	63	3	82	3	1	7	.589	.400
rr, Chuck, Milwaukee†	.274	27	113	106	18	29	40	6	1	1	11	0	1	0	6	0	21	5	4	1	.377	.310
rreon, Mark, Cleveland	.324	38	156	142	16	46	64	12	0	2	14	0	0	3	11	0	9	1	1	4	.451	.385
rter, Joe, Toronto	.253	157	682	625	84	158	297	35	7	30	107	0	6	7	44	2	106	7	6	12	.475	.306
sanova, Raul, Detroit†	.188	25	91	85	6	16	29	1	0	4	9	0	0	6	0		18	0	0	6	.341	.242
deno, Andujar, Detroit	.196	52	186	179	19	35	64	4	2	7	20	3	0	0	4	0	37	2	1	8	.358	.213
deno, Domingo, Tor.-Chi.†	.272	89	329	301	46	82	104	12	2	2	20	8	3	2	15	0	64	6	3	7	.346	.308
illo, Jeff, Milwaukee	.325	138	643	566	101	184	285	46	5	15	83	6	6	7	58	0	69	4	9	14	.504	.391
ark, Phil, Boston	.000	3	3	3	0	0	0	0	0	0	0	0	0	0	0	0	1	0	0	1	.000	.000
ark, Tony, Detroit†	.250	100	411	376	56	94	189	14	0	27	72	0	6	0	29	1	127	0	1	7	.503	.299
ark, Will, Texas*	.284	117	512	436	69	124	190	25	1	13	72	0	7	5	64	5	67	2	1	10	.436	.377
emens, Roger, Boston*	1.000	34	1	1	0	1	1	0	0	0	0	0	0	0	0	0	0	0	0	0	1.000	1.000
le, Alex, Boston*	.222	24	83	72	13	16	23	5	1	0	7	2	1	0	8	0	11	5	3	2	.319	.296
omer, Ron, Minnesota	.296	95	253	233	34	69	119	12	1	12	41	0	3	0	17	1	24	3	0	10	.511	.340
ra, Joey, Seattle†	.291	144	583	530	90	154	221	37	6	6	45	6	5	7	35	1	32	5	5	9	.417	.340
rdero, Wil, Minnesota	.288	59	213	198	29	57	80	14	0	3	37	1	1	2	11	4	31	2	1	8	.404	.330
rdova, Marty, Minnesota	.309	145	640	569	97	176	272	46	1	16	111	0	9	8	53	4	96	11	5	18	.478	.371
espo, Felipe, Toronto†	.184	22	64	49	6	9	13	4	0	0	4	0	0	3	12	0	13	1	0	0	.265	.375
uz, Fausto, Detroit	.237	14	40	38	5	9	11	2	0	0	0	1	0	0	1	0	11	0	0	1	.289	.256
rtis, Chad, Detroit	.263	104	466	400	65	105	157	20	1	10	37	6	6	1	53	0	73	16	10	14	.393	.346
yler, Milt, Boston†	.200	50	134	110	19	22	33	1	2	2	12	7	1	3	13	0	19	7	3	1	.300	.299
mon, Johnny, Kansas City*	.271	145	566	517	61	140	190	22	5	6	50	10	5	3	31	3	64	25	5	4	.368	.313
vis, Chili, California†	.292	145	623	530	73	155	263	24	0	28	95	1	6	0	86	11	99	5	2	18	.496	.387
vis, Russ, Seattle	.234	51	191	167	24	39	63	9	0	5	18	4	0	2	17	1	50	2	0	1	.377	.312
lgado, Alex, Boston	.250	26	24	20	5	5	5	0	0	0	1	1	0	0	3	0	3	0	0	0	.250	.348
lgado, Carlos, Toronto*	.270	138	563	488	68	132	239	28	2	25	92	0	8	9	58	2	139	0	0	13	.490	.353
varez, Cesar, Baltimore	.111	10	19	18	3	2	4	0	1	0	0	0	0	0	1	0	3	0	0	0	.222	.158
vereaux, Mike, Baltimore	.229	127	363	323	49	74	113	11	2	8	34	2	2	2	34	0	53	8	2	8	.350	.305
az, Alex, Seattle†	.241	38	84	79	11	19	24	2	0	1	5	0	1	2	2	0	8	6	3	2	.304	.274
az, Einar, Cleveland	.000	4	1	1	0	0	0	0	0	0	0	0	0	0	0	0	0	0	0	0	.000	.000
Sarcina, Gary, California	.256	150	576	536	62	137	186	26	4	5	48	16	1	2	21	0	36	2	1	16	.347	.286
ncan, Mariano, New York	.340	109	417	400	62	136	200	34	3	8	56	2	5	1	9	1	77	4	3	10	.500	.352
nn, Todd, Milwaukee	.300	6	10	10	2	3	4	1	0	0	1	0	0	0	0	0	3	0	0	1	.400	.300
rant, Mike, Minnesota	.210	40	96	81	15	17	20	3	0	0	5	4	1	0	10	0	15	3	0	2	.247	.293
rham, Ray, Chicago†	.275	156	639	557	79	153	226	33	5	10	65	7	7	10	58	4	95	30	4	6	.406	.350
sley, Damion, Cal.-Det	.268	49	129	112	14	30	44	2	0	4	17	5	1	1	10	0	25	3	1	0	.393	.331
monds, Jim, California*	.304	114	483	431	73	131	246	28	3	27	66	0	2	4	46	2	101	4	0	8	.571	.375
nhoorn, Robert, N.Y.-Cal	.172	18	34	29	3	5	5	0	0	0	2	1	0	2	2	0	5	0	0	0	.172	.212
ster, Kevin, Texas	.252	157	596	515	79	130	238	32	2	24	99	16	11	2	52	1	138	4	1	8	.462	.317
stad, Darin, California*	.284	57	229	208	34	59	78	5	1	4	20	1	3	0	17	1	29	3	3	3	.375	.333
pinoza, Alvaro, Cleveland	.223	59	125	112	12	25	45	4	2	4	11	3	1	3	6	0	18	1	1	4	.402	.279
oregas, Jorge, California*	.287	90	279	254	18	73	85	6	0	2	26	3	5	0	17	3	27	0	1	7	.335	.326
neyte, Rikkert, Texas	.200	8	7	5	0	1	1	0	0	0	0	1	2	0	0	0	0	0	0	0	.200	.200
sano, Sal, Kansas City	.203	51	160	143	20	29	49	2	0	6	19	1	0	2	14	0	25	1	1	3	.343	.283
lder, Cecil, Det.-N.Y	.252	160	688	591	85	149	286	20	0	39	117	0	5	5	87	12	139	2	0	18	.484	.350
herty, John, Detroit	.250	47	165	152	18	38	62	12	0	4	23	3	1	1	8	1	25	1	0	5	.408	.290
x, Andy, New York*	.196	113	219	189	26	37	50	4	0	3	13	9	0	1	20	0	28	11	3	2	.265	.276
anco, Julio, Cleveland	.322	112	499	432	72	139	203	20	1	14	76	0	3	3	61	2	82	8	8	14	.470	.407
azier, Lou, Texas†	.260	30	60	50	5	13	17	2	1	0	5	1	0	1	8	0	10	4	2	2	.340	.373
ve, Jeff, Boston	.286	105	486	419	74	120	163	27	2	4	41	5	3	5	54	0	57	18	4	6	.389	.372
yman, Travis, Detroit	.268	157	688	616	90	165	269	32	3	22	100	1	10	4	57	2	118	4	3	18	.437	.329
rciaparra, Nomar, Boston	.241	24	93	87	11	21	41	2	3	4	16	1	1	0	4	0	14	5	0	0	.471	.272
rrison, Webster, Oakland	.000	5	10	9	0	0	0	0	0	0	0	0	0	0	1	0	0	0	0	0	.000	.100
tes, Brent, Oakland†	.263	64	274	247	26	65	94	19	2	2	30	5	2	2	18	0	35	1	1	9	.381	.316
ambi, Jason, Oakland*	.291	140	598	536	84	156	258	40	1	20	79	1	5	5	51	3	95	0	1	15	.481	.355
, Benji, Texas	.400	5	7	5	0	2	2	0	0	0	1	1	0	0	1	0	1	0	1	0	.400	.500
es, Brian S., Cleveland*	.355	51	143	121	26	43	74	14	1	5	27	0	3	0	19	4	13	3	0	6	.612	.434
ardi, Joe, New York	.294	124	471	422	55	124	158	22	3	2	45	11	3	5	30	1	55	13	4	11	.374	.346
mez, Chris, Detroit	.242	48	150	128	21	31	39	5	0	1	16	3	0	1	18	0	20	1	1	5	.305	.340
nzales, Rene, Texas	.217	51	104	92	19	20	30	4	0	2	5	0	2	0	10	0	11	0	0	3	.326	.288
nzalez, Alex, Toronto	.235	147	587	527	64	124	206	30	5	14	64	7	3	5	45	0	127	16	6	12	.391	.300
nzalez, Juan, Texas	.314	134	592	541	89	170	348	33	2	47	144	0	3	3	45	12	82	2	0	16	.643	.368
odwin, Tom, Kansas City*	.282	143	587	524	80	148	173	14	4	1	35	21	1	2	39	0	79	66	22	3	.330	.334
een, Shawn, Toronto*	.280	132	465	422	52	118	189	32	3	11	45	0	2	8	33	3	75	5	1	9	.448	.342
eene, Todd, California	.190	29	84	79	9	15	22	1	0	2	9	0	0	1	4	0	11	2	0	4	.278	.238
eenwell, Mike, Boston*	.295	77	318	295	35	87	130	20	1	7	44	0	3	2	18	3	27	4	0	11	.441	.336
er, Rusty, Texas*	.332	139	617	542	96	180	287	41	6	18	100	0	10	3	62	4	86	9	0	9	.530	.397
iffey, Ken, Seattle*	.303	140	638	545	125	165	342	26	2	49	140	1	7	7	78	13	104	16	1	7	.628	.392
illen, Ozzie, Chicago*	.263	150	528	499	62	131	183	24	8	4	45	12	7	0	10	0	27	6	5	10	.367	.273
le, Chip, Minnesota*	.276	85	98	87	8	24	32	5	1	0	16	0	1	0	2	0	21	0	0	3	.368	.347
melin, Bob, Kansas City*	.255	89	299	239	31	61	104	14	1	9	40	0	4	2	54	2	58	5	2	7	.435	.391
milton, Darryl, Texas*	.293	148	696	627	94	184	239	29	4	6	51	7	6	2	54	4	66	15	5	15	.381	.348
mmonds, Jeffrey, Balt.	.226	71	282	248	38	56	95	10	1	9	27	6	1	4	23	1	53	3	3	7	.383	.301
ncock, Ryan, California	1.000	11	1	1	1	1	1	0	0	0	0	0	0	0	0	0	0	0	0	0	1.000	1.000

1996 A.L. STATISTICS Batting

Player, Team	Avg.	G	TPA	AB	R	H	TB	2B	3B	HR	RBI	SH	SF	HP	BB	IBB	SO	SB	CS	GDP	Slg.	O
Haselman, Bill, Boston	.274	77	257	237	33	65	104	13	1	8	34	0	0	1	19	3	52	4	2	13	.439	.
Hatteberg, Scott, Boston*	.182	10	14	11	3	2	3	1	0	0	0	0	0	0	3	0	2	0	0	2	.273	.
Hayes, Charlie, New York	.284	20	69	67	7	19	28	3	0	2	13	1	0	0	1	0	12	0	0	1	.418	.2
Herrera, Jose, Oakland*	.269	108	346	320	44	86	121	15	1	6	30	3	0	3	20	1	59	8	2	5	.378	.
Hiatt, Phil, Detroit	.190	7	23	21	3	4	6	0	1	0	1	0	0	0	2	0	11	0	0	1	.286	.2
Higginson, Bob, Detroit*	.320	130	515	440	75	141	254	35	0	26	81	3	6	1	65	7	66	6	3	7	.577	.4
Hocking, Denny, Minnesota†	.197	49	137	127	16	25	34	6	0	1	10	1	1	0	8	0	24	3	3	3	.268	.2
Hoiles, Chris, Baltimore	.258	127	481	407	64	105	193	13	0	25	73	1	7	9	57	1	97	0	1	7	.474	.3
Hollins, Dave, Min.-Sea.†	.262	149	616	516	88	135	212	29	0	16	78	1	2	13	84	7	117	6	6	11	.411	.3
Hosey, Dwayne, Boston†	.218	28	87	78	13	17	26	2	2	1	3	2	0	0	7	0	17	6	3	0	.333	.2
Howard, Dave, Kansas City†	.219	143	485	420	51	92	128	14	5	4	48	17	4	4	40	0	74	5	6	6	.305	.2
Howard, Matt, New York	.204	35	59	54	9	11	15	1	0	1	9	2	1	0	2	0	8	1	0	2	.278	.2
Howell, Jack, California*	.270	66	136	126	20	34	64	4	1	8	21	0	0	0	10	0	30	0	1	3	.508	.3
Hudler, Rex, California	.311	92	317	302	60	94	168	20	3	16	40	2	1	3	9	0	54	14	5	7	.556	.3
Huff, Michael, Toronto	.172	11	30	29	5	5	7	0	1	0	0	0	0	0	1	0	5	0	0	1	.241	.2
Hulse, David, Milwaukee*	.222	81	127	117	18	26	29	3	0	0	6	2	0	0	8	0	16	4	1	2	.248	.2
Hunter, Brian, Seattle	.268	75	221	198	21	53	84	10	0	7	28	1	3	4	15	2	43	0	1	6	.424	.3
Huson, Jeff, Baltimore*	.321	17	30	28	5	9	10	1	0	0	2	0	1	0	1	0	3	0	0	0	.357	.3
Hyers, Tim, Detroit*	.077	17	30	26	1	2	3	1	0	0	0	0	0	0	4	2	5	0	0	1	.115	.2
Ibanez, Raul, Seattle*	.000	4	6	5	0	0	0	0	0	0	0	0	0	0	1	0	1	0	0	0	.000	.1
Incaviglia, Pete, Baltimore	.303	12	35	33	4	10	18	2	0	2	8	0	1	1	0	0	7	0	0	0	.545	.3
Jackson, Damian, Cleveland	.300	5	11	10	2	3	5	2	0	0	1	0	0	0	1	0	4	0	0	0	.500	.3
Jaha, John, Milwaukee	.300	148	636	543	108	163	295	28	1	34	118	0	3	5	85	1	118	3	1	16	.543	.3
James, Dion, New York*	.167	6	13	12	1	2	2	0	0	0	0	0	0	0	1	0	2	1	0	1	.167	.2
Jefferson, Reggie, Boston*	.347	122	418	386	67	134	229	30	4	19	74	0	4	3	25	5	89	0	0	11	.593	.3
Jeter, Derek, New York	.314	157	654	582	104	183	250	25	6	10	78	6	9	9	48	1	102	14	7	13	.430	.3
Johns, Doug, Oakland	.000	42	0	0	1	0	0	0	0	0	0	0	0	0	0	0	0	0	0	0	.000	.0
Jordan, Ricky, Seattle	.250	15	31	28	4	7	10	0	0	1	4	0	1	1	1	0	6	0	0	0	.357	.2
Karkovice, Ron, Chicago	.220	111	389	355	44	78	130	22	0	10	38	7	2	1	24	2	93	0	0	7	.366	.2
Kelly, Pat, New York	.143	13	23	21	4	3	3	0	0	0	2	0	0	0	2	0	9	0	1	1	.143	.2
Kelly, Roberto, Minnesota	.323	98	359	322	41	104	147	17	4	6	47	0	5	7	23	0	53	10	2	17	.457	.3
Kent, Jeff, Cleveland	.265	39	116	102	16	27	43	7	0	3	16	0	3	1	10	0	22	2	1	1	.422	.3
Kirby, Wayne, Cleveland*	.250	27	18	16	3	4	5	1	0	0	1	0	0	0	2	0	2	0	1	1	.313	.3
Knoblauch, Chuck, Minnesota	.341	153	701	578	140	197	299	35	14	13	72	0	6	19	98	6	74	45	14	9	.517	.4
Koslofski, Kevin, Milwaukee*	.214	25	47	42	5	9	16	3	2	0	6	0	0	1	4	1	12	0	0	1	.381	.2
Kreuter, Chad, Chicago†	.219	46	132	114	14	25	42	8	0	3	18	2	1	2	13	0	29	0	0	2	.368	.3
Lawton, Matt, Minnesota*	.258	79	286	252	34	65	92	7	1	6	42	0	2	4	28	1	28	4	4	6	.365	.3
Leius, Scott, Cleveland	.140	27	46	43	3	6	13	4	0	1	3	1	0	0	2	0	8	0	0	1	.302	.1
Lennon, Patrick, Kansas City	.233	14	37	30	5	7	10	3	0	0	1	0	0	0	7	0	10	0	0	0	.333	.3
Lesher, Brian, Oakland	.232	26	90	82	11	19	37	3	0	5	16	1	1	1	5	0	17	0	0	2	.451	.2
Levis, Jesse, Milwaukee*	.236	104	274	233	27	55	66	6	1	1	21	1	0	2	38	0	15	0	0	7	.283	.3
Lewis, Darren, Chicago	.228	141	405	337	55	77	105	12	2	4	53	15	5	3	45	1	40	21	5	9	.312	.3
Lewis, Mark, Detroit	.270	145	599	545	69	147	216	30	3	11	55	4	3	5	42	0	109	6	1	12	.396	.3
Lewis, Richie, Detroit	.000	72	1	1	0	0	0	0	0	0	0	0	0	0	0	0	0	0	0	0	.000	.0
Leyritz, Jim, New York	.264	88	309	265	23	70	101	10	0	7	40	2	3	9	30	1	68	2	0	11	.381	.3
Listach, Pat, Milwaukee†	.240	87	362	317	51	76	99	16	2	1	33	6	2	1	36	0	51	25	5	2	.312	.3
Lockhart, Keith, Kansas City*	.273	138	471	433	49	118	178	33	3	7	55	1	5	2	30	4	40	11	6	7	.411	.3
Lofton, Kenny, Cleveland*	.317	154	736	662	132	210	295	35	4	14	67	7	6	0	61	3	82	75	17	7	.446	.3
Loretta, Mark, Milwaukee	.279	73	170	154	20	43	49	3	0	1	13	2	0	0	14	0	15	2	1	7	.318	.3
Lovullo, Torey, Oakland†	.220	65	99	82	15	18	31	4	0	3	9	3	1	2	11	0	17	1	2	0	.378	.3
Luke, Matt, New York*	.000	1	0	0	1	0	0	0	0	0	0	0	0	0	0	0	0	0	0	0	.000	.0
Macfarlane, Mike, Kansas City	.274	112	419	379	58	104	189	24	2	19	54	0	2	7	31	5	57	3	3	4	.499	.3
Machado, Robert, Chicago	.667	4	6	6	1	4	5	1	0	0	2	0	0	0	0	0	0	0	0	0	.833	.6
Malave, Jose, Boston	.235	41	105	102	12	24	39	3	0	4	17	0	1	2	0		25	0	0	0	.382	.2
Manto, Jeff, Bos.-Sea.	.196	43	120	102	15	20	37	6	1	3	10	0	0	1	17	0	24	0	1	2	.363	.3
Martin, Norberto, Chicago	.350	70	151	140	30	49	59	7	0	1	14	4	1	0	6	0	17	10	2	4	.421	.3
Martinez, Dave, Chicago*	.318	146	498	440	85	140	206	20	8	10	53	2	1	3	52	1	52	15	7	4	.468	.3
Martinez, Edgar, Seattle	.327	139	634	499	121	163	297	52	2	26	103	0	4	8	123	12	84	3	3	15	.595	.4
Martinez, Manny, Seattle	.235	9	20	17	3	4	8	2	1	0	3	0	0	0	3	0	5	2	0	1	.471	.3
Martinez, Sandy, Toronto*	.227	76	251	229	17	52	76	9	3	3	18	1	1	4	16	0	58	0	0	4	.332	.2
Martinez, Tino, New York*	.292	155	671	595	82	174	277	28	0	25	117	1	5	2	68	4	85	2	1	18	.466	.3
Marzano, John, Seattle	.245	41	120	106	8	26	32	6	0	0	6	3	0	4	7	0	15	0	0	2	.302	.3
Mashore, Damon, Oakland	.267	50	124	105	20	28	46	7	1	3	12	1	1	1	16	0	31	4	0	2	.438	.3
Matheny, Mike, Milwaukee	.204	106	341	313	31	64	107	15	2	8	46	7	4	3	14	0	80	3	2	9	.342	.2
McGwire, Mark, Oakland	.312	130	548	423	104	132	306	21	0	52	113	0	1	8	116	16	112	0	0	14	.730	.4
McIntosh, Tim, New York	.000	3	3	3	0	0	0	0	0	0	0	0	0	0	0	0	0	0	0	0	.000	.0
McLemore, Mark, Texas†	.290	147	611	517	84	150	196	23	4	5	46	2	5	0	87	5	69	27	10	16	.379	.3
Meares, Pat, Minnesota	.267	152	554	517	66	138	202	26	7	8	67	4	7	9	17	1	90	9	4	19	.391	.2
Mercedes, Henry, Kansas City	.250	4	4	4	1	1	1	0	0	0	0	0	0	0	0	0	1	0	0	0	.250	.2
Mieske, Matt, Milwaukee	.278	127	409	374	46	104	176	24	3	14	64	1	6	2	26	2	76	1	5	9	.471	.3
Mitchell, Kevin, Boston	.304	27	104	92	9	28	38	4	0	2	13	0	0	1	11	0	14	0	0	3	.413	.3
Molina, Izzy, Oakland	.200	14	26	25	0	5	7	2	0	0	1	0	0	0	1	0	3	0	0	0	.280	.2
Molitor, Paul, Minnesota	.341	161	729	660	99	225	309	41	8	9	113	0	9	3	56	10	72	18	6	21	.468	.3
Moore, Kerwin, Oakland†	.063	22	18	16	4	1	2	1	0	0	0	0	0		2	0	6	1	0	0	.125	.1
Mosquera, Julio, Toronto	.227	8	23	22	2	5	7	2	0	0	2	0	0	1	0	0	6	0	0	0	.318	.2
Mouton, Lyle, Chicago	.294	87	241	214	25	63	94	8	1	7	39	0	3		22	4	50	3	0	3	.439	.3
Munoz, Jose, Chicago†	.259	17	31	27	7	7	7	0	0	0	0	0	0	0	4	0	1	0	0	2	.259	.3
Munoz, Pedro, Minnesota	.256	34	130	121	17	31	54	5	0	6	18	0	0		6		31	0	0	2	.446	.3
Murray, Eddie, Cle.-Bal.†	.260	152	637	566	69	147	236	21	1	22	79	0	10	0	61	6	87	4	0	19	.417	.3
Myers, Greg, Minnesota	.286	97	353	329	37	94	140	22	3	6	47	0	5	0	19	3	52	0	0	11	.426	.3
Myers, Rod, Kansas City*	.286	22	70	63	9	18	28	7	0	1	11	0	0	0	7	0	16	3	2	1	.444	.3
Naehring, Tim, Boston	.288	116	489	430	77	124	191	16	0	17	65	2	4	4	49	4	63	2	1	14	.444	.3
Nevin, Phil, Detroit	.292	38	130	120	15	35	64	5	0	8	19	0	1	1	8	0	39	1	0	1	.533	.3

ayer, Team	Avg.	G	TPA	AB	R	H	TB	2B	3B	HR	RBI	SH	SF	HP	BB	IBB	SO	SB	CS	GDP	Slg.	OBP
wfield, Marc, Milwaukee	.307	49	198	179	21	55	91	15	0	7	31	0	4	4	11	1	26	0	1	1	.508	.354
wson, Warren, Texas*	.255	91	273	235	34	60	106	14	1	10	31	0	1	0	37	1	82	3	0	3	.451	.355
eves, Melvin, Detroit†	.246	120	484	431	71	106	209	23	4	24	60	0	3	6	44	2	158	1	2	10	.485	.322
sson, Dave, Milwaukee* ...	.331	123	516	453	81	150	238	33	2	17	84	0	3	3	57	6	68	2	3	4	.525	.407
kon, Otis, Toronto†	.286	125	575	496	87	142	162	15	1	1	29	7	0	1	71	1	68	54	13	9	.327	.377
kon, Trot, Boston*	.500	2	4	4	2	2	3	1	0	0	0	0	0	0	0	0	1	1	0	0	.750	.500
rman, Les, Kansas City	.122	54	56	49	9	6	6	0	0	0	0	0	0	1	6	0	14	1	1	0	.122	.232
rton, Greg, Chicago†	.217	11	27	23	4	5	11	0	0	2	3	0	0	0	4	0	6	0	1	0	.478	.333
nnally, Jon, Kansas City* ..	.211	35	104	90	16	19	41	5	1	5	17	0	1	0	13	2	25	0	0	0	.456	.308
3rien, Charlie, Toronto	.238	109	375	324	33	77	133	17	0	13	44	3	2	17	29	1	68	0	1	8	.410	.331
erman, Jose, Kansas City†	.303	151	645	561	85	170	234	33	8	5	47	7	2	1	74	3	98	24	10	9	.417	.384
Leary, Troy, Boston*	.260	149	552	497	68	129	212	28	5	15	81	1	3	4	47	3	80	3	2	13	.427	.327
erud, John, Toronto*	.274	125	469	398	59	109	188	25	0	18	61	0	1	10	60	6	37	1	0	10	.472	.382
Neill, Paul, New York*	.302	150	660	546	89	165	259	35	1	19	91	0	8	4	102	8	76	0	1	21	.474	.411
iz, Luis, Texas	.286	3	7	7	1	2	7	0	1	1	1	0	0	0	0	0	1	0	0	0	1.000	.286
meiro, Orlando, California* .	.287	50	98	87	6	25	33	6	1	0	6	1	0	2	8	1	13	0	1	1	.379	.361
meiro, Rafael, Baltimore*..	.289	162	732	626	110	181	342	40	2	39	142	0	3	8	95	12	96	8	0	9	.546	.381
lmer, Dean, Texas	.280	154	652	582	98	163	307	26	2	38	107	0	6	5	59	4	145	2	0	15	.527	.348
quette, Craig, Kansas City ..	.259	118	462	429	61	111	194	15	1	22	67	3	5	2	23	2	101	5	3	11	.452	.296
rent, Mark, Det.-Bal	.226	56	144	137	17	31	65	7	0	9	23	1	1	0	5	0	37	0	0	3	.474	.252
mberton, Rudy, Boston	.512	13	45	41	11	21	32	8	0	1	10	0	0	2	2	0	4	3	1	0	.780	.556
na, Geronimo, Cleveland† ..	.111	5	10	9	1	1	4	0	0	1	2	0	0	1	0	0	4	0	0	2	.444	.200
na, Tony, Cleveland	.195	67	195	174	14	34	41	4	0	1	27	3	3	0	15	0	25	0	1	8	.236	.255
nn, Shannon, Detroit†	.071	6	14	14	0	1	1	0	0	0	1	0	0	0	0	0	3	0	0	0	.071	.071
rcival, Troy, California	.000	62	1	1	0	0	0	0	0	0	0	0	0	0	0	0	1	0	0	0	.000	.000
rez, Danny, Milwaukee	.000	4	4	4	0	0	0	0	0	0	0	0	0	0	0	0	0	0	0	0	.000	.000
rez, Robert, Toronto	.327	86	216	202	30	66	82	10	0	2	21	4	1	1	8	0	17	3	0	6	.406	.354
rez, Tomas, Toronto†	.251	91	328	295	24	74	98	13	4	1	19	6	1	1	25	0	29	1	2	10	.332	.311
rry, Herbert, Cleveland	.083	7	13	12	1	1	2	1	0	0	0	0	0	1	0	0	2	1	0	0	.167	.154
illips, Tony, Chicago†	.277	153	719	581	119	161	232	29	3	12	63	1	8	4	125	9	132	13	8	6	.399	.404
rkl, Greg, Bos.-Sea	.174	9	23	23	2	4	8	1	0	1	1	0	0	0	0	0	4	0	0	1	.348	.174
antier, Phil, Oakland*	.212	73	263	231	29	49	80	8	1	7	31	0	1	3	28	0	56	2	2	5	.346	.304
lonia, Luis, Baltimore*	.240	58	187	175	25	42	54	4	1	2	14	1	0	1	10	0	20	8	6	10	.309	.285
sada, Jorge, New York†	.071	8	15	14	1	1	1	0	0	0	0	0	0	0	1	0	6	0	0	1	.071	.133
azo, Arquimedez, Boston	.172	21	62	58	4	10	18	3	1	1	11	0	1	1	2	0	10	1	0	1	.310	.210
ide, Curtis, Detroit*	.300	95	301	267	52	80	137	17	5	10	31	3	0	0	31	1	63	11	6	2	.513	.372
itchett, Chris, California* ..	.154	5	13	13	1	2	2	0	0	0	1	0	0	0	0	0	3	0	0	0	.154	.154
inlan, Tom, Minnesota	.000	4	6	6	0	0	0	0	0	0	0	0	0	0	0	0	3	0	0	0	.000	.000
abe, Brian, Minnesota	.222	7	10	9	0	2	2	0	0	0	1	0	1	0	0	0	1	0	0	0	.222	.200
ines, Tim, New York†	.284	59	240	201	45	57	94	10	0	9	33	0	4	1	34	1	29	10	1	5	.468	.383
mirez, Manny, Cleveland	.309	152	647	550	94	170	320	45	3	33	112	0	9	3	85	8	104	8	5	18	.582	.399
anda, Joe, Kansas City	.303	110	370	337	36	102	146	24	1	6	47	2	4	1	26	4	47	13	4	10	.433	.351
eboulet, Jeff, Minnesota	.222	107	266	234	20	52	61	9	0	0	23	4	2	1	25	1	34	4	2	10	.261	.298
pken, Billy, Baltimore	.230	57	147	135	19	31	45	8	0	2	12	1	1	1	9	0	18	0	0	4	.333	.281
pken, Cal, Baltimore	.278	163	707	640	94	178	298	40	1	26	102	0	4	4	59	3	78	1	2	28	.466	.341
vera, Ruben, New York	.284	46	106	88	17	25	39	6	1	2	16	1	2	2	13	0	26	6	2	1	.443	.381
oberts, Bip, Kansas City†	.283	90	372	339	39	96	121	21	2	0	52	0	6	2	25	8	38	12	9	8	.357	.331
obertson, Mike, Chicago* ...	.143	6	7	7	0	1	2	1	0	0	0	0	0	0	0	0	1	0	0	0	.286	.143
odriguez, Alex, Seattle	.358	146	677	601	141	215	379	54	1	36	123	6	7	4	59	1	104	15	4	15	.631	.414
odriguez, Ivan, Texas	.300	153	685	639	116	192	302	47	3	19	86	0	4	4	38	7	55	5	0	15	.473	.342
odriguez, Tony, Boston	.239	27	77	67	7	16	20	1	0	1	9	5	0	1	4	0	8	0	0	3	.299	.292
almon, Tim, California	.286	156	681	581	90	166	291	27	4	30	98	0	3	4	93	7	125	4	2	8	.501	.386
amuel, Juan, Toronto	.255	69	207	188	34	48	86	8	3	8	26	0	1	3	15	0	65	9	1	2	.457	.319
chofield, Dick, California	.250	13	17	16	3	4	4	0	0	0	0	0	0	0	1	0	1	1	0	0	.250	.294
eitzer, Kevin, Mil.-Cle	.326	154	675	573	85	187	267	35	3	13	78	5	5	5	87	7	79	6	1	13	.466	.416
elby, Bill, Boston*	.274	40	105	95	12	26	39	4	0	3	6	1	0	0	9	1	11	1	1	3	.411	.333
eets, Andy, Seattle	.191	47	124	110	18	21	29	8	0	0	9	2	1	1	10	0	41	2	0	2	.264	.262
erra, Ruben, N.Y.-Det.†	.247	142	587	518	61	128	194	26	2	12	72	0	9	0	60	12	88	4	4	12	.375	.320
ngleton, Duane, Detroit*	.161	18	61	56	5	9	10	1	0	0	3	0	1	0	4	0	15	0	2	2	.179	.230
aught, Don, Cal.-Chi	.313	76	263	243	25	76	104	10	0	6	36	1	2	2	15	0	22	0	0	16	.428	.355
nith, Mark, Baltimore	.244	27	84	78	9	19	33	2	0	4	10	0	0	3	3	0	20	0	2	0	.423	.298
nopek, Chris, Chicago	.260	46	113	104	18	27	53	6	1	6	18	1	1	1	6	0	16	0	1	5	.510	.304
now, J.T., California†	.257	155	641	575	69	148	221	20	1	17	67	2	3	5	56	6	96	1	6	19	.384	.327
ojo, Luis, Sea.-N.Y	.220	95	308	287	23	63	78	10	1	1	21	8	1	1	11	0	17	2	2	10	.272	.250
orrento, Paul, Seattle*	.289	143	542	471	67	136	239	32	1	23	93	2	5	7	57	10	103	0	2	10	.507	.370
piezio, Scott, Oakland†	.310	9	35	29	6	9	17	2	0	2	8	2	0	0	4	1	4	0	1	0	.586	.394
orague, Ed, Toronto	.247	159	670	591	88	146	293	35	2	36	101	0	7	12	60	3	146	0	0	7	.496	.326
tahoviak, Scott, Minnesota*	.284	130	469	405	72	115	190	30	3	13	61	1	2	2	59	7	114	3	3	9	.469	.376
airs, Matt, Oakland*	.277	61	158	137	21	38	75	5	1	10	23	0	1	1	19	2	23	1	1	2	.547	.367
anley, Mike, Boston	.270	121	473	397	73	107	201	20	1	24	69	0	2	5	69	3	62	2	0	8	.506	.383
teinbach, Terry, Oakland	.272	145	571	514	79	140	272	25	1	35	100	0	2	6	49	5	115	0	1	16	.529	.342
tevens, Lee, Texas*	.231	27	86	78	6	18	35	2	3	3	12	0	1	1	6	0	22	0	0	2	.449	.291
tewart, Shannon, Toronto	.176	7	18	17	2	3	4	1	0	0	2	0	0	0	1	0	4	2	0	1	.235	.222
tillwell, Kurt, Texas†	.273	46	89	77	12	21	28	4	0	1	4	1	0	1	10	0	11	0	0	1	.364	.364
tinnett, Kelly, Milwaukee	.077	14	29	26	1	2	2	0	0	0	3	0	0	0	2	0	11	0	0	0	.077	.172
trange, Doug, Seattle†	.235	88	200	183	19	43	61	7	1	3	23	0	2	1	14	0	31	1	0	3	.333	.292
trawberry, Darryl, New York* .	.262	63	237	202	35	53	99	13	0	11	36	0	3	1	31	5	55	6	5	3	.490	.359
tynes, Chris, Kansas City	.293	36	95	92	8	27	33	6	0	0	6	1	0	0	2	0	5	5	2	1	.359	.309
urhoff, B.J., Baltimore*	.292	143	590	537	74	157	259	27	6	21	82	2	1	3	47	8	79	0	1	7	.482	.352
weeney, Mike, Kansas City ..	.279	50	190	165	23	46	68	10	0	4	24	0	3	4	18	0	21	1	2	7	.412	.358
arasco, Tony, Baltimore*	.238	31	92	84	14	20	26	3	0	1	9	1	0	0	7	0	15	5	3	1	.310	.297
artabull, Danny, Chicago.....	.254	132	541	472	58	120	230	23	3	27	101	0	5	0	64	4	128	1	2	10	.487	.340
atum, Jimmy, Boston	.125	2	8	8	1	1	1	0	0	0	0	0	0	0	0	0	2	0	0	0	.125	.125

Player, Team	Avg.	G	TPA	AB	R	H	TB	2B	3B	HR	RBI	SH	SF	HP	BB	IBB	SO	SB	CS	GDP	Slg.	O
Tettleton, Mickey, Texas†	.246	143	599	491	78	121	221	26	1	24	83	1	9	3	95	8	137	2	1	12	.450	.3
Thomas, Frank, Chicago	.349	141	649	527	110	184	330	26	0	40	134	0	8	5	109	26	70	1	1	25	.626	.4
Thome, Jim, Cleveland*	.311	151	636	505	122	157	309	28	5	38	116	0	2	6	123	8	141	2	2	13	.612	.4
Thompson, Ryan, Cleveland	.318	8	23	22	2	7	10	0	0	1	5	0	0	0	1	0	6	0	0	0	.455	.3
Tinsley, Lee, Boston†	.245	92	209	192	28	47	64	6	1	3	14	1	1	2	13	0	56	6	8	5	.333	.2
Trammell, Alan, Detroit	.233	66	207	193	16	45	50	2	0	1	16	1	3	0	10	0	27	6	0	3	.259	.2
Tucker, Michael, Kansas City*	.260	108	393	339	55	88	150	18	4	12	53	3	4	7	40	1	69	10	4	7	.442	.3
Turner, Chris, California	.333	4	5	3	1	1	1	0	0	0	1	0	1	0	1	0	0	0	0	0	.333	.4
Unroe, Tim, Milwaukee	.188	14	20	16	5	3	3	0	0	0	0	0	0	0	4	0	5	0	1	0	.188	.3
Valentin, John, Boston	.296	131	606	527	84	156	230	29	3	13	59	2	7	7	63	0	59	9	10	15	.436	.3
Valentin, Jose, Milwaukee†	.259	154	628	552	90	143	262	33	7	24	95	6	4	0	66	9	145	17	4	4	.475	.3
Valle, Dave, Texas	.302	42	95	86	14	26	43	6	1	3	17	0	0	9	0	17	0	0	3	.500	.3
Vaughn, Greg, Milwaukee	.280	102	442	375	78	105	214	16	0	31	95	0	5	4	58	4	99	5	2	6	.571	.3
Vaughn, Mo, Boston*	.326	161	752	635	118	207	370	29	1	44	143	0	8	14	95	19	154	2	0	17	.583	.4
Velarde, Randy, California	.285	136	611	530	82	151	226	27	3	14	54	4	2	5	70	0	118	7	7	7	.426	.3
Ventura, Robin, Chicago*	.287	158	674	586	96	168	305	31	2	34	105	0	8	2	78	10	81	1	3	18	.520	.3
Vina, Fernando, Milwaukee*	.283	140	615	554	94	157	217	19	10	7	46	6	4	13	38	3	35	16	7	15	.392	.3
Vitiello, Joe, Kansas City	.241	85	301	257	29	62	103	15	1	8	40	0	3	3	38	2	69	2	0	12	.401	.3
Vizcaino, Jose, Cleveland†	.285	48	191	179	23	51	60	5	2	0	13	4	1	0	7	0	24	6	2	2	.335	.3
Vizquel, Omar, Cleveland†	.297	151	623	542	98	161	226	36	1	9	64	12	9	4	56	0	42	35	9	10	.417	.3
Voigt, Jack, Texas	.111	5	9	9	1	1	1	0	0	0	0	0	0	0	0	0	2	0	0	0	.111	.1
Walbeck, Matt, Minnesota†	.223	63	227	215	25	48	64	10	0	2	24	1	2	0	9	0	34	3	1	6	.298	.2
Walker, Todd, Minnesota*	.256	25	89	82	8	21	27	6	0	0	6	0	3	0	4	0	13	2	0	4	.329	.2
Wallach, Tim, California	.237	57	209	190	23	45	76	7	0	8	20	0	0	1	18	2	47	1	0	3	.400	.3
Ward, Turner, Milwaukee*	.179	43	82	67	7	12	22	2	1	2	10	1	1	0	13	0	17	3	0	3	.328	.3
Whiten, Mark, Seattle†	.300	40	163	140	31	42	85	7	0	12	33	0	0	2	21	4	40	2	1	1	.607	.3
Widger, Chris, Seattle	.182	8	12	11	1	2	2	0	0	0	0	0	0	1	0	0	5	0	0	0	.182	.2
Williams, Bernie, New York†	.305	143	641	551	108	168	295	26	7	29	102	1	7	0	82	8	72	17	4	15	.535	.3
Williams, Eddie, Detroit	.200	77	237	215	22	43	66	5	0	6	26	0	1	2	18	0	50	0	2	8	.307	.2
Williams, George, Oakland†	.152	56	166	132	17	20	34	5	0	3	10	2	1	3	28	1	32	0	0	3	.258	.3
Williams, Gerald, N.Y.-Mil	.252	125	357	325	43	82	124	19	4	5	34	3	5	5	19	3	57	10	9	8	.382	.2
Wilson, Dan, Seattle	.285	138	540	491	51	140	218	24	0	18	83	9	5	3	32	2	88	1	2	15	.444	.3
Wilson, Nigel, Cleveland*	.250	10	13	12	2	3	9	0	0	2	5	0	0	1	0	6	0	0	1	.750	.3
Worthington, Craig, Texas	.158	13	27	19	2	3	6	0	0	1	4	0	2	0	6	0	3	0	0	1	.316	.3
Young, Ernie, Oakland	.242	141	528	462	72	112	196	19	4	19	64	3	4	7	52	1	118	7	5	13	.424	.3
Young, Kevin, Kansas City	.242	55	143	132	20	32	62	6	0	8	23	0	0	11	0	32	3	3	2	.470	.3
Zaun, Greg, Baltimore†	.231	50	123	108	16	25	38	8	1	1	13	0	2	2	11	2	15	0	0	3	.352	.3
Zeile, Todd, Baltimore	.239	29	132	117	17	28	51	8	0	5	19	0	0	0	15	0	16	0	0	2	.436	.3

AWARDED FIRST BASE ON OBSTRUCTION OR CATCHER'S INTERFERENCE—Becker, Minnesota 2 (Martinez, Slaught); Kelly, Minnesota 2 (Martinez, Steinbach); Bonilla, Baltimore (Kreuter); Cordova, Minnesota (Marzano); R. Davis, Seattle (Flaherty); Molitor, Minnesota (Alomar); E. Williams, Detroit (Williams).

PLAYERS WITH TWO OR MORE TEAMS

Player, Team	Avg.	G	TPA	AB	R	H	TB	2B	3B	HR	RBI	SH	SF	HP	BB	IBB	SO	SB	CS	GDP	Slg.	O
Aldrete, Mike, California*	.150	31	46	40	5	6	16	1	0	3	8	0	1	0	5	0	4	0	0	3	.400	.2
Aldrete, Mike, New York*	.250	32	77	68	11	17	31	5	0	3	12	0	0	0	9	0	15	0	1	1	.456	.3
Borders, Pat, California	.228	19	61	57	6	13	22	3	0	2	8	1	0	0	3	0	11	0	1	1	.386	.2
Borders, Pat, Chicago	.277	31	102	94	6	26	36	1	0	3	6	3	0	0	5	0	18	0	0	2	.383	.3
Bragg, Darren, Seattle*	.272	69	235	195	36	53	88	12	1	7	25	1	4	2	33	4	35	8	5	2	.451	.3
Bragg, Darren, Boston*	.252	58	264	222	38	56	81	14	1	3	22	1	3	2	36	2	39	6	4	3	.365	.3
Burnitz, Jeromy, Cleveland*	.281	71	155	128	30	36	67	10	0	7	26	0	0	2	25	1	31	2	1	3	.523	.4
Burnitz, Jeromy, Milwaukee*	.236	23	84	72	8	17	27	4	0	2	14	0	2	2	8	1	16	2	0	1	.375	.3
Cedeno, Domingo, Toronto†	.280	77	307	282	44	79	99	10	2	2	17	7	1	2	15	0	60	5	3	6	.351	.3
Cedeno, Domingo, Chicago†	.158	12	22	19	2	3	5	2	0	0	3	1	2	0	0	0	4	1	0	1	.263	.1
Easley, Damion, California	.156	28	54	45	4	7	14	1	0	2	7	3	0	0	6	0	12	0	0	0	.311	.2
Easley, Damion, Detroit	.343	21	75	67	10	23	30	1	0	2	10	0	2	1	4	0	13	3	1	0	.448	.3
Eenhoorn, Robert, New York	.071	12	19	14	2	1	1	0	0	0	2	1	2	0	2	0	3	0	0	0	.071	.1
Eenhoorn, Robert, California	.267	6	15	15	1	4	4	0	0	0	0	0	0	0	0	0	3	0	0	0	.267	.2
Fielder, Cecil, Detroit	.248	107	460	391	55	97	187	12	0	26	80	0	3	6	63	8	91	2	0	11	.478	.3
Fielder, Cecil, New York	.260	53	228	200	30	52	99	8	0	13	37	0	2	2	24	4	48	0	0	7	.495	.3
Hollins, Dave, Minnesota†	.242	121	503	422	71	102	167	26	0	13	53	0	0	10	71	5	102	6	4	9	.396	.3
Hollins, Dave, Seattle†	.351	28	113	94	17	33	45	3	0	3	25	1	2	3	13	2	15	0	2	2	.479	.4
Manto, Jeff, Boston	.208	22	57	48	8	10	21	3	1	2	6	0	0	1	8	0	12	0	0	0	.438	.3
Manto, Jeff, Seattle	.185	21	63	54	7	10	16	3	0	1	4	0	0	0	9	0	12	0	1	2	.296	.3
Murray, Eddie, Cleveland†	.262	88	374	336	33	88	135	9	1	12	45	0	4	0	34	2	45	3	0	13	.402	.3
Murray, Eddie, Baltimore†	.257	64	263	230	29	59	101	12	0	10	34	0	6	0	27	4	42	1	0	6	.439	.3
Parent, Mark, Detroit	.240	38	108	104	13	25	52	6	0	7	17	0	1	0	3	0	27	0	0	2	.500	.2
Parent, Mark, Baltimore	.182	18	36	33	4	6	13	1	0	2	6	1	0	0	2	0	10	0	0	1	.394	.2
Pirkl, Greg, Boston	.000	2	2	2	0	0	0	0	0	0	0	0	0	0	0	0	1	0	0	0	.000	.0
Pirkl, Greg, Seattle	.190	7	21	21	2	4	8	1	0	1	1	0	0	0	0	0	3	0	0	1	.381	.1
Seitzer, Kevin, Milwaukee	.316	132	577	490	74	155	222	25	3	12	62	5	5	4	73	6	68	6	1	11	.453	.4
Seitzer, Kevin, Cleveland	.386	22	98	83	11	32	45	10	0	1	16	0	0	1	14	1	11	0	0	2	.542	.4
Sierra, Ruben, Milwaukee*	.258	96	407	360	39	93	145	17	1	11	52	0	7	0	40	11	58	1	3	10	.403	.3
Sierra, Ruben, Detroit†	.222	46	180	158	22	35	49	9	1	1	20	0	2	0	20	1	25	3	1	2	.310	.3
Slaught, Don, California	.324	62	224	207	23	67	94	6	0	32	0	2	13	0	28	0	1	0	12	.454	.3
Slaught, Don, Chicago	.250	14	39	36	2	9	10	1	0	0	5	0	0	0	3	0	4	0	4	.278	.2
Sojo, Luis, Seattle	.211	77	264	247	20	52	65	8	1	1	16	6	0	1	10	0	13	2	2	8	.263	.2
Sojo, Luis, New York	.275	18	44	40	3	11	13	2	0	0	5	2	1	0	1	0	4	0	0	2	.325	.2
Williams, Gerald, New York	.270	99	258	233	37	63	101	15	4	5	30	1	5	4	15	2	39	7	8	1	.433	.3
Williams, Gerald, Milwaukee	.207	26	99	92	6	19	23	4	0	0	4	2	0	1	4	1	18	3	1	1	.250	.2

DESIGNATED HITTING

TEAM

am	Avg.	G	TPA	AB	R	H	TB	2B	3B	HR	RBI	SH	SF	HP	BB	IBB	SO	SB	CS	GDP	Slg.	OBP
nnesota	.332	162	740	665	98	221	310	41	9	10	110	0	7	3	64	10	79	16	6	23	.466	.390
attle	.309	161	738	596	134	184	334	50	2	32	111	0	4	10	128	13	105	4	3	18	.560	.436
icago	.307	162	729	632	102	194	305	36	0	25	115	5	3	1	88	8	96	8	4	20	.483	.391
ston	.305	162	748	652	126	199	368	45	5	38	132	0	7	10	79	6	151	4	1	17	.564	.385
eveland	.290	161	717	628	91	182	291	36	2	23	100	0	7	2	80	5	100	9	0	23	.463	.368
lifornia	.278	161	715	612	80	170	288	26	1	30	106	2	7	0	94	12	115	5	2	22	.471	.370
lwaukee	.277	162	731	617	114	171	269	33	1	21	95	3	2	4	105	3	119	4	2	10	.436	.385
xas	.272	163	720	602	103	164	313	33	1	38	110	1	11	2	104	11	149	5	1	10	.520	.376
w York	.272	162	720	629	97	171	292	38	1	27	103	0	8	6	77	15	135	6	5	19	.464	.353
ronto	.260	162	718	628	95	163	295	28	4	32	109	0	9	9	72	2	161	5	0	19	.470	.340
kland	.254	162	709	621	101	158	289	32	0	33	105	1	5	7	75	3	141	1	2	14	.465	.339
ltimore	.248	163	714	629	93	156	241	27	2	18	88	1	10	6	68	7	108	4	5	14	.383	.323
nsas City	.244	161	690	589	70	144	226	33	2	15	92	1	9	10	81	5	139	7	7	14	.384	.341
troit	.229	162	699	620	86	142	239	19	3	24	97	1	4	5	68	6	164	6	8	14	.385	.308
Totals	.277	2266	10088	8720	1390	2419	4060	477	33	366	1473	15	93	75	1183	106	1762	84	46	237	.466	.365

INDIVIDUAL

TOP DESIGNATED HITTERS
Minimum 100 at-bats. *Lefthanded batter. †Switch-hitter.

ayer, Team	Avg.	G	TPA	AB	R	H	TB	2B	3B	HR	RBI	SH	SF	HP	BB	IBB	SO	SB	CS	GDP	Slg.	OBP
fferson, Reggie, Boston*	.389	49	196	180	39	70	119	18	2	9	34	0	3	2	11	1	43	0	0	5	.661	.423
olitor, Paul, Minnesota	.340	143	651	588	85	200	278	38	8	8	100	0	7	3	52	10	65	16	6	21	.473	.392
itzer, Kevin, Mil.-Cle.	.327	73	325	275	40	90	119	18	1	3	35	3	1	3	43	1	43	2	0	6	.433	.422
de, Curtis, Detroit*	.327	31	119	101	20	33	53	4	2	4	12	1	0	0	17	0	22	4	4	1	.525	.424
sson, Dave, Milwaukee*	.325	40	177	151	34	49	80	10	0	7	30	0	1	1	24	3	25	0	1	0	.530	.418
artinez, Edgar, Seattle	.324	134	615	482	117	156	278	49	2	23	93	0	3	8	122	12	82	3	3	15	.577	.465
onzalez, Juan, Texas	.315	32	142	127	24	40	93	5	0	16	34	0	1	0	14	6	22	0	0	1	.732	.380
ines, Harold, Chicago*	.310	141	570	493	80	153	248	29	0	22	94	0	3	1	73	7	62	3	1	19	.503	.398
vis, Chili, California†	.294	143	621	528	73	155	263	24	0	28	95	1	6	0	86	11	98	5	2	18	.498	.389
rroa, Geronimo, Oakland	.287	91	393	356	66	102	187	22	0	21	66	0	4	2	31	0	80	0	2	10	.525	.344
anseco, Jose, Boston	.282	84	381	323	62	91	182	20	1	23	72	0	2	5	51	2	75	3	1	7	.563	.386
lgado, Carlos, Toronto*	.263	108	443	380	51	100	174	21	1	17	63	0	7	8	48	2	111	0	0	10	.458	.352
erra, Ruben, N.Y.-Det.†	.263	81	351	308	39	81	125	16	2	8	47	0	6	0	37	8	46	1	3	6	.406	.336
ttleton, Mickey, Texas†	.259	115	497	405	66	105	189	24	0	20	72	1	9	2	80	5	110	2	1	8	.467	.377
urray, Eddie, Cle.-Bal.†	.258	149	631	561	69	145	234	21	1	22	76	0	9	0	61	6	87	4	0	18	.417	.326

ALL DESIGNATED HITTERS
*Lefthanded batter. †Switch-hitter.

ayer, Team	Avg.	G	TPA	AB	R	H	TB	2B	3B	HR	RBI	SH	SF	HP	BB	IBB	SO	SB	CS	GDP	Slg.	OBP
drete, Mike, Cal.-N.Y.*	.268	15	47	41	10	11	24	4	0	3	10	0	1	0	5	0	8	0	1	3	.585	.340
exander, Manny, Baltimore	.000	1	0	0	1	0	0	0	0	0	0	0	0	0	0	0	0	0	0	0	.000	.000
omar, Roberto, Baltimore†	.333	10	50	42	9	14	20	0	0	2	9	0	0	0	8	0	9	0	0	0	.476	.440
maral, Rich, Seattle	.000	6	0	0	3	0	0	0	0	0	0	0	0	0	0	0	0	0	0	0	.000	.000
nderson, Brady, Baltimore*	.111	2	10	9	0	1	1	0	0	0	0	0	0	0	1	0	3	0	0	0	.111	.200
nderson, Garret, California*	.000	1	3	2	0	0	0	0	0	0	0	0	0	0	1	0	1	0	0	0	.000	.333
rias, George, California	1.000	1	1	1	0	1	1	0	0	0	0	0	0	0	0	0	0	0	0	0	1.000	1.000
aines, Harold, Chicago*	.310	141	570	493	80	153	248	29	0	22	94	0	3	1	73	7	62	3	1	19	.503	.398
artee, Kimera, Detroit	.000	2	0	0	0	0	0	0	0	0	0	0	0	0	0	0	0	0	0	0	.000	.000
atista, Tony, Oakland	.250	4	5	4	0	1	2	1	0	0	1	0	0	0	1	0	2	0	0	0	.500	.400
autista, Danny, Detroit	.333	1	3	3	1	1	1	0	0	0	0	0	0	0	0	0	0	0	0	0	.333	.333
elle, Albert, Cleveland	.190	6	26	21	3	4	7	0	0	1	6	0	0	1	4	0	4	1	0	1	.333	.346
eltre, Esteban, Boston	.000	1	1	1	0	0	0	0	0	0	0	0	0	0	0	0	0	0	0	0	.000	.000
erroa, Geronimo, Oakland	.287	91	393	356	66	102	187	22	0	21	66	0	4	2	31	0	80	0	2	10	.525	.344
oggs, Wade, New York*	.588	4	19	17	2	10	14	4	0	0	2	0	0	0	2	0	1	0	0	0	.824	.632
onilla, Bobby, Baltimore†	.221	44	187	163	24	36	49	7	0	2	19	0	4	2	18	1	28	0	2	5	.301	.299
orders, Pat, Chicago	.333	1	4	3	1	1	2	1	0	0	0	0	1	0	0	0	1	0	0	0	.667	.333
rito, Tilson, Toronto	.000	2	3	2	0	0	0	0	0	0	0	0	0	0	1	0	0	0	0	0	.000	.333
rown, Kevin L., Texas	.000	1	1	1	0	0	0	0	0	0	0	0	0	0	0	0	1	0	0	0	.000	.000
rumfield, Jacob, Toronto	.167	5	12	12	0	2	2	0	0	0	0	0	0	0	0	0	5	0	0	0	.167	.167
uhner, Jay, Seattle	.273	8	36	33	6	9	25	1	0	5	10	0	0	1	2	1	6	0	0	0	.758	.333
urnitz, Jeromy, Cleveland*	.348	15	54	46	13	16	32	4	0	4	15	0	0	0	8	0	13	0	0	1	.696	.444
ameron, Mike, Chicago	.000	2	0	0	1	0	0	0	0	0	0	0	0	0	0	0	0	0	0	0	.000	.000
anseco, Jose, Boston	.282	84	381	323	62	91	182	20	1	23	72	0	2	5	51	2	75	3	1	7	.563	.386
arreon, Mark, Cleveland	.500	2	5	4	0	2	3	1	0	0	0	0	0	0	1	0	0	0	0	0	.750	.600
arter, Joe, Toronto	.203	15	62	59	7	12	22	2	1	2	7	0	1	0	2	0	5	2	0	4	.373	.226
asanova, Raul, Detroit†	.000	3	8	8	0	0	0	0	0	0	0	0	0	0	0	0	3	0	0	2	.000	.000
edeno, Domingo, Oakland†	.000	1	0	0	0	0	0	0	0	0	0	0	0	0	0	0	0	1	0	0	.000	.000
irillo, Jeff, Milwaukee	.250	3	9	8	2	2	5	0	0	1	1	0	0	0	1	0	1	0	0	0	.625	.333
lark, Phil, Boston	.000	1	1	1	0	0	0	0	0	0	0	0	0	0	0	0	1	0	0	0	.000	.000
lark, Tony, Detroit†	.190	12	49	42	6	8	16	2	0	2	7	0	1	0	6	0	15	0	0	1	.381	.286
oomer, Ron, Minnesota	.200	3	5	5	1	1	4	0	0	1	1	0	0	0	0	0	1	0	0	0	.800	.200
ordero, Wil, Boston	.281	13	37	32	7	9	15	3	0	1	7	0	0	1	4	2	7	0	0	2	.469	.378
ruz, Fausto, Detroit	.000	1	1	1	0	0	0	0	0	0	0	0	0	0	0	0	0	0	0	0	.000	.000
uyler, Milt, Boston†	.000	2	1	1	0	0	0	0	0	0	0	0	0	0	0	0	1	0	0	0	.000	.000
amon, Johnny, Kansas City*	.000	1	1	1	0	0	0	0	0	0	0	0	0	0	0	0	0	0	0	0	.000	.000

– 235 –

Player, Team	Avg.	G	TPA	AB	R	H	TB	2B	3B	HR	RBI	SH	SF	HP	BB	IBB	SO	SB	CS	GDP	Slg.	O
Davis, Chili, California†	.294	143	621	528	73	155	263	24	0	28	95	1	6	0	86	11	98	5	2	18	.498	.3
Delgado, Carlos, Toronto*	.263	108	443	380	51	100	174	21	1	17	63	0	7	8	48	2	111	0	0	10	.458	.3
Devereaux, Mike, Baltimore	.243	10	40	37	3	9	11	2	0	0	3	0	0	1	2	0	4	1	1	1	.297	.3
Diaz, Alex, Seattle†	1.000	1	1	1	1	1	1	0	0	0	0	0	0	0	0	0	0	1	0	0	1.000	1.0
Duncan, Mariano, New York	.500	2	8	8	2	4	7	0	0	1	2	0	0	0	0	0	1	0	0	0	.875	.5
Durham, Ray, Chicago†	.000	3	1	1	0	0	0	0	0	0	0	0	0	0	0	0	1	0	1	0	.000	.0
Easley, Damion, Cal.-Det	1.000	3	3	1	0	1	1	0	0	0	0	1	0	0	1	0	0	0	0	0	1.000	1.0
Edmonds, Jim, California*	.000	1	5	4	0	0	0	0	0	0	0	0	0	1	0	1	0	0	0		.000	.0
Espinoza, Alvaro, Cleveland	.000	1	1	1	0	0	0	0	0	0	0	0	0	0	0	0	1	0	0	0	.000	.0
Fabregas, Jorge, California*	.000	1	1	1	0	0	0	0	0	0	0	0	0	0	0	0	0	0	0	0	.000	.0
Faneyte, Rikkert, Texas	.000	2	1	1	0	0	0	0	0	0	0	0	0	0	0	0	0	0	0	0	.000	.0
Fielder, Cecil, Det.-N.Y	.239	79	342	297	46	71	141	10	0	20	65	0	3	4	38	9	82	0	0	8	.475	.3
Fox, Andy, New York*	.000	3	0	0	1	0	0	0	0	0	0	0	0	0	0	0	0	0	0	0	.000	.
Franco, Julio, Cleveland	.347	13	58	49	9	17	20	3	0	0	5	0	0	0	9	0	9	3	0	2	.408	.4
Frazier, Lou, Texas†	.000	13	5	4	2	0	0	0	0	0	0	0	0	0	1	0	2	3	0	0	.000	.2
Frye, Jeff, Boston	.000	1	1	1	0	0	0	0	0	0	0	0	0	0	0	0	1	0	0	0	.000	.
Garciaparra, Nomar, Boston	.000	1	0	0	1	0	0	0	0	0	0	0	0	0	0	0	0	0	0	0	.000	.0
Giambi, Jason, Oakland*	.273	12	51	44	9	12	21	3	0	2	3	0	1	2	4	0	10	0	1	1	.477	.3
Giles, Brian S., Cleveland*	.346	21	90	78	16	27	51	10	1	4	17	0	2	0	10	2	7	2	0	5	.654	.4
Girardi, Joe, New York	.000	2	3	2	0	0	0	0	0	0	0	1	0	0	1	0	0	0	0	0	.000	.3
Gonzalez, Juan, Texas	.315	32	142	127	24	40	93	5	0	16	34	0	1	0	14	6	22	0	0	1	.732	.3
Goodwin, Tom, Kansas City*	.500	5	4	2	2	1	1	0	0	0	0	1	0	0	1	0	1	1	1	0	.500	.6
Green, Shawn, Toronto*	.000	1	4	3	2	0	0	0	0	0	0	0	0	0	1	0	1	0	0	0	.000	.2
Greene, Todd, California	.000	1	4	4	0	0	0	0	0	0	0	0	0	0	0	0	1	0	0	0	.000	.0
Greer, Rusty, Texas*	.000	1	0	0	1	0	0	0	0	0	0	0	0	0	0	0	0	0	0	0	.000	.0
Griffey, Ken, Seattle*	.300	5	21	20	4	6	15	0	0	3	4	0	0	0	1	0	4	0	0	1	.750	.3
Hale, Chip, Minnesota*	.333	10	15	12	3	4	7	0	0	1	3	0	0	0	3	0	0	0	0	0	.583	.4
Hamelin, Bob, Kansas City*	.250	47	173	140	12	35	57	10	0	4	23	0	3	1	29	2	39	3	2	1	.407	.3
Hammonds, Jeffrey, Baltimore	.400	1	5	5	0	2	2	0	0	0	0	0	0	0	0	0	0	0	0	0	.400	.4
Haselman, Bill, Boston	.500	2	2	2	0	1	1	0	0	0	0	1	0	0	0	0	1	0	0	0	.500	.5
Herrera, Jose, Oakland*	.000	1	1	1	0	0	0	0	0	0	0	0	0	0	0	0	1	0	0	0	.000	.0
Hiatt, Phil, Detroit	.250	1	4	4	1	1	1	0	0	0	0	0	0	0	0	0	3	0	0	0	.250	.2
Higginson, Bob, Detroit*	.200	4	11	10	1	2	3	1	0	0	1	0	0	0	1	0	1	0	0	0	.300	.2
Hocking, Denny, Minnesota†	.000	1	3	3	0	0	0	0	0	0	0	0	0	0	0	0	1	0	0	0	.000	.0
Hollins, Dave, Minnesota†	.167	3	13	12	1	2	3	1	0	0	2	0	0	0	1	0	2	0	0	0	.250	.2
Hosey, Dwayne, Boston†	.000	2	1	1	0	0	0	0	0	0	0	0	0	0	0	0	1	0	0	0	.000	.0
Howell, Jack, California*	.375	4	8	8	0	3	3	0	0	0	2	0	0	0	0	0	2	0	0	0	.375	.3
Hudler, Rex, California	.095	8	22	21	2	2	3	1	0	0	0	0	0	0	1	0	5	0	0	1	.143	.1
Hulse, David, Milwaukee*	.000	4	2	2	0	0	0	0	0	0	0	0	0	0	0	0	1	0	0	0	.000	.0
Hunter, Brian, Seattle	.375	2	8	8	1	3	3	0	0	0	0	0	0	0	0	0	3	0	0	0	.375	.3
Hyers, Tim, Detroit*	.000	2	2	2	0	0	0	0	0	0	0	0	0	0	0	0	0	0	0	0	.000	.0
Ibanez, Raul, Seattle*	.000	2	5	4	0	0	0	0	0	0	0	0	0	1	0	0	1	0	0	0	.000	.2
Incaviglia, Pete, Baltimore	.300	4	12	10	1	3	4	1	0	0	2	0	1	1	0	0	3	0	0	0	.400	.3
Jaha, John, Milwaukee	.214	63	273	224	42	48	88	10	0	10	37	0	0	1	48	0	57	1	0	5	.393	.3
James, Dion, New York*	.000	1	3	3	0	0	0	0	0	0	0	0	0	0	0	0	0	0	0	1	.000	.0
Jefferson, Reggie, Boston*	.389	49	196	180	39	70	119	18	2	9	34	0	3	2	11	1	43	0	0	5	.661	.4
Jordan, Ricky, Seattle	.400	2	5	5	0	2	2	0	0	0	0	0	0	0	0	0	1	0	0	0	.400	.4
Kelly, Pat, New York	.000	3	0	0	0	0	0	0	0	0	0	0	0	0	0	0	0	0	1	0	.000	.00
Kelly, Roberto, Minnesota	.400	2	5	5	0	2	3	1	0	0	2	0	0	0	0	0	1	0	0	0	.600	.4
Kent, Jeff, Cleveland	.250	5	17	16	3	4	8	1	0	1	3	0	1	0	0	0	4	0	0	0	.500	.2
Knoblauch, Chuck, Minnesota	.000	2	4	4	0	0	0	0	0	0	0	0	0	0	0	0	0	0	0	0	1.000	.0
Koslofski, Kevin, Milwaukee*	1.000	1	1	1	2	1	2	1	0	0	0	0	0	0	0	0	0	0	0	0	2.000	1.0
Lawton, Matt, Minnesota*	.000	1	1	1	0	0	0	0	0	0	0	0	0	0	0	0	1	0	0	0	.000	.00
Leius, Scott, Cleveland	.000	1	1	1	0	0	0	0	0	0	0	0	0	0	0	0	0	0	0	0	.000	.00
Lennon, Patrick, Kansas City	.500	1	2	2	0	1	1	0	0	0	0	0	0	0	0	0	1	0	0	0	.500	.5
Levis, Jesse, Milwaukee*	.333	6	7	6	0	2	2	0	0	0	0	0	0	0	1	0	0	0	0	0	.333	.4
Lewis, Mark, Detroit	.000	1	3	3	0	0	0	0	0	0	0	0	0	0	0	0	1	0	0	0	.000	.0
Leyritz, Jim, New York	.278	13	42	36	6	10	13	3	0	0	3	0	0	1	5	0	13	1	0	1	.361	.38
Lockhart, Keith, Kansas City*	.000	1	1	0	0	0	0	0	0	0	0	0	0	0	1	0	0	0	0	0	.000	1.0
Lovullo, Torey, Oakland†	.167	4	8	6	0	1	1	0	0	0	1	0	0	0	2	0	0	0	0	0	.167	.3
Luke, Matt, New York*	.000	1	0	0	1	0	0	0	0	0	0	0	0	0	0	0	0	0	0	0	.000	.0
Macfarlane, Mike, Kansas City	.241	9	36	29	6	7	10	0	0	1	4	0	0	3	4	0	5	0	0	0	.345	.38
Manto, Jeff, Seattle	.000	2	5	5	0	0	0	0	0	0	0	0	0	0	0	0	2	0	0	0	.000	.0
Martin, Norberto, Chicago	.333	22	30	24	6	8	13	2	0	1	3	4	0	0	2	0	1	3	1	0	.542	.38
Martinez, Edgar, Seattle	.324	134	615	482	117	156	278	49	2	23	93	0	3	8	122	12	82	3	3	15	.577	.4
Martinez, Tino, New York*	.250	3	14	12	3	3	10	1	0	2	4	0	0	0	2	1	4	0	0	0	.833	.35
Matheny, Mike, Milwaukee	.000	1	2	2	0	0	0	0	0	0	0	0	0	0	0	0	1	0	0	0	.000	.0C
McGwire, Mark, Oakland	.236	18	79	55	10	13	26	1	0	4	10	0	0	3	21	2	16	0	0	1	.473	.46
Mitchell, Kevin, Boston	.333	4	16	15	2	5	5	0	0	0	1	0	0	0	1	0	2	0	0	0	.333	.37
Molina, Izzy, Oakland	.000	1	3	3	0	0	0	0	0	0	0	0	0	0	0	0	0	0	0	0	.000	.0C
Molitor, Paul, Minnesota	.340	143	651	588	85	200	278	38	8	8	100	0	7	3	52	10	65	16	6	21	.473	.39
Moore, Kerwin, Oakland†	.000	2	0	0	1	0	0	0	0	0	0	0	0	0	0	0	0	1	0	0	.000	.0C
Mouton, Lyle, Chicago	.291	28	87	79	7	23	32	3	0	2	9	0	0	8	1	0	23	1	0	1	.405	.3S
Munoz, Jose, Chicago†	.000	2	1	1	0	0	0	0	0	0	0	0	0	0	0	0	1	0	0	0	.000	.0C
Munoz, Pedro, Oakland	.182	18	70	66	6	12	20	2	0	2	9	0	0	0	4	0	17	0	0	1	.303	.22
Murray, Eddie, Cle.-Bal.†	.258	149	631	561	69	145	234	21	1	22	76	0	9	0	61	6	87	4	0	18	.417	.33
Nevin, Phil, Detroit	.000	1	1	1	0	0	0	0	0	0	0	0	0	0	0	0	1	0	0	0	.000	.0C
Newson, Warren, Texas*	.233	9	37	30	5	7	12	2	0	1	1	0	0	0	7	0	10	0	0	0	.400	.37
Nieves, Melvin, Detroit†	.200	11	42	40	6	8	14	0	0	2	5	0	0	1	1	0	15	1	0	1	.350	.23
Nilsson, Dave, Milwaukee*	.325	40	177	151	34	49	80	10	0	7	30	0	1	1	24	3	25	0	1	0	.530	.41
Norman, Les, Kansas City	.000	7	3	3	2	0	0	0	0	0	0	0	0	0	0	0	1	0	0	0	.000	.0C
Norton, Greg, Chicago†	.000	1	0	0	1	0	0	0	0	0	0	0	0	0	0	0	0	0	0	0	.000	.0C
Nunnally, Jon, Kansas City*	.000	4	2	2	0	0	0	0	0	0	0	0	0	0	0	0	2	0	0	0	.000	.0C
Olerud, John, Toronto*	.293	15	70	58	13	17	34	2	0	5	14	0	0	0	12	0	8	0	0	2	.586	.41
O'Neill, Paul, New York*	.111	3	10	9	1	1	1	0	0	0	0	0	0	0	1	0	0	0	0	1	.111	.20
Ortiz, Luis, Texas	.400	1	5	5	1	2	7	0	1	1	1	0	0	0	0	0	0	0	0	0	1.400	.40

yer, Team	Avg.	G	TPA	AB	R	H	TB	2B	3B	HR	RBI	SH	SF	HP	BB	IBB	SO	SB	CS	GDP	Slg.	OBP
meiro, Orlando, California*	.000	4	5	4	0	0	0	0	0	0	0	0	0	0	1	1	0	0	0	0	.000	.200
meiro, Rafael, Baltimore*	.273	3	12	11	1	3	6	0	0	1	2	0	0	0	1	0	1	0	0	1	.545	.333
mer, Dean, Texas	.000	1	4	4	0	0	0	0	0	0	0	0	0	0	0	0	2	0	0	0	.000	.000
quette, Craig, Kansas City	.208	6	25	24	3	5	8	0	0	1	5	0	1	0	0	0	5	0	0	0	.333	.200
in, Shannon, Detroit†	.077	4	13	13	0	1	1	0	0	0	1	0	0	0	0	0	3	0	0	0	.077	.077
ez, Robert, Toronto	.000	2	2	2	0	0	0	0	0	0	0	0	0	0	0	0	0	0	0	0	.000	.000
d, Greg, Seattle	.273	3	11	11	1	3	6	0	0	1	1	0	0	0	0	0	1	0	0	1	.545	.273
ntier, Phil, Oakland*	.000	1	1	0	0	0	0	0	0	0	0	0	0	0	1	0	0	0	0	0	.000	1.000
onia, Luis, Baltimore*	.255	18	59	55	10	14	21	2	1	1	7	0	0	0	4	0	5	2	1	1	.382	.305
sada, Jorge, New York†	.000	3	3	3	0	0	0	0	0	0	0	0	0	0	0	0	2	0	0	0	.000	.000
de, Curtis, Detroit*	.327	31	119	101	20	33	53	4	2	4	12	1	0	0	17	0	22	4	4	1	.525	.424
nes, Tim, New York†	.222	2	10	9	2	2	5	0	0	1	1	0	0	1	0	0	2	0	0	1	.556	.300
nirez, Manny, Cleveland	.273	3	12	11	3	3	8	2	0	1	1	0	0	0	1	0	2	0	0	0	.727	.333
nda, Joe, Kansas City	.250	1	4	4	0	1	1	0	0	0	1	0	0	0	0	0	0	0	0	0	.250	.250
poulet, Jeff, Minnesota	.000	3	3	1	0	0	0	0	0	0	0	0	0	0	2	0	1	0	0	0	.000	.667
berts, Bip, Kansas City†	.259	16	65	58	7	15	19	4	0	0	10	0	2	0	5	1	6	1	2	1	.328	.308
bertson, Mike, Chicago*	.000	2	1	1	0	0	0	0	0	0	0	0	0	0	0	0	0	0	0	0	.000	.000
driguez, Ivan, Texas	.417	6	27	24	3	10	12	2	0	0	2	0	1	0	2	0	2	0	0	0	.500	.444
mon, Tim, California	.500	3	9	8	0	4	6	0	1	0	2	0	0	0	1	0	1	0	0	0	.750	.556
muel, Juan, Toronto	.296	24	79	71	14	21	37	3	2	3	10	0	1	1	6	0	22	2	0	2	.521	.354
nofield, Dick, California	.000	1	0	0	1	0	0	0	0	0	0	0	0	0	0	0	0	0	0	0	.000	.000
tzer, Kevin, Mil.-Cle	.327	73	325	275	40	90	119	18	1	3	35	3	1	3	43	1	43	2	0	6	.433	.422
rra, Ruben, N.Y.-Det.†	.263	81	351	308	39	81	125	16	2	8	47	0	6	0	37	8	46	1	3	6	.406	.336
ught, Don, Cal.-Chi	.500	2	2	2	0	1	1	0	0	0	0	0	0	0	0	0	0	0	0	0	.500	.500
iith, Mark, Baltimore	.200	6	16	15	1	3	6	0	0	1	3	0	0	0	1	0	5	0	0	0	.400	.250
opek, Chris, Chicago	.000	3	2	2	0	0	0	0	0	0	0	0	0	0	0	0	1	0	0	0	.000	.000
iezio, Scott, Oakland†	.333	4	17	15	3	5	12	1	0	2	6	1	0	0	1	1	1	0	0	0	.800	.375
rague, Ed, Toronto	.268	10	43	41	8	11	26	0	0	5	15	0	0	0	2	0	7	0	0	1	.634	.302
ahoviak, Scott, Minnesota*	.387	9	37	31	8	12	15	1	1	0	2	0	0	0	6	0	8	0	0	0	.484	.486
airs, Matt, Oakland*	.375	5	18	16	4	6	13	1	0	2	8	0	0	0	2	0	1	0	0	0	.813	.444
anley, Mike, Boston	.270	10	43	37	6	10	21	2	0	3	9	0	0	1	5	1	10	0	0	0	.568	.372
einbach, Terry, Oakland	.000	4	18	16	1	0	0	0	0	0	1	0	0	0	2	0	4	0	0	0	.000	.111
well, Kurt, Texas†	.000	1	0	0	1	0	0	0	0	0	0	0	0	0	0	0	0	0	0	0	.000	.000
nnett, Kelly, Milwaukee	.000	1	1	1	0	0	0	0	0	0	0	0	0	0	0	0	0	0	0	0	.000	.000
ange, Doug, Seattle†	.148	10	31	27	1	4	4	0	0	0	3	0	1	0	3	0	5	0	0	1	.148	.226
awberry, Darryl, New York*	.270	26	107	89	18	24	41	8	0	3	16	0	1	1	16	3	27	4	0	2	.461	.383
nes, Chris, Kansas City	.000	3	8	8	0	0	0	0	0	0	0	0	0	0	0	0	1	0	0	1	.000	.000
rhoff, B.J., Baltimore*	.306	10	42	36	6	11	19	3	1	1	10	0	0	2	4	2	6	0	0	0	.528	.405
eeney, Mike, Kansas City	.267	22	86	75	8	20	29	3	0	2	10	0	1	3	7	0	9	0	2	2	.387	.349
asco, Tony, Baltimore*	.059	6	20	17	1	1	1	0	0	0	1	0	0	0	2	0	2	0	1	0	.059	.158
tabull, Danny, Chicago	.296	10	32	27	4	8	9	1	0	0	9	0	0	0	5	0	7	0	1	0	.333	.406
tleton, Mickey, Texas†	.259	115	497	405	66	105	189	24	0	20	72	1	9	2	80	5	110	2	1	8	.467	.377
ome, Jim, Cleveland*	.333	1	4	3	1	1	1	0	0	0	0	0	0	0	1	0	2	0	0	0	.333	.500
cker, Michael, Kansas City*	.250	5	4	4	1	1	3	0	1	0	1	0	0	0	0	0	2	0	0	0	.750	.250
roe, Tim, Milwaukee	.000	1	0	0	0	0	0	0	0	0	0	0	0	0	0	0	0	0	1	0	.000	.000
entin, John, Boston	.200	1	5	5	0	1	3	0	1	0	1	0	0	0	0	0	0	0	0	0	.600	.200
le, Dave, Texas	.000	1	1	1	0	0	0	0	0	0	0	0	0	0	0	0	0	0	0	1	.000	.000
ughn, Greg, Milwaukee	.250	1	4	4	0	1	1	0	0	0	1	0	0	0	0	0	1	0	0	0	.250	.250
ughn, Mo, Boston*	.222	15	64	54	8	12	22	2	1	2	7	0	2	1	7	0	10	1	0	3	.407	.313
ello, Joe, Kansas City	.245	70	268	229	27	56	93	14	1	7	36	0	2	3	34	2	67	2	0	9	.406	.347
caino, Jose, Cleveland†	.000	1	0	0	1	0	0	0	0	0	0	0	0	0	0	0	0	0	0	0	.000	.000
lker, Todd, Minnesota*	.000	1	3	3	0	0	0	0	0	0	0	0	0	0	0	0	0	0	0	0	.000	.000
llach, Tim, California	.167	8	19	18	1	3	6	0	0	1	2	0	0	0	1	0	5	0	0	0	.333	.211
ard, Turner, Milwaukee†	.000	1	6	6	0	0	0	0	0	0	0	0	0	0	0	0	1	0	0	1	.000	.000
lliams, Bernie, New York†	.444	2	9	9	1	4	7	0	0	1	4	0	0	0	0	0	1	1	0	0	.778	.444
lliams, Eddie, Detroit	.210	52	204	186	19	39	59	5	0	5	24	0	1	2	14	0	45	0	2	7	.317	.271
lliams, George, Oakland†	.154	11	45	39	1	6	7	1	0	0	0	0	0	0	6	0	10	0	0	1	.179	.267
lliams, Gerald, New York	.000	2	4	3	0	0	0	0	0	0	0	0	0	1	0	0	0	0	0	0	.000	.250
lson, Nigel, Cleveland*	.000	3	3	3	0	0	0	0	0	0	0	0	0	0	0	0	3	0	0	0	.000	.000
ung, Kevin, Kansas City	.250	3	8	8	2	2	4	2	0	0	1	0	0	0	0	0	3	0	0	0	.500	.250

DESIGNATED HITTERS WITH TWO OR MORE TEAMS

ayer, Team	Avg.	G	TPA	AB	R	H	TB	2B	3B	HR	RBI	SH	SF	HP	BB	IBB	SO	SB	CS	GDP	Slg.	OBP
drete, Mike, California*	.167	6	15	12	3	2	6	1	0	1	5	0	1	0	2	0	1	0	0	3	.500	.267
drete, Mike, New York*	.310	9	32	29	7	9	18	3	0	2	5	0	0	0	3	0	7	0	1	0	.621	.375
sley, Damion, California	.000	2	1	0	0	0	0	0	0	0	0	1	0	0	0	0	0	0	0	0	.000	.000
sley, Damion, Detroit	1.000	1	2	1	0	1	1	0	0	0	0	0	0	0	1	0	0	0	0	0	1.000	1.000
elder, Cecil, Detroit	.241	36	156	133	23	32	66	4	0	10	34	0	1	2	20	6	42	0	0	1	.496	.346
elder, Cecil, New York	.238	43	186	164	23	39	75	6	0	10	31	0	2	2	18	3	40	0	0	7	.457	.317
urray, Eddie, Cleveland†	.259	87	370	332	33	86	133	9	1	12	43	0	4	0	34	2	45	3	0	12	.401	.324
urray, Eddie, Baltimore†	.258	62	261	229	36	59	101	12	0	10	33	0	5	0	27	4	42	1	0	6	.441	.330
itzer, Kevin, Milwaukee	.321	56	249	212	31	68	91	12	1	3	25	3	1	2	31	0	34	2	0	4	.429	.411
itzer, Kevin, Cleveland	.349	17	76	63	9	22	28	6	0	0	10	0	0	1	12	1	9	0	0	2	.444	.461
erra, Ruben, New York†	.275	61	270	236	30	65	101	13	1	7	34	0	5	0	29	8	34	0	2	5	.428	.348
erra, Ruben, Detroit†	.222	20	81	72	9	16	24	3	1	1	13	0	1	0	8	0	12	1	1	1	.333	.296
aught, Don, California	.000	1	1	1	0	0	0	0	0	0	0	0	0	0	0	0	0	0	0	0	.000	.000
aught, Don, Chicago	1.000	1	1	1	0	1	1	0	0	0	0	0	0	0	0	0	0	0	0	0	1.000	1.000

PINCH-HITTING

TEAM

Team	Avg.	G	TPA	AB	R	H	TB	2B	3B	HR	RBI	SH	SF	HP	BB	IBB	SO	SB	CS	GDP	Slg.
Minnesota	.310	112	198	174	18	54	77	8	0	5	34	1	1	0	22	1	24	1	0	5	.443
Baltimore	.292	68	84	72	11	21	30	1	1	2	12	1	4	0	7	0	12	1	0	1	.417
Kansas City	.284	91	167	148	11	42	55	7	0	2	26	0	2	0	17	2	33	4	2	7	.372
Cleveland	.274	74	111	95	22	26	51	7	0	6	18	0	0	1	15	1	20	1	0	2	.537
Milwaukee	.264	84	114	106	7	28	43	6	0	3	18	0	0	0	8	1	19	0	0	3	.406
Oakland	.259	81	119	108	11	28	46	4	1	4	15	0	0	0	11	1	35	1	0	0	.426
California	.252	85	143	127	10	32	57	4	0	7	20	3	0	1	12	2	21	0	0	4	.449
Boston	.238	90	150	122	14	29	41	6	0	2	21	1	4	1	22	6	35	0	0	6	.336
New York	.231	65	89	78	7	18	23	2	0	1	17	0	1	0	10	1	22	0	1	0	.295
Seattle	.229	99	180	153	19	35	61	7	2	5	24	1	4	3	19	1	40	1	0	1	.399
Chicago	.216	90	146	125	14	27	34	4	0	1	14	4	1	0	16	3	29	1	0	6	.272
Toronto	.204	74	126	113	15	23	33	4	0	2	12	1	0	0	12	2	37	2	0	2	.292
Detroit	.121	85	117	99	5	12	23	2	0	3	10	2	0	0	16	2	40	1	1	2	.232
Texas	.108	65	86	74	3	8	9	1	0	0	2	0	0	0	12	3	22	0	0	3	.122
Totals	.240	1163	1830	1594	167	383	583	63	4	43	243	14	17	6	199	26	389	13	4	42	.366

TOP PINCH-HITTERS

Minimum 20 at-bats. *Lefthanded batter. †Switch-hitter.

Player, Team	Avg.	G	TPA	AB	R	H	TB	2B	3B	HR	RBI	SH	SF	HP	BB	IBB	SO	SB	CS	GDP	Slg.
Lockhart, Keith, Kansas City*	.400	25	25	20	2	8	9	1	0	0	1	0	0	0	5	0	1	0	0	1	.450
Coomer, Ron, Minnesota	.385	31	30	26	5	10	17	1	0	2	10	0	0	0	4	0	6	0	0	0	.654
Levis, Jesse, Milwaukee*	.306	39	39	36	0	11	11	0	0	0	4	0	0	0	3	0	4	0	0	1	.306
Howell, Jack, California*	.294	39	38	34	5	10	23	1	0	4	9	0	0	0	4	0	10	0	0	1	.676
Hale, Chip, Minnesota*	.292	77	73	65	6	19	25	3	0	1	12	0	1	0	7	1	5	0	0	3	.385
Strange, Doug, Seattle†	.244	49	46	41	3	10	13	1	1	0	5	0	1	0	4	0	9	1	0	1	.317
Perez, Robert, Toronto	.238	23	23	21	4	5	6	1	0	0	2	1	0	0	1	0	2	0	0	1	.286
Burnitz, Jeromy, Cle.-Mil.*	.160	35	32	25	11	4	9	2	0	1	2	0	0	1	6	0	6	0	0	1	.360
Pride, Curtis, Detroit*	.150	27	25	20	1	3	7	1	0	1	4	0	0	0	5	1	10	0	1	1	.350
Aldrete, Mike, Cal.-N.Y.*	.148	30	30	27	2	4	10	0	0	2	4	0	0	0	3	0	3	0	0	2	.370
Jefferson, Reggie, Boston*	.143	24	24	21	2	3	7	1	0	1	3	0	1	0	2	1	9	0	0	0	.333

ALL PINCH-HITTERS

*Lefthanded batter. †Switch-hitter.

Player, Team	Avg.	G	TPA	AB	R	H	TB	2B	3B	HR	RBI	SH	SF	HP	BB	IBB	SO	SB	CS	GDP	Slg.
Aldrete, Mike, Cal.-N.Y.*	.148	30	30	27	2	4	10	0	0	2	4	0	0	0	3	0	3	0	0	2	.370
Alexander, Manny, Baltimore	.000	4	4	4	0	0	0	0	0	0	0	0	0	0	0	0	3	0	0	0	.000
Alomar, Roberto, Baltimore†	.500	3	3	2	0	1	2	1	0	0	1	0	1	0	0	0	0	0	0	1	1.000
Alomar, Sandy, Cleveland	.250	4	4	4	0	1	1	0	0	0	0	0	0	0	0	0	0	0	0	0	.250
Amaral, Rich, Seattle	.222	14	13	9	1	2	2	0	0	0	2	0	0	0	4	0	3	0	0	0	.222
Anderson, Brady, Baltimore*	.333	4	4	3	0	1	1	0	0	0	1	0	0	0	0	0	1	0	0	0	.333
Anderson, Garret, California*	.667	3	3	3	1	2	2	0	0	0	0	0	0	0	0	0	0	0	0	0	.667
Arias, George, California	.500	2	2	2	0	1	1	0	0	0	0	0	0	0	0	0	0	0	0	0	.500
Baines, Harold, Chicago*	.429	15	15	14	2	6	6	0	0	0	5	0	0	0	1	1	3	0	0	2	.429
Banks, Brian, Milwaukee†	.000	1	1	1	0	0	0	0	0	0	0	0	0	0	0	0	1	0	0	0	.000
Bartee, Kimera, Detroit	.000	6	6	5	0	0	0	0	0	0	0	0	0	0	0	0	4	0	0	0	.000
Batista, Tony, Oakland	.000	4	4	4	0	0	0	0	0	0	0	0	0	0	0	0	2	0	0	0	.000
Battle, Allen, Oakland	.000	2	2	2	0	0	0	0	0	0	0	0	0	0	0	0	2	0	0	0	.000
Bautista, Danny, Detroit	.000	2	2	2	0	0	0	0	0	0	0	0	0	0	0	0	1	0	0	0	.000
Becker, Rich, Minnesota*	.286	9	9	7	0	2	2	0	0	0	0	0	0	1	0	1	1	0	0	0	.286
Beltre, Esteban, Boston	.500	2	2	2	0	1	1	0	0	0	0	0	0	0	0	0	0	0	0	0	.500
Berroa, Geronimo, Oakland	.143	7	7	7	0	1	1	0	0	0	1	0	0	0	0	0	2	0	0	0	.143
Boggs, Wade, New York*	.286	7	7	7	1	2	2	0	0	0	1	0	0	0	0	0	2	0	0	0	.286
Bonilla, Bobby, Baltimore†	.000	1	1	1	0	0	0	0	0	0	0	0	0	0	0	0	0	0	0	0	.000
Borders, Pat, California	.000	1	1	0	0	0	0	0	0	0	0	0	1	0	0	0	0	0	0	0	.000
Bordick, Mike, Oakland	1.000	1	1	1	0	1	1	0	0	0	1	0	0	0	0	0	0	0	0	0	1.000
Bournigal, Rafael, Oakland	.200	5	5	5	1	1	1	0	0	0	0	0	0	0	0	0	0	0	0	0	.200
Bragg, Darren, Seattle*	.429	12	11	7	5	3	5	2	0	0	1	0	1	0	3	0	1	0	0	0	.714
Brede, Brent, Minnesota*	.333	3	3	3	0	1	1	0	0	0	0	0	0	0	0	0	2	0	0	0	.333
Brito, Tilson, Toronto	.000	1	1	1	0	0	0	0	0	0	0	0	0	0	0	0	1	0	1	0	.000
Brosius, Scott, Oakland	1.000	1	1	1	0	1	1	0	0	0	0	0	0	0	0	0	0	0	0	0	1.000
Brown, Kevin L., Texas	.000	2	2	2	0	0	0	0	0	0	0	0	0	0	0	0	1	0	0	0	.000
Brumfield, Jacob, Toronto	.167	13	13	12	2	2	2	0	0	0	0	0	0	0	1	0	3	0	0	0	.167
Buford, Damon, Texas	.000	13	13	12	1	0	0	0	0	0	0	0	0	0	1	0	3	0	0	0	.000
Burnitz, Jeromy, Cle.-Mil.*	.160	35	32	25	11	4	9	2	0	1	2	0	0	1	6	0	6	0	0	1	.360
Cameron, Mike, Chicago	.000	1	1	1	0	0	0	0	0	0	0	0	0	0	0	0	0	0	0	0	.000
Candaele, Casey, Cleveland†	.222	9	9	9	1	2	2	0	0	0	0	0	0	0	0	0	2	0	0	0	.222
Canseco, Jose, Boston	.000	5	5	4	0	0	0	0	0	0	0	0	0	0	1	0	2	0	0	0	.000
Carreon, Mark, Cleveland	1.000	2	2	2	1	2	5	1	0	1	1	0	0	0	0	0	0	0	0	0	3.000
Casanova, Raul, Detroit†	.000	2	2	1	0	0	0	0	0	0	0	0	0	0	1	0	1	0	0	0	.000
Cedeno, Andujar, Detroit	.000	1	1	1	0	0	0	0	0	0	0	0	0	0	0	0	1	0	0	0	.000
Cedeno, Domingo, Tor.-Chi.†	.222	9	9	9	1	2	2	0	0	0	0	0	0	3	0	0	0	0	0	0	.222
Cirillo, Jeff, Milwaukee	.333	4	4	3	0	1	2	1	0	0	0	0	0	0	1	0	0	0	0	0	.667
Clark, Phil, Boston	.000	2	2	2	0	0	0	0	0	0	0	0	0	0	0	0	1	0	0	1	.000

Player, Team	Avg.	G	TPA	AB	R	H	TB	2B	3B	HR	RBI	SH	SF	HP	BB	IBB	SO	SB	CS	GDP	Slg.	OBP
lark, Tony, Detroit†	.000	3	3	2	0	0	0	0	0	0	0	0	0	0	1	0	1	0	0	0	.000	.333
lark, Will, Texas*	.000	1	1	0	1	0	0	0	0	0	0	0	0	0	1	0	0	0	0	0	.000	1.000
ole, Alex, Boston*	.000	2	2	2	0	0	0	0	0	0	0	0	0	0	0	0	1	0	0	0	.000	.000
oomer, Ron, Minnesota	.385	31	30	26	5	10	17	1	0	2	10	0	0	0	4	0	6	0	0	0	.654	.467
ora, Joey, Seattle†	.235	22	21	17	2	4	8	2	1	0	1	1	1	0	2	1	1	0	0	0	.471	.300
ordero, Wil, Boston	.417	16	16	12	2	5	6	1	0	0	5	0	1	0	3	3	2	0	0	0	.500	.500
ordova, Marty, Minnesota	.000	1	1	1	0	0	0	0	0	0	0	0	0	0	0	0	0	0	0	0	.000	.000
respo, Felipe, Toronto†	.000	4	4	3	0	0	0	0	0	0	0	0	0	0	1	0	1	0	0	0	.000	.250
ruz, Fausto, Detroit	.000	2	2	2	0	0	0	0	0	0	0	0	0	0	0	0	0	0	0	0	.000	.000
urtis, Chad, Detroit	.000	1	1	1	0	0	0	0	0	0	0	0	0	0	0	0	0	0	0	0	.000	.000
uyler, Milt, Boston†	.000	3	3	3	0	0	0	0	0	0	0	0	0	0	0	0	2	0	0	0	.000	.000
amon, Johnny, Kansas City*	.250	8	8	8	0	2	2	0	0	0	0	0	0	0	0	0	3	1	0	0	.250	.250
avis, Chili, California†	.000	3	3	2	0	0	0	0	0	0	0	0	0	0	1	1	1	0	0	0	.000	.333
avis, Russ, Seattle	.000	2	2	2	0	0	0	0	0	0	0	0	0	0	0	0	2	0	0	0	.000	.000
elgado, Alex, Boston	.167	7	6	6	0	1	1	0	0	0	0	0	0	0	0	0	1	0	0	0	.167	.167
elgado, Carlos, Toronto*	.091	12	12	11	1	1	1	0	0	0	0	0	0	0	1	0	5	0	0	0	.091	.167
evarez, Cesar, Baltimore	.000	1	1	1	0	0	0	0	0	0	0	0	0	0	0	0	0	0	0	0	.000	.000
evereaux, Mike, Baltimore	.412	19	19	17	4	7	12	0	1	1	5	0	0	0	2	0	4	0	0	0	.706	.474
iaz, Alex, Seattle†	.429	7	7	7	0	3	3	0	0	0	1	0	0	0	0	0	2	0	0	0	.429	.429
uncan, Mariano, New York	.500	4	4	4	2	2	2	0	0	0	0	0	0	0	0	0	0	0	0	0	.500	.500
unn, Todd, Milwaukee	1.000	1	1	1	1	1	1	0	0	0	0	0	0	0	0	0	0	0	0	0	1.000	1.000
urant, Mike, Minnesota	.000	2	1	0	0	0	0	0	0	0	0	0	0	0	1	0	0	0	0	0	.000	.000
urham, Ray, Chicago†	.000	2	2	1	0	0	0	0	0	0	0	0	0	0	0	0	0	0	0	0	.000	.500
asley, Damion, Cal.-Det	.000	5	5	3	0	0	0	0	0	0	0	1	0	0	1	0	1	0	0	0	.000	.250
dmonds, Jim, California*	.500	6	6	6	1	3	6	0	0	1	3	0	0	0	0	0	3	0	0	0	1.000	.500
rstad, Darin, California*	.222	9	9	9	0	2	2	0	0	0	2	0	0	0	0	0	0	0	0	0	.222	.222
spinoza, Alvaro, Cleveland	.500	3	3	2	0	1	1	0	0	0	1	0	0	0	1	0	1	0	0	0	.500	.667
abregas, Jorge, California*	.500	2	2	2	0	1	1	0	0	0	0	0	0	0	0	0	0	0	0	0	.500	.500
aneyte, Rikkert, Texas	.000	2	2	2	0	0	0	0	0	0	0	0	0	0	0	0	0	0	0	0	.000	.000
ielder, Cecil, New York	.500	2	2	2	1	1	1	0	0	0	1	0	0	0	0	0	1	0	0	0	.500	.500
laherty, John, Detroit	.000	2	2	1	0	0	0	0	0	0	0	1	0	0	0	0	1	1	0	0	.000	.000
ox, Andy, New York*	.250	4	4	4	0	1	1	0	0	0	0	0	0	0	0	0	0	0	0	0	.250	.250
ranco, Julio, Cleveland	.333	3	3	3	0	1	1	0	0	0	2	0	0	0	0	0	0	0	0	0	.333	.333
razier, Lou, Texas†	.333	3	3	3	0	1	1	0	0	0	0	0	0	0	0	0	0	0	0	0	.333	.333
rye, Jeff, Boston	.000	2	2	1	0	0	0	0	0	0	0	0	0	0	2	0	0	0	0	0	.000	1.000
arciaparra, Nomar, Boston	1.000	1	1	1	1	1	1	0	0	0	0	0	0	0	0	0	0	0	0	0	1.000	1.000
arrison, Webster, Oakland	.000	1	1	1	0	0	0	0	0	0	0	0	0	0	0	0	0	0	0	0	.000	.000
ates, Brent, Oakland†	.000	1	1	1	0	0	0	0	0	0	0	0	0	0	0	0	1	0	0	0	.000	.000
iambi, Jason, Oakland*	.250	4	4	4	1	1	1	0	0	0	1	0	0	0	0	0	3	0	0	0	.250	.250
iles, Brian S., Cleveland*	.286	16	16	14	3	4	8	1	0	1	3	0	0	0	2	0	3	0	0	0	.571	.375
irardi, Joe, New York	.250	6	6	4	1	1	1	0	0	0	3	0	1	0	1	0	0	0	0	0	.250	.333
omez, Chris, Detroit	.000	2	2	1	0	0	0	0	0	0	0	0	0	0	1	0	1	0	0	0	.000	.500
onzales, Rene, Texas	.000	4	4	4	0	0	0	0	0	0	0	0	0	0	0	0	0	0	0	1	.000	.000
oodwin, Tom, Kansas City*	.500	2	2	2	0	1	1	0	0	0	0	0	0	0	0	0	0	0	0	0	.500	.500
reen, Shawn, Toronto*	.231	17	17	13	2	3	4	1	0	0	1	0	0	0	4	1	5	0	0	0	.308	.412
reene, Todd, California	.000	5	4	3	0	0	0	0	0	0	0	0	0	0	0	0	1	0	0	0	.000	.250
reenwell, Mike, Boston*	.000	3	3	2	0	0	0	0	0	0	0	0	0	0	1	0	0	0	0	1	.000	.333
uillen, Ozzie, Chicago*	.000	9	8	6	0	0	0	0	0	0	0	1	0	1	0	0	0	0	0	1	.000	.000
ale, Chip, Minnesota*	.292	77	73	65	6	19	25	3	0	1	12	0	1	0	7	1	5	0	0	3	.385	.356
amelin, Bob, Kansas City*	.188	19	19	16	1	3	8	2	0	1	7	0	1	0	2	0	4	0	0	2	.500	.263
amilton, Darryl, Texas*	.000	2	2	1	0	0	0	0	0	0	0	0	0	0	1	1	0	0	0	0	.000	.500
ammonds, Jeffrey, Baltimore	.500	3	3	2	0	1	1	0	0	0	0	1	0	0	0	0	0	0	0	0	.500	.500
aselman, Bill, Boston	.167	7	7	6	0	1	1	0	0	0	1	0	0	0	1	1	3	0	0	1	.167	.286
atteberg, Scott, Boston*	.000	3	3	2	0	0	0	0	0	0	0	0	0	0	1	0	0	0	0	0	.000	.333
ayes, Charlie, New York	.500	5	4	4	0	2	3	1	0	0	2	0	0	0	0	0	0	0	0	0	.750	.500
errera, Jose, Oakland*	.167	14	14	12	0	2	2	0	0	0	1	0	0	0	2	0	2	0	0	0	.167	.286
iatt, Phil, Detroit	.000	2	2	1	0	0	0	0	0	0	0	0	0	0	1	0	1	0	0	0	.000	.500
igginson, Bob, Detroit*	.333	12	11	9	3	3	9	0	0	2	3	0	0	0	2	0	3	0	0	0	1.000	.455
ocking, Denny, Minnesota†	.000	5	5	5	0	0	0	0	0	0	0	0	0	0	0	0	1	0	0	0	.000	.000
oiles, Chris, Baltimore	.000	4	4	1	0	0	0	0	0	0	0	1	0	1	2	0	1	0	0	0	.000	.500
ollins, Dave, Min.-Sea.†	.000	4	4	3	0	0	0	0	0	0	0	0	0	0	1	0	2	0	0	0	.000	.250
osey, Dwayne, Boston†	.333	3	3	3	0	1	1	0	0	0	0	0	0	0	0	0	2	0	0	0	.333	.333
oward, Dave, Kansas City†	.250	4	4	4	1	1	1	0	0	0	0	0	0	0	0	0	1	1	0	0	.250	.250
oward, Matt, New York	.333	3	3	3	0	1	1	0	0	0	0	0	0	0	0	0	1	0	0	0	.333	.333
owell, Jack, California*	.294	39	38	34	5	10	23	1	0	4	9	0	0	0	4	0	10	0	0	1	.676	.368
udler, Rex, California	.222	11	10	9	1	2	3	1	0	0	1	0	0	0	1	0	2	0	0	0	.333	.300
uff, Michael, Toronto	.500	2	2	2	1	1	1	0	0	0	0	0	0	0	0	0	1	0	0	0	.500	.500
ulse, David, Milwaukee*	.000	2	2	2	0	0	0	0	0	0	0	0	0	0	0	0	0	0	0	0	.000	.000
unter, Brian, Seattle	.211	23	21	19	2	4	8	1	0	1	3	0	0	0	2	0	8	0	0	0	.421	.286
uson, Jeff, Baltimore*	.333	4	4	3	0	1	1	0	0	0	0	0	0	0	1	0	1	0	0	0	.333	.500
yers, Tim, Detroit*	.000	10	10	9	0	0	0	0	0	0	0	0	0	0	1	1	3	0	0	0	.000	.100
banez, Raul, Seattle*	.000	2	2	2	0	0	0	0	0	0	0	0	0	0	0	0	0	0	0	0	.000	.000
ncaviglia, Pete, Baltimore	.333	3	3	3	1	1	1	0	0	0	0	0	0	0	0	0	0	0	0	0	.333	.333
Jackson, Damian, Cleveland	1.000	1	1	1	1	1	2	1	0	0	0	0	0	0	0	0	0	0	0	0	2.000	1.000
Jaha, John, Milwaukee	.000	3	3	3	0	0	0	0	0	0	0	0	0	0	0	0	1	0	0	0	.000	.000
Jefferson, Reggie, Boston*	.143	24	24	21	2	3	7	1	0	1	3	0	1	0	2	1	9	0	0	0	.333	.208
Jordan, Ricky, Seattle	.000	8	8	5	1	0	0	0	0	0	0	2	0	1	1	0	2	0	0	0	.000	.250
Kelly, Pat, New York	.000	1	1	0	1	0	0	0	0	0	0	0	0	0	1	0	0	0	0	0	.000	1.000
Kelly, Roberto, Minnesota	.000	4	3	2	0	0	0	0	0	0	0	1	0	0	0	0	0	0	0	0	.000	.333
Kent, Jeff, Cleveland	.000	2	1	1	0	0	0	0	0	0	0	0	0	0	0	0	0	0	0	0	.000	.000
Kirby, Wayne, Cleveland*	.400	6	6	5	0	2	2	0	0	0	0	0	0	0	1	0	0	0	0	0	.400	.500
Koslofski, Kevin, Milwaukee*	.000	1	1	1	0	0	0	0	0	0	0	0	0	0	0	0	0	0	0	0	.000	.000
Kreuter, Chad, Chicago†	.125	17	17	16	2	2	2	0	0	0	2	0	0	0	1	0	4	0	0	1	.125	.176

1996 A.L. STATISTICS Pinch-hitting

Player, Team	Avg.	G	TPA	AB	R	H	TB	2B	3B	HR	RBI	SH	SF	HP	BB	IBB	SO	SB	CS	GDP	Slg.	OB
Lawton, Matt, Minnesota*	.500	10	10	10	3	5	7	2	0	0	2	0	0	0	0	1	0	0	0	.700	.50
Leius, Scott, Cleveland	.000	8	8	8	0	0	0	0	0	0	0	0	0	0	0	4	0	0	0	.000	.00
Lennon, Patrick, Kansas City	.000	6	6	6	0	0	0	0	0	0	0	0	0	0	0	5	0	0	0	.000	.00
Lesher, Brian, Oakland	.000	5	4	3	1	0	0	0	0	0	0	0	0	1	0	2	0	0	0	.000	.25
Levis, Jesse, Milwaukee*	.306	39	39	36	0	11	11	0	0	0	4	0	0	3	0	4	0	0	1	.306	.35
Leyritz, Jim, New York	.300	11	11	10	0	3	3	0	0	0	5	0	0	1	0	4	0	0	0	.300	.36
Listach, Pat, Milwaukee†	.333	6	6	6	0	2	2	0	0	0	1	0	0	0	0	3	0	0	1	.333	.33
Lockhart, Keith, Kansas City*	.400	25	25	20	2	8	9	1	0	0	1	0	0	5	0	1	0	0	1	.450	.52
Lofton, Kenny, Cleveland*	.000	1	1	0	1	0	0	0	0	0	0	0	0	0	1	0	0	0	0	.000	1.00
Loretta, Mark, Milwaukee	.333	6	6	6	2	2	5	0	0	1	1	0	0	0	0	1	0	0	0	.833	.33
Lovullo, Torey, Oakland†	.111	10	10	9	1	1	1	0	0	0	0	0	0	1	0	4	0	0	0	.111	.20
Macfarlane, Mike, Kansas City	.375	10	10	8	1	3	3	0	0	0	2	0	1	0	1	1	0	0	0	.375	.40
Malave, Jose, Boston	.375	8	8	8	1	3	3	0	0	0	0	0	0	0	0	1	0	0	0	.375	.37
Manto, Jeff, Bos.-Sea	.333	9	9	9	3	3	10	1	0	2	5	0	0	0	0	4	0	0	0	1.111	.33
Martin, Norberto, Chicago	.308	17	17	13	2	4	5	1	0	0	0	4	0	0	0	1	1	0	0	.385	.30
Martinez, Dave, Chicago*	.250	19	18	16	2	4	6	2	0	0	2	0	0	2	0	5	0	0	1	.375	.33
Martinez, Manny, Seattle	.000	1	1	1	0	0	0	0	0	0	0	0	0	0	0	0	0	0	0	.000	.00
Martinez, Sandy, Toronto*	.333	3	3	3	0	1	1	0	0	0	0	0	0	0	0	2	0	0	0	.333	.33
Martinez, Tino, New York*	.000	3	3	1	0	0	0	0	0	0	0	0	0	0	2	0	1	0	0	0	.000	.66
Marzano, John, Seattle	.500	3	3	2	1	1	1	0	0	0	1	0	0	1	0	1	0	0	0	.500	.66
Mashore, Damon, Oakland	.000	7	7	6	1	0	0	0	0	0	1	0	0	1	0	4	0	0	0	.000	.14
Matheny, Mike, Milwaukee	.500	2	2	2	0	1	1	0	0	0	2	0	0	0	0	0	0	0	0	.500	.50
McGwire, Mark, Oakland	.500	5	5	4	1	2	5	0	0	1	1	0	0	1	1	2	0	0	0	1.250	.60
Meares, Pat, Minnesota	.667	3	3	3	0	2	2	0	0	0	1	0	0	0	0	0	0	0	0	.667	.66
Mieske, Matt, Milwaukee	.111	10	10	9	2	1	4	0	0	1	2	0	0	1	0	3	0	0	0	.444	.20
Mitchell, Kevin, Boston	.000	4	4	3	0	0	0	0	0	0	0	0	0	1	0	3	0	0	0	.000	.25
Molina, Izzy, Oakland	.333	3	3	3	0	1	1	0	0	0	0	0	0	0	0	0	0	0	0	.333	.33
Molitor, Paul, Minnesota	1.000	1	1	1	0	1	1	0	0	0	0	0	0	0	0	0	0	0	0	1.000	1.00
Moore, Kerwin, Oakland†	.000	1	1	1	0	0	0	0	0	0	0	0	0	0	0	1	0	0	0	.000	.00
Mouton, Lyle, Chicago	.143	20	19	14	1	2	3	1	0	0	1	0	0	0	5	0	7	0	0	0	.214	.36
Munoz, Jose, Chicago†	.167	7	7	6	1	1	1	0	0	0	0	0	0	0	1	0	1	0	0	0	.167	.28
Munoz, Pedro, Oakland	.500	4	4	4	0	2	3	1	0	0	1	0	0	0	0	2	0	0	0	.750	.50
Murray, Eddie, Cle.-Bal.†	.500	5	5	4	1	2	5	0	0	1	2	0	1	0	0	0	0	0	0	1.250	.40
Myers, Greg, Minnesota*	.375	16	16	16	1	6	7	1	0	0	3	0	0	0	0	1	0	0	0	.438	.37
Myers, Rod, Kansas City*	.250	4	4	4	1	1	4	0	0	1	1	0	0	0	0	0	0	0	1	1.000	.25
Naehring, Tim, Boston	.000	3	3	2	0	0	0	0	0	0	1	0	1	0	0	2	0	0	0	.000	.00
Nevin, Phil, Detroit	.000	3	3	3	0	0	0	0	0	0	0	0	0	0	0	3	0	0	0	.000	.00
Newson, Warren, Texas*	.176	22	20	17	0	3	4	1	0	0	1	0	0	3	0	7	0	0	0	.235	.30
Nieves, Melvin, Detroit†	.250	5	5	4	0	1	1	0	0	0	0	0	0	1	0	2	0	0	0	.250	.40
Nilsson, Dave, Milwaukee*	.500	7	7	6	0	3	5	2	0	0	4	0	0	1	0	0	0	0	1	.833	.57
Norman, Les, Kansas City	.000	11	9	8	0	0	0	0	0	0	0	0	0	0	0	3	0	0	0	.000	.11
Norton, Greg, Chicago†	.333	3	3	3	1	1	1	0	0	0	0	0	0	0	0	1	0	0	0	.333	.33
Nunnally, Jon, Kansas City*	.333	6	6	6	1	2	2	0	0	0	0	0	0	0	0	1	0	0	0	.333	.33
O'Brien, Charlie, Toronto	.308	15	15	13	2	4	8	1	0	1	2	0	0	2	1	3	0	0	0	.615	.40
Offerman, Jose, Kansas City†	.429	7	7	7	0	3	4	1	0	0	0	0	0	0	0	1	0	0	1	.571	.42
O'Leary, Troy, Boston*	.167	18	18	12	4	2	3	1	0	0	3	0	0	6	0	1	0	0	1	.250	.44
Olerud, John, Toronto*	.200	15	15	15	1	3	7	1	0	1	4	0	0	0	0	2	0	0	1	.467	.20
O'Neill, Paul, New York*	.000	2	2	0	0	0	0	0	0	0	0	0	0	0	0	0	0	0	0	.000	.00
Ortiz, Luis, Texas	.000	2	2	2	0	0	0	0	0	0	0	0	0	0	0	1	0	0	0	.000	.00
Palmeiro, Orlando, California*	.235	19	19	17	0	4	5	1	0	0	2	1	0	1	0	3	0	0	0	.294	.27
Paquette, Craig, Kansas City	.250	5	5	4	0	1	1	0	0	0	1	0	0	1	0	1	0	1	0	.250	.25
Parent, Mark, Detroit	.333	4	3	3	0	1	1	0	0	0	0	0	0	0	0	0	0	0	0	.333	.33
Pemberton, Rudy, Boston	.500	2	2	2	0	1	1	0	0	0	0	0	0	0	0	0	0	0	0	.500	.50
Pena, Geronimo, Cleveland†	.000	2	2	2	0	0	0	0	0	0	0	0	0	0	0	1	0	0	1	.000	.00
Penn, Shannon, Detroit†	.000	1	1	1	0	0	0	0	0	0	0	0	0	0	0	1	0	0	0	.000	.00
Perez, Robert, Toronto	.238	23	23	21	4	5	6	1	0	0	2	1	0	1	0	2	0	0	1	.286	.27
Perry, Herbert, Cleveland	.000	3	3	2	0	0	0	0	0	0	0	0	0	1	0	0	0	0	0	.000	.33
Phillips, Tony, Chicago†	.500	4	4	2	1	1	1	0	0	0	0	0	0	2	0	0	0	0	0	.500	.75
Pirkl, Greg, Bos.-Sea	.250	5	4	4	1	1	4	0	0	1	1	0	0	0	0	1	0	0	0	1.000	.25
Plantier, Phil, Oakland*	.000	6	5	3	0	0	0	0	0	0	0	0	0	2	0	2	1	0	0	.000	.40
Polonia, Luis, Baltimore*	.364	13	12	11	2	4	4	0	0	0	1	0	0	1	0	1	1	0	0	.364	.41
Posada, Jorge, New York†	.000	3	3	3	0	0	0	0	0	0	0	0	0	0	0	3	0	0	0	.000	.00
Pozo, Arquimedez, Boston	1.000	1	1	1	0	1	1	0	0	0	0	0	0	0	0	0	0	0	0	1.000	1.00
Pride, Curtis, Detroit*	.150	27	25	20	1	3	7	1	0	1	4	0	0	5	1	10	0	1	1	.350	.32
Raabe, Brian, Minnesota	.333	3	3	3	0	1	1	0	0	0	0	0	0	0	0	1	0	0	0	.333	.33
Raines, Tim, New York†	.000	8	8	7	0	0	0	0	0	0	0	0	0	1	0	0	0	0	0	.000	.12
Ramirez, Manny, Cleveland	.000	3	3	2	0	0	0	0	0	0	0	0	0	1	1	0	0	0	0	.000	.33
Randa, Joe, Kansas City	.300	12	12	10	0	3	3	0	0	0	1	0	0	2	2	2	1	1	0	.300	.41
Reboulet, Jeff, Minnesota	.200	14	12	10	0	2	3	1	0	0	1	0	0	2	0	1	0	1	0	.300	.33
Ripken, Billy, Baltimore	.286	7	7	7	1	2	2	0	0	0	0	0	0	0	0	0	0	0	0	.286	.28
Rivera, Ruben, New York	.500	3	3	2	1	1	4	0	0	1	1	0	0	1	0	1	0	0	0	2.000	.66
Roberts, Bip, Kansas City†	.333	9	9	9	2	3	4	1	0	0	2	0	0	0	0	0	0	0	1	.444	.33
Robertson, Mike, Chicago*	.000	2	2	2	0	0	0	0	0	0	0	0	0	0	0	1	0	0	0	.000	.00
Rodriguez, Alex, Seattle	.000	1	1	1	0	0	0	0	0	0	0	0	0	0	0	0	0	0	0	.000	.00
Rodriguez, Ivan, Texas	.500	5	5	4	0	2	2	0	0	0	1	0	0	1	1	0	0	0	0	.500	.60
Rodriguez, Tony, Boston	.000	2	2	0	1	0	0	0	0	0	0	0	0	1	0	0	0	0	0	.000	1.00
Salmon, Tim, California	.000	1	1	1	0	0	0	0	0	0	0	0	0	0	0	0	0	0	0	.000	.00
Samuel, Juan, Toronto	.111	19	19	18	1	2	2	0	0	0	1	0	0	1	0	8	1	0	0	.111	.15
Seitzer, Kevin, Milwaukee	.667	4	4	3	0	2	3	1	0	0	1	0	0	1	1	0	0	0	0	1.000	.75
Selby, Bill, Boston*	.400	12	12	10	0	4	5	1	0	0	4	0	0	2	1	1	0	0	1	.500	.50
Sheets, Andy, Seattle	.000	3	3	3	0	0	0	0	0	0	0	0	0	0	0	3	0	0	0	.000	.00
Sierra, Ruben, N.Y.-Det.†	.333	9	9	9	1	3	4	1	0	0	4	0	0	0	0	1	0	0	0	.444	.33
Singleton, Duane, Detroit*	.000	3	3	3	0	0	0	0	0	0	0	0	0	0	0	1	0	0	0	.000	.00

yer, Team	Avg.	G	TPA	AB	R	H	TB	2B	3B	HR	RBI	SH	SF	HP	BB	IBB	SO	SB	CS	GDP	Slg.	OBP
ught, Don, Cal.-Chi.	.400	10	10	10	0	4	4	0	0	0	0	0	0	0	0	0	0	0	0	1	.400	.400
ith, Mark, Baltimore	.167	6	6	6	1	1	4	0	0	1	1	0	0	0	0	0	2	0	0	0	.667	.167
opek, Chris, Chicago	.000	6	6	6	0	0	0	0	0	0	0	0	0	0	0	0	1	0	0	0	.000	.000
ow, J.T., California†	.667	3	3	3	0	2	3	1	0	0	0	0	0	0	0	0	0	0	0	1	1.000	.667
o, Luis, Sea.-N.Y.	.000	11	10	9	0	0	0	0	0	0	0	0	0	1	0	0	1	0	0	0	.000	.100
rrento, Paul, Seattle*	.214	16	16	14	1	3	7	1	0	1	3	0	0	1	1	0	4	0	0	0	.500	.313
ague, Ed, Toronto	.000	1	1	1	0	0	0	0	0	0	0	0	0	0	0	0	1	0	0	0	.000	.000
hoviak, Scott, Minnesota*	.333	17	16	12	2	4	10	0	0	2	3	0	0	0	4	0	3	0	0	0	.833	.500
irs, Matt, Oakland*	.471	18	18	17	3	8	18	2	1	2	5	0	0	1	0	1	0	0	0	0	1.059	.500
nley, Mike, Boston	.273	13	13	11	0	3	4	1	0	0	5	0	1	0	1	0	0	0	0	0	.364	.308
inbach, Terry, Oakland	.500	10	10	10	1	5	9	1	0	1	3	0	0	0	1	0	0	0	0	0	.900	.500
vens, Lee, Texas*	.000	5	5	5	0	0	0	0	0	0	0	0	0	0	0	0	4	0	0	0	.000	.000
lwell, Kurt, Texas†	.091	15	15	11	1	1	1	0	0	0	0	0	0	0	4	0	2	0	0	0	.091	.333
nnett, Kelly, Milwaukee	.000	1	1	1	0	0	0	0	0	0	0	0	0	0	0	0	0	0	0	0	.000	.000
ange, Doug, Seattle†	.244	49	46	41	3	10	13	1	1	0	5	0	1	0	4	0	9	1	0	1	.317	.304
awberry, Darryl, New York*	.167	8	8	6	0	1	2	1	0	1	1	0	0	0	2	1	2	0	0	0	.333	.375
nes, Chris, Kansas City	.167	6	6	6	0	1	1	0	0	0	0	0	0	0	0	0	2	0	0	0	.167	.167
hoff, B.J., Baltimore*	.000	3	3	3	0	0	0	0	0	0	0	0	0	0	0	0	0	0	0	0	.000	.000
eeney, Mike, Kansas City	.500	2	2	2	1	1	1	0	0	0	1	0	0	0	0	0	0	0	0	0	.500	.500
asco, Tony, Baltimore*	.167	6	6	6	1	1	1	0	0	0	1	0	0	0	0	0	1	0	0	0	.167	.167
tabull, Danny, Chicago	.000	4	4	4	0	0	0	0	0	0	0	0	0	0	0	0	2	0	0	0	.000	.000
tleton, Mickey, Texas†	.000	5	5	4	0	0	0	0	0	0	0	0	0	0	1	1	2	0	0	1	.000	.000
omas, Frank, Chicago	.500	2	2	2	0	1	1	0	0	0	0	0	0	0	0	0	0	0	0	0	.500	.500
ome, Jim, Cleveland*	.500	5	5	4	0	2	3	1	0	0	0	0	0	1	0	1	0	0	0	0	.750	.600
ompson, Ryan, Cleveland	1.000	2	2	2	1	2	2	0	0	0	1	0	0	0	0	0	0	0	0	0	1.000	1.000
sley, Lee, Boston†	.000	1	1	1	0	0	0	0	0	0	0	0	0	0	0	0	1	0	0	0	.000	.000
mmell, Alan, Detroit	.143	7	7	7	0	1	1	0	0	0	0	0	0	0	0	0	0	0	0	0	.143	.143
cker, Michael, Kansas City*	.400	10	10	10	1	4	4	0	0	0	2	0	0	0	0	0	0	1	0	1	.400	.400
entin, John, Boston	.000	1	1	0	0	0	0	0	0	0	0	0	0	1	0	0	0	0	0	0	.000	1.000
entin, Jose, Milwaukee†	.125	8	8	8	0	1	2	1	0	0	0	0	0	0	0	0	3	0	0	0	.250	.125
le, Dave, Texas	.250	4	4	4	0	1	1	0	0	0	0	0	0	0	0	0	0	0	0	1	.250	.250
ughn, Greg, Milwaukee	.000	1	1	0	0	0	0	0	0	0	0	0	0	0	1	0	0	0	0	0	.000	1.000
arde, Randy, California	.000	3	3	2	0	0	0	0	0	0	0	0	0	0	1	0	0	0	0	0	.000	.333
ntura, Robin, Chicago*	.250	11	11	8	2	2	5	0	0	1	1	0	0	0	3	2	1	0	0	0	.625	.455
a, Fernando, Milwaukee*	.200	5	5	5	0	1	1	0	0	0	0	0	0	0	0	0	0	0	0	0	.200	.200
ello, Joe, Kansas City	.375	12	11	8	0	3	4	1	0	0	3	0	0	0	3	0	2	0	0	0	.500	.545
quel, Omar, Cleveland†	.500	2	2	2	0	1	2	1	0	0	2	0	0	0	0	0	1	0	0	0	1.000	.500
gt, Jack, Texas	.000	2	2	2	0	0	0	0	0	0	0	0	0	0	0	0	1	0	0	0	.000	.000
lbeck, Matt, Minnesota†	.200	5	5	5	1	1	1	0	0	0	0	0	0	0	0	0	2	0	0	0	.200	.200
lker, Todd, Minnesota*	.000	3	3	2	0	0	0	0	0	0	0	0	0	0	0	0	0	0	0	1	.000	.333
llach, Tim, California	.000	7	7	5	0	0	0	0	0	0	0	0	0	1	1	1	1	0	0	0	.000	.286
rd, Turner, Milwaukee†	.200	10	10	10	2	2	6	1	0	1	3	0	0	0	0	0	2	0	0	0	.600	.200
iten, Mark, Seattle†	.667	3	3	3	1	2	5	0	0	1	1	0	0	0	0	0	0	0	0	0	1.667	.667
dger, Chris, Seattle	.000	1	1	1	0	0	0	0	0	0	0	0	0	0	0	0	0	0	0	0	.000	.000
liams, Bernie, New York†	.000	1	1	1	0	0	0	0	0	0	0	0	0	0	0	0	0	0	0	0	.000	.000
liams, Eddie, Detroit	.067	18	17	15	0	1	1	0	0	0	0	0	0	0	2	0	3	0	0	1	.067	.176
liams, George, Oakland†	.000	6	6	5	0	0	0	0	0	0	0	0	0	0	1	0	3	0	0	0	.000	.167
liams, Gerald, New York	.143	8	7	7	0	1	1	0	0	0	0	0	0	0	0	0	1	0	1	0	.143	.143
son, Dan, Seattle	.333	4	4	3	0	1	1	0	0	0	0	0	0	0	0	0	0	0	0	0	.333	.333
son, Nigel, Cleveland*	.250	9	9	8	2	2	8	0	0	2	4	0	0	1	0	4	0	0	0	1.000	.333
rthington, Craig, Texas	.000	1	1	1	0	0	0	0	0	0	0	0	0	0	0	0	0	0	0	0	.000	.000
ung, Ernie, Oakland	.400	6	6	5	1	2	2	0	0	0	0	0	0	0	1	0	0	0	0	0	.400	.400
ung, Kevin, Kansas City	.200	14	12	10	0	2	3	1	0	0	3	0	0	0	2	0	4	0	0	1	.300	.333
un, Greg, Baltimore†	.000	1	1	1	0	0	0	0	0	0	0	0	0	0	0	0	0	0	0	1	.000	.000

PINCH-HITTERS WITH TWO OR MORE TEAMS

ayer, Team	Avg.	G	TPA	AB	R	H	TB	2B	3B	HR	RBI	SH	SF	HP	BB	IBB	SO	SB	CS	GDP	Slg.	OBP
rete, Mike, California*	.150	22	22	20	2	3	9	0	0	2	3	0	0	0	2	0	1	0	0	2	.450	.227
rete, Mike, New York*	.143	8	8	7	0	1	1	0	0	0	1	0	0	0	1	0	2	0	0	0	.143	.250
rnitz, Jeromy, Cleveland*	.182	32	29	22	11	4	9	2	0	1	2	0	0	1	6	0	4	0	0	1	.409	.379
rnitz, Jeromy, Milwaukee*	.000	3	3	3	0	0	0	0	0	0	0	0	0	0	2	0	0	0	0	0	.000	.000
deno, Domingo, Toronto†	1.000	1	1	1	1	1	1	0	0	0	2	0	0	0	0	0	0	0	0	0	1.000	1.000
deno, Domingo, Chicago†	.125	8	8	8	0	1	1	0	0	0	1	0	0	0	0	0	1	0	0	1	.125	.125
sley, Damion, California	.000	2	2	1	0	0	0	0	0	0	0	0	0	1	0	0	0	0	0	0	.000	.000
sley, Damion, Detroit	.000	3	3	2	0	0	0	0	0	0	0	0	0	0	1	0	1	0	0	0	.000	.333
llins, Dave, Minnesota†	.000	3	3	2	0	0	0	0	0	0	0	0	0	0	1	0	2	0	0	0	.000	.333
llins, Dave, Seattle†	.000	1	1	1	0	0	0	0	0	0	0	0	0	0	0	0	0	0	0	0	.000	.000
nto, Jeff, Boston	.500	4	4	4	2	2	6	1	0	1	2	0	0	0	2	0	0	0	0	0	1.500	.500
nto, Jeff, Seattle	.200	5	5	5	1	1	4	0	0	1	3	0	0	0	0	0	2	0	0	0	.800	.200
rray, Eddie, Cleveland†	.500	2	2	2	1	1	4	0	0	1	1	0	0	0	0	0	0	0	0	0	2.000	.500
rray, Eddie, Baltimore†	.500	3	3	2	0	1	1	0	0	0	0	1	0	0	0	0	0	0	0	0	.500	.333
kl, Greg, Boston	.000	2	2	2	0	0	0	0	0	0	0	0	0	0	0	0	0	0	0	0	.000	.000
kl, Greg, Seattle	.500	3	2	2	1	1	4	0	0	1	1	0	0	0	0	0	0	0	0	0	2.000	.500
rra, Ruben, New York†	.333	3	3	3	0	1	1	0	0	0	0	0	0	0	0	0	0	0	0	0	.333	.333
rra, Ruben, Detroit†	.333	6	6	6	1	2	3	1	0	0	3	0	0	0	0	0	0	0	0	0	.500	.333
ught, Don, California	.250	8	8	8	0	2	2	0	0	0	0	0	0	0	0	0	0	0	0	1	.250	.250
ught, Don, Chicago	1.000	2	2	2	0	2	2	0	0	0	0	0	0	0	0	0	0	0	0	0	1.000	1.000
o, Luis, Seattle	.000	10	9	8	0	0	0	0	0	0	0	0	0	0	1	0	1	0	0	0	.000	.111
o, Luis, New York	.000	1	1	1	0	0	0	0	0	0	0	0	0	0	0	0	0	0	0	0	.000	.000

PITCHING

TEAM

Team	W	L	Pct.	ERA	G	ShO	GF	Sv.	IP	H	TBF	R	ER	HR	SH	SF	HB	BB	IBB	SO	WP	B
Clevelandl	99	62	.615	4.34	161	9	161	46	1452.1	1530	6245	769	700	173	39	46	39	484	42	1033	49	
Chicago	85	77	.525	4.52	162	4	162	43	1461.0	1529	6405	794	733	174	41	42	36	616	60	1039	59	
Kansas City	75	86	.466	4.55	161	8	161	35	1450.0	1563	6251	786	733	176	42	51	56	460	32	926	56	
Toronto	74	88	.457	4.57	162	7	162	35	1445.2	1476	6271	809	734	187	31	48	36	610	37	1033	61	
New York	92	70	.568	4.65	162	9	162	52	1440.0	1469	6289	787	744	143	44	45	49	610	35	1139	55	
Texas	90	72	.556	4.65	163	6	163	43	1449.1	1569	6358	799	749	168	33	55	43	582	44	976	38	
Boston	85	77	.525	4.98	162	5	162	37	1458.0	1606	6633	921	807	185	32	67	50	722	41	1165	51	
Milwaukee	80	82	.494	5.14	162	4	162	42	1447.1	1570	6437	899	826	213	43	64	57	635	33	846	56	
Baltimore	88	74	.543	5.14	163	1	163	44	1468.2	1604	6460	903	839	209	44	57	38	597	35	1047	38	
Oakland	78	84	.481	5.20	162	5	162	34	1456.1	1638	6505	900	841	205	52	55	52	644	61	884	60	
Seattle	85	76	.528	5.21	161	4	161	34	1431.2	1562	6351	895	829	216	42	47	60	605	52	1000	37	
Minnesota	78	84	.481	5.28	162	5	162	31	1439.2	1561	6355	900	844	233	41	47	41	581	27	959	49	
California	70	91	.435	5.30	161	8	161	38	1439.0	1546	6461	943	847	219	41	56	84	662	47	1052	80	
Detroit	53	109	.327	6.38	162	4	162	29	1432.2	1699	6713	1103	1015	241	45	72	80	784	63	957	82	
Totals	1132	1132	.500	4.99	1133	79	1133	536	20271.2	21922	89734	12208	11241	2742	570	752	721	8592	609	14056	771	6

NOTE—Totals for earned runs for several clubs do not agree with composite total for all pitchers of each respective club due to instances in which provisions of Secti
10.18(i) of the Scoring Rules were applied. The following differences are to be noted: Cleveland pitchers add to 701; Chicago pitchers add to 735; Toronto pitchers add to 73
Boston pitc hers add to 810; Milwaukee pitchers add to 829; Baltimore pitchers add to 841; Oakland pitchers add to 842; Minnesota pitchers add to 848;
California pitchers add to 849.

INDIVIDUAL

TOP QUALIFIERS FOR EARNED-RUN AVERAGE TITLE

Minimum 162 innings.   *Throws lefthanded.

Pitcher, Team	W	L	Pct.	ERA	G	GS	CG	ShO	GF	Sv.	IP	H	TBF	R	ER	HR	SH	SF	HB	BB	IBB	SO	WP	B
Guzman, Juan, Toronto	11	8	.579	2.93	27	27	4	1	0	0	187.2	158	756	68	61	20	2	2	7	53	3	165	7	
Hentgen, Pat, Toronto	20	10	.667	3.22	35	35	10	3	0	0	265.2	238	1100	105	95	20	5	8	5	94	3	177	8	
Nagy, Charles, Cleveland	17	5	.773	3.41	32	32	5	0	0	0	222.0	217	921	89	84	21	2	4	3	61	2	167	7	
Fernandez, Alex, Chicago	16	10	.615	3.45	35	35	6	1	0	0	258.0	248	1071	110	99	34	5	7	7	72	4	200	5	
Appier, Kevin, Kansas City	14	11	.560	3.62	32	32	5	1	0	0	211.1	192	874	87	85	17	7	4	5	75	2	207	10	
Hill, Ken, Texas	16	10	.615	3.63	35	35	7	3	0	0	250.2	250	1061	110	101	19	4	7	6	95	3	170	5	
Clemens, Roger, Boston	10	13	.435	3.63	34	34	6	2	0	0	242.2	216	1032	106	98	19	4	7	4	106	2	257	8	
Pettitte, Andy, New York*	21	8	.724	3.87	35	35	2	0	1	0	221.0	229	929	105	95	23	7	3	3	72	2	162	6	
McDonald, Ben, Milwaukee	12	10	.545	3.90	35	35	2	0	0	0	221.1	228	951	104	96	25	8	7	6	67	0	146	4	
Belcher, Tim, Kansas City	15	11	.577	3.92	35	35	4	1	0	0	238.2	262	1021	117	104	28	6	10	6	68	4	113	7	
Finley, Chuck, California*	15	16	.484	4.16	35	35	4	1	0	0	238.0	241	1037	124	110	27	7	9	11	94	5	215	17	
Alvarez, Wilson, Chicago*	15	10	.600	4.22	35	35	0	0	0	0	217.1	216	946	106	102	21	5	2	4	97	3	181	2	
Hershiser, Orel, Cleveland	15	9	.625	4.24	33	33	1	0	0	0	206.0	238	908	115	97	21	5	4	12	58	4	125	11	
Baldwin, James, Chicago	11	6	.647	4.42	28	28	0	0	0	0	169.0	168	719	88	83	24	2	2	4	57	3	127	12	
Radke, Brad, Minnesota	11	16	.407	4.46	35	35	3	0	0	0	232.0	231	973	125	115	40	5	6	4	57	2	148	1	

DEPARTMENTAL LEADERS: W—Pettitte, N.Y., 21; L—J. Abbott, Cal., 18; G—Guardado, Min., Myers, Det., 83; GS—Mussina, Bal., 36; CG—Hentgen, Tor., 10; ShO—
Hentgen, Tor.; Hill, Tex., Robertson, Min., 3; GF—Hernandez, Chi., 61; Sv.—Wetteland, N.Y., 43; IP—Hentgen, Tor., 265; H—Haney, K.C., 267; TBF—Hentgen, Tor., 110
R—Wakefield, Bos., 151; ER—Gordon, Bos., 134; HR—Boskie, Cal., Radke, Min., 40; SH—McDowell, Cle., 10; SF—Wells, Bal., 14; HB—Boskie, Cal., Grimsley, Ca
13; BB—Robertson, Min., 116; IBB—Carmona, Sea., R. Lewis, Det., 9; SO—Clemens, Bos., 257; WP—Finley, Cal., 17; Bk.—Hill, Tex., 4.

ALL PITCHERS

*Throws lefthanded.

Pitcher, Team	W	L	Pct.	ERA	G	GS	CG	ShO	GF	Sv.	IP	H	TBF	R	ER	HR	SH	SF	HB	BB	IBB	SO	WP	B
Abbott, Jim, California*	2	18	.100	7.48	27	23	1	0	2	0	142.0	171	654	128	118	23	4	10	4	78	3	58	13	
Abbott, Kyle, California*	0	1	.000	20.25	3	0	0	0	1	0	4.0	10	26	9	9	1	1	0	0	5	0	3	1	
Acre, Mark, Oakland	1	3	.250	6.12	22	0	0	0	11	2	25.0	38	124	17	17	4	1	0	2	9	4	18	0	
Adams, Willie, Oakland	3	4	.429	4.01	12	12	1	1	0	0	76.1	76	329	39	34	11	3	2	5	23	3	68	2	
Aguilera, Rick, Minnesota	8	6	.571	5.42	19	19	2	0	0	0	111.1	124	484	69	67	20	1	3	3	27	1	83	6	
Alberro, Jose, Texas	0	1	.000	5.79	5	1	0	0	1	0	9.1	14	46	6	6	1	0	1	0	7	1	2	0	
Aldred, Scott, Det.-Min.*	6	9	.400	6.21	36	25	0	0	6	0	165.1	194	748	125	114	29	7	7	6	68	4	111	10	
Aldrete, Mike, New York*	0	1	.000	.00	1	0	0	0	1	0	1.0	1	4	0	0	0	1	0	0	0	0	0	0	
Alexander, Manny, Baltimore	0	0	.000	67.50	1	0	0	0	1	0	.2	7	5	5	5	1	0	1	0	0	0	0	0	
Alvarez, Wilson, Chicago*	15	10	.600	4.22	35	35	0	0	0	0	217.1	216	946	106	102	21	5	2	4	97	3	181	2	
Anderson, Brian, Cleveland*	3	1	.750	4.91	10	9	0	0	0	0	51.1	58	215	29	28	9	2	3	0	14	1	21	2	
Andujar, Luis, Chi.-Tor.	3	1	.250	6.99	8	7	0	0	0	0	37.1	46	170	30	29	8	1	4	1	16	0	11	1	
Appier, Kevin, Kansas City	14	11	.560	3.62	32	32	5	1	0	0	211.1	192	874	87	85	17	7	4	5	75	2	207	10	
Assenmacher, Paul, Cleveland*	4	2	.667	3.09	63	0	0	0	25	1	46.2	46	201	18	16	1	4	2	4	14	5	44	2	
Ayala, Bobby, Seattle	6	3	.667	5.88	50	0	0	0	26	3	67.1	65	285	45	44	10	2	2	2	25	3	61	2	
Baldwin, James, Chicago	11	6	.647	4.42	28	28	0	0	0	0	169.0	168	719	88	83	24	2	2	4	57	3	127	12	
Belcher, Tim, Kansas City	15	11	.577	3.92	35	35	4	1	0	0	238.2	262	1021	117	104	28	6	10	6	68	4	113	7	
Belinda, Stan, Boston	2	1	.667	6.59	31	0	0	0	10	2	28.2	31	139	22	21	3	1	0	4	20	1	18	2	
Benitez, Armando, Baltimore	1	0	1.000	3.77	18	0	0	0	8	4	14.1	7	56	6	6	2	0	1	0	6	0	20	1	
Bennett, Erik, Minnesota	2	0	1.000	7.90	24	0	0	0	10	1	27.1	33	130	24	24	7	3	1	2	16	1	13	1	
Bere, Jason, Chicago	0	1	.000	10.26	5	5	0	0	0	0	16.2	26	93	19	19	3	1	1	0	18	1	19	2	
Bertotti, Mike, Chicago*	2	0	1.000	5.14	15	2	0	0	4	0	28.0	28	130	18	16	5	0	1	0	20	3	19	4	
Bevil, Brian, Kansas City	1	0	1.000	5.73	3	1	0	0	1	0	11.0	9	44	7	7	2	0	1	0	5	0	7	0	
Bluma, Jaime, Kansas City	0	0	.000	3.60	7	0	0	0	10	5	5.0	18	82	9	8	2	2	1	2	4	1	14	1	

itcher, Team	W	L	Pct.	ERA	G	GS	CG	ShO	GF	Sv.	IP	H	TBF	R	ER	HR	SH	SF	HB	BB	IBB	SO	WP	Bk.
oehringer, Brian, New York	2	4	.333	5.44	15	3	0	0	1	0	46.1	46	205	28	28	6	3	3	1	21	2	37	1	0
ohanon, Brian, Toronto*	0	1	.000	7.77	20	0	0	0	6	1	22.0	27	112	19	19	4	0	2	2	19	4	17	2	0
ones, Ricky, Mil.-N.Y.	7	14	.333	6.22	36	24	0	0	2	0	152.0	184	699	115	105	30	5	5	10	68	2	63	2	0
osio, Chris, Seattle	4	4	.500	5.93	18	9	0	0	4	0	60.2	72	278	44	40	8	3	6	4	24	1	39	1	0
oskie, Shawn, California	12	11	.522	5.32	37	28	1	0	1	0	189.1	226	860	126	112	40	6	4	13	67	7	133	10	0
oze, Marshall, Milwaukee	0	2	.000	7.79	25	0	0	0	8	1	32.1	47	165	29	28	5	3	1	6	25	4	19	3	0
randenburg, Mark, Tex.-Bos.	5	5	.500	3.43	55	0	0	0	13	0	76.0	76	338	35	29	8	3	4	3	33	2	66	0	1
rewer, Billy, New York*	1	0	1.000	9.53	4	0	0	0	1	0	5.2	7	32	6	6	0	0	0	0	8	0	8	0	0
riscoe, John, Oakland	0	1	.000	3.76	17	0	0	0	8	1	26.1	18	116	11	11	2	2	2	0	24	2	14	3	0
row, Scott, Toronto	1	0	1.000	5.59	18	1	0	0	9	0	38.2	45	180	25	24	5	1	1	0	25	1	23	2	1
urkett, John, Texas	5	2	.714	4.06	10	10	1	1	0	0	68.2	75	289	33	31	4	1	2	2	16	2	47	0	0
urrows, Terry, Milwaukee*	2	0	1.000	2.84	8	0	0	0	4	0	12.2	12	58	4	4	2	1	0	1	10	0	5	0	0
armona, Rafael, Seattle	8	3	.727	4.28	53	1	0	0	15	1	90.1	95	415	47	43	11	7	2	3	55	9	62	4	0
arpenter, Cris, Milwaukee	0	0	.000	7.56	8	0	0	0	2	0	8.1	12	39	8	7	1	0	1	0	2	0	2	0	0
arrara, Giovanni, Toronto	0	1	.000	11.40	11	0	0	0	3	0	15.0	23	76	19	19	5	0	0	0	12	2	10	1	0
astillo, Tony, Tor.-Chi.*	5	4	.556	3.60	55	0	0	0	13	2	95.0	95	398	45	38	10	3	5	3	24	2	57	3	0
harlton, Norm, Seattle*	4	7	.364	4.04	70	0	0	0	50	20	75.2	68	323	37	34	7	3	2	1	38	1	73	9	0
houinard, Bobby, Oakland	4	2	.667	6.10	13	11	0	0	0	0	59.0	75	278	41	40	10	3	3	3	32	3	32	0	0
hristopher, Mike, Detroit	1	1	.500	9.30	13	0	0	0	3	0	30.0	47	149	36	31	12	0	4	0	11	2	19	1	0
lark, Terry, Kansas City	1	1	.500	7.79	12	0	0	0	5	0	17.1	28	87	15	15	3	0	0	0	7	1	12	3	0
lemens, Roger, Boston	10	13	.435	3.63	34	34	6	2	0	0	242.2	216	1032	106	98	19	4	7	4	106	2	257	8	1
one, David, New York	7	2	.778	2.88	11	11	1	0	0	0	72.0	50	295	25	23	3	1	5	2	34	0	71	4	1
ook, Dennis, Texas*	5	2	.714	4.09	60	0	0	0	9	0	70.1	53	298	34	32	2	3	5	7	35	7	64	0	0
oppinger, Rocky, Baltimore	10	6	.625	5.18	23	22	0	0	1	0	125.0	126	548	76	72	25	2	5	2	60	1	104	4	0
orbin, Archie, Baltimore	2	0	1.000	2.30	18	0	0	0	5	0	27.1	22	123	7	7	2	0	1	1	22	0	20	2	0
orsi, Jim, Oakland	6	0	1.000	4.03	56	0	0	0	19	3	73.2	71	312	33	33	6	9	2	3	34	4	43	1	0
rabtree, Tim, Toronto	5	3	.625	2.54	53	0	0	0	21	1	67.1	59	284	26	19	4	2	2	3	22	4	57	3	0
ummings, John, Detroit*	3	3	.500	5.12	21	0	0	0	7	0	31.2	36	152	20	18	3	2	1	2	20	3	24	1	0
'Amico, Jeff, Milwaukee	6	6	.500	5.44	17	17	0	0	0	0	86.0	88	367	53	52	21	3	3	0	31	0	53	1	1
arwin, Jeff, Chicago	0	1	.000	2.93	22	0	0	0	9	0	30.2	26	124	10	10	5	1	0	2	9	1	15	0	0
avis, Tim, Seattle*	2	2	.500	4.01	40	0	0	0	4	0	42.2	43	187	21	19	4	1	1	2	17	1	34	0	0
avison, Scott, Seattle	0	0	.000	9.00	5	0	0	0	3	0	9.0	11	40	9	9	6	0	0	0	3	0	9	0	0
ickson, Jason, California	1	4	.200	4.57	7	7	0	0	0	0	43.1	52	192	22	22	6	2	1	1	18	1	20	1	1
oherty, John, Boston	0	0	.000	5.68	3	0	0	0	1	0	6.1	8	34	10	4	1	0	0	1	4	0	3	0	0
denfield, Ken, California	0	0	.000	10.38	2	0	0	0	0	0	4.1	10	26	5	5	2	0	0	1	2	0	4	0	0
chhorn, Mark, California	1	2	.333	5.04	24	0	0	0	6	0	30.1	36	135	17	17	3	3	2	2	11	3	24	0	1
schen, Joey, Detroit*	1	1	.500	3.24	24	0	0	0	3	0	25.0	27	110	11	9	3	0	1	0	14	3	15	3	0
ldred, Cal, Milwaukee	4	4	.500	4.46	15	15	0	0	0	0	84.2	82	363	43	42	8	0	4	4	38	0	50	1	0
llis, Robert, California	0	0	.000	.00	3	0	0	0	3	0	5.0	0	19	0	0	0	0	0	0	4	0	5	1	0
mbree, Alan, Cleveland*	1	1	.500	6.39	24	0	0	0	2	0	31.0	30	141	26	22	10	1	3	0	21	3	33	3	0
rickson, Scott, Baltimore	13	12	.520	5.02	34	34	6	0	0	0	222.1	262	968	137	124	21	5	5	11	66	4	100	1	0
shelman, Vaughn, Boston*	6	3	.667	7.08	39	10	0	0	1	0	87.2	112	428	79	69	13	3	5	2	58	4	59	4	0
arrell, John, Detroit	0	2	.000	14.21	2	2	0	0	0	0	6.1	11	33	10	10	2	0	0	1	5	0	0	1	0
ernandez, Alex, Chicago	16	10	.615	3.45	35	35	6	1	0	0	258.0	248	1071	110	99	34	5	7	7	72	4	200	5	0
etters, Mike, Milwaukee	3	3	.500	3.38	61	0	0	0	55	32	61.1	65	268	28	23	4	0	4	1	26	4	53	5	0
inley, Chuck, California*	15	16	.484	4.16	35	35	4	1	0	0	238.0	241	1037	124	110	27	7	9	11	94	5	215	17	2
lener, Huck, Toronto*	3	2	.600	4.58	15	11	0	0	0	0	70.2	68	309	40	36	9	0	4	1	33	1	44	1	0
etcher, Paul, Oakland	0	0	.000	20.25	1	0	0	0	0	0	1.1	6	10	3	3	0	0	0	0	1	0	0	0	0
orie, Bryce, Milwaukee	0	1	.000	6.63	15	0	0	0	5	0	19.0	20	90	16	14	3	1	2	0	13	2	12	3	0
reeman, Marvin, Chicago	0	0	.000	13.50	1	1	0	0	0	0	2.0	4	12	3	3	0	0	0	0	1	0	1	0	0
rohwirth, Todd, California	0	0	.000	11.12	4	0	0	0	2	0	5.2	10	33	11	7	1	0	1	1	4	0	1	1	0
arces, Rich, Boston	3	2	.600	4.91	37	0	0	0	9	0	44.0	42	205	26	24	5	0	5	0	33	5	55	0	0
arcia, Ramon, Milwaukee	4	4	.500	6.66	37	2	0	0	14	4	75.2	84	326	58	56	17	1	5	6	21	3	40	2	1
ibson, Paul, New York*	0	0	.000	6.23	4	0	0	0	2	0	4.1	6	19	3	3	1	0	0	0	0	0	3	0	0
ivens, Brian, Milwaukee*	1	3	.250	12.86	4	4	0	0	0	0	14.0	32	81	22	20	3	0	1	0	7	0	10	0	0
ohr, Greg, Det.-Cal.	5	9	.357	7.24	32	16	0	0	7	1	115.2	163	546	96	93	31	1	4	3	44	2	75	6	0
ooden, Dwight, New York	11	7	.611	5.01	29	29	1	1	0	0	170.2	169	756	101	95	19	1	5	9	88	4	126	9	1
ordon, Tom, Boston	12	9	.571	5.59	34	34	4	1	0	0	215.2	249	998	143	134	28	2	11	4	105	5	171	6	1
ranger, Jeff, Kansas City*	0	0	.000	6.61	15	0	0	0	5	0	16.1	21	80	13	12	3	0	1	2	10	0	11	2	0
raves, Danny, Cleveland	2	0	1.000	4.55	15	0	0	0	5	0	29.2	29	129	18	15	2	0	1	0	10	0	22	1	0
rimsley, Jason, California	5	7	.417	6.84	35	20	2	1	4	0	130.1	150	620	110	99	14	4	5	13	74	5	82	11	0
room, Buddy, Oakland*	5	0	1.000	3.84	72	1	0	0	16	2	77.1	85	341	37	33	8	2	0	3	34	3	57	5	0
ross, Kevin, Texas	11	8	.579	5.22	28	19	1	0	4	0	129.1	151	580	78	75	19	3	8	4	50	2	78	4	0
rundt, Ken, Boston*	0	0	.000	27.00	1	0	0	0	0	0	.1	1	2	1	1	0	0	0	0	0	0	0	0	0
uardado, Eddie, Minnesota*	6	5	.545	5.25	83	0	0	0	17	4	73.2	61	313	45	43	12	6	4	3	33	4	74	3	0
ubicza, Mark, Kansas City	4	12	.250	5.13	19	19	2	1	0	0	119.1	132	512	70	68	22	2	5	7	34	0	55	5	0
uetterman, Lee, Seattle*	0	2	.000	4.09	17	0	0	0	1	0	11.0	11	50	8	5	0	0	0	0	10	2	6	0	0
underson, Eric, Boston*	0	1	.000	8.31	28	0	0	0	2	0	17.1	21	82	17	16	5	0	2	2	8	2	7	3	0
uzman, Juan, Toronto	11	8	.579	2.93	27	27	4	1	0	0	187.2	158	756	68	61	20	2	2	7	53	3	165	7	0
ancock, Ryan, California	4	1	.800	7.48	11	4	0	0	4	0	27.2	34	130	23	23	2	0	0	2	17	1	19	2	0
aney, Chris, Kansas City*	10	14	.417	4.70	35	35	4	1	0	0	228.0	267	988	136	119	29	5	8	6	51	0	115	8	0
ansell, Greg, Minnesota	3	0	1.000	5.69	50	0	0	0	23	3	74.1	83	329	48	47	14	3	2	2	31	1	46	9	1
anson, Erik, Toronto	13	17	.433	5.41	35	35	4	1	0	0	214.2	243	955	143	129	26	4	5	2	102	2	156	13	0
arikkala, Tim, Seattle	0	1	.000	12.46	1	1	0	0	0	0	4.1	4	20	6	6	1	1	0	1	2	0	1	0	0
arris, Pep, California	2	0	1.000	3.90	11	3	0	0	0	0	32.1	31	146	16	14	4	0	4	3	17	2	20	4	0
arris, Reggie, Boston	0	0	.000	12.46	4	0	0	0	1	0	4.1	7	24	6	6	2	0	0	1	5	0	4	0	0
awkins, LaTroy, Minnesota	1	1	.500	8.20	7	6	0	0	1	0	26.1	42	124	24	24	8	1	1	0	9	0	24	1	1
aynes, Jimmy, Baltimore	3	6	.333	8.29	26	11	0	0	8	1	89.0	122	435	84	82	14	4	5	2	58	1	65	5	0
elling, Rick, Texas	1	2	.333	7.52	6	2	0	0	2	0	20.1	23	92	17	17	7	0	1	0	9	0	16	1	0
enneman, Mike, Texas	0	7	.000	5.79	49	0	0	0	45	31	42.0	41	182	28	27	6	4	2	0	17	5	34	4	0
entgen, Pat, Toronto	20	10	.667	3.22	35	35	10	3	0	0	265.2	238	1100	105	95	20	5	8	5	94	3	177	8	0
eredia, Gil, Texas	2	5	.286	5.89	44	0	0	0	21	1	73.1	91	320	50	48	12	1	2	1	14	2	43	2	0
ernandez, Roberto, Chicago	6	5	.545	1.91	72	0	0	0	61	38	84.2	65	355	21	18	2	2	2	0	38	5	85	6	0

Pitcher, Team	W	L	Pct.	ERA	G	GS	CG	ShO	GF	Sv.	IP	H	TBF	R	ER	HR	SH	SF	HB	BB	IBB	SO	WP	BK
Hershiser, Orel, Cleveland	15	9	.625	4.24	33	33	1	0	0	0	206.0	238	908	115	97	21	5	4	12	58	4	125	11	
Hill, Ken, Texas	16	10	.615	3.63	35	35	7	3	0	0	250.2	250	1061	110	101	19	4	7	6	95	3	170	5	
Hitchcock, Sterling, Seattle*	13	9	.591	5.35	35	35	0	0	0	0	196.2	245	885	131	117	27	3	8	7	73	4	132	4	
Holtz, Mike, California*	3	3	.500	2.45	30	0	0	0	8	0	29.1	21	127	11	8	1	1	1	3	19	2	31	1	
Holzemer, Mark, California*	1	0	1.000	8.76	25	0	0	0	3	0	24.2	35	119	28	24	7	0	1	3	8	1	20	0	
Howe, Steve, New York*	0	1	.000	6.35	25	0	0	0	4	1	17.0	19	76	12	12	1	2	0	1	6	3	5	2	
Hudson, Joe, Boston	3	5	.375	5.40	36	0	0	0	16	1	45.0	57	214	35	27	4	1	2	0	32	4	19	0	
Huisman, Rick, Kansas City	2	1	.667	4.60	22	0	0	0	5	1	29.1	25	130	15	15	4	2	0	18	2	23	0		
Hurtado, Edwin, Seattle	2	5	.286	7.74	16	4	0	0	6	2	47.2	61	223	42	41	10	0	5	0	30	3	36	2	
Hutton, Mark, New York	2	0	.000	5.04	12	2	0	0	5	0	30.1	32	140	19	17	3	0	2	1	18	1	25	0	
Jackson, Mike, Seattle	1	1	.500	3.63	73	0	0	0	23	6	72.0	61	302	32	29	11	0	1	6	24	3	70	2	
Jacome, Jason, Kansas City*	0	4	.000	4.72	49	2	0	0	21	1	47.2	67	226	27	25	5	3	0	2	22	5	32	1	
James, Mike, California	5	5	.500	2.67	69	0	0	0	23	1	81.0	62	353	27	24	7	6	5	10	42	7	65	5	
Janzen, Marty, Toronto	4	6	.400	7.33	15	11	0	0	3	0	73.2	95	344	65	60	16	1	3	2	38	3	47	7	
Johns, Doug, Oakland*	6	12	.333	5.98	40	23	1	0	4	1	158.0	187	710	112	105	21	2	3	6	69	5	71	9	
Johnson, Dane, Toronto	0	0	.000	3.00	10	0	0	0	2	0	9.0	5	36	3	3	0	0	0	0	5	0	7	0	
Johnson, Randy, Seattle*	5	0	1.000	3.67	14	8	0	0	2	1	61.1	48	256	27	25	8	1	0	2	25	0	85	3	
Jones, Doug, Milwaukee	5	0	1.000	3.41	24	0	0	0	8	1	31.2	31	139	13	12	3	0	2	2	13	2	34	1	
Jones, Stacy, Chicago	0	0	.000	.00	2	0	0	0	1	0	2.0	0	7	0	0	0	0	0	0	1	0	1	0	
Kamieniecki, Scott, New York	1	2	.333	11.12	7	5	0	0	0	0	22.2	36	120	30	28	6	0	0	2	19	1	15	1	
Karchner, Matt, Chicago	7	4	.636	5.76	50	0	0	0	13	1	59.1	61	278	42	38	10	2	4	2	41	8	46	4	
Karl, Scott, Milwaukee*	13	9	.591	4.86	32	32	3	1	0	0	207.1	220	905	124	112	29	2	7	11	72	0	121	5	
Keagle, Greg, Detroit	3	6	.333	7.39	26	6	0	0	5	0	87.2	104	435	76	72	13	2	7	9	68	5	70	2	
Key, Jimmy, New York*	12	11	.522	4.68	30	30	0	0	0	0	169.1	171	715	93	88	21	7	5	2	58	1	116	2	
Keyser, Brian, Chicago	2	2	.333	4.98	28	0	0	0	10	1	59.2	78	275	35	33	3	6	3	0	28	8	19	2	
Kiefer, Mark, Milwaukee	0	0	.000	8.10	7	0	0	0	2	0	10.0	15	48	9	9	1	1	1	0	5	1	5	1	
Klingenbeck, Scott, Minnesota	1	1	.500	7.85	10	3	0	0	2	0	28.2	42	137	28	25	5	1	1	1	10	0	15	1	
Klink, Joe, Seattle*	0	0	.000	3.86	3	0	0	0	1	0	2.1	3	11	1	1	1	0	0	0	1	0	2	0	
Knackert, Brent, Boston	0	1	.000	9.00	8	0	0	0	2	0	10.0	16	53	12	10	1	0	1	0	7	1	5	1	
Krivda, Rick, Baltimore*	3	5	.375	4.96	22	11	0	0	4	0	81.2	89	359	48	45	14	2	2	1	39	2	54	3	
Lacy, Kerry, Boston	2	0	1.000	3.38	11	0	0	0	3	0	10.2	15	54	5	4	2	0	0	1	8	0	9	0	
Langston, Mark, California*	6	5	.545	4.82	18	18	2	0	0	0	123.1	116	518	68	66	18	0	2	2	45	0	83	4	
Leftwich, Phil, California	0	1	.000	7.36	2	2	0	0	0	0	7.1	12	35	9	6	1	0	0	3	0	4	0		
Levine, Al, Chicago	0	1	.000	5.40	16	0	0	0	5	0	18.1	22	85	14	11	1	0	1	1	7	1	12	0	
Lewis, Richie, Detroit	4	6	.400	4.18	72	0	0	0	19	2	90.1	78	412	45	42	9	5	10	4	65	9	78	14	
Lima, Jose, Detroit	5	6	.455	5.70	39	4	0	0	15	3	72.2	87	329	48	46	13	5	3	5	22	4	59	3	
Linton, Doug, Kansas City	7	9	.438	5.02	21	18	0	0	0	0	104.0	111	452	65	58	13	6	2	8	26	1	87	3	
Lira, Felipe, Detroit	6	14	.300	5.22	32	32	3	2	0	0	194.2	204	850	123	113	30	5	11	10	66	2	113	7	
Lloyd, Graeme, Mil.-N.Y.*	2	6	.250	4.29	65	0	0	0	15	0	56.2	61	252	30	27	4	5	3	1	22	4	30	4	
Lopez, Albie, Cleveland	5	4	.556	6.39	13	10	0	0	0	0	62.0	80	282	47	44	14	0	1	2	22	1	45	2	
Maddux, Mike, Boston	3	2	.600	4.48	23	7	0	0	2	0	64.1	76	295	37	32	12	3	2	5	27	2	32	1	
Magnante, Mike, Kansas City*	2	2	.500	5.67	38	0	0	0	9	0	54.0	58	238	38	34	5	0	4	4	24	1	32	3	
Magrane, Joe, Chicago*	1	5	.167	6.88	19	8	0	0	3	0	53.2	70	252	45	41	10	1	3	3	25	1	21	3	
Mahomes, Pat, Min.-Bos.	3	4	.429	6.91	31	5	0	0	10	2	57.1	72	271	46	44	13	2	4	3	33	0	36	2	
Martinez, Dennis, Cleveland	9	6	.600	4.50	20	20	1	1	0	0	112.0	122	483	63	56	12	2	3	2	37	2	48	0	
Mathews, Terry, Baltimore	2	2	.500	3.38	14	0	0	0	5	0	18.2	20	79	7	7	3	1	0	7	1	13	0		
Maxcy, Brian, Detroit	0	0	.000	13.50	2	0	0	0	1	0	3.1	8	19	5	5	2	0	0	2	0	1	0		
May, Darrell, California*	0	0	.000	10.13	5	0	0	0	2	0	2.2	3	13	3	3	1	0	2	0	2	0	1	0	
McCarthy, Greg, Seattle*	0	0	.000	1.86	10	0	0	0	1	0	9.2	8	45	2	2	0	1	1	4	4	0	7	0	
McCaskill, Kirk, Chicago	5	5	.500	6.97	29	4	0	0	13	0	51.2	72	246	41	40	6	3	1	2	31	8	28	1	
McCurry, Jeff, Detroit	0	0	.000	24.30	2	0	0	0	1	0	3.1	9	21	9	9	3	0	0	2	0	0	0		
McDonald, Ben, Milwaukee	12	10	.545	3.90	35	35	2	0	0	0	221.1	228	951	104	96	25	8	7	6	67	0	146	4	
McDowell, Jack, Cleveland	13	9	.591	5.11	30	30	5	1	0	0	192.0	214	846	119	109	22	10	5	4	67	2	141	5	
McDowell, Roger, Baltimore	1	1	.500	4.25	41	0	0	0	11	4	59.1	69	262	32	28	7	3	1	2	23	1	20	0	
McElroy, Chuck, California*	1	1	.833	2.95	40	0	0	0	11	0	36.2	32	151	12	12	2	1	1	2	13	2	32	1	
Meacham, Rusty, Seattle	1	1	.500	5.74	15	5	0	0	3	1	42.1	57	192	28	27	9	0	1	4	13	1	25	1	
Mecir, Jim, New York	1	1	.500	5.13	26	0	0	0	10	0	40.1	42	185	24	23	6	5	4	0	23	4	38	6	
Mendoza, Ramiro, New York	4	5	.444	6.79	12	11	0	0	0	0	53.0	80	249	43	40	5	1	1	4	10	1	34	2	
Menhart, Paul, Seattle	2	2	.500	7.29	11	6	0	0	4	0	42.0	55	196	36	34	9	1	0	2	25	0	18	1	
Mercedes, Jose, Milwaukee	0	2	.000	9.18	11	0	0	0	4	0	16.2	20	74	18	17	0	1	0	5	0	6	2		
Mercker, Kent, Bal.-Cle.*	4	6	.400	6.98	24	12	0	0	2	0	69.2	83	329	60	54	13	3	6	3	38	2	29	3	
Mesa, Jose, Cleveland	2	7	.222	3.73	69	0	0	0	60	39	72.1	69	304	32	30	6	2	2	3	28	4	64	4	
Milacki, Bob, Seattle	1	4	.200	6.86	7	4	0	0	1	0	21.0	30	106	20	16	3	0	0	0	15	3	13	0	
Milchin, Mike, Min.-Bal.*	3	1	.750	7.44	39	0	0	0	7	0	32.2	44	154	28	27	7	1	0	0	17	2	29	1	
Miller, Travis, Minnesota	1	2	.333	9.23	7	7	0	0	0	0	26.1	45	126	29	27	7	1	0	0	9	0	15	0	
Miller, Trever, Detroit*	0	4	.000	9.18	5	4	0	0	0	0	16.2	28	88	17	17	3	2	2	9	0	8	0		
Mills, Alan, Baltimore	3	2	.600	4.28	49	0	0	0	23	5	54.2	40	233	26	26	10	3	2	1	35	2	50	6	
Minchey, Nate, Boston	0	2	.000	15.00	2	2	0	0	0	0	6.0	16	36	11	10	1	0	1	0	5	0	4	1	
Minor, Blas, Seattle	1	1	.000	4.97	11	0	0	0	6	0	25.1	27	109	14	14	6	0	0	11	0	14	2		
Miranda, Angel, Milwaukee*	7	6	.538	4.94	46	12	0	0	5	1	109.1	116	503	68	60	12	5	8	2	69	4	78	10	
Moehler, Brian, Detroit	0	1	.000	4.35	2	2	0	0	0	0	10.1	11	51	10	5	1	1	0	0	8	1	2	1	
Mohler, Mike, Oakland*	7	6	.538	3.67	72	0	0	0	30	7	81.0	79	352	36	33	9	6	4	1	41	6	64	9	
Monteleone, Rich, California	0	3	.000	5.87	12	0	0	0	2	0	15.1	23	69	11	10	5	0	0	1	4	0	5	0	
Montgomery, Jeff, Kansas City	4	6	.400	4.26	48	0	0	0	41	24	63.1	59	261	31	30	14	3	1	3	19	3	45	0	
Montgomery, Steve, Oakland*	1	0	1.000	4.22	8	0	0	0	6	0	13.2	18	71	14	14	5	0	0	2	13	2	9	3	
Moyer, Jamie, Bos.-Sea.*	13	3	.813	3.98	34	21	0	0	1	0	160.2	177	703	86	71	23	7	6	2	46	5	79	3	
Mulholland, Terry, Seattle*	4	5	.444	4.67	12	12	0	0	0	0	69.1	75	300	38	36	5	5	3	2	28	3	34	1	
Mussina, Mike, Baltimore	19	11	.633	4.81	36	36	4	1	0	0	243.1	264	1039	137	130	31	4	4	3	69	0	204	3	
Myers, Jimmy, Baltimore	0	0	.000	7.07	11	0	0	0	5	0	14.0	18	64	13	11	4	0	2	0	3	1	6	1	
Myers, Mike, Detroit*	1	5	.167	5.01	83	0	0	0	25	6	64.2	70	298	41	36	6	2	1	4	34	8	69	2	
Myers, Randy, Baltimore*	4	4	.500	3.53	62	0	0	0	50	31	58.2	60	262	24	23	7	3	1	2	29	4	74	3	
Nagy, Charles, Cleveland	17	5	.773	3.41	32	32	5	0	0	0	222.0	217	921	89	84	21	2	4	3	61	2	167	7	
Naulty, Dan, Minnesota	3	2	.600	3.79	49	0	0	0	15	4	57.0	43	245	26	24	5	2	0	0	35	3	56	2	

tcher, Team	W	L	Pct.	ERA	G	GS	CG	ShO	GF	Sv.	IP	H	TBF	R	ER	HR	SH	SF	HB	BB	IBB	SO	WP	Bk.
lson, Jeff, New York	4	4	.500	4.36	73	0	0	0	27	2	74.1	75	328	38	36	6	3	1	2	36	1	91	4	0
kowski, C.J., Detroit*	2	3	.400	8.08	11	8	0	0	0	0	45.2	62	234	44	41	7	0	2	7	38	1	36	2	0
ea, Chad, Cleveland	10	6	.625	4.79	29	21	1	1	2	0	146.2	151	620	82	78	22	3	3	5	42	3	101	2	0
vares, Omar, Detroit	7	11	.389	4.89	25	25	4	0	0	0	160.0	169	708	90	87	16	3	6	9	75	4	81	4	1
ver, Darren, Texas*	14	6	.700	4.66	30	30	1	1	0	0	173.2	190	777	97	90	20	2	7	10	76	3	112	5	1
son, Gregg, Detroit	3	0	1.000	5.02	43	0	0	0	28	8	43.0	43	196	25	24	6	1	0	1	28	4	29	5	0
osco, Jesse, Baltimore*	3	1	.750	3.40	66	0	0	0	10	0	55.2	42	236	22	21	5	2	1	2	28	4	52	2	0
rra, Jose, Minnesota	5	5	.500	6.04	27	5	0	0	7	0	70.0	88	320	48	47	15	1	3	3	27	0	50	4	1
tterson, Danny, Texas	0	0	.000	.00	7	0	0	0	5	0	8.2	10	38	4	0	0	0	0	3	1	5	0	0
vlas, Dave, New York	0	0	.000	2.35	16	0	0	0	8	1	23.0	23	97	7	6	2	0	1	7	2	18	3	0
vlik, Roger, Texas	15	8	.652	5.19	34	34	7	0	0	0	201.0	216	877	120	116	28	3	4	5	81	5	127	8	0
nnington, Brad, Bos.-Cal.*	0	2	.000	6.20	22	0	0	0	8	0	20.1	11	102	15	14	2	0	1	0	31	1	20	2	0
rcival, Troy, California	0	2	.000	2.31	62	0	0	0	52	36	74.0	38	291	20	19	8	2	1	2	31	4	100	2	0
ttitte, Andy, New York*	21	8	.724	3.87	35	34	2	0	1	0	221.0	229	929	105	95	23	7	3	3	72	2	162	6	1
chardo, Hipolito, Kansas City	3	5	.375	5.43	57	0	0	0	28	3	68.0	74	294	41	41	5	3	2	2	26	5	43	4	0
ink, Eric, Cleveland	3	2	.600	2.43	56	0	0	0	12	2	77.2	56	318	21	21	6	1	4	3	34	2	85	4	1
lley, Dale, New York*	1	2	.333	7.89	32	0	0	0	9	0	21.2	23	103	20	19	5	1	3	11	1	14	0	0
ole, Jim, Cleveland*	4	0	1.000	3.04	32	0	0	0	8	0	26.2	29	121	15	9	3	0	1	0	14	4	19	2	0
tts, Mike, Milwaukee*	1	2	.333	7.15	24	0	0	0	7	1	45.1	58	217	39	36	7	1	4	0	30	2	21	3	1
eto, Ariel, Oakland	6	7	.462	4.15	21	21	2	0	0	0	125.2	130	547	66	58	9	5	5	7	54	2	75	6	2
gh, Tim, Kansas City	0	1	.000	5.45	19	1	0	0	8	0	36.1	42	164	24	22	9	0	1	2	12	1	27	2	0
antrill, Paul, Toronto	5	14	.263	5.43	38	20	0	0	7	0	134.1	172	609	90	81	27	5	7	2	51	3	86	1	1
adke, Brad, Minnesota	11	16	.407	4.46	35	35	3	0	0	0	232.0	231	973	125	115	40	5	6	4	57	2	148	1	0
eyes, Al, Milwaukee	1	0	1.000	7.94	5	0	0	0	2	0	5.2	8	27	5	5	1	0	0	0	2	0	2	2	0
eyes, Carlos, Oakland	7	10	.412	4.78	46	10	0	0	14	0	122.1	134	550	71	65	19	2	8	2	61	8	78	2	1
nodes, Arthur, Baltimore*	9	1	.900	4.08	28	2	0	0	5	1	53.0	48	224	28	24	6	1	1	0	23	3	62	0	0
sley, Bill, Toronto	0	1	.000	3.89	25	0	0	0	11	0	41.2	33	177	20	18	7	1	2	0	25	0	29	1	0
vera, Mariano, New York	8	3	.727	2.09	61	0	0	0	14	5	107.2	73	425	25	25	1	2	1	2	34	3	130	1	0
oa, Joe, Cleveland	0	0	.000	10.80	1	0	0	0	0	0	1.2	4	11	2	2	0	0	0	0	3	0	0	0	0
obertson, Rich, Minnesota*	7	17	.292	5.12	36	31	5	3	1	0	186.1	197	853	113	106	22	2	4	9	116	2	114	7	0
obinson, Ken, Kansas City	1	0	1.000	6.00	5	0	0	0	2	0	6.0	9	30	4	4	0	0	1	0	3	1	5	1	0
odriguez, Frank, Minnesota	13	14	.481	5.05	38	33	3	0	4	2	206.2	218	899	129	116	27	6	8	5	78	1	110	2	0
odriguez, Nerio, Baltimore	0	1	.000	4.32	8	1	0	0	2	0	16.2	18	77	11	8	2	0	1	1	7	0	12	0	0
ogers, Kenny, New York*	12	8	.600	4.68	30	30	2	1	0	0	179.0	179	786	97	93	16	6	3	8	83	2	92	5	0
osado, Jose, Kansas City*	8	6	.571	3.21	16	16	2	1	0	0	106.2	101	441	39	38	7	1	4	4	26	1	64	5	1
iffcorn, Scott, Chicago	0	1	.000	11.37	3	1	0	0	1	0	6.1	10	34	8	8	1	1	0	0	6	0	3	2	0
ussell, Jeff, Texas	3	3	.500	3.38	55	0	0	0	11	3	56.0	58	249	22	21	5	3	4	4	22	3	23	3	0
ckinsky, Brian, Baltimore	0	0	.000	3.86	3	0	0	0	2	0	4.2	6	22	2	2	1	0	0	0	3	0	2	0	1
ger, A.J., Detroit	4	5	.444	5.01	22	9	0	0	1	0	79.0	91	347	46	44	10	3	3	2	29	2	52	1	0
anderson, Scott, California	0	2	.000	7.50	5	4	0	0	0	0	18.0	39	98	21	15	5	1	1	2	4	0	7	0	2
auveur, Rich, Chicago*	0	0	.000	15.00	3	0	0	0	2	0	3.0	3	15	5	5	1	0	1	0	5	0	1	0	0
anlan, Bob, Det.-K.C.	0	1	.000	6.85	17	0	0	0	4	0	22.1	29	105	19	17	2	1	0	2	12	2	6	1	0
hmidt, Jeff, California	2	0	1.000	7.88	9	0	0	0	1	0	8.0	13	42	9	7	2	0	1	0	8	0	2	1	0
le, Aaron, Boston	7	11	.389	5.32	29	29	1	0	0	0	157.1	192	722	110	93	14	6	7	8	67	2	137	2	0
erafini, Dan, Minnesota*	0	1	.000	10.38	1	1	0	0	0	0	4.1	7	23	5	5	1	0	1	1	2	1	0	0	0
lepherd, Keith, Baltimore	0	1	.000	8.71	13	0	0	0	6	0	20.2	31	111	27	20	6	1	1	0	18	1	17	0	0
auey, Paul, Cleveland	5	2	.714	2.85	42	0	0	0	18	4	53.2	45	225	19	17	6	1	3	0	26	3	44	3	1
va, Jose, Toronto	0	0	.000	13.50	2	0	0	0	0	0	2.0	5	11	3	3	1	0	0	0	0	0	0	0	0
nas, Bill, Chicago	2	8	.200	4.58	64	0	0	0	16	2	72.2	75	328	39	37	5	1	2	3	39	6	65	0	0
rotka, Mike, Chicago*	1	2	.333	7.18	15	4	0	0	2	0	26.1	34	122	27	21	3	0	2	0	12	0	11	1	0
ocumb, Heathcliff, Boston	5	5	.500	3.02	75	0	0	0	60	31	83.1	68	368	31	28	2	1	3	3	55	5	88	10	0
mall, Aaron, Oakland	1	3	.250	8.16	12	3	0	0	4	0	28.2	37	144	28	26	3	0	1	1	22	1	17	2	0
nith, Lee, California	0	0	.000	2.45	11	0	0	0	8	0	11.0	8	44	4	3	0	0	2	0	3	0	6	1	0
odowsky, Clint, Detroit	1	3	.250	11.84	7	7	0	0	0	0	24.1	40	132	34	32	5	1	0	3	20	0	9	3	0
parks, Steve, Milwaukee	4	7	.364	6.60	20	13	1	0	2	0	88.2	103	406	66	65	19	3	1	3	52	0	21	6	0
ooljaric, Paul, Toronto*	2	0	.000	3.08	28	0	0	0	12	1	38.0	30	163	17	13	6	1	2	1	19	1	38	0	0
ringer, Dennis, California	5	6	.455	5.51	20	15	2	1	3	0	94.2	91	413	65	58	24	0	1	6	43	0	64	1	0
anton, Mike, Bos.-Tex.*	4	4	.500	3.66	81	0	0	0	28	1	78.2	78	327	32	32	11	4	2	0	27	5	60	3	2
ephenson, Garrett, Baltimore	0	1	.000	12.79	3	0	0	0	0	0	6.1	13	35	9	9	1	1	0	1	3	1	3	0	0
evens, Dave, Minnesota	3	3	.500	4.66	49	0	0	0	38	11	58.0	58	251	31	30	12	3	3	0	25	2	29	1	0
uppan, Jeff, Boston	1	1	.500	7.54	8	4	0	0	2	0	22.2	29	107	19	19	3	1	4	1	13	0	13	3	0
uzuki, Makoto, Seattle	0	0	.000	20.25	1	0	0	0	0	0	1.1	2	8	3	3	0	0	0	0	2	1	0	0	0
vindell, Greg, Cleveland*	1	1	.500	6.59	13	2	0	0	1	0	28.2	31	121	21	21	8	1	1	0	8	0	21	0	0
pani, Kevin, Chicago	13	10	.565	4.59	34	34	1	0	0	0	225.1	236	971	123	115	34	6	8	3	76	5	150	13	0
varez, Julian, Cleveland	4	7	.364	5.36	51	4	0	0	13	0	80.2	101	353	49	48	9	5	4	1	22	5	46	1	0
aylor, Billy, Oakland	6	3	.667	4.33	55	0	0	0	30	17	60.1	52	261	30	29	5	4	3	4	25	4	67	1	0
lgheder, Dave, Oakland	4	7	.364	4.65	16	14	1	1	1	0	79.1	92	348	42	41	12	3	3	1	26	1	43	2	0
iomas, Larry, Chicago*	2	3	.400	3.23	57	0	0	0	11	0	30.2	32	135	11	11	1	4	0	3	14	2	20	1	0
nompson, Justin, Detroit*	1	6	.143	4.58	11	11	0	0	0	0	59.0	62	267	35	30	7	0	2	2	31	2	44	1	0
mlin, Mike, Toronto	1	6	.143	3.65	59	0	0	0	56	31	56.2	47	230	25	23	4	2	3	2	18	4	52	3	0
rres, Salomon, Seattle	3	3	.500	4.59	10	7	1	1	1	0	49.0	44	212	27	25	5	1	3	23	2	36	1	0
ombley, Mike, Minnesota	5	1	.833	3.01	43	0	0	0	19	6	68.2	61	292	24	23	2	0	3	5	25	8	57	4	0
rbani, Tom, Detroit*	2	2	.500	8.37	16	2	0	0	3	0	23.2	31	117	22	22	8	0	1	2	14	0	20	3	0
alera, Julio, Kansas City	3	2	.600	6.46	31	2	0	0	7	1	61.1	75	279	44	44	7	2	4	2	27	3	31	1	1
anEgmond, Tim, Milwaukee	3	5	.375	5.27	12	9	0	0	1	0	54.2	58	242	35	32	6	3	3	1	23	2	33	0	1
an Poppel, Todd, Oak.-Det.	3	9	.250	9.06	37	15	1	1	4	0	99.1	139	491	107	100	24	4	7	3	62	3	53	7	0
anRyn, Ben, California*	0	0	.000	.00	1	0	0	0	1	0	1.0	1	5	0	0	0	0	1	0	0	1	0	0
res, Randy, Detroit	0	4	.000	8.31	25	0	0	0	11	0	30.1	38	153	29	28	6	1	3	2	23	4	28	2	0
llone, Ron, Milwaukee*	1	0	.000	3.28	23	0	0	0	10	2	24.2	14	104	9	9	4	0	2	4	18	0	19	2	0
ola, Frank, Toronto*	1	3	.250	7.71	6	6	0	0	0	0	30.1	43	150	28	26	6	1	3	2	21	3	18	1	0
osberg, Ed, Texas*	1	1	.500	3.27	52	0	0	0	21	8	44.0	51	195	17	16	4	2	1	0	21	4	32	1	0
agner, Matt, Seattle	3	5	.375	6.86	15	14	1	0	0	0	80.0	91	364	62	61	15	0	4	3	38	2	41	0	0
akefield, Tim, Boston	14	13	.519	5.14	32	32	6	0	0	0	211.2	238	963	151	121	38	1	9	12	90	0	140	4	1

- 245 -

Pitcher, Team	W	L	Pct.	ERA	G	GS	CG	ShO	GF	Sv.	IP	H	TBF	R	ER	HR	SH	SF	HB	BB	IBB	SO	WP
Walker, Mike, Detroit..............	0	0	.000	8.46	20	0	0	0	12	1	27.2	40	135	26	26	10	1	2	1	17	1	13	2
Ware, Jeff, Toronto................	1	5	.167	9.09	13	4	0	0	6	0	32.2	35	163	34	33	6	1	0	2	31	1	11	6
Wasdin, John, Oakland..........	8	7	.533	5.96	25	21	1	0	2	0	131.1	145	575	96	87	24	3	6	4	50	5	75	2
Weathers, Dave, New York......	0	2	.000	9.35	11	4	0	0	1	0	17.1	23	90	19	18	1	0	1	2	14	1	13	1
Wells, Bob, Seattle...............	12	7	.632	5.30	36	16	1	1	6	0	130.2	141	574	78	77	25	3	4	6	46	5	94	0
Wells, David, Baltimore*	11	14	.440	5.14	34	34	3	0	0	0	224.1	247	946	132	128	32	8	14	7	51	7	130	4
Wengert, Don, Oakland..........	7	11	.389	5.58	36	25	1	1	2	0	161.1	200	725	102	100	29	3	5	6	60	5	75	4
Wetteland, John, New York......	2	3	.400	2.83	62	0	0	0	58	43	63.2	54	265	23	20	9	1	2	0	21	4	69	1
Whitehurst, Wally, New York ...	1	1	.500	6.75	2	2	0	0	0	0	8.0	11	36	6	6	1	0	0	0	2	0	1	0
Whiteside, Matt, Texas..........	0	1	.000	6.68	14	0	0	0	7	0	32.1	43	148	24	24	8	1	2	0	11	1	15	1
Wickander, Kevin, Milwaukee*	2	0	1.000	4.97	21	0	0	0	6	0	25.1	26	118	16	14	2	1	2	0	17	2	19	2
Wickman, Bob, N.Y.-Mil.........	7	1	.875	4.42	70	0	0	0	18	0	95.2	106	429	50	47	10	2	4	5	44	3	75	4
Williams, Brian, Detroit	3	10	.231	6.77	40	17	2	1	17	2	121.0	145	579	107	91	21	5	6	6	85	2	72	8
Williams, Shad, California	0	2	.000	8.89	13	2	0	0	3	0	28.1	42	150	34	28	7	3	1	2	21	4	26	2
Williams, Woody, Toronto	4	5	.444	4.73	12	10	1	0	0	0	59.0	64	255	33	31	8	2	1	1	21	1	43	2
Witasick, Jay, Oakland...........	1	1	.500	6.23	12	0	0	0	6	0	13.0	12	55	9	9	5	0	1	0	5	0	12	2
Witt, Bobby, Texas................	16	12	.571	5.41	33	32	2	0	1	0	199.2	235	903	129	120	28	2	7	2	96	3	157	4
Wojciechowski, Steve, Oak.* ..	5	5	.500	5.65	16	15	0	0	0	0	79.2	97	356	57	50	10	1	2	2	28	0	30	3
Wolcott, Bob, Seattle.............	7	10	.412	5.73	30	28	1	0	0	0	149.1	179	672	101	95	26	5	3	7	54	5	78	3
Yan, Esteban, Baltimore.........	0	0	.000	5.79	4	0	0	0	2	0	9.1	13	42	7	6	3	0	0	3	1	7	0

COMBINATION SHUTOUTS: **Boston (2)**—Wakefield and Slocumb; Clemens, Brandenburg and Belinda. **California (5)**—Finley and Percival (2); Hancock, James a Percival; Finley, James and Percival; Boskie, Holtz and Percival. **Chicago (3)**—Tapani and Keyser; Alvarez and Hernandez; Baldwin, Castillo and Hernandez. **Cleveland (6)**—Hershiser and Tavarez; Martinez, Assenmacher, Tavarez and Mesa; Nagy, Plunk, Assenmacher and Mesa; Martinez, Swindell, Graves and Shuey; Hershiser a Shuey; McDowell, Plunk and Mesa. **Kansas City (3)**—Appier and Jacome; Appier and Magnante; Rosado and Pichardo. **Milwaukee (3)**—Sparks, Lloyd, Garcia a Fetters; Bones and Villone; McDonald and Miranda. **Minnesota (2)**—Parra, Mahomes, Guardado and Stevens; Aldred, Guardado and Trombley. **New York (7)**—Key, Rivera and Wetteland 2; Gooden, M. Rivera and Wetteland; Rogers and Wetteland; Gooden, M. Rivera and Polley; Cone and M. Rivera; Key and Weathers. **Oakland (2)**— Johns and Corsi; Telgheder and Groom. **Seattle (2)**—Bosio, T. Davis and Wells; Moyer and Ayala. **Texas (1)**—Oliver and Cook. **Toronto (2)**—Hentgen and Timl Williams and Timlin.

PITCHERS WITH TWO OR MORE TEAMS

Pitcher, Team	W	L	Pct.	ERA	G	GS	CG	ShO	GF	Sv.	IP	H	TBF	R	ER	HR	SH	SF	HB	BB	IBB	SO	WP
Aldred, Scott, Detroit*...........	0	4	.000	9.35	11	8	0	0	0	0	43.1	60	217	52	45	9	3	2	3	26	3	36	6
Aldred, Scott, Minnesota*......	6	5	.545	5.09	25	17	0	0	0	0	122.0	134	531	73	69	20	4	5	3	42	1	75	4
Andujar, Luis, Chicago	0	2	.000	8.22	5	5	0	0	0	0	23.0	32	113	22	21	4	1	2	0	15	0	6	0
Andujar, Luis, Toronto	1	1	.500	5.02	3	2	0	0	0	0	14.1	14	57	8	8	4	0	2	1	1	0	5	1
Bones, Ricky, Milwaukee	7	14	.333	5.83	32	23	0	0	2	0	145.0	170	658	104	94	28	4	4	9	62	2	59	2
Bones, Ricky, New York	0	0	.000	14.14	4	1	0	0	0	0	7.0	14	41	11	11	2	1	1	1	6	0	4	0
Brandenburg, Mark, Texas	1	3	.250	3.21	26	0	0	0	8	0	47.2	48	215	22	17	3	3	2	2	25	1	37	0
Brandenburg, Mark, Boston	4	2	.667	3.81	29	0	0	0	5	0	28.1	28	123	13	12	5	0	2	1	8	1	29	0
Castillo, Tony, Toronto*..........	2	3	.400	4.23	40	0	0	0	7	1	72.1	72	304	38	34	9	3	2	2	20	1	48	2
Castillo, Tony, Chicago*	3	1	.750	1.59	15	0	0	0	6	1	22.2	23	94	7	4	1	0	3	1	4	1	9	1
Gohr, Greg, Detroit...............	4	8	.333	7.17	17	16	0	0	0	0	91.2	129	434	76	73	24	1	3	3	34	2	60	6
Gohr, Greg, California............	1	1	.500	7.50	15	0	0	0	7	1	24.0	34	112	20	20	7	0	1	0	10	0	15	0
Lloyd, Graeme, Milwaukee*	2	4	.333	2.82	52	0	0	0	15	0	51.0	49	217	19	16	3	5	1	1	17	3	24	0
Lloyd, Graeme, New York*......	0	2	.000	17.47	13	0	0	0	0	0	5.2	12	35	11	11	1	0	2	0	5	1	6	4
Mahomes, Pat, Minnesota	1	4	.200	7.20	20	5	0	0	5	0	45.0	63	220	38	36	10	0	2	0	27	0	30	2
Mahomes, Pat, Boston	2	0	1.000	5.84	11	0	0	0	5	2	12.1	9	51	8	8	3	2	0	0	6	0	6	0
Mercker, Kent, Baltimore*......	3	6	.333	7.76	14	12	0	0	0	0	58.0	73	283	56	50	12	3	4	3	35	1	22	3
Mercker, Kent, Cleveland*......	1	0	1.000	3.09	10	0	0	0	2	0	11.2	10	46	4	4	1	0	2	0	3	1	7	0
Milchin, Mike, Minnesota*	2	1	.667	8.31	26	0	0	0	7	0	21.2	31	105	21	20	6	2	0	0	12	1	19	1
Milchin, Mike, Baltimore*.......	1	0	1.000	5.73	13	0	0	0	0	0	11.0	13	49	7	7	0	1	3	0	5	1	10	0
Moyer, Jamie, Boston*..........	7	1	.875	4.50	23	10	0	0	1	0	90.0	111	405	50	45	14	4	3	1	27	2	50	2
Moyer, Jamie, Seattle*..........	6	2	.750	3.31	11	11	0	0	0	0	70.2	66	298	36	26	9	3	3	1	19	3	29	1
Pennington, Brad, Boston*.....	0	2	.000	2.77	14	0	0	0	6	0	13.0	6	59	5	4	1	0	1	0	15	1	13	1
Pennington, Brad, California* .	0	0	.000	12.27	8	0	0	0	2	0	7.1	5	43	10	10	1	0	0	0	16	0	7	1
Scanlan, Bob, Detroit	0	0	.000	10.64	8	0	0	0	2	0	11.0	16	57	15	13	1	1	0	1	9	1	3	1
Scanlan, Bob, Kansas City......	0	1	.000	3.18	9	0	0	0	2	0	11.1	13	48	4	4	1	0	1	3	1	3	0
Stanton, Mike, Boston*..........	4	3	.571	3.83	59	0	0	0	19	1	56.1	58	239	24	24	9	3	2	0	23	4	46	3
Stanton, Mike, Texas*...........	0	1	.000	3.22	22	0	0	0	9	0	22.1	20	88	8	8	2	1	0	0	4	1	14	0
Van Poppel, Todd, Oakland	1	5	.167	7.71	28	6	0	0	8	1	63.0	86	301	56	54	13	3	5	2	33	3	37	4
Van Poppel, Todd, Detroit	2	4	.333	11.39	9	9	1	1	0	0	36.1	53	190	51	46	11	1	2	1	29	0	16	3
Wickman, Bob, New York........	4	1	.800	4.67	58	0	0	0	14	0	79.0	94	358	41	41	7	1	4	5	34	1	61	3
Wickman, Bob, Milwaukee	3	0	1.000	3.24	12	0	0	0	4	0	16.2	12	71	9	6	3	1	0	0	10	2	14	1

FIELDING

TEAM

m	Pct.	G	PO	A	E	TC	DP	PB	Team	Pct.	G	PO	A	E	TC	DP	PB
...as	.986	163	4348	1647	87	6082	150	10	Seattle	.982	161	4295	1542	110	5947	155	8
...York	.985	162	4320	1613	91	6024	146	17	Cleveland	.980	161	4357	1765	124	6246	156	11
...timore	.984	163	4406	1730	97	6233	173	14	California	.979	161	4317	1702	128	6147	156	12
...nesota	.984	162	4319	1519	94	5932	142	11	Milwaukee	.978	162	4342	1693	134	6169	180	9
...kland	.984	162	4369	1778	103	6250	195	11	Boston	.978	162	4374	1638	135	6147	152	23
...cago	.982	162	4383	1574	109	6066	145	8	Detroit	.978	162	4298	1727	137	6162	157	7
...sas City	.982	161	4350	1704	111	6165	184	11	Totals	.982	1133	60815	23240	1570	85625	2278	168
...onto	.982	162	4337	1608	110	6055	187	16									

TRIPLE PLAYS: California, Chicago, Kansas City, Oakland.

INDIVIDUAL

FIRST BASEMEN

...TE: All caps denotes fielding-percentage leader based on 72 games for catchers, for all other non-pitchers and 144 innings for pitchers. *Throws lefthanded.

...yer, Team	Pct.	G	PO	A	E	TC	DP
...rete, Mike, Cal.-N.Y.*	1.000	9	38	0	0	38	4
...mar, Sandy, Cleveland	.000	1	0	0	0	0	0
...aral, Rich, Seattle	1.000	10	11	0	0	11	2
...nks, Brian, Milwaukee	1.000	1	14	1	0	15	0
...illa, Bobby, Baltimore	.966	9	27	1	1	29	4
...sius, Scott, Oakland	1.000	10	37	2	0	39	1
...reon, Mark, Cleveland*	.994	34	305	19	2	326	23
...ter, Joe, Toronto	.993	41	249	16	2	267	31
...llo, Jeff, Milwaukee	1.000	2	5	0	0	5	0
...rk, Phil, Boston	1.000	1	2	0	0	2	0
...rk, Tony, Detroit	.993	86	766	54	6	826	82
...rk, Will, Texas*	.996	117	956	73	4	1033	90
...omer, Ron, Minnesota	.993	57	244	39	2	285	26
...dero, Wil, Boston	1.000	1	7	0	0	7	2
...espo, Felipe, Toronto	1.000	2	3	1	0	4	0
...lgado, Alex, Boston	1.000	1	1	1	0	2	0
...lgado, Carlos, Toronto	.983	27	221	13	4	238	21
...inoza, Alvaro, Cleveland	1.000	18	97	8	0	105	10
...der, Cecil, Det.-N.Y.	.990	80	663	63	7	733	59
...nco, Julio, Cleveland	.990	97	852	77	9	938	89
...rrison, Webster, Oakland	1.000	1	1	1	0	2	0
...mbi, Jason, Oakland	.993	45	379	32	3	414	38
...nzales, Rene, Texas	.989	23	88	6	1	95	11
...er, Rusty, Texas*	.000	1	0	0	0	0	0
...e, Chip, Minnesota	1.000	6	7	1	0	8	1
...melin, Bob, Kansas City*	.984	33	232	20	4	256	26
...selman, Bill, Boston	1.000	2	13	0	0	13	2
...cking, Denny, Minnesota	1.000	1	1	0	0	1	0
...iles, Chris, Baltimore	.000	1	0	0	0	0	0
...llins, Dave, Seattle	.000	1	0	0	0	0	0
...ward, Dave, Kansas City	1.000	2	4	0	0	4	0
...well, Jack, California	.917	2	11	0	1	12	1
...dler, Rex, California	.978	7	44	0	1	45	3
...nter, Brian, Seattle*	.991	41	219	7	2	228	19
...ers, Tim, Detroit*	1.000	9	30	1	0	31	6
...na, John, Milwaukee	.992	85	676	58	6	740	84
...ferson, Reggie, Boston*	.993	16	117	16	1	134	8
...rdan, Ricky, Seattle	1.000	9	40	1	0	41	5
...nt, Jeff, Cleveland	.992	20	112	9	1	122	13
...euter, Chad, Chicago	1.000	2	1	0	0	1	0
...us, Scott, Oakland	.976	7	39	2	1	42	1
...sher, Brian, Oakland*	1.000	1	6	0	0	6	0
...yritz, Jim, New York	1.000	5	16	0	0	16	2
...vullo, Torey, Oakland	1.000	42	120	9	0	129	21
...anto, Jeff, Boston	1.000	1	1	0	0	1	0
...artinez, Dave, Chicago*	.980	23	132	12	3	147	8
...artinez, Edgar, Seattle	.967	4	28	1	1	30	3
...ARTINEZ, Tino, New York	.996	151	1238	83	5	1326	118
...cGwire, Mark, Oakland	.990	109	913	60	10	983	118
...cIntosh, Tim, New York	1.000	1	6	1	0	7	1
...olitor, Paul, Minnesota	.993	17	138	13	1	152	13
...urray, Eddie, Cleveland	1.000	1	10	1	0	11	0
...sson, Dave, Milwaukee	.981	24	145	13	3	161	16
...erman, Jose, Kansas City*	.994	96	796	68	5	869	82
...erud, John, Toronto*	.998	101	781	56	2	839	107
...Neill, Paul, New York*	.000	1	0	0	0	0	0
...lmeiro, Rafael, Baltimore*	.995	159	1383	119	8	1510	157
...quette, Craig, Kansas City	1.000	19	148	13	0	161	24
...rent, Mark, Detroit	1.000	1	1	0	0	1	0
...rry, Herbert, Cleveland	1.000	5	29	2	0	31	3

Player, Team	Pct.	G	PO	A	E	TC	DP
Phillips, Tony, Chicago	1.000	1	2	0	0	2	0
Pirkl, Greg, Seattle	1.000	2	14	2	0	16	2
Pritchett, Chris, California	1.000	5	29	1	0	30	3
Randa, Joe, Kansas City	1.000	7	21	3	0	24	2
Reboulet, Jeff, Minnesota	1.000	13	57	8	0	65	7
Ripken, Billy, Baltimore	1.000	1	3	0	0	3	1
Robertson, Mike, Chicago*	1.000	2	11	1	0	12	2
Samuel, Juan, Toronto	.979	17	90	3	2	95	7
Seitzer, Kevin, Mil.-Cle.	.997	70	520	56	2	578	57
Snow, J.T., California*	.993	154	1274	103	10	1387	134
Sorrento, Paul, Seattle	.990	138	957	81	11	1049	112
Stahoviak, Scott, Minnesota	.994	114	801	92	5	898	79
Stairs, Matt, Oakland	1.000	1	6	3	0	9	1
Steinbach, Terry, Oakland	1.000	1	1	0	0	1	0
Stevens, Lee, Texas*	.994	18	152	14	1	167	21
Stillwell, Kurt, Texas	1.000	1	3	0	0	3	0
Strange, Doug, Seattle	1.000	3	4	0	0	4	1
Surhoff, B.J., Baltimore	1.000	2	11	2	0	13	0
Tettleton, Mickey, Texas	.977	23	161	11	4	176	14
Thomas, Frank, Chicago	.992	139	1098	85	9	1192	111
Tucker, Michael, Kansas City	1.000	9	52	3	0	55	6
Unroe, Tim, Milwaukee	.976	11	41	0	1	42	4
Valle, Dave, Texas	1.000	5	5	0	0	5	1
Vaughn, Mo, Boston	.988	146	1207	74	15	1296	123
Ventura, Robin, Chicago	.985	14	56	8	1	65	7
Vitiello, Joe, Kansas City	1.000	9	40	5	0	45	4
Wallach, Tim, California	.958	3	20	3	1	24	2
Williams, Eddie, Detroit	1.000	7	22	1	0	23	7
Worthington, Craig, Texas	1.000	6	16	4	0	20	1

TRIPLE PLAYS: Giambi, Oak.; Hamelin, K.C.; Snow, Cal.; F. Thomas, Chi.

FIRST BASEMEN WITH TWO OR MORE TEAMS

Player, Team	Pct.	G	PO	A	E	TC	DP
Aldrete, Mike, California*	.000	1	0	0	0	0	0
Aldrete, Mike, New York*	1.000	8	38	0	0	38	4
Fielder, Cecil, Detroit	.989	71	589	59	7	655	51
Fielder, Cecil, New York	1.000	9	74	4	0	78	8
Seitzer, Kevin, Milwaukee	.996	65	489	47	2	538	56
Seitzer, Kevin, Cleveland	1.000	5	31	9	0	40	1

SECOND BASEMEN

Player, Team	Pct.	G	PO	A	E	TC	DP
Alexander, Manny, Baltimore	1.000	7	7	4	0	11	1
Alomar, Roberto, Baltimore	.985	141	279	445	11	735	107
Amaral, Rich, Seattle	1.000	15	16	21	0	37	2
Baerga, Carlos, Cleveland	.971	100	191	308	15	514	63
Batista, Tony, Oakland	.988	52	83	162	3	248	36
Beltre, Esteban, Boston	.963	8	16	10	1	27	4
Bournigal, Rafael, Oakland	.993	64	115	175	2	292	40
Brito, Tilson, Toronto	.956	18	36	50	4	90	14
Cairo, Miguel, Toronto	1.000	9	22	18	0	40	5
Candaele, Casey, Cleveland	1.000	11	20	30	0	50	11
Cedeno, Domingo, Tor.-Chi.	.969	64	110	169	9	288	47
Cirillo, Jeff, Milwaukee	1.000	1	2	4	0	6	1
Cora, Joey, Seattle	.979	140	296	314	13	623	88
Cordero, Wil, Boston	.949	37	75	110	10	195	19
Crespo, Felipe, Toronto	.982	10	25	29	1	55	8
Cruz, Fausto, Detroit	.906	8	9	20	3	32	3
Delgado, Alex, Boston	1.000	1	0	1	0	1	0
Duncan, Mariano, New York	.975	104	183	238	11	432	57
Durham, Ray, Chicago	.984	150	236	423	11	670	87
Easley, Damion, Cal.-Det.	.969	17	27	35	2	64	6
Eenhoorn, Robert, N.Y.-Cal.	.971	12	19	15	1	35	6
Espinoza, Alvaro, Cleveland	.941	5	5	11	1	17	5

Player, Team	Pct.	G	PO	A	E	TC	DP
Fox, Andy, New York	.958	72	78	104	8	190	21
Frazier, Lou, Texas	.000	1	0	0	1	1	0
Frye, Jeff, Boston	.983	100	200	317	9	526	70
Garciaparra, Nomar, Boston	1.000	1	2	1	0	3	0
Garrison, Webster, Oakland	.875	3	3	4	1	8	1
Gates, Brent, Oakland	.973	63	140	183	9	332	48
Gonzales, Rene, Texas	1.000	5	2	18	0	20	1
Hale, Chip, Minnesota	1.000	14	8	13	0	21	2
Hocking, Denny, Minnesota	1.000	2	1	2	0	3	1
Howard, Dave, Kansas City	1.000	3	9	10	0	19	3
Howard, Matt, New York	.976	30	14	27	1	42	5
Howell, Jack, California	.000	1	0	0	0	0	0
Hudler, Rex, California	.982	53	97	116	4	217	35
Huson, Jeff, Baltimore	.973	12	20	16	1	37	6
Kelly, Pat, New York	.970	10	8	24	1	33	3
Kent, Jeff, Cleveland	1.000	9	11	30	0	41	2
KNOBLAUCH, Chuck, Minnesota	.988	151	271	390	8	669	93
Leius, Scott, Cleveland	1.000	6	3	8	0	11	2
Lewis, Mark, Detroit	.987	144	264	413	9	686	94
Leyritz, Jim, New York	1.000	2	2	1	0	3	0
Listach, Pat, Milwaukee	.982	12	29	26	1	56	8
Lockhart, Keith, Kansas City	.975	84	110	206	8	324	54
Loretta, Mark, Milwaukee	.989	28	32	61	1	94	13
Lovullo, Torey, Oakland	1.000	2	4	1	0	5	1
Manto, Jeff, Boston	.963	4	10	16	1	27	3
Martin, Norberto, Chicago	.982	10	22	34	1	57	7
McLemore, Mark, Texas	.985	147	313	473	12	798	115
Munoz, Jose, Chicago	.923	7	12	12	2	26	2
Naehring, Tim, Boston	.000	1	0	0	0	0	0
Offerman, Jose, Kansas City	.993	38	64	81	1	146	29
Pena, Geronimo, Cleveland	1.000	1	2	3	0	5	1
Perez, Tomas, Toronto	.970	75	133	226	11	370	64
Phillips, Tony, Chicago	1.000	2	4	5	0	9	2
Pozo, Arquimedez, Boston	.930	10	18	22	3	43	3
Raabe, Brian, Minnesota	.000	1	0	0	0	0	0
Randa, Joe, Kansas City	.976	15	15	26	1	42	5
Reboulet, Jeff, Minnesota	1.000	22	24	22	0	46	4
Ripken, Billy, Baltimore	.968	30	34	57	3	94	15
Roberts, Bip, Kansas City	.986	63	101	189	4	294	42
Schofield, Dick, California	1.000	2	4	6	0	10	1
Selby, Bill, Boston	.980	14	22	28	1	51	5
Sheets, Andy, Seattle	.959	18	18	29	2	49	9
Sojo, Luis, Sea.-N.Y.	.986	41	56	87	2	145	23
Stillwell, Kurt, Texas	.964	21	24	29	2	55	4
Strange, Doug, Seattle	1.000	3	0	1	0	1	0
Stynes, Chris, Kansas City	1.000	5	8	5	0	13	2
Trammell, Alan, Detroit	.950	11	15	23	2	40	6
Velarde, Randy, California	.982	114	236	252	9	497	80
Vina, Fernando, Milwaukee	.979	137	333	412	16	761	116
Vizcaino, Jose, Cleveland	.981	45	79	125	4	208	27
Walker, Todd, Minnesota	1.000	4	5	7	0	12	1

TRIPLE PLAYS: Durham, Chi.; Gates, Oak.; Hudler, Cal.; Roberts, K.C.

SECOND BASEMEN WITH TWO OR MORE TEAMS

Player, Team	Pct.	G	PO	A	E	TC	DP
Cedeno, Domingo, Toronto	.969	62	110	169	9	288	47
Cedeno, Domingo, Chicago	.000	2	0	0	0	0	0
Easley, Damion, California	.960	9	13	11	1	25	2
Easley, Damion, Detroit	.974	8	14	24	1	39	4
Eenhoorn, Robert, New York	1.000	10	15	11	0	26	5
Eenhoorn, Robert, California	.889	2	4	4	1	9	1
Sojo, Luis, Seattle	.981	27	42	59	2	103	15
Sojo, Luis, New York	1.000	14	14	28	0	42	8

THIRD BASEMEN

Player, Team	Pct.	G	PO	A	E	TC	DP
Alexander, Manny, Baltimore	.923	7	3	9	1	13	1
Amaral, Rich, Seattle	.000	1	0	0	0	0	0
Arias, George, California	.960	83	50	190	10	250	19
Batista, Tony, Oakland	.931	18	9	18	2	29	3
Beltre, Esteban, Boston	1.000	13	11	13	0	24	1
Boggs, Wade, New York	.974	123	62	201	7	270	24
Bonilla, Bobby, Baltimore	1.000	4	1	3	0	4	0
Brosius, Scott, Oakland	.969	109	83	232	10	325	25
Candaele, Casey, Cleveland	1.000	3	1	3	0	4	1
Cedeno, Andujar, Detroit	1.000	1	0	2	0	2	0
Cedeno, Domingo, Toronto	1.000	6	5	13	0	18	2
Cirillo, Jeff, Milwaukee	.950	154	105	238	18	361	18
Clark, Phil, Boston	1.000	1	0	1	0	1	0
Coomer, Ron, Minnesota	1.000	9	2	3	0	5	0
Cora, Joey, Seattle	.000	1	0	0	0	0	0
Crespo, Felipe, Toronto	1.000	6	6	8	0	14	2

Player, Team	Pct.	G	PO	A	E	TC
Davis, Russ, Seattle	.933	51	31	67	7	105
Delgado, Alex, Boston	.000	4	0	0	0	0
Duncan, Mariano, New York	.667	3	1	1	1	3
Easley, Damion, Cal.-Det.	.909	5	2	8	1	11
Eenhoorn, Robert, New York	1.000	2	2	1	0	3
Espinoza, Alvaro, Cleveland	.947	20	7	11	1	19
Fox, Andy, New York	.980	31	10	38	1	49
FRYMAN, Travis, Detroit	.979	128	96	271	8	375
Giambi, Jason, Oakland	.932	39	31	79	8	118
Gonzales, Rene, Texas	1.000	15	7	16	0	23
Hale, Chip, Minnesota	1.000	3	2	2	0	4
Hayes, Charlie, New York	1.000	19	14	30	0	44
Hiatt, Phil, Detroit	1.000	3	2	7	0	9
Hollins, Dave, Min.-Sea.	.955	144	102	259	17	378
Howard, Matt, New York	1.000	6	3	4	0	7
Howell, Jack, California	.884	43	17	44	8	69
Huff, Michael, Toronto	1.000	3	1	2	0	3
Huson, Jeff, Baltimore	1.000	3	0	1	0	1
Kent, Jeff, Cleveland	1.000	6	2	7	0	9
Leius, Scott, Cleveland	1.000	8	3	6	0	9
Leyritz, Jim, New York	.778	13	3	11	4	18
Lockhart, Keith, Kansas City	.953	55	27	75	5	107
Loretta, Mark, Milwaukee	1.000	23	9	23	0	32
Lovullo, Torey, Oakland	.952	11	9	11	1	21
Manto, Jeff, Bos.-Sea.	.967	26	15	43	2	60
Martin, Norberto, Chicago	1.000	3	0	1	0	1
Martinez, Edgar, Seattle	1.000	2	1	0	0	1
McIntosh, Tim, New York	.000	1	0	0	0	0
Munoz, Jose, Chicago	.000	1	0	0	0	0
Naehring, Tim, Boston	.963	116	82	206	11	299
Nevin, Phil, Detroit	.943	24	17	49	4	70
Norton, Greg, Chicago	1.000	2	4	2	0	6
Palmer, Dean, Texas	.953	154	105	221	16	342
Paquette, Craig, Kansas City	.891	51	20	70	11	101
Pena, Geronimo, Cleveland	.000	3	0	0	0	0
Perez, Tomas, Toronto	.882	11	1	14	2	17
Perry, Herbert, Cleveland	.000	1	0	0	0	0
Pozo, Arquimedez, Boston	.957	10	5	17	1	23
Quinlan, Tom, Minnesota	.667	4	0	2	1	3
Raabe, Brian, Minnesota	.857	6	2	4	1	7
Randa, Joe, Kansas City	.951	92	44	131	9	184
Reboulet, Jeff, Minnesota	.984	36	19	41	1	61
Ripken, Billy, Baltimore	1.000	25	3	38	0	41
Ripken, Cal, Baltimore	1.000	6	5	16	0	21
Rodriguez, Tony, Boston	.800	5	2	2	1	5
Schofield, Dick, California	1.000	1	0	1	0	1
Seitzer, Kevin, Milwaukee	.903	12	9	19	3	31
Selby, Bill, Boston	.875	14	6	15	3	24
Sheets, Andy, Seattle	.947	25	16	38	3	57
Snopek, Chris, Chicago	.939	27	12	34	3	49
Sojo, Luis, Sea.-N.Y.	.941	34	24	56	5	85
Spiezio, Scott, Oakland	.846	5	6	5	2	13
Sprague, Ed, Toronto	.956	148	108	218	15	341
Stillwell, Kurt, Texas	1.000	6	0	1	0	1
Strange, Doug, Seattle	.961	39	11	38	2	51
Stynes, Chris, Kansas City	.667	2	0	2	1	3
Surhoff, B.J., Baltimore	.948	106	80	175	14	269
Tatum, Jimmy, Boston	1.000	2	3	2	0	5
Thome, Jim, Cleveland	.953	150	86	262	17	365
Trammell, Alan, Detroit	1.000	8	7	13	0	20
Unroe, Tim, Milwaukee	1.000	3	0	10	0	10
Valentin, John, Boston	.947	12	8	10	1	19
Velarde, Randy, California	.906	28	13	45	6	64
Ventura, Robin, Chicago	.974	150	133	239	10	382
Voigt, Jack, Texas	1.000	1	0	1	0	1
Walker, Todd, Minnesota	.956	20	11	32	2	45
Wallach, Tim, California	.941	46	27	85	7	119
Williams, Eddie, Detroit	1.000	3	0	1	0	1
Worthington, Craig, Texas	.917	7	2	9	1	12
Young, Kevin, Kansas City	1.000	7	3	2	0	5
Zeile, Todd, Baltimore	.964	29	24	56	3	83

TRIPLE PLAYS: Howell, Cal.; Randa, K.C.; Ventura, Chi.

THIRD BASEMEN WITH TWO OR MORE TEAMS

Player, Team	Pct.	G	PO	A	E	TC	DP
Easley, Damion, California	1.000	3	0	4	0	4	
Easley, Damion, Detroit	.857	2	2	4	1	7	
Hollins, Dave, Minnesota	.953	116	81	206	14	301	1
Hollins, Dave, Seattle	.961	28	21	53	3	77	
Manto, Jeff, Boston	.960	10	7	17	1	25	
Manto, Jeff, Seattle	.971	16	8	26	1	35	
Sojo, Luis, Seattle	.940	33	24	55	5	84	
Sojo, Luis, New York	1.000	1	0	1	0	1	

SHORTSTOPS

ayer, Team	Pct.	G	PO	A	E	TC	DP
xander, Manny, Baltimore	.940	21	14	33	3	50	6
ista, Tony, Oakland	1.000	4	4	11	0	15	1
tre, Esteban, Boston	1.000	6	4	3	0	7	0
rdick, Mike, Oakland	.979	155	265	476	16	757	121
urnigal, Rafael, Oakland	1.000	23	13	33	0	46	6
to, Tilson, Toronto	1.000	5	6	10	0	16	3
ndaele, Casey, Cleveland	1.000	1	1	0	0	1	0
deno, Andujar, Detroit	.948	51	68	149	12	229	27
deno, Domingo, Tor.-Chi.	.974	7	18	20	1	39	6
iz, Fausto, Detroit	.824	4	4	10	3	17	2
arcina, Gary, California	.971	150	212	460	20	692	93
sley, Damion, Cal.-Det.	.951	21	15	43	3	61	16
nhoorn, Robert, California	.875	4	1	6	1	8	1
ter, Kevin, Texas	.981	157	285	441	14	740	103
pinoza, Alvaro, Cleveland	.978	16	16	29	1	46	12
x, Andy, New York	.889	9	8	16	3	27	3
re, Jeff, Boston	1.000	3	1	0	0	1	0
man, Travis, Detroit	.986	29	53	83	2	138	18
rciaparra, Nomar, Boston	.988	22	35	50	1	86	11
, Benji, Texas	.923	5	5	7	1	13	0
mez, Chris, Detroit	.970	47	77	114	6	197	34
nzales, Rene, Texas	.971	10	12	21	1	34	5
nzalez, Alex, Toronto	.973	147	279	465	21	765	122
illen, Ozzie, Chicago	.981	146	220	348	11	579	69
cking, Denny, Minnesota	1.000	6	3	3	0	6	0
llins, Dave, Minnesota	.000	1	0	0	1	1	0
WARD, Dave, Kansas City	.982	135	197	401	11	609	109
ckson, Damian, Cleveland	1.000	5	3	13	0	16	4
ter, Derek, New York	.969	157	244	444	22	710	83
tach, Pat, Milwaukee	.938	7	5	10	1	16	1
retta, Mark, Milwaukee	.982	21	22	32	1	55	12
vullo, Torey, Oakland	.000	1	0	0	0	0	0
anto, Jeff, Boston	.913	4	7	14	2	23	3
artin, Norberto, Chicago	.943	24	39	44	5	88	17
eares, Pat, Minnesota	.965	150	257	344	22	623	85
unoz, Jose, Chicago	1.000	2	0	1	0	1	0
rton, Greg, Chicago	.778	6	4	3	2	9	0
erman, Jose, Kansas City	.933	36	54	85	10	149	30
quette, Craig, Kansas City	.968	11	14	16	1	31	5
rez, Tomas, Toronto	.931	5	17	10	2	29	4
boulet, Jeff, Minnesota	.987	37	34	41	1	76	13
oken, Cal, Baltimore	.980	158	228	467	14	709	109
driguez, Alex, Seattle	.977	146	238	404	15	657	92
driguez, Tony, Boston	.979	21	30	62	2	94	11
hofield, Dick, California	.889	7	5	3	1	9	1
eets, Andy, Seattle	1.000	7	6	10	0	16	2
opek, Chris, Chicago	.957	12	13	31	2	46	5
jo, Luis, Sea.-N.Y.	.988	23	33	52	1	86	12
llwell, Kurt, Texas	.923	9	3	9	1	13	0
mmell, Alan, Detroit	.976	43	52	108	4	164	15
lentin, John, Boston	.971	118	194	347	16	557	87
lentin, Jose, Milwaukee	.950	151	243	460	37	740	113
arde, Randy, California	.938	7	6	9	1	16	2
caino, Jose, Cleveland	1.000	4	3	10	0	13	4
quel, Omar, Cleveland	.971	150	226	447	20	693	91

SHORTSTOPS WITH TWO OR MORE TEAMS

ayer, Team	Pct.	G	PO	A	E	TC	DP
deno, Domingo, Toronto	1.000	5	12	16	0	28	4
deno, Domingo, Chicago	.909	2	6	4	1	11	2
sley, Damion, California	.943	13	9	24	2	35	10
sley, Damion, Detroit	.962	8	6	19	1	26	6
jo, Luis, Seattle	.987	19	31	44	1	76	10
jo, Luis, New York	1.000	4	2	8	0	10	2

OUTFIELDERS

ayer, Team	Pct.	G	PO	A	E	TC	DP
drete, Mike, Cal.-N.Y.*	.909	15	10	0	1	11	0
exander, Manny, Baltimore	.750	3	2	1	1	4	0
maral, Rich, Seattle	1.000	91	168	3	0	171	0
derson, Brady, Baltimore*	.992	143	341	10	3	354	1
derson, Garret, California*	.979	146	316	5	7	328	1
nks, Brian, Milwaukee	1.000	3	1	0	0	1	0
rtee, Kimera, Detroit	.991	99	217	1	2	220	0
ttle, Allen, Oakland	.988	47	82	2	1	85	1
utista, Danny, Detroit	.974	22	38	0	1	39	0
cker, Rich, Minnesota*	.993	146	391	18	3	412	9
lle, Albert, Cleveland	.970	152	309	11	10	330	0
rroa, Geronimo, Oakland	.980	61	91	6	2	99	1
nilla, Bobby, Baltimore	.975	108	186	8	5	199	1
wers, Brent, Baltimore	1.000	21	22	2	0	24	0
agg, Darren, Sea.-Bos.	.989	121	254	12	3	269	3

Player, Team	Pct.	G	PO	A	E	TC	DP
Brede, Brent, Minnesota*	1.000	7	12	1	0	13	0
Brosius, Scott, Oakland	1.000	4	8	0	0	8	0
Brumfield, Jacob, Toronto	.982	83	159	8	3	170	0
Buford, Damon, Texas	1.000	80	93	3	0	96	0
Buhner, Jay, Seattle	.989	142	251	9	3	263	1
Burnitz, Jeromy, Cle.-Mil.	.988	52	82	1	1	84	0
Cameron, Mike, Chicago	1.000	8	7	0	0	7	0
Canseco, Jose, Boston	1.000	11	17	1	0	18	0
Carr, Chuck, Milwaukee	1.000	27	76	4	0	80	1
Carreon, Mark, Cleveland*	1.000	5	6	0	0	6	0
Carter, Joe, Toronto	.961	115	167	7	7	181	1
Cole, Alex, Boston*	.974	24	37	1	1	39	1
Coomer, Ron, Minnesota	.935	23	29	0	2	31	0
Cordova, Marty, Minnesota	.991	145	328	9	3	340	1
Curtis, Chad, Detroit	.965	104	243	6	9	258	1
Cuyler, Milt, Boston	.972	45	104	0	3	107	0
Damon, Johnny, Kansas City*	.983	144	350	5	6	361	4
Delgado, Alex, Boston	1.000	6	5	1	0	6	0
Devereaux, Mike, Baltimore	.983	112	170	7	3	180	3
Diaz, Alex, Seattle	.982	28	55	1	1	57	0
Duncan, Mariano, New York	1.000	3	3	0	0	3	0
Dunn, Todd, Milwaukee	1.000	6	6	0	0	6	0
Easley, Damion, California	1.000	2	1	0	0	1	0
Edmonds, Jim, California*	.997	111	280	6	1	287	2
Erstad, Darin, California*	.976	48	121	2	3	126	0
Faneyte, Rikkert, Texas	1.000	6	11	0	0	11	0
Fox, Andy, New York	.000	1	0	0	0	0	0
Frazier, Lou, Texas	.971	15	31	3	1	35	0
Frye, Jeff, Boston	1.000	5	10	0	0	10	0
Giambi, Jason, Oakland	1.000	45	68	6	0	74	1
Giles, Brian, Cleveland*	1.000	16	26	0	0	26	0
Gonzales, Rene, Texas	.000	1	0	0	0	0	0
Gonzalez, Juan, Texas	.988	102	163	6	2	171	0
Goodwin, Tom, Kansas City	.984	136	303	7	5	315	1
Green, Shawn, Toronto*	.992	127	254	10	2	266	3
Greenwell, Mike, Boston	.973	76	137	9	4	150	2
Greer, Rusty, Texas*	.984	137	304	6	5	315	0
Griffey, Ken, Seattle*	.990	137	375	10	4	389	1
Guillen, Ozzie, Chicago	1.000	2	2	0	0	2	0
Hale, Chip, Minnesota	.000	3	0	0	0	0	0
HAMILTON, Darryl, Texas	1.000	147	387	2	0	389	0
Hammonds, Jeffrey, Baltimore	.980	70	145	3	3	151	0
Herrera, Jose, Oakland*	.970	100	190	2	6	198	0
Hiatt, Phil, Detroit	1.000	2	1	1	0	2	0
Higginson, Bob, Detroit	.963	123	227	9	9	245	1
Hocking, Denny, Minnesota	.985	33	62	4	1	67	0
Hosey, Dwayne, Boston	.984	26	60	2	1	63	1
Howard, Dave, Kansas City	.000	1	0	0	0	0	0
Hudler, Rex, California	.971	21	32	1	1	34	0
Huff, Michael, Toronto	1.000	9	12	0	0	12	0
Hulse, David, Milwaukee*	.990	68	94	1	1	96	1
Hunter, Brian, Seattle*	.955	29	61	3	3	67	0
Huson, Jeff, Baltimore	.000	1	0	0	0	0	0
Hyers, Tim, Detroit*	1.000	1	3	0	0	3	0
Incaviglia, Pete, Baltimore	1.000	7	9	1	0	10	0
James, Dion, New York*	1.000	4	3	0	0	3	0
Jefferson, Reggie, Boston*	.969	45	61	1	2	64	0
Kelly, Roberto, Minnesota	.990	93	203	4	2	209	0
Kingsale, Gene, Baltimore	1.000	2	2	0	0	2	0
Kirby, Wayne, Cleveland	1.000	18	8	0	0	8	0
Koslofski, Kevin, Milwaukee	.972	22	35	0	1	36	0
Lawton, Matt, Minnesota	.985	75	196	4	3	203	1
Lennon, Patrick, Kansas City	.947	11	18	0	1	19	0
Lesher, Brian, Oakland*	.977	25	40	2	1	43	0
Lewis, Darren, Chicago	.990	138	287	0	3	290	0
Leyritz, Jim, New York	1.000	3	3	0	0	3	0
Listach, Pat, Milwaukee	.982	68	158	6	3	167	1
Lofton, Kenny, Cleveland*	.975	152	376	13	10	399	3
Lovullo, Torey, Oakland	1.000	1	1	0	0	1	0
Malave, Jose, Boston	.978	38	43	1	1	45	0
Manto, Jeff, Seattle	.000	1	0	0	0	0	0
Martinez, Dave, Chicago*	.988	121	236	4	3	243	0
Martinez, Manny, Seattle	1.000	8	12	2	0	14	0
Mashore, Damon, Oakland	.985	48	65	1	1	67	0
McLemore, Mark, Texas	.000	1	0	0	0	0	0
Meares, Pat, Minnesota	.000	1	0	0	0	0	0
Mieske, Matt, Milwaukee	.996	122	250	7	1	258	1
Mitchell, Kevin, Boston	.935	21	29	0	2	31	0
Moore, Kerwin, Oakland	1.000	18	19	0	0	19	0
Mouton, Lyle, Chicago	.970	47	64	1	2	67	0
Munoz, Jose, Chicago	.000	1	0	0	0	0	0
Munoz, Pedro, Oakland	1.000	14	15	0	0	15	0
Myers, Rod, Kansas City*	1.000	19	33	0	0	33	0

Player, Team	Pct.	G	PO	A	E	TC	DP
Nevin, Phil, Detroit	.944	9	16	1	1	18	0
Newfield, Marc, Milwaukee	.990	49	96	3	1	100	1
Newson, Warren, Texas*	.992	66	122	5	1	128	2
Nieves, Melvin, Detroit	.943	105	207	9	13	229	2
Nilsson, Dave, Milwaukee	.965	61	105	5	4	114	1
Nixon, Otis, Toronto	.994	125	342	5	2	349	1
Nixon, Trot, Boston*	1.000	2	3	0	0	3	0
Norman, Les, Kansas City	1.000	38	44	1	0	45	0
Nunnally, Jon, Kansas City	.968	29	61	0	2	63	0
O'Leary, Troy, Boston*	.971	146	227	8	7	242	0
O'Neill, Paul, New York*	1.000	146	293	7	0	300	3
Offerman, Jose, Kansas City	1.000	1	6	0	0	6	0
Palmeiro, Orlando, California	1.000	31	33	0	0	33	0
Paquette, Craig, Kansas City	.976	47	79	3	2	84	1
Pemberton, Rudy, Boston	1.000	13	9	0	0	9	0
Penn, Shannon, Detroit	.000	1	0	0	0	0	0
Perez, Danny, Milwaukee	1.000	3	5	0	0	5	0
Perez, Robert, Toronto	.983	79	114	3	2	119	0
Phillips, Tony, Chicago	.981	150	345	13	7	365	2
Plantier, Phil, Oakland	.973	68	138	8	4	150	2
Polonia, Luis, Baltimore*	.983	34	56	1	1	58	0
Pride, Curtis, Detroit	.967	48	89	0	3	92	0
Raines, Tim, New York	.988	50	79	3	1	83	0
Ramirez, Manny, Cleveland	.970	149	272	19	9	300	4
Reboulet, Jeff, Minnesota	1.000	7	4	2	0	6	0
Rivera, Ruben, New York	1.000	45	77	2	0	79	0
Roberts, Bip, Kansas City	1.000	11	14	1	0	15	1
Salmon, Tim, California	.975	153	299	13	8	320	0
Samuel, Juan, Toronto	1.000	24	27	0	0	27	0
Selby, Bill, Boston	1.000	6	2	0	0	2	0
Sierra, Ruben, N.Y.-Det.	.950	56	108	6	6	120	2
Singleton, Duane, Detroit	1.000	15	29	3	0	32	2
Smith, Mark, Baltimore	.980	20	50	0	1	51	0
Stairs, Matt, Oakland	.985	44	59	8	1	68	3
Stevens, Lee, Texas*	1.000	5	5	0	0	5	0
Stewart, Shannon, Toronto	.800	6	4	0	1	5	0
Strange, Doug, Seattle	1.000	11	11	0	0	11	0
Strawberry, Darryl, New York*	1.000	34	45	1	0	46	0
Stynes, Chris, Kansas City	.939	19	30	1	2	33	0
Surhoff, B.J., Baltimore	.979	27	46	1	1	48	0
Tarasco, Tony, Baltimore	1.000	23	50	1	0	51	0
Tartabull, Danny, Chicago	.973	122	253	4	7	264	1
Thompson, Ryan, Cleveland	1.000	8	5	0	0	5	0
Tinsley, Lee, Boston	.993	83	132	8	1	141	1
Trammell, Alan, Detroit	1.000	1	1	0	0	1	0
Tucker, Michael, Kansas City	.989	98	183	5	2	190	1
Turner, Chris, California	1.000	1	1	0	0	1	0
Unroe, Tim, Milwaukee	.000	1	0	0	0	0	0
Vaughn, Greg, Milwaukee	.980	100	192	5	4	201	1
Vitiello, Joe, Kansas City	.000	1	0	0	0	0	0
Voigt, Jack, Texas	1.000	3	5	0	0	5	0
Ward, Turner, Milwaukee	1.000	32	54	1	0	55	0
Whiten, Mark, Seattle	.969	39	90	4	3	97	0
Williams, Bernie, New York	.986	140	334	10	5	349	3
Williams, Eddie, Detroit	1.000	2	3	0	0	3	0
Williams, Gerald, N.Y.-Mil.	.981	118	207	4	4	215	2
Wilson, Nigel, Cleveland*	.000	1	0	0	0	0	0
Young, Ernie, Oakland	.997	140	353	8	1	362	5
Young, Kevin, Kansas City	.938	17	14	1	1	16	0

TRIPLE PLAY: Young, Oak.

OUTFIELDERS WITH TWO OR MORE TEAMS

Player, Team	Pct.	G	PO	A	E	TC	DP
Aldrete, Mike, California*	.750	6	3	0	1	4	0
Aldrete, Mike, New York*	1.000	9	7	0	0	7	0
Bragg, Darren, Seattle	.992	63	118	7	1	126	1
Bragg, Darren, Boston	.986	58	136	5	2	143	2
Burnitz, Jeromy, Cleveland	1.000	30	44	0	0	44	0
Burnitz, Jeromy, Milwaukee	.975	22	38	1	1	40	0
Sierra, Ruben, New York	.984	33	56	5	1	62	1
Sierra, Ruben, Detroit	.914	23	52	1	5	58	1
Williams, Gerald, New York	.978	92	132	1	3	136	1
Williams, Gerald, Milwaukee	.987	26	75	3	1	79	1

CATCHERS

Player, Team	Pct.	G	PO	A	E	TC	DP	PB
Alomar, Sandy, Cleveland	.988	124	724	48	9	781	5	7
Ausmus, Brad, Detroit	.992	73	452	35	4	491	4	2
Borders, Pat, Cal.-Chi.	.983	49	255	30	5	290	2	3
Brown, Kevin, Texas	1.000	2	11	1	0	12	0	0
Casanova, Raul, Detroit	.978	22	123	12	3	138	0	3
Delgado, Alex, Boston	.889	14	16	0	2	18	1	0
Devarez, Cesar, Baltimore	1.000	10	38	1	0	39	0	1

Player, Team	Pct.	G	PO	A	E	TC	DP
Diaz, Einar, Cleveland	1.000	4	4	0	0	4	0
Durant, Mike, Minnesota	.975	37	183	13	5	201	1
Fabregas, Jorge, California	.989	89	502	46	6	554	3
Fasano, Sal, Kansas City	.984	51	291	14	5	310	2
Flaherty, John, Detroit	.981	46	243	13	5	261	1
Girardi, Joe, New York	.996	120	803	46	3	852	8
Greene, Todd, California	1.000	26	119	19	0	138	1
Haselman, Bill, Boston	.994	69	494	33	3	530	6
Hatteberg, Scott, Boston	1.000	10	32	2	0	34	0
Hoiles, Chris, Baltimore	.992	126	777	42	7	826	3
Karkovice, Ron, Chicago	.993	111	680	45	5	730	5
Kreuter, Chad, Chicago	.990	38	181	12	2	195	4
LEVIS, Jesse, Milwaukee	.998	90	373	26	1	400	5
Leyritz, Jim, New York	.995	55	363	19	2	384	2
Macfarlane, Mike, Kansas City	.993	99	511	35	4	550	2
Machado, Robert, Chicago	1.000	4	6	0	0	6	0
Martinez, Sandy, Toronto	.993	75	413	33	3	449	8
Marzano, John, Seattle	.986	39	194	10	3	207	1
Matheny, Mike, Milwaukee	.985	104	475	40	8	523	5
McIntosh, Tim, New York	.000	1	0	0	0	0	0
McKeel, Walt, Boston	.000	1	0	0	0	0	0
Mercedes, Henry, Kansas City	1.000	4	2	0	0	2	0
Molina, Izzy, Oakland	1.000	12	31	1	0	32	1
Mosquera, Julio, Toronto	1.000	8	48	1	0	49	0
Myers, Greg, Minnesota	.985	90	488	27	8	523	5
Nevin, Phil, Detroit	1.000	4	12	1	0	13	0
Nilsson, Dave, Milwaukee	1.000	2	1	0	0	3	0
O'Brien, Charlie, Toronto	.995	105	613	37	3	653	5
Parent, Mark, Det.-Bal.	.992	51	231	17	2	250	5
Pena, Tony, Cleveland	.992	67	336	27	3	366	6
Posada, Jorge, New York	1.000	4	17	2	0	19	0
Rodriguez, Ivan, Texas	.989	146	850	81	10	941	11
Slaught, Don, Cal.-Chi.	.991	71	408	27	4	439	2
Stanley, Mike, Boston	.985	105	654	19	10	683	3
Steinbach, Terry, Oakland	.991	137	731	46	7	784	7
Stinnett, Kelly, Milwaukee	.960	14	46	2	2	50	1
Sweeney, Mike, Kansas City	.994	26	158	7	1	166	3
Turner, Chris, California	1.000	3	2	0	0	4	0
Valle, Dave, Texas	.994	35	145	13	1	159	2
Walbeck, Matt, Minnesota	.994	61	326	19	2	347	2
Widger, Chris, Seattle	.905	7	18	1	2	21	0
Williams, George, Oakland	.982	43	154	12	3	169	1
Wilson, Dan, Seattle	.996	135	834	58	4	896	5
Zaun, Greg, Baltimore	.987	49	215	10	3	228	3

TRIPLE PLAYS: Fasano, K.C.; Steinbach, Oak.

CATCHERS WITH TWO OR MORE TEAMS

Player, Team	Pct.	G	PO	A	E	TC	DP
Borders, Pat, California	.984	19	111	14	2	127	1
Borders, Pat, Chicago	.982	30	144	16	3	163	1
Parent, Mark, Detroit	.994	33	158	14	1	173	4
Parent, Mark, Baltimore	.987	18	73	3	1	77	1
Slaught, Don, California	.992	59	338	27	3	368	2
Slaught, Don, Chicago	.986	12	70	0	1	71	0

PITCHERS

Player, Team	Pct.	G	PO	A	E	TC
Abbott, Jim, California*	1.000	27	3	27	0	30
Abbott, Kyle, California*	1.000	3	0	1	0	1
Acre, Mark, Oakland	1.000	22	1	2	0	3
Adams, Willie, Oakland	1.000	12	5	6	0	11
Aguilera, Rick, Minnesota	.900	19	13	5	2	20
Alberro, Jose, Texas	1.000	5	1	2	0	3
Aldred, Scott, Det.-Min.*	.875	36	5	16	3	24
Aldrete, Mike, New York*	.000	1	0	0	0	0
Alexander, Manny, Baltimore	.000	1	0	0	0	0
Alvarez, Wilson, Chicago*	1.000	35	11	29	0	40
Anderson, Brian, Cleveland*	.889	10	3	13	2	18
Andujar, Luis, Chi.-Tor.	1.000	8	1	2	0	3
Appier, Kevin, Kansas City	1.000	32	19	15	0	34
Assenmacher, Paul, Cleveland*	1.000	63	0	5	0	5
Ayala, Bobby, Seattle	1.000	50	5	9	0	14
Baldwin, James, Chicago	.903	28	12	16	3	31
Belcher, Tim, Kansas City	.962	35	19	32	2	53
Belinda, Stan, Boston	1.000	31	3	3	0	6
Benitez, Armando, Baltimore	.667	18	1	1	1	3
Bennett, Erik, Minnesota	1.000	24	2	5	0	7
Bere, Jason, Chicago	.800	5	1	3	1	5
Bertotti, Mike, Chicago*	1.000	15	0	6	0	6
Bevil, Brian, Kansas City	1.000	3	2	1	0	3
Bluma, Jaime, Kansas City	1.000	17	1	6	0	7
Boehringer, Brian, New York	1.000	15	2	4	0	6
Bohanon, Brian, Toronto*	1.000	20	2	2	0	4

Player, Team	Pct.	G	PO	A	E	TC	DP
nes, Ricky, Mil.-N.Y.	.963	36	11	15	1	27	4
sio, Chris, Seattle	1.000	18	3	10	0	13	1
skie, Shawn, California	.973	37	7	29	1	37	1
ze, Marshall, Milwaukee	1.000	25	7	5	0	12	0
ndenburg, Mark, Tex.-Bos.	1.000	55	2	7	0	9	0
ewer, Billy, New York*	1.000	4	0	1	0	1	0
scoe, John, Oakland	1.000	17	1	2	0	3	1
ow, Scott, Toronto	1.000	18	3	4	0	7	0
rkett, John, Texas	1.000	10	7	4	0	11	0
rrows, Terry, Milwaukee*	1.000	8	2	1	0	3	0
rmona, Rafael, Seattle	.889	53	2	14	2	18	0
penter, Cris, Milwaukee	.000	8	0	0	0	0	0
rara, Giovanni, Toronto	1.000	11	0	1	0	1	0
stillo, Tony, Tor.-Chi.*	1.000	55	9	15	0	24	1
arlton, Norm, Seattle*	.929	70	4	9	1	14	1
ouinard, Bobby, Oakland	1.000	13	3	13	0	16	3
ristopher, Mike, Detroit	1.000	13	1	3	0	4	0
rk, Terry, Kansas City	1.000	12	2	1	0	3	0
mens, Roger, Boston	.943	34	10	23	2	35	2
ne, David, New York	.917	11	6	5	1	12	1
ok, Dennis, Texas*	1.000	60	4	5	0	9	0
ppinger, Rocky, Baltimore	1.000	23	6	8	0	14	1
rbin, Archie, Baltimore	1.000	18	0	1	0	1	0
rsi, Jim, Oakland	1.000	56	6	17	0	23	2
abtree, Tim, Toronto	.933	53	4	10	1	15	1
mmings, Dennis, Detroit*	1.000	21	0	4	0	4	0
Amico, Jeff, Milwaukee	1.000	17	10	6	0	16	0
rwin, Jeff, Chicago	1.000	22	3	2	0	5	0
vis, Tim, Seattle*	.889	40	3	5	1	9	1
vison, Scott, Seattle	1.000	5	3	0	0	3	0
ckson, Jason, California	.889	7	3	5	1	9	0
herty, John, Boston	1.000	3	1	4	0	5	0
enfield, Ken, California	1.000	2	1	0	0	1	0
hhorn, Mark, California	1.000	24	2	6	0	8	0
chen, Joey, Detroit*	1.000	24	0	7	0	7	1
red, Cal, Milwaukee	1.000	15	4	10	0	14	0
s, Robert, California	.000	3	0	0	0	0	0
abree, Alan, Cleveland*	1.000	24	1	2	0	3	0
ckson, Scott, Baltimore	.973	34	30	43	2	75	6
helman, Vaughn, Boston*	.875	39	5	16	3	24	0
rrell, John, Detroit	1.000	2	1	0	0	1	0
rnandez, Alex, Chicago	.972	35	27	42	2	71	7
ters, Mike, Milwaukee	1.000	61	7	5	0	12	0
ley, Chuck, California*	.925	35	9	28	3	40	4
ner, Huck, Toronto*	.900	15	6	12	2	20	1
tcher, Paul, Oakland	.000	1	0	0	1	1	0
rie, Bryce, Milwaukee	.750	15	1	2	1	4	0
eman, Marvin, Chicago	.000	1	0	0	0	0	0
hwirth, Todd, California	.000	4	0	0	0	0	0
rces, Rich, Boston	.900	37	1	8	1	10	2
rcia, Ramon, Milwaukee	1.000	37	6	10	0	16	2
son, Paul, New York*	1.000	4	1	0	0	1	0
ens, Brian, Milwaukee*	.500	4	1	0	1	2	0
hr, Greg, Det.-Cal.	.944	32	7	10	1	18	0
oden, Dwight, New York	.972	29	9	26	1	36	1
rdon, Tom, Boston	.936	34	14	30	3	47	3
anger, Jeff, Kansas City*	1.000	15	3	1	0	4	0
aves, Danny, Cleveland	1.000	15	2	2	0	4	0
imsley, Jason, California	.953	35	23	18	2	43	2
oom, Buddy, Oakland*	.889	72	2	6	1	9	0
oss, Kevin, Texas	.938	28	11	19	2	32	1
undt, Ken, Boston*	.000	1	0	0	0	0	0
ardado, Eddie, Minnesota*	1.000	83	0	9	0	9	1
bicza, Mark, Kansas City	.969	19	15	16	1	32	1
etterman, Lee, Seattle*	1.000	17	2	3	0	5	0
nderson, Eric, Boston*	.000	28	0	0	0	0	0
zman, Juan, Toronto	.912	27	9	22	3	34	1
ncock, Ryan, California	1.000	11	2	3	0	5	1
ney, Chris, Kansas City*	1.000	35	9	27	0	36	1
nsell, Greg, Minnesota	1.000	50	8	4	0	12	0
erk, Erik, Toronto	.893	35	9	16	3	28	3
rikkala, Tim, Seattle	1.000	1	0	2	0	2	0
ris, Pep, California	1.000	11	1	6	0	7	1
ris, Reggie, Boston	.000	4	0	0	0	0	0
wkins, LaTroy, Minnesota	1.000	7	3	4	0	7	0
ynes, Jimmy, Baltimore	.947	26	6	12	1	19	1
ling, Rick, Texas	1.000	6	2	1	0	3	0
neman, Mike, Texas	.875	49	1	6	1	8	0
ntgen, Pat, Toronto	.977	35	11	31	1	43	6
edia, Gil, Texas	1.000	44	7	7	0	14	0
rnandez, Roberto, Chicago	.900	72	3	6	1	10	0
rshiser, Orel, Cleveland	.971	33	20	47	2	69	3
, Ken, Texas	.983	35	22	37	1	60	5

Player, Team	Pct.	G	PO	A	E	TC	DP
Hitchcock, Sterling, Seattle*	.906	35	6	23	3	32	2
Holtz, Mike, California*	1.000	30	1	5	0	6	0
Holzemer, Mark, California*	.900	25	4	5	1	10	0
Howe, Steve, New York*	.833	25	0	5	1	6	1
Hudson, Joe, Boston	.833	36	1	9	2	12	1
Huisman, Rick, Kansas City	1.000	22	0	5	0	5	0
Hurtado, Edwin, Seattle	1.000	16	3	8	0	11	1
Hutton, Mark, New York	.667	12	2	0	1	3	0
Jackson, Mike, Seattle	.944	73	1	16	1	18	0
Jacome, Jason, Kansas City*	1.000	49	3	14	0	17	3
James, Mike, California	1.000	69	6	12	0	18	2
Janzen, Marty, Toronto	.846	15	5	6	2	13	1
Johns, Doug, Oakland*	.958	40	16	30	2	48	7
Johnson, Dane, Toronto	1.000	10	2	1	0	3	0
Johnson, Randy, Seattle*	.900	14	1	8	1	10	0
Jones, Doug, Milwaukee	1.000	24	1	4	0	5	0
Jones, Stacy, Chicago	.000	2	0	0	0	0	0
Kamieniecki, Scott, New York	1.000	7	0	4	0	4	0
Karchner, Matt, Chicago	.778	50	4	3	2	9	1
Karl, Scott, Milwaukee*	.930	32	13	27	3	43	2
Keagle, Greg, Detroit	1.000	26	7	8	0	15	1
Key, Jimmy, New York*	.975	30	9	30	1	40	1
Keyser, Brian, Chicago	.957	28	6	16	1	23	3
Kiefer, Mark, Milwaukee	.000	7	0	0	0	0	0
Klingenbeck, Scott, Minnesota	1.000	10	6	3	0	9	0
Klink, Joe, Detroit*	1.000	3	0	0	0	0	0
Knackert, Brent, Boston	.000	8	0	4	0	4	1
Krivda, Rick, Baltimore*	1.000	22	1	10	0	11	0
Lacy, Kerry, Boston	.667	11	1	1	1	3	1
Langston, Mark, California*	.971	18	7	27	1	35	0
Leftwich, Phil, California	1.000	2	0	1	0	1	0
Levine, Al, Chicago	1.000	16	0	6	0	6	1
Lewis, Richie, Detroit	1.000	72	4	6	0	10	1
Lima, Jose, Detroit	1.000	39	11	17	0	28	1
Linton, Doug, Kansas City	.905	21	9	10	2	21	0
Lira, Felipe, Detroit	1.000	32	18	33	0	51	4
Lloyd, Graeme, Mil.-N.Y.*	1.000	65	2	7	0	9	1
Lopez, Albie, Cleveland	.833	13	1	9	2	12	0
Maddux, Mike, Boston	1.000	23	7	12	0	19	1
Magnante, Mike, Kansas City*	1.000	38	4	15	0	19	2
Magrane, Joe, Chicago*	.833	19	2	8	2	12	0
Mahomes, Pat, Min.-Bos.	1.000	31	4	8	0	12	0
Martinez, Dennis, Cleveland	.973	20	10	26	1	37	1
Mathews, Terry, Baltimore	1.000	14	3	1	0	4	0
Maxcy, Brian, Detroit	1.000	2	1	1	0	2	0
May, Darrell, California*	.000	5	0	0	0	0	0
McCarthy, Greg, Seattle*	1.000	10	0	3	0	3	1
McCaskill, Kirk, Chicago	1.000	29	3	12	0	15	1
McCurry, Jeff, Detroit	1.000	2	0	4	0	4	0
McDonald, Ben, Milwaukee	.878	35	13	30	6	49	3
McDowell, Jack, Cleveland	.979	30	20	27	1	48	0
McDowell, Roger, Baltimore	.958	41	8	15	1	24	2
McElroy, Chuck, California*	.933	40	3	11	1	15	1
Meacham, Rusty, Seattle	.857	15	3	3	1	7	1
Mecir, Jim, New York	1.000	26	1	13	0	14	0
Mendoza, Ramiro, New York	1.000	12	2	11	0	13	0
Menhart, Paul, Seattle	.923	11	5	7	1	13	2
Mercedes, Jose, Milwaukee	1.000	11	0	2	0	2	0
Mercker, Kent, Bal.-Cle.*	.929	24	9	4	1	14	0
Mesa, Jose, Cleveland	.889	69	5	3	1	9	1
Milacki, Bob, Seattle	1.000	7	3	1	0	4	1
Milchin, Mike, Min.-Bal.*	1.000	39	3	5	0	8	0
Miller, Travis, Minnesota	1.000	7	0	2	0	2	0
Miller, Trever, Detroit*	1.000	5	1	4	0	5	0
Mills, Alan, Baltimore	1.000	49	4	7	0	11	2
Minchey, Nate, Boston	1.000	2	0	1	0	1	0
Minor, Blas, Seattle	1.000	11	0	3	0	3	0
Miranda, Angel, Milwaukee*	.895	46	3	14	2	19	0
Moehler, Brian, Detroit	.500	2	0	1	1	2	0
Mohler, Mike, Oakland*	.952	72	6	14	1	21	3
Monteleone, Rich, California	1.000	12	1	0	0	1	0
Montgomery, Jeff, Kansas City	1.000	48	6	13	0	19	1
Montgomery, Steve, Oakland	.000	8	0	0	0	0	0
Moyer, Jamie, Bos.-Sea.*	.912	34	6	25	3	34	2
Mulholland, Terry, Seattle*	.846	12	1	10	2	13	1
Mussina, Mike, Baltimore	1.000	36	14	34	0	48	3
Myers, Jimmy, Baltimore	.750	11	1	2	1	4	0
Myers, Mike, Detroit*	.944	83	2	15	1	18	2
Myers, Randy, Baltimore	.857	62	2	4	1	7	1
NAGY, Charles, Cleveland	1.000	32	29	35	0	64	3
Naulty, Dan, Minnesota	1.000	49	7	5	0	12	1
Nelson, Jeff, New York	.950	73	4	15	1	20	1
Nitkowski, C.J., Detroit*	1.000	11	2	5	0	7	0

Player, Team	Pct.	G	PO	A	E	TC	DP
Ogea, Chad, Cleveland	.909	29	4	16	2	22	1
Olivares, Omar, Detroit	.971	25	12	22	1	35	2
Oliver, Darren, Texas*	.964	30	4	23	1	28	3
Olson, Gregg, Detroit	1.000	43	3	3	0	6	0
Orosco, Jesse, Baltimore*	1.000	66	2	8	0	10	0
Parra, Jose, Minnesota	1.000	27	7	7	0	14	2
Patterson, Danny, Texas	1.000	7	0	2	0	2	0
Pavlas, Dave, New York	1.000	16	2	3	0	5	0
Pavlik, Roger, Texas	.920	34	9	14	2	25	1
Pennington, Brad, Bos.-Cal.*	1.000	22	0	2	0	2	0
Percival, Troy, California	.833	62	4	1	1	6	0
Pettitte, Andy, New York*	.936	35	6	38	3	47	2
Pichardo, Hipolito, Kansas City	.952	57	7	13	1	21	2
Plunk, Eric, Cleveland	1.000	56	4	7	0	11	0
Polley, Dale, New York*	.800	32	0	4	1	5	0
Poole, Jim, Cleveland*	1.000	32	1	6	0	7	1
Potts, Mike, Milwaukee*	1.000	24	3	2	0	5	0
Prieto, Ariel, Oakland	1.000	21	9	18	0	27	0
Pugh, Tim, Kansas City	1.000	19	3	5	0	8	0
Quantrill, Paul, Toronto	1.000	38	4	23	0	27	1
Radke, Brad, Minnesota	1.000	35	22	15	0	37	0
Reyes, Al, Milwaukee	.000	5	0	0	0	0	0
Reyes, Carlos, Oakland	.895	46	7	10	2	19	2
Rhodes, Arthur, Baltimore*	1.000	28	1	2	0	3	0
Risley, Bill, Toronto	1.000	25	1	3	0	4	1
Rivera, Mariano, New York	1.000	61	4	13	0	17	0
Roa, Joe, Cleveland	.000	1	0	0	0	0	0
Robertson, Rich, Minnesota*	.979	36	15	31	1	47	5
Robinson, Ken, Kansas City	1.000	5	1	0	0	1	0
Rodriguez, Frank, Minnesota	.963	38	23	29	2	54	3
Rodriguez, Nerio, Baltimore	1.000	8	1	0	0	1	0
Rogers, Kenny, New York*	.961	30	15	34	2	51	1
Rosado, Jose, Kansas City*	.947	16	3	15	1	19	1
Ruffcorn, Scott, Chicago	1.000	3	1	0	0	1	0
Russell, Jeff, Texas	1.000	55	1	8	0	9	0
Sackinsky, Brian, Baltimore	.000	3	0	0	0	0	0
Sager, A.J., Detroit	.933	22	5	9	1	15	1
Sanderson, Scott, California	1.000	5	2	3	0	5	0
Sauveur, Rich, Chicago*	1.000	3	0	1	0	1	1
Scanlan, Bob, Det.-K.C.	.556	17	1	4	4	9	0
Schmidt, Jeff, California	.000	9	0	0	0	0	0
Sele, Aaron, Boston	.963	29	8	18	1	27	1
Serafini, Dan, Minnesota*	.000	1	0	0	0	0	0
Shepherd, Keith, Baltimore	1.000	13	1	2	0	3	0
Shuey, Paul, Cleveland	1.000	42	3	5	0	8	1
Silva, Jose, Toronto	1.000	2	0	1	0	1	0
Simas, Bill, Chicago	.933	64	9	5	1	15	1
Sirotka, Mike, Chicago*	.750	15	0	3	1	4	0
Slocumb, Heathcliff, Boston	1.000	75	8	12	0	20	4
Small, Aaron, Oakland	1.000	12	3	4	0	7	0
Smith, Lee, California	1.000	11	1	0	0	1	0
Sodowsky, Clint, Detroit	1.000	7	3	2	0	5	0
Sparks, Steve, Milwaukee	.970	20	9	23	1	33	1
Spoljaric, Paul, Toronto*	1.000	28	1	5	0	6	3
Springer, Dennis, California	.923	20	5	7	1	13	0
Stanton, Mike, Bos.-Tex.*	1.000	81	2	7	0	9	0
Stephenson, Garrett, Baltimore	1.000	3	0	1	0	1	0
Stevens, Dave, Minnesota	1.000	49	7	6	0	13	0
Suppan, Jeff, Boston	1.000	8	0	2	0	2	0
Suzuki, Makoto, Seattle	.000	1	0	0	0	0	0
Swindell, Greg, Cleveland*	1.000	13	1	6	0	7	1
Tapani, Kevin, Chicago	.976	34	15	26	1	42	4
Tavarez, Julian, Cleveland	1.000	51	6	8	0	14	0
Taylor, Billy, Oakland	1.000	55	4	9	0	13	0
Telgheder, Dave, Oakland	1.000	16	3	14	0	17	1
Thomas, Larry, Chicago*	1.000	57	2	4	0	6	1
Thompson, Justin, Detroit*	1.000	11	2	13	0	15	1
Timlin, Mike, Toronto	1.000	59	4	6	0	10	0

Player, Team	Pct.	G	PO	A	E	TC	D
Torres, Salomon, Seattle	1.000	10	6	1	0	7	
Trombley, Mike, Minnesota	1.000	43	6	6	0	12	
Urbani, Tom, Detroit*	1.000	16	0	4	0	4	
Valera, Julio, Kansas City	.923	31	5	7	1	13	
VanEgmond, Tim, Milwaukee	1.000	12	6	7	0	13	
Van Poppel, Todd, Oak.-Det.	.929	37	3	10	1	14	
VanRyn, Ben, California*	1.000	1	0	1	0	1	
Veres, Randy, Detroit	.000	25	0	0	0	0	
Villone, Ron, Milwaukee*	.750	23	2	1	1	4	
Viola, Frank, Toronto*	1.000	6	2	2	0	4	
Vosberg, Ed, Texas*	1.000	52	1	11	0	12	
Wagner, Matt, Seattle	.923	15	4	8	1	13	
Wakefield, Tim, Boston	.941	32	14	18	2	34	
Walker, Mike, Detroit	1.000	20	2	1	0	3	
Ware, Jeff, Toronto	1.000	13	3	5	0	8	
Wasdin, John, Oakland	.955	25	9	12	1	22	
Weathers, Dave, New York	1.000	11	0	3	0	3	
Wells, Bob, Seattle	.909	36	8	12	2	22	
Wells, David, Baltimore*	.982	34	15	39	1	55	
Wengert, Don, Oakland	1.000	36	19	8	0	27	
Wetteland, John, New York	1.000	62	0	6	0	6	
Whitehurst, Wally, New York	1.000	2	1	1	0	2	
Whiteside, Matt, Texas	1.000	14	1	4	0	5	
Wickander, Kevin, Milwaukee*	1.000	21	1	4	0	5	
Wickman, Bob, N.Y.-Mil.	1.000	70	6	24	0	30	
Williams, Brian, Detroit	.917	40	6	16	2	24	
Williams, Shad, California	1.000	13	1	0	0	1	
Williams, Woody, Toronto	1.000	12	7	4	0	11	
Witasick, Jay, Oakland	.000	12	0	0	0	0	
Witt, Bobby, Texas	.974	33	10	28	1	39	
Wojciechowski, Steve, Oakland*	1.000	16	1	10	0	11	
Wolcott, Bob, Seattle	1.000	30	10	19	0	29	
Yan, Esteban, Baltimore	.000	4	0	0	0	0	

PITCHERS WITH TWO OR MORE TEAMS

Player, Team	Pct.	G	PO	A	E	TC	D
Aldred, Scott, Detroit*	.667	11	1	3	2	6	
Aldred, Scott, Minnesota*	.944	25	4	13	1	18	
Andujar, Luis, Chicago	1.000	5	1	2	0	3	
Andujar, Luis, Toronto	.000	3	0	0	0	0	
Bones, Ricky, Milwaukee	.958	32	10	13	1	24	
Bones, Ricky, New York	1.000	4	1	2	0	3	
Brandenburg, Mark, Texas	1.000	26	1	2	0	3	
Brandenburg, Mark, Boston	1.000	29	1	5	0	6	
Castillo, Tony, Toronto*	1.000	40	6	13	0	19	
Castillo, Tony, Chicago*	1.000	15	3	2	0	5	
Gohr, Greg, Detroit	.923	17	6	6	1	13	
Gohr, Greg, California	1.000	15	1	4	0	5	
Lloyd, Graeme, Milwaukee*	1.000	52	2	7	0	9	
Lloyd, Graeme, New York*	.000	13	0	0	0	0	
Mahomes, Pat, Minnesota	1.000	20	3	7	0	10	
Mahomes, Pat, Boston	1.000	11	1	1	0	2	
Mercker, Kent, Baltimore*	.909	14	6	4	1	11	
Mercker, Kent, Cleveland*	1.000	10	3	0	0	3	
Milchin, Mike, Minnesota*	1.000	26	3	2	0	5	
Milchin, Mike, Baltimore*	1.000	13	0	3	0	3	
Moyer, Jamie, Boston*	.950	23	3	16	1	20	
Moyer, Jamie, Seattle*	.857	11	3	9	2	14	
Pennington, Brad, Boston*	1.000	14	0	2	0	2	
Pennington, Brad, California*	.000	8	0	0	0	0	
Scanlan, Bob, Detroit	.500	8	0	3	3	6	
Scanlan, Bob, Kansas City	.667	9	1	1	1	3	
Stanton, Mike, Boston*	1.000	59	2	7	0	9	
Stanton, Mike, Texas*	.000	22	0	0	0	0	
Van Poppel, Todd, Oakland	.833	28	1	4	1	6	
Van Poppel, Todd, Detroit	1.000	9	2	6	0	8	
Wickman, Bob, New York	1.000	58	5	23	0	28	
Wickman, Bob, Milwaukee	1.000	12	1	1	0	2	

MISCELLANEOUS

SHUTOUT GAMES

Read across for wins, down for losses.

am	Cle.	K.C.	Chi.	N.Y.	Cal.	Sea.	Tex.	Min.	Tor.	Oak.	Mil.	Bos.	Det.	Bal.	W	L	Pct.
eveland	..	0	0	0	2	1	0	0	1	0	2	2	1	0	9	1	.900
nsas City	0	..	0	1	0	0	1	0	1	2	0	2	0	1	8	3	.727
icago	1	0	..	0	0	0	1	0	0	0	1	0	1	0	4	2	.667
w York	0	0	1	..	0	1	1	1	1	1	1	1	1	0	9	5	.643
lifornia	0	0	0	3	..	0	0	0	0	1	1	0	1	2	8	6	.571
attle	0	0	0	0	1	..	2	1	0	0	0	0	0	0	4	3	.571
xas	0	1	0	0	0	0	..	0	2	0	0	0	2	1	6	5	.545
nnesota	0	0	0	1	1	1	0	..	1	0	0	1	0	0	5	5	.500
ronto	0	1	1	0	1	0	0	0	..	2	0	0	1	1	7	9	.438
kland	0	0	0	0	0	0	0	1	0	..	1	2	0	1	5	7	.417
lwaukee	0	0	0	0	0	0	0	0	1	1	..	1	1	0	4	7	.364
ston	0	0	0	0	1	0	0	0	1	0	1	..	1	1	5	9	.357
troit	0	1	0	0	0	0	0	2	1	0	0	0	..	0	4	10	.286
ltimore	0	0	0	0	0	0	0	0	0	0	0	0	1	..	1	7	.125
Lost	1	3	2	5	6	3	5	5	9	7	7	9	10	7	79	79	.500

HOME RECORD

Read across for home wins, down for road losses.

am	Cle.	Tex.	N.Y.	Bos.	Chi.	Bal.	Cal.	Sea.	Oak.	Min.	Mil.	K.C.	Tor.	Det.	W	L	Pct.
eveland	..	3	0	6	3	4	6	2	4	6	3	5	3	6	51	29	.638
xas	5	..	5	5	1	5	5	2	3	2	3	4	5	5	50	31	.617
w York	3	4	..	4	5	4	3	2	4	3	5	5	3	4	49	31	.613
ston	1	5	5	..	3	3	4	3	6	4	2	1	5	5	47	34	.580
icago	2	3	4	3	..	4	5	3	1	4	4	2	3	6	44	37	.543
ltimore	3	2	0	4	2	..	3	4	4	2	4	5	4	6	43	38	.531
lifornia	3	2	4	2	5	3	..	4	2	3	4	1	5	5	43	38	.531
attle	1	6	5	3	4	3	5	..	3	1	4	3	1	4	43	38	.531
kland	4	3	1	4	2	2	3	5	..	4	3	5	1	3	40	41	.494
nnesota	2	3	3	4	4	1	5	1	4	..	1	4	4	3	39	43	.476
lwaukee	3	2	5	1	5	1	3	2	4	3	..	3	3	3	38	43	.469
nsas City	4	4	3	4	2	2	2	4	4	3	1	..	2	2	37	43	.463
ronto	2	1	2	3	2	3	4	2	3	3	4	3	..	3	35	46	.432
troit	0	3	2	0	2	1	5	4	1	3	1	2	3	..	27	54	.333
Lost on road	33	41	39	43	40	36	53	38	43	41	39	43	42	55	586	546	.518

ROAD RECORD

Read across for road wins, down for home losses.

am	Cle.	Bal.	Sea.	N.Y.	Mil.	Chi.	Tex.	Min.	Tor.	Bos.	K.C.	Oak.	Cal.	Det.	W	L	Pct.
eveland	..	3	6	3	4	5	1	4	4	5	2	2	3	6	48	33	.593
timore	2	..	3	3	5	2	1	5	4	3	4	5	3	5	45	36	.556
attle	3	2	..	4	5	3	4	5	4	3	2	2	3	2	42	38	.525
w York	6	6	1	..	1	2	1	4	5	2	3	5	3	4	43	39	.524
waukee	3	2	2	1	..	2	4	6	2	4	6	3	2	5	42	39	.519
icago	3	4	2	2	2	..	5	2	4	3	5	4	1	4	41	40	.506
xas	3	5	1	2	4	3	..	3	5	1	2	3	4	4	40	41	.494
nnesota	1	4	5	2	3	3	4	..	4	2	3	2	3	3	39	41	.488
ronto	3	2	5	3	3	3	1	2	..	2	5	5	1	4	39	42	.481
ston	0	3	4	2	5	3	1	2	3	..	2	2	4	7	38	43	.469
nsas City	2	1	3	1	3	4	2	3	3	5	..	1	6	4	38	43	.469
kland	2	2	3	2	2	5	4	3	3	1	2	..	4	5	38	43	.469
ifornia	1	3	1	3	3	1	2	1	2	2	3	4	..	1	27	53	.338
troit	0	1	2	3	3	1	1	3	3	1	4	3	1	..	26	55	.321
Lost at home	29	38	38	31	43	37	31	43	46	34	43	41	38	54	546	586	.482

PITCHING AGAINST EACH CLUB

BALTIMORE—88-74

cher	Bos. W-L	Cal. W-L	Chi. W-L	Cle. W-L	Det. W-L	K.C. W-L	Mil. W-L	Min. W-L	N.Y. W-L	Oak. W-L	Sea. W-L	Tex. W-L	Tor. W-L	Totals W-L
nitez	0-0	0-0	0-0	0-0	0-0	0-0	0-0	1-0	0-0	0-0	0-0	0-0	0-0	1-0
ppinger	1-1	0-1	0-0	0-2	1-0	1-0	1-0	1-0	0-0	0-1	1-1	0-0	4-0	10-6
rbin	0-0	0-0	0-0	0-0	1-0	0-0	1-0	0-0	0-0	0-0	0-0	0-0	0-0	2-0
ckson	0-1	2-1	0-2	1-2	2-0	1-0	2-1	0-1	0-2	1-0	2-0	0-1	2-1	13-12
ynes	0-0	1-1	0-0	0-0	0-0	0-0	0-0	0-3	0-0	0-0	0-0	1-1	1-0	3-6
vda	1-0	0-1	0-0	0-0	1-0	0-2	0-0	0-0	0-0	1-0	0-0	0-0	0-2	3-5
thews	0-0	0-0	0-0	0-0	1-1	0-0	0-1	0-0	1-0	0-0	0-0	0-0	0-0	2-2
Dowell	0-0	0-0	0-0	0-0	0-0	0-0	0-0	0-0	0-0	1-0	0-0	0-1	0-0	1-1
rcker	0-0	0-0	0-1	0-0	0-0	1-1	0-0	1-0	0-1	1-0	0-1	0-2	0-0	3-6
chin	0-0	0-0	0-1	0-0	0-0	0-0	1-0	0-0	0-0	0-0	0-0	0-0	0-0	1-0

Pitcher	Bos. W-L	Cal. W-L	Chi. W-L	Cle. W-L	Det. W-L	K.C. W-L	Mil. W-L	Min. W-L	N.Y. W-L	Oak. W-L	Sea. W-L	Tex. W-L	Tor. W-L	Total W-L
Mills	0-0	0-0	1-1	0-0	1-0	0-0	0-0	0-0	0-1	0-0	1-0	0-0	0-0	3-
Mussina	1-1	2-0	2-2	0-2	2-0	2-0	2-0	3-0	0-3	2-1	2-0	1-1	0-1	19-1
R. Myers	1-1	0-0	0-1	0-0	0-0	0-0	0-0	0-0	0-0	2-0	0-2	0-0	1-0	4-
Orosco	0-0	0-0	0-0	2-0	0-0	0-0	1-0	0-0	0-0	0-0	0-0	0-1	0-0	3
Rhodes	1-0	0-0	0-0	0-0	2-0	3-0	1-0	0-0	1-1	0-0	1-0	0-0	0-0	9
Rodriguez	0-0	0-0	0-0	0-0	0-0	0-0	0-0	0-0	0-0	0-0	0-0	0-0	0-1	0
Shepherd	0-0	0-0	0-0	0-0	0-0	0-0	0-0	0-0	0-1	0-0	0-0	0-0	0-0	0
Stephenson	0-0	0-0	0-0	0-1	0-0	0-0	0-0	0-0	0-0	0-0	0-0	0-0	0-0	0
Wells	2-2	1-2	1-1	2-0	0-1	1-0	0-0	1-1	1-1	1-2	0-1	1-3	0-0	11-
Totals	7-6	6-6	4-8	5-7	11-2	9-3	9-3	7-5	3-10	9-4	7-5	3-10	8-5	88-7

NO DECISIONS—Alexander, J. Myers, Sackinsky, Yan.

BOSTON—85-77

Pitcher	Bal. W-L	Cal. W-L	Chi. W-L	Cle. W-L	Det. W-L	K.C. W-L	Mil. W-L	Min. W-L	N.Y. W-L	Oak. W-L	Sea. W-L	Tex. W-L	Tor. W-L	Total W-L
Belinda	0-0	1-0	0-0	0-0	0-0	0-1	0-0	0-0	0-0	0-0	0-0	0-0	1-0	2-
Brandenburg	0-0	0-1	0-0	0-0	1-0	0-0	0-0	1-0	0-0	1-0	0-1	0-0	0-0	4-
Clemens	0-2	2-0	1-1	0-0	3-0	0-2	2-0	0-2	0-3	1-1	1-1	0-1	0-0	10-1
Eshelman	0-0	0-1	2-0	0-0	1-0	0-1	1-0	1-0	1-0	0-0	0-1	0-0	0-0	6
Garces	0-0	0-0	0-0	1-0	0-0	0-0	1-0	0-0	0-0	1-1	0-1	0-0	0-0	3-
Gordon	1-0	2-0	0-1	0-3	3-0	0-1	0-1	2-0	0-0	1-0	1-1	0-1	2-1	12-
Gunderson	0-0	0-0	0-1	0-0	0-0	0-0	0-0	0-0	0-0	0-0	0-0	0-0	0-0	0-
Hudson	1-0	0-0	1-0	0-0	0-0	0-0	0-2	0-1	0-2	0-0	0-0	1-0	0-0	3-
Knackert	0-0	0-0	0-0	0-0	0-0	0-0	0-0	0-0	0-0	0-0	0-0	0-0	0-1	0-
Lacy	0-0	1-0	0-0	0-0	0-0	0-0	0-0	0-0	0-0	1-0	0-0	0-0	0-0	2-
Maddux	0-1	0-0	0-0	0-0	0-0	0-0	0-0	0-0	1-0	0-1	1-0	0-0	1-0	3-
Mahomes	0-0	0-0	0-0	0-0	0-0	0-0	0-0	0-0	1-0	0-0	1-0	0-0	0-0	2-
Minchey	0-0	0-0	0-0	0-0	0-1	0-0	0-0	0-0	0-0	0-0	0-0	0-1	0-0	0-
Moyer	2-0	1-0	0-0	0-1	1-0	2-0	0-0	0-0	0-0	0-0	0-0	0-0	1-0	7-
Pennington	0-0	0-0	0-0	0-1	0-0	0-1	0-0	0-0	0-0	0-0	0-0	0-0	0-0	0-
Sele	1-1	0-1	0-1	0-2	1-0	0-2	0-1	2-1	1-1	2-0	0-0	0-0	0-1	7-1
Slocumb	0-0	0-0	1-1	0-0	0-0	0-1	0-1	0-0	1-0	0-1	1-0	1-0	1-1	5
Stanton	0-1	0-0	0-0	0-2	0-0	0-0	0-0	0-0	0-0	1-0	0-0	3-0	0-0	4-
Suppan	0-0	0-0	0-0	0-0	0-0	0-0	1-0	0-1	0-0	0-0	0-0	0-0	0-0	1
Wakefield	1-2	1-1	1-1	0-2	2-0	1-0	2-0	0-1	2-0	1-1	1-1	1-3	1-1	14-
Totals	6-7	8-4	6-6	1-11	12-1	3-9	7-5	6-6	7-6	8-5	7-6	6-6	8-5	85-7

NO DECISIONS—Doherty, Grundt, Harris.

CALIFORNIA—70-91

Pitcher	Bal. W-L	Bos. W-L	Chi. W-L	Cle. W-L	Det. W-L	K.C. W-L	Mil. W-L	Min. W-L	N.Y. W-L	Oak. W-L	Sea. W-L	Tex. W-L	Tor. W-L	Total W
J. Abbott	0-2	0-0	0-2	0-0	0-0	0-3	0-1	1-0	0-2	1-0	0-2	0-3	0-3	2-
K. Abbott	0-1	0-0	0-0	0-0	0-0	0-0	0-0	0-0	0-0	0-0	0-0	0-0	0-0	0
Boskie	3-1	1-2	0-0	2-2	0-1	0-0	2-0	1-2	0-0	2-1	1-2	0-0	0-0	12-
Dickson	0-0	0-1	0-0	0-0	0-0	0-1	0-0	0-0	1-1	0-0	0-0	0-1	0-0	1
Eichhorn	0-0	0-0	0-0	0-0	1-0	0-1	0-0	0-0	0-0	0-0	0-1	0-0	0-0	1
Finley	0-0	1-2	2-1	0-3	2-0	0-0	1-2	1-3	4-0	1-1	1-0	0-3	2-1	15-
Gohr	0-0	0-1	0-0	1-0	0-0	0-0	0-0	0-0	0-0	0-0	0-0	0-0	0-0	1
Grimsley	0-1	0-1	0-1	0-0	1-1	0-1	0-0	1-1	1-0	0-0	1-1	0-0	1-0	5-
Hancock	0-0	0-0	2-0	1-0	0-0	0-0	0-0	0-0	0-0	1-1	0-0	0-0	0-0	4
Harris	1-0	0-0	0-0	0-0	0-0	0-0	0-0	0-0	0-0	0-0	0-0	1-0	0-0	2-
Holtz	0-0	1-0	0-0	0-1	0-1	0-0	1-1	0-0	1-0	0-0	0-0	0-0	0-0	3-
Holzemer	0-0	0-0	0-0	0-0	0-0	0-0	0-0	0-0	0-0	0-0	0-0	0-1	0-0	1
James	0-0	0-0	1-1	0-0	1-2	0-0	1-1	0-0	0-0	0-1	0-0	1-0	1-0	5
Langston	1-0	0-0	0-1	0-0	1-0	0-1	1-0	0-1	0-0	1-0	0-0	0-1	2-1	6
Leftwich	0-0	0-0	0-0	0-0	0-1	0-0	0-1	0-0	0-0	0-0	0-0	0-0	0-0	0-
McElroy	0-0	0-0	1-0	0-0	0-0	3-0	0-0	0-0	0-0	0-1	1-0	0-0	0-0	5
Monteleone	0-0	0-0	0-0	0-0	0-0	0-0	0-0	0-0	0-0	0-2	0-1	0-0	0-0	0
Percival	0-0	0-0	0-0	0-2	0-0	0-0	0-0	0-0	0-0	0-0	0-0	0-0	0-0	0
Sanderson	0-0	0-0	0-0	0-1	0-1	0-0	0-0	0-0	0-0	0-0	0-0	0-0	0-0	0
Schmidt	0-0	0-0	0-0	0-0	0-0	0-0	0-0	0-0	0-0	0-0	1-0	1-0	0-0	2
Springer	1-1	1-0	0-0	0-0	0-0	1-0	1-0	0-1	0-2	0-1	1-0	0-1	0-0	5
Williams	0-0	0-1	0-0	0-0	0-0	0-0	0-0	0-0	0-1	0-0	0-0	0-0	0-0	0
Totals	6-6	4-8	6-6	4-9	6-6	4-8	7-5	4-8	7-6	6-7	5-8	4-9	7-5	70-

NO DECISIONS—Edenfield, Ellis, Frohwirth, May, Pennington, Smith, VanRyn.

CHICAGO—85-77

Pitcher	Bal. W-L	Bos. W-L	Cal. W-L	Cle. W-L	Det. W-L	K.C. W-L	Mil. W-L	Min. W-L	N.Y. W-L	Oak. W-L	Sea. W-L	Tex. W-L	Tor. W-L	Total W
Alvarez	0-2	1-1	2-2	1-1	2-0	1-1	2-1	1-1	0-0	0-0	2-1	2-0	1-0	15-
Andujar	0-0	0-0	0-0	0-0	0-0	0-0	0-0	0-1	0-1	0-0	0-0	0-0	0-0	0
Baldwin	2-0	1-1	1-0	1-1	1-0	1-0	1-1	0-0	0-1	1-0	0-0	1-1	1-1	11
Bere	0-0	0-0	0-0	0-0	0-0	0-1	0-0	0-0	0-0	0-0	0-0	0-0	0-0	0
Bertotti	0-0	0-0	0-0	0-0	1-0	0-0	0-0	0-0	1-0	0-0	0-0	0-0	0-0	2
Castillo	0-0	1-0	0-0	0-0	1-0	1-0	0-0	0-1	0-0	0-0	0-0	0-0	0-0	3
Darwin	0-0	0-0	0-0	0-0	0-0	0-0	0-1	0-0	0-0	0-0	0-0	0-0	0-0	0
Fernandez	3-0	1-0	2-0	1-2	0-0	2-1	1-1	3-0	0-1	0-2	0-1	3-0	0-2	16-
Hernandez	0-1	0-1	0-0	0-0	1-1	0-1	0-0	0-1	2-0	0-0	0-0	1-0	2-0	6
Karchner	1-0	0-1	0-0	2-1	0-0	1-0	0-0	0-0	1-0	2-2	0-0	0-0	0-0	7
Keyser	0-0	1-0	0-0	0-0	0-0	0-0	0-1	0-0	0-0	0-0	0-0	0-1	0-0	1
Levine	0-0	0-0	0-0	0-0	0-0	0-0	0-1	0-0	0-0	0-0	0-0	0-0	0-0	0

	Bal. W-L	Bos. W-L	Cal. W-L	Cle. W-L	Det. W-L	K.C. W-L	Mil. W-L	Min. W-L	N.Y. W-L	Oak. W-L	Sea. W-L	Tex. W-L	Tor. W-L	Totals W-L
her														
jrane	0-0	0-2	0-0	0-0	0-0	0-0	0-0	0-0	0-0	0-0	0-0	1-2	0-1	1-5
Caskill	0-0	0-0	0-2	0-1	2-0	0-0	0-0	0-1	1-0	0-0	1-1	0-0	1-0	5-5
corn	0-0	0-0	0-0	0-0	0-0	0-0	0-0	0-0	0-0	0-0	0-0	0-0	0-1	0-1
as	1-0	0-0	0-1	0-0	1-1	0-0	0-0	0-1	0-0	0-3	0-1	0-1	0-0	2-8
tka	0-0	0-0	0-1	0-0	0-0	0-0	0-0	1-1	0-0	0-0	0-0	0-0	0-0	1-2
ani	1-1	1-0	1-0	0-2	1-1	1-1	1-2	1-0	1-2	2-0	1-1	0-0	2-0	13-10
homas	0-0	0-0	0-0	0-0	0-0	0-0	1-0	0-0	0-2	0-0	0-0	1-1	0-0	2-3
otals	8-4	6-6	6-6	5-8	10-3	7-6	6-7	6-7	6-7	5-7	5-7	8-4	7-5	85-77

0 DECISIONS—Freeman, Jones, Sauveur.

CLEVELAND—99-62

	Bal. W-L	Bos. W-L	Cal. W-L	Chi. W-L	Det. W-L	K.C. W-L	Mil. W-L	Min. W-L	N.Y. W-L	Oak. W-L	Sea. W-L	Tex. W-L	Tor. W-L	Totals W-L
her														
erson	1-0	0-0	1-0	1-0	0-0	0-0	0-0	0-0	0-0	0-0	0-0	0-1	0-0	3-1
enmacher	1-1	0-0	1-0	0-0	1-0	0-0	0-0	0-0	0-0	0-1	0-0	0-0	1-0	4-2
oree	0-0	0-1	0-0	0-0	0-0	0-0	0-0	0-0	0-0	0-0	0-0	1-0	0-0	1-1
ves	0-0	0-0	0-0	0-0	0-0	0-0	0-0	2-0	0-0	0-0	0-0	0-0	0-0	2-0
shiser	1-2	2-0	2-0	1-1	2-0	1-2	1-1	1-0	1-0	0-1	1-0	0-1	2-1	15-9
ez	0-0	0-0	0-1	1-0	1-0	0-0	0-0	0-0	0-0	0-1	1-1	1-0	1-1	5-4
tinez	0-0	2-0	0-0	1-0	2-0	0-0	1-0	0-0	0-4	0-0	1-1	0-0	2-1	9-6
Oowell	0-0	2-0	3-1	2-0	1-0	2-0	0-2	2-0	0-2	1-1	0-0	0-3	0-0	13-9
cker	0-0	0-0	0-0	0-0	0-0	1-0	0-0	0-0	0-0	0-0	0-0	0-0	0-0	1-0
sa	1-0	0-0	0-0	0-1	0-0	0-0	0-2	1-0	0-1	0-1	0-2	0-0	0-0	2-7
y	2-0	1-0	0-0	0-0	3-0	0-2	1-0	1-1	1-0	3-1	2-0	2-0	1-1	17-5
a	1-1	1-0	0-1	1-0	1-0	1-1	1-0	2-0	0-1	1-0	1-0	0-1	0-0	10-6
nk	0-0	0-0	0-0	0-0	1-0	0-0	0-1	0-1	0-0	1-0	1-0	0-0	0-0	3-2
le	0-0	0-0	1-0	0-0	0-0	1-0	1-0	0-0	1-0	0-0	0-0	0-0	0-0	4-0
ey	0-0	1-0	0-0	1-1	0-0	0-0	1-0	0-0	1-1	0-0	0-0	0-0	0-0	5-2
ndell	0-0	1-0	0-0	0-1	0-0	0-0	0-0	0-0	0-0	0-0	0-0	0-0	0-0	1-1
rez	0-1	1-0	0-1	0-1	0-0	0-0	1-1	1-0	0-0	0-1	0-0	1-0	0-2	4-7
otals	7-5	11-1	9-4	8-5	12-0	7-6	7-6	10-3	3-9	6-6	8-4	4-8	7-5	99-62

0 DECISIONS—Roa.

DETROIT—53-109

	Bal. W-L	Bos. W-L	Cal. W-L	Chi. W-L	Cle. W-L	K.C. W-L	Mil. W-L	Min. W-L	N.Y. W-L	Oak. W-L	Sea. W-L	Tex. W-L	Tor. W-L	Totals W-L
her														
ed	0-0	0-1	0-0	0-0	0-0	0-0	0-0	0-2	0-0	0-0	0-0	0-1	0-0	0-4
stopher	0-0	0-0	0-1	0-0	0-0	0-0	0-0	0-0	0-0	1-0	0-0	1-0	0-1	1-1
mings	1-1	0-0	0-0	0-0	0-0	0-0	0-1	0-0	1-0	0-0	0-0	1-0	0-1	3-3
hen	0-1	0-0	0-0	0-0	0-0	1-0	0-0	0-0	0-0	0-0	0-0	0-0	0-0	1-1
ell	0-0	0-0	0-0	0-1	0-0	0-1	0-0	0-0	0-0	0-0	0-0	0-0	0-0	0-2
;	0-1	0-0	0-0	0-0	0-1	1-0	0-0	1-0	1-1	0-2	0-1	0-1	1-0	4-8
gle	0-0	0-1	1-1	0-0	0-0	0-0	0-0	0-0	0-1	1-1	1-0	0-1	0-0	3-6
ewis	0-1	0-0	1-1	1-1	0-2	0-0	0-0	0-0	0-0	2-1	0-0	0-0	0-0	4-6
a	0-0	0-1	2-0	1-1	0-1	0-0	1-0	0-0	0-0	0-0	0-0	1-0	0-2	5-6
>	0-2	1-2	0-1	0-1	0-1	0-1	0-0	1-2	0-2	1-1	0-0	2-1	1-0	6-14
r	0-1	0-1	0-0	0-1	0-0	0-1	0-0	0-0	0-0	0-0	0-0	0-0	0-0	0-4
nler	0-0	0-0	0-0	0-0	0-0	0-0	0-1	0-0	0-0	0-0	0-0	0-0	0-0	0-1
s	0-1	0-0	0-1	1-0	0-0	0-1	0-0	0-0	0-0	0-1	0-0	0-0	0-0	1-5
wski	0-0	0-1	1-0	0-0	0-0	0-0	0-0	0-0	0-0	0-0	0-1	0-0	1-1	2-3
res	1-1	0-1	0-1	0-2	0-0	0-1	0-1	1-1	0-0	1-0	3-0	1-1	0-2	7-11
n	0-0	0-0	0-0	0-0	0-0	0-0	0-0	0-0	1-0	0-0	1-0	0-0	1-0	3-0
r	0-0	0-0	0-0	0-0	0-1	1-0	2-1	0-0	0-1	0-0	0-1	0-0	1-1	4-5
wsky	0-0	0-1	0-0	0-0	0-0	0-0	0-0	1-0	0-0	0-1	0-1	0-0	0-0	1-3
pson	0-1	0-1	0-0	0-1	0-2	1-0	0-0	0-0	0-0	0-1	0-0	0-0	0-0	1-6
ni	0-0	0-0	0-0	0-0	0-0	0-0	0-1	1-0	0-0	0-0	0-0	0-0	1-0	2-2
Poppel	0-1	0-0	0-0	0-0	0-0	2-0	0-2	0-0	0-0	0-0	0-0	0-1	0-0	2-4
s	0-0	0-0	0-0	0-0	0-1	0-0	0-0	0-1	0-0	0-0	0-0	0-1	0-0	0-4
lliams	0-0	0-2	1-0	0-0	0-3	0-1	1-1	1-0	0-0	0-0	0-1	0-1	0-1	3-10
tals	2-11	1-12	6-6	3-10	0-12	6-6	4-8	6-6	5-8	4-8	6-6	4-9	6-7	53-109

DECISIONS—Maxcy, McCurry, Scanlan, Walker.

KANSAS CITY—75-86

	Bal. W-L	Bos. W-L	Cal. W-L	Chi. W-L	Cle. W-L	Det. W-L	Mil. W-L	Min. W-L	N.Y. W-L	Oak. W-L	Sea. W-L	Tex. W-L	Tor. W-L	Totals W-L
er														
er	1-1	2-0	1-0	2-1	0-1	0-3	1-1	1-0	0-1	2-1	2-0	1-1	1-1	14-11
ler	0-0	3-0	2-1	1-2	2-1	1-1	0-1	1-1	0-2	1-1	0-1	1-0	3-0	15-11
	0-0	0-0	0-0	0-0	1-0	0-0	0-0	0-0	0-0	0-0	0-0	0-0	0-0	1-0
	0-0	1-0	0-0	0-0	0-0	0-0	0-0	0-1	0-0	0-0	0-0	0-0	0-0	1-1
zza	0-2	0-1	1-0	0-0	0-0	0-0	1-2	0-1	1-0	0-2	0-1	1-1	0-2	4-12
y	0-2	0-1	1-0	1-1	1-1	0-0	1-2	2-0	0-2	2-1	0-1	1-2	1-1	10-14
nan	0-0	0-0	0-0	0-0	0-0	1-0	0-0	0-0	0-0	1-0	0-0	0-0	0-1	2-1
ne	0-1	0-0	0-0	0-0	0-1	0-0	0-1	0-0	0-1	0-0	0-0	0-0	0-0	0-4
n	1-0	0-1	0-0	1-1	0-0	0-0	2-1	0-1	1-1	1-0	0-1	1-2	0-1	7-9
ante	1-0	0-0	0-0	0-0	1-1	0-0	0-0	0-1	0-0	0-0	0-0	0-0	0-0	2-2
jomery	0-1	0-0	0-1	1-0	0-0	1-0	0-0	0-2	1-0	0-0	0-0	1-1	0-1	4-6
rdo	0-1	1-0	1-0	0-1	0-0	0-0	0-0	1-1	0-0	0-1	0-1	0-0	0-0	3-5
	0-0	0-0	0-1	0-0	0-0	0-0	0-0	0-0	0-0	0-0	0-0	0-0	0-0	0-1
son	0-0	1-0	0-0	0-0	0-0	0-0	0-0	0-0	0-0	0-0	0-0	0-0	0-0	1-0

Pitcher	Bal. W-L	Bos. W-L	Cal. W-L	Chi. W-L	Cle. W-L	Det. W-L	Mil. W-L	Min. W-L	N.Y. W-L	Oak. W-L	Sea. W-L	Tex. W-L	Tor. W-L	Tot
Rosado	0-0	1-0	1-0	0-1	1-1	1-1	0-0	1-0	1-1	0-0	2-0	0-0	0-2	
Scanlan	0-0	0-0	0-0	0-0	0-1	0-0	0-0	0-0	0-0	0-0	0-0	0-0	0-0	
Valera	0-1	0-0	1-1	0-0	0-0	0-0	0-0	0-0	0-0	0-0	2-0	0-0	0-0	
Totals	3-9	9-3	8-4	6-7	6-7	6-6	4-9	6-7	4-8	5-7	7-5	6-6	5-8	75

NO DECISIONS—Bluma, Granger.

MILWAUKEE—80-82

Pitcher	Bal. W-L	Bos. W-L	Cal. W-L	Chi. W-L	Cle. W-L	Det. W-L	K.C. W-L	Min. W-L	N.Y. W-L	Oak. W-L	Sea. W-L	Tex. W-L	Tor. W-L	To
Bones	0-2	1-1	0-0	0-2	0-1	0-1	1-1	1-1	1-1	2-1	0-2	1-0	0-1	7
Boze	0-0	0-0	0-0	0-0	0-1	0-0	0-0	0-0	0-0	0-0	0-0	0-0	0-1	
Burrows	0-0	1-0	0-0	0-0	0-0	0-0	1-0	0-0	0-0	0-0	0-0	0-0	0-0	
D'Amico	0-1	0-0	0-1	0-0	0-1	2-1	0-0	1-0	1-0	0-0	0-1	1-0	1-1	
Eldred	0-0	0-2	0-0	1-0	0-0	1-0	0-0	0-0	1-0	1-0	0-1	0-1	0-0	
Fetters	0-0	0-0	1-0	0-0	0-0	1-1	0-0	0-0	0-0	0-1	0-1	0-0	1-0	
Florie	0-0	0-0	0-0	0-0	0-0	0-0	0-0	0-0	0-0	0-0	0-0	0-1	0-0	
Garcia	0-1	1-1	1-0	0-0	1-0	1-0	0-0	0-0	0-0	0-0	0-0	0-1	0-1	
Givens	0-0	0-0	0-1	0-0	0-0	0-0	0-0	0-1	0-0	1-0	0-0	0-1	0-0	
Jones	1-0	0-0	0-0	0-0	2-0	0-0	0-0	2-0	0-0	0-0	0-0	0-0	0-0	
Karl	0-1	1-0	0-0	0-0	2-1	0-1	1-0	2-1	2-2	1-1	2-0	1-0	1-2	1
Lloyd	0-1	1-0	0-2	1-0	0-0	0-0	0-0	0-1	0-0	0-0	0-0	0-0	0-0	
McDonald	1-1	0-1	1-2	0-3	0-1	0-0	3-0	0-0	1-0	1-0	0-1	3-1	2-0	12
Mercedes	0-0	0-0	0-0	0-0	0-0	0-0	0-1	0-0	0-0	0-0	0-1	0-0	0-0	
Miranda	1-0	0-1	1-1	2-0	0-2	0-0	1-0	1-0	0-0	0-0	0-0	0-1	0-1	
Potts	0-1	0-0	0-0	0-0	0-0	0-0	0-0	0-0	0-0	0-0	1-1	0-0	0-0	
Reyes	0-0	0-0	0-0	0-0	0-0	1-0	0-0	0-0	0-0	0-0	0-0	0-0	0-0	
Sparks	0-1	0-0	0-0	1-1	0-0	1-0	1-1	1-0	0-1	0-1	0-1	0-1	0-0	
Vanegmond	0-0	0-1	0-0	2-0	0-0	0-0	0-0	0-1	0-2	0-1	1-0	0-0	0-0	
Wickander	0-0	0-0	1-0	0-0	0-0	0-0	1-0	0-0	0-0	0-0	0-0	0-0	0-0	
Wickman	0-0	0-0	0-0	0-0	1-0	1-0	0-0	1-0	0-0	0-0	0-0	0-0	0-0	
Totals	3-9	5-7	5-7	7-6	6-7	8-4	9-4	9-4	6-6	7-5	4-9	6-7	5-7	80

NO DECISIONS—Carpenter, Kiefer, Koslofski, Villone.

MINNESOTA—78-84

Pitcher	Bal. W-L	Bos. W-L	Cal. W-L	Chi. W-L	Cle. W-L	Det. W-L	K.C. W-L	Mil. W-L	N.Y. W-L	Oak. W-L	Sea. W-L	Tex. W-L	Tor. W-L	To
Aguilera	1-0	1-0	1-0	1-0	0-1	1-1	0-1	0-0	0-0	1-0	0-1	2-0	0-2	
Aldred	0-0	1-0	1-0	1-2	0-0	0-1	0-2	1-0	1-0	0-0	1-0	0-0	0-0	
Bennett	0-0	0-0	0-0	0-0	0-0	1-0	0-0	0-0	1-0	0-0	0-0	0-0	0-0	
Guardado	0-1	0-0	0-0	0-0	1-1	0-0	1-0	0-0	0-2	0-0	1-1	1-0	1-0	
Hansell	0-0	0-0	0-0	0-0	1-0	0-0	1-0	1-0	0-0	0-0	0-0	0-0	0-0	
Hawkins	0-0	0-0	0-1	0-0	0-0	1-0	0-0	0-0	0-0	0-0	0-0	0-0	0-0	
Klingenbeck	0-0	0-1	0-0	0-0	0-0	0-0	0-0	0-0	0-0	1-0	0-0	0-0	0-0	
Mahomes	0-1	0-0	0-0	0-0	0-0	0-0	0-0	0-2	0-0	0-1	0-0	0-0	0-0	
Milchin	0-0	0-0	0-0	0-0	0-0	0-0	0-0	0-0	0-0	0-0	0-0	2-0	0-1	
Miller	0-0	0-0	0-0	0-0	0-0	0-0	1-0	0-0	0-0	0-0	0-1	0-1	0-0	
Naulty	0-0	1-2	0-0	0-0	0-0	0-0	1-0	0-0	0-0	0-0	0-0	0-0	1-0	
Parra	0-0	1-0	0-0	0-0	0-1	0-0	0-0	1-2	0-0	0-1	2-0	0-1	1-0	
Radke	1-0	2-0	2-0	2-2	0-3	1-1	0-2	0-0	0-3	1-2	1-2	0-0	1-1	11
Robertson	1-3	0-1	1-1	0-1	0-1	0-2	0-1	0-2	1-0	1-2	0-1	1-1	2-1	
Rodriguez	2-1	0-2	1-2	0-1	1-1	1-1	1-0	1-2	2-1	2-1	0-0	1-2	1-0	13
Serafini	0-0	0-0	0-0	0-0	0-0	0-0	0-0	0-0	0-1	0-0	0-0	0-0	0-0	
Stevens	0-0	0-0	1-0	0-0	0-2	0-0	1-0	0-1	0-0	1-0	0-0	0-0	0-0	
Trombley	0-1	0-0	1-0	2-0	0-0	0-0	1-0	0-0	0-0	0-0	0-0	0-0	1-0	
Totals	5-7	6-6	8-4	7-6	3-10	6-6	7-6	4-9	5-7	6-7	6-6	7-5	8-5	7

NEW YORK—92-70

Pitcher	Bal. W-L	Bos. W-L	Cal. W-L	Chi. W-L	Cle. W-L	Det. W-L	K.C. W-L	Mil. W-L	Min. W-L	Oak. W-L	Sea. W-L	Tex. W-L	Tor. W-L	To
Boehringer	0-0	0-1	1-0	0-0	0-1	0-0	0-0	0-0	0-1	0-1	0-0	0-0	1-0	
Brewer	0-0	0-0	0-0	0-0	1-0	0-0	0-0	0-0	0-0	0-0	0-0	0-0	0-0	
Cone	0-0	0-0	0-0	1-0	1-0	1-0	1-0	1-1	0-0	1-0	0-0	1-0	0-1	
Gooden	1-0	0-1	0-0	0-0	2-0	2-0	0-0	1-1	0-1	2-0	1-2	1-2	1-0	
Howe	0-0	0-0	0-0	0-0	0-0	0-0	0-0	0-0	0-0	0-0	0-0	0-1	0-0	
Hutton	0-0	0-1	0-0	0-0	0-0	0-0	0-1	0-0	0-0	0-0	0-0	0-0	0-0	
Kamieniecki	0-0	0-0	0-1	0-0	1-0	0-0	0-0	0-0	0-0	0-1	0-0	0-0	0-0	
Key	1-0	2-1	1-1	0-0	0-0	1-2	3-1	1-2	0-0	1-0	0-1	0-2	2-1	1
Lloyd	0-0	0-0	0-0	0-0	0-0	0-0	0-0	0-0	0-0	0-0	0-2	0-0	0-0	
Mecir	0-0	0-0	0-0	0-0	0-0	1-0	0-0	0-0	0-0	0-0	0-1	0-0	0-0	
Mendoza	0-1	1-0	0-1	0-0	1-0	0-0	0-0	0-0	1-1	0-0	1-0	0-0	0-2	
Nelson	2-0	1-0	0-0	0-2	1-0	0-1	0-0	0-0	0-0	0-1	0-0	0-0	0-0	
Pettitte	3-0	0-0	3-0	2-1	2-1	0-1	2-0	1-1	0-1	2-1	1-0	2-1	3-1	
Polley	0-0	0-2	0-0	0-0	0-0	0-0	0-0	0-0	0-0	1-0	0-0	0-0	0-0	
M. Rivera	1-2	1-0	0-0	1-0	0-0	1-0	0-1	1-0	2-0	0-0	0-0	0-0	1-0	
Rogers	2-0	0-0	1-3	1-0	0-1	1-1	1-0	1-1	2-0	2-0	0-1	1-1	0-0	
Weathers	0-0	0-0	0-0	0-1	0-0	0-0	0-1	0-0	0-0	0-0	0-0	0-0	0-0	
Wetteland	0-0	1-1	0-0	0-2	0-0	0-0	1-0	1-0	0-0	0-0	0-0	0-0	0-0	
Whitehurst	0-0	0-0	0-1	0-0	0-0	0-0	0-0	0-0	0-0	1-0	0-0	0-0	0-0	
Wickman	0-0	0-0	0-0	2-0	0-0	1-0	0-0	0-0	1-1	0-0	0-0	0-0	0-0	
Totals	10-3	6-7	6-7	7-6	9-3	8-5	8-4	6-6	7-5	9-3	3-9	5-7	8-5	9

NO DECISIONS—Aldrete, Bones, Gibson, Manto, Pavlas.

OAKLAND—78-84

itcher	Bal. W-L	Bos. W-L	Cal. W-L	Chi. W-L	Cle. W-L	Det. W-L	K.C. W-L	Mil. W-L	Min. W-L	N.Y. W-L	Sea. W-L	Tex. W-L	Tor. W-L	Totals W-L
cre	0-1	0-1	0-0	0-0	0-0	0-0	0-0	0-0	0-0	1-0	0-1	0-0	0-0	1-3
dams	0-1	1-0	0-1	0-0	1-0	0-0	1-0	0-1	0-1	0-0	0-0	0-0	0-0	3-4
riscoe	0-0	0-0	0-0	0-1	0-0	0-0	0-0	0-0	0-0	0-0	0-0	0-0	0-0	0-1
houinard	0-1	0-0	1-0	0-0	0-0	0-0	0-0	0-0	0-0	0-1	1-0	1-0	1-0	4-2
orsi	0-0	0-0	0-0	2-0	0-0	2-0	1-0	0-0	0-0	0-0	1-0	0-0	0-0	6-0
room	0-0	1-0	1-0	1-0	0-0	0-0	0-0	0-0	0-0	0-0	0-0	1-0	1-0	5-0
ohns	1-1	0-2	1-2	0-0	1-1	1-1	0-1	1-1	0-0	0-1	0-0	1-1	0-1	6-12
ohler	0-1	1-1	0-0	0-0	0-0	0-0	0-0	0-0	0-1	1-0	2-0	1-0	1-0	6-3
ontgomery	0-0	0-0	0-0	0-0	1-0	0-0	0-0	0-0	0-0	0-0	0-0	0-0	0-0	1-0
rieto	1-1	0-0	1-1	0-0	0-0	0-0	0-0	1-2	0-0	2-0	0-1	0-0	1-2	6-7
eyes	0-2	0-0	0-0	1-0	1-2	1-1	0-1	1-0	1-0	0-1	0-1	2-1	0-1	7-10
mall	0-0	0-0	0-0	0-0	0-1	0-1	1-0	0-0	0-0	0-0	1-0	0-1	0-0	1-3
aylor	0-0	0-0	2-0	1-0	1-0	0-0	0-0	1-1	0-0	0-1	1-0	0-1	0-0	6-3
elgheder	0-0	1-0	0-0	0-1	0-1	0-0	0-0	1-0	1-1	0-2	1-2	0-1	0-0	4-7
an Poppel	0-0	0-1	0-1	0-1	0-0	1-0	0-0	0-1	0-0	0-0	0-1	0-0	0-0	1-5
asdin	0-1	1-1	1-1	0-1	1-0	2-0	1-1	0-1	1-0	0-0	0-0	1-0	0-1	8-7
engert	2-0	0-1	0-0	1-1	0-1	0-1	2-0	0-0	1-2	0-1	1-1	0-1	0-1	7-11
itasick	0-0	0-0	0-0	1-0	0-0	0-0	0-0	0-0	0-0	0-0	0-0	0-0	0-1	1-1
ojciechowski	0-0	0-1	0-0	0-0	0-0	1-0	1-0	1-1	1-1	1-1	0-0	0-0	0-0	5-5
Totals	4-9	5-8	7-6	7-5	6-6	8-4	7-5	5-7	7-6	3-9	8-5	7-6	4-8	78-84

NO DECISIONS—Fletcher.

SEATTLE—85-76

itcher	Bal. W-L	Bos. W-L	Cal. W-L	Chi. W-L	Cle. W-L	Det. W-L	K.C. W-L	Mil. W-L	Min. W-L	N.Y. W-L	Oak. W-L	Tex. W-L	Tor. W-L	Totals W-L
yala	0-0	0-0	1-1	0-0	0-0	0-1	0-0	1-0	1-0	2-0	1-0	0-0	0-1	6-3
osio	0-1	1-0	0-0	0-1	0-1	1-1	0-0	0-0	0-0	0-0	0-0	1-0	1-0	4-4
armona	0-0	0-1	1-0	1-0	1-0	0-0	0-0	1-1	0-0	0-1	2-0	2-0	0-0	8-3
harlton	2-1	0-0	1-1	0-0	1-1	0-1	0-0	0-0	0-0	0-0	0-2	0-0	0-1	4-7
Davis	0-0	0-0	0-0	0-0	0-0	1-0	0-1	0-1	0-0	0-0	0-0	1-0	0-0	2-2
uetterman	0-1	0-0	0-0	0-1	0-0	0-0	0-0	0-0	0-0	0-0	0-0	0-0	0-0	0-2
arikkala	0-0	0-0	0-0	0-0	0-0	0-0	0-0	0-0	0-0	0-0	0-0	0-0	0-1	0-1
itchcock	0-2	0-1	1-1	2-1	0-1	1-0	1-0	2-0	0-1	2-1	0-1	3-0	1-0	13-9
urtado	0-1	0-0	0-0	1-0	0-0	0-1	0-0	0-1	0-0	1-1	0-0	0-0	0-1	2-5
ackson	0-0	0-0	0-0	0-0	0-0	1-0	0-0	0-0	0-0	0-0	0-0	0-1	0-0	1-1
ohnson	0-0	0-0	1-0	0-0	0-0	1-0	1-0	1-0	0-0	0-0	0-0	0-0	1-0	5-0
eacham	0-0	0-0	1-0	0-0	0-0	0-0	0-0	0-0	0-0	0-0	0-0	0-1	0-0	1-1
enhart	0-0	0-0	0-0	0-0	0-0	1-0	0-1	0-0	0-0	0-0	1-0	0-0	0-1	2-2
ilacki	1-0	0-2	0-0	0-1	0-0	0-0	0-1	0-0	0-0	0-0	0-0	0-0	0-0	1-4
inor	0-0	0-0	0-0	0-0	0-0	0-0	0-0	0-0	0-0	0-0	0-1	0-0	0-0	0-1
oyer	1-0	0-0	0-0	0-0	0-0	0-2	1-0	0-0	0-0	2-0	1-0	1-0	0-0	6-2
ulholland	1-0	0-0	0-0	0-0	0-2	2-0	0-0	0-0	1-0	1-0	0-2	1-0	0-0	5-4
orres	0-0	1-1	1-0	0-0	0-0	0-1	0-0	0-0	1-0	0-0	0-1	0-0	0-0	3-3
agner	0-1	0-1	0-0	1-0	0-0	0-1	0-0	1-0	0-1	0-0	1-0	0-0	0-0	3-5
ells	0-0	2-1	1-2	2-0	1-1	0-0	0-0	2-0	3-2	0-0	0-0	0-1	1-0	12-7
olcott	0-0	2-0	0-0	0-2	0-1	1-0	1-2	0-1	1-2	0-0	0-0	1-0	1-2	7-10
Totals	5-7	6-7	8-5	7-5	4-8	6-6	5-7	9-4	6-6	9-3	5-8	10-3	5-7	85-76

NO DECISIONS—Davison, Klink, McCarthy, Suzuki.

TEXAS—90-72

tcher	Bal. W-L	Bos. W-L	Cal. W-L	Chi. W-L	Cle. W-L	Det. W-L	K.C. W-L	Mil. W-L	Min. W-L	N.Y. W-L	Oak. W-L	Sea. W-L	Tor. W-L	Totals W-L
berro	0-0	0-0	0-0	0-0	0-0	0-0	0-0	0-0	0-0	0-1	0-0	0-0	0-0	0-1
andenburg	1-0	0-0	0-1	0-0	0-0	0-0	0-0	0-0	0-0	0-0	0-2	0-0	0-0	1-3
rkett	0-0	0-0	2-0	0-0	0-1	0-0	1-0	1-0	0-0	0-0	0-0	0-1	1-0	5-2
ook	2-0	0-1	0-0	0-0	1-0	0-0	1-0	0-0	0-0	0-0	1-0	0-1	0-0	5-2
oss	2-1	2-1	1-0	1-0	0-0	2-0	1-1	1-1	0-0	0-1	0-1	0-2	1-0	11-8
illing	0-1	0-0	0-0	0-0	0-0	0-0	1-0	0-0	0-0	0-0	0-0	0-1	0-0	1-2
enneman	0-0	0-2	0-1	0-1	0-0	0-0	0-0	0-0	0-2	0-0	0-0	0-1	0-0	0-7
redia	1-0	0-1	0-0	1-0	0-0	0-1	0-0	0-0	0-1	0-1	0-0	0-1	0-0	2-5
l	0-0	2-0	2-0	0-1	0-0	3-0	2-1	1-3	2-1	2-2	1-0	1-1	0-1	16-10
ver	2-0	0-0	2-0	0-2	3-0	0-1	0-1	1-0	0-1	1-0	1-0	0-1	4-0	14-6
vlik	0-0	2-0	1-0	0-2	3-0	3-1	0-1	1-1	1-1	2-1	1-0	0-1	1-0	15-8
ussell	0-0	0-0	0-0	1-1	0-0	0-0	0-1	0-0	0-0	1-0	0-0	1-0	0-0	3-3
anton	0-0	0-0	0-1	0-0	0-0	0-0	0-0	0-0	0-0	0-0	0-0	0-0	0-0	0-1
sberg	0-0	0-0	0-0	0-0	1-0	0-0	0-0	0-0	0-0	0-0	0-0	0-0	0-1	1-1
hiteside	0-0	0-0	0-0	0-0	0-0	0-0	0-0	0-0	0-0	0-0	0-0	0-0	0-0	1-0
tt	2-1	0-1	1-0	1-1	0-2	1-1	0-1	2-1	2-0	2-0	2-1	0-3	3-0	16-12
Totals	10-3	6-6	9-4	4-8	8-4	9-4	6-6	7-6	5-7	7-5	6-7	3-10	10-2	90-72

NO DECISIONS—Patterson.

TORONTO—74-88

tcher	Bal. W-L	Bos. W-L	Cal. W-L	Chi. W-L	Cle. W-L	Det. W-L	K.C. W-L	Mil. W-L	Min. W-L	N.Y. W-L	Oak. W-L	Sea. W-L	Tex. W-L	Totals W-L
dujar	0-0	0-0	0-0	0-0	0-0	0-0	0-0	0-1	0-0	0-0	0-0	0-0	1-0	1-1
hanon	0-0	0-0	0-0	0-0	0-0	0-0	0-0	0-1	0-0	0-0	0-0	0-0	0-0	0-1
ow	0-0	0-0	0-0	0-0	0-0	1-0	0-0	0-0	0-0	0-0	0-0	0-0	0-0	1-0
rrara	0-0	0-1	0-0	0-0	0-0	0-0	0-0	0-0	0-0	0-0	0-0	0-0	0-0	0-1
stillo	0-0	0-0	0-1	0-0	1-0	0-0	0-0	0-1	0-0	0-1	0-0	1-0	0-0	2-3

Pitcher	Bal. W-L	Bos. W-L	Cal. W-L	Chi. W-L	Cle. W-L	Det. W-L	K.C. W-L	Mil. W-L	Min. W-L	N.Y. W-L	Oak. W-L	Sea. W-L	Tex. W-L	Total W-L
Crabtree	0-0	0-1	0-1	0-0	0-0	0-0	1-0	2-0	0-0	0-0	1-1	1-0	0-0	5-
Flener	1-1	0-0	1-0	0-1	1-0	0-0	0-0	0-0	0-0	0-0	0-0	0-0	0-0	3-
Guzman	2-0	0-1	0-2	0-0	1-0	1-0	1-1	2-1	1-0	0-0	1-0	2-0	0-3	11-
Hanson	0-0	0-1	1-1	2-0	1-3	1-2	1-1	2-1	1-2	1-2	2-0	1-1	0-3	13-1
Hentgen	2-1	2-1	2-0	1-0	1-0	3-0	1-2	1-0	2-1	1-2	3-1	1-1	0-1	20-1
Janzen	0-0	1-0	0-0	1-0	0-1	0-2	0-1	0-1	1-0	1-0	0-0	0-0	0-1	4-
Quantrill	0-1	1-1	1-1	0-0	0-1	0-1	0-0	0-0	0-3	1-3	1-0	0-2	1-1	5-1
Risley	0-0	0-0	0-0	0-0	0-0	0-0	0-0	0-0	0-1	0-0	0-0	0-0	0-0	0-1
Spoljaric	0-1	0-0	0-0	0-1	0-0	1-0	1-0	0-0	0-0	0-0	0-0	0-0	0-0	2-2
Timlin	0-2	0-0	0-0	0-2	0-1	0-0	1-0	0-1	0-0	0-0	0-0	0-0	0-0	1-
Viola	0-0	0-0	0-0	0-1	0-1	0-0	0-0	0-1	0-0	0-0	0-0	0-0	0-0	1-
Ware	0-0	0-0	0-1	0-1	0-0	0-1	0-0	0-0	0-0	0-0	0-1	1-1	0-0	1-
Williams	0-2	1-1	0-0	1-1	0-0	0-0	1-0	0-0	0-0	1-0	0-0	0-0	0-1	4-
Totals	5-8	5-8	5-7	5-7	5-7	7-6	8-5	7-5	5-8	5-8	8-4	7-5	2-10	74-8

NO DECISIONS—Johnson, Silva.

HOME RUNS BY PARKS

	At Bal.	At Bos.	At Cal.	At Chi.	At Cle.	At Det.	At K.C.	At Mil.	At Min.	At N.Y.	At Oak.	At Sea.	At Tex.	At Tor.	Totals 1996	1995
Baltimore	121	6	13	9	7	16	10	13	5	7	10	18	9	13	257	173
Boston	10	121	7	5	5	11	3	7	7	1	7	12	4	9	209	175
California	9	7	104	4	8	8	7	3	6	9	12	6	5	4	192	18
Chicago	9	11	10	76	5	15	8	9	11	4	8	9	10	10	195	14
Cleveland	10	8	9	8	102	13	8	8	14	10	6	6	9	7	218	207
Detroit	6	5	6	8	2	100	13	14	6	9	*11	12	3	9	204	159
Kansas City	1	6	10	9	6	4	50	5	12	1	4	8	1	6	123	11
Milwaukee	10	6	8	5	5	1	11	82	12	3	6	12	9	8	178	12
Minnesota	3	3	5	6	2	6	4	7	61	3	4	3	7	4	118	120
New York	10	8	6	7	8	10	7	2	7	76	10	2	2	7	162	122
Oakland	9	8	17	12	9	19	1	6	12	8	*113	9	13	7	243	16
Seattle	12	9	13	6	5	10	5	13	14	10	8	121	10	9	245	18
Texas	11	11	13	7	8	8	4	7	12	5	7	7	112	9	221	13
Toronto	8	5	6	4	5	9	9	10	3	6	*9	12	4	87	177	14
1996 total	229	214	227	166	177	230	140	186	182	152	*215	237	198	189	2742	
1995 total	174	133	178	132	159	185	117	127	179	145	155	174	154	152	....	216

*There were actually 192 home runs hit at Oakland. The totals include five home runs by the Blue Jays, eight by the Tigers and 10 by the Athletics a Cashman Field, Las Vegas.

AT BALTIMORE (229):

Baltimore (121)—Palmeiro 21, Anderson 19, Alomar 14, Hoiles 13, Surhoff 12, C. Ripken 10, Bonilla 9, Murray 6, Devereaux 5, Hammonds 3, Smith Polonia 2, B. Ripken 1, Zeile 1, Tarasco 1, Zaun 1. **Boston (10)**—Vaughn 3, Canseco 2, Stanley 2, Jefferson 1, Tinsley 1, Malave 1. **California (9)**—Hudler Davis 1, Slaught 1, Velarde 1, Salmon 1, Snow 1, Edmonds 1. **Chicago (9)**—Tartabull 2, F. Thomas 2, Phillips 1, Karkovice 1, Borders 1, Ventura 1, Mouto 1. **Cleveland (10)**—Belle 5, Thome 2, Candaele 1, Burnitz 1, Giles 1. **Detroit (6)**—Higginson 2, Casanova 1, Pride 1, Nevin 1. **Kansas City (1)**—Fasano **Milwaukee (10)**—Cirillo 3, Valentin 2, Vaughn 1, Nilsson 1, Jaha 1, Mieske 1, Burnitz 1. **Minnesota (3)**—Hollins 1, Knoblauch 1, Stahoviak 1. **New York (10)**—Martinez 3, Strawberry 2, O'Neill 1, Leyritz 1, B. Williams 1, G. Williams 1, Jeter 1. **Oakland (9)**—McGwire 2, Batista 2, Steinbach 1, Bordick 1, Munc 1, Stairs 1, Lesher 1. **Seattle (12)**—Buhner 4, Rodriguez 4, E. Martinez 1, Sorrento 1, Whiten 1, Wilson 1. **Texas (11)**—Gonzalez 3, Elster 2, Palmer Gonzales 1, Tettleton 1, Newson 1, Buford 1. **Toronto (8)**—Gonzalez 3, Carter 1, Samuel 1, O'Brien 1, Brumfield 1, Delgado 1.

AT BOSTON (214):

Baltimore (6)—C. Ripken 1, Parent 1, Palmeiro 1, Surhoff 1, Anderson 1, Hoiles 1. **Boston (121)**—Vaughn 27, Canseco 17, Jefferson 12, Stanley 10, O'Lea 10, Naehring 9, Valentin 9, Haselman 5, Greenwell 4, Frye 3, Bragg 3, Garciaparra 3, Manto 2, Cordero 2, Mitchell 1, Tinsley 1, Pemberton 1, Malave 1, Rodriguez 1. **California (7)**—Salmon 2, Davis 1, Howell 1, DiSarcina 1, Edmonds 1, Anderson 1. **Chicago (11)**—F. Thomas 5, Tartabull 2, Ventura 2, Kreute 1, Norton 1. **Cleveland (8)**—Thome 2, Franco 1, Murray 1, Vizquel 1, Belle 1, Lofton 1, Ramirez 1. **Detroit (5)**—Fryman 2, Clark 2, M. Lewis 1. **Kansas Cit (6)**—Macfarlane 2, Paquette 1, Hamelin 1, Lockhart 1, Tucker 1. **Milwaukee (6)**—Cirillo 2, Vaughn 1, Levis 1, Jaha 1, Mieske 1. **Minnesota (3)**—Lawton 1, Kelly 1. **New York (8)**—B. Williams 2, Fielder 1, Duncan 1, O'Neill 1, Sierra 1, Aldrete 1, Jeter 1. **Oakland (8)**—Giambi 3, McGwire 2, Steinbach 1, Bordick 1, Brosius 1. **Seattle (9)**—Griffey 4, Buhner 1, Whiten 1, Bragg 1, R. Davis 1, Rodriguez 1. **Texas (11)**—Tettleton 2, Elster 2, Gonzalez 2, Newson 2, Valle 1, Palmer 1, Buford 1. **Toronto (5)**—Carter 3, Olerud 1, Gonzalez 1.

AT CALIFORNIA (227):

Baltimore (13)—Anderson 3, Zeile 3, Palmeiro 2, Hoiles 2, C. Ripken 1, Bonilla 1, Alomar 1. **Boston (7)**—Vaughn 2, Greenwell 1, Canseco 1, Stanley 1, Naehring 1, O'Leary 1. **California (104)**—Salmon 18, Edmonds 17, Davis 15, Velarde 8, Snow 8, Anderson 7, Hudler 6, Wallach 5, Arias 5, Howell 4, Slaugh 3, Borders 2, DiSarcina 2, Easley 1, Fabregas 1, Greene 1, Erstad 1. **Chicago (10)**—Ventura 3, Tartabull 2, F. Thomas 2, Baines 1, Phillips 1, Durham 1. **Cleveland (9)**—Thome 3, Belle 2, Murray 1, Alomar 1, Lofton 1, Ramirez 1. **Detroit (6)**—Parent 1, Fryman 1, M. Lewis 1, Curtis 1, Nieves 1, Bautista 1. **Kansas City (10)**—Tucker 3, Macfarlane 1, Offerman 1, Howard 1, Randa 1, Vitiello 1, Damon 1, Fasano 1. **Milwaukee (8)**—Vaughn 2, Valentin 2, Seitzer 1, Carr 1, Jaha 1, Cirillo 1. **Minnesota (5)**—Meares 2, Molitor 1, Myers 1, Becker 1. **New York (6)**—Martinez 2, Strawberry 1, Duncan 1, Girardi 1, Leyritz 1. **Oakland (17)**—Steinbach 3, Young 3, Giambi 2, Berroa 2, Brosius 2, McGwire 1, Herrera 1, Mashore 1, Lesher 1. **Seattle (13)**—Griffey 4, Buhner 2, Cora 1, Sorrento 1, Hollins 1, Hunter 1, Wilson 1, Pirkl 1, Rodriguez 1. **Texas (13)**—Gonzalez 5, Palmer 3, Tettleton 1, Valle 1, Hamilton 1, Buford 1, Greer 1. **Toron (6)**—Carter 4, Sprague 1, Brumfield 1.

AT CHICAGO (166):

Baltimore (9)—Anderson 2, C. Ripken 1, Surhoff 1, Murray 1, Devereaux 1, Alomar 1, Hoiles 1, Hammonds 1. **Boston (5)**—Stanley 1, Naehring 1, Jeffersc 1, Valentin 1, Malave 1. **California (4)**—Davis 1, Velarde 1, Salmon 1, Snow 1. **Chicago (76)**—F. Thomas 16, Ventura 13, Tartabull 11, Baines 9, Phillips Karkovice 5, Mouton 4, Martinez 3, Durham 3, Snopek 3, Kreuter 2, Borders 1. **Cleveland (8)**—Ramirez 2, Seitzer 1, Murray 1, Alomar 1, Baerga 1, Leius G. Pena 1. **Detroit (8)**—Fielder 2, Nevin 2, E. Williams 1, Fryman 1, Pride 1, Clark 1. **Kansas City (9)**—Paquette 3, Macfarlane 2, Lockhart 2, Hamelin 1, Rand 1. **Milwaukee (5)**—Mieske 2, Vaughn 1, Valentin 1, Newfield 1. **Minnesota (6)**—Coomer 2, Knoblauch 1, Stahoviak 1, Becker 1, Cordova 1. **New York (7)**—Martinez 3, O'Neill 1, B. Williams 1, G. Williams 1, Jeter 1. **Oakland (12)**—Steinbach 3, McGwire 2, Berroa 2, Bordick 1, Plantier 1, Munoz 1, Giambi 1, Batis 1. **Seattle (6)**—Sorrento 2, Rodriguez 2, E. Martinez 1, Hunter 1. **Texas (7)**—Tettleton 1, Clark 1, Hamilton 1, Gonzalez 1, Palmer 1, Rodriguez 1, Greer 1. **Toronto (4)**—Gonzalez 2, Olerud 1, Sprague 1.

AT CLEVELAND (177):

ltimore (7)—Bonilla 4, Anderson 1, Hoiles 1, Hammonds 1. **Boston (5)**—Canseco 1, Stanley 1, Haselman 1, Vaughn 1, Selby 1. **California (8)**—Snow 2, ught 1, Hudler 1, Velarde 1, Salmon 1, Edmonds 1, Anderson 1. **Chicago (5)**—Baines 2, Martinez 1, Ventura 1, F. Thomas 1. **Cleveland (102)**—Belle 22, mirez 19, Thome 18, Franco 7, Murray 7, Lofton 7, Baerga 5, Burnitz 4, Alomar 3, Vizquel 2, Kent 2, Giles 2, Espinoza 1, Carreon 1, Thompson 1, Wilson Detroit (2)—Nieves 1, Ausmus 1. **Kansas City (6)**—Macfarlane 2, Paquette 2, Randa 1, Sweeney 1. **Milwaukee (5)**—Seitzer 1, Vaughn 1, Nilsson 1, Jaha Valentin 1. **Minnesota (2)**—Cordova 2. **New York (8)**—Sierra 2, B. Williams 2, O'Neill 1, Martinez 1, Jeter 1, Fox 1. **Oakland (9)**—McGwire 5, Steinbach Stairs 1, Young 1. **Seattle (5)**—E. Martinez 2, Buhner 1, Griffey 1, Rodriguez 1. **Texas (8)**—Elster 3, Palmer 2, Hamilton 1, Gonzalez 1, Greer 1. **Toronto** —Olerud 2, Carter 1, Sprague 1, Gonzalez 1.

AT DETROIT (230):

ltimore (16)—C. Ripken 4, Bonilla 4, Palmeiro 2, Anderson 2, Parent 1, Devereaux 1, Hoiles 1, Zeile 1. **Boston (11)**—Stanley 2, Naehring 2, Jefferson 2, ughn 2, Greenwell 1, Haselman 1, Valentin 1. **California (8)**—Davis 3, Edmonds 2, Slaught 1, Howell 1, DiSarcina 1, Greene 1. **Chicago (15)**—Tartabull 3, nes 2, Ventura 2, F. Thomas 2, Lewis 2, Phillips 1, Guillen 1, Martinez 1, Durham 1. **Cleveland (13)**—Belle 5, Thome 3, Lofton 2, Baerga 1, Kent 1, Ramirez Ausmus 2, Trammell 1, Gomez 1, Bautista 1, Casanova 1. **Kansas City (4)**—Vitiello 2, Offerman 1, Paquette 1. **Milwaukee (1)**—Banks 1. **Minnesota (6)**— llins 2, Molitor 1, Hale 1, Stahoviak 1, Cordova 1. **New York (10)**—B. Williams 4, O'Neill 1, Sierra 1, Hayes 1, Martinez 1, Fox 1, Howard 1. **Oakland (19)**— Gwire 3, Steinbach 3, Giambi 3, Berroa 2, Munoz 2, Brosius 2, Plantier 1, Young 1, Williams 1, Batista 1. **Seattle (10)**—Wilson 3, Cora 1, Buhner 1, Jordan Griffey 1, Hunter 1, R. Davis 1, Rodriguez 1. **Texas (8)**—Elster 3, Gonzalez 1, Palmer 1, Newson 1, Rodriguez 1, Greer 1. **Toronto (9)**—Delgado 4, Sprague Carter 1, Olerud 1, Green 1.

AT KANSAS CITY (140):

ltimore (10)—Anderson 5, Hoiles 2, C. Ripken 1, Palmeiro 1, Devereaux 1. **Boston (3)**—Canseco 2, Stanley 1. **California (7)**—Wallach 2, Davis 2, Snow Salmon 1. **Chicago (8)**—Tartabull 2, F. Thomas 2, Baines 1, Karkovice 1, Martinez 1, Snopek 1. **Cleveland (8)**—Belle 2, Ramirez 2, Alomar 1, Vizquel 1, ome 1, Wilson 1. **Detroit (13)**—Fryman 2, Nieves 2, Pride 2, Fielder 1, Curtis 1, Easley 1, Higginson 1, Clark 1, Bartee 1, Casanova 1. **Kansas City (50)**— quette 12, Macfarlane 9, Young 4, Lockhart 4, Howard 3, Vitiello 3, Damon 3, Hamelin 2, Randa 2, Tucker 2, Nunnally 2, Offerman 1, Sweeney 1, Fasano Myers 1. **Milwaukee (11)**—Vaughn 4, Jaha 4, Seitzer 1, Nilsson 1, Mieske 1. **Minnesota (4)**—Lawton 2, Knoblauch 1, Meares 1. **New York (7)**—Fielder O'Neill 2, Leyritz 1, B. Williams 1, Jeter 1. **Oakland (1)**—Giambi 1. **Seattle (5)**—E. Martinez 1, Griffey 1, Hollins 1, Whiten 1, Wilson 1. **Texas (4)**—Elster Gonzalez 1, Palmer 1, Rodriguez 1. **Toronto (9)**—Sprague 3, Samuel 1, Olerud 1, Cedeno 1, Delgado 1, Green 1, Gonzalez 1.

AT MILWAUKEE (186):

ltimore (13)—Palmeiro 3, Hammonds 3, Surhoff 2, Alomar 2, Bonilla 1, Murray 1, Anderson 1. **Boston (7)**—Jefferson 2, Stanley 1, Vaughn 1, Frye 1, sley 1, O'Leary 1. **California (3)**—Wallach 1, Edmonds 1, Erstad 1. **Chicago (9)**—F. Thomas 3, Ventura 2, Guillen 1, Martinez 1, Borders 1, Mouton 1. veland (8)—Ramirez 2, Franco 1, Espinoza 1, Alomar 1, Vizquel 1, Thome 1, Lofton 1. **Detroit (14)**—Nieves 5, Curtis 2, Nevin 2, Clark 2, Fielder 1, Ausmus Higginson 1. **Kansas City (5)**—Fasano 2, Young 1, Hamelin 1, Tucker 1. **Milwaukee (82)**—Jaha 17, Vaughn 16, Valentin 10, Mieske 9, Cirillo 6, Seitzer 5, theny 5, Newfield 4, Nilsson 3, Vina 3, Ward 2, Listach 1, Burnitz 1. **Minnesota (7)**—Coomer 2, Kelly 1, Myers 1, Knoblauch 1, Becker 1, Lawton 1. **New** rk (2)—Sierra 1, B. Williams 1. **Oakland (6)**—Berroa 2, Young 2, McGwire 1, Williams 1. **Seattle (13)**—Buhner 5, Griffey 3, Wilson 2, Rodriguez 2, Hunter exas (7)—Gonzalez 3, Tettleton 1, Hamilton 1, Palmer 1, Rodriguez 1. **Toronto (10)**—O'Brien 3, Delgado 2, R. Perez 2, Carter 1, Olerud 1, Sprague 1.

AT MINNESOTA (182):

timore (5)—Surhoff 2, Bonilla 1, Alomar 1, Hammonds 1. **Boston (7)**—Stanley 2, Vaughn 2, O'Leary 1, Pozo 1, Selby 1. **California (6)**—Salmon 3, Howell Easley 1, Erstad 1. **Chicago (11)**—Tartabull 2, Ventura 2, Durham 2, Baines 1, Martinez 1, Mouton 1, Snopek 1, Norton 1. **Cleveland (14)**—Belle 3, Ramirez Thome 2, Espinoza 1, Carreon 1, Alomar 1, Lofton 1, Burnitz 1, Giles 1. **Detroit (6)**—Fielder 2, Curtis 2, E. Williams 1, Clark 1. **Kansas City (12)**—Tucker Young 2, Hamelin 2, Macfarlane 1, Goodwin 1, Paquette 1, Vitiello 1, Damon 1. **Milwaukee (12)**—Nilsson 6, Jaha 2, Valentin 2, Vina 1, Newfield 1. nnesota (61)—Cordova 10, Stahoviak 8, Becker 8, Knoblauch 7, Molitor 6, Hollins 6, Coomer 5, Kelly 3, Myers 3, Meares 3, Walbeck 1, Lawton 1. **New** rk (7)—B. Williams 3, Sierra 2, O'Neill 1, Leyritz 1. **Oakland (12)**—McGwire 4, Berroa 2, Plantier 2, Lovullo 1, Stairs 1, Gates 1, Young 1, Williams 1, Lesher **Seattle (14)**—Griffey 4, E. Martinez 2, Whiten 2, Wilson 2, Cora 1, Buhner 1, Bragg 1, Rodriguez 1. **Texas (12)**—Palmer 3, Elster 2, Gonzalez 2, Greer 2, le 1, Clark 1, Newson 1. **Toronto (3)**—Sprague 1, Delgado 1, Gonzalez 1.

AT NEW YORK (152):

timore (7)—Palmeiro 3, C. Ripken 1, Bonilla 1, Anderson 1, Alomar 1. **Boston (1)**—Haselman 1. **California (9)**—Davis 3, Velarde 2, Hudler 1, Howell 1, mon 1, Fabregas 1. **Chicago (4)**—Baines 1, Karkovice 1, Ventura 1, Lewis 1. **Cleveland (10)**—Thome 3, Ramirez 2, Murray 1, Vizquel 1, Belle 1, Baerga Burnitz 1. **Detroit (9)**—Fielder 2, Fryman 2, Sierra 1, Cedeno 1, Easley 1, Nieves 1, Higginson 1. **Kansas City (1)**—Offerman 1. **Milwaukee (3)**—Seitzer 1, a 1, Valentin 1. **Minnesota (3)**—Hollins 2, Meares 1. **New York (76)**—B. Williams 12, Fielder 9, Martinez 9, Strawberry 8, Raines 7, O'Neill 7, Duncan 5, rra 4, Leyritz 3, G. Williams 3, Jeter 3, Boggs 2, Aldrete 2, Girardi 1, Fox 1. **Oakland (8)**—Berroa 3, McGwire 2, Lovullo 2, Stairs 1. **Seattle (10)**—Buhner Griffey 2, Sorrento 2, Rodriguez 2, Whiten 1. **Texas (5)**—Palmer 2, Gonzalez 1, Rodriguez 1, Greer 1. **Toronto (6)**—Sprague 3, Carter 1, Gonzalez 1, rtinez 1.

AT OAKLAND (215):

timore (10)—Hoiles 3, Palmeiro 2, Surhoff 2, Bonilla 1, Murray 1, Alomar 1. **Boston (7)**—Mitchell 1, Canseco 1, Vaughn 1, O'Leary 1, Selby 1, Malave 1, ciaparra 1. **California (12)**—Snow 3, Davis 2, Hudler 2, Edmonds 2, Salmon 1, Anderson 1, Erstad 1. **Chicago (8)**—F. Thomas 3, Baines 1, Phillips 1, kovice 1, Durham 1, Snopek 1. **Cleveland (6)**—Belle 3, Thome 2, Lofton 1. **Detroit (11)**—Higginson 5, Fielder 2, Fryman 2, Curtis 1, Nieves 1. **Kansas** y (4)—Macfarlane 1, Randa 1, Nunnally 1, Sweeney 1. **Milwaukee (6)**—Jaha 1, Valentin 1, Newfield 1, Matheny 1, Cirillo 1, Loretta 1. **Minnesota (4)**— ers 1, Knoblauch 1, Coomer 1, Cordova 1. **New York (10)**—O'Neill 3, Martinez 3, Fielder 1, Hayes 1, B. Williams 1, R. Rivera 1. **Oakland (113)**—McGwire Berroa 21, Steinbach 16, Brosius 15, Young 10, Giambi 6, Stairs 5, Plantier 3, Herrera 3, Bordick 2, Munoz 2, Lesher 2, Gates 1, Batista 1, Mashore 1, ezio 1. **Seattle (8)**—Buhner 2, Whiten 2, Griffey 1, Sorrento 1, Hunter 1, Rodriguez 1. **Texas (7)**—Tettleton 2, McLemore 2, Elster 1, Gonzalez 1, Rodriguez oronto (9)—Sprague 3, Samuel 1, Olerud 1, Brumfield 1, Cedeno 1, Delgado 1, Gonzalez 1. **Note:** The Tigers actually hit three home runs at Oakland. ee home runs by Higginson, two by Fryman and one each by Curtis, Fielder and Nieves were hit at Las Vegas. The Athletics actually hit 103 homers at kland. Three home runs by Brosius, two each by Berroa, Plantier and Steinbach, and one by Stairs were hit at Las Vegas. The Blue Jays actually hit four ne runs at Oakland. Cedeno, Delgado, Gonzalez, Olerud and Sprague each hit one homer at Las Vegas.

AT SEATTLE (237):

timore (18)—Anderson 5, C. Ripken 4, Bonilla 4, Incaviglia 2, Palmeiro 1, Murray 1, B. Ripken 1. **Boston (12)**—Greenwell 2, Naehring 2, Cuyler 2, Vaughn Canseco 1, Stanley 1, Jefferson 1, Hosey 1. **California (6)**—Hudler 2, Aldrete 2, Velarde 1, Edmonds 1. **Chicago (9)**—F. Thomas 3, Phillips 1, Guillen 1, kovice 1, Martinez 1, Ventura 1, Durham 1. **Cleveland (6)**—Franco 2, T. Pena 1, Murray 1, Vizquel 1, Belle 1. **Detroit (12)**—Fielder 3, Clark 3, Nieves 2, ent 1, Fryman 1, M. Lewis 1, Higginson 1. **Kansas City (8)**—Macfarlane 1, Offerman 1, Young 1, Paquette 1, Hamelin 1, Tucker 1, Sweeney 1, Fasano 1. waukee (12)—Vaughn 3, Nilsson 3, Jaha 3, Seitzer 2, Matheny 1. **Minnesota (3)**—Hollins 1, Walbeck 1, Meares 1. **New York (2)**—Martinez 1, Jeter 1. kland (9)—McGwire 5, Steinbach 2, Herrera 2, Batista 1, Spiezio 1. **Seattle (121)**—Griffey 26, Buhner 21, Rodriguez 18, E. Martinez 14, Sorrento 13, son 7, Whiten 4, Bragg 4, R. Davis 3, Cora 2, Strange 2, Hunter 2, Sojo 1, Hollins 1, Manto 1, Amaral 1, Diaz 1. **Texas (7)**—Gonzalez 3, Tettleton 1, Elster Rodriguez 1, Greer 1. **Toronto (12)**—Carter 4, Sprague 2, Delgado 2, Samuel 1, Olerud 1, Brumfield 1, Green 1.

AT TEXAS (198):

timore (9)—Anderson 5, Palmeiro 2, C. Ripken 1, Hoiles 1. **Boston (4)**—Canseco 1, Stanley 1, Naehring 1, Vaughn 1. **California (5)**—Hudler 1, DiSarcina almon 1, Anderson 1, Arias 1. **Chicago (10)**—Baines 3, Ventura 3, Tartabull 1, Martinez 1, Martin 1, Durham 1. **Cleveland (9)**—Franco 2, Alomar 2, Belle

2, Baerga 1, Thome 1, Giles 1. **Detroit (3)**—E. Williams 1, Fryman 1, Pride 1. **Kansas City (1)**—Tucker 1. **Milwaukee (9)**—Jaha 2, Vina 2, Vaughn 1, Nilss̲ 1, Valentin 1, Matheny 1, Cirillo 1. **Minnesota (7)**—Stahoviak 2, Molitor 1, Hollins 1, Knoblauch 1, Becker 1, Cordova 1. **New York (2)**—O'Neill 1, B. Willia̲ 1. **Oakland (13)**—McGwire 3, Steinbach 3, Brosius 2, Giambi 2, Berroa 1, Battle 1, Mashore 1. **Seattle (10)**—E. Martinez 4, Buhner 2, Sorrento 2, Bragg̲ Rodriguez 1. **Texas (112)**—Gonzalez 23, Palmer 19, Tettleton 14, Rodriguez 10, Elster 9, Clark 9, Greer 9, Newson 5, McLemore 3, Buford 3, Hamiltor̲ Stevens 2, Gonzales 1, Stillwell 1, Worthington 1, Ortiz 1. **Toronto (4)**—O'Brien 1, Sprague 1, Delgado 1, Green 1.

AT TORONTO (189):

Baltimore (13)—Anderson 5, C. Ripken 2, Bonilla 2, Palmeiro 1, Surhoff 1, Alomar 1, Smith 1. **Boston (9)**—Vaughn 2, Valentin 2, Canseco 1, Stanley̲ Naehring 1, Cordero 1, O'Leary 1. **California (4)**—Davis 1, Aldrete 1, Edmonds 1, Anderson 1. **Chicago (10)**—Ventura 3, Tartabull 2, Baines 1, Phillips̲ Guillen 1, F. Thomas 1, Lewis 1. **Cleveland (7)**—Vizquel 2, Franco 1, Espinoza 1, Alomar 1, Belle 1, Baerga 1. **Detroit (9)**—Fielder 4, Flaherty 2, Paren̲ Curtis 1, Nieves 1. **Kansas City (6)**—Nunnally 2, Paquette 1, Hamelin 1, Vitiello 1, Damon 1. **Milwaukee (8)**—Valentin 3, Seitzer 1, Vaughn 1, Nilsson 1, V̲ 1, Cirillo 1. **Minnesota (4)**—Coomer 2, Kelly 1, Hocking 1. **New York (7)**—Raines 2, Martinez 2, Duncan 1, Jeter 1, R. Rivera 1. **Oakland (7)**—McGwire̲ Steinbach 1, Berroa 1, Stairs 1, Young 1, Giambi 1. **Seattle (9)**—Griffey 2, Cora 1, Buhner 1, E. Martinez 1, Strange 1, Sorrento 1, Wilson 1, Rodriguez̲ **Texas (9)**—Clark 2, Palmer 2, Rodriguez 2, Tettleton 1, Stevens 1, Greer 1. **Toronto (87)**—Sprague 17, Carter 14, Delgado 12, Olerud 9, O'Brien 8, Brumf̲ 8, Green 7, Samuel 4, Gonzalez 3, Martinez 2, Nixon 1, T. Perez 1, Brito 1.

1996 N.L. STATISTICS

atting

inch-hitting

itching

elding

iscellaneous

BATTING

TEAM

Team	Avg.	G	TPA	AB	R	H	TB	2B	3B	HR	RBI	SH	SF	HP	BB	IBB	SO	SB	CS	GDP	LOB	ShO	Slg.	OB
Colorado	.287	162	6333	5590	961	1607	2641	297	37	221	909	81	52	82	527	40	1108	201	66	118	1108	4	.472	.35
Atlanta	.270	162	6293	5614	773	1514	2425	264	28	197	735	69	50	27	530	41	1032	83	43	144	1154	8	.432	.33
New York	.270	162	6220	5618	746	1515	2317	267	47	147	697	75	49	33	445	54	1069	97	48	114	1124	7	.412	.32
St. Louis	.267	162	6177	5502	759	1468	2237	281	31	142	711	88	48	44	495	59	1089	149	58	121	1087	7	.407	.33
Pittsburgh	.266	162	6336	5665	776	1509	2308	319	33	138	738	72	49	40	510	46	989	126	49	107	1181	6	.407	.32
San Diego	.265	162	6419	5655	771	1499	2273	285	24	147	718	59	52	50	601	62	1014	109	55	146	1209	11	.402	.33
Houston	.262	162	6270	5508	753	1445	2187	297	29	129	703	68	55	84	554	61	1057	180	63	115	1172	10	.397	.33
Montreal	.262	162	6171	5505	741	1441	2236	297	27	148	696	79	36	58	492	49	1077	108	34	119	1119	8	.406	.32
Florida	.257	162	6194	5498	688	1413	2163	240	30	150	650	41	45	55	553	51	1122	99	46	138	1171	14	.393	.32
Cincinnati	.256	162	6213	5455	778	1398	2302	259	36	191	733	71	49	34	604	47	1134	171	63	115	1116	6	.422	.33
Philadelphia	.256	162	6171	5499	650	1405	2128	249	39	132	604	54	37	45	536	52	1092	117	41	116	1207	8	.387	.32
San Francisco	.253	162	6316	5533	752	1400	2146	245	21	153	707	77	43	48	615	62	1189	113	53	108	1198	12	.388	.33
Los Angeles	.252	162	6185	5538	703	1396	2127	215	33	150	661	74	35	22	516	59	1190	124	40	112	1113	12	.384	.3?
Chicago	.251	162	6229	5531	772	1388	2218	267	19	175	725	66	48	61	523	48	1090	108	50	126	1078	4	.401	.32
Totals	.262	1134	87527	77711	10623	20398	31708	3782	434	2220	9987	974	648	683	7501	734	15252	1785	709	1699	16037	117	.408	.33

INDIVIDUAL

TOP QUALIFIERS FOR BATTING CHAMPIONSHIP

Minimum 502 plate appearances. *Lefthanded batter. †Switch-hitter.

Player, Team	Avg.	G	TPA	AB	R	H	TB	2B	3B	HR	RBI	SH	SF	HP	BB	IBB	SO	SB	CS	GDP	Slg.	C
Gwynn, Tony, San Diego*‡	.353	116	498	451	67	159	199	27	2	3	50	1	6	1	39	12	17	11	4	17	.441	
Burks, Ellis, Colorado	.344	156	685	613	142	211	392	45	8	40	128	3	2	6	61	2	114	32	6	19	.639	
Piazza, Mike, Los Angeles	.336	148	631	547	87	184	308	16	0	36	105	0	2	1	81	21	93	0	3	21	.563	
Johnson, Lance, New York*	.333	160	724	682	117	227	327	31	21	9	69	3	5	1	33	8	40	50	12	8	.479	
Grace, Mark, Chicago*	.331	142	616	547	88	181	249	39	1	9	75	0	6	1	62	8	41	2	3	18	.455	
Caminiti, Ken, San Diego†	.326	146	639	546	109	178	339	37	2	40	130	0	10	4	78	16	99	11	5	15	.621	
Young, Eric, Colorado	.324	141	643	568	113	184	239	23	4	8	74	2	5	21	47	1	31	53	19	9	.421	
Gilkey, Bernard, New York	.317	153	656	571	108	181	321	44	3	30	117	0	8	4	73	7	125	17	9	18	.562	
Bagwell, Jeff, Houston	.315	162	719	568	111	179	324	48	2	31	120	0	6	10	135	20	114	21	7	15	.570	
Sheffield, Gary, Florida	.314	161	677	519	118	163	324	33	1	42	120	0	6	10	142	19	66	16	9	16	.624	
Bichette, Dante, Colorado	.313	159	694	633	114	198	336	39	3	31	141	0	10	6	45	4	105	31	12	18	.531	
Morris, Hal, Cincinnati*	.313	142	594	528	82	165	253	32	4	16	80	5	6	5	50	5	76	7	5	12	.479	
Jordan, Brian, St. Louis	.310	140	560	513	82	159	248	36	1	17	104	2	9	7	29	4	84	22	5	6	.483	
Jones, Chipper, Atlanta†	.309	157	693	598	114	185	317	32	5	30	110	1	7	0	87	0	88	14	1	14	.530	
Grissom, Marquis, Atlanta	.308	158	723	671	106	207	328	32	10	23	74	4	4	3	41	6	73	28	11	12	.489	
Bonds, Barry, San Francisco*	.308	158	675	517	122	159	318	27	3	42	129	0	6	1	151	30	76	40	7	11	.615	

‡Gwynn's 498 plate appearances were four short of the qualifying mark. If, however, under Rule 10.23 (a), Gwynn were charged with four more at-bats, his subsequent batting average of .349 would still be higher than the next-highest mark of .344, achieved by Ellis Burks.

DEPARTMENTAL LEADERS: G—Bagwell, Hou., Biggio, Hou., 162; AB—Johnson, N.Y., 682; R—Burks, Col., 142; H—Johnson, N.Y., 227; TB—Burks, Col., 392; 1B— Johnson, N.Y., 166; 2B—Bagwell, Hou., 48; 3B—Johnson, N.Y., 21; HR—Galarraga, Col., 47; RBI—Galarraga, Col., 150; SH—Martinez, Mon., Neagle, Pit.-Atl., 16; SF— Bichette, Col., Caminiti, S.D., Wilkins, Hou.-S.F., 10; HP—Biggio, Hou., 27; BB—Bonds, S.F., 151; IBB—Bonds, S.F., 30; SO—Rodriguez, Mon., 160; SB—Young, C... 53; CS—Young, Col., 19; GIDP—Karros, L.A., 27; Slg. Pct.—Burks, Col., .639; OB. Pct.—Sheffield, Fla., .465;

ALL PLAYERS

*Lefthanded batter. †Switch-hitter.

Player, Team	Avg.	G	TPA	AB	R	H	TB	2B	3B	HR	RBI	SH	SF	HP	BB	IBB	SO	SB	CS	GDP	Slg.	O
Abbott, Kurt, Florida	.253	109	349	320	37	81	137	18	7	8	33	4	0	3	22	1	99	3	3	7	.428	.3
Abreu, Bob, Houston*	.227	15	24	22	1	5	6	1	0	0	1	0	0	0	2	0	3	0	0	1	.273	.2
Adams, Terry, Chicago	.000	69	7	6	0	0	0	0	0	0	0	0	0	0	0	1	0	3	0	0	.000	.1
Alfonzo, Edgardo, New York	.261	123	407	368	36	96	127	15	2	4	40	9	5	0	25	2	56	2	0	8	.345	.3
Alicea, Luis, St. Louis†	.258	129	447	380	54	98	145	26	3	5	42	4	6	5	52	10	78	11	3	4	.382	.3
Allensworth, Jermaine, Pit.	.262	61	260	229	32	60	87	9	3	4	31	2	2	4	23	0	50	11	6	2	.380	.3
Alou, Moises, Montreal	.281	143	598	540	87	152	247	28	2	21	96	0	7	2	49	7	83	9	4	15	.457	.3
Alston, Garvin, Colorado	.000	6	1	1	0	0	0	0	0	0	0	0	0	0	0	0	0	0	0	0	.000	.0
Alvarez, Tavo, Montreal	.500	11	5	4	0	2	2	0	0	0	0	1	0	0	0	0	1	0	0	0	.500	.5
Amaro, Ruben, Philadelphia†	.316	61	130	117	14	37	53	10	0	2	15	1	0	3	9	0	18	0	0	3	.453	.3
Andrews, Shane, Montreal	.227	127	414	375	43	85	161	15	2	19	64	0	2	2	35	8	119	3	1	2	.429	.2
Anthony, Eric, Cin.-Col.*	.243	79	218	185	32	45	89	8	0	12	22	0	1	0	32	2	56	0	2	3	.481	.3
Arias, Alex, Florida	.277	100	246	224	27	62	86	11	2	3	26	1	1	3	17	1	28	2	0	2	.384	.3
Ashby, Andy, San Diego	.244	25	55	45	6	11	16	5	0	0	5	9	1	0	0	0	13	0	0	0	.356	.2
Ashley, Billy, Los Angeles	.200	71	133	110	18	22	53	2	1	9	25	0	1	1	21	1	44	0	0	3	.482	.3
Astacio, Pedro, Los Angeles	.088	35	77	68	1	6	6	0	0	0	3	8	0	0	1	0	20	0	0	0	.088	.1
Aude, Rich, Pittsburgh	.250	7	16	16	0	4	4	0	0	0	1	0	0	0	0	0	8	0	0	0	.250	.2
Aurilia, Rich, San Francisco	.239	105	352	318	27	76	94	7	1	3	26	6	2	1	25	2	52	4	1	1	.296	.2
Ausmus, Brad, San Diego	.181	50	166	149	16	27	37	3	0	1	13	1	0	3	13	0	27	1	4	4	.228	.2
Avery, Steve, Atlanta*	.239	24	50	46	5	11	23	4	1	2	11	1	2	0	1	0	12	0	0	1	.500	.2
Ayrault, Joe, Atlanta	.200	7	6	5	0	1	1	0	0	0	0	0	0	0	0	0	1	0	0	1	.200	.3
Baerga, Carlos, New York†	.193	26	91	83	5	16	25	3	0	2	11	0	1	2	5	0	2	0	0	0	.301	.2
Bagwell, Jeff, Houston	.315	162	719	568	111	179	324	48	2	31	120	0	6	10	135	20	114	21	7	15	.570	.4
Bailey, Cory, St. Louis	.000	51	4	1	2	0	0	0	0	0	0	0	0	1	0	2	0	0	0	0	.000	.6
Bailey, Roger, Colorado	.263	24	25	19	4	5	10	0	1	1	5	3	0	0	3	0	4	0	0	0	.526	.3
Barberie, Bret, Chicago†	.034	15	37	29	4	1	4	0	0	1	2	3	0	5	0	0	11	0	1	0	.138	.1

1996 N.L. STATISTICS · Batting

yer, Team	Avg.	G	TPA	AB	R	H	TB	2B	3B	HR	RBI	SH	SF	HP	BB	IBB	SO	SB	CS	GDP	Slg.	OBP
rron, Tony, Montreal	.000	1	1	1	0	0	0	0	0	0	0	0	0	0	0	0	1	0	0	0	.000	.000
cchelor, Richard, St. Louis	.000	11	1	1	0	0	0	0	0	0	0	0	0	0	0	0	1	0	0	0	.000	.000
es, Jason, Colorado†	.206	88	187	160	19	33	46	8	1	1	9	1	1	2	23	1	34	2	1	7	.288	.312
iste, Kim, San Francisco	.208	54	136	130	17	27	42	6	0	3	11	0	1	0	5	1	33	3	3	4	.323	.235
tle, Howard, Philadelphia	.000	5	5	5	0	0	0	0	0	0	0	0	0	0	0	0	2	0	0	0	.000	.000
utista, Danny, Atlanta	.150	17	23	20	1	3	3	0	0	0	1	0	0	1	2	0	5	0	0	3	.150	.261
utista, Jose, San Francisco	.111	37	10	9	1	1	1	0	0	0	0	1	0	0	0	0	4	0	0	0	.111	.111
amon, Trey, Pittsburgh*	.216	24	56	51	7	11	13	2	0	0	6	1	0	0	4	0	6	1	1	0	.255	.273
ck, Rod, San Francisco	.333	63	3	3	0	1	1	0	0	0	0	1	0	0	0	0	2	0	0	0	.333	.333
ech, Matt, Philadelphia*	.071	8	14	14	1	1	1	0	0	0	0	0	0	0	0	0	4	0	0	0	.071	.071
k, Tim, Cincinnati	.200	7	16	15	2	3	3	0	0	0	0	0	0	0	1	0	2	0	0	0	.200	.250
l, David, St. Louis	.214	62	157	145	12	31	40	6	0	1	9	0	1	1	10	2	22	1	1	3	.276	.268
l, Derek, Houston	.263	158	684	627	84	165	262	40	3	17	113	0	9	8	40	8	123	29	3	18	.418	.311
l, Jay, Pittsburgh	.250	151	598	527	65	132	206	29	3	13	71	6	6	5	54	5	108	6	4	10	.391	.323
liard, Rafael, Atlanta	.169	87	148	142	9	24	31	7	0	0	3	3	1	0	2	0	22	3	1	6	.218	.179
hard, Marvin, San Francisco*	.248	135	558	488	89	121	161	17	4	5	27	6	1	4	59	2	84	25	11	8	.330	.333
nes, Alan, St. Louis	.148	34	70	61	4	9	12	3	0	0	5	7	0	0	2	0	25	0	0	1	.197	.175
nes, Andy, St. Louis	.151	36	85	73	5	11	15	4	0	0	6	9	2	0	1	0	37	0	0	0	.205	.158
nitez, Yamil, Montreal	.167	11	12	12	0	2	2	0	0	0	2	0	0	0	0	0	4	0	0	0	.167	.167
njamin, Mike, Philadelphia	.223	35	118	103	13	23	42	5	1	4	13	1	0	2	12	5	21	3	1	2	.408	.316
nnett, Gary, Philadelphia	.250	6	18	16	0	4	4	0	0	0	1	0	0	0	2	1	6	0	0	0	.250	.333
rgman, Sean, San Diego	.100	43	30	30	1	3	6	0	0	1	5	0	0	0	0	0	9	0	0	0	.200	.100
rry, Sean, Houston	.281	132	469	431	55	121	212	38	1	17	95	2	4	9	23	1	58	12	6	11	.492	.328
hette, Dante, Colorado	.313	159	694	633	114	198	336	39	3	31	141	0	10	6	45	4	105	31	12	18	.531	.359
lecki, Mike, Atlanta	.100	40	12	10	1	1	1	0	0	0	1	0	0	0	2	0	5	0	0	0	.100	.250
gio, Craig, Houston	.288	162	723	605	113	174	251	24	4	15	75	8	8	27	75	0	72	25	7	10	.415	.386
ir, Willie, San Diego	.000	60	3	3	0	0	0	0	0	0	0	0	0	0	0	0	1	0	0	0	.000	.000
user, Jeff, Atlanta	.245	83	312	265	48	65	111	14	1	10	35	0	1	6	40	3	54	6	0	7	.419	.356
zier, Ron, Philadelphia	1.000	27	1	1	0	1	1	0	0	0	0	0	0	0	0	0	0	0	0	0	1.000	1.000
wers, Mike, Los Angeles	.265	92	358	317	31	84	125	19	2	6	38	0	3	1	37	2	77	0	0	11	.394	.341
ever, Joe, Pittsburgh	.000	13	1	1	0	0	0	0	0	0	0	0	0	0	0	0	1	0	0	0	.000	.000
gar, Tim, New York	.213	91	104	89	17	19	23	4	0	0	6	3	2	2	8	0	20	1	3	0	.258	.287
nds, Barry, San Francisco*	.308	158	675	517	122	159	318	27	3	42	129	0	6	1	151	30	76	40	7	11	.615	.461
one, Bret, Cincinnati	.233	142	568	520	56	121	184	21	3	12	69	5	9	3	31	0	100	3	2	9	.354	.275
oty, Josh, Florida	.500	2	2	2	1	1	1	0	0	0	0	0	0	0	0	0	0	0	0	1	.500	.500
rbon, Pedro, Atlanta*	1.000	43	1	1	0	1	1	0	0	0	0	0	0	0	0	0	0	0	0	0	1.000	1.000
rders, Pat, St. Louis	.319	26	71	69	3	22	25	3	0	0	4	1	0	0	1	0	14	0	1	1	.362	.329
land, Toby, Philadelphia	.000	69	4	4	0	0	0	0	0	0	0	0	0	0	0	0	2	0	0	0	.000	.000
owski, Joe, Atlanta	.000	22	3	2	0	0	0	0	0	0	0	0	1	0	0	0	1	0	0	0	.000	.000
talico, Ricky, Philadelphia*	.333	61	3	3	0	1	2	1	0	0	0	0	0	0	0	0	2	0	0	0	.667	.333
ttenfield, Kent, Chicago	.500	48	3	2	0	1	1	0	0	0	0	0	0	0	1	0	0	0	0	0	.500	.500
urgeois, Steve, San Francisco	.273	15	14	11	1	3	5	2	0	0	1	1	0	0	2	0	2	0	0	0	.455	.385
dshaw, Terry, St. Louis*	.333	15	25	21	4	7	8	1	0	0	3	1	0	0	3	0	2	0	1	0	.381	.417
nson, Jeff, Cincinnati*	.244	129	353	311	34	76	127	16	4	9	37	7	3	1	31	4	67	2	0	9	.408	.312
ntley, Jeff, Cincinnati	.000	66	2	1	0	0	0	0	0	0	0	0	1	0	0	0	0	0	0	0	.000	.000
to, Jorge, Colorado	.071	8	18	14	1	1	1	0	0	0	0	0	0	2	1	0	8	0	0	0	.071	.235
cail, Doug, Houston*	.000	25	11	11	0	0	0	0	0	0	0	0	0	0	0	0	4	0	0	0	.000	.000
gna, Rico, New York*	.255	55	211	188	18	48	81	10	1	7	30	0	4	0	19	1	50	0	0	4	.431	.318
oks, Jerry, Florida	.400	8	7	5	2	2	4	0	0	1	3	0	0	1	1	0	1	0	0	0	.800	.571
wn, Brant, Chicago*	.304	29	73	69	11	21	37	1	0	5	9	0	1	1	2	1	17	3	3	1	.536	.329
wn, Kevin, Florida	.120	34	85	75	1	9	10	1	0	0	3	4	0	0	6	0	28	0	0	1	.133	.185
mfield, Jacob, Pittsburgh	.250	29	86	80	11	20	35	9	0	2	8	0	1	0	5	1	17	3	1	4	.438	.291
lett, Scott, Chicago*	.212	109	177	165	26	35	49	5	0	3	16	1	1	0	10	0	54	7	3	2	.297	.256
linger, Jim, Chicago	.250	38	41	32	8	8	17	3	0	2	6	3	0	1	5	0	11	0	0	0	.531	.368
ba, Dave, Cincinnati	.104	34	73	67	3	7	13	0	0	2	5	3	0	0	3	0	26	0	0	2	.194	.143
ke, John, Colorado†	.500	11	2	2	0	1	1	0	0	0	1	0	0	0	0	0	0	0	0	0	.500	.500
kett, John, Florida	.173	24	55	52	2	9	11	2	0	0	1	3	0	0	0	0	17	0	0	0	.212	.173
ks, Ellis, Colorado	.344	156	685	613	142	211	392	45	8	40	128	3	2	6	61	2	114	32	6	19	.639	.408
sby, Mike, St. Louis	.500	2	2	2	0	1	1	0	0	0	0	0	0	0	0	0	1	0	0	0	.500	.500
sch, Mike, Los Angeles	.217	38	88	83	8	18	34	4	0	4	17	0	0	0	5	0	33	0	0	2	.410	.261
ler, Brett, Los Angeles*	.267	34	145	131	22	35	38	1	1	0	8	1	3	1	9	0	22	8	3	1	.290	.313
d, Paul, New York	.000	38	2	2	0	0	0	0	0	0	0	0	0	0	0	0	0	0	0	0	.000	.000
niniti, Ken, San Diego†	.326	146	639	546	109	178	339	37	2	40	130	0	10	4	78	16	99	11	5	15	.621	.408
mpbell, Mike, Chicago	.364	13	12	11	2	4	6	2	0	0	1	1	0	0	0	0	5	0	0	0	.545	.364
ndiotti, Tom, Los Angeles	.089	28	56	45	3	4	4	0	0	0	2	9	1	1	0	0	14	0	0	1	.089	.106
ngelosi, John, Houston†	.263	108	313	262	49	69	91	11	4	1	16	1	1	5	44	0	41	17	9	4	.347	.378
nizaro, Jay, San Francisco	.200	43	132	120	11	24	36	4	1	2	8	1	1	1	9	0	38	0	2	5	.300	.260
lson, Dan, San Francisco	.000	5	1	1	0	0	0	0	0	0	0	0	0	0	0	0	1	0	0	0	.000	.000
rara, Giovanni, Cincinnati	.000	8	7	7	1	0	0	0	0	0	0	0	0	0	0	0	1	0	0	0	.000	.000
rasco, Hector, Cincinnati	.200	56	5	5	0	1	1	0	0	0	0	0	0	0	0	0	4	0	0	0	.200	.200
reon, Mark, San Francisco	.260	81	319	292	40	76	131	22	3	9	51	0	2	3	22	2	33	2	3	6	.449	.317
stellano, Pedro, Colorado	.118	13	21	17	1	2	2	0	0	0	2	0	0	1	3	1	6	0	0	0	.118	.286
stilla, Vinny, Colorado	.304	160	673	629	97	191	345	34	0	40	113	0	4	5	35	7	88	7	2	20	.548	.343
stillo, Alberto, New York	.364	6	11	11	1	4	4	0	0	0	0	0	0	0	0	0	4	0	0	0	.364	.364
stillo, Frank, Chicago	.088	33	63	57	1	5	5	0	0	0	2	4	0	0	2	0	21	0	0	0	.088	.119
stillo, Luis, Florida†	.262	41	180	164	26	43	50	2	1	1	8	2	0	0	14	0	46	17	4	0	.305	.320
stro, Juan, Los Angeles	.197	70	146	132	16	26	37	5	3	0	5	4	0	0	10	0	27	1	0	3	.280	.254
deno, Andujar, S.D.-Hou	.231	52	169	156	11	36	49	2	1	3	18	0	1	1	11	2	33	3	2	7	.314	.284
deno, Roger, Los Angeles†.	.246	86	238	211	26	52	71	11	1	2	18	2	0	1	24	0	47	5	1	0	.336	.326
avez, Raul, Montreal	.200	4	6	5	1	1	1	0	0	0	0	0	0	0	1	0	1	1	0	1	.200	.333
istiansen, Jason, Pittsburgh	.000	33	5	4	0	0	0	0	0	0	0	0	1	0	0	0	4	0	0	0	.000	.000
nfrocco, Archi, San Diego	.281	79	204	192	21	54	79	13	3	2	32	0	1	2	8	0	56	1	0	4	.411	.315
rk, Dave, Pit.-L.A.*	.270	107	261	226	28	61	101	12	2	8	36	0	1	0	34	3	53	2	1	6	.447	.364

1996 N.L. STATISTICS Batting

Player, Team	Avg.	G	TPA	AB	R	H	TB	2B	3B	HR	RBI	SH	SF	HP	BB	IBB	SO	SB	CS	GDP	Slg.	O
Clark, Mark, New York	.043	32	81	69	3	3	4	1	0	0	2	10	1	0	1	0	26	0	0	0	.058	.0
Clayton, Royce, St. Louis	.277	129	531	491	64	136	182	20	4	6	35	2	4	1	33	4	89	33	15	13	.371	.3
Clontz, Brad, Atlanta	.000	81	5	2	1	0	0	0	0	0	0	0	1	0	0	2	0	0	0	0	.000	.5
Cockrell, Alan, Colorado	.250	9	9	8	0	2	3	1	0	0	2	0	1	0	0	0	4	0	0	0	.375	.4
Colbrunn, Greg, Florida	.286	141	556	511	60	146	224	26	2	16	69	0	5	14	25	1	76	4	5	22	.438	.3
Coleman, Vince, Cincinnati†	.155	33	94	84	10	13	19	1	1	1	4	1	0	0	9	0	31	12	2	0	.226	.2
Conine, Jeff, Florida	.293	157	670	597	84	175	289	32	2	26	95	0	7	4	62	1	121	1	4	17	.484	.3
Cooke, Steve, Pittsburgh	.000	3	1	1	0	0	0	0	0	0	0	0	0	0	0	0	0	0	0	0	.000	.0
Cordova, Francisco, Pittsburgh	.125	59	18	16	1	2	2	0	0	0	2	2	0	0	0	0	7	0	0	1	.125	.1
Cormier, Rheal, Montreal*	.186	33	56	43	2	8	10	0	1	0	4	11	0	0	2	0	12	0	0	0	.233	.2
Crawford, Carlos, Philadelphia	.000	1	1	1	0	0	0	0	0	0	0	0	0	0	0	0	0	0	0	0	.000	.0
Creek, Doug, San Francisco*	.000	63	2	1	0	0	0	0	0	0	0	0	1	0	0	0	1	0	0	0	.000	.0
Cruz, Jacob, San Francisco*	.234	33	92	77	10	18	30	3	0	3	10	1	0	2	12	0	24	0	1	2	.390	.3
Cummings, Midre, Pittsburgh*	.224	24	87	85	11	19	33	3	1	3	7	1	1	0	0	0	16	0	0	0	.388	.2
Curtis, Chad, Los Angeles	.212	43	121	104	20	22	33	5	0	2	9	0	0	0	17	0	15	2	1	1	.317	.3
Daal, Omar, Montreal*	.000	64	11	11	0	0	0	0	0	0	0	0	0	0	0	0	5	0	0	1	.000	.0
Darwin, Danny, Pit.-Hou	.184	34	56	49	2	9	16	4	0	1	3	7	0	0	0	0	27	1	0	1	.327	.1
Dascenzo, Doug, San Diego†	.111	21	10	9	3	1	1	0	0	0	0	0	0	1	0	0	2	0	1	0	.111	.2
Daulton, Darren, Philadelphia*	.167	5	20	12	3	2	2	0	0	0	0	0	0	1	7	0	5	0	0	1	.167	.5
Davis, Eric, Cincinnati	.287	129	496	415	81	119	217	20	0	26	83	1	4	6	70	3	121	23	9	8	.523	.3
Dawson, Andre, Florida	.276	42	61	58	6	16	24	2	0	2	14	0	0	1	2	0	13	0	0	1	.414	.3
Decker, Steve, S.F.-Col	.245	67	171	147	24	36	45	3	0	2	20	4	2	0	18	4	29	1	0	3	.306	.3
Deer, Rob, San Diego	.180	25	64	50	9	9	24	3	0	4	9	0	0	0	14	0	30	0	0	1	.480	.3
Delgado, Wilson, S.F.†	.364	6	25	22	3	8	8	0	0	0	2	0	0	2	1	0	5	1	0	0	.364	.4
DeLucia, Rich, San Francisco	.250	56	5	4	1	1	1	0	0	0	0	0	0	0	0	0	0	0	0	0	.250	.4
DeShields, Delino, Los Angeles*	.224	154	642	581	75	130	173	12	8	5	41	2	5	1	53	7	124	48	11	12	.298	.2
Dessens, Elmer, Pittsburgh	.400	15	5	5	1	2	2	0	0	0	0	2	0	0	0	0	0	0	0	0	.400	.4
Dewey, Mark, San Francisco	.000	78	8	7	0	0	0	0	0	0	0	0	1	0	0	3	0	0	0	0	.000	.1
Difelice, Mike, St. Louis	.286	4	7	7	0	2	3	1	0	0	2	0	0	0	0	0	1	0	0	0	.429	.2
DiPoto, Jerry, New York	.000	57	1	1	0	0	0	0	0	0	0	0	0	0	0	0	0	0	0	0	.000	.0
Dishman, Glenn, Philadelphia	.000	4	2	0	0	0	0	0	0	0	0	0	2	0	0	0	0	0	0	0	.000	.0
Dorsett, Brian, Chicago	.122	17	46	41	3	5	8	0	0	1	3	0	1	0	4	0	8	0	0	2	.195	.1
Doster, David, Philadelphia	.267	39	113	105	14	28	39	8	0	1	8	1	0	0	7	0	21	0	0	1	.371	.3
Drabek, Doug, Houston	.179	32	63	56	5	10	11	1	0	0	3	7	0	0	0	0	12	0	0	1	.196	.1
Dreifort, Darren, Los Angeles	.000	20	3	3	0	0	0	0	0	0	0	0	0	0	0	0	2	0	0	0	.000	.0
Dunston, Shawon, S.F.	.300	82	307	287	27	86	117	12	2	5	25	5	1	1	13	0	40	8	0	8	.408	.3
Dye, Jermaine, Atlanta	.281	98	306	292	32	82	134	16	0	12	37	0	3	8	8	0	67	1	4	11	.459	.3
Dyer, Mike, Montreal	.000	70	7	7	0	0	0	0	0	0	0	0	0	0	0	0	4	0	0	0	.000	.0
Dykstra, Lenny, Philadelphia*	.261	40	164	134	21	35	56	6	3	3	13	1	1	2	26	2	25	3	1	1	.418	.3
Echevarria, Angel, Colorado	.286	26	26	21	2	6	6	0	0	0	6	0	2	1	2	0	5	0	0	0	.286	.3
Eckersley, Dennis, St. Louis	.000	63	1	1	0	0	0	0	0	0	0	0	0	0	0	0	0	0	0	0	.000	.0
Eischen, Joey, Los Angeles*	.000	28	6	6	0	0	0	0	0	0	0	0	0	0	0	0	2	0	0	0	.000	.0
Eisenreich, Jim, Philadelphia*	.361	113	373	338	45	122	161	24	3	3	41	0	3	1	31	9	32	11	1	7	.476	.4
Encarnacion, Angelo, Pit.	.318	7	22	22	3	7	9	2	0	0	1	0	0	0	0	0	5	0	0	0	.409	.3
Ericks, John, Pittsburgh	.000	28	5	5	0	0	0	0	0	0	0	0	0	0	0	0	1	0	0	1	.000	.0
Espinoza, Alvaro, New York	.306	48	144	134	19	41	64	7	2	4	16	5	1	0	4	0	19	0	2	4	.478	.3
Estalella, Bobby, Philadelphia	.353	7	18	17	5	6	12	0	0	2	4	0	0	0	1	0	6	1	0	0	.706	.3
Estes, Shawn, San Francisco	.158	15	26	19	3	3	3	0	0	0	1	6	0	0	1	0	8	1	0	0	.158	.2
Eusebio, Tony, Houston	.270	58	172	152	15	41	55	7	2	1	19	0	2	0	18	2	20	0	1	5	.362	.3
Everett, Carl, New York†	.240	101	219	192	29	46	59	8	1	1	16	1	1	4	21	2	53	6	4	3	.307	.3
Farmer, Mike, Colorado	.400	7	10	10	1	4	4	0	0	0	0	0	0	0	0	0	1	0	0	0	.400	.4
Fassero, Jeff, Montreal*	.094	34	67	64	5	6	6	0	0	0	4	14	1	0	8	0	32	1	0	0	.094	.1
Fermin, Felix, Chicago	.125	11	19	16	4	2	3	1	0	0	1	1	0	0	2	0	5	0	0	2	.188	.2
Fernandez, Osvaldo, S.F.	.088	33	62	57	0	5	5	0	0	0	1	5	0	0	0	0	25	0	0	0	.088	.0
Fernandez, Sid, Philadelphia*	.105	11	25	19	0	2	3	1	0	0	2	2	1	0	3	0	10	0	0	0	.158	.2
Finley, Steve, San Diego*	.298	161	721	655	126	195	348	45	9	30	95	1	5	4	56	5	87	22	8	20	.531	.3
Flaherty, John, San Diego	.303	72	279	264	22	80	119	12	0	9	41	1	3	2	9	1	36	2	3	8	.451	.3
Fletcher, Darrin, Montreal*	.266	127	432	394	41	105	163	22	0	12	57	1	3	6	27	4	42	0	0	13	.414	.3
Florie, Bryce, San Diego	.000	39	3	3	0	0	0	0	0	0	0	0	0	0	0	1	0	0	0	0	.000	.0
Floyd, Cliff, Montreal*	.242	117	266	227	29	55	96	15	4	6	26	1	3	5	30	1	52	7	1	3	.423	.3
Fonville, Chad, Los Angeles†	.204	103	221	201	34	41	47	4	1	0	13	3	0	0	17	1	31	7	2	1	.234	.2
Fordyce, Brook, Cincinnati	.286	4	10	7	0	2	3	1	0	0	1	0	0	0	3	0	0	0	0	0	.429	.5
Fossas, Tony, St. Louis*	.000	65	1	1	0	0	0	0	0	0	0	0	0	0	0	0	0	0	0	0	.000	.0
Foster, Kevin, Chicago	.296	19	35	27	3	8	14	4	1	0	6	3	0	1	4	0	11	0	0	0	.519	.4
Franco, John, New York*	.000	51	1	1	0	0	0	0	0	0	0	0	0	0	0	0	0	0	0	0	.000	.0
Franco, Matt, New York*	.194	14	34	31	3	6	10	1	0	1	2	0	1	1	1	0	5	0	0	1	.323	.2
Freeman, Marvin, Colorado	.122	26	47	41	3	5	5	0	0	0	4	0	0	2	0	0	21	0	0	1	.122	.1
Gaetti, Gary, St. Louis	.274	141	574	522	71	143	247	27	4	23	80	4	5	8	35	6	97	2	2	10	.473	.3
Gagne, Greg, Los Angeles	.255	128	487	428	48	109	156	13	2	10	55	4	3	2	50	11	93	4	2	6	.364	.3
Galarraga, Andres, Colorado	.304	159	691	626	119	190	376	39	3	47	150	0	8	17	40	3	157	18	8	6	.601	.3
Gallego, Mike, St. Louis	.210	51	159	143	12	30	32	2	0	0	4	3	0	1	12	1	31	0	0	2	.224	.2
Gant, Ron, St. Louis	.246	122	500	419	74	103	211	14	2	30	82	1	4	3	73	5	98	13	4	9	.504	.3
Garcia, Carlos, Pittsburgh	.285	101	422	390	66	111	155	18	4	6	44	3	2	4	23	0	58	16	6	3	.397	.3
Garcia, Karim, Los Angeles*	.000	1	1	1	0	0	0	0	0	0	0	0	0	0	0	0	1	0	0	0	.000	.0
Gardner, Mark, San Francisco	.162	33	79	68	6	11	12	1	0	0	4	8	0	1	2	0	26	0	0	2	.176	.1
Gibralter, Steve, Cincinnati	.000	2	2	2	0	0	0	0	0	0	0	0	0	0	0	0	1	0	0	0	.000	.0
Gilkey, Bernard, New York	.317	153	656	571	108	181	321	44	3	30	117	0	8	4	73	7	125	17	9	18	.562	.3
Giovanola, Ed, Atlanta*	.232	43	94	82	10	19	21	2	0	0	7	2	1	1	8	0	13	1	0	3	.256	.3
Glanville, Doug, Chicago	.241	49	89	83	10	20	30	5	1	1	10	2	1	0	3	0	11	2	0	0	.361	.2
Glavine, Tom, Atlanta*	.289	39	96	76	8	22	26	4	0	0	3	15	0	0	5	0	17	0	0	2	.342	.3
Goff, Jerry, Houston*	.500	1	4	4	1	2	5	0	0	1	2	0	0	0	0	0	1	0	0	0	1.250	.5
Gomez, Chris, San Diego	.262	89	378	328	32	86	113	16	1	3	29	3	2	6	39	1	64	2	2	11	.345	.3
Gomez, Leo, Chicago	.238	136	427	362	44	86	156	19	0	17	56	3	2	7	53	0	94	1	4	8	.431	.3

yer, Team	Avg.	G	TPA	AB	R	H	TB	2B	3B	HR	RBI	SH	SF	HP	BB	IBB	SO	SB	CS	GDP	Slg.	OBP
nzalez, Luis, Chicago*	.271	146	555	483	70	131	214	30	4	15	79	1	6	4	61	8	49	9	6	13	.443	.354
odwin, Curtis, Cincinnati*	.228	49	156	136	20	31	34	3	0	0	5	1	0	0	19	0	34	15	6	1	.250	.323
ce, Mark, Chicago*	.331	142	616	547	88	181	249	39	1	9	75	0	6	1	62	8	41	2	3	18	.455	.396
ce, Mike, Philadelphia	.138	12	33	29	1	4	4	0	0	0	0	1	0	1	2	0	11	0	0	0	.138	.219
ffanino, Tony, Atlanta	.174	22	52	46	7	8	11	1	1	0	2	0	1	1	4	0	13	0	0	1	.239	.250
beck, Craig, Florida	.211	50	103	95	8	20	24	1	0	1	9	1	2	1	4	1	14	0	0	2	.253	.245
ene, Charlie, New York	.000	2	1	1	0	0	0	0	0	0	0	0	0	0	0	0	0	0	0	0	.000	.000
ene, Willie, Cincinnati*	.244	115	325	287	48	70	142	5	5	19	63	1	1	0	36	6	88	0	1	5	.495	.327
ssom, Marquis, Atlanta	.308	158	723	671	106	207	328	32	10	23	74	4	4	3	41	6	73	28	11	12	.489	.349
dzielanek, Mark, Montreal	.306	153	696	657	99	201	261	34	4	6	49	1	3	9	26	3	83	33	7	10	.397	.340
errero, Vladimir, Montreal	.185	9	27	27	2	5	8	0	0	1	1	0	0	0	0	0	3	0	0	1	.296	.185
errero, Wilton, Los Angeles	.000	5	2	2	1	0	0	0	0	0	0	0	0	0	0	0	0	0	0	0	.000	.000
hrie, Mark, Los Angeles	.000	66	3	3	0	0	0	0	0	0	0	0	0	0	0	0	0	0	0	0	.000	.000
ierrez, Ricky, Houston	.284	89	249	218	28	62	75	8	1	1	15	4	1	3	23	3	42	6	1	4	.344	.359
ynn, Chris, San Diego*	.178	81	100	90	8	16	23	4	0	1	10	0	0	0	10	0	28	0	0	2	.256	.260
ynn, Tony, San Diego*	.353	116	498	451	67	159	199	27	2	3	50	1	6	1	39	12	17	11	4	17	.441	.400
oyan, John, Colorado	.000	19	4	3	0	0	0	0	0	0	0	0	0	0	1	0	1	0	0	1	.000	.250
ek, Dave, Houston	.300	8	12	10	3	3	4	1	0	0	0	0	0	0	2	0	0	0	0	3	.400	.417
l, Mel, San Francisco*	.120	25	27	25	3	3	3	0	0	0	5	0	1	0	1	0	4	0	0	0	.120	.148
milton, Joey, San Diego	.162	34	81	68	7	11	16	2	0	1	4	11	0	0	2	0	32	0	0	1	.235	.186
mmond, Chris, Florida*	.067	38	18	15	1	1	1	0	0	0	0	2	0	0	1	0	7	0	0	0	.067	.125
mpton, Mike, Houston	.238	29	54	42	9	10	11	1	0	0	3	7	0	1	4	0	11	0	0	1	.262	.319
ney, Todd, Chicago	.134	49	92	82	11	11	12	1	0	0	3	2	1	0	7	0	15	1	0	1	.146	.200
nsen, Dave, Los Angeles*	.221	80	116	104	7	23	24	1	0	0	6	0	1	0	11	1	22	0	0	4	.231	.293
rdtke, Jason, New York†	.193	19	60	57	3	11	16	5	0	0	6	0	1	0	2	0	12	0	0	1	.281	.233
rnisch, Pete, New York	.091	32	68	55	3	5	6	1	0	0	1	10	1	0	2	0	18	0	0	0	.109	.121
rris, Lenny, Cincinnati*	.285	125	333	302	33	86	122	17	2	5	32	6	3	1	21	1	31	14	6	3	.404	.330
rtgraves, Dean, Hou.-Atl	.000	39	2	1	0	0	0	0	0	0	0	1	0	0	0	0	0	0	0	0	.000	.000
wblitzel, Ryan, Colorado	.000	8	1	1	0	0	0	0	0	0	0	0	0	0	0	0	0	0	0	0	.000	.000
yes, Charlie, Pittsburgh	.248	128	500	459	51	114	169	21	2	10	62	2	3	0	36	4	78	6	0	16	.368	.301
ling, Rick, Florida	.111	5	9	9	1	1	1	0	0	0	0	0	0	0	0	0	3	0	0	0	.111	.111
nderson, Rickey, San Diego	.241	148	602	465	110	112	160	17	2	9	29	0	2	10	125	2	90	37	15	5	.344	.410
nry, Doug, New York	.000	58	5	5	0	0	0	0	0	0	0	0	0	0	0	0	0	0	0	0	.000	.000
rnandez, Carlos, Los Angeles	.286	13	16	14	1	4	4	0	0	0	0	0	0	0	2	0	2	0	0	0	.286	.375
rnandez, Jose, Chicago	.242	131	363	331	52	80	126	14	1	10	41	5	2	1	24	4	97	4	0	10	.381	.293
rnandez, Livan, Florida	1.000	1	1	1	1	1	1	0	0	0	0	0	0	0	0	0	0	0	0	0	1.000	1.000
rnandez, Xavier, Houston*	.000	58	3	2	0	0	0	0	0	0	0	1	0	0	0	0	1	0	0	0	.000	.000
l, Glenallen, San Francisco	.280	98	421	379	56	106	189	26	0	19	67	0	3	6	33	3	95	6	3	6	.499	.344
ffman, Trevor, San Diego	.000	70	9	8	0	0	0	0	0	0	0	1	0	0	0	0	4	0	0	0	.000	.000
bert, Aaron, St. Louis	.000	3	3	3	0	0	0	0	0	0	0	0	0	0	0	0	0	0	0	0	.000	.000
llandsworth, Todd, L.A.*	.291	149	526	478	64	139	209	26	4	12	59	3	2	2	41	1	93	21	6	2	.437	.348
lmes, Darren, Colorado	.000	62	3	2	0	0	0	0	0	0	0	0	0	0	1	0	1	0	0	0	.000	.333
lt, Chris, Houston	.000	4	1	1	0	0	0	0	0	0	0	0	0	0	0	0	0	0	0	0	.000	.000
neycutt, Rick, St. Louis*	.000	61	3	1	0	0	0	0	0	0	0	1	0	0	2	0	1	0	0	0	.000	.667
ok, Chris, San Francisco	.500	10	2	2	0	1	1	0	0	0	1	0	0	0	0	0	1	0	0	0	.500	.500
pe, John, Pittsburgh	.200	5	6	5	0	1	1	0	0	0	0	1	0	0	0	0	1	0	0	0	.200	.200
uston, Tyler, Atl.-Chi.*	.317	79	151	142	21	45	65	9	1	3	27	0	0	9	1	27	3	2	5	.458	.358
ward, Thomas, Cincinnati*	.272	121	386	360	50	98	155	19	10	6	42	2	4	3	17	3	51	6	5	5	.431	.307
bbard, Mark, Florida	.105	21	39	38	1	4	7	0	0	1	4	1	0	0	0	0	15	0	0	1	.184	.103
bbard, Trent, Col.-S.F	.213	55	101	89	15	19	34	5	2	2	14	0	0	1	11	0	27	2	0	3	.382	.307
ndley, Todd, New York†	.259	153	624	540	85	140	297	32	1	41	112	0	2	3	79	15	146	1	3	9	.550	.356
nter, Brian L., Houston	.276	132	553	526	74	145	191	27	2	5	35	1	7	2	17	0	92	35	9	6	.363	.297
nter, Rich, Philadelphia	.167	15	23	18	2	3	4	1	0	0	0	4	0	0	1	0	5	0	0	2	.222	.211
skey, Butch, New York	.278	118	445	414	43	115	180	16	2	15	60	0	4	0	27	3	77	1	2	10	.435	.319
tton, Mark, Florida	.316	13	20	19	2	6	9	0	0	1	1	1	0	0	0	0	6	0	0	1	.474	.316
caviglia, Pete, Philadelphia	.234	99	302	269	33	63	122	7	2	16	42	0	0	3	30	2	82	2	0	6	.454	.318
nghausen, Jason, New York	.255	27	57	51	5	13	21	2	0	2	9	2	1	0	3	0	15	0	0	0	.412	.291
ckson, Danny, St. Louis	.333	13	10	9	1	3	5	2	0	0	4	1	0	0	1	0	0	0	0	5	.556	.333
rvis, Kevin, Cincinnati*	.167	24	44	36	2	6	7	1	0	0	1	8	0	0	0	0	12	0	0	1	.194	.167
vier, Stan, San Francisco†	.270	71	306	274	44	74	105	25	0	2	22	5	0	2	25	0	51	14	2	4	.383	.336
fferies, Gregg, Philadelphia†	.292	104	446	404	59	118	162	17	3	7	51	0	5	1	36	6	21	20	6	9	.401	.348
nnings, Robin, Chicago*	.224	31	62	58	7	13	18	5	0	0	4	0	0	1	3	0	9	1	0	1	.310	.274
nsen, Marcus, San Francisco†	.211	9	27	19	4	4	5	1	0	0	4	0	0	0	8	0	7	0	0	1	.263	.444
hnson, Brian, San Diego	.272	82	257	243	18	66	105	13	1	8	35	2	4	4	2	36	0	0	8	.432	.290
hnson, Charles, Florida	.218	120	435	386	34	84	138	13	1	13	37	2	4	2	40	6	91	1	0	20	.358	.292
hnson, Lance, New York*	.333	160	724	682	117	227	327	31	21	9	69	3	5	1	33	8	40	50	12	8	.479	.362
hnson, Mark, Pittsburgh*	.274	127	396	343	55	94	157	24	0	13	47	0	4	5	44	3	64	6	4	5	.458	.361
nes, Andruw, Atlanta	.217	31	113	106	11	23	47	7	1	5	13	0	0	0	7	0	29	3	0	1	.443	.265
nes, Bobby, New York	.117	31	72	60	6	7	9	2	0	0	2	9	0	0	3	0	20	0	0	1	.150	.159
nes, Chipper, Atlanta†	.309	157	693	598	114	185	317	32	5	30	110	1	7	0	87	0	88	14	1	14	.530	.393
nes, Chris, New York	.242	89	163	149	22	36	55	7	0	4	18	0	0	2	12	1	42	1	0	3	.369	.307
nes, Dax, San Francisco	.172	34	67	58	7	10	17	0	2	1	7	0	1	0	8	0	12	2	2	0	.293	.269
nes, Terry, Colorado†	.300	12	11	10	6	3	3	0	0	0	0	0	0	0	0	0	3	0	0	0	.300	.273
nes, Todd, Houston*	.000	51	1	1	0	0	0	0	0	0	0	0	0	0	0	0	0	0	0	0	.000	.000
rdan, Brian, St. Louis	.310	140	560	513	82	159	248	36	1	17	104	2	9	7	29	4	84	22	5	6	.483	.349
rdan, Kevin, Philadelphia	.282	43	142	131	15	37	56	10	0	3	12	3	2	1	5	0	20	2	1	3	.427	.309
rdan, Ricardo, Philadelphia*	.000	26	1	1	0	0	0	0	0	0	0	0	0	0	0	0	0	0	0	0	.000	.000
yner, Wally, San Diego*	.277	121	510	433	59	120	175	29	1	8	65	1	4	3	69	8	71	5	3	6	.404	.377
den, Jeff, S.F.-Mon.†	.000	58	4	3	0	0	0	0	0	0	0	0	0	0	0	0	2	0	0	0	.000	.000
stice, Dave, Atlanta*	.321	40	164	140	23	45	72	9	0	6	25	0	2	1	21	1	22	1	1	5	.514	.409
rros, Eric, Los Angeles	.260	154	670	608	84	158	291	29	1	34	111	0	8	1	53	2	121	8	0	27	.479	.316
ally, Mike, Cincinnati	.184	19	60	49	5	9	16	4	0	1	7	0	0	2	9	0	11	4	0	2	.327	.333
ndall, Jason, Pittsburgh	.300	130	471	414	54	124	166	23	5	3	42	3	4	15	35	11	30	5	2	7	.401	.372

Player, Team	Avg.	G	TPA	AB	R	H	TB	2B	3B	HR	RBI	SH	SF	HP	BB	IBB	SO	SB	CS	GDP	Slg.	O
Kent, Jeff, New York	.290	89	361	335	45	97	146	20	1	9	39	1	3	1	21	1	56	4	3	7	.436	.3
Kieschnick, Brooks, Chicago*	.345	25	32	29	6	10	15	2	0	1	6	0	0	0	3	0	8	0	0	0	.517	.4
Kile, Darryl, Houston	.137	37	84	73	3	10	14	4	0	0	5	7	1	0	3	0	34	0	0	0	.192	.1
King, Jeff, Pittsburgh	.271	155	672	591	91	160	294	36	4	30	111	1	8	2	70	3	95	15	1	17	.497	.3
Kingery, Mike, Pittsburgh*	.246	117	304	276	32	68	93	12	2	3	27	1	3	1	23	2	29	2	1	5	.337	.3
Kirby, Wayne, Los Angeles*	.271	65	208	188	23	51	66	10	1	1	11	1	1	1	17	1	17	4	2	3	.351	.3
Klesko, Ryan, Atlanta*	.282	153	605	528	90	149	280	21	4	34	93	0	4	2	68	10	129	6	3	10	.530	.3
Knorr, Randy, Houston	.195	37	94	87	7	17	25	5	0	1	7	0	1	1	5	2	18	0	1	1	.287	.2
Lampkin, Tom, San Francisco*	.232	66	204	177	26	41	67	8	0	6	29	0	2	5	20	2	22	1	5	2	.379	.3
Lankford, Ray, St. Louis*	.275	149	635	545	100	150	265	36	8	21	86	1	7	3	79	10	133	35	7	12	.486	.3
Lansing, Mike, Montreal	.285	159	705	641	99	183	260	40	2	11	53	9	1	10	44	1	85	23	8	19	.406	.3
Larkin, Andy, Florida	.000	1	2	2	0	0	0	0	0	0	0	0	0	0	0	0	1	0	0	0	.000	.0
Larkin, Barry, Cincinnati	.298	152	627	517	117	154	293	32	4	33	89	0	7	7	96	3	52	36	10	20	.567	.4
Leiter, Al, Florida*	.100	33	81	70	3	7	7	0	0	0	1	7	0	0	4	0	45	0	0	1	.100	.1
Leiter, Mark, S.F.-Mon.	.119	35	79	67	4	8	9	1	0	0	5	9	0	0	3	0	35	0	0	1	.134	.1
Lemke, Mark, Atlanta†	.255	135	562	498	64	127	159	17	0	5	37	5	6	0	53	1	48	5	2	9	.319	.3
Leskanic, Curt, Colorado	.333	70	4	3	0	1	2	1	0	0	1	1	0	0	0	0	2	0	0	0	.667	.3
Lieber, Jon, Pittsburgh*	.194	51	42	36	4	7	10	3	0	0	3	3	0	0	3	0	11	0	0	2	.278	.2
Lieberthal, Mike, Philadelphia	.253	50	182	166	21	42	71	8	0	7	23	0	4	2	10	0	30	0	0	4	.428	.2
Liriano, Nelson, Pittsburgh†	.267	112	234	217	23	58	85	14	2	3	30	0	3	0	14	2	22	2	0	1	.392	.3
Livingstone, Scott, San Diego*	.297	102	181	172	20	51	63	4	1	2	20	0	0	0	9	0	22	0	1	6	.366	.3
Loaiza, Esteban, Pittsburgh	.118	11	22	17	1	2	2	0	0	0	1	5	0	0	0	0	2	0	0	1	.118	.1
Loiselle, Rich, Pittsburgh	.250	5	8	8	0	2	3	1	0	0	2	0	0	0	0	0	3	0	1	0	.375	.2
Lopez, Javy, Atlanta	.282	138	526	489	56	138	228	19	1	23	69	1	5	3	28	5	84	1	6	17	.466	.3
Lopez, Luis, San Diego†	.180	63	151	139	10	25	34	3	0	2	11	1	1	1	9	1	35	0	0	7	.245	.2
Ludwick, Eric, St. Louis	.000	6	2	2	0	0	0	0	0	0	0	0	0	0	0	0	1	0	0	0	.000	.0
Lukachyk, Rob, Montreal*	.000	2	2	2	0	0	0	0	0	0	0	0	0	0	0	0	1	0	0	0	.000	.0
Lyons, Curt, Cincinnati	.000	3	6	5	0	0	0	0	0	0	0	1	0	0	0	0	2	0	0	0	.000	.0
Mabry, John, St. Louis*	.297	151	591	543	63	161	234	30	2	13	74	3	5	3	37	11	84	3	2	21	.431	.3
Maddux, Greg, Atlanta	.147	35	82	68	6	10	12	2	0	0	2	11	0	0	3	0	12	0	0	1	.176	.1
Maduro, Calvin, Philadelphia	.000	4	4	4	0	0	0	0	0	0	0	0	0	0	0	0	2	0	0	0	.000	.0
Magadan, Dave, Chicago*	.254	78	201	169	23	43	62	10	0	3	17	1	2	0	29	3	23	0	2	3	.367	.3
Magee, Wendell, Philadelphia	.204	38	151	142	9	29	42	7	0	2	14	0	0	0	9	0	33	0	0	2	.296	.2
Mantei, Matt, Florida	.000	14	1	1	0	0	0	0	0	0	0	0	0	0	0	0	1	0	0	0	.000	.0
Manuel, Barry, Montreal	.000	53	9	7	0	0	0	0	0	0	0	1	0	0	1	0	3	0	0	0	.000	.1
Manwaring, Kirt, S.F.-Hou	.229	86	256	227	14	52	64	9	0	1	18	2	2	5	19	1	40	0	1	4	.282	.3
Marrero, Oreste, Los Angeles*	.375	10	9	8	2	3	4	1	0	0	1	0	0	0	1	0	3	0	0	1	.500	.4
Martin, Al, Pittsburgh*	.300	155	694	630	101	189	285	40	1	18	72	1	7	2	54	2	116	38	12	9	.452	.3
Martinez, Manny, Philadelphia	.222	13	39	36	2	8	12	0	2	0	1	0	1	0	1	0	11	2	1	1	.333	.2
Martinez, Pablo, Atlanta†	.500	4	3	2	1	1	1	0	0	0	0	0	0	0	1	0	0	0	0	0	.500	.5
Martinez, Pedro, Montreal	.094	33	85	64	5	6	7	1	0	0	4	16	0	1	4	0	29	0	0	0	.109	.1
Martinez, Ramon, Los Angeles*	.119	30	69	59	3	7	7	0	0	0	2	8	0	0	2	0	22	0	0	1	.119	.1
Mathews, T.J., St. Louis	.000	67	4	4	0	0	0	0	0	0	0	0	0	0	0	0	3	0	0	0	.000	.0
Mathews, Terry, Florida*	.000	57	4	4	0	0	0	0	0	0	0	0	0	0	0	0	0	0	0	0	.000	.0
May, Darrell, Pittsburgh*	.333	5	3	3	1	1	1	0	0	0	0	0	0	0	0	0	1	0	0	0	.333	.3
May, Derrick, Houston*	.251	109	294	259	24	65	98	12	3	5	33	0	3	2	30	8	33	2	2	3	.378	.3
Mayne, Brent, New York*	.263	70	113	99	9	26	35	6	0	1	6	2	0	0	12	1	22	0	1	4	.354	.3
McCarty, Dave, San Francisco	.217	91	197	175	16	38	59	3	0	6	24	0	2	2	18	0	43	2	1	5	.337	.2
McCracken, Quinton, Colorado†	.290	124	329	283	50	82	116	13	6	3	40	12	1	1	32	4	62	17	6	5	.410	.3
McElroy, Chuck, Cincinnati*	.000	12	2	2	0	0	0	0	0	0	0	0	0	0	0	0	0	0	0	0	.000	.0
McGee, Willie, St. Louis†	.307	123	331	309	52	95	129	15	2	5	41	1	1	2	18	2	60	5	2	8	.417	.3
McGriff, Fred, Atlanta*	.295	159	691	617	81	182	305	37	1	28	107	0	4	2	68	12	116	7	3	20	.494	.3
McMillon, Billy, Florida*	.216	28	56	51	4	11	11	0	0	0	4	0	0	1	5	1	14	0	0	1	.216	.2
McRae, Brian, Chicago†	.276	157	716	624	111	172	265	32	5	17	66	2	5	12	73	6	84	37	9	11	.425	.3
Mejia, Miguel, St. Louis	.087	45	23	23	10	2	2	0	0	0	0	0	0	0	0	0	10	6	3	0	.087	.0
Merced, Orlando, Pittsburgh*	.287	120	507	453	69	130	207	24	1	17	80	0	3	0	51	5	74	8	4	9	.457	.3
Miceli, Dan, Pittsburgh	.000	44	13	13	0	0	0	0	0	0	0	0	0	0	0	0	4	0	0	0	.000	.0
Miller, Kurt, Florida	.375	26	9	8	0	3	3	0	0	0	2	1	0	0	0	0	3	0	0	0	.375	.3
Miller, Orlando, Houston	.256	139	496	468	43	120	195	26	2	15	58	1	3	10	14	4	116	3	7	14	.417	.29
Milliard, Ralph, Florida	.161	24	77	62	7	10	12	2	0	0	1	0	1	0	14	1	16	2	0	1	.194	.31
Mimbs, Michael, Philadelphia*	.121	21	35	33	0	4	4	0	0	0	0	2	0	0	0	0	12	0	0	1	.121	.12
Minor, Blas, New York	.000	17	1	1	0	0	0	0	0	0	0	0	0	0	0	0	0	0	0	0	.000	.00
Mirabelli, Doug, San Francisco	.222	9	21	18	2	4	5	1	0	0	1	0	0	0	3	0	4	0	0	0	.278	.33
Mitchell, Keith, Cincinnati	.267	11	16	15	2	4	8	1	0	1	3	0	0	0	1	0	3	0	0	0	.533	.31
Mitchell, Kevin, Cincinnati	.325	37	141	114	18	37	66	11	0	6	26	0	1	0	26	2	16	0	0	5	.579	.44
Mitchell, Larry, Philadelphia	.000	7	2	2	0	0	0	0	0	0	0	0	0	0	0	0	1	0	0	0	.000	.00
Mlicki, Dave, New York	.100	51	11	10	0	1	1	0	0	0	0	0	0	0	1	0	3	0	0	0	.100	.18
Mondesi, Raul, Los Angeles	.297	157	673	634	98	188	314	40	7	24	88	0	2	5	32	9	122	14	7	6	.495	.33
Montgomery, Ray, Houston	.214	12	15	14	4	3	7	1	0	1	4	0	0	0	1	0	5	0	0	0	.500	.26
Moore, Marcus, Cincinnati†	.333	23	3	3	0	1	2	1	0	0	0	0	0	0	0	0	2	0	0	0	.667	.33
Morandini, Mickey, Phi.*	.250	140	606	539	64	135	180	24	6	3	32	5	4	9	49	0	87	26	5	15	.334	.32
Mordecai, Mike, Atlanta	.241	66	122	108	12	26	37	5	0	2	8	4	1	0	9	1	24	1	0	1	.343	.29
Morel, Ramon, Pittsburgh	.000	29	5	4	0	0	0	0	0	0	0	1	0	0	0	0	0	0	0	0	.000	.00
Morgan, Mike, St.L.-Cin	.050	23	51	40	1	2	2	0	0	0	0	11	0	0	0	0	17	0	0	0	.050	.05
Morman, Russ, Florida	.167	6	7	6	0	1	1	0	0	0	0	0	0	1	0	0	1	0	0	0	.333	.28
Morris, Hal, Cincinnati*	.313	142	594	528	82	165	253	32	4	16	80	5	6	5	50	5	76	7	5	12	.479	.37
Mottola, Chad, Cincinnati	.215	35	85	79	10	17	29	3	0	3	6	0	0	1	6	1	16	2	2	0	.367	.27
Mouton, James, Houston	.263	122	343	300	40	79	105	15	1	3	34	2	3	0	38	2	55	21	9	6	.350	.34
Mueller, Bill, San Francisco†	.330	55	228	200	31	66	83	15	1	0	19	1	2	1	24	0	26	0	0	1	.415	.40
Mulholland, Terry, Philadelphia	.178	21	49	45	2	8	12	1	0	1	2	4	0	0	0	0	20	0	0	1	.267	.17
Mulligan, Sean, San Diego	.000	2	1	1	0	0	0	0	0	0	0	0	0	0	0	0	0	0	0	0	.000	.00
Munoz, Bobby, Philadelphia	.143	6	8	7	1	1	2	1	0	0	0	1	0	0	0	0	3	0	0	1	.286	.14
Munoz, Mike, Colorado*	.000	54	1	1	0	0	0	0	0	0	0	0	0	0	0	0	1	0	0	0	.000	.00

yer, Team	Avg.	G	TPA	AB	R	H	TB	2B	3B	HR	RBI	SH	SF	HP	BB	IBB	SO	SB	CS	GDP	Slg.	OBP
rray, Glenn, Philadelphia......	.196	38	104	97	8	19	28	3	0	2	6	0	0	0	7	0	36	1	1	0	.289	.250
ers, Rodney, Chicago..........	.000	45	5	5	0	0	0	0	0	0	0	0	0	0	0	0	4	0	0	0	.000	.000
al, Bob, Florida	.133	44	105	90	4	12	15	1	1	0	2	0	0	0	15	5	31	0	1	3	.167	.257
arro, Jaime, Chicago	.130	35	86	77	1	10	11	1	0	0	3	8	0	1	0	0	26	0	0	1	.143	.141
gle, Denny, Pit.-Atl.*	.174	36	88	69	3	12	13	1	0	0	4	16	1	0	2	0	18	0	0	0	.188	.194
a, Robb, Florida..................	.000	75	2	2	0	0	0	0	0	0	0	0	0	0	0	0	0	0	0	0	.000	.000
vfield, Marc, San Diego......	.251	84	212	191	27	48	74	11	0	5	26	0	3	2	16	1	44	1	1	7	.387	.311
d, Dave, Colorado	.000	6	1	1	0	0	0	0	0	0	0	0	0	0	0	0	1	0	0	0	.000	.000
no, Hideo, Los Angeles.......	.133	33	87	75	1	10	14	4	0	0	3	10	0	0	2	0	38	0	0	1	.187	.156
ando, Sherman, Montreal.......	.247	89	202	178	30	44	77	9	0	8	22	0	1	1	22	1	48	2	0	2	.433	.332
noa, Alex, New York	.294	82	304	282	37	83	120	19	3	4	33	0	3	2	17	0	30	4	3	2	.426	.336
ver, Joe, Cincinnati	.242	106	325	289	31	70	117	12	1	11	46	3	3	2	28	6	54	2	0	8	.405	.311
lonez, Rey, New York	.257	151	530	502	51	129	152	12	4	1	30	4	1	1	22	12	53	1	3	12	.303	.289
ulak, Joe, Florida*	.221	120	234	217	23	48	62	6	1	2	19	0	1	0	16	1	38	1	1	4	.286	.274
borne, Donovan, St. Louis*...	.220	30	72	59	6	13	20	4	0	1	10	10	0	0	3	0	24	0	1	0	.339	.258
k, Keith, Pittsburgh.............	.293	48	156	140	18	41	60	14	1	1	14	1	0	1	14	1	22	1	0	3	.429	.361
na, Al, San Diego...............	.000	10	1	1	0	0	0	0	0	0	0	0	0	0	0	0	0	0	0	0	.000	.000
una, Antonio, Los Angeles....	.000	73	3	1	0	0	0	0	0	0	1	0	1	0	1	0	0	0	0	0	.000	.333
ro, Ricky, Philadelphia†	.273	104	449	411	54	112	143	11	7	2	32	0	2	2	34	0	30	16	10	3	.348	.330
ens, Eric, Cincinnati	.200	88	232	205	26	41	47	6	0	0	9	1	2	1	23	1	38	16	2	2	.229	.281
ens, Jayhawk, Colorado.......	.239	73	213	180	31	43	66	9	1	4	17	3	2	1	27	0	56	4	1	1	.367	.338
gnozzi, Tom, St. Louis	.270	119	440	407	48	110	172	23	0	13	55	3	4	2	24	2	78	4	1	9	.423	.311
nter, Lance, Colorado*	.133	35	15	15	1	2	2	0	0	0	2	0	0	0	0	0	8	0	0	1	.133	.133
l, Donn, Florida.................	.000	12	3	2	0	0	0	0	0	0	0	0	0	0	1	0	0	0	0	0	.000	.333
hiagua, Jose, Montreal	.000	13	14	11	1	0	0	0	0	0	0	1	0	0	2	0	7	0	0	0	.000	.154
k, Chan Ho, Los Angeles	.053	48	23	19	0	1	1	0	0	0	2	3	0	0	1	0	9	0	0	0	.053	.100
ker, Rick, Los Angeles	.286	16	15	14	2	4	5	1	0	0	1	0	0	1	0	0	2	1	0	1	.357	.333
rrett, Jeff, St. Louis.............	.000	33	3	2	1	0	0	0	0	0	0	0	0	0	1	0	1	0	0	0	.000	.333
ris, Steve, Pittsburgh..........	.167	8	9	6	1	1	1	0	0	0	0	2	0	0	1	0	1	0	0	0	.167	.286
terson, Bob, Chicago	.333	79	3	3	0	1	1	0	0	0	0	0	0	0	0	0	2	0	0	0	.333	.333
tier, Dan, San Francisco*	.254	31	67	59	3	15	17	2	0	0	9	0	1	0	7	1	9	0	0	1	.288	.328
ndleton, Terry, Fla.-Atl.†	.238	153	618	568	51	135	196	26	1	11	75	1	5	3	41	6	111	2	3	18	.345	.290
ez, Eddie, Atlanta	.256	68	167	156	19	40	63	9	1	4	17	0	2	1	8	0	19	0	0	6	.404	.293
ez, Eduardo, Cincinnati	.222	18	41	36	8	8	17	0	0	3	5	0	0	0	5	1	9	0	0	2	.472	.317
ez, Mike, Chicago	.000	24	1	1	0	0	0	0	0	0	0	0	0	0	0	0	1	0	0	0	.000	.000
ez, Neifi, Colorado†	.156	17	46	45	4	7	9	2	0	0	3	1	0	0	0	0	8	2	2	2	.200	.156
ez, Yorkis, Florida*	.000	64	1	1	0	0	0	0	0	0	0	0	0	0	1	0	0	0	0	0	.000	.000
rson, Robert, New York	.143	29	26	21	1	3	4	1	0	0	0	5	0	0	0	0	12	0	0	0	.190	.143
tagine, Roberto, New York*...	.232	50	113	99	10	23	38	3	0	4	17	1	1	3	9	1	27	0	2	4	.384	.313
ters, Chris, Pittsburgh*	.211	16	20	19	2	4	5	1	0	0	1	1	0	0	0	0	8	0	0	0	.263	.211
tkovsek, Mark, St. Louis	.188	48	17	16	1	3	3	0	0	0	0	0	0	1	0	0	3	0	0	0	.188	.235
illips, J.R., S.F.-Phi.*	.163	50	116	104	12	17	43	5	0	7	15	0	0	1	11	1	51	0	0	1	.413	.250
zza, Mike, Los Angeles	.336	148	631	547	87	184	308	16	0	36	105	0	2	1	81	21	93	0	3	21	.563	.422
sac, Dan, Pittsburgh*	.000	73	5	5	0	0	0	0	0	0	0	0	0	0	0	0	2	0	0	0	.000	.000
onia, Luis, Atlanta*	.419	22	33	31	3	13	13	0	0	0	2	0	1	0	1	0	3	1	1	0	.419	.424
ole, Jim, San Francisco*	.000	35	2	2	0	0	0	0	0	0	0	0	0	0	0	0	1	0	0	0	.000	.000
rtugal, Mark, Cincinnati	.167	28	56	48	4	8	9	1	0	0	1	7	0	0	1	0	11	0	0	1	.188	.184
well, Jay, Florida.................	.000	67	6	5	0	0	0	0	0	0	0	1	0	0	0	0	4	0	0	0	.000	.000
nce, Tom, Los Angeles	.297	40	77	64	6	19	28	6	0	1	11	3	2	2	6	2	15	0	0	0	.438	.365
gh, Tim, Cincinnati	.000	10	1	0	0	0	0	0	0	0	0	1	0	0	0	0	0	0	0	0	.000	.000
illiam, Harvey, Colorado	.133	10	17	15	2	2	2	0	0	0	0	0	0	0	2	0	6	0	0	1	.133	.235
dinsky, Scott, Los Angeles*..	.000	58	1	1	0	0	0	0	0	0	0	0	0	0	0	0	0	0	0	0	.000	.000
pp, Pat, Florida	.121	30	58	58	2	7	8	1	0	0	2	0	0	0	0	0	21	0	0	1	.138	.121
ed, Jeff, Colorado*	.284	116	395	341	34	97	143	20	1	8	37	6	3	2	43	8	65	2	2	8	.419	.365
ed, Jody, San Diego	.244	146	568	495	45	121	147	20	0	2	49	5	6	3	59	8	53	2	5	15	.297	.325
ed, Steve, Colorado	.333	70	3	3	0	1	1	0	0	0	0	0	0	0	0	0	1	0	0	0	.333	.333
kar, Bryan, Colorado	.267	14	17	15	2	4	5	1	0	0	0	1	0	0	1	0	5	0	0	0	.333	.313
laford, Desi, Philadelphia†....	.175	14	44	40	2	7	9	2	0	0	1	1	0	0	3	0	9	1	0	1	.225	.233
mlinger, Mike, Cincinnati* ...	.143	19	8	7	0	1	1	0	0	0	0	0	0	0	1	0	3	0	0	0	.143	.250
nteria, Edgar, Florida...........	.309	106	471	431	68	133	172	18	3	5	31	2	3	2	33	0	68	16	2	12	.399	.358
ynolds, Shane, Houston	.184	35	93	76	6	14	22	2	0	2	3	14	0	0	3	0	28	0	0	2	.289	.215
ynoso, Armando, Colorado....	.173	30	64	52	4	9	10	1	0	0	2	7	0	0	5	0	25	0	0	1	.192	.246
z, Kevin, Colorado	.231	35	83	65	7	15	20	2	0	1	5	11	0	0	7	0	28	0	0	0	.308	.306
berson, Kevin, New York†	.222	27	46	36	8	8	18	1	0	3	9	0	2	1	7	0	17	0	0	0	.500	.348
driguez, Henry, Montreal*	.276	145	576	532	81	147	299	42	1	36	103	0	4	3	37	7	160	2	0	10	.562	.325
jas, Mel, Montreal...............	.375	74	8	8	0	3	4	1	0	0	3	0	0	0	0	0	2	0	0	0	.500	.375
len, Scott, Philadelphia	.254	37	146	130	10	33	52	7	0	4	18	0	2	1	13	0	27	0	2	4	.400	.322
ebel, Matt, Pittsburgh*.........	.231	26	16	13	0	3	3	0	0	0	0	2	0	0	1	0	4	0	0	0	.231	.286
eter, Kirk, Mon.-S.F.*	.125	20	37	32	2	4	4	0	0	0	3	2	1	0	2	0	5	0	0	1	.125	.171
ffin, Bruce, Colorado†	.000	71	2	1	0	0	0	0	0	0	0	0	0	0	1	0	1	0	0	0	.000	.500
ffin, Johnny, Cincinnati	.500	49	4	4	0	2	2	0	0	0	0	0	0	0	0	0	1	0	0	1	.500	.500
an, Ken, Philadelphia	.143	62	8	7	0	1	1	0	0	0	0	0	0	0	0	0	4	0	0	0	.143	.143
bo, Chris, Cincinnati	.256	54	145	125	15	32	50	7	1	3	16	1	0	1	18	0	27	2	0	4	.400	.354
lkeld, Roger, Cincinnati	.031	29	37	32	1	1	1	0	0	0	0	4	0	0	1	0	21	0	0	0	.031	.061
nchez, Rey, Chicago	.211	95	324	289	28	61	73	9	0	1	12	8	2	3	22	6	42	7	1	6	.253	.272
nchez, Ryne, Chicago	.244	150	621	554	85	135	246	28	4	25	92	1	5	7	54	4	116	12	8	9	.444	.316
nders, Reggie, Cincinnati.....	.251	81	334	287	49	72	133	17	1	14	33	0	1	2	44	4	86	24	8	8	.463	.353
nders, Scott, San Diego	.194	46	41	36	2	7	10	3	0	0	1	4	0	0	1	0	11	0	0	0	.278	.216
antangelo, F.P., Montreal†....	.277	152	467	393	54	109	160	20	5	7	56	9	5	11	49	4	61	5	2	6	.407	.369
ntiago, Benito, Philadelphia ..	.264	136	533	481	71	127	242	21	2	30	85	0	2	1	49	7	104	2	0	8	.503	.332
arsone, Steve, San Francisco..	.219	105	319	283	28	62	91	12	1	5	23	8	1	2	25	0	91	2	3	6	.322	.286
chall, Gene, Philadelphia	.273	28	79	66	7	18	31	5	1	2	10	0	0	1	12	0	15	0	0	2	.470	.392
chilling, Curt, Philadelphia......	.175	28	71	63	1	11	12	1	0	0	4	7	0	0	1	0	24	0	0	1	.190	.188

Player, Team	Avg.	G	TPA	AB	R	H	TB	2B	3B	HR	RBI	SH	SF	HP	BB	IBB	SO	SB	CS	GDP	Slg.	OB
Schmidt, Jason, Atl.-Pit	.032	19	35	31	1	1	1	0	0	0	3	2	0	0	2	0	15	0	0	0	.032	.09
Schourek, Pete, Cincinnati*	.263	13	25	19	1	5	5	0	0	0	2	5	0	0	1	0	5	0	0	0	.263	.30
Schu, Rick, Montreal	.000	1	4	4	0	0	0	0	0	0	0	0	0	0	0	0	0	0	0	0	.000	.00
Scott, Tim, Mon.-S.F.	.000	65	5	5	0	0	0	0	0	0	0	0	0	0	0	0	4	0	0	0	.000	.00
Sefcik, Kevin, Philadelphia	.284	44	130	116	10	33	44	5	3	0	9	1	2	2	9	3	16	3	0	4	.379	.34
Segui, David, Montreal†	.286	115	477	416	69	119	184	30	1	11	58	0	1	0	60	4	54	4	4	8	.442	.37
Servais, Scott, Chicago	.265	129	499	445	42	118	171	20	0	11	63	3	7	14	30	1	75	0	2	18	.384	.32
Service, Scott, Cincinnati	.000	34	5	5	0	0	0	0	0	0	0	0	0	0	0	0	2	0	0	0	.000	.00
Shaw, Jeff, Cincinnati	.000	78	6	5	0	0	0	0	0	0	0	0	0	0	1	0	3	0	0	0	.000	.16
Sheaffer, Danny, St. Louis	.227	79	214	198	10	45	66	9	3	2	20	4	0	3	9	0	25	3	3	13	.333	.27
Sheffield, Gary, Florida	.314	161	677	519	118	163	324	33	1	42	120	0	6	10	142	19	66	16	9	16	.624	.46
Shipley, Craig, San Diego	.315	33	99	92	13	29	37	5	0	1	7	1	2	2	2	1	15	7	0	0	.402	.33
Shumpert, Terry, Chicago	.226	27	35	31	5	7	14	1	0	2	6	0	1	1	2	0	11	0	1	0	.452	.28
Siddall, Joe, Florida*	.149	18	49	47	0	7	8	1	0	0	3	0	0	0	2	0	8	0	0	0	.170	.18
Silvestri, Dave, Montreal	.204	86	200	162	16	33	40	4	0	1	17	3	1	0	34	6	41	2	1	5	.247	.34
Simms, Mike, Houston	.176	49	73	68	6	12	19	2	1	1	8	0	1	1	4	0	16	1	0	1	.279	.23
Small, Mark, Houston	.000	16	1	1	0	0	0	0	0	0	0	0	0	0	0	0	1	0	0	0	.000	.00
Smiley, John, Cincinnati*	.191	35	76	68	1	13	15	2	0	0	6	4	0	0	4	0	22	0	0	1	.221	.23
Smith, Dwight, Atlanta*	.203	101	172	153	16	31	45	5	0	3	16	0	1	1	17	1	42	1	3	2	.294	.28
Smith, Ozzie, St. Louis†	.282	82	261	227	36	64	84	10	2	2	18	7	0	2	25	0	9	7	5	5	.370	.35
Smith, Zane, Pittsburgh*	.154	16	28	26	2	4	4	0	0	0	3	2	0	0	0	0	6	0	0	0	.154	.15
Smoltz, John, Atlanta	.218	35	98	78	3	17	23	3	0	1	12	15	1	1	3	0	26	0	0	0	.295	.25
Soderstrom, Steve, S.F.	.000	3	5	5	0	0	0	0	0	0	0	0	0	0	0	0	3	0	0	0	.000	.00
Sosa, Sammy, Chicago	.273	124	541	498	84	136	281	21	2	40	100	0	4	5	34	6	134	18	5	14	.564	.32
Spehr, Tim, Montreal	.091	63	49	44	4	4	8	1	0	1	3	1	0	1	3	0	15	1	0	1	.182	.16
Spiers, Bill, Houston*	.252	122	242	218	27	55	85	10	1	6	26	1	1	2	20	4	34	7	0	3	.390	.32
Springer, Russ, Philadelphia	.059	51	19	17	1	1	1	0	0	0	0	2	0	0	0	0	12	0	0	1	.059	.05
Stankiewicz, Andy, Montreal	.286	64	88	77	12	22	29	5	1	0	9	1	1	3	6	1	12	1	0	1	.377	.35
Steverson, Todd, San Diego	.000	1	1	1	0	0	0	0	0	0	0	0	0	0	0	0	1	0	0	0	.000	.00
Stocker, Kevin, Philadelphia†	.254	119	452	394	46	100	149	22	6	5	41	3	4	8	43	9	89	6	4	6	.378	.33
Stottlemyre, Todd, St. Louis*	.227	34	82	66	8	15	15	0	0	0	2	9	0	0	7	0	27	1	1	0	.227	.30
Sturtze, Tanyon, Chicago	.000	6	2	1	0	0	0	0	0	0	0	1	0	0	0	0	0	0	0	0	.000	.00
Sullivan, Scott, Cincinnati	.000	7	1	1	0	0	0	0	0	0	1	0	0	0	0	0	0	0	0	0	.000	.00
Sveum, Dale, Pittsburgh†	.353	12	40	34	9	12	20	5	0	1	5	0	0	0	6	0	6	0	0	0	.588	.45
Swartzbaugh, Dave, Chicago	.000	6	7	6	0	0	0	0	0	0	0	0	0	0	1	0	3	0	0	0	.000	.14
Sweeney, Mark, St. Louis*	.265	98	209	170	32	45	63	9	0	3	22	5	0	1	33	2	29	3	0	4	.371	.38
Swift, Bill, Colorado	.333	7	6	6	0	2	2	0	0	0	0	0	0	0	0	0	1	0	0	0	.333	.33
Swindell, Greg, Houston	.333	8	6	6	0	2	3	1	0	0	0	0	0	0	0	0	1	0	0	0	.500	.33
Tabaka, Jeff, Houston	.000	18	1	1	0	0	0	0	0	0	0	0	0	0	0	0	0	0	0	0	.000	.00
Tatum, Jimmy, San Diego	.000	5	3	3	0	0	0	0	0	0	0	0	0	0	0	0	1	0	0	0	.000	.00
Taubensee, Eddie, Cincinnati*	.291	108	359	327	46	95	151	20	0	12	48	1	5	0	26	5	64	3	4	4	.462	.33
Tavarez, Jesus, Florida†	.219	98	124	114	14	25	28	3	0	0	6	3	0	0	7	0	18	5	1	2	.246	.26
Telemaco, Amaury, Chicago	.103	25	34	29	1	3	3	0	0	0	1	4	0	0	1	0	15	0	0	0	.103	.13
Tewksbury, Bob, San Diego	.031	36	76	65	1	2	3	1	0	0	2	8	0	0	3	0	27	0	0	1	.046	.07
Thobe, Tom, Atlanta*	.000	4	1	1	0	0	0	0	0	0	0	0	0	0	0	0	0	0	0	0	.000	.00
Thompson, Jason, San Diego*	.224	13	51	49	4	11	21	4	0	2	6	0	1	0	1	0	14	0	0	0	.429	.23
Thompson, Mark, Colorado	.138	34	64	58	3	8	11	3	0	0	2	5	0	0	1	0	21	0	0	1	.190	.15
Thompson, Milt, L.A.-Col.*	.106	62	73	66	3	7	9	2	0	0	3	0	0	0	7	0	13	1	1	1	.136	.19
Thompson, Robby, S.F.	.211	63	259	227	35	48	76	11	1	5	21	3	0	5	24	0	69	2	2	6	.335	.30
Timmons, Ozzie, Chicago	.200	65	157	140	18	28	53	4	0	7	16	1	0	1	15	0	30	1	0	1	.379	.28
Tinsley, Lee, Philadelphia†	.135	31	57	52	1	7	7	0	0	0	2	1	0	0	4	0	22	2	4	1	.135	.19
Tomberlin, Andy, New York*	.258	63	76	66	12	17	30	4	0	3	10	0	0	1	9	0	27	0	0	0	.455	.35
Trachsel, Steve, Chicago	.106	31	73	66	3	7	12	2	0	1	5	6	0	0	1	0	20	0	0	0	.182	.11
Urbani, Tom, St. Louis*	.167	5	6	6	0	1	1	0	0	0	0	0	0	0	0	0	1	0	0	0	.167	.16
Urbina, Ugueth, Montreal	.103	33	34	29	3	3	3	0	0	0	1	3	0	0	2	0	17	0	0	0	.103	.15
Valdes, Ismael, Los Angeles	.143	33	84	70	6	10	11	1	0	0	2	13	0	0	1	0	25	0	0	1	.157	.15
Valdes, Marc, Florida	.000	11	15	14	0	0	0	0	0	0	0	0	0	0	1	0	2	0	0	0	.000	.06
Valdes, Pedro, Chicago*	.125	9	9	8	2	1	2	1	0	0	1	0	0	0	1	0	5	0	0	0	.250	.22
Valenzuela, Fernando, S.D.*	.143	36	66	63	4	9	11	2	0	0	2	3	0	0	0	0	15	0	0	0	.175	.14
Vander Wal, John, Colorado*	.252	104	173	151	20	38	63	6	2	5	31	0	2	1	19	2	38	2	2	1	.417	.33
VanLandingham, William, S.F.	.131	32	70	61	3	8	9	1	0	0	2	6	1	0	2	0	31	0	0	1	.148	.15
Vaughn, Greg, San Diego	.206	43	167	141	20	29	64	3	1	10	22	0	0	2	24	2	31	4	1	1	.454	.32
Veras, Quilvio, Florida†	.253	73	308	253	40	64	86	8	1	4	14	1	1	2	51	1	42	8	8	3	.340	.38
Veres, Dave, Montreal	.375	68	8	8	1	3	4	1	0	0	1	0	0	0	0	0	4	0	0	0	.500	.37
Vizcaino, Jose, New York†	.303	96	402	363	47	110	137	12	6	1	32	6	2	3	28	0	58	9	5	6	.377	.35
Wade, Terrell, Atlanta*	.154	44	16	13	0	2	2	0	0	0	1	2	0	0	1	0	7	0	0	1	.154	.21
Wagner, Billy, Houston*	.000	37	5	5	0	0	0	0	0	0	0	0	0	0	0	0	2	0	0	0	.000	.00
Wagner, Paul, Pittsburgh	.040	17	30	25	1	1	1	0	0	0	0	3	0	0	2	0	8	0	1	0	.040	.11
Wainhouse, David, Pittsburgh*.	.000	17	1	1	0	0	0	0	0	0	0	0	0	0	0	0	0	0	0	0	.000	.00
Walker, Larry, Colorado*	.276	83	304	272	58	75	155	18	4	18	58	0	3	9	20	2	58	18	2	7	.570	.34
Wall, Donne, Houston	.205	26	54	44	5	9	10	1	0	0	1	8	0	0	2	0	11	0	0	0	.227	.23
Wallach, Tim, Los Angeles	.228	45	175	162	14	37	54	3	1	4	22	0	0	1	12	0	32	0	1	4	.333	.28
Walton, Jerome, Atlanta	.340	37	55	47	9	16	24	5	0	1	4	1	2	0	5	1	8	1	1	1	.511	.38
Watson, Allen, San Francisco*	.231	32	72	65	5	15	18	3	0	0	7	2	0	0	5	0	8	0	0	3	.277	.28
Weathers, Dave, Florida	.158	32	20	19	1	3	6	0	0	1	1	0	0	0	0	0	13	0	0	0	.316	.20
Webster, Lenny, Montreal	.230	78	203	174	18	40	56	10	0	2	17	1	1	2	25	2	21	0	0	10	.322	.33
Wehner, John, Pittsburgh	.259	86	149	139	19	36	53	9	1	2	13	2	0	0	8	1	22	1	5	3	.381	.29
Weiss, Walt, Colorado†	.282	155	624	517	89	146	194	20	2	8	48	14	6	6	80	5	78	10	2	9	.375	.38
Wendell, Turk, Chicago*	.500	70	4	2	0	1	1	0	0	0	0	1	0	0	1	0	0	0	0	0	.500	.66
West, David, Philadelphia*	.286	7	11	7	0	2	2	0	0	0	2	0	0	0	2	0	2	0	0	0	.286	.44
White, Devon, Florida†	.274	146	611	552	77	151	251	37	6	17	84	4	9	8	38	6	99	22	6	8	.455	.32
White, Rondell, Montreal	.293	88	359	334	35	98	143	19	4	6	41	0	1	2	22	0	53	14	6	11	.428	.34
Whiten, Mark, Phi.-Atl.†	.243	96	323	272	45	66	111	13	1	10	38	0	1	1	49	2	87	15	8	11	.408	.35

ayer, Team	Avg.	G	TPA	AB	R	H	TB	2B	3B	HR	RBI	SH	SF	HP	BB	IBB	SO	SB	CS	GDP	Slg.	OBP
ilkins, Marc, Pittsburgh	.222	47	10	9	1	2	2	0	0	0	1	0	0	0	1	0	6	0	0	0	.222	.300
ilkins, Rick, Hou.-S.F.*	.243	136	489	411	53	100	164	18	2	14	59	0	10	1	67	13	121	0	3	5	.399	.344
illiams, Keith, San Francisco	.250	9	20	20	0	5	5	0	0	0	0	0	0	0	0	0	6	0	0	0	.250	.250
illiams, Matt, San Francisco	.302	105	455	404	69	122	206	16	1	22	85	0	6	6	39	9	91	1	2	10	.510	.367
illiams, Mike, Philadelphia	.157	33	59	51	4	8	8	0	0	0	1	6	0	0	2	0	11	1	0	0	.157	.189
ilson, Desi, San Francisco*	.271	41	130	118	10	32	40	2	0	2	12	0	0	0	12	2	27	0	2	2	.339	.338
ilson, Paul, New York	.080	26	56	50	3	4	7	0	0	1	4	4	0	1	1	0	32	0	0	0	.140	.115
ohlers, Mark, Atlanta	.000	77	3	3	0	0	0	0	0	0	0	0	0	0	0	0	3	0	0	0	.000	.000
omack, Tony, Pittsburgh*	.333	17	40	30	11	10	15	3	1	0	7	3	0	1	6	0	1	2	0	0	.500	.459
oodall, Brad, Atlanta†	.200	8	6	5	0	1	1	0	0	0	0	0	0	0	1	0	2	0	0	0	.200	.333
orrell, Tim, San Diego	.150	50	27	20	1	3	3	0	0	0	2	6	0	0	1	0	10	0	0	0	.150	.190
right, Jamey, Colorado	.077	16	33	26	3	2	4	2	0	0	0	5	0	0	2	0	13	0	0	0	.154	.143
oung, Anthony, Houston	.000	28	2	2	0	0	0	0	0	0	0	0	0	0	0	0	2	0	0	0	.000	.000
oung, Dmitri, St. Louis†	.241	16	34	29	3	7	7	0	0	0	2	0	0	1	4	0	5	0	1	1	.241	.353
oung, Eric, Colorado	.324	141	643	568	113	184	239	23	4	8	74	2	5	21	47	1	31	53	19	9	.421	.393
aun, Greg, Florida†	.290	10	35	31	4	9	13	1	0	1	2	1	0	0	3	1	5	1	0	2	.419	.353
ile, Todd, Philadelphia	.268	134	572	500	61	134	218	24	0	20	80	0	4	1	67	4	88	1	1	16	.436	.353
ber, Jon, Philadelphia*	.253	30	99	91	7	23	30	4	0	1	10	1	1	0	6	1	11	1	0	3	.330	.296

AWARDED FIRST BASE ON OBSTRUCTION OR CATCHER'S INTERFERENCE—Klesko, Atlanta 3 (Owens, Osik, Spehr); Caminiti, San Diego (Santiago); Cianfrocco, San ego (Wilkins); Colbrunn, Florida (Taubensee); Fletcher, Montreal (Servais); Johnson, Florida (Osik); Manwaring, S.F.-Hou. (Houston); Weiss, Colorado (Taubensee).

PLAYERS WITH TWO OR MORE TEAMS

ayer, Team	Avg.	G	TPA	AB	R	H	TB	2B	3B	HR	RBI	SH	SF	HP	BB	IBB	SO	SB	CS	GDP	Slg.	OBP
nthony, Eric, Cincinnati*	.244	47	145	123	22	30	60	6	0	8	13	0	0	0	22	2	36	0	1	2	.488	.359
nthony, Eric, Colorado*	.242	32	73	62	10	15	29	2	0	4	9	0	1	0	10	0	20	0	1	1	.468	.342
edeno, Andujar, San Diego	.234	49	165	154	10	36	49	2	1	3	18	0	1	1	9	2	32	3	2	7	.318	.279
edeno, Andujar, Houston	.000	3	4	2	1	0	0	0	0	0	0	0	0	0	2	0	1	0	0	0	.000	.500
ark, Dave, Pittsburgh*	.275	92	243	211	28	58	98	12	2	8	35	0	1	0	31	3	51	2	1	6	.464	.366
ark, Dave, Los Angeles*	.200	15	18	15	0	3	3	0	0	0	1	0	0	0	3	0	2	0	0	0	.200	.333
arwin, Danny, Pittsburgh	.205	19	44	39	2	8	15	4	0	1	3	5	0	0	0	0	19	0	0	1	.385	.205
arwin, Danny, Houston	.100	15	12	10	0	1	1	0	0	0	0	2	0	0	0	0	8	1	0	0	.100	.100
ecker, Steve, San Francisco	.230	57	142	122	16	28	32	1	0	1	12	3	2	0	15	4	26	0	0	3	.262	.309
ecker, Steve, Colorado	.320	10	29	25	8	8	13	2	0	1	8	1	0	0	3	0	3	1	0	0	.520	.393
artgraves, Dean, Houston	.000	19	1	0	0	0	0	0	0	0	0	1	0	0	0	0	0	0	0	0	.000	.000
artgraves, Dean, Atlanta	.000	20	1	1	0	0	0	0	0	0	0	0	0	0	0	0	0	0	0	0	.000	.000
ouston, Tyler, Atlanta*	.222	33	28	27	3	6	13	2	1	1	8	0	0	0	1	0	9	0	0	1	.481	.250
ouston, Tyler, Chicago*	.339	46	123	115	18	39	52	7	0	2	19	0	0	0	8	1	18	3	2	4	.452	.382
ubbard, Trent, Colorado	.217	45	70	60	12	13	23	5	1	1	12	0	0	1	9	0	22	2	0	1	.383	.329
ubbard, Trent, San Francisco	.207	10	31	29	3	6	11	0	1	1	2	0	0	0	2	0	5	0	0	2	.379	.258
den, Jeff, San Francisco†	.000	36	3	3	0	0	0	0	0	0	0	0	0	0	0	0	2	0	0	0	.000	.000
den, Jeff, Montreal†	.000	22	1	0	0	0	0	0	0	0	0	0	1	0	0	0	0	0	0	0	.000	.000
eiter, Mark, San Francisco	.143	23	50	42	2	6	7	1	0	0	2	7	0	0	1	0	20	0	0	1	.167	.163
eiter, Mark, Montreal	.080	12	29	25	2	2	2	0	0	0	3	2	0	0	2	0	15	0	0	0	.080	.148
anwaring, Kirt, San Francisco	.234	49	167	145	9	34	43	6	0	1	14	1	2	3	16	1	24	0	1	2	.297	.319
anwaring, Kirt, Houston	.220	37	89	82	5	18	21	3	0	0	4	1	0	2	3	0	16	0	0	2	.256	.264
organ, Mike, St. Louis	.061	18	42	33	1	2	2	0	0	0	0	9	0	0	0	0	14	0	0	0	.061	.061
organ, Mike, Cincinnati	.000	5	9	7	0	0	0	0	0	0	0	0	2	0	0	0	3	0	0	0	.000	.000
eagle, Denny, Pittsburgh*	.182	30	73	55	3	10	11	1	0	0	2	16	1	0	1	0	15	0	0	0	.200	.193
eagle, Denny, Atlanta*	.143	6	15	14	0	2	2	0	0	0	0	2	0	0	1	0	3	0	0	0	.143	.200
endleton, Terry, Florida†	.251	111	441	406	30	102	145	20	1	7	58	1	5	3	26	5	75	0	2	10	.357	.298
endleton, Terry, Atlanta†	.204	42	177	162	21	33	51	6	0	4	17	0	0	0	15	1	36	2	1	8	.315	.271
hillips, J.R., San Francisco*	.200	15	26	25	3	5	11	0	0	2	5	0	0	0	1	0	13	0	0	0	.440	.231
hillips, J.R., Philadelphia	.152	35	90	79	9	12	32	5	0	5	10	0	0	1	10	1	38	0	0	1	.405	.256
ueter, Kirk, Montreal*	.120	16	29	25	2	3	3	0	0	0	2	2	1	0	1	0	4	0	0	0	.120	.148
ueter, Kirk, San Francisco*	.143	4	8	7	0	1	1	0	0	0	1	0	0	1	0	0	1	0	0	1	.143	.250
chmidt, Jason, Atlanta	.000	13	22	19	1	0	0	0	0	0	1	1	0	0	2	0	9	0	0	0	.000	.095
chmidt, Jason, Pittsburgh	.083	6	13	12	0	1	1	0	0	0	2	1	0	0	0	0	6	0	0	0	.083	.083
cott, Tim, Montreal	.000	45	4	4	0	0	0	0	0	0	0	0	0	0	0	0	3	0	0	0	.000	.000
cott, Tim, San Francisco	.000	20	1	1	0	0	0	0	0	0	0	0	0	0	0	0	1	0	0	0	.000	.000
hompson, Milt, Los Angeles*	.118	48	57	51	2	6	7	1	0	0	1	0	0	0	6	0	10	1	1	1	.137	.211
hompson, Milt, Colorado*	.067	14	16	15	1	1	2	1	0	0	2	0	0	0	1	0	3	0	0	0	.133	.125
hiten, Mark, Philadelphia†	.236	60	216	182	33	43	72	8	0	7	21	0	0	1	33	2	62	13	3	9	.396	.356
hiten, Mark, Atlanta†	.256	36	107	90	12	23	39	5	1	3	17	0	1	0	16	0	25	2	5	2	.433	.364
ilkins, Rick, Houston*	.213	84	306	254	34	54	84	8	2	6	23	0	5	1	46	10	81	0	1	1	.331	.330
ilkins, Rick, San Francisco*	.293	52	183	157	19	46	80	10	0	8	36	0	5	0	21	3	40	0	2	4	.510	.366

1996 N.L. STATISTICS Batting

PINCH-HITTING

TEAM

Team	Avg.	G	TPA	AB	R	H	TB	2B	3B	HR	RBI	SH	SF	HP	BB	IBB	SO	SB	CS	GDP	Slg.	OBP
Pittsburgh	.286	139	292	259	33	74	124	16	2	10	49	5	2	1	25	3	40	1	1	6	.479	.348
St. Louis	.280	130	242	211	26	59	77	11	2	1	36	5	2	1	23	3	44	2	3	4	.365	.350
New York	.250	130	296	248	43	62	84	11	1	3	30	4	4	3	37	2	80	0	0	4	.339	.349
Montreal	.245	120	236	200	22	49	72	9	1	4	30	4	1	1	30	0	54	5	2	3	.360	.345
Atlanta	.243	127	249	218	23	53	82	9	1	6	32	2	5	1	23	3	56	2	3	9	.376	.312
Florida	.237	133	253	236	27	56	83	9	3	4	34	1	0	3	13	0	56	0	0	8	.352	.286
Cincinnati	.231	144	309	268	33	62	110	9	3	11	45	3	4	1	33	2	67	3	2	5	.410	.314
San Diego	.227	141	280	256	20	58	79	9	0	4	33	2	2	0	20	1	71	1	3	11	.309	.281
Los Angeles	.222	137	286	243	29	54	80	5	0	7	29	3	0	4	36	5	71	2	0	6	.329	.332
Philadelphia	.216	136	239	213	22	46	75	10	2	5	25	3	1	0	22	4	77	0	1	4	.352	.288
Chicago	.207	131	316	276	35	57	82	13	0	4	32	4	3	0	33	3	75	6	2	3	.297	.288
San Francisco	.205	132	247	220	24	45	66	3	0	6	31	3	3	1	20	3	59	1	1	6	.300	.270
Colorado	.197	140	277	239	21	47	71	11	2	3	34	3	3	1	31	2	79	2	2	5	.297	.288
Houston	.192	125	248	219	19	42	73	13	0	6	33	3	2	4	20	2	57	2	3	6	.333	.269
Totals	.231	1865	3770	3306	377	764	1158	138	17	74	473	45	32	21	366	33	886	27	23	80	.350	.309

INDIVIDUAL

TOP PINCH-HITTERS

Minimum 20 at-bats. *Lefthanded batter. †Switch-hitter.

Player, Team	Avg.	G	TPA	AB	R	H	TB	2B	3B	HR	RBI	SH	SF	HP	BB	IBB	SO	SB	CS	GDP	Slg.	OBP
Johnson, Mark, Pittsburgh*	.452	36	36	31	9	14	28	2	0	4	9	0	0	1	4	0	7	0	1	1	.903	.52
Howard, Thomas, Cincinnati*	.393	32	31	28	6	11	22	2	0	3	9	0	0	0	3	1	1	0	1	1	.786	.45
Amaro, Ruben, Philadelphia†	.387	35	35	31	5	12	18	3	0	1	10	1	0	0	3	0	4	0	0	2	.581	.44
Arias, Alex, Florida	.357	31	31	28	5	10	15	3	1	0	8	0	0	0	3	0	6	0	0	0	.536	.41
McGee, Willie, St. Louis†	.350	44	43	40	4	14	19	3	1	0	9	0	1	0	2	0	11	0	0	1	.475	.37
Harris, Lenny, Cincinnati*	.347	58	58	49	4	17	27	2	1	2	13	1	2	0	6	1	7	1	1	0	.551	.40
Wehner, John, Pittsburgh	.346	30	27	26	7	9	20	3	1	2	6	0	0	0	1	0	4	0	0	1	.769	.37
Ashley, Billy, Los Angeles	.345	38	38	29	8	10	25	0	0	5	12	0	0	1	8	1	13	0	0	1	.862	.50
Berry, Sean, Houston	.333	22	22	21	1	7	13	3	0	1	10	0	0	0	1	0	4	0	1	0	.619	.36
Stankiewicz, Andy, Montreal	.321	33	32	28	3	9	13	2	1	0	5	1	0	1	2	0	5	0	0	0	.464	.38
Jones, Chris, New York	.318	26	25	22	7	7	8	1	0	0	1	0	0	1	2	1	6	0	0	0	.364	.40
Livingstone, Scott, San Diego*	.311	68	64	61	4	19	24	2	0	1	11	0	0	0	3	0	12	0	0	2	.393	.34
Floyd, Cliff, Montreal*	.303	41	39	33	4	10	19	0	0	3	11	0	1	0	5	0	8	1	0	1	.576	.38
May, Derrick, Houston*	.300	42	39	30	3	9	15	3	0	1	6	0	1	1	7	1	5	0	0	1	.500	.43
Tavarez, Jesus, Florida†	.300	33	33	30	3	9	11	2	0	0	1	1	0	0	2	0	6	0	0	1	.367	.34

ALL PINCH-HITTERS

*Lefthanded batter. †Switch-hitter.

Player, Team	Avg.	G	TPA	AB	R	H	TB	2B	3B	HR	RBI	SH	SF	HP	BB	IBB	SO	SB	CS	GDP	Slg.	OBP
Abbott, Kurt, Florida	.333	15	15	15	4	5	13	0	1	2	3	0	0	0	0	0	3	0	0	1	.867	.333
Abreu, Bob, Houston*	.143	8	7	7	0	1	1	0	0	0	0	0	0	0	0	0	1	0	0	0	.143	.143
Alfonzo, Edgardo, New York	.462	18	18	13	4	6	6	0	0	0	1	2	0	0	3	0	2	0	0	0	.462	.563
Alicea, Luis, St. Louis†	.222	14	14	9	4	2	3	1	0	0	0	1	0	1	3	1	2	1	0	0	.333	.462
Allensworth, Jermaine, Pit.	.000	1	1	0	1	0	0	0	0	0	0	0	0	0	1	0	0	0	0	0	.000	1.000
Alou, Moises, Montreal	1.000	1	1	1	1	1	4	0	0	1	1	0	0	0	0	0	0	0	0	0	4.000	1.000
Amaro, Ruben, Philadelphia†	.387	35	35	31	5	12	18	3	0	1	10	1	0	0	3	0	4	0	0	2	.581	.441
Andrews, Shane, Montreal	.400	5	5	5	0	2	2	0	0	0	2	0	0	0	0	0	3	0	0	0	.400	.400
Anthony, Eric, Cin.-Col.*	.111	24	23	18	2	2	5	0	0	1	2	0	0	0	5	0	5	0	0	1	.278	.304
Arias, Alex, Florida	.357	31	31	28	5	10	15	3	1	0	8	0	0	0	3	0	6	0	0	0	.536	.419
Ashby, Andy, San Diego	.000	1	1	0	0	0	0	0	0	0	0	0	1	0	0	0	0	0	0	0	.000	.000
Ashley, Billy, Los Angeles	.345	38	38	29	8	10	25	0	0	5	12	0	0	1	8	1	13	0	0	1	.862	.500
Aude, Rich, Pittsburgh	.333	3	3	3	0	1	1	0	0	0	0	0	0	0	0	0	1	0	0	0	.333	.333
Aurilia, Rich, San Francisco	.000	3	3	2	0	0	0	0	0	0	0	0	1	0	0	0	1	0	0	0	.000	.333
Ausmus, Brad, San Diego	.250	4	4	4	1	1	1	0	0	0	0	0	0	0	0	0	0	0	0	0	.250	.250
Baerga, Carlos, New York†	.600	6	6	5	2	3	6	0	0	1	2	0	0	0	1	0	0	0	0	0	1.200	.667
Barberie, Bret, Chicago†	.200	8	8	5	2	1	4	0	0	1	2	0	0	0	3	0	2	0	0	0	.800	.500
Barron, Tony, Montreal	.000	1	1	1	0	0	0	0	0	0	0	0	0	0	0	0	1	0	0	0	.000	.000
Bates, Jason, Colorado†	.182	37	37	33	3	6	9	3	0	0	2	0	0	0	4	1	9	0	0	1	.273	.270
Batiste, Kim, San Francisco	.174	24	24	23	5	4	10	0	0	2	5	0	1	0	0	0	10	0	0	1	.435	.167
Battle, Howard, Philadelphia	.000	4	4	4	0	0	0	0	0	0	0	0	0	0	0	0	2	0	0	0	.000	.000
Bautista, Danny, Atlanta	.250	5	5	4	0	1	1	0	0	0	0	0	0	0	1	0	1	0	0	2	.250	.400
Beamon, Trey, Pittsburgh*	.143	10	8	7	1	1	1	0	0	0	0	0	0	0	1	0	2	0	0	0	.143	.250
Belk, Tim, Cincinnati	.000	2	2	2	0	0	0	0	0	0	0	0	0	0	0	0	0	0	0	0	.000	.000
Bell, David, St. Louis	.333	7	6	6	0	2	4	2	0	0	1	0	0	0	0	0	0	0	0	0	.667	.333
Bell, Derek, Houston	.000	1	1	1	0	0	0	0	0	0	0	0	0	0	0	0	1	0	0	0	.000	.000
Bell, Jay, Pittsburgh	1.000	1	1	1	0	1	1	0	0	0	0	0	0	0	0	0	0	0	0	0	1.000	1.000
Belliard, Rafael, Atlanta	.250	4	4	4	0	1	1	0	0	0	0	0	0	0	0	0	0	0	0	0	.250	.250
Benard, Marvin, San Francisco*	.200	5	5	5	1	1	1	0	0	0	0	0	0	0	0	0	0	0	0	1	.200	.200
Benitez, Yamil, Montreal	.143	7	7	7	0	1	1	0	0	0	0	0	0	0	0	0	3	0	0	0	.143	.143
Benjamin, Mike, Philadelphia	.500	3	3	2	0	1	1	0	0	0	0	0	1	0	0	0	1	0	0	0	.500	.500
Bennett, Gary, Philadelphia	.000	1	1	1	0	0	0	0	0	0	0	0	0	0	0	0	1	0	0	0	.000	.000
Bergman, Sean, San Diego	.000	1	1	1	0	0	0	0	0	-0	0	0	0	0	0	0	1	0	0	0	.000	.000
Berry, Sean, Houston	.333	22	22	21	1	7	13	3	0	1	10	0	0	0	1	0	4	0	1	0	.619	.364
Bichette, Dante, Colorado	.000	3	3	3	0	0	0	0	0	0	0	0	0	0	0	0	2	0	0	0	.000	.000
Blauser, Jeff, Atlanta	.000	2	2	1	0	0	0	0	0	0	0	0	0	1	0	0	1	0	0	0	.000	.500

Player, Team	Avg.	G	TPA	AB	R	H	TB	2B	3B	HR	RBI	SH	SF	HP	BB	IBB	SO	SB	CS	GDP	Slg.	OBP
Blowers, Mike, Los Angeles	.000	1	1	1	0	0	0	0	0	0	0	0	0	0	0	0	0	0	0	1	.000	.000
Bogar, Tim, New York	.333	10	10	6	2	2	2	0	0	0	1	0	1	0	3	0	2	0	0	0	.333	.500
Bonds, Barry, San Francisco*	.167	7	7	6	0	1	1	0	0	0	0	0	0	0	1	1	2	0	0	0	.167	.286
Boone, Bret, Cincinnati	.000	1	1	1	0	0	0	0	0	0	0	0	0	0	0	0	1	0	0	0	.000	.000
Booty, Josh, Florida	.500	2	2	2	1	1	1	0	0	0	0	0	0	0	0	0	0	0	0	1	.500	.500
Borders, Pat, St. Louis	.125	8	8	8	0	1	1	0	0	0	0	0	0	0	0	0	2	0	1	0	.125	.125
Bradshaw, Terry, St. Louis*	.429	9	9	7	2	3	3	0	0	0	0	0	0	0	2	0	0	0	1	0	.429	.556
Branson, Jeff, Cincinnati*	.150	24	24	20	2	3	4	1	0	0	2	0	1	0	3	0	6	0	0	1	.200	.250
Brito, Jorge, Colorado	.000	1	1	1	0	0	0	0	0	0	0	0	0	0	0	0	1	0	0	0	.000	.000
Brogna, Rico, New York*	.000	5	5	4	0	0	0	0	0	0	0	0	0	0	1	0	1	0	0	1	.000	.200
Brooks, Jerry, Florida	.250	5	5	4	2	1	3	0	1	0	2	0	0	1	0	0	1	0	0	0	.750	.400
Brown, Brant, Chicago*	.182	13	13	11	1	2	5	0	0	1	2	0	1	0	1	1	4	0	0	1	.455	.231
Brumfield, Jacob, Pittsburgh	.111	10	10	9	0	1	1	0	0	0	0	0	0	0	1	1	3	0	0	0	.111	.200
Bullett, Scott, Chicago*	.203	65	64	59	8	12	13	1	0	0	3	0	1	0	4	0	22	4	1	1	.220	.250
Burks, Ellis, Colorado	.200	6	6	5	0	1	1	0	0	0	0	0	0	0	1	0	1	1	0	0	.200	.333
Busch, Mike, Los Angeles	.214	17	16	14	1	3	7	1	0	1	2	0	0	0	2	0	4	0	0	1	.500	.313
Caminiti, Ken, San Diego†	.000	3	2	2	0	0	0	0	0	0	0	0	0	0	0	0	1	0	0	0	.000	.000
Cangelosi, John, Houston†	.036	34	33	28	3	1	1	0	0	0	0	0	2	3	0	0	8	1	1	0	.036	.182
Canizaro, Jay, San Francisco	.333	3	3	3	0	1	1	0	0	0	0	0	0	0	0	0	2	0	1	0	.333	.333
Carreon, Mark, San Francisco	.667	6	6	6	1	4	5	1	0	0	4	0	0	0	0	0	1	0	0	0	.833	.667
Castellano, Pedro, Colorado	.125	8	8	8	0	1	1	0	0	0	1	0	0	0	0	0	5	0	0	0	.125	.125
Castilla, Vinny, Colorado	1.000	2	2	2	1	2	3	1	0	0	2	0	0	0	0	0	0	0	0	0	1.500	1.000
Castro, Juan, Los Angeles	.000	14	14	11	0	0	0	0	0	0	1	2	0	0	1	0	4	0	0	0	.000	.083
Cedeno, Andujar, San Diego	.500	2	2	2	0	1	1	0	0	0	0	0	0	0	0	0	1	0	0	0	.500	.500
Cedeno, Roger, Los Angeles†	.063	20	20	16	2	1	1	0	0	0	0	0	0	0	4	0	6	0	0	0	.063	.250
Chavez, Raul, Montreal	1.000	1	1	1	0	1	1	0	0	0	0	0	0	0	0	0	0	0	0	0	1.000	1.000
Cianfrocco, Archi, San Diego	.095	22	21	21	0	2	2	0	0	0	2	0	0	0	0	0	8	0	0	1	.095	.095
Clark, Dave, Pit.-L.A.*	.277	54	53	47	4	13	20	2	1	1	6	0	0	0	6	0	10	0	0	0	.426	.358
Clayton, Royce, St. Louis	.231	14	14	13	2	3	3	0	0	0	1	0	0	0	1	1	3	0	1	0	.231	.286
Cockrell, Alan, Colorado	.250	9	9	8	0	2	3	1	0	0	2	0	1	0	0	0	4	0	0	0	.375	.222
Colbrunn, Greg, Florida	.250	8	8	8	1	2	2	0	0	0	1	0	0	0	0	0	1	0	0	0	.250	.250
Coleman, Vince, Cincinnati†	.200	13	13	10	3	2	4	0	1	0	0	0	0	0	3	0	4	1	0	0	.400	.385
Conine, Jeff, Florida	.000	1	1	1	0	0	0	0	0	0	0	0	0	0	0	0	0	0	0	0	.000	.000
Cruz, Jacob, San Francisco*	.125	10	10	8	1	1	1	0	0	0	0	0	0	0	2	0	1	0	0	0	.125	.300
Cummings, Midre, Pittsburgh*	.000	4	4	4	0	0	0	0	0	0	0	0	0	0	0	0	0	0	0	0	.000	.000
Curtis, Chad, Los Angeles	.182	12	12	11	1	2	5	0	0	1	4	0	0	0	1	0	3	0	0	0	.455	.250
Dascenzo, Doug, San Diego†	.200	5	5	5	1	1	1	0	0	0	0	0	0	0	0	0	1	0	0	0	.200	.200
Davis, Eric, Cincinnati	.000	7	7	4	1	0	0	0	0	0	0	2	0	0	3	0	4	0	0	0	.000	.429
Dawson, Andre, Florida	.235	36	36	34	3	8	16	2	0	2	8	0	0	1	1	0	11	0	0	0	.471	.278
Decker, Steve, San Francisco	.200	24	24	20	5	4	5	1	0	0	0	1	0	0	3	1	3	0	0	1	.250	.304
Deer, Rob, San Diego	.222	11	11	9	2	2	6	1	0	1	2	0	0	0	2	0	5	0	0	1	.667	.364
DeShields, Delino, Los Angeles*	.000	3	3	2	0	0	0	0	0	0	0	0	0	0	1	0	0	0	0	0	.000	.333
Dorsett, Brian, Chicago	.000	4	4	2	0	0	0	0	0	0	0	0	0	0	2	0	2	0	0	0	.000	.500
Doster, David, Philadelphia	.308	15	15	13	5	4	4	0	0	0	0	0	0	0	2	0	4	0	0	0	.308	.400
Dreifort, Darren, Los Angeles	.000	1	1	1	0	0	0	0	0	0	0	0	0	0	0	0	0	0	0	0	.000	.000
Dunston, Shawon, S.F.	1.000	3	3	3	0	3	3	0	0	0	1	0	0	0	0	0	0	0	0	0	1.000	1.000
Dye, Jermaine, Atlanta	.571	7	7	7	1	4	4	0	0	0	2	0	0	0	0	0	1	0	1	0	.571	.571
Dykstra, Lenny, Philadelphia*	.333	5	5	3	1	1	1	0	0	0	1	0	1	0	1	0	1	0	0	0	.333	.400
Echevarria, Angel, Colorado	.286	17	17	14	1	4	4	0	0	0	3	0	0	1	2	0	2	0	0	0	.286	.412
Eisenreich, Jim, Philadelphia*	.136	24	24	22	0	3	4	1	0	0	0	0	0	0	2	2	4	0	0	1	.182	.208
Espinoza, Alvaro, New York	.750	4	4	4	1	3	5	0	1	0	1	0	0	0	0	0	1	0	0	0	1.250	.750
Estalella, Bobby, Philadelphia	.000	3	3	3	0	0	0	0	0	0	0	0	0	0	0	0	2	0	0	0	.000	.000
Eusebio, Tony, Houston	.231	15	15	13	2	3	7	1	0	1	5	0	0	0	2	1	4	0	0	1	.538	.333
Everett, Carl, New York†	.256	51	51	43	8	11	14	3	0	0	3	0	0	1	7	0	15	0	0	0	.326	.373
Fermin, Felix, Chicago	.000	5	5	5	0	0	0	0	0	0	0	0	0	0	0	0	0	0	0	1	.000	.000
Finley, Steve, San Diego*	.500	2	2	2	1	1	4	0	0	1	1	0	0	0	0	0	0	0	0	0	2.000	.500
Flaherty, John, San Diego	.667	3	3	3	0	2	2	0	0	0	2	0	0	0	0	0	0	0	0	0	.667	.667
Fletcher, Darrin, Montreal*	.222	22	22	18	2	4	6	2	0	0	1	0	0	0	4	0	2	0	0	0	.333	.364
Floyd, Cliff, Montreal*	.303	41	39	33	4	10	19	0	0	3	11	0	1	0	5	0	8	1	0	1	.576	.385
Fonville, Chad, Los Angeles†	.211	21	21	19	2	4	4	0	0	0	1	1	0	0	1	0	7	1	0	0	.211	.250
Franco, Matt, New York*	.200	6	6	5	1	1	1	0	0	0	1	0	1	0	0	0	1	0	0	0	.200	.167
Gaetti, Gary, St. Louis	1.000	1	1	1	1	1	1	0	0	0	2	0	0	0	0	0	0	0	0	0	1.000	1.000
Gagne, Greg, Los Angeles	.000	1	1	0	0	0	0	0	0	0	0	0	0	0	1	0	0	0	0	0	.000	1.000
Galarraga, Andres, Colorado	.000	1	1	0	0	0	0	0	0	0	0	0	0	0	1	0	0	0	0	0	.000	1.000
Gallego, Mike, St. Louis	.250	4	4	4	1	1	1	0	0	0	0	0	0	0	0	0	2	0	0	0	.250	.250
Gant, Ron, St. Louis	.167	6	6	6	1	1	4	0	0	1	4	0	0	0	0	0	5	0	0	0	.667	.167
Garcia, Carlos, Pittsburgh	.000	2	2	2	0	0	0	0	0	0	0	0	0	0	0	0	0	0	0	0	.000	.000
Garcia, Karim, Los Angeles*	.000	1	1	1	0	0	0	0	0	0	0	0	0	0	0	0	1	0	0	0	.000	.000
Gardner, Mark, San Francisco	.000	3	3	1	0	0	0	0	0	0	0	0	2	0	0	0	0	0	0	0	.000	.000
Gilkey, Bernard, New York	.500	2	2	2	0	1	1	0	0	0	1	0	0	0	0	0	1	0	0	0	.500	.500
Giovanola, Ed, Atlanta*	.357	16	16	14	2	5	6	1	0	0	0	1	0	0	1	0	2	0	0	1	.429	.400
Glanville, Doug, Chicago	.316	23	20	19	1	6	8	2	0	0	1	0	0	0	1	0	4	0	0	0	.421	.364
Glavine, Tom, Atlanta*	.333	3	3	3	0	1	1	0	0	0	0	0	0	0	0	0	0	0	0	0	.333	.333
Gomez, Leo, Chicago	.200	19	17	15	1	3	5	2	0	0	5	0	0	0	2	0	3	0	1	0	.333	.294
Gonzalez, Luis, Chicago*	.111	11	11	9	1	1	2	1	0	0	2	0	0	0	2	0	0	0	0	0	.222	.273
Goodwin, Curtis, Cincinnati*	.000	9	9	8	1	0	0	0	0	0	0	0	0	0	1	0	3	0	0	0	.000	.111
Grace, Mark, Chicago*	.000	2	2	1	0	0	0	0	0	0	0	0	1	0	1	0	0	0	0	0	.000	.000
Graffanino, Tony, Atlanta	.000	5	5	5	0	0	0	0	0	0	0	0	0	0	0	0	1	0	0	0	.000	.000
Grebeck, Craig, Chicago	.294	19	18	17	1	5	5	0	0	0	0	0	0	0	2	0	0	0	0	0	.294	.333
Greene, Charlie, New York	.000	1	1	1	0	0	0	0	0	0	0	0	0	0	0	0	0	0	0	0	.000	.000
Greene, Willie, Cincinnati*	.235	37	35	34	3	8	10	0	1	0	4	0	0	0	1	0	9	0	0	1	.294	.257
Grissom, Marquis, Atlanta	.000	1	1	0	0	0	0	0	0	0	1	0	1	0	0	0	0	0	0	0	.000	.000
Guerrero, Vladimir, Montreal	.000	1	1	1	0	0	0	0	0	0	0	0	0	0	0	0	0	0	0	0	.000	.000

Player, Team	Avg.	G	TPA	AB	R	H	TB	2B	3B	HR	RBI	SH	SF	HP	BB	IBB	SO	SB	CS	GDP	Slg.	OBP
Guerrero, Wilton, Los Angeles..	.000	2	2	2	0	0	0	0	0	0	0	0	0	0	0	0	2	0	0	0	.000	.000
Gutierrez, Ricky, Houston	.000	9	9	6	0	0	0	0	0	0	0	2	0	0	1	0	3	0	0	0	.000	.143
Gwynn, Chris, San Diego*	.151	57	57	53	1	8	12	4	0	0	4	0	0	0	4	0	16	0	0	2	.226	.211
Gwynn, Tony, San Diego*	.400	6	6	5	1	2	2	0	0	0	1	0	0	0	1	1	0	0	1	1	.400	.500
Hajek, Dave, Houston	.500	3	3	2	1	1	2	1	0	0	0	0	0	0	1	0	0	0	0	0	1.000	.667
Hall, Mel, San Francisco*	.105	22	21	19	2	2	2	0	0	0	3	0	1	0	1	0	4	0	0	0	.105	.143
Haney, Todd, Chicago	.118	21	20	17	1	2	3	1	0	0	0	2	0	0	1	0	4	0	0	0	.176	.167
Hansen, Dave, Los Angeles*	.256	58	49	43	5	11	11	0	0	0	4	0	0	0	6	1	12	0	0	1	.256	.347
Hardtke, Jason, New York†	.200	5	5	5	0	1	1	0	0	0	0	0	0	0	0	0	2	0	0	0	.200	.200
Harris, Lenny, Cincinnati*	.347	58	58	49	4	17	27	2	1	2	13	1	2	0	6	1	7	1	1	0	.551	.404
Hayes, Charlie, Pittsburgh	.333	6	6	6	0	2	2	0	0	0	1	0	0	0	0	0	1	0	0	1	.333	.333
Henderson, Rickey, San Diego..	.250	13	13	8	3	2	2	0	0	0	1	0	1	0	4	0	3	1	1	0	.250	.462
Hernandez, Carlos, Los Angeles..	.500	4	4	4	1	2	2	0	0	0	0	0	0	0	0	0	0	0	0	0	.500	.500
Hernandez, Jose, Chicago.........	.167	7	6	6	1	1	1	0	0	0	0	0	0	0	0	0	2	0	0	0	.167	.167
Hollandsworth, Todd, L.A.*	.429	14	14	14	3	6	8	2	0	0	3	0	0	0	0	0	4	0	0	0	.571	.429
Houston, Tyler, Atl.-Chi.*	.207	32	31	29	2	6	11	3	1	0	4	0	0	0	2	1	8	0	0	1	.379	.258
Howard, Thomas, Cincinnati* ...	.393	32	31	28	6	11	22	2	0	3	9	0	0	0	3	1	1	0	1	1	.786	.452
Hubbard, Mike, Chicago	.111	9	9	9	0	1	1	0	0	0	0	0	0	0	0	0	3	0	0	0	.111	.111
Hubbard, Trent, Col.-S.F.	.160	30	30	25	4	4	7	1	1	0	5	0	0	0	5	0	11	0	0	0	.280	.300
Hundley, Todd, New York†	.125	10	10	8	1	1	2	1	0	0	1	0	1	0	1	0	3	0	0	1	.250	.200
Hunter, Brian L., Houston	.125	8	8	8	1	1	1	0	0	0	0	0	0	0	0	0	3	0	0	0	.125	.125
Huskey, Butch, New York...........	.250	4	4	4	0	1	1	0	0	0	0	0	0	0	0	0	2	0	0	0	.250	.250
Incaviglia, Pete, Philadelphia	.077	29	29	26	1	2	3	1	0	0	1	0	0	0	3	1	15	0	0	2	.115	.172
Jefferies, Gregg, Philadelphia† ...	1.000	1	1	1	0	1	1	0	0	0	1	0	0	0	0	0	0	0	0	0	1.000	1.000
Jennings, Robin, Chicago*	.150	20	20	20	1	3	4	1	0	0	1	0	0	0	0	0	6	0	0	0	.200	.150
Jensen, Marcus, San Francisco† .	.000	2	2	1	0	0	0	0	0	0	0	0	0	0	1	0	1	0	0	0	.000	.500
Johnson, Brian, San Diego	.333	15	15	15	0	5	5	0	0	0	3	0	0	0	0	0	3	0	0	0	.333	.333
Johnson, Charles, Florida	.500	2	2	2	0	1	1	0	0	0	0	0	0	0	0	0	0	0	0	0	.500	.500
Johnson, Lance, New York*	.667	4	4	3	2	2	3	1	0	0	0	0	0	0	1	0	0	0	0	0	1.000	.750
Johnson, Mark, Pittsburgh*	.452	36	36	31	9	14	28	2	0	4	9	0	0	1	4	0	7	0	1	1	.903	.528
Jones, Andruw, Atlanta	.250	4	4	4	0	1	2	1	0	0	1	0	0	0	0	0	1	0	0	0	.500	.250
Jones, Chipper, Atlanta†	.000	2	2	1	0	0	0	0	0	0	0	0	0	0	1	0	1	0	0	0	.000	.500
Jones, Chris, New York..............	.318	26	25	22	7	7	8	1	0	0	1	0	0	1	2	1	6	0	0	1	.364	.400
Jones, Dax, San Francisco.........	.000	5	5	5	0	0	0	0	0	0	0	0	0	0	0	0	1	0	0	0	.000	.000
Jones, Terry, Colorado†	.000	1	1	1	0	0	0	0	0	0	0	0	0	0	0	0	0	0	0	0	.000	.000
Jordan, Brian, St. Louis	.600	7	7	5	0	3	4	1	0	0	4	0	1	0	1	1	1	0	0	0	.800	.571
Jordan, Kevin, Philadelphia........	.000	6	6	5	0	0	0	0	0	0	1	0	0	0	0	0	2	0	0	0	.000	.000
Joyner, Wally, San Diego*	.000	4	2	2	0	0	0	0	0	0	0	0	0	0	0	0	0	0	0	0	.000	.000
Kelly, Mike, Cincinnati...............	.000	2	1	1	0	0	0	0	0	0	0	0	0	0	0	0	0	0	0	0	.000	.000
Kendall, Jason, Pittsburgh.........	.667	3	3	3	0	2	2	0	0	0	1	0	0	0	0	0	0	0	0	0	.667	.667
Kieschnick, Brooks, Chicago*...	.353	20	19	17	4	6	8	2	0	0	4	0	0	0	2	0	5	0	0	0	.471	.421
King, Jeff, Pittsburgh................	.200	6	6	5	0	1	1	0	0	0	1	0	0	0	1	0	1	0	0	1	.200	.333
Kingery, Mike, Pittsburgh*	.250	44	43	40	4	10	19	3	0	2	8	0	0	0	3	1	4	0	0	1	.475	.302
Kirby, Wayne, Los Angeles*	.083	14	13	12	0	1	1	0	0	0	1	0	0	0	1	1	1	0	0	0	.083	.154
Klesko, Ryan, Atlanta*	.000	9	9	6	0	0	0	0	0	0	0	0	0	0	3	1	2	1	0	1	.000	.333
Knorr, Randy, Houston	.250	4	4	4	0	1	1	0	0	0	0	0	0	0	0	0	1	0	0	0	.250	.250
Lampkin, Tom, San Francisco*..	.125	17	16	16	0	2	2	0	0	0	0	0	0	0	0	0	3	0	0	0	.125	.125
Lankford, Ray, St. Louis*	.200	7	6	5	0	1	1	0	0	0	0	0	0	0	1	0	1	0	0	0	.200	.333
Larkin, Barry, Cincinnati............	.333	4	4	3	1	1	4	0	0	1	1	0	0	0	1	0	0	0	0	1	1.333	.500
Lemke, Mark, Atlanta†	.500	2	2	2	0	1	1	0	0	0	0	0	0	0	0	0	0	0	0	0	.500	.500
Lieberthal, Mike, Philadelphia	.125	8	8	8	1	1	2	1	0	0	1	0	0	0	0	0	4	0	0	0	.250	.125
Liriano, Nelson, Pittsburgh†	.262	71	71	65	3	17	20	3	0	0	12	0	1	0	5	0	8	1	0	1	.308	.310
Livingstone, Scott, San Diego* ..	.311	68	64	61	4	19	24	2	0	1	11	0	0	0	3	0	12	0	0	2	.393	.344
Loaiza, Esteban, Pittsburgh	.000	1	1	0	0	0	0	0	0	0	0	1	0	0	0	0	0	0	0	0	.000	.000
Lopez, Javy, Atlanta	.167	6	6	6	1	1	4	0	0	1	2	0	0	0	0	0	2	0	0	0	.667	.167
Lopez, Luis, San Diego†	.273	12	12	11	2	3	4	1	0	0	1	0	0	0	1	0	3	0	0	2	.364	.333
Lukachyk, Rob, Montreal*	.000	2	2	2	0	0	0	0	0	0	0	0	0	0	0	0	1	0	0	0	.000	.000
Mabry, John, St. Louis*	.000	2	2	2	0	0	0	0	0	0	0	0	0	0	0	0	1	0	0	0	.000	.000
Magadan, Dave, Chicago*	.444	25	25	18	6	8	12	1	0	1	4	0	0	0	7	1	1	0	0	0	.667	.600
Magee, Wendell, Philadelphia ...	.000	1	1	1	0	0	0	0	0	0	0	0	0	0	0	0	1	0	0	0	.000	.000
Marrero, Oreste, Los Angeles*...	.429	9	8	7	2	3	4	1	0	0	1	0	0	0	1	0	3	0	0	0	.571	.500
Martin, Al, Pittsburgh*	.250	4	4	4	1	1	4	0	0	1	1	0	0	0	0	0	0	0	0	0	1.000	.250
Martinez, Manny, Philadelphia ..	.333	3	3	3	0	1	3	0	1	0	0	0	0	0	0	0	2	0	0	0	1.000	.333
May, Derrick, Houston*	.300	42	39	30	3	9	15	3	0	1	6	0	1	1	7	1	5	0	0	1	.500	.436
Mayne, Brent, New York*	.167	49	48	42	3	7	8	1	0	0	2	2	0	0	4	0	13	0	0	2	.190	.239
McCarty, Dave, San Francisco ..	.167	35	35	30	3	5	11	0	0	2	9	0	1	1	3	0	8	0	0	1	.367	.257
McCracken, Quinton, Colorado†..	.200	40	40	35	1	7	9	2	0	0	2	0	0	3	0	0	10	1	1	2	.257	.263
McGee, Willie, St. Louis†...........	.350	44	43	40	4	14	19	3	1	0	9	0	1	0	2	0	11	0	0	1	.475	.372
McGriff, Fred, Atlanta*	.000	1	1	1	0	0	0	0	0	0	0	0	0	0	0	0	1	0	0	0	.000	.000
McMillon, Billy, Florida*	.000	13	13	13	0	0	0	0	0	0	0	0	0	0	0	0	6	0	0	0	.000	.000
McRae, Brian, Chicago†	.250	4	4	4	0	1	1	0	0	0	2	0	0	0	0	0	0	0	0	0	.250	.250
Mejia, Miguel, St. Louis	.100	10	10	10	0	1	1	0	0	0	0	0	0	0	0	0	6	0	0	0	.100	.100
Merced, Orlando, Pittsburgh* ...	.200	7	7	5	0	1	2	1	0	0	4	0	1	0	1	1	1	0	0	0	.400	.286
Miller, Orlando, Houston..........	.000	7	6	5	0	0	0	0	0	0	0	1	0	0	0	0	3	0	0	0	.000	.000
Milliard, Ralph, Florida.............	.000	1	1	0	0	0	0	0	0	0	0	0	0	0	1	0	0	0	0	0	.000	1.000
Mirabelli, Doug, San Francisco .	.000	1	1	1	0	0	0	0	0	0	0	0	0	0	0	0	0	0	0	0	.000	.000
Mitchell, Keith, Cincinnati	.429	7	7	7	1	3	7	1	0	1	3	0	0	0	0	0	1	0	0	0	1.000	.429
Mitchell, Kevin, Cincinnati.........	.000	3	3	3	0	0	0	0	0	0	0	0	0	0	0	0	2	0	0	0	.000	.000
Mlicki, Dave, New York	.000	1	1	1	0	0	0	0	0	0	0	0	0	0	0	0	1	0	0	0	.000	.000
Montgomery, Ray, Houston	.250	4	4	4	2	1	4	0	0	1	2	0	0	0	0	0	1	0	0	0	1.000	.250
Morandini, Mickey, Phi.*	.000	4	4	4	0	0	0	0	0	0	0	0	0	0	0	0	0	0	0	0	.000	.000
Mordecai, Mike, Atlanta	.212	40	39	33	5	7	8	1	0	0	4	1	1	0	4	1	8	0	0	1	.242	.289
Morman, Russ, Florida	.200	6	6	5	0	1	2	1	0	0	0	0	0	0	1	0	2	0	0	0	.400	.333

er, Team	Avg.	G	TPA	AB	R	H	TB	2B	3B	HR	RBI	SH	SF	HP	BB	IBB	SO	SB	CS	GDP	Slg.	OBP
ris, Hal, Cincinnati*	.333	6	6	6	2	2	6	1	0	1	1	0	0	0	0	0	0	0	0	0	1.000	.333
tola, Chad, Cincinnati	.000	4	4	4	0	0	0	0	0	0	0	0	0	0	0	0	3	0	0	0	.000	.000
ton, James, Houston	.211	20	20	19	0	4	5	1	0	0	2	0	0	1	0	0	5	1	1	2	.263	.250
ller, Bill, San Francisco†	.000	4	4	4	0	0	0	0	0	0	0	0	0	0	0	0	0	0	0	0	.000	.000
igan, Sean, San Diego	.000	2	1	1	0	0	0	0	0	0	0	0	0	0	0	0	0	0	0	0	.000	.000
ray, Glenn, Philadelphia	.154	13	13	13	2	2	6	1	0	1	1	0	0	0	0	0	5	0	0	0	.462	.154
al, Bob, Florida	.000	1	1	1	0	0	0	0	0	0	0	0	0	0	0	0	0	0	0	0	.000	.000
gle, Denny, Pittsburgh*	.500	3	3	2	0	1	2	1	0	0	0	1	0	0	0	0	0	0	0	0	1.000	.500
rfield, Marc, San Diego	.194	37	37	31	3	6	10	1	0	1	5	0	1	0	5	0	11	0	1	2	.323	.297
ndo, Sherman, Montreal	.220	48	47	41	7	9	11	2	0	0	2	0	0	0	6	0	14	0	0	1	.268	.319
oa, Alex, New York	.000	5	5	5	0	0	0	0	0	0	1	0	0	0	0	0	1	0	0	0	.000	.000
er, Joe, Cincinnati	.100	14	14	10	1	1	1	0	0	0	3	0	1	1	2	0	3	0	0	0	.100	.286
onez, Rey, New York	.000	2	2	2	1	0	0	0	0	0	0	0	0	0	0	0	0	0	0	0	.000	.000
ulak, Joe, Florida*	.179	64	61	56	6	10	10	0	0	0	4	0	0	0	5	0	8	0	0	3	.179	.246
k, Keith, Pittsburgh	.000	4	4	2	0	0	0	0	0	0	0	1	0	0	1	0	0	0	0	0	.000	.333
o, Ricky, Philadelphia†	.000	5	5	4	0	0	0	0	0	0	0	0	0	0	1	0	0	0	0	0	.000	.200
ens, Eric, Cincinnati	.154	31	31	26	1	4	4	0	0	0	1	0	0	0	5	0	6	1	0	0	.154	.290
ens, Jayhawk, Colorado	.143	11	11	7	0	1	1	0	0	0	3	1	2	0	1	0	2	0	1	0	.143	.200
nozzi, Tom, St. Louis	1.000	2	2	2	1	2	3	1	0	0	0	0	0	0	0	0	0	0	0	0	1.500	1.000
ater, Lance, Colorado*	.000	2	2	2	0	0	0	0	0	0	0	0	0	0	0	0	0	0	0	0	.000	.000
ker, Rick, Los Angeles	.300	11	11	10	1	3	4	1	0	0	0	0	0	1	0	0	2	1	0	1	.400	.364
ier, Dan, San Francisco*	.357	19	18	14	1	5	5	0	0	0	2	0	0	0	4	0	2	0	0	1	.357	.500
dleton, Terry, Fla.-Atl.†	.000	4	4	4	0	0	0	0	0	0	0	0	0	0	0	0	0	0	0	2	.000	.000
ez, Eddie, Atlanta	.200	8	7	5	0	1	1	0	0	0	1	0	1	0	1	0	0	0	0	0	.200	.286
ez, Eduardo, Cincinnati	.143	8	8	7	1	1	4	0	0	1	1	0	0	0	1	0	3	0	0	1	.571	.250
ez, Neifi, Colorado†	.000	3	3	3	0	0	0	0	0	0	0	0	0	0	0	0	0	0	0	0	.000	.000
agine, Roberto, New York*	.267	18	17	15	1	4	7	0	0	1	4	0	0	2	1	5	0	0	0	.467	.353
lips, J.R., S.F.-Phi.*	.154	15	15	13	2	2	5	0	0	1	3	0	0	0	2	0	10	0	0	0	.385	.242
rza, Mike, Los Angeles	.333	4	4	3	0	1	1	0	0	0	0	0	1	0	1	0	2	0	0	0	.333	.500
onia, Luis, Atlanta*	.267	16	16	15	1	4	4	0	0	0	2	0	1	0	0	0	1	0	0	0	.267	.250
tugal, Mark, Cincinnati	.000	1	1	0	0	0	0	0	0	0	0	1	0	0	0	0	0	0	0	0	.000	.000
vell, Jay, Florida	.000	1	1	1	0	0	0	0	0	0	0	0	0	0	0	0	1	0	0	0	.000	.000
ace, Tom, Los Angeles	.400	7	7	5	1	2	2	0	0	0	0	0	0	2	0	0	1	0	0	0	.400	.571
iam, Harvey, Colorado	.143	8	8	7	2	1	1	0	0	0	0	0	0	0	1	0	2	0	0	1	.143	.250
d, Jeff, Colorado*	.125	8	8	8	0	1	1	0	0	0	2	0	0	0	0	0	4	0	0	0	.125	.125
d, Jody, San Diego	.000	3	3	3	0	0	0	0	0	0	0	0	0	0	0	0	1	0	0	0	.000	.000
aford, Desi, Philadelphia†	.000	5	5	5	0	0	0	0	0	0	0	0	0	0	0	0	2	0	0	0	.000	.000
erson, Kevin, New York†	.250	18	18	12	2	3	7	1	0	1	3	0	1	0	5	0	6	0	0	0	.583	.444
driguez, Henry, Montreal*	.429	7	7	7	1	3	5	2	0	0	1	0	0	0	0	0	3	0	0	0	.714	.429
o, Chris, Cincinnati	.286	16	16	14	2	4	8	1	0	1	3	1	0	0	1	0	4	0	0	0	.571	.333
chez, Rey, Chicago	.000	2	2	0	0	0	0	0	0	0	0	0	2	0	0	0	0	0	0	0	.000	.000
dberg, Ryne, Chicago	.500	5	5	4	1	2	2	0	0	0	1	0	0	0	1	0	1	1	0	0	.500	.600
tangelo, F.P., Montreal†	.231	17	17	13	3	3	3	0	0	0	2	0	0	0	4	0	4	1	0	0	.231	.412
tiago, Benito, Philadelphia	.500	12	12	10	1	5	8	0	0	1	4	0	0	0	2	0	3	0	0	0	.800	.583
rsone, Steve, San Francisco	.222	20	20	18	2	4	5	1	0	0	0	0	0	0	2	0	5	1	0	0	.278	.300
all, Gene, Philadelphia	.625	10	10	8	3	5	11	1	1	1	3	0	0	0	2	0	3	0	0	1	1.375	.700
illing, Curt, Philadelphia	.000	2	2	2	0	0	0	0	0	0	0	0	0	0	0	0	1	0	0	0	.000	.000
ourek, Pete, Cincinnati*	.000	1	1	1	0	0	0	0	0	0	0	0	0	0	0	0	0	0	0	0	.000	.000
cik, Kevin, Philadelphia	.500	4	4	4	0	2	3	1	0	0	0	0	0	0	0	0	1	0	0	0	.750	.500
ui, David, Montreal†	.000	1	1	1	0	0	0	0	0	0	0	0	0	0	0	0	1	0	0	0	.000	.000
vais, Scott, Chicago	.000	3	3	3	0	0	0	0	0	0	0	0	0	0	0	0	1	0	0	0	.000	.000
affer, Danny, St. Louis	.211	21	21	19	0	4	7	1	1	0	5	1	0	0	1	0	3	0	0	2	.368	.250
ffield, Gary, Florida	.000	1	1	1	0	0	0	0	0	0	0	0	0	0	0	0	0	0	0	0	.000	.000
oley, Craig, San Diego	.200	6	6	5	0	1	1	0	0	0	0	0	0	1	0	0	0	0	0	0	.200	.200
mpert, Terry, Chicago	.077	14	13	13	1	1	1	0	0	0	0	0	0	0	0	0	7	0	0	0	.077	.077
dall, Joe, Florida*	.000	1	1	1	0	0	0	0	0	0	0	0	0	0	0	0	1	0	0	0	.000	.000
restri, Dave, Montreal	.263	29	29	19	1	5	6	1	0	0	4	3	0	0	7	0	5	2	1	0	.316	.462
ms, Mike, Houston	.212	35	35	33	2	7	8	1	0	0	2	0	0	1	1	0	7	0	0	1	.242	.257
ith, Dwight, Atlanta*	.232	79	78	69	7	16	28	3	0	3	11	0	1	0	8	1	21	0	1	2	.406	.308
ith, Ozzie, St. Louis†	.250	32	32	28	2	7	8	1	0	0	1	1	0	0	3	0	2	0	0	1	.286	.323
ehr, Tim, Montreal	.250	4	4	4	0	1	1	0	0	0	0	0	0	0	0	0	1	0	0	0	.250	.250
ers, Bill, Houston*	.182	40	37	33	4	6	15	3	0	2	6	0	1	0	3	0	7	0	0	1	.455	.243
nkiewicz, Andy, Montreal	.321	33	32	28	3	9	13	2	1	0	5	1	0	1	2	0	5	0	0	0	.464	.387
werson, Todd, San Diego	.000	1	1	1	0	0	0	0	0	0	0	0	0	0	0	0	1	0	0	0	.000	.000
cker, Kevin, Philadelphia†	.667	4	4	3	1	2	2	0	0	0	0	0	0	0	1	0	1	0	0	0	.667	.750
eum, Dale, Pittsburgh†	.000	2	2	2	0	0	0	0	0	0	0	0	0	0	0	0	1	0	0	0	.000	.000
eeney, Mark, St. Louis*	.243	48	47	37	7	9	10	1	0	0	6	2	0	0	8	0	5	1	0	1	.270	.378
um, Jimmy, San Diego	.000	3	3	3	0	0	0	0	0	0	0	0	0	0	0	0	1	0	0	0	.000	.000
bensee, Eddie, Cincinnati*	.150	22	22	20	2	3	4	1	0	0	1	0	0	0	2	0	7	0	0	1	.200	.227
arez, Jesus, Florida†	.300	33	33	30	3	9	11	2	0	0	1	1	0	0	2	0	6	0	0	1	.367	.344
ompson, Milt, L.A.-Col.*	.054	48	43	37	1	2	2	0	0	0	0	0	0	0	6	0	7	0	0	1	.054	.186
ompson, Robby, S.F.	.000	2	2	2	0	0	0	0	0	0	0	0	0	0	0	0	1	0	0	0	.000	.000
mmons, Ozzie, Chicago	.160	30	30	25	5	4	7	0	0	1	2	0	0	0	5	0	6	1	0	0	.280	.300
sley, Lee, Philadelphia†	.091	11	11	11	0	1	1	0	0	0	0	0	0	0	0	0	6	0	1	0	.091	.091
nberlin, Andy, New York*	.214	51	49	42	8	9	12	3	0	0	7	0	0	1	6	0	19	0	0	0	.286	.327
bani, Tom, St. Louis*	.000	2	2	2	0	0	0	0	0	0	0	0	0	0	0	0	0	0	0	0	.000	.000
des, Pedro, Chicago*	.167	7	7	6	1	1	2	1	0	0	1	0	0	0	1	0	3	0	0	0	.333	.286
enzuela, Fernando, S.D.*	.333	3	3	3	0	1	1	0	0	0	0	0	0	0	0	0	2	0	0	0	.333	.333
nder Wal, John, Colorado*	.286	72	63	56	9	16	30	3	1	3	13	0	0	0	7	1	17	0	0	1	.536	.365
ughn, Greg, San Diego	.200	5	5	5	1	1	1	0	0	0	0	0	0	0	0	0	1	0	0	0	.200	.200
ras, Quilvio, Florida†	.000	6	6	6	0	0	0	0	0	0	0	0	0	0	0	0	3	0	0	0	.000	.000
caino, Jose, New York†	.000	5	5	4	0	0	0	0	0	0	0	0	0	0	1	0	1	0	0	0	.000	.200
gner, Paul, Pittsburgh	.000	1	1	0	0	0	0	0	0	0	0	0	0	0	0	0	1	0	0	0	.000	1.000

- 273 -

Player, Team	Avg.	G	TPA	AB	R	H	TB	2B	3B	HR	RBI	SH	SF	HP	BB	IBB	SO	SB	CS	GDP	Slg.
Wallach, Tim, Los Angeles	1.000	1	1	1	1	1	1	0	0	0	0	0	0	0	0	0	0	0	0	0	1.000
Walton, Jerome, Atlanta	.444	12	11	9	2	4	5	1	0	0	0	0	0	0	2	0	1	0	0	1	.556
Watson, Allen, San Francisco*	.333	3	3	3	0	1	1	0	0	0	0	0	0	0	0	0	0	0	0	1	.333
Webster, Lenny, Montreal	.000	17	17	15	0	0	0	0	0	0	0	0	0	0	2	0	3	0	0	1	.000
Wehner, John, Pittsburgh	.346	30	27	26	7	9	20	3	1	2	6	0	0	0	1	0	4	0	0	1	.769
Weiss, Walt, Colorado†	.500	2	2	2	0	1	1	0	0	0	0	0	0	0	0	0	0	0	0	0	.500
White, Devon, Florida†	.375	8	8	8	1	3	4	1	0	0	5	0	0	0	0	0	3	0	0	0	.500
White, Rondell, Montreal	.000	3	3	3	0	0	0	0	0	0	0	1	0	0	0	0	1	0	1	0	.000
Whiten, Mark, Phi.-Atl.†	.200	19	19	15	2	3	10	1	0	2	5	0	0	0	4	1	9	0	0	0	.667
Wilkins, Rick, Hou.-S.F.*	.231	14	14	13	2	3	9	0	0	2	5	0	0	0	1	0	6	0	0	0	.692
Williams, Keith, San Francisco	.400	5	5	5	0	2	2	0	0	0	0	0	0	0	0	0	1	0	0	0	.400
Williams, Matt, San Francisco	.000	3	3	2	0	0	0	0	0	0	0	0	0	0	1	1	1	0	0	0	.000
Wilson, Desi, San Francisco*	.111	9	9	9	0	1	1	0	0	0	1	0	0	0	0	0	4	0	0	0	.111
Womack, Tony, Pittsburgh*	.167	10	10	6	3	1	2	1	0	0	0	2	0	0	2	0	0	0	0	0	.333
Young, Dmitri, St. Louis†	.571	8	8	7	1	4	4	0	0	0	2	0	0	0	1	0	0	0	0	0	.571
Young, Eric, Colorado	.000	2	2	1	0	0	0	0	0	0	0	0	0	0	1	0	0	0	0	0	.000
Zuber, Jon, Philadelphia*	.100	10	10	10	0	1	1	0	0	0	0	0	0	0	0	0	1	0	0	0	.100

PINCH-HITTERS WITH TWO OR MORE TEAMS

Player, Team	Avg.	G	TPA	AB	R	H	TB	2B	3B	HR	RBI	SH	SF	HP	BB	IBB	SO	SB	CS	GDP	Slg.
Anthony, Eric, Cincinnati*	.200	11	11	10	2	2	5	0	0	1	1	0	0	0	1	0	1	0	0	0	.500
Anthony, Eric, Colorado*	.000	13	12	8	0	0	0	0	0	0	1	0	0	0	4	0	4	0	0	1	.000
Clark, Dave, Pittsburgh*	.306	40	39	36	4	11	18	2	1	1	6	0	0	0	3	0	8	0	0	0	.500
Clark, Dave, Los Angeles*	.182	14	14	11	0	2	2	0	0	0	0	0	0	0	3	0	2	0	0	0	.182
Houston, Tyler, Atlanta*	.190	23	22	21	2	4	8	2	1	0	3	0	0	0	1	0	8	0	0	1	.381
Houston, Tyler, Chicago*	.250	9	9	8	0	2	3	1	0	0	1	0	0	0	1	1	0	0	0	0	.375
Hubbard, Trent, Colorado	.167	29	29	24	4	4	7	1	1	0	5	0	0	0	5	0	10	0	0	0	.292
Hubbard, Trent, San Francisco	.000	1	1	1	0	0	0	0	0	0	0	0	0	0	0	0	1	0	0	0	.000
Pendleton, Terry, Florida†	.000	3	3	3	0	0	0	0	0	0	0	0	0	0	0	0	0	0	0	2	.000
Pendleton, Terry, Atlanta†	.000	1	1	1	0	0	0	0	0	0	0	0	0	0	0	0	0	0	0	0	.000
Phillips, J.R., San Francisco*	.200	5	5	5	0	1	1	0	0	0	0	0	0	0	0	0	4	0	0	0	.200
Phillips, J.R., Philadelphia*	.125	10	10	8	2	1	4	0	0	1	3	0	0	0	2	0	6	0	0	0	.500
Thompson, Milt, Los Angeles*	.077	35	31	26	1	2	2	0	0	0	0	0	0	0	5	0	4	0	0	1	.077
Thompson, Milt, Colorado*	.000	13	12	11	0	0	0	0	0	0	0	0	0	0	1	0	3	0	0	0	.000
Whiten, Mark, Philadelphia†	.125	11	11	8	0	1	2	1	0	0	0	0	0	0	3	1	5	0	0	0	.250
Whiten, Mark, Atlanta†	.286	8	8	7	2	2	8	0	0	2	5	0	0	0	1	0	4	0	0	0	1.143
Wilkins, Rick, Houston*	.000	5	5	5	0	0	0	0	0	0	0	0	0	0	0	0	3	0	0	0	.000
Wilkins, Rick, San Francisco*	.375	9	9	8	2	3	9	0	0	2	5	0	0	0	1	0	3	0	0	0	1.125

PITCHING

TEAM

Team	W	L	Pct.	ERA	G	ShO	GF	Sv.	IP	H	TBF	R	ER	HR	SH	SF	HB	BB	IBB	SO	WP	Bk.
Angeles	90	72	.556	3.46	162	9	162	50	1466.1	1378	6214	652	564	125	77	47	39	534	66	1212	39	22
anta	96	66	.593	3.52	162	9	162	46	1469.0	1372	6132	648	575	120	71	38	19	451	64	1245	49	5
Diego	91	71	.562	3.72	162	11	162	47	1489.0	1395	6292	682	616	138	65	47	45	506	47	1194	59	10
ntreal	88	74	.543	3.78	162	7	162	43	1441.1	1353	6119	668	605	152	67	45	56	482	33	1206	46	9
rida	80	82	.494	3.95	162	12	162	41	1443.0	1386	6183	703	634	113	69	37	57	598	49	1050	49	5
Louis	88	74	.543	3.97	162	11	162	43	1452.1	1380	6184	706	641	173	64	49	35	539	43	1050	44	6
w York	71	91	.438	4.22	162	10	162	41	1440.0	1517	6288	779	675	159	78	48	44	532	73	999	60	12
cinnati	81	81	.500	4.32	162	8	162	52	1443.0	1447	6277	773	692	167	80	58	42	591	66	1089	66	6
cago	76	86	.469	4.36	162	10	162	34	1456.1	1447	6268	771	705	184	61	42	55	546	55	1027	48	8
uston	82	80	.506	4.37	162	4	162	35	1447.0	1541	6364	792	702	154	80	51	70	539	60	1163	65	12
ladelphia	67	95	.414	4.48	162	6	162	42	1423.1	1463	6138	790	708	160	68	45	35	510	49	1044	71	7
tsburgh	73	89	.451	4.61	162	7	162	37	1453.1	1602	6338	833	744	183	59	48	50	479	50	1044	62	8
Francisco	68	94	.420	4.71	162	8	162	35	1442.1	1520	6330	862	755	194	79	48	67	570	60	997	58	10
orado	83	79	.512	5.59	162	4	162	34	1422.2	1597	6391	964	884	198	56	45	69	624	19	932	66	11
Totals	1134	1134	.500	4.21	1134	117	1134	580	20289.0	20398	87518	10623	9500	2220	974	648	683	7501	734	15252	782	131

NOTE—Totals for earned runs for several clubs do not agree with composite total for all pitchers of each respective club due to instances in which provisions of ction 10.18(i) of the Scoring Rules were applied. The following differences are to be noted: Los Angeles pitchers add to 567; Atlanta pitchers add to 577; St. Louis chers add to 642; Cincinnati pitchers add to 695; Houston pitchers add to 704; Philadelphia pitchers add to 709; Pittsburgh pitchers add to 749; San Francisco pitch- add to 757; Colorado pitchers add to 885.

INDIVIDUAL

TOP QUALIFIERS FOR EARNED-RUN AVERAGE TITLE

Minimum 162 innings. *Throws lefthanded.

Pitcher, Team	W	L	Pct.	ERA	G	GS	CG	ShO	GF	Sv.	IP	H	TBF	R	ER	HR	SH	SF	HB	BB	IBB	SO	WP	Bk.
own, Kevin, Florida	17	11	.607	1.89	32	32	5	3	0	0	233.0	187	906	60	49	8	4	16	33	2	159	6	1
addux, Greg, Atlanta	15	11	.577	2.72	35	35	5	1	0	0	245.0	225	978	85	74	11	8	5	28	11	172	4	0
iter, Al, Florida*	16	12	.571	2.93	33	33	2	1	0	0	215.1	153	896	74	70	14	7	3	11	119	3	200	5	0
noltz, John, Atlanta	24	8	.750	2.94	35	35	6	2	0	0	253.2	199	995	93	83	19	12	4	2	55	3	276	10	1
avine, John, Atlanta*	15	10	.600	2.98	36	36	1	0	0	0	235.1	222	994	91	78	14	15	2	0	85	7	181	4	0
achsel, Steve, Chicago	13	9	.591	3.03	31	31	3	2	0	0	205.0	181	845	82	69	30	3	3	8	62	3	132	5	2
hilling, Curt, Philadelphia	9	10	.474	3.19	26	26	8	2	0	0	183.1	149	732	69	65	16	6	4	3	50	5	182	5	0
mo, Hideo, Los Angeles	16	11	.593	3.19	33	33	3	2	0	0	228.1	180	932	93	81	23	12	6	2	85	6	234	11	3
ssero, Jeff, Montreal*	15	11	.577	3.30	34	34	5	1	0	0	231.2	217	967	95	85	20	16	5	3	55	3	222	5	2
ldes, Ismael, Los Angeles	15	7	.682	3.32	33	33	0	0	0	0	225.0	219	945	94	83	20	7	7	3	54	10	173	1	5
artinez, Ramon, Los Angeles	15	6	.714	3.42	28	27	2	2	1	0	168.2	153	723	76	64	12	7	6	8	86	5	133	2	1
ark, Mark, New York	14	11	.560	3.43	32	32	2	0	0	0	212.1	217	883	98	81	20	8	4	3	48	8	142	6	2
tacio, Pedro, Los Angeles	9	8	.529	3.44	35	32	0	0	0	0	211.2	207	885	86	81	18	11	5	9	67	9	130	6	2
eagle, Denny, Pit.-Atl.*	16	9	.640	3.50	33	33	2	0	0	0	221.1	220	910	93	86	26	10	4	3	48	2	149	3	1
sborne, Donovan, St. Louis*	13	9	.591	3.53	30	30	2	1	0	0	198.2	191	822	87	78	22	7	4	1	57	5	134	6	1

DEPARTMENTAL LEADERS: W—Smoltz, Atl., 24; L—Castillo, Chi., Rapp, Fla., 16; G—Clontz, Atl., 81; GS—Glavine, Atl., 36; CG—Schilling, Phi., 8; ShO—Brown, ., 3; GF—Worrell, L.A., 67; Sv.—Brantley, Cin., Worrell, L.A., 44; IP—Smoltz, Atl., 253; H—Navarro, Chi., 244; TBF—Navarro, Chi., 1007; R—Ritz, Col., 135; ER— tz, Col., 125; HR—Leiter, S.F.-Mon., 37; SH—Watson, S.F., 18; SF—Burba, Cin., 12; HB—Brown, Fla., Kile, Hou., Leiter, S.F.-Mon., 16; BB—Leiter, Fla., 119; IBB— una, L.A., 12; SO—Smoltz, Atl., 276; WP—Williams, Phi., 16; Bk.—Valdes, L.A., 5.

ALL PITCHERS

*Throws lefthanded.

Pitcher, Team	W	L	Pct.	ERA	G	GS	CG	ShO	GF	Sv.	IP	H	TBF	R	ER	HR	SH	SF	HB	BB	IBB	SO	WP	Bk.
dams, Terry, Chicago	3	6	.333	2.94	69	0	0	0	22	4	101.0	84	423	36	33	6	7	3	1	49	6	78	5	1
damson, Joel, Florida*	0	0	.000	7.36	9	0	0	0	1	0	11.0	18	56	9	9	1	2	1	1	7	0	7	0	0
ston, Garvin, Colorado	1	0	1.000	9.00	6	0	0	0	4	0	6.0	9	30	6	6	1	0	2	1	3	0	5	1	0
varez, Tavo, Montreal	2	1	.667	3.00	11	5	0	0	3	0	21.0	19	96	10	7	0	2	0	1	12	1	9	0	0
shby, Andy, San Diego	9	5	.643	3.23	24	24	1	0	0	0	150.2	147	612	60	54	7	6	2	3	34	1	85	3	0
stacio, Pedro, Los Angeles	9	8	.529	3.44	35	32	0	0	0	0	211.2	207	885	86	81	18	11	5	9	67	9	130	6	2
ucoin, Derek, Montreal	0	1	.000	3.38	2	0	0	0	0	0	2.2	3	12	1	1	0	1	0	0	1	0	1	0	0
very, Steve, Atlanta*	7	10	.412	4.47	24	23	1	0	0	0	131.0	146	567	70	65	19	7	3	4	40	8	86	5	0
ailey, Cory, St. Louis	5	2	.714	3.00	51	0	0	0	12	0	57.0	57	251	21	19	1	2	1	1	30	3	38	3	0
ailey, Roger, Colorado	2	3	.400	6.24	24	11	0	0	4	1	83.2	94	385	64	58	7	2	4	1	52	0	45	3	0
arber, Brian, St. Louis	0	0	.000	15.00	1	1	0	0	0	0	3.0	4	20	5	5	0	0	2	1	6	0	1	0	0
arton, Shawn, San Francisco*	0	0	.000	9.72	7	0	0	0	2	0	8.1	19	45	12	9	2	1	0	0	1	0	3	1	1
atchelor, Richard, St. Louis	2	0	1.000	1.20	11	0	0	0	7	0	15.0	9	54	2	2	0	1	0	0	1	0	11	0	0
atista, Miguel, Florida	0	0	.000	5.56	9	0	0	0	4	0	11.1	9	49	8	7	0	3	0	0	7	2	6	1	0
autista, Jose, San Francisco	3	4	.429	3.36	37	1	0	0	12	0	69.2	66	289	32	26	10	4	3	2	15	5	28	0	0
eck, Rod, San Francisco	0	9	.000	3.34	63	0	0	0	58	35	62.0	56	248	23	23	9	0	2	1	10	2	48	1	0
eckett, Robbie, Colorado*	0	0	.000	13.50	5	0	0	0	2	0	5.1	6	31	8	8	0	1	0	1	9	0	6	1	0
eech, Matt, Philadelphia*	1	4	.200	6.97	8	8	0	0	0	0	41.1	49	182	32	32	8	2	6	3	11	0	33	0	0
enes, Alan, St. Louis	13	10	.565	4.90	34	32	3	1	1	0	191.0	192	840	120	104	27	15	9	7	87	3	131	5	1
enes, Andy, St. Louis	18	10	.643	3.83	36	34	3	1	1	1	230.1	215	963	107	98	28	2	6	6	77	7	160	6	0
ergman, Sean, San Diego	6	8	.429	4.37	41	14	0	0	11	0	113.1	119	482	63	55	14	8	4	2	33	3	85	7	2
erumen, Andres, San Diego	0	0	.000	5.40	3	0	0	0	1	0	3.1	3	16	2	2	1	0	0	1	2	1	4	0	0
ielecki, Mike, Atlanta	4	3	.571	2.63	40	5	0	0	8	2	75.1	63	317	24	22	8	0	3	0	33	6	71	2	0
lair, Willie, San Diego	2	6	.250	4.60	60	0	0	0	17	1	88.0	80	377	52	45	13	4	3	7	29	5	67	2	0
lazier, Ron, Philadelphia	3	1	.750	5.87	27	0	0	0	9	0	38.1	49	195	30	25	6	3	2	0	10	3	25	3	0

Pitcher, Team	W	L	Pct.	ERA	G	GS	CG	ShO	GF	Sv.	IP	H	TBF	R	ER	HR	SH	SF	HB	BB	IBB	SO	WP	Bk.
Bochtler, Doug, San Diego	2	4	.333	3.02	63	0	0	0	17	3	65.2	45	278	25	22	6	5	2	1	39	8	68	8	2
Boever, Joe, Pittsburgh	0	2	.000	5.40	13	0	0	0	9	2	15.0	17	68	11	9	2	2	0	1	6	0	6	3	0
Borbon, Pedro, Atlanta*	3	0	1.000	2.75	43	0	0	0	19	1	36.0	26	140	12	11	1	4	0	1	7	0	31	0	0
Borland, Toby, Philadelphia	7	3	.700	4.07	69	0	0	0	11	0	90.2	83	399	51	41	9	4	1	3	43	3	76	10	0
Borowski, Joe, Atlanta	2	4	.333	4.85	22	0	0	0	8	0	26.0	33	121	15	14	4	5	0	1	13	4	15	1	0
Bottalico, Ricky, Philadelphia	4	5	.444	3.19	61	0	0	0	56	34	67.2	47	269	24	24	6	4	2	2	23	2	74	3	0
Bottenfield, Kent, Chicago	3	5	.375	2.63	48	0	0	0	10	1	61.2	59	258	25	18	3	5	0	3	19	4	33	2	0
Bourgeois, Steve, San Francisco	1	3	.250	6.30	15	5	0	0	4	0	40.0	60	198	35	28	4	2	2	4	21	4	17	4	0
Brantley, Jeff, Cincinnati	1	2	.333	2.41	66	0	0	0	61	44	71.0	54	288	21	19	7	4	5	0	28	6	76	2	0
Brocail, Doug, Houston	1	5	.167	4.58	23	4	0	0	4	0	53.0	58	231	31	27	7	3	2	2	23	1	34	0	0
Brown, Kevin, Florida	17	11	.607	1.89	32	32	5	3	0	0	233.0	187	906	60	49	8	4	4	16	33	2	159	6	1
Bruske, Jim, Los Angeles	0	0	.000	5.68	11	0	0	0	5	0	12.2	17	58	8	8	2	0	0	1	3	1	12	1	0
Bullinger, Jim, Chicago	6	10	.375	6.54	37	20	1	1	6	1	129.1	144	598	101	94	15	8	5	8	68	5	90	7	0
Burba, Dave, Cincinnati	11	13	.458	3.83	34	33	0	0	0	0	195.0	179	849	96	83	18	5	12	2	97	9	148	9	1
Burke, John, Colorado	2	1	.667	7.47	11	0	0	0	3	0	15.2	21	75	13	13	3	0	1	1	7	0	19	1	0
Burkett, John, Florida	6	10	.375	4.32	24	24	1	0	0	0	154.0	154	645	84	74	15	11	4	3	42	2	108	0	0
Busby, Mike, St. Louis	0	1	.000	18.00	1	1	0	0	0	0	4.0	9	28	13	8	4	1	0	1	4	0	4	0	0
Byrd, Paul, New York	1	2	.333	4.24	38	0	0	0	14	0	46.2	48	204	22	22	7	1	1	0	21	4	31	3	0
Campbell, Mike, Chicago	3	1	.750	4.46	13	5	0	0	4	0	36.1	29	147	19	18	7	2	1	0	10	0	19	0	0
Candiotti, Tom, Los Angeles	9	11	.450	4.49	28	27	1	0	0	0	152.1	172	657	91	76	18	8	5	3	43	3	79	3	1
Carlson, Dan, San Francisco	1	0	1.000	2.70	5	0	0	0	3	0	10.0	13	46	6	3	2	0	2	0	2	0	4	0	0
Carrara, Giovanni, Cincinnati	1	0	1.000	5.87	8	5	0	0	1	0	23.0	31	112	17	15	6	1	0	2	13	1	13	0	0
Carrasco, Hector, Cincinnati	4	3	.571	3.75	56	0	0	0	10	0	74.1	58	325	37	31	6	4	4	1	45	5	59	8	1
Casian, Larry, Chicago*	1	1	.500	1.88	35	0	0	0	4	0	24.0	14	90	5	5	2	2	1	1	11	3	15	1	0
Castillo, Frank, Chicago	7	16	.304	5.28	33	33	1	1	0	0	182.1	209	789	112	107	28	4	5	8	46	4	139	2	1
Christiansen, Jason, Pit.*	3	3	.500	6.70	33	0	0	0	9	0	44.1	56	205	34	33	7	2	3	1	19	2	38	4	1
Clark, Mark, New York	14	11	.560	3.43	32	32	2	0	0	0	212.1	217	883	98	81	20	8	4	3	48	8	142	6	2
Clark, Terry, Houston	0	2	.000	11.37	5	0	0	0	3	0	6.1	16	37	10	8	1	0	0	1	2	1	5	1	0
Clontz, Brad, Atlanta	6	3	.667	5.69	81	0	0	0	11	1	80.2	78	350	53	51	11	5	4	2	33	8	49	0	1
Cooke, Steve, Pittsburgh*	0	0	.000	7.56	3	0	0	0	1	0	8.1	11	41	7	7	1	0	1	0	5	0	7	1	0
Cordova, Francisco, Pittsburgh	4	7	.364	4.09	59	6	0	0	41	12	99.0	103	414	49	45	11	1	0	2	20	6	95	2	1
Cormier, Rheal, Montreal*	7	10	.412	4.17	33	27	1	1	1	0	159.2	165	674	80	74	16	4	8	9	41	3	100	8	0
Crawford, Carlos, Philadelphia	0	1	.000	4.91	1	1	0	0	0	0	3.2	7	22	10	2	1	1	0	1	2	0	4	0	0
Creek, Doug, San Francisco*	0	2	.000	6.52	63	0	0	0	15	0	48.1	45	220	41	35	11	1	0	2	32	2	38	2	0
Cummings, John, Los Angeles*	0	1	.000	6.75	4	0	0	0	1	0	5.1	12	30	7	4	1	1	1	0	2	1	5	0	0
Daal, Omar, Montreal*	4	5	.444	4.02	64	6	0	0	9	0	87.1	74	366	40	39	10	2	2	1	37	3	82	1	1
Darwin, Danny, Pit.-Hou	10	11	.476	3.77	34	25	0	0	1	0	164.2	160	677	79	69	16	8	7	12	27	3	96	3	3
DeLucia, Rich, San Francisco	3	6	.333	5.84	56	0	0	0	20	0	61.2	62	279	44	40	8	4	2	3	31	6	55	7	0
Dessens, Elmer, Pittsburgh	0	2	.000	8.28	15	3	0	0	1	0	25.0	40	112	23	23	2	3	1	0	4	0	13	0	0
Dewey, Mark, San Francisco	6	3	.667	4.21	78	0	0	0	19	0	83.1	79	360	40	39	9	3	4	5	41	9	57	4	0
DiPoto, Jerry, New York	7	2	.778	4.19	57	0	0	0	21	0	77.1	91	364	44	36	5	7	4	3	45	8	52	3	3
Dishman, Glenn, S.D.-Phi.*	0	0	.000	7.71	7	1	0	0	4	0	9.1	12	42	8	8	2	0	1	0	3	0	3	1	0
Dougherty, Jim, Houston	0	2	.000	9.00	12	0	0	0	2	0	13.0	14	64	14	13	2	1	1	1	11	1	6	0	0
Drabek, Doug, Houston	7	9	.438	4.57	30	30	1	0	0	0	175.1	208	786	102	89	21	12	8	7	60	5	137	9	0
Dreifort, Darren, Los Angeles	1	4	.200	4.94	19	0	0	0	5	0	23.2	23	106	13	13	2	3	1	0	12	4	24	2	1
Dyer, Mike, Montreal	5	5	.500	4.40	70	1	0	0	20	2	75.2	79	334	40	37	7	6	4	5	34	4	51	4	0
Eckersley, Dennis, St. Louis	0	6	.000	3.30	63	0	0	0	53	30	60.0	65	251	26	22	8	1	3	4	6	2	49	0	0
Eischen, Joey, Los Angeles*	0	1	.000	4.78	28	0	0	0	11	0	43.1	48	198	25	23	4	3	1	4	20	4	36	1	0
Ericks, John, Pittsburgh	4	5	.444	5.79	28	4	0	0	13	8	46.2	56	213	35	30	11	1	1	0	19	2	46	2	0
Estes, Shawn, San Francisco*	3	5	.375	3.60	11	11	0	0	0	0	70.0	63	305	30	28	3	5	0	2	39	3	60	4	0
Farmer, Mike, Colorado*	0	1	.000	7.71	7	4	0	0	1	0	28.0	32	127	25	24	8	2	0	0	13	0	16	1	0
Fassero, Jeff, Montreal*	15	11	.577	3.30	34	34	5	1	0	0	231.2	217	967	95	85	20	16	5	3	55	3	222	5	2
Fernandez, Osvaldo, S.F.	7	13	.350	4.61	30	28	2	0	1	0	171.2	193	760	95		20	12	5	10	57	4	106	6	2
Fernandez, Sid, Philadelphia*	3	6	.333	3.43	11	11	0	0	0	0	63.0	50	264	25	24	5	2	2	1	26	2	77	1	0
Florie, Bryce, San Diego	2	2	.500	4.01	39	0	0	0	11	0	49.1	45	222	24	22	1	0	1	6	27	3	51	3	1
Fossas, Tony, St. Louis*	0	4	.000	2.68	65	0	0	0	11	2	47.0	43	209	19	14	7	1	1	0	21	3	36	3	0
Foster, Kevin, Chicago	7	6	.538	6.21	17	16	1	0	0	0	87.0	98	386	63	60	16	5	4	2	35	3	53	2	0
Franco, John, New York*	4	3	.571	1.83	51	0	0	0	44	28	54.0	54	235	15	11	2	6	0	0	21	0	48	2	0
Freeman, Marvin, Colorado	7	9	.438	6.04	26	23	0	0	1	0	129.2	151	588	100	87	21	9	3	6	57	1	71	13	1
Frey, Steve, Philadelphia*	0	1	.000	4.72	31	0	0	0	12	0	34.1	38	151	19	18	4	2	2	0	18	3	12	0	0
Fyhrie, Mike, New York	0	1	.000	15.43	2	0	0	0	0	0	2.1	4	14	4	4	0	0	0	0	3	0	0	0	0
Gardner, Mark, San Francisco	12	7	.632	4.42	30	28	4	1	0	0	179.1	200	782	105	88	28	6	5	8	57	3	145	2	0
Glavine, Tom, Atlanta*	15	10	.600	2.98	36	36	1	0	0	0	235.1	222	994	91	78	14	15	2	0	85	7	181	4	0
Grace, Mike, Philadelphia	7	2	.778	3.49	12	12	1	1	0	0	80.0	72	323	33	31	9	4	0	1	16	1	49	0	1
Guthrie, Mark, Los Angeles*	2	3	.400	2.22	66	0	0	0	16	1	73.0	65	302	21	18	3	4	4	1	22	2	56	1	0
Habyan, John, Colorado	1	1	.500	7.13	19	0	0	0	5	0	24.0	34	116	19	19	4	2	1	1	14	1	25	5	1
Hall, Darren, Los Angeles	0	2	.000	6.00	9	0	0	0	3	0	12.0	13	53	9	8	2	0	0	0	5	0	12	0	0
Hamilton, Joey, San Diego	15	9	.625	4.17	34	33	3	1	0	0	211.2	206	908	100	98	19	6	5	9	83	3	184	14	1
Hammond, Chris, Florida*	5	8	.385	6.56	38	9	0	0	5	0	81.0	104	368	65	59	14	3	4	4	27	3	50	1	0
Hampton, Mike, Houston*	10	10	.500	3.59	27	27	2	1	0	0	160.1	175	691	79	64	12	10	3	3	49	1	101	7	2
Hancock, Lee, Pittsburgh*	0	0	.000	6.38	13	0	0	0	3	0	18.1	21	89	18	13	5	1	0	2	10	3	13	1	0
Harnisch, Pete, New York	8	12	.400	4.21	31	31	2	1	0	0	194.2	195	839	103	91	30	13	9	7	61	5	114	7	3
Hartgraves, Dean, Hou.-Atl.*	1	0	1.000	4.78	39	0	0	0	9	0	37.2	34	167	21	20	4	1	2	2	23	3	30	2	0
Hawblitzel, Ryan, Colorado	0	1	.000	6.00	8	0	0	0	3	0	15.0	18	69	12	10	2	0	1	0	6	0	7	1	0
Heflin, Bronson, Philadelphia	0	0	.000	6.75	3	0	0	0	2	0	6.2	11	34	7	5	1	0	1	0	3	0	4	0	0
Helling, Rick, Florida	2	1	.667	1.95	5	4	0	0	0	0	27.2	14	106	6	6	2	1	0	0	7	0	26	0	1
Henry, Doug, New York	2	8	.200	4.68	58	0	0	0	33	9	75.0	82	343	48	39	7	3	3	1	36	6	58	6	1
Heredia, Felix, Florida*	1	1	.500	4.32	21	0	0	0	5	0	16.2	21	78	8	8	1	0	1	0	10	1	10	2	0
Hermanson, Dustin, San Diego	1	0	1.000	8.56	8	0	0	0	4	0	13.2	18	62	15	13	3	2	3	0	4	0	11	0	1
Hernandez, Livan, Florida	0	0	.000	.00	1	0	0	0	0	0	3.0	3	13	0	0	0	0	0	0	2	0	2	0	0
Hernandez, Xavier, Cin.-Hou	5	5	.500	4.62	61	0	0	0	27	6	78.0	77	340	45	40	13	8	3	2	28	5	81	9	0
Hoffman, Trevor, San Diego	9	5	.643	2.25	70	0	0	0	62	42	88.0	50	348	23	22	6	2	2	2	31	5	111	2	0
Holmes, Darren, Colorado	5	4	.556	3.97	62	0	0	0	21	1	77.0	78	333	41	34	8	2	1	1	28	2	73	2	0

tcher, Team	W	L	Pct.	ERA	G	GS	CG	ShO	GF	Sv.	IP	H	TBF	R	ER	HR	SH	SF	HB	BB	IBB	SO	WP	Bk.
lt, Chris, Houston	0	1	.000	5.79	4	0	0	0	3	0	4.2	5	22	3	3	0	0	0	0	3	1	0	1	0
neycutt, Rick, St. Louis*	2	1	.667	2.85	61	0	0	0	13	4	47.1	42	190	15	15	3	5	3	0	7	3	30	1	2
ok, Chris, San Francisco	0	1	.000	7.43	10	0	0	0	3	0	13.1	16	71	13	11	3	2	1	2	14	2	4	1	0
pe, John, Pittsburgh	1	3	.250	6.98	5	4	0	0	0	0	19.1	17	86	18	15	5	2	1	2	11	1	13	2	0
dek, John, Houston	2	0	1.000	2.81	15	0	0	0	6	2	16.0	12	65	5	5	2	2	0	0	5	2	14	1	1
nter, Rich, Philadelphia	3	7	.300	6.49	14	14	0	0	0	0	69.1	84	322	54	50	10	3	4	5	33	2	32	4	0
rst, Bill, Florida	0	0	.000	.00	2	0	0	0	2	0	2.0	3	10	0	0	0	0	0	0	1	0	1	1	0
tton, Mark, Florida	5	1	.833	3.67	13	9	0	0	0	0	56.1	47	234	23	23	6	0	1	3	18	0	31	2	0
inghausen, Jason, New York	6	14	.300	4.77	27	27	2	1	0	0	171.2	190	766	103	91	13	7	9	8	73	5	114	14	0
ckson, Danny, St. Louis*	1	1	.500	4.46	13	4	0	0	3	0	36.1	33	154	18	18	3	0	1	1	16	1	27	0	0
rvis, Kevin, Cincinnati	8	9	.471	5.98	24	20	2	1	2	0	120.1	152	552	93	80	17	6	2	2	43	5	63	3	0
hnstone, John, Houston	1	0	1.000	5.54	9	0	0	0	6	0	13.0	17	60	8	8	2	0	2	0	5	0	5	1	0
nes, Bobby, New York	12	8	.600	4.42	31	31	3	1	0	0	195.2	219	826	102	96	26	12	5	3	46	6	116	2	0
nes, Doug, Chicago	2	2	.500	5.01	28	0	0	0	13	2	32.1	41	143	20	18	4	1	0	1	7	4	26	0	0
nes, Todd, Houston	6	3	.667	4.40	51	0	0	0	37	17	57.1	61	263	30	28	5	2	1	5	32	6	44	3	0
rdan, Ricardo, Philadelphia*	2	2	.500	1.80	26	0	0	0	2	0	25.0	18	103	6	5	0	1	1	0	12	0	17	1	0
den, Jeff, S.F.-Mon	5	0	1.000	3.27	58	0	0	0	16	0	74.1	61	318	35	27	8	3	3	5	34	2	61	5	0
le, Darryl, Houston	12	11	.522	4.19	35	33	4	0	1	0	219.0	233	975	113	102	16	10	9	16	97	8	219	13	3
rkin, Andy, Florida	0	0	.000	1.80	1	1	0	0	0	0	5.0	3	22	1	1	0	0	0	1	4	0	2	0	0
iper, Dave, Phi.-Mon.*	2	1	.667	7.20	33	0	0	0	8	0	25.0	40	120	21	20	4	3	0	0	9	2	13	2	0
iter, Al, Florida*	16	12	.571	2.93	33	33	2	1	0	0	215.1	153	896	74	70	14	7	3	11	119	3	200	5	0
iter, Mark, S.F.-Mon.	8	12	.400	4.92	35	34	2	0	0	0	205.0	219	904	128	112	37	12	6	16	69	8	164	6	4
skanic, Curt, Colorado	7	5	.583	6.23	70	0	0	0	32	6	73.2	82	334	51	51	12	3	3	2	38	1	76	6	2
eber, Jon, Pittsburgh	9	5	.643	3.99	51	15	0	0	6	1	142.0	156	600	70	63	19	7	2	3	28	2	94	0	0
lliquist, Derek, Cincinnati*	0	0	.000	7.36	5	0	0	0	3	0	3.2	5	15	3	3	1	1	0	0	0	0	1	0	0
aiza, Esteban, Pittsburgh	2	3	.400	4.96	10	10	1	1	0	0	52.2	65	236	32	29	11	3	1	2	19	2	32	0	0
iselle, Rich, Pittsburgh	1	0	1.000	3.05	5	3	0	0	0	0	20.2	22	90	8	7	3	0	0	0	8	1	9	3	0
mon, Kevin, Atlanta	0	0	.000	4.91	6	0	0	0	1	0	7.1	7	31	4	4	0	0	1	3	0	1	0	1
dwick, Eric, St. Louis	0	1	.000	9.00	6	1	0	0	2	0	10.0	11	45	11	10	4	0	1	3	0	12	0	0
ons, Curt, Cincinnati	2	0	1.000	4.50	3	3	0	0	0	0	16.0	17	70	8	8	1	0	1	7	0	14	0	0
acDonald, Bob, New York*	0	2	.000	4.26	20	0	0	0	6	0	19.0	16	79	10	9	2	1	1	0	9	0	12	1	0
addux, Greg, Atlanta	15	11	.577	2.72	35	35	5	1	0	0	245.0	225	978	85	74	11	8	5	3	28	11	172	4	0
antei, Matt, Florida	1	0	1.000	6.38	14	0	0	0	1	0	18.1	13	89	13	13	2	1	0	1	21	1	25	2	0
anuel, Barry, Montreal	4	1	.800	3.24	53	0	0	0	7	0	86.0	70	360	34	31	10	6	2	7	26	4	62	4	0
artinez, Pedro, Montreal	13	10	.565	3.70	33	33	4	1	0	0	216.2	189	901	100	89	19	9	6	3	70	3	222	6	0
artinez, Pedro A., N.Y.-Cin.*	0	0	.000	6.30	9	0	0	0	0	0	10.0	13	51	9	7	2	1	0	8	4	9	0	0
artinez, Ramon, Los Angeles	15	6	.714	3.42	28	27	2	2	1	0	168.2	153	723	76	64	12	7	6	8	86	5	133	2	1
athews, T.J., St. Louis	2	6	.250	3.01	67	0	0	0	23	6	83.2	62	345	32	28	8	5	0	2	32	4	80	1	0
athews, Terry, Florida	2	4	.333	4.91	57	0	0	0	19	4	55.0	59	247	33	30	7	2	1	1	27	5	49	0	0
ay, Darrell, Pittsburgh*	0	1	.000	9.35	5	2	0	0	0	0	8.2	15	47	10	9	5	0	1	4	0	5	0	0
cElroy, Chuck, Cincinnati*	2	0	1.000	6.57	12	0	0	0	7	0	12.1	13	59	10	9	2	0	0	10	1	13	0	0
cMichael, Greg, Atlanta	5	3	.625	3.22	73	0	0	0	24	6	86.2	84	366	37	31	4	3	3	1	27	7	78	4	1
iceli, Dan, Pittsburgh	2	10	.167	5.78	44	9	0	0	17	1	85.2	99	398	65	55	15	3	7	3	45	5	66	9	0
iller, Kurt, Florida	1	3	.250	6.80	26	5	0	0	6	0	46.1	57	222	41	35	5	4	1	2	33	8	30	1	1
imbs, Michael, Philadelphia*	3	9	.250	5.53	21	17	0	0	0	0	99.1	116	448	66	61	13	8	3	2	41	1	56	7	0
inor, Blas, New York	0	0	.000	3.51	17	0	0	0	4	0	25.2	23	104	11	10	4	0	1	0	6	2	20	1	0
itchell, Larry, Philadelphia	0	0	.000	4.50	7	0	0	0	2	0	12.0	14	51	6	6	1	0	1	5	1	7	0	0
licki, Dave, New York	6	7	.462	3.30	51	2	0	0	16	1	90.0	95	393	46	33	9	8	3	6	33	8	83	7	0
oore, Marcus, Cincinnati	3	3	.500	5.81	23	0	0	0	11	2	26.1	26	129	21	17	3	3	2	22	1	27	1	1
orel, Ramon, Pittsburgh	2	1	.667	5.36	29	0	0	0	4	0	42.0	57	198	27	25	4	1	1	19	5	22	1	1
organ, Mike, St.L.-Cin	6	11	.353	4.63	23	23	0	0	0	0	130.1	146	567	72	67	16	6	7	1	47	0	74	2	0
orman, Alvin, Houston*	4	1	.800	4.93	53	0	0	0	9	0	42.0	43	192	24	23	8	2	1	0	24	6	31	3	1
ulholland, Terry, Philadelphia*	8	7	.533	4.66	21	21	3	0	0	0	133.1	157	571	74	6	17	6	5	3	21	1	52	5	0
unoz, Bobby, Philadelphia	0	3	.000	7.82	6	6	0	0	0	0	25.1	42	123	28	22	5	2	1	1	7	1	8	0	0
unoz, Mike, Colorado*	2	2	.500	6.65	54	0	0	0	7	0	44.2	55	203	33	33	4	3	1	1	16	2	45	0	0
yers, Rodney, Chicago	2	1	.667	4.68	45	0	0	0	8	0	67.1	61	298	38	35	6	1	5	3	38	3	50	4	1
avarro, Jaime, Chicago	15	12	.556	3.92	35	35	4	1	0	0	236.2	244	1007	116	103	25	10	7	10	72	5	158	10	0
eagle, Denny, Pit.-Atl.*	16	9	.640	3.50	33	33	2	0	0	0	221.1	226	910	93	86	26	10	4	3	48	2	149	3	1
en, Robb, Florida	5	1	.833	1.95	75	0	0	0	66	35	83.0	67	326	21	18	2	5	1	1	21	6	92	4	0
ied, Dave, Colorado	0	0	.000	13.50	6	1	0	0	3	0	5.1	5	29	8	8	1	0	0	0	8	0	4	0	0
omo, Hideo, Los Angeles	16	11	.593	3.19	33	33	3	2	0	0	228.1	180	932	93	81	23	12	6	2	85	6	234	11	3
lson, Gregg, Houston	1	0	1.000	4.82	9	0	0	0	7	0	9.1	12	47	5	5	1	0	1	0	7	2	8	1	0
quist, Mike, San Diego	0	0	.000	2.35	8	0	0	0	3	0	7.2	6	30	2	2	0	0	0	2	0	4	1	0
sborne, Donovan, St. Louis*	13	9	.591	3.53	30	30	2	1	0	0	198.2	191	822	87	78	22	7	4	1	57	5	134	6	1
suna, Al, San Diego*	0	0	.000	2.25	10	0	0	0	4	0	4.0	5	20	1	1	0	1	1	2	1	4	1	0
suna, Antonio, Los Angeles	9	6	.600	3.00	73	0	0	0	21	4	84.0	65	342	33	28	6	7	5	2	32	12	85	3	2
acheco, Alex, Montreal	0	0	.000	11.12	5	0	0	0	2	0	5.2	8	26	7	7	2	0	0	0	5	0	1	0	0
ainter, Lance, Colorado*	4	2	.667	5.86	34	1	0	0	4	0	50.2	56	234	37	33	12	3	3	3	25	3	48	1	0
all, Donn, Florida	1	1	.500	5.79	12	0	0	0	5	0	18.2	16	80	15	12	3	1	1	0	9	1	9	1	0
aniagua, Jose, Montreal	2	4	.333	3.53	13	11	0	0	0	0	51.0	55	223	24	20	7	1	1	3	23	0	27	2	2
ark, Chan Ho, Los Angeles	5	5	.500	3.64	48	10	0	0	7	0	108.2	82	477	48	44	7	8	1	4	71	3	119	4	3
arrett, Jeff, St.L.-Phi.	3	3	.500	3.39	51	0	0	0	23	0	66.1	64	288	25	25	2	2	1	31	4	64	10	0
arris, Steve, Pittsburgh	0	3	.000	7.18	8	4	0	0	0	0	26.1	35	123	22	21	4	1	1	11	0	27	2	0
atterson, Bob, Chicago*	3	3	.500	3.13	79	0	0	0	27	8	54.2	46	230	19	19	6	2	4	1	22	7	53	1	1
ena, Alejandro, Florida	0	1	.000	4.50	4	0	0	0	2	0	4.0	4	18	3	2	0	0	1	0	5	0	0
erez, Mike, Chicago	1	0	1.000	4.67	24	0	0	0	4	0	27.0	29	127	14	14	2	1	0	3	13	1	22	1	0
erez, Yorkis, Florida*	3	4	.429	5.29	64	0	0	0	15	0	47.2	51	222	28	28	2	3	1	4	31	1	47	2	0
erson, Robert, New York	4	5	.444	4.52	27	13	0	0	1	0	89.2	86	390	50	45	16	1	4	2	35	3	76	3	0
eters, Chris, Pittsburgh*	2	4	.333	5.63	16	10	0	0	0	0	64.0	72	283	43	40	9	3	1	25	0	28	4	0
etkovsek, Mark, St. Louis*	11	2	.846	3.55	48	6	0	0	7	0	88.2	83	377	37	35	9	5	1	5	35	2	45	2	1
lesac, Dan, Pittsburgh*	6	5	.545	4.09	73	0	0	0	30	11	70.1	67	300	35	32	4	2	3	0	1	13	3	19	1	0
oole, Jim, San Francisco*	2	1	.667	2.66	35	0	0	0	5	0	23.2	15	97	7	7	2	3	0	1	9	1	22	0	0

Pitcher, Team	W	L	Pct.	ERA	G	GS	CG	ShO	GF	Sv.	IP	H	TBF	R	ER	HR	SH	SF	HB	BB	IBB	SO	WP	Bk
Portugal, Mark, Cincinnati	8	9	.471	3.98	27	26	1	1	0	0	156.0	146	646	77	69	20	7	6	2	42	2	93	6	0
Powell, Jay, Florida	4	3	.571	4.54	67	0	0	0	16	2	71.1	71	321	41	36	5	2	1	4	36	1	52	3	0
Pugh, Tim, Cincinnati	1	1	.500	11.49	10	0	0	0	0	0	15.2	24	83	20	20	3	2	1	1	11	2	9	1	0
Quirico, Rafael, Philadelphia*	0	1	.000	37.80	1	1	0	0	0	0	1.2	4	14	7	7	1	0	0	0	5	0	1	0	1
Radinsky, Scott, Los Angeles*	5	1	.833	2.41	58	0	0	0	19	1	52.1	52	221	19	14	2	4	3	0	17	5	48	0	3
Rapp, Pat, Florida	8	16	.333	5.10	30	29	0	0	1	0	162.1	184	728	95	92	12	15	8	3	91	6	86	13	0
Reed, Steve, Colorado	4	3	.571	3.96	70	0	0	0	7	0	75.0	66	307	38	33	11	2	4	6	19	0	51	1	0
Rekar, Bryan, Colorado	2	4	.333	8.95	14	11	0	0	0	0	58.1	87	289	61	58	11	3	3	5	26	1	25	4	0
Remlinger, Mike, Cincinnati*	0	1	.000	5.60	19	4	0	0	2	0	27.1	24	125	17	17	4	3	1	3	19	2	19	2	2
Reynolds, Shane, Houston	16	10	.615	3.65	35	35	4	1	0	0	239.0	227	981	103	97	20	11	7	8	44	3	204	5	1
Reynoso, Armando, Colorado	8	9	.471	4.96	30	30	0	0	0	0	168.2	195	733	97	93	27	3	3	9	49	0	88	4	3
Ritz, Kevin, Colorado	17	11	.607	5.28	35	35	2	0	0	0	213.0	236	966	135	125	24	8	4	12	105	3	105	10	1
Rojas, Mel, Montreal	7	4	.636	3.22	74	0	0	0	64	36	81.0	56	326	30	29	5	2	4	2	28	3	92	3	0
Ruebel, Matt, Pittsburgh*	1	1	.500	4.60	26	7	0	0	3	1	58.2	64	265	38	30	7	0	3	6	25	0	22	2	0
Rueter, Kirk, Mon.-S.F.*	6	8	.429	3.97	20	19	0	0	0	0	102.0	109	430	50	45	12	4	1	2	27	0	46	2	0
Ruffin, Bruce, Colorado*	7	5	.583	4.00	71	0	0	0	56	24	69.2	55	292	35	31	5	0	3	0	29	3	74	10	0
Ruffin, Johnny, Cincinnati	1	3	.250	5.49	49	0	0	0	13	0	62.1	71	289	42	38	10	4	3	2	37	5	69	8	0
Ryan, Ken, Philadelphia	3	5	.375	2.43	62	0	0	0	26	8	89.0	71	370	32	24	4	5	0	1	45	8	70	4	3
Salkeld, Roger, Cincinnati	8	5	.615	5.20	29	19	1	1	2	0	116.0	114	509	69	67	18	10	3	6	54	2	82	7	1
Sanders, Scott, San Diego	9	5	.643	3.38	46	16	0	0	6	0	144.0	117	594	58	54	10	7	7	2	48	5	157	7	0
Schilling, Curt, Philadelphia	9	10	.474	3.19	26	26	8	2	0	0	183.1	149	732	69	65	16	6	4	3	50	5	182	5	0
Schmidt, Jason, Atl.-Pit.	5	6	.455	5.70	19	17	1	0	0	0	96.1	108	445	67	61	10	4	9	2	53	0	74	8	1
Schourek, Pete, Cincinnati*	4	5	.444	6.01	12	12	0	0	0	0	67.1	79	304	48	45	7	3	4	3	24	1	54	3	0
Schutz, Carl, Atlanta*	0	0	.000	2.70	3	0	0	0	1	0	3.1	3	13	1	1	0	0	0	0	2	1	5	0	0
Scott, Tim, Mon.-S.F.	5	7	.417	4.64	65	0	0	0	16	1	66.0	65	288	36	34	8	4	3	3	30	2	47	3	0
Service, Scott, Cincinnati	1	0	1.000	3.94	34	1	0	0	5	0	48.0	51	213	21	21	7	4	1	6	18	4	46	5	0
Shaw, Jeff, Cincinnati	8	6	.571	2.49	78	0	0	0	24	4	104.2	99	434	34	29	8	5	5	2	29	11	69	0	0
Small, Mark, Houston	0	1	.000	5.92	16	0	0	0	4	0	24.1	33	122	23	16	1	1	0	1	13	3	16	1	1
Smiley, John, Cincinnati*	13	14	.481	3.64	35	34	2	2	0	0	217.1	207	889	100	88	20	16	7	4	54	5	171	7	1
Smith, Lee, Cincinnati	3	4	.429	4.06	43	0	0	0	16	2	44.1	49	201	20	20	4	0	0	1	23	4	35	2	0
Smith, Zane, Pittsburgh*	4	6	.400	5.08	16	16	1	1	0	0	83.1	104	368	53	47	7	3	3	4	21	4	47	0	1
Smoltz, John, Atlanta	24	8	.750	2.94	35	35	6	2	0	0	253.2	199	995	93	83	19	12	4	2	55	3	276	10	1
Soderstrom, Steve, S.F.	2	0	1.000	5.27	3	3	0	0	0	0	13.2	16	63	11	8	1	0	2	2	6	0	9	0	0
Spradlin, Jerry, Cincinnati	0	0	.000	.00	1	0	0	0	1	0	.1	0	1	0	0	0	0	0	0	0	0	0	1	0
Springer, Russ, Philadelphia	3	10	.231	4.66	51	7	0	0	12	0	96.2	106	437	60	50	12	5	3	1	38	6	94	5	0
Stottlemyre, Todd, St. Louis	14	11	.560	3.87	34	33	5	2	0	0	223.1	191	944	100	96	30	12	9	4	93	8	194	8	1
Sturtze, Tanyon, Chicago	1	0	1.000	9.00	6	0	0	0	3	0	11.0	16	51	11	11	3	0	0	0	5	0	7	0	0
Sullivan, Scott, Cincinnati	0	0	.000	2.25	7	0	0	0	4	0	8.0	7	35	2	2	0	1	0	1	5	0	3	1	0
Swartzbaugh, Dave, Chicago	0	2	.000	6.38	6	5	0	0	0	0	24.0	26	110	17	17	3	2	0	0	14	1	13	2	0
Swift, Bill, Colorado	1	1	.500	5.40	7	3	0	0	2	2	18.1	23	81	12	11	1	0	1	0	5	0	5	0	0
Swindell, Greg, Houston*	0	3	.000	7.83	8	4	0	0	3	0	23.0	35	116	25	20	5	0	1	1	11	0	15	0	0
Tabaka, Jeff, Houston*	0	2	.000	6.64	18	0	0	0	5	1	20.1	28	105	18	15	5	1	0	3	14	0	18	3	0
Telemaco, Amaury, Chicago	5	7	.417	5.46	25	17	0	0	2	0	97.1	108	427	67	59	20	5	3	3	31	2	64	3	0
Tewksbury, Bob, San Diego	10	10	.500	4.31	36	33	1	0	0	0	206.2	224	881	116	99	17	10	11	3	43	3	126	2	3
Thobe, Tom, Atlanta*	0	1	.000	1.50	4	0	0	0	3	0	6.0	5	24	2	1	1	0	1	0	0	0	1	0	0
Thompson, Mark, Colorado	9	11	.450	5.30	34	28	3	1	2	0	169.2	189	763	109	100	25	10	3	13	74	1	99	1	1
Trachsel, Steve, Chicago	13	9	.591	3.03	31	31	3	2	0	0	205.0	181	845	82	69	30	3	3	8	62	3	132	5	2
Trlicek, Ricky, New York	0	1	.000	3.38	5	0	0	0	2	0	5.1	3	20	2	2	0	2	0	1	3	1	3	0	0
Urbani, Tom, St. Louis*	1	0	1.000	7.71	3	2	0	0	0	0	11.2	15	53	10	10	3	1	1	0	4	0	1	0	0
Urbina, Ugueth, Montreal	10	5	.667	3.71	33	17	0	0	2	0	114.0	102	484	54	47	18	1	3	1	44	4	108	3	1
Valdes, Ismael, Los Angeles	15	7	.682	3.32	33	33	0	0	0	0	225.0	219	945	94	83	20	7	7	3	54	10	173	1	5
Valdes, Marc, Florida	1	3	.250	4.81	11	8	0	0	0	0	48.2	63	228	32	26	5	1	3	1	23	0	13	3	2
Valenzuela, Fernando, S.D.*	13	8	.619	3.62	33	31	0	0	0	0	171.2	177	741	78	69	17	11	4	0	67	2	95	7	0
VanLandingham, William, S.F.	9	14	.391	5.40	32	32	0	0	0	0	181.2	196	810	123	109	17	7	5	9	78	6	97	7	2
Veras, Dario, San Diego	3	1	.750	2.79	23	0	0	0	6	0	29.0	24	117	10	9	3	1	1	1	10	4	23	1	0
Veres, Dave, Montreal	6	3	.667	4.17	68	0	0	0	22	4	77.2	85	351	39	36	10	3	3	6	32	2	81	3	2
Villone, Ron, San Diego*	1	1	.500	2.95	21	0	0	0	9	0	18.1	17	78	6	6	2	0	0	1	7	0	19	0	0
Wade, Terrell, Atlanta*	5	0	1.000	2.97	44	8	0	0	13	1	69.2	57	305	28	23	9	5	1	1	47	6	79	2	0
Wagner, Billy, Houston*	2	2	.500	2.44	37	0	0	0	20	9	51.2	28	212	16	14	6	7	2	3	30	2	67	1	0
Wagner, Paul, Pittsburgh	4	8	.333	5.40	16	15	1	0	0	0	81.2	86	361	49	49	10	5	1	3	39	2	81	7	0
Wainhouse, David, Pittsburgh	1	0	1.000	5.70	17	0	0	0	6	0	23.2	22	101	16	15	3	1	2	0	10	1	16	2	0
Walker, Pete, San Diego	0	0	.000	.00	1	0	0	0	0	0	.2	0	5	0	0	0	0	0	0	3	0	1	0	0
Wall, Donne, Houston	9	8	.529	4.56	26	23	2	1	1	0	150.0	170	643	84	76	17	4	5	6	34	3	99	3	2
Wallace, Derek, New York	2	3	.400	4.01	19	0	0	0	11	3	24.2	29	115	12	11	2	1	0	0	14	2	15	2	0
Watson, Allen, San Francisco*	8	12	.400	4.61	29	29	2	0	0	0	185.2	189	793	105	95	28	18	9	5	69	2	128	9	2
Weathers, Dave, Florida	2	2	.500	4.54	31	8	0	0	8	0	71.1	85	319	41	36	7	5	1	4	28	4	40	2	0
Wendell, Turk, Chicago	4	5	.444	2.84	70	0	0	0	49	18	79.1	58	339	26	25	8	3	1	3	44	4	75	3	2
West, David, Philadelphia*	2	2	.500	4.76	7	6	0	0	0	0	28.1	31	126	17	15	0	1	0	0	11	0	22	1	1
Wilkins, Marc, Pittsburgh	4	3	.571	3.84	47	2	0	0	11	1	75.0	75	331	36	32	6	3	4	6	36	6	62	5	0
Williams, Mike, Philadelphia	6	14	.300	5.44	32	29	0	0	1	0	167.0	188	732	107	101	25	6	5	6	67	6	103	16	1
Wilson, Paul, New York	5	12	.294	5.38	26	26	1	0	0	0	149.0	157	677	102	89	15	7	3	10	71	11	109	3	3
Wohlers, Mark, Atlanta	2	4	.333	3.03	77	0	0	0	64	39	77.1	71	323	30	26	8	2	2	2	21	3	100	10	0
Woodall, Brad, Atlanta*	2	2	.500	7.32	8	3	0	0	2	0	19.2	28	91	19	16	4	1	2	0	4	0	20	1	0
Worrell, Tim, San Diego	9	7	.563	3.05	50	11	0	0	8	1	121.0	109	510	45	41	9	3	1	6	39	1	99	0	0
Worrell, Todd, Los Angeles	4	6	.400	3.03	72	0	0	0	67	44	65.1	70	285	29	22	5	2	2	2	15	1	66	4	1
Wright, Jamey, Colorado	4	4	.500	4.93	16	15	0	0	0	0	91.1	105	406	60	50	8	4	2	7	41	1	45	1	2
Young, Anthony, Houston	3	3	.500	4.59	28	0	0	0	10	0	33.1	36	158	18	17	4	2	1	4	22	4	19	2	1

COMBINATION SHUTOUTS: **Atlanta (6)**—Smoltz, Clontz, Borbon and Wade; Maddux and McMichael; Glavine and Wohlers; Maddux, McMichael and Wohlers; Smoltz and Wohlers; Maddux, Woodall, Lomon, Hartgraves and Wade. **Chicago (5)**—Trachsel, Adams and Patterson; Trachsel, Bottenfield, Patterson and Wendell; Castillo, Casian and Adams; Navarro and Patterson; Castillo and Adams. **Cincinnati (3)**—Burba, Carrasco and Brantley; Schourek and Shaw; Smiley, Shaw, McElroy and Brantley. **Colorado (3)**—Ritz, S. Reed, Painter and Ruffin; Freeman, Holmes and Hawblitzel; Ritz, Leskanic and Ruffin. **Florida (9)**—Brown and Nen 2; Burkett, Mathews and Perez; Leiter, Mathews and Nen; Rapp, Powell and Nen; Leiter, Powell and Nen; Hutton and Powell; Helling and Hammond; Brown, Hammond, Powell and Nen. **Houston (1)**—

ynolds and Wagner. **Los Angeles (5)**—Astacio and Worrell; Valdes, Radinsky and Worrell; Park, Hall and Worrell; Martinez, Osuna and Worrell; Astacio and Guthrie. ontreal (4)—Fassero, Dyer and Daal; Fassero and Rojas; Martinez and Rojas; Paniagua and Rojas. **New York (7)**— B. Jones and J. Franco 2; Isringhausen and acDonald; Clark and Henry; Wilson and J. Franco; Person and Mlicki; Harnisch and J. Franco. **Philadelphia (3)**—Grace and Bottalico 2; Schilling and Springer. ttsburgh (5)—Darwin, Plesac and Cordova; Wagner, Lieber and Plesac; Darwin, Cordova and Plesac; Neagle, Lieber, Plesac and Cordova; Darwin and Christiansen. **St. uis (6)**—Petkovsek, Fossas, Mathews, Honeycutt, Bailey and Eckersley; A. Benes and Eckersley; Stottlemyre and Petkovsek; Osborne, Mathews and Eckersley; tkovsek, Fossas, Bailey, Honeycutt and Eckersley; Stottlemyre, Mathews, Fossas, Batchelor and Eckersley. **San Diego (10)**—Tewksbury, Bochtler and Hoffman 2; wksbury, Worrell and Hoffman; Tewksbury and Hoffman; Hamilton, Veras and Hoffman; Ashby, Worrell, Bochtler and Hoffman; Worrell, Bochtler and Hoffman; Sanders d Oquist; Tewksbury, Veras and Hoffman; Hamilton and Blair. **San Francisco (7)**—Fernandez and Beck 2; Watson and Beck; Estes and DeLucia; Watson, Dewey and utista; VanLandingham, Poole, Creek and Dewey; VanLandingham, Poole and Beck.

PITCHERS WITH TWO OR MORE TEAMS

tcher, Team	W	L	Pct.	ERA	G	GS	CG	ShO	GF	Sv.	IP	H	TBF	R	ER	HR	SH	SF	HB	BB	IBB	SO	WP	Bk.
arwin, Danny, Pittsburgh	7	9	.438	3.02	19	19	0	0	0	0	122.1	117	493	48	41	9	5	4	6	16	0	69	3	3
arwin, Danny, Houston	3	2	.600	5.95	15	6	0	0	1	0	42.1	43	184	31	28	7	3	3	6	11	3	27	0	0
ishman, Glenn, San Diego*	0	0	.000	7.71	3	0	0	0	2	0	2.1	3	11	2	2	0	0	0	1	0	1	0	1	0
ishman, Glenn, Philadelphia*	0	0	.000	7.71	4	1	0	0	2	0	7.0	9	31	6	6	2	0	1	0	2	0	3	0	0
artgraves, Dean, Houston*	0	0	.000	5.21	19	0	0	0	5	0	19.0	18	89	11	11	1	1	1	1	16	3	16	2	0
artgraves, Dean, Atlanta*	1	0	1.000	4.34	20	0	0	0	4	0	18.2	16	78	10	9	3	0	1	1	7	0	14	0	0
ernandez, Xavier, Cincinnati	0	0	.000	13.50	3	0	0	0	0	0	3.1	8	19	6	5	2	0	0	0	2	0	3	0	0
ernandez, Xavier, Houston	5	5	.500	4.22	58	0	0	0	27	6	74.2	69	321	39	35	11	8	3	2	26	5	78	9	0
iden, Jeff, San Francisco	4	0	1.000	4.10	36	0	0	0	9	0	41.2	39	180	23	19	7	1	2	1	20	2	35	3	0
iden, Jeff, Montreal	1	0	1.000	2.20	22	0	0	0	7	0	32.2	22	138	12	8	1	2	1	4	14	0	26	2	0
eiper, Dave, Houston	2	0	1.000	6.43	26	0	0	0	8	0	21.0	31	97	16	15	4	1	0	0	7	2	10	2	0
eiper, Dave, Montreal*	0	1	.000	11.25	7	0	0	0	0	0	4.0	9	23	5	5	0	2	0	0	2	0	3	0	0
iter, Mark, San Francisco	4	10	.286	5.19	23	22	1	0	0	0	135.1	151	602	93	78	25	7	3	9	50	7	118	2	3
iter, Mark, Montreal	4	2	.667	4.39	12	12	1	0	0	0	69.2	68	302	35	34	12	5	3	7	19	1	46	4	1
artinez, Pedro A., New York*	0	0	.000	6.43	5	0	0	0	0	0	7.0	8	36	7	5	1	1	1	0	7	4	6	0	0
artinez, Pedro A., Cincinnati*	0	0	.000	6.00	4	0	0	0	0	0	3.0	5	15	2	2	1	0	0	0	1	0	3	0	0
organ, Mike, St. Louis	4	8	.333	5.24	18	18	0	0	0	0	103.0	118	452	63	60	14	5	6	0	40	0	55	2	0
organ, Mike, Cincinnati	2	3	.400	2.30	5	5	0	0	0	0	27.1	28	115	9	7	2	1	1	1	7	0	19	0	1
eagle, Denny, Pittsburgh*	14	6	.700	3.05	27	27	1	0	0	0	182.2	186	745	67	62	21	9	3	3	34	2	131	2	1
eagle, Denny, Atlanta*	2	3	.400	5.59	6	6	1	0	0	0	38.2	40	165	26	24	5	1	1	0	14	0	18	1	0
arrett, Jeff, St. Louis	2	2	.500	4.25	33	0	0	0	16	0	42.1	40	186	20	20	2	1	1	1	20	2	42	7	0
arrett, Jeff, Philadelphia	1	1	.500	1.88	18	0	0	0	7	0	24.0	24	102	5	5	0	1	1	0	11	2	22	3	0
ueter, Kirk, Montreal*	5	6	.455	4.58	16	16	0	0	0	0	78.2	91	338	44	40	12	4	1	2	22	0	30	0	0
ueter, Kirk, San Francisco*	1	2	.333	1.93	4	3	0	0	0	0	23.1	18	92	6	5	0	0	0	0	5	0	16	2	0
chmidt, Jason, Atlanta	3	4	.429	6.75	13	11	0	0	0	0	58.2	69	274	48	44	8	3	6	0	32	0	48	5	1
chmidt, Jason, Pittsburgh	2	2	.500	4.06	6	6	1	0	0	0	37.2	39	171	19	17	2	1	3	2	21	0	26	3	0
cott, Tim, Montreal	3	5	.375	3.11	45	0	0	0	14	1	46.1	41	198	18	16	3	1	2	2	21	2	37	1	0
cott, Tim, San Francisco	2	2	.500	8.24	20	0	0	0	2	0	19.2	24	90	18	18	5	3	1	1	9	0	10	2	0

1996 N.L. STATISTICS *Pitching*

FIELDING

TEAM

Team	Pct.	G	PO	A	E	TC	DP	PB
Chicago	.983	162	4369	1767	104	6240	147	13
Florida	.982	162	4329	1796	111	6236	187	12
San Diego	.981	162	4467	1768	118	6353	136	14
Philadelphia	.981	162	4270	1582	116	5968	145	10
Cincinnati	.980	162	4329	1694	121	6144	145	7
Pittsburgh	.980	162	4360	1868	128	6356	144	10
Los Angeles	.980	162	4399	1636	125	6160	143	15
St. Louis	.980	162	4357	1666	125	6148	139	7
Montreal	.980	162	4324	1713	126	6163	121	1
Atlanta	.980	162	4407	1809	130	6346	143	1
San Francisco	.978	162	4327	1637	136	6100	165	1
Houston	.978	162	4341	1692	138	6171	130	1
Colorado	.976	162	4268	1901	149	6318	167	1
New York	.974	162	4320	1717	159	6196	163	1
Totals	.979	1134	60867	24246	1786	86899	2075	16

TRIPLE PLAY: Los Angeles.

INDIVIDUAL

FIRST BASEMEN

NOTE: All caps denotes fielding-percentage leader based on 72 games for catchers, 96 for all other non-pitchers and 144 innings for pitchers. *Throws lefthanded.

Player, Team	Pct.	G	PO	A	E	TC	DP
Amaro, Ruben, Philadelphia	.000	1	0	0	0	0	0
Arias, Alex, Florida	1.000	1	1	0	0	1	0
Aude, Rich, Pittsburgh	.969	4	28	3	1	32	3
Baerga, Carlos, New York	.990	16	98	5	1	104	8
Bagwell, Jeff, Houston	.989	162	1336	136	16	1488	117
Belk, Tim, Cincinnati	1.000	6	28	0	0	28	2
Blowers, Mike, Los Angeles	1.000	6	20	2	0	22	0
Bogar, Tim, New York	1.000	32	77	4	0	81	7
Borders, Pat, St. Louis	.500	1	1	0	1	2	0
Brogna, Rico, New York*	.996	52	440	31	2	473	46
Brooks, Jerry, Florida	.000	1	0	0	1	1	0
Brown, Brant, Chicago*	1.000	18	126	17	0	143	4
Busch, Mike, Los Angeles	1.000	1	2	0	0	2	0
Carreon, Mark, San Francisco*	.986	73	533	37	8	578	64
Cianfrocco, Archi, San Diego	1.000	33	168	15	0	183	13
Colbrunn, Greg, Florida	.995	134	1169	101	6	1276	130
Conine, Jeff, Florida	.991	48	292	40	3	335	33
Davis, Eric, Cincinnati	1.000	1	7	0	0	7	0
Decker, Steve, San Francisco	1.000	3	18	3	0	21	1
Espinoza, Alvaro, New York	.000	1	0	0	0	0	0
Floyd, Cliff, Montreal	.941	2	16	0	1	17	1
Franco, Matt, New York	1.000	2	12	1	0	13	1
Gaetti, Gary, St. Louis	.989	14	85	7	1	93	6
Galarraga, Andres, Colorado	.992	159	1528	116	14	1658	154
Gomez, Leo, Chicago	1.000	8	41	5	0	46	1
Gonzalez, Luis, Chicago	1.000	2	13	1	0	14	0
Grace, Mark, Chicago*	.997	141	1259	107	4	1370	120
Greene, Willie, Cincinnati	1.000	2	1	0	0	1	0
Gwynn, Chris, San Diego*	1.000	1	0	1	0	1	0
Hansen, Dave, Los Angeles	1.000	8	54	4	0	58	3
Harris, Lenny, Cincinnati	.993	16	123	12	1	136	10
Houston, Tyler, Atl.-Chi.	1.000	12	17	2	0	19	1
Huskey, Butch, New York	.984	75	569	43	10	622	57
Jefferies, Gregg, Philadelphia	.998	53	412	38	1	451	38
Johnson, Brian, San Diego	1.000	1	6	0	0	6	1
Johnson, Mark, Pittsburgh*	.994	100	777	72	5	854	64
Jones, Chris, New York	1.000	5	16	1	0	17	1
Jordan, Brian, St. Louis	1.000	1	1	0	0	1	0
Jordan, Kevin, Philadelphia	1.000	30	227	12	0	239	19
JOYNER, Wally, San Diego*	.997	119	1059	89	3	1151	85
Karros, Eric, Los Angeles	.990	154	1314	121	15	1450	133
King, Jeff, Pittsburgh	.997	92	745	47	2	794	60
Klesko, Ryan, Atlanta*	1.000	2	13	2	0	15	2
Livingstone, Scott, San Diego	.993	22	138	10	1	149	15
Mabry, John, St. Louis	.994	146	1170	76	8	1254	107
Magadan, Dave, Chicago	1.000	10	59	4	0	63	4
Marrero, Oreste, Los Angeles*	1.000	1	1	0	0	1	0
McCarty, Dave, San Francisco*	.990	51	269	16	3	288	30
McGee, Willie, St. Louis	1.000	6	23	4	0	27	0
McGriff, Fred, Atlanta*	.992	158	1416	124	12	1552	118
Merced, Orlando, Pittsburgh	1.000	1	1	1	0	2	1
Mitchell, Kevin, Cincinnati	.968	3	28	2	1	31	4
Mordecai, Mike, Atlanta	1.000	1	2	1	0	3	0
Morman, Russ, Pittsburgh	1.000	2	2	0	0	2	1
Morris, Hal, Cincinnati*	.993	140	1129	91	8	1228	103
Newfield, Marc, San Diego	.909	2	9	1	1	11	0
Oliver, Joe, Cincinnati	1.000	3	9	1	0	10	0
Orsulak, Joe, Florida*	1.000	2	4	1	0	5	1
Pagnozzi, Tom, St. Louis	1.000	1	1	0	0	1	0
Peltier, Dan, San Francisco*	1.000	13	87	6	0	93	1
Perez, Eddie, Atlanta	.971	7	31	3	1	35	
Perez, Eduardo, Cincinnati	1.000	8	56	7	0	63	
Petagine, Roberto, New York*	.996	40	209	23	1	233	2
Phillips, J.R., S.F.-Phi.*	.992	21	119	5	1	125	1
Rodriguez, Henry, Montreal*	.989	51	426	28	5	459	2
Santiago, Benito, Philadelphia	.992	14	111	6	1	118	
Scarsone, Steve, San Francisco	1.000	1	1	0	0	1	
Schall, Gene, Philadelphia	.986	19	135	8	2	145	1
Segui, David, Montreal*	.993	113	944	90	7	1041	7
Servais, Scott, Chicago	1.000	1	1	1	0	2	
Sheaffer, Danny, St. Louis	1.000	6	11	0	0	11	
Silvestri, Dave, Montreal	1.000	1	3	0	0	3	
Simms, Mike, Houston	1.000	5	7	1	0	8	
Spiers, Bill, Houston	1.000	4	9	1	0	10	
Sweeney, Mark, St. Louis*	.972	15	67	2	2	71	
Thompson, Jason, San Diego*	.964	13	94	13	4	111	
Tomberlin, Andy, New York*	.000	1	0	0	0	0	
Vander Wal, John, Colorado*	.976	10	38	2	1	41	
Wilkins, Rick, San Francisco	1.000	7	52	5	0	57	
Williams, Matt, San Francisco	.990	13	90	12	1	103	1
Wilson, Desi, San Francisco*	.984	33	236	18	4	258	2
Young, Dmitri, St. Louis	.976	10	39	1	1	41	
Zeile, Todd, Philadelphia	.984	28	223	16	4	243	3
Zuber, Jon, Philadelphia*	.987	22	145	11	2	158	1

TRIPLE PLAY: Karros, L.A.

FIRST BASEMEN WITH TWO OR MORE TEAMS

Player, Team	Pct.	G	PO	A	E	TC	DP
Houston, Tyler, Atlanta	1.000	11	16	1	0	17	
Houston, Tyler, Chicago	1.000	1	1	0	0	2	
Phillips, J.R., San Francisco*	.981	10	49	2	1	52	
Phillips, J.R., Philadelphia*	1.000	11	70	3	0	73	

SECOND BASEMEN

Player, Team	Pct.	G	PO	A	E	TC	DP
Abbott, Kurt, Florida	1.000	20	35	39	0	74	
Alfonzo, Edgardo, New York	.974	66	122	174	8	304	4
Alicea, Luis, St. Louis	.957	125	241	288	24	553	7
Arias, Alex, Florida	1.000	1	0	2	0	2	
Aurilia, Rich, San Francisco	1.000	11	16	18	0	34	
Baerga, Carlos, New York	1.000	1	3	3	0	6	
Barberie, Bret, Chicago	1.000	6	5	17	0	22	
Bates, Jason, Colorado	.978	37	58	78	3	139	1
Bell, David, St. Louis	.987	20	23	54	1	78	
Belliard, Rafael, Atlanta	.951	15	14	25	2	41	
Benjamin, Mike, Philadelphia	1.000	1	1	0	0	1	
Biggio, Craig, Houston	.988	162	361	440	10	811	7
Bogar, Tim, New York	1.000	8	4	11	0	15	
BOONE, Bret, Cincinnati	.991	141	315	381	6	702	8
Branson, Jeff, Cincinnati	.976	31	36	45	2	83	1
Canizaro, Jay, San Francisco	.972	35	60	79	4	143	1
Castellano, Pedro, Colorado	1.000	3	3	10	0	13	
Castillo, Luis, Florida	.986	41	99	118	3	220	3
Castro, Juan, Los Angeles	1.000	9	7	12	0	19	
Cianfrocco, Archi, San Diego	.917	6	5	6	1	12	
DeShields, Delino, Los Angeles	.975	154	274	400	17	691	79
Doster, David, Philadelphia	.973	24	52	56	3	111	12
Espinoza, Alvaro, New York	1.000	2	0	1	0	1	
Fermin, Felix, Chicago	.875	6	2	5	1	8	
Fonville, Chad, Los Angeles	.982	23	20	34	1	55	8
Gallego, Mike, St. Louis	.985	43	84	118	3	205	3
Garcia, Carlos, Pittsburgh	.985	77	131	199	5	335	3

ayer, Team	Pct.	G	PO	A	E	TC	DP
ovanola, Ed, Atlanta	1.000	5	5	10	0	15	2
affanino, Tony, Atlanta	.969	18	24	39	2	65	9
ebeck, Craig, Florida	.985	29	67	65	2	134	24
utierrez, Ricky, Houston	.857	5	3	3	1	7	1
ajek, Dave, Houston	1.000	2	2	1	0	3	0
aney, Todd, Chicago	.978	23	29	60	2	91	12
ardtke, Jason, New York	1.000	18	26	34	0	60	9
arris, Lenny, Cincinnati	.963	8	11	15	1	27	4
ernandez, Jose, Chicago	1.000	1	0	1	0	1	0
olbert, Aaron, St. Louis	1.000	1	0	1	0	1	0
ouston, Tyler, Chicago	1.000	2	2	6	0	8	2
rdan, Kevin, Philadelphia	1.000	7	16	14	0	30	3
ng, Jeff, Pittsburgh	.979	71	145	181	7	333	40
nsing, Mike, Montreal	.985	159	347	393	11	751	85
mke, Mark, Atlanta	.977	133	228	410	15	653	71
riano, Nelson, Pittsburgh	.984	36	50	73	2	125	13
pez, Luis, San Diego	.962	22	19	32	2	53	7
illiard, Ralph, Florida	.955	24	42	65	5	112	14
orandini, Mickey, Philadelphia	.982	137	286	352	12	650	87
ordecai, Mike, Atlanta	.985	20	26	38	1	65	8
ueller, Bill, San Francisco	.949	8	17	20	2	39	8
vens, Eric, Cincinnati	.944	6	10	7	1	18	0
erez, Neifi, Colorado	.933	4	6	8	1	15	3
eed, Jody, San Diego	.987	145	275	411	9	695	86
elaford, Desi, Philadelphia	1.000	4	8	11	0	19	4
andberg, Ryne, Chicago	.991	146	228	421	6	655	82
antangelo, F.P., Montreal	1.000	5	5	7	0	12	2
carsone, Steve, San Francisco	.973	74	161	161	9	331	44
efcik, Kevin, Philadelphia	1.000	1	1	1	0	2	0
hipley, Craig, San Diego	.985	17	26	39	1	66	6
humpert, Terry, Chicago	1.000	4	2	2	0	4	0
lvestri, Dave, Montreal	1.000	1	0	0	0	0	0
iers, Bill, Houston	1.000	7	7	4	0	11	2
ankiewicz, Andy, Montreal	.969	19	12	19	1	32	2
ompson, Robby, San Francisco	.976	62	124	155	7	286	38
eras, Quilvio, Florida	.986	67	174	191	5	370	54
zcaino, Jose, New York	.986	93	179	259	6	444	70
ehner, John, Pittsburgh	.974	12	19	18	1	38	3
omack, Tony, Pittsburgh	.875	4	6	8	2	16	0
ung, Eric, Colorado	.985	139	340	431	12	783	109

TRIPLE PLAY: DeShields, L.A.

THIRD BASEMEN

ayer, Team	Pct.	G	PO	A	E	TC	DP
bbott, Kurt, Florida	.915	33	22	43	6	71	3
fonzo, Edgardo, New York	.957	36	17	50	3	70	5
ndrews, Shane, Montreal	.955	123	64	256	15	335	13
ias, Alex, Florida	.956	59	21	66	4	91	8
erga, Carlos, New York	.667	6	2	4	3	9	0
arberie, Bret, Chicago	1.000	2	1	2	0	3	0
ates, Jason, Colorado	.818	12	0	9	2	11	1
atiste, Kim, San Francisco	.847	25	24	37	11	72	7
attle, Howard, Philadelphia	.000	1	0	0	0	0	0
ell, David, St. Louis	.953	45	22	59	4	85	1
erry, Sean, Houston	.922	110	67	194	22	283	13
owers, Mike, Los Angeles	.951	90	56	120	9	185	9
gar, Tim, New York	.972	25	13	22	1	36	0
oty, Josh, Florida	.000	1	0	0	0	0	0
anson, Jeff, Cincinnati	.932	64	31	93	9	133	12
sch, Mike, Los Angeles	.932	23	16	25	3	44	1
aminiti, Ken, San Diego	.954	145	103	310	20	433	28
astellano, Pedro, Colorado	1.000	1	0	1	0	1	0
astilla, Vinny, Colorado	.960	160	97	389	20	506	43
astro, Juan, Los Angeles	.889	23	5	3	1	9	1
edeno, Andujar, S.D.-Hou.	1.000	3	1	3	0	4	0
anfrocco, Archi, San Diego	.889	11	2	14	2	18	2
ecker, Steve, San Francisco	1.000	2	2	2	0	4	0
oster, David, Philadelphia	1.000	1	0	1	0	1	0
spinoza, Alvaro, New York	.900	38	20	52	8	80	2
nville, Chad, Los Angeles	1.000	2	2	2	0	4	0
anco, Matt, New York	.824	8	3	11	3	17	0
aetti, Gary, St. Louis	.970	133	63	224	9	296	16
alarraga, Andres, Colorado	.000	1	0	0	0	0	0
allego, Mike, St. Louis	1.000	7	3	4	0	7	0
arcia, Carlos, Pittsburgh	.930	14	4	36	3	43	4
ovanola, Ed, Atlanta	1.000	6	1	7	0	8	1
OMEZ, Leo, Chicago	.972	124	69	176	7	252	17
rebeck, Craig, Florida	.000	1	0	0	0	0	0
reene, Willie, Cincinnati	.927	74	45	146	15	206	13
utierrez, Ricky, Houston	1.000	6	1	5	0	6	0
ajek, Dave, Houston	1.000	3	1	6	0	7	0
aney, Todd, Chicago	.889	4	3	5	1	9	0
ansen, Dave, Los Angeles	.962	19	6	19	1	26	1

Player, Team	Pct.	G	PO	A	E	TC	DP
Harris, Lenny, Cincinnati	.935	24	21	37	4	62	2
Hayes, Charlie, Pittsburgh	.950	124	66	275	18	359	24
Hernandez, Jose, Chicago	.978	43	13	32	1	46	2
Houston, Tyler, Chicago	.938	9	6	9	1	16	0
Huskey, Butch, New York	.933	6	5	9	1	15	1
Johnson, Brian, San Diego	.000	1	0	0	0	0	0
Jones, Chipper, Atlanta	.947	118	48	185	13	246	9
Jordan, Kevin, Philadelphia	1.000	1	0	1	0	1	1
Kent, Jeff, New York	.925	89	75	184	21	280	19
King, Jeff, Pittsburgh	.938	17	6	24	2	32	1
Liriano, Nelson, Pittsburgh	1.000	9	4	17	0	21	0
Livingstone, Scott, San Diego	.967	16	5	24	1	30	2
Lopez, Luis, San Diego	1.000	2	1	0	0	1	0
Magadan, Dave, Chicago	.963	51	16	63	3	82	4
Miller, Orlando, Houston	.949	29	14	23	2	39	1
Mordecai, Mike, Atlanta	.941	10	4	12	1	17	0
Mueller, Bill, San Francisco	.966	45	34	79	4	117	10
Osik, Keith, Pittsburgh	1.000	2	1	2	0	3	1
Owens, Eric, Cincinnati	1.000	5	1	4	0	5	0
Pendleton, Terry, Fla.-Atl.	.955	149	110	296	19	425	27
Perez, Eduardo, Cincinnati	1.000	3	3	4	0	7	0
Rolen, Scott, Philadelphia	.954	37	29	54	4	87	4
Sabo, Chris, Cincinnati	.961	43	27	72	4	103	6
Santangelo, F.P., Montreal	.960	23	14	34	2	50	2
Scarsone, Steve, San Francisco	.913	14	5	16	2	23	3
Schu, Rick, Montreal	.667	1	0	2	1	3	0
Sefcik, Kevin, Philadelphia	.872	20	7	34	6	47	3
Sheaffer, Danny, St. Louis	.958	17	6	17	1	24	0
Shipley, Craig, San Diego	1.000	4	1	5	0	6	0
Shumpert, Terry, Chicago	.923	10	8	4	1	13	0
Silvestri, Dave, Montreal	.913	47	20	85	10	115	5
Spiers, Bill, Houston	.959	77	22	94	5	121	9
Stankiewicz, Andy, Montreal	.500	1	0	1	1	2	0
Sveum, Dale, Pittsburgh	.913	10	4	17	2	23	1
Tatum, Jimmy, San Diego	.000	1	0	0	0	0	0
Wallach, Tim, Los Angeles	.971	45	38	62	3	103	3
Wehner, John, Pittsburgh	1.000	24	8	24	0	32	3
Williams, Matt, San Francisco	.951	92	74	179	13	266	18
Zeile, Todd, Philadelphia	.962	106	72	179	10	261	13

THIRD BASEMEN WITH TWO OR MORE TEAMS

Player, Team	Pct.	G	PO	A	E	TC	DP
Cedeno, Andujar, San Diego	1.000	2	1	2	0	3	0
Cedeno, Andujar, Houston	1.000	1	0	1	0	1	0
Pendleton, Terry, Florida	.961	108	83	216	12	311	22
Pendleton, Terry, Atlanta	.939	41	27	80	7	114	5

SHORTSTOPS

Player, Team	Pct.	G	PO	A	E	TC	DP
Abbott, Kurt, Florida	.969	44	66	123	6	195	34
Alfonzo, Edgardo, New York	1.000	15	7	22	0	29	5
Arias, Alex, Florida	.966	20	26	59	3	88	15
Aurilia, Rich, San Francisco	.973	93	126	228	10	364	44
Barberie, Bret, Chicago	.000	1	0	0	0	0	0
Bates, Jason, Colorado	.938	18	8	22	2	32	1
Batiste, Kim, San Francisco	1.000	7	11	4	0	15	4
Bell, David, St. Louis	.000	1	0	0	0	0	0
BELL, Jay, Pittsburgh	.986	151	215	478	10	703	78
Belliard, Rafael, Atlanta	.983	63	51	125	3	179	25
Benjamin, Mike, Philadelphia	.954	31	37	87	6	130	14
Blauser, Jeff, Atlanta	.926	79	83	206	23	312	40
Blowers, Mike, Los Angeles	.000	1	0	0	0	0	0
Bogar, Tim, New York	1.000	19	10	24	0	34	6
Branson, Jeff, Cincinnati	.969	38	30	63	3	96	17
Canizaro, Jay, San Francisco	.889	7	4	12	2	18	4
Castro, Juan, Los Angeles	.982	30	40	69	2	111	21
Cedeno, Andujar, S.D.-Hou.	.948	49	46	137	10	193	31
Cianfrocco, Archi, San Diego	1.000	10	13	16	0	29	2
Clayton, Royce, St. Louis	.972	113	171	347	15	533	68
Delgado, Wilson, San Francisco	.960	6	12	12	1	25	3
Dunston, Shawon, San Francisco	.957	78	116	217	15	348	51
Espinoza, Alvaro, New York	1.000	7	4	13	0	17	3
Fermin, Felix, Chicago	1.000	3	2	3	0	5	0
Fonville, Chad, Los Angeles	.936	20	11	33	3	47	5
Gagne, Greg, Los Angeles	.966	127	184	404	21	609	87
Gallego, Mike, St. Louis	1.000	1	3	4	0	7	1
Garcia, Carlos, Pittsburgh	.961	19	25	49	3	77	13
Giovanola, Ed, Atlanta	.983	25	18	39	1	58	9
Gomez, Chris, San Diego	.967	89	124	261	13	398	54
Gomez, Leo, Chicago	1.000	1	0	1	0	1	1
Grebeck, Craig, Florida	1.000	2	0	1	0	1	0
Greene, Willie, Cincinnati	1.000	1	1	0	0	1	0
Grudzielanek, Mark, Montreal	.959	153	180	453	27	660	78

Player, Team	Pct.	G	PO	A	E	TC	DP
Gutierrez, Ricky, Houston	.953	74	82	141	11	234	33
Haney, Todd, Chicago	.000	3	0	0	0	0	0
Hernandez, Jose, Chicago	.948	87	134	215	19	368	51
Jones, Chipper, Atlanta	.975	38	53	103	4	160	27
Lansing, Mike, Montreal	1.000	2	2	2	0	4	1
Larkin, Barry, Cincinnati	.975	151	230	426	17	673	80
Liriano, Nelson, Pittsburgh	.923	5	4	8	1	13	2
Lopez, Luis, San Diego	.981	35	37	68	2	107	11
Martinez, Pablo, Atlanta	1.000	1	0	2	0	2	1
Miller, Orlando, Houston	.958	117	133	297	19	449	59
Mordecai, Mike, Atlanta	1.000	6	1	1	0	2	0
Ordonez, Rey, New York	.962	150	228	450	27	705	102
Perez, Neifi, Colorado	.972	14	15	20	1	36	8
Relaford, Desi, Philadelphia	.933	9	13	15	2	30	2
Renteria, Edgar, Florida	.979	106	163	344	11	518	77
Sanchez, Rey, Chicago	.977	92	151	307	11	469	55
Santangelo, F.P., Montreal	.000	1	0	0	0	0	0
Scarsone, Steve, San Francisco	.000	1	0	0	0	0	0
Sefcik, Kevin, Philadelphia	.986	21	22	48	1	71	9
Shipley, Craig, San Diego	1.000	7	4	19	0	23	1
Shumpert, Terry, Chicago	1.000	1	1	3	0	4	2
Silvestri, Dave, Montreal	1.000	10	0	7	0	7	0
Smith, Ozzie, St. Louis	.969	52	90	162	8	260	36
Spiers, Bill, Houston	1.000	4	3	9	0	12	1
Stankiewicz, Andy, Montreal	.964	13	4	23	1	28	4
Stocker, Kevin, Philadelphia	.975	119	165	352	13	530	79
Weiss, Walt, Colorado	.957	155	220	450	30	700	90
Williams, Matt, San Francisco	.000	1	0	0	0	0	0

TRIPLE PLAY: Castro, L.A.

SHORTSTOPS WITH TWO OR MORE TEAMS

Player, Team	Pct.	G	PO	A	E	TC	DP
Cedeno, Andujar, San Diego	.946	47	43	131	10	184	28
Cedeno, Andujar, Houston	1.000	2	3	6	0	9	3

OUTFIELDERS

Player, Team	Pct.	G	PO	A	E	TC	DP
Abreu, Bob, Houston	1.000	7	6	0	0	6	0
Allensworth, Jermaine, Pittsburgh	.979	61	139	4	3	146	1
Alou, Moises, Montreal	.989	142	259	8	3	270	2
Amaro, Ruben, Philadelphia	1.000	35	50	0	0	50	0
Anthony, Eric, Cin.-Col.*	.967	56	55	4	2	61	0
Ashley, Billy, Los Angeles	.952	38	38	2	2	42	1
Bautista, Danny, Atlanta	1.000	14	10	0	0	10	0
Beamon, Trey, Pittsburgh	.960	14	24	0	1	25	0
Bell, Derek, Houston	.977	157	283	16	7	306	4
Benard, Marvin, San Francisco*	.984	132	309	7	5	321	0
Benitez, Yamil, Montreal	.500	4	1	0	1	2	0
Bichette, Dante, Colorado	.967	156	255	5	9	269	1
Bonds, Barry, San Francisco*	.980	152	286	10	6	302	1
Bradshaw, Terry, St. Louis	1.000	7	4	0	0	4	0
Brooks, Jerry, Florida	1.000	2	2	0	0	2	0
Brumfield, Jacob, Pittsburgh	.946	22	34	1	2	37	1
Bullett, Scott, Chicago*	.986	58	70	2	1	73	1
Burks, Ellis, Colorado	.983	152	279	6	5	290	2
Butler, Brett, Los Angeles*	.987	34	74	1	1	76	0
Cangelosi, John, Houston*	.975	78	113	5	3	121	0
Carreon, Mark, San Francisco*	1.000	5	6	1	0	7	0
Castellano, Pedro, Colorado	.000	1	0	0	0	0	0
Castro, Juan, Los Angeles	1.000	1	2	0	0	2	0
Cedeno, Roger, Los Angeles	.983	71	117	2	2	121	0
Cianfrocco, Archi, San Diego	1.000	8	7	0	0	7	0
Clark, Dave, Pit.-L.A.	.988	62	80	3	1	84	1
Cockrell, Alan, Colorado	.000	1	0	0	0	0	0
Coleman, Vince, Cincinnati	.968	20	28	2	1	31	0
Conine, Jeff, Florida	.975	128	186	8	5	199	2
Cruz, Jacob, San Francisco*	.977	23	41	1	1	43	0
Cummings, Midre, Pittsburgh	.980	21	49	0	1	50	0
Curtis, Chad, Los Angeles	.985	40	62	2	1	65	1
Dascenzo, Doug, San Diego*	1.000	10	3	0	0	3	0
Daulton, Darren, Philadelphia	1.000	5	6	0	0	6	0
Davis, Eric, Cincinnati	.989	126	272	3	3	278	0
Dawson, Andre, Florida	.833	6	5	0	1	6	0
Deer, Rob, San Diego	1.000	18	26	0	0	26	0
Dye, Jermaine, Atlanta	.950	92	150	2	8	160	1
Dykstra, Lenny, Philadelphia*	1.000	39	103	3	0	106	1
Echevarria, Angel, Colorado	1.000	11	1	0	0	1	0
Eisenreich, Jim, Philadelphia*	.977	91	167	3	4	174	1
Everett, Carl, New York	.935	55	96	4	7	107	1
Finley, Steve, San Diego*	.982	160	385	7	7	399	2
Floyd, Cliff, Montreal	.960	85	93	2	4	99	0
Fonville, Chad, Los Angeles	.964	35	51	2	2	55	1
Gant, Ron, St. Louis	.978	116	216	4	5	225	2

Player, Team	Pct.	G	PO	A	E	TC	D
Gibralter, Steve, Cincinnati	.000	2	0	0	1	1	
Gilkey, Bernard, New York	.982	151	309	18	6	333	
Glanville, Doug, Chicago	.973	35	35	1	1	37	
Gonzalez, Luis, Chicago	.988	139	231	6	3	240	
Goodwin, Curtis, Cincinnati*	.970	42	64	0	2	66	
Greene, Willie, Cincinnati	.909	10	10	0	1	11	
Grissom, Marquis, Atlanta	.997	158	338	10	1	349	
Guerrero, Vladimir, Montreal	1.000	8	11	0	0	11	
Gwynn, Chris, San Diego*	1.000	29	20	0	0	20	
Gwynn, Tony, San Diego*	.989	111	182	2	2	186	
Hall, Mel, San Francisco*	.000	4	0	0	0	0	
Harris, Lenny, Cincinnati	1.000	37	44	2	0	46	
Henderson, Rickey, San Diego*	.975	134	228	3	6	237	
Hernandez, Jose, Chicago	1.000	1	1	0	0	1	
Hill, Glenallen, San Francisco	.960	98	160	6	7	173	
Hollandsworth, Todd, L.A.*	.978	142	217	7	5	229	
Houston, Tyler, Atlanta	.000	1	0	0	0	0	
Howard, Thomas, Cincinnati	.982	103	160	7	3	170	
Hubbard, Trent, Col.-S.F.	1.000	28	51	1	0	52	
Hunter, Brian L., Houston	.960	127	279	11	12	302	
Huskey, Butch, New York	.943	40	64	2	4	70	
Incaviglia, Pete, Philadelphia	.969	71	91	4	3	98	
Javier, Stan, San Francisco	.984	71	180	2	3	185	
Jefferies, Gregg, Philadelphia	1.000	51	110	1	0	111	
Jennings, Robin, Chicago*	1.000	11	19	2	0	21	
Johnson, Lance, New York*	.971	157	391	9	12	412	
Johnson, Mark, Pittsburgh*	.667	1	1	1	1	3	
Jones, Andruw, Atlanta	.975	29	73	4	2	79	
Jones, Chipper, Atlanta	1.000	1	2	0	0	2	
Jones, Chris, New York	.957	66	67	0	3	70	
Jones, Dax, San Francisco	1.000	33	46	1	0	47	
Jones, Terry, Colorado	1.000	4	5	0	0	5	
Jordan, Brian, St. Louis	.994	136	309	9	2	320	
Justice, Dave, Atlanta*	1.000	40	88	3	0	91	
Kelly, Mike, Cincinnati	.972	17	34	1	1	36	
Kieschnick, Brooks, Chicago	.833	8	5	0	1	6	
Kingery, Mike, Pittsburgh*	.985	83	133	2	2	137	
Kirby, Wayne, Los Angeles	.969	53	93	2	3	98	
Klesko, Ryan, Atlanta*	.975	144	191	6	5	202	
LANKFORD, Ray, St. Louis*	.997	144	356	9	1	366	
Mabry, John, St. Louis	1.000	14	12	0	0	12	
Magee, Wendell, Philadelphia	.978	37	88	2	2	92	
Martin, Al, Pittsburgh*	.965	152	217	5	8	230	
Martinez, Manny, Philadelphia	.955	11	20	1	1	22	
May, Derrick, Houston	.970	71	125	5	4	134	
McCarty, Dave, San Francisco*	1.000	20	22	2	0	24	
McCracken, Quinton, Colorado	.957	93	131	3	6	140	
McGee, Willie, St. Louis	.962	83	119	6	5	130	
McMillon, Billy, Florida*	1.000	15	17	0	0	17	
McRae, Brian, Chicago	.986	155	345	2	5	352	
Mejia, Miguel, St. Louis	.933	21	14	0	1	15	
Merced, Orlando, Pittsburgh	.988	115	241	14	3	258	
Mitchell, Keith, Cincinnati	.875	5	7	0	1	8	
Mitchell, Kevin, Cincinnati	.978	31	45	0	1	46	
Mondesi, Raul, Los Angeles	.967	157	337	11	12	360	
Montgomery, Ray, Houston	1.000	6	6	0	0	6	
Mottola, Chad, Cincinnati	1.000	31	42	2	0	44	
Mouton, James, Houston	.971	108	158	7	5	170	
Murray, Glenn, Philadelphia	1.000	27	52	1	0	53	
Newfield, Marc, San Diego	.970	51	64	0	2	66	
Obando, Sherman, Montreal	.962	47	74	2	3	79	
Ochoa, Alex, New York	.966	76	135	8	5	148	
Oliver, Joe, Cincinnati	1.000	3	2	0	0	2	
Orsulak, Joe, Florida*	.956	59	80	6	4	90	
Osik, Keith, Pittsburgh	1.000	2	1	0	0	1	
Otero, Ricky, Philadelphia	.985	100	247	8	4	259	
Owens, Eric, Cincinnati	.986	52	65	3	1	69	
Parker, Rick, Los Angeles	1.000	1	1	0	0	1	
Peltier, Dan, San Francisco*	.000	1	0	0	0	0	
Phillips, J.R., Philadelphia*	.957	15	43	1	2	46	
Polonia, Luis, Atlanta*	.800	7	4	0	1	5	
Pulliam, Harvey, Colorado	1.000	3	4	0	0	4	
Roberson, Kevin, New York	1.000	10	12	0	0	12	
Rodriguez, Henry, Montreal*	.947	89	102	5	6	113	
Sanders, Reggie, Cincinnati	.988	80	160	7	2	169	
Santangelo, F.P., Montreal	.983	124	232	4	4	240	
Sheaffer, Danny, St. Louis	1.000	3	3	0	0	3	
Sheffield, Gary, Florida	.976	161	238	8	6	252	
Shipley, Craig, San Diego	1.000	3	4	1	0	5	
Silvestri, Dave, Montreal	.000	2	0	0	0	0	
Simms, Mike, Houston	1.000	12	17	0	0	17	
Smith, Dwight, Atlanta	.962	29	49	1	2	52	
Sosa, Sammy, Chicago	.964	124	253	15	10	278	

ayer, Team	Pct.	G	PO	A	E	TC	DP
ehr, Tim, Montreal	.000	1	0	0	0	0	0
iers, Bill, Houston	1.000	2	3	0	0	3	0
eeney, Mark, St. Louis*	.984	43	59	1	1	61	0
arez, Jesus, Florida	1.000	65	58	0	0	58	0
ompson, Milt, L.A.-Col.	1.000	18	15	0	0	15	0
mmons, Ozzie, Chicago	1.000	47	65	1	0	66	1
sley, Lee, Philadelphia	.960	22	24	0	1	25	0
nberlin, Andy, New York*	1.000	17	8	1	0	9	0
des, Pedro, Chicago*	1.000	2	1	0	0	1	0
nder Wal, John, Colorado*	1.000	26	34	0	0	34	0
ughn, Greg, San Diego	.974	39	74	2	2	78	0
alker, Larry, Colorado	.994	83	153	4	1	158	0
alton, Jerome, Atlanta	1.000	28	34	0	0	34	0
hner, John, Pittsburgh	.971	29	32	1	1	34	0
aite, Devon, Florida	.987	139	296	5	4	305	1
aite, Rondell, Montreal	.990	86	185	5	2	192	1
aiten, Mark, Phi.-Atl.	.942	80	138	7	9	154	1
illiams, Keith, San Francisco	1.000	4	8	0	0	8	0
omack, Tony, Pittsburgh	1.000	6	5	0	0	5	0

OUTFIELDERS WITH TWO OR MORE TEAMS

ayer, Team	Pct.	G	PO	A	E	TC	DP
thony, Eric, Cincinnati*	.949	37	35	2	2	39	0
thony, Eric, Colorado*	1.000	19	20	2	0	22	0
rk, Dave, Pittsburgh	.988	61	80	3	1	84	1
rk, Dave, Los Angeles	.000	1	0	0	0	0	0
bbard, Trent, Colorado	1.000	19	32	0	0	32	0
bbard, Trent, San Francisco	1.000	9	19	1	0	20	0
ompson, Milt, Los Angeles	1.000	17	13	0	0	13	0
ompson, Milt, Colorado	1.000	1	2	0	0	2	0
hiten, Mark, Philadelphia	.945	51	97	6	6	109	1
hiten, Mark, Atlanta	.933	29	41	1	3	45	0

CATCHERS

ayer, Team	Pct.	G	PO	A	E	TC	DP	PB
smus, Brad, San Diego	.982	46	300	22	6	328	0	5
rault, Joe, Atlanta	1.000	7	14	0	0	14	0	0
nnett, Gary, Philadelphia	1.000	5	35	5	0	40	0	2
rders, Pat, St. Louis	.984	17	116	9	2	127	1	0
to, Jorge, Colorado	1.000	8	36	7	0	43	1	1
stillo, Alberto, New York	1.000	6	23	0	0	23	0	0
avez, Raul, Montreal	1.000	3	14	0	0	14	0	0
nfrocco, Archi, San Diego	.000	1	0	0	0	0	0	0
cker, Steve, S.F.-Col.	1.000	40	234	18	0	252	4	5
elice, Mike, St. Louis	1.000	4	15	1	0	16	0	0
rsett, Brian, Chicago	1.000	15	79	5	0	84	1	1
carnacion, Angelo, Pittsburgh	.951	7	35	4	2	41	0	1
talella, Bobby, Philadelphia	1.000	4	24	1	0	25	0	0
sebio, Tony, Houston	.996	47	255	24	1	280	1	1
herty, John, San Diego	.990	72	471	29	5	505	3	4
tcher, Darrin, Montreal	.992	112	721	30	6	757	5	6
rdyce, Brook, Cincinnati	1.000	4	18	0	0	18	0	0
ff, Jerry, Houston	1.000	1	11	0	0	11	1	6
eene, Charlie, New York	1.000	1	1	0	0	1	0	0
rnandez, Carlos, Los Angeles	1.000	9	31	1	0	32	0	0
uston, Tyler, Chicago	.986	27	130	9	2	141	0	2
bbard, Mike, Chicago	1.000	14	53	3	0	56	1	1
ndley, Todd, New York	.992	150	911	72	8	991	7	10
nsen, Marcus, San Francisco	.955	7	37	5	2	44	1	1
hnson, Brian, San Diego	.989	66	450	21	5	476	3	5
HNSON, Charles, Florida	.995	120	751	70	4	825	12	5
ndall, Jason, Pittsburgh	.980	129	797	71	18	886	10	8
orr, Randy, Houston	1.000	33	204	14	0	218	1	0
mpkin, Tom, San Francisco	.992	53	342	27	3	372	4	0
erthal, Mike, Philadelphia	.990	43	284	20	3	307	4	0
pez, Javy, Atlanta	.994	135	993	81	6	1080	9	11
anwaring, Kirt, S.F.-Hou.	.994	86	439	47	3	489	8	3
ayne, Brent, New York	1.000	21	85	3	0	88	2	0
rabelli, Doug, San Francisco	1.000	8	29	2	0	31	0	0
tal, Bob, Florida	.976	43	187	14	5	206	2	6
ver, Joe, Cincinnati	.992	97	572	44	5	621	7	4
ik, Keith, Pittsburgh	.977	41	235	23	6	264	2	1
vens, Jayhawk, Colorado	.974	68	312	27	9	348	3	7
gnozzi, Tom, St. Louis	.990	116	716	48	8	772	6	6
rez, Eddie, Atlanta	.993	54	250	19	2	271	4	0
azza, Mike, Los Angeles	.992	146	1055	70	9	1134	6	12
nce, Tom, Los Angeles	.994	35	161	11	1	173	2	3
ed, Jeff, Colorado	.982	111	546	51	11	608	4	11
ntiago, Benito, Philadelphia	.987	114	723	61	10	794	5	8
rvais, Scott, Chicago	.988	128	797	72	11	880	11	9
eaffer, Danny, St. Louis	.983	47	257	27	5	289	3	1
ddall, Joe, Florida	.977	18	78	8	2	88	1	1
ehr, Tim, Montreal	.985	58	121	7	2	130	0	1

Player, Team	Pct.	G	PO	A	E	TC	DP	PB
Taubensee, Eddie, Cincinnati	.981	94	538	42	11	591	7	3
Webster, Lenny, Montreal	.998	63	390	25	1	416	3	3
Wehner, John, Pittsburgh	1.000	1	1	0	0	1	0	0
Wilkins, Rick, Hou.-S.F.	.990	124	738	68	8	814	7	11
Zaun, Greg, Florida	1.000	10	60	6	0	66	0	0

CATCHERS WITH TWO OR MORE TEAMS

Player, Team	Pct.	G	PO	A	E	TC	DP	PB
Decker, Steve, San Francisco	1.000	30	183	12	0	195	4	5
Decker, Steve, Colorado	1.000	10	51	6	0	57	0	0
Manwaring, Kirt, San Francisco...	.993	49	268	26	2	296	5	3
Manwaring, Kirt, Houston	.995	37	171	21	1	193	3	0
Wilkins, Rick, Houston	.990	82	550	39	6	595	3	7
Wilkins, Rick, San Francisco	.991	42	188	29	2	219	4	4

PITCHERS

Player, Team	Pct.	G	PO	A	E	TC	DP
Adams, Terry, Chicago	1.000	69	9	11	0	20	1
Adamson, Joel, Florida*	1.000	9	3	2	0	5	0
Alston, Garvin, Colorado	1.000	6	0	1	0	1	0
Alvarez, Tavo, Montreal	1.000	11	2	3	0	5	1
Ashby, Andy, San Diego	.951	24	10	29	2	41	3
Astacio, Pedro, Los Angeles	.946	35	22	31	3	56	2
Aucoin, Derek, Montreal	1.000	2	1	1	0	2	0
Avery, Steve, Atlanta*	.944	24	8	26	2	36	0
Bailey, Cory, St. Louis	1.000	51	6	5	0	11	0
Bailey, Roger, Colorado	.974	24	11	26	1	38	2
Barber, Brian, St. Louis	.000	1	0	0	0	0	0
Barton, Shawn, San Francisco*	1.000	7	1	2	0	3	0
Batchelor, Richard, St. Louis	1.000	11	0	1	0	1	0
Batista, Miguel, Florida	1.000	9	0	1	0	1	0
Bautista, Jose, San Francisco	1.000	37	4	13	0	17	0
Beck, Rod, San Francisco	1.000	63	2	6	0	8	1
Beckett, Robbie, Colorado*	.000	5	0	0	0	0	0
Beech, Matt, Philadelphia*	1.000	8	1	4	0	5	1
Benes, Alan, St. Louis	.900	34	8	19	3	30	3
Benes, Andy, St. Louis	.941	36	8	24	2	34	1
Bergman, Sean, San Diego	1.000	41	11	19	0	30	0
Berumen, Andres, San Diego	.000	3	0	0	0	0	0
Bielecki, Mike, Atlanta	1.000	40	3	14	0	17	0
Blair, Willie, San Diego	.857	60	6	6	2	14	0
Blazier, Ron, Philadelphia	1.000	27	2	3	0	5	0
Bochtler, Doug, San Diego	1.000	63	2	2	0	4	0
Boever, Joe, Pittsburgh	1.000	13	2	1	0	3	0
Borbon, Pedro, Atlanta*	.900	43	4	5	1	10	1
Borland, Toby, Philadelphia	1.000	69	4	7	0	11	1
Borowski, Joe, Atlanta	1.000	22	0	12	0	12	1
Bottalico, Ricky, Philadelphia	1.000	61	1	5	0	6	1
Bottenfield, Kent, Chicago	1.000	48	6	12	0	18	2
Bourgeois, Steve, San Francisco	1.000	15	4	8	0	12	0
Brantley, Jeff, Cincinnati	1.000	66	7	4	0	11	0
Brocail, Doug, Houston	1.000	23	6	5	0	11	0
Brown, Kevin, Florida	.988	32	29	54	1	84	4
Bruske, Jim, Los Angeles	1.000	11	0	2	0	2	0
Bullinger, Jim, Chicago	1.000	37	15	20	0	35	0
Burba, Dave, Cincinnati	.935	34	15	14	2	31	2
Burke, John, Colorado	1.000	11	2	1	0	3	0
Burkett, John, Florida	.971	24	12	21	1	34	1
Busby, Mike, St. Louis	.500	1	0	1	1	2	0
Byrd, Paul, New York	1.000	38	4	6	0	10	0
Campbell, Mike, Chicago	1.000	13	2	1	0	3	0
Candiotti, Tom, Los Angeles	.980	27	14	36	1	51	4
Carlson, Dan, San Francisco	1.000	5	1	1	0	2	0
Carrara, Giovanni, Cincinnati	1.000	8	2	3	0	5	0
Carrasco, Hector, Cincinnati	.882	56	3	12	2	17	1
Casian, Larry, Chicago*	.875	35	2	5	1	8	1
Castillo, Frank, Chicago	.932	33	18	23	3	44	2
Christiansen, Jason, Pittsburgh*	1.000	33	0	7	0	7	0
Clark, Mark, New York	1.000	32	10	24	0	34	1
Clark, Terry, Houston	1.000	5	1	3	0	4	1
Clontz, Brad, Atlanta	.947	81	1	17	1	19	1
Cooke, Steve, Pittsburgh*	.000	3	0	0	0	0	0
Cordova, Francisco, Pittsburgh	.917	59	6	16	2	24	1
Cormier, Rheal, Montreal*	.962	33	15	35	2	52	1
Crawford, Carlos, Philadelphia	.000	1	0	0	1	1	0
Creek, Doug, San Francisco*	1.000	63	3	2	0	5	1
Cummings, John, Los Angeles*	1.000	4	1	1	0	2	0
Daal, Omar, Montreal*	.952	64	4	16	1	21	0
Darwin, Danny, Pit.-Hou.	.974	34	12	25	1	38	3
DeLucia, Rich, San Francisco	1.000	56	4	12	0	16	1
Dessens, Elmer, Pittsburgh	1.000	15	1	2	0	3	0
Dewey, Mark, San Francisco	1.000	78	8	17	0	25	2
DiPoto, Jerry, New York	1.000	57	6	11	0	17	1

1996 N.L. STATISTICS Fielding

Player, Team	Pct.	G	PO	A	E	TC	DP
Dishman, Glenn, S.D.-Phi.*	1.000	7	1	0	0	1	0
Dougherty, Jim, Houston	1.000	12	1	3	0	4	0
Drabek, Doug, Houston	.930	30	17	23	3	43	0
Dreifort, Darren, Los Angeles	1.000	19	3	6	0	9	0
Dyer, Mike, Montreal	1.000	70	7	14	0	21	2
Eckersley, Dennis, St. Louis	.900	63	3	6	1	10	0
Eischen, Joey, Los Angeles*	1.000	28	0	4	0	4	1
Ericks, John, Pittsburgh	1.000	28	1	2	0	3	0
Estes, Shawn, San Francisco*	1.000	11	2	11	0	13	0
Farmer, Mike, Colorado*	1.000	7	1	3	0	4	0
Fassero, Jeff, Montreal*	.982	34	12	44	1	57	2
Fernandez, Osvaldo, San Francisco	.955	30	10	32	2	44	0
Fernandez, Sid, Philadelphia*	1.000	11	1	3	0	4	0
Florie, Bryce, San Diego	.929	39	6	7	1	14	0
Fossas, Tony, St. Louis*	1.000	65	2	8	0	10	0
Foster, Kevin, Chicago	.957	17	6	16	1	23	0
Franco, John, New York*	1.000	51	1	8	0	9	0
Freeman, Marvin, Colorado	.935	26	3	26	2	31	2
Frey, Steve, Philadelphia*	1.000	31	1	8	0	9	1
Fyhrie, Mike, New York	1.000	2	0	1	0	1	0
Gardner, Mark, San Francisco	1.000	30	10	14	0	24	1
Glavine, Tom, Atlanta*	.985	36	15	52	1	68	1
Grace, Mike, Philadelphia	1.000	12	6	17	0	23	0
Guthrie, Mark, Los Angeles*	.917	66	1	10	1	12	1
Habyan, John, Colorado	1.000	19	1	2	0	3	0
Hall, Darren, Los Angeles	.000	9	0	0	0	0	0
Hamilton, Joey, San Diego	.978	34	17	27	1	45	2
Hammond, Chris, Florida*	.905	38	6	13	2	21	1
Hampton, Mike, Houston*	.958	27	13	33	2	48	3
Hancock, Lee, Pittsburgh*	.909	13	3	7	1	11	2
Harnisch, Pete, New York	.897	31	10	16	3	29	1
Hartgraves, Dean, Hou.-Atl.*	1.000	39	3	5	0	8	0
Hawblitzel, Ryan, Colorado	1.000	8	2	2	0	4	0
Heflin, Bronson, Philadelphia	.000	3	0	0	0	0	0
Helling, Rick, Florida	1.000	5	0	2	0	2	0
Henry, Doug, New York	.846	58	4	7	2	13	0
Heredia, Felix, Florida*	.000	21	0	0	0	0	0
Hermanson, Dustin, San Diego	.800	8	2	2	1	5	2
Hernandez, Livan, Florida	.000	1	0	0	0	0	0
Hernandez, Xavier, Cin.-Hou.	1.000	61	2	9	0	11	0
Hoffman, Trevor, San Diego	1.000	70	8	6	0	14	0
Holmes, Darren, Colorado	.786	62	1	10	3	14	0
Holt, Chris, Houston	1.000	4	0	2	0	2	0
Honeycutt, Rick, St. Louis*	.933	61	2	12	1	15	0
Hook, Chris, San Francisco	1.000	10	3	3	0	6	0
Hope, John, Pittsburgh	.778	5	2	5	2	9	0
Hudek, John, Houston	1.000	15	1	5	0	6	0
Hunter, Rich, Philadelphia	.947	14	5	13	1	19	0
Hurst, Bill, Florida	.000	2	0	0	0	0	0
Hutton, Mark, Florida	.875	13	3	4	1	8	0
Isringhausen, Jason, New York	.891	27	13	28	5	46	1
Jackson, Danny, St. Louis*	1.000	13	1	7	0	8	0
Jarvis, Kevin, Cincinnati	.893	24	13	12	3	28	2
Johnstone, John, Houston	1.000	9	1	1	0	2	0
Jones, Bobby, New York	.977	31	11	31	1	43	3
Jones, Doug, Chicago	1.000	28	0	3	0	3	1
Jones, Todd, Houston	1.000	51	4	6	0	10	0
Jordan, Ricardo, Philadelphia*	1.000	26	0	3	0	3	0
Juden, Jeff, S.F.-Mon.	.889	58	1	7	1	9	2
Kile, Darryl, Houston	.930	35	12	28	3	43	6
Larkin, Andy, Florida	1.000	1	1	0	0	1	0
Leiper, Dave, Phi.-Mon.*	.857	33	0	6	1	7	0
Leiter, Al, Florida*	.938	33	8	22	2	32	3
Leiter, Mark, S.F.-Mon.	.943	35	8	25	2	35	1
Leskanic, Curt, Colorado	.917	70	4	7	1	12	0
Lieber, Jon, Pittsburgh	1.000	51	17	25	0	42	0
Lilliquist, Derek, Cincinnati*	1.000	5	1	2	0	3	0
Loaiza, Esteban, Pittsburgh	.947	10	6	12	1	19	0
Loiselle, Rich, Pittsburgh	1.000	5	2	5	0	7	0
Lomon, Kevin, Atlanta	1.000	6	2	2	0	4	2
Ludwick, Eric, St. Louis	.667	6	1	1	1	3	0
Lyons, Curt, Cincinnati	1.000	3	0	2	0	2	0
MacDonald, Bob, New York*	1.000	20	1	2	0	3	0
Maddux, Greg, Atlanta	.991	35	37	71	1	109	6
Maduro, Calvin, Philadelphia	1.000	4	0	1	0	1	0
Mantei, Matt, Florida	1.000	14	3	4	0	7	0
Manuel, Barry, Montreal	1.000	53	1	11	0	12	1
Martinez, Pedro, Montreal	.903	33	11	17	3	31	1
Martinez, Pedro A., N.Y.-Cin.*	1.000	9	0	1	0	1	0
Martinez, Ramon, Los Angeles	.946	28	6	29	2	37	1
Mathews, T.J., St. Louis	.750	67	0	6	2	8	0
Mathews, Terry, Florida	.923	57	7	5	1	13	2
May, Darrell, Pittsburgh*	1.000	5	0	2	0	2	0

Player, Team	Pct.	G	PO	A	E	TC
McElroy, Chuck, Cincinnati*	1.000	12	0	1	0	1
McMichael, Greg, Atlanta	.955	73	4	17	1	22
Miceli, Dan, Pittsburgh	.750	44	6	3	3	12
Miller, Kurt, Florida	.909	26	2	8	1	11
Mimbs, Michael, Philadelphia*	.944	21	3	14	1	18
Minor, Blas, New York	1.000	17	1	4	0	5
Mitchell, Larry, Philadelphia	.500	7	1	0	1	2
Milicki, Dave, New York	.818	51	3	6	2	11
Moore, Marcus, Cincinnati	1.000	23	0	1	0	1
Morel, Ramon, Pittsburgh	1.000	29	4	3	0	7
Morgan, Mike, St.L.-Cin.	.952	23	4	16	1	21
Morman, Alvin, Houston*	.909	53	2	8	1	11
Mulholland, Terry, Philadelphia*	.840	21	5	16	4	25
Munoz, Bobby, Philadelphia	1.000	6	0	3	0	3
Munoz, Mike, Colorado*	.941	54	5	11	1	17
Myers, Rodney, Chicago	.929	45	9	4	1	14
Navarro, Jaime, Chicago	.868	35	8	25	5	38
Neagle, Denny, Pit.-Atl.*	.973	33	6	30	1	37
Nen, Robb, Florida	1.000	75	3	9	0	12
Nied, Dave, Colorado	.000	6	0	0	0	0
Nomo, Hideo, Los Angeles	.971	33	12	22	1	35
Olson, Gregg, Houston	1.000	9	3	0	0	3
Oquist, Mike, San Diego	1.000	8	0	1	0	1
Osborne, Donovan, St. Louis*	.967	30	6	23	1	30
Osuna, Al, San Diego*	1.000	10	1	1	0	2
Osuna, Antonio, Los Angeles	1.000	73	3	11	0	14
Pacheco, Alex, Montreal	.000	5	0	0	0	0
Painter, Lance, Colorado*	.750	34	2	7	3	12
Pall, Donn, Florida	1.000	12	1	1	0	2
Paniagua, Jose, Montreal	1.000	13	3	10	0	13
Park, Chan Ho, Los Angeles	.970	48	10	22	1	33
Parrett, Jeff, St.L.-Phi.	1.000	51	3	9	0	12
Parris, Steve, Pittsburgh	.857	8	2	4	1	7
Patterson, Bob, Chicago*	1.000	79	1	3	0	4
Pena, Alejandro, Florida	.000	4	0	0	0	0
Perez, Mike, Chicago	1.000	24	1	3	0	4
Perez, Yorkis, Florida*	.846	64	2	9	2	13
Person, Robert, New York	.714	27	2	8	4	14
Peters, Chris, Pittsburgh*	.917	16	3	8	1	12
Petkovsek, Mark, St. Louis	.913	48	7	14	2	23
Plesac, Dan, Pittsburgh*	1.000	73	0	1	0	1
Poole, Jim, San Francisco*	.900	35	3	6	1	10
Portugal, Mark, Cincinnati	.931	27	11	16	2	29
Powell, Jay, Florida	1.000	67	3	6	0	9
Pugh, Tim, Cincinnati	1.000	10	2	5	0	7
Quirico, Rafael, Philadelphia	1.000	1	1	0	0	1
Radinsky, Scott, Los Angeles*	1.000	58	3	8	0	11
Rapp, Pat, Florida	.946	30	11	24	2	37
Reed, Steve, Colorado	1.000	70	3	8	0	11
Rekar, Bryan, Colorado	.917	14	2	9	1	12
Remlinger, Mike, Cincinnati*	1.000	19	3	5	0	8
Reynolds, Shane, Houston	1.000	35	19	26	0	45
Reynoso, Armando, Colorado	.941	30	12	36	3	51
RITZ, Kevin, Colorado	1.000	35	18	51	0	69
Rojas, Mel, Montreal	.944	74	4	13	1	18
Ruebel, Matt, Pittsburgh*	.941	26	7	9	1	17
Rueter, Kirk, Mon.-S.F.*	1.000	20	8	25	0	33
Ruffin, Bruce, Colorado*	1.000	71	2	9	0	11
Ruffin, Johnny, Cincinnati	.900	49	4	5	1	10
Ryan, Ken, Philadelphia	1.000	62	8	10	0	18
Salkeld, Roger, Cincinnati	.960	29	8	16	1	25
Sanders, Scott, San Diego	.926	46	15	10	2	27
Schilling, Curt, Philadelphia	.947	26	10	8	1	19
Schmidt, Jason, Atl.-Pit.	.933	19	5	9	1	15
Schourek, Pete, Cincinnati*	1.000	12	2	10	0	12
Schutz, Carl, Atlanta*	.000	3	0	0	0	0
Scott, Tim, Mon.-S.F.	1.000	65	5	7	0	12
Service, Scott, Cincinnati	1.000	34	1	9	0	10
Shaw, Jeff, Cincinnati	.963	78	12	14	1	27
Small, Mark, Houston	1.000	16	1	1	0	2
Smiley, John, Cincinnati*	.946	35	6	29	2	37
Smith, Lee, Cincinnati	1.000	43	2	5	0	7
Smith, Zane, Pittsburgh*	.933	16	1	13	1	15
Smoltz, John, Atlanta	.982	35	27	27	1	55
Soderstrom, Steve, San Francisco	1.000	3	0	1	0	1
Spradlin, Jerry, Cincinnati	.000	1	0	0	0	0
Springer, Russ, Philadelphia	.867	51	3	10	2	15
Stottlemyre, Todd, St. Louis	.957	34	8	37	2	47
Sturtze, Tanyon, Chicago	1.000	6	0	2	0	2
Sullivan, Scott, Cincinnati	1.000	7	0	2	0	2
Swartzbaugh, Dave, Chicago	1.000	6	1	6	0	7
Swift, Bill, Colorado	1.000	7	2	4	0	6
Swindell, Greg, Houston*	.833	8	2	3	1	6

yer, Team	Pct.	G	PO	A	E	TC	DP
aka, Jeff, Houston*	1.000	18	1	0	0	1	0
emaco, Amaury, Chicago	.947	25	9	9	1	19	0
WKSBURY, Bob, San Diego	1.000	36	22	47	0	69	3
obe, Tom, Atlanta*	.000	4	0	0	2	2	0
ompson, Mark, Colorado	.875	34	14	21	5	40	2
chsel, Steve, Chicago	.979	31	16	30	1	47	0
cek, Ricky, New York	1.000	5	0	2	0	2	0
ani, Tom, St. Louis*	.000	3	0	0	0	0	0
oina, Ugueth, Montreal	.941	33	6	10	1	17	2
des, Ismael, Los Angeles	.979	33	19	27	1	47	3
des, Marc, Florida	1.000	11	6	3	0	9	0
enzuela, Fernando, San Diego*	.980	33	11	38	1	50	0
nLandingham, William, S.F.	.935	32	14	15	2	31	0
as, Dario, San Diego	1.000	23	0	6	0	6	0
es, Dave, Montreal	.857	68	3	9	2	14	0
one, Ron, San Diego*	.833	21	1	4	1	6	0
de, Terrell, Atlanta*	.917	44	2	9	1	12	1
gner, Billy, Houston*	1.000	37	2	3	0	5	0
gner, Paul, Pittsburgh	1.000	16	10	14	0	24	1
inhouse, David, Pittsburgh	.909	17	3	7	1	11	0
lker, Pete, San Diego	.000	1	0	0	0	0	0
ll, Donne, Houston	.946	26	17	18	2	37	0
llace, Derek, New York	1.000	19	3	2	0	5	0
tson, Allen, San Francisco*	.964	29	6	21	1	28	2
athers, Dave, Florida	1.000	31	5	9	0	14	0
ndell, Turk, Chicago	1.000	70	9	9	0	18	1
st, David, Philadelphia*	1.000	7	0	3	0	3	0
kins, Marc, Pittsburgh	1.000	47	1	10	0	11	3
liams, Mike, Philadelphia	.981	32	19	32	1	52	4
son, Paul, New York	.917	26	10	12	2	24	2
hlers, Mark, Atlanta	.700	77	4	3	3	10	0
odall, Brad, Atlanta*	1.000	8	0	2	0	2	0
rrell, Tim, San Diego	.895	50	8	9	2	19	0
rrell, Todd, Los Angeles	.900	72	3	6	1	10	0

Player, Team	Pct.	G	PO	A	E	TC	DP
Wright, Jamey, Colorado	.935	16	9	20	2	31	1
Young, Anthony, Houston	1.000	28	1	5	0	6	1

PITCHERS WITH TWO OR MORE TEAMS

Player, Team	Pct.	G	PO	A	E	TC	DP
Darwin, Danny, Pittsburgh	1.000	19	11	21	0	32	3
Darwin, Danny, Houston	.833	15	1	4	1	6	0
Dishman, Glenn, San Diego*	.000	3	0	0	0	0	0
Dishman, Glenn, Philadelphia*	1.000	4	1	0	0	1	0
Hartgraves, Dean, Houston*	1.000	19	2	2	0	4	0
Hartgraves, Dean, Atlanta*	1.000	20	1	3	0	4	0
Hernandez, Xavier, Cincinnati	.000	3	0	0	0	0	0
Hernandez, Xavier, Houston	1.000	58	2	9	0	11	0
Juden, Jeff, San Francisco	1.000	36	1	4	0	5	1
Juden, Jeff, Montreal	.750	22	0	3	1	4	1
Leiper, Dave, Philadelphia*	.833	26	0	5	1	6	0
Leiper, Dave, Montreal*	1.000	7	0	1	0	1	0
Leiter, Mark, San Francisco	.882	23	3	12	2	17	0
Leiter, Mark, Montreal	1.000	12	5	13	0	18	1
Martinez, Pedro A., New York*	1.000	5	0	1	0	1	0
Martinez, Pedro A., Cincinnati*	.000	4	0	0	0	0	0
Morgan, Mike, St. Louis	.941	18	4	12	1	17	0
Morgan, Mike, Cincinnati	1.000	5	0	4	0	4	0
Neagle, Denny, Pittsburgh*	.970	27	6	26	1	33	2
Neagle, Denny, Atlanta*	1.000	6	0	4	0	4	1
Parrett, Jeff, St. Louis	1.000	33	1	8	0	9	1
Parrett, Jeff, Philadelphia	1.000	18	2	1	0	3	0
Rueter, Kirk, Montreal*	1.000	16	7	23	0	30	2
Rueter, Kirk, San Francisco*	1.000	4	1	2	0	3	0
Schmidt, Jason, Atlanta	.875	13	2	5	1	8	0
Schmidt, Jason, Pittsburgh	1.000	6	3	4	0	7	0
Scott, Tim, Montreal	1.000	45	3	2	0	5	0
Scott, Tim, San Francisco	1.000	20	2	5	0	7	1

MISCELLANEOUS

SHUTOUT GAMES

Read across for wins, down for losses.

Team	Chi.	St.L.	N.Y.	Cin.	Pit.	Atl.	S.D.	Col.	Fla.	Mon.	L.A.	Phi.	S.F.	Hou.	W	L
Chicago	..	2	2	1	0	1	0	0	0	0	2	0	1	1	10	4
St. Louis	0	..	0	1	0	2	0	2	0	1	2	1		2	11	7
New York	1	0	..	0	1	0	1	0	2	2	0	0	2	1	10	7
Cincinnati	1	1	0	..	1	0	1	0	0	1	1	1	0	1	8	6
Pittsburgh	0	0	1	0	..	1	2	0	1	0	1	0	1	0	7	6
Atlanta	1	1	0	0	0	..	1	0	1	1	0	2	2	0	9	8
San Diego	0	1	1	2	0	0	..	1	2	2	1	0	0	1	11	11
Colorado	0	0	0	0	1	0	0	..	1	0	1	0	0	1	4	4
Florida	0	0	0	0	1	2	0	2	..	2	2	1	2	1	13	14
Montreal	0	1	1	0	0	0	0	0	1	..	0	1	2	1	7	8
Los Angeles	1	0	1	0	0	1	2	1	2	0	..	0	0	1	9	12
Philadelphia	0	0	0	1	1	1	0	0	1	0	1	..	1	0	6	8
San Francisco	0	1	1	1	0	1	0	0	1	0	2	1	..	0	8	12
Houston	0	0	0	0	1	1	2	0	0	0	0	0	0	..	4	10
Lost	4	7	7	6	6	8	11	4	14	8	12	8	12	10	117	117

HOME RECORD

Read across for home wins, down for road losses.

Team	Atl.	Col.	Fla.	Mon.	Hou.	St.L.	L.A.	Cin.	S.D.	Chi.	N.Y.	S.F.	Pit.	Phi.	W	L
Atlanta	..	4	5	6	4	3	2	5	5	4	4	5	5	4	56	25
Colorado	5	..	5	2	5	6	4	3	5	2	5	4	5	4	55	26
Florida	5	7	..	3	6	3	4	5	1	3	5	4	2	4	52	29
Montreal	2	5	5	..	5	5	1	5	3	4	3	5	5	2	50	31
Houston	4	4	5	2	..	2	4	3	2	5	4	4	4	5	48	33
St. Louis	0	4	3	3	6	..	2	4	4	5	4	3	5	5	48	33
Los Angeles	3	4	5	4	4	4	..	5	1	2	4	4	3	4	47	34
Cincinnati	4	3	2	2	4	3	3	..	5	5	4	4	3	4	46	35
San Diego	3	3	4	5	2	2	3	2	..	4	5	5	3	4	45	36
Chicago	3	1	3	4	4	3	4	4	4	..	4	4	2	3	43	38
New York	4	4	4	3	2	3	2	4	1	3	..	4	4	4	42	39
San Francisco	4	6	5	3	2	3	3	1	1	3	4	..	0	3	38	44
Pittsburgh	2	4	3	4	2	1	3	5	1	5	2	1	..	3	36	44
Philadelphia	2	4	4	2	1	3	3	0	2	3	4	3	4	..	35	46
Lost on road	41	53	53	43	47	41	38	46	35	48	52	50	45	49	641	493

ROAD RECORD

Read across for road wins, down for home losses.

Team	S.D.	L.A.	Atl.	St.L.	Mon.	Pit.	Cin.	Hou.	Chi.	Phi.	S.F.	N.Y.	Col.	Fla.	W	L
San Diego	..	5	1	2	3	6	1	4	2	4	6	5	2	5	46	35
Los Angeles	4	..	4	4	5	3	3	2	3	3	3	4	3	2	43	38
Atlanta	4	3	..	6	4	4	2	2	3	5	2	3	1	1	40	41
St. Louis	4	2	4	..	1	5	4	5	3	3	3	3	0	3	40	41
Montreal	1	2	1	3	..	2	4	4	2	4	4	4	4	3	38	43
Pittsburgh	3	3	1	2	1	..	3	3	4	2	7	3	1	4	37	45
Cincinnati	4	1	1	2	1	2	..	3	3	6	5	2	4	1	35	46
Houston	4	2	2	0	2	4	3	..	3	5	4	1	0	3	34	47
Chicago	2	4	2	2	2	2	1	1	..	4	3	3	4	3	33	48
Philadelphia	2	3	2	1	5	3	2	1	3	..	3	2	2	3	32	49
San Francisco	1	3	1	4	1	4	3	2	2	3	..	2	2	2	30	50
New York	2	2	2	2	3	4	2	2	2	3	2	..	1	2	29	52
Colorado	3	2	2	2	1	2	3	3	5	2	1	2	..	0	28	53
Florida	2	2	2	3	2	3	4	1	3	2	1	2	1	..	28	53
Lost at home	36	34	25	33	31	44	35	33	38	46	44	39	26	29	493	641

PITCHING AGAINST EACH CLUB

ATLANTA—96-66

Pitcher	Chi. W-L	Cin. W-L	Col. W-L	Fla. W-L	Hou. W-L	L.A. W-L	Mon. W-L	N.Y. W-L	Phi. W-L	Pit. W-L	St.L. W-L	S.D. W-L	S.F. W-L	Tota W
Avery	1-0	1-0	1-0	1-2	0-1	0-2	1-1	0-1	1-0	0-2	1-1	0-0	0-0	7-
Bielecki	0-0	0-1	0-1	0-0	1-0	0-0	0-0	0-0	1-0	1-0	0-1	1-0	0-0	3
Borbon	0-0	1-0	0-0	0-0	0-0	1-0	0-0	1-0	0-0	0-0	0-0	0-0	0-0	3
Borowski	1-1	0-0	0-0	0-0	0-0	0-0	0-0	0-2	0-0	1-0	0-0	0-0	0-0	
Clontz	1-0	1-0	1-1	1-0	0-0	0-1	0-0	1-0	0-0	0-0	1-0	0-0	0-0	6
Glavine	2-1	2-1	1-1	1-3	0-0	0-2	2-0	1-0	0-1	1-0	1-0	1-1	3-0	15-
Hartgraves	0-0	0-0	0-0	0-0	0-0	0-0	0-0	0-0	1-0	0-0	0-0	0-0	0-0	1
Maddux	1-0	1-1	0-0	1-0	2-1	1-0	2-1	0-2	1-3	1-0	2-0	1-2	2-1	15-
McMichael	0-0	0-1	0-1	0-0	0-1	0-0	0-0	1-0	1-0	0-0	1-0	1-0	0-0	
Neagle	0-1	0-0	0-1	0-1	0-0	0-0	1-0	1-0	0-0	0-0	0-0	0-0	0-0	

er	Chi. W-L	Cin. W-L	Col. W-L	Fla. W-L	Hou. W-L	L.A. W-L	Mon. W-L	N.Y. W-L	Phi. W-L	Pit. W-L	St.L. W-L	S.D. W-L	S.F. W-L	Totals W-L
idt	0-0	0-0	0-0	0-0	0-1	0-1	0-0	0-1	0-0	0-0	2-0	1-0	0-1	3-4
z	1-0	1-0	2-1	1-1	3-1	2-1	2-0	1-0	3-0	3-1	1-1	3-0	1-2	24-8
e	0-0	0-0	0-0	0-0	0-0	0-0	0-0	0-0	0-0	0-0	0-0	0-1	0-0	0-1
	0-0	0-0	0-0	0-0	0-0	0-0	0-0	0-0	1-0	2-0	1-0	0-0	1-0	5-0
ers	0-2	0-0	0-1	0-0	0-0	0-0	1-1	1-0	0-0	0-0	0-0	0-0	0-0	2-4
all	0-0	0-0	0-0	0-0	0-1	1-0	1-0	0-0	0-0	0-0	0-0	0-0	0-1	2-2
als	7-5	7-5	5-7	6-7	6-6	5-7	10-3	7-6	9-4	9-3	9-4	9-4	7-5	96-66

DECISIONS—Lomon, Schutz.

CHICAGO—76-86

er	Atl. W-L	Cin. W-L	Col. W-L	Fla. W-L	Hou. W-L	L.A. W-L	Mon. W-L	N.Y. W-L	Phi. W-L	Pit. W-L	St.L. W-L	S.D. W-L	S.F. W-L	Totals W-L
s	0-0	0-0	1-0	0-0	0-1	0-1	0-2	0-1	1-0	1-0	0-1	0-0	0-0	3-6
nfield	0-1	0-0	1-0	0-0	0-1	0-0	1-1	0-0	0-1	0-0	1-0	0-0	0-1	3-5
ger	0-1	0-2	1-1	1-0	0-0	1-0	1-1	1-1	1-1	0-0	0-1	0-1	0-1	6-10
bell	1-0	0-0	0-0	0-0	0-0	1-0	0-0	0-0	1-0	0-0	0-1	0-0	0-0	3-1
n	0-1	0-0	0-0	0-0	0-0	0-0	1-0	0-0	0-0	0-0	0-0	0-0	0-0	1-1
o	1-1	0-1	0-2	1-0	0-3	1-0	0-1	0-2	0-2	1-2	0-1	1-1	2-0	7-16
r	2-0	0-1	0-0	1-1	0-0	1-1	1-0	0-0	0-1	0-1	0-0	0-1	2-0	7-6
s	0-0	0-0	0-1	0-0	0-0	1-0	0-0	0-1	0-0	0-0	0-0	1-0	0-0	2-2
	0-0	0-0	0-0	0-0	0-0	0-0	0-0	0-0	0-0	0-0	0-0	1-0	1-1	2-1
ro	0-0	0-1	2-1	2-0	2-2	2-1	0-1	3-0	2-1	0-3	1-0	1-1	0-1	15-12
son	0-0	1-1	0-0	0-1	0-0	0-0	0-0	0-0	1-0	0-0	0-1	1-0	0-0	3-3
	0-0	0-0	0-0	0-0	0-0	0-0	0-0	0-0	0-0	0-0	0-0	0-0	1-0	1-0
e	0-0	1-0	0-0	0-0	0-0	0-0	0-0	0-0	0-0	0-0	0-0	0-0	0-0	1-0
zbaugh	0-0	0-1	0-0	0-0	0-0	0-0	0-0	0-0	0-0	0-1	0-0	0-0	0-0	0-2
aco	1-1	0-0	0-2	0-2	1-0	0-1	1-0	1-0	0-0	1-0	0-0	0-1	0-0	5-7
sel	0-2	2-1	0-0	0-2	2-0	1-1	1-0	1-0	1-0	0-0	2-2	1-0	1-1	13-9
ell	0-0	1-0	0-0	1-1	0-0	0-0	0-0	1-0	0-0	0-2	1-1	0-1	0-0	4-5
als	5-7	5-8	5-7	6-6	5-8	8-5	6-6	7-5	7-6	4-9	5-8	6-6	7-5	76-86

CINCINNATI—81-81

er	Atl. W-L	Chi. W-L	Col. W-L	Fla. W-L	Hou. W-L	L.A. W-L	Mon. W-L	N.Y. W-L	Phi. W-L	Pit. W-L	St.L. W-L	S.D. W-L	S.F. W-L	Totals W-L
ey	0-1	0-0	0-0	0-0	1-1	0-0	0-0	0-0	0-0	0-0	0-0	0-0	0-0	1-2
	1-1	2-1	1-0	0-3	0-0	0-1	0-3	1-0	2-1	2-1	1-0	1-1	0-1	11-13
a	0-0	0-0	0-0	1-0	0-0	0-0	0-0	0-0	0-0	0-0	0-0	0-0	0-0	1-0
sco	1-0	0-1	1-0	0-0	0-0	0-2	0-0	0-0	0-0	0-0	1-0	0-0	1-0	4-3
	0-0	1-0	1-1	1-1	0-0	0-1	0-1	0-1	2-0	1-1	0-0	2-1	2-0	8-9
	0-0	1-0	0-0	0-0	0-0	0-0	0-0	0-0	0-0	0-0	1-0	0-0	0-0	2-0
oy	0-0	0-0	0-0	0-0	0-0	0-0	0-0	0-0	0-0	0-0	0-0	1-0	1-0	2-0
e	0-0	1-0	0-1	0-0	0-1	1-0	0-1	0-0	0-0	0-0	0-0	0-0	1-0	3-3
an	0-0	0-0	0-0	0-0	0-0	0-0	0-0	0-0	0-0	0-1	0-2	1-0	1-0	2-3
gal	1-0	2-1	0-1	0-0	1-2	1-0	0-2	0-1	2-1	1-0	0-1	0-0	0-0	8-9
	0-0	0-0	0-0	0-0	0-0	0-0	0-0	1-0	0-0	0-1	0-0	0-0	0-0	1-1
nger	0-0	0-0	0-0	0-1	0-0	0-0	0-0	0-0	0-0	0-0	0-0	0-0	0-0	0-1
	0-1	0-2	1-0	0-0	0-0	0-0	0-0	0-0	0-0	0-0	0-0	0-0	0-0	1-3
d	1-0	0-0	0-1	0-1	0-0	0-1	1-0	0-1	2-0	1-0	0-1	0-0	3-0	8-5
rek	0-2	0-0	0-1	0-0	1-1	1-0	1-0	1-1	0-0	0-0	0-0	0-0	0-0	4-5
e	0-0	0-0	0-0	0-0	0-0	0-0	0-0	1-0	0-0	0-0	0-0	0-0	0-0	1-0
	1-0	0-0	1-1	0-0	2-1	0-0	1-1	0-1	1-0	0-0	1-2	2-0	1-0	8-6
	0-2	1-0	2-0	1-2	2-0	1-2	0-1	2-1	0-0	0-4	1-1	2-0	1-1	13-14
	0-0	0-0	0-0	0-1	0-0	0-1	0-0	0-0	1-0	0-0	0-1	2-1	0-0	3-4
als	5-7	8-5	7-6	3-9	7-6	4-8	3-9	6-6	10-2	5-8	5-8	9-3	9-4	81-81

DECISIONS—Hernandez, Lilliquist, Martinez, Spradlin, Sullivan.

COLORADO—83-79

er	Atl. W-L	Chi. W-L	Cin. W-L	Fla. W-L	Hou. W-L	L.A. W-L	Mon. W-L	N.Y. W-L	Phi. W-L	Pit. W-L	St.L. W-L	S.D. W-L	S.F. W-L	Totals W-L
	0-0	0-0	0-0	0-0	1-0	0-0	0-0	0-0	0-0	0-0	0-0	0-0	0-0	1-0
	0-0	0-0	0-0	0-0	0-0	0-1	0-1	0-0	0-0	0-0	1-1	0-0	1-0	2-3
	1-0	0-0	0-0	0-0	0-0	1-0	0-0	0-0	0-0	0-0	0-0	0-0	0-1	2-1
er	0-0	0-0	0-0	0-0	0-0	0-0	0-0	0-0	0-0	0-1	0-0	0-0	0-0	0-1
an	0-1	1-1	0-0	1-2	1-0	1-1	0-1	1-0	1-1	0-0	0-0	0-2	1-0	7-9
an	0-0	0-0	0-0	0-0	0-0	0-0	0-0	0-0	0-1	0-0	1-0	0-0	0-0	1-1
itzel	0-0	0-0	0-0	0-0	0-0	0-0	0-0	0-0	0-1	0-0	0-0	0-0	0-0	0-1
es	2-0	0-0	0-0	0-0	1-1	0-0	0-1	0-1	0-0	1-1	0-0	1-0	0-0	5-4
nic	0-1	1-0	1-0	0-2	0-1	0-0	0-0	2-0	0-0	0-0	1-1	1-0	1-0	7-5
z	0-0	0-0	0-1	0-0	0-0	0-0	0-1	0-0	0-0	1-0	1-0	0-0	0-0	2-2
	0-0	0-0	0-0	0-0	0-0	0-0	0-0	0-0	0-0	0-0	0-0	0-0	0-2	0-2
er	1-0	0-0	0-0	0-0	0-0	0-0	1-1	0-0	1-0	0-0	1-0	0-0	0-1	4-2
ed	1-0	0-0	1-1	0-0	1-0	0-0	0-0	1-1	0-1	0-0	0-0	0-0	0-0	4-3
	0-0	1-0	0-0	0-0	0-0	0-1	0-1	0-0	1-1	0-0	0-1	0-0	0-0	2-4
oso	0-1	1-0	1-1	1-0	0-2	0-0	0-2	1-0	1-0	1-1	0-0	1-2	0-0	8-9
field	0-0	1-2	0-1	2-2	3-0	2-1	0-0	1-1	2-0	3-1	1-0	1-1	1-2	17-11
	0-0	0-1	1-1	0-1	0-0	1-1	1-0	1-0	0-1	0-0	0-0	3-0	0-0	7-5
	0-0	0-0	1-0	0-0	0-0	0-1	0-0	0-0	0-0	0-0	0-0	0-0	0-0	1-1
ompson	0-2	1-1	1-2	1-1	1-1	1-0	1-0	0-1	0-1	1-1	1-0	1-0	0-1	9-11
t	2-0	1-0	0-0	0-0	0-1	0-1	0-1	0-0	0-0	0-0	0-1	0-0	1-1	4-4
als	7-5	7-5	6-7	5-8	8-5	6-7	3-9	7-5	6-6	7-5	8-4	8-5	5-8	83-79

DECISIONS—Beckett.

FLORIDA—80-82

Pitcher	Atl. W-L	Chi. W-L	Cin. W-L	Col. W-L	Hou. W-L	L.A. W-L	Mon. W-L	N.Y. W-L	Phi. W-L	Pit. W-L	St.L. W-L	S.D. W-L	S.F. W-L	T
Brown	1-2	3-0	3-0	1-0	1-1	2-1	0-1	0-2	1-2	2-1	0-0	1-1	2-0	
Burkett	1-2	1-0	0-0	0-2	0-0	1-0	1-0	0-1	0-1	0-0	1-1	0-1	1-2	
Hammond	1-0	0-0	0-0	0-1	0-1	1-2	0-0	1-0	1-0	0-0	1-0	0-3	0-1	
Helling	0-0	0-0	0-0	0-0	1-0	0-0	1-1	0-0	0-0	0-0	0-0	0-0	0-0	
Heredia	0-0	0-0	0-0	0-0	1-1	0-0	0-0	0-0	0-0	0-0	0-0	0-0	0-0	
Hutton	0-0	0-1	1-0	1-0	1-0	0-0	1-0	0-0	0-0	0-0	1-0	0-0	0-0	
Leiter	2-1	0-2	2-1	2-1	1-1	1-2	1-1	2-0	0-1	2-0	1-1	2-0	0-1	
Mantei	0-0	1-0	0-0	0-0	0-0	0-0	0-0	0-0	0-0	0-0	0-0	0-0	0-0	
Mathews	0-0	0-1	0-0	0-0	0-1	0-0	0-0	0-0	1-0	0-0	1-0	0-1	0-1	
Miller	0-0	0-0	0-1	1-0	0-0	0-0	0-0	0-0	0-2	0-0	0-0	0-0	0-0	
Nen	0-0	0-0	1-0	1-0	0-0	0-0	1-0	1-0	0-0	0-1	0-0	0-0	1-0	
Pall	0-0	0-0	0-0	0-0	1-0	0-0	0-0	0-0	0-0	0-0	0-0	0-1	0-0	
Pena	0-0	0-0	0-0	0-0	0-0	0-0	0-0	0-0	0-0	0-1	0-0	0-0	0-0	
Perez	0-1	0-0	0-0	0-1	1-0	0-0	0-0	1-0	0-0	1-1	0-0	0-1	0-0	
Powell	0-0	0-0	0-0	1-0	0-0	1-0	0-2	1-0	0-0	0-0	1-0	0-0	1-0	
Rapp	2-0	0-2	1-0	1-0	0-0	0-1	0-2	1-1	3-1	0-3	0-3	0-1	0-2	
Valdes	0-0	1-0	0-1	0-0	0-0	0-0	0-1	0-1	0-1	0-0	0-0	0-0	0-0	
Weathers	0-0	0-0	1-0	0-0	0-0	0-1	0-0	0-1	0-0	0-0	1-0	0-0	0-0	
Totals	7-6	6-6	9-3	8-5	7-5	6-7	5-8	7-6	6-7	5-7	6-6	3-9	5-7	8

NO DECISIONS—Adamson, Batista, Hernandez, Hurst, Larkin.

HOUSTON—82-80

Pitcher	Atl. W-L	Chi. W-L	Cin. W-L	Col. W-L	Fla. W-L	L.A. W-L	Mon. W-L	N.Y. W-L	Phi. W-L	Pit. W-L	St.L. W-L	S.D. W-L	S.F. W-L	T
Brocail	0-0	0-1	1-0	0-0	0-0	0-1	0-1	0-0	0-0	0-0	0-1	0-1	0-0	
Clark	0-0	0-0	0-1	0-0	0-0	0-1	0-0	0-0	0-0	0-0	0-0	0-0	0-0	
Darwin	0-0	0-0	0-0	0-0	1-0	2-0	0-1	0-0	0-0	0-1	0-0	0-0	0-0	
Dougherty	0-0	0-0	0-0	0-0	0-0	0-0	0-2	0-0	0-0	0-0	0-0	0-0	0-0	
Drabek	0-0	1-1	0-1	0-2	1-0	1-1	1-1	1-2	1-0	0-0	0-1	0-0	1-0	
Hampton	1-2	1-0	1-2	1-0	1-0	1-0	0-1	0-1	1-0	0-1	0-1	0-2	3-0	1
Hernandez	1-0	0-0	0-1	1-1	0-0	0-1	0-1	1-0	0-0	1-0	0-1	1-0	0-0	
Holt	0-0	0-0	0-0	0-0	0-0	0-0	0-0	0-0	0-1	0-0	0-0	0-0	0-0	
Hudek	0-0	0-0	0-0	0-0	1-0	0-0	0-0	1-0	0-0	0-0	0-0	0-0	0-0	
Johnstone	0-0	0-0	0-0	0-0	1-0	0-0	0-0	0-0	0-0	0-0	0-0	0-0	0-0	
Jones	0-2	1-0	2-0	0-0	0-1	1-0	0-0	0-0	0-0	1-0	0-0	1-0	0-0	
Kile	2-1	1-1	0-0	1-0	0-2	0-0	1-1	2-0	2-0	1-0	0-3	1-1	1-2	
Morman	0-0	1-0	0-0	0-0	0-0	0-0	0-0	0-0	1-0	2-0	0-0	0-1	0-0	
Olson	0-0	1-0	0-0	0-0	0-0	0-0	0-0	0-0	0-0	0-0	0-0	0-0	0-0	
Reynolds	1-0	1-2	1-0	0-2	0-2	0-2	2-0	3-0	2-0	1-0	1-2	2-0	2-0	
Small	0-0	0-0	0-0	0-0	0-0	0-0	0-0	0-0	0-0	0-0	0-0	0-1	0-0	
Swindell	0-0	0-0	0-0	0-0	0-0	0-0	0-0	0-0	0-0	0-1	0-1	0-1	0-0	
Tabaka	0-0	0-0	0-0	0-0	0-0	0-0	0-0	0-0	0-1	0-0	0-0	0-0	0-1	
Wagner	1-0	0-0	0-0	0-0	0-1	0-0	0-0	0-0	1-0	0-1	0-0	0-0	0-0	
Wall	0-1	1-0	0-1	2-2	0-1	1-0	0-1	0-1	0-0	2-0	1-1	1-0	1-0	
Young	0-0	0-0	1-1	0-1	0-0	0-0	0-0	0-0	2-0	0-1	0-0	0-0	0-0	
Totals	6-6	8-5	6-7	5-8	5-7	6-6	4-9	8-4	10-2	8-5	2-11	6-6	8-4	8

NO DECISIONS—Hartgraves.

LOS ANGELES—90-72

Pitcher	Atl. W-L	Chi. W-L	Cin. W-L	Col. W-L	Fla. W-L	Hou. W-L	Mon. W-L	N.Y. W-L	Phi. W-L	Pit. W-L	St.L. W-L	S.D. W-L	S.F. W-L	T
Astacio	0-2	1-1	0-0	0-4	2-0	0-0	1-0	1-0	2-0	1-1	0-0	1-0	0-0	
Candiotti	2-1	0-2	1-0	0-0	0-0	0-1	2-1	1-2	0-0	1-1	1-0	1-1	0-2	
Cummings	0-0	0-0	0-0	0-0	0-0	0-1	0-0	0-0	0-0	0-0	0-0	0-0	0-0	
Dreifort	0-0	0-0	0-0	0-0	0-1	0-0	0-0	0-1	1-0	0-0	0-0	0-1	0-0	
Eischen	0-0	0-0	0-0	0-0	0-0	0-0	0-1	0-0	0-0	0-0	0-0	0-0	0-0	
Guthrie	0-1	0-0	0-0	0-0	0-0	0-1	0-0	0-0	1-0	0-0	0-1	1-0	0-0	
Hall	0-0	0-0	0-0	0-0	0-2	0-0	0-0	0-0	0-0	0-0	0-0	0-0	0-0	
Martinez	0-1	1-0	2-0	0-1	1-0	2-0	3-0	2-0	0-0	0-1	1-1	1-2	2-0	
Nomo	2-0	0-1	2-0	3-0	1-2	1-2	1-0	0-1	1-1	2-1	2-1	0-1	1-1	1
Osuna	1-0	0-2	1-0	1-0	1-0	1-0	1-0	0-0	0-1	1-0	0-0	0-2	2-1	
Park	0-0	2-1	0-1	0-0	1-0	0-0	0-1	0-0	0-0	1-0	1-0	0-1	0-1	
Radinsky	1-0	0-0	0-0	0-0	0-0	0-0	0-0	2-0	0-1	0-0	1-0	0-0	1-0	
Valdes	1-0	1-1	1-2	3-0	1-1	1-0	0-0	2-0	2-1	0-1	1-1	1-0	1-0	
Worrell	0-0	0-0	1-1	0-0	0-0	1-0	1-1	0-0	0-2	0-0	1-0	0-0	0-1	
Totals	7-5	5-8	8-4	7-6	7-6	6-6	9-3	8-4	7-6	6-6	8-4	5-8	7-6	9

NO DECISIONS—Bruske.

MONTREAL—88-74

Pitcher	Atl. W-L	Chi. W-L	Cin. W-L	Col. W-L	Fla. W-L	Hou. W-L	L.A. W-L	N.Y. W-L	Phi. W-L	Pit. W-L	St.L. W-L	S.D. W-L	S.F. W-L	T
Alvarez	1-0	0-0	0-0	1-0	0-0	0-0	0-0	0-1	0-0	0-0	0-0	0-0	0-0	
Aucoin	0-0	0-0	0-0	0-0	0-0	0-0	0-0	0-0	0-0	0-0	0-0	0-0	0-1	
Cormier	1-0	1-1	1-1	1-0	1-0	0-2	0-1	1-0	0-2	0-1	1-0	0-1	0-1	
Daal	0-1	0-1	0-0	0-1	0-1	0-0	0-1	0-0	1-0	0-0	0-1	1-0	2-0	
Dyer	0-0	0-1	1-1	2-0	0-1	1-0	0-0	1-0	0-0	0-1	0-0	0-0	0-1	
Fassero	0-2	1-0	0-1	2-0	1-1	3-0	0-2	2-2	1-1	0-1	2-0	1-1	2-0	1
Juden	0-0	0-0	0-0	0-0	0-0	0-0	0-0	0-0	1-0	0-0	0-0	0-0	0-0	
Leiper	0-1	0-0	0-0	0-0	0-0	0-0	0-0	0-0	0-0	0-0	0-0	0-0	0-0	

tcher	Atl. W-L	Chi. W-L	Cin. W-L	Col. W-L	Fla. W-L	Hou. W-L	L.A. W-L	N.Y. W-L	Phi. W-L	Pit. W-L	St.L. W-L	S.D. W-L	S.F. W-L	Totals W-L
eiter	0-2	0-0	0-0	0-0	1-0	2-0	1-0	0-0	0-0	0-0	0-0	0-0	0-0	4-2
anuel	0-1	0-0	0-0	0-0	1-0	0-0	1-0	0-0	0-0	1-0	0-0	0-0	1-0	4-1
artinez	0-0	1-1	3-0	0-0	1-1	1-1	0-1	2-0	0-1	2-2	0-1	0-1	3-1	13-10
aniagua	0-0	0-1	1-0	0-0	0-0	0-0	0-0	0-0	0-1	0-0	0-1	1-0	1-0	2-4
ojas	0-0	1-0	0-0	0-0	0-0	0-0	1-1	0-0	2-1	1-1	2-0	0-1	0-0	7-4
eter	0-1	0-1	1-0	1-1	0-1	0-1	0-0	0-1	0-0	2-0	1-0	0-0	0-0	5-6
cott	0-2	0-0	0-0	0-1	1-0	0-0	0-0	0-1	1-0	0-0	1-0	0-1	0-0	3-5
bina	1-0	1-0	1-0	2-0	0-0	1-0	0-1	1-1	0-1	0-0	1-1	2-1	0-0	10-5
res	0-0	1-0	1-0	0-0	2-0	1-0	0-2	0-0	0-0	1-0	0-0	0-1	0-0	6-3
Totals	3-10	6-6	9-3	9-3	8-5	9-4	3-9	7-6	6-7	7-5	8-4	4-8	9-4	88-74

NO DECISIONS—Pacheco.

NEW YORK—71-91

tcher	Atl. W-L	Chi. W-L	Cin. W-L	Col. W-L	Fla. W-L	Hou. W-L	L.A. W-L	Mon. W-L	Phi. W-L	Pit. W-L	St.L. W-L	S.D. W-L	S.F. W-L	Totals W-L
rd	0-1	0-0	0-0	0-1	0-0	0-0	0-0	0-0	1-0	0-0	0-0	0-0	0-0	1-2
ark	2-0	0-2	1-1	0-1	2-1	2-0	1-3	0-2	2-0	0-1	1-0	1-0	2-0	14-11
Poto	1-0	1-1	1-0	0-0	0-0	0-0	0-0	1-0	1-1	1-0	1-0	0-0	0-0	7-2
Franco	0-0	0-0	0-0	1-1	0-0	0-1	0-0	0-0	1-0	1-0	0-1	1-0		4-3
hrie	0-0	0-0	0-0	0-0	0-0	0-0	0-0	0-0	0-1	0-0	0-0	0-0	0-0	0-1
rnisch	0-1	0-1	0-0	1-1	1-1	1-0	1-1	1-2	0-2	1-0	1-1	1-0	0-2	8-12
enry	0-1	1-0	1-0	0-2	0-3	0-0	0-1	0-0	0-0	0-1	0-0	0-0		2-8
ringhausen	0-0	0-1	1-0	1-0	2-1	0-2	0-0	1-2	0-0	1-2	0-2	0-2	0-2	6-14
Jones	1-1	3-0	1-2	1-0	0-0	1-1	1-1	1-0	0-1	1-0	0-2	1-0	1-0	12-8
acDonald	0-1	0-0	0-1	0-0	0-0	0-0	0-0	0-0	0-0	0-0	0-0	0-0	0-0	0-2
icki	0-1	0-0	0-0	1-1	1-0	0-1	0-0	0-1	1-0	3-2	0-0	0-1	0-0	6-7
rson	0-0	0-0	0-1	0-0	0-0	0-1	0-0	1-0	1-0	0-0	1-1	0-1	1-1	4-5
icek	0-0	0-0	0-0	0-0	0-0	0-1	0-0	0-0	0-0	0-0	0-0	0-0	0-0	0-1
allace	1-0	0-0	0-0	0-0	0-0	0-0	1-0	0-0	0-1	0-0	0-0	0-0	0-0	2-3
ilson	1-1	0-2	1-1	0-0	0-1	0-1	0-1	1-0	1-0	0-0	0-0	0-4	1-1	5-12
Totals	6-7	5-7	6-6	5-7	6-7	4-8	4-8	6-7	7-6	8-5	5-7	3-10	6-6	71-91

NO DECISIONS—Martinez, Minor.

PHILADELPHIA—67-95

tcher	Atl. W-L	Chi. W-L	Cin. W-L	Col. W-L	Fla. W-L	Hou. W-L	L.A. W-L	Mon. W-L	N.Y. W-L	Pit. W-L	St.L. W-L	S.D. W-L	S.F. W-L	Totals W-L
ech	1-1	0-0	0-0	0-0	0-1	0-0	0-0	0-0	0-0	0-0	0-0	0-2	0-0	1-4
azier	0-0	0-0	0-0	1-0	1-0	0-0	0-0	0-0	1-0	0-1	0-0	0-0	0-0	3-1
rland	0-0	0-1	0-1	2-0	2-0	0-0	1-0	0-0	0-0	0-1	0-0	1-0	1-0	7-3
ttalico	0-0	0-0	0-0	0-0	0-0	0-0	0-1	1-1	1-0	1-1	0-2	0-0	1-0	4-5
awford	0-0	0-0	0-0	0-0	0-0	0-1	0-0	0-0	0-0	0-0	0-0	0-0	0-0	0-1
rnandez	0-0	1-0	0-0	1-2	0-0	0-0	0-1	0-0	0-0	1-0	0-2	0-0	0-1	3-6
ey	0-0	0-0	0-0	0-0	0-0	0-0	0-0	0-0	0-1	0-0	0-0	0-0	0-0	0-1
ace	1-0	0-0	1-0	1-0	1-0	0-0	0-0	1-1	0-0	1-0	1-0	0-1	0-0	7-2
unter	0-1	1-1	0-1	0-0	0-0	0-1	0-0	0-0	0-1	1-0	1-0	1-1	0-1	3-7
Jordan	0-0	0-0	0-0	0-0	0-1	0-0	1-0	0-0	1-0	0-0	0-0	0-0	0-1	2-2
iper	0-0	0-0	1-0	0-0	0-0	0-0	1-0	0-0	0-0	0-0	0-0	0-0	0-0	2-0
aduro	0-0	0-0	0-0	0-0	0-0	0-0	0-0	0-0	0-1	0-0	0-0	0-0	0-0	0-1
mbs	0-1	1-1	0-2	0-0	0-1	0-0	0-1	1-0	0-0	0-1	1-1	0-0		3-9
ulholland	1-1	0-1	0-1	1-1	0-0	0-0	0-0	3-0	0-0	1-1	0-1	1-1	1-0	8-7
unoz	0-1	0-1	0-0	0-1	0-0	0-0	0-0	0-0	0-0	0-0	0-0	0-0	0-0	0-3
rrett	0-0	0-0	0-0	0-0	0-0	1-0	0-1	0-0	0-0	0-0	0-0	0-0	0-0	1-1
irico	0-0	0-0	0-1	0-0	0-0	0-0	0-0	0-0	0-0	0-0	0-0	0-0	0-0	0-1
an	0-1	0-2	0-1	0-0	1-0	1-0	0-0	0-0	0-1	0-0	1-0	0-0	0-0	3-5
hilling	0-1	2-0	0-1	0-1	1-0	0-2	1-1	1-2	1-1	1-0	0-0	0-0	2-1	9-10
ringer	0-1	0-0	0-0	0-1	0-1	0-2	0-0	0-1	1-1	1-1	1-1	0-1	0-0	3-10
est	1-0	0-0	0-0	0-0	0-0	0-1	0-0	1-0	0-0	0-0	0-0	0-1	0-0	2-2
lliams	0-1	1-0	0-2	0-0	1-2	0-3	1-1	0-2	1-0	1-0	1-0	0-0	1-2	6-14
Totals	4-9	6-7	2-10	6-6	7-6	2-10	6-7	7-6	6-7	7-5	4-8	4-8	6-6	67-95

NO DECISIONS—Dishman, Heflin, Mitchell.

PITTSBURGH—73-89

tcher	Atl. W-L	Chi. W-L	Cin. W-L	Col. W-L	Fla. W-L	Hou. W-L	L.A. W-L	Mon. W-L	N.Y. W-L	Phi. W-L	St.L. W-L	S.D. W-L	S.F. W-L	Totals W-L
ever	0-0	0-1	0-0	0-0	0-0	0-0	0-0	0-0	0-0	0-0	0-0	0-1	0-0	0-2
ristiansen	0-0	0-0	0-0	0-1	1-0	0-0	0-0	0-1	1-0	0-1	0-0	1-0	0-0	3-3
rdova	0-1	1-0	1-0	0-0	0-1	1-0	0-0	0-1	0-3	0-0	0-0	1-0	0-1	4-7
rwin	0-2	1-0	0-1	0-0	1-1	0-1	1-1	1-1	1-0	1-0	0-2	1-0	0-0	7-9
ssens	0-0	0-0	0-0	0-0	0-0	0-0	0-0	0-1	0-0	0-0	0-1	0-0	0-0	0-2
cks	0-0	0-0	0-0	0-1	0-1	0-1	0-0	1-1	0-0	2-0	0-1	0-1	1-0	4-5
pe	0-0	0-0	1-0	0-0	0-1	0-0	0-1	0-0	0-0	0-0	0-0	0-0	0-1	1-3
ber	0-1	1-0	1-1	2-0	1-0	0-2	1-0	1-0	0-1	0-0	1-0	0-0	0-0	9-5
aiza	0-1	1-0	0-0	0-1	0-0	0-0	0-0	0-0	0-0	0-0	0-1	0-0	1-0	2-3
iselle	0-0	1-0	0-0	0-0	0-0	0-0	0-0	0-0	0-0	0-0	0-0	0-0	0-0	1-0
ay	0-0	0-0	0-0	0-0	0-0	0-0	0-0	0-0	0-0	0-0	0-0	0-1	0-0	0-1
celi	0-1	0-1	0-1	0-0	0-0	1-1	0-1	0-0	0-1	1-1	0-2	0-1	0-0	2-10
orel	0-0	0-0	0-0	0-0	0-0	0-1	0-0	0-0	1-0	0-0	0-0	0-0	0-0	2-1
agle	3-1	2-0	3-0	1-1	1-1	1-0	1-0	1-0	0-0	0-2	0-1	0-0	1-0	14-6
rris	0-0	0-0	0-0	0-0	0-0	0-0	0-1	0-0	0-0	0-1	0-0	0-1	0-0	0-3

Pitcher	Atl. W-L	Chi. W-L	Cin. W-L	Col. W-L	Fla. W-L	Hou. W-L	L.A. W-L	Mon. W-L	N.Y. W-L	Phi. W-L	St.L. W-L	S.D. W-L	S.F. W-L	Tota W-
Peters	0-0	0-0	1-0	0-1	0-0	0-1	0-0	0-0	0-1	0-0	0-0	0-1	1-0	2
Plesac	0-0	2-0	0-0	0-0	2-0	0-0	1-0	0-1	1-1	0-1	0-0	0-1	0-1	6
Ruebel	0-1	0-0	0-0	1-0	0-0	0-0	0-0	0-0	0-0	0-0	0-0	0-0	0-0	1
Schmidt	0-0	0-1	1-0	0-0	0-0	0-0	0-1	0-0	0-0	0-0	0-0	0-0	1-0	2
Smith	0-0	0-0	0-0	1-1	0-0	0-1	0-0	0-1	1-0	0-0	1-2	1-0	0-1	4
Wagner	0-1	0-1	0-2	0-1	1-0	0-0	1-0	1-0	0-1	0-1	1-0	0-1	0-0	4
Wainhouse	0-0	0-0	0-0	0-0	0-0	1-0	0-0	0-0	0-0	0-0	0-0	0-0	0-0	1
Wilkins	0-0	0-0	0-0	0-0	0-0	1-0	1-1	0-0	0-0	1-0	0-0	0-1	1-0	4
Totals	3-9	9-4	8-5	5-7	7-5	5-8	6-6	5-7	5-8	5-7	3-10	4-9	8-4	73-8

NO DECISIONS—Cooke, Hancock.

ST. LOUIS—88-74

Pitcher	Atl. W-L	Chi. W-L	Cin. W-L	Col. W-L	Fla. W-L	Hou. W-L	L.A. W-L	Mon. W-L	N.Y. W-L	Phi. W-L	Pit. W-L	S.D. W-L	S.F. W-L	Tota W
Bailey	1-0	1-0	0-0	0-1	0-1	1-0	0-0	0-0	0-0	1-0	1-0	0-0	0-0	5
Batchelor	0-0	0-0	1-0	0-0	0-0	0-0	1-0	0-0	0-0	0-0	0-0	0-0	0-0	2
A. Benes	1-1	2-0	0-2	1-0	0-0	2-1	1-1	1-0	1-2	1-0	2-0	1-1	0-2	13-
A. Benes	1-1	1-1	1-0	1-2	2-1	2-0	0-1	1-0	0-1	3-1	2-1	1-0	3-1	18-
Busby	0-1	0-0	0-0	0-0	0-0	0-0	0-0	0-0	0-0	0-0	0-0	0-0	0-0	0-
Eckersley	0-0	0-1	0-0	0-1	0-0	0-0	0-2	0-1	0-1	0-0	0-0	0-0	0-0	0-
Fossas	0-0	0-0	0-0	0-0	0-0	0-0	0-0	0-0	0-1	0-1	0-0	0-1	0-1	0-
Honeycutt	0-0	0-0	1-0	0-0	0-0	0-0	0-0	0-0	0-0	0-0	1-0	0-0	0-1	2-
Jackson	0-0	0-0	1-1	0-0	0-0	0-0	0-0	0-0	0-0	0-0	0-0	0-0	0-0	1-
Ludwick	0-0	0-0	0-1	0-0	0-0	0-0	0-0	0-0	0-0	0-0	0-0	0-0	0-0	0-
Mathews	0-1	0-0	0-1	0-2	1-0	0-0	0-0	0-1	0-0	1-1	0-0	0-0	0-0	2-
Morgan	0-1	0-1	1-0	0-1	1-1	0-0	0-2	1-0	1-0	0-0	0-1	0-0	0-1	4-
Osborne	0-1	1-1	2-0	0-0	0-1	3-0	1-1	0-3	0-0	1-1	2-0	2-1	1-0	13-
Parrett	1-0	0-0	0-0	0-0	0-0	0-0	0-0	0-1	0-0	0-0	0-0	0-0	0-0	2-
Petkovsek	0-0	1-1	0-0	2-0	0-0	0-0	1-0	1-1	2-0	0-0	0-0	3-0	1-0	11-
Stottlemyre	0-3	2-0	1-0	0-1	2-1	3-1	0-1	0-1	3-0	0-0	2-1	1-1	0-1	14-
Urbani	0-0	0-0	0-0	0-0	0-0	0-0	0-0	0-0	0-0	1-0	0-0	0-0	0-0	1
Totals	4-9	8-5	8-5	4-8	6-6	11-2	4-8	4-8	7-5	8-4	10-3	8-4	6-7	88-7

NO DECISIONS—Barber.

SAN DIEGO—91-71

Pitcher	Atl. W-L	Chi. W-L	Cin. W-L	Col. W-L	Fla. W-L	Hou. W-L	L.A. W-L	Mon. W-L	N.Y. W-L	Phi. W-L	Pit. W-L	St.L. W-L	S.F. W-L	Tota W
Ashby	1-0	0-0	0-1	1-0	1-0	0-1	1-0	0-1	2-0	1-0	1-0	0-2	1-0	9-
Bergman	0-2	0-0	0-1	0-0	1-0	1-1	0-0	0-0	1-1	1-1	1-1	0-1	1-0	6-
Blair	0-0	0-2	0-0	0-2	0-1	0-0	0-0	0-0	1-0	0-0	0-1	0-0	1-0	2-
Bochtler	0-1	0-0	0-1	0-1	0-0	0-0	0-0	0-0	0-0	0-0	1-0	0-1	1-0	2-
Florie	0-0	0-0	0-2	1-0	0-0	0-0	1-0	0-0	0-0	0-0	0-0	0-0	0-0	2-
Hamilton	1-2	3-0	1-2	0-1	1-1	1-1	2-0	1-0	2-1	2-1	0-0	1-0	0-0	15-
Hermanson	0-0	0-0	0-0	0-0	0-0	0-0	0-0	0-0	0-0	1-0	0-0	0-0	0-0	1-
Hoffman	0-0	1-1	0-0	0-2	2-0	1-0	0-1	2-0	0-0	0-1	1-0	1-0	1-0	9-
Sanders	0-0	0-0	0-0	1-1	1-1	1-1	0-1	2-0	0-0	3-0	1-1	0-0	0-0	9-
Tewksbury	0-2	1-1	1-1	1-0	1-0	1-0	1-0	1-1	0-0	0-0	1-1	0-3	2-1	10-1
Valenzuela	1-1	0-1	0-1	1-1	1-0	0-0	0-2	1-2	3-0	1-0	1-0	1-0	3-0	13-
Veras	0-0	0-0	1-0	0-0	0-0	0-0	1-0	0-0	0-0	1-0	0-0	0-0	0-1	3-
Villone	0-0	0-0	0-0	0-0	1-0	0-1	0-0	0-0	0-0	0-0	0-0	0-0	0-0	1-
Worrell	1-1	1-1	0-0	0-0	0-0	1-1	2-1	1-0	1-1	0-1	0-0	1-1	1-0	9-
Totals	4-9	6-6	3-9	5-8	9-3	6-6	8-5	8-4	10-3	8-4	9-4	4-8	11-2	91-7

NO DECISIONS—Berumen, Dishman, Oquist, Osuna, Walker.

SAN FRANCISCO—68-94

Pitcher	Atl. W-L	Chi. W-L	Cin. W-L	Col. W-L	Fla. W-L	Hou. W-L	L.A. W-L	Mon. W-L	N.Y. W-L	Phi. W-L	Pit. W-L	St.L. W-L	S.D. W-L	Tota W
Bautista	0-0	1-0	0-1	0-0	1-0	0-0	1-0	0-1	0-0	0-1	0-0	0-0	0-1	3-
Beck	0-1	0-0	0-1	0-1	0-1	0-0	0-0	0-1	0-1	0-1	0-0	0-0	0-2	0-
Bourgeois	0-0	0-0	0-1	0-0	1-0	0-0	0-0	0-0	0-0	0-0	0-0	0-0	0-1	1-
Carlson	0-0	0-0	0-0	1-0	0-0	0-0	0-0	0-0	0-0	0-0	0-0	0-0	0-0	1-
Creek	0-0	0-0	0-1	0-0	0-0	0-0	0-0	0-1	0-0	0-0	0-0	0-0	0-0	0-
DeLucia	0-0	0-1	0-0	0-0	0-0	1-0	0-2	0-1	0-0	0-0	1-1	1-0	0-1	3-
Dewey	0-0	0-0	0-0	0-0	0-1	0-0	1-0	2-0	1-0	1-0	1-1	0-1	0-0	6-
Estes	1-0	0-0	0-0	0-0	0-0	0-0	1-1	0-2	1-0	0-0	0-1	0-0	0-0	3-
Fernandez	0-1	1-0	1-0	0-1	2-1	1-1	0-1	1-1	0-1	0-2	0-1	1-1	0-2	7-1
Gardner	2-1	1-0	2-0	2-0	0-0	0-1	1-0	0-1	1-0	2-1	0-0	1-1	0-2	12-
Hook	0-0	0-0	0-0	0-0	0-0	0-0	0-0	0-0	0-0	0-0	0-1	0-0	0-0	0-
Juden	0-0	1-0	0-0	1-0	1-0	0-1	0-0	0-0	0-0	0-0	0-0	0-0	0-0	4-
Leiter	0-2	1-0	0-1	0-1	1-1	1-1	0-1	2-0	0-1	0-0	0-0	0-0	0-1	4-1
Poole	0-0	0-0	0-0	0-0	0-0	0-0	0-0	0-0	0-0	0-0	0-1	1-0	1-0	2-
Rueter	0-0	0-0	0-0	1-0	0-0	0-0	0-0	0-0	0-0	0-0	0-1	0-1	0-0	1-
Scott	0-0	0-0	0-1	0-0	0-0	0-0	0-0	0-0	1-1	0-0	0-0	1-0	0-0	2-
Soderstrom	0-0	0-0	0-0	2-0	0-0	0-0	0-0	0-0	0-0	0-0	0-0	0-0	0-0	2-
VanLandingham	0-1	0-3	1-2	1-0	1-0	0-3	2-0	0-1	1-1	2-0	1-1	0-1	0-1	9-1
Watson	2-1	0-3	0-1	0-1	0-1	0-1	0-1	0-0	1-1	1-1	1-0	2-1	1-0	8-1
Totals	5-7	5-7	4-9	8-5	7-5	4-8	6-7	4-9	6-6	6-6	4-8	7-6	2-11	68-9

NO DECISIONS—Barton.

HOME RUNS BY PARKS

	At Atl.	At Chi.	At Cin.	At Col.	At Fla.	At Hou.	At L.A.	At Mon.	At N.Y.	At Phi.	At Pit.	At St.L.	At S.D.	At S.F.	Totals 1996	1995
anta	106	2	14	8	1	8	4	10	3	6	10	9	7	9	197	168
icago	5	97	5	12	5	5	3	3	10	5	3	7	9	6	175	158
cinnati	7	9	89	17	4	7	5	9	4	11	6	6	7	10	191	161
orado	7	7	11	149	1	4	1	4	7	9	6	7	6	2	221	200
rida	7	7	4	10	73	5	5	7	3	6	6	8	5	4	150	144
uston	3	5	10	4	2	60	3	5	10	7	3	4	6	7	129	109
s Angeles	5	6	8	15	3	5	62	4	7	5	9	7	8	6	150	140
ntreal	5	3	7	12	0	4	2	81	7	3	5	5	2	12	148	118
w York	4	5	4	10	5	3	6	6	64	10	8	10	*4	8	147	125
ladelphia	7	11	1	8	4	3	5	13	4	55	8	2	4	7	132	94
tsburgh	4	6	7	8	3	3	3	4	6	4	74	6	5	5	138	125
Louis	6	15	7	7	4	5	2	4	5	5	4	70	3	5	142	107
Diego	1	6	4	8	4	4	2	6	4	5	7	4	*75	17	147	116
Francisco	5	9	4	3	8	7	8	1	2	6	6	6	6	82	153	152
1996 total	172	188	175	271	117	123	111	157	136	137	155	151	*147	180	2220	....
1995 total	160	166	134	241	128	89	110	98	131	129	136	114	127	154	....	1917

* There were actually 138 home runs hit at San Diego. The totals include one home run by the Mets and eight by the Padres at Monterrey Stadium, Mexico.

AT ATLANTA (172):

anta (106)—Klesko 20, C. Jones 18, McGriff 17, Grissom 11, Lopez 10, Justice 5, Blauser 4, Dye 4, Lemke 3, A. Jones 3, Pendleton 2, Smith 2, Perez 2, oltz 1, Walton 1, Avery 1, Whiten 1, Houston 1. **Chicago (5)**—Sandberg 1, Dorsett 1, Grace 1, Gonzalez 1, Hernandez 1. **Cincinnati (7)**—Davis 2, K. Mitchell _arkin 1, Harris 1, Branson 1, Boone 1. **Colorado (7)**—Galarraga 2, Burks 2, Castilla 2, J. Reed 1. **Florida (7)**—Sheffield 3, Conine 2, Abbott 1, Johnson 1. **uston (3)**—Bagwell 2, Berry 1. **Los Angeles (5)**—Piazza 3, Mondesi 1, Cedeno 1. **Montreal (5)**—Segui 1, Alou 1, Rodriguez 1, Andrews 1, Guerrero 1. **New k (4)**—Hundley 2, Gilkey 1, C. Jones 1. **Philadelphia (7)**—Santiago 5, Incaviglia 1, K. Jordan 1. **Pittsburgh (4)**—Hayes 2, King 1, Cummings 1. **St. Louis** —Gant 3, Jordan 2, Mabry 1. **San Diego (1)**—Thompson 1. **San Francisco (5)**—Dunston 1, Thompson 1, Hill 1, Batiste 1, Phillips 1.

AT CHICAGO (188):

anta (2)—Klesko 1, Mordecai 1. **Chicago (97)**—Sosa 26, Sandberg 12, Gomez 10, McRae 9, Gonzalez 6, Servais 6, Timmons 6, Grace 4, Hernandez 4, wn 3, Magadan 2, Shumpert 2, Bullett 2, Barberie 1, Sanchez 1, Trachsel 1, Hubbard 1, Glanville 1. **Cincinnati (9)**—Larkin 3, Davis 1, Harris 1, Anthony 1oward 1, Taubensee 1, Branson 1. **Colorado (7)**—Burks 3, Galarraga 2, Castilla 2. **Florida (5)**—Sheffield 2, Colbrunn 2, White 1, Conine 1, Johnson 1. **uston (5)**—Biggio 2, Bell 2, Berry 1. **Los Angeles (6)**—Gagne 1, Prince 1, DeShields 1, Karros 1, Mondesi 1, Cedeno 1. **Montreal (3)**—Segui 1, Alou 1, 1rews 1. **New York (5)**—Johnson 2, Espinoza 1, Hundley 1, Kent 1. **Philadelphia (11)**—Santiago 4, Incaviglia 2, Benjamin 2, Jefferies 1, Otero 1, Schall 1. **Pittsburgh (6)**—Sveum 1, King 1, Garcia 1, Johnson 1, Kendall 1, Osik 1. **St. Louis (15)**—Lankford 5, Jordan 4, Gaetti 2, Gant 2, Pagnozzi 1, Mabry 1. **n Diego (6)**—T. Gwynn 1, Joyner 1, Caminiti 1, Finley 1, Cianfrocco 1, Ausmus 1. **San Francisco (9)**—Bonds 3, M. Williams 2, Carreon 2, Decker 1, 1rsone 1.

AT CINCINNATI (175):

anta (14)—McGriff 3, Grissom 2, Perez 2, Dye 2, Pendleton 1, Blauser 1, Lopez 1, C. Jones 1, A. Jones 1. **Chicago (5)**—Gonzalez 2, Sosa 1, McRae 1, 1schnick 1. **Cincinnati (89)**—Larkin 14, Greene 11, Davis 8, Morris 7, Sanders 7, Boone 7, Oliver 6, Taubensee 6, K. Mitchell 5, Branson 5, Anthony 3, Perez 1arris 2, Coleman 1, Howard 1, Burba 1, K. Mitchell 1, Mottola 1. **Colorado (11)**—Bichette 3, Walker 3, Burks 2, Galarraga 1, Weiss 1, Castilla 1. **Florida** —White 1, Sheffield 1, Weathers 1, Castillo 1. **Houston (10)**—Bagwell 2, Bell 2, Miller 2, Biggio 1, Spiers 1, Wilkins 1, Reynolds 1. **Los Angeles (8)**— 1zza 3, Hollandsworth 2, Wallach 1, Karros 1, Busch 1. **Montreal (7)**—Alou 2, Andrews 2, Fletcher 1, Rodriguez 1, Grudzielanek 1. **New York (4)**—Hundley 1ilkey 1. **Philadelphia (1)**—Santiago 1. **Pittsburgh (7)**—King 2, Merced 2, Kingery 1, Brumfield 1, Johnson 1. **St. Louis (7)**—Lankford 2, Mabry 2, Gaetti 1ant 1, Jordan 1. **San Diego (4)**—Joyner 1, Caminiti 1, Cianfrocco 1, Johnson 1. **San Francisco (4)**—Bonds 1, Hill 1, M. Williams 1, Wilson 1.

AT COLORADO (271):

anta (8)—Klesko 3, Lopez 2, McGriff 1, Blauser 1, Dye 1. **Chicago (12)**—Sosa 2, McRae 2, Gomez 2, Servais 2, Gonzalez 1, Hernandez 1, Bullinger 1, 1uston 1. **Cincinnati (17)**—Davis 5, Morris 3, Oliver 2, Taubensee 2, Harris 1, Howard 1, Sanders 1, Boone 1, Greene 1. **Colorado (149)**—Galarraga 32, 1tilla 27, Burks 23, Bichette 22, Walker 12, J. Reed 7, Young 7, Weiss 5, Vander Wal 5, Owens 3, Mccracken 2, Anthony 1, Decker 1, Hubbard 1, Bates 1. 1rida (10)**—Conine 4, Sheffield 3, Grebeck 1, Arias 1, Johnson 1. **Houston (4)**—Berry 2, Spiers 1, Bell 1. **Los Angeles (15)**—Karros 4, Piazza 4, Mondesi 1ollandsworth 2, Wallach 1, Gagne 1, Ashley 1. **Montreal (12)**—Lansing 3, Andrews 3, Segui 2, Fletcher 1, Alou 1, Rodriguez 1, Santangelo 1. **New York**)—Gilkey 4, Hundley 2, Huskey 2, Kent 1, Isringhausen 1. **Philadelphia (8)**—Stocker 3, Incaviglia 1, Zeile 1, Whiten 1, Lieberthal 1, Otero 1. **Pittsburgh** —Bell 2, Hayes 2, King 2, Clark 1, Liriano 1. **St. Louis (7)**—Pagnozzi 2, Lankford 2, Gaetti 1, Jordan 1, Mabry 1. **San Diego (8)**—Caminiti 3, Newfield 3, 1ngstone 1, Gomez 1. **San Francisco (3)**—M. Williams 1, Wilkins 1, Batiste 1.

AT FLORIDA (117):

anta (1)—Blauser 1. **Chicago (5)**—Sandberg 2, Sosa 1, McRae 1, Servais 1. **Cincinnati (4)**—Larkin 2, Taubensee 1, Greene 1. **Colorado (1)**—Galarraga 1orida (73)**—Sheffield 19, Conine 16, Colbrunn 9, White 5, Pendleton 4, Dawson 2, Orsulak 2, Renteria 2, Arias 1, Veras 1. **Houston** —Bell 1, Miller 1. **Los Angeles (3)**—Karros 2, Piazza 1. **New York (5)**—Hundley 2, Espinoza 1, Baerga 1, Gilkey 1. **Philadelphia (4)**—Incaviglia 1, Santiago 1eile 1, Stocker 1. **Pittsburgh (3)**—King 1, Garcia 1, Wehner 1. **St. Louis (4)**—Sweeney 2, McGee 1, Lankford 1. **San Diego (4)**—Deer 1, Finley 1, 1ngstone 1, Flaherty 1. **San Francisco (8)**—Carreon 2, Javier 1, Dunston 1, Bonds 1, Thompson 1, Phillips 1, Aurilia 1.

AT HOUSTON (123):

anta (8)—Klesko 3, McGriff 2, Grissom 2, C. Jones 1. **Chicago (5)**—Gonzalez 2, Sandberg 1, Grace 1, Sosa 1. **Cincinnati (7)**—Davis 2, Sabo 2, Larkin 1, 1rris 1, Sanders 1. **Colorado (4)**—Galarraga 2, Bichette 1, Castilla 1. **Florida (5)**—Sheffield 2, Colbrunn 1, Hutton 1, Zaun 1. **Houston (60)**—Bagwell 16, 8, Biggio 7, Miller 7, Berry 4, Spiers 3, Wilkins 3, May 2, Mouton 2, Cangelosi 1, Simms 1, Eusebio 1, Knorr 1, Reynolds 1, Gutierrez 1, Hunter 1, 1tgomery 1. **Los Angeles (5)**—Gagne 2, Ashley 2, Karros 1. **Montreal (4)**—Fletcher 2, Rodriguez 2. **New York (3)**—Johnson 1, Huskey 1, M. Franco 1. 1adelphia (3)**—Eisenreich 2, Benjamin 1. **Pittsburgh (3)**—King 2, Martin 1. **St. Louis (5)**—Mabry 2, McGee 1, Lankford 1, Jordan 1. **San Diego (4)**— 1ley 1, Caminiti 1, Newfield 1, Johnson 1. **San Francisco (5)**—Bonds 3, Hill 2, Carreon 1, Wilkins 1.

AT LOS ANGELES (111):

anta (4)—Lopez 2, Justice 1, Klesko 1. **Chicago (3)**—Gomez 2, Servais 1. **Cincinnati (5)**—Davis 1, Larkin 1, Morris 1, Howard 1, Greene 1. **Colorado** —Young 1. **Florida (5)**—Sheffield 3, Colbrunn 1, Veras 1. **Houston (3)**—Bagwell 2, Miller 1. **Los Angeles (62)**—Karros 16, Piazza 14, Mondesi 11, Ashley 1lowers 4, Gagne 3, DeShields 3, Wallach 2, Hollandsworth 2, Curtis 1, Busch 1. **Montreal (2)**—White 1, Andrews 1. **New York (6)**—Gilkey 3, Hundley 1, 1gna 1, Petagine 1. **Philadelphia (5)**—Santiago 2, Rolen 2, Amaro 1. **Pittsburgh (3)**—Martin 2, King 1. **St. Louis (2)**—Gaetti 1, Gant 1. **San Diego (2)**— 1initi 1, Finley 1. **San Francisco (8)**—Benard 2, Bonds 1, Hill 1, M. Williams 1, Lampkin 1, Wilkins 1, Wilson 1.

AT MONTREAL (157):

Atlanta (10)—Grissom 2, Lopez 2, C. Jones 2, Dye 2, Avery 1, Mordecai 1. **Chicago (3)**—Sandberg 2, Grace 1. **Cincinnati (9)**—Davis 2, Sanders 2, Larkin 1, Sabo 1, Morris 1, Anthony 1, Taubensee 1. **Colorado (4)**—Castilla 2, Galarraga 1, Burks 1. **Florida (7)**—Conine 2, White 1, Sheffield 1, Colbrunn 1, Johns 1, Renteria 1. **Houston (5)**—Berry 2, Biggio 1, Goff 1, Hunter 1. **Los Angeles (4)**—Piazza 2, Gagne 1, Karros 1. **Montreal (81)**—Rodriguez 20, Alou 14, Andre 8, Fletcher 7, Segui 6, Obando 6, Grudzielanek 5, Santangelo 5, Lansing 3, Floyd 3, White 2, Webster 1, Spehr 1. **New York (6)**—Hundley 3, Baerga 1, Petago 1, Ochoa 1. **Philadelphia (13)**—Zeile 4, Santiago 3, Incaviglia 2, Dykstra 1, Whiten 1, Morandini 1, Lieberthal 1. **Pittsburgh (4)**—King 2, Liriano 1, Martir 1. **St. Louis (4)**—Gaetti 1, Sheaffer 1, Lankford 1, Mabry 1. **San Diego (6)**—Henderson 2, Finley 2, Cedeno 1, Lopez 1. **San Francisco (1)**—Bonds 1.

AT NEW YORK (136):

Atlanta (3)—McGriff 2, Pendleton 1. **Chicago (10)**—Sandberg 2, Grace 2, Magadan 1, McRae 1, Gonzalez 1, Hernandez 1. **Cincinnati (4)**—Mo 1, Sanders 1, Boone 1, Greene 1. **Colorado (7)**—Galarraga 2, Bichette 2, Burks 1, Walker 1, Castilla 1. **Florida (3)**—White 2, Renteria 1. **Houston (10)**—Mi 3, May 2, Bagwell 2, Bell 2, Berry 1. **Los Angeles (7)**—Blowers 2, Karros 2, Piazza 1, Mondesi 1, Hollandsworth 1. **Montreal (7)**—Rodriguez 2, Lansing Floyd 2, Andrews 1. **New York (64)**—Hundley 20, Gilkey 14, Huskey 9, Brogna 5, Espinoza 2, C. Jones 2, Kent 2, Tomberlin 2, Petagine 2, Alfonzo 2, Johns 1, Vizcaino 1, Everett 1, Ochoa 1. **Philadelphia (4)**—Estalella 2, Santiago 1, Stocker 1. **Pittsburgh (6)**—Martin 2, Clark 1, Bell 1, Liriano 1, King 1. **St. Louis (5)**—Gant 2, Gaetti 1, McGee 1, Mabry 1. **San Diego (4)**—Caminiti 2, Finley 1, Johnson 1. **San Francisco (2)**—Wilkins 1, Benard 1.

AT PHILADELPHIA (137):

Atlanta (6)—Blauser 2, Grissom 2, Whiten 1, C. Jones 1. **Chicago (5)**—Sandberg 1, Sosa 1, McRae 1, Bullett 1, Timmons 1. **Cincinnati (11)**—Larkin 3, Da 2, Oliver 1, Anthony 1, Taubensee 1, Sanders 1, Greene 1, Kelly 1. **Colorado (9)**—Burks 4, Castilla 2, Bichette 1, Walker 1, Owens 1. **Florida (6)**—White Conine 1, Colbrunn 1, Abbott 1, Renteria 1. **Houston (7)**—Bagwell 4, Berry 1, Mouton 1, Hunter 1. **Los Angeles (5)**—Mondesi 2, Piazza 1, Ashley Hollandsworth 1. **Montreal (3)**—Rodriguez 1, Lansing 1, Floyd 1. **New York (10)**—Huskey 2, Alfonzo 2, Ochoa 2, Johnson 1, Gilkey 1, Ordonez 1, Wilsor **Philadelphia (55)**—Zeile 9, Santiago 8, Incaviglia 6, Jefferies 4, Whiten 4, Phillips 4, Lieberthal 4, Morandini 2, K. Jordan 2, Murray 2, Rolen 2, Magee Eisenreich 1, Dykstra 1, Amaro 1, Schall 1, Zuber 1, Doster 1. **Pittsburgh (4)**—King 1, Brumfield 1, Martin 1, Johnson 1. **St. Louis (5)**—Gant 2, Gaett Jordan 1, Mabry 1. **San Diego (5)**—Finley 2, Caminiti 1, Vaughn 1, Johnson 1. **San Francisco (6)**—Bonds 2, M. Williams 2, Hill 1, Jones 1.

AT PITTSBURGH (155):

Atlanta (10)—Klesko 2, Lopez 2, Dye 2, Blauser 1, Grissom 1, C. Jones 1, A. Jones 1. **Chicago (3)**—Gonzalez 1, Gomez 1, Brown 1. **Cincinnati (6)**—Lar 2, Morris 1, Oliver 1, Burba 1, Sanders 1. **Colorado (6)**—Galarraga 1, Burks 1, Weiss 1, Bichette 1, Ritz 1, Castilla 1. **Florida (6)**—Sheffield 3, White 2, Ve 1. **Houston (3)**—Bagwell 2, Biggio 1. **Los Angeles (9)**—Piazza 3, Mondesi 3, Gagne 1, Karros 1, Busch 1. **Montreal (5)**—Alou 1, Rodriguez 1, Obando White 1, Andrews 1. **New York (8)**—Gilkey 2, Kent 2, Johnson 1, C. Jones 1, Roberson 1, Isringhausen 1. **Philadelphia (8)**—Santiago 3, Jefferies 2, Dyks 1, Zeile 1, Whiten 1. **Pittsburgh (74)**—King 14, Johnson 10, Merced 9, Martin 8, Bell 7, Clark 6, Hayes 5, Allensworth 4, Garcia 3, Kingery 2, Cummings Kendall 2, Darwin 1, Wehner 1. **St. Louis (4)**—Jordan 2, Gaetti 1, Pagnozzi 1. **San Diego (7)**—Caminiti 3, Finley 2, Vaughn 2. **San Francisco (6)**—Bonds Hill 2, M. Williams 1, Wilkins 1.

AT ST. LOUIS (151):

Atlanta (9)—McGriff 2, Grissom 2, Lopez 2, Whiten 1, Klesko 1, C. Jones 1. **Chicago (7)**—McRae 2, Sandberg 1, Sosa 1, Gonzalez 1, Servais 1, Hernand 1. **Cincinnati (6)**—Larkin 3, Oliver 1, Howard 1, Greene 1. **Colorado (7)**—Galarraga 2, Anthony 2, Burks 1, Walker 1, Castilla 1. **Florida (8)**—Colbrunn White 2, Sheffield 2, Arias 1. **Houston (4)**—Berry 2, Hunter 2. **Los Angeles (7)**—Hollandsworth 2, Gagne 1, Karros 1, Curtis 1, Piazza 1, Mondesi 1. **Montr (5)**—Rodriguez 2, Fletcher 1, White 1, Andrews 1. **New York (10)**—Johnson 2, Hundley 2, Kent 2, Gilkey 1, Mayne 1, Roberson 1, Huskey 1. **Philadelp (2)**—Zeile 1, Phillips 1. **Pittsburgh (6)**—Merced 3, Martin 2, Bell 1. **St. Louis (70)**—Gant 17, Gaetti 13, Pagnozzi 9, Lankford 8, Clayton 6, Alicea 4, Jor 3, Mabry 3, Smith 2, McGee 2, Sheaffer 1, Osborne 1, Bell 1. **San Diego (4)**—Caminiti 2, Joyner 1, Vaughn 1. **San Francisco (6)**—Bonds 2, Hill 1, M. Willia 1, McCarty 1, Canizaro 1.

AT SAN DIEGO (147):

Atlanta (7)—Lemke 2, Klesko 2, C. Jones 2, Lopez 1. **Chicago (9)**—Sosa 3, Hernandez 2, Sandberg 1, Gomez 1, Bullinger 1, Brown 1. **Cincinnati (7** Mottola 2, Davis 1, Morris 1, Branson 1, Boone 1, Greene 1. **Colorado (6)**—Galarraga 1, Burks 1, Weiss 1, Bichette 1, Bailey 1, Mccracken 1. **Florida (5** Pendleton 2, White 1, Conine 1, Veras 1. **Houston (6)**—Berry 2, May 1, Bagwell 1, Bell 1, Miller 1. **Los Angeles (8)**—Karros 3, Piazza 3, Mondesi Hollandsworth 1. **Montreal (2)**—Silvestri 1, Lansing 1. **New York (4)**—Hundley 1, Gilkey 1, Kent 1, Tomberlin 1. **Philadelphia (4)**—Incaviglia 1, Santiago Mulholland 1, Zeile 1. **Pittsburgh (5)**—Merced 2, King 1, Garcia 1, Martin 1. **St. Louis (3)**—Gaetti 1, Gant 1, Jordan 1. **San Diego (75)**—Caminiti 20, Fin 15, Henderson 6, Vaughn 6, Flaherty 6, Joyner 5, Deer 3, Johnson 3, T. Gwynn 2, Cedeno 2, Reed 1, Bergman 1, Newfield 1, Gomez 1, Lopez 1, Hamiltor Thompson 1. **San Francisco (6)**—Bonds 3, Thompson 1, Hill 1, Aurilia 1. **Note:** The Mets actually hit three home runs at San Diego. The home run Tomberlin was hit at Monterrey, Mexico. The Padres actually hit 67 homers at San Diego. Three home runs by Caminiti and one each by Finley, Flahe Hamilton, Johnson and Vaughn were hit at Monterrey, Mexico.

AT SAN FRANCISCO (180):

Atlanta (9)—C. Jones 3, McGriff 1, Smith 1, Grissom 1, Klesko 1, Lopez 1, Dye 1. **Chicago (6)**—Sandberg 2, Sosa 2, Gomez 1, Houston 1. **Cincinnati (10** Davis 2, Larkin 2, Anthony 2, Howard 1, Branson 1, Boone 1, Greene 1. **Colorado (2)**—Burks 1, Anthony 1. **Florida (4)**—Sheffield 3, Pendleton 1. **Hous (7)**—Biggio 3, Wilkins 2, Spiers 1, Berry 1. **Los Angeles (6)**—DeShields 1, Karros 1, Kirby 1, Mondesi 1, Hollandsworth 1, Busch 1. **Montreal (12** Rodriguez 6, Webster 1, Segui 1, Alou 1, Obando 1, Lansing 1, White 1, Santangelo 1. **New York (8)**—Hundley 4, Johnson 1, Gilkey 1, Brogna 1, Robers 1. **Philadelphia (7)**—Incaviglia 2, Zeile 2, Santiago 1, Benjamin 1, Lieberthal 1. **Pittsburgh (5)**—Bell 2, Hayes 1, King 1, Merced 1. **St. Louis (5)**—Gan Alicea 1, Lankford 1, Jordan 1, Sweeney 1. **San Diego (17)**—Caminiti 5, Finley 5, Flaherty 2, Henderson 1, C. Gwynn 1, Reed 1, Gomez 1, Johnson 1. **S Francisco (82)**—Bonds 23, M. Williams 13, Hill 9, Lampkin 5, McCarty 5, Carreon 4, Scarsone 4, Dunston 3, Wilkins 3, Cruz 3, Thompson 2, Benard 2, Ja 1, Manwaring 1, Batiste 1, Hubbard 1, Aurilia 1, Canizaro 1.

HISTORY

ALL-TIME RESULTS

AMERICAN LEAGUE CHAMPIONS

Year	Team	Manager	Year	Team	Manager
1901—Chicago	Clark Griffith		1950—New York	Casey Steng
1902—Philadelphia	Connie Mack		1951—New York	Casey Steng
1903—Boston	Jimmy Collins		1952—New York	Casey Sten
1904—Boston	Jimmy Collins		1953—New York	Casey Sten
1905—Philadelphia	Connie Mack		1954—Cleveland	Al Lop
1906—Chicago	Fielder Jones		1955—New York	Casey Steng
1907—Detroit	Hugh Jennings		1956—New York	Casey Steng
1908—Detroit	Hugh Jennings		1957—New York	Casey Steng
1909—Detroit	Hugh Jennings		1958—New York	Casey Steng
1910—Philadelphia	Connie Mack		1959—Chicago	Al Lop
1911—Philadelphia	Connie Mack		1960—New York	Casey Steng
1912—Boston	Jake Stahl		1961—New York	Ralph Ho
1913—Philadelphia	Connie Mack		1962—New York	Ralph Ho
1914—Philadelphia	Connie Mack		1963—New York	Ralph Ho
1915—Boston	Bill Carrigan		1964—New York	Yogi Ber
1916—Boston	Bill Carrigan		1965—Minnesota	Sam Me
1917—Chicago	Pants Rowland		1966—Baltimore	Hank Bau
1918—Boston	Ed Barrow		1967—Boston	Dick Willian
1919—Chicago	Kid Gleason		1968—Detroit	Mayo Sm
1920—Cleveland	Tris Speaker		1969—Baltimore (East Division)	Earl Weav
1921—New York	Miller Huggins		1970—Baltimore (East Division)	Earl Weav
1922—New York	Miller Huggins		1971—Baltimore (East Division)	Earl Weav
1923—New York	Miller Huggins		1972—Oakland (West Division)	Dick Willian
1924—Washington	Bucky Harris		1973—Oakland (West Division)	Dick Willian
1925—Washington	Bucky Harris		1974—Oakland (West Division)	Al Da
1926—New York	Miller Huggins		1975—Boston (East Division)	Darrell Johns
1927—New York	Miller Huggins		1976—New York (East Division)	Billy Mar
1928—New York	Miller Huggins		1977—New York (East Division)	Billy Mar
1929—Philadelphia	Connie Mack		1978—New York (East Division)	Billy Martin, Bob Lem
1930—Philadelphia	Connie Mack		1979—Baltimore (East Division)	Earl Weav
1931—Philadelphia	Connie Mack		1980—Kansas City (West Division)	Jim F
1932—New York	Joe McCarthy		1981—New York (East Division)... Gene Michael, Bob Lem
1933—Washington	Joe Cronin		1982—Milwaukee (East Division). Buck Rodgers, Harvey Kue
1934—Detroit	Mickey Cochrane		1983—Baltimore (East Division)	Joe Altobe
1935—Detroit	Mickey Cochrane		1984—Detroit (East Division)	Sparky Anders
1936—New York	Joe McCarthy		1985—Kansas City (West Division)	Dick Hows
1937—New York	Joe McCarthy		1986—Boston (East Division)	John McNama
1938—New York	Joe McCarthy		1987—Minnesota (West Division)	Tom Ke
1939—New York	Joe McCarthy		1988—Oakland (West Division)	Tony La Rus
1940—Detroit	Del Baker		1989—Oakland (West Division)	Tony La Rus
1941—New York	Joe McCarthy		1990—Oakland (West Division)	Tony La Rus
1942—New York	Joe McCarthy		1991—Minnesota (West Division)	Tom Ke
1943—New York	Joe McCarthy		1992—Toronto (East Division)	Cito Gast
1944—St. Louis	Luke Sewell		1993—Toronto (East Division)	Cito Gast
1945—Detroit	Steve O'Neill		1994—None†	
1946—Boston	Joe Cronin		1995—Cleveland (Central Division)	Mike Hargro
1947—New York	Bucky Harris		1996—New York (East Division)	Joe Tor
1948—Cleveland*	Lou Boudreau		*Defeated Boston in one-game playoff. †New York finished
1949—New York	Casey Stengel		the strike-shortened season with the league's best record.

NATIONAL LEAGUE CHAMPIONS

Year	Team	Manager	Year	Team	Manager
1876—Chicago	Albert Spalding		1894—Baltimore	Edward Hanl
1877—Boston	Harry Wright		1895—Baltimore	Edward Hanl
1878—Boston	Harry Wright		1896—Baltimore	Edward Hanl
1879—Providence	George Wright		1897—Boston	Frank Sel
1880—Chicago	Adrian Anson		1898—Boston	Frank Sel
1881—Chicago	Adrian Anson		1899—Brooklyn	Edward Hanl
1882—Chicago	Adrian Anson		1900—Brooklyn	Edward Hanl
1883—Boston	John Morrill		1901—Pittsburgh	Fred Clar
1884—Providence	Frank Bancroft		1902—Pittsburgh	Fred Clar
1885—Chicago	Adrian Anson		1903—Pittsburgh	Fred Clar
1886—Chicago	Adrian Anson		1904—New York	John McGra
1887—Detroit	William Watkins		1905—New York	John McGra
1888—New York	James Mutrie		1906—Chicago	Frank Chan
1889—New York	James Mutrie		1907—Chicago	Frank Chan
1890—Brooklyn	William McGunnigle		1908—Chicago	Frank Chan
1891—Boston	Frank Selee		1909—Pittsburgh	Fred Clar
1892—Boston	Frank Selee		1910—Chicago	Frank Chan
1893—Boston	Frank Selee		1911—New York	John McGra

Year	Team	Manager	Year	Team	Manager
1912—New York		John McGraw	1957—Milwaukee		Fred Haney
1913—New York		John McGraw	1958—Milwaukee		Fred Haney
1914—Boston		George Stallings	1959—Los Angeles‡		Walter Alston
1915—Philadelphia		Pat Moran	1960—Pittsburgh		Danny Murtaugh
1916—Brooklyn		Wilbert Robinson	1961—Cincinnati		Fred Hutchinson
1917—New York		John McGraw	1962—San Francisco§		Al Dark
1918—Chicago		Fred Mitchell	1963—Los Angeles		Walter Alston
1919—Cincinnati		Pat Moran	1964—St. Louis		Johnny Keane
1920—Brooklyn		Wilbert Robinson	1965—Los Angeles		Walter Alston
1921—New York		John McGraw	1966—Los Angeles		Walter Alston
1922—New York		John McGraw	1967—St. Louis		Red Schoendienst
1923—New York		John McGraw	1968—St. Louis		Red Schoendienst
1924—New York		John McGraw	1969—New York (East Division)		Gil Hodges
1925—Pittsburgh		Bill McKechnie	1970—Cincinnati (West Division)		Sparky Anderson
1926—St. Louis		Rogers Hornsby	1971—Pittsburgh (East Division)		Danny Murtaugh
1927—Pittsburgh		Donie Bush	1972—Cincinnati (West Division)		Sparky Anderson
1928—St. Louis		Bill McKechnie	1973—New York (East Division)		Yogi Berra
1929—Chicago		Joe McCarthy	1974—Los Angeles (West Division)		Walter Alston
1930—St. Louis		Gabby Street	1975—Cincinnati (West Division)		Sparky Anderson
1931—St. Louis		Gabby Street	1976—Cincinnati (West Division)		Sparky Anderson
1932—Chicago		Charlie Grimm	1977—Los Angeles (West Division)		Tommy Lasorda
1933—New York		Bill Terry	1978—Los Angeles (West Division)		Tommy Lasorda
1934—St. Louis		Frank Frisch	1979—Pittsburgh (East Division)		Chuck Tanner
1935—Chicago		Charlie Grimm	1980—Philadelphia (East Division)		Dallas Green
1936—New York		Bill Terry	1981—Los Angeles (West Division)		Tommy Lasorda
1937—New York		Bill Terry	1982—St. Louis (East Division)		Whitey Herzog
1938—Chicago		Gabby Hartnett	1983—Philadelphia (East Division)		Pat Corrales, Paul Owens
1939—Cincinnati		Bill McKechnie	1984—San Diego (West Division)		Dick Williams
1940—Cincinnati		Bill McKechnie	1985—St. Loius (East Division)		Whitey Herzog
1941—Brooklyn		Leo Durocher	1986—New York (East Division)		Dave Johnson
1942—St. Louis		Billy Southworth	1987—St. Louis (East Division)		Whitey Herzog
1943—St. Louis		Billy Southworth	1988—Los Angeles (West Division)		Tommy Lasorda
1944—St. Louis		Billy Southworth	1989—San Francisco (West Division)		Roger Craig
1945—Chicago		Charlie Grimm	1990—Cincinnati (West Division)		Lou Piniella
1946—St. Louis*		Eddie Dyer	1991—Atlanta (West Division)		Bobby Cox
1947—Brooklyn		Burt Shotton	1992—Atlanta (West Division)		Bobby Cox
1948—Boston		Billy Southworth	1993—Philadelphia (East Division)		Jim Fregosi
1949—Brooklyn		Burt Shotton	1994—None∞		
1950—Philadelphia		Eddie Sawyer	1995—Atlanta (East Division)		Bobby Cox
1951—New York†		Leo Durocher	1996—Atlanta (East Division)		Bobby Cox
1952—Brooklyn		Charlie Dressen			
1953—Brooklyn		Charlie Dressen			
1954—New York		Leo Durocher			
1955—Brooklyn		Walter Alston			
1956—Brooklyn		Walter Alston			

*Defeated Brooklyn, two games to none, in playoff for pennant.
†Defeated Brooklyn, two games to one, in playoff for pennant.
‡Defeated Milwaukee, two games to none, in playoff for pennant.
§Defeated Los Angeles, two games to one, in playoff for pennant.
∞Montreal finished the strike-shortened season with the league's best record.

WORLD SERIES

Year	Winner	Loser	Games	Year	Winner	Loser	Games
1903—Boston A.L.		Pittsburgh N.L.	5-3	1931—St. Louis N.L.		Philadelphia A.L.	4-3
1904—No Series				1932—New York A.L.		Chicago N.L.	4-0
1905—New York N.L.		Philadelphia A.L.	4-1	1933—New York N.L.		Washington A.L.	4-1
1906—Chicago A.L.		Chicago N.L.	4-2	1934—St. Louis N.L.		Detroit A.L.	4-3
1907—Chicago N.L.		Detroit A.L.	*4-0	1935—Detroit A.L.		Chicago N.L.	4-2
1908—Chicago N.L.		Detroit A.L.	4-1	1936—New York A.L.		New York N.L.	4-2
1909—Pittsburgh N.L.		Detroit A.L.	4-3	1937—New York A.L.		New York N.L.	4-1
1910—Philadelphia A.L.		Chicago N.L.	4-1	1938—New York A.L.		Chicago N.L.	4-0
1911—Philadelphia A.L.		New York N.L.	4-2	1939—New York A.L.		Cincinnati N.L.	4-0
1912—Boston A.L.		New York N.L.	*4-3	1940—Cincinnati N.L.		Detroit A.L.	4-3
1913—Philadelphia A.L.		New York N.L.	4-1	1941—New York A.L.		Brooklyn N.L.	4-1
1914—Boston N.L.		Philadelphia A.L.	4-0	1942—St. Louis N.L.		New York A.L.	4-1
1915—Boston A.L.		Philadelphia N.L.	4-1	1943—New York A.L.		St. Louis N.L.	4-1
1916—Boston A.L.		Brooklyn N.L.	4-1	1944—St. Louis N.L.		St. Louis A.L.	4-2
1917—Chicago A.L.		New York N.L.	4-2	1945—Detroit A.L.		Chicago N.L.	4-3
1918—Boston A.L.		Chicago N.L.	4-2	1946—St. Louis N.L.		Boston A.L.	4-3
1919—Cincinnati N.L.		Chicago A.L.	5-3	1947—New York A.L.		Brooklyn, N.L.	4-3
1920—Cleveland A.L.		Brooklyn N.L.	5-2	1948—Cleveland A.L.		Boston N.L.	4-2
1921—New York N.L.		New York A.L.	5-3	1949—New York A.L.		Brooklyn N.L.	4-1
1922—New York N.L.		New York A.L.	*4-0	1950—New York A.L.		Philadelphia N.L.	4-0
1923—New York A.L.		New York N.L.	4-2	1951—New York A.L.		New York N.L.	4-2
1924—Washington A.L.		New York N.L.	4-3	1952—New York A.L.		Brooklyn N.L.	4-3
1925—Pittsburgh N.L.		Washington A.L.	4-3	1953—New York A.L.		Brooklyn N.L.	4-2
1926—St. Louis N.L.		New York A.L.	4-3	1954—New York N.L.		Cleveland A.L.	4-0
1927—New York A.L.		Pittsburgh, N.L.	4-0	1955—Brooklyn N.L.		New York A.L.	4-3
1928—New York A.L.		St. Louis N.L.	4-0	1956—New York A.L.		Brooklyn N.L.	4-3
1929—Philadelphia A.L.		Chicago N.L.	4-1	1957—Milwaukee N.L.		New York A.L.	4-3
1930—Philadelphia A.L.		St. Louis N.L.	4-2	1958—New York A.L.		Milwaukee N.L.	4-3

Year	Winner	Loser	Games	Year	Winner	Loser	Game
1959	Los Angeles N.L.	Chicago A.L.	4-2	1979	Pittsburgh N.L.	Baltimore A.L.	4-
1960	Pittsburgh N.L.	New York A.L.	4-3	1980	Philadelphia N.L.	Kansas City A.L.	4-
1961	New York A.L.	Cincinnati N.L.	4-1	1981	Los Angeles N.L.	New York A.L.	4-
1962	New York A.L.	San Francisco N.L.	4-3	1982	St. Louis N.L.	Milwaukee A.L.	4-
1963	Los Angeles N.L.	New York A.L.	4-0	1983	Baltimore A.L.	Philadelphia N.L.	4-
1964	St. Louis N.L.	New York A.L.	4-3	1984	Detroit A.L.	San Diego N.L.	4-
1965	Los Angeles N.L.	Minnesota A.L.	4-3	1985	Kansas City A.L.	St. Louis N.L.	4-
1966	Baltimore A.L.	Los Angeles N.L.	4-0	1986	New York N.L.	Boston A.L.	4-
1967	St. Louis N.L.	Boston A.L.	4-3	1987	Minnesota A.L.	St. Louis N.L.	4-
1968	Detroit A.L.	St. Louis N.L.	4-3	1988	Los Angeles N.L.	Oakland A.L.	4-
1969	New York N.L.	Baltimore A.L.	4-1	1989	Oakland A.L.	San Francisco N.L.	4-
1970	Baltimore A.L.	Cincinnati N.L.	4-1	1990	Cincinnati N.L.	Oakland A.L.	4-
1971	Pittsburgh N.L.	Baltimore A.L.	4-3	1991	Minnesota A.L.	Atlanta N.L.	4-
1972	Oakland A.L.	Cincinnati N.L.	4-3	1992	Toronto A.L.	Atlanta N.L.	4-
1973	Oakland A.L.	New York N.L.	4-3	1993	Toronto A.L.	Philadelphia N.L.	4-
1974	Oakland A.L.	Los Angeles N.L.	4-1	1994	No Series		
1975	Cincinnati N.L.	Boston A.L.	4-3	1995	Atlanta N.L.	Cleveland A.L.	4-
1976	Cincinnati N.L.	New York A.L.	4-0	1996	New York A.L.	Atlanta N.L.	4-
1977	New York A.L.	Los Angeles N.L.	4-2	*Includes tie game.			
1978	New York A.L.	Los Angeles N.L.	4-2				

DIVISION SERIES

AMERICAN LEAGUE

Year	Winner (Division)	Loser (Division)	Games
1981	New York (East)	Milwaukee (East)	3-2
	Oakland (West)	Kansas City (West)	3-0
1995	Cleveland (Central)	Boston (East)	3-0
	Seattle (West)	New York* (East)	3-2
1996	New York (East)	Texas (West)	3-1
	Baltimore (East)*	Cleveland (Central)	3-1

NATIONAL LEAGUE

Year	Winner (Division)	Loser (Division)	Game
1981	Montreal (East)	Philadelphia (East)	3-
	Los Angeles (West)	Houston (West)	3-
1995	Atlanta (East)	Colorado* (West)	3-
	Cincinnati (Central)	Los Angeles (West)	3-
1996	Atlanta (East)	Los Angeles (West)*	3-
	St. Louis (Central)	San Diego (West)	3-

*Wild-card team.

CHAMPIONSHIP SERIES

AMERICAN LEAGUE

Year	Winner (Division)	Loser (Division)	Games
1969	Baltimore (East)	Minnesota (West)	3-0
1970	Baltimore (East)	Minnesota (West)	3-0
1971	Baltimore (East)	Oakland (West)	3-0
1972	Oakland (West)	Detroit (East)	3-2
1973	Oakland (West)	Baltimore (East)	3-2
1974	Oakland (West)	Baltimore (East)	3-1
1975	Boston (East)	Oakland (West)	3-0
1976	New York (East)	Kansas City (West)	3-2
1977	New York (East)	Kansas City (West)	3-2
1978	New York (East)	Kansas City (West)	3-1
1979	Baltimore (East)	California (West)	3-1
1980	Kansas City (West)	New York (East)	3-0
1981	New York (East)	Oakland (West)	3-0
1982	Milwaukee (East)	California (West)	3-2
1983	Baltimore (East)	Chicago (West)	3-1
1984	Detroit (East)	Kansas City (West)	3-0
1985	Kansas City (West)	Toronto (East)	4-3
1986	Boston (East)	California (West)	4-3
1987	Minnesota (West)	Detroit (East)	4-1
1988	Oakland (West)	Boston (East)	4-0
1989	Oakland (West)	Toronto (East)	4-1
1990	Oakland (West)	Boston (East)	4-0
1991	Minnesota (West)	Toronto (East)	4-1
1992	Toronto (East)	Oakland (West)	4-2
1993	Toronto (East)	Chicago (West)	4-2
1994	No series		
1995	Cleveland (Central)	Seattle (West)	4-2
1996	New York (East)	Baltimore (East)*	4-1

NATIONAL LEAGUE

Year	Winner (Division)	Loser (Division)	Game
1969	New York (East)	Atlanta (West)	3-
1970	Cincinnati (West)	Pittsburgh (East)	3-
1971	Pittsburgh (East)	San Francisco (West)	3-
1972	Cincinnati (West)	Pittsburgh (East)	3-
1973	New York (East)	Cincinnati (West)	3-
1974	Los Angeles (West)	Pittsburgh (East)	3-
1975	Cincinnati (West)	Pittsburgh (East)	3-
1976	Cincinnati (West)	Philadelphia (East)	3-
1977	Los Angeles (West)	Philadelphia (East)	3-
1978	Los Angeles (West)	Philadelphia (East)	3-
1979	Pittsburgh (East)	Cincinnati (West)	3-
1980	Philadelphia (East)	Houston (West)	3-
1981	Los Angeles (West)	Montreal (East)	3-
1982	St. Louis (East)	Atlanta (West)	3-
1983	Philadelphia (East)	Los Angeles (West)	3-
1984	San Diego (West)	Chicago (East)	3-
1985	St. Louis (East)	Los Angeles (West)	4-
1986	New York (East)	Houston (West)	4-
1987	St. Louis (East)	San Francisco (West)	4-
1988	Los Angeles (West)	New York (East)	4-
1989	San Francisco (West)	Chicago (East)	4-
1990	Cincinnati (West)	Pittsburgh (East)	4-
1991	Atlanta (West)	Pittsburgh (East)	4-
1992	Atlanta (West)	Pittsburgh (East)	4-
1993	Philadelphia (East)	Atlanta (West)	4-
1994	No series		
1995	Atlanta (East)	Cincinnati (Central)	4-
1996	Atlanta (East)	St. Louis (Central)	4-

*Wild-card team.

ALL-STAR GAME

Date	Site	Score (Winner)	Winning pitcher (Losing pitcher)	Winning manager (Losing manager)	Att.
7-6-33	Comiskey Park Chicago	4-2 (A.L.)	Lefty Gomez, Yankees (Bill Hallahan, Cardinals)	Connie Mack, Athletics (John McGraw, Giants)	47,595
7-10-34	Polo Grounds New York	9-7 (A.L.)	Mel Harder, Indians (Van Mungo, Dodgers)	Joe Cronin, Senators (Bill Terry, Giants)	48,363

ate	Site	Score (Winner)	Winning pitcher (Losing pitcher)	Winning manager (Losing manager)	Att.
8-35	Municipal Stadium Cleveland	4-1 (A.L.)	Lefty Gomez, Yankees (Bill Walker, Cardinals)	Mickey Cochrane, Tigers (Frankie Frisch, Cardinals)	69,831
7-36	Braves Field Boston	4-3 (N.L.)	Dizzy Dean, Cardinals (Lefty Grove, Red Sox)	Charlie Grimm, Cubs (Joe McCarthy, Yankees)	25,556
7-37	Griffith Stadium Washington	8-3 (A.L.)	Lefty Gomez, Yankees (Dizzy Dean, Cardinals)	Joe McCarthy, Yankees (Bill Terry, Giants)	31,391
6-38	Crosley Field Cincinnati	4-1 (N.L.)	Johnny Vander Meer, Reds (Lefty Gomez, Yankees)	Bill Terry, Giants (Joe McCarthy, Yankees)	27,067
11-39	Yankee Stadium New York	3-1 (A.L.)	Tommy Bridges, Tigers (Bill Lee, Cubs)	Joe McCarthy, Yankees (Gabby Hartnett, Cubs)	62,892
9-40	Sportsman's Park St. Louis	4-0 (N.L.)	Paul Derringer, Reds (Red Ruffing, Yankees)	Bill McKechnie, Reds (Joe Cronin, Red Sox)	32,373
8-41	Briggs Stadium Detroit	7-5 (A.L.)	Ed Smith, White Sox (Claude Passeau, Cubs)	Del Baker, Tigers (Bill McKechnie, Reds)	54,674
6-42	Polo Grounds New York	3-1 (A.L.)	Spud Chandler, Yankees (Mort Cooper, Cardinals)	Joe McCarthy, Yankees (Leo Durocher, Dodgers)	34,178
13-43	Shibe Park Philadelphia	5-3 (A.L.)	Dutch Leonard, Senators (Mort Cooper, Cardinals)	Joe McCarthy, Yankees (Billy Southworth, Cardinals)	31,938
11-44	Forbes Field Pittsburgh	7-1 (N.L.)	Ken Raffensberger, Phillies (Tex Hughson, Red Sox)	Billy Southworth, Cardinals (Joe McCarthy, Yankees)	29,589
45	No game played.				
9-46	Fenway Park Boston	12-0 (A.L.)	Bob Feller, Indians (Claude Passeau, Cubs)	Steve O'Neill, Tigers (Charlie Grimm, Cubs)	34,906
8-47	Wrigley Field Chicago	2-1 (A.L.)	Frank Shea, Yankees (Johnny Sain, Braves)	Joe Cronin, Red Sox (Eddie Dyer, Cardinals)	41,123
13-48	Sportsman's Park St. Louis	5-2 (A.L.)	Vic Raschi, Yankees (Johnny Schmitz, Cubs)	Bucky Harris, Yankees (Leo Durocher, Dodgers)	34,009
12-49	Ebbets Field Brooklyn	11-7 (A.L.)	Virgil Trucks, Tigers (Don Newcombe, Dodgers)	Lou Boudreau, Indians (Billy Southworth, Braves)	32,577
11-50	Comiskey Park Chicago	4-3* (N.L.)	Ewell Blackwell, Reds (Ted Gray, Tigers)	Burt Shotton, Dodgers (Casey Stengel, Yankees)	46,127
10-51	Briggs Stadium Detroit	8-3 (N.L.)	Sal Maglie, Giants (Ed Lopat, Yankees)	Eddie Sawyer, Phillies (Casey Stengel, Yankees)	52,075
8-52	Shibe Park Philadelphia	3-2† (N.L.)	Bob Rush, Cubs (Bob Lemon, Indians)	Leo Durocher, Giants (Casey Stengel, Yankees)	32,785
14-53	Crosley Field Cincinnati	5-1 (N.L.)	Warren Spahn, Braves (Allie Reynolds, Yankees)	Chuck Dressen, Dodgers (Casey Stengel, Yankees)	30,846
13-54	Municipal Stadium Cleveland	11-9 (A.L.)	Dean Stone, Senators (Gene Conley, Braves)	Casey Stengel, Yankees (Walter Alston, Dodgers)	68,751
12-55	Milwaukee Co. Stadium Milwaukee	6-5‡ (N.L.)	Gene Conley, Braves (Frank Sullivan, Red Sox)	Leo Durocher, Giants (Al Lopez, Indians)	45,643
10-56	Griffith Stadium Washington	7-3 (N.L.)	Bob Friend, Pirates (Billy Pierce, White Sox)	Walter Alston, Dodgers (Casey Stengel, Yankees)	28,843
9-57	Busch Stadium St. Louis	6-5 (A.L.)	Jim Bunning, Tigers (Curt Simmons, Phillies)	Casey Stengel, Yankees (Walter Alston, Dodgers)	30,693
8-58	Memorial Stadium Baltimore	4-3 (A.L.)	Early Wynn, White Sox (Bob Friend, Pirates)	Casey Stengel, Yankees (Fred Haney, Braves)	48,829
7-59	Forbes Field Pittsburgh	5-4 (N.L.)	Johnny Antonelli, Giants (Whitey Ford, Yankees)	Fred Haney, Braves (Casey Stengel, Yankees)	35,277
3-59	Memorial Coliseum Los Angeles	5-3 (A.L.)	Jerry Walker, Orioles (Don Drysdale, Dodgers)	Casey Stengel, Yankees (Fred Haney, Braves)	55,105
11-60	Municipal Stadium Kansas City	5-3 (N.L.)	Bob Friend, Pirates (Bill Monbouquette, Red Sox)	Walter Alston, Dodgers (Al Lopez, White Sox)	30,619
13-60	Yankee Stadium New York	6-0 (N.L.)	Vernon Law, Pirates (Whitey Ford, Yankees)	Walter Alston, Dodgers (Al Lopez, White Sox)	38,362
11-61	Candlestick Park San Francisco	5-4§ (N.L.)	Stu Miller, Giants (Hoyt Wilhelm, Orioles)	Danny Murtaugh, Pirates (Paul Richards, Orioles)	44,115
31-61	Fenway Park Boston	1-1 (tie)		Paul Richards, Orioles (A.L.) Danny Murtaugh, Pirates (N.L.)	31,851
10-62	District of Col. Stad. Washington	3-1 (N.L.)	Juan Marichal, Giants (Camilo Pascual, Twins)	Fred Hutchinson, Reds (Ralph Houk, Yankees)	45,480
30-62	Wrigley Field Chicago	9-4 (A.L.)	Ray Herbert, White Sox (Art Mahaffey, Phillies)	Ralph Houk, Yankees (Fred Hutchinson, Reds)	38,359
9-63	Municipal Stadium Cleveland	5-3 (N.L.)	Larry Jackson, Cubs (Jim Bunning, Tigers)	Alvin Dark, Giants (Ralph Houk, Yankees)	44,160
7-64	Shea Stadium New York	7-4 (N.L.)	Juan Marichal, Giants (Dick Radatz, Red Sox)	Walter Alston, Dodgers (Al Lopez, White Sox)	50,850
13-65	Metropolitan Stadium Bloomington, Minn.	6-5 (N.L.)	Sandy Koufax, Dodgers (Sam McDowell, Indians)	Gene Mauch, Phillies (Al Lopez, White Sox)	46,706
12-66	Busch Stadium St. Louis	2-1§ (N.L.)	Gaylord Perry, Giants (Pete Richert, Senators)	Walter Alston, Dodgers (Sam Mele, Twins)	49,936
11-67	Anaheim Stadium Anaheim, Calif.	2-1∞ (N.L.)	Don Drysdale, Dodgers (Jim Hunter, Athletics)	Walter Alston, Dodgers (Hank Bauer, Orioles)	46,309
9-68	Astrodome Houston	1-0 (N.L.)	Don Drysdale, Dodgers (Luis Tiant, Indians)	Red Schoendienst, Cardinals (Dick Williams, Red Sox)	48,321

Date	Site	Score (Winner)	Winning pitcher (Losing pitcher)	Winning manager (Losing manager)	Att.
7-23-69	R.F.K. Stadium Washington	9-3 (N.L.)	Steve Carlton, Cardinals (Mel Stottlemyre, Yankees)	Red Schoendienst, Cardinals (Mayo Smith, Tigers)	45,259
7-14-70	Riverfront Stadium Cincinnati	5-4‡ (N.L.)	Claude Osteen, Dodgers (Clyde Wright, Angels)	Gil Hodges, Mets (Earl Weaver, Orioles)	51,838
7-13-71	Tiger Stadium Detroit	6-4 (A.L.)	Vida Blue, Athletics (Dock Ellis, Pirates)	Earl Weaver, Orioles (Sparky Anderson, Reds)	53,559
7-25-72	Atlanta Stadium Atlanta	4-3∞ (N.L.)	Tug McGraw, Mets (Dave McNally, Orioles)	Danny Murtaugh, Pirates (Earl Weaver, Orioles)	53,107
7-24-73	Royals Stadium Kansas City	7-1 (N.L.)	Rick Wise, Cardinals (Bert Blyleven, Twins)	Sparky Anderson, Reds (Dick Williams, Athletics)	40,849
7-23-74	Three Rivers Stadium Pittsburgh	7-2 (N.L.)	Ken Brett, Pirates (Luis Tiant, Red Sox)	Yogi Berra, Mets (Dick Williams, Athletics)	50,706
7-15-75	Milwaukee Co. Stadium Milwaukee	6-3 (N.L.)	Jon Matlack, Mets (Jim Hunter, Yankees)	Walter Alston, Dodgers (Alvin Dark, Athletics)	51,480
7-13-76	Veterans Stadium Philadelphia	7-1 (N.L)	Randy Jones, Padres (Mark Fidrych, Tigers)	Sparky Anderson, Reds (Darrell Johnson, Red Sox)	63,974
7-19-77	Yankee Stadium New York	7-5 (N.L.)	Don Sutton, Dodgers (Jim Palmer, Orioles)	Sparky Anderson, Reds (Billy Martin, Yankees)	56,683
7-11-78	San Diego Stadium San Diego	7-3 (N.L.)	Bruce Sutter, Cubs (Rich Gossage, Yankees)	Tommy Lasorda, Dodgers (Billy Martin, Yankees)	51,549
7-17-79	Kingdome Seattle	7-6 (N.L.)	Bruce Sutter, Cubs (Jim Kern, Rangers)	Tommy Lasorda, Dodgers (Bob Lemon, Yankees)	58,905
7-8-80	Dodger Stadium Los Angeles	4-2 (N.L.)	Jerry Reuss, Dodgers (Tommy John, Yankees)	Chuck Tanner, Pirates (Earl Weaver, Orioles)	56,088
8-9-81	Municipal Stadium Cleveland	5-4 (N.L.)	Vida Blue, Giants (Rollie Fingers, Brewers)	Dallas Green, Phillies (Jim Frey, Royals)	72,086
7-13-82	Olympic Stadium Montreal	4-1 (N.L.)	Steve Rogers, Expos (Dennis Eckersley, Red Sox)	Tommy Lasorda, Dodgers (Billy Martin, Athletics)	59,057
7-6-83	Comiskey Park Chicago	13-3 (A.L.)	Dave Stieb, Blue Jays (Mario Soto, Reds)	Harvey Kuenn, Brewers (Whitey Herzog, Cardinals)	43,801
7-10-84	Candlestick Park San Francisco	3-1 (N.L.)	Charlie Lea, Expos (Dave Stieb, Blue Jays)	Paul Owens, Phillies (Joe Altobelli, Orioles)	57,756
7-16-85	Metrodome Minneapolis	6-1 (N.L.)	LaMarr Hoyt, Padres (Jack Morris, Tigers)	Dick Williams, Padres (Sparky Anderson, Tigers)	54,960
7-15-86	Astrodome Houston	3-2 (A.L.)	Roger Clemens, Red Sox (Dwight Gooden, Mets)	Dick Howser, Royals (Whitey Herzog, Cardinals)	45,774
7-14-87	Oak.-Alameda Co. Col. Oakland	2-0▲ (N.L.)	Lee Smith, Cubs (Jay Howell, Athletics)	Dave Johnson, Mets (John McNamara, Red Sox)	49,671
7-12-88	Riverfront Stadium Cincinnati	2-1 (A.L.)	Frank Viola, Twins (Dwight Gooden, Mets)	Tom Kelly, Twins (Whitey Herzog, Cardinals)	55,837
7-11-89	Anaheim Stadium Anaheim, Calif.	5-3 (A.L.)	Nolan Ryan, Rangers (John Smoltz, Braves)	Tony La Russa, Athletics (Tommy Lasorda, Dodgers)	64,036
7-10-90	Wrigley Field Chicago	2-0 (A.L.)	Bret Saberhagen, Royals (Jeff Brantley, Giants)	Tony La Russa, Athletics (Roger Craig, Giants)	39,071
7-9-91	SkyDome Toronto	4-2 (A.L.)	Jimmy Key, Blue Jays (Dennis Martinez, Expos)	Tony La Russa, Athletics (Lou Piniella, Reds)	52,383
7-14-92	Jack Murphy Stadium San Diego	13-6 (A.L.)	Kevin Brown, Rangers (Tom Glavine, Braves)	Tom Kelly, Twins (Bobby Cox, Braves)	59,372
7-13-93	Oriole Park at Camden Yards, Baltimore	9-3 (A.L.)	Jack McDowell, White Sox (John Burkett, Giants)	Cito Gaston, Blue Jays (Bobby Cox, Braves)	48,147
7-12-94	Three Rivers Stadium Pittsburgh	8-7§ (N.L.)	Doug Jones, Phillies (Jason Bere, White Sox)	Jim Fregosi, Phillies (Cito Gaston, Blue Jays)	59,568
7-11-95	Ballpark in Arlington Arlington, Texas	3-2 (N.L.)	Heathcliff Slocumb, Phillies (Steve Ontiveros, A's)	Felipe Alou, Expos (Buck Showalter, Yankees)	50,920
7-9-96	Veterans Stadium Philadelphia	6-0 (N.L.)	John Smoltz, Braves (Charles Nagy, Indians)	Bobby Cox, Braves (Mike Hargrove, Indians)	62,670

*14 innings. †5 innings (rain). ‡12 innings. §10 innings. ∞15 innings. ▲13 innings.

AWARD WINNERS

THE SPORTING NEWS

MOST VALUABLE PLAYER

	AMERICAN LEAGUE					NATIONAL LEAGUE			
Year	Player	Team	Pos.	Points	Year	Player	Team	Pos.	Points
1929	Al Simmons	Philadelphia	OF	40	1929	No selection			
1930	Joe Cronin	Washington	SS	52	1930	Bill Terry	New York	1B	47
1931	Lou Gehrig	New York	1B	40	1931	Chuck Klein	Philadelphia	OF	40
1932	Jimmie Foxx	Philadelphia	1B	46	1932	Chuck Klein	Philadelphia	OF	46
1933	Jimmie Foxx	Philadelphia	1B	49	1933	Carl Hubbell	New York	P	64
1934	Lou Gehrig	New York	1B	51	1934	Dizzy Dean	St. Louis	P	57
1935	Hank Greenberg	Detroit	1B	64	1935	Arky Vaughan	Pittsburgh	SS	42
1936	Lou Gehrig	New York	1B	55	1936	Carl Hubbell	New York	P	61
1937	Charley Gehringer	Detroit	2B	78	1937	Joe Medwick	St. Louis	OF	70
1938	Jimmie Foxx	Boston	1B	304	1938	Ernie Lombardi	Cincinnati	C	229
1939	Joe DiMaggio	New York	OF	280	1939	Bucky Walters	Cincinnati	P	303
1940	Hank Greenberg	Detroit	OF	292	1940	Frank McCormick	Cincinnati	1B	274
1941	Joe DiMaggio	New York	OF	291	1941	Dolf Camilli	Brooklyn	1B	300
1942	Joe Gordon	New York	2B	270	1942	Mort Cooper	St. Louis	P	263
1943	Spud Chandler	New York	P	246	1943	Stan Musial	St. Louis	OF	267
1944	Bobby Doerr	Boston	2B		1944	Marty Marion	St. Louis	SS	
1945	Eddie Mayo	Detroit	2B		1945	Tommy Holmes	Boston	OF	

PLAYER AND PITCHER OF THE YEAR

	AMERICAN LEAGUE				NATIONAL LEAGUE		
Year	Player	Team	Pos.	Year	Player	Team	Pos.
1944	Bobby Doerr	Boston	2B	1944	Marty Marion	St. Louis	SS
	Hal Newhouser	Detroit	P		Bill Voiselle	New York	P
1945	Eddie Mayo	Detroit	2B	1945	Tommy Holmes	Boston	OF
	Hal Newhouser	Detroit	P		Hank Borowy	Chicago	P
1946	No selections			1946	No selections		
1947	No selections			1947	No selections		
1948	Lou Boudreau	Cleveland	SS	1948	Stan Musial	St. Louis	OF-1B
	Bob Lemon	Cleveland	P		Johnny Sain	Boston	P
1949	Ted Williams	Boston	OF	1949	Enos Slaughter	St. Louis	OF
	Ellis Kinder	Boston	P		Howard Pollet	St. Louis	P
1950	Phil Rizzuto	New York	SS	1950	Ralph Kiner	Pittsburgh	OF
	Bob Lemon	Cleveland	P		Jim Konstanty	Philadelphia	P
1951	Ferris Fain	Philadelphia	1B	1951	Stan Musial	St. Louis	OF
	Bob Feller	Cleveland	P		Preacher Roe	Brooklyn	P
1952	Luke Easter	Cleveland	1B	1952	Hank Sauer	Chicago	OF
	Bobby Shantz	Philadelphia	P		Robin Roberts	Philadelphia	P
1953	Al Rosen	Cleveland	3B	1953	Roy Campanella	Brooklyn	C
	Bob Porterfield	Washington	P		Warren Spahn	Milwaukee	P
1954	Bobby Avila	Cleveland	2B	1954	Willie Mays	New York	OF
	Bob Lemon	Cleveland	P		Johnny Antonelli	New York	P
1955	Al Kaline	Detroit	OF	1955	Duke Snider	Brooklyn	OF
	Whitey Ford	New York	P		Robin Roberts	Philadelphia	P
1956	Mickey Mantle	New York	OF	1956	Hank Aaron	Milwaukee	OF
	Billy Pierce	Chicago	P		Don Newcombe	Brooklyn	P
1957	Ted Williams	Boston	OF	1957	Stan Musial	St. Louis	1B
	Billy Pierce	Chicago	P		Warren Spahn	Milwaukee	P
1958	Jackie Jensen	Boston	OF	1958	Ernie Banks	Chicago	SS
	Bob Turley	New York	P		Warren Spahn	Milwaukee	P
1959	Nellie Fox	Chicago	2B	1959	Ernie Banks	Chicago	SS
	Early Wynn	Chicago	P		Sam Jones	San Francisco	P
1960	Roger Maris	New York	OF	1960	Dick Groat	Pittsburgh	SS
	Chuck Estrada	Baltimore	P		Vern Law	Pittsburgh	P
1961	Roger Maris	New York	OF	1961	Frank Robinson	Cincinnati	OF
	Whitey Ford	New York	P		Warren Spahn	Milwaukee	P
1962	Mickey Mantle	New York	OF	1962	Maury Wills	Los Angeles	SS
	Dick Donovan	Cleveland	P		Don Drysdale	Los Angeles	P
1963	Al Kaline	Detroit	OF	1963	Hank Aaron	Milwaukee	OF
	Whitey Ford	New York	P		Sandy Koufax	Los Angeles	P
1964	Brooks Robinson	Baltimore	3B	1964	Ken Boyer	St. Louis	3B
	Dean Chance	Los Angeles	P		Sandy Koufax	Los Angeles	P
1965	Tony Oliva	Minnesota	OF	1965	Willie Mays	San Francisco	OF
	Jim Grant	Minnesota	P		Sandy Koufax	Los Angeles	P
1966	Frank Robinson	Baltimore	OF	1966	Roberto Clemente	Pittsburgh	OF
	Jim Kaat	Minnesota	P		Sandy Koufax	Los Angeles	P
1967	Carl Yastrzemski	Boston	OF	1967	Orlando Cepeda	St. Louis	1B
	Jim Lonborg	Boston	P		Mike McCormick	San Francisco	P

HISTORY *Award winners*

Year	Player	Team	Pos.	Year	Player	Team	Pos.
1968—Ken Harrelson	Boston	OF		1968— Pete Rose	Cincinnati	OF	
Denny McLain	Detroit	P		Bob Gibson	St. Louis	P	
1969—Harmon Killebrew	Minnesota	1B-3B		1969— Willie McCovey	San Francisco	1B	
Denny McLain	Detroit	P		Tom Seaver	New York	P	
1970—Harmon Killebrew	Minnesota	3B		1970— Johnny Bench	Cincinnati	C	
Sam McDowell	Cleveland	P		Bob Gibson	St. Louis	P	
1971—Tony Oliva	Minnesota	OF		1971— Joe Torre	St. Louis	3B	
Vida Blue	Oakland	P		Ferguson Jenkins	Chicago	P	
1972—Dick Allen	Chicago	1B		1972— Billy Williams	Chicago	OF	
Wilbur Wood	Chicago	P		Steve Carlton	Philadelphia	P	
1973—Reggie Jackson	Oakland	OF		1973— Bobby Bonds	San Francisco	OF	
Jim Palmer	Baltimore	P		Ron Bryant	San Francisco	P	
1974—Jeff Burroughs	Texas	OF		1974— Lou Brock	St. Louis	OF	
Jim Hunter	Oakland	P		Mike Marshall	Los Angeles	P	
1975—Fred Lynn	Boston	OF		1975— Joe Morgan	Cincinnati	2B	
Jim Palmer	Baltimore	P		Tom Seaver	New York	P	
1976—Thurman Munson	New York	C		1976— George Foster	Cincinnati	OF	
Jim Palmer	Baltimore	P		Randy Jones	San Diego	P	
1977—Rod Carew	Minnesota	1B		1977— George Foster	Cincinnati	OF	
Nolan Ryan	California	P		Steve Carlton	Philadelphia	P	
1978—Jim Rice	Boston	OF		1978— Dave Parker	Pittsburgh	OF	
Ron Guidry	New York	P		Vida Blue	San Francisco	P	
1979—Don Baylor	California	OF		1979— Keith Hernandez	St. Louis	1B	
Mike Flanagan	Baltimore	P		Joe Niekro	Houston	P	
1980—George Brett	Kansas City	3B		1980— Mike Schmidt	Philadelphia	3B	
Steve Stone	Baltimore	P		Steve Carlton	Philadelphia	P	
1981—Tony Armas	Oakland	OF		1981— Andre Dawson	Montreal	OF	
Jack Morris	Detroit	P		Fernando Valenzuela	Los Angeles	P	
1982—Robin Yount	Milwaukee	SS		1982— Dale Murphy	Atlanta	OF	
Dave Stieb	Toronto	P		Steve Carlton	Philadelphia	P	
1983—Cal Ripken Jr.	Baltimore	SS		1983— Dale Murphy	Atlanta	OF	
LaMarr Hoyt	Chicago	P		John Denny	Philadelphia	P	
1984—Don Mattingly	New York	1B		1984— Ryne Sandberg	Chicago	2B	
Willie Hernandez	Detroit	P		Rick Sutcliffe	Chicago	P	
1985—Don Mattingly	New York	1B		1985— Willie McGee	St. Louis	OF	
Bret Saberhagen	Kansas City	P		Dwight Gooden	New York	P	
1986—Don Mattingly	New York	1B		1986— Mike Schmidt	Philadelphia	3B	
Roger Clemens	Boston	P		Mike Scott	Houston	P	
1987—George Bell	Toronto	OF		1987— Andre Dawson	Chicago	OF	
Jimmy Key	Toronto	P		Rick Sutcliffe	Chicago	P	
1988—Jose Canseco	Oakland	OF		1988— Andy Van Slyke	Pittsburgh	OF	
Frank Viola	Minnesota	P		Orel Hershiser	Los Angeles	P	
1989—Ruben Sierra	Texas	OF		1989— Kevin Mitchell	San Francisco	OF	
Bret Saberhagen	Kansas City	P		Mark Davis	San Diego	P	
1990—Cecil Fielder	Detroit	1B		1990— Barry Bonds	Pittsburgh	OF	
Bob Welch	Oakland	P		Doug Drabek	Pittsburgh	P	
1991—Cal Ripken Jr.	Baltimore	SS		1991— Barry Bonds	Pittsburgh	OF	
Roger Clemens	Boston	P		Tom Glavine	Atlanta	P	

PITCHER OF THE YEAR

	AMERICAN LEAGUE			NATIONAL LEAGUE	
Year	Pitcher	Team	Year	Pitcher	Team
1992—Dennis Eckersley	Oakland		1992— Greg Maddux	Chicago	
1993—Jack McDowell	Chicago		1993— Greg Maddux	Atlanta	
1994—Jimmy Key	New York		1994— Greg Maddux	Atlanta	
1995—Randy Johnson	Seattle		1995— Greg Maddux	Atlanta	
1996—Pat Hentgen	Toronto		1996— John Smoltz	Atlanta	

ROOKIE OF THE YEAR

1946—Combined selection—Del Ennis, Philadelphia N.L., OF
1947—Combined selection—Jackie Robinson, Brooklyn N.L., 1B
1948—Combined selection—Richie Ashburn, Philadelphia N.L., OF

	AMERICAN LEAGUE			NATIONAL LEAGUE		
Year	Player	Team	Pos.	Year	Player	Team	Pos.
1949—Roy Sievers	St. Louis	OF		1949—Don Newcombe	Brooklyn	P	
1950—Whitey Ford	New York	P		1950—Combined A.L.-N.L. selection			
1951—Minnie Minoso	Chicago	OF		1951— Willie Mays	New York	OF	
1952—Clint Courtney	St. Louis	C		1952— Joe Black	Brooklyn	P	
1953—Harvey Kuenn	Detroit	SS		1953— Jim Gilliam	Brooklyn	2B	
1954—Bob Grim	New York	P		1954— Wally Moon	St. Louis	OF	
1955—Herb Score	Cleveland	P		1955— Bill Virdon	St. Louis	OF	
1956—Luis Aparicio	Chicago	SS		1956— Frank Robinson	Cincinnati	OF	
1957—Tony Kubek	New York	IF-OF		1957— Ed Bouchee	Philadelphia	1B	
(No pitcher named)				Jack Sanford	Philadelphia	P	

ear	Player	Team	Pos.	Year	Player	Team	Pos.
958—	Albie Pearson	Washington	OF	1958—	Orlando Cepeda	San Francisco	1B
	Ryne Duren	New York	P		Carlton Willey	Milwaukee	P
959—	Bob Allison	Washington	OF	1959—	Willie McCovey	San Francisco	1B
960—	Ron Hansen	Baltimore	SS	1960—	Frank Howard	Los Angeles	OF
961—	Dick Howser	Kansas City	SS	1961—	Billy Williams	Chicago	OF
	Don Schwall	Boston	P		Ken Hunt	Cincinnati	P
962—	Tom Tresh	New York	OF-SS	1962—	Ken Hubbs	Chicago	2B
963—	Pete Ward	Chicago	3B	1963—	Pete Rose	Cincinnati	2B
	Gary Peters	Chicago	P		Ray Culp	Philadelphia	P
964—	Tony Oliva	Minnesota	OF	1964—	Dick Allen	Philadelphia	3B
	Wally Bunker	Baltimore	P		Billy McCool	Cincinnati	P
965—	Curt Blefary	Baltimore	OF	1965—	Joe Morgan	Houston	2B
	Marcelino Lopez	California	P		Frank Linzy	San Francisco	P
966—	Tommie Agee	Chicago	OF	1966—	Tommy Helms	Cincinnati	3B
	Jim Nash	Kansas City	P		Don Sutton	Los Angeles	P
967—	Rod Carew	Minnesota	2B	1967—	Lee May	Cincinnati	1B
	Tom Phoebus	Baltimore	P		Dick Hughes	St. Louis	P
968—	Del Unser	Washington	OF	1968—	Johnny Bench	Cincinnati	C
	Stan Bahnsen	New York	P		Jerry Koosman	New York	P
969—	Carlos May	Chicago	OF	1969—	Coco Laboy	Montreal	3B
	Mike Nagy	Boston	P		Tom Griffin	Houston	P
970—	Roy Foster	Cleveland	OF	1970—	Bernie Carbo	Cincinnati	OF
	Bert Blyleven	Minnesota	P		Carl Morton	Montreal	P
971—	Chris Chambliss	Cleveland	1B	1971—	Earl Williams	Atlanta	C
	Bill Parsons	Milwaukee	P		Reggie Cleveland	St. Louis	P
972—	Carlton Fisk	Boston	C	1972—	Dave Rader	San Francisco	C
	Dick Tidrow	Cleveland	P		Jon Matlack	New York	P
973—	Al Bumbry	Baltimore	OF	1973—	Gary Matthews	San Francisco	OF
	Steve Busby	Kansas City	P		Steve Rogers	Montreal	P
974—	Mike Hargrove	Texas	1B	1974—	Greg Gross	Houston	OF
	Frank Tanana	California	P		John D'Acquisto	San Francisco	P
975—	Fred Lynn	Boston	OF	1975—	Gary Carter	Montreal	OF-C
	Dennis Eckersley	Cleveland	P		John Montefusco	San Francisco	P
976—	Butch Wynegar	Minnesota	C	1976—	Larry Herndon	San Francisco	OF
	Mark Fidrych	Detroit	P		Butch Metzger	San Diego	P
977—	Mitchell Page	Oakland	OF	1977—	Andre Dawson	Montreal	OF
	Dave Rozema	Detroit	P		Bob Owchinko	San Diego	P
978—	Paul Molitor	Milwaukee	2B	1978—	Bob Horner	Atlanta	3B
	Rich Gale	Kansas City	P		Don Robinson	Pittsburgh	P
979—	Pat Putnam	Texas	1B	1979—	Jeff Leonard	Houston	OF
	Mark Clear	California	P		Rick Sutcliffe	Los Angeles	P
980—	Joe Charboneau	Cleveland	OF	1980—	Lonnie Smith	Philadelphia	OF
	Britt Burns	Chicago	P		Bill Gullickson	Montreal	P
981—	Rich Gedman	Boston	C	1981—	Tim Raines	Montreal	OF
	Dave Righetti	New York	P		Fernando Valenzuela	Los Angeles	P
982—	Cal Ripken Jr.	Baltimore	SS-3B	1982—	Johnny Ray	Pittsburgh	2B
	Ed Vande Berg	Seattle	P		Steve Bedrosian	Atlanta	P
983—	Ron Kittle	Chicago	OF	1983—	Darryl Strawberry	New York	OF
	Mike Boddicker	Baltimore	P		Craig McMurtry	Atlanta	P
984—	Alvin Davis	Seattle	1B	1984—	Juan Samuel	Philadelphia	2B
	Mark Langston	Seattle	P		Dwight Gooden	New York	P
985	Ozzie Gullen	Chicago	SS	1985—	Vince Coleman	St. Louis	OF
	Teddy Higuera	Milwaukee	P		Tom Browning	Cincinnati	P
986—	Jose Canseco	Oakland	OF	1986—	Robby Thompson	San Francisco	2B
	Mark Eichhorn	Toronto	P		Todd Worrell	St. Louis	P
987—	Mark McGwire	Oakland	1B	1987—	Benito Santiago	San Diego	C
	Mike Henneman	Detroit	P		Mike Dunne	Pittsburgh	P
988—	Walt Weiss	Oakland	SS	1988—	Mark Grace	Chicago	1B
	Bryan Harvey	California	P		Tim Belcher	Los Angeles	P
989—	Craig Worthington	Baltimore	3B	1989—	Jerome Walton	Chicago	OF
	Tom Gordon	Kansas City	P		Andy Benes	San Diego	P
990—	Sandy Alomar Jr.	Cleveland	C	1990—	David Justice	Atlanta	OF
	Kevin Appier	Kansas City	P		Mike Harkey	Chicago	P
991—	Chuck Knoblauch	Minnesota	2B	1991—	Jeff Bagwell	Houston	1B
	Juan Guzman	Toronto	P		Al Osuna	Houston	P
992—	Pat Listach	Milwaukee	SS	1992—	Eric Karros	Los Angeles	1B
	Cal Eldred	Milwaukee	P		Tim Wakefield	Pittsburgh	P
993—	Tim Salmon	California	OF	1993—	Mike Piazza	Los Angeles	C
	Aaron Sele	Boston	P		Kirk Rueter	Montreal	P
994—	Bob Hamelin	Kansas City	DH	1994—	Raul Mondesi	Los Angeles	OF
	Brian Anderson	California	P		Steve Trachsel	Chicago	P
995—	Garret Anderson	California	OF	1995—	Chipper Jones	Atlanta	3B
	Julian Tavarez	Cleveland	P		Hideo Nomo	Los Angeles	P
996—	Derek Jeter	New York	SS	1996—	Jason Kendall	Pittsburgh	C
	James Baldwin	Chicago	P		Alan Benes	St. Louis	P

HISTORY *Award winners*

FIREMAN OF THE YEAR

AMERICAN LEAGUE

Year	Pitcher	Team
1960	Mike Fornieles	Boston
1961	Luis Arroyo	New York
1962	Dick Radatz	Boston
1963	Stu Miller	Baltimore
1964	Dick Radatz	Boston
1965	Eddie Fisher	Chicago
1966	Jack Aker	Kansas City
1967	Minnie Rojas	California
1968	Wilbur Wood	Chicago
1969	Ron Perranoski	Minnesota
1970	Ron Perranoski	Minnesota
1971	Ken Sanders	Milwaukee
1972	Sparky Lyle	New York
1973	John Hiller	Detroit
1974	Terry Forster	Chicago
1975	Rich Gossage	Chicago
1976	Bill Campbell	Minnesota
1977	Bill Campbell	Boston
1978	Rich Gossage	New York
1979	Mike Marshall	Minnesota
	Jim Kern	Texas
1980	Dan Quisenberry	Kansas City
1981	Rollie Fingers	Milwaukee
1982	Dan Quisenberry	Kansas City
1983	Dan Quisenberry	Kansas City
1984	Dan Quisenberry	Kansas City
1985	Dan Quisenberry	Kansas City
1986	Dave Righetti	New York
1987	Dave Righetti	New York
	Jeff Reardon	Minnesota
1988	Dennis Eckersley	Oakland
1989	Jeff Russell	Texas
1990	Bobby Thigpen	Chicago
1991	Dennis Eckersley	Oakland
	Bryan Harvey	California
1992	Dennis Eckersley	Oakland
1993	Jeff Montgomery	Kansas City
1994	Lee Smith	Baltimore
1995	Jose Mesa	Cleveland
1996	John Wetteland	New York

NATIONAL LEAGUE

Year	Pitcher	Team
1960	Lindy McDaniel	St. Louis
1961	Stu Miller	San Francisco
1962	Roy Face	Pittsburgh
1963	Lindy McDaniel	Chicago
1964	Al McBean	Pittsburgh
1965	Ted Abernathy	Chicago
1966	Phil Regan	Los Angeles
1967	Ted Abernathy	Cincinnati
1968	Phil Regan	L.A.-Chicago
1969	Wayne Granger	Cincinnati
1970	Wayne Granger	Cincinnati
1971	Dave Giusti	Pittsburgh
1972	Clay Carroll	Cincinnati
1973	Mike Marshall	Montreal
1974	Mike Marshall	Los Angeles
1975	Al Hrabosky	St. Louis
1976	Rawly Eastwick	Cincinnati
1977	Rollie Fingers	San Diego
1978	Rollie Fingers	San Diego
1979	Bruce Sutter	Chicago
1980	Rollie Fingers	San Diego
	Tom Hume	Cincinnati
1981	Bruce Sutter	St. Louis
1982	Bruce Sutter	St. Louis
1983	Al Holland	Philadelphia
	Lee Smith	Chicago
1984	Bruce Sutter	St. Louis
1985	Jeff Reardon	Montreal
1986	Todd Worrell	St. Louis
1987	Steve Bedrosian	Philadelphia
1988	John Franco	Cincinnati
1989	Mark Davis	San Diego
1990	John Franco	New York
1991	Lee Smith	St. Louis
1992	Doug Jones	Houston
	Lee Smith	St. Louis
1993	Randy Myers	Chicago
1994	John Franco	New York
1995	Randy Myers	Chicago
1996	Trevor Hoffman	San Diego

MAJOR LEAGUE PLAYER OF THE YEAR

Year	Player	Team	Year	Player	Team	Year	Player	Team
1936	Carl Hubbell	New York N.L.	1957	Ted Williams	Boston A.L.	1977	Rod Carew	Minnesota A.L.
1937	Johnny Allen	Cleveland A.L.	1958	Bob Turley	New York A.L.	1978	Ron Guidry	New York A.L.
1938	Johnny Vander Meer	Cincinnati N.L.	1959	Early Wynn	Chicago A.L.	1979	Willie Stargell	Pittsburgh N.L.
1939	Joe DiMaggio	New York A.L.	1960	Bill Mazeroski	Pittsburgh N.L.	1980	George Brett	Kansas City A.L.
1940	Bob Feller	Cleveland A.L.	1961	Roger Maris	New York A.L.	1981	Fernando Valenzuela	Los Angeles N.L.
1941	Ted Williams	Boston A.L.	1962	Maury Wills	Los Angeles N.L.	1982	Robin Yount	Milwaukee A.L.
1942	Ted Williams	Boston A.L.		Don Drysdale	Los Angeles N.L.	1983	Cal Ripken Jr.	Baltimore A.L.
1943	Spud Chandler	New York A.L.	1963	Sandy Koufax	Los Angeles N.L.	1984	Ryne Sandberg	Chicago N.L.
1944	Marty Marion	St. Louis N.L.	1964	Ken Boyer	St. Louis N.L.	1985	Don Mattingly	New York A.L.
1945	Hal Newhouser	Detroit A.L.	1965	Sandy Koufax	Los Angeles N.L.	1986	Roger Clemens	Boston A.L.
1946	Stan Musial	St. Louis N.L.	1966	Frank Robinson	Baltimore A.L.	1987	George Bell	Toronto A.L.
1947	Ted Williams	Boston A.L.	1967	Carl Yastrzemski	Boston A.L.	1988	Orel Hershiser	Los Angeles N.L.
1948	Lou Boudreau	Cleveland A.L.	1968	Denny McLain	Detroit A.L.	1989	Kevin Mitchell	San Francisco N.L.
1949	Ted Williams	Boston A.L.	1969	Willie McCovey	San Francisco N.L.	1990	Barry Bonds	Pittsburgh N.L.
1950	Phil Rizzuto	New York A.L.	1970	Johnny Bench	Cincinnati N.L.	1991	Cal Ripken Jr.	Baltimore A.L.
1951	Stan Musial	St. Louis N.L.	1971	Joe Torre	St. Louis N.L.	1992	Gary Sheffield	San Diego N.L.
1952	Robin Roberts	Philadelphia N.L.	1972	Billy Williams	Chicago N.L.	1993	Frank Thomas	Chicago A.L.
1953	Al Rosen	Cleveland A.L.	1973	Reggie Jackson	Oakland A.L.	1994	Jeff Bagwell	Houston N.L.
1954	Willie Mays	New York N.L.	1974	Lou Brock	St. Louis N.L.	1995	Albert Belle	Cleveland A.L.
1955	Duke Snider	Brooklyn N.L.	1975	Joe Morgan	Cincinnati N.L.	1996	Alex Rodriguez	Seattle A.L.
1956	Mickey Mantle	New York A.L.	1976	Joe Morgan	Cincinnati N.L.			

MAJOR LEAGUE MANAGER OF THE YEAR

Year	Manager	Team	Year	Manager	Team	Year	Manager	Team
1936	Joe McCarthy	New York A.L.	1940	Bill McKechnie	Cincinnati N.L.	1944	Luke Sewell	St. Louis A.L.
1937	Bill McKechnie	Boston N.L.	1941	Billy Southworth	St. Louis N.L.	1945	Ossie Bluege	Washington A.L.
1938	Joe McCarthy	New York A.L.	1942	Billy Southworth	St. Louis N.L.	1946	Eddie Dyer	St. Louis N.L.
1939	Leo Durocher	Brooklyn N.L.	1943	Joe McCarthy	New York A.L.	1947	Bucky Harris	New York A.L.

Year	Manager	Team	Year	Manager	Team	Year	Manager	Team
1948	Bill Meyer	Pittsburgh N.L.	1969	Gil Hodges	New York N.L.	1988	Tony La Russa	Oakland A.L.
1949	Casey Stengel	New York A.L.	1970	Danny Murtaugh	Pittsburgh N.L.		Tom Lasorda	L.A. N.L. (tie)
1950	Red Rolfe	Detroit A.L.	1971	Charlie Fox	San Francisco N.L.		Jim Leyland	Pit. N.L. (tie)
1951	Leo Durocher	New York N.L.	1972	Chuck Tanner	Chicago A.L.	1989	Frank Robinson	Baltimore A.L.
1952	Eddie Stanky	St. Louis N.L.	1973	Gene Mauch	Montreal N.L.		Don Zimmer	Chicago N.L.
1953	Casey Stengel	New York A.L.	1974	Bill Virdon	New York A.L.	1990	Jeff Torborg	Chicago A.L.
1954	Leo Durocher	New York N.L.	1975	Darrell Johnson	Boston A.L.		Jim Leyland	Pittsburgh N.L.
1955	Walter Alston	Brooklyn N.L.	1976	Danny Ozark	Philadelphia N.L.	1991	Tom Kelly	Minnesota A.L.
1956	Birdie Tebbetts	Cincinnati N.L.	1977	Earl Weaver	Baltimore A.L.		Bobby Cox	Atlanta N.L.
1957	Fred Hutchinson	St. Louis N.L.	1978	George Bamberger	Milwaukee A.L.	1992	Tony La Russa	Oakland A.L.
1958	Casey Stengel	New York A.L.	1979	Earl Weaver	Baltimore A.L.		Jim Leyland	Pittsburgh N.L.
1959	Walter A.L.ston	Los Angeles N.L.	1980	Bill Virdon	Houston N.L.	1993	Johnny Oates	Baltimore A.L.
1960	Danny Murtaugh	Pittsburgh N.L.	1981	Billy Martin	Oakland A.L.		Bobby Cox	Atlanta N.L.
1961	Ralph Houk	New York A.L.	1982	Whitey Herzog	St. Louis N.L.	1994	Buck Showalter	New York A.L.
1962	Bill Rigney	Los Angeles A.L.	1983	Tony La Russa	Chicago A.L.		Felipe Alou	Montreal N.L.
1963	Walter Alston	Los Angeles N.L.	1984	Jim Frey	Chicago N.L.	1995	Mike Hargrove	Cleveland A.L.
1964	Johnny Keane	St. Louis N.L.	1985	Bobby Cox	Toronto A.L.		Don Baylor	Colorado N.L.
1965	Sam Mele	Minnesota A.L.	1986	John McNamara	Boston A.L.	1996	Johnny Oates	Texas A.L.
1966	Hank Bauer	Baltimore A.L.		Hal Lanier	Houston N.L.		Bruce Bochy	San Diego N.L.
1967	Dick Williams	Boston A.L.	1987	Sparky Anderson	Detroit A.L.			
1968	Mayo Smith	Detroit A.L.		Buck Rodgers	Montreal N.L.			

MAJOR LEAGUE EXECUTIVE OF THE YEAR

Year	Executive	Team	Year	Executive	Team	Year	Executive	Team
1936	Branch Rickey	St. Louis N.L.	1957	Frank Lane	St. Louis N.L.	1978	Spec Richardson	San Francisco N.L.
1937	Ed Barrow	New York A.L.	1958	Joe Brown	Pittsburgh N.L.	1979	Hank Peters	Baltimore A.L.
1938	Warren Giles	Cincinnati N.L.	1959	Buzzie Bavasi	L.A. N.L.	1980	Tal Smith	Houston N.L.
1939	Larry MacPhail	Brooklyn N.L.	1960	George Weiss	New York A.L.	1981	John McHale	Montreal N.L.
1940	Walter Briggs Sr.	Detroit A.L.	1961	Dan Topping	New York A.L.	1982	Harry Dalton	Milwaukee A.L.
1941	Ed Barrow	New York A.L.	1962	Fred Haney	Los Angeles A.L.	1983	Hank Peters	Baltimore A.L.
1942	Branch Rickey	St. Louis N.L.	1963	Bing Devine	St. Louis N.L.	1984	Dallas Green	Chicago N.L.
1943	Clark Griffith	Washington A.L.	1964	Bing Devine	St. Louis N.L.	1985	John Schuerholz	Kansas City A.L.
1944	Billy DeWitt	St. Louis A.L.	1965	Cal Griffith	Minnesota A.L.	1986	Frank Cashen	New York N.L.
1945	Phil Wrigley	Chicago N.L.	1966	Lee MacPhail	Commissioner's Office	1987	Al Rosen	San Francisco N.L.
1946	Tom Yawkey	Boston A.L.	1967	Dick O'Connell	Boston A.L.	1988	Fred Claire	Los Angeles N.L.
1947	Branch Rickey	Brooklyn N.L.	1968	Jim Campbell	Detroit A.L.	1989	Roland Hemond	Baltimore A.L.
1948	Bill Veeck	Cleveland A.L.	1969	John Murphy	New York N.L.	1990	Bob Quinn	Cincinnati N.L.
1949	Bob Carpenter	Philadelphia N.L.	1970	Harry Dalton	Baltimore A.L.	1991	Andy MacPhail	Minnesota A.L.
1950	George Weiss	New York A.L.	1971	Cedric Tallis	Kansas City A.L.	1992	Dan Duquette	Montreal N.L.
1951	George Weiss	New York A.L.	1972	Roland Hemond	Chicago A.L.	1993	Lee Thomas	Philadelphia N.L.
1952	George Weiss	New York A.L.	1973	Bob Howsam	Cincinnati N.L.	1994	John Hart	Cleveland A.L.
1953	Lou Perini	Milwaukee N.L.	1974	Gabe Paul	New York A.L.	1995	John Hart	Cleveland A.L.
1954	Horace Stoneham	New York N.L.	1975	Dick O'Connell	Boston A.L.	1996	Doug Melvin	Texas A.L.
1955	Walter O'Malley	Brooklyn N.L.	1976	Joe Burke	Kansas City A.L.			
1956	Gabe Paul	Cincinnati N.L.	1977	Bill Veeck	Chicago A.L.			

GOLD GLOVE TEAMS

1957
MAJORS
P— Bobby Shantz, New York A.L.
C— Sherm Lollar, Chicago A.L.
1B— Gil Hodges, Brooklyn N.L.
2B— Nellie Fox, Chicago A.L.
3B— Frank Malzone, Boston A.L.
SS— Roy McMillan, Cincinnati N.L.
OF— Minnie Minoso, Chicago A.L.
OF— Willie Mays, New York N.L.
OF— Al Kaline, Detroit A.L.

1958
AMERICAN LEAGUE
P— Bobby Shantz, New York
C— Sherm Lollar, Chicago
1B— Vic Power, Cleveland
2B— Frank Bolling, Detroit
3B— Frank Malzone, Boston
SS— Luis Aparicio, Chicago
OF— Norm Siebern, New York
OF— Jimmy Piersall, Boston
OF— Al Kaline, Detroit

NATIONAL LEAGUE
P— Harvey Haddix, Cincinnati
C— Del Crandall, Milwaukee
1B— Gil Hodges, Los Angeles
2B— Bill Mazeroski, Pittsburgh
3B— Ken Boyer, St. Louis
SS— Roy McMillan, Cincinnati
OF— Frank Robinson, Cincinnati

OF— Willie Mays, San Francisco
OF— Hank Aaron, Milwaukee

1959
AMERICAN LEAGUE
P— Bobby Shantz, New York
C— Sherm Lollar, Chicago
1B— Vic Power, Cleveland
2B— Nellie Fox, Chicago
3B— Frank Malzone, Boston
SS— Luis Aparicio, Chicago
OF— Minnie Minoso, Cleveland
OF— Al Kaline, Detroit
OF— Jackie Jensen, Boston

NATIONAL LEAGUE
P— Harvey Haddix, Pittsburgh
C— Del Crandall, Milwaukee
1B— Gil Hodges, Los Angeles
2B— Charley Neal, Los Angeles
3B— Ken Boyer, St. Louis
SS— Roy McMillan, Cincinnati
OF— Jackie Brandt, San Francisco
OF— Willie Mays, San Francisco
OF— Hank Aaron, Milwaukee

1960
AMERICAN LEAGUE
P— Bobby Shantz, New York
C— Earl Battey, Washington
1B— Vic Power, Cleveland
2B— Nellie Fox, Chicago
3B— Brooks Robinson, Baltimore

SS— Luis Aparicio, Chicago
OF— Minnie Minoso, Chicago
OF— Jim Landis, Chicago
OF— Roger Maris, New York

NATIONAL LEAGUE
P— Harvey Haddix, Pittsburgh
C— Del Crandall, Milwaukee
1B— Bill White, St. Louis
2B— Bill Mazeroski, Pittsburgh
3B— Ken Boyer, St. Louis
SS— Ernie Banks, Chicago
OF— Wally Moon, Los Angeles
OF— Willie Mays, San Francisco
OF— Hank Aaron, Milwaukee

1961
AMERICAN LEAGUE
P— Frank Lary, Detroit
C— Earl Battey, Chicago
1B— Vic Power, Cleveland
2B— Bobby Richardson, New York
3B— Brooks Robinson, Baltimore
SS— Luis Aparicio, Chicago
OF— Al Kaline, Detroit
OF— Jimmy Piersall, Cleveland
OF— Jim Landis, Chicago

NATIONAL LEAGUE
P— Bobby Shantz, Pittsburgh
C— John Roseboro, Los Angeles
1B— Bill White, St. Louis
2B— Bill Mazeroski, Pittsburgh

3B— Ken Boyer, St. Louis
SS— Maury Wills, Los Angeles
OF— Willie Mays, San Francisco
OF— Roberto Clemente, Pittsburgh
OF— Vada Pinson, Cincinnati

1962
AMERICAN LEAGUE
P— Jim Kaat, Minnesota
C— Earl Battey, Minnesota
1B— Vic Power, Minnesota
2B— Bobby Richardson, New York
3B— Brooks Robinson, Baltimore
SS— Luis Aparicio, Chicago
OF— Jim Landis, Chicago
OF— Mickey Mantle, New York
OF— Al Kaline, Detroit

NATIONAL LEAGUE
P— Bobby Shantz, St. Louis
C— Del Crandall, Milwaukee
1B— Bill White, St. Louis
2B— Ken Hubbs, Chicago
3B— Jim Davenport, San Francisco
SS— Maury Wills, Los Angeles
OF— Willie Mays, San Francisco
OF— Roberto Clemente, Pittsburgh
OF— Bill Virdon, Pittsburgh

1963
AMERICAN LEAGUE
P— Jim Kaat, Minnesota
C— Elston Howard, New York
1B— Vic Power, Minnesota
2B— Bobby Richardson, New York
3B— Brooks Robinson, Baltimore
SS— Zoilo Versalles, Minnesota
OF— Al Kaline, Detroit
OF— Carl Yastrzemski, Boston
OF— Jim Landis, Chicago

NATIONAL LEAGUE
P— Bobby Shantz, St. Louis
C— Johnny Edwards, Cincinnati
1B— Bill White, St. Louis
2B— Bill Mazeroski, Pittsburgh
3B— Ken Boyer, St. Louis
SS— Bobby Wine, Philadelphia
OF— Willie Mays, San Francisco
OF— Roberto Clemente, Pittsburgh
OF— Curt Flood, St. Louis

1964
AMERICAN LEAGUE
P— Jim Kaat, Minnesota
C— Elston Howard, New York
1B— Vic Power, Los Angeles
2B— Bobby Richardson, New York
3B— Brooks Robinson, Baltimore
SS— Luis Aparicio, Baltimore
OF— Al Kaline, Detroit
OF— Jim Landis, Chicago
OF— Vic Davalillo, Cleveland

NATIONAL LEAGUE
P— Bobby Shantz, Philadelphia
C— Johnny Edwards, Cincinnati
1B— Bill White, St. Louis
2B— Bill Mazeroski, Pittsburgh
3B— Ron Santo, Chicago
SS— Ruben Amaro, Philadelphia
OF— Willie Mays, San Francisco
OF— Roberto Clemente, Pittsburgh
OF— Curt Flood, St. Louis

1965
AMERICAN LEAGUE
P— Jim Kaat, Minnesota
C— Bill Freehan, Detroit
1B— Joe Pepitone, New York
2B— Bobby Richardson, New York
3B— Brooks Robinson, Baltimore
SS— Zoilo Versalles, Minnesota
OF— Al Kaline, Detroit

OF— Tom Tresh, New York
OF— Carl Yastrzemski, Boston

NATIONAL LEAGUE
P— Bob Gibson, St. Louis
C— Joe Torre, Atlanta
1B— Bill White, St. Louis
2B— Bill Mazeroski, Pittsburgh
3B— Ron Santo, Chicago
SS— Leo Cardenas, Cincinnati
OF— Willie Mays, San Francisco
OF— Roberto Clemente, Pittsburgh
OF— Curt Flood, St. Louis

1966
AMERICAN LEAGUE
P— Jim Kaat, Minnesota
C— Bill Freehan, Detroit
1B— Joe Pepitone, New York
2B— Bobby Knoop, California
3B— Brooks Robinson, Baltimore
SS— Luis Aparicio, Baltimore
OF— Al Kaline, Detroit
OF— Tommie Agee, Chicago
OF— Tony Oliva, Minnesota

NATIONAL LEAGUE
P— Bob Gibson, St. Louis
C— John Roseboro, Los Angeles
1B— Bill White, Philadelphia
2B— Bill Mazeroski, Pittsburgh
3B— Ron Santo, Chicago
SS— Gene Alley, Pittsburgh
OF— Willie Mays, San Francisco
OF— Curt Flood, St. Louis
OF— Roberto Clemente, Pittsburgh

1967
AMERICAN LEAGUE
P— Jim Kaat, Minnesota
C— Bill Freehan, Detroit
1B— George Scott, Boston
2B— Bobby Knoop, California
3B— Brooks Robinson, Baltimore
SS— Jim Fregosi, California
OF— Carl Yastrzemski, Boston
OF— Paul Blair, Baltimore
OF— Al Kaline, Detroit

NATIONAL LEAGUE
P— Bob Gibson, St. Louis
C— Randy Hundley, Chicago
1B— Wes Parker, Los Angeles
2B— Bill Mazeroski, Pittsburgh
3B— Ron Santo, Chicago
SS— Gene Alley, Pittsburgh
OF— Roberto Clemente, Pittsburgh
OF— Curt Flood, St. Louis
OF— Willie Mays, San Francisco

1968
AMERICAN LEAGUE
P— Jim Kaat, Minnesota
C— Bill Freehan, Detroit
1B— George Scott, Boston
2B— Bobby Knoop, California
3B— Brooks Robinson, Baltimore
SS— Luis Aparicio, Chicago
OF— Mickey Stanley, Detroit
OF— Carl Yastrzemski, Boston
OF— Reggie Smith, Boston

NATIONAL LEAGUE
P— Bob Gibson, St. Louis
C— Johnny Bench, Cincinnati
1B— Wes Parker, Los Angeles
2B— Glenn Beckert, Chicago
3B— Ron Santo, Chicago
SS— Dal Maxvill, St. Louis
OF— Willie Mays, San Francisco
OF— Roberto Clemente, Pittsburgh
OF— Curt Flood, St. Louis

1969
AMERICAN LEAGUE
P— Jim Kaat, Minnesota
C— Bill Freehan, Detroit
1B— Joe Pepitone, New York
2B— Dave Johnson, Baltimore
3B— Brooks Robinson, Baltimore
SS— Mark Belanger, Baltimore
OF— Paul Blair, Baltimore
OF— Mickey Stanley, Detroit
OF— Carl Yastrzemski, Boston

NATIONAL LEAGUE
P— Bob Gibson, St. Louis
C— Johnny Bench, Cincinnati
1B— Wes Parker, Los Angeles
2B— Felix Millan, Atlanta
3B— Clete Boyer, Atlanta
SS— Don Kessinger, Chicago
OF— Roberto Clemente, Pittsburgh
OF— Curt Flood, St. Louis
OF— Pete Rose, Cincinnati

1970
AMERICAN LEAGUE
P— Jim Kaat, Minnesota
C— Ray Fosse, Cleveland
1B— Jim Spencer, California
2B— Dave Johnson, Baltimore
3B— Brooks Robinson, Baltimore
SS— Luis Aparicio, Chicago
OF— Mickey Stanley, Detroit
OF— Paul Blair, Baltimore
OF— Ken Berry, Chicago

NATIONAL LEAGUE
P— Bob Gibson, St. Louis
C— Johnny Bench, Cincinnati
1B— Wes Parker, Los Angeles
2B— Tommy Helms, Cincinnati
3B— Doug Rader, Houston
SS— Don Kessinger, Chicago
OF— Roberto Clemente, Pittsburgh
OF— Tommie Agee, New York
OF— Pete Rose, Cincinnati

1971
AMERICAN LEAGUE
P— Jim Kaat, Minnesota
C— Ray Fosse, Cleveland
1B— George Scott, Boston
2B— Dave Johnson, Baltimore
3B— Brooks Robinson, Baltimore
SS— Mark Belanger, Baltimore
OF— Paul Blair, Baltimore
OF— Amos Otis, Kansas City
OF— Carl Yastrzemski, Boston

NATIONAL LEAGUE
P— Bob Gibson, St. Louis
C— Johnny Bench, Cincinnati
1B— Wes Parker, Los Angeles
2B— Tommy Helms, Cincinnati
3B— Doug Rader, Houston
SS— Bud Harrelson, New York
OF— Roberto Clemente, Pittsburgh
OF— Bobby Bonds, San Francisco
OF— Willie Davis, Los Angeles

1972
AMERICAN LEAGUE
P— Jim Kaat, Minnesota
C— Carlton Fisk, Boston
1B— George Scott, Milwaukee
2B— Doug Griffin, Boston
3B— Brooks Robinson, Baltimore
SS— Ed Brinkman, Detroit
OF— Paul Blair, Baltimore
OF— Bobby Murcer, New York
OF— Ken Berry, California

NATIONAL LEAGUE
P— Bob Gibson, St. Louis
C— Johnny Bench, Cincinnati
1B— Wes Parker, Los Angeles
2B— Felix Millan, Atlanta
3B— Doug Rader, Houston
SS— Larry Bowa, Philadelphia
OF— Roberto Clemente, Pittsburgh
OF— Cesar Cedeno, Houston
OF— Willie Davis, Los Angeles

1973
AMERICAN LEAGUE
P— Jim Kaat, Chicago
C— Thurman Munson, New York
1B— George Scott, Milwaukee
2B— Bobby Grich, Baltimore
3B— Brooks Robinson, Baltimore
SS— Mark Belanger, Baltimore
OF— Paul Blair, Baltimore
OF— Amos Otis, Kansas City
OF— Mickey Stanley, Detroit

NATIONAL LEAGUE
P— Bob Gibson, St. Louis
C— Johnny Bench, Cincinnati
1B— Mike Jorgensen, Montreal
2B— Joe Morgan, Cincinnati
3B— Doug Rader, Houston
SS— Roger Metzger, Houston
OF— Bobby Bonds, San Francisco
OF— Cesar Cedeno, Houston
OF— Willie Davis, Los Angeles

1974
AMERICAN LEAGUE
P— Jim Kaat, Chicago
C— Thurman Munson, New York
1B— George Scott, Milwaukee
2B— Bobby Grich, Baltimore
3B— Brooks Robinson, Baltimore
SS— Mark Belanger, Baltimore
OF— Paul Blair, Baltimore
OF— Amos Otis, Kansas City
OF— Joe Rudi, Oakland

NATIONAL LEAGUE
P— Andy Messersmith, Los Angeles
C— Johnny Bench, Cincinnati
1B— Steve Garvey, Los Angeles
2B— Joe Morgan, Cincinnati
3B— Doug Rader, Houston
SS— Dave Concepcion, Cincinnati
OF— Cesar Cedeno, Houston
OF— Cesar Geronimo, Cincinnati
OF— Bobby Bonds, San Francisco

1975
AMERICAN LEAGUE
P— Jim Kaat, Chicago
C— Thurman Munson, New York
1B— George Scott, Milwaukee
2B— Bobby Grich, Baltimore
3B— Brooks Robinson, Baltimore
SS— Mark Belanger, Baltimore
OF— Paul Blair, Baltimore
OF— Joe Rudi, Oakland
OF— Fred Lynn, Boston

NATIONAL LEAGUE
P— Andy Messersmith, Los Angeles
C— Johnny Bench, Cincinnati
1B— Steve Garvey, Los Angeles
2B— Joe Morgan, Cincinnati
3B— Ken Reitz, St. Louis
SS— Dave Concepcion, Cincinnati
OF— Cesar Cedeno, Houston
OF— Cesar Geronimo, Cincinnati
OF— Garry Maddox, Philadelphia

1976
AMERICAN LEAGUE
P— Jim Palmer, Baltimore
C— Jim Sundberg, Texas

1B— George Scott, Milwaukee
2B— Bobby Grich, Baltimore
3B— Aurelio Rodriguez, Detroit
SS— Mark Belanger, Baltimore
OF— Joe Rudi, Oakland
OF— Dwight Evans, Boston
OF— Rick Manning, Cleveland

NATIONAL LEAGUE
P— Jim Kaat, Philadelphia
C— Johnny Bench, Cincinnati
1B— Steve Garvey, Los Angeles
2B— Joe Morgan, Cincinnati
3B— Mike Schmidt, Philadelphia
SS— Dave Concepcion, Cincinnati
OF— Cesar Cedeno, Houston
OF— Cesar Geronimo, Cincinnati
OF— Garry Maddox, Philadelphia

1977
AMERICAN LEAGUE
P— Jim Palmer, Baltimore
C— Jim Sundberg, Texas
1B— Jim Spencer, Chicago
2B— Frank White, Kansas City
3B— Graig Nettles, New York
SS— Mark Belanger, Baltimore
OF— Juan Beniquez, Texas
OF— Carl Yastrzemski, Boston
OF— Al Cowens, Kansas City

NATIONAL LEAGUE
P— Jim Kaat, Philadelphia
C— Johnny Bench, Cincinnati
1B— Steve Garvey, Los Angeles
2B— Joe Morgan, Cincinnati
3B— Mike Schmidt, Philadelphia
SS— Dave Concepcion, Cincinnati
OF— Cesar Geronimo, Cincinnati
OF— Garry Maddox, Philadelphia
OF— Dave Parker, Pittsburgh

1978
AMERICAN LEAGUE
P— Jim Palmer, Baltimore
C— Jim Sundberg, Texas
1B— Chris Chambliss, New York
2B— Frank White, Kansas City
3B— Graig Nettles, New York
SS— Mark Belanger, Baltimore
OF— Fred Lynn, Boston
OF— Dwight Evans, Boston
OF— Rick Miller, California

NATIONAL LEAGUE
P— Phil Niekro, Atlanta
C— Bob Boone, Philadelphia
1B— Keith Hernandez, St. Louis
2B— Dave Lopes, Los Angeles
3B— Mike Schmidt, Philadelphia
SS— Larry Bowa, Philadelphia
OF— Garry Maddox, Philadelphia
OF— Dave Parker, Pittsburgh
OF— Ellis Valentine, Montreal

1979
AMERICAN LEAGUE
P— Jim Palmer, Baltimore
C— Jim Sundberg, Texas
1B— Cecil Cooper, Milwaukee
2B— Frank White, Kansas City
3B— Buddy Bell, Texas
SS— Rick Burleson, Boston
OF— Dwight Evans, Boston
OF— Sixto Lezcano, Milwaukee
OF— Fred Lynn, Boston

NATIONAL LEAGUE
P— Phil Niekro, Atlanta
C— Bob Boone, Philadelphia
1B— Keith Hernandez, St. Louis
2B— Manny Trillo, Philadelphia

3B— Mike Schmidt, Philadelphia
SS— Dave Concepcion, Cincinnati
OF— Garry Maddox, Philadelphia
OF— Dave Parker, Pittsburgh
OF— Dave Winfield, San Diego

1980
AMERICAN LEAGUE
P— Mike Norris, Oakland
C— Jim Sundberg, Texas
1B— Cecil Cooper, Milwaukee
2B— Frank White, Kansas City
3B— Buddy Bell, Texas
SS— Alan Trammell, Detroit
OF— Fred Lynn, Boston
OF— Dwayne Murphy, Oakland
OF— Willie Wilson, Kansas City

NATIONAL LEAGUE
P— Phil Niekro, Atlanta
C— Gary Carter, Montreal
1B— Keith Hernandez, St. Louis
2B— Doug Flynn, New York
3B— Mike Schmidt, Philadelphia
SS— Ozzie Smith, San Diego
OF— Andre Dawson, Montreal
OF— Garry Maddox, Philadelphia
OF— Dave Winfield, San Diego

1981
AMERICAN LEAGUE
P— Mike Norris, Oakland
C— Jim Sundberg, Texas
1B— Mike Squires, Chicago
2B— Frank White, Kansas City
3B— Buddy Bell, Texas
SS— Alan Trammell, Detroit
OF— Dwayne Murphy, Oakland
OF— Dwight Evans, Boston
OF— Rickey Henderson, Oakland

NATIONAL LEAGUE
P— Steve Carlton, Philadelphia
C— Gary Carter, Montreal
1B— Keith Hernandez, St. Louis
2B— Manny Trillo, Philadelphia
3B— Mike Schmidt, Philadelphia
SS— Ozzie Smith, San Diego
OF— Andre Dawson, Montreal
OF— Garry Maddox, Philadelphia
OF— Dusty Baker, Los Angeles

1982
AMERICAN LEAGUE
P— Ron Guidry, New York
C— Bob Boone, California
1B— Eddie Murray, Baltimore
2B— Frank White, Kansas City
3B— Buddy Bell, Texas
SS— Robin Yount, Milwaukee
OF— Dwight Evans, Boston
OF— Dave Winfield, New York
OF— Dwayne Murphy, Oakland

NATIONAL LEAGUE
P— Phil Niekro, Atlanta
C— Gary Carter, Montreal
1B— Keith Hernandez, St. Louis
2B— Manny Trillo, Philadelphia
3B— Mike Schmidt, Philadelphia
SS— Ozzie Smith, St. Louis
OF— Andre Dawson, Montreal
OF— Dale Murphy, Atlanta
OF— Garry Maddox, Philadelphia

1983
AMERICAN LEAGUE
P— Ron Guidry, New York
C— Lance Parrish, Detroit
1B— Eddie Murray, Baltimore
2B— Lou Whitaker, Detroit
3B— Buddy Bell, Texas
SS— Alan Trammell, Detroit

OF— Dwight Evans, Boston
OF— Dave Winfield, New York
OF— Dwayne Murphy, Oakland

NATIONAL LEAGUE
P— Phil Niekro, Atlanta
C— Tony Pena, Pittsburgh
1B— Keith Hernandez, St.L.-N.Y.
2B— Ryne Sandberg, Chicago
3B— Mike Schmidt, Philadelphia
SS— Ozzie Smith, St. Louis
OF— Andre Dawson, Montreal
OF— Dale Murphy, Atlanta
OF— Willie McGee, St. Louis

1984
AMERICAN LEAGUE
P— Ron Guidry, New York
C— Lance Parrish, Detroit
1B— Eddie Murray, Baltimore
2B— Lou Whitaker, Detroit
3B— Buddy Bell, Texas
SS— Alan Trammell, Detroit
OF— Dwight Evans, Boston
OF— Dave Winfield, New York
OF— Dwayne Murphy, Oakland

NATIONAL LEAGUE
P— Joaquin Andujar, St. Louis
C— Tony Pena, Pittsburgh
1B— Keith Hernandez, New York
2B— Ryne Sandberg, Chicago
3B— Mike Schmidt, Philadelphia
SS— Ozzie Smith, St. Louis
OF— Dale Murphy, Atlanta
OF— Bob Dernier, Chicago
OF— Andre Dawson, Montreal

1985
AMERICAN LEAGUE
P— Ron Guidry, New York
C— Lance Parrish, Detroit
1B— Don Mattingly, New York
2B— Lou Whitaker, Detroit
3B— George Brett, Kansas City
SS— Alfredo Griffin, Oakland
OF— Gary Pettis, California
OF— Dave Winfield, New York
OF— Dwight Evans, Boston (tie)
     Dwayne Murphy, Oakland (tie)

NATIONAL LEAGUE
P— Rick Reuschel, Pittsburgh
C— Tony Pena, Pittsburgh
1B— Keith Hernandez, New York
2B— Ryne Sandberg, Chicago
3B— Tim Wallach, Montreal
SS— Ozzie Smith, St. Louis
OF— Willie McGee, St. Louis
OF— Dale Murphy, Atlanta
OF— Andre Dawson, Montreal

1986
AMERICAN LEAGUE
P— Ron Guidry, New York
C— Bob Boone, California
1B— Don Mattingly, New York
2B— Frank White, Kansas City
3B— Gary Gaetti, Minnesota
SS— Tony Fernandez, Toronto
OF— Gary Pettis, California
OF— Jesse Barfield, Toronto
OF— Kirby Puckett, Minnesota

NATIONAL LEAGUE
P— Fernando Valenzuela, Los Angeles
C— Jody Davis, Chicago
1B— Keith Hernandez, New York
2B— Ryne Sandberg, Chicago
3B— Mike Schmidt, Philadelphia
SS— Ozzie Smith, St. Louis
OF— Tony Gwynn, San Diego
OF— Dale Murphy, Atlanta
OF— Willie McGee, St. Louis

1987
AMERICAN LEAGUE
P— Mark Langston, Seattle
C— Bob Boone, California
1B— Don Mattingly, New York
2B— Frank White, Kansas City
3B— Gary Gaetti, Minnesota
SS— Tony Fernandez, Toronto
OF— Jesse Barfield, Toronto
OF— Kirby Puckett, Minnesota
OF— Dave Winfield, New York

NATIONAL LEAGUE
P— Rick Reuschel, Pit.-S.F.
C— Mike LaValliere, Pittsburgh
1B— Keith Hernandez, New York
2B— Ryne Sandberg, Chicago
3B— Terry Pendleton, St. Louis
SS— Ozzie Smith, St. Louis
OF— Eric Davis, Cincinnati
OF— Tony Gwynn, San Diego
OF— Andre Dawson, Chicago

1988
AMERICAN LEAGUE
P— Mark Langston, Seattle
C— Bob Boone, California
1B— Don Mattingly, New York
2B— Harold Reynolds, Seattle
3B— Gary Gaetti, Minnesota
SS— Tony Fernandez, Toronto
OF— Kirby Puckett, Minnesota
OF— Devon White, California
OF— Gary Pettis, Detroit

NATIONAL LEAGUE
P— Orel Hershiser, Los Angeles
C— Benito Santiago, San Diego
1B— Keith Hernandez, New York
2B— Ryne Sandberg, Chicago
3B— Tim Wallach, Montreal
SS— Ozzie Smith, St. Louis
OF— Andy Van Slyke, Pittsburgh
OF— Eric Davis, Cincinnati
OF— Andre Dawson, Chicago

1989
AMERICAN LEAGUE
P— Bret Saberhagen, Kansas City
C— Bob Boone, Kansas City
1B— Don Mattingly, New York
2B— Harold Reynolds, Seattle
3B— Gary Gaetti, Minnesota
SS— Tony Fernandez, Toronto
OF— Kirby Puckett, Minnesota
OF— Devon White, California
OF— Gary Pettis, Detroit

NATIONAL LEAGUE
P— Ron Darling, New York
C— Benito Santiago, San Diego
1B— Andres Galarraga, Montreal
2B— Ryne Sandberg, Chicago
3B— Terry Pendleton, St. Louis
SS— Ozzie Smith, St. Louis
OF— Andy Van Slyke, Pittsburgh
OF— Tony Gwynn, San Diego
OF— Eric Davis, Cincinnati

1990
AMERICAN LEAGUE
P— Mike Boddicker, Boston
C— Sandy Alomar Jr., Cleveland
1B— Mark McGwire, Oakland
2B— Harold Reynolds, Seattle
3B— Kelly Gruber, Toronto
SS— Ozzie Guillen, Chicago
OF— Ken Griffey Jr., Seattle
OF— Ellis Burks, Boston
OF— Gary Pettis, Texas

NATIONAL LEAGUE
P— Greg Maddux, Chicago
C— Benito Santiago, San Diego
1B— Andres Galarraga, Montreal
2B— Ryne Sandberg, Chicago
3B— Tim Wallach, Montreal
SS— Ozzie Smith, St. Louis
OF— Barry Bonds, Pittsburgh
OF— Andy Van Slyke, Pittsburgh
OF— Tony Gwynn, San Diego

1991
AMERICAN LEAGUE
P— Mark Langston, California
C— Tony Pena, Boston
1B— Don Mattingly, New York
2B— Roberto Alomar, Toronto
3B— Robin Ventura, Chicago
SS— Cal Ripken, Baltimore
OF— Ken Griffey Jr., Seattle
OF— Kirby Puckett, Minnesota
OF— Devon White, Toronto

NATIONAL LEAGUE
P— Greg Maddux, Chicago
C— Tom Pagnozzi, St. Louis
1B— Will Clark, San Francisco
2B— Ryne Sandberg, Chicago
3B— Matt Williams, San Francisco
SS— Ozzie Smith, St. Louis
OF— Barry Bonds, Pittsburgh
OF— Andy Van Slyke, Pittsburgh
OF— Tony Gwynn, San Diego

1992
AMERICAN LEAGUE
P— Mark Langston, California
C— Ivan Rodriguez, Texas
1B— Don Mattingly, New York
2B— Roberto Alomar, Toronto
3B— Robin Ventura, Chicago
SS— Cal Ripken, Baltimore
OF— Ken Griffey Jr., Seattle
OF— Kirby Puckett, Minnesota
OF— Devon White, Toronto

NATIONAL LEAGUE
P— Greg Maddux, Chicago
C— Tom Pagnozzi, St. Louis
1B— Mark Grace, Chicago
2B— Jose Lind, Pittsburgh
3B— Terry Pendleton, Atlanta
SS— Ozzie Smith, St. Louis
OF— Barry Bonds, Pittsburgh
OF— Andy Van Slyke, Pittsburgh
OF— Larry Walker, Montreal

1993
AMERICAN LEAGUE
P— Mark Langston, California
C— Ivan Rodriguez, Texas
1B— Don Mattingly, New York
2B— Roberto Alomar, Toronto
3B— Robin Ventura, Chicago
SS— Omar Vizquel, Seattle
OF— Ken Griffey Jr., Seattle
OF— Kenny Lofton, Cleveland
OF— Devon White, Toronto

NATIONAL LEAGUE
P— Greg Maddux, Atlanta
C— Kirt Manwaring, San Francisco
1B— Mark Grace, Chicago
2B— Robby Thompson, San Fran.
3B— Matt Williams, San Francisco
SS— Jay Bell, Pittsburgh
OF— Barry Bonds, San Francisco
OF— Marquis Grissom, Montreal
OF— Larry Walker, Montreal

1994
AMERICAN LEAGUE
P— Mark Langston, California
C— Ivan Rodriguez, Texas
1B— Don Mattingly, New York
2B— Roberto Alomar, Toronto
3B— Wade Boggs, New York
SS— Omar Vizquel, Cleveland
OF— Ken Griffey Jr., Seattle
OF— Kenny Lofton, Cleveland
OF— Devon White, Toronto

NATIONAL LEAGUE
P— Greg Maddux, Atlanta
C— Tom Pagnozzi, St. Louis
1B— Jeff Bagwell, Houston
2B— Craig Biggio, Houston
3B— Matt Williams, San Francisco
SS— Barry Larkin, Cincinnati
OF— Barry Bonds, San Francisco
OF— Marquis Grissom, Montreal
OF— Darren Lewis, San Francisco

1995
AMERICAN LEAGUE
P— Mark Langston, California
C— Ivan Rodriguez, Texas
1B— J.T. Snow, California
2B— Roberto Alomar, Toronto
3B— Wade Boggs, New York
SS— Omar Vizquel, Cleveland
OF— Ken Griffey Jr., Seattle
OF— Kenny Lofton, Cleveland
OF— Devon White, Toronto

NATIONAL LEAGUE
P— Greg Maddux, Atlanta
C— Charles Johnson, Florida
1B— Mark Grace, Chicago
2B— Craig Biggio, Houston
3B— Ken Caminiti, San Diego
SS— Barry Larkin, Cincinnati
OF— Raul Mondesi, Los Angeles
OF— Marquis Grissom, Atlanta
OF— Steve Finley, San Diego

1996
AMERICAN LEAGUE
P— Mike Mussina, Baltimore
C— Ivan Rodriguez, Texas
1B— J.T. Snow, California
2B— Roberto Alomar, Baltimore
3B— Robin Ventura, Chicago
SS— Omar Vizquel, Cleveland
OF— Jay Buhner, Seattle
OF— Ken Griffey Jr., Seattle
OF— Kenny Lofton, Cleveland

NATIONAL LEAGUE
P— Greg Maddux, Atlanta
C— Charles Johnson, Florida
1B— Mark Grace, Chicago
2B— Craig Biggio, Houston
3B— Ken Caminiti, San Diego
SS— Barry Larkin, Cincinnati
OF— Barry Bonds, San Francisco
OF— Marquis Grissom, Atlanta
OF— Steve Finley, San Diego

SILVER SLUGGER TEAMS

1980
AMERICAN LEAGUE
1B— Cecil Cooper, Milwaukee
2B— Willie Randolph, New York
3B— George Brett, Kansas City
SS— Robin Yount, Milwaukee
OF— Ben Oglivie, Milwaukee
OF— Al Oliver, Texas
OF— Willie Wilson, Kansas City
C— Lance Parrish, Detroit
DH— Reggie Jackson, New York

NATIONAL LEAGUE
1B— Keith Hernandez, St. Louis
2B— Manny Trillo, Philadelphia
3B— Mike Schmidt, Philadelphia
SS— Garry Templeton, St. Louis
OF— Dusty Baker, Los Angeles
OF— Andre Dawson, Montreal
OF— George Hendrick, St. Louis
C— Ted Simmons, St. Louis
P— Bob Forsch, St. Louis

1981
AMERICAN LEAGUE
1B— Cecil Cooper, Milwaukee
2B— Bobby Grich, California
3B— Carney Lansford, Boston
SS— Rick Burleson, California
OF— Rickey Henderson, Oakland
OF— Dwight Evans, Boston
OF— Dave Winfield, New York
C— Carlton Fisk, Chicago
DH— Al Oliver, Texas

NATIONAL LEAGUE
1B— Pete Rose, Philadelphia
2B— Manny Trillo, Philadelphia
3B— Mike Schmidt, Philadelphia
SS— Dave Concepcion, Cincinnati
OF— Andre Dawson, Montreal
OF— George Foster, Cincinnati
OF— Dusty Baker, Los Angeles
C— Gary Carter, Montreal
P— Fernando Valenzuela, Los Angeles

1982
AMERICAN LEAGUE
1B— Cecil Cooper, Milwaukee
2B— Damaso Garcia, Toronto
3B— Doug DeCinces, California
SS— Robin Yount, Milwaukee
OF— Dave Winfield, New York
OF— Willie Wilson, Kansas City
OF— Reggie Jackson, California
C— Lance Parrish, Detroit
DH— Hal McRae, Kansas City

NATIONAL LEAGUE
1B— Al Oliver, Montreal
2B— Joe Morgan, San Francisco
3B— Mike Schmidt, Philadelphia
SS— Dave Concepcion, Cincinnati
OF— Dale Murphy, Atlanta
OF— Pedro Guerrero, Los Angeles
OF— Leon Durham, Chicago
C— Gary Carter, Montreal
P— Don Robinson, Pittsburgh

1983
AMERICAN LEAGUE
1B— Eddie Murray, Baltimore
2B— Lou Whitaker, Detroit
3B— Wade Boggs, Boston
SS— Cal Ripken Jr., Baltimore
OF— Jim Rice, Boston
OF— Dave Winfield, New York
OF— Lloyd Moseby, Toronto
C— Lance Parrish, Detroit
DH— Don Baylor, New York

NATIONAL LEAGUE
1B— George Hendrick, St. Louis
2B— Johnny Ray, Pittsburgh
3B— Mike Schmidt, Philadelphia
SS— Dickie Thon, Houston
OF— Andre Dawson, Montreal
OF— Dale Murphy, Atlanta
OF— Jose Cruz, Houston
C— Terry Kennedy, San Diego
P— Fernando Valenzuela, Los Angeles

1984
AMERICAN LEAGUE
1B— Eddie Murray, Baltimore
2B— Lou Whitaker, Detroit
3B— Buddy Bell, Texas
SS— Cal Ripken Jr., Baltimore
OF— Tony Armas, Boston
OF— Jim Rice, Boston
OF— Dave Winfield, New York
C— Lance Parrish, Detroit
DH— Andre Thornton, Cleveland

NATIONAL LEAGUE
1B— Keith Hernandez, New York
2B— Ryne Sandberg, Chicago
3B— Mike Schmidt, Philadelphia
SS— Garry Templeton, San Diego
OF— Dale Murphy, Atlanta
OF— Jose Cruz, Houston
OF— Tony Gwynn, San Diego
C— Gary Carter, Montreal
P— Rick Rhoden, Pittsburgh

1985
AMERICAN LEAGUE
1B— Don Mattingly, New York
2B— Lou Whitaker, Detroit
3B— George Brett, Kansas City
SS— Cal Ripken Jr., Baltimore
OF— Rickey Henderson, New York
OF— Dave Winfield, New York
OF— George Bell, Toronto
C— Carlton Fisk, Chicago
DH— Don Baylor, New York

NATIONAL LEAGUE
1B— Jack Clark, St. Louis
2B— Ryne Sandberg, Chicago
3B— Tim Wallach, Montreal
SS— Hubie Brooks, Montreal
OF— Willie McGee, St. Louis
OF— Dale Murphy, Atlanta
OF— Dave Parker, Cincinnati
C— Gary Carter, New York
P— Rick Rhoden, Pittsburgh

1986
AMERICAN LEAGUE
1B— Don Mattingly, New York
2B— Frank White, Kansas City
3B— Wade Boggs, Boston
SS— Cal Ripken Jr., Baltimore
OF— George Bell, Toronto
OF— Kirby Puckett, Minnesota
OF— Jesse Barfield, Toronto
C— Lance Parrish, Detroit
DH— Don Baylor, Boston

NATIONAL LEAGUE
1B— Glenn Davis, Houston
2B— Steve Sax, Los Angeles
3B— Mike Schmidt, Philadelphia
SS— Hubie Brooks, Montreal
OF— Tony Gwynn, San Diego
OF— Tim Raines, Montreal
OF— Dave Parker, Cincinnati
C— Gary Carter, New York
P— Rick Rhoden, Pittsburgh

1987
AMERICAN LEAGUE
1B— Don Mattingly, New York
2B— Lou Whitaker, Detroit
3B— Wade Boggs, Boston
SS— Alan Trammell, Detroit
OF— George Bell, Toronto
OF— Dwight Evans, Boston
OF— Kirby Puckett, Minnesota
C— Matt Nokes, Detroit
DH— Paul Molitor, Milwaukee

NATIONAL LEAGUE
1B— Jack Clark, St. Louis
2B— Juan Samuel, Philadelphia
3B— Tim Wallach, Montreal
SS— Ozzie Smith, St. Louis
OF— Andre Dawson, Chicago
OF— Eric Davis, Cincinnati
OF— Tony Gwynn, San Diego
C— Benito Santiago, San Diego
P— Bob Forsch, St. Louis

1988
AMERICAN LEAGUE
1B— George Brett, Kansas City
2B— Julio Franco, Cleveland
3B— Wade Boggs, Boston
SS— Alan Trammell, Detroit
OF— Kirby Puckett, Minnesota
OF— Jose Canseco, Oakland
OF— Mike Greenwell, Boston
C— Carlton Fisk, Chicago
DH— Paul Molitor, Milwaukee

NATIONAL LEAGUE
1B— Andres Galarraga, Montreal
2B— Ryne Sandberg, Chicago
3B— Bobby Bonilla, Pittsburgh
SS— Barry Larkin, Cincinnati
OF— Darryl Strawberry, New York
OF— Andy Van Slyke, Pittsburgh
OF— Kirk Gibson, Los Angeles
C— Benito Santiago, San Diego
P— Tim Leary, Los Angeles

1989
AMERICAN LEAGUE
1B— Fred McGriff, Toronto
2B— Julio Franco, Texas
3B— Wade Boggs, Boston
SS— Cal Ripken Jr., Baltimore
OF— Kirby Puckett, Minnesota
OF— Ruben Sierra, Texas
OF— Robin Yount, Milwaukee
C— Mickey Tettleton, Baltimore
DH— Harold Baines, Chi.-Tex.

NATIONAL LEAGUE
1B— Will Clark, San Francisco
2B— Ryne Sandberg, Chicago
3B— Howard Johnson, New York
SS— Barry Larkin, Cincinnati
OF— Kevin Mitchell, San Francisco
OF— Tony Gwynn, San Diego
OF— Eric Davis, Cincinnati
C— Craig Biggio, Houston
P— Don Robinson, San Francisco

1990
AMERICAN LEAGUE
1B— Cecil Fielder, Detroit
2B— Julio Franco, Texas
3B— Kelly Gruber, Toronto
SS— Alan Trammell, Detroit
OF— Rickey Henderson, Oakland
OF— Jose Canseco, Oakland
OF— Ellis Burks, Boston
C— Lance Parrish, California
DH— Dave Parker, Milwaukee

NATIONAL LEAGUE
1B— Eddie Murray, Los Angeles
2B— Ryne Sandberg, Chicago
3B— Matt Williams, San Francisco
SS— Barry Larkin, Cincinnati

OF— Barry Bonds, Pittsburgh
OF— Bobby Bonilla, Pittsburgh
OF— Darryl Strawberry, New York
C— Benito Santiago, San Diego
P— Don Robinson, San Francisco

1991
AMERICAN LEAGUE
1B— Cecil Fielder, Detroit
2B— Julio Franco, Texas
3B— Wade Boggs, Boston
SS— Cal Ripken Jr., Baltimore
OF— Jose Canseco, Oakland
OF— Joe Carter, Toronto
OF— Ken Griffey Jr., Seattle
C— Mickey Tettleton, Detroit
DH— Frank Thomas, Chicago

NATIONAL LEAGUE
1B— Will Clark, San Francisco
2B— Ryne Sandberg, Chicago
3B— Howard Johnson, New York
SS— Barry Larkin, Cincinnati
OF— Barry Bonds, Pittsburgh
OF— Bobby Bonilla, Pittsburgh
OF— Ron Gant, Atlanta
C— Benito Santiago, San Diego
P— Tom Glavine, Atlanta

1992
AMERICAN LEAGUE
1B— Mark McGwire, Oakland
2B— Roberto Alomar, Toronto
3B— Edgar Martinez, Seattle
SS— Travis Fryman, Detroit
OF— Joe Carter, Toronto
OF— Juan Gonzalez, Texas
OF— Kirby Puckett, Minnesota
C— Mickey Tettleton, Detroit
DH— Dave Winfield, Toronto

NATIONAL LEAGUE
1B— Fred McGriff, San Diego
2B— Ryne Sandberg, Chicago
3B— Gary Sheffield, San Diego
SS— Barry Larkin, Cincinnati
OF— Barry Bonds, Pittsburgh
OF— Andy Van Slyke, Pittsburgh
OF— Larry Walker, Montreal
C— Darren Daulton, Philadelphia
P— Dwight Gooden, New York

1993
AMERICAN LEAGUE
1B— Frank Thomas, Chicago
2B— Carlos Baerga, Cleveland
3B— Wade Boggs, New York
SS— Cal Ripken Jr., Baltimore
OF— Albert Belle, Cleveland
OF— Juan Gonzalez, Texas
OF— Ken Griffey Jr., Seattle
C— Mike Stanley, New York
DH— Paul Molitor, Toronto

NATIONAL LEAGUE
1B— Fred McGriff, S.D.-Atl.
2B— Robby Thompson, San Fran.
3B— Matt Williams, San Francisco
SS— Jay Bell, Pittsburgh
OF— Barry Bonds, San Francisco
OF— Lenny Dykstra, Philadelphia
OF— David Justice, Atlanta
C— Mike Piazza, Los Angeles
P— Orel Hershiser, Los Angeles

1994
AMERICAN LEAGUE
1B— Frank Thomas, Chicago
2B— Carlos Baerga, Cleveland
3B— Wade Boggs, New York
SS— Cal Ripken Jr., Baltimore
OF— Albert Belle, Cleveland
OF— Ken Griffey Jr., Seattle
OF— Kirby Puckett, Minnesota
C— Ivan Rodriguez, Texas
DH— Julio Franco, Chicago

NATIONAL LEAGUE
1B— Jeff Bagwell, Houston
2B— Craig Biggio, Houston
3B— Matt Williams, San Francisco
SS— Wil Cordero, Montreal
OF— Moises Alou, Montreal
OF— Barry Bonds, San Francisco
OF— Tony Gwynn, San Diego
C— Mike Piazza, Los Angeles
P— Mark Portugal, San Francisco

1995
AMERICAN LEAGUE
1B— Mo Vaughn, Boston
2B— Chuck Knoblauch, Minnesota
3B— Gary Gaetti, Kansas City
SS— John Valentin, Boston
OF— Albert Belle, Cleveland
OF— Tim Salmon, California
OF— Manny Ramirez, Cleveland
C— Ivan Rodriguez, Texas
DH— Edgar Martinez, Seattle

NATIONAL LEAGUE
1B— Eric Karros, Los Angeles
2B— Craig Biggio, Houston
3B— Vinny Castilla, Colorado
SS— Barry Larkin, Cincinnati
OF— Dante Bichette, Colorado
OF— Tony Gwynn, San Diego
OF— Sammy Sosa, Chicago
C— Mike Piazza, Los Angeles
P— Tom Glavine, Atlanta

1996
AMERICAN LEAGUE
1B— Mark McGwire, Oakland
2B— Roberto Alomar, Baltimore
3B— Jim Thome, Cleveland
SS— Alex Rodriguez, Seattle
OF— Albert Belle, Cleveland
OF— Juan Gonzalez, Texas
OF— Ken Griffey Jr., Seattle
C— Ivan Rodriguez, Texas
DH— Paul Molitor, Minnesota

NATIONAL LEAGUE
1B— Andres Galarraga, Colorado
2B— Eric Young, Colorado
3B— Ken Caminiti, San Diego
SS— Barry Larkin, Cincinnati
OF— Barry Bonds, San Francisco
OF— Ellis Burks, Colorado
OF— Gary Sheffield, Florida
C— Mike Piazza, Los Angeles
P— Tom Glavine, Atlanta

MAJOR LEAGUE ALL-STAR TEAMS

1925
1B— Jim Bottomley, St. Louis N.L.
2B— Rogers Hornsby, St. Louis N.L.
SS— Glenn Wright, Pittsburgh N.L.
3B— Pie Traynor, Pittsburgh N.L.
OF— Kiki Cuyler, Pittsburgh N.L.

OF— Max Carey, Pittsburgh N.L.
OF— Goose Goslin, Washington A.L.
C— Mickey Cochrane, Phil. A.L.
P— Walter Johnson, Washington A.L.
P— Ed Rommel, Philadelphia A.L.
P— Dazzy Vance, Brooklyn N.L.

1926
1B— George Burns, Cleveland A.L.
2B— Rogers Hornsby, St. Louis N.L.
SS— Joe Sewell, Cleveland A.L.
3B— Pie Traynor, Pittsburgh N.L.
OF— Goose Goslin, Washington A.L.

OF— John Mostil, Chicago A.L.
OF— Babe Ruth, New York A.L.
C— Bob O'Farrell, St. Louis N.L.
P— Herb Pennock, New York A.L.
P— George Uhle, Cleveland A.L.
P— Grover Alexander, St. Louis N.L.

1927
1B— Lou Gehrig, New York A.L.
2B— Rogers Hornsby, New York N.L.
SS— Travis Jackson, New York N.L.
3B— Pie Traynor, Pittsburgh A.L.
OF— Babe Ruth, New York A.L.
OF— Al Simmons, Philadelphia A.L.
OF— Paul Waner, Pittsburgh N.L.
C— Gabby Hartnett, Chicago N.L.
P— Charley Root, Chicago N.L.
P— Ted Lyons, Chicago A.L.

1928
1B— Lou Gehrig, New York A.L.
2B— Rogers Hornsby, Boston N.L.
SS— Travis Jackson, New York N.L.
3B— Fred Lindstrom, New York N.L.
OF— Babe Ruth, New York A.L.
OF— Heinie Manush, St. Louis A.L.
OF— Paul Waner, Pittsburgh N.L.
C— Mickey Cochrane, Phil. A.L.
P— Lefty Grove, Philadelphia A.L.
P— Waite Hoyt, New York A.L.

1929
1B— Jimmie Foxx, Philadelphia A.L.
2B— Rogers Hornsby, Chicago N.L.
SS— Travis Jackson, New York N.L.
3B— Pie Traynor, Pittsburgh, N.L.
OF— Al Simmons, Philadelphia A.L.
OF— Hack Wilson, Chicago N.L.
OF— Babe Ruth, New York A.L.
C— Mickey Cochrane, Phil. A.L.
P— Lefty Grove, Philadelphia A.L.
P— Burleigh Grimes, Pittsburgh N.L.

1930
1B— Bill Terry, New York N.L.
2B— Frank Frisch, St. Louis N.L.
SS— Joe Cronin, Washington A.L.
3B— Fred Lindstrom, New York N.L.
OF— Al Simmons, Philadelphia A.L.
OF— Hack Wilson, Chicago N.L.
OF— Babe Ruth, New York A.L.
C— Mickey Cochrane, Phil. A.L.
P— Lefty Grove, Philadelphia A.L.
P— Wes Ferrell, Cleveland A.L.

1931
1B— Lou Gehrig, New York A.L.
2B— Frank Frisch, St. Louis N.L.
SS— Joe Cronin, Washington A.L.
3B— Pie Traynor, Pittsburgh N.L.
OF— Al Simmons, Philadelphia A.L.
OF— Earl Averill, Cleveland A.L.
OF— Babe Ruth, New York A.L.
C— Mickey Cochrane, Phil. A.L.
P— Lefty Grove, Philadelphia A.L.
P— George Earnshaw, Phil. A.L.

1932
1B— Jimmie Foxx, Philadelphia A.L.
2B— Tony Lazzeri, New York A.L.
SS— Joe Cronin, Washington A.L.
3B— Pie Traynor, Pittsburgh N.L.
OF— Lefty O'Doul, Brooklyn N.L.
OF— Earl Averill, Cleveland A.L.
OF— Chuck Klein, Philadelphia N.L.
C— Bill Dickey, New York A.L.
P— Lefty Grove, Philadelphia A.L.
P— Lon Warneke, Chicago N.L.

1933
1B— Jimmie Foxx, Philadelphia A.L.
2B— Charley Gehringer, Detroit A.L.

SS— Joe Cronin, Washington A.L.
3B— Pie Traynor, Pittsburgh N.L.
OF— Al Simmons, Chicago A.L.
OF— Wally Berger, Boston N.L.
OF— Chuck Klein, Philadelphia N.L.
C— Bill Dickey, New York A.L.
P— Alvin Crowder, Washington A.L.
P— Carl Hubbell, New York N.L.

1934
1B— Lou Gehrig, New York A.L.
2B— Charley Gehringer, Detroit A.L.
SS— Joe Cronin, Washington A.L.
3B— Mike Higgins, Philadelphia A.L.
OF— Al Simmons, Chicago A.L.
OF— Earl Averill, Cleveland A.L.
OF— Mel Ott, New York N.L.
C— Mickey Cochrane, Detroit A.L.
P— Lefty Gomez, New York A.L.
P— Schoolboy Rowe, Detroit A.L.
P— Dizzy Dean, St. Louis N.L.

1935
1B— Hank Greenberg, Detroit A.L.
2B— Charley Gehringer, Detroit A.L.
SS— Arky Vaughan, Pittsburgh N.L.
3B— Pepper Martin, St. Louis N.L.
OF— Joe Medwick, St. Louis N.L.
OF— Doc Cramer, Philadelphia A.L.
OF— Mel Ott, New York N.L.
C— Mickey Cochrane, Detroit A.L.
P— Carl Hubbell, New York N.L.
P— Dizzy Dean, St. Louis N.L.

1936
1B— Lou Gehrig, New York A.L.
2B— Charley Gehringer, Detroit A.L.
SS— Luke Appling, Chicago A.L.
3B— Mike Higgins, Philadelphia A.L.
OF— Joe Medwick, St. Louis N.L.
OF— Earl Averill, Cleveland A.L.
OF— Mel Ott, New York N.L.
C— Bill Dickey, New York A.L.
P— Carl Hubbell, New York N.L.
P— Dizzy Dean, St. Louis N.L.

1937
1B— Lou Gehrig, New York A.L.
2B— Charley Gehringer, Detroit A.L.
SS— Dick Bartell, New York N.L.
3B— Red Rolfe, New York A.L.
OF— Joe Medwick, St. Louis N.L.
OF— Joe DiMaggio, New York A.L.
OF— Paul Waner, Pittsburgh N.L.
C— Gabby Hartnett, Chicago N.L.
P— Carl Hubbell, New York N.L.
P— Red Ruffing, New York A.L.

1938
1B— Jimmie Foxx, Boston A.L.
2B— Charley Gehringer, Detroit A.L.
SS— Joe Cronin, Boston A.L.
3B— Red Rolfe, New York A.L.
OF— Joe Medwick, St. Louis N.L.
OF— Joe DiMaggio, New York A.L.
OF— Mel Ott, New York N.L.
C— Bill Dickey, New York A.L.
P— Red Ruffing, New York A.L.
P— Lefty Gomez, New York A.L.
P— Johnny Vander Meer, Cin. N.L.

1939
1B— Jimmie Foxx, Boston A.L.
2B— Joe Gordon, New York A.L.
SS— Joe Cronin, Boston A.L.
3B— Red Rolfe, New York A.L.
OF— Joe Medwick, St. Louis N.L.
OF— Joe DiMaggio, New York A.L.
OF— Ted Williams, Boston A.L.
C— Bill Dickey, New York A.L.

P— Red Ruffing, New York A.L.
P— Bob Feller, Cleveland A.L.
P— Bucky Walters, Cincinnati N.L.

1940
1B— Frank McCormick, Cincinnati N.L.
2B— Joe Gordon, New York A.L.
SS— Luke Appling, Chicago A.L.
3B— Stan Hack, Chicago N.L.
OF— Hank Greenberg, Detroit A.L.
OF— Joe DiMaggio, New York A.L.
OF— Ted Williams, Boston A.L.
C— Harry Danning, New York N.L.
P— Bob Feller, Cleveland A.L.
P— Bucky Walters, Cincinnati N.L.
P— Paul Derringer, Cincinnati N.L.

1941
1B— Dolf Camilli, Brooklyn N.L.
2B— Joe Gordon, New York A.L.
SS— Cecil Travis, Washington A.L.
3B— Stan Hack, Chicago N.L.
OF— Ted Williams, Boston A.L.
OF— Joe DiMaggio, New York A.L.
OF— Pete Reiser, Brooklyn N.L.
C— Bill Dickey, New York A.L.
P— Bob Feller, Cleveland A.L.
P— Whitlow Wyatt, Brooklyn N.L.
P— Thornton Lee, Chicago A.L.

1942
1B— Johnny Mize, New York N.L.
2B— Joe Gordon, New York A.L.
SS— Johnny Pesky, Boston A.L.
3B— Stan Hack, Chicago N.L.
OF— Ted Williams, Boston A.L.
OF— Joe DiMaggio, New York A.L.
OF— Enos Slaughter, St. Louis N.L.
C— Mickey Owen, Brooklyn N.L.
P— Mort Cooper, St. Louis N.L.
P— Tiny Bonham, New York A.L.
P— Tex Hughson, Boston A.L.

1943
1B— Rudy York, Detroit A.L.
2B— Billy Herman, Brooklyn N.L.
SS— Luke Appling, Chicago A.L.
3B— Billy Johnson, New York A.L.
OF— Dick Wakefield, Detroit A.L.
OF— Stan Musial, St. Louis N.L.
OF— Bill Nicholson, Chicago N.L.
C— Walker Cooper, St. Louis N.L.
P— Spud Chandler, New York A.L.
P— Mort Cooper, St. Louis N.L.
P— Rip Sewell, Pittsburgh N.L.

1944
1B— Ray Sanders, St. Louis N.L.
2B— Bobby Doerr, Boston A.L.
SS— Marty Marion, St. Louis N.L.
3B— Bob Elliott, Pittsburgh N.L.
OF— Stan Musial, St. Louis N.L.
OF— Dick Wakefield, Detroit A.L.
OF— Dixie Walker, Brooklyn, N.L.
C— Walker Cooper, St. Louis N.L.
P— Hal Newhouser, Detroit A.L.
P— Mort Cooper, St. Louis N.L.
P— Dizzy Trout, Detroit A.L.

1945
1B— Phil Cavarretta, Chicago N.L.
2B— George Stirnweiss, N.Y. A.L.
SS— Marty Marion, St. Louis N.L.
3B— Whitey Kurowski, St. Louis N.L.
OF— Tommy Holmes, Boston N.L.
OF— Andy Pafko, Chicago N.L.
OF— Goody Rosen, Brooklyn N.L.
C— Paul Richards, Detroit A.L.
P— Hal Newhouser, Detroit A.L.
P— Boo Ferriss, Boston A.L.
P— Hank Borowy, Chicago N.L.

HISTORY *Award winners*

1946

1B— Stan Musial, St. Louis N.L.
2B— Bobby Doerr, Boston A.L.
SS— Johnny Pesky, Boston A.L.
3B— George Kell, Detroit A.L.
OF— Ted Williams, Boston A.L.
OF— Dom DiMaggio, Boston A.L.
OF— Enos Slaughter, St. Louis N.L.
C— Aaron Robinson, New York A.L.
P— Hal Newhouser, Detroit A.L.
P— Bob Feller, Cleveland A.L.
P— Boo Ferriss, Boston A.L.

1947

1B— Johnny Mize, New York N.L.
2B— Joe Gordon, Cleveland A.L.
SS— Lou Boudreau, Cleveland A.L.
3B— George Kell, Detroit A.L.
OF— Ted Williams, Boston A.L.
OF— Joe DiMaggio, New York A.L.
OF— Ralph Kiner, Pittsburgh N.L.
C— Walker Cooper, New York N.L.
P— Ewell Blackwell, Cincinnati N.L.
P— Bob Feller, Cleveland A.L.
P— Ralph Branca, Brooklyn N.L.

1948

1B— Johnny Mize, New York N.L.
2B— Joe Gordon, Cleveland A.L.
SS— Lou Boudreau, Cleveland A.L.
3B— Bob Elliott, Boston N.L.
OF— Ted Williams, Boston A.L.
OF— Joe DiMaggio, New York A.L.
OF— Stan Musial, St. Louis N.L.
C— Birdie Tebbetts, Boston A.L.
P— Johnny Sain, Boston N.L.
P— Bob Lemon, Cleveland A.L.
P— Harry Brecheen, St. Louis N.L.

1949

1B— Tommy Henrich, New York A.L.
2B— Jackie Robinson, Brooklyn N.L.
SS— Phil Rizzuto, New York A.L.
3B— George Kell, Detroit A.L.
OF— Ted Williams, Boston A.L.
OF— Stan Musial, St. Louis N.L.
OF— Ralph Kiner, Pittsburgh N.L.
C— Roy Campanella, Brooklyn N.L.
P— Mel Parnell, Boston A.L.
P— Ellis Kinder, Boston A.L.
P— Joe Page, New York A.L.

1950

1B— Walt Dropo, Boston A.L.
2B— Jackie Robinson, Brooklyn N.L.
SS— Phil Rizzuto, New York A.L.
3B— George Kell, Detroit A.L.
OF— Stan Musial, St. Louis N.L.
OF— Ralph Kiner, Pittsburgh N.L.
OF— Larry Doby, Cleveland A.L.
C— Yogi Berra, New York A.L.
P— Vic Raschi, New York A.L.
P— Bob Lemon, Cleveland A.L.
P— Jim Konstanty, Phil. N.L.

1951

1B— Ferris Fain, Philadelphia A.L.
2B— Jackie Robinson, Brooklyn N.L.
SS— Phil Rizzuto, New York A.L.
3B— George Kell, Detroit A.L.
OF— Stan Musial, St. Louis N.L.
OF— Ted Williams, Boston A.L.
OF— Ralph Kiner, Pittsburgh N.L.
C— Roy Campanella, Brooklyn N.L.
P— Sal Maglie, New York N.L.
P— Preacher Roe, Brooklyn N.L.
P— Allie Reynolds, New York A.L.

1952

1B— Ferris Fain, Philadelphia A.L.
2B— Jackie Robinson, Brooklyn N.L.
SS— Phil Rizzuto, New York A.L.
3B— George Kell, Boston A.L.

OF— Stan Musial, St. Louis N.L.
OF— Hank Sauer, Chicago N.L.
OF— Mickey Mantle, New York A.L.
C— Yogi Berra, New York A.L.
P— Robin Roberts, Philadelphia N.L.
P— Bobby Shantz, Philadelphia A.L.
P— Allie Reynolds, New York A.L.

1953

1B— Mickey Vernon, Washington A.L.
2B— Red Schoendienst, St. Louis N.L.
SS— Pee Wee Reese, Brooklyn N.L.
3B— Al Rosen, Cleveland A.L.
OF— Stan Musial, St. Louis N.L.
OF— Duke Snider, Brooklyn N.L.
OF— Carl Furillo, Brooklyn N.L.
C— Roy Campanella, Brooklyn N.L.
P— Robin Roberts, Philadelphia N.L.
P— Warren Spahn, Milwaukee N.L.
P— Bob Porterfield, Washington A.L.

1954

1B— Ted Kluszewski, Cincinnati N.L.
2B— Bobby Avila, Cleveland A.L.
SS— Alvin Dark, New York N.L.
3B— Al Rosen, Cleveland A.L.
OF— Willie Mays, New York N.L.
OF— Stan Musial, St. Louis N.L.
OF— Duke Snider, Brooklyn N.L.
C— Yogi Berra, New York A.L.
P— Bob Lemon, Cleveland A.L.
P— Johnny Antonelli, New York N.L.
P— Robin Roberts, Philadelphia N.L.

1955

1B— Ted Kluszewski, Cincinnati N.L.
2B— Nellie Fox, Chicago A.L.
SS— Ernie Banks, Chicago N.L.
3B— Ed Mathews, Milwaukee N.L.
OF— Duke Snider, Brooklyn N.L.
OF— Ted Williams, Boston A.L.
OF— Al Kaline, Detroit A.L.
C— Roy Campanella, Brooklyn N.L.
P— Robin Roberts, Philadelphia N.L.
P— Don Newcombe, Brooklyn N.L.
P— Whitey Ford, New York A.L.

1956

1B— Ted Kluszewski, Cincinnati N.L.
2B— Nellie Fox, Chicago A.L.
SS— Harvey Kuenn, Detroit A.L.
3B— Ken Boyer, St. Louis N.L.
OF— Mickey Mantle, New York A.L.
OF— Hank Aaron, Milwaukee N.L.
OF— Ted Williams, Boston A.L.
C— Yogi Berra, New York A.L.
P— Don Newcombe, Brooklyn N.L.
P— Whitey Ford, New York A.L.
P— Billy Pierce, Chicago A.L.

1957

1B— Stan Musial, St. Louis N.L.
2B— Red Schoendienst, N.Y.-Mil. N.L.
SS— Gil McDougald, New York A.L.
3B— Ed Mathews, Milwaukee N.L.
OF— Mickey Mantle, New York A.L.
OF— Ted Williams, Boston A.L.
OF— Willie Mays, New York N.L.
C— Yogi Berra, New York A.L.
P— Warren Spahn, Milwaukee N.L.
P— Billy Pierce, Chicago A.L.
P— Jim Bunning, Detroit A.L.

1958

1B— Stan Musial, St. Louis N.L.
2B— Nellie Fox, Chicago A.L.
SS— Ernie Banks, Chicago N.L.
3B— Frank Thomas, Pittsburgh N.L.
OF— Ted Williams, Boston A.L.
OF— Willie Mays, San Francisco N.L.
OF— Hank Aaron, Milwaukee N.L.
C— Del Crandall, Milwaukee N.L.
P— Bob Turley, New York A.L.

P— Warren Spahn, Milwaukee N.L.
P— Bob Friend, Pittsburgh N.L.

1959

1B— Orlando Cepeda, S.F. N.L.
2B— Nellie Fox, Chicago A.L.
SS— Ernie Banks, Chicago N.L.
3B— Ed Mathews, Milwaukee N.L.
OF— Minnie Minoso, Cleveland A.L.
OF— Willie Mays, San Francisco N.L.
OF— Hank Aaron, Milwaukee N.L.
C— Sherm Lollar, Chicago A.L.
P— Early Wynn, Chicago A.L.
P— Sam Jones, San Francisco N.L.
P— Johnny Antonelli, S.F. N.L.

1960

1B— Bill Skowron, New York A.L.
2B— Bill Mazeroski, Pittsburgh N.L.
SS— Ernie Banks, Chicago N.L.
3B— Ed Mathews, Milwaukee N.L.
OF— Minnie Minoso, Chicago A.L.
OF— Willie Mays, San Francisco N.L.
OF— Roger Maris, New York A.L.
C— Del Crandall, Milwaukee N.L.
P— Vernon Law, Pittsburgh N.L.
P— Warren Spahn, Milwaukee N.L.
P— Ernie Broglio, St. Louis N.L.

1961
AMERICAN LEAGUE

1B— Norm Cash, Detroit
2B— Bobby Richardson, New York
SS— Tony Kubek, New York
3B— Brooks Robinson, Baltimore
OF— Mickey Mantle, New York
OF— Roger Maris, New York
OF— Rocky Colavito, Detroit
C— Elston Howard, New York
P— Whitey Ford, New York
P— Frank Lary, Detroit

NATIONAL LEAGUE

1B— Orlando Cepeda, San Francisco
2B— Frank Bolling, Milwaukee
SS— Maury Wills, Los Angeles
3B— Ken Boyer, St. Louis
OF— Willie Mays, San Francisco
OF— Frank Robinson, Cincinnati
OF— Roberto Clemente, Pittsburgh
C— Smoky Burgess, Pittsburgh
P— Joey Jay, Cincinnati
P— Warren Spahn, Milwaukee

1962
AMERICAN LEAGUE

1B— Norm Siebern, Kansas City
2B— Bobby Richardson, New York
SS— Tom Tresh, New York
3B— Brooks Robinson, Baltimore
OF— Leon Wagner, Los Angeles
OF— Mickey Mantle, New York
OF— Al Kaline, Detroit
C— Earl Battey, Minnesota
P— Ralph Terry, New York
P— Dick Donovan, Cleveland

NATIONAL LEAGUE

1B— Orlando Cepeda, San Francisco
2B— Bill Mazeroski, Pittsburgh
SS— Maury Wills, Los Angeles
3B— Ken Boyer, St. Louis
OF— Tommy Davis, Los Angeles
OF— Willie Mays, San Francisco
OF— Frank Robinson, Cincinnati
C— Del Crandall, Milwaukee
P— Don Drysdale, Los Angeles
P— Bob Purkey, Cincinnati

1963
AMERICAN LEAGUE
1B— Joe Pepitone, New York
2B— Bobby Richardson, New York
SS— Luis Aparicio, Baltimore
3B— Frank Malzone, Boston
OF— Carl Yastrzemski, Boston
OF— Albie Pearson, Los Angeles
OF— Al Kaline, Detroit
C— Elston Howard, New York
P— Whitey Ford, New York
P— Gary Peters, Chicago

NATIONAL LEAGUE
1B— Bill White, St. Louis
2B— Jim Gilliam, Los Angeles
SS— Dick Groat, St. Louis
3B— Ken Boyer, St. Louis
OF— Tommy Davis, Los Angeles
OF— Willie Mays, San Francisco
OF— Hank Aaron, Milwaukee
C— John Edwards, Cincinnati
P— Sandy Koufax, Los Angeles
P— Juan Marichal, San Francisco

1964
AMERICAN LEAGUE
1B— Dick Stuart, Boston
2B— Bobby Richardson, New York
SS— Jim Fregosi, Los Angeles
3B— Brooks Robinson, Baltimore
OF— Harmon Killebrew, Minnesota
OF— Mickey Mantle, New York
OF— Tony Oliva, Minnesota
C— Elston Howard, New York
P— Dean Chance, Los Angeles
P— Gary Peters, Chicago

NATIONAL LEAGUE
1B— Bill White, St. Louis
2B— Ron Hunt, New York
SS— Dick Groat, St. Louis
3B— Ken Boyer, St. Louis
OF— Billy Williams, Chicago
OF— Willie Mays, San Francisco
OF— Roberto Clemente, Pittsburgh
C— Joe Torre, Milwaukee
P— Sandy Koufax, Los Angeles
P— Jim Bunning, Philadelphia

1965
AMERICAN LEAGUE
1B— Fred Whitfield, Cleveland
2B— Bobby Richardson, New York
SS— Zoilo Versalles, Minnesota
3B— Brooks Robinson, Baltimore
OF— Carl Yastrzemski, Boston
OF— Jimmie Hall, Minnesota
OF— Tony Oliva, Minnesota
C— Earl Battey, Minnesota
P— Jim Grant, Minnesota
P— Mel Stottlemyre, New York

NATIONAL LEAGUE
1B— Willie McCovey, San Francisco
2B— Pete Rose, Cincinnati
SS— Maury Wills, Los Angeles
3B— Deron Johnson, Cincinnati
OF— Willie Stargell, Pittsburgh
OF— Willie Mays, San Francisco
OF— Hank Aaron, Milwaukee
C— Joe Torre, Milwaukee
P— Sandy Koufax, Los Angeles
P— Juan Marichal, San Francisco

1966
AMERICAN LEAGUE
1B— Boog Powell, Baltimore
2B— Bobby Richardson, New York
SS— Luis Aparicio, Baltimore
3B— Brooks Robinson, Baltimore
OF— Frank Robinson, Baltimore
OF— Al Kaline, Detroit
OF— Tony Oliva, Minnesota
C— Paul Casanova, Washington
P— Jim Kaat, Minnesota
P— Earl Wilson, Detroit

NATIONAL LEAGUE
1B— Felipe Alou, Atlanta
2B— Pete Rose, Cincinnati
SS— Gene Alley, Pittsburgh
3B— Ron Santo, Chicago
OF— Willie Stargell, Pittsburgh
OF— Willie Mays, San Francisco
OF— Roberto Clemente, Pittsburgh
C— Joe Torre, Atlanta
P— Sandy Koufax, Los Angeles
P— Juan Marichal, San Francisco

1967
AMERICAN LEAGUE
1B— Harmon Killebrew, Minnesota
2B— Rod Carew, Minnesota
SS— Jim Fregosi, California
3B— Brooks Robinson, Baltimore
OF— Carl Yastrzemski, Boston
OF— Al Kaline, Detroit
OF— Frank Robinson, Baltimore
C— Bill Freehan, Detroit
P— Jim Lonborg, Boston
P— Earl Wilson, Detroit

NATIONAL LEAGUE
1B— Orlando Cepeda, St. Louis
2B— Bill Mazeroski, Pittsburgh
SS— Gene Alley, Pittsburgh
3B— Ron Santo, Chicago
OF— Hank Aaron, Atlanta
OF— Jim Wynn, Houston
OF— Roberto Clemente, Pittsburgh
C— Tim McCarver, St. Louis
P— Mike McCormick, San Francisco
P— Ferguson Jenkins, Chicago

1968
AMERICAN LEAGUE
1B— Boog Powell, Baltimore
2B— Rod Carew, Minnesota
SS— Luis Aparicio, Chicago
3B— Brooks Robinson, Baltimore
OF— Ken Harrelson, Boston
OF— Willie Horton, Detroit
OF— Frank Howard, Washington
C— Bill Freehan, Detroit
P— Dave McNally, Baltimore
P— Denny McLain, Detroit

NATIONAL LEAGUE
1B— Willie McCovey, San Francisco
2B— Tommy Helms, Cincinnati
SS— Don Kessinger, Chicago
3B— Ron Santo, Chicago
OF— Billy Williams, Chicago
OF— Curt Flood, St. Louis
OF— Pete Rose, Cincinnati
C— Johnny Bench, Cincinnati
P— Bob Gibson, St. Louis
P— Juan Marichal, San Francisco

1969
AMERICAN LEAGUE
1B— Boog Powell, Baltimore
2B— Rod Carew, Minnesota
SS— Rico Petrocelli, Boston
3B— Harmon Killebrew, Minnesota
OF— Frank Howard, Washington
OF— Paul Blair, Baltimore
OF— Reggie Jackson, Oakland
C— Bill Freehan, Detroit
RHP— Denny McLain, Detroit
LHP— Mike Cuellar, Baltimore

NATIONAL LEAGUE
1B— Willie McCovey, San Francisco
2B— Glenn Beckert, Chicago
SS— Don Kessinger, Chicago
3B— Ron Santo, Chicago
OF— Cleon Jones, New York
OF— Matty Alou, Pittsburgh
OF— Hank Aaron, Atlanta
C— Johnny Bench, Cincinnati
RHP— Tom Seaver, New York
LHP— Steve Carlton, St. Louis

1970
AMERICAN LEAGUE
1B— Boog Powell, Baltimore
2B— Dave Johnson, Baltimore
SS— Luis Aparicio, Chicago
3B— Harmon Killebrew, Minnesota
OF— Frank Howard, Washington
OF— Reggie Smith, Boston
OF— Tony Oliva, Minnesota
C— Ray Fosse, Cleveland
RHP— Jim Perry, Minnesota
LHP— Sam McDowell, Cleveland

NATIONAL LEAGUE
1B— Willie McCovey, San Francisco
2B— Glenn Beckert, Chicago
SS— Don Kessinger, Chicago
3B— Tony Perez, Cincinnati
OF— Billy Williams, Chicago
OF— Bobby Tolan, Cincinnati
OF— Hank Aaron, Atlanta
C— Johnny Bench, Cincinnati
RHP— Bob Gibson, St. Louis
LHP— Jim Merritt, Cincinnati

1971
AMERICAN LEAGUE
1B— Norm Cash, Detroit
2B— Cookie Rojas, Kansas City
SS— Leo Cardenas, Minnesota
3B— Brooks Robinson, Baltimore
OF— Merv Rettenmund, Baltimore
OF— Bobby Murcer, New York
OF— Tony Oliva, Minnesota
C— Bill Freehan, Detroit
RHP— Jim Palmer, Baltimore
LHP— Vida Blue, Oakland

NATIONAL LEAGUE
1B— Lee May, Cincinnati
2B— Glenn Beckett, Chicago
SS— Bud Harrelson, New York
3B— Joe Torre, St. Louis
OF— Willie Stargell, Pittsburgh
OF— Willie Davis, Los Angeles
OF— Hank Aaron, Atlanta
C— Manny Sanguillen, Pittsburgh
RHP— Ferguson Jenkins, Chicago
LHP— Steve Carlton, St. Louis

1972
AMERICAN LEAGUE
1B— Dick Allen, Chicago
2B— Rod Carew, Minnesota
SS— Luis Aparicio, Boston
3B— Brooks Robinson, Baltimore
OF— Joe Rudi, Oakland
OF— Bobby Murcer, New York
OF— Richie Scheinblum, Kansas City
C— Carlton Fisk, Boston
RHP— Gaylord Perry, Cleveland
LHP— Wilbur Wood, Chicago

NATIONAL LEAGUE
1B— Willie Stargell, Pittsburgh
2B— Joe Morgan, Cincinnati
SS— Chris Speier, San Francisco
3B— Ron Santo, Chicago
OF— Billy Williams, Chicago
OF— Cesar Cedeno, Houston

OF— Roberto Clemente, Pittsburgh
C— Johnny Bench, Cincinnati
RHP— Ferguson Jenkins, Chicago
LHP— Steve Carlton, Philadelphia

1973
AMERICAN LEAGUE
1B— John Mayberry, Kansas City
2B— Rod Carew, Minnesota
SS— Bert Campaneris, Oakland
3B— Sal Bando, Oakland
OF— Reggie Jackson, Oakland
OF— Amos Otis, Kansas City
OF— Bobby Murcer, New York
C— Thurman Munson, New York
RHP— Jim Palmer, Baltimore
LHP— Ken Holtzman, Oakland

NATIONAL LEAGUE
1B— Tony Perez, Cincinnati
2B— Dave Johnson, Atlanta
SS— Bill Russell, Los Angeles
3B— Darrell Evans, Atlanta
OF— Bobby Bonds, San Francisco
OF— Cesar Cedeno, Houston
OF— Pete Rose, Cincinnati
C— Johnny Bench, Cincinnati
RHP— Tom Seaver, New York
LHP— Ron Bryant, San Francisco

1974
AMERICAN LEAGUE
1B— Dick Allen, Chicago
2B— Rod Carew, Minnesota
SS— Bert Campaneris, Oakland
3B— Sal Bando, Oakland
OF— Joe Rudi, Oakland
OF— Paul Blair, Baltimore
OF— Jeff Burroughs, Texas
C— Thurman Munson, New York
DH— Tommy Davis, Baltimore
RHP— Jim Hunter, Oakland
LHP— Mike Cuellar, Baltimore

NATIONAL LEAGUE
1B— Steve Garvey, Los Angeles
2B— Joe Morgan, Cincinnati
SS— Dave Concepcion, Cincinnati
3B— Mike Schmidt, Philadelphia
OF— Lou Brock, St. Louis
OF— Jim Wynn, Los Angeles
OF— Richie Zisk, Pittsburgh
C— Johnny Bench, Cincinnati
RHP— Andy Messersmith, Los Angeles
LHP— Don Gullett, Cincinnati

1975
AMERICAN LEAGUE
1B— John Mayberry, Kansas City
2B— Rod Carew, Minnesota
SS— Toby Harrah, Texas
3B— Graig Nettles, New York
OF— Jim Rice, Boston
OF— Fred Lynn, Boston
OF— Reggie Jackson, Oakland
C— Thurman Munson, New York
DH— Willie Horton, Detroit
RHP— Jim Palmer, Baltimore
LHP— Jim Kaat, Chicago

NATIONAL LEAGUE
1B— Steve Garvey, Los Angeles
2B— Joe Morgan, Cincinnati
SS— Larry Bowa, Philadelphia
3B— Bill Madlock, Chicago
OF— Greg Luzinski, Philadelphia
OF— Al Oliver, Pittsburgh
OF— Dave Parker, Pittsburgh
C— Johnny Bench, Cincinnati
RHP— Tom Seaver, New York
LHP— Randy Jones, San Diego

1976
AMERICAN LEAGUE
1B— Chris Chambliss, New York
2B— Bobby Grich, Baltimore
3B— George Brett, Kansas City
SS— Mark Belanger, Baltimore
OF— Joe Rudi, Oakland
OF— Mickey Rivers, New York
OF— Reggie Jackson, Baltimore
C— Thurman Munson, New York
DH— Hal McRae, Kansas City
RHP— Jim Palmer, Baltimore
LHP— Frank Tanana, California

NATIONAL LEAGUE
1B— Willie Montanez, S.F.-Atl.
2B— Joe Morgan, Cincinnati
3B— Mike Schmidt, Philadelphia
SS— Dave Concepcion, Cincinnati
OF— George Foster, Cincinnati
OF— Cesar Cedeno, Houston
OF— Ken Griffey, Cincinnati
C— Bob Boone, Philadelphia
RHP— Don Sutton, Los Angeles
LHP— Randy Jones, San Diego

1977
AMERICAN LEAGUE
1B— Rod Carew, Minnesota
2B— Willie Randolph, New York
3B— Graig Nettles, New York
SS— Rick Burleson, Boston
OF— Jim Rice, Boston
OF— Larry Hisle, Minnesota
OF— Bobby Bonds, California
C— Carlton Fisk, Boston
DH— Hal McRae, Kansas City
RHP— Nolan Ryan, California
LHP— Frank Tanana, California

NATIONAL LEAGUE
1B— Steve Garvey, Los Angeles
2B— Joe Morgan, Cincinnati
3B— Mike Schmidt, Philadelphia
SS— Garry Templeton, St. Louis
OF— George Foster, Cincinnati
OF— Dave Parker, Pittsburgh
OF— Greg Luzinski, Philadelphia
C— Ted Simmons, St. Louis
RHP— Rick Reuschel, Chicago
LHP— Steve Carlton, Philadelphia

1978
AMERICAN LEAGUE
1B— Rod Carew, Minnesota
2B— Frank White, Kansas City
3B— Graig Nettles, New York
SS— Robin Yount, Milwaukee
OF— Jim Rice, Boston
OF— Larry Hisle, Milwaukee
OF— Fred Lynn, Boston
C— Jim Sundberg, Texas
DH— Rusty Staub, Detroit
RHP— Jim Palmer, Baltimore
LHP— Ron Guidry, New York

NATIONAL LEAGUE
1B— Steve Garvey, Los Angeles
2B— Dave Lopes, Los Angeles
3B— Pete Rose, Cincinnati
SS— Larry Bowa, Philadelphia
OF— George Foster, Cincinnati
OF— Dave Parker, Pittsburgh
OF— Jack Clark, San Francisco
C— Ted Simmons, St. Louis
RHP— Gaylord Perry, San Diego
LHP— Vida Blue, San Francisco

1979
AMERICAN LEAGUE
1B— Cecil Cooper, Milwaukee
2B— Bobby Grich, California

3B— George Brett, Kansas City
SS— Roy Smalley, Minnesota
OF— Jim Rice, Boston
OF— Fred Lynn, Boston
OF— Ken Singleton, Baltimore
C— Darrell Porter, Kansas City
DH— Don Baylor, California
RHP— Jim Kern, Texas
LHP— Mike Flanagan, Baltimore

NATIONAL LEAGUE
1B— Keith Hernandez, St. Louis
2B— Dave Lopes, Los Angeles
3B— Mike Schmidt, Philadelphia
SS— Garry Templeton, St. Louis
OF— Dave Kingman, Chicago
OF— Omar Moreno, Pittsburgh
OF— Dave Winfield, San Diego
C— Ted Simmons, St. Louis
RHP— Joe Niekro, Houston
LHP— Steve Carlton, Philadelphia

1980
AMERICAN LEAGUE
1B— Cecil Cooper, Milwaukee
2B— Willie Randolph, New York
3B— George Brett, Kansas City
SS— Robin Yount, Milwaukee
OF— Ben Oglivie, Milwaukee
OF— Al Bumbry, Baltimore
OF— Reggie Jackson, New York
DH— Reggie Jackson, New York
C— Rick Cerone, New York
RHP— Steve Stone, Baltimore
LHP— Tommy John, New York

NATIONAL LEAGUE
1B— Keith Hernandez, St. Louis
2B— Manny Trillo, Philadelphia
3B— Mike Schmidt, Philadelphia
SS— Garry Templeton, St. Louis
OF— Dusty Baker, Los Angeles
OF— Cesar Cedeno, Houston
OF— George Hendrick, St. Louis
C— Gary Carter, Montreal
RHP— Jim Bibby, Pittsburgh
LHP— Steve Carlton, Philadelphia

1981
AMERICAN LEAGUE
1B— Cecil Cooper, Milwaukee
2B— Bobby Grich, California
3B— Buddy Bell, Texas
SS— Rick Burleson, California
OF— Rickey Henderson, Oakland
OF— Dwayne Murphy, Oakland
OF— Tony Armas, Oakland
C— Jim Sundberg, Texas
DH— Richie Zisk, Seattle
RHP— Jack Morris, Detroit
LHP— Ron Guidry, New York

NATIONAL LEAGUE
1B— Pete Rose, Philadelphia
2B— Manny Trillo, Philadelphia
3B— Mike Schmidt, Philadelphia
SS— Dave Concepcion, Cincinnati
OF— George Foster, Cincinnati
OF— Andre Dawson, Montreal
OF— Pedro Guerrero, Los Angeles
C— Gary Carter, Montreal
RHP— Tom Seaver, Cincinnati
LHP— Fernando Valenzuela, Los Angel

1982
AMERICAN LEAGUE
1B— Cecil Cooper, Milwaukee
2B— Damaso Garcia, Toronto
3B— Doug DeCinces, California
SS— Robin Yount, Milwaukee
OF— Dave Winfield, New York
OF— Gorman Thomas, Milwaukee

OF— Dwight Evans, Boston
C— Lance Parrish, Detroit
DH— Hal McRae, Kansas City
RHP— Dave Stieb, Toronto
LHP— Geoff Zahn, California

NATIONAL LEAGUE
1B— Al Oliver, Montreal
2B— Manny Trillo, Philadelphia
3B— Mike Schmidt, Philadelphia
SS— Ozzie Smith, St. Louis
OF— Lonnie Smith, St. Louis
OF— Dale Murphy, Atlanta
OF— Pedro Guerrero, Los Angeles
C— Gary Carter, Montreal
RHP— Steve Rogers, Montreal
LHP— Steve Carlton, Philadelphia

1983
AMERICAN LEAGUE
1B— Eddie Murray, Baltimore
2B— Lou Whitaker, Detroit
3B— Wade Boggs, Boston
SS— Cal Ripken, Baltimore
OF— Jim Rice, Boston
OF— Dave Winfield, New York
OF— Lloyd Moseby, Toronto
C— Carlton Fisk, Chicago
DH— Greg Luzinski, Chicago
RHP— LaMarr Hoyt, Chicago
LHP— Ron Guidry, New York

NATIONAL LEAGUE
1B— George Hendrick, St. Louis
2B— Glenn Hubbard, Atlanta
3B— Mike Schmidt, Philadelphia
SS— Dickie Thon, Houston
OF— Dale Murphy, Atlanta
OF— Andre Dawson, Montreal
OF— Tim Raines, Montreal
C— Tony Pena, Pittsburgh
RHP— John Denny, Philadelphia
LHP— Larry McWilliams, Pittsburgh

1984
AMERICAN LEAGUE
1B— Don Mattingly, New York
2B— Lou Whitaker, Detroit
3B— Buddy Bell, Texas
SS— Cal Ripken, Baltimore
OF— Tony Armas, Boston
OF— Dwight Evans, Boston
OF— Dave Winfield, New York
C— Lance Parrish, Detroit
DH— Dave Kingman, Oakland
RHP— Mike Boddicker, Baltimore
LHP— Willie Hernandez, Detroit

NATIONAL LEAGUE
1B— Keith Hernandez, New York
2B— Ryne Sandberg, Chicago
3B— Mike Schmidt, Philadelphia
SS— Ozzie Smith, St. Louis
OF— Dale Murphy, Atlanta
OF— Jose Cruz, Houston
OF— Tony Gwynn, San Diego
C— Gary Carter, Montreal
RHP— Rick Sutcliffe, Chicago
LHP— Mark Thurmond, San Diego

1985
AMERICAN LEAGUE
1B— Don Mattingly, New York
2B— Damaso Garcia, Toronto
3B— Wade Boggs, Boston
SS— Cal Ripken, Baltimore
OF— Rickey Henderson, New York
OF— Harold Baines, Chicago
OF— Phil Bradley, Seattle
C— Carlton Fisk, Chicago
DH— Don Baylor, New York
RHP— Bret Saberhagen, Kansas City
LHP— Ron Guidry, New York

NATIONAL LEAGUE
1B— Keith Hernandez, New York
2B— Tom Herr, St. Louis
3B— Tim Wallach, Montreal
SS— Ozzie Smith, St. Louis
OF— Dave Parker, Cincinnati
OF— Willie McGee, St. Louis
OF— Dale Murphy, Atlanta
C— Gary Carter, New York
RHP— Dwight Gooden, New York
LHP— John Tudor, St. Louis

1986
AMERICAN LEAGUE
1B— Don Mattingly, New York
2B— Tony Bernazard, Cleveland
3B— Wade Boggs, Boston
SS— Tony Fernandez, Toronto
OF— Jim Rice, Boston
OF— George Bell, Toronto
OF— Kirby Puckett, Minnesota
C— Rich Gedman, Boston
DH— Don Baylor, Boston
RHP— Roger Clemens, Boston
LHP— Teddy Higuera, Milwaukee

NATIONAL LEAGUE
1B— Keith Hernandez, New York
2B— Steve Sax, Los Angeles
3B— Mike Schmidt, Philadelphia
SS— Ozzie Smith, St. Louis
OF— Tim Raines, Montreal
OF— Tony Gwynn, San Diego
OF— Dave Parker, Cincinnati
C— Gary Carter, New York
RHP— Mike Scott, Houston
LHP— Fernando Valenzuela, Los Angeles

1987
AMERICAN LEAGUE
1B— Don Mattingly, New York
2B— Willie Randolph, New York
3B— Wade Boggs, Boston
SS— Alan Trammell, Detroit
OF— George Bell, Toronto
OF— Kirby Puckett, Minnesota
OF— Dwight Evans, Boston
C— Matt Nokes, Detroit
DH— Paul Molitor, Milwaukee
RHP— Roger Clemens, Boston
LHP— Jimmy Key, Toronto

NATIONAL LEAGUE
1B— Jack Clark, St. Louis
2B— Juan Samuel, Philadelphia
3B— Tim Wallach, Montreal
SS— Ozzie Smith, St. Louis
OF— Andre Dawson, Chicago
OF— Tony Gwynn, San Diego
OF— Eric Davis, Cincinnati
C— Benito Santiago, San Diego
RHP— Rick Sutcliffe, Chicago
LHP— Zane Smith, Atlanta

1988
AMERICAN LEAGUE
1B— George Brett, Kansas City
2B— Johnny Ray, California
3B— Wade Boggs, Boston
SS— Alan Trammell, Detroit
OF— Kirby Puckett, Minnesota
OF— Mike Greenwell, Boston
OF— Jose Canseco, Oakland
C— Ernie Whitt, Toronto
DH— Harold Baines, Chicago
RHP— Dave Stewart, Oakland
LHP— Frank Viola, Minnesota

NATIONAL LEAGUE
1B— Will Clark, San Francisco
2B— Ryne Sandberg, Chicago
3B— Bobby Bonilla, Pittsburgh
SS— Barry Larkin, Cincinnati

OF— Darryl Strawberry, New York
OF— Andy Van Slyke, Pittsburgh
OF— Kevin McReynolds, New York
C— Mike LaValliere, Pittsburgh
RHP— Orel Hershiser, Los Angeles
LHP— Danny Jackson, Cincinnati

1989
AMERICAN LEAGUE
1B— Fred McGriff, Toronto
2B— Julio Franco, Texas
3B— Carney Lansford, Oakland
SS— Cal Ripken, Baltimore
OF— Ruben Sierra, Texas
OF— Kirby Puckett, Minnesota
OF— Robin Yount, Milwaukee
C— Mickey Tettleton, Baltimore
DH— Harold Baines, Chi.-Tex.
RHP— Bret Saberhagen, Kansas City
LHP— Chuck Finley, California

NATIONAL LEAGUE
1B— Will Clark, San Francisco
2B— Ryne Sandberg, Chicago
3B— Howard Johnson, New York
SS— Shawon Dunston, Chicago
OF— Tony Gwynn, San Diego
OF— Kevin Mitchell, San Francisco
OF— Eric Davis, Cincinnati
C— Benito Santiago, San Diego
RHP— Mike Scott, Houston
LHP— Mark Davis, San Diego

1990
AMERICAN LEAGUE
1B— Cecil Fielder, Detroit
2B— Julio Franco, Texas
3B— Kelly Gruber, Toronto
SS— Alan Trammell, Detroit
OF— Rickey Henderson, Oakland
OF— Jose Canseco, Oakland
OF— Ellis Burks, Boston
C— Carlton Fisk, Chicago
DH— Dave Parker, Milwaukee
RHP— Bob Welch, Oakland
LHP— Chuck Finley, California

NATIONAL LEAGUE
1B— Eddie Murray, Los Angeles
2B— Ryne Sandberg, Chicago
3B— Matt Williams, San Francisco
SS— Barry Larkin, Cincinnati
OF— Barry Bonds, Pittsburgh
OF— Bobby Bonilla, Pittsburgh
OF— Darryl Strawberry, New York
C— Mike Scioscia, Los Angeles
RHP— Doug Drabek, Pittsburgh
LHP— Frank Viola, New York

1991
AMERICAN LEAGUE
1B— Cecil Fielder, Detroit
2B— Julio Franco, Texas
3B— Wade Boggs, Boston
SS— Cal Ripken, Baltimore
OF— Jose Canseco, Oakland
OF— Joe Carter, Toronto
OF— Ken Griffey Jr., Seattle
C— Mickey Tettleton, Detroit
RHP— Roger Clemens, Boston
LHP— Jim Abbott, California

NATIONAL LEAGUE
1B— Will Clark, San Francisco
2B— Ryne Sandberg, Chicago
3B— Terry Pendleton, Atlanta
SS— Barry Larkin, Cincinnati
OF— Barry Bonds, Pittsburgh
OF— Bobby Bonilla, Pittsburgh
OF— Ron Gant, Atlanta
C— Benito Santiago, San Diego

RHP— Jose Rijo, Cincinnati
LHP— Tom Glavine, Atlanta

1992
AMERICAN LEAGUE
1B— Mark McGwire, Oakland
2B— Roberto Alomar, Toronto
3B— Edgar Martinez, Seattle
SS— Travis Fryman, Detroit
OF— Joe Carter, Toronto
OF— Mike Devereaux, Baltimore
OF— Kirby Puckett, Minnesota
C— Mickey Tettleton, Detroit
RHP— Jack McDowell, Chicago
LHP— Dave Fleming, Seattle

NATIONAL LEAGUE
1B— Fred McGriff, San Diego
2B— Ryne Sandberg, Chicago
3B— Gary Sheffield, San Diego
SS— Barry Larkin, Cincinnati
OF— Barry Bonds, Pittsburgh
OF— Andy Van Slyke, Pittsburgh
OF— Larry Walker, Montreal
C— Darren Daulton, Philadelphia
RHP— Greg Maddux, Chicago
LHP— Tom Glavine, Atlanta

1993
AMERICAN LEAGUE
1B— Frank Thomas, Chicago
2B— Carlos Baerga, Cleveland
3B— Travis Fryman, Detroit
SS— Cal Ripken Jr., Baltimore
OF— Albert Belle, Cleveland
OF— Juan Gonzalez, Texas
OF— Ken Griffey Jr., Seattle
C— Mike Stanley, New York
DH— Paul Molitor, Toronto
RHP— Jack McDowell, Chicago
LHP— Jimmy Key, New York

NATIONAL LEAGUE
1B— Fred McGriff, S.D.-Atl.
2B— Robby Thompson, San Francisco

3B— Matt Williams, San Francisco
SS— Jay Bell, Pittsburgh
OF— Barry Bonds, San Francisco
OF— Lenny Dykstra, Philadelphia
OF— David Justice, Atlanta
C— Mike Piazza, Los Angeles
RHP— Greg Maddux, Atlanta
LHP— Steve Avery, Atlanta

1994
AMERICAN LEAGUE
1B— Frank Thomas, Chicago
2B— Chuck Knoblauch, Minnesota
3B— Wade Boggs, New York
SS— Cal Ripken Jr., Baltimore
OF— Albert Belle, Cleveland
OF— Ken Griffey Jr., Seattle
OF— Kirby Puckett, Minnesota
C— Ivan Rodriguez, Texas
DH— Paul Molitor, Toronto
RHP— David Cone, Kansas City
LHP— Jimmy Key, New York

NATIONAL LEAGUE
1B— Jeff Bagwell, Houston
2B— Craig Biggio, Houston
3B— Matt Williams, San Francisco
SS— Barry Larkin, Cincinnati
OF— Moises Alou, Montreal
OF— Barry Bonds, San Francisco
OF— Tony Gwynn, San Diego
C— Mike Piazza, Los Angeles
RHP— Greg Maddux, Atlanta
LHP— Danny Jackson, Philadelphia

1995
AMERICAN LEAGUE
1B— Mo Vaughn, Boston
2B— Carlos Baerga, Cleveland
3B— Jim Thome, Cleveland
SS— Cal Ripken Jr., Baltimore
OF— Albert Belle, Cleveland
OF— Tim Salmon, California
OF— Jim Edmonds, California
C— Ivan Rodriguez, Texas
DH— Edgar Martinez, Seattle

RHP— Mike Mussina, Baltimore
LHP— Randy Johnson, Seattle

NATIONAL LEAGUE
1B— Eric Karros, Los Angeles
2B— Craig Biggio, Houston
3B— Vinny Castilla, Colorado
SS— Barry Larkin, Cincinnati
OF— Reggie Sanders, Cincinnati
OF— Dante Bichette, Colorado
OF— Sammy Sosa, Chicago
C— Mike Piazza, Los Angeles
RHP— Greg Maddux, Atlanta
LHP— Pete Schourek, Cincinnati

1996
AMERICAN LEAGUE
1B— Mark McGwire, Oakland
2B— Roberto Alomar, Baltimore
3B— Jim Thome, Cleveland
SS— Alex Rodriguez, Seattle
OF— Albert Belle, Cleveland
OF— Juan Gonzalez, Texas
OF— Ken Griffey Jr., Seattle
C— Ivan Rodriguez, Texas
DH— Paul Molitor, Minnesota
RHP— Pat Hentgen, Toronto
LHP— Andy Pettitte, New York

NATIONAL LEAGUE
1B— Jeff Bagwell, Houston
2B— Eric Young, Colorado
3B— Ken Caminiti, San Diego
SS— Barry Larkin, Cincinnati
OF— Barry Bonds, San Francisco
OF— Ellis Burks, Colorado
OF— Gary Sheffield, Florida
C— Mike Piazza, Los Angeles
RHP— John Smoltz, Atlanta
LHP— Al Leiter, Florida

MINOR LEAGUE PLAYER OF THE YEAR

Year	Player, Team, League
1936	John Vander Meer, Durham, Piedmont
1937	Charlie Keller, Newark, International
1938	Fred Hutchinson, Seattle, Pacific Coast
1939	Lou Novikoff, Tulsa, Texas; Los Angeles, Pacific Coast
1940	Phil Rizzuto, Kansas City, American Association
1941	John Lindell, Newark, International
1942	Dick Barrett, Seattle, Pacific Coast
1943	Chet Covington, Scranton, Eastern
1944	Rip Collins, Albany, Eastern
1945	Gil Coan, Chattanooga, Southern
1946	Sibby Sisti, Indianapolis, American Association
1947	Hank Sauer, Syracuse, International
1948	Gene Woodling, San Francisco, Pacific Coast
1949	Orie Arntzen, Albany, Eastern
1950	Frank Saucier, San Antonio, Texas
1951	Gene Conley, Hartford, Eastern
1952	Bill Skowron, Kansas City, American Association
1953	Gene Conley, Toledo, American Association
1954	Herb Score, Indianapolis, American Association
1955	John Murff, Dallas, Texas
1956	Steve Bilko, Los Angeles, Pacific Coast
1957	Norm Siebern, Denver, American Association
1958	Jim O'Toole, Nashville, Southern
1959	Frank Howard, Victoria-Spokane
1960	Willie Davis, Spokane, Pacific Coast
1961	Howie Koplitz, Birmingham, Southern
1962	Bob Bailey, Columbus, International
1963	Don Buford, Indianapolis, International
1964	Mel Stottlemyre, Richmond, International
1965	Joe Foy, Toronto, International
1966	Mike Epstein, Rochester, International
1967	Johnny Bench, Buffalo, International

Year	Player, Team, League
1968	Merv Rettenmund, Rochester, International
1969	Danny Walton, Oklahoma City, American Association
1970	Don Baylor, Rochester, International
1971	Bobby Grich, Rochester, International
1972	Tom Paciorek, Albuquerque, Pacific Coast
1973	Steve Ontiveros, Phoenix, Pacific Coast
1974	Jim Rice, Pawtucket, International
1975	Hector Cruz, Tulsa, American Association
1976	Pat Putnam, Asheville, Western Carolina
1977	Ken Landreaux, S.L.C., Pacific Coast; El Paso, Texas
1978	Champ Summers, Indianapolis, American Association
1979	Mark Bomback, Vancouver, Pacific Coast
1980	Tim Raines, Denver, American Association
1981	Mike Marshall, Albuquerque, Pacific Coast
1982	Ron Kittle, Edmonton, Pacific Coast
1983	Kevin McReynolds, Las Vegas, Pacific Coast
1984	Alan Knicely, Wichita, American Association
1985	Jose Canseco, Hunt., Southern-Tac., Pacific Coast
1986	Tim Pyznarski, Las Vegas, Pacific Coast
1987	Randy Milligan, Tidewater, International
1988	Sandy Alomar Jr., Las Vegas, Pacific Coast; Gary Sheffield, Denver, American Association (tie)
1989	Sandy Alomar Jr., Las Vegas, Pacific Coast
1990	Jose Offerman, Albuquerque, Pacific Coast
1991	Pedro Martinez, Albuquerque, Pacific Coast
1992	Tim Salmon, Edmonton, Pacific Coast
1993	Cliff Floyd, Harrisburg, Eastern
1994	Derek Jeter, Tampa, Florida State; Albany, Eastern; Columbus, International
1995	Karim Garcia, Albuquerque, Pacific Coast
1996	Vladimir Guerrero, West Palm Beach, Florida State; Harrisburg, Eastern

MINOR LEAGUE MANAGER OF THE YEAR

Year	Manager, Team, League	Year	Manager, Team, League
1936	Al Sothoron, Milwaukee, American Association	1967	Bob Skinner, San Diego, Pacific Coast
1937	Jake Flowers, Salisbury, Eastern Shore	1968	Jack Tighe, Toledo, International
1938	Paul Richards, Atlanta, Southern	1969	Clyde McCullough, Tidewater, International
1939	Bill Meyer, Kansas City, American Association	1970	Tom Lasorda, Spokane, Pacific Coast
1940	Larry Gilbert, Nashville, Southern	1971	Del Rice, Salt Lake City, Pacific Coast
1941	Burt Shotton, Columbus, American Association	1972	Hank Bauer, Tidewater, International
1942	Eddie Dyer, Columbus, American Association	1973	Joe Morgan, Charleston, International
1943	Nick Cullop, Columbus, American Association	1974	Joe Altobelli, Rochester, International
1944	Al Thomas, Baltimore, International	1975	Joe Frazier, Tidewater, International
1945	Lefty O'Doul, San Francisco, Pacific Coast	1976	Vern Rapp, Denver, American Association
1946	Clay Hopper, Montreal, International	1977	Tommy Thompson, Arkan., Texas
1947	Nick Cullop, Milwaukee, American Association	1978	Les Moss, Evansville, American Association
1948	Casey Stengel, Oakland, Pacific Coast	1979	Vern Benson, Syracuse, International
1949	Fred Haney, Hollywood, Pacific Coast	1980	Hal Lanier, Springfield, American Association
1950	Rollie Hemsley, Columbus, American Association	1981	Del Crandall, Albuquerque, Pacific Coast
1951	Charlie Grimm, Milwaukee, American Association	1982	George Scherger, Indianapolis, American Association
1952	Luke Appling, Memphis, Southern	1983	Bill Dancy, Reading, Eastern
1953	Bobby Bragan, Hollywood, Pacific Coast	1984	Bob Rodgers, Indianapolis, American Association
1954	Kerby Farrell, Indianapolis, American Association	1985	Jim Fregosi, Louisville, American Association
1955	Bill Rigney, Minneapolis, American Association	1986	Joe Sparks, Indianapolis, American Association
1956	Kerby Farrell, Indianapolis, American Association	1987	Terry Collins, Albuquerque, Pacific Coast
1957	Ben Geraghty, Wichita, American Association	1988	Joe Sparks, Indianapolis, American Association
1958	Cal Ermer, Birmingham, Southern	1989	Bob Bailor, Syracuse, International
1959	Pete Reiser, Victoria, Texas	1990	Sal Rende, Omaha, American Association
1960	Mel McGaha, Toronto, International	1991	Chris Chambliss, Greenville, Southern
1961	Kerby Farrell, Buffalo, International	1992	Grady Little, Greenville, Southern
1962	Ben Geraghty, Jacksonville, International	1993	Jim Tracy, Harrisburg, Eastern
1963	Rollie Hemsley, Indianapolis, International	1994	Mike Jirschele, Wilmington, Carolina
1964	Harry Walker, Jacksonville, International	1995	Pete Mackanin, Ottawa, International
1965	Grady Hatton, Oklahoma City, Pacific Coast	1996	John Mizerock, Wilmington, Carolina
1966	Bob Lemon, Seattle, Pacific Coast		

MINOR LEAGUE EXECUTIVE OF THE YEAR (HIGHER CLASSIFICATIONS, 1936-1992)

(Restricted to Class AAA starting in 1963)

Year	Executive, Team, League	Year	Executive, Team, League
1936	Earl Mann, Atlanta, Southern	1965	Harold Cooper, Columbus, International
1937	Robert LaMotte, Savannah, Sally	1966	John Quinn Jr., Hawaii, Pacific Coast
1938	Louis McKenna, St. Paul, American Association	1967	Hillman Lyons, Richmond, International
1939	Bruce Dudley, Louisville, American Association	1968	Gabe Paul Jr., Tulsa, Pacific Coast
1940	Roy Hamey, Kansas City, American Association	1969	Bill Gardner, Louisville, International
1941	Emil Sick, Seattle, Pacific Coast	1970	Dick King, Wichita, American Association
1942	Bill Veeck, Milwaukee, American Association	1971	Carl Steinfeldt Jr., Rochester, International
1943	Clarence Rowland, Los Angeles, Pacific Coast	1972	Don Labbruzzo, Evansville, American Association
1944	William Mulligan, Seattle, Pacific Coast	1973	Merle Miller, Tucson, Pacific Coast
1945	Bruce Dudley, Louisville, American Association	1974	John Carbray, Sacramento, Pacific Coast
1946	Earl Mann, Atlanta, Southern	1975	Stan Naccarato, Tacoma, Pacific Coast
1947	William Purnhage, Waterloo, I.I.I.	1976	Art Teece, Salt Lake City, Pacific Coast
1948	Edward Glennon, Birmingham, Southern	1977	George Sisler Jr., Columbus, International
1949	Ted Sullivan, Indianapolis, American Association	1978	Willie Sanchez, Albuquerque, Pacific Coast
1950	Clearnce (Brick) Laws, Oakland, Pacific Coast	1979	George Sisler Jr., Columbus, International
1951	Robert Howsam, Denver, West	1980	Jim Burris, Denver, American Association
1952	Jack Cooke, Toronto, International	1981	Pat McKernan, Albuquerque, Pacific Coast
1953	Richard Burnett, Dallas, Texas	1982	A. Ray Smith, Louisville, American Association
1954	Edward Stumpf, Indianapolis, American Association	1983	A. Ray Smith, Louisville, American Association
1955	Dewey Soriano, Seattle, Pacific Coast	1984	Mike Tamburro, Pawtucket, International
1956	Robert Howsam, Denver American Association	1985	Patty Cox Hampton, Oklahoma City, American Association
1957	John Stiglmeier, Buffalo, International	1986	Bob Goughan, Rochester, International
1958	Edward Glennon, Birmingham, Southern	1987	Stu Kehoe, Vancouver, Pacific Coast
1959	Edward Leishman, Salt Lake City, Pacific Coast	1988	Bob Rich, Buffalo, American Association
1960	Ray Winder, Little Rock, Southern	1989	Larry Schmittou, Nashville, American Association
1961	Elten Schiller, Omaha, American Association	1990	Greg Corns, Phoenix, Pacific Coast
1962	George Sisler Jr., Rochester, International	1991	Tom Maloney, Denver, American Association
1963	Lewis Matlin, Hawaii, Pacific Coast	1992	Lou Schwechheimer, Pawtucket, International
1964	Edward Leishman, San Diego, Pacific Coast		

MINOR LEAGUE EXECUTIVE OF THE YEAR (LOWER CLASSIFICATIONS, 1950-1990)

(Separate awards for Class AA and Class A started in 1963; for Short Class A in 1988)

Year	Executive, Team, League	Year	Executive, Team, League
1950	H. Cooper, Hutchinson, Western Association	1956	Marvin Milkes, Fresno, California
1951	O. W. (Bill) Hayes, Triple, B.S.	1957	Richard Wagner, Lincoln, West.
1952	Hillman Lyons, Danville, MOV	1958	Gerald Waring, Macon, Sally
1953	Carl Roth, Peoria, I.I.I.	1959	Clay Dennis, Des Moines, I.I.I.
1954	James Meagham, Cedar Rapids, I.I.I.	1960	Hubert Kittle, Yakima, Northwest
1955	John Petrakis, Dubuque, MOV	1961	David Steele, Fresno, California

Year	Executive, Team, League	Year	Executive, Team, League
1962—John Quinn Jr., San Jose, California		1978—Larry Schmittou, Nashville, Southern	
1963—Hugh Finnerty, Tulsa, Texas		Dave Hersh, Appleton, Midwest	
Ben Jewell, M. Valley, Pioneer		1979—Bill Rigney Jr., Midland, Texas	
1964—Glynn West, Birmingham, Southern		Tom Romenesko, Greensboro, W.C.	
James Bayens, Rock Hill, W. Carolina		1980—Frances Crockett, Charlotte, Southern	
1965—Dick Butler, Dallas-Ft. Worth, Texas		Tom Romenesko, Greensboro, W.C.	
Ken. Blackman, Quad Cities, Midwest		1981—Allie Prescott, Memphis, Southern	
1966—Tom Fleming, Evansville, Southern		Dan Overstreet, Hagerstown, Caro.	
Cappy Harada, Lodi, California		1982—Art Clarkson, Birmingham, Southern	
1967—Robert Quinn, Reading, Eastern		Bob Carruesco, Stockton, California	
Pat Williams, Spar'burg, W.C.		1983—Edward Kenney, New Britain, Eastern	
1968—Phil Howser, Charlotte, Southern		Terry Reynolds, Vero Beach, Florida State	
Merle Miller, Burlington, Midwest		1984—Bruce Baldwin, Greenville, Southern	
1969—Charlie Blaney, Albuquerque, Texas		Dave Tarrolly, Beloit, Midwest	
Bill Gorman, Visalia, California		1985—Ben Bernard, Albany-Colonie, Eastern	
1970—Carl Sawatski, Arkansas, Texas		Pete Vonachen, Peoria, Midwest	
Bob Williams, Bakersfield, California		1986—Bill Davidson, Midland, Texas	
1971—Miles Wolff, Savannah, Dixie Association		Rob Dlugozima, Durham, Carolina	
Ed Holtz, Appleton, Midwest		1987—Joe Preseren, Tulsa, Texas	
1972—John Begzos, S. Antonio, Texas		Skip Weisman, Greensboro, South Atlantic	
Bob Piccinini, Modesto, California		1988—Bill Valentine, Arkansas, Texas	
1973—Dick Kravitz, Jacksonville, Southern		Dennis Bastien, Charleston (W.Va.), South Atlantic	
Fritz Colschen, Clinton, Midwest		Bob Beban, Eugene, Northwest	
1974—Jim Paul, El Paso, Texas		1989—Chuck Domino, Reading, Eastern	
Bing Russell, Portland, Northwest		John Baxter, South Bend, Midwest	
1975—Jim Paul, El Paso, Texas		Bill Pereira, Boise, Northwest	
Cordy Jensen, Eugene, Northwest		1990—Joe Preseren, Tulsa, Texas	
1976—Woodrow Reid, Chattanooga, Southern		Dan Chapman, Stockton, California	
Don Buchheister, Cedar Rapids, Midwest		Dave Baggott, Salt Lake City, Pioneer	
1977—Jim Paul, El Paso, Texas			
Harry Pells, Quad Cities, Midwest			

MINOR LEAGUE EXECUTIVE OF THE YEAR

Year	Executive, Team, League	Year	Executive, Team, League
1993—Todd Vander Woude, Harrisburg, Eastern (AA)		1995—Jack and Mary Cain, Portland, Northwest (A)	
1994—Scott Lane, West Michigan, Midwest (A)		1996—Wayne Hodes, Trenton, Eastern (AA)	

BASEBALL WRITERS' ASSOCIATION OF AMERICA

MOST VALUABLE PLAYER

<table>
<tr><th colspan="5">AMERICAN LEAGUE</th><th colspan="5">NATIONAL LEAGUE</th></tr>
<tr><th>Year</th><th>Player</th><th>Team</th><th>Pos.</th><th>Points</th><th>Year</th><th>Player</th><th>Team</th><th>Pos.</th><th>Point</th></tr>
<tr><td>1931—Lefty Grove</td><td></td><td>Philadelphia</td><td>P</td><td>78</td><td>1931—Frank Frisch</td><td></td><td>St. Louis</td><td>2B</td><td>6</td></tr>
<tr><td>1932—Jimmie Foxx</td><td></td><td>Philadelphia</td><td>1B</td><td>75</td><td>1932—Chuck Klein</td><td></td><td>Philadelphia</td><td>OF</td><td>7</td></tr>
<tr><td>1933—Jimmie Foxx</td><td></td><td>Philadelphia</td><td>1B</td><td>74</td><td>1933—Carl Hubbell</td><td></td><td>New York</td><td>P</td><td>7</td></tr>
<tr><td>1934—Mickey Cochrane</td><td></td><td>Detroit</td><td>C</td><td>67</td><td>1934—Dizzy Dean</td><td></td><td>St. Louis</td><td>P</td><td>7</td></tr>
<tr><td>1935—Hank Greenberg</td><td></td><td>Detroit</td><td>1B</td><td>*80</td><td>1935—Gabby Hartnett</td><td></td><td>Chicago</td><td>C</td><td>7</td></tr>
<tr><td>1936—Lou Gehrig</td><td></td><td>New York</td><td>1B</td><td>73</td><td>1936—Carl Hubbell</td><td></td><td>New York</td><td>P</td><td>6</td></tr>
<tr><td>1937—Charley Gehringer</td><td></td><td>Detroit</td><td>2B</td><td>78</td><td>1937—Joe Medwick</td><td></td><td>St. Louis</td><td>OF</td><td>7</td></tr>
<tr><td>1938—Jimmie Foxx</td><td></td><td>Boston</td><td>1B</td><td>305</td><td>1938—Ernie Lombardi</td><td></td><td>Cincinnati</td><td>C</td><td>22</td></tr>
<tr><td>1939—Joe DiMaggio</td><td></td><td>New York</td><td>OF</td><td>280</td><td>1939—Bucky Walters</td><td></td><td>Cincinnati</td><td>P</td><td>30</td></tr>
<tr><td>1940—Hank Greenberg</td><td></td><td>Detroit</td><td>OF</td><td>292</td><td>1940—Frank McCormick</td><td></td><td>Cincinnati</td><td>1B</td><td>27</td></tr>
<tr><td>1941—Joe DiMaggio</td><td></td><td>New York</td><td>OF</td><td>291</td><td>1941—Dolf Camilli</td><td></td><td>Brooklyn</td><td>1B</td><td>30</td></tr>
<tr><td>1942—Joe Gordon</td><td></td><td>New York</td><td>2B</td><td>270</td><td>1942—Mort Cooper</td><td></td><td>St. Louis</td><td>P</td><td>26</td></tr>
<tr><td>1943—Spud Chandler</td><td></td><td>New York</td><td>P</td><td>246</td><td>1943—Stan Musial</td><td></td><td>St. Louis</td><td>OF</td><td>26</td></tr>
<tr><td>1944—Hal Newhouser</td><td></td><td>Detroit</td><td>P</td><td>236</td><td>1944—Marty Marion</td><td></td><td>St. Louis</td><td>SS</td><td>19</td></tr>
<tr><td>1945—Hal Newhouser</td><td></td><td>Detroit</td><td>P</td><td>236</td><td>1945—Phil Cavarretta</td><td></td><td>Chicago</td><td>1B</td><td>27</td></tr>
<tr><td>1946—Ted Williams</td><td></td><td>Boston</td><td>OF</td><td>224</td><td>1946—Stan Musial</td><td></td><td>St. Louis</td><td>1B</td><td>31</td></tr>
<tr><td>1947—Joe DiMaggio</td><td></td><td>New York</td><td>OF</td><td>202</td><td>1947—Bob Elliott</td><td></td><td>Boston</td><td>3B</td><td>20</td></tr>
<tr><td>1948—Lou Boudreau</td><td></td><td>Cleveland</td><td>SS</td><td>324</td><td>1948—Stan Musial</td><td></td><td>St. Louis</td><td>OF</td><td>30</td></tr>
<tr><td>1949—Ted Williams</td><td></td><td>Boston</td><td>OF</td><td>272</td><td>1949—Jackie Robinson</td><td></td><td>Brooklyn</td><td>2B</td><td>26</td></tr>
<tr><td>1950—Phil Rizzuto</td><td></td><td>New York</td><td>SS</td><td>284</td><td>1950—Jim Konstanty</td><td></td><td>Philadelphia</td><td>P</td><td>28</td></tr>
<tr><td>1951—Yogi Berra</td><td></td><td>New York</td><td>C</td><td>184</td><td>1951—Roy Campanella</td><td></td><td>Brooklyn</td><td>C</td><td>24</td></tr>
<tr><td>1952—Bobby Shantz</td><td></td><td>Philadelphia</td><td>P</td><td>280</td><td>1952—Hank Sauer</td><td></td><td>Chicago</td><td>OF</td><td>22</td></tr>
<tr><td>1953—Al Rosen</td><td></td><td>Cleveland</td><td>3B</td><td>*336</td><td>1953—Roy Campanella</td><td></td><td>Brooklyn</td><td>C</td><td>29</td></tr>
<tr><td>1954—Yogi Berra</td><td></td><td>New York</td><td>C</td><td>230</td><td>1954—Willie Mays</td><td></td><td>New York</td><td>OF</td><td>28</td></tr>
<tr><td>1955—Yogi Berra</td><td></td><td>New York</td><td>C</td><td>218</td><td>1955—Roy Campanella</td><td></td><td>Brooklyn</td><td>C</td><td>22</td></tr>
<tr><td>1956—Mickey Mantle</td><td></td><td>New York</td><td>OF</td><td>*336</td><td>1956—Don Newcombe</td><td></td><td>Brooklyn</td><td>P</td><td>22</td></tr>
<tr><td>1957—Mickey Mantle</td><td></td><td>New York</td><td>OF</td><td>233</td><td>1957—Hank Aaron</td><td></td><td>Milwaukee</td><td>OF</td><td>23</td></tr>
<tr><td>1958—Jackie Jensen</td><td></td><td>Boston</td><td>OF</td><td>233</td><td>1958—Ernie Banks</td><td></td><td>Chicago</td><td>SS</td><td>28</td></tr>
<tr><td>1959—Nellie Fox</td><td></td><td>Chicago</td><td>2B</td><td>295</td><td>1959—Ernie Banks</td><td></td><td>Chicago</td><td>SS</td><td>2321/</td></tr>
<tr><td>1960—Roger Maris</td><td></td><td>New York</td><td>OF</td><td>225</td><td>1960—Dick Groat</td><td></td><td>Pittsburgh</td><td>SS</td><td>27</td></tr>
<tr><td>1961—Roger Maris</td><td></td><td>New York</td><td>OF</td><td>202</td><td>1961—Frank Robinson</td><td></td><td>Cincinnati</td><td>OF</td><td>21</td></tr>
<tr><td>1962—Mickey Mantle</td><td></td><td>New York</td><td>OF</td><td>234</td><td>1962—Maury Wills</td><td></td><td>Los Angeles</td><td>SS</td><td>20</td></tr>
<tr><td>1963—Elston Howard</td><td></td><td>New York</td><td>C</td><td>248</td><td>1963—Sandy Koufax</td><td></td><td>Los Angeles</td><td>P</td><td>23</td></tr>
</table>

HISTORY *Award winners*

ar	Player	Team	Pos.	Points	Year	Player	Team	Pos.	Points
64—Brooks Robinson	Baltimore	3B	269		1964—Ken Boyer	St. Louis	3B	243	
65—Zoilo Versalles	Minnesota	SS	275		1965—Willie Mays	San Francisco	OF	224	
66—Frank Robinson	Baltimore	OF	*280		1966—Roberto Clemente	Pittsburgh	OF	218	
67—Carl Yastrzemski	Boston	OF	275		1967—Orlando Cepeda	St. Louis	1B	*280	
68—Denny McLain	Detroit	P	*280		1968—Bob Gibson	St. Louis	P	242	
69—Harmon Killebrew	Minnesota	1B-3B	294		1969—Willie McCovey	San Francisco	1B	265	
70—Boog Powell	Baltimore	1B	234		1970—Johnny Bench	Cincinnati	C	326	
71—Vida Blue	Oakland	P	268		1971—Joe Torre	St. Louis	3B	318	
72—Dick Allen	Chicago	1B	321		1972—Johnny Bench	Cincinnati	C	263	
73—Reggie Jackson	Oakland	OF	*336		1973—Pete Rose	Cincinnati	OF	274	
74—Jeff Burroughs	Texas	OF	248		1974—Steve Garvey	Los Angeles	1B	270	
75—Fred Lynn	Boston	OF	326		1975—Joe Morgan	Cincinnati	2B	321½	
76—Thurman Munson	New York	C	304		1976—Joe Morgan	Cincinnati	2B	311	
77—Rod Carew	Minnesota	1B	273		1977—George Foster	Cincinnati	OF	291	
78—Jim Rice	Boston	OF	352		1978—Dave Parker	Pittsburgh	OF	320	
79—Don Baylor	California	OF	347		1979—Willie Stargell	Pittsburgh	1B	216	
					Keith Hernandez	St. Louis	1B	216	
80—George Brett	Kansas City	3B	335		1980—Mike Schmidt	Philadelphia	3B	*336	
81—Rollie Fingers	Milwaukee	P	319		1981—Mike Schmidt	Philadelphia	3B	321	
82—Robin Yount	Milwaukee	SS	385		1982—Dale Murphy	Atlanta	OF	283	
83—Cal Ripken Jr.	Baltimore	SS	322		1983—Dale Murphy	Atlanta	OF	318	
84—Willie Hernandez	Detroit	P	306		1984—Ryne Sandberg	Chicago	2B	326	
85—Don Mattingly	New York	1B	367		1985—Willie McGee	St. Louis	OF	280	
86—Roger Clemens	Boston	P	339		1986—Mike Schmidt	Philadelphia	3B	287	
87—George Bell	Toronto	OF	332		1987—Andre Dawson	Chicago	OF	269	
88—Jose Canseco	Oakland	OF	*392		1988—Kirk Gibson	Los Angeles	OF	272	
89—Robin Yount	Milwaukee	OF	256		1989—Kevin Mitchell	San Francisco	OF	314	
90—Rickey Henderson	Oakland	OF	317		1990—Barry Bonds	Pittsburgh	OF	331	
91—Cal Ripken Jr.	Baltimore	SS	318		1991—Terry Pendleton	Atlanta	3B	274	
92—Dennis Eckersley	Oakland	P	306		1992—Barry Bonds	Pittsburgh	OF	304	
93—Frank Thomas	Chicago	1B	*392		1993—Barry Bonds	San Francisco	OF	372	
94—Frank Thomas	Chicago	1B	372		1994—Jeff Bagwell	Houston	1B	*392	
95—Mo Vaughn	Boston	1B	308		1995—Barry Larkin	Cincinnati	SS	281	
96—Juan Gonzalez	Texas	OF	290		1996—Ken Caminiti	San Diego	3B	*392	

*Unanimous selection.

CY YOUNG MEMORIAL AWARD

ar	Pitcher	Team	Votes	Year	Pitcher	Team	Votes
56—Don Newcombe	Brooklyn	10		1980—A.L.—Steve Stone	Baltimore	100	
57—Warren Spahn	Milwaukee	15		N.L.—Steve Carlton	Philadelphia	118	
58—Bob Turley	New York A.L.	5		1981—A.L.—Rollie Fingers	Milwaukee	126	
59—Early Wynn	Chicago A.L.	13		N.L.—Fernando Valenzuela	Los Angeles	70	
60—Vernon Law	Pittsburgh	8		1982—A.L.—Pete Vuckovich	Milwaukee	87	
61—Whitey Ford	New York A.L.	9		N.L.—Steve Carlton	Philadelphia	112	
62—Don Drysdale	Los Angeles N.L.	14		1983—A.L.—LaMarr Hoyt	Chicago	116	
63—Sandy Koufax	Los Angeles N.L.	*20		N.L.—John Denny	Philadelphia	103	
64—Dean Chance	Los Angeles A.L.	17		1984—A.L.—Willie Hernandez	Detroit	88	
65—Sandy Koufax	Los Angeles N.L.	*20		N.L.—Rick Sutcliffe	Chicago	*120	
66—Sandy Koufax	Los Angeles N.L.	*20		1985—A.L.—Bret Saberhagen	Kansas City	127	
67—A.L.—Jim Lonborg	Boston	18		N.L.—Dwight Gooden	New York	*120	
N.L.—Mike McCormick	San Francisco	18		1986—A.L.—Roger Clemens	Boston	*140	
68—A.L.—Denny McLain	Detroit	*20		N.L.—Mike Scott	Houston	98	
N.L.—Bob Gibson	St. Louis	*20		1987—A.L.—Roger Clemens	Boston	124	
69—A.L.—Denny McLain	Detroit	10		N.L.—Steve Bedrosian	Philadelphia	57	
Mike Cuellar	Baltimore	10		1988—A.L.—Frank Viola	Minnesota	138	
N.L.—Tom Seaver	New York	23		N.L.—Orel Hershiser	Los Angeles	*120	
70—A.L.—Jim Perry	Minnesota	55		1989—A.L.—Bret Saberhagen	Kansas City	138	
N.L.—Bob Gibson	St. Louis	118		N.L.—Mark Davis	San Diego	107	
71—A.L.—Vida Blue	Oakland	98		1990—A.L.—Bob Welch	Oakland	107	
N.L.—Fergie Jenkins	Chicago	97		N.L.—Doug Drabek	Pittsburgh	118	
72—A.L.—Gaylord Perry	Cleveland	64		1991—A.L.—Roger Clemens	Boston	119	
N.L.—Steve Carlton	Philadelphia	*120		N.L.—Tom Glavine	Atlanta	110	
73—A.L.—Jim Palmer	Baltimore	88		1992—A.L.—Dennis Eckersley	Oakland	107	
N.L.—Tom Seaver	New York	71		N.L.—Greg Maddux	Chicago	112	
74—A.L.—Jim Hunter	Oakland	90		1993—A.L.—Jack McDowell	Chicago	124	
N.L.—Mike Marshall	Los Angeles	96		N.L.—Greg Maddux	Atlanta	119	
75—A.L.—Jim Palmer	Baltimore	98		1994—A.L.—David Cone	Kansas City	108	
N.L.—Tom Seaver	New York	98		N.L.—Greg Maddux	Atlanta	*140	
76—A.L.—Jim Palmer	Baltimore	108		1995—A.L.—Randy Johnson	Seattle	136	
N.L.—Randy Jones	San Diego	96		N.L.—Greg Maddux	Atlanta	*140	
77—A.L.—Sparky Lyle	New York	56½		1996—A.L.—Pat Hentgen	Toronto	110	
N.L.—Steve Carlton	Philadelphia	*104		N.L.—John Smoltz	Atlanta	136	
78—A.L.—Ron Guidry	New York	*140					
N.L.—Gaylord Perry	San Diego	116					
79—A.L.—Mike Flanagan	Baltimore	136					
N.L.—Bruce Sutter	Chicago	72					

*Unanimous selection.

HISTORY Award winners

ROOKIE OF THE YEAR

1947—Combined selection—Jackie Robinson, Brooklyn N.L., 1B
1948—Combined selection—Alvin Dark, Boston N.L., SS

AMERICAN LEAGUE

Year	Player	Team	Pos.	Votes
1949	Roy Sievers	St. Louis	OF	10
1950	Walt Dropo	Boston	1B	15
1951	Gil McDougald	New York	3B	13
1952	Harry Byrd	Philadelphia	P	9
1953	Harvey Kuenn	Detroit	SS	23
1954	Bob Grim	New York	P	15
1955	Herb Score	Cleveland	P	18
1956	Luis Aparicio	Chicago	SS	22
1957	Tony Kubek	New York	IF-OF	23
1958	Albie Pearson	Washington	OF	14
1959	Bob Allison	Washington	OF	18
1960	Ron Hansen	Baltimore	SS	22
1961	Don Schwall	Boston	P	7
1962	Tom Tresh	New York	OF-SS	13
1963	Gary Peters	Chicago	P	10
1964	Tony Oliva	Minnesota	OF	19
1965	Curt Blefary	Baltimore	OF	12
1966	Tommie Agee	Chicago	OF	16
1967	Rod Carew	Minnesota	2B	19
1968	Stan Bahnsen	New York	P	17
1969	Lou Piniella	Kansas City	OF	9
1970	Thurman Munson	New York	C	23
1971	Chris Chambliss	Cleveland	1B	11
1972	Carlton Fisk	Boston	C	*24
1973	Al Bumbry	Baltimore	OF	13½
1974	Mike Hargrove	Texas	1B	16½
1975	Fred Lynn	Boston	OF	23
1976	Mark Fidrych	Detroit	P	22
1977	Eddie Murray	Baltimore	DH-1B	12½
1978	Lou Whitaker	Detroit	2B	21
1979	John Castino	Minnesota	3B	7
	Alfredo Griffin	Toronto	SS	7
1980	Joe Charboneau	Cleveland	OF	103
1981	Dave Righetti	New York	P	127
1982	Cal Ripken	Baltimore	SS-3B	132
1983	Ron Kittle	Chicago	OF	104
1984	Alvin Davis	Seattle	1B	134
1985	Ozzie Guillen	Chicago	SS	101
1986	Jose Canseco	Oakland	OF	110
1987	Mark McGwire	Oakland	1B	*140
1988	Walt Weiss	Oakland	SS	103
1989	Gregg Olson	Baltimore	P	136
1990	Sandy Alomar Jr.	Cleveland	C	*140
1991	Chuck Knoblauch	Minnesota	2B	136
1992	Pat Listach	Milwaukee	SS	122
1993	Tim Salmon	California	OF	*140
1994	Bob Hamelin	Kansas City	DH	134
1995	Marty Cordova	Minnesota	3B	105
1996	Derek Jeter	New York	SS	140

*Unanimous selection. †Three writers did not vote.

NATIONAL LEAGUE

Year	Player	Team	Pos.	Vot
1949	Don Newcombe	Brooklyn	P	
1950	Sam Jethroe	Boston	OF	
1951	Willie Mays	New York	OF	
1952	Joe Black	Brooklyn	P	
1953	Jim Gilliam	Brooklyn	2B	
1954	Wally Moon	St. Louis	OF	
1955	Bill Virdon	St. Louis	OF	
1956	Frank Robinson	Cincinnati	OF	*
1957	Jack Sanford	Philadelphia	P	
1958	Orlando Cepeda	San Francisco	1B	*†
1959	Willie McCovey	San Francisco	1B	*
1960	Frank Howard	Los Angeles	OF	
1961	Billy Williams	Chicago	OF	
1962	Ken Hubbs	Chicago	2B	
1963	Pete Rose	Cincinnati	2B	
1964	Dick Allen	Philadelphia	3B	
1965	Jim Lefebvre	Los Angeles	2B	
1966	Tommy Helms	Cincinnati	3B	
1967	Tom Seaver	New York	P	
1968	Johnny Bench	Cincinnati	C	10
1969	Ted Sizemore	Los Angeles	2B	
1970	Carl Morton	Montreal	P	
1971	Earl Williams	Atlanta	C	
1972	Jon Matlack	New York	P	
1973	Gary Matthews	San Francisco	OF	
1974	Bake McBride	St. Louis	OF	
1975	John Montefusco	San Francisco	P	
1976	Butch Metzger	San Diego	P	
	Pat Zachry	Cincinnati	P	
1977	Andre Dawson	Montreal	OF	
1978	Bob Horner	Atlanta	3B	12
1979	Rick Sutcliffe	Los Angeles	P	
1980	Steve Howe	Los Angeles	P	
1981	Fernando Valenzuela	Los Angeles	P	1
1982	Steve Sax	Los Angeles	2B	
1983	Darryl Strawberry	New York	OF	1
1984	Dwight Gooden	New York	P	1
1985	Vince Coleman	St. Louis	OF	*1
1986	Todd Worrell	St. Louis	P	1
1987	Benito Santiago	San Diego	C	*1
1988	Chris Sabo	Cincinnati	3B	
1989	Jerome Walton	Chicago	OF	1
1990	Dave Justice	Atlanta	OF	1
1991	Jeff Bagwell	Houston	1B	1
1992	Eric Karros	Los Angeles	1B	1
1993	Mike Piazza	Los Angeles	C	*1
1994	Raul Mondesi	Los Angeles	OF	*1
1995	Hideo Nomo	Los Angeles	P	1
1996	Todd Hollandsworth	Los Angeles	OF	1

MANAGER OF THE YEAR

AMERICAN LEAGUE

Year	Manager	Team	Points
1983	Tony La Russa	Chicago	17
1984	Sparky Anderson	Detroit	96
1985	Bobby Cox	Toronto	104
1986	John McNamara	Boston	95
1987	Sparky Anderson	Detroit	90
1988	Tony La Russa	Oakland	103
1989	Frank Robinson	Baltimore	125
1990	Jeff Torborg	Chicago	128
1991	Tom Kelly	Minnesota	138
1992	Tony La Russa	Oakland	132
1993	Gene Lamont	Chicago	72
1994	Buck Showalter	New York	132
1995	Lou Piniella	Seattle	86
1996	Johnny Oates	Texas	89
	Joe Torre	New York	89

NATIONAL LEAGUE

Year	Manager	Team	Poir
1983	Tommy Lasorda	Los Angeles	
1984	Jim Frey	Chicago	10
1985	Whitey Herzog	St. Louis	8
1986	Hal Lanier	Houston	10
1987	Buck Rodgers	Montreal	9
1988	Tommy Lasorda	Los Angeles	10
1989	Don Zimmer	Chicago	11
1990	Jim Leyland	Pittsburgh	9
1991	Bobby Cox	Atlanta	9
1992	Jim Leyland	Pittsburgh	10
1993	Dusty Baker	San Francisco	10
1994	Felipe Alou	Montreal	13
1995	Don Baylor	Colorado	12
1996	Bruce Bochy	San Diego	7

HISTORY *Award winners*

EARLY MOST VALUABLE PLAYER AWARDS

CHALMERS AWARD

	AMERICAN LEAGUE					NATIONAL LEAGUE			
ar	Player	Team	Pos.	Points	Year	Player	Team	Pos.	Points
1—Ty Cobb	Detroit	OF	64		1911—Frank Schulte	Chicago	OF	29
2—Tris Speaker	Boston	OF	59		1912—Larry Doyle	New York	2B	48
3—Walter Johnson	Washington	P	54		1913—Jake Daubert	Brooklyn	1B	50
4—Eddie Collins	Philadelphia	2B	63		1914—Johnny Evers	Boston	2B	50

LEAGUE AWARDS

	AMERICAN LEAGUE					NATIONAL LEAGUE			
ar	Player	Team	Pos.	Points	Year	Player	Team	Pos.	Points
22—George Sisler	St. Louis	1B	59		1922—No selection			
23—Babe Ruth	New York	OF	64		1923—No selection			
24—Walter Johnson	Washington	P	55		1924—Dazzy Vance	Brooklyn	P	74
25—Roger Peckinpaugh	Washington	SS	45		1925—Rogers Hornsby	St. Louis	2B	73
26—George Burns	Cleveland	1B	63		1926—Bob O'Farrell	St. Louis	C	79
27—Lou Gehrig	New York	1B	56		1927—Paul Waner	Pittsburgh	OF	72
28—Mickey Cochrane	Philadelphia	C	53		1928—Jim Bottomley	St. Louis	1B	76
29—No selection					1929—Rogers Hornsby	Chicago	2B	60

Name	Des.*	Elec. year	Votes rec.†	Votes cast‡	% of vote	Teams as player
Aaron, Hank	P	1982	406	415	97.8	Milwaukee NL, Atlanta NL, Milwaukee AL
Alexander, Grover C.	P	1938	212	262	80.9	Philadelphia NL, Chicago NL, St. Louis NL
Alston, Walter	M	1983	CV	—	—	St. Louis NL
Anson, Cap	P	1939	C1	—	—	Chicago NL
Aparicio, Luis	P	1984	341	403	84.6	Chicago AL, Baltimore AL, Boston AL
Appling, Luke	P	1964	189	225	84	Chicago AL
Ashburn, Richie	P	1995	CV	—	—	Philadelphia NL, Chicago NL, New York NL
Averill, Earl	P	1975	CV	—	—	Cleveland AL, Detroit AL, Boston AL
Baker, Home Run	P	1955	CV	—	—	Philadelphia NL, New York AL
Bancroft, Dave	P	1971	CV	—	—	Philadelphia NL, New York NL, Boston NL, Brooklyn
Banks, Ernie	P	1977	321	383	83.8	Chicago NL
Barlick, Al	U	1989	CV	—	—	
Barrow, Ed	E	1953	CV	—	—	
Beckley, Jake	P	1971	CV	—	—	Pittsburgh NL, Pittsburgh PL, New York NL, Cincinnati NL, St. Louis NL
Bell, Cool Papa	P	1974	SCNL	—	—	Negro Leagues
Bench, Johnny	P	1989	431	447	96.4	Cincinnati NL
Bender, Chief	P	1953	CV	—	—	Philadelphia AL, Philadelphia NL, Chicago AL
Berra, Yogi	P	1972	339	396	85.6	New York AL, New York NL
Bottomley, Jim	P	1974	CV	—	—	St. Louis NL, Cincinnati NL, St. Louis AL
Boudreau, Lou	P	1970	232	300	77.3	Cleveland AL, Boston AL
Bresnahan, Roger	P	1945	C2	—	—	Washington NL, Chicago NL, Baltimore AL, New York NL, St. Louis NL
Brock, Lou	P	1985	315	395	79.7	Chicago NL, St. Louis NL
Brouthers, Dan	P	1945	C2	—	—	Troy NL, Buffalo NL, Detroit NL, Boston NL, Boston PL, Boston AA,Brooklyn NL, Baltimore NL,Louis NL, Philadelphia NL, New York NL
Brown, Three Finger	P	1949	C2	—	—	St. Louis NL, Chicago NL, Cincinnati NL
Bulkeley, Morgan	E	1937	CC	—	—	
Bunning, Jim	P	1996	CV	—	—	Detroit AL, Philadelphia NL, Pittsburgh NL, Los Angeles NL
Burkett, Jesse	P	1946	C2	—	—	New York NL, Cleveland NL, St. Louis NL, St. L AL, Boston AL
Campanella, Roy	P	1969	270	340	79.4	Brooklyn NL
Carew, Rod	P	1991	401	447	89.7	Minnesota AL, California AL
Carey, Max	P	1961	CV	—	—	Pittsburgh NL, Brooklyn NL
Carlton, Steve	P	1994	436	455	95.8	St. Louis NL, Philadelphia NL, San Francisco N Chicago AL, Cleveland AL, Minnesota AL
Cartwright, Alexander	O	1938	CC	—	—	
Chadwick, Henry	O	1938	CC	—	—	
Chance, Frank	P	1946	C2	—	—	Chicago NL, New York AL
Chandler, Happy	E	1982	CV	—	—	
Charleston, Oscar	P	1976	SCNL	—	—	Negro Leagues
Chesbro, Jack	P	1946	C2	—	—	Pittsburgh NL, New York AL, Boston AL
Clarke, Fred	P	1945	C2	—	—	Louisville NL, Pittsburgh NL
Clarkson, John	P	1963	CV	—	—	Worcester NL, Chicago NL, Boston NL, Cleveland
Clemente, Roberto	P	1973	393	424	92.7	Pittsburgh NL
Cobb, Ty	P	1936	222	226	98.2	Detroit AL, Philadelphia AL
Cochrane, Mickey	P	1947	128	161	79.5	Philadelphia AL, Detroit AL
Collins, Eddie	P	1939	213	274	77.7	Philadelphia AL, Chicago AL
Collins, Jimmy	P	1945	C2	—	—	Boston NL, Louisville NL, Boston AL, Philadelph
Combs, Earle	P	1970	CV	—	—	New York AL
Comiskey, Charley	F/P	1939	C1	—	—	St. Louis AA, Chicago PL, Cincinnati NL
Conlan, Jocko	U	1974	CV	—	—	Chicago AL
Connolly, Tommy	U	1953	CV	—	—	
Connor, Roger	P	1976	CV	—	—	Troy NL, New York NL, New York PL, Philadelp NL, St. Louis NL
Coveleski, Stan	P	1969	CV	—	—	Philadelphia AL, Cleveland AL, Washington AL, New York AL
Crawford, Sam	P	1957	CV	—	—	Cincinnati NL, Detroit AL
Cronin, Joe	P	1956	152	193	78.8	Pittsburgh NL, Washington AL, Boston AL
Cummings, Candy	P	1939	C1	—	—	Hartford NL, Cincinnati NL
Cuyler, Kiki	P	1968	CV	—	—	Pittsburgh NL, Chicago NL, Cincinnati NL, Brooklyn
Dandridge, Ray	P	1987	CV	—	—	Negro Leagues
Day, Leon	P	1995	CV	—	—	Negro Leagues
Dean, Dizzy	P	1953	209	264	79.2	St. Louis NL, Chicago NL, St. Louis AL
Delahanty, Ed	P	1945	C2	—	—	Philadelphia NL, Cleveland PL, Washington AL
Dickey, Bill	P	1954	202	252	80.2	New York AL
Dihigo, Martin	P	1977	SCNL	—	—	Negro Leagues
DiMaggio, Joe	P	1955	223	251	88.8	New York AL

ame	Des.*	Elec. year	Votes rec.†	Votes cast‡	% of vote	Teams as player
oerr, Bobby	P	1986	CV	—	—	Boston AL
rysdale, Don	P	1984	316	403	78.4	Brooklyn NL, Los Angeles NL
uffy, Hugh	P	1945	C2	—	—	Chicago NL, Chicago PL, Boston AA, Boston NL, Milwaukee AL, Philadelphia NL
urocher, Leo	M	1994	CV	—	—	New York AL, Cincinnati NL, St. Louis NL, Brooklyn NL
vans, Billy	U	1973	CV	—	—	
vers, Johnny	P	1946	C2	—	—	Chicago NL, Boston NL, Philadelphia NL, Chicago AL
wing, Buck	P	1939	C1	—	—	Troy NL, New York NL, New York PL, Cleveland NL, Cincinnati NL
aber, Red	P	1964	CV	—	—	Chicago AL
eller, Bob	P	1962	150	160	93.8	Cleveland AL
errell, Rick	P	1984	CV	—	—	St. Louis AL, Boston AL, Washington AL
ngers, Rollie	P	1992	349	430	81.2	Oakland AL, San Diego NL, Milwaukee AL
ick, Elmer	P	1963	CV	—	—	Philadelphia NL, Philadelphia AL, Cleveland AL
ord, Whitey	P	1974	284	365	77.8	New York AL
oster, Bill	P	1996	CV	—	—	Negro Leagues
oster, Rube	P	1981	CV	—	—	Negro Leagues
oxx, Jimmie	P	1951	179	226	79.2	Philadelphia AL, Boston AL, Chicago NL, Philadelphia NL
ick, Ford	E	1970	CV	—	—	
isch, Frank	P	1947	136	161	84.5	New York NL, St. Louis NL
alvin, Pud	P	1965	CV	—	—	Buffalo NL, Pittsburgh AA, Pittsburgh NL, Pittsburgh PL, St. Louis NL
ehrig, Lou	P	1939	SE	—	—	New York AL
ehringer, Charley	P	1949	159	187	85.0	Detroit AL
bson, Bob	P	1981	337	401	84.0	St. Louis NL
bson, Josh	P	1972	SCNL	—	—	Negro Leagues
les, Warren	E	1979	CV	—	—	
omez, Lefty	P	1972	CV	—	—	New York AL, Washington AL
oslin, Goose	P	1968	CV	—	—	Washington AL, St. Louis AL, Detroit AL
reenberg, Hank	P	1956	164	193	85.0	Detroit AL, Pittsburgh NL
riffith, Clark	M	1946	C2	—	—	St. Louis AA, Boston AA, Chicago AL, Chicago NL, New York AL, Cincinnati NL, Washington AL
rimes, Burleigh	P	1964	CV	—	—	Pittsburgh NL, Brooklyn NL, New York NL, Boston NL, St. Louis NL, Chicago NL, New York AL
rove, Lefty	P	1947	123	161	76.4	Philadelphia AL, Boston AL
afey, Chick	P	1971	CV	—	—	St. Louis NL, Cincinnati NL
aines, Jesse	P	1970	CV	—	—	Cincinnati NL, St. Louis NL
amilton, Billy	P	1961	CV	—	—	Kansas City AA, Philadelphia NL, Boston NL
anlon, Ned	M	1996	CV	—	—	Cleveland NL, Detroit NL, Pittsburgh NL, Pittsburgh PL, Baltimore NL
arridge, Will	E	1972	CV	—	—	
arris, Bucky	M	1975	CV	—	—	Washington AL, Detroit AL
artnett, Gabby	P	1955	195	251	77.7	Chicago NL, New York NL
eilmann, Harry	P	1952	203	234	86.8	Detroit AL, Cincinnati NL
erman, Billy	P	1975	CV	—	—	Chicago NL, Brooklyn NL, Boston NL, Pittsburgh NL
ooper, Harry	P	1971	CV	—	—	Boston AL, Chicago AL
ornsby, Rogers	P	1942	182	233	78.1	St. Louis NL, New York NL, Boston NL, Chicago NL, St. Louis AL
oyt, Waite	P	1969	CV	—	—	New York NL, Boston AL, New York AL, Detroit AL, Philadelphia AL, Brooklyn NL, Pittsburgh NL
ubbard, Cal	U	1976	CV	—	—	
ubbell, Carl	P	1947	140	161	87.0	New York NL
uggins, Miller	M	1964	CV	—	—	Cincinnati NL, St. Louis NL
ulbert, William	F	1995	CV	—	—	
unter, Catfish	P	1987	315	413	76.3	Kansas City AL, Oakland AL, New York AL
vin, Monte	P	1973	SCNL	—	—	New York NL, Chicago NL, Negro Leagues
ckson, Reggie	P	1993	396	423	93.6	Kansas City AL, Oakland AL, Baltimore AL, New York AL, California AL
ckson, Travis	P	1982	CV	—	—	New York NL
nkins, Ferguson	P	1991	334	447	74.7	Philadelphia NL, Chicago NL, Texas AL, Boston AL
nnings, Hugh	P	1945	C2	—	—	Louisville AA, Louisville NL, Baltimore NL, Brooklyn NL, Philadelphia NL, Detroit AL
hnson, Ban	E	1937	CC	—	—	
hnson, Judy	P	1975	SCNL	—	—	Negro Leagues
hnson, Walter	P	1936	189	226	83.6	Washington AL
ss, Addie	P	1978	CV	—	—	Cleveland AL
line, Al	P	1980	340	385	88.3	Detroit AL
efe, Tim	P	1964	CV	—	—	Troy NL, New York AA, New York NL, New York PL, Philadelphia NL
eler, Willie	P	1939	207	274	75.5	New York NL, Brooklyn, NL, Baltimore NL, New York AL
ll, George	P	1983	CV	—	—	Philadelphia AL, Detroit AL, Boston AL, Chicago AL, Baltimore AL
lley, Joe	P	1971	CV	—	—	Boston NL, Pittsburgh NL, Baltimore NL, Brooklyn NL, Baltimore AL, Cincinnati NL

Name	Des.*	Elec. year	Votes rec.†	Votes cast‡	% of vote	Teams as player
Kelly, George	P	1973	CV	—	—	New York NL, Pittsburgh NL, Cincinnati NL, Chicago NL, Brooklyn NL
Kelly, Mike	P	1945	C2	—	—	Cincinnati NL, Chicago NL, Boston NL, Boston PL, Cincinnati AA, Boston AA, New York NL
Killebrew, Harmon	P	1984	335	403	83.1	Washington AL, Minnesota AL, Kansas City AL
Kiner, Ralph	P	1975	273	362	75.4	Pittsburgh NL, Chicago NL, Cleveland AL
Klein, Chuck	P	1980	CV	—	—	Philadelphia NL, Chicago NL, Pittsburgh NL
Klem, Bill	U	1953	CV	—	—	
Koufax, Sandy	P	1972	344	396	86.9	Brooklyn NL, Los Angeles NL
Lajoie, Nap	P	1937	168	201	83.6	Philadelphia NL, Philadelphia AL, Cleveland AL
Landis, Kenesaw M.	E	1944	C2	—	—	
Lazzeri, Tony	P	1991	CV	—	—	New York AL, Chicago NL, Brooklyn NL, New York N
Lemon, Bob	P	1976	305	388	78.6	Cleveland AL
Leonard, Buck	P	1972	SCNL	—	—	Negro Leagues
Lindstrom, Fred	P	1976	CV	—	—	New York NL, Pittsburgh NL, Chicago NL, Brooklyn N
Lloyd, John Henry	P	1977	SCNL	—	—	Negro Leagues
Lombardi, Ernie	P	1986	CV	—	—	Brooklyn NL, Cincinnati NL, Boston NL, New York NL
Lopez, Al	M	1977	CV	—	—	Brooklyn NL, Boston NL, Pittsburgh NL, Cleveland AL
Lyons, Ted	P	1955	217	251	86.5	Chicago AL
Mack, Connie	M	1937	CC	—	—	Washington NL, Buffalo PL, Pittsburgh NL
MacPhail, Larry	E	1978	CV	—	—	
Mantle, Mickey	P	1974	322	365	88.2	New York AL
Manush, Heinie	P	1964	CV	—	—	Detroit AL, St. Louis AL, Washington AL, Boston AL, Brooklyn NL, Pittsburgh NL
Maranville, Rabbit	P	1954	209	252	82.9	Boston NL, Pittsburgh NL, Chicago NL, Brooklyn NL, St. Louis NL
Marichal, Juan	P	1983	313	374	83.7	San Francisco NL, Boston AL, Los Angeles NL
Marquard, Rube	P	1971	CV	—	—	New York NL, Brooklyn NL, Cincinnati NL, Boston N
Mathews, Eddie	P	1978	301	379	79.4	Boston NL, Milwaukee NL, Atlanta NL, Houston NL, Detroit AL
Mathewson, Christy	P	1936	205	226	90.7	New York NL, Cincinnati NL
Mays, Willie	P	1979	409	432	94.7	New York (Giants)NL, San Francisco NL, New York (Mets)NL
McCarthy, Joe	M	1957	CV	—	—	
McCarthy, Tommy	P	1946	C2	—	—	Boston UA, Boston NL, Philadelphia NL, St. Louis AA, Brooklyn NL
McCovey, Willie	P	1986	346	425	81.4	San Francisco NL, San Diego NL, Oakland AL
McGinnity, Joe	P	1946	C2	—	—	Baltimore NL, Brooklyn NL, Baltimore AL, New York N
McGowan, Bill	U	1992	CV	—	—	
McGraw, John	M	1937	CC	—	—	Baltimore AA, Baltimore NL, St. Louis NL, Baltimore AL, New York NL
McKechnie, Bill	M	1962	CV	—	—	Pittsburgh NL, Boston NL, New York AL, New York NL, Cincinnati
Medwick, Joe	P	1968	240	283	84.8	St. Louis NL, Brooklyn NL, New York NL, Boston N
Mize, Johnny	P	1981	CV	—	—	St. Louis NL, New York NL, New York AL
Morgan, Joe	P	1990	363	444	81.8	Houston NL, Cincinnati NL, San Francisco NL, Philadelphia NL, Oakland AL
Musial, Stan	P	1969	317	340	93.2	St. Louis NL
Newhouser, Hal	P	1992	CV	—	—	Detroit AL, Cleveland AL
Nichols, Kid	P	1949	C2	—	—	Boston NL, St. Louis NL, Philadelphia NL
Niekro, Phil	P	1997	380	473	80.3	Milwaukee NL, Atlanta NL, New York AL, Cleveland AL, Toronto AL
O'Rourke, Jim	P	1945	C2	—	—	Boston NL, Providence NL, Buffalo NL, New York NL, Washington NL, New York PL
Ott, Mel	P	1951	197	226	87.2	New York NL
Paige, Satchel	P	1971	SCNL	—	—	Cleveland AL, St. Louis AL, Kansas City AL, Negro Leagues
Palmer, Jim	P	1990	411	444	92.6	Baltimore AL
Pennock, Herb	P	1948	94	121	77.7	Philadelphia AL, Boston AL, New York AL
Perry, Gaylord	P	1991	342	447	76.5	San Francisco NL, Cleveland AL, Texas AL, San Diego NL, New York AL, Atlanta AL, Seattle AL, Kansas City AL
Plank, Eddie	P	1946	C2	—	—	Philadelphia AL, St. Louis AL
Radbourn, Hoss	P	1939	C1	—	—	Buffalo NL, Providence NL, Boston NL, Boston PL, Cincinnati NL
Reese, Pee Wee	P	1984	CV	—	—	Brooklyn NL, Los Angeles NL
Rice, Sam	P	1963	CV	—	—	Washington AL, Cleveland AL
Rickey, Branch	E	1967	CV	—	—	St. Louis AL, New York AL
Rixey, Eppa	P	1963	CV	—	—	Philadelphia NL, Cincinnati NL
Rizzuto, Phil	P	1994	CV	—	—	New York AL
Roberts, Robin	P	1976	337	388	86.9	Philadelphia NL, Baltimore AL, Houston NL, Chicago NL
Robinson, Brooks	P	1983	344	374	92.0	Baltimore AL
Robinson, Frank	P	1982	370	415	89.2	Cincinnati NL, Baltimore AL, Los Angeles NL, California AL, Cleveland AL
Robinson, Jackie	P	1962	124	160	77.5	Brooklyn NL

me	Des.*	Elec. year	Votes rec.†	Votes cast‡	% of vote	Teams as player
ɔinson, Wilbert	M	1945	C2	—	—	Philadelphia AA, Baltimore AA, Baltimore NL, St. Louis NL, Baltimore AL
ʋsh, Edd	P	1962	CV	—	—	Chicago AL, New York NL, Cincinnati NL
ffing, Red	P	1967	266	306	86.9	Boston AL, New York AL, Chicago AL
sie, Amos	P	1977	CV	—	—	Indianapolis NL, New York NL, Cincinnati NL
th, Babe	P	1936	215	226	95.1	Boston AL, New York AL, Boston NL
ʋalk, Ray	P	1955	CV	—	—	Chicago AL, New York NL
ʋmidt, Mike	P	1995	444	460	96.5	Philadelphia NL
ʋoendienst, Red	P	1989	CV	—	—	St. Louis NL, New York (Giants) NL, Milwaukee NL
ıver, Tom	P	1992	425	430	98.8	New York NL, Cincinnati NL, Chicago AL, Boston AL
ʋell, Joe	P	1977	CV	—	—	Cleveland AL, New York AL
ʋmons, Al	P	1953	199	264	75.4	Philadelphia AL, Chicago AL, Detroit AL, Washington AL, Boston AL, Cincinnati NL, Boston AL
ʋler, George	P	1939	235	274	85.8	St. Louis AL, Washington AL, Boston NL
ʋughter, Enos	P	1985	CV	—	—	St. Louis NL, New York AL, Kansas City AL, Milwaukee NL
ʋder, Duke	P	1980	333	385	86.5	Brooklyn NL, Los Angeles NL, New York NL, San Francisco NL
ʋahn, Warren	P	1973	316	380	83.2	Boston NL, Milwaukee NL, New York NL, San Francisco NL
ʋalding, Al	P	1939	C1	—	—	Chicago NL
ʋeaker, Tris	P	1937	165	201	82.1	Boston AL, Cleveland AL, Washington AL, Philadelphia AL
ʋrgell, Willie	P	1988	352	427	82.4	Pittsburgh NL
ʋngel, Casey	M	1966	CV	—	—	Brooklyn NL, Pittsburgh NL, Philadelphia NL, New York NL, Boston NL
ʋry, Bill	P	1954	195	252	77.4	New York NL
ʋompson, Sam	P	1974	CV	—	—	Detroit NL, Philadelphia NL, Detroit AL
ʋker, Joe	P	1946	C2	—	—	Chicago NL, Cincinnati NL
ʋynor, Pie	P	1948	93	121	76.9	Pittsburgh NL
ʋnce, Dazzy	P	1955	205	251	81.7	Pittsburgh NL, New York AL, Brooklyn NL, St. Louis NL, Cincinnati NL
ʋughan, Arky	P	1985	CV	—	—	Pittsburgh NL, Brooklyn NL
ʋeck, Bill	E	1991	CV	—	—	
ʋddell, Rube	P	1946	C2	—	—	Louisville NL, Pittsburgh NL, Chicago NL, Philadelphia AL, St. Louis AL
ʋgner, Honus	P	1936	215	226	95.1	Louisville NL, Pittsburgh NL
ʋllace, Bobby	P	1953	CV	—	—	Cleveland NL, St. Louis NL, St. Louis AL
ʋlsh, Ed	P	1946	C2	—	—	Chicago AL, Boston NL
ʋner, Lloyd	P	1967	CV	—	—	Pittsburgh NL, Boston NL, Cincinnati NL, Philadelphia NL, Brooklyn NL
ʋner, Paul	P	1952	195	234	83.3	Pittsburgh NL, Brooklyn NL, Boston NL, New York AL
ʋrd, John Montgomery	P	1964	CV	—	—	Providence NL, New York NL, Brooklyn PL, Brooklyn NL
ʋaver, Earl	M	1996	CV	—	—	
ʋeiss, George	E	1971	CV	—	—	
ʋelch, Mickey	P	1973	CV	—	—	Troy NL, New York NL
ʋeat, Zack	P	1959	CV	—	—	Brooklyn NL, Philadelphia AL
ʋhelm, Hoyt	P	1985	331	395	83.8	New York NL, St. Louis NL, Cleveland AL, Baltimore AL, Chicago AL California AL, Atlanta NL, Chicago NL, Los Angeles NL
ʋlliams, Billy	P	1987	354	413	85.7	Chicago NL, Oakland AL
ʋlliams, Ted	P	1966	282	302	93.4	Boston AL
ʋllis, Vic	P	1995	CV	—	—	Boston NL, Pittsburgh NL, St. Louis NL
ʋlson, Hack	P	1979	CV	—	—	New York NL, Chicago NL, Brooklyn NL, Philadelphia NL
ʋright, George	M	1937	CC	—	—	Boston NL, Providence NL
ʋright, Harry	M	1953	CV	—	—	Boston NL
ʋnn, Early	P	1972	301	396	76.0	Washington AL, Cleveland AL, Chicago AL
ʋstrzemski, Carl	P	1989	423	447	94.6	Boston AL
ʋwkey, Tom	E	1980	CV	—	—	
ʋung, Cy	P	1937	153	201	76.1	Cleveland NL, St. Louis NL, Boston AL, Cleveland AL, Boston NL
ʋungs, Ross	P	1972	CV	—.	—	New York NL

*Designation for which he was honored. Abbreviations: E—executive; F—founder; M—manager; O—organizer; P—player; U—umpire.
†Where an abbreviation is listed rather than a vote total, the enshrinee was selected by one of the following groups: Centennial Commission (CC), committee of old-time players and writers (C1), committee on old-timers (C2), Committee on Veterans (CV), special election by Baseball Writers' Association of America (SE) or Special Committee on Negro Leagues (SCNL).
‡Votes cast by eligible members of the Baseball Writers' Association of America.
League abbreviations: AA—American Association; AL—American League; NL—National League; PL—Players League; UA—Union Association.

TEAM BY TEAM

AMERICAN LEAGUE

YEARLY FINISHES

Year	Position	W	L	Pct.	*GB	Manager	Attendanc
1901†	8th	48	89	.350	35 1/2	Hugh Duffy	139,03
1902‡	2nd	78	58	.574	5	Jimmy McAleer	272,28
1903‡	6th	65	74	.468	26 1/2	Jimmy McAleer	380,40
1904‡	6th	65	87	.428	29	Jimmy McAleer	318,10
1905‡	8th	54	99	.354	40 1/2	Jimmy McAleer	339,11
1906‡	5th	76	73	.510	16	Jimmy McAleer	389,15
1907‡	6th	69	83	.454	24	Jimmy McAleer	419,02
1908‡	4th	83	69	.546	6 1/2	Jimmy McAleer	618,94
1909‡	7th	61	89	.407	36	Jimmy McAleer	366,27
1910‡	8th	47	107	.305	57	John O'Connor	249,88
1911‡	8th	45	107	.296	56 1/2	Bobby Wallace	207,98
1912‡	7th	53	101	.344	53	Bobby Wallace, George Stovall	214,07
1913‡	8th	57	96	.373	39	George Stovall, Branch Rickey	250,33
1914‡	5th	71	82	.464	28 1/2	Branch Rickey	244,71
1915‡	6th	63	91	.409	39 1/2	Branch Rickey	150,35
1916‡	5th	79	75	.513	12	Fielder Jones	335,74
1917‡	7th	57	97	.370	43	Fielder Jones	210,48
1918‡	5th	58	64	.475	15	Fielder Jones, Jimmy Austin, Jimmy Burke	122,07
1919‡	5th	67	72	.482	20 1/2	Jimmy Burke	349,35
1920‡	4th	76	77	.497	21 1/2	Jimmy Burke	419,31
1921‡	3rd	81	73	.526	17 1/2	Lee Fohl	355,97
1922‡	2nd	93	61	.604	1	Lee Fohl	712,91
1923‡	5th	74	78	.487	24	Lee Fohl, Jimmy Austin	430,29
1924‡	4th	74	78	.487	17	George Sisler	533,34
1925‡	3rd	82	71	.536	15	George Sisler	462,89
1926‡	7th	62	92	.403	29	George Sisler	283,98
1927‡	7th	59	94	.336	50 1/2	Dan Howley	247,87
1928‡	3rd	82	72	.532	19	Dan Howley	339,49
1929‡	4th	79	73	.520	26	Dan Howley	280,69
1930‡	6th	64	90	.416	38	Bill Killefer	152,08
1931‡	5th	63	91	.409	45	Bill Killefer	179,12
1932‡	6th	63	91	.409	44	Bill Killefer	112,55
1933‡	8th	55	96	.364	43 1/2	Bill Killefer, Allen Sothoron, Rogers Hornsby	88,11
1934‡	6th	67	85	.441	33	Rogers Hornsby	115,3C
1935‡	7th	65	87	.428	28 1/2	Rogers Hornsby	80,92
1936‡	7th	57	95	.375	44 1/2	Rogers Hornsby	93,26
1937‡	8th	46	108	.299	56	Rogers Hornsby, Jim Bottomley	123,12
1938‡	7th	55	97	.362	44	Gabby Street	130,41
1939‡	8th	43	111	.279	64 1/2	Fred Haney	109,15
1940‡	6th	67	87	.435	23	Fred Haney	239,59
1941‡	6th (tied)	70	84	.455	31	Fred Haney, Luke Sewell	176,24
1942‡	3rd	82	69	.543	19 1/2	Luke Sewell	255,61
1943‡	6th	72	80	.474	25	Luke Sewell	214,39
1944‡	1st	89	65	.578	+1	Luke Sewell	508,64
1945‡	3rd	81	70	.536	6	Luke Sewell	482,98
1946‡	7th	66	88	.429	38	Luke Sewell, Zack Taylor	526,43
1947‡	8th	59	95	.383	38	Muddy Ruel	320,47
1948‡	6th	59	94	.386	37	Zack Taylor	335,54
1949‡	7th	53	101	.344	44	Zack Taylor	270,93
1950‡	7th	58	96	.377	40	Zack Taylor	247,13
1951‡	8th	52	102	.338	46	Zack Taylor	293,79
1952‡	7th	64	90	.416	31	Rogers Hornsby, Marty Marion	518,79
1953‡	8th	54	100	.351	46 1/2	Marty Marion	297,23
1954	7th	54	100	.351	57	Jimmie Dykes	1,060,91
1955	7th	57	97	.370	39	Paul Richards	852,03
1956	6th	69	85	.448	28	Paul Richards	901,2C
1957	5th	76	76	.500	21	Paul Richards	1,029,58
1958	6th	74	79	.484	17 1/2	Paul Richards	829,99
1959	6th	74	80	.481	20	Paul Richards	891,92
1960	2nd	89	65	.578	8	Paul Richards	1,187,84
1961	3rd	95	67	.586	14	Paul Richards, Luman Harris	951,0
1962	7th	77	85	.475	19	Billy Hitchcock	790,2
1963	4th	86	76	.531	18 1/2	Billy Hitchcock	774,34
1964	3rd	97	65	.599	2	Hank Bauer	1,116,2
1965	3rd	94	68	.580	8	Hank Bauer	781,6
1966	1st	97	63	.606	+9	Hank Bauer	1,203,3

ar	Position	W	L	Pct.	*GB	Manager	Attendance
67	6th (tied)	76	85	.472	15½	Hank Bauer	955,053
68	2nd	91	71	.562	12	Hank Bauer, Earl Weaver	943,977

EAST DIVISION

ar	Position	W	L	Pct.	*GB	Manager	Attendance
69	1st§	109	53	.673	+19	Earl Weaver	1,058,168
70	1st§	108	54	.667	+15	Earl Weaver	1,057,069
71	1st§	101	57	.639	+12	Earl Weaver	1,023,037
72	3rd	80	74	.519	5	Earl Weaver	899,950
73	1st∞	97	65	.599	+8	Earl Weaver	958,667
74	1st∞	91	71	.562	+2	Earl Weaver	962,572
75	2nd	90	69	.566	4½	Earl Weaver	1,002,157
76	2nd	88	74	.543	10½	Earl Weaver	1,058,609
77	2nd (tied)	97	64	.602	2½	Earl Weaver	1,195,769
78	4th	90	71	.559	9	Earl Weaver	1,051,724
79	1st§	102	57	.642	+8	Earl Weaver	1,681,009
80	2nd	100	62	.617	3	Earl Weaver	1,797,438
81	2nd/4th	59	46	.562	▲	Earl Weaver	1,024,652
82	2nd	94	68	.580	1	Earl Weaver	1,613,031
83	1st§	98	64	.605	+6	Joe Altobelli	2,042,071
84	5th	85	77	.525	19	Joe Altobelli	2,045,784
85	4th	83	78	.516	16	Joe Altobelli, Earl Weaver	2,132,387
86	7th	73	89	.451	22½	Earl Weaver	1,973,176
87	6th	67	95	.414	31	Cal Ripken Sr.	1,835,692
88	7th	54	107	.335	34½	Cal Ripken Sr., Frank Robinson	1,660,738
89	2nd	87	75	.537	2	Frank Robinson	2,535,208
90	5th	76	85	.472	11½	Frank Robinson	2,415,189
91	6th	67	95	.414	24	Frank Robinson, Johnny Oates	2,552,753
92	3rd	89	73	.549	7	Johnny Oates	3,567,819
93	3rd (tied)	85	77	.525	10	Johnny Oates	3,644,965
94	2nd	63	49	.563	6½	Johnny Oates	2,535,359
95	3rd	71	73	.493	15	Phil Regan	3,098,475
96	2nd♦	88	74	.543	4	Dave Johnson	3,646,950

*Games behind winner. †Milwaukee Brewers. ‡St. Louis Browns. §Won championship series. ∞Lost championship series. ▲First 31-23; second half 28-23. ♦Lost division series.

MANAGERIAL RECORDS

Joe Altobelli 212-167, Jimmy Austin 29-38, Hank Bauer 407-318, Jim Bottomley 21-56, Jimmy Burke 172-180, Hugh Duffy 48-89, Jimmie Dykes 54-100, Lee Fohl 226-183, Fred Haney 125-227, Lum Harris 17-10, Billy Hitchcock 163-161, Rogers Hornsby 255-381, Dan Howley 220-239, Dave Johnson 88-74, Fielder Jones 158-196, Bill Killefer 224-329, Marty Marion 96-161, Jimmy McAleer 551-532, Johnny Oates 291-270, Jack O'Connor 47-107, Phil Regan 71-73, Paul Richards 517-539, Branch Rickey 139-179, Cal Ripken Sr. 68-101, Frank Robinson 230-285, Luke Sewell 432-410, George Sisler 218-241, Al Sothoron 2-6, George Stovall 91-158, Gabby Street 53-97, Zack Taylor 235-410, Bobby Wallace 57-134, Earl Weaver 1,481-1,060.

BOSTON RED SOX

YEARLY FINISHES

ar	Position	W	L	Pct.	*GB	Manager	Attendance
01	2nd	79	57	.581	4	Jimmy Collins	289,448
02	3rd	77	60	.562	6½	Jimmy Collins	348,567
03	1st	91	47	.659	+14½	Jimmy Collins	379,338
04	1st	95	59	.617	+1½	Jimmy Collins	623,295
05	4th	78	74	.513	16	Jimmy Collins	468,828
06	8th	49	105	.318	45½	Jimmy Collins, Chick Stahl	410,209
07	7th	59	90	.396	32½	George Huff, Bob Unglaub, Deacon McGuire	436,777
08	5th	75	79	.487	15½	Deacon McGuire, Fred Lake	473,048
09	3rd	88	63	.583	9½	Fred Lake	668,965
10	4th	81	72	.529	22½	Patsy Donovan	584,619
11	5th	78	75	.510	24	Patsy Donovan	503,961
12	1st	105	47	.691	+14	Jake Stahl	597,096
13	4th	79	71	.527	15½	Jake Stahl, Bill Carrigan	437,194
14	2nd	91	62	.595	8½	Bill Carrigan	481,359
15	1st	101	50	.669	+2½	Bill Carrigan	539,885
16	1st	91	63	.591	+2	Bill Carrigan	496,397
17	2nd	90	62	.592	9	Jack Barry	387,856
18	1st	75	51	.595	+2½	Ed Barrow	249,513
19	6th	66	71	.482	20½	Ed Barrow	417,291
20	5th	72	81	.471	25½	Ed Barrow	402,445
21	5th	75	79	.487	23½	Hugh Duffy	279,273
22	8th	61	93	.396	33	Hugh Duffy	259,184
23	8th	61	91	.401	37	Frank Chance	229,668
24	7th	67	87	.435	25	Lee Fohl	448,556
25	8th	47	105	.309	49½	Lee Fohl	267,782
26	8th	46	107	.301	44½	Lee Fohl	285,155
27	8th	51	103	.331	59	Bill Carrigan	305,275

Year	Position	W	L	Pct.	*GB	Manager	Attendanc
1928	8th	57	96	.373	43 1/2	Bill Carrigan	396,92
1929	8th	58	96	.377	48	Bill Carrigan	394,62
1930	8th	52	102	.338	50	Heinie Wagner	444,04
1931	6th	62	90	.408	45	Shano Collins	350,97
1932	8th	43	111	.279	64	Shano Collins, Marty McManus	182,15
1933	7th	63	86	.423	34 1/2	Marty McManus	268,71
1934	4th	76	76	.500	24	Bucky Harris	610,64
1935	4th	78	75	.510	16	Joseph Cronin	558,56
1936	6th	74	80	.481	28 1/2	Joe Cronin	626,89
1937	5th	80	72	.526	21	Joe Cronin	559,65
1938	2nd	88	61	.591	9 1/2	Joe Cronin	646,45
1939	2nd	89	62	.589	17	Joe Cronin	573,07
1940	4th (tied)	82	72	.532	8	Joe Cronin	716,23
1941	2nd	84	70	.545	17	Joe Cronin	718,49
1942	2nd	93	59	.612	9	Joe Cronin	730,34
1943	7th	68	84	.447	29	Joe Cronin	358,27
1944	4th	77	77	.500	12	Joe Cronin	506,97
1945	7th	71	83	.461	17 1/2	Joe Cronin	603,79
1946	1st	104	50	.675	+12	Joe Cronin	1,416,94
1947	3rd	83	71	.539	14	Joe Cronin	1,427,31
1948	2nd†	96	59	.619	1	Joe McCarthy	1,558,79
1949	2nd	96	58	.623	1	Joe McCarthy	1,596,65
1950	3rd	94	60	.610	4	Joe McCarthy, Steve O'Neill	1,344,08
1951	3rd	87	67	.565	11	Steve O'Neill	1,312,28
1952	6th	76	78	.494	19	Lou Boudreau	1,115,75
1953	4th	84	69	.549	16	Lou Boudreau	1,026,13
1954	4th	69	85	.448	42	Lou Boudreau	931,12
1955	4th	84	70	.545	12	Pinky Higgins	1,203,20
1956	4th	84	70	.545	13	Pinky Higgins	1,137,15
1957	3rd	82	72	.532	16	Pinky Higgins	1,181,08
1958	3rd	79	75	.513	13	Pinky Higgins	1,077,04
1959	5th	75	79	.487	19	Pinky Higgins, Billy Jurges	984,10
1960	7th	65	89	.422	32	Billy Jurges, Pinky Higgins	1,129,86
1961	6th	76	86	.469	33	Pinky Higgins	850,58
1962	8th	76	84	.475	19	Pinky Higgins	733,08
1963	7th	76	85	.472	28	Johnny Pesky	942,64
1964	8th	72	90	.444	27	Johnny Pesky, Billy Herman	883,27
1965	9th	62	100	.383	40	Billy Herman	652,20
1966	9th	72	90	.444	26	Billy Herman, Pete Runnels	811,17
1967	1st	92	70	.568	+1	Dick Williams	1,727,83
1968	4th	86	76	.531	17	Dick Williams	1,940,78

EAST DIVISION

Year	Position	W	L	Pct.	*GB	Manager	Attendanc
1969	3rd	87	75	.537	22	Dick Williams, Eddie Popowski	1,833,24
1970	3rd	87	75	.537	21	Eddie Kasko	1,595,27
1971	3rd	85	77	.525	18	Eddie Kasko	1,678,73
1972	2nd	85	70	.548	1/2	Eddie Kasko	1,441,71
1973	2nd	89	73	.549	8	Eddie Kasko	1,481,00
1974	3rd	84	78	.519	7	Darrell Johnson	1,556,41
1975	1st‡	95	65	.594	+4 1/2	Darrell Johnson	1,748,58
1976	3rd	83	79	.512	15 1/2	Darrell Johnson, Don Zimmer	1,895,84
1977	2nd (tied)	97	64	.602	2 1/2	Don Zimmer	2,074,54
1978	2nd§	99	64	.607	1	Don Zimmer	2,320,64
1979	3rd	91	69	.569	11 1/2	Don Zimmer	2,353,11
1980	4th	83	77	.519	19	Don Zimmer, Johnny Pesky	1,956,09
1981	5th/2nd (tied)	59	49	.546	∞	Ralph Houk	1,060,37
1982	3rd	89	73	.549	6	Ralph Houk	1,950,12
1983	6th	78	84	.481	20	Ralph Houk	1,782,28
1984	4th	86	76	.531	18	Ralph Houk	1,661,61
1985	5th	81	81	.500	18 1/2	John McNamara	1,786,63
1986	1st‡	95	66	.590	+5 1/2	John McNamara	2,147,64
1987	5th	78	84	.481	20	John McNamara	2,231,55
1988	1st▲	89	73	.549	+1	John McNamara, Joe Morgan	2,464,85
1989	3rd	83	79	.512	6	Joe Morgan	2,510,01
1990	1st▲	88	74	.543	+2	Joe Morgan	2,528,98
1991	2nd (tied)	84	78	.519	7	Joe Morgan	2,562,43
1992	7th	73	89	.451	23	Butch Hobson	2,468,57
1993	5th	80	82	.494	15	Butch Hobson	2,422,02
1994	4th	54	61	.470	17	Butch Hobson	1,775,81
1995	1st◆	86	58	.597	+7	Kevin Kennedy	2,164,41
1996	3rd	85	77	.525	7	Kevin Kennedy	2,315,23

*Games behind winner. †Lost pennant playoff. ‡Won championship series. §Lost division playoff. ∞First half 30-26; second h 29-23. ▲Lost championship series. ◆Lost division series.

MANAGERIAL RECORDS

Ed Barrow 213-203, Jack Barry 90-62, Lou Boudreau 229-232, Bill Carrigan 489-500, Frank Chance 61-91, Jimmy Collins 455-376, ano Collins 73-134, Joe Cronin 1,071-916, Patsy Donovan 159-147, Hugh Duffy 136-172, Lee Fohl 160-299, Bucky Harris 76-76, ly Herman 128-182, Pinky Higgins 560-556, Butch Hobson 207-232, Ralph Houk 312-282, George Huff 2-6, Darrell Johnson 220-8, Billy Jurges 59-63, Eddie Kasko 346-295, Kevin Kennedy 171-135, Fred Lake 110-80, Joe McCarthy 223-145, Deacon McGuire -123, Marty McManus 95-153, John McNamara 297-273, Joe Morgan 301-262, Steve O'Neill 150-99, Johnny Pesky 147-179, Eddie powski 5-4, Pete Runnels 8-8, Chick Stahl 14-26, Jake Stahl 144-88, Bob Unglaub 9-20, Heinie Wagner 52-102, Dick Williams 260-7, Don Zimmer 411-304.

CALIFORNIA ANGELS

YEARLY FINISHES

ar	Position	W	L	Pct.	*GB	Manager	Attendance
61†	8th	70	91	.435	38 1/2	Bill Rigney	603,510
62†	3rd	86	76	.531	10	Bill Rigney	1,144,063
63†	9th	70	91	.435	34	Bill Rigney	821,015
64†	5th	82	80	.506	17	Bill Rigney	760,439
65†	7th	75	87	.463	27	Bill Rigney	566,727
66	6th	80	82	.494	18	Bill Rigney	1,400,321
67	5th	84	77	.522	7 1/2	Bill Rigney	1,317,713
68	8th	67	95	.414	36	Bill Rigney	1,025,956

WEST DIVISION

ar	Position	W	L	Pct.	*GB	Manager	Attendance
69	3rd	71	91	.438	26	Bill Rigney, Lefty Phillips	758,388
70	3rd	86	76	.531	12	Lefty Phillips	1,077,741
71	4th	76	86	.469	25 1/2	Lefty Phillips	926,373
72	5th	75	80	.484	18	Del Rice	744,190
73	4th	79	83	.488	15	Bobby Winkles	1,058,206
74	6th	68	94	.420	22	Bobby Winkles, Dick Williams	917,269
75	6th	72	89	.447	25 1/2	Dick Williams	1,058,163
76	4th (tied)	76	86	.469	14	Dick Williams, Norm Sherry	1,006,774
77	5th	74	88	.457	28	Norm Sherry, Dave Garcia	1,432,633
78	2nd (tied)	87	75	.537	5	Dave Garcia, Jim Fregosi	1,755,386
79	1st‡	88	74	.543	+3	Jim Fregosi	2,523,575
80	6th	65	95	.406	31	Jim Fregosi	2,297,327
81	4th/7th	51	59	.464	§	Jim Fregosi, Gene Mauch	1,441,545
82	1st‡	93	69	.574	+3	Gene Mauch	2,807,360
83	5th (tied)	70	92	.432	29	John McNamara	2,555,016
84	2nd (tied)	81	81	.500	3	John McNamara	2,402,997
85	2nd	90	72	.556	1	Gene Mauch	2,567,427
86	1st‡	92	70	.568	+5	Gene Mauch	2,655,872
87	6th (tied)	75	87	.463	10	Gene Mauch	2,696,299
88	4th	75	87	.463	29	Cookie Rojas	2,340,925
89	3rd	91	71	.562	8	Doug Rader	2,647,291
90	4th	80	82	.494	23	Doug Rader	2,555,688
91	7th	81	81	.500	14	Doug Rader, Buck Rodgers	2,416,236
92	5th (tied)	72	90	.444	24	Buck Rodgers	2,065,444
93	5th (tied)	71	91	.438	23	Buck Rodgers	2,057,460
94	4th	47	68	.409	5	Buck Rodgers, Marcel Lachemann	1,512,622
95	2nd	78	67	.538	1	Marcel Lachemann	1,748,680
96	4th	70	91	.435	19 1/2	Marcel Lachemann, John McNamara, Joe Maddon	1,820,521

*Games behind winner. †Los Angeles Angels through September 1, 1965. ‡Lost championship series. §First half 31-29; second f 20-30.

MANAGERIAL RECORDS

Jim Fregosi 237-249, Dave Garcia 60-66, Marcel Lachemann 161-170, Joe Maddon 8-14, Gene Mauch 379-332, John McNamara 1-191, Lefty Phillips 222-225, Doug Rader 232-216, Del Rice 75-80, Bill Rigney 625-707, Buck Rodgers 179-223, Cookie Rojas 75-Norm Sherry 76-71, Dick Williams 147-194, Bobby Winkles 109-127.

CHICAGO WHITE SOX

YEARLY FINISHES

ar	Position	W	L	Pct.	*GB	Manager	Attendance
01	1st	83	53	.610	+4	Clark Griffith	354,350
02	4th	74	60	.552	8	Clark Griffith	337,898
03	7th	60	77	.438	30 1/2	Nixey Callahan	286,183
04	3rd	89	65	.578	6	Nixey Callahan, Fielder Jones	557,123
05	2nd	92	60	.605	2	Fielder Jones	687,419
06	1st	93	58	.616	+3	Fielder Jones	585,202
07	3rd	87	64	.576	5 1/2	Fielder Jones	666,307
08	3rd	88	64	.579	1 1/2	Fielder Jones	636,096

Year	Position	W	L	Pct.	*GB	Manager	Attendanc
1909	4th	78	74	.513	20	Billy Sullivan	478,40
1910	6th	68	85	.444	35 1/2	Hugh Duffy	552,08
1911	4th	77	74	.510	24	Hugh Duffy	583,20
1912	4th	78	76	.506	28	Nixey Callahan	602,24
1913	5th	78	74	.513	17 1/2	Nixey Callahan	644,50
1914	6th (tied)	70	84	.455	30	Nixey Callahan	469,29
1915	3rd	93	61	.604	9 1/2	Pants Rowland	539,46
1916	2nd	89	65	.578	2	Pants Rowland	679,92
1917	1st	100	54	.649	+9	Pants Rowland	684,52
1918	6th	57	67	.460	17	Pants Rowland	195,08
1919	1st	88	52	.629	+3 1/2	Kid Gleason	627,18
1920	2nd	96	58	.623	2	Kid Gleason	833,49
1921	7th	62	92	.403	36 1/2	Kid Gleason	543,65
1922	5th	77	77	.500	17	Kid Gleason	602,86
1923	7th	69	85	.448	30	Kid Gleason	573,77
1924	8th	66	87	.431	25 1/2	Johnny Evers	606,65
1925	5th	79	75	.513	18 1/2	Eddie Collins	832,23
1926	5th	81	72	.529	9 1/2	Eddie Collins	710,33
1927	5th	70	83	.458	29 1/2	Ray Schalk	614,42
1928	5th	72	82	.468	29	Ray Schalk, Lena Blackburne	494,15
1929	7th	59	93	.388	46	Lena Blackburne	426,79
1930	7th	62	92	.403	40	Donie Bush	406,12
1931	8th	56	97	.366	51	Donie Bush	403,55
1932	7th	49	102	.325	56 1/2	Lew Fonseca	233,19
1933	6th	67	83	.447	31	Lew Fonseca	397,78
1934	8th	53	99	.349	47	Lew Fonseca, Jimmie Dykes	236,55
1935	5th	74	78	.487	19 1/2	Jimmie Dykes	470,28
1936	3rd	81	70	.536	20	Jimmie Dykes	440,81
1937	3rd	86	68	.558	16	Jimmie Dykes	589,24
1938	6th	65	83	.439	32	Jimmie Dykes	338,27
1939	4th	85	69	.552	22 1/2	Jimmie Dykes	594,10
1940	4th (tied)	82	72	.532	8	Jimmie Dykes	660,33
1941	3rd	77	77	.500	24	Jimmie Dykes	677,07
1942	6th	66	82	.446	34	Jimmie Dykes	425,73
1943	4th	82	72	.532	16	Jimmie Dykes	508,96
1944	7th	71	83	.461	18	Jimmie Dykes	563,53
1945	6th	71	78	.477	15	Jimmie Dykes	657,98
1946	5th	74	80	.481	30	Jimmie Dykes, Ted Lyons	983,40
1947	6th	70	84	.455	27	Ted Lyons	876,94
1948	8th	51	101	.336	44 1/2	Ted Lyons	777,84
1949	6th	63	91	.409	34	Jack Onslow	937,15
1950	6th	60	94	.390	38	Jack Onslow, Red Corriden	781,33
1951	4th	81	73	.526	17	Paul Richards	1,328,23
1952	3rd	81	73	.526	14	Paul Richards	1,231,67
1953	3rd	89	65	.578	11 1/2	Paul Richards	1,191,35
1954	3rd	94	60	.610	17	Paul Richards, Marty Marion	1,231,62
1955	3rd	91	63	.591	5	Marty Marion	1,175,68
1956	3rd	85	69	.552	12	Marty Marion	1,000,09
1957	2nd	90	64	.584	8	Al Lopez	1,135,66
1958	2nd	82	72	.532	10	Al Lopez	797,45
1959	1st	94	60	.610	+5	Al Lopez	1,423,14
1960	3rd	87	67	.565	10	Al Lopez	1,644,46
1961	4th	86	76	.531	23	Al Lopez	1,146,01
1962	5th	85	77	.525	11	Al Lopez	1,131,56
1963	2nd	94	68	.580	10 1/2	Al Lopez	1,158,84
1964	2nd	98	64	.605	1	Al Lopez	1,250,05
1965	2nd	95	67	.586	7	Al Lopez	1,130,51
1966	4th	83	79	.512	15	Eddie Stanky	990,01
1967	4th	89	73	.549	3	Eddie Stanky	985,63
1968	8th (tied)	67	95	.414	36	Eddie Stanky, Al Lopez	803,77

WEST DIVISION

Year	Position	W	L	Pct.	*GB	Manager	Attendanc
1969	5th	68	94	.420	29	Al Lopez, Don Gutteridge	589,54
1970	6th	56	106	.346	42	Don Gutteridge, Chuck Tanner	495,35
1971	3rd	79	83	.488	22 1/2	Chuck Tanner	833,89
1972	2nd	87	67	.565	5 1/2	Chuck Tanner	1,177,31
1973	5th	77	85	.475	17	Chuck Tanner	1,302,52
1974	4th	80	80	.500	9	Chuck Tanner	1,149,59
1975	5th	75	86	.466	22 1/2	Chuck Tanner	750,80
1976	6th	64	97	.398	25 1/2	Paul Richards	914,94
1977	3rd	90	72	.556	12	Bob Lemon	1,657,13
1978	5th	71	90	.441	20 1/2	Bob Lemon, Larry Doby	1,491,10
1979	5th	73	87	.456	14	Don Kessinger, Tony La Russa	1,280,70
1980	5th	70	90	.438	26	Tony La Russa	1,200,36
1981	3rd/6th	54	52	.509	†	Tony La Russa	946,65

ar	Position	W	L	Pct.	*GB	Manager	Attendance
82	3rd	87	75	.537	6	Tony La Russa	1,567,787
83	1st‡	99	63	.611	+20	Tony La Russa	2,132,821
84	5th (tied)	74	88	.457	10	Tony La Russa	2,136,988
85	3rd	85	77	.525	6	Tony La Russa	1,669,888
86	5th	72	90	.444	20	Tony La Russa, Jim Fregosi	1,424,313
87	5th	77	85	.475	8	Jim Fregosi	1,208,060
88	5th	71	90	.441	32 1/2	Jim Fregosi	1,115,749
89	7th	69	92	.429	29 1/2	Jeff Torborg	1,045,651
90	2nd	94	68	.580	9	Jeff Torborg	2,002,357
91	2nd	87	75	.537	8	Jeff Torborg	2,934,154
92	3rd	86	76	.531	10	Gene Lamont	2,681,156
93	1st‡	94	68	.580	+8	Gene Lamont	2,581,091

CENTRAL DIVISION

ar	Position	W	L	Pct.	*GB	Manager	Attendance
94	1st	67	46	.593	+1	Gene Lamont	1,697,398
95	3rd	68	76	.472	32	Gene Lamont, Terry Bevington	1,609,773
96	2nd	85	77	.525	14 1/2	Terry Bevington	1,676,403

*Games behind winner. †First half 31-22; second half 23-30. ‡Lost championship series.

MANAGERIAL RECORDS

Terry Bevington 142-133, Lena Blackburne 99-133, Donie Bush 118-189, Nixey Callahan 309-329, Eddie Collins 160-147, Red rriden 52-72, Larry Doby 37-50, Hugh Duffy 145-159, Jimmie Dykes 899-940, Johnny Evers 66-87, Lew Fonseca 120-196, Jim egosi 193-226, Kid Gleason 392-364, Clark Griffith 157-113, Don Gutteridge 109-172, Fielder Jones 426-293, Don Kessinger 46-60, ny La Russa 522-510, Gene Lamont 258-210, Bob Lemon 124-112, Al Lopez 840-650, Ted Lyons 185-245, Marty Marion 179-138, ck Onslow 71-133, Paul Richards 406-362, Pants Rowland 339-247, Ray Schalk 102-125, Eddie Stanky 206-197, Billy Sullivan 78-, Chuck Tanner 401-414, Jeff Torborg 250-235.

CLEVELAND INDIANS

YEARLY FINISHES

ar	Position	W	L	Pct.	*GB	Manager	Attendance
01	7th	54	82	.397	29	James McAleer	131,380
02	5th	69	67	.507	14	Bill Armour	275,395
03	3rd	77	63	.550	15	Bill Armour	311,280
04	4th	86	65	.570	7 1/2	Bill Armour	264,749
05	5th	76	78	.494	19	Nap Lajoie	316,306
06	3rd	89	64	.582	5	Nap Lajoie	325,733
07	4th	85	67	.559	8	Nap Lajoie	382,046
08	2nd	90	64	.584	1/2	Nap Lajoie	422,242
09	6th	71	82	.464	27 1/2	Nap Lajoie, Deacon McGuire	354,627
10	5th	71	81	.467	32	Deacon McGuire	293,456
11	3rd	80	73	.523	22	Deacon McGuire, George Stovall	406,296
12	5th	75	78	.490	30 1/2	Harry Davis, J.L. Birmingham	336,844
13	3rd	86	66	.566	9 1/2	J.L. Birmingham	541,000
14	8th	51	102	.333	48 1/2	J.L. Birmingham	185,997
15	7th	57	95	.375	44 1/2	J.L. Birmingham, Lee Fohl	159,285
16	6th	77	77	.500	14	Lee Fohl	492,106
17	3rd	88	66	.571	12	Lee Fohl	477,298
18	2nd	73	54	.575	2 1/2	Lee Fohl	295,515
19	2nd	84	55	.604	3 1/2	Lee Fohl, Tris Speaker	538,135
20	1st	98	56	.636	+2	Tris Speaker	912,832
21	2nd	94	60	.610	4 1/2	Tris Speaker	748,705
22	4th	78	76	.507	16	Tris Speaker	528,145
23	3rd	82	71	.536	16 1/2	Tris Speaker	558,856
24	6th	67	86	.438	24 1/2	Tris Speaker	481,905
25	6th	70	84	.455	27 1/2	Tris Speaker	419,005
26	2nd	88	66	.571	3	Tris Speaker	627,426
27	6th	66	87	.431	43 1/2	Jack McAllister	373,138
28	7th	62	92	.403	39	Roger Peckinpaugh	375,907
29	3rd	81	71	.533	24	Roger Peckinpaugh	536,210
30	4th	81	73	.536	21	Roger Peckinpaugh	528,657
31	4th	78	76	.506	30	Roger Peckinpaugh	483,027
32	4th	87	65	.572	19	Roger Peckinpaugh	468,953
33	4th	75	76	.497	23 1/2	Roger Peckinpaugh, Walter Johnson	387,936
34	3rd	85	69	.552	16	Walter Johnson	391,338
35	3rd	82	71	.536	12	Walter Johnson, Steve O'Neill	397,615
36	5th	80	74	.519	22 1/2	Steve O'Neill	500,391
37	4th	83	71	.539	19	Steve O'Neill	564,849
38	3rd	86	66	.566	13	Ossie Vitt	652,006
39	3rd	87	67	.565	20 1/2	Ossie Vitt	563,926
40	2nd	89	65	.578	1	Ossie Vitt	902,576

Year	Position	W	L	Pct.	*GB	Manager	Attendanc
1941	4th (tied)	75	79	.487	26	Roger Peckinpaugh	745,94
1942	4th	75	79	.487	28	Lou Boudreau	459,44
1943	3rd	82	71	.536	15 1/2	Lou Boudreau	438,89
1944	5th (tied)	72	82	.468	17	Lou Boudreau	475,27
1945	5th	73	72	.503	11	Lou Boudreau	558,18
1946	6th	68	86	.442	36	Lou Boudreau	1,057,28
1947	4th	80	74	.519	17	Lou Boudreau	1,521,97
1948	1st†	97	58	.626	+1	Lou Boudreau	2,620,62
1949	3rd	89	65	.578	8	Lou Boudreau	2,233,77
1950	4th	92	62	.597	6	Lou Boudreau	1,727,46
1951	2nd	93	61	.604	5	Al Lopez	1,704,98
1952	2nd	93	61	.604	2	Al Lopez	1,444,60
1953	2nd	92	62	.597	8 1/2	Al Lopez	1,069,17
1954	1st	111	43	.721	+8	Al Lopez	1,335,47
1955	2nd	93	61	.604	3	Al Lopez	1,221,78
1956	2nd	88	66	.571	9	Al Lopez	865,46
1957	6th	76	77	.497	21 1/2	Kerby Farrell	722,25
1958	4th	77	76	.503	14 1/2	Bobby Bragan, Joe Gordon	663,80
1959	2nd	89	65	.578	5	Joe Gordon	1,497,97
1960	4th	76	78	.494	21	Joe Gordon, Jimmie Dykes	950,98
1961	5th	78	83	.484	30 1/2	Jimmie Dykes	725,54
1962	6th	80	82	.494	16	Mel McGaha	716,07
1963	5th (tied)	79	83	.488	25 1/2	Birdie Tebbetts	562,50
1964	6th (tied)	79	83	.488	20	Birdie Tebbetts	653,29
1965	5th	87	75	.537	15	Birdie Tebbetts	934,78
1966	5th	81	81	.500	17	Birdie Tebbetts, George Strickland	903,35
1967	8th	75	87	.463	17	Joe Adcock	662,98
1968	3rd	86	75	.534	16 1/2	Alvin Dark	857,99

EAST DIVISION

Year	Position	W	L	Pct.	*GB	Manager	Attendanc
1969	6th	62	99	.385	46 1/2	Alvin Dark	619,97
1970	5th	76	86	.469	32	Alvin Dark	729,75
1971	6th	60	102	.370	43	Alvin Dark, John Lipon	591,36
1972	5th	72	84	.462	14	Ken Aspromonte	626,35
1973	6th	71	91	.438	26	Ken Aspromonte	615,10
1974	4th	77	85	.475	14	Ken Aspromonte	1,114,26
1975	4th	79	80	.497	15 1/2	Frank Robinson	977,03
1976	4th	81	78	.509	16	Frank Robinson	948,77
1977	5th	71	90	.441	28 1/2	Frank Robinson, Jeff Torborg	900,36
1978	6th	69	90	.434	29	Jeff Torborg	800,58
1979	6th	81	80	.503	22	Jeff Torborg, Dave Garcia	1,011,64
1980	6th	79	81	.494	23	Dave Garcia	1,033,82
1981	6th/5th	52	51	.504	‡	Dave Garcia	661,39
1982	6th (tied)	78	84	.481	17	Dave Garcia	1,044,02
1983	7th	70	92	.432	28	Mike Ferraro, Pat Corrales	768,94
1984	6th	75	87	.463	29	Pat Corrales	734,07
1985	7th	60	102	.370	39 1/2	Pat Corrales	655,18
1986	5th	84	78	.519	11 1/2	Pat Corrales	1,471,80
1987	7th	61	101	.377	37	Pat Corrales, Doc Edwards	1,077,89
1988	6th	78	84	.481	11	Doc Edwards	1,411,61
1989	6th	73	89	.451	16	Doc Edwards, John Hart	1,285,54
1990	4th	77	85	.475	11	John McNamara	1,225,24
1991	7th	57	105	.352	34	John McNamara, Mike Hargrove	1,051,86
1992	4th (tied)	76	86	.469	20	Mike Hargrove	1,224,27
1993	6th	76	86	.469	19	Mike Hargrove	2,177,90

CENTRAL DIVISION

Year	Position	W	L	Pct.	*GB	Manager	Attendanc
1994	2nd	66	47	.584	1	Mike Hargrove	1,995,17
1995	1st§∞	100	44	.694	+30	Mike Hargrove	2,842,74
1996	1st▲	99	62	.615	14 1/2	Mike Hargrove	3,318,17

*Games behind winner. †Won pennant playoff. ‡First half 26-24; second half 26-27. §Won division series. ∞Won championship serie ▲Lost division series.

MANAGERIAL RECORDS

Joe Adcock 75-87, Bill Armour 232-195, Ken Aspromonte 220-260, Joe Birmingham 170-191, Lou Boudreau 728-649, Bobby Brag 31-36, Pat Corrales 280-355, Alvin Dark 266-321, Harry Davis 54-71, Jimmie Dykes 103-115, Doc Edwards 173-207, Kerby Farrell 7 77, Mike Ferraro 40-60, Lee Fohl 327-310, Dave Garcia 247-244, Joe Gordon 184-151, Mike Hargrove 449-378, John Hart 8-11, Walt Johnson 179-168, Nap Lajoie 377-309, Johnny Lipon 18-41, Al Lopez 570-354, Jimmy McAleer 54-82, Jack McCallister 66-87, M McGaha 80-82, Deacon McGuire 91-117, John McNamara 102-137, Steve O'Neill 199-168, Roger Peckinpaugh 490-481, Fra Robinson 186-189, Tris Speaker 617-520, George Stovall 74-62, George Strickland 15-24, Birdie Tebbetts 269-298, Jeff Torborg 1 201, Oscar Vitt 262-198.

YEARLY FINISHES

ar	Position	W	L	Pct.	*GB	Manager	Attendance
01	3rd	74	61	.548	8 1/2	George Stallings	259,430
02	7th	52	83	.385	30 1/2	Frank Dwyer	189,469
03	5th	65	71	.478	25	Ed Barrow	224,523
04	7th	62	90	.408	32	Ed Barrow, Bobby Lowe	177,796
05	3rd	79	74	.516	15 1/2	Bill Armour	193,384
06	6th	71	78	.477	21	Bill Armour	174,043
07	1st	92	58	.613	+1 1/2	Hughey Jennings	297,079
08	1st	90	63	.588	+ 1/2	Hughey Jennings	436,199
09	1st	98	54	.645	+3 1/2	Hughey Jennings	490,490
10	3rd	86	68	.558	18	Hughey Jennings	391,288
11	2nd	89	65	.578	13 1/2	Hughey Jennings	484,988
12	6th	69	84	.451	36 1/2	Hughey Jennings	402,870
13	6th	66	87	.431	30	Hughey Jennings	398,502
14	4th	80	73	.523	19 1/2	Hughey Jennings	416,225
15	2nd	100	54	.649	2 1/2	Hughey Jennings	476,105
16	3rd	87	67	.565	4	Hughey Jennings	616,772
17	4th	78	75	.510	21 1/2	Hughey Jennings	457,289
18	7th	55	71	.437	20	Hughey Jennings	203,719
19	4th	80	60	.571	8	Hughey Jennings	643,805
20	7th	61	93	.396	37	Hughey Jennings	579,650
21	6th	71	82	.464	27	Ty Cobb	661,527
22	3rd	79	75	.513	15	Ty Cobb	861,206
23	2nd	83	71	.539	16	Ty Cobb	911,377
24	3rd	86	68	.558	6	Ty Cobb	1,015,136
25	4th	81	73	.526	16 1/2	Ty Cobb	820,766
26	6th	79	75	.513	12	Ty Cobb	711,914
27	4th	82	71	.536	27 1/2	George Moriarty	773,716
28	6th	68	86	.442	33	George Moriarty	474,323
29	6th	70	84	.455	36	Bucky Harris	869,318
30	5th	75	79	.487	27	Bucky Harris	649,450
31	7th	61	93	.396	47	Bucky Harris	434,056
32	5th	76	75	.503	29 1/2	Bucky Harris	397,157
33	5th	75	79	.487	25	Del Baker	320,972
34	1st	101	53	.656	+7	Mickey Cochrane	919,161
35	1st	93	58	.616	+3	Mickey Cochrane	1,034,929
36	2nd	83	71	.539	19 1/2	Mickey Cochrane	875,948
37	2nd	89	65	.578	13	Mickey Cochrane	1,072,276
38	4th	84	70	.545	16	Mickey Cochrane, Del Baker	799,557
39	5th	81	73	.526	26 1/2	Del Baker	836,279
40	1st	90	64	.584	+1	Del Baker	1,112,693
41	4th (tied)	75	79	.487	26	Del Baker	684,915
42	5th	73	81	.474	30	Del Baker	580,087
43	5th	78	76	.506	20	Steve O'Neill	606,287
44	2nd	88	66	.571	1	Steve O'Neill	923,176
45	1st	88	65	.575	+1 1/2	Steve O'Neill	1,280,341
46	2nd	92	62	.597	12	Steve O'Neill	1,722,590
47	2nd	85	69	.552	12	Steve O'Neill	1,398,093
48	5th	78	76	.506	18 1/2	Steve O'Neill	1,743,035
49	4th	87	67	.565	10	Red Rolfe	1,821,204
50	2nd	95	59	.617	3	Red Rolfe	1,951,474
51	5th	73	81	.474	25	Red Rolfe	1,132,641
52	8th	50	104	.325	45	Red Rolfe, Fred Hutchinson	1,026,846
53	6th	60	94	.390	40 1/2	Fred Hutchinson	884,658
54	5th	68	86	.442	43	Fred Hutchinson	1,079,847
55	5th	79	75	.513	17	Bucky Harris	1,181,838
56	5th	82	72	.532	15	Bucky Harris	1,051,182
57	4th	78	76	.506	20	Jack Tighe	1,272,346
58	5th	77	77	.500	15	Jack Tighe, Bill Norman	1,098,924
59	4th	76	78	.494	18	Bill Norman, Jimmie Dykes	1,221,221
60	6th	71	83	.461	26	Jimmie Dykes, Billy Hitchcock, Joe Gordon	1,167,669
61	2nd	101	61	.623	8	Bob Scheffing	1,600,710
62	4th	85	76	.528	10 1/2	Bob Scheffing	1,207,881
63	5th (tied)	79	83	.488	25 1/2	Bob Scheffing, Charlie Dressen	821,952
64	4th	85	77	.525	14	Charlie Dressen	816,139
65	4th	89	73	.549	13	Charlie Dressen, Bob Swift	1,029,645
66	3rd	88	74	.543	10	Charlie Dressen, Bob Swift, Frank Skaff	1,124,293
67	2nd	91	71	.562	1	Mayo Smith	1,447,143
68	1st	103	59	.636	+12	Mayo Smith	2,031,847

Year	Position	W	L	Pct.	*GB	Manager	Attendanc
1969	2nd	90	72	.556	19	Mayo Smith	1,577,48
1970	4th	79	83	.488	29	Mayo Smith	1,501,29
1971	2nd	91	71	.562	12	Billy Martin	1,591,07
1972	1st†	86	70	.551	+ 1/2	Billy Martin	1,892,38
1973	3rd	85	77	.525	12	Billy Martin, Joe Schultz	1,724,14
1974	6th	72	90	.444	19	Ralph Houk	1,243,08
1975	6th	57	102	.358	37 1/2	Ralph Houk	1,058,83
1976	5th	74	87	.460	24	Ralph Houk	1,467,02
1977	4th	74	88	.457	26	Ralph Houk	1,359,85
1978	5th	86	76	.531	13 1/2	Ralph Houk	1,714,89
1979	5th	85	76	.528	18	Les Moss, Dick Tracewski, Sparky Anderson	1,630,92
1980	5th	84	78	.519	19	Sparky Anderson	1,785,29
1981	4th/2nd (tied)	60	49	.550	‡	Sparky Anderson	1,149,14
1982	4th	83	79	.512	12	Sparky Anderson	1,636,05
1983	2nd	92	70	.568	6	Sparky Anderson	1,829,63
1984	1st§	104	58	.642	+15	Sparky Anderson	2,704,79
1985	3rd	84	77	.522	15	Sparky Anderson	2,286,60
1986	3rd	87	75	.537	8 1/2	Sparky Anderson	1,899,43
1987	1st†	98	64	.605	+2	Sparky Anderson	2,061,83
1988	2nd	88	74	.543	1	Sparky Anderson	2,081,16
1989	7th	59	103	.364	30	Sparky Anderson	1,543,65
1990	3rd	79	83	.488	9	Sparky Anderson	1,495,78
1991	2nd	84	78	.519	7	Sparky Anderson	1,641,66
1992	6th	75	87	.463	21	Sparky Anderson	1,423,96
1993	3rd (tied)	85	77	.525	10	Sparky Anderson	1,971,42
1994	5th	53	62	.461	18	Sparky Anderson	1,184,78
1995	4th	60	84	.417	26	Sparky Anderson	1,180,97
1996	5th	53	109	.327	39	Buddy Bell	1,168,61

*Games behind winner. †Lost championship series. ‡First half 31-26; second half 29-23. §Won championship series.

MANAGERIAL RECORDS

Sparky Anderson 1,431-1,248, Bill Armour 150-152, Del Baker 392-336, Ed Barrow 97-117, Buddy Bell 53-109, Ty Cobb 479-44 Mickey Cochrane 379-278, Chuck Dressen 221-189, Frank Dwyer 52-83, Jimmie Dykes 118-115, Joe Gordon 26-31, Bucky Harris 51 557, Ralph Houk 366-443, Fred Hutchinson 155-235, Hugh Jennings 1,131-972, Bobby Lowe 30-44, Billy Martin 248-204, Geor Moriarty 150-157, Les Moss 27-26, Bill Norman 58-64, Steve O'Neill 509-414, Red Rolfe 278-256, Bob Scheffing 210-173, Joe Schu 14-14, Frank Skaff 40-39, Mayo Smith 363-285, George Stallings 74-61, Bob Swift 56-43, Jack Tighe 99-104.

KANSAS CITY ROYALS

YEARLY FINISHES

WEST DIVISION

Year	Position	W	L	Pct.	*GB	Manager	Attendanc
1969	4th	69	93	.429	28	Joe Gordon	902,414
1970	4th (tied)	65	97	.401	33	Charlie Metro, Bob Lemon	693,047
1971	2nd	85	76	.528	16	Bob Lemon	910,784
1972	4th	76	78	.494	16 1/2	Bob Lemon	707,656
1973	2nd	88	74	.543	6	Jack McKeon	1,345,34
1974	5th	77	85	.475	13	Jack McKeon	1,173,29
1975	2nd	91	71	.562	7	Jack McKeon, Whitey Herzog	1,151,83
1976	1st†	90	72	.556	+2 1/2	Whitey Herzog	1,680,26
1977	1st†	102	60	.630	+8	Whitey Herzog	1,852,60
1978	1st†	92	70	.568	+5	Whitey Herzog	2,255,49
1979	2nd	85	77	.525	3	Whitey Herzog	2,261,84
1980	1st‡	97	65	.599	+14	Jim Frey	2,288,71
1981	5th/1st∞	50	53	.485	§	Jim Frey, Dick Howser	1,279,40
1982	2nd	90	72	.556	3	Dick Howser	2,284,46
1983	2nd	79	83	.488	20	Dick Howser	1,963,87
1984	1st†	84	78	.519	+3	Dick Howser	1,810,01
1985	1st‡	91	71	.562	+1	Dick Howser	2,162,71
1986	3rd (tied)	76	86	.469	16	Dick Howser, Mike Ferraro	2,320,79
1987	2nd	83	79	.512	2	Billy Gardner, John Wathan	2,392,47
1988	3rd	84	77	.522	19 1/2	John Wathan	2,350,18
1989	2nd	92	70	.568	7	John Wathan	2,477,70
1990	6th	75	86	.466	27 1/2	John Wathan	2,244,95
1991	6th	82	80	.506	13	John Wathan, Hal McRae	2,161,53
1992	5th (tied)	72	90	.444	24	Hal McRae	1,867,68
1993	3rd	84	78	.519	10	Hal McRae	1,934,57

CENTRAL DIVISION

Year	Position	W	L	Pct.	*GB	Manager	Attendance
1994	3rd	64	51	.557	4	Hal McRae	1,400,494
1995	2nd	70	74	.486	30	Bob Boone	1,233,530
1996	5th	75	86	.466	24	Bob Boone	1,435,997

*Games behind winner. †Lost championship series. ‡Won championship series. §First half 20-30; second half 30-23. ∞Lost division
ries.

MANAGERIAL RECORDS

Bob Boone 145-160, Mike Ferraro 36-38, Jim Frey 127-105, Billy Gardner 62-64, Joe Gordon 69-93, Whitey Herzog 410-304, Dick ɔwser 404-365, Bob Lemon 207-218, Jack McKeon 215-205, Hal McRae 286-277, Charlie Metro 19-33, John Wathan 288-270.

MILWAUKEE BREWERS

YEARLY FINISHES

WEST DIVISION

ear	Position	W	L	Pct.	*GB	Manager	Attendance
ɔ69†	6th	64	98	.395	33	Joe Schultz	677,944
ʲ70	4th	65	97	.401	33	Dave Bristol	933,690
ʲ71	6th	69	92	.429	32	Dave Bristol	731,531

EAST DIVISION

ɛar	Position	W	L	Pct.	*GB	Manager	Attendance
ʲ72	6th	65	91	.417	21	Dave Bristol, Del Crandall	600,440
ʲ73	5th	74	88	.457	23	Del Crandall	1,092,158
ʲ74	5th	76	86	.469	15	Del Crandall	955,741
ʲ75	5th	68	94	.420	28	Del Crandall	1,213,357
ʲ76	6th	66	95	.410	32	Alex Grammas	1,012,164
ʲ77	6th	67	95	.414	33	Alex Grammas	1,114,938
ʲ78	3rd	93	69	.574	6 1/2	George Bamberger	1,601,406
ʲ79	2nd	95	66	.590	8	George Bamberger	1,918,343
ʲ80	3rd	86	76	.531	17	George Bamberger, Buck Rodgers	1,857,408
ʲ81	3rd/1st§	62	47	.569	‡	Buck Rodgers	878,432
ʲ82	1st∞	95	67	.586	+1	Buck Rodgers, Harvey Kuenn	1,978,896
ʲ83	5th	87	75	.537	11	Harvey Kuenn	2,397,131
ʲ84	7th	67	94	.416	36 1/2	Rene Lachemann	1,608,509
ʲ85	6th	71	90	.441	28	George Bamberger	1,360,265
ʲ86	6th	77	84	.478	18	George Bamberger, Tom Trebelhorn	1,265,041
ʲ87	3rd	91	71	.562	7	Tom Trebelhorn	1,909,244
ʲ88	3rd (tied)	87	75	.537	2	Tom Trebelhorn	1,923,238
ʲ89	4th	81	81	.500	8	Tom Trebelhorn	1,970,735
ʲ90	6th	74	88	.457	14	Tom Trebelhorn	1,752,900
ʲ91	4th	83	79	.512	8	Tom Trebelhorn	1,478,729
ʲ92	2nd	92	70	.568	4	Phil Garner	1,857,314
ʲ93	7th	69	93	.426	26	Phil Garner	1,688,080

CENTRAL DIVISION

ɛar	Position	W	L	Pct.	*GB	Manager	Attendance
ʲ94	5th	53	62	.461	15	Phil Garner	1,268,399
ʲ95	4th	65	79	.451	35	Phil Garner	1,087,560
ʲ96	3rd	80	82	.494	19 1/2	Phil Garner	1,327,155

*Games behind winner. †Seattle Pilots. ‡First half 31-25; second half 31-22. §Lost division series. ∞Won championship series.

MANAGERIAL RECORDS

George Bamberger 377-351, Dave Bristol 144-209, Del Crandall 271-338, Phil Garner 359-386, Alex Grammas 133-190, Harvey ɹenn 160-118, Rene Lachemann 67-94, Buck Rodgers 124-102, Joe Schultz 64-98, Tom Trebelhorn 422-397.

MINNESOTA TWINS

YEARLY FINISHES

ear	Position	W	L	Pct.	*GB	Manager	Attendance
ɔ01†	6th	61	72	.459	20 1/2	Jimmy Manning	161,661
ɔ02†	6th	61	75	.449	22	Tom Loftus	188,158
ʲ03†	8th	43	94	.314	47 1/2	Tom Loftus	128,878
ʲ04†	8th	38	113	.251	55 1/2	Patsy Donovan	131,744
ʲ05†	7th	64	87	.421	29 1/2	Jake Stahl	252,027
ʲ06†	7th	55	95	.367	37 1/2	Jake Stahl	129,903
ʲ07†	8th	49	102	.325	43 1/2	Joe Cantillon	221,929
ʲ08†	7th	67	85	.441	22 1/2	Joe Cantillon	264,252
ʲ09†	8th	42	110	.276	56	Joe Cantillon	205,199
ʲ10†	7th	66	85	.437	36 1/2	Jimmy McAleer	254,591
ʲ11†	7th	64	90	.416	38 1/2	Jimmy McAleer	244,884
ʲ12†	2nd	91	61	.599	14	Clark Griffith	350,663
ʲ13†	2nd	90	64	.584	6 1/2	Clark Griffith	325,831
ʲ14†	3rd	81	73	.526	19	Clark Griffith	243,888
ʲ15†	4th	85	68	.556	17	Clark Griffith	167,332

Year	Position	W	L	Pct.	*GB	Manager	Attendance
1916†	7th	76	77	.497	14 1/2	Clark Griffith	177,26:
1917†	5th	74	79	.484	25 1/2	Clark Griffith	89,68:
1918†	3rd	72	56	.563	4	Clark Griffith	182,12:
1919†	7th	56	84	.400	32	Clark Griffith	234,09(
1920†	6th	68	84	.447	29	Clark Griffith	359,26(
1921†	4th	80	73	.523	18	George McBride	456,06(
1922†	6th	69	85	.448	25	Clyde Milan	458,55:
1923†	4th	75	78	.490	23 1/2	Donie Bush	357,40(
1924†	1st	92	62	.597	+2	Bucky Harris	534,31(
1925†	1st	96	55	.636	+8 1/2	Bucky Harris	817,19!
1926†	4th	81	69	.540	8	Bucky Harris	551,58(
1927†	3rd	85	69	.552	25	Bucky Harris	528,97(
1928†	4th	75	79	.487	26	Bucky Harris	378,50
1929†	5th	71	81	.467	34	Walter Johnson	355,50(
1930†	2nd	94	60	.610	8	Walter Johnson	614,47
1931†	3rd	92	62	.597	16	Walter Johnson	492,65
1932†	3rd	93	61	.604	14	Walter Johnson	371,39(
1933†	1st	99	53	.651	+7	Joe Cronin	437,53:
1934†	7th	66	86	.434	34	Joe Cronin	330,07
1935†	6th	67	86	.438	27	Bucky Harris	255,01
1936†	4th	82	71	.536	20	Bucky Harris	379,52!
1937†	6th	73	80	.477	28 1/2	Bucky Harris	397,79!
1938†	5th	75	76	.497	23 1/2	Bucky Harris	522,69
1939†	6th	65	87	.428	41 1/2	Bucky Harris	339,25
1940†	7th	64	90	.416	26	Bucky Harris	381,24
1941†	6th (tied)	70	84	.455	31	Bucky Harris	415,66:
1942†	7th	62	89	.411	39 1/2	Bucky Harris	403,49:
1943†	2nd	84	69	.549	13 1/2	Ossie Bluege	574,694
1944†	8th	64	90	.416	25	Ossie Bluege	525,23!
1945†	2nd	87	67	.565	1 1/2	Ossie Bluege	652,66(
1946†	4th	76	78	.494	28	Ossie Bluege	1,027,21(
1947†	7th	64	90	.416	33	Ossie Bluege	850,758
1948†	7th	56	97	.366	40	Joe Kuhel	795,254
1949†	8th	50	104	.325	47	Joe Kuhel	770,745
1950†	5th	67	87	.435	31	Bucky Harris	699,697
1951†	7th	62	92	.403	36	Bucky Harris	695,167
1952†	5th	78	76	.506	17	Bucky Harris	699,457
1953†	5th	76	76	.500	23 1/2	Bucky Harris	595,594
1954†	6th	66	88	.429	45	Bucky Harris	503,542
1955†	8th	53	101	.344	43	Chuck Dressen	425,238
1956†	7th	59	95	.383	38	Chuck Dressen	431,647
1957†	8th	55	99	.357	43	Chuck Dressen, Cookie Lavagetto	457,079
1958†	8th	61	93	.396	31	Cookie Lavagetto	475,288
1959†	8th	63	91	.409	31	Cookie Lavagetto	615,372
1960†	5th	73	81	.474	24	Cookie Lavagetto	743,404
1961	7th	70	90	.438	38	Cookie Lavagetto, Sam Mele	1,256,723
1962	2nd	91	71	.562	5	Sam Mele	1,433,116
1963	3rd	91	70	.565	13	Sam Mele	1,406,652
1964	6th (tied)	79	83	.488	20	Sam Mele	1,207,514
1965	1st	102	60	.630	+7	Sam Mele	1,463,258
1966	2nd	89	73	.549	9	Sam Mele	1,259,374
1967	2nd (tied)	91	71	.562	1	Sam Mele, Cal Ermer	1,483,547
1968	7th	79	83	.488	24	Cal Ermer	1,143,257

WEST DIVISION

Year	Position	W	L	Pct.	*GB	Manager	Attendance
1969	1st‡	97	65	.599	+9	Billy Martin	1,349,328
1970	1st‡	98	64	.605	+9	Bill Rigney	1,261,887
1971	5th	74	86	.463	26 1/2	Bill Rigney	940,858
1972	3rd	77	77	.500	15 1/2	Bill Rigney, Frank Quilici	797,901
1973	3rd	81	81	.500	13	Frank Quilici	907,499
1974	3rd	82	80	.506	8	Frank Quilici	662,401
1975	4th	76	83	.478	20 1/2	Frank Quilici	737,156
1976	3rd	85	77	.525	5	Gene Mauch	715,394
1977	4th	84	77	.522	17 1/2	Gene Mauch	1,162,727
1978	4th	73	89	.451	19	Gene Mauch	787,878
1979	4th	82	80	.506	6	Gene Mauch	1,070,521
1980	3rd	77	84	.478	19 1/2	Gene Mauch, Johnny Goryl	769,206
1981	7th/4th	41	68	.376	§	Johnny Goryl, Billy Gardner	469,090
1982	7th	60	102	.370	33	Billy Gardner	921,186
1983	5th (tied)	70	92	.432	29	Billy Gardner	858,939
1984	2nd (tied)	81	81	.500	3	Billy Gardner	1,598,422
1985	4th (tied)	77	85	.475	14	Billy Gardner, Ray Miller	1,651,814
1986	6th	71	91	.438	21	Ray Miller, Tom Kelly	1,255,453

Year	Position	W	L	Pct.	*GB	Manager	Attendance
1987	1st∞	85	77	.525	+2	Tom Kelly	2,081,976
1988	2nd	91	71	.562	13	Tom Kelly	3,030,672
1989	5th	80	82	.494	19	Tom Kelly	2,277,438
1990	7th	74	88	.457	29	Tom Kelly	1,751,584
1991	1st∞	95	67	.586	+8	Tom Kelly	2,293,842
1992	2nd	90	72	.556	6	Tom Kelly	2,482,428
1993	5th (tied)	71	91	.438	23	Tom Kelly	2,048,673

CENTRAL DIVISION

Year	Position	W	L	Pct.	*GB	Manager	Attendance
1994	4th	53	60	.469	14	Tom Kelly	1,398,565
1995	5th	56	88	.389	44	Tom Kelly	1,057,667
1996	4th	78	84	.481	21 1/2	Tom Kelly	1,437,352

*Games behind winner. †Washington Senators (original club). ‡Lost championship series. §First half 17-39; second half 24-29. ∞Won championship series.

MANAGERIAL RECORDS

Ossie Bluege 375-394, Donie Bush 75-78, Joe Cantillon 158-297, Joe Cronin 165-139, Patsy Donovan 38-113, Chuck Dressen 116-212, Cal Ermer 145-129, Billy Gardner 268-353, Johnny Goryl 34-38, Clark Griffith 693-646, Bucky Harris 1,336-1,416, Walter Johnson 350-264, Tom Kelly 785-791, Joe Kuhel 106-201, Cookie Lavagetto 271-384, Tom Loftus 104-169, Jimmy Manning 61-72, Billy Martin 97-65, Gene Mauch 378-394, Jimmy McAleer 130-175, George McBride 80-73, Sam Mele 524-436, Clyde Milan 69-85, Ray Miller 109-130, Frank Quilici 280-287, Bill Rigney 208-184, Jake Stahl 119-182.

NEW YORK YANKEES

YEARLY FINISHES

Year	Position	W	L	Pct.	*GB	Manager	Attendance
1901†	5th	68	65	.511	13 1/2	John McGraw	141,952
1902	8th	50	88	.362	34	John McGraw, Wilbert Robinson	174,606
1903	4th	72	62	.537	17	Clark Griffith	211,808
1904	2nd	92	59	.609	1 1/2	Clark Griffith	438,919
1905	6th	71	78	.477	21 1/2	Clark Griffith	309,100
1906	2nd	90	61	.596	3	Clark Griffith	434,709
1907	5th	70	78	.473	21	Clark Griffith	350,020
1908	8th	51	103	.331	39 1/2	Clark Griffith, Kid Elberfeld	305,500
1909	5th	74	77	.490	23 1/2	George Stallings	501,000
1910	2nd	88	63	.583	14 1/2	George Stallings, Hal Chase	355,857
1911	6th	76	76	.500	25 1/2	Hal Chase	302,444
1912	8th	50	102	.329	55	Harry Wolverton	242,194
1913	7th	57	94	.377	38	Frank Chance	357,551
1914	6th (tied)	70	84	.455	30	Frank Chance, Roger Peckinpaugh	359,477
1915	5th	69	83	.454	32 1/2	Bill Donovan	256,035
1916	4th	80	74	.519	11	Bill Donovan	469,211
1917	6th	71	82	.464	28 1/2	Bill Donovan	330,294
1918	4th	60	63	.488	13 1/2	Miller Huggins	282,047
1919	3rd	80	59	.576	7 1/2	Miller Huggins	619,164
1920	3rd	95	59	.617	3	Miller Huggins	1,289,422
1921	1st	98	55	.641	+4 1/2	Miller Huggins	1,230,696
1922	1st	94	60	.610	+1	Miller Huggins	1,026,134
1923	1st	98	54	.645	+16	Miller Huggins	1,007,066
1924	2nd	89	63	.586	2	Miller Huggins	1,053,533
1925	7th	69	85	.448	30	Miller Huggins	697,267
1926	1st	91	63	.591	+3	Miller Huggins	1,027,095
1927	1st	110	44	.714	+19	Miller Huggins	1,164,015
1928	1st	101	53	.656	+2 1/2	Miller Huggins	1,072,132
1929	2nd	88	66	.571	18	Miller Huggins, Art Fletcher	960,148
1930	3rd	86	68	.558	16	Bob Shawkey	1,169,230
1931	2nd	94	59	.614	13 1/2	Joe McCarthy	912,437
1932	1st	107	47	.695	+13	Joe McCarthy	962,320
1933	2nd	91	59	.607	7	Joe McCarthy	728,014
1934	2nd	94	60	.610	7	Joe McCarthy	854,682
1935	2nd	89	60	.597	3	Joe McCarthy	657,508
1936	1st	102	51	.667	+19 1/2	Joe McCarthy	976,913
1937	1st	102	52	.662	+13	Joe McCarthy	998,148
1938	1st	99	53	.651	+9 1/2	Joe McCarthy	970,916
1939	1st	106	45	.702	+17	Joe McCarthy	859,785
1940	3rd	88	66	.571	2	Joe McCarthy	988,975
1941	1st	101	53	.656	+17	Joe McCarthy	964,722
1942	1st	103	51	.669	+9	Joe McCarthy	988,251
1943	1st	98	56	.636	+13 1/2	Joe McCarthy	645,006
1944	3rd	83	71	.539	6	Joe McCarthy	822,864
1945	4th	81	71	.533	6 1/2	Joe McCarthy	881,846

Year	Position	W	L	Pct.	*GB	Manager	Attendance
1946	3rd	87	67	.565	17	Joe McCarthy, Bill Dickey, Johnny Neun	2,265,512
1947	1st	97	57	.630	+12	Bucky Harris	2,178,937
1948	3rd	94	60	.610	2½	Bucky Harris	2,373,901
1949	1st	97	57	.630	+1	Casey Stengel	2,281,676
1950	1st	98	56	.636	+3	Casey Stengel	2,081,380
1951	1st	98	56	.636	+5	Casey Stengel	1,950,107
1952	1st	95	59	.617	+2	Casey Stengel	1,629,665
1953	1st	99	52	.656	+8½	Casey Stengel	1,537,811
1954	2nd	103	51	.669	8	Casey Stengel	1,475,171
1955	1st	96	58	.623	+3	Casey Stengel	1,490,138
1956	1st	97	57	.630	+9	Casey Stengel	1,491,784
1957	1st	98	56	.636	+8	Casey Stengel	1,497,134
1958	1st	92	62	.597	+10	Casey Stengel	1,428,438
1959	3rd	79	75	.513	15	Casey Stengel	1,552,030
1960	1st	97	57	.630	+8	Casey Stengel	1,627,349
1961	1st	109	53	.673	+8	Ralph Houk	1,747,725
1962	1st	96	66	.593	+5	Ralph Houk	1,493,574
1963	1st	104	57	.646	+10½	Ralph Houk	1,308,920
1964	1st	99	63	.611	+1	Yogi Berra	1,305,638
1965	6th	77	85	.475	25	Johnny Keane	1,213,552
1966	10th	70	89	.440	26½	Johnny Keane, Ralph Houk	1,124,648
1967	9th	72	90	.444	20	Ralph Houk	1,259,514
1968	5th	83	79	.512	20	Ralph Houk	1,185,666

EAST DIVISION

Year	Position	W	L	Pct.	*GB	Manager	Attendance
1969	5th	80	81	.497	28½	Ralph Houk	1,067,996
1970	2nd	93	69	.574	15	Ralph Houk	1,136,879
1971	4th	82	80	.506	21	Ralph Houk	1,070,771
1972	4th	79	76	.510	6½	Ralph Houk	966,328
1973	4th	80	82	.494	17	Ralph Houk	1,262,103
1974	2nd	89	73	.549	2	Bill Virdon	1,273,075
1975	3rd	83	77	.519	12	Bill Virdon, Billy Martin	1,288,048
1976	1st‡	97	62	.610	+10½	Billy Martin	2,012,434
1977	1st‡	100	62	.617	+2½	Billy Martin	2,103,092
1978	1st§‡	100	63	.613	+1	Billy Martin, Bob Lemon	2,335,871
1979	4th	89	71	.556	13½	Bob Lemon, Billy Martin	2,537,765
1980	1st∞	103	59	.636	+3	Dick Howser	2,627,417
1981	1st/6th♦‡	59	48	.551	▲	Gene Michael, Bob Lemon	1,614,533
1982	5th	79	83	.488	16	Bob Lemon, Gene Michael, Clyde King	2,041,219
1983	3rd	91	71	.562	7	Billy Martin	2,257,976
1984	3rd	87	75	.537	17	Yogi Berra	1,821,815
1985	2nd	97	64	.602	2	Yogi Berra, Billy Martin	2,214,587
1986	2nd	90	72	.556	5½	Lou Piniella	2,268,030
1987	4th	89	73	.549	9	Lou Piniella	2,427,672
1988	5th	85	76	.528	3½	Billy Martin, Lou Piniella	2,633,701
1989	5th	74	87	.460	14½	Dallas Green, Bucky Dent	2,170,485
1990	7th	67	95	.414	21	Bucky Dent, Stump Merrill	2,006,436
1991	5th	71	91	.438	20	Stump Merrill	1,863,733
1992	4th (tied)	76	86	.469	20	Buck Showalter	1,748,733
1993	2nd	88	74	.543	7	Buck Showalter	2,416,965
1994	1st	70	43	.619	+6½	Buck Showalter	1,675,556
1995	2nd■	79	65	.549	7	Buck Showalter	1,705,263
1996	1st♦‡	92	70	.568	+4	Joe Torre	2,250,877

*Games behind winner. †Baltimore Orioles. ‡Won championship series. §Won pennant playoff. ∞Lost championship series. ▲First half 34-22; second half 25-26. ♦Won division series. ■Lost division series.

MANAGERIAL RECORDS

Yogi Berra 192-148, Frank Chance 117-168, Hal Chase 86-80, Bucky Dent 36-53, Bill Dickey 57-48, Bill Donovan 220-239, Kid Elberfeld 27-71, Art Fletcher 6-5, Dallas Green 56-65, Clark Griffith 419-370, Bucky Harris 191-117, Ralph Houk 944-806, Dick Howser 103-59, Miller Huggins 1,067-719, Johnny Keane 81-101, Clyde King 29-33, Bob Lemon 99-73, Billy Martin 501-385, Joe McCarthy 1,460-867, John McGraw 94-96, Stump Merrill 120-155, Gene Michael 92-76, Johnny Neun 8-6, Roger Peckinpaugh 10-10, Lou Piniella 224-193, Wilbert Robinson 24-57, Bob Shawkey 86-68, Buck Showalter 311-268, George Stallings 152-136, Casey Stengel 1,149-696, Joe Torre 92-70, Bill Virdon 142-124, Harry Wolverton 50-102.

OAKLAND ATHLETICS

YEARLY FINISHES

Year	Position	W	L	Pct.	*GB	Manager	Attendance
1901†	4th	74	62	.544	9	Connie Mack	206,329
1902†	1st	83	53	.610	+5	Connie Mack	442,473
1903†	2nd	75	60	.556	14½	Connie Mack	420,078
1904†	5th	81	70	.536	12½	Connie Mack	512,294

Year	Position	W	L	Pct.	*GB	Manager	Attendance
05†	1st	92	56	.622	+2	Connie Mack	554,576
06†	4th	78	67	.538	12	Connie Mack	489,129
07†	2nd	88	57	.607	1 1/2	Connie Mack	625,581
08†	6th	68	85	.444	22	Connie Mack	455,062
09†	2nd	95	58	.621	3 1/2	Connie Mack	674,915
10†	1st	102	48	.680	+14 1/2	Connie Mack	588,905
11†	1st	101	50	.669	+13 1/2	Connie Mack	605,749
12†	3rd	90	62	.592	15	Connie Mack	517,653
13†	1st	96	57	.627	+6 1/2	Connie Mack	571,896
14†	1st	99	53	.651	+8 1/2	Connie Mack	346,641
15†	8th	43	109	.283	58 1/2	Connie Mack	146,223
16†	8th	36	117	.235	54 1/2	Connie Mack	184,471
17†	8th	55	98	.359	44 1/2	Connie Mack	221,432
18†	8th	52	76	.406	24	Connie Mack	177,926
19†	8th	36	104	.257	52	Connie Mack	225,209
20†	8th	48	106	.312	50	Connie Mack	287,888
21†	8th	53	100	.346	45	Connie Mack	344,430
22†	7th	65	89	.422	29	Connie Mack	425,356
23†	6th	69	83	.454	29	Connie Mack	534,122
24†	5th	71	81	.467	20	Connie Mack	531,992
25†	2nd	88	64	.579	8 1/2	Connie Mack	869,703
26†	3rd	83	67	.553	6	Connie Mack	714,308
27†	2nd	91	63	.591	19	Connie Mack	605,529
28†	2nd	98	55	.641	2 1/2	Connie Mack	689,756
29†	1st	104	46	.693	+18	Connie Mack	839,176
30†	1st	102	52	.662	+8	Connie Mack	721,663
31†	1st	107	45	.704	+13 1/2	Connie Mack	627,464
32†	2nd	94	60	.610	13	Connie Mack	405,500
33†	3rd	79	72	.523	19 1/2	Connie Mack	297,138
34†	5th	68	82	.453	31	Connie Mack	305,847
35†	8th	58	91	.389	34	Connie Mack	233,173
36†	8th	53	100	.346	49	Connie Mack	285,173
37†	7th	54	97	.358	46 1/2	Connie Mack	430,733
38†	8th	53	99	.349	46	Connie Mack	385,357
39†	7th	55	97	.362	51 1/2	Connie Mack	395,022
40†	8th	54	100	.351	36	Connie Mack	432,145
41†	8th	64	90	.416	37	Connie Mack	528,894
42†	8th	55	99	.357	48	Connie Mack	423,487
43†	8th	49	105	.318	49	Connie Mack	376,735
44†	5th (tied)	72	82	.468	17	Connie Mack	505,322
45†	8th	52	98	.347	34 1/2	Connie Mack	462,631
46†	8th	49	105	.318	55	Connie Mack	621,793
47†	5th	78	76	.506	19	Connie Mack	911,566
48†	4th	84	70	.545	12 1/2	Connie Mack	945,076
49†	5th	81	73	.526	16	Connie Mack	816,514
50†	8th	52	102	.338	46	Connie Mack	309,805
51†	6th	70	84	.455	28	Jimmie Dykes	465,469
52†	4th	79	75	.513	16	Jimmie Dykes	627,100
53†	7th	59	95	.383	41 1/2	Jimmie Dykes	362,113
54†	8th	51	103	.331	60	Ed Joost	304,666
55‡	6th	63	91	.409	33	Lou Boudreau	1,393,054
56‡	8th	52	102	.338	45	Lou Boudreau	1,015,154
57‡	7th	59	94	.386	38 1/2	Lou Boudreau, Harry Craft	901,067
58‡	7th	73	81	.474	19	Harry Craft	925,090
59‡	7th	66	88	.429	28	Harry Craft	963,683
60‡	8th	58	96	.377	39	Bob Elliot	774,944
61‡	9th (tied)	61	100	.379	47 1/2	Joe Gordon, Hank Bauer	683,817
62‡	9th	72	90	.444	24	Hank Bauer	635,675
63‡	8th	73	89	.451	31 1/2	Ed Lopat	762,364
64‡	10th	57	105	.352	42	Ed Lopat, Mel McGaha	642,478
65‡	10th	59	103	.364	43	Mel McGaha, Haywood Sullivan	528,344
66‡	7th	74	86	.463	23	Alvin Dark	773,929
67‡	10th	62	99	.385	29 1/2	Alvin Dark, Luke Appling	726,639
68	6th	82	80	.506	21	Bob Kennedy	837,466

WEST DIVISION

Year	Position	W	L	Pct.	*GB	Manager	Attendance
69	2nd	88	74	.543	9	Hank Bauer, John McNamara	778,232
70	2nd	89	73	.549	9	John McNamara	778,355
71	1st§	101	60	.627	+16	Dick Williams	914,993
72	1st∞	93	62	.600	+5 1/2	Dick Williams	921,323
73	1st∞	94	68	.580	+6	Dick Williams	1,000,763
74	1st∞	90	72	.556	+5	Alvin Dark	845,693
75	1st§	98	64	.605	+7	Alvin Dark	1,075,518
76	2nd	87	74	.540	2 1/2	Chuck Tanner	780,593
77	7th	63	98	.391	38 1/2	Jack McKeon, Bobby Winkles	495,599

– 337 –

HISTORY Team by team

Year	Position	W	L	Pct.	*GB	Manager	Attendan
1978	6th	69	93	.426	23	Bobby Winkles, Jack McKeon	526,9
1979	7th	54	108	.333	34	Jim Marshall	306,7
1980	2nd	83	79	.512	14	Billy Martin	842,2
1981	1st/2nd♦§	64	45	.587	▲	Billy Martin	1,304,0
1982	5th	68	94	.420	25	Billy Martin	1,735,4
1983	4th	74	88	.457	25	Steve Boros	1,294,9
1984	4th	77	85	.475	7	Steve Boros, Jackie Moore	1,353,2
1985	4th (tied)	77	85	.475	14	Jackie Moore	1,334,5
1986	3rd (tied)	76	86	.469	16	Jackie Moore, Tony La Russa	1,314,6
1987	3rd	81	81	.500	4	Tony La Russa	1,678,9
1988	1st∞	104	58	.642	+13	Tony La Russa	2,287,3
1989	1st∞	99	63	.611	+7	Tony La Russa	2,667,2
1990	1st∞	103	59	.636	+9	Tony La Russa	2,900,2
1991	4th	84	78	.519	11	Tony La Russa	2,713,4
1992	1st§	96	66	.593	+6	Tony La Russa	2,494,16
1993	7th	68	94	.420	26	Tony La Russa	2,035,02
1994	2nd	51	63	.447	1	Tony La Russa	1,242,69
1995	4th	67	77	.465	11 1/2	Tony La Russa	1,174,31
1996	3rd	78	84	.481	12	Art Howe	1,148,38

*Games behind winner. †Philadelphia Athletics. ‡Kansas City Athletics. §Lost championship series. ∞Won championsh series. ▲First half 37-23; second half 27-22. ♦Won division series.

MANAGERIAL RECORDS

Luke Appling 10-30, Hank Bauer 187-226, Steve Boros 94-112, Lou Boudreau 151-260, Harry Craft 162-196, Alvin Dark 314-2? Jimmie Dykes 198-254, Bob Elliott 58-96, Joe Gordon 26-33, Art Howe 78-84, Eddie Joost 51-103, Bob Kennedy 82-80, Tony La Rus 695-614, Eddie Lopat 90-124, Connie Mack 3,582-3,814, Jim Marshall 54-108, Billy Martin 215-218, Mel McGaha 45-91, Jack McKe 71-105, John McNamara 97-78, Jackie Moore 163-190, Haywood Sullivan 54-82, Chuck Tanner 87-74, Dick Williams 288-190, Bob Winkles 61-86.

SEATTLE MARINERS

YEARLY FINISHES

WEST DIVISION

Year	Position	W	L	Pct.	*GB	Manager	Attendanc
1977	6th	64	98	.395	38	Darrell Johnson	1,338,51
1978	7th	56	104	.350	35	Darrell Johnson	877,44
1979	6th	67	95	.414	21	Darrell Johnson	844,44
1980	7th	59	103	.364	38	Darrell Johnson, Maury Wills	836,20
1981	6th/5th	44	65	.404	†	Maury Wills, Rene Lachemann	636,27
1982	4th	76	86	.469	17	Rene Lachemann	1,070,40
1983	7th	60	102	.370	39	Rene Lachemann, Del Crandall	813,53
1984	5th (tied)	74	88	.457	10	Del Crandall, Chuck Cottier	870,37
1985	6th	74	88	.457	17	Chuck Cottier	1,128,69
1986	7th	67	95	.414	25	Chuck Cottier, Marty Martinez, Dick Williams	1,029,04
1987	4th	78	84	.481	7	Dick Williams	1,134,25
1988	7th	68	93	.422	35 1/2	Dick Williams, Jim Snyder	1,022,39
1989	6th	73	89	.451	26	Jim Lefebvre	1,298,44
1990	5th	77	85	.475	26	Jim Lefebvre	1,509,72
1991	5th	83	79	.512	12	Jim Lefebvre	2,147,90
1992	7th	64	98	.395	32	Bill Plummer	1,651,39
1993	4th	82	80	.506	12	Lou Piniella	2,051,85
1994	3rd	49	63	.438	2	Lou Piniella	1,104,20
1995	1st‡§	79	66	.545	+1	Lou Piniella	1,643,20
1996	2nd	85	76	.528	4 1/2	Lou Piniella	2,723,85

*Games behind winner. †First half 21-36; second half 23-29. ‡Won division series. §Lost championship series.

MANAGERIAL RECORDS

Chuck Cottier 98-120, Del Crandall 93-141, Darrell Johnson 226-362, Rene Lachemann 140-180, Jim Lefebvre 233-253, Lou Pinie 295-285, Bill Plummer 64-98, Jimmy Snyder 45-60, Dick Williams 159-192, Maury Wills 26-56.

TEXAS RANGERS

YEARLY FINISHES

Year	Position	W	L	Pct.	*GB	Manager	Attendanc
1961†	9th (tied)	61	100	.379	47 1/2	Mickey Vernon	597,28
1962†	10th	60	101	.373	35 1/2	Mickey Vernon	729,77
1963†	10th	56	106	.346	48 1/2	Mickey Vernon, Gil Hodges	535,60
1964†	9th	62	100	.383	37	Gil Hodges	600,10
1965†	8th	70	92	.432	32	Gil Hodges	560,08
1966†	8th	71	88	.447	25 1/2	Gil Hodges	576,26
1967†	6th (tied)	76	85	.472	15 1/2	Gil Hodges	770,86
1968†	10th	65	96	.404	37 1/2	Jim Lemon	546,66

EAST DIVISION

Year	Position	W	L	Pct.	*GB	Manager	Attendance
969†	4th	86	76	.531	23	Ted Williams	918,106
970†	6th	70	92	.432	38	Ted Williams	824,789
971†	5th	63	96	.396	38 1/2	Ted Williams	655,156

WEST DIVISION

Year	Position	W	L	Pct.	*GB	Manager	Attendance
972	6th	54	100	.351	38 1/2	Ted Williams	662,974
973	6th	57	105	.352	37	Whitey Herzog, Del Wilber, Billy Martin	686,085
974	2nd	84	76	.525	5	Billy Martin	1,193,902
975	3rd	79	83	.488	19	Billy Martin, Frank Lucchesi	1,127,924
976	4th (tied)	76	86	.469	14	Frank Lucchesi	1,164,982
977	2nd	94	68	.580	8	Frank Lucchesi, Eddie Stanky, Connie Ryan, Billy Hunter	1,250,722
978	2nd (tied)	87	75	.537	5	Billy Hunter, Pat Corrales	1,447,963
979	3rd	83	79	.512	5	Pat Corrales	1,519,671
980	4th	76	85	.472	20 1/2	Pat Corrales	1,198,175
981	2nd/3rd	57	48	.543	‡	Don Zimmer	850,076
982	6th	64	98	.395	29	Don Zimmer, Darrell Johnson	1,154,432
983	3rd	77	85	.475	22	Doug Rader	1,363,469
984	7th	69	92	.429	14 1/2	Doug Rader	1,102,471
985	7th	62	99	.385	28 1/2	Doug Rader, Bobby Valentine	1,112,497
986	2nd	87	75	.537	5	Bobby Valentine	1,692,002
987	6th (tied)	75	87	.463	10	Bobby Valentine	1,763,053
988	6th	70	91	.435	33 1/2	Bobby Valentine	1,581,901
989	4th	83	79	.512	16	Bobby Valentine	2,043,993
990	3rd	83	79	.512	20	Bobby Valentine	2,057,911
991	3rd	85	77	.525	10	Bobby Valentine	2,297,720
992	4th	77	85	.475	19	Bobby Valentine, Toby Harrah	2,198,231
993	2nd	86	76	.531	8	Kevin Kennedy	2,244,616
994	1st	52	62	.456	+1	Kevin Kennedy	2,503,198
995	3rd	74	70	.514	4 1/2	Johnny Oates	1,985,910
996	1st§	90	72	.556	+4 1/2	Johnny Oates	2,889,020

*Games behind winner. †Washington Senators (second club). ‡First half 33-22; second half 24-26. §Lost division series.

MANAGERIAL RECORDS

Pat Corrales 160-164, Toby Harrah 32-44, Whitey Herzog 47-91, Gil Hodges 321-444, Billy Hunter 146-108, Darrell Johnson 26-40, evin Kennedy 138-138, Jim Lemon 65-96, Frank Lucchesi 142-149, Billy Martin 137-141, Johnny Oates 164-142, Doug Rader 155-00, Connie Ryan 2-4, Eddie Stanky 1-0, Bobby Valentine 581-605, Mickey Vernon 135-227, Del Wilber 1-0, Ted Williams 273-364, on Zimmer 95-106.

TORONTO BLUE JAYS

YEARLY FINISHES

EAST DIVISION

Year	Position	W	L	Pct.	*GB	Manager	Attendance
977	7th	54	107	.335	45 1/2	Roy Hartsfield	1,701,052
978	7th	59	102	.366	40	Roy Hartsfield	1,562,585
979	7th	53	109	.327	50 1/2	Roy Hartsfield	1,431,651
980	7th	67	95	.414	36	Bobby Mattick	1,400,327
981	7th/7th	37	69	.349	†	Bobby Mattick	755,083
982	6th (tied)	78	84	.481	17	Bobby Cox	1,275,978
983	4th	89	73	.549	9	Bobby Cox	1,930,415
984	2nd	89	73	.549	15	Bobby Cox	2,110,009
985	1st‡	99	62	.615	+2	Bobby Cox	2,468,925
986	4th	86	76	.531	9 1/2	Jimy Williams	2,455,477
987	2nd	96	66	.593	2	Jimy Williams	2,778,429
988	3rd (tied)	87	75	.537	2	Jimy Williams	2,595,175
989	1st‡	89	73	.549	+2	Jimy Williams, Cito Gaston	3,375,883
990	2nd	86	76	.531	2	Cito Gaston	3,885,284
991	1st‡	91	71	.562	+7	Cito Gaston	4,001,527
992	1st§	96	66	.593	+4	Cito Gaston	4,028,318
993	1st§	95	67	.586	+7	Cito Gaston	4,057,947
994	3rd	55	60	.478	16	Cito Gaston	2,907,933
995	5th	56	88	.389	30	Cito Gaston	2,826,483
996	4th	74	88	.457	18	Cito Gaston	2,559,573

*Games behind winner. †First half 16-42; second half 21-27. ‡Lost championship series. §Won championship series.

MANAGERIAL RECORDS

Bobby Cox 355-292, Cito Gaston 630-565, Roy Hartsfield 166-318, Bobby Mattick 104-164, Jimy Williams 281-241.

ATLANTA BRAVES

YEARLY FINISHES

Year	Position	W	L	Pct.	*GB	Manager	Attendance
1901†	5th	69	69	.500	20 1/2	Frank Selee	146,502
1902†	3rd	73	64	.533	29	Al Buckenberger	116,960
1903†	6th	58	80	.420	32	Al Buckenberger	143,155
1904†	7th	55	98	.359	51	Al Buckenberger	140,694
1905†	7th	51	103	.331	54 1/2	Fred Tenney	150,003
1906†	8th	49	102	.325	66 1/2	Fred Tenney	143,280
1907†	7th	58	90	.392	47	Fred Tenney	203,221
1908†	6th	63	91	.409	36	Joe Kelley	253,750
1909†	8th	45	108	.294	65 1/2	Frank Bowerman, Harry Smith	195,188
1910†	8th	53	100	.346	50 1/2	Fred Lake	149,027
1911†	8th	44	107	.291	54	Fred Tenney	116,000
1912†	8th	52	101	.340	52	Johnny Kling	121,000
1913†	5th	69	82	.457	31 1/2	George Stallings	208,000
1914†	1st	94	59	.614	+10 1/2	George Stallings	382,913
1915†	2nd	83	69	.546	7	George Stallings	376,283
1916†	3rd	89	63	.586	4	George Stallings	313,495
1917†	6th	72	81	.471	25 1/2	George Stallings	174,253
1918†	7th	53	71	.427	28 1/2	George Stallings	84,938
1919†	6th	57	82	.410	38 1/2	George Stallings	167,401
1920†	7th	62	90	.408	30	George Stallings	162,483
1921†	4th	79	74	.516	15	Fred Mitchell	318,627
1922†	8th	53	100	.346	39 1/2	Fred Mitchell	167,965
1923†	7th	54	100	.351	41 1/2	Fred Mitchell	227,802
1924†	8th	53	100	.346	40	Dave Bancroft	117,478
1925†	5th	70	83	.458	25	Dave Bancroft	313,528
1926†	7th	66	86	.434	22	Dave Bancroft	303,598
1927†	7th	60	94	.390	34	Dave Bancroft	288,685
1928†	7th	50	103	.327	44 1/2	Jack Slattery, Rogers Hornsby	227,001
1929†	8th	56	98	.364	43	Emil Fuchs	372,351
1930†	6th	70	84	.455	22	Bill McKechnie	464,835
1931†	7th	64	90	.416	37	Bill McKechnie	515,005
1932†	5th	77	77	.500	13	Bill McKechnie	507,606
1933†	4th	83	71	.539	9	Bill McKechnie	517,803
1934†	4th	78	73	.517	16	Bill McKechnie	303,205
1935†	8th	38	115	.248	61 1/2	Bill McKechnie	232,754
1936†	6th	71	83	.461	21	Bill McKechnie	340,585
1937†	5th	79	73	.520	16	Bill McKechnie	385,339
1938†	5th	77	75	.507	12	Casey Stengel	341,149
1939†	7th	63	88	.417	32 1/2	Casey Stengel	285,994
1940†	7th	65	87	.428	34 1/2	Casey Stengel	241,616
1941†	7th	62	92	.403	38	Casey Stengel	263,680
1942†	7th	59	89	.399	44	Casey Stengel	285,332
1943†	6th	68	85	.444	36 1/2	Casey Stengel	271,289
1944†	6th	65	89	.422	40	Bob Coleman	208,691
1945†	6th	67	85	.441	30	Bob Coleman, Del Bissonette	374,178
1946†	4th	81	72	.529	15 1/2	Billy Southworth	969,673
1947†	3rd	86	68	.558	8	Billy Southworth	1,277,361
1948†	1st	91	62	.595	+6 1/2	Billy Southworth	1,455,439
1949†	4th	75	79	.487	22	Billy Southworth	1,081,795
1950†	4th	83	71	.539	8	Billy Southworth	944,391
1951†	4th	76	78	.494	20 1/2	Billy Southworth, Tommy Holmes	487,475
1952†	7th	64	89	.418	32	Tommy Holmes, Charlie Grimm	281,278
1953‡	2nd	92	62	.597	13	Charlie Grimm	1,826,397
1954‡	3rd	89	65	.578	8	Charlie Grimm	2,131,388
1955‡	2nd	85	69	.552	13 1/2	Charlie Grimm	2,005,836
1956‡	2nd	92	62	.597	1	Charlie Grimm, Fred Haney	2,046,331
1957‡	1st	95	59	.617	+8	Fred Haney	2,215,404
1958‡	1st	92	62	.597	+8	Fred Haney	1,971,101
1959‡	2nd§	86	70	.551	2	Fred Haney	1,749,112
1960‡	2nd	88	66	.571	7	Chuck Dressen	1,497,799
1961‡	4th	83	71	.539	10	Chuck Dressen, Birdie Tebbetts	1,101,441
1962‡	5th	86	76	.531	15 1/2	Birdie Tebbetts	766,921
1963‡	6th	84	78	.519	15	Bobby Bragan	773,018
1964‡	5th	88	74	.543	5	Bobby Bragan	910,911
1965‡	5th	86	76	.531	11	Bobby Bragan	555,584
1966	5th	85	77	.525	10	Bobby Bragan, Billy Hitchcock	1,539,801
1967	7th	77	85	.475	24 1/2	Billy Hitchcock, Ken Silvestri	1,389,222
1968	5th	81	81	.500	16	Lum Harris	1,126,540

WEST DIVISION

ear	Position	W	L	Pct.	*GB	Manager	Attendance
069	1st∞	93	69	.574	+3	Lum Harris	1,458,320
070	5th	76	86	.469	26	Lum Harris	1,078,848
071	3rd	82	80	.506	8	Lum Harris	1,006,320
072	4th	70	84	.455	25	Lum Harris, Eddie Mathews	752,973
073	5th	76	85	.472	22 1/2	Eddie Mathews	800,655
074	3rd	88	74	.543	14	Eddie Mathews, Clyde King	981,085
075	5th	67	94	.416	40 1/2	Clyde King, Connie Ryan	534,672
076	6th	70	92	.432	32	Dave Bristol	818,179
077	6th	61	101	.377	37	Dave Bristol, Ted Turner	872,464
978	6th	69	93	.426	26	Bobby Cox	904,494
979	6th	66	94	.413	23 1/2	Bobby Cox	769,465
980	4th	81	80	.503	11	Bobby Cox	1,048,411
981	4th/5th	50	56	.472	▲	Bobby Cox	535,418
982	1st∞	89	73	.549	+1	Joe Torre	1,801,985
983	2nd	88	74	.543	3	Joe Torre	2,119,935
984	2nd (tied)	80	82	.494	12	Joe Torre	1,724,892
985	5th	66	96	.407	29	Eddie Haas, Bobby Wine	1,350,137
986	6th	72	89	.447	23 1/2	Chuck Tanner	1,387,181
987	5th	69	92	.429	20 1/2	Chuck Tanner	1,217,402
988	6th	54	106	.338	39 1/2	Chuck Tanner, Russ Nixon	848,089
989	6th	63	97	.394	28	Russ Nixon	984,930
990	6th	65	97	.401	26	Russ Nixon, Bobby Cox	980,129
991	1st◆	94	68	.580	+1	Bobby Cox	2,140,217
992	1st◆	98	64	.605	+8	Bobby Cox	3,077,400
993	1st∞	104	58	.642	+1	Bobby Cox	3,884,725

EAST DIVISION

ear	Position	W	L	Pct.	*GB	Manager	Attendance
994	2nd	68	46	.596	6	Bobby Cox	2,539,240
995	1st■◆	90	54	.625	+21	Bobby Cox	2,561,831
996	1st■◆	96	66	.593	+8	Bobby Cox	2,901,242

*Games behind winner. †Boston Braves. ‡Milwaukee Braves. §Lost pennant playoff. ∞Lost championship series. ▲First half 25-29; ɛcond half 25-27. ◆Won championship series. ■Won division series.

MANAGERIAL RECORDS

Dave Bancroft 249-363, Del Bissonette 25-34, Frank Bowerman 23-55, Bobby Bragan 310-287, Dave Bristol 131-192, Al uckenberger 186-242, Bob Coleman 107-140, Bobby Cox 856-736, Chuck Dressen 159-124, Emil Fuchs 56-98, Charlie Grimm 341-85, Eddie Haas 50-71, Fred Haney 341-231, Lum Harris 379-373, Billy Hitchcock 110-100, Tommy Holmes 61-69, Rogers Hornsby 9-83, Joe Kelley 63-91, Clyde King 96-101, Johnny Kling 52-101, Fred Lake 53-100, Eddie Mathews 149-161, Bill McKechnie 560-66, Fred Mitchell 186-274, Russ Nixon 130-216, Connie Ryan 9-18, Frank Selee 69-69, Ken Silvestri 0-3, Jack Slattery 11-20, Harry mith 22-53, Billy Southworth 424-358, George Stallings 579-597, Casey Stengel 394-516, Chuck Tanner 153-208, Birdie Tebbetts 98-9, Fred Tenney 202-402, Joe Torre 257-229, Ted Turner 0-1, Bobby Wine 16-25.

CHICAGO CUBS

YEARLY FINISHES

ear	Position	W	L	Pct.	*GB	Manager	Attendance
901	6th	53	86	.381	37	Tom Loftus	205,071
902	5th	68	69	.496	34	Frank Selee	263,700
903	3rd	82	56	.594	8	Frank Selee	386,205
904	2nd	93	60	.608	13	Frank Selee	439,100
905	3rd	92	61	.601	13	Frank Selee, Frank Chance	509,900
906	1st	116	36	.763	+20	Frank Chance	654,300
907	1st	107	45	.704	+17	Frank Chance	422,550
908	1st	99	55	.643	+1	Frank Chance	665,325
909	2nd	104	49	.680	6 1/2	Frank Chance	633,480
910	1st	104	50	.675	+13	Frank Chance	526,152
911	2nd	92	62	.597	7 1/2	Frank Chance	576,000
912	3rd	91	59	.607	11 1/2	Frank Chance	514,000
913	3rd	88	65	.575	13 1/2	Johnny Evers	419,000
914	4th	78	76	.506	16 1/2	Hank O'Day	202,516
915	4th	73	80	.477	17 1/2	Roger Bresnahan	217,058
916	5th	67	86	.438	26 1/2	Joe Tinker	453,685
917	5th	74	80	.481	24	Fred Mitchell	360,218
918	1st	84	45	.651	+10 1/2	Fred Mitchell	337,256
919	3rd	75	65	.536	21	Fred Mitchell	424,430
950	5th (tied)	75	79	.487	18	Fred Mitchell	480,783
921	7th	64	89	.418	30	Johnny Evers, Bill Killefer	410,107
922	5th	80	74	.519	13	Bill Killefer	542,283
923	4th	83	71	.539	12 1/2	Bill Killefer	703,705
924	5th	81	72	.529	12	Bill Killefer	716,922
925	8th	68	86	.442	27 1/2	Bill Killefer, Rabbit Maranville, George Gibson	622,610
926	4th	82	72	.532	7	Joe McCarthy	885,063

Year	Position	W	L	Pct.	*GB	Manager	Attendance
1927	4th	85	68	.556	8 1/2	Joe McCarthy	1,159,168
1928	3rd	91	63	.591	4	Joe McCarthy	1,143,740
1929	1st	98	54	.645	+10 1/2	Joe McCarthy	1,485,166
1930	2nd	90	64	.584	2	Joe McCarthy, Rogers Hornsby	1,463,624
1931	3rd	84	70	.545	17	Rogers Hornsby	1,086,422
1932	1st	90	64	.584	+4	Rogers Hornsby, Charlie Grimm	974,688
1933	3rd	86	68	.558	6	Charlie Grimm	594,112
1934	3rd	86	65	.570	8	Charlie Grimm	707,525
1935	1st	100	54	.649	+4	Charlie Grimm	692,604
1936	2nd (tied)	87	67	.565	5	Charlie Grimm	699,370
1937	2nd	93	61	.604	3	Charlie Grimm	895,020
1938	1st	89	63	.586	+2	Charlie Grimm, Gabby Hartnett	951,640
1939	4th	84	70	.545	13	Gabby Hartnett	726,663
1940	5th	75	79	.487	25 1/2	Gabby Hartnett	534,878
1941	6th	70	84	.455	30	Jimmy Wilson	545,159
1942	6th	68	86	.442	38	Jimmy Wilson	590,872
1943	5th	74	79	.484	30 1/2	Jimmy Wilson	508,247
1944	4th	75	79	.487	30	Jimmy Wilson, Charlie Grimm	640,110
1945	1st	98	56	.636	+3	Charlie Grimm	1,036,386
1946	3rd	82	71	.536	14 1/2	Charlie Grimm	1,342,970
1947	6th	69	85	.448	25	Charlie Grimm	1,364,039
1948	8th	64	90	.416	27 1/2	Charlie Grimm	1,237,792
1949	8th	61	93	.396	36	Charlie Grimm, Frankie Frisch	1,143,139
1950	7th	64	89	.418	26 1/2	Frankie Frisch	1,165,944
1951	8th	62	92	.403	34 1/2	Frankie Frisch, Phil Cavarretta	894,415
1952	5th	77	77	.500	19 1/2	Phil Cavarretta	1,024,826
1953	7th	65	89	.422	40	Phil Cavarretta	763,658
1954	7th	64	90	.416	33	Stan Hack	748,183
1955	6th	72	81	.471	26	Stan Hack	875,800
1956	8th	60	94	.390	33	Stan Hack	720,118
1957	7th (tied)	62	92	.403	33	Bob Scheffing	670,629
1958	5th (tied)	72	82	.468	20	Bob Scheffing	979,904
1959	5th (tied)	74	80	.481	13	Bob Scheffing	858,255
1960	7th	60	94	.390	35	Charlie Grimm, Lou Boudreau	809,770
1961	7th	64	90	.416	29	Vedie Himsl, Harry Craft, Elvin Tappe, Lou Klein	673,057
1962	9th	59	103	.364	42 1/2	Charlie Metro, Elvin Tappe, Lou Klein	609,802
1963	7th	82	80	.506	17	Bob Kennedy	979,551
1964	8th	76	86	.469	17	Bob Kennedy	751,647
1965	8th	72	90	.444	25	Bob Kennedy, Lou Klein	641,361
1966	10th	59	103	.364	36	Leo Durocher	635,891
1967	3rd	87	74	.540	14	Leo Durocher	977,226
1968	3rd	84	78	.519	13	Leo Durocher	1,043,409

EAST DIVISION

Year	Position	W	L	Pct.	*GB	Manager	Attendance
1969	2nd	92	70	.568	8	Leo Durocher	1,674,993
1970	2nd	84	78	.519	5	Leo Durocher	1,642,705
1971	3rd (tied)	83	79	.512	14	Leo Durocher	1,653,007
1972	2nd	85	70	.548	11	Leo Durocher, Whitey Lockman	1,299,163
1973	5th	77	84	.478	5	Whitey Lockman	1,351,705
1974	6th	66	96	.407	22	Whitey Lockman, Jim Marshall	1,015,378
1975	5th (tied)	75	87	.463	17 1/2	Jim Marshall	1,034,819
1976	4th	75	87	.463	26	Jim Marshall	1,026,217
1977	4th	81	81	.500	20	Herman Franks	1,439,834
1978	3rd	79	83	.488	11	Herman Franks	1,525,311
1979	5th	80	82	.494	18	Herman Franks, Joe Amalfitano	1,648,587
1980	6th	64	98	.395	27	Preston Gomez, Joe Amalfitano	1,206,776
1981	6th/5th	38	65	.369	†	Joe Amalfitano	565,637
1982	5th	73	89	.451	19	Lee Elia	1,249,278
1983	5th	71	91	.438	19	Lee Elia, Charlie Fox	1,479,717
1984	1st‡	96	65	.596	+6 1/2	Jim Frey	2,104,219
1985	4th	77	84	.478	23 1/2	Jim Frey	2,161,534
1986	5th	70	90	.438	37	Jim Frey, John Vukovich, Gene Michael	1,859,102
1987	6th	76	85	.472	18 1/2	Gene Michael, Frank Lucchesi	2,035,130
1988	4th	77	85	.475	24	Don Zimmer	2,089,034
1989	1st‡	93	69	.574	+6	Don Zimmer	2,491,942
1990	4th	77	85	.475	18	Don Zimmer	2,243,791
1991	4th	77	83	.481	20	Don Zimmer, Joe Altobelli, Jim Essian	2,314,250
1992	4th	78	84	.481	18	Jim Lefebvre	2,126,720
1993	4th	84	78	.519	13	Jim Lefebvre	2,653,763

CENTRAL DIVISION

Year	Position	W	L	Pct.	*GB	Manager	Attendance
1994	5th	49	64	.434	16 1/2	Tom Trebelhorn	1,845,208
1995	3rd	73	71	.507	12	Jim Riggleman	1,918,265
1996	4th	76	86	.469	12	Jim Riggleman	2,219,110

*Games behind winner. †First half 15-37; second half 23-28. ‡Lost championship series.

MANAGERIAL RECORDS

Joe Amalfitano 66-116, Lou Boudreau 54-83, Roger Bresnahan 73-80, Phil Cavarretta 169-213, Frank Chance 753-379, Harry Craft 9, Leo Durocher 535-526, Lee Elia 127-158, Jim Essian 59-63, Johnny Evers 130-121, Charlie Fox 17-22, Herman Franks 238-241, n Frey 196-182, Frank Frisch 141-196, George Gibson 12-14, Preston Gomez 38-52, Charlie Grimm 946-784, Stan Hack 196-265, abby Hartnett 203-176, Vedie Himsl 10-21, Rogers Hornsby 141-114, Roy Johnson 0-1, Bob Kennedy 182-198, Bill Killefer 299-292, u Klein 65-83, Jim Lefebvre 162-162, Whitey Lockman 157-162, Tom Loftus 53-86, Frank Lucchesi 8-17, Rabbit Maranville 23-30, n Marshall 175-218, Joe McCarthy 442-321, Charlie Metro 43-69, Gene Michael 114-124, Fred Mitchell 308-269, Hank O'Day 78-76, n Riggleman 149-157, Bob Scheffing 208-254, Frank Selee 295-223, Elvin Tappe 46-69, Joe Tinker 67-86, Tom Trebelhorn 49-64, hn Vukovich 1-1, Jimmy Wilson 213-258, Don Zimmer 265-259.

CINCINNATI REDS

YEARLY FINISHES

ar	Position	W	L	Pct.	*GB	Manager	Attendance
01	8th	52	87	.374	38	Bid McPhee	205,728
02	4th	70	70	.500	33 1/2	Bid McPhee, Frank Bancroft, Joe Kelley	217,300
03	4th	74	65	.532	16 1/2	Joe Kelley	351,680
04	3rd	88	65	.575	18	Joe Kelley	391,915
05	5th	79	74	.516	26	Joe Kelley	313,927
06	6th	64	87	.424	51 1/2	Ned Hanlon	330,056
07	6th	66	87	.431	41 1/2	Ned Hanlon	317,500
08	5th	73	81	.474	26	John Ganzel	399,200
09	4th	77	76	.503	33 1/2	Clark Griffith	424,643
10	5th	75	79	.487	29	Clark Griffith	380,622
11	6th	70	83	.458	29	Clark Griffith	300,000
12	4th	75	78	.490	29	Hank O'Day	344,000
13	7th	64	89	.418	37 1/2	Joe Tinker	258,000
14	8th	60	94	.390	34 1/2	Buck Herzog	100,791
15	7th	71	83	.461	20	Buck Herzog	218,878
16	7th (tied)	60	93	.392	33 1/2	Buck Herzog, Christy Mathewson	255,846
17	4th	78	76	.506	20	Christy Mathewson	269,056
18	3rd	68	60	.531	15 1/2	Christy Mathewson, Heinie Groh	163,009
19	1st	96	44	.686	+9	Pat Moran	532,501
20	3rd	82	71	.536	10 1/2	Pat Moran	568,107
21	6th	70	83	.458	24	Pat Moran	311,227
22	2nd	86	68	.558	7	Pat Moran	493,754
23	2nd	91	63	.591	4 1/2	Pat Moran	575,063
24	4th	83	70	.542	10	Jack Hendricks	437,707
25	3rd	80	73	.523	15	Jack Hendricks	464,920
26	2nd	87	67	.565	2	Jack Hendricks	672,987
27	5th	75	78	.490	18 1/2	Jack Hendricks	442,164
28	5th	78	74	.513	16	Jack Hendricks	490,490
29	7th	66	88	.429	33	Jack Hendricks	295,040
30	7th	59	95	.383	33	Dan Howley	386,727
31	8th	58	96	.377	43	Dan Howley	263,316
32	8th	60	94	.390	30	Dan Howley	356,950
33	8th	58	94	.382	33	Donie Bush	218,281
34	8th	52	99	.344	42	Bob O'Farrell, Chuck Dressen	206,773
35	6th	68	85	.444	31 1/2	Chuck Dressen	448,247
36	5th	74	80	.481	18	Chuck Dressen	466,245
37	8th	56	98	.364	40	Chuck Dressen, Bobby Wallace	411,221
38	4th	82	68	.547	6	Bill McKechnie	706,756
39	1st	97	57	.630	+4 1/2	Bill McKechnie	981,443
40	1st	100	53	.654	+12	Bill McKechnie	850,180
41	3rd	88	66	.571	12	Bill McKechnie	643,513
42	4th	76	76	.500	29	Bill McKechnie	427,031
43	2nd	87	67	.565	18	Bill McKechnie	379,122
44	3rd	89	65	.578	16	Bill McKechnie	409,567
45	7th	61	93	.396	37	Bill McKechnie	290,070
46	6th	67	87	.435	30	Bill McKechnie	715,751
47	5th	73	81	.474	21	Johnny Neun	899,975
48	7th	64	89	.418	27	Johnny Neun, Bucky Walters	823,386
49	7th	62	92	.403	35	Bucky Walters	707,782
50	6th	66	87	.431	24 1/2	Luke Sewell	538,794
51	6th	68	86	.442	28 1/2	Luke Sewell	588,268
52	6th	69	85	.448	27 1/2	Luke Sewell, Rogers Hornsby	604,197
53	6th	68	86	.442	37	Rogers Hornsby, Buster Mills	548,086
54	5th	74	80	.481	23	Birdie Tebbetts	704,167
55	5th	75	79	.487	23 1/2	Birdie Tebbetts	693,662
56	3rd	91	63	.591	2	Birdie Tebbetts	1,125,928
57	4th	80	74	.519	15	Birdie Tebbetts	1,070,850

Year	Position	W	L	Pct.	*GB	Manager	Attendance
1958	4th	76	78	.494	16	Birdie Tebbetts, Jimmie Dykes	788,582
1959	5th (tied)	74	80	.481	13	Mayo Smith, Fred Hutchinson	801,289
1960	6th	67	87	.435	28	Fred Hutchinson	663,486
1961	1st	93	61	.604	+4	Fred Hutchinson	1,117,603
1962	3rd	98	64	.605	3 1/2	Fred Hutchinson	982,085
1963	5th	86	76	.531	13	Fred Hutchinson	858,805
1964	2nd (tied)	92	70	.549	1	Fred Hutchinson, Dick Sisler	862,466
1965	4th	89	73	.549	8	Dick Sisler	1,047,824
1966	7th	76	84	.475	18	Don Heffner, Dave Bristol	742,958
1967	4th	87	75	.537	14 1/2	Dave Bristol	958,300
1968	4th	83	79	.512	14	Dave Bristol	733,354

WEST DIVISION

Year	Position	W	L	Pct.	*GB	Manager	Attendance
1969	3rd	89	73	.549	4	Dave Bristol	987,991
1970	1st†	102	60	.630	+14 1/2	Sparky Anderson	1,803,568
1971	4th (tied)	79	83	.488	11	Sparky Anderson	1,501,122
1972	1st†	95	59	.617	+10 1/2	Sparky Anderson	1,611,459
1973	1st‡	99	63	.611	+3 1/2	Sparky Anderson	2,017,601
1974	2nd	98	64	.605	4	Sparky Anderson	2,164,307
1975	1st†	108	54	.667	+20	Sparky Anderson	2,315,603
1976	1st†	102	60	.630	+10	Sparky Anderson	2,629,708
1977	2nd	88	74	.543	10	Sparky Anderson	2,519,670
1978	2nd	92	69	.571	2 1/2	Sparky Anderson	2,532,497
1979	1st‡	90	71	.559	+1 1/2	John McNamara	2,356,933
1980	3rd	89	73	.549	3 1/2	John McNamara	2,022,450
1981	2nd/2nd	66	42	.611	§	John McNamara	1,093,730
1982	6th	61	101	.377	28	John McNamara, Russ Nixon	1,326,528
1983	6th	74	88	.457	17	Russ Nixon	1,190,419
1984	5th	70	92	.432	22	Vern Rapp, Pete Rose	1,275,887
1985	2nd	89	72	.553	5 1/2	Pete Rose	1,834,619
1986	2nd	86	76	.531	10	Pete Rose	1,692,432
1987	2nd	84	78	.519	6	Pete Rose	2,185,205
1988	2nd	87	74	.540	7	Pete Rose	2,072,528
1989	5th	75	87	.463	17	Pete Rose, Tommy Helms	1,979,320
1990	1st†	91	71	.562	+5	Lou Piniella	2,400,892
1991	5th	74	88	.457	20	Lou Piniella	2,372,377
1992	2nd	90	72	.556	8	Lou Piniella	2,315,946
1993	5th	73	89	.451	31	Tony Perez, Dave Johnson	2,453,232

CENTRAL DIVISION

Year	Position	W	L	Pct.	*GB	Manager	Attendance
1994	1st	66	48	.579	+ 1/2	Dave Johnson	1,897,68
1995	1st∞‡	85	59	.590	+9	Dave Johnson	1,837,649
1996	3rd	81	81	.500	7	Ray Knight	1,861,428

*Games behind winner. †Won championship series. ‡Lost championship series. §First half 35-21; second half 31-21. ∞Won division series.

MANAGERIAL RECORDS

Sparky Anderson 863-586, Frank Bancroft 9-7, Dave Bristol 298-265, Donie Bush 58-94, Chuck Dressen 214-282, Jimmie Dykes 2-17, John Ganzel 73-81, Clark Griffith 222-238, Heinie Groh 7-3, Ned Hanlon 130-174, Don Heffner 37-46, Tommy Helms 14-21, Ja Hendricks 469-450, Buck Herzog 165-226, Rogers Hornsby 91-106, Dan Howley 177-285, Fred Hutchinson 443-372, Dave Johnson 204-172, Joe Kelley 275-230, Ray Knight 81-81, Christy Mathewson 164-176, Bill McKechnie 747-632, John McNamara 279-244, B McPhee 79-124, Buster Mills 4-4, Pat Moran 425-329, Johnny Neun 117-137, Russ Nixon 101-131, Hank O'Day 75-78, Bob O'Farre 30-60, Tony Perez 20-24, Lou Piniella 255-231, Vern Rapp 51-70, Pete Rose 426-388, Luke Sewell 176-234, Dick Sisler 121-94, May Smith 35-45, Birdie Tebbetts 372-357, Joe Tinker 64-89, Bobby Wallace 5-20, Bucky Walters 81-123.

COLORADO ROCKIES

YEARLY FINISHES

WEST DIVISION

Year	Position	W	L	Pct.	*GB	Manager	Attendance
1993	6th	67	95	.414	37	Don Baylor	4,483,350
1994	3rd	53	64	.453	6 1/2	Don Baylor	3,281,51
1995	2nd†	77	67	.535	1	Don Baylor	3,390,03
1996	3rd	83	79	.512	8	Don Baylor	3,891,01

*Games behind winner. †Lost division series.

MANAGERIAL RECORDS

Don Baylor 280-305.

YEARLY FINISHES

EAST DIVISION

Year	Position	W	L	Pct.	*GB	Manager	Attendance
93	6th	64	98	.395	33	Rene Lachemann	3,064,847
94	5th	51	64	.443	23½	Rene Lachemann	1,937,467
95	4th	67	76	.469	22½	Rene Lachemann	1,700,466
96	3rd	80	82	.494	16	Rene Lachemann, John Boles	1,746,767

*Games behind winner.

MANAGERIAL RECORDS

John Boles 40-35, Rene Lachemann 222-285.

HOUSTON ASTROS

YEARLY FINISHES

Year	Position	W	L	Pct.	*GB	Manager	Attendance
62†	8th	64	96	.400	36½	Harry Craft	924,456
63†	9th	66	96	.407	33	Harry Craft	719,502
64†	9th	66	96	.407	27	Harry Craft, Luman Harris	725,773
65	9th	65	97	.401	32	Luman Harris	2,151,470
66	8th	72	90	.444	23	Grady Hatton	1,872,108
67	9th	69	93	.426	32½	Grady Hatton	1,348,303
68	10th	72	90	.444	25	Grady Hatton, Harry Walker	1,312,887

WEST DIVISION

Year	Position	W	L	Pct.	*GB	Manager	Attendance
69	5th	81	81	.500	12	Harry Walker	1,442,995
70	4th	79	83	.488	23	Harry Walker	1,253,444
71	4th (tied)	79	83	.488	11	Harry Walker	1,261,589
72	2nd	84	69	.549	10½	Harry Walker, Leo Durocher, Salty Parker	1,469,247
73	4th	82	80	.506	17	Leo Durocher, Preston Gomez	1,394,004
74	4th	81	81	.500	21	Preston Gomez	1,090,728
75	6th	64	97	.398	43½	Preston Gomez, Bill Virdon	858,002
76	3rd	80	82	.494	22	Bill Virdon	886,146
77	3rd	81	81	.500	17	Bill Virdon	1,109,560
78	5th	74	88	.457	21	Bill Virdon	1,126,145
79	2nd	89	73	.549	1½	Bill Virdon	1,900,312
80	1st‡§	93	70	.571	+1	Bill Virdon	2,278,217
81	3rd/1st▲	61	49	.555	∞	Bill Virdon	1,321,282
82	5th	77	85	.475	12	Bill Virdon, Bob Lillis	1,558,555
83	3rd	85	77	.525	6	Bob Lillis	1,351,962
84	2nd (tied)	80	82	.494	12	Bob Lillis	1,229,862
85	3rd (tied)	83	79	.512	12	Bob Lillis	1,184,314
86	1st§	96	66	.593	+10	Hal Lanier	1,734,276
87	3rd	76	86	.469	14	Hal Lanier	1,909,902
88	5th	82	80	.506	12½	Hal Lanier	1,933,505
89	3rd	86	76	.531	6	Art Howe	1,834,908
90	4th (tied)	75	87	.463	16	Art Howe	1,310,927
91	6th	65	97	.401	29	Art Howe	1,196,152
92	4th	81	81	.500	17	Art Howe	1,211,412
93	3rd	85	77	.525	19	Art Howe	2,084,546

CENTRAL DIVISION

Year	Position	W	L	Pct.	*GB	Manager	Attendance
94	2nd	66	49	.574	½	Terry Collins	1,561,136
95	2nd	76	68	.528	9	Terry Collins	1,363,801
96	2nd	82	80	.506	6	Terry Collins	1,975,888

*Games behind winner. †Houston Colt .45s. ‡Won division playoff. §Lost championship series. ∞First half 28-29; second half 33-20. ▲Lost division series.

MANAGERIAL RECORDS

Terry Collins 224-197, Harry Craft 191-280, Leo Durocher 98-95, Preston Gomez 128-161, Lum Harris 70-105, Grady Hatton 164-1, Art Howe 392-418, Hal Lanier 254-232, Bob Lillis 276-261, Bill Virdon 544-522, Harry Walker 355-353.

LOS ANGELES DODGERS

YEARLY FINISHES

Year	Position	W	L	Pct.	*GB	Manager	Attendance
01†	3rd	79	57	.581	9½	Ned Hanlon	189,200
02†	2nd	75	63	.543	27½	Ned Hanlon	199,868

HISTORY Team by team

Year	Position	W	L	Pct.	*GB	Manager	Attendance
1903†	5th	70	66	.515	19	Ned Hanlon	224,670
1904†	6th	56	97	.366	50	Ned Hanlon	214,600
1905†	8th	48	104	.316	56 1/2	Ned Hanlon	227,924
1906†	5th	66	86	.434	50	Patsy Donovan	227,400
1907†	5th	65	83	.439	40	Patsy Donovan	312,500
1908†	7th	53	101	.344	46	Patsy Donovan	275,600
1909†	6th	55	98	.359	55 1/2	Harry Lumley	321,300
1910†	6th	64	90	.416	40	Bill Dahlen	279,321
1911†	7th	64	86	.427	33 1/2	Bill Dahlen	269,000
1912†	7th	58	95	.379	46	Bill Dahlen	243,000
1913†	6th	65	84	.436	34 1/2	Bill Dahlen	347,000
1914†	5th	75	79	.487	19 1/2	Wilbert Robinson	122,671
1915†	3rd	80	72	.526	10	Wilbert Robinson	297,766
1916†	1st	94	60	.610	+2 1/2	Wilbert Robinson	447,747
1917†	7th	70	81	.464	26 1/2	Wilbert Robinson	221,619
1918†	5th	57	69	.452	25 1/2	Wilbert Robinson	83,831
1919†	5th	69	71	.493	27	Wilbert Robinson	360,721
1920†	1st	93	61	.604	+7	Wilbert Robinson	808,722
1921†	5th	77	75	.507	16 1/2	Wilbert Robinson	613,245
1922†	6th	76	78	.494	17	Wilbert Robinson	498,856
1923†	6th	76	78	.494	19 1/2	Wilbert Robinson	564,666
1924†	2nd	92	62	.597	1 1/2	Wilbert Robinson	818,883
1925†	6th (tied)	68	85	.444	27	Wilbert Robinson	659,435
1926†	6th	71	82	.464	17 1/2	Wilbert Robinson	650,819
1927†	6th	65	88	.425	28 1/2	Wilbert Robinson	637,230
1928†	6th	77	76	.503	17 1/2	Wilbert Robinson	664,863
1929†	6th	70	83	.458	28 1/2	Wilbert Robinson	731,886
1930†	4th	86	68	.558	6	Wilbert Robinson	1,097,339
1931†	4th	79	73	.520	21	Wilbert Robinson	753,133
1932†	3rd	81	73	.526	9	Max Carey	681,827
1933†	6th	65	88	.425	26 1/2	Max Carey	526,815
1934†	6th	71	81	.467	23 1/2	Casey Stengel	434,188
1935†	5th	70	83	.458	29 1/2	Casey Stengel	470,517
1936†	7th	67	87	.435	25	Casey Stengel	489,618
1937†	6th	62	91	.405	33 1/2	Burleigh Grimes	482,481
1938†	7th	69	80	.463	18 1/2	Burleigh Grimes	663,087
1939†	3rd	84	69	.549	12 1/2	Leo Durocher	955,668
1940†	2nd	88	65	.575	12	Leo Durocher	975,978
1941†	1st	100	54	.649	+2 1/2	Leo Durocher	1,214,910
1942†	2nd	104	50	.675	2	Leo Durocher	1,037,765
1943†	3rd	81	72	.529	23 1/2	Leo Durocher	661,739
1944†	7th	63	91	.409	42	Leo Durocher	605,905
1945†	3rd	87	67	.565	11	Leo Durocher	1,059,220
1946†	2nd‡	96	60	.615	2	Clyde Sukeforth, Burt Shotton	1,796,824
1947†	1st	94	60	.610	+5	Clyde Sukeforth, Burt Shotton	1,807,526
1948†	3rd	84	70	.545	7 1/2	Leo Durocher, Burt Shotton	1,398,967
1949†	1st	97	57	.630	+1	Burt Shotton	1,633,747
1950†	2nd	89	65	.578	2	Burt Shotton	1,185,896
1951†	2nd‡	97	60	.618	1	Chuck Dressen	1,282,628
1952†	1st	96	57	.627	+4 1/2	Chuck Dressen	1,088,704
1953†	1st	105	49	.682	+13	Chuck Dressen	1,163,419
1954†	2nd	92	62	.597	5	Walter Alston	1,020,531
1955†	1st	98	55	.641	+13 1/2	Walter Alston	1,033,589
1956†	1st	93	61	.604	+1	Walter Alston	1,213,562
1957†	3rd	84	70	.545	11	Walter Alston	1,028,258
1958	7th	71	83	.461	21	Walter Alston	1,845,556
1959	1st§	88	68	.564	+2	Walter Alston	2,071,045
1960	4th	82	72	.532	13	Walter Alston	2,253,887
1961	2nd	89	65	.578	4	Walter Alston	1,804,250
1962	2nd‡	102	63	.618	1	Walter Alston	2,755,184
1963	1st	99	63	.611	+6	Walter Alston	2,538,602
1964	6th (tied)	80	82	.494	13	Walter Alston	2,228,751
1965	1st	97	65	.599	+2	Walter Alston	2,553,577
1966	1st	95	67	.586	+1 1/2	Walter Alston	2,617,029
1967	8th	73	89	.451	28 1/2	Walter Alston	1,664,362
1968	7th	76	86	.469	21	Walter Alston	1,581,093

WEST DIVISION

Year	Position	W	L	Pct.	*GB	Manager	Attendance
1969	4th	85	77	.525	8	Walter Alston	1,784,527
1970	2nd	87	74	.540	14 1/2	Walter Alston	1,697,142
1971	2nd	89	73	.549	1	Walter Alston	2,064,594
1972	3rd	85	70	.548	10 1/2	Walter Alston	1,860,858
1973	2nd	95	66	.590	3 1/2	Walter Alston	2,136,192

Year	Position	W	L	Pct.	*GB	Manager	Attendance
1974	1st∞	102	60	.630	+4	Walter Alston	2,632,474
1975	2nd	88	74	.543	20	Walter Alston	2,539,349
1976	2nd	92	70	.568	10	Walter Alston, Tommy Lasorda	2,386,301
1977	1st∞	98	64	.605	+10	Tommy Lasorda	2,955,087
1978	1st∞	95	67	.586	+2 1/2	Tommy Lasorda	3,347,845
1979	3rd	79	83	.488	11 1/2	Tommy Lasorda	2,860,954
1980	2nd▲	92	71	.564	1	Tommy Lasorda	3,249,287
1981	1st/4th§∞	63	47	.573	◆	Tommy Lasorda	2,381,292
1982	2nd	88	74	.543	1	Tommy Lasorda	3,608,881
1983	1st▼	91	71	.652	+3	Tommy Lasorda	3,510,313
1984	4th	79	83	.488	13	Tommy Lasorda	3,134,824
1985	1st▼	95	67	.586	+5 1/2	Tommy Lasorda	3,264,593
1986	5th	73	89	.451	23	Tommy Lasorda	3,023,208
1987	4th	73	89	.451	17	Tommy Lasorda	2,797,409
1988	1st∞	94	67	.584	+7	Tommy Lasorda	2,980,262
1989	4th	77	83	.481	14	Tommy Lasorda	2,944,653
1990	2nd	86	76	.531	5	Tommy Lasorda	3,002,396
1991	2nd	93	69	.574	1	Tommy Lasorda	3,348,170
1992	6th	63	99	.389	35	Tommy Lasorda	2,473,266
1993	4th	81	81	.500	23	Tommy Lasorda	3,170,392
1994	1st	58	56	.509	+3 1/2	Tommy Lasorda	2,279,355
1995	1st@	78	66	.542	+1	Tommy Lasorda	2,766,251
1996	2nd@	90	72	.556	1	Tommy Lasorda, Bill Russell	3,188,454

*Games behind winner. †Brooklyn Dodgers. ‡Lost pennant playoff. §Won division series. ∞Won championship series. ▲Lost division playoff. ◆First half 36-21; second half 27-26. ■Won division series. ▼Lost championship series. @Lost division series.

MANAGERIAL RECORDS

Walter Alston 2,040-1,613, Max Carey 146-161, Bill Dahlen 251-355, Patsy Donovan 184-270, Chuck Dressen 298-166, Leo Durocher 738-565, Burleigh Grimes 131-171, Ned Hanlon 328-387, Tommy Lasorda 1,599-1,439, Harry Lumley 55-98, Wilbert Robinson 1,375-1,341, Bill Russell 49-37, Burt Shotton 326-215, Casey Stengel 208-251, Clyde Sukeforth 2-0.

MONTREAL EXPOS

YEARLY FINISHES
EAST DIVISION

Year	Position	W	L	Pct.	*GB	Manager	Attendance
1969	6th	52	110	.321	48	Gene Mauch	1,212,608
1970	6th	73	89	.451	16	Gene Mauch	1,424,683
1971	5th	71	90	.441	25 1/2	Gene Mauch	1,290,963
1972	5th	70	86	.449	26 1/2	Gene Mauch	1,142,145
1973	4th	79	83	.488	3 1/2	Gene Mauch	1,246,863
1974	4th	79	82	.491	8 1/2	Gene Mauch	1,019,134
1975	5th (tied)	75	87	.463	17 1/2	Gene Mauch	908,292
1976	6th	55	107	.340	46	Karl Kuehl, Charlie Fox	646,704
1977	5th	75	87	.463	26	Dick Williams	1,433,757
1978	4th	76	86	.469	14	Dick Williams	1,427,007
1979	2nd	95	65	.594	2	Dick Williams	2,102,173
1980	2nd	90	72	.556	1	Dick Williams	2,208,175
1981	3rd/1st‡§	60	48	.556	†	Dick Williams, Jim Fanning	1,534,564
1982	3rd	86	76	.531	6	Jim Fanning	2,318,292
1983	3rd	82	80	.506	8	Bill Virdon	2,320,651
1984	5th	78	83	.484	18	Bill Virdon, Jim Fanning	1,606,531
1985	3rd	84	77	.522	16 1/2	Buck Rodgers	1,502,494
1986	4th	78	83	.484	29 1/2	Buck Rodgers	1,128,981
1987	3rd	91	71	.562	4	Buck Rodgers	1,850,324
1988	3rd	81	81	.500	20	Buck Rodgers	1,478,659
1989	4th	81	81	.500	12	Buck Rodgers	1,783,533
1990	3rd	85	77	.525	10	Buck Rodgers	1,373,087
1991	6th	71	90	.441	26 1/2	Buck Rodgers, Tom Runnells	934,742
1992	2nd	87	75	.537	9	Tom Runnells, Felipe Alou	1,669,077
1993	2nd	94	68	.580	3	Felipe Alou	1,641,437
1994	1st	74	40	.649	+6	Felipe Alou	1,276,250
1995	5th	66	78	.458	24	Felipe Alou	1,309,618
1996	2nd	88	74	.543	8	Felipe Alou	1,616,709

*Games behind winner. †First half 30-25; second half 30-23. ‡Won division series. §Lost championship series.

MANAGERIAL RECORDS

Felipe Alou 392-315, Jim Fanning 116-103, Charlie Fox 12-22, Karl Kuehl 43-85, Gene Mauch 499-627, Buck Rodgers 520-499, Tom Runnells 68-81, Bill Virdon 146-147, Dick Williams 380-347.

YEARLY FINISHES

Year	Position	W	L	Pct.	*GB	Manager	Attendance
1962	10th	40	120	.250	60 1/2	Casey Stengel	922,530
1963	10th	51	111	.315	48	Casey Stengel	1,080,108
1964	10th	53	109	.327	40	Casey Stengel	1,732,597
1965	10th	50	112	.309	47	Casey Stengel, Wes Westrum	1,768,389
1966	9th	66	95	.410	28 1/2	Wes Westrum	1,932,693
1967	10th	61	101	.377	40 1/2	Wes Westrum, Salty Parker	1,565,492
1968	9th	73	89	.451	24	Gil Hodges	1,781,657

EAST DIVISION

Year	Position	W	L	Pct.	*GB	Manager	Attendance
1969	1st†	100	62	.617	+8	Gil Hodges	2,175,373
1970	3rd	83	79	.512	6	Gil Hodges	2,697,479
1971	3rd (tied)	83	79	.512	14	Gil Hodges	2,266,680
1972	3rd	83	73	.532	13 1/2	Yogi Berra	2,134,185
1973	1st†	82	79	.509	+1 1/2	Yogi Berra	1,912,390
1974	5th	71	91	.438	17	Yogi Berra	1,722,209
1975	3rd (tied)	82	80	.506	10 1/2	Yogi Berra, Roy McMillan	1,730,566
1976	3rd	86	76	.531	15	Joe Frazier	1,468,754
1977	6th	64	98	.395	37	Joe Frazier, Joe Torre	1,066,825
1978	6th	66	96	.407	24	Joe Torre	1,007,328
1979	6th	63	99	.389	35	Joe Torre	788,905
1980	5th	67	95	.414	24	Joe Torre	1,192,073
1981	5th/4th	41	62	.398	‡	Joe Torre	704,244
1982	6th	65	97	.401	27	George Bamberger	1,323,036
1983	6th	68	94	.420	22	George Bamberger, Frank Howard	1,112,774
1984	2nd	90	72	.556	6 1/2	Dave Johnson	1,842,695
1985	2nd	98	64	.605	3	Dave Johnson	2,761,601
1986	1st†	108	54	.667	+21 1/2	Dave Johnson	2,767,601
1987	2nd	92	70	.568	3	Dave Johnson	3,034,129
1988	1st§	100	60	.625	+15	Dave Johnson	3,055,445
1989	2nd	87	75	.537	6	Dave Johnson	2,918,710
1990	2nd	91	71	.562	4	Dave Johnson, Bud Harrelson	2,732,747
1991	5th	77	84	.478	20 1/2	Bud Harrelson, Mike Cubbage	2,284,484
1992	5th	72	90	.444	24	Jeff Torborg	1,779,534
1993	7th	59	103	.364	38	Jeff Torborg, Dallas Green	1,873,183
1994	3rd	55	58	.487	18 1/2	Dallas Green	1,151,471
1995	2nd (tied)	69	75	.479	21	Dallas Green	1,273,183
1996	4th	71	91	.438	25	Dallas Green, Bobby Valentine	1,588,322

*Games behind winner. †Won championship series. ‡First half 17-34; second half 24-28. §Lost championship series.

MANAGERIAL RECORDS

George Bamberger 81-127, Yogi Berra 292-296, Mike Cubbage 3-4, Joe Frazier 101-106, Dallas Green 229-283, Bud Harrelson 148-129, Gil Hodges 339-309, Frank Howard 52-64, Davey Johnson 595-417, Roy McMillan 26-27, Salty Parker 4-7, Casey Stengel 175-404, Jeff Torborg 85-115, Joe Torre 286-420, Bobby Valentine 12-19, Wes Westrum 142-237.

YEARLY FINISHES

Year	Position	W	L	Pct.	*GB	Manager	Attendance
1901	2nd	83	57	.593	7 1/2	Bill Shettsline	234,937
1902	7th	56	81	.409	46	Bill Shettsline	112,066
1903	7th	49	86	.363	39 1/2	Chief Zimmer	151,729
1904	8th	52	100	.342	53 1/2	Hugh Duffy	140,771
1905	4th	83	69	.546	21 1/2	Hugh Duffy	317,932
1906	4th	71	82	.464	45 1/2	Hugh Duffy	294,680
1907	3rd	83	64	.565	21 1/2	Bill Murray	341,216
1908	4th	83	71	.539	16	Bill Murray	420,660
1909	5th	74	79	.484	36 1/2	Bill Murray	303,177
1910	4th	78	75	.510	25 1/2	Red Dooin	296,597
1911	4th	79	73	.520	19 1/2	Red Dooin	416,000
1912	5th	73	79	.480	30 1/2	Red Dooin	250,000
1913	2nd	88	63	.583	12 1/2	Red Dooin	470,000
1914	6th	74	80	.481	20 1/2	Red Dooin	138,474
1915	1st†	90	62	.592	+7	Pat Moran	449,898
1916	2nd	91	62	.595	2 1/2	Pat Moran	515,365
1917	2nd	87	65	.572	10	Pat Moran	354,428
1918	6th	55	68	.447	26	Pat Moran	122,266
1919	8th	47	90	.343	47 1/2	Jack Coombs, Gavvy Cravath	240,424

Year	Position	W	L	Pct.	*GB	Manager	Attendance
20	8th	62	91	.405	30½	Gavvy Cravath	330,998
21	8th	51	103	.331	43½	Bill Donovan, Kaiser Wilhelm	273,961
22	7th	57	96	.373	35½	Kaiser Wilhelm	232,471
23	8th	50	104	.325	45½	Art Fletcher	228,168
24	7th	55	96	.364	37	Art Fletcher	299,818
25	6th (tied)	68	85	.444	27	Art Fletcher	304,905
26	8th	58	93	.384	29½	Art Fletcher	240,600
27	8th	51	103	.331	43	Stuffy McInnis	305,420
28	8th	43	109	.283	51	Burt Shotton	182,168
29	5th	71	82	.464	27½	Burt Shotton	281,200
30	8th	52	102	.338	40	Burt Shotton	299,007
31	6th	66	88	.429	35	Burt Shotton	284,849
32	4th	78	76	.506	12	Burt Shotton	268,914
33	7th	60	92	.395	31	Burt Shotton	156,421
34	7th	56	93	.376	37	Jimmy Wilson	169,885
35	7th	64	89	.418	35½	Jimmy Wilson	205,470
36	8th	54	100	.351	38	Jimmy Wilson	249,219
37	7th	61	92	.399	34½	Jimmy Wilson	212,790
38	8th	45	105	.300	43	Jimmy Wilson, Hans Lobert	166,111
39	8th	45	106	.298	50½	Doc Prothro	277,973
40	8th	50	103	.327	50	Doc Prothro	207,177
41	8th	43	111	.279	57	Doc Prothro	231,401
42	8th	42	109	.278	62½	Hans Lobert	230,183
43	7th	64	90	.416	41	Bucky Harris, Fred Fitzsimmons	466,975
44	8th	61	92	.399	43½	Fred Fitzsimmons	369,586
45	8th	46	108	.299	52	Fred Fitzsimmons, Ben Chapman	285,057
46	5th	69	85	.448	28	Ben Chapman	1,045,247
47	7th (tied)	62	92	.403	32	Ben Chapman	907,332
48	6th	66	88	.429	25½	Ben Chapman, Dusty Cooke, Eddie Sawyer	767,429
49	3rd	81	73	.526	16	Eddie Sawyer	819,698
50	1st	91	63	.591	+2	Eddie Sawyer	1,217,035
51	5th	73	81	.474	23½	Eddie Sawyer	937,658
52	4th	87	67	.565	9½	Eddie Sawyer, Steve O'Neill	775,417
53	3rd (tied)	83	71	.539	22	Steve O'Neill	853,644
54	4th	75	79	.487	22	Steve O'Neill, Terry Moore	738,991
55	4th	77	77	.500	21½	Mayo Smith	922,886
56	5th	71	83	.461	22	Mayo Smith	934,798
57	5th	77	77	.500	19	Mayo Smith	1,146,230
58	8th	69	85	.448	23	Mayo Smith, Eddie Sawyer	931,110
59	8th	64	90	.416	23	Eddie Sawyer	802,815
60	8th	59	95	.383	36	Eddie Sawyer, Andy Cohen, Gene Mauch	862,205
61	8th	47	107	.305	46	Gene Mauch	590,039
62	7th	81	80	.503	20	Gene Mauch	762,034
63	4th	87	75	.537	12	Gene Mauch	907,141
64	2nd (tied)	92	70	.568	1	Gene Mauch	1,425,891
65	6th	85	76	.528	11½	Gene Mauch	1,166,376
66	4th	87	75	.537	8	Gene Mauch	1,108,201
67	5th	82	80	.506	19½	Gene Mauch	828,888
68	7th (tied)	76	86	.469	21	Gene Mauch, George Myatt, Bob Skinner	664,546

EAST DIVISION

Year	Position	W	L	Pct.	*GB	Manager	Attendance
69	5th	63	99	.389	37	Bob Skinner, George Myatt	519,414
70	5th	73	88	.453	15½	Frank Lucchesi	708,247
71	6th	67	95	.414	30	Frank Lucchesi	1,511,223
72	6th	59	97	.378	37½	Frank Lucchesi, Paul Owens	1,343,329
73	6th	71	91	.438	11½	Danny Ozark	1,475,934
74	3rd	80	82	.494	8	Danny Ozark	1,808,648
75	2nd	86	76	.531	6½	Danny Ozark	1,909,233
76	1st†	101	61	.623	+9	Danny Ozark	2,480,150
77	1st†	101	61	.623	+5	Danny Ozark	2,700,070
78	1st†	90	72	.556	+1½	Danny Ozark	2,583,389
79	4th	84	78	.519	14	Danny Ozark, Dallas Green	2,775,011
80	1st‡	91	71	.562	+1	Dallas Green	2,651,650
81	1st/3rd∞	59	48	.551	§	Dallas Green	1,638,752
82	2nd	89	73	.549	3	Pat Corrales	2,376,394
83	1st‡	90	72	.556	+6	Pat Corrales, Paul Owens	2,128,339
84	4th	81	81	.500	15½	Paul Owens	2,062,693
85	5th	75	87	.463	26	John Felske	1,830,350
86	2nd	86	75	.534	21½	John Felske	1,933,335
87	4th (tied)	80	82	.494	15	John Felske, Lee Elia	2,100,110
88	6th	65	96	.404	35½	Lee Elia, John Vukovich	1,990,041
89	6th	67	95	.414	26	Nick Leyva	1,861,985
90	4th (tied)	77	85	.475	18	Nick Leyva	1,992,484
91	3rd	78	84	.481	20	Nick Leyva, Jim Fregosi	2,050,012

HISTORY *Team by team*

Year	Position	W	L	Pct.	*GB	Manager	Attendanc
1992	6th	70	92	.432	26	Jim Fregosi	1,927,44
1993	1st‡	97	65	.599	+3	Jim Fregosi	3,137,67
1994	4th	54	61	.470	20 1/2	Jim Fregosi	2,290,97
1995	2nd (tied)	69	75	.479	21	Jim Fregosi	2,043,59
1996	5th	67	95	.414	29	Jim Fregosi	1,801,67

*Games behind winner. †Lost championship series. ‡Won championship series. §First half 34-21; second half 25-27. ∞Lost divisio series.

MANAGERIAL RECORDS

Ben Chapman 197-277, Andy Cohen 1-0, Dusty Cooke 6-6, Jack Coombs 18-44, Pat Corrales 132-115, Gavvy Cravath 91-137, Donovan 31-71, Red Dooin 392-370, Hugh Duffy 206-251, Lee Elia 111-142, John Felske 190-194, Fred Fitzsimmons 102-179, Fletcher 231-378, Jim Fregosi 431-463, Dallas Green 169-130, Bucky Harris 40-53, Nick Leyva 148-189, Hans Lobert 42-111, Fra Lucchesi 166-233, Gene Mauch 645-684, Stuffy McInnis 51-103, Terry Moore 35-42, Pat Moran 323-257, Bill Murray 240-214, Geor Myatt 21-35, Steve O'Neill 182-140, Paul Owens 161-158, Danny Ozark 594-510, Doc Prothro 138-320, Eddie Sawyer 390-424, Shettsline 139-138, Burt Shotton 370-549, Bob Skinner 92-123, Mayo Smith 264-281, John Vukovich 5-4, Kaiser Wilhelm 77-12 Jimmy Wilson 280-477, Chief Zimmer 49-86.

PITTSBURGH PIRATES

YEARLY FINISHES

Year	Position	W	L	Pct.	*GB	Manager	Attendanc
1901	1st	90	49	.647	+7 1/2	Fred Clarke	251,95
1902	1st	103	36	.741	+27 1/2	Fred Clarke	243,82
1903	1st	91	49	.650	+6 1/2	Fred Clarke	326,85
1904	4th	87	66	.569	19	Fred Clarke	340,61
1905	2nd	96	57	.627	9	Fred Clarke	369,12
1906	3rd	93	60	.608	23 1/2	Fred Clarke	394,87
1907	2nd	91	63	.591	17	Fred Clarke	319,50
1908	2nd	98	56	.636	1	Fred Clarke	382,44
1909	1st	110	42	.724	+6 1/2	Fred Clarke	534,95
1910	3rd	86	67	.562	17 1/2	Fred Clarke	436,58
1911	3rd	85	69	.552	14 1/2	Fred Clarke	432,00
1912	2nd	93	58	.616	10	Fred Clarke	384,00
1913	4th	78	71	.523	21 1/2	Fred Clarke	296,00
1914	7th	69	85	.448	25 1/2	Fred Clarke	139,62
1915	5th	73	81	.474	18	Fred Clarke	225,74
1916	6th	65	89	.422	29	Jimmy Callahan	289,13
1917	8th	51	103	.331	47	Jimmy Callahan, Honus Wagner, Hugo Bezdek	192,80
1918	4th	65	60	.520	17	Hugo Bezdek	213,61
1919	4th	71	68	.511	24 1/2	Hugo Bezdek	276,81
1920	4th	79	75	.513	14	George Gibson	429,03
1921	2nd	90	63	.588	4	George Gibson	701,56
1922	3rd (tied)	85	69	.552	8	George Gibson, Bill McKechnie	523,67
1923	3rd	87	67	.565	8 1/2	Bill McKechnie	611,08
1924	3rd	90	63	.588	3	Bill McKechnie	736,88
1925	1st	95	58	.621	+8 1/2	Bill McKechnie	804,35
1926	3rd	84	69	.549	4 1/2	Bill McKechnie	798,54
1927	1st	94	60	.610	+1 1/2	Donie Bush	869,72
1928	4th	85	67	.559	9	Donie Bush	495,07
1929	2nd	88	65	.575	10 1/2	Donie Bush, Jewel Ens	491,37
1930	5th	80	74	.519	12	Jewel Ens	357,79
1931	5th	75	79	.487	26	Jewel Ens	260,39
1932	2nd	86	68	.558	4	George Gibson	287,26
1933	2nd	87	67	.565	5	George Gibson	288,74
1934	5th	74	76	.493	19 1/2	George Gibson, Pie Traynor	322,62
1935	4th	86	67	.562	13 1/2	Pie Traynor	352,88
1936	4th	84	70	.545	8	Pie Traynor	372,52
1937	3rd	86	68	.558	10	Pie Traynor	459,67
1938	2nd	86	64	.573	2	Pie Traynor	641,03
1939	6th	68	85	.444	28 1/2	Pie Traynor	376,73
1940	4th	78	76	.506	22 1/2	Frankie Frisch	507,93
1941	4th	81	73	.526	19	Frankie Frisch	482,24
1942	5th	66	81	.449	36 1/2	Frankie Frisch	448,89
1943	4th	80	74	.519	25	Frankie Frisch	604,27
1944	2nd	90	63	.588	14 1/2	Frankie Frisch	498,74
1945	4th	82	72	.532	16	Frankie Frisch	604,69
1946	7th	63	91	.409	34	Frankie Frisch, Spud Davis	749,96
1947	7th (tied)	62	92	.403	32	Billy Herman, Bill Burwell	1,283,53
1948	4th	83	71	.539	8 1/2	Billy Meyer	1,517,02
1949	6th	71	83	.461	26	Billy Meyer	1,499,43
1950	8th	57	96	.373	33 1/2	Billy Meyer	1,166,26
1951	7th	64	90	.416	32 1/2	Billy Meyer	980,59
1952	8th	42	112	.273	54 1/2	Billy Meyer	686,67

Position	W	L	Pct.	*GB	Manager	Attendance
8th	50	104	.325	55	Fred Haney	572,757
8th	53	101	.344	44	Fred Haney	475,494
8th	60	94	.390	38 1/2	Fred Haney	469,397
7th	66	88	.429	27	Bobby Bragan	949,878
7th (tied)	62	92	.403	33	Bobby Bragan, Danny Murtaugh	850,732
2nd	84	70	.545	8	Danny Murtaugh	1,311,988
4th	78	76	.506	9	Danny Murtaugh	1,359,917
1st	95	59	.617	+7	Danny Murtaugh	1,705,828
6th	75	79	.487	18	Danny Murtaugh	1,199,128
4th	93	68	.578	8	Danny Murtaugh	1,090,648
8th	74	88	.457	25	Danny Murtaugh	783,648
6th (tied)	80	82	.494	13	Danny Murtaugh	759,496
3rd	90	72	.556	7	Harry Walker	909,279
3rd	92	70	.568	3	Harry Walker	1,196,618
6th	81	81	.500	20 1/2	Harry Walker, Danny Murtaugh	907,012
6th	80	82	.494	17	Larry Shepard	693,485

EAST DIVISION

Position	W	L	Pct.	*GB	Manager	Attendance
3rd	88	74	.543	12	Larry Shepard, Alex Grammas	769,369
1st†	89	73	.549	+5	Danny Murtaugh	1,341,947
1st‡	97	65	.599	+7	Danny Murtaugh	1,501,132
1st†	96	59	.619	+11	Bill Virdon	1,427,460
3rd	80	82	.494	2 1/2	Bill Virdon, Danny Murtaugh	1,319,913
1st†	88	74	.543	+1 1/2	Danny Murtaugh	1,110,552
1st†	92	69	.571	+6 1/2	Danny Murtaugh	1,270,018
2nd	92	70	.568	9	Danny Murtaugh	1,025,945
2nd	96	66	.593	5	Chuck Tanner	1,237,349
2nd	88	73	.547	1 1/2	Chuck Tanner	964,106
1st‡	98	64	.605	+2	Chuck Tanner	1,435,454
3rd	83	79	.512	8	Chuck Tanner	1,646,757
4th/6th	46	56	.451	§	Chuck Tanner	541,789
4th	84	78	.519	8	Chuck Tanner	1,024,106
2nd	84	78	.519	6	Chuck Tanner	1,225,916
6th	75	87	.463	21 1/2	Chuck Tanner	773,500
6th	57	104	.354	43 1/2	Chuck Tanner	735,900
6th	64	98	.395	44	Jim Leyland	1,000,917
4th (tied)	80	82	.494	15	Jim Leyland	1,161,193
2nd	85	75	.531	15	Jim Leyland	1,866,713
5th	74	88	.457	19	Jim Leyland	1,374,141
1st†	95	67	.586	+4	Jim Leyland	2,049,908
1st†	98	64	.605	+14	Jim Leyland	2,065,302
1st†	96	66	.593	+9	Jim Leyland	1,829,395
5th	75	87	.463	22	Jim Leyland	1,650,593

CENTRAL DIVISION

Position	W	L	Pct.	*GB	Manager	Attendance
3rd (tied)	53	61	.465	13	Jim Leyland	1,222,520
5th	58	86	.403	27	Jim Leyland	905,517
5th	73	89	.451	15	Jim Leyland	1,332,150

*Games behind winner. †Lost championship series. ‡Won championship series. §First half 25-23; second half 21-33.

MANAGERIAL RECORDS

ugo Bezdek 166-187, Bobby Bragan 102-155, Bill Burwell 1-0, Donie Bush 246-178, Jimmy Callahan 85-129, Fred Clarke 1,343-Spud Davis 1-2, Jewel Ens 176-167, Frank Frisch 539-528, George Gibson 401-330, Alex Grammas 4-1, Fred Haney 163-299, Billy an 61-92, Jim Leyland 851-863, Bill McKechnie 409-293, Billy Meyer 317-452, Danny Murtaugh 1,115-950, Larry Shepard 164-Chuck Tanner 711-685, Pie Traynor 457-406, Bill Virdon 163-128, Honus Wagner 1-4, Harry Walker 224-184.

ST. LOUIS CARDINALS

YEARLY FINISHES

Position	W	L	Pct.	*GB	Manager	Attendance
4th	76	64	.543	14 1/2	Patsy Donovan	379,988
6th	56	78	.418	44 1/2	Patsy Donovan	226,417
8th	43	94	.314	46 1/2	Patsy Donovan	226,538
5th	75	79	.487	31 1/2	Kid Nichols	386,750
6th	58	96	.377	47 1/2	Kid Nichols, Jimmy Burke, Matt Robison	292,800
7th	52	98	.347	63	John McCloskey	283,770
8th	52	101	.340	55 1/2	John McCloskey	185,377
8th	49	105	.318	50	John McCloskey	205,129
7th	54	98	.355	56	Roger Bresnahan	299,982
7th	63	90	.412	40 1/2	Roger Bresnahan	355,668
5th	75	74	.503	22	Roger Bresnahan	447,768

Year	Position	W	L	Pct.	*GB	Manager	Attendan
1912	6th	63	90	.412	41	Roger Bresnahan	241,7
1913	8th	51	99	.340	49	Miller Huggins	203,5
1914	3rd	81	72	.529	13	Miller Huggins	256,0
1915	6th	72	81	.471	18 1/2	Miller Huggins	252,6
1916	7th (tied)	60	93	.392	33 1/2	Miller Huggins	224,3
1917	3rd	82	70	.539	15	Miller Huggins	288,4
1918	8th	51	78	.395	33	Jack Hendricks	110,5
1919	7th	54	83	.394	40 1/2	Branch Rickey	167,0
1920	5th (tied)	75	79	.487	18	Branch Rickey	326,8
1921	3rd	87	66	.569	7	Branch Rickey	384,7
1922	3rd (tied)	85	69	.552	8	Branch Rickey	536,9
1923	5th	79	74	.516	16	Branch Rickey	338,5
1924	6th	65	89	.422	28 1/2	Branch Rickey	272,8
1925	4th	77	76	.503	18	Branch Rickey, Rogers Hornsby	404,9
1926	1st	89	65	.578	+2	Rogers Hornsby	668,4
1927	2nd	92	61	.601	1 1/2	Bob O'Farrell	749,3
1928	1st	95	59	.617	+2	Bill McKechnie	761,5
1929	4th	78	74	.513	20	Bill McKechnie, Billy Southworth	399,8
1930	1st	92	62	.597	+2	Gabby Street	508,5
1931	1st	101	53	.656	+13	Gabby Street	608,5
1932	6th (tied)	72	82	.468	18	Gabby Street	279,2
1933	5th	82	71	.536	9 1/2	Gabby Street, Frankie Frisch	256,1
1934	1st	95	58	.621	+2	Frankie Frisch	325,0
1935	2nd	96	58	.623	4	Frankie Frisch	506,0
1936	2nd (tied)	87	67	.565	5	Frankie Frisch	448,0
1937	4th	81	73	.526	15	Frankie Frisch	430,8
1938	6th	71	80	.470	17 1/2	Frankie Frisch, Mike Gonzalez	291,4
1939	2nd	92	61	.601	4 1/2	Ray Blades	400,2
1940	3rd	84	69	.549	16	Ray Blades, Mike Gonzalez, Billy Southworth	324,0
1941	2nd	97	56	.634	2 1/2	Billy Southworth	633,6
1942	1st	106	48	.688	+2	Billy Southworth	553,5
1943	1st	105	49	.682	+18	Billy Southworth	517,1
1944	1st	105	49	.682	+14 1/2	Billy Southworth	461,9
1945	2nd	95	59	.617	3	Billy Southworth	594,6
1946	1st†	98	58	.628	+2	Eddie Dyer	1,061,
1947	2nd	89	65	.578	5	Eddie Dyer	1,247,
1948	2nd	85	69	.552	6 1/2	Eddie Dyer	1,111,
1949	2nd	96	58	.623	1	Eddie Dyer	1,430,
1950	5th	78	75	.510	12 1/2	Eddie Dyer	1,093,
1951	3rd	81	73	.526	15 1/2	Marty Marion	1,013,
1952	3rd	88	66	.571	8 1/2	Eddie Stanky	913,
1953	3rd (tied)	83	71	.539	22	Eddie Stanky	880,
1954	6th	72	82	.468	25	Eddie Stanky	1,039,
1955	7th	68	86	.442	30 1/2	Eddie Stanky, Harry Walker	849,
1956	4th	76	78	.494	17	Fred Hutchinson	1,029,
1957	2nd	87	67	.565	8	Fred Hutchinson	1,183,
1958	5th (tied)	72	82	.468	20	Fred Hutchinson, Stan Hack	1,063,
1959	7th	71	83	.461	16	Solly Hemus	929,
1960	3rd	86	68	.558	9	Solly Hemus	1,096,
1961	5th	80	74	.519	13	Solly Hemus, Johnny Keane	855,
1962	6th	84	78	.519	17 1/2	Johnny Keane	953,
1963	2nd	93	69	.574	6	Johnny Keane	1,170,
1964	1st	93	69	.574	+1	Johnny Keane	1,143,
1965	7th	80	81	.497	16 1/2	Red Schoendienst	1,241,
1966	6th	83	79	.512	12	Red Schoendienst	1,712,
1967	1st	101	60	.627	+10 1/2	Red Schoendienst	2,090,
1968	1st	97	65	.599	+9	Red Schoendienst	2,011,

EAST DIVISION

Year	Position	W	L	Pct.	*GB	Manager	Attenda
1969	4th	87	75	.537	13	Red Schoendienst	1,682,
1970	4th	76	86	.469	13	Red Schoendienst	1,629,
1971	2nd	90	72	.556	7	Red Schoendienst	1,604,
1972	4th	75	81	.481	21 1/2	Red Schoendienst	1,196,
1973	2nd	81	81	.500	1 1/2	Red Schoendienst	1,574,
1974	2nd	86	75	.534	1 1/2	Red Schoendienst	1,838,
1975	3rd (tied)	82	80	.506	10 1/2	Red Schoendienst	1,695,
1976	5th	72	90	.444	29	Red Schoendienst	1,207,
1977	3rd	83	79	.512	18	Vern Rapp	1,659,
1978	5th	69	93	.426	21	Vern Rapp, Jack Krol, Ken Boyer	1,278,
1979	3rd	86	76	.531	12	Ken Boyer	1,627,
1980	4th	74	88	.457	17	Ken Boyer, Jack Krol, Whitey Herzog, Red Schoendienst	1,385,
1981	2nd/2nd	59	43	.578	‡	Whitey Herzog	1,010,

– 352 –

ear	Position	W	L	Pct.	*GB	Manager	Attendance
982	1st§	92	70	.568	+3	Whitey Herzog	2,111,906
983	4th	79	83	.488	11	Whitey Herzog	2,317,914
984	3rd	84	78	.519	12½	Whitey Herzog	2,037,448
985	1st§	101	61	.623	+3	Whitey Herzog	2,637,563
986	3rd	79	82	.491	28½	Whitey Herzog	2,471,974
987	1st§	95	67	.586	+3	Whitey Herzog	3,072,122
988	5th	76	86	.469	25	Whitey Herzog	2,892,799
989	3rd	86	76	.531	7	Whitey Herzog	3,080,980
990	6th	70	92	.432	25	Whitey Herzog, Red Schoendienst, Joe Torre	2,573,225
991	2nd	84	78	.519	14	Joe Torre	2,448,699
992	3rd	83	79	.512	13	Joe Torre	2,418,483
993	3rd	87	75	.537	10	Joe Torre	2,844,328

CENTRAL DIVISION

ear	Position	W	L	Pct.	*GB	Manager	Attendance
994	3rd (tied)	53	61	.465	13	Joe Torre	1,866,544
995	4th	62	81	.434	22½	Joe Torre, Mike Jorgensen	1,756,727
996	1st∞▲	88	74	.543	+6	Tony La Russa	2,654,718

*Games behind winner. †Won pennant playoff. ‡First half 30-20; second half 29-23. §Won championship series. ∞Won division
ories. ▲Lost championship series.

MANAGERIAL RECORDS

Ray Blades 106-85, Ken Boyer 166-190, Roger Bresnahan 255-352, Jimmy Burke 17-32, Patsy Donovan 175-236, Eddie Dyer 446-
25, Frank Frisch 458-354, Mike Gonzalez 9-13, Stan Hack 3-7, Solly Hemus 190-192, Jack Hendricks 51-78, Whitey Herzog 835-739,
ogers Hornsby 153-116, Miller Huggins 346-415, Fred Hutchinson 232-220, Mike Jorgensen 42-54, Johnny Keane 317-249, Tony La
issa 88-74, Marty Marion 81-73, John McCloskey 153-304, Bill McKechnie 129-88, Kid Nichols 94-108, Bob O'Farrell 92-61, Vern
app 89-90, Branch Rickey 458-485, Stanley Robison 22-35, Red Schoendienst 1,028-944, Billy Southworth 620-346, Eddie Stanky
70-238, Gabby Street 312-242, Joe Torre 351-354, Harry Walker 51-67.

SAN DIEGO PADRES

YEARLY FINISHES

WEST DIVISION

ar	Position	W	L	Pct.	*GB	Manager	Attendance
69	6th	52	110	.321	41	Preston Gomez	512,970
70	6th	63	99	.389	39	Preston Gomez	643,679
71	6th	61	100	.379	28½	Preston Gomez	557,513
72	6th	58	95	.379	36½	Preston Gomez, Don Zimmer	644,273
73	6th	60	102	.370	39	Don Zimmer	611,826
74	6th	60	102	.370	42	John McNamara	1,075,399
75	4th	71	91	.438	37	John McNamara	1,281,747
76	5th	73	89	.451	29	John McNamara	1,458,478
77	5th	69	93	.426	29	John McNamara, Bob Skinner, Alvin Dark	1,376,269
78	4th	84	78	.519	11	Roger Craig	1,670,107
79	5th	68	93	.422	22	Roger Craig	1,456,967
80	6th	73	89	.451	19½	Jerry Coleman	1,139,026
81	6th/6th	41	69	.373	†	Frank Howard	519,161
82	4th	81	81	.500	8	Dick Williams	1,607,516
83	4th	81	81	.500	10	Dick Williams	1,539,815
84	1st†	92	70	.568	+12	Dick Williams	1,983,904
85	3rd (tied)	83	79	.512	12	Dick Williams	2,210,352
86	4th	74	88	.457	22	Steve Boros	1,805,716
87	6th	65	97	.401	25	Larry Bowa	1,454,061
88	3rd	83	78	.516	11	Larry Bowa, Jack McKeon	1,506,896
89	2nd	89	73	.549	3	Jack McKeon	2,009,031
90	4th (tied)	75	87	.463	16	Jack McKeon, Greg Riddoch	1,856,396
91	3rd	84	78	.519	10	Greg Riddoch	1,804,289
92	3rd	82	80	.506	16	Greg Riddoch, Jim Riggleman	1,722,102
93	7th	61	101	.377	43	Jim Riggleman	1,375,432
94	4th	47	70	.402	12½	Jim Riggleman	953,857
95	3rd	70	74	.486	8	Bruce Bochy	1,041,805
96	1st§	91	71	.562	+1	Bruce Bochy	2,187,886

*Games behind winner. †First half 23-33; second half 18-36. ‡Won championship series. §Lost division series.

MANAGERIAL RECORDS

Bruce Bochy 161-145, Steve Boros 74-88, Larry Bowa 81-127, Jerry Coleman 73-89, Roger Craig 152-171, Alvin Dark 49-65,
eston Gomez 180-316, Frank Howard 41-69, Jack McKeon 193-164, John McNamara 224-310, Greg Riddoch 200-194, Jim
ggleman 112-179, Dick Williams 337-311, Don Zimmer 114-190.

YEARLY FINISHES

Year	Position	W	L	Pct.	*GB	Manager	Attendance
1901†	7th	52	85	.380	37	George Davis	297,650
1902†	8th	48	88	.353	53 1/2	Horace Fogel, Heinie Smith, John McGraw	302,875
1903†	2nd	84	55	.604	6 1/2	John McGraw	579,530
1904†	1st	106	47	.693	+13	John McGraw	609,826
1905†	1st	105	48	.686	+9	John McGraw	552,700
1906†	2nd	96	56	.632	20	John McGraw	402,850
1907†	4th	82	71	.536	25 1/2	John McGraw	538,350
1908†	2nd (tied)	98	56	.636	1	John McGraw	910,000
1909†	3rd	92	61	.601	18 1/2	John McGraw	783,700
1910†	2nd	91	63	.591	13	John McGraw	511,785
1911†	1st	99	54	.647	+7 1/2	John McGraw	675,000
1912†	1st	103	48	.682	+10	John McGraw	638,000
1913†	1st	101	51	.664	+12 1/2	John McGraw	630,000
1914†	2nd	84	70	.545	10 1/2	John McGraw	364,313
1915†	8th	69	83	.454	21	John McGraw	391,850
1916†	4th	86	66	.566	7	John McGraw	552,056
1917†	1st	98	56	.636	+10	John McGraw	500,264
1918†	2nd	71	53	.573	10 1/2	John McGraw	256,618
1919†	2nd	87	53	.621	9	John McGraw	708,857
1920†	2nd	86	68	.558	7	John McGraw	929,609
1921†	1st	94	59	.614	+4	John McGraw	773,477
1922†	1st	93	61	.604	+7	John McGraw	945,809
1923†	1st	95	58	.621	+4 1/2	John McGraw	820,780
1924†	1st	93	60	.608	+1 1/2	John McGraw	844,068
1925†	2nd	86	66	.566	8 1/2	John McGraw	778,993
1926†	5th	74	77	.490	13 1/2	John McGraw	700,362
1927†	3rd	92	62	.597	2	John McGraw	858,190
1928†	2nd	93	61	.604	2	John McGraw	916,191
1929†	3rd	84	67	.556	13 1/2	John McGraw	868,806
1930†	3rd	87	67	.565	5	John McGraw	868,714
1931†	2nd	87	65	.572	13	John McGraw	812,163
1932†	6th (tied)	72	82	.468	18	John McGraw, Bill Terry	484,868
1933†	1st	91	61	.599	+5	Bill Terry	604,471
1934†	2nd	93	60	.608	2	Bill Terry	730,851
1935†	3rd	91	62	.595	8 1/2	Bill Terry	748,748
1936†	1st	92	62	.597	+5	Bill Terry	837,952
1937†	1st	95	57	.625	+3	Bill Terry	926,887
1938†	3rd	83	67	.553	5	Bill Terry	799,633
1939†	5th	77	74	.510	18 1/2	Bill Terry	702,457
1940†	6th	72	80	.474	27 1/2	Bill Terry	747,852
1941†	5th	74	79	.484	25 1/2	Bill Terry	763,098
1942†	3rd	85	67	.559	20	Mel Ott	779,621
1943†	8th	55	98	.359	49 1/2	Mel Ott	466,095
1944†	5th	67	87	.435	38	Mel Ott	674,083
1945†	5th	78	74	.513	19	Mel Ott	1,016,468
1946†	8th	61	93	.396	36	Mel Ott	1,219,873
1947†	4th	81	73	.526	13	Mel Ott	1,600,793
1948†	5th	78	76	.506	13 1/2	Mel Ott, Leo Durocher	1,459,269
1949†	5th	73	81	.474	24	Leo Durocher	1,218,446
1950†	3rd	86	68	.558	5	Leo Durocher	1,008,876
1951†	1st‡	98	59	.624	+1	Leo Durocher	1,059,539
1952†	2nd	92	62	.597	4 1/2	Leo Durocher	984,940
1953†	5th	70	84	.455	35	Leo Durocher	811,518
1954†	1st	97	57	.630	+5	Leo Durocher	1,155,067
1955†	3rd	80	74	.519	18 1/2	Leo Durocher	824,112
1956†	6th	67	87	.435	26	Bill Rigney	629,179
1957†	6th	69	85	.448	26	Bill Rigney	653,923
1958	3rd	80	74	.519	12	Bill Rigney	1,272,625
1959	3rd	83	71	.539	4	Bill Rigney	1,422,130
1960	5th	79	75	.513	16	Bill Rigney, Tom Sheehan	1,795,356
1961	3rd	85	69	.552	8	Alvin Dark	1,390,679
1962	1st‡	103	62	.624	+1	Alvin Dark	1,592,594
1963	3rd	88	74	.543	11	Alvin Dark	1,571,306
1964	4th	90	72	.556	3	Alvin Dark	1,504,364
1965	2nd	95	67	.586	2	Herman Franks	1,546,075
1966	2nd	93	68	.578	1 1/2	Herman Franks	1,657,192
1967	2nd	91	71	.562	10 1/2	Herman Franks	1,242,480
1968	2nd	88	74	.543	9	Herman Franks	837,220

WEST DIVISION

ar	Position	W	L	Pct.	*GB	Manager	Attendance
69	2nd	90	72	.556	3	Clyde King	873,603
70	3rd	86	76	.531	16	Clyde King, Charlie Fox	740,720
71	1st§	90	72	.556	+1	Charlie Fox	1,106,043
72	5th	69	86	.445	26 1/2	Charlie Fox	647,744
73	3rd	88	74	.543	11	Charlie Fox	834,193
74	5th	72	90	.444	30	Charlie Fox, Wes Westrum	519,987
75	3rd	80	81	.497	27 1/2	Wes Westrum	522,919
76	4th	74	88	.457	28	Bill Rigney	626,868
77	4th	75	87	.463	23	Joe Altobelli	700,056
78	3rd	89	73	.549	6	Joe Altobelli	1,740,477
79	4th	71	91	.438	19 1/2	Joe Altobelli, Dave Bristol	1,456,402
80	5th	75	86	.466	17	Dave Bristol	1,096,115
81	5th/3rd	56	55	.505	∞	Frank Robinson	632,274
82	3rd	87	75	.537	2	Frank Robinson	1,200,948
83	5th	79	83	.488	12	Frank Robinson	1,251,530
84	6th	66	96	.407	26	Frank Robinson, Danny Ozark	1,001,545
85	6th	62	100	.383	33	Jim Davenport, Roger Craig	818,697
86	3rd	83	79	.512	13	Roger Craig	1,528,748
87	1st§	90	72	.556	+6	Roger Craig	1,917,168
88	4th	83	79	.512	11 1/2	Roger Craig	1,785,297
89	1st▲	92	70	.568	+3	Roger Craig	2,059,701
90	3rd	85	77	.525	6	Roger Craig	1,975,528
91	4th	75	87	.463	19	Roger Craig	1,737,478
92	5th	72	90	.444	26	Roger Craig	1,561,987
93	2nd	103	59	.636	1	Dusty Baker	2,606,354
94	2nd	55	60	.478	3 1/2	Dusty Baker	1,704,608
95	4th	67	77	.465	11	Dusty Baker	1,241,500
96	4th	68	94	.420	23	Dusty Baker	1,413,922

*Games behind winner. †New York Giants. ‡Won pennant playoff. §Lost championship series. ∞First half 27-32; second half 29-23. ▲Won championship series.

MANAGERIAL RECORDS

Joe Altobelli 225-239, Dusty Baker 293-290, Dave Bristol 85-98, Roger Craig 586-566, Alvin Dark 366-277, Jim Davenport 56-88, orge Davis 52-85, Leo Durocher 637-523, Horace Fogel 18-23, Charlie Fox 348-327, Herman Franks 367-280, Clyde King 109-95, n McGraw 2,604-1,801, Mel Ott 464-530, Danny Ozark 24-32, Bill Rigney 406-430, Frank Robinson 264-277, Tom Sheehan 46-50, nie Smith 5-27, Bill Terry 823-661, Wes Westrum 118-129.

MINOR LEAGUES

Farm systems

American Association

International League

Mexican League

Pacific Coast League

Eastern League

Southern League

Texas League

California League

Carolina League

Florida State League

Midwest League

New York-Pennsylvania League

Northwest League

South Atlantic League

Appalachian League

Arizona League

Dominican Summer League

Gulf Coast League

Pioneer League

Minor league index

FARM SYSTEMS

ANAHEIM (6): AAA—Vancouver. AA—Midland. A—Cedar Rapids, Lake Elsinore, Boise. Rookie—Butte.
BALTIMORE (6): AAA—Rochester. AA—Bowie. A—Delmarva, Frederick. Rookie—Bluefield, Gulf Coast Orioles.
BOSTON (6): AAA—Pawtucket. AA—Trenton. A—Sarasota, Michigan, Lowell. Rookie—Gulf Coast Red Sox.
CHICAGO (6): AAA—Nashville. AA—Birmingham. A—Hickory, Winston-Salem. Rookie—Bristol, Gulf Coast White Sox.
CLEVELAND (6): AAA—Buffalo. AA—Akron. A—Kinston, Columbus, Watertown. Rookie—Burlington.
DETROIT (6): AAA—Toledo. AA—Jacksonville. A—Lakeland, Jamestown, West Michigan. Rookie—Gulf Coast Tigers.
KANSAS CITY (6): AAA—Omaha. AA—Wichita. A—Lansing, Wilmington, Spokane. Rookie—Gulf Coast Royals.
MILWAUKEE (6): AAA—Tucson. AA—El Paso. A—Stockton, Beloit. Rookie—Helena, Ogden.
MINNESOTA (6): AAA—Salt Lake. AA—New Britain. A—Fort Myers, Fort Wayne. Rookie—Elizabethton, Gulf Coast Twins.
NEW YORK (6): AAA—Columbus. AA—Norwich. A—Tampa, Greensboro, Oneonta. Rookie—Gulf Coast Yankees.
OAKLAND (6): AAA—Edmonton. AA—Huntsville. A—Modesto, Visalia, Southern Oregon. Rookie—Scottsdale A's.
SEATTLE (6): AAA—Tacoma. AA—Memphis. A—Lancaster, Wisconsin, Everett. Rookie—Peoria Mariners.
TEXAS (5): AAA—Oklahoma City. AA—Tulsa. A—Charlotte, Pulaski. Rookie—Gulf Coast Rangers.
TORONTO (6): AAA—Syracuse. AA—Knoxville. A—Dunedin, Hagerstown, St. Catharines. Rookie—Medicine Hat.

ATLANTA (7): AAA—Richmond. AA—Greenville. A—Durham, Macon, Eugene. Rookie—Danville, Gulf Coast Braves.
CHICAGO (6): AAA—Iowa. AA—Orlando. A—Daytona, Rockford, Williamsport. Rookie—Mesa Cubs.
CINCINNATI (5): AAA—Indianapolis. AA—Chattanooga. A—Burlington, Charleston (WV). Rookie—Billings.
COLORADO (6): AAA—Colorado Springs. AA—New Haven. A—Salem, Asheville, Portland. Rookie—Mesa Rockies.
FLORIDA (6): AAA—Charlotte. AA—Portland. A—Brevard County, Kane County, Utica. Rookie—Gulf Coast Marlins.
HOUSTON (6): AAA—New Orleans. AA—Jackson. A—Kissimmee, Quad City, Auburn. Rookie—Gulf Coast Astros.
LOS ANGELES (7): AAA—Albuquerque. AA—San Antonio. A—San Bernardino, Savannah, Vero Beach, Yakima. Rookie—Great Falls.
MONTREAL (6): AAA—Ottawa. AA—Harrisburg. A—West Palm Beach, Cape Fear, Vermont. Rookie—Gulf Coast Expos.
NEW YORK (7): AAA—Norfolk. AA—Binghamton. A—St. Lucie, Capital City, Pittsfield. Rookie—Kingsport, Gulf Coast Mets.
PHILADELPHIA (6): AAA—Scranton/Wilkes-Barre. AA—Reading. A—Clearwater, Piedmont, Batavia. Rookie—Martinsville.
PITTSBURGH (6): AAA—Calgary. AA—Carolina. A—Lynchburg, Augusta, Erie. Rookie—Gulf Coast Pirates.
ST. LOUIS (6): AAA—Louisville. AA—Arkansas. A—Prince William, Peoria (IL), New Jersey. Rookie—Johnson City.
SAN DIEGO (6): AAA—Las Vegas. AA—Mobile. A—Rancho Cucamonga, Clinton. Rookie—Idaho Falls, Peoria (AZ) Padres.
SAN FRANCISCO (5): AAA—Phoenix. AA—Shreveport. A—San Jose, Bakersfield. Rookie—Salem-Keizer.

MINOR LEAGUES Farm systems

AMERICAN ASSOCIATION

LEAGUE OFFICE

esident
Branch Rickey

Address
6801 Miami Ave., Suite 3
Cincinnati, OH 45243

Phone
513-271-4800

TEAMS

BUFFALO BISONS
eneral manager
Mike Buczowski
anager
Brian Graham
Ilpark (capacity, surface)
North AmeriCore Park (21,050, grass)
filiation
Indians
ddress
P.O. Box 450
Buffalo, NY 14205
none
716-846-2003

INDIANAPOLIS INDIANS
eneral manager
Max Schumacher
anager
Dave Miley
Ilpark (capacity, surface)
Victory Field (15,000, grass)
filiation
Reds
ddress
501 W. Maryland St.
Indianapolis, IN 42225
none
317-269-3545

IOWA CUBS
eneral manager
Sam Bernabe
anager
Tim Johnson
Ilpark (capacity, surface)
Sec Taylor Stadium (10,500, grass)
filiation
Cubs

Address
350 SW 1 St.
Des Moines, IA 50309
Phone
515-243-6111

LOUISVILLE REDBIRDS
General manager
Dale Owens
Manager
Gaylen Pitts
Ballpark (capacity, surface)
Cardinal Stadium (33,000, artificial)
Affiliation
Cardinals
Address
P.O. Box 36407
Louisville, KY 40233
Phone
502-367-9121

NASHVILLE SOUNDS
General manager
Larry Schmittou
Manager
Tom Spencer
Ballpark (capacity, surface)
Greer Stadium (17,000, grass)
Affiliation
White Sox
Address
P.O. Box 23290
Nashville, TN 37202
Phone
615-242-4371

NEW ORLEANS ZEPHYRS
General manager
Jay Miller
Manager
Steve Swisher

Ballpark (capacity, surface)
Jefferson Ball Park (10,000, grass)
Affiliation
Astros
Address
600 Airline Highway
Metairie, LA 70003
Phone
504-734-5155

OKLAHOMA CITY 89ERS
General Manager
To be announced
Manager
Greg Biagini
Ballpark (capacity, surface)
All Sports Stadium (12,000, grass)
Affiliation
Rangers
Address
P.O. Box 75089
Oklahoma City, OK 73147
Phone
405-946-8989

OMAHA ROYALS
Vice president/general manager
Bill Gorman
Manager
Mike Jirschele
Ballpark (capacity, surface)
Rosenblatt Stadium (23,000, grass)
Affiliation
Royals
Address
P.O. Box 3665
Omaha, NE 68103
Phone
402-734-2550

1996 FINAL STANDINGS

EASTERN DIVISION

am	W	L	T	Pct.	GB
ffalo (Indians)	84	60	0	.583	....
dianapolis (Reds)	78	66	0	.542	6
shville (White Sox)	77	67	0	.535	7
uisville (Cardinals)	60	84	0	.417	24

WESTERN DIVISION

Team	W	L	T	Pct.	GB
Omaha (Royals)	79	65	0	.549	....
Oklahoma City (Rangers)	74	70	0	.514	5
Iowa (Cubs)	64	78	0	.451	14
New Orleans (Brewers)	58	84	0	.408	20

COMPOSITE

am	Buf.	Oma.	Ind.	Nash.	O.C.	Iowa	Lou.	N.O.	W	L	T	Pct.	GB
ffalo (Indians)	....	9	13	11	9	11	19	12	84	60	0	.583	....
naha (Royals)	9	....	12	10	11	15	9	13	79	65	0	.549	5
dianapolis (Reds)	11	6	....	14	11	13	14	9	78	66	0	.542	6
shville (White Sox)	13	8	10	....	8	14	13	11	77	67	0	.535	7
lahoma City (Rangers)	9	13	7	10	....	11	9	15	74	70	0	.514	10
wa (Cubs)	7	9	5	4	13	....	10	16	64	78	0	.451	19
uisville (Cardinals)	5	9	10	11	9	8	....	8	60	84	0	.417	24
w Orleans (Brewers)	6	11	9	7	9	6	10	....	58	84	0	.408	25

Major league affiliations in parentheses.
Iowa club represented Des Moines, Iowa.

PLAYOFFS: Oklahoma City defeated Omaha, three games to one; Indianapolis defeated Buffalo, three games to two; Oklahoma City defeated Indianapolis, ree games to one, to win league championship.

REGULAR-SEASON ATTENDANCE: Buffalo, 825,530; Indianapolis, 537,325; Iowa, 453,630; Louisville, 494,929; Nashville, 303,407; New Orlean 180,485; Oklahoma City, 267,784; Omaha, 421,994. Total—3,485,084. Playoffs (13 games)—79,613. Class AAA All-Star Game at Salt Lake City—15,50

MANAGERS: Buffalo, Brian Graham; Indianapolis, Dave Miley; Iowa, Ron Clark; Louisville, Joe Pettini; Nashville, Rick Renick; New Orleans, Tim Irelan Oklahoma City, Greg Biagini; Omaha, Mike Jirschele.

ALL-STAR TEAM: 1B—Dmitri Young, Louisville; 2B—Casey Candaele, Buffalo; 3B—Eduardo Perez, Indianapolis; SS—Damian Jackson, Buffalo; OF—Je Abbott, Nashville; Nigel Wilson, Buffalo; Brian Giles, Buffalo; C—Kelly Stinnett, New Orleans; DH—Lee Stevens, Oklahoma City; RHP—Rick Hellin Oklahoma City; LHP—Brian Anderson, Buffalo; Relief Pitcher—Jaime Bluma, Omaha; Most Valuable Player—Lee Stevens, Oklahoma City; Rookie of th Year—Jeff Abbott, Nashville; Manager of the Year—Rick Renick, Nashville.

1996 BATTING

TEAM

Team	Avg.	G	TPA	AB	R	H	TB	2B	3B	HR	RBI	SH	SF	HP	BB	IBB	SO	SB	CS	GDP	LOB	SHO	Sig.	OBI
Buffalo	.273	144	5469	4870	723	1330	2128	245	32	163	676	33	48	62	456	43	885	65	41	99	1024	5	.437	.34
Omaha	.266	144	5409	4740	712	1263	2021	258	28	148	663	63	34	73	497	34	887	106	57	107	980	8	.426	.34
Okla. City	.266	144	5473	4821	658	1282	2010	271	20	139	620	33	56	45	516	33	952	77	64	111	1053	14	.417	.33
Indianapolis	.263	144	5366	4806	689	1263	1992	258	39	131	634	30	40	30	460	31	988	131	49	103	956	7	.414	.32
Iowa	.262	142	5238	4771	593	1250	1889	226	25	121	554	43	36	26	362	19	820	64	35	111	940	9	.396	.31
Nashville	.254	144	5195	4708	624	1194	1859	237	28	124	583	45	27	44	368	23	772	78	48	105	877	13	.395	.31
Louisville	.250	144	5195	4708	583	1178	1902	215	37	145	545	39	25	36	387	31	912	100	60	113	877	16	.404	.31
New Orleans	.244	142	5332	4750	606	1160	1859	217	28	142	552	26	38	53	465	23	999	79	44	117	940	5	.391	.31

INDIVIDUAL

TOP QUALIFIERS FOR BATTING CHAMPIONSHIP
Minimum 389 plate appearances. *Lefthanded batter. †Switch-hitter.

Player, Team	Avg.	G	TPA	AB	R	H	TB	2B	3B	HR	RBI	SH	SF	HP	BB	IBB	SO	SB	CS	GDP	Sig.	OB
Young, Dmitri, Louisville#	.333	122	498	459	90	153	245	31	8	15	64	0	3	1	34	8	67	16	5	5	.534	.37
Abbott, Jeff, Nashville	.325	113	475	440	64	143	214	27	1	14	60	1	0	2	32	1	50	12	4	12	.486	.37
Stevens, Lee, Oklahoma City*	.325	117	498	431	84	140	277	37	2	32	94	0	6	3	58	8	90	3	0	8	.643	.4C
Ortiz, Luis, Oklahoma City	.317	124	533	501	70	159	226	25	0	14	73	0	6	4	22	2	36	0	5	17	.451	.34
Candaele, Casey, Buffalo#	.311	94	426	392	66	122	166	22	2	6	37	3	3	1	27	2	35	3	5	6	.423	.35
Glanville, Doug, Iowa	.308	90	397	373	53	115	153	23	3	3	34	7	3	2	12	1	35	15	10	2	.410	.33
Bradshaw, Terry, Louisville*	.303	102	435	389	56	118	179	23	1	12	44	0	2	2	42	1	64	21	9	6	.460	.37
Lee, Derek, Oklahoma City*	.301	120	469	409	59	123	198	32	2	13	62	0	6	2	50	7	69	6	9	13	.484	.37
Mitchell, Keith, Indianapolis	.300	112	428	357	60	107	182	21	3	16	66	0	6	1	64	2	68	9	1	7	.510	.4C
Wilson, Nigel, Buffalo*	.299	128	552	482	88	144	269	23	6	30	95	1	7	12	50	7	117	4	4	9	.558	.37
Voigt, Jack, Oklahoma City	.297	127	530	445	77	132	223	26	1	21	80	2	6	1	76	4	103	5	5	11	.501	.39
Sparks, Don, Buffalo	.295	137	580	511	69	151	217	32	5	8	68	1	12	2	54	4	72	2	2	14	.425	.35
Valdes, Pedro, Iowa*	.295	103	435	397	61	117	185	23	0	15	60	1	5	1	31	1	57	2	0	12	.466	.34
Perez, Eduardo, Indianapolis	.293	122	509	451	84	132	234	29	5	21	84	0	1	6	51	5	69	11	0	11	.519	.37
Myers, Rod, Omaha*	.292	112	481	411	68	120	197	27	1	16	54	9	3	9	49	6	106	37	8	6	.479	.37

DEPARTMENTAL LEADERS: G—M. Robertson, Thompson, Valrie, 138; AB—Thompson, 540; R—D. Young, 90; H—L. Ortiz, 159; TB—Stevens, 277; 2B—Steven 37; 3B—Mejia, 9; HR—Stevens, 32; RBI—N. Wilson, 95; SH—R. Martinez, 13; SF—D. Sparks, 12; HP—(tie) Saenz, Stinnett, 13; BB—Voigt, 76; IBB—Several playe tied with 8; SO—Felder, 129; SB—Goodwin, 40; CS—Holbert, 14; GIDP—L. Ortiz, 17; Slg.—Stevens, .643; OBP—Stevens, .404.

ALL PLAYERS
*Lefthanded batter. †Switch-hitter.

Player, Team	Avg.	G	TPA	AB	R	H	TB	2B	3B	HR	RBI	SH	SF	HP	BB	IBB	SO	SB	CS	GDP	Sig.	O
Abbott, Jeff, Nashville	.325	113	475	440	64	143	214	27	1	14	60	1	0	2	32	1	50	12	4	12	.486	.3
Anthony, Eric, Indianapolis*	.238	7	28	21	4	5	12	1	0	2	7	0	0	0	7	0	8	0	1	0	.571	.4
Arias, Amador, Indianapolis†	.000	1	3	3	0	0	0	0	0	0	0	0	0	0	0	0	1	0	0	0	.000	.0
Arrandale, Matt, Louisville	.000	63	1	1	0	0	0	0	0	0	0	0	0	0	0	0	0	0	0	0	.000	.0
Aven, Bruce, Buffalo	.667	3	11	9	5	6	9	0	0	1	2	0	0	1	1	0	1	0	1	0	1.000	.7
Aybar, Manuel, Louisville	.000	5	4	3	0	0	0	0	0	0	0	1	0	0	0	0	0	0	0	0	.000	.0
Badorek, Mike, Louisville	.500	20	2	2	0	1	1	0	0	0	0	0	0	0	0	0	0	0	0	0	.500	.5
Banks, Brian, New Orleans†	.271	137	564	487	71	132	223	29	7	16	64	2	7	2	66	3	105	17	8	6	.458	.3
Barber, Brian, Louisville	.000	11	3	3	0	0	0	0	0	0	0	0	0	0	0	0	0	0	0	1	.000	.0
Barberie, Bret, Iowa†	.233	68	246	210	26	49	72	8	0	5	24	0	2	3	31	1	23	3	2	5	.343	.3
Belk, Tim, Indianapolis	.287	120	472	436	63	125	203	27	3	15	63	1	6	2	27	1	72	5	2	7	.466	.3
Bell, David, Louisville	.176	42	143	136	9	24	31	5	1	0	7	0	0	0	7	1	15	1	2	4	.228	.2
Beltran, Rigo, Louisville*	.400	39	12	10	2	4	7	1	1	0	1	1	0	0	1	0	3	0	0	0	.700	.4
Bradshaw, Terry, Louisville*	.303	102	435	389	56	118	179	23	1	12	44	0	2	2	42	1	64	21	9	6	.460	.3
Brady, Doug, Nashville†	.241	115	468	427	59	103	153	18	7	6	42	6	2	2	31	1	61	20	6	4	.358	.2
Brown, Brant, Iowa*	.304	94	364	342	48	104	165	25	3	10	43	0	3	19	1	65	6	6	10	.482	.3
Bryant, Pat, Buffalo	.172	27	71	64	6	11	12	1	0	0	1	0	0	1	5	0	20	0	2	2	.188	.2
Bryant, Scott, Oklahoma City	.268	12	46	41	4	11	14	3	0	0	3	0	1	0	4	0	10	0	0	3	.341	.3
Buckley, Travis, Indianapolis	.000	23	14	10	0	0	0	0	0	0	0	4	0	0	0	0	3	0	0	0	.000	.0
Burlingame, Ben, Iowa	.000	27	7	7	0	0	0	0	0	0	0	0	0	0	0	0	2	0	0	0	.000	.0
Burton, Darren, Omaha†	.270	129	541	463	75	125	208	28	5	15	67	9	4	6	59	6	82	7	7	10	.449	.3
Busby, Mike, Louisville	.000	14	8	8	0	0	0	0	0	0	0	0	0	0	7	0	0	0	0	0	.000	.0
Caceres, Edgar, New Orleans†...	.270	115	429	397	40	107	133	0	2	4	29	5	2	2	23	3	32	8	5	9	.335	.3
Campbell, Mike, Iowa	.100	16	11	10	0	1	1	0	0	0	0	1	0	0	0	0	2	0	0	0	.100	.1
Campos, Miguel, Iowa	.250	2	4	4	0	1	1	0	0	0	0	0	0	0	0	0	2	0	0	0	.250	.2
Candaele, Casey, Buffalo†	.311	94	426	392	66	122	166	22	2	6	37	3	3	1	27	2	35	3	5	6	.423	.3
Cappuccio, Carmine, Nashville*.	.273	120	443	407	55	111	169	22	3	10	61	3	2	6	25	7	48	1	3	15	.415	.3
Cardenas, Johnny, O.C.	.169	30	78	77	8	13	18	5	0	0	2	0	0	1	0	23	0	0	2	.234	.1
Carr, Chuck, New Orleans†	.385	4	15	13	2	5	6	1	0	0	1	0	0	0	2	0	1	2	0	0	.462	.4
Carrara, Giovanni, Indianapolis ..	.000	9	5	5	0	0	0	0	0	0	0	0	0	0	0	0	1	0	0	0	.000	.0
Carrasco, Hector, Indianapolis...1.000		13	1	1	1	1	4	0	0	1	0	0	0	0	0	0	0	0	0	0	4.000	1.0

Player, Team	Avg.	G	TPA	AB	R	H	TB	2B	3B	HR	RBI	SH	SF	HP	BB	IBB	SO	SB	CS	GDP	Slg.	OBP
arter, Mike, Iowa	.266	113	401	384	41	102	123	13	1	2	18	5	1	1	10	0	42	4	6	5	.320	.285
asian, Larry, Iowa	.500	24	2	2	0	1	1	0	0	0	1	0	0	0	0	0	1	0	0	0	.500	.500
narles, Frank, Oklahoma City ...	.186	35	120	113	10	21	35	7	2	1	8	0	2	1	4	0	29	0	3	3	.310	.217
nolowsky, Dan, Lou.-Iowa	.176	43	125	108	13	19	35	7	0	3	11	1	0	1	15	0	34	1	2	1	.324	.282
oleman, Vince, Indianapolis† ..	.077	7	27	26	2	2	2	0	0	0	1	0	0	0	1	0	5	0	0	0	.077	.111
orreia, Rod, Louisville	.159	35	117	113	7	18	27	3	0	2	8	1	0	0	3	0	22	1	2	3	.239	.181
osto, Tim, Buffalo	.214	83	276	252	25	54	90	12	0	8	28	4	1	0	19	4	59	1	2	7	.357	.268
omer, Tripp, Louisville	.225	80	272	244	28	55	79	4	4	4	25	3	1	2	22	2	47	3	1	12	.324	.294
abney, Fred, Iowa	.000	33	1	1	0	0	0	0	0	0	0	0	0	0	0	0	0	0	0	0	.000	.000
eak, Darrel, Louisville†	.232	70	190	164	19	38	66	4	0	8	18	0	1	1	24	4	47	2	1	3	.402	.332
iaz, Lino, Omaha	.271	75	291	266	32	72	98	13	2	3	28	1	1	6	17	0	29	0	3	9	.368	.328
felice, Mike, Louisville	.285	79	269	246	25	70	110	13	0	9	33	0	2	1	20	1	43	0	3	15	.447	.338
iggs, Tony, Louisville†	.205	92	354	308	35	63	102	14	2	7	23	11	0	2	33	1	49	5	5	6	.331	.286
Sarcina, Glenn, Nashville*	.237	38	103	97	8	23	32	9	0	0	11	1	0	0	5	0	20	1	1	2	.330	.275
orsett, Brian, Iowa	.207	9	29	29	2	6	11	2	0	1	2	0	0	0	0	0	4	0	0	1	.379	.207
oyle, Tom, Indianapolis*	.000	1	1	1	0	0	0	0	0	0	0	0	0	0	0	0	0	0	0	0	.000	.000
unn, Steve, Buffalo*	.290	92	335	300	35	87	145	20	1	12	48	0	3	2	30	7	74	2	1	3	.483	.355
iland, Dave, Louisville	.000	8	1	1	0	0	0	0	0	0	0	0	0	0	0	0	1	0	0	0	.000	.000
rdman, Brad, Iowa	.175	57	193	171	18	30	42	6	0	2	16	3	2	1	16	0	38	1	0	8	.246	.247
strada, Osmani, Oklahoma City	.262	50	147	130	15	34	45	6	1	1	13	1	1	1	14	0	26	3	1	3	.346	.336
aneyte, Rikkert, Oklahoma City.	.236	93	413	364	53	86	134	15	0	11	44	5	5	5	34	1	65	14	9	7	.368	.306
aries, Paul, Iowa-N.O.-Buf.	.247	121	450	397	45	98	129	14	4	3	31	9	3	4	37	2	49	10	3	6	.325	.315
asano, Sal, Omaha	.231	29	112	104	12	24	40	4	0	4	15	0	1	1	6	0	21	0	1	3	.385	.277
elder, Ken, New Orleans	.216	122	466	430	55	93	166	20	1	17	45	0	1	7	28	3	129	2	4	12	.386	.275
elix, Lauro, New Orleans	.000	2	4	4	0	0	0	0	0	0	0	0	0	0	0	0	2	0	0	0	.000	.000
ermin, Felix, Iowa	.286	39	123	119	8	34	40	4	1	0	8	1	0	0	3	0	7	1	0	5	.336	.303
nn, John, Iowa	.273	17	64	55	10	15	19	1	0	1	5	2	1	2	4	0	7	1	1	2	.345	.339
ordyce, Brook, Indianapolis	.275	107	405	374	48	103	177	20	3	16	64	1	4	1	25	3	56	2	1	5	.473	.319
ortugno, Tim, Indianapolis*	.167	41	6	6	0	1	1	0	0	0	0	0	0	0	0	0	5	0	0	0	.167	.167
oster, Kevin, Iowa	.176	20	17	17	3	3	4	1	0	0	0	0	0	0	0	0	11	0	0	0	.235	.176
ranklin, Micah, Louisville†	.232	86	341	289	43	67	136	18	3	15	53	1	3	8	40	2	71	2	3	4	.471	.338
ascatore, John, Louisville	.125	36	13	8	0	1	1	0	0	0	1	4	0	0	1	0	3	0	0	0	.125	.222
azier, Lou, Oklahoma City†	.245	58	227	208	28	51	74	8	3	3	16	3	1	1	14	2	42	13	4	3	.356	.295
azier, Ron, Indianapolis	.000	2	3	3	0	0	0	0	0	0	0	0	0	0	0	0	0	0	0	0	.000	.000
ye, Jeff, Oklahoma City	.238	49	211	181	25	43	56	10	0	1	18	2	1	3	24	1	21	10	1	5	.309	.335
anote, Joe, New Orleans	.000	41	1	1	0	0	0	0	0	0	0	0	0	0	0	0	1	0	0	0	.000	.000
arcia, Guillermo, Indianapolis ..	.255	16	49	47	4	12	14	2	0	0	0	0	0	0	2	0	6	0	0	5	.298	.286
bralter, Steve, Indianapolis	.255	126	479	447	58	114	180	29	2	11	54	1	3	2	26	6	114	2	3	10	.403	.297
al, Benji, Oklahoma City	.223	84	322	292	32	65	100	15	1	6	28	4	3	2	21	0	90	4	6	10	.342	.277
les, Brian, Buffalo*	.314	83	366	318	65	100	189	17	6	20	64	1	3	2	42	6	29	1	0	4	.594	.395
vens, Brian, New Orleans	.000	29	1	1	0	0	0	0	0	0	0	0	0	0	0	0	0	0	0	1	.000	.000
lanville, Doug, Iowa	.308	90	397	373	53	115	153	23	3	3	34	7	3	2	12	1	35	15	10	2	.410	.331
onzales, Rene, Oklahoma City..	.260	42	186	154	21	40	61	8	2	3	13	2	2	2	26	2	23	1	1	5	.396	.370
oodwin, Curtis, Indianapolis* ..	.261	91	398	337	57	88	121	19	4	2	30	5	1	1	54	2	67	40	12	2	.359	.364
otewold, Jeff, Omaha*	.278	98	407	338	63	94	144	20	0	10	51	1	2	8	58	3	84	1	3	11	.426	.394
ulan, Mike, Louisville	.255	123	456	419	47	107	193	27	4	17	55	1	2	7	26	1	119	7	2	10	.461	.308
uzman, Jose, Iowa	.500	8	4	4	1	2	4	0	1	0	1	0	0	0	0	0	1	0	0	0	1.000	.500
all, Mel, Nashville*	.267	4	16	15	1	4	7	0	0	1	1	0	0	0	1	0	1	0	0	0	.467	.313
alter, Shane, Omaha	.258	93	341	299	43	77	110	24	0	3	33	8	1	2	31	0	49	7	2	6	.368	.330
amelin, Bob, Omaha*	.313	4	17	16	4	5	8	1	1	0	0	0	0	0	1	0	4	1	0	0	.500	.353
aney, Todd, Iowa	.246	66	267	240	20	59	78	13	0	2	19	6	2	0	19	0	24	3	1	6	.325	.299
ansen, Jed, Omaha	.232	29	116	99	14	23	36	4	0	3	9	1	1	3	12	0	22	2	0	1	.364	.330
are, Shawn, Louisville*	.163	15	52	49	3	8	12	1	0	1	1	0	0	0	3	0	11	1	0	2	.245	.212
arris, Mike, New Orleans*	.193	40	161	150	17	29	39	2	1	2	11	1	2	2	6	0	30	1	2	4	.260	.231
elfand, Eric, Buffalo*	.209	90	320	258	31	54	79	10	0	5	22	3	2	11	46	8	51	0	3	2	.306	.350
emond, Scott, Louisville	.260	50	165	150	15	39	60	10	1	3	15	1	1	0	13	0	35	1	2	2	.400	.317
olbert, Aaron, Louisville	.264	112	468	436	54	115	155	16	6	4	32	5	4	2	21	0	61	20	14	8	.356	.298
oward, Tom, Indianapolis†	.400	1	5	5	2	2	5	0	0	1	2	0	0	0	0	0	0	0	0	0	1.000	.400
owitt, Dann, Lou.-Ind.*	.266	96	333	297	38	79	119	12	2	8	40	2	2	2	30	4	66	4	4	6	.401	.335
ubbard, Mike, Iowa	.293	67	249	232	38	68	101	12	0	7	33	3	1	3	10	1	56	2	0	6	.435	.329
ughes, Bobby, New Orleans	.200	37	132	125	11	25	42	5	0	4	15	0	0	3	4	0	31	1	1	2	.336	.242
ulse, David, New Orleans*	.276	8	30	29	2	8	10	2	0	0	1	0	0	0	1	0	6	0	0	1	.345	.300
urst, Jimmy, Nashville	.333	3	7	6	2	2	6	1	0	1	2	0	0	0	1	0	3	0	0	0	1.000	.429
ackson, Damian, Buffalo	.257	133	521	452	77	116	169	15	1	12	49	8	6	7	48	0	78	24	7	7	.374	.333
ames, Dion, New Orleans*	.290	11	35	31	0	9	9	0	0	0	3	0	1	0	3	0	5	0	1	1	.290	.343
arvis, Kevin, Indianapolis*	.000	8	5	4	0	0	0	0	0	0	0	0	1	0	0	0	0	0	0	0	.000	.000
enkins, Brett, New Orleans	.225	26	77	71	9	16	37	3	0	6	11	0	2	1	3	0	17	0	1	2	.521	.260
ennings, Robin, Iowa*	.284	86	367	331	53	94	175	15	6	18	56	0	3	1	32	1	53	2	0	6	.529	.346
elly, Mike, Indianapolis	.209	88	329	292	43	61	97	10	1	8	30	1	3	3	30	0	80	13	2	2	.332	.287
ennedy, Darryl, Oklahoma City .	.286	2	7	7	0	2	2	0	0	0	0	0	0	0	0	0	2	0	0	0	.286	.286
essinger, Keith, Iowa†	.239	55	214	184	19	44	64	8	0	4	26	5	3	0	22	3	30	0	1	6	.348	.316
ieschnick, Brooks, Iowa*	.259	117	480	441	47	114	190	20	1	18	64	0	2	0	37	4	108	0	1	8	.431	.315
rnak, Joe, Indianapolis	.280	48	171	143	20	40	49	3	0	2	19	1	0	1	26	1	35	3	0	4	.343	.394
osco, Bryn, Iowa*	.253	29	85	79	8	20	28	2	0	2	7	0	1	0	5	1	22	1	0	1	.354	.294
oslofski, Kevin, New Orleans*..	.231	75	275	238	39	55	81	8	3	4	25	2	2	2	31	1	64	5	2	5	.340	.322
remblas, Frank, Indianapolis	.198	23	99	91	14	18	23	5	0	0	8	1	0	0	7	0	30	3	1	1	.253	.255
adell, Cleveland, Indianapolis ...	.000	8	8	8	0	0	2	0	0	0	0	0	0	0	0	0	2	0	0	0	.000	.125
andry, Todd, New Orleans	.240	113	431	391	41	94	132	19	2	5	44	2	3	3	32	0	61	14	4	15	.338	.301
ee, Derek, Oklahoma City*	.301	120	469	409	59	123	198	32	2	13	62	0	6	2	50	7	69	6	9	13	.484	.375
eius, Scott, Buffalo	.268	35	138	122	22	33	50	3	1	4	17	0	1	2	12	1	16	0	0	4	.407	.341
lliquist, Derek, Indianapolis*	.250	47	4	4	1	1	1	0	0	0	0	0	0	0	0	0	0	0	0	0	.250	.250
s, Joe, Buffalo	.233	51	167	146	21	34	60	8	0	6	22	1	1	1	18	0	19	0	0	5	.411	.319

Player, Team	Avg.	G	TPA	AB	R	H	TB	2B	3B	HR	RBI	SH	SF	HP	BB	IBB	SO	SB	CS	GDP	Slg.	OB
Lopez, Pedro, New Orleans	.218	34	100	87	7	19	23	4	0	0	3	0	0	0	13	1	22	0	0	5	.264	.32
Lopez, Roberto, New Orleans†	.233	129	515	438	50	102	149	20	3	7	39	8	3	4	62	4	67	8	6	4	.340	.33
Loretta, Mark, New Orleans	.254	19	85	71	10	18	25	5	1	0	11	1	2	2	9	0	8	1	1	1	.352	.34
Lowe, Sean, Louisville	.000	25	10	9	0	0	0	0	0	0	0	1	0	0	0	0	2	0	0	0	.000	.00
Ludwick, Eric, Louisville	.000	11	6	6	0	0	0	0	0	0	0	0	0	0	0	0	3	0	0	0	.000	.00
Luebbers, Larry, Indianapolis	.250	14	6	4	0	1	1	0	0	0	0	2	0	0	0	0	1	0	0	0	.250	.25
Maas, Kevin, New Orleans*	.256	36	133	117	18	30	62	8	0	8	22	0	1	1	14	2	18	0	0	2	.530	.33
Magadan, Dave, Iowa*	.222	3	10	9	0	2	3	1	0	0	1	0	0	0	1	0	2	0	0	0	.333	.30
Marsh, Tom, Buffalo	.235	112	419	395	45	93	141	16	1	10	49	2	2	4	16	0	58	9	5	14	.357	.27
Martin, Norberto, Nashville†	.206	17	75	68	9	14	23	3	0	2	8	1	1	1	4	0	10	1	0	1	.338	.27
Martinez, Felix, Omaha†	.235	118	454	395	54	93	127	13	3	5	35	10	0	5	44	0	79	18	10	11	.322	.32
Martinez, Ramon, Omaha	.253	85	357	320	35	81	117	12	3	6	41	13	0	3	21	1	34	3	2	6	.366	.30
Matheny, Mike, New Orleans	.227	20	69	66	3	15	22	4	0	1	6	0	1	0	2	0	17	1	0	1	.333	.24
Maxcy, Brian, Louisville	.000	36	1	1	0	0	0	0	0	0	0	0	0	0	0	0	0	0	0	0	.000	.00
McElroy, Chuck, Indianapolis*	.000	5	2	1	0	0	0	0	0	0	0	0	1	0	0	0	1	0	0	0	.000	.00
McFarlin, Jason, O.C.*	.167	3	13	12	0	2	3	1	0	0	1	0	0	0	1	0	2	0	0	1	.250	.23
McNeely, Jeff, Louisville	.125	3	8	8	0	1	1	0	0	0	1	0	0	0	0	0	2	0	0	0	.125	.12
Mejia, Roberto, Indianapolis	.291	101	410	374	55	109	190	24	9	13	58	1	5	1	29	1	79	13	5	7	.508	.34
Mercedes, Henry, Omaha	.215	72	259	223	28	48	83	9	1	8	35	6	2	0	28	0	60	0	0	7	.372	.30
Merchant, Mark, Nash.-Oma.†	.245	80	293	249	39	61	98	13	0	8	36	2	1	2	39	1	55	2	1	12	.394	.35
Merullo, Matt, Iowa*	.236	30	99	89	8	21	32	8	0	1	10	0	1	1	8	0	15	1	0	1	.360	.30
Mitchell, Keith, Indianapolis	.300	112	428	357	60	107	182	21	3	16	66	0	6	1	64	2	68	9	1	7	.510	.40
Moore, Marcus, Indianapolis†	.091	15	11	11	0	1	2	1	0	0	0	0	0	0	0	0	7	0	0	0	.182	.09
Morgan, Mike, Louisville	.000	4	4	3	0	0	0	0	0	0	0	0	1	0	0	0	1	0	0	0	.000	.00
Morris, Hal, Indianapolis*	.500	1	4	4	1	2	6	1	0	1	1	0	0	0	0	0	0	0	0	0	1.500	.50
Morris, Matt, Louisville	.000	1	2	2	0	0	0	0	0	0	0	0	0	0	0	0	1	0	0	0	.000	.00
Mota, Jose, Omaha†	.245	72	248	229	24	56	74	5	2	3	20	1	1	0	17	1	28	7	6	1	.323	.29
Moten, Scott, Iowa	.000	21	3	2	1	0	0	0	0	0	0	0	0	0	1	0	1	0	0	0	.000	.33
Mottola, Chad, Indianapolis	.262	103	391	362	45	95	152	24	3	9	47	0	4	4	21	3	93	9	6	10	.420	.30
Munoz, Jose, Nashville†	.234	78	320	295	30	69	106	17	1	6	34	2	2	1	20	2	37	8	1	10	.359	.28
Mutis, Jeff, Louisville*	.000	32	1	1	0	0	0	0	0	0	0	0	0	0	0	0	0	0	0	0	.000	.00
Myers, Rod, Omaha*	.292	112	481	411	68	120	197	27	1	16	54	9	3	9	49	6	106	37	8	6	.479	.37
Nilsson, Dave, New Orleans*	.269	7	30	26	3	7	11	1	0	1	2	0	0	0	4	0	3	0	0	1	.423	.36
Norman, Les, Omaha	.260	24	85	77	8	20	29	6	0	1	13	0	1	1	6	0	8	0	1	2	.377	.31
Norton, Greg, Nashville†	.287	43	183	164	28	47	86	14	2	7	26	0	2	0	17	3	42	2	3	1	.524	.35
Nunnally, Jon, Omaha*	.281	103	406	345	76	97	201	21	4	25	77	0	6	8	47	8	100	10	9	2	.583	.37
Ojala, Kirt, Indianapolis*	.273	22	13	11	0	3	4	1	0	0	3	2	0	0	0	0	0	0	0	0	.364	.27
Oliva, Jose, Louisville	.242	118	449	413	53	100	206	13	0	31	86	0	1	1	34	5	101	3	3	11	.499	.30
Orie, Kevin, Iowa	.208	14	54	48	5	10	17	1	0	2	6	0	0	0	6	1	10	0	0	1	.354	.29
Ortega, Hector, New Orleans	.556	5	18	18	2	10	12	0	1	0	2	0	0	0	0	0	2	0	0	1	.667	.55
Ortiz, Hector, Iowa	.241	27	83	79	6	19	21	2	0	0	3	0	1	0	3	1	16	0	0	5	.266	.26
Ortiz, Luis, Oklahoma City	.317	124	533	501	70	159	226	25	0	14	73	0	6	4	22	2	36	0	5	17	.451	.34
Osborne, Donovan, Louisville*	.000	1	3	3	0	0	0	0	0	0	0	0	0	0	0	0	0	0	0	0	.000	.00
Owen, Spike, Oklahoma City†	.000	2	4	4	0	0	0	0	0	0	0	0	0	0	0	0	0	0	0	0	.000	.00
Owens, Eric, Indianapolis	.320	33	140	128	24	41	65	8	2	4	14	0	0	1	11	3	16	6	3	3	.508	.37
Pagnozzi, Tom, Louisville	.154	8	29	26	5	4	10	0	0	2	3	0	0	0	3	1	2	0	0	0	.385	.24
Pappas, Erik, Oklahoma City	.206	107	404	330	38	68	98	15	0	5	36	3	7	1	63	3	69	3	8	7	.297	.32
Paquette, Craig, Omaha	.333	18	72	63	9	21	36	3	0	4	13	0	1	0	8	1	14	1	0	3	.571	.40
Pemberton, Rudy, O.C.	.254	17	74	71	6	18	27	3	0	2	11	0	1	1	1	0	10	1	4	0	.380	.27
Pena, Geronimo, Lou.-Buf.†	.313	51	220	195	32	61	112	15	3	10	35	0	1	0	24	2	52	0	0	4	.574	.38
Perez, Danny, New Orleans	.187	65	233	198	25	37	48	5	0	2	15	1	1	1	32	1	57	4	2	2	.242	.30
Perez, Eduardo, Indianapolis	.293	122	509	451	84	132	234	29	5	21	84	0	1	6	51	5	69	11	0	11	.519	.37
Perez, Mike, Iowa	.000	23	1	1	0	0	0	0	0	0	0	0	0	0	0	0	0	0	0	0	.000	.00
Perry, Herb, Buffalo	.338	40	161	151	21	51	75	7	1	5	30	1	0	2	7	2	19	4	0	0	.497	.37
Petersen, Chris, Iowa	.247	63	210	194	12	48	66	6	3	2	23	2	1	1	12	1	46	1	2	4	.340	.29
Powell, Ross, Lou.-Ind.*	.250	18	11	8	1	2	2	0	0	0	1	3	0	0	0	0	1	0	0	0	.250	.25
Pugh, Tim, Indianapolis	.200	4	5	5	1	1	1	0	0	0	0	0	0	0	0	0	2	0	0	0	.200	.20
Pulido, Carlos, Iowa*	.111	28	9	9	0	1	1	0	0	0	0	0	0	0	0	0	3	0	0	0	.111	.11
Ramsey, Fernando, Nashville	.218	110	414	395	42	86	110	3	0	7	24	6	0	3	10	0	57	12	10	9	.278	.24
Randa, Joe, Omaha	.111	3	10	9	1	1	3	0	1	0	0	0	0	0	1	0	1	0	0	0	.333	.20
Ratliff, Jon, Iowa	.000	32	4	4	0	0	0	0	0	0	0	0	0	0	0	0	1	0	0	0	.000	.00
Reese, Pokey, Indianapolis	.232	79	313	280	26	65	84	16	0	1	23	4	3	5	21	0	46	5	2	10	.300	.29
Remlinger, Mike, Indianapolis*	.000	28	5	5	0	0	0	0	0	0	0	0	0	0	0	0	1	0	0	0	.000	.00
Renko, Steve, Iowa	.000	3	3	3	0	0	0	0	0	0	0	0	0	0	0	0	2	0	0	0	.000	.00
Robertson, Mike, Nashville*	.258	138	504	450	64	116	203	16	4	21	74	9	2	5	38	4	83	1	2	10	.451	.32
Robledo, Nilson, Nashville	.100	9	12	10	0	1	1	0	0	0	1	0	0	1	1	0	7	0	0	1	.100	.25
Sabo, Chris, Indianapolis	.290	8	32	31	0	9	10	1	0	0	1	0	1	0	0	0	6	0	0	3	.323	.28
Saenz, Olmedo, Nashville	.261	134	545	476	86	124	209	29	1	18	63	2	1	13	53	1	80	4	2	5	.439	.35
Sagmoen, Marc, O.C.*	.293	32	122	116	16	34	55	6	0	5	16	0	1	1	4	0	20	1	0	1	.474	.32
Sanchez, Rey, Iowa	.167	3	13	12	2	2	2	0	0	0	0	1	0	0	0	0	2	0	0	1	.167	.23
Sanchez, Yuri, Indianapolis	.000	1	4	4	0	0	0	0	0	0	0	0	0	0	0	0	2	0	0	0	.000	.00
Sanders, Reggie, Indianapolis	.417	4	14	12	3	5	7	2	0	0	1	0	0	0	1	0	4	0	1	0	.583	.50
Santana, Ruben, Indianapolis	.118	6	20	17	4	2	3	1	0	0	2	0	0	0	3	0	3	0	0	1	.176	.25
Shave, Jon, Oklahoma City	.266	116	473	414	54	110	155	20	2	7	41	4	4	10	41	0	97	8	6	7	.374	.34
Shumpert, Terry, Iowa	.276	72	279	246	45	68	104	13	4	5	32	4	3	2	24	0	44	13	3	5	.423	.34
Simmons, Scott, Louisville	.100	30	13	10	1	1	1	0	0	0	1	2	0	0	1	0	4	0	0	0	.100	.18
Slusarski, Joseph, New Orleans	.000	40	1	1	0	0	0	0	0	0	0	0	0	0	0	0	0	0	0	0	.000	.00
Smith, Alex, Oklahoma City	.225	81	230	200	22	45	75	12	0	6	20	3	1	4	22	0	53	4	2	5	.375	.31
Snopek, Chris, Nashville	.248	40	176	153	18	38	52	8	0	2	12	1	0	1	21	1	24	2	2	0	.340	.34
Sparks, Don, Buffalo	.295	137	580	511	69	151	217	32	5	8	68	1	12	2	54	4	72	2	2	14	.425	.35
Spradlin, Jerry, Indianapolis†	.000	49	7	7	0	0	0	0	0	0	0	0	0	0	0	0	5	0	0	0	.000	.00
Steenstra, Kennie, Iowa	.000	26	16	16	0	0	0	0	0	0	0	0	0	0	0	0	7	0	0	0	.000	.00
Stefanski, Mike, Louisville	.206	53	141	126	11	26	41	7	1	2	9	1	2	1	11	1	11	1	2	4	.325	.27

ayer, Team	Avg.	G	TPA	AB	R	H	TB	2B	3B	HR	RBI	SH	SF	HP	BB	IBB	SO	SB	CS	GDP	Slg.	OBP
evens, Lee, Oklahoma City*	.325	117	498	431	84	140	277	37	2	32	94	0	6	3	58	8	90	3	0	8	.643	.404
ewart, Andy, Omaha	.215	50	202	181	23	39	59	10	2	2	13	0	1	5	15	0	25	0	2	9	.326	.292
llwell, Kurt, Oklahoma City†	.235	4	17	17	1	4	4	0	0	0	1	0	0	0	0	0	0	0	0	0	.235	.235
nnett, Kelly, New Orleans	.287	95	382	334	63	96	200	21	1	27	70	0	4	13	31	2	83	3	3	6	.599	.366
urtze, Tanyon, Iowa	.250	51	4	4	0	1	1	0	0	0	0	0	0	0	0	0	1	0	0	0	.250	.250
ynes, Chris, Omaha	.356	72	311	284	50	101	157	22	2	10	40	0	3	4	18	2	17	7	3	7	.553	.398
llivan, Scott, Indianapolis	.200	53	5	5	0	1	1	0	0	0	0	1	0	0	0	0	3	0	0	0	.200	.200
artzbaugh, Dave, Iowa	.000	44	4	4	0	0	0	0	0	0	0	0	0	0	0	0	0	0	0	0	.000	.000
veeney, Mike, Omaha	.257	25	111	101	14	26	44	9	0	3	16	1	0	3	6	0	13	0	0	0	.436	.318
anoa, Scott, New Orleans	.188	32	90	80	9	15	22	1	0	2	11	0	0	2	8	0	26	2	0	5	.275	.275
xis, Fernando, Oklahoma City†	.500	2	4	4	0	2	3	1	0	0	0	0	0	0	0	0	1	0	0	0	.750	.500
lemaco, Amaury, Iowa	.000	8	1	1	0	0	0	0	0	0	0	0	0	0	0	0	1	0	0	0	.000	.000
omas, Brian, Oklahoma City*	.263	88	287	247	30	65	108	14	4	7	36	4	2	3	31	3	63	1	0	2	.437	.350
ompson, Ryan, Buffalo	.259	138	574	540	79	140	237	26	4	21	83	2	4	7	21	1	119	12	5	14	.439	.294
mmons, Ozzie, Iowa	.249	59	246	213	32	53	111	7	0	17	40	0	2	3	28	0	42	1	1	9	.521	.341
amie, Paul, Louisville	.500	1	2	2	0	1	1	0	0	0	0	0	0	0	0	0	0	1	0	0	.500	.500
emie, Chris, Nashville	.219	70	244	215	17	47	59	10	1	0	26	6	3	2	18	0	48	2	0	4	.274	.282
cker, Scooter, Omaha	.162	24	83	74	5	12	17	2	0	1	4	2	3	2	2	0	12	0	0	3	.230	.198
roe, Tim, New Orleans	.270	109	448	404	72	109	218	26	4	25	67	0	4	4	36	2	121	8	3	10	.540	.333
bani, Tom, Louisville*	.167	8	6	6	1	1	1	0	0	0	0	0	0	0	0	0	2	0	0	0	.167	.167
ldes, Pedro, Iowa*	.295	103	435	397	61	117	185	23	0	15	60	1	5	1	31	1	57	2	0	12	.466	.343
ldez, Trovin, Indianapolis†	.000	1	1	1	0	0	0	0	0	0	0	0	0	0	0	0	0	0	0	0	.000	.000
alrie, Kerry, Nashville	.273	138	536	498	59	136	217	32	5	13	66	1	6	3	28	0	94	10	9	12	.436	.312
nRyn, Ben, Louisville*	.200	19	5	5	0	1	1	0	0	0	0	0	0	0	0	0	3	0	0	0	.200	.200
nas, Julio, Nashville	.237	104	380	338	48	80	135	18	2	11	52	0	4	2	36	2	63	1	4	8	.399	.311
tiello, Joe, Omaha	.280	36	152	132	26	37	71	7	0	9	31	0	1	3	16	1	32	1	0	1	.538	.368
igt, Jack, Oklahoma City	.297	127	530	445	77	132	223	26	1	21	80	2	6	1	76	4	103	5	5	11	.501	.396
ard, Turner, New Orleans†	.348	9	31	23	4	8	12	1	0	1	1	0	0	1	7	0	4	0	0	0	.522	.516
eger, Wes, New Orleans	.210	64	230	210	23	44	67	11	0	4	23	1	0	1	18	0	33	0	0	10	.319	.275
hite, Gabe, Indianapolis*	.000	11	5	5	1	0	0	0	0	0	0	0	0	0	0	0	2	0	0	1	.000	.000
illiamson, Antone, N.O.*	.261	55	221	199	23	52	79	10	1	5	23	0	2	1	19	1	40	1	0	9	.397	.326
ilson, Brandon, Indianapolis ...	.233	95	347	305	48	71	96	7	3	4	31	1	2	0	39	0	53	10	6	8	.315	.318
ilson, Craig, Nashville	.179	44	139	123	13	22	31	4	1	1	6	5	1	0	10	0	15	0	0	6	.252	.239
ilson, Enrique, Buffalo†	.500	3	9	8	1	4	5	1	0	0	0	0	0	0	0	1	0	1	0	2	.625	.556
ilson, Nigel, Buffalo*	.299	128	552	482	88	144	269	23	6	30	95	1	7	12	50	7	117	4	4	9	.558	.374
ilson, Tom, Buffalo	.269	72	250	208	28	56	101	14	2	9	30	1	0	6	35	0	66	0	1	4	.486	.390
immer, Chris, Louisville	.249	112	372	345	40	86	107	11	2	2	23	3	2	6	16	0	41	11	3	11	.310	.293
oodson, Tracy, Iowa	.184	10	41	38	2	7	16	3	0	2	8	0	1	0	2	0	4	0	0	1	.421	.220
orthington, Craig, O.C.	.264	15	58	53	5	14	19	2	0	1	4	0	0	0	5	0	6	0	0	2	.358	.328
ung, Dmitri, Louisville†	.333	122	498	459	90	153	245	31	8	15	64	0	3	1	34	8	67	16	5	5	.534	.378
ung, Kevin, Omaha	.306	50	204	186	29	57	109	11	1	13	46	0	2	4	12	5	41	3	0	1	.586	.358
pcic, Bob, Louisville	.143	4	8	7	1	1	1	0	0	0	1	0	0	0	0	0	1	0	0	1	.143	.250

GRAND SLAMS: N. Wilson, 3; Burton, Mejia, Mitchell, Nunnally, Oliva, 2; Abbott, Brady, Cromer, Franklin, L. Frazier, Gulan, Kessinger, Leius, Shumpert, Stinnett, lanoa, Thomas, Vinas, 1 each.
AWARDED FIRST BASE ON CATCHER'S INTERFERENCE: Lee 2 (Stinnett 2); Stynes 2 (Helfand, Stefanski); Gulan (Cardenas); D. Young (Tremie).

PLAYERS WITH TWO OR MORE TEAMS

ayer, Team	Avg.	G	TPA	AB	R	H	TB	2B	3B	HR	RBI	SH	SF	HP	BB	IBB	SO	SB	CS	GDP	Slg.	OBP
olowsky, Dan, Louisville	.179	17	61	56	3	10	15	2	0	1	6	0	0	1	4	0	16	1	2	1	.268	.246
olowsky, Dan, Iowa	.173	26	64	52	10	9	20	5	0	2	5	1	0	0	11	0	18	0	0	0	.385	.317
ries, Paul, Iowa	.261	37	134	115	14	30	38	4	2	0	8	2	1	2	14	2	12	6	1	2	.330	.348
ries, Paul, New Orleans	.227	35	125	110	7	25	31	1	1	1	8	3	0	1	11	0	13	1	1	2	.282	.303
ries, Paul, Buffalo	.250	49	191	172	24	43	60	9	1	2	15	4	2	1	12	0	24	3	1	2	.349	.299
owitt, Dann, Louisville*	.255	46	161	141	19	36	56	6	1	4	18	2	1	1	16	2	31	4	1	2	.397	.333
witt, Dann, Indianapolis*	.276	50	172	156	19	43	63	6	1	4	22	0	1	1	14	2	35	0	3	4	.404	.337
erchant, Mark, Nashville†	.214	42	152	131	21	28	46	6	0	4	15	1	1	2	17	1	29	1	1	6	.351	.311
erchant, Mark, Omaha†	.280	38	141	118	18	33	52	7	0	4	21	1	0	0	22	0	26	1	0	6	.441	.393
na, Geronimo, Louisville†	.283	27	118	106	17	30	58	6	2	6	18	0	0	0	12	1	25	0	0	3	.547	.356
na, Geronimo, Buffalo†	.348	24	102	89	15	31	54	9	1	4	17	0	1	0	12	1	27	0	0	1	.607	.422
well, Ross, Louisville	.000	5	1	1	0	0	0	0	0	0	0	0	0	0	0	0	1	0	0	0	.000	.000
well, Ross, Indianapolis*	.286	13	10	7	1	2	2	0	0	0	0	0	3	0	0	0	0	1	0	0	.286	.286

1996 PITCHING

TEAM

am	W	L	Pct.	ERA	G	CG	ShO	Sv.	IP	H	TBF	R	ER	HR	SH	SF	HB	BB	IBB	SO	WP	Bk.
dianapolis	78	66	.542	3.53	144	6	13	39	1245.0	1171	5233	578	489	130	37	32	40	394	24	942	53	4
klahoma City	74	70	.514	3.60	144	11	10	25	1250.1	1249	5313	595	500	97	35	33	48	381	18	943	57	11
ashville	77	67	.535	3.77	144	13	12	40	1234.2	1167	5255	590	517	129	36	38	38	472	33	880	55	3
uffalo	84	60	.583	3.97	144	11	9	40	1252.2	1198	5342	632	552	126	35	38	50	454	12	935	54	8
maha	79	65	.549	4.21	144	5	10	42	1245.0	1299	5367	668	582	164	31	33	48	412	19	912	54	10
ew Orleans	58	84	.408	4.30	142	8	11	32	1253.0	1278	5397	708	598	159	50	44	51	526	45	871	59	7
wa	64	78	.451	4.46	142	8	7	36	1232.1	1261	5281	676	611	170	48	46	39	405	36	837	55	6
uisville	60	84	.417	4.76	144	8	5	36	1234.0	1297	5398	741	652	138	40	40	55	467	50	895	64	8

INDIVIDUAL

TOP QUALIFIERS FOR EARNED-RUN AVERAGE TITLE

Minimum 115 innings. *Lefthanded pitcher.

tcher, Team	W	L	Pct.	ERA	G	GS	CG	ShO	GF	Sv.	IP	H	TBF	R	ER	HR	SH	SF	HB	BB	IBB	SO	WP	Bk.
elling, Rick, Oklahoma City...	12	4	.750	2.96	23	22	2	1	1	0	140.0	124	574	54	46	10	3	5	7	38	1	157	4	2
vens, Brian, New Orleans*	10	9	.526	3.02	29	22	3	2	1	1	137.0	124	591	60	46	11	4	3	3	57	1	117	7	0

Pitcher, Team	W	L	Pct.	ERA	G	GS	CG	ShO	GF	Sv.	IP	H	TBF	R	ER	HR	SH	SF	HB	BB	IBB	SO	WP
Roa, Joe, Buffalo	11	8	.579	3.27	26	24	5	0	0	0	165.1	161	676	66	60	19	5	3	6	36	0	82	6
Fordham, Tom, Nashville*	10	8	.556	3.45	22	22	3	2	0	0	140.2	117	589	60	54	15	4	2	4	69	1	118	7
Alberro, Jose, Oklahoma City	9	9	.500	3.47	29	27	4	2	0	0	171.0	154	720	73	66	12	6	0	8	57	1	140	9
Anderson, Brian, Buffalo*	11	5	.688	3.59	19	19	2	0	0	0	128.0	125	531	57	51	14	3	3	2	28	0	85	4
Ojala, Kirt, Indianapolis*	7	7	.500	3.77	22	21	3	0	0	0	133.2	143	569	67	56	15	2	6	6	31	0	92	3
Ruffcorn, Scott, Nashville	13	4	.765	3.87	24	24	2	1	0	0	149.0	142	649	71	64	18	6	4	5	61	1	129	7
Swartzbaugh, Dave, Iowa	8	11	.421	3.88	44	13	0	0	11	0	118.1	106	491	61	51	22	5	4	3	33	1	103	5
Dreyer, Steve, Oklahoma City	6	8	.429	3.89	29	14	0	0	9	2	118.0	130	500	55	51	6	1	3	4	31	1	79	2
Sanford, Mo, Oklahoma City	6	10	.375	3.97	30	24	0	0	0	0	143.0	155	627	77	63	18	3	4	3	49	2	130	2
Rusch, Glendon, Omaha*	11	9	.550	3.98	28	28	1	0	0	0	169.2	177	723	88	75	15	7	8	6	40	3	117	3
Santana, Julio, Oklahoma City	11	12	.478	4.02	29	29	4	1	0	0	185.2	171	787	102	83	12	5	9	5	66	1	113	12
Foster, Kevin, Iowa	7	6	.538	4.30	18	18	3	1	0	0	115.0	106	484	56	55	23	2	0	2	46	2	87	6
Beltran, Rigo, Louisville*	8	6	.571	4.35	38	16	3	1	5	0	130.1	132	548	67	63	17	2	4	5	24	1	132	8

DEPARTMENTAL LEADERS: W—Ruffcorn, 13; L—Frascatore, 13; Pct.—Lopez, .833; G—Arrandale, 63; GS—Santana, 29; CG—Roa, 5; ShO—Sparks, Lewis, Giv...Fordham, Alberro, 2; GF—Bluma, 47; Sv.—Batchelor, 28; IP—Santana, 185.2; H—Bunch, 181; TBF—Santana, 787; R—Bunch, Frascatore, 106; ER—Bunch, 99; HR—Bunch, 32; SH—several players tied with 7; SF—Santana, Steenstra, 9; HB—Lopez, 10; BB—Browne, 73; IBB—Arrandale, 9; SO—Helling, 157; WP—Remlinger, 1... BK—Several pitchers tied with 3.

ALL PITCHERS

*Lefthanded pitcher.

Pitcher, Team	W	L	Pct.	ERA	G	GS	CG	ShO	GF	Sv.	IP	H	TBF	R	ER	HR	SH	SF	HB	BB	IBB	SO	WP
Alberro, Jose, Oklahoma City	9	9	.500	3.47	29	27	4	2	0	0	171.0	154	720	73	66	12	6	0	8	57	1	140	9
Anderson, Brian, Buffalo*	11	5	.688	3.59	19	19	2	0	0	0	128.0	125	531	57	51	14	3	3	2	28	0	85	4
Anderson, Mike, O.C.	3	4	.429	6.34	11	4	0	0	3	0	32.2	45	154	32	23	7	1	1	0	11	1	21	2
Andujar, Luis, Nashville*	1	4	.200	5.92	8	7	1	0	0	0	38.0	50	171	26	25	4	0	2	2	8	0	24	1
Archer, Kurt, New Orleans	1	3	.250	5.46	23	0	0	0	11	0	31.1	39	133	20	19	5	1	3	0	9	3	15	1
Arrandale, Matt, Louisville	5	4	.556	4.78	63	0	0	0	22	3	79.0	83	351	51	42	6	0	2	4	33	9	38	4
Aybar, Manuel, Louisville	2	2	.500	3.23	5	5	0	0	0	0	30.2	26	123	12	11	1	0	1	0	7	0	25	3
Badorek, Mike, Louisville	4	0	.000	5.29	20	6	0	0	6	0	49.1	52	216	34	29	3	4	2	4	18	2	22	1
Bailey, Cory, Louisville	2	4	.333	5.82	22	0	0	0	8	1	34.0	29	151	22	22	1	3	1	0	20	5	27	4
Baldwin, James, Nashville	1	1	.500	0.64	2	2	1	0	0	0	14.0	5	48	1	1	0	1	0	0	4	0	15	1
Barber, Brian, Louisville	0	6	.000	5.62	11	11	1	0	0	0	49.2	49	222	37	31	12	0	1	3	26	1	33	2
Batchelor, Rich, Louisville	5	2	.714	4.12	51	0	0	0	44	28	54.2	59	246	29	25	5	4	2	2	19	5	57	5
Beltran, Rigo, Louisville*	8	6	.571	4.35	38	16	3	1	5	0	130.1	132	548	67	63	17	2	4	5	24	1	132	8
Bere, Jason, Nashville	0	0	.000	1.42	3	3	0	0	0	0	12.2	9	48	2	2	1	0	0	0	4	0	9	1
Bertotti, Mike, Nashville*	5	3	.625	4.37	28	9	1	0	5	1	82.1	80	365	43	40	10	5	4	2	42	3	73	3
Bevil, Brian, Omaha	7	5	.583	4.12	12	12	0	0	0	0	67.2	62	289	36	31	10	0	5	1	19	0	73	6
Bluma, Jaime, Omaha	1	2	.333	3.12	52	0	0	0	47	25	57.2	57	251	22	20	7	0	1	3	20	3	40	5
Bottenfield, Kent, Iowa	1	2	.333	2.19	28	0	0	0	26	18	24.2	19	99	9	6	0	0	0	1	8	1	14	1
Bowen, Ryan, New Orleans	2	2	.500	4.94	6	6	0	0	0	0	27.1	27	125	18	15	4	0	1	1	19	0	23	3
Boze, Marshall, New Orleans	4	3	.571	4.89	25	2	0	0	12	3	38.2	35	180	22	21	6	3	2	1	29	5	32	2
Browne, Byron, New Orleans	3	9	.250	6.20	23	21	1	0	0	0	107.1	104	489	79	74	18	3	5	7	73	1	80	7
Buckley, Travis, Indianapolis*	11	7	.611	4.50	22	20	1	0	0	0	122.0	126	518	68	61	23	2	3	4	32	0	58	2
Bunch, Mel, Omaha	9	8	.471	6.08	33	27	0	0	2	0	146.2	181	663	106	99	32	1	4	7	59	1	94	8
Burlingame, Ben, Iowa	5	6	.455	4.30	27	11	0	0	5	0	98.1	104	410	49	47	13	0	4	3	20	3	66	1
Burrows, Terry, New Orleans*	3	0	1.000	2.21	18	0	0	0	9	6	28.2	19	108	9	8	1	0	1	0	8	0	17	1
Busby, Mike, Louisville	2	5	.286	6.38	14	14	0	0	0	0	72.0	89	343	57	51	11	3	1	6	44	1	53	7
Butcher, Mike, Buffalo	1	2	.333	8.18	12	2	0	0	5	0	22.0	31	115	24	20	4	0	4	1	13	0	21	2
Caceres, Edgar, New Orleans	0	0	.000	0.00	1	0	0	0	0	0	1.0	3	3	0	0	0	0	0	0	0	0	1	0
Cadaret, Greg, Buffalo*	1	5	.167	3.66	32	3	0	0	9	2	64.0	59	274	28	26	3	3	2	2	29	2	44	4
Campbell, Mike, Iowa	8	2	.800	2.73	16	16	1	0	0	0	95.2	75	381	31	29	8	4	4	1	23	2	87	2
Carpenter, Cris, New Orleans	1	0	1.000	2.52	40	0	0	0	17	8	50.0	46	201	16	14	4	1	1	2	7	3	41	0
Carrara, Giovanni, Indianapolis	4	0	1.000	0.76	9	6	1	1	2	1	47.2	25	177	6	4	2	0	1	3	9	0	45	0
Carrasco, Hector, Indianapolis	0	1	.000	2.14	13	2	0	0	4	0	21.0	18	97	7	5	1	2	0	1	13	1	17	2
Carter, Mike, Iowa	0	0	.000	0.00	1	0	0	0	0	0	1.0	1	5	0	0	0	0	0	0	2	0	1	0
Casian, Larry, Iowa*	3	2	.600	1.71	24	0	0	0	5	1	47.1	37	187	13	9	3	1	1	0	11	4	32	2
Clark, Terry, Omaha	3	1	.750	2.56	16	2	0	0	4	2	45.2	42	190	15	13	5	1	2	4	13	1	36	1
Colon, Bart, Buffalo	0	0	.000	0.00	8	0	0	0	0	0	15.0	16	69	10	10	2	1	1	0	8	0	19	2
Cornelius, Reid, Buffalo	5	7	.417	5.60	20	18	0	0	2	0	90.0	101	422	64	56	6	4	2	5	49	1	62	3
Curtis, Chris, Oklahoma City	2	5	.286	5.11	41	2	0	0	13	1	75.2	91	344	50	43	6	4	3	3	34	3	38	10
Dabney, Fred, Iowa*	2	3	.400	4.34	33	3	1	0	5	0	64.1	76	287	38	31	9	2	0	3	24	1	33	2
Darwin, Jeff, Nashville	5	2	.714	3.55	25	6	0	0	11	3	63.1	52	256	31	25	8	0	1	1	17	1	33	5
Davis, Clint, Oklahoma City	0	0	.000	3.46	8	0	0	0	0	0	13.0	14	60	5	5	1	1	0	3	6	0	16	0
Dixon, Steve, Louisville*	0	0	.000	10.38	5	0	0	0	4	0	4.1	4	20	5	5	2	1	1	1	3	1	2	0
Doyle, Tom, Indianapolis*	0	1	.000	3.86	1	0	0	0	0	0	2.1	2	10	1	1	0	1	0	1	1	1	0	0
Drahman, Brian, Indianapolis	0	0	.000	7.20	3	0	0	0	0	0	5.0	7	27	4	4	0	0	0	4	0	1	1	0
Dreyer, Steve, Oklahoma City	6	8	.429	3.89	29	14	0	0	9	2	118.0	130	500	55	51	6	1	3	4	31	1	79	2
Eddy, Chris, New Orleans*	0	0	.000	9.72	12	0	0	0	6	0	8.1	13	49	9	9	3	0	0	0	11	0	11	1
Eiland, Dave, Louisville	0	1	.000	5.55	8	6	0	0	0	0	24.1	27	110	17	15	2	2	1	2	8	0	17	0
Eldred, Cal, New Orleans	2	2	.500	3.34	6	6	0	0	0	0	32.1	24	135	12	12	2	0	1	1	7	0	30	1
Ellis, Robert, Nashville	3	8	.273	6.01	19	13	1	0	2	0	70.1	78	327	49	47	6	5	3	7	45	3	35	8
Embree, Alan, Buffalo*	4	1	.800	3.93	20	0	0	0	15	0	34.1	26	142	16	15	1	0	3	1	14	0	46	5
Estrada, Osmani, O.C.	0	0	.000	0.00	2	0	0	0	0	0	2.0	2	9	0	0	0	0	0	0	0	0	0	0
Eversgerd, Bryan, O.C.*	3	3	.500	2.74	38	5	0	0	14	4	65.2	57	266	21	20	3	2	1	4	14	0	60	3
Farrell, John, Buffalo	3	0	1.000	3.67	4	4	0	0	0	0	27.0	20	106	11	11	2	0	1	2	7	0	14	0
Farrell, Mike, New Orleans*	1	3	.250	4.60	29	4	0	0	9	2	64.1	72	276	31	30	7	4	5	0	13	3	39	0
Fordham, Tom, Nashville*	10	8	.556	3.45	22	22	3	2	0	0	140.2	117	589	60	54	15	4	2	4	69	1	118	7
Fortugno, Tim, Indianapolis*	5	5	.500	3.41	41	5	0	0	19	2	58.0	55	253	22	22	9	2	3	2	25	3	46	3
Foster, Kevin, Iowa	7	6	.538	4.30	18	18	3	1	0	0	115.0	106	484	56	55	23	2	0	2	46	2	87	6
Frascatore, John, Louisville	6	13	.316	5.18	36	21	3	0	0	0	156.1	180	692	106	90	22	7	6	7	42	2	95	5
Frazier, Ron, Indianapolis	0	1	.000	11.05	2	2	0	0	0	0	7.1	8	34	11	9	2	1	0	0	3	0	4	0

cher, Team	W	L	Pct.	ERA	G	GS	CG	ShO	GF	Sv.	IP	H	TBF	R	ER	HR	SH	SF	HB	BB	IBB	SO	WP	Bk.
jkowski, Steve, Nashville	5	6	.455	3.94	49	8	0	0	17	2	107.1	113	472	61	47	11	4	5	5	41	5	47	6	0
note, Joe, New Orleans	6	11	.353	5.19	41	12	0	0	9	0	109.1	121	484	77	63	17	7	4	6	44	8	65	6	1
rcia, Ramon, New Orleans	2	1	.667	1.88	11	5	0	0	2	0	38.1	31	155	10	8	2	2	2	2	12	0	32	0	0
vens, Brian, New Orleans*	10	9	.526	3.02	29	22	3	2	1	1	137.0	124	591	60	46	11	4	3	3	57	1	117	7	0
anger, Jeff, Omaha*	5	3	.625	2.34	45	0	0	0	25	4	77.0	65	314	24	20	10	2	2	2	29	2	68	3	0
aves, Danny, Buffalo	4	3	.571	1.48	43	0	0	0	32	19	79.0	57	308	14	13	1	5	3	2	24	2	46	1	0
'gsby, Benji, Buffalo	0	0	.000	5.40	8	0	0	0	4	0	13.1	18	63	13	8	6	0	0	0	4	0	3	0	0
oss, Kevin, Oklahoma City	0	0	.000	6.75	1	1	0	0	0	0	4.0	6	18	4	3	0	0	2	0	2	0	3	0	0
zman, Jose, Iowa	1	6	.143	8.45	8	8	0	0	0	0	38.1	51	185	39	36	9	3	0	1	19	1	24	5	0
lter, Shane, Omaha	0	0	.000	9.00	1	0	0	0	1	0	1.0	2	6	1	1	0	0	1	0	1	0	0	0	0
ney, Todd, Iowa	0	0	.000	0.00	1	0	0	0	1	0	1.0	2	6	0	0	0	0	0	0	0	0	0	0	0
lling, Rick, Oklahoma City	12	4	.750	2.96	23	22	2	1	1	0	140.0	124	574	54	46	10	3	5	7	38	1	157	4	2
redia, Gil, Oklahoma City	0	0	.000	1.86	6	0	0	0	3	0	9.2	11	38	3	2	0	0	0	0	0	0	4	0	0
isman, Rick, Omaha	2	4	.333	4.87	27	4	0	0	6	0	57.1	54	243	32	31	9	0	1	2	24	0	50	0	1
ckson, Danny, Louisville*	0	0	.000	3.46	8	1	0	0	1	0	13.0	14	56	6	5	2	0	1	1	5	0	10	0	0
rvis, Kevin, Indianapolis	4	3	.571	5.06	8	8	0	0	0	0	42.2	45	186	27	24	3	0	2	1	12	0	32	3	0
an, Domingo, Indianapolis	1	1	.500	8.68	7	0	0	0	2	0	9.1	13	49	11	9	2	0	0	0	8	1	5	0	0
hnson, Barry, Nashville	7	2	.778	2.80	38	8	0	0	8	0	103.0	93	430	38	32	11	2	3	1	39	3	68	4	0
hnson, Jonathan, O.C.	1	0	1.000	0.00	1	1	1	1	0	0	9.0	2	29	0	0	0	0	0	0	1	0	6	0	0
nes, Doug, New Orleans	0	3	.000	3.75	13	0	0	0	9	6	24.0	28	106	10	10	2	2	0	1	6	4	17	0	0
nes, Stacy, N.O.-Nash.	3	1	.750	3.15	28	0	0	0	20	12	34.1	35	145	13	12	2	1	2	2	13	3	28	1	0
rchner, Matt, Nashville	0	0	.000	0.00	1	0	0	0	0	0	0.2	0	2	0	0	0	0	0	0	0	0	0	0	0
yser, Brian, Nashville	3	3	.500	2.01	6	6	2	1	0	0	44.2	38	178	11	10	2	2	3	0	13	1	22	0	0
efer, Mark, N.O.-Oma.	6	8	.429	4.56	30	17	1	0	3	0	118.1	109	506	71	60	22	5	4	5	42	1	99	4	0
oek, Kevin, New Orleans	0	0	.000	9.00	1	0	0	0	0	0	1.0	3	6	1	1	1	0	0	0	1	0	0	0	0
cy, Kerry, Oklahoma City	3	3	.500	2.89	37	0	0	0	28	6	56.0	48	232	21	18	2	2	0	0	15	2	31	2	0
vine, Alan, Nashville	4	5	.444	3.65	43	0	0	0	28	12	61.2	58	267	27	25	4	2	2	3	24	6	45	1	0
wis, James, Buffalo	9	6	.600	5.01	21	21	2	2	0	0	120.1	134	530	79	67	10	5	5	7	49	0	71	10	1
liquist, Derek, Indianapolis*	4	1	.800	2.60	47	0	0	0	17	1	52.0	47	208	17	15	3	5	0	2	7	1	51	0	0
nton, Doug, Omaha	1	1	.500	4.76	4	4	0	0	0	0	22.2	26	99	13	12	1	0	1	2	7	0	14	2	0
pez, Albie, Buffalo	10	2	.833	3.87	17	17	2	0	0	0	104.2	90	444	54	45	13	1	3	10	40	0	89	1	3
we, Sean, Louisville	8	9	.471	4.70	25	18	0	0	1	0	115.0	127	515	72	60	7	4	6	7	51	7	76	6	0
dwick, Eric, Louisville	3	4	.429	2.83	11	11	0	0	0	0	60.1	55	253	24	19	4	2	2	1	24	2	73	2	0
ebbers, Larry, Indianapolis	5	4	.556	3.91	14	11	0	0	0	0	71.1	76	301	44	31	8	1	2	1	23	2	35	1	0
agnante, Mike, Omaha*	1	0	1.000	0.00	1	0	0	0	1	0	3.0	3	12	1	0	0	0	0	0	0	0	6	0	0
agrane, Joe, Nashville*	1	1	.500	5.47	21	1	0	0	8	1	26.1	29	115	17	16	5	0	1	1	8	0	26	2	0
anning, David, O.C.	0	0	.000	5.40	1	1	0	0	0	0	5.0	6	21	3	3	0	0	1	0	2	0	1	0	0
auser, Tim, Oklahoma City	1	1	.500	2.16	8	0	0	0	4	0	8.1	8	37	3	2	1	0	0	0	2	0	11	0	0
axcy, Brian, Louisville	4	2	.667	4.79	36	3	0	0	8	1	62.0	63	274	34	33	5	2	3	4	32	6	52	5	0
cDill, Allen, Omaha*	0	1	.000	54.00	2	0	0	0	0	0	0.1	3	5	2	2	0	0	0	0	1	0	1	2	0
cElroy, Chuck, Indianapolis*	1	1	.500	2.70	5	3	0	0	0	0	13.1	11	53	4	4	0	0	0	0	4	0	10	1	0
eacham, Rusty, Omaha	3	3	.500	4.82	23	4	0	0	8	2	52.1	56	233	30	28	6	4	2	1	18	0	39	2	1
ercedes, Henry, Omaha	0	0	.000	0.00	2	0	0	0	2	0	1.1	0	4	0	0	0	0	0	0	0	0	0	0	0
ercedes, Jose, New Orleans	3	7	.300	3.56	25	15	0	0	3	1	101.0	109	439	58	40	14	3	5	7	28	1	47	4	1
ercker, Kent, Buffalo*	0	2	.000	3.94	3	3	0	0	0	0	16.0	11	70	7	7	3	0	1	3	9	0	11	1	0
suraca, Mike, New Orleans	2	7	.222	4.13	23	12	0	0	5	2	80.2	93	358	42	37	11	4	0	3	31	3	57	5	1
ontoya, Norm, New Orleans*	0	0	.000	8.53	11	0	0	0	6	2	12.2	23	63	16	12	3	0	0	0	5	1	8	0	0
oore, Marcus, Indianapolis	4	7	.364	3.45	15	15	0	0	0	0	88.2	72	369	41	34	8	1	2	3	38	1	70	2	0
organ, Mike, Louisville	1	3	.250	7.04	4	4	1	0	0	0	23.0	29	106	18	18	2	0	0	2	11	1	10	2	0
orris, Matt, Louisville	0	1	.000	3.38	1	1	0	0	0	0	8.0	8	32	3	3	0	0	0	0	1	0	9	0	0
oten, Scott, Iowa	1	2	.333	9.21	21	1	0	0	9	0	42.0	55	199	47	43	9	4	4	4	18	1	18	8	0
utis, Jeff, Louisville*	2	3	.400	5.87	32	0	0	0	12	1	38.1	44	174	26	25	4	1	1	3	19	2	21	0	0
chting, Chris, Oklahoma City	1	0	1.000	1.00	4	1	0	0	1	0	9.0	9	37	1	1	0	0	0	0	3	0	7	0	0
ea, Chad, Buffalo	0	1	.000	5.26	5	5	0	0	0	0	25.2	27	108	15	15	4	0	0	1	6	0	20	0	0
ala, Kirt, Indianapolis*	7	7	.500	3.77	22	21	3	0	0	0	133.2	143	569	67	56	15	2	6	6	31	0	92	3	0
sen, Steve, Omaha	7	4	.636	5.07	24	4	1	1	6	0	65.2	70	283	39	37	7	2	1	4	23	4	41	6	0
son, Gregg, Indianapolis	0	0	.000	4.26	7	0	0	0	7	4	6.1	6	33	4	3	1	0	0	1	6	0	4	0	0
borne, Donovan, Louisville*	1	0	1.000	2.57	1	1	0	0	0	0	7.0	6	24	2	2	1	0	0	0	2	0	3	0	0
tterson, Danny, O.C.	6	2	.750	1.68	44	0	0	0	34	10	80.1	79	334	22	15	5	2	0	7	15	3	53	5	0
tterson, Ken, Omaha*	0	1	.000	1.80	16	0	0	0	2	1	20.0	16	79	5	4	2	1	0	0	4	0	13	1	0
rez, Mike, Iowa	0	4	.000	6.53	23	0	0	0	6	0	30.1	42	146	24	22	4	2	3	1	15	3	19	2	1
tkovsek, Mark, Louisville	0	1	.000	9.00	2	1	0	0	0	0	3.0	5	16	4	3	0	0	0	0	1	0	4	1	0
illips, Tony, New Orleans	2	1	.667	2.92	20	6	0	0	4	0	52.1	51	214	25	17	6	0	3	4	7	0	32	2	0
tsley, Jim, Omaha	7	1	.875	3.97	13	13	0	0	0	0	70.1	74	312	34	31	8	3	2	1	39	0	53	0	0
antenberg, Erik, Buffalo*	2	2	.500	3.74	17	1	0	0	7	1	33.2	35	148	16	14	2	0	1	0	14	0	29	0	0
tts, Mike, New Orleans*	0	1	.000	6.75	11	1	0	0	0	0	16.0	23	78	15	12	2	0	2	0	11	0	8	1	0
well, Ross, Lou.-Ind.*	6	3	.667	5.56	17	11	0	0	4	0	68.0	82	307	43	42	9	3	3	0	28	0	61	2	3
gh, Tim, Indianapolis	2	1	.667	2.45	4	4	1	1	0	0	25.2	19	102	7	7	1	0	0	2	4	0	18	1	0
lido, Carlos, Iowa*	2	8	.200	5.31	28	17	0	0	3	0	101.2	133	461	64	60	17	6	3	3	36	3	48	5	1
in, Steve, Iowa	2	1	.667	3.12	26	0	0	0	26	10	26.0	17	103	9	9	3	3	3	0	8	3	23	1	0
lston, Kris, Omaha	0	0	.000	3.00	1	0	0	0	0	0	3.0	3	12	1	1	0	0	0	0	0	0	1	0	0
tliff, Jon, Iowa	4	8	.333	5.28	32	13	0	0	5	1	93.2	107	419	63	55	10	3	6	6	31	2	59	3	0
mlinger, Mike, Indianapolis*	4	3	.571	2.52	28	13	0	0	3	0	89.1	64	365	29	25	4	3	0	2	44	0	97	18	0
nko, Steve, Iowa	2	0	1.000	2.57	3	3	1	0	0	0	21.0	16	82	6	6	1	0	1	0	5	0	11	1	0
vera, Roberto, Iowa*	1	0	1.000	2.70	35	0	0	0	13	2	33.1	26	130	10	10	3	3	0	0	8	1	18	0	0
a, Joe, Buffalo	11	8	.579	3.27	26	24	5	0	0	0	165.1	161	676	66	60	19	5	3	6	36	0	82	6	1
berson, Sid, New Orleans*	0	1	.000	4.91	2	2	0	0	0	0	11.0	10	48	6	6	2	0	1	0	9	0	3	1	0
binson, Ken, Omaha	2	0	1.000	0.79	6	0	0	0	0	0	11.1	7	43	1	1	1	0	1	0	4	0	9	1	0
driguez, Frankie, N.O.	0	2	.000	6.75	13	1	0	0	7	0	18.2	24	87	15	14	1	1	1	0	11	3	16	0	0
driguez, Rich, Omaha*	2	3	.400	3.99	47	0	0	0	22	3	70.0	75	304	40	31	11	1	1	3	20	1	68	2	0
sado, Jose, Omaha*	8	3	.727	3.17	15	15	1	0	0	0	96.2	80	399	38	34	16	3	1	2	38	0	82	4	1
ffcorn, Scott, Nashville	13	4	.765	3.87	24	24	2	1	0	0	149.0	142	649	71	64	18	6	4	5	61	1	129	7	0

CLASS AAA — American Association

Pitcher, Team	W	L	Pct.	ERA	G	GS	CG	ShO	GF	Sv.	IP	H	TBF	R	ER	HR	SH	SF	HB	BB	IBB	SO	WP
Rusch, Glendon, Omaha*	11	9	.550	3.98	28	28	1	0	0	0	169.2	177	723	88	75	15	7	8	6	40	3	117	3
Russell, Jeff, Oklahoma City	1	0	1.000	1.04	5	1	0	0	4	2	8.2	8	32	2	1	0	0	1	0	1	0	5	0
Sanford, Mo, Oklahoma City	6	10	.375	3.97	30	24	0	0	0	0	143.0	155	627	77	63	18	3	4	3	49	2	130	2
Santana, Julio, Oklahoma City	11	12	.478	4.02	29	29	4	1	0	0	185.2	171	787	102	83	12	5	9	5	66	1	113	12
Sauveur, Rich, Nashville*	4	3	.571	3.70	61	3	0	0	20	8	73.0	63	311	34	30	8	2	3	3	28	4	69	3
Scanlan, Bob, Omaha	0	0	.000	0.73	12	0	0	0	12	5	12.1	10	45	2	1	0	0	0	0	3	0	9	0
Schrenk, Steve, Nashville	4	10	.286	4.42	16	15	1	0	1	0	95.2	93	395	54	47	12	3	1	3	29	2	58	3
Scott, Darryl, Buffalo	3	5	.375	2.89	50	1	0	0	30	9	81.0	61	323	29	26	11	4	2	0	24	4	73	2
Service, Scott, Indianapolis	1	4	.200	3.00	35	1	0	0	26	15	48.0	34	193	18	16	5	2	1	1	10	2	58	2
Shuey, Paul, Buffalo	3	2	.600	0.81	19	0	0	0	14	4	33.1	14	121	4	3	1	0	1	0	9	2	57	1
Simmons, Scott, Louisville*	5	6	.455	4.15	30	8	0	0	10	1	99.2	98	416	51	46	17	1	1	0	35	5	58	4
Sirotka, Mike, Nashville*	7	5	.583	3.60	15	15	1	1	0	0	90.0	90	381	44	36	10	0	3	1	24	0	58	0
Slusarski, Joseph, N.O.	2	4	.333	4.95	40	0	0	0	19	1	60.0	70	280	38	33	4	6	3	3	24	5	36	1
Smith, Chuck, Nashville	0	0	.000	27.00	1	0	0	0	0	0	0.2	2	5	2	2	0	0	0	0	1	0	1	0
Smith, Dan, Oklahoma City*	0	2	.000	9.00	5	5	0	0	0	0	15.0	27	78	19	15	4	0	1	1	7	0	12	1
Sparks, Steve, New Orleans	2	6	.250	4.99	11	10	3	2	0	0	57.2	64	267	43	32	8	1	4	2	35	0	27	6
Spradlin, Jerry, Indianapolis	6	8	.429	3.33	49	8	0	0	28	15	100.0	94	415	49	37	14	3	1	4	23	3	79	3
Steenstra, Kennie, Iowa	8	12	.400	5.01	26	26	1	0	0	0	158.0	170	686	96	88	24	5	9	9	47	4	101	2
Stefanski, Mike, Louisville	0	0	.000	0.00	2	0	0	0	2	0	1.1	1	7	0	0	0	0	1	1	0	0	0	0
Sturtze, Tanyon, Iowa	6	4	.600	4.85	51	1	0	0	18	4	72.1	80	315	42	39	7	3	0	3	33	2	51	6
Sullivan, Scott, Indianapolis	5	2	.714	2.73	53	3	0	0	12	1	108.2	95	452	38	33	10	1	2	4	37	3	77	5
Swartzbaugh, Dave, Iowa	8	11	.421	3.88	44	13	0	0	11	0	118.1	106	491	61	51	22	5	4	3	33	1	103	5
Talanoa, Scott, New Orleans	0	0	.000	16.20	2	0	0	0	2	0	3.1	8	20	6	6	4	0	0	0	3	0	1	1
Tavarez, Julian, Buffalo	1	0	1.000	1.29	2	2	0	0	0	0	14.0	10	54	2	2	0	0	0	1	3	0	10	0
Telemaco, Amaury, Iowa	3	1	.750	3.06	8	8	1	0	0	0	50.0	38	205	19	17	5	2	2	2	18	2	42	3
Thigpen, Bobby, Nashville	0	1	.000	7.11	4	0	0	0	0	0	6.1	8	27	5	5	2	0	0	0	2	0	6	1
Torres, Dilson, Omaha	4	7	.364	4.60	16	14	2	1	0	0	86.0	102	376	54	44	11	3	1	3	19	2	36	3
Toth, Robert, Omaha	3	3	.500	7.04	11	8	0	0	0	0	46.0	63	214	40	36	6	1	2	3	17	1	20	2
Urbani, Tom, Louisville*	2	2	.500	3.27	7	7	0	0	0	0	44.0	40	180	19	16	5	1	1	2	12	0	26	2
Valera, Julio, Omaha	1	3	.250	5.17	6	2	0	0	1	0	15.2	22	72	13	9	0	0	0	0	5	1	9	3
VanEgmond, Tim, N.O.	5	1	.833	1.50	7	7	0	0	0	0	48.0	28	180	8	8	2	2	0	1	11	0	32	1
VanRyn, Ben, Louisville*	4	6	.400	4.88	19	10	0	0	4	1	66.1	69	288	43	36	9	2	3	0	27	0	42	2
Vierra, Joey, Oklahoma City*	1	0	1.000	9.64	4	0	0	0	2	0	4.2	7	23	7	5	2	0	1	0	2	1	4	0
Warren, Brian, Indianapolis	2	3	.400	3.90	50	0	0	0	17	0	64.2	68	277	30	28	7	2	4	2	25	3	40	4
Weger, Wes, New Orleans	0	0	.000	0.00	1	0	0	0	1	0	1.0	1	4	0	0	0	0	1	0	0	0	0	0
Wertz, Bill, Buffalo	1	2	.333	4.71	17	1	0	0	11	0	28.2	32	133	16	15	3	1	1	2	19	1	22	0
White, Gabe, Indianapolis*	6	3	.667	2.77	11	11	0	0	0	0	68.1	69	273	25	21	6	2	2	1	9	3	51	1
Whiteside, Matt, O.C.	9	6	.600	3.45	36	7	0	0	14	0	94.0	95	393	41	36	8	5	2	3	24	2	52	4
Whitten, Casey, Buffalo*	3	4	.429	8.04	12	10	0	0	1	0	43.2	54	209	47	39	8	0	3	1	24	0	35	3
Wickander, Kevin, N.O.*	0	1	.000	12.79	8	0	0	0	1	0	6.1	9	34	12	9	2	1	0	0	5	2	9	3
Williams, Jimmy, Buffalo*	12	3	.800	4.04	35	13	0	0	2	0	113.2	116	496	60	51	13	3	3	1	45	0	96	9
Worrell, Steve, Nashville*	1	1	.500	3.15	11	2	0	0	7	0	20.0	19	84	8	7	2	0	0	5	1	11	2		
Zappelli, Mark, Nashville	0	0	.000	0.68	9	0	0	0	6	1	13.1	11	54	3	1	0	0	0	2	0	9	1	

COMBINATION SHUTOUTS: **Buffalo (7)**—Anderson-Scott, Tavarez-Scott, Roa-Graves, Lopez-Wertz-Cadaret, Roa-Wertz, Whitten-Wertz-Scott, Lopez-Graves-Shue **Indianapolis (11)**—Pugh-Fortugno-Spradlin, Luebbers-Sullivan-Spradlin, Fortugno-Sullivan-Lilliquist-Spradlin, Moore-Spradlin, Remlinger-Lilliquist, White-Service-Lilliqui Ojala-Warren-Fortugno, White-Service, Powell-Carrasco, Buckley-Jean-Service-Olson, Jarvis-Remlinger-Drahman-Olson. **Iowa (5)**—Swartzbaugh-Rain, Swartzbaugh-Dabne Ratliff-Rain, Campbell-Ratliff-Rivera, Steenstra-Rivera-Sturtze, Casian-Perez-Pulido. **Louisville (4)**—Aybar-Maxcy-Frascatore-Badorek, VanRyn-Arrandale-Batchelor, Ludwic Simmons-Arrandale, Frascatore-Arrandale. **Nashville (7)**—Fordham-Karchner-Zappelli, Fordham-Levine, Gajkowski-Magrane-Levine, Ellis-Levine-Sauveur, Ruffcorn-Sauve Darwin, Sirotka-Gajkowski-Sauveur-Levine, Baldwin-Levine-Bertotti. **New Orleans (7)**—Givens-Phillips, Givens-Ganote-Eddy-Carpenter-Boze, Browne-Jones, Vanegmon Slusarski, Eldred-Misuraca, Browne-Carpenter-Kiefer-Archer, Bowen-Garcia-Boze. **Oklahoma City (5)**—Whiteside-Nichting-Mauser, Dreyer-Heredia, Sanford-Eversgerd, Curti Patterson, Eversgerd-Dreyer. **Omaha (8)**—Pittsley-Olsen-Rodriguez, Bevil-Patterson-Scanlan, Kiefer-Patterson-Granger, Rusch-Meacham, Bunch-Huisman-Bluma, Rusc Meacham-Granger, Toth-Bluma, Rusch-Robinson-Granger.
NO-HIT GAMES: Helling, Oklahoma City, defeated Nashville, 4-0, August 13.

PITCHERS WITH TWO OR MORE TEAMS

Pitcher, Team	W	L	Pct.	ERA	G	GS	CG	ShO	GF	Sv.	IP	H	TBF	R	ER	HR	SH	SF	HB	BB	IBB	SO	WP	Bk
Jones, Stacy, New Orleans	0	1	.000	7.11	9	0	0	0	2	0	12.2	18	64	10	10	2	1	1	2	7	1	10	1	
Jones, Stacy,	3	0	1.000	0.83	19	0	0	0	18	12	21.2	17	81	3	2	0	0	1	0	6	2	18	0	
Kiefer, Mark, New Orleans		6	.833	4.33	22	10	1	0	3	0	72.2	60	310	40	35	15	3	3	3	33	1	66	4	
Kiefer, Mark, Omaha	3	2	.600	4.93	8	7	0	0	0	0	45.2	49	196	31	25	7	2	1	2	9	0	33	0	
Powell, Ross, Louisville*	0	0	.000	2.16	5	0	0	0	4	0	8.1	8	35	2	2	0	1	0	0	2	0	10	1	
Powell, Ross, Indianapolis	6	3	.667	6.03	12	11	0	0	0	0	59.2	74	272	41	40	9	2	3	0	26	0	51	1	

1996 FIELDING
TEAM

Team	Pct.	G	PO	A	E	TC	DP	PB	Team	Pct.	G	PO	A	E	TC	DP	PB
Iowa	.978	142	3697	1428	114	5239	125	9	Omaha	.972	144	3735	1423	147	5305	147	
Nashville	.977	144	3704	1451	119	5274	120	10	New Orleans	.971	142	3759	1585	160	5504	154	
Buffalo	.977	144	3758	1454	125	5337	130	24	Indianapolis	.971	144	3735	1398	145	5289	119	
Louisville	.974	144	3702	1597	140	5439	129	15	Oklahoma City	.970	144	3751	1579	164	5494	149	

TRIPLE PLAYS: None.

INDIVIDUAL

FIRST BASEMEN

NOTE: All caps denotes fielding-percentage leader based on 72 games for catchers, 96 for all other non-pitchers and 144 innings for pitchers. *Throws lefthanded.

Player, Team	Pct.	G	PO	A	E	TC	DP
Belk, Tim, Indianapolis	.986	113	930	44	14	988	75
Brown, Brant, Iowa*	.990	92	762	66	8	836	74

Player, Team	Pct.	G	PO	A	E	TC	D..
Caceres, Edgar, New Orleans	1.000	2	12	0	0	12	
Cardenas, Johnny, O.C.	.800	1	4	0	1	5	
Charles, Frank, Oklahoma City	.947	2	15	3	1	19	
Cholowsky, Dan, Louisville	1.000	1	2	0	0	2	
Costo, Tim, Buffalo	.998	54	417	35	1	453	3
Deak, Darrel, Louisville	1.000	8	43	1	0	44	
Dunn, Steve, Buffalo*	.995	52	385	27	2	414	3

Player, Team	Pct.	G	PO	A	E	TC	DP
Erdman, Brad, Iowa	1.000	1	11	0	0	11	2
Estrada, Osmani, Oklahoma City	1.000	1	2	0	0	2	0
Fasano, Sal, Omaha	1.000	2	18	1	0	19	5
Fordyce, Brook, Indianapolis	1.000	2	10	0	0	10	1
Garcia, Guillermo, Indianapolis	.824	2	11	3	3	17	3
Gonzales, Rene, Oklahoma City	1.000	1	9	4	0	13	1
Grotewold, Jeff, Omaha	.993	32	259	14	2	275	25
Gulan, Mike, Louisville	1.000	2	3	1	0	4	0
Hamelin, Bob, Omaha*	1.000	4	37	1	0	38	6
Harris, Mike, New Orleans*	1.000	4	20	1	0	21	1
Helfand, Eric, Buffalo	1.000	1	4	0	0	4	1
Howitt, Dann, Indianapolis	.979	6	44	3	1	48	6
Kieschnick, Brooks, Iowa	.984	52	417	23	7	447	34
Kosco, Bryn, Iowa	1.000	3	23	0	0	23	1
Landry, Todd, New Orleans*	.992	91	756	86	7	849	79
Lee, Derek, Oklahoma City	1.000	5	24	3	0	27	0
Leius, Scott, Buffalo	.979	14	92	3	2	97	8
Maas, Kevin, New Orleans*	.989	12	85	7	1	93	8
Merchant, Mark, Omaha	1.000	8	40	3	0	43	6
Mitchell, Keith, Indianapolis	.989	27	172	13	2	187	21
Morris, Hal, Indianapolis*	1.000	1	2	0	0	2	0
Nilsson, Dave, New Orleans	1.000	3	25	3	0	28	4
Norman, Les, Omaha	.923	3	23	1	2	26	1
Oliva, Jose, Louisville	.989	21	163	17	2	182	11
Ortiz, Luis, Oklahoma City	.995	100	912	49	5	966	92
Pappas, Erik, Oklahoma City	1.000	2	23	1	0	24	5
Paquette, Craig, Omaha	1.000	2	13	2	0	15	2
Pena, Geronimo, Buffalo	1.000	5	41	1	0	42	5
Perez, Eduardo, Indianapolis	1.000	6	35	4	0	39	2
Perry, Herb, Buffalo	.987	29	209	19	3	231	20
ROBERTSON, Mike, Nashville*	.996	137	1074	54	4	1132	89
Robledo, Nilson, Nashville	1.000	5	9	0	0	9	0
Shumpert, Terry, Iowa	1.000	1	4	0	0	4	0
Sparks, Don, Buffalo	1.000	10	81	7	0	88	8
Stefanski, Mike, Louisville	1.000	1	7	0	0	7	1
Stevens, Lee, Oklahoma City*	.994	36	315	22	2	339	37
Stewart, Andy, Omaha	.996	28	240	20	1	261	30
Talanoa, Scott, New Orleans	1.000	1	2	0	0	2	0
Torres, Paul, Louisville	1.000	1	2	0	0	2	0
Tucker, Scooter, Omaha	1.000	1	6	0	0	6	1
Unroe, Tim, New Orleans	.966	22	104	11	4	119	15
Vinas, Julio, Nashville	.992	16	120	8	1	129	17
Vitiello, Joe, Omaha	.990	36	281	20	3	304	27
Voigt, Jack, Oklahoma City	1.000	4	9	0	0	9	0
Williamson, Antone, N.O.	.979	29	268	16	6	290	26
Young, Dmitri, Louisville	.993	122	1091	83	8	1182	102
Young, Kevin, Omaha	.990	31	269	21	3	293	23

SECOND BASEMEN

Player, Team	Pct.	G	PO	A	E	TC	DP
Barberie, Bret, Iowa	.990	20	35	61	1	97	14
Bell, David, Louisville	.970	34	64	95	5	164	19
Brady, Doug, Louisville	.971	109	227	273	15	515	65
Caceres, Edgar, New Orleans	1.000	5	8	9	0	17	2
Candaele, Casey, Buffalo	.979	56	98	131	5	234	37
Carter, Mike, Iowa	.667	1	1	1	1	3	0
Cholowsky, Dan, Iowa	1.000	5	8	13	0	21	4
Costo, Tim, Buffalo	.833	1	1	4	1	6	0
Cromer, Tripp, Louisville	1.000	2	12	5	0	17	4
Deak, Darrel, Louisville	1.000	5	10	13	0	23	4
Estrada, Osmani, Oklahoma City	1.000	3	1	2	0	3	1
Faries, Paul, Ia.-N.O.-Buf.	.972	61	120	153	8	281	39
Fermin, Felix, Iowa	.750	1	1	2	1	4	0
Finn, John, Iowa	.900	2	4	5	1	10	0
Frazier, Lou, New Orleans	.778	2	3	4	2	9	0
Frye, Jeff, Oklahoma City	.972	39	86	124	6	216	22
Garcia, Guillermo, Indianapolis	.913	5	7	14	2	23	2
Halter, Shane, Omaha	1.000	7	15	13	0	28	4
Haney, Todd, Iowa	.963	53	95	138	9	242	28
Hansen, Jed, Omaha	.953	29	66	75	7	148	21
Hemond, Scott, Louisville	1.000	2	2	7	0	9	1
Holbert, Aaron, Louisville	.948	65	119	211	18	348	31
Jenkins, Brett, New Orleans	.875	3	2	5	1	8	1
Kessinger, Keith, Iowa	.857	2	3	3	1	7	0
Kremblas, Frank, Indianapolis	.990	22	52	50	1	103	8
Leius, Scott, Buffalo	.957	10	16	28	2	46	9
Lis, Joe, Buffalo	.985	36	68	63	2	133	24
LOPEZ, Roberto, New Orleans	.976	121	252	307	14	573	88
Martin, Norberto, Nashville	.957	9	19	26	2	47	7
Martinez, Ramon, Omaha	.969	85	163	207	12	382	53
Mejia, Roberto, Indianapolis	.975	98	208	261	12	481	52
Mota, Jose, Omaha	.952	22	37	43	4	84	13
Munoz, Jose, Nashville	.974	25	49	63	3	115	12
Owens, Eric, Indianapolis	1.000	8	17	20	0	37	7
Pena, Geronimo, Lou.-Buf.	.938	31	64	72	9	145	14
Petersen, Chris, Iowa	1.000	7	15	22	0	37	4
Shave, Jon, Oklahoma City	.982	65	97	176	5	278	36
Shumpert, Terry, Iowa	.982	46	97	127	4	228	31
Smith, Alex, Oklahoma City	.984	48	77	110	3	190	28
Sparks, Don, Buffalo	.900	3	7	2	1	10	1
Stillwell, Kurt, Oklahoma City	.900	4	9	9	2	20	4
Stynes, Chris, Omaha	.971	7	18	15	1	34	6
Weger, Wes, New Orleans	.979	26	35	60	2	97	11
Wilson, Brandon, Indianapolis	.944	17	37	48	5	90	10
Wilson, Craig, Nashville	1.000	5	9	6	0	15	4
Wilson, Tom, Buffalo	1.000	1	1	0	0	1	0
Wimmer, Chris, Louisville	.982	29	47	62	2	111	14

SECOND BASEMEN WITH TWO OR MORE TEAMS

Player, Team	Pct.	G	PO	A	E	TC	DP
Faries, Paul, Iowa	.935	14	33	39	5	77	8
Faries, Paul, New Orleans	1.000	3	8	7	0	15	3
Faries, Paul, Buffalo	.984	44	79	107	3	189	28
Pena, Geronimo, Louisville	.945	20	51	52	6	109	14
Pena, Geronimo, Buffalo	.917	11	13	20	3	36	0

THIRD BASEMEN

Player, Team	Pct.	G	PO	A	E	TC	DP
Banks, Brian, New Orleans	.778	6	1	6	2	9	1
Barberie, Bret, Iowa	.951	38	25	72	5	102	7
Belk, Tim, Indianapolis	.000	2	0	0	3	3	0
Bell, David, Louisville	1.000	8	1	19	0	20	0
Caceres, Edgar, New Orleans	1.000	4	1	2	0	3	1
Cholowsky, Dan, Iowa	.818	11	7	20	6	33	1
Costo, Tim, Buffalo	.778	4	2	5	2	9	1
Diaz, Lino, Omaha	.959	65	42	120	7	169	6
DiSarcina, Glenn, Nashville	.938	5	2	13	1	16	1
Estrada, Osmani, Oklahoma City	.971	36	10	58	2	70	8
Faries, Paul, Ia.-N.O.-Buf.	.954	24	21	61	4	86	5
Fasano, Sal, Omaha	1.000	1	1	2	0	3	0
Fermin, Felix, Iowa	.944	11	3	14	1	18	0
Finn, John, Iowa	.943	14	8	25	2	35	2
Frye, Jeff, Oklahoma City	1.000	2	0	1	0	1	0
Gonzales, Rene, Oklahoma City	.852	8	7	16	4	27	2
Gulan, Mike, Louisville	.927	111	64	239	24	327	15
Halter, Shane, Omaha	.846	20	9	24	6	39	3
Haney, Todd, Iowa	.857	8	4	8	2	14	1
Howitt, Dann, Indianapolis	1.000	1	2	3	0	5	0
Hubbard, Mike, Iowa	1.000	3	2	2	0	4	0
Hughes, Bobby, New Orleans	.800	1	1	3	1	5	0
Jenkins, Brett, New Orleans	.833	8	1	9	2	12	1
Kessinger, Keith, Iowa	1.000	5	2	4	0	6	1
Kosco, Bryn, Iowa	.920	17	5	18	2	25	1
Leius, Scott, Buffalo	.750	3	1	5	2	8	0
Lis, Joe, Buffalo	.909	4	0	10	1	11	0
Magadan, Dave, Iowa	.333	3	3	3	0	6	2
Martin, Norberto, Nashville	1.000	2	3	1	0	4	0
Mota, Jose, Omaha	.962	26	12	39	2	53	6
Munoz, Jose, Nashville	.931	8	7	20	2	29	3
Norton, Greg, Nashville	.889	3	1	7	1	9	1
Oliva, Jose, Louisville	.951	29	21	57	4	82	5
Orie, Kevin, Iowa	.974	14	11	26	1	38	0
Ortega, Hector, New Orleans	1.000	5	3	6	0	9	1
Owens, Eric, Indianapolis	.778	9	5	9	4	18	1
Paquette, Craig, Omaha	.857	4	5	7	2	14	1
Pena, Geronimo, Buffalo	.950	5	5	14	1	20	1
Perez, Eduardo, Indianapolis	.932	114	75	211	21	307	19
Perry, Herb, Buffalo	.889	7	3	5	1	9	0
Petersen, Chris, Iowa	1.000	3	2	1	0	3	0
Randa, Joe, Iowa	1.000	3	1	10	0	11	1
Reese, Pokey, Indianapolis	.880	7	9	13	3	25	1
Sabo, Chris, Indianapolis	1.000	8	6	16	0	22	1
Saenz, Olmedo, Nashville	.939	120	97	244	22	363	24
Santana, Ruben, Indianapolis	.909	5	4	6	1	11	0
Shave, Jon, Oklahoma City	.899	39	33	65	11	109	6
Shumpert, Terry, Iowa	.945	24	14	38	3	55	2
Smith, Alex, Oklahoma City	.844	11	9	18	5	32	3
Snopek, Chris, Nashville	1.000	5	5	15	0	20	1
SPARKS, Don, Buffalo	.952	129	66	250	16	332	21
Stinnett, Kelly, New Orleans	.800	4	0	4	1	5	0
Stynes, Chris, Omaha	.934	28	13	58	5	76	2
Tatis, Fernando, Oklahoma City	1.000	1	0	1	0	1	0
Unroe, Tim, New Orleans	.932	94	68	218	21	307	22
Vinas, Julio, Nashville	.909	5	3	7	1	11	1

Player, Team	Pct.	G	PO	A	E	TC	DP
Voigt, Jack, Oklahoma City	.917	59	35	109	13	157	11
Weger, Wes, New Orleans	.904	25	15	32	5	52	2
Williamson, Antone, N.O.	.778	5	3	4	2	9	1
Wilson, Brandon, Indianapolis	.889	7	2	6	1	9	2
Wilson, Enrique, Buffalo	.667	2	0	2	1	3	0
Wilson, Tom, Buffalo	.500	1	1	1	2	4	0
Wimmer, Chris, Louisville	.833	2	1	4	1	6	0
Woodson, Tracy, Iowa	.963	10	6	20	1	27	1
Worthington, Craig, O.C.	.915	15	10	33	4	47	1
Young, Kevin, Omaha	.946	11	11	24	2	37	3

THIRD BASEMEN WITH TWO OR MORE TEAMS

Player, Team	Pct.	G	PO	A	E	TC	DP
Faries, Paul, Iowa	1.000	2	2	4	0	6	0
Faries, Paul, New Orleans	.945	19	17	52	4	73	4
Faries, Paul, Buffalo	1.000	3	2	5	0	7	1

SHORTSTOPS

Player, Team	Pct.	G	PO	A	E	TC	DP
Arias, Amador, Indianapolis	1.000	1	0	3	0	3	0
Bell, David, Louisville	1.000	1	1	0	0	1	0
CACERES, Edgar, New Orleans	.964	105	147	308	17	472	65
Candaele, Casey, Buffalo	.949	13	15	41	3	59	8
Correia, Rod, Louisville	.953	12	16	25	2	43	8
Cromer, Tripp, Louisville	.986	76	112	233	5	350	45
DiSarcina, Glenn, Nashville	.952	27	40	78	6	124	16
Estrada, Osmani, Oklahoma City	.964	11	13	41	2	56	11
Faries, Paul, Ia.-N.O.-Buf.	.980	36	56	91	3	150	23
Felix, Lauro, New Orleans	1.000	2	4	5	0	9	1
Fermin, Felix, Iowa	.989	22	31	63	1	95	16
Frye, Jeff, Oklahoma City	.935	5	6	23	2	31	3
Gil, Benji, Oklahoma City	.949	83	121	267	21	409	57
Gonzales, Rene, Oklahoma City	.964	34	39	122	6	167	24
Halter, Shane, Omaha	.921	18	25	33	5	63	5
Haney, Todd, Iowa	1.000	6	9	12	0	21	3
Holbert, Aaron, Louisville	.942	49	66	129	12	207	28
Jackson, Damian, Buffalo	.954	131	203	403	29	635	84
Kessinger, Keith, Iowa	.979	45	61	123	4	188	27
Lopez, Roberto, New Orleans	.882	2	10	5	2	17	2
Loretta, Mark, New Orleans	.948	19	31	60	5	96	15
Martin, Norberto, Nashville	1.000	6	5	16	0	21	0
Martinez, Felix, Omaha	.929	117	177	374	42	593	79
Mota, Jose, Omaha	.949	12	18	38	3	59	14
Munoz, Jose, Nashville	.930	10	14	26	3	43	5
Norton, Greg, Nashville	.915	37	42	88	12	142	10
Owen, Spike, Oklahoma City	1.000	1	2	1	0	3	0
Owens, Eric, Indianapolis	.980	14	15	34	1	50	5
Pena, Geronimo, Buffalo	1.000	1	2	2	0	4	0
Petersen, Chris, Iowa	.979	53	91	140	5	236	30
Reese, Pokey, Indianapolis	.948	73	122	226	19	367	48
Sanchez, Rey, Iowa	.933	3	4	10	1	15	2
Sanchez, Yuri, Indianapolis	1.000	1	2	2	0	4	0
Shave, Jon, Oklahoma City	.921	17	28	42	6	76	13
Shumpert, Terry, Iowa	1.000	1	4	0	0	4	0
Snopek, Chris, Nashville	.954	34	33	92	6	131	16
Unroe, Tim, New Orleans	1.000	3	1	1	0	2	0
Weger, Wes, New Orleans	.884	13	11	27	5	43	3
Wilson, Brandon, Indianapolis	.935	63	74	141	15	230	27
Wilson, Craig, Nashville	.933	40	43	97	10	150	19
Wilson, Enrique, Buffalo	1.000	1	1	0	0	1	0
Wimmer, Chris, Louisville	.986	20	21	47	1	69	10

SHORTSTOPS WITH TWO OR MORE TEAMS

Player, Team	Pct.	G	PO	A	E	TC	DP
Faries, Paul, Iowa	.988	20	32	47	1	80	12
Faries, Paul, New Orleans	.967	14	19	39	2	60	10
Faries, Paul, Buffalo	1.000	2	5	5	0	10	1

OUTFIELDERS

Player, Team	Pct.	G	PO	A	E	TC	DP
Abbott, Jeff, Nashville*	.990	104	186	5	2	193	1
Anthony, Eric, Indianapolis*	.750	3	3	0	1	4	0
Aven, Bruce, Buffalo	1.000	3	7	0	0	7	0
Banks, Brian, New Orleans	.977	130	248	12	6	266	3
Belk, Tim, Indianapolis	1.000	6	2	0	0	2	0
Bradshaw, Terry, Louisville	.967	101	203	5	7	215	1
Bryant, Pat, Buffalo	.979	22	45	2	1	48	0
Bryant, Scott, Oklahoma City	1.000	8	8	2	0	10	0
Burton, Darren, Omaha	.986	121	262	11	4	277	3
Candaele, Casey, Buffalo	1.000	35	75	3	0	78	0
Cappuccio, Carmine, Nashville	.991	104	215	11	2	228	2
Carr, Chuck, New Orleans	1.000	4	6	2	0	8	1

Player, Team	Pct.	G	PO	A	E	TC	DP
Carter, Mike, Iowa	.977	82	169	3	4	176	1
Cholowsky, Dan, Louisville	.952	14	19	1	1	21	0
Coleman, Vince, Indianapolis	1.000	6	6	0	0	6	0
Correia, Rod, Louisville	1.000	24	46	2	0	48	0
Costo, Tim, Buffalo	.667	3	2	0	1	3	0
Deak, Darrel, Louisville	1.000	12	14	0	0	14	0
Diggs, Tony, Louisville	.994	89	153	4	1	158	1
Dunn, Steve, Buffalo*	1.000	1	3	0	0	3	0
Faneyte, Rikkert, Oklahoma City	.970	86	186	9	6	201	2
Felder, Ken, New Orleans	.962	114	163	14	7	184	5
Franklin, Micah, Louisville	.977	85	159	11	4	174	2
Frazier, Lou, Oklahoma City	.981	53	101	4	2	107	1
Frye, Jeff, Oklahoma City	1.000	4	2	0	0	2	0
Gibralter, Steve, Indianapolis	.975	113	262	10	7	279	2
Giles, Brian, Buffalo*	.986	83	132	5	2	139	0
Glanville, Doug, Iowa	.987	86	217	6	3	226	3
Goodwin, Curtis, Indianapolis*	.978	82	172	4	4	180	1
Halter, Shane, Omaha	.977	51	81	5	2	88	0
Hare, Shawn, Louisville*	1.000	14	24	0	0	24	0
Harris, Mike, New Orleans*	.973	38	72	0	2	74	0
Hemond, Scott, Louisville	1.000	1	2	0	0	2	0
Howard, Tom, Indianapolis	1.000	1	3	0	0	3	0
Howitt, Dann, Lou.-Ind.	.980	61	93	7	2	102	4
Hulse, David, New Orleans*	1.000	5	11	0	0	11	0
Hurst, Jimmy, Nashville	1.000	3	2	0	0	2	0
James, Dion, New Orleans*	.958	10	23	0	1	24	0
Jenkins, Brett, New Orleans	1.000	1	1	0	0	1	0
Jennings, Robin, Iowa*	.982	77	156	5	3	164	1
Kelly, Mike, Indianapolis	.971	72	132	2	4	138	1
Kieschnick, Brooks, Iowa	.989	52	81	5	1	87	0
Koslofski, Kevin, New Orleans	.988	71	154	4	2	160	2
Ladell, Cleveland, Indianapolis	1.000	2	1	0	0	1	0
Landry, Todd, New Orleans*	.935	27	27	2	2	31	0
Lee, Derek, Oklahoma City	.959	86	133	7	6	146	1
Leius, Scott, Buffalo	.500	1	1	0	1	2	0
Marsh, Tom, Buffalo	.986	107	203	11	3	217	0
McNeely, Jeff, Louisville	1.000	3	4	0	0	4	0
Merchant, Mark, Nash.-Oma.	.667	5	2	0	1	3	0
Mitchell, Keith, Indianapolis	.963	46	75	4	3	82	0
Mota, Jose, Omaha	1.000	5	9	0	0	9	0
Mottola, Chad, Indianapolis	.968	95	176	8	6	190	1
Munoz, Jose, Nashville	1.000	1	1	0	0	1	0
MYERS, Rod, Omaha*	.993	112	263	5	2	270	2
Norman, Les, Omaha	.943	16	33	0	2	35	0
Nunnally, Jon, Omaha	.980	99	182	12	4	198	5
Oliva, Jose, Louisville	1.000	10	8	0	0	8	0
Owens, Eric, Indianapolis	.889	3	7	1	1	9	0
Pappas, Erik, Oklahoma City	.667	6	4	0	2	6	0
Paquette, Craig, Omaha	.857	2	6	0	1	7	0
Pemberton, Rudy, O.C.	.939	15	29	2	2	33	0
Perez, Danny, New Orleans	.976	63	120	1	3	124	0
Perry, Herb, Buffalo	1.000	4	5	0	0	5	0
Ramsey, Fernando, Nashville	.980	107	232	7	5	244	4
Sagmoen, Marc, Oklahoma City*	.964	29	52	2	2	56	0
Sanders, Reggie, Indianapolis	1.000	3	4	1	0	5	0
Smith, Alex, Oklahoma City	1.000	8	11	1	0	12	0
Stefanski, Mike, Louisville	.750	3	3	0	1	4	0
Stevens, Lee, Oklahoma City*	.972	24	33	2	1	36	0
Stynes, Chris, Omaha	.959	35	67	4	3	74	0
Thomas, Brian, Oklahoma City	.979	76	132	6	3	141	0
Thompson, Ryan, Buffalo	.973	136	317	8	9	334	3
Timmons, Ozzie, Iowa	.971	50	98	1	3	102	0
Unroe, Tim, New Orleans	1.000	2	2	1	0	3	0
Valdes, Pedro, Iowa*	.974	88	183	7	5	195	1
Valrie, Kerry, Nashville	.981	123	309	7	6	322	2
Voigt, Jack, Oklahoma City	.973	74	105	4	3	112	0
Wilson, Brandon, Indianapolis	.833	5	5	0	1	6	0
Wilson, Nigel, Buffalo*	.982	65	104	4	2	110	1
Wimmer, Chris, Louisville	.987	58	74	4	1	79	0
Zupcic, Bob, Omaha	1.000	3	6	1	0	7	0

OUTFIELDERS WITH TWO OR MORE TEAMS

Player, Team	Pct.	G	PO	A	E	TC	DP
Howitt, Dann, Louisville	.975	45	73	6	2	81	3
Howitt, Dann, Indianapolis	1.000	16	20	1	0	21	1
Merchant, Mark, Nashville	1.000	2	1	0	0	1	0
Merchant, Mark, Omaha	.500	3	1	0	1	2	0

CATCHERS

Player, Team	Pct.	G	PO	A	E	TC	DP	PB
Banks, Brian, New Orleans	1.000	3	7	0	0	7	0	1
Campos, Miguel, Iowa*	1.000	2	10	2	0	12	0	0

ayer, Team	Pct.	G	PO	A	E	TC	DP	PB
rdenas, Johnny, O.C.	.981	29	141	10	3	154	0	3
arles, Frank, Oklahoma City	.968	31	173	11	6	190	4	3
olowsky, Dan, Iowa	1.000	3	1	0	0	1	0	0
elice, Mike, Louisville	.984	77	455	48	8	511	2	7
rsett, Brian, Iowa	1.000	7	46	2	0	48	1	0
lman, Brad, Iowa	.991	52	310	20	3	333	2	3
sano, Sal, Omaha	.980	25	179	18	4	201	4	1
RDYCE, Brook, Ind.	.994	96	610	49	4	663	9	4
rcia, Guillermo, Ind.	1.000	8	48	2	0	50	0	2
fand, Eric, Buffalo	.992	87	573	34	5	612	3	16
mond, Scott, Louisville	.982	37	196	18	4	218	3	4
bbard, Mike, Iowa	.988	62	370	25	5	400	5	5
ghes, Bobby, New Orleans	.980	32	175	24	4	203	3	4
nnedy, Darryl, O.C.	1.000	2	12	0	0	12	0	0
nak, Joe, Indianapolis	.988	46	313	30	4	347	3	7
mblas, Frank, Indianapolis	1.000	1	5	3	0	8	0	0
pez, Pedro, New Orleans	.988	27	151	14	2	167	3	6
theny, Mike, New Orleans	1.000	18	87	6	0	93	0	5
rcedes, Henry, Omaha	.993	66	400	49	3	452	8	6
rullo, Matt, Iowa	1.000	1	3	0	0	3	0	0
tiz, Hector, Iowa	.987	25	139	9	2	150	0	1
gnozzi, Tom, Louisville	1.000	8	36	5	0	41	1	1
ppas, Erik, Oklahoma City	.992	100	656	51	6	713	4	2
bledo, Nilson, Nashville	1.000	1	1	0	0	1	0	0
efanski, Mike, Louisville	.981	45	233	20	5	258	6	3
ewart, Andy, Omaha	1.000	14	83	6	0	89	1	0
nnett, Kelly, New Orleans	.982	81	485	48	10	543	9	6
veeney, Mike, Omaha	1.000	23	167	8	0	175	2	3
mie, Chris, Nashville	.996	70	433	52	2	487	6	5
cker, Scooter, Omaha	.992	23	122	10	1	133	1	3
as, Julio, Nashville	.992	82	461	46	4	511	1	5
lson, Tom, Buffalo	.988	66	386	26	5	417	3	8

PITCHERS

ayer, Team	Pct.	G	PO	A	E	TC	DP
erro, Jose, Oklahoma City	.977	29	14	28	1	43	3
derson, Brian, Buffalo*	.960	19	8	16	1	25	1
derson, Mike, Oklahoma City	1.000	11	0	2	0	2	0
dujar, Luis, Nashville	.778	8	2	5	2	9	0
cher, Kurt, New Orleans	1.000	23	5	3	0	8	0
andale, Matt, Louisville	1.000	63	9	17	0	26	2
oar, Manuel, Louisville	1.000	5	2	2	0	4	0
dorek, Mike, Louisville	.800	20	1	7	2	10	0
ley, Cory, Louisville	.900	22	3	6	1	10	0
dwin, James, Nashville	1.000	2	2	0	0	2	0
ber, Brian, Louisville	.909	11	5	5	1	11	0
tchelor, Rich, Louisville	1.000	51	2	3	0	5	0
tran, Rigo, Louisville*	1.000	38	8	10	0	18	0
e, Jason, Nashville	.667	3	1	1	1	3	0
totti, Mike, Nashville*	1.000	28	4	13	0	17	1
vil, Brian, Omaha	1.000	12	4	2	0	6	0
ma, Jaime, Omaha	.909	52	5	5	1	11	2
ttenfield, Kent, Iowa	1.000	28	1	3	0	4	0
wen, Ryan, New Orleans	1.000	6	3	3	0	6	0
ze, Marshall, New Orleans	1.000	25	5	5	0	10	0
wne, Byron, New Orleans	1.000	23	7	13	0	20	0
ckley, Travis, Indianapolis	1.000	22	9	13	0	22	0
nch, Mel, Omaha	1.000	33	13	11	0	24	3
lingame, Ben, Iowa	.958	27	9	14	1	24	1
rows, Terry, New Orleans*	.778	18	4	3	2	9	1
sby, Mike, Louisville	.933	14	5	9	1	15	1
tcher, Mike, Buffalo	1.000	12	1	1	0	2	0
daret, Greg, Buffalo*	1.000	32	5	14	0	19	1
mpbell, Mike, Iowa	1.000	16	7	8	0	15	0
rpenter, Cris, New Orleans	1.000	40	2	3	0	5	0
rrara, Giovanni, Indianapolis	.857	9	4	2	1	7	0
rrasco, Hector, Indianapolis	1.000	13	2	3	0	5	1
sian, Larry, Iowa*	.909	24	0	10	1	11	2
rk, Terry, Omaha	.818	16	3	6	2	11	0
lon, Bart, Buffalo	1.000	8	2	3	0	5	0
rnelius, Reid, Buffalo	.750	20	5	7	4	16	0
rtis, Chris, Oklahoma City	.929	41	1	12	1	14	0
bney, Fred, Iowa*	.923	33	3	9	1	13	2
rwin, Jeff, Nashville	1.000	25	1	9	0	10	1
vis, Clint, Oklahoma City	1.000	8	0	1	0	1	0
on, Steve, Louisville*	1.000	5	1	2	0	3	1
yle, Tom, Indianapolis*	1.000	1	0	1	0	1	0
ahman, Brian, Indianapolis	1.000	3	0	1	0	1	0
yer, Steve, Oklahoma City	.909	29	6	14	2	22	2
nd, Dave, Louisville	1.000	8	4	3	0	7	0
red, Cal, New Orleans	1.000	6	3	2	0	5	1
s, Robert, Nashville	1.000	19	3	20	0	23	2

Player, Team	Pct.	G	PO	A	E	TC	DP
Embree, Alan, Buffalo*	1.000	20	1	2	0	3	0
Estrada, Osmani, Oklahoma City	1.000	2	1	0	0	1	0
Eversgerd, Bryan, O.C.*	1.000	38	3	6	0	9	2
Farrell, John, Buffalo	1.000	4	3	2	0	5	1
Farrell, Mike, New Orleans*	1.000	29	5	8	0	13	0
Fordham, Tom, Nashville*	1.000	22	4	12	0	16	1
Fortugno, Tim, Indianapolis*	.889	41	2	6	1	9	0
Foster, Kevin, Iowa	.912	18	10	21	3	34	2
Frascatore, John, Louisville	.844	36	10	17	5	32	1
Frazier, Ron, Indianapolis	1.000	2	1	1	0	2	0
Gajkowski, Steve, Nashville	.973	49	6	30	1	37	3
Ganote, Joe, New Orleans	.923	41	7	17	2	26	1
Garcia, Ramon, New Orleans	1.000	11	1	8	0	9	0
Givens, Brian, Iowa	.909	29	11	19	3	33	2
Granger, Jeff, Omaha*	.800	45	6	6	3	15	1
GRAVES, Danny, Buffalo	1.000	43	11	23	0	34	2
Grigsby, Benji, Buffalo	1.000	8	0	1	0	1	0
Guzman, Jose, Iowa	1.000	8	5	6	0	11	0
Helling, Rick, Oklahoma City	.760	23	5	14	6	25	1
Heredia, Gil, Oklahoma City	1.000	6	1	0	0	1	0
Huisman, Rick, Omaha	1.000	27	1	4	0	5	1
Jackson, Danny, Louisville*	.800	8	1	3	1	5	2
Jarvis, Kevin, Indianapolis	1.000	8	3	8	0	11	0
Jean, Domingo, Indianapolis	1.000	7	1	0	0	1	0
Johnson, Barry, Nashville	1.000	38	4	12	0	16	0
Johnson, Jonathan, O.C.	1.000	1	1	2	0	3	0
Jones, Doug, New Orleans	1.000	13	3	3	0	6	0
Jones, Stacy, N.O.-Nash.	1.000	28	3	1	0	4	0
Karchner, Matt, Louisville	1.000	1	1	0	0	1	0
Keyser, Brian, Nashville	.818	6	4	5	2	11	0
Kiefer, Mark, N.O.-Oma.	.957	30	9	13	1	23	2
Lacy, Kerry, Oklahoma City	1.000	37	3	16	0	19	2
Levine, Alan, Nashville	1.000	43	3	11	0	14	1
Lewis, James, Buffalo	.952	21	6	14	1	21	0
Lilliquist, Derek, Indianapolis*	.833	47	0	5	1	6	0
Linton, Doug, Omaha	1.000	4	1	4	0	5	0
Lopez, Albie, Buffalo	.909	17	6	14	2	22	2
Lowe, Sean, Louisville	.920	25	8	15	2	25	2
Ludwick, Eric, Louisville	.667	11	1	3	2	6	0
Luebbers, Larry, Indianapolis	1.000	14	4	4	0	8	1
Magrane, Joe, Nashville*	1.000	21	1	3	0	4	0
Manning, David, Oklahoma City	1.000	1	0	1	0	1	0
Mauser, Tim, Oklahoma City	.000	8	0	0	1	1	0
Maxcy, Brian, Louisville	1.000	36	4	13	0	17	1
McElroy, Chuck, Indianapolis*	1.000	5	0	4	0	4	0
Meacham, Rusty, Omaha	1.000	23	1	14	0	15	0
Mercedes, Henry, Omaha	1.000	2	1	0	0	1	0
Mercedes, Jose, New Orleans	.958	25	16	7	1	24	0
Mercker, Kent, Buffalo*	1.000	3	1	1	0	2	0
Misuraca, Mike, New Orleans	.909	23	7	13	2	22	1
Montoya, Norm, New Orleans*	1.000	11	3	2	0	5	0
Moore, Marcus, Indianapolis	.846	15	4	7	2	13	0
Morgan, Mike, Louisville	.800	4	3	1	1	5	1
Morris, Matt, Louisville	1.000	1	0	1	0	1	0
Moten, Scott, Iowa	.750	21	2	4	2	8	0
Mutis, Jeff, Louisville*	1.000	32	1	13	0	14	1
Nichting, Chris, Oklahoma City	1.000	4	1	1	0	2	1
Ogea, Chad, Buffalo	1.000	5	1	3	0	4	0
Ojala, Kirt, Indianapolis*	.962	22	5	20	1	26	1
Olsen, Steve, Omaha	1.000	24	5	5	0	10	0
Olson, Gregg, Indianapolis	1.000	7	0	1	0	1	0
Osborne, Donovan, Louisville*	1.000	1	0	2	0	2	0
Patterson, Danny, Oklahoma City	1.000	44	9	6	0	15	1
Patterson, Ken, Omaha*	1.000	16	2	2	0	4	0
Perez, Mike, Iowa	1.000	23	3	4	0	7	0
Phillips, Tony, New Orleans	.875	20	3	4	1	8	2
Pittsley, Jim, Omaha	.909	13	5	5	1	11	0
Plantenberg, Erik, Buffalo*	1.000	17	0	3	0	3	0
Potts, Mike, New Orleans*	.875	11	2	5	1	8	0
Powell, Ross, Lou.-Ind.*	.889	17	4	4	1	9	1
Pugh, Tim, Indianapolis	1.000	4	0	2	0	2	0
Pulido, Carlos, Iowa*	1.000	28	4	13	0	17	1
Rain, Steve, Iowa	1.000	26	2	4	0	6	0
Ratliff, Jon, Iowa	.941	32	2	14	1	17	1
Remlinger, Mike, Indianapolis*	.880	28	2	20	3	25	1
Renko, Steve, Iowa	1.000	3	2	2	0	4	1
Rivera, Roberto, Iowa*	1.000	35	3	6	0	9	0
Roa, Joe, Buffalo	.962	26	24	27	2	53	2
Roberson, Sid, New Orleans*	1.000	2	0	3	0	3	0
Robinson, Ken, Omaha	1.000	6	1	1	0	2	0
Rodriguez, Frankie, New Orleans	.857	13	1	5	1	7	1
Rodriguez, Rich, Omaha*	.875	47	1	6	1	8	0

Player, Team	Pct.	G	PO	A	E	TC	DP
Rosado, Jose, Omaha*	1.000	15	5	13	0	18	2
Ruffcorn, Scott, Nashville	1.000	24	10	22	0	32	2
Rusch, Glendon, Omaha*	.957	28	4	18	1	23	2
Russell, Jeff, Oklahoma City	.667	5	1	1	1	3	0
Sanford, Mo, Oklahoma City	.926	30	7	18	2	27	0
Santana, Julio, Oklahoma City	.953	29	15	26	2	43	1
Sauveur, Rich, Nashville*	.909	61	7	13	2	22	0
Scanlan, Bob, Omaha	1.000	12	1	4	0	5	1
Schrenk, Steve, Nashville	.952	16	4	16	1	21	1
Scott, Darryl, Buffalo	1.000	50	2	10	0	12	0
Service, Scott, Indianapolis	.833	35	2	3	1	6	0
Shuey, Paul, Buffalo	1.000	19	1	1	0	2	0
Simmons, Scott, Louisville*	1.000	30	9	21	0	30	0
Sirotka, Mike, Nashville*	1.000	15	2	14	0	16	1
Slusarski, Joseph, New Orleans	.963	40	8	18	1	27	1
Smith, Dan, Oklahoma City*	.500	5	0	1	1	2	0
Sparks, Steve, New Orleans	1.000	11	5	7	0	12	1
Spradlin, Jerry, Indianapolis	.955	49	3	18	1	22	1
Steenstra, Kennie, Iowa	.951	26	10	29	2	41	3
Stefanski, Mike, Louisville	1.000	2	0	1	0	1	0
Sturtze, Tanyon, Iowa	.957	51	7	15	1	23	1
Sullivan, Scott, Indianapolis	.947	53	2	16	1	19	0
Swartzbaugh, Dave, Iowa	1.000	44	4	24	0	28	1
Tavarez, Julian, Buffalo	1.000	2	2	3	0	5	0
Telemaco, Amaury, Iowa	1.000	8	5	7	0	12	0
Thigpen, Bobby, Nashville	1.000	4	0	1	0	1	0

Player, Team	Pct.	G	PO	A	E	TC	D
Torres, Dilson, Omaha	.947	16	9	9	1	19	
Toth, Robert, Omaha	1.000	11	2	8	0	10	
Urbani, Tom, Louisville*	1.000	7	0	9	0	9	
Valera, Julio, Omaha	1.000	6	2	0	0	2	
VanEgmond, Tim, New Orleans	.917	7	7	4	1	12	
VanRyn, Ben, Louisville*	1.000	19	4	9	0	13	
Warren, Brian, Indianapolis	1.000	50	2	8	0	10	
Weger, Wes, New Orleans	1.000	1	0	1	0	1	
Wertz, Bill, Buffalo	1.000	17	1	3	0	4	
White, Gabe, Indianapolis*	1.000	11	0	7	0	7	
Whiteside, Matt, Oklahoma City	.913	36	6	15	2	23	
Whitten, Casey, Buffalo*	.818	12	3	6	2	11	
Wickander, Kevin, New Orleans*	.000	8	0	0	2	2	
Williams, Jimmy, Buffalo*	.941	35	4	12	1	17	
Worrell, Steve, Nashville*	1.000	11	1	1	0	2	
Zappelli, Mark, Nashville	1.000	9	1	1	0	2	

PITCHERS WITH TWO OR MORE TEAMS

Player, Team	Pct.	G	PO	A	E	TC	D
Jones, Stacy, New Orleans	1.000	9	3	1	0	4	
Jones, Stacy, Nashville	.000	19	0	0	0	0	
Kiefer, Mark, New Orleans	1.000	22	6	7	0	13	
Kiefer, Mark, Omaha	.900	8	3	6	1	10	
Powell, Ross, Louisville*	1.000	5	0	1	0	1	
Powell, Ross, Indianapolis*	.875	12	4	3	1	8	

The following players did not have any fielding statistics at the positions indicated or appeared only as a designated hitter, pinch-hitter or pinch-runner: P. Bryant, 3b; Cacer p; Carter, p; Deak, 3b; Eddy, p; Erdman, 3b; Estrada, of; Gross, p; Hall, dh; Halter, p; Haney, p-of; Hubbard, of; Hughes, 1b; Kloek, p; Kmak, 1b; Magnante, p; McDill, p; McFar dh; Mejia, 3b; Petkovsek, p; Ralston, p; C. Smith, p; Talanoa, p; Valdez, ph; Vierra, p; Wakamatsu, c; Ward, dh-ph; T. Wilson, ss.

LEAGUE CHAMPIONS

Year Team	Pct.
1902— Indianapolis	.683
1903— St. Paul	.657
1904— St. Paul	.646
1905— Columbus	.658
1906— Columbus	.615
1907— Columbus	.584
1908— Indianapolis	.601
1909— Louisville	.554
1910— Minneapolis	.637
1911— Minneapolis	.600
1912— Minneapolis	.636
1913— Milwaukee	.599
1914— Milwaukee	.590
1915— Minneapolis	.597
1916— Louisville	.605
1917— Indianapolis	.588
1918— Kansas City	.589
1919— St. Paul	.610
1920— St. Paul	.701
1921— Louisville	.583
1922— St. Paul	.641
1923— Kansas City	.675
1924— St. Paul	.578
1925— Louisville	.635
1926— Louisville	.629
1927— Toledo	.601
1928— Indianapolis	.593
1929— Kansas City	.665
1930— Louisville	.608
1931— St. Paul	.623
1932— Minneapolis	.595
1933— Columbus*	.604
Minneapolis	.562
1934— Minneapolis	.570
Columbus*	.556
1935— Minneapolis	.591
1936— Milwaukee†	.584
1937— Columbus†	.584
1938— St. Paul	.596
Kansas City (2nd)‡	.556
1939— Kansas City	.695
Louisville (4th)‡	.490
1940— Kansas City	.625
Louisville (4th)‡	.500
1941— Columbus†	.621
1942— Kansas City	.549
Columbus (3rd)‡	.532

Year Team	Pct.
1943— Milwaukee	.596
Columbus (3rd)‡	.532
1944— Milwaukee	.667
Louisville (3rd)‡	.574
1945— Milwaukee	.604
Louisville (3rd)‡	.545
1946— Louisville†	.601
1947— Kansas City	.608
Milwaukee (3rd)†	.513
1948— Indianapolis	.649
St. Paul (3rd)‡	.558
1949— St. Paul	.608
Indianapolis (2nd)‡	.604
1950— Minneapolis	.584
Columbus (3rd)‡	.549
1951— Milwaukee†	.623
1952— Milwaukee	.656
Kansas City (2nd)‡	.578
1953— Toledo	.584
Kansas City (2nd)‡	.571
1954— Indianapolis	.625
Louisville (2nd)‡	.556
1955— Minneapolis†	.597
1956— Indianapolis†	.597
1957— Wichita	.604
Denver (2nd)†	.584
1958— Charleston	.589
Minneapolis (3rd)‡	.536
1959— Louisville§	.599
Omaha§	.516
Minneapolis (2nd)‡	.586
1960— Denver	.571
Louisville (2nd)‡	.556
1961— Indianapolis	.573
Louisville (2nd)‡	.553
1962— Indianapolis	.605
Louisville (4th)‡	.486
1963-1968—Did not operate.	
1969— Omaha	.607
1970— Omaha*	.529
Denver	.504
1971— Indianapolis	.604
Denver*	.521
1972— Wichita	.621
Evansville*	.593
1973— Iowa	.610
Tulsa*	.504

Year Team	Pc
1974— Indianapolis	.57
Tulsa*	.56
1975— Evansville*	.56
Denver	.56
1976— Denver*	.63
Omaha	.57
1977— Omaha	.56
Denver*	.52
1978— Indianapolis	.57
Omaha*	.48
1979— Evansville*	.57
Oklahoma City	.53
1980— Denver	.67
Springfield*	.55
1981— Omaha	.58
Denver*	.55
1982— Indianapolis*	.55
Omaha	.51
1983— Louisville	.57
Denver‡	.54
1984— Denver	.51
Louisville‡	.51
1985— Oklahoma City	.55
Louisville*	.52
1986— Indianapolis*	.56
Denver	.53
1987— Denver	.56
Indianapolis‡	.53
1988— Indianapolis	.62
Omaha	.5
1989— Indianapolis*	.59
Omaha	.50
1990— Omaha*	.58
Nashville	.58
1991— Buffalo	.56
Denver*	.54
1992— Buffalo	.60
Oklahoma City*	.51
1993— Iowa*	.59
Nashville	.56
1994— Indianapolis‡	.60
Nashville	.57
1995— Louisville	.61
Louisville‡	.51
1996— Buffalo	.58
Oklahoma City‡	.5

*Won playoff (East vs. West). †Won championship and four-team playoff. ‡Won four-team playoff. §Respective Eastern and Western division winners.

INTERNATIONAL LEAGUE

LEAGUE OFFICE

President
Randy Mobley

Address
55 S. High St., Suite 202
Dublin, OH 43017

Phone
614-791-9300

TEAMS

CHARLOTTE KNIGHTS

General manager
Pete Moore

Manager
Carlos Tosca

Ballpark (capacity, surface)
Knights Stadium (10,000, grass)

Affiliation
Marlins

Address
P.O. Box 1207
Fort Mill, SC 29716

Phone
803-548-8050

COLUMBUS CLIPPERS

General manager
Ken Schnacke

Manager
Stump Merrill

Ballpark (capacity, surface)
Cooper Stadium (15,000, artificial)

Affiliation
Yankees

Address
1155 W. Mound St.
Columbus, OH 43223

Phone
614-462-5250

NORFOLK TIDES

General manager
Dave Rosenfield

Manager
Rick Dempsey

Ballpark (capacity, surface)
Harbor Park (12,059, grass)

Affiliation
Mets

Address
150 Park Ave.
Norfolk, VA 23510

Phone
804-622-2222

OTTAWA LYNX

Director of baseball operations
Joe Bohringer

Manager
Pat Kelly

Ballpark (capacity, surface)
Ottawa Stadium (10,332, grass)

Affiliation
Expos

Address
300 Coventry Rd.
Ottawa, Ontario K1K 4P5

Phone
613-747-5969

PAWTUCKET RED SOX

General manager
Lou Schwechheimer

Manager
Ken Macha

Ballpark (capacity, surface)
McCoy Stadium (7,002, grass)

Affiliation
Red Sox

Address
P.O. Box 2365
Pawtucket, RI 02861

Phone
401-724-7300

RICHMOND BRAVES

General manager
Bruce Baldwin

Manager
Bill Dancy

Ballpark (capacity, surface)
The Diamond (12,156, grass)

Affiliation
Braves

Address
P.O. Box 6667
Richmond, VA 23230

Phone
804-359-4444

ROCHESTER RED WINGS

General manager
Dan Mason

Manager
Marv Foley

Ballpark (capacity, surface)
Frontier Field (10,600, grass)

Affiliation
Orioles

Address
1 Morrie Silver Way
Rochester, NY 14608

Phone
716-454-1001

SCRANTON/WILKES-BARRE BARONS

General manager
Bill Terlecky

Manager
Marc Bombard

Ballpark (capacity, surface)
Lackawanna County Stadium (10,832, artificial)

Affiliation
Phillies

Address
P.O. Box 3449
Scranton, PA 18505

Phone
717-969-2255

SYRACUSE SKY CHIEFS

General manager
John Simone

Manager
Garth Iorg

Ballpark (capacity, surface)
P&C Stadium (11,100, grass)

Affiliation
Blue Jays

Address
P&C Stadium
Syracuse, NY 13208

Phone
315-474-7833

TOLEDO MUD HENS

General manager
Gene Cook

Manager
Glenn Ezell

Ballpark (capacity, surface)
Ned Skeldon Stadium (10,025, grass)

Affiliation
Tigers

Address
P.O. Box 6212
Toledo, OH 43614

Phone
419-893-9483

1996 FINAL STANDINGS

EAST DIVISION

Team	W	L	T	Pct.	GB
Pawtucket (Red Sox)	78	64	0	.549	....
Rochester (Orioles)	72	69	0	.511	5$^{1}/_{2}$
Scranton/Wilkes-Barre (Phillies)	70	72	0	.493	8
Syracuse (Blue Jays)	67	75	0	.472	11
Ottawa (Expos)	60	82	0	.423	18

WEST DIVISION

Team	W	L	T	Pct.	GB
Columbus (Yankees)	85	57	0	.599	....
Norfolk (Mets)	82	59	0	.582	2$^{1}/_{2}$
Toledo (Tigers)	70	72	0	.493	15
Richmond (Braves)	62	79	1	.440	22$^{1}/_{2}$
Charlotte (Marlins)	62	79	1	.440	22$^{1}/_{2}$

COMPOSITE

Team	Col.	Nor.	Paw.	Roch.	Tol.	SWB	Syr.	Rich.	Char.	Ott.	W	L	T	Pct.	GB
Columbus (Yankees)	....	8	8	8	11	8	10	14	10	8	85	57	0	.599	....
Norfolk (Mets)	10	....	10	7	9	9	8	11	9	8	82	59	0	.582	2$^{1}/_{2}$
Pawtucket (Red Sox)	6	4	....	11	9	12	7	8	7	14	78	64	0	.549	7
Rochester (Orioles)	6	6	7	....	8	7	13	8	5	12	72	69	0	.511	12$^{1}/_{2}$
Toledo (Tigers)	7	9	5	6	....	6	9	9	8	11	70	72	0	.493	15
Scranton/Wilkes-Barre (Phillies)	6	5	6	11	8	....	10	8	8	8	70	72	0	.493	15
Syracuse (Blue Jays)	4	6	11	5	5	8	....	8	10	10	67	75	0	.472	18
Richmond (Braves)	4	7	6	6	9	6	6	....	12	6	62	79	1	.440	22$^{1}/_{2}$
Charlotte (Marlins)	8	9	7	9	10	6	4	5	....	4	62	79	1	.440	22$^{1}/_{2}$
Ottawa (Expos)	6	5	4	6	3	10	8	8	10	....	60	82	0	.423	25

Major league affiliations in parentheses.

PLAYOFFS: Columbus defeated Norfolk, three games to none; Rochester defeated Pawtucket, three games to one; Columbus defeated Rochester, three games to none, to win league championship.

REGULAR-SEASON ATTENDANCE: Charlotte, 326,761; Columbus, 526,599; Norfolk, 506,965; Ottawa, 347,050; Pawtucket, 461,181; Richmond 500,035; Rochester, 375,781; Scranton/Wilkes-Barre, 458,033; Syracuse, 300,410; Toledo, 316,126. Total—4,487,154. Playoffs (10 games)—32,821. Class AAA All-Star Game at Salt Lake City—15,500.

MANAGERS: Charlotte, Sal Rende; Columbus, Stump Merrill; Norfolk, Bobby Valentine (through August 25) and Bruce Benedict (August 26 through end of season); Ottawa, Pete Mackanin; Pawtucket, Buddy Bailey; Richmond, Bill Dancy; Rochester, Harv Foley; Scranton/Wilkes-Barre, Butch Hobson (through May 5) and Ramon Aviles (May 7 through end of season); Syracuse, Richie Hebner; Toledo, Tom Runnells. Managerial record of teams with more than one manager: Norfolk, Valentine, 76-57, Benedict, 6-2; Scranton/Wilkes-Barre, Hobson, 13-14, Aviles, 57-58.

ALL-STAR TEAM: 1B—Ivan Cruz, Columbus; 2B—Jason Hardtke, Norfolk; 3B—Phil Hiatt, Toledo; SS—Clay Bellinger, Rochester; OF—Rudy Pemberton, Pawtucket; Billy McMillon, Charlotte; Phil Clark, Charlotte; C—Jorge Posada, Columbus; DH—Jerry Brooks, Charlotte; Starting pitcher—Mike Fyhrie, Norfolk; Relief pitcher—Derek Wallace, Norfolk; Most Valuable Player—Phil Hiatt, Toledo; Most Valuable Pitcher—Mike Fyhrie, Norfolk; Rookie of the Year— Billy McMillon, Charlotte; Manager of the Year—Buddy Bailey, Pawtucket.

1996 BATTING

TEAM

Team	Avg.	G	TPA	AB	R	H	TB	2B	3B	HR	RBI	SH	SF	HP	BB	IBB	SO	SB	CS	GDP	LOB	ShO	Slg.	OB
Charlotte	.284	142	5153	4656	722	1320	2116	271	15	165	681	35	35	35	391	17	832	99	59	117	877	3	.454	.34
Pawtucket	.282	142	5407	4782	840	1350	2350	301	36	209	790	28	40	60	497	13	932	84	49	116	942	3	.491	.35
Rochester	.281	141	5234	4641	727	1304	2067	258	56	131	675	17	54	33	488	11	855	117	55	96	974	6	.445	.35
Columbus	.272	142	5279	4665	766	1268	2111	298	46	151	713	25	52	51	483	18	858	100	49	98	914	6	.453	.34
Ottawa	.269	142	5176	4618	606	1240	1855	241	34	102	.565	69	36	48	404	29	798	160	64	103	936	3	.402	.33
Norfolk	.267	141	5250	4645	643	1238	1910	258	42	110	605	69	43	56	437	27	900	109	63	77	977	6	.411	.33
Richmond	.264	142	5080	4604	593	1215	1808	253	20	100	543	50	32	34	360	22	966	92	68	94	888	13	.393	.32
Syracuse	.263	142	5295	4624	694	1215	1863	236	47	106	620	40	48	49	532	19	815	167	74	90	975	7	.403	.34
Scr./Wil.-Bar.	.258	142	5270	4692	640	1210	1851	240	49	101	583	43	41	43	450	14	819	92	49	118	954	9	.395	.32
Toledo	.256	142	5275	4675	716	1195	1989	221	39	165	670	28	38	43	490	12	1086	130	62	95	912	6	.425	.32

INDIVIDUAL

TOP QUALIFIERS FOR BATTING CHAMPIONSHIP

Minimum 383 plate appearances. *Lefthanded batter. †Switch-hitter.

Player, Team	Avg.	G	TPA	AB	R	H	TB	2B	3B	HR	RBI	SH	SF	HP	BB	IBB	SO	SB	CS	GDP	Slg.	OB
McMillon, Billy, Charlotte*	.352	97	390	347	72	122	209	32	2	17	70	0	2	5	36	0	76	5	3	8	.602	.41
Pemberton, Rudy, Pawtucket	.326	102	429	396	77	129	244	28	3	27	92	0	1	14	18	0	63	16	7	12	.616	.37
Clark, Phil, Charlotte	.325	97	399	369	57	120	196	36	2	12	66	0	3	10	17	4	32	3	6	10	.531	.36
Franco, Matt, Norfolk*	.323	133	557	508	74	164	229	40	2	7	81	1	9	3	36	3	55	5	2	10	.451	.36
Bieser, Steve, Ottawa#	.322	123	448	382	63	123	158	24	4	1	32	23	2	6	35	4	55	27	7	6	.414	.38
Olmeda, Jose, Charlotte*	.320	115	404	375	52	120	175	26	1	9	49	4	3	1	21	0	58	7	6	7	.467	.35
Barron, Tony, Ottawa	.320	105	427	394	58	126	201	29	2	14	59	3	1	9	20	1	74	9	4	12	.510	.36
Zuber, Jon, Scr./W.-B.*	.311	118	477	412	62	128	172	22	5	4	59	2	4	1	58	3	50	4	2	15	.417	.39
Bellinger, Clay, Rochester	.301	125	510	459	68	138	225	34	4	15	78	1	7	6	39	0	90	8	4	6	.490	.34
Stewart, Shannon, Syracuse	.298	112	485	420	77	125	185	26	8	6	42	5	4	2	54	0	61	35	8	6	.440	.37
Hosey, Dwayne, Pawtucket#	.297	93	415	367	77	109	184	25	4	14	53	0	5	3	40	2	67	20	7	3	.501	.36
Pecorilli, Aldo, Richmond	.290	122	441	403	61	117	189	27	0	15	62	1	3	3	31	1	87	5	6	8	.469	.34
Schall, Gene, Scr./W.-B.	.288	104	433	371	66	107	184	16	5	17	67	0	5	9	48	2	92	1	0	9	.496	.37
Hall, Joe, Rochester	.288	131	554	479	96	138	241	26	10	19	95	0	6	2	67	3	69	15	9	8	.503	.37
Woodson, Tracy, Columbus	.288	114	450	420	53	121	224	34	3	21	81	0	11	3	16	2	52	4	0	5	.533	.33
Brooks, Jerry, Charlotte	.288	136	502	466	72	134	269	29	2	34	107	0	2	2	32	3	78	5	5	17	.577	.33

DEPARTMENTAL LEADERS: G—Hiatt, 142; AB—Hiatt, 555; R—Hiatt, 99; H—Franco, 164; TB—Hiatt, 304; 2B—Franco, 40; 3B—Hall, 10; HR—Hiatt, 42; RBI—Hiatt, 119; SH—Bieser, 23; SF—Bellinger, Woodson, 11; HP—Pemberton, Penn, 14; BB—Posada, 79; IBB—Petagine, 7; SO—Hiatt, 180; SB—Stewart, 35; CS—Pose, GIDP—Brooks, 17; Slg.—Pemberton, .616; OBP—McMillon, .418.

*Lefthanded batter. †Switch-hitter.

Player, Team	Avg.	G	TPA	AB	R	H	TB	2B	3B	HR	RBI	SH	SF	HP	BB	IBB	SO	SB	CS	GDP	Slg.	OBP
bbott, Kurt, Charlotte	.377	18	78	69	20	26	53	10	1	5	11	0	1	1	7	0	18	2	0	1	.768	.436
cevedo, Juan, Norfolk	.077	19	16	13	0	1	1	0	0	0	0	2	0	0	1	0	7	0	0	0	.077	.143
damson, Joel, Charlotte*	.125	44	12	8	1	1	1	0	0	0	0	3	0	0	1	0	2	0	0	0	.125	.222
driana, Sharnol, Syracuse	.281	90	326	292	48	82	134	12	5	10	37	2	0	8	24	1	72	18	7	5	.459	.352
gbayani, Benny, Norfolk	.278	99	372	331	43	92	144	13	9	7	56	3	5	3	30	3	57	14	5	5	.435	.339
hearne, Pat, Norfolk	.000	5	4	4	0	0	0	0	0	0	0	0	0	0	0	0	3	0	0	0	.000	.000
fonseca, Antonio, Charlotte	.190	14	23	21	3	4	5	1	0	0	1	2	0	0	0	0	6	0	0	1	.238	.190
varez, Tavo, Ottawa	.067	20	15	15	1	1	1	0	0	0	0	0	0	0	0	0	1	1	0	0	.067	.067
maro, Ruben, Syr-Scr/W.B.†	.270	68	264	230	36	62	85	11	3	2	24	2	0	7	24	0	40	13	3	4	.370	.356
ucoin, Derek, Ottawa	.500	52	3	2	0	1	1	0	0	0	0	0	0	0	1	0	1	0	0	0	.500	.667
usanio, Joe, Norfolk	.000	35	1	1	0	0	0	0	0	0	0	0	0	0	0	0	1	0	0	0	.000	.000
vila, Rolo, Rochester	.298	12	51	47	7	14	18	2	1	0	6	0	0	1	3	0	4	2	0	0	.383	.353
yrault, Joe, Richmond	.229	98	349	314	23	72	102	15	0	5	34	2	4	3	26	4	57	1	1	12	.325	.291
aez, Kevin, Toledo	.245	98	337	302	34	74	125	12	3	11	44	5	4	2	24	0	53	3	0	6	.414	.301
akkum, Scott, Paw-Scr/W.B.	.000	44	2	2	0	0	0	0	0	0	0	0	0	0	0	0	2	0	0	0	.000	.000
ark, Brian, Norfolk*	.000	13	2	2	0	0	0	0	0	0	0	0	0	0	0	0	0	0	0	0	.000	.000
arker, Glen, Toledo	.250	24	91	80	13	20	24	2	1	0	2	2	0	0	9	0	25	6	6	1	.300	.326
arker, Tim, Columbus	.266	116	466	402	71	107	156	27	8	2	45	2	4	2	56	1	57	24	8	3	.388	.356
arron, Tony, Ottawa	.320	105	427	394	58	126	201	29	2	14	59	3	1	9	20	1	74	9	4	12	.510	.366
atista, Miguel, Charlotte	.000	47	4	4	1	0	0	0	0	0	0	0	0	0	0	0	3	0	0	0	.000	.000
attle, Howard, Scr./W-B	.228	115	422	391	37	89	139	24	1	8	44	2	6	2	21	0	53	3	8	15	.355	.267
axter, Bob, Ottawa*	.250	54	5	4	0	1	1	0	0	0	2	1	0	0	0	0	2	0	0	0	.250	.250
eech, Matt, Scr./W-B.*	.250	2	8	8	0	2	3	1	0	0	1	0	0	0	0	0	3	0	0	0	.375	.250
ell, Juan, Pawtucket†	.248	68	239	210	28	52	84	13	2	5	23	5	2	0	22	0	43	2	2	5	.400	.316
ellinger, Clay, Rochester	.301	125	510	459	68	138	225	34	4	15	78	1	11	6	33	0	90	8	4	6	.490	.348
eltre, Esteban, Scr/W.B.-Rich.	.209	14	44	43	4	9	12	3	0	0	1	0	0	0	1	0	3	0	0	2	.279	.227
enavides, Freddie, Columbus	.000	1	4	4	0	0	0	0	0	0	0	1	0	0	0	0	0	0	0	0	.000	.000
enbow, Lou, Richmond	.232	91	270	250	21	58	69	8	0	1	23	1	3	0	16	1	65	3	4	6	.276	.275
enitez, Yamil, Ottawa	.278	114	474	439	56	122	215	20	2	23	81	0	6	1	28	5	120	11	4	5	.490	.319
enjamin, Mike, Scr./W.-B.	.385	4	17	13	2	5	7	2	0	0	4	0	1	0	3	2	0	0	0	1	.538	.471
ennett, Gary, Scr./W-B	.248	91	319	286	37	71	112	15	1	8	37	3	3	3	24	2	43	1	0	10	.392	.310
eser, Steve, Ottawa†	.322	123	448	382	63	123	158	24	4	1	32	23	2	6	35	4	55	27	7	6	.414	.386
azier, Ron, Scr./W-B.	.000	33	3	2	0	0	0	0	0	0	0	0	1	0	0	0	1	0	0	0	.000	.000
osser, Greg, Rochester*	.235	38	127	115	11	27	41	6	1	2	12	0	0	0	12	0	29	2	1	3	.357	.307
orowski, Joe, Richmond	.000	34	3	3	0	0	0	0	0	0	0	0	0	0	0	0	2	0	0	0	.000	.000
oston, D.J., Syracuse*	.247	26	100	85	12	21	40	7	0	4	12	0	1	0	14	0	23	0	1	3	.471	.350
oucher, Denis, Ottawa	.429	17	8	7	2	3	3	0	0	0	0	0	1	0	0	0	2	0	0	0	.429	.429
owers, Brent, Rochester*	.325	49	223	206	40	67	95	8	4	4	19	3	0	0	14	0	41	9	3	1	.461	.368
rito, Mario, Charlotte	1.000	6	1	1	1	1	4	0	0	1	1	0	0	0	0	0	0	0	0	0	4.000	1.000
rito, Tilson, Syracuse	.278	108	450	400	63	111	179	22	8	10	54	3	4	5	38	1	65	11	10	8	.448	.345
rock, Chris, Norfolk	.241	30	34	29	2	7	8	1	0	0	2	2	0	1	2	0	6	0	0	0	.276	.313
rooks, Jerry, Charlotte	.288	136	502	466	72	134	269	29	2	34	107	0	2	2	32	3	78	5	5	17	.577	.335
rown, Jarvis, Rochester	.211	57	228	204	28	43	73	6	6	4	19	0	3	2	19	0	36	9	1	5	.358	.281
rown, Randy, Pawtucket	.167	3	7	6	0	1	1	0	0	0	1	0	0	0	1	0	1	0	0	1	.167	.286
uccheri, Jim, Ottawa	.257	65	244	206	40	53	67	2	4	1	12	1	2	2	33	0	28	33	6	1	.325	.362
urrows, Terry, Columbus*	.000	23	1	1	0	0	0	0	0	0	0	0	0	0	0	0	1	0	0	0	.000	.000
urton, Essex, Norfolk	.172	16	66	58	4	10	13	3	0	0	1	0	0	1	7	0	16	5	3	1	.224	.273
utler, Robert, Scr./W-B.*	.255	91	321	298	39	76	119	15	8	4	34	2	0	1	20	1	45	3	5	6	.399	.304
yrd, Paul, Norfolk	.500	5	2	2	0	1	1	0	0	0	0	0	0	0	0	0	1	0	0	0	.500	.500
airo, Miguel, Syracuse	.277	120	509	465	71	129	160	14	4	3	48	5	5	8	26	1	44	27	9	5	.344	.323
anseco, Jose, Pawtucket	.200	2	5	5	0	1	1	0	0	0	0	0	0	0	0	0	3	0	0	0	.200	.200
arpenter, Bubba, Columbus*	.245	132	517	466	55	114	164	23	3	7	48	2	1	0	48	1	80	10	7	7	.352	.315
asanova, Raul, Toledo	.273	49	188	161	23	44	79	11	0	8	28	1	4	2	20	0	24	0	1	11	.491	.353
astillo, Alberto, Norfolk	.208	113	394	341	34	71	118	12	1	11	39	7	3	4	39	1	67	2	2	3	.346	.295
astleberry, Kevin, Ottawa*	.280	66	222	193	27	54	77	8	3	3	22	6	2	0	21	4	27	9	5	2	.399	.347
hamberlain, Wes, Syracuse	.344	37	153	131	20	45	80	5	0	10	37	0	1	0	19	2	19	2	1	5	.611	.424
havez, Raul, Ottawa	.247	60	214	198	15	49	65	10	0	2	24	4	0	1	11	0	31	0	2	7	.328	.290
hergey, Dan, Charlotte	.000	47	4	3	0	0	0	0	0	0	0	1	0	0	0	0	1	0	0	0	.000	.000
himelis, Joel, Norfolk	.382	25	83	76	9	29	35	6	0	4	22	0	0		5	1	12	1	0	4	.461	.420
apinski, Chris, Charlotte†	.285	105	426	362	74	103	155	20	1	10	39	8	5	3	47	0	54	13	6	7	.428	.367
ark, Phil, Pawtucket	.325	97	399	369	57	120	196	36	2	12	69	0	3	10	17	4	32	3	6	10	.531	.368
ark, Tony, Toledo†	.299	55	225	194	42	58	109	7	1	14	36	0	0		31	0	58	1	1	3	.562	.396
ole, Alex, Pawtucket*	.296	82	362	304	57	90	132	14	8	4	39	4	2	2	50	1	47	11	7	3	.434	.397
ookson, Brent, Paw.-Roch.	.269	103	411	368	73	99	196	20	1	25	71	0	3	7	33	1	92	4	5	14	.533	.338
oolbaugh, Scott, Ottawa	.208	58	201	173	20	36	59	12	1	3	22	1	4	0	23	1	37	2	2	7	.341	.295
ordero, Wil, Pawtucket	.300	4	12	10	2	3	7	1	0	1	2	0	0	0	3	0	3	0	0	1	.700	.417
otton, John, Toledo*	.187	50	182	171	14	32	53	7	1	4	19	2	0	2	7	0	64	4	4	1	.310	.228
ox, Darron, Richmond	.238	55	180	168	19	40	58	9	0	3	20	2	2	3	5	0	22	1	0	5	.345	.270
radle, Rickey, Syracuse	.200	40	147	130	22	26	61	5	3	8	22	0	2	1	14	1	39	1	0	2	.469	.279
rawford, Carlos, Scr./W-B.	.091	28	26	22	0	2	2	0	0	0	0	0	0	0	2	0	6	0	0	0	.091	.167
rawford, Joe, Norfolk*	.429	24	24	21	2	9	13	2	1	0	3	1	0	1	0	0	6	0	0	0	.619	.478
respo, Felipe, Syracuse†	.282	98	426	355	53	100	149	25	2	6	58	2	4	9	56	2	39	10	11	7	.420	.389
ruz, Fausto, Toledo	.250	107	422	384	49	96	154	18	2	12	59	2	2	1	33	0	81	11	10	7	.401	.310
ruz, Ivan, Columbus*	.258	130	513	446	86	115	225	26	0	28	96	2	9	8	48	3	99	2	4	9	.504	.335
alesandro, Mark, Columbus	.282	78	279	255	34	72	115	29	4	2	38	0	2	5	17	0	31	2	0	9	.451	.337
aubach, Brian, Norfolk*	.204	17	61	54	7	11	13	2	0	0	6	0	1	0	6	0	14	1	1	1	.241	.279
elgado, Alex, Pawtucket	.216	27	95	88	15	19	25	3	1	0	6	0	0	0	7	0	11	0	0	5	.284	.274
elvecchio, Nick, Columbus*	1.000	2	4	1	0	1	1	0	0	0	0	0	0	0	3	0	0	0	0	0	1.000	1.000
enson, Drew, Rochester	.350	16	67	60	14	21	36	7	1	2	10	0	0	0	7	0	12	0	0	1	.600	.418

CLASS AAA International League

Player, Team	Avg.	G	TPA	AB	R	H	TB	2B	3B	HR	RBI	SH	SF	HP	BB	IBB	SO	SB	CS	GDP	Slg.	OB
Dettmer, John, Richmond	.000	19	5	4	1	0	0	0	0	0	0	1	0	0	0	0	1	0	0	0	.000	.000
Devarez, Cesar, Rochester	.287	67	239	223	24	64	87	9	1	4	27	2	4	1	9	0	26	5	1	7	.390	.312
Diaz, Mario, Col.-Scr./W.B.	.274	62	256	241	29	66	90	9	0	5	33	1	1	1	12	0	15	0	2	8	.373	.310
Dismuke, Jamie, Syracuse*	.167	19	48	42	3	7	8	1	0	0	5	0	1	0	5	0	5	1	0	1	.190	.250
Dodd, Robert, Scr./W.-B.*	.333	8	4	3	0	1	1	0	0	0	0	1	0	0	0	1	0	0	0	0	.333	.333
Dodson, Bo, Pawtucket*	.344	82	313	276	37	95	148	20	0	11	43	1	3	1	32	1	50	4	0	7	.536	.410
Dorlarque, Aaron, Ottawa	.000	14	1	1	0	0	0	0	0	0	0	0	0	0	0	0	0	0	0	0	.000	.000
Doster, David, Scr./W.-B.	.258	89	358	322	37	83	124	20	0	7	48	3	5	2	26	1	54	7	3	8	.385	.313
Duncan, Mariano, Columbus..	.200	2	6	5	0	1	1	0	0	0	2	0	1	0	0	0	2	0	0	0	.200	.167
Dye, Jermaine, Richmond	.232	36	148	142	25	33	60	7	1	6	19	0	1	0	5	0	25	3	0	3	.423	.264
Eenhoorn, Robert, Columbus.	.337	55	200	172	28	58	77	14	1	1	16	3	3	1	21	0	18	7	2	3	.448	.406
Elliott, Donnie, Scr./W.-B.	.050	21	22	20	0	1	1	0	0	0	1	1	0	0	1	0	5	0	1	0	.050	.095
Estalella, Bobby, Scr./W.-B.	.250	11	41	36	7	9	21	3	0	3	8	0	0	0	5	0	10	0	0	1	.583	.341
Fagley, Dan, Charlotte	.000	2	1	1	1	0	0	0	0	0	0	0	0	0	0	0	0	0	0	0	.000	.000
Falteisek, Steve, Ottawa	.500	12	7	6	0	3	4	1	0	0	0	1	0	0	0	0	2	0	0	0	.667	.500
Fermin, Felix, Columbus	.211	7	25	19	3	4	4	0	0	0	3	0	1	2	3	0	1	0	0	1	.211	.360
Figga, Mike, Columbus	.273	4	12	11	3	3	4	1	0	0	0	0	0	0	1	0	3	0	0	0	.364	.333
Figueroa, Bien, Rochester	.312	50	169	154	25	48	58	7	0	1	16	1	0	0	14	0	11	3	1	5	.377	.369
Fisher, David, Scr./W.-B.	.156	26	72	64	6	10	14	1	0	1	3	0	0	1	7	0	15	1	1	0	.219	.250
Flora, Kevin, Norfolk	.222	46	150	135	20	30	49	8	1	3	15	0	0	4	11	2	40	9	2	5	.363	.300
Flores, Jose, Scr./W.-B.	.257	26	86	70	10	18	19	1	0	0	3	1	1	2	12	0	10	0	1	2	.271	.376
Floyd, Cliff, Ottawa*	.303	20	84	76	7	23	31	3	1	1	8	0	0	1	7	1	20	2	2	0	.408	.369
Fox, Chad, Richmond	.000	18	21	19	0	0	0	0	0	0	0	1	0	0	1	0	10	0	0	1	.000	.095
Franco, Matt, Norfolk*	.323	133	557	508	74	164	229	40	2	7	81	0	9	3	36	3	55	5	2	10	.451	.365
Franklin, Micah, Toledo†	.246	53	209	179	32	44	77	10	1	7	21	0	3	0	27	0	60	3	2	1	.430	.354
Fuller, Aaron, Pawtucket†	.500	1	2	2	0	1	1	0	0	0	0	0	0	0	0	0	0	0	0	0	.500	.500
Fyhrie, Mike, Norfolk	.111	28	28	27	1	3	5	2	0	0	1	0	0	0	1	0	10	0	0	0	.185	.143
Garcia, Omar, Richmond	.264	93	325	311	36	82	111	15	1	4	35	2	2	1	9	1	32	4	4	6	.357	.285
Garciaparra, Nomar, Paw.	.343	43	191	172	40	59	126	15	2	16	46	0	4	1	14	0	21	3	1	6	.733	.387
Gardiner, Mike, Norfolk†	.105	24	23	19	0	2	3	1	0	0	5	2	1	0	1	0	4	0	0	1	.158	.143
Gilbert, Shawn, Norfolk	.256	131	562	493	76	126	183	28	1	9	50	14	4	5	46	0	97	17	9	5	.371	.323
Giovanola, Ed, Richmond*	.295	62	252	210	29	62	88	15	1	3	16	4	0	1	37	3	34	2	6	2	.419	.403
Gordon, Keith, Rochester	.250	33	113	104	15	26	47	4	1	5	19	0	0	0	9	0	27	0	3	3	.452	.310
Graffanino, Tony, Richmond	.283	96	396	353	57	100	154	29	2	7	33	5	1	3	34	2	72	11	7	3	.436	.350
Greene, Tommy, Scr./W.-B.	.167	5	6	6	0	1	2	1	0	0	0	0	0	0	0	0	0	0	0	0	.333	.167
Greenwell, Mike, Pawtucket*	.273	3	12	11	3	3	9	0	0	2	2	0	0	0	1	0	1	0	0	0	.818	.333
Gregg, Tommy, Charlotte*	.286	119	461	405	69	116	206	24	0	22	80	0	4	3	49	3	62	10	1	8	.509	.364
Grijak, Kevin, Richmond*	.367	13	36	30	3	11	17	3	0	1	8	0	0	1	5	0	7	0	1	1	.567	.472
Grott, Matt, Scr./W.B.-Roch.*	.083	32	12	12	0	1	1	0	0	0	1	0	0	0	0	0	4	0	0	1	.083	.083
Hall, Joe, Rochester	.288	131	554	499	96	138	241	26	10	19	95	0	6	2	67	3	69	15	9	8	.503	.374
Halter, Shane, Charlotte	.293	16	45	41	3	12	13	1	0	0	4	0	2	0	2	0	8	0	0	0	.317	.311
Hammond, Chris, Charlotte*..	.500	1	2	2	1	1	2	1	0	0	0	0	0	0	0	0	0	0	0	0	1.000	.500
Hammonds, Jeffrey, Roch.	.272	34	148	125	24	34	51	4	2	3	19	0	3	1	19	0	19	3	1	2	.408	.365
Hansen, Terrel, Toledo	.125	5	20	16	2	2	5	0	0	1	1	0	0	3	1	0	8	1	0	0	.313	.300
Hardtke, Jason, Norfolk†	.300	71	292	257	49	77	125	17	2	9	35	4	2	0	29	1	29	4	6	4	.486	.368
Hatteberg, Scott, Pawtucket*	.268	90	351	287	52	77	129	16	0	12	49	1	3	2	58	0	66	1	1	6	.449	.391
Heffernan, Bert, Ottawa*	.303	64	215	198	20	60	73	8	1	1	27	0	2	1	14	0	15	1	4	5	.369	.349
Heflin, Bronson, Scr./W.-B.	.000	30	2	1	0	0	0	0	0	0	0	0	1	0	0	0	0	0	0	0	.000	.000
Held, Dan, Scr./W.-B.	.000	4	16	14	1	0	0	0	0	0	0	0	0	1	1	0	6	0	0	0	.000	.125
Henderson, Rod, Ottawa	.000	25	17	12	0	0	0	0	0	0	0	3	0	0	2	0	4	0	0	0	.000	.143
Hernandez, Livan, Charlotte	.400	10	5	5	1	2	2	0	0	0	1	0	0	0	0	0	2	0	0	0	.400	.400
Hiatt, Phil, Toledo	.261	142	611	555	99	145	304	27	3	42	119	0	4	2	50	3	180	17	6	13	.548	.322
Higginson, Bob, Toledo*	.308	3	16	13	4	4	6	0	1	0	3	0	0	0	3	0	0	0	0	0	.462	.438
Hinds, Rob, Columbus	.087	11	32	23	4	2	2	0	0	0	1	3	1	1	4	0	3	1	0	0	.087	.241
Holifield, Rick, Pawtucket*	.069	9	30	29	1	2	3	1	0	0	1	0	0	0	1	0	12	1	1	0	.103	.100
Hollins, Damon, Richmond	.199	42	163	146	16	29	38	9	0	0	8	1	0	0	16	1	37	2	3	2	.260	.278
Holman, Craig, Scr./W.-B.†	.000	36	1	0	0	0	0	0	0	0	0	0	0	0	1	0	0	0	0	0	.000	1.000
Hosey, Dwayne, Pawtucket†	.297	90	415	367	77	109	184	25	4	14	53	0	5	3	40	2	67	20	7	3	.501	.366
Hostetler, Mike, Richmond	.091	27	27	22	2	2	2	0	0	0	0	1	0	0	3	0	6	0	0	0	.091	.167
Howard, Chris, Norfolk	.160	56	130	119	8	19	31	6	0	2	15	5	1	0	5	1	30	0	0	2	.260	.192
Howard, Matt, Columbus	.347	51	225	202	36	70	92	12	2	2	16	3	1	1	18	0	9	9	3	5	.455	.401
Huff, Mike, Syracuse	.290	78	281	248	40	72	122	20	3	8	42	0	4	1	28	0	39	8	3	5	.492	.359
Hunter, Rich, Scr./W.-B.	.000	8	9	7	0	0	0	0	0	0	0	2	0	0	0	0	4	0	0	0	.000	.000
Huson, Jeff, Rochester*	.250	2	8	8	0	2	2	0	0	0	1	0	0	0	0	0	2	0	0	1	.250	.250
Hyers, Tim, Toledo*	.259	117	486	437	55	113	163	17	6	7	59	1	5	3	40	2	57	7	1	8	.373	.322
Ilsley, Blaise, Ott.-Scr./W.B.*	.000	27	11	9	0	0	0	0	0	0	0	1	0	0	1	0	3	0	0	0	.000	.100
Jackson, Gavin, Pawtucket	.250	15	48	44	5	11	13	2	0	0	1	1	0	0	3	0	8	0	1	0	.295	.298
Jefferies, Gregg, Scr./W.-B.†..	.118	4	18	17	1	2	4	0	1	0	0	0	0	0	1	0	0	0	0	2	.235	.167
Johnson, Erik, Charlotte	.178	67	196	185	19	33	39	6	0	0	10	1	1	1	8	0	35	4	0	7	.211	.215
Jones, Andruw, Richmond	.378	12	46	45	11	17	37	3	1	5	12	0	0	0	1	0	9	2	2	0	.822	.391
Jose, Felix, Paw.-Syr.†	.253	99	396	359	50	91	166	17	2	18	66	0	2	0	35	4	73	3	0	9	.462	.318
Juelsgaard, Jarod, Charlotte ..	.000	26	1	1	0	0	0	0	0	0	0	0	0	0	0	0	0	0	0	0	.000	.000
Karp, Ryan, Scr./W.-B.*	.000	7	6	5	0	0	0	0	0	0	0	0	0	0	0	0	3	0	0	0	.000	.000
Katzaroff, Robbie, Columbus .	.444	2	9	9	0	4	4	0	0	0	0	0	0	0	0	0	1	0	0	1	.444	.444
Kelly, Pat, Columbus	.378	8	40	37	8	14	23	1	1	2	7	0	0	0	2	0	11	3	0	0	.622	.400
Knorr, Randy, Syracuse	.278	12	42	36	1	10	15	0	0	0	5	1	0	0	5	0	9	0	0	1	.417	.366
Kowitz, Brian, Tol.-Syr.*	.222	58	200	176	23	39	59	11	3	1	22	4	0	0	18	0	32	4	4	4	.335	.291
Leach, Jalal, Ottawa*	.317	37	109	101	12	32	45	4	0	3	9	0	0	0	8	1	17	0	0	1	.446	.364
Ledee, Ricky, Columbus*	.282	96	407	358	79	101	198	22	6	21	64	0	2	3	44	2	95	6	3	4	.553	.360
Leiper, Dave, Ottawa*	.000	25	1	1	0	0	0	0	0	0	0	0	0	0	0	0	0	0	0	0	.000	.000
Levangie, Dana, Pawtucket	.250	2	6	4	1	1	1	0	0	0	0	1	0	0	1	0	0	0	0	0	.250	.400
Lewis, T.R., Pawtucket	.314	79	313	274	55	86	153	23	1	14	52	1	2	2	34	1	50	2	2	8	.558	.391

ayer, Team	Avg.	G	TPA	AB	R	H	TB	2B	3B	HR	RBI	SH	SF	HP	BB	IBB	SO	SB	CS	GDP	Slg.	OBP
mon, Kevin, Richmond	.091	26	25	22	0	2	2	0	0	0	0	2	0	0	1	0	4	0	1	0	.091	.130
ng, R.D., Columbus†........	.226	61	141	124	18	28	35	3	2	0	9	1	0	1	15	0	36	5	2	4	.282	.314
wery, Terrell, Norfolk	.233	62	221	193	25	45	68	7	2	4	21	3	2	1	22	0	44	6	3	1	.352	.312
cca, Lou, Charlotte...........	.260	87	291	273	26	71	108	14	1	7	35	0	3	4	11	0	62	0	3	11	.396	.296
kachyk, Rob, Ottawa*	.264	70	267	246	38	65	115	15	4	9	39	2	2	3	13	1	54	10	2	4	.467	.307
ke, Matt, Columbus*	.280	74	293	264	46	74	149	14	2	19	70	1	5	6	17	0	52	1	1	9	.564	.332
acDonald, Bob, Norfolk*	.000	27	3	3	0	0	0	0	0	0	0	0	0	0	0	0	1	0	0	0	.000	.000
agee, Wendell, Scr./W.-B....	.284	44	178	155	31	44	87	9	2	10	32	0	2	0	21	0	31	3	1	2	.561	.365
ahalik, John, Norfolk...........	.235	8	18	17	1	4	4	0	0	0	0	1	0	0	1	0	1	0	0	0	.235	.235
alave, Jose, Pawtucket.......	.271	41	170	155	30	42	72	6	0	8	29	0	1	2	12	1	37	2	1	5	.465	.329
alloy, Marty, Richmond*.....	.203	18	72	64	7	13	17	2	1	0	8	2	1	0	5	1	7	3	0	1	.266	.257
anahan, Anthony, Scr./W.-B..	.105	17	41	38	3	4	6	2	0	0	0	1	0	0	2	0	9	0	0	1	.158	.150
antei, Matt, Charlotte	.000	7	2	2	0	0	0	0	0	0	0	0	0	0	0	0	2	0	0	0	.000	.000
anto, Jeff, Pawtucket	.244	12	51	45	6	11	22	5	0	2	6	0	0	1	5	0	8	1	0	1	.489	.333
arini, Marc, Columbus*.......	.267	46	151	135	23	36	53	11	0	2	23	1	3	2	10	1	23	1	0	4	.393	.320
artin, Chris, Ottawa	.264	122	502	451	68	119	175	30	1	8	54	6	5	7	33	0	54	25	12	16	.388	.321
artindale, Ryan, Columbus..	.263	7	22	19	3	5	9	2	1	0	3	0	0	0	3	0	5	0	0	0	.474	.364
artinez, Domingo, Roch.......	.362	29	129	116	18	42	70	7	0	7	38	0	3	0	10	0	17	0	1	5	.603	.403
artinez, Manuel, Scr./W.-B...	.209	17	72	67	8	14	17	1	1	0	5	0	0	1	4	0	17	3	0	0	.254	.264
artinez, Pablo, Richmond†..	.270	77	288	263	29	71	92	12	3	1	18	11	1	1	12	0	58	14	7	3	.350	.303
artinez, Pedro, Norfolk*......	.167	34	7	6	0	1	1	0	0	0	0	1	1	0	0	0	3	0	0	0	.167	.167
atos, Francisco, Ottawa......	.238	100	331	307	30	73	100	15	3	2	23	3	2	3	16	0	35	4	5	14	.326	.280
cClain, Scott, Rochester.....	.281	131	532	463	76	130	212	23	4	17	69	0	7	1	61	1	109	8	6	6	.458	.361
cCoy, Trey, Norfolk...........	.191	25	58	47	2	9	13	1	0	1	7	0	1	2	8	0	5	0	0	2	.277	.328
cCready, Jim, Norfolk	.000	6	1	1	0	0	0	0	0	0	0	0	0	0	0	0	0	0	0	0	.000	.000
cDavid, Ray, Ottawa*........	.155	18	68	58	7	9	10	1	0	0	2	1	0	0	9	1	11	6	2	0	.172	.269
cGriff, Terry, Syracuse	.186	27	70	59	7	11	15	1	0	1	6	1	1	1	8	0	9	0	0	1	.254	.290
cGuire, Ryan, Ottawa*	.257	134	516	451	62	116	177	21	2	12	60	1	3	2	59	4	80	11	4	12	.392	.344
Intosh, Tim, Columbus........	.277	67	227	206	30	57	100	11	1	10	28	2	2	6	11	1	40	0	0	6	.485	.329
Millon, Billy, Charlotte*	.352	97	390	347	72	122	209	32	2	17	70	0	2	5	36	0	76	5	3	8	.602	.418
Nair, Fred, Scr./W.-B..........	.160	14	34	25	3	4	4	0	0	0	3	1	0	0	8	0	12	0	0	0	.160	.364
jia, Roberto, Pawtucket	.257	21	81	74	9	19	23	4	0	0	4	0	1	1	5	0	18	4	1	3	.311	.309
ndoza, Reynol, Charlotte ...	.067	15	16	15	0	1	1	0	0	0	0	0	1	0	0	0	2	0	0	1	.067	.067
rloni, Lou, Pawtucket	.252	38	132	115	19	29	38	6	0	1	12	4	0	3	10	0	20	0	1	1	.330	.328
ler, Kurt, Charlotte	.222	12	10	9	0	2	2	0	0	0	0	0	0	0	0	0	3	0	0	1	.222	.222
liard, Ralph, Charlotte	.276	69	295	250	47	69	106	15	2	6	26	1	1	5	38	0	43	8	4	5	.424	.381
nbs, Mike, Scr./W.-B.*	.000	7	9	8	0	0	0	0	0	0	0	0	1	0	0	0	3	0	0	0	.000	.000
chell, Kevin, Pawtucket	.125	5	17	16	1	2	2	0	0	0	0	0	0	1	0	0	5	0	0	0	.125	.176
chell, Tony, Toledo†	.278	82	333	288	45	80	134	10	4	12	43	0	2	1	41	1	89	3	2	8	.465	.367
x, Greg, Charlotte..............	.500	4	2	2	0	1	1	0	0	0	0	0	0	0	0	0	1	0	0	0	.500	.500
ntoyo, Charlie, Ottawa.......	.351	22	66	57	10	20	27	5	1	0	5	2	0	0	7	0	6	0	0	1	.474	.422
ore, Bobby, Richmond.......	.270	67	217	200	29	54	73	10	0	3	14	1	1	0	15	0	11	9	2	3	.365	.319
rdecai, Mike, Richmond	.182	3	12	11	2	2	5	0	0	1	2	0	1	0	0	0	3	0	0	0	.455	.167
rgan, Kevin, Norfolk	.134	29	98	82	7	11	14	3	0	0	3	4	1	2	9	0	14	3	1	0	.171	.234
rman, Russ, Charlotte	.332	80	323	289	59	96	170	18	1	18	77	0	4	1	29	2	51	2	4	10	.588	.390
squera, Julio, Syracuse.....	.250	23	79	72	6	18	19	1	0	0	5	0	0	1	6	0	14	0	0	1	.264	.316
tuzas, Jeff, Columbus	.250	5	12	12	1	3	5	0	1	0	1	0	0	0	0	0	7	0	0	0	.417	.250
mmau, Bob, Syracuse.......	.000	4	3	3	1	0	0	0	0	0	0	0	0	0	0	0	0	0	0	0	.000	.000
noz, Bobby, Scr./W.-B.	.200	8	5	5	1	1	2	1	0	0	1	0	0	0	0	0	1	0	0	1	.400	.200
rray, Glenn, Scr./W.-B.	.366	41	166	142	31	52	87	10	2	7	22	0	1	1	22	0	29	7	0	1	.613	.452
rray, Matt, Scr./W.B.-Rich.*	.250	18	5	4	0	1	1	0	0	0	0	0	1	0	0	0	0	0	0	0	.250	.250
hols, Rod, Richmond	.500	57	3	2	0	1	1	0	0	0	0	0	0	0	1	0	0	0	0	0	.500	.667
thrup, Kevin, Columbus......	.286	56	181	168	22	48	75	13	1	4	20	0	1	0	12	0	25	4	2	7	.446	.331
e, Ryan, Scr./W.-B............	.091	14	14	11	2	1	1	0	0	0	0	0	1	0	0	0	2	0	0	0	.091	.231
hoa, Alex, Norfolk	.339	67	269	233	45	79	123	12	4	8	39	0	2	2	32	3	22	5	11	8	.528	.420
neda, Jose, Charlotte†	.320	115	404	375	52	120	175	26	1	9	49	4	3	1	21	0	58	7	6	7	.467	.355
ro, Ricky, Scr./W.-B.†........	.299	46	208	177	38	53	81	9	8	1	9	2	1	0	28	1	13	15	6	2	.458	.393
ens, Billy, Rochester†	.254	61	214	201	19	51	80	14	0	5	30	0	2	1	10	0	35	2	2	6	.398	.290
heco, Alex, Ottawa	.000	33	2	1	0	0	0	0	0	0	0	0	0	0	0	0	0	0	0	0	.000	.000
l, Donn, Charlotte	.000	38	4	3	0	0	0	0	0	0	0	0	0	1	0	0	2	0	0	0	.000	.250
iagua, Jose, Ottawa.........	.125	5	8	8	0	1	1	0	0	0	0	0	0	0	0	0	4	0	0	0	.125	.125
ton, Jay, Norfolk..............	.307	55	168	153	30	47	77	6	3	6	26	0	1	3	11	1	25	10	1	3	.503	.363
orilli, Aldo, Richmond	.290	122	441	403	61	117	189	27	0	15	62	1	3	3	31	1	87	5	6	8	.469	.343
ues, Steve, Richmond.......	.341	52	178	167	31	57	90	10	1	7	30	0	1	4	6	0	43	0	0	4	.539	.376
nberton, Rudy, Pawtucket...	.326	102	429	396	77	129	244	28	3	27	92	0	1	14	18	0	63	16	7	12	.616	.375
n, Shannon, Toledo†	.287	97	402	356	65	102	140	12	4	6	42	3	3	14	26	0	59	22	11	5	.393	.356
ez, Tomas, Syracuse	.276	40	134	123	15	34	49	10	1	1	13	3	1	0	7	0	19	8	1	2	.398	.313
ez, Yorkis, Charlotte*	.000	9	1	1	0	0	0	0	0	0	0	0	0	0	0	0	1	0	0	0	.000	.000
son, Robert, Norfolk.........	.500	10	4	4	1	2	2	0	0	0	0	0	0	0	0	0	2	0	0	0	.500	.500
agine, Roberto, Norfolk*....	.318	95	375	314	49	100	166	24	3	12	65	0	3	7	51	7	75	4	1	3	.529	.421
lips, J.R., Scr./W.-B.*	.285	53	222	200	33	57	114	14	2	13	42	0	2	1	19	0	53	2	2	9	.570	.347
onia, Luis, Rochester*	.240	13	57	50	9	12	14	2	0	0	3	0	0	0	7	0	8	5	0	1	.280	.333
ada, Jorge, Columbus†......	.271	104	440	354	76	96	163	22	6	11	62	1	3	3	79	3	86	3	3	13	.460	.405
e, Scott, Syracuse*	.272	113	493	419	71	114	137	11	6	0	39	9	4	3	58	0	71	30	16	3	.327	.362
gh, Pork Chop, Paw.	.236	74	276	242	43	57	114	17	2	12	40	0	1	1	32	0	68	2	2	7	.471	.326
o, Arquimedez, Paw.	.243	11	42	37	6	9	13	1	0	1	3	0	0	2	3	0	6	0	0	1	.351	.333
e, Curtis, Toledo*	.231	9	36	26	4	6	10	1	0	1	2	0	0	1	9	0	7	4	1	1	.385	.444
rico, Rafael, Scr./W.-B.*.....	.222	13	9	9	0	2	2	0	0	0	0	0	0	0	0	0	3	0	0	0	.222	.222
nes, Tim, Columbus†........	.250	4	13	12	3	3	4	1	0	0	0	0	0	0	1	0	3	1	0	0	.333	.308
nirez, Hector, Norfolk	.000	3	2	2	0	0	0	0	0	0	0	0	0	0	0	0	0	0	0	0	.000	.000
nos, John, Syracuse	.243	89	365	317	38	77	117	16	0	8	42	0	7	0	41	1	51	1	1	9	.369	.323
p, Pat, Charlotte...............	.000	2	1	1	0	0	0	0	0	0	0	0	0	0	0	0	0	0	0	0	.000	.000

Player, Team	Avg.	G	TPA	AB	R	H	TB	2B	3B	HR	RBI	SH	SF	HP	BB	IBB	SO	SB	CS	GDP	Slg.	O
Reed, Rick, Norfolk	.179	29	33	28	2	5	10	2	0	1	3	4	1	0	0	0	11	1	0	0	.357	.1
Relaford, Desi, Scr./W.-B.†	.235	21	96	85	12	20	29	4	1	1	11	1	1	1	8	0	19	7	1	0	.341	.3
Renteria, Edgar, Charlotte	.280	35	143	132	17	37	51	8	0	2	16	2	0	0	9	0	17	10	4	5	.386	.3
Reyes, Gilberto, Ottawa	.182	17	53	44	5	8	20	3	0	3	5	0	0	1	8	0	12	0	0	0	.455	.3
Riley, Marquis, Charlotte	.227	92	333	300	43	68	78	10	0	0	13	4	2	1	26	1	31	16	5	8	.260	.2
Rivera, Ben, Ottawa	.000	31	9	5	0	0	0	0	0	0	0	0	0	0	2	0	2	0	0	0	.000	.2
Rivera, Luis, Norfolk	.225	114	401	356	34	80	127	23	3	6	39	8	3	3	31	1	58	1	3	10	.357	.2
Rivera, Ruben, Columbus	.235	101	412	362	59	85	143	20	4	10	46	1	1	8	40	4	96	15	10	4	.395	.3
Roberson, Kevin, Norfolk†	.265	70	239	215	26	57	97	13	3	7	33	1	2	7	14	2	65	0	1	4	.451	.3
Robertson, Jason, Charlotte*	.040	11	27	25	2	1	4	0	0	1	2	0	0	0	2	0	12	0	1	0	.160	.1
Rodarte, Raul, Richmond	.338	61	243	219	30	74	117	12	2	9	46	0	4	1	19	1	43	4	2	6	.534	.3
Rodriguez, Steve, Toledo	.285	96	367	333	49	95	129	18	2	4	30	7	2	2	23	0	43	18	3	8	.387	.3
Rodriguez, Tony, Pawtucket	.245	72	293	265	37	65	90	14	1	3	28	10	0	3	15	1	32	3	1	10	.340	.2
Rogers, Bryan, Norfolk	.000	20	2	2	0	0	0	0	0	0	0	0	0	0	0	0	1	0	0	0	.000	.0
Rolen, Scott, Scr./W.-B.	.274	45	197	168	23	46	69	17	0	2	19	0	1	0	28	0	28	4	5	9	.411	.3
Romano, Scott, Columbus	.150	18	46	40	5	6	8	2	0	0	4	1	0	0	5	0	6	1	0	1	.200	.2
Rosario, Marc, Charlotte*	.305	79	240	220	23	67	89	10	0	4	20	0	2	2	16	2	37	3	4	4	.405	.3
Rosario, Mel, Rochester†	.000	3	2	2	0	0	0	0	0	0	0	0	0	0	0	0	1	0	0	0	.000	.0
Rowland, Rich, Syracuse	.226	96	348	288	43	65	117	24	2	8	45	2	4	4	50	3	79	1	1	9	.406	.3
Rueter, Kirk, Ottawa*	.000	3	3	3	0	0	0	0	0	0	0	0	0	0	0	0	0	0	0	0	.000	.0
Schall, Gene, Scr./W.-B.	.288	104	433	371	66	107	184	16	5	17	67	0	5	9	48	2	92	1	0	9	.496	.3
Schilling, Curt, Scr./W.-B.	.000	2	3	3	0	0	0	0	0	0	0	0	0	0	0	0	2	0	0	0	.000	.0
Schmidt, Curt, Ottawa	.000	54	1	0	0	0	0	0	0	0	0	0	0	0	1	0	0	0	0	0	.000	1.0
Schmidt, Jason, Richmond	.000	7	8	7	1	0	0	0	0	0	0	0	0	1	0	3	0	0	0	0	.000	.12
Schu, Rick, Ottawa	.271	116	449	395	48	107	173	24	3	12	54	0	4	9	41	5	51	9	3	5	.438	.3
Schutz, Carl, Richmond*	.000	41	5	5	0	0	0	0	0	0	0	0	0	0	0	0	1	0	0	0	.000	.0
Seelbach, Chris, Charlotte	.000	25	28	24	0	0	0	0	0	0	1	2	0	0	2	0	5	0	0	1	.000	.07
Sefcik, Kevin, Scr./W.-B.	.333	45	203	180	34	60	77	7	5	0	19	3	2	3	15	0	20	11	3	4	.428	.39
Selby, Bill, Pawtucket*	.254	71	288	260	39	66	123	14	5	11	47	0	4	2	22	0	39	0	3	5	.473	.3
Sheff, Chris, Charlotte	.264	92	306	284	41	75	128	15	1	12	49	0	1	0	21	1	55	7	1	10	.451	.3
Siddall, Joe, Charlotte*	.280	65	205	189	22	53	77	13	1	3	20	2	0	3	11	1	36	1	2	2	.407	.3
Singleton, Duane, Toledo*	.221	88	335	294	42	65	116	15	6	8	30	1	3	1	36	4	84	17	7	4	.395	.3
Smith, Mark, Rochester	.348	39	151	132	24	46	86	14	1	8	32	0	1	4	14	0	22	10	1	0	.652	.4
Smith, Robert, Richmond	.256	124	486	445	49	114	165	27	0	8	58	2	3	4	32	0	114	15	9	12	.371	.3
Spencer, Shane, Columbus	.355	9	37	31	7	11	24	4	0	3	6	0	0	1	5	0	5	0	1	0	.774	.4
Steph, Rod, Richmond	.000	38	3	3	0	0	0	0	0	0	0	0	0	0	0	0	1	0	0	0	.000	.0
Stewart, Shannon, Syracuse	.298	112	485	420	77	125	185	26	8	6	42	5	4	2	54	0	61	35	6	8	.440	.3
Stocker, Kevin, Scr./W.-B.†	.227	12	46	44	5	10	19	3	0	2	6	1	0	1	0	0	4	1	0	1	.432	.2
Strawberry, Darryl, Columbus*	.375	2	8	8	3	3	12	0	0	3	5	0	0	0	3	0	0	0	1	0	1.500	.3
Stull, Everett, Ottawa	.167	13	17	12	0	2	2	0	0	0	0	4	0	0	1	0	4	0	0	0	.167	.2
Swann, Pedro, Richmond*	.250	93	327	296	42	74	105	11	4	4	35	2	3	4	22	2	56	7	7	5	.355	.3
Tackett, Jeff, Toledo	.237	89	331	283	41	67	104	10	3	7	49	2	4	6	36	1	54	4	2	7	.367	.3
Tarasco, Tony, Rochester*	.262	29	122	103	18	27	39	6	0	2	9	1	1	0	17	2	20	4	4	2	.379	.3
Tatum, Jim, Pawtucket	.273	19	74	66	11	18	35	2	0	5	16	0	0	1	7	0	12	2	0	3	.530	.3
Telford, Anthony, Ottawa	.364	31	23	22	0	8	12	2	1	0	3	1	0	0	0	0	2	0	0	1	.545	.3
Thobe, Tom, Richmond*	.000	31	3	3	0	0	0	0	0	0	0	0	0	0	0	0	1	0	0	0	.000	.0
Thurman, Gary, Norfolk	.267	127	500	449	81	120	183	24	6	9	39	3	1	7	40	0	108	25	12	4	.408	.3
Tokheim, David, Scr./W.-B.*	.212	92	276	255	35	54	75	10	4	1	21	4	1	5	11	1	37	5	5	3	.294	.2
Tomberlin, Andy, Norfolk*	.326	38	142	129	17	42	74	6	1	8	18	3	0	2	8	1	29	1	3	2	.574	.3
Torres, Jaime, Columbus	.270	12	40	37	5	10	16	3	0	1	7	1	0	0	2	0	4	1	0	1	.432	.3
Torres, Tomas, Charlotte	.250	5	4	4	0	1	1	0	0	0	1	0	0	0	0	0	0	0	0	0	.250	.2
Trammell, Bubba, Toledo	.294	51	203	180	32	53	87	14	1	6	24	0	1	0	22	1	44	5	1	1	.483	.3
Trlicek, Rick, Norfolk	.000	62	1	1	0	0	0	0	0	0	0	0	0	0	0	0	1	0	0	0	.000	.0
Troutman, Keith, Scr./W.-B.	.000	8	1	1	0	0	0	0	0	0	0	0	0	0	0	0	0	0	0	0	.000	.0
Turang, Brian, Syracuse	.172	37	106	93	13	16	23	2	1	1	8	3	0	1	9	0	14	3	0	3	.247	.2
Tyler, Brad, Rochester*	.270	118	458	382	68	103	180	18	10	13	52	1	3	5	67	2	95	19	7	2	.471	.3
Urbina, Ugueth, Ottawa	.000	5	3	2	0	0	0	0	0	0	0	1	0	0	0	0	1	0	0	0	.000	.0
Valdes, Marc, Charlotte	.200	8	5	5	0	1	1	0	0	0	0	0	0	0	0	0	0	0	0	0	.200	.2
Veras, Quilvio, Charlotte†	.327	28	118	104	22	34	49	5	2	2	8	0	1	1	13	2	14	8	3	1	.471	.4
Walton, Jerome, Richmond	.444	6	20	18	3	8	15	2	1	1	5	0	0	1	1	0	5	0	0	0	.833	.5
Ward, Daryle, Toledo*	.174	6	23	23	1	4	4	0	0	0	1	0	0	0	0	0	6	0	0	0	.174	.1
Warner, Mike, Richmond*	.207	7	30	29	4	6	7	1	0	0	1	0	0	0	1	0	8	1	2	0	.241	.2
Waszgis, B.J., Rochester	.266	96	352	304	37	81	130	16	0	11	48	1	1	4	41	0	87	2	3	7	.428	.3
Wawruck, Jim, Rochester*	.284	59	224	204	31	58	84	14	6	0	15	4	1	1	14	1	29	4	2	2	.412	.3
Wedge, Eric, Toledo	.235	96	332	302	43	78	148	26	0	15	57	1	4	0	43	0	81	2	2	5	.446	.3
Weinke, Chris, Syracuse*	.186	51	182	161	21	30	49	8	1	3	18	0	1	1	19	2	49	0	1	6	.304	.2
Weston, Mickey, Charlotte	.111	31	11	9	1	1	1	0	0	0	0	2	0	0	0	0	2	0	0	0	.111	.1
Whisenant, Matt, Charlotte†	.333	28	19	15	2	5	8	0	0	1	4	1	0	0	3	0	8	0	0	0	.533	.4
Whitehurst, Wally, Ott.-Col.	.000	28	5	5	0	0	0	0	0	0	0	0	0	0	0	0	3	0	0	0	.000	.0
Whitmore, Darrell, Charlotte*	.304	55	214	204	27	62	108	13	0	11	36	0	2	1	7	2	43	2	5	2	.529	.3
Wiegandt, Scott, Scr./W.-B.*	.333	46	3	3	1	1	1	0	0	0	1	0	0	0	0	0	1	0	0	0	.333	.3
Williams, Juan, Richmond*	.272	119	413	357	55	97	168	22	2	15	52	3	2	0	51	5	127	5	4	10	.471	.3
Williams, Mitch, Scr./W.-B.*	.000	9	1	1	0	0	0	0	0	0	0	0	0	0	0	0	0	0	0	0	.000	.0
Wilson, Tom, Columbus	.000	1	2	1	0	0	0	0	0	0	0	0	0	0	0	0	1	0	0	0	.000	.5
Withem, Shannon, Norfolk	.143	8	7	7	0	1	1	0	0	0	0	0	0	0	0	0	2	0	0	0	.143	.1
Woodall, Brad, Richmond†	.313	22	22	16	2	5	8	0	0	1	2	3	0	0	3	0	3	0	0	0	.500	.4
Woodson, Tracy, Columbus	.288	114	450	420	53	121	224	34	3	21	81	0	11	3	16	2	52	4	0	5	.533	.3
Wrona, Rick, Scr./W.-B.	.229	61	191	175	10	40	63	8	0	5	20	4	2	3	7	0	41	1	1	4	.360	.2
Yan, Julian, Ottawa	.184	48	149	136	17	25	42	3	1	4	21	0	1	2	10	1	40	0	0	4	.309	.2
Zambrano, Eduardo, Paw.	.111	3	9	9	0	1	1	0	0	0	0	0	0	0	0	0	0	0	0	1	.111	.1
Zaun, Greg, Rochester†	.319	14	59	47	11	15	17	2	0	0	4	0	1	0	11	1	6	0	2	0	.362	.4
Zinter, Alan, Pawtucket†	.269	108	424	357	78	96	203	19	5	26	69	0	5	4	58	2	123	5	1	3	.569	.3

yer, Team	Avg.	G	TPA	AB	R	H	TB	2B	3B	HR	RBI	SH	SF	HP	BB	IBB	SO	SB	CS	GDP	Slg.	OBP
sky, Eddie, Rochester........	.256	95	372	340	42	87	126	22	4	3	34	3	6	2	21	1	40	5	2	8	.371	.298
ʁer, Jon, Scr./W.-B.*	.311	118	477	412	62	128	172	22	5	4	59	2	4	1	58	3	50	4	2	15	.417	.394
ɔcic, Bob, Scr./W.-B...........	.235	44	134	119	12	28	39	5	0	2	16	0	2	0	13	1	20	1	0	0	.328	.306

GRAND SLAMS: Brooks, I. Cruz, Luke, Pemberton, 2 each; Adriana, Barron, Bowers, Chamberlain, Cradle, F. Cruz, Doster, Gordon, Grijak, Hosey, Huff, Lucca, Magee ᴵave, D. Martinez, McClain, Morman, Penn, Roberson, Schall, Singleton, M. Smith, Stewart, Tyler, Waszgis, Ju. Williams, Woodson, 1 each.

AWARDED FIRST BASE ON CATCHER'S INTERFERENCE: Chamberlain 2 (Brooks, Castillo); Amaro (Waszgis); Clapinski (Tackett); A. Mitchell (Mosquera); Waszgis ᵢlesandro).

PLAYERS WITH TWO OR MORE TEAMS

yer, Team	Avg.	G	TPA	AB	R	H	TB	2B	3B	HR	RBI	SH	SF	HP	BB	IBB	SO	SB	CS	GDP	Slg.	OBP
ᵃaro, Ruben, Syracuse†	.240	16	65	50	8	12	13	1	0	0	2	1	0	4	10	0	11	6	2	0	.260	.406
ᵃaro, Ruben, Scr./W.-B.†	.278	52	199	180	28	50	72	10	3	2	22	1	0	3	14	0	29	7	1	4	.400	.340
ᵏkum, Scott, Pawtucket	.000	14	0	0	0	0	0	0	0	0	0	0	0	0	0	0	0	0	0	0	.000	.000
ᵏkum, Scott, Scr./W.-B.......	.000	30	2	2	0	0	0	0	0	0	0	0	0	0	0	0	2	0	0	0	.000	.000
tre, Esteban, Scr./W.-B.	.133	4	15	15	1	2	2	0	0	0	1	0	0	0	0	0	1	0	0	2	.133	.133
tre, Esteban, Richmond......	.250	10	29	28	3	7	10	3	0	0	0	0	0	1	0	0	2	0	0	0	.357	.276
ɔkson, Brent, Pawtucket	.271	73	286	255	51	69	141	13	1	19	50	0	2	5	24	1	72	2	4	9	.553	.343
ɔkson, Brent, Rochester	.265	30	125	113	22	30	55	7	0	6	21	0	1	2	9	0	20	2	1	5	.487	.328
z, Mario, Columbus...........	.262	16	63	61	9	16	25	3	0	2	11	1	0	0	1	0	6	0	2	3	.410	.274
z, Mario, Scr./W.-B............	.278	46	193	180	20	50	65	6	0	3	22	0	1	1	11	0	9	0	0	5	.361	.321
ᵒtt, Matt, Scr./W.-B.*.........	.083	27	12	12	0	1	1	0	0	0	0	1	0	0	0	0	4	0	0	1	.083	.083
ᵒtt, Matt, Rochester*	.000	5	0	0	0	0	0	0	0	0	0	0	0	0	0	0	0	0	0	0	.000	.000
ᵉy, Blaise, Ottawa*	.000	22	9	7	0	0	0	0	0	0	0	1	1	0	1	0	1	0	0	0	.000	.125
ᵉy, Blaise, Scr./W.-B.*	.000	5	2	2	0	0	0	0	0	0	0	0	0	0	0	0	0	0	0	0	.000	.000
ᵉe, Felix, Pawtucket†	.219	11	35	32	3	7	16	3	0	2	5	0	0	0	3	0	10	0	0	0	.500	.286
ᵉe, Felix, Syracuse†	.257	88	361	327	47	84	150	14	2	16	61	0	2	0	32	4	63	3	0	9	.459	.321
ᵛitz, Brian, Toledo*	.191	24	78	68	9	13	18	5	0	0	3	1	0	0	9	0	12	2	2	3	.265	.286
ᵛitz, Brian, Syracuse*	.241	34	122	108	14	26	41	6	3	1	19	3	2	0	9	0	20	2	2	1	.380	.294
ʳray, Matt, Scr./W.-B.*	.250	13	5	4	0	1	1	0	0	0	1	0	0	0	0	0	2	0	0	0	.250	.250
ʳray, Matt, Richmond*	.000	5	0	0	0	0	0	0	0	0	0	0	0	0	0	0	0	0	0	0	.000	.000
ᵢtehurst, Wally, Ottawa......	.000	15	5	5	0	0	0	0	0	0	0	0	0	0	0	0	3	0	0	0	.000	.000
ᵢtehurst, Wally, Columbus.	.000	13	0	0	0	0	0	0	0	0	0	0	0	0	0	0	0	0	0	0	.000	.000

1996 PITCHING

TEAM

ʳm	W	L	Pct.	ERA	G	CG	ShO	Sv.	IP	H	TBF	R	ER	HR	SH	SF	HB	BB	IBB	SO	WP	Bk.
folk	82	59	.582	3.51	141	9	12	46	1221.0	1122	5071	545	476	120	43	43	40	356	20	921	47	9
ᵤmbus.........	85	57	.599	4.02	142	14	6	38	1210.1	1176	5175	628	540	113	34	35	69	420	10	912	70	4
ʰmond.........	62	79	.440	4.17	142	14	7	34	1195.2	1190	5136	640	554	102	50	52	33	432	17	826	65	3
ᶜhester	72	69	.511	4.57	141	7	3	33	1178.2	1248	5143	684	599	145	37	49	42	458	10	888	66	10
ᵛtucket........	78	64	.549	4.61	142	16	9	33	1215.1	1255	5250	704	622	169	21	37	40	417	12	944	75	6
ᵃcuse.........	67	75	.472	4.64	142	10	4	28	1205.2	1265	5265	709	622	122	42	56	45	470	21	890	62	8
ᵃnton/W.-B..	70	72	.493	4.67	142	6	4	36	1218.2	1271	5365	712	633	145	48	43	40	509	37	860	62	10
ᵉdo	70	72	.493	4.95	142	9	4	34	1213.2	1317	5309	761	668	130	38	24	41	457	17	920	75	9
ᵃwa	60	82	.423	5.10	142	10	10	36	1200.2	1327	5326	751	680	138	40	33	56	476	20	862	60	2
ᵣrlotte.........	62	79	.440	5.49	142	7	3	41	1181.0	1384	5378	813	720	156	51	47	46	537	18	838	93	9

INDIVIDUAL

TOP QUALIFIERS FOR EARNED-RUN AVERAGE TITLE

Minimum 114 innings. *Lefthanded pitcher.

ᶜher, Team	W	L	Pct.	ERA	G	GS	CG	ShO	GF	Sv.	IP	H	TBF	R	ER	HR	SH	SF	HB	BB	IBB	SO	WP	Bk.
ʳie, Mike, Norfolk..............	15	6	.714	3.04	27	27	2	2	0	0	169.0	150	678	61	57	16	2	2	5	33	1	103	8	2
ᵈ, Rick, Norfolk.................	8	10	.444	3.16	28	28	1	0	0	0	182.0	164	726	72	64	13	6	8	4	33	2	128	5	2
ᵈiner, Mike, Norfolk..........	13	3	.813	3.21	24	24	2	2	0	0	146.0	125	590	58	52	18	3	5	2	38	1	125	3	0
ᵖan, Jeff, Pawtucket	10	6	.625	3.22	22	22	7	1	0	0	145.1	130	593	66	52	16	0	3	6	25	1	142	9	1
ᵒdall, Brad, Richmond*	9	7	.563	3.38	21	21	5	1	0	0	133.1	124	555	59	50	10	7	3	1	36	1	74	3	0
ᵒwsky, Clint, Toledo	6	8	.429	3.94	19	19	1	0	0	0	118.2	128	525	67	52	8	6	3	6	51	0	59	3	2
ʰringer, Brian, Columbus..	11	7	.611	4.00	25	25	3	1	0	0	153.0	155	664	79	68	13	2	5	11	56	1	132	4	1
ᵒrd, Anthony, Ottawa	7	2	.778	4.11	30	15	1	1	0	0	118.1	128	506	62	54	12	6	1	5	34	1	69	4	0
ᵢndow, Derek, Syracuse ...	8	7	.533	4.28	24	20	2	0	0	0	124.0	118	539	64	59	14	4	5	3	57	0	103	8	0
ʰon, Kevin, Richmond	9	8	.529	4.33	26	26	2	0	0	0	141.1	151	607	82	68	11	5	4	4	44	2	102	6	1
ᵗetler, Mike, Richmond	9	9	.500	4.38	27	24	2	0	1	0	148.0	168	632	80	72	8	7	9	5	41	1	81	8	0
ʷford, Carlos, Scr./W.-B...	9	10	.474	4.54	28	25	3	1	3	0	158.2	169	695	87	80	15	5	4	4	63	5	89	3	2
ᶜk, Chris, Richmond	10	11	.476	4.67	26	26	3	0	0	0	150.1	137	652	95	78	20	3	8	6	61	0	112	9	0
ᵒhenson, Garrett, Roch.....	7	6	.538	4.81	23	21	3	1	1	0	121.2	123	515	66	65	13	2	5	10	44	0	86	3	2
ᵉr, Trever, Toledo*	13	6	.684	4.90	27	27	0	0	0	0	165.1	167	722	98	90	19	4	1	9	65	1	115	3	2

ᵂEPARTMENTAL LEADERS: W—Fyhrie, 15; L—Seelbach, 13; Pct.—Gardiner, .813; G—Trlicek, 62; GS—Reed, 28; CG—Suppan, 7; ShO—Gardiner, Fyhrie, 2; GF—
ᵢnols, 51; Sv.—D. Wallace, 26; IP—Reed, 182; H—Baptist, 187; TBF—Reed, 726; R—Seelbach, 123; ER—Seelbach, 113; HR—Seelbach, 26; SH—Several pitchers
with 8; SF—Baptist, 10; HB—Boehringer, 11; IBB—Wiegandt, 7; SO—Suppan, 146; WP—Whisenant, 30; BK—Hernandez, 4.

ALL PITCHERS

*Lefthanded pitcher.

ʰer, Team	W	L	Pct.	ERA	G	GS	CG	ShO	GF	Sv.	IP	H	TBF	R	ER	HR	SH	SF	HB	BB	IBB	SO	WP	Bk.
ᵛedo, Juan, Norfolk..........	4	8	.333	5.96	19	19	2	1	0	0	102.2	116	472	70	68	15	3	7	8	53	0	83	11	1
ᵐson, Joel, Charlotte*	6	6	.500	3.78	44	8	0	0	14	3	97.2	108	424	48	41	15	3	3	3	28	2	84	1	0
ᵃrne, Pat, Norfolk.............	1	2	.333	4.62	5	4	0	0	0	0	25.1	26	108	14	13	1	3	0	1	9	1	14	0	1
ᵢnseca, Antonio, Charlotte.	4	4	.500	5.53	14	13	0	0	1	1	71.2	86	321	47	44	6	1	4	3	22	0	51	2	0

Pitcher, Team	W	L	Pct.	ERA	G	GS	CG	ShO	GF	Sv.	IP	H	TBF	R	ER	HR	SH	SF	HB	BB	IBB	SO	WP	BK
Alvarez, Tavo, Ottawa	4	9	.308	4.70	20	20	2	1	0	0	113.0	128	485	66	59	12	3	0	2	25	1	86	5	
Andujar, Luis, Syracuse*	0	0	.000	2.25	2	2	0	0	0	0	12.0	17	55	7	3	1	0	2	0	2	0	10	0	
Aucoin, Derek, Ottawa	3	5	.375	3.96	52	0	0	0	24	3	75.0	74	351	37	33	6	2	2	7	53	4	69	11	
Ausanio, Joe, Norfolk	3	3	.500	5.86	35	0	0	0	17	4	43.0	38	197	31	28	8	2	4	2	29	1	40	2	
Austin, Jim, Pawtucket	0	1	.000	9.00	10	0	0	0	6	0	14.0	15	64	14	14	6	1	1	0	9	2	7	2	
Baez, Kevin, Toledo	0	0	.000	0.00	1	0	0	0	1	0	1.1	0	5	0	0	0	0	0	0	1	0	1	0	
Bakkum, Scott, Paw.-Scr./W.B..	5	7	.417	6.08	44	4	0	0	19	6	93.1	119	429	77	63	16	1	2	3	28	6	50	1	
Baptist, Travis, Syracuse*	7	6	.538	5.43	30	21	2	0	1	0	141.0	187	633	91	85	15	5	10	2	48	2	77	7	
Bark, Brian, Norfolk*	1	0	1.000	4.63	12	0	0	0	2	0	11.2	9	51	6	6	2	1	0	1	6	0	13	0	
Barnes, Brian, Toledo*	6	6	.500	3.99	14	13	2	0	0	0	88.0	85	373	49	39	8	0	1	4	29	0	70	6	
Batista, Miguel, Charlotte	4	3	.571	5.38	47	2	0	0	14	4	77.0	93	360	57	46	4	4	4	6	39	0	56	16	
Baxter, Bob, Ottawa*	3	3	.500	5.51	54	2	0	0	23	3	81.2	104	362	55	50	8	1	3	3	23	2	60	5	
Beech, Matt, Scr./W.-B.*	2	0	1.000	2.40	2	2	0	0	0	0	15.0	9	57	6	4	3	0	0	0	1	0	14	0	
Belinda, Stan, Pawtucket	1	0	1.000	0.00	6	0	0	0	2	0	7.2	2	30	2	0	0	0	0	2	0	7	0		
Benitez, Armando, Rochester.	0	0	.000	2.25	2	0	0	0	0	0	4.0	3	17	1	1	1	0	0	1	0	5	1		
Bieser, Steve, Ottawa	0	0	.000	18.00	1	0	0	0	0	0	1.0	3	10	4	2	1	0	0	0	3	0	1	0	
Blazier, Ron, Scr./W.-B.	4	0	1.000	2.57	33	0	0	0	23	12	42.0	33	168	15	12	1	1	2	2	9	2	38	1	
Blomdahl, Ben, Toledo	2	6	.250	6.22	53	0	0	0	27	2	59.1	77	271	42	41	9	1	1		18	1	34	9	
Boehringer, Brian, Columbus.	11	7	.611	4.00	25	25	3	1	0	0	153.0	155	664	79	68	13	2	5	11	56	1	132	4	
Bohanon, Brian, Syracuse*...	4	3	.571	3.86	31	0	0	0	10	0	58.1	56	245	29	25	4	2	2	6	17	2	38	2	
Borowski, Joe, Richmond	1	5	.167	3.71	34	0	0	0	19	7	53.1	42	224	25	22	4	4	0	30	1	40	1		
Boucher, Denis, Ottawa*	3	7	.300	9.30	17	11	0	0	4	0	61.0	90	306	63	63	17	2	3	1	40	0	24	1	
Brandow, Derek, Syracuse	8	7	.533	4.28	24	20	2	0	0	0	124.0	118	539	64	59	14	4	5	3	57	0	103	8	
Brewer, Billy, Columbus*	0	2	.000	7.20	13	4	0	0	6	0	25.0	27	122	21	20	4	0	2	2	19	0	27	3	
Brito, Mario, Charlotte	1	0	1.000	1.80	6	0	0	0	6	4	5.0	3	21	1	1	1	0	0	2	0	10	0		
Brock, Chris, Richmond	10	11	.476	4.67	26	25	3	0	0	0	150.1	137	652	95	78	20	3	8	6	61	0	112	9	
Brock, Russ, Columbus	0	0	.000	9.00	1	0	0	0	0	0	1.0	2	5	1	1	0	0	0	0	0	0	2	0	
Brow, Scott, Syracuse	5	4	.556	4.93	18	11	0	0	2	0	76.2	84	331	49	42	6	0	3	0	26	1	52	1	
Brumley, Duff, Scr./W.-B.	2	1	.667	5.85	20	0	0	0	7	0	20.0	19	104	18	13	1	0	1	0	22	1	15	6	
Buccheri, Jim, Ottawa	0	0	.000	0.00	1	0	0	0	0	0	2.0	2	8	0	0	0	1	0	0	0	0	0	0	
Bullard, Jason, Norfolk	0	3	.000	4.89	24	0	0	0	7	0	38.2	45	178	23	21	2	2	2	6	16	1	24	6	
Bullinger, Kirk, Ottawa	2	1	.667	3.52	10	0	0	0	4	0	15.1	10	62	6	6	3	0	0	0	9	1	9	1	
Burrows, Terry, Columbus*...	1	0	1.000	5.96	23	0	0	0	5	0	22.2	24	102	16	15	1	1	1	2	11	0	20	1	
Byrd, Paul, Norfolk	2	1	1.000	3.52	5	0	0	0	1	1	7.2	4	32	3	3	0	0	1	0	4	1	8	0	
Cain, Tim, Pawtucket	1	0	1.000	1.86	11	0	0	0	1	0	19.1	15	80	4	4	1	0	0	2	6	1	10	0	
Carper, Mark, Columbus	1	2	.333	6.62	15	4	0	0	2	0	35.1	43	163	30	26	7	0	0	3	16	0	16	4	
Carrara, Giovanni, Syracuse...	4	4	.500	3.58	9	6	1	0	1	0	37.2	37	159	16	15	2	0	1	0	12	1	28	1	
Cederblad, Brett, Pawtucket...	0	0	.000	3.60	10	0	0	0	2	0	20.0	26	90	10	8	4	0	0	1	4	0	19	3	
Chergey, Dan, Charlotte	0	1	.000	6.21	45	1	0	0	11	1	75.1	86	333	55	52	16	0	6	1	28	0	43	2	
Christopher, Mike, Toledo	4	1	.800	3.92	39	0	0	0	38	22	39.0	50	168	21	17	5	1	0	0	5	1	40	5	
Clapinski, Chris, Pawtucket...	0	0	.000	4.50	1	0	0	0	0	0	2.0	1	7	1	1	1	0	0	0	0	0	2	0	
Cole, Alex, Pawtucket*	0	0	.000	9.00	1	0	0	0	1	0	1.0	2	6	1	1	0	0	0	0	1	0	2	1	
Coppinger, Rocky, Rochester.	6	4	.600	4.19	12	12	0	0	0	0	73.0	65	315	36	34	6	1	2	0	39	1	81	4	
Corbin, Archie, Rochester....	0	2	.000	4.74	20	5	0	0	10	1	43.2	44	197	25	23	5	1	1	1	25	0	47	4	
Cox, Darron, Richmond	0	0	.000	0.00	1	0	0	0	1	0	1.0	2	4	0	0	0	0	0	0	0	0	0	0	
Crawford, Carlos, Scr./W.-B..	9	10	.474	4.54	28	25	3	1	3	1	158.2	169	695	87	80	15	5	5	4	63	5	89	3	
Crawford, Joe, Norfolk*	6	5	.545	3.44	20	16	2	1	2	0	96.2	98	403	45	37	10	3	1	4	20	1	68	0	
Croghan, Andy, Columbus	2	0	1.000	8.46	14	0	0	0	3	0	22.1	27	108	24	21	6	3	1	2	13	0	21	3	
Cumberland, Chris, Col.*	2	7	.222	6.52	12	12	1	0	0	0	58.0	86	272	45	42	9	4	1	4	23	0	35	3	
Czajkowski, Jim, Syracuse....	6	4	.600	3.83	48	2	0	0	20	1	89.1	85	395	52	38	4	6	9	3	37	6	71	3	
Darensbourg, Vic, Charlotte*.	1	5	.167	3.69	47	0	0	0	25	7	63.1	61	280	30	26	7	3	2	2	32	3	66	3	
Dedrick, Jim, Rochester	6	3	.667	6.51	39	3	0	0	20	4	66.1	88	316	59	48	14	2	4	1	41	0	37	5	
DeJesus, Jose, Columbus	0	0	.000	14.40	3	0	0	0	0	0	5.0	9	26	8	8	1	0	0	0	1	0	6	1	
DeSilva, John, Pawtucket*	4	3	.571	5.21	16	16	0	0	0	0	84.2	99	373	55	49	12	2	1	0	27	0	68	1	
Dettmer, John, Richmond	3	5	.375	3.92	19	6	0	0	3	0	59.2	69	249	27	26	8	4	2	1	9	1	26	2	
Dixon, Darron, Rochester*	0	2	.000	3.41	32	0	0	0	9	2	34.1	27	147	15	13	1	1	3	3	23	0	32	2	
Dodd, Robert, Scr./W.-B.*	0	0	.000	8.10	8	2	0	0	2	0	20.0	32	101	21	18	4	0	0	1	9	0	12	1	
Dodson, Bo, Pawtucket*	0	0	.000	0.00	1	0	0	0	1	0	1.0	0	3	0	0	0	0	0	0	0	0	0	0	
Doherty, John, Toledo	1	4	.200	6.62	19	7	0	0	5	1	50.1	79	235	39	37	4	1	0	2	8	0	13	1	
Doolan, Blake, Scr./W.-B.	1	1	.500	6.50	18	0	0	0	3	1	18.0	26	87	15	13	1	3	1	2	7	1	8	2	
Dorlarque, Aaron, Ottawa	1	1	.500	13.27	14	0	0	0	1	0	19.2	39	108	30	29	6	0	1	2	11	1	13	0	
Drews, Matt, Columbus	0	4	.000	8.41	7	7	0	0	0	0	20.1	18	113	27	19	4	1	5	7	27	0	7	8	
Dunbar, Matt, Columbus*	2	0	1.000	1.74	14	0	0	0	1	0	20.2	12	84	6	4	0	0	1	2	13	0	16	0	
Edenfield, Ken, Columbus	4	1	.800	2.34	33	0	0	0	13	3	42.1	32	172	12	11	1	4	0	4	15	1	28	2	
Edens, Tom, Rochester	4	6	.400	5.19	20	10	0	0	4	0	67.2	73	300	43	39	9	2	4	4	23	1	36	2	
Eiland, Dave, Columbus	8	4	.667	2.92	15	15	3	0	0	0	92.1	77	360	37	30	9	3	3	2	13	0	76	2	
Elliott, Donnie, Scr./W.-B.	5	11	.313	4.79	21	19	1	0	1	0	103.1	105	466	62	55	12	7	5	5	59	3	93	9	
Eshelman, Vaughn, Paw.*	1	2	.333	4.33	7	7	1	0	0	0	43.2	40	190	21	21	6	3	3	19	1	28	1		
Falteisek, Steve, Ottawa	2	5	.286	6.36	12	12	0	0	0	0	58.0	75	272	45	41	10	1	0	5	25	0	26	3	
Farrell, John, Toledo	2	4	.333	8.10	6	6	1	0	0	0	30.0	38	135	29	27	8	1	1	3	9	0	21	3	
Finnvold, Gar, Pawtucket	3	2	.600	6.62	8	8	0	0	0	0	35.1	50	167	29	26	7	0	4	3	11	0	35	5	
Flener, Huck, Syracuse*	7	3	.700	2.28	14	14	0	0	0	0	86.2	73	350	27	22	3	3	3	3	23	1	62	2	
Florence, Don, Rochester*	4	4	.500	6.14	36	8	0	0	10	0	85.0	111	388	62	58	11	2	7	0	30	1	53	3	
Flynt, Will, Rochester*	1	1	.500	8.27	4	4	0	0	0	0	16.1	26	86	15	15	2	1	1	0	13	0	9	1	
Fox, Chad, Richmond	3	10	.231	4.73	18	18	1	0	0	0	93.1	91	415	57	49	9	8	6	3	49	1	87	8	
Frey, Steve, Scr./W.-B.*	2	2	.500	5.40	10	0	0	0	2	0	13.1	11	57	8	8	1	1	0	0	8	0	9	0	
Frohwirth, Todd, Rochester...	2	2	.500	4.50	9	0	0	0	3	0	16.0	11	61	8	8	2	0	0	0	5	1	16	1	
Fyhrie, Mike, Norfolk	15	6	.714	3.04	27	27	2	2	0	0	169.0	150	678	61	57	16	2	2	5	33	1	103	8	
Gallaher, Kevin, Toledo	0	0	.000	21.00	2	0	0	0	2	0	3.0	9	22	7	7	0	0	0	0	4	1	4	1	
Garces, Rich, Pawtucket	0	0	.000	2.30	10	0	0	0	4	0	15.2	10	58	4	4	2	0	0	5	0	13	1		
Gardiner, Mike, Norfolk	13	3	.813	3.21	24	24	2	2	0	0	146.0	125	590	58	52	18	3	5	2	38	3	125	3	
Gibson, Paul, Columbus*	1	0	1.000	7.04	9	0	0	0	2	0	7.2	8	38	6	6	3	1	0	0	9	1	4	0	

tcher, Team	W	L	Pct.	ERA	G	GS	CG	ShO	GF	Sv.	IP	H	TBF	R	ER	HR	SH	SF	HB	BB	IBB	SO	WP	Bk.
hr, Greg, Toledo	0	0	.000	7.50	2	2	0	0	0	0	12.0	17	57	10	10	1	0	1	0	5	0	15	2	0
nzalez, Gabe, Charlotte*	0	0	.000	3.00	2	0	0	0	1	0	3.0	4	15	1	1	0	0	0	0	2	0	3	0	0
ay, Dennis, Ottawa*	0	1	.000	6.75	3	0	0	0	2	0	5.1	9	32	4	4	1	0	0	2	5	0	3	1	0
eene, Tommy, Scr./W.-B.	2	0	1.000	3.77	5	5	0	0	0	0	31.0	31	129	13	13	3	0	2	0	7	0	26	0	0
ott, Matt, Scr./W.B.-Roch.*	1	3	.250	4.78	32	13	0	0	5	0	96.0	105	411	58	51	21	4	4	1	29	2	68	4	1
undt, Ken, Pawtucket*	9	4	.692	4.20	44	0	0	0	16	2	64.1	72	274	32	30	4	3	2	1	16	0	46	5	0
ilfoyle, Michael, Toledo*	5	5	.500	5.14	54	0	0	0	12	1	49.0	59	230	35	28	7	4	1	0	31	4	42	6	0
nderson, Eric, Pawtucket*	2	1	.667	3.48	26	1	0	0	3	2	33.2	38	144	15	13	2	0	1	0	9	1	34	3	0
byan, John, Ottawa	0	1	.000	2.45	7	0	0	0	2	1	7.1	7	29	2	2	1	0	0	0	2	0	8	0	0
mmond, Chris, Charlotte*	1	0	1.000	7.20	1	1	0	0	0	0	5.0	5	20	4	4	0	0	0	0	3	0	0	0	0
nsen, Brent, Pawtucket	1	0	1.000	6.23	2	2	0	0	0	0	8.2	8	41	6	6	1	0	0	0	8	0	3	0	0
rris, Doug, Roch.-Char.	2	3	.400	3.92	10	3	0	0	2	0	20.2	25	98	20	9	3	0	1	5	6	0	5	1	0
rrison, Tommy, Richmond	0	0	.000	5.21	10	0	0	0	3	0	19.0	16	87	12	11	5	0	2	2	12	0	12	3	0
rtgraves, Dean, Rich.*	0	0	.000	2.08	4	0	0	0	1	0	8.2	4	32	2	2	1	0	0	1	2	0	8	0	0
ynes, Jimmy, Rochester	1	1	.500	5.65	5	5	0	0	0	0	28.2	31	130	19	18	5	1	0	0	18	0	24	2	1
flin, Bronson, Scr./W.-B.	4	0	1.000	2.61	30	0	0	0	27	12	38.0	25	140	11	11	4	0	3	1	3	1	23	1	0
nderson, Rod, Ottawa	4	11	.267	5.19	25	23	3	1	0	0	121.1	117	528	75	70	12	1	4	4	52	1	83	2	0
nry, Dwayne, Toledo	0	1	.000	7.23	18	0	0	0	5	1	18.2	21	92	19	15	3	0	0	1	12	0	23	0	0
rnandez, Livan, Charlotte	2	4	.333	5.14	10	10	0	0	0	0	49.0	61	239	32	28	3	2	4	1	34	1	45	2	4
nes, Rich, Columbus*	6	3	.667	5.16	32	5	0	0	7	0	66.1	70	303	42	38	7	4	0	5	37	0	48	8	2
lman, Craig, Scr./W.-B.	3	2	.600	5.89	36	3	0	0	9	0	62.2	77	291	44	41	10	6	5	4	34	5	36	6	1
rsman, Vince, Syracuse*	0	3	.000	5.40	29	0	0	0	15	0	35.0	37	150	22	21	7	1	0	1	11	0	21	3	0
stetler, Rich, Richmond	11	9	.550	4.38	27	24	2	0	1	0	148.0	168	632	80	72	8	7	9	5	41	1	81	8	0
dson, Joe, Pawtucket	1	1	.500	3.51	25	0	0	0	15	5	33.1	29	151	19	13	0	0	1	1	21	0	18	4	0
nter, Rich, Scr./W.-B.	2	4	.333	6.69	8	7	1	0	0	0	40.1	39	182	31	30	5	4	1	3	22	0	22	3	0
tton, Mark, Columbus	0	0	.000	0.00	2	0	0	0	1	0	2.0	0	8	0	0	0	0	0	0	0	0	3	1	0
ey, Blaise, Ott.-Scr./W.B.*	6	4	.600	5.43	25	7	0	0	2	0	61.1	73	273	39	37	11	2	1	1	19	0	31	3	0
zen, Marty, Syracuse	3	4	.429	7.76	10	10	0	0	0	0	55.2	74	257	54	48	12	1	4	2	24	2	34	2	0
zembeck, Mike, Columbus	0	0	.000	5.40	1	0	0	0	0	0	1.2	1	7	1	1	0	0	0	0	1	0	0	0	0
nson, Dane, Syracuse	3	2	.600	2.45	43	0	0	0	42	22	51.1	37	201	14	14	4	2	2		17	1	51	2	1
nson, Erik, Charlotte	0	0	.000	0.00	1	0	0	0	1	0	1.0	1	4	0	0	0	0	0	0	0	0	0	0	0
rdan, Ricardo, Scr./W.-B.*	3	3	.500	5.26	32	0	0	0	15	1	39.1	40	180	30	23	5	3	0	1	22	1	40	2	0
elsgaard, Jarod, Charlotte	4	2	.667	3.48	26	5	0	0	9	1	44.0	43	192	23	17	1	1	2	0	21	0	29	3	0
nieniecki, Scott, Col.	2	1	.667	5.64	5	5	2	0	0	0	30.1	33	131	21	19	4	0	1		8	0	27	2	0
rp, Ryan, Scr./W.-B.*	1	1	.500	3.07	7	7	0	0	0	0	41.0	35	168	14	14	1	1	0	0	14	1	30	3	0
agle, Greg, Toledo	2	3	.400	10.00	6	6	0	0	0	0	27.0	42	135	32	30	7	1	2	4	11	0	24	0	1
ackert, Brent, Pawtucket	2	3	.400	5.17	19	5	0	0	4	2	47.0	48	209	32	27	11	0	2	2	26	0	34	4	0
arski, Mike, Columbus*	0	0	.000	6.75	1	1	0	0	0	0	4.0	3	18	4	3	0	0	1	0	2	0	5	1	0
vda, Rick, Rochester*	3	1	.750	4.30	8	8	0	0	0	0	44.0	51	191	24	21	6	0	1	1	15	0	34	2	2
y, Kerry, Pawtucket	0	0	.000	0.00	7	0	0	0	6	4	8.0	1	26	0	0	0	0	0		2	0	8	0	0
e, Aaron, Rochester*	1	0	1.000	5.64	9	0	0	0	2	1	22.1	31	104	16	14	0	0	1	2	8	0	13	1	0
son, Toby, Norfolk	1	0	1.000	4.76	1	1	0	0	0	0	5.2	6	23	3	3	1	0	0		1	0	1	0	0
, Mark, Nor.-Rich.*	4	5	.444	2.69	53	0	0	0	18	1	67.0	69	277	23	20	6	3	3	2	17	2	71	2	0
oer, Dave, Ottawa*	3	1	.750	1.93	25	0	0	0	19	6	32.2	29	125	7	7	3	0	0		6	3	26	1	0
vis, Richie, Toledo	0	0	.000	2.25	2	0	0	0	0	0	4.0	1	13	1	1	1	0	0	0	1	0	4	0	0
la, Jose, Toledo	5	4	.556	6.78	12	12	0	0	0	0	69.0	93	303	53	52	11	1	1	0	12	0	57	2	0
non, Kevin, Toledo	9	8	.529	4.33	26	26	2	0	0	0	141.1	151	607	82	68	11	5	4	4	44	2	102	6	1
ney, Brian, Pawtucket*	5	6	.455	4.81	27	9	1	1	7	1	82.1	78	357	55	44	14	0	2	4	27	2	78	3	0
cDonald, Bob, Norfolk*	4	1	.800	3.13	27	0	0	0	5	0	31.2	27	135	14	11	3	1	3	1	12	1	36	0	0
ddux, Mike, Pawtucket	2	0	1.000	3.21	3	3	0	0	0	0	14.0	13	56	5	5	2	1	0	0	2	0	9	0	0
duro, Calvin, Rochester	5	3	.375	4.74	8	8	0	0	0	0	43.2	49	197	25	23	8	1	1	3	18	0	40	2	0
ntei, Matt, Charlotte	0	2	.000	4.70	7	0	0	0	6	2	7.2	6	36	4	4	1	0	1	0	7	0	8	3	0
shall, Randy, Toledo*	3	5	.375	4.15	29	11	0	0	8	0	95.1	97	400	49	44	7	3	5	3	25	2	60	0	0
rtin, Chris, Ottawa	0	0	.000	67.50	1	0	0	0	0	0	0.2	4	7	5	5	0	0	0		2	0	0	1	0
rtinez, Pedro, Norfolk*	4	4	.500	3.02	34	5	0	0	7	2	56.2	45	236	29	19	4	5	1	2	20	1	37	1	0
xcy, Brian, Toledo	3	1	.750	3.97	15	0	0	0	6	0	22.2	24	97	11	10	2	3	2	0	9	2	8	2	0
Cready, Jim, Norfolk	0	0	.000	4.15	6	0	0	0	2	0	8.2	11	36	4	4	0	0	0	0	6	0	0	0	0
Curry, Jeff, Toledo	1	4	.200	4.76	39	0	0	0	13	2	58.2	66	264	37	31	2	0	0	1	26	1	56	9	0
cir, Jim, Columbus	3	3	.500	2.27	33	0	0	0	19	7	47.2	37	195	14	12	2	3	1	3	15	2	52	3	0
endez, Jose, Columbus	1	0	1.000	6.52	8	1	0	0	2	0	9.2	9	43	10	7	4	0	0	1	2	0	7	0	0
ndoza, Ramiro, Columbus.	6	2	.750	2.51	15	15	0	0	0	0	97.0	96	392	30	27	3	4	5		19	0	61	1	0
ndoza, Reynol, Charlotte	7	4	.636	5.64	15	14	2	0	1	0	91.0	112	413	67	57	18	6	2	4	33	0	41	8	0
er, Kurt, Charlotte	3	5	.375	4.66	12	12	0	0	0	0	65.2	77	294	39	34	7	8	3	2	26	2	38	4	1
er, Trever, Toledo*	13	6	.684	4.90	27	27	0	0	0	0	165.1	167	722	98	90	19	4	1	9	65	1	115	3	2
nbs, Mike, Scr./W.-B.*	2	1	.667	2.48	7	3	0	0	2	0	29.0	27	115	8	8	2	2	1	0	5	0	20	1	0
chey, Nate, Pawtucket	7	4	.636	2.96	14	13	6	1	0	0	97.1	89	394	32	32	8	2	2	0	21	0	61	6	0
chell, Larry, Scr./W.-B.	1	1	.500	2.55	11	0	0	0	2	1	24.2	19	99	8	7	2	1	2	0	10	0	24	1	1
, Greg, Charlotte	1	3	.250	6.87	4	0	0	0	0	0	18.1	27	87	15	14	4	2	2		7	1	9	1	0
nteleone, Rich, Columbus.	4	3	.571	3.60	21	1	0	0	6	0	35.0	42	151	17	14	1	1	0		7	2	21	0	0
ntoyo, Charlie, Ottawa	0	0	.000	0.00	1	0	0	0	0	0	2.0	0	6	0	0	0	0	0	0	0	0	0	0	0
noz, Bobby, Scr./W.-B.	0	0	.000	3.91	8	8	0	0	0	0	50.2	50	207	24	22	6	1	1	0	7	0	34	2	0
noz, Oscar, Rochester	6	7	.462	4.23	21	17	1	0	2	0	112.2	100	465	60	53	17	2	6	2	37	1	85	7	1
ray, Matt, Scr./W.-B.-Rich.	2	10	.167	7.38	18	15	0	0	1	0	68.1	75	339	60	56	13	2	3	5	63	0	43	7	0
ers, Jimmy, Rochester	7	5	.583	2.89	39	0	0	0	35	12	53.0	53	220	19	17	1	8	0	2	12	4	21	5	0
ols, Rod, Richmond	3	3	.500	1.99	57	0	0	0	51	20	72.1	54	294	20	16	5	3	2	2	20	1	64	3	1
owski, C.J., Toledo*	4	6	.400	4.46	19	19	1	0	0	0	111.0	104	471	60	55	13	4	1	3	53	1	103	6	1
, Ryan, Scr./W.-B.	5	2	.714	5.02	14	14	0	0	0	0	80.2	97	362	52	45	10	0	2	3	30	0	51	1	1
ares, Omar, Toledo	1	0	1.000	8.44	1	1	0	0	0	0	5.1	4	23	5	5	1	0	0		3	0	5	0	0
eda, Jose, Charlotte	0	0	.000	31.50	2	0	0	0	2	0	2.0	11	16	7	7	1	0	0	0	0	0	0	0	0
lano, Rafael, Pawtucket*	4	11	.267	7.88	22	20	0	0	0	0	99.1	124	476	94	87	20	2	9	6	62	0	66	10	1
e, Scotty, Syracuse*	3	3	.500	5.05	20	5	1	0	11	0	51.2	53	221	37	29	4	0	1	2	27	0	35	4	0
neco, Alex, Ottawa	2	2	.500	6.48	33	0	0	0	12	6	41.2	47	191	32	30	6	5	1	6	18	0	34	2	0

CLASS AAA International League

Pitcher, Team	W	L	Pct.	ERA	G	GS	CG	ShO	GF	Sv.	IP	H	TBF	R	ER	HR	SH	SF	HB	BB	IBB	SO	WP
Pall, Donn, Charlotte	3	3	.500	2.96	38	0	0	0	33	17	51.2	42	208	21	17	3	1	4	4	12	0	53	2
Paniagua, Jose, Ottawa	9	5	.643	3.18	15	14	2	1	0	0	85.0	72	352	39	30	7	2	4	3	23	0	61	4
Pavlas, Dave, Columbus	8	2	.800	1.99	57	0	0	0	46	26	77.0	64	306	20	17	5	1	0	0	13	1	65	3
Perez, Yorkis, Charlotte*	3	0	1.000	4.22	9	0	0	0	1	0	10.2	6	41	5	5	1	0	0	0	3	0	13	0
Person, Robert, Norfolk	5	0	1.000	3.35	8	8	0	0	0	0	43.0	33	178	16	16	7	0	1	1	21	0	32	1
Pett, Jose, Syracuse	2	9	.182	5.83	20	18	1	0	0	0	109.2	134	503	81	71	10	4	4	10	42	1	50	6
Pierce, Jeff, Pawtucket	2	1	.667	4.94	12	3	0	0	2	0	31.0	37	136	18	17	6	2	1	0	8	0	22	2
Polley, Dale, Columbus*	2	2	.500	3.13	31	0	0	0	6	1	31.2	29	130	11	11	1	0	0	0	9	0	29	2
Pose, Scott, Syracuse	0	0	.000	13.50	2	0	0	0	2	0	2.0	4	12	3	3	0	0	1	0	2	0	3	0
Powell, Dennis, Rochester*	0	0	.000	1.35	5	0	0	0	2	1	6.2	4	24	1	1	0	0	0	0	1	0	4	1
Quirico, Rafael, Scr./W.-B.*	4	4	.500	3.32	13	13	1	0	0	0	65.0	48	273	29	24	8	3	1	7	26	0	51	3
Ramirez, Hector, Norfolk	1	0	1.000	3.38	3	1	0	0	1	0	10.2	13	49	7	4	1	1	1	0	3	0	8	1
Rapp, Pat, Charlotte	1	1	.500	8.18	2	2	0	0	0	0	11.0	18	58	12	10	3	0	0	0	4	0	9	1
Reed, Rick, Norfolk	8	10	.444	3.16	28	28	1	0	0	0	182.0	164	726	72	64	13	6	8	4	33	2	128	5
Revenig, Todd, Rochester	2	0	1.000	7.50	3	0	0	0	0	0	6.0	8	25	5	5	2	0	0	0	0	0	4	0
Ricci, Chuck, Pawtucket	8	4	.667	3.01	60	0	0	0	43	13	80.2	56	326	30	27	12	2	3	1	32	2	79	9
Ricken, Ray, Columbus	4	5	.444	4.76	20	11	1	0	2	1	68.0	62	301	44	36	4	1	3	3	37	2	58	8
Rios, Dan, Columbus	4	1	.800	1.95	24	0	0	0	6	0	27.2	22	111	7	6	1	0	2	4	6	0	22	1
Risley, Bill, Syracuse	0	0	.000	0.00	2	0	0	0	0	0	1.0	0	6	1	0	0	0	0	0	1	0	0	0
Rivera, Ben, Ottawa	4	9	.308	6.46	31	15	0	0	2	1	100.1	112	458	74	72	7	2	2	8	47	2	87	8
Robinson, Ken, Syracuse	3	7	.300	4.64	47	0	0	0	18	1	64.0	52	278	37	33	14	4	4	1	39	3	78	6
Rodriguez, Nerio, Rochester	1	0	1.000	1.80	2	2	0	0	0	0	15.0	10	58	3	3	0	0	0	0	2	0	6	2
Rogers, Bryan, Norfolk	0	2	.000	3.38	20	0	0	0	9	0	24.0	20	103	11	9	2	2	0	0	11	2	23	2
Rogers, Jimmy, Syracuse	1	3	.250	6.04	8	3	0	0	0	0	22.1	28	102	16	15	4	2	0	1	7	0	15	1
Rojas, Euclides, Charlotte	0	0	.000	6.00	6	0	0	0	3	0	9.0	12	42	6	6	2	0	0	1	3	0	8	2
Rowland, Rich, Syracuse	0	0	.000	9.00	1	0	0	0	1	0	1.0	2	5	1	1	1	0	0	0	0	0	0	0
Rueter, Kirk, Ottawa*	1	2	.333	4.20	3	3	1	0	0	0	15.0	21	67	7	7	3	1	0	0	3	0	3	0
Rumer, Tim, Columbus*	3	1	.750	2.72	12	8	0	0	1	0	49.2	39	204	20	15	3	1	1	2	14	0	35	5
Sackinsky, Brian, Rochester	7	3	.700	3.46	14	13	1	0	1	0	67.2	75	276	28	26	12	4	3	0	15	0	38	1
Sager, A.J., Toledo	1	0	1.000	2.63	18	2	0	0	6	0	37.2	38	149	14	11	5	0	0	1	3	0	24	0
Scanlan, Bob, Toledo	1	3	.250	7.50	14	5	0	0	3	0	36.0	46	171	35	30	5	2	1	3	15	0	18	5
Schilling, Curt, Scr./W.-B.	1	0	1.000	1.38	2	2	0	0	0	0	13.0	9	50	2	2	0	0	0	0	5	0	10	1
Schmidt, Curt, Ottawa	1	5	.167	2.43	54	0	0	0	31	13	70.1	60	283	27	19	2	5	6	1	22	3	45	1
Schmidt, Jason, Richmond	3	0	1.000	2.56	7	7	0	0	0	0	45.2	36	184	17	13	2	1	0	0	19	1	41	4
Schullstrom, Erik, Pawtucket	1	4	.200	5.01	15	10	0	0	1	0	55.2	57	246	37	31	9	2	2	2	28	1	62	3
Schutz, Carl, Richmond*	4	3	.571	5.30	41	7	0	0	13	3	69.2	86	320	46	41	4	7	4	0	26	3	52	8
Schwarz, Jeff, Richmond	0	1	.000	27.00	2	0	0	0	1	0	1.1	4	12	4	4	0	0	0	0	4	0	1	0
Seelbach, Chris, Charlotte	6	13	.316	7.35	25	25	1	0	0	0	138.1	167	650	123	113	26	2	5	5	76	3	98	9
Sele, Aaron, Pawtucket	0	0	.000	6.00	1	1	0	0	0	0	3.0	3	13	2	2	0	0	0	0	1	0	4	0
Shepherd, Keith, Rochester	4	7	.364	4.01	27	11	2	0	15	9	94.1	91	414	54	42	12	2	4	4	37	0	98	5
Shouse, Brian, Rochester*	1	2	.333	4.50	32	0	0	0	10	2	50.0	53	217	27	25	6	2	2	1	16	1	45	5
Sievert, Mark, Syracuse	2	5	.286	5.93	10	10	1	0	0	0	54.2	62	256	40	36	6	4	1	1	33	0	46	4
Sodowsky, Clint, Toledo	6	8	.429	3.94	19	19	1	0	0	0	118.2	128	525	67	52	8	8	3	6	51	0	59	3
Spoljaric, Paul, Syracuse*	3	0	1.000	3.27	17	0	0	0	9	4	22.0	20	91	9	8	2	2	1	1	6	1	24	1
Steph, Rod, Richmond	2	3	.400	3.84	38	0	0	0	16	1	79.2	75	324	34	34	6	0	2	3	17	2	41	5
Stephenson, Garrett, Roch.	7	6	.538	4.81	23	21	3	1	1	0	121.2	123	515	66	65	13	2	5	10	44	0	86	3
Stull, Everett, Ottawa	2	6	.250	6.33	13	13	1	0	0	0	69.2	87	331	57	49	7	3	3	3	39	1	69	5
Suppan, Jeff, Pawtucket	10	6	.625	3.22	22	22	7	1	0	0	145.1	130	593	66	52	16	0	3	6	25	1	142	9
Telford, Anthony, Ottawa	7	2	.778	4.11	30	15	1	1	0	0	118.1	128	506	62	54	12	6	1	5	34	1	69	4
Thobe, Tom, Richmond*	1	8	.111	6.13	31	6	1	0	9	3	72.0	89	345	60	49	6	1	5	2	37	2	40	4
Thompson, Justin, Toledo*	6	3	.667	3.42	13	13	3	1	0	0	84.1	74	338	36	32	2	1	2	1	26	0	69	2
Tomlin, Randy, Pawtucket*	0	2	.000	8.31	5	2	0	0	3	1	13.0	17	58	12	12	5	0	0	0	5	0	5	1
Trlicek, Rick, Norfolk	4	5	.444	1.87	62	0	0	0	26	10	77.0	52	289	18	16	1	2	2	1	16	3	54	3
Troutman, Keith, Scr./W.-B.	1	1	.500	5.14	8	0	0	0	4	0	14.0	19	65	9	8	1	1	0	1	5	1	9	1
Urbani, Thomas, Toledo*	0	3	.000	6.43	4	3	0	0	0	0	14.0	18	64	15	10	2	0	1	0	7	0	10	1
Urbina, Ugueth, Ottawa	2	0	1.000	2.66	5	5	0	0	0	0	23.2	17	94	9	7	2	0	0	1	6	0	28	0
Valdes, Marc, Charlotte	2	4	.333	5.12	8	8	1	0	0	0	51.0	66	229	32	29	10	3	0	6	15	1	24	3
VanEgmond, Tim, Pawtucket	5	3	.625	4.38	11	11	1	0	0	0	61.2	66	262	37	30	9	0	2	3	24	1	46	1
Walker, Mike, Toledo	3	2	.600	3.83	28	0	0	0	14	6	44.2	37	194	23	19	4	3	0	1	27	1	37	8
Wallace, Derek, Norfolk	5	2	.714	1.72	49	0	0	0	39	26	57.2	37	227	20	11	4	2	2	1	17	1	52	0
Wallace, Kent, Columbus	4	2	.667	4.68	13	12	2	0	0	0	67.1	69	284	37	35	15	1	1	2	15	0	34	1
Ware, Jeff, Syracuse	3	7	.300	5.68	13	13	1	1	0	0	77.2	83	347	54	49	6	2	3	6	32	0	59	6
Weathers, David, Char.-Col.	0	2	.000	5.68	4	4	0	0	0	0	19.0	25	91	15	12	1	0	4	2	8	0	7	2
Welch, Mike, Norfolk	0	1	.000	4.15	10	0	0	0	5	2	8.2	8	36	4	4	0	0	0	0	2	0	6	0
West, Dave, Scr./W.-B.*	1	0	1.000	5.25	2	2	0	0	0	0	12.0	14	52	8	7	3	0	0	0	2	0	12	2
Weston, Mickey, Charlotte	5	9	.357	5.78	31	14	0	0	5	1	104.1	131	472	73	67	11	7	3	3	39	2	47	1
Whisenant, Matt, Charlotte*	8	10	.444	6.92	28	22	1	0	1	0	121.0	149	590	107	93	15	8	2	3	101	3	97	30
Whitehurst, Wally, Ott.-Col.	8	7	.533	3.08	28	18	2	0	5	3	108.0	101	437	42	37	7	1	1	4	25	0	83	5
Wiegandt, Scott, Scr./W.-B.*	5	6	.455	2.71	46	0	0	0	13	2	63.0	63	276	21	19	3	4	3	2	33	7	46	1
Williams, Brian, Toledo	1	2	.333	5.49	3	3	1	0	0	0	19.2	22	87	13	12	1	0	0	0	9	1	21	3
Williams, Jeff, Rochester	1	1	.500	1.13	8	0	0	0	5	0	8.0	11	42	7	1	0	0	0	1	4	0	4	2
Williams, Mitch, Scr./W.-B.*	2	2	.500	10.20	9	0	0	0	2	0	15.0	25	79	20	17	3	0	0	0	11	1	15	0
Williams, Woody, Syracuse	3	1	.750	1.41	7	7	1	1	0	0	32.0	22	123	5	5	3	0	0	1	7	0	33	3
Withem, Shannon, Norfolk	3	3	.500	4.64	8	8	0	0	0	0	42.2	56	188	25	22	6	2	1	0	6	0	30	2
Woodall, Brad, Richmond*	9	7	.563	3.38	21	21	5	1	0	0	133.1	124	555	59	50	10	7	3	1	36	1	74	3
Wrona, Rick, Scr./W.-B.	0	0	.000	0.00	1	0	0	0	1	0	1.0	2	5	0	0	0	0	0	0	0	0	2	0
Yan, Esteban, Rochester	5	4	.556	4.27	22	10	0	0	3	1	71.2	75	306	37	34	6	3	4	2	18	0	61	4
Yan, Julian, Ottawa	0	0	.000	27.00	1	0	0	0	1	0	0.1	2	3	1	1	1	0	0	0	0	0	0	0

COMBINATION SHUTOUTS: **Charlotte (3)**—Adamson-Batista-Darensbourg-Mantei-Pall, Hernandez-Chergey-Pall, Seelbach-Perez-Brito. **Columbus (5)**—Rum Dunbar-Ricken-Mecir, Mendoza-Melendez-Burrows-Rios-Brewer, Rumer-Rios-Mecir, Whitehurst-Ricken-Brewer, Boehringer-Brewer. **Norfolk (6)**—Fyhrie-Trlicek, Re Byrd-Wallace, Person-Trlicek-Wallace-Martinez, Fyhrie-Trlicek, Fyhrie-Trlicek-Bark-Wallace, Gardiner-Trlicek. **Ottawa (6)**—Rivera-Schmidt-Leiper, Paniagua-Schm Rivera-Leiper, Ilsley-Aucoin-Pacheco, Falteisek-Bullinger-Aucoin, Alvarez-Aucoin. **Pawtucket (6)**—Knackert-Ricci-Lacy, Hansen-Knackert-Lacy, Maddux-Orella erderblad-Looney, Doherty-Hudson, Suppan-Bakkum, Suppan-Minchey-Hudson. **Richmond (6)**—Schutz-Nichols, Dettmer-Nichols, Hostetler-Nichols, Hostetler-Borowski, Schmidt-Thobe-Borowski, Fox-Borowski-Schutz. **Rochester (2)**—Munoz-Shepard, Edens-Shepard. **Scranton/Wilkes-Barre (3)**—Munoz-Mitchell, Quirico-Wiegandt-Jordan, Schilling-Grott-Brumley-Wiegandt. **Syracuse (2)**—Sievert-Robinson, Carrara-Robinson. **Toledo (3)**—Farrell-Sager, Thompson-Guilfoyle-Blomdahl, Thompson-Maxcy-Blomdahl-Sager-McCurry.

NO-HIT GAMES: None.

PITCHERS WITH TWO OR MORE TEAMS

Pitcher, Team	W	L	Pct.	ERA	G	GS	CG	ShO	GF	Sv.	IP	H	TBF	R	ER	HR	SH	SF	HB	BB	IBB	SO	WP	Bk.
Bakkum, Scott, Pawtucket	4	2	.667	6.09	14	2	0	0	4	0	44.1	51	192	33	30	8	0	1	3	8	0	25	0	0
Bakkum, Scott, Scr./W.-B.	1	5	.167	6.06	30	2	0	0	15	6	49.0	68	237	44	33	8	1	1	0	20	6	25	1	0
Scott, Matt, Scr./W.-B.*	1	3	.250	4.88	27	12	0	0	4	0	86.2	92	365	48	47	18	2	4	1	22	2	63	4	1
Scott, Matt, Rochester	0	0	.000	3.86	5	1	0	0	1	0	9.1	13	46	10	4	3	2	0	0	7	0	5	0	0
Harris, Doug, Rochester	2	3	.400	4.08	7	3	0	0	1	0	17.2	22	86	19	8	3	0	0	5	6	0	4	1	0
Harris, Doug, Charlotte	0	0	.000	3.00	3	0	0	0	1	0	3.0	3	12	1	1	0	0	1	0	0	0	1	0	0
Ilsley, Blaise, Ottawa*	5	2	.714	5.16	20	4	0	0	1	0	45.1	49	198	27	26	9	2	1	1	15	0	22	2	0
Ilsley, Blaise, Scr./W.-B.*	1	2	.333	6.19	5	1	0	0	1	0	16.0	24	75	12	11	2	0	0	0	4	0	9	1	0
Lee, Mark, Norfolk*	2	1	.667	2.53	33	0	0	0	9	1	32.0	39	136	11	9	3	3	2	1	6	1	35	2	0
Lee, Mark, Richmond*	2	4	.333	2.83	20	0	0	0	9	0	35.0	30	141	12	11	3	0	1	1	11	1	36	0	0
Murray, Matt, Scr./W.-B.	1	8	.111	7.67	13	13	0	0	0	0	56.1	63	280	52	48	13	2	3	3	49	0	34	6	0
Murray, Matt, Richmond	1	2	.333	6.00	5	2	0	0	1	0	12.0	12	59	8	8	0	0	2	14	0	9	1	0
Weathers, David, Charlotte	0	0	.000	7.71	1	1	0	0	0	0	2.1	5	14	2	2	0	0	1	0	3	0	0	0	0
Weathers, David, Columbus	0	2	.000	5.40	3	3	0	0	0	0	16.2	20	77	13	10	1	0	3	2	5	0	7	2	0
Whitehurst, Wally, Ottawa	2	4	.333	4.37	15	5	0	0	5	3	35.0	41	152	17	17	2	1	1	2	13	0	35	4	0
Whitehurst, Wally, Columbus	6	3	.667	2.47	13	13	2	0	0	0	73.0	60	285	25	20	5	0	0	2	12	0	48	1	0

1996 FIELDING

TEAM

Team	Pct.	G	PO	A	E	TC	DP	PB	Team	Pct.	G	PO	A	E	TC	DP	PB
Ottawa	.977	142	3602	1461	117	5180	117	11	Rochester	.975	141	3536	1402	128	5066	111	9
Toledo	.976	142	3641	1609	128	5378	149	15	Norfolk	.974	141	3663	1480	139	5282	108	11
Charlotte	.976	142	3543	1493	125	5161	110	20	Pawtucket	.973	142	3646	1406	140	5192	117	17
Scr./W.-B.	.975	142	3656	1444	130	5230	101	13	Richmond	.969	142	3587	1301	157	5045	113	15
Columbus	.975	142	3631	1526	132	5289	114	14	Syracuse	.969	142	3617	1411	162	5190	155	14

TRIPLE PLAYS: Ottawa 2, Syracuse.

INDIVIDUAL

FIRST BASEMEN

NOTE: All caps denotes fielding-percentage leader based on 71 games for catchers, for all other non-pitchers and 142 innings for pitchers. *Throws lefthanded.

Player, Team	Pct.	G	PO	A	E	TC	DP
Ariana, Sharnol, Syracuse	1.000	8	33	4	0	37	7
Abayani, Benny, Norfolk	1.000	3	27	1	0	28	3
Battle, Howard, Scr./W.-B.	1.000	2	8	0	0	8	0
Bellinger, Clay, Rochester	.992	42	338	13	3	354	27
Bnbow, Lou, Richmond	1.000	1	1	0	0	1	0
Boston, D.J., Syracuse*	.987	26	194	27	3	224	25
Brooks, Jerry, Charlotte	.974	20	168	16	5	189	13
Chimelis, Joel, Norfolk	1.000	2	6	1	0	7	1
Clark, Phil, Pawtucket	.974	4	37	0	1	38	4
Clark, Tony, Toledo	.993	44	400	28	3	431	36
Colbaugh, Scott, Ottawa	1.000	3	11	2	0	13	1
Cox, Darron, Richmond	1.000	3	9	0	0	9	1
Crespo, Felipe, Syracuse	.981	7	50	2	1	53	5
CRUZ, Ivan, Columbus*	.996	125	1028	94	5	1127	88
Daubach, Brian, Norfolk	1.000	9	72	3	0	75	7
Delgado, Alex, Pawtucket	1.000	1	4	1	0	5	0
DeSmuke, Jamie, Syracuse	1.000	15	114	20	0	134	10
Dodson, Bo, Pawtucket*	.995	73	562	48	3	613	51
Figueroa, Bien, Rochester	.971	5	30	4	1	35	0
Franco, Matt, Norfolk	.994	42	330	29	2	361	25
Garcia, Omar, Richmond	.997	83	604	35	2	641	57
Gregg, Tommy, Charlotte*	.996	65	522	45	2	569	46
Hajak, Kevin, Richmond	1.000	9	69	7	0	76	5
Halter, Shane, Charlotte	1.000	1	4	0	0	4	0
Held, Dan, Scr./W.-B.	.968	4	28	2	1	31	2
Huff, Mike, Syracuse	.973	17	98	11	3	112	15
Jacobsen, Tim, Toledo*	.996	88	786	68	3	857	85
Jefferies, Gregg, Scr./W.-B.	.962	3	22	3	1	26	0
Johnson, Erik, Charlotte	1.000	1	7	2	0	9	0
Lewis, T.R., Pawtucket	1.000	2	7	1	0	8	0
Luke, Matt, Columbus*	.989	10	87	6	1	94	3
Makachyk, Rob, Ottawa	1.000	6	31	4	0	35	4
Martinez, Domingo, Rochester	.992	29	233	13	2	248	24
McCoy, Trey, Norfolk	1.000	3	18	3	0	21	0
McGuire, Ryan, Ottawa*	.993	120	984	73	7	1064	86
McIntosh, Tim, Columbus	1.000	11	73	3	0	76	5
McNair, Fred, Scr./W.-B.	1.000	3	19	2	0	21	5
Morman, Russ, Charlotte	.993	61	533	25	4	562	40
Oneda, Jose, Charlotte	1.000	1	6	2	0	8	1
Owens, Billy, Rochester	.998	53	416	26	1	443	35

Player, Team	Pct.	G	PO	A	E	TC	DP
Pecorilli, Aldo, Richmond	.984	59	394	32	7	433	36
Petagine, Roberto, Norfolk*	.982	94	743	67	15	825	60
Phillips, J.R., Scr./W.-B.*	.889	2	6	2	1	9	1
Pose, Scott, Syracuse	1.000	1	1	0	0	1	0
Pough, Pork Chop, Pawtucket	1.000	26	206	10	0	216	19
Ramos, John, Syracuse	.982	38	248	24	5	277	33
Rowland, Rich, Syracuse	.976	8	37	4	1	42	6
Schall, Gene, Scr./W.-B.	.996	80	626	67	3	696	42
Schu, Rick, Ottawa	1.000	6	23	1	0	24	4
Tackett, Jeff, Toledo	.909	2	9	1	1	11	0
Tatum, Jim, Pawtucket	1.000	1	7	0	0	7	1
Torres, Jaime, Columbus	1.000	1	2	0	0	2	0
Tyler, Brad, Rochester	1.000	8	49	3	0	52	8
Ward, Daryle, Toledo*	.979	6	42	5	1	48	5
Waszgis, B.J., Rochester	1.000	10	68	7	0	75	5
Wedge, Eric, Toledo	.970	5	62	2	2	66	5
Weinke, Chris, Syracuse	.986	45	318	33	5	356	41
Woodson, Tracy, Columbus	1.000	10	58	4	0	62	5
Yan, Julian, Ottawa	.969	23	144	13	5	162	10
Zinter, Alan, Pawtucket	.989	49	407	24	5	436	37
Zuber, Jon, Scr./W.-B.*	.990	60	457	46	5	508	44

TRIPLE PLAYS: McGuire, Weinke.

SECOND BASEMEN

Player, Team	Pct.	G	PO	A	E	TC	DP
Abbott, Kurt, Charlotte	.929	5	10	16	2	28	6
Adriana, Sharnol, Syracuse	1.000	2	1	4	0	5	0
Amaro, Ruben, Scr./W.-B.	1.000	3	3	8	0	11	1
Baez, Kevin, Toledo	.981	42	74	135	4	213	28
Barker, Tim, Columbus	.976	67	133	193	8	334	43
Bell, Juan, Pawtucket	.981	57	108	146	5	259	31
Bellinger, Clay, Rochester	.916	25	40	58	9	107	9
Benbow, Lou, Richmond	.969	18	27	35	2	64	13
Bieser, Steve, Ottawa	1.000	1	0	1	0	1	0
Brito, Tilson, Syracuse	.963	6	14	12	1	27	6
Buccheri, Jim, Syracuse	1.000	8	9	6	0	15	1
Burton, Essex, Scr./W.-B.	.957	16	32	35	3	70	12
Cairo, Miguel, Syracuse	.963	84	165	222	15	402	64
Castleberry, Kevin, Ottawa	.974	60	94	166	7	267	27
Chimelis, Joel, Norfolk	.958	6	9	14	1	24	4
Clapinski, Chris, Charlotte	1.000	4	8	11	0	19	1
Cordero, Wil, Pawtucket	1.000	3	2	6	0	8	1
Cotton, John, Toledo	.917	8	9	13	2	24	3

Player, Team	Pct.	G	PO	A	E	TC	DP
Crespo, Felipe, Syracuse	.955	39	99	94	9	202	26
Cruz, Fausto, Toledo	.974	7	17	21	1	39	7
Dalesandro, Mark, Columbus	.980	11	19	30	1	50	5
Diaz, Mario, Col.-Scr./W.B.	1.000	29	56	69	0	125	12
Doster, David, Scr./W.-B.	.985	87	197	203	6	406	40
Duncan, Mariano, Columbus	1.000	2	1	5	0	6	1
Eenhoorn, Robert, Columbus	1.000	1	3	2	0	5	0
Fermin, Felix, Columbus	1.000	5	9	21	0	30	5
Figueroa, Bien, Rochester	.975	32	49	67	3	119	11
Fisher, David, Scr./W.-B.	1.000	1	0	3	0	3	0
Flores, Jose, Scr./W.-B.	.978	13	17	28	1	46	5
Gilbert, Shawn, Norfolk	.976	48	90	113	5	208	22
Giovanola, Ed, Richmond	.959	17	30	41	3	74	11
Graffanino, Tony, Richmond	.977	93	215	216	10	441	47
Halter, Shane, Charlotte	1.000	3	1	6	0	7	0
Hardtke, Jason, Norfolk	.985	70	149	175	5	329	39
Heffernan, Bert, Ottawa	1.000	2	0	2	0	2	0
Hinds, Rob, Columbus	.957	11	27	18	2	47	3
Howard, Matt, Columbus	1.000	7	15	17	0	32	3
Johnson, Erik, Charlotte	.991	24	49	64	1	114	15
Kelly, Pat, Columbus	1.000	8	19	19	0	38	2
Long, R.D., Columbus	.952	40	63	96	8	167	21
Mahalik, John, Norfolk	1.000	2	2	2	0	4	1
Malloy, Marty, Richmond	.973	17	33	39	2	74	8
Manahan, Anthony, Scr./W.-B.	1.000	1	1	0	0	1	0
Manto, Jeff, Pawtucket	1.000	2	4	8	0	12	1
Martin, Chris, Ottawa	1.000	1	2	6	0	8	1
Matos, Francisco, Ottawa	.977	72	108	150	6	264	37
Mejia, Roberto, Pawtucket	.963	20	25	52	3	80	9
Merloni, Lou, Pawtucket	.962	11	21	30	2	53	3
Milliard, Ralph, Columbus	.986	67	154	188	5	347	37
Morgan, Kevin, Norfolk	.976	26	49	73	3	125	15
Olmeda, Jose, Charlotte	.973	20	31	42	2	75	9
Penn, Shannon, Toledo	.931	5	14	13	2	29	2
Perez, Tomas, Syracuse	.976	8	21	19	1	41	8
Rodriguez, Steve, Toledo	.984	90	176	252	7	435	63
Rodriguez, Tony, Pawtucket	1.000	5	13	13	0	26	2
Romano, Scott, Columbus	1.000	6	7	17	0	24	1
Schu, Rick, Ottawa	.978	26	42	46	2	90	13
Sefcik, Kevin, Scr./W.-B.	1.000	1	4	6	0	10	2
Selby, Bill, Pawtucket	.942	50	82	113	12	207	31
Tatum, Jim, Pawtucket	1.000	6	8	18	0	26	2
Turang, Brian, Syracuse	.953	10	20	21	2	43	6
Tyler, Brad, Rochester	.954	92	161	229	19	409	59
Veras, Quilvio, Charlotte	.973	25	44	66	3	113	13
Zosky, Eddie, Rochester	.944	5	8	9	1	18	3

TRIPLE PLAYS: Cairo, Matos (2).

SECOND BASEMEN WITH TWO OR MORE TEAMS

Player, Team	Pct.	G	PO	A	E	TC	DP
Diaz, Mario, Columbus	1.000	1	0	2	0	2	1
Diaz, Mario, Scr./W.-B.	1.000	28	56	67	0	123	11

THIRD BASEMEN

Player, Team	Pct.	G	PO	A	E	TC	DP
Abbott, Kurt, Charlotte	1.000	2	0	1	0	1	0
Adriana, Sharnol, Syracuse	.891	54	28	86	14	128	5
Baez, Kevin, Toledo	1.000	2	1	3	0	4	0
Barker, Tim, Columbus	1.000	4	1	2	0	3	0
Battle, Howard, Scr./W.-B.	.919	88	58	146	18	222	9
Beltre, Esteban, Richmond	.833	2	2	3	1	6	0
Benbow, Lou, Richmond	.913	44	28	67	9	104	5
Brito, Tilson, Syracuse	.923	7	4	8	1	13	1
Cairo, Miguel, Syracuse	.925	32	24	62	7	93	6
Castleberry, Kevin, Ottawa	1.000	4	0	2	0	2	0
Chimelis, Joel, Norfolk	1.000	3	3	0	0	3	0
Clapinski, Chris, Charlotte	.917	12	6	16	2	24	1
Clark, Phil, Pawtucket	.872	38	23	52	11	86	5
Coolbaugh, Scott, Ottawa	.971	51	37	95	4	136	6
Crespo, Felipe, Syracuse	.878	26	20	45	9	74	6
Dalesandro, Mark, Columbus	.887	20	10	37	6	53	0
Delgado, Alex, Pawtucket	1.000	1	1	1	0	2	0
Diaz, Mario, Col.-Scr./W.B.	.968	20	20	41	2	63	2
Figueroa, Bien, Rochester	.909	11	6	14	2	22	2
Fisher, David, Scr./W.-B.	1.000	2	1	2	0	3	0
Franco, Matt, Norfolk	.905	91	53	138	20	211	9
Gilbert, Shawn, Norfolk	.930	61	33	127	12	172	6
Giovanola, Ed, Richmond	1.000	8	5	24	0	29	3
Halter, Shane, Charlotte	1.000	2	0	2	0	2	0
Heffernan, Bert, Ottawa	.857	4	2	4	1	7	1
Hiatt, Phil, Toledo	.943	141	85	345	26	456	39
Huff, Mike, Syracuse	1.000	14	6	28	0	34	2
Johnson, Erik, Charlotte	.974	16	6	31	1	38	2

Player, Team	Pct.	G	PO	A	E	TC	DP
Long, R.D., Columbus	.714	5	0	5	2	7	
Lucca, Lou, Charlotte	.913	85	38	151	18	207	
Manahan, Anthony, Scr./W.-B.	1.000	2	1	2	0	3	
Manto, Jeff, Pawtucket	.938	10	9	21	2	32	
Martin, Chris, Ottawa	.917	11	7	15	2	24	
Martinez, Pablo, Richmond	1.000	14	4	22	0	26	
Matos, Francisco, Ottawa	1.000	1	2	4	0	6	
McClain, Scott, Rochester	.954	131	96	255	17	368	
McIntosh, Tim, Columbus	.778	10	7	14	6	27	
Merloni, Lou, Pawtucket	.917	17	6	38	4	48	
Montoyo, Charlie, Ottawa	.917	5	6	5	1	12	
Northrup, Kevin, Columbus	1.000	1	0	3	0	3	
Olmeda, Jose, Charlotte	.929	46	33	84	9	126	
Pecorilli, Aldo, Richmond	.875	2	2	5	1	8	
Pough, Pork Chop, Pawtucket	.909	46	27	83	11	121	
Pozo, Arquimedez, Pawtucket	.886	11	11	20	4	35	
Rivera, Luis, Norfolk	.833	2	1	4	1	6	
Rodarte, Raul, Richmond	.714	9	2	8	4	14	
Rodriguez, Tony, Pawtucket	1.000	1	1	0	0	1	
Rolen, Scott, Scr./W.-B.	.952	45	32	88	6	126	
Romano, Scott, Columbus	1.000	4	0	6	0	6	
Schu, Rick, Ottawa	.928	79	52	140	15	207	
Sefcik, Kevin, Scr./W.-B.	1.000	1	3	3	0	6	
Selby, Bill, Pawtucket	.902	14	10	27	4	41	
Siddall, Joe, Charlotte	.667	1	0	2	1	3	
Smith, Robert, Richmond	.935	77	63	125	13	201	
Tatum, Jim, Pawtucket	.875	12	5	16	3	24	
Turang, Brian, Syracuse	.879	15	8	21	4	33	
Tyler, Brad, Rochester	.667	2	0	2	1	3	
Weinke, Chris, Syracuse	.600	3	3	3	4	10	
WOODSON, Tracy, Columbus	.956	108	73	188	12	273	
Zosky, Eddie, Rochester	1.000	1	0	3	0	3	

TRIPLE PLAY: Martin (2).

THIRD BASEMEN WITH TWO OR MORE TEAMS

Player, Team	Pct.	G	PO	A	E	TC	D
Diaz, Mario, Columbus	1.000	8	5	19	0	24	
Diaz, Mario, Scr./W.-B.	.949	12	15	22	2	39	

SHORTSTOPS

Player, Team	Pct.	G	PO	A	E	TC	D
Abbott, Kurt, Charlotte	1.000	11	21	43	0	64	
Adriana, Sharnol, Syracuse	.955	12	8	34	2	44	
Baez, Kevin, Toledo	.934	51	69	157	16	242	
Barker, Tim, Columbus	.947	43	64	133	11	208	
Battle, Howard, Scr./W.-B.	.963	27	35	70	4	109	
Bell, Juan, Pawtucket	.964	13	15	39	2	56	
Bellinger, Clay, Rochester	.959	55	77	157	10	244	
Beltre, Esteban, Scr./W.B.-Rich.	.907	11	14	25	4	43	
Benavides, Freddie, Columbus	.667	1	0	2	1	3	
Benbow, Lou, Richmond	.853	12	11	18	5	34	
Benjamin, Mike, Scr./W.-B.	1.000	3	4	12	0	15	
Brito, Tilson, Syracuse	.932	98	138	270	30	438	
Brown, Randy, Pawtucket	.833	2	2	3	1	6	
Burton, Essex, Scr./W.-B.	1.000	1	1	4	0	5	
Cairo, Miguel, Syracuse	.938	5	4	11	1	16	
Chimelis, Joel, Norfolk	.943	13	15	35	3	53	
Clapinski, Chris, Charlotte	.963	85	122	238	14	374	
Cotton, John, Toledo	1.000	1	1	0	0	1	
Cruz, Fausto, Toledo	.954	93	161	296	22	479	
Diaz, Mario, Scr./W.-B.	.000	1	0	0	1	1	
Eenhoorn, Robert, Columbus	.947	53	73	158	13	244	
Fermin, Felix, Columbus	1.000	2	4	5	0	9	
Figueroa, Bien, Rochester	1.000	1	2	5	0	7	
Fisher, David, Scr./W.-B.	.883	20	22	46	9	77	
Flores, Jose, Scr./W.-B.	.929	12	13	26	3	42	
Garciaparra, Nomar, Pawtucket	.973	43	63	120	5	188	
Gilbert, Shawn, Norfolk	.942	29	41	72	7	120	
Giovanola, Ed, Richmond	.941	28	37	90	8	135	
Howard, Matt, Columbus	.962	46	53	147	8	208	
Jackson, Gavin, Pawtucket	.947	15	21	50	4	75	
Johnson, Erik, Charlotte	.939	12	14	17	2	33	
Long, R.D., Columbus	.875	2	3	4	1	8	
Mahalik, John, Norfolk	.750	3	3	6	3	12	
Malloy, Marty, Richmond	1.000	1	1	1	0	2	
Manahan, Anthony, Scr./W.-B.	1.000	9	13	24	0	37	
MARTIN, Chris, Ottawa	.965	110	178	341	19	538	
Martinez, Pablo, Richmond	.933	62	79	158	17	254	
Matos, Francisco, Ottawa	.977	24	27	57	2	86	
Merloni, Lou, Pawtucket	.915	11	12	31	4	47	
Montoyo, Charlie, Ottawa	.939	13	26	36	4	66	
Mordecai, Mike, Richmond	1.000	3	3	13	0	16	
Mummau, Bob, Syracuse	1.000	1	1	2	0	3	

er, Team	Pct.	G	PO	A	E	TC	DP
eda, Jose, Charlotte	.917	4	4	7	1	12	0
z, Tomas, Syracuse	.958	32	59	78	6	143	20
ford, Desi, Scr./W.-B.	.938	21	25	65	6	96	7
eria, Edgar, Charlotte	.959	35	48	114	7	169	15
ra, Luis, Norfolk	.958	110	125	326	20	471	56
iguez, Tony, Pawtucket	.976	69	83	198	7	288	39
a, Rick, Ottawa	.933	4	3	11	1	15	1
k, Kevin, Scr./W.-B.	.950	43	56	134	10	200	18
h, Robert, Richmond	.934	43	53	103	11	167	21
ker, Kevin, Scr./W.-B.	.982	12	17	39	1	57	7
y, Eddie, Rochester	.952	89	151	245	20	416	36

SHORTSTOPS WITH TWO OR MORE TEAMS

er, Team	Pct.	G	PO	A	E	TC	DP
e, Esteban, Scr./W.-B.	.905	4	7	12	2	21	3
e, Esteban, Richmond	.909	7	7	13	2	22	4

OUTFIELDERS

er, Team	Pct.	G	PO	A	E	TC	DP
ana, Sharnol, Syracuse	.951	17	39	0	2	41	0
ayani, Benny, Norfolk	.987	81	145	7	2	154	2
ro, Ruben, Syr.-Scr./W.B.	.993	63	130	3	1	134	0
, Rolo, Rochester	1.000	12	29	3	0	32	0
er, Glen, Toledo	.982	22	51	3	1	55	0
on, Tony, Ottawa	1.000	92	154	7	0	161	0
ez, Yamil, Ottawa	.968	111	197	14	7	218	2
er, Steve, Ottawa	.973	81	178	5	5	188	1
ser, Greg, Rochester*	.895	19	15	2	2	19	0
ers, Brent, Rochester	.979	43	89	3	2	94	0
ks, Jerry, Charlotte	.989	52	82	9	1	92	1
n, Jarvis, Rochester	.992	57	124	5	1	130	2
n, Randy, Pawtucket	1.000	1	0	1	0	1	0
heri, Jim, Ottawa	1.000	55	121	2	0	123	0
r, Robert, Scr./W.-B.*	1.000	71	130	4	0	134	1
enter, Bubba, Columbus*	.987	123	225	8	3	236	1
nberlain, Wes, Syracuse	1.000	15	23	0	0	23	0
nski, Chris, Charlotte	1.000	3	7	0	0	7	0
, Phil, Pawtucket	1.000	2	2	0	0	2	0
Alex, Pawtucket*	.964	79	153	6	6	165	1
son, Brent, Paw.-Roch.	1.000	75	117	4	0	121	0
n, John, Toledo	.975	36	75	4	2	81	1
e, Rickey, Syracuse	.947	40	67	5	4	76	0
oo, Felipe, Syracuse	1.000	31	51	2	0	53	0
sandro, Mark, Columbus	.938	13	13	2	1	16	0
Jermaine, Richmond	.955	36	83	2	4	89	0
Kevin, Norfolk	.978	34	43	2	1	46	0
, Cliff, Ottawa	.951	19	38	1	2	41	0
lin, Micah, Toledo	1.000	52	93	2	0	95	1
, Aaron, Pawtucket	1.000	1	1	0	0	1	0
t, Shawn, Norfolk	.909	6	10	0	1	11	0
nola, Ed, Richmond	1.000	5	5	0	0	5	0
on, Keith, Columbus	.970	26	64	1	2	67	0
well, Mike, Pawtucket	1.000	2	3	0	0	3	0
g, Tommy, Charlotte*	.980	32	47	1	1	49	0
Joe, Rochester	.978	119	203	15	5	223	0
s, Shane, Charlotte	.923	7	10	2	1	13	0
monds, Jeffrey, Rochester	.987	28	75	1	1	77	0
en, Terrel, Toledo	1.000	4	2	1	0	3	0
nson, Bob, Toledo	1.000	3	3	0	0	3	0
eld, Rick, Pawtucket*	.929	9	13	0	1	14	0
s, Damon, Richmond*	.976	41	116	6	3	125	0
y, Dwayne, Pawtucket	.985	91	197	4	3	204	0
Mike, Syracuse	1.000	51	99	3	0	102	2
n, Jeff, Rochester	1.000	2	4	0	0	4	0
, Tim, Toledo*	.947	28	35	1	2	38	0
s, Andruw, Richmond	.972	12	34	1	1	36	0
Felix, Paw.-Syr.	.909	10	18	2	2	22	0
z, Brian, Tol.-Syr.*	.976	55	80	1	2	83	1
, Jalal, Ottawa	1.000	21	27	1	0	28	0
, Ricky, Columbus*	.952	68	97	3	5	105	0
, T.R., Pawtucket	.991	67	111	3	1	115	0
ry, Terrell, Norfolk	.991	57	106	4	1	111	1
shyk, Rob, Ottawa	.971	57	99	3	3	105	0
Matt, Columbus*	.987	50	72	2	1	75	1
e, Wendell, Scr./W.-B.	.959	44	92	2	4	98	0
e, Jose, Pawtucket	.986	34	68	0	1	69	0
i, Marc, Columbus	.975	24	38	1	1	40	0
nez, Manuel, Scr./W.-B.	.976	17	40	0	1	41	0
vid, Ray, Ottawa	1.000	17	29	0	0	29	0
ire, Ryan, Ottawa*	.750	3	3	0	1	4	0
osh, Tim, Columbus	1.000	4	4	0	0	4	0
llon, Billy, Charlotte*	.973	94	135	10	4	149	0

Player, Team	Pct.	G	PO	A	E	TC	DP
Mejia, Roberto, Pawtucket	1.000	1	2	0	0	2	0
Mitchell, Kevin, Pawtucket	.667	2	2	0	1	3	0
Mitchell, Tony, Toledo	.983	59	108	5	2	115	2
Moore, Bobby, Richmond	.983	59	117	2	2	121	1
Murray, Glenn, Scr./W.-B.	.973	37	72	1	2	75	0
Northrup, Kevin, Columbus	.973	50	67	6	2	75	1
Ochoa, Alex, Norfolk	.960	62	110	9	5	124	3
Olmeda, Jose, Charlotte	1.000	37	55	1	0	56	0
Otero, Ricky, Scr./W.-B.	.977	46	121	4	3	128	1
Payton, Jay, Norfolk	1.000	6	7	1	0	8	0
Pecorilli, Aldo, Richmond	.960	20	23	1	1	25	0
Pegues, Steve, Richmond	.973	36	68	3	2	73	0
Pemberton, Rudy, Pawtucket	.973	95	180	1	5	186	0
Penn, Shannon, Toledo	.969	84	117	6	4	127	0
Phillips, J.R., Scr./W.-B.*	.965	52	106	4	4	114	0
Polonia, Luis, Rochester*	1.000	8	18	0	0	18	0
POSE, Scott, Syracuse	.990	110	193	9	2	204	2
Pride, Curtis, Toledo	1.000	3	3	0	0	3	0
Raines, Tim, Columbus	1.000	2	2	0	0	2	0
Ramos, John, Syracuse	1.000	12	12	1	0	13	0
Riley, Marquis, Charlotte	.990	86	184	5	2	191	0
Rivera, Ruben, Columbus	.972	101	239	6	7	252	1
Roberson, Kevin, Norfolk	.981	55	99	3	2	104	2
Robertson, Jason, Charlotte*	.933	10	14	0	1	15	0
Rodarte, Raul, Richmond	.944	52	94	7	6	107	3
Rodriguez, Steve, Toledo	1.000	1	2	0	0	2	0
Romano, Scott, Columbus	1.000	5	2	0	0	2	0
Schall, Gene, Scr./W.-B.	1.000	1	1	0	0	1	0
Schu, Rick, Ottawa	1.000	1	2	0	0	2	0
Selby, Bill, Pawtucket	1.000	2	3	0	0	3	0
Sheff, Chris, Charlotte	.986	83	133	8	2	143	0
Singleton, Duane, Toledo	.973	83	134	8	4	146	0
Smith, Mark, Rochester	.966	32	55	1	2	58	0
Spencer, Shane, Columbus	.963	9	25	1	1	27	1
Stewart, Shannon, Syracuse	.983	111	274	7	5	286	2
Swann, Pedro, Richmond	.983	86	171	5	3	179	0
Tarasco, Tony, Rochester	1.000	3	4	0	0	4	0
Tatum, Jim, Pawtucket	.857	2	6	0	1	7	0
Thurman, Gary, Norfolk	.982	122	262	7	5	274	2
Tokheim, David, Scr./W.-B.*	1.000	75	118	2	0	120	0
Tomberlin, Andy, Norfolk*	.985	32	66	1	1	68	0
Trammell, Bubba, Toledo	.987	47	72	5	1	78	1
Turang, Brian, Syracuse	1.000	8	8	0	0	8	0
Tyler, Brad, Rochester	1.000	9	20	1	0	21	0
Walton, Jerome, Richmond	1.000	5	12	0	0	12	0
Warner, Mike, Richmond*	1.000	7	14	0	0	14	0
Wawruck, Jim, Rochester*	1.000	47	85	1	0	86	0
Whitmore, Darrell, Charlotte	.943	54	114	2	7	123	0
Williams, Juan, Richmond	.965	111	239	8	9	256	0
Zambrano, Eduardo, Pawtucket	.909	3	9	1	1	11	0
Zuber, Jon, Scr./W.-B.*	.985	42	65	0	1	66	0
Zupcic, Bob, Scr./W.-B.*	1.000	38	50	5	0	55	1

TRIPLE PLAY: Stewart.

OUTFIELDERS WITH TWO OR MORE TEAMS

Player, Team	Pct.	G	PO	A	E	TC	DP
Amaro, Ruben, Syracuse	1.000	15	23	2	0	25	0
Amaro, Ruben, Scr./W.-B.	.991	48	107	1	1	109	0
Cookson, Brent, Pawtucket	1.000	47	73	4	0	77	0
Cookson, Brent, Rochester	1.000	28	44	0	0	44	0
Jose, Felix, Pawtucket	.889	3	8	0	1	9	0
Jose, Felix, Syracuse	.923	7	10	2	1	13	0
Kowitz, Brian, Toledo*	.913	22	20	1	2	23	1
Kowitz, Brian, Syracuse*	1.000	33	60	0	0	60	0

CATCHERS

Player, Team	Pct.	G	PO	A	E	TC	DP	PB
Ayrault, Joe, Richmond	.982	97	548	61	11	620	7	11
Bennett, Gary, Scr./W.-B.	.988	85	517	61	7	585	5	8
Bieser, Steve, Ottawa	.983	33	159	17	3	179	1	2
Brooks, Jerry, Charlotte	.982	31	155	11	3	169	0	4
Casanova, Raul, Toledo	.992	36	234	15	2	251	2	5
Castillo, Alberto, Norfolk	.990	111	747	72	8	827	9	7
Chavez, Raul, Ottawa	.990	60	363	50	4	417	3	4
Clark, Phil, Pawtucket	.965	15	72	10	3	85	0	2
Cox, Darron, Richmond	1.000	49	310	29	0	339	5	4
Dalesandro, Mark, Columbus	.979	15	86	6	2	94	0	1
Delgado, Alex, Pawtucket	.990	25	174	16	2	192	1	2
Devarez, Cesar, Rochester	.991	61	421	44	4	469	3	3
Estalella, Bobby, Scr./W.-B.	.968	10	55	6	2	63	0	0
Fagley, Dan, Charlotte	1.000	1	1	0	0	1	0	0
Figga, Mike, Columbus	1.000	3	17	2	0	19	1	0
Hatteberg, Scott, Pawtucket	.990	86	566	42	6	614	0	10

Player, Team	Pct.	G	PO	A	E	TC	DP	PB
Heffernan, Bert, Ottawa	.993	48	277	19	2	298	1	2
Howard, Chris, Norfolk	.992	51	213	22	2	237	2	4
Knorr, Randy, Syracuse	1.000	10	53	2	0	55	0	1
Levangie, Dana, Pawtucket	.923	2	11	1	1	13	0	1
Martindale, Ryan, Columbus	.973	7	35	1	1	37	0	1
McGriff, Terry, Syracuse	1.000	25	95	6	0	101	1	2
McIntosh, Tim, Columbus	.993	24	139	11	1	151	1	2
Mosquera, Julio, Syracuse	.983	23	164	9	3	176	0	1
Motuzas, Jeff, Columbus	.955	5	19	2	1	22	0	0
Pecorilli, Aldo, Richmond	.714	2	5	0	2	7	0	0
Posada, Jorge, Columbus	.985	94	598	51	10	659	3	10
Ramos, John, Syracuse	.987	21	139	15	2	156	2	4
Reyes, Gilberto, Ottawa	1.000	15	85	15	0	100	1	3
Ronan, Marc, Charlotte	.991	74	389	49	4	442	4	10
Rosario, Mel, Rochester	.875	3	7	0	1	8	0	0
ROWLAND, Rich, Syracuse	.994	83	476	38	3	517	5	6
Siddall, Joe, Charlotte	.984	62	316	43	6	365	4	6
Tackett, Jeff, Toledo	.993	86	561	35	4	600	7	7
Torres, Jaime, Columbus	1.000	7	30	3	0	33	1	0
Waszgis, B.J., Rochester	.988	75	443	46	6	495	2	6
Wedge, Eric, Toledo	1.000	27	147	13	0	160	0	3
Wrona, Rick, Scr./W.-B.	.980	56	311	27	7	345	1	5
Zaun, Greg, Rochester	.965	8	52	3	2	57	0	0
Zinter, Alan, Pawtucket	.993	25	140	9	1	150	1	2

PITCHERS

Player, Team	Pct.	G	PO	A	E	TC	DP
Acevedo, Juan, Norfolk	.955	19	11	10	1	22	2
Adamson, Joel, Charlotte*	.913	44	3	18	2	23	0
Aherne, Pat, Norfolk	1.000	5	3	3	0	6	0
Alfonseca, Antonio, Charlotte	.929	14	7	6	1	14	2
Alvarez, Tavo, Ottawa	.875	20	8	13	3	24	1
Andujar, Luis, Syracuse	1.000	2	1	0	0	1	0
Aucoin, Derek, Ottawa	1.000	52	4	3	0	7	0
Ausanio, Joe, Norfolk	.800	35	1	3	1	5	0
Austin, Jim, Pawtucket	1.000	10	0	2	0	2	0
Baez, Kevin, Toledo	1.000	1	0	1	0	1	0
Bakkum, Scott, Paw.-Scr./W.B.	.952	44	9	11	1	21	3
Baptist, Travis, Syracuse*	.951	30	15	24	2	41	4
Bark, Brian, Norfolk*	1.000	12	1	2	0	3	0
Barnes, Brian, Toledo*	.850	14	5	12	3	20	2
Batista, Miguel, Charlotte	.941	47	5	11	1	17	2
Baxter, Bob, Ottawa*	.960	54	8	16	1	25	1
Beech, Matt, Scr./W.-B.*	1.000	2	0	1	0	1	0
Belinda, Stan, Pawtucket	1.000	6	1	2	0	3	0
Blazier, Ron, Scr./W.-B.	1.000	33	2	1	0	3	0
Blomdahl, Ben, Toledo	1.000	53	4	7	0	11	1
Boehringer, Brian, Columbus	.964	25	9	18	1	28	2
Bohanon, Brian, Syracuse*	.750	31	4	2	2	8	0
Borowski, Joe, Richmond	1.000	34	2	7	0	9	0
Boucher, Denis, Ottawa*	1.000	17	4	5	0	9	0
Brandow, Derek, Syracuse	.957	24	8	14	1	23	3
Brewer, Billy, Columbus*	1.000	10	0	4	0	4	0
Brock, Chris, Richmond	.889	26	13	11	3	27	2
Brow, Scott, Syracuse	.962	18	17	8	1	26	1
Brumley, Duff, Scr./W.-B.	1.000	20	2	1	0	3	0
Bullard, Jason, Norfolk	1.000	24	5	5	0	10	0
Bullinger, Kirk, Ottawa	.857	10	0	6	1	7	0
Burrows, Terry, Columbus*	1.000	23	0	7	0	7	0
Cain, Tim, Pawtucket	1.000	11	1	3	0	4	0
Carper, Mark, Columbus	.889	15	5	3	1	9	0
Carrara, Giovanni, Syracuse	1.000	9	2	5	0	7	2
Cederlane, Brett, Pawtucket	1.000	10	1	1	0	2	0
Chergey, Dan, Charlotte	1.000	45	5	2	0	7	0
Christopher, Mike, Toledo	1.000	39	2	1	0	3	0
Coppinger, Rocky, Rochester	1.000	12	1	10	0	11	1
Corbin, Archie, Rochester	1.000	20	3	4	0	7	0
Crawford, Carlos, Scr./W.-B.	.917	28	13	20	3	36	1
Crawford, Joe, Norfolk*	.955	20	3	18	1	22	0
Croghan, Andy, Columbus	1.000	14	1	1	0	2	0
Cumberland, Chris, Columbus*	.786	12	2	9	3	14	0
Czajkowski, Jim, Syracuse	.960	48	12	12	1	25	2
Darensbourg, Vic, Charlotte*	1.000	47	2	6	0	8	0
Dedrick, Jim, Rochester	.952	39	2	18	1	21	0
DeSilva, John, Pawtucket	.917	16	5	6	1	12	0
Dettmer, John, Richmond	1.000	19	4	3	0	7	1
Dixon, Steve, Rochester*	1.000	32	3	7	0	10	1
Dodd, Robert, Scr./W.-B.*	1.000	8	0	2	0	2	0
Doherty, John, Pawtucket	1.000	19	5	7	0	12	1
Doolan, Blake, Scr./W.-B.	.857	18	2	4	1	7	0
Dorlarque, Aaron, Ottawa	1.000	14	1	0	0	1	0
Drews, Matt, Columbus	.667	7	2	2	2	6	0

Player, Team	Pct.	G	PO	A	E	TC
Dunbar, Matt, Columbus*	1.000	14	0	2	0	2
Edenfield, Ken, Columbus	1.000	33	1	7	0	8
Edens, Tom, Rochester	.875	20	6	8	2	16
Eiland, Dave, Columbus	1.000	15	7	19	0	26
Elliott, Donnie, Scr./W.-B.	.926	21	10	15	2	27
Eshelman, Vaughn, Pawtucket*	1.000	7	2	9	0	11
Falteisek, Steve, Ottawa	1.000	12	5	15	0	20
Farrell, John, Toledo	1.000	6	4	1	0	5
Finnvold, Gar, Pawtucket	1.000	8	1	1	0	2
Flener, Huck, Syracuse*	.930	14	9	31	3	43
Florence, Don, Rochester*	1.000	36	2	16	0	18
Flynt, Will, Rochester*	1.000	4	1	1	0	2
Fox, Chad, Richmond	.842	18	8	8	3	19
Frey, Steve, Scr./W.-B.*	1.000	10	2	2	0	4
Frohwirth, Todd, Rochester	1.000	9	1	0	0	1
Fyhrie, Mike, Norfolk	.950	27	13	25	2	40
Garces, Rich, Pawtucket	1.000	10	0	2	0	2
Gardiner, Mike, Norfolk	.931	24	14	13	2	29
Gibson, Paul, Columbus*	1.000	9	0	2	0	2
Gohr, Greg, Toledo	1.000	2	2	0	0	2
Gonzalez, Gabe, Charlotte*	1.000	2	0	3	0	3
Gray, Dennis, Ottawa*	1.000	3	0	2	0	2
Greene, Tommy, Scr./W.-B.	1.000	5	1	3	0	4
Grott, Matt, Scr./W.B.-Roch.*	1.000	32	3	12	0	15
Grundt, Ken, Pawtucket*	1.000	44	3	9	0	12
Guilfoyle, Michael, Toledo*	.750	54	1	5	2	8
Gunderson, Eric, Pawtucket*	1.000	26	1	8	0	9
Hansen, Brent, Pawtucket	1.000	2	0	2	0	2
Harris, Doug, Roch.-Char.	.800	10	0	4	1	5
Harrison, Tommy, Richmond	1.000	10	1	1	0	2
Hartgraves, Dean, Richmond*	1.000	4	1	1	0	2
Haynes, Jimmy, Rochester	1.000	5	5	2	0	7
Heflin, Bronson, Scr./W.-B.	1.000	30	4	3	0	7
Henderson, Rod, Ottawa	.917	25	3	8	1	12
Henry, Dwayne, Toledo	.750	18	3	0	1	4
Hernandez, Livan, Charlotte	.900	10	2	7	1	10
Hines, Rich, Columbus*	1.000	32	5	11	0	16
Holman, Craig, Scr./W.-B.	.842	36	5	11	3	19
Horsman, Vince, Syracuse*	1.000	29	3	4	0	7
Hostetler, Mike, Richmond	.935	27	9	20	2	31
Hudson, Joe, Pawtucket	1.000	25	5	5	0	10
Hunter, Rich, Scr./W.-B.	.938	8	9	6	1	16
Hutton, Mark, Columbus	1.000	2	0	1	0	1
Ilsley, Blaise, Ott.-Scr./W.B.*	.938	25	7	8	1	16
Janzen, Marty, Syracuse	.938	10	7	8	1	16
Johnson, Dane, Syracuse	.889	43	3	5	1	9
Jordan, Ricardo, Scr./W.-B.*	.900	32	6	3	1	10
Juelsgaard, Jarod, Charlotte	1.000	26	4	10	0	14
Kamieniecki, Scott, Columbus	1.000	5	2	4	0	6
Karp, Ryan, Scr./W.-B.*	1.000	7	0	4	0	4
Keagle, Greg, Toledo	1.000	6	2	5	0	7
Knackert, Brent, Pawtucket	1.000	19	4	5	0	9
Kotarski, Mike, Columbus*	1.000	1	1	1	0	2
Krivda, Rick, Rochester*	1.000	8	2	4	0	6
Lacy, Kerry, Pawtucket	1.000	7	1	2	0	3
Lane, Aaron, Rochester*	.900	9	0	9	1	10
Larson, Toby, Norfolk	1.000	1	2	0	0	2
Lee, Mark, Nor.-Rich.*	.938	53	3	12	1	16
Leiper, Dave, Ottawa*	1.000	25	2	4	0	6
Lewis, Richie, Toledo	1.000	2	0	1	0	1
Lima, Jose, Toledo	1.000	12	5	6	0	11
Lomon, Kevin, Richmond	.900	26	13	14	3	30
Looney, Brian, Pawtucket*	.733	27	2	9	4	15
MacDonald, Bob, Norfolk*	1.000	27	2	4	0	6
Maddux, Mike, Richmond	1.000	3	0	3	0	3
Maduro, Calvin, Rochester	.833	8	2	3	1	6
Mantei, Matt, Charlotte	1.000	7	1	1	0	2
Marshall, Randy, Toledo*	.913	29	3	18	2	23
Martinez, Pedro, Norfolk*	1.000	34	3	6	0	9
Maxcy, Brian, Toledo	1.000	15	1	6	0	7
McCready, Jim, Norfolk	1.000	6	1	2	0	3
McCurry, Jeff, Toledo	1.000	39	4	5	0	9
Mecir, Jim, Columbus	.929	33	4	9	1	14
Melendez, Jose, Columbus	1.000	8	0	1	0	1
Mendoza, Ramiro, Columbus	1.000	15	8	18	0	26
Mendoza, Reynol, Charlotte	1.000	15	9	14	0	23
Miller, Kurt, Charlotte	.929	12	1	12	1	14
Miller, Trever, Toledo*	.939	27	9	22	2	33
Mimbs, Mike, Scr./W.-B.*	1.000	7	2	9	0	11
Minchey, Nate, Pawtucket	.875	14	7	7	2	16
Mitchell, Larry, Scr./W.-B.	1.000	11	1	1	0	2
Mix, Greg, Charlotte	.667	4	1	1	1	3

Player, Team	Pct.	G	PO	A	E	TC	DP
?onteleone, Rich, Columbus	.833	21	3	2	1	6	0
?ontoyo, Charlie, Ottawa	1.000	1	1	0	0	1	0
?unoz, Bobby, Scr./W.-B.	1.000	8	5	6	0	11	0
?unoz, Oscar, Rochester	.952	21	8	12	1	21	1
?urray, Matt, Scr./W.B.-Rich.	.867	18	6	7	2	15	1
?yers, Jimmy, Rochester	.955	39	5	16	1	22	2
?ichols, Rod, Richmond	.929	57	2	11	1	14	0
?ITKOWSKI, C.J., Toledo*	1.000	19	8	19	0	27	0
?ye, Ryan, Scr./W.-B.	1.000	14	8	12	0	20	0
?rellano, Rafael, Pawtucket*	.875	22	6	8	2	16	1
?ace, Scotty, Syracuse*	.909	20	1	9	1	11	1
?acheco, Alex, Ottawa	.875	33	0	7	1	8	0
?all, Donn, Charlotte	.900	38	5	4	1	10	1
?aniagua, Jose, Ottawa	.941	15	7	9	1	17	0
?avlas, Dave, Columbus	1.000	57	6	8	0	14	0
?erez, Yorkis, Charlotte*	.667	9	2	0	1	3	0
?erson, Robert, Norfolk	.833	8	3	2	1	6	0
?ett, Jose, Syracuse	1.000	20	9	16	0	25	1
?ierce, Jeff, Pawtucket	1.000	12	0	9	0	9	1
?olley, Dale, Columbus*	.889	31	4	4	1	9	1
?ose, Scott, Syracuse	1.000	2	1	0	0	1	0
?owell, Dennis, Rochester*	1.000	5	1	0	0	1	0
?uirico, Rafael, Scr./W.-B.*	.923	13	2	10	1	13	0
?amirez, Hector, Norfolk	1.000	3	0	2	0	2	0
?app, Pat, Charlotte	1.000	2	1	5	0	6	0
?eed, Rick, Norfolk	.979	28	12	34	1	47	1
?icci, Chuck, Pawtucket	1.000	60	4	6	0	10	1
?icken, Ray, Columbus	1.000	20	7	9	0	16	0
?ios, Dan, Columbus	1.000	24	0	4	0	4	0
?isley, Bill, Syracuse	.000	2	0	0	1	1	0
?ivera, Ben, Ottawa	1.000	31	5	3	0	8	1
?obinson, Ken, Syracuse	1.000	47	7	3	0	10	0
?odriguez, Nerio, Rochester	1.000	2	0	3	0	3	0
?ogers, Bryan, Norfolk	.833	20	0	5	1	6	0
?ogers, Jimmy, Syracuse	.833	8	5	0	1	6	0
?ojas, Euclides, Charlotte	1.000	6	0	1	0	1	0
?owland, Rich, Syracuse	1.000	1	1	0	0	1	0
?eter, Kirk, Ottawa*	1.000	3	5	5	0	10	1
?mer, Tim, Columbus*	1.000	12	4	6	0	10	1
?ackinsky, Brian, Rochester	1.000	14	3	8	0	11	1
?ager, A.J., Toledo	1.000	18	0	10	0	10	0
?canlan, Bob, Toledo	.818	14	6	3	2	11	0
?hilling, Curt, Scr./W.-B.	1.000	2	0	4	0	4	1
?hmidt, Curt, Ottawa	.938	54	3	12	1	16	0
?hmidt, Jason, Richmond	1.000	7	2	2	0	4	0
?hullstrom, Erik, Pawtucket	1.000	15	4	3	0	7	1
?hutz, Carl, Richmond*	1.000	41	1	3	0	4	0
?eelbach, Chris, Charlotte	.889	25	5	11	2	18	0
?hepherd, Keith, Rochester	.944	27	3	14	1	18	0
?house, Brian, Rochester*	.875	32	2	5	1	8	0
?evert, Mark, Syracuse	1.000	10	1	7	0	8	0
?idowsky, Clint, Toledo	.971	19	11	23	1	35	0

Player, Team	Pct.	G	PO	A	E	TC	DP
Spoljaric, Paul, Syracuse*	1.000	17	2	4	0	6	0
Steph, Rod, Richmond	1.000	38	5	7	0	12	1
Stephenson, Garrett, Rochester	1.000	23	7	19	0	26	3
Stull, Everett, Ottawa	.900	13	4	5	1	10	1
Suppan, Jeff, Pawtucket	.950	22	7	12	1	20	0
Telford, Anthony, Ottawa	.943	30	11	22	2	35	2
Thobe, Tom, Richmond*	.923	31	3	9	1	13	0
Thompson, Justin, Toledo*	1.000	13	1	10	0	11	0
Tomlin, Randy, Pawtucket*	1.000	5	3	5	0	8	0
Trilicek, Rick, Norfolk	.941	62	6	10	1	17	0
Troutman, Keith, Scr./W.-B.	1.000	8	0	2	0	2	0
Urbani, Thomas, Toledo*	1.000	4	1	4	0	5	1
Urbina, Ugueth, Ottawa	.667	5	1	1	1	3	0
Valdes, Marc, Charlotte	1.000	8	3	11	0	14	0
VanEgmond, Tim, Pawtucket	.846	11	3	8	2	13	0
Walker, Mike, Toledo	1.000	28	6	9	0	15	0
Wallace, Derek, Norfolk	1.000	49	3	6	0	9	0
Wallace, Kent, Columbus	1.000	13	10	6	0	16	1
Ware, Jeff, Syracuse	1.000	13	7	9	0	16	0
Weathers, David, Char.-Col.	.500	4	0	1	1	2	0
Welch, Mike, Norfolk	1.000	10	0	2	0	2	0
West, Dave, Scr./W.-B.*	1.000	2	0	2	0	2	0
Weston, Mickey, Charlotte	.967	31	8	21	1	30	0
Whisenant, Matt, Charlotte*	.931	28	8	19	2	29	3
Whitehurst, Wally, Ott.-Col.	1.000	28	6	16	0	22	2
Wiegandt, Scott, Scr./W.-B.*	1.000	46	5	9	0	14	0
Williams, Brian, Toledo	.750	3	0	3	1	4	0
Williams, Jeff, Rochester	1.000	8	0	2	0	2	1
Williams, Mitch, Scr./W.-B.*	.857	9	0	6	1	7	0
Williams, Woody, Syracuse	.800	7	0	4	1	5	0
Withem, Shannon, Norfolk	.750	8	1	5	2	8	0
Woodall, Brad, Richmond*	.864	21	4	15	3	22	0
Yan, Esteban, Rochester	.800	22	3	1	1	5	0

PITCHERS WITH TWO OR MORE TEAMS

Player, Team	Pct.	G	PO	A	E	TC	DP
Bakkum, Scott, Pawtucket	.900	14	4	5	1	10	2
Bakkum, Scott, Scr./W.-B.	1.000	30	5	6	0	11	1
Grott, Matt, Scr./W.-B.*	1.000	27	3	12	0	15	0
Grott, Matt, Rochester*	.000	5	0	0	0	0	0
Harris, Doug, Rochester	.800	7	0	4	1	5	0
Harris, Doug, Charlotte	.000	3	0	0	0	0	0
Ilsley, Blaise, Ottawa*	.933	20	7	7	1	15	1
Ilsley, Blaise, Scr./W.-B.*	1.000	5	0	1	0	1	0
Lee, Mark, Norfolk*	.889	33	2	6	1	9	0
Lee, Mark, Richmond*	1.000	20	1	6	0	7	0
Murray, Matt, Scr./W.-B.	.833	13	6	4	2	12	1
Murray, Matt, Richmond	1.000	5	0	3	0	3	0
Weathers, David, Charlotte	.000	1	0	0	0	0	0
Weathers, David, Columbus	.500	3	0	1	1	2	0
Whitehurst, Wally, Ottawa	1.000	15	3	4	0	7	0
Whitehurst, Wally, Columbus	1.000	13	3	12	0	15	2

The following players did not have any fielding statistics at the positions indicated or appeared only as a designated hitter, pinch-hitter or pinch-runner: Amaro, 3b; ?ll, 3b; Benitez, p; Bieser, p; Brito, p; R. Brock, p; Brooks, 3b; Buccheri, p; Byrd, p; Canseco, dh-ph; Clapinski, p; P. Clark, 2b; Cole, p; Coolbaugh, ss; Cotton, 3b; Cox, DeJesus, p; Delvecchio, dh-ph; Denson, dh; Dismuke, p; Dodson, p; Floyd, 3b; Gallaher, p; Grijak, of; Habyan, p; Hammond, p; Heffernan, of; C. Howard, 1b; ?rzembeck, p; E. Johnson, p; Martin, p-1b; Montoyo, 2b; Mummau, of; Olivares, p; Olmeda, p; Posada, of; Revenig, p; Schwarz, p; Sele, p; Strawberry, dh; T. Torres, ?-ss; Wilson, dh; Wrona, p; J. Yan, p; Zinter, 3b.

LEAGUE CHAMPIONS

Year Team	Pct.	Year Team	Pct.	Year Team	Pct.
?84— Trenton	.520	1902— Toronto	.669	1922— Baltimore	.689
?85— Syracuse	.584	1903— Jersey City	.742	1923— Baltimore	.677
?86— Utica	.646	1904— Buffalo	.657	1924— Baltimore	.709
?87— Toronto	.644	1905— Providence	.638	1925— Baltimore	.633
?88— Syracuse	.723	1906— Buffalo	.607	1926— Toronto	.657
?89— Detroit	.649	1907— Toronto	.619	1927— Buffalo	.667
?90— Detroit	.617	1908— Baltimore	.593	1928— Rochester	.549
?91— Buffalo (reg. season)	.727	1909— Rochester	.596	1929— Rochester	.613
Buffalo (supplemental)	.680	1910— Rochester	.601	1930— Rochester	.629
?92— Providence	.615	1911— Rochester	.645	1931— Rochester	.601
Binghamton*	.667	1912— Toronto	.595	1932— Newark	.649
?93— Erie	.606	1913— Newark	.625	1933— Newark	.622
?94— Providence	.696	1914— Providence	.617	Buffalo (4th)†	.494
?95— Springfield	.687	1915— Buffalo	.632	1934— Newark	.608
?96— Providence	.602	1916— Buffalo	.586	Toronto (3rd)†	.559
?97— Syracuse	.632	1917— Toronto	.604	1935— Montreal	.597
?98— Montreal	.586	1918— Toronto	.693	Syracuse (2nd)†	.565
?99— Rochester	.624	1919— Baltimore	.671	1936— Buffalo‡	.610
?00— Providence	.616	1920— Baltimore	.719	1937— Newark‡	.717
?01— Rochester	.642	1921— Baltimore	.717	1938— Newark‡	.684

Year	Team	Pct.	Year	Team	Pct.	Year	Team	Pct.
1939—	Jersey City	.582	1959—	Buffalo	.582	1978—	Charleston	.607
	Rochester (2nd)†	.556		Havana (3rd)†	.523		Richmond (4th)†	.511
1940—	Rochester	.611	1960—	Toronto‡	.649	1979—	Columbus‡	.612
	Newark (2nd)†	.594	1961—	Columbus	.597	1980—	Columbus‡	.593
1941—	Newark	.649		Buffalo (3rd)†	.559	1981—	Columbus‡	.633
	Montreal (2nd)†	.584	1962—	Jacksonville	.610	1982—	Richmond	.590
1942—	Newark	.601		Atlanta (3rd)†	.539		Tidewater (3rd)†	.540
	Syracuse (3rd)†	.513	1963—	Syracuse∞	.533	1983—	Columbus	.593
1943—	Toronto	.625		Indianapolis‡	.562		Tidewater (4th)†	.511
	Syracuse (3rd)†	.536	1964—	Jacksonville	.589	1984—	Columbus	.590
1944—	Baltimore‡	.553		Rochester (4th)†	.532		Pawtucket (4th)†	.536
1945—	Montreal	.621	1965—	Columbus	.582	1985—	Syracuse	.564
	Newark (2nd)†	.582		Toronto (3rd)†	.556		Tidewater (4th)†	.540
1946—	Montreal‡	.649	1966—	Rochester	.565	1986—	Richmond‡	.571
1947—	Jersey City	.610		Toronto (2nd-tied)†	.558	1987—	Tidewater	.579
	Syracuse (3rd)†	.575	1967—	Richmond	.574		Columbus†	.550
1948—	Montreal‡	.614		Toledo (3rd)†	.525	1988—	Rochester♦	.546
1949—	Buffalo	.584	1968—	Toledo	.565		Tidewater	.546
	Montreal (3rd)†	.545		Jacksonville (4th)†	.514	1989—	Syracuse	.572
1950—	Rochester	.609	1969—	Tidewater	.563		Richmond♦	.555
	Baltimore (3rd)†	.556		Syracuse (3rd)†	.536	1990—	Rochester♦	.614
1951—	Montreal‡	.617	1970—	Syracuse‡	.600		Columbus	.596
1952—	Montreal	.629	1971—	Rochester‡	.614	1991—	Columbus♦	.590
	Rochester (3rd)†	.619	1972—	Louisville	.563		Pawtucket	.552
1953—	Rochester	.630		Tidewater (3rd)†	.545	1992—	Columbus♦	.660
	Montreal (2nd)†	.586	1973—	Charleston	.586		Scr. W.B.	.592
1954—	Toronto	.630		Pawtucket▲†	.534	1993—	Charlotte♦	.610
	Syracuse (4th)§	.510	1974—	Memphis	.613		Rochester	.525
1955—	Montreal	.617		Rochester ∞‡	.611	1994—	Richmond♦	.567
	Rochester (4th)†	.497	1975—	Tidewater‡	.610		Pawtucket	.549
1956—	Toronto	.566	1976—	Rochester	.638	1995—	Norfolk	.606
	Rochester (2nd)†	.553		Syracuse (2nd)†	.590		Ottawa♦	.507
1957—	Toronto	.575	1977—	Pawtucket	.571	1996—	Columbus♦	.599
	Buffalo (2nd)†	.571		Charleston (2nd)‡	.557		Rochester	.511
1958—	Montreal‡	.588						

*Won split-season playoff. †Won four-team playoff. ‡Won championship and four-team playoff. §Defeated Havana in game to decide fourth place, the won four-team playoff. ∞League was divided into Northern, Southern divisions. ▲League divided into American, National divisions. ♦League divided in Eastern, Western divisions; won playoffs. (NOTE—Known as Eastern League in 1884, New York State League in 1885, International League in 1886-8 International Association in 1888, International League in 1889-90, Eastern Association in 1891 and Eastern League from 1892 until 1912.)

MEXICAN LEAGUE

1996 FINAL STANDINGS

FIRST HALF

NORTHERN ZONE

Team	W	L	T	Pct.	GB
...nterrey	43	15	1	.741	...
...ynosa	31	27	1	.534	12
...evo Laredo	28	31	0	.475	15$^{1}/_{2}$
...nclova	28	31	0	.475	15$^{1}/_{2}$
...rreon	24	33	2	.421	18$^{1}/_{2}$
...tillo	20	38	1	.345	23

CENTRAL ZONE

Team	W	L	T	Pct.	GB
...xico City Tigers	38	19	1	.667	....
...uascalientes	31	28	0	.525	8
...xico City Red Devils	31	28	0	.525	8
...za Rica	28	29	1	.491	10
...xaca	20	38	0	.345	18$^{1}/_{2}$

SOUTHERN ZONE

Team	W	L	T	Pct.	GB
...mpeche	30	28	1	.517	....
...catan	30	29	0	.508	$^{1}/_{2}$
...ntana Roo	29	29	0	.500	1
...asco	28	30	1	.483	2
...aatitlan	26	32	1	.448	4

SECOND HALF

NORTHERN ZONE

Team	W	L	T	Pct.	GB
Monterrey	39	18	0	.684	....
Monclova	30	25	1	.545	8
Torreon	26	29	1	.473	12
Reynosa	25	29	1	.463	12$^{1}/_{2}$
Saltillo	21	32	3	.396	16
Nuevo Laredo	20	34	3	.370	17$^{1}/_{2}$

CENTRAL ZONE

Team	W	L	T	Pct.	GB
Mexico City Red Devils	39	15	1	.722	....
Poza Rica	35	21	1	.625	5
Mexico City Tigers	30	26	0	.536	10
Oaxaca	26	26	5	.500	12
Aguascalientes	27	29	0	.482	13

SOUTHERN ZONE

Team	W	L	T	Pct.	GB
Yucatan	28	27	1	.509	....
Quintana Roo	26	26	5	.500	$^{1}/_{2}$
Campeche	23	31	2	.426	4$^{1}/_{2}$
Tabasco	20	33	3	.377	7
Minatitlan	19	33	1	.365	7$^{1}/_{2}$

COMPOSITE

NORTHERN ZONE

Team	W	L	T	Pct.	GB
...nterrey	82	33	1	.713	....
...nclova	58	56	1	.509	23$^{1}/_{2}$
...ynosa	56	56	2	.500	24$^{1}/_{2}$
...reon	50	62	3	.446	30$^{1}/_{2}$
...evo Laredo	48	65	3	.424	33
...tillo	41	70	4	.369	39

CENTRAL ZONE

Team	W	L	T	Pct.	GB
Mexico City Red Devils	70	43	1	.619	....
Mexico City Tigers	68	45	1	.602	2
Poza Rica	63	50	2	.558	7
Aguascalientes	58	57	0	.504	13
Oaxaca	46	64	5	.418	22$^{1}/_{2}$

SOUTHERN ZONE

Team	W	L	T	Pct.	GB
Yucatan	58	56	1	.509	....
Quintana Roo	55	55	5	.500	1
Campeche	53	59	3	.473	4
Tabasco	48	63	4	.432	8$^{1}/_{2}$
Minatitlan	45	65	2	.409	11

...LAYOFFS—Mexico City Red Devils defeated Aguascalientes, four games to three; Mexico City Tigers defeated Poza Rica, four games to one; Monterrey defeated ...nclova, four games to two; Yucatan defeated Campeche, four games to one, in the first round. Mexico City Red Devils defeated Mexico City Tigers, four games to ... Monterrey defeated Yucatan, four games to two, in the second round. Monterrey defeated Mexico City Red Devils, four games to one, in final series to capture ...ue championship.

(Compiled by Ana Luisa Perea Talarico, League Statistician, Mexico, D.F.)

1996 BATTING

TEAM

...m	Avg.	G	TPA	AB	R	H	TB	2B	3B	HR	RBI	SH	SF	HP	BB	IBB	SO	SB	CS	GDP	LOB	ShO	Slg.	OBP
...nterrey	.297	116	4453	3863	663	1146	1584	193	34	59	602	49	51	30	460	29	519	127	69	60	830	..	.410	.371
...Red Devils	.293	114	4419	3870	595	1135	1623	175	29	85	546	33	38	30	448	35	467	100	47	115	878	..	.419	.368
...nosa	.284	114	4451	3783	586	1075	1565	188	28	82	540	57	26	49	536	34	508	37	21	92	948	..	.414	.378
...Tigers	.278	114	4432	3890	560	1083	1567	166	12	98	504	62	40	36	404	42	691	82	46	78	851	..	.403	.349
...eon	.277	115	4475	3836	567	1063	1495	158	29	72	527	64	28	36	511	24	568	21	19	111	921	..	.390	.365
...ascalientes	.275	115	4306	3787	509	1043	1468	179	21	68	457	57	23	45	394	31	456	41	39	102	851	..	.388	.349
...clova	.272	115	4501	3787	581	1031	1507	171	16	91	537	80	35	24	575	36	460	30	17	116	942	..	.398	.369
...llo	.270	115	4369	3745	498	1012	1339	160	25	39	462	53	37	36	498	28	541	42	39	111	916	..	.358	.358
...aca	.270	115	4208	3663	453	990	1302	151	22	39	397	70	27	37	411	34	460	64	38	107	849	..	.355	.348
...vo Laredo	.266	116	4516	3803	510	1011	1406	166	14	67	466	57	23	45	588	26	510	51	44	120	982	..	.370	.369
...a Rica	.259	115	4285	3772	418	977	1258	123	28	34	375	79	25	29	380	39	404	59	13	94	848	..	.344	.330
...atitlan	.253	112	4154	3547	420	899	1153	140	15	28	370	65	34	39	469	28	482	34	32	121	824	..	.325	.344
...peche	.251	115	4086	3476	425	874	1204	131	17	55	383	106	32	56	416	41	497	72	48	95	797	..	.346	.338
...sco	.248	115	3995	3568	341	886	1083	106	11	23	297	77	23	36	470	68	47	90	760	..	.304	.310	
...tan	.248	115	4256	3649	399	904	1159	124	13	35	350	78	24	48	457	45	499	91	40	96	872	..	.318	.337
...tana Roo	.243	115	4257	3655	415	887	1184	126	12	49	360	96	33	31	442	35	475	40	26	111	840	..	.324	.327

INDIVIDUAL

TOP QUALIFIERS FOR BATTING CHAMPIONSHIP

Minimum 313 plate appearances.

CLASS AAA *Mexican League*

Player, Team	Avg.	G	TPA	AB	R	H	TB	2B	3B	HR	RBI	SH	SF	HP	BB	IBB	SO	SB	CS	GDP	Slg.	O
Carrillo, G. Matias, Tig.	.368	108	464	391	77	144	240	31	1	21	86	2	4	4	57	9	34	11	7	14	.614	
Tellez, J. Alonso, Rey.	.365	80	337	293	54	107	149	19	1	7	49	3	0	3	38	3	19	1	1	13	.509	.4
Gonzalez, Jose, Mont.	.354	107	453	384	84	136	197	21	5	10	71	2	7	2	58	1	68	34	11	5	.513	.4
Garcia Ch., Cornelio, Mont.	.345	103	472	374	87	129	162	21	6	0	50	2	4	0	92	8	49	30	21	2	.433	.4
Chance, Tony, Monc.	.338	115	513	435	84	147	217	31	0	13	78	2	5	1	70	4	53	4	3	14	.499	.4
Magallanes, Everardo, Mont.	.338	82	330	287	60	97	123	16	2	2	46	3	2	3	35	2	27	7	2	3	.429	.4
Chimelis, Joel, Oax	.327	113	483	416	72	136	196	33	3	7	51	11	2	7	47	5	28	4	4	14	.471	.4
Stark, Matt, Rey	.321	103	457	358	66	115	181	24	0	14	72	0	3	6	90	2	24	2	0	9	.506	.4
Martinez, L. Domingo, Rey	.320	114	490	413	75	132	216	22	4	18	91	0	4	6	67	5	51	1	1	13	.523	.4
Felix S., Junior, Rey	.319	95	408	335	73	107	190	20	3	19	50	3	3	5	62	11	71	3	3	6	.567	.4

DEPARTMENTAL LEADERS: G—B. Rodriquez, G. Sanchez, 116; AB—Aganza, 452; R—C. Garcia, 87; H—Chance,147; 2B—E. Zambrano, 34; 3B—Three players t with 7; HR—Horn, 30; RBI—G. Velazquez, 12; SH—A. Castro, 31; SF—Tolentino, G. Velazquez, 9; HP—Cervera, 17; BB—Horn, 124; IBB—E. Castro, Horn, 13; SO Horn, 92; SB—Jo. Gonzalez, 34; CS—Garcia, C., 21; GIDP—Aganza, 23; Slg.—M. Carrillo, 614.

ALL PLAYERS

Player, Team	Avg.	G	TPA	AB	R	H	TB	2B	3B	HR	RBI	SH	SF	HP	BB	IBB	SO	SB	CS	GDP	Slg.	C
Abrego, M. Jesus, Oax	.206	83	284	238	23	49	67	9	0	3	28	5	0	1	40	4	30	1	1	4	.282	.3
Aganza, E. Ruben, Monc.	.277	115	505	452	67	125	204	19	0	20	80	1	4	1	47	4	44	1	0	23	.451	.3
Aguilar, Enrique, Agua.	.277	96	360	328	41	91	119	13	0	5	40	1	0	4	27	6	28	2	2	9	.363	.3
Aguilera, Antonio, Mex	.276	102	451	387	61	107	134	11	2	4	55	1	5	3	55	5	39	7	5	8	.346	.3
Aguilera, Armando, Sal	.225	76	199	182	15	41	50	5	2	0	10	4	1	2	10	1	31	2	2	5	.275	.2
Almeida, Shammar, Sal	.214	59	156	131	16	28	38	1	0	3	18	0	2	1	24	2	42	0	0	2	.290	
Almendra, Gregorio, Tab	.158	16	25	19	6	3	3	0	0	0	1	0	1	1	4	0	1	0	0	0	.158	
Alvarez, Hector, Q.R.	.253	96	399	363	39	92	124	15	1	5	38	9	4	0	23	2	36	5	5	9	.342	
Alvarez, Luis, Yuc	.273	10	36	33	2	9	13	4	0	0	4	2	0	0	1	0	2	2	0	1	.394	
Amador, Alfonso, Agua.	.000	1	1	0	0	0	0	0	0	0	0	0	0	0	1	0	0	0	0	0	.000	1.
Arano, Wilfredo, Lar	.320	51	209	172	22	55	67	6	3	0	11	2	0	4	23	0	13	4	5	3	.390	
Arauz, E. Ignacio, P.R.	.193	39	60	57	5	11	17	3	0	1	4	0	0	1	2	0	13	0	0	2	.298	
Arce Francisco, Javier, Tab	.222	6	10	9	0	2	2	0	0	0	1	0	1	0	0	0	2	0	0	2	.222	
Arevalo, Guadalupe, Agua.	.255	63	191	165	15	42	54	10	1	0	20	4	3	1	18	0	12	0	3	3	.327	
Arias, Everardo, Q.R.	.186	30	52	43	5	8	10	2	0	0	2	2	0	0	7	0	9	1	1	3	.233	
Armas, Marcos, Tab	.247	26	84	81	6	20	28	5	0	1	6	0	0	3	0	0	19	0	0	1	.346	
Armenta, Fernando, Min	.273	3	11	11	0	3	4	1	0	0	2	0	0	0	0	0	3	0	0	0	.364	
Armenta, Guillermo, Mex	.247	41	92	81	9	20	22	2	0	0	8	2	1	0	8	0	12	3	2	1	.272	
Arredondo, Jesus, Agua.	.262	86	380	317	53	83	95	3	3	1	20	8	2	4	49	1	32	11	7	3	.300	
Arredondo, Luis, Mex	.292	106	484	418	75	122	167	19	7	4	47	6	3	0	57	1	50	32	12	9	.400	
Arvizu, Javier, Cam	.087	12	26	23	1	2	2	0	0	0	1	0	0	0	3	0	1	0	0	0	.087	
Attwell, Sergio, Monc.	.500	2	2	2	0	1	1	0	0	0	0	0	0	0	0	0	1	0	0	0	.500	
Avila, G. Roberto, Min	.095	32	47	42	1	4	4	0	0	0	7	3	0	0	2	0	9	0	0	0	.095	
Avila, Ruben, Tor	.278	100	387	335	46	93	135	13	1	9	51	6	2	3	41	0	53	1	0	14	.403	
Aviles, Alejandro, Sal	.162	16	45	37	3	6	6	0	0	0	2	1	1	0	6	0	10	0	1	2	.162	
Azocar, Oscar, P.R.	.312	115	469	443	52	138	197	15	7	10	56	3	2	1	20	5	20	4	2	17	.445	
Balderas, S. Abelardo, Min	.192	43	97	78	8	15	15	0	0	0	11	6	2	0	11	0	11	1	0	3	.192	
Barrera, Jesus Antonio, Q.R.	.171	46	88	76	8	13	15	2	0	0	5	3	0	0	9	0	6	0	0	2	.197	
Barrera, R. Nelson, Mont.	.304	110	444	398	48	121	177	23	0	11	78	2	5	6	33	5	48	7	2	19	.445	
Basse, Mike, P.R.	.259	27	115	85	15	22	27	3	1	0	6	5	0	0	25	2	13	8	2	1	.318	
Beltran, P. Gerardo, Min	.264	85	286	250	31	66	97	7	3	6	21	8	1	5	22	0	39	0	4	7	.388	
Beristran, R. Gregorio, Min	.265	23	43	34	5	9	10	1	0	0	3	0	0	0	9	0	3	0	0	5	.294	
Bojorquez, Victor, Mex	.417	38	28	24	16	10	17	0	2	1	7	0	0	0	4	0	4	1	1	0	.708	
Bolick, Frank, Oax	.308	89	371	299	56	92	140	19	1	9	64	1	6	0	65	9	51	1	1	8	.468	
Bowie, Jim, Agua.	.309	76	306	262	33	81	102	12	0	3	37	1	4	0	39	9	18	3	1	7	.389	
Cabreja, Alexis, Min	.313	16	78	67	11	21	22	1	0	0	8	1	1	4	6	0	9	4	0	3	.328	
Cabrera, Francisco, Monc.	.262	35	146	130	11	34	39	5	0	0	14	1	1	0	14	2	18	1	0	12	.300	
Camacho, Adulfo, Sal	.214	81	259	210	35	45	57	8	2	0	18	9	3	4	42	0	50	0	3	4	.271	
Camacho, C. Adrian, Sal	.000	1	1	0	0	0	0	0	0	0	0	0	0	0	0	0	0	0	0	0	.000	
Campo, Oscar, P.R.	.143	12	16	14	1	2	2	0	0	0	0	0	0	1	1	0	9	0	0	0	.143	
Canizalez, Juan Carlos, Mont.	.313	114	469	422	71	132	198	25	7	9	62	3	4	3	37	7	37	3	6	3	.469	
Cantu, Gerardo, Q.R.	.121	19	37	33	2	4	4	0	0	0	1	0	0	0	4	0	6	0	1	1	.121	
Carranza, Pedro, Mex	.400	8	12	10	2	4	5	1	0	0	2	0	0	0	2	0	1	0	2	0	.500	
Carrasco, Ernesto, Lar	.245	112	428	367	43	90	103	13	0	0	28	15	1	4	41	4	31	3	4	6	.281	
Carrillo, G. Matias, Tig.	.368	108	464	391	77	144	240	31	1	21	86	2	4	4	57	9	34	11	7	14	.614	
Castaldo, Vince, Oax	.211	18	74	57	9	12	15	3	0	0	6	0	1	1	15	0	13	0	0	2	.263	
Castaneda, Hector, Min	.237	88	295	257	28	61	82	13	1	2	28	2	3	4	29	3	27	2	2	8	.319	
Castaneda, Rafael, Tig.	.295	100	412	352	34	104	129	12	2	3	41	10	2	0	48	2	26	3	4	17	.366	
Castillejos, Luis, Tab	.000	1	1	0	0	0	0	0	0	0	0	0	0	0	0	0	0	0	0	0	.000	
Castillo, Braulio, Tab	.260	49	199	173	23	45	71	9	1	5	28	0	2	2	22	1	36	0	0	6	.410	
Castillo, Juan, Q.R.	.191	13	53	47	3	9	9	0	0	0	4	1	0	0	5	0	12	0	1	2	.191	
Castro, C. Arnoldo, Q.R.	.230	108	480	404	49	93	106	10	0	1	30	31	3	1	41	1	35	4	1	11	.262	
Castro, R. Eddie, Min	.285	106	418	319	43	91	127	18	0	6	46	1	4	4	90	13	49	1	2	12	.398	
Cazarin, Manuel, Yuc	.260	97	363	335	36	87	107	14	0	2	37	1	1	1	18	1	28	1	8	2	.319	
Cervera, Francisco, Cam	.265	106	399	302	39	80	122	19	1	7	54	15	6	17	59	4	54	12	7	14	.404	
Chan Q., Armando, Monc.	.305	75	222	190	25	58	75	7	2	2	26	1	1	2	28	6	21	1	1	4	.395	
Chance, Tony, Monc.	.338	115	513	435	84	147	217	31	0	13	78	2	5	1	70	4	53	4	3	14	.499	
Chimelis, Joel, Oax	.327	113	483	416	72	136	196	33	3	7	51	11	2	7	47	5	28	4	4	14	.471	
Clark, Tim, Sal	.280	112	479	411	68	115	194	26	4	15	85	0	8	5	55	5	57	1	3	16	.472	

yer, Team	Avg.	G	TPA	AB	R	H	TB	2B	3B	HR	RBI	SH	SF	HP	BB	IBB	SO	SB	CS	GDP	Slg	OBP
ɔos, P. Rogelio, Oax	.257	74	226	202	25	52	70	10	1	2	17	5	1	1	17	0	38	0	4	11	.347	.317
on, Cristobal, P.R.	.249	61	252	229	26	57	74	11	3	0	15	2	2	1	18	3	26	2	0	7	.323	.304
ntreras, Jose, Mont.	.300	17	22	20	3	6	6	0	0	0	1	0	0	0	2	0	2	0	1	0	.300	.364
rrales, Virgilio, P.R.	.000	4	3	3	0	0	0	0	0	0	0	0	0	0	0	0	0	0	0	0	.000	.000
z, Juan Diego, Yuc	.000	1	0	0	1	0	0	0	0	0	0	0	0	0	0	0	0	0	0	0	.000	.000
z, Marco Antonio, Lar	.265	74	262	238	21	63	84	9	0	4	27	2	1	3	18	1	22	0	1	15	.353	.323
z, Luis Alfonso, Rey	.269	101	408	357	34	96	127	14	1	5	48	5	4	7	35	6	40	0	2	9	.356	.342
eto, Raul, Min	.173	29	63	52	3	9	11	2	0	0	5	0	0	1	10	0	5	0	1	2	.212	.317
La Nuez, Rex, Lar	.269	67	300	227	60	61	105	14	0	10	33	5	0	3	65	0	50	2	1	7	.463	.437
Lima, Rafael, Min	.228	28	120	101	14	23	28	3	1	0	9	3	1	1	17	1	15	4	0	2	.277	.342
gado, R. Tomas, Min	.222	6	11	9	2	2	3	1	0	0	4	0	1	0	1	0	1	0	0	0	.333	.231
nson, Drew, Mex	.314	82	332	277	41	87	149	18	1	14	50	0	3	8	35	5	42	0	2	10	.538	.402
z, Pedro, Tig.	.000	1	1	0	0	0	0	0	0	0	0	0	0	0	1	0	0	0	0	0	.000	1.000
z, Luis Fernando, Tig.	.300	103	419	360	58	108	176	18	1	16	62	0	6	0	53	9	86	9	8	7	.489	.384
z, R. Remigio, Mont.	.290	100	342	307	41	89	102	6	2	1	35	8	1	0	26	1	25	12	5	8	.332	.344
minguez, Fausto, P.R.	.280	19	28	25	1	7	8	1	0	0	2	1	0	1	0	0	4	0	0	0	.320	.296
minguez, J. David, Tab	.277	110	449	365	44	101	123	16	0	2	46	5	5	4	70	4	53	2	7	10	.337	.394
arte, C. Rene J., Tab	.282	69	219	188	23	53	69	11	1	1	25	8	3	1	19	1	22	2	2	4	.367	.346
ran, B. Felipe, Oax	.272	103	391	364	32	99	125	10	5	2	34	8	3	5	11	0	49	4	0	9	.343	.300
ira, Honorio, Tab	.256	23	44	43	2	11	12	1	0	0	4	0	0	0	1	0	10	0	0	1	.279	.273
iquez, Graciano, Agua.	.144	40	112	97	3	14	21	1	3	0	3	4	0	0	11	0	21	1	3	5	.216	.231
iquez, Martin, Agua.	.000	1	1	1	0	0	0	0	0	0	0	0	0	0	0	0	0	0	0	0	.000	.000
calante, Marcelo, Sal	.209	49	91	86	7	18	22	2	1	0	6	4	0	1	4	1	25	0	2	2	.256	.253
ino, Daniel, Agua.	.091	9	12	11	0	1	1	0	0	0	0	0	0	0	1	0	2	0	0	0	.091	.167
inoza, Jose M., Monc	.200	7	12	10	1	2	2	0	0	0	2	0	0	0	2	0	4	0	0	0	.200	.333
inoza, Ramon, Tor	.300	4	12	10	2	3	3	0	0	0	3	0	0	0	2	0	3	0	1	0	.300	.357
inoza, E. Javier, Cam	.250	73	214	168	23	42	54	1	1	3	19	8	2	1	35	3	16	3	2	3	.321	.379
quer, E. Ramon, Rey	.263	109	472	399	61	105	137	17	6	1	40	8	3	2	60	3	50	8	0	6	.343	.360
rada, Hector, Q.R.	.264	115	455	409	32	108	143	20	0	5	41	5	1	7	33	5	48	3	3	14	.350	.329
rada, Ruben, Lar	.289	24	41	38	3	11	12	1	0	0	5	1	0	1	1	0	7	0	0	0	.316	.325
x, Arturo, Yuc	.228	102	346	298	23	68	83	12	0	1	23	14	1	2	31	1	47	3	1	3	.279	.304
x, S. Junior Fco., Rey	.319	94	408	335	73	107	190	20	3	19	50	3	3	5	62	11	71	3	3	6	.567	.430
tanes, Oscar, Tab	.288	108	406	375	42	108	133	11	4	2	38	5	3	6	17	3	48	3	8	6	.355	.327
nandez, Daniel, Mex	.313	105	477	402	84	126	164	17	6	3	27	3	3	2	67	2	39	26	5	8	.408	.411
nandez, J. Fabian, Mex	.246	26	62	57	6	14	19	1	2	0	6	1	0	0	4	0	10	0	1	1	.333	.295
ueroa, Bienvenido, Mex.	.364	14	37	33	8	12	17	3	1	0	4	0	0	0	4	0	5	0	1	0	.515	.432
es, Miguel, Mont.	.280	107	463	407	81	114	146	18	4	2	41	4	4	5	43	1	39	27	8	11	.359	.353
nes, G. Daniel, Rey	.174	16	29	23	3	4	4	0	0	0	2	3	0	1	2	0	1	0	1	1	.174	.269
, Eric, P.R.	.235	60	265	238	30	56	74	6	3	2	19	2	2	2	21	2	30	2	3	3	.311	.300
nco, Manuel, Yuc	.250	55	182	164	15	41	55	8	0	2	20	3	2	0	13	1	30	6	1	4	.335	.302
ney, Ty, Mex	.345	71	302	235	54	81	155	17	0	19	61	0	6	5	56	10	37	3	1	9	.660	.470
nboa, Jose A., P.R.	.125	9	9	8	1	1	1	0	0	0	2	0	0	0	1	0	1	0	0	0	.125	.222
cia, Heriberto, P.R.	.252	103	411	361	33	91	106	9	3	0	32	17	3	2	28	0	18	7	1	7	.294	.307
cia, Cornelio, Mont.	.345	103	472	374	87	129	162	21	6	0	50	2	4	0	92	8	49	30	21	2	.433	.470
cia, Hector, Tor	.308	100	407	354	58	109	129	6	4	2	29	11	1	1	40	2	32	7	2	7	.364	.379
ibay, Roberto, Q.R.	.000	1	2	2	0	0	0	0	0	0	0	0	0	0	0	0	0	0	0	0	.000	.000
za, Alejandro, Agua.	.000	1	0	0	0	0	0	0	0	0	0	0	0	0	0	0	0	0	0	0	.000	.000
za, G. Gerardo, Tor	.276	106	389	352	35	97	121	11	2	3	54	8	4	2	23	1	31	0	2	9	.344	.320
zon, Eliseo, Tab	.261	89	301	253	20	66	84	10	1	2	21	6	2	3	37	3	32	0	1	5	.332	.359
telum, G. Carlos, Monc	.283	79	246	212	21	60	69	9	0	0	25	13	2	1	18	0	22	0	0	7	.325	.339
telum, G. Sergio Omar., Tig.	.238	48	92	80	14	19	20	1	0	0	4	3	1	1	7	0	9	1	2	1	.250	.303
ia, A. Jesus, Min	.176	42	78	74	3	13	16	1	1	0	7	2	0	0	2	0	12	0	1	5	.216	.197
nez, Ever, Tab	.154	6	14	13	1	2	2	0	0	0	1	0	0	1	0	0	5	1	0	0	.154	.214
nez, R. Martin, Min	.000	1	1	1	0	0	0	0	0	0	0	0	0	0	0	0	0	0	0	0	.000	.000
zalez, Hector, P.R.	.000	2	2	2	0	0	0	0	0	0	0	0	0	0	0	0	2	0	0	0	.000	.000
zalez, Jesus, Cam	.292	90	344	308	38	90	129	21	0	6	37	4	1	3	28	5	33	9	0	9	.419	.356
zalez, Jose, Mont.	.354	107	453	384	84	136	197	21	5	10	71	2	7	2	58	1	68	34	11	5	.513	.435
zalez, F. Mauricio, Cam	.143	4	15	14	0	2	2	0	0	0	0	0	0	1	0	0	4	0	1	0	.143	.200
ak, Kevin Scott, Tig.	.288	89	363	323	41	93	139	13	0	11	42	0	5	5	30	8	44	3	4	7	.430	.352
rrero, Jaime, P.R.	.168	64	137	125	12	21	25	4	0	0	9	4	1	1	6	0	21	2	0	3	.200	.211
rrero, Javier, Agua.	.186	35	74	70	5	13	18	2	0	1	4	0	0	0	4	1	23	0	1	0	.257	.230
rrero, Juan, Tab	.290	115	498	442	56	128	172	26	3	4	69	6	1	4	45	4	50	5	4	13	.389	.360
rrero, M. Francisco, Q.R.	.290	99	389	317	43	92	114	12	2	2	30	16	5	1	50	2	37	14	4	10	.360	.383
rrero, Q. Jose, Q.R.	.000	7	11	11	0	0	0	0	0	0	0	0	0	0	0	0	4	0	0	0	.000	.000
zar, V. Hector, Cam	.226	103	345	305	25	69	84	15	0	0	29	8	3	3	26	0	22	5	7	10	.275	.291
man, Marco Antonio, Q.R.	.210	24	69	62	5	13	16	3	0	0	2	2	0	1	4	0	6	0	0	2	.258	.269
ht, Steve, Oax	.227	5	24	22	3	5	5	0	0	0	1	0	1	0	1	0	5	0	0	0	.227	.250
nandez, Gerardo, Tig.	.282	96	241	206	32	58	82	11	2	3	18	2	0	3	30	1	57	2	3	2	.398	.381
nandez, A. Martin, Cam	.304	24	78	69	6	21	26	3	1	0	7	1	1	2	5	0	13	1	1	0	.377	.364
nandez, B. Juan Carlos, P.R.	.600	9	6	5	3	3	3	0	0	0	0	0	0	0	1	0	0	1	0	0	.600	.667
nandez, S. Miguel, P.R.	.195	77	185	159	9	31	35	2	1	0	11	10	0	2	14	0	12	0	0	3	.220	.269
rera, Enrique, Tab	.000	1	1	1	0	0	0	0	0	0	0	0	0	0	0	0	0	0	0	0	.000	.000
rera, V. Isidro, Oax	.275	109	478	385	79	106	120	7	2	1	16	5	3	7	78	4	40	21	11	7	.312	.404
zo, Tommy, Mex	.235	55	232	204	31	48	59	9	1	0	7	0	2	7	19	1	22	7	3	3	.289	.322
d, Dennis, Tab	.000	2	7	7	0	0	0	0	0	0	0	0	0	0	0	0	2	0	0	0	.000	.000
n, Sam, Tor	.265	113	492	359	78	95	204	19	0	30	90	1	6	2	124	13	92	1	0	8	.568	.450
vell, Pat, Tig.	.300	71	316	293	52	88	106	7	4	1	19	9	2	4	8	3	37	13	6	1	.362	.326
cado, Hector, Cam	.157	78	223	198	11	31	51	5	0	5	26	10	0	2	13	1	59	0	1	3	.258	.216
ra, I.J. Alberto, Min	.000	3	6	5	0	0	0	0	0	0	0	0	0	0	0	0	1	0	0	0	.000	.167
nte, Alexis, Tab	.290	90	341	303	26	88	94	3	0	1	24	15	0	3	20	1	18	1	3	7	.310	.340
be, Pedro, Tab	.236	108	388	347	38	82	112	16	1	4	34	12	3	6	20	6	51	28	7	2	.323	.287
enez, Eduardo, Yuc	.244	80	327	271	34	66	108	12	0	10	35	0	1	2	53	12	48	4	1	6	.399	.370
enez, Jesus, Tor	.333	1	4	3	1	1	1	0	0	0	3	0	1	0	0	0	0	0	0	0	.667	.250

Player, Team	Avg.	G	TPA	AB	R	H	TB	2B	3B	HR	RBI	SH	SF	HP	BB	IBB	SO	SB	CS	GDP	Slg.
Jimenez, Ulises, Tor	.275	17	46	40	9	11	18	1	0	2	9	1	2	0	3	0	10	0	0	1	.450
Jimenez, G. Alfonso, Sal	.286	100	451	378	68	108	143	22	2	3	39	7	3	4	59	0	37	13	3	8	.378
Landrum, Ced, Tab	.259	52	229	201	28	52	69	5	3	2	14	3	0	0	25	0	23	9	7	4	.343
Leal, P.J. Guadalupe, Cam	.260	87	275	231	28	60	77	6	1	3	28	9	4	2	29	6	42	5	1	7	.333
Leyva, V. German, Monc	.267	113	489	409	62	109	141	14	3	4	37	17	3	3	57	7	24	3	2	14	.345
Lopez, Gonzalo, Monc	.167	13	14	12	0	2	2	0	0	0	0	0	0	0	2	0	2	0	0	0	.167
Lopez, Miguel, Yuc	.242	37	103	95	13	23	24	1	0	0	8	2	0	2	4	0	18	3	2	6	.253
Lopez, Rodrigo, P.R.	.000	1	1	1	0	0	0	0	0	0	0	0	0	0	0	0	0	0	0	0	.000
Lopez, Salvador, Yuc	.165	53	114	97	10	16	20	2	1	0	4	4	0	0	13	0	12	1	3	2	.206
Lopez, Victor M., Oax	.266	60	169	158	15	42	51	4	1	1	16	2	1	1	7	0	16	2	0	4	.323
Lopez, H. Fabian, Oax	.244	47	85	78	8	19	27	4	2	0	10	1	0	0	6	0	8	0	0	1	.346
Loredo, M. Jorge Luis, Cam	.244	102	417	344	48	84	109	14	1	3	22	13	1	13	46	2	52	5	6	9	.317
Luna, G. Jose Luis, Sal	.186	77	194	172	8	32	36	4	0	0	17	4	1	0	17	0	13	1	1	7	.209
Machiria, Pablo, Agua	.289	107	437	401	36	116	146	15	3	3	61	5	5	6	20	1	27	1	3	14	.364
Mack, Quinn, Lar	.318	114	479	421	53	134	189	24	2	9	78	3	4	3	48	5	38	14	11	11	.449
Magallanes, Everardo, Mont	.338	82	330	287	60	97	123	16	2	2	46	3	2	3	35	2	27	7	2	3	.429
Magallanes, E. Roberto, Mex	.282	113	475	411	59	116	178	24	1	12	71	3	5	3	53	1	61	8	5	11	.433
Magana, Gabriel, Yuc	.250	15	13	12	4	3	4	1	0	0	0	1	0	0	0	0	2	0	0	0	.333
Malpica, Enrique, P.R.	.167	38	60	54	13	9	15	2	2	0	3	0	1	0	5	1	11	1	0	1	.278
Marrujo, Hector, Min	.200	8	14	10	2	2	2	0	0	0	1	0	0	0	4	0	1	0	0	1	.200
Martinez, Abel, P.R.	.154	23	28	26	8	4	5	1	0	0	2	1	0	0	1	0	8	0	1	1	.192
Martinez, Carlos, P.R.	.282	94	381	330	34	93	128	9	1	8	53	2	5	4	40	6	31	1	1	9	.388
Martinez, Jose Antonio, Cam	.000	1	0	0	1	0	0	0	0	0	0	0	0	0	0	0	0	0	0	0	.000
Martinez, Ray, Rey	.303	91	405	353	60	107	156	21	5	6	44	4	1	3	44	2	42	7	4	8	.442
Martinez, E. Raul, Sal	.301	53	150	136	12	41	59	9	0	3	15	0	1	0	13	1	17	0	0	7	.434
Martinez, G. Grimaldo, Monc	.265	104	461	370	67	98	123	13	3	2	33	13	2	3	73	0	42	13	2	10	.332
Martinez, L. Domingo, Rey	.320	114	490	413	75	132	216	22	4	18	91	0	4	6	67	5	51	1	1	13	.523
Mata, Noe, P.R.	.000	5	5	4	0	0	0	0	0	0	0	1	1	0	0	0	3	0	0	0	.000
Medina, D.J. Ramon, Cam	.255	72	184	161	28	41	48	0	2	1	8	4	2	3	14	1	27	6	6	1	.298
Mendez, Jesus, P.R.	.264	115	486	435	42	115	138	16	2	1	35	7	4	1	39	4	19	2	1	16	.317
Mendez, Ramon, Agua	.200	29	58	50	3	10	11	1	0	0	1	3	0	0	5	0	9	0	0	1	.220
Mendez, N. Roberto, Oax	.266	101	392	335	30	89	122	16	1	5	38	9	3	0	45	9	42	12	5	5	.364
Mendiola, Juan Carlos, P.R.	.222	6	10	9	1	2	2	0	0	0	0	0	0	1	0	0	2	0	0	0	.222
Mendoza, Omar, Lar	.205	58	147	132	14	27	39	7	1	1	10	0	1	1	13	0	21	1	1	3	.295
Mercedes, Luis, Tab	.235	30	101	85	10	20	21	1	0	0	8	3	0	1	12	0	4	6	2	2	.247
Mere, Pedro, P.R.	.257	114	452	377	52	97	120	15	4	0	28	11	2	3	59	3	53	6	1	9	.318
Meza, P. Alfredo, Mont	.272	93	258	232	24	63	77	8	0	2	33	6	6	0	14	1	35	0	1	4	.332
Michel, Domingo, Cam	.280	111	436	350	63	98	172	19	2	17	55	5	3	4	74	6	43	15	5	6	.491
Milligan, Randy, Oax	.214	12	53	42	4	9	11	2	0	0	5	0	0	1	10	0	9	1	0	1	.262
Monroy, Victor Hugo, Rey	.219	52	77	73	4	16	19	3	0	0	3	0	1	1	2	0	9	1	0	3	.260
Montalvo, R. Ivan Vladimir, Tig	.260	110	446	389	50	101	139	13	2	7	42	6	2	3	46	4	89	8	3	7	.357
Montanez, Daniel, Lar	.188	7	20	16	2	3	3	0	0	0	0	3	0	0	1	0	5	0	0	0	.188
Mora, Andres, Lar	.000	6	6	3	0	0	0	0	0	0	1	0	0	0	3	0	0	0	0	0	.000
Morales, Florentino, Lar	.255	91	387	314	39	80	101	17	2	0	26	7	2	7	57	2	26	3	3	7	.322
Moreno, F. David, Monc	.171	32	42	35	2	6	6	0	0	0	3	1	0	1	5	0	7	0	0	1	.171
Moreno, R. Leonardo, Oax	.279	79	256	219	30	61	75	6	4	0	14	12	1	4	20	0	20	4	3	6	.342
Morones, Martin, P.R.	.244	70	205	180	24	44	60	6	2	2	19	2	0	3	20	2	24	4	0	2	.333
Motley, Darryl, P.R.	.253	47	192	162	27	41	59	6	0	4	24	1	0	2	27	4	24	0	1	3	.364
Murillo, M. Felipe, Monc	.000	1	1	0	0	0	0	0	0	0	0	1	0	0	0	0	0	0	0	0	.000
Munoz, Jose De Jesus, Lar	.203	42	79	69	6	14	15	1	0	0	5	1	1	0	8	0	19	0	1	3	.217
Munoz, Leonardo, Mont.	.000	1	0	0	0	0	0	0	0	0	0	0	0	0	0	0	0	0	0	0	.000
Munoz, Noe, Rey.	.333	51	200	168	24	56	85	11	3	4	35	4	3	1	24	1	20	0	3	7	.506
Munoz, Pablo, Q.R.	.000	1	0	0	1	0	0	0	0	0	0	0	0	0	0	0	0	0	0	0	.000
Naveda, Edgar, Oax	.246	36	142	126	8	31	31	0	0	0	10	1	1	1	13	1	11	0	2	5	.246
Noris, V. Rogelio, Rey	.224	81	273	245	33	55	75	14	0	2	20	8	0	2	18	0	36	5	2	5	.306
Nunez Garcia, Jose Juan, Oax	.200	19	49	45	5	9	11	2	0	0	1	1	0	1	2	0	6	1	0	2	.244
Ochoa, M. Edgar, Tig.	.257	65	170	152	17	39	51	6	0	2	9	0	2	1	15	0	35	2	3	2	.336
O'Halloran, Greg, Q.R.	.271	101	412	365	44	99	146	17	3	8	51	4	3	1	39	6	47	3	0	15	.400
Ojeda, Miguel, Mex	.311	71	266	251	43	78	114	10	1	8	29	0	3	1	11	1	34	3	0	11	.454
Olvera, Sergio, Monc	.286	18	16	14	3	4	5	1	0	0	3	0	0	0	2	0	5	0	0	0	.357
Orantes, R. Ramon, Agua	.255	77	240	212	29	54	74	9	4	1	19	4	6	0	18	1	34	1	5	5	.349
Ortega, Antonio, Rey	.250	10	18	16	4	4	5	1	0	0	0	0	0	1	1	0	2	0	0	0	.313
Ortega, Roberto, Q.R.	.000	1	2	2	0	0	0	0	0	0	0	0	0	0	0	0	0	0	0	0	.000
Ortiz, Alejandro, Q.R.	.226	106	393	327	26	74	109	9	1	8	34	10	3	4	49	5	38	1	2	13	.333
Ortiz, Raymond, Cam	.269	89	349	312	38	84	115	14	1	5	43	3	4	2	28	8	42	5	2	13	.369
Osuna, Hector, Yuc	.259	24	60	54	8	14	15	1	0	0	2	1	1	0	4	0	5	0	1	1	.278
Pacho, Juan Jose, Yuc	.260	113	438	393	31	102	115	9	2	0	36	17	0	3	25	1	27	5	4	11	.293
Paez, Raul, Mex	.284	51	121	102	11	29	44	5	2	2	17	0	2	1	16	7	11	0	0	5	.431
Pardo, Victor Manuel, Oax	.200	83	256	225	20	45	48	3	0	0	9	7	1	2	21	0	39	1	3	6	.213
Payro, O. Edison, Cam	.249	104	404	350	36	87	101	12	1	0	23	8	1	0	45	6	49	6	6	7	.289
Pegues, Steven, Tab	.286	2	8	7	2	2	2	0	0	0	0	0	0	0	1	0	1	0	0	0	.286
Peralta, Amado, Sal	.203	61	164	128	15	26	35	4	1	1	12	5	2	2	27	5	39	1	1	2	.273
Perez, Alejandro, Lar	.092	35	83	65	6	6	7	1	0	0	3	2	0	2	14	0	9	0	0	5	.108
Perez, Francisco, Mex	.302	60	146	139	17	42	73	10	0	7	35	1	2	1	3	0	26	2	2	2	.525
Perez D., Juan Luis, Tor	.170	28	55	47	7	8	10	0	1	0	4	2	0	1	5	0	15	0	1	2	.213
Perezchica, Antonio, Tig.	.274	49	202	179	27	49	64	9	0	2	15	2	2	3	16	2	30	0	0	6	.358
Pena, Carlos, Yuc	.051	27	43	39	0	2	2	0	0	0	2	0	0	0	4	0	7	0	0	2	.051
Pena, Luis Alberto, Yuc	.148	60	177	155	5	23	27	4	0	0	8	1	1	0	20	3	24	0	0	5	.174
Precichi, Jorge, Sal	.205	22	85	73	17	15	16	1	0	0	4	1	1	0	10	0	11	1	0	3	.219
Pulido, Jesus, Lar	.192	29	59	52	7	10	19	0	0	3	4	0	0	0	7	0	15	0	0	0	.365
Quijada, G. Mario, Tor.	.000	1	0	0	1	0	0	0	0	0	0	0	0	0	0	0	0	0	0	0	.000
Quintana, Carlos, Q.R.	.280	69	263	218	25	61	80	7	0	4	26	0	2	2	41	3	19	1	1	10	.367
Quintero, Guillermo, Mont.	.272	80	184	158	23	43	51	6	1	0	13	7	2	0	17	0	25	4	7	2	.323

ayer, Team	Avg.	G	TPA	AB	R	H	TB	2B	3B	HR	RBI	SH	SF	HP	BB	IBB	SO	SB	CS	GDP	Slg.	OBP
iroz, Jose Julian, Agua.	.333	3	4	3	0	1	1	0	0	0	0	0	0	0	1	0	1	0	0	0	.333	.500
ben, Luis, Yuc....................	.256	24	96	90	7	23	52	0	1	9	0	0	0	6	0	2	2	1	1	4	.344	.302
mirez, Efren, Agua.	.226	101	363	310	38	70	105	12	1	7	34	14	1	15	23	0	41	5	1	15	.339	.309
mirez, Jesus, P.R.	.278	84	225	194	18	54	64	3	2	1	16	8	0	1	22	1	25	8	3	4	.330	.355
mirez, U. Enrique, Monc.....	.249	114	398	353	52	88	99	11	0	0	17	21	1	2	21	0	15	3	1	10	.280	.294
nteria, Ricardo, Mex	.256	23	102	86	13	22	36	4	2	2	16	0	1	2	13	1	9	0	0	1	.419	.363
yes, Gilberto, Mont.	.173	35	112	98	8	17	22	5	0	0	10	3	0	1	10	0	14	0	1	4	.224	.257
era, D. German, Tab..........	.252	58	241	206	28	52	68	7	0	3	27	3	3	0	29	1	32	0	0	9	.330	.340
obinson, Don, Sal..............	.259	21	90	81	10	21	34	4	0	3	13	3	0	0	6	0	22	1	1	0	.420	.310
bles, Gerardo, Rey..........	.176	40	57	51	11	9	9	0	0	0	4	3	0	0	3	0	19	1	0	0	.176	.222
bles, Ricardo, Sal..........	.147	18	40	34	4	5	7	0	1	0	1	1	0	1	4	0	12	1	0	1	.206	.256
bles, A. Javier, Tig..........	.272	112	480	427	64	116	196	18	1	20	72	7	5	2	39	1	73	16	5	9	.459	.332
bles, A. Trinidad, Lar	.223	111	442	386	46	86	116	12	0	6	39	4	1	6	45	0	84	13	8	5	.301	.313
driguez, Boi, Lar..............	.302	116	505	397	79	120	208	23	1	21	82	0	7	3	98	9	74	2	1	7	.524	.438
driguez, Jose Luis, Q.R.	.190	12	23	21	2	4	4	0	0	0	1	1	0	0	1	0	4	0	0	0	.190	.227
driguez, Serafin, Q.R.	.242	77	238	215	36	52	59	5	1	0	9	7	1	2	13	0	32	8	0	4	.274	.290
driguez, O. Hector, Rey	.195	96	312	267	35	52	71	8	1	3	32	8	2	2	33	0	69	1	0	4	.266	.286
driguez, R. Fernando, Tor ...	.303	94	356	320	44	97	146	25	3	6	50	2	0	8	26	2	37	1	3	18	.456	.370
jas, Francisco, Tab	.229	49	116	105	8	24	27	3	0	0	7	3	0	4	4	1	17	2	1	5	.257	.283
jas, Homar, Mex	.247	83	321	287	34	71	87	14	1	0	34	2	4	3	25	2	22	2	0	13	.303	.310
mero, Israel, Lar..............	.169	39	96	89	7	15	19	1	0	1	11	0	0	1	6	0	31	0	1	3	.213	.229
mero, Oscar, Min..............	.261	97	390	352	38	92	129	16	0	7	31	3	3	2	30	1	50	5	6	11	.366	.320
bio, Sergio, Yuc..............	.269	86	323	271	36	73	90	8	3	1	23	16	2	7	27	1	35	11	6	3	.332	.349
iz, Demetrio, Cam..............	.091	23	41	33	0	3	3	0	0	0	1	6	0	0	2	0	2	0	0	2	.091	.143
iz L., Juan De Dios, Tor	.244	70	273	242	40	59	70	6	1	1	30	6	1	2	22	2	20	3	0	10	.289	.311
ssell, Omar, Min	.167	10	13	12	0	2	2	0	0	0	0	0	0	1	0	0	4	0	0	0	.167	.231
enz, Ricardo, Monc..........	.326	64	261	224	40	73	114	18	1	7	47	1	3	0	33	4	35	0	0	5	.509	.408
as, B. Heriberto, Tor..........	.301	109	474	415	62	125	164	19	4	4	53	11	3	5	40	0	46	2	3	3	.395	.367
gado, Eduardo, Min	.000	2	1	1	0	0	0	0	0	0	0	0	0	0	0	0	0	0	0	0	.000	.000
inas, Rogelio, Yuc..........	.259	60	224	205	15	53	74	9	0	4	23	2	2	2	13	1	25	0	1	4	.361	.306
naniego, Manuel, Monc.	.174	19	24	23	0	4	5	1	0	0	1	0	0	1	0	2	0	0	2	.217	.208
nchez, Gerardo, Lar	.288	116	509	406	57	117	165	17	2	9	69	2	4	9	88	2	44	6	3	20	.406	.422
nchez, Raul, Q.R.	.216	28	40	37	8	8	8	0	0	0	2	0	1	1	1	0	7	0	0	1	.216	.250
nchez, Roque, Cam..........	.189	58	135	127	9	24	30	4	1	0	8	6	1	0	1	0	12	1	0	4	.236	.194
nchez, S. Armando, Mont. ..	.258	64	156	124	15	32	39	5	1	0	23	1	3	0	28	1	10	0	0	4	.315	.387
ndoval, Benjamin, Cam	.000	3	3	3	0	0	0	0	0	0	0	0	0	0	0	0	1	0	0	0	.000	.000
doval, Jose Luis, Mex........	.261	101	383	352	39	92	130	12	1	8	45	6	1	2	22	0	51	4	3	7	.369	.308
ndoval, Octavio A., Tig......	.239	68	158	142	22	34	40	6	0	0	12	2	2	4	8	0	34	2	2	2	.282	.295
atana, C. Miguel, Min	.282	32	141	117	18	33	67	1	0	11	1	2	2	18	2	1	3	4	4	4	.316	.381
atana, J. Mario Ivan, Mont.	.182	28	51	44	3	8	10	2	0	0	3	2	0	0	5	0	6	1	0	1	.227	.265
sser, Mackey, Tab	.177	37	134	124	9	22	26	4	0	0	10	0	1	0	9	4	9	0	0	5	.210	.231
ott, Bryant, Tab	.226	13	56	53	5	12	18	3	0	1	6	0	0	1	2	0	14	0	0	1	.340	.268
erman, Darrell, Yuc..........	.305	74	325	266	40	81	93	10	1	0	20	4	3	7	45	5	27	17	3	3	.350	.414
rra, Ruben, Cam	.000	1	0	0	1	0	0	0	0	0	0	0	0	0	0	0	0	0	0	0	.000	.000
vers, Carlos, Yuc..............	.180	27	64	50	2	9	10	1	0	0	1	1	0	4	9	4	8	0	1	4	.200	.349
verio, S. Nelson, Cam	.218	28	114	101	9	22	30	2	0	2	14	4	1	1	7	0	16	0	0	3	.297	.273
der, Van, Tor	.239	98	418	352	40	84	121	14	1	7	37	3	2	3	58	1	76	3	2	8	.344	.349
mmers, Jesus, P.R.............	.237	68	213	194	9	46	56	7	0	1	26	3	1	2	13	3	28	0	0	4	.289	.290
iano, Ricardo, Tor..............	.171	17	50	41	5	7	7	0	0	0	4	1	0	0	8	1	0	1	0	1	.171	.306
o, Emison, Q.R.	.211	82	303	256	31	54	68	8	0	2	22	7	2	3	35	5	50	3	3	7	.266	.311
, Cecil, Oax	.195	38	141	123	9	24	27	1	1	0	10	2	1	0	15	0	21	3	2	3	.220	.281
rk, Matt, Rey..............	.321	103	457	358	66	115	181	24	0	14	72	0	3	6	90	2	24	2	0	9	.506	.462
s, Bernardo, Yuc..............	.269	115	495	416	48	112	145	11	5	4	46	2	4	1	72	11	48	27	11	13	.349	.375
eda, Arturo, Oax	.000	6	10	9	1	0	0	0	0	0	0	0	0	0	1	0	4	0	0	0	.000	.100
ez, J. Alonso, Rey	.365	80	337	293	54	107	149	19	1	7	49	3	0	3	38	1	9	1	1	13	.509	.443
mas, Keith, P.R.	.270	20	98	89	16	24	34	2	1	2	10	0	1	1	7	0	21	8	1	1	.382	.327
utsis, Paul, Yuc..............	.000	1	4	4	0	0	0	0	0	0	0	0	0	0	0	0	0	0	0	0	.000	.000
urcio, Freddy, Cam	.305	84	348	311	44	95	137	11	5	7	35	5	3	5	24	3	49	3	3	9	.441	.362
uet, Lazaro, Tab	.250	74	233	216	16	54	63	7	1	0	27	5	1	2	9	0	29	1	1	4	.292	.285
antino, F. Jose, Mont..........	.288	85	352	306	44	88	136	17	2	9	67	0	9	8	29	2	37	2	3	1	.444	.355
res, Raymundo, Yuc..........	.221	83	330	258	35	57	105	14	2	10	34	0	3	7	62	2	80	2	1	6	.407	.382
res, M. Eduardo, Monc.	.199	112	430	342	52	68	129	12	2	15	50	4	0	7	77	3	81	4	4	7	.377	.357
rton, Todd, Yuc..............	.279	102	422	359	54	100	142	19	1	7	42	1	3	5	54	2	62	0	2	9	.396	.378
paga, M. Julio Miguel, Tig....	.259	88	308	270	28	70	92	11	1	3	27	12	1	3	22	0	54	7	0	0	.341	.321
dez, Francisco J., Rey	.266	82	293	237	27	63	77	9	1	1	24	6	0	8	42	1	24	3	2	5	.325	.394
dez, Jesus, Yuc..............	.263	12	21	19	2	5	5	0	0	0	0	0	0	1	1	1	3	0	0	0	.263	.333
dez, Ramon, Min..............	.239	38	108	92	9	22	27	3	1	0	1	0	0	1	15	0	12	0	2	2	.293	.352
encia, Carlos, Agua..........	.267	96	360	329	34	88	107	13	0	2	21	2	3	2	24	0	20	1	2	11	.325	.318
encia, Jorge, Sal	.000	1	1	1	0	0	0	0	0	0	0	0	0	0	0	0	1	0	0	0	.000	.000
enzuela, Eduardo, Sal..........	.313	109	384	339	31	106	124	15	0	1	43	5	2	2	36	1	40	1	4	10	.366	.380
enzuela, Jose Luis, Tab	.379	21	31	29	8	11	14	0	0	1	2	0	0	0	2	0	7	0	0	1	.483	.419
enzuela, M. Horacio, Tab.....	.111	25	40	36	1	4	4	0	0	0	3	0	0	0	4	0	7	0	0	0	.111	.200
enzuela, S. Joel, Tor..........	.125	12	17	16	4	2	2	0	0	0	1	0	0	0	1	0	3	0	0	0	.125	.176
enzuela, V. Armando, Rey ..	.213	18	66	61	4	13	14	1	0	0	4	1	0	0	4	0	6	2	0	2	.230	.262
e D., Jorge Luis, Tor..........	.284	97	332	285	40	81	100	7	3	2	31	4	1	4	38	0	42	0	2	17	.351	.375
e G., Jose Luis, Min..........	.275	111	411	374	38	103	125	10	3	2	31	10	2	2	23	0	32	3	1	16	.334	.319
verde, L. J. Raul, Oax..........	.240	17	51	50	2	12	16	2	1	0	4	0	0	0	1	0	10	1	0	1	.320	.255
gas, Hector, Min	.267	99	403	344	41	92	108	12	2	0	32	3	4	4	48	2	42	11	9	11	.314	.360
gas, Jose A., Tig..............	.200	12	28	25	1	5	5	0	0	0	1	3	0	0	3	0	5	0	0	0	.200	.286
gas, Trinidad, Tab	.212	45	123	113	4	24	25	1	0	0	8	4	0	0	6	0	17	0	0	4	.221	.252
quez, Felipe, Mex..............	.226	38	98	93	7	21	25	1	0	1	10	2	0	0	3	0	17	1	1	5	.269	.250
a, V. Edgar, Tig..............	.232	98	266	228	26	53	56	3	0	0	23	11	2	1	24	0	35	3	1	6	.246	.306

Player, Team	Avg.	G	TPA	AB	R	H	TB	2B	3B	HR	RBI	SH	SF	HP	BB	IBB	SO	SB	CS	GDP	Slg.	O
Velazquez, Ernesto S., Monc. .	.333	1	3	3	2	1	1	0	0	0	0	0	0	0	0	0	1	0	0	0	.333	.3
Velazquez, Guillermo, Mont. ...	.286	110	477	423	78	121	216	30	1	21	112	0	9	1	44	4	75	3	3	9	.511	.3
Verdugo, Vicente, Mex............	.316	111	402	370	33	117	139	10	3	2	45	8	1	0	23	0	23	10	6	15	.376	.3
Villaescusa, Fernando, Cam	.182	4	11	11	1	2	2	0	0	0	0	0	0	0	0	0	0	0	0	0	.182	.1
Villanueva, Hector, Monc.	.287	114	500	394	69	113	206	16	1	25	94	0	8	0	98	6	47	1	1	12	.523	.4
Villapudua, Israel, Monc.	.000	3	1	1	0	0	0	0	0	0	0	0	0	0	0	0	1	0	0	0	.000	.0
Villarreal, Alejandro, Lar	.233	85	237	215	21	50	65	10	1	1	10	4	1	0	17	1	20	1	2	13	.302	.2
Villegas, Fernando, Sal	.300	75	279	243	32	73	96	7	5	2	32	1	3	2	30	1	33	3	3	10	.395	.3
Vizcarra, Marco Antonio, Sal ..	.284	93	394	345	51	98	113	11	2	0	24	5	4	6	34	0	26	4	4	6	.328	.3
Vizcarra, Roberto, Agua..........	.299	108	488	435	70	130	196	28	1	12	60	7	2	5	39	3	20	12	8	5	.451	.3
Wong M., Julian, Monc.	.302	69	189	149	21	45	65	11	0	3	18	6	3	2	29	1	23	0	0	5	.436	.4
Wood, Ted, Agua.	.299	112	479	398	82	119	193	27	4	13	55	2	2	3	74	5	61	3	1	11	.485	.4
Wright, George, Sal	.309	105	444	356	61	110	149	17	2	6	63	0	5	1	82	7	38	8	7	10	.419	.4
Yuriar, A. Jesus, Min..............	.254	101	357	307	46	78	95	14	0	1	36	8	4	0	38	2	41	0	2	11	.309	.3
Zambrano, Eduardo, Agua.......	.288	113	479	427	56	123	205	34	0	16	74	2	3	2	45	5	89	2	2	10	.480	.3
Zambrano, Jose Luis, Min........	.281	59	214	178	19	50	70	8	0	4	21	0	2	7	27	0	43	3	1	5	.393	.3
Zambrano, Roberto, Q.R.	.278	102	418	352	44	98	159	14	4	13	52	0	5	7	54	5	51	1	2	5	.452	.3
Zamudio, L. Rafael, Mont.	.305	68	184	164	26	50	69	10	3	1	22	6	0	4	10	0	42	3	0	2	.421	.3
Zazueta, Juan Carlos, Tab	.206	79	296	262	22	54	58	1	0	1	8	9	1	2	22	1	20	7	6	6	.221	.2
Zazueta, F. Maurico, Tor.........	.279	102	435	391	50	109	142	17	8	0	45	7	3	0	34	2	49	2	1	6	.363	.3

GRAND SLAMS: M. Carillo, Ro. Magallanes, 2 each; Aganza, Almeida, Chance, A. Felix, Infante, Leal, Michel, Paez, B. Rodriguez, G. Sanchez, E. Torres, G. Velazqu
R. Vizcarra, Wright, 1 each.

AWARDED FIRST BASE ON CATCHER'S INTERFERENCE: Jo. Gonzalez (H. Rojas); F. Guerrero (V. Lopez); Payro (Campos); M. Vizcarra (Cabrera).

1996 PITCHING

TEAM

Team	W	L	Pct.	ERA	G	CG	ShO	Sv.	IP	H	TBF	R	ER	HR	SH	SF	HB	BB	IBB	SO	WP	B
Poza Rica	63	50	.558	2.72	115	18	7	27	1011.0	913	3695	377	306	43	68	35	42	416	38	455	40	
Quintana Roo	55	55	.500	2.99	115	28	12	20	998.0	912	3675	384	332	50	88	24	36	363	29	475	47	
Tabasco	48	63	.432	3.08	115	12	3	31	961.2	917	3588	401	329	40	81	30	38	327	37	440	41	
Monterrey	82	33	.713	3.20	116	5	3	36	1016.2	944	3793	434	362	54	54	22	37	513	29	513	41	
Yucatan	58	56	.509	3.24	115	4	1	29	993.1	953	3677	435	358	26	94	34	44	455	62	486	53	
Campeche	53	59	.473	3.26	115	28	12	20	951.2	898	3506	423	345	59	91	24	39	422	38	425	37	
M.C.R.D.	70	43	.619	3.42	114	16	3	29	992.0	983	3749	450	377	57	54	30	36	400	11	590	63	
M.C. Tigers	68	45	.602	3.83	114	4	1	31	1017.1	994	3844	496	433	71	54	27	35	443	20	589	67	
Aguascalientes ..	58	57	.504	4.16	115	9	1	29	985.0	1080	3829	529	455	51	61	27	37	398	46	437	31	
Minatitlan	45	65	.409	4.21	112	13	5	21	963.1	1036	3693	508	451	53	71	34	37	432	30	467	33	
Monclova	58	56	.509	4.32	115	13	4	25	994.0	1029	3804	556	477	77	47	32	33	541	30	574	49	
Oaxaca	46	64	.418	4.33	115	32	5	10	959.2	1000	3642	547	462	53	71	42	31	487	44	526	68	
Nuevo Laredo	48	65	.425	4.57	116	8	5	22	995.0	1110	3894	607	505	74	59	33	35	469	36	513	46	
Reynosa	56	56	.500	4.61	114	22	2	20	971.2	1050	3767	569	498	53	54	30	42	482	27	577	49	
Torreon	50	62	.446	4.75	115	16	3	19	990.1	1084	3783	590	523	81	69	35	40	526	28	478	57	
Saltillo	41	70	.369	5.20	115	14	3	13	972.0	1113	3755	634	562	82	67	40	45	606	29	462	58	

INDIVIDUAL

TOP QUALIFIERS FOR EARNED-RUN AVERAGE TITLE

Minimum 93 innings.

Pitcher, Team	W	L	Pct.	ERA	G	GS	CG	ShO	GF	Sv.	IP	H	TBF	R	ER	HR	SH	SF	HB	BB	IBB	SO	WP	E
Baez, Sixto, P.R.	7	5	.583	1.54	41	9	1	0	32	9	105.1	79	361	30	18	3	12	3	2	59	7	30	4	
Jimenez, C. Isaac, P.R...........	10	6	.625	1.70	20	19	7	3	1	1	127.1	96	448	35	24	3	9	1	7	43	2	68	3	
Gonzalez, M. Arturo, Mont.	12	2	.857	1.78	20	20	1	1	0	0	12.1	86	434	29	24	6	5	3	5	35	4	42	2	
Lopez, Emigdio, Tab	15	4	.789	2.15	25	25	3	1	0	0	159.1	135	584	46	38	5	9	5	6	41	2	68	4	
Valdez, Efrain, Q.R	11	5	.688	2.23	20	20	6	3	0	0	149.1	123	535	49	37	7	14	1	8	44	1	69	2	
Diaz, Rafael, Mont..................	14	1	.933	2.41	22	22	2	2	0	0	134.2	108	492	42	36	5	3	1	4	78	2	68	4	
Villarreal, Antonio, Yuc..........	10	6	.625	2.45	22	22	1	0	0	0	143.1	141	534	46	39	3	10	2	7	53	5	67	6	
Campos, M. Francisco, Cam ...	10	3	.769	2.49	23	22	7	3	1	0	144.2	120	512	44	40	8	13	1	10	52	3	60	1	
Perez, G. Vladimir, Ags...........	8	5	.615	2.59	55	0	0	0	55	3	100.2	92	365	37	29	0	7	6	3	50	6	52	7	
Miranda, Julio Cesar, Yuc........	9	4	.692	2.66	49	1	0	0	48	12	101.2	79	364	38	30	4	8	2	4	26	7	56	2	

DEPARTMENTAL LEADERS: W—Figueroa, E. Lopez, 15; L—Galvez, I. Velazquez, 13; Pct—R. Diaz, .933; G—V. Perez, 55; GS—Ramirez, 28; CG—Flynt, 14; ShO—
Chapa, Ra. Rodriguez, 4; GF—V. Perez, 55; Sv.—Mauser, 25; IP—Ro. Ramirez 190.1; H—Palafox, 190; TBF—Bennett, 703; R—Palafox, Montano, 86; HR—Rios,
SH—Figueroa, Saenz, 16; SF—Gomez, 8; HB—Palafox, 13; BB—Ignacio Flores, 108; IBB—R. Garibay, 11; SO—Flynt, 137; WP—Kelley, 15; Bk.—Orozco, 3.

ALL PITCHERS

Pitcher, Team	W	L	Pct.	ERA	G	GS	CG	ShO	GF	Sv.	IP	H	TBF	R	ER	HR	SH	SF	HB	BB	IBB	SO	WP	E
Acosta, A. Gerardo, Rey	7	6	.538	5.00	39	2	0	0	37	5	75.2	80	289	43	42	4	8	1	1	43	5	39	6	
Acosta, R. Aaron, Tor	4	8	.333	4.16	22	21	1	0	1	0	119.0	120	446	61	55	9	12	5	8	60	3	64	7	
Aguilar, Miguel, Tab...............	1	5	.167	2.18	23	7	1	1	16	0	57.2	43	211	23	14	2	6	0	2	16	0	23	4	
Aguirre, Gaudencio, Tab	4	4	.500	4.25	21	6	0	0	15	0	42.1	40	164	28	20	0	4	1	5	17	1	12	3	
Alicea, Miguel, Monc...............	1	6	.143	6.00	27	0	0	0	27	9	33.0	42	131	22	22	2	3	2	0	21	7	17	0	
Alvarez, Juan Carlos, Min........	2	6	.250	3.86	27	11	2	1	16	0	84.0	86	324	37	36	7	8	1	2	25	0	20	2	
Alvarez, O. Juan Jesus, Tig......	6	5	.545	2.73	23	23	1	1	0	0	142.0	131	538	51	43	10	8	1	4	41	3	84	3	
Antunez, S. Martin, Ags	2	3	.400	5.40	30	1	0	0	29	0	23.1	35	99	14	14	0	8	1	2	12	2	11	3	
Austin, James, Ags	3	4	.429	3.29	48	0	0	0	48	18	52.0	48	195	20	19	3	2	0	2	38	3	43	5	
Baez, Sixto, P.R.	7	5	.583	1.54	41	9	1	0	32	9	105.1	79	361	30	18	3	12	3	2	59	7	30	4	
Barfield, John, Lar..................	4	1	.800	4.81	22	0	0	0	22	8	24.1	26	97	18	13	2	3	1	0	10	3	12	3	

cher, Team	W	L	Pct.	ERA	G	GS	CG	ShO	GF	Sv.	IP	H	TBF	R	ER	HR	SH	SF	HB	BB	IBB	SO	WP	Bk.
rojas, Salome, Mex	0	0	.000	5.79	3	0	0	0	3	0	4.2	7	22	4	3	1	0	1	0	2	1	4	0	0
rraza, R. Ernesto, Tig	9	7	.563	4.21	21	20	1	0	1	0	115.1	119	439	65	54	5	5	1	1	58	3	62	8	0
rron, Q. Avelino, Cam	3	6	.333	4.65	30	1	0	0	29	4	50.1	45	179	31	26	5	8	3	4	29	5	19	1	0
uer, Matt, Monc	1	1	.500	3.57	14	0	0	0	14	0	22.2	23	84	10	9	1	1	2	0	20	2	18	2	0
nnett, Chris, Rey	13	6	.684	3.78	26	26	9	0	0	0	181.0	189	703	92	76	5	8	4	9	66	3	106	10	0
immet, Greg, Rey	1	6	.143	5.87	8	7	1	0	1	0	38.1	59	166	30	25	2	3	0	2	14	2	17	1	0
rgos, John, Tig	5	2	.714	2.66	46	0	0	0	46	3	74.1	56	258	25	22	6	4	2	0	26	2	53	3	0
orales, Gabriel, Min	1	2	.333	5.85	26	0	0	0	26	0	32.1	41	130	23	21	3	4	2	1	7	1	9	2	0
deron, G. Manaces, Min	1	0	1.000	4.82	4	1	0	0	3	0	9.1	7	33	5	5	0	1	0	0	10	1	3	0	0
macho, C. Adrian, Sal	0	0	.000	10.38	4	0	0	0	4	0	4.1	10	24	5	5	1	0	0	0	5	0	2	2	0
mara, Pedro, Min	0	0	.000	5.56	15	0	0	0	15	0	11.1	44	8	7	2	2	1	1	0	11	0	8	2	0
mpos, Frank, Lar	9	3	.750	5.20	38	4	0	0	34	0	71.0	91	293	46	41	7	4	4	0	55	6	24	7	0
mpos, M. Francisco, Cam	10	3	.769	2.49	23	22	7	3	1	0	144.2	120	512	44	40	8	13	1	10	52	3	60	1	1
no, Jose, Yuc	4	6	.400	2.46	13	13	2	1	0	0	84.0	58	297	29	23	0	6	5	5	45	1	19	1	0
ranza, Javier, Rey	1	3	.250	7.81	18	6	0	0	12	0	27.2	39	113	32	24	1	3	1	2	24	2	14	0	1
rrasco, Alejandro, Oax	4	10	.286	3.50	30	19	5	0	11	1	138.2	135	518	62	54	11	7	5	4	53	4	66	2	1
stillo, Felipe, Tor	0	1	.000	7.00	7	0	0	0	7	1	9.0	15	39	7	7	3	0	0	0	3	0	5	0	0
stro, C. Leonel, Oax	0	0	.000	4.24	6	2	0	0	4	0	17.0	19	70	11	8	3	1	1	1	9	1	9	6	0
zares, Juan, Monc	0	1	.000	8.10	17	0	0	0	17	0	10.0	16	45	11	9	2	0	1	1	5	1	3	1	0
zares, Rosario, Tab	4	3	.571	1.64	54	0	0	0	54	5	66.0	41	228	18	12	2	6	1	5	27	2	39	1	0
cena, Jose Isabel, Sal	5	11	.313	5.67	33	9	1	0	24	2	85.2	87	317	60	54	5	7	2	3	59	4	64	9	0
rros, R. Juan, Rey	4	1	.800	4.22	28	1	0	0	27	0	79.0	78	297	42	37	5	0	2	4	47	5	34	7	0
apa, M. Javier, Oax	7	12	.368	3.23	24	24	7	4	0	0	150.2	145	553	68	54	8	9	6	3	63	4	72	12	0
nde, Ricardo, Oax	0	0	.000	5.40	9	0	0	0	9	0	8.1	9	32	6	5	0	0	2	1	9	0	1	2	1
rbin, Archie, Rey	0	0	.000	9.31	9	0	0	0	9	2	9.2	10	36	10	10	0	1	0	3	7	1	13	1	0
ta, Marino, Sal	2	2	.500	6.67	34	2	0	0	32	1	55.1	71	227	46	41	4	5	0	0	27	4	30	3	2
uoh, H. Enrique, Tig	9	6	.600	4.03	24	23	2	0	1	0	31.2	143	504	66	59	12	9	6	2	66	0	74	10	1
uz, Juan Diego, Yuc	0	0	.000	5.40	12	0	0	0	12	0	8.1	9	32	7	5	0	2	0	0	10	2	4	2	0
uz, Miguel, Lar	2	1	.667	4.50	19	1	0	0	18	0	22.0	25	86	13	11	1	1	0	0	12	0	10	1	0
uz, O. Javier, Rey	10	7	.588	4.79	29	22	3	1	7	0	50.1	161	579	89	80	7	8	4	2	69	3	103	9	0
ervo, F. Bernardo, Cam	7	5	.583	2.68	19	19	2	2	0	0	121	117	454	48	36	5	11	2	4	47	4	42	6	1
La Hoya, Javier, Min	4	8	.333	3.05	13	12	1	0	1	0	65	62	242	27	22	2	4	1	2	42	0	48	3	1
La Rosa, Francisco, Cam	4	8	.333	2.32	23	11	2	1	12	4	81.1	62	286	28	21	0	13	2	3	38	3	51	4	1
Leon, Danilo, Ags	1	2	.333	6.57	12	0	0	0	12	0	12.1	15	48	10	9	2	1	0	4	8	1	13	0	0
Toro, Miguel, Oax	1	1	.500	4.11	32	0	0	0	32	7	46	45	161	27	21	2	1	4	7	36	1	29	3	0
fin, L. Adolfo, Sal	1	1	.500	7.34	23	0	0	0	23	0	38	46	148	33	31	1	3	3	4	33	4	15	1	1
ssens, Elmer, Mex	7	0	1.000	1.26	7	7	1	0	0	0	50	44	188	12	7	1	1	2	1	10	0	17	3	0
ttmer, John F., Tig	0	0	.000	8.31	4	0	0	0	4	0	4.1	6	18	4	4	0	0	1	0	3	0	3	0	0
az, Alejandro, Oax	4	3	.571	3.34	31	2	0	0	29	0	59.1	63	229	28	22	4	6	1	3	17	3	23	0	1
az, Cesar, Lar	2	2	.500	4.56	43	1	0	0	42	1	71	72	267	39	36	5	3	4	1	32	2	38	0	0
az, Rafael, Mont	14	1	.933	2.41	22	22	2	2	0	0	134.2	108	492	42	36	5	3	1	4	78	2	68	4	2
az, R. Marco A., Tor	3	3	.500	6.19	26	6	0	0	20	0	56.2	77	231	43	39	4	1	3	0	38	1	26	4	0
minguez, G. Herminio, Cam	3	0	1.000	1.86	20	2	1	1	18	1	19.1	20	71	5	4	1	2	2	0	5	1	5	1	0
ahman, Bryan, Lar	2	1	.667	2.65	22	0	0	0	22	8	34	22	122	12	10	1	1	0	1	10	2	29	2	0
aper, Mike, Rey	0	3	.000	5.79	10	0	0	0	10	1	9.1	16	42	7	6	1	1	0	1	3	0	4	1	0
ncan, Chip, Tig	5	2	.714	2.95	27	4	0	0	22	1	55	51	198	21	18	4	2	1	1	22	2	32	6	0
ra, Narciso, Mont	4	1	.800	1.16	8	5	0	0	3	0	31	22	109	10	4	0	0	1	0	18	0	21	3	0
riquez, Martin, Ags	2	10	.167	5.70	21	13	1	0	8	0	77.1	102	305	59	49	3	7	7	2	35	5	37	3	0
pinoza, Mario, Yuc	0	0	.000	0.00	1	0	0	0	1	0	0	0	2	0	0	0	0	0	0	0	0	0	0	0
quer, L.L. Mercedes, Mont	7	6	.538	4.09	18	18	0	0	0	0	92.1	97	362	57	42	9	6	6	2	39	3	37	2	0
ardo, Hector, Mex	1	0	1.000	5.87	4	4	0	0	0	0	15.1	25	67	12	10	0	0	1	0	7	0	7	2	0
derico, M. Gustavo A., Mont	2	3	.400	5.80	15	4	0	0	11	2	35.2	43	135	24	23	3	4	0	2	29	1	6	0	0
ix, Leopoldo, P.R.	1	1	.500	5.70	14	3	0	0	11	0	23.2	25	96	19	15	2	0	1	0	13	0	8	2	0
ueroa, G. Fernando, Tor	15	4	.789	2.98	25	24	8	2	1	0	184	170	677	71	61	9	15	6	5	73	1	93	8	0
res, Ignacio, Tor	1	1	.500	5.83	18	2	0	0	16	0	29.1	24	108	22	19	4	3	2	2	27	1	21	3	0
res, J. Ignacio, Sal	5	10	.333	5.09	26	25	3	1	1	0	141.1	144	535	92	80	8	10	1	8	108	3	82	14	1
nt, Will, Oax	11	8	.579	3.11	22	22	14	0	0	0	168	149	619	64	58	5	10	6	4	89	5	137	5	0
ntes, Agustin, Tab	0	0	.000	0.00	5	0	0	0	5	0	3	3	16	2	0	0	1	0	4	0	1	1	0
lvez, Rosario, Lar	3	13	.188	5.53	31	18	0	0	13	0	84.2	97	330	66	52	4	4	2	3	69	1	42	7	2
mez, Francisco, Mont	2	2	.500	5.47	28	6	0	0	22	0	54.1	62	217	39	33	6	1	1	3	36	0	19	1	0
rcia, Apolinar, Sal	4	4	.500	3.99	13	13	0	0	0	0	67.2	69	252	31	30	3	10	0	5	36	1	33	5	0
rcia, C. Jose Luis, Lar	1	4	.200	4.02	36	4	1	1	32	2	65	65	255	35	29	7	7	1	3	18	2	35	4	0
rcia, Francisco, Mex	3	5	.375	5.05	20	10	0	0	10	0	51.2	53	202	37	29	2	2	1	0	29	1	26	5	0
rcia, P. Zenon, Oax	1	2	.333	5.50	27	1	0	0	26	0	34.1	42	130	30	21	5	1	5	3	13	2	7	2	0
rcia, R. Miguel, Min	4	8	.333	3.87	29	10	2	2	19	0	102.1	93	372	48	44	2	10	3	1	56	3	34	2	0
rcia, V. David, Monc	0	0	.000	4.50	3	0	0	0	3	0	4	5	16	2	2	1	0	0	0	3	0	4	0	0
ribay, Roberto, Q.R.	9	5	.643	3.54	45	0	0	0	45	11	63.2	48	210	19	18	2	11	3	3	34	11	28	6	0
ribay, Salvador, Ags	0	0	.000	20.25	2	0	0	0	2	0	1.1	5	13	9	3	0	0	0	0	1	0	0	0	0
ribay, Daniel, Tig	2	4	.333	4.98	20	10	0	0	10	0	59.2	64	239	39	33	3	1	2	8	32	1	36	6	0
za, Roberto, Lar	2	4	.333	6.50	30	11	0	0	19	1	63.2	87	258	51	46	8	4	2	2	38	1	24	2	0
rza, Ch. Alejandro, Ags	0	1	.000	6.41	17	1	0	0	16	1	26.2	31	107	27	19	3	2	1	3	27	2	14	2	0
mez, R. Martin, Min	2	6	.250	5.22	29	10	0	0	19	0	79.1	104	311	53	46	1	4	8	4	47	4	27	0	0
nzalez, Gilberto, Tor	5	3	.625	3.86	16	13	0	0	3	0	65.1	71	249	37	28	4	2	0	2	40	0	30	5	1
nzalez, M. Arturo, Mont	12	2	.857	1.78	20	20	1	1	0	0	121.1	86	434	29	24	6	5	3	5	35	4	42	2	0
nzalez, N. Juan Raul, Oax	0	0	.000	24.30	5	0	0	0	5	0	3.1	9	18	9	9	0	0	1	0	3	0	2	0	0
nzalez, T. Victor, P.R.	3	0	1.000	1.69	36	2	1	0	34	2	64	56	234	20	12	2	0	2	0	21	1	35	3	1
acia, Edmundo, Sal	0	1	.000	5.36	21	2	0	0	19	0	42	46	153	32	25	5	2	5	2	39	0	12	3	0
ajales, G. Norberto, Tor	6	2	.750	5.60	42	0	0	0	42	2	62.2	84	254	43	39	3	5	1	1	28	2	22	3	0
em, Otis, Mont	5	3	.625	2.01	40	0	0	0	40	10	49.1	28	167	13	11	2	4	0	1	37	2	52	4	0
ereca, G. Guillermo, Oax	1	4	.200	5.92	15	3	0	0	12	0	38	47	149	25	25	1	3	4	2	20	1	14	6	1
errero, P. Omar, Rey	1	2	.333	4.43	22	1	0	0	21	2	61	64	237	32	30	4	0	7	0	26	1	24	1	1
rrison, Brian, Tig	1	1	.500	5.16	8	4	0	0	4	0	22.2	22	83	16	13	3	0	3	2	21	0	10	3	0
redia, H. Hector, Mont	4	5	.444	5.64	23	17	0	0	6	1	97.1	133	404	68	61	7	8	2	2	29	3	39	6	0

– 393 –

Pitcher, Team	W	L	Pct.	ERA	G	GS	CG	ShO	GF	Sv.	IP	H	TBF	R	ER	HR	SH	SF	HB	BB	IBB	SO	WP	Bk
Hernandez, Dimas C., Monc....	0	0	.000	0.00	1	0	0	0	1	0	0.1	1	4	0	0	0	0	0	0	0	0	0	0	0
Hernandez, Encarnacion, P.R. .	2	0	1.000	4.54	21	0	0	0	21	0	35.2	42	141	19	18	4	1	2	1	7	2	9	0	
Hernandez, J. Manuel, Lar	4	10	.286	4.00	27	23	1	0	4	0	123.2	160	497	73	55	6	14	7	2	43	2	47	4	
Hernanado, Julio, P.R.	6	3	.667	2.81	22	18	3	0	4	0	118.1	109	429	46	37	5	13	3	5	60	3	48	8	
Hernandez, Martin, Q.R.	9	5	.643	3.02	20	20	5	3	0	0	128	120	473	49	43	4	14	4	1	41	2	63	14	
Herrera, Enrique, Tab	1	1	.500	1.93	19	0	0	0	19	0	32.2	35	122	12	7	2	4	0	2	17	7	18	6	
Herrera, H. Calixto, Monc.	4	3	.571	3.13	44	0	0	0	44	2	63.1	52	225	26	22	5	1	2	6	44	0	48	3	
Holman, Shawn, Mex	14	6	.700	3.30	35	19	0	0	16	3	141.2	165	559	61	52	6	8	4	5	48	1	61	7	
Huerta, Luis Enrique, Sal	4	12	.250	4.87	24	23	3	1	1	0	133	160	529	83	72	13	8	6	8	58	2	50	2	
Hurst, Jonathan, Mont.	4	2	.667	2.28	45	0	0	0	45	18	55.1	41	199	20	14	2	3	0	3	28	3	42	1	
Jimenez, Danilo, Monc.	3	1	.750	2.48	5	5	0	0	0	0	29	21	102	10	8	4	2	0	0	10	1	12	0	
Jimenez, German, Ags	10	5	.667	3.38	17	17	1	0	0	0	90.2	104	361	41	34	2	6	0	2	24	4	32	2	
Jimenez, Jesus, Tor	1	1	.500	8.80	22	4	0	0	18	0	30.2	46	121	31	30	4	1	2	1	29	0	12	1	
Jimenez, C. Isaac, P.R.	10	6	.625	1.70	20	19	7	3	1	1	127.1	96	448	35	24	3	9	1	7	43	2	68	3	
Johnston, Joe, Sal	0	0	.000	14.40	8	0	0	0	8	1	5	4	17	8	8	0	1	0	1	12	1	4	0	
Juarez, B. Fernando, Tor	1	1	.500	5.40	32	0	0	0	32	0	18.1	21	72	12	11	1	1	4	1	6	1	9	1	
Kelly, Richard, Monc.	6	10	.375	3.74	23	21	4	0	2	0	125	116	462	63	52	10	6	3	3	86	4	52	15	
Kutzler, Jerry, Oax	0	1	.000	1.50	1	1	0	0	0	0	6	7	24	2	1	0	2	0	1	0	0	1	0	
Lancaster, Lest W., Oax	2	4	.333	6.26	6	6	1	0	0	0	41.2	57	168	32	29	4	2	0	0	19	1	15	1	
Lara, Hugo, P.R.	7	5	.583	3.38	26	16	2	2	10	0	117.1	108	439	50	44	7	4	5	7	46	3	54	3	
Lara, E. Jorge, Monc.	2	4	.333	5.28	31	0	0	0	31	3	44.1	55	190	29	26	6	1	1	7	21	2	35	1	
Larranaga, Miguel, P.R.	0	0	.000	6.23	2	0	0	0	2	0	4.1	8	21	6	3	1	0	0	1	1	0	3	1	
Leal, P. Gerardo. Monc.	3	1	.750	3.74	33	4	0	0	29	1	67.1	77	265	32	28	6	3	2	0	37	6	40	3	
Leon, Juan A., Tor	0	0	.000	4.05	5	0	0	0	5	0	6.2	7	24	3	3	0	1	0	0	5	0	2	1	
Leyva, Carlos, Tig	0	0	.000	10.80	5	0	0	0	5	0	1.2	4	9	2	2	0	1	0	0	2	0	0	0	
Linares, Efrain, Q.R.	2	2	.500	3.49	11	2	0	0	9	2	28.1	20	97	13	11	1	5	1	0	21	0	23	3	
Lizarraga, Andres, Lar	0	1	.000	10.80	6	1	0	0	5	0	3.1	7	17	7	4	0	0	0	0	7	0	0	2	
Lizarraga, J. Hugo, Cam	1	4	.200	9.69	10	4	0	0	6	0	26	43	118	31	28	3	2	1	0	24	4	11	0	
Llanes, Emeterio, Yuc	0	1	.000	1.99	6	1	0	0	5	0	22.2	14	76	6	5	0	3	2	0	11	2	12	2	
Loaiza, Esteban, Mex	2	0	1.000	2.43	5	5	0	0	0	0	33.1	28	123	12	9	1	3	0	2	14	0	16	1	
Loaiza, R. Sabino, Cam	5	2	.714	3.75	18	9	1	1	9	0	69.2	83	265	33	29	3	6	2	4	33	4	23	4	
Long, Steve, Lar	0	1	.000	9.82	2	2	0	0	0	0	3.2	6	16	7	4	0	1	1	0	6	0	0	0	
Lopez, Emigdio, Tab	15	4	.789	2.15	25	25	3	1	0	0	159.1	135	584	46	38	5	9	5	6	41	2	68	4	
Lopez, Gilberto, P.R.	0	2	.000	8.10	6	1	0	0	5	0	13.1	20	55	12	12	1	2	3	1	5	1	5	1	
Lopez, Jonas, Ags	8	6	.571	3.83	23	22	2	1	1	1	124.2	122	480	62	53	7	8	4	2	54	2	38	2	
Lopez, Rodrigo, P.R.	1	1	.500	3.54	7	3	0	0	4	1	20.1	15	70	8	8	2	4	0	0	16	3	22	1	
Lopez, C. Jesus Juan, Rey	1	1	.500	5.60	5	3	0	0	2	0	17.2	16	65	15	11	0	3	2	0	13	0	8	1	
Lopez, De La T. Jose Juan, Oax	4	8	.333	5.07	38	1	0	0	37	9	65.2	89	272	49	37	4	8	2	3	27	9	41	2	
Luevano, Juan, P.R.	5	3	.625	2.23	34	7	0	0	27	6	72.2	67	271	20	18	2	4	0	3	26	3	25	2	
Lupercio, Hector M.,Sal	1	0	1.000	6.57	12	0	0	0	12	0	24.2	33	96	18	18	4	1	2	3	11	0	11	0	
Lynch, David, Tig	7	5	.583	4.32	17	17	0	0	0	0	98	93	371	52	47	6	1	5	2	51	0	84	8	
Manzano, Adrian, Tig	0	1	.000	5.48	11	3	0	0	8	0	21.1	26	85	13	13	1	0	1	2	7	0	9	2	
Marquez, Jose A., Tor	0	1	.000	9.00	17	0	0	0	17	0	17	26	69	18	17	1	1	1	0	13	0	7	3	
Marquez, E. Isidro, Tig	9	4	.692	3.46	48	0	0	0	48	23	67.2	55	244	30	26	4	5	2	4	21	2	44	2	
Martinez, Filberto, Sal	1	0	1.000	6.00	6	0	0	0	6	0	3	4	12	2	2	1	0	0	0	2	0	1	0	
Martinez, Jose Antonio, Cam ..	0	2	.000	2.42	22	2	0	0	20	1	48.1	46	177	15	13	2	4	2	2	8	0	21	0	
Martinez, Mauricio, Sal	0	0	.000	6.75	16	0	0	0	16	0	21.1	30	86	16	16	3	1	0	0	13	2	12	0	
Mauser, Tim, Tab	1	6	.143	2.72	47	0	0	0	47	25	56.1	45	199	18	17	3	11	3	1	25	8	36	4	
Maysey, Matt, Cam	2	3	.400	3.05	15	5	0	0	10	2	41.1	40	157	17	14	5	0	0	0	16	1	25	3	
Melendez, Jose, Yuc	5	4	.556	1.65	35	3	0	0	32	11	82	61	290	21	15	1	6	3	7	27	5	63	8	
Mendez, G. Luis Fernando, Rey .	6	6	.500	5.73	20	19	1	0	1	0	92.2	95	358	64	59	9	6	5	4	49	1	64	3	
Menendez, Tony, Mex	1	3	.250	4.40	28	0	0	0	28	4	28.2	33	115	17	14	1	2	1	1	13	1	30	0	
Metoyer, Tony, Oax	4	2	.667	1.64	29	0	0	0	29	8	38.1	24	125	11	7	3	4	1	2	23	6	31	2	
Meza, Leobardo, P.R.	0	0	.000	4.50	3	2	0	0	1	0	12	14	46	6	6	1	0	1	0	6	0	6	3	
Miranda, Julio Cesar, Yuc	9	4	.692	2.66	49	1	0	0	48	12	101.2	79	364	38	30	4	8	2	4	26	7	56	2	
Molina, Joaquin, Tor	0	0	.000	1.93	7	0	0	0	7	0	9.1	6	34	3	2	0	0	1	7	1	4	0		
Montalvo, Rafael, Cam	4	2	.667	4.00	16	0	0	0	16	1	18	23	73	9	8	3	1	0	1	5	1	6	1	
Montano, Francisco, Monc.	7	7	.500	7.04	25	23	0	0	2	0	110	149	448	93	86	8	5	4	3	61	3	47	6	
Mora, Eleazar, P.R.	5	7	.417	3.34	30	19	1	1	11	1	102.1	118	405	42	38	6	3	4	3	36	2	69	2	
Mora, Jose Luis, Sal	0	0	.000	9.00	2	0	0	0	2	0	2	3	9	2	2	0	0	0	0	1	0	0	0	
Moreno, Agustin, Tig	10	6	.625	2.90	23	24	3	0	0	0	152	134	562	59	49	8	6	1	3	60	2	88	3	
Moreno, Jesus, Yuc	0	1	.000	11.57	3	3	0	0	0	0	4.2	8	22	7	6	1	1	0	2	4	0	0	0	
Moreno, Leobardo, Mex	6	7	.462	2.93	25	18	5	1	7	0	129	111	474	58	42	10	9	5	4	48	1	99	9	
Moreno, V. Ricardo, Oax	0	1	.000	14.66	9	1	0	0	8	0	11.2	18	51	19	19	2	1	1	1	10	2	7	2	
Murillo, M. Felipe, Monc.	4	5	.444	4.53	39	0	0	0	39	15	45.2	54	184	29	23	2	4	0	0	17	2	14	0	
Munoz, Jaime, Tig	3	3	.500	3.69	23	2	0	0	21	0	39	35	141	17	16	2	6	0	1	18	1	19	2	
Munoz, Leonardo, Mont.	3	0	1.000	1.84	37	1	0	0	36	0	49	43	168	11	10	0	8	4	1	26	1	18	2	
Munoz, Pablo, Q.R.	0	0	.000	13.50	3	0	0	0	3	0	0.2	2	3	1	1	0	0	1	0	1	0	0	0	
Munoz, Ricardo, Tab	7	10	.412	3.17	24	23	2	0	1	1	144.2	154	560	62	51	5	8	4	8	37	3	56	3	
Munoz, G. Miguel, Rey	0	0	.000	4.50	3	0	0	0	3	0	4	7	18	2	2	0	0	0	0	1	0	0	1	
Navarro, Luis Alberto, Lar	0	0	.000	9.45	6	0	0	0	6	0	6.2	12	33	7	7	2	0	1	4	0	3	0		
Neri, Braulio, Q.R.	1	2	.333	3.58	42	1	0	0	41	0	27.2	31	105	14	11	3	2	0	3	21	6	12	0	
Neri, Eduardo, P.R.	6	5	.545	2.70	53	0	0	0	53	5	86.2	70	310	32	26	6	8	5	4	37	6	36	3	
Nunez, Edwin, Mex	2	0	1.000	2.25	14	0	0	0	14	6	16	18	64	4	4	1	3	0	4	0	12	2		
Nunez, Avina Jose Juan, Oax ..	0	0	.000	7.62	19	0	0	0	19	2	13	14	52	12	11	1	1	0	0	17	1	14	3	
Ochoa, Pablo, Mex	0	0	.000	10.13	3	0	0	0	3	0	2.2	4	13	4	3	0	0	0	0	1	0	0	0	
Olague, Jesus, Mont.	3	2	.600	4.24	32	3	0	0	29	1	63.2	60	236	34	30	3	2	0	4	52	5	37	5	
Orea, Flavio, Mont.	0	0	.000	6.75	13	0	0	0	13	0	13.1	17	55	12	10	0	1	1	0	8	0	1	2	
Orozco, Jaime, Min	6	8	.429	5.31	23	21	0	0	2	0	101.2	125	409	66	60	7	7	1	8	36	1	49	3	
Ortega, Roberto, Q.R.	0	0	.000	4.22	35	0	0	0	35	2	21.1	16	78	11	10	1	2	0	0	20	1	22	2	
Ortega, Wilbert, Yuc	0	0	.000	3.73	26	3	0	0	23	0	31.1	22	104	16	13	1	5	3	2	23	3	22	2	
Osuna, Gabriel, Yuc	4	5	.444	2.53	10	4	0	0	19	5	32	35	123	17	9	2	1	2	0	8	2	20	0	
Osuna, Ricardo, Tab	2	7	.222	3.58	14	14	0	0	0	0	78	83	295	39	31	1	7	2	4	30	3	32	5	

cher, Team	W	L	Pct.	ERA	G	GS	CG	ShO	GF	Sv.	IP	H	TBF	R	ER	HR	SH	SF	HB	BB	IBB	SO	WP	Bk.
una, Roberto, Lar	6	5	.545	4.24	51	6	0	0	44	3	121	130	467	68	57	9	9	5	2	49	4	70	2	1
lacios, Vicente, Ags	2	1	.667	3.77	11	0	0	0	11	2	14.1	13	53	6	6	1	2	0	0	4	2	15	1	0
lafox, Juan M., Tor	7	11	.389	4.16	24	24	7	1	0	0	166.2	190	646	93	77	14	10	2	13	54	8	58	1	0
tterson, Kent, Monc	0	1	.000	1.42	6	0	0	0	6	0	6.1	4	23	2	1	0	0	0	0	6	0	2	0	0
lcastregui, Leonardo, Cam ..	0	0	.000	2.25	6	0	0	0	6	0	4	1	12	1	1	0	0	0	0	7	1	0	2	0
rez, David, Mont.	13	4	.765	2.68	21	19	1	0	2	0	127.2	126	473	41	38	6	7	1	7	48	2	58	3	0
rez, Edgar, Min	0	0	.000	7.71	3	0	0	0	3	0	2.1	4	10	2	2	0	0	1	1	0	1	0	1	1
rez, Leonardo, Ags	4	6	.400	5.81	16	13	0	0	3	0	74.1	85	291	51	48	4	3	0	8	49	8	39	3	0
rez, G. Vladimir, Ags	8	5	.615	2.59	55	0	0	0	55	3	100.2	92	365	37	29	0	7	6	3	50	6	52	7	0
rschke, Greg, Tor	3	5	.375	2.81	23	0	0	0	23	7	32	33	115	13	10	2	9	0	0	16	3	22	6	0
cota, Lenin, Oax	6	5	.545	3.66	19	18	4	1	0	0	120.1	123	454	59	49	3	13	4	6	59	5	67	10	0
nentel, V. Roberto, Monc. ..	0	2	.000	6.98	43	0	0	0	43	0	40	50	165	35	31	4	2	1	1	35	0	23	2	0
neda, Gabriel, Oax	5	3	.625	3.66	27	6	1	0	21	2	71.1	55	254	37	29	3	4	3	1	50	7	39	6	0
na, Rafael, Mex	7	4	.636	3.09	39	6	0	0	33	4	84.1	72	307	33	29	2	4	3	3	49	1	56	14	0
well, Dennis, Mont.	5	1	.833	1.53	38	1	0	0	37	4	47	30	166	11	8	1	1	2	2	21	1	48	1	0
ig, Benny, Tor	0	1	.000	9.95	1	1	0	0	0	0	6.1	12	29	7	7	3	0	0	0	3	0	2	1	0
rata, A. Julio, Rey	11	11	.500	3.37	25	25	8	1	0	0	152.1	148	569	63	57	11	10	2	3	68	2	97	6	1
iijada, G. Mario, Tor	3	8	.273	4.59	32	11	0	0	21	1	98	88	349	54	50	10	4	2	4	73	4	55	8	1
intanilla, Enrique, Lar	6	7	.462	5.64	41	10	0	0	31	1	107	120	424	77	67	10	5	5	12	40	5	58	8	1
airoz, Aaron, Lar	4	6	.400	3.82	18	14	2	1	4	0	68.1	65	258	38	29	2	2	3	3	34	3	45	3	2
airoz, Jose Julian, Ags	0	2	.000	6.97	22	0	0	0	22	1	20.2	30	91	18	16	3	0	0	1	7	0	11	3	0
iinones, Enrique, Ags	9	2	.818	3.20	23	14	1	0	8	0	109.2	115	423	47	39	7	4	0	1	29	1	42	4	0
mirez, Roberto, Mex	14	9	.609	2.84	28	28	8	1	0	0	190.1	179	698	70	60	10	9	4	10	74	2	132	9	0
mos, Jorge, Q.R.	1	2	.333	2.04	38	0	0	0	38	3	57.1	52	209	13	13	2	3	1	3	18	0	24	2	0
aygoza, V. Martin, P.R.	7	8	.467	3.18	22	21	3	1	1	0	130	136	490	56	46	4	9	6	4	33	5	63	3	0
anteria, Hilario, Tor.	5	8	.385	3.01	22	22	5	2	0	0	140.1	139	535	56	47	6	6	2	3	28	1	52	4	0
esendez, Oscar, Rey	0	0	.000	15.00	4	1	0	0	3	0	3	4	12	6	5	0	0	0	0	7	0	2	0	0
etes, Lorenzo, Tab	2	2	.500	5.66	31	1	0	0	30	0	20.2	27	78	16	13	2	1	4	0	14	3	8	1	0
yes, B. Flavio, Min	0	0	.000	5.03	20	0	0	0	20	0	19.2	23	76	13	11	2	4	0	1	10	2	11	2	1
ncon, Ricardo, Mex	5	3	.625	2.97	50	0	0	0	50	10	78.2	58	275	28	26	2	7	2	0	27	2	60	2	0
os, V. Jesus, Monc	6	6	.500	4.50	24	24	2	0	0	0	140	127	515	80	70	16	8	5	6	66	3	104	4	0
vera, Francisco J., Tor	1	1	.500	6.37	15	3	0	0	12	0	29.2	31	121	22	21	3	1	2	2	23	0	14	2	0
vera, Hector, Tab	1	4	.200	5.20	26	6	0	0	20	0	64	76	251	38	37	3	3	4	0	29	5	27	2	0
vera, Oscar, Mex	0	0	.000	3.60	11	0	0	0	11	0	20	21	76	8	8	2	1	2	1	3	0	5	0	0
vera, Paul, Ags	0	0	.000	17.36	4	0	0	0	4	0	4.2	10	24	11	9	0	0	0	4	1	0	1	0	0
driguez, Rene, Lar	0	0	.000	7.88	5	0	0	0	5	0	8	13	35	7	7	1	0	0	2	0	4	1	0
driguez, Rosario, P.R.	0	1	0.000	11	1	0	0	0	10	0	17	13	59	8	7	1	1	1	0	3	11	0	3	4	0
driguez, Salvador, Yuc	4	0	1.000	3.23	28	4	0	0	24	0	75.1	83	293	36	27	1	4	2	0	43	7	44	5	0
driguez, T. Raul, Monc	13	8	.619	3.15	26	24	7	4	2	0	171.2	148	637	67	60	7	5	3	6	71	0	121	7	0
jo, R. Oscar, Rey	0	3	.000	3.71	15	1	0	0	14	2	17	25	78	14	7	0	1	0	0	10	0	4	2	0
man, Porfirio, P.R.	0	0	.000	9.00	1	0	0	0	0	0	1	1	3	1	1	0	0	1	1	1	0	1	0	0
mero, Juan, Tab	2	6	.250	4.70	27	7	3	0	20	0	59.1	76	241	37	31	7	6	1	2	19	2	20	1	0
mo, Guillermo, Tor	1	3	.250	9.89	16	6	0	0	10	1	33.2	46	139	41	37	5	0	4	0	24	0	16	3	0
sario, David, Tig	0	0	.000	0.00	1	0	0	0	1	0	.1	2	2	0	0	0	0	0	0	0	0	0	0	0
yal, Thomas, Tig	1	1	.500	5.25	3	3	0	0	0	0	12	18	52	9	7	1	1	0	0	4	0	4	1	0
iz, Cecilio, Tab	8	9	.471	3.06	23	23	3	1	0	0	144.1	137	534	51	49	8	14	4	3	36	2	82	2	2
enz, Alfredo, Q.R.	5	8	.385	3.11	21	21	5	2	0	0	133	131	498	53	46	4	15	5	3	44	2	57	6	0
ldana, Edgardo, Tig	4	2	.667	2.89	39	2	0	0	37	1	71.2	63	263	28	23	6	3	1	3	27	1	23	7	0
lgado, Eduardo, Min	0	0	.000	5.71	20	0	0	0	20	0	34.2	40	137	23	22	4	3	1	1	17	0	13	1	0
nchez, Alejandro, Q.R.	0	0	.000	0.00	1	0	0	0	1	0	1	0	4	0	0	0	0	0	0	1	0	0	0	0
nchez, C. Efrain, Cam	0	3	.000	2.89	14	2	1	0	12	0	43.2	38	151	19	14	3	5	1	1	18	0	25	1	0
nchez, S. Hector, Ags	3	4	.429	3.09	27	14	1	0	13	0	107.2	98	400	42	37	4	5	4	0	24	2	37	1	1
ndoval, Guillermo, Yuc	4	8	.333	4.17	23	23	0	0	0	0	123	149	478	68	57	4	14	5	2	52	7	44	13	0
ndoval, Ch. Carlos, Min	1	0	1.000	5.66	25	0	0	0	25	1	20.2	25	86	18	13	1	2	1	0	17	0	11	2	0
ngeado, A. Juan Carlos, Oax .	1	5	.167	8.64	12	7	0	0	5	0	33.1	44	135	37	32	3	2	1	0	27	0	17	4	0
rna, Ramon, Sal	2	4	.333	4.83	19	11	0	0	8	0	63.1	73	244	40	34	6	4	3	7	35	2	21	2	0
erra, F. Abel, Cam	8	12	.400	3.53	23	23	10	3	0	0	155.1	158	591	74	61	11	11	3	3	50	2	75	4	0
ohui M., David, Oax	0	1	.000	13.50	4	1	0	0	3	0	3.1	6	17	5	5	0	2	0	0	4	0	2	1	0
tano M., Julio Cesar, P.R.	1	3	.250	5.06	20	0	0	0	20	2	21.1	30	89	13	12	4	1	0	1	10	3	12	1	0
arte S., Jose A, Min	8	2	.800	1.39	54	0	0	0	54	15	84	67	299	21	13	2	5	2	2	24	7	65	6	0
lis, Ricardo, Yuc	9	8	.529	2.83	20	20	1	0	0	0	114.2	122	434	47	36	12	0	0	41	5	47	1	0
mbra, Francisco, Sal	5	12	.294	4.28	31	17	5	1	14	0	109.1	126	425	56	52	5	9	4	1	46	1	50	4	0
to, Daniel, Mex	0	1	.000	9.16	8	0	0	0	8	0	18.2	24	79	20	19	4	0	1	2	10	1	8	1	0
to M., Fernando, Q.R.	10	12	.455	3.51	26	24	9	2	2	1	159	176	622	72	62	6	10	5	6	33	5	73	3	0
to P., Cruz Antonio, Q.R.	2	8	.200	4.29	31	7	1	0	24	1	63	52	232	33	30	3	7	3	3	41	2	53	5	1
eed, Ricky, Tig	0	0	.000	5.40	3	0	0	0	3	0	3.1	2	12	2	2	0	0	0	0	5	1	6	0	0
range, Donald T., Sal	4	5	.444	2.91	38	2	0	0	36	12	52.2	41	190	20	17	4	4	2	1	28	3	58	7	0
lu, Mario, Cam	0	1	.000	2.45	3	0	0	0	3	0	3.2	4	14	4	1	0	1	0	0	5	0	1	0	0
eda, Arturo, Oax	0	0	.000	0.00	1	0	0	0	1	0	1	1	4	1	0	0	0	0	0	1	0	0	0	0
eda S., Juan, Cam	1	1	.500	5.14	12	0	0	0	12	1	7	6	26	4	4	1	0	0	2	4	1	1	0	0
noco M., Ruben, Cam	0	0	.000	11.37	6	0	0	0	8	0	6.1	12	30	9	8	3	1	1	0	3	1	1	0	0
edo, Mario, Oax	0	0	.000	0.00	1	0	0	0	1	0	1	0	4	0	0	0	0	1	0	0	0	1	0	0
liver, Fred, Yuc	1	3	.250	5.31	8	8	0	0	0	0	40.2	40	151	25	24	3	4	0	2	32	1	32	1	2
rres, M. Eduardo, Monc. ...	0	0	.000	5.00	1	0	0	0	0	0	.1	0	1	0	0	0	0	0	0	0	0	0	0	0
be, Juan Carlos, Yuc	5	3	.625	4.97	33	1	0	0	32	1	54.1	59	199	33	30	1	7	5	5	25	10	25	4	0
dez, Efrain, Q.R.	11	5	.688	2.23	20	20	6	3	0	0	149.1	123	535	49	37	7	14	1	8	44	1	69	2	0
dez, R. Rodolfo, Monc	3	2	.600	4.37	27	9	0	0	18	0	55.2	69	224	37	27	5	4	2	31	1	28	2	0
lencia, Jorge, Sal	2	8	.200	5.97	36	3	0	0	33	0	75.1	93	294	57	50	9	5	6	2	55	2	25	3	0
lenzuela, Lorenzo, Yuc	1	2	.333	9.82	7	1	0	0	6	0	11	17	45	13	12	1	0	1	2	13	3	5	2	1
lenzuela, Saul, Q.R.	8	7	.533	3.61	21	21	3	2	0	0	122	118	457	53	49	14	5	2	9	42	1	44	0	0
rgas, Ignacio, Min	1	2	.333	5.16	31	1	0	0	30	0	45.1	58	182	27	26	3	0	5	1	22	0	22	3	0
rgas, Joel, Tab	0	2	.000	2.78	12	3	0	0	9	0	35.2	29	120	11	11	1	3	0	1	17	0	18	4	0
zquez, Aguedo, Ags	5	6	.455	4.50	18	15	1	0	0	0	92	114	369	49	46	5	5	3	2	30	6	45	0	0

Pitcher, Team	W	L	Pct.	ERA	G	GS	CG	ShO	GF	Sv.	IP	H	TBF	R	ER	HR	SH	SF	HB	BB	IBB	SO	WP
Vazquez, Jose A., Monc.	0	0	.000	10.80	1	0	0	0	1	0	1.2	4	9	2	2	0	0	0	0	0	0	1	0
Vazquez, A. Adrian, Cam	6	7	.462	4.02	19	19	4	1	0	0	112	100	414	58	50	10	9	4	4	68	3	48	8
Vazquez, De Aza Lioner, Oax...	0	2	.000	18.00	2	2	0	0	0	0	5	6	19	13	10	0	0	0	0	10	0	3	0
Vega, Obed, Lar.....................	1	3	.250	5.50	25	6	0	0	19	0	52.1	66	211	39	32	6	4	2	4	33	4	22	4
Velazquez, Ernesto S., Monc...	0	0	.000	8.53	6	0	0	0	6	0	6.1	17	33	6	6	1	0	0	4	0	5	2	
Velazquez G., Israel, Min.......	7	13	.350	4.19	29	25	2	0	4	0	150.1	147	566	76	70	13	8	5	6	73	5	83	5
Verdugo, Orlando, Yuc..........	0	2	.000	1.27	9	2	0	0	7	0	21.1	13	72	3	3	1	2	0	2	11	1	3	1
Villanueva, Luis, Ags............	1	0	1.000	3.18	15	0	0	0	15	0	5.2	6	23	2	2	0	0	0	4	2	0	1	0
Villarreal, Antonio, Yuc........	10	6	.625	2.45	22	22	1	0	0	0	143.1	141	534	46	39	3	10	2	7	53	5	67	6
Villegas, Jose Angel, Ags......	2	6	.250	3.22	31	5	2	0	26	3	95	99	361	39	34	6	8	3	5	25	3	31	2
Williams, Jeff, Mex.................	5	1	.833	2.28	12	7	2	1	5	2	51.1	45	189	14	13	1	2	2	1	16	0	23	3
Zappelli, Mark, Sal................	7	4	.636	3.92	14	14	2	0	0	0	96.1	96	353	47	42	9	7	4	8	61	2	32	3
Zavala, Marcos, Tig	0	0	.000	6.75	6	0	0	0	6	0	8.2	10	36	6	6	1	0	0	5	0	4	3

COMBINATION SHUTOUTS: A total of 154 combination shutouts were pitched in the Mexican League in 1996. Poza Rica led the league with 16.
NO-HIT GAME: Ramirez, Mexico City Red Devils, defeated Tabasco, 2-0, July 10.

1996 FIELDING

TEAM

Team	Pct.	G	PO	A	E	TC	DP	PB	Team	Pct.	G	PO	A	E	TC	DP
Quintana Roo	.980	115	2994	1257	87	4338	102	11	Yucatan	.973	115	2980	1324	119	4423	97
Monterrey..............	.979	116	3050	1352	96	4498	88	14	Reynosa	.971	114	2915	1244	126	4285	123
Torreon.................	.977	115	2971	1300	101	4372	127	9	Aguascalientes	.971	115	2955	1328	126	4409	123
Poza Rica	.977	115	3034	1352	103	4489	102	10	Nuevo Laredo	.970	116	2985	1279	134	4398	123
Minatitlan	.977	112	2890	1233	98	4221	90	8	Saltillo..................	.970	115	2916	1355	134	4405	128
Mex. City R.D.	.975	114	2976	1308	108	4392	106	12	Monclova...............	.970	115	2982	1207	131	4320	110
Oaxaca.................	.975	115	2878	1393	111	4382	121	10	Campeche..............	.969	115	2855	1195	130	4180	105
Mexico City Tigers..	.974	114	3052	1324	116	4492	103	15	Tabasco	.968	115	2885	1348	141	4374	112

TRIPLE PLAYS: Monterrey, Oaxaca, Poza Rica, Saltillo, Torreon.

INDIVIDUAL

FIRST BASEMEN

Player, Team	Pct.	G	PO	A	E	TC	DP
Aganza, Ruben, Mva......................	.988	106	920	70	12	1002	89
Almeida, Shammar, Sal	.990	43	294	17	3	314	39
Alvarez, Luis, Yuc	1.000	2	16	1	0	17	2
Arias, Everardo, Q.R.	1.000	1	1	0	0	1	0
Arvizu, Javier, Cam	.982	9	51	4	1	56	2
Aviles, Alejandro, Sal	1.000	1	2	1	0	3	0
Azocar, Oscar, P.R......................	1.000	1	9	0	0	9	2
Barrera, Nelson, Oax...................	.991	55	491	49	5	545	53
Beltran, Gerardo, Min	.989	34	263	6	3	272	14
Bojorquez, Victor, M.C.R.D.	1.000	7	15	0	0	15	1
Bolick, Frank, Oax......................	1.000	11	66	5	0	71	5
Bowie, Jim, Agua........................	.992	37	338	34	3	375	31
Cabrera, Francisco, Mva	1.000	4	35	4	0	39	2
Carrasco, Ernesto, Lar	1.000	1	1	0	0	1	0
Carrillo, Matias, M.C.Tig..............	.987	25	152	5	2	159	15
Castaneda, Hector, Min...............	1.000	6	30	1	0	31	2
Castaneda, Rafael, M.C.Tig..........	1.000	8	47	4	0	51	2
Castro, Eddie, Min	.987	56	505	42	7	554	49
Clark, Tim, Sal	.987	45	281	30	4	315	34
Cobos, Rogelio, Oax...................	.971	5	31	2	1	34	1
Colon, Cristobal, P.R...................	.947	5	16	2	1	19	1
Denson, Drew, M.C.R.D...............	.991	42	389	34	4	427	30
Diaz, Luis Fernando, M.C.Tig........	.987	12	71	3	1	75	8
Duarte, Rene, Tab	.986	7	64	5	1	70	3
Estrada, Ruben, Lar	.833	3	5	0	1	6	0
Fentanes, Oscar, Tab...................	1.000	4	27	5	0	32	2
Gavia, Jesus, Min	.974	10	34	3	1	38	5
Gonzalez, Jesus, Cam	.991	62	589	38	6	633	46
Grijak, Kevin Scott, M.C.R.D........	.995	21	180	17	1	198	6
Guerrero, Javier, Agua.	1.000	21	147	7	0	154	14
Guzman, Marco Antonio, Q.R.	.976	4	38	3	1	42	8
Hernandez, Martin, Cam	.975	9	74	4	2	80	8
Iturbe, Pedro, Tab	.992	13	111	6	1	118	6
Jimenez, Eduardo, Yuc	1.000	2	17	1	0	18	1
Jimenez, Ulises, Tor....................	1.000	5	33	3	0	36	2
Leal, P.J. Guadalupe, Cam	1.000	9	57	4	0	61	2
Lopez, Victor, Oax......................	.984	9	59	3	1	63	5
Machiria, Pablo, Agua..................	.987	62	573	24	8	605	54
Martinez, Domingo, Rey...............	.991	111	989	74	10	1073	110
Martinez, Raul, Lar	.981	19	144	13	3	160	14
Mendez, Jesus, P.R.....................	.995	114	1188	74	6	1268	76
Mercedes, Luis, Tab....................	.900	1	8	1	1	10	1
Michel, Domingo, Cam	.991	93	752	33	7	792	75
Milligan, Randy, Oax...................	1.000	2	22	0	0	22	4
Monroy, Victor Hugo, Rey	1.000	2	6	0	0	6	1
Mora, Andres, Lar.......................	.667	1	2	0	1	3	1
Naveda, Edgar, Oax.....................	1.000	8	56	5	0	61	10

Player, Team	Pct.	G	PO	A	E	TC	D
Ochoa, Edgar, M.C.Tig..................	.952	2	19	1	1	21	
O'Halloran, Greg, Q.R.	.982	26	211	12	4	227	2
Orantes, Ramon, Agua.	1.000	2	4	0	0	4	
Ortiz, Alejandro, Q.R.	.966	5	24	4	1	29	
Pardo, Victor Manuel, Oax............	.988	103	291	27	4	322	2
Pena, Carlos, Yuc	1.000	1	1	0	0	1	
Pena, Luis Alberto, Yuc	.989	27	176	4	2	182	
Peralta, Amado, Oax....................	.992	44	327	27	3	357	3
Perez, Francisco, M.c.r.d.	1.000	10	52	5	0	57	
Perezchica, Antonio, M.C.Tig........	1.000	3	29	0	0	29	
Quintana, Carlos, Q.R.	.992	67	581	45	5	631	4
Quiroz, Jose Julian, Agua.	1.000	1	1	0	0	1	
Raben, Luis, Yuc........................	.991	11	101	9	1	111	1
Rivera, German, Tab	1.000	2	18	0	0	18	
Rodriguez, Boi, Lar......................	.977	49	405	21	10	436	4
Rojas, Homar, M.C.R.D.................	.986	18	131	7	2	140	1
Romero, Marco Antonio, M.C.Tig...	.992	70	603	46	5	654	5
Romero, Oscar, Min.....................	.970	4	26	6	1	33	
Salinas, Rogelio, Yuc...................	.989	59	477	39	6	522	3
Sanchez, Armando, Mont.	1.000	3	14	1	0	15	
Sanchez, Gerardo, Lar	.988	27	224	15	3	242	2
Sasser, Mackey, Tab	.990	34	271	25	3	299	3
Scott, Bryant, Tab	1.000	9	88	6	0	94	
Sievers, Carlos, Yuc....................	.987	18	147	4	2	153	1
Snider, Van, Tor	.991	28	209	5	2	216	1
Stark, Matt, Rey.........................	.971	3	30	4	1	35	
Tatis, Bernardo, Yuc	.993	18	116	19	1	136	
Tolentino, Jose, Mont.	1.000	43	412	23	0	435	3
Valdez, Jesus, Yuc	1.000	7	26	0	0	26	
Valenzuela, Horacio, Tab	1.000	1	11	0	0	11	
Valverde, Raul, Oax	1.000	2	9	1	0	10	
Vargas, Hector, Min	.990	33	282	16	3	301	3
Vega, Edgar, M.C.Tig...................	1.000	1	1	0	0	1	
Velazquez, Guillermo, Mont.	.992	65	576	42	5	623	3
Villanueva, Hector, Mva	.988	11	76	6	1	83	
Villarreal, Alejandro, Lar	.995	50	359	30	2	391	4
Zambrano, Eduardo, Agua............	1.000	4	40	5	0	45	
Zambrano, Roberto, Q.R.	1.000	1	2	0	0	2	
Zamudio, Rafael, Mont.	.974	13	73	3	2	78	

TRIPLE PLAYS: Villanueva, Ru. Avila.

SECOND BASEMEN

Player, Team	Pct.	G	PO	A	E	TC	D
Arevalo, Guadalupe, Agua............	1.000	17	46	61	0	107	1
Arias, Everardo, Q.R.	.900	4	4	5	1	10	
Armenta, Guillermo, M.C.R.D.	.954	27	45	59	5	109	1
Balderas, Abelardo, Min	.972	33	64	75	4	143	2
Barrera, Jesus Antonio, Q.R.	.950	6	9	10	1	20	

– 396 –

Player, Team	Pct.	G	PO	A	E	TC	DP
eristain, Gregorio, Min	.976	21	39	41	2	82	6
amacho, Adulfo, Sal	.986	45	95	121	3	219	27
arrasco, Ernesto, Lar	.976	49	116	125	6	247	37
astaneda, Rafael, M.C.Tig.	1.000	2	1	1	0	2	0
astro, Arnoldo, Q.R.	.982	108	304	337	12	653	64
ervera, Francisco, Cam	.958	6	12	11	1	24	5
himelis, Joel, Oax	.981	112	285	334	12	631	93
olon, Cristobal, P.R.	.991	24	53	60	1	114	10
ontreras, Jose, Mont.	1.000	1	1	1	0	2	0
az R., Remigio, Mont.	1.000	1	1	2	0	3	0
riquez, Graciano, Agua.	1.000	1	1	5	0	6	0
squer, Ramon, Rey	.965	107	219	306	19	544	78
strada, Ruben, Lar	1.000	1	3	0	0	3	0
lix, Arturo, Yuc	.965	55	132	141	10	283	31
rnandez, Fabian, Rey	.985	16	33	32	1	66	12
gueroa, Bienvenido, M.C.R.D.	.750	3	1	5	2	8	0
ores, Miguel, Mont.	.976	105	264	301	14	579	60
anco, Manuel, Yuc	.556	3	1	4	4	9	0
astelum, Sergio Omar, M.C.Tig.	1.000	23	42	52	0	94	10
onzalez, Hector, P.R.	1.000	1	0	1	0	1	0
uerrero, Jaime, P.R.	1.000	4	7	12	0	19	1
uerrero, Juan, Sal	1.000	4	5	12	0	17	3
ernandez, Juan Carlos, P.R.	1.000	7	2	1	0	3	0
nzo, Tommy, Min	.962	55	118	134	10	262	25
fante, Alexis, Tab	.964	29	60	75	5	140	16
opez, Magali, Yuc	.935	31	64	80	10	154	15
opez H., Fabian, Oax	1.000	6	10	14	0	24	6
oredo, Jorge Luis, Cam	.976	102	240	257	12	509	57
agallanes, Everardo, Mont.	1.000	2	9	6	0	15	1
agana, Gabriel, Yuc	1.000	2	1	0	0	1	0
arrujo, Hector, Min	1.000	1	1	1	0	2	1
artinez, Abel, Q.R.	1.000	3	0	1	0	1	0
artinez, Grimaldo, Mva	.971	101	234	264	15	513	75
endiola, Juan Carlos, P.R.	1.000	5	2	6	0	8	1
endoza, Omar, Lar	.967	39	63	82	5	150	19
ere, Pedro, P.R.	.983	112	254	326	10	590	53
ontalvo, Ivan Vladimir, M.C.Tig.	1.000	6	12	20	0	32	3
orales, Florentino, Lar	.972	48	115	97	6	218	29
nez Garcia, Jose Juan, Oax	.750	2	5	1	2	8	0
ardo, Victor Manuel, Oax	.975	37	74	81	4	159	21
rez, Alejandro, Lar	.967	9	16	13	1	30	2
erezchica, Antonio, M.C.Tig.	.972	28	70	71	4	145	14
ecichi, Jorge, Sal	.969	21	63	61	4	128	15
intero, Guillermo, Mont.	.957	18	19	26	2	47	4
amirez, Enrique, Mva	1.000	1	0	1	0	1	0
obles A., Trinidad Adrian, Lar	1.000	7	7	13	0	20	3
odriquez, Hector, Rey	1.000	1	1	0	0	1	0
uiz, Juan De Dios, Tor	.990	17	43	53	1	97	10
algado, Eduardo, Min	.500	1	1	0	1	2	0
anchez, Armando, Mont.	1.000	13	23	26	0	49	4
anchez, Rogue, Cam	.940	14	16	31	3	50	6
ndoval, Benjamin, Cam	1.000	3	2	3	0	5	0
andoval, Jose Luis, M.C.R.D.	.900	1	2	7	1	10	1
oriano, Ricardo, Tor	1.000	1	1	0	0	1	0
tis, Bernardo, Yuc	.980	10	31	19	1	51	3
apaga, Julio Miguel, M.C.Tig.	.975	78	181	204	10	395	42
lenzuela S., Joel, Tor	1.000	6	14	8	0	22	4
lle D., Jorge Luis, Tor	1.000	3	2	4	0	6	2
rgas, Hector, Min	1.000	1	3	2	0	5	0
rgas, Trinidad, Tab	1.000	3	4	9	0	13	3
rdugo, Vicente, M.C.R.D.	.978	98	202	290	11	503	59
zcarra, Marco Antonio, Sal	.967	73	207	232	15	454	62
zcarra, Roberto, Agua.	.979	100	230	334	12	576	64
ong, Julian, Mva	.955	22	38	47	4	89	7
mbrano, Eduardo, Agua.	1.000	1	1	0	0	1	0
zueta, Juan Carlos, Tab	.978	76	181	218	9	408	54
zueta, Mauricio, Tab	.986	98	281	285	8	574	80

TRIPLE PLAYS: Chimelis, Flores, M. Zazueta.

THIRD BASEMEN

ayer, Team	Pct.	G	PO	A	E	TC	DP
janza, Ruben, Mva	1.000	6	6	13	0	19	1
juilar, Enrique, Agua.	.864	17	10	28	6	44	2
ce, Francisco Javier, Tab	.857	4	2	4	1	7	1
evalo, Guadalupe, Agua.	.885	31	24	45	9	78	1
ias, Everardo, Q.R.	1.000	7	5	4	0	9	2
menta, Guillermo, M.C.R.D.	1.000	1	0	2	0	2	0
redondo, Jesus, Agua.	1.000	1	2	1	0	3	0
vila, Roberto, Min	1.000	12	12	15	0	27	0
iles, Alejandro, Sal	.921	14	13	22	3	38	3
lderas, Abelardo, Min	.875	7	4	10	2	16	1
rrera, Jesus Antonio, Q.R.	.966	26	10	18	1	29	0
rrera, Nelson, Oax	1.000	2	1	2	0	3	0

Player, Team	Pct.	G	PO	A	E	TC	DP
Bolick, Frank, Oax	.957	44	34	100	6	140	5
Camacho, Adulfo, Sal	.947	36	37	71	6	114	8
Carranza, Pedro, M.C.R.D.	1.000	2	2	6	0	8	0
Carrasco, Ernesto, Lar	.940	50	65	122	12	199	17
Castaldo, Vince, Oax	.922	18	16	43	5	64	8
Castaneda, Hector, Min	1.000	2	0	7	0	7	0
Castaneda. Rafael, M.C.Tig.	.969	78	76	173	8	257	21
Castillo, Juan, Q.R.	.778	9	11	10	6	27	0
Colon, Cristobal, P.R.	1.000	35	38	71	0	109	11
Contreras, Jose, Mont.	.955	16	7	14	1	22	2
Cruz, Luis Alfonso, Rey	.750	2	1	2	1	4	0
Diaz, Pedro, M.C.Tig.	.500	1	0	1	1	2	0
Diaz, Remigio, Mont.	1.000	17	8	38	0	46	17
Duarte, Rene J., Taba	1.000	3	0	3	0	3	0
Duran, Felipe, Oax	1.000	2	1	3	0	4	1
Enriquez, Graciano, Agua.	.964	15	13	14	1	28	1
Felix, Arturo, Yuc	.959	18	16	31	2	49	3
Fentanes, Oscar, Tab	.901	33	20	62	9	91	4
Fernandez, Fabian, Rey	.667	2	1	3	2	6	0
Figueroa, Bienvenido, M.C.R.D.	1.000	9	4	11	0	15	1
Franco, Manuel, Yuc	.921	45	43	73	10	126	5
Garcia, Heriberto, P.R.	1.000	1	0	2	0	2	1
Gastelum, Sergio Omar, M.C.Tig.	1.000	5	1	3	0	4	0
Gonzalez, Hector, P.R.	1.000	1	0	1	0	1	0
Guerrero, Jaime, P.R.	1.000	13	7	11	0	18	3
Guerrero, Javier, Agua.	1.000	1	4	0	0	4	0
Guerrero, Juan, Sal	.919	74	56	148	18	222	13
Hecht, Steve, Oax	.905	4	3	16	2	21	3
Infante, Alexis, Tab	.950	7	6	13	1	20	1
Jimenez, Jesus, Tor	1.000	1	0	2	0	2	0
Jimenez, Ulises, Tor	1.000	3	1	0	0	1	0
Leyva, German, Mva	.939	107	118	188	20	326	26
Lopez, Fabian, Oax	.900	14	5	13	2	20	0
Lopez, Javier, Oax	1.000	1	1	0	0	1	0
Lopez, Miguel, Yuc	1.000	1	0	2	0	2	0
Magallanes, Everardo, Mont.	.925	80	62	160	18	240	10
Magallanes, Roberto, M.C.R.D.	.929	86	71	165	18	254	5
Malpica, Enrique, P.R.	.880	25	17	27	6	50	4
Marrujo, Hector, Min	1.000	3	4	2	0	6	1
Martinez, Abel, Q.R.	.875	10	4	10	2	16	0
Martinez, Carlos, P.R.	.904	50	33	89	13	135	3
Martinez, Ray, Rey	.981	19	13	39	1	53	4
Mendoza, Omar, Lar	.000	1	0	0	1	1	0
Mercedes, Luis, Tab	.947	5	6	12	1	19	3
Mere, Pedro, P.R.	.000	3	0	0	1	1	0
Michel, Domingo, Cam	1.000	5	6	6	0	12	0
Montalvo, Ivan Vladimir, M.C.Tig.	.931	99	68	229	22	319	13
Montanez, Daniel, Lar	1.000	2	4	9	0	13	0
Naveda, Edgar, Oax	.987	30	24	50	1	75	3
Orantes, Ramon, Agua.	.948	61	57	107	9	173	10
Ortiz, Alejandro, Q.R.	.942	104	88	188	17	293	13
Pardo, Victor Manuel, Oax	1.000	14	11	27	0	38	1
Peralta, Amado, Sal	1.000	1	2	0	0	2	0
Perez, Alejandro, Lar	.840	9	8	13	4	25	1
Perezchica, Antonio, M.C.Tig.	1.000	1	1	0	0	1	0
Quintero, Guillermo, Mont.	1.000	2	1	7	0	8	0
Renteria, Ricardo, M.C.R.D.	.970	23	19	45	2	66	2
Rivera, German, Tab	.941	56	46	130	11	187	18
Robles, Gerardo, Rey	.932	28	9	32	3	44	1
Robles, Javier, M.C.Tig.	1.000	2	1	1	0	2	0
Robles, Trinidad Adrian, Lar	1.000	3	1	6	0	7	1
Rodriguez, Hector, Rey	.924	91	75	167	20	262	18
Rojas, Francisco, Oax	.909	15	15	25	4	44	4
Romero, Marco Antonio, M.C.Tig.	.333	1	1	0	2	3	0
Romero, Oscar, Min	.947	91	79	209	16	304	10
Ruiz, Juan De Dios, Tor	.939	54	57	111	11	179	12
Salas, Heriberto, Tor	1.000	2	2	2	0	4	0
Sanchez, Armando, Mont.	1.000	6	1	8	0	9	0
Sanchez, Roque, Cam	.933	34	20	50	5	75	7
Sommers, Jesus, P.R.	1.000	1	0	2	0	2	0
Tatis, Bernardo, Yuc	.961	65	65	159	9	233	19
Trapaga, Julio Miguel, M.C.Tig.	1.000	6	4	5	0	9	2
Valle, Jorge Luis, Tor	.947	66	49	146	11	206	18
Vargas, Hector, Min	1.000	7	3	8	0	11	1
Vargas, Trinidad, Tab	1.000	1	1	1	0	2	0
Villarreal, Alejandro, Lar	.500	2	0	1	1	2	0
Wong, Julian, Mva	.700	7	7	0	3	10	0
Zambrano, Eduardo, Agua.	.822	13	12	25	8	45	1

TRIPLE PLAYS: Bolick.

SHORTSTOPS

Player, Team	Pct.	G	PO	A	E	TC	DP
Arevalo, Guadalupe, Agua.	.880	6	5	17	3	25	1
Arias, Everado, Q.R.	.940	17	14	33	3	50	5

Player, Team	Pct.	G	PO	A	E	TC	DP
Armenta, Guillermo, M.C.R.D.	1.000	3	3	6	0	9	0
Arredondo, Jesus, Agua.	.951	85	168	278	23	469	51
Avila, Roberto, Min	.955	13	8	13	1	22	2
Barrera, Jesus Antonio, Q.R.	.979	13	16	30	1	47	4
Bolick, Frank, Oax	1.000	2	1	4	0	5	0
Carrasco, Ernesto, Lar	.955	15	19	45	3	67	11
Castaneda, Rafael, M.C.Tig.	1.000	1	4	0	0	4	0
Cervera, Francisco, Cam	.943	13	14	19	2	35	3
Diaz, Remigio, Mont.	.984	84	144	235	6	385	35
Duran, Felipe, Oax	.946	101	165	345	29	539	72
Enriquez, Graciano, Agua.	.926	16	36	39	6	81	11
Felix, Arturo, Yuc	1.000	3	1	8	0	9	1
Figueroa, Bienvenido, M.C.R.D.	1.000	2	3	11	0	14	0
Franco, Manuel, Yuc	.833	4	4	6	2	12	2
Garcia, Hector, Tor	1.000	1	3	0	0	3	0
Garcia, Heriberto, P.R.	.975	102	192	344	14	550	47
Gomez, Ever, Tab	.850	6	6	11	3	20	3
Gonzalez, Mauricio, Cam	.875	4	6	8	2	16	1
Guerrero, Francisco, Q.R.	.970	97	182	302	15	499	60
Guerrero, Jaime, P.R.	.962	26	34	67	4	105	10
Guizar, Hector, Cam	.942	102	216	283	31	530	65
Infante, Alexis, Oax	.909	62	96	185	28	309	38
Jimenez, Alfonso, Sal	.964	100	196	307	19	522	83
Leyva, German, Mva	1.000	3	1	3	0	4	0
Lopez, Fabian, Oax	.900	7	6	12	2	20	3
Lopez, Gonzalo, Mva	1.000	8	5	5	0	10	3
Loredo, Jorge Luis, Cam	1.000	1	2	0	0	2	0
Magallanes, Everardo, Mont.	1.000	1	2	2	0	4	0
Magallanes, Roberto, M.C.R.D.	.946	22	35	70	6	111	14
Magana, Gabriel, Yuc	1.000	7	2	10	0	12	2
Marrujo, Hector, Min	1.000	2	2	8	0	10	0
Martinez, Ray, Rey	.945	72	145	201	20	366	51
Montanez, Daniel, Lar	.800	3	6	6	3	15	0
Nunez, Garcia Jose Juan, Oax	.952	16	25	55	4	84	13
Olivera, Sergio, Mva	1.000	13	5	11	0	16	3
Pacho, Juan Jose, Yuc	.970	113	195	317	16	528	54
Perez, Alejandro, Lar	.909	8	0	10	1	11	0
Quintero, Guillermo, Mont.	.952	53	90	150	12	252	19
Ramirez, Enrique, Mva	.960	114	209	321	22	552	51
Ramirez, Jesus,P.R.	.667	1	1	1	1	3	0
Robles, Gerardo, Rey	.923	4	6	6	1	13	1
Robles, Javier, M.C.Tig.	.957	111	164	331	22	517	58
Robles, Trinidad Adrian, Lar	.952	100	182	293	24	499	56
Rodriquez, Hector, Rey	1.000	3	3	3	0	6	0
Rojas, Francisco, Tab	.933	33	30	54	6	90	10
Salas, Heriberto, Tor	.955	107	183	323	24	530	67
Sandoval, Jose Luis, M.C.R.D.	.963	99	180	320	19	519	60
Trapaga, Julio Miguel, M.C.Tig.	.952	7	8	12	1	21	2
Valenzuela, Armando, Rey	.960	18	31	41	3	75	9
Valle, Jorge Luis, Tor	.943	12	11	22	2	35	5
Valle, Jose Luis, Min	.975	110	179	296	12	487	46
Vargas, Trinidad, Tab	.945	41	69	103	10	182	24
Verdugo, Vicente, M.C.R.D.	.952	15	16	44	3	63	14
Vizcarra, Marco Antonio, Sal	1.000	19	39	48	0	87	13
Vizcarra, Roberto, Agua.	.932	6	14	27	3	44	12
Wong, Julian, Mva	.893	12	7	18	3	28	1
Zambrano, Eduardo, Agua.	.900	1	1	8	1	10	0

TRIPLE PLAYS: R. Diaz, En. Ramirez, Salas.

OUTFIELDERS

Player, Team	Pct.	G	PO	A	E	TC	DP
Abrego, Jesus, Oax	.982	36	53	3	1	57	0
Aguilar, Antonio, M.C.R.D.	.958	101	155	5	7	167	2
Aguilera, Armando, Sal	.958	13	23	0	1	24	0
Almendra, Gregorio, Tab	1.000	7	3	1	0	4	0
Alvarez, Hector, Q.R.	.979	92	215	13	5	233	3
Alvarez, Luis, Yuc	.944	7	17	0	1	18	0
Arano, Wilfredo, Lar	1.000	28	31	5	0	36	1
Armenta, Fernando, Min	1.000	3	6	0	0	6	0
Arredondo, Luis, M.C.R.D.	.975	103	186	8	5	199	1
Azocar, Oscar, P.R.	.945	108	198	10	12	220	1
Basse, Mike, P.R.	1.000	26	66	0	0	66	0
Beltran, Gerardo, Min	.959	33	46	1	2	49	0
Bojorquez, Victor, M.C.R.D.	.938	23	15	0	1	16	0
Bolick, Frank, Oax	.978	19	41	4	1	46	1
Bowie, Jim, Agua.	.977	27	41	2	1	44	0
Cabreja, Alexis, Min	.909	12	20	0	2	22	0
Canizalez, Juan Carlos, Mont.	.984	113	236	8	4	248	1
Carrillo, Matias, M.C.Tig.	.985	95	194	9	3	206	2
Castillo, Braulio, Tab	.947	38	66	5	4	75	1
Castillo, Juan, Q.R.	1.000	5	9	3	0	12	1
Chan, Armando, Mva	.938	38	55	5	4	64	0
Chance, Tony, Mva	.960	115	233	10	10	253	
Clark, Tim, Sal	.961	82	106	16	5	127	
Corbin, Archie, Rey	1.000	1	1	0	0	1	
Cruz, Luis Alfonso, Rey	.981	101	201	5	4	210	
De La Nuez, Rex, Lar	.915	57	103	4	10	117	
Delgado, Thomas, Min	1.000	3	4	1	0	5	
DeLima, Rafael, Min	.982	28	55	1	1	57	
Diaz, Luis Fernando, M.C.Tig.	.978	91	169	12	4	185	
Dominguez, David, Tab	.993	73	145	5	1	151	
Enriquez, Graciano, Agua.	.875	7	7	0	1	8	
Escalante, Marcelo, Sal	.948	38	51	4	3	58	
Espinoza, Javier, Cam	.992	60	124	2	1	127	
Espinoza, Jose, Mva	1.000	4	3	0	0	3	
Espy, Cecil, Oax	1.000	38	69	1	0	70	
Estrada, Ruben, Lar	.857	11	6	0	1	7	
Felix, Arturo, Yuc	.932	34	51	4	4	59	
Felix, Junior Francisco, Rey	.966	88	164	6	6	176	
Fentanes, Oscar, Tab	.948	59	103	6	6	115	
Fernandez, Daniel, M.C.R.D.	.992	101	233	11	2	246	
Figueroa, Bienvenido, M.C.R.D.	1.000	1	1	0	0	1	
Fornes, Daniel, Rey	.882	14	14	1	2	17	
Fox, Eric, P.R.	.986	58	131	5	2	138	
Gainey, Ty, M.C.R.D.	1.000	8	14	1	0	15	
Gamboa, Jose, P.R.	1.000	4	1	0	0	1	
Garcia, Cornelio, Mont.	.978	101	175	7	4	186	
Garcia, Hector, Tor	.980	95	186	11	4	201	
Gastelum, Sergio Omar, M.C.Tig.	1.000	17	10	1	0	11	
Gonzalez, Jose, Mont.	.987	103	212	9	3	224	
Grijak, Kevin Scott, M.C.Tig.	1.000	3	4	0	0	4	
Guerrero, Juan, Sal	.975	41	77	0	2	79	
Hernandez, Gerardo, M.C.Tig.	.970	83	121	10	4	135	
Hernandez, Juan Carlos, P.R.	1.000	1	1	0	0	1	
Herrera, Isidro, Oax	.977	109	162	7	4	173	
Howell, Pat, M.C.Tig.	.961	69	118	5	5	128	
Iturbe, Pedro, Tab	.974	93	173	12	5	190	
Jimenez, Eduardo, Yuc	.978	54	86	5	2	93	
Jimenez, Ulises, Tor	.833	9	10	0	2	12	
Landrum, Ced, Tab	.952	51	114	5	6	125	
Leal, P.J. Guadalupe, Cam	.990	56	99	3	1	103	
Lopez, Gonzalo, Mva	1.000	2	2	0	0	2	
Lopez, Salvador, Yuc	1.000	48	55	4	0	59	
Lopez, Victor, Oax	1.000	1	4	1	0	5	
Machiria, Pablo, Agua.	.981	44	49	2	1	52	
Mack, Quinn, Lar	.970	113	254	7	8	269	
Martinez, Abel, Q.R.	1.000	6	1	0	0	1	
Martinez, Domingo, Rey	1.000	2	1	0	0	1	
Mata, Noe, Q.R.	1.000	5	5	0	0	5	
Medina, D.J. Ramon, Cam	.992	67	125	7	1	133	
Mendez, Roberto Carlos, Oax	.971	98	156	10	5	171	
Mendoza, Omar, Lar	1.000	3	1	0	0	1	
Mercedes, Luis, Cam	1.000	20	40	3	0	43	
Montalvo, Ivan Vladimir, M.C.Tig.	1.000	6	9	0	0	9	
Moreno, David, Mva	1.000	27	15	2	0	17	
Moreno, Leonardo, Oax	.972	71	131	7	4	142	
Morones, Martin, P.R.	.979	53	89	3	2	94	
Motley, Darryl, P.R.	.936	46	70	3	5	78	
Munoz, Jose De Jesus, Sal	.975	39	39	0	1	40	
Naveda, Edgar, Oax	1.000	1	1	0	0	2	
Noris, Rogelio, Rey	.992	78	120	4	1	125	
O'Halloran, Greg, Q.R.	1.000	55	108	3	0	111	
Ojeda, Miguel, M.C.R.D.	1.000	14	19	0	0	19	
Orantes, Ramon, Agua.	.867	10	13	0	2	15	
Ortiz, Raymond, Cam	.775	23	29	2	9	40	
Payro, Edison, Cam	.968	101	200	14	7	221	
Perez, Alejandro, Lar	1.000	3	3	0	0	3	
Perez, Francisco, M.C.R.D.	.935	22	29	0	2	31	
Quintero, Alan, Yuc	1.000	6	15	0	0	15	
Quintero, Guillermo, Mont.	1.000	1	4	0	0	4	
Raben, Luis, Yuc	1.000	3	8	1	0	9	
Ramirez, Jesus, P.R.	.960	69	115	5	5	125	
Robinson, Don, Sal	.933	7	13	1	1	15	
Robles, Trinidad Adrian, Lar	1.000	1	1	0	0	1	
Rodriguez, Boi, Oax	.978	60	127	8	3	138	
Rodriguez, Fernando, Tor	.976	91	151	11	4	166	
Rodriguez, Jose Luis, Q.R.	1.000	3	4	0	0	4	
Rodriguez, Serafin, Q.R.	.992	65	117	4	1	122	
Roman, Porfirio, P.R.	1.000	1	3	0	0	3	
Rubio, Sergio, Yuc	.955	84	139	8	7	154	
Saenz, Ricardo, Mva	.944	64	132	2	8	142	
Sanchez, Gerardo, Lar	.967	88	165	12	6	183	
Sanchez, Raul, Q.R.	1.000	21	22	1	0	23	
Sandoval, Octavio Augusto, M.C.Tig.	.962	49	48	2	2	52	
Santana, Miguel, Min	.946	30	61	9	4	74	

Player, Team	Pct.	G	PO	A	E	TC	DP
Scott, Bryant, Tab	1.000	1	1	0	0	1	0
Sherman, Darrell, Yuc	.970	74	158	5	5	168	0
Snider, Van, Tor	.993	75	135	16	1	152	0
Soriano, Ricardo, Tor	.917	15	20	2	2	24	0
Soto, Emison, Q.R.	1.000	19	42	6	0	48	3
Tatis, Bernardo, Yuc	.987	32	75	2	1	78	0
Tejeda, Arturo, Oax	1.000	2	1	0	0	1	0
Tellez, Alonso, Rey	.973	75	103	6	3	112	1
Thomas, Keith, P.R.	.980	20	47	1	1	49	0
Thoutsis, Paul, Yuc	1.000	1	3	0	0	3	0
Tiburcio, Freddy, Cam	.976	85	159	6	4	169	0
Tiquet, Lazaro, Tab	.988	57	78	4	1	83	0
Tolentino, Jose, Mont.	.600	1	3	0	2	5	0
Torres, Edgar, Mva	.982	106	217	7	4	228	0
Torres, Raymundo, Yuc	1.000	27	38	6	0	44	0
Trafton, Todd, Yuc	.981	83	146	6	3	155	2
Trapaga, Julio Miguel, M.C.Tig.	1.000	1	2	0	0	2	0
Valdez, Francisco, Rey	.974	16	34	3	1	38	1
Valdez, Jesus, Yuc	1.000	4	3	0	0	3	0
Valdez, Ramon, Min	.986	34	68	5	1	74	1
Valencia, Carlos, Agua	.993	81	139	7	1	147	0
Valenzuela, Jose Luis, Tab	.867	16	13	0	2	15	0
Valle, Jorge Luis, Tor	.944	14	14	3	1	18	0
Valverde, L.J. Raul, Oax	.900	8	9	0	1	10	0
Vargas, Hector, Min	.992	62	121	8	1	130	0
Verdugo, Orlando, Yuc	1.000	1	1	0	0	1	0
Villaescusa, Fernando, Cam	1.000	1	2	0	0	2	0
Villarreal, Alejandro, Lar	1.000	4	1	0	0	1	0
Villegas, Fernando, Sal	.963	67	116	13	5	134	2
Wood, Ted, Agua	.983	111	226	11	4	241	1
Wright, George, Sal	.979	105	229	5	5	239	0
Yuriar, Jesus, Min	.985	97	188	8	3	199	1
Zambrano, Eduardo, Agua	1.000	77	165	10	0	175	0
Zambrano, Jose Luis, Min	.974	56	107	4	3	114	2
Zambrano, Roberto, Q.R.	.990	95	193	9	2	204	2
Zamudio, Rafael, Mont.	.973	46	70	2	2	74	0

TRIPLE PLAY: Chance.

CATCHERS

Player, Team	Pct.	G	PO	A	E	TC	DP	PB
Abrego, Jesus, Oax	.979	29	118	19	3	140	1	3
Aguilera, Armando, Sal	.965	67	180	41	8	229	2	4
Arauz, Ignacio, P.R.	.991	37	89	16	1	106	0	1
Avila, Ruben, Tor	1.000	1	5	0	0	5	0	0
Cabrera, Francisco, Mva	.931	5	24	3	2	29	0	2
Campos, Oscar, P.R.	.895	12	13	4	2	19	1	0
Cantu, Gerardo, Q.R.	1.000	8	20	0	0	20	0	0
Castaneda, Hector, Min	.985	66	278	52	5	335	3	2
Castaneda, Rafael, M.C.Tig.	.985	14	60	5	1	66	1	3
Cazarin, Manuel, Yuc	.982	92	403	77	9	489	4	7
Cobos, Rogelio, Oax	.990	67	269	40	3	312	1	7
Corrales, Virgilio, P.R.	1.000	4	3	0	0	3	0	0
Cruz, Marco Antonio, Lar	.992	74	348	22	3	373	2	7
Cueto, Raul, Min	.987	25	74	4	1	79	0	0
Dominguez, Fausto, P.R.	1.000	19	26	5	0	31	0	0
Duarte, Rene, Tab	.978	38	152	25	4	181	1	3
Elvira, Honorio, Tab	1.000	22	64	8	0	72	0	0
Espinoza, Ramon, Tor	1.000	4	13	0	0	13	0	0
Garza, Gerardo, Tor	.987	103	462	60	7	529	7	9
Garzon, Eliseo, Tab	.989	79	331	40	4	375	1	6
Gastelum, Carlos, Mva	.989	79	404	55	5	464	6	5
Gavia, Jesus, Min	.977	24	78	7	2	87	0	4
Gonzalez, Jesus, Cam	.969	24	83	11	3	97	3	0
Guerrero, Jose, Q.R.	1.000	3	9	2	0	11	0	0
Guzman, Marco Antonio, Q.R.	1.000	14	47	7	0	54	0	0
Hernandez, Miguel, P.R.	.991	77	277	42	3	322	2	6
Hurtado, Hector, Cam	.966	77	276	39	11	326	3	5
Lopez, Victor, Oax	.979	39	167	18	4	189	0	2
Luna, Jose Luis, Sal	.984	77	255	51	5	311	4	3
Martinez, Raul, Sal	.949	10	33	4	2	39	0	0
Mendez, Ramon, Agua	.973	25	65	7	2	74	1	0
Meza, Alfredo, Mont.	.992	90	320	56	3	379	4	2
Monroy, Victor Hugo, Rey	1.000	6	16	5	0	21	0	0
Munoz, Noe, Rey	.994	47	286	30	2	318	2	4
Ochoa, Edgar, M.C.Tig.	.987	56	215	13	3	231	1	6
Ojeda, Antonio, M.C.R.D.	.994	28	139	16	1	156	0	3
Ortega, Antonio, Rey	.967	9	24	5	1	30	1	2
Osuna, Hector, Yuc	.966	21	75	11	3	89	1	0
Pena, Carlos, Rey	.969	23	56	7	2	65	0	2
Perez, Juan Luis, Tor	.984	20	55	5	1	61	0	0
Pulido, Jesus, Lar	.949	18	45	11	3	59	0	1
Ramirez, Efren, Agua	.987	100	416	56	6	478	5	2
Reyes, Gilberto, Mont.	.987	34	125	25	2	152	0	1

Player, Team	Pct.	G	PO	A	E	TC	DP	PB
Rojas, Homar, M.C.R.D.	.978	68	317	35	8	360	2	5
Romero, Israel, Lar	1.000	35	120	15	0	135	4	3
Ruiz, Demetrio, Cam	1.000	20	55	6	0	61	1	1
Russell, Omar, Min	1.000	7	12	2	0	14	1	0
Samaniego, Manuel, Mva	1.000	19	27	5	0	32	1	0
Santana, Mario Ivan, Mont.	.988	24	64	16	1	81	0	2
Silverio, Nelson, Cam	.975	28	134	20	4	158	5	6
Soto, Emison, Q.R.	.980	53	212	27	5	244	3	9
Valdez, Francisco, Rey	.974	65	297	42	9	348	6	4
Valenzuela, Eduardo, Sal	1.000	9	29	4	0	33	1	0
Vargas, Jose, M.C.Tig.	1.000	4	8	1	0	9	0	2
Vazquez, Felipe, M.C.R.D.	.995	38	172	26	1	199	2	4
Vega, Edgar, M.C.Tig.	.989	99	406	59	5	470	4	7
Villanueva, Hector, Mva	.978	37	154	22	4	180	3	3
Villapudua, Israel, Mva	1.000	3	4	1	0	5	0	1

TRIPLE PLAYS: Hurtado, V. Lopez.

PITCHERS

Player, Team	Pct.	G	PO	A	E	TC	DP
Acosta, Aaron, Tor	.943	22	7	26	2	35	1
Acosta, Gerardo, Rey	1.000	39	4	14	0	18	0
Aguilar, Miguel, Tab	.900	23	5	13	2	20	0
Aguirre, Gaudencio, Tab	.941	21	3	13	1	17	0
Alicea, Miguel, Mva	1.000	27	1	3	0	1	4
Alvarez, Juan Carlos, Min	.931	27	5	22	2	29	1
Alvarez, Juan Jesus, M.C.Tig.	.944	23	8	26	2	36	2
Antunez, Martin, Agua	.833	30	1	4	1	6	1
Austin, James, Agua	1.000	48	4	7	0	11	1
Baez, Sixto, Rey	.976	41	7	34	1	42	3
Barfield, John, Lar	1.000	22	1	5	0	6	6
Barojas, Salome, M.C.R.D.	1.000	3	0	2	0	2	0
Barraza, Ernesto, M.C.Tig.	.935	21	19	24	3	46	1
Barron, Avelino, Cam	1.000	30	2	10	0	12	0
Bauer, Matt, Mva	1.000	14	0	2	0	2	2
Bennett, Chris, Rey	.977	26	16	26	1	43	3
Brummet, Greg, Rey	1.000	8	4	8	0	12	1
Burgos, John, M.C.Tig.	1.000	46	1	7	0	8	8
Cabrales, Gabriel, Min	1.000	26	1	10	0	11	0
Calderon, Manaces, Min	1.000	4	1	0	0	1	0
Camacho, Adrian, Sal	1.000	4	0	1	0	1	1
Camara, Pedro, Min	1.000	15	3	2	0	5	5
Campos, Francisco, Cam	.941	23	8	40	3	51	4
Campos, Frank, Lar	.923	38	5	7	1	13	0
Cano, Jose, Yuc	.970	13	10	22	1	33	0
Carranza, Javier, Rey	1.000	18	4	3	0	7	7
Carrasco, Alejandro, Oax	1.000	30	11	28	0	39	0
Castillo, Felipe, Tor	1.000	7	3	1	0	4	0
Castro, Leonel, Oax	.833	7	1	4	1	6	1
Cazares, Rosario, Tab	.895	52	2	15	2	19	0
Cecena, Jose Isabel, Sal	.857	3	3	15	3	21	1
Cerros, Juan, Rey	1.000	28	4	8	0	12	1
Chapa, Juan, Rey	.913	24	17	25	4	46	2
Corbin, Archie, Rey	1.000	9	1	0	0	1	0
Cota, Marino, Sal	.900	34	4	5	1	10	0
Couoh, Enrique, M.C.Tig.	.900	24	10	17	3	30	3
Cruz, Javier, Rey	.950	28	16	22	2	40	3
Cruz, Juan Diego, Yuc	1.000	12	0	3	0	3	3
Cruz, Miguel, Lar	1.000	20	1	2	0	3	0
Cuervo, Bernardo, Cam	.930	19	11	29	3	43	3
De La Hoya, Javier, Min	.875	13	4	10	2	16	1
De La Rosa, Francisco, Cam	.818	23	7	11	4	22	0
De Leon, Danilo, Agua	1.000	12	2	0	0	2	2
Delfin, Adolfo, Sal	1.000	23	2	9	0	11	1
Del Toro, Miguel, Rey	1.000	32	4	7	0	11	1
Dessens, Elmer, M.C.R.D.	1.000	7	5	7	0	12	0
Dettmer, John, M.C.Tig.	1.000	4	0	1	0	1	1
Diaz, Alejandro, Oax	1.000	31	8	8	0	16	0
Diaz, Cesar, Lar	1.000	43	9	15	0	24	3
Diaz, Marco, Tor	1.000	26	5	6	0	11	1
Diaz, Rafael, Min	.893	22	9	16	3	28	1
Dominguez, Herminio, Cam	1.000	19	0	3	0	3	0
Drahman, Bryan, Lar	1.000	22	1	0	0	1	0
Draper, Mike, Rey	1.000	10	0	1	0	1	1
Duncan, Chip, M.C.Tig.	.867	25	1	12	2	15	1
Elvira, Narciso, Mont.	.600	8	0	3	2	5	0
Enriquez, Martin, Agua	1.000	21	7	22	0	29	2
Esquer, Mercedes, Mont.	.929	18	1	12	1	14	0
Fajardo, Hector, M.C.R.D.	1.000	4	0	1	0	1	1
Federico, Gustavo, Mont.	1.000	15	1	7	0	8	0
Felix, Leopoldo, P.R.	1.000	14	1	0	0	1	0
Figueroa, Fernando, Tor	.979	24	11	36	1	48	3
Flores, Ignacio, Sal	.955	27	10	32	2	44	3
Flores, Ignacio, Tor	1.000	18	1	2	0	3	0

Player, Team	Pct.	G	PO	A	E	TC	DP
Flynt, Will, Oax	.912	22	2	29	3	34	0
Fontes, Agustin, Tab	1.000	5	0	1	0	0	1
Galvez, Rosario, Lar	.957	31	6	16	1	23	0
Gamez, Francisco, Mont.	1.000	28	8	1	0	0	9
Garcia, Apolinar, Yuc	.913	13	8	13	2	23	0
Garcia, Francisco, M.C.R.D.	.909	20	3	7	1	11	0
Garcia, Jose Luis, Lar	.933	36	1	13	1	15	0
Garcia, Miguel, Min	1.000	29	10	22	0	32	2
Garcia, Zenon, Oax	1.000	27	5	7	0	12	0
Garibay, Daniel, M.C.Tig.	.846	19	4	7	2	13	0
Garibay, Roberto, Q.R.	1.000	43	5	12	0	17	1
Garibay, Salvador, Agua.	1.000	2	0	1	0	0	1
Garza, Alejandro, Agua.	.857	16	2	4	1	7	0
Garza, Roberto, Lar	.867	29	3	10	2	15	0
Gomez, Martin, Min	.941	29	4	12	1	17	1
Gonzalez, Arturo, Mont.	1.000	19	6	25	0	31	1
Gonzalez, Gilberto, Tor	1.000	16	1	11	0	12	2
Gonzalez, Victor Manuel, P.R.	1.000	36	5	11	0	16	0
Gracia, Edmundo, Sal	.900	21	2	7	1	10	0
Grajales, Norberto, Tor	.846	42	4	7	2	13	2
Green, Otis, Mont.	1.000	40	5	8	0	13	0
Guereca, Guillermo, Oax	1.000	15	1	9	0	10	1
Guerrero, Omar, Rey	1.000	22	2	5	0	0	7
Harrison, Brian, M.C.Tig.	1.000	8	1	1	0	2	0
Heredia, Hector, Mont.	1.000	23	5	13	0	18	0
Hernandez, Encarnacion, P.R.	1.000	21	2	2	0	0	4
Hernandez, Julio, P.R.	.893	22	6	19	3	28	1
Hernandez, Manuel, Lar	.919	27	4	30	3	37	2
Hernandez, Martin, Q.R.	.941	20	5	11	1	17	1
Herrera, Calixto, Mva	.857	44	2	10	2	14	1
Herrera, Enrique, Tab	.889	19	8	8	2	18	0
Holman, Shawn, M.C.R.D.	1.000	35	9	32	0	41	1
Huerta, Luis Enrique, Sal	1.000	24	14	19	0	33	3
Hurst, Jonathan, Mont.	1.000	45	6	6	0	12	0
Jimenez, Danilo, Mva	1.000	5	0	1	0	1	0
Jimenez, German, Agua.	1.000	17	3	17	0	20	4
Jimenez, Isaac, P.R.	.933	20	1	27	2	30	1
Jimenez, Jesus, Tor	.857	22	0	6	1	7	1
Johnston, Joe, Sal	.500	8	1	0	1	2	0
Juarez, Fernando, Tor	1.000	32	1	3	0	0	4
Kelly, Richard, Mva	1.000	23	1	19	0	20	1
Kutzler, Jerry, Oax	1.000	1	0	2	0	2	0
Lancaster, Lest, Oax	1.000	6	2	8	0	10	0
Lara, Hugo, P.R.	.971	26	13	21	1	35	3
Lara, Jorge, Mva	.900	31	2	7	1	10	0
Leal, Gerardo, Mva	1.000	33	0	5	0	0	5
Leon, Juan, Tor	1.000	5	1	0	0	1	0
Leyva, Carlos, M.C.Tig.	1.000	5	0	1	0	0	1
Linares, Efrain, Q.R.	1.000	11	0	7	0	0	7
Lizarraga, Andres, Lar	.500	6	0	1	1	2	0
Lizarraga, Hugo, Cam	1.000	10	1	5	0	1	6
Llanes, Emeterio, Yuc	1.000	6	0	3	0	3	0
Loaiza, Esteban, M.C.R.D.	1.000	5	2	9	0	11	0
Loaiza, Sabino, Cam	1.000	18	6	24	0	30	3
Long, Steve, Lar	1.000	2	0	1	0	1	0
Lopez, Emigdio, Tab	.983	25	16	41	1	58	3
Lopez, Gilberto, P.R.	1.000	6	2	3	0	5	0
Lopez, Jesus Nain, Rey	1.000	5	0	6	0	6	0
Lopez, Jonas, Agua.	.976	23	13	28	1	42	3
Lopez, Jose Juan, Oax	.885	38	7	16	3	26	1
Lopez, Rodrigo, P.R.	.833	7	0	5	1	6	1
Luevano, Juan, P.R.	1.000	34	5	12	0	17	0
Lupercio, Hector, Sal	1.000	12	1	2	0	0	3
Lynch, Dave, M.C.Tig.	.941	17	2	14	1	17	0
Marquez, Isidro, M.C.Tig.	1.000	48	4	11	0	15	0
Marquez, Jose, Tor	1.000	17	0	1	0	0	1
Martinez, Jose Antonio, Cam	1.000	22	4	7	0	11	1
Martinez, Mauricio, Sal	1.000	16	0	2	0	0	2
Mauser, Tim, Tab	.833	47	3	12	3	18	1
Maysey, Matt, Cam	1.000	15	2	3	0	1	5
Melendez, Jose, Yuc	.909	35	3	7	1	11	0
Mendez, Luis Fernando, Rey	.826	20	3	16	4	23	0
Menendez, Tony, M.C.R.D.	1.000	28	2	4	0	0	6
Metoyer, Tony, Oax	1.000	29	2	11	0	13	2
Meza, Leobardo, P.R.	1.000	3	2	5	0	7	0
Miranda, Julio Cesar, Yuc	.913	49	9	12	2	23	0
Molina, Joaquin, Tor	.500	7	1	0	1	2	0
Montalvo, Rafael, Cam	1.000	16	0	7	0	1	7
Montano, Francisco, Mva	.926	25	3	22	2	27	0
Mora, Eleazar, P.R.	1.000	30	4	13	0	17	0
Moreno, Angel, M.C.Tig.	.973	23	10	26	1	37	3
Moreno, Jesus, Yuc	1.000	3	1	1	0	0	2
Moreno, Leobardo, M.C.R.D.	.968	26	7	23	1	31	1
Moreno, Ricardo, Oax	1.000	9	1	1	0	2	0
Munoz, Jaime, M.C.Tig.	1.000	23	1	7	0	0	8
Munoz, Leonardo, Mont.	1.000	37	1	7	0	0	8
Munoz, Ricardo, Tab	1.000	24	11	41	0	52	1
Murillo, Felipe, Mva	1.000	39	1	4	0	0	5
Neri, Braulio, Q.R.	.636	42	1	6	4	11	0
Neri, Eduardo, P.R.	1.000	53	4	24	0	28	0
Nunez, Aviva Jose Juan, Oax	1.000	19	0	3	0	0	3
Nunez, Edwin, M.C.R.D.	1.000	14	2	1	0	0	3
Olague, Jesus, Mont.	1.000	32	1	9	0	10	0
Orea, Flavio, Mont.	1.000	13	0	5	0	0	5
Orozco, Jaime, Min.	1.000	23	8	13	0	21	1
Ortega, Roberto, Q.R.	1.000	36	1	8	0	9	0
Ortega, Wilbert, Yuc	.750	26	0	3	1	4	0
Osuna, Gabriel, Yuc	1.000	20	2	3	0	0	5
Osuna, Ricardo, Tab	.952	14	2	18	1	21	2
Osuna, Roberto, Lar	.960	51	11	13	1	25	2
Palacios, Vicente, Agua.	1.000	11	3	3	0	0	6
Palafox, Juan Manuel, Tor	.926	24	6	19	2	27	2
Patterson, Kent, Mva	1.000	6	1	1	0	0	2
Pelcastregui, Leonardo, Cam	1.000	7	0	1	0	0	1
Perez, David, Mont.	.920	21	3	20	2	25	1
Perez, Leonardo, Agua.	.952	16	8	12	1	21	0
Perez, Vladimir, Agua.	.864	55	9	10	3	22	0
Perschke, Greg,	.667	22	0	2	1	3	0
Picota, Lenin, Oax	.966	19	7	21	1	29	0
Pimentel, Roberto, Mva	.800	43	2	2	1	5	1
Pina, Rafael, M.C.R.D.	.875	39	7	7	2	16	2
Pineda, Gabriel, Oax	.941	26	5	11	1	17	2
Powell, Dennis, Mont.	.909	38	3	7	1	11	0
Purata, Julio, Rey	1.000	24	8	29	0	37	1
Quijada, Mario, Tor	.875	32	5	9	2	16	0
Quinones, Enrique, Agua.	1.000	23	3	9	0	12	1
Quintanilla, Enrique, Lar	1.000	41	5	15	0	20	2
Quiroz, Aaron, Lar	1.000	18	3	12	0	15	2
Quiroz, Jose Julian, Agua.	1.000	21	1	3	0	0	4
Ramirez, Roberto, M.C.R.D.	.981	28	11	41	1	53	6
Ramos, Jorge, Q.R.	1.000	37	4	3	0	1	7
Raygoza, Martin, P.R.	1.000	22	7	35	0	42	1
Renteria, Hilario, Q.R.	.917	21	2	20	2	24	1
Retes, Lorenzo, Tab	1.000	30	3	2	0	0	5
Reyes, Flavio, Min	1.000	20	1	3	0	0	4
Rincon, Ricardo, M.C.R.D.	1.000	50	4	13	0	17	1
Rios, Jesus, Mva	.917	24	2	20	2	24	1
Rivera, Francisco, Tor	.000	15	0	0	1	1	0
Rivera, Hector, Tab	.947	26	3	15	1	19	3
Rivera, Oscar, M.C.R.D.	1.000	11	3	0	0	0	3
Rodriguez, Raul, Mva	.919	26	6	28	3	37	0
Rodriguez, Rosario, P.R.	.857	11	2	4	1	7	0
Rodriguez, Salvador, Yuc	.950	28	3	16	1	20	3
Rojo, Oscar, Rey	.000	15	0	0	2	2	0
Romero, Juan, Tab	.875	27	2	12	2	16	2
Romo, Guillermo, Tor	1.000	16	2	4	0	1	6
Royal, Thomas, M.C.Tig.	1.000	3	3	2	0	5	0
Ruiz, Cecilio, Tab	1.000	23	10	32	0	42	2
Saenz, Alfredo, Q.R.	1.000	21	7	21	0	28	0
Saldana, Edgardo, M.C.Tig.	1.000	39	5	9	0	14	1
Salgado, Eduardo, Min	1.000	20	5	6	0	11	0
Sanchez, Alejandro, Q.R.	1.000	1	0	1	0	0	1
Sanchez, Efrain, Cam	.905	14	2	17	2	21	1
Sanchez, Hector, Agua.	.935	27	9	20	2	31	4
Sandoval, Carlos, Min.	.833	25	1	4	1	6	0
Sandoval, Guillermo, Yuc	.966	23	5	23	1	29	3
Sangeado, Juan Carlos, Oax.	1.000	12	3	5	0	0	8
Serna, Ramon, Lar	.933	19	7	7	1	15	0
Sierra, Abel, Cam	.975	23	7	32	1	40	3
Sinohui, David, Oax	1.000	4	1	1	0	0	2
Solano, Julio Cesar, P.R.	1.000	20	1	4	0	0	5
Solarte, Jose, Min.	.947	54	4	14	1	19	2
Solis, Ricardo, Yuc	.967	20	7	22	1	30	4
Sombra, Francisco, Sal.	.971	31	11	23	1	35	1
Soto, Daniel, M.C.R.D.	1.000	7	0	5	0	5	0
Soto, Fernando, Q.R.	.933	26	9	19	2	30	0
Soto Cruz, Antonio, Q.R.	1.000	31	5	19	0	24	1
Steed, Ricky, M.C.Tig.	.000	3	0	0	1	1	0
Strange, Donald, Sal	1.000	38	3	9	0	12	0
Sulu, Mario, Cam	.667	3	0	2	1	3	0
Tinoco, Ruben, Cam	1.000	8	0	1	0	1	0
Tolliver, Fred, Yuc	1.000	8	2	8	0	10	1
Uribe, Juan Carlos, Yuc	1.000	33	2	17	0	19	0
Valdez, Efrain, Q.R.	1.000	20	15	37	0	52	3
Valdez, Rodolfo, Mva	.857	27	2	10	2	14	0
Valencia, Jorge, Sal	.895	36	3	14	2	19	2

er, Team	Pct.	G	PO	A	E	TC	DP
enzuela, Saul, Q.R.	1.000	20	14	15	0	29	2
gas, Ignacio, Min	1.000	31	5	7	0	12	2
gas, Joel, Tab	1.000	12	3	13	0	16	1
quez, Adrian, Cam	.935	19	4	25	2	31	0
quez, Aguedo, Agua.	1.000	15	6	15	0	21	1
quez, Lioner, Oax.	1.000	2	0	2	0	2	0
a, Obed, Lar	.909	24	3	7	1	11	1
azquez, Israel, Min	.979	29	14	32	1	47	0

Player, Team	Pct.	G	PO	A	E	TC	DP
Verdugo, Orlando, Yuc	1.000	9	4	5	0	9	0
Villanueva, Luis, Agua.	1.000	16	3	1	0	0	4
Villarreal, Antonio, Yuc	.975	22	7	32	1	40	1
Villegas, Jose Angel, Agua.	1.000	31	4	19	0	23	0
Williams, Jeff, M.C.R.D.	.929	12	3	10	1	14	0
Zappelli, Mark, Sal	.950	14	10	9	1	20	0
Zavala, Marcos, M.C.Tig.	1.000	6	0	1	0	0	1

LEAGUE CHAMPIONS

r	Team	Pct.	Year	Team	Pct.	Year	Team	Pct.
5—	Mexico City Tigers*	.539	1973—	Saltillo	.656	1986—	Puebla◆	.682
6—	Mexico City Reds	.692		Mexico City Reds∞	.590		Monclova	.598
7—	Yucatan	.567	1974—	Jalisco	.627	1987—	Mexico City Reds◆	.605
	Mex. C. Reds (2nd)†	.550		Mexico City Reds∞	.551		Monterrey	.536
8—	Nuevo Laredo	.625	1975—	Tampico∞	.541	1988—	Mexico City Reds◆	.646
9—	Poza Rica	.575		Cordoba	.649		Nuevo Laredo	.602
	Mex. C. Reds (3rd)†	.507	1976—	Mexico City Reds∞	.543	1989—	Nuevo Laredo◆	.621
0—	Mexico City Tigers	.538		Union Laguna	.547		Yucatan	.539
1—	Veracruz	.575	1977—	Mexico City Reds	.623	1990—	Nuevo Laredo	.618
2—	Monterrey	.592		Nuevo Laredo∞	.507		Leon◆	.565
3—	Puebla	.606	1978—	Aguascalientes∞	.589	1991—	Monterrey◆	.683
4—	Mexico City Reds	.586		Union Laguna	.523		Mexico City Reds	.627
5—	Mexico City Tigers	.590	1979—	Saltillo	.704	1992—	Mexico City Tigers◆	.594
6—	Mexico City Tigers‡	.614		Puebla∞	.628		Nuevo Laredo	.538
	Mexico City Reds	.571	1980—	No champion▲		1993—	Nuevo Laredo	.589
7—	Jalisco	.607	1981—	Mexico City Reds	.615		Tabasco◆	.528
8—	Mexico City Reds	.586		Reynosa	.492	1994—	Mexico City Red Devils◆	.646
9—	Reynosa	.591	1982—	Ciudad Juarez∞	.570		Monterrey Sultans	.608
0—	Aguila§	.580		Mexico City Tigers	.508	1995—	Mexico City Red Devils	.708
	Mexico City Reds	.607	1983—	Campeche◆	.614		Monterrey Sultans◆	.570
1—	Jalisco§	.558		Ciudad Juarez	.535	1996—	Monterrey Sultans	.713
	Saltillo	.593	1984—	Yucatan◆	.560		Mexico City Reds◆	.619
2—	Saltillo	.636		Ciudad Juarez	.509			
	Cordoba§	.541	1985—	Mexico City Reds◆	.606			
				Nuevo Laredo	.5275			

*Defeated Nuevo Laredo, two games to none, in playoff for pennant. †Won four-team playoff. ‡Won split-season playoff. §League divided into Northern, uthern divisions; won two-team playoff. ∞League divided into Northern, Southern zones; sub-divided into Eastern, Western divisions, won eight-team play-
▲A players strike on July 1 forced the cancellation of the regular season and playoff schedule. ◆League divided into Northern, Southern zones; four bs from each zone qualified for postseason play. Won final series for league championship.

PACIFIC COAST LEAGUE

LEAGUE OFFICE

President/secretary-treasurer
Bill Cutler

Address
2345 S. Alma School Rd., Suite 110
Mesa, AZ 85210

Phone
602-838-2171

TEAMS

ALBUQUERQUE DUKES

General manager
Pat McKernan

Manager
Glenn Hoffman

Ballpark (capacity, surface)
Albuquerque Sports Stadium (10,510, grass)

Affiliation
Dodgers

Address
1601 Stadium Blvd. SE
Albuquerque, NM 87106

Phone
505-243-1791

CALGARY CANNONS

Vice president, baseball operations
John Traub

Manager
Trent Jewett

Ballpark (capacity, surface)
Burn Stadium (7,500, grass)

Affiliation
Pirates

Address
2255 Crowchild Trail N.W.
Calgary, Alberta T2M 4S7

Phone
403-284-1111

COLORADO SPRINGS SKY SOX

General manager/president
Robert Goughan

Manager
Paul Zuvella

Ballpark (capacity, surface)
Sky Sox Stadium (8,500, grass)

Affiliation
Rockies

Address
4385 Tutt Blvd.
Colorado Springs, CO 80922

Phone
719-597-1449

EDMONTON TRAPPERS

President/general manager
Mel Kowalchuk

Manager
Gary Jones

Ballpark (capacity, surface)
Teluf Field (10,000; artificial infield, grass outfield)

Affiliation
Athletics

Address
10233 96th Ave.
Edmonton, Alberta T5K 0A5

Phone
403-429-2934

LAS VEGAS STARS

General manager
Don Logan

Manager
Jerry Royster

Ballpark (capacity, surface)
Cashman Field (9,370, grass)

Affiliation
Padres

Address
850 Las Vegas Blvd. N
Las Vegas, NV 89101

Phone
702-386-7200

PHOENIX FIREBIRDS

Vice president/general manager
Craig Pletenik

Manager
Ron Wotus

Ballpark (capacity, surface)
Scottsdale Stadium (11,200, grass)

Affiliation
Giants

Address
P.O. Box 8528
Scottsdale, AZ 85252

Phone
602-275-0500

SALT LAKE BUZZ

Vice president/general manager
Tammy Felker-White

Manager
Phil Roof

Ballpark (capacity, surface)
Franklin-Quest Field (15,500, grass)

Affiliation
Twins

Address
P.O. Box 4108
Salt Lake City, UT 84110

Phone
801-485-3800

TACOMA RAINIERS

Director of marketing
Mel Taylor

Manager
Dave Myers

Ballpark (capacity, surface)
Cheney Stadium (10,106, grass)

Affiliation
Mariners

Address
P.O. Box 11087
Tacoma, WA 98411

Phone
206-752-7707

TUCSON TOROS

General manager
Mike Feder

Manager
Tim Ireland

Ballpark (capacity, surface)
Hi Corbett Field (8,000, grass)

Affiliation
Brewers

Address
P.O. Box 27045
Tucson, AZ 85716

Phone
520-325-2621

VANCOUVER CANADIANS

Vice president/general manager
Brent Imlach

Manager
Don Long

Ballpark (capacity, surface)
Nat Bailey Stadium (6,500, grass)

Affiliation
Angels

Address
4601 Ontario St.
Vancouver, B.C. V5V 3H4

Phone
604-872-5232

1996 FINAL STANDINGS

FIRST HALF

NORTHERN DIVISION

Team	W	L	T	Pct.	GB
Edmonton (Athletics)	39	31	0	.557	....
Tacoma (Mariners)	40	32	0	.556	....
Vancouver (Angels)	35	32	0	.522	2½
Calgary (Pirates)	37	34	0	.521	2½
Salt Lake (Twins)	35	37	0	.486	5

SOUTHERN DIVISION

Team	W	L	T	Pct.	G
Phoenix (Giants)	39	33	0	.542	....
Tucson (Astros)	35	37	0	.486	4
Albuquerque (Dodgers)	33	39	0	.458	6
Las Vegas (Padres)	31	37	0	.456	6
Colorado Springs (Rockies)	29	41	0	.414	9

SECOND HALF

NORTHERN DIVISION						SOUTHERN DIVISION					
am	W	L	T	Pct.	GB	Team	W	L	T	Pct.	GB
as Vegas (Padres)	42	30	0	.583	....	Edmonton (Athletics)	45	27	0	.625	....
cson (Astros)	35	37	0	.486	7	Salt Lake (Twins)	43	29	0	.597	2
buquerque (Dodgers)	34	37	0	.479	7½	Calgary (Pirates)	37	34	1	.521	7½
oenix (Giants)	30	42	0	.417	12	Vancouver (Angels)	33	38	0	.465	11½
olorado Springs (Rockies)	29	42	1	.408	12½	Tacoma (Mariners)	29	41	0	.414	15

COMPOSITE

am	Edm.	SLC	L.V.	Cal.	Van.	Tuc.	Tac.	Phx.	Alb.	C.S.	W	L	T	Pct.	GB
dmonton (Athletics)	....	9	9	10	8	10	8	11	10	9	84	58	0	.592	....
alt Lake (Twins)	7	....	10	7	7	11	7	9	8	12	78	66	0	.542	7
as Vegas (Padres)	6	6	....	8	8	9	9	8	11	8	73	67	0	.521	10
algary (Pirates)	5	9	8	....	12	8	9	8	6	9	74	68	1	.521	10
ancouver (Angels)	8	9	5	4	....	8	7	9	10	8	68	70	0	.493	14
cson (Astros)	6	5	7	8	8	....	11	7	7	11	70	74	0	.486	15
acoma (Mariners)	8	9	7	7	8	5	....	9	7	9	69	73	0	.486	15
hoenix (Giants)	5	7	8	8	7	9	7	....	7	11	69	75	0	.479	16
buquerque (Dodgers)	6	8	5	10	6	9	8	9	....	6	67	76	0	.469	17½
olorado Springs (Rockies)	7	4	8	6	6	5	7	5	10	....	58	83	1	.411	25½

Major league affiliations in parentheses.

PLAYOFFS: Edmonton defeated Salt Lake, three games to one; Phoenix defeated Las Vegas, three games to none; Edmonton defeated Phoenix, three ames to one, to win league championship.

REGULAR-SEASON ATTENDANCE: Albuquerque, 307,445; Calgary, 273,545; Colorado Springs, 237,826; Edmonton, 463,684; Las Vegas, 313,212; hoenix, 267,649; Salt Lake, 621,027; Tacoma, 338,500; Tucson, 307,091; Vancouver, 334,800. Total—3,464,779. Playoffs (11 games)—29,667. Class AAA ll-Star Game at Salt Lake City—15,500.

MANAGERS: Albuquerque, Phil Regan; Calgary, Trent Jewett; Colorado Springs, Brad Mills; Edmonton, Gary Jones; Las Vegas, Jerry Royster; Phoenix, on Wotus; Salt Lake, Phil Roof; Tacoma, Dave Myers; Tucson, Tim Tolman; Vancouver, Don Long.

ALL-STAR TEAM: 1B—Jason Thompson, Las Vegas; 2B—Brian Raabe, Salt Lake; 3B—Todd Walker, Salt Lake; SS—Neifi Perez, Colorado Springs; OF— ermaine Allensworth, Calgary; Brent Brede, Salt Lake; Ray Montgomery, Tucson; C—Angelo Encarnacion, Calgary; DH—James Bonnici, Tacoma; RHP—Bob ilacki, Tacoma; LHP—Shawn Estes, Phoenix; Relief pitcher—Steve Mintz, Phoenix; Most Valuable Player—Steve Mintz, Phoenix; Manager of the Year— ary Jones, Edmonton.

1996 BATTING

TEAM

am	Avg.	G	TPA	AB	R	H	TB	2B	3B	HR	RBI	SH	SF	HP	BB	IBB	SO	SB	CS	GDP	LOB	ShO	Slg.	OBP
alt Lake	.293	144	5775	5085	855	1490	2360	319	49	151	797	29	61	70	530	48	892	141	71	107	1076	2	.464	.364
algary	.290	143	5433	4870	764	1413	2069	288	40	96	695	65	48	60	390	46	844	119	56	111	967	5	.425	.347
cson	.282	144	5496	4893	742	1380	2120	250	62	122	689	32	46	27	491	40	912	103	75	104	1006	4	.433	.348
olo. Springs.	.282	142	5496	4863	719	1370	2055	264	35	117	665	37	39	38	519	34	879	81	65	129	1062	9	.423	.353
buquerque	.278	143	5545	4940	712	1372	2040	237	46	113	646	61	34	36	474	46	1076	104	72	98	1035	8	.413	.343
coma	.276	142	5390	4852	665	1341	2081	245	33	164	612	39	48	39	412	16	789	72	63	122	970	12	.429	.335
dmonton	.276	142	5456	4728	785	1306	2082	245	45	147	729	42	46	56	582	24	968	123	59	108	1021	7	.440	.359
ancouver	.276	138	5372	4732	677	1304	1857	285	35	66	617	51	53	47	488	30	775	89	52	102	1042	12	.392	.346
hoenix	.275	144	5598	4984	700	1371	1991	273	58	77	632	41	47	49	477	38	900	77	58	114	1058	6	.399	.341
as Vegas	.264	140	5329	4669	654	1232	1930	272	24	126	597	57	33	39	531	51	949	74	59	117	1018	4	.413	.342

INDIVIDUAL

TOP QUALIFIERS FOR BATTING CHAMPIONSHIP

Minimum 389 plate appearances. *Lefthanded batter. †Switch-hitter.

layer, Team	Avg.	G	TPA	AB	R	H	TB	2B	3B	HR	RBI	SH	SF	HP	BB	IBB	SO	SB	CS	GDP	Slg.	OBP
aabe, Brian, Salt Lake	.351	116	539	482	103	169	270	39	4	18	69	2	4	4	47	2	19	8	8	12	.560	.410
ede, Brent, Salt Lake*	.348	132	582	483	102	168	255	38	8	11	86	4	5	3	87	9	87	14	6	4	.528	.446
uerrero, Wilton, Albuquerque..	.344	98	463	425	79	146	193	17	12	2	38	11	0	1	26	2	48	26	15	6	.454	.383
alker, Todd, Salt Lake*	.339	135	625	551	94	187	330	41	9	28	111	2	10	5	57	11	91	13	8	17	.599	.400
ilson, Desi, Phoenix*	.339	113	431	407	56	138	193	26	7	5	59	0	3	3	18	3	80	15	4	9	.474	.369
chevarria, Angel, Col. Springs .	.337	110	460	415	67	140	211	19	2	16	74	0	4	3	38	3	81	4	3	4	.508	.393
astellano, Pedro, Col. Springs .	.337	94	409	362	56	122	197	30	3	13	59	0	3	4	40	4	46	0	2	8	.544	.406
llensworth, Jermaine, Calgary ..	.330	95	400	352	77	116	175	23	6	8	43	1	1	7	39	6	61	25	5	4	.497	.406
all, Jeff, Tucson	.324	116	465	429	64	139	231	31	2	19	73	0	1	1	34	1	83	10	8	12	.538	.374
ajek, Dave, Tucson	.317	121	539	508	81	161	214	31	5	4	64	1	4	1	25	5	36	9	6	17	.421	.348
erez, Neifi, Colorado Springs†	.316	133	607	570	77	180	253	28	12	7	72	4	10	2	21	4	48	16	13	13	.444	.337
ecrist, Reed, Calgary*	.307	128	484	420	68	129	210	30	0	17	66	3	5	4	52	11	105	2	4	8	.500	.385
ontgomery, Ray, Tucson	.306	100	423	359	70	110	196	20	0	22	75	0	2	3	59	7	54	7	1	12	.546	.407
rstad, Darin, Vancouver*	.305	85	401	351	63	107	157	22	5	6	41	1	2	3	44	4	53	11	6	5	.447	.385
edesma, Aaron, Vancouver	.305	109	482	440	60	134	172	27	4	1	51	2	1	7	32	2	59	2	3	18	.391	.360

DEPARTMENTAL LEADERS: G—Spiezio, 140; AB—Perez, 570; R—Raabe, 103; H—T. Walker, 187; TB—T. Walker, 330; 2B—T. Walker, 41; 3B—Abreu, 16; HR—T. alker, 28; RBI—T. Walker, 111; SH—Womack, 14; SF—Ja. Cruz, 11; HP—McDonald, Quinlan, 15; BB—Moore, 95; IBB—Pritchett, Secrist, T. Walker, 11each; SO— ott, 124; SB—Moore, 38; CS—Abreu, 18; GIDP—Ledesma, 18; Slg.—T. Walker, .599; OBP—Brede, .446.

*Lefthanded batter. †Switch-hitter.

CLASS AAA *Pacific Coast League*

Player, Team	Avg.	G	TPA	AB	R	H	TB	2B	3B	HR	RBI	SH	SF	HP	BB	IBB	SO	SB	CS	GDP	Slg.	OB
Abreu, Bob, Tucson*	.283	132	573	484	86	137	222	14	16	13	68	2	2	2	83	3	111	24	18	6	.459	.389
Acre, Mark, Edmonton	.000	39	1	1	0	0	0	0	0	0	0	0	0	0	0	0	1	0	0	0	.000	.000
Allensworth, Jermaine, Calgary	.330	95	400	352	77	116	175	23	6	8	43	1	1	7	39	6	61	25	5	4	.497	.406
Anderson, Cliff, Albuquerque*	.269	64	214	186	19	50	75	9	2	4	17	2	1	4	21	2	53	3	3	3	.403	.354
Arias, George, Vancouver	.337	59	268	243	49	82	133	24	0	9	55	0	2	3	20	2	38	2	1	5	.547	.392
Ashley, Billy, Albuquerque	.348	7	30	23	6	8	12	1	0	1	9	0	0	0	7	0	9	2	0	0	.522	.500
Aude, Rich, Calgary	.292	103	429	394	69	115	195	29	0	17	81	0	5	4	26	2	69	4	4	10	.495	.338
Aurilia, Rich, Phoenix	.433	7	32	30	9	13	20	7	0	0	4	0	0	0	2	0	3	1	1	1	.667	.469
Ausanio, Joe, Col. Springs	.000	13	1	1	0	0	0	0	0	0	0	0	0	0	0	0	0	0	0	0	.000	.000
Backlund, Brett, Calgary	.000	7	6	5	0	0	0	0	0	0	0	1	0	0	0	0	4	0	0	0	.000	.000
Bailey, Roger, Col. Springs	.214	10	17	14	2	3	3	0	0	0	2	2	0	0	1	0	2	0	0	1	.214	.267
Ball, Jeff, Tucson	.324	116	465	429	64	139	231	31	2	19	73	0	1	1	34	1	83	10	8	12	.538	.374
Barry, Jeff, Las Vegas†	.083	4	15	12	1	1	1	0	0	0	0	0	0	0	3	0	0	0	0	0	.083	.267
Barton, Shawn, Phoenix	.000	44	3	3	0	0	0	0	0	0	0	0	0	0	0	0	2	0	0	0	.000	.000
Batista, Tony, Edmonton	.322	57	224	205	33	66	115	17	4	8	40	1	1	2	15	0	30	2	1	8	.561	.372
Batiste, Kim, Phoenix	.297	42	173	165	32	49	105	8	3	14	44	0	1	1	6	3	25	1	1	7	.636	.324
Battle, Allen, Edmonton	.304	62	272	224	53	68	97	12	4	3	33	6	2	3	37	0	37	9	3	5	.433	.406
Bautista, Jose, Phoenix	.125	6	8	8	1	1	1	0	0	0	0	0	0	0	0	0	2	0	0	0	.125	.125
Beamon, Trey, Calgary*	.288	111	447	378	62	109	145	15	3	5	52	3	5	6	55	6	63	16	3	12	.384	.383
Bell, Eric, Tucson*	.053	30	23	19	1	1	1	0	0	0	1	3	0	0	1	0	5	0	0	0	.053	.100
Benard, Marvin, Phoenix*	.368	4	21	19	2	7	7	0	0	0	4	0	0	0	2	0	2	1	0	0	.368	.429
Berumen, Andres, Las Vegas	.000	50	3	3	0	0	0	0	0	0	0	0	0	0	0	0	3	0	0	0	.000	.000
Blanco, Henry, Albuquerque	.167	2	6	6	1	1	1	0	0	0	0	0	0	0	0	0	3	0	0	0	.167	.167
Boever, Joe, Calgary	.083	44	13	12	1	1	2	1	0	0	2	1	0	0	0	0	6	0	0	2	.167	.083
Bolton, Tom, Calgary*	.222	40	21	18	2	4	6	2	0	0	4	1	0	0	2	0	5	0	0	0	.333	.300
Bonnici, James, Tacoma	.292	139	562	497	76	145	248	25	0	26	74	1	3	2	59	4	100	1	3	13	.499	.367
Bourgeois, Steve, Phoenix	.043	23	24	23	2	1	1	0	0	0	3	1	0	0	0	0	6	0	0	1	.043	.043
Bragg, Darren, Tacoma*	.282	20	87	71	17	20	37	8	0	3	8	0	0	2	14	0	14	1	0	1	.521	.414
Brede, Brent, Salt Lake*	.348	132	582	483	102	168	255	38	8	11	86	4	5	3	87	9	87	14	6	4	.528	.446
Brewer, Billy, Albuquerque*	.500	31	2	2	0	1	1	0	0	0	1	0	0	0	0	0	0	0	0	0	.500	.500
Brewington, Jamie, Phoenix	.217	37	24	23	3	5	6	1	0	0	0	1	0	0	0	0	2	1	0	0	.261	.217
Bridges, Kary, Tucson*	.314	42	152	140	24	44	58	9	1	1	21	0	2	1	9	1	8	1	3	3	.414	.355
Brito, Jorge, Colorado Springs	.340	53	188	159	32	54	92	17	0	7	31	0	1	4	24	1	37	0	1	7	.579	.436
Brosius, Scott, Edmonton	.625	3	11	8	5	5	6	1	0	0	0	0	0	0	3	0	1	0	0	0	.750	.727
Brumley, Mike, Tucson†	.234	88	323	278	40	65	102	11	7	4	28	1	2	2	40	4	79	9	3	5	.367	.332
Bruno, Julio, Las Vegas	.273	80	322	297	36	81	105	16	1	2	30	5	1	2	17	3	33	6	5	3	.354	.315
Brunson, William, Alb.*	.000	9	10	9	0	0	0	0	0	0	0	0	0	0	1	0	5	0	0	0	.000	.100
Bruske, Jim, Albuquerque	.143	36	7	7	0	1	1	0	0	0	0	0	0	0	0	0	2	0	0	1	.143	.143
Bryant, Scott, Tacoma	.266	58	229	214	21	57	79	10	3	2	19	1	1	0	13	1	41	0	3	5	.369	.307
Burke, Jamie, Vancouver	.250	41	167	156	12	39	47	5	0	1	14	1	2	1	7	0	18	2	1	5	.301	.283
Burke, John, Col. Springs†	.158	26	19	19	3	3	9	0	0	2	4	0	0	0	0	0	5	0	0	0	.474	.158
Busch, Mike, Albuquerque	.303	38	166	142	30	43	87	6	1	12	36	0	0	2	22	4	45	0	1	1	.613	.404
Bush, Homer, Las Vegas	.362	32	126	116	24	42	61	11	1	2	3	5	0	2	3	1	33	3	5	2	.526	.385
Bustillos, Albert, Col. Springs	.083	33	27	24	2	2	2	0	0	0	1	1	0	0	2	0	5	0	0	1	.083	.154
Cadaret, Greg, Albuquerque*	.000	9	2	2	0	0	0	0	0	0	0	0	0	0	0	0	1	0	0	0	.000	.000
Canizaro, Jay, Phoenix	.262	102	419	363	50	95	141	21	2	7	64	1	5	4	46	2	77	14	4	7	.388	.347
Carlson, Dan, Phoenix	.143	35	35	28	6	4	5	1	0	0	1	3	0	0	4	0	13	0	0	1	.179	.250
Carter, Andy, Phoenix*	.250	38	9	8	1	2	2	0	0	0	0	1	0	0	0	0	2	0	0	0	.250	.333
Carter, Jeff, Colorado Springs†	.255	50	186	161	19	41	53	9	0	1	12	1	0	1	23	0	33	3	6	3	.329	.351
Carvajal, Jovino, Vancouver†	.239	77	296	272	29	65	87	6	2	4	31	6	3	1	14	2	38	17	7	8	.320	.276
Castellano, Pedro, Col. Springs	.337	94	409	362	56	122	197	30	3	13	59	0	3	4	40	4	46	0	2	8	.544	.406
Castro, Juan, Albuquerque	.375	17	63	56	12	21	32	4	2	1	8	0	0	1	6	0	7	1	1	0	.571	.444
Cedeno, Roger, Albuquerque†	.224	33	142	125	16	28	39	2	3	1	10	2	0	0	15	1	22	6	5	2	.312	.307
Christiansen, Jason, Calgary	.000	2	3	1	0	0	0	0	0	0	0	1	1	0	0	0	1	0	0	0	.000	.500
Christopherson, Eric, Tucson	.287	67	250	223	31	64	103	15	3	6	36	1	4	1	21	2	47	2	0	1	.462	.345
Clark, Jerald, Calgary	.266	75	266	248	33	66	112	20	1	8	45	0	2	4	12	0	43	0	1	10	.452	.308
Cockrell, Alan, Col. Springs	.300	109	414	357	55	107	180	25	3	14	60	0	4	1	52	3	88	1	2	14	.504	.386
Colbert, Craig, Las Vegas	.250	65	212	200	18	50	73	8	0	5	19	0	4	0	8	0	48	3	1	4	.365	.274
Coleman, Vince, Vancouver†	.207	21	96	87	9	18	22	2	1	0	5	0	0	0	9	0	15	4	1	0	.253	.281
Correa, Ramser, Albuquerque	.000	23	2	2	0	0	0	0	0	0	0	0	0	0	0	0	1	0	0	0	.000	.000
Correia, Rod, Edmonton	.087	8	23	23	1	2	2	0	0	0	0	0	0	0	0	0	2	0	0	1	.087	.087
Counsell, Craig, Col. Springs*	.240	25	99	75	17	18	27	3	0	2	10	0	0	0	24	1	7	4	3	2	.360	.424
Cruz, Jacob, Phoenix*	.285	121	520	435	60	124	179	26	4	7	75	2	11	10	62	5	77	5	9	16	.411	.378
Cruz, Jose, Tacoma†	.237	22	95	76	15	18	41	1	2	6	15	1	0	0	18	1	12	1	1	2	.539	.383
Cummings, John, Alb.*	.400	27	12	10	1	4	4	0	0	0	1	2	0	0	0	0	6	0	0	0	.400	.400
Cummings, Midre, Calgary*	.304	97	397	368	60	112	166	24	3	8	55	4	3	1	21	3	60	6	4	6	.451	.344
Dandridge, Brad, Albuquerque	.263	30	84	80	14	21	31	4	0	2	7	0	0	1	3	0	7	0	0	4	.388	.298
Dascenzo, Doug, Las Vegas†	.284	86	366	320	48	91	114	17	3	0	20	10	2	2	32	2	38	15	13	6	.356	.351
Dault, Donnie, Tucson	.000	1	1	1	0	0	0	0	0	0	0	0	0	0	0	0	1	0	0	0	.000	.000
Davis, Jay, Tucson*	.337	33	109	101	18	34	46	7	1	1	17	0	2	1	5	0	16	4	1	0	.455	.367
Decker, Steve, Col. Springs	.400	7	30	25	4	10	11	1	0	0	3	0	0	1	4	1	3	0	0	1	.440	.500
Deer, Rob, Las Vegas	.224	84	317	259	43	58	136	14	2	20	47	0	1	1	56	2	118	5	1	7	.525	.363
DeJean, Mike, Col. Springs	.500	30	2	2	0	1	1	0	0	0	0	0	0	0	0	0	0	0	0	0	.500	.500
DeLeon, Roberto, Phoenix	.194	19	36	36	1	7	9	2	0	0	2	0	0	0	0	0	7	0	0	1	.250	.194
Delgado, Wilson, Phoenix†	.140	12	46	43	1	6	8	0	1	0	1	0	0	0	3	1	7	0	1	1	.186	.196
Demetral, Chris, Albuquerque*	.263	99	259	209	30	55	75	8	0	4	26	5	5	0	40	5	35	4	3	6	.359	.374
Dessens, Elmer, Calgary	.000	6	5	4	0	0	0	0	0	0	0	1	0	0	0	0	3	0	0	0	.000	.200
Diaz, Alex, Tacoma†	.244	44	187	176	19	43	48	5	0	0	7	3	1	0	7	0	20	5	6	9	.273	.272
Diaz, Eddy, Tacoma	.280	107	454	422	63	118	193	28	4	13	58	5	2	10	15	1	38	3	4	9	.457	.318
Diaz, Freddy, Vancouver†	.260	34	143	123	19	32	54	9	2	3	23	3	3	0	14	0	25	0	0	1	.439	.329

layer, Team	Avg.	G	TPA	AB	R	H	TB	2B	3B	HR	RBI	SH	SF	HP	BB	IBB	SO	SB	CS	GDP	Slg.	OBP
ishman, Glenn, Las Vegas	.250	27	25	24	4	6	8	2	0	0	0	0	0	1	0	0	6	1	0	0	.333	.280
ougherty, Jim, Tucson	.000	46	3	3	0	0	0	0	0	0	0	0	0	0	0	0	1	0	0	0	.000	.000
reifort, Darren, Albuquerque	.250	20	16	16	2	4	5	1	0	0	1	0	0	0	0	0	9	0	0	0	.313	.250
rinkwater, Sean, Tacoma	.258	9	32	31	2	8	9	1	0	0	1	0	0	0	1	0	5	0	0	0	.290	.281
uncan, Andres, Phoenix†	.226	42	116	106	11	24	38	7	2	1	12	0	0	2	8	0	22	2	0	1	.358	.293
urant, Mike, Salt Lake	.287	31	117	101	21	29	39	7	0	1	12	1	0	4	11	1	21	7	2	3	.386	.379
asley, Damion, Vancouver	.313	12	59	48	13	15	25	2	1	2	8	0	1	1	9	0	6	4	1	0	.521	.424
chevarria, Angel, Col. Springs	.337	110	460	415	67	140	211	19	2	16	74	0	4	3	38	3	81	4	3	4	.508	.393
dge, Tim, Calgary	.333	12	39	36	6	12	21	3	0	2	11	1	0	0	2	0	9	0	0	2	.583	.368
hmann, Kurt, Phoenix	.201	50	151	134	14	27	37	6	2	0	12	2	0	3	12	1	35	0	2	0	.276	.282
vira, Narciso, Albuquerque*	.000	3	6	6	1	0	0	0	0	0	0	0	0	0	0	0	1	0	0	0	.000	.000
ncarnacion, Angelo, Calgary	.319	75	278	263	38	84	114	18	0	4	31	0	2	3	10	2	19	6	2	10	.433	.349
ricks, John, Calgary	.000	14	4	4	0	0	0	0	0	0	1	0	0	0	0	0	1	0	0	0	.000	.000
rstad, Darin, Vancouver*	.305	85	401	351	63	107	157	22	5	6	41	1	2	3	44	4	53	11	6	5	.447	.385
spinosa, Ramon, Calgary	.282	78	256	245	37	69	93	8	8	0	25	3	0	2	6	3	28	2	3	6	.380	.304
stes, Shawn, Phoenix	.080	18	27	25	2	2	2	0	0	0	2	2	0	0	0	0	9	1	0	0	.080	.080
usebio, Tony, Tucson	.415	15	55	53	8	22	26	4	0	0	14	0	0	0	2	1	7	0	0	0	.491	.436
vans, Dave, Tucson	.000	43	10	10	0	0	0	0	0	0	0	0	0	0	0	0	4	0	0	0	.000	.000
abregas, Jorge, Vancouver*	.297	10	43	37	4	11	14	3	0	0	5	1	0	1	4	1	4	0	0	1	.378	.381
armer, Mike, Col. Springs†	.167	10	8	6	0	1	1	0	0	0	2	1	1	0	0	0	0	0	0	0	.167	.143
elder, Mike, Calgary†	.284	21	86	81	14	23	29	3	0	1	5	1	1	0	3	1	8	0	0	1	.358	.306
gueroa, Bien, Col. Springs	.207	10	31	29	2	6	8	2	0	0	6	0	1	0	1	0	3	0	0	2	.276	.226
nn, John, Calgary	.255	69	228	192	24	49	64	13	1	0	32	2	6	3	25	4	28	2	5	4	.333	.341
letcher, Paul, Edmonton	.000	39	2	2	0	0	0	0	0	0	0	0	0	0	0	0	1	0	0	0	.000	.000
lorez, Tim, Phoenix	.290	113	413	366	42	106	155	31	3	4	39	0	3	10	34	4	56	0	5	12	.423	.363
onville, Chad, Albuquerque†	.240	25	110	96	17	23	24	1	0	0	5	4	2	0	8	0	13	7	0	0	.250	.292
orbes, P.J., Vancouver	.274	117	471	409	58	112	140	24	2	0	46	10	4	5	42	3	44	4	3	13	.342	.346
ox, Eric, Albuquerque†	.330	30	95	91	8	30	38	6	1	0	2	0	0	0	4	1	20	1	2	2	.418	.358
redrickson, Scott, Col. Springs	.000	55	3	3	0	0	0	0	0	0	0	0	0	0	0	0	3	0	0	0	.000	.000
riedman, Jason, Tacoma*	.164	20	78	73	9	12	23	6	1	1	4	0	2	1	2	0	14	0	1	0	.315	.192
agne, Greg, Albuquerque	.273	4	13	11	1	3	4	1	0	0	1	0	0	1	1	0	1	0	0	1	.364	.385
ainer, Jay, Colorado Springs*	.234	109	372	333	51	78	136	16	0	14	49	0	3	0	36	4	71	6	2	9	.408	.306
allaher, Kevin, Tucson	.154	35	13	13	0	2	2	0	0	0	0	0	0	0	0	0	5	0	0	0	.154	.154
arcia, Carlos, Calgary	.333	2	6	6	0	2	4	0	1	0	0	0	0	0	0	0	0	0	0	0	.667	.333
arcia, Jose, Albuquerque	.333	44	3	3	1	1	1	0	0	0	0	0	0	0	0	0	2	0	0	0	.333	.333
arcia, Karim, Albuquerque*	.297	84	360	327	54	97	173	17	10	13	58	0	3	1	29	8	67	6	4	9	.529	.353
arrison, Webster, Edmonton	.303	80	338	294	56	89	137	18	0	10	49	1	2	0	41	2	47	2	1	11	.466	.386
iannelli, Ray, S.L.-C.S.*	.230	54	176	148	16	34	49	9	0	2	17	0	1	2	25	1	27	1	2	3	.331	.347
lenn, Darrin, Phoenix	.056	12	20	18	3	1	1	0	0	0	1	0	0	1	1	0	8	0	0	1	.056	.150
off, Jerry, Tucson*	.236	96	333	275	39	65	110	14	2	9	52	0	1	2	55	9	97	1	0	5	.400	.366
onzalez, Pedro, Col. Springs	.174	36	106	86	10	15	28	7	0	2	13	0	1	2	17	0	20	1	1	1	.326	.321
rebeck, Brian, Vancouver	.232	78	280	237	25	55	74	10	3	1	27	4	4	1	34	0	27	1	1	2	.312	.326
reene, Todd, Vancouver	.305	60	245	223	27	68	101	18	0	5	33	0	5	1	16	0	36	0	2	6	.453	.347
reer, Ken, Calgary	.000	46	4	3	0	0	0	0	0	0	0	1	0	0	0	0	1	0	0	0	.000	.000
roppuso, Mike, Tucson	.255	50	157	145	15	37	57	3	1	5	18	0	2	2	8	0	45	2	0	3	.393	.299
ubanich, Creighton, Edm	.248	34	125	117	14	29	50	7	1	4	19	0	1	1	6	0	33	3	0	5	.427	.288
uerrero, Wilton, Albuquerque	.344	98	463	425	79	146	193	17	12	2	38	11	0	1	26	2	48	26	15	6	.454	.383
ajek, Dave, Tucson	.317	121	539	508	81	161	214	31	5	4	64	1	4	1	25	5	36	9	6	17	.421	.348
ancock, Lee, Cal.-Pho.*	.000	26	5	4	0	0	0	0	0	0	0	1	0	0	0	0	1	0	0	0	.000	.000
arkey, Mike, Albuquerque	.200	49	12	10	1	2	3	1	0	0	2	1	1	0	0	0	3	0	0	0	.300	.182
arriger, Denny, Las Vegas	.167	26	29	24	3	4	4	0	0	0	0	3	0	0	2	0	6	0	0	0	.167	.231
arris, Greg W., Las Vegas	.000	1	1	1	0	0	0	0	0	0	0	0	0	0	0	0	1	0	0	0	.000	.000
atcher, Chris, Tucson	.302	95	372	348	53	105	188	21	4	18	61	0	5	5	14	1	87	10	8	9	.540	.333
awblitzel, Ryan, Col. Springs	.238	29	25	21	1	5	5	0	0	0	3	1	0	0	3	0	4	0	0	0	.238	.333
azlett, Steve, Salt Lake	.203	101	346	301	44	61	113	14	4	10	41	2	5	5	33	1	85	7	2	6	.375	.288
elton, Todd, Col. Springs*	.352	21	82	71	13	25	37	4	1	2	13	0	0	0	11	0	12	0	0	3	.521	.439
enry, Dwayne, Col. Springs	.000	28	1	1	0	0	0	0	0	0	0	0	0	0	0	0	0	0	0	0	.000	.000
eredia, Julian, Phoenix	.125	52	9	8	0	1	1	0	0	0	1	0	0	0	1	0	5	0	0	0	.125	.222
erges, Matt, Albuquerque	.000	10	3	2	0	0	0	0	0	0	0	1	0	0	0	0	1	0	0	0	.000	.000
ermanson, Dustin, Las Vegas	.000	42	2	2	0	0	0	0	0	0	0	0	0	0	0	0	1	0	0	0	.000	.000
ernandez, Carlos, Alb.	.240	66	250	233	19	56	82	11	0	5	30	1	3	2	11	0	49	5	4	4	.352	.277
ill, Glenallen, Phoenix	.353	5	17	17	4	6	13	1	0	2	2	0	0	0	0	0	3	1	0	0	.765	.353
ocking, Denny, Salt Lake†	.277	37	146	130	18	36	55	6	2	3	22	2	2	2	10	2	17	2	2	4	.423	.333
olbert, Ray, Tucson	.247	28	107	97	13	24	31	3	2	0	10	0	1	2	7	0	19	4	1	3	.320	.308
olt, Chris, Tucson	.121	28	38	33	0	4	4	0	0	0	0	4	0	1	0	0	3	0	0	1	.121	.147
ook, Chris, Phoenix†	.000	32	23	18	1	0	0	0	0	0	1	3	1	0	1	0	16	0	0	0	.000	.050
ope, John, Calgary	.217	23	28	23	2	5	5	0	0	0	3	4	1	0	0	0	8	0	1	0	.217	.208
orn, Jeff, Salt Lake	.337	25	101	83	14	28	42	5	0	3	13	2	2	2	12	1	5	0	1	4	.506	.424
orne, Tyrone, Edmonton*	.230	67	239	204	28	47	70	7	2	4	16	0	2	1	32	1	53	5	3	6	.343	.335
ubbard, Trent, Col. Springs	.314	50	219	188	41	59	102	15	5	6	16	0	1	2	28	0	14	6	8	4	.543	.406
ubbs, Dan, Albuquerque	.000	49	9	7	0	0	0	0	0	0	1	0	0	1	1	0	3	0	0	0	.000	.222
uckaby, Ken, Albuquerque	.276	103	309	286	37	79	108	16	2	3	41	3	1	2	17	1	35	0	0	10	.378	.320
unter, Brian, Tacoma	.348	25	104	92	19	32	61	6	1	7	24	0	3	0	9	0	11	1	0	3	.663	.394
unter, Brian, Tucson	.357	3	15	14	3	5	7	0	1	0	1	0	1	0	0	0	2	3	0	0	.500	.333
uson, Jeff, Col. Springs*	.295	14	68	61	10	18	22	4	0	0	8	2	0	2	3	0	1	6	0	0	.361	.348
banez, Raul, Tacoma*	.284	111	456	405	59	115	174	20	3	11	47	0	5	2	44	2	56	7	7	4	.430	.353
ngram, Garey, Albuquerque	.100	6	11	10	1	1	1	0	0	0	0	0	0	0	1	0	2	0	0	1	.100	.182
ngram, Riccardo, Las Vegas	.249	124	463	409	54	102	149	21	1	8	51	0	2	3	49	7	64	6	6	11	.364	.333
ensen, Marcus, Phoenix†	.264	120	458	405	41	107	152	22	4	5	53	2	4	3	44	4	95	1	1	10	.375	.338
ohnson, J.J., Salt Lake	.339	13	59	56	8	19	27	3	1	1	13	1	0	1	1	0	11	0	1	1	.482	.362
ohnson, Keith, Albuquerque	.250	4	17	16	2	4	5	1	0	0	2	0	0	0	1	0	1	0	0	0	.313	.294
ohnstone, John, Tucson	.000	45	2	2	0	0	0	0	0	0	0	0	0	0	0	0	1	0	0	0	.000	.000
ones, Bobby, Col. Springs	.333	60	7	6	3	2	2	0	0	0	1	0	0	0	1	0	3	0	0	0	.333	.429

Player, Team	Avg.	G	TPA	AB	R	H	TB	2B	3B	HR	RBI	SH	SF	HP	BB	IBB	SO	SB	CS	GDP	Slg.	OBP
Jones, Dax, Phoenix	.309	74	319	298	52	92	142	20	6	6	41	1	0	1	19	1	21	13	8	7	.477	.352
Jones, Terry, Col. Springs†	.288	128	541	497	75	143	158	7	4	0	33	4	2	1	37	3	80	26	14	5	.318	.337
Jordan, Ricky, Tacoma	.200	13	56	50	3	10	16	0	0	2	7	0	1	0	5	1	6	0	0	1	.320	.268
Kellner, Frank, Tucson†	.272	96	289	254	37	69	94	12	5	1	31	7	6	0	22	1	43	3	6	7	.370	.323
Kennedy, Darryl, Phoenix	.307	64	215	192	27	59	82	11	3	2	24	4	4	3	12	3	25	2	2	5	.427	.351
Kennedy, David, Col. Springs	.255	117	371	333	46	85	145	27	0	11	50	0	0	2	36	1	82	1	2	16	.435	.332
Kester, Tim, Tucson	.000	1	1	1	0	0	0	0	0	0	0	0	0	0	0	0	1	0	0	0	.000	.000
Kirkpatrick, Jay, Albuquerque*	.243	51	119	107	12	26	31	5	0	0	9	0	2	0	10	2	35	0	0	4	.290	.303
Knapp, Mike, Tacoma	.190	59	209	184	12	35	56	10	1	3	18	3	1	0	21	0	51	1	2	3	.304	.272
Konerko, Paul, Albuquerque	.429	4	15	14	2	6	9	0	0	1	2	0	0	0	1	0	2	0	1	0	.643	.467
Kramer, Tom, Col. Springs	.118	41	20	17	1	2	2	0	0	0	0	3	0	0	0	0	2	0	0	0	.118	.118
Latham, Chris, Salt Lake†	.274	115	421	376	59	103	158	16	6	9	50	4	3	2	36	1	91	26	9	5	.420	.338
Lawton, Matt, Salt Lake*	.297	53	243	212	40	63	102	16	1	7	33	0	2	3	26	0	34	2	4	2	.481	.379
Ledesma, Aaron, Vancouver	.305	109	482	440	60	134	172	27	4	1	51	2	1	7	32	2	59	2	3	18	.391	.366
Lee, Derek, Edmonton*	.200	9	31	25	3	5	6	1	0	0	1	0	0	0	6	1	0	0	1	2	.240	.355
Lennon, Patrick, Edmonton	.327	68	281	251	37	82	138	16	2	12	42	0	0	2	28	2	82	3	3	9	.550	.399
Leonard, Mark, Salt Lake*	.250	59	238	192	25	48	73	6	2	5	27	0	3	2	41	4	39	0	2	6	.380	.382
Lesher, Brian, Edmonton	.287	109	462	414	57	119	206	29	2	18	75	2	3	7	36	0	108	6	5	9	.498	.352
Lewis, Scott, Las Vegas	.158	29	20	19	0	3	3	0	0	0	1	1	0	0	0	0	6	0	0	1	.158	.158
List, Lou, Colorado Springs	.083	7	12	12	1	1	1	0	0	0	1	0	0	0	0	0	6	0	0	0	.083	.083
Loaiza, Esteban, Calgary	.077	12	14	13	1	1	1	0	0	0	0	1	0	0	0	0	3	0	0	0	.077	.143
Loiselle, Rich, Tuc.-Cal.	.100	13	12	10	0	1	1	0	0	0	1	2	0	0	0	0	3	0	0	0	.100	.100
Long, Joey, Las Vegas	.000	32	1	1	0	0	0	0	0	0	0	0	0	0	0	0	0	0	0	0	.000	.000
Lopez, Luis, Las Vegas†	.206	18	71	68	4	14	20	3	0	1	12	1	0	0	2	0	15	0	0	0	.294	.229
Lopez, Rene, Salt Lake	.241	22	68	58	5	14	18	4	0	0	4	2	3	0	5	0	10	1	0	2	.310	.288
Lott, Billy, Albuquerque	.266	114	469	418	67	111	190	20	1	19	66	0	0	5	46	1	124	6	7	6	.455	.345
Lovullo, Torey, Edmonton†	.280	26	114	93	18	26	42	4	0	4	19	1	1	1	18	1	12	0	0	3	.452	.398
Luce, Roger, Tucson	.300	20	52	50	8	15	25	2	1	2	8	0	0	0	2	0	17	0	0	0	.500	.327
Luzinski, Ryan, Albuquerque	.143	9	14	14	0	2	2	0	0	0	1	0	0	0	0	0	6	0	0	0	.143	.143
Manwaring, Kirt, Phoenix	.182	4	13	11	1	2	2	0	0	0	1	0	0	0	2	0	0	0	0	1	.182	.308
Marrero, Oreste, Albuquerque*	.283	121	482	441	50	125	195	29	1	13	76	0	4	1	36	1	119	2	6	12	.442	.336
Martinez, Manny, Tacoma	.314	66	308	277	54	87	116	15	1	4	24	3	3	2	23	1	41	14	10	6	.419	.367
Martinez, Ray, Vancouver	.253	24	96	87	8	22	31	5	2	0	10	3	3	2	1	0	13	1	0	4	.356	.269
Marx, Tim, Calgary	.324	95	336	296	50	96	121	20	1	1	37	3	6	2	29	1	50	6	2	8	.409	.381
Mashore, Damon, Edmonton	.268	50	211	183	32	49	84	9	1	8	29	2	2	5	19	0	48	6	2	3	.459	.349
Maurer, Ron, Albuquerque	.275	80	262	222	32	61	92	14	1	5	30	4	3	3	30	2	50	2	4	5	.414	.364
May, Darrell, Calgary*	.053	23	28	19	1	1	1	0	0	0	1	6	0	0	3	0	13	0	0	1	.053	.182
McCarty, Dave, Phoenix	.400	6	28	25	4	10	16	1	1	1	7	0	1	0	2	0	4	0	0	0	.640	.429
McDonald, Jason, Edmonton†	.238	137	573	479	71	114	155	7	5	8	46	10	6	15	63	0	82	33	13	8	.324	.341
Melendez, Dan, Albuquerque*	.152	31	55	46	5	7	9	2	0	0	2	0	1	0	8	0	14	0	0	1	.196	.273
Miller, Damian, Salt Lake	.286	104	422	385	54	110	160	27	1	7	55	2	4	6	25	2	58	1	4	13	.416	.336
Miller, Roger, Col. Springs	.000	1	2	2	0	0	0	0	0	0	0	0	0	0	0	0	0	0	0	0	.000	.000
Millette, Joe, Calgary	.213	53	120	108	7	23	31	8	0	0	7	1	0	2	9	0	19	0	2	8	.287	.286
Mimbs, Mark, Albuquerque*	.231	35	32	26	3	6	9	1	1	0	5	3	0	0	3	0	6	0	0	0	.346	.310
Mintz, Steve, Phoenix*	.333	61	4	3	0	1	1	0	0	0	0	1	0	0	0	0	2	0	0	0	.333	.333
Mirabelli, Doug, Phoenix	.298	14	52	47	10	14	21	7	0	0	7	0	0	1	4	0	7	0	0	1	.447	.365
Mlicki, Doug, Tucson	.080	26	27	25	0	2	2	0	0	0	1	1	0	0	1	0	2	0	0	0	.080	.115
Molina, Izzy, Edmonton	.263	98	377	342	45	90	144	12	3	12	56	5	2	3	25	4	55	2	5	9	.421	.317
Montgomery, Ray, Tucson	.306	100	423	359	70	110	196	20	0	22	75	0	2	3	59	7	54	7	1	12	.546	.407
Moore, Kerwin, Edmonton†	.230	119	558	452	90	104	144	12	11	2	32	4	5	2	95	2	115	38	12	2	.319	.363
Mora, Melvin, Tucson	.281	62	253	228	35	64	88	11	2	3	26	3	4	1	17	1	27	3	5	7	.386	.328
Mouton, James, Tucson	.250	1	5	4	1	1	1	0	0	0	0	0	0	0	1	0	0	0	0	0	.250	.400
Mueller, Bill, Phoenix†	.302	106	488	440	73	133	171	14	6	4	36	0	3	1	44	4	40	2	5	11	.389	.365
Mulligan, Sean, Las Vegas	.288	102	397	358	55	103	190	24	3	19	75	0	2	7	30	4	68	1	2	8	.531	.353
Munoz, Mike, Col. Springs*	.000	70	1	1	0	0	0	0	0	0	0	0	0	0	0	0	1	0	0	0	.000	.000
Murray, Calvin, Phoenix	.244	83	363	311	50	76	113	16	6	3	28	5	1	3	43	0	60	12	6	1	.363	.341
Neill, Mike, Edmonton*	.150	6	23	20	4	3	7	1	0	1	4	1	0	0	2	0	3	0	0	0	.350	.227
Nied, David, Col. Springs	.250	16	9	8	2	2	3	1	0	0	1	1	0	0	0	0	3	0	0	0	.375	.250
Ogden, Jamie, Salt Lake*	.263	123	499	448	80	118	198	22	2	18	74	2	2	2	45	6	105	17	2	9	.442	.332
Oquist, Mike, Las Vegas	.212	27	36	33	2	7	7	0	0	0	2	0	0	0	3	0	6	1	0	1	.212	.278
Orton, John, Vancouver	.056	6	20	18	0	1	1	0	0	0	0	0	0	0	2	0	5	0	0	0	.056	.150
Osuna, Al, Las Vegas	.000	11	1	1	0	0	0	0	0	0	0	0	0	0	0	0	1	0	0	0	.000	.000
Owens, Jayhawk, Col. Springs	.227	6	26	22	6	5	8	3	0	0	6	1	0	0	3	0	6	0	0	1	.364	.320
Palmeiro, Orlando, Vancouver*	.306	62	289	245	40	75	96	13	4	0	33	5	5	4	30	1	19	7	3	4	.392	.384
Parker, Rick, Albuquerque	.303	50	207	175	26	53	66	7	3	0	23	4	2	3	23	1	27	7	6	2	.377	.389
Patrick, Bronswell, Tucson	.235	33	18	17	4	4	5	1	0	0	1	0	0	0	1	0	3	0	0	0	.294	.278
Pedraza, Rod, Col. Springs	.000	6	5	5	0	0	0	0	0	0	0	0	0	0	0	0	1	0	0	0	.000	.000
Peguero, Julio, Tacoma†	.280	100	365	328	41	92	112	15	1	1	21	11	5	1	20	1	47	7	7	10	.341	.319
Peltier, Dan, Phoenix*	.285	70	299	267	40	76	90	8	3	0	27	1	2	1	28	3	39	0	2	7	.337	.352
Pennyfeather, William, Van.	.283	108	440	413	56	117	174	36	3	5	63	5	2	1	19	0	71	19	11	7	.421	.315
Perez, Neifi, Colorado Springs†	.316	133	607	570	77	180	253	28	12	7	72	4	10	2	21	4	48	16	13	13	.444	.337
Peters, Chris, Calgary*	.250	4	5	4	0	1	1	0	0	0	0	1	0	0	0	0	0	0	0	0	.250	.250
Phoenix, Steve, Phoenix	.000	10	1	1	0	0	0	0	0	0	0	0	0	0	0	0	0	0	0	0	.000	.000
Pirkl, Greg, Tacoma	.302	88	371	348	50	105	194	22	2	21	75	0	3	6	14	2	58	1	1	13	.557	.337
Pisciotta, Marc, Calgary	.500	57	2	2	0	1	1	0	0	0	1	0	0	0	0	0	1	0	0	0	.500	.500
Plantier, Phil, Edmonton*	.352	34	139	122	25	43	79	7	1	9	45	0	3	2	12	1	25	1	0	1	.648	.410
Poe, Charles, Edmonton	.200	3	17	15	2	3	3	0	0	0	1	0	0	0	1	1	5	0	0	0	.200	.250
Polcovich, Kevin, Calgary	.274	104	375	336	53	92	122	21	3	1	46	5	2	14	18	3	49	7	6	9	.363	.335
Powell, Dante, Phoenix	.250	2	10	8	0	2	4	0	1	0	1	0	0	0	1	0	5	0	0	0	.500	.400
Pozo, Arquimedez, Tacoma	.279	95	419	365	55	102	169	12	5	15	64	1	8	6	39	1	40	3	5	11	.463	.352
Pozo, Yohel, Col. Springs	.277	20	52	47	8	13	18	2	0	1	6	1	1	1	2	0	8	0	0	5	.383	.314
Prieto, Chris, Las Vegas*	.000	5	7	7	1	0	0	0	0	0	0	0	0	0	0	0	0	0	0	0	.000	.000

ayer, Team	Avg.	G	TPA	AB	R	H	TB	2B	3B	HR	RBI	SH	SF	HP	BB	IBB	SO	SB	CS	GDP	Slg.	OBP
ince, Tom, Albuquerque	.411	32	112	95	24	39	67	5	1	7	22	0	0	2	15	2	14	0	2	1	.705	.500
itchett, Chris, Vancouver*	.295	130	568	485	78	143	232	39	1	16	73	0	6	6	71	11	96	5	4	7	.478	.387
obst, Alan, Tucson	.286	2	8	7	0	2	3	1	0	0	1	0	0	0	1	0	3	0	0	0	.429	.375
illiam, Harvey, Col. Springs	.276	79	322	283	46	78	123	13	1	10	58	0	4	3	32	4	49	2	3	12	.435	.351
rc, Dave, Albuquerque*	.167	13	7	6	1	1	1	0	0	0	3	1	0	0	0	1	0	0	0	0	.167	.167
e, Eddie, Tucson	.258	92	310	275	39	71	104	15	6	2	25	2	3	1	29	2	41	5	3	8	.378	.328
ainlan, Tom, Salt Lake	.283	121	552	491	81	139	224	38	1	15	81	0	8	15	38	2	121	4	8	8	.456	.348
aabe, Brian, Salt Lake	.351	116	539	482	103	169	270	39	4	18	69	2	4	4	47	2	19	8	8	12	.560	.410
amos, Ken, Tucson*	.270	104	440	385	54	104	144	22	3	4	34	3	4	0	41	2	41	6	9	3	.374	.337
ath, Gary, Albuquerque*	.135	30	40	37	2	5	5	0	0	0	2	2	0	0	1	0	17	0	0	1	.135	.158
atliff, Darryl, Calgary	.336	38	145	131	19	44	47	3	0	0	12	1	2	0	11	1	19	4	1	5	.359	.382
eady, Randy, Las Vegas	.324	35	131	105	19	34	50	7	0	3	11	0	2	1	23	0	13	0	1	2	.476	.443
eimer, Kevin, S.L.-Tac.*	.283	78	312	286	38	81	132	12	0	13	44	0	4	8	14	3	43	4	1	7	.462	.330
ekar, Bryan, Col. Springs	.130	19	31	23	1	3	5	2	0	0	3	7	0	0	1	0	11	0	0	0	.217	.167
elaford, Desi, Tacoma†	.205	93	348	317	27	65	89	12	0	4	32	4	3	1	23	0	58	10	6	7	.281	.259
chardson, Brian, Albuquerque	.245	105	398	355	52	87	135	17	2	9	43	4	4	3	32	6	89	4	1	5	.380	.310
ley, Marquis, Vancouver	.234	12	50	47	8	11	13	2	0	0	0	0	0	0	3	0	12	3	0	2	.277	.280
os, Eduardo, Albuquerque	.069	15	34	29	3	2	2	0	0	0	1	0	1	1	3	1	6	1	0	1	.069	.176
oberge, J.P., Albuquerque	.321	53	174	156	17	50	70	6	1	4	17	3	0	1	14	1	28	3	0	1	.449	.380
odriguez, Alex, Tacoma	.200	2	7	5	0	1	1	0	0	0	0	0	0	0	2	1	1	0	0	0	.200	.429
odriguez, Felix, Albuquerque	.200	27	27	25	2	5	5	0	0	0	1	2	0	0	0	0	10	0	0	1	.200	.200
omero, Willie, Albuquerque	.385	4	14	13	1	5	8	0	0	1	3	0	0	0	1	0	1	1	0	0	.615	.429
ossy, Rico, Las Vegas	.252	130	503	413	56	104	141	21	2	4	35	9	5	6	70	7	63	6	6	11	.341	.364
uebel, Matt, Calgary*	.000	13	11	10	1	0	0	0	0	0	0	0	1	0	0	0	4	0	0	0	.000	.000
ueter, Kirk, Phoenix*	.000	5	4	4	0	0	0	0	0	0	0	0	0	0	0	0	3	0	0	0	.000	.000
usso, Paul, Las Vegas	.252	80	252	226	16	57	88	15	2	4	33	0	2	1	23	1	53	2	1	7	.389	.321
van, Matt, Calgary	.000	51	2	2	0	0	0	0	0	0	0	0	0	0	0	0	2	0	0	0	.000	.000
aunders, Doug, Tacoma	.252	40	153	131	16	33	48	6	0	3	13	3	0	0	19	0	22	1	0	1	.366	.347
chwenke, Matt, Las Vegas	.250	11	17	16	0	4	4	0	0	0	2	0	0	1	0	0	7	0	0	0	.250	.294
ott, Gary, Las Vegas	.272	65	249	217	24	59	85	16	2	2	27	0	1	0	31	1	47	0	2	6	.392	.361
anez, Rudy, Albuquerque	.000	20	1	1	0	0	0	0	0	0	0	0	0	0	0	0	1	0	0	0	.000	.000
crist, Reed, Calgary*	.307	128	484	420	68	129	210	30	4	17	66	3	5	4	52	11	105	2	4	8	.500	.385
arperson, Mike, Las Vegas	.304	32	133	112	17	34	45	8	0	1	21	0	0	1	20	1	11	1	0	6	.402	.414
eets, Andy, Tacoma	.358	62	260	232	44	83	124	16	5	5	33	0	3	0	25	0	56	6	4	6	.534	.415
eldon, Scott, Edmonton	.300	98	404	350	61	105	168	27	3	10	60	3	4	4	43	3	83	5	3	8	.480	.379
ipley, Craig, Las Vegas	.000	1	2	2	1	0	0	0	0	0	0	0	0	0	0	0	0	0	0	0	.000	.000
ouse, Brian, Calgary*	.000	12	2	2	0	0	0	0	0	0	0	0	0	0	0	0	1	0	0	0	.000	.000
mms, Mike, Tucson	.297	17	74	64	11	19	43	3	0	7	19	0	1	0	9	0	17	0	3	1	.672	.392
mons, Doug, Tucson*	.250	8	9	8	0	2	2	0	0	0	1	1	0	0	0	0	0	0	0	0	.250	.250
mons, Mitch, Salt Lake	.264	129	570	512	76	135	193	27	8	5	59	3	4	8	43	3	59	35	11	7	.377	.328
monton, Benji, Phoenix	.750	1	5	4	1	3	6	0	0	1	2	0	0	1	0	0	0	0	0	0	1.500	.800
ngleton, Christopher, Phoenix*	.125	9	34	32	3	4	4	0	0	0	1	0	0	1	0	2	0	0	0	.125	.152
nall, Mark, Tucson	.000	32	1	1	0	0	0	0	0	0	0	0	0	0	0	0	1	0	0	0	.000	.000
nith, Demond, Edmonton†	.333	2	3	3	0	1	1	0	0	0	0	0	0	0	0	0	2	0	0	0	.333	.333
nith, Ira, Las Vegas	.242	72	279	252	37	61	94	16	1	5	25	5	1	1	20	0	27	3	3	9	.373	.299
nith, Pete, Las Vegas	.148	26	32	27	2	4	4	0	0	0	1	5	0	0	0	0	7	0	2	0	.148	.148
nderstrom, Steve, Phoenix	.125	29	40	32	1	4	4	0	0	0	2	6	0	0	2	0	9	0	0	0	.125	.176
niezio, Scott, Edmonton†	.262	140	593	523	87	137	235	30	4	20	91	3	5	4	56	6	66	6	5	7	.449	.335
airs, Matt, Edmonton*	.344	51	208	180	35	62	104	16	1	8	41	1	6	0	21	0	34	0	0	4	.578	.401
everson, Todd, Las Vegas	.239	100	355	301	42	72	130	16	3	12	50	1	5	1	47	5	87	6	5	8	.432	.339
rittmatter, Mark, Col. Springs	.233	58	184	159	21	37	53	8	1	2	18	1	0	7	17	3	30	2	1	5	.333	.333
veum, Dale, Calgary†	.300	101	381	343	62	103	204	28	2	23	84	0	2	3	33	3	71	2	1	2	.595	.365
van, Russ, Las Vegas*	.040	25	27	25	1	1	1	0	0	0	0	2	0	0	0	0	15	0	0	2	.040	.040
vingle, Paul, Vancouver	.000	16	3	3	0	0	0	0	0	0	0	0	0	0	0	0	0	0	0	0	.000	.000
kayoshi, Todd, Vancouver*	.286	3	7	7	1	2	2	0	0	0	2	0	0	0	0	0	0	0	0	0	.286	.286
tum, Jimmy, Las Vegas	.343	64	260	233	40	80	138	20	1	12	56	0	1	3	23	6	53	4	0	9	.592	.408
jero, Fausto, Vancouver	.200	54	184	155	21	31	40	4	1	1	12	6	0	1	22	0	41	0	1	6	.258	.303
ompson, Jason, Las Vegas*	.300	111	446	387	80	116	206	27	0	21	57	0	3	5	51	9	93	7	5	10	.532	.386
omson, John, Col. Springs	.154	11	16	13	0	2	2	0	0	0	1	1	1	0	1	0	6	0	0	0	.154	.200
mberlin, Andy, Edmonton*	.283	17	70	60	12	17	21	2	1	0	5	0	0	2	8	0	15	1	0	0	.350	.386
ammell, Gary, Tucson*	.400	3	12	10	3	4	7	0	0	1	2	0	0	0	2	0	2	0	1	0	.700	.500
eadwell, Jody, Albuquerque	.000	6	6	5	0	0	0	0	0	0	1	1	0	0	0	0	1	0	0	1	.000	.000
edaway, Chad, Las Vegas†	.224	76	220	196	26	44	73	10	2	5	19	5	1	1	17	2	25	4	1	4	.372	.288
rner, Chris, Vancouver	.256	113	461	390	51	100	127	19	1	2	47	1	4	5	61	2	85	1	3	5	.326	.361
rso, Sal, Tacoma	.000	46	1	1	0	0	0	0	0	0	0	0	0	0	0	0	0	0	0	0	.000	.250
ldez, Carlos, Phoenix	.000	44	5	3	0	0	0	0	0	0	0	0	1	0	1	0	3	0	0	0	.000	.250
anderweele, Doug, Phoenix*	.222	41	12	9	1	2	2	0	0	0	1	2	0	1	0	0	2	0	0	0	.222	.300
azquez, Ramon, Tacoma*	.224	18	54	49	7	11	15	2	1	0	4	0	0	1	4	0	12	0	0	2	.306	.296
entura, Wilfredo, Edmonton	.250	2	4	4	1	1	1	0	0	0	0	0	0	0	0	0	1	0	0	0	.250	.250
eras, Dario, Las Vegas	.000	20	8	4	0	0	0	0	0	0	0	3	0	0	1	0	1	0	0	0	.000	.200
ano, Jake, Colorado Springs	.500	7	2	2	1	1	1	0	0	0	0	0	0	0	0	0	0	0	0	0	.500	.500
agner, Billy, Tucson*	.182	13	14	11	3	2	2	0	0	0	0	0	0	0	2	0	2	0	0	0	.182	.308
akamatsu, Don, Tacoma	.000	1	3	3	0	0	0	0	0	0	0	0	0	0	0	0	0	0	0	0	.000	.000
alker, Larry, Col. Springs*	.364	3	13	11	2	4	10	0	0	2	8	0	1	0	1	0	4	0	0	0	.909	.385
alker, Pete, Las Vegas	.000	26	1	0	0	0	0	0	0	0	0	1	0	0	0	0	0	0	0	0	.000	.000
alker, Todd, Salt Lake*	.339	135	625	551	94	187	330	41	5	28	111	2	10	5	57	11	91	13	8	17	.599	.400
all, Donne, Tucson	.133	9	16	15	1	2	2	0	0	0	1	0	0	0	0	0	7	0	0	0	.133	.133
alters, Dan, Edmonton	.250	25	69	64	5	16	24	5	0	1	8	1	0	0	4	0	7	0	0	5	.375	.294
eaver, Eric, Vancouver	.143	13	7	7	1	1	1	0	0	0	0	0	0	0	0	0	3	0	0	0	.143	.143
ite, Billy, Colorado Springs	.243	103	322	284	24	69	93	11	2	3	26	4	1	1	32	1	80	2	2	7	.327	.321
idger, Chris, Tacoma	.304	97	385	352	42	107	170	20	2	13	48	2	2	2	27	0	62	7	1	13	.483	.355
illiams, George, Edmonton†	.404	14	66	57	10	23	43	5	0	5	18	0	1	2	6	0	11	0	1	2	.754	.470

Player, Team	Avg.	G	TPA	AB	R	H	TB	2B	3B	HR	RBI	SH	SF	HP	BB	IBB	SO	SB	CS	GDP	Slg.	OB
Williams, Keith, Phoenix............	.274	108	456	398	63	109	179	25	3	13	63	1	5	0	52	4	96	2	2	9	.450	.354
Williams, Reggie, Albuquerque† ..	.287	92	396	352	60	101	148	25	2	6	42	5	1	1	37	5	72	17	7	6	.420	.358
Wilson, Desi, Phoenix*	.339	113	431	407	56	138	193	26	7	5	59	0	3	3	18	3	80	15	4	9	.474	.369
Wilson, Gary, Calgary	.059	27	41	34	2	2	2	0	0	0	1	5	0	0	2	0	11	0	0	0	.059	.111
Wojciechowski, Steve, Edm.*.....	.000	11	1	1	0	0	0	0	0	0	0	0	0	0	0	0	1	0	0	0	.000	.000
Wolff, Mike, Vancouver..............	.250	71	303	256	46	64	115	15	3	10	38	3	6	4	34	2	69	6	4	3	.449	.340
Womack, Tony, Calgary*	.300	131	559	506	75	152	196	19	11	1	47	14	5	3	31	0	79	37	12	3	.387	.341
Wood, Jason, Edmonton	.000	3	17	12	0	0	0	0	0	0	0	0	0	0	5	0	6	0	1	0	.000	.294
Woods, Ken, Phoenix	.279	56	231	208	32	58	78	12	1	2	13	0	3	1	19	0	29	3	4	6	.375	.343
Wright, Jamey, Col. Springs......	.200	9	17	15	2	3	3	0	0	0	0	2	0	0	0	0	4	0	0	1	.200	.200
Yelding, Eric, Tacoma	.267	19	67	60	5	16	20	2	1	0	5	1	1	0	5	0	12	3	4	0	.333	.318
Young, Anthony, Tucson............	.000	4	1	1	0	0	0	0	0	0	0	0	0	0	0	0	0	0	0	0	.000	.000
Young, Eric, Colorado Springs ..	.261	7	28	23	4	6	9	1	1	0	3	0	0	0	5	0	1	0	0	1	.391	.393

GRAND SLAMS: Busch, Marrero, Molina, Ramos, 2 each; Arias, Batista, Batiste, Bonnici, Brede, Brito, Christopherson, Cockrell, Ja. Cruz, M. Cummings, Goff, Hazle Hernandez, Dav. Kennedy, Lawton, Lennon, Lesher, Lovullo, Ogden, Pennyfeather, Pirkl, Spiezio, Stairs, White, G. Williams, Wolff, 1 each.
AWARDED FIRST BASE ON CATCHER'S INTERFERENCE: Ramos 7 (Mirabelli, Jensen, Brito, Strittmatter, Turner 2, Knapp); Spiezio 2 (Brito, Goff); Forbes (Goff).

PLAYERS WITH TWO OR MORE TEAMS

Player, Team	Avg.	G	TPA	AB	R	H	TB	2B	3B	HR	RBI	SH	SF	HP	BB	IBB	SO	SB	CS	GDP	Slg.	OB
Giannelli, Ray, Salt Lake*	.258	10	35	31	2	8	9	1	0	0	4	0	1	1	2	0	8	0	0	0	.290	.314
Giannelli, Ray, Col. Springs*	.222	44	141	117	14	26	40	8	0	2	13	0	0	1	23	1	19	1	2	3	.342	.355
Hancock, Lee, Calgary*	.000	9	0	0	0	0	0	0	0	0	0	0	0	0	0	0	0	0	0	0	.000	.000
Hancock, Lee, Phoenix*	.000	17	5	4	0	0	0	0	0	0	0	1	0	0	0	0	1	0	0	0	.000	.000
Loiselle, Rich, Tucson...............	.000	5	3	2	0	0	0	0	0	0	0	1	0	0	0	0	0	0	0	0	.000	.000
Loiselle, Rich, Phoenix*	.125	8	9	8	0	1	1	0	0	0	1	1	0	0	0	0	3	0	0	0	.125	.125
Reimer, Kevin, Salt Lake*	.285	54	212	193	29	55	94	9	0	10	33	0	3	5	11	3	31	4	1	4	.487	.335
Reimer, Kevin, Tacoma*	.280	24	100	93	9	26	38	3	0	3	11	0	1	3	3	0	12	0	0	3	.409	.320

1996 PITCHING

TEAM

Team	W	L	Pct.	ERA	G	CG	ShO	Sv.	IP	H	TBF	R	ER	HR	SH	SF	HB	BB	IBB	SO	WP	Bk
Edmonton.........	84	58	.592	4.03	142	6	9	28	1226.1	1259	5279	628	549	100	31	34	36	406	44	840	60	6
Vancouver.........	68	70	.493	4.10	138	25	5	29	1215.1	1175	5253	639	554	105	55	38	55	530	17	840	66	14
Tucson.............	70	74	.486	4.21	144	7	7	28	1247.1	1401	5533	732	583	70	54	56	39	439	38	987	74	5
Calgary	74	68	.521	4.30	143	4	6	31	1240.0	1397	5492	691	593	114	51	51	50	461	57	788	55	4
Tacoma	69	73	.486	4.36	142	10	8	28	1254.1	1344	5506	699	608	115	39	42	56	485	21	978	62	18
Las Vegas	73	67	.521	4.62	140	11	7	35	1221.1	1328	5333	711	627	126	44	50	39	441	55	897	66	4
Phoenix	69	75	.479	4.67	144	5	10	40	1276.2	1354	5586	734	662	121	51	43	54	513	24	818	77	10
Albuquerque	67	76	.469	4.81	143	5	6	30	1262.0	1409	5675	799	675	116	49	47	49	598	66	981	60	13
Salt Lake	78	66	.542	5.09	144	13	6	31	1285.0	1501	5707	798	727	140	42	49	41	486	24	946	83	8
Col. Springs......	58	83	.411	5.57	142	3	6	31	1225.2	1411	5526	842	759	151	38	52	44	535	27	909	59	8

INDIVIDUAL

TOP QUALIFIERS FOR EARNED-RUN AVERAGE TITLE

Minimum 115 innings. *Lefthanded pitcher.

Pitcher, Team	W	L	Pct.	ERA	G	GS	CG	ShO	GF	Sv.	IP	H	TBF	R	ER	HR	SH	SF	HB	BB	IBB	SO	WP	Bk
Milacki, Bob, Tacoma..............	13	3	.813	2.74	23	23	5	2	0	0	164.1	131	653	62	50	12	3	1	4	39	1	117	4	1
Oquist, Mike, Las Vegas	9	4	.692	2.89	27	20	2	0	4	1	140.1	136	586	55	45	12	6	6	3	44	2	110	4	0
Klingenbeck, Scott, Salt Lake...	9	3	.750	3.11	22	22	5	2	0	0	150.2	159	635	64	52	8	4	6	3	41	2	100	9	1
Carlson, Dan, Phoenix	13	6	.684	3.44	33	15	2	0	3	1	146.2	135	604	61	56	18	5	5	2	46	0	123	3	0
Patrick, Bronswell, Tucson.......	7	3	.700	3.51	33	15	0	0	2	1	118.0	137	521	59	46	7	1	14	0	33	4	82	1	0
Holt, Chris, Tucson.................	9	6	.600	3.72	28	27	4	1	0	0	186.1	209	782	87	77	11	11	0	5	38	1	137	6	1
Dickson, Jason, Vancouver......	7	11	.389	3.80	18	18	7	0	0	0	130.1	134	553	73	55	9	2	4	5	40	1	70	4	4
Hawkins, Latroy, Salt Lake	8	8	.529	3.92	20	20	4	1	0	0	137.2	138	563	66	60	11	0	4	3	31	3	99	6	0
Bolton, Tom, Calgary*	12	5	.706	4.02	40	14	0	0	11	2	116.1	121	517	64	52	7	4	2	7	47	5	92	6	0
May, Darrell, Calgary*	7	6	.538	4.10	22	22	1	1	0	0	131.2	146	568	64	60	17	3	5	0	36	6	75	3	1
Rath, Gary, Albuquerque*........	10	11	.476	4.19	30	30	1	1	0	0	180.1	177	784	97	84	13	9	4	3	89	8	125	8	0
Harriger, Denny, Las Vegas	10	7	.588	4.22	26	25	1	0	0	0	164.1	183	711	91	77	12	3	8	7	51	1	102	4	1
Small, Aaron, Edmonton	8	6	.571	4.29	25	19	1	1	4	1	119.2	111	492	65	57	9	2	2	5	28	0	83	9	0
Soderstrom, Steve, Phoenix	7	8	.467	4.41	29	29	0	0	0	0	171.1	178	728	94	84	13	8	4	7	58	1	80	9	5
Rekar, Bryan, Col. Springs.......	8	8	.500	4.46	19	19	0	0	0	0	123.0	138	534	68	61	13	2	8	1	36	1	75	9	0

DEPARTMENTAL LEADERS: W—Carlson, 13; L—Bell, 14; Pct.—Boever, .923; G—Mintz, 59; GS—Roberts, Rath, 30; CG—Dickson, 7; ShO—Edsell, Klingenbeck, Milacki, 2; GF—Mintz, 45; SV—Mintz, 27; IP—Holt, 186.1; H—Roberts, 211; TBF—Rath, 784; R—Roberts, 115; ER—Roberts, 101; HR—Roberts, 28; SH—Holt, 1 SF—Patrick, 14; HB—Janicki, 13; BB—Rath, 89; IBB—Hubbs, 12; SO—Berumen, 143; WP—Berumen, 17; Bk.—Urso, 6.

ALL PITCHERS

*Lefthanded pitcher.

Pitcher, Team	W	L	Pct.	ERA	G	GS	CG	ShO	GF	Sv.	IP	H	TBF	R	ER	HR	SH	SF	HB	BB	IBB	SO	WP	Bk
Abbott, Jim, Vancouver*	0	2	.000	3.41	4	4	1	0	0	0	29.0	16	118	12	11	3	1	0	0	20	0	20	2	0
Abbott, Paul, Las Vegas	4	2	.667	4.18	28	0	0	0	14	7	28.0	27	124	14	13	4	3	1	1	12	4	37	4	0
Acre, Mark, Edmonton	6	2	.750	2.09	39	0	0	0	28	6	43.0	33	175	11	10	1	3	1	0	16	5	50	1	1
Adams, Willie, Edmonton.........	10	4	.714	3.78	19	19	3	1	0	0	112.0	95	466	49	47	12	1	1	6	39	2	80	4	1
Agosto, Juan, Calgary*............	0	0	.000	3.67	24	0	0	0	7	0	27.0	28	123	16	11	4	1	1	1	12	3	10	1	1
Alston, Garvin, Col. Springs.....	1	4	.200	5.77	35	0	0	0	26	14	34.1	47	171	23	22	3	1	0	1	27	0	36	2	0
Ausanio, Joe, Col. Springs.......	1	1	.500	4.34	13	1	0	0	6	0	18.2	18	84	10	9	2	0	2	0	10	2	18	2	0
Ayala, Bobby, Tacoma	0	0	.000	0.00	1	0	0	0	0	0	1.0	0	4	0	0	0	0	0	0	1	0	1	0	0
Backlund, Brett, Calgary	3	2	.600	6.00	7	7	0	0	0	0	39.0	47	179	26	26	4	0	3	1	16	1	16	7	0

tcher, Team	W	L	Pct.	ERA	G	GS	CG	ShO	GF	Sv.	IP	H	TBF	R	ER	HR	SH	SF	HB	BB	IBB	SO	WP	Bk.
ailey, Roger, Col. Springs	4	4	.500	6.29	9	9	0	0	0	0	48.2	60	214	34	34	5	0	3	2	20	0	27	2	0
arcelo, Marc, Salt Lake	2	2	.500	6.52	12	9	0	0	1	0	59.1	82	267	45	43	8	4	3	3	17	1	34	4	0
arton, Shawn, Phoenix*	4	4	.500	4.74	44	0	0	0	15	2	49.1	52	213	27	26	1	4	0	1	19	4	27	1	0
autista, Jose, Phoenix	2	2	.500	4.35	6	6	0	0	0	0	39.1	41	159	19	19	1	0	1	4	5	0	18	0	0
eckett, Robbie, Col. Springs*	0	2	.000	2.19	12	0	0	0	4	1	12.1	6	55	6	3	0	1	0	1	11	0	15	2	0
ell, Eric, Tucson*	4	14	.222	5.65	30	21	1	0	4	0	127.1	177	599	114	80	7	6	9	1	48	4	58	4	0
ennett, Erik, Salt Lake	3	1	.750	6.38	17	0	0	0	4	0	24.0	27	114	17	17	4	0	2	2	14	1	10	0	0
erumen, Andres, Las Vegas	4	7	.364	6.11	50	0	0	0	20	1	70.2	73	342	53	48	4	4	3	6	58	9	59	17	0
ever, Joe, Calgary	12	1	.923	2.15	44	0	0	0	12	4	83.2	78	341	24	20	1	5	0	0	19	2	66	2	0
olton, Tom, Calgary*	12	5	.706	4.02	40	14	0	0	11	2	116.1	121	517	64	52	7	4	2	7	47	5	92	6	0
osio, Chris, Tacoma	0	0	.000	0.00	2	1	0	0	0	0	4.0	2	13	0	0	0	0	0	0	0	0	3	0	0
ourgeois, Steve, Phoenix	8	6	.571	3.62	20	18	2	1	0	0	97.0	112	435	50	39	6	2	4	6	42	1	65	5	1
rewer, Billy, Albuquerque*	2	2	.500	3.13	31	0	0	0	12	2	31.2	28	141	13	11	5	1	0	0	22	6	33	3	3
rewington, Jamie, Phoenix	6	9	.400	7.02	35	17	0	0	7	1	110.1	130	526	93	86	14	5	3	6	72	1	75	15	0
iscoe, John, Edmonton	5	2	.714	4.77	30	1	0	0	10	1	54.2	69	256	33	29	6	2	2	2	23	3	62	5	1
ocail, Doug, Tucson	0	1	.000	7.36	5	1	0	0	0	0	7.1	12	34	6	6	1	1	0	0	1	0	4	0	0
osnan, Jason, Tacoma*	3	1	.750	2.84	12	2	0	0	3	1	31.2	19	125	14	10	2	1	1	3	15	1	26	2	0
umley, Mike, Tucson	0	0	.000	0.00	1	0	0	0	1	0	1.0	1	4	0	0	0	0	0	0	0	0	1	0	0
unson, William, Alb.*	3	4	.429	4.47	9	9	1	0	0	0	54.1	53	239	29	27	7	2	1	2	23	1	47	2	0
ruske, Jim, Albuquerque	5	2	.714	4.06	36	0	0	0	21	4	62.0	63	270	34	28	3	3	4	3	21	6	51	1	0
urke, John, Col. Springs	2	4	.333	5.24	9	4	0	0	1	0	63.2	75	293	46	42	3	1	5	2	28	0	54	5	0
ustillos, Albert, Col. Springs	6	10	.375	5.23	33	22	1	1	2	1	144.2	167	629	91	84	26	5	2	6	44	2	95	1	2
itcher, Mike, Tacoma	1	4	.200	11.79	14	8	0	0	3	0	42.0	70	223	59	55	14	0	3	7	27	0	42	3	0
adaret, Greg, Calgary	3	0	.000	6.57	9	0	0	0	3	0	12.1	19	69	18	9	2	2	1	1	12	2	10	4	0
arlson, Dan, Phoenix	13	6	.684	3.44	33	15	2	0	3	1	146.2	135	604	61	56	18	5	5	2	46	0	123	3	0
armona, Rafael, Tacoma	0	0	.000	1.42	4	1	0	0	2	0	6.1	5	29	1	1	1	0	0	0	5	0	9	0	1
arter, Andy, Phoenix*	1	5	.167	5.54	37	8	0	0	8	0	79.2	98	373	61	49	5	2	4	5	36	2	50	7	0
ouinard, Bobby, Edmonton	10	2	.833	2.77	15	15	0	0	0	0	84.1	70	344	32	26	7	1	2	1	24	2	45	1	0
ristiansen, Jason, Calgary*	1	0	1.000	3.27	2	2	0	0	0	0	11.0	9	40	4	4	1	1	0	0	1	0	10	0	0
orrea, Ramser, Albuquerque	0	3	.000	5.75	23	0	0	0	15	1	36.0	44	170	29	23	3	1	2	0	22	4	30	3	1
orreia, Rod, Edmonton	0	0	.000	5.40	1	0	0	0	1	0	1.2	1	6	1	1	0	0	1	0	0	0	0	0	0
ummings, John, Alb.*	2	6	.250	4.14	27	9	0	0	8	2	78.1	91	342	47	36	5	5	4	3	28	1	49	3	0
spit, Jamie, Edmonton	4	5	.444	4.12	33	9	0	0	5	0	89.2	96	394	50	41	5	1	4	4	29	9	76	6	0
ault, Donnie, Tucson	0	0	.000	9.00	1	0	0	0	1	0	2.0	4	10	2	2	1	0	0	0	0	0	2	0	0
vis, Tim, Tacoma*	0	1	.000	5.29	8	1	0	0	1	0	17.0	19	78	12	10	1	3	1	0	10	2	19	1	0
avison, Scott, Tacoma	1	1	.500	0.39	17	0	0	0	16	9	23.0	13	90	2	1	0	1	0	1	6	1	23	3	0
Jean, Mike, Col. Springs	0	2	.000	5.13	30	0	0	0	17	1	40.1	52	186	24	23	3	0	0	2	21	3	31	2	0
ssens, Elmer, Calgary	2	2	.500	3.15	6	6	0	0	0	0	34.1	40	150	14	12	5	2	1	1	15	1	15	2	1
ckson, Jason, Vancouver	7	11	.389	3.81	18	18	7	0	0	0	130.1	134	553	73	55	9	2	4	5	40	1	70	4	4
shman, Glenn, Las Vegas*	6	8	.429	5.57	26	26	3	1	0	0	155.0	177	669	103	96	17	3	9	3	43	5	115	7	1
ougherty, Jim, Tucson	4	3	.571	3.50	46	0	0	0	23	1	61.2	65	269	35	24	0	1	1	2	27	3	53	2	1
ahman, Brian, Las Vegas	1	0	1.000	1.00	9	0	0	0	4	0	9.0	4	33	1	1	0	1	0	0	4	0	10	0	0
eifort, Darren, Albuquerque	5	6	.455	4.17	18	18	0	0	0	0	86.1	88	387	49	40	6	3	2	6	52	3	75	6	2
essendorfer, Kirk, Edm.	0	1	.000	5.54	10	0	0	0	2	0	13.0	23	66	11	8	1	0	0	0	3	1	10	3	0
enfield, Ken, Vancouver	2	4	.333	2.81	19	0	0	0	7	0	32.0	26	139	13	10	1	3	2	1	20	5	18	2	1
sell, Geoff, Vancouver	4	6	.400	3.43	15	15	3	2	0	0	105.0	93	437	45	40	7	5	4	3	45	1	48	2	2
s, Robert, Vancouver	2	3	.400	3.25	7	7	1	0	0	0	44.1	30	186	19	16	2	2	2	0	28	0	29	5	0
vira, Narciso, Albuquerque*	1	1	.500	4.76	3	3	0	0	0	0	17.0	19	76	12	9	1	0	1	0	9	0	14	0	0
icks, John, Calgary	1	2	.333	4.20	14	4	0	0	5	1	30.0	31	131	15	14	3	1	2	1	15	1	40	2	1
tes, Shawn, Phoenix*	9	3	.750	3.43	18	18	0	0	0	0	110.1	92	446	43	42	7	2	0	2	38	1	95	4	0
ans, Dave, Tucson	6	12	.333	5.24	43	15	0	0	12	1	111.2	120	511	77	65	8	8	3	12	47	3	80	11	0
rmer, Mike, Col. Springs*	3	3	.500	3.30	9	9	2	1	0	0	57.1	51	245	27	21	4	2	3	2	25	2	28	2	0
rnandez, Osvaldo, Tacoma*	0	0	.000	5.40	1	1	0	0	0	0	3.1	4	15	2	2	0	0	0	0	0	0	4	0	0
tcher, Paul, Edmonton	4	6	.400	2.70	38	0	0	0	6	1	83.1	66	349	28	25	8	2	1	2	41	6	76	3	0
edrickson, Scott, Col. Springs	2	2	.500	6.64	55	0	0	0	17	2	63.2	71	303	56	47	9	3	6	3	40	6	66	8	0
eehill, Mike, Vancouver	1	1	.500	9.90	7	0	0	0	3	0	10.0	16	53	11	11	1	0	1	1	8	1	5	4	0
eitas, Mike, Las Vegas	0	1	.000	3.18	3	0	0	0	2	0	5.2	8	25	2	2	1	0	0	0	1	1	1	0	0
ohwirth, Todd, Vancouver	0	1	.000	3.21	9	0	0	0	8	2	14.0	11	55	5	5	1	1	2	1	3	0	13	1	0
llaher, Kevin, Tucson	4	2	.667	4.66	35	3	0	0	6	1	87.0	88	392	50	45	5	5	6	3	45	3	81	11	1
rcia, Jose, Albuquerque	6	1	.857	4.71	44	0	0	0	17	0	78.1	97	361	49	41	10	4	1	2	40	10	34	2	0
rrison, Webster, Edmonton	0	1	1.000	0.00	1	0	0	0	1	0	1.0	1	4	0	0	0	0	0	0	0	0	0	0	0
uld, Clint, Tacoma	0	0	.000	4.50	1	1	0	0	0	0	4.0	4	20	3	2	0	0	1	2	2	0	2	0	0
eer, Ken, Calgary	5	4	.556	3.97	46	1	0	0	19	3	68.0	74	294	34	30	9	5	2	3	17	5	36	2	0
igsby, Benji, Edmonton	0	3	.000	7.25	11	3	0	0	5	0	22.1	29	104	20	18	2	0	1	2	7	2	15	4	0
msley, Jason, Vancouver	2	0	1.000	1.20	2	2	1	0	0	0	15.0	8	55	2	2	0	1	1	1	3	0	11	0	1
etterman, Lee, Tacoma*	2	2	.500	3.77	25	0	0	0	11	0	28.2	27	121	14	12	2	3	0	2	10	0	28	2	0
zman, Jose, Tacoma	0	1	.000	3.52	5	2	0	0	0	0	15.1	14	64	7	6	0	0	1	1	6	0	11	0	0
byan, John, Col. Springs	0	0	.000	4.50	1	1	0	0	0	0	4.0	2	15	2	2	1	0	0	0	1	0	4	0	0
jek, Dave, Tucson	0	0	.000	0.00	1	0	0	0	0	0	1.0	1	4	0	0	0	0	0	0	0	0	0	0	0
ncock, Lee, Cal.-Pho.*	0	2	.000	3.58	26	4	0	0	9	0	50.1	51	217	22	20	0	4	1	0	17	2	28	5	0
ncock, Ryan, Vancouver	4	6	.400	3.70	19	11	1	0	1	0	80.1	69	347	38	33	7	7	0	5	38	0	65	1	1
rikkala, Tim, Tacoma	8	12	.400	4.83	27	27	1	1	0	0	158.1	204	715	98	85	12	3	6	5	48	2	115	5	1
rkey, Mike, Albuquerque	7	11	.389	5.38	49	13	0	0	28	13	118.2	146	530	79	71	11	3	2	1	39	4	90	3	0
rriger, Denny, Las Vegas	10	7	.588	4.22	26	25	1	0	0	0	164.1	183	711	91	77	12	3	8	7	51	1	102	4	1
rris, Greg W., Las Vegas	0	0	.000	18.00	1	1	0	0	0	0	4.0	11	26	9	8	3	0	0	0	3	0	2	0	0
rris, Pep, Vancouver	9	3	.750	4.56	18	18	1	0	0	0	118.1	135	517	67	60	12	6	2	3	46	0	61	2	2
rtgraves, Dean, Tucson*	2	1	.667	1.89	18	0	0	0	9	4	19.0	17	79	6	4	1	0	1	0	8	1	13	1	0
wblitzel, Mike, Col. Springs	7	6	.538	5.00	26	18	0	0	5	1	117.0	131	501	76	65	17	4	4	5	27	2	75	2	0
wkins, Latroy, Salt Lake	9	8	.529	3.92	26	20	4	1	0	0	137.2	138	563	66	60	11	0	4	3	31	3	99	6	0
nderson, Ryan, Alb.	0	0	.000	7.94	3	0	0	0	1	0	5.2	5	31	9	5	0	0	1	0	6	0	7	1	2
nry, Dwayne, Col. Springs	1	4	.200	7.71	28	0	0	0	10	0	39.2	43	188	38	34	6	2	2	3	30	0	33	5	1
redia, Julian, Phoenix	0	5	.000	4.91	52	2	1	0	27	4	69.2	71	299	40	38	12	3	7	6	23	1	59	3	0

Pitcher, Team	W	L	Pct.	ERA	G	GS	CG	ShO	GF	Sv.	IP	H	TBF	R	ER	HR	SH	SF	HB	BB	IBB	SO	WP
Herges, Matt, Albuquerque	4	1	.800	2.60	10	4	2	1	1	0	34.2	33	140	11	10	2	2	2	0	14	0	15	1
Hermanson, Dustin, Las Vegas	1	4	.200	3.13	42	0	0	0	35	21	46.0	41	208	20	16	3	1	0	1	27	7	54	2
Holdridge, David, Vancouver	2	1	.667	4.63	29	0	0	0	17	1	35.0	39	163	19	18	4	0	2	2	23	2	26	3
Holt, Chris, Tucson	9	6	.600	3.72	28	27	4	1	0	0	186.1	209	782	87	77	11	11	0	5	38	1	137	6
Hook, Chris, Phoenix	7	10	.412	4.78	32	20	0	0	3	0	128.0	139	560	75	68	18	7	3	6	51	1	70	9
Hope, John, Calgary	4	7	.364	4.82	23	21	0	0	0	0	125.0	147	561	74	67	11	6	11	7	49	3	71	6
Hubbs, Dan, Albuquerque	7	1	.875	4.76	49	0	0	0	15	2	75.2	89	356	51	40	4	0	3	3	47	12	82	2
Hudek, John, Tucson	1	0	1.000	3.10	17	2	0	0	13	4	20.1	17	86	8	7	2	1	0	1	8	0	26	1
Humphrey, Rich, Tucson	1	1	.500	10.80	10	0	0	0	7	0	13.1	23	71	20	16	3	0	2	1	7	0	8	4
Hurtado, Edwin, Tacoma	1	2	.333	3.73	5	4	0	0	1	0	31.1	23	123	13	13	5	1	1	0	12	1	26	3
Janicki, Pete, Vancouver	2	9	.182	6.75	31	14	0	0	10	1	104.0	135	485	82	78	15	5	4	13	37	1	86	4
Johnstone, John, Tucson	3	3	.500	3.42	45	1	0	0	17	5	55.1	59	249	27	21	2	3	3	1	22	2	70	3
Jones, Bobby, Col. Springs*	2	8	.200	4.97	57	0	0	0	17	3	88.2	88	410	54	49	8	5	2	4	63	4	78	7
Jones, Calvin, Albuquerque	0	0	.000	4.50	10	0	0	0	5	0	12.0	11	58	6	6	0	0	0	1	12	1	15	1
Jones, Todd, Tucson	0	0	.000	0.00	1	0	0	0	0	0	2.0	1	7	1	0	0	0	0	0	2	0	0	1
Kellner, Frank, Tucson	0	0	.000	0.00	1	0	0	0	1	0	1.0	0	3	0	0	0	0	0	0	0	0	2	0
Kester, Tim, Tucson	0	1	.000	43.20	1	1	0	0	0	0	1.2	8	15	8	8	1	1	1	0	1	0	1	0
Klingenbeck, Scott, Salt Lake	9	3	.750	3.11	22	22	5	2	0	0	150.2	159	635	64	52	8	4	6	3	41	2	100	9
Klink, Joe, Tacoma*	1	0	1.000	4.05	7	0	0	0	3	0	6.2	9	32	3	3	0	1	1	1	3	0	4	0
Konieczki, Dom, Salt Lake*	0	0	.000	18.00	4	0	0	0	2	0	3.0	8	23	7	6	0	0	0	0	5	0	2	2
Konuszewski, Dennis, Calgary	0	0	.000	24.30	3	0	0	0	2	0	3.1	13	28	11	9	0	0	0	0	5	0	0	0
Kramer, Tom, Col. Springs	8	4	.667	5.37	41	10	0	0	17	4	112.1	129	512	74	67	16	5	5	0	47	3	79	4
Kubinski, Tim, Edmonton*	0	0	.000	0.00	1	0	0	0	1	0	1.0	1	4	0	0	0	0	0	0	1	0	0	0
Lagarde, Joe, Albuquerque	0	0	.000	5.25	10	0	0	0	4	0	12.0	14	59	7	7	2	1	0	2	9	2	11	4
Leftwich, Phil, Vancouver	6	6	.500	5.15	19	19	3	0	0	0	110.0	113	477	75	63	14	3	6	8	41	1	87	7
Legault, Kevin, Salt Lake	5	4	.556	5.36	50	0	0	0	13	0	80.2	100	353	51	48	10	3	3	0	24	2	57	4
Leskanic, Curt, Col. Springs	0	0	.000	3.00	3	0	0	0	2	0	3.0	5	14	1	1	0	0	0	0	1	0	2	0
Lewis, Scott, Las Vegas	3	9	.250	5.34	29	21	2	1	2	0	150.0	174	645	96	89	22	6	4	6	36	3	109	3
Loaiza, Esteban, Calgary	3	4	.429	4.02	12	11	1	1	0	0	69.1	61	288	34	31	5	3	6	3	25	2	38	0
Loiselle, Rich, Tuc.-Cal.	4	4	.500	3.43	13	13	1	1	0	0	84.0	92	379	48	32	4	3	0	4	27	1	72	0
Long, Joey, Las Vegas*	3	3	.500	4.24	32	0	0	0	13	1	34.0	39	156	21	16	2	2	3	0	23	3	23	5
Lopez, Rene, Salt Lake	0	0	.000	0.00	1	0	0	0	1	0	1.0	2	5	0	0	0	0	0	0	0	0	0	0
Lorraine, Andrew, Edmonton*	8	10	.444	5.68	30	25	0	0	0	0	141.0	181	640	95	89	19	4	5	4	46	2	73	5
Lovullo, Torey, Edmonton	0	0	.000	4.50	2	0	0	0	1	0	4.0	3	19	2	2	0	1	0	1	3	0	0	1
Lowe, Derek, Tacoma	6	9	.400	4.54	17	16	1	1	0	0	105.0	118	463	64	53	7	4	5	3	37	1	54	1
Mahomes, Pat, Salt Lake	3	1	.750	3.74	22	2	0	0	20	7	33.2	32	143	14	14	0	1	0	2	12	0	41	1
Martin, Tom, Tucson*	0	0	.000	0.00	5	0	0	0	3	0	6.0	6	25	0	0	0	0	0	0	2	2	1	0
May, Darrell, Calgary*	7	6	.538	4.10	23	22	1	1	0	0	131.2	146	558	64	60	17	3	5	0	36	6	75	3
McCarthy, Greg, Tacoma*	4	2	.667	3.29	39	0	0	0	14	4	68.1	58	317	31	25	2	3	1	5	53	2	90	11
Meacham, Rusty, Tacoma	2	1	.667	2.29	7	2	0	0	2	2	19.2	13	78	7	5	0	0	0	1	5	0	20	1
Menhart, Paul, Tacoma	0	3	.000	11.08	6	6	0	0	0	0	26.0	53	142	33	32	4	0	3	1	16	0	12	3
Milacki, Bob, Tacoma	13	3	.813	2.74	23	23	5	2	0	0	164.1	131	653	62	50	12	3	1	4	39	1	117	4
Milchin, Mike, Salt Lake*	0	0	.000	3.68	19	0	0	0	6	2	22.0	21	99	9	9	0	1	2	1	11	3	18	4
Miller, Travis, Salt Lake*	8	10	.444	4.83	27	27	1	0	0	0	160.1	187	709	97	86	17	2	6	7	57	1	143	6
Mimbs, Mark, Albuquerque*	8	8	.500	4.59	34	23	1	1	1	0	151.0	165	656	93	77	14	4	2	3	43	2	136	7
Minor, Blas, Tacoma	1	2	.333	8.38	7	0	0	0	6	1	9.2	15	45	11	9	1	0	1	0	3	1	8	0
Mintz, Steve, Phoenix	3	5	.375	5.37	59	0	0	0	45	27	57.0	63	256	39	34	6	1	3	2	25	3	35	5
Misuraca, Mike, Salt Lake	1	2	.333	6.27	18	2	0	0	4	1	37.1	50	173	33	26	4	1	3	0	16	2	25	3
Mlicki, Doug, Tucson	5	11	.313	4.72	26	26	0	0	0	0	137.1	171	624	89	72	9	4	9	4	41	2	98	12
Montgomery, Steve, Edm.	2	0	1.000	2.89	36	0	0	0	14	1	56.0	51	230	19	18	7	2	0	1	12	1	40	1
Munoz, Mike, Col. Springs*	1	1	.500	2.03	10	0	0	0	4	3	13.1	8	52	3	3	0	1	0	0	6	0	13	0
Nied, David, Col. Springs	3	8	.273	12.27	16	16	0	0	0	0	62.1	116	334	92	85	16	1	8	3	32	0	53	1
Norris, Joe, Salt Lake	1	1	.500	5.79	21	0	0	0	5	2	37.1	48	174	27	24	3	3	1	0	17	0	38	4
Novoa, Rafael, Vancouver*	1	1	.500	7.11	13	0	0	0	6	1	12.2	19	63	10	10	3	0	0	2	5	0	10	0
Oquist, Mike, Las Vegas	9	4	.692	2.89	27	20	2	0	4	1	140.1	136	586	55	45	12	6	6	3	44	2	110	4
Osuna, Al, Las Vegas*	1	0	1.000	2.30	11	0	0	0	3	0	15.2	9	64	6	4	2	0	0	0	5	0	17	1
Osuna, Antonio, Albuquerque	0	0	.000	0.00	1	0	0	0	1	0	1.0	2	4	0	0	0	0	0	0	0	0	1	0
Parra, Jose, Salt Lake	5	3	.625	5.11	23	1	0	0	11	8	44.0	51	192	25	25	2	3	2	1	13	2	26	1
Patrick, Bronswell, Tucson	7	3	.700	3.51	33	15	0	0	2	1	118.0	137	521	59	46	7	1	14	0	33	4	82	1
Pedraza, Rod, Col. Springs	1	1	.500	8.36	6	5	0	0	0	0	28.0	39	125	26	26	3	1	0	2	4	0	13	0
Pennington, Brad, Van.*	3	0	1.000	4.23	11	2	0	0	1	1	27.2	20	124	20	13	2	0	1	0	22	0	43	1
Peters, Chris, Calgary*	1	1	.500	0.98	4	4	0	0	0	0	27.2	18	102	3	3	0	1	1	0	8	1	16	1
Phillips, Tony, Tacoma	1	3	.250	6.40	21	3	0	0	9	1	52.0	70	233	40	37	10	1	4	3	9	1	24	0
Phoenix, Steve, Calgary	1	1	.500	1.69	10	1	0	0	3	0	16.0	16	68	8	3	3	0	3	1	5	1	9	0
Pickett, Ricky, Phoenix*	0	3	.000	8.64	8	0	0	0	2	0	8.1	12	43	8	8	1	0	0	1	5	0	7	1
Pirkl, Greg, Tacoma	0	0	.000	0.00	2	0	0	0	2	0	5.2	1	19	0	0	0	0	0	0	0	0	2	0
Pisciotta, Marc, Calgary	2	7	.222	4.11	57	0	0	0	27	1	65.2	71	308	38	30	3	1	2	2	46	8	46	7
Prieto, Ariel, Edmonton	3	0	1.000	0.57	3	3	0	0	0	0	15.2	11	61	1	1	0	0	0	0	6	0	18	1
Pyc, Dave, Albuquerque*	2	3	.400	9.17	13	4	0	0	2	0	35.1	53	179	39	36	4	1	1	5	19	3	27	2
Rath, Gary, Albuquerque*	10	11	.476	4.19	30	30	1	1	0	0	180.1	177	784	97	84	13	9	4	3	89	8	125	8
Redman, Mark, Salt Lake*	0	0	.000	9.00	1	1	0	0	0	0	4.0	7	21	4	4	1	0	0	1	2	0	4	0
Rekar, Bryan, Col. Springs	8	8	.500	4.46	19	19	0	0	0	0	123.0	138	534	68	61	13	2	8	1	36	1	75	9
Ritchie, Todd, Salt Lake	0	4	.000	5.47	16	0	0	0	4	0	24.2	27	113	15	15	5	2	1	1	11	0	19	4
Roberts, Brett, Salt Lake	9	7	.563	5.40	31	30	2	1	1	0	168.1	211	772	115	101	28	2	5	9	71	0	86	7
Rodriguez, Felix, Albuquerque	3	9	.250	5.53	27	19	0	0	1	0	107.1	111	476	70	66	17	7	4	9	60	1	65	5
Rose, Scott, Edmonton	4	4	.500	2.91	50	0	0	0	41	10	55.2	57	239	21	18	2	4	2	1	16	4	20	4
Rosselli, Joe, Vancouver*	2	3	.400	2.91	47	0	0	0	18	3	58.2	53	253	22	19	3	5	2	0	26	3	37	4
Ruebel, Matt, Calgary*	5	3	.625	4.60	13	13	1	0	0	0	76.1	89	338	43	39	8	4	3	3	28	2	48	0
Rueter, Kirk, Phoenix*	1	2	.333	3.51	5	5	0	0	0	0	25.2	25	112	12	10	2	0	1	0	12	0	15	1
Ryan, Matt, Calgary	2	6	.250	5.30	51	0	0	0	44	20	52.2	70	259	39	31	4	3	1	6	28	8	35	6
Rychel, Kevin, Calgary	2	0	1.000	8.18	11	0	0	0	1	0	11.0	15	56	11	10	2	0	0	1	8	1	5	2
Schmidt, Jeff, Vancouver	0	1	.000	2.87	35	0	0	0	30	19	37.2	29	164	12	12	0	2	4	2	25	0	19	7

tcher, Team	W	L	Pct.	ERA	G	GS	CG	ShO	GF	Sv.	IP	H	TBF	R	ER	HR	SH	SF	HB	BB	IBB	SO	WP	Bk.
chmitt, Todd, Las Vegas	0	0	.000	4.50	4	0	0	0	1	0	4.0	2	22	2	2	1	0	1	1	6	0	6	0	1
anez, Rudy, Albuquerque	0	2	.000	6.52	20	0	0	0	13	6	19.1	27	98	18	14	0	1	2	1	11	1	20	3	0
rafini, Dan, Salt Lake*	7	7	.500	5.58	25	23	1	0	1	0	130.2	164	588	84	81	20	5	6	2	58	1	109	9	2
aw, Curtis, Edmonton*	0	0	.000	18.00	1	1	0	0	0	0	3.0	6	17	6	6	0	1	0	0	2	0	1	2	1
ouse, Brian, Calgary*	1	0	1.000	10.66	12	1	0	0	2	0	12.2	22	65	15	15	4	0	1	0	4	1	12	1	0
mons, Doug, Tucson*	3	4	.429	5.40	8	6	0	0	1	0	41.2	53	187	25	25	1	2	2	1	15	2	27	2	0
mons, Mitch, Salt Lake	0	0	36.00		1	0	0	0	1	0	1.0	3	8	4	4	2	0	0	0	2	0	0	0	0
nall, Aaron, Edmonton	8	6	.571	4.29	25	19	1	1	4	1	119.2	111	492	65	57	9	2	2	5	28	0	83	9	0
nall, Mark, Tucson	3	3	.500	2.08	32	0	0	0	20	7	39.0	32	166	17	9	3	3	0	0	18	4	36	4	1
nith, Pete, Las Vegas	11	9	.550	4.95	26	26	2	1	0	0	169.0	192	723	106	93	17	5	10	3	42	8	95	5	2
derstrom, Steve, Phoenix	7	8	.467	4.41	29	29	0	0	0	0	171.1	178	728	94	84	13	8	4	7	58	1	80	9	5
ringer, Dennis, Vancouver	10	3	.769	2.72	16	12	6	0	1	0	109.1	89	437	35	33	9	4	0	4	36	1	78	10	1
dham, Phil, Salt Lake	10	5	.667	6.78	33	7	0	0	8	0	78.1	100	366	63	59	8	3	2	4	40	1	54	10	1
zuki, Mac, Tacoma	0	3	.000	7.25	13	2	0	0	6	0	22.1	31	110	19	18	3	2	0	0	12	2	14	3	0
van, Russ, Las Vegas*	5	6	.455	5.08	25	20	1	0	0	0	125.2	148	565	80	71	17	4	6	4	47	6	71	10	1
vingle, Paul, Vancouver	2	2	.500	3.00	15	0	0	0	6	1	24.0	20	104	10	8	1	1	0	1	11	0	24	1	0
baka, Jeff, Tucson*	6	2	.750	2.93	41	0	0	0	16	4	43.0	40	186	16	14	2	4	1	1	21	5	51	2	0
ylor, Billy, Edmonton	0	0	.000	0.79	7	0	0	0	5	4	11.1	10	45	1	1	0	1	0	0	3	0	13	0	0
lgheder, Dave, Edmonton	8	6	.571	4.17	17	17	1	0	0	0	101.1	102	421	53	47	7	0	4	2	23	1	59	1	0
omson, John, Col. Springs	4	7	.364	5.04	11	11	0	0	0	0	69.2	76	305	45	39	6	3	1	4	26	2	62	4	1
rres, Salomon, Tacoma	7	10	.412	5.29	22	21	3	1	0	0	134.1	150	605	87	79	16	4	4	7	52	1	121	7	2
eadwell, Jody, Albuquerque	1	1	.500	7.85	5	3	0	0	0	0	18.1	30	93	18	16	4	0	3	0	10	1	16	0	0
edaway, Chad, Las Vegas	0	1	.000	0.00	1	0	0	0	1	0	0.0	1	3	1	1	0	0	0	0	2	0	0	0	0
ombley, Mike, Salt Lake	2	2	.500	2.45	24	0	0	0	20	10	36.2	24	145	12	10	3	3	0	0	10	0	38	6	0
so, Sal, Tacoma*	6	2	.750	2.35	46	0	0	0	19	3	72.2	69	302	22	19	5	4	1	1	32	1	45	2	6
ldez, Carlos, Phoenix	4	3	.571	4.98	44	0	0	0	17	5	59.2	63	276	38	33	4	4	2	4	34	5	38	6	1
nderweele, Doug, Phoenix	4	2	.667	5.36	41	3	0	0	6	0	89.0	101	397	55	53	13	4	5	2	35	4	42	4	0
nRyn, Ben, Vancouver*	3	3	.500	3.89	18	1	0	0	4	0	34.2	35	154	17	15	2	3	1	1	13	1	28	3	0
ras, Dario, Las Vegas	6	2	.750	2.90	19	1	0	0	9	1	40.1	41	165	17	13	1	3	1	0	2	2	30	2	0
no, Jake, Col. Springs	2	0	10.89		7	3	0	0	1	0	20.2	33	104	25	25	7	1	0	1	13	0	12	0	0
lone, Ron, Las Vegas*	2	1	.667	1.64	23	0	0	0	10	3	22.0	13	90	5	4	0	2	0	2	9	0	29	2	1
agner, Billy, Tucson*	6	2	.750	3.28	12	12	1	1	0	0	74.0	62	318	32	27	2	2	1	6	33	0	86	5	1
agner, Matt, Tacoma	9	2	.818	2.41	15	15	0	0	0	0	93.1	89	384	30	25	8	2	2	2	30	0	82	4	1
alker, Pete, Las Vegas	5	1	.833	6.83	26	0	0	0	8	0	27.2	37	129	22	21	7	1	4	0	14	2	23	0	0
ll, Donne, Tucson	3	3	.500	4.13	8	8	0	0	0	0	52.1	67	224	30	24	2	1	3	0	6	0	36	3	0
asdin, John, Edmonton	2	1	.667	4.14	9	9	0	0	0	0	50.0	52	214	23	23	6	1	0	1	17	2	30	0	1
shburn, Jarrod, Van.*	0	2	.000	10.80	2	2	0	0	0	0	8.1	12	48	16	10	1	0	0	0	12	0	5	1	0
atkins, Scott, Salt Lake*	4	6	.400	7.69	47	0	0	0	29	1	50.1	60	244	46	43	6	5	3	2	34	5	43	3	1
eaver, Eric, Albuquerque	1	4	.200	5.40	13	8	0	0	0	0	46.2	63	225	39	28	5	2	1	3	22	0	38	3	0
eber, Weston, Las Vegas	2	1	.667	6.30	7	0	0	0	3	0	10.0	12	47	7	7	1	0	0	0	8	2	4	0	0
ertz, Bill, Tacoma	0	3	.000	5.01	16	2	0	0	8	0	32.1	46	162	21	18	2	0	0	1	23	2	25	3	0
nite, Billy, Col. Springs	0	0	.000	13.50	1	0	0	0	1	0	0.2	3	6	1	1	0	0	0	0	1	0	0	0	0
lliams, Shad, Vancouver	6	2	.750	3.96	15	13	1	1	1	0	75.0	73	321	36	33	8	4	0	2	28	0	57	2	0
lliams, Todd, Edmonton	5	3	.625	5.50	35	10	0	0	7	0	91.2	125	427	71	56	4	2	5	3	37	3	33	3	0
lson, Gary, Calgary	6	9	.400	5.08	27	27	1	0	0	0	161.1	209	725	105	91	18	6	6	9	44	1	88	2	1
tasick, Jay, Edmonton	0	0	.000	4.15	6	0	0	0	5	2	8.2	9	39	4	4	1	1	1	1	6	0	9	2	1
tte, Trey, Tacoma	2	2	.500	2.15	35	0	0	0	20	7	46.0	47	191	12	11	2	3	3	1	13	2	22	1	0
ojciechowski, Steve, Edm.*	4	3	.571	3.73	11	11	1	1	0	0	60.1	56	257	32	25	3	2	2	2	21	1	46	4	0
olcott, Bob, Tacoma	0	2	.000	7.30	3	3	0	0	0	0	12.1	17	58	13	10	5	0	1	0	3	0	16	1	0
ood, Jason, Edmonton	0	0	.000	0.00	1	0	0	0	0	0	2.0	1	10	0	0	0	0	0	0	3	0	1	0	0
right, Jamey, Col. Springs	9	4	.667	2.72	9	9	0	0	0	0	59.2	53	246	20	18	3	0	1	2	22	0	40	1	0
ung, Anthony, Tucson	1	0	1.000	3.86	4	1	0	0	0	0	4.2	3	22	3	2	1	0	0	0	5	2	3	0	0
nmerman, Mike, Tacoma	1	1	.500	9.17	13	0	0	0	6	0	17.2	23	92	19	18	1	0	2	4	13	0	13	2	0

COMBINATION SHUTOUTS: **Albuquerque (3)**—Rath-Gargia, Rath-Hubbs-Seanez, Brunson-Harkey. **Calgary (4)**—May-Hancock, Peters-Boever-Bolton, Bolton-ever-Ericks, Loiselle-Boever-Agosto-Ryan. **Colorado Springs (4)**—Burke-Bustillos, Burke-Jones-Henry-Alston, Write-Jones, Thomson-Alston. **Edmonton (6)**—ouinard-Taylor, Wasdin-Fletcher-Rose, Telgheder-Rose, Daspit-Fletcher, Small-Fletcher-Acre, Prieto-Daspit-Montgomery-Acre. **Las Vegas (4)**—Smith-Long-manson, Oquist-Harriger-Berumen, Harriger-Walker-Drahman, Swan-Osuna-Hermanson. **Phoenix (9)**—Estes-Hook-Barton-Heredia, Estes-Heredia, Estes-Barton, ok-Carlson, Brewington-Carlson-Barton-Mintz, Brewington-Carlson, Estes-Carter-Carlson-Barton-Heredia, Brewington-Barton-Vanderweele-Mintz, Soderstrom-ncock. **Salt Lake (1)**—Parra-Norris. **Tacoma (3)**—Milacki-Klink, Davis-Witte-Urso-Davidson, Meacham-Guetterman. **Tucson (4)**—Evans-Dougherty-Humphrey, icki-Gallaher-Tabaka, Holt-Tabaka-Hudek, Patrick-Dougherty. **Vancouver (2)**—Grimsley-Schmidt, Springer-Frohwirth.

NO-HIT GAMES: Small, Edmonton, defeated Vancouver, 6-0, August 8.

PITCHERS WITH TWO OR MORE TEAMS

tcher, Team	W	L	Pct.	ERA	G	GS	CG	ShO	GF	Sv.	IP	H	TBF	R	ER	HR	SH	SF	HB	BB	IBB	SO	WP	Bk.
ncock, Lee, Calgary*	0	0	.000	1.80	9	1	0	0	3	0	15.0	9	58	3	3	0	0	0	5	2	9	1	0	
ncock, Lee, Phoenix*	0	2	.000	4.33	17	3	0	0	6	0	35.1	42	159	19	17	0	4	1	0	12	0	19	4	0
selle, Rich, Tucson	2	2	.500	2.43	5	5	1	1	0	0	33.1	28	145	20	9	1	0	0	1	11	0	31	0	0
iselle, Rich, Calgary	2	2	.500	4.09	8	8	0	0	0	0	50.2	64	234	28	23	3	3	0	3	16	1	41	0	0

1996 FIELDING

TEAM

am	Pct.	G	PO	A	E	TC	DP	PB	Team	Pct.	G	PO	A	E	TC	DP	PB
t Lake	.978	144	3855	1661	125	5641	137	10	Calgary	.973	143	3720	1625	146	5491	128	10
s Vegas	.977	140	3664	1552	123	5339	133	17	Tacoma	.973	142	3763	1508	145	5416	136	12
ncouver	.977	138	3646	1520	124	5290	145	13	Col. Springs	.970	142	3677	1491	158	5326	137	11
oenix	.976	144	3830	1616	133	5579	164	7	Albuquerque	.966	143	3786	1674	193	5653	156	15
monton	.974	142	3679	1581	141	5401	125	14	Tucson	.960	144	3742	1593	224	5559	124	23

TRIPLE PLAYS: None.

INDIVIDUAL

FIRST BASEMEN

NOTE: All caps denotes fielding-percentage leader based on 72 games for catchers, 96 for all other non-pitchers and 144 innings for pitchers. *Throws lefthanded.

Player, Team	Pct.	G	PO	A	E	TC	DP
Aude, Rich, Calgary	.991	97	872	52	8	932	75
Ball, Jeff, Tucson	.986	94	773	64	12	849	72
Batiste, Kim, Phoenix	1.000	1	16	1	0	17	5
Bonnici, James, Tacoma	.989	90	777	35	9	821	75
Brede, Brent, Salt Lake*	.996	28	249	20	1	270	28
Brumley, Mike, Tucson	.970	12	88	10	3	101	5
Busch, Mike, Albuquerque	.987	25	216	15	3	234	22
Deer, Rob, Las Vegas	.986	16	132	10	2	144	12
Diaz, Eddy, Tacoma	1.000	1	2	0	0	2	0
Drinkwater, Sean, Tacoma	1.000	1	11	0	0	11	1
Durant, Mike, Salt Lake	1.000	1	1	0	0	1	0
Ehmann, Kurt, Phoenix	1.000	1	8	1	0	9	1
Erstad, Darin, Vancouver*	1.000	3	25	6	0	31	5
Fabregas, Jorge, Vancouver	1.000	1	14	1	0	15	0
Friedman, Jason, Tacoma*	1.000	2	11	2	0	13	2
Gainer, Jay, Col. Springs*	.984	59	467	29	8	504	41
Garrison, Webster, Edmonton	.983	24	211	15	4	230	16
Giannelli, Ray, S.L.-C.S.	1.000	3	21	3	0	24	4
Glenn, Darrin, Phoenix	1.000	2	3	0	0	3	1
Goff, Jerry, Tucson	.994	19	142	11	1	154	14
Groppuso, Mike, Tucson	1.000	4	31	1	0	32	2
Gubanich, Creighton, Edmonton	.983	9	52	5	1	58	4
Helton, Todd, Col. Springs*	.988	20	143	16	2	161	16
Hernandez, Carlos, Albuquerque	.933	2	11	3	1	15	3
Hocking, Denny, Salt Lake	1.000	1	10	0	0	10	0
Hunter, Brian, Tacoma*	1.000	4	22	2	0	24	3
Ibanez, Raul, Tacoma	1.000	2	4	0	0	4	0
Kellner, Frank, Tucson	1.000	11	53	4	0	57	8
Kennedy, David, Col. Springs	.987	78	582	42	8	632	64
Kirkpatrick, Jay, Albuquerque	.987	27	145	12	2	159	18
Konerko, Paul, Albuquerque	1.000	4	30	0	0	30	2
Lesher, Brian, Edmonton*	.990	71	634	41	7	682	52
Lovullo, Torey, Edmonton	.991	13	96	11	1	108	8
Marrero, Oreste, Albuquerque*	.991	89	689	63	7	759	71
Marx, Tim, Calgary	1.000	7	20	1	0	21	2
Maurer, Ron, Albuquerque	1.000	7	42	4	0	46	2
McCarty, Dave, Phoenix*	1.000	2	24	0	0	24	3
Melendez, Dan, Albuquerque*	.985	27	119	9	2	130	13
Miller, Damian, Salt Lake	1.000	2	11	1	0	12	1
Molina, Izzy, Edmonton	.955	4	20	1	1	22	2
Montgomery, Ray, Tucson	1.000	2	10	1	0	11	1
Ogden, Jamie, Salt Lake*	.990	83	759	44	8	811	58
Parker, Rick, Albuquerque	.875	2	13	1	2	16	4
Peltier, Dan, Phoenix*	.993	46	407	33	3	443	46
Pirkl, Greg, Tacoma	.990	46	385	32	4	421	37
PRITCHETT, Chris, Vancouver	.995	125	1107	98	6	1211	107
Quinlan, Tom, Salt Lake	.997	38	333	22	1	356	28
Ready, Randy, Las Vegas	.909	1	10	0	1	11	0
Reimer, Kevin, Tacoma	.972	4	33	2	1	36	2
Roberge, J.P., Albuquerque	1.000	2	5	3	0	8	2
Russo, Paul, Las Vegas	.986	9	68	3	1	72	13
Scott, Gary, Las Vegas	1.000	1	4	0	0	4	0
Secrist, Reed, Calgary	.993	30	271	16	2	289	26
Sheldon, Scott, Edmonton	.977	19	163	10	4	177	19
Simms, Mike, Tucson	.967	17	138	9	5	152	12
Simonton, Benji, Phoenix	1.000	1	9	0	0	9	1
Spiezio, Scott, Edmonton	.966	11	83	2	3	88	5
Stairs, Matt, Edmonton	.947	4	17	1	1	19	2
Sveum, Dale, Calgary	.994	28	150	10	1	161	6
Tatum, Jimmy, Las Vegas	1.000	18	121	13	0	134	10
Tejero, Fausto, Vancouver	1.000	1	10	0	0	10	0
Thompson, Jason, Las Vegas*	.992	109	952	62	8	1022	88
Tredaway, Chad, Las Vegas	1.000	2	9	1	0	10	0
Turner, Chris, Vancouver	1.000	9	85	6	0	91	9
Wilson, Desi, Phoenix*	.991	98	842	52	8	902	92
Wood, Jason, Edmonton	.976	3	39	1	1	41	3

FIRST BASEMEN WITH TWO OR MORE TEAMS

Player, Team	Pct.	G	PO	A	E	TC	DP
Giannelli, Ray, Salt Lake	1.000	1	8	1	0	9	2
Giannelli, Ray, Col. Springs	1.000	2	13	2	0	15	2

SECOND BASEMEN

Player, Team	Pct.	G	PO	A	E	TC	DP
Bridges, Kary, Tucson	.957	34	54	81	6	141	21
Brumley, Mike, Tucson	1.000	1	3	1	0	4	1

Player, Team	Pct.	G	PO	A	E	TC	D
Bruno, Julio, Las Vegas	.976	71	127	195	8	330	3
Bush, Homer, Las Vegas	.969	31	67	88	5	160	2
Canizaro, Jay, Phoenix	.986	56	123	167	4	294	4
Carter, Jeff, Col. Springs	.967	41	76	99	6	181	2
Castro, Juan, Albuquerque	1.000	1	5	1	0	6	
Counsell, Craig, Col. Springs	.962	16	27	48	3	78	
Demetral, Chris, Albuquerque	.971	56	75	123	6	204	2
DeLeon, Roberto, Phoenix	.750	1	2	1	1	4	
Diaz, Eddy, Tacoma	.972	21	38	66	3	107	1
Diaz, Freddy, Vancouver	.981	9	24	29	1	54	
Easley, Damion, Vancouver	1.000	2	6	4	0	10	
Finn, John, Calgary	.987	50	85	139	3	227	2
Florez, Tim, Phoenix	.982	87	186	256	8	450	7
Fonville, Chad, Albuquerque	.958	6	9	14	1	24	
FORBES, P.J., Vancouver	.986	107	221	281	7	509	6
Garcia, Carlos, Calgary	1.000	1	2	2	0	4	
Garrison, Webster, Edmonton	1.000	17	33	41	0	74	
Giannelli, Ray, Col. Springs	1.000	1	0	1	0	1	
Grebeck, Brian, Vancouver	1.000	15	30	44	0	74	1
Guerrero, Wilton, Albuquerque	.973	66	137	188	9	334	4
Hajek, Dave, Tucson	.959	73	146	225	16	387	5
Hocking, Denny, Salt Lake	1.000	1	0	1	0	1	
Hubbard, Trent, Col. Springs	.963	17	29	48	3	80	1
Huson, Jeff, Col. Springs	1.000	9	24	27	0	51	
Ingram, Garey, Albuquerque	.800	2	3	1	1	5	
Kellner, Frank, Tucson	.957	7	11	11	1	23	
Lopez, Luis, Las Vegas	.983	13	32	26	1	59	
Lovullo, Torey, Edmonton	.970	8	10	22	1	33	
Martinez, Ray, Vancouver	.981	10	26	26	1	53	1
Maurer, Ron, Albuquerque	1.000	6	15	14	0	29	
McDonald, Jason, Edmonton	.962	122	254	352	24	630	7
Millette, Joe, Calgary	.920	15	22	24	4	50	
Mora, Melvin, Tucson	1.000	2	3	3	0	6	
Mueller, Bill, Phoenix	1.000	12	25	30	0	55	
Parker, Rick, Albuquerque	.959	20	34	60	4	98	2
Polcovich, Kevin, Calgary	.993	37	56	88	1	145	
Pozo, Arquimedez, Tacoma	.989	18	29	62	1	92	
Pye, Eddie, Tucson	.969	46	74	113	6	193	2
Quinlan, Tom, Salt Lake	.965	12	22	33	2	57	1
Raabe, Brian, Salt Lake	.995	83	163	252	2	417	5
Ready, Randy, Las Vegas	.962	12	24	27	2	53	
Relaford, Desi, Tacoma	.964	73	148	249	15	412	5
Richardson, Brian, Albuquerque	1.000	3	1	1	0	2	
Rios, Eduardo, Albuquerque	.955	12	15	27	2	44	
Sheets, Andy, Tacoma	1.000	5	4	16	0	20	
Sheldon, Scott, Edmonton	1.000	3	6	10	0	16	
Simons, Mitch, Salt Lake	.978	19	41	49	2	92	1
Sveum, Dale, Calgary	.976	28	49	75	3	127	1
Tredaway, Chad, Las Vegas	.957	27	49	63	5	117	1
Vazquez, Ramon, Tacoma	1.000	13	20	31	0	51	1
Walker, Todd, Salt Lake	.977	36	72	99	4	175	1
White, Billy, Col. Springs	.954	63	89	160	12	261	2
Womack, Tony, Calgary	.968	40	88	93	6	187	2
Yelding, Eric, Tacoma	.909	17	35	25	6	66	
Young, Eric, Col. Springs	.917	7	15	18	3	36	

THIRD BASEMEN

Player, Team	Pct.	G	PO	A	E	TC	D
Arias, George, Vancouver	.969	59	50	135	6	191	
Ball, Jeff, Tucson	.878	21	9	34	6	49	
Batiste, Kim, Phoenix	.878	20	12	31	6	49	
Bonnici, James, Tacoma	.733	7	5	6	4	15	
Brosius, Scott, Edmonton	.667	3	0	4	2	6	
Brumley, Mike, Tucson	.917	15	3	19	2	24	
Bruno, Julio, Las Vegas	.889	3	2	6	1	9	
Bryant, Scott, Tacoma	.889	5	1	7	1	9	
Burke, Jamie, Vancouver	.938	21	9	52	4	65	
Busch, Mike, Albuquerque	1.000	3	3	19	0	22	
Canizaro, Jay, Phoenix	.900	3	2	7	1	10	
Castellano, Pedro, Col. Springs	.963	49	49	185	9	243	
Castro, Juan, Albuquerque	.931	12	6	21	2	29	
Counsell, Craig, Col. Springs	1.000	6	2	9	0	11	
Dandridge, Brad, Albuquerque	.000	1	0	0	1	1	
DeLeon, Roberto, Phoenix	.944	11	2	15	1	18	
Diaz, Alex, Tacoma	1.000	1	2	0	0	2	
Diaz, Eddy, Tacoma	1.000	12	10	18	0	28	
Diaz, Freddy, Vancouver	.960	10	5	19	1	25	
Drinkwater, Sean, Tacoma	.941	6	2	14	1	17	
Duncan, Andres, Phoenix	1.000	2	1	4	0	5	
Ehmann, Kurt, Phoenix	.957	9	5	17	1	23	

yer, Team	Pct.	G	PO	A	E	TC	DP
ueroa, Bien, Col. Springs	.929	9	2	11	1	14	1
n, John, Calgary	.935	16	9	20	2	31	2
rez, Tim, Phoenix	.957	16	13	31	2	46	5
bes, P.J., Vancouver	.938	8	10	20	2	32	3
rison, Webster, Edmonton	.947	9	4	14	1	19	1
nnelli, Ray, S.L.-C.S.	.857	19	11	25	6	42	2
ebeck, Brian, Vancouver	.978	27	19	69	2	90	2
ppuso, Mike, Tucson	.880	39	27	68	13	108	8
ek, Dave, Tucson	.903	26	19	46	7	72	6
cking, Denny, Salt Lake	.667	1	0	2	1	3	0
bard, Trent, Col. Springs	.750	4	0	3	1	4	0
lner, Frank, Tucson	.929	10	2	11	1	14	0
nnedy, Darryl, Phoenix	.750	12	3	15	6	24	3
lesma, Aaron, Vancouver	.917	3	3	8	1	12	2
t, Billy, Albuquerque	1.000	1	0	1	0	1	0
ullo, Torey, Edmonton	1.000	3	4	6	0	10	0
urer, Ron, Albuquerque	.951	32	10	48	3	61	6
lette, Joe, Calgary	.907	19	10	29	4	43	0
ra, Melvin, Tucson	.889	33	16	64	10	90	2
eller, Bill, Phoenix	.975	85	50	180	6	236	25
ker, Rick, Albuquerque	.833	7	3	7	2	12	1
zo, Arquimedez, Tacoma	.930	74	44	115	12	171	17
nce, Tom, Albuquerque	1.000	3	2	2	0	4	0
e, Eddie, Tucson	.952	31	13	46	3	62	3
nlan, Tom, Salt Lake	.949	52	43	126	9	178	7
abe, Brian, Salt Lake	1.000	5	5	6	0	11	1
ady, Randy, Las Vegas	.500	1	1	0	1	2	0
hardson, Brian, Albuquerque	.908	95	63	183	25	271	14
s, Eduardo, Albuquerque	1.000	1	1	3	0	4	1
erge, J.P., Albuquerque	.900	4	1	8	1	10	1
ssy, Rico, Las Vegas	1.000	1	1	1	0	2	0
sso, Paul, Las Vegas	.943	47	31	68	6	105	11
nders, Doug, Tacoma	.951	36	36	81	6	123	5
tt, Gary, Las Vegas	.918	57	29	106	12	147	8
rist, Reed, Calgary	.910	83	43	169	21	233	16
rperson, Mike, Las Vegas	.941	29	21	75	6	102	8
ets, Andy, Tacoma	1.000	2	3	7	0	10	0
ldon, Scott, Edmonton	1.000	3	2	7	0	9	1
EZIO, Scott, Edmonton	.970	129	91	302	12	405	18
um, Dale, Calgary	.963	41	27	76	4	107	9
im, Jimmy, Las Vegas	1.000	4	0	6	0	6	0
daway, Chad, Las Vegas	.915	22	13	30	4	47	3
ner, Chris, Vancouver	.875	12	6	22	4	32	4
ker, Todd, Salt Lake	.940	87	57	177	15	249	12
te, Billy, Col. Springs	.953	25	8	33	2	43	3
ds, Ken, Phoenix	1.000	7	4	15	0	19	1
ing, Eric, Tacoma	.500		0	1	1	2	1

THIRD BASEMEN WITH TWO OR MORE TEAMS

yer, Team	Pct.	G	PO	A	E	TC	DP
nnelli, Ray, Salt Lake	1.000	5	1	7	0	8	1
nnelli, Ray, Col. Springs	.824	14	10	18	6	34	1

SHORTSTOPS

yer, Team	Pct.	G	PO	A	E	TC	DP
erson, Cliff, Albuquerque	.951	60	74	180	13	267	36
lia, Rich, Phoenix	.972	7	10	25	1	36	6
sta, Tony, Edmonton	.973	57	75	213	8	296	41
ste, Kim, Phoenix	.894	12	16	26	5	47	8
nley, Mike, Tucson	.916	49	57	129	17	203	23
izaro, Jay, Phoenix	.958	41	69	134	9	212	30
tro, Juan, Albuquerque	1.000	4	6	11	0	17	2
eia, Rod, Edmonton	.963	6	16	10	1	27	2
nsell, Craig, Col. Springs	.929	5	6	7	1	14	0
ado, Wilson, Phoenix	.975	12	30	47	2	79	13
y, Eddy, Tacoma	.962	65	87	193	11	291	37
, Freddy, Vancouver	.900	8	12	24	4	40	8
kwater, Sean, Tacoma	1.000	1	3	5	0	8	2
can, Andres, Phoenix	.906	30	33	83	12	128	12
ey, Damion, Vancouver	.947	10	14	22	2	38	4
ann, Kurt, Phoenix	.933	29	39	72	8	119	12
, John, Calgary	.938	2	4	11	1	16	4
ez, Tim, Phoenix	1.000	1	0	1	0	1	0
ville, Chad, Albuquerque	.944	18	30	55	5	90	7
, Eddy, Tacoma	1.000	1	4	7	0	11	1
es, P.J., Vancouver	1.000	1	4	7	0	11	1
ne, Greg, Albuquerque	1.000	4	7	9	0	16	5
cia, Carlos, Calgary	1.000	1	1	3	0	4	0
ison, Webster, Edmonton	.938	15	15	46	4	65	8
beck, Brian, Vancouver	.951	22	33	64	5	102	20
rrero, Wilton, Albuquerque	.943	34	46	118	10	174	24
k, Dave, Tucson	.901	27	39	61	11	111	15
ing, Denny, Salt Lake	.978	22	26	65	2	93	12

Player, Team	Pct.	G	PO	A	E	TC	DP
Holbert, Ray, Tucson	.919	27	37	65	9	111	10
Huson, Jeff, Col. Springs	.964	5	12	15	1	28	3
Johnson, Keith, Albuquerque	1.000	4	8	11	0	19	1
Kellner, Frank, Tucson	.944	64	79	173	15	267	36
Ledesma, Aaron, Vancouver	.955	93	147	253	19	419	55
Lopez, Luis, Las Vegas	.960	9	7	17	1	25	3
Martinez, Ray, Vancouver	.857	12	17	25	7	49	6
Maurer, Ron, Albuquerque	.932	35	50	115	12	177	28
Millette, Joe, Calgary	1.000	2	0	1	0	1	0
Mueller, Bill, Phoenix	.919	16	17	40	5	62	10
Perez, Neifi, Col. Springs	.963	132	244	409	25	678	91
Polcovich, Kevin, Calgary	.948	70	109	204	17	330	28
Pye, Eddie, Tucson	.750	2	2	4	2	8	2
Quinlan, Tom, Salt Lake	.921	17	31	51	7	89	13
Raabe, Brian, Salt Lake	.961	11	12	37	2	51	7
Relaford, Desi, Tacoma	.943	19	26	57	5	88	13
Richardson, Brian, Albuquerque	1.000	1	2	2	0	4	1
Rios, Eduardo, Albuquerque	.875	1	3	4	1	8	1
Rodriguez, Alex, Tacoma	.833	2	1	4	1	6	2
Rossy, Rico, Las Vegas	.969	127	163	405	18	586	76
Scott, Gary, Las Vegas	1.000	2	1	0	0	1	0
Sheets, Andy, Tacoma	.945	55	88	153	14	255	29
Sheldon, Scott, Edmonton	.954	65	86	203	14	303	39
Shipley, Craig, Las Vegas	1.000	1	0	2	0	2	0
SIMONS, Mitch, Salt Lake	.970	101	153	329	15	497	66
Tredaway, Chad, Las Vegas	.944	11	9	25	2	36	4
Vazquez, Ramon, Tacoma	.938	4	1	14	1	16	1
White, Billy, Col. Springs	.923	4	5	7	1	13	2
Womack, Tony, Calgary	.952	79	138	241	19	398	50
Woods, Ken, Phoenix	.913	14	22	41	6	69	9

OUTFIELDERS

Player, Team	Pct.	G	PO	A	E	TC	DP
Abreu, Bob, Tucson	.969	128	202	15	7	224	2
Allensworth, Jermaine, Calgary	.971	88	196	4	6	206	0
Ashley, Billy, Albuquerque	.917	7	11	0	1	12	0
Barry, Jeff, Las Vegas	.923	4	12	0	1	13	0
Batiste, Kim, Phoenix	1.000	10	4	0	0	4	0
Battle, Allen, Edmonton	.952	62	116	3	6	125	0
Beamon, Trey, Calgary	.928	99	161	7	13	181	0
Benard, Marvin, Phoenix*	1.000	4	10	0	0	10	0
Bragg, Darren, Tacoma	1.000	20	32	2	0	34	0
Brede, Brent, Salt Lake*	.964	97	155	4	6	165	1
Brumley, Mike, Tucson	.933	6	14	0	1	15	0
Bryant, Scott, Tacoma	.976	49	80	3	2	85	0
Burke, Jamie, Vancouver	1.000	7	8	0	0	8	0
Carter, Jeff, Col. Springs	1.000	4	6	1	0	7	1
Carvajal, Jovino, Vancouver	.955	61	102	4	5	111	2
Cedeno, Roger, Albuquerque	1.000	32	71	2	0	73	1
Clark, Jerald, Calgary	.937	56	99	5	7	111	1
Cockrell, Alan, Col. Springs	.973	95	173	7	5	185	2
Colbert, Craig, Las Vegas	1.000	1	1	0	0	1	0
Coleman, Vince, Vancouver	.960	12	24	0	1	25	0
Cruz, Jacob, Phoenix*	.989	116	249	11	3	263	2
Cruz, Jose, Tacoma	1.000	22	36	4	0	40	0
Cummings, Midre, Calgary	.974	80	176	9	5	190	1
Dandridge, Brad, Calgary	1.000	11	12	0	0	12	0
Dascenzo, Doug, Las Vegas*	.994	85	168	6	1	175	0
Davis, Jay, Tucson*	.958	26	45	1	2	48	0
Deer, Rob, Las Vegas	.956	58	83	3	4	90	0
Diaz, Alex, Tacoma	.975	42	74	5	2	81	0
Diaz, Eddy, Tacoma	1.000	5	6	0	0	6	0
Diaz, Freddy, Vancouver	1.000	1	6	0	0	6	0
Echevarria, Angel, Col. Springs	.978	105	168	8	4	180	0
Ehmann, Kurt, Phoenix	1.000	2	3	0	0	3	0
Erstad, Darin, Vancouver*	.994	81	159	4	1	164	1
Espinosa, Ramon, Calgary	.969	67	114	9	4	127	1
Felder, Mike, Calgary	.970	20	30	2	1	33	0
Fonville, Chad, Albuquerque	1.000	2	3	1	0	4	0
Fox, Eric, Albuquerque*	.980	28	46	2	1	49	0
Friedman, Jason, Tacoma*	1.000	2	3	0	0	3	0
Gainer, Jay, Col. Springs*	.857	8	6	0	1	7	0
Garcia, Karim, Albuquerque*	.921	80	148	4	13	165	0
Garrison, Webster, Edmonton	1.000	3	2	0	0	2	0
Giannelli, Ray, S.L.-C.S.	1.000	10	17	0	0	17	0
Grebeck, Brian, Vancouver	1.000	4	11	1	0	12	0
Hatcher, Chris, Tucson	.984	75	122	4	2	128	0
Hazlett, Steve, Salt Lake	.975	99	137	17	4	158	2
Helton, Todd, Col. Springs*	1.000	2	1	1	0	2	0
Hill, Glenallen, Phoenix	1.000	5	8	0	0	8	0
Hocking, Denny, Salt Lake	1.000	13	15	1	0	16	0
Horne, Tyrone, Edmonton	.978	45	86	1	2	89	1

Player, Team	Pct.	G	PO	A	E	TC	DP
Hubbard, Trent, Col. Springs	1.000	27	59	3	0	62	1
Hunter, Brian, Tacoma*	.963	22	23	3	1	27	0
Hunter, Brian, Tucson	1.000	3	8	0	0	8	0
Ibanez, Raul, Tacoma	.950	109	197	12	11	220	1
INGRAM, Riccardo, Las Vegas	1.000	106	198	10	0	208	3
Johnson, J.J., Salt Lake	.952	12	20	0	1	21	0
Jones, Dax, Phoenix	1.000	70	178	9	0	187	0
Jones, Terry, Col. Springs	.949	124	281	14	16	311	2
Latham, Chris, Salt Lake	.964	110	235	9	9	253	2
Lawton, Matt, Salt Lake	.936	41	88	0	6	94	0
Lee, Derek, Edmonton	.846	9	11	0	2	13	0
Lennon, Patrick, Edmonton	.939	37	57	5	4	66	0
Leonard, Mark, Salt Lake	.971	23	32	2	1	35	1
Lesher, Brian, Edmonton*	.971	44	65	3	2	70	2
List, Lou, Col. Springs	1.000	2	1	0	0	1	0
Lott, Billy, Albuquerque	.940	112	196	6	13	215	1
Lovullo, Torey, Edmonton*	.667	2	2	0	1	3	0
Marrero, Oreste, Albuquerque*	.970	28	31	1	1	33	0
Martinez, Manny, Tacoma	.975	65	181	11	5	197	3
Mashore, Damon, Edmonton	.988	48	74	7	1	82	1
Maurer, Ron, Albuquerque	1.000	3	3	0	0	3	0
McCarty, Dave, Phoenix*	1.000	4	5	1	0	6	0
McDonald, Jason, Edmonton	.980	18	48	0	1	49	0
Montgomery, Ray, Tucson	.978	93	172	7	4	183	1
Moore, Kerwin, Edmonton	.977	118	284	8	7	299	1
Mora, Melvin, Tucson	.941	29	61	3	4	68	0
Mouton, James, Tucson	1.000	1	2	0	0	2	0
Murray, Calvin, Phoenix	.991	79	207	3	2	212	2
Neill, Mike, Edmonton*	1.000	4	10	0	0	10	0
Ogden, Jamie, Salt Lake*	.977	44	81	3	2	86	0
Palmeiro, Orlando, Vancouver	.959	62	113	4	5	122	0
Parker, Rick, Albuquerque	.972	24	32	3	1	36	0
Peguero, Julio, Tacoma	.995	99	195	6	1	202	3
Peltier, Dan, Phoenix*	1.000	17	25	2	0	27	0
Pennyfeather, William, Vancouver	.972	90	198	13	6	217	6
Plantier, Phil, Edmonton	.864	20	18	1	3	22	0
Poe, Charles, Edmonton	1.000	3	5	1	0	6	0
Powell, Dante, Phoenix	1.000	2	4	0	0	4	0
Prieto, Chris, Las Vegas*	1.000	5	12	2	0	14	2
Pritchett, Chris, Vancouver	1.000	3	9	0	0	9	0
Pulliam, Harvey, Col. Springs	.935	74	124	6	9	139	0
Ramos, Ken, Tucson*	.956	92	165	10	8	183	0
Ratliff, Darryl, Calgary	.955	33	61	3	3	67	2
Ready, Randy, Las Vegas	1.000	1	2	0	0	2	0
Reimer, Kevin, S.L.-Tac.	.955	41	61	2	3	66	0
Riley, Marquis, Vancouver	1.000	12	18	1	0	19	0
Roberge, J.P., Albuquerque	.970	45	60	4	2	66	1
Romero, Willie, Albuquerque	1.000	4	10	0	0	10	0
Secrist, Reed, Calgary	1.000	1	4	0	0	4	0
Sheldon, Scott, Edmonton	1.000	1	2	0	0	2	0
Simons, Mitch, Salt Lake	1.000	8	13	0	0	13	0
Singleton, Christopher, Phoenix*	1.000	8	18	1	0	19	0
Smith, Demond, Edmonton	1.000	2	3	0	0	3	0
Smith, Ira, Las Vegas	.984	64	124	1	2	127	0
Stairs, Matt, Edmonton	.943	18	32	1	2	35	0
Steverson, Todd, Las Vegas	.980	86	140	9	3	152	2
Tatum, Jimmy, Las Vegas	.960	45	64	8	3	75	0
Tomberlin, Andy, Edmonton*	.963	17	25	1	1	27	1
Trammell, Gary, Tucson	1.000	3	4	0	0	4	0
Turner, Chris, Vancouver	1.000	22	38	2	0	40	0
Walker, Larry, Col. Springs	1.000	3	6	2	0	8	0
Williams, Keith, Phoenix	.988	96	160	6	2	168	2
Williams, Reggie, Albuquerque	.981	89	197	10	4	211	5
Wilson, Desi, Phoenix*	1.000	3	5	0	0	5	0
Wolff, Mike, Vancouver	.985	67	130	5	2	137	1
Womack, Tony, Calgary	1.000	16	32	1	0	33	1
Woods, Ken, Phoenix	1.000	34	50	3	0	53	0

OUTFIELDERS WITH TWO OR MORE TEAMS

Player, Team	Pct.	G	PO	A	E	TC	DP
Giannelli, Ray, Salt Lake	1.000	1	2	0	0	2	0
Giannelli, Ray, Col. Springs	1.000	9	15	0	0	15	0
Reimer, Kevin, Salt Lake	.953	27	40	1	2	43	0
Reimer, Kevin, Tacoma	.957	14	21	1	1	23	0

CATCHERS

Player, Team	Pct.	G	PO	A	E	TC	DP	PB
Blanco, Henry, Albuquerque	1.000	2	11	1	0	12	0	0
Bonnici, James, Tacoma	1.000	2	13	0	0	13	0	0
Brito, Jorge, Col. Springs	.977	50	313	25	8	346	1	3
Burke, Jamie, Vancouver	.969	5	28	3	1	32	2	0
Christopherson, Eric, Tucson	.990	61	450	34	5	489	3	6
Colbert, Craig, Las Vegas	.986	54	307	33	5	345	2	
Dandridge, Brad, Albuquerque	.967	8	28	1	1	30	1	
Decker, Steve, Col. Springs	.984	7	56	4	1	61	0	
Durant, Mike, Salt Lake	.982	17	100	12	2	114	1	
Edge, Tim, Calgary	.981	11	46	7	1	54	0	
Ehmann, Kurt, Phoenix	.955	4	20	1	1	22	0	
Encarnacion, Angelo, Calgary	.990	63	314	63	4	381	0	
Eusebio, Tony, Tucson	1.000	10	45	1	0	46	0	
Fabregas, Jorge, Vancouver	1.000	3	13	1	0	14	0	
Glenn, Darrin, Phoenix	1.000	2	5	0	0	5	0	
Goff, Jerry, Tucson	.978	74	440	49	11	500	4	
Gonzalez, Pedro, Col. Springs	.985	34	179	16	3	198	2	
Greene, Todd, Vancouver	.988	42	219	37	3	259	6	
Gubanich, Creighton, Edmonton	.992	18	113	13	1	127	1	
Hernandez, Carlos, Albuquerque	.978	50	320	35	8	363	5	
Horn, Jeff, Salt Lake	.994	24	155	13	1	169	1	
Hubbard, Trent, Col. Springs	1.000	1	1	1	0	2	0	
Huckaby, Ken, Albuquerque	.990	94	557	63	6	626	11	
Jensen, Marcus, Phoenix	.988	102	568	65	8	641	7	
Kennedy, Darryl, Phoenix	.982	31	156	10	3	169	0	
Knapp, Mike, Tacoma	.988	57	369	32	5	406	3	
Lopez, Rene, Salt Lake	.989	16	88	6	1	95	2	
Luce, Roger, Tucson	1.000	16	75	7	0	82	1	
Luzinski, Ryan, Albuquerque	1.000	2	2	0	0	2	0	
Manwaring, Kirt, Phoenix	1.000	4	15	3	0	18	0	
MARX, Tim, Calgary	.994	76	464	51	3	518	10	
Miller, Damian, Salt Lake	.991	95	619	70	6	695	9	
Miller, Roger, Col. Springs	1.000	1	7	0	0	7	0	
Mirabelli, Doug, Phoenix	.982	14	97	10	2	109	1	
Molina, Izzy, Edmonton	.991	95	562	64	6	632	7	
Mulligan, Sean, Las Vegas	.989	90	582	58	7	647	5	
Orton, John, Vancouver	1.000	3	21	2	0	23	2	
Owens, Jayhawk, Col. Springs	1.000	5	35	3	0	38	0	
Pozo, Yohel, Col. Springs	.971	13	62	4	2	68	1	
Prince, Tom, Albuquerque	.990	19	86	18	1	105	2	
Probst, Alan, Tucson	1.000	1	10	2	0	12	0	
Schwenke, Matt, Las Vegas	.962	5	22	3	1	26	0	
Strittmatter, Mark, Col. Springs	.982	56	302	34	6	342	4	
Takayoshi, Todd, Vancouver	1.000	3	15	0	0	15	0	
Tejero, Fausto, Vancouver	.988	49	287	49	4	340	7	
Turner, Chris, Vancouver	.987	42	267	27	4	298	3	
Ventura, Wilfredo, Edmonton	1.000	1	4	2	0	6	0	
Wakamatsu, Don, Tacoma	1.000	1	8	1	0	9	0	
Walters, Dan, Edmonton	1.000	21	96	6	0	102	1	
Widger, Chris, Tacoma	.988	89	622	41	8	671	9	
Williams, George, Edmonton	1.000	12	76	0	0	76	0	

PITCHERS

Player, Team	Pct.	G	PO	A	E	TC
Abbott, Jim, Vancouver*	1.000	4	1	6	0	7
Abbott, Paul, Las Vegas	1.000	28	1	7	0	8
Acre, Mark, Edmonton	1.000	39	2	6	0	8
Adams, Willie, Edmonton	.882	19	8	7	2	17
Agosto, Juan, Calgary*	.857	24	0	6	1	7
Alston, Garvin, Col. Springs	1.000	35	3	2	0	5
Ausanio, Joe, Col. Springs	.750	13	0	3	1	4
Backlund, Brett, Calgary	1.000	7	2	7	0	9
Bailey, Roger, Col. Springs	1.000	9	6	16	0	22
Barcelo, Marc, Salt Lake	1.000	12	4	8	0	12
Barton, Shawn, Phoenix*	.917	44	3	8	1	12
Bautista, Jose, Phoenix	1.000	6	3	3	0	6
Beckett, Robbie, Col. Springs*	1.000	12	0	1	0	1
Bell, Eric, Tucson*	.853	30	11	18	5	34
Bennett, Erik, Salt Lake	1.000	17	3	4	0	7
Berumen, Andres, Las Vegas	.950	50	10	9	1	20
Boever, Joe, Calgary	1.000	44	8	12	0	20
Bolton, Tom, Calgary*	1.000	40	5	27	0	32
Bourgeois, Steve, Phoenix	.923	20	8	16	2	26
Brewer, Billy, Albuquerque*	.750	31	4	2	2	8
Brewington, Jamie, Phoenix	.900	35	5	13	2	20
Briscoe, John, Edmonton	.800	30	4	0	1	5
Brocail, Doug, Tucson	1.000	5	1	1	0	2
Brosnan, Jason, Tacoma*	1.000	12	2	4	0	6
Brunson, William, Albuquerque*	1.000	9	2	8	0	10
Bruske, Jim, Albuquerque	1.000	36	2	8	0	10
Burke, John, Col. Springs	1.000	24	8	6	0	14
Bustillos, Albert, Col. Springs	.964	33	7	20	1	28
Butcher, Mike, Tacoma	.600	14	1	2	2	5
Cadaret, Greg, Calgary*	1.000	9	0	1	0	1
Carlson, Dan, Phoenix	.968	33	10	20	1	31
Carter, Andy, Phoenix*	1.000	37	4	9	0	13
Chouinard, Bobby, Edmonton	1.000	15	5	13	0	18

r, Team	Pct.	G	PO	A	E	TC	DP
iansen, Jason, Calgary*	1.000	2	1	1	0	2	0
a, Ramser, Albuquerque	1.000	23	3	2	0	5	0
nings, John, Albuquerque*	1.000	27	2	13	0	15	0
t, Jamie, Edmonton	.833	33	8	2	2	12	0
, Donnie, Tucson	1.000	1	1	2	0	3	0
, Tim, Tacoma*	1.000	8	0	3	0	3	0
on, Scott, Tacoma	1.000	17	2	0	0	2	0
an, Mike, Col. Springs	1.000	30	1	6	0	7	2
ens, Elmer, Calgary	1.000	6	0	6	0	6	1
on, Jason, Vancouver	1.000	18	17	18	0	35	1
nan, Glenn, Las Vegas*	.957	26	6	16	1	23	0
herty, Jim, Tucson	.933	46	3	11	1	15	3
nan, Brian, Las Vegas	1.000	9	2	0	0	2	0
rt, Darren, Albuquerque	.818	18	6	12	4	22	1
endorfer, Kirk, Edmonton	.800	10	1	3	1	5	1
ield, Ken, Vancouver	.900	19	4	5	1	10	0
l, Geoff, Vancouver	.929	15	7	19	2	28	2
Robert, Vancouver	1.000	7	2	8	0	10	0
, Narciso, Albuquerque*	.667	3	1	1	1	3	0
s, John, Calgary	1.000	14	0	2	0	2	0
, Shawn, Phoenix*	.935	18	10	19	2	31	2
s, Dave, Tucson	.808	43	5	16	5	26	1
er, Mike, Col. Springs*	.938	9	6	9	1	16	2
ndez, Osvaldo, Tacoma*	1.000	1	0	1	0	1	0
er, Paul, Edmonton	1.000	38	3	15	0	18	0
ckson, Scott, Col. Springs	.929	55	4	9	1	14	0
ll, Mike, Vancouver	1.000	7	0	1	0	1	1
s, Mike, Las Vegas	1.000	3	1	1	0	2	0
irth, Todd, Vancouver	1.000	9	0	3	0	3	0
er, Kevin, Tucson	1.000	35	5	15	0	20	0
a, Jose, Albuquerque	.893	44	9	16	3	28	2
, Clint, Tacoma	1.000	1	1	0	0	1	0
Ken, Calgary	1.000	46	1	16	0	17	2
oy, Benji, Edmonton	1.000	11	0	2	0	2	0
ley, Jason, Vancouver*	1.000	2	2	4	0	6	0
erman, Lee, Tacoma*	1.000	25	2	2	0	4	0
an, Jose, Tacoma	1.000	5	2	4	0	6	0
n, John, Col. Springs	1.000	1	1	0	0	1	0
Dave, Tucson	1.000	1	0	1	0	1	0
ck, Lee, Cal.-Pho.*	1.000	26	4	10	0	14	0
ck, Ryan, Vancouver	.966	19	14	14	1	29	1
ala, Tim, Tacoma	.897	27	6	20	3	29	4
y, Mike, Albuquerque	.824	49	8	20	6	34	0
er, Denny, Las Vegas	.960	26	17	31	2	50	2
, Greg W., Las Vegas	1.000	1	1	1	0	2	0
, Pep, Vancouver	.889	18	7	9	2	18	0
aves, Dean, Tucson*	1.000	18	2	1	0	3	0
itzel, Ryan, Col. Springs	1.000	26	9	11	0	20	2
ns, Latroy, Salt Lake	.964	20	5	22	1	28	2
Dwayne, Col. Springs	1.000	28	6	4	0	10	1
a, Julian, Phoenix	.778	52	1	6	2	9	0
s, Matt, Albuquerque	1.000	10	3	9	0	12	1
anson, Dustin, Las Vegas	1.000	42	3	4	0	7	0
dge, David, Vancouver	.900	29	6	3	1	10	0
Chris, Tucson	.932	28	15	40	4	59	0
Chris, Phoenix	.895	32	6	11	2	19	0
John, Calgary	1.000	23	5	20	0	25	2
, Dan, Albuquerque	1.000	49	1	6	0	7	0
, John, Tucson	1.000	17	0	1	0	1	0
hrey, Rich, Tucson	.600	10	2	1	2	5	1
o, Edwin, Tacoma	1.000	5	0	4	0	4	0
, Pete, Vancouver	.933	31	5	9	1	15	0
one, John, Tucson	.944	45	6	11	1	18	0
Bobby, Col. Springs*	.923	57	1	11	1	13	1
Calvin, Albuquerque	1.000	10	0	1	0	1	0
Todd, Tucson	.500	1	1	0	1	2	0
nbeck, Scott, Salt Lake	.879	22	10	19	4	33	0
Joe, Tacoma*	1.000	7	1	2	0	3	1
zki, Dom, Salt Lake*	1.000	4	1	0	0	1	0
r, Tom, Col. Springs	.909	41	2	18	2	22	3
le, Joe, Albuquerque	1.000	10	1	1	0	2	1
ch, Phil, Vancouver	.893	19	13	12	3	28	1
t, Kevin, Salt Lake	.967	50	12	17	1	30	1
ic, Curt, Col. Springs	1.000	3	0	1	0	1	0
Scott, Las Vegas	.971	29	1	33	1	35	1
, Esteban, Calgary	1.000	12	8	13	0	21	1
e, Rich, Tuc.-Cal.	.968	13	11	19	1	31	0
Joey, Las Vegas*	1.000	32	1	5	0	6	0
ne, Andrew, Edmonton*	.947	30	6	30	2	38	3
Derek, Tacoma	1.000	17	8	22	0	30	2
es, Pat, Salt Lake	.833	22	3	2	1	6	0
, Tom, Tucson*	.750	5	0	3	1	4	0

Player, Team	Pct.	G	PO	A	E	TC	DP
May, Darrell, Calgary*	.960	23	1	23	1	25	1
McCarthy, Greg, Tacoma*	1.000	39	2	11	0	13	0
Meacham, Rusty, Tacoma	1.000	7	1	3	0	4	1
Menhart, Paul, Tacoma	1.000	6	3	3	0	6	0
Milacki, Bob, Tacoma	.963	23	19	33	2	54	5
Milchin, Mike, Salt Lake*	1.000	19	1	1	0	2	0
Miller, Travis, Salt Lake*	.963	27	2	24	1	27	0
Mimbs, Mark, Albuquerque*	.828	34	5	19	5	29	1
Minor, Blas, Tacoma	1.000	7	0	1	0	1	0
Mintz, Steve, Phoenix	1.000	59	4	2	0	6	1
Misuraca, Mike, Salt Lake	1.000	18	4	7	0	11	1
Mlicki, Doug, Tucson	.839	26	11	15	5	31	2
Montgomery, Steve, Edmonton	.909	36	3	7	1	11	0
Munoz, Mike, Col. Springs*	1.000	10	2	1	0	3	0
Nied, David, Col. Springs	.875	16	1	6	1	8	0
Norris, Joe, Salt Lake	1.000	21	3	5	0	8	0
Novoa, Rafael, Vancouver*	1.000	13	0	2	0	2	0
Oquist, Mike, Las Vegas	.947	27	13	23	2	38	1
Osuna, Al, Las Vegas*	1.000	11	1	2	0	3	0
Parra, Jose, Salt Lake	1.000	23	2	5	0	7	0
Patrick, Bronswell, Tucson	.875	33	9	19	4	32	1
Pedraza, Rod, Col. Springs	1.000	6	2	10	0	12	1
Peters, Chris, Calgary*	1.000	4	4	8	0	12	1
Phillips, Tony, Tacoma	.923	21	4	8	1	13	0
Phoenix, Steve, Calgary	1.000	10	0	1	0	1	0
Pirkl, Greg, Tacoma	1.000	2	1	0	0	1	0
Pisciotta, Marc, Calgary	1.000	57	4	3	0	7	0
Prieto, Ariel, Edmonton	1.000	3	2	0	0	2	1
Pyc, Dave, Albuquerque*	.900	13	3	6	1	10	0
Rath, Gary, Albuquerque	.963	30	12	40	2	54	3
Redman, Mark, Salt Lake*	1.000	1	0	1	0	1	0
Rekar, Bryan, Col. Springs	.964	19	8	19	1	28	2
Ritchie, Todd, Salt Lake	1.000	16	0	1	0	1	0
Roberts, Brett, Salt Lake	.970	31	9	23	1	33	1
Rodriguez, Felix, Albuquerque	.926	27	12	13	2	27	2
Rose, Scott, Edmonton	.909	50	4	6	1	11	1
Rosselli, Joe, Vancouver*	.833	47	1	9	2	12	0
Ruebel, Matt, Calgary*	1.000	13	3	5	0	8	0
Rueter, Kirk, Phoenix*	1.000	5	1	9	0	10	0
Ryan, Matt, Calgary	.933	51	6	8	1	15	0
Rychel, Kevin, Calgary	1.000	11	0	1	0	1	0
Schmidt, Jeff, Vancouver	.625	35	2	3	3	8	0
Seanez, Rudy, Albuquerque	1.000	20	1	1	0	2	0
Serafini, Dan, Salt Lake*	.980	25	5	43	1	49	1
Shaw, Curtis, Edmonton*	1.000	1	0	1	0	1	0
Simons, Doug, Tucson*	1.000	8	2	9	0	11	0
Small, Aaron, Edmonton	1.000	25	8	13	0	21	1
Small, Mark, Tucson	1.000	32	3	3	0	6	0
Smith, Pete, Las Vegas	.971	26	7	26	1	34	1
Soderstrom, Steve, Phoenix	.938	29	7	23	2	32	2
Springer, Dennis, Vancouver	.824	16	4	10	3	17	0
Stidham, Phil, Salt Lake	.929	33	6	7	1	14	1
Suzuki, Mac, Tacoma	1.000	13	0	2	0	2	1
Swan, Russ, Las Vegas*	.889	25	5	19	3	27	1
Swingle, Paul, Vancouver	1.000	15	3	2	0	5	1
Tabaka, Jeff, Tucson*	.833	41	4	6	2	12	0
Taylor, Billy, Edmonton	1.000	7	0	1	0	1	0
Telgheder, Dave, Edmonton	1.000	17	7	11	0	18	0
Thomson, John, Col. Springs	1.000	11	5	6	0	11	1
Torres, Salomon, Tacoma	.926	22	4	21	2	27	1
Treadwell, Jody, Albuquerque	1.000	5	2	4	0	6	1
Trombley, Mike, Salt Lake	.833	24	3	2	1	6	0
Urso, Sal, Tacoma*	.920	46	5	18	2	25	0
Valdez, Carlos, Phoenix	.750	44	1	5	2	8	0
Vanderweele, Doug, Phoenix	.952	41	5	15	1	21	1
VanRyn, Ben, Vancouver*	.833	18	1	4	1	6	1
Veras, Dario, Las Vegas	1.000	19	3	7	0	10	0
Viano, Jake, Col. Springs	1.000	7	2	5	0	7	1
Villone, Ron, Las Vegas*	.500	23	0	1	1	2	0
Wagner, Billy, Tucson*	.947	12	4	14	1	19	1
Wagner, Matt, Tacoma	1.000	15	5	8	0	13	0
Walker, Pete, Las Vegas	1.000	26	4	2	0	6	0
Wall, Donne, Tucson	1.000	8	5	11	0	16	0
Wasdin, John, Edmonton	.875	9	2	5	1	8	0
Washburn, Jarrod, Vancouver*	1.000	13	0	2	0	2	0
Watkins, Scott, Salt Lake*	.938	47	5	10	1	16	0
Weaver, Eric, Albuquerque	1.000	13	5	5	0	10	1
Weber, Weston, Las Vegas	1.000	7	0	3	0	3	0
Wertz, Bill, Tacoma	.667	16	0	2	1	3	0
White, Billy, Col. Springs	1.000	1	0	1	0	1	0
Williams, Shad, Vancouver	1.000	15	14	10	0	24	1
Williams, Todd, Edmonton	.962	35	10	15	1	26	2

CLASS AAA Pacific Coast League

Player, Team	Pct.	G	PO	A	E	TC	DP
WILSON, Gary, Calgary	1.000	27	14	36	0	50	1
Witasick, Jay, Edmonton	1.000	6	0	1	0	1	0
Witte, Trey, Tacoma	1.000	35	1	11	0	12	1
Wojciechowski, Steve, Edmonton*	1.000	11	3	10	0	13	0
Wolcott, Bob, Tacoma	1.000	3	2	2	0	4	0
Wood, Jason, Edmonton	1.000	1	1	0	0	1	0
Wright, Jamey, Col. Springs	.882	9	5	10	2	17	1
Young, Anthony, Tucson	.000	4	0	0	1	1	0
Zimmerman, Mike, Tacoma	1.000	13	3	3	0	6	0

PITCHERS WITH TWO OR MORE TEAMS

Player, Team	Pct.	G	PO	A	E	TC
Hancock, Lee, Calgary*	1.000	9	2	3	0	5
Hancock, Lee, Phoenix*	1.000	17	2	7	0	9
Loiselle, Rich, Tucson	.941	5	8	8	1	17
Loiselle, Rich, Calgary	1.000	8	3	11	0	14

The following players did not have any fielding statistics at the positions indicated or appeared only as a designated hitter, pinch-hitter or pinch-runner: Aurili Ayala, p; Bosio, p; Brumley, p; Carmona, p; Colbert, 3b; Correia, p; Demetral, 3b; Easley, 3b; Fletcher, of; Forbes, of; Garrison, p; Gonzalez, 3b; Henderson, p; Herna 3b; Jordan, dh; Kellner, p; Kester, p; Kirkpatrick, c; Konuszewski, p; Kubinski, p; Lopez, p; Lovullo, ss-p; Millette, of; An. Osuna, p; Parker, ss; Pennington, p; Pick Prince, of; Schmitt, p; Scott, of-2b; Secrist, c; Sharperson, 2b; Shouse, p; M. Simons, p; Tredaway, p; G. Williams, of; Yelding, of.

LEAGUE CHAMPIONS

Year	Team	Pct.	Year	Team	Pct.	Year	Team
1903—	Los Angeles	.630	1939—	Seattle	.589	1973—	Tucson
1904—	Tacoma	.589		Sacramento (4th)†	.500		Spokane•
	Tacoma§	.571	1940—	Seattle‡	.629	1974—	Spokane•
	Los Angeles§	.571	1941—	Seattle‡	.598		Albuquerque
1905—	Tacoma	.583	1942—	Sacramento	.590	1975—	Salt Lake City
	Los Angeles*	.604		Seattle (3rd)†	.539		Hawaii•
1906—	Portland	.657	1943—	Los Angeles	.710	1976—	Salt Lake City
1907—	Los Angeles	.608		S. Francisco (2nd)†	.574		Hawaii•
1908—	Los Angeles	.585	1944—	Los Angeles	.586	1977—	Phoenix•
1909—	San Francisco	.623		S. Francisco (3rd)†	.509		Hawaii
1910—	Portland	.567	1945—	Portland	.622	1978—	Tacoma††
1911—	Portland	.589		S. Francisco (4th)†	.525		Albuquerque††
1912—	Oakland	.591	1946—	San Francisco‡	.628	1979—	Albuquerque
1913—	Portland	.559	1947—	Los Angeles▲	.567		Salt Lake City‡‡
1914—	Portland	.574	1948—	Oakland‡	.606	1980—	Albuquerque
1915—	San Francisco	.570	1949—	Hollywood‡	.583		Hawaii
1916—	Los Angeles	.601	1950—	Oakland	.590	1981—	Albuquerque*
1917—	San Francisco	.561	1951—	Seattle‡	.593		Tacoma
1918—	Vernon	.569	1952—	Hollywood	.606	1982—	Albuquerque*
	Los Angeles (2nd)◆	.548	1953—	Hollywood	.589		Spokane
1919—	Vernon	.613	1954—	San Diego■	.604	1983—	Albuquerque
1920—	Vernon	.556	1955—	Seattle	.552		Portland*
1921—	Los Angeles	.574	1956—	Los Angeles	.637	1984—	Hawaii
1922—	San Francisco	.638	1957—	San Francisco	.601		Edmonton*
1923—	San Francisco	.617	1958—	Phoenix	.578	1985—	Vancouver*
1924—	Seattle	.545	1959—	Salt Lake City	.552		Phoenix
1925—	San Francisco	.643	1960—	Spokane	.601	1986—	Vancouver
1926—	Los Angeles	.599	1961—	Tacoma	.630		Las Vegas*
1927—	Oakland	.615	1962—	San Diego	.604	1987—	Calgary
1928—	San Francisco*	.630	1963—	Spokane	.620		Albuquerque*
	Sacramento∞	.626		Oklahoma City•	.632	1988—	Vancouver
	San Francisco∞	.626	1964—	Arkansas	.609		Las Vegas*
1929—	Mission	.643		San Diego•	.576	1989—	Albuquerque
	Hollywood*	.592	1965—	Oklahoma City a	.628		Vancouver*
1930—	Los Angeles	.576		Portland	.547	1990—	Albuquerque*
	Hollywood*	.650	1966—	Seattle•	.561		Edmonton
1931—	Hollywood	.626		Tulsa	.578	1991—	Albuquerque
	San Francisco*	.608	1967—	San Diego•	.574		Tucson*
1932—	Portland	.587		Spokane	.541	1992—	Colorado Springs*
1933—	Los Angeles	.610	1968—	Tulsa•	.642		Portland
1934—	Los Angeles▼	.786		Spokane	.586	1993—	Portland
	Los Angeles▼	.689	1969—	Tacoma•	.589		Tucson*
1935—	Los Angeles	.648		Eugene	.603	1994—	Albuquerque*
	San Francisco*	.608	1970—	Spokane•	.644		Vancouver
1936—	Portland‡	.549		Hawaii	.671	1995—	Salt Lake
1937—	Sacramento	.573	1971—	Salt Lake City	.534		Colorado Springs*
	San Diego (3rd)†	.545		Tacoma	.545	1996—	Edmonton*
1938—	Los Angeles	.590	1972—	Albuquerque	.622		Phoenix
	Sacramento (3rd)†	.537		Eugene	.534		

*Won split-season playoff. †Won four-team playoff. ‡Won pennant and four-team playoff. §Tied for second-half title with Tacoma winning playoff. for second-half title, with Sacramento winning playoff. ▲Ended regular season in tie with San Francisco and won one-game playoff for pennant, the four-club playoff. ◆Won playoff from first-place Vernon and awarded championship. ■Defeated Hollywood in one-game playoff for pennant. ▼Wo halves, no playoff. •League was divided into Northern, Southern divisions in 1963, 1969-70-71, and Eastern, Western divisions in 1964 through 196 1972 through 1977, won two-team playoff. ††League divided into Eastern and Western divisions, Tacoma and Albuquerque declared co-champions f ing cancellation of four-team playoff due to continuing rain and wet grounds. ‡‡Won second-half title and defeated Hawaii in four-team playoff.

EASTERN LEAGUE

LEAGUE OFFICE

President
Bill Troubh

Address
P.O. Box 9711
Portland, ME 04104

Phone
207-761-2700

TEAMS

AKRON AEROS

General manager/vice president
Jeff Auman

Manager
Jeff Datz

Ballpark (capacity, surface)
Canal Park (8,800, grass)

Affiliation
Indians

Address
300 S. Main St.
Akron, OH 44308

Phone
216-456-5100

BINGHAMTON METS

General manager
R.C. Reuteman

Manager
Rick Sweet

Ballpark (capacity, surface)
Binghamton Municipal Stadium (6,064, grass)

Affiliation
Mets

Address
P.O. Box 598
Binghamton, NY 13902

Phone
607-723-6387

BOWIE BAYSOX

General manager
Jon Danos

Manager
Joe Ferguson

Ballpark (capacity, surface)
Prince George's Stadium (10,000, grass)

Affiliation
Orioles

Address
P.O. Box 1661
Bowie, MD 20717

Phone
301-805-6000

HARRISBURG SENATORS

General manager
Todd Vander Woude

Manager
Rick Sofield

Ballpark (capacity, surface)
RiverSide Stadium (6,300, grass)

Affiliation
Expos

Address
P.O. Box 15757
Harrisburg, PA 17105

Phone
717-231-4444

NEW BRITAIN ROCK CATS

General manager
Gerry Berthiaume

Manager
Al Newman

Ballpark (capacity, surface)
New Britain Stadium (6,146, grass)

Affiliation
Twins

Address
P.O. Box 1718
New Britain, CT 06050

Phone
860-224-8383

NEW HAVEN RAVENS

General manager
Charles Dowd

Manager
Bill Hayes

Ballpark (capacity, surface)
Yale Field (6,200, grass)

Affiliation
Rockies

Address
252 Darby Ave.
West Haven, CT 06516

Phone
1-800-728-3671

NORWICH NAVIGATORS

General manager
Brian Mahoney

Manager
Trey Hillman

Ballpark (capacity, surface)
Dodd Stadium (7,000, grass)

Affiliation
Yankees

Address
P.O. Box 6003
Yantic, CT 06389

Phone
860-887-7962

PORTLAND SEA DOGS

General manager
Charles Eshbach

Manager
Fredi Gonzalez

Ballpark (capacity, surface)
Hadlock Field (6,000, grass)

Affiliation
Marlins

Address
P.O. Box 636
Portland, ME 04104

Phone
207-874-9300

READING PHILLIES

General manager
Chuck Domino

Manager
Al LeBoeuf

Ballpark (capacity, surface)
Municipal Memorial Stadium (8,500, grass)

Affiliation
Phillies

Address
P.O. Box 15050
Reading, PA 19612

Phone
610-375-8469

TRENTON THUNDER

General manager
Wayne Hodes

Manager
DeMarlo Hale

Ballpark (capacity, surface)
Mercer County Waterfront Park (6,300, grass)

Affiliation
Red Sox

Address
One Thunder Road
Trenton, NJ 08611

Phone
609-394-8326

CLASS AA *Eastern League*

NORTHERN DIVISION

Team	W	L	T	Pct.	GB
Portland (Marlins)	83	58	0	.589	....
Binghamton (Mets)	76	66	0	.535	7½
Norwich (Yankees)	71	70	0	.504	12
New Haven (Rockies)	66	75	0	.468	17
New Britain (Twins)	61	81	0	.430	22½

SOUTHERN DIVISION

Team	W	L	T	Pct.	GB
Trenton (Red Sox)	86	56	0	.606	....
Harrisburg (Expos)	74	68	0	.521	12
Canton-Akron (Indians)	71	71	0	.500	15
Reading (Phillies)	66	75	0	.468	19
Bowie (Orioles)	54	88	0	.380	32

COMPOSITE

Team	Tre.	Por.	Bin.	Har.	Nor.	C.A.	Rea.	N.H.	N.B.	Bow.	W	L	T	Pct.	GB
Trenton (Red Sox)	....	9	8	12	6	10	11	9	9	12	86	56	0	.606	....
Portland (Marlins)	5	....	8	10	14	7	8	10	12	9	83	58	0	.589	2
Binghamton (Mets)	6	10	....	4	8	7	8	11	15	7	76	66	0	.535	10
Harrisburg (Expos)	6	4	10	....	9	10	11	5	8	11	74	68	0	.521	12
Norwich (Yankees)	8	4	10	5	....	9	6	8	10	11	71	70	0	.504	14
Canton-Akron (Indians)	8	7	7	8	5	....	11	8	8	9	71	71	0	.500	15
Reading (Phillies)	7	5	6	7	8	7	....	7	8	11	66	75	0	.468	19
New Haven (Rockies)	5	8	7	9	9	6	7	....	6	9	66	75	0	.468	19
New Britain (Twins)	5	6	3	6	8	6	6	12	....	9	61	81	0	.430	25
Bowie (Orioles)	6	5	7	7	3	9	7	5	5	....	54	88	0	.380	32

Major league affiliations in parentheses.

PLAYOFFS: Portland defeated Binghamton, three games to two; Harrisburg defeated Trenton, three games to two; Harrisburg defeated Portland, three games to one, to win league championship.

REGULAR-SEASON ATTENDANCE: Binghamton, 202,461; Bowie, 396,086; Canton-Akron, 213,278; Harrisburg, 230,744; New Britain, 160,765; New Hav 254,084; Norwich, 269,022; Portland, 408,503; Reading, 375,326; Trenton, 437,396. Total—2,947,665. Playoffs (14 games)—51,801. Class AA All-Star Gar at Trenton—8,369.

MANAGERS: Binghamton, John Tamargo; Bowie, Bob Miscik (through April 14), Moe Drabowsky (April 15) and Tim Blackwell (April 16 through end o' season); Canton-Akron, Jeff Datz; Harrisburg, Pat Kelly; New Britain, Al Newman; New Haven, Bill Hayes; Norwich, Jim Essian; Portland, Carlos Toss Reading, Bill Robinson; Trenton, Ken Macha. Managerial record of teams with more than one manager: Bowie, Miscik, 4-4, Drabowsky, 0-1, Blackwell, 5 83.

ALL-STAR TEAM: 1B—Todd Helton, New Haven; 2B—Luis Castillo, Portland; 3B—Scott Rolen, Reading; SS—Enrique Wilson, Canton-Akron; OF—T Dunwoody, Portland; Vladimir Guerrero, Harrisburg; Adam Hyzdu, Trenton; C—Walt McKeel, Trenton; DH—Rod McCall, Canton-Akron; P—Carl Pava Trenton; Mike Welch, Binghamton; Matt Bleech, Reading; Tony Saunders, Portland; Most Valuable Player—Vladimir Guerrero, Harrisburg; Pitcher of ' Year—Carl Pavano, Trenton; Rookie of the Year—Vladimir Guerrero, Harrisburg; Manager of the Year—Carlos Tosca, Portland.

TEAM

Team	Avg.	G	TPA	AB	R	H	TB	2B	3B	HR	RBI	SH	SF	HP	BB	IBB	SO	SB	CS	GDP	LOB	ShO	Slg.	O
Canton/Akron	.280	142	5468	4913	768	1377	2143	248	46	142	709	11	41	71	431	27	896	105	54	91	1016	6	.436	.3
Portland	.275	141	5353	4726	694	1301	1955	260	38	106	643	52	38	61	476	35	907	153	101	93	993	10	.414	.3
Trenton	.269	142	5382	4677	751	1259	2003	228	33	150	689	49	37	51	566	44	924	134	92	76	979	4	.428	.3
Harrisburg	.261	142	5245	4580	620	1195	1816	233	29	110	580	73	37	37	515	38	881	72	67	104	985	9	.397	.3
Norwich	.258	141	5263	4619	675	1193	1848	235	21	126	619	51	32	40	521	29	1016	82	49	101	966	6	.400	.3
New Britain	.255	142	5163	4605	617	1174	1864	227	26	137	563	35	37	40	446	26	950	71	88	102	896	12	.405	.3
Binghamton	.253	142	5329	4582	662	1160	1727	204	27	103	597	75	47	52	572	38	867	109	66	97	1006	11	.377	.3
Bowie	.252	142	5277	4730	582	1193	1810	227	24	114	527	38	33	59	417	21	968	86	77	93	941	8	.383	.3
Reading	.252	141	5423	4686	684	1179	1879	226	39	132	603	58	36	88	554	27	1056	130	83	84	1018	6	.401	.3
New Haven	.241	141	5109	4502	510	1084	1556	193	24	77	457	70	31	40	465	36	893	41	48	115	983	11	.346	.3

INDIVIDUAL

TOP QUALIFIERS FOR BATTING CHAMPIONSHIP

Minimum 383 plate appearances. *Lefthanded batter. †Switch-hitter.

Player, Team	Avg.	G	TPA	AB	R	H	TB	2B	3B	HR	RBI	SH	SF	HP	BB	IBB	SO	SB	CS	GDP	Slg.	O
Guerrero, Vladimir, Harrisburg	.360	118	479	417	84	150	255	32	8	19	78	0	2	9	51	13	42	17	10	8	.612	.4
Hyzdu, Adam, Trenton	.337	109	434	374	71	126	231	24	3	25	80	0	2	2	56	6	75	1	8	7	.618	.4
Ramirez, Alex, Canton/Akron	.329	131	534	513	79	169	263	28	12	14	85	1	1	3	16	1	74	18	10	8	.513	.3
Millar, Kevin, Portland	.318	130	523	472	69	150	236	32	0	18	86	0	5	9	37	4	53	6	5	13	.500	.3
Castillo, Luis, Portland†	.317	109	495	420	83	133	165	15	7	1	35	6	1	2	66	4	68	51	28	2	.393	.4
Woods, Tyrone, Trenton	.312	99	415	356	75	111	206	16	2	25	71	0	2	0	56	3	66	5	4	6	.579	.4
Burton, Essex, Reading	.304	102	438	381	66	116	148	19	5	1	30	16	2	2	37	0	56	40	12	4	.388	.3
Wilson, Enrique, Can./Akron†	.304	117	526	484	70	147	189	17	5	5	50	0	7	4	31	2	46	23	16	9	.390	.3
Berg, David, Portland	.302	109	475	414	64	125	190	28	5	9	73	8	6	5	42	1	60	17	7	10	.459	.3
McKeel, Walt, Trenton	.302	128	543	464	86	140	209	19	1	16	78	5	7	7	60	3	52	2	4	13	.450	.3
McCall, Rod, Canton/Akron*	.300	120	498	440	80	132	246	29	2	27	85	0	0	6	52	4	118	2	0	4	.559	.3
Saffer, Jon, Harrisburg*	.300	134	579	487	96	146	210	26	4	10	52	5	3	6	78	1	77	8	16	8	.431	.4
Saunders, Chris, Binghamton	.298	141	604	510	82	152	236	27	3	17	105	2	11	8	73	3	88	5	4	11	.463	.3
Aven, Bruce, Canton/Akron	.297	131	545	481	91	143	251	31	4	23	79	0	3	17	43	0	101	22	6	9	.522	.3
Daubach, Brian, Binghamton*	.296	122	521	436	80	129	221	24	1	22	76	0	4	7	74	9	103	7	9	8	.507	.4

DEPARTMENTAL LEADERS: G—C. Saunders, 141; AB—Dunwoody, 552; R—Saffer, 96; H—A. Ramirez, 169; TB—Dunwoody, 267; 2B—Carey, 34; 3B—A. Ra 12; HR—Spencer, 29; RBI—C. Saunders, 105; SH—Burton, 16; SF—C. Saunders, 11; HP—Held, 22; BB—Riggs, 81; IBB—Guerrero, 13; SO—Dunwoody, 149; S Castillo, 51; CS—Castillo, 28; GIDP—Donato, 19; Slg.—Hyzdu, .618; OBP—Guerrero, .438.

CLASS AA *Eastern League*

ALL PLAYERS

*Lethanded batter. †Switch-hitter.

er, Team	Avg.	G	TPA	AB	R	H	TB	2B	3B	HR	RBI	SH	SF	HP	BB	IBB	SO	SB	CS	GDP	Slg.	OBP
d, Andy, Trenton*	.277	65	249	213	33	59	95	22	1	4	39	0	3	0	33	2	41	5	3	4	.446	.369
ayani, Benny, Binghamton...	.170	21	67	53	7	9	16	1	0	2	8	1	1	1	11	0	13	1	0	2	.302	.318
ntara, Israel, Harrisburg	.211	62	234	218	26	46	75	5	0	8	19	0	1	1	14	0	62	1	1	5	.344	.261
re, Jeff, Portland	.000	11	1	1	0	0	0	0	0	0	0	0	0	0	0	0	0	0	0	0	.000	.000
on, Chris, Trenton	.230	109	392	357	49	82	91	7	1	0	22	4	0	3	28	0	61	14	11	7	.255	.291
ador, Manuel, Reading†	.278	10	23	18	5	5	10	2	0	1	3	0	0	0	5	0	4	0	0	1	.556	.435
erson, Marlon, Reading*	.274	75	345	314	38	86	115	14	3	3	28	3	1	1	26	2	44	17	9	5	.366	.330
eli, Doug, Reading	.235	56	218	187	24	44	77	9	0	8	29	6	2	2	20	3	43	3	2	1	.412	.313
n, Bruce, Canton/Akron	.297	131	545	481	91	143	251	31	4	23	79	0	3	17	43	0	101	22	6	9	.522	.373
sa, Joe, Bing.-Por.†	.234	67	204	167	25	39	47	8	0	0	22	5	1	1	30	0	30	2	3	4	.281	.352
a, Rolo, Bowie	.266	60	263	233	31	62	82	12	1	2	17	1	2	8	19	0	34	8	5	4	.352	.340
aje, Jesus, Binghamton	.237	86	300	249	36	59	81	16	0	2	26	3	1	1	45	1	33	5	6	5	.325	.355
on, Tony, Harrisburg	.284	18	73	67	12	19	39	3	1	5	12	0	0	0	6	1	19	1	0	1	.582	.342
ista, Juan, Bowie	.234	129	477	441	35	103	136	18	3	3	33	8	2	5	21	1	102	15	12	6	.308	.275
kett, Robbie, Por.-N.H.	.250	33	5	4	0	1	1	0	0	0	1	0	0	0	1	0	3	0	0	0	.250	.400
ch, Matt, Reading*	.043	21	27	23	1	1	1	0	0	0	0	2	0	1	1	0	5	0	0	0	.043	.120
nett, Shayne, Harrisburg	.000	53	6	6	0	0	0	0	0	0	0	0	0	0	0	0	1	0	0	0	.000	.000
i, David, Portland	.302	109	475	414	64	125	190	28	5	9	73	8	6	5	42	1	60	17	7	10	.459	.368
hardt, Steve, New Haven	.286	32	93	84	5	24	27	3	0	0	10	1	2	2	4	1	14	0	2	1	.321	.326
ios, Harry, Bowie	.187	37	147	123	19	23	45	4	0	6	17	1	1	6	16	1	24	7	2	3	.366	.308
y, Mike, Bowie	.143	2	8	7	1	1	1	0	0	0	2	0	1	0	0	0	4	0	0	0	.143	.125
s, Todd, Canton/Akron*	.252	77	285	238	35	60	76	13	0	1	26	0	4	5	38	2	51	0	1	6	.319	.361
sold, James, Canton/Akron.	.239	84	306	268	35	64	94	11	5	3	35	1	1	6	30	1	74	4	1	3	.351	.328
n, Geoffrey, Harrisburg†	.240	120	472	396	47	95	124	22	2	1	41	11	3	3	59	2	51	6	7	11	.313	.341
ero, Richie, Trenton	.310	26	80	71	12	22	40	5	2	3	26	1	0	0	8	0	16	2	1	2	.563	.380
, Heath, New Haven	.000	4	1	1	0	0	0	0	0	0	0	0	0	0	0	0	1	0	0	0	.000	.000
cher, Denis, Harrisburg	.500	1	2	2	0	1	2	1	0	0	0	0	0	0	0	0	0	0	0	0	1.000	.500
ers, Brent, Bowie*	.311	58	250	228	37	71	111	11	1	9	25	3	0	2	17	2	40	10	4	1	.487	.364
vn, Randy, Trenton	.298	72	278	245	46	73	125	15	2	11	38	1	0	5	27	2	56	9	4	3	.510	.379
vn, Ron, Portland	.100	4	11	10	1	1	3	0	1	0	1	0	0	0	1	0	1	0	0	0	.300	.182
vnson, Mark, New Haven	.222	37	19	18	3	4	5	1	0	0	0	1	0	0	0	0	2	0	0	2	.278	.222
nt, Pat, Canton/Akron	.193	34	133	109	13	21	34	2	1	3	17	1	2	4	17	1	24	8	2	1	.312	.318
nger, Kirk, New Haven	.000	47	2	1	0	0	0	0	0	0	0	0	0	0	1	0	1	0	0	0	.000	.500
on, Essex, Reading	.304	102	438	381	66	116	148	19	5	1	30	16	2	2	37	0	56	40	12	4	.388	.367
, Anthony, New Britain†	.247	59	217	194	23	48	61	8	1	1	10	3	1	1	18	1	35	11	9	3	.314	.313
era, Jolbert, Harrisburg	.240	107	387	354	40	85	116	18	2	3	29	5	4	1	23	3	63	10	5	9	.328	.285
pos, Jesus, Harrisburg	.260	73	221	208	15	54	58	4	0	0	17	1	0	2	9	2	17	5	9	5	.279	.297
ballo, Gary, New Britain	.240	85	327	292	32	70	107	16	0	7	32	1	5	2	27	0	62	1	3	7	.366	.304
y, Todd, Trenton*	.250	125	497	440	78	110	210	34	3	20	78	3	3	3	48	9	123	4	4	3	.477	.326
er, John, Binghamton	.176	19	22	17	1	3	4	1	0	0	3	3	0	0	2	0	4	0	0	1	.235	.263
ajal, Jhonny, Binghamton	.300	16	67	60	7	18	25	3	2	0	4	1	0	1	5	0	10	1	1	1	.417	.364
aneda, Hector, Bowie*	.216	14	55	51	6	11	15	1	0	1	5	0	1	3	0		12	2	0	0	.294	.273
llo, Luis, Portland†	.317	109	495	420	83	133	165	15	7	1	35	6	1	2	66	4	68	51	28	2	.393	.411
gey, Dan, Portland	.000	13	1	1	0	0	0	0	0	0	0	0	0	0	0	0	1	0	0	0	.000	.000
nski, Chris, Portland†	.260	23	90	73	15	19	35	7	0	3	11	1	1	2	13	1	13	3	1	2	.479	.382
, Howie, Bowie*	.272	127	527	449	55	122	169	29	3	4	52	10	7	2	59	1	54	2	8	8	.376	.354
urn, Danny, Bowie	.252	95	390	365	51	92	170	14	5	18	55	0	4	4	17	1	88	4	3	5	.466	.290
er, Dan, Trenton	.213	28	104	94	12	20	35	3	0	4	9	1	0	0	9	1	36	2	1	4	.372	.282
er, Scott, Bowie	.000	21	1	1	0	0	0	0	0	0	0	0	0	0	0	0	0	0	0	0	.000	.000
, Hayward, Portland	.304	14	50	46	7	14	17	3	0	0	2	0	0	4	0	1	11	2	1	1	.370	.360
a, Tony, Reading	.176	30	19	17	3	3	3	0	0	0	0	0	0	0	2	0	8	0	0	0	.176	.263
hlin, Kevin, Trenton*	.271	52	203	170	24	46	50	2	1	0	18	4	3	3	22	4	24	5	4	2	.294	.359
ford, Joe, Binghamton*	.500	7	8	8	1	4	7	0	0	1	3	0	0	0	0	0	1	0	0	0	.875	.500
by, Mike, New Haven*	.202	31	107	99	3	20	27	4	0	1	6	2	3	0	3	1	25	0	0	3	.273	.219
ther, Brent, New Haven...	.111	25	12	9	1	1	1	0	0	0	0	0	2	0	1	0	2	0	0	0	.111	.200
ane, Will, Portland	.091	25	25	22	3	2	4	0	1	0	2	1	0	0	2	0	3	0	0	1	.182	.167
s, Kevin, Bowie	.246	129	518	460	69	113	192	21	2	18	58	0	1	3	54	4	95	2	1	10	.417	.328
ach, Brian, Binghamton*	.296	122	521	436	80	129	221	24	1	22	76	0	4	7	74	9	103	7	9	8	.507	.403
s, Tommy, Bowie	.261	137	581	524	75	137	215	32	2	14	54	3	3	10	41	4	113	5	8	16	.410	.325
kins, Walt, Reading	.268	77	292	254	40	68	102	16	3	4	28	1	0	0	37	0	48	4	4	3	.402	.361
rry, Joe, Norwich*	.154	9	26	26	1	4	4	0	0	0	6	0	0	0	0	0	7	0	0	1	.154	.154
ick, Jim, Bowie†	.000	13	1	1	0	0	0	0	0	0	0	0	0	0	0	0	1	0	0	0	.000	.000
rt, Rick, Harrisburg*	.000	30	4	1	0	0	0	0	0	0	0	0	0	0	2	0	1	0	0	0	.000	.500
n, Mike, New Haven	1.000	16	2	1	0	1	2	1	0	0	0	0	0	0	0	0	0	0	0	0	2.000	1.000
eld, Wil, Norwich	.196	22	48	46	3	9	10	1	0	0	3	0	0	0	2	0	15	1	1	1	.217	.229
ado, Alex, Trenton	.222	21	93	81	7	18	31	4	0	3	14	1	1	1	9	1	8	1	0	1	.383	.304
cci, David, Portland*	.291	66	283	251	27	73	95	14	1	2	33	2	1	1	28	1	56	2	7	4	.378	.363
ccchio, Nick, Norwich*	.278	12	47	36	7	10	19	3	0	2	7	0	0	5	6	0	9	1	0	2	.528	.447
Einar, Canton/Akron	.281	104	418	395	47	111	150	26	2	3	35	1	1	9	12	0	22	3	2	11	.380	.317
, Robert, Reading*	.000	18	4	4	0	0	0	0	0	0	0	0	0	0	0	0	2	0	0	0	.000	.000
to, Daniel, Norwich*	.285	134	506	459	47	131	166	27	1	2	48	5	1	7	34	2	51	5	6	19	.362	.343
rque, Aaron, Harrisburg	.000	13	2	2	0	0	0	0	0	0	0	0	0	0	0	0	1	0	0	0	.000	.000
roody, Todd, Portland*	.277	138	609	552	88	153	267	30	6	24	93	0	5	7	45	6	149	24	19	10	.484	.337
Bill, New Haven*	.000	29	3	1	0	0	0	0	0	0	0	0	0	0	0	0	0	0	0	0	.000	.500
endson, Brian, Binghamton	.308	39	16	13	1	4	4	0	0	0	2	0	0	0	0	0	3	0	0	0	.308	.308
ella, Bobby, Reading	.244	111	442	365	48	89	176	14	2	23	72	1	4	5	67	5	104	2	4	7	.482	.365
il, Mauricio, Reading*	.000	20	1	1	0	0	0	0	0	0	0	0	0	0	0	0	0	0	0	0	.000	.000
sek, Steve, Harrisburg	.118	19	19	17	2	2	3	1	0	0	4	2	0	0	0	0	7	0	0	0	.176	.118
son, Jeff, New Britain	.285	89	325	284	46	81	116	16	2	5	20	0	1	3	37	2	67	5	4	2	.408	.372
Tony, Reading	.125	5	9	8	1	1	1	0	0	0	1	0	0	0	0	0	4	0	0	0	.125	.125
, David, Reading	.269	57	189	171	21	46	67	9	0	4	24	4	2	0	12	1	18	5	3	7	.392	.314

CLASS AA Eastern League

Player, Team	Avg.	G	TPA	AB	R	H	TB	2B	3B	HR	RBI	SH	SF	HP	BB	IBB	SO	SB	CS	GDP	Slg.	OB
Fithian, Grant, Norwich	.197	63	195	178	19	35	59	7	1	5	26	4	1	1	11	1	46	1	0	4	.331	.2
Fleming, Carlton, Norwich†	.321	15	33	28	4	9	9	0	0	0	1	0	0	0	5	0	1	0	1	1	.321	.4
Forster, Scott, Harrisburg	.053	28	26	19	1	1	1	0	0	0	0	0	4	0	3	0	11	0	0	0	.053	.1
Foster, Jim, Bowie	.303	9	41	33	7	10	18	0	1	2	9	0	1	0	7	0	6	0	0	0	.545	.4
Foster, Mark, Reading*	.333	50	6	6	1	2	3	1	0	0	0	0	0	0	0	0	3	0	0	0	.500	.3
Fuller, Mark, Binghamton*	.000	51	5	5	1	0	0	0	0	0	0	0	0	0	0	0	2	0	0	0	.000	.0
Fullmer, Brad, Harrisburg*	.276	24	103	98	11	27	45	4	1	4	14	0	0	2	3	0	8	0	0	3	.459	.3
Garcia, Vicente, New Haven	.214	87	336	295	32	63	84	10	1	3	18	6	2	5	28	1	43	1	2	7	.285	.2
Geisler, Phil, Binghamton*	.251	107	397	355	47	89	143	17	2	11	59	1	5	3	33	6	96	5	4	7	.403	.3
Gentile, Scott, Harrisburg	.000	15	2	2	0	0	0	0	0	0	0	0	0	0	0	0	0	0	0	0	.000	.0
Gibson, Derrick, New Haven	.256	122	493	449	58	115	189	21	4	15	62	1	4	8	31	1	125	3	12	15	.421	.3
Giudice, John, New Haven	.254	32	130	118	13	30	48	4	1	4	13	0	2	0	10	2	25	2	4	2	.407	.3
Goligoski, Jason, New Haven*	.172	30	76	64	6	11	13	0	1	0	3	3	0	1	8	2	12	0	2	2	.203	.2
Gonzalez, Alex, Portland	.235	11	37	34	4	8	10	0	1	0	1	0	0	1	2	2	10	0	0	2	.294	.2
Gonzalez, Pete, New Haven	.185	42	137	119	9	22	29	1	0	2	8	2	0	2	14	1	19	1	2	8	.244	.2
Gordon, Keith, Bowie	.261	82	330	306	38	80	112	13	2	5	28	1	0	1	22	0	80	13	11	5	.366	.3
Greene, Charlie, Binghamton	.244	100	359	336	35	82	105	17	0	2	27	2	4	0	17	0	52	2	0	8	.313	.2
Gresham, Kris, Bowie	.202	42	146	129	12	26	33	7	0	0	6	1	1	5	10	1	28	1	2	2	.256	.2
Grifol, Pedro, Binghamton	.238	64	223	202	22	48	72	3	0	7	28	8	0	0	13	2	29	0	0	6	.356	.2
Grunewald, Keith, New Haven†	.227	111	392	352	27	80	106	13	2	3	28	7	3	5	25	3	98	2	1	3	.301	.2
Guerra, Mark, Binghamton	.231	27	17	13	2	3	7	1	0	1	1	2	0	1	1	0	6	0	0	0	.538	.3
Guerrero, Vladimir, Harrisburg	.360	118	479	417	84	150	255	32	8	19	78	0	2	9	51	13	42	17	10	8	.612	.4
Guiliano, Matt, Reading	.200	74	252	220	19	44	59	9	3	0	19	3	1	3	25	1	59	0	0	4	.268	.2
Gutierrez, Ricky, Canton/Akron	.252	119	532	484	69	122	160	11	3	7	55	4	5	2	37	0	56	18	9	8	.331	.3
Gyselman, Jeff, Reading	.172	49	149	128	9	22	24	2	0	0	12	5	1	1	14	0	36	0	2	3	.188	.2
Hardtke, Jason, Binghamton†	.263	35	154	137	23	36	56	11	0	3	16	1	0	0	16	1	16	0	1	3	.409	.3
Harris, Doug, Bow.-Por.	.000	23	2	2	0	0	0	0	0	0	0	0	0	0	0	0	0	0	0	0	.000	.0
Harvey, Ray, Canton/Akron*	.353	5	19	17	3	6	9	3	0	0	0	0	0	0	2	1	2	0	0	1	.529	.4
Hastings, Lionel, Portland	.232	97	327	293	30	68	100	12	1	6	44	10	1	8	15	2	50	5	2	8	.341	.2
Haws, Scott, Reading*	1.000	1	3	1	0	1	1	0	0	0	0	0	0	0	2	0	0	0	0	0	1.000	1.0
Heflin, Bronson, Reading	.000	25	2	1	0	0	0	0	0	0	0	0	0	0	1	0	0	0	0	0	.000	.3
Held, Dan, Reading	.243	136	585	497	77	121	226	17	5	26	92	0	6	22	60	4	141	3	8	10	.455	.3
Helton, Todd, New Haven*	.332	93	375	319	46	106	155	24	2	7	51	3	1	1	51	5	37	2	5	8	.486	.4
Henley, Bob, Harrisburg	.228	103	374	289	33	66	89	12	1	3	27	9	2	3	70	1	78	1	2	14	.308	.3
Heredia, Felix, Portland*	.000	55	1	1	0	0	0	0	0	0	0	0	0	0	0	0	1	0	0	0	.000	.0
Hernandez, Livan, Portland	.250	15	12	12	0	3	5	2	0	0	2	0	0	0	0	0	3	0	0	1	.417	.2
Herrmann, Gary, Reading	.111	24	10	9	0	1	1	0	0	0	0	0	0	0	1	0	1	0	0	0	.111	.2
Higgins, Mike, New Haven	.181	22	74	72	6	13	17	2	1	0	5	0	0	0	2	0	14	1	1	1	.236	.2
Hilt, Scott, New Britain*	.194	70	218	180	19	35	48	5	1	2	19	2	1	1	34	1	53	3	2	7	.267	.3
Hinds, Rob, Norwich	.228	85	212	180	25	41	52	3	1	2	15	10	2	0	20	0	48	9	5	1	.289	.3
Holdren, Nate, New Haven	.167	10	38	36	3	6	10	1	0	1	6	0	0	2	0	0	11	1	1	0	.278	.2
Holifield, Rick, Portland*	.267	109	448	375	73	100	158	20	4	10	38	9	3	9	52	3	98	35	18	2	.421	.3
Holman, Craig, Reading†	.000	10	13	11	0	0	0	0	0	0	0	1	2	0	0	0	2	0	0	0	.000	.0
Horn, Jeff, New Britain	.267	12	51	45	4	12	14	2	0	0	3	0	0	0	6	1	7	0	1	0	.311	.3
Horne, Tyrone, Binghamton*	.272	43	141	125	17	34	53	10	0	3	19	0	0	1	15	4	39	3	0	4	.424	.3
Hunter, Rich, Reading	.222	10	9	9	0	2	2	0	0	0	1	0	0	0	0	0	0	0	0	1	.222	.2
Hunter, Torii, New Britain	.263	99	387	342	49	90	137	20	3	7	33	9	1	7	28	1	60	7	7	7	.401	.3
Hurst, William, Portland	1.000	45	2	2	0	2	2	0	0	0	1	0	0	0	0	0	0	0	0	0	1.000	1.
Huson, Jeff, Bowie*	.385	3	14	13	3	5	7	2	0	0	0	0	0	0	1	0	0	0	0	0	.538	.4
Hyzdu, Adam, Trenton	.337	109	434	374	71	126	231	24	3	25	80	0	2	2	56	6	75	1	8	7	.618	.4
Imrisek, Jason, Norwich	.333	2	7	6	2	2	3	1	0	0	2	1	0	0	1	0	1	0	0	0	.500	.4
Jackson, Gavin, Trenton	.250	6	22	20	2	5	7	2	0	0	2	0	0	0	2	0	3	0	1	0	.350	.3
Jarrett, Link, New Haven†	.195	56	182	164	18	32	41	6	0	1	9	3	1	0	14	0	23	1	1	5	.250	.2
Johnson, J.J., New Britain*	.273	119	492	440	62	120	197	23	3	16	59	2	3	7	40	3	90	10	11	4	.448	.3
Katzaroff, Robbie, Norwich	.274	23	91	84	11	23	27	4	0	0	5	0	0	0	7	0	9	0	2	1	.321	.3
Kelly, Pat, Norwich	.294	4	17	17	3	5	9	2	1	0	0	0	0	0	0	0	0	0	0	0	.529	.2
Kendall, Jeremey, Reading	.168	35	157	131	23	22	32	5	1	1	10	3	0	11	12	0	35	5	5	4	.244	.3
Knowles, Eric, Norwich	.245	126	445	396	56	97	143	23	1	7	42	8	5	4	32	1	92	9	6	8	.361	.3
Koeyers, Ramsey, Harrisburg	.208	25	84	77	6	16	22	3	0	1	9	3	1	1	2	0	27	0	1	1	.286	.2
Kusiewicz, Mike, New Haven	.000	14	8	8	0	0	0	0	0	0	0	0	0	0	0	0	4	0	0	0	.000	.0
Lane, Ryan, New Britain	.222	33	128	117	13	26	39	5	1	2	12	2	1	0	8	0	29	3	4	1	.333	.2
Larkin, Andy, Portland	.143	8	7	7	0	1	1	0	0	0	0	0	0	0	0	0	2	0	0	0	.143	.
Larson, Toby, Binghamton	.111	11	11	9	1	1	2	1	0	0	1	1	0	0	0	0	2	0	0	0	.222	.
Leach, Jalal, Harrisburg*	.328	83	295	268	38	88	134	22	3	6	48	2	4	0	21	4	55	3	7	6	.500	.3
Ledee, Ricky, Norwich*	.365	39	160	137	27	50	87	11	1	8	37	1	5	1	16	0	25	2	2	4	.635	.4
Leiper, Tim, Binghamton*	.167	6	7	6	0	1	1	0	0	0	0	0	0	0	1	0	0	0	0	0	.167	.
Levangie, Dana, Trenton	.382	23	69	55	5	21	21	3	0	2	7	2	0	0	12	0	11	2	2	2	.382	.
Lewis, Anthony, New Britain*	.253	134	512	458	58	116	207	15	2	24	95	0	6	1	47	4	99	6	9	9	.452	.3
Lidle, Cory, Binghamton	.120	28	34	25	3	3	3	0	0	0	1	7	0	0	2	0	7	0	0	0	.120	.
Loewer, Carlton, Reading†	.143	27	23	21	1	3	7	1	0	1	1	1	0	0	1	0	5	0	0	0	.333	.
Long, R.D., Norwich†	.300	6	14	10	4	3	3	0	0	0	3	0	0	0	4	0	2	0	0	0	.300	.
Lopez, Rene, New Britain	.233	61	203	180	23	42	60	9	0	3	16	0	2	0	21	1	28	0	3	2	.333	.
Lowery, Terrell, Binghamton	.275	62	262	211	34	58	100	13	4	7	32	2	3	2	44	2	44	5	6	4	.474	.
Lukachyk, Rob, Harrisburg*	.326	27	106	92	22	30	51	6	0	5	24	1	1	0	12	0	18	4	1	0	.554	.
Macca, Chris, New Haven	.000	28	2	1	0	0	0	0	0	0	0	0	0	0	1	0	1	0	0	0	.000	.
Mack, Quinn, Portland*	.216	36	121	111	12	24	38	5	0	3	19	3	0	0	7	0	20	3	3	4	.342	.
Magee, Wendell, Reading	.293	71	295	270	38	79	122	15	5	6	30	0	0	1	24	1	40	10	6	8	.452	.
Mahalik, John, Binghamton	.241	75	234	216	37	52	76	11	2	3	22	6	3	2	27	0	35	6	2	3	.352	.
Maness, Dwight, Binghamton	.243	130	471	399	65	97	143	14	7	6	47	7	5	8	52	2	80	25	8	2	.358	.
Manto, Jeff, Trenton	.286	6	24	21	3	6	6	0	0	0	5	0	1	1	1	0	5	0	0	1	.286	.
Martin, Chandler, New Haven	.000	1	2	2	0	0	0	0	0	0	0	0	0	0	0	0	1	0	0	0	.000	.
Martinez, Ramiro, Harrisburg*	.000	8	9	9	0	0	0	0	0	0	0	0	0	0	0	0	2	0	0	2	.000	.
Masteller, Dan, Harrisburg*	.328	44	148	128	21	42	59	11	0	2	21	1	1	0	18	3	11	0	0	3	.461	.
McCall, Rod, Canton/Akron*	.300	120	498	440	80	132	246	29	2	27	85	0	0	6	52	4	118	2	0	4	.559	.

ayer, Team	Avg.	G	TPA	AB	R	H	TB	2B	3B	HR	RBI	SH	SF	HP	BB	IBB	SO	SB	CS	GDP	Slg.	OBP
:Common, Jason, Harrisburg	.235	31	18	17	2	4	5	1	0	0	0	1	0	0	0	0	5	0	0	0	.294	.235
:Connell, Chad, Reading	.247	116	449	385	70	95	151	18	1	12	50	3	2	19	40	0	119	6	5	8	.392	.345
:Keel, Walt, Trenton	.302	128	543	464	86	140	209	19	1	16	78	5	7	60	3	52	2	4	13	.450	.385	
:Nair, Fred, Norwich	.276	69	261	246	31	68	101	10	1	7	43	1	3	0	11	0	53	2	0	7	.411	.304
adows, Brian, Portland	.000	4	4	2	0	0	0	0	0	0	0	0	0	0	2	0	1	0	0	0	.000	.500
ndoza, Reynol, Portland	.091	10	13	11	1	1	1	0	0	0	2	1	1	0	0	0	3	0	0	1	.091	.083
erloni, Lou, Trenton	.232	28	110	95	11	22	39	6	1	3	16	1	0	5	9	1	18	0	2	2	.411	.330
etheney, Nelson, Reading	.000	26	1	1	0	0	0	0	0	0	0	0	0	0	0	0	1	0	0	0	.000	.000
lar, Kevin, Portland	.318	130	523	472	69	150	236	32	0	18	86	0	5	9	37	4	53	6	5	13	.500	.375
lares, Jose, Bowie	.186	25	79	70	3	13	16	3	0	0	1	2	0	3	4	0	6	1	1	0	.229	.260
ller, Roger, New Haven	.242	85	293	256	23	62	81	8	1	3	29	6	3	2	26	0	32	0	1	11	.316	.314
lliard, Ralph, Portland	.200	6	21	20	2	4	6	0	1	0	2	0	0	0	1	0	5	1	0	0	.300	.238
llion, Doug, New Haven*	.143	10	8	7	0	1	1	0	0	0	0	1	0	0	0	0	2	0	0	0	.143	.143
tchell, Larry, Reading	.000	34	3	2	1	0	0	0	0	0	0	0	0	0	1	0	1	0	0	0	.000	.333
x, Greg, Portland	.333	25	14	12	1	4	4	0	0	0	1	0	0	0	2	0	3	0	0	1	.333	.429
iler, Jason, Reading	.246	109	438	374	59	92	168	22	0	18	59	1	5	4	54	3	50	4	5	7	.449	.343
ntoyo, Charlie, Harrisburg	.224	74	220	183	21	41	46	3	1	0	18	2	1	2	32	0	23	1	0	6	.251	.344
ore, Joel, New Haven*	.000	6	4	4	0	0	0	0	0	0	0	0	0	0	0	0	3	0	0	0	.000	.000
rgan, Kevin, Binghamton	.252	107	478	409	61	103	136	11	2	6	35	10	3	3	53	2	59	13	4	15	.333	.340
otuzas, Jeff, Norwich	.333	5	9	9	1	3	3	0	0	0	2	0	0	0	0	0	4	0	0	0	.333	.333
noz, Bobby, Reading	.200	4	6	5	1	1	3	0	1	0	0	0	0	0	1	0	0	0	0	0	.600	.333
rrow, John, New Haven	.251	122	447	406	46	102	131	11	3	4	36	6	2	2	30	3	61	11	3	14	.323	.305
ehring, Tim, Trenton	.222	3	10	9	2	2	6	1	0	1	2	0	0	0	1	0	3	0	0	1	.667	.300
al, Mike, Canton/Akron	.224	94	306	254	42	57	84	9	3	4	32	2	6	5	39	0	53	2	3	3	.331	.332
er, Chris, New Haven	.000	55	2	2	0	0	0	0	0	0	0	0	0	0	0	0	1	0	0	0	.000	.000
vers, Tom, New Britain	.264	127	513	459	65	121	183	27	7	7	44	2	3	3	46	1	87	3	10	18	.399	.333
ton, Trot, Trenton*	.251	123	502	438	55	110	162	11	4	11	63	6	5	3	50	3	65	7	9	6	.370	.329
thrup, Kevin, Norwich	.243	63	267	235	36	57	92	10	2	7	37	3	2	1	26	2	36	3	1	14	.391	.318
ton, Chris, Norwich	.279	47	188	172	24	48	83	12	1	7	28	0	0	1	15	0	43	3	2	3	.483	.340
nez, Clemente, Portland	.000	32	8	8	0	0	0	0	0	0	0	0	0	0	0	0	3	0	0	0	.000	.000
e, Ryan, Reading	.222	14	10	9	0	2	3	1	0	0	0	0	0	0	1	0	3	0	0	0	.333	.300
eill, Doug, Portland	.257	72	273	241	39	62	97	10	2	7	26	2	2	2	26	1	64	8	4	3	.402	.332
z, Nick, Trenton	.223	38	144	130	20	29	42	4	0	3	13	1	0	0	13	2	28	2	2	3	.323	.294
nez, Willis, Bowie	.265	138	559	506	60	134	237	27	2	24	75	2	5	1	45	2	97	3	7	17	.468	.323
oole, Bobby, Bowie	.000	6	10	10	0	0	0	0	0	0	0	0	0	0	0	0	5	0	0	0	.000	.000
heco, Alexander, Harrisburg	.000	18	2	2	0	0	0	0	0	0	0	0	0	0	0	0	1	0	0	0	.000	.000
ano, Scott, Binghamton†	.259	126	525	464	63	120	144	15	3	1	46	9	2	7	43	3	55	26	16	11	.310	.329
iagua, Jose, Harrisburg	.250	3	4	4	0	1	2	1	0	0	1	0	0	0	0	0	1	0	0	0	.500	.250
ton, Greg, Trenton	.188	6	20	16	3	3	4	1	0	0	1	0	0	0	4	0	4	0	1	0	.250	.350
ton, Jay, Binghamton	.200	4	14	10	0	2	2	0	0	0	2	0	2	0	2	1	2	0	1	0	.200	.286
raza, Rodney, New Haven	.063	19	20	16	0	1	2	1	0	0	0	3	0	0	1	0	7	0	0	0	.125	.118
lps, Tom, Harrisburg*	.200	8	5	5	0	1	1	0	0	0	0	0	0	0	0	0	1	0	0	0	.200	.200
hardo, Sandy, Norwich†	.353	6	19	17	3	6	10	1	0	1	3	1	0	0	1	0	5	1	0	0	.588	.389
rson, Jason, Binghamton	.000	34	4	4	0	0	0	0	0	0	0	0	0	0	0	0	1	0	0	0	.000	.000
ciotta, Scott, Harrisburg	.000	27	2	1	0	0	0	0	0	0	0	1	0	0	0	0	0	0	0	0	.000	.000
iger, Kinnis, Norwich*	.265	131	513	445	80	118	214	27	6	19	67	1	0	2	65	7	123	20	5	4	.481	.361
al, Matt, New Haven†	.000	4	2	1	0	0	0	0	0	0	0	0	0	0	0	0	0	0	0	0	.000	.000
e, Lou, Harrisburg	.000	25	17	15	0	0	0	0	0	0	0	1	0	0	1	0	11	0	0	0	.000	.063
ico, Rafael, Rea.-Nor.*	.000	9	2	2	0	0	0	0	0	0	0	0	0	0	0	0	2	0	0	0	.000	.000
manovich, Ryan, N.B.*	.280	125	510	453	77	127	237	31	2	25	86	3	2	3	49	6	122	4	11	12	.523	.353
nes, Tim, Norwich†	.185	8	37	27	8	5	9	1	0	1	1	0	0	1	9	3	2	2	0	0	.333	.405
eigh, Matt, Bowie	.250	4	9	8	0	2	3	1	0	0	2	0	0	0	1	0	3	0	0	0	.375	.333
nirez, Alex, Canton/Akron	.329	131	534	513	99	169	263	28	12	14	85	1	1	3	16	1	74	18	10	8	.513	.353
nirez, Hector, Binghamton	.250	38	4	4	1	1	1	0	0	0	1	2	0	0	0	0	0	0	0	0	.250	.250
poli, Paul, Trenton*	.212	69	231	193	16	41	58	8	0	3	22	4	4	3	27	1	54	4	5	4	.301	.313
en, Luis, Canton/Akron	.302	74	309	268	57	81	161	17	0	21	64	0	2	1	38	6	73	0	0	6	.601	.388
mond, Mike, Portland	.287	120	435	394	43	113	147	22	0	4	44	5	5	5	26	2	45	3	4	12	.373	.335
dina, Mike, Harrisburg*	.143	16	46	42	4	6	8	2	0	0	0	1	0	0	3	0	11	0	0	1	.190	.200
teria, Dave, Harrisburg	.236	24	80	72	7	17	23	6	0	0	4	2	0	1	5	0	13	0	0	1	.319	.295
e, Lance, Bowie†	.213	55	182	164	8	35	45	4	0	2	17	3	2	0	13	1	19	0	0	4	.274	.268
gs, Kevin, Norwich*	.290	118	497	403	75	117	149	24	1	2	37	2	5	6	81	4	66	9	9	7	.370	.412
erts, Chris, Binghamton	.000	9	2	2	0	0	0	0	0	0	0	0	0	0	0	0	1	0	0	0	.000	.000
ertson, Jason, Portland*	.272	99	375	338	65	92	151	17	3	12	48	0	4	2	31	2	91	12	6	3	.447	.333
riguez, Maximo, Portland	.176	6	18	17	1	3	3	0	0	0	1	0	0	0	1	0	6	0	1	1	.176	.222
en, Scott, Reading	.361	61	274	230	44	83	136	22	2	9	42	0	5	5	34	3	32	8	3	5	.591	.445
ano, Scott, Tren.-Nor.	.283	31	127	113	14	32	45	4	0	3	8	1	0	2	11	0	26	2	0	2	.398	.357
er, Chad, New Britain	.251	128	514	466	59	117	169	18	2	10	48	1	2	3	42	4	73	4	7	12	.363	.316
ue, Rafael, Binghamton*	.125	13	10	8	1	1	1	0	0	0	1	0	0	0	2	0	4	0	0	0	.125	.300
ario, Melvin, Bowie†	.210	47	176	162	14	34	50	10	0	2	17	1	2	5	6	1	43	3	2	4	.309	.257
kos, John, Portland	.275	121	470	396	53	109	168	26	3	9	58	0	2	5	67	4	102	3	4	5	.424	.385
ster, Aaron, Reading	.257	65	269	230	42	59	82	11	0	4	20	3	1	5	30	2	56	4	5	3	.357	.353
p, Chad, New Britain	.252	77	303	278	38	70	138	14	0	18	48	3	5	4	13	0	56	3	2	8	.496	.290
er, Donnie, Trenton	.267	115	507	454	68	121	175	20	8	6	46	6	3	6	38	3	75	34	8	6	.385	.329
er, Jon, Harrisburg*	.300	134	579	487	96	146	210	26	4	10	52	5	3	6	78	1	77	8	16	8	.431	.401
e, Mike, New Haven	.222	32	21	18	0	4	6	2	0	0	3	2	0	0	1	0	6	0	0	1	.333	.263
erbeck, Scott, Binghamton..	.167	8	8	6	1	1	1	0	0	0	1	0	0	0	2	0	1	0	0	0	.167	.375
nders, Chris, Binghamton	.298	141	604	510	82	152	236	27	3	17	105	2	11	8	73	3	88	5	4	11	.463	.387
nders, Tony, Portland*	.120	26	27	25	2	3	3	0	0	0	1	0	0	1	0	0	7	0	0	1	.120	.154
zitti, Will, New Haven	.231	7	27	26	1	6	8	2	0	0	1	0	0	0	0	0	3	0	0	2	.308	.231
fried, Tate, Norwich*	.208	115	412	361	52	75	134	17	0	14	47	2	1	1	47	3	128	2	3	9	.371	.300
son, Richie, Canton/Akron	.276	133	568	518	85	143	230	33	3	16	76	0	5	6	39	5	118	2	1	13	.444	.331
on, Chris, New Haven	.216	127	526	444	50	96	112	12	2	0	28	7	3	1	71	2	68	8	5	10	.252	.324
f, Chris, Portland	.295	27	118	105	16	31	53	12	2	2	17	0	0	0	13	3	23	3	2	3	.505	.373
es, Scott, Reading	.229	120	457	398	52	91	159	19	8	11	51	3	4	6	46	2	133	19	10	3	.399	.315

Player, Team	Avg.	G	TPA	AB	R	H	TB	2B	3B	HR	RBI	SH	SF	HP	BB	IBB	SO	SB	CS	GDP	Slg.	OB
Smith, Mark, Bowie	.091	6	25	22	1	2	5	0	0	1	2	0	0	2	1	0	6	0	0	1	.227	.20
Smith, Sloan, Norwich†	.218	60	235	202	27	44	64	10	2	2	20	3	0	0	30	2	96	4	1	0	.317	.31
Soliz, Steve, Canton/Akron	.259	46	158	143	18	37	51	4	2	2	15	0	2	2	11	0	28	1	2	1	.357	.31
Spencer, Shane, Norwich	.253	126	528	450	70	114	220	19	0	29	89	1	5	4	68	2	99	4	2	6	.489	.35
Stanifer, Robby, Portland	.500	18	2	2	0	1	2	1	0	0	1	0	0	0	0	0	1	0	0	0	1.000	.50
Stovall, Darond, Harrisburg†	.221	74	310	272	38	60	99	7	1	10	36	4	0	2	32	1	86	10	5	5	.364	.30
Strange, Don, Bowie	.000	12	1	1	0	0	0	0	0	0	0	0	0	0	0	0	0	0	0	0	.000	.00
Stull, Everett, Harrisburg	.111	14	11	9	1	1	2	1	0	0	0	2	0	0	0	0	4	0	0	0	.222	.11
Talanoa, Scott, Harrisburg	.210	50	171	138	20	29	67	5	0	11	23	0	0	1	31	3	50	0	0	4	.486	.35
Tam, Jeff, Binghamton	1.000	49	1	1	0	1	1	0	0	0	0	0	0	0	0	0	0	0	0	0	1.000	1.00
Taylor, Jamie, New Haven*	.243	124	418	362	46	88	134	20	1	8	37	3	5	3	45	6	74	1	2	12	.370	.32
Thomas, Greg, Canton/Akron*	.279	97	331	301	44	84	145	14	4	13	55	1	2	1	26	4	56	2	1	8	.482	.33
Thompson, Fletcher, Bowie*	.256	59	204	172	30	44	53	4	1	1	19	0	0	0	32	1	52	8	4	3	.308	.37
Thomson, John, New Haven	.056	18	23	18	0	1	1	0	0	0	2	4	1	0	0	0	5	0	0	0	.056	.05
Thornton, Paul, Portland	.333	52	3	3	1	1	1	0	0	0	0	0	0	0	0	0	1	0	0	0	.333	.33
Thoutsis, Paul, Harrisburg*	.200	5	23	20	1	4	7	3	0	0	3	0	1	0	2	0	6	0	0	0	.350	.26
Torres, Jaime, Norwich	.251	100	368	334	42	84	125	19	2	6	40	7	2	4	21	2	28	1	3	7	.374	.30
Torres, Tony, Portland	.270	47	146	126	21	34	48	11	0	1	13	1	0	5	14	0	24	3	1	2	.381	.36
Troilo, Jason, Norwich	.500	3	8	8	3	4	10	0	0	2	2	0	0	0	0	0	1	0	0	0	1.250	.50
Troutman, Keith, Reading	.000	52	3	3	0	0	0	0	0	0	0	0	0	0	0	0	0	0	0	0	.000	.00
Turner, Brian, Bing.-N.B.*	.228	80	278	241	27	55	96	13	2	8	30	5	6	4	22	2	53	6	3	6	.398	.29
Valdes, Marc, Portland	.231	10	14	13	1	3	3	0	0	0	0	0	0	0	1	0	4	0	0	0	.231	.28
Valentin, Jose, New Britain†	.236	48	185	165	22	39	56	8	0	3	14	3	0	1	16	1	35	0	3	2	.339	.30
Valette, Ramon, New Britain	.239	23	74	71	7	17	26	2	2	1	6	0	0	3	0	0	11	6	0	2	.366	.27
Velazquez, Edgard, New Haven	.290	132	543	486	72	141	235	29	4	19	62	0	4	4	53	5	114	6	2	7	.484	.36
Viano, Jake, New Haven	.000	23	4	3	0	0	0	0	0	0	0	1	0	0	0	0	1	0	0	0	.000	.00
Vidro, Jose, Harrisburg†	.259	126	502	452	57	117	202	25	3	18	82	9	10	2	29	3	71	3	1	6	.447	.30
Voisard, Mark, New Haven	.000	8	1	1	0	0	0	0	0	0	0	0	0	0	0	0	1	0	0	0	.000	.00
Walbeck, Matt, New Britain*	.208	7	25	24	1	5	5	0	0	0	0	0	0	0	1	0	1	0	0	1	.208	.24
Ward, Bryan, Portland*	.250	28	29	28	4	7	13	3	0	1	3	1	0	0	0	0	5	0	0	2	.464	.25
Weber, Neil, Harrisburg*	.091	18	12	11	0	1	2	1	0	0	1	0	0	0	1	0	6	0	0	0	.182	.09
Welch, Mike, Binghamton*	.000	46	2	0	0	0	0	0	0	0	0	0	0	0	1	0	0	0	0	0	.000	1.00
Wells, Forry, New Haven*	.230	108	358	304	44	70	112	19	1	7	43	2	2	4	46	4	73	1	2	4	.368	.33
White, Don, Binghamton	.192	82	250	219	29	42	68	6	1	6	22	1	1	3	26	0	61	5	4	5	.311	.28
White, Rondell, Harrisburg	.350	5	21	20	5	7	17	1	0	3	6	0	0	1	0	1	1	1	1	1	.850	.38
Wilson, Enrique, Can./Akron†	.304	117	526	484	70	147	189	17	5	5	50	0	7	4	31	2	46	23	16	9	.390	.34
Wilson, Pookie, Portland*	.256	113	429	375	46	96	140	16	5	6	35	9	4	8	33	3	49	7	10	4	.373	.32
Withem, Shannon, Binghamton	.143	12	17	14	0	2	2	0	0	0	1	2	0	0	1	0	4	0	0	0	.143	.20
Woods, Tyrone, Trenton	.312	99	415	356	75	111	206	16	2	25	71	0	2	0	56	3	66	5	4	6	.579	.40
Wright, Jamey, New Haven	.231	7	15	13	0	3	5	2	0	0	3	2	0	0	0	0	5	0	0	0	.385	.23
Young, Eric, New Haven	.067	3	15	15	0	1	1	0	0	0	0	0	0	0	0	0	3	0	0	0	.067	.06
Zolecki, Mike, New Haven	.000	47	5	5	0	0	0	0	0	0	0	0	0	0	1	0	1	0	0	0	.000	.00

GRAND SLAMS: Radmanovich, 4; R. Brown, Held, C. Saunders, 2 each; Abad, Aven, Estalella, Gibson, Grifol, Johnson, Lewis, Lukachyk, Mahalik, McCall, Millar, Nixon, Northrup, Pledger, Sexson, Shores, S. Smith, Vidro.

AWARDED FIRST BASE ON CATCHER'S INTERFERENCE: Angeli (Norton); Aven (Miller); Azuaje (Torres); Campos (Torres); Coughlin (Norton); Henley (Miller); Myrow (Grifol); Talanoa (Miller); Woods (Torres).

PLAYERS WITH TWO OR MORE TEAMS

Player, Team	Avg.	G	TPA	AB	R	H	TB	2B	3B	HR	RBI	SH	SF	HP	BB	IBB	SO	SB	CS	GDP	Slg.	O
Aversa, Joe, Binghamton†	.188	13	42	32	3	6	6	0	0	0	1	2	0	1	7	0	8	0	0	1	.188	.3
Aversa, Joe, Portland†	.244	54	162	135	22	33	41	8	0	0	21	3	1	0	23	0	22	2	3	3	.304	.3
Beckett, Robbie, Portland	.500	3	3	2	0	1	1	0	0	0	1	0	0	0	1	0	1	0	0	0	.500	.6
Beckett, Robbie, New Haven	.000	30	2	2	0	0	0	0	0	0	0	0	0	0	0	0	2	0	0	0	.000	.0
Harris, Doug, Bowie	.000	3	0	0	0	0	0	0	0	0	0	0	0	0	0	0	0	0	0	0	.000	.0
Harris, Doug, Portland	.000	20	2	2	0	0	0	0	0	0	0	0	0	0	0	0	2	0	0	0	.000	.0
Quirico, Rafael, Reading*	.000	5	2	2	0	0	0	0	0	0	0	0	0	0	0	0	2	0	0	0	.000	.0
Quirico, Rafael, Norwich*	.000	4	0	0	0	0	0	0	0	0	0	0	0	0	0	0	0	0	0	0	.000	.
Romano, Scott, Trenton	.167	1	7	6	0	1	2	1	0	0	0	0	0	0	1	0	1	0	0	0	.333	.2
Romano, Scott, Norwich	.290	30	120	107	14	31	43	3	0	3	8	1	0	2	10	0	24	2	0	2	.402	.3
Turner, Brian, Binghamton*	.202	32	99	84	8	17	32	5	2	2	12	1	2	3	9	2	18	1	1	1	.381	.2
Turner, Brian, New Britain*	.242	48	179	157	19	38	64	8	0	6	18	4	4	1	13	0	35	5	2	5	.408	.2

1996 PITCHING

TEAM

Team	W	L	Pct.	ERA	G	CG	ShO	Sv.	IP	H	TBF	R	ER	HR	SH	SF	HB	BB	IBB	SO	WP	B
Norwich	71	70	.504	3.63	141	11	11	33	1208.2	1154	5268	633	488	92	52	36	51	523	36	979	79	
Harrisburg	74	68	.521	3.63	142	6	10	44	1219.0	1169	5250	592	498	117	48	30	58	529	23	813	51	
Portland	83	58	.589	3.72	141	12	7	45	1232.2	1206	5210	609	509	132	58	34	46	387	37	986	57	
New Haven	66	75	.468	3.84	141	7	14	37	1199.2	1151	5153	609	512	107	50	33	41	496	52	1016	61	
Binghamton	76	66	.535	4.05	142	17	8	40	1224.2	1268	5223	626	551	123	63	32	40	412	30	851	44	
Trenton	86	56	.606	4.11	142	15	8	39	1231.2	1170	5303	644	563	135	49	45	67	494	44	896	63	
Canton/Akron	71	71	.500	4.15	142	8	4	33	1228.0	1190	5330	663	566	101	55	35	47	530	33	1020	63	
Reading	66	75	.468	4.37	141	6	8	26	1236.0	1221	5461	717	600	140	43	37	65	576	35	1026	86	
New Britain	61	81	.430	4.61	142	13	7	24	1207.1	1278	5397	726	619	104	47	46	73	513	22	886	83	
Bowie	54	88	.380	4.71	142	8	8	25	1234.1	1308	5417	744	646	146	47	41	51	503	9	885	66	

INDIVIDUAL

TOP QUALIFIERS FOR EARNED-RUN AVERAGE TITLE

Minimum 114 innings. *Lefthanded pitcher.

itcher, Team	W	L	Pct.	ERA	G	GS	CG	ShO	GF	Sv.	IP	H	TBF	R	ER	HR	SH	SF	HB	BB	IBB	SO	WP	Bk.
avano, Carl, Trenton..............	16	5	.762	2.63	27	26	6	2	1	0	185.0	154	741	66	54	16	5	7	11	47	2	146	7	1
aunders, Tony, Portland* ..	13	4	.765	2.63	26	26	2	0	0	0	167.2	121	669	51	49	10	8	4	0	62	3	156	8	1
edraza, Rodney, New Haven ..	7	3	.700	2.95	19	18	3	2	0	0	122.0	115	488	49	40	10	2	4	2	21	1	74	1	1
aipe, Mike, New Haven	10	7	.588	3.07	32	19	1	1	5	3	138.0	114	562	53	47	12	4	3	4	42	6	126	4	4
eech, Matt, Reading*	11	6	.647	3.17	21	21	0	0	0	0	133.1	108	547	57	47	16	2	5	4	32	0	132	9	0
aduro, Calvin, Bowie	9	7	.563	3.26	19	19	4	3	0	0	124.1	116	507	50	45	8	4	1	2	36	0	87	4	2
dle, Cory, Binghamton	14	10	.583	3.31	27	27	6	1	0	0	190.1	186	779	78	70	13	6	2	3	49	4	141	14	3
rownson, Mark, New Haven..	8	13	.381	3.50	37	19	1	0	10	3	144.0	141	619	73	56	10	6	3	6	43	5	155	7	2
uerra, Mark, Binghamton	7	6	.538	3.53	27	20	1	0	3	0	140.1	143	577	60	55	23	5	2	2	34	3	84	1	1
riskill, Travis, Cant./Akron ..	13	7	.650	3.61	29	24	4	2	0	0	172.0	169	732	89	69	8	6	6	3	63	0	148	10	2
unnane, Will, Portland	10	12	.455	3.74	25	25	4	0	0	0	151.2	156	631	73	63	15	5	2	1	30	6	101	4	0
rster, Scott, Harrisburg* ..	10	7	.588	3.78	28	28	0	0	0	0	176.1	164	755	92	74	15	3	4	7	67	2	97	5	0
alteisek, Steve, Harrisburg ..	6	5	.545	3.81	17	17	1	0	0	0	115.2	111	492	60	49	9	7	0	5	48	1	62	5	3
inidad, Hector, New Britain ..	6	6	.500	3.84	25	24	1	1	0	0	138.1	137	583	75	59	6	4	1	7	31	0	93	7	0
eLaRosa, Maximo, C./A.	11	5	.688	3.91	40	15	0	0	17	3	119.2	104	530	60	52	7	2	4	3	81	3	109	12	2

DEPARTMENTAL LEADERS: W—Pavano, 16; L—Hale, 13; Pct.—Betti, .900; G—Gomes, 67; GS—Fernandez, 29; CG—Pavano, Lidle, 6; ShO—Maduro, 3; GF—omes, 55; SV—Hurst, 30; IP—Lidle, 190.1; H—Loewer, 191; TBF—Fernandez, 798; R—Loewer, Fernandez, 115; ER—Fernandez, 101; HR—Loewer, 24; SH—Kline,); SF—Fernandez, 9; HB—Costa, 14; BB—Costa, 92; IBB—Neier, Vaught, 9; SO—A. Saunders, 156; WP—Chavez, 19; BK—Several players tied with 4 each.

ALL PITCHERS

*Lefthanded pitcher.

tcher, Team	W	L	Pct.	ERA	G	GS	CG	ShO	GF	Sv.	IP	H	TBF	R	ER	HR	SH	SF	HB	BB	IBB	SO	WP	Bk.
kire, Jeff, Portland*	0	2	.000	6.41	11	0	0	0	4	0	19.2	26	93	15	14	4	1	0	1	7	1	24	1	0
arcelo, Marc, New Britain	3	8	.273	5.06	14	13	3	1	1	0	80.0	98	377	53	45	7	2	5	4	38	0	59	5	0
arkley, Brian, Trenton*	8	8	.500	5.72	22	21	0	0	0	0	119.2	126	535	79	76	17	6	5	5	56	4	89	7	2
uckett, Robbie, Port.-N.H.*	7	3	.700	5.11	33	7	0	0	11	0	61.2	55	285	39	35	8	5	5	1	59	5	62	4	0
eech, Matt, Reading*	11	6	.647	3.17	21	21	0	0	0	0	133.1	108	547	57	47	16	2	5	4	32	0	132	9	0
ll, Jason, New Britain	2	6	.250	4.40	16	16	2	1	0	0	94.0	93	410	54	46	13	5	2	5	38	1	94	6	1
nitez, Armando, Bowie	0	0	.000	4.50	4	4	0	0	0	0	6.0	7	23	3	3	0	0	0	0	0	0	8	0	0
nnett, Joel, Tren.-Bow.	3	3	.500	3.66	13	8	0	0	1	0	59.0	39	229	25	24	7	0	0	1	19	0	56	0	0
nnett, Shayne, Harrisburg ..	8	8	.500	2.53	53	0	0	0	27	12	92.2	83	393	32	26	6	3	3	5	35	2	89	2	2
nz, Jake, Harrisburg*	1	4	.200	5.97	34	0	0	0	20	4	37.2	42	181	30	25	7	3	2	2	27	3	25	4	0
tti, Rick, Trenton*	9	1	.900	3.67	31	8	0	0	1	0	81.0	70	361	39	33	7	2	1	3	44	5	65	5	0
verlin, Jason, Norwich	0	3	.000	8.44	8	4	0	0	1	0	16.0	25	81	21	15	2	0	2	0	6	1	17	0	0
ais, Mike, Trenton	10	3	.769	3.94	53	0	0	0	27	5	77.2	74	323	37	34	10	5	1	2	23	4	52	3	0
ost, Heath, New Haven	1	0	1.000	1.50	4	0	0	0	2	0	6.0	5	24	1	1	0	0	0	0	2	0	7	0	0
ucher, Denis, Harrisburg*	1	0	1.000	1.50	1	1	0	0	0	0	6.0	2	22	1	1	0	1	0	0	2	0	6	0	0
wers, Shane, New Britain ..	6	8	.429	4.19	27	22	1	0	1	0	131.0	134	569	71	61	15	2	3	6	42	1	96	11	0
ewer, Brian, Bowie*	2	4	.333	4.89	11	11	0	0	0	0	57.0	61	253	40	31	10	1	2	2	27	0	35	2	2
ock, Russ, Norwich	0	1	.000	8.18	4	0	0	0	0	0	11.0	14	48	10	10	1	1	0	0	5	0	14	0	0
own, Charlie, Norwich	0	0	.000	0.00	1	0	0	0	0	0	2.1	1	9	0	0	0	0	0	0	1	0	1	0	0
own, Dickie, Cant./Akron ..	0	2	.000	8.03	6	0	0	0	1	0	12.1	13	62	12	11	3	0	0	1	9	1	11	0	0
ownson, Mark, New Haven..	8	13	.381	3.50	37	19	1	0	10	3	144.0	141	619	73	56	10	6	3	6	43	5	155	7	2
ddie, Mike, Norwich	7	12	.368	4.45	29	26	4	0	0	0	159.2	176	708	101	79	10	8	5	8	71	5	103	16	0
llard, Jason, Bing.-C/A	1	1	.500	2.57	17	0	0	0	8	0	21.0	18	91	7	6	1	3	0	1	11	3	22	0	0
llinger, Kirk, Harrisburg ..	3	4	.429	4.17	47	0	0	0	40	22	45.2	46	193	40	16	10	5	3	1	18	3	29	3	0
brera, Jose, Cant./Akron ..	4	3	.571	5.63	15	9	1	0	0	0	62.1	78	278	45	39	10	2	3	1	17	2	40	4	0
faro, Rocco, Bowie	4	8	.333	4.96	27	15	1	0	1	0	103.1	130	467	67	57	14	3	5	5	36	0	55	5	2
ridad, Ron, Norwich	2	2	.500	5.01	20	0	0	0	5	0	32.1	29	148	21	18	3	1	2	2	24	0	21	7	1
rrasco, Troy, New Britain* ..	6	9	.400	5.07	34	17	1	1	8	0	110.0	113	504	74	62	9	5	2	9	66	1	69	15	1
rter, John, Binghamton	9	3	.750	4.23	19	19	3	1	0	0	110.2	120	485	60	52	10	6	3	6	54	1	48	6	0
derblad, Brett, Trenton	1	3	.250	3.72	27	3	0	0	9	2	58.0	59	245	27	24	8	1	3	3	16	3	49	5	1
avez, Carlos, Bowie.............	4	6	.400	4.34	56	1	0	0	27	7	83.0	69	369	44	40	8	1	3	6	52	0	80	19	0
ergey, Dan, Portland	0	2	.000	4.00	13	0	0	0	8	2	18.0	18	80	9	8	1	1	0	0	6	2	16	0	0
morelli, Frank, New Haven ..	0	1	.000	9.00	5	0	0	0	3	0	9.0	10	39	6	5	1	1	0	1	1	1	8	0	0
ark, Howie, Bowie	0	0	.000	0.00	1	0	0	0	0	0	0.1	0	1	0	0	0	0	0	0	0	0	0	0	0
ayton, Royal, Bowie	0	1	.000	10.80	3	2	0	0	0	0	11.2	8	12	38	10	10	3	0	4	5	0	0		
lon, Bartolo, Cant./Akron ..	2	2	.500	1.74	13	12	0	0	0	0	62.0	44	253	17	12	2	0	1	2	25	0	56	3	1
ne, David, Norwich	0	0	.000	0.90	2	2	0	0	0	0	10.0	9	38	3	1	1	0	0	0	1	0	13	0	0
nner, Scott, Bowie	1	5	.167	5.05	21	11	0	0	1	0	82.0	86	362	54	46	12	2	3	3	36	0	59	3	3
sta, Tony, Reading	5	13	.278	4.81	27	26	1	0	0	0	153.1	150	702	107	82	20	5	4	14	92	2	112	16	3
urtright, John, N.B.-Bow.* ...	1	1	.500	6.56	23	3	0	0	6	0	48.0	61	229	40	35	4	4	1	2	24	1	22	1	2
awford, Joe, Binghamton* ..	5	1	.833	1.45	7	7	1	1	0	0	49.2	34	190	10	8	4	2	0	0	9	1	34	1	2
oghan, Andy, Norwich	9	5	.643	3.07	35	0	0	0	19	4	41.0	41	181	23	14	4	2	0	1	16	3	49	5	0
owther, Brent, New Haven ..	3	7	.300	6.20	25	12	0	0	2	1	85.2	109	385	64	59	10	8	1	1	30	5	54	2	2
mberland, Chris, Norwich*..	5	7	.417	5.27	16	16	2	1	0	0	95.2	112	427	73	56	13	2	5	4	37	2	44	4	0
nnane, Will, Portland	10	12	.455	3.74	25	25	4	0	0	0	151.2	156	631	73	63	15	5	2	1	30	6	101	4	0
an, Greg, Bowie	0	3	.000	8.53	3	3	0	0	0	0	12.2	21	70	15	12	2	0	1	0	13	0	4	1	0
drick, Jim, Bowie	1	1	.500	3.38	13	0	0	0	4	2	26.2	28	116	10	10	3	0	1	4	11	1	21	1	0
Hart, Rick, Harrisburg*	1	2	.333	2.68	30	2	0	0	14	1	43.2	46	196	19	13	4	1	2	3	18	0	38	4	0
ean, Mike, New Haven	0	0	.000	3.22	16	0	0	0	15	11	22.1	20	90	9	8	2	0	1	0	19	0	12	2	0
LaMaza, Roland, C./A.	9	7	.563	4.38	40	14	0	0	9	1	139.2	122	587	75	68	15	6	1	1	49	3	132	3	2
LaRosa, Maximo, C./A.	11	5	.688	3.91	40	15	0	0	17	3	119.2	104	530	60	52	7	2	4	3	81	3	109	12	2
xon, Steve, Binghamton* ..	0	1	.000	5.40	5	0	0	0	4	0	8.1	10	41	5	5	0	1	0	1	8	1	11	0	1
dd, Robert, Reading*	2	3	.400	3.56	18	5	0	0	4	0	43.0	41	185	21	17	4	2	4	3	24	2	35	0	1

CLASS AA Eastern League

Pitcher, Team	W	L	Pct.	ERA	G	GS	CG	ShO	GF	Sv.	IP	H	TBF	R	ER	HR	SH	SF	HB	BB	IBB	SO	WP
Doherty, John, Trenton	1	1	.500	1.85	4	4	0	0	0	0	24.1	20	95	8	5	0	1	1	3	2	0	14	0
Dorlarque, Aaron, Harrisburg	1	0	1.000	6.00	13	0	0	0	3	0	24.0	32	111	17	16	4	2	1	2	7	1	14	0
Dougherty, Anthony, C./A.	0	0	.000	9.00	3	0	0	0	0	0	5.0	3	26	5	5	1	0	0	0	8	1	6	0
Drews, Matt, Norwich	1	3	.250	4.50	9	9	0	0	0	0	46.0	40	210	26	23	4	1	0	5	33	1	37	1
Driskill, Travis, Cant./Akron	13	7	.650	3.61	29	24	4	2	0	0	172.0	169	732	89	69	8	6	6	3	63	0	148	10
Dunbar, Matt, Norwich*	4	2	.667	1.78	33	6	0	0	11	1	70.2	59	306	33	14	3	6	4	5	28	3	59	2
Eden, Bill, New Haven*	1	1	.500	5.23	29	0	0	0	10	0	41.1	48	197	26	24	6	2	4	2	24	2	41	6
Edmondson, Brian, Bing.	6	6	.500	4.25	39	13	1	0	9	0	114.1	130	502	69	54	16	7	7	4	38	5	83	3
Emerson, Scott, Trenton*	1	0	1.000	5.85	19	0	0	0	6	0	32.1	34	154	24	21	4	0	1	1	26	0	23	7
Estavil, Mauricio, Reading*	0	3	.000	11.57	20	0	0	0	6	0	18.2	30	110	28	24	3	0	0	1	22	1	19	4
Eversgerd, Bryan, Trenton*	1	0	1.000	2.57	4	0	0	0	2	0	7.0	6	31	2	2	0	1	0	1	4	1	2	0
Falteisek, Steve, Harrisburg	6	5	.545	3.81	17	17	1	0	0	0	115.2	111	492	60	49	9	7	0	5	48	1	62	5
Fernandez, Jared, Trenton	9	9	.500	5.08	30	29	3	0	0	0	179.0	185	798	115	101	19	5	9	10	83	5	94	10
Fiore, Tony, Reading	1	2	.333	4.35	5	5	0	0	0	0	31.0	32	146	21	15	2	0	1	1	18	0	19	6
Fisher, David, Reading	0	0	.000	0.00	1	0	0	0	1	0	1.0	1	4	0	0	0	0	0	0	0	0	0	1
Fleetham, Ben, Harrisburg	0	0	.000	0.00	4	0	0	0	3	1	6.0	2	23	0	0	0	0	0	0	5	0	6	0
Forster, Scott, Harrisburg*	10	7	.588	3.78	28	28	0	0	0	0	176.1	164	755	92	74	15	3	4	7	67	2	97	5
Foster, Mark, Reading*	4	5	.444	5.80	50	8	0	0	12	0	76.0	84	349	54	49	6	4	4	4	45	6	56	4
Fuller, Mark, Binghamton	5	4	.556	4.18	51	0	0	0	17	1	75.1	86	332	41	35	7	5	2	3	22	3	43	2
Gavaghan, Sean, New Britain	2	2	.500	6.46	28	0	0	0	16	6	39.0	42	187	28	28	5	1	3	4	29	1	44	3
Gentile, Scott, Harrisburg	2	2	.500	2.63	15	0	0	0	6	1	24.0	14	100	8	7	2	2	0	3	14	1	23	0
Gomes, Wayne, Reading	0	4	.000	4.48	67	0	0	0	55	24	64.1	53	291	35	32	7	1	3	1	48	3	79	14
Gray, Dennis, Harrisburg*	0	0	.000	7.59	9	0	0	0	1	0	10.2	12	54	9	9	1	0	0	0	14	0	10	0
Grigsby, Benji, Cant./Akron	1	2	.333	1.26	16	0	0	0	8	2	28.2	22	120	11	4	0	4	2	3	11	1	21	1
Grott, Matt, Bowie*	2	1	.667	4.98	9	0	0	0	3	0	21.2	26	93	15	12	3	0	2	0	5	0	15	2
Grundt, Ken, Trenton*	1	0	1.000	0.00	12	0	0	0	3	0	12.2	6	48	0	0	0	1	0	0	6	0	13	1
Guerra, Mark, Binghamton	7	6	.538	3.53	27	20	1	0	3	0	140.1	143	577	60	55	23	5	2	2	34	3	84	1
Hale, Shane, Bowie*	5	13	.278	5.00	24	24	0	0	0	0	135.0	146	591	81	75	18	6	3	6	51	2	86	4
Harris, Doug, Bow.-Port.	6	5	.545	5.59	23	3	0	0	10	1	48.1	50	219	31	30	6	3	2	3	21	3	31	2
Harris, Reggie, Trenton	2	1	.667	1.46	33	0	0	0	30	17	37.0	17	144	6	6	2	0	3	0	19	2	43	1
Hecker, Doug, Trenton	0	1	.000	2.25	13	0	0	0	7	2	20.0	18	82	5	5	1	2	2	1	5	2	12	2
Heflin, Bronson, Reading	2	2	.500	5.22	25	0	0	0	12	1	29.1	37	139	20	17	3	2	0	2	15	2	27	2
Henthorne, Kevin, Norwich	5	3	.625	2.26	12	8	0	0	2	0	59.2	50	252	25	15	3	1	2	2	22	2	47	3
Heredia, Felix, Portland*	8	1	.889	1.50	55	0	0	0	17	5	60.0	48	236	11	10	3	4	1	1	15	2	42	1
Hernandez, Livan, Portland	9	2	.818	4.34	15	15	0	0	0	0	93.1	81	380	48	45	14	3	0	3	34	1	95	3
Herrmann, Gary, Reading*	1	5	.167	4.99	23	5	0	0	7	0	39.2	43	185	25	22	7	1	3	3	27	2	31	1
Hill, Milt, Bowie	5	7	.417	6.67	25	16	2	0	4	1	87.2	126	400	73	65	15	1	3	3	18	0	66	2
Hmielewski, Chris, Har.*	1	2	.333	12.00	3	0	0	0	1	0	3.0	4	17	4	4	0	1	0	2	3	1	2	1
Holman, Craig, Reading	6	1	.857	3.50	8	8	0	0	0	0	46.1	42	186	21	18	6	4	0	2	13	0	34	3
Hostetler, Marcus, Bowie	3	0	1.000	3.32	32	0	0	0	9	1	57.0	51	243	29	21	4	4	1	3	22	0	44	5
Hubbard, Mark, Norwich*	2	0	1.000	5.49	4	4	0	0	0	0	19.2	19	89	13	12	2	1	0	1	10	1	14	0
Hunter, Rich, Reading	4	3	.571	3.17	10	10	2	0	0	0	71.0	69	290	26	25	7	1	1	7	12	0	40	3
Hurst, William, Portland	2	3	.400	2.20	45	0	0	0	42	30	49.0	45	218	22	12	3	1	2	1	31	0	46	6
Jarvis, Matt, Bowie*	1	3	.250	7.45	6	4	0	0	0	0	19.1	31	91	17	16	2	0	2	1	7	0	13	4
Jerzembeck, Mike, Norwich	3	6	.333	4.52	14	13	1	1	0	0	69.2	74	303	38	35	9	4	2	3	26	0	65	2
Juhl, Mike, Reading*	1	1	.500	2.79	9	0	0	0	1	0	9.2	8	40	3	3	0	0	0	1	5	0	4	0
Kendrena, Ken, Harrisburg	1	0	1.000	4.63	7	0	0	0	3	0	11.2	10	46	6	6	3	0	0	1	2	0	4	0
Kline, Steven, Cant./Akron*	8	12	.400	5.46	25	24	0	0	0	0	146.2	168	658	98	89	16	10	4	6	55	2	107	5
Knackert, Brent, Trenton	0	0	.000	1.38	11	0	0	0	10	10	13.0	6	50	2	2	0	2	0	0	6	1	21	2
Konieczki, Dom, New Britain*	1	3	.250	4.98	28	0	0	0	11	2	34.1	32	159	19	19	2	1	2	4	23	2	23	3
Kotarski, Mike, Norwich*	1	2	.333	4.35	42	1	0	0	14	3	72.1	73	320	40	35	3	2	4	4	29	4	66	8
Kusiewicz, Mike, New Haven*	2	4	.333	3.30	14	14	0	0	0	0	76.1	83	326	38	28	4	2	3	2	27	2	64	0
Lane, Aaron, Bowie*	3	5	.375	4.59	13	8	1	1	2	2	51.0	44	224	37	26	7	6	3	0	24	4	35	1
Lankford, Frank, Norwich	7	8	.467	2.66	61	0	0	0	25	4	88.0	82	392	42	26	4	9	1	2	40	6	61	3
Larkin, Andy, Portland	4	1	.800	3.10	8	8	0	0	0	0	49.1	45	195	18	17	6	2	0	2	10	0	40	3
Larson, Toby, Binghamton	2	4	.333	6.00	11	8	1	0	1	0	48.0	57	209	36	32	5	6	3	1	14	0	25	2
Lemp, Chris, Bowie	1	3	.250	4.72	27	1	0	0	12	1	47.2	53	219	27	25	4	1	6	4	24	0	35	3
Lewis, Anthony, New Britain*	0	0	.000	13.50	2	0	0	0	2	0	2.0	1	9	3	3	1	0	0	0	2	0	0	0
Lidle, Cory, Binghamton	14	10	.583	3.31	27	27	6	1	0	0	190.1	186	779	78	70	13	6	2	3	49	4	141	14
Linebarger, Keith, New Britain	7	5	.583	3.27	42	4	1	0	19	4	99.0	98	428	53	36	9	7	4	7	32	6	69	2
Loewer, Carlton, Reading	7	10	.412	5.26	27	27	3	1	0	0	171.0	191	753	115	100	24	7	3	8	57	3	119	9
Macca, Chris, New Haven	3	1	.750	1.30	28	0	0	0	28	15	34.2	18	139	6	5	0	2	1	3	18	2	34	2
Maduro, Calvin, Bowie	9	7	.563	3.26	19	19	4	3	0	0	124.1	116	507	50	45	8	4	1	2	36	0	87	4
Maeda, Katsuhiro, Norwich	3	2	.600	4.05	9	9	1	1	0	0	53.1	49	221	25	24	4	1	2	1	21	0	30	4
Mahay, Ron, Trenton*	0	1	.000	29.45	1	1	0	0	0	0	3.2	12	29	13	12	1	0	0	0	6	0	0	1
Maine, Dalton, Bowie	0	1	.000	5.06	11	0	0	0	5	0	21.1	24	98	14	12	3	2	0	2	11	0	18	0
Martin, Chandler, New Haven	1	0	1.000	7.20	1	1	0	0	0	0	5.0	6	22	4	4	2	0	1	1	3	0	4	0
Martinez, Johnny, Cant./Akron	0	1	.000	5.40	5	0	0	0	2	0	8.1	9	39	6	5	1	0	0	2	4	0	3	0
Martinez, Ramiro, Harrisburg*	0	4	.000	4.50	8	5	0	0	3	0	24.0	23	109	13	12	2	3	0	2	15	0	10	2
Matthews, Mike, Cant./Akron*	9	11	.450	4.66	27	27	3	0	0	0	162.1	178	713	96	84	13	6	7	5	74	3	112	6
McCommon, Jason, Har.	10	10	.500	3.94	30	24	1	0	2	1	153.0	169	663	88	67	13	2	8	7	44	1	92	5
McCormack, Andy, C./A.*	0	1	.000	27.00	1	0	0	0	0	0	0.1	0	2	1	1	0	1	0	0	1	0	0	0
McCready, Jim, Binghamton	0	0	.000	0.00	1	0	0	0	0	0	1.0	0	3	0	0	0	0	0	0	0	0	0	0
McGraw, Tom, Trenton*	3	4	.429	3.18	30	0	0	0	12	1	34.0	34	149	15	12	1	3	0	0	19	7	32	1
Meadows, Brian, Portland	0	1	.000	4.33	4	4	1	0	0	0	27.0	26	108	15	13	1	3	1	1	4	0	13	0
Medina, Rafael, Norwich	5	8	.385	3.06	19	19	1	0	0	0	103.0	78	446	48	35	7	5	1	6	55	2	112	11
Mendoza, Reynol, Portland	4	2	.667	3.43	10	10	2	2	0	0	63.0	60	255	27	24	7	0	0	3	14	0	41	5
Merrill, Ethan, Trenton*	3	6	.333	7.05	13	10	1	0	0	0	60.0	71	279	55	47	12	1	1	3	26	0	42	5
Metheney, Nelson, Reading	0	2	.000	5.59	26	0	0	0	5	0	38.2	50	180	30	24	8	0	1	1	19	3	17	2
Meyer, David, Norwich*	0	0	.000	4.71	19	0	0	0	9	1	21.0	20	95	12	11	1	0	1	1	11	1	13	3
Million, Doug, New Haven*	3	3	.500	3.15	10	10	0	0	0	0	54.1	54	247	23	19	2	1	1	1	40	1	40	8
Mitchell, Larry, Reading	3	6	.333	5.21	34	2	0	0	7	0	57.0	55	267	39	33	2	4	2	1	44	2	71	3

tcher, Team	W	L	Pct.	ERA	G	GS	CG	ShO	GF	Sv.	IP	H	TBF	R	ER	HR	SH	SF	HB	BB	IBB	SO	WP	Bk.
ix, Greg, Portland	3	0	1.000	4.52	25	5	0	0	8	1	65.2	80	296	40	33	8	4	5	5	19	5	57	6	2
oler, Jason, Reading	0	0	.000	0.00	1	0	0	0	1	0	1.0	3	6	0	0	0	0	0	0	0	0	1	0	0
ontoya, Wilmer, Cant./Akron	2	5	.286	3.38	43	0	0	0	38	23	50.2	41	225	24	19	2	4	3	8	28	3	42	2	3
oore, Joel, New Haven	0	5	.000	4.60	6	6	0	0	0	0	31.1	35	134	18	16	4	2	1	3	5	0	15	1	0
orse, Paul, New Britain	6	4	.600	5.34	35	1	0	0	23	4	55.2	55	249	36	33	5	4	4	1	26	2	48	4	1
otuzas, Jeff, Norwich	0	0	.000	0.00	1	0	0	0	1	0	2.0	2	8	0	0	0	0	0	0	1	0	0	0	0
unoz, Bobby, Reading	0	1	.000	2.93	4	4	0	0	0	0	27.2	24	113	13	9	3	1	0	1	8	0	29	2	1
usselwhite, Jim, Norwich	2	1	.667	2.25	5	5	1	0	0	0	36.0	28	144	9	9	4	1	2	0	10	0	25	1	0
eier, Chris, New Haven	1	7	.125	4.98	55	0	0	0	20	2	81.1	99	388	63	45	9	7	1	2	44	9	54	9	3
inez, Clemente, Portland	2	7	.222	5.47	32	10	0	0	2	0	97.0	119	441	74	59	18	6	4	9	31	4	52	7	1
ye, Ryan, Reading	8	2	.800	3.84	14	14	0	0	0	0	86.2	76	365	41	37	9	1	3	6	30	1	90	3	1
'Donoghue, John, Bowie*	1	3	.250	4.38	7	7	0	0	0	0	37.0	42	162	21	18	6	4	2	2	16	0	26	0	0
ıme, Kevin, New Britain*	5	6	.455	4.33	51	0	0	0	22	3	81.0	83	363	49	39	7	6	4	6	33	5	42	5	2
acheco, Alexander, Har.	5	2	.714	2.73	18	0	0	0	4	0	26.1	26	113	10	8	2	1	1	1	12	1	27	0	0
aniagua, Jose, Harrisburg	3	0	1.000	0.00	3	3	0	0	0	0	18.0	12	66	1	0	0	1	0	1	2	0	16	1	0
avano, Carl, Trenton	16	5	.762	2.63	27	26	6	2	1	0	185.0	154	741	66	54	16	5	7	11	47	2	146	7	1
edraza, Rodney, New Haven	7	3	.700	2.95	19	18	3	2	0	0	122.0	115	488	49	40	10	2	4	2	21	3	74	1	1
erez, Melido, Norwich	1	0	1.000	0.00	1	1	0	0	0	0	8.0	4	27	0	0	0	0	0	0	1	0	7	0	0
helps, Tom, Harrisburg*	2	2	.500	2.47	8	8	2	2	0	0	47.1	43	195	16	13	3	2	0	1	19	2	23	0	0
erce, Jeff, Trenton	0	0	.000	1.00	4	0	0	0	1	0	9.0	6	38	1	1	0	0	0	1	4	1	5	1	0
erson, Jason, Binghamton*	5	3	.625	3.38	34	5	0	0	12	1	53.1	56	227	21	20	6	2	1	2	15	2	42	0	0
sciotta, Scott, Harrisburg	2	1	.667	5.50	27	0	0	0	5	1	36.0	35	165	22	22	4	3	0	3	27	2	18	3	1
antenberg, Erik, C./A.*	0	0	.000	3.00	19	0	0	0	9	0	21.0	21	84	7	7	3	1	0	0	2	1	26	2	0
aster, Allen, Bowie	0	0	.000	13.50	1	0	0	0	0	0	2.0	5	12	3	3	0	0	0	0	1	0	3	1	0
ool, Matt, New Haven	0	1	.000	2.70	4	0	0	0	3	0	6.2	9	30	2	2	0	1	0	2	1	0	7	1	0
ote, Lou, Harrisburg	1	7	.125	5.07	25	18	0	0	3	1	104.2	114	467	66	59	15	3	2	2	48	2	61	8	0
uirico, Rafael, Read.-Nor.*	2	0	1.000	2.21	9	5	0	0	4	0	36.2	27	151	9	9	3	0	2	2	14	1	32	1	1
amirez, Hector, Binghamton	1	5	.167	5.14	38	0	0	0	17	6	56.0	51	245	34	32	3	5	3	6	23	5	49	4	2
edman, Mark, New Britain*	7	7	.500	3.81	16	16	3	0	0	0	106.1	101	467	51	45	5	1	6	8	50	1	96	4	1
esz, Greg, Norwich	1	1	.500	2.54	19	2	0	0	9	2	39.0	38	172	17	11	1	1	0	1	18	1	37	3	0
evenig, Todd, Bowie	3	4	.429	2.63	38	0	0	0	29	7	61.2	42	238	18	18	6	0	2	2	18	0	39	2	0
hodes, Joey, Bowie	2	1	.667	1.50	4	1	0	0	1	0	12.0	6	46	2	2	0	0	0	1	5	0	9	1	0
cken, Ray, Norwich	5	2	.714	4.47	8	8	1	1	0	0	46.1	42	201	26	23	7	1	3	1	20	0	42	5	0
os, Dan, Norwich	3	1	.750	2.09	38	0	0	0	29	17	43.0	34	183	14	10	0	2	0	3	21	1	38	3	2
tchie, Todd, New Britain	3	7	.300	5.44	29	10	0	0	14	4	82.2	101	376	55	50	6	3	4	5	30	1	53	4	0
oberts, Chris, Binghamton*	2	7	.222	7.24	9	9	1	0	0	0	46.0	55	225	40	37	6	6	2	1	37	0	30	1	0
oque, Rafael, Binghamton*	0	4	.000	7.27	13	13	0	0	0	0	60.2	71	291	57	49	8	2	1	2	39	0	46	4	0
ose, Brian, Trenton	12	7	.632	4.01	27	27	4	2	0	0	163.2	157	687	82	73	21	6	4	13	45	3	115	1	1
umer, Tim, Norwich*	3	1	.750	2.25	8	7	0	0	0	0	40.0	32	165	12	10	3	2	0	0	18	0	44	1	0
yan, Kevin, Bowie	0	1	.000	9.00	2	1	0	0	0	0	3.0	7	17	4	3	0	0	0	1	1	0	2	0	0
aipe, Mike, New Haven	10	7	.588	3.07	32	19	1	1	5	3	138.0	114	562	53	47	12	4	3	4	42	6	126	4	4
ampson, Benj, New Britain*	5	7	.417	5.73	16	16	1	0	0	0	75.1	108	353	54	48	8	0	2	2	25	0	51	2	1
auerbeck, Scott, Bing.*	3	3	.500	3.47	8	8	2	0	0	0	46.2	48	191	24	18	4	1	2	1	12	0	30	0	0
aunders, Tony, Portland*	13	4	.765	2.63	26	26	2	0	0	0	167.2	121	669	51	49	10	8	4	0	62	3	156	8	1
chuermann, Lance, Bowie*	0	0	.000	3.18	6	0	0	0	4	0	5.2	7	28	5	2	2	0	0	0	2	0	6	0	0
chullstrom, Erik, Trenton	3	0	1.000	2.54	19	0	0	0	8	1	28.1	23	124	11	8	1	2	4	4	13	2	22	3	0
enior, Shawn, Trenton*	5	6	.455	4.72	16	13	1	0	0	0	82.0	89	372	53	43	13	6	3	6	42	2	49	1	0
exton, Jeff, Cant./Akron	2	4	.333	5.11	9	9	1	0	0	0	49.1	45	210	29	28	6	2	0	2	23	1	34	1	0
obkoviak, Jeff, New Haven	0	1	.000	5.40	4	0	0	0	1	0	6.2	7	32	5	4	0	0	0	0	5	1	4	2	0
tanifer, Robby, Portland	3	1	.750	1.57	18	0	0	0	10	2	34.1	27	137	15	6	3	1	2	1	9	0	33	2	0
tidham, Phil, New Britain	1	0	1.000	2.63	12	0	0	0	4	1	13.2	11	61	5	4	1	2	1	2	8	1	16	4	0
trange, Don, Bowie	2	1	.667	2.45	12	0	0	0	9	3	14.2	11	58	4	4	0	2	0	0	5	0	10	2	0
tull, Everett, Harrisburg	6	3	.667	3.15	14	14	0	0	0	0	80.0	64	345	31	28	8	3	2	2	52	1	81	6	0
utherland, John, Norwich	3	2	.600	2.74	26	0	0	0	6	1	42.2	37	187	15	13	3	2	1	3	19	3	31	3	0
alanoa, Scott, Harrisburg	0	0	.000	0.00	1	0	0	0	1	0	1.0	0	3	0	0	0	0	0	0	0	0	0	0	0
am, Jeff, Binghamton	6	2	.750	2.44	49	0	0	0	18	2	62.2	51	241	19	17	6	2	1	2	16	3	48	2	4
homson, John, New Haven	9	4	.692	2.86	16	16	1	0	0	0	97.2	82	389	35	31	8	2	2	1	27	1	86	2	1
hornton, Paul, Portland	3	6	.333	4.17	52	0	0	0	28	4	77.2	74	357	45	36	6	7	2	8	44	5	64	7	0
hurman, Mike, Harrisburg	3	1	.750	5.11	4	4	1	0	0	0	24.2	25	101	14	14	6	1	1	3	5	0	14	0	0
olar, Kevin, Cant./Akron*	1	3	.250	2.62	50	0	0	0	15	1	44.2	42	201	19	13	1	4	2	3	26	2	39	5	0
ranbarger, Mark, Bowie*	3	3	.500	5.40	40	2	0	0	17	3	55.0	67	263	37	33	5	5	2	3	35	1	45	2	1
rinidad, Hector, New Britain	6	6	.500	3.84	25	24	1	1	0	0	138.1	137	583	75	59	6	4	1	7	31	0	93	7	0
routman, Keith, Reading	6	3	.667	3.31	52	1	0	0	13	1	73.1	62	323	36	27	7	3	2	3	40	3	73	3	1
urrentine, Rich, Binghamton	1	1	.500	2.89	8	0	0	0	7	3	9.1	12	43	3	3	0	0	1	0	5	0	10	0	0
aldes, Marc, Portland	6	2	.750	2.66	10	10	1	0	0	0	64.1	60	263	25	19	5	1	2	3	12	2	49	2	0
aught, Jay, Cant./Akron	5	4	.556	4.77	51	0	0	0	26	3	94.1	101	415	58	50	10	5	2	4	35	9	78	6	1
ano, Jake, New Haven	4	3	.571	4.84	23	5	0	0	11	0	44.2	39	196	28	24	6	1	0	2	24	2	32	2	0
oisard, Mark, New Haven	0	2	.000	9.35	8	0	0	0	3	0	8.2	10	43	9	9	1	1	0	1	5	1	7	0	1
allace, Kent, Norwich	0	0	.000	6.00	1	1	0	0	0	0	6.0	10	28	4	4	2	0	1	0	0	0	1	0	0
ard, Bryan, Portland*	9	9	.500	4.91	28	25	2	0	0	0	146.2	170	633	97	80	23	9	6	7	32	3	124	0	2
eber, Neil, Harrisburg*	7	4	.636	3.03	18	18	1	0	0	0	107.0	90	440	37	36	8	3	3	5	44	0	74	5	0
elch, Mike, Binghamton	4	2	.667	4.59	46	0	0	0	37	27	51.0	55	216	29	26	4	3	1	3	10	0	53	0	0
estbrook, Destry, Reading	4	3	.571	3.97	25	0	0	0	11	0	34.0	40	156	19	15	4	3	0	0	14	4	15	1	0
hitten, Casey, Cant./Akron*	3	1	.750	1.67	8	8	0	0	0	0	37.2	23	150	8	7	2	0	0	2	13	0	44	3	0
ilson, Paul, Binghamton	0	1	.000	7.20	1	1	0	0	0	0	5.0	6	25	4	4	0	0	1	0	5	0	5	2	0
ithem, Shannon, Bing.	6	3	.667	3.24	12	12	1	1	0	0	86.0	86	355	32	31	8	3	0	3	17	0	59	2	0
right, Jamey, New Haven	5	1	.833	0.81	7	7	1	1	0	0	44.2	27	167	7	4	0	3	0	2	12	0	54	1	1
an, Esteban, Bowie	0	2	.000	5.63	9	1	0	0	3	0	16.0	18	75	12	10	2	1	1	0	8	0	16	1	1
olecki, Mike, New Haven	2	8	.200	5.46	47	10	0	0	10	2	90.2	82	417	60	55	13	1	4	4	68	6	83	8	0

COMBINATION SHUTOUTS: **Binghamton (2)**—Lidle-Welch, Carter-Guerra. **Bowie (3)**—Hale-Hill, Cafaro-Tranbarger, Bennett-Revenig. **Canton/Akron (2)**—Sexton-aught-Tolar-Martinez, DeLaRosa-DeLaMaza. **Harrisburg (7)**—Paniagua-Bennett-Benz, Paniagua-Bennett, Stull-Bennett-Bullinger, Weber-Bennett, Forster-Bennett, alteisek-DeHart, McCommon-Gentile. **New Britain (2)**—Sampson-Bowers-Gavaghan, Bowers-Caridad. **New Haven (10)**—Wright-Saipe, Wright-Pedraza-Zolecki,

Wright-Saipe, Thomson-Dejean, Thomson-Neier-Dejean, Saipe-Bost, Thomson-Macca, Saipe-Neier-Macca, Brownson-Macca, Viano-Brownson-Neier. **Norwich (7)**—Henthrone-Resz, Jerzembeck-Resz-Beverlin-Kotarski, Drews-Kotarski-Lankford, Maeda-Croghan-Rios, Perez-Meyer, Dunbar-Lankford-Rios, Maeda-Kotarski-Crogha Rios. **Portland (4)**—Cunnane-Heredia-Hurst, Valdes-Heredia-Hurst, Saunders-Heredia, Saunders-Heredia-Hurst. **Reading (6)**—Costa-Heflin-Gomes, Beech-Juhl-Foste Beech-Gomes, Beech-Mitchell-Gomes, Beech-Metheney, Hunter-Foster-Gomes. **Trenton (2)**—Rose-Blais, Fernandez-Cederblad-Gomes.

NO-HIT GAMES: Crawford, Binghamton, defeated Trenton, 1-0, May 5; Maduro, Bowie, defeated Portland, 5-0, May 28; Lane, Bowie, defeated Norwich, 2-0, June

PITCHERS WITH TWO OR MORE TEAMS

Pitcher, Team	W	L	Pct.	ERA	G	GS	CG	ShO	GF	Sv.	IP	H	TBF	R	ER	HR	SH	SF	HB	BB	IBB	SO	WP	Bk
Beckett, Robbie, Portland*	1	0	1.000	6.23	3	3	0	0	0	0	13.0	17	66	9	9	1	1	2	0	13	0	7	1	0
Beckett, Robbie, New Haven*	6	3	.667	4.81	30	4	0	0	11	0	48.2	38	219	30	26	7	4	3	1	46	5	55	3	0
Bennett, Joel, Trenton	1	0	1.000	8.31	3	0	0	0	1	0	4.1	3	18	4	4	2	0	0	0	2	0	8	0	0
Bennett, Joel, Bowie	2	3	.400	3.29	10	8	0	0	0	0	54.2	36	211	21	20	5	0	0	1	17	0	48	0	0
Bullard, Jason, Binghamton	0	0	.000	2.70	8	0	0	0	3	0	10.0	11	46	4	3	0	1	0	0	5	2	10	0	0
Bullard, Jason, Cant./Akron	1	1	.500	2.45	9	0	0	0	5	0	11.0	7	45	3	3	1	2	0	1	6	1	12	0	0
Courtright, John, New Britain*	1	1	.500	6.61	14	3	0	0	3	0	32.2	42	154	25	24	2	3	1	1	16	0	12	1	2
Courtright, John, Bowie*	0	0	.000	6.46	9	0	0	0	3	0	15.1	19	75	15	11	2	1	0	1	8	1	10	0	0
Harris, Doug, Bowie	0	2	.000	11.08	3	3	0	0	0	0	13.0	17	67	16	16	2	2	1	3	7	0	5	1	0
Harris, Doug, Portland	6	3	.667	3.57	20	0	0	0	10	1	35.1	33	152	15	14	4	1	1	0	14	3	26	1	0
Quirico, Rafael, Reading*	1	0	1.000	1.80	5	5	0	0	0	0	30.0	22	124	6	6	2	0	2	2	11	1	23	0	1
Quirico, Rafael, Norwich*	1	0	1.000	4.05	4	0	0	0	4	0	6.2	5	27	3	3	1	0	0	0	3	0	9	1	0

1996 FIELDING

TEAM

Team	Pct.	G	PO	A	E	TC	DP	PB	Team	Pct.	G	PO	A	E	TC	DP	P
Binghamton	.976	142	3674	1684	133	5491	137	8	New Haven	.970	141	3599	1480	159	5238	117	1
Trenton	.972	142	3695	1510	148	5353	135	26	Reading	.969	141	3708	1482	165	5355	129	2
Bowie	.972	142	3703	1509	151	5363	99	16	Canton-Akron	.969	142	3684	1502	167	5353	127	1
Portland	.972	141	3698	1662	157	5517	155	15	New Britain	.968	142	3622	1455	168	5245	109	1
Harrisburg	.971	142	3657	1587	158	5402	137	17	Norwich	.962	141	3626	1521	205	5352	109	2

TRIPLE PLAYS: None.

INDIVIDUAL

FIRST BASEMEN

NOTE: All caps denotes fielding-percentage leader based on 71 games for catchers, 95 for all other non-pitchers and 142 innings for pitchers. *Throws lefthanded.

Player, Team	Pct.	G	PO	A	E	TC	DP
Abad, Andy, Trenton*	.997	41	326	18	1	345	33
Barron, Tony, Harrisburg	.964	3	26	1	1	28	3
Berg, David, Portland	1.000	1	1	0	0	1	0
Bernhardt, Steve, New Haven	1.000	2	14	1	0	15	1
Betts, Todd, Canton/Akron	1.000	1	3	0	0	3	0
Blum, Geoffrey, Harrisburg	1.000	1	2	0	0	2	0
Caraballo, Gary, New Britain	.981	18	140	13	3	156	10
Carey, Todd, Trenton	.976	16	121	2	3	126	9
Clark, Howie, Bowie	1.000	1	1	0	0	1	0
Coughlin, Kevin, Trenton*	.995	25	196	14	1	211	17
Curtis, Kevin, Bowie	1.000	8	78	1	0	79	5
Daubach, Brian, Binghamton	.991	121	1108	115	11	1234	109
DAVIS, Tommy, Bowie	.995	134	1158	95	6	1259	79
DeBerry, Joe, Norwich*	.968	3	25	5	1	31	2
Delgado, Alex, Trenton	1.000	6	67	2	0	69	7
Delvecchio, Nick, Norwich	1.000	1	2	0	0	2	0
Donato, Daniel, Norwich	1.000	1	2	0	0	2	1
Fisher, David, Reading	.983	7	53	4	1	58	2
Fullmer, Brad, Harrisburg	.923	1	11	1	1	13	1
Geisler, Phil, Binghamton*	.984	9	55	7	1	63	6
Grunewald, Keith, New Haven	1.000	13	102	7	0	109	9
Held, Dan, Reading	.990	134	1115	81	12	1208	111
Helton, Todd, New Haven*	.994	92	788	61	5	854	58
Holdren, Nate, New Haven	.987	9	68	6	1	75	9
Leach, Jalal, Harrisburg*	1.000	1	2	1	0	3	0
Lewis, Anthony, New Britain*	.991	16	104	3	1	108	10
Lukachyk, Rob, Harrisburg	.978	24	206	21	5	232	19
Masteller, Dan, Harrisburg*	.993	39	286	13	2	301	28
McCall, Rod, Canton/Akron	.993	34	250	19	2	271	25
McConnell, Chad, Reading	.667	2	2	0	1	3	1
McKeel, Walt, Trenton	.984	38	283	23	5	311	26
McNair, Fred, Norwich	.982	38	285	38	6	329	24
Merloni, Lou, Trenton	1.000	1	7	1	0	8	0
Millar, Kevin, Portland	.987	87	739	48	10	797	79
Millares, Jose, Bowie	1.000	1	1	1	0	2	0
Moler, Jason, Reading	1.000	11	36	3	0	39	5
Montoyo, Charlie, Harrisburg	.991	32	224	9	2	235	21
Norton, Chris, Norwich	.962	15	89	11	4	104	15
Patton, Greg, Trenton	1.000	1	1	1	0	2	0
Raleigh, Matt, Bowie	1.000	1	1	0	0	1	0
Rappoli, Paul, Trenton	1.000	2	3	2	0	5	1
Raven, Luis, Canton/Akron	.929	3	13	0	1	14	1

Player, Team	Pct.	G	PO	A	E	TC	DP
Rendina, Mike, Harrisburg*	1.000	14	99	5	0	104	1
Riggs, Kevin, Norwich	1.000	1	6	0	0	6	
Romano, Scott, Trenton	1.000	1	15	0	0	15	
Roper, Chad, New Britain	.979	6	45	2	1	48	
Roskos, John, Portland	.987	67	572	39	8	619	6
Rupp, Chad, New Britain	.985	68	573	35	9	617	47
Saunders, Chris, Binghamton	1.000	2	8	1	0	9	
Seefried, Tate, Norwich	.985	88	659	58	11	728	41
Sexson, Richie, Canton/Akron	.989	104	892	76	11	979	9
Spencer, Shane, Norwich	1.000	12	86	5	0	91	
Talanoa, Scott, Harrisburg	.983	42	308	31	6	345	3
Taylor, Jamie, New Haven	1.000	1	2	0	0	2	
Thomas, Greg, Canton/Akron*	.953	3	36	5	2	43	
Thoutsis, Paul, Harrisburg	1.000	5	44	2	0	46	
Torres, Jaime, Norwich	.964	9	51	2	2	55	
Turner, Brian, Bing.-N.B.*	.994	59	473	50	3	526	3
Vidro, Jose, Harrisburg	1.000	1	8	1	0	9	
Wells, Forry, New Haven	.980	27	218	22	5	245	2
Wilson, Pookie, Portland*	1.000	1	9	2	0	11	2
Woods, Tyrone, Trenton	1.000	27	220	14	0	234	2

FIRST BASEMEN WITH TWO OR MORE TEAMS

Player, Team	Pct.	G	PO	A	E	TC	DP
Turner, Brian, Binghamton*	1.000	18	163	16	0	179	1
Turner, Brian, New Britain*	.991	41	310	34	3	347	2

SECOND BASEMEN

Player, Team	Pct.	G	PO	A	E	TC	DP
Allison, Chris, Trenton	.959	106	237	253	21	511	63
Amador, Manuel, Reading	1.000	1	0	2	0	2	
Anderson, Marlon, Reading	.957	75	166	239	18	423	67
Aversa, Joe, Bing.-Port.	1.000	3	3	9	0	12	
Azuaje, Jesus, Binghamton	.978	79	154	249	9	412	54
Bautista, Juan, Bowie	.000	1	0	0	1	1	
Bernhardt, Steve, New Haven	1.000	5	4	8	0	12	
Blum, Geoffrey, Harrisburg	.984	85	223	207	7	437	57
Brown, Randy, Trenton	.910	19	29	32	6	67	
Burton, Essex, Reading	.950	64	124	162	15	301	27
Caraballo, Gary, New Britain	.951	24	48	49	5	102	
Carey, Todd, Trenton	.895	4	8	9	2	19	
Carvajal, Jhonny, Harrisburg	.980	16	42	57	2	101	1
CASTILLO, Luis, Portland	.975	108	217	326	14	557	8
Clark, Howie, Bowie	.974	123	249	286	14	549	53
Donato, Daniel, Norwich	1.000	1	1	4	0	5	
Ferguson, Jeff, New Britain	.966	88	170	229	14	413	4
Fisher, David, Reading	.900	4	5	4	1	10	
Fleming, Carlton, Norwich	1.000	7	5	6	0	11	

– 426 –

ayer, Team	Pct.	G	PO	A	E	TC	DP
arcia, Vicente, New Haven	.985	72	148	182	5	335	42
oligoski, Jason, New Haven	1.000	10	10	21	0	31	8
runewald, Keith, New Haven	.966	20	37	49	3	89	10
utierrez, Ricky, Canton/Akron	.975	99	197	263	12	472	63
ardtke, Jason, Binghamton	.964	34	61	100	6	167	25
astings, Lionel, Portland	.981	19	49	52	2	103	18
nds, Rob, Norwich	.932	60	112	108	16	236	32
arrett, Link, New Haven	.966	47	77	96	6	179	17
elly, Pat, New Haven	.952	4	7	13	1	21	3
nowles, Eric, Norwich	1.000	13	14	30	0	44	3
ane, Ryan, New Britain	.966	12	25	31	2	58	7
eiper, Tim, Binghamton	1.000	1	1	3	0	4	1
ong, R.D., Norwich	.750	2	2	1	1	4	0
ahalik, John, Binghamton	.987	33	69	85	2	156	18
anto, Jeff, Trenton	.000	1	0	0	2	2	0
erloni, Lou, Trenton	.947	7	10	8	1	19	1
illares, Jose, Bowie	.975	17	44	33	2	79	10
illiard, Ralph, Portland	1.000	5	12	18	0	30	6
ontoyo, Charlie, Harrisburg	.959	10	27	20	2	49	11
eal, Mike, Canton/Akron	.973	43	76	101	5	182	24
evers, Tom, New Britain	1.000	20	43	39	0	82	7
rtiz, Nick, Trenton	.971	20	35	31	2	68	9
atton, Greg, Trenton	.833	1	1	4	1	6	1
enteria, Dave, Harrisburg	.962	6	13	12	1	26	1
iggs, Kevin, Norwich	.958	79	125	174	13	312	36
omano, Scott, Norwich	1.000	5	9	6	0	15	1
hompson, Fletcher, Bowie	1.000	6	6	4	0	10	0
orres, Tony, Portland	.924	13	29	32	5	66	7
alette, Ramon, New Britain	1.000	7	16	12	0	28	1
dro, Jose, Harrisburg	.987	34	78	74	2	154	21
ilson, Enrique, Canton/Akron	1.000	1	0	2	0	2	1
oung, Eric, New Haven	1.000	3	9	5	0	14	0

SECOND BASEMEN WITH TWO OR MORE TEAMS

layer, Team	Pct.	G	PO	A	E	TC	DP
versa, Joe, Binghamton	1.000	1	1	4	0	5	0
versa, Joe, Portland	1.000	2	2	5	0	7	0

THIRD BASEMEN

layer, Team	Pct.	G	PO	A	E	TC	DP
cantara, Israel, Harrisburg	.912	57	33	133	16	182	12
mador, Manuel, Reading	1.000	1	1	2	0	3	0
versa, Joe, Portland	.911	34	15	57	7	79	8
erg, David, Portland	.903	19	20	45	7	72	4
ernhardt, Steve, New Britain	.881	21	12	40	7	59	3
etts, Todd, Canton/Akron	.899	72	34	117	17	168	12
own, Randy, Trenton	.895	8	6	11	2	19	1
abrera, Jolbert, Harrisburg	1.000	1	0	1	0	1	0
araballo, Gary, New Britain	.945	25	19	67	5	91	7
AREY, Todd, Trenton	.941	103	67	238	19	324	21
ark, Howie, Bowie	1.000	1	0	1	0	1	0
elgado, Alex, Norwich	1.000	2	0	4	0	4	0
az, Einar, Canton/Akron	1.000	3	3	1	0	4	0
onato, Daniel, Norwich	.911	107	54	201	25	280	10
sher, David, Reading	.944	27	19	48	4	71	4
thian, Grant, Norwich	1.000	1	1	2	0	3	0
eming, Carlton, Norwich	.500	3	0	1	1	2	0
runewald, Keith, New Haven	.898	27	13	40	6	59	1
astings, Lionel, Portland	.902	68	33	152	20	205	16
nds, Rob, Norwich	.583	6	2	5	5	12	0
uson, Jeff, Bowie	1.000	1	1	4	0	5	1
nowles, Eric, Norwich	.816	13	5	26	7	38	2
ong, R.D., Norwich	1.000	3	2	6	0	8	1
ahalik, John, Binghamton	.933	9	1	13	1	15	3
anto, Jeff, Trenton	1.000	3	3	2	0	5	1
cKeel, Walt, Trenton	1.000	2	0	1	0	1	0
cNair, Fred, Norwich	.867	7	3	10	2	15	0
erloni, Lou, Trenton	.923	20	22	50	6	78	5
illar, Kevin, Portland	.952	34	14	86	5	105	9
oler, Jason, Reading	.898	57	37	112	17	166	12
ontoyo, Charlie, Harrisburg	.970	16	8	24	1	33	1
aehring, Tim, Portland	.750	2	1	2	1	4	0
eal, Mike, Canton/Akron	.898	24	12	41	6	59	5
evers, Tom, New Britain	.667	3	2	6	4	12	0
orton, Chris, Norwich	.750	3	1	2	1	4	1
rtiz, Nick, Trenton	.947	10	9	9	1	19	0
anez, Willis, Bowie	.941	133	106	278	24	408	18
atton, Greg, Trenton	1.000	3	2	6	0	8	1
aven, Luis, Canton/Akron	.885	64	32	114	19	165	9
enteria, Dave, Harrisburg	.500	1	0	1	1	2	0
olen, Scott, Reading	.949	61	41	125	9	175	10
omano, Scott, Norwich	.866	21	19	39	9	67	3
oper, Chad, New Britain	.918	108	64	205	24	293	16

Player, Team	Pct.	G	PO	A	E	TC	DP
Saunders, Chris, Binghamton	.941	137	74	327	25	426	25
Spencer, Shane, Norwich	1.000	4	2	9	0	11	0
Taylor, Jamie, New Haven	.934	110	79	258	24	361	30
Thompson, Fletcher, Bowie	.920	12	6	17	2	25	2
Torres, Jaime, Norwich	1.000	1	0	1	0	1	0
Torres, Tony, Portland	.881	13	7	30	5	42	1
Valentin, Jose, New Britain	.970	15	11	21	1	33	5
Vidro, Jose, Harrisburg	.952	77	46	193	12	251	17

SHORTSTOPS

Player, Team	Pct.	G	PO	A	E	TC	DP
Amador, Manuel, Reading	.857	3	3	3	1	7	1
Angeli, Doug, Reading	.929	56	79	156	18	253	38
Aversa, Joe, Bing.-Port.	.927	24	35	66	8	109	13
Azuaje, Jesus, Binghamton	1.000	1	1	3	0	4	0
Bautista, Juan, Bowie	.951	127	203	354	29	586	55
Berg, David, Portland	.958	90	123	313	19	455	65
Betts, Todd, Canton/Akron	1.000	2	2	3	0	5	0
Blum, Geoffrey, Harrisburg	.982	30	34	74	2	110	19
Brown, Randy, Trenton	.941	46	61	115	11	187	27
Burton, Essex, Reading	.750	2	3	6	3	12	1
Cabrera, Jolbert, Harrisburg	.950	102	173	305	25	503	59
Caraballo, Gary, New Britain	.842	5	4	12	3	19	1
Carey, Todd, Trenton	1.000	4	7	16	0	23	7
Clapinski, Chris, Portland	.980	23	29	68	2	99	13
Donato, Daniel, Norwich	.935	39	55	88	10	153	16
Fisher, David, Reading	.957	9	10	12	1	23	7
Fleming, Carlton, Norwich	1.000	3	5	4	0	9	0
Goligoski, Jason, New Haven	1.000	10	10	23	0	33	1
Gonzalez, Alex, Portland	.887	11	17	38	7	62	12
Grunewald, Keith, New Haven	.935	19	20	38	4	62	6
Guiliano, Matt, Reading	.969	73	77	177	8	262	29
Gutierrez, Ricky, Canton/Akron	.969	20	26	68	3	97	10
Hastings, Lionel, Portland	.750	1	1	2	1	4	0
Hinds, Rob, Norwich	.947	7	7	11	1	19	1
Jackson, Gavin, Trenton	.957	6	8	14	1	23	3
Jarrett, Link, New Haven	1.000	7	6	16	0	22	4
Knowles, Eric, Norwich	.940	103	131	262	25	418	53
Lane, Ryan, New Britain	.894	22	30	46	9	85	7
Long, R.D., Norwich	.875	1	3	4	1	8	1
Mahalik, John, Binghamton	.933	24	28	69	7	104	15
Manto, Jeff, Trenton	.833	1	2	3	1	6	0
Merloni, Lou, Trenton	.889	2	0	8	1	9	1
Millares, Jose, Bowie	.800	2	1	3	1	5	0
Moler, Jason, Reading	.944	10	14	20	2	36	6
MORGAN, Kevin, Binghamton	.956	107	170	330	23	523	65
Neal, Mike, Canton/Akron	.860	12	19	30	8	57	7
Nevers, Tom, New Britain	.951	106	153	310	24	487	54
Ortiz, Nick, Trenton	.981	11	10	41	1	52	3
Otanez, Willis, Bowie	1.000	1	0	1	0	1	0
Pichardo, Sandy, Norwich	.853	6	14	15	5	34	6
Renteria, Dave, Harrisburg	.895	15	23	28	6	57	4
Romano, Scott, Norwich	1.000	2	1	6	0	7	0
Roper, Chad, New Britain	.933	5	4	10	1	15	2
Sadler, Donnie, Trenton	.930	79	117	231	26	374	42
Sexton, Chris, New Haven	.954	116	178	294	23	495	58
Thompson, Fletcher, Bowie	.933	20	26	57	6	89	8
Torres, Tony, Portland	.811	9	7	23	7	37	3
Valette, Ramon, New Britain	.947	15	21	33	3	57	3
Vidro, Jose, Harrisburg	.857	2	3	3	1	7	1
Wilson, Enrique, Canton/Akron	.949	113	179	342	28	549	74

SHORTSTOPS WITH TWO OR MORE TEAMS

Player, Team	Pct.	G	PO	A	E	TC	DP
Aversa, Joe, Binghamton	.940	12	16	31	3	50	5
Aversa, Joe, Portland	.915	12	19	35	5	59	8

OUTFIELDERS

Player, Team	Pct.	G	PO	A	E	TC	DP
Abad, Andy, Trenton*	1.000	28	42	2	0	44	1
Agbayani, Benny, Binghamton	.952	11	19	1	1	21	0
Aven, Bruce, Canton/Akron	.979	130	280	3	6	289	0
Aversa, Joe, Portland	1.000	7	12	2	0	14	0
Avila, Rolo, Bowie	.977	58	127	3	3	133	0
Barron, Tony, Harrisburg	1.000	11	18	4	0	22	0
Berrios, Harry, Bowie	.946	34	52	1	3	56	0
Betzsold, James, Canton/Akron	.966	84	140	4	5	149	0
Bowers, Brent, Bowie	.992	55	116	4	1	121	0
Brown, Ron, Portland	1.000	2	2	0	0	2	0
Bryant, Pat, Canton/Akron	.980	33	47	1	1	49	0
Byrd, Anthony, New Britain	.952	49	98	2	5	105	1
Cabrera, Jolbert, Harrisburg	1.000	3	6	0	0	6	0
Campos, Jesus, Harrisburg	.961	58	117	6	5	128	2

CLASS AA *Eastern League*

Player, Team	Pct.	G	PO	A	E	TC	DP
Caraballo, Gary, New Britain	.900	8	26	1	3	30	0
Clyburn, Danny, Bowie	.899	59	103	4	12	119	0
Collier, Dan, Trenton	1.000	9	14	1	0	15	0
Cook, Hayward, Portland	1.000	13	18	1	0	19	0
Coughlin, Kevin, Trenton*	1.000	20	29	2	0	31	1
Curtis, Kevin, Bowie	.984	90	179	11	3	193	1
Dawkins, Walt, Reading	.962	70	147	4	6	157	2
DeBerry, Joe, Norwich*	.500	3	1	0	1	2	0
Delafield, Wil, Norwich	1.000	19	15	2	0	17	0
Dellucci, David, Bowie*	.979	60	134	5	3	142	0
DUNWOODY, Todd, Portland*	.996	138	254	2	1	257	2
Fisher, David, Reading	1.000	5	2	1	0	3	0
Fullmer, Brad, Harrisburg	.970	19	32	0	1	33	0
Geisler, Phil, Binghamton*	.990	70	93	5	1	99	1
Gibson, Derrick, New Haven	.932	117	168	10	13	191	0
Giudice, John, New Haven	.944	30	46	5	3	54	0
Goligoski, Jason, New Haven	1.000	2	2	0	0	2	0
Gordon, Keith, Bowie	.938	73	117	5	8	130	1
Grunewald, Keith, New Haven	1.000	1	2	0	0	2	0
Guerrero, Vladimir, Harrisburg	.961	106	184	13	8	205	3
Harvey, Ray, Canton/Akron*	1.000	4	6	0	0	6	0
Hastings, Lionel, Portland	1.000	6	2	0	0	2	0
Hinds, Rob, Norwich	1.000	4	2	0	0	2	0
Holifield, Rick, Trenton*	.984	104	240	8	4	252	1
Horne, Tyrone, Binghamton	1.000	22	23	2	0	25	0
Hunter, Torii, New Britain	.982	96	207	11	4	222	0
Huson, Jeff, Bowie	1.000	2	3	0	0	3	0
Hyzdu, Adam, Trenton	.979	79	132	9	3	144	1
Johnson, J.J., New Britain	.959	115	201	9	9	219	1
Katzaroff, Robbie, Norwich	.967	21	27	2	1	30	1
Kendall, Jeremey, Reading	.984	35	62	1	1	64	0
Leach, Jalal, Harrisburg*	.976	61	121	2	3	126	0
Ledee, Ricky, Norwich*	.980	35	48	2	1	51	0
Lewis, Anthony, New Britain*	.947	41	71	1	4	76	0
Lowery, Terrell, Binghamton	.971	53	97	3	3	103	0
Lukachyk, Rob, Harrisburg	1.000	2	6	1	0	7	0
Mack, Quinn, Portland*	.929	28	39	0	3	42	0
Magee, Wendell, Reading	.973	71	101	8	3	112	0
Maness, Dwight, Binghamton	.981	122	244	9	5	258	0
McConnell, Chad, Reading	.967	104	199	8	7	214	2
McNair, Fred, Norwich	.846	10	10	1	2	13	0
Moler, Jason, Reading	.846	9	11	0	2	13	0
Myrow, John, New Haven	.939	107	159	10	11	180	2
Neal, Mike, Canton/Akron	1.000	7	11	0	0	11	0
Nixon, Trot, Trenton*	.979	120	224	14	5	243	4
Northrup, Kevin, Norwich	1.000	63	109	4	0	113	2
Norton, Chris, Norwich	.923	10	11	1	1	13	0
O'Neill, Doug, Portland	.960	68	96	1	4	101	1
Pagano, Scott, Binghamton	.976	116	194	10	5	209	0
Pledger, Kinnis, Norwich	.969	122	244	3	8	255	0
Radmanovich, Ryan, New Britain	.984	118	246	3	4	253	0
Raines, Tim, Norwich	1.000	7	4	0	0	4	0
Raleigh, Matt, Bowie	1.000	1	1	0	0	1	0
Ramirez, Alex, Canton/Akron	.977	131	209	4	5	218	0
Rappoli, Paul, Trenton	1.000	60	75	3	0	78	1
Riggs, Kevin, Norwich	1.000	3	2	0	0	2	0
Robertson, Jason, Portland*	.949	54	74	0	4	78	0
Romano, Scott, Norwich	1.000	4	4	0	0	4	0
Royster, Aaron, Reading	.992	65	114	5	1	120	1
Sadler, Donnie, Trenton	.987	30	68	6	1	75	2
Saffer, Jon, Harrisburg	.940	106	154	3	10	167	0
Seefried, Tate, Norwich	.938	8	15	0	1	16	0
Sexton, Chris, New Haven	1.000	10	12	0	0	12	0
Sheff, Chris, Portland	1.000	27	37	0	0	37	0
Shores, Scott, Reading	.989	88	170	13	2	185	4
Smith, Sloan, Norwich	.975	58	116	3	3	122	0
Spencer, Shane, Norwich	.979	95	130	10	3	143	1
Stovall, Darond, Harrisburg*	.983	72	171	4	3	178	1
Thomas, Greg, Canton/Akron*	.989	67	83	7	1	91	1
Thompson, Fletcher, Bowie	.750	4	3	0	1	4	0
Turner, Brian, New Britain*	1.000	10	12	0	0	12	0
Velazquez, Edgard, New Haven	.978	123	215	9	5	229	1
Wells, Forry, New Haven	.962	47	75	1	3	79	1
White, Don, Binghamton	.941	62	91	4	6	101	0
White, Rondell, Harrisburg	1.000	5	12	0	0	12	0
Wilson, Pookie, Portland*	.982	104	153	8	3	164	0

CATCHERS

Player, Team	Pct.	G	PO	A	E	TC	DP	PB
Borrero, Richie, Trenton	.982	25	157	9	3	169	1	7
Castaneda, Hector, Bowie	1.000	8	59	3	0	62	0	0
Clark, Howie, Bowie	1.000	1	1	0	0	1	0	0

Player, Team	Pct.	G	PO	A	E	TC	DP
Crosby, Mike, Harrisburg	.988	27	142	17	2	161	1
Delgado, Alex, Trenton	1.000	13	94	11	0	105	1
Diaz, Einar, Canton/Akron	.983	103	762	87	15	864	4
Estalella, Bobby, Reading	.984	106	775	84	14	873	5
Fithian, Grant, Norwich	.986	42	259	30	4	293	4
Foster, Jim, Bowie	.988	8	77	5	1	83	1
Gonzalez, Pete, New Haven	.966	37	231	24	9	264	0
Greene, Charlie, Binghamton	.995	98	550	75	3	628	8
Gresham, Kris, Bowie	.993	41	239	38	2	279	7
Grifol, Pedro, Binghamton	.987	53	336	32	5	373	2
Gyselman, Jeff, Reading	.987	47	268	29	4	301	3
Henley, Bob, Harrisburg	.986	99	565	92	9	666	11
Higgins, Mike, New Haven	.987	21	140	13	2	155	0
Hilt, Scott, New Britain	.985	54	307	29	5	341	4
Horn, Jeff, New Britain	1.000	12	75	9	0	84	0
Hyzdu, Adam, Trenton	1.000	1	3	0	0	3	0
Imrisek, Jason, Norwich	.923	2	11	1	1	13	0
Koeyers, Ramsey, Harrisburg	.965	24	131	8	5	144	0
Levangie, Dana, Trenton	.993	23	129	14	1	144	2
Lopez, Rene, New Britain	.987	59	330	43	5	378	8
McKeel, Walt, Trenton	.992	93	552	76	5	633	11
Miller, Roger, New Haven	.991	82	611	69	6	686	8
Motuzas, Jeff, Norwich	.941	4	12	4	1	17	1
Norton, Chris, Norwich	.981	20	92	9	2	103	0
O'Toole, Bobby, Bowie	1.000	6	19	0	0	19	0
REDMOND, Mike, Portland	.996	119	814	88	4	906	10
Rice, Lance, Bowie	.994	52	302	45	2	349	2
Rodriguez, Maximo, Portland	1.000	6	44	5	0	49	0
Rosario, Melvin, Bowie	.973	38	219	38	7	264	3
Roskos, John, Portland	.988	29	147	11	2	160	0
Scalzitti, Will, New Haven	.984	6	58	3	1	62	0
Soliz, Steve, Canton/Akron	.987	45	276	31	4	311	6
Torres, Jaime, Norwich	.983	90	624	75	12	711	6
Troilo, Jason, Norwich	1.000	3	13	2	0	15	0
Valentin, Jose, New Britain	.980	31	177	15	4	196	0
Walbeck, Matt, New Britain	1.000	3	11	2	0	13	0

PITCHERS

Player, Team	Pct.	G	PO	A	E	TC
Alkire, Jeff, Portland*	1.000	11	0	2	0	2
Barcelo, Marc, New Britain	.889	14	6	10	2	18
Barkley, Brian, Trenton*	.900	22	4	14	2	20
Beckett, Robbie, Port.-N.H.*	.929	33	4	9	1	14
Beech, Matt, Reading*	1.000	21	9	14	0	23
Bell, Jason, New Britain	.833	16	8	7	3	18
Benitez, Armando, Bowie	1.000	4	0	1	0	1
Bennett, Joel, Bowie	.944	13	11	6	1	18
Bennett, Shayne, Harrisburg	.944	53	5	12	1	18
Benz, Jake, Harrisburg*	1.000	34	0	5	0	5
Betti, Rick, Trenton*	1.000	31	6	10	0	16
Beverlin, Jason, Norwich	1.000	8	1	2	0	3
Blais, Mike, Trenton	.952	53	4	16	1	21
Bost, Heath, New Haven	1.000	4	3	0	0	3
Boucher, Denis, Harrisburg*	1.000	1	0	2	0	2
Bowers, Shane, New Britain	1.000	27	7	7	0	14
Brewer, Brian, Bowie*	.923	11	2	10	1	13
Brock, Russ, Norwich	.750	4	0	3	1	4
Brown, Charlie, Norwich	1.000	1	1	0	0	1
Brown, Dickie, Canton/Akron	1.000	6	2	2	0	4
Brownson, Mark, New Haven	.889	37	16	16	4	36
Buddie, Mike, Norwich	.963	29	13	39	2	54
Bullard, Jason, Bing.-C./A.	1.000	17	1	5	0	6
Bullinger, Kirk, New Haven	.947	47	2	16	1	19
Cabrera, Jose, Canton/Akron	.875	15	3	4	1	8
Cafaro, Rocco, Bowie	.920	27	7	16	2	25
Caridad, Ron, New Britain	1.000	20	3	8	0	11
Carrasco, Troy, New Britain*	1.000	34	3	18	0	21
Carter, John, Binghamton	.943	19	16	17	2	35
Cederblad, Brett, Trenton	1.000	27	1	5	0	6
Chavez, Carlos, Bowie	.867	56	4	9	2	15
Chergey, Dan, Portland	.667	13	0	2	1	3
Cimorelli, Frank, New Haven	1.000	5	1	4	0	5
Clayton, Royal, Bowie	1.000	3	0	1	0	1
Colon, Bartolo, Canton/Akron	.727	13	2	6	3	11
Cone, David, Norwich	.000	2	0	0	2	2
Conner, Scott, Bowie	.909	21	6	4	1	11
Costa, Tony, Reading	.943	27	17	16	2	35
Courtright, John, N.B.-Bow.*	.944	23	1	16	1	18
Crawford, Joe, Binghamton*	.900	7	2	7	1	10
Croghan, Andy, Norwich	.900	36	1	6	0	7
Crowther, Brent, New Haven	.857	25	7	17	4	28
Cumberland, Chris, Norwich*	.968	16	10	20	1	31

ayer, Team	Pct.	G	PO	A	E	TC	DP
nnane, Will, Portland	.950	25	19	19	2	40	2
an, Greg, Bowie	1.000	3	2	4	0	6	0
drick, Jim, Bowie	1.000	13	1	7	0	8	0
Hart, Rick, Harrisburg*	.800	30	1	3	1	5	0
jean, Mike, New Haven	1.000	16	3	3	0	6	1
LaMaza, Roland, Canton/Akron	1.000	40	15	24	0	39	3
LaRosa, Maximo, Canton/Akron.	.917	40	7	15	2	24	2
kon, Steve, Binghamton*	1.000	5	0	2	0	2	0
dd, Robert, Reading*	.917	18	1	10	1	12	0
herty, John, Trenton	.875	4	0	7	1	8	0
rlarque, Aaron, Harrisburg	1.000	13	2	5	0	7	1
ugherty, Anthony, Canton/Akron	1.000	3	0	2	0	2	0
ews, Matt, Norwich	.933	9	5	9	1	15	1
iskill, Travis, Canton/Akron	.919	29	17	17	3	37	1
nbar, Matt, Norwich*	.941	33	3	13	1	17	0
en, Bill, New Haven*	1.000	29	2	7	0	9	0
mondson, Brian, Binghamton	.921	39	11	24	3	38	2
nerson, Scott, Trenton*	.857	19	2	4	1	7	1
tavil, Mauricio, Reading*	1.000	20	2	1	0	3	0
ersgerd, Bryan, Trenton*	1.000	4	0	3	0	3	0
teisek, Steve, Harrisburg	.973	17	4	32	1	37	2
RNANDEZ, Jared, Trenton	1.000	30	10	31	0	41	1
re, Tony, Reading	1.000	5	2	4	0	6	1
rster, Scott, Harrisburg*	.964	28	13	41	2	56	3
ster, Mark, Reading*	.867	50	1	12	2	15	0
ller, Mark, Binghamton	.920	51	10	13	2	25	0
vaghan, Sean, New Britain	1.000	28	3	11	0	14	0
ntile, Scott, Harrisburg	1.000	15	1	3	0	4	0
mes, Wayne, Reading	.714	67	1	4	2	7	0
ay, Dennis, Harrisburg*	1.000	9	0	3	0	3	1
igsby, Benji, Canton/Akron	.889	16	3	5	1	9	0
ott, Matt, Bowie*	1.000	9	0	4	0	4	1
undt, Ken, Trenton*	1.000	12	0	6	0	6	1
erra, Mark, Binghamton	.971	27	20	14	1	35	2
le, Shane, Bowie*	.964	24	5	22	1	28	0
rris, Doug, Bow.-Port.	1.000	23	4	6	0	10	1
rris, Reggie, Trenton	1.000	33	1	4	0	5	0
cker, Doug, Trenton	1.000	13	1	3	0	4	1
flin, Bronson, Reading	.929	25	1	12	1	14	1
nthorne, Kevin, Norwich	1.000	12	7	9	0	16	0
redia, Felix, Portland*	.938	55	5	10	1	16	1
rnandez, Livan, Portland	.955	15	5	16	1	22	1
rrmann, Gary, Reading*	.857	23	0	6	1	7	0
ll, Milt, Bowie	.955	25	5	16	1	22	0
nielewski, Chris, Harrisburg*	1.000	3	0	2	0	2	0
lman, Craig, Reading*	.909	8	0	10	1	11	0
stetler, Marcus, Bowie	1.000	32	3	8	0	11	0
bbard, Mark, Norwich*	1.000	4	0	4	0	4	0
nter, Rich, Reading	.944	10	8	9	1	18	2
rst, William, Portland	1.000	45	3	9	0	12	3
rvis, Matt, Bowie*	.778	6	1	6	2	9	0
rzembeck, Mike, Norwich	1.000	14	5	8	0	13	0
hl, Mike, Reading*	1.000	9	1	2	0	3	0
ndrena, Ken, Harrisburg	1.000	7	0	4	0	4	0
ne, Steven, Canton/Akron*	.932	25	14	27	3	44	0
ackert, Brent, Trenton	1.000	11	0	3	0	3	0
nieczki, Dom, New Britain*	1.000	28	6	2	0	8	1
tarski, Mike, Norwich*	1.000	42	4	15	0	19	1
siewicz, Mike, New Haven*	.885	14	6	17	3	26	1
ne, Aaron, Bowie*	.889	13	2	14	2	18	0
nkford, Frank, Norwich	.969	61	10	21	1	32	0
rkin, Andy, Portland	.917	8	3	8	1	12	0
rson, Toby, Binghamton	1.000	11	3	5	0	8	1
mp, Chris, Bowie	.667	27	0	4	2	6	0
dle, Cory, Binghamton	.969	27	31	32	2	65	3
nebarger, Keith, New Britain	.941	42	3	13	1	17	0
ewer, Carlton, Reading	1.000	27	12	23	0	35	1
acca, Chris, New Haven	1.000	28	3	8	0	11	2
aduro, Calvin, Bowie	.889	19	6	26	4	36	2
aeda, Katsuhiro, Norwich	.929	9	6	7	1	14	0
aine, Dalton, Bowie	1.000	11	0	4	0	4	1
artinez, Johnny, Canton/Akron	1.000	5	0	1	0	1	0
artinez, Ramiro, Harrisburg	.857	8	3	3	1	7	0
atthews, Mike, Canton/Akron*	.980	27	10	39	1	50	3
cCommon, Jason, Harrisburg	.929	30	16	23	3	42	1
cGraw, Tom, Trenton*	.778	30	2	5	2	9	0
eadows, Brian, Portland	.857	4	5	1	1	7	0
edina, Rafael, Norwich	.806	19	7	18	6	31	0
endoza, Reynol, Portland	1.000	10	9	8	0	17	3
errill, Ethan, Trenton*	.889	13	2	6	1	9	0
etheney, Nelson, Reading	1.000	26	1	12	0	13	2
eyer, David, Norwich*	1.000	19	1	4	0	5	0
illion, Doug, New Haven*	.900	10	0	9	1	10	1

Player, Team	Pct.	G	PO	A	E	TC	DP
Mitchell, Larry, Reading	.875	34	0	7	1	8	0
Mix, Greg, Portland	1.000	25	5	5	0	10	2
Montoya, Wilmer, Canton/Akron.	1.000	43	5	7	0	12	0
Moore, Joel, New Haven	1.000	6	1	3	0	4	1
Morse, Paul, New Britain	1.000	35	8	6	0	14	0
Munoz, Bobby, Reading	.667	4	1	1	1	3	0
Musselwhite, Jim, Norwich	1.000	5	9	5	0	14	1
Neier, Chris, New Haven	.846	55	1	10	2	13	0
Nunez, Clemente, Portland	1.000	32	4	19	0	23	1
Nye, Ryan, Reading	1.000	14	5	10	0	15	2
O'Donoghue, John, Bowie*	1.000	7	3	16	0	19	0
Ohme, Kevin, New Britain*	.917	51	4	18	2	24	0
Pacheco, Alexander, Harrisburg.	.857	18	2	4	1	7	0
Paniagua, Jose, Harrisburg	1.000	3	1	4	0	5	0
Pavano, Carl, Trenton	.967	27	15	14	1	30	3
Pedraza, Rodney, New Haven	.920	19	6	17	2	25	2
Perez, Melido, Norwich	1.000	1	1	0	0	1	0
Phelps, Tom, Harrisburg*	.857	8	3	9	2	14	0
Pierce, Jeff, Trenton	1.000	4	1	1	0	2	0
Pierson, Jason, Binghamton*	1.000	34	4	6	0	10	1
Pisciotta, Scott, Harrisburg	.875	27	1	6	1	8	2
Plantenberg, Erik, Canton/Akron*	1.000	19	1	4	0	5	1
Pote, Lou, Harrisburg	1.000	25	14	12	0	26	2
Quirico, Rafael, Read.-Nor.*	.923	9	2	10	1	13	0
Ramirez, Hector, Binghamton	.800	38	2	6	2	10	0
Redman, Mark, New Britain*	.941	16	4	12	1	17	0
Resz, Greg, Norwich	1.000	19	0	5	0	5	0
Revenig, Todd, Bowie	1.000	38	4	6	0	10	0
Ricken, Ray, Norwich	1.000	8	2	7	0	9	1
Rios, Dan, Norwich	1.000	38	1	9	0	10	0
Ritchie, Todd, New Britain	.920	29	6	17	2	25	0
Roberts, Chris, Binghamton*	1.000	9	3	12	0	15	2
Roque, Rafael, Binghamton*	.909	13	1	9	1	11	0
Rose, Brian, Trenton	1.000	27	9	29	0	38	1
Rumer, Tim, Norwich*	1.000	8	2	8	0	10	0
Saipe, Mike, New Haven	1.000	32	16	17	0	33	0
Sampson, Benj, New Britain*	.917	16	3	8	1	12	1
Sauerbeck, Scott, Binghamton*	1.000	8	1	8	0	9	2
Saunders, Tony, Portland*	1.000	26	4	23	0	27	1
Schullstrom, Erik, Trenton	1.000	19	0	5	0	5	1
Senior, Shawn, Trenton*	.933	16	4	24	2	30	4
Sexton, Jeff, Canton/Akron	1.000	9	3	7	0	10	0
Stanifer, Robby, Portland	.667	18	1	1	1	3	1
Stidham, Phil, New Britain	1.000	12	0	5	0	5	0
Strange, Don, Bowie	1.000	12	1	4	0	5	0
Stull, Everett, Harrisburg	.857	14	4	8	2	14	0
Sutherland, John, Norwich	1.000	26	3	6	0	9	0
Talanoa, Scott, Harrisburg	1.000	1	0	1	0	1	0
Tam, Jeff, Binghamton	1.000	49	7	11	0	18	0
Thomson, John, New Haven	1.000	16	7	9	0	16	0
Thornton, Paul, Portland	1.000	52	13	16	0	29	0
Thurman, Mike, Harrisburg	1.000	4	1	2	0	3	0
Tolar, Kevin, Canton/Akron*	.857	50	3	3	1	7	1
Tranbarger, Mark, Bowie*	1.000	40	5	11	0	16	0
Trinidad, Hector, New Britain	.972	25	14	21	1	36	3
Troutman, Keith, Reading	1.000	52	5	8	0	13	0
Turrentine, Rich, Binghamton	1.000	8	0	1	0	1	0
Valdes, Marc, Portland	.941	10	9	7	1	17	0
Vaught, Jay, Canton/Akron	.957	51	8	14	1	23	2
Viano, Jake, New Haven	1.000	23	3	3	0	6	0
Voisard, Mark, New Haven	1.000	8	1	1	0	2	0
Ward, Bryan, Portland*	.889	28	2	22	3	27	1
Weber, Neil, Harrisburg*	.963	18	6	20	1	27	1
Welch, Mike, Binghamton	.818	46	0	9	2	11	1
Westbrook, Destry, Reading	.889	25	5	3	1	9	0
Whitten, Casey, Canton/Akron*	1.000	8	2	3	0	5	0
Withem, Shannon, Binghamton	1.000	12	6	12	0	18	0
Wright, Jamey, New Haven	1.000	7	4	13	0	17	1
Yan, Esteban, Bowie	1.000	9	3	3	0	6	0
Zolecki, Mike, New Haven	1.000	47	2	9	0	11	0

PITCHERS WITH TWO OR MORE TEAMS

Player, Team	Pct.	G	PO	A	E	TC	DP
Beckett, Robbie, Portland*	1.000	3	1	3	0	4	0
Beckett, Robbie, New Haven*	.900	30	3	6	1	10	0
Bullard, Jason, Binghamton	1.000	8	0	2	0	2	0
Bullard, Jason, Canton/Akron	1.000	9	1	3	0	4	0
Courtright, John, New Britain*	1.000	14	1	10	0	11	0
Courtright, John, Bowie*	.857	9	0	6	1	7	1
Harris, Doug, Bowie	1.000	3	1	4	0	5	0
Harris, Doug, Portland	1.000	20	3	2	0	5	1
Quirico, Rafael, Reading*	1.000	5	2	9	0	11	0
Quirico, Rafael, Norwich*	.500	4	0	1	1	2	0

The following players did not have any fielding statistics at the positions indicated or appeared only as a designated hitter, pinch-hitter or pinch-runner: Berry, Betts, 2b; Blum, of; Ra. Brown, of; Castaneda, 3B; Clark, of, ss, p; Daubach, 3b; Davis, of; Fisher, p; Fithian, of; Fleetham, p; Foster, of; Haws, dh; Leiper, 3b; Mahay; Martin, p; McCormack, p; McCready, p; Millares, 3b, of; Moler, p; Motuzas, p; Payton, dh, ph; Plaster, p; Pool, p; Rhodes, p; Ryan, p; Schuermann, p; M. Smith, Sobkoviak, p; Wallace, p; Wilsson, p.

LEAGUE CHAMPIONS

Year	Team	Pct.	Year	Team	Pct.	Year	Team	P
1923—	Williamsport	.661	1952—	Albany	.603	1977—	West Haven‡‡	.62
1924—	Williamsport	.654		Binghamton (2nd)‡	.562		Three Rivers	.55
1925—	York§	.583	1953—	Reading	.682	1978—	Reading	.64
	Williamsport§	.583		Binghamton (2nd)‡	.636		Bristol*	.58
1926—	Scranton	.627	1954—	Wilkes-Barre	.576	1979—	West Haven§§	.59
1927—	Harrisburg	.630		Albany (3rd)‡	.540	1980—	Holyoke*	.56
1928—	Harrisburg	.603	1955—	Reading	.613		Waterbury	.54
1929—	Binghamton	.597		Allentown (2nd)‡	.565	1981—	Glens Falls	.61
1930—	Wilkes-Barre	.572	1956—	Schenectady†	.609		Bristol*	.57
1931—	Harrisburg	.597	1957—	Binghamton	.607	1982—	West Haven*	.61
1932—	Wilkes-Barre	.561		Reading (3rd)‡	.529		Lynn	.59
1933—	Binghamton	.690	1958—	Lancaster∞	.568	1983—	Lynn	.55
1934—	Binghamton	.694		Binghamton (6th)‡	.493		New Britain†	.51
	Williamsport*	.603	1959—	Springfield†	.607	1984—	Waterbury	.54
1935—	Scranton	.657	1960—	Williamsport▲	.551		Vermont‡	.53
	Binghamton*	.580		Springfield (3rd)▲	.496	1985—	Albany	.54
1936—	Scranton*	.609	1961—	Springfield	.612		Vermont‡	.51
	Elmira	.629	1962—	Williamsport	.593	1986—	Reading	.56
1937—	Elmira†	.622		Elmira (2nd)‡	.514		Vermont‡	.55
1938—	Binghamton	.622	1963—	Charleston	.593	1987—	Pittsfield	.63
	Elmira (3rd)‡	.522	1964—	Elmira	.586		Harrisburg‡	.55
1939—	Scranton†	.571	1965—	Pittsfield	.607	1988—	Glens Falls	.58
1940—	Scranton	.568	1966—	Elmira	.633		Albany‡	.52
	Binghamton (2nd)‡	.554	1967—	Binghamton♦	.586	1989—	Albany‡	.65
1941—	Wilkes-Barre	.630		Elmira	.532		Harrisburg	.52
	Elmira (3rd)‡	.514	1968—	Pittsfield	.604	1990—	Albany	.56
1942—	Albany	.600		Reading (2nd)‡	.579		London†	.54
	Scranton (2nd)‡	.593	1969—	York	.640	1991—	Harrisburg	.62
1943—	Scranton	.630	1970—	Waterbury■	.560		Albany‡	.54
	Elmira (2nd)‡	.568		Reading■	.553	1992—	Canton/Akron	.58
1944—	Hartford	.723	1971—	Three Rivers	.569		Binghamton‡	.57
	Binghamton (4th)‡	.474		Elmira▼	.561	1993—	Harrisburg‡	.66
1945—	Utica	.615	1972—	West Haven▼	.600		Canton/Akron	.54
	Albany (3rd)‡	.564		Three Rivers	.559	1994—	Harrisburg	.63
1946—	Scranton†	.691	1973—	Reading▼	.551		Binghamton‡	.58
1947—	Utica†	.652		Pittsfield	.551	1995—	New Haven	.55
1948—	Scranton†	.636	1974—	Thetford Miners (2nd)•	.536		Reading‡	.51
1949—	Albany	.664		Pittsfield (2nd)	.496	1996—	Portland	.58
	Binghamton (4th)‡	.500	1975—	Reading	.613		Harrisburg‡	.52
1950—	Wilkes-Barre‡	.652		Bristol*	.587			
1951—	Wilkes-Barre‡	.612	1976—	Three Rivers	.601			
	Scranton (2nd)†	.562		West Haven††	.576			

*Won split-season playoff. †Won championship and four-team playoff. ‡Won four-team playoff. §Tied for pennant, York winning playoff. ∞League w[as] divided into Northern, Southern divisions and played a split season; Lancaster was overall season leader. ▲Playoff finals canceled after one game because [of] rain with Williamsport and Springfield declared playoff co-champions. ♦League was divided into Eastern, Western divisions; Binghamton won playoff. ■T[ied] for pennant, Waterbury winning playoff. ▼League was divided into American, National divisions; won playoff. •League was divided into American and Natio[nal] divisions; won four-team playoff. ††League was divided into Northern, Southern divisions, won playoff. ‡‡League was divided into New England and Canadi[an] American divisions; won playoff. §§Won both halves of split season (no playoffs). (NOTE—Known as New York-Pennsylvania League prior to 1938.)

CLASS AA Eastern League

SOUTHERN LEAGUE

LEAGUE OFFICE

President/secretary-treasurer
Arnold Fielkow

Address
1 Depot St., Suite 300
Marietta, GA 30060

Phone
770-428-4749

TEAMS

BIRMINGHAM BARONS

President/general manager
Bill Hardekopf

Manager
Dave Huppert

Ballpark (capacity, surface)
Hoover Metropolitan Stadium (10,500, grass)

Affiliation
White Sox

Address
P.O. Box 360007
Birmingham, AL 35236

Phone
205-988-3200

CAROLINA MUDCATS

General manager
Joe Kremer

Manager
Marc Hill

Ballpark (capacity, surface)
Five County Stadium (6,000, grass)

Affiliation
Pirates

Address
P.O. Drawer 1218
Zebulon, NC 27597

Phone
919-269-2287

CHATTANOOGA LOOKOUTS

President/general manager
J. Frank Burke

Manager
Mark Berry

Ballpark (capacity, surface)
Historic Engel Stadium (7,500, grass)

Affiliation
Reds

Address
P.O. Box 11002
Chattanooga, TN 37401

Phone
423-267-2208

GREENVILLE BRAVES

General manager
Steve DeSalvo

Manager
Randy Ingle

Ballpark (capacity, surface)
Greenville Municipal Stadium (7,027, grass)

Affiliation
Braves

Address
P.O. Box 16683
Greenville, SC 29606

Phone
864-299-3456

HUNTSVILLE STARS

President/general manager
Don Mincher

Manager
Mike Quade

Ballpark (capacity, surface)
Joe W. Davis Stadium (10,400, grass)

Affiliation
Athletics

Address
P.O. Box 2769
Huntsville, AL 35804

Phone
205-882-2562

JACKSONVILLE SUNS

Vice president/general manager
Peter Bragan Jr.

Manager
Dave Anderson

Ballpark (capacity, surface)
Wolfson Park (8,200, grass)

Affiliation
Tigers

Address
P.O. Box 4756
Jacksonville, FL 32201

Phone
904-358-2846

KNOXVILLE SMOKIES

General manager
Dan Rajkowski

Manager
Omar Malave

Ballpark (capacity, surface)
Bill Meyer Stadium (6,412, grass)

Affiliation
Blue Jays

Address
633 Jessamine St.
Knoxville, TN 37917

Phone
423-637-9494

MEMPHIS CHICKS

President/general manager
David Hersh

Manager
Dave Brundage

Ballpark (capacity, surface)
Tim McCarver Stadium (10,000, artificial infield, grass outfield)

Affiliation
Mariners

Address
800 Home Run Lane
Memphis, TN 38104

Phone
901-272-1687

MOBILE BAYBEARS

General manager
Bill Shanahan

Manager
Mike Ramsey

Ballpark (capacity, surface).
Hank Aaron Stadium (6,000, grass)

Affiliation
Padres

Address
P.O. Box 161663
Mobile, AL 36616

Phone
334-476-2287

ORLANDO RAYS

General manager
Roger Wexelberg

Manager
Dave Trembley

Ballpark (capacity, surface)
Tinker Field (6,000, grass)

Affiliation
Cubs

Address
287 S. Tampa Ave.
Orlando, FL 32805

Phone
407-245-2827

CLASS AA *Southern League*

FIRST HALF

EAST DIVISION

Team	W	L	T	Pct.	GB
Jacksonville (Tigers)	39	30	0	.565	....
Carolina (Pirates)	37	32	0	.536	2
Orlando (Cubs)	31	39	0	.443	8½
Port City (Mariners)	28	42	0	.400	11½
Greenville (Braves)	28	42	0	.400	11½

WEST DIVISION

Team	W	L	T	Pct.	GB
Memphis (Padres)	47	23	0	.671	...
Knoxville (Blue Jays)	41	29	0	.586	6
Huntsville (Athletics)	33	37	0	.471	14
Chattanooga (Reds)	33	37	0	.471	14
Birmingham (White Sox)	32	38	0	.457	15

SECOND HALF

EAST DIVISION

Team	W	L	T	Pct.	GB
Jacksonville (Tigers)	36	33	0	.522	....
Carolina (Pirates)	33	37	0	.471	3½
Orlando (Cubs)	30	39	0	.435	6
Greenville (Braves)	30	40	0	.429	6½
Port City (Mariners)	28	42	0	.400	8½

WEST DIVISION

Team	W	L	T	Pct.	GB
Chattanooga (Reds)	48	22	0	.686	....
Birmingham (White Sox)	42	27	0	.609	5½
Memphis (Padres)	34	35	0	.493	13½
Knoxville (Blue Jays)	34	36	0	.486	14
Huntsville (Athletics)	33	37	0	.471	15

COMPOSITE

Team	Mem.	Chat.	Jax.	Knx.	Bir.	Car.	Hun.	Orl.	Grn.	P.C.	W	L	T	Pct.	G.B.
Memphis (Padres)	....	11	3	11	14	6	9	4	16	7	81	58	0	.583	....
Chattanooga (Reds)	10	....	5	11	12	10	6	4	12	11	81	59	0	.579	½
Jacksonville (Tigers)	7	5	....	6	8	13	9	12	6	9	75	63	0	.543	5½
Knoxville (Blue Jays)	9	7	6	....	4	8	12	12	8	9	75	65	0	.536	6½
Birmingham (White Sox)	10	6	9	6	....	4	11	11	8	9	74	65	0	.532	7
Carolina (Pirates)	2	6	8	10	5	....	6	9	9	15	70	69	0	.504	11
Huntsville (Athletics)	11	7	6	10	7	10	....	8	6	1	66	74	0	.471	15½
Orlando (Cubs)	4	4	12	4	2	6	8	....	9	12	61	78	0	.439	20
Greenville (Braves)	4	5	6	2	6	6	6	12	....	11	58	82	0	.414	23½
Port City (Mariners)	1	8	8	5	7	6	7	6	8	....	56	84	0	.400	25½

Carolina's home games played in Zebulon, N.C.

Port City's home games played in Wilmington, N.C.

Major league affiliations in parentheses.

PLAYOFFS: Jacksonville defeated Carolina, three games to two; Chattanooga defeated Memphis, three games to one; Jacksonville defeated Chattanooga, three games to one, to win league championship.

REGULAR-SEASON ATTENDANCE: Birmingham, 296,131; Carolina, 278,361; Chattanooga, 227,885; Greenville, 230,124; Huntsville, 255,139; Jacksonville, 219,947; Knoxville, 142,537; Memphis, 197,084; Orlando, 175,399; Port City, 68,463. Total—2,091,070. Playoffs (13 games)—26,536. Class AA All-Star Game at Trenton—8,369.

MANAGERS: Birmingham, Mike Heath; Carolina, Marc Hill; Chattanooga, Mark Berry; Greenville, Jeff Cox; Huntsville, Dick Scott; Jacksonville, Bill Plummer (through June 19) and Larry Parrish (June 20 through end of season); Knoxville, Omar Malave; Memphis, Ed Romero; Orlando, Bruce Kimm; Port City, Orlando Gomez. Managerial record of team with more than one manager: Jacksonville, Plummer, 39-30, Parrish, 36-33.

ALL-STAR TEAM: 1B—Derek Lee, Memphis; 2B—Frank Catalanotto, Jacksonville; 3B—Aaron Boone, Chattanooga; SS—Lou Collier, Carolina; OF—T. Staton, Carolina; Bubba Trammell, Jacksonville; Mike Cameron, Birmingham; C—Willie Morales, Huntsville; DH—Dan Rohrmeier, Memphis; Utility—Tom Beasley, Carolina; RHP—Curt Lyons, Chattanooga; LHP—Heath Murray, Memphis; Most Valuable Player—Derek Lee, Memphis; Most Outstanding Pitcher—Curt Lyons, Chattanooga; Manager of the Year—Mark Berry, Chattanooga.

1996 BATTING

TEAM

Team	Avg.	G	TPA	AB	R	H	TB	2B	3B	HR	RBI	SH	SF	HP	BB	IBB	SO	SB	CS	GDP	LOB	ShO	Slg.	OBP
Chattanooga ..	.273	140	5293	4700	687	1284	1930	270	32	104	625	37	36	51	469	36	897	139	75	101	987	2	.411	.343
Knoxville	.270	140	5435	4685	708	1264	1948	263	41	113	635	27	38	61	620	28	1028	103	73	84	1081	6	.416	.360
Jacksonville ...	.266	138	5211	4617	725	1227	2135	238	35	200	686	30	31	79	451	36	1081	103	71	97	907	4	.462	.339
Birmingham ...	.266	139	5314	4676	670	1242	1914	260	26	120	624	35	38	57	502	27	896	93	66	99	1001	8	.409	.342
Memphis	.265	139	5240	4563	714	1208	1931	245	35	136	648	41	54	32	550	38	981	107	79	105	907	7	.423	.344
Huntsville	.262	140	5408	4646	748	1219	1870	229	31	120	673	58	47	72	584	28	993	98	51	106	1007	1	.402	.351
Greenville	.262	140	5225	4625	667	1210	1828	250	25	106	611	56	33	50	461	33	958	84	69	99	949	12	.395	.333
Carolina	.259	139	5216	4550	617	1178	1685	220	40	69	546	43	39	44	540	39	968	175	86	98	986	11	.370	.341
Orlando	.252	139	5271	4593	643	1158	1701	223	34	84	574	36	43	40	557	30	912	116	74	106	998	10	.370	.335
Port City	.252	140	5407	4717	591	1189	1635	234	34	48	510	44	32	59	551	32	833	142	71	115	1066	14	.347	.336

INDIVIDUAL

TOP QUALIFIERS FOR BATTING CHAMPIONSHIP

Minimum 378 plate appearances. *Lefthanded batter. †Switch-hitter.

Player, Team	Avg.	G	TPA	AB	R	H	TB	2B	3B	HR	RBI	SH	SF	HP	BB	IBB	SO	SB	CS	GDP	Slg.	OBP
Rohrmeier, Dan, Memphis	.344	134	554	471	98	162	279	29	2	28	95	0	4	2	77	10	76	2	5	12	.592	.435
Brown, Ray, Chattanooga*	.327	115	422	364	68	119	194	26	5	13	52	0	3	3	52	7	62	2	1	11	.533	.412
Malloy, Marty, Greenville*	.312	111	495	429	82	134	177	27	2	4	36	6	2	4	54	6	50	11	10	11	.413	.393
Santana, Ruben, Chattanooga..	.309	98	378	343	47	106	155	21	2	8	56	0	4	5	26	1	39	5	3	7	.452	.362
Staton, T.J., Carolina*	.308	112	454	386	72	119	194	24	3	15	57	0	4	6	58	1	99	17	7	4	.503	.403
Patzke, Jeff, Knoxville†	.303	124	517	429	70	130	181	31	4	4	66	0	2	6	80	6	103	6	5	2	.422	.418
Cameron, Mike, Birmingham ...	.300	123	563	473	120	142	284	34	12	28	77	3	4	12	71	6	117	39	15	5	.600	.402

ayer, Team	Avg.	G	TPA	AB	R	H	TB	2B	3B	HR	RBI	SH	SF	HP	BB	IBB	SO	SB	CS	GDP	Slg.	OBP
talanotto, Frank, Jac.*	.298	132	588	497	105	148	245	34	6	17	67	3	3	11	74	8	69	15	14	8	.493	.398
ll, Billy, Chattanooga†	.295	117	524	461	80	136	172	24	3	2	43	4	2	0	57	5	72	34	11	9	.373	.371
ko, Paul, Chattanooga	.294	110	419	360	53	106	157	27	0	8	48	2	4	5	48	5	93	1	0	5	.436	.381
vin, Phil, Jacksonville	.294	98	413	344	77	101	193	18	1	24	69	0	6	3	60	4	83	6	2	9	.561	.397
orales, William, Huntsville	.292	108	432	377	54	110	188	24	0	18	73	4	6	7	38	2	67	0	2	11	.499	.362
enechino, Frank, Birm.	.292	125	497	415	77	121	188	25	3	12	62	3	6	8	64	0	84	7	9	5	.453	.391
one, Aaron, Chattanooga	.288	136	596	548	86	158	267	44	7	17	95	1	4	5	38	4	77	21	10	5	.487	.338
ashore, Justin, Jacksonville..	.285	120	499	453	67	129	193	27	8	7	50	7	2	4	33	1	97	17	13	10	.426	.337

DEPARTMENTAL LEADERS: G—Jorgensen, 137; AB—Boone, 548; R—Cameron, 120; H—Rohrmeier, 162; TB—Lee, 285; 2B—Boone, 44; 3B—D. Smith, 14; HR—e, 34; RBI—Lee, 104; SH—Francisco, 12; SF—Wood, 11; HP—Hansen, 24; BB—Evans, 115; IBB—Rohrmeier, Jorgensen, 10; SO—Lee, 170; SB—Cameron, 39; —Cameron, Gipson, D. Smith, 15; GIDP—Petersen, 18; Slg.—Cameron, .600; OBP—Evans, .452.

ALL PLAYERS
*Lefthanded batter. †Switch-hitter.

ayer, Team	Avg.	G	TPA	AB	R	H	TB	2B	3B	HR	RBI	SH	SF	HP	BB	IBB	SO	SB	CS	GDP	Slg.	OBP
en, Cedric, Chattanooga*	.333	13	3	3	0	1	1	0	0	0	0	0	0	0	0	0	0	0	0	0	.333	.333
arez, Gabe, Memphis	.247	104	438	368	58	91	140	23	1	8	40	0	3	3	64	1	87	2	3	10	.380	.361
derson, Jimmy, Carolina*	.111	17	9	9	0	1	1	0	0	0	0	0	0	0	0	0	3	0	0	1	.111	.111
as, Amador, Chattanooga†	.000	1	1	1	0	0	0	0	0	0	0	0	0	0	0	0	0	0	0	0	.000	.000
nold, Jamie, Greenville	.250	23	20	16	2	4	5	1	0	0	3	0	0	1	0	6	0	0	1	.313	.294	
cklund, Brett, Carolina	.143	26	7	7	1	1	1	0	0	0	0	0	0	0	0	0	3	0	0	0	.143	.143
ko, Paul, Chattanooga*	.294	110	419	360	53	106	157	27	0	8	48	2	4	5	48	5	93	1	0	5	.436	.381
rger, Mike, Port City	.205	108	405	366	45	75	100	17	4	0	26	7	0	6	26	0	47	19	4	9	.273	.269
rker, Glen, Jacksonville	.158	43	130	120	9	19	23	2	1	0	8	2	0	0	8	0	36	6	4	2	.192	.211
rry, Jeff, Memphis†	.243	91	263	226	29	55	71	7	0	3	25	1	6	1	29	5	48	3	7	6	.314	.324
asley, Tony, Carolina	.312	96	307	269	40	84	123	17	5	4	30	2	4	2	30	4	33	10	9	5	.457	.380
atty, Blaine, Carolina*	.273	23	25	22	3	6	10	1	0	1	3	2	0	0	1	0	1	0	1	0	.455	.304
lhorn, Mark, Huntsville*	.250	131	556	468	84	117	181	24	5	10	71	7	4	4	73	7	124	19	2	7	.387	.353
tran, Alonso, Chattanooga	.000	3	3	3	0	0	0	0	0	0	0	0	0	0	0	0	0	0	0	0	.000	.000
ck, Jeff, Greenville	.176	20	18	17	0	3	3	0	0	0	1	1	0	0	0	0	4	0	0	0	.176	.176
nifay, Ken, Carolina*	.243	95	319	272	33	66	106	18	2	6	42	2	0	4	41	2	68	4	3	4	.390	.350
one, Aaron, Chattanooga	.288	136	596	548	86	158	267	44	7	17	95	1	4	5	38	4	77	21	10	5	.487	.338
ston, D.J., Carolina*	.280	93	377	321	47	90	138	16	4	8	48	0	4	3	49	3	61	5	3	7	.430	.377
wles, Justin, Huntsville*	.333	3	13	12	1	4	4	0	0	0	2	0	0	1	0	5	0	0	0	.333	.385	
eam, Scott, Jacksonville†	.241	36	122	108	18	26	40	3	1	3	12	3	0	1	10	0	31	2	1	0	.370	.311
ggs, Stoney, Memphis	.274	133	525	452	72	124	196	24	6	12	80	4	3	4	62	4	123	28	11	18	.434	.365
nkley, Darryl, Memphis	.296	60	230	203	36	60	96	9	0	9	29	1	1	3	22	2	33	13	5	2	.473	.371
to, Luis, Greenville†	.116	19	46	43	4	5	5	0	0	0	4	2	0	0	1	0	6	1	1	2	.116	.136
ach, Donald, Chattanooga	.261	110	405	349	58	91	123	10	2	6	37	5	1	11	39	2	51	20	9	7	.352	.353
ock, Tarrik, Jacksonville*	.127	37	113	102	14	13	15	2	0	0	6	0	0	1	10	0	36	3	3	0	.147	.212
osnan, Jason, Port City*	.000	30	1	1	0	0	0	0	0	0	0	0	0	0	0	0	0	0	0	0	.000	.000
own, Adrian, Carolina†	.296	84	373	341	48	101	127	11	3	3	25	5	1	1	25	3	40	27	11	4	.372	.345
own, Ray, Chattanooga*	.327	115	422	364	68	119	194	26	5	13	52	0	3	3	52	7	62	2	1	11	.533	.412
ano, Julio, Memphis	.238	27	92	84	11	20	30	8	1	0	9	1	1	0	6	1	18	1	2	2	.357	.286
ckley, Travis, Chattanooga	.286	8	8	7	0	2	2	0	0	0	1	0	0	0	1	0	1	0	0	0	.286	.286
lett, Scott, Orlando*	.182	3	12	11	2	2	2	0	0	0	0	0	0	0	1	0	2	0	0	1	.182	.250
rlingame, Ben, Orlando	.000	11	2	2	0	0	0	0	0	0	0	0	0	0	0	0	1	0	0	0	.000	.000
rd, Matt, Greenville†	.167	51	13	12	2	2	6	1	0	1	3	1	0	0	0	0	7	0	0	0	.500	.167
rne, Earl, Orlando*	.111	11	9	9	0	1	1	0	0	0	0	0	0	0	0	0	4	0	0	0	.111	.111
meron, Mike, Birmingham	.300	123	563	473	120	142	284	34	12	28	77	3	4	12	71	6	117	39	15	5	.600	.402
ndelaria, Ben, Knoxville*	.278	55	184	162	16	45	69	11	2	3	14	2	0	2	18	0	40	3	3	7	.426	.357
rdenas, John, Port City	.189	27	77	74	4	14	17	0	0	1	6	2	0	0	1	0	16	1	0	5	.230	.200
sanova, Papo, Jacksonville	.333	8	32	30	5	10	24	2	0	4	9	0	0	0	2	0	7	0	0	0	.800	.375
talanotto, Frank, Jacksonville*	.298	132	588	497	105	148	245	34	6	17	67	3	3	11	74	8	69	15	14	8	.493	.398
cher, Mike, Greenville	.125	53	8	8	1	1	2	1	0	0	0	0	0	0	0	0	5	0	0	0	.250	.125
aves, Rafael, Carolina	.000	19	1	1	0	0	0	0	0	0	0	0	0	0	0	0	0	0	0	0	.000	.000
olowsky, Dan, Orlando	.238	45	170	143	21	34	50	4	0	4	14	0	1	3	23	0	38	2	4	3	.350	.353
ark, Dera, Memphis	.200	9	5	5	0	1	1	0	0	0	1	0	0	0	0	0	1	0	0	0	.200	.200
llier, Lou, Carolina	.280	119	506	443	76	124	159	20	3	3	49	2	6	7	48	4	73	29	9	11	.359	.355
nger, Jeff, Carolina*	.230	66	202	178	19	41	59	7	1	3	17	4	0	3	17	1	52	12	4	3	.331	.308
nnolly, Matt, Orlando	.333	31	5	3	2	1	1	0	0	0	0	1	0	0	0	0	1	0	0	0	.333	.500
oke, Steve, Carolina	.375	12	9	8	1	3	3	0	0	0	1	0	0	0	1	0	1	0	0	0	.375	.444
rrea, Miguel, Greenville†	.222	64	242	225	20	50	82	13	2	5	25	5	0	1	11	2	65	2	2	3	.364	.262
rreia, Rod, Carolina	.253	64	283	241	38	61	78	9	1	2	30	3	4	7	28	1	24	11	1	8	.324	.343
tton, John, Jacksonville*	.240	63	239	217	34	52	106	7	4	13	39	0	1	2	19	2	66	15	3	2	.488	.305
urtright, John, Chattanooga*	.167	9	13	12	1	2	2	0	0	0	2	0	0	0	1	0	3	0	1	1	.167	.231
x, Steve, Huntsville*	.281	104	443	381	59	107	166	21	1	12	61	2	3	6	51	6	65	2	2	10	.436	.372
adle, Rickey, Knoxville*	.282	92	412	333	59	94	157	23	2	12	47	7	7	10	55	1	65	15	11	2	.471	.393
anford, Jay, Carolina	.269	90	321	268	34	72	97	15	2	2	37	0	3	3	47	4	68	6	4	3	.362	.380
omer, Brandon, Huntsville*	.277	98	385	318	56	88	140	15	8	7	32	2	2	3	60	3	84	3	6	2	.440	.392
uz, Jose, Port City†	.282	47	209	181	39	51	74	10	2	3	31	0	1	0	27	4	38	5	0	8	.409	.373
bney, Fred, Orlando	.000	12	1	0	0	0	0	0	0	0	0	0	0	0	1	0	0	0	0	0	.000	1.000
boer, Rob, Huntsville	.279	44	150	122	24	34	55	6	0	5	21	1	1	1	25	0	45	1	3	3	.451	.403
LaCruz, Lorenzo, Knoxville	.247	122	488	441	60	109	195	24	4	18	79	0	4	7	36	1	123	8	4	11	.442	.311
lossantos, Mariano, Carolina.	.000	52	1	1	0	0	0	0	0	0	0	0	0	0	0	0	0	0	0	0	.000	.000
nnis, Shane, Memphis	.050	19	22	20	1	1	1	0	0	0	0	0	0	0	2	0	6	0	0	0	.050	.136
ssens, Elmer, Carolina	.000	5	1	0	0	0	0	0	0	0	0	0	1	0	0	0	0	0	0	0	.000	.000
ttmer, John, Greenville	.000	26	4	3	0	0	0	0	0	0	0	0	0	1	0	0	0	0	0	0	.000	.000
Sarcina, Glenn, Birmingham*	.366	43	185	175	25	64	101	10	3	7	36	0	2	1	7	1	45	4	0	3	.577	.389
smuke, Jamie, Jacksonville*..	.266	29	95	79	7	21	39	4	1	4	12	0	0	2	14	2	14	0	0	3	.494	.389
con, Bubba, Memphis*	.000	42	2	2	0	0	0	0	0	0	0	0	0	0	0	0	0	0	0	0	.000	.000
nnelly, Brendan, Chatt.	.000	22	3	2	0	0	0	0	0	0	0	0	0	0	1	0	1	0	0	0	.000	.333

Player, Team	Avg.	G	TPA	AB	R	H	TB	2B	3B	HR	RBI	SH	SF	HP	BB	IBB	SO	SB	CS	GDP	Slg.	OB
Dowler, Dee, Orlando	.278	113	410	352	59	98	143	15	6	6	47	6	2	3	47	2	42	25	5	10	.406	.36
Doyle, Tom, Chattanooga*	.500	54	6	6	1	3	5	2	0	0	0	0	0	0	0	0	1	0	0	0	.833	.50
Dressendorfer, Kirk, Huntsville	.000	30	1	1	0	0	0	0	0	0	0	0	0	0	0	0	0	0	0	0	.000	.00
Drinkwater, Sean, Port City	.267	32	115	101	10	27	39	9	0	1	13	0	1	0	13	0	18	1	3	0	.386	.34
Duross, Gabe, Orl.-Birm.*	.202	54	211	198	16	40	45	3	1	0	21	0	1	3	9	3	20	1	1	6	.227	.24
Edge, Tim, Carolina	.242	53	173	153	18	37	59	10	0	4	21	1	1	2	16	1	44	1	0	4	.386	.32
Etheridge, Roger, Greenville*	.333	49	3	3	1	1	4	0	0	1	1	0	0	0	0	0	0	0	0	0	1.333	.33
Evans, Tom, Knoxville	.282	120	522	394	87	111	191	27	1	17	65	0	2	9	115	0	113	4	0	7	.485	.45
Eyre, Scott, Birmingham*	.000	27	1	1	0	0	0	0	0	0	0	0	0	0	0	0	0	0	0	0	.000	.00
Farrell, Jon, Carolina	.216	22	60	51	6	11	14	3	0	0	3	0	1	2	6	2	22	0	0	0	.275	.31
Fesh, Sean, Memphis*	.000	7	1	0	0	0	0	0	0	0	0	1	0	0	0	0	0	0	0	0	.000	.00
Forkerway, Trey, Orlando	.242	59	180	161	22	39	59	9	1	3	20	1	3	4	11	0	24	0	2	8	.366	.30
Francisco, David, Huntsville	.259	114	437	386	59	100	123	12	1	3	28	12	2	9	28	0	72	13	4	6	.319	.32
Frazier, Ron, Chattanooga	.111	32	9	9	1	1	1	0	0	0	0	0	0	0	0	0	4	0	0	1	.111	.11
Freeman, Sean, Jacksonville*	.267	124	489	412	72	110	205	18	1	25	74	1	4	6	66	2	117	3	4	8	.498	.37
Freitas, Mike, Memphis	1.000	44	3	1	0	1	1	0	0	0	0	2	0	0	0	0	0	0	0	0	1.000	1.00
Friedman, Jason, Port City*	.188	45	142	133	7	25	39	5	3	1	11	0	0	1	8	1	16	0	0	2	.293	.23
Fryman, Troy, Birm.-Orl.*	.225	68	282	249	35	56	82	18	1	2	28	2	3	3	25	1	61	2	2	1	.329	.30
Garcia, Al, Orlando†	.188	23	16	16	0	3	4	1	0	0	1	0	0	0	0	0	9	0	0	0	.250	.18
Garcia, Guillermo, Chattanooga	.315	60	219	203	25	64	94	12	0	6	36	2	1	1	12	2	32	3	3	3	.463	.35
Garcia, Luis, Jacksonville	.245	131	545	522	68	128	185	22	4	9	46	7	2	2	12	1	90	15	12	9	.354	.26
Garrison, Webster, Huntsville	.281	47	202	178	28	50	87	12	2	7	31	0	1	1	22	0	33	1	1	4	.489	.36
Gipson, Charles, Port City	.268	119	462	407	54	109	130	12	3	1	30	6	0	7	41	1	62	26	15	9	.319	.34
Gonzalez, Jeremi, Orlando	.077	17	17	13	1	1	1	0	0	0	0	0	0	3	0	0	1	0	0	0	.077	.14
Gray, Dennis, P.C.-Green.*	.000	28	1	0	0	0	0	0	0	0	0	0	0	0	1	0	0	0	0	0	.000	1.00
Grieve, Ben, Huntsville*	.237	63	272	232	34	55	89	8	1	8	32	0	3	2	35	5	53	0	3	3	.384	.33
Griffey, Craig, Port City	.222	120	457	396	43	88	122	14	7	2	35	2	6	6	46	0	88	20	7	6	.308	.30
Gubanich, Creighton, Huntsville	.276	62	257	217	40	60	106	19	0	9	43	3	2	4	31	1	71	1	0	5	.488	.37
Guevara, Giomar, Port City†	.266	119	485	414	60	110	138	18	2	2	41	9	4	4	54	1	102	21	7	12	.333	.35
Hall, Billy, Chattanooga†	.295	117	524	461	80	136	172	24	3	2	43	4	2	0	57	5	72	34	11	9	.373	.37
Hanel, Marcus, Carolina	.178	101	362	332	22	59	95	19	1	5	36	3	4	7	16	4	57	2	2	9	.286	.22
Hansen, Terrel, Jacksonville	.264	104	416	367	49	97	194	18	2	25	66	0	5	24	19	4	107	5	2	8	.529	.33
Harmes, Kris, Knoxville*	.213	44	136	122	16	26	42	8	1	2	8	0	1	1	13	1	17	1	0	4	.344	.29
Harrison, Tommy, Greenville	.050	20	23	20	1	1	4	0	0	1	1	1	0	0	2	0	7	0	1	2	.200	.13
Hart, Jason, Orlando	.250	51	4	4	0	1	1	0	0	0	0	0	0	0	0	0	2	0	0	0	.250	.2
Haught, Gary, Huntsville†	.000	45	1	1	0	0	0	0	0	0	0	0	0	0	0	0	1	0	0	0	.000	.00
Helms, Wes, Greenville	.255	64	249	231	24	59	88	13	2	4	22	1	0	4	13	2	48	2	1	6	.381	.30
Henry, Santiago, Knoxville	.270	110	399	371	37	100	138	15	7	3	32	4	2	3	19	1	66	11	7	5	.372	.30
Hernandez, Fernando, Memphis	.158	27	19	19	0	3	3	0	0	0	0	0	0	0	0	0	7	0	0	0	.158	.15
Herrera, Jose, Huntsville*	.286	23	100	84	18	24	31	4	0	1	7	0	2	0	14	1	15	3	2	2	.369	.38
Hickey, Mike, Port City†	.255	75	315	247	35	63	86	14	3	1	23	5	2	1	58	3	51	9	6	4	.348	.33
Hicks, Jamie, Greenville	.167	3	6	6	0	1	1	0	0	0	0	0	0	0	0	0	0	0	0	0	.167	.16
Hightower, Vee, Orlando†	.067	19	79	75	2	5	5	0	0	0	4	0	0	0	4	0	24	3	0	1	.067	.1
Hollinger, Adrian, Greenville*	.000	20	1	1	0	0	0	0	0	0	0	0	0	0	0	0	1	0	0	0	.000	.0
Howard, Tom, Chattanooga†	.333	8	32	30	4	10	14	1	0	1	2	0	0	0	2	0	7	1	1	0	.467	.3
Hughes, Troy, Orlando	.273	123	503	450	75	123	209	26	3	18	93	0	2	1	50	4	86	3	4	8	.464	.34
Hurst, Jimmy, Birmingham	.265	126	539	472	62	125	204	23	1	18	88	0	8	3	53	2	128	19	11	10	.432	.33
Hust, Gary, Huntsville	.223	60	220	197	22	44	64	11	0	3	26	4	0	1	18	0	64	3	0	6	.325	.28
Hutcheson, David, Orlando	.000	19	10	7	2	0	0	0	0	0	0	1	0	0	2	0	3	0	0	0	.000	.2
Ibanez, Raul, Port City*	.368	19	85	76	12	28	41	8	1	1	13	0	1	0	8	1	7	3	2	1	.539	.42
Jacobs, Ryan, Greenville	.167	21	18	12	2	2	3	1	0	0	1	0	1	5	0	0	5	0	0	0	.250	.23
Jimenez, Manny, Greenville	.274	131	515	474	68	130	164	21	2	3	57	4	3	6	28	3	67	12	7	18	.346	.32
Johnson, Earl, Memphis†	.252	82	364	337	50	85	113	10	6	2	33	5	3	1	18	1	59	15	13	5	.335	.2
Jones, Andruw, Greenville	.369	38	176	157	39	58	106	10	1	12	37	0	1	1	17	0	34	12	4	3	.675	.4
Jones, Ryan, Knoxville	.271	134	580	506	70	137	229	26	3	20	97	0	6	6	60	6	88	2	2	6	.453	.35
Jorgensen, Randy, Port City*	.280	137	535	460	61	129	187	32	1	8	81	5	5	7	58	10	75	2	1	15	.407	.33
Kaufman, Brad, Memphis	.143	29	25	21	2	3	8	2	0	1	3	4	0	0	0	0	7	0	0	0	.381	.1
Keefe, Jamie, Memphis	.176	12	22	17	2	3	3	0	0	0	1	0	1	1	3	0	6	1	0	0	.176	.2
Kilgo, Rusty, Memphis*	.000	48	2	2	0	0	0	0	0	0	0	0	0	0	0	0	0	0	0	0	.000	.0
Killeen, Tim, Memphis*	.259	83	259	224	44	58	113	10	6	11	51	1	6	1	27	1	57	0	2	4	.504	.3
Kimsey, Keith, Jacksonville	.179	31	119	106	8	19	27	0	1	2	6	0	0	0	13	0	50	2	4	2	.255	.2
King, Andre, Chattanooga	.070	13	45	43	1	3	5	0	1	0	3	0	0	1	1	0	21	0	1	1	.116	.1
Kingston, Mark, Orlando†	.205	60	150	122	21	25	43	9	0	3	17	2	1	2	22	0	39	1	1	0	.352	.33
Koller, Jerry, Greenville	.267	14	16	15	0	4	4	0	0	0	2	0	1	0	0	0	7	1	0	0	.267	.2
Konuszewski, Dennis, Carolina	.000	32	6	5	0	0	0	0	0	0	0	1	0	0	0	0	2	0	0	0	.000	.0
Koppe, Clint, Chattanooga	.125	10	9	8	0	1	1	0	0	0	0	0	0	0	1	0	4	0	0	0	.125	.2
Kroon, Marc, Memphis†	.000	44	2	2	0	0	0	0	0	0	0	0	0	0	0	0	1	0	0	0	.000	.0
Ladell, Cleveland, Chattanooga	.252	121	446	405	59	102	143	15	7	4	41	4	1	5	31	5	88	31	14	11	.353	.3
Ladjevich, Rick, Port City	.283	115	466	414	44	117	163	23	1	7	48	1	1	15	35	1	58	1	4	14	.394	.3
LaRocca, Greg, Memphis	.274	128	516	445	66	122	172	22	5	6	42	5	5	10	51	4	58	5	9	9	.387	.3
Larregui, Ed, Orl.-Birm.	.245	82	308	282	38	69	88	14	1	1	19	3	1	0	22	2	40	1	3	7	.312	.2
Lawrence, Sean, Carolina*	.167	37	7	6	0	1	1	0	0	0	0	1	0	0	0	0	4	0	0	0	.167	.2
Leary, Rob, Carolina*	.183	32	133	109	13	20	38	4	1	4	12	0	0	2	22	3	31	2	2	2	.349	.3
Lee, Derrek, Memphis	.280	134	575	500	98	140	285	39	2	34	104	0	8	2	65	3	170	13	6	8	.570	.3
LeRoy, John, Greenville	.455	8	14	11	0	5	6	1	0	0	2	0	0	0	1	0	5	0	0	0	.545	.5
Lidle, Kevin, Jacksonville	.250	4	9	8	2	2	5	0	0	1	2	0	0	0	1	0	1	0	0	0	.625	.3
Lister, Martin, Chattanooga*	.000	19	1	1	0	0	0	0	0	0	0	0	0	0	0	0	0	0	0	0	.000	.00
Livsey, Shawn, Orlando†	.257	75	297	257	36	66	91	15	2	2	33	3	5	5	27	0	39	13	8	9	.354	.3
Luebbers, Larry, Chattanooga	.300	15	11	10	2	3	4	1	0	0	3	0	0	0	1	0	5	0	1	0	.400	.3
Lyons, Curt, Chattanooga	.056	24	19	18	0	1	1	0	0	0	1	0	0	0	1	0	9	0	0	0	.056	.1
Machado, Robert, Birmingham	.239	87	343	309	35	74	108	16	0	6	28	10	1	3	20	1	56	1	4	9	.350	.2
Magdaleno, Ricky, Chattanooga	.222	132	498	424	60	94	168	21	1	17	63	5	4	1	64	4	135	2	7	8	.396	.3
Makarewicz, Scott, Jacksonville	.314	83	290	258	42	81	141	16	1	14	49	3	3	7	18	2	46	4	3	9	.547	.3

Player, Team	Avg.	G	TPA	AB	R	H	TB	2B	3B	HR	RBI	SH	SF	HP	BB	IBB	SO	SB	CS	GDP	Slg.	OBP
Malloy, Marty, Greenville*	.312	111	495	429	82	134	177	27	2	4	36	6	2	4	54	6	50	11	10	11	.413	.393
Martinez, Angel, Knoxville*	.188	4	16	16	2	3	3	0	0	0	0	0	0	0	0	0	5	0	0	0	.188	.188
Martinez, Pablo, Greenville†	.324	9	41	37	7	12	21	2	2	1	11	1	1	0	2	0	6	3	0	1	.568	.350
Martins, Eric, Huntsville	.255	111	450	388	61	99	129	23	2	1	34	8	1	5	47	0	77	7	7	6	.332	.342
Mashore, Justin, Jacksonville	.285	120	499	453	67	129	193	27	8	7	50	7	2	4	33	1	97	17	13	10	.426	.337
Massarelli, John, Memphis	.263	65	221	205	26	54	82	16	3	2	15	2	1	0	13	0	32	9	4	1	.400	.306
Mattson, Rob, Memphis*	.138	28	32	29	3	4	5	1	0	0	3	3	0	0	0	0	8	0	0	0	.172	.138
Maurer, Mike, Huntsville	.000	52	1	1	0	0	0	0	0	0	0	0	0	0	0	0	0	0	0	0	.000	.000
Maxwell, Jason, Orlando	.266	126	502	433	64	115	164	20	1	9	45	4	3	6	56	3	77	19	4	5	.379	.355
McBride, Charles, Greenville	.268	85	324	291	38	78	117	17	5	4	50	0	3	3	27	1	75	4	3	3	.402	.333
McFarlin, Jason, Greenville*	.230	79	280	244	40	56	82	14	0	4	21	2	2	3	29	1	60	6	2	6	.336	.317
McKenzie, Scott, Chattanooga	.000	27	2	2	0	0	0	0	0	0	0	0	0	0	0	0	0	0	0	0	.000	.000
Meggers, Mike, Chattanooga	.198	38	130	111	13	22	43	6	0	5	18	0	2	1	16	0	33	1	2	1	.387	.300
Melhuse, Adam, Knoxville†	.213	32	110	94	13	20	26	3	0	1	6	1	1	0	14	1	29	0	1	3	.277	.312
Menechino, Frank, Birmingham	.292	125	497	415	77	121	188	25	3	12	62	3	6	8	64	0	84	7	9	5	.453	.391
Miceli, Danny, Carolina	.000	3	3	3	0	0	0	0	0	0	0	0	0	0	0	0	2	0	0	0	.000	.000
Michalak, Chris, Huntsville*	.000	22	1	1	0	0	0	0	0	0	0	0	0	0	0	0	1	0	0	0	.000	.000
Mitchell, Tony, Jacksonville†	.312	51	200	173	30	54	100	13	0	11	41	1	2	2	21	2	45	1	0	4	.578	.389
Monds, Wonderful, Greenville	.300	32	120	110	17	33	50	9	1	2	14	0	1	0	9	0	17	7	3	2	.455	.350
Moore, Vince, Memphis*	.206	44	162	141	24	29	47	11	2	1	11	0	1	0	20	0	47	7	4	1	.333	.302
Morales, William, Huntsville	.292	108	432	377	54	110	188	24	0	18	73	4	6	7	38	2	67	0	2	11	.499	.362
Morel, Ramon, Carolina	.400	11	14	10	1	4	4	0	0	0	0	4	0	0	0	0	1	0	0	0	.400	.400
Morris, Bobby, Orlando*	.262	131	544	463	72	122	181	29	3	8	62	0	8	6	65	4	73	12	14	12	.389	.355
Morrow, Nick, Chattanooga	1.000	1	1	1	1	1	1	0	0	0	0	0	0	0	0	0	0	0	0	0	1.000	1.000
Mosquera, Julio, Knoxville	.230	92	355	318	36	73	96	17	0	2	31	3	1	4	29	1	55	6	5	16	.302	.301
Moss, Damian, Greenville	.167	11	7	6	0	1	2	1	0	0	1	1	0	0	0	0	3	0	0	0	.333	.167
Moten, Scott, Orlando	.333	18	8	6	1	2	2	0	0	0	0	0	0	0	2	0	0	0	0	0	.333	.500
Mummau, Bob, Knoxville	.279	47	177	154	23	43	60	11	0	2	22	3	2	3	15	1	25	1	4	6	.390	.351
Munoz, Omer, Carolina	1.000	1	1	1	0	1	1	0	0	0	0	0	0	0	0	0	0	0	0	0	1.000	1.000
Murray, Heath, Memphis*	.190	27	26	21	1	4	4	0	0	0	2	3	0	0	2	0	7	0	0	1	.190	.261
Nevin, Phil, Jacksonville	.294	98	413	344	77	101	193	18	1	24	69	0	6	3	60	4	83	6	2	9	.561	.397
Newell, Brett, Greenville	.219	103	326	297	23	65	73	5	0	1	21	7	1	2	19	0	98	0	6	4	.246	.270
Nix, Jim, Chattanooga*	1.000	62	2	1	0	1	1	0	0	0	0	0	0	0	1	0	0	0	0	0	1.000	1.000
Norton, Greg, Birmingham†	.282	76	323	287	40	81	125	14	3	8	44	1	1	1	33	5	55	5	5	5	.436	.357
Nunez, Raymond, Greenville	.201	58	182	169	15	34	52	6	0	4	26	1	2	1	9	1	43	1	2	2	.308	.243
Ordonez, Magglio, Birmingham	.263	130	529	479	66	126	221	41	0	18	67	1	0	9	39	1	74	9	10	16	.461	.330
Orie, Kevin, Orlando	.314	82	351	296	42	93	142	25	0	8	58	0	6	0	48	3	52	2	0	7	.480	.403
Ortiz, Hector, Orlando	.218	78	246	216	16	47	55	8	0	0	15	1	3	0	26	2	23	1	2	12	.255	.298
Parris, Steve, Carolina	.000	5	5	5	0	0	0	0	0	0	0	0	0	0	0	0	2	0	0	0	.000	.000
Patel, Manny, Port City*	.220	126	437	369	48	81	95	9	1	1	32	4	4	4	56	1	51	12	6	5	.257	.326
Patzke, Jeff, Knoxville†	.303	124	517	429	70	130	181	31	4	4	66	0	2	6	80	6	103	6	5	2	.422	.418
Pearson, Eddie, Birmingham*	.223	85	360	323	38	72	116	20	0	8	40	0	3	2	31	3	57	2	2	6	.359	.292
Peters, Chris, Carolina*	.167	10	20	18	0	3	3	0	0	0	1	0	1	0	1	0	3	0	0	1	.167	.200
Peters, Chris, Carolina*	.125	14	18	16	0	2	3	1	0	0	1	0	2	0	0	0	2	1	0	1	.188	.125
Petersen, Chris, Orlando	.296	47	176	152	21	45	62	3	4	2	12	0	1	5	18	0	31	3	5	5	.408	.386
Peterson, Charles, Carolina	.275	125	516	462	71	127	176	24	2	7	63	3	1	0	50	5	104	33	10	18	.381	.345
Phoenix, Steve, Carolina	.000	20	1	1	0	0	0	0	0	0	0	0	0	0	0	0	1	0	0	0	.000	.000
Pobe, Charles, Huntsville	.264	122	476	416	74	110	170	18	3	12	68	4	2	8	46	2	99	5	4	14	.409	.347
Polidor, Wil, Birmingham†	.235	25	84	81	7	19	22	3	0	0	6	1	0	0	2	0	13	0	0	1	.272	.253
Pontbriant, Matt, Carolina*	.500	45	2	2	0	1	1	0	0	0	0	0	0	0	0	0	0	0	0	0	.500	.500
Pough, Pork Chop, Jacksonville	.500	2	5	4	1	2	2	0	0	0	0	0	0	1	0	0	2	0	0	0	.500	.600
Prieto, Chris, Memphis*	.333	7	13	12	1	4	6	0	1	0	3	0	0	0	1	0	2	2	0	0	.500	.385
Rackley, Keifer, Port City*	.158	6	20	19	0	3	4	1	0	0	1	0	0	0	1	0	5	0	0	0	.211	.200
Ramirez, Angel, Knoxville	.281	102	418	392	64	110	164	25	7	5	51	1	4	6	15	1	69	16	6	9	.418	.314
Ramirez, Roberto, Port City	.225	52	199	182	19	41	64	12	1	3	19	2	0	0	15	1	37	1	1	6	.352	.284
Ratliff, Darryl, Carolina	.274	82	301	270	39	74	85	11	0	0	36	4	2	0	25	0	50	13	8	7	.315	.333
Reed, Chris, Chattanooga	.120	28	26	25	1	3	3	0	0	0	2	0	0	0	1	0	7	0	0	1	.120	.154
Reynolds, Chance, Carolina†	.167	4	6	6	0	1	1	0	0	0	1	0	0	0	0	0	2	0	0	0	.167	.167
Repplemeyer, Brad, Greenville	.067	7	16	15	2	1	1	0	0	0	1	0	0	0	1	0	6	0	0	1	.067	.125
Rivera, Roberto, Orlando*	.000	9	3	3	0	0	0	0	0	0	0	0	0	0	0	0	0	0	0	0	.000	.000
Robbins, Jason, Chattanooga	.188	25	20	16	2	3	5	2	0	0	5	2	0	0	2	0	9	0	0	0	.313	.278
Roberts, David, Jacksonville*	.222	3	10	9	0	2	2	0	0	0	0	0	0	0	1	0	0	1	0	0	.222	.300
Roberts, Lonell, Knoxville†	.291	58	272	237	35	69	73	1	0	1	12	3	0	0	32	1	39	24	14	1	.308	.375
Robledo, Nilson, Birmingham	.231	7	30	26	3	6	10	1	0	1	6	0	1	0	3	0	2	0	0	0	.385	.300
Rodarte, Raul, Car.-Green.	.306	68	253	219	39	67	97	12	0	6	34	2	3	1	28	2	35	2	4	7	.443	.382
Rohrmeier, Dan, Memphis	.344	134	554	471	98	162	279	29	2	28	95	0	4	2	77	10	76	2	5	12	.592	.435
Romero, Mandy, Memphis†	.269	88	342	297	40	80	125	15	0	10	46	1	2	1	41	2	52	3	1	15	.421	.358
Rose, Pete, Birmingham*	.243	108	441	394	40	97	121	13	1	3	44	5	3	2	32	1	54	1	3	9	.303	.300
Rumfield, Toby, Chattanooga	.280	113	416	364	49	102	156	25	1	9	53	3	6	6	37	1	51	2	1	12	.429	.351
Russell, Lagrande, Port City	.000	44	1	1	1	0	0	0	0	0	0	0	0	0	0	0	0	0	0	0	.000	.000
Ryan, Jay, Orlando†	.000	7	2	2	0	0	0	0	0	0	0	0	0	0	0	0	0	0	0	0	.000	.000
Rychel, Kevin, Carolina	.000	27	1	1	0	0	0	0	0	0	0	0	0	0	0	0	0	0	0	0	.000	.000
Samuels, Scott, Orlando*	.260	106	408	342	62	89	124	19	5	2	33	3	1	0	62	2	81	21	10	3	.363	.373
Sanders, Anthony, Knoxville	.271	38	143	133	16	36	47	8	0	1	18	1	0	2	7	0	33	1	3	0	.353	.317
Sanford, Chance, Carolina*	.245	131	551	470	62	115	169	16	13	4	56	2	7	0	72	2	108	11	11	9	.360	.341
Santana, Ruben, Chattanooga	.309	98	378	343	47	106	155	21	2	8	56	0	4	5	26	1	39	5	3	7	.452	.362
Sawkiw, Warren, Birmingham†	.232	20	68	56	7	13	15	2	0	0	5	0	1	1	11	1	17	2	3	0	.268	.368
Schmidt, Tom, Jacksonville	.221	115	422	385	45	85	146	24	2	11	45	2	2	2	31	1	91	4	1	12	.379	.281
Schmitt, Todd, Memphis	.000	38	1	1	0	0	0	0	0	0	0	0	0	0	0	0	1	0	0	0	.000	.000
Sealy, Scot, Port City	.085	18	69	59	2	5	6	1	0	0	1	1	1	0	8	0	24	0	2	1	.102	.191
Simon, Randall, Greenville*	.279	134	543	498	74	139	223	26	2	18	77	0	4	4	37	7	61	4	9	13	.448	.331
Smith, Demond, Huntsville†	.260	123	526	447	75	116	188	17	14	9	62	8	5	11	55	1	89	30	15	6	.421	.351
Smith, Ryan, Port City	.000	50	1	1	0	0	0	0	0	0	0	0	0	0	0	0	0	0	0	0	.000	.000

Player, Team	Avg.	G	TPA	AB	R	H	TB	2B	3B	HR	RBI	SH	SF	HP	BB	IBB	SO	SB	CS	GDP	Slg.	OBP
Staton, T.J., Carolina*	.308	112	454	386	72	119	194	24	3	15	57	0	4	6	58	1	99	17	7	4	.503	.403
Steed, Rick, Greenville	.000	33	14	10	0	0	0	0	0	0	0	3	0	0	1	0	9	0	0	0	.000	.091
Stephenson, Brian, Orlando	.167	32	15	12	0	2	2	0	0	0	1	2	0	0	1	0	4	0	0	0	.167	.231
Stewart, Rachaad, Greenville*	.091	24	12	11	2	1	3	0	1	0	0	0	0	0	1	0	6	0	0	1	.273	.167
Stricklin, Scott, Greenville*	.145	45	152	131	14	19	23	4	0	0	11	3	1	1	16	1	29	1	1	0	.176	.242
Sturdivant, Marcus, Port City*	.284	63	271	243	34	69	94	11	4	2	23	0	2	0	26	1	33	13	7	2	.387	.351
Swann, Pedro, Greenville*	.310	35	152	129	15	40	54	5	0	3	20	1	1	3	18	2	23	4	4	3	.419	.404
Sweet, Jon, Carolina*	.100	20	42	40	2	4	6	2	0	0	1	2	0	0	0	0	3	0	0	5	.150	.100
Taylor, Scott, Carolina	.091	29	27	22	2	2	2	0	0	0	1	2	1	1	1	0	10	0	0	0	.091	.160
Thomas, Keith, Chattanooga†	.095	9	21	21	3	2	3	1	0	0	3	0	0	0	0	0	8	0	0	0	.143	.091
Thomas, Royal, Green.-Orl.	.154	10	14	13	0	2	2	0	0	0	0	1	0	0	0	0	6	0	0	0	.154	.154
Thompson, Billy, Jacksonville	.232	41	123	112	9	26	40	5	0	3	10	1	0	3	7	1	31	1	2	0	.357	.295
Thurston, Jerrey, Orlando	.209	67	194	177	16	37	54	6	1	3	23	3	0	0	14	0	57	0	0	5	.305	.267
Tomko, Brett, Chattanooga	.316	27	28	19	4	6	6	0	0	0	2	6	0	0	3	0	5	0	0	0	.316	.409
Toth, David, Greenville	.266	120	450	376	63	100	163	31	1	10	55	1	4	11	58	0	61	2	3	4	.434	.376
Trachsel, Steve, Orlando	.000	2	2	2	0	0	0	0	0	0	0	0	0	0	0	0	1	0	0	0	.000	.000
Trammell, Bubba, Jacksonville	.328	83	352	311	63	102	210	23	2	27	75	0	1	8	32	6	61	3	2	11	.675	.403
Twiggs, Greg, Orlando	.000	44	3	3	0	0	0	0	0	0	0	0	0	0	0	0	2	0	0	0	.000	.000
Valdez, Mario, Birmingham*	.274	50	208	168	22	46	69	10	2	3	28	0	3	5	32	2	34	0	0	3	.411	.399
Varitek, Jason, Port City†	.262	134	577	503	63	132	204	34	1	12	67	0	4	4	66	7	93	7	6	14	.406	.351
Vazquez, Archie, Birmingham	.000	31	1	1	0	0	0	0	0	0	0	0	0	0	0	0	1	0	0	0	.000	.000
Velandia, Jorge, Memphis	.240	122	439	392	42	94	140	19	0	9	48	5	8	3	31	3	65	3	7	10	.357	.295
Veras, Dario, Memphis	.000	29	1	1	0	0	0	0	0	0	0	0	0	0	0	0	1	0	0	0	.000	.000
Vollmer, Scott, Birmingham	.260	98	399	361	41	94	127	21	0	4	31	1	1	4	32	0	60	0	0	8	.352	.327
Wagner, Bret, Huntsville*	.000	28	3	3	0	0	0	0	0	0	0	0	0	0	0	0	1	0	0	1	.000	.000
Wakamatsu, Don, Port City	.314	24	78	70	10	22	32	4	0	2	9	0	0	4	4	0	11	1	0	2	.457	.385
Walker, Steve, Orlando†	.254	54	245	224	31	57	84	7	4	4	21	1	1	1	18	2	65	6	9	1	.375	.311
Walker, Wade, Orlando	.263	29	22	19	1	5	9	2	0	1	2	0	0	1	0	1	0	0	0	1	.474	.304
Walton, Jerome, Greenville	.200	3	8	5	0	1	3	0	1	0	0	0	0	0	3	0	1	0	0	1	.600	.500
Warner, Mike, Greenville*	.259	64	259	205	39	53	94	19	2	6	33	3	0	4	47	0	45	10	7	4	.459	.400
Watkins, Pat, Chattanooga	.276	127	535	492	63	136	195	31	2	8	59	2	4	7	30	0	64	15	11	17	.396	.323
Weinke, Chris, Knoxville*	.264	75	321	265	48	70	137	18	2	15	55	0	4	0	52	4	74	2	2	3	.517	.384
White, Jimmy, Chattanooga*	.132	15	42	38	5	5	8	1	1	0	2	0	0	4	0	12	0	0	1	.211	.217
Wilkins, Marc, Carolina	.000	11	2	2	0	0	0	0	0	0	0	0	0	0	0	0	1	0	0	0	.000	.000
Williams, Gregory, Orlando*	.000	12	2	2	0	0	0	0	0	0	0	0	0	0	0	0	0	0	0	0	.000	.000
Williams, Harold, Birm.-Orl.*	.266	94	337	301	36	80	120	10	0	10	40	1	1	3	31	5	67	2	3	10	.399	.333
Wilson, Craig, Birmingham	.282	58	253	202	36	57	75	9	0	3	26	6	4	1	40	1	28	1	1	7	.371	.399
Winslett, Dax, Orlando	.000	4	1	1	0	0	0	0	0	0	0	0	0	0	0	0	1	0	0	0	.000	.000
Wood, Jason, Huntsville	.261	133	581	491	77	128	211	21	1	20	84	2	11	5	72	2	87	2	5	14	.430	.352
Woodridge, Dickie, Memphis*	.154	34	84	65	10	10	10	0	0	0	11	1	2	0	16	1	6	1	0	1	.154	.313
Wright, Ron, Green.-Car.	.248	67	291	246	40	61	122	11	1	16	52	0	3	2	40	5	80	1	1	2	.496	.355
Zancanaro, Dave, Huntsville†	.000	10	3	2	0	0	0	0	0	0	0	0	0	0	1	0	0	0	0	0	.000	.333

GRAND SLAMS: Romero, 3; Correia, Evans, Morales, D. Smith, H. Williams, 2 each; Beasley, Bellhorn, Boone, Cameron, Dowler, Gubanich, Hurst, Hust, R. Jones, Jorgensen, Lee, Magdaleno, Makarewicz, McBride, Ordonez, Peterson, Poe, Rohrmeier, Trammell, Wakamatsu, Weinke, 1 each.

AWARDED FIRST BASE ON CATCHER'S INTERFERENCE: Evans (Kingston); Hurst (Kingston); Mitchell (Machado); Pearson (Nevin).

PLAYERS WITH TWO OR MORE TEAMS

Player, Team	Avg.	G	TPA	AB	R	H	TB	2B	3B	HR	RBI	SH	SF	HP	BB	IBB	SO	SB	CS	GDP	Slg.	OBP
Duross, Gabe, Orlando*	.155	17	62	58	2	9	11	0	1	0	6	0	1	1	2	2	3	0	0	2	.190	.194
Duross, Gabe, Birmingham*	.221	37	149	140	14	31	34	3	0	0	15	0	0	2	7	1	17	1	1	4	.243	.264
Fryman, Troy, Birmingham*	.204	14	56	49	8	10	15	2	0	1	3	1	0	1	5	0	11	0	0	0	.306	.291
Fryman, Troy, Orlando*	.230	54	226	200	27	46	67	16	1	1	25	1	3	2	20	1	50	2	2	1	.335	.304
Gray, Dennis, Port City*	.000	21	0	0	0	0	0	0	0	0	0	0	0	0	0	0	0	0	0	0	.000	.000
Gray, Dennis, Greenville*	.000	7	1	0	0	0	0	0	0	0	0	0	0	1	0	0	0	0	0	0	.000	1.000
Larregui, Ed, Orlando	.261	17	75	69	12	18	26	5	0	1	5	0	0	0	6	1	9	0	2	3	.377	.333
Larregui, Ed, Birmingham	.239	65	233	213	26	51	62	9	1	0	14	3	1	0	16	1	31	1	1	4	.291	.291
Rodarte, Raul, Carolina	.209	20	57	43	6	9	10	1	0	0	6	1	0	1	12	0	12	2	1	1	.233	.393
Rodarte, Raul, Greenville	.330	48	196	176	33	58	87	11	0	6	28	1	3	0	16	2	23	0	3	6	.494	.379
Thomas, Royal, Greenville	.000	2	0	0	0	0	0	0	0	0	0	0	0	0	0	0	0	0	0	0	.000	.000
Thomas, Royal, Orlando	.154	8	14	13	0	2	2	0	0	0	0	1	0	0	0	0	6	0	0	0	.154	.154
Williams, Harold, Birm.*	.283	14	52	46	3	13	17	4	0	0	4	0	0	2	4	1	12	1	1	1	.370	.346
Williams, Harold, Orlando*	.263	80	285	255	33	67	103	6	0	10	36	1	1	1	27	4	55	1	2	9	.404	.331
Wright, Ron, Greenville	.254	63	275	232	39	59	120	11	1	16	52	0	3	2	38	5	73	1	0	2	.517	.359
Wright, Ron, Carolina	.143	4	16	14	1	2	2	0	0	0	0	0	0	0	2	0	7	0	1	0	.143	.250

1996 PITCHING

TEAM

Team	W	L	Pct.	ERA	G	CG	ShO	Sv.	IP	H	TBF	R	ER	HR	SH	SF	HB	BB	IBB	SO	WP	BK
Memphis	81	58	.583	3.69	139	8	11	40	1219.0	1125	5256	599	500	109	35	34	50	510	22	1106	79	17
Birmingham	74	65	.532	3.94	139	9	7	40	1222.1	1190	5253	624	535	121	36	42	53	493	32	1017	49	15
Chattanooga	81	59	.579	4.00	140	7	11	51	1218.1	1153	5213	637	542	111	30	42	52	520	24	1013	85	11
Jacksonville	75	63	.543	4.06	138	6	10	37	1198.1	1219	5259	683	541	98	42	33	49	550	33	859	86	10
Carolina	70	69	.504	4.18	139	1	10	35	1208.2	1226	5237	641	562	106	39	32	63	456	44	969	66	12
Knoxville	75	65	.536	4.22	140	2	12	40	1214.2	1223	5323	673	570	100	39	31	46	582	30	1013	88	17
Port City	56	84	.400	4.34	140	5	5	31	1239.0	1221	5434	702	600	105	49	42	58	591	22	869	81	13
Orlando	61	78	.439	4.37	139	6	5	27	1199.1	1259	5323	699	582	121	46	46	60	503	35	910	69	10
Huntsville	66	74	.471	4.58	140	8	9	22	1208.1	1257	5346	743	615	106	36	39	57	526	59	950	92	12
Greenville	58	82	.414	5.14	140	2	1	35	1192.1	1306	5376	769	681	123	55	50	57	554	26	841	103	18

INDIVIDUAL

TOP QUALIFIERS FOR EARNED-RUN AVERAGE TITLE

Minimum 112 innings. *Lefthanded pitcher.

itcher, Team	W	L	Pct.	ERA	G	GS	CG	ShO	GF	Sv.	IP	H	TBF	R	ER	HR	SH	SF	HB	BB	IBB	SO	WP	Bk.
ennis, Shane, Memphis*	9	1	.900	2.27	19	19	1	0	0	0	115.0	83	471	35	29	11	4	2	5	45	0	131	8	1
yons, Curt, Chattanooga	13	4	.765	2.41	24	24	1	0	0	0	141.2	113	577	48	38	8	1	1	10	52	0	176	6	0
ruz, Nelson, Birmingham	6	6	.500	3.20	37	18	2	1	8	1	149.0	150	627	65	53	10	7	6	8	41	2	142	3	1
urray, Heath, Memphis*	13	9	.591	3.21	27	27	1	1	0	0	174.0	154	728	83	62	13	4	3	6	60	2	156	7	3
eatty, Blaine, Carolina*	11	5	.688	3.29	23	22	1	1	0	0	145.0	135	594	58	53	15	3	3	4	34	6	117	3	2
Moehler, Brian, Jacksonville	15	6	.714	3.48	28	28	1	0	0	0	173.1	186	744	80	67	9	3	2	4	50	2	120	11	2
alperin, Mike, Knoxville*	13	7	.650	3.48	28	28	0	0	0	0	155.0	156	658	67	60	6	8	2	6	71	3	112	11	4
aufman, Brad, Memphis	12	10	.545	3.63	29	29	3	1	0	0	178.1	161	768	84	72	18	8	4	4	83	4	163	8	0
ratt, Rich, Birmingham*	13	9	.591	3.86	27	27	5	2	0	0	177.1	180	732	87	76	24	3	7	6	40	2	122	5	1
omko, Brett, Chattanooga	11	7	.611	3.88	27	27	0	0	0	0	157.2	131	647	73	68	20	3	4	5	54	4	164	6	5
arpenter, Chris, Knoxville	7	9	.438	3.94	28	28	1	0	0	0	171.1	161	755	94	75	13	9	3	8	91	4	150	8	2
igby, Brad, Huntsville	9	12	.429	3.95	26	26	3	0	0	0	159.1	161	682	89	70	13	3	3	7	59	8	127	13	2
ranklin, Ryan, Port City	6	12	.333	4.01	28	27	2	0	0	0	182.0	186	764	99	81	23	6	3	16	37	0	127	4	2
eathcott, Mike, Birmingham	11	8	.579	4.02	23	23	1	0	0	0	147.2	138	625	72	66	9	5	5	4	55	3	108	5	0
arlyle, Ken, Jacksonville	8	5	.615	4.05	27	26	1	1	0	0	155.2	167	671	92	70	8	7	6	9	51	2	89	6	0

DEPARTMENTAL LEADERS: W—Moehler, 15; L—Walker, 14; Pct.—Dennis, .900; G—Nix, 62; GS—Kaufman, Walker, 29; CG—Pratt, 5; ShO—Hollins, Pratt, 3; GF—Crow, 49; V—Jean, 31; IP—Walker, 187.2; H—Walker, 205; TBF—Walker, 833; R—Walker, 112; ER—Walker, 92; HR—Pratt, 24; SH—Ry. Smith, 10; SF—Rossiter, 10; HB—Franklin, 6; BB—Carpenter, 91; IBB—Maurer, 9; SO—Lyons, 176; WP—Wagner, 19; BK—Drumright, 6.

ALL PITCHERS

*Lefthanded pitcher.

itcher, Team	W	L	Pct.	ERA	G	GS	CG	ShO	GF	Sv.	IP	H	TBF	R	ER	HR	SH	SF	HB	BB	IBB	SO	WP	Bk.
len, Cedric, Chattanooga*	1	2	.333	6.51	12	3	1	1	1	0	27.2	31	126	23	20	4	0	0	4	11	0	12	2	0
manzar, Carlos, Knoxville	7	8	.467	4.85	54	0	0	0	29	9	94.2	106	418	58	51	13	1	2	3	33	6	105	3	0
nderson, Jimmy, Carolina*	8	3	.727	3.34	17	16	0	0	0	0	97.0	92	411	40	36	3	1	0	3	44	3	79	13	5
bana, Matt, Port City	3	8	.273	5.33	18	18	0	0	0	0	96.1	86	431	58	57	8	2	6	4	69	0	55	13	0
rnold, Jamie, Greenville	7	7	.500	4.92	23	23	2	0	0	0	128.0	149	573	79	70	17	0	5	10	44	1	64	6	1
very, Steve, Greenville*	0	0	.000	0.00	1	1	0	0	0	0	0.2	0	2	0	0	0	0	0	0	0	0	0	0	0
yala, Bobby, Port City	0	0	.000	0.00	2	1	0	0	0	0	1.2	0	7	0	0	0	0	0	1	0	2	0	0
acklund, Brett, Carolina	4	6	.400	5.13	26	9	0	0	3	0	80.2	77	342	47	46	14	1	2	5	28	2	84	3	2
arnes, Brian, Jacksonville*	4	6	.400	3.74	13	12	1	1	0	0	74.2	74	320	37	31	8	6	1	4	25	1	74	3	0
easley, Tony, Carolina	1	0	1.000	0.00	2	0	0	0	2	0	2.1	1	8	0	0	0	0	0	0	1	0	1	0	0
eatty, Blaine, Carolina*	11	5	.688	3.29	23	22	1	1	0	0	145.0	135	594	58	53	15	3	3	4	34	6	117	3	2
eltran, Alonso, Chattanooga	0	1	.000	8.10	3	3	0	0	0	0	13.1	18	62	13	12	2	0	0	1	6	0	10	0	0
ennett, Bob, Huntsville	5	3	.625	5.27	38	2	0	0	12	0	83.2	92	380	55	49	10	6	1	4	36	7	83	4	0
ere, Jason, Birmingham	0	0	.000	4.15	1	1	0	0	0	0	4.1	4	21	2	2	2	0	0	0	4	0	5	1	0
ock, Jeff, Greenville	6	5	.545	5.35	20	19	0	0	0	0	106.0	136	474	67	63	10	5	4	0	41	0	51	4	0
eever, Joe, Carolina	0	0	.000	0.00	1	0	0	0	1	0	1.0	0	3	0	0	0	0	0	0	0	0	1	0	0
ogle, Sean, Orlando	0	0	.000	0.00	4	0	0	0	1	0	5.2	2	24	0	0	0	0	0	1	6	1	6	1	0
ogott, Kurtiss, Knoxville*	2	2	.500	5.33	33	0	0	0	9	3	54.0	64	256	34	32	2	0	2	5	29	2	56	12	1
orbon, Pedro, Greenville*	0	0	.000	0.00	1	0	0	0	0	0	1.0	0	3	0	0	0	0	0	0	0	0	0	0	0
randow, Derek, Knoxville	1	2	.333	7.71	5	1	0	0	3	0	11.2	11	50	10	10	3	2	2	0	5	0	6	2	1
rosnan, Jason, Port City*	5	6	.455	3.62	30	9	1	1	7	1	77.0	71	327	33	31	8	2	2	1	32	1	76	2	0
own, Chad, Knoxville*	2	4	.333	4.06	46	0	0	0	23	7	64.1	72	285	33	29	2	1	1	1	23	1	63	6	1
umley, Duff, Port City	0	1	.000	3.86	6	5	0	0	0	0	28.0	27	127	13	12	1	0	2	0	21	0	17	6	3
ryant, Adam, Chattanooga	0	0	.000	0.00	1	0	0	0	0	0	1.0	0	3	0	0	0	0	0	0	0	0	1	0	0
uckley, Travis, Chattanooga	3	4	.429	4.86	8	8	2	1	0	0	53.2	57	234	40	29	6	3	2	2	13	1	41	3	0
urlingame, Ben, Orlando	1	1	.500	3.71	11	0	0	0	5	0	17.0	21	82	7	7	1	2	2	0	16	2	0
utler, Adam, Greenville*	1	4	.200	5.09	38	0	0	0	31	17	35.1	36	161	22	20	6	5	3	2	16	3	31	3	0
rd, Matt, Greenville	4	9	.308	6.97	14	14	0	0	0	0	90.1	108	421	77	70	12	8	5	2	40	4	66	11	0
yrne, Earl, Orlando*	1	2	.333	5.59	11	6	1	0	2	0	37.0	36	170	28	23	5	1	1	0	26	1	30	1	2
arlyle, Ken, Jacksonville	8	5	.615	4.05	27	26	1	1	0	0	155.2	167	671	92	70	8	7	6	9	51	2	89	6	0
arpenter, Chris, Knoxville	7	9	.438	3.94	28	28	1	0	0	0	171.1	161	755	94	75	13	9	3	8	91	4	150	8	2
arper, Mark, Greenville	0	0	.000	0.00	4	0	0	0	2	0	6.1	4	27	1	0	0	0	0	0	5	1	0	0
ather, Mike, Greenville	3	4	.429	3.70	53	0	0	0	18	5	87.2	89	384	42	36	2	6	2	8	29	5	61	2	1
edeno, Blas, Jacksonville	0	0	.000	5.40	26	2	0	0	8	0	46.2	63	219	34	28	7	2	3	3	26	0	30	3	0
naves, Rafael, Carolina	1	2	.333	1.37	19	0	0	0	7	0	26.1	21	109	5	4	1	1	0	0	8	3	15	2	0
ccarella, Joe, Orlando*	0	0	.000	0.00	1	0	0	0	0	0	1.1	1	7	0	0	0	0	0	0	2	0	0	0	0
ark, Dera, Memphis	4	3	.571	3.13	9	9	0	0	0	0	46.0	47	199	24	16	6	2	2	2	13	0	42	3	0
ayton, Craig, Memphis	0	0	.000	5.59	5	0	0	0	0	0	9.2	14	52	12	6	3	0	1	0	5	0	9	3	0
emons, Chris, Birmingham	5	2	.714	3.15	19	16	1	0	2	0	94.1	91	400	39	33	7	0	1	6	40	2	69	1	1
ole, Victor, Memphis	1	0	1.000	1.20	8	1	0	0	4	1	15.0	11	65	3	2	0	0	0	1	8	0	13	0	0
onnolly, Matt, Orlando	7	3	.700	3.31	31	10	1	0	9	2	87.0	79	374	45	32	8	2	4	6	35	1	80	3	0
ooke, Steve, Carolina*	1	5	.167	4.53	12	12	0	0	0	0	53.2	56	240	34	27	3	4	1	3	26	3	45	3	1
ourtright, John, Chattanooga*	8	0	1.000	2.39	9	9	0	0	0	0	60.1	52	236	18	16	3	1	3	2	11	0	36	2	1
row, Dean, Port City	2	3	.400	3.18	60	0	0	0	49	26	68.0	64	285	35	24	4	5	1	1	20	1	43	6	0
ruz, Nelson, Birmingham	6	6	.500	3.20	37	18	2	1	8	1	149.0	150	627	65	53	10	7	6	8	41	2	142	3	1
abney, Fred, Orlando*	0	0	.000	2.57	12	0	0	0	2	0	14.0	15	62	5	4	1	2	0	0	5	1	16	0	0
aniels, Lee, Greenville	2	0	1.000	2.65	16	0	0	0	15	9	17.0	10	73	5	5	1	0	0	0	14	0	23	4	0
eboer, Rob, Huntsville	0	0	.000	27.00	1	0	0	0	0	0	1.0	5	8	3	3	0	0	0	0	0	0	0	0	1
elossantos, Mariano, Carolina	4	5	.375	3.53	52	0	0	0	15	1	66.1	67	288	28	26	1	3	4	10	23	4	79	3	0
ennis, Shane, Memphis*	9	1	.900	2.27	19	19	1	0	0	0	115.0	83	471	35	29	11	4	2	5	45	0	131	8	1
essens, Elmer, Carolina	0	1	.000	5.40	5	1	0	0	0	0	11.2	15	54	8	7	1	0	0	1	4	0	7	1	0
ettmer, John, Greenville	3	3	.500	2.88	26	0	0	0	4	0	40.2	43	173	19	13	3	0	1	3	6	1	28	1	0
smuke, Jamie, Jacksonville	0	0	.000	0.00	1	0	0	0	1	0	1.0	1	5	0	0	0	0	0	0	1	0	0	0	0

CLASS AA *Southern League*

Pitcher, Team	W	L	Pct.	ERA	G	GS	CG	ShO	GF	Sv.	IP	H	TBF	R	ER	HR	SH	SF	HB	BB	IBB	SO	WP	B
Dixon, Bubba, Memphis*	2	3	.400	4.12	42	0	0	0	12	3	63.1	53	267	32	29	6	2	1	2	28	2	77	4	
Doman, Roger, Knoxville	1	1	.500	5.49	17	1	0	0	6	0	39.1	51	177	30	24	2	0	0	0	14	0	30	5	
Donnelly, Brendan, Chattanooga	1	2	.333	5.52	22	0	0	0	10	0	29.1	27	133	21	18	4	0	1	1	17	2	22	1	
Doyle, Tom, Chattanooga*	4	2	.667	4.80	53	0	0	0	14	0	54.1	54	246	34	29	1	2	4	3	39	3	32	8	
Dressendorfer, Kirk, Huntsville...	4	4	.500	4.99	30	1	0	0	14	2	52.1	54	233	38	29	3	1	1	4	21	1	43	6	
Drews, Matt, Jacksonville	0	4	.000	4.35	6	6	1	0	0	0	31.0	26	138	18	15	3	0	0	4	19	0	40	2	
Drumright, Mike, Jacksonville....	6	4	.600	3.97	18	18	1	1	0	0	99.2	80	418	51	44	11	1	3	3	48	0	109	10	
Duncan, Chip, Greenville	0	0	.000	11.48	8	1	0	0	2	0	13.1	23	69	17	17	2	1	1	0	11	1	10	0	
Duran, Roberto, Knoxville*	4	6	.400	5.13	19	16	0	0	1	0	80.2	72	366	52	46	8	1	1	3	61	1	74	13	
Ellis, Robert, Birmingham	0	1	.000	11.05	2	2	0	0	0	0	7.1	6	35	9	9	1	0	1	1	8	0	8	1	
Escobar, Kelvim, Knoxville	3	4	.429	5.33	10	10	0	0	0	0	54.0	61	238	36	32	7	0	1	1	24	0	44	6	
Etheridge, Roger, Greenville*	4	2	.667	6.89	49	1	0	0	16	2	66.2	71	324	55	51	8	3	4	3	55	2	43	8	
Eyre, Scott, Birmingham*	12	7	.632	4.38	27	27	0	0	0	0	158.1	170	709	90	77	12	3	6	8	79	3	137	12	
Farson, Bryan, Carolina*	0	0	.000	16.20	4	0	0	0	1	0	5.0	9	29	10	9	3	0	0	0	4	0	3	0	
Fermin, Ramon, Jacksonville	6	6	.500	4.50	46	6	0	0	13	3	84.0	82	378	56	42	5	2	3	5	46	2	48	11	
Fesh, Sean, Memphis*	1	1	.500	5.63	7	0	0	0	2	0	8.0	7	36	5	5	2	0	0	0	7	1	5	0	
Fordham, Tom, Birmingham*	2	1	.667	2.65	6	6	0	0	0	0	37.1	26	147	13	11	4	0	2	0	14	1	37	2	
Fortugno, Tim, Chattanooga*	2	0	1.000	0.00	11	0	0	0	9	6	11.1	4	38	0	0	0	1	0	0	4	0	10	0	
Franklin, Ryan, Port City	6	12	.333	4.01	28	27	2	0	0	0	182.0	186	764	99	81	23	6	3	16	37	1	127	4	
Frazier, Ron, Chattanooga	2	5	.286	5.83	31	4	0	0	10	0	71.0	91	333	51	46	11	0	6	3	25	1	54	1	
Freeman, Chris, Knoxville	6	1	.857	3.35	26	0	0	0	8	0	45.2	45	200	23	17	3	0	3	1	23	3	54	1	
Freitas, Mike, Memphis	3	0	1.000	5.11	44	0	0	0	6	0	68.2	78	307	41	39	8	3	0	3	26	2	36	6	
Friedman, Jason, Port City*	0	0	.000	9.00	1	0	0	0	1	0	1.0	1	5	1	1	1	0	0	0	0	0	0	0	
Gaillard, Eddie, Jacksonville	9	6	.600	3.38	56	0	0	0	24	1	88.0	82	389	40	33	8	4	3	5	50	7	76	10	
Gambs, Chris, Orlando	0	0	.000	5.40	2	0	0	0	1	0	5.0	3	23	3	3	0	0	1	0	5	0	3	1	
Garcia, Al, Orlando	6	7	.462	4.85	23	16	1	0	3	0	118.2	149	528	71	64	17	6	5	7	32	1	66	4	
Gipson, Charles, Port City	0	1	.000	1.93	4	0	0	0	4	0	4.2	3	20	1	1	0	0	0	0	4	1	3	0	
Giron, Emiliano, Chattanooga.....	0	0	.000	2.25	4	0	0	0	1	0	8.0	5	33	3	2	1	0	1	1	5	1	8	0	
Gogolin, Al, Huntsville	0	0	.000	0.00	5	0	0	0	3	0	6.0	3	23	0	0	0	1	0	0	2	1	4	1	
Gonzalez, Jeremi, Orlando	6	3	.667	3.34	17	14	0	0	2	0	97.0	95	415	39	36	6	1	2	4	28	1	85	2	
Gould, Clint, Port City	0	1	.000	3.38	11	0	0	0	4	0	21.1	17	89	11	8	2	0	1	0	6	0	9	1	
Graves, Ryan, Orlando*	2	0	1.000	12.00	4	1	0	0	3	1	9.0	16	52	15	12	0	2	0	1	9	0	3	2	
Gray, Dennis, P.C.-Green.*	3	2	.600	6.99	28	1	0	0	9	0	46.1	45	226	40	36	2	4	1	1	51	4	37	5	
Greene, Rick, Jacksonville	2	7	.222	4.98	57	0	0	0	48	30	56.0	67	275	44	31	8	6	2		39	4	42	2	
Gutierrez, Jim, Jacksonville	8	6	.571	3.76	51	10	0	0	10	1	105.1	98	452	55	44	6	3	5	1	54	5	71	6	
Halperin, Mike, Knoxville*	13	7	.650	3.48	28	28	0	0	0	0	155.0	156	658	67	60	6	8	2	6	71	3	112	11	
Hansen, Terrel, Jacksonville	0	0	.000	9.00	1	0	0	0	1	0	1.0	2	6	1	1	0	0	0	1	0	0	1	0	
Hanson, Craig, Port City	0	0	.000	3.86	5	0	0	0	2	0	9.1	5	38	4	4	1	0	0	0	6	0	9	1	
Harmes, Kris, Knoxville	0	0	.000	3.38	1	0	0	0	1	0	2.2	3	12	1	1	0	0	0	0	2	0	1	0	
Harris, Gene, Carolina	0	2	.000	16.20	4	0	0	0	2	0	3.1	6	19	6	6	2	0	0	0	3	1	7	0	
Harrison, Tommy, Greenville	8	4	.667	4.71	20	16	0	0	3	0	99.1	88	421	55	52	11	2	6	3	34	0	82	7	
Hart, Jason, Orlando	3	5	.375	3.21	51	0	0	0	22	4	73.0	59	300	29	26	11	2	0	1	28	4	78	5	
Haught, Gary, Huntsville	3	2	.600	3.90	45	0	0	0	18	4	67.0	67	295	33	29	4	2	1	7	24	4	52	2	
Heathcott, Mike, Birmingham	11	8	.579	4.02	23	23	1	0	0	0	147.2	138	625	72	66	9	5	5	4	55	3	108	5	
Hernandez, Fernando, Memphis.	11	10	.524	4.64	27	27	0	0	0	0	147.1	128	655	83	76	8	3	8	8	85	4	161	11	
Hollinger, Adrian, Greenville	2	1	.667	5.46	20	0	0	0	3	0	29.2	30	136	19	18	6	2	0	5	17	0	24	2	
Hollins, Stacy, Huntsville	9	9	.500	5.11	28	26	3	2	0	0	141.0	149	623	100	80	18	3	2	6	56	6	102	13	
Holman, Shawn, Carolina	1	0	1.000	3.12	5	1	0	0	1	0	8.2	11	43	4	3	0	0	1		6	1	6	0	
Hust, Gary, Huntsville	0	0	.000	9.00	1	0	0	0	1	0	1.0	2	6	1	1	0	0	0	1	0	0	1	0	
Hutcheson, David, Orlando	4	3	.571	3.51	19	13	0	0	2	0	84.2	82	363	43	33	8	2	5	5	28	2	60	3	
Jacobs, Ryan, Greenville*	3	9	.250	6.68	21	21	0	0	0	0	99.2	127	468	83	74	19	3	4	4	57	1	64	8	
Jean, Domingo, Chattanooga	2	3	.400	4.08	39	0	0	0	37	31	39.2	34	169	19	18	1	3	0	0	17	2	33	5	
Jimenez, Miguel, Huntsville	0	4	.000	8.84	19	2	0	0	5	0	37.2	43	180	37	37	7	0	4	2	27	2	28	5	
Johnson, Barry, Birmingham	0	0	.000	0.00	9	0	0	0	7	4	10.2	2	35	0	0	0	1	0	0	1	0	15	0	
Jones, Stacy, Birmingham	1	1	.500	2.57	27	0	0	0	24	14	28.0	25	115	11	8	0	2	0	2	6	1	31	0	
Kaufman, Brad, Memphis	12	10	.545	3.63	29	29	3	1	0	0	178.1	161	768	84	72	18	8	4	4	83	4	163	8	
Kelly, John, Jacksonville	2	2	.500	4.58	9	9	1	1	0	0	55.0	54	243	38	28	2	1	1	1	35	1	29	5	
Kilgo, Rusty, Memphis*	1	4	.200	3.65	48	0	0	0	24	2	74.0	80	314	35	30	6	1	2	5	18	0	58	2	
Kimsey, Keith, Jacksonville	0	0	.000	0.00	1	0	0	0	1	0	1.0	0	3	0	0	0	0	0	0	0	0	0	0	
Kingston, Mark, Orlando	0	0	.000	9.00	1	0	0	0	1	0	1.0	3	5	1	1	0	0	0	1	0	0	0	0	
Koller, Jerry, Greenville	2	10	.167	5.50	14	13	0	0	0	0	73.2	83	321	50	45	7	5	2	1	27	1	45	5	
Konuszewski, Dennis, Carolina..	2	8	.200	6.30	32	10	0	0	8	0	80.0	103	362	61	56	12	3	4	6	36	0	59	3	
Koppe, Clint, Chattanooga	4	2	.667	3.49	10	9	1	0	1	1	56.2	54	232	27	22	3	1	3	0	18	0	30	4	
Kroon, Marc, Memphis	2	4	.333	2.89	44	0	0	0	43	22	46.2	33	208	19	15	4	1	4	3	28	1	56	6	
Kubinski, Tim, Huntsville*	8	7	.533	2.38	43	3	0	0	15	3	102.0	84	418	41	27	7	4	3	3	36	6	78	8	
Lawrence, Sean, Carolina*	3	5	.375	3.95	37	9	0	0	13	2	82.0	80	362	40	36	11	2	1	3	36	1	81	0	
LeRoy, John, Greenville	1	1	.500	2.98	8	8	0	0	0	0	45.1	43	193	18	15	5	2	2	2	18	1	38	4	
Lister, Martin, Chattanooga*	0	1	.000	5.31	19	0	0	0	9	0	20.1	25	94	13	12	2	1	1	1	11	1	10	3	
Long, Joey, Memphis*	2	0	1.000	2.00	10	0	0	0	6	0	18.0	16	79	4	4	0	1	0	0	11	1	14	3	
Lowe, Derek, Port City	5	3	.625	3.05	10	10	0	0	0	0	65.0	56	258	27	22	7	0	2	1	17	0	33	0	
Luebbers, Larry, Chattanooga	3	5	.375	3.63	11	11	0	0	0	0	69.1	64	292	32	28	6	3	1	3	26	0	38	5	
Lyons, Curt, Chattanooga	13	4	.765	2.41	24	24	1	0	0	0	141.2	113	577	48	38	8	1	1	10	52	0	176	6	
Manning, Derek, Huntsville*	4	6	.400	6.75	18	12	0	0	1	1	72.0	96	324	59	54	10	2	3	1	22	1	51	2	
Martins, Eric, Huntsville	1	0	1.000	3.86	2	0	0	0	2	0	2.1	4	14	1	1	0	0	0		3	0	2	0	
Mattson, Rob, Memphis	13	8	.619	4.33	27	27	3	1	0	0	164.1	172	708	87	79	19	2	4	7	54	2	88	5	
Maurer, Mike, Huntsville	4	6	.400	3.76	52	0	0	0	41	8	64.2	67	298	31	27	3	3	2	3	35	9	46	5	
McKenzie, Scott, Chattanooga	2	4	.333	3.40	27	0	0	0	7	0	47.2	51	214	25	18	7	0	2	0	23	3	28	4	
Miceli, Danny, Carolina	1	0	1.000	1.00	3	0	0	0	2	1	9.0	4	33	1	1	0	0	2	0	1	0	17	0	
Michalak, Chris, Huntsville*	1	0	1.000	7.71	21	0	0	0	4	0	23.1	32	123	29	20	2	1	1	1	26	4	15	4	
Moehler, Brian, Jacksonville	15	6	.714	3.48	28	28	1	0	0	0	173.1	186	744	80	67	9	3	2	4	50	2	120	11	
Montane, Ivan, Port City	3	8	.273	5.20	18	18	0	0	0	0	100.1	96	461	67	58	6	1	2	9	75	0	81	16	
Moore, Tim, Birmingham	1	4	.200	8.54	9	6	0	0	2	0	26.1	43	127	31	25	6	0	1	1	6	1	23	0	
Moore, Trey, Port City*	1	6	.143	7.71	11	11	0	0	0	0	53.2	73	265	54	46	6	2	5	0	33	0	42	4	

CLASS AA Southern League

cher, Team	W	L	Pct.	ERA	G	GS	CG	ShO	GF	Sv.	IP	H	TBF	R	ER	HR	SH	SF	HB	BB	IBB	SO	WP	Bk.
rel, Ramon, Carolina	2	5	.286	5.09	11	11	0	0	0	0	63.2	75	283	42	36	3	3	2	5	16	3	44	4	0
ss, Damian, Greenville*	2	5	.286	4.97	11	10	0	0	0	0	58.0	57	262	41	32	5	0	3	3	35	0	48	12	0
ten, Scott, Orlando	2	6	.250	5.63	18	7	1	0	5	1	54.1	59	252	40	34	8	2	5	2	31	3	35	3	0
rray, Heath, Memphis*	13	9	.591	3.21	27	27	1	1	0	0	174.0	154	728	83	62	13	4	3	6	60	2	156	7	3
well, Brett, Greenville	0	0	.000	9.00	1	0	0	0	1	0	1.0	2	5	1	1	0	0	0	0	0	0	0	0	0
wton, Geronimo, Port City*	4	1	.800	2.76	33	1	0	0	9	0	45.2	45	195	16	14	6	2	1	1	22	4	25	0	1
, Jim, Chattanooga	7	2	.778	3.34	62	0	0	0	25	11	89.0	80	378	43	33	5	4	1	2	46	2	93	5	0
rman, Scott, Jacksonville	6	5	.545	4.82	27	14	0	0	5	0	97.0	122	437	58	52	8	4	1	4	37	4	30	5	1
se, Scotty, Knoxville*	2	0	1.000	3.00	4	1	0	0	0	0	12.0	8	49	4	4	2	0	1	0	6	0	5	1	0
ris, Steve, Carolina	2	0	1.000	3.04	5	5	0	0	0	0	26.2	24	108	11	9	1	0	0	0	6	0	22	2	0
schke, Greg, Orlando	2	1	.667	2.25	9	0	0	0	6	0	12.0	12	52	6	3	0	0	0	0	3	0	12	1	2
ers, Chris, Carolina*	7	3	.700	2.64	14	14	0	0	0	0	92.0	73	378	37	27	4	4	2	0	34	2	69	4	0
t, Jose, Knoxville	4	2	.667	4.09	7	7	1	1	0	0	44.0	37	169	20	20	4	1	0	0	10	0	38	1	1
enix, Steve, Carolina	2	2	.500	4.98	20	0	0	0	15	5	21.2	31	102	12	12	3	0	2	1	6	2	16	4	0
ce, Mike, Birmingham	2	3	.400	7.09	22	0	0	0	9	1	33.0	43	154	26	26	9	1	0	1	18	2	20	2	0
e, Charles, Huntsville	0	0	.000	0.00	1	0	0	0	1	0	1.0	0	3	0	0	0	0	0	0	0	0	0	0	0
ntbriant, Matt, Carolina*	2	2	.500	5.56	45	0	0	0	12	0	56.0	73	261	40	37	5	3	2	2	25	1	36	3	0
tt, Rich, Birmingham*	13	9	.591	3.86	27	27	5	2	0	0	177.1	180	732	87	76	24	3	7	6	40	2	122	5	1
ido, Carlos, Orlando*	2	2	.500	7.45	6	0	0	0	1	0	9.2	17	50	9	8	0	0	0	0	3	0	12	3	0
n, Steve, Orlando	1	0	1.000	2.56	35	0	0	0	29	10	38.2	32	163	15	11	4	0	0	3	12	1	48	2	1
ed, Brandon, Jacksonville	1	0	1.000	2.08	7	3	0	0	1	1	26.0	18	94	6	6	1	0	1	1	3	0	18	0	0
ed, Chris, Chattanooga	13	10	.565	4.09	28	27	2	0	1	1	176.0	157	752	89	80	15	5	9	9	91	1	135	17	0
ne, Kendall, Knoxville	0	0	.000	9.56	11	0	0	0	2	0	12.1	12	62	8	8	1	0	1	3	11	1	9	3	0
by, Brad, Huntsville	9	12	.429	3.95	26	26	3	0	0	0	159.1	161	682	89	70	13	3	3	7	59	8	127	13	2
era, Roberto, Orlando*	1	2	.333	6.35	9	0	0	0	4	1	17.0	20	81	13	12	2	2	0	2	8	5	14	1	0
zo, Todd, Birmingham	4	4	.500	2.75	46	0	0	0	19	10	68.2	61	300	28	21	0	3	2	1	40	7	48	7	0
obins, Jason, Chattanooga	5	3	.625	4.72	25	12	0	0	8	1	76.1	81	342	46	40	9	1	3	3	43	1	72	12	0
mano, Michael, Knoxville	9	9	.500	4.98	34	21	0	0	5	1	130.0	148	600	98	72	17	5	8	5	72	1	92	5	2
ber, John, Chattanooga	2	0	.000	9.75	3	3	0	0	0	0	12.0	19	62	18	13	2	1	0	2	7	2	6	1	0
sengren, John, Jacksonville*	5	1	.833	4.55	60	0	0	0	15	1	55.1	48	249	36	28	9	2	1	3	37	1	47	4	0
ssiter, Michael, Huntsville	8	9	.471	4.84	27	25	2	1	1	0	145.0	167	636	92	78	15	2	10	7	44	4	116	5	0
ssell, Lagrande, Port City	7	7	.500	4.34	42	9	1	0	12	2	118.1	127	526	70	57	8	8	4	2	50	1	89	3	0
n, Jay, Orlando	2	5	.286	5.71	7	7	0	0	0	0	34.2	39	169	30	22	6	1	0	4	24	0	25	2	0
hel, Kevin, Carolina	1	1	.500	4.46	26	0	0	0	8	1	36.1	32	156	21	18	2	1	3	6	11	3	21	7	0
azar, Michael, Jacksonville*	2	5	.286	4.30	16	4	0	0	2	0	29.1	34	137	25	14	3	1	1	0	14	1	19	4	0
midt, Jason, Greenville	0	0	.000	9.00	1	1	0	0	0	0	2.0	4	9	2	2	0	0	0	0	0	0	2	1	0
mitt, Todd, Memphis	4	4	.500	3.43	38	0	0	0	25	11	39.1	39	181	26	15	1	3	0	1	21	1	47	4	4
vert, Mark, Knoxville	9	2	.818	2.58	17	17	0	0	0	0	101.1	79	415	32	29	6	2	0	3	51	0	75	3	0
a, Jose, Knoxville	2	3	.400	4.91	22	6	0	0	4	0	44.0	45	196	27	24	3	1	3	2	22	2	26	4	0
a, Luis, Huntsville	0	0	.000	13.50	1	0	0	0	0	0	2.2	5	14	4	4	1	0	1	0	2	0	2	0	1
amons, Scott, Port City*	1	1	.500	3.79	11	0	0	0	3	0	19.0	19	79	8	8	1	1	0	0	6	1	12	3	0
metta, Matt, Jacksonville	0	0	.000	4.50	4	0	0	0	1	0	6.0	4	27	3	3	0	0	1	0	5	1	7	1	0
th, Brian, Knoxville	3	5	.375	3.81	54	0	0	0	43	16	75.2	76	333	42	32	7	6	3	4	31	6	58	4	0
th, Chuck, Birmingham	2	1	.667	2.64	7	3	0	0	2	1	30.2	25	124	11	9	1	0	1	0	15	2	30	0	1
th, Ryan, Port City	6	9	.400	3.13	50	0	0	0	22	2	97.2	92	420	42	34	5	10	4	9	37	5	65	6	3
der, John, Birmingham	3	5	.375	4.83	9	9	0	0	0	0	54.0	59	236	35	29	10	2	2	1	16	1	58	4	3
rks, Jeff, Chattanooga	0	0	.000	4.50	3	0	0	0	0	0	2.0	5	10	1	1	1	0	0	1	1	0	2	0	0
ier, Justin, Orlando	4	1	.800	2.05	24	0	0	0	19	6	26.1	23	110	7	6	2	1	1	2	5	1	14	0	0
ed, Rick, Greenville	6	9	.400	3.92	33	9	0	0	7	0	101.0	100	449	51	44	4	5	4	11	44	2	70	11	1
oh, Rod, Greenville	0	0	.000	0.00	2	0	0	0	0	0	3.1	1	10	0	0	0	0	0	0	0	0	3	1	0
ohenson, Brian, Orlando	5	13	.278	4.69	32	20	0	0	3	1	128.2	130	574	82	67	13	4	9	5	61	3	106	10	1
wart, Rachaad, Greenville*	3	5	.375	6.06	24	13	0	0	2	0	71.1	89	348	55	48	4	6	3	0	48	2	74	12	2
uki, Mac, Port City	3	6	.333	4.72	16	16	0	0	0	0	74.1	69	320	41	39	10	2	1	2	32	0	66	0	0
or, Scott, Carolina	11	7	.611	4.61	29	25	0	0	1	0	158.0	170	692	94	81	16	4	5	6	62	4	100	10	1
mas, Royal, Green.-Orl.	3	2	.600	6.35	10	8	0	0	1	0	45.1	57	208	39	32	3	1	2	2	18	0	20	5	0
nko, Brett, Birmingham	11	7	.611	3.88	27	27	0	0	0	0	157.2	131	647	73	68	20	3	4	5	54	4	164	6	5
hsel, Steve, Orlando	0	1	.000	2.77	2	2	0	0	0	0	13.0	11	51	6	4	0	1	0	0	0	0	12	1	0
ggs, Greg, Orlando*	4	2	.667	3.95	44	0	0	0	15	1	54.2	53	243	27	24	2	3	4	0	33	5	40	2	0
quez, Archie, Birmingham	0	6	.000	6.61	31	1	0	0	9	1	65.1	68	313	53	48	11	4	9	6	48	3	51	4	0
as, Dario, Memphis	3	1	.750	2.32	29	0	0	0	8	1	42.2	38	172	14	11	4	1	2	1	9	2	47	2	1
a, Frank, Knoxville*	0	0	.000	1.64	4	4	0	0	0	0	22.0	16	84	4	4	1	0	0	0	3	0	15	0	0
gner, Bret, Huntsville*	8	8	.500	4.23	27	27	0	0	0	0	134.0	125	597	77	63	6	5	5	7	77	3	98	19	2
nhouse, Dave, Carolina.	5	3	.625	3.16	45	0	0	0	40	25	51.1	43	226	22	18	3	4	1	4	31	3	34	2	0
ker, Wade, Orlando	8	14	.364	4.41	29	29	2	0	0	0	187.2	205	833	112	92	20	9	4	13	76	2	117	11	1
d, Duane, Orlando	0	1	.000	27.00	1	0	0	0	0	0	1.1	4	10	4	4	1	0	0	2	0	0	0	0	1
tz, Bill, Port City	2	2	.500	2.57	6	5	1	0	1	0	28.0	28	120	10	8	1	1	1	0	9	0	26	1	0
te, Rick, Carolina	0	1	.000	11.37	2	1	0	0	0	0	6.1	9	30	8	8	2	0	1	1	0	0	7	0	1
teside, Sean, Jacksonville*	1	0	1.000	5.84	8	0	0	0	3	0	12.1	11	54	9	8	2	0	0	0	9	0	9	3	0
kins, Marc, Carolina	2	3	.400	4.01	11	3	0	0	3	0	24.2	19	103	12	11	1	2	0	2	11	2	19	0	0
iams, Gregory, Orlando*	0	0	.000	4.26	12	2	0	0	0	0	19.0	21	89	12	9	0	1	1	1	13	1	11	3	0
slett, Dax, Chattanooga	1	3	.250	7.84	4	4	0	0	0	0	20.2	31	97	19	18	4	1	1	1	7	0	13	2	0
asick, Jay, Huntsville	0	3	.000	2.30	25	6	0	0	12	4	66.2	47	274	21	17	3	3	1	3	26	2	63	2	2
od, Jason, Huntsville	0	0	.000	0.00	2	0	0	0	0	0	2.1	0	9	0	0	0	0	0	0	3	0	3	0	0
odridge, Dickie, Memphis	0	0	.000	9.00	1	0	0	0	1	0	1.0	2	6	1	1	0	0	1	0	1	0	1	0	0
ods, Brian, Birmingham	5	5	.500	3.76	53	0	0	0	26	5	67.0	59	301	32	28	11	4	0	7	38	2	46	1	0
rley, Robert, Port City	2	5	.286	3.93	35	1	0	0	13	0	66.1	66	298	40	29	3	2	4	4	39	6	40	9	0
rrell, Steve, Birmingham*	5	1	.833	2.12	35	0	0	0	16	3	51.0	28	200	14	12	1	1	0	1	21	0	55	0	0
a, Tsuyoshi, Memphis	0	0	.000	11.42	9	0	0	0	5	0	7.2	9	40	11	10	0	0	1	1	8	0	3	6	1
canaro, Dave, Huntsville*	3	3	.500	5.61	10	10	0	0	0	0	43.1	54	206	32	27	4	0	1	2	26	1	36	3	0
nerman, Mike, Port City	4	4	.500	6.94	14	8	0	0	2	0	48.0	56	231	40	37	3	2	2	7	33	0	25	2	0

CLASS AA Southern League

COMBINATION SHUTOUTS: **Birmingham (2)**—Fordham-Vazquez, Moore-Woods-Worrell. **Carolina (2)**—Peters-Chaves, Peters, Wainhouse. **Greenville (1)**—Arnold-Catl Etheridge-Hollinger-Daniels. **Huntsville (4)**—Hollins-Kubinski, Rigby-Haught-Maurer, Rossiter-Witasick, Wagner-Dressendorfer. **Jacksonville (3)**—Reed-Gutierrez-Gree Drumright-Gutierrez-Greene, Drumright-Whiteside-Greene. **Knoxville (6)**—Halperin-Romano, Pett-Romano-Brown, Pett-Freeman, Halperin-Almanzar, Sievert-Romano, Halpe Brown. **Memphis (4)**—Kaufman-Dixon-Kroon, Clark-Frietas-Kilgo, Murray-Veras-Kilgo, Hernandez-Kilgo-Kroon-Dixon. **Orlando (4)**—Gonzalez-Hutchenson-Twiggs, Gonza Dabney-Rain, Gonzalez-Rain, Gonzalez-Twiggs.

NO-HIT GAMES: Buckley, Chattanooga, defeated Huntsville, 6-0, June 1.

PITCHERS WITH TWO OR MORE TEAMS

Pitcher, Team	W	L	Pct.	ERA	G	GS	CG	ShO	GF	Sv.	IP	H	TBF	R	ER	HR	SH	SF	HB	BB	IBB	SO	WP
Gray, Dennis, Port City*	2	0	1.000	7.83	21	1	0	0	6	0	33.1	34	168	32	29	1	3	1	1	42	2	24	4
Gray, Dennis, Greenville*.........	1	2	.333	4.85	7	0	0	0	3	0	13.0	11	58	8	7	1	1	0	0	9	2	13	1
Thomas, Royal, Greenville	0	0	.000	9.00	2	0	0	0	1	0	2.0	2	12	2	2	0	1	1	0	4	0	0	0
Thomas, Royal, Orlando	3	2	.600	6.23	8	8	0	0	0	0	43.1	55	196	37	30	3	0	1	2	14	0	20	5

1996 FIELDING

TEAM

Team	Pct.	G	PO	A	E	TC	DP	PB	Team	Pct.	G	PO	A	E	TC	DP
Knoxville	.972	140	3644	1508	148	5300	152	26	Greenville	.970	140	3577	1414	153	5144	119
Port City.......	.972	140	3717	1607	153	5477	146	25	Memphis...........	.968	139	3657	1407	169	5233	107
Chattanooga......	.972	140	3655	1435	147	5237	131	13	Jacksonville	.967	138	3595	1645	177	5417	147
Birmingham	.972	139	3667	1452	148	5267	109	21	Orlando	.967	139	3598	1370	170	5138	113
Carolina............	.970	139	3626	1499	156	5281	131	17	Huntsville.........	.966	140	3625	1529	182	5336	128

TRIPLE PLAYS: Carolina, Jacksonville.

INDIVIDUAL

FIRST BASEMEN

NOTE: All caps denotes fielding-percentage leader based on 72 games for catchers, 96 for all other non-pitchers and 144 innings for pitchers. *Throws lefthanded.

Player, Team	Pct.	G	PO	A	E	TC	DP
Barry, Jeff, Memphis	.902	5	33	4	4	41	3
Bonifay, Ken, Carolina..................	.990	11	98	3	1	102	9
Boston, D.J., Carolina*	.994	87	743	53	5	801	57
Brown, Ray, Chattanooga	.981	72	584	50	12	646	47
Cholowsky, Dan, Orlando	.992	15	114	12	1	127	11
Correia, Rod, Huntsville.................	1.000	2	18	4	0	22	0
Cotton, John, Jacksonville.............	1.000	1	7	0	0	7	1
Cox, Steve, Huntsville*	.985	101	909	72	15	996	79
DiSarcina, Glenn, Birmingham.......	1.000	3	19	3	0	22	2
Dismuke, Jamie, Jacksonville........	1.000	3	26	1	0	27	2
Duross, Gabe, Orl.-Birm.*	.990	45	374	34	4	410	29
Edge, Tim, Carolina	1.000	1	9	3	0	12	0
Evans, Tom, Knoxville....................	1.000	1	6	0	0	6	0
Farrell, Jon, Carolina.....................	1.000	1	8	0	0	8	0
FREEMAN, Sean, Jacksonville*	.994	116	1064	81	7	1152	106
Friedman, Jason, Port City*	1.000	5	30	2	0	32	4
Fryman, Troy, Orlando	1.000	10	58	5	0	63	4
Garcia, Guillermo, Chattanooga	1.000	2	4	0	0	4	0
Gubanich, Creighton, Huntsville	1.000	7	41	9	0	50	5
Hanel, Marcus, Carolina................	1.000	7	42	6	0	48	5
Hansen, Terrel, Jacksonville..........	.996	24	200	27	1	228	22
Harmes, Kris, Knoxville	1.000	10	82	7	0	89	6
Ibanez, Raul, Port City..................	1.000	1	9	1	0	10	1
Jimenez, Manny, Greenville	1.000	1	3	0	0	3	0
Jones, Ryan, Knoxville...................	.992	121	1054	76	9	1139	116
Jorgensen, Randy, Port City*	.991	132	1118	106	11	1235	116
Killeen, Tim, Memphis....................	1.000	2	5	0	0	5	0
Kingston, Mark, Orlando................	1.000	4	23	1	0	24	3
Ladjevich, Rick, Port City	1.000	12	84	2	0	86	5
Leary, Rob, Carolina*	.982	32	306	16	6	328	28
Lee, Derrek, Memphis....................	.991	133	1121	76	11	1208	91
Morales, William, Huntsville..........	.976	11	74	6	2	82	7
Morris, Bobby, Orlando	.982	73	564	38	11	613	49
Mummau, Bob, Knoxville................	1.000	1	2	0	0	2	1
Nevin, Phil, Jacksonville	1.000	1	7	0	0	7	1
Newell, Brett, Greenville	1.000	1	8	0	0	8	0
Nunez, Raymond, Greenville	1.000	6	60	2	0	62	8
Pearson, Eddie, Birmingham	.984	68	529	42	9	580	32
Perez, Richard, Orlando	.973	5	31	5	1	37	3
Robledo, Nilson, Birmingham........	.941	3	27	5	2	34	1
Rohrmeier, Dan, Memphis..............	1.000	2	13	0	0	13	1
Rose, Pete, Birmingham................	.967	8	58	1	2	61	7
Rumfield, Toby, Chattanooga.........	.992	73	554	56	5	615	71
Schmidt, Tom, Jacksonville............	1.000	1	2	1	0	3	0
Sealy, Scot, Port City	1.000	1	1	0	0	1	0
Simon, Randall, Greenville	.983	81	664	50	12	726	61
Thompson, Billy, Jacksonville........	1.000	1	2	0	0	2	0
Valdez, Mario, Birmingham...........	.993	33	273	25	2	300	31
Wakamatsu, Don, Port City	1.000	7	35	2	0	37	0

Player, Team	Pct.	G	PO	A	E	TC
Weinke, Chris, Knoxville	1.000	11	78	13	0	91
Williams, Harold, Orlando*	.980	34	232	19	5	256
Wood, Jason, Huntsville.................	1.000	27	225	18	0	243
Wright, Ron, Green.-Car.	.985	58	466	45	8	519

TRIPLE PLAYS: Freeman, Leary.

SECOND BASEMEN

Player, Team	Pct.	G	PO	A	E	TC
Arias, Amador, Chattanooga	1.000	1	2	1	0	3
Barry, Jeff, Memphis	1.000	1	1	0	0	1
Beasley, Tony, Carolina..................	.953	16	26	35	3	64
Bellhorn, Mark, Huntsville	.961	57	114	158	11	283
Bream, Scott, Jacksonville.............	.950	5	8	11	1	20
Brito, Luis, Greenville	1.000	2	3	3	0	6
Bruno, Julio, Memphis....................	.958	19	25	44	3	72
Catalanotto, Frank, Jacksonville	.968	132	246	421	22	689
Cotton, John, Jacksonville.............	.926	6	7	18	2	27
Cromer, Brandon, Knoxville............	1.000	1	0	1	0	1
DiSarcina, Glenn, Birmingham.......	1.000	5	12	10	0	22
Forkerway, Trey, Orlando	1.000	11	13	34	0	47
Garcia, Guillermo, Chattanooga	.933	14	24	32	4	60
Garrison, Webster, Huntsville	.968	37	51	99	5	155
Guevara, Giomar, Port City	.971	24	44	57	3	104
Hall, Billy, Chattanooga.................	.971	117	223	314	16	553
Henry, Santiago, Knoxville.............	.966	26	47	65	4	116
Hickey, Mike, Port City	.949	50	75	110	10	195
Jimenez, Manny, Greenville	.968	35	58	91	5	154
Keefe, Jamie, Memphis	.944	7	3	14	1	18
LaRocca, Greg, Memphis	.959	107	171	274	19	464
Livsey, Shawn, Orlando	.963	63	118	167	11	296
Malloy, Marty, Greenville	.972	105	209	278	14	501
Martins, Eric, Huntsville	.967	48	89	116	7	212
Maxwell, Jason, Orlando	.947	26	39	68	6	113
MENECHINO, Frank, Birmingham...	.978	123	273	308	13	594
Morris, Bobby, Orlando	.915	36	41	66	10	117
Patel, Manny, Port City	.980	88	175	256	9	440
Patzke, Jeff, Knoxville....................	.973	120	223	343	16	582
Perez, Richard, Orlando.................	.833	2	2	3	1	6
Petersen, Chris, Orlando................	.982	24	48	60	2	110
Polidor, Wil, Birmingham...............	1.000	5	8	11	0	19
Rose, Pete, Birmingham................	1.000	2	1	4	0	5
Sanford, Chance, Carolina.............	.961	127	213	336	22	571
Santana, Ruben, Chattanooga	1.000	16	27	44	0	71
Sawkiw, Warren, Birmingham........	.947	5	6	12	1	19
Vollmer, Scott, Birmingham...........	1.000	1	1	0	0	1
Wilson, Craig, Birmingham............	.909	2	4	6	1	11
Woodridge, Dickie, Memphis.........	.973	21	34	38	2	74

TRIPLE PLAYS: Catalanotto, Sanford.

THIRD BASEMEN

Player, Team	Pct.	G	PO	A	E	TC
Alvarez, Gabe, Memphis	.878	96	59	156	30	245
Barry, Jeff, Memphis	.915	42	21	76	9	106

– 440 –

yer, Team	Pct.	G	PO	A	E	TC	DP
sley, Tony, Carolina	.833	5	2	3	1	6	1
horn, Mark, Huntsville	.848	12	6	22	5	33	1
ifay, Ken, Carolina	.945	59	30	125	9	164	8
ne, Aaron, Chattanooga	.939	126	101	225	21	347	28
am, Scott, Jacksonville	.750	5	4	8	4	16	0
no, Julio, Memphis	1.000	6	4	7	0	11	1
lowsky, Dan, Orlando	.884	21	13	25	5	43	3
ton, John, Jacksonville	.838	23	7	24	6	37	2
nford, Jay, Carolina	.928	73	46	159	16	221	9
mer, Brandon, Knoxville	.976	27	15	66	2	83	8
arcina, Glenn, Birmingham	.941	25	16	48	4	68	3
nkwater, Sean, Port City	.906	32	15	62	8	85	5
ns, Tom, Knoxville	.941	72	46	146	12	204	13
kerway, Trey, Orlando	.913	14	3	18	2	23	2
cia, Guillermo, Chattanooga	1.000	7	4	11	0	15	3
banich, Creighton, Huntsville	.875	5	5	9	2	16	2
nel, Marcus, Carolina	.500	2	0	1	1	2	0
mes, Kris, Knoxville	.500	2	0	2	2	4	0
ms, Wes, Greenville	.924	64	50	96	12	158	6
key, Mike, Port City	.928	36	22	55	6	83	7
nenez, Manny, Greenville	.917	44	29	82	10	121	5
efe, Jamie, Memphis	1.000	3	0	1	0	1	1
gston, Mark, Orlando	.912	32	20	32	5	57	2
jevich, Rick, Port City	.893	70	42	117	19	178	12
, Derrek, Memphis	1.000	1	0	1	0	1	0
le, Kevin, Jacksonville	1.000	2	0	1	0	1	0
rtins, Eric, Huntsville	.884	50	31	106	18	155	9
xwell, Jason, Orlando	1.000	5	3	10	0	13	2
rris, Bobby, Orlando	.909	4	2	8	1	11	1
mmau, Bob, Knoxville	.961	45	31	93	5	129	11
rin, Phil, Jacksonville	.943	12	7	26	2	35	3
vell, Brett, Greenville	1.000	4	3	8	0	11	0
nez, Raymond, Greenville	.848	23	10	29	7	46	2
el, Kevin, Orlando	.936	79	60	144	14	218	14
el, Manny, Port City	.941	24	19	45	4	68	3
dor, Wil, Birmingham	.941	6	4	12	1	17	2
gh, Pork Chop, Jacksonville	1.000	2	0	2	0	2	0
plemeyer, Brad, Greenville	.667	2	0	2	1	3	0
larte, Raul, Car.-Green.	.907	35	28	60	9	97	7
rrmeier, Dan, Memphis	1.000	1	1	0	0	1	0
SE, Pete, Birmingham	.942	97	73	201	17	291	12
tana, Ruben, Chattanooga	.893	14	9	16	3	28	2
midt, Tom, Jacksonville	.904	109	80	230	33	343	21
mer, Scott, Jacksonville	1.000	7	2	14	0	16	1
son, Craig, Birmingham	.939	11	6	25	2	33	3
od, Jason, Huntsville	.943	82	62	187	15	264	22
odridge, Dickie, Memphis	.750	3	1	5	2	8	1

TRIPLE PLAYS: Bonifay, Schmidt.

THIRD BASEMEN WITH TWO OR MORE TEAMS

yer, Team	Pct.	G	PO	A	E	TC	DP
larte, Raul, Carolina	.913	16	10	32	4	46	3
larte, Raul, Greenville	.902	19	18	28	5	51	4

SHORTSTOPS

yer, Team	Pct.	G	PO	A	E	TC	DP
rez, Gabe, Memphis	.889	3	3	5	1	9	1
sley, Tony, Carolina	.923	15	24	36	5	65	7
horn, Mark, Huntsville	.940	55	88	164	16	268	27
ne, Aaron, Chattanooga	.982	14	22	32	1	55	9
am, Scott, Jacksonville	.955	4	9	12	1	22	0
o, Luis, Greenville	.936	13	13	31	3	47	6
ier, Lou, Carolina	.943	117	189	310	30	529	71
reia, Rod, Huntsville	.925	62	104	180	23	307	40
on, John, Jacksonville	1.000	9	6	15	0	21	5
nford, Jay, Carolina	.955	17	23	41	3	67	12
mer, Brandon, Knoxville	.947	73	79	172	14	265	36
arcina, Glenn, Birmingham	.941	4	7	9	1	17	1
kerway, Trey, Orlando	.966	28	35	79	4	118	15
cia, Luis, Jacksonville	.947	131	205	435	36	676	93
son, Charles, Port City	.945	43	71	151	13	235	21
vara, Giomar, Port City	.932	99	143	293	32	468	73
ry, Santiago, Knoxville	.932	80	135	224	26	385	68
nenez, Manny, Greenville	.939	56	78	139	14	231	27
locca, Greg, Memphis	.926	28	17	46	5	68	10
gdaleno, Ricky, Chattanooga	.937	131	187	337	35	559	74
tinez, Pablo, Greenville	.957	9	9	35	2	46	7
xwell, Jason, Orlando	.946	97	146	258	23	427	40
vell, Brett, Greenville	.955	84	116	201	15	332	44
ton, Greg, Birmingham	.949	76	104	214	17	335	34
el, Manny, Port City	.894	13	14	28	5	47	7
rsen, Chris, Orlando	.904	24	43	61	11	115	15
dor, Wil, Birmingham	.975	12	9	30	1	40	5

Player, Team	Pct.	G	PO	A	E	TC	DP
Rose, Pete, Birmingham	.750	1	1	2	1	4	0
Sawkiw, Warren, Birmingham	.929	12	16	23	3	42	5
Schmidt, Tom, Jacksonville	.923	3	9	3	1	13	1
Velandia, Jorge, Memphis	.943	121	173	368	33	574	66
Wilson, Craig, Birmingham	.930	40	57	117	13	187	28
Wood, Jason, Huntsville	.965	26	50	87	5	142	14

OUTFIELDERS

Player, Team	Pct.	G	PO	A	E	TC	DP
BARGER, Mike, Port City	1.000	97	207	7	0	214	0
Barker, Glen, Jacksonville	.979	41	91	2	2	95	0
Barry, Jeff, Memphis	1.000	30	35	1	0	36	0
Beasley, Tony, Carolina	.885	26	23	0	3	26	0
Bonifay, Ken, Carolina	1.000	9	10	1	0	11	1
Bowles, Justin, Huntsville*	1.000	3	2	0	0	2	0
Bream, Scott, Jacksonville	1.000	18	20	2	0	22	0
Briggs, Stoney, Memphis	.963	133	217	15	9	241	3
Brinkley, Darryl, Memphis	.989	51	89	1	1	91	0
Broach, Donald, Chattanooga	.983	104	165	12	3	180	0
Brock, Tarrik, Jacksonville*	.930	34	48	5	4	57	0
Brown, Adrian, Carolina	.990	81	185	5	2	192	2
Bullett, Scott, Orlando*	1.000	2	1	0	0	1	0
Cameron, Mike, Birmingham	.973	120	249	8	7	264	1
Candelaria, Ben, Knoxville	.962	38	47	3	2	52	0
Conger, Jeff, Carolina*	.981	27	49	2	1	52	0
Correa, Miguel, Greenville	.981	60	150	6	3	159	1
Cotton, John, Jacksonville	1.000	35	42	5	0	47	0
Cradle, Rickey, Knoxville	.973	88	135	8	4	147	1
Cruz, Jose, Port City	.990	46	90	6	1	97	2
DeLaCruz, Lorenzo, Knoxville	.955	116	184	9	9	202	1
Dismuke, Jamie, Jacksonville	1.000	7	6	0	0	6	0
Dowler, Dee, Orlando	.991	101	209	5	2	216	0
Farrell, Jon, Carolina	.955	13	21	0	1	22	0
Forkerway, Trey, Orlando	1.000	4	1	0	0	1	0
Francisco, David, Huntsville	.978	108	217	7	5	229	1
Friedman, Jason, Port City*	1.000	8	7	0	0	7	0
Fryman, Troy, Birm.-Orl.	.966	54	81	4	3	88	0
Garrison, Webster, Huntsville	1.000	4	2	0	0	2	0
Gipson, Charles, Port City	.987	75	139	11	2	152	4
Grieve, Ben, Huntsville	.953	59	79	2	4	85	0
Griffey, Craig, Port City	1.000	112	179	13	0	192	3
Hanel, Marcus, Carolina	1.000	3	2	0	0	2	0
Hansen, Terrel, Jacksonville	1.000	46	50	1	0	51	0
Henry, Santiago, Knoxville	1.000	3	4	0	0	4	0
Herrera, Jose, Huntsville*	.972	20	34	1	1	36	1
Hightower, Vee, Orlando	.978	18	44	0	1	45	0
Howard, Tom, Chattanooga	1.000	5	8	0	0	8	0
Hughes, Troy, Orlando	.961	113	211	11	9	231	3
Hurst, Jimmy, Birmingham	.972	119	234	11	7	252	2
Hust, Gary, Huntsville	.973	44	67	6	2	75	0
Ibanez, Raul, Port City	.871	15	26	1	4	31	0
Johnson, Earl, Memphis	.986	82	204	9	3	216	3
Jones, Andruw, Greenville	.993	38	129	7	1	137	1
Jorgenson, Randy, Port City*	1.000	4	1	0	0	1	0
Kimsey, Keith, Jacksonville	.966	31	50	6	2	58	4
King, Andre, Chattanooga	1.000	13	28	0	0	28	0
Ladell, Cleveland, Chattanooga	.977	117	246	7	6	259	3
Larregui, Ed, Orl.-Birm.	.988	58	80	2	1	83	0
Mashore, Justin, Jacksonville	.984	113	228	19	4	251	3
Massarelli, John, Memphis	.978	47	84	6	2	92	1
McBride, Charles, Greenville*	.977	80	127	3	3	133	0
McFarlin, Jason, Greenville*	.983	71	111	3	2	116	1
Meggers, Mike, Chattanooga	.981	27	50	1	1	52	0
Mitchell, Tony, Jacksonville	.949	27	35	2	2	39	0
Monds, Wonderful, Greenville	.970	32	62	2	2	66	1
Moore, Vince, Memphis*	.983	40	58	0	1	59	0
Morrow, Nick, Chattanooga	1.000	1	1	0	0	1	0
Nevin, Phil, Jacksonville	1.000	11	16	0	0	16	0
Ordonez, Magglio, Birmingham	.976	129	231	12	6	249	3
Peterson, Charles, Carolina	.948	120	186	16	11	213	5
Poe, Charles, Huntsville	.957	84	127	5	6	138	0
Prieto, Chris, Memphis*	1.000	5	6	0	0	6	0
Rackley, Keifer, Port City	1.000	6	7	0	0	7	0
Ramirez, Angel, Huntsville	.979	95	180	5	4	189	1
Ramirez, Roberto, Port City	.958	27	44	2	2	48	0
Ratliff, Darryl, Carolina	.992	57	108	9	1	118	1
Rippelmeyer, Brad, Greenville	1.000	1	3	0	0	3	0
Roberts, David, Jacksonville*	1.000	3	5	0	0	5	0
Roberts, Lonell, Knoxville	.991	58	102	4	1	107	1
Rodarte, Raul, Greenville	.980	26	42	7	1	50	2
Rohrmeier, Dan, Memphis	.990	63	93	9	1	103	2
Rumfield, Toby, Chattanooga	.984	4	4	1	0	5	0

Player, Team	Pct.	G	PO	A	E	TC	DP
Samuels, Scott, Orlando	.981	96	149	7	3	159	1
Sanders, Anthony, Knoxville	.957	38	66	1	3	70	0
Santana, Ruben, Chattanooga	1.000	40	60	0	0	60	0
Sawkiw, Warren, Birmingham	1.000	2	2	0	0	2	0
Simon, Randall, Greenville*	.941	36	59	5	4	68	0
Smith, Demond, Huntsville	.955	111	187	4	9	200	1
Staton, T.J., Carolina*	.979	106	178	7	4	189	1
Sturdivant, Marcus, Port City*	.986	61	136	8	2	146	0
Swann, Pedro, Greenville	.949	34	55	1	3	59	0
Thomas, Keith, Chattanooga	1.000	5	10	0	0	10	0
Thompson, Billy, Jacksonville	.947	15	16	2	1	19	0
Toth, David, Greenville	1.000	1	1	0	0	1	0
Trammell, Bubba, Jacksonville	.955	70	100	6	5	111	1
Valdez, Mario, Birmingham	1.000	7	11	1	0	12	0
Varitek, Jason, Port City	1.000	1	1	0	0	1	0
Walker, Steve, Orlando	.975	54	114	5	3	122	0
Walton, Jerome, Greenville	1.000	3	2	0	0	2	0
Warner, Mike, Greenville*	.994	60	153	6	1	160	3
Watkins, Pat, Chattanooga	.984	126	220	21	4	245	2
Weinke, Chris, Knoxville	1.000	3	3	0	0	3	0
White, Jimmy, Chattanooga	.833	6	4	1	1	6	1

OUTFIELDERS WITH TWO OR MORE TEAMS

Player, Team	Pct.	G	PO	A	E	TC	DP
Fryman, Troy, Birmingham	1.000	8	14	0	0	14	0
Fryman, Troy, Orlando	.959	46	67	4	3	74	0
Larregui, Ed, Orlando	1.000	13	24	1	0	25	0
Larregui, Ed, Birmingham	.983	45	56	1	1	58	0

CATCHERS

Player, Team	Pct.	G	PO	A	E	TC	DP	PB
Bako, Paul, Chattanooga	.984	102	694	84	13	791	8	7
Cardenas, John, Port City	.992	18	115	4	1	120	2	4
Casanova, Papo, Jacksonville	1.000	4	21	1	0	22	0	1
Cholowsky, Dan, Orlando	.940	16	61	2	4	67	0	4
Deboer, Rob, Huntsville	.980	32	172	26	4	202	4	6
Edge, Tim, Carolina	.994	44	278	39	2	319	9	4
Garcia, Guillermo, Chatt.	.993	32	248	22	2	272	3	4
Gubanich, Creighton, Hunts.	.982	29	198	16	4	218	1	11
Hanel, Marcus, Carolina	.989	91	621	80	8	709	10	12
Harmes, Kris, Knoxville	.980	30	182	17	4	203	1	1
Hicks, Jamie, Greenville	1.000	1	1	0	0	1	0	0
Ibanez, Raul, Port City	1.000	1	1	0	0	1	0	0
Killeen, Tim, Memphis	.987	66	424	40	6	470	2	6
Kingston, Mark, Orlando	.971	13	60	7	2	69	1	1
Lidle, Kevin, Jacksonville	1.000	1	5	0	0	5	0	0
Machado, Robert, Birm.	.991	70	502	67	5	574	10	11
Makarewicz, Scott, Jackson.	.987	66	392	51	6	449	4	12
Martinez, Angel, Knoxville	.950	3	17	2	1	20	1	0
Massarelli, John, Memphis	1.000	9	32	5	0	37	0	0
Melhuse, Adam, Knoxville	.989	31	162	15	2	179	2	6
Morales, William, Huntsville	.982	86	577	77	12	666	4	17
Mosquera, Julio, Knoxville	.991	92	679	63	7	749	6	19
Nevin, Phil, Jacksonville	.978	62	354	50	9	413	6	17
Ortiz, Hector, Orlando	.988	76	475	32	6	513	2	5
Reynolds, Chance, Carolina	1.000	4	10	0	0	10	0	0
Ripplemeyer, Brad, Greenville	1.000	1	2	0	0	2	0	0
Robledo, Nilson, Birmingham	1.000	2	8	3	0	11	0	0
Romero, Mandy, Memphis	.983	78	657	52	12	721	5	12
Rumfield, Toby, Chattanooga	1.000	15	80	7	0	87	0	2
Sealy, Scot, Port City	1.000	8	57	4	0	61	0	4
Stricklin, Scott, Greenville	.996	44	238	30	1	269	5	4
Sweet, Jon, Carolina	1.000	16	78	11	0	89	2	1
Thompson, Billy, Jacksonville	.977	23	118	11	3	132	1	5
Thurston, Jerrey, Orlando	.987	63	354	21	5	380	5	8
Toth, David, Greenville	.981	107	600	83	13	696	5	9
VARITEK, Jason, Port City	.993	108	662	79	5	746	10	16
Vollmer, Scott, Birmingham	.975	71	543	46	15	604	2	10
Wakamatsu, Don, Port City	.985	11	62	3	1	66	0	1

PITCHERS

Player, Team	Pct.	G	PO	A	E	TC	DP
Allen, Cedric, Chattanooga*	.875	12	1	6	1	8	0
Almanzar, Carlos, Knoxville	.875	54	7	7	2	16	0
Anderson, Jimmy, Carolina*	.970	17	9	23	1	33	3
Apana, Matt, Port City	1.000	18	5	9	0	14	0
Arnold, Jamie, Greenville	.963	23	11	15	1	27	0
Ayala, Bobby, Port City	1.000	2	1	0	0	1	0
Backlund, Brett, Carolina	.944	26	7	10	1	18	0
Barnes, Brian, Jacksonville*	.950	13	5	14	1	20	0
Beatty, Blaine, Carolina*	1.000	23	10	13	0	23	0
Beltran, Alonso, Chattanooga	.800	3	2	2	1	5	1

Player, Team	Pct.	G	PO	A	E	TC
Bennett, Bob, Huntsville	.950	38	7	12	1	20
Bere, Jason, Birmingham	1.000	1	1	0	0	1
Bock, Jeff, Greenville	1.000	20	6	9	0	15
Bogle, Sean, Orlando	1.000	4	1	1	0	2
Bogott, Kurtiss, Knoxville	.938	33	5	10	1	16
Brosnan, Jason, Port City*	.875	30	2	5	1	8
Brown, Chad, Knoxville*	.923	46	2	10	1	13
Brumley, Duff, Port City	1.000	6	0	3	0	3
Buckley, Travis, Chattanooga	1.000	8	2	5	0	7
Burlingame, Ben, Orlando	1.000	11	2	1	0	3
Butler, Adam, Greenville*	1.000	38	1	4	0	5
Byrd, Matt, Greenville	1.000	51	5	8	0	13
Byrne, Earl, Orlando*	.889	11	2	6	1	9
Carlyle, Ken, Jacksonville	.893	27	15	35	6	56
Carpenter, Chris, Knoxville	.943	28	8	25	2	35
Carper, Mark, Greenville	1.000	4	0	2	0	2
Cather, Mike, Greenville	.944	53	6	11	1	18
Cedeno, Blas, Jacksonville	1.000	26	6	3	0	9
Chaves, Rafael, Carolina	1.000	19	2	4	0	6
Clark, Dera, Memphis	1.000	9	1	9	0	10
Clayton, Craig, Memphis	1.000	5	0	2	0	2
Clemons, Chris, Birmingham	.955	19	8	13	1	22
Cole, Victor, Memphis	1.000	8	1	1	0	2
Connolly, Matt, Orlando	.875	31	3	4	1	8
Cooke, Steve, Carolina*	.714	12	1	4	2	7
Courtright, John, Chattanooga*	.909	9	0	10	1	11
Crow, Dean, Port City	.933	60	4	10	1	15
Cruz, Nelson, Birmingham	.867	37	11	15	4	30
Dabney, Fred, Orlando*	.750	12	2	1	1	4
Daniels, Lee, Greenville	1.000	16	1	2	0	3
Delossantos, Mariano, Carolina	.909	52	2	8	1	11
Dennis, Shane, Memphis*	.913	19	3	15	0	18
Dettmer, John, Greenville	.889	26	2	6	1	9
Dismuke, Jamie, Jacksonville	1.000	1	1	0	0	1
Dixon, Bubba, Memphis*	1.000	42	1	7	0	8
Doman, Roger, Knoxville	.875	17	2	5	1	8
Donnelly, Brendan, Chattanooga	1.000	22	3	3	0	6
Doyle, Tom, Chattanooga*	.933	53	3	11	1	15
Dressendorfer, Kirk, Huntsville	.800	30	4	4	2	10
Drews, Matt, Jacksonville	1.000	6	2	4	0	6
Drumright, Mike, Jacksonville	.852	18	10	13	4	27
Duncan, Chip, Greenville	.857	8	4	2	1	7
Duran, Roberto, Knoxville*	.857	19	5	7	2	14
Ellis, Robert, Birmingham	1.000	2	0	2	0	2
Escobar, Kelvim, Knoxville	.846	10	8	3	2	13
Etheridge, Roger, Greenville*	.917	49	1	10	1	12
Eyre, Scott, Birmingham*	1.000	27	7	17	0	24
Farson, Bryan, Carolina*	.000	4	0	0	1	1
Fermin, Ramon, Jacksonville	.769	46	5	5	3	13
Fesh, Sean, Memphis*	.500	7	0	1	1	2
Fordham, Tom, Birmingham*	1.000	6	0	5	0	5
Fortugno, Tim, Chattanooga*	1.000	11	0	4	0	4
Franklin, Ryan, Port City	.950	28	13	25	2	40
Frazier, Ron, Chattanooga	.900	31	7	11	2	20
Freeman, Chris, Knoxville	1.000	26	4	6	0	10
Freitas, Mike, Memphis	.955	44	6	15	1	22
Gaillard, Eddie, Jacksonville	.944	56	7	10	1	18
Garcia, Al, Orlando	1.000	23	13	18	0	31
Giron, Emiliano, Chattanooga	1.000	4	0	1	0	1
Gogolin, Al, Huntsville	1.000	5	2	1	0	3
Gonzalez, Jeremi, Orlando	.905	17	9	10	2	21
Gould, Clint, Port City	1.000	11	1	5	0	6
Graves, Ryan, Orlando*	1.000	4	1	0	0	1
Gray, Dennis, P.C.-Green.*	1.000	28	2	8	0	10
Greene, Rick, Orlando	1.000	57	5	9	0	14
Gutierrez, Jim, Jacksonville	.923	51	2	10	1	13
Halperin, Mike, Knoxville*	.962	28	7	43	2	52
Hanson, Craig, Port City	1.000	5	0	1	0	1
Harmes, Kris, Knoxville	1.000	1	0	1	0	1
Harrison, Tommy, Greenville	1.000	20	7	9	0	16
Hart, Jason, Orlando	.944	51	5	12	1	18
Haught, Gary, Huntsville	1.000	45	4	8	0	12
Heathcott, Mike, Birmingham	.949	23	17	20	2	39
Hernandez, Fernando, Memphis	.880	27	5	17	3	25
Hollinger, Adrian, Greenville	.857	20	2	4	1	7
Hollins, Stacy, Huntsville	1.000	28	15	13	0	28
Holman, Shawn, Carolina	.800	5	3	1	1	5
Hust, Gary, Huntsville	1.000	1	0	1	0	1
Hutcheson, David, Orlando	.846	19	3	8	2	13
Jacobs, Ryan, Greenville*	.909	21	2	8	1	11
Jean, Domingo, Chattanooga	1.000	39	5	6	0	11
Jimenez, Miguel, Huntsville	.889	19	4	4	1	9
Johnson, Barry, Birmingham	1.000	9	0	1	0	1

Player, Team	Pct.	G	PO	A	E	TC	DP
es, Stacy, Birmingham	.750	27	1	2	1	4	0
ufman, Brad, Memphis	.914	29	12	20	3	35	0
ly, John, Jacksonville	.909	9	4	6	1	11	0
go, Rusty, Memphis*	1.000	48	15	7	0	22	2
ler, Jerry, Greenville	1.000	14	2	10	0	12	1
nuszewski, Dennis, Carolina	.900	32	2	7	1	10	0
ope, Clint, Chattanooga	.750	10	3	6	3	12	1
oon, Marc, Memphis	1.000	44	4	3	0	7	1
inski, Tim, Huntsville*	.964	43	5	22	1	28	0
wrence, Sean, Carolina*	.714	37	1	9	4	14	0
Roy, John, Greenville	1.000	8	5	5	0	10	0
ter, Martin, Chattanooga*	.667	19	2	0	1	3	0
ng, Joey, Memphis*	1.000	10	2	4	0	6	0
we, Derek, Port City	1.000	10	10	11	0	21	3
ebbers, Larry, Chattanooga	.926	11	11	14	2	27	0
ons, Curt, Chattanooga	.926	24	7	18	2	27	1
nning, Derek, Huntsville*	.957	18	5	17	1	23	0
rtins, Eric, Huntsville	1.000	2	1	0	0	1	0
ttson, Rob, Memphis	.973	27	12	24	1	37	2
urer, Mike, Huntsville	1.000	52	5	8	0	13	0
Kenzie, Scott, Chattanooga	.800	27	3	1	1	5	1
celi, Danny, Carolina	1.000	3	0	1	0	1	0
chalak, Chris, Huntsville*	1.000	21	2	5	0	7	0
ehler, Brian, Jacksonville	.953	28	17	24	2	43	3
ntane, Ivan, Port City	.818	18	7	11	4	22	0
ore, Tim, Birmingham	.600	9	0	3	2	5	0
ore, Trey, Port City*	1.000	11	5	10	0	15	1
rel, Ramon, Carolina	1.000	11	3	10	0	13	0
ss, Damian, Greenville*	.889	11	2	6	1	9	0
ten, Scott, Orlando	.923	18	5	7	1	13	0
rray, Heath, Memphis*	.963	27	8	18	1	27	0
wton, Geronimo, Port City*	1.000	33	2	12	0	14	0
, Jim, Chattanooga	.952	62	8	12	1	21	2
rman, Scott, Jacksonville	.889	27	14	18	4	36	1
ce, Scotty, Knoxville*	.667	4	1	1	1	3	0
ris, Steve, Carolina	.800	5	3	1	1	5	0
schke, Greg, Birmingham	1.000	9	1	0	0	1	0
ers, Chris, Carolina*	1.000	14	3	24	0	27	2
, Jose, Knoxville	.875	7	2	5	1	8	1
enix, Steve, Carolina	1.000	20	2	0	0	2	0
ce, Mike, Birmingham	1.000	22	3	2	0	5	0
ntbriant, Matt, Carolina*	1.000	45	5	11	0	16	0
ATT, Rich, Birmingham*	1.000	27	8	39	0	47	0
do, Carlos, Orlando*	1.000	6	0	1	0	1	0
n, Steve, Orlando	1.000	35	0	4	0	4	1
d, Brandon, Jacksonville	1.000	7	3	1	0	4	0
d, Chris, Chattanooga	.958	28	17	29	2	48	2
ne, Kendall, Knoxville	1.000	11	3	1	0	4	1
by, Brad, Huntsville	1.000	26	19	13	0	32	0
era, Roberto, Orlando*	1.000	9	1	4	0	5	0
to, Todd, Birmingham*	.933	46	1	13	1	15	2
obins, Jason, Chattanooga	.929	25	6	7	1	14	1
nano, Michael, Knoxville	.906	34	10	19	3	32	1

Player, Team	Pct.	G	PO	A	E	TC	DP
Roper, John, Chattanooga	.800	3	3	1	1	5	1
Rosengren, John, Jacksonville*	1.000	60	3	6	0	9	1
Rossiter, Michael, Huntsville	1.000	27	11	10	0	21	0
Russell, Lagrande, Port City	.963	42	8	18	1	27	2
Ryan, Jay, Orlando	1.000	7	3	2	0	5	0
Rychel, Kevin, Carolina	1.000	26	3	7	0	10	1
Salazar, Michael, Jacksonville*	1.000	16	2	5	0	7	0
Schmidt, Jason, Greenville	1.000	1	0	1	0	1	0
Schmitt, Todd, Memphis	.750	38	2	4	2	8	0
Sievert, Mark, Knoxville	.941	17	7	9	1	17	1
Silva, Jose, Knoxville	.929	22	5	8	1	14	0
Simmons, Scott, Port City*	.778	11	1	6	2	9	0
Smith, Brian, Knoxville	.944	54	5	12	1	18	2
Smith, Chuck, Birmingham	.667	7	0	2	1	3	0
Smith, Ryan, Port City	.967	50	6	23	1	30	0
Snyder, John, Birmingham	1.000	9	4	6	0	10	0
Speier, Justin, Orlando	.667	24	0	4	2	6	0
Steed, Rick, Greenville	.882	33	15	15	4	34	2
Steph, Rod, Greenville	1.000	2	1	0	0	1	0
Stephenson, Brian, Orlando	.926	32	13	12	2	27	1
Stewart, Rachaad, Greenville*	.938	24	4	11	1	16	1
Suzuki, Mac, Port City	.917	16	5	6	1	12	0
Taylor, Scott, Carolina	.955	29	17	25	2	44	5
Thomas, Royal, Orlando	.857	10	4	2	1	7	0
Tomko, Brett, Chattanooga	1.000	27	13	14	0	27	1
Trachsel, Steve, Orlando	1.000	2	2	3	0	5	0
Twiggs, Greg, Orlando*	1.000	44	0	10	0	10	0
Vazquez, Archie, Birmingham	1.000	31	1	5	0	6	0
Veras, Dario, Memphis	.875	29	1	6	1	8	1
Viola, Frank, Knoxville*	1.000	4	4	1	0	5	0
Wagner, Bret, Huntsville	.906	27	8	21	3	32	3
Wainhouse, Dave, Carolina	1.000	45	1	7	0	8	2
Walker, Wade, Orlando	.920	29	19	27	4	50	1
Ward, Duane, Orlando	1.000	2	0	1	0	1	0
Wertz, Bill, Port City	.857	6	3	3	1	7	0
White, Rick, Carolina	1.000	2	1	0	0	1	0
Whiteside, Sean, Jacksonville*	1.000	8	1	3	0	4	0
Wilkins, Marc, Carolina	1.000	11	1	5	0	6	0
Williams, Gregory, Orlando*	1.000	12	1	7	0	8	0
Winslett, Dax, Orlando	1.000	4	1	5	0	6	1
Witasick, Jay, Huntsville	.917	25	2	9	1	12	0
Woods, Brian, Birmingham	.923	53	3	9	1	13	0
Worley, Robert, Port City	.941	35	7	9	1	17	0
Worrell, Steve, Birmingham*	.889	35	3	5	1	9	0
Yoda, Tsuyoshi, Memphis	.500	9	0	1	1	2	0
Zancanaro, Dave, Huntsville*	.667	10	2	0	1	3	0
Zimmerman, Mike, Port City	1.000	14	4	10	0	14	0

PITCHERS WITH TWO OR MORE TEAMS

Player, Team	Pct.	G	PO	A	E	TC	DP
Gray, Dennis, Port City*	1.000	21	2	5	0	7	0
Gray, Dennis, Greenville*	1.000	7	0	3	0	3	0

LEAGUE CHAMPIONS

r	Team	Pct.	Year	Team	Pct.	Year	Team	Pct.
4—	Macon	.598	1921—	Columbia	.642	1941—	Macon	.643
5—	Macon	.625	1922—	Charleston	.625		Columbia (2nd)†	.636
6—	Savannah	.637	1923—	Charlotte*	.653	1942—	Charleston	.620
7—	Charleston	.620		Macon	.580		Macon (2nd)†	.585
8—	Jacksonville	.694	1924—	Augusta	.612	1943-45—Did not operate.		
9—	Chattanooga*	.738	1925—	Spartanburg	.620	1946—	Columbus	.568
	Augusta	.702	1926—	Greenville	.662		Augusta (4th)†	.547
0—	Columbus	.588	1927—	Greenville	.622	1947—	Columbus	.575
1—	Columbus*	.681	1928—	Asheville	.664		Savannah (2nd)†	.563
	Columbia	.710	1929—	Asheville	.605	1948—	Charleston	.572
2—	Jacksonville*	.679		Knoxville*	.634		Greenville (3rd)†	.549
	Columbus	.632	1930—	Greenville*	.620	1949—	Macon‡	.623
3—	Savannah	.754		Macon	.643	1950—	Macon‡	.588
	Savannah	.593	1931-35—Did not operate.			1951—	Montgomery	.607
4—	Savannah*	.667	1936—	Jacksonville	.652	1952—	Columbia	.649
	Albany	.650		Columbus*	.650		Montgomery (3rd)†	.558
5—	Macon	.588	1937—	Columbus	.572	1953—	Jacksonville	.679
	Columbus*	.686		Savannah (3rd)†	.565		Savannah (2nd)†	.571
6—	Augusta*	.617	1938—	Savannah	.574	1954—	Jacksonville	.593
	Columbia	.631		Macon (2nd)†	.570		Savannah (2nd)†	.571
7—	Charleston	.741	1939—	Columbus	.601	1955—	Greenville	.636
	Columbia*	.667		Augusta (2nd)†	.597		Augusta (3rd)†	.543
8—	Did not operate.		1940—	Savannah	.627	1956—	Jacksonville‡	.621
9—	Columbia	.585		Columbus (2nd)†	.583	1957—	Augusta	.636
0—	Columbia	.633					Charlotte (2nd)†	.562

Year	Team	Pct.	Year	Team	Pct.	Year	Team	Pc
1958—	Augusta	.550	1974—	Jacksonville	.565	1986—	Huntsville	.55
	Macon (3rd)†	.500		Knoxville§	.533		Columbus∞	.50
1959—	Knoxville	.557	1975—	Orlando	.587	1987—	Charlotte	.58
	Gastonia (4th)†	.504		Montgomery§	.545		Birmingham∞	.47
1960—	Columbia	.597	1976—	Montgomery∞	.591	1988—	Greenville	.60
	Savannah (3rd)†	.561		Orlando	.540		Chattanooga∞	.56
1961—	Asheville	.635	1977—	Montgomery∞	.628	1989—	Birmingham∞	.61
1962—	Savannah	.662		Jacksonville	.522		Greenville	.50
	Macon (3rd)†	.576	1978—	Knoxville∞	.611	1990—	Orlando	.59
1963—	Augusta*	.661		Savannah	.500		Memphis∞	.50
	Lynchburg	.662	1979—	Columbus	.587	1991—	Greenville	.61
1964—	Lynchburg	.579		Nashville∞	.576		Orlando∞	.53
1965—	Columbus	.572	1980—	Memphis	.576	1992—	Greenville∞	.69
1966—	Mobile	.629		Charlotte∞	.500		Chattanooga	.62
1967—	Birmingham	.604	1981—	Nashville	.566	1993—	Birmingham∞	.54
1968—	Asheville	.614		Orlando∞	.556		Knoxville	.50
1969—	Charlotte	.579	1982—	Jacksonville	.576	1994—	Huntsville∞	.58
1970—	Columbus	.569		Nashville∞	.535		Carolina	.52
1971—	Did not operate as league—clubs were members of Dixie Association.		1983—	Birmingham∞	.628	1995—	Carolina∞	.61
				Jacksonville	.531		Chattanooga	.58
1972—	Asheville	.583	1984—	Charlotte∞	.510	1996—	Chattanooga	.57
	Montgomery§	.561		Knoxville	.483		Jacksonville∞	.54
1973—	Montgomery§	.580	1985—	Charlotte	.545			
	Jacksonville	.559		Huntsville∞	.542			

*Won split season playoff. †Won four-club playoff. ‡Won championship and four-club playoff. §League was divided into Eastern and Western division won playoff. ∞League was divided into Eastern and Western divisions and played split season; won playoff.

TEXAS LEAGUE

President/treasurer
Tom Kayser

Address
2442 Facet Oak
San Antonio, TX 78232

Phone
210-545-5297

TEAMS

ARKANSAS TRAVELERS
General manager
Bill Valentine
Manager
Rick Mahler
Ballpark (capacity, surface)
Ray Winder Field (6,089, grass)
Affiliation
Cardinals
Address
P.O. Box 55066
Little Rock, AR 72215
Phone
501-664-1555

EL PASO DIABLOS
General manager
Rick Parr
Manager
Dave Machemer
Ballpark (capacity, surface)
Cohen Stadium (9,765, grass)
Affiliation
Brewers
Address
P.O. Drawer 4797
El Paso, TX 79914
Phone
915-755-2000

JACKSON GENERALS
General manager
Bill Blackwell
Manager
Gary Allenson
Ballpark (capacity, surface)
Smith-Wills Stadium (5,200, grass)
Affiliation
Astros

Address
P.O. Box 4209
Jackson, MS 39296
Phone
601-981-4664

MIDLAND ANGELS
General manager
Monty Hoppel
Manager
Mario Mendoza
Ballpark (capacity, surface)
Christensen Stadium (5,000, grass)
Affiliation
Angels
Address
P.O. Box 51187
Midland, TX 79710
Phone
915-683-4251

SAN ANTONIO MISSIONS
General manager
Burl Yarbrough
Manager
Ron Roenicke
Ballpark (capacity, surface)
Nelson Wolf Stadium (6,300, grass)
Affiliation
Dodgers
Address
5757 Highway 90 West
San Antonio, TX 78227
Phone
210-675-7275

SHREVEPORT CAPTAINS
General manager
Gilbert Little
Manager
Carlos Lezcano

Ballpark (capacity, surface)
Fair Grounds Field (6,200, grass)
Affiliation
Giants
Address
P.O. Box 3448
Shreveport, LA 71133
Phone
318-636-5555

TULSA DRILLERS
Executive v.p./general manager
Chuck Lamson
Manager
Bobby Jones
Ballpark (capacity, surface)
Drillers Stadium (10,813, grass)
Affiliation
Rangers
Address
P.O. Box 4448
Tulsa, OK 74159
Phone
918-744-5998

WICHITA WRANGLERS
General manager
Lance Deckinger
Manager
Ron Johnson
Ballpark (capacity, surface)
Lawrence-Dumont Stadium (6,067, artificial infield, grass outfield)
Affiliation
Royals
Address
P.O. Box 1420
Wichita, KS 67201
Phone
316-267-3372

CLASS AA *Texas League*

1996 FINAL STANDINGS

FIRST HALF

EAST DIVISION

Team	W	L	T	Pct.	GB
Jackson (Astros)	37	31	0	.544	....
Tulsa (Rangers)	36	32	0	.529	1
Shreveport (Giants)	36	32	0	.529	1
Arkansas (Cardinals)	30	38	0	.441	7

WEST DIVISION

Team	W	L	T	Pct.	GB
Wichita (Royals)	38	30	0	.559	....
El Paso (Brewers)	34	34	0	.500	4
Midland (Angels)	31	37	0	.456	7
San Antonio (Dodgers)	30	38	0	.441	8

SECOND HALF

EAST DIVISION

Team	W	L	T	Pct.	GB
Tulsa (Rangers)	39	32	0	.549	....
Shreveport (Giants)	37	34	0	.521	2
Arkansas (Cardinals)	37	35	0	.514	2½
Jackson (Astros)	33	39	0	.458	6½

WEST DIVISION

Team	W	L	T	Pct.	GB
El Paso (Brewers)	42	29	0	.592	....
San Antonio (Dodgers)	39	32	0	.549	3
Wichita (Royals)	32	40	0	.444	10½
Midland (Angels)	27	45	0	.375	15½

COMPOSITE

Team	E.P.	Tul.	Shr.	Wch.	Jac.	S.A.	Ark.	Mid.	W	L	T	Pct.	G.B.
El Paso (Brewers)	....	6	7	15	7	17	4	20	76	63	0	.547	....
Tulsa (Rangers)	4	....	19	8	19	4	16	5	75	64	0	.540	1
Shreveport (Giants)	5	12	....	4	14	7	23	8	73	66	0	.525	3
Wichita (Royals)	17	4	6	....	4	18	3	18	70	70	0	.500	6½
Jackson (Astros)	5	13	18	6	....	6	15	7	70	70	0	.500	6½
San Antonio (Dodgers)	14	8	3	14	4	....	7	19	69	70	0	.496	7
Arkansas (Cardinals)	6	16	9	9	17	5	....	5	67	73	0	.479	9½
Midland (Angels)	12	5	4	14	5	13	5	....	58	82	0	.414	18½

Arkansas club represented Little Rock, Ark.

Major league affiliations in parentheses.

PLAYOFFS: Jackson defeated Tulsa, three games to one; Wichita defeated El Paso, three games to one; Jackson defeated Wichita, four games to none, win league championship.

REGULAR-SEASON ATTENDANCE: Arkansas, 209,535; El Paso, 292,074; Jackson, 179,423; Midland, 203,011; San Antonio, 381,001; Shreveport, 179,58█ Tulsa, 343,196; Wichita, 186,074. Total—1,973,908; Playoffs (12 games)–19,807; Class AA All-Star Game at Trenton–8,369; Texas League All-Star Game Midland—5,135.

MANAGERS: Arkansas, Rick Mahler; El Paso, Dave Machemer; Jackson, Dave Engle; Midland, Mario Mendoza; San Antonio, John Shelby; Shreveport, Fran Cacciatore; Tulsa, Bobby Jones; Wichita, Ron Johnson.

ALL-STAR TEAM: 1B—Paul Konerko, San Antonio; 2B—Ronnie Belliard, El Paso; 3B—Brad Seitzer, El Paso; SS—Russ Johnson, Jackson; OF—Todd Dunn, El Paso; Richard Hidalgo, Jackson; Bo Ortiz, Midland; C—Eli Marrero, Arkansas; DH—Bubba Smith, Tulsa; Utility—Jeff Berblinger, Arkansas; Jon Hamlin, El Paso; P—Kris Detmers, Arkansas; Keith Foulke, Shreveport; Jonathan Johnson, Tulsa; Sean Maloney, El Paso; Matt Norris, Arkansas; Bra█ Raggio, Arkansas; Cree Weaver, San Antonio; Player of the Year—Bubba Smith, Tulsa; Pitcher of the Year—Keith Foulke, Shreveport; Manager of the Year—Dave Machemer, El Paso.

1996 BATTING

TEAM

Team	Avg.	G	TPA	AB	R	H	TB	2B	3B	HR	RBI	SH	SF	HP	BB	IBB	SO	SB	CS	GDP	LOB	ShO	Slg.	OB
El Paso	.291	139	5334	4664	809	1356	2108	265	68	117	716	61	55	50	504	13	871	129	80	108	944	3	.452	.36
Jackson	.278	140	5301	4753	647	1319	1932	229	30	108	587	55	31	56	406	20	697	60	45	143	997	6	.406	.33
Wichita	.277	140	5351	4797	713	1331	2046	279	32	124	648	44	38	49	423	9	669	124	66	122	967	5	.427	.34
San Antonio	.273	139	5166	4645	616	1267	1876	244	43	93	554	50	46	48	376	24	773	112	72	110	926	7	.404	.33
Tulsa	.268	139	5345	4745	699	1274	2085	271	36	156	641	34	33	54	478	21	1006	64	57	98	996	5	.439	.34
Midland	.266	140	5290	4711	670	1254	1903	274	42	97	594	38	37	39	462	12	824	67	62	115	960	10	.404	.33
Shreveport	.264	139	5326	4622	692	1219	1889	235	33	123	634	56	43	52	553	21	889	143	89	97	1004	7	.409	.34
Arkansas	.257	140	5109	4495	610	1154	1724	214	34	96	561	51	34	38	487	19	724	106	70	111	928	8	.384	.34

INDIVIDUAL

TOP QUALIFIERS FOR BATTING CHAMPIONSHIP

Minimum 367 plate appearances. *Lefthanded batter. †Switch-hitter.

Player, Team	Avg.	G	TPA	AB	R	H	TB	2B	3B	HR	RBI	SH	SF	HP	BB	IBB	SO	SB	CS	GDP	Slg.	O
Dunn, Todd, El Paso	.340	98	412	359	72	122	213	24	5	19	78	2	4	2	45	1	84	13	4	11	.593	
Bridges, Kary, Jackson*	.325	87	381	338	51	110	138	12	2	4	33	7	3	1	32	1	14	4	5	11	.408	
Seitzer, Brad, El Paso	.319	115	498	433	78	138	222	31	1	17	87	2	5	7	51	0	67	6	4	9	.513	
Shockey, Greg, Midland*	.317	98	379	325	58	103	162	26	6	7	49	0	2	3	47	1	56	2	2	5	.498	
Johnson, Russ, Jackson	.310	132	563	496	86	154	233	24	5	15	74	5	3	3	56	1	50	9	4	16	.470	
Christian, Eddie, Midland†	.305	107	469	426	59	130	185	30	5	5	46	4	3	0	36	0	72	7	9	8	.434	
Rupp, Brian, Arkansas	.303	114	395	353	46	107	140	17	2	4	41	5	4	0	33	4	44	5	6	14	.397	
Konerko, Paul, San Antonio	.300	133	557	470	78	141	255	23	2	29	86	0	7	8	72	6	85	1	3	7	.543	
Singleton, Chris, Shreveport*	.298	129	541	500	68	149	213	31	9	5	72	3	8	6	24	2	58	27	12	12	.426	
Sisco, Steve, Wichita	.297	122	515	462	80	137	202	24	1	13	74	5	5	3	40	0	69	4	2	14	.437	
Sutton, Larry, Wichita*	.296	125	554	463	84	137	229	22	2	22	84	0	6	8	77	3	66	4	1	11	.495	
Ortiz, Bo, Midland	.296	127	550	507	73	150	225	32	5	11	64	4	4	2	32	0	80	12	7	9	.444	
Romero, Willie, San Antonio	.295	122	492	444	66	131	197	36	6	6	48	2	8	3	34	2	52	21	15	11	.444	
Mirabelli, Doug, Shreveport	.295	115	464	380	60	112	198	23	0	21	70	1	1	6	76	0	49	0	1	9	.521	
Hidalgo, Richard, Jackson	.294	130	561	513	66	151	231	34	2	14	78	1	7	11	29	2	55	11	7	24	.450	

DEPARTMENTAL LEADERS: G—Simonton, 137; AB—Luuloa, 531; R—L. Powell, 92; H—W. Johnson, 154; TB—C. Smith, 274; 2B—Romero, 36; 3B—Frias, HR—C. Smith, 32; RBI—C. Smith, Hamlin, 94; SH—B. King, 17; SF—Hamlin, 10; HP—Carr, 12; BB—Simonton, 101; IBB—Fick, 8; SO—K. Brown, 150; SB—L. Pow█ 43; CS—L. Powell, 23; GIDP—Hidalgo, 24; Slg.—Dunn, .593; OBP—Mirabelli, .419.

ALL PLAYERS

*Lefthanded batter. †Switch-hitter.

Player, Team	Avg.	G	TPA	AB	R	H	TB	2B	3B	HR	RBI	SH	SF	HP	BB	IBB	SO	SB	CS	GDP	Slg.	O
Ahearne, Pat, San Antonio	.000	8	3	3	0	0	0	0	0	0	0	0	0	0	0	0	2	0	0	0	.000	
Alfonzo, Edgar, Midland	.274	83	342	310	37	85	121	22	1	4	40	1	4	3	24	2	45	1	2	10	.390	
Alguacil, Jose, Shreveport*	.208	13	28	24	2	5	5	0	0	0	0	0	0	1	3	0	9	0	0	0	.208	
Anderson, Charlie, Arkansas	.000	2	2	1	0	0	0	0	0	0	0	0	0	0	1	0	0	0	0	0	.000	
Anderson, Cliff, San Antonio*	.231	7	30	26	2	6	8	0	1	0	2	2	0	1	0	0	7	0	1	0	.308	
Arnold, Ken, Tulsa	.138	22	64	58	9	8	9	1	0	0	7	0	1	0	5	0	24	0	0	2	.155	
Aybar, Manuel, Arkansas	.143	20	16	14	0	2	3	1	0	0	1	2	0	0	0	0	3	0	0	0	.214	
Barrios, Manuel, Jackson	.000	60	1	1	0	0	0	0	0	0	0	0	0	0	0	0	1	0	0	0	.000	
Bell, Mike, Tulsa	.267	128	533	484	62	129	214	31	3	16	59	4	0	3	42	1	75	3	1	13	.442	
Belliard, Ronnie, El Paso	.279	109	487	416	73	116	161	20	8	3	57	4	3	4	60	1	51	26	10	11	.387	
Berblinger, Jeff, Arkansas	.288	134	570	500	78	144	223	32	7	11	53	3	7	8	52	0	66	23	10	9	.446	
Bess, Johnny, Shreveport†	.246	57	200	175	25	43	80	10	3	7	30	1	3	2	19	1	63	1	1	1	.457	

er, Team	Avg.	G	TPA	AB	R	H	TB	2B	3B	HR	RBI	SH	SF	HP	BB	IBB	SO	SB	CS	GDP	Slg.	OBP
en, Randy, Midland	.171	28	88	82	5	14	16	2	0	0	5	1	0	0	5	0	19	3	1	2	.195	.218
r, Brian, Tulsa*	.245	113	433	379	47	93	136	28	3	3	29	6	1	2	45	2	86	7	8	6	.359	.328
co, Henry, San Antonio	.267	92	343	307	39	82	113	14	1	5	40	3	5	0	28	2	38	2	3	8	.368	.324
kin, Tyrone, Midland	.252	49	168	127	27	32	62	10	1	6	30	4	1	0	36	0	28	0	2	2	.488	.415
ges, Kary, Jackson*	.325	87	381	338	51	110	138	12	2	4	33	7	3	1	32	1	14	4	5	11	.408	.382
awn, Troy, Shreveport*	.121	28	35	33	2	4	4	0	0	0	3	1	0	0	1	0	4	0	0	3	.121	.147
wn, Kevin, Tulsa	.263	128	550	460	77	121	228	27	1	26	86	0	6	11	73	0	150	0	3	5	.496	.373
nson, William, San Antonio*	.125	11	9	8	0	1	1	0	0	0	0	1	0	0	0	0	6	0	0	0	.125	.125
ant, Ralph, Midland*	.208	60	237	216	33	45	88	16	0	9	26	0	2	0	19	1	75	1	1	7	.407	.270
ke, Jamie, Midland	.319	45	167	144	24	46	64	8	2	2	16	1	0	2	20	1	22	1	1	1	.444	.410
eron, Stanton, Wichita	.143	2	7	7	0	1	1	0	0	0	2	0	0	0	0	0	0	0	0	0	.143	.143
enter, Brian, Arkansas	.167	37	6	6	0	1	1	0	0	0	0	0	0	0	0	0	2	0	0	1	.167	.167
, Jeremy, Wichita	.260	129	518	453	68	118	163	23	2	6	40	3	3	12	47	1	64	41	9	15	.360	.344
rajal, Jovino, Midland†	.269	41	171	160	20	43	58	5	2	2	22	1	0	0	10	1	24	7	7	4	.363	.312
illo, Marino, Shreveport	.000	38	3	3	0	0	0	0	0	0	0	0	0	0	0	0	0	0	0	0	.000	.000
les, Frank, Tulsa	.265	41	157	147	18	39	60	6	0	5	15	0	0	0	10	0	28	2	0	1	.408	.312
stian, Eddie, Midland†	.305	107	469	426	59	130	185	30	5	5	46	4	3	0	36	0	72	7	9	8	.434	.357
k, Will, Tulsa*	.222	3	11	9	3	2	2	0	0	0	0	0	0	0	2	0	0	0	0	0	.222	.364
n, Dennis, Jackson*	.280	127	453	432	49	121	182	23	1	12	58	0	0	0	21	6	49	0	3	19	.421	.313
n, Julio, San Antonio	.000	6	2	1	0	0	0	0	0	0	0	0	0	1	0	0	1	0	0	0	.000	.500
baugh, Mike, Tulsa	.348	7	27	23	6	8	17	3	0	2	9	0	0	2	2	0	3	1	0	0	.739	.444
os, Edwin, Shreveport	.000	38	6	3	1	0	0	0	0	0	0	1	1	0	0	2	0	0	0	0	.000	.400
ea, Ramser, San Antonio	.500	31	2	2	0	1	2	1	0	0	0	0	0	0	0	0	0	0	0	0	1.000	.500
sins, Tim, Tulsa	.500	3	7	4	0	2	2	0	0	0	0	1	0	0	3	0	0	0	0	0	.500	.714
k, Ryan, Jackson	.045	29	26	22	1	1	1	0	0	0	1	3	0	1	0	0	9	0	0	0	.045	.087
ushore, Rick, Arkansas	.211	34	20	19	1	4	4	0	0	0	2	1	0	0	0	0	6	0	0	0	.211	.211
e, Derek, Jackson*	.000	1	1	1	0	0	0	0	0	0	0	0	0	0	0	0	0	0	0	0	.000	.000
n, Dee, Arkansas	.238	113	394	345	38	82	121	17	2	6	42	6	3	2	38	2	61	4	4	10	.351	.314
dridge, Brad, San Antonio	.282	47	193	177	22	50	66	7	0	3	25	0	3	1	12	1	19	4	3	3	.373	.326
alillo, David, Midland	.171	25	90	82	6	14	15	1	0	0	5	3	0	1	4	0	16	2	0	2	.183	.218
s, Ray, Arkansas	.000	12	1	1	0	0	0	0	0	0	0	0	0	0	0	0	1	0	0	0	.000	.000
ney, Sean, Wichita	.208	23	54	48	5	10	19	3	0	2	5	1	0	0	5	0	15	2	0	1	.396	.283
on, Roberto, Shreveport	.236	85	291	263	30	62	93	11	4	4	34	1	3	1	23	3	43	0	2	5	.354	.297
ers, Kris, Arkansas†	.148	27	31	27	1	4	4	0	0	0	4	4	0	0	0	0	18	0	0	0	.148	.148
Edwin, Tulsa	.265	121	545	499	70	132	225	33	6	16	65	8	4	9	25	4	122	8	9	9	.451	.309
Freddy, Midland†	.199	54	176	156	23	31	51	7	2	3	18	4	3	0	13	1	43	1	1	3	.327	.256
Lino, Wichita	.252	44	170	159	18	40	59	8	1	3	19	0	0	2	9	0	11	2	1	7	.371	.300
s, Tony, Arkansas†	.304	35	155	138	23	42	64	7	3	3	22	1	3	1	12	0	16	7	4	0	.464	.357
rolsky, Bill, El Paso	.282	68	230	202	26	57	76	11	1	2	21	3	3	5	17	0	37	1	4	5	.376	.348
Derrin, Midland	.272	50	190	158	32	43	74	10	3	5	25	1	3	3	25	1	29	3	5	2	.468	.347
an, Andres, Shreveport†	.264	68	215	193	33	51	67	6	2	2	10	2	0	0	20	0	38	8	3	6	.347	.333
, Todd, El Paso	.340	98	412	359	72	122	213	24	5	19	78	2	4	2	45	1	84	13	4	11	.593	.412
n, Chris, San Antonio*	.300	8	34	30	6	9	14	2	0	1	3	0	0	0	4	0	9	0	0	0	.467	.382
ey, Damion, Midland	.429	4	14	14	1	6	8	2	0	0	2	0	0	0	0	0	0	0	0	0	.571	.429
Paul, Arkansas*	.255	65	182	157	16	40	54	5	0	3	26	0	0	3	22	0	20	0	0	3	.344	.357
da, Osmani, Tulsa	.259	27	96	85	12	22	32	4	0	2	5	0	1	1	9	0	13	1	1	2	.376	.333
Lauro, El Paso	.269	101	399	301	71	81	130	15	2	10	59	12	6	6	74	1	69	11	5	4	.432	.416
Chris, Arkansas*	.257	134	524	448	64	115	201	25	2	19	74	0	5	4	67	8	93	2	5	16	.449	.355
z, Tim, Midland	.273	18	74	66	9	18	25	1	0	2	8	0	0	1	7	1	11	2	0	0	.379	.351
ner, Tim, Jackson*	.293	114	444	379	55	111	158	20	3	7	46	4	2	4	55	1	47	0	4	10	.417	.386
ke, Keith, Shreveport	.323	30	37	31	2	10	15	2	0	1	3	4	0	1	1	0	6	0	0	0	.484	.364
, Hanley, Tulsa†	.287	134	543	505	73	145	199	24	12	2	41	5	3	0	30	2	73	9	9	19	.394	.325
a, Karim, San Antonio*	.248	35	138	129	21	32	55	6	1	5	22	0	0	0	9	0	38	1	1	1	.426	.297
, Darrin, Shreveport	.182	7	13	11	1	2	5	0	0	1	4	0	1	0	1	0	3	0	0	0	.455	.231
, Leon, Midland*	.213	94	346	319	30	68	116	14	2	10	53	0	2	2	23	2	86	8	9	8	.364	.269
alez, Jimmy, Jackson	.200	2	6	5	1	1	1	0	0	0	0	0	0	0	1	0	1	0	0	0	.200	.333
alez, Raul, Wichita	.286	23	90	84	17	24	34	5	1	1	9	0	0	1	5	0	12	1	2	3	.405	.333
n, Scarborough, Arkansas	.200	92	345	300	45	60	81	6	3	3	24	3	1	3	38	1	58	21	8	3	.270	.295
puso, Mike, Jackson	.252	33	125	111	17	28	41	0	2	3	12	0	0	3	11	1	35	1	1	6	.369	.336
nich, Mike, Jackson	.000	57	5	5	0	0	0	0	0	0	0	0	0	0	0	0	3	0	0	0	.000	.000
, Aaron, Midland*	.269	129	508	439	72	118	191	29	7	10	48	2	1	10	56	0	71	11	7	6	.435	.364
na, John, Jackson*	.280	27	30	25	2	7	8	1	0	0	5	0	0	0	0	0	9	0	0	0	.320	.280
in, Jonas, El Paso	.283	131	568	515	81	146	260	35	8	21	94	1	10	5	37	0	101	9	7	14	.505	.332
en, Jed, Wichita	.286	99	444	405	60	116	187	27	4	12	50	4	2	4	29	0	72	14	8	6	.462	.339
s, Mike, El Paso*	.308	76	296	260	47	80	126	15	5	7	35	2	3	2	29	3	29	5	2	5	.485	.378
ner, Chris, Jackson	.308	41	170	156	29	48	98	9	1	13	36	0	1	4	9	2	39	2	1	5	.628	.359
erson, Ryan, San Antonio	.000	39	1	1	0	0	0	0	0	0	0	0	0	0	0	0	0	0	0	0	.000	.000
es, Matt, San Antonio	.000	30	3	1	0	0	0	0	0	0	0	2	0	0	0	0	1	0	0	0	.000	.000
go, Richard, Jackson	.294	130	561	513	66	151	231	34	2	14	78	1	7	11	29	2	55	11	7	24	.450	.341
s, Erik, Arkansas	.300	10	11	10	2	3	6	0	0	1	1	0	0	0	1	0	4	0	0	0	.600	.364
s, Ron, San Antonio*	.000	25	1	1	0	0	0	0	0	0	0	0	0	0	0	0	0	0	0	0	.000	.000
y, Bobby, Shreveport*	.290	28	34	31	1	9	10	1	0	0	6	1	0	0	2	0	8	0	1	1	.323	.333
es, Bobby, El Paso	.304	67	272	237	43	72	137	18	1	15	39	0	3	2	30	1	40	3	3	5	.578	.382
ohrey, Rich, Jackson	.000	43	3	3	0	0	0	0	0	0	0	1	0	0	0	0	3	0	0	0	.000	.000
, Rich, Shreveport	.200	19	5	5	1	1	1	0	0	0	1	0	0	0	0	0	3	0	0	0	.200	.200
ns, Geoff, El Paso*	.286	22	92	77	17	22	38	5	4	1	11	0	1	2	12	1	21	1	2	2	.494	.391
s, Keith, Arkansas	.246	127	508	447	52	110	132	17	1	1	40	7	1	4	47	0	61	8	9	17	.295	.323
son, Keith, San Antonio	.274	127	554	521	74	143	213	28	6	10	57	9	3	4	17	1	82	15	8	15	.409	.301
son, Russ, Jackson	.310	132	563	496	86	154	233	24	5	15	74	5	3	3	56	1	50	9	4	16	.470	.382
edy, Darryl, Tulsa	.302	15	49	43	11	13	21	3	1	1	10	1	0	1	4	0	5	0	1	2	.488	.375
r, Tim, Jackson	.143	48	8	7	0	1	1	0	0	0	0	0	0	0	1	0	4	0	0	0	.143	.250
Brett, Shreveport	.233	127	532	459	61	107	159	23	4	7	48	17	1	6	49	0	116	19	9	5	.346	.315
atrick, Jay, San Antonio*	.242	30	102	91	6	22	35	4	0	3	10	0	0	0	11	3	26	1	0	5	.385	.324

Player, Team	Avg.	G	TPA	AB	R	H	TB	2B	3B	HR	RBI	SH	SF	HP	BB	IBB	SO	SB	CS	GDP	Slg.
Konerko, Paul, San Antonio	.300	133	557	470	78	141	255	23	2	29	86	0	7	8	72	6	85	1	3	7	.543
Krause, Scott, El Paso	.318	24	89	85	16	27	45	5	2	3	11	1	0	1	2	0	19	2	0	1	.529
Little, Mark, Tulsa	.291	101	475	409	69	119	186	24	2	13	50	5	3	10	48	0	88	22	10	5	.455
Loiselle, Rich, Jackson	.222	17	21	18	0	4	5	1	0	0	2	2	0	0	1	0	6	0	0	0	.278
Long, Kevin, Wichita*	.273	128	500	436	62	119	165	31	3	3	48	3	5	0	56	1	36	9	14	11	.378
Long, Ryan, Wichita	.283	122	467	442	64	125	216	29	1	20	78	1	2	5	17	0	71	6	5	9	.489
Lopez, Mendy, Wichita	.281	93	360	327	47	92	140	20	5	6	32	2	1	4	26	1	67	14	4	6	.428
Lopez, Pedro, El Paso	.306	46	166	144	22	44	62	10	1	2	20	3	2	0	17	1	24	2	2	2	.431
Lovingier, Kevin, Arkansas*	.000	60	1	1	0	0	0	0	0	0	0	0	0	0	0	0	0	0	0	0	.000
Lowe, Sean, Arkansas	.500	6	4	4	1	2	2	0	0	0	0	0	0	0	0	0	0	0	0	0	.500
Luce, Roger, Jackson	.255	69	256	243	29	62	105	11	4	8	36	1	2	0	10	0	52	0	0	12	.432
Luuloa, Keith, Midland	.260	134	595	531	80	138	187	24	2	7	44	8	3	6	47	0	54	4	6	14	.352
Luzinski, Ryan, San Antonio	.291	32	116	103	12	30	36	6	0	0	10	1	0	1	11	0	19	2	0	6	.350
Macey, Fausto, Shreveport	.174	27	29	23	2	4	4	0	0	0	4	3	1	0	2	0	3	0	0	1	.174
Magallanes, Bobby, Jackson	.268	12	45	41	7	11	19	2	0	2	4	0	0	2	2	0	8	0	0	2	.463
Marrero, Elieser, Arkansas	.270	116	414	374	65	101	181	17	3	19	65	0	2	6	32	1	55	9	6	7	.484
Martin, Jim, San Antonio*	.211	38	128	114	9	24	35	6	1	1	8	0	2	3	9	1	42	2	2	2	.307
Martin, Tom, Jackson*	.000	57	3	2	0	0	0	0	0	0	0	0	1	0	0	0	1	0	0	0	.000
Martinez, Gabby, El Paso†	.251	91	375	338	44	85	112	11	8	0	37	13	4	2	18	1	57	8	9	8	.331
Martinez, Greg, El Paso†	.313	41	189	166	27	52	61	2	2	1	21	6	1	3	13	0	19	14	4	4	.367
Martinez, Jesus, San Antonio*	.167	27	20	18	2	3	4	1	0	0	4	2	0	0	0	0	7	0	0	1	.222
Martinez, Ramon, Wichita	.344	26	107	93	16	32	41	4	1	1	8	7	0	0	7	0	8	4	1	4	.441
Matranga, Jeff, Arkansas	.500	62	2	2	0	1	1	0	0	0	0	0	0	0	0	0	0	0	0	0	.500
Matulevich, Jeff, Arkansas	.000	41	1	1	0	0	0	0	0	0	0	0	0	0	0	0	1	0	0	0	.000
Maurer, Ron, San Antonio	.263	6	22	19	3	5	5	0	0	0	0	0	0	0	3	0	7	0	0	0	.263
Mayes, Craig, Shreveport*	.400	10	45	40	5	16	18	2	0	0	3	0	0	0	5	1	2	0	1	0	.450
McEwing, Joe, Arkansas	.208	106	235	216	27	45	64	7	3	2	14	5	1	0	13	0	32	2	4	8	.296
McFarlin, Jason, Tulsa*	.273	2	11	11	1	3	4	1	0	0	2	0	0	0	0	0	1	0	1	0	.364
McNabb, Buck, Jackson*	.301	88	325	279	38	84	109	15	5	0	26	1	2	2	41	1	37	10	6	3	.391
McNeely, Jeff, Midland	.240	36	146	125	11	30	40	8	1	0	18	0	2	0	19	0	27	2	1	7	.320
Medrano, Anthony, Wichita	.274	125	503	474	59	130	182	26	1	8	55	7	2	2	18	0	36	10	8	8	.384
Melendez, Dan, San Antonio*	.238	67	215	189	19	45	58	10	0	1	29	0	3	3	20	4	31	0	0	3	.307
Meluskey, Mitch, Jackson†	.313	38	155	134	18	42	53	11	0	0	21	1	1	1	18	0	24	0	0	6	.396
Mirabelli, Doug, Shreveport	.295	115	464	380	60	112	198	23	0	21	70	1	1	6	76	0	49	0	1	9	.521
Mitchell, Donovan, Jackson*	.252	120	450	408	57	103	138	22	2	3	32	4	2	3	33	2	51	11	4	8	.338
Moeder, Tony, Midland	.224	23	98	85	19	19	39	3	1	5	7	0	0	1	12	0	30	0	0	3	.459
Molina, Ben, Midland	.274	108	405	365	45	100	149	21	2	8	54	4	5	6	25	1	25	0	1	16	.408
Monzon, Jose, Midland	.279	43	151	140	15	39	52	4	3	3	22	0	2	0	9	1	22	1	0	6	.371
Moore, Mike, San Antonio	.240	64	220	200	21	48	72	10	4	2	21	0	1	2	17	0	64	8	4	4	.360
Mora, Melvin, Shreveport	.286	70	278	255	36	73	96	6	1	5	23	1	2	6	14	1	23	4	7	4	.376
Morillo, Cesar, Wichita†	.235	45	131	119	8	28	39	3	1	2	7	5	0	0	7	0	18	3	0	3	.328
Morris, Matt, Arkansas	.115	27	32	26	3	3	3	0	0	0	2	1	1	0	4	0	6	0	0	0	.115
Mota, Gary, Jackson	.240	12	29	25	3	6	6	0	0	0	0	0	0	0	4	0	2	0	0	3	.240
Murphy, Jeffrey, Arkansas†	.571	2	7	7	3	4	5	1	0	0	1	0	0	0	0	0	2	0	0	0	.714
Murphy, Mike, Tulsa	.231	34	147	121	22	28	51	7	2	4	16	1	1	3	21	0	29	1	0	2	.421
Murray, Calvin, Shreveport	.260	50	202	169	32	44	72	7	0	7	24	3	4	1	25	0	33	6	5	5	.426
Narcisse, Tyrone, Jackson	.050	27	25	20	1	1	1	0	0	0	0	3	0	0	2	0	8	0	0	0	.050
Nicholas, Darrell, El Paso	.274	70	270	237	46	65	91	12	4	2	24	4	1	1	27	2	57	7	5	6	.384
O'Neill, Doug, Tulsa	.307	20	88	75	8	23	41	3	0	5	15	1	0	1	11	0	19	1	2	2	.547
Ortega, Hector, El Paso	.242	99	390	351	52	85	126	12	4	7	53	3	4	5	27	1	74	11	6	12	.359
Ortiz, Bo, Midland	.296	127	550	507	73	150	225	32	5	11	64	4	4	2	32	0	80	12	7	9	.444
Pages, Javier, Arkansas	.261	26	49	46	3	12	17	2	0	1	7	0	0	0	3	0	11	0	0	0	.370
Perez, Danny, El Paso	.351	38	168	154	31	54	88	16	6	2	19	0	0	1	13	0	30	5	1	6	.571
Peterson, Mark, Shreveport*	.167	42	6	6	2	1	1	0	0	0	1	0	0	0	0	0	1	0	0	0	.167
Peterson, Nate, Jackson*	.278	114	362	324	36	90	115	19	0	2	34	1	4	6	27	1	49	1	1	5	.355
Phillips, Gary, Shreveport	.246	111	373	337	37	83	115	18	4	2	43	3	5	6	22	0	71	1	6	12	.341
Phillips, Randy, Shreveport*	.250	35	10	8	1	2	3	1	0	0	1	1	0	0	1	0	1	0	0	0	.375
Pickett, Ricky, Shreveport*	.000	29	6	5	0	0	0	0	0	0	0	0	0	0	0	0	2	0	0	0	.000
Pincavitch, Kevin, San Antonio	.000	11	1	1	0	0	0	0	0	0	0	0	0	0	0	0	0	0	0	0	.000
Powell, Dante, Shreveport	.280	135	586	508	92	142	236	27	2	21	78	1	2	3	72	4	92	43	23	6	.465
Prado, Jose, San Antonio	.333	18	4	3	1	1	1	0	0	0	0	0	0	0	1	0	1	0	0	0	.333
Price, Tom, San Antonio*	.000	7	1	1	0	0	0	0	0	0	0	0	0	0	0	0	1	0	0	0	.000
Probst, Alan, Jackson	.244	63	202	180	20	44	76	9	1	7	33	2	2	2	16	1	43	1	0	1	.422
Pyc, Dave, San Antonio*	.000	14	5	5	0	0	0	0	0	0	0	0	0	0	0	0	2	0	0	0	.000
Raggio, Brady, Arkansas	.115	26	32	26	1	3	3	0	0	0	1	6	0	0	0	0	7	0	0	0	.115
Ramirez, Hiram, Shreveport	1.000	1	3	3	2	3	4	1	0	0	0	0	0	0	0	0	0	0	0	0	1.333
Ramos, Edgar, Jackson	.091	13	12	11	1	1	1	0	0	0	1	0	0	0	0	0	3	0	0	0	.091
Reid, Derek, Shreveport	.246	30	135	118	16	29	45	4	0	4	18	0	3	3	11	1	18	2	2	3	.381
Richardson, Brian, San Antonio	.323	19	66	62	10	20	23	1	1	0	7	0	0	2	2	0	10	0	2	0	.371
Riggs, Adam, San Antonio	.283	134	562	506	68	143	228	31	6	14	66	5	5	4	37	1	82	16	6	13	.451
Rios, Armando, Shreveport*	.283	92	381	329	62	93	155	22	2	12	49	3	4	1	44	3	42	9	9	2	.471
Rios, Eddie, San Antonio	.277	75	263	242	29	67	97	11	2	5	37	0	1	0	20	0	32	2	2	7	.401
Roach, Petie, San Antonio*	.667	13	6	3	0	2	2	0	0	0	1	3	0	0	0	0	0	0	0	0	.667
Roberge, J.P., San Antonio	.293	62	252	232	28	68	104	14	2	6	27	2	2	2	14	1	39	9	3	5	.448
Rodriguez, Boi, Wichita*	.063	16	36	32	0	2	3	1	0	0	1	0	0	0	4	0	15	0	0	0	.094
Rodriques, Cecil, El Paso	.283	119	433	389	63	110	160	23	6	5	50	5	5	2	32	0	92	5	8	3	.411
Romero, Willie, San Antonio	.295	122	492	444	66	131	197	36	6	6	48	2	8	3	34	2	52	21	15	11	.444
Ross, Tony, Jackson	.175	34	94	80	13	14	16	0	1	0	3	4	0	3	7	0	11	2	1	0	.200
Rupp, Brian, Arkansas	.303	114	395	353	46	107	140	17	2	4	41	5	4	0	33	4	44	5	6	14	.397
Sagmoen, Marc, Tulsa*	.282	96	429	387	58	109	172	21	6	10	62	0	7	2	33	4	58	5	8	7	.444
Sanchez, Victor, Jackson	.219	86	229	210	30	46	94	9	0	13	34	0	4	0	15	0	58	4	1	7	.448
Sanders, Tracy, Tulsa*	.232	52	203	168	31	39	70	10	0	7	20	0	2	0	33	2	49	2	1	3	.417
Santucci, Steve, Arkansas	.150	11	20	20	2	3	3	0	0	0	0	0	0	0	0	0	5	0	1	0	.150

Player, Team	Avg.	G	TPA	AB	R	H	TB	2B	3B	HR	RBI	SH	SF	HP	BB	IBB	SO	SB	CS	GDP	Slg.	OBP
brocco, Jon, Shreveport*	.247	23	97	81	16	20	27	2	1	1	5	2	1	2	11	0	10	5	0	2	.333	.347
chneider, Dan, Shreveport	.238	7	23	21	3	5	12	1	0	2	6	0	0	2	0	0	11	0	0	0	.571	.304
eitzer, Brad, El Paso	.319	115	498	433	78	138	222	31	1	17	87	2	5	7	51	0	67	6	4	9	.513	.395
heppard, Don, Wichita	.216	45	108	97	12	21	32	2	0	3	12	1	1	0	9	1	24	3	4	0	.330	.280
hockey, Greg, Midland*	.317	98	379	325	58	103	162	26	6	7	49	0	2	3	47	1	56	2	2	5	.498	.406
mons, Doug, Jackson*	.105	21	26	19	1	2	2	0	0	0	6	0	0	1	0	0	3	0	0	0	.105	.150
monton, Benji, Shreveport	.249	137	577	469	86	117	213	25	1	23	76	1	0	6	101	4	144	6	4	12	.454	.389
ngleton, Chris, Shreveport*	.298	129	541	500	68	149	213	31	9	5	72	3	8	6	24	2	58	27	12	12	.426	.333
sco, Steve, Wichita	.297	122	515	462	80	137	202	24	1	13	74	5	5	3	40	0	69	4	2	14	.437	.353
mith, Bubba, Tulsa	.292	134	570	513	82	150	274	28	0	32	94	0	3	5	48	5	121	0	1	10	.534	.357
pearman, Vernon, San Ant.	.257	123	521	471	66	121	157	15	9	1	30	7	3	5	35	0	38	26	17	10	.333	.313
are, Lonny, San Antonio	.224	32	81	67	7	15	17	2	0	0	4	2	0	1	11	0	11	2	2	3	.254	.342
eed, Dave, San Antonio	.118	7	18	17	0	2	3	1	0	0	2	0	0	0	1	0	6	0	0	1	.176	.167
tewart, Andy, Wichita	.302	58	224	202	29	61	93	17	3	3	32	2	2	4	14	1	25	3	2	9	.460	.356
rickland, Chad, Wichita	.226	77	264	239	35	54	88	15	2	5	34	3	4	2	16	0	23	1	1	10	.368	.276
utton, Larry, Wichita*	.296	125	554	463	84	137	229	22	2	22	84	0	6	8	77	3	66	4	1	11	.495	.401
weeney, Mike, Wichita	.319	66	273	235	45	75	137	18	1	14	51	0	4	2	32	1	29	3	2	5	.583	.399
ulbee, Andy, Shreveport	.200	27	32	30	2	6	6	0	0	0	2	2	0	0	0	0	12	0	0	0	.200	.200
xidor, Jose, Tulsa	.256	85	325	301	34	77	125	15	0	11	37	3	3	0	18	1	44	2	1	8	.415	.295
homas, Brian, Tulsa*	.222	3	11	9	0	2	2	0	0	0	0	0	0	2	0	0	5	0	1	0	.222	.364
rres, Paul, Arkansas	.262	102	358	309	38	81	130	16	0	11	44	0	1	2	44	1	62	1	1	3	.421	.357
cker, Michael, Wichita*	.450	6	26	20	4	9	16	1	3	0	7	0	1	0	5	0	4	0	2	0	.800	.538
rat, Chris, Tulsa*	.182	20	71	55	6	10	15	2	0	1	7	0	0	0	16	0	13	0	0	2	.273	.366
lez, Jose, Arkansas†	.273	86	284	264	36	72	93	11	2	2	32	3	2	1	14	0	29	8	4	10	.352	.310
llano, Mike, Shreveport	.000	2	4	3	2	0	0	0	0	0	0	0	0	0	1	1	0	0	0	1	.000	.250
alker, Jamie, Jackson*	.300	45	12	10	0	3	4	1	0	0	1	2	0	0	0	0	3	0	0	1	.400	.300
arner, Ron, Arkansas	.300	84	276	233	36	70	118	22	4	6	39	2	2	1	38	1	25	5	1	4	.506	.398
atts, Brandon, San Antonio*	.143	22	14	14	0	2	2	0	0	0	1	0	0	0	0	0	3	0	0	0	.143	.143
eaver, Eric, San Antonio	.143	18	9	7	0	1	1	0	0	0	0	0	0	0	0	0	0	0	0	0	.143	.143
eaver, Terry, Shreveport	.125	5	9	8	1	1	1	0	0	0	1	0	0	0	1	0	1	0	0	0	.125	.222
olfe, Joel, Arkansas	.215	72	234	200	29	43	70	11	2	4	26	2	1	3	28	1	36	11	7	5	.350	.319
oods, Kenny, Shreveport	.279	83	330	287	36	80	102	17	1	1	29	4	6	4	29	0	35	14	10	11	.355	.347
rd, Bruce, San Antonio*	.314	48	170	153	25	48	68	15	1	1	13	5	3	2	7	2	11	0	0	5	.444	.345
rbe, Chad, San Antonio*	.667	17	8	6	2	4	4	0	0	0	1	0	0	0	1	0	0	0	0	0	.667	.714

GRAND SLAMS: Bell, Boykin, K. Brown, Bryant, Estrada, K. Garcia, Hamlin, B. King, P. Lopez, Medrano, Mirabella, Ortega, Probst, Riggs, C. Smith, P. Torres, Velez, 1 each.
AWARDED FIRST ON CATCHER'S INTERFERENCE: Johns 2 (Monzon 2); P. Torres 2 (K. Brown, Meluskey); Shockey 2 (Hughes, Steed); B. Ortiz (P. Lopez); C. Smith (Ellis); mero (Molina).

1996 PITCHING

TEAM

am	W	L	Pct.	ERA	G	CG	ShO	Sv.	IP	H	TBF	R	ER	HR	SH	SF	HB	BB	IBB	SO	WP	Bk.
ckson	70	70	.500	3.78	140	5	10	36	1220.0	1199	5308	631	513	100	52	35	76	513	15	894	70	3
ansas	67	73	.479	3.80	140	10	8	28	1187.1	1180	5132	597	501	108	55	32	25	470	26	888	57	5
n Antonio	69	70	.496	3.87	139	6	5	37	1205.1	1229	5252	625	518	82	60	40	34	534	2	764	80	10
reveport	73	66	.525	4.01	139	5	6	43	1211.0	1211	5160	635	540	129	51	32	51	395	30	675	43	10
sa	75	64	.540	4.38	139	12	8	42	1224.0	1306	5302	677	596	126	36	49	57	403	18	721	38	5
chita	70	70	.500	4.67	140	9	10	34	1225.1	1344	5329	737	636	154	47	49	38	432	17	785	86	3
Paso	76	63	.547	4.74	139	9	2	47	1201.2	1353	5362	746	633	92	41	41	46	465	16	872	61	9
dland	58	82	.414	5.06	140	11	2	28	1206.2	1352	5377	808	679	123	47	39	59	477	15	854	89	8

INDIVIDUAL

TOP QUALIFIERS FOR EARNED-RUN AVERAGE TITLE

Minimum 109 innings. *Lefthanded pitcher.

cher, Team	W	L	Pct.	ERA	G	GS	CG	ShO	GF	Sv.	IP	H	TBF	R	ER	HR	SH	SF	HB	BB	IBB	SO	WP	Bk.
lke, Keith, Shreveport	12	7	.632	2.76	27	27	4	2	0	0	182.2	149	712	61	56	16	6	7	3	35	0	129	6	1
ar, Manuel, Arkansas	8	6	.571	3.05	20	20	0	0	0	0	121.0	120	507	53	41	10	6	3	0	34	0	83	3	3
ama, John, Jackson*	9	10	.474	3.21	27	27	0	0	0	0	162.2	151	691	77	58	10	7	7	8	59	0	110	7	0
gio, Brady, Arkansas	9	10	.474	3.22	26	24	4	1	0	0	162.1	160	667	68	58	17	8	2	3	40	2	123	3	2
aver, Eric, San Antonio	10	5	.667	3.30	18	18	1	1	0	0	122.2	106	509	51	45	6	7	2	3	44	0	69	2	1
ners, Kris, Arkansas*	12	8	.600	3.35	27	27	0	0	0	0	163.2	154	698	72	61	15	6	3	4	70	0	97	8	0
ons, Doug, Jackson*	8	7	.533	3.48	20	19	1	1	0	0	126.2	132	520	53	49	11	7	2	3	30	0	75	5	0
nson, Jonathan, Tulsa	13	10	.565	3.56	26	25	6	0	1	0	174.1	176	728	86	69	15	3	5	6	41	1	97	2	3
rison, Brian, Wichita	9	2	.818	3.66	49	7	0	0	17	6	118.0	118	472	54	48	11	1	5	2	14	3	60	0	0
rris, Matt, Arkansas	12	12	.500	3.88	27	27	4	4	0	0	167.0	178	711	79	72	14	8	4	2	48	1	120	9	0
ey, Fausto, San Antonio	11	7	.588	4.30	27	26	1	0	0	0	157.0	165	673	86	75	22	4	5	8	47	0	62	7	2
tinez, Jesus, San Antonio*	10	13	.435	4.40	27	27	0	0	0	0	161.2	157	700	90	79	7	5	7	5	92	0	124	20	0
ts, Brandon, San Antonio*	6	10	.375	4.50	22	22	2	1	0	0	126.0	136	561	69	63	21	8	4	2	70	0	79	4	2
taker, Steve, El Paso*	11	7	.611	4.58	25	24	2	0	0	0	145.1	157	672	92	74	9	7	5	5	87	3	85	7	1
hawn, Troy, Shreveport*	9	10	.474	4.60	28	28	0	0	0	0	156.2	163	668	99	80	30	7	3	6	49	0	82	3	3

DEPARTMENTAL LEADERS: W—Johnson, 13; L—Beaumont, 16; Pct.—Bevil, Harrison, .818; G—Matranga, 62; GS—Brohawn, Beaumont, 28; CG—Johnson, 6; ShO—rris, 4; GF—Barrios, 53; SV—Maloney, 38; IP—Foulke, 182.2; H—Bovee, 223; TBF—Bovee, 783; R—Beaumont, 124; ER—Beaumont, 105; HR—Brohawn, 30; SH—Pyc, 10; -Bovee, 8; HB—Beaumont, 12; BB—Creek, 121; IBB—Lovingier, Manning, 6; SO—Beaumont, 132; WP—J. Martinez, 20; BK—Roach, 4.

CLASS AA Texas League

ALL PITCHERS
*Lefthanded pitcher.

Pitcher, Team	W	L	Pct.	ERA	G	GS	CG	ShO	GF	Sv.	IP	H	TBF	R	ER	HR	SH	SF	HB	BB	IBB	SO	WP	B
Abbott, Kyle, Midland*	3	5	.375	4.50	15	15	0	0	0	0	88.0	93	377	52	44	11	6	2	3	34	1	48	5	
Ahearne, Pat, San Antonio	2	4	.333	5.76	8	8	0	0	0	0	45.1	59	208	34	29	3	2	2	1	18	0	21	4	
Alfonzo, Edgar, Midland	0	0	.000	9.00	1	0	0	0	0	0	1.0	2	5	1	1	0	0	0	0	0	0	0	0	
Aybar, Manuel, Arkansas	8	6	.571	3.05	20	20	0	0	0	0	121.0	120	507	53	41	10	6	3	0	34	0	83	3	
Barrios, Manuel, Jackson	6	4	.600	2.37	60	0	0	0	53	23	68.1	60	298	29	18	4	4	2	3	29	5	69	3	
Beaumont, Matt, Midland*	7	16	.304	5.85	28	28	2	0	0	0	161.2	198	746	124	105	20	4	6	12	71	0	132	5	
Bevil, Brian, Wichita	9	2	.818	2.02	13	13	2	0	0	0	75.2	56	301	22	17	4	1	3	2	26	0	74	6	
Bonanno, Rob, Midland	1	2	.333	5.32	23	6	1	0	7	2	64.1	79	289	44	38	8	1	1	3	23	1	52	5	
Bovee, Mike, Wichita	10	11	.476	4.84	27	27	3	2	0	0	176.2	223	783	113	95	21	9	8	6	40	1	102	10	
Brocail, Doug, Jackson	0	0	.000	0.00	2	2	0	0	0	0	5.0	1	15	0	0	0	0	1	1	5	0	5	0	
Brohawn, Troy, Shreveport*	9	10	.474	4.60	28	28	0	0	0	0	156.2	163	668	99	80	30	7	3	6	49	0	82	8	
Brower, Jim, Tulsa	3	2	.600	3.78	5	5	1	1	0	0	33.1	35	140	16	14	4	0	1	1	10	0	16	1	
Brown, Willard, Midland	0	6	.000	11.61	9	8	0	0	1	0	33.1	58	170	45	43	8	2	1	4	9	0	16	1	
Brunson, William, San Ant.*	3	1	.750	2.14	11	5	0	0	1	0	42.0	32	166	13	10	2	2	0	1	15	0	38	2	
Byrdak, Tim, Wichita*	5	7	.417	6.91	15	15	0	0	0	0	84.2	112	388	73	65	15	5	1	0	44	0	47	8	
Camacho, Dan, San Antonio	1	1	.500	2.70	4	2	0	0	0	0	16.2	11	73	5	5	0	1	0	17	0	11	1	
Carpenter, Brian, Arkansas	1	2	.333	3.16	37	6	0	0	3	0	74.0	63	305	26	26	6	2	7	1	26	3	53	2	
Castillo, Carlos, Midland	2	3	.400	4.26	25	0	0	0	8	1	38.0	37	169	19	18	4	2	0	2	21	2	15	6	
Castillo, Juan, Tulsa	6	6	.500	5.04	19	17	0	0	0	0	89.1	94	408	64	50	11	2	3	10	49	0	37	6	
Castillo, Marino, Shreveport	5	5	.500	3.58	38	0	0	0	26	3	50.1	48	208	21	20	7	3	0	3	14	2	53	2	
Charles, Frank, Tulsa	0	0	.000	9.00	1	0	0	0	1	0	1.0	1	4	1	1	0	0	0	0	0	0	0	0	
Chavez, Tony, Midland	2	4	.333	4.21	31	0	0	0	16	1	72.2	81	322	40	34	4	6	7	2	24	2	55	3	
Colon, Julio, San Antonio	2	3	.400	4.46	6	6	0	0	0	0	36.1	35	159	20	18	2	1	2	3	17	0	14	6	
Corps, Edwin, Shreveport	2	3	.400	4.48	38	3	0	0	6	1	70.1	74	305	46	35	6	1	1	3	26	2	39	2	
Correa, Ramser, San Antonio	4	1	.800	2.88	31	0	0	0	27	9	34.1	26	140	12	11	2	1	0	0	16	0	29	3	
Creek, Ryan, Jackson	7	15	.318	5.26	27	26	1	0	1	0	142.0	139	674	95	83	9	3	7	11	121	0	119	14	
Croushore, Rick, Arkansas	5	10	.333	4.92	34	17	2	0	11	3	108.0	113	486	75	59	18	4	1	2	51	1	85	7	
Dace, Derek, Jackson*	0	0	.000	2.25	1	1	0	0	0	0	4.0	5	21	1	1	0	0	0	5	0	0	0	
D'Amico, Jeff, El Paso	5	4	.556	3.19	13	13	3	0	0	0	96.0	89	387	42	34	10	0	2	13	0	76	0	
Dault, Donnie, Jackson	0	0	.000	0.00	1	0	0	0	1	0	2.0	2	9	0	0	0	0	0	2	1	0	
Davis, Clint, Tulsa	3	3	.500	1.88	32	0	0	0	24	10	48.0	31	186	11	10	3	4	1	3	12	1	40	1	
Davis, Jeff, Tulsa	7	2	.778	4.59	16	15	3	0	0	0	98.0	110	420	57	50	10	2	6	2	20	1	51	1	
Davis, Ray, Arkansas	0	1	.000	5.16	12	3	0	0	4	0	22.2	25	105	15	13	2	1	0	10	0	15	0	
DeClue, Jon, Midland*	6	9	.400	5.32	32	15	2	0	5	0	111.2	137	512	83	66	11	4	2	51	1	76	6	
Detmers, Kris, Arkansas*	12	8	.600	3.35	27	27	0	0	0	0	163.2	154	698	72	61	15	6	3	4	70	0	97	8	
Diaz, Freddy, Midland	0	0	.000	0.00	2	0	0	0	2	0	2.1	1	8	0	0	0	0	0	0	0	1	0	
Dickson, Jason, Midland	5	2	.714	3.58	8	8	3	1	0	0	55.1	55	228	27	22	3	2	0	0	10	40	3	
Doorneweerd, Dave, Midland	1	2	.333	5.79	9	1	0	0	3	0	18.2	25	94	15	12	2	1	0	1	12	0	20	5	
Eddy, Chris, Wichita*	0	0	.000	2.97	30	0	0	0	16	0	30.1	33	138	16	10	6	1	0	1	18	1	22	3	
Edsell, Geoff, Midland	5	5	.500	4.70	14	14	0	0	0	0	88.0	84	382	53	46	10	3	5	6	47	0	60	5	
Evans, Bart, Wichita	1	2	.333	11.84	9	7	0	0	0	0	24.1	31	146	38	32	7	3	2	6	36	0	16	12	
Farrell, Mike, El Paso*	1	0	1.000	0.66	11	0	0	0	3	1	13.2	6	51	3	1	1	0	0	2	0	13	0	
Foulke, Keith, Shreveport	12	7	.632	2.76	27	27	4	2	0	0	182.2	149	712	61	56	16	6	7	3	35	0	129	6	
Freehill, Mike, Midland	7	6	.538	3.42	47	0	0	0	45	17	50.0	49	224	25	19	4	3	1	1	21	1	48	10	
Gamboa, Javier, Wichita	5	5	.500	5.93	15	15	0	0	0	0	91.0	118	414	68	60	19	3	5	2	33	0	39	2	
Ganote, Joe, El Paso	0	0	.000	5.79	1	1	0	0	0	0	4.2	9	23	3	3	0	0	0	1	0	5	0	
Garcia, Frank, Arkansas	0	0	.000	3.72	11	0	0	0	2	0	19.1	20	84	11	8	1	1	1	7	0	12	1	
Garcia, Jose, San Antonio	2	0	1.000	0.00	8	0	0	0	5	2	11.1	4	38	0	0	0	0	1	0	8	1	
Gavaghan, Sean, El Paso	4	1	.800	5.11	24	0	0	0	9	0	37.0	48	175	27	21	3	3	2	2	15	1	24	0	
Geeve, Dave, Tulsa	7	6	.538	5.55	18	17	0	0	0	0	82.2	105	364	53	51	12	2	3	2	23	0	60	7	
Goedhart, Darrell, Midland	0	1	.000	3.86	3	2	0	0	1	0	14.0	15	57	9	6	0	1	1	0	4	0	5	3	
Golden, Matt, Arkansas	3	4	.429	4.14	52	0	0	0	41	18	63.0	74	285	40	29	1	2	1	0	26	3	43	10	
Grundy, Phillip, Wichita	1	0	1.000	1.29	1	1	0	0	0	0	7.0	4	26	1	1	0	0	0	2	0	1	
Grzanich, Mike, Jackson	5	4	.556	3.98	57	0	0	0	19	6	72.1	60	316	47	32	10	4	2	8	43	2	80	6	
Halama, John, Jackson*	9	10	.474	3.21	27	27	0	0	0	0	162.2	151	691	77	58	10	7	7	8	59	0	110	7	
Harris, Pep, Midland	2	2	.500	5.31	6	6	1	0	0	0	39.0	47	177	27	23	2	1	0	2	9	1	28	0	
Harrison, Brian, Wichita	9	2	.818	3.66	49	7	0	0	17	6	118.0	118	472	54	48	11	1	5	2	14	3	80	0	
Henderson, Ryan, San Antonio	3	3	.500	3.82	39	0	0	0	19	6	63.2	59	275	29	27	2	4	5	29	0	46	4	
Herges, Matt, San Antonio	3	2	.600	2.71	30	6	0	0	10	3	83.0	83	355	38	25	3	2	5	2	28	0	45	5	
Hiljus, Erik, Arkansas	3	5	.375	6.11	10	10	0	0	0	0	45.2	62	221	37	31	6	3	2	0	30	1	21	4	
Hollinger, Adrian, Midland	1	1	.500	4.32	13	0	0	0	10	2	16.2	18	80	11	8	0	2	1	3	11	1	8	6	
Hollis, Ron, San Antonio	0	3	.000	3.43	25	0	0	0	13	1	39.1	38	175	21	15	2	1	1	0	19	0	36	1	
Holtz, Mike, Midland*	1	2	.333	4.17	33	0	0	0	13	2	41.0	52	188	34	19	6	1	1	1	9	1	41	4	
Howry, Bobby, Shreveport	10	8	.556	4.65	27	27	0	0	0	0	156.2	163	682	90	81	17	6	4	9	56	3	57	3	
Humphrey, Rich, Jackson	4	2	.667	2.51	43	0	0	0	22	1	64.2	53	257	21	18	6	3	1	3	15	0	37	2	
Hyde, Rich, Shreveport	1	2	.333	5.94	19	0	0	0	5	1	33.1	36	150	26	22	4	6	1	0	12	4	25	2	
Ingram, Todd, Midland	0	1	.000	7.94	15	0	0	0	6	0	22.2	35	114	22	20	1	1	1	3	21	0	11	7	
Jacobsen, Joe, San Antonio	1	4	.200	4.19	38	0	0	0	23	5	58.0	62	256	33	27	4	4	3	1	24	2	39	7	
Janicki, Pete, Midland	1	3	.250	6.39	5	5	0	0	0	0	31.0	37	136	28	22	4	0	2	10	0	17	4	
Johnson, Jonathan, Tulsa	13	10	.565	3.56	26	25	6	0	1	0	174.1	176	728	86	69	15	3	6	41	1	97	2	
Keling, Korey, Midland	0	1	.000	6.90	17	1	0	0	4	1	30.0	42	140	29	23	4	0	3	0	14	0	13	1	
Kell, Rob, Tulsa*	0	0	.000	0.00	2	0	0	0	1	0	0.2	3	0	0	0	0	0	0	0	0	0	
Kester, Tim, Jackson	2	4	.333	7.28	48	4	0	0	7	0	103.2	105	435	52	43	8	4	6	16	0	55	8	
Keusch, Joe, Tulsa	0	0	.000	17.18	8	0	0	0	4	0	11.0	25	64	21	21	5	0	0	2	5	1	8	0	
King, Curtis, Arkansas	0	1	.000	19.80	5	0	0	0	3	0	5.0	15	37	12	11	1	0	0	1	3	0	2	0	
Kloek, Kevin, El Paso	3	1	.750	4.02	9	9	0	0	0	0	53.2	58	230	29	24	7	2	1	2	18	0	46	3	
Kolb, Danny, Tulsa	1	0	1.000	0.77	2	2	0	0	0	0	11.2	5	45	1	1	0	0	1	8	0	7	0	
Kramer, Jeff, El Paso	3	4	.429	6.34	21	5	0	0	7	1	59.2	76	280	57	42	5	2	6	3	29	1	36	5	
Lacy, Kerry, Tulsa	0	0	.000	0.00	2	0	0	0	2	0	4.0	3	15	0	0	0	6	0	1	0	10	0	
LaGarde, Joseph, San Antonio	3	1	.750	1.74	24	0	0	0	21	9	31.0	28	129	7	6	0	1	0	8	0	22	4	

– 450 –

tcher, Team	W	L	Pct.	ERA	G	GS	CG	ShO	GF	Sv.	IP	H	TBF	R	ER	HR	SH	SF	HB	BB	IBB	SO	WP	Bk.
ftwich, Phil, Midland	4	2	.667	2.90	6	6	1	0	0	0	40.1	33	154	14	13	4	1	0	1	4	0	33	1	0
iselle, Rich, Jackson	7	4	.636	3.47	16	16	2	0	0	0	98.2	107	429	46	38	6	0	1	4	27	0	65	3	0
ng, Kevin, Wichita*	0	0	.000	0.00	1	0	0	0	1	0	1.0	0	3	0	0	0	0	0	0	0	0	0	0	0
vingier, Kevin, Arkansas*	2	3	.400	4.10	60	0	0	0	19	1	63.2	60	295	30	29	4	6	2	1	48	6	73	3	0
we, Sean, Arkansas	2	3	.400	6.00	6	6	0	0	0	0	33.0	32	150	24	22	2	1	1	2	15	1	25	1	0
acey, Fausto, Shreveport	10	7	.588	4.30	27	26	1	0	0	0	157.0	165	673	86	75	22	4	5	8	47	0	62	7	2
aloney, Sean, El Paso	3	2	.600	1.43	51	0	0	0	49	38	56.2	49	230	11	9	1	2	1	1	12	1	57	6	1
anning, David, Tulsa	6	5	.545	3.26	39	5	0	0	13	3	91.0	89	394	36	33	5	3	5	2	45	6	48	5	0
artin, Jerry, Tulsa	5	4	.556	4.94	36	6	0	0	13	5	85.2	98	385	56	47	11	0	5	1	42	2	49	0	1
artin, Tom, Jackson*	6	2	.750	3.24	57	0	0	0	18	3	75.0	71	338	35	27	8	5	3	4	42	4	58	4	0
artinez, Jesus, San Antonio*	10	13	.435	4.40	27	27	0	0	0	0	161.2	157	706	90	79	7	5	7	5	92	0	124	20	0
artinez, Ramiro, Tulsa*	0	2	.000	8.56	11	0	0	0	3	0	13.2	23	65	13	13	2	0	0	0	5	0	7	0	0
artinez, Ramon, San Antonio	0	0	.000	0.00	1	1	0	0	0	0	2.2	0	11	0	0	0	0	0	0	0	3	0	1	0	0
atranga, Jeff, Arkansas	6	5	.545	2.15	62	0	0	0	31	4	79.2	56	327	22	19	6	5	2	8	30	3	82	0	0
atulevich, Jeff, Arkansas	4	3	.571	3.64	41	0	0	0	16	1	59.1	48	254	33	24	5	2	3	1	29	4	51	6	0
cDill, Allen, Wichita*	1	5	.167	5.54	54	0	0	0	30	11	65.0	79	288	43	40	10	2	4	4	21	3	62	7	0
ontoya, Norm, El Paso*	9	8	.529	4.67	24	17	1	0	4	1	125.1	153	545	74	65	6	3	2	2	28	2	73	4	1
ody, Eric, Tulsa	8	4	.667	3.57	44	5	0	0	29	16	95.2	92	395	40	38	4	1	3	1	23	2	80	4	0
orillo, Cesar, Wichita	0	0	.000	27.00	1	0	0	0	1	0	1.0	2	6	3	3	1	0	0	0	1	0	1	0	0
orones, Geno, Wichita	1	5	.167	6.93	13	4	1	0	4	0	37.2	50	178	32	29	6	3	1	1	19	0	24	5	1
orris, Matt, Arkansas	12	12	.500	3.88	27	27	4	4	0	0	167.0	178	711	79	72	14	8	4	2	48	1	120	9	0
ervay, Joe, Tulsa	2	2	.500	6.26	24	1	0	0	11	2	46.0	55	213	32	32	3	5	2	4	20	2	27	2	0
llins, Greg, El Paso*	1	5	.167	7.07	23	1	0	0	6	2	28.0	30	130	25	22	7	3	0	1	17	2	28	0	1
rcisse, Tyrone, Jackson	7	12	.368	5.54	27	26	0	0	0	0	126.2	151	572	92	78	15	9	4	6	55	2	88	9	1
voa, Rafael, Wichita*	0	1	.000	6.66	19	0	0	0	8	2	24.1	28	113	20	18	0	1	3	1	12	2	16	5	0
Donoghue, John, Tulsa*	2	4	.333	4.18	27	9	0	0	4	0	79.2	89	355	47	37	9	3	3	6	23	1	46	2	0
en, Steve, Wichita	6	0	1.000	2.77	15	3	0	0	3	1	55.1	40	213	18	17	9	1	2	0	14	0	39	3	0
iz, Russ, Shreveport	1	2	.333	4.05	26	0	0	0	20	13	26.2	22	123	14	12	0	0	0	2	21	3	29	1	0
ul, Andy, El Paso	5	6	.455	4.72	38	7	0	0	16	3	95.1	105	426	60	50	4	5	1	1	43	2	72	8	2
isho, Matt, Midland*	3	2	.600	3.21	8	8	0	0	0	0	53.1	48	222	22	19	4	4	1	2	20	0	50	1	0
erson, Mark, Shreveport*	5	3	.625	3.21	41	0	0	0	16	2	56.0	58	235	23	20	5	1	2	4	8	2	32	0	0
llips, Randy, Shreveport	1	4	.200	3.23	35	2	0	0	9	4	69.2	77	308	34	25	5	5	2	3	21	5	31	4	1
kett, Ricky, Shreveport*	4	1	.800	2.77	29	0	0	0	12	2	48.2	35	214	21	15	4	3	2	3	35	3	51	2	0
cavitch, Kevin, San Antonio	0	0	.000	5.63	11	0	0	0	8	0	16.0	26	82	14	10	1	0	1	2	10	0	11	3	1
sley, Jim, Wichita	3	0	1.000	0.41	3	3	0	0	0	0	22.0	9	78	1	1	0	0	1	0	5	0	7	0	0
vell, John, Tulsa	3	8	.273	4.89	39	10	0	0	16	4	114.0	121	486	71	62	18	3	5	11	31	0	79	4	0
do, Jose, San Antonio	2	1	.667	5.01	18	1	0	0	5	1	32.1	32	149	21	18	3	3	1	0	24	0	20	6	0
e, Tom, San Antonio*	0	4	.000	9.36	7	5	0	0	0	0	25.0	50	125	30	26	5	1	1	0	3	0	11	2	0
bst, Alan, Jackson	0	0	.000	0.00	1	0	0	0	1	0	1.0	2	7	2	0	1	0	0	0	1	0	1	0	0
dy, Shawn, Shreveport	5	4	.556	3.10	54	0	0	0	37	16	52.1	46	218	23	18	3	4	1	1	16	4	23	4	0
, Dave, San Antonio*	7	5	.583	2.98	14	14	1	1	0	0	96.2	106	415	45	32	5	10	1	2	24	0	62	4	0
gio, Brady, Arkansas	9	10	.474	3.22	26	24	4	1	0	0	162.1	160	667	68	58	17	8	2	3	40	2	123	3	2
nos, Edgar, Jackson	4	5	.444	4.88	12	12	1	1	0	0	66.1	63	293	41	36	2	3	1	11	29	0	52	7	0
vitzer, Kevin, Wichita*	0	6	.000	4.74	42	0	0	0	17	3	68.1	77	314	52	36	8	2	2	5	39	1	48	3	0
Ken, Wichita	4	12	.250	6.12	22	22	1	0	0	0	120.2	151	553	94	82	17	5	6	1	57	1	79	15	1
ch, Petie, San Antonio*	6	3	.667	3.82	13	13	1	0	0	0	75.1	81	336	41	32	5	3	5	3	34	0	40	5	4
riguez, Frank, El Paso	3	4	.429	6.82	16	7	0	0	3	0	34.1	45	169	32	26	1	0	2	2	24	0	39	1	0
ado, Jose, Wichita*	2	0	1.000	0.00	2	0	0	0	0	0	13.0	10	48	0	0	0	1	0	0	1	0	12	0	0
sell, Jeff, Tulsa	0	0	.000	0.00	2	2	0	0	0	0	5.0	0	15	0	0	0	0	0	0	5	0	0	0	0
ler, Aldren, El Paso	3	3	.500	4.71	26	0	0	0	10	1	42.0	39	207	28	22	3	2	1	3	40	2	31	4	0
zar, Luis, El Paso	1	0	1.000	11.81	3	0	0	0	2	0	5.1	14	32	8	7	2	1	0	2	1	0	2	0	0
chez, Victor, Jackson	0	0	.000	54.00	1	0	0	0	0	0	1.0	3	9	6	6	2	0	0	0	1	0	0	0	0
ders, Tracy, Tulsa	0	0	.000	0.00	2	0	0	0	0	0	2.0	2	8	0	0	0	0	0	0	0	0	1	0	0
tos, Henry, El Paso*	7	7	.500	6.10	35	12	0	0	11	0	100.1	126	468	76	68	11	3	7	2	50	0	74	13	1
ach, Kyle, Midland	2	0	1.000	7.59	4	4	0	0	0	0	21.1	31	109	20	18	2	0	1	3	15	2	11	2	0
a, John, Tulsa*	0	1	.000	13.97	9	0	0	0	1	0	9.2	23	56	15	15	2	0	1	0	5	1	4	3	1
, Ted, Tulsa	7	2	.778	2.99	11	11	2	1	0	0	75.1	72	314	27	25	5	4	2	2	16	0	27	0	0
ons, Doug, Jackson*	8	7	.533	3.48	20	19	1	1	0	0	126.2	132	520	53	49	11	7	2	3	30	0	75	5	0
th, Dan, Tulsa*	2	3	.400	4.29	9	9	0	0	0	0	50.1	53	227	27	24	6	3	3	1	21	0	29	0	0
th, Toby, Wichita	4	2	.667	4.13	42	0	0	0	30	8	52.1	46	221	25	24	7	4	2	2	19	4	44	7	0
th, Travis, El Paso	7	4	.636	4.18	17	17	3	1	0	0	107.2	119	478	56	50	6	4	5	6	39	0	68	2	0
bee, Andy, Shreveport	6	10	.375	5.00	27	24	0	0	3	0	138.2	169	617	87	77	10	5	6	4	47	2	55	2	1
or, Tommy, El Paso	2	1	.667	4.67	14	0	0	0	5	0	17.1	24	79	9	9	0	0	2	0	6	0	20	2	0
heder, Jim, Wichita	0	2	.000	3.43	13	0	0	0	4	0	21.0	23	92	9	8	2	0	0	1	6	1	11	1	0
dor, Jose, Tulsa	0	0	.000	13.50	2	0	0	0	0	0	2.0	3	12	3	3	1	0	0	0	3	0	3	0	0
erg, Brian, El Paso	7	5	.583	4.90	26	26	0	0	0	0	154.1	183	660	94	84	15	2	3	10	23	0	109	4	1
es, Dilson, Wichita	5	3	.625	3.88	9	8	0	0	1	1	55.2	62	234	27	24	6	1	2	3	13	2	27	0	1
, Robert, Wichita	4	6	.400	3.78	19	13	2	0	5	4	104.2	100	433	48	44	5	5	3	2	34	0	81	0	0
no, Mike, Shreveport	2	0	1.000	3.00	2	2	0	0	0	0	12.0	6	47	4	4	0	0	0	0	2	0	6	0	0
ker, Jamie, Jackson*	5	1	.833	2.50	45	7	0	0	13	2	101.0	94	424	34	28	7	3	1	8	35	2	79	2	0
hburn, Jarrod, Midland*	5	5	.500	4.40	13	13	1	0	0	0	88.0	77	361	44	43	11	1	2	5	20	0	58	1	1
ts, Brandon, San Antonio*	6	10	.375	4.50	22	22	1	1	0	0	126.0	136	561	69	63	21	8	4	2	70	0	79	4	2
ver, Eric, San Antonio	10	5	.667	3.30	18	18	1	1	0	0	122.2	106	509	51	45	6	7	2	3	44	0	69	2	1
b, Doug, El Paso	0	0	.000	6.75	10	0	0	0	3	0	8.0	4	38	6	6	0	0	0	0	10	0	3	1	0
aker, Steve, El Paso*	11	7	.611	4.58	25	24	2	0	0	0	145.1	157	672	92	74	9	7	5	5	87	3	85	7	1
tead, Judd, El Paso	0	1	.000	8.47	7	0	0	0	3	0	17.0	19	79	18	16	1	0	2	1	7	0	11	1	0
e, Chad, San Antonio*	4	4	.500	4.50	17	11	1	0	1	0	86.0	90	384	52	43	9	5	2	2	37	0	38	4	0

OMBINATION SHUTOUTS: **Arkansas (3)**—Raggio-Matranga-Lovingier-Matulevich-Golden, Lowe-Matranga, Aybar-Lovingier-Carpenter. **El Paso (1)**—Whitaker-er-Montoya-Maloney. **Jackson (8)**—Creek-Kester-Barrios, Loiselle-Humphrey, Loiselle-Grzanich-Barrios, Brocail-Creek, Narcisse-Martin-Grzanich, Ramos-Barrios, er-Barrios, Kester-Martin. **Midland (1)**—Edsell-Keling-Holtz-Freehill. **San Antonio (2)**—Weaver-Henderson, Herges-Prado-Henderson. **Shreveport (4)**—Howry-y, Macey-Purdy, Foulke-Ortiz, Howry-Phillips. **Tulsa (6)**—Johnson-Morvay, Russell-Johnson, Davis-Manning-Powell, Castillo-Powell, Manning-Moody, Johnson-dy. **Wichita (8)**—Rosado-Rawitzer, Bevil-McDill-Olsen, Torres-Rawitzer, Bovee-Rawitzer, Bovee-Eddy-Smith-Harrison, Pittsley-Eddy, Bevil-Harrison-Eddy.

O-HIT GAMES: Ramos, Jackson, defeated Shreveport, 3-0, August 6.

TEAM

Team	Pct.	G	PO	A	E	TC	DP	PB
Arkansas	.974	140	3562	1416	134	5112	118	11
Tulsa	.971	139	3672	1540	154	5366	139	10
Wichita	.970	140	3676	1538	160	5374	148	11
Shreveport	.970	139	3633	1446	157	5236	125	5
San Antonio	.969	139	3616	1683	168	5467	145	
Jackson	.966	140	3660	1607	185	5452	137	
Midland	.965	140	3620	1542	186	5348	149	
El Paso	.962	139	3605	1550	202	5357	152	

TRIPLE PLAY: San Antonio.

INDIVIDUAL

FIRST BASEMEN

NOTE: All caps denotes fielding-percentage leader based on 68 games for catchers, 91 for all other non-pitchers and 136 innings for pitchers. *Throws lefthanded.

Player, Team	Pct.	G	PO	A	E	TC	DP
Arnold, Ken, Tulsa	.875	5	7	0	1	8	0
Betten, Randy, Midland	1.000	3	30	1	0	31	2
Blair, Brian, Tulsa*	1.000	1	8	0	0	8	2
Boykin, Tyrone, Midland	.981	33	246	18	5	269	22
Bridges, Kary, Jackson	1.000	1	2	0	0	2	0
Brown, Kevin, Tulsa	.966	6	53	3	2	58	3
Burke, Jamie, Midland	.969	5	31	0	1	32	2
Charles, Frank, Tulsa	1.000	3	11	0	0	11	1
Clark, Will, Tulsa*	1.000	3	21	3	0	24	2
Colon, Dennis, Jackson	.982	120	966	97	19	1082	92
Coolbaugh, Mike, Tulsa	1.000	2	19	2	0	21	4
Estrada, Osmani, Tulsa	1.000	1	2	0	0	2	0
Forkner, Tim, Jackson	.974	4	32	6	1	39	1
Glenn, Leon, Midland	.991	90	716	45	7	768	82
Groppuso, Mike, Jackson	.833	2	14	1	3	18	0
Hamlin, Jonas, El Paso	.988	127	1189	71	15	1275	122
Harris, Mike, El Paso*	1.000	1	11	1	0	12	1
Kirkpatrick, Jay, San Antonio	1.000	6	47	4	0	51	2
Konerko, Paul, San Antonio	.9885	120	1114	92	14	1220	107
Melendez, Dan, San Antonio*	.994	19	162	9	1	172	21
Mirabelli, Doug, Shreveport	1.000	4	31	1	0	32	2
Moeder, Tony, Midland	.966	23	217	11	8	236	20
Ortega, Hector, El Paso	.957	5	44	0	2	46	4
Peterson, Nate, Jackson	1.000	1	3	0	0	3	1
Phillips, Gary, Shreveport	1.000	2	11	0	0	11	1
Roberge, J.P., San Antonio	1.000	1	1	0	0	1	0
Rupp, Brian, Arkansas	.996	90	711	56	3	770	65
Sanchez, Victor, Jackson	.979	34	263	22	6	291	26
Seitzer, Brad, El Paso	.957	7	61	6	3	70	6
Simonton, Benji, Shreveport	.988	136	1171	79	15	1265	109
Sisco, Steve, Wichita	.988	17	157	3	2	162	18
Smith, Bubba, Tulsa	.986	128	1193	100	18	1311	121
SUTTON, Larry, Wichita*	.9891	124	1105	76	13	1194	118
Torres, Paul, Arkansas	.973	20	137	6	4	147	18
Tucker, Michael, Wichita	1.000	2	6	1	0	7	1
Wolfe, Joel, Arkansas	.985	44	359	23	6	388	27

TRIPLE PLAY: Konerko.

SECOND BASEMEN

Player, Team	Pct.	G	PO	A	E	TC	DP
Alfonzo, Edgar, Midland	1.000	2	3	3	0	6	2
Alguacil, Jose, Shreveport	1.000	5	4	10	0	14	4
Arnold, Ken, Tulsa	.966	10	14	14	1	29	3
Belliard, Ronnie, El Paso	.972	107	246	314	16	576	89
Berblinger, Jeff, Arkansas	.952	127	241	310	28	579	73
Bridges, Kary, Jackson	.953	82	130	196	16	342	52
Colon, Dennis, Jackson	1.000	2	2	4	0	6	1
Coolbaugh, Mike, Tulsa	1.000	5	12	21	0	33	4
Dalton, Dee, Arkansas	.973	7	14	22	1	37	9
Davalillo, David, Midland	1.000	4	8	5	0	13	3
DeLeon, Roberto, Shreveport	.962	69	138	167	12	317	39
Diaz, Edwin, Tulsa	.967	121	238	322	19	579	80
Duncan, Andres, Shreveport	.964	30	45	63	4	112	8
Estrada, Osmani, Tulsa	.961	8	22	27	2	51	8
Felix, Lauro, El Paso	.943	26	50	66	7	123	21
Florez, Tim, Shreveport	.972	18	45	60	3	108	10
Guiel, Aaron, Midland	.957	38	72	85	7	164	24
HANSEN, Jed, Wichita	.979	96	196	276	10	482	72
Luuloa, Keith, Midland	.968	100	267	278	18	563	83
Magallanes, Bobby, Jackson	1.000	10	15	23	0	38	5
Martinez, Ramon, Wichita	.956	26	47	84	6	137	20
McEwing, Joe, Arkansas	.889	2	4	4	1	9	1
Mitchell, Donavan, Jackson	.962	47	76	101	7	184	25
Mora, Melvin, Jackson	.946	10	12	23	2	37	4
Morillo, Cesar, Wichita	1.000	8	9	21	0	30	5

CATCHERS (continued)

Player, Team	Pct.	G	PO	A	E	TC	DP
Ortiz, Bo, Midland	1.000	3	5	6	0	11	
Riggs, Adam, San Antonio	.962	125	295	395	27	717	
Rios, Eddie, San Antonio	.970	13	25	39	2	66	
Roberge, J.P., San Antonio	.933	3	5	9	1	15	
Sbrocco, Jon, Shreveport	.960	23	49	46	4	99	
Seitzer, Brad, El Paso	1.000	17	28	41	0	69	
Sisco, Steve, Wichita	1.000	16	34	37	0	71	
Warner, Ron, Arkansas	1.000	10	15	27	0	42	
Woods, Kenny, Shreveport	.968	13	39	21	2	62	

THIRD BASEMEN

Player, Team	Pct.	G	PO	A	E	TC	DP
Alfonzo, Edgar, Midland	.929	39	21	84	8	113	
Alguacil, Jose, Shreveport	1.000	3	0	1	0	1	
Arnold, Ken, Tulsa	1.000	8	4	10	0	14	
BELL, Mike, Tulsa	.936	126	90	277	25	392	
Bess, Johnny, Shreveport	1.000	1	1	0	0	1	
Betten, Randy, Midland	.935	14	9	34	3	46	
Burke, Jamie, Midland	.929	16	14	25	3	42	
Dalton, Dee, Arkansas	.936	93	58	162	15	235	
DeLeon, Roberto, Shreveport	1.000	2	1	0	0	1	
Diaz, Freddy, Midland	.000	2	0	0	1	1	
Diaz, Lino, Wichita	.922	44	36	82	10	128	
Dobrolsky, Bill, El Paso	.857	5	1	5	1	7	
Duncan, Andres, Shreveport	1.000	8	6	14	0	20	
Easley, Damion, Midland	.833	2	2	3	1	6	
Estrada, Osmani, Tulsa	.964	10	6	21	1	28	
Felix, Lauro, El Paso	1.000	3	3	4	0	7	
Forkner, Tim, Jackson	.924	100	60	256	26	342	
Glenn, Darrin, Shreveport	1.000	1	1	4	0	5	
Glenn, Leon, Midland	.800	4	1	3	1	5	
Groppuso, Mike, Jackson	.879	20	13	38	7	58	
Guiel, Aaron, Midland	.914	81	55	169	21	245	
Hamlin, Jonas, El Paso	.333	1	0	1	2	3	
Johnson, Keith, San Antonio	.964	43	34	101	5	140	
Lopez, Mendy, Wichita	.933	91	75	261	24	360	
Mitchell, Donavan, Jackson	.944	22	18	50	4	72	
Mora, Melvin, Jackson	.900	5	3	15	2	20	
Morillo, Cesar, Wichita	.909	6	1	9	1	11	
Ortega, Hector, El Paso	.913	61	37	131	16	184	
Phillips, Gary, Shreveport	.947	93	66	183	14	263	
Richardson, Brian, San Antonio	.925	19	11	38	4	53	
Rios, Eddie, San Antonio	.886	41	18	83	13	114	
Roberge, J.P., San Antonio	.948	41	17	93	6	116	
Rupp, Brian, Arkansas	.900	5	3	6	1	10	
Seitzer, Brad, El Paso	.928	79	52	205	20	277	
Sisco, Steve, Wichita	.929	10	10	16	2	28	
Smith, Bubba, Tulsa	.833	3	1	4	1	6	
Warner, Ron, Arkansas	.948	52	39	125	9	173	
Weaver, Terry, Shreveport	1.000	3	0	1	0	1	
Woods, Kenny, Shreveport	.883	53	26	87	15	128	
Yard, Bruce, San Antonio	1.000	2	1	4	0	5	

SHORTSTOPS

Player, Team	Pct.	G	PO	A	E	TC
Alfonzo, Edgar, Midland	.945	36	45	110	9	164
Alguacil, Jose, Shreveport	1.000	1	1	1	0	2
Anderson, Cliff, San Antonio	.956	7	10	33	2	45
Arnold, Ken, Tulsa	.889	4	8	8	2	18
Betten, Randy, Midland	.944	9	8	26	2	36
Dalton, Dee, Arkansas	1.000	9	13	34	0	47
Davalillo, David, Midland	.947	21	33	57	5	95
Diaz, Freddy, Midland	.943	42	63	118	11	192
Duncan, Andres, Shreveport	.930	13	16	24	3	43
Easley, Damion, Midland	1.000	2	3	9	0	12
Estrada, Osmani, Tulsa	1.000	3	3	4	0	7
Felix, Lauro, El Paso	.923	59	82	159	20	261
Florez, Tim, Shreveport	1.000	1	2	1	0	3

yer, Team	Pct.	G	PO	A	E	TC	DP
IAS, Hanley, Tulsa	.964	133	197	417	23	637	84
ppuso, Mike, Jackson	1.000	3	1	5	0	6	1
ins, Keith, Arkansas	.951	127	199	348	28	575	72
nson, Keith, San Antonio	.964	86	128	301	16	445	54
nson, Russ, Jackson	.949	132	219	411	34	664	87
g, Brett, Shreveport	.945	126	198	353	32	583	66
ez, Mendy, Wichita	1.000	2	5	4	0	9	1
lloa, Keith, Midland	.903	39	40	119	17	176	27
gallanes, Bobby, Jackson	1.000	1	2	3	0	5	0
rtinez, Gabby, El Paso	.914	85	102	239	32	373	48
drano, Anthony, Wichita	.934	121	188	324	36	548	79
chell, Donovan, Jackson	1.000	2	2	2	0	4	2
ra, Melvin, Jackson	.955	6	4	17	1	22	0
rillo, Cesar, Wichita	.943	26	23	59	5	87	11
ega, Hector, El Paso	1.000	1	0	2	0	2	0
s, Eddie, San Antonio	.955	4	5	16	1	22	1
zer, Brad, El Paso	.917	3	5	6	1	12	1
co, Steve, Wichita	1.000	1	1	1	0	2	1
rner, Ron, Arkansas	.821	10	9	14	5	28	3
ods, Kenny, Shreveport	.946	11	25	28	3	56	6
d, Bruce, Jackson	.934	45	67	146	15	228	32

TRIPLE PLAY: Anderson.

OUTFIELDERS

yer, Team	Pct.	G	PO	A	E	TC	DP
acil, Jose, Shreveport	1.000	3	3	0	0	3	0
s, Johnny, Shreveport	1.000	6	7	1	0	8	0
r, Brian, Tulsa*	.981	111	195	10	4	209	2
kin, Tyrone, Midland	1.000	3	2	0	0	2	0
ant, Ralph, Midland	.897	18	26	0	3	29	0
ke, Jamie, Midland	.970	16	30	2	1	33	1
, Jeremy, Wichita	.982	127	262	12	5	279	5
ajal, Jovino, Midland*	1.000	38	66	2	0	68	0
stian, Eddie, Midland*	.968	97	172	8	6	186	0
dridge, Brad, San Antonio	.982	38	52	3	1	56	0
gs, Tony, Arkansas	.988	34	81	1	1	83	0
r, Derrin, Midland	.947	39	51	3	3	57	0
can, Andres, Shreveport	.958	7	22	1	1	24	0
n, Todd, El Paso	.940	72	108	2	7	117	0
kin, Chris, San Antonio*	1.000	5	10	1	0	11	1
x, Lauro, El Paso	1.000	17	37	2	0	39	0
, Chris, Arkansas	.965	119	183	8	7	198	1
cia, Karim, San Antonio*	.971	33	60	6	2	68	1
zalez, Raul, Wichita	.969	23	30	1	1	32	0
en, Scarborough, Arkansas	.990	89	194	7	2	203	3
el, Aaron, Midland	1.000	6	11	0	0	11	0
is, Mike, El Paso*	.971	54	96	4	3	103	1
cher, Chris, Jackson	.947	33	53	1	3	57	0
algo, Richard, Jackson	.981	127	302	14	6	322	6
nse, Scott, El Paso	1.000	24	36	4	0	40	2
e, Mark, Tulsa	.968	94	263	9	9	281	3
g, Kevin, Wichita*	.980	121	238	11	5	254	1
g, Ryan, Wichita	.969	74	150	6	5	161	1
tin, Jim, San Antonio	.974	34	35	2	1	38	0
tinez, Greg, El Paso	.980	41	99	0	2	101	0
WING, Joe, Arkansas	.993	98	130	11	1	142	2
labb, Buck, Jackson	1.000	77	111	4	0	115	0
eely, Jeff, Midland	.986	31	67	2	1	70	1
endez, Dan, San Antonio*	1.000	1	2	0	0	2	0
hell, Donovan, Jackson	.946	44	66	4	4	74	0
re, Mike, Jackson	.960	47	111	8	5	124	2
a, Melvin, Jackson	.978	46	89	1	2	92	0
llo, Cesar, Wichita	1.000	1	1	0	0	1	0
a, Gary, Jackson	1.000	8	7	0	0	7	0
phy, Mike, Tulsa	.973	34	72	1	2	75	0
ray, Calvin, Shreveport	.969	41	89	4	3	96	1
olas, Darrell, El Paso	.962	67	144	6	6	156	0
ill, Doug, Tulsa	.960	20	48	0	2	50	0
ga, Hector, El Paso	.857	14	12	0	2	14	0
, Bo, Midland	.985	122	252	6	4	262	1
z, Danny, El Paso	.947	38	67	5	4	76	1
rson, Nate, Jackson	.923	94	137	7	12	156	1
ell, Dante, Shreveport	.977	127	331	8	8	347	2
, Derek, Shreveport	1.000	30	56	0	0	56	0
, Armando, Shreveport*	.963	85	165	15	7	187	3
erge, J.P., San Antonio	.960	20	22	2	1	25	0
iguez, Boi, Wichita	1.000	5	9	0	0	9	0
iques, Cecil, El Paso	.947	113	170	8	10	188	3
ero, Willie, San Antonio	.970	120	246	14	8	268	3
s, Tony, Jackson	.956	32	39	4	2	45	1
, Brian, Arkansas	1.000	10	9	0	0	9	0
noen, Marc, Tulsa*	.981	93	198	7	4	209	0

Player, Team	Pct.	G	PO	A	E	TC	DP
Sanders, Tracy, Tulsa	1.000	4	4	0	0	4	0
Santucci, Steve, Arkansas	1.000	9	9	0	0	9	0
Sheppard, Don, Wichita	.972	38	65	5	2	72	1
Shockey, Greg, Midland*	.992	61	118	8	1	127	4
Singleton, Chris, Shreveport*	.986	123	262	10	4	276	2
Sisco, Steve, Wichita	.967	61	115	4	4	123	1
Spearman, Vernon, San Antonio*	.963	118	250	7	10	267	2
Stare, Lonny, San Antonio	1.000	24	29	1	0	30	0
Stewart, Andy, Wichita	1.000	1	1	0	0	1	0
Strickland, Chad, Wichita	1.000	5	8	1	0	9	0
Texidor, Jose, Tulsa	.986	65	139	2	2	143	1
Torres, Paul, Arkansas	.971	53	62	4	2	68	0
Tucker, Michael, Wichita	1.000	6	11	0	0	11	0
Velez, Jose, Arkansas*	.978	76	127	7	3	137	0
Woods, Kenny, Shreveport	.967	12	28	1	1	30	0

CATCHERS

Player, Team	Pct.	G	PO	A	E	TC	DP	PB
Bess, Johnny, Shreveport	.984	23	106	14	2	122	3	1
Blanco, Henry, San Antonio	.979	91	532	65	13	610	8	17
Brown, Kevin, Tulsa	.982	104	541	66	11	618	3	8
Burke, Jamie, Midland	1.000	8	42	6	0	48	0	0
Charles, Frank, Tulsa	1.000	7	31	2	0	33	0	0
Cossins, Tim, Tulsa	1.000	3	7	2	0	9	1	1
Dandridge, Brad, San Antonio	1.000	10	46	5	0	51	0	3
Delaney, Sean, Wichita	.976	23	75	7	2	84	1	2
Dobrolsky, Bill, El Paso	.983	59	369	37	7	413	0	5
Ellis, Paul, Arkansas	.991	40	197	18	2	217	1	5
Glenn, Darrin, Shreveport	.933	6	13	1	1	15	1	0
Glenn, Leon, Midland	1.000	1	1	0	0	1	0	2
Gonzalez, Jimmy, Jackson	1.000	2	19	2	0	21	0	0
Hughes, Bobby, El Paso	.979	44	250	32	6	288	4	9
Kennedy, Darryl, Tulsa	.987	13	67	11	1	79	0	0
Lopez, Pedro, El Paso	.969	45	248	32	9	289	5	5
Luce, Roger, Jackson	.990	66	366	37	4	407	7	7
Luzinski, Ryan, San Antonio	.995	32	173	22	1	196	3	2
MARRERO, Elieser, Arkansas	.996	107	676	67	3	746	4	4
Maurer, Ron, San Antonio	1.000	6	23	2	0	25	0	0
Mayes, Craig, Shreveport	.981	10	48	3	1	52	1	0
Meluskey, Mitch, Jackson	.978	30	207	18	5	230	1	4
Mirabelli, Doug, Shreveport	.988	106	517	55	7	579	8	4
Molina, Ben, Midland	.990	97	615	81	7	703	9	10
Monzon, Jose, Midland	.967	40	214	48	9	271	4	11
Murphy, Jeffrey, Arkansas	1.000	1	8	0	0	8	0	1
Pages, Javier, Arkansas	1.000	5	23	0	0	23	0	1
Probst, Alan, Jackson	.983	51	323	32	6	361	7	3
Ramirez, Hiram, Shreveport	1.000	1	2	1	0	3	0	0
Schneider, Dan, Shreveport	.971	7	33	0	1	34	0	0
Steed, Dave, San Antonio	.960	6	23	1	1	25	0	0
Stewart, Andy, Wichita	.977	43	216	35	6	257	3	4
Strickland, Chad, Wichita	.986	64	317	48	5	370	6	3
Sweeney, Mike, Wichita	.995	30	201	13	1	215	0	2
Unrat, Chris, Tulsa	.956	17	101	8	5	114	1	1

PITCHERS

Player, Team	Pct.	G	PO	A	E	TC	DP
Abbott, Kyle, Midland*	.929	15	4	9	1	14	0
Ahearne, Pat, San Antonio	.786	8	3	8	3	14	0
Aybar, Manuel, Arkansas	1.000	20	5	15	0	20	1
Barrios, Manuel, Jackson	.947	60	6	12	1	19	1
Beaumont, Matt, Midland*	.917	28	8	25	3	36	1
Bevil, Brian, Wichita	1.000	13	4	13	0	17	0
Bonanno, Rob, Midland	.929	23	5	8	1	14	0
Bovee, Mike, Wichita	.935	27	11	18	2	31	0
Brocail, Doug, Jackson	1.000	2	0	2	0	2	0
Brohawn, Troy, Shreveport*	.952	28	9	31	2	42	1
Brower, Jim, Tulsa	1.000	5	5	1	0	6	0
Brown, Willard, Midland	1.000	9	1	1	0	2	0
Brunson, William, San Antonio*	1.000	11	4	7	0	11	0
Byrdak, Tim, Wichita*	.929	15	10	16	2	28	0
Camacho, Dan, San Antonio	.857	4	2	4	1	7	1
Carpenter, Brian, Arkansas	1.000	37	4	12	0	16	0
Castillo, Carlos, Midland	.889	25	2	6	1	9	0
Castillo, Juan, Tulsa	.900	19	3	15	2	20	1
Castillo, Marvin, Shreveport	1.000	38	1	5	0	6	0
Chavez, Tony, Midland	.870	31	6	14	3	23	1
Colon, Julio, San Antonio	1.000	6	1	1	0	2	0
Corps, Edwin, Shreveport	.923	38	1	11	1	13	2
Correa, Ramser, San Antonio	1.000	31	3	3	0	6	0
Creek, Ryan, Jackson	.955	27	9	12	1	22	2
Croushore, Rick, Arkansas	1.000	34	6	3	0	9	0
Dace, Derek, Jackson*	1.000	1	1	0	0	1	0

Player, Team	Pct.	G	PO	A	E	TC	DP
D'Amico, Jeff, El Paso	1.000	13	3	3	0	6	0
Dault, Donnie, Jackson	1.000	1	0	1	0	1	0
Davis, Clint, Tulsa	1.000	32	4	4	0	8	3
Davis, Jeff, Tulsa	.897	16	11	15	3	29	2
Davis, Ray, Arkansas	1.000	12	0	3	0	3	0
DeClue, Jon, Midland*	.933	32	5	23	2	30	2
Detmers, Kris, Arkansas*	.926	27	4	21	2	27	0
Diaz, Freddy, Midland	1.000	2	1	0	0	1	0
Dickson, Jason, Midland	.933	8	5	9	1	15	1
Doorneweerd, Dave, Midland	.750	9	1	2	1	4	0
Eddy, Chris, Wichita*	1.000	30	0	6	0	6	1
Edsell, Geoff, Midland	.913	14	6	15	2	23	1
Evans, Bart, Wichita	1.000	9	4	1	0	5	0
Farrell, Mike, El Paso*	1.000	11	2	2	0	4	0
Foulke, Keith, Shreveport	.976	27	11	29	1	41	1
Freehill, Mike, Midland	.857	47	4	8	2	14	0
Gamboa, Javier, Wichita	.950	15	7	12	1	20	0
Garcia, Frank, Arkansas	1.000	11	3	2	0	5	1
Garcia, Jose, San Antonio	1.000	8	2	2	0	4	0
Gavaghan, Sean, El Paso	1.000	24	3	7	0	10	1
Geeve, Dave, Tulsa	1.000	18	6	12	0	18	0
Golden, Matt, Arkansas	.769	52	2	8	3	13	0
Grzanich, Mike, Jackson	.813	57	5	8	3	16	2
Halama, John, Jackson*	.957	27	12	33	2	47	0
Harris, Pep, Midland	.667	6	1	3	2	6	0
Harrison, Brian, Wichita	.905	49	7	12	2	21	0
Henderson, Ryan, San Antonio	.923	39	4	8	1	13	0
Herges, Matt, San Antonio	.778	30	4	10	4	18	0
Hiljus, Erik, Arkansas	1.000	10	2	3	0	5	1
Hollinger, Adrian, Midland	1.000	13	2	4	0	6	0
Hollis, Ron, San Antonio	1.000	25	2	7	0	9	1
Holtz, Mike, Midland*	.900	33	2	7	1	10	1
Howry, Bobby, Shreveport	.923	27	14	22	3	39	2
Humphrey, Rich, Jackson	1.000	43	11	11	0	22	2
Hyde, Rich, Shreveport	.889	19	3	5	1	9	0
Ingram, Todd, Midland	1.000	15	1	4	0	5	0
Jacobsen, Joe, San Antonio	1.000	38	3	11	0	14	0
Janicki, Pete, Midland	1.000	5	0	3	0	3	0
Johnson, Jonathan, Tulsa	.833	26	15	30	9	54	2
Keling, Korey, Midland	.833	17	2	3	1	6	0
Kester, Tim, Jackson	.909	48	10	10	2	22	2
Keusch, Joe, Tulsa	.667	8	1	1	1	3	0
King, Curtis, Arkansas	1.000	5	1	2	0	3	1
Kloek, Kevin, El Paso	1.000	9	1	8	0	9	1
Kolb, Danny, Tulsa	1.000	2	1	2	0	3	1
Kramer, Jeff, El Paso	.750	21	1	5	2	8	0
Lacy, Kerry, Tulsa	1.000	2	0	3	0	3	0
LaGarde, Joseph, San Antonio	.833	24	0	5	1	6	0
Leftwich, Phil, Midland	1.000	6	1	5	0	6	0
Loiselle, Rich, Jackson	.971	16	14	20	1	35	2
Long, Kevin, Wichita*	1.000	1	0	1	0	1	0
Lovingier, Kevin, Arkansas*	1.000	60	4	8	0	12	0
Lowe, Sean, Arkansas	1.000	6	5	4	0	9	0
Macey, Fausto, Shreveport	.943	27	12	21	2	35	3
Maloney, Sean, El Paso	1.000	51	5	10	0	15	0
Manning, David, Tulsa	1.000	39	7	14	0	21	2
Martin, Jerry, Tulsa	1.000	36	5	8	0	13	1
Martin, Tom, Jackson*	1.000	57	5	12	0	17	1
Martinez, Jesus, San Antonio*	.920	27	3	20	2	25	0
Martinez, Ramiro, Tulsa*	.667	11	0	2	1	3	0

Player, Team	Pct.	G	PO	A	E	TC	DP
Matranga, Jeff, Arkansas	.933	62	8	20	2	30	
Matulevich, Jeff, Arkansas	.875	41	2	5	1	8	
McDill, Allen, Wichita*	.875	54	3	4	1	8	
Montoya, Norm, El Paso*	.931	24	8	19	2	29	
Moody, Eric, Tulsa	1.000	44	7	18	0	25	
Morillo, Cesar, Wichita	1.000	1	1	0	0	1	
Morones, Geno, Wichita	.923	13	1	11	1	13	
Morris, Matt, Arkansas	.923	27	7	17	2	26	
Morvay, Joe, Tulsa	.944	24	5	12	1	18	
Mullins, Greg, El Paso*	1.000	23	0	5	0	5	
NARCISSE, Tyrone, Jackson	1.000	27	9	28	0	37	
Novoa, Rafael, Midland*	.800	19	1	3	1	5	
O'Donoghue, John, Tulsa*	.950	27	3	16	1	20	
Olsen, Steve, Wichita	1.000	15	5	6	0	11	
Ortiz, Russ, Shreveport	1.000	26	2	4	0	6	
Paul, Andy, El Paso	1.000	38	10	13	0	23	
Perisho, Matt, Midland*	.857	8	0	6	1	7	
Peterson, Mark, Shreveport*	1.000	41	3	12	0	15	
Phillips, Randy, Shreveport	1.000	35	3	15	0	18	
Pickett, Ricky, Shreveport*	.667	29	1	1	1	3	
Pincavitch, Kevin, San Antonio	.667	11	2	0	1	3	
Pittsley, Jim, Wichita	1.000	3	1	2	0	3	
Powell, John, Tulsa	1.000	39	10	19	0	29	
Prado, Jose, San Antonio	1.000	18	2	7	0	9	
Price, Tom, San Antonio*	1.000	7	1	6	0	7	
Probst, Alan, Jackson	1.000	1	0	1	0	1	
Purdy, Shawn, Shreveport	1.000	54	7	10	0	17	
Pyc, Dave, San Antonio*	.939	14	7	24	2	33	
Raggio, Brady, Arkansas	.953	26	8	33	2	43	
Ramos, Edgar, Jackson	.923	12	3	9	1	13	
Rawitzer, Kevin, Wichita*	.846	42	8	3	2	13	
Ray, Ken, Wichita	.889	22	12	13	3	27	
Roach, Petie, San Antonio*	.923	13	1	11	1	13	
Rodriguez, Frank, El Paso	.889	16	0	8	1	9	
Rosado, Jose, Wichita*	.500	2	0	1	1	2	
Russell, Jeff, Tulsa	1.000	2	1	0	0	1	
Sadler, Aldren, El Paso	1.000	26	1	4	0	5	
Salazar, Luis, El Paso	1.000	3	0	1	0	1	
Santos, Henry, El Paso*	.867	35	2	11	2	15	
Sebach, Kyle, Midland	1.000	4	2	2	0	4	
Silva, Ted, Tulsa	1.000	11	8	10	0	18	
Simons, Doug, Jackson*	.974	20	6	32	1	39	
Smith, Dan, Tulsa*	.923	9	5	7	1	13	
Smith, Toby, Wichita	1.000	42	2	4	0	6	
Smith, Travis, El Paso	1.000	17	3	14	0	17	
Taulbee, Andy, Shreveport	.933	27	8	20	2	30	
Telgheder, Jim, Midland	1.000	13	1	0	0	1	
Tollberg, Brian, El Paso	.974	26	12	25	1	38	
Torres, Dilson, Wichita	1.000	9	1	6	0	7	
Toth, Robert, Wichita	1.000	19	6	13	0	19	
Villano, Mike, Shreveport	.667	2	0	2	1	3	
Walker, Jamie, Jackson*	.972	45	13	22	1	36	
Washburn, Jarrod, Midland*	1.000	13	3	7	0	10	
Watts, Brandon, San Antonio*	1.000	22	5	22	0	27	
Weaver, Eric, San Antonio	.895	18	6	11	2	19	
Webb, Doug, El Paso	1.000	10	1	0	0	1	
Whitaker, Steve, El Paso*	.923	25	5	31	3	39	
Wilstead, Judd, El Paso	1.000	7	1	1	0	2	
Zerbe, Chad, San Antonio*	1.000	17	7	14	0	21	

TRIPLE PLAY: Weaver.

The following players did not have any fielding statistics at the positions indicated or appeared only as a designated hitter, pinch-hitter or pinch-runner: Alfonzo, Anderson, ph; Blanco, 3b; Cameron, of; Charles, p; Diaz, 2B, of; Estrada, of; Ganote, p; Glenn, of; Goedhart, p; Grundy, p; Hansen, of; Jenkins, dh; Kell, p; Ramon Marti, p; McFarlin, dh; McKamie, pr; Pages, of; Probst, 1b; Sanchez, of; Sanchez, p; Sanders, p; Shea, p; Stewart, 1b; Sutton, of; Taylor, p; Texidor, p; Thomas, dh; Wolfe, Yard, c.

LEAGUE CHAMPIONS

Year	Team	Pct.	Year	Team	Pct.	Year	Team	P
1888—	Dallas	.671	1899—	Galveston	.632	1908—	San Antonio	.6
1889—	Houston	.551		Galveston	.762	1909—	Houston	.6
1890—	Galveston	.705	1900-01—	Did not operate.		1910—	Dallas†	.5
1892—	Houston	.741	1902—	Corsicana	.866		Houston†	.5
	Houston	.613		Corsicana	.682	1911—	Austin	.5
1895—	Dallas	.754	1903—	Paris-Waco	.615	1912—	Houston	.6
	Fort Worth*	.750		Dallas*	.648	1913—	Houston	.6
1896—	Fort Worth	.757	1904—	Corsicana*	.615	1914—	Houston†	.6
	Houston*	.679		Fort Worth	.800		Waco†	.6
	Galveston	.548	1905—	Fort Worth	.545	1915—	Waco	.5
1897—	San Antonio†	.657	1906—	Fort Worth	.677	1916—	Waco	.5
	Galveston†	.717		Cleburne∞	.609	1917—	Dallas	.6
1898—	League disbanded.		1907—	Austin	.629	1918—	Dallas	.5

Year	Team	Pct.	Year	Team	Pct.	Year	Team	Pct.
19—	Shreveport*	.677	1949—	Fort Worth	.649	1975—	Lafayette▼	.558
	Fort Worth	.651		Tulsa (2nd)§	.584		Midland▼	.604
20—	Fort Worth	.703	1950—	Beaumont	.595	1976—	Amarillo■	.600
	Fort Worth	.750		San Antonio (4th)§	.513		Shreveport	.515
21—	Fort Worth	.691	1951—	Houston‡	.619	1977—	El Paso	.600
	Fort Worth	.662	1952—	Dallas	.571		Arkansas•	.485
22—	Fort Worth	.694		Shreveport (3rd)§	.522	1978—	El Paso•	.593
	Fort Worth	.711	1953—	Dallas‡	.571		Jackson	.567
23—	Fort Worth	.632	1954—	Shreveport	.559	1979—	Arkansas•	.571
	Fort Worth	.689		Houston (2nd)§	.553		Midland	.563
24—	Fort Worth	.763	1955—	Dallas	.581	1980—	Arkansas•	.596
	Fort Worth	.711		Shreveport (3rd)§	.540		San Antonio	.544
25—	Fort Worth	.711	1956—	Houston‡	.623	1981—	San Antonio	.571
	Fort Worth▲	.653	1957—	Dallas	.662		Jackson•	.507
26—	Dallas	.574		Houston (2nd)§	.630	1982—	El Paso	.559
27—	Wichita Falls	.654	1958—	Fort Worth	.582		Tulsa•	.515
28—	Houston*	.679		Cor. Christi (3rd)§	.507	1983—	Jackson	.507
	Wichita Falls	.731	1959—	Victoria	.589		Beaumont•	.500
29—	Dallas*	.588		Austin (2nd)§	.548	1984—	Beaumont	.654
	Wichita Falls	.620	1960—	Rio Grande Valley	.590		Jackson•	.610
30—	Wichita Falls	.697		Tulsa (3rd)	.528	1985—	El Paso	.632
	Fort Worth*	.632	1961—	Amarillo	.643		Jackson•	.537
31—	Houston♦	.625		San Antonio (3rd)§	.532	1986—	El Paso•	.630
	Houston	.734	1962—	El Paso	.571		Jackson	.533
32—	Beaumont*	.640		Tulsa (2nd)§	.550	1987—	Wichita•	.515
	Dallas	.727	1963—	San Antonio	.564		Jackson	.515
33—	Houston	.623		Tulsa (3rd)§	.529	1988—	El Paso	.552
	San Antonio (4th)§	.523	1964—	San Antonio‡	.607		Tulsa•	.522
34—	Galveston‡	.579	1965—	Tulsa	.574	1989—	Arkansas•	.585
35—	Oklahoma City‡	.590		Albuquerque■	.550		Wichita	.537
36—	Dallas	.604	1966—	Arkansas	.579	1990—	San Antonio	.582
	Tulsa (3rd)§	.519	1967—	Albuquerque	.557		Shreveport•	.489
37—	Oklahoma City	.635	1968—	Arkansas	.586	1991—	Shreveport•	.632
	Fort Worth (3rd)§	.535		El Paso■	.562		El Paso	.596
38—	Beaumont	.635	1969—	Amarillo	.593	1992—	Shreveport	.566
39—	Houston	.606		Memphis■	.504		Wichita•	.515
	Fort Worth (4th)§	.540	1970—	Albuquerque♦	.615	1993—	El Paso	.563
40—	Houston‡	.652		Memphis	.507		Jackson•	.541
41—	Houston	.673	1971—Did not operate as league—clubs			1994—	El Paso•	.647
	Dallas (4th)§	.519	were members of Dixie Association.				Jackson	.548
42—	Beaumont	.605	1972—	Alexandria	.600	1995—	Shreveport•	.652
	Shreveport (2nd)§	.576		El Paso■	.557		Midland	.485
43-44-45—Did not operate.			1973—	San Antonio	.590	1996—	Jackson•	.547
46—	Fort Worth	.656		Memphis■	.558		Wichita	.500
	Dallas (2nd)§	.591	1974—	Victoria■	.581			
47—	Houston‡	.623		El Paso	.555			
48—	Fort Worth‡	.601						

*Won split-season playoff. †Won playoff for title. ‡Finished first and won four-club playoff. §Won four-club playoff. ∞Title to Cleburne by default. ▲Tied with Dallas in second half and won playoff for championship. ♦Tied with Beaumont at end of first half and won title in best-of-five series played as part of second-half schedule. ■League divided into Eastern, Western divisions; won two-team playoff. ▼League divided into Eastern, Western divisions; declared co-champions when playoffs were not completed. •League divided into Eastern and Western divisions and played split-season; won playoffs. NOTE—Championship awarded to winner of four-team playoff, 1933-51; first-place team and playoff winner co-champions, 1952-64.

CLASS AA Texas League

– 455 –

CALIFORNIA LEAGUE

LEAGUE OFFICE

President/treasurer
Joe Gagliardi
Address
2380 S. Bascom Ave., Suite 200
Campbell, CA 95008
Phone
408-369-8038

Teams (affiliation)
Bakersfield Blaze (Giants)
High Desert Mavericks (Diamondbacks)
Lake Elsinore Storm (Angels)
Modesto A's (A's)
Rancho Cucamonga Quakes (Padres)
Lancaster Jethawks (Mariners)

San Bernardino Stampede (Dodgers)
San Jose Giants (Giants)
Stockton Ports (Brewers)
Visalia Oaks (A's)

1996 FINAL STANDINGS

FIRST HALF

NORTHERN DIVISION

Team	W	L	T	Pct.	GB
San Jose (Giants)	44	26	0	.629	....
Stockton (Brewers)	40	30	0	.571	4
Modesto (Athletics)	37	33	0	.529	7
Visalia (Co-op)	27	43	0	.386	17
Bakersfield (Co-op)	24	46	0	.343	20

SOUTHERN DIVISION

Team	W	L	T	Pct.	GB
Rancho Cucamonga (Padres)	38	32	0	.543	....
Lancaster (Mariners)	36	34	0	.514	2
Lake Elsinore (Angels)	35	35	0	.500	3
High Desert (Orioles)	35	35	0	.500	3
San Bernardino (Dodgers)	34	36	0	.486	4

SECOND HALF

NORTHERN DIVISION

Team	W	L	T	Pct.	GB
San Jose (Giants)	45	25	0	.643	....
Modesto (Athletics)	45	25	0	.643	....
Stockton (Brewers)	39	31	0	.557	6
Visalia (Co-op)	23	47	0	.329	22
Bakersfield (Co-op)	15	55	0	.214	30

SOUTHERN DIVISION

Team	W	L	T	Pct.	GB
High Desert (Orioles)	41	29	0	.586	....
Lake Elsinore (Angels)	40	30	0	.571	1
San Bernardino (Dodgers)	36	34	0	.514	5
Lancaster (Mariners)	35	35	0	.500	6
Rancho Cucamonga (Padres)	31	39	0	.443	10

COMPOSITE

Team	S.J.	Mod.	Stk.	H.D.	L.E.	Lan.	S.B.	R.C.	Vis.	Bak.	W	L	T	Pct.	G.B.
San Jose (Giants)	....	9	13	4	8	7	9	5	16	18	89	51	0	.636	....
Modesto (Athletics)	11	....	12	7	5	6	8	6	12	15	82	58	0	.586	7
Stockton (Brewers)	7	8	....	5	6	8	7	4	17	17	79	61	0	.564	10
High Desert (Orioles)	8	5	7	....	8	11	9	12	6	10	76	64	0	.543	13
Lake Elsinore (Angels)	4	7	6	12	....	11	11	9	6	9	75	65	0	.536	14
Lancaster (Mariners)	5	6	4	9	9	....	10	10	8	10	71	69	0	.507	18
San Bernardino (Dodgers)	3	4	5	11	9	10	....	12	7	9	70	70	0	.500	19
Rancho Cucamonga (Padres)	7	6	8	8	11	10	8	....	7	4	69	71	0	.493	20
Visalia (Co-op)	4	8	3	6	6	4	5	5	....	9	50	90	0	.357	39
Bakersfield (Co-op)	2	5	3	2	3	2	3	8	11	....	39	101	0	.279	50

High Desert home games played in Adelanto, Calif.

Major league affiliations in parentheses.

PLAYOFFS: Lake Elsinore defeated Rancho Cucamonga, two games to one; Stockton defeated Modesto, two games to none; Lake Elsinore defeated High Desert, three games to none; San Jose defeated Stockton, three games to one; Lake Elsinore defeated San Jose, three games to two, to win league champ onship.

REGULAR-SEASON ATTENDANCE: Bakersfield, 83,246; High Desert, 143,852; Lake Elsinore, 360,392; Lancaster, 316,390; Modesto, 98,795; Ranch Cucamonga, 410,214; San Bernardino, 148,363; San Jose, 144,782; Stockton, 101,555; Visalia, 67,798. Total—1,875,387. Playoffs (17 games)—23,67 All-Star Game at Rancho Cucamonga—6,671.

MANAGERS: Bakersfield, Graig Nettles; High Desert, Joe Ferguson; Lake Elsinore, Mitch Seoane; Lancaster, Dave Brundage; Modesto, Jim Colborn; Ranch Cucamonga, Mike Basso; San Bernardino, Del Crandall; San Jose, Carlos Lezcano; Stockton, Greg Mahlberg; Visalia, Tim Torricelli.

ALL-STAR TEAM: 1B—Chris Kirgan, High Desert; 2B—Jason Cook, Lancaster; 3B—Mike Berry, High Desert; SS—Miguel Tejada, Modesto; OF—Mike Nei Modesto; Mike Renhack, Stockton; Ben Grieve, Modesto; C—Craig Mayes, San Jose; DH—D.T. Cromer, Modesto; P—Bill King, Modesto; Ken Cloud Lancaster; Rich Linares, San Bernardino; Most Valuable Player—D.T. Cromer, Modesto; Pitcher of the Year—Darin Blood, San Jose; Rookie of the Year— Darin Blood, San Jose; Manager of the Year—Carlos Lezcano, San Jose.

1996 BATTING

TEAM

Team	Avg.	G	TPA	AB	R	H	TB	2B	3B	HR	RBI	SH	SF	HP	BB	IBB	SO	SB	CS	GDP	LOB	ShO	Slg.	OB
High Desert	.292	140	5749	4957	924	1446	2234	274	38	146	842	58	40	76	617	7	1034	119	66	110	1104	3	.451	.37
San Jose	.289	140	5619	4950	771	1433	2010	241	45	82	679	49	41	58	518	17	902	185	71	99	1111	4	.406	.36
Stockton	.286	140	5489	4759	767	1359	1974	225	42	102	689	56	52	84	536	9	894	147	91	103	1062	1	.415	.36
Modesto	.285	140	5667	4858	952	1386	2271	242	41	187	832	50	46	63	650	18	1192	219	102	86	1005	1	.467	.37
Lancaster	.278	140	5621	4899	852	1362	2100	275	59	115	775	28	53	93	544	8	1019	120	48	84	1056	6	.429	.35
San Bernardino	.278	140	5470	4853	807	1349	2092	243	22	152	711	48	41	71	456	9	1074	208	128	76	915	7	.431	.34
R. Cucamonga	.275	140	5558	4826	779	1327	1978	269	47	96	699	24	44	65	599	13	1096	124	61	110	1090	1	.410	.36
Lake Elsinore	.274	140	5672	4846	805	1327	2054	286	33	125	736	50	43	52	681	22	930	113	68	118	1121	3	.424	.36
Visalia	.254	140	5528	4786	738	1216	1856	254	34	106	655	29	54	56	598	5	1249	179	79	93	1015	5	.388	.34
Bakersfield	.250	140	5509	4821	682	1205	1833	256	15	114	595	51	35	76	517	11	1256	127	55	105	1023	9	.380	.35

INDIVIDUAL

TOP QUALIFIERS FOR BATTING CHAMPIONSHIP

Minimum 378 plate appearances. *Lefthanded batter. †Switch-hitter.

Player, Team	Avg.	G	TPA	AB	R	H	TB	2B	3B	HR	RBI	SH	SF	HP	BB	IBB	SO	SB	CS	GDP	Slg.	OBP
Berry, Mike, High Desert	.361	121	572	463	109	167	260	44	5	13	113	0	3	7	99	3	67	7	4	9	.562	.477
Reid, Derek, San Jose	.343	88	394	350	71	120	185	15	4	14	58	3	3	3	35	2	68	23	2	4	.529	.404
Neill, Mike, Modesto*	.339	114	518	442	101	150	239	20	6	19	78	2	2	4	68	4	123	28	7	3	.541	.430
Cromer, D.T., Modesto*	.329	124	550	505	100	166	316	40	10	30	130	3	4	6	32	4	67	20	7	5	.626	.373
Mayes, Craig, San Jose*	.328	114	507	472	56	155	198	26	4	3	68	2	4	0	29	2	43	6	8	5	.419	.364
Wingate, Ervan, San Bern.	.324	115	431	383	60	124	176	16	0	12	55	4	6	6	32	1	75	7	9	7	.460	.379
Rennhack, Mike, Stockton†	.320	121	522	456	67	146	237	32	4	17	103	2	7	4	53	1	66	8	10	11	.520	.390
Bogle, Bryan, High Desert	.317	126	545	495	86	157	267	32	6	22	92	2	8	5	35	0	142	14	9	7	.539	.363
Newstrom, Doug, H. Desert*	.313	122	484	403	84	126	195	30	3	11	75	2	6	0	73	0	62	15	8	9	.484	.413
Garland, Tim, San Jose	.311	132	625	550	96	171	218	18	7	5	61	5	6	10	54	1	77	51	18	6	.396	.379
Sbrocco, Jon, San Jose	.310	95	444	358	76	111	139	12	5	2	48	8	3	8	67	1	36	29	11	6	.388	.427
Takayoshi, Todd, Lk. Elsinore*	.310	99	389	310	58	96	147	18	0	11	61	0	2	3	74	5	50	0	1	13	.474	.445
Fernandez, Antonio, R. C.	.308	121	530	471	77	145	199	27	0	9	73	1	5	10	43	1	96	2	2	17	.423	.374
Moeder, Tony, Lake Elsinore	.307	94	383	339	57	104	171	21	2	14	66	0	3	3	38	1	92	3	3	9	.504	.379
Richardson, Scott, San Bern.	.306	128	516	458	80	140	209	30	0	13	69	4	4	4	46	0	71	31	14	9	.456	.371

DEPARTMENTAL LEADERS: G—Espinal, Garcia, 137; AB—Monahan, 584; R—D. Roberts, 112; H—Garland, 171; TB—Cromer, 316; 2B—Urso, 47; 3B—Monahan, 12; HR—Kirgan, 35; RBI—Kirgan, 131; SH—Garcia, 20; SF—Durkac, 16; HP—Cook, Krause, 16; BB—Berry, 99; IBB—Van Burkleo, 6; SO—Kirgan, 162; SB—Roberts, 65; CS—E. Davis, 23; GIDP—Lamb, 19; Slg.—Cromer, .626; OBP—Berry, .477.

ALL PLAYERS

*Lefthanded batter. †Switch-hitter.

Player, Team	Avg.	G	TPA	AB	R	H	TB	2B	3B	HR	RBI	SH	SF	HP	BB	IBB	SO	SB	CS	GDP	Slg.	OBP
Akins, Carlos, High Desert	.208	11	31	24	4	5	6	1	0	0	2	0	0	1	6	0	8	1	0	0	.250	.387
Alguacil, Jose, San Jose*	.265	79	315	272	53	72	92	11	3	1	31	1	0	2	24	1	53	18	7	8	.338	.338
Allen, Dustin, Rancho Cuca.	.298	55	251	208	41	62	109	15	1	10	45	0	3	2	38	1	65	3	2	3	.524	.406
Anderson, Cliff, San Bern.*	.296	55	251	230	43	68	121	16	2	11	44	4	2	6	15	0	50	7	5	2	.526	.352
Andreopoulos, Alex, Stockton*	.302	87	342	291	52	88	124	17	2	5	41	2	4	5	40	2	33	10	3	5	.426	.391
Arano, Eloy, Visalia†	.229	43	158	140	19	32	38	6	0	0	16	1	0	0	17	0	30	4	2	5	.271	.312
Ardoin, Danny, Modesto	.262	91	378	317	55	83	120	13	3	6	34	3	2	9	47	0	81	5	7	9	.379	.371
Augustine, Andy, Lancaster	.278	41	142	115	16	32	39	5	1	0	12	1	1	3	22	0	40	2	0	4	.339	.404
Avila, Rolando, High Desert	.331	68	327	296	54	98	131	17	2	4	33	4	2	3	22	0	32	15	7	5	.443	.381
Baker, Jason, San Bernardino	.103	19	29	29	2	3	3	0	0	0	0	1	0	0	0	0	10	0	0	1	.103	.103
Barajas, Rod, Visalia	.162	27	82	74	6	12	15	3	0	0	8	0	0	1	7	0	21	0	0	3	.203	.244
Batiste, Kim, San Jose	.167	2	6	6	0	1	1	0	0	0	0	0	0	0	0	0	2	0	0	0	.167	.167
Baugh, Gavin, Bakersfield†	.150	6	24	20	3	3	4	1	0	0	1	0	0	0	3	0	9	0	0	1	.200	.261
Bazzani, Matt, Bakersfield	.203	20	78	69	5	14	23	3	0	2	8	0	1	1	7	0	21	0	0	3	.333	.282
Beltre, Adrian, San Bernardino	.261	63	268	238	40	62	107	13	1	10	40	1	5	5	19	0	44	3	4	3	.450	.322
Bentley, Kevin, Bakersfield	.274	22	99	84	19	23	43	3	1	5	21	0	2	3	9	0	30	7	1	2	.512	.357
Berry, Mike, High Desert	.361	121	572	463	109	167	260	44	5	13	113	0	3	7	99	3	67	7	4	9	.562	.477
Betances, Junior, Stockton	.253	125	525	458	69	116	142	9	7	1	41	4	6	6	51	0	61	14	11	9	.310	.332
Betten, Barry, Lake Elsinore	.259	74	303	274	32	71	101	15	3	3	34	3	1	3	22	1	49	11	3	6	.369	.320
Bilderback, Ty, Lake Elsinore*	.267	42	172	150	21	40	59	10	0	3	22	0	1	4	17	1	38	4	2	1	.393	.355
Bogle, Bryan, High Desert	.317	126	545	495	86	157	267	32	6	22	92	2	8	5	35	0	142	14	9	7	.539	.363
Bonds, Bobby, San Jose	.248	110	469	420	65	104	163	16	5	11	51	1	3	2	43	0	126	21	5	15	.388	.318
Brinkley, Darryl, Rancho Cuca.	.363	65	290	259	52	94	153	28	2	9	59	0	6	2	23	2	37	18	10	13	.591	.410
Brissey, Jason, Visalia	.226	83	262	234	32	53	95	15	3	7	34	2	5	3	18	0	80	2	4	4	.406	.285
Brown, Emil, Modesto	.303	57	251	211	50	64	106	10	1	10	47	0	2	6	32	1	51	13	5	5	.502	.406
Bryant, Chris, High Desert	.299	68	276	234	53	70	99	10	2	5	41	4	2	4	32	0	55	3	2	6	.423	.390
Bucci, Carmen, Rancho Cuca.†	.000	9	17	16	1	0	0	0	0	0	0	1	0	0	0	0	5	0	0	0	.000	.000
Buhner, Shawn, Lancaster	.209	69	270	239	28	50	80	19	1	3	25	1	1	9	20	0	55	0	0	10	.335	.294
Buxbaum, Danny, Lake Elsinore	.292	74	333	298	53	87	150	17	2	14	60	0	2	2	31	2	41	1	0	8	.503	.360
Cabrera, Alex, Bakersfield	.281	89	374	345	45	97	162	18	1	15	53	0	4	11	14	0	80	0	1	13	.470	.326
Campillo, Rob, Stockton	.241	46	167	145	11	35	41	4	1	0	18	4	2	1	15	0	27	2	3	6	.283	.313
Carney, Bartt, High Desert†	.250	47	137	116	31	29	41	3	3	1	11	2	0	4	15	0	26	6	4	1	.353	.356
Carpentier, Mike, San Bern.	.214	15	48	42	5	9	12	1	1	0	7	2	0	0	4	0	4	2	3	3	.286	.283
Carroll, Doug, Bak.-Lan.*	.285	90	375	326	55	93	154	21	2	10	53	1	3	6	39	2	83	3	2	5	.472	.369
Carter, Cale, Lake Elsinore*	.292	38	129	113	12	33	45	9	0	1	15	2	0	0	14	1	21	4	4	3	.398	.370
Castro, Jose, Modesto†	.226	95	419	363	58	82	124	16	1	8	48	8	3	3	42	0	124	25	12	4	.342	.309
Cesar, Dionys, Modesto	.200	22	73	60	5	12	14	2	0	0	4	6	0	0	7	0	19	1	3	0	.233	.284
Christian, Eddie, Lake Elsinore†	.397	16	73	58	10	23	34	5	0	2	9	1	0	2	12	0	10	1	2	0	.586	.514
Clayton, Craig, Rancho Cuca.	.000	11	1	1	0	0	0	0	0	0	0	0	0	0	0	0	0	0	0	0	.000	.000
Clifford, Jim, Lancaster*	.257	112	468	389	78	100	191	19	6	20	85	0	7	15	53	2	92	4	4	3	.491	.362
Cochrane, Chris, Modesto	.000	22	5	5	0	0	0	0	0	0	0	0	0	0	0	0	2	0	0	0	.000	.000
Collier, Dan, Bakersfield	.274	56	229	212	22	58	90	15	1	5	40	2	2	7	6	0	63	9	3	2	.425	.313
Cook, Jason, Lancaster	.289	124	563	450	95	130	175	22	5	4	58	4	4	16	89	0	68	5	2	6	.389	.420
Cooney, Kyle, San Bernardino	.273	107	453	406	57	111	173	20	0	14	67	0	5	14	28	1	78	9	8	8	.426	.338
Corujo, Rey, San Jose	.271	57	212	188	26	51	77	12	1	4	28	0	3	2	19	0	43	1	0	4	.410	.340
Cromer, D.T., Modesto*	.329	124	550	505	100	166	316	40	10	30	130	3	4	6	32	4	67	20	7	5	.626	.373
Cruz, Jose, Lancaster†	.325	53	248	203	38	66	103	17	1	6	43	0	6	0	39	1	33	7	1	4	.507	.432
Cuevas, Eduardo, Rancho C.	.348	7	26	23	3	8	8	0	0	0	1	0	0	0	2	0	4	0	0	1	.348	.385
Curtis, Randy, Rancho Cuca.*	.267	104	451	359	63	96	135	14	5	5	52	4	8	4	76	2	94	22	6	2	.376	.394
Daedelow, Craig, Bakersfield	.235	86	339	298	37	70	92	17	1	1	28	4	2	4	31	0	60	10	4	6	.309	.313
Dalton, Jed, Lake Elsinore	.256	38	137	121	19	31	42	4	2	1	15	2	1	2	11	0	19	6	3	3	.347	.326
D'Amico, Jeffrey, Modesto	.267	47	197	172	28	46	67	7	1	4	21	1	1	4	19	0	31	3	1	3	.390	.352
Danapilis, Eric, Visalia	.257	105	452	377	58	97	158	29	1	10	64	0	1	8	66	0	122	2	1	6	.419	.378

CLASS A California League

Player, Team	Avg.	G	TPA	AB	R	H	TB	2B	3B	HR	RBI	SH	SF	HP	BB	IBB	SO	SB	CS	GDP	Slg.	OB
D'Aquila, Tom, High Desert	.063	6	17	16	2	1	3	0	1	0	1	0	0	0	1	0	7	0	0	0	.188	.11
Darnell, Bryce, Visalia*	.077	7	14	13	1	1	1	0	0	0	1	0	1	0	0	0	2	0	0	0	.077	.07
Dauphin, Phil, Lake Elsinore*	.229	67	291	245	43	56	95	13	1	8	38	1	5	4	36	1	52	8	3	2	.388	.33
Davis, Ben, Rancho Cuca.†	.201	98	390	353	35	71	101	10	1	6	41	4	2	0	31	0	89	1	1	8	.286	.26
Davis, Eddie, San Bernardino	.256	136	623	546	107	140	265	34	2	29	89	3	4	8	62	1	150	31	23	8	.485	.33
Dean, Chris, Lancaster†	.276	48	195	174	30	48	75	10	1	5	22	1	1	3	16	0	31	7	1	3	.431	.34
Deberry, Joe, Stockton*	.268	54	217	190	33	51	83	7	2	7	25	0	3	1	23	0	55	3	0	0	.437	.34
DeBoer, Rob, Modesto	.285	73	329	249	68	71	127	8	6	12	52	0	2	4	74	0	75	12	5	5	.510	.45
DeJesus, Malvin, Visalia	.241	124	564	485	66	117	167	24	4	6	51	7	3	6	63	0	107	34	13	4	.344	.33
DelaRosa, Elvis, Visalia	.221	69	237	204	33	45	75	10	1	6	27	3	1	5	24	0	76	2	2	1	.368	.31
DeLeon, Roberto, San Jose	.091	3	11	11	0	1	1	0	0	0	0	0	0	0	0	0	2	0	1	0	.091	.09
Delgado, Wilson, San Jose†	.268	121	520	462	59	124	161	19	6	2	54	4	4	2	48	0	89	8	2	8	.348	.33
Demetral, Chris, San Bern.*	.281	11	38	32	5	9	15	3	0	1	4	0	0	0	6	1	5	0	3	0	.469	.39
Denbow, Don, San Jose	.371	26	116	97	19	36	68	8	3	6	19	0	1	1	17	1	30	1	1	2	.701	.46
Dilone, Juan, Modesto†	.265	111	468	404	78	107	168	17	1	14	66	8	5	6	45	0	138	31	10	11	.416	.34
Dunlop, Steve, Visalia	.225	23	80	71	12	16	19	3	0	0	3	1	0	3	5	0	20	2	1	2	.268	.30
Durkac, Bo, Visalia†	.298	126	550	453	67	135	180	29	2	4	81	0	16	2	79	0	84	6	3	14	.397	.39
Eaddy, Keith, H.D.-R.C.	.194	52	150	129	14	25	41	5	1	3	10	1	0	2	18	0	48	3	4	2	.318	.30
Edmonds, Jim, Lake Elsinore*	.400	5	17	15	4	6	11	2	0	1	4	0	0	1	1	1	1	0	0	0	.733	.47
Espinal, Juan, Bakersfield	.274	137	609	522	81	143	259	38	0	26	98	1	6	6	74	2	126	1	4	11	.496	.36
Facione, Chris, Visalia	.258	78	337	310	50	80	129	16	6	7	38	1	1	3	22	0	60	9	11	7	.416	.31
Failla, Paul, Lake Elsinore†	.207	91	345	285	39	59	81	11	4	1	32	7	3	0	50	0	66	13	8	7	.284	.32
Faircloth, Kevin, San Bern.	.298	56	200	171	30	51	75	6	3	4	23	5	0	4	20	0	30	9	8	1	.439	.38
Felix, Lauro, Stockton	.182	12	53	33	5	6	12	0	0	2	5	1	0	1	18	0	9	1	2	0	.364	.48
Fernandez, Antonio, Rancho C.	.308	121	530	471	77	145	199	27	0	9	73	1	5	10	43	1	96	2	2	17	.423	.37
Figueroa, Luis, Lancaster	.387	9	33	31	5	12	18	4	1	0	6	0	0	0	2	0	6	0	1	0	.581	.42
Galarza, Joel, San Jose	.289	81	330	291	39	84	125	17	0	8	50	0	3	9	25	1	60	10	3	9	.430	.36
Gama, Ricardo, Rancho Cuca.	.271	108	467	417	59	113	166	28	2	7	50	5	4	4	37	1	57	13	5	10	.398	.33
Garcia, Jesse, High Desert	.266	137	548	459	94	122	183	21	5	10	66	20	4	8	57	0	81	25	7	8	.399	.35
Garland, Tim, San Jose	.311	132	625	550	96	171	218	18	7	5	61	5	6	10	54	1	77	51	18	6	.396	.37
Glenn, Darrin, San Jose	.222	3	11	9	2	2	5	0	0	1	1	0	0	0	2	0	4	0	0	0	.556	.36
Gonzalez, Manuel, San Bern.†	.304	43	182	168	29	51	64	7	3	0	21	2	0	0	12	0	32	10	8	2	.381	.35
Gonzalez, Mauricio, Bakersfld†	.278	97	444	418	48	116	159	29	1	4	48	9	2	2	13	1	63	2	5	15	.380	.30
Greene, Eric, Bakersfield*	.222	2	9	9	1	2	2	0	0	0	0	0	0	0	0	0	3	0	0	0	.222	.22
Greer, Ryan, Bakersfield	.000	2	5	5	0	0	0	0	0	0	0	0	0	0	0	0	3	0	0	0	.000	.00
Gresham, Kris, High Desert	.375	2	8	8	2	3	9	0	0	2	4	0	0	0	0	0	1	0	0	0	1.125	.37
Grieve, Ben, Modesto*	.356	72	324	281	61	100	155	20	1	11	51	1	3	1	38	2	52	8	7	5	.552	.43
Gross, Rafael, San Bernardino	.235	112	389	362	58	85	125	18	2	6	43	5	2	2	18	0	68	31	14	5	.345	.27
Guzman, Edwards, San Jose*	.270	106	423	367	41	99	131	19	5	1	40	6	5	5	39	4	60	3	5	6	.357	.34
Harmer, Frank, Bak.-H.D.†	.216	64	197	162	26	35	51	7	0	3	20	4	1	0	30	0	41	1	1	1	.315	.33
Harrison, Adonis, Lancaster*	.350	16	48	40	7	14	18	4	0	0	5	0	0	0	8	0	13	4	1	0	.450	.45
Hemphill, Bret, Lake Elsinore†	.263	108	462	399	64	105	183	21	3	17	64	6	1	4	52	1	93	4	3	7	.459	.35
Henderson, Juan, Lake Elsinore	.197	50	188	147	24	29	40	7	2	0	17	5	1	4	31	0	47	13	8	2	.272	.35
Hendricks, Ryan, H.D.-Bak.*	.179	44	145	123	16	22	34	3	0	3	12	2	1	2	17	0	42	2	0	2	.276	.28
Herider, Jeremy, Vis.-Bak.†	.218	78	314	252	40	55	68	10	0	1	26	1	0	2	59	1	68	3	7	5	.270	.37
Herrick, Jason, Lake Elsinore*	.319	58	239	210	35	67	102	13	2	6	30	2	2	0	25	2	52	5	4	5	.486	.38
Hodge, Roy, High Desert	.280	112	455	393	71	110	159	21	2	8	54	8	4	2	47	0	58	9	7	8	.405	.35
Howell, Jack, Lake Elsinore	.167	4	15	12	2	2	6	1	0	1	3	0	0	0	3	0	4	0	0	1	.500	.33
Hugo, Sean, High Desert*	.154	18	45	39	3	6	13	1	0	2	5	1	0	1	4	0	11	0	2	1	.333	.25
Hunter, Andy, Rancho Cuca.	.222	4	10	9	2	2	2	0	0	0	0	0	0	1	0	0	2	0	0	0	.222	.30
Hust, Gary, Modesto	.238	12	53	42	6	10	18	2	0	2	10	0	0	1	10	0	14	0	2	2	.429	.35
Ibarra, Jesus, San Jose†	.283	126	566	498	74	141	230	38	0	17	95	0	2	3	63	3	108	5	1	12	.462	.36
James, Dion, Stockton*	.188	4	21	16	5	3	3	0	0	0	1	0	0	0	5	0	3	3	0	0	.188	.38
Javier, Stan, San Jose	.400	3	7	5	1	2	2	0	0	0	1	0	0	1	1	0	1	0	0	0	.400	.57
Jenkins, Geoff, Stockton*	.348	37	165	138	27	48	73	8	4	3	25	1	3	3	20	1	32	3	3	3	.529	.43
Johnson, Todd, Bakersfield	.238	110	407	369	45	88	117	23	0	2	31	1	0	5	32	0	90	1	1	6	.317	.30
Jones, Jack, San Bernardino	.241	10	36	29	5	7	13	3	0	1	6	0	0	1	6	0	8	1	1	1	.448	.38
Jordan, Ricky, Lancaster	.323	7	33	31	7	10	14	1	0	1	4	0	0	2	0	5	0	0	0	.452	.36
Joyner, Wally, Rancho Cuca.*	.300	3	11	10	1	3	4	1	0	0	2	0	0	0	1	0	1	0	0	0	.400	.36
Keefe, Jamie, Rancho Cuca.	.234	24	79	64	12	15	28	5	1	2	10	0	2	2	11	0	26	1	0	3	.438	.35
Kenady, Jake, San Bernardino*	.000	45	1	1	0	0	0	0	0	0	0	0	0	0	0	0	0	0	0	0	.000	.00
Kimsey, Keith, Visalia	.274	99	442	394	64	108	194	17	3	21	72	0	3	2	43	2	140	13	4	7	.492	.34
Kinard, Kirk, Bakersfield	.198	37	137	116	16	23	30	3	2	0	5	5	0	3	13	1	44	3	1	4	.259	.29
Kirgan, Chris, High Desert*	.297	136	591	529	96	157	287	23	1	35	131	1	2	5	54	3	162	2	3	9	.543	.36
Klassen, Danny, Stockton	.269	118	484	432	58	116	152	22	4	2	46	5	2	10	34	0	77	14	8	12	.352	.33
Kliner, Josh, Bakersfield†	.308	43	205	156	37	48	71	6	1	5	33	0	1	8	37	1	25	0	3	1	.455	.44
Kominek, Toby, Stockton	.296	100	423	358	76	106	158	17	7	7	47	4	3	8	49	1	97	10	7	7	.441	.39
Krause, Scott, Stockton	.300	108	479	427	82	128	215	22	4	19	83	1	3	16	32	0	101	25	6	9	.504	.36
Lackey, Steve, Visalia	.266	46	205	184	27	49	74	11	1	4	29	2	2	1	16	0	44	7	1	7	.402	.32
Lamb, David, Lake Desert†	.257	116	527	460	63	118	157	24	3	3	55	5	2	10	50	1	68	5	6	20	.341	.34
Lampkin, Tom, San Jose*	.286	2	8	7	2	2	4	0	1	0	2	0	0	0	1	0	2	0	0	0	.571	.37
Landrum, Tito, San Bernardino	.268	51	181	157	29	42	58	7	0	3	20	0	1	2	21	0	38	8	4	2	.369	.35
Landry, Lonny, Visalia	.215	51	207	191	23	41	58	7	2	2	10	4	0	3	9	0	54	10	2	0	.304	.24
Lanza, Mike, Lancaster	.263	109	409	380	53	100	133	12	6	3	42	4	4	3	18	0	73	3	4	7	.350	.29
Lemonis, Chris, Visalia*	.278	126	534	482	69	134	209	27	3	14	82	2	4	6	35	1	99	12	5	10	.434	.33
Lewis, Andreaus, Bakersfield†	.244	62	237	205	40	50	72	7	3	0	13	0	3	16	1	0	9	22	0	78	9	2	7	.351	.3
Lewis, Tyrone, San Bernardino	.263	67	237	217	30	57	90	14	2	5	30	4	1	1	14	0	51	6	2	4	.415	.3
LeCronier, Jason, High Desert*	.237	52	146	135	17	32	49	13	1	4	25	2	1	1	6	0	37	1	0	5	.363	.2
Lopez, Mickey, Stockton†	.281	64	254	217	30	61	73	10	1	0	25	9	1	4	23	0	36	6	4	4	.336	.3
Lukasiewicz, Mark, Bakersfield*	.167	9	8	6	0	1	2	1	0	0	0	0	0	0	3	0	0	0	0	0	.333	.3
Luzinski, Ryan, San Bernardino	.347	30	133	118	24	41	66	10	0	5	21	2	1	0	11	0	33	6	1	2	.559	.4
Madsen, Dave, Modesto	.241	52	213	174	25	42	61	7	0	4	19	3	1	4	31	0	31	2	0	5	.351	.3
Marine, Del, Visalia	.257	105	442	378	58	97	167	20	1	16	69	0	7	10	47	1	121	8	2	6	.442	.3

– 458 –

Player, Team	Avg.	G	TPA	AB	R	H	TB	2B	3B	HR	RBI	SH	SF	HP	BB	IBB	SO	SB	CS	GDP	Slg.	OBP
arquez, Jesus, Lancaster*	.300	126	557	490	84	147	258	31	10	20	106	4	9	9	45	1	78	19	8	5	.527	.363
artin, Jeff, Bakersfield	.182	5	22	22	2	4	4	0	0	0	1	0	0	0	0	0	10	0	0	0	.182	.182
artin, Jim, San Bernardino*	.243	50	174	152	26	37	58	1	1	6	23	3	2	1	16	1	53	9	4	1	.382	.316
artinez, Greg, Stockton†	.287	73	325	286	51	82	89	5	1	0	26	8	2	0	29	0	34	30	9	3	.311	.350
artinez, Tony, Visalia	.193	31	94	83	7	16	22	6	0	0	11	0	3	1	7	0	20	0	0	5	.265	.255
arval, Raul, San Jose	.234	39	152	137	19	32	38	6	0	0	19	4	1	1	9	0	13	0	0	3	.277	.284
assarelli, John, Rancho Cuca.	.296	26	125	108	24	32	47	9	3	0	17	0	0	2	15	1	14	6	1	3	.435	.392
atthews, Gary, R. Cuca.†	.271	123	507	435	65	118	182	21	11	7	54	4	2	6	60	1	102	7	8	11	.418	.366
axwell, Pat, Modesto*	.455	4	14	11	1	5	6	1	0	0	0	1	0	1	1	1	1	0	0	0	.545	.538
ayes, Craig, San Jose*	.328	114	507	472	56	155	198	26	4	3	68	2	4	0	29	2	43	6	8	5	.419	.364
cCarty, Matt, San Bernardino	.236	38	130	110	30	26	50	2	2	6	19	1	1	4	14	1	35	5	2	1	.455	.341
cGonigle, Bill, Stockton	.269	74	256	227	29	61	76	12	0	1	25	4	6	1	18	0	27	2	4	8	.335	.317
cGuire, Matt, San Jose	.333	4	6	6	1	2	3	1	0	0	0	0	0	0	0	0	1	0	0	0	.500	.333
cKinnis, Leroy, Rancho Cuca.	.268	87	370	328	49	88	124	20	2	4	39	0	1	3	38	0	74	2	3	6	.378	.349
elo, Juan, Rancho Cuca.†	.304	128	536	503	75	153	216	27	6	8	75	0	1	10	22	0	102	6	8	10	.429	.345
erullo, Matt, Lake Elsinore*	.222	9	42	36	8	8	13	2	0	1	6	0	1	0	5	0	7	0	0	1	.361	.310
ichael, Jeff, High Desert	.286	3	9	7	2	2	2	0	0	0	0	0	0	0	2	0	1	0	1	0	.286	.444
ikesell, Steve, San Bernardino	.067	6	19	15	2	1	3	0	1	0	1	0	1	1	2	0	6	0	0	2	.200	.211
oeder, Tony, Lake Elsinore	.307	94	383	339	57	104	171	21	2	14	66	0	3	3	38	1	92	3	3	9	.504	.379
olina, Luis, Lancaster	.254	37	142	122	13	31	35	4	0	0	10	2	2	2	14	0	24	3	2	2	.287	.336
onahan, Shane, Lancaster*	.281	132	630	584	107	164	261	31	12	14	97	4	8	4	30	2	124	19	5	8	.447	.316
oore, Mark, Modesto	.179	31	115	95	13	17	35	6	0	4	24	0	2	1	17	0	37	0	0	2	.368	.304
oore, Vince, Rancho Cuca.*	.288	63	265	219	49	63	104	13	2	8	38	0	0	4	42	1	78	12	1	4	.475	.411
orales, Alex, San Jose	.167	17	68	54	9	9	14	2	0	1	5	1	0	0	13	1	17	5	2	0	.259	.328
orimoto, Ken, San Bernardino	.250	24	111	92	13	23	26	3	0	0	8	5	1	1	12	0	28	14	3	0	.283	.340
orreale, John, Stockton	.236	50	173	148	19	35	48	7	0	2	19	4	1	4	16	0	33	3	3	4	.324	.325
orris, Greg, Lake Elsinore	.252	62	258	234	26	59	87	20	1	2	31	0	1	0	23	0	50	1	3	9	.372	.318
oultrie, Pat, Bakersfield*	.209	48	203	158	19	33	46	4	0	3	15	9	3	0	29	0	37	15	5	0	.291	.326
aikirk, Derick, Visalia	.148	9	29	27	3	4	4	0	0	0	2	0	0	0	2	0	9	0	0	1	.148	.207
eill, Mike, Modesto*	.339	114	518	442	101	150	239	20	6	19	78	2	2	4	68	4	123	28	7	3	.541	.430
ewhan, David, Modesto*	.301	117	527	455	96	137	245	27	3	25	75	6	2	2	62	1	106	17	8	8	.538	.384
ewstrom, Doug, High Desert*	.313	122	484	403	84	126	195	30	3	11	75	2	6	0	73	0	62	15	8	9	.484	.413
dham, Bob, Bakersfield	.091	47	22	22	1	2	2	0	0	0	0	0	0	0	0	0	7	0	0	2	.091	.091
opeza, Igor, Bakersfield	.000	24	4	4	0	0	0	0	0	0	0	0	0	0	0	0	0	0	0	0	.000	.000
tega, Randy, Modesto	.246	23	76	65	8	16	23	2	1	1	5	1	0	1	9	1	11	1	2	1	.354	.347
tiz, Jose, Modesto	.250	1	4	4	0	1	1	0	0	0	0	0	0	0	1	0	1	0	0	0	.250	.250
Toole, Bobby, High Desert	.171	16	45	35	8	6	7	1	0	0	3	0	0	2	8	0	10	0	0	3	.200	.356
arker, Allan, Lake Elsinore	.194	51	147	134	13	26	32	3	0	1	10	2	0	1	10	0	29	1	2	0	.239	.255
xton, Chris, Bakersfield*	.249	85	311	269	30	67	114	14	0	11	39	2	2	3	35	0	89	0	0	6	.424	.340
z, Richard, High Desert	.176	7	20	17	2	3	4	1	0	0	0	2	0	0	1	0	4	0	0	1	.235	.222
rez, Mickey, Bakersfield	.176	6	21	17	1	3	3	0	0	0	1	0	0	0	3	0	8	0	0	0	.176	.300
lanco, Juan, Modesto	.214	8	31	28	4	6	11	2	0	1	2	0	0	3	0	0	7	1	2	1	.393	.290
ieto, Chris, Rancho Cuca.*	.241	55	257	216	36	52	73	11	2	2	23	2	0	0	39	1	36	23	8	2	.338	.357
ajotte, Jason, Modesto*	.167	48	6	6	0	1	1	0	0	0	0	0	0	0	0	0	1	0	0	0	.167	.167
leigh, Matt, High Desert	.286	27	99	84	17	24	51	6	0	7	13	0	1	0	14	0	33	2	0	2	.607	.384
ese, Mat, Lake Elsinore*	.500	2	2	2	0	1	1	0	0	0	0	0	0	0	0	0	0	0	0	0	.500	.500
ich, Steve, High Desert*	.000	3	3	2	0	0	0	0	0	0	0	0	0	0	1	0	1	0	0	0	.000	.333
id, Derek, San Jose	.343	88	394	350	71	120	185	15	4	14	58	3	3	3	35	2	68	23	2	4	.529	.404
nnhack, Mike, Stockton†	.320	121	522	456	67	146	237	32	4	17	103	2	7	4	53	1	66	8	10	11	.520	.390
ynolds, Chance, Stockton†	.164	20	79	67	3	11	13	2	0	0	7	0	0	4	8	0	10	1	2	4	.194	.291
chardson, Scott, San Bern.	.306	128	516	458	80	140	209	30	0	13	69	4	4	4	46	0	71	31	14	9	.456	.371
berge, J.P., Bakersfield	.364	12	50	44	8	16	24	3	1	1	6	0	1	2	3	0	9	1	2	0	.545	.420
berts, David, Visalia*	.272	126	591	482	112	131	184	24	7	5	37	3	7	1	98	0	105	65	21	6	.382	.391
berts, John, Rancho Cuca.	.164	23	85	73	11	12	24	4	1	2	6	0	0	1	11	1	27	4	1	0	.329	.282
sario, Melvin, R.C.-H.D.†	.311	52	229	196	42	61	114	12	1	13	44	0	0	9	24	0	53	5	0	3	.582	.402
nion, Tony, Rancho Cuca.	.000	8	1	1	0	0	0	0	0	0	0	0	0	0	0	0	0	0	0	0	.000	.000
ssin, Tom, High Desert	.000	6	6	6	0	0	0	0	0	0	0	0	0	0	0	0	2	0	0	0	.000	.000
nchez, Yuri, Visalia*	.237	18	69	59	9	14	24	1	0	3	6	3	0	0	7	0	19	1	1	0	.407	.318
rocco, Jon, San Jose	.310	95	444	358	76	111	139	12	5	2	48	8	3	8	67	1	36	29	11	6	.388	.427
hofield, Dick, Lake Elsinore	.250	2	6	4	1	1	1	0	0	0	0	0	0	0	1	0	1	0	1	0	.250	.500
hwenke, Matt, Rancho Cuca.	.207	10	34	29	2	6	9	0	0	1	7	2	2	0	1	2	13	0	0	1	.310	.281
aly, Scot, Lancaster	.272	75	306	254	47	69	124	22	3	9	49	2	1	8	41	0	63	3	2	7	.488	.388
ll, Chip, San Bernardino*	.280	95	357	321	47	90	105	12	0	1	23	3	1	5	27	2	68	13	5	6	.327	.345
aw, Curtis, Modesto	.000	39	1	1	0	0	0	0	0	0	0	0	0	0	0	0	1	0	0	0	.000	.000
effield, Tony, Bakersfield*	.233	49	189	172	14	40	59	8	1	3	13	4	0	0	13	3	73	8	5	4	.343	.286
xes, Ken, San Bernardino	.000	17	2	2	0	0	0	0	0	0	0	0	0	0	0	0	1	0	0	0	.000	.000
emmer, Dave, Modesto	.294	26	99	85	17	25	43	9	0	3	13	1	1	1	10	1	15	2	2	4	.506	.378
ith, Chris, Lake Elsinore	.266	63	271	241	38	64	110	12	2	10	45	0	3	3	24	0	35	1	1	9	.456	.336
ith, Dave, Bakersfield	.239	35	146	117	25	28	48	9	1	3	18	2	2	4	20	1	36	1	0	0	.410	.364
ith, Scott, Lancaster	.298	61	276	252	52	75	124	19	0	10	52	0	3	5	16	0	74	9	2	5	.492	.348
riano, Fred, Modesto†	.262	33	148	126	21	33	42	3	0	2	19	4	4	0	14	0	33	14	3	1	.333	.326
wards, Ryan, San Bern.*	.000	5	4	2	0	0	0	0	0	0	0	0	0	0	0	0	1	0	0	0	.000	.500
ed, David, San Bernardino	.299	28	103	87	11	26	35	6	0	1	13	0	1	1	14	0	19	2	3	1	.402	.398
inmann, Scott, Lancaster†	.200	5	10	10	2	2	2	0	0	0	0	0	0	0	0	0	4	0	0	0	.200	.200
ner, Mike, Bakersfield	.293	36	156	147	25	43	69	6	1	3	20	3	1	0	8	1	18	1	1	4	.469	.327
rdivant, Marcus, Lancaster*	.284	68	328	292	54	83	114	19	6	0	31	0	1	3	32	1	35	23	9	3	.390	.360
plee, Ray, High Desert	.298	112	400	352	54	105	143	16	2	6	56	0	4	12	32	0	72	3	3	7	.406	.373
inton, Jermaine, Stockton	.280	40	179	164	30	46	85	9	0	10	35	0	1	1	13	0	72	0	0	4	.518	.335
mmonds, Maika, Bakersfld*	.500	9	7	6	1	3	3	2	0	0	0	0	0	0	1	0	3	0	0	0	.833	.571
kayoshi, Todd, Lk. Elsinore*	.310	99	389	310	58	96	147	18	0	11	61	0	2	3	74	5	50	0	1	13	.474	.445
asley, Ken, Bakersfield†	.158	21	63	57	4	9	10	1	0	0	2	1	0	1	4	0	19	0	0	2	.175	.226
ada, Miguel, Modesto	.279	114	521	458	97	128	210	12	5	20	72	1	7	4	51	3	93	27	16	9	.459	.352
elen, D.J., San Jose	.273	6	26	22	4	6	10	1	0	1	4	1	0	0	3	0	8	0	1	1	.455	.360

CLASS A California League

Player, Team	Avg.	G	TPA	AB	R	H	TB	2B	3B	HR	RBI	SH	SF	HP	BB	IBB	SO	SB	CS	GDP	Slg.	O
Thompson, Fletcher, H. Desert*	.292	25	83	72	10	21	27	4	1	0	8	1	0	0	10	0	6	3	2	2	.375	.3
Tingley, Ron, Lake Elsinore	.308	13	51	39	6	12	18	1	1	1	10	0	2	1	9	0	6	0	0	1	.462	.4
Torrealba, Yorvit, San Jose	.000	2	6	5	0	0	0	0	0	0	0	0	0	0	1	0	1	0	0	0	.000	.1
Towner, Kyle, Bakersfield†	.229	90	414	349	65	80	106	12	1	4	17	4	2	4	55	0	80	53	13	4	.304	.3
Townsend, Chad, San Bern.*	.295	116	476	421	63	124	210	18	1	22	72	0	2	3	50	1	100	3	2	7	.499	.3
Tredaway, Chad, Rancho C.†	.250	21	94	84	13	21	30	3	0	2	13	0	3	0	7	0	7	1	0	1	.357	.2
Twist, Jeff, Bakersfield†	.115	7	27	26	0	3	3	0	0	0	1	0	0	0	1	0	8	0	0	1	.115	.1
Tyler, Josh, Stockton	.322	75	318	273	42	88	112	14	2	2	33	7	2	11	25	0	35	4	8	6	.410	.3
Urso, Joe, Lake Elsinore	.291	125	577	474	106	138	216	47	2	9	66	12	8	8	75	0	57	6	2	17	.456	.3
Van Burkleo, Ty, Lake Elsinore*	.312	61	264	202	44	63	125	14	3	14	50	0	2	2	58	6	42	4	1	5	.619	.4
Van Rossum, Chris, San Jose*	.258	11	38	31	7	8	10	2	0	0	4	0	0	1	6	0	10	1	2	0	.323	.3
Ventura, Wilfredo, Modesto	.260	32	112	100	15	26	43	3	1	4	23	1	2	1	8	0	37	1	0	2	.430	.3
Villalobos, Carlos, Lancaster	.292	111	474	415	69	121	167	21	5	5	63	2	3	4	50	0	89	9	4	9	.402	.3
Wallach, Tim, San Bernardino	.300	5	22	20	3	6	9	0	0	1	6	0	0	0	2	0	7	0	0	0	.450	.3
Wathan, Dusty, Lancaster†	.260	74	282	246	41	64	100	10	1	8	40	3	1	6	26	0	65	1	1	5	.407	.3
Watkins, Sean, Rancho C.*	.273	97	431	363	57	99	146	21	4	6	51	0	5	7	56	0	104	0	2	11	.402	.3
Watts, Josh, Bak.-Lan.*	.278	55	227	205	30	57	89	7	2	7	34	0	1	0	21	1	53	4	3	3	.434	.3
Weaver, Terry, San Jose	.214	6	15	14	1	3	3	0	0	0	0	0	0	0	1	0	1	0	0	0	.214	.2
White, Derrick, Modesto	.294	54	233	197	45	58	96	15	1	7	39	0	3	4	29	1	41	8	3	1	.487	.3
Williams, Drew, Stockton*	.305	112	507	433	78	132	238	28	3	24	85	0	6	4	64	4	86	8	8	12	.550	.3
Wilson, Todd, San Jose	.305	90	344	318	50	97	132	18	1	5	40	4	1	3	18	0	47	3	2	10	.415	.3
Wingate, Ervan, San Bern.	.324	115	431	383	60	124	176	16	0	12	55	4	6	6	32	1	75	7	9	7	.460	.3
Wolff, Mike, Lake Elsinore	.286	12	51	42	12	12	21	3	0	2	7	0	0	0	9	0	10	3	0	1	.500	.4
Wolger, Michael, Bakersfield*	.000	1	3	3	0	0	0	0	0	0	0	0	0	0	0	0	1	0	0	0	.000	.0
Woodridge, Dickie, Rancho C.*	.298	36	171	141	32	42	58	4	3	2	23	0	1	5	24	1	14	1	0	3	.411	.4
Young, Kevin, Lake Elsinore	.290	114	527	462	78	134	163	17	3	2	39	7	4	4	50	0	58	24	14	8	.353	.3
Zancanaro, Dave, Modesto†	.000	20	2	2	0	0	0	0	0	0	0	0	0	0	0	0	0	0	0	0	.000	.0

GRAND SLAMS: Fernandez, Kirgan, Rennhack, S. Smith, 2; Bogle, Bonds, Brinkley, J. Castro, J. Clifford, Collier, Cromer, Curtis, E. Davis, Espinal, Garcia, Hemph[ill] Kliner, Lanza, Marine, Ja. Martin, M. Moore, Takayoshi, Urso, Van Burkleo, 1 each.

AWARDED FIRST BASE ON CATCHER'S INTERFERENCE: Lemonis 5 (DeBoer, Galarza, Hemphill, T. Johnson, Mayes); Clifford 4 (DelaRosa, Hemphill, Mikes[?] Takayoshi); Moultrie 4 (DelaRosa 2, Marine, Newstrom); Kliner 3 (DelaRosa 2, Marine); Galarza 2 (T. Johnson, Marine); Bentley (Hemphill); Guzman (Wathan); Hod[?] (Ardoin); Klassen (DelaRosa); Kominek (DeBoer); Luzinski (Newstrom); D. Smith (Ardoin).

PLAYERS WITH TWO OR MORE TEAMS

Player, Team	Avg.	G	TPA	AB	R	H	TB	2B	3B	HR	RBI	SH	SF	HP	BB	IBB	SO	SB	CS	GDP	Slg.	O
Carroll, Doug, Bakersfield*	.298	58	249	215	35	64	106	17	2	7	39	1	3	3	27	1	53	3	2	3	.493	.3
Carroll, Doug, Lancaster*	.261	32	126	111	20	29	48	4	0	5	14	0	3	12	1	30	0	0	2	.432	.3	
Eaddy, Keith, High Desert	.080	12	26	25	1	2	2	0	0	0	0	0	0	1	0	0	7	2	1	1	.080	.1
Eaddy, Keith, Rancho Cuca.	.221	40	124	104	13	23	39	5	1	3	10	1	0	1	18	0	41	1	3	1	.375	.3
Harmer, Frank, Bakersfield†	.179	28	78	67	6	12	14	2	0	0	4	2	1	0	8	0	16	0	1	3	.209	.2
Harmer, Frank, High Desert†	.242	36	119	95	20	23	37	5	0	3	16	2	0	0	22	0	25	1	0	2	.389	.3
Hendricks, Ryan, H. Desert*	.241	14	37	29	3	7	9	2	0	0	4	2	0	1	5	0	11	1	0	1	.310	.3
Hendricks, Ryan, Bakersfield*	.160	30	108	94	13	15	25	1	0	3	8	0	1	1	12	0	31	1	0	1	.266	.2
Herider, Jeremy, Visalia†	.234	49	179	145	22	34	43	6	0	1	14	0	0	1	33	1	36	2	6	3	.297	.3
Herider, Jeremy, Rancho C.*	.196	29	135	107	18	21	25	4	0	0	12	1	0	1	26	0	32	1	1	2	.234	.3
Rosario, Melvin, R. Cuca.†	.273	10	36	33	7	9	21	3	0	3	10	0	0	3	0	8	1	0	0	.636	.3	
Rosario, Melvin, High Desert†	.319	42	193	163	35	52	93	9	1	10	34	0	0	9	21	0	45	4	0	3	.571	.4
Watts, Josh, Bakersfield*	.313	34	146	134	24	42	68	6	1	6	23	0	0	12	1	36	2	2	2	.507	.3	
Watts, Josh, Lancaster*	.211	21	81	71	6	15	21	1	1	1	11	0	1	0	9	0	17	2	1	1	.296	.2

1996 PITCHING

TEAM

Team	W	L	Pct.	ERA	G	CG	ShO	Sv.	IP	H	TBF	R	ER	HR	SH	SF	HB	BB	IBB	SO	WP	Bk
San Jose	89	51	.636	3.54	140	4	16	40	1262.1	1154	5393	594	497	76	53	34	68	494	12	1236	101	10
Modesto	82	58	.586	4.22	140	0	6	39	1251.0	1318	5507	749	587	100	38	35	70	487	8	1048	89	17
Lancaster	71	69	.507	4.24	140	5	3	36	1241.0	1301	5488	747	585	124	40	45	74	504	13	1070	96	16
Lake Elsinore	75	65	.536	4.25	140	7	5	28	1250.0	1292	5445	717	590	111	44	54	64	469	5	1111	72	21
Stockton	79	61	.564	4.27	140	6	4	39	1228.0	1244	5345	686	582	113	42	33	60	497	9	995	69	18
R. Cucamonga	69	71	.493	4.80	140	1	4	30	1229.0	1381	5525	775	655	119	47	46	87	513	8	1112	98	13
San Bernardino	70	70	.500	5.04	140	1	3	45	1248.1	1282	5739	864	699	109	42	40	74	738	15	1165	131	22
Visalia	50	90	.357	5.47	140	2	1	26	1241.2	1467	5697	926	755	148	44	55	68	566	17	936	116	15
High Desert	76	64	.543	5.54	140	3	3	29	1244.2	1372	5709	881	766	153	44	49	63	702	28	965	138	28
Bakersfield	39	101	.279	6.77	140	11	1	20	1238.1	1599	6034	1138	931	172	49	58	66	746	4	1008	129	14

INDIVIDUAL

TOP QUALIFIERS FOR EARNED-RUN AVERAGE TITLE

Minimum 112 innings. *Lefthanded pitcher.

Pitcher, Team	W	L	Pct.	ERA	G	GS	CG	ShO	GF	Sv.	IP	H	TBF	R	ER	HR	SH	SF	HB	BB	IBB	SO	WP	B
Blood, Darin, San Jose	17	6	.739	2.65	27	25	2	2	0	0	170.0	140	717	59	50	4	5	2	10	71	0	193	26	
Oropesa, Eddie, San Bern.*	11	6	.647	3.34	33	19	0	0	2	1	156.1	133	669	74	58	8	1	3	6	77	1	133	8	
Rector, Bobby, San Jose	12	8	.600	3.59	28	26	1	0	1	0	165.1	161	694	77	66	14	4	5	8	40	0	145	4	
Woodard, Steve, Stockton	12	9	.571	4.02	28	28	3	0	0	0	181.1	201	762	89	81	14	4	6	3	33	1	142	7	
VanDeWeg, Ryan, Rancho Cuca.	9	6	.600	4.06	26	26	0	0	0	0	146.1	164	636	78	66	15	1	2	10	52	1	129	8	
Gardner, Scott, Stockton	10	8	.556	4.13	27	21	3	1	0	0	144.0	127	608	77	66	11	4	0	7	52	0	148	19	
Reyes, Dennis, San Bernardino*	11	12	.478	4.17	29	28	0	0	0	0	166.0	166	731	106	77	11	4	2	6	77	0	176	9	

tcher, Team	W	L	Pct.	ERA	G	GS	CG	ShO	GF	Sv.	IP	H	TBF	R	ER	HR	SH	SF	HB	BB	IBB	SO	WP	Bk.
rrisho, Matt, Lake Elsinore*	7	5	.583	4.20	21	18	1	1	1	0	128.2	131	565	72	60	9	8	7	7	58	0	97	5	4
oper, Brian, Lake Elsinore	7	9	.438	4.21	26	23	1	1	0	0	162.1	177	702	100	76	17	6	8	10	39	0	155	4	1
oude, Ken, Lancaster	15	4	.789	4.22	28	28	1	0	0	0	168.1	167	727	94	79	15	4	6	8	60	0	161	6	1
nchliffe, Brett, Lancaster	11	10	.524	4.24	27	26	0	0	0	0	163.1	179	731	105	77	19	6	5	9	64	1	146	10	1
ale, Carl, Modesto	8	2	.800	4.28	26	24	0	0	0	0	128.1	124	565	79	61	11	2	5	5	72	0	102	12	0
alters, Brett, R. Cucamonga	9	9	.500	4.32	24	24	0	0	0	0	135.1	150	575	73	65	16	10	6	7	39	0	89	1	0
oshiba, Takahisa, Visalia	8	6	.571	4.43	21	16	0	0	2	1	126.0	151	552	77	62	22	4	2	2	39	1	108	8	0
ntenot, Joe, San Jose	9	4	.692	4.44	26	23	0	0	1	0	144.0	137	642	87	71	7	10	6	11	74	0	124	13	1

DEPARTMENTAL LEADERS: W—Blood, 17; L—K. Davis, Knighton, Santana, 15; Pct.—Bailey, .818; G—Linares, 60; GS—several players tied at 28; CG—Oropeza, 4; ShO—Blood, 2; GF—Linares, Tuttle, 52; SV—Linares, 33; IP—Woodard, 181.1; H—Oldham, 224; TBF—Oldham, 774; R—Oldham, 187; ER—Oldham, 154; HR—Oropeza, 30; SH—Fontenot, Walters, 10; SF—Kelly, 11; HB—Davis, 18; BB—Oldham, 105; IBB—Olszewski, Tuttle, 5; SO—Blood, 193; WP—Blood, 26; BK—Santana, 6.

ALL PITCHERS
*Lefthanded pitcher.

tcher, Team	W	L	Pct.	ERA	G	GS	CG	ShO	GF	Sv.	IP	H	TBF	R	ER	HR	SH	SF	HB	BB	IBB	SO	WP	Bk.
rffa, Steve, Bakersfield*	5	6	.455	6.81	15	11	1	0	0	0	72.2	98	338	61	55	18	2	4	5	22	0	71	3	0
abineaux, Darrin, San Bern.	1	3	.250	14.29	5	5	0	0	0	0	17.0	34	97	27	27	3	0	0	0	14	0	16	3	0
ackowski, Lance, San Bern.	0	0	.000	18.00	1	0	0	0	1	0	1.0	2	7	2	2	0	0	0	1	2	0	0	2	0
ailey, Philip, San Jose*	9	2	.818	3.05	35	6	0	0	9	0	73.2	76	308	30	25	4	4	2	7	22	1	53	6	0
aker, Jason, San Bernardino	0	0	.000	45.00	1	0	0	0	0	0	1.0	1	9	5	5	1	0	1	0	4	0	0	0	0
aron, Jim, Rancho Cuca.*	6	3	.667	3.00	54	0	0	0	17	1	87.0	87	383	44	29	9	2	3	1	35	0	85	7	2
ates, Shawn, Bakersfield*	1	1	.500	12.60	4	0	0	0	2	0	5.0	13	32	8	7	0	2	0	1	4	0	1	1	0
azzani, Matt, Bakersfield	0	0	.000	3.97	5	0	0	0	5	0	11.1	14	51	5	5	3	2	0	1	3	0	1	0	0
eck, Chris, Lancaster	6	5	.545	3.53	23	11	0	0	4	1	86.2	90	381	45	34	7	3	4	2	43	3	57	5	1
eck, Greg, Stockton	9	11	.450	6.14	28	28	0	0	0	0	152.1	197	695	119	104	18	8	7	12	53	1	96	7	0
ood, Darin, San Jose	17	6	.739	2.65	27	25	2	2	0	0	170.0	140	717	59	50	4	5	2	10	71	0	193	26	2
onanno, Rob, Lake Elsinore	3	2	.600	2.20	13	2	0	0	9	1	32.2	34	131	11	8	0	1	1	1	10	1	34	1	0
osio, Chris, Lancaster	0	0	.000	1.13	2	2	0	0	0	0	8.0	6	31	3	1	0	0	2	0	0	0	7	0	0
ray, Chris, Bakersfield	0	2	.000	12.68	17	0	0	0	8	1	22.0	28	134	34	31	1	1	2	6	38	0	15	5	1
ewer, Brian, High Desert*	5	4	.556	5.16	18	13	0	0	1	0	75.0	77	345	53	43	8	4	4	4	48	0	57	11	2
own, Alvin, San Bernardino	2	4	.333	3.80	42	2	0	0	16	2	68.2	43	306	40	29	2	5	2	2	62	0	84	17	1
own, Dickie, Stockton	0	0	.000	5.68	5	0	0	0	0	0	6.1	9	31	5	4	1	0	0	1	4	0	7	0	0
ucci, Carmen, Rancho Cuca.	0	0	.000	9.00	1	0	0	0	1	0	1.0	3	5	1	1	0	0	0	0	0	0	1	2	0
urt, Chris, Stockton	0	0	.000	54.00	1	0	0	0	0	0	0.1	3	5	2	2	0	0	0	0	1	0	0	0	0
ush, Craig, Bakersfield	4	6	.400	4.98	41	0	0	0	28	8	72.1	84	332	44	40	8	4	2	3	36	0	80	5	0
ussa, Todd, Rancho Cuca.	0	1	.000	9.72	16	0	0	0	5	0	16.2	27	93	20	18	3	1	0	1	16	1	19	0	0
abrera, Jose, Bakersfield	2	2	.500	3.92	7	7	0	0	0	0	41.1	40	183	25	18	7	2	2	1	21	0	52	5	0
amacho, Lance, San Bernardino	4	5	.444	6.69	14	13	0	0	1	1	74.0	81	343	56	55	12	0	3	3	52	1	72	11	2
ana, Nelson, Stockton*	4	4	.500	4.44	29	0	0	0	13	2	52.2	47	239	30	26	4	7	2	1	36	2	36	2	2
andiotti, Tom, San Bernardino	0	1	.000	5.00	2	2	0	0	0	0	9.0	11	41	6	5	0	0	1	4	0	10	1	1	
aridad, Ron, Stockton	1	0	1.000	1.50	18	0	0	0	5	1	30.0	29	130	9	5	2	1	1	2	13	0	19	1	0
arroll, Doug, Lancaster	0	0	.000	12.46	4	0	0	0	4	0	4.1	12	25	6	6	1	0	1	0	4	0	4	2	0
astillo, Carlos, Lake Elsinore	2	3	.400	3.68	27	0	0	0	26	13	29.1	26	122	16	12	2	1	0	0	8	0	27	6	0
astillo, Aaron, Lake Elsinore	3	0	1.000	0.79	10	0	0	0	8	1	11.1	8	42	1	1	1	0	0	0	0	0	19	0	0
astro, Nelson, San Bernardino	2	4	.333	6.30	12	0	0	0	6	1	20.0	25	92	14	14	3	0	1	0	9	4	22	3	1
avez, Tony, Lake Elsinore	3	0	1.000	1.98	10	0	0	0	8	4	13.2	8	53	4	3	0	0	0	3	3	0	16	0	0
ayton, Craig, Rancho Cuca.	2	3	.400	4.76	11	3	0	0	2	0	28.1	34	127	18	15	4	0	0	2	8	0	29	5	0
ement, Matt, Rancho Cuca.	4	5	.444	5.59	11	11	0	0	0	0	56.1	61	261	40	35	8	5	3	9	26	0	75	5	1
ifford, Eric, Lancaster	0	0	.000	5.25	11	0	0	0	5	1	24.0	21	99	14	14	2	0	4	4	5	0	11	4	0
oude, Ken, Lancaster	15	4	.789	4.22	28	28	1	0	0	0	168.1	167	727	94	79	15	4	6	8	60	0	161	6	1
ochrane, Chris, Modesto	5	4	.556	4.00	21	10	0	0	2	0	74.1	74	314	38	33	6	3	1	1	21	2	68	2	2
onnelly, Steven, Modesto	4	7	.364	3.76	52	0	0	0	42	14	64.2	58	283	33	27	5	1	1	5	32	1	65	5	2
ooper, Brian, Lake Elsinore	7	9	.438	4.21	26	23	1	1	0	0	162.1	177	702	100	76	17	6	8	10	39	0	155	4	1
orsi, Jim, Modesto	0	0	.000	0.00	1	1	0	0	0	0	1.0	0	3	0	0	0	0	0	0	0	0	2	0	0
ills, Brad, High Desert	2	4	.333	4.68	14	14	1	0	0	0	77.0	79	332	45	40	10	2	2	5	26	3	45	3	1
aedelow, Craig, Bakersfield	0	0	.000	9.00	1	0	0	0	1	0	1.0	3	6	1	1	0	0	0	0	0	0	1	0	0
aigle, Tim, High Desert*	1	0	1.000	9.82	4	0	0	0	2	0	3.2	7	19	4	4	1	0	0	0	1	0	2	1	0
ale, Carl, Modesto	8	2	.800	4.28	26	24	0	0	0	0	128.1	124	565	79	61	11	2	5	5	72	0	102	12	0
alton, Brian, Stock.-Vis.	1	2	.333	5.84	19	0	0	0	6	0	37.0	38	172	25	24	7	1	1	1	29	0	28	6	1
Amico, Jeffrey, Modesto	0	0	.000	18.00	1	0	0	0	0	0	1.0	3	7	3	2	0	0	0	1	0	0	0	0	0
aniels, John, Lancaster	3	5	.375	3.30	43	0	0	0	23	6	95.1	91	412	51	35	9	3	2	8	30	1	100	3	0
arley, Ned, High Desert	2	1	.667	6.38	30	1	0	0	12	1	42.1	44	196	34	30	4	2	3	3	29	2	34	8	0
avis, Eddie, San Bernardino	0	0	.000	20.25	1	0	0	0	0	0	1.1	4	13	7	3	0	0	0	0	4	0	3	0	0
avis, Keith, Rancho Cuca.	6	15	.286	5.75	28	28	0	0	0	0	153.1	180	719	119	98	14	3	6	18	78	0	123	18	2
eakman, Josh, Lake Elsinore	8	10	.444	5.02	27	25	2	0	0	0	163.0	188	734	109	91	16	3	1	13	56	1	115	14	3
ean, Greg, High Desert	10	7	.588	4.36	37	12	0	0	10	3	105.1	110	493	68	51	5	4	1	8	71	2	76	23	1
eLaCruz, Fernando, L Elsinore	0	0	.000	8.59	5	0	0	0	3	0	7.1	8	40	12	7	2	0	0	1	10	0	3	2	1
eLucia, Rich, San Jose	0	0	.000	2.45	5	4	0	0	0	0	7.1	5	28	2	2	0	0	0	3	0	0	11	0	0
ennis, Shane, Rancho Cuca.*	4	2	.667	3.20	9	9	1	0	0	0	59.0	57	247	22	21	6	1	1	1	19	0	54	2	0
eskins, Casey, San Bern.*	3	3	.500	6.07	12	7	0	0	0	0	43.0	61	198	38	29	5	3	1	0	12	0	26	2	0
xon, Bubba, Rancho Cuca.*	1	0	1.000	7.16	11	0	0	0	3	0	16.1	20	73	16	13	3	0	1	0	4	0	20	1	0
orneweerd, Dave, L. Elsinore	1	0	1.000	6.00	11	2	0	0	2	0	21.0	23	105	17	14	3	1	1	2	18	0	24	2	0
ysdale, Brooks, Stockton	6	1	.857	5.13	35	0	0	0	9	0	59.2	61	266	35	34	10	2	2	4	28	1	61	3	0
uffy, Ryan, Visalia*	0	0	.000	9.00	6	0	0	0	2	0	15.1	16	60	3	2	0	0	2	6	0	9	1	0	
dwards, Wayne, Bakersfield*	0	2	.000	10.80	3	2	0	0	1	0	18.1	38	108	30	22	4	1	0	1	13	0	13	2	0
oey, Scott, High Desert	1	0	1.000	8.49	11	0	0	0	3	0	11.2	17	65	16	11	0	0	1	0	10	2	7	2	0
chhorn, Mark, Lake Elsinore	1	0	1.000	4.70	12	4	0	0	1	0	15.1	16	60	8	8	1	2	1	0	2	0	21	0	0
dos, Todd, Rancho Cuca.	3	3	.500	3.74	55	0	0	0	41	17	67.1	63	305	33	28	2	7	6	3	37	3	82	6	0
trada, Horacio, Stockton*	1	3	.250	4.59	29	0	0	0	11	3	51.0	43	214	29	26	7	1	1	2	21	2	62	3	0
lkenborg, Brian, High Desert	0	0	.000	0.00	1	0	0	0	0	0	1.0	1	3	0	0	0	0	0	0	0	0	1	0	0

CLASS A California League

Pitcher, Team	W	L	Pct.	ERA	G	GS	CG	ShO	GF	Sv.	IP	H	TBF	R	ER	HR	SH	SF	HB	BB	IBB	SO	WP	Bk
Fontenot, Joe, San Jose	9	4	.692	4.44	26	23	0	0	1	0	144.0	137	642	87	71	7	10	6	11	74	0	124	13	
Foster, Kris, San Bernardino	3	5	.375	3.86	30	8	0	0	9	2	81.2	66	355	46	35	5	3	4	3	54	3	78	10	
Fultz, Aaron, San Jose*	9	5	.643	3.96	36	12	0	0	11	1	104.2	101	460	52	46	7	9	3	8	54	2	103	13	
Gardner, Mark, San Jose	0	0	.000	3.18	1	1	0	0	0	0	5.2	4	21	2	2	0	1	0	0	0	0	7	0	
Gardner, Scott, Stockton	10	8	.556	4.13	27	21	3	1	0	0	144.0	127	608	77	66	11	4	0	7	52	0	148	19	
Garrett, Hal, Rancho Cuca.	4	1	.800	1.94	24	1	0	0	3	0	51.0	41	214	12	11	3	1	2	3	20	0	56	6	
Gaspar, Cade, Rancho Cuca.	7	4	.636	5.05	24	19	0	0	2	0	112.1	121	502	69	63	13	3	3	8	50	0	106	11	
Goedhart, Darrell, Lake Elsinore	2	1	.667	1.35	4	2	0	0	2	0	13.1	17	59	6	2	0	0	0	0	4	0	12	0	
Goldsmith, Gary, Visalia	10	11	.476	4.98	28	27	0	0	0	0	170.0	188	752	108	94	23	4	10	7	76	1	120	2	
Gomez, Dennys, Bak.-S.J.	4	1	.800	5.44	32	0	0	0	13	0	51.1	52	239	39	31	2	0	3	9	28	0	38	7	
Gomez, Javier, Visalia	1	3	.250	3.68	22	0	0	0	4	0	36.2	32	163	17	15	3	1	1	4	18	1	40	1	
Gould, Clint, Bak.-Lan.	3	2	.600	3.38	26	0	0	0	15	2	34.2	36	165	23	13	0	1	0	2	19	1	18	4	
Granger, Greg, Visalia	2	0	1.000	4.87	4	4	0	0	0	0	20.1	24	95	12	11	1	0	0	3	10	0	13	3	
Green, Blake, Bakersfield	0	1	.000	16.20	1	1	0	0	0	0	1.2	0	12	4	3	0	0	0	0	8	0	1	2	
Hacen, Abraham, High Desert	0	0	.000	32.40	3	0	0	0	0	0	3.1	12	29	13	12	4	0	0	0	7	0	2	1	
Hackett, Jason, High Desert*	0	0	.000	4.70	5	0	0	0	0	0	7.2	9	43	4	4	0	0	0	0	15	0	4	1	
Hammerschmidt, Andy, R. C.*	6	4	.600	5.25	35	7	0	0	6	2	82.1	102	366	59	48	6	3	3	5	20	1	59	3	
Harmer, Frank, High Desert	0	0	.000	1.80	4	0	0	0	3	0	5.0	3	18	1	1	1	0	0	0	0	0	4	0	
Harper, David, Visalia	0	0	.000	19.73	12	0	0	0	3	0	8.2	15	52	19	19	3	1	0	2	10	0	5	0	
Harris, Bryan, Lake Elsinore*	0	7	.000	4.38	20	2	0	0	7	0	37.0	29	164	20	18	3	3	3	2	26	1	31	5	
Harris, Greg W., Rancho Cuca.	1	3	.250	5.94	13	4	0	0	3	0	33.1	44	158	28	22	5	0	2	4	11	0	34	2	
Hartvigson, Chad, San Jose*	4	7	.364	3.23	36	10	0	0	7	2	103.0	94	427	46	37	10	1	4	1	30	0	114	4	
Hause, Brendan, Modesto*	0	0	.000	13.50	1	0	0	0	0	0	2.0	4	12	3	3	1	0	0	1	1	0	2	1	
Haynes, Heath, Lake Elsinore	5	1	.833	1.64	31	0	0	0	11	2	38.1	29	142	9	7	1	1	0	3	2	0	44	1	
Henderson, Juan, Lake Elsinore	0	0	.000	18.00	1	0	0	0	1	0	1.0	3	6	2	2	0	1	0	0	0	0	0	0	
Henderson, Kenny, R. Cuca.	1	1	.500	5.71	4	4	0	0	0	0	17.1	19	81	14	11	1	1	3	2	10	0	14	0	
Herider, Jeremy, Bakersfield	0	0	.000	9.00	1	0	0	0	0	0	2.0	5	15	6	2	0	0	0	0	3	0	0	1	
Hermanson, Mike, Lake Elsinore	0	3	.000	4.11	29	0	0	0	11	0	35.0	40	166	25	16	6	0	1	2	22	0	30	3	
Hernandez, Jeremy, Visalia	2	9	.182	5.96	24	15	0	0	3	0	102.2	133	471	89	68	15	3	2	3	30	0	88	8	
Hill, Jason, Lake Elsinore	4	3	.571	2.50	32	0	0	0	8	0	39.2	39	167	16	11	4	1	0	2	14	0	28	0	
Hill, Tyrone, Stockton*	0	2	.000	5.03	5	5	0	0	0	0	19.2	18	87	14	11	1	0	0	0	9	1	11	0	
Hinchliffe, Brett, Lancaster	11	10	.524	4.24	27	26	0	0	0	0	163.1	179	731	105	77	19	6	5	9	64	1	146	10	
Holden, Jason, Modesto	0	0	.000	13.50	1	0	0	0	0	0	2.0	5	12	3	3	1	0	0	2	0	0	1	0	
Holdridge, David, Lake Elsinore	0	0	.000	2.08	12	0	0	0	12	6	13.0	11	53	3	3	1	0	0	1	2	0	21	0	
Hollinger, Adrian, Lake Elsinore	1	0	1.000	1.56	12	0	0	0	4	0	17.1	15	77	6	3	1	1	1	1	11	0	15	1	
Holzemer, Mark, Lake Elsinore*	0	1	.000	2.38	9	3	0	0	2	0	11.1	10	47	3	3	0	0	0	1	4	0	10	0	
Hommel, Brian, Stockton*	0	0	.000	0.00	4	0	0	0	1	0	5.0	2	21	1	0	0	1	0	0	4	0	4	0	
Hoshiba, Takahisa, Visalia	8	6	.571	4.43	21	16	0	0	2	1	126.0	151	552	77	62	22	4	2	2	39	1	108	8	
Hritz, Derrick, Bakersfield*	4	6	.400	5.86	31	7	0	0	14	2	81.1	100	386	68	53	10	6	4	0	50	1	60	5	
Huber, Jeff, Stockton*	1	1	.500	1.83	18	0	0	0	13	6	19.2	24	84	9	4	0	0	2	1	3	0	12	0	
Huntsman, Brandon, H. Desert	1	3	.250	9.55	13	2	0	0	2	0	27.1	36	142	29	29	6	2	1	3	27	1	25	1	
Huntsman, Scott, Stockton	4	3	.571	2.79	43	0	0	0	29	12	48.1	37	213	21	15	3	0	3	2	27	0	56	2	
Ito, Makoto, Visalia*	0	1	.000	3.94	34	0	0	0	8	0	32.0	34	139	16	14	1	3	0	0	12	2	26	1	
Jimenez, Miguel, Modesto	7	1	.875	4.58	13	12	0	0	0	0	70.2	87	320	40	36	6	0	2	1	28	0	75	10	
Johnson, Carl, Visalia	3	5	.375	15.55	15	5	0	0	3	0	22.0	35	137	44	38	5	1	2	3	35	0	16	11	
Johnson, Todd, Bakersfield	1	1	.500	5.30	21	1	0	0	16	3	35.2	54	174	28	21	8	2	1	4	13	1	27	1	
Jordan, Jason, Visalia	6	10	.375	4.85	30	20	1	0	2	0	144.2	175	650	89	78	14	5	6	6	54	2	110	17	
Karsay, Steve, Modesto	0	1	.000	2.65	14	14	0	0	0	0	34.0	35	141	16	10	2	0	0	3	1	0	31	3	
Keling, Korey, Lake Elsinore	0	1	.000	6.60	10	2	0	0	2	0	15.0	21	77	15	11	2	1	3	0	14	0	10	0	
Kell, Rob, Bakersfield*	5	3	.625	3.78	13	13	1	1	0	0	88.0	94	376	43	37	6	2	0	3	22	0	103	3	
Kelly, John, Visalia	2	10	.167	7.13	19	18	1	0	1	1	96.0	115	475	100	76	10	5	11	13	63	1	89	16	
Kenady, Jake, San Bernardino*	2	3	.400	6.40	45	0	0	0	12	0	70.1	83	375	65	50	6	4	2	9	68	3	81	10	
Keppen, Jeffrey, San Bernardino	3	1	.750	5.82	24	1	0	0	7	0	55.2	56	274	44	36	3	0	1	5	46	0	45	11	
King, Bill, Modesto	16	4	.800	4.75	29	27	0	0	1	1	163.0	193	716	102	86	11	3	8	8	40	0	100	8	
Kirgan, Chris, High Desert*	0	0	.000	7.20	4	0	0	0	3	0	5.0	8	27	4	4	2	0	1	0	4	0	3	1	
Knighton, Toure, Bakersfield	5	15	.250	6.54	25	24	1	0	0	0	150.0	197	705	134	109	18	5	7	4	67	1	108	18	
Kramer, Jeff, Stockton	6	4	.600	4.42	15	7	0	0	2	0	59.0	62	272	43	29	4	2	1	4	31	0	46	6	
Langston, Mark, Lake Elsinore	0	0	.000	0.00	1	1	0	0	0	0	4.0	3	13	0	0	0	0	0	0	0	0	5	0	
Lehman, Toby, High Desert	1	2	.333	6.46	6	5	0	0	0	0	23.2	24	112	19	17	1	1	1	1	22	0	18	3	
Lemke, Steve, Modesto	4	5	.444	5.68	12	6	0	0	1	0	44.1	65	209	34	28	2	2	2	3	17	0	29	2	
Linares, Rich, San Bernardino	4	3	.571	3.36	60	0	0	0	52	33	61.2	59	266	30	23	2	2	1	6	19	0	59	2	
Logan, Chris, Rancho Cuca.	5	2	.714	4.90	53	0	0	0	26	6	71.2	80	322	44	39	4	3	3	4	36	1	56	9	
Lukasiewicz, Mark, Bakersfield*	0	2	.000	9.24	7	0	0	0	3	0	12.2	17	66	14	13	2	1	0	1	11	0	9	1	
Maine, Dalton, Bak.-H.D.	3	3	.500	2.88	33	2	0	0	24	8	59.1	50	249	27	19	5	2	2	1	16	0	67	6	
Marenghi, Matt, High Desert	9	7	.563	5.85	33	23	1	0	3	1	170.2	205	750	119	111	27	3	4	6	54	1	114	9	
Martin, Jeff, San Jose	2	4	.333	4.62	42	0	0	0	17	3	60.1	52	268	36	31	4	4	3	4	29	3	54	6	
McDonald, Matt, San Bern.*	0	0	.000	12.00	4	0	0	0	1	0	9.0	14	53	14	12	3	0	1	0	12	0	11	1	
McGonigle, Bill, Stockton	0	0	.000	15.00	3	0	0	0	3	0	3.0	7	17	5	5	2	0	0	0	2	0	1	1	
Michalak, Chris, Modesto*	2	2	.500	3.03	21	0	0	0	13	4	38.2	37	173	21	13	4	0	2	2	17	0	39	0	
Montane, Ivan, Lancaster	2	2	.500	3.64	11	11	0	0	0	0	59.1	57	273	37	24	2	5	3	2	43	0	54	9	
Montgomery, Steve, H. Desert	5	6	.455	5.27	44	3	0	0	17	2	71.2	85	331	54	42	8	0	2	8	34	3	79	7	
Moore, Trey, Lancaster*	7	5	.583	4.10	15	15	2	0	0	0	94.1	106	413	57	43	10	2	0	7	31	0	77	7	
Moore, Vince, Rancho Cuca.*	0	0	.000	9.00	1	0	0	0	1	0	1.0	2	5	1	1	0	0	0	0	0	0	0	0	
Moreno, Claudio, San Bern.	1	2	.333	7.82	6	6	0	0	0	0	25.1	41	132	28	22	1	3	1	1	9	0	27	1	
Morgan, Eric, Lancaster	0	1	.000	4.26	10	0	0	0	3	1	12.2	13	64	7	6	2	1	1	3	12	0	5	0	
Mullins, Greg, Stockton*	0	0	.000	3.97	10	0	0	0	3	1	11.1	13	51	5	5	0	0	0	1	4	0	12	0	
Myers, Jason, San Jose*	8	7	.533	4.89	33	16	1	1	10	1	119.2	140	529	74	65	10	3	2	3	38	1	82	7	
Nartker, Mike, Visalia	1	1	.500	6.75	3	3	0	0	0	0	12.0	22	64	10	9	3	0	0	0	7	0	11	4	
Neill, Mike, Modesto*	0	0	.000	18.00	1	0	0	0	1	0	1.0	0	7	2	2	0	0	0	0	5	0	0	1	
Nelson, Chris, Modesto	3	5	.375	5.40	14	13	0	0	0	0	63.1	86	292	50	38	7	1	3	4	17	0	62	6	
Niemeier, Todd, Lancaster*	0	2	.000	4.65	41	0	0	0	12	0	40.2	42	194	30	21	2	3	0	2	30	2	30	3	
Novoa, Rafael, Lake Elsinore*	2	2	.500	4.39	16	0	0	0	5	1	26.2	29	118	14	13	6	2	1	0	12	1	31	2	

Pitcher, Team	W	L	Pct.	ERA	G	GS	CG	ShO	GF	Sv.	IP	H	TBF	R	ER	HR	SH	SF	HB	BB	IBB	SO	WP	Bk.
unez, Vladimir, Visalia	1	6	.143	5.43	12	10	0	0	0	0	53.0	64	233	45	32	10	1	3	3	17	0	37	3	2
dell, Jacob, Modesto	1	0	1.000	5.40	1	1	0	0	0	0	5.0	6	22	4	3	1	0	1	0	4	0	4	0	1
ldham, Bob, Bakersfield	2	10	.167	9.69	41	17	0	0	6	0	143.0	224	774	187	154	25	3	9	9	105	0	107	19	0
lszewski, Tim, High Desert	6	3	.667	6.61	49	0	0	0	16	0	64.0	78	307	53	47	5	3	5	3	41	5	38	2	3
ntiveros, Steve, Lake Elsinore..	1	1	.500	2.25	2	2	0	0	0	0	8.0	12	35	3	2	0	0	0	0	0	0	8	1	0
ropesa, Eddie, San Bern.*	11	6	.647	3.34	33	19	0	0	2	1	156.1	133	669	74	58	8	1	3	6	77	1	133	8	4
ropeza, Igor, Bakersfield	1	14	.067	6.80	23	21	4	0	1	0	137.2	160	641	113	104	30	3	7	9	92	0	94	15	1
rtiz, Russ, San Jose	0	0	.000	0.25	34	0	0	0	31	23	36.2	16	145	2	1	0	0	0	2	20	0	63	0	0
almer, Brett, Bakersfield*	2	6	.250	7.42	12	11	2	0	0	0	60.2	91	317	63	50	8	3	3	4	45	0	37	5	1
aluk, Jeff, San Bernardino	4	3	.571	5.06	50	0	0	0	21	5	69.1	79	318	47	39	11	5	3	2	31	1	70	5	2
asqualicchio, Michael, Stcktn*.	3	3	.500	3.53	18	17	0	0	0	0	71.1	67	307	35	28	3	1	0	2	36	0	69	2	4
earce, Jeff, Lancaster*	0	0	.000	2.08	21	0	0	0	4	0	21.2	13	102	7	5	0	0	0	5	23	1	17	4	2
ena, Alex, Visalia	1	3	.250	5.73	44	2	0	0	14	0	70.2	94	334	53	45	8	3	6	1	31	3	30	4	0
ennington, Brad, Lk Elsinore*..	0	0	.000	0.00	2	2	0	0	0	0	3.0	0	11	0	0	0	0	0	0	2	0	5	0	0
erez, Juan, Modesto*	2	4	.333	5.02	38	8	0	0	15	4	98.2	120	445	68	55	12	5	3	2	34	0	89	5	1
erisho, Matt, Lake Elsinore*	7	5	.583	4.20	21	18	1	1	1	0	128.2	131	565	72	60	9	8	7	7	58	0	97	5	4
erpetuo, Nelson, Bakersfield* ..	0	0	.000	5.75	8	7	0	0	0	0	40.2	35	203	31	26	0	3	3	7	38	0	45	4	0
incavitch, Kevin, San Bern.	8	8	.500	4.88	20	17	0	0	2	0	101.1	95	479	66	55	10	3	3	16	75	1	79	23	4
rice, Tom, San Bernardino*	5	3	.625	3.84	15	11	1	0	1	0	82.0	94	344	42	35	8	5	1	3	5	0	60	1	0
rieto, Ariel, Modesto	0	0	.000	3.00	2	1	0	0	1	1	9.0	9	38	4	3	0	0	0	1	2	0	8	2	0
adinsky, Scott, San Bern.*	0	0	.000	2.08	3	0	0	0	0	0	4.1	2	17	1	1	0	0	0	0	2	0	4	0	0
ajotte, Jason, Modesto*	3	6	.333	2.52	47	0	0	0	29	7	75.0	50	295	24	21	4	1	0	2	28	2	57	1	0
aleigh, Matt, High Desert	0	0	.000	67.50	1	0	0	0	0	0	0.2	6	9	7	5	2	0	0	0	1	0	1	1	0
ector, Bobby, San Jose	12	8	.600	3.59	28	26	1	0	1	0	165.1	161	694	77	66	14	4	5	8	43	0	145	4	0
eed, Dan, Bak.-H.D.*	6	4	.600	4.90	37	13	0	0	4	0	119.1	136	541	80	65	11	5	2	2	58	1	91	2	1
eich, Steve, High Desert*	0	0	.000	10.80	2	2	0	0	0	0	6.2	14	37	11	8	2	0	0	2	0	0	3	0	0
eyes, Dennis, San Bernardino*	11	12	.478	4.17	29	28	0	0	0	0	166.0	166	731	106	77	11	4	2	6	77	0	176	9	3
hodes, Joe, High Desert	5	9	.357	5.11	25	21	0	0	1	0	123.1	133	564	85	70	13	4	10	2	66	1	81	11	2
odriguez, Larry, Visalia	2	5	.286	5.24	13	10	0	0	0	0	56.2	72	265	49	33	8	2	1	3	19	1	37	5	0
uch, Rob, Visalia	2	7	.222	4.13	37	5	0	0	14	3	96.0	94	424	57	44	5	3	4	2	47	0	75	19	2
union, Tony, Bakersfield	0	6	.000	11.36	7	6	1	0	0	0	35.2	61	197	56	45	5	2	2	3	27	0	20	9	0
adler, Al, Stockton	1	2	.333	2.70	18	0	0	0	17	7	20.0	12	79	7	6	3	1	0	0	7	0	19	1	0
ak, James, R. Cucamonga	0	3	.000	6.32	4	4	0	0	0	0	15.2	21	78	13	11	2	1	0	2	12	0	14	0	0
alazar, Luis, Stockton	3	2	.600	3.49	44	0	0	0	27	6	56.2	46	227	23	22	9	2	5	2	16	1	34	3	0
alazar, Mike, Visalia	0	0	.000	5.40	6	4	0	0	1	0	25.0	31	116	19	15	1	1	2	3	11	0	14	1	0
anchez, Mike, San Bernardino..	0	0	.000	8.22	11	0	0	0	2	0	23.0	23	124	30	21	2	2	3	2	28	1	29	6	1
anderson, Scott, Lake Elsinore.	1	0	1.000	3.00	1	1	0	0	0	0	3.0	8	26	3	2	0	0	0	0	4	0	0	0	0
aneaux, Francisco, High Desert	4	5	.444	5.56	20	19	0	0	0	0	102.0	98	474	71	63	13	4	0	7	91	4	101	17	2
antana, Marino, Lancaster	8	15	.348	5.03	28	28	1	0	0	0	157.1	164	688	105	88	26	5	8	8	57	0	167	18	6
auritch, Chris, High Desert	4	1	.800	5.68	35	0	0	0	11	0	52.1	52	244	33	33	10	2	6	4	33	2	41	6	3
chlutt, Jason, R. Cucamonga* .	0	0	.000	5.63	7	0	0	0	3	0	8.0	10	34	5	5	2	0	1	0	2	0	6	4	0
chmitt, Todd, R. Cucamonga	0	1	.000	6.75	7	0	0	0	7	4	6.2	6	33	6	5	1	1	1	4	3	0	8	1	1
choeneweis, Scott, L Elsinore*	8	3	.727	3.94	14	12	0	0	1	0	93.2	86	387	47	41	6	3	2	2	27	0	83	2	1
chramm, Carl, San Jose	7	3	.700	3.45	39	0	0	0	10	1	70.1	64	303	31	27	5	8	0	5	25	1	66	4	1
eaver, Mark, High Desert	2	1	.667	3.42	4	4	0	0	0	0	23.2	19	99	12	9	1	1	0	1	10	0	16	6	1
ebach, Kyle, Lake Elsinore	8	4	.667	5.58	26	13	0	0	5	0	109.2	124	477	73	68	15	1	7	4	31	0	105	2	0
ellner, Aaron, Bak.-H.D.	0	3	.000	7.68	20	0	0	0	8	0	34.0	44	175	41	29	6	2	3	2	25	0	31	8	1
haw, Curtis, Modesto*	10	5	.667	3.77	39	10	0	0	11	1	107.1	101	481	63	45	5	8	2	10	63	0	89	9	2
ick, David, Lake Elsinore	1	0	1.000	7.15	16	0	0	0	3	1	22.2	25	112	19	18	2	0	1	5	14	1	17	1	0
kes, Ken, San Bernardino	6	3	.667	4.81	17	17	0	0	0	0	91.2	89	410	58	49	12	2	6	4	56	0	65	2	2
lva, Luis, Modesto	0	0	.000	0.00	1	0	0	0	0	0	1.0	0	4	0	0	0	0	0	0	1	0	1	0	0
kuse, Nicholas, Lake Elsinore...	0	3	.000	6.47	6	6	0	0	0	0	32.0	36	155	27	23	1	6	3	0	22	0	18	7	2
mith, Hut, High Desert	3	4	.429	5.36	10	7	1	0	0	0	50.1	59	216	34	30	7	1	1	3	16	0	34	6	3
mith, Lee, Lake Elsinore	0	0	.000	9.00	1	1	0	0	0	0	1.0	1	5	2	1	0	0	1	0	1	0	1	1	0
mith, Travis, Stockton	6	1	.857	1.84	14	6	0	0	3	1	58.2	56	241	17	12	4	1	0	4	21	0	48	2	4
nyder, Matt, High Desert	6	2	.750	3.75	58	0	0	0	49	20	72.0	60	317	34	30	6	5	2	1	38	2	93	9	1
oden, Chad, Lancaster	0	1	.000	10.64	9	0	0	0	1	0	11.0	17	59	14	13	1	1	0	0	9	1	8	1	0
outhall, Pete, Visalia	1	1	.500	9.17	32	0	0	0	26	0	54.0	83	273	64	55	7	3	3	7	27	0	26	7	0
owards, Ryan, San Bernardino.	0	1	.000	60.75	1	1	0	0	0	0	1.1	6	14	9	9	1	0	0	1	4	0	0	2	0
teed, David, San Bernardino	0	0	.000	4.50	2	0	0	0	1	0	2.0	2	9	1	1	0	0	0	0	2	0	0	0	0
teinert, Rob, Bakersfield	0	0	.000	27.00	4	1	0	0	1	0	3.0	4	27	9	9	0	0	1	0	14	0	5	5	0
mmonds, Maika, Bakersfield*	0	0	.000	8.88	7	2	1	0	2	0	24.1	34	127	32	24	1	0	0	0	21	0	21	3	3
zimanski, Tom, Lancaster	2	2	.500	4.22	35	0	0	0	21	9	42.2	55	194	24	20	3	1	4	1	12	1	46	2	2
elgheder, Dave, Modesto	1	0	1.000	1.50	1	1	0	0	0	0	6.0	4	24	3	1	0	0	0	0	1	0	3	0	1
homas, Carlos, R. Cucamonga.	1	1	.500	11.42	9	0	0	0	2	0	8.2	13	50	12	11	1	0	0	0	10	1	10	1	0
hompson, Fletcher, H. Desert.	0	0	.000	18.00	1	0	0	0	1	0	2.0	5	13	4	4	1	0	0	1	0	0	2	0	0
hompson, John, Lancaster	3	8	.273	6.13	50	0	0	0	41	14	61.2	72	287	50	42	12	3	4	5	29	1	53	6	1
hompson, Justin, Visalia*	0	0	.000	0.00	1	1	0	0	0	0	2.0	2	13	0	0	0	0	0	0	0	0	7	1	0
hurmond, Travis, Lake Elsinore	2	2	.500	3.93	6	5	0	0	0	0	36.2	36	159	18	16	4	0	2	2	17	0	39	2	1
awick, Tim, Lancaster	0	2	.000	6.39	16	0	0	0	4	0	31.0	43	139	26	22	4	0	2	2	9	0	20	3	1
ucker, Benjamin, San Jose	1	4	.200	6.25	13	13	0	0	0	0	67.2	71	301	54	47	8	3	1	3	36	0	30	6	4
ttle, Dave, Visalia	7	9	.438	3.71	55	0	0	0	52	21	70.1	71	308	39	29	3	3	1	3	33	5	56	1	0
rbina, Dan, San Bernardino	0	0	.000	5.91	3	3	0	0	0	0	10.2	11	55	8	7	0	0	1	0	9	0	13	1	0
anDeWeg, Ryan, R. Cuca.	9	6	.600	4.06	26	26	0	0	0	0	146.1	164	636	78	66	15	1	2	10	52	1	129	8	0
ermillion, Grant, Lake Elsinore .	2	1	.667	7.78	18	0	0	0	8	0	19.2	29	91	18	17	4	0	3	0	7	0	9	2	0
llano, Mike, San Jose	7	1	.875	0.72	39	2	0	0	21	8	88.0	48	341	12	7	2	1	1	0	33	4	133	7	1
agner, Joe, Stockton	12	6	.667	4.79	28	28	0	0	0	0	167.1	171	745	102	89	16	6	3	12	86	0	103	7	0
alsh, Matthew, Modesto	3	1	.750	3.49	38	0	0	0	10	4	69.2	54	293	38	27	5	1	1	6	31	1	68	7	1
alters, Brett, R. Cucamonga	9	9	.500	4.32	24	24	0	0	0	0	135.1	150	575	73	65	16	10	6	7	39	0	89	1	0
ashburn, Jarrod, Lk Elsinore*.	6	3	.667	3.30	14	14	3	0	0	0	92.2	79	384	38	34	5	2	2	2	33	0	93	8	0
atson, Allen, San Jose*	0	0	.000	1.42	2	2	0	0	0	0	6.1	7	25	1	1	0	0	0	0	0	0	12	0	0
atts, Josh, Lancaster	0	0	.000	13.50	1	0	0	0	1	0	2.0	5	16	7	3	0	0	0	0	4	0	2	1	0

CLASS A California League

Pitcher, Team	W	L	Pct.	ERA	G	GS	CG	ShO	GF	Sv.	IP	H	TBF	R	ER	HR	SH	SF	HB	BB	IBB	SO	WP	Bk
Whitaker, Ryan, Modesto	6	8	.429	4.99	37	9	0	0	8	0	113.2	142	520	83	63	8	7	3	9	39	2	87	10	1
White, Darell, R. Cucamonga	1	1	.500	6.50	38	0	0	0	17	0	54.0	76	258	48	39	1	4	4	0	25	0	43	6	0
White, Gary, High Desert*	4	2	.667	5.82	16	8	0	0	1	0	51.0	62	232	36	33	10	0	3	1	26	0	34	3	2
Wingate, Ervan, San Bernardino	0	0	.000	0.00	2	0	0	0	2	0	1.2	1	8	0	0	0	0	0	0	2	0	0	0	0
Wolcott, Bob, Lancaster	0	1	.000	10.50	1	1	0	0	0	0	6.0	9	27	7	7	3	0	0	0	6	0	6	0	0
Wolger, Michael, Bakersfield * ..	0	0	.000	40.50	1	0	0	0	0	0	1.1	4	13	7	6	1	0	1	1	4	0	1	0	0
Woodard, Steve, Stockton........	12	9	.571	4.02	28	28	3	0	0	0	181.1	201	762	89	81	14	4	6	3	33	1	142	7	2
Wooten, Greg, Lancaster............	8	4	.667	3.80	14	14	1	0	0	0	97.0	101	408	47	41	7	1	2	3	25	1	71	9	0
Worley, Robert, Lancaster	3	0	1.000	0.34	4	4	0	0	0	0	26.1	20	100	2	1	0	1	1	0	5	0	17	3	0
Zancanaro, Dave, Modesto*	7	3	.700	3.38	20	3	0	0	6	3	77.1	61	331	38	29	9	4	2	3	37	0	66	5	1

COMBINATION SHUTOUTS: **High Desert (3)**—White-Hackett-Snyder-Montgomery, Reed-Snyder, Reed-Maine. **Lake Elsinore (3)**—Pennington-Cooper-Haynes, Hermanson-Castillo, Sebach-Hayes-Castillo, Sebach-Holzemer-Hollinger-Holdridge. **Modesto (6)**—Whitaker-Zancanaro-Rajotte, Dale-Silva-Shaw-Rajotte, Dale-Zancanaro, Karsay-Zancanaro, Dale-Rajotte, Nelson-Perez. **Rancho Cucamonga (4)**—VanDeWeg-Hammerschmidt, Dennis-White-Thomas, Gaspar-Garrett, Walters-Baron-Logan. **San Bernardino (3)**—Oropesa-Kenady, Reyes-Paluk, Camacho-Linares. **San Jose (13)**—Blood-Fultz-Ortiz, Rector-DeLucia-Villano, Tucker-Rector-Ortiz, Rector-Villano, Blood-Fultz-Ortiz, Blood-Villano-Ortiz, Fultz-Martin-Villano, Rector-Castillo, Bailey-Hartvigson-Martin, Bailey-Schramm-Gomez, Fontenot-Myers-Martin-Castillo, Bailey-Fontenot-Schramm-Castillo. **Stockton (3)**—Beck-Drysdale-Cana-Sadler, Smith-Hommel-Salazar, Pasqualicchio-Kramer. **Lancaster (3)**—Worley-Daniels, Montane-Daniels, Beck-Thompson-Niemeier. **Visalia (1)**—Goldsmith-Jordan-Tuttle.

NO-HIT GAMES: None.

PITCHERS WITH TWO OR MORE TEAMS

Pitcher, Team	W	L	Pct.	ERA	G	GS	CG	ShO	GF	Sv.	IP	H	TBF	R	ER	HR	SH	SF	HB	BB	IBB	SO	WP	Bk.
Dalton, Brian, Stockton............	0	1	.000	6.97	6	0	0	0	2	0	10.1	12	51	9	8	1	1	0	0	10	0	9	3	0
Dalton, Brian, Visalia................	1	1	.500	5.40	13	0	0	0	4	0	26.2	26	121	16	16	6	0	1	1	19	0	19	3	1
Gomez, Dennys, Bakersfield	3	1	.750	3.52	10	0	0	0	3	0	23.0	22	97	11	9	2	0	0	1	12	0	11	2	1
Gomez, Dennys, San Jose........	1	0	1.000	6.99	22	0	0	0	10	0	28.1	30	142	28	22	0	0	3	8	16	0	27	5	0
Gould, Clint, Bakersfield	0	0	.000	9.00	2	0	0	0	1	0	1.0	1	6	1	1	0	0	0	0	2	0	1	1	0
Gould, Clint, Lancaster	3	2	.600	3.21	24	0	0	0	14	2	33.2	35	159	22	12	0	1	0	2	17	1	17	3	0
Maine, Dalton, Bakersfield	2	3	.400	3.23	23	2	0	0	16	8	47.1	42	204	25	17	4	2	0	1	14	0	58	5	2
Maine, Dalton, High Desert......	1	0	1.000	1.50	10	0	0	0	6	2	12.0	8	45	2	2	1	0	2	0	2	0	9	1	0
Reed, Dan, Bakersfield*	2	4	.333	5.00	20	7	0	0	3	0	68.1	83	316	52	38	4	3	2	0	36	1	48	1	1
Reed, Dan, High Desert............	4	0	1.000	4.76	17	6	0	0	1	0	51.0	53	225	28	27	7	2	0	2	22	0	43	1	0
Sellner, Aaron, Bakersfield......	0	2	.000	7.71	16	0	0	0	8	0	25.2	30	135	32	22	5	0	3	1	20	0	26	5	0
Sellner, Aaron, High Desert......	0	1	.000	7.56	4	0	0	0	2	0	8.1	11	40	9	7	1	2	0	1	5	0	5	3	1

1996 FIELDING

TEAM

Team	Pct.	G	PO	A	E	TC	DP	PB	Team	Pct.	G	PO	A	E	TC	DP	PB
San Jose	.971	140	3787	1517	159	5463	130	20	Visalia	.961	140	3725	1561	216	5502	120	6
Stockton	.969	140	3684	1634	171	5489	138	13	San Bernardino	.961	140	3745	1491	214	5450	104	2
High Desert..........	.969	140	3734	1564	171	5469	122	46	Lancaster	.959	140	3723	1473	224	5420	130	2
Lake Elsinore	.968	140	3750	1520	173	5443	105	24	Modesto	.956	140	3753	1680	253	5686	143	2
Rancho Cucamonga...	.966	140	3687	1409	177	5273	141	34	Bakersfield................	.954	140	3715	1386	246	5347	111	3

TRIPLE PLAYS: Bakersfield, Lancaster, San Jose.

INDIVIDUAL

FIRST BASEMEN

NOTE: All caps denotes fielding-percentage leader based on 70 games for catchers, 93 for all other non-pitchers and 140 innings for pitchers. *Throws lefthanded.

Player, Team	Pct.	G	PO	A	E	TC	DP
Alguacil, Jose, San Jose	1.000	4	13	1	0	14	2
Allen, Dustin, R. Cucamonga	.989	44	333	26	4	363	37
Ardoin, Danny, Modesto	.944	4	31	3	2	36	5
Betten, Randy, Lake Elsinore..........	1.000	2	15	1	0	16	2
Bryant, Chris, High Desert	1.000	1	6	1	0	7	0
Buhner, Shawn, Lancaster	.991	50	419	27	4	450	32
Buxbaum, Danny, Lake Elsinore ..	.993	73	672	58	5	735	43
Cabrera, Alex, Bakersfield	.987	37	273	26	4	303	24
Carroll, Doug, Bakersfield	.949	11	68	7	4	79	4
Clifford, Jim, Lancaster*	.982	93	782	57	15	854	79
Cromer, D.T., Modesto*	.986	59	491	63	8	562	49
Danapilis, Eric, Visalia	.984	96	830	81	15	926	76
Deberry, Joe, Stockton*	.990	32	293	16	3	312	18
Dilone, Juan, Modesto	.978	14	118	18	3	139	10
Durkac, Bo, Visalia	.955	3	20	1	1	22	2
Fernandez, Antonio, R. Cuca.	1.000	3	17	1	0	18	2
Galarza, Joel, San Jose	.750	3	6	0	2	8	0
Glenn, Darrin, San Jose	1.000	1	9	1	0	10	0
Hendricks, Ryan, H.D.-Bak.	.981	32	244	12	5	261	18
Herider, Jeremy, Visalia	1.000	1	5	0	0	5	1
Ibarra, Jesus, San Jose	.981	109	928	82	20	1030	95
Jordan, Ricky, Lancaster	.953	4	39	2	2	43	5
Joyner, Wally, R. Cucamonga*	1.000	3	14	2	0	16	2
Keefe, Jamie, R. Cucamonga	.667	1	2	0	1	3	0
Kirgan, Chris, High Desert*	.989	135	1168	105	14	1287	104
Kliner, Josh, Bakersfield	1.000	3	22	1	0	23	1
Krause, Scott, Stockton	1.000	7	61	4	0	65	12

Player, Team	Pct.	G	PO	A	E	TC	DP
Madsen, Dave, Modesto	.979	30	245	40	6	291	28
Marine, Del, Visalia	.979	28	214	20	5	239	15
Martinez, Tony, Visalia	.994	23	164	9	1	174	14
McKinnis, Leroy, R. Cucamonga	.857	3	12	0	2	14	3
Michael, Jeff, High Desert..............	1.000	1	4	1	0	5	0
Moeder, Tony, Lake Elsinore	.990	22	186	14	2	202	15
Moore, Mark, Modesto	.961	10	92	6	4	102	10
Morris, Greg, Lake Elsinore	.978	24	210	8	5	223	24
Newstrom, Doug, High Desert..........	1.000	2	1	2	0	3	1
Ortega, Randy, Modesto	.938	3	14	1	1	16	1
Paxton, Chris, Bakersfield	.937	20	128	6	9	143	11
Raleigh, Matt, High Desert	1.000	5	33	5	0	38	3
Richardson, Scott, San Bern.	1.000	1	14	0	0	14	1
Roberge, J.P., San Bernardino	.986	9	62	8	1	71	3
Russin, Tom, High Desert	1.000	4	3	0	0	3	1
Sealy, Scot, Lancaster	.929	1	11	2	1	14	1
Sell, Chip, San Bernardino	.990	22	171	21	2	194	18
Smith, Dave, Bakersfield	.993	18	127	11	1	139	11
Sowards, Ryan, San Bernardino	1.000	1	1	0	0	1	0
Stoner, Mike, Bakersfield	.987	36	276	25	4	305	35
Takayoshi, Todd, Lake Elsinore	.965	12	78	4	3	85	6
Tingley, Ron, Lake Elsinore	1.000	1	2	1	0	3	0
Townsend, Chad, San Bern.*	.990	87	724	66	8	798	58
Tyler, Josh, Stockton	1.000	1	5	2	0	7	0
Van Burkleo, Ty, Lake Elsinore*	.980	7	44	5	1	50	3
Ventura, Wilfredo, Modesto	1.000	2	14	1	0	15	3
Wathan, Dusty, Lancaster	1.000	1	12	1	0	13	0
Watkins, Sean, R. Cucamonga*	.979	92	740	71	17	828	82
White, Derrick, Modesto	.994	30	272	36	2	310	24
WILLIAMS, Drew, Stockton	.991	102	934	102	9	1045	96
Wilson, Todd, San Jose	.993	33	252	16	2	270	20

ayer, Team	Pct.	G	PO	A	E	TC	DP
ngate, Ervan, San Bernardino	.981	36	222	30	5	257	13
olff, Mike, Lake Elsinore	.976	5	36	5	1	42	2

TRIPLE PLAY: Clifford.

FIRST BASEMEN WITH TWO OR MORE TEAMS

ayer, Team	Pct.	G	PO	A	E	TC	DP
ndricks, Ryan, High Desert	1.000	6	41	4	0	45	5
ndricks, Ryan, Bakersfield	.977	26	203	8	5	216	13

SECOND BASEMEN

ayer, Team	Pct.	G	PO	A	E	TC	DP
juacil, Jose, San Jose	.983	60	113	169	5	287	38
derson, Cliff, San Bernardino	.952	5	11	9	1	21	6
ano, Eloy, Visalia	.911	9	21	30	5	56	4
rry, Mike, High Desert	.958	8	12	11	1	24	5
tances, Junior, Stockton	1.000	2	9	4	0	13	0
ssey, Jason, Visalia	1.000	3	7	8	0	15	1
yant, Chris, High Desert	1.000	1	0	1	0	1	0
rpentier, Mike, San Bern.	.917	10	16	17	3	36	3
stro, Jose, Modesto	.960	22	42	55	4	101	15
sar, Dionys, Modesto	.947	21	34	55	5	94	9
ok, Jason, Lancaster	.980	76	126	215	7	348	42
evas, Eduardo, R. Cucamonga	1.000	4	4	8	0	12	2
Amico, Jeffrey, Modesto	.950	5	6	13	1	20	4
edelow, Craig, Bakersfield	1.000	1	1	5	0	6	2
an, Chris, Lancaster	.966	48	94	135	8	237	31
metral, Chris, San Bernardino	1.000	2	4	9	0	13	1
Leon, Roberto, San Jose	1.000	3	3	5	0	8	0
one, Juan, Modesto	.974	30	60	87	4	151	23
nlop, Steve, Visalia	.949	13	23	33	3	59	9
lla, Paul, Lake Elsinore	.973	66	104	152	7	263	29
rcloth, Kevin, San Bernardino	.909	4	5	5	1	11	0
ix, Lauro, Stockton	.963	4	8	18	1	27	6
rna, Ricardo, R. Cucamonga	.962	103	213	244	18	475	52
RCIA, Jesse, High Desert	.968	137	263	409	22	694	81
nzalez, Mauricio, Bakersfield	.962	77	151	205	14	370	31
oss, Rafael, San Bernardino	.947	85	147	209	20	376	33
rrison, Adonis, Lancaster	.969	14	27	36	2	65	8
nderson, Juan, Lake Elsinore	.970	20	44	53	3	100	7
rider, Jeremy, Vis.-Bak.	.978	18	38	52	2	92	13
nnson, Todd, Bakersfield	1.000	6	16	16	0	32	2
efe, Jamie, R. Cucamonga	1.000	5	8	12	0	20	6
ard, Kirk, Bakersfield	.929	20	41	51	7	99	11
ner, Josh, Bakersfield	.980	24	39	59	2	100	17
ckey, Steve, Visalia	.939	28	51	73	8	132	17
aza, Mike, Lancaster	.927	11	21	30	4	55	4
nonis, Chris, Visalia	.943	77	127	234	22	383	38
wis, Tyrone, San Bernardino	.927	26	50	64	9	123	13
pez, Mickey, Stockton	.970	60	118	177	9	304	45
dsen, Dave, Modesto	1.000	1	1	2	0	3	1
rval, Raul, San Jose	1.000	19	28	48	0	76	7
xwell, Pat, Modesto	1.000	3	5	4	0	9	1
ore, Mark, Modesto	1.000	1	1	1	0	2	1
rreale, John, Stockton	.986	49	81	128	3	212	24
whan, David, Modesto	.955	27	43	83	6	132	14
iz, Jose, Modesto	1.000	1	2	5	0	7	1
ker, Allan, Lake Elsinore	1.000	2	0	4	0	4	1
ez, Mickey, Bakersfield	.900	6	16	20	4	40	2
hardson, Scott, San Bern.	.933	4	5	9	1	15	2
occo, Jon, San Jose	.966	61	117	171	10	298	49
mmer, Dave, Bakersfield	.979	12	24	22	1	47	8
ith, Chris, Lake Elsinore	.934	27	50	64	8	122	18
ith, Dave, Bakersfield	.853	9	20	9	5	34	2
riano, Fred, Modesto	.964	31	70	93	6	169	18
ompson, Fletcher, High Desert.	1.000	4	6	10	0	16	4
vner, Kyle, Bakersfield	1.000	2	2	6	0	8	1
daway, Chad, R. Cucamonga	.967	5	12	17	1	30	7
er, Josh, Stockton	.933	37	66	100	12	178	23
o, Joe, Lake Elsinore	.973	37	56	89	4	149	16
aver, Terry, San Jose	.800	3	2	2	1	5	0
ngate, Ervan, San Bernardino	.980	23	36	62	2	100	10
odridge, Dickie, R. Cuca.	.982	28	39	71	2	112	15
ng, Kevin, Lake Elsinore	1.000	1	1	1	0	2	0

TRIPLE PLAY: Kliner.

SECOND BASEMEN WITH TWO OR MORE TEAMS

yer, Team	Pct.	G	PO	A	E	TC	DP
ider, Jeremy, Visalia	.977	17	36	49	2	87	10
ider, Jeremy, Bakersfield	1.000	1	2	3	0	5	3

THIRD BASEMEN

yer, Team	Pct.	G	PO	A	E	TC	DP
uacil, Jose, San Jose	.750	2	1	2	1	4	0
no, Eloy, Visalia	1.000	6	4	8	0	12	0

Player, Team	Pct.	G	PO	A	E	TC	DP
Ardoin, Danny, Modesto	.800	8	1	3	1	5	0
Batiste, Kim, San Jose	1.000	1	0	1	0	1	0
Beltre, Adrian, San Bernardino	.953	58	32	110	7	149	6
BERRY, Mike, High Desert	.936	98	72	178	17	267	12
Betances, Junior, Stockton	.902	113	57	237	32	326	28
Betten, Randy, Lake Elsinore	.953	36	28	73	5	106	3
Bogle, Bryan, High Desert	.500	8	3	2	5	10	0
Bryant, Chris, High Desert	.918	31	16	40	5	61	5
Bucci, Carmen, R. Cucamonga	.778	3	2	5	2	9	0
Buhner, Shawn, Lancaster	1.000	1	2	0	0	2	0
Castro, Jose, Modesto	.861	48	26	92	19	137	9
Cesar, Dionys, Modesto	1.000	1	0	1	0	1	0
Cook, Jason, Lancaster	.934	31	15	42	4	61	3
Cuevas, Eduardo, R. Cucamonga	1.000	2	1	3	0	4	0
D'Amico, Jeffrey, Modesto	.882	39	27	85	15	127	9
Demetral, Chris, San Bernardino	1.000	2	0	3	0	3	0
Dilone, Juan, Modesto	.880	12	3	19	3	25	0
Dunlop, Steve, Visalia	1.000	1	1	0	0	1	0
Durkac, Bo, Visalia	.916	122	86	221	28	335	16
Espinal, Juan, Bakersfield	.888	129	117	200	40	357	13
Fernandez, Antonio, R.Cuca.	.932	118	57	202	19	278	25
Figueroa, Luis, Lancaster	.875	9	1	20	3	24	1
Gonzalez, Mauricio, Bakersfield	.824	11	6	22	6	34	7
Gross, Rafael, San Bernardino	.923	22	14	46	5	65	5
Guzman, Edwards, San Jose	.919	105	69	213	25	307	14
Herider, Jeremy, Vis.-Bak.	1.000	6	3	8	0	11	0
Howell, Jack, Lake Elsinore	.917	3	3	8	1	12	1
Keefe, Jamie, R. Cucamonga	.800	9	5	7	3	15	1
Kinard, Kirk, Bakersfield	.800	2	2	2	1	5	0
Lackey, Steve, Visalia	1.000	4	3	5	0	8	1
Lanza, Mike, Lancaster	1.000	6	3	12	0	15	2
Lemonis, Chris, Visalia	.700	3	4	3	3	10	0
Madsen, Dave, Modesto	.918	15	13	32	4	49	5
Marine, Del, Visalia	1.000	2	1	2	0	3	0
Martinez, Tony, Visalia	1.000	4	2	2	0	4	1
Marval, Raul, San Jose	.929	4	1	12	1	14	1
Massarelli, John, R. Cucamonga	1.000	1	0	1	0	1	0
McCarty, Matt, San Bernardino	.826	35	12	45	12	69	2
Michael, Jeff, High Desert	.800	2	0	4	1	5	2
Morris, Greg, Lake Elsinore	.941	38	28	67	6	101	3
Ortega, Randy, Modesto	.667	3	0	2	1	3	0
Parker, Allan, Lake Elsinore	1.000	2	1	0	0	1	1
Polanco, Juan, Modesto	.857	2	0	6	1	7	0
Raleigh, Matt, High Desert	1.000	2	0	3	0	3	0
Reynolds, Chance, Stockton	.778	3	0	7	2	9	0
Sell, Chip, San Bernardino	1.000	1	1	1	0	2	0
Slemmer, Dave, Modesto	.917	13	9	24	3	36	1
Smith, Chris, Lake Elsinore	.889	25	17	39	7	63	4
Sowards, Ryan, San Bernardino	1.000	1	0	1	0	1	0
Tejada, Miguel, Modesto	.800	1	2	2	1	5	0
Thompson, Fletcher, High Desert	.957	17	2	20	1	23	0
Tredaway, Chad, R. Cucamonga	.906	10	5	24	3	32	1
Tyler, Josh, Stockton	.930	30	21	59	6	86	5
Urso, Joe, Lake Elsinore	.944	47	37	97	8	142	11
Villalobos, Carlos, Lancaster	.848	100	64	175	43	282	17
Wallach, Tim, San Bernardino	.917	5	6	5	1	12	0
Weaver, Terry, San Jose	1.000	3	1	3	0	4	0
White, Derrick, Modesto	.956	17	10	33	2	45	6
Williams, Drew, Stockton	.750	2	1	2	1	4	0
Wilson, Todd, San Jose	.924	35	14	47	5	66	6
Wingate, Ervan, San Bernardino	.940	23	11	36	3	50	1
Woodridge, Dickie, R. Cuca.	.833	4	2	8	2	12	1

TRIPLE PLAY: Espinal.

THIRD BASEMEN WITH TWO OR MORE TEAMS

Player, Team	Pct.	G	PO	A	E	TC	DP
Herider, Jeremy, Visalia	1.000	5	2	7	0	9	0
Herider, Jeremy, Bakersfield	1.000	1	1	1	0	2	0

SHORTSTOPS

Player, Team	Pct.	G	PO	A	E	TC	DP
Alguacil, Jose, San Jose	.979	9	19	28	1	48	6
Anderson, Cliff, San Bernardino	.937	52	70	138	14	222	25
Arano, Eloy, Visalia	.928	20	35	55	7	97	16
Batiste, Kim, San Jose	1.000	1	0	3	0	3	0
Baugh, Gavin, Bakersfield	.935	6	14	15	2	31	8
Betances, Junior, Stockton	.943	13	11	39	3	53	8
Betten, Randy, Lake Elsinore	.965	22	34	49	3	86	8
Brissey, Jason, Visalia	.929	64	108	193	23	324	46
Bryant, Chris, High Desert	.889	22	21	51	9	81	9
Bucci, Carmen, R. Cucamonga	.600	2	0	3	2	5	0
Carpentier, Mike, San Bernardino	1.000	3	1	6	0	7	0
Castro, Jose, Modesto	.921	31	50	89	12	151	21

CLASS A California League

Player, Team	Pct.	G	PO	A	E	TC	DP
Cook, Jason, Lancaster	.916	19	29	47	7	83	11
D'Amico, Jeffrey, Modesto	.667	3	3	3	3	9	0
Daedelow, Craig, Bakersfield	.926	84	126	224	28	378	40
Delgado, Wilson, San Jose	.957	121	192	343	24	559	70
Dunlop, Steve, Visalia	.882	8	13	17	4	34	4
Failla, Paul, Lake Elsinore	.882	20	30	60	12	102	9
Faircloth, Kevin, San Bernardino	.915	52	75	130	19	224	23
Felix, Lauro, Stockton	.875	8	8	20	4	32	3
Fernandez, Antonio, R. Cucamonga	1.000	1	1	0	0	1	0
Gonzalez, Mauricio, Bakersfield	1.000	7	15	17	0	32	5
Gross, Rafael, San Bernardino	1.000	5	5	11	0	16	2
Henderson, Juan, Lake Elsinore	.913	27	35	81	11	127	8
Herider, Jeremy, Vis.-Bak.	.951	48	93	121	11	225	25
Jones, Jack, San Bernardino	.981	10	18	34	1	53	6
Keefe, Jamie, Rancho Cucamonga	.885	8	12	11	3	26	4
Kinard, Kirk, Bakersfield	.877	16	23	41	9	73	6
Klassen, Danny, Stockton	.944	118	186	373	33	592	73
Lackey, Steve, Visalia	.864	14	20	37	9	66	8
LAMB, David, High Desert	.969	116	202	356	18	576	75
Lanza, Mike, Lancaster	.940	90	127	251	24	402	48
Lopez, Mickey, Stockton	.944	4	4	13	1	18	0
Marval, Raul, San Jose	.906	15	16	42	6	64	10
Maxwell, Pat, Modesto	1.000	1	3	4	0	7	2
Melo, Juan, Rancho Cucamonga	.958	128	209	378	26	613	92
Molina, Luis, Lancaster	.916	37	61	80	13	154	22
Morimoto, Ken, San Bernardino	.847	24	35	70	19	124	11
Morreale, John, Stockton	1.000	1	0	2	0	2	0
Parker, Allan, Lake Elsinore	.957	45	52	104	7	163	24
Paz, Richard, High Desert	.944	7	7	10	1	18	3
Sanchez, Yuri, Visalia	.958	17	20	49	3	72	5
Schofield, Dick, Lake Elsinore	1.000	2	1	4	0	5	0
Smith, Dave, Bakersfield	.810	6	11	6	4	21	2
Soriano, Fred, Modesto	1.000	1	1	6	0	7	1
Tejada, Miguel, Modesto	.926	110	192	356	44	592	67
Thompson, Fletcher, High Desert	1.000	4	7	8	0	15	2
Tredaway, Chad, R. Cucamonga	.941	6	9	23	2	34	4
Urso, Joe, Lake Elsinore	.974	42	65	126	5	196	25
Wingate, Ervan, San Bernardino	.889	4	2	6	1	9	1

TRIPLE PLAYS: Delgado, Lanza.

SHORTSTOPS WITH TWO OR MORE TEAMS

Player, Team	Pct.	G	PO	A	E	TC	DP
Herider, Jeremy, Visalia	.973	24	48	61	3	112	10
Herider, Jeremy, Bakersfield	.929	24	45	60	8	113	15

OUTFIELDERS

Player, Team	Pct.	G	PO	A	E	TC	DP
Akins, Carlos, High Desert	1.000	10	16	0	0	16	0
Alguacil, Jose, San Jose	1.000	5	10	0	0	10	0
Allen, Dustin, R. Cucamonga	.882	10	15	0	2	17	2
Arano, Eloy, Visalia	1.000	8	11	1	0	12	0
Avila, Rolando, High Desert	.976	68	160	5	4	169	1
Baker, Jason, San Bernardino*	1.000	16	14	1	0	15	0
Bazzani, Matt, Bakersfield	1.000	6	13	2	0	15	0
Bentley, Kevin, Bakersfield	.959	19	44	3	2	49	1
Betten, Randy, Lake Elsinore	1.000	11	23	4	0	27	0
Bilderback, Ty, Lake Elsinore*	1.000	38	67	3	0	70	0
Bogle, Bryan, High Desert	.956	111	184	10	9	203	0
Bonds, Bobby, San Jose	.963	101	166	14	7	187	1
Brinkley, Darryl, R. Cucamonga	.979	30	45	1	1	47	1
Brown, Emil, Modesto	.962	56	97	5	4	106	1
Cabrera, Alex, Bakersfield	.980	46	91	6	2	99	1
Carney, Bartt, High Desert	1.000	46	65	2	0	67	0
Carroll, Doug, Bak.-Lan.	.951	49	74	3	4	81	1
Carter, Cale, Lake Elsinore	.978	34	42	3	1	46	0
Castro, Jose, Modesto	1.000	1	1	0	0	1	0
Christian, Eddie, Lake Elsinore*	.974	16	35	2	1	38	0
Clifford, Jim, Lancaster*	1.000	2	3	0	0	3	0
Collier, Dan, Bakersfield	.910	46	69	2	7	78	0
Cook, Jason, Lancaster	1.000	6	6	2	0	8	1
Corujo, Rey, San Jose	.967	43	57	1	2	60	1
Cromer, D.T., Modesto*	.912	46	58	4	6	68	0
Cruz, Jose, Lancaster	.986	42	62	7	1	70	1
Curtis, Randy, R. Cucamonga*	.959	96	175	11	8	194	1
D'Aquila, Tom, High Desert	.778	5	6	1	2	9	0
Dalton, Jed, Lake Elsinore	.959	34	46	1	2	49	0
Danapilis, Eric, Visalia	1.000	3	6	2	0	8	0
Dauphin, Phil, Lake Elsinore*	.941	67	104	7	7	118	1
Davis, Eddie, San Bernardino	.973	135	246	7	7	260	2
Denbow, Don, San Jose	.906	20	28	1	3	32	0
DeJesus, Malvin, Visalia	.985	85	177	15	3	195	2

Player, Team	Pct.	G	PO	A	E	TC	D..
Dilone, Juan, Modesto	.958	50	88	4	4	96	
Eaddy, Keith, H.D.-R.C.	.980	36	49	0	1	50	
Edmonds, Jim, Lake Elsinore*	1.000	3	5	0	0	5	
Facione, Chris, Visalia	.994	78	166	4	1	171	
Galarza, Joel, San Jose	.900	7	9	0	1	10	
Garland, Tim, San Jose	.976	130	187	14	5	206	
Gonzalez, Manuel, San Bern.	.975	43	74	5	2	81	
Greene, Eric, Bakersfield	.800	2	4	0	1	5	
Grieve, Ben, Modesto	.956	69	104	5	5	114	
Herider, Jeremy, Bakersfield	.933	4	14	0	1	15	
Herrick, Jason, Lake Elsinore*	.970	57	86	10	3	99	
Hodge, Roy, High Desert	.956	106	206	9	10	225	
Hugo, Sean, High Desert*	1.000	2	2	0	0	2	
Hunter, Andy, R. Cucamonga	1.000	2	2	0	0	2	
Hust, Gary, Modesto	.889	12	16	0	2	18	
James, Dion, Stockton*	1.000	4	5	0	0	5	
Javier, Stan, San Jose	1.000	2	1	0	0	1	
Jenkins, Geoff, Stockton*	1.000	3	2	0	0	2	
Johnson, Todd, Bakersfield	.750	1	3	0	1	4	
Kimsey, Keith, Visalia	.954	99	177	11	9	197	
Kliner, Josh, Bakersfield	.939	17	30	1	2	33	
KOMINEK, Toby, Stockton	.984	95	169	13	3	185	
Krause, Scott, Stockton	.969	99	148	8	5	161	
Landrum, Tito, San Bernardino	.973	38	66	7	2	75	
Landry, Lonny, Visalia	.960	51	113	6	5	124	
Lewis, Andreaus, Bakersfield	.962	38	71	4	3	78	
LeCronier, Jason, High Desert	.960	39	47	1	2	50	
Marquez, Jesus, Lancaster*	.914	106	171	10	17	198	
Martin, Jim, San Bernardino	.917	22	22	0	2	24	
Martinez, Greg, Stockton	1.000	69	141	5	0	146	
Massarelli, John, R. Cucamonga	.986	26	69	1	1	71	
Matthews, Gary, R. Cucamonga	.934	122	218	7	16	241	
McGonigle, Bill, Stockton	.973	64	102	5	3	110	
Moeder, Tony, Lake Elsinore	.949	68	68	7	4	79	
Monahan, Shane, Lancaster	.974	127	248	10	7	265	
Moore, Vince, R. Cucamonga*	.956	46	79	8	4	91	
Morales, Alex, San Jose	.939	17	31	0	2	33	
Moultrie, Pat, Bakersfield*	.965	42	80	2	3	85	
Neill, Mike, Modesto*	.973	98	136	6	4	146	
Newhan, David, Modesto	.964	93	128	5	5	138	
Newstrom, Doug, High Desert	1.000	1	1	0	0	1	
Oldham, Bob, Bakersfield	.923	7	12	0	1	13	
Oropeza, Igor, Bakersfield	1.000	1	3	0	0	3	
Polanco, Juan, Modesto	1.000	6	8	1	0	9	
Prieto, Chris, R. Cucamonga*	.992	54	108	9	1	118	
Reese, Mat, Lake Elsinore*	1.000	1	1	0	0	1	
Reid, Derek, San Jose	.994	88	171	8	1	180	
Rennhack, Mike, Stockton	.974	95	141	11	4	156	
Richardson, Scott, San Bern.	.962	114	166	11	7	184	
Roberge, J.P., San Bernardino	1.000	4	5	0	0	5	
Roberts, David, Visalia*	.977	99	201	8	5	214	
Roberts, John, R. Cucamonga	1.000	21	26	2	0	28	
Sell, Chip, San Bernardino	.980	57	93	7	2	102	
Sheffield, Tony, Bakersfield*	.955	39	80	4	4	88	
Smith, Dave, Bakersfield	1.000	2	4	0	0	4	
Smith, Scott, Lancaster	.929	58	85	6	7	98	
Stoner, Mike, Bakersfield	1.000	1	1	0	0	1	
Sturdivant, Marcus, Lancaster*	.961	63	118	4	5	127	
Suplee, Ray, High Desert	.966	82	109	6	4	119	
Swinton, Jermaine, Stockton	.889	7	8	0	1	9	
Symmonds, Maika, Bakersfield*	1.000	1	1	0	0	1	
Teasley, Ken, Bakersfield	.850	12	17	0	3	20	
Thielen, D.J., San Jose	.818	6	9	0	2	11	
Towner, Kyle, Bakersfield	.966	88	211	17	8	236	
Tyler, Josh, Stockton	1.000	1	1	0	0	1	
Van Rossum, Chris, San Jose*	1.000	11	20	0	0	20	
Villalobos, Carlos, Lancaster	1.000	2	1	2	0	3	
Watts, Josh, Bak.-Lan.	.951	46	74	4	4	82	
White, Derrick, San Jose	.875	6	7	0	1	8	
Wilson, Todd, San Jose	1.000	1	1	0	0	1	
Wingate, Ervan, San Bernardino	1.000	22	24	0	0	24	
Wolff, Mike, Lake Elsinore	1.000	7	13	0	0	13	
Young, Kevin, Lake Elsinore	.979	113	217	12	5	234	

OUTFIELDERS WITH TWO OR MORE TEAMS

Player, Team	Pct.	G	PO	A	E	TC	
Carroll, Doug, Bakersfield	.967	35	56	3	2	61	
Carroll, Doug, Lancaster	.900	14	18	0	2	20	
Eaddy, Keith, High Desert	1.000	9	10	0	0	10	
Eaddy, Keith, Rancho Cucamonga	.975	27	39	0	1	40	
Watts, Josh, Bakersfield	.952	33	55	4	3	62	
Watts, Josh, Lancaster	.950	13	19	0	1	20	

ayer, Team	Pct.	G	PO	A	E	TC	DP	PB
adreopoulos, Alex, Stockton	.990	86	582	78	7	667	1	6
doin, Danny, Modesto	.971	76	545	56	18	619	5	13
gustine, Andy, Lancaster	.981	39	240	25	5	270	0	9
rajas, Rod, Visalia	1.000	17	83	14	0	97	1	8
zzani, Matt, Bakersfield	.907	10	43	6	5	54	0	2
mpillo, Rob, Stockton	.979	46	288	37	7	332	3	6
oney, Kyle, San Bernardino	.979	92	787	67	18	872	8	20
rnell, Bryce, Visalia	1.000	5	24	2	0	26	1	3
vis, Ben, Rancho Cucamonga	.987	77	642	51	9	702	7	12
laRosa, Elvis, Visalia	.973	66	406	62	13	481	2	34
Boer, Rob, Modesto	.974	43	297	42	9	348	2	5
larza, Joel, San Jose	.982	36	307	16	6	329	2	12
enn, Darrin, San Jose	1.000	1	5	0	0	5	0	0
esham, Kris, High Desert	1.000	2	12	4	0	16	0	0
rmer, Frank, Bak.-H.D.	.986	58	310	44	5	359	4	15
mphill, Bret, Lake Elsinore	.982	108	879	92	18	989	5	16
arra, Jesus, San Jose	1.000	6	26	2	0	28	0	1
hnson, Todd, Bakersfield	.983	73	555	69	11	635	3	10
mpkin, Tom, San Jose	1.000	2	10	1	0	11	1	0
zinski, Ryan, San Bernardino	.995	20	161	24	1	186	0	4
arine, Del, Visalia	.977	67	411	63	11	485	3	17
artin, Jeff, Modesto	.982	5	45	10	1	56	0	1
AYES, Craig, San Jose	.994	101	850	77	6	933	5	6
cGuire, Matt, San Jose	1.000	3	7	0	0	7	0	1
cKinnis, Leroy, R. Cucamonga	.993	53	396	32	3	431	3	17
errullo, Matt, Lake Elsinore	.973	8	63	8	2	73	0	4
kesell, Steve, San Bernardino	.977	5	38	5	1	44	0	0
oore, Mark, Modesto	.967	6	29	0	1	30	0	0
ikirk, Derick, Visalia	.950	6	16	3	1	20	0	1
ewstrom, Doug, High Desert	.966	79	486	56	19	561	2	27
Toole, Bobby, High Desert	.980	14	82	15	2	99	1	2
tega, Randy, Modesto	.989	13	86	4	1	91	0	2
xton, Chris, Bakersfield	.988	39	225	14	3	242	2	9
eynolds, Chance, Stockton	.992	17	116	5	1	122	1	1
sario, Melvin, R.C.-H.D.	.984	37	260	41	5	306	5	13
hwenke, Matt, R. Cucamonga	.986	9	63	10	1	74	0	1
aly, Scot, Lancaster	.988	49	371	43	5	419	6	6
ed, David, San Bernardino	.973	27	191	25	6	222	1	4
einmann, Scott, Lancaster	1.000	3	13	1	0	14	0	0
kayoshi, Todd, Lake Elsinore	.976	15	111	12	3	126	0	3
asley, Ken, Bakersfield	1.000	4	1	0	0	1	0	0
ngley, Ron, Lake Elsinore	.951	10	73	4	4	81	0	1
rrealba, Yorvit, San Jose	1.000	2	16	1	0	17	0	0
ist, Jeff, Bakersfield	1.000	7	32	3	0	35	0	4
er, Josh, Stockton	1.000	1	2	0	0	2	0	0
ntura, Wilfredo, Modesto	.968	16	107	13	4	124	2	1
athan, Dusty, Lancaster	.984	60	451	49	8	508	3	13

TRIPLE PLAY: Johnson.

CATCHERS WITH TWO OR MORE TEAMS

ayer, Team	Pct.	G	PO	A	E	TC	DP	PB
rmer, Frank, Bakersfield	.988	25	141	18	2	161	3	7
rmer, Frank, High Desert	.985	33	169	26	3	198	1	8
sario, Melvin, R. Cucamonga	1.000	5	37	10	0	47	2	4
sario, Melvin, High Desert	.981	32	223	31	5	259	3	9

PITCHERS

ayer, Team	Pct.	G	PO	A	E	TC	DP
ffa, Steve, Bakersfield*	.941	15	3	13	1	17	1
bineaux, Darrin, San Bern.	.778	5	4	3	2	9	1
ckowski, Lance, San Bern.	1.000	1	1	0	0	1	0
iley, Philip, San Jose*	.966	35	9	19	1	29	5
ron, Jim, Rancho Cucamonga*	.933	54	4	10	1	15	1
tes, Shawn, Bakersfield*	1.000	4	0	3	0	3	0
zzani, Matt, Bakersfield	1.000	5	0	1	0	1	0
ck, Chris, Lancaster	1.000	23	4	16	0	20	1
ck, Greg, Stockton	.900	28	18	18	4	40	0
ood, Darin, San Jose	.867	27	8	18	4	30	3
nanno, Rob, Lake Elsinore	1.000	13	1	5	0	6	0
sio, Chris, Lancaster	1.000	2	0	2	0	2	0
ay, Chris, Bakersfield	1.000	17	2	2	0	4	1
ewer, Brian, High Desert*	.905	18	4	15	2	21	1
own, Alvin, San Bernardino	.955	42	12	9	1	22	0
own, Dickie, Stockton	1.000	5	0	3	0	3	0
sh, Craig, Bakersfield	.882	41	4	11	2	17	0
ssa, Todd, Rancho Cucamonga	1.000	16	0	1	0	1	0
brera, Jose, Bakersfield	.909	7	2	8	1	11	0
macho, Dan, San Bernardino	.917	14	5	6	1	12	0
na, Nelson, Stockton*	1.000	29	1	12	0	13	1
ndiotti, Tom, San Bernardino	1.000	2	1	1	0	2	0

Player, Team	Pct.	G	PO	A	E	TC	DP
Caridad, Ron, Stockton	1.000	18	2	1	0	3	1
Carroll, Doug, Bakersfield	1.000	4	1	0	0	1	0
Castillo, Carlos, Lake Elsinore	1.000	27	5	5	0	10	0
Castillo, Marino, San Jose	1.000	10	1	0	0	1	0
Castro, Nelson, San Bernardino	1.000	12	0	2	0	2	0
Chavez, Tony, Lake Elsinore	1.000	10	0	3	0	3	0
Clayton, Craig, R.Cucamonga	1.000	11	2	3	0	5	0
Clement, Matt, R.Cucamonga	.800	11	1	7	2	10	1
Clifford, Eric, Lancaster	.857	11	1	5	1	7	1
Cloude, Ken, Lancaster	.907	28	14	25	4	43	2
Cochrane, Chris, Modesto	.933	21	13	15	2	30	1
Connelly, Steven, Modesto	.923	52	6	6	1	13	1
Cooper, Brian, Lake Elsinore	.875	26	13	22	5	40	2
Crills, Brad, High Desert	.964	14	6	21	1	28	1
Daigle, Tim, High Desert*	1.000	4	1	0	0	1	0
Dale, Carl, Modesto	.897	26	14	21	4	39	5
Dalton, Brian, Stock.-Vis.	1.000	19	5	2	0	7	0
Daniels, John, Lancaster	.842	43	7	9	3	19	1
Darley, Ned, High Desert	1.000	30	7	5	0	12	1
Davis, Keith, Rancho Cucamonga	.765	28	10	3	4	17	0
Deakman, Josh, Lake Elsinore	.955	27	17	25	2	44	3
Dean, Greg, High Desert	.929	37	9	17	2	28	2
Dennis, Shane, R.Cucamonga*	.933	9	2	12	1	15	0
Deskins, Casey, San Bernardino*	.944	12	6	11	1	18	0
DeLaCruz, Fernando, Lk Elsinore	1.000	5	0	1	0	1	0
DeLucia, Rich, San Jose	1.000	5	1	1	0	2	1
Dixon, Bubba, R.Cucamonga*	1.000	11	0	3	0	3	0
Doorneweerd, Dave, Lk Elsinore	.800	11	1	3	1	5	1
Drysdale, Brooks, Stockton	1.000	35	6	4	0	10	1
Duffy, Ryan, Visalia*	.750	15	1	2	1	4	0
Edwards, Wayne, Bakersfield*	1.000	3	1	3	0	4	0
Eibey, Scott, High Desert*	1.000	11	1	1	0	2	0
Eichhorn, Mark, Lake Elsinore	1.000	12	1	2	0	3	0
Erdos, Todd, Rancho Cucamonga	.900	55	2	7	1	10	0
Estrada, Horacio, Stockton*	.941	29	7	9	1	17	1
Fontenot, Joe, San Jose	.975	26	14	25	1	40	0
Foster, Kris, San Bernardino	.923	30	5	7	1	13	0
Fultz, Aaron, San Jose*	.875	36	3	18	3	24	1
Gardner, Mark, San Jose	1.000	1	0	2	0	2	0
Gardner, Scott, Stockton	.821	27	15	17	7	39	0
Garrett, Hal, Rancho Cucamonga	.500	24	2	6	0	8	2
Gaspar, Cade, R.Cucamonga	.935	24	11	18	2	31	2
Goedhart, Darrell, Lake Elsinore	1.000	4	1	2	0	3	0
Goldsmith, Gary, Visalia	.929	28	11	28	3	42	1
Gomez, Dennys, Bak.-S.J.	1.000	32	7	10	0	17	1
Gomez, Javier, Visalia	.875	22	2	5	1	8	1
Gould, Clint, Bak.-Lan.	.875	26	2	5	1	8	1
Hackett, Jason, High Desert*	1.000	5	0	1	0	1	0
Hammerschmidt, Andy, R.Cuca.*	.970	35	14	18	1	33	0
Harris, Bryan, Lake Elsinore	.875	20	3	4	1	8	0
Harris, Greg W., R.Cucamonga	.714	13	1	4	2	7	1
Hartvigson, Chad, San Jose*	1.000	36	3	20	0	23	0
Hause, Brendan, Modesto*	1.000	1	0	1	0	1	0
Haynes, Heath, Lake Elsinore	1.000	31	1	6	0	7	0
Henderson, Juan, Lake Elsinore	1.000	1	0	1	0	1	0
Henderson, Kenny, R.Cucamonga	.750	5	2	1	1	4	0
Herider, Jeremy, Bakersfield	1.000	1	1	0	0	1	0
Hermanson, Mike, Lake Elsinore	1.000	29	2	4	0	6	2
Hernandez, Jeremy, Visalia	.818	24	5	4	2	11	0
Hill, Jason, Lake Elsinore*	.900	32	2	7	1	10	1
Hill, Tyrone, Stockton*	1.000	5	2	2	0	4	0
Hinchliffe, Brett, Lancaster	.828	27	6	18	5	29	2
Holdridge, David, Lake Elsinore	1.000	12	2	1	0	3	0
Hollinger, Adrian, Lake Elsinore	1.000	12	2	2	0	4	0
Holzemer, Mark, Lake Elsinore*	.750	9	1	2	1	4	0
Hommel, Brian, Stockton*	1.000	4	0	3	0	3	0
Hoshiba, Takahisa, Visalia	.909	21	2	8	1	11	1
Hritz, Derrick, Bakersfield*	.895	31	3	14	2	19	1
Huber, Jeff, Stockton*	1.000	18	1	1	0	2	0
Huntsman, Brandon, High Desert	1.000	13	3	6	0	9	0
Huntsman, Scott, Stockton	.769	43	6	4	3	13	0
Ito, Makoto, Visalia*	1.000	34	1	7	0	8	2
Jimenez, Miguel, Modesto	.875	13	7	7	2	16	0
Johnson, Carl, Visalia	.875	15	4	5	1	10	0
Johnson, Todd, Bakersfield	1.000	21	5	4	0	9	1
Jordan, Jason, Visalia	.828	30	8	16	5	29	0
Karsay, Steve, Modesto	.889	14	3	5	1	9	0
Keling, Korey, Lake Elsinore	1.000	10	0	2	0	2	0
Kell, Rob, Bakersfield*	.875	13	2	12	2	16	1
Kelly, John, Visalia	.947	19	6	12	1	19	0
Kenady, Jake, San Bernardino*	.846	45	2	9	2	13	0
Keppen, Jeffrey, San Bernardino	.933	24	8	6	1	15	0

CLASS A   California League

Player, Team	Pct.	G	PO	A	E	TC	DP
KING, Bill, Modesto	1.000	29	21	18	0	39	3
Knighton, Toure, Bakersfield	.900	25	13	23	4	40	1
Kramer, Jeff, Stockton	.889	15	6	10	2	18	1
Langston, Mark, Lake Elsinore*	1.000	1	0	1	0	1	0
Lehman, Toby, High Desert	1.000	6	0	2	0	2	1
Lemke, Steve, Modesto	.947	12	6	12	1	19	0
Linares, Rich, San Bernardino	.875	60	0	7	1	8	0
Logan, Chris, R.Cucamonga	.867	53	5	8	2	15	1
Lukasiewicz, Mark, Bakersfield*	1.000	7	1	3	0	4	0
Maine, Dalton, Bak.-H.D.	1.000	33	0	5	0	5	0
Marenghi, Matt, High Desert	.925	33	13	24	3	40	2
Martin, Jeff, San Jose	.833	42	4	11	3	18	1
McDonald, Matt, San Bern.*	1.000	4	1	1	0	2	0
Michalak, Chris, Modesto*	.941	21	4	12	1	17	0
Montane, Ivan, Lancaster	.882	11	7	8	2	17	0
Montgomery, Steve, High Desert	1.000	44	4	8	0	12	2
Moore, Trey, Lancaster*	.826	15	6	13	4	23	2
Moore, Vince, R.Cucamonga*	1.000	1	1	0	0	1	0
Moreno, Claudio, San Bernardino	.889	6	2	6	1	9	0
Morgan, Eric, Lancaster	1.000	10	0	4	0	4	0
Mullins, Greg, Stockton*	1.000	10	0	2	0	2	0
Myers, Jason, San Jose*	.966	33	8	20	1	29	0
Nartker, Mike, Visalia	1.000	3	1	2	0	3	0
Nelson, Chris, Modesto	.850	14	9	8	3	20	0
Niemeier, Todd, Lancaster*	1.000	41	3	5	0	8	0
Novoa, Rafael, Lake Elsinore*	1.000	16	5	4	0	9	0
Nunez, Vladimir, Visalia	.867	12	3	10	2	15	0
Odell, Jacob, Modesto	1.000	1	1	0	0	1	0
Oldham, Bob, Bakersfield	.857	41	6	12	3	21	2
Olszewski, Tim, High Desert	1.000	49	4	7	0	11	0
Ontiveros, Steve, Lake Elsinore	1.000	2	1	1	0	2	0
Oropesa, Eddie, San Bernardino*	.904	33	17	30	5	52	3
Oropeza, Igor, Bakersfield	.833	23	8	12	4	24	1
Ortiz, Russ, San Jose	.900	34	5	4	1	10	1
Palmer, Brett, Bakersfield*	.667	12	0	4	2	6	0
Paluk, Jeff, San Bernardino	1.000	50	7	14	0	21	1
Pasqualicchio, Michael, Stckton*	1.000	18	5	14	0	19	2
Pearce, Jeff, Lancaster*	.800	21	0	4	1	5	0
Pena, Alex, Visalia	.909	44	5	15	2	22	1
Perez, Juan, Modesto*	.875	38	9	12	3	24	1
Perisho, Matt, Lake Elsinore*	.929	21	7	32	3	42	0
Perpetuo, Nelson, Bakersfield*	.750	8	1	5	2	8	0
Pincavitch, Kevin, San Bern.	.857	20	15	15	5	35	0
Price, Tom, San Bernardino*	1.000	15	2	13	0	15	0
Prieto, Ariel, Modesto	.833	2	3	2	1	6	0
Rajotte, Jason, Modesto*	1.000	47	6	17	0	23	0
Raleigh, Matt, High Desert	1.000	1	1	0	0	1	0
Rector, Bobby, San Jose	.909	28	17	23	4	44	2
Reed, Dan, Bak.-H.D.*	1.000	37	7	23	0	30	1
Reich, Steve, High Desert*	.667	2	0	2	1	3	0
Reyes, Dennis, San Bernardino*	.794	29	2	25	7	34	1
Rhodes, Joe, High Desert	.857	25	5	13	3	21	1
Rodriguez, Larry, Visalia	.833	13	13	7	4	24	0
Ruch, Rob, Visalia	.968	37	11	19	1	31	2
Runion, Tony, Bakersfield	.909	7	7	3	1	11	0
Sadler, Al, Stockton	1.000	18	3	1	0	4	0
Sak, James, Rancho Cucamonga	1.000	4	1	2	0	3	0
Salazar, Luis, Stockton	.944	44	9	8	1	18	0
Salazar, Mike, Visalia*	.833	6	0	5	1	6	1
Sanchez, Mike, San Bernardino	.750	11	2	1	1	4	0
Saneaux, Francisco, High Desert	.857	20	10	14	4	28	1

Player, Team	Pct.	G	PO	A	E	TC	D
Santana, Marino, Lancaster	.841	28	10	27	7	44	
Sauritch, Chris, High Desert	1.000	35	5	10	0	15	
Schlutt, Jason, R. Cucamonga*	1.000	7	0	2	0	2	
Schmitt, Todd, R. Cucamonga	.500	7	1	0	1	2	
Schoeneweis, Scott, Lk Elsinore*	.947	14	6	12	1	19	
Schramm, Carl, San Jose	.889	39	3	13	2	18	
Seaver, Mark, High Desert	1.000	4	2	1	0	3	
Sebach, Kyle, Lake Elsinore	1.000	26	7	12	0	19	
Sellner, Aaron, Bak.-H.D.	1.000	20	1	7	0	8	
Shaw, Curtis, Modesto*	.912	39	10	21	3	34	
Sick, David, Lake Elsinore	1.000	16	1	3	0	4	
Sikes, Ken, San Bernardino	.923	17	11	13	2	26	
Skuse, Nicholas, Lake Elsinore	1.000	6	2	2	0	4	
Smith, Hut, High Desert	.909	10	3	7	1	11	
Smith, Travis, Stockton	1.000	14	5	12	0	17	
Snyder, Matt, High Desert	1.000	58	4	10	0	14	
Soden, Chad, Lancaster*	1.000	9	1	3	0	4	
Southall, Pete, Visalia	1.000	32	7	9	0	16	
Steed, David, San Bernardino	1.000	1	1	0	0	1	
Symmonds, Maika, Bakersfield*	1.000	7	1	3	0	4	
Szimanski, Tom, Lancaster	1.000	35	4	6	0	10	
Telgheder, Dave, Modesto	.000	1	0	0	1	1	
Thomas, Carlos, R.Cucamonga	1.000	9	0	1	0	1	
Thompson, John, Lancaster	.944	50	7	10	1	18	
Thurmond, Travis, Lake Elsinore	.500	6	0	2	2	4	
Trawick, Tim, Lancaster	1.000	16	2	4	0	6	
Tucker, Benjamin, San Jose	.938	13	7	8	1	16	
Tuttle, Dave, Visalia	.960	55	7	17	1	25	
Urbina, Dan, San Bernardino	1.000	3	4	2	0	6	
VanDeWeg, Ryan, R.Cucamonga	.903	26	7	21	3	31	
Vermillion, Grant, Lake Elsinore	1.000	18	1	10	0	11	
Villano, Mike, San Jose	1.000	39	4	8	0	12	
Wagner, Joe, Stockton	.943	28	11	22	2	35	
Walsh, Matthew, Modesto	.882	38	7	8	2	17	
Walters, Brett, R.Cucamonga	1.000	24	8	19	0	27	
Washburn, Jarrod, Lk Elsinore*	.900	14	6	12	2	20	
Watts, Josh, Bakersfield	1.000	1	0	1	0	1	
Whitaker, Ryan, Modesto	.939	37	15	16	2	33	
White, Darell, R. Cucamonga	.750	38	2	4	2	8	
White, Gary, High Desert*	1.000	16	5	6	0	11	
Wolcott, Bob, Lancaster	1.000	1	1	1	0	2	
Woodard, Steve, Stockton	.976	28	16	25	1	42	
Wooten, Greg, Lancaster	1.000	14	8	12	0	20	
Worley, Robert, Lancaster	1.000	4	1	5	0	6	
Zancanaro, Dave, Modesto*	1.000	20	7	9	0	16	

TRIPLE PLAY: Myers.

PITCHERS WITH TWO OR MORE TEAMS

Player, Team	Pct.	G	PO	A	E	TC	DP
Dalton, Brian, Stockton	1.000	6	3	1	0	4	
Dalton, Brian, Visalia	1.000	13	2	1	0	3	
Gomez, Dennys, Bakersfield	1.000	10	2	7	0	9	
Gomez, Dennys, San Jose	1.000	22	5	3	0	8	
Gould, Clint, Bakersfield	.000	2	0	0	0	0	
Gould, Clint, Lancaster	.875	24	2	5	1	8	
Maine, Dalton, Bakersfield	1.000	23	0	3	0	3	
Maine, Dalton, High Desert	1.000	10	0	2	0	2	
Reed, Dan, Bakersfield*	1.000	20	6	21	0	27	
Reed, Dan, High Desert*	1.000	17	1	2	0	3	
Sellner, Aaron, Bakersfield	1.000	16	0	4	0	4	
Sellner, Aaron, High Desert	1.000	4	1	3	0	4	

The following players did not have any fielding statistics at the positions indicated or appeared only as a designated hitter, pinch-hitter or pinch-runner: Baker, p; Briss of; Bucci, 2b, p; Burt, p; Carpentier, 3b; Cooney, 1b, of, ss; Corsi, p; Daedelow, p; E. Davis, p; DeBoer, of; D'Amico, p; Falkenborg, p; Garcia, ss; Mau. Gonzalez, Granger, p; Green, p; Greene, 2b; Greer, of; Guzman, of; Hacen, p; Harmer, p; Harper, p; Holden, p; Kirgan, of, p; Kliner, 3b; Lecronier, 2b; Lukasiewicz, of; Mayes, McGonigle, p; Neill, p; Pennington, p; Radinsky, p; Reich, of; Reynolds, of; Runion, of; Sanderson, p; Sealy, 3b, of; Silva, p; L. Smith, p; Sowards, p; Steinert, p; Supl, 2b; F. Thompson, p; Ju. Thompson, p; Watson, p; Wingate, p; Wolger, of, p; Woodridge, ss.

LEAGUE CHAMPIONS

Year Team	Pct.	Year Team	Pct.	Year Team	Pct.
1914— Fresno	.571	1949— Bakersfield	.612	1957— Visalia∞	.62
1915— Modesto	.857	San Jose (4th)*	.543	Salinas (4th)*	.50
1916-40—Did not operate.		1950— Ventura	.607	1958— Fresno*	.63
1941— Fresno	.643	Modesto (2nd)*	.586	Bakersfield	.67
Santa Barbara (2nd)*	.597	1951— Santa Barbara‡	.599	1959— Bakersfield	.59
1942— Santa Barbara†	.642	1952— Fresno‡	.629	Modesto§	.64
1943-44-45—Did not operate.		1953— San Jose‡	.664	1960— Reno	.61
1946— Stockton‡	.600	1954— Modesto‡	.623	Reno	.65
1947— Stockton‡	.679	1955— Stockton	.733	1961— Reno	.74
1948— Fresno	.607	Fresno§	.718	Reno	
Santa Barbara (3rd)*	.529	1956— Fresno§	.650	1962— San Jose§	.68

Year	Team	Pct.
	Reno	.587
*1963—	Modesto	.589
	Stockton§	.687
*1964—	Fresno	.638
	Fresno	.600
1965—	San Jose	.586
	Stockton§	.614
1966—	Modesto	.577
	Modesto	.671
*1967—	San Jose§	.676
	Modesto	.586
*1968—	San Jose	.629
	Fresno§	.623
1969—	Stockton§	.600
	Visalia	.614
1970—	Bakersfield	.667
	Bakersfield	.671
1971—	Visalia§	.583
	Fresno	.500
*1972—	Modesto§	.547
	Bakersfield	.629
*1973—	Lodi§	.657
	Bakersfield	.571
1974—	Fresno§	.607
	San Jose	.579
1975—	Reno	.614
	Reno	.614
1976—	Salinas	.650
	Reno§	.547
1977—	Salinas	.564
	Lodi§	.579
1978—	Visalia§	.698
	Lodi	.607
1979—	San Jose§	.636
	Reno	.525
1980—	Stockton§	.638
	Visalia	.507
1981—	Visalia	.621
	Lodi§	.521
1982—	Modesto§	.671
	Visalia	.586
1983—	Visalia	.621
	Redwood§	.529
1984—	Modesto§	.597
	Bakersfield	.486
1985—	Fresno§	.575
	Stockton	.566
1986—	Palm Springs	.613
	Stockton§	.585
1987—	Fresno§	.559
	Reno	.535
1988—	Stockton	.657
	Riverside§	.599
1989—	Stockton	.627
	Bakersfield§	.577
1990—	Visalia	.638
	Stockton§	.582
1991—	San Jose	.676
	High Desert§	.537
1992—	Stockton§	.610
	Visalia	.551
1993—	High Desert§	.620
	Modesto	.529
1994—	Modesto	.706
	Rancho Cucamonga§	.566
1995—	San Bernardino§	.612
	San Jose	.550
1996—	San Jose	.636
	Lake Elsinore‡	.550

*Won four-club playoff. †League disbanded June 28. ‡Won championship and four-club playoff. §Won split-season playoff. ∞Won both halves of split season.

CAROLINA LEAGUE

LEAGUE OFFICE

President/treasurer
John Hopkins
Address
P.O. Box 9503
Greensboro, NC 27429
Phone
910-691-9030

Teams (affiliation)
Durham Bulls (Braves)
Frederick Keys (Orioles)
Kinston Indians (Indians)
Lynchburg Hillcats (Pirates)
Prince William Cannons (Cardinals)
Salem Avalanche (Rockies)

Wilmington Blue Rocks (Royals)
Winston-Salem Warthogs (White Sox)

1996 FINAL STANDINGS

FIRST HALF

NORTHERN DIVISION

Team	W	L	T	Pct.	GB
Wilmington (Royals)	40	30	0	.571	....
Frederick (Orioles)	34	36	0	.486	6
Prince William (White Sox)	31	37	0	.456	8
Lynchburg (Pirates)	26	43	0	.377	13½

SOUTHERN DIVISION

Team	W	L	T	Pct.	GB
Durham (Braves)	38	31	0	.551	....
Kinston (Indians)	37	32	0	.536	1
Winston-Salem (Reds)	37	33	0	.529	1
Salem (Rockies)	34	35	0	.493	4

SECOND HALF

NORTHERN DIVISION

Team	W	L	T	Pct.	GB
Wilmington (Royals)	40	30	0	.571	....
Lynchburg (Pirates)	39	31	0	.557	1
Frederick (Orioles)	33	36	0	.478	6½
Prince William (White Sox)	27	43	0	.386	13

SOUTHERN DIVISION

Team	W	L	T	Pct.	GB
Kinston (Indians)	39	30	0	.565	....
Winston-Salem (Reds)	37	32	0	.536	2
Durham (Braves)	35	35	0	.500	4
Salem (Rockies)	28	41	0	.406	11

COMPOSITE

Team	Wil.	Kin.	W.S.	Dur.	Fre.	Lyn.	Sal.	P.W.	W	L	T	Pct.	GB
Wilmington (Royals)	...	12	5	16	10	13	12	12	80	60	0	.571	....
Kinston (Indians)	8	....	11	11	10	11	12	13	76	62	0	.551	3
Winston-Salem (Reds)	15	8	....	8	13	11	10	9	74	65	0	.532	5
Durham (Braves)	4	9	12	...	16	10	10	12	73	66	0	.525	6
Frederick (Orioles)	10	10	7	4	....	11	12	13	67	72	0	.482	12
Lynchburg (Pirates)	7	8	9	10	9	...	9	13	65	74	0	.468	14
Salem (Rockies)	8	8	10	10	7	11	...	8	62	76	0	.449	17
Prince William (White Sox)	8	7	11	7	7	7	11	....	58	80	0	.420	21

Major league affiliations in parentheses.

PLAYOFFS: Kinston defeated Durham, two games to one; Wilmington defeated Kinston, three games to one, to win league championship.

REGULAR-SEASON ATTENDANCE: Durham, 365,445; Frederick, 258,427; Kinston, 145,493; Lynchburg, 100,016; Prince William, 190,055; Salem 173,703; Wilmington, 335,309; Winston-Salem, 154,132. Total—1,722,580. Playoffs (6 games)—10,340. All-Star Game at High Desert—6,671.

MANAGERS: Durham, Randy Ingle; Frederick, Tim Blackwell (through April 14) and Julio Gargia (April 16 through end of season); Kinston, Jack Mu Lynchburg, Jeff Banister; Prince William, Dave Huppert; Salem, Bill McGuire; Wilmington, John Mizerock; Winston-Salem, Phillip Wellman. Managerial reco of teams with more than one manager: Frederick, Blackwell, 3-5, Garcia, 64-67.

ALL-STAR TEAM: 1B—Sean Casey, Kinston; 2B—Sergio Nunez, Wilmington; 3B—Freddy Garcia, Lynchburg; SS—Alejandro Prieto, Wilmington; Utili Inf.—Rick Short, Frederick; OF—Jose Guillen, Frederick; Johnny Isom, Frederick; Decomba Conner, Winston-Salem; Utility OF—Mike Asche, Lynchbur C—Blake Barthol, Salem; DH—Juan Thomas, Prince William; SP—Noe Najera, Kinston; RP—Steve Prihoda, Wilmington; Most Valuable Player—Jos Guillen, Lynchburg; Pitcher of the Year—Noe Majera, Kingston; Manager of the Year—Jack Mull, Kingston.

1996 BATTING

TEAM

Team	Avg.	G	TPA	AB	R	H	TB	2B	3B	HR	RBI	SH	SF	HP	BB	IBB	SO	SB	CS	GDP	LOB	ShO	Slg.	OE
Lynchburg	.283	139	5229	4673	730	1323	1959	253	34	105	649	47	48	55	405	17	965	155	80	97	908	10	.419	.34
Durham	.262	139	5263	4701	702	1232	1993	245	30	152	637	35	33	49	425	14	1007	168	74	71	919	8	.424	.3
Wilmington	.259	140	5253	4609	637	1195	1740	234	34	81	579	39	52	57	493	19	958	160	72	67	985	12	.378	.3
Frederick	.259	139	5199	4568	648	1184	1739	226	25	93	574	36	37	63	495	34	819	150	81	112	950	4	.381	.3
Kinston	.257	138	5173	4529	635	1166	1705	245	24	82	584	65	35	54	490	25	812	86	51	85	986	12	.376	.3
Salem	.256	138	5173	4539	585	1164	1683	216	18	89	527	68	28	61	477	19	835	154	89	98	961	8	.371	.3
Winston-Salem	.252	139	5157	4493	641	1131	1734	192	24	121	581	57	40	39	524	16	1070	219	88	90	914	11	.386	.3
Prince William	.248	138	5201	4583	603	1138	1686	224	30	88	538	39	28	44	504	10	930	81	45	113	983	10	.368	.3

INDIVIDUAL

TOP QUALIFIERS FOR BATTING CHAMPIONSHIP

Minimum 378 plate appearances. *Lefthanded batter. †Switch-hitter.

Player, Team	Avg.	G	TPA	AB	R	H	TB	2B	3B	HR	RBI	SH	SF	HP	BB	IBB	SO	SB	CS	GDP	Slg.	OÉ
Casey, Sean, Kinston*	.331	92	388	344	62	114	187	31	3	12	57	0	2	6	36	3	47	1	1	5	.544	.4
Guillen, Jose, Lynchburg	.322	136	571	528	78	170	263	30	0	21	94	1	8	13	20	1	73	24	13	16	.498	.3

yer, Team	Avg.	G	TPA	AB	R	H	TB	2B	3B	HR	RBI	SH	SF	HP	BB	IBB	SO	SB	CS	GDP	Slg.	OBP
rt, Rick, Frederick	.312	126	517	474	68	148	190	33	0	3	54	5	4	5	29	2	44	12	7	14	.401	.355
cia, Freddy, Lynchburg	.306	129	531	474	79	145	253	39	3	21	86	0	12	1	44	2	86	4	2	10	.534	.358
lker, Shon, Lynchburg*	.303	97	378	323	61	98	165	19	3	14	70	0	4	2	49	6	99	3	4	7	.511	.394
gee, Danny, Durham	.299	95	383	344	59	103	164	19	3	12	40	4	1	14	20	0	70	17	5	6	.477	.361
omas, Juan, Prince William	.299	134	556	495	88	148	248	28	6	20	71	0	2	5	54	3	129	9	3	15	.501	.372
nbill, Chad, Salem	.296	115	449	406	61	120	167	22	2	7	41	6	1	3	33	2	83	6	6	4	.411	.352
she, Mike, Lynchburg	.295	129	553	498	79	147	205	25	6	7	54	8	7	2	38	1	92	26	5	11	.412	.343
ndez, Wilmington	.293	109	441	406	40	119	162	25	3	4	59	3	7	3	22	4	39	3	1	6	.399	.329
dice, John, Salem	.292	101	431	373	58	109	189	30	1	16	67	3	3	7	45	6	66	10	8	11	.507	.376
udio, Patricio, Kinston	.291	100	419	361	67	105	127	15	2	1	38	2	3	6	47	2	74	36	14	2	.352	.379
ry, Chan, Frederick	.291	96	402	358	44	104	163	27	1	10	62	3	3	2	36	3	33	2	3	9	.455	.356
m, Johnny, Frederick	.290	124	539	486	69	141	228	27	3	18	104	0	6	7	40	4	87	8	6	15	.469	.349
s, Amador, Winston-Salem†	.288	116	428	378	53	109	158	17	1	10	57	5	3	2	40	1	72	30	10	6	.418	.357

DEPARTMENTAL LEADERS: G—Eddie, 137; AB—Guillen, 528; R—J. Thomas, 88; H—Guillen, 170; TB—Guillen, 263; 2B—Garcia, 39; 3B—Glass, 9; HR—Guillen, ...cia, 21; RBI—Isom, 104; SH—Mercedes, 14; SF—M. Allen, Garcia, 12; HP—Eaglin, 18; BB—Towle, 93; IBB—Giudice, V. Walker, 6; SO—Shirley, 149; SB—S. Nunez, ...CS—Swafford, 18; GIDP—Guillen, 16; Slg.—Casey, .544; OBP—Towle, .416.

ALL PLAYERS
*Lefthanded batter. †Switch-hitter.

yer, Team	Avg.	G	TPA	AB	R	H	TB	2B	3B	HR	RBI	SH	SF	HP	BB	IBB	SO	SB	CS	GDP	Slg.	OBP
ns, Carlos, Frederick	.290	42	182	145	36	42	66	7	1	5	14	0	1	2	34	0	31	9	5	3	.455	.429
n, Marlon, Winston-Salem	.237	121	476	426	57	101	173	19	1	17	82	1	12	5	32	2	133	8	2	3	.406	.291
onte, Wady, Frederick	.286	85	319	287	45	82	134	12	2	12	44	4	1	6	21	2	59	1	5	12	.467	.346
czak, Chuck, Frederick	.091	5	13	11	2	1	1	0	0	0	0	0	0	1	1	0	2	0	0	0	.091	.231
s, Amador, Winston-Salem†	.288	116	428	378	53	109	158	17	1	10	57	5	3	2	40	1	72	30	10	6	.418	.357
he, Mike, Lynchburg	.295	129	553	498	79	147	205	25	6	7	54	8	7	2	38	1	92	26	5	11	.412	.343
ry, Mark, Prince William	.237	75	308	270	33	64	111	16	2	9	31	1	2	3	32	0	66	0	0	11	.411	.322
hol, Blake, Salem	.285	109	430	375	58	107	167	17	2	13	67	6	1	12	36	0	48	12	5	5	.445	.366
nhardt, Steve, Salem	.300	63	223	203	17	61	80	12	2	1	19	5	1	2	12	0	23	4	4	4	.394	.344
rios, Harry, Fred.-Kin.	.218	67	263	234	32	51	85	14	1	6	31	2	3	3	21	0	37	10	3	7	.363	.287
ry, Mike, Frederick	.125	3	12	8	2	1	4	0	0	1	1	0	0	0	4	0	2	0	0	1	.500	.417
lware, Ben, Prince William	.253	117	479	443	41	112	147	18	1	5	52	4	2	2	28	0	51	16	6	9	.332	.299
o, Luis, Durham†	.286	81	335	315	35	90	117	16	1	3	34	6	1	3	10	0	33	6	3	5	.371	.313
rey, Dustin, Wilmington	.000	34	1	1	0	0	0	0	0	0	0	0	0	0	0	0	0	1	0	0	.000	.000
oks, Eddie, Lynchburg	.267	85	296	270	41	72	109	23	1	4	28	4	3	4	15	1	73	4	2	7	.404	.312
oks, Eddie, Lynchburg	.251	111	417	363	54	91	164	24	2	15	66	2	7	0	45	0	80	4	3	10	.452	.328
wn, Adrian, Lynchburg†	.321	52	232	215	39	69	96	9	3	4	25	1	0	2	14	1	24	18	9	1	.447	.368
ant, Chris, Frederick	.000	3	9	8	0	0	0	0	0	0	0	0	0	1	0	0	4	0	0	0	.000	.111
ke, Stoney, Lynchburg	.207	37	101	92	10	19	23	4	0	0	9	1	1	0	7	0	24	0	0	3	.250	.260
gton, Jimmie, Wilmington	.296	105	332	297	46	88	115	20	2	1	32	6	5	5	19	0	44	12	8	4	.387	.344
ne, Rick, Wilmington	.111	7	31	27	1	3	7	1	0	1	3	1	0	0	3	0	7	0	1	1	.259	.200
ey, Sean, Kinston*	.331	92	388	344	62	114	187	31	3	12	57	0	2	6	36	3	47	1	1	5	.544	.402
horn, Gerad, Kinston	.236	53	206	174	29	41	63	14	1	2	23	6	1	3	22	0	35	2	1	3	.362	.330
eno, Eduardo, Wilmington	.209	78	184	163	28	34	44	7	0	1	18	2	2	3	14	0	65	11	5	2	.270	.280
vez, Eric, Frederick	.279	122	498	416	60	116	201	29	1	18	64	2	5	3	72	5	101	5	3	10	.483	.385
dio, Patricio, Kinston	.291	100	419	361	67	105	127	15	2	1	38	2	3	6	47	2	74	36	14	2	.352	.379
ner, Decomba, Winston-Salem	.281	129	566	512	77	144	232	18	5	20	63	5	4	2	43	1	117	33	11	6	.453	.340
dero, Edward, Durham	.198	68	199	177	27	35	43	6	1	0	12	4	1	2	15	1	59	1	3	1	.243	.267
ea, Miguel, Durham†	.258	65	267	248	39	64	106	17	2	7	27	2	1	2	14	2	46	15	6	2	.427	.302
, Brian, Salem	.198	36	140	121	8	24	31	4	0	1	15	0	2	1	16	0	14	3	1	2	.256	.293
ingham, Earl, Salem	.172	29	100	87	9	15	19	1	0	1	6	1	1	2	9	0	24	3	0	0	.218	.263
delow, Craig, Frederick	.208	26	81	72	13	15	19	4	0	0	8	2	0	1	6	1	9	2	0	0	.264	.278
quila, Tom, Frederick	.146	45	161	130	21	19	25	3	0	1	11	1	2	3	25	1	55	9	4	3	.192	.294
ney, Donovan, Wilmington	.272	124	417	386	45	105	142	17	4	4	38	4	3	3	21	0	63	18	7	6	.368	.312
icci, David, Frederick*	.324	59	224	185	33	60	85	11	1	4	28	0	1	0	38	3	34	5	6	2	.459	.438
in, Mike, Durham	.253	131	542	466	84	118	180	25	2	11	54	4	4	18	50	0	88	23	12	1	.386	.346
e, Steve, Winston-Salem	.272	137	556	497	56	135	189	23	2	9	64	6	4	4	45	3	78	14	9	14	.380	.335
s, Jason, Prince William†	.264	95	394	329	41	87	127	24	2	4	41	2	3	2	58	1	80	4	3	7	.386	.375
s, Michael, Wilmington*	.191	98	340	278	36	53	94	9	1	10	40	1	1	4	56	2	78	1	2	1	.338	.333
s, Pat, Kinston†	.259	21	32	27	5	7	12	3	1	0	6	1	0	0	4	0	12	0	1	0	.444	.355
auzzi, John, Salem*	.284	62	117	95	10	27	37	10	0	0	11	2	0	3	17	1	25	2	0	3	.389	.409
ell, Jon, Lynchburg	.359	24	101	78	8	28	34	3	0	1	11	0	1	3	19	1	16	0	0	1	.436	.495
er, Jim, Frederick	.252	82	324	278	35	70	115	20	2	7	42	0	3	4	39	1	32	1	6	3	.414	.349
ler, Maleke, Frederick	.182	5	14	11	3	2	2	0	0	0	1	0	0	0	3	0	2	1	1	0	.182	.357
accio, Dan, Prince William	.275	44	164	149	16	41	50	9	0	0	20	2	0	1	12	0	20	1	0	5	.336	.333
ch, Anton, Durham†	.248	52	225	210	25	52	81	10	0	2	22	5	0	0	13	0	42	23	3	0	.386	.291
riel, Denio, Frederick†	.180	40	147	133	12	24	27	1	1	0	5	1	1	1	11	0	29	6	9	1	.203	.247
nbill, Chad, Salem	.296	115	449	406	61	120	167	22	2	7	41	6	1	3	33	2	83	6	6	4	.411	.352
ia, Freddy, Lynchburg	.306	129	531	474	79	145	253	39	3	21	86	0	12	1	44	2	86	4	2	10	.534	.358
iulo, Mike, Frederick*	.199	51	182	161	14	32	47	9	0	2	16	1	1	4	15	2	35	2	1	5	.292	.282
ice, John, Salem	.292	101	431	373	58	109	189	30	1	16	67	3	3	7	45	6	66	10	8	11	.507	.376
, Chip, Kinston*	.267	134	529	479	64	128	179	18	9	5	52	5	1	4	40	2	67	11	6	8	.374	.328
on, Gary, Salem	.371	10	38	35	5	13	16	3	0	0	6	0	0	0	3	0	6	2	1	0	.457	.421
ndy, Phillip, Wilmington	1.000	28	2	2	0	2	2	0	0	0	1	0	0	0	0	0	0	0	0	0	1.000	1.000
ewald, Keith, Salem†	.243	10	42	37	1	9	10	1	0	0	4	1	1	1	2	0	12	0	3	0	.270	.293
en, Jose, Lynchburg	.322	136	571	528	78	170	263	30	0	21	94	1	8	13	20	1	73	24	13	16	.498	.357
, Gary, Kinston	.218	74	227	174	30	38	65	10	1	5	22	5	5	3	40	2	50	4	3	1	.374	.363
Ronnie, Salem	.151	14	58	53	7	8	10	2	0	0	2	0	0	1	4	0	9	0	3	2	.189	.224
lin, Mark, Salem	.143	9	33	28	1	4	7	0	0	1	4	1	0	0	3	0	6	0	0	2	.250	.273
son, Kenny, Lynchburg*	.120	18	54	50	2	6	9	3	0	0	3	0	0	0	0	0	8	0	1	2	.180	.185
ss, Robin, Kinston	.218	89	298	262	25	57	81	7	1	5	32	12	3	5	16	1	57	1	2	8	.309	.273

CLASS A Carolina League

Player, Team	Avg.	G	TPA	AB	R	H	TB	2B	3B	HR	RBI	SH	SF	HP	BB	IBB	SO	SB	CS	GDP	Slg.	O
Harvey, Raymond, Kinston*	.281	32	128	114	14	32	45	7	0	2	16	0	1	1	12	1	26	0	0	2	.395	.3
Hayes, Darren, Prince William	.212	66	236	189	28	40	55	8	2	1	19	8	0	10	29	0	64	5	2	1	.291	.3
Helms, Wes, Durham	.322	67	278	258	40	83	145	19	2	13	54	0	1	7	12	0	51	1	1	7	.562	.3
Hermansen, Chad, Lynchburg	.275	66	287	251	40	69	116	11	3	10	46	0	4	3	29	1	56	5	1	8	.462	.3
Higgins, Mike, Salem	.237	66	249	219	24	52	78	11	0	5	18	3	1	2	24	2	50	1	4	6	.356	.3
Hodge, Roy, Frederick	.000	4	16	12	2	0	0	0	0	0	0	0	0	1	3	0	5	1	0	0	.000	.2
Holdren, Nate, Salem	.277	114	466	426	53	118	190	24	0	16	64	1	5	5	29	3	109	15	5	6	.446	.3
Houser, Kyle, Salem	.239	117	513	436	59	104	125	12	3	1	48	5	3	1	68	1	47	13	9	12	.287	.3
Huson, Jeff, Frederick*	.438	4	18	16	4	7	12	2	0	1	1	0	0	0	2	0	0	0	0	0	.750	.5
Isom, Johnny, Frederick	.290	124	539	486	69	141	228	27	3	18	104	0	6	7	40	4	87	8	6	15	.469	.3
Jarrett, Link, Salem†	.224	38	110	98	9	22	27	3	1	0	8	3	0	1	8	0	14	1	2	3	.276	.2
Jenkins, Dee, Winston-Salem*	.268	108	441	380	58	102	153	20	2	9	59	3	3	1	54	1	96	15	7	11	.403	.3
Johnson, Mark, Prince William*	.241	18	72	58	9	14	17	3	0	0	3	0	0	1	13	0	6	0	0	0	.293	.3
Jones, Andruw, Durham	.313	66	289	243	65	76	147	14	3	17	43	0	1	3	42	3	54	16	4	5	.605	.4
Jones, Pookie, Salem	.281	102	376	335	45	94	132	18	1	6	40	7	4	1	29	0	76	16	6	12	.394	.3
Jorgensen, Tim, Kinston*	.216	119	463	412	56	89	164	24	0	17	64	1	3	6	41	2	103	1	2	7	.398	.2
Kelley, Erskine, Lynchburg	.282	111	378	344	61	97	144	22	5	5	43	2	3	4	25	2	93	13	8	8	.419	.3
Kennedy, Gus, Durham	.210	116	411	348	52	73	145	11	2	19	50	0	2	3	58	2	124	6	6	3	.417	.3
King, Andre, Winston-Salem	.192	82	312	261	43	50	89	9	3	8	29	4	2	10	34	0	88	16	7	2	.341	.3
Kingsale, Eugene, Frederick†	.271	49	196	166	26	45	59	6	4	0	9	3	2	6	19	1	32	23	4	1	.355	.3
Kopriva, Dan, Prince William	.252	91	406	337	53	85	132	21	1	8	39	0	3	4	59	2	44	0	0	12	.392	.3
Larkin, Stephen, Winston-Salem*	.179	39	133	117	13	21	32	2	0	3	6	1	1	0	14	2	25	6	1	6	.274	.2
Lawrence, Chip, Frederick	.235	43	145	132	9	31	34	1	1	0	14	4	0	1	8	0	13	6	3	3	.258	.2
LeCronier, Jason, Frederick*	.228	29	105	92	13	21	36	3	0	4	12	2	0	1	10	4	29	0	0	0	.391	.3
Levias, Andres, Prince William†	.100	15	46	40	3	4	5	1	0	0	1	1	1	0	4	0	15	0	1	2	.125	.1
Lewis, Marc, Durham	.298	68	292	262	43	78	112	12	2	6	26	3	1	2	24	2	37	25	9	5	.427	.3
Liefer, Jeff, Prince William*	.224	37	159	147	17	33	42	6	0	1	13	0	1	0	11	2	27	0	0	6	.286	.2
Light, Tal, Salem	.235	64	259	234	29	55	104	10	0	13	36	0	1	5	19	0	59	3	1	6	.444	.
Lofton, James, Winston-Salem†	.224	82	312	277	27	62	80	9	0	3	33	5	2	1	27	1	55	14	8	7	.289	.2
Magee, Danny, Durham	.299	95	383	344	59	103	164	19	3	12	40	4	1	14	20	0	70	17	5	6	.477	.3
Mahoney, Mike, Durham	.259	101	401	363	52	94	149	24	2	9	46	4	4	7	23	0	64	4	3	8	.410	.3
Martin, Lincoln, Frederick†	.266	114	488	421	77	112	149	17	7	2	31	7	2	8	50	2	66	22	7	9	.354	.3
Martinez, Eddy, Frederick	.221	74	269	244	21	54	64	4	0	2	25	1	1	2	21	0	48	13	8	5	.262	.2
Martinez, Ramon, Lynchburg†	.307	91	341	306	58	94	117	10	5	1	30	9	0	2	24	0	53	12	5	4	.382	.
Mathews, Del, Durham*	.000	43	1	0	0	0	0	0	0	0	0	0	0	0	1	0	0	0	0	0	.000	1.
Matos, Pascual, Durham	.224	67	230	219	24	49	82	9	3	6	28	0	1	3	7	0	70	6	0	2	.374	.
Mayber, Chan, Salem	.208	97	310	264	38	55	63	5	0	1	20	11	3	5	27	0	50	22	9	2	.239	.
McBride, Gator, Durham	.245	14	54	49	7	12	22	4	0	2	6	0	0	0	5	0	14	1	0	3	.449	.
McCollough, Adam, Frederick	.000	4	10	10	0	0	0	0	0	0	0	0	0	0	0	0	4	0	0	0	.000	.
McKinnon, Sandy, Prince William	.263	113	446	410	56	108	170	28	5	8	60	9	2	2	23	0	68	20	10	4	.415	.3
McNally, Sean, Wilmington	.276	126	499	428	49	118	171	27	1	8	63	1	8	5	57	2	83	3	3	8	.400	.3
Mendez, Carlos, Wilmington	.293	109	441	406	40	119	162	25	3	4	59	3	7	3	22	4	39	3	1	6	.399	.3
Mendez, Sergio, Lynchburg	.277	39	145	137	19	38	61	9	1	4	17	0	1	1	6	0	24	0	1	2	.445	.
Mercedes, Guillermo, Kinston†	.246	117	432	382	45	94	108	12	1	0	27	14	1	5	30	1	41	3	3	14	.283	.
Miller, David, Kinston*	.254	129	533	488	71	124	170	23	1	7	54	2	5	0	38	4	94	14	7	7	.348	.
Montilla, Julio, Wilmington†	.260	49	163	150	22	39	49	10	0	0	12	2	0	2	9	0	18	3	1	3	.327	.
Moore, Brandon, Prince William	.241	125	529	439	56	106	126	13	2	1	41	2	3	3	82	1	70	9	11	14	.287	.
Morrow, Nick, Winston-Salem	.258	123	492	422	78	109	188	19	3	18	54	3	3	5	59	1	93	28	6	6	.445	.
Moyle, Mike, Kinston	.269	61	233	197	37	53	88	12	1	7	34	1	1	4	30	1	32	3	2	3	.447	.
Munoz, Omer, Lynchburg	.300	3	11	10	0	3	3	0	0	0	1	1	0	0	0	0	1	0	0	0	.300	.
Neubart, Garrett, Salem	.365	24	102	85	16	31	37	2	2	0	6	1	0	4	12	0	13	8	6	0	.435	.
Nunez, Raymond, Durham	.309	65	264	243	30	75	125	18	1	10	55	1	7	1	12	1	45	2	2	5	.514	.
Nunez, Sergio, Wilmington	.271	105	452	402	60	109	153	23	6	3	40	6	2	4	38	0	52	44	11	2	.381	.
O'Toole, Bobby, Frederick	.143	3	7	7	0	1	1	0	0	0	0	0	0	0	0	0	2	0	0	0	.143	.
Parsons, Jason, Winston-Salem†	.348	14	49	46	4	16	19	3	0	0	7	0	0	1	2	0	5	0	2	0	.413	.
Pena, Elvis, Salem†	.223	102	419	341	48	76	93	9	4	0	28	13	1	3	61	2	70	30	16	12	.273	.
Perry, Chan, Kinston	.291	96	402	358	44	104	163	27	1	10	62	3	2	2	36	3	33	2	3	9	.455	.
Polidor, Wil, Prince William†	.232	72	300	276	26	64	83	7	3	2	26	5	4	0	15	0	34	2	4	13	.301	.
Prieto, Alejandro, Wilmington†	.284	119	494	447	65	127	161	19	6	1	40	8	5	3	31	0	66	26	15	7	.360	.
Rackley, Keifer, Wilmington*	.279	95	347	290	47	81	128	13	2	10	47	0	3	7	46	2	55	4	2	5	.441	.
Raleigh, Matt, Frederick	.228	21	73	57	8	13	18	0	1	1	8	0	2	2	12	0	22	3	0	0	.316	.
Ramirez, Omar, Kinston	.400	2	6	5	1	2	5	0	0	1	3	0	0	0	1	0	0	0	0	1	1.000	.
Robinson, Tony, Lynchburg	.172	31	115	93	13	16	19	3	0	0	7	3	0	2	17	0	17	5	3	2	.204	.
Robledo, Nilson, Prince William	.259	80	338	313	37	81	121	16	0	8	46	0	2	2	21	0	55	0	0	2	.387	.
Russin, Tom, Frederick	.200	19	66	65	2	13	17	4	0	0	6	0	0	0	1	0	16	2	2	1	.262	.
Sanchez, Yuri, Winston-Salem*	.215	100	409	353	48	76	112	15	3	5	39	10	3	0	43	0	103	9	6	10	.317	.
Scalzitti, Will, Salem	.196	81	287	270	24	53	85	14	0	6	23	0	0	1	16	2	33	0	2	5	.315	.
Sharp, Scott, Winston-Salem	.232	34	116	95	14	22	30	8	0	0	8	6	0	2	13	0	39	3	1	2	.316	.
Shirley, Al, Wilmington	.229	116	407	340	54	78	146	13	2	17	47	0	1	9	57	3	149	8	7	1	.429	.
Short, Rick, Frederick	.312	126	517	474	68	148	190	33	0	3	54	5	4	5	29	2	44	12	7	14	.401	.
Simmons, Brian, Prince William†	.198	33	141	131	17	26	48	4	3	4	14	1	0	0	9	1	39	2	0	3	.366	.
Smith, Mark, Frederick	.000	1	1	1	0	0	0	0	0	0	0	0	0	0	0	0	0	0	0	1	.000	.
Smith, Matt, Wilmington*	.248	125	508	451	48	112	148	17	2	5	59	1	7	5	42	5	110	3	4	6	.328	.
Smith, Sean, Lynchburg	.227	87	315	278	18	63	98	9	1	8	34	2	1	2	32	0	59	3	1	3	.353	.
Strasser, John, Prince William	.200	18	66	55	7	11	14	0	0	1	2	2	0	1	8	0	18	0	0	1	.255	.
Strickland, Chad, Wilmington	.061	11	38	33	2	2	3	1	0	0	2	0	0	3	0	5	1	0	1	.091	.
Swafford, Derek, Lynchburg*	.259	116	502	433	77	112	144	18	4	2	48	12	1	8	48	0	107	35	18	2	.333	.
Sweet, Jonathan, Lynchburg*	.274	72	239	212	16	58	68	10	0	0	35	5	3	2	17	1	26	2	4	0	.321	.
Tarasco, Tony, Frederick*	.229	9	40	35	6	8	14	3	0	1	5	0	0	1	4	1	4	0	1	2	.400	.
Taylor, Jerry, Kinston	.260	64	201	146	19	38	52	9	1	1	19	4	0	3	48	2	37	1	1	2	.356	.
Teeters, Brian, Wilmington*	.215	61	211	172	41	37	58	9	3	2	17	1	1	4	33	1	50	19	3	5	.337	.
Thobe, Steve, Lynchburg	.228	109	394	359	49	82	130	15	0	11	42	0	0	6	29	0	93	4	4	13	.362	.
Thomas, Juan, Prince William	.299	134	556	495	88	148	248	28	6	20	71	0	2	5	54	3	129	9	3	15	.501	.

yer, Team	Avg.	G	TPA	AB	R	H	TB	2B	3B	HR	RBI	SH	SF	HP	BB	IBB	SO	SB	CS	GDP	Slg.	OBP
ɔmas, Rod, Winston-Salem.........	.000	3	7	7	0	0	0	0	0	0	0	0	0	0	0	0	4	0	0	2	.000	.000
vle, Justin, Winston-Salem	.256	116	454	351	60	90	159	19	1	16	47	2	1	4	93	3	96	17	3	12	.453	.416
ɔpy, Joe, Durham*	.250	5	22	20	3	5	8	0	0	1	3	0	0	0	2	0	3	1	2	2	.400	.318
ing, Andrew, Frederick†	.333	1	3	3	0	1	1	0	0	0	1	0	0	0	0	0	1	0	0	0	.333	.333
dez, Trovin, Winston-Salem†	.254	90	374	342	49	87	113	11	3	3	30	6	2	2	22	1	62	26	14	3	.330	.302
lker, Joe, Prince William†	.199	54	182	161	22	32	56	9	0	5	14	1	1	1	18	0	65	0	0	0	.348	.282
lker, Larry, Salem*	.500	2	8	8	3	4	10	3	0	1	1	0	0	0	0	0	1	0	0	1	1.250	.500
lker, Shon, Lynchburg*	.303	97	378	323	61	98	165	19	3	14	70	0	4	2	49	6	99	3	4	7	.511	.394
rner, Bryan, Kinston*	.225	43	121	111	9	25	30	2	0	1	12	1	1	0	8	0	23	2	1	1	.270	.275
rner, Mike, Durham*	.111	3	12	9	1	1	2	1	0	0	2	0	0	1	2	0	2	1	0	0	.222	.333
atley, Gabe, Durham*	.331	49	195	160	29	53	73	11	0	3	26	2	0	1	32	1	23	7	6	2	.456	.446
ite, Eric, Kinston......................	.239	114	471	422	50	101	141	26	1	4	52	7	4	6	32	1	65	3	4	10	.334	.300
ittaker, Jerry, Prince William	.257	83	335	303	50	78	126	12	3	10	42	0	2	6	24	0	70	13	4	7	.416	.322
lff, Mike, Frederick*	.253	105	374	352	44	89	131	21	0	7	50	2	3	1	16	5	32	6	3	12	.372	.285
od, Tony, Durham	.144	60	124	118	11	17	18	1	0	0	5	1	0	0	5	0	38	5	4	3	.153	.179
ght, Ron, Durham	.275	66	284	240	47	66	145	15	2	20	62	0	7	0	37	2	71	1	0	5	.604	.363
ght, Terry, W.S.-Dur.*	.200	58	172	160	15	32	38	4	1	0	11	0	0	1	12	0	18	4	5	2	.238	.256
ing, Eric, Salem	.300	3	13	10	2	3	6	3	0	0	0	0	0	0	3	0	1	2	0	0	.600	.462

GRAND SLAMS: Eddie, 3; Giudice, J. Thomas, 2; Berrios, R. Brooks, M. Evans, Guillen, Harriss, Holdren, Matos, McKinnon, Moyle, Rackley, V. Walker, 1 each.
AWARDED FIRST BASE ON CATCHER'S INTERFERENCE: Kopriva 3 (Barthol 2, Cedeno); Towle 3 (Barthol 3); Mat. Smith 2 (Scalzitti, Towle); Guillen (Gargiulo); A. g (Harriss); Rackley (M. Johnson).

PLAYERS WITH TWO OR MORE TEAMS

er, Team	Avg.	G	TPA	AB	R	H	TB	2B	3B	HR	RBI	SH	SF	HP	BB	IBB	SO	SB	CS	GDP	Slg.	OBP
os, Harry, Frederick	.230	43	179	161	25	37	60	9	1	4	20	1	2	3	12	0	21	8	3	5	.373	.292
os, Harry, Kinston.................	.192	24	84	73	7	14	25	5	0	2	11	1	1	0	9	0	16	2	0	2	.342	.277
ht, Terry, Winston-Salem* ..	.241	9	32	29	4	7	7	0	0	0	3	0	0	0	3	0	4	0	1	0	.241	.313
ht, Terry, Durham*	.191	49	140	131	11	25	31	4	1	0	8	0	0	0	9	0	14	4	4	2	.237	.243

1996 PITCHING

TEAM

m	W	L	Pct.	ERA	G	CG	ShO	Sv.	IP	H	TBF	R	ER	HR	SH	SF	HB	BB	IBB	SO	WP	Bk.
nington	80	60	.571	3.53	140	5	8	41	1221.0	1158	5134	595	479	95	47	26	44	395	26	835	64	6
ton	76	62	.551	3.56	138	3	14	37	1188.2	1095	5074	566	470	81	44	33	62	534	19	869	75	9
ham	73	66	.525	3.82	139	6	12	36	1216.2	1178	5235	630	517	99	54	52	53	499	13	1054	72	11
ston-Salem	74	65	.532	4.02	139	11	7	27	1203.0	1255	5196	643	538	143	30	46	51	423	9	746	70	7
m	62	76	.449	4.10	138	7	9	33	1205.1	1167	5253	656	549	75	53	44	49	558	19	969	84	13
ce William	58	80	.420	4.15	138	14	9	19	1193.0	1164	5189	668	550	101	52	45	68	479	32	923	61	14
hburg	65	74	.468	4.20	139	11	7	20	1192.2	1249	5303	704	557	99	55	25	69	459	21	896	87	15
erick...............	67	72	.482	4.41	139	6	9	37	1200.0	1237	5264	719	588	118	51	30	46	466	15	1104	75	11

INDIVIDUAL

TOP QUALIFIERS FOR EARNED-RUN AVERAGE TITLE

Minimum 112 innings. *Lefthanded pitcher.

er, Team	W	L	Pct.	ERA	G	GS	CG	ShO	GF	Sv.	IP	H	TBF	R	ER	HR	SH	SF	HB	BB	IBB	SO	WP	Bk.
ra, Noe, Kinston*	12	2	.857	2.70	24	24	1	0	0	0	140.0	124	576	52	42	12	0	3	0	62	1	131	9	0
well, David, Wilmington	13	9	.591	3.30	23	23	0	0	0	0	139.0	142	582	66	51	11	4	4	1	37	0	80	1	2
ert, Russ, Prince William	6	10	.375	3.38	25	25	1	0	0	0	144.0	129	609	73	54	12	8	11	6	62	3	148	3	2
ey, Dustin, Wilmington.............	10	5	.667	3.44	34	12	1	0	8	1	115.0	109	490	58	44	4	7	6	8	41	3	38	4	0
eno, Julio, Frederick	9	10	.474	3.50	28	26	0	0	1	0	162.0	167	682	80	63	14	8	0	9	38	0	147	9	3
y, Allen, Prince William.............	7	12	.368	3.54	24	24	4	0	0	0	137.1	123	568	69	54	16	3	1	7	49	2	131	7	4
dy, Phillip, Wilmington	7	11	.389	3.55	27	26	3	2	0	0	164.2	155	679	87	65	17	8	4	6	49	3	117	5	2
rson, Eric, Wilmington	12	5	.706	3.69	27	26	1	1	0	0	158.1	161	665	81	65	19	4	4	6	44	1	69	6	0
ger, John, Lynchburg	10	5	.667	3.74	33	15	2	0	0	0	132.1	101	554	65	55	11	3	3	4	58	0	113	11	1
t, Derrin, Durham*	12	9	.571	4.00	27	27	2	0	0	0	166.1	189	711	102	74	13	8	9	4	37	1	99	5	0
h, Chuck, Prince William	6	6	.500	4.01	20	20	2	1	0	0	123.1	125	545	65	55	7	3	2	10	49	1	99	13	1
, Matthew, Wilmington	9	9	.500	4.03	26	26	0	0	0	0	134.0	136	585	74	60	9	4	0	6	52	0	129	9	2
ord, Kevin, Lynchburg*	11	11	.500	4.07	28	28	4	1	0	0	172.1	195	749	99	78	15	7	6	11	25	0	100	4	1
wood, Kevin, Durham	6	9	.400	4.28	30	20	1	0	3	1	149.1	138	638	77	71	17	9	6	8	50	0	139	8	3
s, Kane, Lynchburg	11	9	.550	4.29	26	26	3	1	0	0	157.1	160	684	84	75	12	12	3	10	56	0	116	11	2

DEPARTMENTAL LEADERS: W—Caldwell, 13; L—Halley, 12; Pct.—Moss, .900; G—Spade, 53; GS—Caruthers, Pickford, 28; CG—Castillo, Halley, Pickford, 4; ShO—dy, 2; GF—Lightenberg, 42; SV—Prihoda, 25; IP—Pickford, 172.1; H—Pickford, 195; TBF—Pickford, 749; R—Warrecker, 105; ER—Warrecker, 88; HR—thers, 20; SH—Davis, 12; SF—Herbert, 11; HB—Caruthers, 13; BB—Warrecker, 88; IBB—Dixon, 8; SO—Herbert, 148; WP—Dyess, 15; BK—Halley, 4.

ALL PITCHERS

*Lefthanded pitcher.

er, Team	W	L	Pct.	ERA	G	GS	CG	ShO	GF	Sv.	IP	H	TBF	R	ER	HR	SH	SF	HB	BB	IBB	SO	WP	Bk.
, Cedric, Winston-Salem*..........	7	3	.700	3.82	12	12	1	1	0	0	68.1	73	293	37	29	10	4	3	0	28	0	40	4	0
rson, Eric, Wilmington	12	5	.706	3.69	27	26	1	1	0	0	158.1	161	665	81	65	19	4	4	6	44	1	69	6	0
rson, Jimmy, Lynchburg*	5	3	.625	1.93	11	11	1	1	0	0	65.1	51	267	25	14	2	2	0	2	21	0	56	1	0
ey, Justin, Winston-Salem*	3	3	.500	5.09	12	12	0	0	0	0	69.0	74	290	48	39	13	3	3	2	16	0	50	2	0
y, Ben, Winston-Salem	7	4	.636	2.85	16	15	2	0	0	0	101.0	91	409	34	32	10	1	1	4	32	0	78	3	0
es, Keith, Salem*	1	0	1.000	3.38	4	0	0	0	1	0	8.0	10	34	3	3	0	0	0	0	2	0	9	1	0

Pitcher, Team	W	L	Pct.	ERA	G	GS	CG	ShO	GF	Sv.	IP	H	TBF	R	ER	HR	SH	SF	HB	BB	IBB	SO	WP
Beltran, Alonso, Winston-Salem	2	1	.667	1.88	14	1	0	0	4	0	38.1	26	148	9	8	2	2	0	1	10	1	26	1
Bigham, Dave, Frederick*	4	6	.400	5.64	29	9	0	0	7	2	68.2	82	307	52	43	13	6	4	5	14	1	56	5
Blyleven, Todd, Lynchburg	2	1	.667	2.09	23	3	0	0	4	1	56.0	49	224	18	13	4	2	1	0	14	1	33	5
Bowie, Micah, Durham*	3	6	.333	3.66	13	13	0	0	0	0	66.1	55	283	29	27	4	6	3	7	33	0	65	2
Brabant, Dan, Kinston	1	1	.500	4.35	26	1	0	0	11	2	60.0	52	257	34	29	8	0	1	4	29	0	50	3
Briggs, Anthony, Durham	9	10	.474	4.40	31	18	1	0	3	0	124.2	131	548	84	61	10	7	9	3	60	1	76	9
Brixey, Dustin, Wilmington	10	5	.667	3.44	34	12	1	0	8	1	115.0	109	490	58	44	4	7	6	8	41	3	38	4
Brooks, Antone, Durham*	0	0	.000	0.00	2	0	0	0	1	0	3.0	1	10	0	0	0	0	0	0	0	0	0	0
Broome, Curtis, Prince William	3	3	.500	5.46	27	2	0	0	12	0	56.0	68	271	41	34	6	4	1	8	38	3	33	1
Brown, Derek, Frederick	0	1	.000	9.00	1	1	0	0	0	0	4.0	6	18	4	4	0	0	0	0	3	0	0	0
Brown, Michael, Lynchburg*	1	5	.167	7.14	34	11	0	0	6	0	69.1	91	356	66	55	6	2	4	8	52	1	62	8
Bryant, Adam, Winston-Salem	4	3	.571	2.38	28	0	0	0	23	8	34.0	39	149	13	9	1	0	3	2	10	0	16	0
Burke, John, Salem	0	1	.000	6.00	3	3	0	0	0	0	12.0	10	54	12	8	1	1	0	0	9	0	12	4
Burke, Stoney, Lynchburg	0	0	.000	0.00	2	0	0	0	1	0	2.0	2	9	0	0	0	0	0	0	0	0	1	0
Buteaux, Shane, Prince William	2	3	.400	3.35	23	0	0	0	17	2	40.1	34	171	18	15	3	7	1	3	22	1	29	2
Butler, Adam, Durham*	0	0	.000	0.00	9	0	0	0	9	5	11.0	2	41	0	0	0	0	0	1	7	0	14	0
Byington, Jimmie, Wilmington	0	0	.000	0.00	1	1	0	0	0	0	1.0	0	3	0	0	0	0	0	0	0	0	1	0
Cabrera, Jose, Kinston	1	1	.500	1.02	4	3	0	0	0	0	17.2	7	68	2	2	0	1	1	1	8	0	19	3
Cafaro, Rocco, Frederick	1	3	.250	4.50	8	0	0	0	7	2	20.0	19	85	10	10	2	0	0	1	6	0	16	0
Caldwell, David, Kinston*	13	9	.591	3.30	23	23	0	0	0	0	139.0	142	582	66	51	11	4	4	1	37	0	80	1
Carter, Lance, Wilmington	3	6	.333	6.34	16	12	0	0	3	0	65.1	81	292	50	46	8	1	0	2	17	2	49	3
Caruthers, Clay, Winston-Salem	10	10	.500	4.37	28	28	2	0	0	0	169.0	179	745	93	82	20	3	7	13	60	1	105	11
Castillo, Carlos, Prince William	2	4	.333	3.95	6	6	4	0	0	0	43.1	45	180	22	19	0	3	5	2	4	1	30	1
Chaves, Rafael, Lynchburg	1	3	.250	2.53	30	0	0	0	28	5	32.0	35	139	18	9	3	3	0	3	8	6	20	1
Christman, Scott, Prince William*	1	0	1.000	0.00	1	1	0	0	0	0	5.0	4	21	0	0	0	0	0	0	3	0	4	0
Clemons, Chris, Prince William	1	4	.200	2.25	6	6	0	0	0	0	36.0	36	150	16	9	6	0	3	0	8	0	26	1
Collie, Tim, Lynchburg	4	1	.800	3.60	24	0	0	0	17	1	25.0	26	110	10	10	2	3	0	1	10	4	14	1
Colmenares, Luis, Salem	4	5	.444	5.23	32	0	0	0	25	12	32.2	28	156	21	19	4	5	2	2	22	1	45	6
Conner, Scott, Frederick	1	2	.333	3.65	12	10	0	0	0	0	61.2	52	260	29	25	7	2	0	4	27	0	47	5
Crowther, Brent, Salem	3	3	.500	4.03	8	8	1	1	0	0	51.1	52	210	23	23	2	4	0	3	14	0	28	2
Cruz, Charlie, Durham*	1	1	.500	5.79	8	0	0	0	1	0	18.2	15	82	12	12	2	0	3	0	7	0	12	0
Davis, Kane, Lynchburg	11	9	.550	4.29	26	26	3	1	0	0	157.1	160	684	84	75	12	3	10	56	0	116	11	
Desrosiers, Erik, Prince William	1	4	.200	5.63	7	7	1	0	0	0	40.0	47	174	29	25	7	3	1	1	9	0	25	0
Dillinger, John, Lynchburg	10	5	.667	3.74	33	15	2	0	0	0	132.1	101	554	65	55	11	3	4	58	0	113	11	
Dixon, Jim, Prince William	5	7	.417	4.79	38	2	0	0	27	4	73.1	71	320	46	39	6	5	3	4	31	8	56	8
Donovan, Scot, Kinston	2	2	.500	5.26	28	0	0	0	12	0	53.0	60	236	39	31	6	4	3	1	25	1	36	3
Dougherty, Tony, Kinston	3	1	.750	1.62	18	0	0	0	15	8	33.1	29	135	6	6	2	3	0	1	11	2	32	3
Duncan, Sean, Prince William*	0	0	.000	5.74	6	0	0	0	6	1	15.2	17	75	11	10	3	1	1	0	9	1	13	2
Dyess, Todd, Frederick	4	7	.364	5.25	20	17	0	0	1	0	96.0	99	411	63	56	7	1	2	4	39	2	90	15
Dykhoff, Radhames, Frederick*	2	6	.250	5.66	33	0	0	0	15	3	62.0	77	290	45	39	7	4	4	1	22	2	75	0
Ebert, Derrin, Durham*	12	9	.571	4.00	27	27	2	0	0	0	166.1	189	711	102	74	13	8	9	4	37	1	99	5
Eden, Bill, Salem*	0	1	.000	2.70	11	0	0	0	7	1	13.1	8	56	4	4	0	0	1	1	7	1	15	2
Etler, Todd, Winston-Salem	4	5	.444	3.49	33	1	0	0	16	2	77.1	72	321	30	30	7	3	2	5	17	0	59	2
Flury, Pat, Wilmington	7	2	.778	1.92	45	0	0	0	19	5	84.1	66	339	22	18	2	1	0	4	29	4	67	9
Ford, Jack, Prince William*	3	4	.429	4.18	36	0	0	0	15	1	75.1	78	332	40	35	9	2	4	29	2	59	4	
France, Aaron, Lynchburg	0	8	.000	6.41	13	13	0	0	0	0	60.1	79	286	53	43	6	1	0	3	32	1	40	8
Fussell, Chris, Frederick	5	2	.714	2.81	15	14	1	1	0	0	86.1	71	369	36	27	8	1	1	5	44	0	94	5
Gamboa, Javier, Wilmington	3	1	.750	3.15	6	6	0	0	0	0	34.1	36	138	12	12	3	1	0	1	2	0	24	1
Garrett, Neil, Salem	0	1	.000	5.14	1	1	0	0	0	0	7.0	8	29	4	4	1	1	0	0	2	0	8	1
Genke, John, Salem	8	7	.533	3.53	41	1	0	0	13	3	86.2	88	372	41	34	7	8	3	3	28	1	55	5
Giard, Ken, Durham	3	5	.375	5.16	42	0	0	0	15	1	68.0	69	310	44	39	9	4	2	1	43	3	93	5
Giron, Emiliano, Winston-Salem	0	0	.000	7.41	12	0	0	0	3	0	17.0	21	80	14	14	7	0	0	2	11	0	17	0
Granata, Chris, Kinston	7	6	.538	4.34	35	6	1	1	6	0	95.1	105	417	51	46	5	2	4	6	43	4	57	9
Grieve, Tim, Wilmington	4	1	.800	1.31	22	0	0	0	13	4	34.1	28	143	9	5	1	2	1	0	13	3	30	1
Grundy, Phillip, Wilmington	7	11	.389	3.55	27	26	3	2	0	0	164.2	155	679	87	65	17	8	4	6	49	3	117	5
Hackman, Luther, Salem	5	7	.417	4.24	21	21	1	0	0	0	110.1	93	484	60	52	2	4	7	5	69	1	83	6
Hagy, Gary, Kinston	0	0	.000	0.00	3	0	0	0	2	0	3.0	3	11	0	0	0	0	0	0	0	0	0	0
Halley, Allen, Prince William	7	12	.368	3.54	24	24	4	0	0	0	137.1	123	568	69	54	16	3	1	7	49	2	131	7
Hanson, Kris, Winston-Salem	2	5	.286	5.36	9	8	0	0	0	0	47.0	46	204	31	28	6	1	0	4	16	0	26	1
Harrison, Kenny, Lynchburg	0	0	.000	0.00	1	0	0	0	0	0	1.1	1	6	0	0	0	0	0	1	0	1	1	
Harvey, Terry, Kinston	2	4	.333	4.00	12	12	0	0	0	0	69.2	80	293	38	31	5	4	2	3	16	0	34	2
Hasselhoff, Derek, Prince William	0	0	.000	5.23	5	0	0	0	4	1	10.1	14	49	7	6	1	0	0	6	2	9	0	
Herbert, Russ, Prince William	6	10	.375	3.38	25	25	1	0	0	0	144.0	129	609	73	54	12	8	11	6	62	3	148	3
Hernandez, Francisco, Frederick	4	3	.571	4.57	37	0	0	0	30	12	45.1	44	197	26	23	6	5	1	1	21	7	39	2
Hodges, Kevin, Winston-Salem	2	4	.333	5.35	8	8	0	0	0	0	38.2	45	172	30	23	2	1	3	18	0	15	5	
Johnson, Jason, Lynchburg	1	0	.200	6.50	15	5	0	0	1	0	44.1	56	204	37	32	6	5	1	12	0	27	0	
Jones, Mike, Durham*	0	2	.000	4.79	7	3	0	0	2	0	20.2	21	94	14	11	2	0	2	1	14	0	16	6
Kelly, Jeff, Lynchburg*	4	5	.444	3.60	13	13	0	0	0	0	75.0	77	335	45	30	7	0	0	0	26	0	57	6
Kelly, John, Lynchburg	0	0	.000	3.68	7	0	0	0	4	0	7.1	11	35	4	3	0	0	0	5	0	3	2	
King, Raymond, Durham*	3	6	.333	4.46	14	14	2	0	0	0	82.2	104	364	54	41	3	4	4	3	15	2	52	2
Kirkreit, Daron, Kinston	2	0	1.000	1.93	6	6	0	0	0	0	32.2	23	125	7	7	3	1	1	2	10	0	19	3
Koppe, Clint, Winston-Salem	8	2	.800	3.30	16	15	3	1	0	0	95.1	87	388	41	35	10	3	3	4	25	0	46	7
Kusiewicz, Mike, Salem*	0	1	.000	5.09	5	3	0	0	2	1	23.0	19	100	15	13	2	1	1	1	12	0	18	2
LaRock, Scott, Salem	3	2	.600	3.65	39	1	0	0	13	1	81.1	72	341	38	33	4	2	3	0	31	3	57	2
Lee, David, Salem	0	2	.000	2.25	4	0	0	0	5	1	12.0	14	56	6	3	0	0	2	6	0	10	2	
Leroy, John, Durham	7	4	.636	3.50	19	19	0	0	0	0	110.2	91	463	47	43	6	4	5	2	52	0	94	10
Ligtenberg, Kerry, Durham*	4	4	.636	2.41	49	0	0	0	42	20	59.2	58	255	20	16	3	3	2	3	16	3	76	4
Lister, Martin, Winston-Salem*	0	0	.000	5.40	7	0	0	0	3	0	10.0	9	47	7	6	1	2	1	0	9	0	9	0
Lott, Brian, Winston-Salem	8	11	.421	4.34	26	26	2	0	0	0	147.1	169	659	99	71	19	1	5	3	49	0	85	8
Lundquist, David, Prince William	0	2	.000	5.67	5	5	0	0	0	0	27.0	31	125	17	17	2	1	0	1	14	1	23	2
Magre, Pete, Winston-Salem	2	2	.500	2.58	37	0	0	0	14	1	59.1	44	255	22	17	5	1	3	2	32	2	33	4
Martin, Chandler, Salem	2	8	.200	5.87	13	13	1	0	0	0	69.0	80	333	56	45	5	4	0	5	53	1	59	12
Martin, Jeffrey, Wilmington	0	1	.000	4.87	5	5	0	0	0	0	20.1	24	87	11	11	3	1	0	5	0	12	0	

tcher, Team	W	L	Pct.	ERA	G	GS	CG	ShO	GF	Sv.	IP	H	TBF	R	ER	HR	SH	SF	HB	BB	IBB	SO	WP	Bk.
askivish, Joe, Lynchburg	1	2	.333	6.75	12	0	0	0	10	4	10.2	17	56	9	8	1	1	0	2	5	0	10	2	1
athews, Del, Durham*	4	3	.571	4.43	42	2	0	0	26	5	65.0	74	292	39	32	9	1	3	6	26	0	46	6	0
attson, Craig, Lynchburg	0	0	.000	7.71	6	0	0	0	2	0	7.0	10	36	6	6	3	0	1	0	5	0	4	0	0
cClinton, Patrick, Salem*	3	1	.750	2.09	39	0	0	0	20	1	64.2	58	278	28	15	2	3	6	3	21	1	47	2	2
cCormack, Andy, Kinston*	0	0	.000	.000	5	0	0	0	3	1	10.1	4	35	0	0	0	0	0	0	2	0	8	0	0
cDade, Neal, Durham*	0	1	.000	9.00	1	1	0	0	0	0	5.0	6	23	6	5	1	1	0	1	1	0	2	0	0
esa, Rafael, Kinston	8	3	.727	2.32	45	1	0	0	34	15	81.1	58	330	26	21	4	5	1	8	28	5	56	1	1
illion, Doug, Salem*	7	5	.583	2.53	17	16	1	1	0	0	106.2	84	443	37	30	1	2	0	2	60	1	99	8	1
illwood, Kevin, Durham	6	9	.400	4.28	33	20	1	0	3	1	149.1	138	638	77	71	17	9	6	8	58	0	139	8	3
ontoya, Wilmer, Kinston	1	2	.333	1.20	11	0	0	0	10	2	15.0	10	64	5	2	0	1	1	6	12	1	0	0	0
oreno, Julio, Frederick	9	10	.474	3.50	28	26	0	0	1	0	162.0	167	682	80	63	14	8	0	9	38	0	147	9	3
orones, Geno, Wilmington	6	3	.667	3.09	19	14	0	0	1	0	96.0	86	393	40	33	8	2	1	4	27	0	60	3	1
orseman, Robert, Frederick*	3	0	1.000	6.10	29	0	0	0	18	3	48.2	56	234	36	33	4	3	2	1	31	1	50	4	0
oss, Damian, Durham*	9	1	.900	2.25	14	14	0	0	0	0	84.0	52	333	25	21	9	3	3	2	40	0	89	7	2
urphy, Chris, Winston-Salem*	8	11	.421	5.09	29	19	1	1	3	1	123.2	164	550	87	70	19	2	5	1	36	1	80	10	0
urphy, Sean, Salem	0	1	.000	5.68	3	0	0	0	2	1	6.1	9	29	5	4	0	1	0	1	4	0	4	0	1
ajera, Noe, Kinston*	12	2	.857	2.70	24	24	1	0	0	0	140.0	124	576	52	42	12	0	3	0	62	1	131	9	0
egrette, Richard, Kinston	0	1	.000	23.14	1	1	0	0	0	0	2.1	9	20	7	6	0	0	0	0	4	0	0	0	0
ed, David, Salem	3	3	.500	2.95	7	6	1	1	1	0	42.2	37	183	25	14	3	1	1	1	18	0	42	3	0
eto, Tony, Winston-Salem	3	2	.600	5.14	37	0	0	0	16	4	56.0	66	259	37	32	4	3	5	6	22	2	30	6	0
sen, Jason, Prince William	6	4	.600	3.87	12	12	0	0	0	0	79.0	74	343	39	34	5	0	2	5	31	1	55	3	0
szewski, Eric, Durham	2	2	.500	1.88	32	0	0	0	15	0	52.2	34	212	12	11	3	2	2	4	21	0	69	5	0
opeza, Igor, Kinston	1	2	.333	3.81	8	4	0	0	2	0	26.0	23	120	13	11	3	0	0	4	18	0	20	4	1
ironto, Chad, Frederick	0	1	.000	4.80	8	1	0	0	2	0	15.0	11	63	9	8	0	2	0	0	8	0	6	2	0
ugh, Rick, Lynchburg*	1	4	.200	3.81	45	0	0	0	17	0	52.0	48	230	33	22	1	4	0	2	20	0	41	6	0
ona, Alex, Frederick	0	0	.000	13.50	2	0	0	0	1	0	2.0	3	10	3	3	0	0	0	0	1	0	1	0	0
rez, Julio, Kinston	1	2	.333	3.09	24	0	0	0	13	3	43.2	44	186	22	15	3	3	1	3	17	3	21	3	0
illips, Jason, Lynchburg	5	6	.455	4.52	13	13	1	1	0	0	73.2	82	343	47	37	3	2	2	5	35	0	63	6	1
illips, Marc, Wilmington*	2	0	1.000	5.26	31	0	0	0	14	0	49.2	59	219	33	29	4	3	2	3	19	0	19	4	0
ckford, Kevin, Lynchburg*	11	11	.500	4.07	28	28	4	1	0	0	172.1	199	749	99	78	15	7	6	11	25	0	100	4	1
tsley, Jim, Wilmington	0	1	.000	11.00	2	2	0	0	0	0	9.0	13	42	12	11	4	0	0	5	1	0	10	0	0
ace, Mike, Prince William	6	2	.750	2.31	23	0	0	0	20	7	39.0	30	161	17	10	1	4	3	7	0	31	1	0		
nson, Sidney, Frederick	7	6	.538	3.45	18	16	3	0	2	0	107.0	98	443	56	41	6	3	4	5	28	0	110	6	3
ol, Matt, Salem	5	6	.455	4.64	27	21	0	0	3	0	135.2	158	591	80	70	8	6	2	6	41	3	93	10	0
rtillo, Alex, Prince William*	1	1	.500	5.29	25	0	0	0	11	2	49.1	55	211	35	29	6	1	0	1	16	2	30	1	1
est, Eddie, Winston-Salem*	1	0	1.000	0.73	4	4	0	0	0	0	12.1	5	48	2	1	1	0	0	0	6	0	9	1	0
hoda, Stephen, Wilmington*	6	6	.500	1.47	47	0	0	0	40	25	79.1	50	313	17	13	1	6	1	3	22	4	89	3	0
irk, John, Prince William*	1	2	.333	6.21	18	3	0	0	10	0	42.0	52	206	34	29	3	0	4	2	28	1	22	4	0
cker, John, Durham*	4	3	.571	3.39	9	9	0	0	0	0	58.1	63	245	24	22	4	0	1	25	0	43	4	0	
driguez, Nerio, Frederick	8	7	.533	2.26	24	17	3	0	7	2	111.1	83	462	42	28	10	5	0	4	40	0	114	6	1
gers, Jason, Frederick*	7	8	.467	5.48	31	18	1	0	1	0	115.0	136	540	87	70	8	3	4	62	0	87	5	2	
se, Brian, Salem	0	0	.000	6.14	5	0	0	0	1	0	7.1	10	32	7	5	0	0	0	0	3	0	2	1	1
nion, Tony, Kinston	1	1	.500	5.79	6	1	0	0	2	0	14.0	16	71	10	9	0	1	0	3	14	0	11	3	0
nyan, Paul, Winston-Salem	3	1	.750	2.41	6	5	0	0	0	0	37.1	38	151	11	10	2	0	1	8	0	11	2	0	
er, Matthew, Wilmington	9	9	.500	4.03	26	26	0	0	0	0	134.0	136	585	74	60	9	4	6	52	2	129	9	2	
neaux, Francisco, Frederick	0	0	.000	37.13	2	1	0	0	0	0	2.2	9	23	11	11	3	0	0	1	6	0	3	0	0
wyer, Zack, Salem	0	1	.000	13.50	4	0	0	0	4	1	2.0	6	13	3	3	1	0	0	0	1	0	2	1	0
hmitt, Chris, Durham*	3	1	.750	4.40	42	0	0	0	14	0	73.2	80	347	47	36	5	3	2	4	45	0	65	5	1
epherd, Alvie, Frederick	6	5	.545	5.59	41	6	0	0	19	10	96.2	112	445	67	60	13	3	4	2	47	2	104	5	0
oemaker, Stephen, Salem	2	7	.222	4.69	25	13	0	0	1	0	86.1	63	371	49	45	6	1	5	4	63	0	105	1	1
ith, Chuck, Prince William	6	6	.500	4.01	20	20	2	1	0	0	123.1	125	545	65	55	7	3	2	10	49	1	99	13	1
okoviak, Jeff, Salem	6	6	.500	3.14	46	1	0	0	26	9	77.1	67	331	31	27	7	7	1	6	26	6	52	0	1
omon, David, Winston-Salem*	3	2	.600	4.56	38	0	0	0	16	0	53.1	56	240	32	27	4	1	5	3	27	2	28	3	0
ade, Matt, Lynchburg	6	4	.600	3.02	53	0	0	0	17	2	80.1	88	353	38	27	7	6	3	1	27	6	71	10	1
ift, Bill, Salem	0	0	.000	4.50	2	2	0	0	0	0	6.0	9	29	4	3	0	1	2	0	1	0	4	0	0
gheder, Jim, Wilmington	8	3	.727	2.42	31	2	0	0	9	2	74.1	60	294	24	20	8	3	1	2	14	2	50	5	0
ple, Jason, Lynchburg	2	2	.500	4.76	21	0	0	0	16	3	22.2	24	115	14	12	0	1	0	3	19	1	18	1	0
odile, Robert, Prince William	7	9	.438	4.30	25	22	1	1	1	0	132.0	133	571	73	63	5	6	5	7	56	3	91	8	1
narco, Mike, Frederick	5	3	.625	4.94	43	0	0	0	21	3	78.1	96	351	52	43	10	2	5	1	23	0	47	6	0
eedlie, Brad, Winston-Salem	1	5	.167	6.67	33	0	0	0	30	11	29.2	35	144	23	22	6	1	2	1	22	0	22	6	0
rek, Mike, Salem*	10	8	.556	4.87	26	25	2	1	0	0	149.2	167	658	92	81	15	6	8	5	59	0	103	10	0
lls, Doug, Salem	0	0	.000	7.07	5	3	0	0	1	1	14.0	17	70	12	11	3	0	0	1	13	0	13	0	0
recker, Teddy, Kinston	9	11	.450	6.03	27	26	1	1	0	0	131.1	137	616	105	88	12	3	7	11	88	0	88	14	1
oer, Lenny, Kinston	2	4	.333	1.83	36	0	0	0	25	6	59.0	44	250	12	12	0	6	1	1	36	5	49	2	0
glarz, John, Frederick	0	0	.000	7.71	2	0	0	0	1	0	2.1	3	10	2	2	0	0	0	0	1	0	4	0	0
gmann, Tom, Frederick	1	0	1.000	1.80	3	3	0	0	0	0	15.0	13	64	9	3	0	0	0	0	6	0	16	0	0
iams, Matt, Lynchburg*	0	0	.000	5.23	23	0	0	0	5	0	41.1	40	189	27	24	9	0	1	2	28	1	45	3	1
ff, Bryan, Wilmington	1	2	.333	3.61	42	0	0	0	28	4	62.1	49	280	35	25	2	3	1	3	38	1	56	6	0
ght, Jaret, Kinston	7	4	.636	2.50	19	19	0	0	0	0	101.0	65	413	32	28	1	6	3	7	55	0	109	7	1
ght, Scott, Winston-Salem	0	0	.000	7.71	1	1	0	0	0	0	4.2	7	24	4	4	0	0	0	0	4	0	5	0	0
ght, Terry, Durham*	0	0	.000	0.00	2	0	0	0	2	0	2.0	1	7	0	0	0	0	0	0	0	0	0	0	0
pelli, Mark, Prince William	0	2	.000	5.84	4	3	0	0	1	0	24.2	28	107	16	16	3	1	0	0	9	0	19	3	0
iri, Jon, Kinston	1	1	.500	3.21	3	0	0	0	2	0	14.0	14	65	8	5	0	0	1	9	1	11	3	0	

OMBINATION SHUTOUTS: **Durham (12)**—Bowie-Millwood-Briggs-Lightenberg, Bowie-Cruz-Lightenberg-Mathews, Leroy-Olszewski-Cruz-Mathews, Briggs-Giard-tenberg, Leroy-Mathews, Briggs-Schmitt, Leroy-Schmitt-Olszewski, Millwood-Schmitt-Butler, Moss-Lightenberg, Leroy-Schmitt, Millwood-Giard, Millwood-ewski. **Frederick (8)**—Dyess-Dykhoff, Rodriguez-Dykhoff-Bigham, Rodriguez-Trimarco, Dyess-Rogers-Morseman, Rodriguez-Morsemen-Hernandez, Moreno-son, Rodriguez-Dykhoff, Rogers-Trimarco. **Kinston (12)**—Najera-Mesa-Montoya, Granata-McCormick, Oropeza-Weber, Mesa-Weber, Cabrera-Mesa, Wright-Perez-ovan-Weber, Wright-Brabant, Harvey-Weber-Mesa, Caldwell-Dougherty, Najera-Dougherty, Kirkeit-Dougherty, Najera-Weber-Mesa. **Lynchburg (3)**—Anderson-Spade-kivish, Davis-Temple, Davis Chaves. **Prince William (7)**—Smith-Portillo, Halley-Theodile, Theodile-Dixon, Herbert-Ford, Theodile-Dixon-Place, Smith-Ford, Christman-eaux. **Salem (4)**—Hackman-LaRock, Million-Shoemaker, Sobboviak-Murphy, Pool-Sobkoviak. **Wilmington (5)**—Anderson-Prihoda, Gamboa-Telgheder-Prihoda, er-Brixey-Phillips-Flury, Carter-Phillips-Wolff, Grundy-Grieve. **Winston-Salem (4)**—Caruthers-Tweedlie, Bailey-Tweedlie, Murphy-Solomon, Caruthers-Bryant.

O-HIT GAMES: Hackman, Salem, defeated Kinston, 4-1, August 4.

TEAM

Team	Pct.	G	PO	A	E	TC	DP	PB
Kinston	.973	138	3566	1494	143	5203	124	18
Prince William	.967	138	3579	1445	173	5197	111	14
Durham	.966	139	3650	1397	180	5227	116	23
Wilmington	.965	140	3663	1568	190	5421	139	19
Winston-Salem	.964	139	3609	1520	190	5319	140	2
Salem	.964	138	3616	1607	195	5418	113	2
Frederick	.962	139	3600	1396	196	5192	105	2
Lynchburg	.959	139	3578	1511	220	5309	111	3

TRIPLE PLAY: Winston-Salem.

INDIVIDUAL

FIRST BASEMEN

NOTE: All caps denotes fielding-percentage leader based on 70 games for catchers, 93 for all other non-pitchers and 140 innings for pitchers. *Throws lefthanded.

Player, Team	Pct.	G	PO	A	E	TC	DP
Allen, Marlon, Winston-Salem	.984	117	1030	44	18	1092	94
Asche, Mike, Lynchburg	.889	2	16	0	2	18	2
Brooks, Eddie, Lynchburg	1.000	1	12	0	0	12	2
Casey, Sean, Kinston	.991	70	632	15	6	653	60
Chavez, Eric, Frederick	.989	35	240	24	3	267	23
Eddie, Steve, Winston-Salem	1.000	1	7	1	0	8	1
Evans, Michael, Wilmington	1.000	1	5	0	0	5	0
Fantauzzi, John, Salem*	.991	58	294	20	3	317	22
Farrell, Jon, Lynchburg	1.000	4	43	0	0	43	4
Hagy, Gary, Kinston	1.000	5	42	4	0	46	3
Harrison, Kenny, Lynchburg	.991	12	109	3	1	113	6
Harvey, Raymond, Kinston*	1.000	6	39	8	0	47	4
HOLDREN, Nate, Salem	.987	94	788	64	11	863	68
Kopriva, Dan, Prince William	.950	2	18	1	1	20	2
Larkin, Stephen, Win.-Salem*	.962	19	169	8	7	184	18
Light, Tal, Salem	1.000	4	15	2	0	17	1
Martinez, Ramon, Lynchburg	1.000	1	2	0	0	2	0
Mendez, Carlos, Wilmington	.992	28	220	15	2	237	19
Miller, David, Kinston*	.983	35	265	17	5	287	24
Nunez, Raymond, Durham	.982	60	478	22	9	509	47
Parsons, Jason, Winston-Salem	.989	9	87	6	1	94	15
Perry, Chan, Kinston	.996	27	212	21	1	234	24
Raleigh, Matt, Frederick	1.000	14	112	6	0	118	6
Robledo, Nilson, Prince William	.989	18	169	10	2	181	16
Russin, Tom, Frederick	.986	18	129	9	2	140	13
Scalzitti, Will, Salem	.981	23	145	7	3	155	11
Smith, Matt, Wilmington*	.986	120	1039	61	16	1116	108
Smith, Sean, Durham	.960	5	22	2	1	25	2
Thobe, Steve, Lynchburg	.990	91	702	24	7	733	45
Thomas, Juan, Prince William	.983	118	982	76	18	1076	83
Towle, Justin, Winston-Salem	1.000	1	11	0	0	11	1
Walker, Shon, Lynchburg*	.990	50	394	19	4	417	37
Whatley, Gabe, Durham	1.000	7	35	4	0	39	4
White, Eric, Kinston	1.000	1	0	1	0	1	0
Wolff, Mike, Frederick*	.990	88	619	52	7	678	44
Wood, Tony, Durham	.984	14	58	5	1	64	6
Wright, Ron, Durham	.987	66	494	34	7	535	37
Wright, Terry, Durham*	1.000	2	3	0	0	3	0

TRIPLE PLAY: Allen.

SECOND BASEMEN

Player, Team	Pct.	G	PO	A	E	TC	DP
Arias, Amador, Winston-Salem	.964	66	129	163	11	303	41
Asche, Mike, Lynchburg	1.000	1	1	0	0	1	0
Boulware, Ben, Prince William	.956	87	158	211	17	386	44
Brito, Luis, Durham	.900	2	4	5	1	10	1
Brooks, Eddie, Lynchburg	.961	29	55	68	5	128	11
Byington, Jimmie, Wilmington	1.000	4	4	5	0	9	1
Cawhorn, Gerad, Kinston	.924	43	79	91	14	184	23
Cedeno, Eduardo, Wilmington	.956	36	59	92	7	158	22
Cordero, Edward, Durham	.939	11	22	24	3	49	1
Daedelow, Craig, Frederick	1.000	14	24	31	0	55	7
EAGLIN, Mike, Durham	.9719	128	317	271	17	605	83
Fowler, Maleke, Frederick	1.000	2	2	3	0	5	0
Gabriel, Denio, Frederick	.893	24	49	43	11	103	12
Grunewald, Keith, Salem	1.000	10	21	38	0	59	4
Hagy, Gary, Kinston	.982	28	60	49	2	111	9
Jarrett, Link, Salem	.989	19	48	42	1	91	11
Jenkins, Dee, Winston-Salem	.946	22	44	62	6	112	20
Lofton, James, Winston-Salem	.964	58	120	144	10	274	36
Martin, Lincoln, Frederick	.948	85	157	207	20	384	46
Martinez, Ramon, Lynchburg	1.000	1	1	1	0	2	0
Mayber, Chan, Salem	.985	15	24	42	1	67	6
Montilla, Julio, Wilmington	.917	8	8	14	2	24	4
Moore, Brandon, Prince William	.957	7	13	9	1	23	2
Munoz, Omer, Lynchburg	1.000	3	5	7	0	12	3

Player, Team	Pct.	G	PO	A	E	TC	D
Nunez, Raymond, Durham	1.000	1	0	1	0	1	
Nunez, Sergio, Wilmington	.9718	103	228	254	14	496	6
Pena, Elvis, Salem	.960	97	211	245	19	475	6
Polidor, Wil, Prince William	.975	39	70	89	4	163	1
Short, Rick, Frederick	.950	20	26	31	3	60	
Strasser, John, Prince William	.962	13	26	25	2	53	
Swafford, Derek, Lynchburg	.957	111	234	281	23	538	6
White, Eric, Kinston	.965	81	175	188	13	376	4
Wood, Tony, Durham	1.000	4	7	4	0	11	
Young, Eric, Salem	.875	3	8	6	2	16	

TRIPLE PLAY: Arias.

THIRD BASEMEN

Player, Team	Pct.	G	PO	A	E	TC	D
Arias, Amador, Winston-Salem	.800	4	1	3	1	5	
Asche, Mike, Lynchburg	.875	25	9	54	9	72	
Bernhardt, Steve, Salem	.931	61	39	150	14	203	1
Berry, Mike, Frederick	1.000	2	0	3	0	3	
Brito, Luis, Durham	1.000	1	1	2	0	3	
Brooks, Eddie, Lynchburg	.885	10	6	17	3	26	
Bryant, Chris, Frederick	.818	2	2	7	2	11	
Byington, Jimmie, Wilmington	.946	10	6	29	2	37	
Cawhorn, Gerad, Kinston	.857	11	1	23	4	28	
Cedeno, Eduardo, Wilmington	.909	20	7	23	3	33	
Chavez, Eric, Frederick	.943	41	17	82	6	105	
Cordero, Edward, Durham	.944	10	7	10	1	18	
Daedelow, Craig, Frederick	1.000	1	0	1	0	1	
Eddie, Steve, Winston-Salem	.928	134	98	315	32	445	2
Fraraccio, Dan, Prince William	.929	21	12	40	4	56	
Gabriel, Denio, Frederick	1.000	3	0	2	0	2	
Garcia, Freddy, Lynchburg	.916	109	96	285	35	416	2
Hagy, Gary, Kinston	.833	3	1	4	1	6	
Helms, Wes, Durham	.920	67	40	133	15	188	
Jarrett, Link, Salem	1.000	7	2	7	0	9	
Jenkins, Dee, Winston-Salem	.800	1	0	4	1	5	
JORGENSEN, Tim, Kinston	.949	118	105	268	20	393	2
Kopriva, Dan, Prince William	.920	89	57	196	22	275	1
Light, Tal, Salem	.827	58	33	120	32	185	
Lofton, James, Winston-Salem	.750	1	2	1	1	4	
Magee, Danny, Durham	.878	43	22	86	15	123	
Mayber, Chan, Salem	.932	27	15	53	5	73	
McNally, Sean, Wilmington	.936	124	84	282	25	391	2
Montilla, Julio, Wilmington	.900	5	1	8	1	10	
Perry, Chan, Kinston	1.000	1	0	3	0	3	
Polidor, Wil, Prince William	.968	30	25	65	3	93	
Raleigh, Matt, Frederick	.875	2	4	3	1	8	
Short, Rick, Frederick	.906	99	75	195	28	298	
Whatley, Gabe, Durham	.836	17	9	37	9	55	
White, Eric, Kinston	.935	12	10	33	3	46	
Wood, Tony, Durham	.865	17	7	25	5	37	

SHORTSTOPS

Player, Team	Pct.	G	PO	A	E	TC	
Arias, Amador, Winston-Salem	.923	40	57	123	15	195	
Brito, Luis, Durham	.943	67	77	171	15	263	
Brooks, Eddie, Lynchburg	.897	32	35	87	14	136	
Byington, Jimmie, Wilmington	.875	2	3	4	1	8	
Cedeno, Eduardo, Wilmington	.955	5	6	15	1	22	
Cordero, Edward, Durham	.931	40	36	99	10	145	
Daedelow, Craig, Frederick	.854	11	11	24	6	41	
Eddie, Steve, Winston-Salem	.800	2	2	6	2	10	
Fraraccio, Dan, Prince William	.880	16	27	39	9	75	
Gabriel, Denio, Frederick	.872	13	17	24	6	47	
Hagy, Gary, Kinston	.946	37	50	73	7	130	
Hermansen, Chad, Lynchburg	.897	64	75	168	28	271	
Houser, Kyle, Salem	.961	117	151	342	20	513	
Jarrett, Link, Salem	.952	10	9	31	2	42	
Lawrence, Chip, Frederick	.924	42	42	115	13	170	

ayer, Team	Pct.	G	PO	A	E	TC	DP
agee, Danny, Durham	.888	39	39	88	16	143	15
artinez, Eddy, Frederick	.941	74	94	209	19	322	32
artinez, Ramon, Lynchburg	.896	18	24	45	8	77	8
ayber, Chan, Salem	.932	18	21	47	5	73	5
RCEDES, Guillermo, Kinston	.978	117	178	354	12	544	66
antilla, Julio, Wilmington	.869	31	40	73	17	130	14
oore, Brandon, Prince William	.955	117	177	307	23	507	56
lidor, Wil, Prince William	.902	8	9	28	4	41	8
eto, Alejandro, Wilmington	.929	119	163	364	40	567	79
binson, Tony, Lynchburg	.910	30	33	98	13	144	13
nchez, Yuri, Winston-Salem	.957	100	120	300	19	439	64
ort, Rick, Frederick	.917	7	5	17	2	24	2
asser, John, Prince William	.800	2	0	4	1	5	1
od, Tony, Durham	.824	7	4	10	3	17	1

TRIPLE PLAY: Sanchez.

OUTFIELDERS

ayer, Team	Pct.	G	PO	A	E	TC	DP
ns, Carlos, Frederick	.970	42	93	4	3	100	0
nonte, Wady, Frederick	.953	84	147	17	8	172	4
che, Mike, Lynchburg	.926	82	108	5	9	122	1
rios, Harry, Fred.-Kin	.985	65	125	9	2	136	2
ulware, Ben, Prince William	.966	33	49	7	2	58	2
to, Luis, Durham	1.000	8	15	2	0	17	0
wn, Adrian, Lynchburg	.981	50	99	4	2	105	1
ngton, Jimmie, Wilmington	.976	90	163	2	4	169	0
leno, Eduardo, Wilmington	1.000	4	2	1	0	3	0
avez, Eric, Frederick	.667	3	1	1	1	3	0
udio, Patricio, Kinston	.995	79	185	2	1	188	1
ner, Decomba, Win.-Salem	.978	123	308	6	7	321	1
rea, Miguel, Durham	.988	63	160	5	2	167	2
o, Brian, Salem	.833	13	10	0	2	12	0
ningham, Earl, Salem	1.000	22	28	3	0	31	0
quila, Tom, Frederick	.930	42	50	3	4	57	1
aney, Donovan, Wilmington	.966	121	214	15	8	237	0
ucci, David, Frederick*	.972	55	100	4	3	107	2
ns, Jason, Prince William	.960	94	158	11	7	176	1
ns, Michael, Wilmington	.947	37	69	2	4	75	2
ell, Jon, Lynchburg	1.000	8	13	1	0	14	0
ler, Maleke, Frederick	1.000	2	2	0	0	2	0
accio, Dan, Prince William	1.000	4	6	1	0	7	0
ich, Anton, Durham	1.000	45	79	2	0	81	0
bill, Chad, Salem	.976	114	197	8	5	210	1
lice, John, Salem*	.970	100	210	16	7	233	3
s, Chip, Kinston*	.977	131	229	27	6	262	4
don, Gary, Salem	1.000	10	23	0	0	23	0
en, Jose, Lynchburg	.949	125	224	16	13	253	6
Ronnie, Salem	1.000	5	9	0	0	9	0
lin, Mark, Salem	1.000	5	7	0	0	7	0
ey, Raymond, Kinston*	1.000	2	1	0	0	1	0
es, Darren, Prince William	.985	65	120	13	2	135	3
ge, Roy, Frederick	1.000	3	6	0	0	6	0
on, Jeff, Frederick	1.000	4	6	0	0	6	0
s, Johnny, Frederick	.992	85	116	3	1	120	0
s, Andruw, Durham	.963	66	174	9	7	190	2
es, Pookie, Salem	.927	97	108	7	9	124	1
LEY, Erskine, Lynchburg	.988	101	156	7	2	165	1
edy, Gus, Durham	.950	106	121	12	7	140	1
, Andre, Winston-Salem	.969	75	150	7	5	162	2
sale, Eugene, Frederick	.962	49	100	1	4	105	0
in, Stephen, Win.-Salem*	.957	15	21	1	1	23	0
as, Andres, Prince William	1.000	14	29	1	0	30	0
s, Marcus, Durham	.985	67	122	7	2	131	1
onier, Jason, Frederick	.953	20	39	2	2	43	0
on, James, Winston-Salem	1.000	1	1	0	0	1	0
nez, Ramon, Lynchburg	.963	69	146	8	6	160	2
er, Chan, Salem	.976	37	33	7	1	41	1
ide, Gator, Durham	1.000	13	21	0	0	21	0
nnon, Sandy, Prince William	.977	107	241	12	6	259	2
r, David, Kinston*	.950	88	141	10	8	159	0
ow, Nick, Winston-Salem	.969	115	232	16	8	256	0
art, Garrett, Salem	1.000	23	54	4	0	58	0
ns, Jason, Winston-Salem	1.000	1	1	0	0	1	0
, Chan, Kinston	.973	19	35	1	1	37	0
ley, Keifer, Wilmington	.984	65	120	5	2	127	0
tti, Will, Salem	.900	20	24	3	3	30	0
ey, Al, Wilmington	.941	111	182	8	12	202	0
ons, Brian, Prince William	.973	33	70	2	2	74	1
r, Jerry, Kinston	.987	53	69	5	1	75	0
rs, Brian, Wilmington*	.950	48	92	4	5	101	1
as, Rod, Winston-Salem	1.000	1	2	0	0	2	0
Joe, Durham*	1.000	5	5	1	0	6	0

Player, Team	Pct.	G	PO	A	E	TC	DP
Valdez, Trovin, Winston-Salem	.954	89	180	8	9	197	3
Walker, Shon, Lynchburg*	1.000	4	2	0	0	2	0
Warner, Bryan, Kinston*	.930	39	61	5	5	71	0
Warner, Mike, Durham*	1.000	1	3	0	0	3	0
Whatley, Gabe, Durham	1.000	28	44	4	0	48	2
White, Eric, Kinston	.909	19	20	0	2	22	0
Whittaker, Jerry, Prince William	.981	82	143	9	3	155	3
Wood, Tony, Durham	1.000	5	4	1	0	5	0
Wright, Terry, W.S.-Dur.*	.989	49	82	6	1	89	1

OUTFIELDERS WITH TWO OR MORE TEAMS

Player, Team	Pct.	G	PO	A	E	TC	DP
Berrios, Harry, Frederick	.978	43	85	4	2	91	2
Berrios, Harry, Kinston	1.000	22	40	5	0	45	0
Wright, Terry, Winston-Salem*	1.000	7	12	2	0	14	0
Wright, Terry, Durham*	.987	42	70	4	1	75	1

CATCHERS

Player, Team	Pct.	G	PO	A	E	TC	DP	PB
Antczak, Chuck, Prince William	.929	3	11	2	1	14	1	2
Avery, Mark, Prince William	.978	37	242	23	6	271	2	1
Barthol, Blake, Salem	.979	92	668	80	16	764	5	15
Brooks, Ramy, Wilmington	.987	105	605	76	9	690	7	15
Burke, Stoney, Lynchburg	.978	34	163	18	4	185	1	7
Byington, Jimmie, Wilmington	1.000	1	1	0	0	1	0	0
Carone, Rick, Prince William	1.000	7	51	6	0	57	2	0
Chavez, Eric, Frederick	.978	13	76	12	2	90	1	2
Evans, Michael, Wilmington	1.000	8	10	0	0	10	0	0
Evans, Pat, Kinston	.972	20	60	10	2	72	2	1
FOSTER, Jim, Frederick	.999	78	641	67	1	709	8	12
Gargiulo, Mike, Frederick	.971	51	405	30	13	448	2	12
Harriss, Robin, Kinston	.981	87	498	74	11	583	4	12
Higgins, Mike, Salem	.966	47	323	44	13	380	1	11
Johnson, Mark, Prince William	.992	16	112	8	1	121	0	0
Mahoney, Mike, Durham	.990	90	674	83	8	765	7	16
Matos, Pascual, Durham	.982	55	394	54	8	456	3	5
McCollough, Adam, Frederick	.889	3	13	3	2	18	0	0
Mendez, Carlos, Wilmington	.970	34	198	25	7	230	1	3
Mendez, Sergio, Lynchburg	.988	36	226	26	3	255	4	6
Moyle, Mike, Kinston	.992	54	339	49	3	391	5	5
O'Toole, Bobby, Frederick	.857	3	6	0	1	7	0	0
Robledo, Nilson, Prince Wm.	.969	40	277	40	10	327	4	7
Scalzitti, Will, Salem	.931	5	25	2	2	29	0	0
Sharp, Scott, Winston-Salem	.953	34	169	13	9	191	2	5
Smith, Sean, Durham	1.000	3	17	1	0	18	0	2
Strickland, Chad, Wilmington	1.000	10	62	7	0	69	0	1
Sweet, Jonathan, Lynchburg	.988	65	370	41	5	416	3	6
Thobe, Steve, Lynchburg	.979	27	169	18	4	191	3	18
Towle, Justin, Winston-Salem	.982	112	594	100	13	707	6	20
Walker, Joe, Prince William	.989	40	262	20	3	285	3	4

PITCHERS

Player, Team	Pct.	G	PO	A	E	TC	DP
Allen, Cedric, Winston-Salem*	.923	12	8	16	2	26	3
ANDERSON, Eric, Wilmington	1.000	27	15	22	0	37	5
Anderson, Jimmy, Lynchburg*	.955	11	2	19	1	22	2
Atchley, Justin, Winston-Salem*	.923	12	2	10	1	13	0
Bailey, Ben, Winston-Salem	1.000	16	3	23	0	26	1
Barnes, Keith, Salem*	1.000	4	1	2	0	3	0
Beltran, Alonso, Winston-Salem	1.000	14	0	5	0	5	0
Bigham, Dave, Frederick*	.929	29	1	12	1	14	0
Blyleven, Todd, Lynchburg	1.000	23	0	5	0	5	0
Bowie, Micah, Durham*	1.000	13	5	10	0	15	0
Brabant, Dan, Kinston	1.000	26	4	6	0	10	0
Briggs, Anthony, Durham	.892	31	13	20	4	37	2
Brixey, Dustin, Wilmington	.926	34	6	19	2	27	0
Brooks, Antone, Durham*	1.000	2	0	1	0	1	0
Broome, Curtis, Prince William	.938	27	1	14	1	16	3
Brown, Derek, Frederick	1.000	1	1	1	0	2	0
Brown, Michael, Lynchburg*	1.000	34	1	14	0	15	2
Bryant, Adam, Winston-Salem	.750	28	0	3	1	4	1
Burke, John, Salem	.600	3	0	3	2	5	1
Buteaux, Shane, Prince William	.917	23	7	4	1	12	1
Butler, Adam, Durham*	1.000	9	0	1	0	1	0
Cabrera, Jose, Kinston	1.000	4	0	4	0	4	0
Cafaro, Rocco, Frederick	1.000	8	0	1	0	1	0
Caldwell, David, Kinston*	.967	23	3	26	1	30	0
Carter, Lance, Wilmington	1.000	16	1	15	0	16	2
Caruthers, Clay, Winston-Salem	.912	28	7	24	3	34	1
Castillo, Carlos, Prince William	.857	6	0	6	1	7	0
Chaves, Rafael, Lynchburg	.900	30	2	7	1	10	1
Christman, Scott, Prince Wm.*	1.000	0	1	0	0	1	0

Player, Team	Pct.	G	PO	A	E	TC	DP
Clemons, Chris, Prince William	.875	6	2	5	1	8	0
Collie, Tim, Lynchburg	1.000	24	3	6	0	9	0
Colmenares, Luis, Salem	1.000	32	1	9	0	10	0
Conner, Scott, Frederick	.857	12	2	4	1	7	1
Crowther, Brent, Salem	.913	8	5	16	2	23	2
Cruz, Charlie, Durham*	1.000	8	0	3	0	3	0
Davis, Kane, Lynchburg	.938	26	8	37	3	48	1
Desrosiers, Erik, Prince William	1.000	7	1	11	0	12	0
Dillinger, John, Lynchburg	.867	33	7	19	4	30	0
Dixon, Jim, Prince William	.929	38	2	11	1	14	2
Donovan, Scot, Kinston	1.000	28	4	13	0	17	0
Dougherty, Tony, Kinston	1.000	18	0	2	0	2	0
Duncan, Sean, Prince William*	1.000	6	1	1	0	2	0
Dyess, Todd, Frederick	.762	20	6	10	5	21	1
Dykhoff, Radhames, Frederick*	.933	33	5	9	1	15	1
Ebert, Derrin, Durham*	.952	27	3	37	2	42	1
Eden, Bill, Salem*	1.000	11	0	1	0	1	1
Etler, Todd, Winston-Salem	1.000	33	5	10	0	15	2
Flury, Pat, Wilmington	1.000	45	6	15	0	21	1
Ford, Jack, Prince William*	1.000	36	1	8	0	9	0
France, Aaron, Lynchburg	.917	13	4	7	1	12	0
Fussell, Chris, Frederick	.938	15	4	11	1	16	0
Gamboa, Javier, Wilmington	1.000	6	2	6	0	8	0
Genke, Todd, Salem	1.000	41	3	20	0	23	1
Giard, Ken, Durham	1.000	42	4	9	0	13	1
Giron, Emiliano, Winston-Salem	1.000	12	3	3	0	6	0
Granata, Chris, Kinston	1.000	35	6	11	0	17	1
Grieve, Tim, Wilmington	1.000	22	1	6	0	7	0
Grundy, Phillip, Wilmington	.966	27	11	17	1	29	2
Hackman, Luther, Salem	.947	21	3	15	1	19	1
Hagy, Gary, Kinston	1.000	2	0	1	0	1	0
Halley, Allen, Prince William	.868	24	12	21	5	38	4
Hanson, Kris, Kinston	1.000	9	1	7	0	8	0
Harvey, Terry, Kinston	.824	12	7	7	3	17	0
Herbert, Russ, Prince William	.909	25	11	29	4	44	0
Hernandez, Francisco, Frederick	1.000	37	3	4	0	7	0
Hodges, Kevin, Wilmington	1.000	8	4	7	0	11	0
Johnson, Jason, Lynchburg	.857	15	4	8	2	14	0
Jones, Mike, Durham*	.800	7	2	2	1	5	0
Kelly, Jeff, Lynchburg*	.941	13	3	13	1	17	0
Kelly, John, Lynchburg	1.000	7	0	2	0	2	0
King, Raymond, Durham*	1.000	14	0	15	0	15	0
Kirkreit, Daron, Kinston	1.000	6	1	1	0	2	0
Koppe, Clint, Winston-Salem	1.000	16	4	7	0	11	2
Kusiewicz, Mike, Salem*	1.000	5	0	6	0	6	0
LaRock, Scott, Salem	.950	39	5	14	1	20	0
Lee, David, Salem	1.000	8	2	1	0	3	0
Leroy, John, Durham	.947	19	3	15	1	19	1
Ligtenberg, Kerry, Durham	1.000	49	3	6	0	9	0
Lister, Martin, Winston-Salem*	1.000	7	0	1	0	1	0
Lott, Brian, Winston-Salem	.938	26	16	14	2	32	0
Lundquist, David, Prince William	1.000	5	0	3	0	3	0
Magre, Pete, Winston-Salem	1.000	37	3	13	0	16	1
Martin, Chandler, Salem	1.000	13	2	7	0	9	0
Martin, Jeffrey, Wilmington	1.000	5	2	4	0	6	0
Maskivish, Joe, Lynchburg	1.000	12	0	1	0	1	0
Mathews, Del, Durham*	.929	42	4	9	1	14	1
Mattson, Craig, Lynchburg	1.000	6	0	2	0	2	0
McClinton, Patrick, Salem*	.900	39	9	9	2	20	0
McCormack, Andy, Kinston*	1.000	5	0	2	0	2	0
McDade, Neal, Lynchburg	.000	1	0	0	1	1	0
Mesa, Rafael, Kinston	.818	45	1	8	2	11	0

Player, Team	Pct.	G	PO	A	E	TC
Million, Doug, Salem*	.929	17	4	22	2	28
Millwood, Kevin, Durham	.941	33	12	20	2	34
Montoya, Wilmer, Kinston	.800	11	0	4	1	5
Moreno, Julio, Frederick	.875	28	11	17	4	32
Morones, Geno, Wilmington	1.000	19	4	18	0	22
Morseman, Robert, Frederick*	1.000	29	3	10	0	13
Moss, Damian, Durham*	.833	14	6	9	3	18
Murphy, Chris, Winston-Salem*	.941	29	2	14	1	17
Murphy, Sean, Salem	1.000	3	1	2	0	3
Najera, Noe, Kinston*	1.000	24	2	19	0	21
Negrette, Richard, Kinston	.500	1	0	1	1	2
Nied, David, Salem	.889	7	1	7	1	9
Nieto, Tony, Winston-Salem	.917	37	6	16	2	24
Olsen, Jason, Prince William	1.000	12	5	6	0	11
Olszewski, Eric, Durham	1.000	32	4	5	0	9
Oropeza, Igor, Kinston	.750	8	0	3	1	4
Paronto, Chad, Frederick	1.000	8	2	2	0	4
Paugh, Rick, Lynchburg*	.846	45	1	10	2	13
Pena, Alex, Frederick	1.000	2	0	1	0	1
Perez, Julio, Kinston	.909	24	3	7	1	11
Phillips, Jason, Lynchburg	.857	13	3	9	2	14
Phillips, Marc, Wilmington*	.909	31	4	6	1	11
Pickford, Kevin, Lynchburg*	.973	28	10	26	1	37
Place, Mike, Prince William	1.000	23	3	5	0	8
Ponson, Sidney, Frederick	.950	18	6	13	1	20
Pool, Matt, Salem	.960	27	16	32	2	50
Portillo, Alex, Prince William*	1.000	25	2	10	0	12
Priest, Eddie, Winston-Salem*	1.000	4	1	1	0	2
Prihoda, Stephen, Wilmington*	1.000	47	4	13	0	17
Quirk, John, Prince William	1.000	18	1	3	0	4
Rocker, John, Durham*	1.000	9	3	6	0	9
Rodriguez, Nerio, Frederick	.900	24	8	19	3	30
Rogers, Jason, Frederick*	.968	31	16	14	1	31
Rose, Brian, Salem	.600	5	1	2	2	5
Runion, Tony, Kinston	1.000	6	0	2	0	2
Runyan, Paul, Winston-Salem	1.000	6	0	10	0	10
Saier, Matthew, Wilmington	.870	26	6	14	3	23
Schmitt, Chris, Frederick*	.824	42	3	11	3	17
Shepherd, Alvie, Frederick	.952	41	10	10	1	21
Shoemaker, Stephen, Salem	1.000	25	4	9	0	13
Smith, Chuck, Prince William	.919	20	9	25	3	37
Sobkoviak, Jeff, Salem	1.000	46	0	8	0	8
Solomon, David, Win.-Salem*	.833	38	1	9	2	12
Spade, Matt, Lynchburg	.950	53	1	18	1	20
Swift, Bill, Salem	1.000	2	0	2	0	2
Telgheder, Jim, Wilmington	.923	31	3	9	1	13
Temple, Jason, Lynchburg	1.000	21	1	5	0	6
Theodile, Robert, Prince William	.938	25	7	23	2	32
Trimarco, Mike, Frederick	.964	43	11	16	1	28
Tweedlie, Brad, Winston-Salem	1.000	33	1	7	0	8
Vavrek, Mike, Salem*	.913	26	13	29	4	46
Walls, Doug, Salem	1.000	5	2	1	0	3
Warrecker, Teddy, Kinston	.750	27	3	12	5	20
Weber, Lenny, Kinston	1.000	36	2	6	0	8
Weglarz, John, Frederick	1.000	2	0	1	0	1
Wegmann, Tom, Frederick	1.000	3	0	2	0	2
Williams, Matt, Lynchburg*	1.000	23	0	2	0	2
Wolff, Bryan, Wilmington	1.000	42	3	13	0	16
Wright, Jaret, Kinston	1.000	19	1	11	0	12
Wright, Scott, Winston-Salem	1.000	1	0	1	0	1
Zappelli, Mark, Prince William	1.000	4	0	4	0	4
Zubiri, Jon, Kinston	1.000	3	1	1	0	2

The following players did not have any fielding statistics at the positions indicated or appeared only as a designated hitter, pinch-hitter or pinch-runner: S. Burk... Byington, 1b, p; Cordero, of; Garrett, p; Harrison, p; Hasselhoff, p; Liefer, dh; McDade, p; E. Pena, 3b; Pittsley, p; Ramirez, dh; Saneaux, p; Sawyer, p; Scalzitti, 3b; S... 1b; Mark Smith, dh; Tarasco, dh; Utting, dh; L. Walker, dh; T. Wright, p.

LEAGUE CHAMPIONS

Year	Team	Pct.	Year	Team	Pct.	Year	Team	Pct.
1945—	Danville	.681	1951—	Durham	.600	1957—	Durham	
1946—	Greensboro	.599		Winston-Salem (2nd)†	.583		HP-Thomasville	
	Raleigh (2nd)†	.563	1952—	Raleigh	.581	1958—	Danville	
1947—	Burlington	.613		Reidsville (4th)†	.536		Burlington (4th)†	
	Raleigh (3rd)†	.574	1953—	Raleigh	.593	1959—	Raleigh	
1948—	Raleigh	.592		Danville (2nd)†	.572		Wilson (2nd)†	
	Martinsville (2nd)†	.570	1954—	Fayetteville*	.628	1960—	Greensboro‡	
1949—	Danville	.601	1955—	HP-Thomasville	.580		Burlington	
	Burlington (4th)†	.500		Danville (2nd)†	.533	1961—	Wilson	
1950—	Winston-Salem*	.693	1956—	HP-Thomasville	.591	1962—	Durham	
				Fayetteville (4th)§	.523		Wilson	

r	Team	Pct.	Year	Team	Pct.	Year	Team	Pct.
	Kinston (2nd)†	.593	1972—	Salem‡	.657	1985—	Lynchburg	.679
3—	Kinston§	.538		Burlington	.632		Winston-Salem‡	.417
	Greensboro§	.590	1973—	Lynchburg	.588	1986—	Hagerstown	.655
	Wilson (2nd)†	.535		Winston-Salem‡	.557		Winston-Salem‡	.594
4—	Kinston§	.572	1974—	Salem	.671	1987—	Salem‡	.576
	Winston-Salem§†	.590		Salem	.582		Kinston	.536
5—	Peninsula§	.597	1975—	Rocky Mount	.667	1988—	Kinston§	.629
	Durham§	.580		Rocky Mount	.614		Lynchburg	.486
	Tidewater†	.528	1976—	Winston-Salem	.618	1989—	Durham	.609
6—	Kinston§	.547		Winston-Salem	.551		Prince William‡	.522
	Winston-Salem§	.586	1977—	Lynchburg	.591	1990—	Kinston	.652
	Rocky Mount†	.533		Peninsula‡	.556		Frederick‡	.544
7—	Durham∞(West.)	.536	1978—	Peninsula	.696	1991—	Kinston‡	.645
	Raleigh (East.)	.542		Lynchburg‡	.614		Lynchburg	.482
8—	Salem (West.)	.607	1979—	Winston-Salem■	.607	1992—	Lynchburg	.570
	Ral-Dur (East.)	.597	1980—	Peninsula‡	.714		Peninsula‡	.536
	HP-Thom.▲(W.)	.493		Durham	.600	1993—	Wilmington	.532
9—	Rocky M (East.)	.569	1981—	Peninsula	.522		Winston-Salem‡	.514
	Salem (West.)	.542		Hagerstown‡	.507	1994—	Wilmington‡	.681
	Ral-Dur◆(East.)	.560	1982—	Alexandria‡	.597		Winston-Salem	.555
0—	Winston-Salem‡	.586		Durham	.588	1995—	Wilmington	.601
	Burlington	.597	1983—	Lynchburg‡	.691		Kinston‡	.591
1—	Peninsula‡	.647		Winston-Salem	.529	1996—	Wilmington▼	.571
	Kinston	.623	1984—	Lynchburg‡	.645		Kinston	.551
				Durham	.486			

■Won championship and four-club playoff. †Won four-club playoff. ‡Won split-season playoff. §League was divided into Eastern, Western divisions. ∞Won ▲-club, two-division playoff. sWon eight-club, two-division playoff against Raleigh-Durham. uWon eight-club, two-division playoff against Burlington. ▼n both halves of split season (no playoffs). tLeague divided into Northern and Southern Divisions and played a split-season, won playoffs.

CLASS A *Carolina League*

FLORIDA STATE LEAGUE

LEAGUE OFFICE

President
Chuck Murphy
Address
P.O. Box 349
Daytona Beach, FL 32115
Phone
904-252-7479

Teams (affiliation)
Brevard County Manatees (Marlins)
Charlotte Rangers (Rangers)
Clearwater Phillies (Phillies)
Daytona Cubs (Cubs)
Dunedin Blue Jays (Blue Jays)
Fort Myers Miracle (Twins)
Kissimmee Cobras (Astros)

Lakeland Tigers (Tigers)
St. Lucie Mets (Mets)
St. Petersburg Devil Rays (Devil Ray
Sarasota Red Sox (Red Sox)
Tampa Yankees (Yankees)
Vero Beach Dodgers (Dodgers)
West Palm Beach Expos (Expos)

1996 FINAL STANDINGS

FIRST HALF

EAST DIVISION

Team	W	L	T	Pct.	GB
Vero Beach (Dodgers)	39	24	0	.619	....
West Palm Beach (Expos)	34	33	0	.507	7
St. Lucie (Mets)	32	34	0	.485	8½
Daytona (Cubs)	31	37	0	.456	10½
Kissimmee (Astros)	28	38	0	.424	12½
Brevard County (Marlins)	25	45	0	.357	17½

WEST DIVISION

Team	W	L	T	Pct.	G
Clearwater (Phillies)	44	26	0	.629	.
Tampa (Yankees)	41	25	0	.621	
Dunedin (Blue Jays)	40	29	0	.580	
Fort Myers (Twins)	36	32	1	.529	
St. Petersburg (Cardinals)	35	34	1	.507	
Lakeland (Tigers)	33	36	0	.478	
Charlotte (Rangers)	31	38	0	.449	
Sarasota (Red Sox)	25	43	0	.368	

SECOND HALF

EAST DIVISION

Team	W	L	T	Pct.	GB
St. Lucie (Mets)	39	28	0	.582	....
Daytona (Cubs)	40	29	0	.580	....
West Palm Beach (Expos)	34	34	0	.500	5½
Kissimmee (Astros)	32	37	0	.464	8
Vero Beach (Dodgers)	26	42	0	.382	13½
Brevard County (Marlins)	22	47	0	.319	18

WEST DIVISION

Team	W	L	T	Pct.	G
Tampa (Yankees)	43	25	0	.632	
Fort Myers (Twins)	43	26	0	.623	
Sarasota (Red Sox)	42	26	0	.618	
St. Petersburg (Cardinals)	40	29	0	.580	
Clearwater (Phillies)	31	36	0	.463	
Charlotte (Rangers)	32	38	0	.457	
Lakeland (Tigers)	28	41	0	.406	
Dunedin (Blue Jays)	27	41	0	.397	

COMPOSITE

Team	Tam.	Ft.M.	Clw.	St.P.	StL	Day.	WPB	V.B.	Sar.	Dun.	Char.	Kis.	Lak.	B.C.	W	L	T	Pct.	.
Tampa (Yankees)	....	9	10	8	6	5	5	4	5	5	9	4	9	5	84	50	0	.627	
Fort Myers (Twins)	3	....	5	7	3	3	4	7	6	8	14	6	8	5	79	58	1	.577	
Clearwater (Phillies)	4	7	....	6	5	4	4	3	8	8	5	7	9	5	75	62	0	.547	
St. Petersburg (Cardinals)	8	4	7	....	3	4	4	6	7	6	6	6	9	5	75	63	1	.543	
St. Lucie (Mets)	2	5	1	5	....	8	6	9	4	6	4	6	2	13	71	62	0	.534	
Daytona (Cubs)	3	4	4	4	8	....	5	5	6	7	5	6	4	10	71	66	0	.518	
West Palm Beach (Expos)	2	4	4	4	7	9	....	5	4	3	5	9	3	9	68	67	0	.504	
Vero Beach (Dodgers)	1	1	5	2	7	9	10	....	3	2	5	5	4	11	65	66	0	.496	
Sarasota (Red Sox)	7	9	4	5	4	2	4	2	....	6	8	3	7	6	67	69	0	.493	
Dunedin (Blue Jays)	8	4	8	8	2	0	5	6	6	....	2	4	7	7	67	70	0	.489	
Charlotte (Rangers)	3	2	7	6	4	3	3	2	4	10	....	6	8	5	63	76	0	.453	
Kissimmee (Astros)	3	2	1	2	7	9	7	8	5	3	2	....	3	8	60	75	0	.444	
Lakeland (Tigers)	3	4	3	3	5	4	5	4	9	5	8	5	....	3	61	77	0	.442	
Brevard County (Marlins)	3	3	3	3	1	6	5	5	2	1	3	8	4	....	47	92	0	.338	

Brevard County played home games in Melbourne, Fla.

Charlotte played home games in Port Charlotte, Fla.

Major league affiliations in parentheses.

PLAYOFFS: St. Lucie defeated Vero Beach, two games to none; Clearwater defeated Tampa, two games to none; St. Lucie defeated Clearwater, three g
to one, to win league championship.

REGULAR-SEASON ATTENDANCE: Brevard County, 140,724; Charlotte, 70,941; Clearwater, 75,118; Daytona, 97,098; Dunedin, 66,567; Fort Myers, 7?
Kissimmee, 29,482; Lakeland, 24,165; St. Lucie, 74,728; St. Petersburg, 124,174; Sarasota, 69,487; Tampa, 124,619; Vero Beach, 76,196; West Palm E
76,172; Total—1,126,652. Playoffs (8 games)—4,826. All-Star Game—6,904.

MANAGERS: Brevard County, Fredi Gonzales; Charlotte, Butch Wynegar; Clearwater, Al LeBoeuf; Daytona, Dave Trembley; Dunedin, Dennis Holmberg
Myers, John Russell; Kissimmee, Alan Ashby; Lakeland, Dave Anderson; St. Lucie, John Gibbons; St. Petersburg, Chris Maloney; Sarasota, DeMarlo
Tampa, Trey Hillman; Vero Beach, Jon Debus; West Palm Beach, Rick Sofield.

ALL-STAR TEAM: 1B—Chris Richard, St. Petersburg; 2B—Richard Almanzar, Lakeland; 3B—Jose Lopez, St. Lucie; SS—Mike Coolbaugh, Charlotte;
Inf.—Placido Polanco, St. Petersburg; LF—Aaron Fuller, Sarasota; CF—Anthony Sanders, Dunedin; RF—Mike Murphy, Charlotte; Utility OF—Kurk E
Tampa; C—Paul LoDuca, Vero Beach; Pat Cline, Daytona; DH—Daryle Ward, Lakeland; RHP—Blake Stein, St. Petersburg; Roy Halladay, Dunedin; L
Anthony Mounce, Kissimmee; Tommy Phelps, West Palm Beach; Relievers—Jay Tessmer, Tampa; Curtis King, St. Petersburg; Most Valuable Players
Tessmer, Tampa; Manager—Trey Hillman, Tampa; Coaches—Al LeBoeuf, Clearwater; Chris Maloney, St. Petersburg.

1996 BATTING

TEAM

Team	Avg.	G	TPA	AB	R	H	TB	2B	3B	HR	RBI	SH	SF	HP	BB	IBB	SO	SB	CS	GDP	LOB	ShO	Slg.	OBP
aytona	.267	137	5051	4510	660	1205	1787	234	36	92	585	19	33	81	404	15	795	181	76	91	915	7	.396	.336
harlotte	.264	139	5321	4713	678	1246	1758	253	32	65	595	41	42	69	456	22	890	110	73	108	948	10	.373	.335
arasota	.262	136	5069	4476	566	1171	1662	215	42	64	512	52	33	64	439	12	915	159	64	88	969	7	.371	.334
Vst Palm Bch	.260	135	5060	4450	587	1156	1585	214	34	49	508	47	45	89	428	11	815	142	83	76	952	10	.356	.334
akeland	.257	138	5160	4650	578	1197	1703	233	42	63	517	28	37	66	379	12	919	144	61	98	946	10	.366	.320
ampa	.257	134	5080	4407	587	1131	1629	212	32	74	542	54	37	56	526	19	892	110	62	114	984	11	.370	.341
ero Beach	.255	131	4889	4280	598	1092	1501	171	41	52	514	53	28	36	490	19	859	139	67	86	907	13	.351	.335
issimmee	.254	135	4851	4348	500	1105	1533	206	33	52	441	52	31	40	376	18	746	121	65	93	893	13	.353	.317
t. Petersburg	.252	139	5073	4508	533	1138	1508	185	37	37	480	45	44	38	436	19	745	82	54	116	957	10	.335	.321
learwater	.252	137	5228	4534	629	1144	1636	208	31	74	559	60	43	83	508	17	902	152	49	101	996	8	.361	.336
unedin	.252	137	5135	4500	629	1135	1740	229	35	102	552	52	27	49	506	19	1056	102	78	94	943	8	.387	.333
ort Myers	.250	138	5258	4538	641	1134	1603	202	42	61	565	45	46	58	570	15	834	148	77	66	1001	8	.353	.338
t. Lucie	.249	133	4858	4356	517	1083	1459	161	31	51	461	37	31	54	378	16	863	177	84	91	878	8	.335	.314
revard County	.246	139	5219	4611	520	1134	1518	192	36	40	449	45	36	58	467	18	896	128	86	99	1000	11	.329	.321

INDIVIDUAL

TOP QUALIFIERS FOR BATTING CHAMPIONSHIP

Minimum 378 plate appearances. *Lefthanded batter. †Switch-hitter.

Player, Team	Avg.	G	TPA	AB	R	H	TB	2B	3B	HR	RBI	SH	SF	HP	BB	IBB	SO	SB	CS	GDP	Slg.	OBP
urphy, Mike, Charlotte	.332	87	396	358	73	119	174	20	7	7	52	3	0	3	32	1	94	22	9	5	.486	.392
manzar, Richard, Lakeland	.306	124	543	471	81	144	173	22	2	1	36	12	3	8	49	0	49	53	19	5	.367	.379
Duca, Paul, Vero Beach	.305	124	515	439	54	134	165	22	0	3	66	0	4	2	70	2	38	8	2	14	.376	.400
eeman, Ricky, Daytona	.304	127	525	477	70	145	232	36	6	13	64	0	2	10	36	2	72	10	8	9	.486	.364
llmer, Brad, W. Palm Beach*	.303	102	431	380	52	115	161	29	1	5	63	0	8	11	32	2	43	4	6	9	.424	.367
ller, Aaron, Sarasota†	.300	115	513	434	74	130	175	20	5	5	49	4	5	4	63	0	60	33	12	4	.403	.389
eeves, Glenn, Brevard County	.299	123	554	478	72	143	198	29	4	6	41	4	4	5	63	0	82	8	5	6	.414	.384
pez, Jose, St. Lucie	.291	121	470	419	63	122	182	17	5	11	60	1	2	9	39	2	103	18	10	7	.434	.362
ard, Daryle, Lakeland*	.291	128	531	464	65	135	202	29	4	10	68	0	4	6	57	6	77	1	1	9	.435	.373
lanco, Placido, St. Petersburg	.291	137	582	540	65	157	196	29	5	0	51	6	7	5	24	1	34	4	4	31	.363	.323
entkiewicz, Doug, Ft Myers*	.291	133	568	492	69	143	202	36	4	5	79	1	6	3	66	3	47	12	2	10	.411	.374
ammell, Gary, Kissimmee*	.289	118	429	402	48	116	148	16	8	0	39	3	4	0	20	0	52	11	3	5	.368	.319
olbaugh, Mike, Charlotte	.287	124	502	449	76	129	215	33	4	15	75	0	3	8	42	4	80	8	10	10	.479	.357
rkett, Andy, Charlotte	.286	115	458	392	57	112	158	22	3	6	54	0	4	5	57	2	59	3	1	6	.403	.380
ralter, David, Sarasota	.285	120	497	452	47	129	205	34	3	12	70	0	4	9	30	3	101	8	7	9	.454	.339

DEPARTMENTAL LEADERS: G—Polanco, 137; AB—Polanco, 540; R—Almanzar, 81; H—Polanco, 157; TB—Freeman, 232; 2B—Freeman, Mientkiewicz, , 3B—Gibbs, 11; HR—Curl, 18; RBI—Ellis, 89; SH—Freel, 14; SF—Vessel, 11; HP—Kendall, 19; BB—Robles, 74; IBB—Carver, 7; SO—Curl, 133; SB— obs, 60; CS—Almanzar, Gibbs, 19; GIDP—Polanco, 31; Slg.—Freeman, Murphy, .486; OBP—LoDuca, .400.

ALL PLAYERS

*Lefthanded batter. †Switch-hitter.

Player, Team	Avg.	G	TPA	AB	R	H	TB	2B	3B	HR	RBI	SH	SF	HP	BB	IBB	SO	SB	CS	GDP	Slg.	OBP
d, Andy, Sarasota*	.287	58	246	202	28	58	81	15	1	2	41	2	2	3	37	1	28	10	3	6	.401	.402
ms, Tommy, Charlotte	.257	53	213	183	28	47	61	8	0	2	21	0	1	3	26	1	39	8	3	2	.333	.357
mo, Jason, Brevard County	.238	6	22	21	1	5	5	0	0	0	0	0	0	0	1	0	4	0	0	2	.238	.273
antara, Israel, W. Palm Beach	.311	15	66	61	11	19	33	2	0	4	14	0	1	1	3	0	13	0	0	1	.541	.348
manzar, Richard, Lakeland	.306	124	543	471	81	144	173	22	2	1	36	12	3	8	49	0	49	53	19	5	.367	.379
arez, Rafael, Fort Myers*	.136	6	24	22	1	3	3	0	0	0	1	0	1	0	1	0	7	0	1	0	.136	.167
ador, Manuel, Clearwater†	.273	52	196	172	24	47	72	10	0	5	21	2	1	2	19	0	46	1	1	5	.419	.351
ezcua, Adan, Kissimmee	.284	88	303	264	24	75	93	16	1	0	29	8	3	3	25	0	42	0	1	2	.352	.349
erson, Marlon, Clearwater*	.272	60	277	257	37	70	92	10	3	2	22	4	0	2	14	1	18	26	1	4	.358	.315
no, Eloy, Lakeland†	.232	46	166	155	15	36	41	3	1	0	7	1	1	1	8	0	23	0	1	2	.265	.273
old, Ken, Charlotte	.243	52	165	144	23	35	41	4	1	0	12	3	0	2	16	0	42	2	3	1	.285	.327
ncio, Alex, Vero Beach*	.266	115	436	402	56	107	137	12	6	2	49	3	0	2	29	2	68	15	6	11	.341	.319
y, Chris, Tampa	.246	100	403	325	55	80	126	28	0	6	46	1	1	5	71	1	78	16	4	5	.388	.388
los, Gilbert, Daytona	.253	90	319	285	38	72	84	12	0	0	25	3	2	7	20	0	49	23	8	5	.295	.315
in, Brady, Brevard County	.200	2	5	5	0	1	1	0	0	0	0	0	0	0	0	0	2	0	0	0	.200	.200
y, Edward, W. Palm Beach†	.281	128	551	484	62	136	154	9	3	1	34	12	3	10	42	0	93	42	17	2	.318	.349
e, Ryan, Lakeland†	.277	92	379	347	48	96	152	21	1	11	65	0	3	5	24	2	66	3	0	13	.438	.330
kett, Andy, Charlotte*	.286	115	458	392	57	112	158	22	3	6	54	0	4	5	57	2	59	3	1	6	.403	.380
ksdale, Shane, Kissimmee*	.133	9	16	15	1	2	5	0	0	1	2	1	0	0	0	0	7	0	0	1	.333	.133
ok, Todd, Vero Beach	.258	116	450	384	63	99	138	19	4	4	47	1	2	8	55	3	94	7	6	7	.359	.361
gh, Gavin, Brevard County†	.121	19	35	33	5	4	5	1	0	0	1	0	0	0	2	0	17	1	2	0	.152	.171
zani, Matt, Sarasota	.270	12	41	37	5	10	16	1	1	1	4	0	0	2	2	0	6	0	0	0	.432	.341
ney, Ryan, Tampa	.205	13	47	39	7	8	9	1	0	0	4	0	0	1	7	0	12	0	0	0	.231	.340
amin, Mike, Clearwater	.174	8	26	23	3	4	5	1	0	0	2	0	0	0	3	0	4	1	0	1	.217	.269
tley, Kevin, Daytona	.272	78	276	254	32	69	97	9	2	5	30	0	1	2	19	1	79	9	3	9	.382	.326
ek, Kurt, Tampa*	.303	88	370	320	48	97	148	14	7	11	55	0	3	6	41	3	40	6	3	5	.463	.389
nann, Steve, St. Petersburg†	.123	52	93	81	13	10	13	3	0	0	4	1	3	0	8	0	23	0	1	0	.160	.196
eney, Mo, W. Palm Beach	.176	7	19	17	1	3	5	0	1	0	2	2	0	0	0	0	6	0	0	0	.294	.176
achica, Hiram, W. Palm Beach	.337	71	313	267	50	90	123	17	5	2	26	3	3	6	34	0	47	21	3	6	.461	.419
emeier, Matt, Charlotte†	.274	131	544	503	74	138	183	31	4	2	62	3	7	3	28	6	81	18	2	15	.364	.312
el, Jamie, Lakeland	.227	31	51	44	10	10	11	1	0	0	1	0	0	0	7	0	8	1	2	0	.250	.333
ego, Ramon, Fort Myers†	.196	16	63	56	10	11	15	2	1	0	5	1	0	2	4	0	13	1	4	1	.268	.274

Player, Team	Avg.	G	TPA	AB	R	H	TB	2B	3B	HR	RBI	SH	SF	HP	BB	IBB	SO	SB	CS	GDP	Slg.	OB
Borrero, Richie, Sarasota	.250	27	100	92	15	23	37	5	0	3	13	1	0	1	6	0	17	1	1	3	.402	.30
Boryczewski, Marty, Lakeland	.188	13	21	16	1	3	4	1	0	0	2	0	0	1	4	0	7	0	0	0	.250	.38
Bowers, R.J., Kissimmee	.246	40	143	122	19	30	49	2	1	5	14	0	1	4	16	1	32	5	2	0	.402	.35
Bowles, John, Sarasota*	.183	33	109	93	17	17	23	3	0	1	8	2	1	0	13	0	18	2	2	1	.247	.28
Braddy, Junior, Sarasota	.241	98	378	345	37	83	134	20	5	7	36	2	2	3	26	1	97	7	2	5	.388	.29
Bravo, Danny, W. Palm Beach†	.197	48	155	137	15	27	33	2	2	0	12	3	0	1	14	0	30	3	4	0	.241	.27
Brinkley, Josh, W. Palm Beach	.261	87	316	268	34	70	100	11	2	5	27	5	3	14	26	0	44	1	2	6	.373	.35
Brock, Tarrik, Lakeland*	.278	53	237	212	42	59	93	11	4	5	27	0	3	5	17	0	61	9	2	4	.439	.34
Brown, Armann, Fort Myers	.248	112	483	403	75	100	139	14	8	3	27	7	3	5	65	0	75	36	15	5	.345	.35
Brown, Nate, W. Palm Beach*	.214	95	322	285	39	61	84	12	1	3	25	0	3	4	30	2	68	12	4	7	.295	.29
Brown, Vick, Tampa	.202	35	107	89	17	18	21	3	0	0	7	2	0	2	14	0	22	2	0	3	.236	.32
Brunson, Matt, Brevard County†	.205	127	476	396	51	81	96	13	1	0	29	7	3	4	66	0	89	28	11	6	.242	.32
Buchanan, Brian, Tampa	.260	131	575	526	65	137	197	22	4	10	58	1	1	10	37	6	108	23	8	14	.375	.32
Bustos, Saul, Daytona	.188	100	328	298	35	56	82	7	2	5	29	4	2	2	22	1	76	5	4	7	.275	.24
Butler, Rich, Dunedin*	.071	10	33	28	1	2	2	0	0	0	0	0	0	0	5	0	9	4	1	1	.071	.21
Cady, Todd, Brevard County†	.215	101	387	340	34	73	106	10	1	7	34	2	1	4	38	3	83	3	6	9	.312	.30
Camfield, Eric, Tampa*	.220	13	43	41	4	9	10	1	0	0	0	0	0	0	2	0	7	0	1	1	.244	.25
Camilo, Jose, Brevard County*	.182	12	49	44	6	8	16	0	1	2	4	1	1	0	3	0	11	2	0	0	.364	.22
Campos, Jesus, W. Palm Beach	.250	44	165	148	24	37	45	6	1	0	20	1	2	2	12	0	24	8	3	1	.304	.31
Campos, Miguel, Daytona	.417	8	14	12	1	5	5	0	0	0	1	0	0	1	1	0	1	0	0	0	.417	.50
Candelaria, Ben, Dunedin*	.200	39	138	125	13	25	33	5	0	1	6	1	0	0	12	0	25	1	4	1	.264	.27
Carpentier, Mike, Vero Beach	.226	64	231	208	28	47	68	9	0	4	23	2	1	1	19	1	34	3	4	3	.327	.29
Carvajal, Jhonny, W. Palm Beach	.237	114	487	426	50	101	125	18	0	2	38	7	4	6	44	0	73	14	16	9	.293	.3
Carver, Steve, Clearwater*	.278	117	493	436	59	121	204	32	0	17	79	0	4	1	52	7	89	1	1	12	.468	.35
Castro, Dennis, Brevard County*	.258	67	248	225	15	58	82	11	2	3	27	1	3	3	16	0	56	0	4	5	.364	.31
Cline, Pat, Daytona	.279	124	502	434	75	121	206	30	2	17	76	0	2	12	54	2	79	10	2	6	.475	.37
Coleman, Michael, Sarasota	.246	110	463	407	54	100	133	20	5	1	36	7	3	8	38	1	86	24	5	10	.327	.31
Contreras, Efrain, St. Petersburg*	.152	31	92	79	6	12	21	4	1	1	12	0	1	2	10	1	20	0	0	0	.266	.2
Cook, Hayward, Brevard County	.292	80	321	284	45	83	133	11	9	7	47	1	1	6	29	1	87	14	7	5	.468	.3
Coolbaugh, Mike, Charlotte	.287	124	502	449	76	129	215	33	4	15	75	0	3	8	42	4	80	8	10	10	.479	.3
Coquillette, Trace, W. Palm Beach	.252	72	304	266	39	67	95	17	4	1	27	0	3	8	27	1	72	9	7	5	.357	.3
Cora, Alex, Vero Beach*	.257	61	233	214	26	55	68	5	4	0	26	4	0	3	12	0	36	5	5	1	.318	.3
Cossins, Tim, Charlotte	.244	67	254	234	34	57	82	16	0	3	32	3	2	2	13	0	44	1	1	11	.350	.2
Costello, Brian, Clearwater	.206	81	311	282	28	58	81	13	2	2	31	4	4	4	17	0	84	6	4	3	.287	.2
Coston, Sean, Vero Beach†	.227	10	24	22	4	5	6	1	0	0	0	0	0	1	1	0	9	0	0	1	.273	.2
Cox, Chuck, Clearwater	.100	4	13	10	0	1	2	1	0	0	2	1	1	0	1	0	4	0	0	1	.200	.1
Cranford, Joe, Fort Myers	.219	30	115	105	9	23	28	3	1	0	17	2	1	0	7	0	21	3	1	0	.267	.2
Crespo, Felipe, Dunedin†	.324	9	36	34	3	11	18	1	0	2	6	0	0	0	2	1	6	0	0	0	.529	.3
Curl, John, Dunedin*	.246	125	499	447	52	110	188	20	2	18	62	2	5	1	44	1	133	7	4	6	.421	.3
Daly, Bob, St. Lucie	.273	53	197	183	18	50	64	8	0	2	24	0	2	0	12	0	22	1	3	9	.350	.3
Darden, Tony, Brevard County	.241	108	437	390	37	94	126	21	4	1	43	4	8	7	28	1	55	6	11	7	.323	.2
Darr, Mike, Lakeland*	.248	85	342	311	26	77	105	14	7	0	38	0	3	0	28	0	64	7	3	7	.338	.3
Daulton, Darren, Clearwater*	.000	1	2	1	1	0	0	0	0	0	0	0	0	0	1	0	0	0	0	0	.000	.5
Davila, Vic, Dunedin*	.269	122	443	398	54	107	161	26	2	8	72	2	8	33	3	76	1	3	15		.405	.3
Dawkins, Walt, Clearwater	.293	47	199	174	22	51	74	13	2	2	23	1	1	3	20	0	38	4	5	3	.425	.3
Delvecchio, Nick, Tampa	.269	17	72	52	9	14	22	2	0	2	4	0	0	3	17	1	15	2	1	2	.423	.4
Depastino, Joe, Sarasota	.262	97	380	344	35	90	128	16	2	6	44	0	4	3	29	1	71	2	3	7	.372	.3
Derosso, Tony, Sarasota	.257	116	462	416	64	107	178	19	5	14	60	0	2	5	31	2	84	15	2	10	.428	.3
Diaz, Cesar, St. Lucie	.239	74	271	247	29	59	97	15	1	7	34	0	3	3	18	1	72	9	2	12	.393	.3
Dowler, Dee, Daytona	.404	12	56	47	5	19	22	3	0	0	8	2	1	1	5	0	5	4	1	1	.468	.4
Dukart, Derek, Tampa*	.314	59	212	194	19	61	84	17	0	2	27	5	3	2	8	0	28	1	2	9	.433	.3
Durkin, Chris, Vero Beach*	.267	56	233	202	49	54	113	11	0	16	34	0	1	1	28	3	54	4	0	3	.559	.3
Ellis, Kevin, Daytona	.272	128	518	481	69	131	206	23	2	16	89	0	5	7	25	1	64	5	4	15	.428	.3
Emmons, Scott, Tampa	.204	36	113	98	6	20	27	2	1	1	10	3	0	2	10	1	26	0	1	1	.276	.2
Encarnacion, Juan, Lakeland	.240	131	538	499	54	120	200	31	2	15	58	0	3	12	24	2	104	11	5	10	.401	.2
Ephan, Larry, Charlotte	.226	9	39	31	3	7	9	2	0	0	8	0	0	0	8	1	6	0	0	2	.290	.3
Erwin, Mat, Brevard County	.278	60	240	212	24	59	77	13	1	1	31	0	1	5	22	4	30	0	2	3	.363	.3
Evans, Stan, Clearwater*	.241	80	288	241	42	58	73	5	2	2	23	9	3	2	33	1	36	12	5	8	.303	.3
Faggett, Ethan, Sarasota*	.275	110	457	408	48	112	152	12	3	8	35	7	1	6	35	0	118	24	10	9	.373	.3
Fagley, Dan, Brevard County	.094	20	61	53	1	5	7	2	0	0	2	1	0	2	5	0	19	0	0	3	.132	.1
Faircloth, Kevin, Vero Beach	.333	4	12	9	4	3	6	0	0	1	3	0	0	1	2	0	1	0	0	0	.667	.5
Falciglia, Tony, St. Petersburg	.233	16	46	43	5	10	13	3	0	0	4	0	0	1	1	0	16	0	2	0	.302	.2
Farley, Cordell, St. Petersburg	.000	5	6	4	1	0	0	0	0	0	0	0	0	0	1	0	1	0	0	0	.000	.
Farrell, Jon, St. Lucie	.000	1	2	1	0	0	0	0	0	0	0	0	0	0	0	0	0	0	0	0	.000	.5
Fenton, Cary, Charlotte	.272	87	336	290	47	79	90	9	1	0	22	7	2	6	31	0	49	21	11	5	.310	.3
Flora, Kevin, St. Lucie	.154	11	48	39	8	6	10	0	2	0	3	0	0	0	9	1	14	2	0	0	.256	.3
Flores, Jose, Clearwater	.228	84	324	281	39	64	83	6	5	1	39	5	1	3	34	0	42	15	2	6	.295	.3
Forkerway, Trey, Daytona	.280	49	165	143	27	40	48	6	1	0	13	1	1	3	17	0	17	7	6	0	.336	.
Fortin, Troy, Fort Myers	.249	104	401	358	40	89	125	11	2	7	52	6	4	4	29	0	29	1	1	10	.349	.3
Foster, Jeff, W. Palm Beach*	.154	3	14	13	0	2	2	0	0	0	1	0	0	1	0	0	6	1	0	0	.154	.
Freel, Ryan, Dunedin	.255	104	435	381	64	97	138	23	3	4	41	14	2	5	33	0	76	19	15	4	.362	.
Freeman, Ricky, Daytona	.304	127	525	477	70	145	232	36	6	13	64	0	2	10	36	2	72	10	8	9	.486	.
Freire, Alejandro, Kissimmee	.255	115	418	384	40	98	160	24	1	12	42	1	2	7	24	1	66	11	7	11	.417	.
French, Anton, Lakeland†	.277	61	268	253	36	70	92	10	6	0	14	0	1	2	12	0	37	24	10	2	.364	.
Fuller, Aaron, Sarasota†	.300	115	513	434	74	130	175	20	4	5	49	4	5	4	63	0	60	33	12	4	.403	.
Fullmer, Brad, W. Palm Beach*	.303	102	435	380	52	115	161	29	1	5	63	0	8	11	32	2	43	4	6	9	.424	.
Gallego, Mike, St. Petersburg	.294	14	59	51	7	15	15	0	0	0	5	0	0	1	7	1	4	0	0	2	.294	.
Garcia, Carlos, Fort Myers	.144	26	97	90	10	13	18	2	0	1	8	0	1	0	6	0	26	9	2	0	.200	.2
Gazarek, Marty, Daytona	.278	129	518	472	68	131	203	31	4	11	77	0	5	12	28	0	52	15	13	10	.430	.3
Giardi, Mike, Tam.-W.P.B.	.245	53	202	163	22	40	63	6	1	5	20	0	2	5	31	1	36	2	1	5	.387	.
Gibbs, Kevin, Vero Beach†	.270	118	502	423	69	114	145	9	11	0	33	6	4	4	65	0	80	60	19	6	.343	.
Gibralter, David, Sarasota	.285	120	497	452	47	129	205	34	3	12	70	0	4	9	30	3	101	8	7	9	.454	.
Gil, Benji, Charlotte	.258	11	34	31	2	8	17	6	0	1	7	0	0	0	3	0	7	0	0	0	.548	

yer, Team	Avg.	G	TPA	AB	R	H	TB	2B	3B	HR	RBI	SH	SF	HP	BB	IBB	SO	SB	CS	GDP	Slg.	OBP
zier, Larry, Brevard County	.154	5	14	13	0	2	2	0	0	0	0	0	0	0	1	0	3	1	0	0	.154	.214
igoski, Jason, Sarasota*	.385	4	16	13	1	5	5	0	0	0	3	1	0	0	2	0	2	0	1	0	.385	.467
nez, Paul, St. Lucie	.375	7	27	24	3	9	17	2	0	2	7	0	0	1	2	0	5	0	0	0	.708	.444
nez, Rudy, Tampa	.292	40	163	130	15	38	52	9	1	1	24	4	3	0	26	0	12	4	1	8	.400	.403
nzalez, Jimmy, Kissimmee	.168	73	242	208	19	35	59	4	1	6	17	2	3	3	25	0	59	1	0	8	.284	.264
odell, Steve, Brevard County	.250	1	4	4	0	1	1	0	0	0	0	0	0	0	0	0	0	0	0	0	.250	.250
don, Herman, Dunedin†	.133	20	33	30	4	4	7	1	1	0	2	0	0	0	3	0	11	1	0	1	.233	.212
ecki, Ryan, Charlotte*	.288	82	319	288	26	83	88	5	0	0	28	10	1	0	20	0	6	1	3	8	.306	.333
en, Scarborough, St. Petersbrg	.293	36	165	140	26	41	50	4	1	1	11	2	0	2	21	1	22	13	9	1	.357	.393
irrero, Rafael, St. Lucie	.246	83	283	260	32	64	82	12	0	2	26	0	2	1	20	0	37	4	0	9	.315	.300
irrero, Vladimir, W. Palm Beach	.363	20	85	80	16	29	52	8	0	5	18	0	1	1	3	0	10	2	2	1	.650	.388
iliano, Matt, Clearwater	.229	55	187	166	13	38	54	9	2	1	14	6	3	6	6	0	46	2	3	3	.325	.276
nderson, Shane, Fort Myers	.251	117	495	410	61	103	148	20	5	5	50	6	2	14	63	2	85	12	8	5	.361	.368
s, Matt, W. Palm Beach*	.266	77	235	207	22	55	67	7	1	1	26	0	3	3	22	1	27	4	2	2	.324	.340
opian, Derek, W. Palm Beach...	.268	43	176	157	23	42	60	12	0	2	22	0	3	3	13	1	11	0	3	2	.382	.330
, Ryan, St. Petersburg*	.213	66	195	174	7	37	47	10	0	0	11	1	1	0	19	2	37	0	0	2	.270	.289
vey, Aaron, Brevard County*...	.261	99	368	360	37	94	133	18	3	5	40	4	2	1	21	6	55	13	8	3	.369	.302
kins, Kraig, Tampa†	.299	75	315	268	41	80	95	2	5	1	21	9	1	2	35	0	41	13	6	2	.354	.382
vs, Scott, Clearwater*	.184	37	139	114	15	21	25	1	0	1	11	1	1	1	22	2	21	0	0	7	.219	.319
es, Chris, Dunedin	.236	32	127	106	14	25	34	6	0	1	12	4	1	5	11	0	21	1	2	6	.321	.333
ntower, Vee, Daytona†	.324	87	354	293	59	95	136	13	5	6	27	0	1	8	52	1	44	25	7	3	.464	.438
an, Todd, St. Petersburg	.333	2	6	6	1	2	2	0	0	0	0	0	0	0	0	0	3	0	0	0	.333	.333
i, Larry, Clearwater	.275	128	563	483	73	133	160	17	5	0	37	10	4	6	60	1	65	37	11	4	.331	.360
ter, Scott, St. Lucie	.257	127	527	475	71	122	149	19	1	2	38	3	3	8	38	4	68	49	12	6	.314	.321
ter, Torii, Fort Myers	.188	4	18	16	1	3	3	0	0	0	1	0	0	0	2	0	5	1	1	0	.188	.278
sek, Jason, Tampa	.000	4	3	3	0	0	0	0	0	0	0	0	0	0	0	0	1	0	0	0	.000	.000
son, Gavin, Sarasota	.239	87	327	276	26	66	83	13	2	0	24	8	3	7	33	0	47	4	6	6	.301	.332
kson, Jeff, Daytona	.245	16	62	53	5	13	17	2	1	0	4	0	1	0	8	0	18	7	1	1	.321	.339
son, Ryan, Brevard County*...	.308	6	27	26	4	8	13	2	0	1	4	0	0	0	1	0	7	1	0	0	.500	.333
ne, Angel, St. Lucie	.257	99	337	288	38	74	95	10	1	3	21	6	3	6	34	0	47	12	6	5	.330	.344
es, Ben, Fort Myers	.210	56	184	162	22	34	35	1	0	0	8	4	1	0	17	0	26	17	3	4	.216	.283
es, Ivory, Fort Myers*	.236	48	170	144	20	34	43	7	1	0	10	3	1	1	21	0	32	9	7	2	.299	.333
es, Jacque, Fort Myers*	.667	1	3	3	0	2	3	1	0	0	1	0	0	0	0	0	0	0	1	0	1.000	.667
onville, Joe, St. Petersburg	.158	41	110	101	10	16	21	3	1	0	7	0	0	1	8	1	22	0	0	5	.208	.227
, Pat, Tampa	.273	6	24	22	6	6	9	0	0	1	2	0	0	1	1	0	7	0	0	0	.409	.333
iall, Jeremy, Clearwater	.244	81	348	291	42	71	100	15	1	4	40	2	2	19	34	0	86	22	5	2	.344	.358
Jeff, Clearwater*	.244	101	378	348	53	85	117	15	4	3	34	3	1	10	16	1	82	15	3	5	.336	.296
, Brion, Dunedin	.071	7	16	14	1	1	1	0	0	0	1	1	0	1	0	0	5	0	0	2	.071	.133
ss, Tom, Fort Myers	.188	36	130	117	11	22	38	1	0	5	12	0	0	1	12	0	28	2	1	1	.325	.269
ers, Ramsey, W. Palm Beach .	.121	10	33	33	2	4	6	2	0	0	2	0	0	0	0	0	8	0	0	4	.182	.121
kie, Corey, Fort Myers*	.260	95	384	338	43	88	142	19	4	9	55	1	3	1	40	0	76	1	1	4	.420	.338
rde, Joe, Vero Beach	.000	14	1	1	0	0	0	0	0	0	0	0	0	0	0	0	0	0	0	0	.000	.000
aker, Dave, Kissimmee	.194	41	126	108	10	21	23	2	0	0	7	2	0	1	15	0	23	1	3	1	.213	.298
rum, Tito, Vero Beach	.238	44	137	122	12	29	40	5	0	2	14	2	2	1	10	1	33	2	0	0	.328	.296
ry, Jacques, Lakeland	.086	11	39	35	2	3	4	1	0	0	2	0	1	0	3	0	15	0	0	0	.114	.154
ry, Lonny, Lakeland	.236	75	326	292	35	69	101	9	7	3	21	2	0	8	24	1	72	19	3	4	.346	.312
, Ryan, Fort Myers	.272	106	459	404	74	110	171	20	7	9	62	6	9	6	60	0	96	21	9	2	.423	.367
aigne, Selwyn, Dunedin*	.222	31	132	117	16	26	34	2	3	0	4	4	0	2	9	0	30	1	3	5	.291	.289
gua, Eddie, Daytona	.196	43	147	143	10	28	44	1	0	5	14	0	0	1	3	1	31	3	1	3	.308	.218
viere, Jason, St. Petersburg	.300	41	165	140	27	42	57	6	0	3	18	4	1	0	18	1	19	1	1	1	.407	.377
ee, Keith, Fort Myers*	.273	58	247	198	39	54	81	8	2	5	37	0	2	5	42	2	52	2	2	2	.409	.409
Kevin, Lakeland	.216	97	354	320	37	69	113	18	1	8	41	0	1	3	30	0	90	1	1	4	.353	.288
es, Sendry, Kissimmee	.250	2	4	4	0	1	1	0	0	0	0	0	0	0	0	0	0	0	0	0	.250	.250
y, Shawn, Daytona†	.325	50	224	194	39	63	89	14	3	2	28	1	3	2	24	2	32	17	6	1	.459	.399
ton, Jose, Tampa	.232	113	432	375	39	87	128	16	5	5	37	11	4	8	34	1	74	11	7	6	.341	.306
ca, Paul, Vero Beach	.305	124	515	439	54	134	165	22	0	3	66	0	4	2	70	2	38	8	2	14	.376	.400
z, Jose, St. Lucie	.291	121	470	419	63	122	182	17	5	11	60	1	2	9	39	2	103	18	10	7	.434	.362
il, Mike, Tampa	.282	24	85	78	8	22	27	5	0	0	11	1	3	0	3	0	13	1	1	2	.346	.298
Jesus, St. Petersburg	.203	19	65	64	5	13	15	2	0	0	3	0	0	1	0	1	7	1	2	1	.234	.215
Matthew, Tampa*	.286	2	8	7	1	2	2	0	0	0	1	0	0	0	1	0	1	0	0	0	.286	.375
n, Leland, Charlotte	.249	99	397	338	45	84	108	12	3	2	31	3	4	13	39	2	74	9	12	7	.320	.345
dan, Dave, Daytona*	.300	7	27	20	5	6	7	1	0	0	3	0	0	0	7	0	2	0	0	1	.350	.481
ski, Brian, Vero Beach	.249	69	243	205	30	51	62	9	1	0	14	5	1	3	29	0	56	16	7	1	.302	.349
varren, Mark, Kissimmee	.190	74	181	158	16	30	40	7	0	1	10	3	0	5	15	1	58	17	2	1	.253	.281
nez, Rafael, Vero Beach*	.198	116	407	354	38	70	99	8	3	5	45	6	2	5	40	2	105	1	5	9	.280	.287
ews, Byron, W. Palm Beach†	.263	10	24	19	4	5	5	0	0	0	0	0	0	1	4	0	5	0	0	0	.263	.417
ey, Mike, St. Petersburg	.256	127	465	407	51	104	123	10	3	1	40	2	5	4	47	2	90	3	6	8	.302	.335
lay, John, Charlotte	.197	49	154	122	15	24	37	7	0	2	11	4	1	4	23	0	38	0	0	2	.303	.340
lmont, Jim, Fort Myers	.202	30	96	89	8	18	21	3	0	0	6	2	0	1	4	0	15	1	0	2	.236	.245
rmick, Andrew, Dunedin	.214	55	154	126	15	27	32	3	1	0	7	3	1	3	20	1	36	4	0	1	.254	.333
vid, Ray, W. Palm Beach*	.375	4	20	16	2	6	11	2	0	1	3	0	0	1	3	2	1	1	0	0	.688	.500
nald, Keith, St. Petersburg ...	.271	114	455	410	30	111	142	25	0	2	52	1	5	3	34	1	65	1	3	18	.346	.330
mb, Brian, Tampa†	.211	85	300	266	31	56	75	13	0	2	25	4	3	4	23	1	62	7	5	5	.282	.280
llen, Jon, Clearwater*	.185	51	132	119	10	22	32	4	0	2	9	0	0	1	12	0	26	0	0	7	.269	.265
bb, Buck, Kissimmee*	.346	7	29	26	4	9	10	1	0	0	3	0	0	0	3	1	5	3	0	0	.385	.414
Miguel, St. Petersburg	.115	8	28	26	2	3	3	0	0	0	1	0	0	1	0	0	12	0	0	0	.115	.148
se, Adam, Dunedin†	.248	97	391	315	50	78	144	23	2	13	51	0	4	3	69	2	68	3	1	5	.457	.384
key, Mitch, Kissimmee†	.333	74	267	231	29	77	99	19	0	1	31	1	5	1	29	5	26	1	1	9	.429	.402
lfe, Mike, Vero Beach	.000	2	5	5	0	0	0	0	0	0	0	0	0	0	0	0	0	0	0	0	.000	.000
er, Erik, Sarasota	.333	1	3	3	0	1	1	0	0	0	0	0	0	0	0	0	0	0	0	0	.333	.333
, Travis, Vero Beach	.242	12	36	33	6	8	18	1	0	3	8	0	0	0	3	0	6	0	0	2	.545	.306
ci, Mike, Daytona*	.183	39	89	82	6	15	15	0	0	0	3	1	0	1	5	0	16	0	3	1	.183	.239
kiewicz, Doug, Fort Myers* ..	.291	133	568	492	69	143	202	36	4	5	79	1	6	3	66	3	47	12	2	10	.411	.374

CLASS A   Florida State League

Player, Team	Avg.	G	TPA	AB	R	H	TB	2B	3B	HR	RBI	SH	SF	HP	BB	IBB	SO	SB	CS	GDP	Slg.
Millan, Adan, Clearwater	.270	101	409	348	55	94	150	21	1	11	55	0	6	3	52	2	52	1	2	15	.431
Miller, Logan, Dunedin	.174	10	26	23	2	4	4	0	0	0	1	0	0	0	3	0	8	0	0	0	.174
Miller, Ryan, St. Lucie	.255	86	349	310	32	79	99	8	3	2	23	13	1	3	22	1	51	8	5	5	.319
Moore, Tris, Lakeland	.152	11	43	33	6	5	7	2	0	0	4	3	0	0	7	0	11	2	0	1	.212
Morales, Francisco, St.P.-W.P.B.	.261	96	362	326	38	85	128	25	3	4	48	3	2	7	24	0	104	3	1	6	.393
Morgan, Dave, Dunedin	.261	39	109	88	13	23	40	3	1	4	15	0	0	3	18	0	24	0	1	3	.455
Moriarty, Mike, Fort Myers	.250	133	504	428	76	107	138	18	2	3	39	5	4	8	59	0	67	14	15	2	.322
Morimoto, Ken, Vero Beach	.000	6	12	11	1	0	0	0	0	0	0	0	0	0	1	0	4	0	0	0	.000
Mota, Gary, Kissimmee	.329	45	161	152	17	50	70	8	3	2	20	3	0	1	5	0	31	0	3	2	.461
Mota, Guillermo, St. Lucie	.234	102	348	304	34	71	90	10	3	1	21	7	2	1	34	0	90	8	8	6	.296
Motuzas, Jeff, Tampa	.000	2	3	3	0	0	0	0	0	0	0	0	0	0	0	0	3	0	0	0	.000
Mucker, Kelcey, Fort Myers*	.239	100	371	331	34	79	100	9	3	2	32	1	1	2	36	4	66	5	2	11	.302
Mummau, Rob, Dunedin	.208	36	125	106	10	22	25	3	0	0	10	7	0	0	12	0	22	2	4	2	.236
Munoz, Juan, St. Petersburg*	.242	90	375	330	41	80	101	12	3	1	46	3	3	1	38	0	35	6	5	8	.306
Murphy, Mike, Charlotte	.332	87	396	358	73	119	174	20	7	7	52	3	0	3	32	1	94	22	9	5	.486
Naples, Brandon, St. Lucie	.000	3	8	8	0	0	0	0	0	0	0	0	0	0	0	0	0	0	0	0	.000
Neal, Billy, Vero Beach	1.000	51	1	1	0	1	1	0	0	0	0	0	0	0	0	0	0	0	0	0	1.000
Nelson, Bry, Kissimmee†	.252	89	370	345	38	87	129	21	6	3	52	1	4	1	19	3	27	8	2	13	.374
Northeimer, Jamie, Clearwater	.254	101	411	327	52	83	134	21	0	10	42	4	4	16	60	1	69	0	2	7	.410
O'Connor, Rick, Clearwater	.240	12	31	25	3	6	7	1	0	0	2	2	1	0	3	0	5	0	0	0	.280
Ordaz, Luis, St. Petersburg	.272	126	467	423	46	115	143	13	3	3	49	7	6	1	30	0	53	10	5	10	.338
Ottavinia, Paul, W. Palm Beach*	.213	45	157	141	15	30	37	2	1	1	10	3	1	0	12	0	20	2	1	2	.262
Owen, Andy, Vero Beach*	.272	101	384	342	35	93	127	21	2	3	54	4	2	1	34	3	63	5	5	8	.371
Owen, Tom, Brevard County	.210	49	157	124	14	26	33	2	1	1	9	1	0	5	27	0	22	2	2	4	.266
Ozorio, Yudith, St. Petersburg	.242	136	573	505	67	122	156	11	10	1	42	8	2	1	57	1	110	30	8	5	.309
Ozuna, Rafael, Vero Beach†	.221	33	131	113	16	25	28	1	1	0	9	3	1	0	14	0	21	3	2	5	.248
Pachot, John, W. Palm Beach	.190	44	166	163	8	31	40	9	0	0	19	1	0	0	2	0	19	0	1	1	.245
Padilla, Roy, Sarasota	.296	8	29	27	2	8	10	2	0	0	2	0	0	0	1	0	3	4	0	1	.370
Pages, Javier, St. Petersburg	.226	39	131	106	14	24	42	7	1	3	8	2	0	1	22	1	29	1	1	3	.396
Parra, Jose, Charlotte†	.333	3	7	6	1	2	2	0	0	0	1	0	0	0	1	0	3	0	0	0	.333
Patterson, Jarrod, St. Lucie*	.180	17	66	61	6	11	16	2	0	1	6	0	1	1	3	0	19	1	0	0	.262
Patton, Greg, Sarasota	.244	80	317	275	31	67	96	16	2	3	24	1	2	4	35	1	64	2	3	5	.349
Payton, Jay, St. Lucie	.308	9	30	26	4	8	10	2	0	0	1	0	0	0	4	1	5	2	1	1	.385
Perez, Jhonny, Kissimmee	.270	90	356	322	54	87	147	20	2	12	49	3	0	2	26	1	70	16	16	3	.457
Perez, Richard, Daytona	.228	52	202	184	20	42	51	7	1	0	8	3	0	3	12	0	24	4	3	6	.277
Perez, Santiago, Lakeland†	.251	122	446	418	33	105	130	18	2	1	27	7	2	3	16	1	88	6	5	9	.311
Pichardo, Sandy, Tampa†	.252	84	328	294	40	74	101	7	7	2	33	8	2	3	21	0	49	4	6	6	.344
Pico, Brandon, Daytona*	.194	19	73	67	10	13	18	0	1	1	8	1	0	0	5	0	9	1	0	0	.269
Podsednik, Scott, Brevard Cnty*	.261	108	438	383	39	100	113	9	2	0	30	7	0	3	45	0	65	20	10	8	.295
Polanco, Placido, St. Petersburg	.291	137	582	540	65	157	196	29	5	0	51	6	7	5	24	1	34	4	4	31	.363
Porter, Bo, Daytona	.175	20	71	63	9	11	17	4	1	0	6	2	0	0	6	0	24	5	1	0	.270
Post, Dave, W. Palm Beach	.279	79	309	258	42	72	114	15	6	5	35	5	4	5	37	1	32	8	4	6	.442
Pratt, Wes, Kissimmee	.176	48	158	142	18	25	37	6	0	2	15	4	1	2	9	0	33	2	1	3	.261
Pullen, Shane, Clearwater*	.267	23	87	75	11	20	22	2	0	0	8	2	2	0	8	0	20	1	0	0	.293
Raines, Tim, Tampa†	.361	9	44	36	9	13	21	2	0	2	11	0	0	0	8	1	3	0	0	0	.583
Ramirez, Julio, Brevard County	.246	17	66	61	11	15	17	0	1	0	2	0	1	0	4	0	18	2	3	1	.279
Rascon, Rene, Brevard County*	.258	10	38	31	3	8	12	1	0	1	5	1	0	0	6	0	10	0	2	1	.387
Raynor, Mark, Clearwater	.200	18	75	55	8	11	14	1	1	0	4	1	2	0	17	0	9	2	1	1	.255
Reeves, Glenn, Brevard County	.299	123	554	478	72	143	198	29	4	6	41	4	4	5	63	0	82	8	5	6	.414
Renteria, David, W. Palm Beach	.187	31	118	107	10	20	24	2	1	0	5	2	0	0	9	0	20	2	3	3	.224
Reynoso, Ismael, Brevard County..	.114	11	37	35	5	4	4	0	0	0	1	1	0	0	1	0	11	2	1	2	.114
Richard, Chris, St. Petersburg*	.283	129	531	460	65	130	212	28	6	14	82	0	5	9	57	6	50	7	3	11	.461
Richards, Rowan, Charlotte	.162	34	127	117	10	19	27	3	1	1	10	1	2	2	5	0	33	2	1	1	.231
Rivera, Santiago, Daytona†	.150	10	24	20	3	3	6	1	1	0	1	0	0	0	4	0	5	0	0	2	.250
Rivers, Jonathan, Dunedin	.249	97	374	333	46	83	121	14	3	6	43	1	1	1	38	3	67	8	9	10	.363
Roberts, John, W. Palm Beach	.134	28	76	67	7	9	20	1	2	2	8	0	1	1	7	0	26	1	0	0	.299
Robles, Oscar, Kissimmee*	.269	125	517	427	57	115	132	13	2	0	29	8	2	6	74	3	37	10	8	13	.309
Rodriguez, Adam, Lakeland	.238	57	188	160	18	38	56	7	1	3	25	1	6	1	20	0	37	0	0	7	.350
Rodriguez, Maximo, Brevard Cnty	.227	84	300	273	19	62	87	16	0	3	39	2	4	3	18	2	62	3	3	17	.319
Rodriguez, Noel, Kissimmee	.251	82	323	291	24	73	106	16	1	5	38	2	1	3	26	1	31	0	1	9	.364
Rodriguez, Tony, Sarasota	.286	8	22	21	0	6	6	0	0	0	0	0	0	0	1	0	2	0	0	2	.286
Rodriguez, Victor, Brevard County	.274	114	483	438	54	120	142	14	4	0	26	8	3	2	32	0	42	20	7	13	.324
Rojas, Mo, Sarasota	.000	2	5	5	0	0	0	0	0	0	0	0	0	0	0	0	2	0	0	0	.000
Rose, Mike, Kissimmee	.000	2	1	1	0	0	0	0	0	0	0	0	0	0	0	0	1	0	0	0	.000
Ross, Tony, Kissimmee	.223	57	214	193	22	43	58	8	2	1	17	4	2	0	15	0	42	10	2	2	.301
Royster, Aaron, Clearwater	.280	72	320	289	35	81	128	10	2	11	60	3	2	3	23	1	56	4	3	7	.443
Salzano, Jerry, Lakeland	.263	123	479	426	52	112	166	28	4	6	60	2	4	9	38	0	66	6	7	10	.390
Samboy, Nelson, Kissimmee	.253	105	397	372	43	94	118	20	2	0	21	3	1	1	20	1	61	17	7	7	.317
Sampson, Benj, Fort Myers*	.000	11	1	1	0	0	0	0	0	0	0	0	0	0	0	0	0	0	0	0	.000
Sanchez, Omar, Dunedin†	.230	45	147	126	17	29	38	1	4	0	12	5	1	1	14	1	36	3	3	3	.302
Sanchez, Orlando, Sarasota	.333	5	18	15	2	5	7	2	0	0	4	0	0	0	2	0	5	0	0	0	.467
Sanders, Anthony, Dunedin	.259	102	457	417	75	108	184	25	0	17	50	0	0	6	34	0	93	16	12	5	.441
Sanderson, David, St. Lucie*	.239	50	189	163	17	39	50	2	3	1	13	3	0	1	22	1	42	8	3	2	.307
Santucci, Steven, St. Petersburg	.229	111	387	349	38	80	112	10	2	6	29	6	4	1	27	0	96	5	3	5	.321
Saylor, Jamie, Kissimmee*	.204	59	196	181	17	37	49	3	3	1	6	3	2	0	10	0	43	8	6	3	.271
Schaaf, Bob, Vero Beach	.220	61	201	186	23	41	51	8	1	0	11	3	0	1	12	1	47	4	2	1	.274
Seidel, Ryan, Daytona	.118	9	21	17	0	2	3	1	0	0	0	0	0	0	4	0	6	0	0	3	.176
Shanahan, Jason, Brevard Cnty†	.205	102	419	371	39	76	105	19	2	2	32	0	4	8	36	1	63	2	1	4	.283
Simpson, Jeramie, St. Lucie*	.216	59	244	222	25	48	65	7	5	0	19	1	0	4	17	1	55	21	11	2	.293
Smith, David, Sarasota	.250	45	151	124	24	31	45	3	1	2	14	0	1	1	23	0	27	6	3	2	.363
Smith, Sloan, Tampa†	.222	61	243	194	25	43	67	10	1	4	21	1	2	0	46	2	60	5	6	6	.345
Snyder, Jared, Daytona	.207	12	31	29	5	6	6	0	0	0	4	0	0	2	0	0	6	0	0	3	.207
Sotelo, Danilo, Vero Beach	.238	72	281	239	39	57	91	14	4	4	32	7	4	3	28	0	56	3	2	4	.381

yer, Team	Avg.	G	TPA	AB	R	H	TB	2B	3B	HR	RBI	SH	SF	HP	BB	IBB	SO	SB	CS	GDP	Slg.	OBP
wards, Ryan, Vero Beach*	.200	7	18	15	0	3	4	1	0	0	2	0	0	0	3	0	5	0	0	0	.267	.333
ed, David, Vero Beach	.288	23	80	73	6	21	27	3	0	1	10	1	0	0	6	0	15	1	0	1	.370	.342
ne, Craig, Dunedin	.263	61	253	228	26	60	97	25	0	4	22	0	2	3	20	3	55	0	0	3	.425	.328
vall, Darond, W. Palm Beach†	.452	8	37	31	8	14	21	4	0	1	8	0	0	0	6	0	7	2	2	1	.677	.541
ange, Mike, Dunedin	.318	51	185	154	25	49	57	4	2	0	13	5	0	0	26	0	42	5	5	3	.370	.417
ner, Paul, St. Petersburg	.000	1	2	2	0	0	0	0	0	0	0	0	0	0	0	0	2	0	0	0	.000	.000
is, Fernando, Charlotte†	.286	85	366	325	46	93	154	25	0	12	53	1	4	6	30	4	48	9	3	9	.474	.353
bs, Nathan, Sarasota†	.250	116	458	420	44	105	123	11	2	1	34	10	1	3	24	1	68	17	4	7	.293	.295
mpson, Andy, Dunedin	.282	129	490	425	64	120	189	26	5	11	50	1	3	1	60	1	108	16	4	5	.445	.370
erina, Tony, St. Lucie*	.071	19	48	42	1	3	5	0	1	0	3	0	0	1	5	1	7	1	0	0	.119	.188
sley, Lee, Clearwater†	.294	4	19	17	4	5	7	0	1	0	3	0	0	0	2	0	4	2	0	0	.412	.368
mmell, Gary, Kissimmee*	.289	118	429	402	48	116	148	16	8	0	39	3	4	0	20	0	52	11	3	5	.368	.319
ilo, Jason, Tampa	.200	11	27	25	2	5	9	1	0	1	5	0	0	1	1	0	7	0	0	1	.360	.259
ner, Brian, St. Lucie*	.202	33	112	99	15	20	29	3	0	2	15	0	1	1	11	0	27	1	0	1	.293	.286
ombley, Dennis, Tampa	.276	28	89	76	7	21	28	4	0	1	8	0	0	1	12	0	18	0	0	7	.368	.382
abria, Jose, Dunedin	.188	6	17	16	1	3	3	0	0	0	2	0	0	0	1	0	3	0	0	0	.188	.235
derwood, Devin, Sarasota	.269	27	77	67	12	18	24	3	0	1	13	1	0	1	8	0	9	0	0	1	.358	.355
rat, Chris, Charlotte*	.274	41	162	135	18	37	51	8	0	2	11	0	0	0	27	1	28	2	3	4	.378	.395
entin, Jose, Fort Myers†	.263	87	379	338	34	89	138	26	1	7	54	0	5	4	32	4	65	1	0	5	.408	.330
ette, Ramon, Daytona	.194	14	37	31	5	6	10	2	1	0	2	2	1	0	3	0	5	1	0	0	.323	.257
squez, Danny, Charlotte	.199	77	268	256	30	51	87	14	2	6	30	1	0	4	7	0	62	3	5	6	.340	.232
ssel, Andrew, Charlotte	.229	126	549	484	63	111	157	25	6	3	67	2	11	7	45	0	94	1	6	14	.324	.298
gt, Jack, Charlotte	.407	7	31	27	7	11	17	3	0	1	8	0	0	1	3	0	3	0	0	0	.630	.484
ggoner, James, Charlotte*	.237	64	209	194	17	46	53	7	0	0	21	0	2	2	11	0	44	1	2	11	.273	.282
lbeck, Matt, Fort Myers†	.273	9	40	33	4	9	12	1	1	0	9	0	2	1	4	0	2	0	1	0	.364	.350
lkanoff, A.J., Vero Beach	.282	29	96	85	15	24	42	5	2	3	19	0	0	0	11	0	15	0	0	1	.494	.365
lker, Steve, Daytona†	.316	58	252	225	39	71	119	17	2	9	39	1	2	7	17	3	53	21	4	4	.529	.378
rd, Daryle, Lakeland*	.291	128	531	464	65	135	202	29	4	10	68	0	4	6	57	6	77	1	1	9	.435	.373
rner, Randy, St. Lucie	.277	109	421	386	43	107	157	20	3	8	69	0	6	6	23	1	65	5	1	6	.407	.323
atley, Gabe, Daytona*	.226	56	216	186	24	42	64	14	1	2	25	0	2	1	26	1	27	9	1	2	.344	.321
ite, Rondell, W. Palm Beach	.200	3	10	10	0	2	3	1	0	0	2	0	0	0	0	0	4	0	1	0	.300	.200
cox, Luke, Tampa*	.283	119	523	470	72	133	208	32	5	11	76	4	6	3	40	1	71	14	10	14	.443	.339
kes, Brian, Brevard County	.364	4	13	11	4	4	4	0	0	0	2	0	0	0	2	0	3	0	1	0	.364	.462
liams, Bryan, Dunedin	.000	6	17	17	0	0	0	0	0	0	0	0	0	0	0	0	9	0	0	0	.000	.000
son, Preston, St. Lucie	.176	23	95	85	6	15	21	3	0	1	7	0	0	2	8	0	21	1	1	3	.247	.263
son, Vance, St. Lucie	.244	93	354	311	29	76	112	14	2	6	44	0	4	6	31	2	41	2	4	7	.360	.321
t, Kevin, Dunedin*	.271	124	498	446	63	121	190	18	6	13	70	2	5	6	39	3	96	9	4	9	.426	.335
d, Bruce, Vero Beach*	.266	59	220	192	24	51	65	7	2	1	15	6	4	0	18	1	19	2	2	7	.339	.322
o, Carlos, Tampa*	.227	131	533	463	58	105	161	21	1	11	55	0	4	2	64	1	131	1	0	15	.348	.321
rilla, Julio, St. Lucie†	.248	110	432	403	43	100	109	7	1	0	27	3	1	0	25	0	72	24	17	10	.270	.291

GRAND SLAMS: Cline, Curl, T. Raines, 2; Barlock, A. Brown, Buchanan, Carver, Ellis, Fortin, Gibralter, Harvey, Je. Key, Lidle, Morales, Mucker, Murphy, J. Perez, Pico, ster, Shanahan, Valentin, Witt, 1 each.

AWARDED FIRST BASE ON CATCHER'S INTERFERENCE: Fuller 3 (Amezcua, Brinkley, Pages); J. Perez 3 (Lidle, Melhuse, Pachot); Avalos 2 (Bowles, M. Rodriquez); ly 2 (Ji. Gonzalez, Tijerina); Gibralter 2 (Pages, Tijerina); LaRiviere 2 (Cline 2); V. Wilson 2 (Cossins, Haas); Durkin (McDonald); Gazarek (C. Stone); Giardi (Cossins); Gonzalez (LoDuca); Koskie (Unrat); McCormick (Ashby); A. Owen (Unrat).

PLAYERS WITH TWO OR MORE TEAMS

yer, Team	Avg.	G	TPA	AB	R	H	TB	2B	3B	HR	RBI	SH	SF	HP	BB	IBB	SO	SB	CS	GDP	Slg.	OBP
rdi, Mike, Tampa	.154	5	18	13	3	2	2	0	0	0	1	0	1	0	4	0	3	0	0	2	.154	.333
rdi, Mike, W. Palm Beach	.253	48	184	150	19	38	61	6	1	5	19	0	1	5	27	1	33	2	1	3	.407	.383
rales, Francisco, St. Petersburg	.209	21	75	67	6	14	24	5	1	1	6	0	1	2	5	0	25	0	0	1	.358	.280
ales, Francisco, W. Palm Beach	.274	75	287	259	32	71	104	20	2	3	42	3	1	5	19	0	79	3	1	5	.402	.335

1996 PITCHING

TEAM

m	W	L	Pct.	ERA	G	CG	ShO	Sv.	IP	H	TBF	R	ER	HR	SH	SF	HB	BB	IBB	SO	WP	Bk.
Petersburg	75	63	.543	3.04	139	5	13	44	1200.1	1111	5031	474	406	47	49	36	59	451	13	892	51	11
Lucie	71	62	.534	3.15	133	9	12	41	1156.0	1045	4834	505	404	53	43	28	37	431	22	852	82	8
pa	84	50	.627	3.15	134	4	8	49	1180.2	1123	4942	522	413	63	43	26	51	337	18	912	48	8
arwater	75	62	.547	3.49	137	7	8	37	1208.1	1149	5168	568	468	54	43	36	47	478	25	837	57	10
: Myers	79	58	.577	3.50	138	10	10	37	1213.0	1115	5119	541	472	66	47	37	66	478	6	966	98	7
simmee	60	75	.444	3.54	135	11	9	30	1150.2	1125	5044	603	453	56	45	41	74	491	12	793	77	5
st Palm Beach	68	67	.504	3.55	135	5	9	35	1176.2	1170	5081	581	464	52	46	34	60	420	12	841	94	7
o Beach	65	66	.496	3.57	131	4	9	27	1124.1	1046	4829	554	446	67	41	29	54	469	17	894	86	18
eland	61	77	.442	3.65	138	10	14	34	1200.0	1106	5146	582	487	60	53	43	64	543	7	911	72	11
edin	67	70	.489	3.71	137	6	11	35	1187.1	1166	5190	654	490	63	35	32	78	489	21	924	76	11
rlotte	63	76	.453	3.93	139	14	9	21	1228.1	1256	5292	636	537	82	48	52	38	442	10	844	64	13
tona	71	66	.518	4.01	137	6	7	38	1162.1	1146	5124	648	518	72	56	43	69	488	24	912	101	14
ard County	47	92	.338	4.14	139	5	5	23	1212.2	1277	5256	669	558	86	46	38	87	364	26	715	66	5
asota	67	69	.493	4.39	136	8	10	35	1180.0	1236	5196	686	576	55	35	38	57	482	19	834	65	18

INDIVIDUAL

TOP QUALIFIERS FOR EARNED-RUN AVERAGE TITLE

Minimum 112 innings. *Lefthanded pitcher.

Pitcher, Team	W	L	Pct.	ERA	G	GS	CG	ShO	GF	Sv.	IP	H	TBF	R	ER	HR	SH	SF	HB	BB	IBB	SO	WP	BK
Stein, Blake, St. Petersburg	16	5	.762	2.15	28	27	2	1	1	1	172.0	122	667	48	41	4	3	4	5	54	0	159	4	
Mounce, Tony, Kissimmee*	9	9	.500	2.25	25	25	4	2	0	0	155.2	139	675	65	39	7	6	3	10	68	1	102	7	
Gooch, Arnold, St. Lucie	12	12	.500	2.58	26	26	2	0	0	0	167.2	131	680	74	48	7	6	4	4	51	3	141	11	
Cobb, Trevor, Fort Myers*	7	3	.700	2.64	31	14	1	1	5	0	126.1	101	520	44	37	1	4	6	5	43	0	98	12	
Halladay, Roy, Dunedin	15	7	.682	2.73	27	27	2	2	0	0	164.2	158	688	75	50	7	5	1	6	46	0	109	1	
Press, Gregg, Brevard County	9	9	.500	2.75	28	23	0	0	1	0	150.1	134	604	62	46	9	6	1	4	37	4	90	10	
Silva, Ted, Charlotte	10	2	.833	2.86	16	16	4	0	0	0	113.1	98	463	39	36	9	1	2	3	27	1	95	3	
Roberts, Willis, Lakeland	9	7	.563	2.89	23	22	2	0	0	0	149.1	133	636	60	48	5	8	9	9	69	0	105	13	
Phelps, Tommy, W. Palm Beach*	10	2	.833	2.89	18	18	1	1	0	0	112.0	105	468	42	36	5	4	1	2	35	0	71	8	
Dixon, Timothy, W. Palm Beach*	5	11	.313	2.90	37	16	0	0	8	2	124.0	126	528	55	40	10	8	5	6	35	3	87	7	
Corn, Chris, Tampa	12	4	.750	2.91	26	25	2	1	0	0	170.1	145	686	67	55	10	5	3	9	38	0	109	6	
Logan, Marcus, St. Petersburg	7	7	.500	2.91	30	19	0	0	2	0	133.0	125	556	49	43	9	4	6	8	49	1	99	7	
Wood, Kerry, Daytona	10	2	.833	2.91	22	22	0	0	0	0	114.1	72	495	51	37	6	5	4	14	70	0	136	10	
Elarton, Scott, Kissimmee	12	7	.632	2.92	27	27	3	1	0	0	172.1	154	715	67	56	13	7	6	8	54	0	130	5	
Perkins, Dan, Fort Myers	13	7	.650	2.96	39	13	3	1	10	2	136.2	125	557	52	45	5	4	6	11	37	1	111	9	

DEPARTMENTAL LEADERS: W—Neal, Stein, 16; L—Lock, 18; Pct.—Silva, Wood, Phelps, .833; G—Tessmer, 68; GS—Bair, 28; CG—W. Powell, 5; ShO—Ke Sauerbeck, Munro, Mounce, Halladay, 2; GF—Tessmer, 63; SV—Tessmer, 35; IP—Bair, W. Powell, 174.1; H—W. Powell, 195; TBF—W. Powell, 746; R—Lock, 10 ER—W. Powell, 95; HR—Schlomann, Meadows, Elarton, 13; BB—Whiteman, 89; IBB—Tatis, 8; SO—Stein, 159; WP—Dowhower, 17; BK—Wood, 7.

ALL PITCHERS

*Lefthanded pitcher.

Pitcher, Team	W	L	Pct.	ERA	G	GS	CG	ShO	GF	Sv.	IP	H	TBF	R	ER	HR	SH	SF	HB	BB	IBB	SO	WP	BK
Abad, Andy, Sarasota*	0	0	.000	0.00	1	0	0	0	1	0	0.2	0	2	0	0	0	0	0	0	0	0	0	0	
Adkins, Tim, Dunedin*	7	9	.438	3.92	39	11	0	0	14	2	103.1	88	475	68	45	4	3	1	8	73	1	91	2	
Aguilera, Rick, Fort Myers	2	0	1.000	3.75	2	2	0	0	0	0	12.0	13	50	5	5	1	1	0	1	0	0	12	1	
Ahearne, Pat, Vero Beach	3	2	.600	2.11	6	6	1	1	0	0	47.0	38	179	16	11	1	2	1	1	5	0	26	2	
Alejo, Nigel, Brevard County	1	6	.143	4.58	37	0	0	0	26	11	39.1	47	183	23	20	1	5	0	3	13	3	35	3	
Altman, Heath, Brevard County	0	1	.000	11.96	16	0	0	0	7	0	23.1	31	137	38	31	2	0	6	9	27	2	7	7	
Arffa, Steve, St. Lucie*	1	2	.333	3.31	11	4	0	0	5	1	32.2	29	132	14	12	2	0	2	1	8	1	18	0	
Arroyo, Luis, St. Lucie*	1	0	1.000	3.00	12	0	0	0	4	2	42.0	36	170	17	14	1	0	3	1	15	1	28	3	
Atwater, Joe, St. Lucie*	2	6	.250	4.38	19	16	1	1	0	0	86.1	79	365	47	42	3	3	2	3	39	0	66	2	
Babineaux, Darrin, Vero Beach	1	7	.125	3.29	10	10	1	0	0	0	63.0	56	267	30	23	6	2	0	2	23	0	41	8	
Bair, Dennis, Daytona	9	8	.529	3.67	29	28	2	1	1	0	174.1	167	737	82	71	8	3	5	13	42	2	127	7	
Barbao, Joe, Clearwater	4	2	.667	3.35	28	0	0	0	10	1	40.1	49	170	19	15	0	2	2	1	5	2	14	0	
Barker, Richie, Daytona	4	0	1.000	5.67	17	0	0	0	7	0	27.0	34	135	23	17	0	2	1	2	18	0	14	10	
Barksdale, Joe, Sarasota	2	7	.222	7.79	19	11	0	0	4	0	64.2	88	320	62	56	9	0	1	8	41	1	37	3	
Belinda, Stan, Sarasota	0	1	.000	45.00	1	1	0	0	0	0	1.0	6	9	5	5	0	0	0	1	0	1	1	1	
Bell, Jason, Fort Myers	6	3	.667	1.69	13	13	0	0	0	0	90.1	61	350	20	17	1	4	2	6	22	0	83	3	
Bell, Mike, W. Palm Beach*	0	1	.000	8.80	13	0	0	0	5	0	15.1	27	82	19	15	1	2	0	1	11	1	11	1	
Benz, Jacob, W. Palm Beach*	2	4	.333	2.21	16	0	0	0	8	2	20.1	19	93	10	5	0	4	0	0	11	1	14	7	
Betti, Rick, Sarasota*	0	2	.000	2.87	13	0	0	0	13	7	15.2	13	70	6	5	0	0	1	3	7	2	21	0	
Beverlin, Jason, Tampa	2	0	1.000	3.50	25	1	0	0	6	1	46.1	43	194	22	18	5	1	1	1	17	2	38	4	
Bland, Nate, Vero Beach*	10	4	.714	3.09	17	17	0	0	0	0	96.0	99	414	42	33	3	4	2	4	35	0	69	5	
Bogle, Sean, Daytona	3	1	.750	7.13	13	0	0	0	0	0	17.2	28	92	17	14	0	1	2	0	13	1	18	3	
Bogott, Kurtiss, Dunedin*	1	1	.500	1.78	19	0	0	0	8	4	30.1	22	133	16	6	2	0	0	3	20	1	41	8	
Booker, Chris, Daytona	0	0	.000	0.00	1	1	0	0	0	0	2.1	1	11	1	0	0	0	0	0	3	0	2	1	
Boucher, Denis, W. Palm Beach*	1	0	1.000	2.84	2	2	0	0	0	0	12.2	12	50	4	4	1	0	0	1	2	0	5	1	
Bowen, Mitchel, Brevard County	0	2	.000	4.67	29	0	0	0	13	2	54.0	66	244	33	28	3	1	0	4	14	2	29	1	
Box, Shawn, Daytona	6	2	.750	4.27	14	9	0	0	0	0	52.2	50	218	28	25	4	3	0	1	12	0	32	2	
Boyd, Jason, Clearwater	11	8	.579	3.90	26	26	2	0	0	0	161.2	160	674	75	70	12	3	6	3	49	1	120	7	
Bracho, Alejandro, Tampa*	0	0	.000	5.40	2	0	0	0	0	0	1.2	2	9	1	1	0	0	0	0	2	0	0	0	
Braddy, Junior, Sarasota	0	0	.000	13.50	1	0	0	0	0	0	1.1	3	9	2	2	0	0	0	0	3	0	1	1	
Brower, Jim, Charlotte	9	8	.529	3.79	23	21	2	0	0	2	145.0	148	607	67	61	11	5	4	4	40	0	86	7	
Brown, Charlie, Tampa	0	0	.000	3.45	12	0	0	0	8	0	15.2	16	69	9	6	2	0	1	1	5	0	16	0	
Brown, Darold, Daytona*	4	4	.500	2.73	35	0	0	0	11	4	52.2	42	221	20	16	3	7	2	3	20	4	43	2	
Buckles, Bucky, Charlotte	1	4	.200	3.60	21	3	0	0	9	0	55.0	55	228	25	22	3	5	1	2	13	1	43	2	
Bullock, Craig, St. Lucie	0	2	.000	7.94	7	0	0	0	5	0	5.2	8	30	6	5	0	1	0	0	5	1	4	1	
Byrne, Earl, Daytona*	1	4	.200	3.38	18	3	1	0	6	1	45.1	44	201	22	17	5	2	0	1	21	2	47	4	
Camacho, Dan, Vero Beach	5	1	.833	2.48	10	10	0	0	0	0	54.1	38	227	16	15	4	3	1	5	29	0	50	4	
Cannon, Kevan, Sarasota*	0	0	.000	0.00	2	0	0	0	1	0	1.0	1	3	0	0	0	0	0	0	0	0	3	0	
Caravelli, Mike, Brevard County*	4	3	.571	2.27	47	0	0	0	23	1	71.1	69	297	20	18	2	4	2	5	16	0	46	2	
Carl, Todd, Daytona	0	1	.000	7.27	5	0	0	0	0	0	8.2	19	49	11	7	0	3	1	0	6	0	2	1	
Carter, John, St. Lucie	1	2	.333	7.20	4	4	0	0	0	0	20.0	26	93	18	16	2	1	0	1	11	1	6	3	
Cedeno, Blas, Lakeland	1	1	.500	5.51	10	0	0	0	4	0	16.1	17	72	10	10	3	0	0	1	7	0	11	2	
Censale, Silvio, Clearwater*	8	9	.471	3.92	24	22	1	1	1	0	126.1	118	546	65	55	5	3	6	7	54	1	100	4	
Centeno, Jose, W. Palm Beach*	4	4	.500	3.90	37	0	0	0	13	4	60.0	64	261	30	26	4	2	3	1	19	2	47	1	
Chambers, Scott, Vero Beach*	0	0	.000	2.25	10	0	0	0	3	0	12.0	7	50	6	3	1	0	0	3	1	0	20	1	
Chavarria, David, Charlotte	1	6	.143	3.94	38	4	0	0	22	7	81.2	76	364	46	28	4	3	8	4	43	0	76	14	
Cobb, Trevor, Fort Myers*	7	3	.700	2.64	31	14	1	1	5	0	126.1	101	520	44	37	1	4	6	5	43	0	98	12	
Cole, Jason, W. Palm Beach	6	1	.857	2.31	39	0	0	0	24	3	62.1	57	256	25	16	2	3	1	2	20	0	40	1	
Colon, Julio, Vero Beach	3	2	.600	2.61	8	8	0	0	0	0	41.1	44	182	21	12	2	0	2	1	19	0	49	2	
Conway, Keith, St. Petersburg*	7	3	.700	2.08	19	0	0	0	21	2	69.1	63	294	18	16	1	4	1	1	25	1	67	3	
Cook, Jake, Sarasota	2	9	.182	5.38	20	13	1	0	3	1	85.1	100	406	67	51	3	2	5	3	44	3	49	7	
Cook, Rodney, Charlotte	6	4	.600	2.94	39	0	0	0	25	8	79.2	78	332	30	26	2	5	1	2	26	2	48	2	
Coolbaugh, Mike, Charlotte	0	0	.000	36.00	1	0	0	0	1	0	1.0	5	8	4	4	0	0	0	0	0	0	2	0	

Pitcher, Team	W	L	Pct.	ERA	G	GS	CG	ShO	GF	Sv.	IP	H	TBF	R	ER	HR	SH	SF	HB	BB	IBB	SO	WP	Bk.
orn, Chris, Tampa	12	4	.750	2.91	26	25	2	1	0	0	170.1	145	686	67	55	10	5	3	9	38	0	109	6	0
ornett, Brad, Dunedin	0	1	.000	8.59	4	0	0	0	2	0	7.1	15	41	7	7	1	0	0	1	3	0	5	1	1
osman, Jeff, St. Lucie	0	1	.000	8.59	3	2	0	0	0	0	7.1	11	35	7	7	2	0	0	0	2	0	5	0	0
ox, Robert, St. Lucie	1	0	1.000	6.75	4	0	0	0	3	0	5.1	4	23	4	4	1	0	0	0	3	0	6	0	0
ace, Derek, Kissimmee*	0	0	.000	2.95	12	0	0	0	3	1	18.1	19	77	6	6	0	0	0	0	7	0	11	1	0
arensbourg, Vic, Brevard County*	0	0	.000	0.00	2	0	0	0	1	0	3.0	1	10	0	0	0	0	0	1	0	5	0	0	
aSilva, Fernando, W. Palm Beach	4	2	.667	2.57	40	0	0	0	10	0	66.2	58	275	23	19	4	3	2	3	20	3	45	2	0
ault, Donnie, Kissimmee	2	2	.500	5.08	29	0	0	0	14	3	39.0	33	166	24	22	4	2	0	2	20	2	42	1	1
az, Jairo, Daytona	1	1	.500	3.08	8	3	0	0	1	0	26.1	31	126	14	9	1	0	2	1	14	1	18	5	0
nyar, Eric, Lakeland	3	3	.500	1.92	58	0	0	0	56	27	65.2	45	281	20	14	0	5	3	12	35	2	55	4	0
xon, Timothy, W. Palm Beach*	5	11	.313	2.90	37	16	0	0	8	2	124.0	126	528	55	40	10	8	5	6	35	3	87	7	0
oman, Roger, Dunedin	0	1	.000	3.30	18	0	0	0	9	0	30.0	36	148	22	11	2	1	2	1	14	2	19	0	0
owhower, Deron, Fort Myers	2	4	.333	3.70	39	2	0	0	9	1	75.1	63	329	37	31	5	3	2	5	45	0	83	17	0
ews, Matt, Tampa	0	3	.000	7.13	4	4	0	0	0	0	17.2	26	93	20	14	0	2	1	3	12	2	12	1	0
umheller, Al, Tampa*	9	3	.750	2.28	36	0	0	0	7	1	51.1	34	215	15	13	2	4	0	0	33	2	57	2	0
uran, Roberto, Dunedin*	3	1	.750	1.12	8	8	1	1	0	0	48.1	31	188	9	6	1	1	1	2	19	0	54	5	0
urocher, Jayson, W. Palm Beach	7	6	.538	3.34	23	23	1	1	0	0	129.1	118	557	65	48	5	4	3	7	44	0	101	15	3
addy, Brad, Vero Beach*	0	1	.000	5.91	12	0	0	0	5	0	10.2	9	44	8	7	1	2	0	1	4	1	8	2	1
oy, Mike, Lakeland*	0	0	.000	4.50	17	0	0	0	5	0	28.0	28	132	16	14	0	1	2	2	24	1	27	3	0
aler, Daniel, Brevard County	5	16	.238	4.74	28	23	1	0	0	0	150.0	176	658	80	79	10	5	4	10	41	2	88	9	0
arton, Scott, Kissimmee	12	7	.632	2.92	27	27	3	1	0	0	172.1	154	715	67	56	13	7	6	8	54	0	130	5	0
erson, Scott, Sarasota*	0	0	.000	5.40	4	0	0	0	0	0	6.2	11	37	4	4	0	1	0	1	6	1	7	1	0
ard, Tony, Brevard County	0	1	.000	5.79	2	0	0	0	0	0	4.2	2	19	3	3	1	0	1	0	4	0	6	0	0
camilla, Jaime, Charlotte*	3	3	.500	4.09	37	0	0	0	18	1	61.2	68	272	31	28	4	2	3	3	28	3	39	2	0
cobar, Kelvim, Dunedin	9	5	.643	2.69	18	18	1	0	0	0	110.1	101	460	44	33	5	2	1	3	33	0	113	7	2
tavil, Mauricio, Clearwater*	5	3	.625	3.44	29	0	0	0	12	3	34.0	20	140	15	13	0	2	1		20	0	25	1	0
ans, Stan, Clearwater	0	0	.000	54.00	2	0	0	0	1	0	1.0	5	11	6	6	0	0	0	0	4	0	0	1	0
rrell, Jim, Sarasota	9	8	.529	3.51	21	21	3	1	0	0	133.1	116	539	58	52	11	4	5	4	34	0	92	9	0
ulkner, Neal, Daytona	1	1	.500	7.82	11	0	0	0	5	2	12.2	17	61	11	11	0	0	1	1	5	0	10	1	0
rnandez, Sid, Clearwater*	0	0	.000	0.00	1	1	0	0	0	0	3.0	3	9	0	0	0	0	0	0	0	0	5	0	0
sta, Chris, Sarasota	0	2	.000	8.55	6	2	0	0	2	0	20.0	37	109	24	19	2	2	1	1	11	0	12	2	0
beck, Ryan, Brevard County	1	1	.500	8.44	9	0	0	0	6	0	10.2	16	54	13	10	1	0	0		5	1	9	1	0
re, Tony, Clearwater	8	4	.667	3.16	22	22	3	1	0	0	128.0	102	533	61	45	4	1	1	5	56	1	80	13	1
terer, Scott, Dunedin	2	3	.400	6.23	20	0	0	0	13	5	26.0	43	126	21	18	0	0	1	1	8	1	15	3	0
etham, Ben, W. Palm Beach	0	1	.000	2.05	31	0	0	0	29	17	30.2	15	122	8	7	0	0	1	0	15	0	48	9	2
anko, Kris, W. Palm Beach*	2	1	.667	3.75	9	0	0	0	6	0	12.0	10	46	6	5	1	0	0	4	0	3	1	0	
mbs, Chris, Daytona	0	2	.000	6.26	13	0	0	0	3	0	23.0	28	115	22	16	2	0	1	1	21	1	17	1	0
ndarillas, Gus, Fort Myers	0	0	.000	9.00	4	0	0	0	3	1	6.0	9	35	7	6	0	0	1	0	8	0	3	1	0
agozzo, Keith, Brevard County*	0	1	.000	10.80	2	2	0	0	0	0	5.0	9	25	6	6	2	0	0	1	4	0	1	0	0
rcia, Al, Daytona	4	1	.800	2.87	7	7	0	0	0	0	47.0	48	187	20	15	1	3	1	2	5	0	28	2	0
rcia, Frank, St. Petersburg	2	0	1.000	2.53	28	0	0	0	5	0	32.0	35	147	11	9	1	1	0	1	18	2	24	2	0
rcia, Garbriel, Kissimmee	0	0	.000	0.00	3	0	0	0	3	0	8.2	6	37	2	0	0	1	0	1	4	0	0		
ntile, Scott, W. Palm Beach	0	0	.000	0.00	7	0	0	0	5	1	10.0	8	39	0	0	0	0	0	2	0	5	1	0	
lden, Matt, St. Petersburg	0	0	.000	0.90	8	0	0	0	7	7	10.0	5	36	1	1	0	1	0	1	1	0	7	1	0
mez, Miguel, Dunedin	5	4	.556	3.38	33	0	0	0	14	5	50.2	45	218	27	19	5	4	3	3	17	1	35	7	1
nzalez, Gabe, Brevard County	2	7	.222	1.77	47	0	0	0	32	9	76.1	56	308	20	15	2	9	1	3	23	7	62	2	0
nzalez, Generoso, Lakeland	0	0	.000	4.50	1	0	0	0	1	0	2.0	3	12	5	1	2	0	1	0	2	0	1	0	0
nzalez, Juan, Brevard County	1	9	.100	5.32	23	17	0	0	2	0	86.1	102	385	57	51	6	5	3	7	27	0	48	12	1
och, Arnold, St. Lucie	12	12	.500	2.58	26	26	2	0	0	0	167.2	131	680	74	48	7	6	4	4	51	3	141	11	0
rdon, Mike, Dunedin	3	12	.200	3.44	24	24	0	0	0	0	133.1	127	588	70	51	7	2	5	7	64	1	102	15	1
urdin, Tom, Fort Myers	4	6	.400	4.26	52	1	0	0	32	16	63.1	64	277	30	30	6	6	1	3	29	3	44	7	1
aham, Rich, Sarasota	2	0	1.000	3.57	11	0	0	0	4	0	22.2	23	99	13	9	1	0	0	2	7	1	21	1	1
anger, Greg, Lakeland	1	0	1.000	1.42	5	0	0	0	0	0	6.1	7	29	1	1	0	1	0	0	3	0	4	0	0
aves, Ryan, Daytona*	0	0	.000	5.25	4	0	0	0	6	0	12.0	16	56	8	7	2	0	1	0	5	0	9	2	0
een, Jason, Daytona	0	3	.000	10.93	5	4	0	0	1	0	14.0	13	82	17	17	0	0	1	0	29	0	13	8	0
eene, Brian, Daytona	5	2	.714	3.07	26	1	0	0	10	1	55.2	51	244	26	19	5	2	2	10	18	3	37	6	2
eene, Tommy, Clearwater	1	1	.500	2.00	7	4	0	0	1	0	27.0	25	108	8	6	2	3	2	1	4	0	23	0	0
zman, Jose, Daytona	1	0	1.000	2.45	2	2	0	0	0	0	11.0	8	44	3	3	0	0	0	0	7	0	14	1	0
e, Chad, Sarasota*	3	0	1.000	3.12	42	0	0	0	19	7	60.2	56	260	33	21	2	2	5	1	17	1	37	2	3
l, Billy, Kissimmee	0	0	.000	0.00	2	0	0	0	0	0	3.0	2	12	0	0	0	0	0	0	0	0	1	0	0
l, Yates, St. Petersburg	1	10	.091	5.44	26	17	0	0	6	1	89.1	93	411	62	54	6	5	4	4	58	0	58	10	2
lladay, Roy, Dunedin	15	7	.682	2.73	27	27	2	2	0	0	164.2	158	688	75	50	7	5	1	6	46	0	109	1	2
nmack, Brandon, Daytona	2	1	.667	2.30	27	0	0	0	25	16	31.1	27	132	10	8	1	4	2	0	10	0	36	0	0
nmond, Chris, Brevard County*	0	0	.000	0.00	1	1	0	0	0	0	4.0	3	14	0	0	0	0	0	0	0	0	8	1	0
ndy, Russell, W. Palm Beach	2	4	.333	9.09	14	5	0	0	3	0	31.2	43	168	40	32	3	1	1	7	28	0	12	5	0
nsen, Brent, Sarasota	2	4	.333	5.51	8	8	1	1	0	0	47.1	54	220	36	29	1	4	1	4	21	0	25	3	0
nisch, Pete, St. Lucie	1	0	1.000	2.77	2	2	0	0	0	0	13.0	11	49	4	4	1	0	0	0	12	0	12	0	0
ris, D.J., Dunedin	4	3	.571	5.19	35	0	0	0	19	1	43.1	49	203	30	25	3	3	4		19	1	31	3	0
tgrove, Lyle, Sarasota	2	0	1.000	4.66	15	0	0	0	6	0	19.1	30	86	12	10	2	0	1	0	3	1	7	1	2
cker, Doug, Sarasota	2	2	.500	4.97	26	3	0	0	15	6	41.2	46	180	25	23	0	1	1		12	0	39	3	3
serman, Rick, St. Petersburg	10	8	.556	3.24	26	26	1	1	0	0	155.1	168	663	68	56	8	6	3	9	41	0	104	4	0
nriquez, Oscar, Kissimmee	0	4	.000	3.97	37	0	0	0	33	15	34.0	28	162	18	15	0	1	3		29	2	40	4	0
athorne, Kevin, Tampa	7	4	.636	2.60	19	13	0	0	0	0	93.1	88	360	31	27	4	3	2		12	0	82	1	2
lis, Ron, Vero Beach	0	1	.000	2.95	19	0	0	0	17	11	21.1	20	89	10	7	1	0	0	6	0	12	1	0	
bbard, Mark, Tampa*	1	2	.333	5.73	4	4	0	0	0	0	22.0	27	96	17	14	1	0	0	3	6	0	12	0	0
dek, John, Kissimmee	0	0	.000	0.00	2	1	0	0	0	0	3.0	2	14	0	0	0	0	0	0	0	0	3	0	0
f, Larry, Clearwater	0	0	.000	9.00	2	0	0	0	1	0	2.0	3	10	2	2	0	0	0	0	0	0	2	0	0
nphrey, Rich, Kissimmee	0	1	.000	2.08	5	0	0	0	5	0	8.2	6	34	3	2	0	0	2	0	1	0	5	1	0
mphry, Trevor, Clearwater	2	0	1.000	1.87	16	0	0	0	9	0	33.2	21	134	8	7	1	1	1		17	0	12	1	0
ton, Mark, Tampa	0	0	.000	1.80	3	2	0	0	0	0	5.0	2	18	1	1	0	0	0	1	0	4	0	0	
sias, Mike, Vero Beach	5	8	.385	5.11	31	16	0	0	14	7	104.0	112	463	68	59	9	1	4	5	37	1	101	6	1
kson, Danny, St. Petersburg*	0	0	.000	0.00	1	1	0	0	0	0	4.0	2	14	0	0	0	0	0	0	0	0	3	0	0
obson, K.J., Lakeland	0	4	.000	3.67	26	3	0	0	12	1	56.1	53	257	30	23	0	3	5	4	36	0	44	12	2

Pitcher, Team	W	L	Pct.	ERA	G	GS	CG	ShO	GF	Sv.	IP	H	TBF	R	ER	HR	SH	SF	HB	BB	IBB	SO	WP
Jarvis, Jason, Dunedin	7	3	.700	4.89	36	13	2	1	8	1	112.1	117	485	66	61	5	4	3	10	40	1	65	6
Jerzembeck, Mike, Tampa	4	2	.667	2.95	12	12	0	0	0	0	73.1	67	297	26	24	4	1	1	0	13	0	60	3
Kamieniecki, Scott, Tampa	2	1	.667	1.17	3	3	1	0	0	0	23.0	20	92	6	3	1	0	0	0	4	0	17	1
Kell, Rob, Charlotte*	6	4	.600	3.81	11	11	3	2	0	0	78.0	71	317	39	33	4	2	5	3	17	0	61	3
Kelly, John, St. Lucie	0	0	.000	3.00	1	0	0	0	0	0	3.0	3	13	1	1	1	0	0	1	0	0	6	0
Key, Jimmy, Tampa	0	0	.000	2.77	2	2	0	0	0	0	13.0	10	53	4	4	1	0	0	0	1	0	11	0
King, Curtis, St. Petersburg	3	3	.500	2.75	48	0	0	0	46	30	55.2	41	232	20	17	0	5	2	5	24	4	27	2
Knight, Brandon, Charlotte	4	10	.286	5.12	19	17	2	0	0	0	102.0	118	463	65	58	9	4	7	2	45	0	74	6
Knighton, Tore, Charlotte	0	2	.000	2.82	5	2	0	0	2	0	22.1	15	88	11	7	3	0	1	0	11	0	11	2
Knoll, Randy, Clearwater	1	0	1.000	3.05	4	4	0	0	0	0	20.2	17	79	8	7	2	0	1	0	2	0	19	0
Kolb, Danny, Charlotte	2	2	.500	4.26	6	6	0	0	0	0	38.0	38	162	18	18	1	1	0	1	14	0	28	2
Konieczki, Dom, Fort Myers*	0	0	.000	0.64	14	0	0	0	8	1	14.0	7	54	1	1	0	0	0	0	6	0	22	2
Kosek, Kory, Clearwater	3	4	.429	3.77	42	4	0	0	9	1	74.0	84	339	43	31	5	5	2	6	32	4	50	1
Lagarde, Joe, Vero Beach	4	3	.571	2.44	14	4	0	0	5	1	44.1	41	194	17	12	0	2	1	4	22	1	46	1
Lail, Denny, Tampa	4	0	1.000	2.55	31	0	0	0	8	1	35.1	37	152	11	10	0	1	0	1	14	2	21	2
Larkin, Andy, Brevard County	0	4	.000	4.23	6	6	0	0	0	0	27.2	34	126	20	13	0	0	1	7	7	0	18	3
Larson, Toby, St. Lucie	4	3	.571	4.69	9	9	1	0	0	0	48.0	60	210	28	25	4	0	1	3	10	0	36	1
Leaman, Jeff, Clearwater	1	0	1.000	3.60	3	0	0	0	0	0	5.0	8	26	4	2	0	0	0	0	2	0	3	1
Lee, Jeremy, Dunedin	2	4	.333	4.97	10	10	0	0	0	0	50.2	69	235	38	28	2	2	1	6	19	2	27	0
Licciardi, Ron, Daytona*	1	0	1.000	1.13	2	1	0	0	1	0	8.0	3	31	2	1	0	0	1	1	2	0	3	0
Lincoln, Mike, Fort Myers	5	2	.714	4.07	12	11	0	0	0	0	59.2	64	263	31	27	5	2	4	3	25	0	24	4
Link, Bryan, Charlotte	5	4	.556	4.10	15	10	1	0	1	0	74.2	79	318	41	34	8	3	2	1	18	0	62	2
Lock, Dan, Kissimmee*	5	18	.217	4.75	27	27	1	0	0	0	147.2	166	672	109	78	3	9	8	7	62	0	72	8
Logan, Marcus, St. Petersburg	7	7	.500	2.91	30	19	0	0	2	0	133.0	125	556	49	43	9	4	3	6	49	1	99	7
Lopez, Johann, Kissimmee	3	10	.231	3.75	19	19	2	1	0	0	98.1	114	434	50	41	5	0	5	1	35	1	70	9
Lukasiewicz, Mark, Dunedin*	2	1	.667	4.60	23	0	0	0	5	1	31.1	28	144	20	16	1	1	1	4	22	1	31	1
Maeda, Katsuhiro, Tampa	0	0	.000	4.22	2	2	0	0	0	0	10.2	11	50	5	5	0	1	0	2	6	0	8	0
Mahay, Ronald, Sarasota*	2	2	.500	3.82	31	4	0	0	13	2	70.2	61	295	33	30	5	1	0	0	35	0	68	4
Manning, Len, Clearwater*	3	7	.300	3.69	20	18	1	0	1	0	102.1	94	448	51	42	6	5	1	4	63	1	77	10
Marquardt, Scott, St. Lucie	0	0	.000	0.00	1	0	0	0	1	0	1.0	1	5	0	0	0	0	0	0	1	1	1	0
Marquez, Robert, W. Palm Beach	1	1	.500	7.36	11	0	0	0	7	6	11.0	14	54	10	9	0	0	0	4	5	0	8	0
Marrero, Kenny, Lakeland	0	3	.000	2.30	34	0	0	0	13	0	66.2	60	282	26	17	1	0	2	1	25	1	82	6
Martinez, Cesar, Sarasota	3	4	.429	4.72	35	0	0	0	16	1	68.2	82	325	40	36	1	2	3	6	40	2	50	7
Martinez, Ramiro, W. Palm Beach	1	0	1.000	3.40	9	7	0	0	1	0	42.1	47	185	20	16	1	1	3	1	14	0	44	2
Martinez, Ramon, Vero Beach	1	0	1.000	0.00	1	1	0	0	0	0	7.0	5	28	1	0	0	0	0	0	0	0	10	0
McAulay, John, Charlotte	0	0	.000	0.00	1	0	0	0	1	0	0.1	0	1	0	0	0	0	0	0	0	0	0	0
McCready, Jim, St. Lucie	1	2	.333	3.86	10	0	0	0	3	0	16.1	18	65	8	7	1	1	0	0	2	0	12	2
McFerrin, Chris, Kissimmee	0	0	.000	10.13	4	0	0	0	1	0	2.2	7	19	7	3	0	0	0	2	3	0	2	1
McNeely, Mitch, Vero Beach*	1	1	.500	2.08	23	1	1	0	11	2	47.2	32	188	13	11	0	1	3	2	12	2	34	0
McNeese, John, Daytona*	1	1	.500	5.14	9	0	0	0	2	0	14.0	18	66	8	8	0	0	2	1	7	0	10	3
McNeill, Kevin, St. Petersburg*	4	2	.667	2.95	45	0	0	0	8	0	61.0	56	256	28	20	1	8	1	5	18	0	44	3
McNichol, Brian, Daytona*	1	2	.333	4.67	8	7	0	0	0	0	34.2	39	162	24	18	4	0	1	0	14	0	22	1
Meadows, Brian, Brevard County	8	7	.533	3.58	24	23	3	1	1	0	146.0	129	600	73	58	13	3	4	10	25	1	69	4
Medina, Tomas, Kissimmee	1	0	1.000	7.50	9	0	0	0	4	0	12.0	16	65	11	10	0	0	1	6	9	0	7	8
Meiners, Doug, Dunedin	1	1	.500	3.26	17	3	0	0	6	0	38.2	37	165	21	14	2	0	2	4	8	1	16	0
Mendez, Manuel, St. Petersburg*	4	3	.571	2.87	59	0	0	0	9	0	69.0	61	290	25	22	3	3	2	5	36	2	53	0
Mercado, Hector, Kissimmee*	3	5	.375	4.16	56	0	0	0	18	3	80.0	78	353	43	37	4	3	1	4	48	1	68	6
Merrill, Ethan, Sarasota*	5	6	.455	4.31	14	14	0	0	0	0	87.2	96	383	50	42	1	3	4	5	26	2	54	5
Metheney, Nelson, Clearwater	1	0	1.000	0.79	21	0	0	0	5	1	34.0	29	134	4	3	0	2	0	1	6	4	19	0
Meyer, David, Tampa*	3	2	.600	2.11	11	6	0	0	0	0	38.1	46	177	16	9	2	2	2	1	17	1	18	1
Miles, Chad, Brevard County*	1	5	.167	5.48	27	7	0	0	12	0	70.2	90	328	57	43	8	4	4	3	31	3	37	7
Miller, David, Brevard County	4	5	.444	4.76	26	11	0	0	5	0	85.0	94	374	51	45	12	2	4	9	26	0	40	1
Miranda, Walter, Brevard County	0	1	.000	9.95	2	2	0	0	0	0	6.1	8	31	7	7	0	0	0	1	6	0	1	1
Mitchell, Kendrick, Vero Beach	3	8	.273	5.47	39	6	0	0	12	1	80.2	75	365	61	49	9	5	3	9	51	1	58	12
Mittauer, Casey, Tampa	1	1	.500	2.01	21	0	0	0	11	4	31.1	28	126	10	7	0	4	1	1	5	1	23	2
Montelongo, Joe, Daytona	6	6	.500	3.10	19	14	1	0	1	0	101.2	84	432	53	35	5	4	0	5	36	2	77	10
Moody, Ritchie, Charlotte*	1	1	.500	4.05	18	1	0	0	11	1	33.1	34	156	17	15	1	1	2	2	22	0	25	3
Moraga, David, W. Palm Beach*	7	10	.412	4.58	29	20	1	0	1	0	125.2	138	560	74	64	6	4	7	4	50	0	96	12
Morgan, Mike, St. Petersburg	1	0	1.000	0.00	1	1	0	0	0	0	5.2	4	21	0	0	0	0	0	0	1	0	4	0
Morillo, Donald, Charlotte	2	3	.400	4.76	32	0	0	0	17	2	51.0	51	234	33	27	2	1	7	2	40	2	34	6
Morse, Paul, Fort Myers	1	0	1.000	2.57	13	0	0	0	12	9	14.0	8	50	4	4	1	0	0	0	5	0	10	0
Mosley, Tim, Daytona	0	3	.000	11.42	6	0	0	0	3	0	8.2	16	47	15	11	1	1	0	0	6	2	7	2
Mott, Tom, Fort Myers	7	5	.583	4.82	14	14	0	0	0	0	74.2	80	328	43	40	5	3	0	3	37	0	48	10
Mounce, Tony, Kissimmee*	9	9	.500	2.25	25	25	4	2	0	0	155.2	139	675	65	39	7	6	3	10	68	1	102	7
Munoz, Bobby, Clearwater	1	1	.500	1.93	2	2	0	0	1	0	14.0	15	58	4	3	0	1	0	0	2	0	7	0
Munro, Peter, Sarasota	11	6	.647	3.60	27	25	2	2	1	1	155.0	153	667	76	62	4	3	2	7	62	1	115	7
Murray, Dan, St. Lucie	7	5	.583	4.25	33	13	0	0	5	0	101.2	114	465	60	48	2	3	3	8	53	3	56	11
Musselwhite, Jim, Tampa	0	2	.000	7.80	3	3	0	0	0	0	15.0	24	77	16	13	2	0	0	2	5	0	5	0
Nakashima, Tony, Vero Beach*	0	0	.000	0.00	2	0	0	0	1	1	3.0	4	14	1	0	0	0	0	0	0	0	2	0
Neal, Billy, Vero Beach	16	6	.727	2.28	51	0	0	0	12	1	110.2	94	455	37	28	4	4	3	5	39	4	75	6
O'Flynn, Gardner, Charlotte*	8	9	.471	4.61	28	17	1	0	7	0	109.1	130	483	71	56	9	9	2	6	31	0	37	6
Oliver, Darren, Charlotte*	0	1	.000	3.00	2	1	0	0	0	0	12.0	8	47	4	4	1	0	0	2	3	0	9	0
Olson, Phillip, St. Lucie	1	5	.167	4.32	15	7	0	0	2	1	50.0	63	220	26	24	5	1	3	4	18	0	27	5
Osborne, Donovan, St. Petersburg*	1	0	1.000	0.00	1	1	0	0	0	0	6.0	2	19	0	0	0	0	0	0	0	0	2	0
Owen, Tom, Brevard County	0	0	.000	0.00	1	0	0	0	1	0	0.1	2	3	0	0	0	0	0	0	0	0	0	0
Pace, Scotty, Dunedin*	0	0	.000	1.78	19	0	0	0	12	6	30.1	24	123	7	6	0	2	0	3	13	1	20	3
Pack, Steve, St. Lucie	0	0	.000	3.63	23	0	0	0	7	0	34.2	41	151	20	14	3	1	4	0	10	1	16	2
Parisi, Michael, Brevard County	6	8	.429	4.15	21	19	1	0	0	0	119.1	117	515	59	55	9	2	4	10	39	1	65	1
Parra, Julio, Vero Beach	0	0	.000	1.27	12	0	0	0	7	1	21.1	12	79	3	3	1	0	0	0	5	0	17	0
Pavicich, Paul, Fort Myers*	2	3	.400	5.06	29	0	0	0	8	0	42.2	49	190	30	24	4	1	2	0	13	0	29	3
Perkins, Dan, Fort Myers	13	7	.650	2.96	39	13	3	1	10	2	136.2	125	557	52	45	5	4	6	11	37	1	111	9
Peters, Tim, Fort Myers*	0	3	.000	3.54	28	0	0	0	16	1	28.0	31	120	11	11	2	1	2	2	5	2	23	2
Peterson, Dean, Sarasota	7	2	.778	3.05	26	3	0	0	11	3	62.0	45	252	30	21	5	3	1	2	21	1	58	0

itcher, Team	W	L	Pct.	ERA	G	GS	CG	ShO	GF	Sv.	IP	H	TBF	R	ER	HR	SH	SF	HB	BB	IBB	SO	WP	Bk.
eterson, Jay, Daytona	0	2	.000	6.51	8	7	0	0	0	0	27.2	35	134	29	20	3	0	3	1	21	0	15	4	0
etkovsek, Mark, St. Petersburg	0	0	.000	4.50	3	0	0	0	0	0	6.0	6	25	3	3	0	0	1	1	0	0	5	0	0
helps, Tommy, W. Palm Beach*	10	2	.833	2.89	18	18	1	1	0	0	112.0	105	468	42	36	5	4	1	2	35	0	71	8	0
ivaral, Hugo, Vero Beach	1	1	.500	4.44	7	6	0	0	0	0	26.1	34	122	15	13	1	1	0	1	16	0	16	10	0
ontes, Dan, St. Petersburg	7	8	.467	3.81	27	22	1	0	2	0	120.1	120	495	56	51	8	3	5	3	34	0	73	3	1
owell, Brian, Lakeland	8	13	.381	4.90	29	27	5	0	2	0	174.1	195	746	106	95	12	9	2	7	47	0	84	1	2
owell, Jay, Brevard County	0	0	.000	0.00	1	1	0	0	0	0	2.0	0	6	0	0	0	0	0	0	0	0	4	0	0
ress, Gregg, Brevard County	9	9	.500	2.75	28	23	0	0	1	0	150.1	134	604	62	46	9	6	1	4	37	4	90	10	0
uirico, Rafael, Clearwater*	0	1	.000	7.84	2	2	0	0	0	0	10.1	13	45	9	9	2	0	1	1	1	0	12	0	4
adlosky, Rob, Fort Myers	4	6	.400	5.45	28	16	1	1	5	1	104.0	116	467	70	63	11	2	3	9	46	0	80	10	0
aines, Ken, Charlotte*	0	4	.000	5.64	23	0	0	0	13	2	30.1	44	144	20	19	4	0	1	0	14	1	23	0	0
ama, Shelby, Clearwater	7	3	.700	2.92	34	7	0	0	5	0	83.1	88	356	41	27	4	4	1	4	25	1	38	2	0
amirez, Felix, Sarasota*	1	0	1.000	3.27	5	0	0	0	3	0	11.0	10	49	8	4	0	0	0	1	8	0	7	1	0
amos, Edgar, Kissimmee	9	0	1.000	1.51	11	11	1	0	0	0	77.2	51	298	17	13	4	3	1	6	15	0	81	4	0
amsay, Robert, Sarasota*	2	2	.500	6.09	12	7	0	0	0	0	34.0	42	165	23	23	1	1	1	1	27	0	32	2	2
ath, Fred, Fort Myers	2	5	.286	2.79	22	0	0	0	16	4	29.0	25	123	10	9	1	1	0	2	10	0	29	3	0
edman, Mark, Fort Myers*	3	4	.429	1.85	13	13	1	0	0	0	82.2	63	335	24	17	1	6	3	5	34	0	75	4	1
eed, Brian, St. Petersburg	5	4	.556	3.04	58	0	0	0	27	3	68.0	55	295	26	23	2	2	6	7	35	2	76	5	1
esz, Greg, Tampa	0	1	.000	2.52	20	0	0	0	9	4	25.0	20	108	11	7	0	1	2	0	12	1	31	2	0
hine, Kendall, Dunedin	1	0	1.000	3.91	20	0	0	0	11	3	23.0	20	104	11	10	1	0	3	11	2	25	2	0
hodriguez, Rory, W. Palm Beach	5	2	.714	4.10	35	2	0	0	10	0	68.0	57	292	33	31	2	2	2	4	37	1	48	10	0
icabal, Dan, Vero Beach	0	2	.000	1.20	13	1	0	0	8	1	30.0	14	119	7	4	1	0	0	17	4	36	0	1
ichardson, Kasey, Fort Myers*	1	0	1.000	6.32	3	3	0	0	0	0	15.2	18	69	11	11	2	0	1	0	8	0	12	2	0
oach, Peter, Vero Beach*	3	4	.429	3.65	17	10	0	0	2	0	69.0	56	273	30	28	6	1	1	1	17	1	52	3	2
oberts, Chris, St. Lucie	1	0	1.000	0.00	1	1	0	0	0	0	6.0	1	21	0	0	0	0	0	3	0	2	0	0
oberts, Willis, Lakeland	9	7	.563	2.89	23	22	2	0	0	0	149.1	133	636	60	48	5	8	9	9	69	0	105	13	3
obertson, Jeriome, Kissimmee	0	0	.000	2.57	1	1	0	0	0	0	7.0	4	27	4	2	0	0	0	0	1	0	2	0	0
ogers, Bryan, St. Lucie	2	0	1.000	1.54	9	0	0	0	4	0	11.2	12	50	2	2	0	0	0	4	0	11	0	1
olocut, Brian, Vero Beach	1	7	.125	5.51	33	6	0	0	12	0	65.1	69	320	50	40	6	3	1	6	53	1	52	9	0
oque, Rafael, St. Lucie	6	4	.600	2.12	14	12	1	0	1	0	76.1	57	311	22	18	2	5	0	3	39	0	59	8	0
ushing, Will, Fort Myers*	13	6	.684	3.49	28	25	2	1	1	1	165.0	157	699	72	64	10	8	3	9	74	0	111	5	2
ussell, Jeff, Charlotte	0	0	.000	0.00	2	2	0	0	0	0	3.0	0	9	0	0	0	0	0	0	0	0	6	0	0
yan, Jason, Daytona	1	8	.111	5.24	17	10	0	0	3	1	67.0	72	298	42	39	8	5	2	4	33	0	49	1	0
. Pierre, Bob, Tampa	12	6	.667	3.21	29	22	0	0	3	1	140.1	133	579	69	50	5	3	6	38	1	107	7	2
alazar, Mike, Lakeland*	1	1	.500	2.50	19	1	0	0	4	0	36.0	31	143	16	10	1	1	1	6	1	24	0	0
ampson, Benj, Fort Myers*	7	1	.875	3.47	11	11	2	0	0	0	70.0	55	282	28	27	5	1	2	1	26	0	65	1	0
anchez, Jesus, St. Lucie*	9	3	.750	1.96	16	16	1	0	0	0	92.0	53	344	22	20	6	3	1	1	24	0	81	4	2
antiago, Sandi, Tampa	0	1	.000	5.11	9	1	0	0	3	1	12.1	18	60	9	7	1	2	0	4	0	11	1	0
antos, Victor, Lakeland	2	2	.500	2.22	5	4	0	0	0	0	28.1	19	114	11	7	2	2	1	4	9	0	25	2	0
auerbeck, Scott, St. Lucie*	6	6	.500	2.27	17	16	2	2	0	0	99.1	101	406	37	25	1	3	0	1	27	0	62	4	1
canlan, Bob, Lakeland	0	1	.000	5.00	2	2	0	0	0	0	9.0	9	39	6	5	0	1	0	0	3	0	4	2	0
chaaf, Bob, Vero Beach	0	0	.000	0.00	2	0	0	0	2	0	0.2	0	3	0	0	0	0	0	1	0	0	0	0
cheffler, Craig, Vero Beach*	0	0	.000	6.53	31	1	0	0	16	1	41.1	50	197	33	30	1	2	4	3	27	1	23	5	1
chilling, Curt, Clearwater	2	0	1.000	1.29	2	2	0	0	0	0	14.0	9	53	2	2	0	0	0	0	1	0	17	0	0
chlomann, Brett, Tampa	11	8	.579	4.26	26	26	1	1	0	0	145.2	152	628	81	69	13	3	4	8	49	2	103	10	1
haver, Tony, Kissimmee	4	4	.500	2.39	42	0	0	0	24	4	64.0	57	275	24	17	3	6	1	1	23	1	35	2	0
helby, Anthony, Tampa	2	2	.500	1.80	24	0	0	0	8	1	30.0	26	124	12	6	1	1	1	7	1	18	1	0
hort, Barry, St. Lucie	6	2	.750	2.34	58	0	0	0	24	10	88.1	70	350	28	23	5	4	1	1	18	1	70	1	0
humaker, Anthony, Clearwater*	5	3	.625	5.10	31	0	0	0	13	3	30.0	39	136	17	17	1	0	0	12	5	24	1	0
ier, Jeff, Lakeland*	6	3	.667	2.64	37	0	0	0	7	1	58.0	52	237	20	17	3	4	1	1	18	0	45	0	1
iva, Ted, Charlotte	10	2	.833	2.86	16	16	4	0	0	0	113.1	98	463	39	36	9	1	2	3	27	1	95	3	1
inclair, Steve, Dunedin*	0	1	.000	3.38	3	0	0	0	1	0	2.2	4	12	2	1	1	0	0	0	0	1	0	0
krmetta, Matt, Lakeland	5	5	.500	3.59	40	0	0	0	20	5	52.2	44	223	23	21	5	2	0	2	19	1	52	2	1
mith, Cam, Lakeland	5	8	.385	4.59	22	21	0	0	1	0	113.2	93	500	64	58	10	1	5	7	71	0	114	8	0
mith, Dan, Charlotte	3	7	.300	5.07	18	18	1	0	0	0	87.0	100	403	61	49	6	5	5	4	38	0	55	3	0
mith, Danny, Charlotte*	0	1	.000	2.74	5	5	0	0	0	0	23.0	21	92	7	7	1	0	0	0	8	0	16	1	1
mith, Keilan, Dunedin	0	3	.000	5.04	23	1	0	0	9	2	44.2	50	205	32	25	3	3	4	2	22	4	37	5	0
obik, Trad, Lakeland	4	6	.400	4.43	13	13	2	0	0	2	81.1	79	362	51	40	5	8	2	6	48	1	49	3	0
eier, Justin, Daytona	2	4	.333	3.76	33	0	0	0	29	13	38.1	32	168	19	16	3	3	2	2	19	3	34	5	0
ence, Michael, Tampa	2	4	.333	5.80	8	8	0	0	0	0	40.1	51	181	31	26	3	0	3	2	12	0	20	2	1
achler, Eric, Kissimmee	4	3	.571	3.83	30	0	0	0	11	0	56.1	50	257	35	24	3	1	4	3	39	2	41	3	0
anifer, Robert, Brevard County	4	2	.667	2.39	22	0	0	0	4	0	49.0	54	206	17	13	3	0	1	1	9	0	32	1	0
ein, Blake, St. Petersburg	16	5	.762	2.15	28	27	1	1	1	1	172.0	122	667	48	41	4	3	4	5	54	0	159	4	0
einke, Brock, Kissimmee	4	3	.571	6.41	16	8	0	0	2	1	46.1	62	227	39	33	2	0	4	6	31	0	22	6	1
ephens, Shannon, Brevard County	0	4	.000	6.29	4	4	0	0	0	0	24.1	33	114	22	17	2	0	2	0	9	0	12	0	0
evenson, Jason, Daytona	8	5	.615	3.54	27	17	2	1	5	0	122.0	136	519	56	48	7	6	5	5	22	2	86	8	1
ewart, Stan, Tampa	0	0	.000	2.70	14	0	0	0	9	2	26.2	29	117	14	8	1	1	2	1	5	0	23	1	1
one, Ricky, Vero Beach	8	6	.571	3.83	21	21	1	0	0	0	112.2	115	488	58	48	9	4	3	3	46	0	74	10	0
ubbs, Jerry, W. Palm Beach	1	0	1.000	6.00	7	0	0	0	0	0	9.0	11	46	7	6	0	0	0	3	0	5	0	0
umpf, Brian, Clearwater	1	6	.143	3.36	56	0	0	0	50	26	59.0	54	260	25	22	3	5	2	0	32	3	48	2	0
van, Tyrone, Clearwater	3	2	.600	3.54	10	6	0	0	1	0	40.2	38	170	21	16	1	2	1	3	12	0	22	1	0
tar, Jason, Fort Myers	0	0	.000	9.82	4	0	0	0	3	0	3.2	6	21	4	4	0	0	0	0	4	0	4	2	0
tis, Ramon, St. Lucie*	4	2	.667	3.39	46	1	0	0	20	6	74.1	71	325	35	28	4	7	2	2	38	8	46	14	1
ssmer, Jay, Tampa	12	4	.750	1.48	68	0	0	0	63	35	97.1	68	381	18	16	2	6	0	6	19	3	104	1	0
ornton, Paul, Brevard County	0	0	.000	0.00	1	0	0	0	0	0	2.2	4	12	0	0	0	0	0	0	0	0	2	0	0
urman, Michael, W. Palm Beach	6	8	.429	3.40	19	19	1	0	0	0	113.2	122	479	53	43	3	5	2	3	23	0	68	7	1
lmon, Darrell, Sarasota	7	6	.538	3.20	18	18	1	1	0	0	112.1	104	450	41	40	4	3	2	28	0	59	3	0
eend, Patrick, Brevard County	1	0	1.000	0.00	1	0	0	0	0	0	1.0	0	3	0	0	0	0	0	0	0	0	1	0	0
cker, Julien, Kissimmee	4	8	.333	4.27	32	16	0	0	6	1	116.0	131	525	79	55	8	4	6	12	41	1	55	9	1
rrentine, Rich, St. Lucie	4	4	.500	2.28	45	0	0	0	40	21	51.1	31	232	18	13	0	4	1	2	45	1	63	9	0
eedle, Brad, Sarasota	2	0	1.000	0.79	11	0	0	0	11	7	11.1	6	45	1	1	0	0	0	1	3	1	9	0	0
rrell, Jim, Sarasota*	1	2	.333	5.27	8	0	0	0	3	0	13.2	11	60	9	8	1	0	0	1	8	1	14	1	0
derwood, Devin, Sarasota	0	0	.000	7.71	3	0	0	0	2	0	2.1	4	12	2	2	0	0	0	1	0	1	0	1	0

CLASS A Florida State League

Pitcher, Team	W	L	Pct.	ERA	G	GS	CG	ShO	GF	Sv.	IP	H	TBF	R	ER	HR	SH	SF	HB	BB	IBB	SO	WP	Bk
Urbina, Ugueth, W. Palm Beach....	1	1	.500	1.29	3	3	0	0	0	0	14.0	13	58	3	2	0	2	0	2	3	0	21	0	
Vandemark, John, Clearwater*	0	2	.000	2.39	27	0	0	0	5	3	26.1	21	114	10	7	0	2	0	1	14	0	27	3	
Veniard, Jay, Dunedin*	4	5	.444	4.04	14	14	0	0	0	0	64.2	63	270	37	29	7	0	2	5	19	0	40	4	
Waggoner, James, Lakeland	1	0	1.000	0.00	1	0	0	0	0	1	3.0	0	9	0	0	0	0	0	0	0	0	0	0	
Wallace, B.J., Clearwater*	3	4	.429	5.83	15	12	0	0	0	0	63.1	71	299	47	41	3	1	3	8	41	0	37	3	
Ward, Duane, Daytona	0	1	.000	6.35	6	0	0	0	6	0	5.2	5	25	4	4	2	2	0	0	4	0	3	1	
Weidert, Chris, W. Palm Beach	3	8	.273	3.40	20	20	1	0	0	0	106.0	106	462	54	40	4	3	3	7	37	1	64	4	
West, David, Clearwater.........	1	0	1.000	3.13	5	5	0	0	0	0	23.0	21	99	8	8	1	0	0	1	11	0	17	3	
Westbrook, Destry, Clearwater	3	3	.500	2.08	34	0	0	0	12	0	43.1	35	180	12	10	3	0	1	1	11	2	35	2	
Whatley, Gabe, Daytona	0	0	.000	0.00	1	0	0	0	1	0	0.2	0	2	0	0	0	0	0	0	0	0	0	0	
Whiteman, Greg, Lakeland*.........	11	10	.524	3.71	27	27	1	0	0	0	150.1	134	640	66	62	5	4	6	7	89	0	122	8	
Whiteside, Sean, Lakeland*.........	4	10	.286	3.86	19	18	0	0	0	0	102.2	104	432	51	44	6	3	3	0	32	0	63	6	
Wiley, Chad, Charlotte............	2	1	.667	2.03	5	5	0	0	0	0	26.2	19	101	7	6	0	1	1	1	4	0	14	0	
Williams, Mitch, Clearwater*.........	0	0	.000	2.25	6	0	0	0	1	0	8.0	10	37	3	2	0	0	1	1	6	0	6	0	
Williams, Woody, Dunedin...........	0	2	.000	8.22	2	2	0	0	0	0	7.2	9	34	7	7	1	0	0	0	2	0	11	0	
Wilson, Paul, St. Lucie.............	0	1	.000	3.38	2	2	0	0	0	0	8.0	6	36	5	3	0	1	0	0	4	0	5	0	
Wimberly, Larry, Sarasota*.........	2	4	.333	6.90	6	6	0	0	0	0	30.0	38	142	26	23	2	1	2	2	16	1	16	1	
Windham, Mike, St. Petersburg.....	7	10	.412	3.13	25	25	1	0	0	0	143.2	153	610	59	50	4	4	4	6	57	1	87	7	
Winslett, Dax, Daytona	0	1	.000	13.50	2	1	0	0	0	0	6.0	10	34	10	9	1	0	1	1	5	1	3	0	
Withem, Shannon, St. Lucie	1	0	1.000	1.29	2	2	0	0	0	0	14.0	8	53	2	2	0	0	0	1	1	0	13	1	
Wood, Kerry, Daytona.............	10	2	.833	2.91	22	22	0	0	0	0	114.1	72	495	51	37	6	5	4	14	70	0	136	10	
Yocum, David, Vero Beach*.........	0	2	.000	6.14	7	7	0	0	0	0	14.2	22	69	11	10	1	0	0	1	7	0	8	0	
Young, Joe, Dunedin.............	1	3	.250	5.88	6	6	0	0	0	0	33.2	30	145	24	22	3	2	1	2	17	1	36	3	

COMBINATION SHUTOUTS: **Clearwater (6)**—Fiore-Kosek-Estavil, Rama-Kosek-Estavil, Censale-Kosek, Boyd-Greene-Barbao, Boyd-Shumaker, Knoll-Swan-Barba Stumpf-Shumaker. **Daytona (5)**—Garcia-Faulkner, Wood-Green-Speier, Diaz-Hammack, Wood-Brown-Hammack, Wood-Greene-Hammack. **Dunedin (7)**—Duran-Pac Halladay-Fitterer-Doman, Escobar-Lukasiewicz, Veniard-Meiners-Jarvis-Gomez, Escobar-Rhine, Halladay-Meiners-Smith, Adkins-Jarvis-Gomez. **Fort Myers (6)**— Rushing-Pavicich-Morse, Bell-Gourdin, Rushing-Gourdin-Konieczki-Morse, Redman-Dowhower-Konieczki, Bell-Dowhower, Rushing-Peters. **Kissimmee (5)**—Ramc Dault-Mercado-Henriquez, Elarton-Stachler, Tucker-Dault, Elarton-Humphrey, Elarton-Shaver-Stachler. **Lakeland (14)**—Whiteman-Jacobson-Marrero-Skrmett Roberts-Marrero-Cedeno, Roberts-Cedeno-Dinyar, Salazar-Siler-Marrero-Dinyar, Whiteside-Siler-Skrmetta-Dinyar, Whiteman-Salazar-Dinyar, Whiteside-Siler-Diny Whiteside-Marrero, Roberts-Diyar, Smith-Eby, Whiteman-Dinyar, Smith-Siler-Dinyar-Waggoner, Santos-Siler-Skrmetta, Whiteside-Jacobson. **St. Lucie (8)**— Sauerbec Short-Pack, Gooch-Short, Sauerbeck-Olson, Sanchez-Short, Sanchez-Rogers-Turrentine, Roberts-Turrentine, Larson-Short, Roque-Short. **St. Petersburg (11)**—Stei Conway-Reed-Golden, Osborne-Hall, Stein-King, Windham-McNeill-Reed-Conway, Heiserman-King, Heiserman-Mendez-Conway-King, Stein-King, Windham-McNe Heiserman-McNeill-Hall, Windham-King, Logan-Reed-Mendez-King. **Sarasota (5)**—Munro-Mahay, Farrell-Mahay-Munro, Cook-Martinez-Tweedlie, Tillmon-Tweedl Tillmon-Ramirez-Cannon-Peterson. **Tampa (6)**—Henthorne-Stewart-Tessmer, Corn-Tessmer, Hutton-Beverlin-Drumheller-Tessmer, Schlomann-Mittauer-Tessm Jerzembeck-Resz-Santiago, St. Pierre-Drumheller-Resz. **Vero Beach (8)**—Colon-Neal-Eaddy-Hollis, Camacho-Rolocut-Roach, Camacho-Neal, Iglesias-Mitche Scheffler, Bland-Parra, Roach-Mitchell, Bland-Parra, Stone-McNeely-Iglesias. **West Palm Beach (7)**—Urbina-Moraga-Rhodriquez, Thurman-DaSilva, Dixon-DaSilv Fleetham, Phelps-Gentile, Durocher-Cole-Rhodriquez, Dixon-Cole, Martinez-DaSilva.

NO-HIT GAMES: Atwater, St. Lucie, defeated Daytona, 1-0, June 10.

1996 FIELDING

TEAM

Team	Pct.	G	PO	A	E	TC	DP	PB	Team	Pct.	G	PO	A	E	TC	DP
St. Petersburg......	.981	139	3601	1453	100	5154	130	25	Clearwater.........	.967	137	3625	1595	178	5398	114
Fort Myers..........	.975	138	3639	1612	134	5385	141	13	Brevard County.....	.966	139	3638	1657	185	5480	131
Sarasota............	.971	136	3540	1378	149	5067	111	34	Vero Beach.........	.964	131	3373	1458	179	5010	112
Charlotte	.970	139	3685	1541	161	5387	118	27	W. Palm Beach..	.964	135	3528	1477	189	5194	102
Lakeland............	.969	138	3600	1499	164	5263	123	23	Daytona.............	.961	137	3487	1405	198	5090	104
St. Lucie.............	.969	133	3468	1669	167	5304	138	20	Kissimmee..........	.958	137	3452	1467	213	5132	115
Tampa	.967	134	3542	1429	168	5139	106	27	Dunedin.............	.958	137	3562	1594	227	5383	127

TRIPLE PLAYS: Charlotte 2.

INDIVIDUAL

FIRST BASEMEN

NOTE: All caps denotes fielding-percentage leader based on 69 games for catchers, 92 for all other non-pitchers and 138 innings for pitchers. *Throws lefthanded.

Player, Team	Pct.	G	PO	A	E	TC	DP
Abad, Andy, Sarasota*	.989	29	252	17	3	272	22
Barkett, Andy, Charlotte*...............	.993	102	822	72	6	900	87
Bokemeier, Matt, Charlotte	1.000	4	36	2	0	38	0
Braddy, Junior, Sarasota..............	.500	1	1	0	1	2	0
Brinkley, Josh, W. Palm Beach	.976	6	40	1	1	42	0
Brown, Nate, W. Palm Beach*........	.990	63	479	32	5	516	44
Cady, Todd, Brevard County	.985	56	548	32	9	589	48
Campos, Jesus, W. Palm Beach	1.000	1	6	0	0	6	2
Carver, Steve, Clearwater.............	.987	67	639	44	9	692	60
Castro, Dennis, Brevard County.......	1.000	1	4	1	0	5	0
Coolbaugh, Mike, Charlotte	.991	36	303	29	3	335	19
Cossins, Tim, Charlotte	1.000	1	10	1	0	11	1
Curl, John, Dunedin...................	.990	108	972	94	11	1077	83
Daly, Bob, St. Lucie	.994	50	494	27	3	524	54
Daulton, Darren, Clearwater	1.000	1	5	1	0	6	0
Davila, Vic, Dunedin	.958	3	22	1	1	24	2
Delvecchio, Nick, Tampa..............	1.000	1	2	1	0	3	1
Depastino, Joe, Sarasota..............	1.000	1	2	1	0	3	1
Derosso, Tony, Sarasota................	.985	18	115	13	2	130	15

Player, Team	Pct.	G	PO	A	E	TC	D
Ellis, Kevin, Daytona	.989	46	340	28	4	372	
Emmons, Scott, Tampa	1.000	3	35	4	0	39	
Fortin, Troy, Fort Myers	1.000	13	108	11	0	119	
Freeman, Ricky, Daytona	.994	95	808	60	5	873	
Freire, Alejandro, Kissimmee	.984	46	356	22	6	384	
Fullmer, Brad, W. Palm Beach	.975	9	70	7	2	79	
Giardi, Mike, Tampa-W.P.B.	1.000	8	53	3	0	56	
Gibralter, David, Sarasota	.988	93	804	67	11	882	
Gonzalez, Jimmy, Kissimmee	1.000	3	29	6	0	35	
Guerrero, Rafael, St. Lucie	1.000	3	9	0	0	9	
Gunderson, Shane, Fort Myers	1.000	2	7	1	0	8	
Haas, Matt, West Palm Beach	.993	18	127	10	1	138	
Hacopian, Derek, W. Palm Beach ...	.993	29	257	23	2	282	
Hall, Ryan, St. Petersburg..............	.994	19	151	4	0	155	
Hayes, Chris, Dunedin	1.000	5	36	2	0	38	
Jackson, Ryan, Brevard County*......	.938	5	28	2	2	32	
Jumonville, Joe, St. Petersburg........	1.000	5	45	3	0	48	
Landaker, Dave, Kissimmee...........	1.000	2	5	0	0	5	
LoDuca, Paul, Vero Beach	.990	12	93	8	1	102	
Martinez, Rafael, Vero Beach*.........	.987	112	904	91	13	1008	
McLamb, Brian, Tampa..................	.962	4	22	3	1	26	
Melhuse, Adam, Dunedin	.985	8	59	5	1	65	
MIENTKIEWICZ, Doug, Ft. Myers......	.998	126	1183	85	3	1271	1

FIRST BASEMEN (continued)

Player, Team	Pct.	G	PO	A	E	TC	DP
Iillan, Adan, Clearwater	.984	74	635	49	11	695	45
Morales, Francisco, W. Palm Beach	.727	1	6	2	3	11	0
Iummau, Rob, Dunedin	1.000	2	24	0	0	24	3
aples, Brandon, St. Lucie*	1.000	3	19	0	0	19	0
wen, Tom, Brevard County	1.000	1	16	0	0	16	1
atterson, Jarrod, St. Lucie	.968	14	137	12	5	154	15
atton, Greg, Sarasota	1.000	2	4	0	0	4	1
ost, Dave, West Palm Beach	.994	20	156	16	1	173	7
ullen, Shane, Clearwater	1.000	2	9	1	0	10	0
ichard, Chris, St. Petersburg*	.994	120	1124	57	7	1188	106
odriguez, Adam, Lakeland	1.000	8	16	1	0	17	2
odriguez, Noel, Kissimmee	.988	77	662	55	9	726	58
alzano, Jerry, Lakeland	1.000	1	4	1	0	5	0
chaaf, Bob, Vero Beach	.987	23	141	11	2	154	8
hanahan, Jason, Brevard County	.993	83	765	84	6	855	70
tone, Craig, Dunedin	.981	17	147	10	3	160	17
rammell, Gary, Kissimmee	.985	15	119	13	2	134	10
urner, Brian, St. Lucie*	.995	20	188	18	1	207	18
nrat, Chris, Charlotte	1.000	1	8	0	0	8	1
asquez, Danny, Charlotte	1.000	1	2	0	0	2	0
oigt, Jack, Charlotte	1.000	5	43	6	0	49	2
Vaggoner, James, Lakeland	.992	23	110	17	1	128	8
Vard, Daryle, Lakeland*	.993	123	1055	103	8	1166	98
Varner, Randy, St. Lucie	.995	55	497	48	3	548	46
edo, Carlos, Tampa*	.979	130	1105	83	25	1213	88

TRIPLE PLAYS: Barkett, Coolbaugh.

FIRST BASEMEN WITH TWO OR MORE TEAMS

Player, Team	Pct.	G	PO	A	E	TC	DP
iardi, Mike, Tampa	1.000	1	11	0	0	11	1
iardi, Mike, West Palm Beach	1.000	7	42	3	0	45	2

SECOND BASEMEN

Player, Team	Pct.	G	PO	A	E	TC	DP
manzar, Richard, Lakeland	.971	124	257	378	19	654	70
mador, Manuel, Clearwater	.939	12	24	38	4	66	5
nderson, Marlon, Clearwater	.958	60	142	221	16	379	43
rano, Eloy, Lakeland	.965	19	38	45	3	86	10
rnold, Ken, Charlotte	.938	2	7	8	1	16	3
valos, Gilbert, Daytona	.966	73	115	171	10	296	26
eeney, Ryan, Tampa	.917	2	6	5	1	12	1
ermann, Steve, St. Petersburg	1.000	5	2	7	0	9	1
orrego, Ramon, Fort Myers	1.000	7	14	21	0	35	7
owles, John, Sarasota	.980	11	22	26	1	49	2
avo, Danny, West Palm Beach	.974	44	80	110	5	195	22
own, Vick, Tampa	.922	24	33	61	8	102	7
unson, Matt, Brevard County	.953	117	255	367	31	653	82
arpentier, Mike, Vero Beach	.945	32	60	78	8	146	18
arvajal, Jhonny, W. Palm Beach	.987	33	64	88	2	154	17
oquillette, Trace, W. Palm Beach	.958	36	68	90	7	165	16
anford, Joe, Fort Myers	.966	25	31	81	4	116	15
espo, Felipe, Dunedin	.947	9	18	18	2	38	5
arden, Tony, Brevard County	.959	20	45	49	4	98	9
avila, Vic, Dunedin	1.000	3	3	3	0	6	0
nton, Cary, Charlotte	.970	74	153	197	11	361	41
ores, Jose, Clearwater	.976	26	40	81	3	124	15
rkerway, Trey, Daytona	1.000	6	12	9	0	21	2
eel, Ryan, Dunedin	.958	94	189	267	20	476	64
allego, Mike, St. Petersburg	.967	12	17	41	2	60	7
rcia, Carlos, Fort Myers	1.000	1	0	1	0	1	0
ardi, Mike, West Palm Beach	1.000	2	6	6	0	12	2
ozier, Larry, Brevard County	1.000	3	5	4	0	9	0
omez, Rudy, Tampa	.961	40	65	107	7	179	16
recki, Ryan, Charlotte	.986	71	133	217	5	355	43
ayes, Chris, Dunedin	.750	1	2	1	1	4	0
uff, Larry, Clearwater	.979	41	80	107	4	191	20
ackson, Gavin, Sarasota	1.000	10	16	24	0	40	4
elly, Pat, Tampa	.923	6	15	9	2	26	1
ane, Ryan, Fort Myers	.964	105	219	296	19	534	79
rsey, Shawn, Daytona	.964	46	77	111	7	195	22
atvey, Mike, St. Petersburg	1.000	1	1	0	0	1	0
cCalmont, Jim, Fort Myers	.867	4	5	8	2	15	1
iller, Ryan, St. Lucie	.948	32	52	94	8	154	14
ummau, Rob, Dunedin	.960	12	22	26	2	50	2
Connor, Rick, Clearwater	.967	6	13	16	1	30	4
wen, Tom, Brevard County	.941	7	11	5	1	17	3
una, Rafael, Vero Beach	.909	33	52	78	13	143	12
rra, Jose, Charlotte	.800	1	1	3	1	5	0
rez, Richard, Daytona	.975	20	28	49	2	79	11
chardo, Sandy, Tampa	.967	71	118	175	10	303	38
LANCO, Placido, St. Petersburg	.993	126	198	383	4	585	79
Post, Dave, W. Palm Beach	.985	30	49	83	2	134	15
Reynoso, Ismael, Brevard County	.941	2	4	12	1	17	1
Rivera, Santiago, Daytona	1.000	2	2	1	0	3	0
Robles, Oscar, Kissimmee	.979	29	70	73	3	146	15
Rodriguez, Tony, Sarasota	1.000	3	3	13	0	16	2
Salzano, Jerry, Lakeland	1.000	3	0	2	0	2	0
Samboy, Nelson, Kissimmee	.954	96	209	269	23	501	64
Sanchez, Orlando, Sarasota	1.000	5	6	13	0	19	2
Saylor, Jamie, Kissimmee	1.000	3	9	8	0	17	4
Schaaf, Bob, Vero Beach	.933	3	6	8	1	15	1
Smith, David, Sarasota	.969	24	41	54	3	98	11
Sotelo, Danilo, Vero Beach	.961	67	120	199	13	332	41
Strange, Mike, Dunedin	.933	30	62	92	11	165	22
Tebbs, Nathan, Sarasota	.976	88	148	257	10	415	50
Trammell, Gary, Kissimmee	.946	16	30	40	4	74	11
Yard, Bruce, Vero Beach	1.000	1	2	2	0	4	0
Zorrilla, Julio, St. Lucie	.966	108	219	317	19	555	92

TRIPLE PLAYS: Gorecki 2.

THIRD BASEMEN

Player, Team	Pct.	G	PO	A	E	TC	DP
Alcantara, Israel, W. Palm Beach	.897	14	11	24	4	39	2
Amador, Manuel, Clearwater	.945	26	18	51	4	73	4
Arano, Eloy, Lakeland	.867	7	4	9	2	15	0
Avalos, Gilbert, Daytona	.806	15	9	20	7	36	1
Balfe, Ryan, Lakeland	.946	81	51	140	11	202	19
Barlok, Todd, Vero Beach	.904	110	84	171	27	282	12
Baugh, Gavin, Brevard County	.833	2	0	5	1	6	0
Beeney, Ryan, Tampa	1.000	3	3	5	0	8	0
Biermann, Steve, St. Petersburg	1.000	8	2	16	0	18	2
Bokemeier, Matt, Charlotte	.943	35	34	66	6	106	4
Borrego, Ramon, Fort Myers	.885	8	4	19	3	26	2
Brinkley, Josh, W. Palm Beach	.919	30	15	42	5	62	1
Brown, Vick, Tampa	.857	5	5	7	2	14	1
Cady, Todd, Brevard County	1.000	1	0	1	0	1	0
Carpentier, Mike, Vero Beach	.917	11	15	18	3	36	3
Carvajal, Jhonny, W. Palm Beach	.931	22	15	52	5	72	5
Carver, Steve, Clearwater	.889	30	25	47	9	81	6
Castro, Dennis, Brevard County	.896	50	36	110	17	163	10
Coolbaugh, Mike, Charlotte	.840	28	14	49	12	75	3
Coquillette, Trace, W. Palm Beach	.848	33	32	52	15	99	4
Cranford, Joe, Fort Myers	.875	6	4	10	2	16	1
Darden, Tony, Brevard County	.961	65	55	165	9	229	8
Davila, Vic, Dunedin	1.000	1	1	13	0	14	0
Derosso, Tony, Sarasota	.944	83	58	162	13	233	7
Dukart, Derek, Tampa	.931	54	42	106	11	159	8
Fenton, Cary, Charlotte	1.000	2	1	1	0	2	1
Flores, Jose, Clearwater	.833	2	3	2	1	6	0
Forkerway, Trey, Daytona	.921	16	10	25	3	38	2
Foster, Jeff, West Palm Beach	.857	2	1	5	1	7	0
Freel, Ryan, Dunedin	1.000	5	4	9	0	13	3
Freeman, Ricky, Daytona	.855	35	32	68	17	117	5
Gallego, Mike, St. Petersburg	1.000	1	1	2	0	3	0
Garcia, Carlos, Fort Myers	.843	19	5	38	8	51	3
Giardi, Mike, Tampa-W.P.B.	.930	33	32	48	6	86	2
Gibralter, David, Sarasota	.870	17	13	27	6	46	3
Hayes, Chris, Dunedin	.500	1	1	0	1	2	0
Huff, Larry, Clearwater	.941	87	65	173	15	253	19
Jumonville, Joe, St. Petersburg	.950	16	10	9	1	20	0
Koskie, Corey, Fort Myers	.926	87	62	176	19	257	15
Landaker, Dave, Kissimmee	1.000	1	0	1	0	1	0
Landry, Jacques, Lakeland	.885	11	6	17	3	26	2
Lantigua, Eddie, Daytona	.932	37	28	68	7	103	4
Lopez, Jose, St. Lucie	.910	118	74	299	37	410	23
Lowell, Mike, Tampa	.954	24	22	40	3	65	6
LoDuca, Paul, Vero Beach	1.000	3	1	2	0	3	0
Magadan, Dave, Daytona	.857	4	0	6	1	7	1
MATVEY, Mike, St. Petersburg	.956	122	78	247	15	340	23
McCalmont, Jim, Fort Myers	.911	18	11	30	4	45	1
McLamb, Brian, Tampa	.899	56	39	103	16	158	5
Melhuse, Adam, Dunedin	.857	2	0	6	1	7	1
Mota, Guillermo, St. Lucie	.933	22	14	42	4	60	6
Mummau, Rob, Dunedin	.962	8	8	17	1	26	2
Nelson, Bry, Kissimmee	.888	86	52	169	28	249	18
O'Connor, Rick, Clearwater	1.000	1	0	2	0	2	0
Owen, Tom, Brevard County	.862	36	21	73	15	109	9
Parra, Jose, Charlotte	1.000	1	1	1	0	2	0
Patton, Greg, Sarasota	.915	42	37	71	10	118	5
Perez, Richard, Daytona	.894	29	20	56	9	85	2
Post, Dave, W. Palm Beach	.955	14	5	16	1	22	4
Renteria, David, W. Palm Beach	.500	1	1	0	1	2	0

CLASS A *Florida State League*

Player, Team	Pct.	G	PO	A	E	TC	DP
Robles, Oscar, Kissimmee	.952	7	7	13	1	21	2
Rodriguez, Tony, Sarasota	1.000	2	3	1	0	4	0
Salzano, Jerry, Lakeland	.835	42	37	54	18	109	6
Saylor, Jamie, Kissimmee	.905	39	26	88	12	126	12
Schaaf, Bob, Vero Beach	.966	12	7	21	1	29	1
Strange, Mike, Dunedin	.929	4	3	10	1	14	0
Tatis, Fernando, Charlotte	.893	81	53	148	24	225	11
Thompson, Andy, Dunedin	.877	114	75	259	47	381	21
Trammell, Gary, Kissimmee	.867	7	4	9	2	15	0
Valentin, Jose, Fort Myers	.889	6	5	11	2	18	0
Whatley, Gabe, Daytona	.860	16	16	27	7	50	1
Yard, Bruce, Vero Beach	1.000	4	3	4	0	7	1

THIRD BASEMEN WITH TWO OR MORE TEAMS

Player, Team	Pct.	G	PO	A	E	TC	DP
Giardi, Mike, Tampa	1.000	3	4	1	0	5	0
Giardi, Mike, West Palm Beach	.926	30	28	47	6	81	2

SHORTSTOPS

Player, Team	Pct.	G	PO	A	E	TC	DP
Amador, Manuel, Clearwater	.870	5	6	14	3	23	3
Arano, Eloy, Lakeland	.933	16	22	48	5	75	6
Arnold, Ken, Charlotte	.971	50	50	115	5	170	23
Babin, Brady, Brevard County	1.000	2	4	3	0	7	1
Baugh, Gavin, Brevard County	.848	10	10	29	7	46	4
Beeney, Ryan, Tampa	.929	8	12	27	3	42	4
Benjamin, Mike, Clearwater	.935	8	9	20	2	31	4
Biermann, Steve, St. Petersburg	.933	23	23	47	5	75	10
Bocachica, Hiram, W. Palm Beach	.833	27	37	83	24	144	14
Bokemeier, Matt, Charlotte	.961	56	79	166	10	255	35
Bowles, John, Sarasota	1.000	1	0	2	0	2	0
Bravo, Danny, W. Palm Beach	1.000	4	6	14	0	20	2
Brown, Vick, Tampa	.833	2	3	2	1	6	0
Brunson, Matt, Brevard County	.914	13	19	34	5	58	5
Bustos, Saul, Daytona	.958	100	182	295	21	498	50
Carpentier, Mike, Vero Beach	.959	20	31	63	4	98	11
Carvajal, Jhonny, W. Palm Beach	.951	64	110	198	16	324	38
Coolbaugh, Mike, Charlotte	.955	37	47	101	7	155	20
Cora, Alex, Vero Beach	.940	58	86	164	16	266	31
Faircloth, Kevin, Vero Beach	.818	3	3	6	2	11	1
Fenton, Cary, Charlotte	1.000	7	10	14	0	24	3
Flores, Jose, Clearwater	.939	56	97	179	18	294	30
Forkerway, Trey, Daytona	.903	30	43	69	12	124	15
Gallego, Mike, St. Petersburg	1.000	1	1	1	0	2	0
Garcia, Carlos, Fort Myers	1.000	4	6	13	0	19	1
Gil, Benji, Charlotte	.931	10	6	21	2	29	3
Glozier, Larry, Brevard County	.750	1	2	1	1	4	0
Goligoski, Jason, Sarasota	.950	4	11	8	1	20	4
Goodell, Steve, Brevard County	.778	1	2	5	2	9	1
Guiliano, Matt, Clearwater	.929	55	65	158	17	240	28
Jackson, Gavin, Sarasota	.950	78	130	215	18	363	47
Jaime, Angel, St. Lucie	.778	6	2	5	2	9	1
Lane, Ryan, Fort Myers	1.000	2	4	4	0	8	1
Lobaton, Jose, Tampa	.960	113	169	335	21	525	66
Matvey, Mike, St. Petersburg	.933	4	4	10	1	15	1
McLamb, Brian, Tampa	.892	15	23	43	8	74	2
Miller, Ryan, St. Lucie	.963	58	90	172	10	272	50
MORIARTY, Mike, Fort Myers	.967	133	239	458	24	721	96
Mota, Guillermo, St. Lucie	.955	81	113	251	17	381	38
Mummau, Rob, Dunedin	.952	13	20	40	3	63	2
Nelson, Bry, Kissimmee	1.000	1	2	1	0	3	0
O'Connor, Rick, Clearwater	.941	5	5	11	1	17	0
Ordaz, Luis, St. Petersburg	.963	123	228	317	21	566	62
Patton, Greg, Sarasota	.941	30	47	96	9	152	16
Perez, Jhonny, Kissimmee	.929	44	73	124	15	212	21
Perez, Richard, Daytona	.889	2	3	5	1	9	0
Perez, Santiago, Lakeland	.924	122	192	310	41	543	63
Post, Dave, West Palm Beach	.945	15	19	50	4	73	7
Raynor, Mark, Clearwater	.968	18	37	55	3	95	8
Renteria, David, W. Palm Beach	.944	30	45	91	8	144	13
Reynoso, Ismael, Brevard County	1.000	9	13	26	0	39	4
Rivera, Santiago, Daytona	.826	8	10	9	4	23	4
Robles, Oscar, Kissimmee	.949	90	140	273	22	435	54
Rodriguez, Tony, Sarasota	1.000	1	2	6	0	8	1
Rodriguez, Victor, Brevard County	.958	114	166	319	21	506	56
Salzano, Jerry, Lakeland	1.000	2	3	1	0	4	0
Saylor, Jamie, Kissimmee	1.000	3	0	6	0	6	2
Strange, Mike, Dunedin	.975	11	14	25	1	40	4
Tebbs, Nathan, Sarasota	.944	25	40	44	5	89	12
Valette, Ramon, Daytona	.907	13	10	29	4	43	3
Witt, Kevin, Dunedin	.917	119	161	369	48	578	76
Yard, Bruce, Vero Beach	.938	55	89	169	17	275	30

OUTFIELDERS

Player, Team	Pct.	G	PO	A	E	TC	DP
Abad, Andy, Sarasota*	.963	26	46	6	2	54	
Adams, Tommy, Charlotte	.953	32	60	1	3	64	
Alvarez, Rafael, Fort Myers*	1.000	5	9	1	0	10	
Arano, Eloy, Lakeland	1.000	2	2	0	0	2	
Asencio, Alex, Vero Beach*	.973	108	174	8	5	187	
Bady, Edward, W. Palm Beach	.970	127	312	14	10	336	
Barksdale, Shane, Kissimmee	1.000	8	3	0	0	3	
Bentley, Kevin, Daytona	.952	64	95	4	5	104	
Bierek, Kurt, Tampa	1.000	58	80	8	0	88	
Blakeney, Mo, W. Palm Beach	.923	6	12	0	1	13	
Borel, Jamie, Lakeland	1.000	17	24	1	0	25	
Bowers, R.J., Kissimmee	.985	37	66	1	1	68	
Braddy, Junior, Sarasota	.969	73	122	5	4	131	
Brinkley, Josh, W. Palm Beach	1.000	10	22	1	0	23	
Brock, Tarrik, Lakeland*	.969	51	89	5	3	97	
Brown, Armann, Fort Myers	.976	95	202	4	5	211	
Brown, Nate, W. Palm Beach*	1.000	33	38	4	0	42	
Buchanan, Brian, Tampa	.969	96	178	11	6	195	
Camfield, Eric, Tampa*	1.000	3	3	1	0	4	
Camilo, Jose, Brevard County*	.964	10	27	0	1	28	
Campos, Jesus, W. Palm Beach	.972	43	62	7	2	71	
Candelaria, Ben, Dunedin	.980	36	41	7	1	49	
Carver, Steve, Clearwater	1.000	5	6	3	0	9	
COLEMAN, Michael, Sarasota	.993	108	261	9	2	272	
Contreras, Efrain, St. Petersburg	.950	16	17	2	1	20	
Cook, Hayward, Brevard County	.992	77	122	3	1	126	
Coolbaugh, Mike, Charlotte	1.000	3	2	1	0	3	
Costello, Brian, Clearwater	.974	79	143	4	4	151	
Coston, Sean, Vero Beach	1.000	3	1	0	0	1	
Darden, Tony, Brevard County	.976	23	39	2	1	42	
Darr, Mike, Lakeland	.978	82	128	8	3	139	
Davila, Vic, Dunedin	.991	70	103	5	1	109	
Dawkins, Walt, Clearwater	.974	47	74	2	2	78	
Derosso, Tony, Sarasota	1.000	3	2	0	0	2	
Dowler, Dee, Daytona	.964	12	26	1	1	28	
Durkin, Chris, Vero Beach*	1.000	20	26	2	0	28	
Ellis, Kevin, Daytona	.933	8	14	0	1	15	
Encarnacion, Juan, Lakeland	.976	125	233	12	6	251	
Evans, Stan, Clearwater	.974	77	136	11	4	151	
Faggett, Ethan, Sarasota*	.957	92	171	6	8	185	
Farley, Cordell, St. Petersburg	1.000	1	2	0	0	2	
Farrell, Jon, St. Lucie	1.000	1	1	0	0	1	
Flora, Kevin, St. Lucie	1.000	11	21	0	0	21	
Freire, Alejandro, Kissimmee	.934	70	111	2	8	121	
French, Anton, Lakeland	.977	59	122	5	3	130	
Fuller, Aaron, Sarasota	.988	108	225	12	3	240	
Fullmer, Brad, W. Palm Beach	.963	81	127	3	5	135	
Gazarek, Marty, Daytona	.979	126	217	12	5	234	
Giardi, Mike, West Palm Beach	1.000	9	17	2	0	19	
Gibbs, Kevin, Vero Beach	.985	115	252	11	4	267	
Gordon, Herman, Dunedin	.895	14	17	0	2	19	
Green, Scarborough, St. Petersburg	.979	36	90	4	2	96	
Guerrero, Rafael, St. Lucie	.960	74	94	3	4	101	
Guerrero, Vladimir, W. Palm Beach	.917	20	28	5	3	36	
Gunderson, Shane, Fort Myers	.982	112	146	14	3	163	
Haas, Matt, West Palm Beach	.966	18	28	0	1	29	
Harvey, Aaron, Brevard County	.955	75	122	5	6	133	
Hawkins, Kraig, Tampa	.990	72	185	5	2	192	
Hayes, Chris, Dunedin	.958	23	22	1	1	24	
Hightower, Vee, Daytona	.993	81	143	4	1	148	
Hunter, Scott, St. Lucie	.952	121	167	13	9	189	
Hunter, Torii, Fort Myers	1.000	4	9	0	0	9	
Jackson, Jeff, Daytona	.958	16	23	0	1	24	
Jaime, Angel, St. Lucie	.968	86	111	9	4	124	
Jones, Ben, Fort Myers	1.000	42	61	4	0	65	
Jones, Ivory, Fort Myers*	.943	36	62	4	4	70	
Kendall, Jeremy, Clearwater	.970	81	183	9	6	198	
Key, Jeff, Clearwater	1.000	39	51	2	0	53	
King, Brion, Dunedin	1.000	6	7	0	0	7	
Knauss, Tom, Fort Myers	.941	13	15	1	1	17	
Landaker, Dave, Kissimmee	.966	37	55	2	2	59	
Landrum, Tito, Vero Beach	.971	23	31	3	1	35	
Landry, Lonny, Lakeland	.976	65	119	2	3	124	
Langaigne, Selwyn, Dunedin*	.984	30	59	3	1	63	
LaRiviere, Jason, St. Petersburg	.977	24	41	2	1	44	
Legree, Keith, Fort Myers	.969	49	57	6	2	65	
Linares, Sendry, Kissimmee	1.000	1	2	0	0	2	
Lugo, Jesus, St. Petersburg	1.000	12	17	1	0	18	
Luke, Matthew, Tampa*	1.000	2	3	0	0	3	
Macon, Leland, Charlotte	.976	94	191	11	5	207	
Majeski, Brian, Vero Beach	.979	55	89	5	2	96	

ayer, Team	Pct.	G	PO	A	E	TC	DP
anwarren, Mark, Kissimmee	.966	63	110	4	4	118	0
athews, Byron, W. Palm Beach	1.000	8	16	0	0	16	0
cCormick, Andrew, Dunedin	.930	48	63	3	5	71	0
cDavid, Ray, W. Palm Beach	1.000	4	12	0	0	12	0
cLamb, Brian, Tampa	1.000	4	2	0	0	2	0
cNabb, Buck, Kissimmee	1.000	7	9	1	0	10	0
ejia, Miguel, St. Petersburg	1.000	6	14	0	0	14	0
elhuse, Adam, Dunedin	1.000	1	2	0	0	2	0
oore, Tris, Lakeland	1.000	10	17	0	0	17	0
orimoto, Ken, Vero Beach	1.000	4	2	0	0	2	0
ota, Gary, Kissimmee	.979	30	47	0	1	48	0
ucker, Kelcey, Fort Myers	.977	84	119	7	3	129	0
unoz, Juan, St. Petersburg*	.986	89	132	10	2	144	0
urphy, Mike, Charlotte	.981	84	206	1	4	211	0
tavinia, Paul, W. Palm Beach*	.989	45	86	2	1	89	0
wen, Andy, Vero Beach*	.991	83	99	7	1	107	0
zorio, Yudith, St. Petersburg	.981	135	243	11	5	259	0
adilla, Roy, Sarasota*	.944	8	17	0	1	18	0
chardo, Sandy, Tampa	1.000	5	14	1	0	15	0
co, Brandon, Daytona*	.970	18	31	1	1	33	0
odsednik, Scott, Brevard County*	.984	105	231	10	4	245	4
orter, Bo, Daytona	.922	19	44	3	4	51	1
ost, Dave, West Palm Beach	1.000	4	5	1	0	6	0
ratt, Wes, Kissimmee	.955	47	103	2	5	110	0
ullen, Shane, Clearwater	.962	20	23	2	1	26	0
aines, Tim, Tampa	1.000	7	10	2	0	12	0
amirez, Julio, Brevard County	.950	17	34	4	2	40	0
ascon, Rene, Brevard County*	.933	9	12	2	1	15	0
eves, Glenn, Brevard County	.984	114	181	9	3	193	1
chard, Chris, St. Petersburg*	1.000	9	14	1	0	15	0
chards, Rowan, Charlotte	1.000	26	54	1	0	55	0
vers, Jonathan, Dunedin	.941	87	105	7	7	119	2
oberts, John, W. Palm Beach	.925	24	36	1	3	40	0
odriguez, Noel, Kissimmee	.667	3	2	0	1	3	0
ojas, Mo, Sarasota	1.000	1	2	0	0	2	0
oss, Tony, Kissimmee	.990	53	96	6	1	103	1
oyster, Aaron, Clearwater	.972	72	132	7	4	143	0
lzano, Jerry, Lakeland	.958	14	19	4	1	24	2
nchez, Omar, Dunedin	.968	42	57	4	2	63	1
nders, Anthony, Dunedin	.982	100	209	8	4	221	2
nderson, David, St. Lucie*	1.000	47	79	3	0	82	0
ntucci, Steven, St. Petersburg	.989	106	157	15	2	174	2
ylor, Jamie, Kissimmee	.950	13	19	0	1	20	0
haaf, Bob, Vero Beach	.955	13	20	1	1	22	1
idel, Ryan, Daytona	.800	9	4	0	1	5	0
anahan, Jason, Brevard County	1.000	1	1	0	0	1	0
mpson, Jeramie, St. Lucie	1.000	56	101	5	0	106	0
nith, Sloan, Tampa	.967	59	111	5	4	120	1
ovall, Darond, W. Palm Beach*	.950	8	19	0	1	20	0
obs, Nathan, Sarasota	1.000	4	5	0	0	5	0
nsley, Lee, Clearwater	1.000	4	12	0	0	12	0
ammell, Gary, Kissimmee	.966	83	139	2	5	146	0
rner, Brian, St. Lucie*	1.000	4	3	0	0	3	0
squez, Danny, Charlotte	.975	70	153	5	4	162	1
ssel, Andrew, Charlotte	.988	121	241	14	3	258	1
igt, Jack, Charlotte	1.000	2	3	1	0	4	0
alker, Steve, Daytona	.963	55	99	6	4	109	3
arner, Randy, St. Lucie	1.000	1	1	0	0	1	0
hatley, Gabe, Daytona	1.000	24	51	2	0	53	0
hite, Rondell, W. Palm Beach	1.000	1	2	0	0	2	0
lcox, Luke, Tampa	.986	106	209	10	3	222	1
lson, Preston, St. Lucie	.956	20	39	4	2	45	0

TRIPLE PLAYS: Vessel, Voigt.

CATCHERS

ayer, Team	Pct.	G	PO	A	E	TC	DP	PB
imo, Jason, Brevard County	.966	6	27	1	1	29	0	0
nezcua, Adan, Kissimmee	.957	35	180	40	10	230	1	10
hby, Chris, Tampa	.980	85	581	47	13	641	0	18
zzani, Matt, Sarasota	1.000	10	59	2	0	61	0	3
rrero, Richie, Sarasota	.984	24	165	14	3	182	0	10
ryczewski, Marty, Lakeland	.976	13	39	2	1	42	0	2
wles, John, Sarasota	.857	8	21	3	4	28	0	4
nkley, Josh, W. Palm Beach	.962	23	123	5	5	133	0	5
dy, Todd, Brevard County	.909	2	9	1	1	11	0	1
mpos, Miguel, Daytona	1.000	7	22	0	0	22	0	1
ne, Pat, Daytona	.980	104	697	70	16	783	4	18
ssins, Tim, Charlotte	.986	65	378	41	6	425	1	16
x, Chuck, Clearwater	1.000	4	15	4	0	19	0	4
Pastino, Joe, Sarasota	.980	82	490	60	11	561	1	11
az, Cesar, St. Lucie	.982	44	290	33	6	329	0	9
mons, Scott, Tampa	.959	30	144	18	7	169	1	6
win, Mat, Brevard County	.984	45	221	30	4	255	1	4

Player, Team	Pct.	G	PO	A	E	TC	DP	PB
Fagley, Dan, Brevard County	.990	20	92	9	1	102	1	5
Falciglia, Tony, St. Petersburg	1.000	10	37	7	0	44	0	3
FORTIN, Troy, Fort Myers	.990	76	529	61	6	596	7	3
Gonzalez, Jimmy, Kissimmee	.982	63	321	51	7	379	1	16
Gorecki, Ryan, Charlotte	1.000	1	2	0	0	2	0	0
Haas, Matt, West Palm Beach	.992	27	113	7	1	121	0	3
Hall, Ryan, St. Petersburg	1.000	2	2	0	0	2	0	0
Haws, Scott, Clearwater	.995	33	166	25	1	192	1	4
Imrisek, Jason, Tampa	1.000	4	6	0	0	6	0	1
Koeyers, Ramsey, W. Palm Beach	.985	9	60	6	1	67	0	3
Lidle, Kevin, Lakeland	.989	96	608	107	8	723	11	17
LoDuca, Paul, Vero Beach	.978	98	651	106	17	774	2	15
McAulay, John, Charlotte	.984	48	269	37	5	311	2	7
McDonald, Keith, St. Petersburg	.986	99	679	76	11	766	4	14
Melhuse, Adam, Dunedin	.978	81	512	73	13	598	6	18
Meluskey, Mitch, Kissimmee	.974	52	315	27	9	351	2	8
Meyer, Travis, Vero Beach	.984	11	60	3	1	64	0	0
Micucci, Mike, Daytona	.982	37	151	13	3	167	1	4
Mientkiewicz, Doug, Ft. Myers	.981	8	46	6	1	53	0	2
Millan, Adan, Clearwater	.992	17	121	8	1	130	1	2
Miller, Logan, Dunedin	.980	10	47	1	1	49	0	2
Morales, Francisco, St.P.-W.P.B.	.985	70	390	56	7	453	1	16
Morgan, Dave, Dunedin	.960	29	153	13	7	173	0	10
Motuzas, Jeff, Tampa	1.000	1	4	0	0	4	0	0
Northeimer, Jamie, Clearwater	.984	89	558	58	10	626	4	22
Pachot, John, W. Palm Beach	.983	40	244	51	5	300	2	4
Pages, Javier, St. Petersburg	.979	22	125	14	3	142	1	7
Rodriguez, Adam, Lakeland	.982	43	305	22	6	333	3	4
Rodriguez, Maximo, Brev. Cnty	.986	77	369	56	6	431	5	10
Rose, Mike, Kissimmee	1.000	1	4	1	0	5	0	0
Snyder, Jared, Daytona	.979	10	45	2	1	48	0	4
Steed, David, Vero Beach	.992	20	109	18	1	128	3	1
Stone, Craig, Dunedin	.977	27	154	19	4	177	0	13
Tijerina, Tony, St. Lucie	.958	16	60	8	3	71	1	0
Troilo, Jason, Tampa	.974	6	31	6	1	38	2	2
Twombley, Dennis, Tampa	.990	28	177	13	2	192	2	0
Umbria, Jose, Dunedin	.972	6	29	6	1	36	0	1
Underwood, Devin, Sarasota	.977	20	122	6	3	131	0	6
Unrat, Chris, Charlotte	.968	36	222	22	8	252	1	4
Valentin, Jose, Fort Myers	.995	53	355	60	2	417	2	8
Walbeck, Matt, Fort Myers	1.000	7	46	6	0	52	1	0
Walkanoff, A.J., Vero Beach	.988	15	74	11	1	86	0	3
Wilkes, Brian, Brevard County	.964	4	26	1	1	28	0	3
Williams, Bryan, Dunedin	.979	6	45	2	1	48	0	1
Wilson, Vance, St. Lucie	.987	81	502	87	8	597	1	11

CATCHERS WITH TWO OR MORE TEAMS

Player, Team	Pct.	G	PO	A	E	TC	DP	PB
Morales, Francisco, St. Petersburg	1.000	15	81	15	0	96	1	1
Morales, Francisco, W. Palm Beach	.980	55	309	41	7	357	0	15

PITCHERS

Player, Team	Pct.	G	PO	A	E	TC	DP
Adkins, Tim, Dunedin*	.909	39	7	13	2	22	2
Aguilera, Rick, Fort Myers	1.000	2	1	2	0	3	0
Ahearne, Pat, Vero Beach	.944	6	8	9	1	18	0
Alejo, Nigel, Brevard County	1.000	37	4	9	0	13	0
Altman, Heath, Brevard County	1.000	16	4	2	0	6	0
Arffa, Steve, St. Lucie*	1.000	11	4	7	0	11	0
Arroyo, Luis, St. Lucie*	1.000	22	3	10	0	13	0
Atwater, Joe, St. Lucie*	.913	19	7	14	2	23	1
Babineaux, Darrin, Vero Beach	1.000	10	4	11	0	15	0
Bair, Dennis, Daytona	.880	29	10	12	3	25	1
Barbao, Joe, Clearwater	.900	28	5	4	1	10	1
Barker, Richie, Daytona	1.000	17	2	9	0	11	2
Barksdale, Joe, Sarasota	.846	19	5	6	2	13	1
Bell, Jason, Fort Myers	.917	13	10	12	2	24	1
Bell, Mike, West Palm Beach*	1.000	13	0	3	0	3	0
Benz, Jacob, West Palm Beach*	.700	16	2	5	3	10	0
Betti, Rick, Sarasota*	1.000	13	0	2	0	2	0
Beverlin, Jason, Tampa	1.000	25	2	2	0	4	0
Bland, Nate, Vero Beach*	.833	17	6	19	5	30	1
Bogle, Sean, Daytona	1.000	13	0	5	0	5	1
Bogott, Kurtiss, Dunedin*	1.000	19	0	5	0	5	0
Booker, Chris, Daytona	.500	1	0	1	1	2	0
Boucher, Denis, W. Palm Beach*	1.000	2	0	2	0	2	0
Bowen, Mitchel, Brevard County	.929	29	4	9	1	14	1
Box, Shawn, Daytona	1.000	14	8	9	0	17	2
Boyd, Jason, Clearwater	.956	26	15	28	2	45	4
Braddy, Junior, Sarasota	1.000	1	0	1	0	1	1
Brower, Jim, Charlotte	.933	23	10	18	2	30	1
Brown, Charlie, Tampa	1.000	12	1	2	0	3	0

CLASS A *Florida State League*

Player, Team	Pct.	G	PO	A	E	TC	DP	Player, Team	Pct.	G	PO	A	E	TC
Brown, Darold, Daytona*	.875	35	2	12	2	16	0	Hecker, Doug, Sarasota	1.000	26	1	5	0	6
Buckles, Bucky, Charlotte	1.000	21	4	15	0	19	0	Heiserman, Rick, St. Petersburg	.880	26	8	14	3	25
Byrne, Earl, Daytona*	.714	18	3	7	4	14	0	Henriquez, Oscar, Kissimmee	.600	37	2	1	2	5
Camacho, Dan, Vero Beach	.938	10	5	10	1	16	1	Henthorne, Kevin, Tampa	.968	19	9	21	1	31
Caravelli, Mike, Brevard County*	.947	47	5	13	1	19	0	Hollis, Ron, Vero Beach	1.000	19	4	7	0	11
Carl, Todd, Daytona	.750	5	1	2	1	4	0	Hubbard, Mark, Tampa*	1.000	4	2	8	0	10
Carter, John, St. Lucie	.900	4	2	7	1	10	0	Hudek, John, Kissimmee	1.000	2	0	1	0	1
Cedeno, Blas, Lakeland	1.000	10	2	1	0	3	0	Humphrey, Rich, Kissimmee	1.000	5	0	1	0	1
Censale, Silvio, Clearwater*	1.000	24	8	13	0	21	0	Humphry, Trevor, Clearwater	.909	16	3	7	1	11
Centeno, Jose, W. Palm Beach*	1.000	37	4	13	0	17	0	Hutton, Mark, Tampa	1.000	3	1	2	0	3
Chambers, Scott, Vero Beach*	1.000	10	0	2	0	2	0	Iglesias, Mike, Vero Beach	.957	31	10	12	1	23
Chavarria, David, Charlotte	.692	38	6	3	4	13	0	Jackson, Danny, St. Petersburg*	1.000	1	0	1	0	1
Cobb, Trevor, Fort Myers*	.824	31	11	17	6	34	3	Jacobson, K.J., Lakeland	1.000	26	6	4	0	10
Cole, Jason, West Palm Beach	1.000	39	3	13	0	16	0	Jarvis, Jason, Dunedin	1.000	36	12	22	0	34
Colon, Julio, Vero Beach	1.000	8	0	5	0	5	0	Jerzembeck, Mike, Tampa	1.000	12	4	12	0	16
Conway, Keith, St. Petersburg*	1.000	59	2	11	0	13	0	Kamieniecki, Scott, Tampa	1.000	3	1	3	0	4
Cook, Jake, Sarasota	.813	20	5	8	3	16	1	Kell, Rob, Charlotte*	.889	11	5	3	1	9
Cook, Rodney, Charlotte	.872	39	5	29	5	39	0	Key, Jimmy, Tampa*	1.000	2	1	1	0	2
CORN, Chris, Tampa	1.000	26	8	33	0	41	1	King, Curtis, St. Petersburg	.857	48	2	10	2	14
Cornett, Brad, Dunedin	1.000	4	1	1	0	2	0	Knight, Brandon, Charlotte	.879	19	13	16	4	33
Cosman, Jeff, St. Lucie	1.000	3	0	1	0	1	0	Knighton, Tore, Charlotte	1.000	5	2	1	0	3
Dace, Derek, Kissimmee*	1.000	12	1	7	0	8	1	Knoll, Randy, Clearwater	1.000	4	3	3	0	6
DaSilva, Fernando, W. Palm Beach	.941	40	6	10	1	17	0	Kolb, Danny, Charlotte	1.000	6	1	5	0	6
Dault, Donnie, Kissimmee	.800	29	0	4	1	5	0	Konieczki, Dom, Fort Myers*	1.000	14	0	3	0	3
Diaz, Jairo, Daytona	1.000	8	4	1	0	5	0	Kosek, Kory, Clearwater	.913	42	6	15	2	23
Dinyar, Eric, Lakeland	.913	58	5	16	2	23	1	Lagarde, Joe, Vero Beach	1.000	14	5	7	0	12
Dixon, Timothy, W. Palm Beach*	.862	37	8	17	4	29	0	Lail, Denny, Tampa	.889	31	2	6	1	9
Doman, Roger, Dunedin	.833	18	1	4	1	6	0	Larkin, Andy, Brevard County	1.000	6	6	5	0	11
Dowhower, Deron, Fort Myers	.933	39	8	6	1	15	0	Larson, Toby, St. Lucie	.833	9	3	2	1	6
Drews, Matt, Tampa	1.000	4	2	5	0	7	1	Leaman, Jeff, Clearwater	1.000	3	1	2	0	3
Drumheller, Al, Tampa*	1.000	36	2	6	0	8	1	Lee, Jeremy, Dunedin	.818	10	3	6	2	11
Duran, Roberto, Dunedin*	1.000	8	5	11	0	16	3	Licciardi, Ron, Daytona*	1.000	2	0	1	0	1
Durocher, Jayson, W. Palm Beach	.900	23	8	10	2	20	1	Lincoln, Mike, Fort Myers	1.000	12	7	12	0	19
Eaddy, Brad, Vero Beach*	.500	12	1	1	2	4	2	Link, Bryan, Charlotte*	1.000	15	6	15	0	21
Eby, Mike, Lakeland*	1.000	17	0	6	0	6	1	Lock, Dan, Kissimmee*	.879	27	9	20	4	33
Ehler, Daniel, Brevard County	.920	28	11	12	2	25	0	Logan, Marcus, St. Petersburg	.941	30	5	11	1	17
Elarton, Scott, Kissimmee	.905	27	18	20	4	42	1	Lopez, Johann, Kissimmee	1.000	19	8	9	0	17
Emerson, Scott, Sarasota*	1.000	4	0	2	0	2	0	Lukasiewicz, Mark, Dunedin*	1.000	23	2	4	0	6
Enard, Tony, Brevard County	1.000	2	1	0	0	1	0	Maeda, Katsuhiro, Tampa	1.000	2	1	1	0	2
Escamilla, Jaime, Charlotte*	.933	37	5	9	1	15	1	Mahay, Ronald, Sarasota*	.882	31	6	9	2	17
Escobar, Kelvim, Dunedin	.950	18	7	12	1	20	0	Manning, Len, Clearwater*	.806	20	5	20	6	31
Estavil, Mauricio, Clearwater*	1.000	29	3	5	0	8	0	Marquez, Robert, W. Palm Beach	1.000	11	1	3	0	4
Farrell, Jim, Sarasota	1.000	21	13	16	0	29	0	Marrero, Kenny, Lakeland	1.000	34	7	2	0	9
Faulkner, Neal, Daytona	1.000	11	2	1	0	3	0	Martinez, Cesar, Sarasota*	.929	35	3	10	1	14
Festa, Chris, Sarasota	1.000	6	2	2	0	4	0	Martinez, Ramiro, W. Palm Beach*	1.000	9	1	6	0	7
Filbeck, Ryan, Brevard County	.833	9	5	0	1	6	0	Martinez, Ramon, Vero Beach	1.000	1	2	3	0	5
Fiore, Tony, Clearwater	.900	22	13	23	4	40	2	McCready, Jim, St. Lucie	1.000	10	2	4	0	6
Fitterer, Scott, Dunedin	1.000	20	1	3	0	4	0	McNeely, Mitch, Vero Beach*	.778	23	2	5	2	9
Fleetham, Ben, W. Palm Beach	.333	31	1	0	2	3	0	McNeese, John, Daytona*	1.000	9	1	3	0	4
Franko, Kris, W. Palm Beach*	1.000	9	0	3	0	3	0	McNeill, Kevin, St. Petersburg	.905	45	3	16	2	21
Gambs, Chris, Daytona	1.000	13	1	3	0	4	0	McNichol, Brian, Daytona*	1.000	8	3	7	0	10
Gandarillas, Gus, Fort Myers	1.000	4	0	3	0	3	0	Meadows, Brian, Brevard County	.905	24	16	22	4	42
Garagozzo, Keith, Brev. County*	1.000	2	1	2	0	3	0	Medina, Tomas, Kissimmee	1.000	9	0	1	0	1
Garcia, Al, Daytona	1.000	7	5	11	0	16	1	Meiners, Doug, Dunedin	.889	17	4	4	1	9
Garcia, Frank, St. Petersburg	1.000	28	3	3	0	6	1	Mendez, Manuel, St. Petersburg*	.917	59	5	6	1	12
Garcia, Garbriel, Kissimmee	1.000	3	0	2	0	2	0	Mercado, Hector, Kissimmee*	1.000	56	4	13	0	17
Gentile, Scott, W. Palm Beach	1.000	7	0	2	0	2	0	Merrill, Ethan, Sarasota*	1.000	14	4	12	0	16
Golden, Matt, St. Petersburg	1.000	8	1	1	0	2	0	Metheney, Nelson, Clearwater	1.000	21	2	4	0	6
Gomez, Miguel, Dunedin	.938	33	7	8	1	16	0	Meyer, David, Tampa*	.909	11	2	8	1	11
Gonzalez, Gabe, Brev. County*	1.000	47	8	20	1	28	1	Miles, Chad, Brevard County*	.857	27	1	11	2	14
Gonzalez, Generoso, Lakeland	1.000	1	2	0	0	2	1	Miller, David, Brevard County	.950	26	8	11	1	20
Gonzalez, Juan, Brevard County	.880	23	7	15	3	25	1	Miranda, Walter, Brevard County	1.000	2	0	1	0	1
Gooch, Arnold, St. Lucie	.894	26	13	29	5	47	2	Mitchell, Kendrick, Vero Beach	.636	39	2	5	4	11
Gordon, Mike, Dunedin	.848	24	13	15	5	33	0	Mittauer, Casey, Tampa	1.000	21	0	4	0	4
Gourdin, Tom, Fort Myers	.952	52	10	10	1	21	0	Montelongo, Joe, Daytona	.909	19	8	12	2	22
Graham, Rich, Sarasota	1.000	11	0	1	0	1	0	Moody, Ritchie, Charlotte*	.800	18	2	2	1	5
Granger, Greg, Lakeland	1.000	5	1	1	0	2	0	Moraga, David, W. Palm Beach*	.900	29	10	17	3	30
Graves, Ryan, Daytona*	.667	6	1	1	1	3	0	Morillo, Donald, Charlotte	.833	32	4	6	2	12
Green, Jason, Daytona	.667	5	1	1	1	3	0	Morse, Paul, Fort Myers	1.000	13	1	1	0	2
Greene, Brian, Daytona	.933	26	2	12	1	15	0	Mosley, Tim, Daytona	1.000	6	1	1	0	2
Greene, Tommy, Clearwater	1.000	7	1	4	0	5	0	Mott, Tom, Fort Myers	.895	14	4	13	2	19
Guzman, Jose, Daytona	1.000	2	0	2	0	2	0	Mounce, Tony, Kissimmee*	.875	25	8	20	4	32
Hale, Chad, Sarasota*	.909	42	4	6	1	11	0	Munoz, Bobby, Clearwater	1.000	2	0	4	0	4
Hall, Billy, Kissimmee	1.000	2	1	0	0	1	0	Munro, Peter, Sarasota	.970	27	15	17	1	33
Hall, Yates, St. Petersburg	.875	26	8	13	3	24	1	Murray, Dan, St. Lucie	.919	33	15	19	3	37
Halladay, Roy, Dunedin	.921	27	12	23	3	38	0	Musselwhite, Jim, Tampa	.500	3	0	1	1	2
Hammack, Brandon, Daytona	.900	27	2	7	1	10	0	Neal, Billy, Vero Beach	.921	51	14	21	3	38
Hammond, Chris, Brev. County*	1.000	1	1	0	0	1	0	O'Flynn, Gardner, Charlotte*	.870	28	10	30	6	46
Handy, Russell, W. Palm Beach	.800	14	4	8	3	15	0	Oliver, Darren, Charlotte*	1.000	2	1	0	0	1
Hansen, Brent, Sarasota	1.000	8	3	6	0	9	0	Olson, Phillip, St. Lucie	.938	15	4	11	1	16
Harnisch, Pete, St. Lucie	1.000	2	2	3	0	5	0	Pace, Scotty, Dunedin*	1.000	19	5	9	0	14
Harris, D.J., Dunedin	.900	35	3	6	1	10	1	Pack, Steve, St. Lucie	.750	23	1	2	1	4
Hartgrove, Lyle, Sarasota	1.000	15	3	3	0	6	1	Parisi, Michael, Brev. County	.976	21	14	26	1	41

Player, Team	Pct.	G	PO	A	E	TC	DP	Player, Team	Pct.	G	PO	A	E	TC	DP
Parra, Julio, Vero Beach	1.000	12	0	4	0	4	1	Skrmetta, Matt, Lakeland	1.000	40	1	5	0	6	0
Pavicich, Paul, Fort Myers*	1.000	29	1	8	0	9	0	Smith, Cam, Lakeland	.958	22	8	15	1	24	2
Perkins, Dan, Fort Myers	1.000	39	4	18	0	22	0	Smith, Dan, Charlotte	.800	19	4	8	3	15	0
Peters, Tim, Fort Myers*	1.000	28	3	6	0	9	1	Smith, Danny, Charlotte*	1.000	4	1	5	0	6	0
Peterson, Dean, Sarasota	.867	26	7	6	2	15	0	Smith, Keilan, Dunedin	.917	23	4	7	1	12	0
Peterson, Jay, Daytona	1.000	8	3	3	0	6	1	Sobik, Trad, Lakeland	.808	13	6	15	5	26	1
Petkovsek, Mark, St. Petersburg	1.000	3	0	1	0	1	0	Speier, Justin, Daytona	1.000	33	0	2	0	2	0
Phelps, Tommy, W. Palm Beach*	1.000	18	7	20	0	27	1	Spence, Michael, Tampa	1.000	8	1	2	0	3	0
Pivaral, Hugo, Vero Beach	1.000	7	0	7	0	7	1	St. Pierre, Bob, Tampa	.925	29	14	23	3	40	1
Pontes, Dan, St. Petersburg	.955	27	6	15	1	22	1	Stachler, Eric, Kissimmee	1.000	30	4	5	0	9	1
Powell, Brian, Lakeland	.964	29	20	34	2	56	2	Stanifer, Robert, Brevard County	.917	22	6	5	1	12	0
Press, Gregg, Brevard County	.956	28	13	30	2	45	3	Stein, Blake, St. Petersburg	.958	28	8	15	1	24	0
Quirico, Rafael, Clearwater*	.667	2	0	2	1	3	0	Steinke, Brock, Kissimmee	.813	16	4	9	3	16	0
Radlosky, Rob, Fort Myers	1.000	28	5	12	0	17	0	Stephens, Shannon, Brev. County	.833	4	1	4	1	6	1
Raines, Ken, Charlotte*	1.000	23	1	3	0	4	0	Stevenson, Jason, Daytona	.909	27	8	22	3	33	0
Rama, Shelby, Clearwater	1.000	34	4	10	0	14	1	Stewart, Stan, Tampa	1.000	14	2	1	0	3	0
Ramos, Edgar, Kissimmee	.793	11	5	18	6	29	1	Stone, Ricky, Vero Beach	.958	21	5	18	1	24	1
Ramsay, Robert, Sarasota*	.900	12	2	7	1	10	0	Stubbs, Jerry, W. Palm Beach	.500	7	1	0	1	2	0
Rath, Fred, Fort Myers	1.000	22	1	3	0	4	0	Stumpf, Brian, Clearwater	.933	56	2	12	1	15	0
Redman, Mark, Fort Myers*	.938	13	2	13	1	16	0	Swan, Tyrone, Lakeland	.800	10	6	6	3	15	0
Reed, Brian, St. Petersburg	.875	58	3	4	1	8	0	Tatis, Ramon, St. Lucie*	.905	46	8	11	2	21	1
Resz, Greg, Tampa	.667	20	2	0	1	3	0	Tessmer, Jay, Tampa	.957	68	4	18	1	23	1
Rhine, Kendall, Dunedin	.857	20	2	4	1	7	0	Thurman, Michael, W. Palm Beach	.929	19	11	15	2	28	1
Rhodriguez, Rory, W. Palm Beach	.947	35	6	12	1	19	1	Tillmon, Darrell, Sarasota*	1.000	18	3	13	0	16	1
Ricabal, Dan, Vero Beach	1.000	13	3	9	0	12	1	Tucker, Julien, Kissimmee	.909	32	5	15	2	22	1
Richardson, Kasey, Fort Myers*	.500	3	1	0	1	2	0	Turrentine, Rich, St. Lucie	1.000	45	2	9	0	11	0
Roach, Peter, Vero Beach*	1.000	17	5	19	0	24	0	Tweedlie, Brad, Sarasota	1.000	11	1	1	0	2	0
Roberts, Willis, Lakeland	.936	23	20	24	3	47	1	Tyrrell, Jim, Sarasota*	.500	8	0	1	1	2	0
Robertson, Jeriome, Kissimmee*	1.000	1	2	1	0	3	0	Underwood, Devin, Sarasota	1.000	3	0	1	0	1	0
Rogers, Bryan, St. Lucie	1.000	9	0	4	0	4	0	Urbina, Ugueth, W. Palm Beach	1.000	3	0	4	0	4	0
Rolocut, Brian, Vero Beach	.938	33	5	10	1	16	0	Vandemark, John, Clearwater*	.900	27	2	7	1	10	0
Roque, Rafael, St. Lucie*	.964	14	3	24	1	28	0	Veniard, Jay, Dunedin*	.882	14	3	12	2	17	0
Rushing, Will, Fort Myers*	.949	28	6	31	2	39	2	Wallace, B.J., Clearwater*	.895	15	5	12	2	19	1
Ryan, Jason, Daytona	.833	17	4	11	3	18	3	Ward, Duane, Daytona	1.000	6	1	2	0	3	1
Salazar, Mike, Lakeland	.846	19	3	8	2	13	1	Weidert, Chris, W. Palm Beach	1.000	20	11	19	0	30	0
Sampson, Benj, Fort Myers*	.857	11	1	5	1	7	0	West, David, Clearwater*	1.000	5	0	2	0	2	0
Sanchez, Jesus, St. Lucie*	.906	16	8	21	3	32	1	Westbrook, Destry, Clearwater	1.000	34	3	2	0	5	0
Santiago, Sandi, Tampa	1.000	9	0	5	0	5	1	Whiteman, Greg, Lakeland*	1.000	26	3	21	0	24	3
Santos, Victor, Lakeland	.750	5	2	1	1	4	0	Whiteside, Sean, Lakeland	.975	20	8	31	1	40	1
Sauerbeck, Scott, St. Lucie*	.963	17	3	23	1	27	2	Wiley, Chad, Charlotte	1.000	5	3	4	0	7	1
Scanlan, Bob, Lakeland	1.000	2	1	4	0	5	0	Williams, Mitch, Clearwater*	1.000	6	0	1	0	1	0
Scheffler, Craig, Vero Beach*	.800	31	4	4	2	10	0	Williams, Woody, Dunedin	1.000	2	1	1	0	2	0
Schlomann, Brett, Tampa	.917	26	8	14	2	24	1	Wilson, Paul, St. Lucie	.500	2	1	0	1	2	0
Shaver, Tony, Kissimmee	.773	42	6	11	5	22	0	Wimberly, Larry, Sarasota*	.750	6	0	3	1	4	0
Shelby, Anthony, Tampa*	1.000	24	1	7	0	8	0	Windham, Mike, St. Petersburg	.953	25	11	30	2	43	2
Short, Barry, St. Lucie	1.000	58	9	15	0	24	0	Winslett, Dax, Daytona	.667	2	2	0	1	3	0
Shumaker, Anthony, Clearwater*	1.000	31	1	4	0	5	0	Withem, Shannon, St. Lucie	1.000	2	1	3	0	4	0
Siler, Jeff, Lakeland	.917	37	5	17	2	24	0	Wood, Kerry, Daytona	.727	22	3	21	9	33	1
Silva, Ted, Charlotte	.962	16	8	17	1	26	0	Yocum, David, Vero Beach*	.750	7	1	2	1	4	0
Sinclair, Steve, Dunedin*	1.000	3	1	0	0	1	0	Young, Joe, Dunedin	1.000	5	0	5	0	5	0

The following players did not have any fielding statistics at the positions indicated or appeared only as a designated hitter, pinch-hitter or pinch-runner: Abad, p; Arnold, 3b; Belinda, p; Bracho, p; N. Brown, c; Bullock, p; Butler, dh; Cannon, p; L. Carter, of; Coolbaugh, p; Cora, of; Cox, p; Darensbourg, p; Ephan, dh; Evans, 3B, p; Hernandez, p; Fortin, of; Gibbs, 2b; P. Gomez, 3b; Hogan, dh; Huff, p; J. Jones; of; Kelly, p; Marquardt, p; McAulay, p; McFerrin, p; McLamb, 2b; McMullen, dh; Metcalfe, dh, ph; Metzger, dh; Morgan, p; Nakashima, p; Neal, of; Osborne, p; Owen, p; Ozuna, ss; Jo. Parra, ss; Payton, dh, ph; J. Powell, p; Ramirez, p; C. Roberts, p; L. Rodriguez, of; M. Rodriguez, of; Russell, p; Samboy, of; Schaaf, p; Schilling, p; Shanahan, 3b; Dav. Smith, 3b; Sowards, dh, pr; Strange, of; Tanner, 3b; Tatar, of; Thornton, p; Treend, p; Troilo, 3b; Waggoner, p; Whatley, p.

LEAGUE CHAMPIONS

Year	Team	Pct.	Year	Team	Pct.	Year	Team†	Pct.
1919—	Sanford*	.605		Gainesville (2nd)‡	.615		Lakeland†	.594
	Orlando*	.703	1939—	Sanford§	.787	1955—	Orlando	.671
1920—	Tampa	.654	1940—	Daytona Beach	.619		Orlando	.643
	Tampa	.722		Orlando (4th)‡	.507	1956—	Cocoa	.614
1921—	Orlando	.635	1941—	St. Augustine	.659		Cocoa	.671
1922—	St. Petersburg	.503		Leesburg (4th)‡	.488	1957—	Palatka	.629
	St. Petersburg	.618	1942-45—Did not operate.				Tampa†	.681
1923—	Orlando	.667	1946—	Orlando§	.681	1958—	St. Petersburg	.732
	Orlando	.678	1947—	St. Augustine	.625		St. Petersburg	.681
1924—	Lakeland	.695		Gainesville (2nd)‡	.584	1959—	Tampa	.591
	Lakeland	.683	1948—	Orlando	.643		St. Petersburg†	.612
1925—	St. Petersburg	.667		Daytona Beach (2nd)‡	.616	1960—	Lakeland	.731
	Tampa†	.696	1949—	Gainesville	.635		Palatka†	.614
1926—	Sanford	.647		St. Augustine (3rd)‡	.556	1961—	Tampa†	.710
	Sanford	.623	1950—	Orlando	.629		Sarasota	.696
1927—	Orlando†	.600		DeLand (3rd)‡	.590	1962—	Sarasota	.689
	Miami	.661	1951—	DeLand§	.643		Fort Lauderdale†	.623
1928-35—Did not operate.			1952—	DeLand∞	.704	1963—	Sarasota	.645
1936—	Gainesville	.542		Palatka (3rd)‡	.569		Sarasota	.667
	St. Augustine (4th)†	.492	1953—	Daytona Beach†	.657	1964—	Fort Lauderdale†	.629
1937—	Gainesville§	.616		DeLand	.703		St. Petersburg	.594
1938—	Leesburg	.626	1954—	Jacksonville Beach	.629	1965—	Fort Lauderdale	.627

CLASS A Florida State League

Year	Team	Pct.	Year	Team	Pct.	Year	Team	Pct.
	Fort Lauderdale	.634	1976—	Tampa	.559		West Palm Beach	.593
1966—	Leesburg†	.781		Lakeland††	.536	1987—	Fort Lauderdale∞∞∞	.616
	St. Petersburg	.700	1977—	Lakeland††	.616		Osceola	.576
1967—	St. Petersburg▲	.691		West Palm Beach	.583	1988—	Osceola	.606
	Orlando	.638	1978—	Lakeland	.565		St. Lucie▲▲	.532
1968—	Miami	.613		Miami§	.539	1989—	Port Charlotte▲▲	.540
	Orlando◆	.579	1979—	Fort Lauderdale	.643		St. Petersburg	.540
1969—	Miami■	.606		Winter Haven‡‡	.577	1990—	West Palm Beach	.697
	Orlando	.606	1980—	Daytona Beach	.628		Vero Beach▲▲	.585
1970—	Miami▼	.662		Fort Lauderdale††	.606	1991—	Clearwater	.623
	St. Petersburg	.600	1981—	Fort Myers	.554		West Palm Beach▲▲	.550
1971—	Miami▼	.667		Daytona Beach§§	.504	1992—	Sarasota	.639
	Daytona Beach	.586	1982—	Fort Lauderdale§§	.621		Lakeland◆◆	.530
1972—	Miami•	.562		Tampa	.546	1993—	St. Lucie	.600
	Daytona Beach	.606	1983—	Daytona Beach	.634		Clearwater§§	.556
1973—	St. Petersburg††	.575		Vero Beach§§	.515	1994—	Tampa§§	.606
	West Palm Beach	.580	1984—	Tampa	.532		Brevard County	.561
1974—	West Palm Beach††	.598		Fort Lauderdale§§	.521	1995—	Daytona§§	.644
	Fort Lauderdale	.626	1985—	Fort Myers	.590		Fort Myers	.577
1975—	St. Petersburg††	.652		Fort Lauderdale	.550	1996—	Tampa	.627
	Miami	.581	1986—	St. Petersburg∞∞∞	.647		St. Lucie§§	.534

*Split-season playoff abandoned after each team won three games. †Won split-season playoff. ‡Won four-club playoff. §Won championship and four-club playoff. ∞Won both halves of split season. ▲League divided into Eastern and Western divisions with split season. St. Petersburg and Orlando won both halves of split season; St. Petersburg won playoff. ◆League divided into Eastern and Western divisions. Miami won regular-season pennant on basis of highest won-lost percentage. Orlando won four-club playoff involving first two teams in each division. ■League divided into Southern and Central divisions. Miami won playoff between division leaders. (NOTE—Pennant awarded to playoff winner in 1936.) ▼League divided into Eastern and Western divisions. Miami won regular-season pennant on basis of highest won-loss percentage, and also won four-club playoff involving first two teams in each division. •League divided into Eastern and Western divisions. Won four-club playoff involving first two teams in each division. ††League divided into Northern and Southern divisions. Won four-club playoff involving first two teams in each division. ‡‡League divided into Northern and Southern divisions. Same two clubs won both halves; won playoffs. §§Won split-season playoff. ∞∞∞League divided into Western, Central and Southern divisions. Won four-club playoff. ▲▲League divided into Eastern, Western and Central divisions; played split-season. Won six-club playoff. ◆◆League divided into Eastern, Western and Central divisions; played split season. Won eight-club playoff.

MIDWEST LEAGUE

'esident
George H. Spelius

Idress
P.O. Box 936
Beloit, WI 53512

1one
608-364-1188

Teams (affiliation)
Beloit Snappers (Brewers)
Burlington Bees (Reds)
Cedar Rapids Kernels (Angels)
Clinton Lumber Kings (Padres)
Fort Wayne Wizards (Twins)
Kane County Cougars (Marlins)
Lansing Lugnuts (Royals)

Michigan Battle Cats (Red Sox)
Peoria Chiefs (Cardinals)
Quad City River Bandits (Astros)
Rockford Cubbies (Cubs)
South Bend Silver Hawks
 (Diamondbacks)
West Michigan Whitecaps (Tigers)
Wisconsin Timber Rattlers (Mariners)

1996 FINAL STANDINGS

FIRST HALF

EASTERN DIVISION

am	W	L	T	Pct.	GB
est Michigan (Athletics)	38	30	0	.559	....
rt Wayne (Twins)	34	32	0	.515	3
uth Bend (White Sox)	30	36	0	.455	7
chigan (Red Sox)	31	38	0	.449	7½
nsing (Royals)	29	40	0	.420	9½

CENTRAL DIVISION

am	W	L	T	Pct.	GB
sconsin (Mariners)	46	21	0	.687	....
oria (Cardinals)	37	29	0	.561	8½
ne County (Marlins)	30	33	0	.476	14
oit (Brewers)	31	35	0	.470	14½
ckford (Cubs)	30	36	0	.455	15½

WESTERN DIVISION

am	W	L	T	Pct.	GB
ad City (Astros)	34	28	0	.548	....
rlington (Giants)	34	34	0	.500	3
nton (Padres)	31	34	0	.477	4½
dar Rapids (Angels)	29	38	0	.433	7½

SECOND HALF

EASTERN DIVISION

Team	W	L	T	Pct.	GB
West Michigan (Athletics)	39	31	0	.557	....
Lansing (Royals)	39	31	0	.557	....
Fort Wayne (Twins)	35	35	0	.500	4
Michigan (Red Sox)	29	40	0	.420	9½
South Bend (White Sox)	24	46	0	.343	15

CENTRAL DIVISION

Team	W	L	T	Pct.	GB
Peoria (Cardinals)	42	28	0	.600	....
Rockford (Cubs)	40	29	0	.580	1½
Beloit (Brewers)	38	32	0	.543	4
Kane County (Marlins)	35	35	0	.500	7
Wisconsin (Mariners)	31	37	0	.456	10

WESTERN DIVISION

Team	W	L	T	Pct.	GB
Quad City (Astros)	36	33	0	.522	....
Cedar Rapids (Angels)	34	34	0	.500	1½
Clinton (Padres)	33	36	0	.478	3
Burlington (Giants)	31	39	0	.443	5½

COMPOSITE

am	Peo.	Wis.	W.M.	Q.C.	Rck.	F.W.	Bel.	Lan.	K.C.	Cln.	Bur.	C.R.	Mch.	S.B.	W	L	T	Pct.	GB
oria (Cardinals)	....	7	5	4	11	7	12	3	7	3	4	4	5	7	79	57	0	.581	....
sconsin (Mariners)	9	....	4	4	9	4	11	3	10	4	5	5	5	4	77	58	0	.570	1½
est Michigan (Athletics)	3	4	....	3	2	11	5	10	6	5	4	4	10	10	77	61	0	.558	3
ad City (Astros)	3	3	3	....	3	5	1	4	3	12	12	8	7	6	70	61	0	.534	6½
ckford (Cubs)	7	9	6	4	....	5	8	3	8	6	4	4	3	3	70	65	0	.519	8½
rt Wayne (Twins)	1	4	5	3	3	....	3	8	6	2	6	5	11	12	69	67	0	.507	10
loit (Brewers)	3	7	3	7	7	4	....	8	10	6	3	3	3	5	69	67	0	.507	10
nsing (Royals)	5	4	8	4	5	8	0	....	3	4	2	4	11	10	68	71	0	.489	12½
ne County (Marlins)	11	6	2	1	8	2	7	5	....	5	3	5	6	4	65	68	0	.489	12½
nton (Padres)	5	3	3	8	2	3	2	4	3	....	10	15	2	4	64	70	0	.478	14
rlington (Giants)	4	3	4	8	3	2	5	6	4	10	....	6	5	5	65	73	0	.471	15
dar Rapids (Angels)	2	2	4	12	3	3	5	4	3	5	14	....	1	5	63	72	0	.467	15½
chigan (Red Sox)	3	3	6	1	5	7	5	7	2	5	3	6	....	7	60	78	0	.435	20
uth Bend (White Sox)	1	3	8	2	4	6	3	6	3	3	3	3	9	....	54	82	0	.397	25

Kane County's home games played in Geneva, Ill.

Michigan's home games played in Battle Creek, Mich.

Quad City's home games played in Davenport, Ia.

West Michigan's home games played in Comstock Park, Mich.

Major league affiliations in parentheses.

PLAYOFFS: Rockford defeated Beloit, two games to one; Quad City defeated Cedar Rapids, two games to one; West Michigan defeated Lansing, two games
one; Wisconsin defeated Peoria, two games to one; West Michigan defeated Rockford, two games to none; Wisconsin defeated Quad City, two games to
e; West Michigan defeated Wisconsin, three games to one, to win league championship.

REGULAR-SEASON ATTENDANCE: Beloit, 73,552; Burlington, 52,726; Cedar Rapids, 127,379; Clinton, 57,120; Fort Wayne, 226,740; Kane County,
6,076; Lansing, 538,325; Michigan, 161,520; Peoria, 187,283; Quad City, 209,513; Rockford, 102,479; South Bend, 214,721; West Michigan, 547,401;
sconsin, 233,797; Total—3,168,632; Playoffs (21 games)—46,831; All-Star Game at Wisconsin—4,204.

MANAGERS: Beloit, Luis Salazar; Burlington, Glenn Tufts; Cedar Rapids, Tom Lawless; Clinton, Mike Ramsey; Fort Wayne, Dan Rohn; Kane County, Lynn
nes; Lansing, Brian Polberg; Michigan, Tommie Barrett; Peoria, Roy Silver; Quad City, Jim Pankovits; Rockford, Steve Roadcap; South Bend, Dave Keller;
est Michigan, Mike Quade; Wisconsin, Mike Goff.

ALL-STAR TEAM: 1B—Larry Barnes, Cedar Rapids; 2B—Andy Hall, Peoria; 3B—Mike Kinkade, Beloit; SS—Deivi Cruz, Burlington; OF—Kerry Robinson,
oria; Brian Simmons, South Bend; Don Denbow, Burlington; C—Ramon Hernandez, West Michigan; DH—Jeff Liefer, South Bend; LHP—Valerio
ossantos, Beloit; RHP—Britt Reames, Peoria; LH Reliever—Armando Almanza, Peoria; RH Reliever—Santos Hernandez, Burlington; Most Valuable
ayer—Larry Barnes, Cedar Rapids; Prospect of the Year—Britt Reames, Peoria; Manager of the Year—Roy Silver, Peoria.

CLASS A *Midwest League*

TEAM

Team	Avg.	G	TPA	AB	R	H	TB	2B	3B	HR	RBI	SH	SF	HP	BB	IBB	SO	SB	CS	GDP	LOB	SHO	Slg.	O
Wisconsin	.269	135	5199	4561	731	1228	1788	250	29	84	649	39	39	92	466	17	925	95	78	91	967	9	.392	.3
Lansing	.266	139	5526	4824	727	1285	1813	233	41	71	645	49	44	79	528	16	893	161	67	98	1081	3	.376	.3
Quad City	.265	131	4913	4391	629	1162	1701	212	30	89	555	39	43	45	394	15	845	153	100	96	844	6	.387	.3
Fort Wayne	.263	136	5177	4552	632	1196	1669	229	35	58	566	36	46	72	470	25	911	96	65	95	988	5	.367	.3
Peoria	.261	136	5143	4402	696	1148	1572	214	45	40	584	60	56	63	561	19	933	159	95	81	982	3	.357	.3
Michigan	.259	138	5276	4693	638	1216	1799	261	35	84	567	32	50	56	443	11	945	83	50	87	990	7	.383	.3
Rockford	.256	135	5141	4392	694	1126	1587	207	43	56	605	47	44	90	561	16	979	211	88	88	1000	5	.361	.3
Cedar Rapids	.255	135	5130	4491	645	1146	1779	218	41	111	587	44	38	77	477	14	1049	153	77	78	948	6	.396	.3
Beloit	.255	136	5056	4434	637	1131	1593	210	36	60	549	45	38	81	456	13	835	150	93	99	895	4	.359	.3
W. Michigan	.249	138	5348	4559	639	1133	1603	199	29	71	551	30	47	52	653	14	920	117	67	131	1083	2	.352	.3
South Bend	.245	136	5040	4450	566	1090	1584	213	34	71	494	52	44	45	445	25	947	117	84	80	897	11	.356	.3
Kane County	.240	133	4927	4280	580	1026	1569	215	26	92	518	46	35	69	496	17	1137	101	67	86	913	15	.367	.3
Burlington	.236	138	5260	4479	572	1055	1536	207	20	78	501	53	29	58	641	23	972	108	44	124	1075	8	.343	.3
Clinton	.230	134	4938	4240	529	974	1404	180	35	60	472	31	27	57	583	15	964	153	69	92	958	9	.331	.3

INDIVIDUAL

TOP QUALIFIERS FOR BATTING CHAMPIONSHIP

Minimum 378 plate appearances. *Lefthanded batter. †Switch-hitter.

Player, Team	Avg.	G	TPA	AB	R	H	TB	2B	3B	HR	RBI	SH	SF	HP	BB	IBB	SO	SB	CS	GDP	Slg.	C
Robinson, Kerry, Peoria*	.359	123	506	440	98	158	209	17	14	2	47	4	8	3	51	5	51	50	27	2	.475	
Vieira, Scott, Rockford	.324	134	563	442	81	143	205	30	4	8	81	2	9	26	84	7	89	9	8	6	.464	
Sapp, Damian, Michigan	.322	90	380	335	55	108	191	21	4	18	52	0	3	4	38	1	88	3	2	5	.570	
Arias, David, Wisconsin*	.322	129	548	485	89	156	248	34	2	18	93	2	4	5	52	8	108	3	4	5	.511	
Amado, Jose, Wis.-Lan.	.318	118	505	444	82	141	204	31	1	10	83	3	5	16	37	3	37	14	9	11	.459	
Barnes, Larry, Ced. Rapids*	.317	131	560	489	84	155	282	36	5	27	112	1	6	6	58	5	101	9	6	8	.577	
Tinoco, Luis, Wisconsin	.313	120	509	431	71	135	212	31	5	12	71	1	6	18	53	1	85	4	9	14	.492	
Joseph, Terry, Rockford	.305	128	554	449	98	137	199	23	6	9	94	2	9	25	69	0	88	28	15	7	.443	
Kinkade, Mike, Beloit	.304	135	583	496	104	151	237	33	4	15	100	3	6	32	46	7	68	23	12	10	.478	
Alvarez, Rafael, Ft. Wayne*	.302	119	522	473	61	143	199	30	7	4	58	2	1	3	43	5	55	11	9	5	.421	
Quinn, Mark, Lansing	.302	113	491	437	63	132	188	23	3	9	71	0	6	5	43	2	54	14	8	12	.430	
Hall, Andy, Peoria†	.300	128	551	446	80	134	185	29	5	4	68	10	5	15	75	1	90	21	7	6	.415	
Simmons, Brian, So. Bend†	.298	92	412	356	73	106	198	29	6	17	58	1	4	2	48	2	69	14	9	3	.556	
Gordon, Adrian, Fort Wayne	.297	110	407	343	58	102	134	15	7	1	47	3	9	5	47	1	90	9	9	5	.391	
Lugo, Julio, Quad City	.295	101	436	393	60	116	168	18	2	10	50	4	4	3	32	0	75	24	11	7	.427	
Febles, Carlos, Lansing	.295	102	451	363	84	107	155	23	5	5	43	7	4	11	66	0	64	30	14	8	.427	

DEPARTMENTAL LEADERS: G—Kinkade, J. Cepeda, 135; AB—J. Cepeda, 558; R—Kinkade, 104; H—J. Cepeda, 161; TB—Larry R. Barnes, 282; 2B—Larry R. Barnes, K. Thompson, 36; 3B—Hutchins, 16; HR—Larry R. Barnes, 27; RBI—Larry R. Barnes, 112; SH—Baughman, 15; SF—McNally, 11; HP—Kinkade, 32; BB—D. Walton, 112; IBB—Denbow, 12; SO—Booty, 195; SB—K. Robinson, Baughman, 50 each; CS—K. Robinson, 27; GIDP—R. Hernandez, 22; Slg.—Larry R. Barnes, .577; OBP—Vieira, .451.

ALL PLAYERS

*Lefthanded batter. †Switch-hitter.

Player, Team	Avg.	G	TPA	AB	R	H	TB	2B	3B	HR	RBI	SH	SF	HP	BB	IBB	SO	SB	CS	GDP	Slg.	C
Abernathy, Matt, Clinton*	.199	60	232	211	23	42	65	6	1	5	36	2	2	6	11	0	53	0	1	4	.308	
Adams, Jason, Quad City	.265	74	261	226	35	60	80	14	0	2	27	2	4	0	29	2	36	6	6	6	.354	
Agnoly, Earl, Kane County	.246	63	225	203	19	50	65	8	2	1	20	1	0	7	14	0	40	2	4	5	.320	
Alexander, Chad, Quad City	.264	118	497	435	68	115	187	25	4	13	69	0	3	2	57	4	108	16	11	11	.430	
Allen, Chad, Fort Wayne	.429	7	25	21	2	9	9	0	0	0	2	0	1	0	3	1	2	1	1	0	.429	
Allen, Justin, Clinton	.267	77	317	243	46	65	111	10	3	10	46	0	3	4	67	1	59	4	7	7	.457	
Almond, Greg, Peoria	.231	90	309	273	28	63	83	14	0	2	41	5	0	0	26	0	75	2	0	8	.304	
Alvarez, Rafael, Ft. Wayne*	.302	119	522	473	61	143	199	30	7	4	58	2	1	3	43	5	55	11	9	5	.421	
Amado, Jose, Wis.-Lan.	.318	118	505	444	82	141	204	31	1	10	83	3	5	16	37	3	37	14	9	11	.459	
Amerson, Gordon, Clinton*	.203	116	460	394	47	80	129	14	4	9	48	0	3	3	60	4	113	9	5	6	.327	
Anderson, Frank, So. Bend	.155	68	230	213	8	33	56	5	3	4	19	3	2	2	10	0	89	1	2	3	.263	
Antczak, Chuck, So. Bend	.097	16	35	31	3	3	5	2	0	0	1	1	0	2	1	0	9	0	0	1	.161	
Arias, David, Wisconsin*	.322	129	548	485	89	156	248	34	2	18	93	2	4	5	52	8	108	3	4	5	.511	
Arrollado, Courtney, Lansing	.256	17	46	39	5	10	11	1	0	0	5	3	0	0	7	0	13	2	1	1	.282	
Baeza, Art, Burlington	.093	17	51	43	4	4	8	1	0	1	5	2	0	1	5	0	7	0	0	2	.186	
Barnes, Kelvin, Rockford	.235	125	482	429	59	101	169	19	8	11	63	1	6	4	42	2	100	23	3	16	.394	
Barnes, Larry, Ced. Rapids*	.317	131	560	489	84	155	282	36	5	27	112	1	6	6	58	5	101	9	6	8	.577	
Baughman, Justin, Ced. Rapids	.248	127	534	464	78	115	163	17	8	5	48	15	1	6	45	2	78	50	17	13	.351	
Beltran, Carlos, Lansing†	.143	11	43	42	3	6	8	2	0	0	0	0	0	0	1	0	11	1	0	0	.190	
Bess, Johnny, Burlington†	.140	15	55	43	5	6	16	1	0	3	11	0	0	2	10	0	12	0	1	0	.372	
Betancourt, Rafael, Michigan	.167	62	187	168	14	28	42	1	2	3	14	3	2	2	12	0	39	5	2	7	.250	
Blosser, Doug, Lansing*	.205	36	137	117	14	24	44	5	0	5	18	0	4	1	15	0	38	2	0	0	.376	
Bly, Derrick, Rockford	.286	4	11	7	1	2	5	0	0	1	4	0	1	1	2	0	5	0	0	0	.714	
Booty, Josh, Kane County	.206	128	529	475	62	98	188	25	1	21	87	1	6	1	46	0	195	2	3	11	.396	
Borrero, Richie, Michigan	.167	11	32	30	3	5	6	1	0	0	1	0	0	0	2	0	5	0	1	1	.200	
Bovender, Andy, Quad City	.260	76	305	269	41	70	116	18	2	8	36	1	0	4	31	0	61	4	7	6	.431	
Bowers, R.J., Peoria	.257	64	263	226	35	58	93	23	0	4	20	1	2	1	33	2	59	6	10	5	.412	
Bowness, Brian, So. Bend	.202	65	223	203	19	41	47	4	1	0	18	0	1	1	18	1	36	1	2	8	.232	
Brown, Roosevelt, Kane Co.*	.150	11	42	40	1	6	8	2	0	0	3	0	0	1	1	0	10	0	1	0	.200	
Bucci, Carmen, Clinton†	.169	28	75	65	9	11	12	1	0	0	5	1	0	1	8	0	22	3	0	2	.185	
Bunkley, Antuan, Ft. Wayne	.233	58	196	172	19	40	56	11	1	1	12	1	0	7	16	1	39	1	0	6	.326	

Player, Team	Avg.	G	TPA	AB	R	H	TB	2B	3B	HR	RBI	SH	SF	HP	BB	IBB	SO	SB	CS	GDP	Slg.	OBP
alderon, Ricardo, Burlington*	.143	19	69	63	8	9	15	0	0	2	4	0	0	0	6	0	16	0	0	1	.238	.217
amilo, Jose, Kane Co.*	.177	30	109	96	10	17	36	0	2	5	14	2	0	1	10	0	26	7	0	0	.375	.262
ampusano, Carlos, Beloit	.246	108	358	337	33	83	111	17	4	1	20	5	1	5	10	0	63	4	3	7	.329	.278
ancel, David, South Bend†	.251	96	340	315	30	79	96	7	2	2	29	7	5	0	13	2	37	12	8	7	.305	.276
ancel, Robinson, Beloit	.220	72	239	218	26	48	56	3	1	1	29	5	1	1	14	0	31	13	5	7	.257	.269
armona, Cesarin, Clinton†	.197	104	367	315	38	62	79	7	2	2	21	6	1	1	44	0	104	8	6	6	.251	.296
arrasquel, Domingo, Beloit†	.168	73	214	190	16	32	38	6	0	0	10	3	0	0	21	0	14	1	1	1	.200	.251
arroll, Doug, Wisconsin*	.206	22	77	68	12	14	19	2	0	1	7	0	1	0	8	0	10	1	1	5	.279	.286
astro, Jose, Wisconsin*	.216	37	124	111	12	24	27	3	0	0	10	2	1	1	9	0	22	2	5	4	.243	.279
astro, Ramon, Quad City	.248	96	350	314	38	78	114	15	0	7	43	0	3	2	31	1	61	2	0	12	.363	.317
atlett, David, Rockford	.232	78	261	224	31	52	75	18	1	1	30	2	0	5	23	0	73	5	3	6	.335	.317
epeda, Jose, Lansing	.289	135	624	558	87	161	205	29	3	3	81	9	8	11	38	0	44	10	3	8	.367	.341
epeda, Malcolm, Burlington	.158	82	261	209	20	33	44	9	1	0	15	3	1	7	41	1	73	1	2	3	.211	.314
ey, Dan, Ft. Wayne	.259	27	93	85	8	22	26	4	0	0	6	0	0	0	8	6	0	11	2	1	2	.306	.323
hamblee, James, Michigan	.218	100	335	303	31	66	88	15	2	1	39	4	4	7	16	0	75	2	2	1	.290	.270
havera, Arnie, Quad City*	.245	77	205	184	22	45	72	16	1	3	34	0	1	1	19	0	46	0	1	4	.391	.317
hevalier, Virgil, Michigan	.248	126	523	483	61	120	181	31	3	8	62	1	5	1	33	1	69	11	4	11	.375	.295
hristenson, Ryan, W. Mich.	.311	33	143	122	21	38	50	2	2	2	18	1	3	4	13	0	22	2	4	2	.410	.387
lark, Kevin, Michigan	.276	126	521	474	53	131	199	32	3	10	56	1	4	12	30	2	94	4	5	11	.420	.333
oe, Ryan, Quad City	.293	77	279	246	38	72	126	10	1	14	47	3	2	10	18	0	56	0	0	6	.512	.362
offee, Gary, Lansing	.232	105	454	393	52	91	145	17	2	11	59	0	3	5	53	2	141	6	1	11	.369	.328
olon, Jose, Rockford	.250	8	15	12	1	3	3	0	0	0	1	0	0	0	3	0	5	0	2	0	.250	.400
ordero, Pablo, Burlington	.089	33	88	79	5	7	10	3	0	0	4	1	1	1	6	0	17	2	0	2	.127	.161
ruz, Deivi, Burlington	.294	127	563	517	72	152	210	27	2	9	64	4	3	4	35	3	49	12	5	20	.406	.342
uevas, Eduardo, Clinton	.276	88	343	312	33	86	114	15	5	1	34	4	3	2	22	0	47	19	5	7	.365	.324
alton, Jed, Cedar Rapids	.280	79	341	304	52	85	139	16	1	12	47	0	2	12	23	0	38	20	8	10	.457	.352
arcuiel, Faruq, Wisconsin*	.213	74	245	211	28	45	57	6	3	0	30	4	2	10	18	1	46	6	4	5	.270	.303
avalillo, David, Ced. Rapids	.275	98	415	378	63	104	135	22	0	3	34	3	3	3	28	0	51	4	6	4	.357	.328
aVanon, Jeff, W. Michigan†	.242	89	343	289	43	70	97	13	4	2	33	2	1	1	49	2	66	5	7	6	.336	.353
avidson, Cleatus, Ft. Wayne†	.177	59	229	203	20	36	50	8	3	0	30	1	2	0	23	0	45	2	3	4	.246	.259
avis, Josh, Clinton	.056	9	18	18	0	1	1	0	0	0	0	0	0	0	0	0	5	0	0	0	.056	.056
awsey, Jason, Beloit*	.000	35	1	1	0	0	0	0	0	0	0	0	0	0	0	0	0	0	0	0	.000	.000
ean, Chris, Wisconsin†	.271	53	236	210	32	57	81	8	2	4	32	1	1	4	18	1	46	11	7	5	.386	.339
enbow, Don, Burlington	.278	92	394	302	64	84	168	17	2	21	62	1	2	8	81	12	123	19	5	5	.556	.440
ishington, Nate, Peoria*	.226	75	244	208	22	47	74	12	3	3	30	0	4	7	25	0	73	1	1	6	.356	.324
rent, Brian, South Bend	.189	93	344	291	37	55	80	17	1	2	23	6	2	1	44	1	107	12	6	5	.275	.296
unn, Nathan, Clinton	.253	50	198	166	20	42	57	11	2	0	23	0	2	1	29	0	44	10	1	7	.343	.364
urrington, Trent, Ced. Rapids	.250	25	114	76	12	19	20	1	0	0	4	2	1	2	33	0	20	15	2	2	.263	.482
obert, Chad, Clinton	.182	27	82	77	5	14	17	1	1	0	6	1	0	2	2	0	13	0	0	3	.221	.222
liott, David, Beloit	.268	112	438	365	65	98	152	12	3	12	58	0	4	7	62	4	80	17	10	10	.416	.381
llison, Tony, Rockford	.170	31	99	94	7	16	25	3	0	2	7	0	0	2	3	0	30	0	2	1	.266	.212
ncarnacion, Mario, W. Mich.	.229	118	459	401	55	92	133	14	3	7	43	4	0	5	49	0	131	23	8	13	.332	.321
scandon, Emiliano, Lansing†	.272	107	431	372	50	101	141	18	5	4	52	6	2	3	46	3	47	8	5	3	.379	.355
spada, Josue, W. Michigan	.270	23	89	74	9	20	22	2	0	0	4	0	0	2	13	0	11	3	1	2	.297	.393
arley, Cordell, Peoria	.232	29	86	82	10	19	22	1	1	0	7	0	0	0	4	0	23	1	4	3	.268	.267
ebles, Carlos, Lansing	.295	102	451	363	84	107	155	23	5	5	43	7	4	11	66	0	64	30	14	8	.427	.414
elix, Pedro, Burlington	.265	93	343	321	36	85	116	12	2	5	36	0	3	1	18	0	65	5	2	11	.361	.303
elston, Anthony, Ft. Wayne*	.313	62	251	201	53	63	69	4	1	0	18	2	1	4	43	0	36	22	4	2	.343	.442
erguson, Dwight, Michigan*	.111	10	40	36	2	4	4	0	0	0	0	0	0	0	4	0	14	0	1	0	.111	.200
gueroa, Luis, Wisconsin	.290	37	150	138	18	40	55	9	0	2	19	1	2	3	6	0	14	1	1	6	.399	.329
ichner, Duane, W. Michigan*	.264	133	564	477	66	126	177	24	3	7	82	1	10	3	73	5	82	2	0	5	.371	.359
nnieston, Adam, Lansing	.181	60	207	193	19	35	50	3	3	2	13	0	1	0	13	1	61	4	1	3	.259	.232
aser, Joe, Fort Wayne	.224	101	375	331	42	74	111	17	1	6	43	8	2	8	26	2	60	7	2	7	.335	.294
riedrich, Steve, So. Bend	.264	133	582	545	51	144	190	25	6	3	46	4	4	7	20	3	114	18	11	11	.349	.297
unaro, Joe, Kane County	.309	89	347	291	57	90	135	20	2	7	43	5	4	7	40	2	42	5	3	5	.464	.401
arcia, Amaury, Kane County	.263	106	471	395	65	104	155	19	7	6	36	7	2	5	62	2	84	37	19	8	.392	.369
arcia, Carlos, Fort Wayne	.211	40	151	128	18	27	32	2	0	1	9	0	1	2	20	0	24	14	5	5	.250	.325
arcia, Luis, South Bend	.217	58	232	221	23	48	62	9	1	1	16	0	1	1	9	2	29	3	4	5	.281	.250
arcia, Ossie, Peoria	.237	120	437	359	70	85	101	14	1	0	38	14	4	14	46	0	68	20	13	6	.281	.343
lozier, Larry, Kane County	.215	26	104	79	13	17	22	3	1	0	4	3	1	3	18	0	17	1	3	4	.278	.376
onzalez, Alex, Kane Co.	.200	4	14	10	2	2	2	0	0	0	0	1	0	1	2	0	4	0	0	1	.200	.385
oodell, Steve, Kane Co.	.280	86	332	282	34	79	127	17	2	9	39	2	5	13	30	2	68	1	1	8	.450	.370
oodwin, Keith, Michigan	.273	66	274	238	40	65	86	18	0	1	28	6	3	2	25	0	52	11	6	0	.361	.343
ordon, Adrian, Fort Wayne	.297	110	407	343	58	102	134	15	7	1	47	3	9	5	47	1	90	9	9	5	.391	.381
raves, Bryan, Ced. Rapids	.224	83	283	228	27	51	72	5	2	4	27	1	3	5	46	0	59	4	2	3	.316	.362
uillen, Carlos, Quad City†	.330	29	131	112	23	37	55	7	1	3	17	0	3	0	16	2	25	13	6	1	.491	.405
ulseth, Mark, Burlington*	.262	125	520	423	61	111	169	35	4	5	41	4	3	1	89	3	95	4	2	11	.400	.390
aas, Chris, Peoria*	.240	124	496	421	56	101	155	19	1	11	63	1	3	7	64	3	169	3	2	4	.368	.347
all, Andy, Peoria†	.300	128	551	446	80	134	185	29	5	4	68	10	5	15	75	1	90	21	7	6	.415	.414
allmark, Patrick, Lansing	.280	118	497	453	68	127	163	23	5	1	53	6	1	3	34	2	80	33	9	3	.360	.334
am, Kevin, Cedar Rapids	.215	100	369	326	38	70	114	14	0	10	35	5	3	6	29	0	102	4	4	7	.350	.288
amilton, Joe, Michigan*	.262	108	437	389	54	102	165	20	2	13	58	0	1	2	45	1	117	3	5	10	.424	.341
arris, Jeff, Fort Wayne	.000	42	1	1	0	0	0	0	0	0	0	0	0	0	0	1	0	0	0	0	.000	.000
arrison, Adonis, Wisconsin*	.265	54	217	196	29	52	74	15	2	1	24	1	0	1	19	0	36	5	3	3	.378	.333
ayes, Darren, South Bend	.071	9	38	28	5	2	5	0	0	1	3	0	2	4	0	0	14	1	1	0	.179	.263
eintz, Chris, South Bend	.265	64	258	230	25	61	78	12	1	1	22	1	3	1	23	1	46	1	1	3	.339	.339
erdman, Eli, Fort Wayne*	.190	7	30	21	2	4	7	0	0	1	5	1	0	1	8	0	7	0	1	1	.333	.367
ernandez, Carlos, Quad City	.270	112	501	456	67	123	167	15	7	5	49	9	5	4	27	0	71	41	14	6	.366	.313
ernandez, Ramon, W. Mich.	.255	123	528	447	62	114	180	26	2	12	68	1	7	4	69	1	62	2	3	22	.403	.355
ickey, Mike, Wisconsin†	.329	26	110	85	15	28	35	7	0	0	11	1	1	0	20	0	7	1	1	1	.412	.468
ills, Rich, Clinton	.249	124	498	433	42	108	163	34	0	7	58	0	3	12	50	2	69	4	4	11	.376	.341
uls, Steve, Fort Wayne†	.214	60	222	201	21	43	51	3	1	1	11	6	2	1	12	1	53	2	2	3	.254	.259
utchins, Norm, Ced. Rapids†	.225	126	510	466	59	105	156	13	16	2	52	8	2	6	28	0	110	22	8	5	.335	.277

CLASS A *Midwest League*

Player, Team	Avg.	G	TPA	AB	R	H	TB	2B	3B	HR	RBI	SH	SF	HP	BB	IBB	SO	SB	CS	GDP	Slg.	OB
Iapoce, Anthony, Beloit†	.290	78	323	269	63	78	93	6	3	1	11	3	0	7	44	0	54	23	13	4	.346	.40
Inzunza, Miguel, Peoria	.197	26	77	61	10	12	13	1	0	0	8	3	2	0	11	0	8	0	0	2	.213	.31
Izquierdo, Sergio, Sou. Bend	.000	2	2	2	0	0	0	0	0	0	0	0	0	0	0	0	1	0	0	0	.000	.00
Jasco, Elinton, Rockford	.293	120	545	464	95	136	164	11	7	1	43	12	2	5	62	1	97	48	14	1	.353	.38
Jefferson, David, Rockford	.233	93	345	301	35	70	85	8	2	1	40	1	2	4	37	0	53	15	6	6	.282	.32
Johnson, Heath, Ft. Wayne*	.160	8	32	25	4	4	5	1	0	0	1	0	0	1	6	0	9	0	0	0	.200	.34
Johnson, James, Clinton	.252	118	496	428	67	108	126	12	3	0	26	11	2	2	53	1	67	44	15	8	.294	.33
Johnson, Jeffrey, So. Bend	.180	102	381	345	27	62	81	13	0	2	39	10	4	0	22	1	49	10	7	3	.235	.22
Johnson, Mark, South Bend	.257	67	262	214	29	55	81	14	3	2	27	4	4	1	39	2	25	3	3	8	.379	.36
Johnson, Ric, Quad City	.236	95	353	318	36	75	99	9	3	3	39	4	6	8	16	0	47	10	4	12	.311	.28
Johnson, Travis, Ft. Wayne*	.328	57	228	183	32	60	91	18	2	3	18	1	1	11	32	0	49	5	5	4	.497	.45
Jones, Jaime, Kane Co.*	.249	62	261	237	29	59	102	17	1	8	45	0	5	0	19	0	74	7	2	6	.430	.29
Joseph, Terry, Rockford	.305	128	554	449	98	137	199	23	6	9	94	2	9	25	69	0	88	28	15	7	.443	.41
Juarez, Raul, Fort Wayne	.224	54	195	170	24	38	50	6	0	2	21	1	1	3	20	1	51	1	2	4	.294	.3
Kane, Ryan, Cedar Rapids	.258	125	538	485	56	125	200	29	2	14	75	1	8	4	40	3	120	5	5	9	.412	.3
Keefe, Jamie, Clinton	.302	32	141	106	25	32	46	5	0	3	15	0	1	34	0	18	8	1	1	.434	.47	
Kinkade, Mike, Beloit	.304	135	583	496	104	151	237	33	4	15	100	3	6	32	46	7	68	23	12	10	.478	.39
Kinnie, Donald, Rockford	.231	31	68	65	12	15	19	4	0	0	3	0	0	0	3	0	20	7	0	3	.292	.26
Klee, Charles, South Bend	.236	18	64	55	8	13	19	0	0	2	4	1	1	0	7	0	13	2	2	2	.345	.31
Knauss, Tom, Fort Wayne	.300	56	239	207	30	62	105	18	2	7	39	1	4	2	25	3	46	1	0	8	.507	.37
Kotsay, Mark, Kane Co.*	.283	17	79	60	16	17	28	5	0	2	8	0	1	1	16	0	8	3	0	3	.467	.43
Kuilan, Hector, Kane Co.	.201	94	338	308	28	62	94	12	1	6	30	3	2	3	22	0	52	1	3	7	.305	.26
Lakovic, Greg, Fort Wayne*	.255	36	118	94	12	24	27	3	0	0	11	4	0	4	16	0	22	2	2	3	.287	.38
Lara, Edward, W. Michigan	.216	87	296	259	29	56	65	7	1	0	16	5	2	5	25	0	39	16	6	9	.251	.29
Lariviere, Jason, Peoria	.249	64	256	225	33	56	74	13	1	1	36	2	3	0	25	0	31	6	5	5	.329	.32
Layne, Jason, Lansing*	.253	25	104	91	11	23	30	4	0	1	16	0	0	0	13	0	23	1	0	1	.330	.34
Lebron, Ruben, Michigan†	.178	38	117	107	17	19	24	5	0	0	6	1	0	2	7	0	18	3	0	3	.224	.24
Lewis, Jeremy, Rockford	.247	105	415	365	50	90	136	23	4	5	61	1	2	1	46	1	85	13	3	9	.373	.33
Liefer, Jeff, South Bend	.325	74	316	277	60	90	149	14	0	15	58	0	4	5	30	3	62	6	5	3	.538	.39
Lindsey, Rodney, Clinton	.161	23	102	87	11	14	16	2	0	0	4	0	1	3	11	0	30	12	8	2	.184	.27
Liniak, Cole, Michigan	.263	121	517	437	65	115	154	26	2	3	46	3	8	10	59	1	59	7	6	12	.352	.35
Listach, Pat, Beloit†	.400	1	5	5	2	2	2	0	0	0	0	0	0	0	0	0	1	0	0	0	.400	.40
Longueira, Tony, Lansing	.190	45	175	153	14	29	36	2	1	1	15	5	1	2	14	0	23	4	3	6	.235	.26
Lopez, Mickey, Beloit†	.271	61	275	236	35	64	78	10	2	0	14	10	0	1	28	0	36	12	8	8	.331	.35
Lopiccolo, Jamie, Beloit	.263	96	363	304	44	80	115	19	2	4	57	2	9	8	39	0	48	4	6	8	.378	.3
Lowry, Curt, Clinton	.186	32	79	70	9	13	20	2	1	1	7	0	0	1	8	0	21	0	1	0	.286	.27
Loyd, Brian, Clinton	.297	10	39	37	3	11	13	2	0	0	2	0	0	2	0	0	6	0	0	0	.351	.33
Lugo, Julio, Quad City	.295	101	436	393	60	116	168	18	2	10	50	4	4	3	32	0	75	24	11	7	.427	.3
Maleski, Tom, Rockford	.125	6	10	8	1	1	1	0	0	0	1	0	0	0	2	0	3	0	0	1	.125	.3
Manning, Brian, Burlington	.297	33	138	111	16	33	50	4	2	3	22	0	1	4	22	1	18	2	1	2	.450	.42
Martin, Mike, Clinton*	.175	77	243	206	16	36	46	7	0	1	23	2	3	3	29	2	33	1	0	3	.223	.28
Marval, Raul, Burlington	.201	44	174	159	13	32	42	10	0	0	9	4	2	3	6	0	12	3	1	7	.264	.24
Mathis, Joe, Wisconsin*	.285	126	518	473	79	135	185	19	8	5	47	3	2	4	36	0	75	19	6	4	.391	.34
McAninch, John, Ced. Rapids	.248	86	329	298	43	74	122	16	1	10	42	0	4	6	21	1	81	0	2	3	.409	.3
McCartney, Sommer, Kane Co.	.300	51	180	160	21	48	77	14	0	5	19	1	1	4	10	0	50	1	1	3	.481	.36
McClendon, Travis, Peoria	.194	60	181	155	23	30	38	4	0	0	23	4	1	4	17	1	27	1	4	5	.245	.28
McDonald, Ashanti, Rockford*	.233	76	231	202	19	47	57	6	2	0	17	4	1	3	21	2	40	6	2	5	.282	.3
McHugh, Ryan, Peoria	.253	76	272	237	46	60	103	17	4	6	40	1	1	0	33	1	46	7	4	10	.435	.34
McNally, Shawn, Peoria	.278	123	505	431	59	120	170	19	5	7	75	2	11	4	57	3	60	9	8	7	.394	.36
Mealing, Al, Beloit*	.259	88	295	274	41	71	112	15	4	6	24	0	0	1	20	0	66	13	12	5	.409	.3
Medrano, Teodoro, Wisconsin	.203	63	194	172	20	35	58	9	1	4	22	2	2	3	15	1	58	3	3	1	.337	.2
Melito, Mark, Lansing	.254	59	234	201	29	51	68	12	1	1	18	1	0	5	27	0	28	8	3	5	.338	.3
Miranda, Alex, W. Michigan*	.222	123	513	414	57	92	129	18	2	5	48	4	4	5	86	1	84	3	0	15	.312	.3
Miranda, Tony, Lansing	.287	39	159	136	28	39	53	6	1	2	23	2	1	3	17	1	24	3	0	9	.390	.3
Molina, Jose, Rockford	.226	96	355	305	35	69	87	10	1	2	27	7	4	3	36	0	71	2	4	8	.285	.3
Montas, Ricardo, Lansing	.292	8	26	24	1	7	7	0	0	0	0	2	0	0	0	0	4	0	0	0	.292	.3
Morales, Alex, Burlington	.225	41	173	138	26	31	57	6	1	6	17	4	0	4	27	0	37	15	2	0	.413	.38
Moreno, Juan, W. Michigan*	.000	38	1	1	0	0	0	0	0	0	0	0	0	0	0	0	0	0	0	0	.000	.00
Morgan, Steve, Michigan*	.143	7	7	7	1	1	1	0	0	0	0	0	0	0	0	0	2	0	0	0	.143	.14
Mosley, Tim, Rockford	.500	38	2	2	0	1	1	0	0	0	0	0	0	0	0	0	0	0	0	0	.500	.50
Mota, Alfonso, Ced. Rapids*	.222	35	76	63	7	14	23	3	0	2	4	0	0	1	12	0	15	1	2	2	.365	.35
Mueller, Brett, Peoria	.212	12	36	33	5	7	10	3	0	0	3	0	0	0	3	0	9	1	1	3	.303	.2
Munoz, Juan, Peoria*	.355	30	124	107	19	38	47	9	0	0	18	0	2	1	14	0	13	4	1	2	.439	.42
Murray, Doug, Lansing*	.143	18	38	35	2	5	5	0	0	0	4	0	0	2	1	0	9	0	1	0	.143	.21
Niedermaier, Brad, Ft. Wayne	1.000	38	2	1	0	1	1	0	0	0	0	0	0	0	0	0	0	0	0	0	1.000	1.00
Nieves, Jose, Rockford	.242	113	441	396	55	96	139	20	4	5	57	4	3	5	33	1	59	17	9	8	.351	.3
Noriega, Kevin, Beloit†	.268	115	461	414	55	111	149	22	2	4	59	0	6	2	39	0	69	5	5	10	.360	.3
Nunez, Isaias, Peoria*	.221	108	304	271	33	60	77	12	1	1	27	3	3	1	26	4	53	2	3	3	.284	.2
O'Neal, Troy, Beloit	.243	74	234	206	18	50	54	4	0	0	20	4	2	6	16	0	28	1	2	8	.262	.3
O'Quinn, James, Ced. Rapids*	.000	41	1	1	0	0	0	0	0	0	0	0	0	0	0	0	0	0	0	0	.000	.0
Ortega, Randy, W. Michigan	.252	49	169	139	15	35	45	4	0	2	21	0	3	1	25	0	34	0	1	3	.324	.3
Ortiz, Nick, Michigan	.302	73	269	242	37	73	101	14	4	2	25	1	1	5	20	1	44	1	1	4	.417	.38
Oyola, Carlos, Burlington†	.160	7	26	25	1	4	6	2	0	0	3	1	0	0	0	0	5	0	0	1	.240	.16
Padilla, Roy, Michigan*	.280	103	426	386	58	108	146	20	6	2	40	1	2	2	34	2	56	21	8	5	.378	.34
Paez, Israel, Fort Wayne	.266	128	514	451	86	120	167	22	5	5	50	4	3	5	51	2	76	11	8	18	.370	.34
Parent, Gerald, Beloit*	.211	40	114	95	12	20	28	6	1	0	12	1	0	0	18	0	19	2	3	1	.295	.33
Paulino, Arturo, W. Michigan	.221	87	263	231	27	51	66	7	1	2	23	1	1	6	24	0	46	9	10	8	.286	.29
Perez, Richard, Rockford	.253	33	101	83	12	21	36	6	0	3	13	5	1	2	10	0	17	2	0	3	.434	.34
Peterman, Tommy, Ft. Wayne*	.251	58	190	175	17	44	64	11	0	3	28	0	3	2	10	3	30	0	1	1	.366	.26
Peters, Tony, Beloit	.257	71	199	179	20	46	71	13	3	2	23	1	1	0	18	0	47	5	1	3	.397	.32
Phair, Kelly, Beloit	.212	30	117	99	16	21	26	5	0	0	12	1	2	2	13	0	18	3	1	1	.263	.3
Pico, Brandon, Rockford*	.314	12	39	35	3	11	13	0	1	0	7	0	1	0	3	0	5	0	0	0	.371	.3
Pierzynski, A.J., Ft. Wayne*	.274	114	461	431	48	118	175	36	3	7	70	0	6	2	22	1	53	0	4	10	.406	.3

ayer, Team	Avg.	G	TPA	AB	R	H	TB	2B	3B	HR	RBI	SH	SF	HP	BB	IBB	SO	SB	CS	GDP	Slg.	OBP
tts, Rick, Lansing	.208	13	53	48	7	10	11	1	0	0	2	0	0	0	5	0	14	2	1	1	.229	.283
oor, Jeff, Burlington	.242	104	414	359	27	87	107	17	0	1	40	2	2	2	49	1	54	1	0	14	.298	.335
orter, Bo, Rockford	.241	105	458	378	83	91	140	22	3	7	44	3	4	1	72	1	107	30	14	7	.370	.360
owers, John, Clinton*	.257	64	281	237	29	61	80	8	4	1	21	3	3	4	34	0	38	1	4	5	.338	.356
odanov, Peter, Michigan	.231	44	167	147	21	34	52	7	1	3	14	0	2	0	18	1	23	2	1	3	.354	.311
ospero, Teo, Burlington	.167	10	28	24	0	4	4	0	0	0	2	1	0	1	2	0	9	0	0	0	.167	.259
uinn, Mark, Lansing	.302	113	491	437	63	132	188	23	3	9	71	0	6	5	43	2	54	14	8	12	.430	.367
aifstanger, John, Michigan	.290	111	416	345	55	100	134	17	1	5	41	6	2	1	62	1	48	5	4	3	.388	.398
amirez, Hiram, Burlington	.245	101	387	327	42	80	130	17	0	11	55	2	3	3	52	1	94	2	1	13	.398	.351
amirez, Joel, Wisconsin	.239	110	409	364	53	87	104	14	0	1	52	4	1	10	30	0	45	5	6	10	.286	.314
andolph, Edward, Wisconsin†	.179	70	224	196	23	35	49	9	1	1	13	3	1	1	23	2	43	3	0	7	.250	.267
ascon, Rene, Kane Co.*	.170	56	210	188	23	32	50	6	0	4	20	1	3	1	17	1	61	0	1	7	.266	.239
athmell, Lance, Michigan	.130	20	58	54	5	7	14	2	1	1	5	0	1	0	3	0	9	0	0	0	.259	.172
auer, Troy, West Michigan	.045	13	25	22	3	1	1	0	0	0	1	0	0	0	3	0	13	0	0	0	.045	.160
eese, Mat, Cedar Rapids*	.071	9	14	14	0	1	1	0	0	0	0	0	0	0	0	0	5	0	0	0	.071	.071
chardson, Kasey, Ft. Wayne*	.500	30	2	2	0	1	1	0	0	0	0	0	0	0	0	0	1	0	0	0	.500	.500
tter, Ryan, Beloit	.239	99	381	347	43	83	128	12	6	7	42	5	2	3	24	0	103	20	6	4	.369	.293
vera, Miguel, Peoria	.224	72	235	210	26	47	62	10	1	1	22	6	2	3	14	0	33	2	3	3	.295	.279
vera, Wilfredo, Michigan	.248	65	160	149	17	37	56	9	2	2	18	1	2	1	7	0	32	1	0	5	.376	.283
oberts, Ryan, Peoria	.200	9	23	20	0	4	4	0	0	0	0	1	0	1	1	0	4	1	0	0	.200	.273
obertson, Ryan, Kane Co.*	.231	55	203	160	21	37	54	8	0	3	16	2	3	1	37	1	31	0	1	3	.338	.373
obinson, Hassan, Quad City	.271	106	398	373	53	101	119	11	2	1	38	5	3	3	14	2	35	15	6	4	.319	.300
obinson, Kerry, Peoria*	.359	123	506	440	98	158	209	17	14	2	47	4	8	3	51	5	51	50	27	2	.475	.422
obles, Juan, Lansing	.269	27	75	67	11	18	25	4	0	1	5	1	0	1	6	0	10	2	0	1	.373	.338
ocha, Juan, Lansing	.268	131	546	459	79	123	203	22	8	14	83	5	9	5	68	2	116	15	9	8	.442	.362
oche, Marlon, Quad City	.273	85	305	275	34	75	100	5	4	4	25	2	0	2	26	1	60	5	12	7	.364	.340
odriguez, Juan, Ced. Rapids†	.240	8	26	25	3	6	8	0	1	0	3	0	0	0	1	0	6	2	1	1	.320	.269
odriguez, Noel, Quad City	.271	39	159	144	26	39	61	10	0	4	19	0	0	1	14	0	18	1	0	1	.424	.340
olison, Nate, Kane County*	.243	131	549	474	63	115	187	28	1	14	75	1	0	8	66	9	170	3	3	9	.395	.345
omboli, Curtis, Michigan*	.000	41	1	0	0	0	0	0	0	0	0	1	0	0	0	0	0	0	0	0	.000	.000
ondon, Alex, W. Michigan	.213	19	55	47	3	10	13	1	1	0	7	1	2	1	4	0	15	1	0	2	.277	.278
yder, Derek, Cedar Rapids	.235	62	183	153	11	36	45	5	2	0	11	6	1	2	21	0	31	0	2	5	.294	.333
anchez, Marcos, Clinton†	.203	42	138	123	14	25	42	6	1	3	13	0	0	0	15	2	49	2	0	4	.341	.290
app, Damian, Michigan	.322	90	380	335	55	108	191	21	4	18	52	0	3	4	38	1	88	3	2	5	.570	.395
aucedo, Robert, Ced. Rapids	.000	3	3	3	0	0	0	0	0	0	0	0	0	0	0	0	1	0	0	0	.000	.000
auve, Jeff, Michigan	.000	37	1	1	0	0	0	0	0	0	0	0	0	0	0	0	1	0	0	0	.000	.000
aylor, Jamie, Quad City*	.121	23	67	58	8	7	8	1	0	0	5	2	2	2	3	0	13	4	2	0	.138	.185
chafer, Brett, Lansing	.255	15	56	47	5	12	16	2	1	0	3	0	1	1	7	0	7	3	2	3	.340	.357
chroeder, John, Ft. Wayne*	.264	111	461	425	54	112	178	20	2	14	58	0	5	12	18	3	119	3	5	3	.419	.309
chwenke, Matt, Clinton	.151	28	95	86	4	13	16	3	0	0	2	0	0	3	6	0	28	0	1	3	.186	.232
eidel, Ryan, Rockford	.190	47	115	105	14	20	23	3	0	0	10	3	0	1	6	1	25	6	3	1	.219	.241
heffer, Chad, Wisconsin†	.196	101	389	316	60	62	85	11	0	4	35	2	2	6	63	0	79	13	10	0	.269	.339
effield, Tony, Michigan*	.233	48	151	133	20	31	58	10	1	5	31	0	5	1	12	0	38	3	2	4	.436	.291
heppard, Greg, So. Bend	.268	54	158	142	17	38	45	5	1	0	9	4	0	1	11	1	40	5	2	3	.317	.325
mmons, Brian, So. Bend†	.298	92	412	356	73	106	198	29	6	17	58	1	4	2	48	2	69	14	9	3	.556	.380
mith, Jeff, Fort Wayne*	.236	63	233	208	20	49	61	6	0	2	26	1	2	0	22	0	32	2	1	4	.293	.306
mith, Rick, Beloit*	.245	114	424	372	41	91	141	27	1	7	57	2	4	6	39	2	81	4	5	9	.379	.323
mith, Scott, Wisconsin	.332	67	277	241	43	80	129	11	4	10	49	2	2	8	24	1	74	11	7	1	.535	.407
oriano, Jose, W. Michigan	.247	126	476	434	57	107	145	20	3	4	44	2	4	5	31	1	86	20	11	15	.334	.302
orrow, Michael, Burlington	.241	61	273	224	30	54	63	7	1	0	13	1	1	5	42	0	33	0	1	5	.281	.371
rasser, John, So. Bend	.125	2	8	8	0	1	1	0	0	0	0	0	0	0	0	0	4	0	0	0	.125	.125
uart, Rich, Ced. Rapids	.286	39	146	133	19	38	51	5	1	2	15	0	0	2	11	0	33	5	1	2	.383	.349
ompson, Bruce, Burlington*	.197	116	440	365	47	72	81	6	0	1	20	12	1	1	61	1	107	17	11	7	.222	.313
ompson, Karl, Wisconsin	.290	119	493	441	76	128	193	36	1	9	66	6	5	6	35	1	79	1	2	9	.438	.347
hoco, Luis, Wisconsin	.313	120	509	431	71	135	212	31	5	12	71	1	6	18	53	1	85	4	9	14	.492	.406
opin, Greg, Michigan*	.271	93	257	229	29	62	97	12	1	7	31	3	5	4	16	0	62	1	0	2	.424	.323
pham, Ryan, So. Bend*	.232	114	456	392	50	91	137	17	7	5	39	5	3	3	53	0	106	18	9	4	.349	.326
pping, Dan, Burlington	.229	45	151	131	16	30	46	4	0	4	22	1	0	0	19	0	24	0	1	3	.351	.327
rrealba, Yorvit, Burlington	.000	1	4	4	0	0	0	0	0	0	0	0	0	0	0	0	1	0	0	1	.000	.000
tman, Jason, Clinton	.215	39	149	121	15	26	37	7	2	0	11	1	0	5	22	0	17	2	1	1	.306	.358
eanor, Matt, Lansing	.260	119	439	384	56	100	140	18	2	6	33	6	1	13	35	1	63	5	3	9	.365	.342
uby, Chris, Quad City	.251	109	403	362	45	91	136	15	3	8	37	6	5	2	28	1	74	6	10	8	.376	.305
rlais, John, Rockford*	.154	11	31	26	2	4	5	1	0	0	2	0	1	0	4	0	9	0	0	1	.192	.258
ldez, Mario, South Bend*	.376	61	249	202	46	76	125	19	0	10	43	0	2	6	36	2	42	2	4	3	.619	.480
lenti, Jon, West Michigan	.260	125	504	462	46	120	180	19	4	11	57	1	3	5	33	0	91	5	3	12	.390	.314
llone, Gar, Cedar Rapids†	.225	66	187	151	21	34	41	4	0	1	14	2	1	3	30	0	55	2	5	2	.272	.362
anderGriend, Jon, C. Rapids*	.263	122	501	434	72	114	207	32	2	19	64	0	3	13	51	3	142	10	5	2	.477	.355
zquez, Ramon, Wisconsin*	.300	3	12	10	1	3	4	1	0	0	1	0	0	0	2	0	2	0	0	1	.400	.417
ckers, Randy, Wisconsin	.249	51	202	181	27	45	78	12	0	7	31	2	3	4	12	0	63	1	4	5	.431	.305
eira, Scott, Rockford	.324	134	563	442	81	143	205	30	4	8	81	2	9	26	84	7	89	9	8	6	.464	.451
alker, Dane, W. Mich.*	.277	127	603	477	97	132	184	25	3	7	47	3	3	3	112	2	75	14	10	11	.386	.415
atkins, Sean, Clinton*	.200	16	64	55	7	11	17	3	0	1	6	0	0	0	9	0	17	0	0	2	.309	.313
atson, John, Burlington	.261	81	366	318	46	83	102	15	2	0	25	4	3	10	31	0	38	23	5	7	.321	.343
atson, Kevin, Burlington	.115	32	90	78	8	9	27	1	1	5	11	2	0	0	10	0	34	0	0	3	.346	.216
eaver, Terry, Burlington	.208	72	252	216	25	45	65	13	2	1	20	4	3	0	29	0	49	2	4	6	.301	.298
hite, Derrick, W. Michigan	.262	73	317	263	49	69	116	17	0	10	43	0	4	6	44	2	63	12	3	7	.441	.375
hite, Walter, Kane County	.175	95	353	308	26	54	78	15	3	1	24	5	1	4	35	0	90	1	4	3	.253	.267
ilders, Paul, Peoria	.230	25	76	61	10	14	21	4	0	1	9	1	1	1	12	0	13	0	0	3	.344	.360
lhelm, Brent, South Bend	.242	107	450	380	55	92	129	21	2	4	38	3	4	6	57	4	55	8	8	8	.339	.347
nn, Randy, Kane County	.270	130	581	514	90	139	161	16	3	0	35	11	1	8	47	0	115	30	18	3	.313	.340
oolf, Jason, Peoria†	.257	108	425	362	68	93	124	12	8	1	27	3	1	2	57	1	87	28	12	3	.343	.360
ulfert, Mark, Clinton	.251	127	521	450	66	113	197	24	6	16	65	0	1	1	69	3	111	26	9	10	.438	.351
visler, Josh, Beloit	.074	8	32	27	3	2	2	0	0	0	1	0	0	0	5	0	9	0	0	1	.074	.219

GRAND SLAMS: Amerson, Larry R. Barnes, R. Johnson, Kane, Pierzynski, VanderGriend, 2 each; Amado, Booty, Coffee, Dishington, Elliott, Filchner, Fraser, Haas, Herdn... Joseph, Liefer, Lopiccolo, McHugh, Medrano, Noriega, Ortiz, Paez, Paulino, Porter, Quinn, H. Ramirez, Robles, Schroeder, Sheffer, S. Smith, Valdez. Walker, K. Watson, 1 ea...

AWARDED FIRST BASE ON CATCHER'S INTERFFERENCE: Catlett 7 (Chevalier, Medrano, O'Neal, Pierzynski, Schwenke, K. Thompson, Topping); D. Walker 5 (Graves. Johnson, Kuilan, O'Neal, K. Thompson); Baughman 3 (R. Castro, R. Hernandez, Rondon); Valdez 3 (Chevalier, R. Hernandez, Rondon); Dean 2 (Pierzynski 2); Escando (Anderson, R. Castro); Chamblee (Ryder); DaVanon (O'Neal); R. Johnson (Anderson); Kotsay (Medrano); Lariviere (O'Neal); Lopiccolo (Pierzynski); Ortega (McClendon); Pa (R. Hernandez); Simmons (R. Hernandez); Schroeder (O'Neal); R. Smith (Graves).

1996 PITCHING

TEAM

Team	W	L	Pct.	ERA	G	CG	ShO	Sv.	IP	H	TBF	R	ER	HR	SH	SF	HB	BB	IBB	SO	WP	B
Peoria	79	57	.581	3.30	136	7	13	31	1165.0	991	4901	533	427	56	36	32	52	445	10	1065	57	1
West Michigan	77	61	.558	3.42	138	0	9	45	1219.0	1121	5245	561	463	62	45	44	43	495	31	1090	52	2
Kane County	65	68	.489	3.65	133	12	7	30	1148.2	1099	4985	596	466	49	46	36	91	459	14	941	91	1
Beloit	69	67	.507	3.75	136	13	11	29	1178.2	1147	5145	610	491	70	52	42	47	538	31	1000	93	2
Burlington	65	73	.471	3.81	138	5	9	42	1202.2	1086	5104	604	509	112	49	42	48	499	8	982	86	1
Quad City	70	61	.534	3.87	131	3	5	36	1147.1	1068	4983	599	493	74	32	43	83	502	12	948	85	2
South Bend	54	82	.397	3.92	136	7	2	22	1176.2	1174	5119	665	512	78	46	45	56	426	0	825	72	2
Rockford	70	65	.519	4.02	135	11	4	31	1149.0	1170	5071	663	513	78	35	42	75	457	13	886	80	2
Fort Wayne	69	67	.507	4.09	136	7	8	28	1187.0	1224	5165	661	539	67	38	56	50	440	9	969	75	1
Clinton	64	70	.478	4.11	134	6	7	34	1143.2	1095	5061	643	522	66	40	49	78	536	13	1013	116	1
Cedar Rapids	63	72	.467	4.14	135	7	4	29	1172.0	1123	5188	657	539	94	41	47	87	610	33	855	103	2
Michigan	60	78	.435	4.16	138	13	4	26	1211.0	1147	5315	675	560	75	40	38	71	573	26	901	121	1
Lansing	68	71	.489	4.28	139	3	6	27	1239.1	1336	5490	739	589	82	64	30	89	521	9	806	110	2
Wisconsin	77	58	.570	4.61	135	9	4	33	1172.2	1135	5302	709	601	62	39	34	66	673	31	974	120	2

INDIVIDUAL

TOP QUALIFIERS FOR EARNED-RUN AVERAGE TITLE

Minimum 112 innings. *Lefthanded pitcher.

Pitcher, Team	W	L	Pct.	ERA	G	GS	CG	ShO	GF	Sv.	IP	H	TBF	R	ER	HR	SH	SF	HB	BB	IBB	SO	WP
Reames, Britt, Peoria	15	7	.682	1.90	25	25	2	1	0	0	161.0	97	620	43	34	5	3	2	4	41	0	167	7
Politte, Cliff, Peoria	14	6	.700	2.59	25	25	0	0	0	0	149.2	108	603	50	43	8	3	2	7	47	0	151	5
Mlodik, Kevin, West Michigan	8	6	.571	2.77	31	22	0	0	6	1	136.1	118	581	53	42	3	4	6	5	53	1	135	5
Jimenez, Jose, Peoria	12	9	.571	2.92	28	27	3	1	0	0	172.1	158	720	75	56	6	5	6	9	53	0	129	8
Pena, Juan, Michigan	12	10	.545	2.97	26	26	4	0	0	0	187.2	149	743	70	62	16	9	5	10	34	2	156	10
Thorn, Todd, Lansing*	11	5	.688	3.11	27	27	2	0	0	0	170.2	161	695	70	59	13	6	4	5	34	0	107	8
Sikorski, Brian, Quad City	11	8	.579	3.13	26	25	1	0	0	0	166.2	140	704	79	58	12	4	7	10	70	2	150	7
Mull, Blaine, Lansing	15	8	.652	3.25	28	28	1	0	0	0	174.2	186	734	91	63	9	7	5	9	40	0	114	6
Hurtado, Victor, Kane County	15	7	.682	3.27	27	27	5	0	0	0	176.0	167	748	79	64	10	5	4	19	56	0	126	14
O'Malley, Paul, Quad City	11	9	.550	3.44	26	26	1	0	0	0	178.0	173	753	80	66	10	7	9	11	51	0	111	15
Vardijan, Daniel, Kane County	7	7	.500	3.35	24	24	2	1	0	0	145.0	128	603	71	54	5	5	2	16	55	4	92	13
Robbins, Michael, Lansing*	9	6	.600	3.40	25	15	0	0	3	0	116.1	122	497	56	44	5	7	5	6	37	1	76	6
Kolb, Brandon, Clinton	16	9	.640	3.42	27	27	3	0	0	0	181.1	170	776	84	69	7	6	7	8	76	1	138	19
Yoder, Jeff, Rockford	12	5	.706	3.44	25	24	2	0	0	0	154.1	139	640	70	59	10	2	4	10	48	1	124	12
Baez, Benito, West Michigan*	8	4	.667	3.47	32	20	0	0	4	4	129.2	123	557	60	50	6	5	6	2	52	1	92	4

DEPARTMENTAL LEADERS: W—Kolb, 16; L—Getz, 14; Pct.—Fieldbinder, .818; G—Hernandez, 61; GS—Rivette, Bishop, 29 each; CG—Castillo, Delossan... Hurtado, 5 each; ShO—Several players tied at 1; GF—Hernandez, 58; Sv.—Hernandez, 35; IP—Pena, 187.2; H—Yennaco, 195; TBF—Kolb, 776; R—W. Smith, 1... ER—Yennaco, 87; HR—Barcelo, 19; SH—Duncan, 10; SF—Camp, O'Malley, Castillo, 9 each; HB—S. DeWitt, Hurtado, 19 each; BB—Vanhof, 105; IBB—Cana, Scut... 6 each; SO—Reames, 167; WP—Yennaco, Vanhof, 20 each; Bk.—Sikorski, 9.

ALL PITCHERS

*Lefthanded pitcher.

Pitcher, Team	W	L	Pct.	ERA	G	GS	CG	ShO	GF	Sv.	IP	H	TBF	R	ER	HR	SH	SF	HB	BB	IBB	SO	WP
Abbott, Todd, West Michigan	11	7	.611	3.98	32	13	0	0	4	1	131.0	135	560	66	58	8	2	7	5	41	1	104	4
Adam, Justin, Lansing	3	7	.300	5.18	46	0	0	0	18	1	80.0	84	371	59	46	7	4	2	3	58	0	61	14
Adams, Juan, Quad City	0	0	.000	0.00	1	0	0	0	1	0	1.0	0	3	0	0	0	0	0	0	0	0	1	0
Agosto, Stevenson, Cedr Rpds*	8	10	.444	4.42	28	28	1	0	0	0	156.2	143	680	91	77	12	8	6	7	86	2	121	8
Almanza, Armando, Peoria*	8	6	.571	2.76	52	1	0	0	18	0	62.0	50	271	27	19	2	3	2	2	32	5	67	8
Alvarez, Juan, Cedar Rapids*	1	2	.333	3.40	40	0	0	0	14	3	53.0	50	238	25	20	0	3	1	7	30	1	53	4
Ames, Skip, Rockford	3	3	.500	5.95	22	0	0	0	17	9	19.2	25	104	16	13	1	2	1	2	17	0	18	2
Arias, Wagner, Beloit	3	4	.429	2.74	21	5	0	0	6	2	69.0	52	276	26	21	2	2	3	3	24	1	58	8
Arrollado, Courtney, Lansing	0	0	.000	9.00	1	0	0	0	1	0	2.0	4	12	2	2	0	0	0	0	2	0	0	0
Avrard, Corey, Peoria	9	9	.357	4.24	21	21	2	0	0	0	110.1	105	489	73	52	6	6	2	8	58	0	103	5
Baez, Benito, West Michigan*	8	4	.667	3.47	32	20	0	0	4	4	129.2	123	557	60	50	6	5	6	2	52	1	92	4
Barcelo, Lorenzo, Burlington	12	10	.545	3.54	26	26	1	0	0	0	152.2	138	633	70	60	19	5	5	5	46	0	139	5
Barker, Richie, Rockford	1	1	.500	5.18	19	0	0	0	9	1	33.0	42	156	24	19	2	1	4	0	15	0	23	3
Barksdale, Joe, Michigan	2	5	.286	5.32	8	8	0	0	0	0	44.0	42	210	30	26	3	2	1	7	33	0	16	9
Barnes, Larry, Beloit	0	5	.000	7.02	9	9	0	0	0	0	33.1	30	163	30	26	1	0	3	3	34	1	34	12
Bartels, Todd, Fort Wayne	3	2	.400	4.10	11	10	0	0	0	0	52.2	51	220	29	24	5	0	2	2	11	0	34	9
Beirne, Kevin, South Bend	4	11	.267	4.15	26	25	1	0	0	0	145.1	153	627	85	67	5	5	5	9	60	0	110	12
Benes, Adam, Peoria	2	2	.500	3.74	43	0	0	0	15	0	65.0	58	278	31	27	4	2	0	2	28	0	64	2
Bennett, Tom, West Michigan	0	1	.000	3.92	6	5	0	0	0	0	20.2	17	96	11	9	1	0	1	2	18	0	17	0
Benny, Peter, Beloit	7	10	.412	3.79	26	26	2	0	0	0	156.2	136	674	80	66	11	4	2	6	87	2	150	11
Bermudez, Manuel, Burlington	10	9	.526	4.39	26	26	1	1	0	0	135.1	119	589	73	66	13	2	4	7	73	0	95	7

tcher, Team	W	L	Pct.	ERA	G	GS	CG	ShO	GF	Sv.	IP	H	TBF	R	ER	HR	SH	SF	HB	BB	IBB	SO	WP	Bk.
rnal, Manuel, Lansing	2	4	.333	4.55	34	6	0	0	7	2	95.0	123	417	55	48	7	6	2	3	16	0	41	2	1
rninger, Darren, Beloit	2	3	.400	5.40	41	0	0	0	22	5	61.2	69	278	48	37	7	3	4	2	28	1	39	5	1
sner, Roark, Rockford	0	0	.000	12.46	5	0	0	0	4	0	4.1	6	24	6	6	1	0	0	0	5	0	4	0	0
shop, Joshua, Beloit	12	9	.571	3.86	29	29	4	0	0	0	170.0	177	737	84	73	14	8	8	7	62	3	111	11	1
anco, Alberto, Quad City*	2	2	.500	3.47	11	11	0	0	0	0	46.2	42	198	25	18	3	0	2	3	15	0	58	3	0
asingim, Joseph, Burlington	1	4	.200	4.86	27	4	0	0	4	0	66.2	54	285	39	36	11	6	2	1	35	0	60	4	1
ggs, Robert, Fort Wayne	9	12	.429	4.02	28	27	1	1	1	0	150.0	153	660	81	67	8	6	7	13	64	0	134	4	0
gle, Sean, Rockford	0	0	.000	4.24	16	0	0	0	5	0	23.1	26	125	23	11	1	0	1	4	24	0	15	6	0
nilla, Denys, Wisconsin*	6	1	.857	2.19	45	0	0	0	14	4	70.0	56	292	21	17	1	1	1	0	25	2	62	4	0
ring, Richard, Lansing	0	0	.000	3.00	3	0	0	0	3	0	3.0	4	14	1	1	0	0	1	0	2	0	2	0	0
ester, Jason, Burlington*	10	9	.526	3.96	27	27	0	0	0	0	157.0	139	659	78	69	14	4	7	3	64	0	143	13	1
yant, Chris, Rockford*	4	7	.364	5.65	43	4	0	0	11	1	71.2	87	341	54	45	6	5	2	4	37	2	51	6	1
rgus, Travis, Kane County*	5	4	.556	1.78	30	7	1	0	11	4	96.1	80	404	29	19	1	4	3	5	39	1	111	9	1
sh, Craig, Michigan	1	1	.500	3.38	4	0	0	0	0	0	8.0	11	36	3	3	0	0	0	0	2	0	7	1	0
ssa, Todd, Clinton	1	0	1.000	1.30	32	0	0	0	31	18	34.2	22	140	7	5	0	1	0	3	7	0	50	1	0
teaux, Shane, South Bend	3	4	.429	3.23	25	0	0	0	11	2	39.0	37	178	21	14	0	1	3	2	15	0	33	4	1
mp, Jared, Beloit	3	5	.375	5.43	11	11	0	0	0	0	53.0	56	251	42	32	4	3	9	2	39	0	47	10	1
mpbell, Tim, Clinton	0	3	.000	3.13	42	0	0	0	21	3	63.1	44	260	27	22	4	5	1	4	18	3	67	6	0
mpusano, Carlos, Beloit	0	0	.000	3.86	2	0	0	0	2	0	2.1	3	11	1	1	0	1	0	0	1	0	3	1	1
na, Nelson, Beloit*	3	0	1.000	2.83	21	0	0	0	12	4	35.0	34	157	15	11	2	1	1	0	21	6	38	2	2
nnon, Kevan, Michigan*	2	6	.250	2.59	37	0	0	0	17	5	73.0	70	308	24	21	0	5	3	4	21	4	72	5	1
rmody, Brian, Clinton*	7	4	.636	3.52	13	13	1	0	0	0	76.2	79	325	42	30	4	5	4	1	22	1	46	4	4
stillo, Carlos, South Bend	9	9	.500	4.05	20	19	5	0	1	0	133.1	131	557	74	60	12	3	9	5	29	0	128	9	6
stro, Antonio, Kane County	6	7	.462	3.53	39	0	0	0	16	7	66.1	55	287	38	26	2	4	3	1	31	0	63	7	3
amblee, James, Michigan	0	0	.000	0.00	1	0	0	0	1	0	0.2	0	3	0	0	0	0	0	0	0	0	0	0	0
antres, Carlos, South Bend	4	5	.444	3.60	10	10	1	0	0	0	65.0	61	274	31	26	3	1	2	2	19	0	41	3	1
apman, Walker, Fort Wayne	6	8	.429	4.73	19	18	1	0	0	0	97.0	107	436	61	51	3	1	4	4	41	0	61	6	1
itron, Jose, Cedar Rapids	10	8	.556	3.88	28	28	1	0	0	0	178.2	192	754	88	77	15	5	7	7	41	2	127	6	3
rk, Chris, Clinton	3	8	.273	5.05	24	11	0	0	7	1	82.0	96	385	58	46	5	4	3	7	51	1	74	9	1
rk, Kevin, Michigan	0	0	.000	9.00	1	0	0	0	1	0	1.0	1	5	1	1	0	0	0	0	1	0	1	0	0
yton, Craig, Clinton	2	1	.667	1.45	27	0	0	0	18	9	37.1	27	154	10	6	1	0	1	3	8	0	29	3	0
ment, Matt, Clinton	8	3	.727	2.80	16	16	1	1	0	0	96.1	66	410	31	30	3	1	3	9	52	0	109	15	0
e, Keith, Cedar Rapids	0	1	.000	10.80	6	0	0	0	3	0	6.2	9	43	10	8	0	2	2	2	9	3	5	0	0
llett, Andy, Wisconsin	2	2	.500	3.65	22	0	0	0	8	0	37.0	32	169	18	15	2	2	2	5	23	1	31	6	1
llins, Edward, Beloit	6	5	.545	4.70	38	3	0	0	16	3	67.0	79	315	44	35	1	4	1	7	37	4	50	7	0
awford, Paxton, Michigan	6	11	.353	3.58	22	22	1	0	0	0	128.1	120	548	62	51	5	2	5	8	42	1	105	8	1
wsey, Jason, Beloit*	6	4	.600	1.51	31	14	1	1	4	2	101.1	71	411	21	17	4	4	0	1	42	0	119	2	1
LaCruz, Fernando, Cdr Rpds	0	5	.000	8.00	6	6	0	0	0	0	27.0	35	139	25	24	1	1	3	7	21	0	18	4	3
ossantos, Valerio, Beloit*	10	8	.556	3.55	33	23	5	1	10	4	164.2	164	715	83	65	11	8	5	3	59	4	137	8	3
mpster, Ryan, Kane County	2	1	.667	2.73	4	4	1	1	0	0	26.1	18	109	10	8	0	1	0	1	18	0	16	2	0
srosiers, Erik, South Bend	3	5	.375	4.72	14	12	0	0	2	1	68.2	68	293	41	36	8	1	0	2	19	0	39	1	1
Witt, Chris, Rockford	6	4	.600	4.00	15	13	0	0	0	0	81.0	88	357	48	36	3	3	4	6	21	1	45	4	3
Witt, Scott, Kane County*	10	11	.476	4.72	27	27	1	1	0	0	148.2	151	667	96	78	8	5	4	19	59	0	119	2	2
az, Jairo, Rockford	6	3	.667	3.16	25	11	0	0	6	0	88.1	80	363	33	31	6	2	2	6	26	0	84	1	5
nnelly, Robert, Peoria	2	2	.500	3.43	46	0	0	0	16	0	60.1	45	246	27	23	3	1	1	2	24	1	76	3	0
ncan, Sean, South Bend*	2	5	.286	3.38	43	0	0	0	16	3	56.0	43	238	29	21	3	10	1	2	23	0	54	5	0
vall, Michael, Kane County*	4	1	.800	2.06	41	0	0	0	28	8	48.0	43	210	20	11	0	2	0	0	21	2	46	3	0
ard, Tony, Kane County	0	0	.000	6.75	3	0	0	0	1	0	2.2	1	16	2	2	0	0	1	2	4	0	1	4	0
rada, Horacio, Beloit*	2	1	.667	1.23	17	0	0	0	9	1	29.1	21	113	8	4	2	2	0	0	11	1	34	5	1
ans, Mike, Kane County	0	0	.000	10.80	2	0	0	0	0	0	1.2	3	12	2	2	0	0	0	0	4	0	1	3	0
fan, David, Cedar Rapids	0	1	.000	2.35	5	0	0	0	4	1	7.2	8	37	9	2	0	0	1	1	6	0	6	2	0
nsworth, Kyle, Rockford	9	6	.600	3.70	20	20	1	0	0	0	112.0	122	495	62	46	7	2	4	9	35	0	82	8	1
rrell, Jim, Michigan	6	1	.857	2.45	7	7	2	0	0	0	44.0	39	185	15	12	2	1	0	1	17	1	32	1	0
ldbinder, Mick, Beloit	9	2	.818	3.39	12	12	1	0	0	0	77.0	74	312	33	29	2	1	2	1	18	2	66	5	1
eck, Ryan, South Bend	1	4	.200	3.63	19	2	0	0	12	3	34.2	27	142	16	14	2	2	2	4	11	0	20	0	0
deraro, Kevin, Peoria	1	0	1.000	3.97	32	3	0	0	5	0	56.2	54	245	25	25	3	3	2	1	26	1	41	5	1
rber, Joel, South Bend*	0	5	.000	5.10	14	7	0	0	4	0	47.2	60	224	40	27	6	3	5	2	15	0	27	1	6
rcia, Ariel, South Bend	6	10	.375	4.58	26	26	0	0	0	0	151.1	159	659	96	77	11	5	6	7	48	0	76	5	3
rcia, Freddy, Quad City	5	4	.556	3.12	13	13	0	0	0	0	60.2	57	265	27	21	3	1	1	4	27	0	50	5	5
rcia, Rick, Kane County	0	4	.000	6.28	32	2	0	0	9	0	57.1	63	273	48	40	3	3	4	7	41	1	47	6	0
rrett, Hal, Clinton	2	3	.400	4.53	25	3	0	0	11	1	49.2	45	229	28	25	4	2	2	5	31	2	60	3	0
tz, Rod, Kane County	3	14	.176	5.01	25	25	1	0	0	0	120.1	146	546	79	67	8	4	3	6	41	0	85	9	4
ian, Charlie, Fort Wayne	0	0	.000	3.18	20	0	0	0	19	5	22.2	24	91	9	8	3	0	1	2	5	1	14	1	0
uber, Keith, Peoria	3	3	.500	3.09	54	0	0	0	36	14	64.0	54	276	31	22	2	2	5	1	26	2	80	2	1
oda, David, Beloit*	1	3	.250	10.43	4	4	0	0	0	0	14.2	24	81	21	17	1	0	1	2	11	0	6	0	3
uld, Clint, Wisconsin	1	0	1.000	3.48	6	0	0	0	3	1	10.1	8	44	4	4	0	1	1	0	5	0	10	3	1
enert, Geoff, Cedar Rapids	3	7	.300	5.88	14	12	1	0	1	0	67.1	73	304	52	44	10	0	3	6	30	0	57	6	0
eve, Tim, Lansing	0	1	.000	3.00	3	0	0	0	3	0	3.0	0	15	1	1	0	1	0	0	6	1	5	1	0
ote, Jason, Burlington	11	9	.550	4.38	28	26	1	1	0	0	139.2	146	604	80	68	18	3	5	0	55	0	103	11	3
yboski, Kevin, Wisconsin	10	5	.667	4.74	32	21	3	0	5	1	138.2	146	630	90	73	7	9	6	12	62	2	100	12	0
nderson, Mike, Quad City	4	4	.500	5.15	34	7	0	0	11	3	80.1	80	380	60	46	7	5	3	5	64	0	59	6	0
nther, Kevin, West Michigan	5	5	.500	2.92	43	0	0	0	21	6	95.2	83	398	37	31	6	7	2	1	25	4	90	3	0
zman, Domingo, Clinton	0	5	.000	12.63	6	5	0	0	1	0	20.2	32	112	33	29	2	0	1	2	19	0	18	5	0
gler, Phil, Fort Wayne	4	3	.571	5.27	15	13	0	0	0	0	68.1	80	305	42	40	3	1	3	6	25	0	35	1	3
mmack, Brandon, Rockford	2	3	.400	2.27	30	0	0	0	28	13	31.2	22	140	13	8	0	2	0	1	19	1	45	1	0
mmons, Matt, Rockford	1	3	.250	6.12	5	5	0	0	0	0	25.0	24	105	19	17	3	1	0	3	8	1	22	3	0
rris, Jeff, Fort Wayne	8	3	.727	3.11	42	0	0	0	15	3	89.2	90	387	35	31	4	3	8	4	33	1	85	10	1
sselhoff, Derek, South Bend	6	3	.667	3.02	35	0	0	0	29	10	47.2	46	205	18	16	4	4	1	2	17	0	39	5	0
nderson, Juan, Cedar Rapids	3	0	1.000	3.15	19	0	0	0	9	2	34.1	25	150	14	12	3	1	2	4	19	2	22	3	1
nderson, Kenny, Clinton	0	3	.000	2.33	7	7	0	0	0	0	27.0	30	116	13	7	0	1	1	2	5	0	26	5	0
manson, Mike, Cedar Rpds	0	0	.000	5.74	4	3	0	0	0	0	15.2	15	66	11	10	2	0	0	1	9	0	12	3	0
rnandez, Santos, Burlington	3	3	.500	1.89	61	0	0	0	58	35	66.2	39	249	15	14	4	3	1	2	13	0	79	7	1
, Chris, Quad City	3	5	.375	6.24	18	5	0	0	4	0	49.0	48	212	39	34	7	3	1	8	15	0	39	1	2

Pitcher, Team	W	L	Pct.	ERA	G	GS	CG	ShO	GF	Sv.	IP	H	TBF	R	ER	HR	SH	SF	HB	BB	IBB	SO	WP	B
Hill, Jason, Cedar Rapids*	2	2	.500	3.09	18	6	0	0	2	1	43.2	38	197	19	15	2	3	1	5	31	1	26	4	
Hodges, Kevin, Lansing	1	2	.333	4.66	9	9	0	0	0	0	48.1	47	208	32	25	3	2	1	6	19	0	23	3	
Hooten, David, Fort Wayne	4	1	.800	2.41	21	0	0	0	14	2	37.1	30	155	11	10	0	2	4	2	13	1	39	3	
Housley, Adam, Beloit	2	4	.333	2.99	34	0	0	0	18	4	69.1	74	315	33	23	5	7	2	9	28	5	49	1	
Hurtado, Victor, Kane County	15	7	.682	3.27	27	27	5	0	0	0	176.0	167	748	79	64	10	5	4	19	56	0	126	14	
Hutzler, Jeff, Burlington	8	7	.533	3.81	25	25	2	0	0	0	139.1	133	580	71	59	7	2	7	5	33	0	79	11	
Iddon, Brent, Wisconsin	11	4	.733	2.78	50	0	0	0	22	11	97.0	82	409	32	30	4	6	4	6	41	3	114	3	
Jacobs, Russell, Wisconsin	4	4	.500	5.27	24	10	0	0	4	2	68.1	67	313	48	40	2	2	3	2	53	0	63	13	
Jimenez, Jose, Peoria	12	9	.571	2.92	28	27	3	1	0	0	172.1	158	720	75	56	6	5	6	9	53	0	129	8	
Jones, Scott, Michigan	0	3	.000	5.44	48	0	0	0	42	18	44.2	32	219	33	27	3	3	3	5	45	2	41	14	
Kast, Nick, Peoria*	0	1	.000	17.36	5	0	0	0	2	0	4.2	6	28	11	9	0	0	0	2	8	0	8	0	
Kaysner, Brent, Lansing	3	4	.400	5.08	38	0	0	0	19	0	44.1	38	234	34	25	3	1	0	13	57	0	39	14	
Kazmirski, Robert, W Michigan	3	5	.375	2.68	51	0	0	0	48	28	53.2	45	234	19	16	2	6	1	1	28	5	37	3	
Keith, Jeff, Burlington*	1	2	.333	3.78	35	0	0	0	19	1	52.1	45	239	32	22	5	5	2	5	40	0	41	2	
Key, Scott, Lansing	1	5	.167	5.40	42	0	0	0	22	5	61.2	51	285	45	37	4	4	1	13	46	4	60	14	
Knoll, Brian, Burlington	3	8	.273	3.65	52	0	0	0	16	1	79.0	76	342	43	32	5	6	2	4	34	2	56	4	
Kolb, Brandon, Clinton	16	9	.640	3.42	27	27	3	0	0	0	181.1	170	776	84	69	7	6	7	8	76	1	138	19	
Kown, John, Peoria	4	9	.692	3.09	26	11	0	0	5	0	78.2	80	329	32	27	2	1	3	0	19	0	46	1	
Kraus, Tim, South Bend	3	4	.429	2.67	35	5	0	0	13	0	81.0	82	355	42	24	4	4	2	2	31	0	48	1	
Kruse, Kelly, South Bend	1	2	.333	4.89	26	0	0	0	11	2	35.0	36	163	21	19	2	2	2	6	20	0	16	1	
Kurtz, Danny, Wisconsin	2	5	.286	8.10	38	4	0	0	18	0	53.1	51	289	51	48	1	1	1	11	74	3	37	15	
Lake, Kevin, Burlington*	3	7	.300	4.45	43	4	0	0	11	0	97.0	107	421	57	48	11	5	4	5	38	2	85	11	
LaRosa, Tom, Fort Wayne*	7	3	.700	3.53	15	13	2	0	0	0	89.1	77	367	46	35	7	1	2	4	33	0	90	7	
Leach, Jarman, Clinton*	1	1	.500	4.97	10	0	0	0	3	0	12.2	17	61	8	7	1	0	0	1	6	0	3	5	
Lloyd, John, Cedar Rapids	8	7	.533	3.97	27	17	1	1	3	1	99.2	98	445	62	44	13	1	4	6	58	1	63	11	
Loiz, Miguel, Quad City	8	6	.571	4.93	28	14	1	0	7	1	115.0	121	508	75	63	8	0	5	5	53	0	75	11	
Lopez, Orlando, Rockford*	0	0	.000	10.80	1	0	0	0	0	0	1.2	6	12	5	2	0	0	0	0	0	0	1	1	
Lynch, Jim, Quad City	1	1	.500	4.01	31	1	0	0	15	1	60.2	51	276	28	27	3	1	0	4	50	0	51	7	
Mahaffey, Alan, Fort Wayne*	7	10	.412	4.84	30	19	2	0	1	0	126.1	139	545	84	68	13	8	6	3	35	1	75	4	
Markey, Barry, Rockford	6	2	.750	3.15	15	13	2	1	0	0	97.0	97	403	43	34	8	4	3	7	16	0	39	3	
Marshall, Gary, Rockford*	4	1	.800	3.33	50	0	0	0	18	2	46.0	39	192	20	17	3	2	6	0	19	3	35	1	
Marte, Damaso, Wisconsin*	8	6	.571	4.49	26	26	2	1	0	0	142.1	134	626	82	71	8	1	3	6	75	5	115	4	
Martin, Mike, Clinton	0	0	.000	9.00	1	0	0	0	1	0	1.0	3	6	1	1	0	0	0	0	0	0	1	0	
Martinez, Javier, Rockford	4	3	.571	3.36	10	10	3	0	0	0	59.0	49	250	26	22	5	2	2	1	30	0	53	9	
Martinez, Uriel, Clinton	1	1	.000	13.50	1	0	0	0	0	0	2.0	3	12	4	3	0	0	1	0	3	0	1	2	
Matos, Luis, Lansing	1	1	.500	6.35	8	0	0	0	2	0	17.0	23	81	13	12	2	1	0	0	9	0	10	7	
Mayer, Aaron, Cedar Rapids	1	4	.200	4.13	18	0	0	0	8	4	48.0	53	210	28	22	2	4	3	20	2	31	7	
McBride, Rodney, Fort Wayne	0	5	.000	8.08	16	10	0	0	3	0	45.2	69	235	47	41	5	1	2	3	24	0	44	2	
McKenzie, Jason, Fort Wayne	1	1	.500	5.17	17	0	0	0	2	0	38.1	38	165	24	22	2	1	0	14	1	29	2	
McLaughlin, Denis, Michigan	2	4	.333	6.25	39	0	0	0	22	0	59.0	59	280	47	41	6	2	0	3	43	5	45	9	
McMullen, Mike, Burlington	0	2	.000	2.88	38	0	0	0	7	0	56.1	47	241	22	18	3	4	2	5	28	0	33	5	
Mlodik, Kevin, West Michigan	8	6	.571	2.77	31	22	0	0	6	1	136.1	118	581	53	42	3	4	6	5	53	1	135	5	
Montgomery, Greg, Peoria	0	0	.000	2.75	14	0	0	0	3	0	19.2	11	79	6	6	0	2	2	1	9	0	22	1	
Moreno, Juan, West Michigan*	4	6	.400	4.37	38	11	0	0	5	0	107.0	98	475	60	52	6	6	6	2	69	5	97	6	
Morgan, Steve, Michigan*	0	1	.000	5.87	5	1	0	0	1	0	15.1	16	72	13	10	1	1	0	2	12	0	3	0	
Morrison, Chris, W Michigan	5	5	.500	4.32	40	0	0	0	20	1	58.1	64	262	38	28	7	5	4	1	20	4	51	1	
Mosley, Tim, Rockford	3	4	.429	5.02	37	0	0	0	5	1	57.1	74	282	47	32	1	1	3	6	32	1	36	6	
Mull, Blaine, Lansing	15	8	.652	3.25	28	28	1	0	0	0	174.2	186	734	91	63	9	7	5	9	40	0	114	6	
Nelson, Chris, West Michigan	3	1	.750	2.42	16	9	0	0	3	1	70.2	53	275	19	19	3	3	1	1	20	0	79	4	
Newman, Eric, Clinton	5	7	.417	4.29	34	14	0	0	6	1	113.1	101	501	71	54	9	3	7	7	67	0	108	13	
Niedermaier, Brad, Fort Wayne	6	4	.600	3.25	32	3	0	0	14	2	69.1	64	295	39	25	3	4	0	29	2	72	11	
Noffke, Andrew, Michigan	5	3	.625	4.86	28	7	0	0	6	3	74.0	74	347	51	40	2	1	5	7	57	1	34	7	
Olsen, Jason, South Bend	4	1	.800	1.75	9	9	0	0	0	0	56.2	39	220	16	11	3	2	1	2	13	0	55	3	
O'Malley, Paul, Quad City	11	9	.550	3.34	26	26	1	0	0	0	178.0	173	753	80	66	10	7	9	11	51	0	111	15	
O'Quinn, James, Cedar Rpds*	2	4	.333	5.66	41	0	0	0	9	0	55.2	52	271	40	35	5	4	2	6	41	3	58	18	
Pailthorpe, Bob, Kane County	4	5	.444	3.48	43	0	0	0	18	2	72.1	76	321	36	28	2	2	3	2	30	3	74	7	
Paredes, Carlos, Lansing	7	8	.467	4.85	23	23	0	0	0	0	118.2	138	549	75	64	2	5	1	7	69	0	72	15	
Parent, Gerald, Beloit	0	0	.000	5.68	3	0	0	0	1	0	6.1	7	27	4	4	0	0	0	0	3	0	1	1	
Pavlovich, Tony, Beloit	2	4	.400	3.21	28	0	0	0	15	4	33.2	26	141	12	12	1	4	0	0	15	1	31	2	
Pena, Juan, Michigan	12	10	.545	2.97	26	26	4	0	0	0	187.2	149	743	70	62	16	9	5	10	34	2	156	10	
Peters, Tim, Fort Wayne*	2	0	1.000	1.31	13	0	0	0	6	1	20.2	13	75	5	3	1	1	1	4	0	12	0	
Peterson, Jayson, Rockford	4	7	.364	3.45	15	15	2	1	0	0	94.0	82	406	50	36	8	0	2	4	39	0	87	4	
Petroff, Daniel, Cedar Rapids	2	3	.400	3.81	9	9	2	0	0	0	49.2	44	227	34	21	3	2	3	4	34	0	29	5	
Politte, Cliff, Peoria	14	6	.700	2.59	25	25	0	0	0	0	149.2	108	603	50	43	8	3	2	7	47	0	151	5	
Portillo, Alex, South Bend*	0	0	.000	2.89	7	0	0	0	7	0	9.1	9	39	4	3	0	0	0	1	0	9	1	
Price, Jamey, West Michigan	6	1	.857	1.71	20	16	0	0	1	0	89.1	80	360	22	17	1	0	2	1	19	1	88	2	
Quirk, John, South Bend*	0	0	.000	4.26	5	0	0	0	3	0	6.1	8	33	3	3	0	1	0	7	0	1	1	
Randolph, Edward, Wisconsin	0	0	.000	9.00	1	0	0	0	1	0	1.0	1	6	1	1	0	0	0	2	0	1	0	
Rath, Fred, Fort Wayne	1	2	.333	1.51	32	0	0	0	29	14	41.2	26	163	12	7	1	0	2	0	10	0	63	3	
Rathmell, Lance, Michigan	0	0	.000	0.00	1	0	0	0	1	0	1.0	1	7	4	0	1	0	0	1	0	1	0	
Reames, Britt, Peoria	15	7	.682	1.90	25	25	2	1	0	0	161.0	97	603	43	34	5	3	2	4	41	0	167	7	
Remington, Jake, Clinton	6	7	.462	5.19	27	7	1	0	7	0	85.0	98	381	60	49	3	4	2	4	25	3	59	8	
Reyes, Alberto, Beloit	1	0	1.000	1.83	13	0	0	0	4	0	19.2	17	81	7	4	1	0	0	6	0	22	1	
Richardson, Kasey, Ft Wayne*	6	8	.429	3.47	30	13	1	0	7	1	111.2	113	481	56	43	5	5	5	39	1	81	12	
Ricketts, Chad, Rockford	8	3	.273	5.03	37	9	0	0	17	4	87.2	89	389	60	49	8	5	2	7	29	2	70	5	
Ritter, Jason, Lansing	0	0	.000	9.53	13	0	0	0	8	0	17.0	35	95	24	18	4	0	0	10	0	8	0	
Rivera, Wilfredo, Michigan	1	4	.200	4.86	16	5	0	0	3	0	46.1	42	213	27	25	4	2	1	2	36	0	28	7	
Rivette, Scott, West Michigan	8	9	.471	3.52	32	29	0	0	1	1	153.1	145	667	80	60	7	2	3	12	51	0	142	9	
Robbins, Michael, Lansing*	9	6	.600	3.40	25	15	0	0	3	0	116.1	122	497	56	44	5	7	5	6	37	1	76	6	
Roettgen, Mark, Clinton	2	1	.667	5.13	6	6	0	0	0	0	26.1	27	127	22	15	5	1	2	1	24	0	18	6	
Romboli, Curtis, Michigan*	3	5	.375	4.22	41	2	0	0	11	0	79.0	78	351	43	37	4	2	3	2	45	3	75	12	
Root, Derek, Quad City*	5	3	.625	3.00	40	2	0	0	22	7	63.0	55	272	25	21	1	4	4	26	4	47	6	
Runyan, Sean, Quad City*	9	4	.692	3.88	29	17	0	0	3	1	132.1	128	551	61	57	10	1	5	14	30	0	104	4	

– 504 –

Pitcher, Team	W	L	Pct.	ERA	G	GS	CG	ShO	GF	Sv.	IP	H	TBF	R	ER	HR	SH	SF	HB	BB	IBB	SO	WP	Bk.
ak, Jim, Clinton	3	4	.429	3.56	21	7	0	0	6	0	65.2	46	291	31	26	2	4	2	4	45	1	72	4	0
anders, Allen, Lansing	3	0	1.000	4.31	5	5	0	0	0	0	31.1	38	130	18	15	3	2	0	3	2	0	5	0	0
anders, Craig, Lansing	2	1	.667	4.80	8	0	0	0	0	0	15.0	10	71	13	8	0	1	1	3	17	0	15	3	1
antiago, Jose, Lansing	7	6	.538	2.57	54	0	0	0	46	19	77.0	78	331	34	22	4	7	1	5	21	3	55	3	1
antoro, Gary, Kane County	1	2	.333	2.76	31	0	0	0	29	9	32.2	30	137	13	10	0	2	5	2	12	2	35	2	0
auve, Jeff, Michigan	0	3	.000	4.09	36	0	0	0	17	0	61.2	51	258	34	28	4	4	0	2	26	4	55	3	0
cheer, Greg, Wisconsin*	3	1	.750	6.79	35	0	0	0	14	0	54.1	60	258	43	41	3	2	1	4	33	1	55	2	0
cheffer, Aaron, Wisconsin	8	1	.889	3.72	45	1	0	0	28	14	67.2	55	292	35	28	5	2	2	3	34	4	89	16	5
cutero, Brian, Cedar Rapids	10	5	.667	3.27	53	0	0	0	21	3	88.0	74	366	38	32	9	3	3	3	43	6	52	5	0
ecoda, Jason, South Bend	6	12	.333	3.97	31	21	0	0	6	1	133.2	132	605	84	59	9	2	3	3	75	0	94	18	1
neffer, Chad, Wisconsin	0	0	.000	18.00	1	0	0	0	1	0	1.0	4	9	3	2	1	0	0	0	1	0	0	2	0
heppard, Greg, South Bend	0	0	.000	27.00	1	0	0	0	1	0	1.0	4	8	3	3	0	0	1	1	0	0	0	0	0
ck, Dave, Cedar Rapids	1	2	.333	2.00	26	0	0	0	21	0	27.0	27	124	10	6	1	2	1	6	13	4	19	5	0
korski, Brian, Quad City	11	8	.579	3.13	26	25	1	0	0	0	166.2	140	704	79	58	12	4	7	10	70	2	150	7	9
kuse, Nick, Cedar Rapids	5	6	.455	4.09	18	16	0	0	1	0	94.2	77	415	47	43	10	2	0	5	58	2	50	7	4
mith, Andy, West Michigan	10	7	.588	4.58	37	13	0	0	3	0	116.0	112	527	71	59	8	3	4	7	68	5	94	8	1
mith, Eric, Quad City	6	3	.667	3.11	26	7	0	0	5	1	75.1	66	320	32	26	4	3	2	3	26	1	59	6	0
mith, Roy, Wisconsin	6	13	.316	5.12	27	27	0	0	0	0	146.0	164	679	113	83	9	6	4	8	73	3	99	11	2
oden, Chad, Wisconsin*	3	0	1.000	1.57	19	1	0	0	4	0	28.2	26	126	10	5	2	0	0	0	10	1	21	1	0
ear, Russell, Clinton	4	3	.571	6.10	11	10	0	0	0	1	51.2	60	257	43	35	3	1	4	4	42	0	44	8	1
iers, Corey, Fort Wayne*	0	1	.000	6.75	2	1	0	0	1	0	4.0	6	23	3	3	0	0	0	0	5	0	2	0	0
inelli, Michael, Michigan*	3	4	.429	5.25	11	11	0	0	0	0	60.0	58	275	43	35	1	3	1	4	39	1	41	9	0
littorff, Jamie, Fort Wayne	2	1	.667	4.23	8	6	0	0	1	0	27.2	28	124	14	13	2	0	1	1	12	0	21	3	0
einert, Rob, Beloit	0	0	.000	4.50	3	0	0	0	2	0	2.0	2	12	1	1	0	0	0	0	4	0	1	1	0
einke, Brock, Quad City	2	4	.333	6.10	24	3	0	0	2	0	48.2	53	235	38	33	3	1	3	4	36	4	55	5	0
ephens, Jason, Cedar Rapids	2	3	.400	3.46	21	0	0	0	20	6	26.0	27	118	12	10	1	1	2	3	14	2	19	2	0
ephens, Shannon, Kane Co	8	3	.727	2.88	17	17	1	1	0	0	106.1	92	432	41	34	8	6	1	7	25	0	85	7	1
oops, Jim, Burlington	3	3	.500	2.52	46	0	0	0	18	5	60.2	43	262	24	17	2	4	1	6	40	4	69	6	1
mter, Kevin, Cedar Rapids	0	0	.000	6.75	3	0	0	0	0	0	2.2	4	14	2	2	0	0	0	1	1	0	4	0	0
mmonds, Maika, Michigan*	0	0	.000	11.88	5	0	0	0	3	0	8.1	12	46	11	11	1	0	0	1	10	0	4	3	0
nksley, Scott, Fort Wayne	2	1	.667	3.14	16	0	0	0	6	0	28.2	24	124	16	10	0	3	0	0	8	0	25	1	0
orn, Todd, Lansing*	11	5	.688	3.11	27	27	2	0	0	0	170.2	161	695	70	59	13	6	4	5	34	0	107	8	0
urmond, Travis, Cedar Rpds	2	0	1.000	1.55	4	4	1	0	0	0	29.0	20	120	6	5	1	0	0	1	14	0	29	2	0
kell, Brian, Quad City	0	2	.000	9.72	7	0	0	0	3	0	8.1	17	45	10	9	0	0	0	1	5	0	4	2	0
erina, Tano, Beloit	0	0	.000	11.37	5	0	0	0	2	0	12.2	31	75	17	16	1	0	1	1	8	0	4	0	1
mon, Darrell, Michigan*	4	3	.571	5.21	7	7	0	0	0	0	38.0	38	170	25	22	4	0	1	2	17	1	27	2	0
pin, Greg, Michigan*	0	0	.000	0.00	1	0	0	0	0	0	1.0	1	4	0	0	0	0	0	0	0	0	0	0	0
res, Luis, Clinton	2	2	.500	5.08	35	1	0	0	16	1	67.1	76	306	46	38	9	2	4	5	26	1	65	5	3
wick, Tim, Wisconsin	5	5	.500	4.29	15	13	1	0	1	0	79.2	87	347	42	38	4	4	2	1	28	3	51	4	2
end, Patrick, Kane County	0	2	.000	4.44	27	0	0	0	4	0	48.2	46	220	32	24	2	2	4	3	23	1	40	3	2
be, Byron, Rockford	0	0	.000	2.45	9	1	0	0	4	0	14.2	10	64	4	4	0	0	2	1	12	1	22	2	0
nderbush, Matt, Ft Wayne*	2	1	.667	5.32	35	3	0	0	12	1	66.0	92	314	47	39	2	1	3	0	35	1	55	5	0
ahof, John, Wisconsin*	1	10	.091	7.88	27	19	0	0	3	0	93.2	104	477	89	82	10	1	2	3	105	1	58	20	3
dijan, Daniel, Kane County	7	7	.500	3.35	24	24	2	1	0	0	145.0	128	603	71	54	5	5	2	16	55	4	92	13	0
million, Grant, Cedar Rapids	3	2	.600	4.72	38	1	0	0	12	2	61.0	59	270	34	32	4	1	2	2	32	2	54	1	0
arreal, Modesto, Lansing	0	5	.000	6.21	15	5	0	0	2	0	42.0	54	191	37	29	6	2	3	4	12	0	29	2	0
egas, Ismael, Rockford	2	5	.286	5.13	10	10	1	0	0	0	47.1	63	223	40	27	5	1	2	3	25	0	30	3	1
a, Michael, South Bend	2	2	.500	4.57	34	0	0	0	13	0	65.0	79	299	41	33	6	1	1	5	23	0	35	2	0
gner, Matthew, Peoria	4	2	.667	5.88	16	12	0	0	1	0	64.1	80	295	47	42	4	2	1	6	26	0	38	2	3
ker, Kevin, Clinton	4	6	.400	4.74	13	13	0	0	0	0	76.0	80	339	46	40	9	1	6	9	33	0	43	1	0
lace, Jeff, Lansing*	4	9	.308	5.30	30	21	0	0	2	0	122.1	140	560	79	72	10	8	3	7	66	0	84	12	7
ter, Michael, Quad City	3	6	.333	2.04	52	0	0	0	48	21	61.2	37	261	20	14	3	2	1	7	34	1	85	7	1
bl, Clint, Peoria	1	2	.333	4.85	5	5	0	0	0	0	29.2	27	122	16	16	2	0	1	2	7	0	21	0	0
inberg, Todd, W Michigan*	6	4	.600	3.45	43	0	0	0	16	1	57.1	48	253	25	22	4	2	1	3	31	4	64	3	0
ch, Travis, Peoria	1	3	.250	3.12	34	0	0	0	28	17	40.1	31	173	17	14	4	2	1	4	17	1	34	2	2
mberly, Larry, Michigan*	3	4	.429	2.85	14	14	2	1	0	0	66.1	58	272	27	21	5	1	3	4	24	1	41	1	2
oten, Greg, Wisconsin	7	1	.875	2.47	13	13	3	1	0	0	83.2	58	336	27	23	3	1	2	5	29	0	68	4	1
nnaco, Jay, Michigan	10	10	.500	4.61	28	28	4	1	0	0	169.2	195	763	112	87	13	2	7	6	68	0	117	20	1
er, Jeff, Rockford	12	5	.706	3.44	25	24	2	0	0	0	154.1	139	640	70	59	10	2	2	6	68	1	124	12	5

COMBINATION SHUTOUTS: **Beloit (9)**—Benny-Collins-Estrada, Benny-Berninger, Bishop-Pavlovich-Estrada, Bishop-Estrada-Berninger, Dawsey-Arias, Dawsey-es-Delossantos, Arias-Delossantos, Bishop-Reyes-Pavlovich-Cana, Arias-Reyes. **Burlington (7)**—Barcelo-Lake-Stoops, Grote-Knoll-Hernandez, Brester-Knoll-nandez, Lake-Hernandez, Barcelo-McMullen-Hernandez, Hutzler-Hernandez, Bermudez-Lake. **Cedar Rapids (3)**—Lloyd-Alvarez-Sick, Clintron-Vermillion-Sick, Lloyd-derson-Mayer. **Clinton (6)**—Clement-Campbell-Bussa, Kolb-Bussa, Carmody-Sak-Bussa, Carmody-Torres, Sak-Bussa, Walker-Campbell-Bussa. **Fort Wayne (7)**—ttorff-Peters-Rath, Boggs-Mahaffey-McBride, Chapman-Mahaffey-Niedermaier-Rath, Mahaffey-Harris, Bartels-Harris, Chapman-Niedermaier-Gillian, Mahaffey-ten. **Kane County (3)**—Getz-Duvall, Vardijan-Castro-Santoro, Hurtado-Santoro. **Lansing (6)**—Thorn-Wallace, Mull-Villarreal, Mull-Ritter, Thorn-Key, Mull-Santiago, rn-Bernal. **Michigan (2)**—Yennaco-Rombolo, Wimberly-Cannon-McLaughlin. **Peoria (11)**—Jimenez-Benes, Reames-Glauber, Reames-Almanza, Foderaro-Donnelly-es-Welch, Roettgen-Foderaro-Almanza-Welch, Politte-Donnely, Reames-Glauber-Welch, Reames-Benes, Reames-Kown-Benes, Politte-Montgomery-Benes, Reames-uber. **Quad City (5)**—Garcia-Lynch-Tickell, Sikorski-Loiz, Gunderson-Lynch-Root, Garcia-Sikorski-Lynch, Smith-Hill-Root-Lynch. **Rockford (2)**—Villegas-Hammack, rson-Diaz. **South Bend (2)**—Desrosiers-Hasselhoff, Garcia-Secoda-Hasselhoff. **West Michigan (9)**—Mlodik-Price-Gunther, Smith-Weinberg-Kazmirski, Baez-ther, Nelson-Abbott, Rivette-Gunther, Rivette-Gunther, Smith-Moreno-Kazmirski, Mlodik-Moreno-Gunther, Price-Smith. **Wisconsin (2)**—Marte-Iddon, Trawick-eer-Iddon.

NO-HIT GAMES: Dawsey, Beloit, defeated Burlington, 5-0, July 26; Grote, Burlington, defeated Clinton, 8-0, August 5.

1996 FIELDING

TEAM

Team	Pct.	G	PO	A	E	TC	DP	PB	Team	Pct.	G	PO	A	E	TC	DP	PB
ington	.972	138	3608	1573	147	5328	121	20	Michigan	.963	138	3633	1511	197	5341	117	30
ar Rapids	.969	135	3516	1461	159	5136	137	17	Fort Wayne	.963	136	3561	1463	194	5218	126	28
d City	.963	131	3442	1447	186	5075	128	18	Beloit	.962	136	3536	1454	198	5188	122	38

CLASS A Midwest League

Team	Pct.	G	PO	A	E	TC	DP	PB
Lansing	.962	139	3718	1743	218	5679	171	25
Peoria	.961	136	3495	1418	198	5111	107	15
Kane County	.961	133	3446	1497	202	5145	132	11
Wisconsin	.961	135	3518	1575	209	5302	103	23
Clinton	.960	134	3431	1402	199	5032	102	24
Rockford	.960	135	3447	1427	203	5077	125	
West Michigan	.958	138	3657	1498	224	5379	113	
South Bend	.953	136	3530	1401	242	5173	109	

TRIPLE PLAYS: Kane County, Rockford, Wisconsin.

INDIVIDUAL

FIRST BASEMEN

NOTE: All caps denotes fielding-percentage leader based on 70 games for catchers, 93 for all other non-pitchers and 144 innings for pitchers. *Throws lefthanded.

Player, Team	Pct.	G	PO	A	E	TC	DP
Agnoly, Earl, Kane County	.966	4	27	1	1	29	1
Allen, Dustin, Clinton	.990	76	651	44	7	702	59
Amado, Jose, Wis.-Lan.	.949	4	35	2	2	39	5
Arias, David, Wisconsin*	.989	121	1126	78	13	1217	82
Arrollado, Courtney, Lansing	1.000	2	13	1	0	14	1
Barnes, Larry, Cedar Rapids*	.990	122	1059	80	11	1150	108
Blosser, Doug, Lansing	1.000	7	61	1	0	62	8
Bovender, Andy, Quad City	.985	27	256	15	4	275	23
Bowness, Brian, South Bend	.983	51	428	25	8	461	41
Bunkley, Antuan, Fort Wayne	.971	6	29	4	1	34	4
Carroll, Doug, Wisconsin	1.000	2	25	0	0	25	3
Castro, Jose, Wisconsin*	1.000	3	16	0	0	16	1
Catlett, David, Rockford	.979	24	124	14	3	141	16
Cepeda, Jose, Lansing	.973	7	66	6	2	74	8
Cepeda, Malcolm, Burlington	1.000	1	5	0	0	5	0
Chavera, Arnie, Quad City	.991	18	109	7	1	117	15
Chevalier, Virgil, Michigan	.985	23	177	14	3	194	18
Clark, Kevin, Michigan	.984	72	623	36	11	670	53
Coffee, Gary, Lansing	.982	100	1000	44	19	1063	106
Davis, Josh, Clinton	1.000	2	14	0	0	14	0
DaVanon, Jeff, West Michigan	.923	4	10	2	1	13	1
Dishington, Nate, Peoria	.955	24	159	10	8	177	10
Dunn, Nathan, Clinton	.970	34	305	19	10	334	18
Felix, Pedro, Burlington	.933	2	12	2	1	15	1
Filchner, Duane, West Michigan*	1.000	1	1	0	0	1	0
Garcia, Carlos, Fort Wayne	1.000	1	10	0	0	10	1
GULSETH, Mark, Burlington	.997	121	1122	77	4	1203	88
Heintz, Chris, South Bend	.990	11	97	6	1	104	8
Hernandez, Ramon, West Michigan	1.000	5	40	1	0	41	3
Hills, Rich, Clinton	1.000	4	25	0	0	25	2
Kinkade, Mike, Beloit	1.000	1	1	0	0	1	0
Layne, Jason, Lansing	.992	25	253	9	2	264	26
Lewis, Jeremy, Rockford	1.000	1	4	0	0	4	1
McAninch, John, Cedar Rapids	.987	9	69	5	1	75	8
McDonald, Ashanti, Rockford	1.000	1	4	1	0	5	0
McNally, Shawn, Peoria	.991	40	308	17	3	328	26
Miranda, Alex, West Michigan*	.985	118	1029	57	16	1102	80
Noriega, Kevin, Beloit	.985	56	433	23	7	463	43
Nunez, Isaias, Peoria*	.987	102	697	40	10	747	50
Ortega, Randy, West Michigan	.954	11	78	5	4	87	5
Perez, Richard, Rockford	1.000	4	15	1	0	16	1
Peterman, Tommy, Fort Wayne*	.979	31	214	23	5	242	30
Peters, Tony, Beloit	1.000	5	32	1	0	33	5
Prodanov, Peter, Michigan	.769	2	10	0	3	13	1
Raifstanger, John, Michigan	1.000	8	72	4	0	76	5
Ramirez, Hiram, Burlington	.989	16	168	7	2	177	15
Randolph, Edward, Wisconsin	1.000	2	0	1	0	1	0
Rathmell, Lance, Michigan	.983	7	50	7	1	58	6
Roberts, Ryan, Peoria	.000	1	0	0	0	0	0
Robertson, Ryan, Kane County	1.000	1	3	0	0	3	0
Rodriguez, Noel, Quad City	.984	36	296	19	5	320	22
Rolison, Nate, Kane County	.990	131	1161	80	13	1254	114
Sanchez, Marcos, Clinton	1.000	6	34	0	0	34	5
Sapp, Damian, Michigan	.987	9	71	3	1	75	3
Schroeder, John, Fort Wayne	.991	106	894	57	9	960	80
Sheppard, Greg, South Bend	.985	26	183	13	3	199	12
Smith, Jeff, Fort Wayne	1.000	1	4	2	0	6	0
Smith, Rick, Beloit	.988	83	681	40	9	730	55
Tippin, Greg, Michigan*	.996	39	262	14	1	277	17
Truby, Chris, Quad City	.986	61	515	29	8	552	57
Valdez, Mario, South Bend	.984	52	438	41	8	487	29
Valenti, Jon, West Michigan	1.000	3	5	0	0	5	0
Vallone, Gar, Cedar Rapids	1.000	1	1	0	0	1	0
VanderGriend, Jon, Cedar Rapids	1.000	8	69	3	0	72	4
Vickers, Randy, Wisconsin	.991	13	102	6	1	109	4
Vieira, Scott, Rockford	.981	121	1061	65	22	1148	89
Watkins, Sean, Clinton*	.972	16	131	10	4	145	9
White, Derrick, West Michigan	1.000	13	108	3	0	111	13
Wilders, Paul, Peoria	1.000	8	51	3	0	54	1
Wilhelm, Brent, South Bend	1.000	6	45	3	0	48	5
Wulfert, Mark, Clinton	1.000	1	15	0	0	15	
Zwisler, Josh, Beloit	1.000	2	12	0	0	12	

TRIPLE PLAYS: Arias, Catlett, Rolison.

FIRST BASEMEN WITH TWO OR MORE TEAMS

Player, Team	Pct.	G	PO	A	E	TC
Amado, Jose, Wisconsin	.667	1	2	0	1	3
Amado, Jose, Lansing	.972	3	33	2	1	36

SECOND BASEMEN

Player, Team	Pct.	G	PO	A	E	TC
Adams, Jason, Quad City	.962	20	48	53	4	105
Amado, Jose, Wisconsin	1.000	1	1	2	0	3
Arrollado, Courtney, Lansing	1.000	5	9	10	0	19
Betancourt, Rafael, Michigan	.980	14	26	24	1	51
Bucci, Carmen, Clinton	.926	9	8	17	2	27
Campusano, Carlos, Beloit	.981	24	53	49	2	104
Carrasquel, Domingo, Beloit	.973	36	56	89	4	149
Cepeda, Jose, Lansing	.950	4	6	13	1	20
Cuevas, Eduardo, Clinton	.952	18	19	40	3	62
Davalillo, David, Cedar Rapids	.980	87	175	224	8	407
Dean, Chris, Wisconsin	.954	51	76	131	10	217
Durrington, Trent, Cedar Rapids	.969	24	46	48	3	97
Escandon, Emiliano, Lansing	.960	43	97	97	8	202
Febles, Carlos, Lansing	.963	96	205	289	19	513
FRASER, Joe, Fort Wayne	.986	97	187	231	6	424
Friedrich, Steve, South Bend	.938	109	203	282	32	517
Funaro, Joe, Kane County	1.000	4	8	11	0	19
Garcia, Amaury, Kane County	.964	106	219	286	19	524
Garcia, Carlos, Fort Wayne	1.000	1	1	4	0	5
Glozier, Larry, Kane County	.975	24	38	80	3	121
Graves, Bryan, Cedar Rapids	1.000	1	4	0	0	4
Hall, Andy, Peoria	.949	108	169	260	23	452
Harrison, Adonis, Wisconsin	.959	51	106	127	10	243
Hernandez, Carlos, Quad City	.970	106	234	315	17	566
Huls, Steve, Fort Wayne	.902	14	17	29	5	51
Inzunza, Miguel, Peoria	.973	17	23	49	2	74
Jasco, Elinton, Rockford	.955	120	258	319	27	604
Johnson, Jeffrey, South Bend	.982	28	42	69	2	113
Keefe, Jamie, Clinton	.959	27	54	64	5	123
Lara, Edward, West Michigan	.960	17	25	23	2	50
Lebron, Ruben, Michigan	.947	33	66	96	9	171
Liniak, Cole, Michigan	1.000	1	1	0	0	1
Longueira, Tony, Lansing	.968	6	11	19	1	31
Lopez, Mickey, Beloit	.968	58	112	162	9	283
Lugo, Julio, Quad City	.974	8	16	21	1	38
Marval, Raul, Burlington	.951	33	66	89	8	163
McDonald, Ashanti, Rockford	1.000	7	10	3	0	13
Montas, Ricardo, Lansing	1.000	2	0	1	0	1
Mota, Alfonso, Cedar Rapids	.976	15	18	23	1	42
Nieves, Jose, Rockford	.976	12	20	21	1	42
Ortiz, Nick, Michigan	.971	43	87	144	7	238
Paez, Israel, Fort Wayne	.963	35	69	111	7	187
Paulino, Arturo, West Michigan	.974	11	17	20	1	38
Perez, Richard, Rockford	.818	3	2	7	2	11
Powers, John, Clinton	.980	52	99	142	5	246
Prodanov, Peter, Michigan	.917	5	4	7	1	12
Prospero, Teo, Burlington	1.000	1	1	2	0	3
Raifstanger, John, Michigan	.966	54	104	123	8	235
Ramirez, Joel, Wisconsin	.964	37	56	76	5	137
Rathmell, Lance, Michigan	.938	4	6	9	1	16
Ritter, Ryan, Beloit	.894	35	66	69	16	151
Rivera, Miguel, Peoria	.988	20	34	51	1	86
Roberts, Ryan, Peoria	1.000	1	2	2	0	4
Sheppard, Greg, South Bend	1.000	1	0	1	0	1
Sorrow, Michael, Burlington	.941	7	3	13	1	17
Totman, Jason, Clinton	.980	32	67	79	3	149
Vallone, Gar, Cedar Rapids	.939	21	47	46	6	99
Walker, Dane, West Michigan	.947	120	215	302	29	546
Watson, John, Burlington	.969	44	90	127	7	224
Weaver, Terry, Burlington	.963	60	131	131	10	272
Wilhelm, Brent, South Bend	.889	5	7	9	2	18

TRIPLE PLAY: Jasco.

THIRD BASEMEN

yer, Team	Pct.	G	PO	A	E	TC	DP
ims, Jason, Quad City	.870	44	13	81	14	108	4
ado, Jose, Wis.-Lan.	.922	97	67	216	24	307	24
czak, Chuck, South Bend	1.000	2	0	1	0	1	0
ollado, Courtney, Lansing	1.000	3	0	5	0	5	0
za, Art, Burlington	.889	3	3	5	1	9	1
nes, Kelvin, Rockford	.864	117	69	204	43	316	18
ancourt, Rafael, Michigan	.889	6	2	6	1	9	1
ity, Josh, Kane County	.918	121	62	252	28	342	20
ender, Andy, Quad City	.924	45	20	90	9	119	14
ci, Carmen, Clinton	.833	6	1	4	1	6	0
kley, Antuan, Fort Wayne	.775	20	3	28	9	40	1
npusano, Carlos, Beloit	1.000	4	5	10	0	15	0
asquel, Domingo, Beloit	1.000	4	1	3	0	4	0
eda, Jose, Lansing	.904	88	65	235	32	332	25
mblee, James, Michigan	1.000	1	1	3	0	4	1
istenson, Ryan, West Michigan	.500	1	1	0	1	2	0
k, Kevin, Michigan	.800	7	2	2	1	5	0
z, Deivi, Burlington	.958	7	6	17	1	24	5
vas, Eduardo, Clinton	.800	3	2	2	1	5	0
alillo, David, Cedar Rapids	1.000	4	2	4	0	6	0
s, Josh, Clinton	.667	2	0	2	1	3	0
n, Nathan, Clinton	.830	15	3	36	8	47	2
andon, Emiliano, Lansing	.875	7	8	6	2	16	0
k, Pedro, Burlington	.937	91	54	184	16	254	18
eroa, Luis, Wisconsin	.906	37	32	94	13	139	7
er, Joe, Fort Wayne	1.000	1	1	3	0	4	0
drich, Steve, South Bend	.824	5	6	8	3	17	0
cia, Carlos, Fort Wayne	.943	26	15	51	4	70	3
zier, Larry, Kane County	1.000	1	0	3	0	3	0
dell, Steve, Kane County	.800	7	2	14	4	20	2
s, Chris, Peoria	.883	114	75	241	42	358	11
mark, Patrick, Lansing	.714	4	3	7	4	14	1
tz, Chris, South Bend	.909	50	41	89	13	143	8
dman, Eli, Fort Wayne	.643	7	3	6	5	14	0
ey, Mike, Wisconsin	.846	24	19	58	14	91	3
, Rich, Peoria	.919	104	67	195	23	285	12
, Steve, Fort Wayne	.500	1	0	2	2	4	0
nza, Miguel, Peoria	1.000	1	1	1	0	2	0
e, Ryan, Cedar Rapids	.914	120	62	267	31	360	28
ade, Mike, Beloit	.912	129	94	301	38	433	27
Charles, South Bend	.889	2	2	6	1	9	2
vic, Greg, Fort Wayne	.857	7	4	14	3	21	2
s, Jeremy, Rockford	.500	2	0	2	2	4	0
r, Jeff, South Bend	.802	36	31	62	23	116	6
AK, Cole, Michigan	.967	116	78	248	11	337	13
jueira, Tony, Lansing	1.000	4	3	11	0	14	2
, Julio, Quad City	.800	1	2	2	1	5	1
in, Mike, Clinton	.571	3	1	3	3	7	1
al, Raul, Burlington	.783	8	3	15	5	23	0
onald, Ashanti, Rockford	.778	3	1	6	2	9	1
o, Mark, Lansing	1.000	1	1	3	0	4	0
es, Jose, Rockford	.789	11	4	11	4	19	0
ga, Randy, West Michigan	1.000	1	0	1	0	1	0
, Nick, Michigan	.929	5	2	11	1	14	1
, Israel, Fort Wayne	.944	89	75	146	13	234	15
no, Arturo, West Michigan	.915	23	14	40	5	59	6
z, Richard, Rockford	.907	28	7	42	5	54	1
ers, John, Clinton	.950	8	6	13	1	20	1
anov, Peter, Michigan	.947	13	10	26	2	38	3
pero, Teo, Burlington	.500	1	0	1	1	2	0
stanger, John, Michigan	1.000	1	0	1	0	1	0
mell, Lance, Michigan	.889	5	3	5	1	9	2
r, Ryan, Beloit	.957	7	16	6	1	23	0
a, Miguel, Peoria	.905	6	4	15	2	21	1
rts, Ryan, Peoria	1.000	6	1	10	0	11	0
fer, Brett, Lansing	.867	2	6	7	2	15	2
er, Chad, Wisconsin	.818	15	6	30	8	44	1
pard, Greg, South Bend	.667	2	0	4	2	6	0
ow, Michael, Burlington	.875	3	0	7	1	8	2
an, Jason, Clinton	1.000	2	0	1	0	1	0
y, Chris, Quad City	.935	45	30	99	9	138	8
ti, Jon, West Michigan	.891	113	74	252	40	366	17
ne, Gar, Cedar Rapids	.971	17	7	27	1	35	3
uez, Ramon, Wisconsin	.818	3	4	5	2	11	0
rs, Randy, Wisconsin	.923	9	4	20	2	26	1
on, John, Burlington	.920	36	25	56	7	88	4
e, Derrick, West Michigan	.882	12	8	22	4	34	1
e, Walter, Kane County	1.000	5	4	8	0	12	0
rs, Paul, Peoria	.929	14	3	23	2	28	0
lm, Brent, South Bend	.897	43	49	82	15	146	2

THIRD BASEMEN WITH TWO OR MORE TEAMS

Player, Team	Pct.	G	PO	A	E	TC	DP
Amado, Jose, Wisconsin	.904	58	35	126	17	178	11
Amado, Jose, Lansing	.946	39	32	90	7	129	13

SHORTSTOPS

Player, Team	Pct.	G	PO	A	E	TC	DP
Arrollado, Courtney, Lansing	1.000	4	3	10	0	13	2
Baughman, Justin, Cedar Rapids	.943	126	201	360	34	595	81
Betancourt, Rafael, Michigan	.932	46	56	95	11	162	14
Bucci, Carmen, Clinton	.982	12	11	43	1	55	9
Campusano, Carlos, Beloit	.910	79	84	198	28	310	38
Carmona, Cesarin, Clinton	.915	104	90	287	35	412	50
Carrasquel, Domingo, Beloit	.958	34	47	68	5	120	17
Cepeda, Jose, Lansing	.947	30	53	90	8	151	23
Cey, Dan, Fort Wayne	.912	27	41	62	10	113	20
Chamblee, James, Michigan	.937	92	112	257	25	394	41
CRUZ, Deivi, Burlington	.980	121	153	427	12	592	63
Davalillo, David, Cedar Rapids	.966	8	7	21	1	29	2
Davidson, Cleatus, Fort Wayne	.919	59	86	185	24	295	36
Escandon, Emiliano, Lansing	.926	18	22	66	7	95	9
Espada, Josue, West Michigan	.926	23	19	56	6	81	8
Febles, Carlos, Lansing	1.000	1	1	3	0	4	0
Friedrich, Steve, South Bend	.889	19	28	52	10	90	10
Funaro, Joe, Kane County	.500	1	0	1	1	2	0
Garcia, Carlos, Fort Wayne	1.000	4	4	12	0	16	0
Glozier, Larry, Kane County	1.000	1	1	1	0	2	1
Gonzalez, Alex, Kane County	1.000	4	2	10	0	12	3
Goodell, Steve, Kane County	.871	41	70	112	27	209	27
Guillen, Carlos, Quad City	.929	29	47	71	9	127	11
Hernandez, Carlos, Quad City	.926	5	4	21	2	27	1
Hills, Rich, Clinton	.933	19	24	32	4	60	6
Huls, Steve, Fort Wayne	.946	47	49	160	12	221	31
Inzunza, Miguel, Peoria	.750	4	3	3	2	8	0
Johnson, Jeffrey, South Bend	.933	74	102	204	22	328	37
Keefe, Jamie, Clinton	.935	7	8	21	2	31	4
Klee, Charles, South Bend	.878	16	23	42	9	74	8
Lara, Edward, West Michigan	.932	69	85	202	21	308	35
Liniak, Cole, Michigan	.000	1	0	0	1	1	0
Listach, Pat, Beloit	.833	1	2	3	1	6	0
Longueira, Tony, Lansing	.947	34	57	120	10	187	32
Lopez, Mickey, Beloit	.897	7	11	15	3	29	3
Lugo, Julio, Quad City	.932	82	104	266	27	397	54
Marval, Raul, Burlington	.778	2	2	5	2	9	1
McDonald, Ashanti, Rockford	.942	51	77	119	12	208	24
Melito, Mark, Lansing	.975	55	87	191	7	285	45
Montas, Ricardo, Lansing	.903	6	4	24	3	31	2
Nieves, Jose, Rockford	.929	97	132	286	32	450	47
Ortiz, Nick, Michigan	.904	21	30	55	9	94	10
Oyola, Carlos, Burlington	.818	7	5	13	4	22	2
Paez, Israel, Fort Wayne	.911	9	16	25	4	45	6
Paulino, Arturo, West Michigan	.907	48	51	143	20	214	26
Perez, Richard, Rockford	.941	4	5	11	1	17	4
Phair, Kelly, Beloit	.939	30	48	60	7	115	11
Ramirez, Joel, Wisconsin	.927	67	80	200	22	302	29
Rivera, Miguel, Peoria	.914	32	48	79	12	139	21
Saylor, Jamie, Quad City	.964	18	26	54	3	83	15
Sheffer, Chad, Wisconsin	.925	78	101	233	27	361	33
Strasser, John, South Bend	.923	2	4	8	1	13	2
Valenti, Jon, West Michigan	.884	9	11	27	5	43	3
Vallone, Gar, Cedar Rapids	.909	2	4	6	1	11	1
Weaver, Terry, Burlington	.931	11	12	42	4	58	6
White, Walter, Kane County	.933	90	126	295	30	451	58
Wilhelm, Brent, South Bend	.938	33	31	104	9	144	20
Woolf, Jason, Peoria	.916	106	128	295	39	462	53

TRIPLE PLAYS: Nieves, Ramirez, White.

SHORTSTOPS

Player, Team	Pct.	G	PO	A	E	TC	DP
Abernathy, Matt, Clinton	.959	50	89	5	4	98	0
Agnoly, Earl, Kane County	.941	23	31	1	2	34	0
Alexander, Chad, Quad City	.958	96	176	6	8	190	2
Allen, Chad, Fort Wayne	1.000	4	4	1	0	5	0
Allen, Dustin, Clinton	1.000	3	1	0	0	1	0
Alvarez, Rafael, Fort Wayne*	.974	115	293	6	8	307	1
Amado, Jose, Lansing	1.000	1	2	0	0	2	0
Amerson, Gordon, Clinton*	.961	113	161	12	7	180	0
Baeza, Art, Burlington	.938	10	15	0	1	16	0
Barnes, Larry, Cedar Rapids*	1.000	3	3	1	0	4	0
Beltran, Carlos, Lansing	.938	11	28	2	2	32	0
Bess, Johnny, Burlington	1.000	3	6	2	0	8	2
Bowers, R.J., Quad City	.899	52	87	2	10	99	2

CLASS A Midwest League

Player, Team	Pct.	G	PO	A	E	TC	DP
Brown, Roosevelt, Kane County	.933	11	13	1	1	15	0
Calderon, Ricardo, Burlington*	.923	18	36	0	3	39	0
Camilo, Jose, Kane County*	.952	22	38	2	2	42	1
Cancel, David, South Bend	.966	79	164	5	6	175	2
Carroll, Doug, Wisconsin	1.000	6	3	1	0	4	0
Castro, Jose, Wisconsin*	.948	29	53	2	3	58	1
Cepeda, Malcolm, Burlington	.932	30	37	4	3	44	0
Chamblee, James, Michigan	.867	7	10	3	2	15	1
Chevalier, Virgil, Michigan	.833	8	5	0	1	6	0
Christenson, Ryan, West Michigan.	.970	32	63	1	2	66	0
Colon, Jose, Rockford	1.000	7	8	1	0	9	0
Cordero, Pablo, Burlington	.977	29	42	1	1	44	1
Dalton, Jed, Cedar Rapids	.985	76	122	6	2	130	1
Darcuiel, Faruq, Wisconsin*	.952	68	76	3	4	83	1
DaVanon, Jeff, West Michigan	.986	51	62	7	1	70	1
Denbow, Don, Burlington	.990	92	184	7	2	193	3
Dishington, Nate, Peoria	.000	2	0	0	0	0	0
Drent, Brian, South Bend	.958	78	130	6	6	142	0
Elliott, David, Beloit	.975	110	185	12	5	202	2
Ellison, Tony, Rockford	1.000	27	40	0	0	40	0
Encarnacion, Mario, W. Michigan	.949	112	192	13	11	216	4
Escandon, Emiliano, Lansing	1.000	6	8	1	0	9	0
Farley, Cordell, Peoria	.977	24	39	3	1	43	1
Felston, Anthony, Fort Wayne*	1.000	59	117	6	0	123	0
Ferguson, Dwight, Michigan*	.857	10	18	0	3	21	0
Filchner, Duane, West Michigan*	.969	82	90	4	3	97	0
Finnieston, Adam, Lansing	.930	39	37	3	3	43	0
Friedrich, Steve, South Bend	1.000	1	1	0	0	1	0
Funaro, Joe, Kane County	.962	80	146	5	6	157	1
Garcia, Carlos, Fort Wayne	.857	7	10	2	2	14	0
Garcia, Luis, South Bend	.975	48	112	7	3	122	1
Garcia, Ossie, Peoria	.948	118	199	20	12	231	4
Goodell, Steve, Kane County	.929	22	23	3	2	28	0
Goodwin, Keith, Michigan	.943	62	106	9	7	122	0
Gordon, Adrian, Fort Wayne	.930	80	117	2	9	128	0
Hallmark, Patrick, Lansing	.973	101	203	15	6	224	2
Ham, Kevin, Cedar Rapids	.977	83	114	15	3	132	0
Hamilton, Joe, Michigan	.974	102	134	15	4	153	2
Hayes, Darren, South Bend	1.000	9	15	1	0	16	0
Hutchins, Norm, Cedar Rapids*	.956	124	303	2	14	319	1
Iapoce, Anthony, Beloit*	.985	77	126	5	2	133	0
Jefferson, David, Rockford	.977	93	169	3	4	176	1
Johnson, Heath, Fort Wayne	1.000	6	8	0	0	8	0
Johnson, James, Clinton	.960	114	200	14	9	223	2
Johnson, Ric, Quad City	.983	88	170	4	3	177	2
Johnson, Travis, Fort Wayne	.976	51	75	5	2	82	1
Jones, Jaime, Kane County*	.932	59	80	2	6	88	2
Joseph, Terry, Rockford	.966	126	196	4	7	207	0
Juarez, Raul, Fort Wayne	.956	50	80	7	4	91	1
Kinnie, Donald, Rockford	1.000	20	26	1	0	27	1
Knauss, Tom, Fort Wayne	.944	56	81	3	5	89	1
Kotsay, Mark, Kane County*	1.000	17	37	2	0	39	0
Lariviere, Jason, Peoria	.946	45	52	1	3	56	0
Lewis, Jeremy, Rockford	1.000	9	10	1	0	11	1
Lindsey, Rodney, Clinton	.926	23	50	0	4	54	0
Longueira, Tony, Lansing	1.000	3	2	0	0	2	0
Lopiccolo, Jamie, Beloit	1.000	56	69	2	0	71	0
Lowry, Curt, Clinton	1.000	23	21	1	0	22	1
Manning, Brian, Burlington	.985	33	61	4	1	66	3
Mathis, Joe, Wisconsin	.975	124	227	10	6	243	1
McHugh, Ryan, Peoria	1.000	34	30	3	0	33	1
McNally, Shawn, Peoria	.984	88	114	6	2	122	2
Mealing, Al, Beloit	.983	69	112	3	2	117	1
Miranda, Tony, Lansing	.929	18	25	1	2	28	0
Morales, Alex, Burlington	.984	40	59	2	1	62	0
Morgan, Steve, Michigan*	1.000	2	2	0	0	2	0
Mota, Alfonso, Cedar Rapids	1.000	3	1	0	0	1	0
Mueller, Brett, Peoria	1.000	2	4	0	0	4	0
Munoz, Juan, Peoria*	1.000	30	45	3	0	48	2
Noriega, Kevin, Beloit	.947	43	69	2	4	75	1
Ortega, Randy, West Michigan	1.000	4	5	0	0	5	0
Padilla, Roy, Michigan*	.966	98	225	5	8	238	1
Paez, Israel, Fort Wayne	1.000	3	5	0	0	5	0
Parent, Gerald, Beloit	.971	35	61	5	2	68	0
Paulino, Arturo, West Michigan	1.000	3	6	0	0	6	0
Peters, Tony, Beloit	.960	61	91	6	4	101	1
Pico, Brandon, Rockford*	1.000	3	2	0	0	2	0
Pierzynski, A.J., Fort Wayne	.667	3	2	0	1	3	0
Pitts, Rick, Lansing	.958	12	21	2	1	24	0
PORTER, Bo, Rockford	.984	105	172	8	3	183	7
Prodanov, Peter, Michigan	.914	24	28	4	3	35	1
Quinn, Mark, Lansing	.958	111	143	15	7	165	0
Raifstanger, John, Michigan	.980	38	47	2	1	50	0
Randolph, Edward, Wisconsin	.929	21	24	2	2	28	
Rascon, Rene, Kane County*	.966	49	80	5	3	88	
Rauer, Troy, West Michigan	.714	6	5	0	2	7	
Reese, Mat, Cedar Rapids*	1.000	2	1	0	0	1	
Ritter, Ryan, Beloit	.800	9	7	1	2	10	
Rivera, Wilfredo, Michigan	.932	41	64	4	5	73	
Robinson, Hassan, Quad City	.967	96	136	11	5	152	
Robinson, Kerry, Peoria*	.962	115	168	7	7	182	
Rocha, Juan, Lansing	.936	127	233	16	17	266	
Roche, Marlon, Quad City	.951	68	114	3	6	123	
Rodriguez, Juan, Cedar Rapids	.923	8	12	0	1	13	
Saylor, Jamie, Quad City	1.000	2	1	0	0	1	
Schafer, Brett, Lansing	.864	14	18	1	3	22	
Seidel, Ryan, Rockford	1.000	43	59	3	0	62	
Sheffield, Tony, Michigan*	.957	48	78	10	4	92	
Sheppard, Greg, South Bend	1.000	10	13	1	0	14	
Simmons, Jason, South Bend	.968	91	204	10	7	221	
Smith, Scott, Wisconsin	.977	65	118	9	3	130	
Soriano, Jose, West Michigan	.958	118	218	11	10	239	
Sorrow, Michael, Burlington	1.000	53	82	1	0	83	
Stuart, Rich, Cedar Rapids	.982	27	49	5	1	55	
Thompson, Bruce, Burlington	.953	113	156	7	8	171	
Tinoco, Luis, Wisconsin	.962	116	164	14	7	185	
Tippin, Greg, Michigan*	.966	22	54	2	2	58	
Topham, Ryan, South Bend*	.969	102	183	6	6	195	
Treanor, Matt, Lansing	1.000	2	2	0	0	2	
VanderGriend, Jon, Cedar Rapids	.975	91	182	12	5	199	
Vieira, Scott, Rockford	1.000	8	7	0	0	7	
Walker, Dane, West Michigan	.000	2	0	0	1	1	
Watson, Kevin, Burlington	1.000	27	24	2	0	26	
White, Derrick, West Michigan	1.000	23	34	1	0	35	
Winn, Randy, Kane County	.970	128	260	2	8	270	
Wulfert, Mark, Clinton	.974	88	177	11	5	193	
Zwisler, Josh, Beloit	.750	6	3	0	1	4	

CATCHERS

Player, Team	Pct.	G	PO	A	E	TC	DP
ALMOND, Greg, Peoria	.990	89	700	58	8	766	2
Anderson, Frank, South Bend	.958	68	396	42	19	457	3
Antczak, Chuck, South Bend	.904	11	43	4	5	52	1
Bess, Johnny, Burlington	1.000	3	19	2	0	21	0
Borrero, Richie, Michigan	.972	11	66	3	2	71	0
Cancel, Robinson, Beloit	.979	72	483	81	12	576	7
Castro, Ramon, Quad City	.987	96	660	82	10	752	7
Chavera, Arnie, Quad City	.960	10	45	3	2	50	0
Chevalier, Virgil, Michigan	.972	76	431	57	14	502	5
Clark, Kevin, Michigan	.941	8	43	5	3	51	0
Coe, Ryan, Quad City	.984	45	269	31	5	305	2
Davalillo, David, Cedar Rapids	1.000	1	7	1	0	8	0
Davis, Josh, Clinton	1.000	3	8	0	0	8	0
Ebbert, Chad, Clinton	.995	27	183	17	1	201	0
Graves, Bryan, Cedar Rapids	.984	81	502	41	9	552	5
Hallmark, Patrick, Lansing	.987	13	63	13	1	77	0
Hernandez, Ramon, W Michigan	.980	109	877	84	20	981	8
Izquierdo, Sergio, South Bend	1.000	1	2	0	0	2	0
Johnson, Mark, South Bend	.980	65	408	37	9	454	1
Kinkade, Mike, Beloit	.984	7	53	9	1	63	1
Kuilan, Hector, Kane County	.985	94	612	105	11	728	6
Lakovic, Greg, Fort Wayne	.714	3	5	0	2	7	0
Lewis, Jeremy, Rockford	.989	37	234	24	3	261	4
Loyd, Brian, Clinton	.955	10	74	10	4	88	0
Maleski, Tom, Rockford	.500	3	1	0	1	2	0
Martin, Mike, Clinton	.988	73	465	49	6	520	4
McAninch, John, Cedar Rapids	.980	13	44	4	1	49	1
McCartney, Sommer, Kane Co	.952	7	20	0	1	21	0
McClendon, Travis, Peoria	.984	55	334	43	6	383	9
McNally, Shawn, Peoria	1.000	13	47	7	0	54	0
Medrano, Teodoro, Wisconsin	.966	45	277	40	11	328	5
Molina, Jose, Rockford	.985	96	620	98	11	729	10
Murray, Doug, Lansing	1.000	15	50	4	0	54	0
O'Neal, Troy, Beloit	.976	74	447	74	13	534	7
Ortega, Randy, West Michigan	.995	24	176	10	1	187	1
Peters, Tony, Beloit	1.000	3	12	3	0	15	0
Pierzynski, A.J., Fort Wayne	.974	95	656	80	20	756	6
Poor, Jeff, Burlington	.987	89	596	80	9	685	2
Prodanov, Peter, Michigan	1.000	3	5	0	0	5	0
Ramirez, Hiram, Burlington	.978	24	156	23	4	183	2
Randolph, Edward, Wisconsin	1.000	7	15	0	0	15	0
Robertson, Ryan, Kane County	.985	40	304	30	5	339	2
Robles, Juan, Lansing	.991	24	102	14	1	117	0
Rondon, Alex, West Michigan	.965	13	75	8	3	86	2
Ryder, Derek, Cedar Rapids	.982	62	321	60	7	388	8

yer, Team	Pct.	G	PO	A	E	TC	DP	PB
...chez, Marcos, Clinton	.982	16	94	13	2	109	1	4
...p, Damian, Michigan	.984	55	388	40	7	435	7	16
...wenke, Matt, Clinton	.954	28	205	23	11	239	2	6
...eppard, Greg, South Bend.	1.000	4	11	1	0	12	1	3
...ith, Jeff, Fort Wayne	.989	50	314	31	4	349	3	6
...mpson, Karl, Wisconsin	.989	101	700	99	9	808	5	17
...ping, Dan, Burlington	.981	29	189	23	4	216	1	3
...realba, Yorvit, Burlington	1.000	1	7	1	0	8	0	0
...anor, Matt, Lansing	.978	110	626	96	16	738	5	17
...lais, John, Rockford	1.000	7	35	7	0	42	0	1

PITCHERS

yer, Team	Pct.	G	PO	A	E	TC	DP
...ott, Todd, West Michigan	.931	33	6	21	2	29	0
...am, Justin, Lansing	1.000	46	4	13	0	17	1
...osto, Stevenson, Cedar Rapids*	.952	28	11	29	2	42	2
...anza, Armando, Peoria*	.833	52	1	9	2	12	0
...arez, Juan, Cedar Rapids*	1.000	40	6	13	0	19	2
...es, Skip, Rockford	.667	22	1	1	1	3	0
...as, Wagner, Beloit	1.000	21	5	6	0	11	0
...ollado, Courtney, Lansing	1.000	1	0	1	0	1	0
...ard, Corey, Peoria	.913	21	3	18	2	23	1
...z, Benito, West Michigan*	.967	32	6	23	1	30	0
...celo, Lorenzo, Burlington	.923	26	9	27	3	39	3
...ker, Richie, Rockford	1.000	19	4	4	0	8	2
...xsdale, Joe, Michigan	1.000	8	6	2	0	8	0
...nes, Larry, Beloit	.909	9	2	8	1	11	0
...els, Todd, Fort Wayne	.889	11	5	3	1	9	0
...RNE, Kevin, South Bend	1.000	26	9	25	0	34	0
...es, Adam, Peoria	1.000	43	4	11	0	15	0
...nett, Tom, West Michigan	1.000	6	2	2	0	4	0
...ny, Peter, Beloit	.909	26	4	16	2	22	1
...mudez, Manuel, Burlington	.973	26	14	22	1	37	1
...nal, Manuel, Lansing	.840	34	4	17	4	25	1
...ninger, Darren, Beloit	.833	41	4	6	2	12	0
...nop, Joshua, Beloit	.955	29	13	29	2	44	3
...nco, Alberto, Quad City*	1.000	11	0	9	0	9	1
...ingim, Joseph, Burlington	.857	27	3	15	3	21	1
...gs, Robert, Fort Wayne	.972	28	11	24	1	36	1
...le, Sean, Rockford	1.000	16	2	3	0	5	0
...illa, Denys, Wisconsin*	.938	45	4	11	1	16	0
...ster, Jason, Burlington*	.963	27	7	19	1	27	1
...ant, Chris, Rockford*	1.000	43	5	14	0	19	2
...gus, Travis, Kane County*	.923	30	0	12	1	13	1
...h, Craig, Michigan	1.000	4	0	1	0	1	0
...sa, Todd, Clinton	1.000	32	1	4	0	5	0
...eaux, Shane, South Bend	1.000	25	2	4	0	6	0
...p, Jared, Beloit	.889	11	2	6	1	9	0
...pbell, Tim, Clinton	1.000	42	4	14	0	18	0
...pusano, Carlos, Beloit	1.000	2	0	1	0	1	0
...a, Nelson, Beloit*	.833	21	2	3	1	6	0
...non, Kevan, Michigan*	.963	37	8	18	1	27	2
...mody, Brian, Clinton*	.913	13	3	18	2	23	0
...tillo, Carlos, South Bend	.806	20	7	18	6	31	0
...tro, Antonio, Kane County	.895	39	6	11	2	19	1
...ntres, Carlos, South Bend	1.000	10	7	8	0	15	0
...pman, Walker, Fort Wayne	.750	19	5	13	6	24	1
...ron, Jose, Cedar Rapids	.964	28	6	21	1	28	1
...k, Chris, Clinton	.818	24	6	12	4	22	0
...ton, Craig, Clinton	.929	27	7	6	1	14	0
...ment, Matt, Clinton	.913	16	9	12	2	23	0
..., Keith, Cedar Rapids	.400	6	0	2	3	5	0
...ett, Andy, Wisconsin	1.000	22	3	7	0	10	0
...ins, Edward, Beloit	.941	38	5	11	1	17	0
...vford, Paxton, Michigan	.920	22	8	15	2	25	1
...sey, Jason, Beloit*	.909	31	8	12	2	22	0
...aCruz, Fernando, Cedar Rapids..	1.000	6	3	8	0	11	1
...ossantos, Valerio, Beloit*	.913	33	4	17	2	23	2
...pster, Ryan, Kane County*	.800	4	4	0	1	5	0
...rosiers, Erik, South Bend	1.000	14	3	8	0	11	1
...Vitt, Chris, Rockford	.917	15	4	7	1	12	0
...Vitt, Scott, Kane County*	.857	27	5	19	4	28	1
..., Jairo, Rockford	1.000	25	4	13	0	17	0
...nelly, Robert, Peoria	1.000	46	6	7	0	13	1
...can, Sean, South Bend*	.941	43	5	11	1	17	1
...all, Michael, Kane County*	.842	41	3	13	3	19	2
...rd, Tony, Kane County	1.000	3	1	0	0	1	0
...ada, Horacio, Beloit*	1.000	17	3	10	0	13	0
...an, David, Cedar Rapids	1.000	5	0	3	0	3	0
...sworth, Kyle, Rockford	.882	20	1	14	2	17	0
...ell, Jim, Michigan	.909	7	3	7	1	11	1
...lbinder, Mick, Beloit	1.000	12	4	7	0	11	1

Player, Team	Pct.	G	PO	A	E	TC	DP
Filbeck, Ryan, South Bend	1.000	19	2	7	0	9	0
Foderaro, Kevin, Peoria	1.000	32	4	10	0	14	0
Garber, Joel, South Bend*	.941	14	4	12	1	17	0
Garcia, Ariel, South Bend	.902	26	19	18	4	41	0
Garcia, Freddy, Quad City	.909	13	4	6	1	11	0
Garcia, Rick, Kane County	.824	32	5	9	3	17	3
Garrett, Hal, Clinton	.923	25	5	7	1	13	1
Getz, Rod, Kane County	.895	25	7	27	4	38	1
Gillian, Charlie, Fort Wayne	1.000	20	2	1	0	3	0
Glauber, Keith, Peoria	1.000	54	3	3	0	6	0
Gooda, David, Beloit*	.600	4	1	2	2	5	0
Gould, Clint, Wisconsin	1.000	6	1	5	0	6	0
Grenert, Geoff, Cedar Rapids	.938	14	6	9	1	16	0
Grieve, Tim, Lansing	1.000	3	0	1	0	1	0
Grote, Jason, Burlington	.974	28	7	30	1	38	0
Gryboski, Kevin, Wisconsin	.897	32	12	23	4	39	1
Gunderson, Mike, Quad City	.889	34	6	10	2	18	0
Gunther, Kevin, West Michigan	1.000	43	7	21	0	28	0
Guzman, Domingo, Clinton	.714	6	0	5	2	7	0
Haigler, Phil, Fort Wayne	1.000	15	9	11	0	20	1
Hammack, Brandon, Rockford	.778	30	1	6	2	9	0
Hammons, Matt, Rockford	.800	5	2	2	1	5	0
Harris, Jeff, Fort Wayne	1.000	42	6	11	0	17	2
Hasselhoff, Derek, South Bend	1.000	35	1	6	0	7	0
Henderson, Juan, Cedar Rapids	1.000	19	2	3	0	5	0
Henderson, Kenny, Cedar Rapids	.667	7	1	3	2	6	0
Hermanson, Mike, Cedar Rapids	1.000	4	1	4	0	5	0
Hernandez, Santos, Burlington	.900	61	3	6	1	10	0
Hill, Chris, Quad City	.955	18	4	17	1	22	1
Hill, Jason, Cedar Rapids*	.917	18	2	9	1	12	0
Hodges, Kevin, Lansing	1.000	9	0	11	0	11	0
Hooten, David, Fort Wayne	1.000	21	6	4	0	10	1
Housley, Adam, Beloit	.824	34	2	12	3	17	0
Hurtado, Victor, Kane County	.933	27	10	18	2	30	3
Hutzler, Jeff, Burlington	.925	25	13	24	3	40	2
Iddon, Brent, Wisconsin	1.000	50	6	15	0	21	1
Jacobs, Russell, Wisconsin	1.000	24	6	12	0	18	2
Jimenez, Jose, Peoria	.929	28	5	34	3	42	1
Jones, Scott, Michigan	1.000	48	5	2	0	7	0
Kast, Nick, Peoria*	.667	5	1	1	1	3	0
Kaysner, Brent, Lansing	.778	38	3	4	2	9	0
Kazmirski, Robert, West Michigan..	1.000	51	3	11	0	14	2
Keith, Jeff, Burlington*	.714	35	7	3	4	14	1
Key, Scott, Lansing	.800	42	4	8	3	15	2
Knoll, Brian, Burlington	.950	52	8	11	1	20	0
Kolb, Brandon, Clinton	.922	27	10	37	4	51	1
Kown, John, Peoria	1.000	26	3	6	0	9	0
Kraus, Tim, South Bend	.955	35	6	15	1	22	0
Kruse, Kelly, South Bend	.909	26	3	7	1	11	0
Kurtz, Danny, Wisconsin	.917	38	3	8	1	12	1
Lake, Kevin, Burlington*	1.000	43	2	21	0	23	2
LaRosa, Tom, Fort Wayne*	.913	15	2	19	2	23	1
Leach, Jarman, Clinton*	1.000	10	1	1	0	2	0
Lloyd, John, Cedar Rapids	1.000	27	17	16	0	33	5
Loiz, Niuman, Quad City	.889	28	7	9	2	18	0
Lynch, Jim, Quad City	.917	31	4	7	1	12	0
Mahaffey, Alan, Fort Wayne*	.842	30	4	12	3	19	0
Markey, Barry, Rockford	.974	15	14	24	1	39	2
Marshall, Gary, Rockford	1.000	50	3	5	0	8	2
Marte, Damaso, Wisconsin*	.938	26	6	24	2	32	0
Martinez, Javier, Rockford	.900	10	2	7	1	10	1
Matos, Luis, Lansing	1.000	8	0	2	0	2	0
Mayer, Aaron, Cedar Rapids	1.000	18	2	4	0	6	0
McBride, Rodney, Fort Wayne	1.000	16	4	5	0	9	0
McKenzie, Jason, Fort Wayne	.889	17	1	7	1	9	0
McLaughlin, Denis, Michigan	.833	39	2	8	2	12	0
McMullen, Mike, Burlington	.778	38	2	12	4	18	0
Mlodik, Kevin, West Michigan	.926	31	7	18	2	27	0
Montgomery, Greg, Peoria	1.000	14	0	5	0	5	0
Moreno, Juan, West Michigan*	.880	38	4	18	3	25	1
Morgan, Steve, Michigan*	1.000	5	0	2	0	2	0
Morrison, Chris, West Michigan	.917	40	2	9	1	12	0
Mosley, Tim, Rockford	.800	37	6	6	3	15	3
Mull, Blaine, Lansing	1.000	28	9	21	0	30	1
Nelson, Chris, West Michigan	.909	16	7	13	2	22	1
Newman, Eric, Clinton	.889	34	2	14	2	18	2
Niedermaier, Brad, Fort Wayne	.900	32	2	7	1	10	2
Noffke, Andrew, Michigan	.818	28	6	12	4	22	1
Olsen, Jason, South Bend	1.000	9	1	8	0	9	1
O'Malley, Paul, Quad City	.900	26	12	33	5	50	4
O'Quinn, James, Cedar Rapids*	.900	41	5	13	2	20	1
Pailthorpe, Bob, Kane County	.826	43	9	10	4	23	3
Paredes, Carlos, Lansing	.861	23	4	27	5	36	2

CLASS A Midwest League

Player, Team	Pct.	G	PO	A	E	TC	DP
Pavlovich, Tony, Beloit	.857	28	2	4	1	7	0
Pena, Juan, Michigan	.926	26	9	16	2	27	0
Peters, Tim, Fort Wayne*	1.000	13	2	4	0	6	0
Peterson, Jayson, Rockford	.824	15	5	9	3	17	0
Petroff, Daniel, Cedar Rapids	1.000	9	3	13	0	16	0
Politte, Cliff, Peoria	.963	25	5	21	1	27	3
Portillo, Alex, South Bend*	1.000	7	0	1	0	1	0
Price, Jamey, West Michigan	1.000	20	5	21	0	26	3
Quirk, John, South Bend*	1.000	5	1	0	0	1	0
Rath, Fred, Fort Wayne	.667	32	0	2	1	3	0
Reames, Britt, Peoria	.935	25	11	18	2	31	1
Remington, Jake, Clinton	.870	27	6	14	3	23	1
Reyes, Alberto, Beloit	1.000	13	1	1	0	2	0
Richardson, Kasey, Fort Wayne*	.964	30	3	24	1	28	3
Ricketts, Chad, Rockford	.957	37	6	16	1	23	1
Ritter, Jason, Lansing	.833	13	2	3	1	6	1
Rivera, Wilfredo, Michigan	1.000	16	0	3	0	3	0
Rivette, Scott, West Michigan	.862	32	2	23	4	29	0
Robbins, Michael, Lansing*	.941	25	3	13	1	17	0
Roettgen, Mark, Peoria	1.000	6	3	3	0	6	0
Romboli, Curtis, Michigan*	1.000	41	8	14	0	22	2
Root, Derek, Quad City*	1.000	40	2	10	0	12	0
Runyan, Sean, Quad City*	.955	29	1	20	1	22	0
Sak, Jim, Clinton	.929	21	4	9	1	14	0
Sanders, Allen, Lansing	.889	5	1	7	1	9	0
Sanders, Craig, Lansing	.800	8	3	1	1	5	0
Santiago, Jose, Lansing	.952	54	3	17	1	21	1
Santoro, Gary, Kane County	1.000	31	1	2	0	3	0
Sauve, Jeff, Michigan	1.000	36	4	8	0	12	0
Scheer, Greg, Wisconsin*	.833	35	3	12	3	18	1
Scheffer, Aaron, Wisconsin	1.000	46	3	11	0	14	1
Scutero, Brian, Cedar Rapids	.913	53	1	20	2	23	2
Secoda, Jason, South Bend	.912	31	13	18	3	34	0
Sick, Dave, Cedar Rapids	.909	26	3	7	1	11	0
Sikorski, Brian, Quad City	.857	26	12	18	5	35	3
Skuse, Nick, Cedar Rapids	.950	18	8	11	1	20	2
Smith, Andy, West Michigan	1.000	37	7	14	0	21	0
Smith, Eric, Quad City	.875	26	4	10	2	16	0
Smith, Roy, Wisconsin	.912	27	6	25	3	34	1
Soden, Chad, Wisconsin*	1.000	19	2	5	0	7	
Spear, Russell, Clinton	.929	11	2	11	1	14	
Spiers, Corey, Fort Wayne*	1.000	2	0	1	0	1	
Spinelli, Michael, Michigan*	.800	11	2	10	3	15	
Splittorff, Jamie, Fort Wayne	1.000	8	3	2	0	5	
Steinert, Rob, Beloit	1.000	3	0	1	0	1	
Steinke, Brock, Quad City	.778	24	2	5	2	9	
Stephens, Jason, Cedar Rapids	.667	21	0	2	1	3	
Stephens, Shannon, Kane County	.974	17	16	21	1	38	
Stoops, Jim, Burlington	.875	46	3	4	1	8	
Symmonds, Maika, Michigan*	1.000	5	2	0	0	2	
Tanksley, Scott, Fort Wayne	1.000	16	4	6	0	10	
Thorn, Todd, Lansing*	.972	27	9	26	1	36	
Thurmond, Travis, Cedar Rapids	.750	4	2	4	2	8	
Tickell, Brian, Quad City	.667	7	1	1	1	3	
Tijerina, Tano, Beloit	1.000	5	2	2	0	4	
Tillmon, Darrell, Michigan*	1.000	7	1	7	0	8	
Torres, Luis, Clinton	.909	35	3	7	1	11	
Trawick, Tim, Wisconsin	1.000	15	6	19	0	25	
Treend, Patrick, Kane County	.909	27	2	8	1	11	
Tribe, Byron, Rockford	1.000	9	0	1	0	1	
Vanderbush, Matt, Fort Wayne*	.923	35	3	9	1	13	
Vanhof, John, Wisconsin*	.842	27	5	11	3	19	
Vardijan, Daniel, Kane County	.938	24	10	35	3	48	
Vermillion, Grant, Cedar Rapids	.938	38	6	9	1	16	
Villarreal, Modesto, Lansing	1.000	15	2	7	0	9	
Villegas, Ismael, Rockford	.929	10	1	12	1	14	
Vota, Michael, South Bend	1.000	34	5	4	0	9	
Wagner, Matthew, Peoria	.875	16	4	10	2	16	
Walker, Kevin, Clinton	.958	13	4	19	1	24	
Wallace, Jeff, Lansing*	.867	30	5	21	4	30	
Walter, Michael, Quad City	1.000	52	5	7	0	12	
Weibl, Clint, Peoria	1.000	5	1	7	0	8	
Weinberg, Todd, West Michigan*	1.000	43	5	9	0	14	
Welch, Travis, Peoria	1.000	34	3	5	0	8	
Wimberly, Larry, Michigan*	.875	14	2	12	2	16	
Wooten, Greg, Wisconsin	.923	13	4	20	2	26	
Yennaco, Jay, Michigan	.892	28	7	26	4	37	
Yoder, Jeff, Rockford	.972	25	14	21	1	36	

The following players did not have any fielding statistics at the positions indicated or appeared only as a designated hitter, pinch-hitter or pinch-runner: Adams; Arrollando, of; Birsner, p; Bly, 3b; Boring, p; M. Cepeda, 2b; Chamblee, p; K. Clark, p; DaVanon, 2b; Dishington, of; Evans, p; Fraser, of; Hall, of; Hallmark, 2b; Lewis, O. Lopez, p; Martin, p; U. Martinez, p; Melito, 2b; Nunez, of; Parent, p; Prodanov, ss; Randolph, p; Rathmell, p; Saucedo, ph; Sheffer, 1b, p; Sheppard, p; Sumter; Tinoco, 3b; Tippin, p; Vieira, ss; J. Watson, of; W. White, 2b; Wilders, 2b.

LEAGUE CHAMPIONS

Year	Team	Pct.	Year	Team	Pct.	Year	Team	P
1947—	Belleville	.667	1965—	Burlington	.667	1981—	Wausau■	.6
	Belleville	.672		Burlington	.677		Quad Cities	.5
1948—	West Frankfort*	.708	1966—	Fox Cities◆	.689	1982—	Madison	.6
1949—	Centralia	.627		Cedar Rapids	.762		Appleton▼	.5
	Paducah (4th)†	.454	1967—	Wisconsin Rapids	.685	1983—	Appleton•	.6
1950—	Centralia‡	.675		Appleton◆	.587		Springfield	.5
1951—	Paris§	.700	1968—	Decatur	.656	1984—	Appleton•	.6
	Danville (4th)†	.432		Quad Cities◆	.648		Springfield	.5
1952—	Danville∞	.685	1969—	Appleton	.648	1985—	Kenosha▼	.5
	Decatur (3rd)†	.584		Appleton	.690		Peoria	.5
1953—	Decatur*	.576	1970—	Quincy◆	.691	1986—	Springfield	.6
1954—	Decatur	.587		Quad Cities	.581		Waterloo▼	.5
	Danville (2nd)‡	.528	1971—	Appleton	.642	1987—	Springfield	.6
1955—	Dubuque*	.587		Quad Cities■	.548		Kenosha▼	.5
1956—	Paris▲	.656	1972—	Appleton	.598	1988—	Cedar Rapids■	.6
	Dubuque	.603		Danville■	.584		Kenosha	.5
1957—	Decatur▲	.683	1973—	Wisconsin Rapids■	.562	1989—	South Bend■	.6
	Clinton	.623		Danville	.537		Springfield	.5
1958—	Michigan City	.623	1974—	Appleton■	.593	1990—	Cedar Rapids	.6
	Waterloo◆	.613		Danville■	.517		Quad City■	.5
1959—	Waterloo	.613	1975—	Waterloo■	.727	1991—	Clinton■	.5
	Waterloo	.613		Quad Cities	.624		Madison	.5
1960—	Waterloo	.629	1976—	Waterloo■	.600	1992—	Quad City	.6
	Waterloo	.677		Cedar Rapids	.595		Cedar Rapids■	.5
1961—	Waterloo	.613	1977—	Waterloo	.580	1993—	Clinton	.5
	Quincy◆	.594		Burlington■	.511		South Bend■	.5
1962—	Dubuque◆	.667	1978—	Appleton■	.708	1994—	Rockford	.6
	Waterloo	.625		Burlington	.500		Cedar Rapids■	.5
1963—	Clinton	.710	1979—	Waterloo	.600	1995—	Beloit††	.6
	Clinton	.629		Quad Cities■	.579		Michigan	.5
1964—	Clinton	.667	1980—	Waterloo■	.610	1996—	Wisconsin	.5
	Fox Cities◆	.667		Quad Cities	.532		West Michigan††	.5

*Won championship and four-club playoff. †Won four-club playoff. ‡Playoff finals canceled because of bad weather. §Won both halves of split season. ∞ first half of split season and tied Paris for second-half title. ▲Won first-half title and four-team playoff. ◆Won split season playoff. ■League divided Northern and Southern divisions and played split season. Playoff winner. ▼League divided into Northern, Central and Southern divisions. Playoff win •League divided into Northern, Central and Southern divisions; regular season and playoff winner. ††League divided into Eastern, Central and Western divisi regular season and playoff winner. (NOTE—Known as Illinois State League in 1947-48 and Mississippi-Ohio Valley League from 1949 through 1955.)

NEW YORK-PENN LEAGUE

LEAGUE OFFICE

sident
ob Julian
ress
629 Oneida St.
tica, NY 13501
ne
15-733-8036

Teams (affiliation)
Auburn Doubledays (Astros)
Batavia Clippers (Phillies)
Erie SeaWolves (Pirates)
Hudson Valley Renegades (Devil Rays)
Jamestown Jammers (Tigers)
Lowell Spinners (Red Sox)
New Jersey Cardinals (Cardinals)

Oneonta Yankees (Yankees)
Pittsfield Mets (Mets)
St. Catharines Stompers (Blue Jays)
Utica Blue Sox (Marlins)
Vermont Expos (Expos)
Watertown Indians (Indians)
Williamsport Cubs (Cubs)

1996 FINAL STANDINGS

McNAMARA DIVISION

	W	L	T	Pct.	GB
nont (Expos)	48	26	0	.649	....
field (Mets)	46	29	0	.613	2½
ell (Red Sox)	33	41	0	.446	15
son Valley (Co-op)	32	44	0	.421	17
Jersey (Cardinals)	28	47	0	.373	20½

PINCKNEY DIVISION

Team	W	L	T	Pct.	GB
Watertown (Indians)	45	30	0	.600	....
Williamsport (Cubs)	43	32	1	.573	2
Auburn (Astros)	37	39	0	.487	8½
Oneonta (Yankees)	31	45	0	.408	14½
Utica (Marlins)	29	47	0	.382	16½

STEDLER DIVISION

Team	W	L	T	Pct.	GB
St. Catharines (Blue Jays)	44	32	0	.579	....
Batavia (Phillies)	42	33	0	.560	1½
Jamestown (Tigers)	39	36	1	.520	4½
Erie (Pirates)	30	46	0	.395	14

COMPOSITE

	Ver.	Pit.	Wat.	St.C.	Wpt.	Bat.	Jam.	Aub.	Low.	H.V.	One.	Erie	Uti.	N.J.	W	L	T	Pct.	GB
ont (Expos)	....	4	3	2	3	1	1	3	4	7	4	3	2	11	48	26	0	.649	....
ield (Mets)	6	....	2	2	1	1	1	1	7	8	3	4	6	4	46	29	0	.613	2½
rtown (Indians)	1	1	....	3	5	1	3	7	4	2	5	4	7	2	45	30	0	.600	3½
atharines (Blue Jays)	2	2	1	....	3	6	7	3	3	2	3	5	4	3	44	32	0	.579	5
msport (Cubs)	0	3	5	1	....	1	4	5	4	4	7	3	5	1	43	32	1	.573	5½
ia (Phillies)	3	3	3	6	3	....	5	2	1	3	3	6	3	1	42	33	0	.560	6½
stown (Tigers)	1	3	1	5	2	7	....	1	1	2	3	10	1	2	39	36	1	.520	9½
rn (Astros)	1	3	5	1	3	2	3	....	4	2	5	2	4	2	37	39	0	.487	12
ll (Red Sox)	3	3	2	1	0	3	2	2	....	5	2	2	3	5	33	41	0	.446	15
on Valley (Co-op)	3	2	2	2	2	1	2	3	....	3	2	2	6	32	44	0	.421	17
nta (Yankees)	0	1	3	1	3	1	1	5	2	1	....	2	7	4	31	45	0	.408	18
Pirates)	1	0	0	7	1	6	2	2	2	2	2	....	1	4	30	46	0	.395	19
(Marlins)	2	0	1	0	5	1	3	4	3	2	3	3	....	2	29	47	0	.382	20
Jersey (Cardinals)	3	4	2	1	1	1	2	2	3	4	2	0	2	....	28	47	0	.373	20½

dson Valley home games played in Fishkill, N.J.
w Jersey home games played in Augusta, N.J.
rmont home games played in Winooski, Vt.
jor league affiliations in parentheses.

AYOFFS: Vermont defeated Pittsfield, two games to none; St. Catherines defeated Watertown, two games to none; Vermont defeated St. Catherines, two s to one, to win league championship.

GULAR SEASON ATTENDANCE: Auburn, 44,813; Bativia, 39,025; Erie, 187,794; Hudson Valley, 152,626; Jamestown, 60,114; Lowell, 95,986; New /, 172,314; Oneonta, 50,509; Pittsfield, 63,533; St. Catharines, 56,546; Utica, 51,432; Vermont, 124,496; Watertown, 40,681; Williamsport, 65,089; —1,204,958; Playoffs (7 games)—12,617.

NAGERS: Auburn, Manny Acta; Batavia, Floyd Rayford; Erie, Jeff Richardson; Hudson Valley, Bump Wills; Jamestown, Bruce Fields; Lowell, Billy er Jr.; New Jersey, Scott Melvin; Oneonta, Gary Tuck; Pittsfield, Dug Davis; St. Catharines, Rocket Wheeler; Utica, Steve McFarland; Vermont, Kevin ns; Watertown, Ted Kubiak; Williamsport, Ruben Amaro Sr.

-STAR TEAM: 1B—Kevin Burns, Auburn; 2B—Will Skett, St. Catherines; 3B—Aramis Ramirez, Erie; SS—Abraham Nunez, St. Catharines; Utility Inf.— Pond, Vermont; OF—Donzell McDonald, Oneonta; Danny Ramirez, Pittsfield; Christopher Stowers, Vermont; Chris Wakeland, Jamestown; C—Nilson a, Erie; Michael Rose, Auburn; DH—Joe Pomierski, Hudson Valley; RHP—Courtney Duncan, Williamsport; Jared Camp, Watertown; LHP—Derek Dace, n; Time Young, Vermont; Manager—Rocket Wheller, St. Catharines; Most Valuable Player—Christopher Stowers, Vermont; Manager of the Year—Kevin s, Vermont.

1996 BATTING

TEAM

	Avg.	G	TPA	AB	R	H	TB	2B	3B	HR	RBI	SH	SF	HP	BB	IBB	SO	SB	CS	GDP	LOB	ShO	Slg.	OBP
nt	.265	74	2735	2406	373	637	865	116	26	20	312	17	21	23	268	16	437	95	58	47	504	7	.360	.341
	.256	76	2834	2530	334	647	913	111	22	37	283	26	24	31	220	3	510	66	43	59	501	4	.361	.320
own	.255	76	2904	2491	391	634	974	117	29	55	344	34	23	38	318	9	609	91	48	38	541	6	.391	.345
harines	.254	76	2819	2493	347	634	948	113	24	51	296	29	23	41	232	9	535	84	39	28	537	7	.380	.325
	.252	75	2797	2516	348	635	899	116	26	32	313	22	17	35	207	6	510	57	35	34	510	3	.357	.316
ld	.250	75	2765	2401	360	600	854	82	26	40	299	13	23	27	301	10	593	93	46	38	516	5	.356	.337

Team	Avg.	G	TPA	AB	R	H	TB	2B	3B	HR	RBI	SH	SF	HP	BB	IBB	SO	SB	CS	GDP	LOB	ShO	Slg.
New Jersey........	.250	75	2891	2541	347	634	886	114	30	26	300	28	24	28	269	6	604	56	23	50	566	4	.349
Williamsport.......	.244	76	2808	2482	342	606	814	96	20	24	289	25	18	44	238	7	582	104	44	38	517	6	.328
Watertown.........	.239	75	2885	2424	359	580	792	105	13	27	301	38	21	43	358	9	581	75	38	44	591	10	.327
Auburn	.238	76	2800	2499	308	596	860	123	21	33	261	18	25	37	221	8	522	80	32	49	506	5	.344
Lowell...............	.238	74	2754	2458	306	586	826	108	9	38	246	7	14	37	233	6	575	51	24	48	524	5	.336
Oneonta............	.236	76	2821	2471	319	584	761	70	25	19	258	31	28	32	257	9	661	126	34	28	514	4	.308
Utica.................	.235	76	2832	2426	299	570	784	112	18	22	264	21	34	43	308	8	641	64	33	44	574	3	.323
Hudson Valley ...	.228	76	2957	2581	356	588	910	127	27	47	303	10	28	54	280	9	720	120	48	42	515	3	.353

INDIVIDUAL

TOP QUALIFIERS FOR BATTING CHAMPIONSHIP

Minimum 205 plate appearances. *Lefthanded batter. †Switch-hitter.

Player, Team	Avg.	G	TPA	AB	R	H	TB	2B	3B	HR	RBI	SH	SF	HP	BB	IBB	SO	SB	CS	GDP	Slg.
Freitas, Joe, New Jersey	.344	45	194	163	29	56	84	10	3	4	37	0	6	0	25	0	35	0	1	4	.515
Stowers, Christopher, Vermont* ..	.319	72	305	282	58	90	150	21	9	7	44	0	0	2	21	6	37	16	5	4	.532
Manning, Nate, Williamsport........	.317	62	258	240	28	76	104	14	1	4	32	0	2	2	14	2	62	4	0	3	.433
Hillenbrand, Shea, Lowell...........	.315	72	308	279	33	88	116	18	2	2	38	0	2	8	18	1	32	4	3	6	.416
Pratt, Wes, Auburn......................	.313	70	288	246	43	77	116	22	1	5	35	0	1	2	39	2	37	11	3	8	.472
Mazurek, Brian, New Jersey*......	.310	69	300	274	31	85	111	18	1	2	48	5	3	2	16	0	39	0	2	8	.405
Wakeland, Chris, Jamestown*......	.309	70	271	220	38	68	122	14	5	10	49	1	3	4	43	0	83	8	3	1	.555
Ramirez, Aramis, Erie..................	.305	61	263	223	37	68	117	14	4	9	42	0	2	7	31	1	41	0	0	7	.525
Naples, Brandon, Pittsfield..........	.304	71	294	263	44	80	95	7	4	0	29	0	1	2	28	0	45	13	5	8	.361
Pond, Simon, Vermont*...............	.300	69	286	253	37	76	103	16	1	3	40	1	3	3	26	2	26	9	3	7	.407
Cameron, Ken, New Jersey*........	.289	53	231	190	43	55	77	10	6	0	20	0	1	6	34	2	37	8	4	4	.405
Francia, David, Batavia*..............	.289	69	298	280	45	81	117	14	5	4	29	2	2	6	8	0	25	16	6	1	.418
Hernandez, Alexander, Erie*........	.289	61	249	225	38	65	98	13	4	4	30	1	2	0	20	1	47	7	8	1	.436
Lopez, Luis, St. Catharines	.285	74	301	260	36	74	116	17	2	7	40	4	3	7	27	1	31	2	3	4	.446
Ellison, Tony, Williamsport..........	.284	63	255	229	33	65	98	10	1	7	35	1	1	4	20	1	51	4	0	2	.428

DEPARTMENTAL LEADERS: G—Shatley, 76; AB—Nunez, 297; R—Stowers, 58; H—Stowers, 90; TB—Stowers, 150; 2B—Pomierski, 25; 3B—D. McDonald, HR—Skett, 15; RBI—K. Burns, 55; SH—J. McDonald, 11; SF—Pomierski, Freitas, Dennis, 6 each; HP—Kleinz, 13; BB—Venghaus, 60; IBB—Stowers, 6; SO—Pom, 91; SB—D. McDonald, 54; CS—Sollman, Nunez, 14 each; GIDP—Veras, 9; Slg.—Wakeland, .555; OBP—Wakeland, .426.

ALL PLAYERS

*Lefthanded batter. †Switch-hitter.

Player, Team	Avg.	G	TPA	AB	R	H	TB	2B	3B	HR	RBI	SH	SF	HP	BB	IBB	SO	SB	CS	GDP	Slg.
Abell, Antonio, New Jersey	.120	7	29	25	4	3	3	0	0	0	1	0	0	0	4	0	11	1	0	1	.120
Afenir, Tom, Watertown................	.222	3	10	9	0	2	2	0	0	0	1	0	1	0	0	0	3	0	0	0	.222
Airoso, Kurt, Jamestown..............	.282	27	92	78	12	22	37	5	2	2	12	0	2	2	10	0	31	3	1	1	.474
Alayon, Elvis, Lowell*.................	.277	63	231	213	28	59	76	3	1	4	20	1	2	4	11	3	37	10	3	4	.357
Alvarado, Basilio, Vermont...........	.234	49	180	171	16	40	53	8	1	1	22	1	1	4	3	0	37	0	3	4	.310
Ammirato, Zak, Utica†.................	.221	74	310	262	26	58	93	13	2	6	36	1	5	3	39	4	80	3	2	3	.355
Andersen, Ryan, Williamsport.......	.267	25	85	75	6	20	22	2	0	0	8	1	1	3	5	0	11	2	2	2	.293
Anderson, Chris, Hudson Valley....	.147	52	176	156	17	23	44	4	1	5	18	0	1	4	15	0	70	2	0	1	.282
Antigua, Nilson, Erie...................	.273	57	205	187	24	51	72	9	0	4	26	7	2	0	9	0	26	5	3	7	.385
Antrim, Pat, Oneonta†.................	.224	14	55	49	4	11	11	0	0	0	2	1	0	0	5	0	14	3	3	0	.224
Arenas, Pete, Utica*..................	.192	66	219	182	25	35	40	5	0	0	12	4	2	0	31	0	61	1	3	4	.220
Aylor, Brian, Oneonta*................	.440	8	30	25	9	11	20	3	3	0	5	0	1	2	2	1	5	3	1	1	.800
Ayotte, Scott, Oneonta*..............	.202	27	99	89	9	18	25	5	1	0	8	0	2	0	8	0	32	2	1	0	.281
Barlow, Ethan, Vermont*.............	.250	42	135	116	18	29	30	1	0	0	8	2	0	3	14	0	20	8	5	3	.259
Barner, Doug, Hudson Valley	.218	46	182	147	21	32	45	7	0	2	17	0	1	4	30	2	42	3	3	2	.306
Barr, Tucker, Auburn	.218	44	173	165	16	36	60	12	0	4	22	0	2	1	5	0	39	1	1	2	.364
Batts, Rodney, Batavia................	.144	41	171	153	20	22	29	5	1	0	15	2	2	2	12	0	36	7	2	0	.190
Beaumont, Hamil, Oneonta	.000	1	4	3	0	0	0	0	0	0	0	0	0	1	0	0	1	0	0	0	.000
Beeney, Ryan, Oneonta	.500	2	4	4	1	2	2	0	0	0	0	0	0	0	0	0	0	0	0	0	.500
Bellenger, Butch, Erie.................	.238	52	207	193	21	46	63	8	0	3	15	2	2	1	9	0	33	9	4	5	.326
Bennett, Ryan, Pittsfield..............	.241	27	94	79	11	19	23	2	1	0	14	0	2	0	13	1	21	0	0	1	.291
Betts, Darrell, New Jersey†..........	.102	21	68	59	6	6	7	1	0	0	3	0	0	1	8	0	18	1	0	1	.119
Bishop, Tim, Pittsfield.................	.000	3	6	6	1	0	0	0	0	0	1	0	0	0	0	0	1	0	0	0	.000
Blandford, Paul, Vermont.............	.247	64	276	231	39	57	85	11	7	1	39	4	5	2	34	0	37	11	9	2	.368
Blessing, Chad, Williamsport........	.238	38	124	105	15	25	31	3	0	1	12	2	0	3	14	0	25	5	2	1	.295
Braughler, Matt, Utica*...............	.216	42	136	125	15	27	34	4	0	1	5	0	0	0	11	1	33	0	0	2	.272
Britt, Bryan, New Jersey..............	.239	69	292	268	28	64	99	12	1	7	42	1	1	2	19	2	86	3	5	4	.369
Buirley, Matthew, Vermont...........	.174	35	126	115	10	20	27	4	0	1	8	1	0	1	9	0	46	1	2	4	.235
Burns, Kevin, Auburn*.................	.264	71	293	269	27	71	129	19	3	11	55	0	5	4	15	1	77	2	1	1	.480
Burns, Xavier, Erie......................	.158	14	43	38	6	6	7	1	0	0	2	0	0	2	3	0	12	2	1	1	.184
Butler, Allen, Oneonta*...............	.217	72	289	249	32	54	68	7	2	1	24	4	1	3	32	4	66	0	1	6	.273
Butler, Garrett, Oneonta†............	.280	69	246	207	36	58	63	3	1	0	16	7	1	1	30	0	46	29	7	2	.304
Cameron, Ken, New Jersey*........	.289	53	231	190	43	55	77	10	6	0	20	0	1	6	34	2	37	8	4	4	.405
Campos, Miguel, Williamsport.......	.150	6	20	20	1	3	4	1	0	0	1	0	0	0	0	0	11	0	0	0	.200
Carroll, Jamey, Vermont..............	.276	54	237	203	40	56	64	6	1	0	17	3	2	0	29	0	25	16	11	1	.315
Cedeno, Jesus, Jamestown..........	.280	74	286	236	43	66	113	16	2	9	39	6	3	10	31	0	57	7	6	4	.479
Charles, Steve, St. Catharines * ..	.205	68	226	200	22	41	55	7	2	1	15	3	1	3	18	0	48	5	2	3	.275
Chatman, Karl, Williamsport.........	.265	72	296	260	47	69	89	11	3	1	38	0	5	4	27	1	52	16	6	5	.342
Ciminiello, Michael, Jamestown....	.111	10	18	18	1	2	2	0	0	0	1	0	0	0	0	0	3	0	0	1	.111
Clark, Kirby, Batavia*.................	.262	51	203	183	25	48	70	11	1	3	24	0	0	4	16	1	39	1	1	3	.383
Coats, Nathan, Watertown...........	.265	31	120	102	13	27	34	5	1	0	7	4	0	6	8	0	20	1	1	2	.333
Cole, Abdul, Utica......................	.213	67	241	202	21	43	66	15	1	2	27	4	3	8	24	1	78	7	2	5	.327
Cole, Eric, Auburn......................	.172	46	165	151	9	26	33	4	0	1	10	1	4	3	6	0	46	3	1	7	.219
Colon, Jose, Williamsport............	.216	36	140	125	13	27	34	5	1	0	13	0	0	5	1	1	10	0	3	2	.272

Player, Team	Avg.	G	TPA	AB	R	H	TB	2B	3B	HR	RBI	SH	SF	HP	BB	IBB	SO	SB	CS	GDP	Slg.	OBP
Connell, Jerry, Williamsport	.000	2	6	6	0	0	0	0	0	0	0	0	0	0	0	0	0	0	0	0	.000	.000
Cook, John, Auburn	.086	10	35	35	0	3	3	0	0	0	1	0	0	0	0	0	7	1	0	0	.086	.086
Cooley, Shannon, Batavia*	.275	62	249	229	30	63	84	9	3	2	23	2	0	1	17	2	40	6	6	3	.367	.328
Cox, Robert, Pittsfield	.000	4	11	8	0	0	0	0	0	0	0	0	0	0	0	0	5	0	0	0	.000	.273
Crane, Todd, Batavia	.239	36	153	138	21	33	56	10	2	3	18	1	1	2	11	0	31	3	4	0	.406	.303
Crawford, Marty, Batavia*	.269	63	243	219	26	59	75	8	1	2	30	3	1	2	18	1	22	5	2	4	.342	.329
Crede, Bradley, Batavia	.275	75	317	280	44	77	118	15	1	8	51	1	3	3	30	1	85	0	5	6	.421	.348
Dallimore, Brian, Auburn	.266	74	322	290	50	77	115	17	3	5	30	0	4	10	18	0	38	7	5	5	.397	.326
Dedonatis, Don, Jamestown*	.298	42	160	141	21	42	46	4	0	0	17	1	0	1	17	0	15	9	4	2	.326	.377
Deman, Lou, New Jersey	.143	8	23	21	2	3	5	2	0	0	3	0	0	0	2	0	6	0	0	1	.238	.217
Dennis, Les, Oneonta	.243	72	321	276	36	67	74	3	2	0	43	5	6	1	33	1	76	20	9	2	.268	.320
DeLaCruz, Wilfredo, Oneonta	.400	4	16	15	3	6	7	1	0	0	0	0	0	0	1	0	2	0	0	0	.467	.438
De La Rosa, Tomas, Vermont	.250	3	8	8	1	2	2	0	0	0	1	0	0	0	0	0	3	0	0	1	.250	.250
Diaz, Alain, Utica	.213	46	162	141	14	30	41	6	1	1	11	2	1	2	16	0	25	1	1	5	.291	.300
Dransfeldt, Kelly, Hudson Valley	.236	75	321	284	42	67	107	17	1	7	29	1	3	4	27	1	76	13	4	2	.377	.308
Edwards, Aaron, Erie	.170	12	50	47	4	8	8	0	0	0	3	0	1	0	2	0	6	2	0	1	.170	.200
Elliott, Dawan, Erie*	.148	39	134	115	17	17	28	5	0	2	6	2	0	1	16	0	42	3	3	2	.243	.258
Ellis, John, Hudson Valley	.244	64	234	221	22	54	74	13	2	1	23	3	3	2	5	0	45	2	1	5	.335	.264
Ellison, Tony, Williamsport	.284	63	255	229	33	65	98	10	1	7	35	1	1	4	20	1	51	4	0	2	.428	.350
Erickson, Corey, Pittsfield	.264	73	309	258	49	68	122	19	1	11	49	0	4	4	43	2	71	6	3	3	.473	.372
Fagley, Dan, Utica	.000	1	4	3	0	0	0	0	0	0	0	0	0	0	1	0	2	0	0	0	.000	.250
Falciglia, Tony, New Jersey	.171	15	44	41	3	7	12	2	0	1	6	0	0	1	2	0	13	0	0	1	.293	.227
Farraez, Jesus, Auburn	.225	42	141	129	13	29	47	4	4	2	11	1	1	0	10	0	34	2	2	0	.364	.279
Fick, Rob, Jamestown*	.248	43	147	133	18	33	42	6	0	1	14	0	2	0	12	1	25	3	1	4	.316	.306
Finnerty, Keith, New Jersey*	.209	55	195	172	21	36	51	7	1	2	16	2	3	1	17	0	31	7	0	4	.297	.280
Florchic, Derek, Utica*	.287	27	96	87	12	25	38	5	1	2	10	0	3	1	5	0	20	0	0	1	.437	.323
Fortin, Blaine, St. Catharines	.220	29	89	82	14	18	29	2	0	3	10	1	0	0	6	1	7	0	1	1	.354	.273
Foster, Quincy, Utica*	.221	73	281	240	34	53	65	7	1	1	22	3	4	4	30	0	71	24	6	3	.271	.313
Francia, David, Batavia*	.289	69	298	280	45	81	117	14	5	4	29	2	2	6	8	0	25	16	6	1	.418	.321
Freitas, Joe, New Jersey	.344	45	194	163	29	56	84	10	3	4	37	0	6	0	25	0	35	0	1	4	.515	.418
Frias, Ovidio, Erie	.283	12	49	46	5	13	14	1	0	0	3	2	0	0	1	0	7	0	0	0	.304	.298
Fuentes, Javier, Lowell	.287	46	184	157	21	45	59	6	1	2	21	0	0	2	21	0	23	2	1	4	.376	.378
Gallagher, Shawn, Hudson Valley	.273	44	186	176	15	48	74	10	2	4	29	0	1	2	7	0	48	8	5	5	.420	.306
Garrett, Jason, Utica	.276	68	277	243	34	67	95	8	4	4	35	0	4	5	25	0	53	1	2	5	.391	.350
Glozier, Larry, Utica	.000	2	4	3	0	0	0	0	0	0	0	0	0	0	1	0	2	0	0	0	.000	.250
Gonzalez, Freddy, Vermont	.209	14	50	43	7	9	13	2	1	0	6	0	0	0	7	0	12	2	0	2	.302	.320
Gordon, Buck, Williamsport	.223	32	100	94	13	21	27	6	0	0	7	0	0	0	6	0	35	1	3	0	.287	.270
Gordon, Herman, St. Catharines†	.150	13	46	40	5	6	11	2	0	1	9	0	2	1	3	0	9	1	0	0	.275	.217
Hall, Doug, Williamsport	.264	67	257	227	35	60	77	5	3	2	19	5	4	1	20	0	58	12	11	3	.339	.321
Haltiwanger, Garrick, Pittsfield	.256	60	234	203	36	52	92	9	2	9	37	1	2	4	24	3	55	9	4	3	.453	.343
Hampton, Robby, St. Catharines	.262	34	141	130	17	34	58	6	3	4	17	0	1	1	9	1	48	5	1	2	.446	.312
Harris, Mike, Utica	.238	38	107	92	9	26	37	8	0	1	8	0	1	3	11	0	23	0	0	3	.402	.374
Hernandez, Alexander, Erie*	.289	61	249	225	38	65	98	13	4	4	30	1	2	1	20	1	47	7	8	1	.436	.344
Hillenbrand, Shea, Lowell	.315	72	308	279	33	88	116	18	2	2	38	0	2	8	18	1	32	4	3	6	.416	.371
Hine, Steve, Lowell*	.217	27	83	73	5	20	22	2	0	0	3	0	0	0	10	0	6	0	0	3	.301	.361
Huelsmann, Mike, Watertown†	.262	41	152	130	21	34	41	5	1	0	21	3	0	2	17	0	14	14	4	0	.315	.356
Huff, B.J., Pittsfield	.196	42	148	138	19	27	41	4	2	2	14	1	1	1	7	0	36	3	1	2	.297	.238
Huffman, Ryan, Oneonta	.197	23	75	61	8	12	18	4	1	0	6	0	0	6	6	0	24	0	0	0	.295	.329
Hundt, Bo, Erie†	.164	20	61	55	8	9	14	0	1	1	4	1	0	1	4	0	11	1	0	0	.255	.233
Ivers, Matt, Auburn*	.255	63	272	231	50	59	77	13	1	1	20	3	2	0	36	2	50	14	4	3	.333	.361
Jefferies, Daryl, Williamsport*	.257	34	115	101	12	26	30	2	1	0	11	0	1	3	10	0	18	12	2	1	.297	.339
Jenkins, Corey, Lowell	.224	65	258	228	37	51	86	7	2	8	29	0	1	1	28	0	81	5	0	8	.377	.310
Jimenez, Ruben, New Jersey†	.229	64	294	236	53	54	67	5	4	0	12	8	1	8	41	0	51	20	3	2	.284	.360
Johnson, Damon, St. Catharines	.241	19	63	58	12	14	20	6	0	0	3	1	0	1	3	0	17	0	1	0	.345	.290
Johnson, Rontrez, Lowell	.222	35	158	135	27	30	46	4	0	4	12	0	2	0	21	1	30	7	3	2	.341	.323
Jones, Jay, Utica*	.284	37	125	116	9	33	39	6	0	0	9	2	1	0	6	0	17	0	1	5	.336	.317
Jones, Kevin, Oneonta	.250	4	4	4	1	1	1	0	0	0	0	0	0	0	0	0	1	0	0	0	.250	.250
Kavaney, Jeff, Lowell	.249	49	189	169	15	42	69	13	1	4	20	0	1	9	10	1	65	1	1	1	.408	.323
Kennedy, Brad, New Jersey*	.211	64	232	199	24	42	72	10	4	4	24	0	3	0	30	0	48	8	0	2	.362	.310
Kent, Troy, Watertown	.251	72	304	263	34	66	99	20	2	3	32	2	2	4	33	2	54	1	5	5	.376	.341
Kiefer, Dax, Williamsport	.227	64	265	229	36	52	74	7	3	3	20	2	1	3	27	0	50	12	2	2	.323	.314
King, Brad, Williamsport	.171	23	79	70	7	12	16	2	1	0	8	0	1	4	4	0	20	0	0	1	.229	.253
Kingsbury, Willy, Lowell*	.159	19	67	63	3	10	14	1	0	1	5	0	2	0	2	0	28	0	1	0	.222	.179
Kleiner, Stacy, New Jersey	.294	56	189	177	24	52	72	10	2	2	23	2	0	1	9	0	32	2	1	5	.407	.332
Klinz, Larry, Utica	.242	73	294	256	21	62	78	14	1	0	34	2	3	13	20	0	44	1	0	6	.305	.325
Kupfer, Jason, Batavia	.280	66	252	218	32	61	71	5	1	1	24	3	2	4	25	0	43	5	5	4	.326	.361
Koehler, Jason, St. Catharines	.230	47	155	135	21	31	49	6	0	4	18	0	0	1	19	0	40	2	1	2	.363	.329
Kofler, Eric, Oneonta*	.227	46	191	176	18	40	57	8	0	3	22	1	3	1	10	2	33	3	1	0	.324	.268
Kurady, Dennis, Watertown*	.251	60	234	183	23	46	61	10	1	1	30	5	3	1	42	0	32	2	5	1	.333	.389
Kwiatkowicz, Derek, Jamestown	.236	68	274	242	34	57	103	7	4	7	40	1	5	5	21	2	74	2	5	5	.426	.304
...tochvil, Tim, Lowell	.304	44	169	158	20	48	68	11	0	3	19	1	1	1	8	0	31	1	0	3	.430	.339
...dstad, Rob, Watertown*	.300	6	22	20	3	6	10	2	1	0	3	0	0	0	2	0	6	0	0	1	.500	.364
...kin, Garrett, Erie*	.208	19	60	53	6	11	13	2	0	0	4	0	0	0	7	0	8	0	1	1	.245	.300
Lawrence, Joe, St. Catharines	.224	29	118	98	23	22	33	7	2	0	11	1	3	2	14	1	17	1	1	0	.337	.325
Lebron, Ruben, Lowell†	.220	46	172	159	24	35	42	5	1	0	11	0	1	1	7	0	31	11	3	3	.264	.271
...n, Jose, New Jersey	.286	7	30	28	4	8	16	3	1	1	3	0	0	2	0	0	7	0	0	0	.571	.333
Lavis, Keith, Williamsport†	.191	60	214	188	25	36	44	4	2	0	13	4	1	4	17	0	46	10	3	3	.234	.271
Lindstrom, David, Jamestown	.248	52	182	165	19	41	66	10	0	5	13	6	3	1	10	0	29	1	0	3	.400	.299
...anti, Bob, Williamsport	.193	43	136	119	10	23	30	7	0	0	15	3	0	1	13	0	27	0	3	2	.252	.278
...nasney, Steve, Lowell	.139	59	177	173	26	24	46	10	0	4	21	0	0	2	42	0	53	2	0	2	.266	.313
Long, Garrett, Erie	.286	20	82	70	5	20	24	2	1	0	9	0	1	1	9	0	17	1	2	3	.343	.370
Lopez, Luis, St. Catharines	.285	74	301	260	36	74	116	17	2	7	40	1	3	7	27	1	31	2	3	4	.446	.364
Lopez, Pee Wee, Pittsfield	.429	5	15	14	2	6	8	0	1	0	3	0	0	0	1	0	1	0	0	0	.571	.467

CLASS A New York-Pennsylvania League

Player, Team	Avg.	G	TPA	AB	R	H	TB	2B	3B	HR	RBI	SH	SF	HP	BB	IBB	SO	SB	CS	GDP	Slg.	OB
Lorenzana, Luis, Erie	.195	44	154	128	19	25	35	8	1	0	12	4	3	3	16	0	26	1	4	4	.273	.2
MacKay, Tripp, Vermont†	.244	46	201	172	29	42	49	4	0	1	12	1	1	2	25	2	29	9	7	1	.285	.3
Majcherek, Matt, Hudson Valley	.188	40	102	80	16	15	21	4	1	0	9	0	1	1	20	0	24	5	1	2	.263	.3
Maloney, Jeff, St. Catharines	.250	1	4	4	0	1	1	0	0	0	1	0	0	0	0	0	2	0	0	0	.250	.2
Manning, Nate, Williamsport	.317	62	258	240	28	76	104	14	1	4	32	0	2	2	14	2	62	4	0	3	.433	.3
Mansavage, Jay, Auburn†	.169	49	171	148	17	25	39	7	2	1	17	1	1	3	18	0	33	5	2	1	.264	.2
Marsters, Brandon, Batavia	.232	42	160	151	15	35	50	8	2	1	13	0	0	1	8	0	46	1	0	1	.331	.2
Martinez, Roger, Pittsfield	.246	41	150	126	14	31	43	4	1	2	14	0	0	2	22	0	40	1	5	1	.341	.3
May, Scott, Erie*	.250	25	47	40	5	10	12	2	0	0	0	0	0	0	7	0	11	0	0	1	.300	.3
Mazurek, Brian, New Jersey*	.310	69	300	274	31	85	111	18	1	2	48	5	3	2	16	0	39	0	2	8	.405	.3
McDonald, Donzell, Oneonta†	.277	74	332	282	57	78	112	8	10	2	30	3	2	2	43	0	62	54	4	1	.397	.3
McDonald, John, Watertown	.270	75	327	278	48	75	92	11	0	2	26	11	1	5	32	0	49	11	1	3	.331	.3
McDougal, Mike, New Jersey*	.161	27	37	31	2	5	8	0	0	1	5	0	1	0	5	1	15	0	0	1	.258	.2
McKinley, Michael, Lowell	.188	30	74	64	10	12	16	4	0	0	6	0	1	0	9	0	22	1	4	1	.250	.2
McNeal, Pepe, New Jersey	.278	19	57	54	4	15	22	2	1	1	4	0	0	3	0	0	14	0	0	3	.407	.3
Mejia, Marlon, Auburn	.206	34	110	107	11	22	32	3	2	1	8	2	0	1	0	0	20	1	0	5	.299	.2
Metzger, Erik, Lowell	.115	9	32	26	2	3	10	1	0	2	3	0	0	2	4	0	6	0	1	0	.385	.2
Meyers, Chad, Williamsport	.243	67	272	230	46	56	75	9	2	2	26	2	1	5	33	0	39	27	6	2	.326	.3
Mitchell, Derek, Jamestown	.245	56	213	184	25	45	65	10	2	2	25	7	2	2	18	0	38	7	4	1	.353	.3
Monroe, Craig, Hudson Valley	.276	67	297	268	53	74	117	16	6	5	29	0	2	2	23	0	63	21	7	4	.437	.3
Moore, Tris, Jamestown	.271	13	55	48	9	13	18	2	0	1	13	0	1	1	5	0	10	2	3	0	.375	.3
Morrison, Ryan, Pittsfield*	.151	39	101	86	11	13	16	3	0	0	6	0	2	2	11	1	26	4	2	2	.186	.2
Motley, Mel, Watertown	.246	61	229	199	24	49	64	8	2	1	27	0	3	3	24	0	55	5	5	8	.322	.3
Myers, Adrian, Hudson Valley	.169	54	169	142	22	24	40	5	4	1	15	0	2	8	17	0	44	19	2	2	.282	.2
Naples, Brandon, Pittsfield	.304	71	294	263	44	80	95	7	4	0	29	0	1	2	28	0	45	13	5	8	.361	.3
Niethammer, Marc, Hudson Val.*	.208	67	245	212	21	44	78	8	1	8	27	1	2	9	21	1	80	2	5	2	.368	.3
Nolte, Bruce, Pittsfield	.319	31	99	91	16	29	33	2	1	0	10	1	1	0	6	0	23	1	0	1	.363	.3
Nova, Jose, Williamsport	.232	60	232	203	27	47	72	7	3	4	38	1	1	2	25	2	62	5	2	7	.355	.3
Nunez, Abraham, St. Catharines†	.279	75	342	297	43	83	106	6	4	3	26	8	2	4	31	0	43	37	14	2	.357	.3
Oliveros, Leonardo, Batavia	.248	42	135	121	12	30	37	7	0	0	18	1	1	1	11	1	22	1	1	1	.306	.3
Olmeda, Jose, Lowell	.225	27	103	89	6	20	28	2	0	2	10	2	0	0	12	0	27	1	2	1	.315	.3
Oropeza, William, Vermont	.297	37	135	128	13	38	52	9	1	1	26	2	2	0	3	0	20	1	1	1	.406	.3
Osik, Keith, Erie	.300	3	12	10	1	3	4	1	0	0	2	0	0	1	1	0	2	0	0	0	.400	.4
Owens-Bragg, Luke, Hudson Vl.†	.182	67	257	214	22	39	50	7	2	0	13	3	2	2	36	3	53	12	8	1	.234	.3
Parsons, Jeff, Pittsfield	.241	72	318	274	46	66	76	5	1	1	14	3	1	1	39	1	60	20	7	2	.277	.3
Pena, Adelis, Erie	.282	66	273	252	31	71	87	11	1	1	26	4	2	0	15	0	41	7	4	7	.345	.3
Pena, Alex, Erie	.267	74	298	281	31	75	103	10	3	4	33	0	1	2	14	0	52	10	4	5	.367	.3
Peoples, Daniel, Watertown	.239	35	149	117	20	28	44	7	0	3	26	0	1	2	28	2	36	3	1	2	.376	.3
Perez, Jersen, Pittsfield	.333	1	4	3	1	1	1	0	0	0	0	0	0	0	1	0	1	0	0	0	.333	.3
Petke, Jonathan, Watertown	.246	63	276	224	35	55	68	10	0	1	26	1	4	3	44	1	36	8	4	4	.304	.3
Phillips, Blaine, Oneonta	.209	47	163	148	12	31	33	2	0	0	12	2	1	1	11	0	51	0	2	3	.223	.2
Pinto, Rene, Oneonta	.206	53	221	199	15	41	52	1	2	2	20	3	3	3	13	0	54	1	1	4	.261	.2
Pointer, Corey, Erie	.190	5	22	21	1	4	5	1	0	0	2	0	0	1	0	0	9	0	0	1	.238	.2
Pomierski, Joe, Hudson Valley*	.260	74	330	285	45	74	129	25	3	8	54	0	6	4	35	1	91	2	4	6	.453	.3
Pond, Simon, Vermont*	.300	69	286	253	37	76	103	16	1	3	40	1	3	3	26	2	26	9	3	7	.407	.3
Pratt, Wes, Auburn	.313	70	288	246	43	77	116	22	1	5	35	0	1	2	39	2	37	11	3	8	.472	.3
Ramirez, Aramis, Erie	.305	61	263	223	37	68	117	14	4	9	42	0	2	7	31	1	41	0	0	7	.525	.3
Ramirez, Danny, Pittsfield	.281	70	284	260	28	73	91	5	5	1	22	4	2	4	14	0	45	24	9	3	.350	.3
Ramirez, Frank, Jamestown	.054	19	40	37	5	2	3	1	0	0	3	0	0	1	2	0	17	1	0	0	.081	.3
Raymondi, Michael, Hudson Val.	.040	16	32	25	1	1	1	0	0	0	1	0	0	3	4	0	10	0	0	0	.040	.3
Redman, Julian, Erie*	.294	43	192	170	31	50	72	4	6	2	21	2	3	0	17	0	30	7	3	2	.424	.3
Reeder, Jim, Auburn*	.282	69	273	241	24	68	84	8	4	0	25	1	4	4	23	2	32	6	1	5	.349	.3
Restovich, George, Jamestown*	.179	48	184	151	25	27	50	5	0	6	22	0	2	1	30	2	55	1	1	1	.331	.3
Rice, Charles, Erie†	.251	54	226	187	24	47	73	12	1	4	19	0	4	10	23	0	39	6	4	4	.390	.3
Richards, Rowan, Hudson Valley	.274	30	136	113	18	31	52	6	0	5	18	0	2	5	16	0	33	4	1	4	.460	.3
Rios, Brian, Jamestown	.304	36	122	102	19	31	44	6	2	1	17	0	1	0	19	0	15	4	1	3	.431	.3
Rivero, Eddie, Batavia*	.255	13	58	55	7	14	22	1	2	1	6	1	0	0	2	0	14	1	2	1	.400	.2
Roberts, Ryan, New Jersey	.226	50	215	190	28	43	57	8	3	0	18	4	2	1	18	0	49	1	2	3	.300	.2
Rodriguez, Chris, Watertown†	.000	2	5	5	0	0	0	0	0	0	0	0	0	0	0	0	1	0	0	0	.000	.0
Rodriguez, Mike, St. Catharines	.269	46	155	145	14	39	43	2	1	0	12	0	2	1	7	3	14	4	4	4	.297	.3
Rodriguez, Sammy, Pittsfield	.194	32	106	93	8	18	24	3	0	1	10	0	1	1	11	0	25	1	0	3	.258	.2
Rodriquez, Gary, Watertown*	.235	67	305	247	45	58	65	7	0	0	17	8	1	5	44	1	70	20	7	1	.263	.3
Rose, Michael, Auburn	.250	61	215	180	20	45	58	5	1	2	11	4	0	1	30	0	41	9	3	5	.322	.3
Saffer, Jeff, Oneonta	.249	53	228	197	18	49	67	4	1	4	27	0	5	4	22	1	62	2	1	1	.340	.3
Sanchez, Orlando, Lowell	.183	33	128	115	15	21	23	2	0	0	5	0	0	3	10	0	29	3	0	4	.200	.2
Schmidt, David, New Jersey*	.254	57	210	189	17	48	64	9	2	1	23	3	2	0	16	0	55	1	1	2	.339	.3
Schofield, Andy, New Jersey	.185	11	31	27	1	5	7	0	1	0	1	0	0	0	4	0	8	1	1	1	.259	.2
Seabol, Scott, Oneonta	.211	43	165	142	16	30	50	9	1	3	10	2	0	6	15	0	30	2	3	1	.352	.3
Shadburne, Adam, Batavia*	.182	32	38	33	4	6	9	0	0	1	2	4	0	0	1	0	13	0	0	0	.273	.2
Shatley, Andy, St. Catharines	.281	76	287	256	34	72	108	17	2	5	36	2	2	6	21	1	64	4	3	3	.422	.3
Shipp, Skip, Erie	.254	55	207	189	19	48	64	7	0	3	26	0	1	1	16	1	50	3	2	7	.339	.3
Sime, Rafael, Utica*	.241	67	247	216	26	52	80	9	5	3	31	0	3	0	28	1	62	10	4	1	.370	.3
Skett, Will, St. Catharines	.276	75	324	272	47	75	135	13	1	15	52	5	4	10	33	0	73	13	3	2	.496	.3
Snelling, Allen, St. Catharines	.144	39	113	104	10	15	16	1	0	0	5	1	0	2	6	0	23	2	0	0	.154	.1
Snusz, Christopher, Batavia	.161	13	38	31	6	5	5	0	0	0	6	0	0	1	6	0	9	0	0	0	.161	.3
Sollman, Scott, Jamestown*	.281	67	302	253	49	71	86	5	5	0	19	6	2	7	34	1	47	35	14	2	.340	.3
Stanton, Robert, Watertown	.185	44	165	146	19	27	41	5	0	3	20	0	1	3	15	1	49	0	0	5	.281	.2
Stewart, Paxton, St. Catharines*	.277	65	220	206	21	57	73	13	0	1	8	1	0	1	12	0	40	3	2	3	.354	.3
Stowers, Christopher, Vermont*	.319	72	305	282	58	90	150	21	9	7	44	0	2	2	21	0	37	16	5	4	.532	.3
Swaino, Shannon, Vermont*	.284	50	178	155	20	44	56	10	1	0	21	0	0	0	23	0	31	0	2	3	.361	.3
Tagliaferri, Jeff, Jamestown*	.246	72	295	252	42	62	107	12	3	9	36	0	0	4	42	1	61	2	2	5	.425	.3
Tamargo, John, Pittsfield†	.223	55	225	184	26	41	52	5	3	0	19	1	3	2	35	0	34	5	3	5	.283	.3
Taylor, Adam, Watertown	.184	49	186	147	25	27	53	5	0	7	27	0	0	3	36	1	57	1	0	2	.361	.3

ayer, Team	Avg.	G	TPA	AB	R	H	TB	2B	3B	HR	RBI	SH	SF	HP	BB	IBB	SO	SB	CS	GDP	Slg.	OBP
ylor, Gregory, Batavia	.245	19	58	53	5	13	19	0	3	0	5	0	1	1	3	0	9	1	0	1	.358	.293
ompson, Andre, Lowell	.168	35	115	107	12	18	30	4	1	2	8	0	0	1	7	0	35	1	0	1	.280	.226
ler, Brad, Watertown	.233	55	220	202	26	47	67	5	3	3	24	2	3	3	10	0	50	7	5	6	.332	.275
rti, Mike, Batavia	.250	59	251	216	35	54	91	14	4	5	44	1	2	5	27	0	55	7	0	3	.421	.344
acy, Andrew, Vermont*	.269	57	212	175	26	47	72	11	1	4	24	1	2	2	32	2	37	1	1	8	.411	.384
cci, Peter, St. Catharines	.254	54	234	205	28	52	95	8	7	7	33	2	3	1	23	1	58	5	3	1	.463	.328
ombley, Dennis, Oneonta	.211	6	23	19	2	4	8	1	0	1	3	0	0	0	4	0	5	0	0	0	.421	.348
jueto, Hector, New Jersey	.247	52	186	170	22	42	46	4	0	0	11	3	1	3	9	1	40	4	2	2	.271	.295
lencia, Victor, Oneonta	.195	72	288	261	30	51	68	8	0	3	25	3	3	0	21	0	86	3	0	4	.261	.253
zquez, Manny, Hudson Valley*	.240	73	290	258	41	62	78	5	4	1	21	2	2	4	24	1	41	27	7	6	.302	.313
nghaus, Jeff, Utica†	.229	75	329	258	53	59	78	12	2	1	24	3	4	4	60	1	70	16	12	2	.302	.377
ras, Wilton, Lowell	.240	67	266	250	22	60	75	15	0	0	19	1	2	0	13	0	29	2	1	9	.300	.275
ckers, Randy, Pittsfield	.241	35	140	133	22	32	72	5	1	11	30	0	0	3	4	0	52	1	1	0	.541	.279
akeland, Chris, Jamestown*	.309	70	271	220	38	68	122	14	5	10	49	1	3	4	43	0	83	8	3	1	.555	.426
are, Jeremy, Vermont	.191	32	110	94	12	18	20	2	0	0	6	1	0	0	15	0	25	5	3	1	.213	.303
esemann, Jason, Batavia	.218	49	173	156	21	34	46	9	0	1	11	4	2	3	8	0	30	3	1	1	.295	.266
esson, Barry, Auburn	.159	55	193	176	11	28	35	7	0	0	12	1	3	1	12	1	46	5	3	5	.199	.214
heeler, Ryan, Oneonta	.308	24	67	65	12	20	25	3	1	0	5	0	0	1	1	0	11	4	0	1	.385	.328
itlock, Brian, Watertown	.217	47	181	152	23	33	51	5	2	3	14	2	1	3	23	0	49	2	0	5	.336	.330
lders, Paul, New Jersey	.185	10	34	27	1	5	6	1	0	0	0	0	0	0	7	0	9	0	1	1	.222	.353
der, P.J., Pittsfield*	.242	63	227	182	26	44	65	9	3	2	27	2	3	1	39	2	52	5	6	4	.357	.373
ung, Randel, Auburn	.229	40	149	131	17	30	32	2	0	0	4	4	0	5	9	0	22	13	6	1	.244	.303
ata, Alexis, Jamestown	.283	15	56	53	8	15	26	1	2	2	7	0	0	3	2	0	19	0	0	0	.491	.321
vershnik, Mike, St. Catharines...	.000	25	1	1	0	0	0	0	0	0	0	0	0	0	0	0	1	0	0	0	.000	.000
oeda, Jesse, Jamestown†	.208	54	207	178	23	37	44	3	2	0	17	7	0	1	21	0	31	6	3	5	.247	.295
eta, Julio, Williamsport	.258	62	250	221	35	57	76	12	2	1	29	0	2	8	19	2	36	7	4	8	.344	.336

GRAND SLAMS: Wakeland, 2; Antigua, Erickson, Fuentes, S. Gallagher, Garrett, H. Gordon, Jenkins, Kent, Lomasney, Manning, Olmeda, Skett, Stanton, Torti, 1 each.

AWARDED FIRST BASE ON CATCHER'S INTERFERENCE: Fuentes 4 (Falciglia, Fick, Marsters, Schmidt); Dransfeldt 2 (Alvarado, Falciglia); Huffman 2 (Jason S. Koehler, se); Monroe 2 (Fortin, S. Rodriguez); Rice 2 (Jason S. Koehler, Schmidt); Britt (Ellis); Charles (Antigua); Hernandez (Jason S. Koehler); Hillenbrand (May); C. Meyers rr); Peoples (King).

1996 PITCHING

TEAM

m	W	L	Pct.	ERA	G	CG	ShO	Sv.	IP	H	TBF	R	ER	HR	SH	SF	HB	BB	IBB	SO	WP	Bk.
rmont	48	26	.649	3.07	74	7	7	20	630.0	541	2601	256	215	29	18	15	30	194	1	575	43	12
ertown	45	30	.600	3.11	75	4	13	20	651.1	552	2732	283	225	36	14	14	20	246	11	661	44	17
nestown	39	36	.520	3.21	76	1	2	14	658.1	595	2802	319	239	47	21	23	39	245	1	547	52	11
sfield	46	29	.613	3.37	75	6	8	19	635.1	575	2694	274	238	23	24	20	38	221	3	559	44	13
avia	42	33	.560	3.57	75	2	8	20	650.0	606	2738	304	258	32	27	20	36	207	5	523	42	9
amsport	43	32	.573	3.59	76	3	4	18	654.2	560	2836	326	261	30	17	18	27	322	12	585	50	23
onta	31	45	.408	3.69	76	4	7	18	655.2	565	2889	364	269	20	25	29	32	338	5	576	49	21
ell	33	41	.446	3.91	74	4	3	18	637.1	603	2860	372	277	31	27	29	55	297	11	592	83	14
Catharines	44	32	.579	4.01	76	5	7	24	651.0	599	2813	361	290	43	19	26	40	262	6	542	61	11
urn	37	39	.487	4.02	76	2	4	24	661.0	639	2944	371	295	30	21	23	60	317	13	519	64	15
a	30	46	.395	4.10	76	4	2	13	658.2	670	2912	373	300	35	32	29	49	272	8	573	48	15
	29	47	.382	4.19	76	4	2	15	646.2	648	2822	360	301	44	15	19	33	236	16	567	58	19
Jersey	28	47	.373	4.25	75	0	5	16	654.0	692	2914	399	309	37	33	30	30	270	10	608	52	14
son Valley	32	44	.421	4.31	76	1	2	13	688.1	686	3045	427	330	34	26	26	24	283	13	653	84	23

INDIVIDUAL

TOP QUALIFIERS FOR EARNED-RUN AVERAGE TITLE

Minimum 61 innings. *Lefthanded pitcher.

her, Team	W	L	Pct.	ERA	G	GS	CG	ShO	GF	Sv.	IP	H	TBF	R	ER	HR	SH	SF	HB	BB	IBB	SO	WP	Bk.
es, Ken, Hudson Valley*	6	2	.750	1.07	38	0	0	0	23	5	67.0	51	273	19	8	1	5	0	1	21	3	64	2	1
erol, Beiker, St. Catharines	9	1	.900	1.50	14	13	1	1	0	0	84.0	59	330	24	14	6	3	3	4	21	0	66	2	1
p, Jared, Watertown	10	2	.833	1.69	15	15	1	1	0	0	95.2	68	380	29	18	2	1	1	7	30	0	99	6	0
gers, Bobby, Lowell	7	4	.636	1.90	14	14	2	1	0	0	90.0	60	363	33	19	3	2	2	3	31	0	108	9	2
er, Brian, Batavia	8	3	.727	2.07	17	10	1	1	2	0	82.2	70	332	22	19	4	3	0	0	25	0	43	3	1
can, Courtney, Williamsport	7	1	.917	2.19	15	15	1	0	0	0	90.1	58	360	28	22	6	3	0	5	34	0	91	8	0
an, Corey, Pittsfield	8	3	.727	2.30	14	14	2	0	0	0	98.0	74	390	30	25	2	5	1	4	20	0	84	5	2
ada, Edward, Vermont	6	5	.545	2.33	14	14	2	0	0	0	92.2	82	378	32	24	3	3	1	7	20	0	79	7	0
inez, Willie, Watertown	6	5	.545	2.40	14	14	1	1	0	0	90.0	79	358	25	24	5	2	0	0	21	2	92	6	0
z, Luis, Auburn	5	5	.500	2.45	15	15	4	0	0	0	99.0	85	416	38	27	4	2	2	3	31	2	73	3	1
er, Christian, Vermont	7	1	.875	2.48	14	14	2	1	0	0	80.0	63	322	26	22	1	2	1	4	22	0	61	8	3
on, Phillip, Williamsport*	7	4	.636	2.54	15	13	2	1	1	0	85.0	68	364	33	24	1	3	2	3	32	3	77	7	3
ey, Matt, Lowell	3	9	.250	2.68	15	15	0	0	0	0	87.1	68	387	51	26	0	3	3	9	44	2	72	13	1
nas, Evan, Batavia	10	2	.833	2.78	13	13	0	0	0	0	81.0	60	321	29	25	3	1	3	5	23	0	75	6	0
es, Aaron, Utica	8	2	.750	2.81	18	9	1	0	3	0	73.2	60	301	28	23	2	3	5	2	18	2	77	5	4

PARTMENTAL LEADERS: W—C. Duncan, 11; L—O'Connor, 10; Pct.—C. Duncan, .917; G—Raines, 38; GS—Several players tied at 15; CG—Delossantos, McDade, h; ShO—Delossantos, 2; GF—McFerrin, 32; Sv.—Kawabata, McFerrin, 20 each; IP—Beebe, Yanez, 99.0 each; H—Lara, 95; TBF—Yanez, 416; R—O'Connor, 60; Lara, 48; HR—Johannsen, 9; SH—Beebe, 6; SF—Tilton, 9; HB—Braswell, 11; BB—V. Rodriguez, 54; IBB—G. Duncan, 5; SO—Rodgers, 108; WP—Yount, 15; Licciardi, 7.

CLASS A New York-Pennsylvania League

ALL PITCHERS

*Lefthanded pitcher.

Pitcher, Team	W	L	Pct.	ERA	G	GS	CG	ShO	GF	Sv.	IP	H	TBF	R	ER	HR	SH	SF	HB	BB	IBB	SO	WP
Aguilar, Carlos, Oneonta	0	4	.000	3.62	23	0	0	0	7	0	49.2	44	221	29	20	0	2	2	4	27	0	43	6
Ah Yat, Paul, Erie*	1	1	.500	3.25	26	0	0	0	4	1	27.2	24	114	15	10	1	1	0	0	6	0	34	0
Albrecht, Daniel, Utica*	0	0	.000	7.59	13	0	0	0	4	0	21.1	25	113	19	18	2	0	1	0	25	0	19	3
Allen, Brandon, Batavia*	2	6	.250	3.52	13	11	0	0	1	0	64.0	69	268	36	25	2	2	1	4	10	0	39	2
Aquino, Julio, Hudson Valley	3	1	.750	2.60	22	0	0	0	10	3	45.0	36	183	16	13	2	2	1	2	7	0	46	5
Armas, Antonio, Oneonta	1	1	.500	5.74	3	3	0	0	0	0	15.2	14	73	12	10	1	0	1	0	11	0	14	4
Austin, Kevie, Lowell	2	0	1.000	5.87	8	0	0	0	3	0	15.1	14	68	11	10	3	0	1	0	10	0	15	0
Avila, Jose, Erie	4	3	.571	4.04	14	14	0	0	0	0	78.0	75	337	37	35	4	1	4	5	33	0	74	2
Bale, John, St. Catharines*	3	2	.600	4.86	8	8	0	0	0	0	33.1	39	148	21	18	2	0	1	0	11	0	35	4
Bauer, Chris, Jamestown	3	4	.429	4.08	11	11	0	0	0	0	57.1	65	250	31	26	2	3	4	1	15	0	35	6
Beach, Scott, Erie	0	1	.000	1.64	17	0	0	0	5	0	22.0	16	98	7	4	0	2	0	3	14	0	25	2
Beagle, Chad, Utica*	0	1	.000	81.00	1	0	0	0	0	0	0.1	3	5	3	3	0	0	0	0	2	0	0	0
Beale, Chuck, Lowell	0	0	.000	1.24	28	0	0	0	26	16	29.0	16	112	7	4	1	2	0	1	7	0	33	2
Beebe, Hans, Pittsfield*	6	5	.545	3.09	14	14	2	1	0	0	99.0	94	398	39	34	3	6	4	4	17	0	74	1
Bernhard, David, Auburn	3	2	.600	4.78	24	2	0	0	8	1	49.0	56	223	31	26	4	4	3	7	23	2	27	6
Berry, Jason, Hudson Valley	4	7	.364	5.50	28	0	0	0	21	4	37.2	41	180	28	23	4	5	2	1	20	3	48	4
Biehle, Michael, Oneonta*	2	3	.400	3.96	20	0	0	0	12	0	36.1	37	171	22	16	1	4	1	2	18	2	42	2
Billingsley, Brent, Utica*	4	5	.444	4.01	15	15	0	0	0	0	89.2	83	373	46	40	6	0	4	3	28	0	82	5
Birsner, Roark, Williamsport	2	4	.333	5.47	31	0	0	0	8	1	51.0	53	238	33	31	3	1	0	5	27	2	58	7
Booker, Chris, Williamsport	4	6	.400	5.31	14	14	0	0	0	0	61.0	57	292	51	36	2	0	6	3	51	1	52	7
Bracho, Alejandro, Oneonta*	0	2	.000	7.20	4	1	0	0	2	1	10.0	8	49	8	8	0	1	0	1	13	0	11	3
Bradford, Josh, St. Catharines	5	4	.556	3.35	18	7	0	0	3	1	53.2	49	232	27	20	1	1	3	4	17	0	63	8
Brammer, John, Watertown	5	0	1.000	3.55	17	0	0	0	5	1	38.0	27	173	22	15	0	0	3	3	28	1	49	8
Brand, Scott, Oneonta	1	2	.333	3.70	9	1	0	0	1	0	24.1	20	114	17	10	0	0	2	4	19	1	22	2
Braswell, Bryan, Auburn*	4	8	.333	4.32	15	14	0	0	1	0	73.0	70	325	40	35	2	1	2	11	29	2	77	9
Brittan, Corey, Pittsfield	8	3	.727	2.30	14	14	2	0	0	0	98.0	74	390	30	25	2	5	1	4	20	0	84	5
Brookens, Casey, Williamsport	3	1	.750	3.33	25	1	0	0	8	2	51.1	50	219	20	19	1	1	1	0	20	2	42	4
Brooks, Wyatt, Erie*	1	0	1.000	1.54	15	0	0	0	2	1	23.1	20	96	5	4	1	4	1	2	7	1	24	1
Browning, Tom, Jamestown*	0	1	.000	8.10	5	1	0	0	2	0	6.2	13	38	7	6	0	0	0	0	6	1	5	0
Cafferty, Jason, Batavia	3	4	.429	6.42	14	6	0	0	2	0	40.2	44	183	30	29	4	2	0	5	14	0	35	4
Cain, Travis, Hudson Valley	2	5	.286	4.60	15	15	0	0	0	0	76.1	67	337	50	39	2	0	5	3	44	0	87	12
Calmus, Lance, Watertown	1	3	.250	6.41	11	11	0	0	0	0	46.1	53	212	40	33	8	2	0	0	18	1	51	2
Cames, Aaron, Utica	6	2	.750	2.81	18	9	1	0	3	0	73.2	60	301	28	23	2	3	5	2	18	2	77	5
Camp, Jared, Watertown	10	2	.833	1.69	15	15	1	1	0	0	95.2	68	380	29	18	2	1	1	7	30	0	99	6
Campbell, Tedde, Erie	3	4	.429	3.34	27	0	0	0	15	4	32.1	24	140	17	12	2	2	1	6	16	0	30	3
Cannon, Jon, Williamsport*	6	4	.600	3.02	14	13	0	0	1	0	83.1	61	329	31	28	6	0	0	3	26	0	66	2
Chaney, Michael, Erie*	1	1	.500	5.28	10	5	0	0	2	0	29.0	27	125	20	17	1	2	3	1	14	1	21	1
Clark, Brian, New Jersey*	3	5	.375	2.86	32	0	0	0	14	1	44.0	42	188	21	14	3	2	3	0	15	3	29	3
Coleman, Billy, Oneonta	1	0	1.000	14.73	3	0	0	0	0	0	3.2	4	23	6	6	1	0	0	3	6	0	4	1
Cook, John, Auburn	0	0	.000	36.00	1	0	0	0	1	0	1.0	5	9	4	4	0	0	0	0	1	0	1	0
Cordero, Francisco, Jamestown.	0	0	.000	0.82	2	2	0	0	0	0	11.0	5	39	1	1	0	0	0	0	2	0	10	0
Cotton, Joseph, Batavia	2	4	.333	4.27	9	9	0	0	0	0	46.1	43	196	23	22	2	3	1	1	19	0	37	4
Crafton, Kevin, New Jersey	2	3	.400	2.18	23	0	0	0	10	2	33.0	28	132	8	8	1	3	1	1	6	2	43	2
Crane, John, Batavia*	1	0	1.000	3.86	21	0	0	0	8	0	35.0	38	157	20	15	0	2	1	1	17	0	31	5
Crawford, Chris, Auburn	2	4	.333	4.12	12	9	0	0	0	0	59.0	51	252	28	27	1	0	4	5	29	0	36	9
Crawford, Jim, Williamsport	0	3	.000	9.67	21	0	0	0	6	1	27.0	40	142	35	29	4	2	0	2	20	1	31	3
Cressend, Jack, Lowell	3	2	.600	2.36	9	8	0	0	1	0	45.2	37	189	15	12	0	2	2	4	17	1	57	6
Cutchins, Todd, Pittsfield*	2	1	.667	4.62	6	3	0	0	1	0	25.1	24	108	15	13	0	2	1	2	10	0	29	0
Dace, Derek, Auburn*	9	4	.692	3.25	15	15	0	0	0	0	97.0	89	400	41	35	7	2	1	2	35	2	87	1
Daniels, David, Erie	1	3	.250	2.72	31	0	0	0	19	7	36.1	33	150	12	11	3	3	1	4	5	3	45	0
Davenport, Joe, St. Catharines	2	4	.333	5.13	20	8	0	0	3	0	66.2	71	295	44	38	5	4	3	5	23	0	43	8
Dellamano, Anthony, Hudson V.	4	7	.364	6.17	18	10	0	0	2	1	65.2	83	311	54	45	5	1	1	4	33	2	61	13
Delossantos, Luis, Oneonta	4	4	.500	3.72	10	10	3	2	0	0	58.0	44	240	28	24	3	0	3	3	21	0	62	2
DePaula, Sean, Watertown	0	0	.000	0.00	1	0	0	0	0	0	2.0	0	6	0	0	0	0	0	0	0	0	5	0
Dingman, Craig, Oneonta	0	2	.000	2.04	20	0	0	0	15	9	35.1	17	137	11	8	0	1	1	1	9	0	52	0
Draeger, Mark, Hudson Valley	1	2	.333	6.12	17	0	0	0	3	0	32.1	44	166	35	22	1	1	2	2	17	1	28	7
Duffy, John, Lowell*	3	4	.429	5.66	29	0	0	0	10	0	41.1	56	207	32	26	3	4	3	3	27	4	32	3
Duncan, Courtney, Williamsport	11	1	.917	2.19	15	15	1	0	0	0	90.1	58	360	28	22	6	3	0	5	34	0	91	8
Duncan, Geoff, Utica	2	5	.286	3.79	24	1	0	0	8	2	40.1	46	191	23	17	3	0	1	4	19	5	52	5
Eason, Michael, Utica	0	1	.000	6.75	9	0	0	0	5	1	14.2	21	71	12	11	2	1	1	2	7	2	9	3
Edwards, Jon, Watertown	1	3	.250	3.15	23	0	0	0	17	4	34.1	26	141	12	12	2	2	0	2	14	2	37	2
Ellison, Jason, Oneonta	0	0	.000	9.00	1	0	0	0	1	0	1.0	2	5	1	1	0	0	0	0	0	0	2	0
Elmore, George, Erie	1	0	1.000	4.78	19	0	0	0	6	0	32.0	38	155	22	17	1	1	4	3	21	0	17	9
Falciglia, Tony, New Jersey	0	0	.000	0.00	1	0	0	0	1	0	2.0	3	10	2	0	0	0	1	0	0	0	0	0
Feliz, Bienvenido, Watertown	5	6	.455	3.89	13	11	2	1	1	0	71.2	59	297	37	31	7	0	1	1	26	1	56	4
Ferrell, Dan, Utica*	2	5	.286	4.71	14	13	1	1	1	1	70.2	74	298	40	37	6	0	2	0	17	0	61	4
Ferullo, Matt, Pittsfield	4	1	.800	4.68	11	4	0	0	5	2	32.2	38	146	20	17	1	2	0	2	9	1	22	2
Festa, Chris, Lowell	2	5	.286	5.10	20	9	1	0	3	0	72.1	94	341	53	41	6	3	2	5	20	1	43	8
Figueroa, Julio, Vermont	5	3	.625	3.30	14	14	1	0	0	0	79.0	78	334	37	29	6	1	2	4	32	0	59	3
Fleetwood, Tony, Watertown*	0	0	.000	5.00	12	0	0	0	5	1	18.0	22	83	13	10	1	0	1	1	6	0	19	0
Fortune, Peter, Vermont*	0	1	.000	3.86	2	0	0	0	1	0	2.1	3	12	2	1	0	0	1	0	2	0	2	0
Fowler, Jered, Hudson Valley	0	0	.000	2.25	2	0	0	0	1	0	4.0	2	15	2	1	1	0	0	0	0	0	1	0
Frace, Ryan, Batavia	4	1	.800	2.68	25	1	0	0	11	0	53.2	49	221	19	16	5	3	1	2	14	0	57	6
Frazier, Harold, Oneonta*	2	1	.667	2.70	5	0	0	0	1	0	6.2	2	24	2	2	0	0	0	0	2	0	7	0
Fuller, Duane, Auburn	1	0	1.000	8.66	11	2	0	0	1	0	17.2	17	92	18	17	1	1	0	5	21	0	16	4
Fuller, Stephen, Auburn	2	6	.250	5.66	18	9	0	0	4	0	70.0	80	324	52	44	4	5	3	8	38	0	45	9
Gallagher, Keith, New Jersey	1	7	.125	7.22	12	12	0	0	0	0	52.1	64	244	51	42	1	1	2	1	28	0	28	6
Garsky, Brian, Vermont	5	1	.833	3.18	25	0	0	0	10	1	28.1	25	129	13	10	1	2	2	1	15	1	34	2
Gaskill, Derek, St. Catharines	4	4	.500	4.76	19	6	1	0	6	1	58.2	61	258	37	31	7	2	6	9	18	1	51	6
Gonzalez, Generoso, Jamestwn.	0	0	.000	5.40	6	0	0	0	1	0	10.0	16	49	8	6	3	0	0	1	4	0	10	0

cher, Team	W	L	Pct.	ERA	G	GS	CG	ShO	GF	Sv.	IP	H	TBF	R	ER	HR	SH	SF	HB	BB	IBB	SO	WP	Bk.
nzalez, Luis, Erie	1	4	.200	5.68	21	1	0	0	8	0	25.1	32	113	19	16	2	0	1	0	6	0	19	1	1
rdon, Andrew, New Jersey	0	0	.000	4.22	25	5	0	0	0	0	49.0	67	222	33	23	3	2	4	1	9	0	46	9	3
aterol, Beiker, St. Catharines	9	1	.900	1.50	14	13	1	1	0	0	84.0	59	330	24	14	6	3	3	4	21	0	66	2	1
aves, Ryan, Williamsport*	0	0	.000	0.00	4	0	0	0	2	0	5.0	4	20	0	0	0	0	0	0	2	0	3	0	1
een, Jason, Auburn	0	0	.000	0.00	2	2	0	0	0	0	6.0	4	22	1	0	0	0	0	0	1	0	2	0	0
iffiths, Everard, Hudson Val.	1	1	.500	3.06	11	4	0	0	4	0	32.1	26	137	12	11	2	0	0	2	13	0	39	6	0
rt, Lendon, Williamsport*	2	3	.400	1.44	28	0	0	0	13	2	31.1	15	129	6	5	0	2	0	0	24	1	26	1	0
ynie, Jason, Erie*	3	4	.429	3.25	16	12	1	0	2	0	80.1	86	345	36	29	2	5	4	3	22	2	74	4	3
ffernan, Greg, New Jersey	0	1	.000	3.42	18	0	0	0	4	0	23.2	24	110	16	9	2	2	1	1	13	0	22	1	2
ndrikx, Brandon, Oneonta	3	2	.600	1.33	17	0	0	0	10	1	27.0	17	109	6	4	3	1	1	2	15	0	23	2	0
rbison, Brett, Pittsfield	0	1	.000	22.50	1	1	0	0	0	0	2.0	4	15	6	5	0	0	0	0	4	0	1	1	0
lobinko, Mike, Williamsport*	1	0	1.000	1.56	4	2	0	0	0	0	17.1	11	69	4	3	0	0	1	0	7	0	9	2	1
rton, Aaron, Hudson Valley*	0	3	.000	12.43	9	7	0	0	0	0	25.1	55	154	46	35	2	1	2	3	15	0	15	7	2
eda, Alejandro, St. Cathrns	0	3	.000	8.71	12	5	0	0	1	0	31.0	41	151	33	30	5	0	1	2	16	0	17	2	1
jerick, Rhett, Oneonta	1	1	.500	5.85	11	0	0	0	7	0	20.0	26	97	16	13	0	0	0	0	11	0	21	3	0
hannsen, Jeffrey, Utica*	4	5	.444	4.33	14	14	0	0	0	0	79.0	68	324	40	38	9	2	2	6	22	0	73	2	3
uflin, David, Jamestown	6	2	.750	3.09	22	7	0	0	3	0	64.0	55	266	25	22	5	0	3	3	26	0	56	10	0
wabata, Kyle, Batavia	1	2	.333	1.93	25	0	0	0	25	20	28.0	21	115	7	6	2	2	0	1	7	1	24	2	0
ssel, Kyle, Pittsfield*	2	6	.250	4.74	13	13	0	0	0	0	79.2	80	332	44	42	6	0	1	4	19	0	67	4	2
ney, Matt, Lowell	3	9	.250	2.68	15	15	0	0	0	0	87.1	68	387	51	26	0	3	3	9	44	2	72	13	1
ght, Brandon, Hudson Valley	2	2	.500	4.42	9	9	0	0	0	0	53.0	59	236	29	26	1	2	1	1	21	0	52	2	1
all, Eric, Oneonta*	0	5	.000	2.42	15	6	0	0	6	0	44.2	43	203	27	12	2	3	2	1	25	1	29	1	2
chapelle, Yan, St. Catharines	0	0	.000	0.00	3	0	0	0	1	0	4.0	0	12	0	0	0	0	0	0	0	0	8	0	0
ra, Giovanni, Vermont	6	3	.667	4.68	15	15	2	0	0	0	92.1	95	392	54	48	5	3	3	4	27	0	63	7	1
vrence, Clint, St. Catharines*	4	1	.800	2.50	9	8	2	1	0	0	57.2	53	230	18	16	1	1	2	1	11	0	25	5	0
e, Corey, Hudson Valley*	1	4	.200	3.29	9	9	0	0	0	0	54.2	42	226	24	20	1	2	3	1	21	1	59	1	2
an, Scott, Hudson Valley	3	5	.375	4.70	15	15	1	0	0	0	88.0	82	378	54	46	4	2	4	4	36	2	73	9	6
lie, Sean, Vermont*	2	4	.333	4.12	17	7	0	0	5	0	54.2	52	232	28	25	3	1	2	2	14	0	46	3	0
vis, Ron, Utica	2	2	.500	3.96	20	0	0	0	8	2	36.1	36	159	17	16	3	1	0	2	15	2	42	6	1
ciardi, Ronald, Williamsport*	3	5	.375	4.50	15	15	0	0	0	0	76.0	78	338	51	38	4	0	4	2	38	0	53	5	7
e, Jeff, New Jersey	2	2	.500	6.46	17	5	0	0	2	0	39.0	47	187	35	28	4	2	1	1	19	2	29	0	4
cherek, Matt, Hudson Valley	0	1	.000	0.00	3	0	0	0	3	0	2.0	3	12	1	0	0	0	0	0	3	0	0	0	0
donado, Esteban, Auburn	0	1	.000	5.17	6	6	0	0	0	0	15.2	20	76	14	9	1	1	1	1	9	0	9	0	2
enfant, Dave, Jamestown	0	0	.000	0.00	2	0	0	0	0	0	3.0	1	12	1	0	0	0	1	0	0	0	0	0	1
nn, James, St. Catharines	2	1	.667	3.62	26	0	0	0	23	17	27.1	22	117	12	11	3	2	2	3	10	1	37	0	1
nsavage, Jay, Auburn	0	1	.000	3.00	2	0	0	0	2	0	3.0	4	18	4	1	0	0	0	0	3	0	1	0	0
tinez, Dennis, Watertown	4	2	.667	2.44	12	6	0	0	2	0	44.1	30	177	14	12	1	1	1	0	20	1	37	4	1
tinez, Jose, Hudson Valley	2	3	.400	3.79	16	5	0	0	4	0	54.2	56	233	35	23	3	3	2	0	11	0	38	6	3
tinez, Willie, Watertown*	6	5	.545	2.44	14	14	1	1	0	0	90.0	79	358	25	24	5	2	0	0	21	2	92	6	0
z, Brian, Vermont*	5	3	.625	2.60	14	9	0	0	3	0	55.1	41	224	20	16	3	1	0	2	18	0	53	2	0
vs, Jarrod, Watertown	5	2	.714	3.34	12	12	0	0	0	0	59.1	62	257	29	22	1	0	4	2	18	1	56	5	3
Bride, Chris, St. Catharines	3	1	.750	2.51	6	6	1	0	0	0	43.0	37	169	14	12	2	0	0	4	7	0	28	2	0
ade, Neal, Erie	7	3	.700	3.40	13	13	3	0	0	0	76.2	76	319	33	29	3	3	4	6	21	0	67	5	2
Dougal, Mike, New Jersey	1	1	.500	7.08	14	0	0	0	4	0	20.1	20	87	17	16	4	1	1	1	4	0	25	1	0
errin, Chris, Auburn	4	2	.667	1.71	33	0	0	0	32	20	42.0	23	175	16	8	2	1	0	5	24	1	45	3	0
sink, Brian, Batavia	3	1	.750	3.75	8	8	1	1	0	0	50.1	48	211	22	21	4	1	0	3	16	0	35	5	0
ers, Ryan, St. Catharines	3	0	1.000	1.50	7	1	0	0	1	0	12.0	6	43	2	2	0	1	1	0	5	0	9	0	0
er, Brian, Batavia	8	3	.727	2.07	17	10	1	1	2	0	82.2	70	332	22	19	4	3	0	0	25	0	43	3	1
er, Matt, Jamestown*	1	3	.250	4.62	6	6	0	0	0	0	25.1	33	115	16	13	0	1	0	3	13	0	21	6	2
er, Wade, Auburn	1	1	.500	5.00	2	2	0	0	0	0	9.0	8	41	9	5	0	0	0	0	4	0	11	0	1
er, Matthew, Watertown*	2	1	.667	3.60	21	3	0	0	5	3	36.0	29	151	14	10	2	1	0	0	13	0	38	2	0
hell, Christopher, Jamestwn	1	5	.167	3.97	25	7	0	0	7	1	56.2	54	249	33	25	6	3	3	4	30	0	43	3	1
hell, Courtney, Batavia*	0	1	.000	1.88	24	0	0	0	8	0	43.0	38	183	14	9	0	3	2	1	17	1	49	2	0
atemayor, Humberto, Lowell	1	2	.333	6.20	5	5	0	0	0	0	24.2	30	109	20	17	1	2	4	1	6	0	19	2	0
tgomery, Greg, New Jersey	1	0	1.000	1.23	11	0	0	0	5	1	14.2	9	60	5	2	0	1	1	0	4	0	22	2	0
re, Joe, Utica	0	5	.000	3.78	11	0	0	0	6	1	16.2	22	85	15	7	0	1	1	0	10	0	14	4	0
gan, Steve, Lowell*	1	1	.500	4.76	13	1	0	0	3	0	22.2	25	119	18	12	3	2	1	3	20	2	19	4	1
ris, Chad, Vermont	2	1	.667	3.69	20	0	0	0	6	0	31.2	20	124	13	13	4	1	0	2	10	0	44	1	0
a, Daniel, Oneonta	0	1	.000	4.50	10	0	0	0	8	7	10.0	10	42	5	5	0	0	0	2	0	0	11	0	1
grave, Brian, Lowell*	0	0	.000	0.00	2	0	0	0	2	0	4.0	4	23	1	0	0	0	1	0	2	0	7	0	0
John, Williamsport*	0	0	.000	6.08	9	0	0	0	5	0	13.1	13	60	11	9	1	1	1	1	3	0	9	1	0
le, Chad, St. Catharines	0	1	.000	5.13	20	0	0	0	5	0	26.1	24	129	22	15	5	0	1	0	28	1	26	6	0
on, Phillip, Williamsport*	7	4	.636	2.54	15	13	2	1	0	0	85.0	68	364	33	24	1	3	2	3	33	2	77	7	3
sbeck, Mark, New Jersey	6	3	.667	2.94	16	14	0	0	1	0	79.2	72	325	31	26	4	2	2	4	16	0	74	3	3
ey, Matt, Jamestown	4	2	.667	2.22	24	1	0	0	6	1	48.2	30	218	18	12	3	4	2	4	34	0	54	5	0
nnor, Brian, Erie*	4	10	.286	5.85	15	15	0	0	0	0	67.2	75	329	60	44	4	3	2	3	47	0	60	10	1
, Rosario, Jamestown	2	0	1.000	0.00	6	0	0	0	0	0	8.0	3	31	0	0	0	0	0	1	6	0	6	0	0
her, Brett, Watertown*	1	1	.500	2.53	2	2	0	0	0	0	10.2	6	45	3	3	2	0	0	0	6	0	12	0	0
er, Christian, Vermont	7	1	.875	2.48	14	14	2	1	0	0	80.0	63	322	26	22	1	2	1	4	22	0	61	8	3
erson, Casey, Pittsfield	1	3	.250	5.32	17	0	0	0	12	0	23.2	30	111	14	14	2	2	0	2	10	0	20	4	0
, Jesus, Erie*	2	5	.286	4.79	21	3	0	0	5	0	35.2	32	164	24	19	3	2	0	2	24	1	34	2	0
ails, Mark, Jamestown	1	4	.200	4.24	13	13	0	0	0	0	63.2	53	295	35	30	6	1	6	0	29	0	37	6	0
ps, Ben, Oneonta	3	4	.429	2.97	14	14	0	0	0	0	78.2	58	337	40	26	1	2	5	2	41	0	56	4	6
ck, Jason, New Jersey	3	7	.300	4.89	18	10	0	0	1	0	57.0	59	265	37	31	4	4	1	5	36	0	61	4	0
art, Melvin, Pittsfield	3	4	.429	3.14	23	0	0	0	20	7	28.2	25	127	12	10	2	2	5	1	14	1	30	4	0
ey, Kirk, Pittsfield	1	0	1.000	3.00	5	5	0	0	0	0	18.0	19	80	9	6	0	0	0	1	10	0	14	4	0
phrey, Kenny, Pittsfield	7	2	.778	3.21	14	14	1	1	0	0	87.0	68	373	41	31	1	2	4	4	41	0	61	10	2
e, Joe, Pittsfield	0	0	.000	3.45	8	0	0	0	5	0	15.2	18	68	8	6	1	1	0	4	0	17	1	0
ada, Edward, Vermont	6	5	.545	2.33	14	14	2	0	0	0	92.2	82	378	32	24	3	3	1	7	20	0	79	7	0
tal, Craig, Jamestown	4	8	.333	3.44	15	15	0	0	0	0	86.1	93	374	51	33	5	2	5	5	23	0	49	5	4
es, Ken, Hudson Valley*	0	0	.000	1.07	38	0	0	0	23	5	67.0	51	273	19	8	1	5	0	1	21	3	64	2	1
el, Julio, Oneonta	7	2	.778	2.96	15	14	0	0	1	0	85.0	64	355	35	28	2	3	4	5	36	0	79	4	1
nent, Justin, Oneonta*	0	1	.000	18.00	1	1	0	0	0	0	2.0	3	12	4	4	0	0	1	0	3	0	0	0	0

CLASS A New York-Pennsylvania League

Pitcher, Team	W	L	Pct.	ERA	G	GS	CG	ShO	GF	Sv.	IP	H	TBF	R	ER	HR	SH	SF	HB	BB	IBB	SO	WP
Reames, Jay, New Jersey	2	2	.500	3.32	31	0	0	0	20	10	43.1	42	187	20	16	4	3	1	2	18	0	48	2
Reinfelder, Dave, Jamestown*	2	2	.500	2.83	28	0	0	0	8	2	57.1	46	233	24	18	4	1	0	5	14	0	52	0
Rigdon, Paul, Watertown	2	2	.500	4.08	22	0	0	0	21	6	39.2	41	174	24	18	4	1	0	2	10	0	46	1
Rijo, Jose, Auburn	1	3	.250	3.54	33	0	0	0	15	3	53.1	65	241	29	21	0	2	3	6	16	1	39	8
Risley, Bill, St. Catharines	0	0	.000	1.29	3	1	0	0	0	0	7.0	3	25	1	1	0	0	0	0	2	0	10	0
Robbins, Jake, Oneonta	3	4	.429	4.50	11	11	0	0	0	0	66.0	64	298	42	33	3	5	1	2	35	1	47	6
Robinson, Martin, Oneonta*	3	6	.333	3.90	15	15	1	0	0	0	80.2	83	370	49	35	3	3	5	2	43	0	50	9
Rodgers, Bobby, Lowell	7	4	.636	1.90	14	14	2	1	0	0	90.0	60	363	33	19	3	2	2	3	31	0	108	9
Rodriguez, Victor, St. Cathrns.	2	7	.222	5.91	21	8	0	0	7	2	64.0	50	296	55	42	2	3	2	6	54	2	54	8
Romo, Gregory, Jamestown	4	2	.667	2.35	6	6	1	0	0	0	38.1	35	155	17	10	3	0	1	1	6	0	39	3
Roque, Jorge, New Jersey	1	2	.333	7.02	13	0	0	0	7	2	16.2	15	90	15	13	1	1	2	2	23	0	18	7
Rosado, Juan, Vermont*	1	0	1.000	3.32	12	0	0	0	6	0	19.0	20	84	9	7	0	1	2	0	9	0	19	2
Rosenbohm, Jim, Pittsfield	1	1	.500	3.38	20	0	0	0	7	1	26.2	22	134	10	10	0	1	2	5	26	0	37	4
Santiago, Derek, Utica	2	2	.500	4.45	12	10	0	0	1	0	54.2	57	245	30	27	4	1	0	3	28	0	41	8
Santos, Rafael, Erie	1	2	.333	3.79	18	4	0	0	3	0	54.2	55	238	31	23	5	2	0	3	19	0	32	4
Schroeder, Chad, Jamestown	5	0	1.000	1.40	31	0	0	0	26	6	38.2	29	153	15	6	1	1	3	0	6	0	41	0
Seabury, Jaron, St. Catharines	3	1	.750	3.26	19	0	0	0	6	1	30.1	29	135	16	11	1	2	1	0	10	1	24	5
Shadburne, Adam, Batavia	2	0	1.000	3.18	20	0	0	0	11	0	34.0	34	143	16	12	3	1	2	3	8	2	37	0
Shaffer, Trevor, Williamsport	2	0	1.000	1.69	25	0	0	0	19	8	32.0	25	134	6	6	0	3	3	1	16	1	29	0
Sheredy, Kevin, New Jersey	1	0	1.000	4.30	8	5	0	0	0	0	23.0	21	100	15	11	2	2	1	1	13	0	13	1
Siciliano, Jess, Erie	0	0	.000	6.75	4	0	0	0	2	0	5.1	7	28	5	4	0	1	0	1	4	0	4	1
Siegel, Justin, Hudson Valley*	1	0	1.000	5.68	5	0	0	0	1	0	6.1	8	30	5	4	1	1	0	5	1	8	0
Smatana, Steve, Lowell*	5	0	1.000	1.45	19	0	0	0	9	2	31.0	22	116	5	5	1	2	1	0	3	0	33	1
Snusz, Christopher, Batavia	0	0	.000	3.00	1	0	0	0	1	0	3.0	2	11	1	1	0	0	1	0	0	0	2	0
Spear, Russ, Jamestown	2	1	.667	5.19	8	7	0	0	0	0	34.2	39	158	24	20	5	1	2	2	15	0	28	4
Splawn, Matthew, Pittsfield	4	1	.800	0.99	22	0	0	0	15	8	36.1	26	145	5	4	0	1	0	0	10	1	44	0
Spoljaric, Paul, St. Catharines*	0	0	.000	0.00	2	2	0	0	0	0	5.0	3	18	0	0	0	0	0	0	0	0	7	1
Stadelhofer, Michael, Utica	0	0	.000	9.31	4	0	0	0	0	0	9.2	15	51	12	10	2	1	0	2	5	0	9	3
Stechschulte, Gene, New Jersey	1	2	.333	3.27	20	1	0	0	6	0	33.0	41	159	17	12	0	2	1	2	16	2	27	4
Stevens, Kris, Batavia*	1	1	.500	8.10	3	3	0	0	0	0	13.1	16	61	12	12	2	1	0	0	6	0	11	0
Stevenson, Rodney, Vermont*	5	2	.714	2.84	22	0	0	0	5	1	31.2	24	133	11	10	1	1	0	1	13	0	46	2
Stewart, Paxton, St. Catharines	0	0	.000	0.00	1	0	0	0	1	0	1.0	0	5	0	0	0	0	0	1	1	0	2	1
Symmonds, Maika, Lowell*	0	1	1.000	10.45	5	0	0	0	1	0	10.1	11	60	12	12	1	1	2	4	15	0	10	3
Taylor, Mark, Watertown*	1	0	1.000	3.54	12	0	0	0	3	0	20.1	18	90	9	8	0	1	2	0	16	1	17	1
Thomas, Evan, Batavia	10	2	.833	2.78	13	13	0	0	0	0	81.0	60	321	29	25	3	1	3	5	23	0	75	6
Thompson, Chris, Lowell	2	5	.286	4.40	25	0	0	0	12	0	47.0	43	214	34	23	2	1	4	5	20	1	51	8
Tilton, Ira, Batavia	5	6	.455	5.48	14	14	0	0	0	0	69.0	66	302	47	42	1	3	9	26	0	43	3
Tober, Dave, Batavia	0	2	.000	6.00	4	0	0	0	1	0	6.0	8	34	6	4	0	0	1	1	5	1	8	0
Townsend, Dave, Utica	3	6	.333	3.59	14	14	2	0	0	0	77.2	69	320	38	31	4	1	1	4	18	0	51	4
Tribe, Byron, Williamsport	2	1	.667	2.49	15	0	0	0	10	4	21.2	16	97	10	6	2	1	2	13	2	33	2
Trunk, Todd, Oneonta	0	0	.000	36.00	1	0	0	0	1	0	1.0	5	9	4	4	0	0	0	1	0	1	0
Turley, Jason, Auburn	3	0	1.000	5.56	19	0	0	0	7	0	43.2	39	217	35	27	4	2	2	5	36	2	31	7
Velez, Jeff, Williamsport	0	0	.000	13.50	1	1	0	0	0	0	2.0	4	14	4	3	0	0	0	4	0	1	0
Viegas, Randy, Erie*	0	0	.000	7.36	2	0	0	0	1	0	3.2	4	19	3	3	0	0	1	0	4	0	3	2
Villafuerte, Brandon, Pittsfield	8	3	.727	3.02	18	7	1	0	4	1	62.2	53	267	21	21	5	2	3	6	27	0	59	4
Villar, Maximo, Erie	0	5	.000	7.22	9	9	0	0	0	0	28.2	46	142	27	23	3	0	3	7	9	0	10	1
Villegas, Ismael, Williamsport	0	0	.000	2.57	2	2	0	0	0	0	7.0	7	31	3	2	0	0	0	4	0	5	1
Wagner, Ken, Watertown	2	3	.400	2.20	21	1	0	0	12	5	45.0	32	188	12	11	1	3	1	2	20	1	47	3
Ward, Jon, New Jersey	1	6	.143	5.80	9	9	0	0	0	0	35.2	56	178	35	23	1	0	3	2	21	1	29	2
Welch, Robb, Lowell	2	7	.222	5.09	14	14	1	1	0	0	81.1	85	371	50	46	7	2	1	7	37	0	63	9
West, Adam, New Jersey*	5	4	.556	3.70	15	14	0	0	0	0	87.2	82	370	41	36	3	5	3	5	29	0	94	5
Westover, Richard, Vermont	3	2	.600	2.41	18	1	0	0	5	0	33.2	24	131	10	9	1	0	0	1	8	0	23	6
Whitson, Eric, Hudson Valley	3	0	1.000	2.86	19	2	0	0	8	0	44.0	31	174	17	14	4	1	3	0	16	0	34	10
Williams, Woody, St. Catharines	0	0	.000	3.68	2	2	0	0	0	0	7.1	7	30	3	3	0	0	0	0	4	0	12	1
Wilmot, Toby, Auburn*	2	2	.500	3.57	13	0	0	0	3	0	22.2	23	113	11	9	0	0	2	1	17	1	19	5
Wyckoff, Travis, Utica*	2	5	.286	2.95	24	0	0	0	10	1	36.2	39	166	21	12	1	3	0	2	14	2	16	4
Yanez, Luis, Auburn	5	5	.500	2.45	15	15	2	0	0	0	99.0	85	416	38	27	4	2	2	3	31	2	73	3
Young, Tim, Vermont*	1	0	1.000	0.31	27	0	0	0	26	18	29.1	14	106	1	1	2	1	2	4	0	46	0
Yount, Andy, Lowell	1	2	.333	6.29	8	8	0	0	0	0	34.1	38	181	30	24	0	1	3	9	38	0	30	15
Zaleski, Kevin, Utica	2	3	.400	3.91	26	0	0	0	26	7	25.1	30	120	16	11	0	1	1	2	8	3	21	2
Zamarripa, Mark, Jamestown	4	2	.667	2.03	29	0	0	0	22	4	48.2	25	187	13	11	4	3	2	14	0	61	4
Zavershnik, Mike, St. Cathrns.*	4	2	.667	6.28	25	1	0	0	14	2	38.2	45	190	32	27	3	0	0	1	24	0	25	2

COMBINATION SHUTOUTS: **Auburn (4)**—Yanez-Rijo, Yanez-Bernhard-Turley, Bernhard-Wilmot, Braswell-Wilmot-McFerrin. **Batavia (6)**—Thomas-Crane-Shadbu.. Miller-Kawabata, Thomas-Crane. Miller-Kawabata, Cafferty-Frace-Mitchell, Tilton-Tober. **Erie (2)**—McDade-Santos-Campbell, O'Connor-Gonzalez-Campbell. **Hu.. Valley (2)**—Cain-Aquino, Cain-Aquino-Berry. **Jamestown (2)**—Quintal-Reinfelder-Kauflin-Zamarripa, Miller-Kauflin-Zamarripa. **Lowell (1)**—Cressend-Festa-Smat.. Beale. **New Jersey (3)**—Pollock-Reames-Stechschulte, West-Heffernan-Reames, Nussbeck-Stechschulte-McDougal. **Oneonta (5)**—Robbins-Aguilar-Dingman, Phi.. Aguilar-Krall, Delossantos-Bracho, Rangel-Dingman, Robbins-Dingman. **Pittsfield (6)**—Brittan-Rosenbohm-Villafuerte-Poupart, Presley-Villafuerte, Ferullo-Patte.. Pumphrey-Pyrtle, Brittan-Splawn, Brittan-Splawn. **St. Catharines (5)**—Graterol-Davenport-Mann, Bradford-Hueda-Seasbury-Mann, Spoljaric-Graterol-Mann, Grat.. Mann, Graterol-Needle. **Utica (1)**—Cames-Ferrell. **Vermont (6)**—Matz-Westover-Stevenson, Quezada-Stevenson, Leslie-Stevenson-Garsky, Quezada-Rosado-Yo.. Quezada-Westover, Figueroa-Leslie-Steveson-Young. **Watertown (10)**—Mays-Fleetwood, Camp-Rigdon, Camp-Taylor-Edwards, Calmus-Brammer, Martinez-Edw.. Feliz-Rigdon, Minter-Brammer-Edwards, Martinez-Edwards, Martinez-Rigdon, Martinez-DePaula-Minter-Wagner. **Williamsport (3)**—Duncan-Shaffer-Brook.. Crawford-Birsner, Cannon-Brookens, Licciardi-Hart.

1996 FIELDING

TEAM

Team	Pct.	G	PO	A	E	TC	DP	PB	Team	Pct.	G	PO	A	E	TC	DP
Batavia	.969	75	1950	788	87	2825	58	6	Jamestown	.964	76	1975	845	106	2926	60
Pittsfield	.969	75	1906	807	87	2800	51	13	Watertown	.962	76	1954	753	106	2813	49
Vermont	.968	74	1890	734	86	2710	65	14	St. Catharines	.962	76	1953	811	109	2873	57
Utica	.967	76	1940	721	90	2751	38	21	Auburn	.961	76	1983	843	114	2940	63

am	Pct.	G	PO	A	E	TC	DP	PB		Team	Pct.	G	PO	A	E	TC	DP	PB
w Jersey	.960	75	1962	778	114	2854	46	14		Hudson Valley	.952	76	2065	877	148	3090	58	23
lliamsport	.957	76	1964	752	121	2837	66	24		Oneonta	.950	76	1967	797	147	2911	53	22
e	.957	76	1976	805	125	2906	55	25		Lowell	.945	74	1912	692	151	2755	57	29

TRIPLE PLAY: Lowell.

INDIVIDUAL

FIRST BASEMEN

TE: All caps denotes fielding-percentage leader based on 38 games for catchers, for all other non-pitchers and 76 innings for pitchers. *Throws lefthanded.

iyer, Team	Pct.	G	PO	A	E	TC	DP
mirato, Zak, Utica	.980	11	92	4	2	98	2
tigua, Nilson, Erie	1.000	5	32	2	0	34	3
llenger, Butch, Erie	1.000	3	23	1	0	24	0
ssing, Chad, Williamsport	1.000	31	205	20	0	225	20
rns, Kevin, Auburn*	.988	67	634	22	8	664	53
niniello, Michael, Jamestown	.979	6	45	1	1	47	1
le, Eric, Auburn	.989	11	84	5	1	90	8
x, Robert, Pittsfield	1.000	1	6	0	0	6	0
de, Bradley, Batavia	.984	74	632	46	11	689	48
s, John, Hudson Valley	1.000	2	10	0	0	10	1
tin, Blaine, St. Catharines	1.000	2	10	0	0	10	1
entes, Javier, Lowell	.963	7	47	5	2	54	3
lagher, Shawn, Hudson Valley	.981	42	402	15	8	425	31
rrett, Jason, Utica	.985	66	563	40	9	612	29
rdon, Buck, Williamsport	1.000	4	27	2	0	29	2
rnandez, Alexander, Erie*	.979	29	262	17	6	285	16
enbrand, Shea, Lowell	.963	52	424	24	17	465	31
ffman, Ryan, Oneonta	.952	6	20	0	1	21	2
ndt, Bo, Erie	.889	1	8	0	1	9	0
nes, Jay, Utica	.917	3	9	2	1	12	2
nnedy, Brad, New Jersey	1.000	2	3	0	0	3	0
nt, Troy, Watertown	.991	71	600	45	6	651	42
g, Brad, Williamsport	1.000	1	1	0	0	1	0
ehler, Jason, St. Catharines	.833	1	5	0	1	6	1
nrady, Dennis, Watertown	.970	6	30	2	1	33	3
atochvil, Tim, Lowell	.959	18	138	4	6	148	13
dstrom, David, Jamestown	1.000	4	26	0	0	26	2
ng, Garrett, Erie	.984	20	173	13	3	189	17
PEZ, Luis, St. Catharines	.995	68	565	50	3	618	49
ez, Pee Wee, Pittsfield	.929	1	12	1	1	14	2
nning, Nate, Williamsport	.969	7	30	1	1	32	2
zurek, Brian, New Jersey*	.993	65	538	44	4	586	36
Dougal, Mike, New Jersey	.979	11	87	8	2	97	4
Neal, Pepe, New Jersey	1.000	2	12	2	0	14	0
jia, Marlon, Auburn	1.000	1	5	0	0	5	0
oles, Brandon, Pittsfield*	.992	55	444	44	4	492	30
thammer, Marc, Hudson Val.	.985	10	62	4	1	67	6
peza, William, Vermont	.988	22	160	10	2	172	19
ke, Jonathan, Watertown	1.000	3	7	0	0	7	1
nierski, Joe, Hudson Valley	.964	27	223	19	9	251	16
fer, Jeff, Oneonta	.980	53	449	31	10	490	33
bol, Scott, Oneonta	.969	22	177	10	6	193	11
adburne, Adam, Batavia	.923	2	9	3	1	13	0
atley, Andy, St. Catharines	1.000	3	17	3	0	20	0
pp, Skip, Erie	.984	24	169	10	3	182	14
wart, Paxton, St. Catharines	.950	7	55	2	3	60	3
aino, Shannon, Vermont	1.000	6	28	0	0	28	0
liaferri, Jeff, Jamestown	.987	72	643	45	9	697	51
cy, Andrew, Vermont	.987	52	426	33	6	465	41
kers, Randy, Pittsfield	.983	20	164	14	3	181	13
ler, P.J., Pittsfield	1.000	1	12	0	0	12	0
eta, Julio, Williamsport	.989	43	338	25	4	367	30

TRIPLE PLAY: Fuentes.

SECOND BASEMEN

yer, Team	Pct.	G	PO	A	E	TC	DP
mirato, Zak, Utica	1.000	1	1	4	0	5	1
rim, Pat, Oneonta	.912	13	20	32	5	57	5
nas, Pete, Utica	1.000	2	0	4	0	4	0
ner, Doug, Hudson Valley	1.000	1	0	2	0	2	0
ts, Rodney, Batavia	.952	40	83	96	9	188	18
ney, Ryan, Oneonta	.667	2	1	1	1	3	1
enger, Butch, Erie	.963	31	72	84	6	162	21
ts, Darrell, New Jersey	1.000	2	3	6	0	9	0
NDFORD, Paul, Vermont	.969	56	122	158	9	289	31
roll, Jamey, Vermont	1.000	2	2	3	0	5	0
wford, Marty, Batavia	.977	11	22	21	1	44	6
imore, Brian, Auburn	.960	19	43	54	4	101	10
onatis, Don, Jamestown	.937	39	77	87	11	175	20
kson, Corey, Pittsfield	1.000	2	6	4	0	10	0

Player, Team	Pct.	G	PO	A	E	TC	DP
Finnerty, Keith, New Jersey	.977	43	78	130	5	213	23
Frias, Ovidio, Erie	1.000	7	9	15	0	24	2
Glozier, Larry, Utica	1.000	2	6	4	0	10	2
Hine, Steve, Lowell	.930	22	41	39	6	86	14
Hyers, Matt, Auburn	.961	16	25	49	3	77	5
Jefferies, Daryl, Williamsport	1.000	9	13	18	0	31	4
Kane, Kevin, Oneonta	1.000	1	1	0	0	1	0
Kleiner, Stacy, New Jersey	.975	34	53	63	3	119	7
Konrady, Dennis, Watertown	.927	11	14	24	3	41	6
Larkin, Garrett, Erie	.909	4	5	15	2	22	3
Lebron, Ruben, Lowell	.981	38	71	88	3	162	16
Lewis, Keith, Williamsport	.963	19	41	38	3	82	10
MacKay, Tripp, Vermont	.933	18	29	41	5	75	12
Majcherek, Matt, Hudson Valley	.933	15	21	35	4	60	9
Maloney, Jeff, Watertown	1.000	1	0	2	0	2	1
Mansavage, Jay, Auburn	.955	41	80	131	10	221	29
Meyers, Chad, Williamsport	.953	57	106	136	12	254	33
Nolte, Bruce, Pittsfield	.950	23	43	53	5	101	15
Nova, Jose, Williamsport	1.000	2	2	1	0	3	0
Nunez, Abraham, St. Catharines	.978	24	48	85	3	136	12
Owens-Bragg, Luke, Hudson Val	.932	66	127	176	22	325	26
Parsons, Jeff, Pittsfield	.875	4	3	11	2	16	2
Pena, Adelis, Erie	.970	39	71	89	5	165	13
Phillips, Blaine, Oneonta	.925	40	78	106	15	199	21
Roberts, Ryan, New Jersey	1.000	4	8	8	0	16	2
Sanchez, Orlando, Lowell	.907	23	38	50	9	97	5
Seabol, Scott, Oneonta	.936	15	13	31	3	47	6
Skett, Will, St. Catharines	.943	38	52	96	9	157	19
Snelling, Allen, St. Catharines	.988	21	30	52	1	83	12
Tamargo, John, Pittsfield	.983	49	71	106	3	180	17
Taylor, Gregory, Batavia	.973	9	13	23	1	37	3
Tiller, Brad, Watertown	.949	55	87	137	12	236	26
Venghaus, Jeff, Utica	.961	74	100	149	10	259	16
Wesemann, Jason, Batavia	.962	18	32	44	3	79	8
Wheeler, Ryan, Oneonta	.917	13	26	29	5	60	7
Whitlock, Brian, Watertown	.957	14	16	28	2	46	5
Zepeda, Jesse, Jamestown	.968	45	75	104	6	185	24

THIRD BASEMEN

Player, Team	Pct.	G	PO	A	E	TC	DP
Ammirato, Zak, Utica	.938	6	3	12	1	16	1
Andersen, Ryan, Williamsport	1.000	1	1	0	0	1	0
Barner, Doug, Hudson Valley	.870	32	24	70	14	108	6
Bellenger, Butch, Erie	.936	17	6	38	3	47	1
Blessing, Chad, Williamsport	1.000	3	2	1	0	3	0
Butler, Allen, Oneonta	.877	71	39	125	23	187	9
Carroll, Jamey, Vermont	1.000	2	4	3	0	7	0
Cole, Eric, Auburn	.853	25	12	46	10	68	4
Dallimore, Brian, Auburn	.883	52	37	106	19	162	8
ERICKSON, Corey, Pittsfield	.937	70	56	168	15	239	12
Fuentes, Javier, Lowell	.938	6	8	7	1	16	3
Harris, Mike, Utica	1.000	1	1	1	0	2	1
Hillenbrand, Shea, Lowell	.833	4	3	7	2	12	1
Hundt, Bo, Erie	.500	1	0	2	2	4	0
Jefferies, Daryl, Williamsport	1.000	2	0	1	0	1	0
Kennedy, Brad, New Jersey	.877	29	16	41	8	65	4
Kent, Troy, Watertown	.500	2	0	2	2	4	0
Kleinz, Larry, Utica	.934	72	48	150	14	212	9
Konrady, Dennis, Watertown	.938	42	33	72	7	112	4
Kopacz, Derek, Jamestown	.934	61	48	122	12	182	6
Larkin, Garrett, Erie	.000	1	0	0	0	0	0
Lawrence, Joe, St. Catharines	.857	2	3	3	1	7	0
Leon, Jose, New Jersey	.833	6	6	9	3	18	1
Lindstrom, David, Jamestown	.667	1	1	1	1	3	0
Lopez, Luis, St. Catharines	1.000	3	2	2	0	4	0
Majcherek, Matt, Hudson Valley	.846	12	6	16	4	26	0
Manning, Nate, Williamsport	.843	37	28	63	17	108	6
May, Scott, Erie	.667	2	0	4	2	6	0
Mejia, Marlon, Auburn	1.000	1	0	1	0	1	0
Mitchell, Derek, Jamestown	.786	11	5	17	6	28	1
Nolte, Bruce, Pittsfield	1.000	6	2	6	0	8	0
Nova, Jose, Williamsport	.918	42	23	66	8	97	6
Oropeza, William, Vermont	.944	7	1	16	1	18	2
Pena, Adelis, Erie	1.000	2	2	3	0	5	0

CLASS A — *New York-Pennsylvania League*

Player, Team	Pct.	G	PO	A	E	TC	DP
Phillips, Blaine, Oneonta	1.000	2	1	4	0	5	0
Pomierski, Joe, Hudson Valley	.874	36	27	84	16	127	4
Pond, Simon, Vermont	.877	67	40	110	21	171	9
Ramirez, Aramis, Erie	.896	61	39	107	17	163	7
Roberts, Ryan, New Jersey	.881	37	23	73	13	109	6
Rodriguez, Chris, Watertown	.000	1	0	0	1	1	0
Seabol, Scott, Oneonta	.833	3	2	3	1	6	0
Shatley, Andy, St. Catharines	.878	74	49	138	26	213	7
Snelling, Allen, St. Catharines	1.000	3	1	1	0	2	0
Torti, Mike, Batavia	.908	54	32	106	14	152	3
Ugueto, Hector, New Jersey	1.000	2	2	4	0	6	0
Veras, Wilton, Lowell	.931	65	57	106	12	175	11
Vickers, Randy, Pittsfield	.818	3	4	5	2	11	0
Wesemann, Jason, Batavia	.973	23	20	51	2	73	3
Whitlock, Brian, Watertown	.928	37	28	62	7	97	6
Wilders, Paul, New Jersey	.826	7	3	16	4	23	0
Zepeda, Jesse, Jamestown	1.000	5	2	6	0	8	0

SHORTSTOPS

Player, Team	Pct.	G	PO	A	E	TC	DP
Andersen, Ryan, Williamsport	.853	20	17	41	10	68	8
Antrim, Pat, Oneonta	.857	2	1	5	1	7	0
Arenas, Pete, Utica	.936	64	75	129	14	218	16
Betts, Darrell, New Jersey	.950	13	12	26	2	40	3
Carroll, Jamey, Vermont	.958	49	73	131	9	213	29
Dallimore, Brian, Auburn	.833	1	4	1	1	6	1
De La Rosa, Tomas, Vermont	.833	3	1	4	1	6	1
Dennis, Les, Oneonta	.952	72	95	204	15	314	35
Dransfeldt, Kelly, Hudson Valley	.946	75	117	253	21	391	45
Fuentes, Javier, Lowell	.933	27	39	73	8	120	12
Harris, Mike, Utica	.942	28	28	53	5	86	8
Hillenbrand, Shea, Lowell	.736	11	13	26	14	53	3
Hyers, Matt, Auburn	.934	46	64	150	15	229	25
Jefferies, Daryl, Williamsport	.942	24	23	58	5	86	12
Jimenez, Ruben, New Jersey	.883	61	76	143	29	248	20
Kleiner, Stacy, New Jersey	1.000	3	4	8	0	12	2
Kleinz, Larry, Utica	.800	2	1	3	1	5	0
Knupfer, Jason, Batavia	.947	65	101	185	16	302	38
Larkin, Garrett, Erie	.894	9	10	32	5	47	1
Lawrence, Joe, St. Catharines	.902	24	28	64	10	102	13
Lebron, Ruben, Lowell	.800	4	1	3	1	5	1
Lewis, Keith, Williamsport	.943	41	55	109	10	174	20
Lorenzana, Luis, Erie	.931	43	59	104	12	175	18
MacKay, Tripp, Vermont	.927	26	33	68	8	109	15
Majcherek, Matt, Hudson Valley	.750	7	1	8	3	12	1
McDonald, John, Watertown	.946	75	85	228	18	331	35
Mejia, Marlon, Auburn	.929	32	48	83	10	141	16
Mitchell, Derek, Jamestown	.936	45	51	170	15	236	27
Nolte, Bruce, Pittsfield	1.000	2	2	6	0	8	0
Nova, Jose, Williamsport	.857	2	3	3	1	7	0
NUNEZ, Abraham, St. Catharines	.953	52	88	154	12	254	30
Olmeda, Jose, Lowell	.894	26	43	58	12	113	8
Parsons, Jeff, Pittsfield	.919	68	75	197	24	296	26
Pena, Adelis, Erie	.904	26	39	64	11	114	14
Perez, Jensen, Pittsfield	.800	1	4	0	1	5	0
Rios, Brian, Jamestown	.914	32	31	96	12	139	12
Sanchez, Orlando, Lowell	.875	10	13	29	6	48	6
Seabol, Scott, Oneonta	.900	3	3	6	1	10	1
Shatley, Andy, St. Catharines	1.000	2	2	2	0	4	1
Tamargo, John, Pittsfield	.941	5	4	12	1	17	3
Taylor, Gregory, Batavia	.905	8	9	10	2	21	3
Wesemann, Jason, Batavia	1.000	4	9	10	0	19	3
Zepeda, Jesse, Jamestown	1.000	3	1	7	0	8	0

TRIPLE PLAY: Olmeda.

OUTFIELDERS

Player, Team	Pct.	G	PO	A	E	TC	DP
Abell, Antonio, New Jersey	.923	7	11	1	1	13	0
Airoso, Kurt, Jamestown	1.000	17	24	1	0	25	1
Alayon, Elvis, Lowell	.922	61	108	10	10	128	0
Ammirato, Zak, Utica	.979	27	46	1	1	48	1
Anderson, Chris, Hudson Valley	.930	28	38	2	3	43	0
Arenas, Pete, Utica	.000	1	0	0	0	0	0
Aylor, Brian, Oneonta*	.938	8	12	3	1	16	0
Ayotte, Scott, Oneonta*	.940	25	47	0	3	50	0
Barlow, Ethan, Vermont*	.986	39	68	1	1	70	0
Betts, Darrell, New Jersey	1.000	3	3	0	0	3	0
Bishop, Tim, Pittsfield	1.000	3	5	0	0	5	0
Britt, Bryan, New Jersey	.989	53	89	3	1	93	0
Buirley, Matthew, Vermont	1.000	5	5	0	0	5	0
Burns, Xavier, Erie	1.000	4	2	0	0	2	0
Butler, Garrett, Oneonta	.983	69	116	2	2	120	0

Player, Team	Pct.	G	PO	A	E	TC	D
Cameron, Ken, New Jersey*	.960	53	94	1	4	99	
Cedeno, Jesus, Jamestown	.966	71	111	4	4	119	
Charles, Steve, St. Catharines	.967	64	83	5	3	91	
Chatman, Karl, Vermont	.963	72	103	2	4	109	
Clark, Kirby, Batavia	1.000	10	11	0	0	11	
Cole, Abdul, Utica	.939	62	105	2	7	114	
Colon, Jose, Williamsport	.970	36	63	2	2	67	
Connell, Jerry, Williamsport	1.000	2	5	0	0	5	
Cooley, Shannon, Batavia	.960	60	115	5	5	125	
Crane, Todd, Batavia	1.000	35	64	0	0	64	
Crawford, Marty, Batavia	.973	43	70	2	2	74	
Dennis, Les, Oneonta	.000	1	0	0	0	0	
DeLaCruz, Wilfredo, Oneonta	1.000	2	5	0	0	5	
Diaz, Alain, Utica	1.000	23	23	1	0	24	
Edwards, Aaron, Erie	1.000	12	23	2	0	25	
Elliott, Dawan, Erie*	.910	37	58	3	6	67	
Ellison, Tony, Williamsport	.947	57	88	1	5	94	
Farraez, Jesus, Auburn	1.000	41	48	2	0	50	
Finnerty, Keith, New Jersey	.900	7	8	1	1	10	
Foster, Quincy, Utica	.958	72	133	4	6	143	
Francia, David, Batavia*	.987	67	149	7	2	158	
Freitas, Joe, New Jersey	.969	40	62	1	2	65	
Frias, Ovidio, Erie	1.000	2	2	0	0	2	
Gonzalez, Freddy, Vermont	.950	13	18	1	1	20	
Gordon, Buck, Williamsport	1.000	2	1	0	0	1	
Gordon, Herman, St. Catharines	1.000	13	26	0	0	26	
Hall, Doug, Williamsport*	.979	67	133	6	3	142	
Haltiwanger, Garrick, Pittsfield*	.946	55	84	3	5	92	
Hampton, Robby, St. Catharines	.955	30	59	5	3	67	
Hernandez, Alexander, Erie*	.978	31	43	2	1	46	
Huelsmann, Mike, Watertown	.976	26	40	1	1	42	
Huff, B.J., Pittsfield	.984	36	54	6	1	61	
Huffman, Ryan, Oneonta	.893	15	24	1	3	28	
Hundt, Bo, Erie	1.000	7	6	0	0	6	
Jenkins, Corey, Lowell	.956	65	83	3	4	90	
Johnson, Damon, St. Catharines	1.000	16	33	2	0	35	
Johnson, Rontrez, Lowell	.947	35	70	1	4	75	
Keaveney, Jeff, Lowell	.824	17	13	1	3	17	
Kennedy, Brad, New Jersey	.840	19	19	2	4	25	
Kiefer, Dax, Williamsport	.934	64	123	5	9	137	
Kofler, Eric, Oneonta*	.902	37	55	0	6	61	
Kratochvil, Tim, Lowell	1.000	1	3	0	0	3	
Landstad, Rob, Watertown	.750	1	3	0	1	4	
McDonald, Donzell, Oneonta	.966	74	169	4	6	179	
McKinley, Michael, Lowell	.975	28	37	2	1	40	
Meyers, Chad, Williamsport	1.000	11	17	0	0	17	
Monroe, Craig, Hudson Valley	.938	62	86	5	6	97	
Moore, Tris, Jamestown	1.000	9	14	1	0	15	
Morrison, Ryan, Pittsfield	.974	27	36	2	1	39	
Motley, Mel, Watertown	.907	52	75	3	8	86	
Myers, Adrian, Hudson Valley	1.000	49	74	2	0	76	
Niethammer, Marc, Hudson Val.	.893	26	25	0	3	28	
Nova, Jose, Williamsport	1.000	2	0	1	0	1	
Pena, Alex, Erie	.961	73	131	15	6	152	
Petke, Jonathan, Watertown	.980	59	92	6	2	100	
Phillips, Blaine, Oneonta	1.000	2	3	0	0	3	
Pointer, Corey, Erie	1.000	5	12	2	0	14	
Pratt, Wes, Auburn	.963	61	127	2	5	134	
Ramirez, Danny, Pittsfield	.980	70	138	6	3	147	
Ramirez, Frank, Jamestown	.800	6	4	0	1	5	
Redman, Julian, Erie*	.920	43	79	1	7	87	
Reeder, Jim, Auburn	1.000	49	76	5	0	81	
Rice, Charles, Erie	.941	19	14	2	1	17	
Richards, Rowan, Hudson Valley	1.000	24	31	1	0	32	
Rivero, Eddie, Batavia*	1.000	13	15	0	0	15	
Rodriguez, Chris, Watertown	1.000	1	3	0	0	3	
Rodriguez, Mike, St. Catharines	1.000	2	4	0	0	4	
Rodriguez, Gary, Watertown	.966	66	110	2	4	116	
Schofield, Andy, New Jersey	1.000	6	6	0	0	6	
Sime, Rafael, Utica*	.934	63	96	3	7	106	
Skett, Will, St. Catharines	.947	42	68	3	4	75	
Snelling, Allen, St. Catharines	1.000	10	9	0	0	9	
Sollman, Scott, Jamestown*	.984	65	123	3	2	128	
Stanton, Robert, Watertown	.891	33	39	2	5	46	
Stewart, Paxton, St. Catharines	.909	13	19	1	2	22	
Stowers, Christopher, Vermont*	.976	70	112	9	3	124	
Thompson, Andre, Lowell	.959	34	45	2	2	49	
TUCCI, Peter, St. Catharines	1.000	54	90	3	0	93	
Ugueto, Hector, New Jersey	.969	47	93	2	3	98	
Vazquez, Manny, Hudson Valley*	.959	67	113	4	5	122	
Wakeland, Chris, Jamestown*	.978	59	79	9	2	90	
Ware, Jeremy, Vermont	.983	31	54	3	1	58	
Wesson, Barry, Auburn	.943	51	76	6	5	87	

Player, Team	Pct.	G	PO	A	E	TC	DP
Wheeler, Ryan, Oneonta	.800	6	7	1	2	10	0
oder, P.J., Pittsfield	.949	44	55	1	3	59	1
oung, Randel, Auburn	.973	36	65	6	2	73	0
apata, Alexis, Jamestown	.913	14	21	0	2	23	0

TRIPLE PLAY: Alayon.

CATCHERS

Player, Team	Pct.	G	PO	A	E	TC	DP	PB
enir, Tom, Watertown	.963	3	23	3	1	27	0	0
varado, Basilio, Vermont	.981	48	365	40	8	413	1	8
nderson, Chris, Hudson Val.	.972	23	157	18	5	180	0	5
ntigua, Nilson, Erie	.980	47	339	60	8	407	5	10
arr, Tucker, Auburn	.975	22	148	11	4	163	0	5
ennett, Ryan, Pittsfield	.995	25	182	15	1	198	1	6
aughler, Matt, Utica	.982	30	202	16	4	222	0	9
uirley, Matthew, Vermont	.991	14	105	9	1	115	1	3
ampos, Miguel, Williamsport	.982	6	49	5	1	55	1	3
miniello, Michael, Jamestn	.800	3	4	0	1	5	0	0
lark, Kirby, Batavia	.974	10	68	8	2	78	1	1
oats, Nathan, Watertown	.979	29	252	29	6	287	1	6
ook, John, Auburn	.917	4	15	7	2	24	0	3
eman, Lou, New Jersey	1.000	2	14	1	0	15	0	1
llis, John, Hudson Valley	.985	56	415	53	7	475	1	14
agley, Dan, Utica	1.000	1	6	0	0	6	0	1
alciglia, Tony, New Jersey	.953	11	67	14	4	85	0	1
ck, Rob, Jamestown	.982	23	155	13	3	171	1	7
rchic, Derek, Utica	1.000	18	135	12	0	147	1	5
rtin, Blaine, St. Catharines	.995	24	163	18	1	182	0	4
rdon, Buck, Williamsport	1.000	18	100	6	0	106	0	2
nes, Jay, Utica	.992	32	228	25	2	255	2	6
ng, Brad, Williamsport	.980	22	133	15	3	151	0	9
ngsbury, Willy, Lowell	.985	10	59	8	1	68	0	4
aehler, Jason, St. Catharines	.984	27	168	16	3	187	1	8
atochvil, Tim, Lowell	.970	9	92	6	3	101	1	2
NDSTROM, David, Jamestn	.994	42	315	43	2	360	3	6
santi, Bob, Williamsport	.976	43	291	35	8	334	3	10
masney, Steve, Lowell	.980	54	402	47	9	458	4	21
pez, Pee Wee, Pittsfield	1.000	1	5	0	0	5	0	0
arsters, Brandon, Batavia	.987	39	275	34	4	313	1	2
artinez, Roger, Pittsfield	.990	38	267	27	3	297	3	1
ay, Scott, Erie	.978	15	42	3	1	46	0	3
cNeal, Pepe, New Jersey	.981	15	93	12	2	107	3	0
etzger, Erik, Lowell	.970	7	29	3	1	33	0	2
veros, Leonardo, Batavia	.982	26	147	19	3	169	4	3
ik, Keith, Erie	1.000	3	19	2	0	21	0	3
illips, Blaine, Oneonta	1.000	3	10	1	0	11	0	1
nto, Rene, Oneonta	.987	26	212	23	3	238	2	8
ymondi, Michael, Hudson V	.985	16	62	4	1	67	0	4
stovich, George, Jamestn	.970	15	82	16	3	101	0	7
adriguez, Mike, St. Cathrn.s	.972	35	229	14	7	250	2	8
adriguez, Sammy, Pittsfield	.978	16	125	9	3	137	2	6
se, Michael, Auburn	.984	56	364	62	7	433	3	10
hmidt, David, New Jersey	.980	56	429	55	10	494	4	12
ipp, Skip, Erie	.985	26	183	10	3	196	1	9
elling, Allen, St. Catharines	1.000	1	3	0	0	3	0	0
usz, Christopher, Batavia	.981	9	45	8	1	54	1	0
vaino, Shannon, Vermont	1.000	17	109	12	0	121	1	3
ylor, Adam, Watertown	.986	45	379	38	6	423	2	9
ombley, Dennis, Oneonta	1.000	2	9	0	0	9	0	0
lencia, Victor, Oneonta	.985	47	338	50	6	394	2	13

PITCHERS

Player, Team	Pct.	G	PO	A	E	TC	DP
uilar, Carlos, Oneonta	.778	23	5	9	4	18	0
Yat, Paul, Erie*	.909	26	5	5	1	11	1
brecht, Daniel, Utica*	1.000	13	0	2	0	2	0
en, Brandon, Batavia*	.947	13	1	17	1	19	1
uino, Julio, Hudson Valley	1.000	22	2	8	0	10	0
mas, Antonio, Oneonta	1.000	3	4	1	0	5	0
stin, Kevie, Lowell	1.000	8	2	3	0	5	0
la, Jose, Erie	1.000	14	1	13	0	14	0
le, St. Catharines*	.875	8	0	7	1	8	1
uer, Chris, Jamestown	.941	11	3	13	1	17	0
ach, Scott, Erie	.750	17	1	5	2	8	0
ale, Chuck, Lowell	1.000	28	1	5	0	6	0
ebe, Hans, Pittsfield*	1.000	14	5	20	0	25	1
rnhard, David, Auburn	.900	24	1	8	1	10	0
rry, Jason, Hudson Valley	1.000	28	2	6	0	8	0
ahle, Michael, Oneonta*	.833	20	1	9	2	12	0
ingsley, Brent, Utica*	1.000	15	7	17	0	24	2
sner, Roark, Williamsport	.750	31	1	5	2	8	0
oker, Chris, Williamsport	.833	14	2	3	1	6	0

Player, Team	Pct.	G	PO	A	E	TC	DP
Bracho, Alejandro, Oneonta*	1.000	4	0	3	0	3	0
Bradford, Josh, St. Catharines	.909	18	1	9	1	11	0
Brammer, John, Watertown	.833	17	0	5	1	6	0
Brand, Scott, Oneonta	.833	9	2	3	1	6	0
Braswell, Bryan, Auburn*	.900	15	2	7	1	10	0
BRITTAN, Corey, Pittsfield	1.000	14	11	18	0	29	0
Brookens, Casey, Williamsport	1.000	25	3	6	0	9	0
Brooks, Wyatt, Erie*	1.000	15	2	1	0	3	0
Browning, Tom, Jamestown*	1.000	5	1	0	0	1	0
Cafferty, Jason, Batavia	.909	14	2	8	1	11	1
Cain, Travis, Hudson Valley	.875	15	5	9	2	16	1
Calmus, Lance, Watertown	1.000	11	4	4	0	8	0
Cames, Aaron, Utica	1.000	18	7	13	0	20	0
Camp, Jared, Watertown	1.000	15	3	8	0	11	2
Campbell, Tedde, Erie	1.000	27	1	8	0	9	0
Cannon, Jon, Williamsport*	.864	14	6	13	3	22	1
Chaney, Michael, Erie*	1.000	10	1	5	0	6	0
Clark, Brian, New Jersey*	.909	32	1	9	1	11	0
Cordero, Francisco, Jamestown	.857	2	0	6	1	7	0
Cotton, Joseph, Batavia	.917	9	2	9	1	12	0
Crafton, Kevin, New Jersey	1.000	23	0	3	0	3	0
Crane, John, Batavia*	1.000	21	2	7	0	9	1
Crawford, Chris, Auburn	.875	12	1	6	1	8	0
Crawford, Jim, Williamsport	.818	21	6	3	2	11	0
Cressend, Jack, Lowell	1.000	9	1	6	0	7	1
Cutchins, Todd, Pittsfield*	1.000	6	2	5	0	7	0
Dace, Derek, Auburn*	1.000	15	4	19	0	23	0
Daniels, David, Erie	1.000	31	1	5	0	6	0
Davenport, Joe, St. Catharines	.769	20	5	5	3	13	0
Dellamano, Anthony, Hudson Val.	1.000	18	3	8	0	11	0
Delossantos, Luis, Oneonta	.667	10	4	6	5	15	2
DePaula, Sean, Watertown	1.000	1	0	1	0	1	0
Dingman, Craig, Oneonta	.800	20	1	3	1	5	0
Draeger, Mark, Hudson Valley	.667	17	1	3	2	6	1
Duffy, John, Lowell*	.923	29	1	11	1	13	0
Duncan, Courtney, Williamsport	.897	15	11	15	3	29	1
Duncan, Geoff, Erie	1.000	24	3	3	0	6	1
Eason, Michael, Utica	1.000	9	1	1	0	2	0
Edwards, Jon, Watertown	.667	23	0	2	1	3	0
Elmore, George, Erie	1.000	19	1	5	0	6	0
Falciglia, Tony, New Jersey	1.000	1	1	0	0	1	0
Feliz, Bienvenido, Watertown	.840	13	7	14	4	25	0
Ferrell, Dan, Utica*	1.000	14	2	10	0	12	1
Ferullo, Matt, Pittsfield	1.000	11	3	6	0	9	1
Festa, Chris, Lowell	.786	20	3	8	3	14	0
Figueroa, Julio, Vermont	1.000	14	3	10	0	13	0
Frace, Ryan, Batavia	1.000	25	3	6	0	9	0
Fuller, Duane, Auburn	1.000	11	1	4	0	5	0
Fuller, Stephen, Auburn	.867	18	2	11	2	15	0
Gallagher, Keith, New Jersey	1.000	12	6	12	0	18	2
Garsky, Brian, Vermont	.750	25	1	5	2	8	1
Gaskill, Derek, St. Catharines	.933	19	5	9	1	15	1
Gonzalez, Generoso, Jamestown	1.000	6	1	1	0	2	1
Gonzalez, Luis, Erie	.875	21	4	3	1	8	0
Gordon, Andrew, New Jersey	1.000	25	3	8	0	11	1
Graterol, Beiker, St. Catharines	1.000	14	5	6	0	11	0
Graves, Ryan, Williamsport*	1.000	4	2	0	0	2	0
Green, Jason, Auburn	.500	2	0	1	1	2	0
Griffiths, Everard, Hudson Valley	.750	11	1	2	1	4	0
Hart, Lendon, Williamsport*	1.000	28	1	3	0	4	0
Haynie, Jason, Erie*	1.000	16	6	13	0	19	0
Heffernan, Greg, New Jersey	1.000	18	3	6	0	9	0
Hendrikx, Brandon, Oneonta	1.000	17	1	5	0	6	0
Holobinko, Mike, Williamsport*	1.000	4	0	3	0	3	0
Horton, Aaron, Hudson Valley*	1.000	9	1	3	0	4	0
Hueda, Alejandro, St. Catharines	.818	12	2	7	2	11	0
Ingerick, Rhett, Oneonta	1.000	11	0	4	0	4	0
Johannsen, Jeffrey, Utica*	.800	14	0	4	1	5	0
Kauflin, David, Jamestown	1.000	22	3	4	0	7	0
Kawabata, Kyle, Batavia	1.000	25	2	6	0	8	1
Kessel, Kyle, Pittsfield*	.913	13	7	14	2	23	2
Kinney, Matt, Lowell	.800	15	7	9	4	20	0
Knight, Brandon, Hudson Valley	.867	17	7	6	2	15	0
Krall, Eric, Oneonta*	.688	15	1	10	5	16	1
Lara, Giovanni, Vermont	1.000	15	4	6	0	10	0
Lawrence, Clint, St. Catharines*	.950	9	7	12	1	20	0
Lee, Corey, Hudson Valley*	.923	9	1	11	1	13	1
Leon, Scott, Hudson Valley	.875	15	6	15	3	24	0
Leslie, Sean, Vermont*	.909	17	3	7	1	11	0
Lewis, Ron, Utica	1.000	20	3	9	0	12	1
Licciardi, Ronald, Williamsport*	.857	15	3	9	2	14	1
Love, Jeff, New Jersey	1.000	17	5	3	0	8	0
Maldonado, Esteban, Auburn	.833	6	2	3	1	6	0

CLASS A *New York-Pennsylvania League*

Player, Team	Pct.	G	PO	A	E	TC	DP
Mann, James, St. Catharines	.800	26	0	4	1	5	0
Mansavage, Jay, Auburn	1.000	2	0	1	0	1	0
Martinez, Dennis, Watertown	.750	12	1	5	2	8	0
Martinez, Jose, Hudson Valley	.857	16	2	10	2	14	0
Martinez, Willie, Watertown	.905	14	10	9	2	21	0
Matz, Brian, Vermont*	1.000	14	3	7	0	10	0
Mays, Jarrod, Watertown	.857	12	5	1	1	7	0
McBride, Chris, St. Catharines	.833	6	3	2	1	6	0
McDade, Neal, Erie	.875	13	4	10	2	16	0
McDougal, Mike, New Jersey	1.000	14	3	2	0	5	0
McFerrin, Chris, Auburn	1.000	33	4	7	0	11	1
Mensink, Brian, Batavia	1.000	8	1	9	0	10	1
Meyers, Ryan, St. Catharines	1.000	7	2	3	0	5	0
Miller, Chris, Batavia	1.000	17	1	13	0	14	0
Miller, Matt, Jamestown*	.778	6	3	4	2	9	1
Miller, Wade, Jamestown	1.000	2	0	1	0	1	0
Minter, Matthew, Watertown*	1.000	21	2	7	0	9	0
Mitchell, Christopher, Jamestn.	1.000	25	4	7	0	11	3
Mitchell, Courtney, Batavia*	.875	24	0	7	1	8	0
Montemayor, Humberto, Lowell	.000	5	0	0	1	1	0
Montgomery, Greg, New Jersey	.500	11	0	1	1	2	0
Moore, Joe, Utica	.600	11	1	2	2	5	0
Morgan, Steve, Lowell*	1.000	13	0	7	0	7	0
Morris, Chad, Vermont	1.000	20	0	2	0	2	0
Mota, Daniel, Oneonta	1.000	10	0	3	0	3	0
Musgrave, Brian, Lowell*	1.000	2	0	1	0	1	0
Nall, John, Williamsport*	.000	9	0	0	1	1	0
Needle, Chad, St. Catharines	1.000	20	4	3	0	7	1
Norton, Phillip, Williamsport*	.914	15	8	24	3	35	1
Nussbeck, Mark, New Jersey	.933	16	6	8	1	15	0
Oakley, Matt, Jamestown	.917	24	1	10	1	12	0
O'Connor, Brian, Erie*	.833	15	8	7	3	18	0
Ortiz, Rosario, Jamestown	1.000	6	0	2	0	2	0
Palmer, Brett, Watertown*	1.000	2	0	1	0	1	0
Parker, Christian, Vermont	.960	14	6	18	1	25	6
Patterson, Casey, Pittsfield	1.000	17	0	5	0	5	0
Pena, Jesus, Erie*	.833	21	2	8	2	12	0
Persails, Mark, Jamestown	1.000	13	7	7	0	14	1
Phillips, Ben, Oneonta	.810	14	3	14	4	21	0
Pollock, Jason, New Jersey	.833	18	2	8	2	12	1
Poupart, Melvin, Pittsfield	1.000	23	1	4	0	5	0
Presley, Kirk, Pittsfield	1.000	5	3	4	0	7	0
Pumphrey, Kenny, Pittsfield	.889	14	10	14	3	27	0
Pyrtle, Joe, Pittsfield	1.000	8	0	2	0	2	0
Quezada, Edward, Vermont	.947	14	8	10	1	19	0
Quintal, Craig, Jamestown	.800	15	5	7	3	15	1
Raines, Ken, Hudson Valley*	.912	38	9	22	3	34	1
Rangel, Julio, Oneonta	.900	15	4	23	3	30	2
Reames, Jay, New Jersey	.909	31	4	6	1	11	0
Reinfelder, Dave, Jamestown*	.846	28	2	9	2	13	1
Rigdon, Paul, Watertown	1.000	22	1	7	0	8	0
Rijo, Jose, Auburn	1.000	33	1	10	0	11	1
Risley, Bill, St. Catharines	1.000	3	1	0	0	1	0

Player, Team	Pct.	G	PO	A	E	TC
Robbins, Jake, Oneonta	.950	11	3	16	1	20
Robinson, Martin, Oneonta*	.913	15	5	16	2	23
Rodgers, Bobby, Lowell	.900	14	8	10	2	20
Rodriguez, Victor, St. Catharines	.833	21	4	11	3	18
Romo, Gregory, Jamestown	1.000	6	2	5	0	7
Roque, Jorge, New Jersey	1.000	13	0	3	0	3
Rosado, Juan, Vermont*	1.000	12	2	5	0	7
Rosenbohm, Jim, Pittsfield	.889	20	1	7	1	9
Santiago, Derek, Utica	1.000	12	5	12	0	17
Santos, Rafael, Erie	.929	18	3	10	1	14
Schroeder, Chad, Jamestown	1.000	31	2	6	0	8
Seabury, Jaron, St. Catharines	.909	19	5	5	1	11
Shadburne, Adam, Batavia	.917	20	2	9	1	12
Shaffer, Trevor, Williamsport	.875	25	1	6	1	8
Sheredy, Kevin, New Jersey	1.000	8	5	8	0	13
Siciliano, Jess, Erie	.500	4	1	0	1	2
Siegel, Justin, Hudson Valley*	1.000	5	1	0	0	1
Smatana, Steve, Lowell*	1.000	19	1	9	0	10
Spear, Russ, Jamestown	.889	8	0	8	1	9
Splawn, Matthew, Pittsfield	1.000	22	1	1	0	2
Spoljaric, Paul, St. Catharines*	1.000	2	0	1	0	1
Stadelhofer, Michael, Utica	1.000	4	0	4	0	4
Stechschulte, Gene, New Jersey	.800	20	4	4	2	10
Stevens, Kris, Batavia*	1.000	3	1	2	0	3
Stevenson, Rodney, Vermont	1.000	22	1	2	0	3
Symmonds, Maika, Lowell*	1.000	5	1	0	0	1
Taylor, Mark, Watertown*	.800	12	3	1	1	5
Thomas, Evan, Batavia	1.000	13	7	9	0	16
Thompson, Chris, Lowell	.889	25	2	6	1	9
Tilton, Ira, Batavia	.867	14	5	8	2	15
Tober, Dave, Batavia	.000	4	0	0	1	1
Townsend, Dave, Utica	.933	14	4	10	1	15
Tribe, Byron, Williamsport	.800	15	2	2	1	5
Turley, Jason, Auburn	.800	19	0	4	1	5
Viegas, Randy, Erie*	1.000	2	0	1	0	1
Villafuerte, Brandon, Pittsfield	1.000	18	3	11	0	14
Villar, Maximo, Erie	.875	9	3	4	1	8
Villegas, Ismael, Williamsport	1.000	2	0	1	0	1
Wagner, Ken, Watertown	.857	21	2	4	1	7
Ward, Jon, New Jersey	1.000	9	0	4	0	4
Welch, Robb, Lowell	1.000	14	7	9	0	16
West, Adam, New Jersey*	.963	15	7	19	1	27
Westover, Richard, Vermont	1.000	18	0	3	0	3
Whitson, Eric, Hudson Valley	1.000	19	3	3	0	6
Williams, Woody, St. Catharines	1.000	2	0	1	0	1
Wilmot, Toby, Auburn*	1.000	13	2	2	0	4
Wyckoff, Travis, Utica*	.900	24	5	13	2	20
Yanez, Luis, Auburn	1.000	15	8	10	0	18
Young, Tim, Vermont*	1.000	27	1	5	0	6
Yount, Andy, Lowell	.778	8	1	6	2	9
Zaleski, Kevin, Utica	1.000	26	1	2	0	3
Zamarripa, Mark, Jamestown	.875	29	4	10	2	16
Zavershnik, Mike, St. Cath.*	.714	5	0	5	2	7

The following players did not have any fielding statistics at the positions indicated or appeared only as a designated hitter, pinch-hitter or pinch-runner: Beagle Beaumont, dh; Bellenger, ss; Coleman, p; Cook, p; Cox, 3b; Ellis, of; J. Ellison, p; Fleetwood, p; Fortune, p; Fowler, p; Frazier, p; Herbison, p; Kleiner, 3b; Lachapelle Lindstrom, of; L. Lopez, of; Majcherek, p; Malenfant, p; Maloney, ss; Mansavage, ss; Morrison, c; Naples, of; Owens-Bragg, ss; Peoples, dh, ph; Rayment, p; Snusz Stewart, p; Tracy, 3b; Trunk, p; Ugueto, 2b; Velez, p; Venghaus, of.

LEAGUE CHAMPIONS

Year	Team	Pct.
1939—	Olean*	.631
1940—	Olean*	.625
1941—	Jamestown	.618
	Bradford (2nd)†	.549
1942—	Jamestown*	.672
1943—	Lockport	.591
	Wellsville (3rd)†	.532
1944—	Lockport	.608
	Jamestown (2nd)†	.565
1945—	Batavia*	.677
1946—	Jamestown‡	.672
	Batavia‡	.672
1947—	Jamestown*	.690
1948—	Lockport*	.603
1949—	Bradford*	.635
1950—	Hornell	.653
	Olean (2nd)†	.568
1951—	Olean	.622
	Hornell (3rd)†	.568
1952—	Hamilton	.659

Year	Team	Pct.
	Jamestown (2nd)†	.643
1953—	Jamestown*	.704
1954—	Corning*	.621
1955—	Hamilton*	.656
1956—	Wellsville*	.617
1957—	Wellsville	.632
	Erie (2nd)†	.598
1958—	Wellsville	.556
	Geneva (2nd)†	.548
1959—	Wellsville†	.635
1960—	Erie	.643
	Wellsville (2nd)†	.535
1961—	Geneva	.616
	Olean (4th)†	.512
1962—	Jamestown	.580
	Auburn (3rd)†	.521
1963—	Auburn	.585
	Batavia (3rd)†	.485
1964—	Auburn§	.622
1965—	Binghamton	.677

Year	Team	Pc
	Binghamton	.60
1966—	Auburn∞	.62
	Binghamton	.64
1967—	Auburn	.66
1968—	Auburn	.64
	Oneonta (2nd)*	.55
1969—	Oneonta	.66
1970—	Auburn	.62
1971—	Oneonta	.66
1972—	Niagara Falls	.68
1973—	Auburn	.66
1974—	Oneonta	.76
1975—	Newark	.68
	Newark	.71
1976—	Elmira	.72
	Elmira	.70
1977—	Oneonta▲	.67
	Batavia	.60
1978—	Oneonta	.72
	Geneva◆	.71

Year	Team	Pct.	Year	Team	Pct.	Year	Team	Pct.
979—	Geneva	.725	1985—	Oneonta*	.705	1991—	Pittsfield	.662
	Oneonta♦	.618		Auburn	.603		Jamestown■	.654
980—	Oneonta▲	.662	1986—	Oneonta	.766	1992—	Hamilton	.737
	Geneva	.649		St. Catharines♦	.632		Geneva▼	.547
981—	Oneonta▲	.658	1987—	Geneva▲	.632	1993—	Niagara Falls▼	.603
	Jamestown	.649		Watertown	.579		Pittsfield	.533
982—	Oneonta	.566	1988—	Oneonta▲	.632	1994—	Auburn	.592
	Niagara Falls▲	.553		Jamestown	.618		New Jersey▼	.573
983—	Utica▲	.649	1989—	Pittsfield	.697	1995—	Vermont	.645
	Newark	.649		Jamestown▲	.579		Watertown▼	.630
984—	Newark	.622	1990—	Oneonta■	.667	1996—	Vermont▼	.649
	Little Falls▲	.587		Geneva	.662		St. Catharines	.579

*Won championship and four-club playoff. †Won four-club playoff. ‡Jamestown and Batavia declared co-champions; Batavia defeated Jamestown in final of ur-club playoff. §Won championship and two-club playoff. ∞Won split-season playoff. ▲League divided into Eastern and Western divisions; won playoff. League vided into Wrigley and Yawkey divisions; won playoff. ■League divided into Eastern, Western and Stedler divisions; won playoff. ▼League divided into :Namara, Pinckney and Stedler divisions; won playoff. (NOTE—Known as Pennsylvania-Ontario-New York League from 1939 through 1956.)

NORTHWEST LEAGUE

President/treasurer
Bob Richmond
Address
P.O. Box 4941
Scottsdale, AZ 85261
Phone
602-483-8224

Teams (affiliation)
Boise Hawks (Angels)
Eugene Emeralds (Braves)
Everett AquaSox (Mariners)
Portland Rockies (Rockies)
Salem-Keizer (Giants)
Southern Oregon Timberjacks (A's)

Spokane Indians (Royals)
Yakima Bears (Dodgers)

1996 FINAL STANDINGS

NORTH DIVISION

Team	W	L	T	Pct.	GB
Yakima (Dodgers)	40	36	0	.526	....
Bellingham (Giants)	39	36	0	.520	1/2
Spokane (Royals)	37	39	0	.487	3
Everett (Mariners)	33	42	0	.440	6 1/2

SOUTH DIVISION

Team	W	L	T	Pct.	G
Eugene (Braves)	49	27	0	.645	....
Boise (Angels)	43	33	0	.566	6
Portland (Rockies)	33	43	0	.434	16
Southern Oregon (Athletics)	29	47	0	.382	20

COMPOSITE

Team	Eug.	Boi.	Yak.	Bell.	Spo.	Ever.	Port.	S.O.	W	L	T	Pct.	GB
Eugene (Braves)	....	5	6	5	6	5	10	12	49	27	0	.645	....
Boise (Angels)	9	....	7	2	3	4	7	11	43	33	0	.566	6
Yakima (Dodgers)	2	1	....	8	9	9	5	6	40	36	0	.526	9
Bellingham (Giants)	3	6	7	....	8	8	3	4	39	36	0	.520	9
Spokane (Royals)	2	5	5	7	....	10	4	4	37	39	0	.487	12
Everett (Mariners)	3	4	6	5	5	....	5	5	33	42	0	.440	15
Portland (Rockies)	5	8	3	5	4	3	....	5	33	43	0	.434	16
Southern Oregon (Athletics)	3	4	2	4	4	3	9	....	29	47	0	.382	20

Southern Oregon played home games in Medford, Ore.

Major league affiliations in parentheses.

PLAYOFFS: Yakima defeated Eugene, two games to none, to win league championship.

REGULAR SEASON ATTENDANCE: Bellingham, 48,417; Boise, 164,231; Eugene, 148,282; Everett, 87,846; Portland, 249,995; Southern Oregon, 77,4. Spokane, 180,903; Yakima, 82,313; Total—1,039,424; Playoffs (2 games)—8,022.

MANAGERS: Bellingham, Ozzie Virgil (through July 27), Shane Turner (July 28 through end of season); Boise, Tom Kotchman; Eugene, Jim Saul; Ever Roger Hansen; Portland, Ron Gideon; Southern Oregon, Tony DeFrancesco; Spokane, Bob Herold; Yakima, Joe Vavra. Managerial records of teams with me than one manager: Bellingham, Ozzie Virgil, 20-18, Shane Turner, 19-18.

ALL-STAR TEAM: 1B—Rob Zachmann, Everett; 2B—Doug Livingston, Portland and Tony Zuniga, Bellingham; 3B—Brian Rust, Eugene; SS—Mike Caru Bellingham; OF—Justin Bowles, Southern Oregon; Adam Johnson, Eugene; Nate Murphy, Boise; C—Matt Curtis, Boise and Dax Norris, Eugene; DH—Ste Hacker, Eugene; RHP—Brandon Leese, Bellingham; LHP—Ken Vining, Bellingham; RHRP—Mick Pageler, Bellingham; LHRP—Jeff Kubenka, Yakima; M Valuable Player—Rob Zachmann, Everett; Manager of the Year—Joe Vavra, Yakima.

1996 BATTING

TEAM

Team	Avg.	G	TPA	AB	R	H	TB	2B	3B	HR	RBI	SH	SF	HP	BB	IBB	SO	SB	CS	GDP	LOB	ShO	Slg.	O
Boise	.270	76	3194	2764	477	747	1105	149	25	53	414	12	30	40	347	13	561	79	31	64	627	3	.400	.3
Eugene	.266	76	3017	2669	447	710	1174	150	28	86	399	12	27	36	273	19	607	51	30	44	545	2	.440	.3
Spokane	.254	76	3056	2623	433	667	1041	122	18	72	385	30	31	46	326	5	563	122	30	55	576	4	.397	.3
Bellingham	.252	75	2882	2560	355	646	943	110	17	51	318	22	29	33	237	12	636	55	37	43	510	5	.368	.3
Portland	.248	76	2968	2628	367	653	917	128	23	30	311	31	24	35	250	10	544	59	23	47	551	2	.349	.3
Yakima	.245	76	2932	2597	337	635	924	120	20	43	301	17	16	36	266	7	703	79	36	34	570	7	.356	.3
South. Oregon	.244	76	2972	2587	374	631	978	136	11	63	326	29	22	38	295	9	644	101	45	40	541	3	.378	.3
Everett	.231	75	2897	2519	344	581	848	100	16	45	311	14	16	28	319	10	738	56	29	45	570	3	.337	.3

INDIVIDUAL

TOP QUALIFIERS FOR BATTING CHAMPIONSHIP

Minimum 205 plate appearances. *Lefthanded batter. †Switch-hitter.

Player, Team	Avg.	G	TPA	AB	R	H	TB	2B	3B	HR	RBI	SH	SF	HP	BB	IBB	SO	SB	CS	GDP	Slg.	C
Johnson, Adam, Eugene*	.314	76	344	318	58	100	161	22	9	7	56	1	2	4	19	3	32	4	1	4	.506	.3
Berger, Brandon, Spokane	.307	71	320	283	46	87	140	12	1	13	58	1	3	2	31	0	64	17	5	7	.495	.3
Curtis, Matt, Boise†	.305	75	354	305	57	93	164	29	3	12	62	0	4	8	37	0	47	2	1	7	.538	.3
Meyer, Matt, Yakima*	.302	66	269	235	40	71	109	14	6	4	28	1	1	5	27	1	73	6	0	1	.464	.3
Zuniga, Jose, Bellingham	.299	69	304	264	36	79	98	11	1	2	35	4	2	0	34	2	47	0	5	2	.371	.3
Livingston, Doug, Portland	.299	57	258	224	36	67	108	18	4	5	34	6	2	3	23	1	45	6	0	4	.482	.3
Rodriguez, Juan, Boise†	.297	52	209	192	24	57	72	9	0	2	28	1	4	0	12	3	52	3	3	5	.375	.3
Sankey, Brian, Yakima*	.294	72	294	255	40	75	131	19	2	11	52	0	3	2	34	2	53	2	0	1	.514	.3
Caruso, Michael, Bellingham†	.292	73	339	312	48	91	112	13	1	2	24	3	6	2	16	2	23	24	10	2	.359	.3
Zachmann, Rob, Everett	.291	74	318	285	49	83	155	13	1	19	64	0	2	1	30	3	87	4	0	3	.544	.3

CLASS A Northwest League

Player, Team	Avg.	G	TPA	AB	R	H	TB	2B	3B	HR	RBI	SH	SF	HP	BB	IBB	SO	SB	CS	GDP	Slg.	OBP
Norris, Dax, Eugene	.289	60	257	232	31	67	105	17	0	7	37	3	1	3	18	0	32	2	0	4	.453	.346
Rust, Brian, Eugene	.287	71	298	275	52	79	139	24	3	10	43	0		3	20	2	74	4	2	4	.505	.342
Pellow, Kit, Spokane	.287	71	315	279	48	80	156	18	2	18	66	1	7	8	20	0	52	8	3	5	.559	.344
Murphy, Nate, Boise*	.286	67	311	266	58	76	117	18	1	7	41	0	1	1	41	1	63	12	4	4	.440	.382
Bowles, Justin, So. Oregon*	.285	56	246	214	41	61	116	20	1	11	45	0	0	1	31	2	53	8	3	1	.542	.378

DEPARTMENTAL LEADERS: G—A. Johnson, 76; AB—A. Johnson, 318; R—A. Johnson, Murphy, Giambi, 58 each; H—A. Johnson, 100; TB—Curtis, 164; 2B—Curtis, 29; 3B—A. Johnson, 9; HR—Hacker, 21; RBI—Pellow, 66; SH—Cesar, 7; SF—Pellow, 7; HP—Durrington, 13; BB—Giambi, 61; IBB—Minor, Pointer, 4 each; SO—Sachse, 94; SB—Caruso, Durrington, 24; CS—Caruso, 10; GIDP—Derosa, 10; Slg.—Pellow, .559; OBP—Giambi, .440.

ALL PLAYERS

*Lefthanded batter. †Switch-hitter.

Player, Team	Avg.	G	TPA	AB	R	H	TB	2B	3B	HR	RBI	SH	SF	HP	BB	IBB	SO	SB	CS	GDP	Slg.	OBP
Abbott, Chuck, Boise	.198	70	305	268	41	53	66	9	2	0	20	4	4	5	24	0	59	11	5	8	.246	.272
Anderson, Blake, Portland†	.231	39	162	134	24	31	49	5	2	3	16	0	1	1	26	2	27	1	1	3	.366	.358
Anthony, Brian, Portland*	.140	30	117	107	6	15	23	5	0	1	5	0	0	0	10	0	30	1	0	3	.215	.214
Arias, Rogelio, Portland	.238	44	181	168	15	40	48	3	1	1	15	4	2	2	5	0	24	1	1	4	.286	.266
Arnold, John, Eugene	.256	31	93	78	16	20	40	5	0	5	19	1	0	0	14	2	25	1	0	2	.513	.370
Arrollado, Courtney, Spokane	.213	22	49	47	2	10	11	1	0	0	2	0	1	0	1	0	13	2	0	2	.234	.224
Baeza, Art, Bellingham	.198	25	104	86	11	17	25	2	0	2	9	3	1	4	10	0	24	2	0	4	.291	.307
Bair, Rod, Portland	.217	56	254	221	34	48	75	11	2	4	33	5	4	7	17	2	29	9	4	2	.339	.289
Beltran, Carlos, Spokane†	.270	59	251	215	29	58	93	8	3	7	29	3	2	0	31	0	65	10	2	4	.433	.359
Berger, Brandon, Spokane	.307	71	320	283	46	87	140	12	1	13	58	1	3	2	31	0	64	17	5	7	.495	.376
Bergeron, Peter, Yakima*	.254	61	263	232	36	59	85	5	3	5	21	3	0	0	28	0	59	13	9	2	.366	.335
Blosser, Doug, Spokane*	.255	16	54	47	10	12	27	4	1	3	8	0	0	1	6	1	14	0	0	0	.574	.352
Bowles, Justin, So. Oregon*	.285	56	246	214	41	61	116	20	1	11	45	0	0	1	31	2	53	8	3	1	.542	.378
Brown, Eric, Yakima	.234	53	191	171	19	40	70	9	0	7	21	0	2	2	16	1	68	5	2	4	.409	.304
Brown, Gavin, Eugene	.262	58	233	206	31	54	80	6	1	6	34	0	3	2	22	0	33	0	2	5	.388	.335
Burrows, Mike, Everett*	.211	43	170	147	18	31	53	9	2	3	19	0	1	1	21	0	41	5	3	2	.361	.312
Byers, MacGregor, So. Oregon	.302	34	155	126	28	38	52	9	1	1	20	0	2	4	23	1	32	5	2	2	.413	.419
Byers, Scott, Boise*	.280	66	287	257	31	72	111	19	1	6	39	0	2	1	27	1	21	0	0	4	.432	.348
Calderon, Ricardo, Bellingham*	.222	43	122	108	10	24	40	5	1	3	11	0	2	1	11	0	42	3	2	2	.370	.295
Caruso, Michael, Bellingham†	.292	73	339	342	48	91	112	13	1	2	24	3	6	2	16	2	23	24	10	2	.359	.324
Castro, Jose, Everett*	.250	1	4	4	0	1	1	0	0	0	0	0	0	0	0	0	1	0	0	0	.250	.250
Castro, Nelson, Boise†	.000	1	1	1	0	0	0	0	0	0	0	0	0	0	0	0	0	0	0	0	.000	.000
Cesar, Dionys, So. Oregon†	.271	52	234	203	37	55	73	7	4	1	12	7	1	4	19	0	46	18	6	3	.360	.344
Cespedes, Angel, Portland†	.188	27	92	80	8	15	21	1	1	1	3	1	1	0	10	0	28	1	1	0	.263	.275
Christenson, Ryan, So. Oregon	.287	36	158	136	31	39	65	11	0	5	21	1	1	1	19	1	21	8	6	3	.478	.376
Clark, John, Portland	.204	58	230	211	17	43	63	8	3	2	19	2	1	4	12	0	62	0	2	4	.299	.259
Cross, Adam, Eugene	.255	55	230	196	34	50	71	12	0	3	24	1	2	4	27	1	41	9	5	0	.362	.354
Cruz, Cirilo, Everett	.270	44	174	163	12	44	50	6	0	0	21	0	1	2	8	0	34	1	5	3	.307	.310
Curtis, Matt, Boise†	.305	54	305	305	57	93	164	29	3	12	62	0	4	8	37	0	47	2	1	7	.538	.390
DeRosa, Mark, Eugene	.259	70	300	255	43	66	87	13	1	2	28	0	2	5	38	1	48	3	4	10	.341	.363
Didion, Kristopher, Spokane	.219	61	236	201	30	44	77	7	4	6	32	0	6	3	26	0	60	7	2	8	.383	.309
Durrington, Trent, Boise	.279	40	198	154	38	43	54	7	2	0	14	0	0	13	31	1	32	24	5	4	.351	.439
Ellison, Skeeter, Eugene†	.350	7	25	20	4	7	15	3	1	1	6	0	1	1	3	0	6	0	1	1	.750	.440
Escamilla, Roman, Spokane	.217	46	165	152	11	33	46	7	0	2	21	1	0	0	12	0	22	1	0	1	.303	.274
Espada, Angel, Eugene	.245	24	103	98	5	24	28	4	0	0	5	0	0	1	3	0	11	13	5	2	.286	.272
Espada, Josue, So. Oregon	.222	15	61	54	7	12	16	1	0	1	5	1	0	1	5	0	10	0	0	1	.296	.300
Esfee, Theo, Boise*	.301	41	168	156	23	47	65	3	3	3	25	2	3	0	7	1	44	1	2	3	.417	.325
Ferrer, Eduardo, Boise†	.262	54	219	183	31	48	63	8	2	2	19	3	1	0	32	1	21	4	4	7	.344	.370
Figueroa, Luis, Everett	.462	4	15	13	4	6	9	1	1	0	3	0	0	0	2	0	1	0	0	1	.692	.533
Fjach, Jason, Eugene	.000	27	1	1	0	0	0	0	0	0	0	0	0	0	0	0	0	0	0	0	.000	.000
Flores, Eric, Yakima	.190	38	117	100	7	19	23	4	0	0	8	1	1	3	12	0	42	0	0	1	.230	.293
Freeman, Terrance, So. Oregon†	.234	56	199	167	26	39	46	5	1	0	18	4	0	5	23	0	29	21	7	5	.275	.344
Galloway, Paul, Bellingham	.277	47	198	177	22	49	79	11	2	5	24	1	1	4	15	3	35	1	1	3	.446	.345
Giambi, Jeremy, Spokane*	.273	67	300	231	58	63	98	17	0	6	39	0	0	8	61	2	32	22	5	5	.424	.440
Gillespie, Eric, Boise*	.276	61	222	192	28	53	83	11	5	3	38	1	3	1	25	1	50	0	1	4	.432	.357
Glassey, Josh, Yakima*	.219	50	163	137	11	30	35	5	0	0	20	0	0	0	26	1	44	0	0	3	.255	.344
Glendinning, Michael, Bellingham	.260	73	308	265	54	69	132	19	4	12	48	1	2	0	39	0	80	4	6	6	.498	.355
Hacker, Steve, Eugene	.250	75	330	292	45	73	153	15	1	21	61	0	6	6	26	3	64	0	0	2	.524	.318
Halleab, John, Portland*	.243	52	202	181	22	44	56	9	0	1	23	3	0		15	1	42	6	1	1	.309	.296
Hamlin, Mark, Portland	.272	54	223	202	25	55	79	8	2	4	26	2	0	3	16	0	53	5	3	3	.391	.335
Harp, Scott, Spokane	.275	55	209	178	31	49	67	10	1	2	16	5	1	4	21	0	28	6	1	7	.376	.335
Hines, Pooh, Eugene	.352	21	99	88	20	31	52	5	5	2	8	3	1	0	7	0	18	3	4	1	.591	.396
Hobbie, Matt, Boise*	.252	51	148	127	26	32	46	6	1	2	22	0	1	0	20	1	24	5	1	2	.362	.351
Horner, Jim, Everett	.150	18	71	60	6	9	17	2	0	2	5	0	0	1	10	1	16	0	0	1	.283	.282
Hutchison, Bernard, Portland	.260	51	214	192	29	50	56	6	0	0	13	2	1	3	16	0	34	20	3	3	.292	.325
Jackson, Wade, Boise	.282	43	139	117	17	33	48	5	2	2	25	0	3	2	17	0	25	5	1	3	.410	.374
Johnson, Adam, Eugene*	.314	76	344	318	58	100	161	22	9	7	56	1	2	4	19	3	32	4	1	4	.506	.359
Johnson, Duan, Everett	.262	51	212	202	32	53	67	7	2	1	19	1	1	1	7	0	26	3	3	8	.332	.289
Johnson, Jace, So. Oregon	.228	36	131	114	13	26	38	9	0	1	8	1	0	0	14	0	29	3	1	0	.333	.310
Johnson, Patrick, Boise	.200	27	84	75	2	15	15	0	0	0	4	0	0	1	8	0	12	0	0	3	.200	.200
Jones, Tim, Southern Oregon*	.202	62	206	173	25	35	61	8	0	6	18	2	2	2	27	0	69	7	5	2	.353	.314
Jordan, Ricky, Everett	.357	3	15	14	2	5	6	1	0	0	2	0	0	0	1	0	4	0	0	0	.429	.400
Katz, Jason, Eugene†	.179	7	32	28	3	5	6	1	0	0	2	0	0	0	4	0	11	0	0	0	.214	.293
Keck, Brian, Portland	.263	43	183	156	29	41	46	1	2	0	20	0	3	1	22	0	23	7	2	1	.295	.356
Kenna, David, Bellingham*	.217	56	204	180	11	39	57	9	3	1	25	0	2	2	20	1	78	2	0	1	.317	.299
Keffer, Brian, So. Oregon*	.000	2	5	2	0	0	0	0	0	0	0	0	0	0	3	1	2	0	0	0	.000	.600
King, William M., Yakima*	.154	24	46	39	4	6	6	0	0	0	1	0	0	0	7	0	16	0	0	0	.154	.283
Okinda, Steven, Everett*	.146	16	57	48	7	7	9	2	0	0	3	0	0	1	8	0	16	0	0	0	.188	.281
Payne, Jason, Spokane*	.286	41	148	126	24	36	66	9	3	5	27	0	0	5	17	1	34	0	0	0	.524	.392

CLASS A Northwest League

Player, Team	Avg.	G	TPA	AB	R	H	TB	2B	3B	HR	RBI	SH	SF	HP	BB	IBB	SO	SB	CS	GDP	Slg.	O
Linder, Brian, Everett	.206	64	294	248	27	51	67	8	1	?	?7	?	0	2	42	0	67	6	1	9	.270	.3
Lindsey, John, Portland	.255	57	238	208	32	53	72	11	1	2	22	0	0	4	26	0	63	1	1	3	.346	.3
Livingston, Doug, Portland	.299	57	258	224	36	67	108	18	4	5	34	6	2	3	23	1	45	6	0	4	.482	.3
Lopez, Luis, Bellingham	.000	1	2	2	0	0	0	0	0	0	0	0	0	0	0	0	2	0	0	0	.000	.0
Malave, Jaime, Yakima	.204	40	115	108	14	22	43	6	0	5	16	1	0	0	6	0	33	0	0	2	.398	.2
Manning, Brian, Bellingham	.297	35	158	138	26	41	60	6	2	3	22	0	1	6	13	0	27	0	3	2	.435	.3
Marcinczyk, T.R., So. Oregon	.222	63	252	216	29	48	86	13	2	7	38	5	4	5	22	0	57	3	3	3	.398	.3
Marnell, Dean, Portland	.298	38	144	131	20	39	46	7	0	0	23	2	1	1	9	0	12	0	1	4	.351	.3
Marshall, Monte, Yakima†	.191	17	79	68	9	13	16	1	1	0	7	2	0	2	7	0	14	0	1	1	.235	.2
McGuire, Matt, Bellingham	.133	7	17	15	1	2	2	0	0	0	0	1	0	0	1	0	4	1	0	0	.133	.1
McKay, Cody, So. Oregon*	.268	69	289	254	33	68	90	13	0	3	30	1	3	6	25	0	42	0	5	7	.354	.3
Mensik, Todd, So. Oregon*	.240	59	217	192	21	46	54	8	0	0	14	0	4	2	19	2	39	2	0	6	.281	.3
Meyer, Bobby, Yakima	.213	33	94	80	12	17	25	5	0	1	7	1	1	0	12	0	25	2	0	3	.313	.3
Meyer, Matt, Yakima*	.302	66	269	235	40	71	109	14	6	4	28	1	1	5	27	1	73	6	0	1	.464	.3
Minor, Damon, Bellingham*	.242	75	323	269	44	65	114	11	1	12	55	1	1	5	47	4	86	0	2	5	.424	.3
Miranda, Tony, Spokane	.170	21	66	53	11	9	18	3	0	2	8	1	1	2	9	0	13	2	1	1	.340	.3
Miskolczi, Levi, Bellingham	.214	57	195	187	19	40	46	6	0	0	17	1	2	1	3	0	36	4	2	3	.246	.2
Moore, Kenderick, Spokane	.260	52	237	204	37	53	67	6	1	2	25	5	2	3	23	0	29	19	3	4	.328	.3
Morrison, Scott, Yakima	.207	60	225	184	22	38	54	11	1	1	26	0	2	7	32	0	42	2	1	2	.293	.3
Mota, Tony, Yakima†	.276	60	243	225	29	62	88	11	3	3	29	3	1	1	13	0	37	13	7	0	.391	.3
Murphy, Nate, Boise*	.286	67	311	266	58	76	117	18	1	7	41	0	1	1	41	1	63	12	4	4	.440	.3
Myers, Aaron, Portland	.276	72	327	290	52	80	125	24	3	5	46	1	5	6	25	2	48	1	2	9	.431	.3
Neal, Rob, Boise	.289	47	200	173	36	50	80	13	1	5	35	0	2	5	20	0	40	3	1	3	.462	.3
Nelson, Brian, Everett	.184	30	122	98	11	18	26	5	0	1	11	0	0	5	19	0	32	0	0	1	.265	.3
Newton, Kimani, Yakima	.156	33	54	45	8	7	8	1	0	0	3	0	1	2	6	0	13	1	2	1	.178	.2
Norris, Dax, Eugene	.289	60	257	232	31	67	105	17	0	7	37	3	1	3	18	0	32	2	0	4	.453	.3
Oliva, Osvaldo, Bellingham	.000	3	5	4	0	0	0	0	0	0	0	0	0	0	1	0	2	0	0	0	.000	.2
Pellow, Kit, Spokane	.287	71	315	279	48	80	156	18	2	18	66	1	7	8	20	0	52	8	3	5	.559	.3
Pickett, Eric, Eugene*	.224	61	240	214	32	48	81	7	4	6	25	0	1		25	3	77	1	4	2	.379	.3
Pitts, Rick, Spokane†	.193	55	159	135	23	26	34	2	0	2	11	2	1	3	18	0	37	14	1	0	.252	.2
Pointer, Corey, Eugene	.245	65	278	233	46	57	117	12	3	14	39	0	5	5	35	4	88	10	2	3	.502	.3
Polanco, Juan, So. Oregon	.216	56	230	208	22	45	68	7	2	4	24	1	2	2	15	0	57	13	3	0	.327	.2
Prospero, Teo, Bellingham	.211	26	81	76	7	16	28	1	1	3	8	0	2	1	2	0	28	0	3	0	.368	.2
Quesada, Travis, Boise	.100	10	27	20	3	2	4	0	1	0	0	0	0	0	7	0	7	0	1	0	.200	.3
Rand, Ian, Bellingham	.215	53	161	149	23	32	40	3	1	1	8	2	0	2	8	0	48	5	1	2	.268	.2
Rauer, Troy, Southern Oregon	.205	62	241	215	29	44	78	10	0	8	24	2	0	3	21	0	85	7	1	3	.363	.2
Regan, Jason, Everett	.210	40	157	124	17	26	46	11	0	3	22	2	4	4	25	0	47	3	3	1	.371	.3
Robles, Juan, Spokane	.275	53	200	178	27	49	63	6	1	2	20	0	4	1	17	1	37	4	1	4	.354	.3
Rodriguez, Guillermo, Bellingham	.000	3	4	4	1	0	0	0	0	0	0	0	0	0	0	0	1	0	0	0	.000	.0
Rodriguez, Juan, Boise†	.297	52	209	192	24	57	72	9	0	2	28	1	4	0	12	3	52	3	3	5	.375	.3
Rolls, Damian, Yakima	.265	66	270	257	31	68	93	11	1	4	27	2	1	3	7	0	46	8	3	5	.362	.2
Rondon, Alex, Southern Oregon	.213	49	192	174	15	37	62	10	0	5	20	2	1	1	14	2	43	0	1	2	.356	.2
Rowson, James, Everett	.221	53	211	181	30	40	65	9	2	4	24	0	1	3	26	2	68	4	2	1	.359	.2
Rust, Brian, Eugene	.287	71	298	275	52	79	139	24	3	10	43	0	3	3	20	2	74	4	2	4	.505	.3
Sachse, Matt, Everett*	.236	67	256	237	24	56	82	9	1	5	27	1	2	2	14	2	94	4	2	6	.346	.2
Saitta, Rich, Yakima	.248	48	181	165	17	41	49	5	0	1	17	2	1	2	11	0	34	7	5	5	.297	.3
Sankey, Brian, Yakima*	.294	72	294	255	40	75	131	19	2	11	52	0	3	2	34	2	53	2	0	1	.514	.3
Saucedo, Robert, Boise	.500	1	5	2	2	1	1	0	0	0	1	0	0	0	3	0	0	0	0	1	.500	.8
Sees, Eric, Spokane	.202	59	201	168	25	34	43	7	1	0	8	5	2	5	21	0	36	8	5	5	.256	.2
Serrano, Danny, Boise†	.143	8	11	7	3	1	1	0	0	0	1	0	0	2	2	0	0	0	0	1	.143	.4
Simonton, Cy Leon, Everett*	.213	40	155	136	18	29	33	1	0	1	8	0	0	0	19	1	37	3	3	1	.243	.2
Skeels, David, Everett	.286	51	81	77	8	22	28	3	0	1	8	0	0	1	3	0	13	2	1	3	.364	.2
Slemmer, Dave, So. Oregon	.273	35	157	139	17	38	73	5	0	10	29	1	1	1	15	0	30	6	2	2	.525	.3
Soriano, Jacobo, Boise	.000	1	1	1	0	0	0	0	0	0	0	0	0	0	0	0	1	0	0	0	.000	.0
Sorrow, Michael, Bellingham	.333	2	5	3	1	1	1	0	0	0	0	0	0	1	0	0	0	0	0	0	.333	.6
Stearns, Randy, Yakima*	.257	57	202	183	29	47	61	8	3	0	10	1	1	0	17	2	60	17	6	2	.333	.3
Steinmann, Scott, Everett†	.140	30	118	100	13	14	20	4	1	0	4	0	0	1	15	1	33	0	0	0	.200	.2
Stewart, Keith, Everett*	.144	32	102	90	13	13	20	1	0	2	6	3	1	0	8	0	47	3	2	0	.222	.2
Stuart, Rich, Boise	.312	22	107	93	36	29	61	6	1	8	24	0	2	0	12	2	15	8	2	1	.656	.3
Taft, Brett, Spokane	.190	42	146	126	21	24	35	5	0	2	15	6	1	1	12	0	27	2	1	2	.278	.2
't Hoen, E.J., Boise	.200	18	66	60	6	12	19	1	0	2	4	1	0	1	4	0	17	0	0	2	.317	.2
Topaum, Tom, Bellingham	.271	38	138	129	15	35	56	9	0	4	18	1	3	1	4	0	34	0	0	4	.434	.2
Torrealba, Yoruit, Bellingham	.267	48	165	150	23	40	47	4	0	0	10	4	2	0	9	0	27	4	1	7	.313	.3
Ussery, Brian, Boise†	.261	33	133	115	15	30	35	5	0	0	12	0	0	0	18	1	31	1	0	3	.304	.3
Valera, Ramon, Everett	.229	50	206	166	28	38	47	3	0	3	12	3	0	2	35	0	48	11	2	2	.283	.3
VanRossum, Chris, Bellingham	.143	23	49	42	3	6	6	0	0	0	4	0	2	2	0	0	12	5	1	0	.143	.2
Vazquez, Ramon, Everett*	.278	33	160	126	25	35	47	5	2	1	18	2	5	1	26	0	26	7	2	3	.373	.2
Vecchioni, Jerry, Eugene	.137	26	63	51	7	7	12	2	0	1	4	2	2	0	8	0	21	0	0	0	.235	.2
Vidal, Carlos, Portland	.226	32	126	106	16	24	37	8	1	1	11	0	2	0	18	2	20	0	1	3	.349	.2
Wilson, Steve, Yakima	.177	43	126	113	9	20	28	5	0	1	9	1	0	1	7	5	44	3	0	1	.248	.2
Wong, Jerrod, Eugene*	.262	28	91	84	10	22	27	2	0	1	8	1	1	1	4	0	26	1	0	4	.321	.2
Zachmann, Rob, Everett	.291	74	318	285	49	83	155	13	1	19	64	0	2	4	30	3	87	4	0	5	.544	.3
Zuniga, Juan, Spokane	.299	69	304	264	36	79	98	11	1	2	35	4	2	0	34	2	47	0	5	2	.371	.3
Zweifel, Kent, Portland	.471	4	17	17	5	8	13	3	1	0	4	0	0	0	0	0	4	0	0	0	.765	.4

GRAND SLAMS: Zachmann, 3; Beltran, Bowles, Escamilla, Giambi, A. Johnson, Livingston, Marcinczyk, M. Meyer, Moore, Morrison, Pellow, Rowson, Sachse, 1 ea.

AWARDED FIRST BASE ON CATCHER'S INTERFERENCE: Miskolczi (Escamilla); Murphy (Norris); Polanco (Topaum); Steinmann (Rondon).

TEAM

Team	W	L	Pct.	ERA	G	CG	ShO	Sv.	IP	H	TBF	R	ER	HR	SH	SF	HB	BB	IBB	SO	WP	Bk.
Bellingham	39	36	.520	3.41	75	0	5	19	673.1	575	2898	318	255	57	17	14	25	316	4	691	58	8
Yakima	40	36	.526	3.45	76	0	6	25	677.1	588	2893	333	260	38	19	26	16	283	10	689	58	17
Eugene	49	27	.645	3.67	76	0	4	33	686.2	634	2999	365	280	36	25	19	29	272	12	682	46	6
Portland	33	43	.434	4.10	76	0	4	18	678.1	656	2964	386	309	66	17	26	45	250	5	585	43	10
Everett	33	42	.440	4.19	75	0	4	19	657.1	658	2877	390	306	53	22	18	28	254	2	657	80	19
Boise	43	33	.566	4.43	76	2	2	16	699.1	695	3142	440	344	61	29	32	53	334	29	585	57	6
Spokane	37	39	.487	4.50	76	0	2	19	681.1	718	3019	418	341	64	20	34	53	264	3	567	44	10
Southern Oregon	29	47	.382	5.29	76	0	2	14	677.2	746	3126	484	398	68	18	26	43	340	20	540	50	22

INDIVIDUAL

TOP QUALIFIERS FOR EARNED-RUN AVERAGE TITLE

Minimum 61 innings. *Lefthanded pitcher.

Pitcher, Team	W	L	Pct.	ERA	G	GS	CG	ShO	GF	Sv.	IP	H	TBF	R	ER	HR	SH	SF	HB	BB	IBB	SO	WP	Bk.
Mayo, Blake, Yakima	5	2	.714	1.20	20	6	0	0	8	1	67.1	44	256	15	9	1	0	1	0	12	0	68	5	1
Culmo, Kevin, Yakima	4	2	.667	2.27	17	5	0	0	5	2	63.1	47	262	18	16	2	1	2	1	22	0	60	5	0
Chapman, Jake, Spokane*	7	1	.875	2.37	19	7	0	0	3	1	68.1	44	274	19	18	2	2	2	6	20	1	71	3	1
Calero, Enrique, Spokane	4	2	.667	2.52	17	11	0	0	3	1	75.0	77	318	34	21	5	0	6	3	18	0	61	2	2
Hueston, Stephen, Spokane	3	2	.600	3.08	13	13	0	0	0	0	64.1	54	272	27	22	8	3	2	5	31	0	60	5	2
Mays, Joe, Everett	4	4	.500	3.08	13	10	0	0	0	0	64.1	55	271	33	22	3	3	2	2	22	0	56	9	1
Leese, Brandon, Bellingham	5	6	.455	3.25	16	15	0	0	0	0	80.1	59	341	39	29	6	0	2	5	37	0	90	8	0
Darrell, Tommy, Boise	8	1	.889	3.48	15	15	1	1	0	0	101.0	114	433	56	39	11	2	2	4	13	2	76	2	0
Noriega, Ray, Southern Oregon*	4	4	.500	3.54	17	14	0	0	0	0	61.0	61	263	28	24	3	2	0	2	22	0	50	4	0
Giuliano, Joe, Eugene	4	5	.444	3.55	26	1	0	0	11	3	66.0	61	298	39	26	1	3	3	3	26	4	58	5	0
Koehler, P.K., Eugene*	4	2	.667	3.63	17	11	0	0	2	0	74.1	74	320	38	30	6	0	4	0	23	0	54	5	2
Simon, Benjamin, Yakima	2	6	.250	3.66	15	10	0	0	1	1	66.1	59	275	34	27	5	3	5	3	21	2	62	0	1
Stepka, Tom, Portland	5	4	.556	3.71	12	12	0	0	0	0	68.0	74	291	42	28	8	1	0	2	10	0	48	2	1
Sebring, Jeffrey, Portland*	5	5	.500	3.79	16	12	0	0	3	0	76.0	78	337	38	32	6	2	5	7	28	1	49	3	0
Mullen, Scott, Spokane*	5	6	.455	3.92	15	15	0	0	0	0	80.1	78	352	45	35	6	1	2	8	29	0	78	1	0

DEPARTMENTAL LEADERS: W—Darrell, 8; L—Blanco, Volkman, 8 each; Pct.—Darrell, .889; G—Pageler, Patino, 30 each; GS—Bell, Leese, 16 each; CG—Riggan, Darrell, 1 each; ShO—Darrell, 1; GF—Pageler, 25; Sv.—Kubenka, 14; IP—Darrell, 101.0; H—Darrell, 114; TBF—Darrell, 433; R—Volkman, 66; ER—Volkman, 50; HR—Matcuk, Darrell, 11 each; SH—Volkman, 50; SF—several pitchers tied with 6 each; HB—Delacruz, 13; BB—Blevins, 58; IBB—Robertson, 6; SO—Leese, 90; WP—Blevins, 13; Bk.—Kramer, 7.

ALL PITCHERS

*Lefthanded pitcher.

Pitcher, Team	W	L	Pct.	ERA	G	GS	CG	ShO	GF	Sv.	IP	H	TBF	R	ER	HR	SH	SF	HB	BB	IBB	SO	WP	Bk.
Abreu, Jose, Bellingham	1	0	1.000	4.20	8	0	0	0	3	0	15.0	15	73	8	7	0	1	1	1	14	0	14	2	0
Aguilar, Alonzo, Spokane	2	2	.500	4.05	15	0	0	0	9	1	20.0	20	93	14	9	1	1	1	1	11	0	22	5	0
Allen, Rodney, Eugene	1	0	1.000	3.50	22	1	0	0	12	6	43.2	47	190	21	17	1	1	0	2	13	1	39	5	0
Ayala, Julio, Everett*	1	3	.250	3.48	12	6	0	0	2	0	44.0	43	185	20	17	2	2	1	4	10	0	28	2	2
Baird, Brandon, Spokane*	1	1	.500	4.76	5	1	0	0	2	0	11.1	10	52	8	6	1	0	0	1	8	0	13	2	0
Batchelder, Bill, So. Oregon	0	0	.000	8.71	6	0	0	0	1	0	10.1	19	64	17	10	3	0	1	0	12	0	10	1	0
Bauldree, Joe, Eugene	0	0	.000	9.00	3	1	0	0	0	0	7.0	10	37	8	7	0	0	1	1	4	0	5	2	0
Beasley, Raymond, Eugene*	0	0	.000	0.00	3	0	0	0	0	0	4.0	4	19	2	0	0	0	0	0	2	0	7	0	0
Bell, Rob, Eugene	5	6	.455	5.11	16	16	0	0	0	0	81.0	89	356	49	46	5	5	3	3	29	1	74	2	0
Blanco, Roger, Ever.-Eug.	3	8	.273	6.23	16	14	0	0	1	0	65.0	79	314	59	45	6	1	1	6	40	0	47	7	0
Blasingim, Joseph, Bellingham	1	1	.500	0.78	4	4	0	0	0	0	23.0	16	92	5	2	0	0	0	3	5	0	23	1	0
Blevins, Jeremy, Boise	2	3	.400	6.60	14	13	0	0	0	0	58.2	54	283	49	43	4	1	6	5	58	0	39	13	1
Blumenstock, Brad, So. Oregon	3	1	.750	9.87	23	1	0	0	5	0	34.2	48	190	49	38	7	1	3	5	34	1	20	5	5
Bond, Jason, Everett*	2	0	1.000	1.87	20	1	0	0	4	4	43.1	24	165	10	9	3	1	0	1	12	0	52	4	1
Bosio, Chris, Everett	0	0	.000	2.25	1	1	0	0	0	0	4.0	3	15	1	1	0	0	0	0	0	0	8	0	0
Brewer, Ryan, Spokane	3	2	.600	3.35	17	2	0	0	11	5	43.0	41	182	20	16	4	4	2	1	16	0	39	3	0
Brown, Gavin, Eugene	0	0	.000	18.00	1	0	0	0	0	0	1.0	2	9	3	2	0	0	0	0	3	0	1	0	0
Brueggemann, Dean, Portland*	1	1	.500	4.37	8	2	0	0	0	0	22.2	21	96	15	11	2	0	0	1	8	0	12	0	0
Brzozoski, Marc, Portland	1	3	.250	4.56	18	0	0	0	13	4	25.2	27	115	15	13	2	1	2	3	10	0	22	4	0
Burton, Jamie, Spokane*	1	1	.500	5.40	11	0	0	0	5	0	13.1	11	67	11	8	2	0	1	3	13	0	12	4	0
Calero, Enrique, Spokane	4	2	.667	2.52	17	11	0	0	3	1	75.0	77	318	34	21	5	0	6	3	18	0	61	2	2
Carcamo, Kevin, Spokane	0	0	.000	6.33	10	0	0	0	3	0	21.1	31	101	19	15	3	0	0	4	7	0	13	1	0
Castillo, Alberto, Bellingham*	0	1	.000	1.88	9	7	0	0	1	0	24.0	20	102	5	5	2	0	3	0	12	0	18	2	1
Chacon, Shawn, Portland	0	2	.000	6.86	4	4	0	0	0	0	19.2	24	92	18	15	2	0	1	9	0	17	5	0
Chapman, Jake, Spokane*	7	1	.875	2.37	19	7	0	0	3	1	68.1	44	274	19	18	2	2	2	6	20	1	71	3	1
Chen, Bruce, Eugene*	4	1	.800	2.27	11	8	0	0	0	0	35.2	23	151	13	9	1	0	3	14	0	55	2	1
Christman, Tim, Portland*	1	2	.333	4.28	21	0	0	0	7	2	40.0	30	176	23	19	6	1	3	1	23	0	56	2	1
Clifford, Eric, Everett	0	0	.000	6.00	2	0	0	0	1	0	3.0	4	15	2	2	0	1	0	1	4	0	1	1	0
Cochran, Andrew, Eugene*	6	0	1.000	3.55	15	7	0	0	1	0	58.1	54	262	33	23	4	0	1	7	26	0	51	6	2
Cortes, David, Eugene	2	1	.667	0.73	15	0	0	0	11	4	24.2	13	95	2	2	0	1	0	0	6	0	33	0	0
Costello, T.J., Southern Oregon*	0	0	.000	6.00	9	0	0	0	8	0	12.0	15	58	8	8	2	0	0	0	11	0	9	0	0
Cowsill, Brendon, Boise	1	0	1.000	1.57	16	0	0	0	9	0	23.0	19	100	5	4	1	1	2	5	9	2	26	0	0
Crabtree, Robert, Bellingham	3	3	.500	2.77	28	0	0	0	13	4	52.0	38	206	18	16	8	2	1	0	14	1	72	3	0
Culmo, Kevin, Yakima	4	2	.667	2.27	17	5	0	0	5	2	63.1	47	262	18	16	2	1	2	1	22	0	60	5	0
Darrell, Tommy, Boise	8	1	.889	3.48	15	15	1	1	0	0	101.0	114	433	56	39	11	2	2	4	13	2	76	2	0
Davis, Tim, Everett*	0	0	.000	0.00	1	1	0	0	0	0	2.0	0	7	0	0	0	0	0	0	1	0	5	0	0
Delacruz, Fernando, Boise	6	3	.667	4.94	15	15	0	0	0	0	85.2	85	400	55	47	5	0	1	13	51	3	61	6	2
Della Ratta, Pete, So. Oregon	0	5	.000	7.19	22	0	0	0	0	0	41.1	46	194	34	33	10	2	2	4	24	4	41	3	1

CLASS A Northwest League

Pitcher, Team	W	L	Pct.	ERA	G	GS	CG	ShO	GF	Sv.	IP	H	TBF	R	ER	HR	SH	SF	HB	BB	IBB	SO	WP	Bk.
Deskins, Casey, Yakima*	4	5	.444	4.76	15	9	0	0	2	0	62.1	69	279	40	33	6	4	2	2	20	1	43	0	0
Druckrey, Chris, Portland	1	0	.000	7.94	6	0	0	0	2	0	17.0	29	90	20	15	3	1	1	0	12	0	19	5	1
Ellison, Skeeter, Eugene	0	0	.000	0.00	1	0	0	0	0	0	1.0	0	3	0	0	0	0	0	0	0	0	0	0	0
Estrella, Luis, Bellingham	4	0	1.000	1.79	23	0	0	0	6	1	55.1	35	213	13	11	3	1	0	0	22	1	52	6	0
Farnsworth, Jeff, Everett	3	3	.500	4.12	10	7	0	0	1	0	39.1	33	158	19	18	4	0	1	0	13	0	42	6	5
Fitzgerald, Brian, Everett*	1	2	.333	6.46	21	1	0	0	8	1	39.0	56	181	36	28	2	1	1	0	8	0	31	1	2
Flach, Jason, Eugene	4	1	.800	2.26	27	0	0	0	14	11	59.2	45	238	18	15	2	3	1	1	17	1	68	2	0
Flores, Eric, Yakima	0	0	.000	0.00	1	0	0	0	1	0	0.0	0	0	0	0	0	0	0	0	0	0	0	0	0
Ford, Jason, Portland*	0	2	.000	10.13	13	0	0	0	5	1	18.2	22	93	21	21	4	0	0	1	14	0	29	4	0
Franklin, Wayne, Yakima*	1	0	1.000	2.52	20	0	0	0	5	1	25.0	32	115	10	7	2	0	0	0	12	3	22	3	1
Fuentes, Brian, Everett*	4	4	.439	4.39	13	2	0	0	3	0	26.2	23	114	14	13	2	0	1	0	13	0	26	5	0
Giuliano, Joe, Eugene	4	5	.444	3.55	26	1	0	0	11	3	66.0	61	298	39	26	1	3	3	3	26	4	58	5	0
Glaze, Randy, Southern Oregon...	1	2	.333	6.35	19	1	0	0	12	3	28.1	23	138	22	20	4	0	1	3	23	0	26	2	4
Gogolin, Al, Southern Oregon	1	1	.500	8.68	6	0	0	0	2	0	9.1	10	49	9	9	1	0	1	2	14	1	3	1	
Greene, Danny, Boise	0	3	.000	3.86	9	0	0	0	7	1	11.2	12	54	6	5	2	3	0	0	8	4	12	0	0
Gutierrez, Javier, Everett	4	1	.800	5.56	7	7	0	0	0	0	34.0	43	158	25	21	6	0	1	2	12	0	35	2	0
Hall, Darren, Yakima	0	1	.000	3.00	2	2	0	0	0	0	3.0	5	13	2	1	0	0	0	0	0	0	4	0	0
Hannah, Michael, Yakima	1	1	.500	5.70	18	0	0	0	3	1	23.2	25	119	26	15	1	1	2	2	22	0	13	3	0
Harriger, Mark, Boise	0	0	.000	8.31	7	0	0	0	1	0	4.1	9	26	5	4	1	1	0	0	3	0	3	1	1
Herrera, Ivan, Bellingham	0	1	.000	12.71	6	0	0	0	3	0	5.2	10	34	11	8	0	0	1	4	0	0	1	1	
Hilton, Willy, Southern Oregon	2	1	.667	5.84	26	2	0	0	8	2	61.2	71	291	44	40	4	4	0	6	27	1	38	6	3
Hinchy, Brian, Portland	0	3	.000	7.36	9	0	0	0	6	0	11.0	13	58	16	9	1	1	1	1	9	1	5	0	1
Holden, Jason, Southern Oregon	3	5	.375	5.79	9	8	0	0	0	0	32.2	39	156	27	21	2	0	0	2	14	0	21	2	1
Hueston, Stephen, Spokane	3	2	.600	3.08	13	13	0	0	0	0	64.1	54	272	27	22	8	3	2	5	31	0	60	5	2
Hughes, Michael, Boise	0	0	.000	4.86	13	0	0	0	4	1	16.2	16	79	12	9	1	0	1	1	13	1	20	1	0
Humphreys, Kevin, Boise	3	2	.600	1.99	19	0	0	0	9	0	45.1	32	190	17	10	4	1	1	4	15	3	34	6	
Jensen, Ryan, Bellingham	2	4	.333	4.98	13	11	0	0	0	0	47.0	35	208	30	26	4	1	0	1	38	0	31	7	
Jimenez, Jhonny, Everett	1	3	.250	4.60	24	0	0	0	16	5	31.1	34	138	20	16	3	4	2	1	12	1	26	3	2
Johnson, Gregory, Boise	0	0	.000	10.24	8	0	0	0	5	0	9.2	17	47	11	11	2	0	1	0	2	1	6	0	
Johnson, Randy, Everett*	0	0	.000	0.00	1	1	0	0	0	0	2.0	0	6	0	0	0	0	0	0	0	0	5	0	
Jones, Michael, Eugene*	5	4	.556	3.98	13	2	0	0	2	0	40.2	40	186	24	18	3	2	1	3	17	0	41	1	
Kennison, Kyle, Everett	2	2	.333	8.24	12	2	0	0	5	0	19.2	25	95	18	18	3	0	2	3	11	0	25	4	
Kjos, Ryan, Southern Oregon	0	3	.000	3.72	24	1	0	0	6	0	48.1	41	217	33	20	6	1	3	3	26	3	64	5	
Knickerbocker, Tom, So. Oregon*	1	1	.500	4.71	12	1	0	0	5	1	21.0	22	102	11	11	2	0	0	2	17	0	11	4	
Koehler, P.K., Eugene*	4	2	.667	3.63	17	11	0	0	2	0	74.1	74	320	38	30	6	0	4	0	23	0	54	5	
Kramer, Matthew, Yakima	2	0	1.000	2.61	12	5	0	0	2	0	38.0	36	164	13	11	3	0	2	0	21	0	31	7	
Kubenka, Jeff, Yakima*	5	1	.833	2.51	28	0	0	0	24	14	32.1	20	127	11	9	2	0	0	0	10	1	61	4	
Lagattuta, Rico, So. Oregon*	3	3	.500	2.82	28	0	0	0	14	3	54.1	49	230	23	17	4	2	1	1	23	2	31	1	
Larreal, Guillermo, Bellingham	3	2	.600	1.44	22	0	0	0	9	1	50.0	46	205	15	8	4	0	2	0	10	1	48	0	
Laxton, Brett, Southern Oregon	0	5	.000	7.71	13	8	0	0	1	0	32.2	39	162	34	28	4	1	1	3	26	1	38	5	3
Lee, David, Portland	5	1	.833	0.78	17	0	0	0	16	7	23.0	13	96	3	2	0	1	0	3	16	3	24	1	
Leese, Brandon, Bellingham	5	6	.455	3.25	16	15	0	0	0	0	80.1	59	341	39	29	6	0	2	5	37	0	90	8	
Lilly, Theodore, Yakima*	4	0	1.000	0.84	13	8	0	0	1	0	53.2	25	200	9	5	0	0	1	1	14	1	75	0	
Lineweaver, Aaron, Spokane	3	4	.429	7.53	21	5	0	0	5	1	49.0	62	227	43	41	6	1	3	2	23	0	34	3	
Lovinger, Eric, Yakima	0	1	.000	1.80	4	0	0	0	3	0	5.0	4	24	3	1	0	0	0	0	2	0	3	1	
Luce, Robert, Everett	3	4	.429	4.39	23	0	0	0	16	7	41.0	45	187	26	20	6	3	1	1	16	1	47	6	
Maestas, Mickey, Yakima	0	6	.000	9.20	14	6	0	0	1	0	30.1	44	149	34	31	7	0	2	1	17	0	25	8	
Mahlberg, John, Portland	2	7	.222	5.43	17	10	0	0	2	1	56.1	67	263	43	34	5	1	4	9	15	0	47	3	
Malloy, William, Bellingham	2	3	.400	5.82	15	7	0	0	3	0	34.0	34	155	27	22	0	2	3	3	15	0	41	7	
Matcuk, Steven, Portland	5	3	.625	4.29	10	10	0	0	0	0	56.2	52	238	31	27	11	1	2	4	15	0	49	1	
Mayer, Aaron, Boise	2	0	1.000	1.00	5	0	0	0	2	0	9.0	6	39	2	1	0	0	0	3	3	1	11	3	
Mayo, Blake, Yakima	5	2	.714	1.20	20	6	0	0	8	1	67.1	44	256	15	9	1	0	1	0	12	0	68	5	
Mays, Joe, Everett	4	4	.500	3.08	13	10	0	0	0	0	64.1	55	271	33	22	3	3	2	2	22	0	56	9	
McGlinchy, Kevin, Eugene	0	0	.000	5.40	2	2	0	0	0	0	6.2	7	31	5	4	2	1	0	1	0	1	5	0	
Milburn, Adam, Eugene*	3	1	.750	2.98	24	0	0	0	16	7	42.1	28	176	17	14	1	2	3	1	21	4	33	4	
Mitchell, Dean, Yakima	2	2	.500	3.44	15	5	0	0	3	2	52.1	53	233	25	20	4	1	5	0	25	1	61	3	
Morgan, Eric, Everett	0	1	.000	4.70	4	4	0	0	0	0	15.1	20	74	14	8	2	0	0	2	12	0	11	4	
Mullen, Scott, Spokane*	5	6	.455	3.92	15	15	0	0	0	0	80.1	78	352	45	35	6	1	2	8	29	0	78	1	
Nelson, Joe, Eugene	5	3	.625	4.37	14	13	0	0	0	0	70.0	69	309	43	34	5	3	1	5	29	1	67	6	
Nicholson, John, Portland	0	1	.000	4.20	3	3	0	0	0	0	15.0	12	68	8	7	0	2	1	0	10	0	11	0	
Nogowski, Brandon, Everett*	0	0	.000	4.44	19	0	0	0	10	1	26.1	27	128	18	13	1	0	2	2	25	0	31	7	
Noriega, Ray, Southern Oregon*	4	4	.500	3.54	17	14	0	0	0	0	61.0	61	263	28	24	3	2	0	2	22	0	50	4	
O'Dell, Jake, Southern Oregon	2	3	.400	3.33	13	10	0	0	0	0	48.2	41	205	25	18	2	1	3	1	16	1	46	2	
Ortiz, Ramon, Boise	1	1	.500	3.66	3	3	0	0	0	0	19.2	21	89	10	8	3	2	0	1	6	0	18	0	
O'Shaughnessy, Jay, Yakima	4	3	.571	3.23	13	11	0	0	1	1	55.2	26	231	24	20	2	2	3	3	36	0	85	8	
Osting, Jimmy, Eugene*	2	1	.667	2.59	5	5	0	0	0	0	24.1	14	99	11	7	1	0	0	0	13	0	35	1	
Pageler, Mick, Bellingham	2	0	1.000	1.57	30	0	0	0	25	12	34.1	22	137	9	6	2	2	2	0	10	0	55	2	
Paluk, Brian, Yakima	4	1	.800	3.40	20	5	0	0	5	0	45.0	36	185	24	17	1	3	2	1	17	1	37	4	
Patino, Leonardo, Boise*	6	5	.545	1.61	30	0	0	0	14	6	56.0	37	228	15	10	7	4	0	2	21	2	71	3	
Paulino, Jose, Southern Oregon..	4	1	.800	3.10	10	8	0	0	0	0	40.2	43	175	20	14	3	0	2	2	9	0	21	3	
Perez, Odalis, Eugene*	2	1	.667	3.80	10	6	0	0	0	0	23.2	26	110	16	10	2	2	0	0	11	0	38	3	
Pinales, Aquiles, Eugene	0	0	.000	3.38	3	0	0	0	3	1	5.1	4	20	3	2	1	1	0	0	2	0	4	0	
Plooy, Eric, Boise	1	1	.500	4.63	16	0	0	0	6	0	35.0	39	156	23	18	2	1	1	1	15	0	31	3	
Pohl, Jeff, Bellingham	3	5	.375	3.94	17	0	0	0	3	0	32.0	33	146	17	14	1	2	0	0	19	1	19	2	
Puffer, Brandon, Boise	2	0	1.000	4.45	16	0	0	0	7	0	30.1	27	129	19	15	3	1	1	1	11	0	22	3	
Quigley, Donald, Spokane	0	1	.000	6.26	19	0	0	0	6	0	27.1	41	142	24	19	0	2	4	1	18	1	18	6	
Riggan, Jerrod, Boise	3	5	.375	4.63	15	15	1	0	0	0	89.1	90	395	62	46	10	3	6	5	38	0	80	6	
Riley, Michael, Bellingham*	1	3	.250	4.17	17	3	0	0	2	0	36.2	38	181	26	17	3	1	2	1	29	0	38	5	
Rivera, Rafael, Everett	4	1	.800	2.19	24	0	0	0	9	3	49.1	47	203	19	12	1	1	0	1	10	0	61	2	
Robertson, Doug, So. Oregon	2	3	.400	6.02	23	4	0	0	7	3	52.1	69	242	44	35	5	3	2	1	17	6	48	2	
Rodriguez, Chad, Spokane	0	2	.000	5.23	14	0	0	0	13	3	20.2	22	95	16	12	2	1	0	0	8	1	24	1	
Rodriguez, Hector, Boise	1	1	.500	3.70	20	0	0	0	6	0	24.1	27	109	13	10	2	2	3	1	11	0	25	2	
Rodriguez, Luis, Bellingham*	0	0	.000	0.00	1	0	0	0	0	0	0.0	1	1	0	0	0	0	0	0	0	0	0	0	

tcher, Team	W	L	Pct.	ERA	G	GS	CG	ShO	GF	Sv.	IP	H	TBF	R	ER	HR	SH	SF	HB	BB	IBB	SO	WP	Bk.
omine, Jason, Portland	4	1	.800	2.73	16	5	0	0	6	2	59.1	48	246	18	18	6	1	2	2	20	0	53	4	0
osa, Cristy, Portland	0	1	.000	6.75	3	3	0	0	0	0	9.1	14	47	10	7	2	0	0	1	3	0	5	1	0
ust, Brian, Eugene	0	0	.000	36.00	1	0	0	0	1	0	1.0	7	12	7	4	1	0	0	1	0	1	1	1	0
inders, Allen, Spokane	5	2	.714	4.53	13	5	0	0	2	0	43.2	49	183	25	22	3	1	4	3	9	0	19	1	0
inders, Craig, Spokane	0	1	.000	10.32	6	0	0	0	1	1	11.1	14	64	16	13	3	0	2	2	15	0	5	4	0
hmidt, Donnie, Portland	2	2	.500	3.36	19	5	0	0	7	0	59.0	53	251	31	22	6	0	3	3	20	0	51	1	1
hroeffel, Scott, Portland	1	1	.500	1.66	16	6	0	0	7	1	59.2	36	235	15	11	1	2	2	4	17	0	61	4	1
ebring, Jeffrey, Portland*	5	5	.500	3.79	16	12	0	0	3	0	76.0	78	337	38	32	6	2	5	7	28	1	49	3	0
lva, Luis, Southern Oregon	1	3	.250	9.50	5	4	0	0	0	0	18.0	25	89	22	19	3	1	0	1	10	0	18	2	0
mon, Benjamin, Yakima	2	6	.250	3.66	15	10	0	0	1	1	66.1	59	275	34	27	5	3	5	3	21	2	62	0	1
montacchi, Jason, Spokane	2	5	.286	5.17	14	6	0	0	3	2	47.0	59	214	37	27	8	3	3	3	15	0	43	1	0
ark, Dennis, Everett	1	3	.250	4.45	12	4	0	0	4	0	30.1	25	133	19	15	2	3	1	1	17	0	49	5	1
ein, Ethan, Spokane	0	3	.000	6.34	9	8	0	0	0	0	38.1	48	174	27	27	5	1	1	3	12	0	20	2	1
ephens, Jason, Boise	2	0	1.000	8.10	3	0	0	0	2	1	3.1	4	16	3	3	1	0	0	1	0	0	5	0	0
epka, Tom, Portland	5	4	.556	3.71	12	12	0	0	0	0	68.0	74	291	42	28	8	1	0	2	10	0	48	2	1
ockstill, Jason, Boise*	0	0	.000	12.38	2	2	0	0	0	0	8.0	12	42	11	11	2	0	0	0	10	0	7	1	0
over, C.D., Yakima	1	4	.200	5.57	15	4	0	0	4	1	32.1	36	151	23	20	1	3	0	2	16	0	25	4	0
czy, Craig, Yakima*	1	1	.500	7.48	16	0	0	0	7	1	21.2	27	110	22	18	1	1	1	0	16	0	14	3	0
kahashi, Kurt, Bellingham	1	2	.333	4.00	16	6	0	0	2	1	54.0	45	230	25	24	7	1	0	3	20	0	55	4	0
ompson, Travis, Portland	0	2	.000	5.94	9	0	0	0	2	0	16.2	21	73	11	11	0	2	0	0	6	8	1	1	0
icchioni, Jerry, Eugene	0	0	.000	0.00	1	0	0	0	1	1	1.0	0	5	0	0	0	0	0	0	2	0	1	0	0
ctery, Joe, Everett	5	4	.556	3.14	13	8	0	0	2	1	51.2	43	218	22	18	4	2	1	2	15	0	45	4	3
larreal, Modesto, Spokane	2	4	.333	5.74	19	3	0	0	10	3	47.0	57	209	33	30	5	1	1	4	11	0	35	5	0
ning, Kenneth, Bellingham*	4	2	.667	2.09	12	11	0	0	0	0	60.1	45	238	16	14	4	1	0	1	23	0	69	5	0
lkman, Keith, Boise*	5	8	.385	6.59	16	13	0	0	1	0	68.1	74	327	66	50	0	6	2	7	46	3	38	7	0
illace, Flint, Southern Oregon..	2	6	.250	4.22	17	14	0	0	1	0	70.1	86	301	34	33	3	0	6	5	15	0	45	2	0
ells, Matt, Bellingham	2	4	.333	7.05	12	11	0	0	0	0	44.2	57	220	38	35	9	1	2	2	30	0	41	0	0
estbrook, Jake, Portland	1	1	.500	2.55	4	4	0	0	0	0	24.2	22	99	8	7	1	0	0	1	5	0	19	2	0
eymouth, Marty, Everett	2	3	.400	4.83	10	10	0	0	0	0	41.0	46	185	28	22	3	0	2	0	16	0	35	9	0
oodrow, James, Bellingham	2	0	1.000	3.96	17	0	0	0	5	0	25.0	26	116	16	11	4	2	0	0	14	0	25	3	0

COMBINATION SHUTOUTS: **Bellingham (5)**—Castillo-Pageler, Blasingim-Riley-Pageler, Riley-Pageler, Leese-Crabtree-Pageler, Malloy-Takahashi. **Boise (1)**—Darrell-ino-Humphreys-Mayer. **Eugene (4)**—Koehler-Allen, Bell-Cortes, Nelson-Cortes, Bell-Allen. **Everett (4)**—Weymouth-Fitzgerald, Johnson-Victery-Rivera-Bond, Blanco-nd, Mays-Jimenez-Fuentes. **Portland (4)**—Mahlberg-Druckrey-Schmidt, Westbrook-Romine, Sebring-Romine, Westbrook-Brzozoski. **Southern Oregon (2)**—O'Dell-on, Silva-Kjos-Knickerbocker. **Spokane (2)**—Calero-Lineweaver-Quigley, Mullen-Villarreal. **Yakima (6)**—O'Saughnessy-Mayo-Franklin-Kubenka, Mayo-haughnessy, O'Shaughnessy-Stiver, Lilly-Mitchell, O'Shaughnessy-Deskins-Kubenka, Lilly-Mitchell.

NO-HIT GAMES: None.

PITCHERS WITH TWO OR MORE TEAMS

cher, Team	W	L	Pct.	ERA	G	GS	CG	ShO	GF	Sv.	IP	H	TBF	R	ER	HR	SH	SF	HB	BB	IBB	SO	WP	Bk.
nco, Roger, Everett	1	7	.125	6.16	11	11	0	0	0	0	49.2	62	241	46	34	6	1	0	6	28	0	35	6	0
nco, Roger, Eugene	2	1	.667	6.46	5	3	0	0	1	0	15.1	17	73	13	11	0	0	1	0	12	0	12	1	0

1996 FIELDING

TEAM

am	Pct.	G	PO	A	E	TC	DP	PB	Team	Pct.	G	PO	A	E	TC	DP	PB
lingham	.962	75	2020	788	112	2920	63	22	Southern Oregon	.955	76	2033	862	138	3033	51	14
kima	.959	76	2032	801	120	2953	55	17	Spokane	.954	76	2044	883	141	3068	78	10
erett	.959	75	1972	827	119	2918	42	34	Portland	.954	76	2035	763	136	2934	52	18
gene	.958	76	2060	797	125	2982	51	38	TRIPLE PLAYS: None.								
se	.955	76	2098	885	139	3122	68	14									

INDIVIDUAL

FIRST BASEMEN

TE: All caps denotes fielding-percentage leader based on 38 games for catchers, for all other non-pitchers and 76 innings for pitchers. *Throws lefthanded.

yer, Team	Pct.	G	PO	A	E	TC	DP
derson, Blake, Portland	1.000	3	14	1	0	15	0
thony, Brian, Portland	.990	23	177	14	2	193	13
ollado, Courtney, Spokane	1.000	4	9	1	0	10	2
rger, Brandon, Spokane	1.000	1	11	1	0	12	2
sser, Doug, Spokane	.950	8	71	5	4	80	6
rs, Scott, Boise*	.990	64	570	30	6	606	49
deron, Ricardo, Bellingham*	.929	3	10	3	1	14	2
z, Cirilo, Everett	1.000	1	3	0	0	3	0
rtis, Matt, Boise	.960	12	118	3	5	126	8
ion, Kristopher, Spokane	1.000	1	16	1	0	17	2
CKER, Steve, Eugene	.995	64	545	38	3	586	39
inson, Duan, Everett	1.000	1	1	0	0	1	0
g, William M., Yakima	.949	11	36	1	2	39	5
kinda, Steven, Everett	.986	15	135	6	2	143	7
ne, Jason, Spokane	.970	26	203	20	7	230	21
dsey, John, Portland	.977	50	394	39	10	443	29
ave, Jaime, Yakima	.971	6	34	0	1	35	1
rcinczyk, T.R., So. Oregon	.987	46	318	48	5	371	21
nsik, Todd, Southern Oregon*	.994	38	301	29	2	332	23
yer, Matt, Yakima	1.000	1	15	0	0	15	1
or, Damon, Bellingham*	.993	75	650	38	5	693	56

Player, Team	Pct.	G	PO	A	E	TC	DP
Myers, Aaron, Portland	1.000	1	10	0	0	10	0
Pellow, Kit, Spokane	.983	44	374	33	7	414	39
Polanco, Juan, Southern Oregon	1.000	3	6	1	0	7	0
Rodriguez, Juan, Boise	.965	12	52	3	2	57	4
Rust, Brian, Eugene	1.000	6	18	1	0	19	0
Sankey, Brian, Yakima*	.992	71	581	40	5	626	45
Simonton, Cy Leon, Everett*	.917	2	10	1	1	12	1
Skeels, David, Everett	1.000	3	19	1	0	20	0
Vidal, Carlos, Portland	.969	3	28	3	1	32	3
Wong, Jerrod, Eugene*	.963	14	94	9	4	107	7
Zachmann, Rob, Everett	.993	59	529	21	4	554	29

SECOND BASEMEN

Player, Team	Pct.	G	PO	A	E	TC	DP
Abbott, Chuck, Boise	.938	13	14	31	3	48	5
Arrollado, Courtney, Spokane	.952	5	4	16	1	21	2
Cesar, Dionys, Southern Oregon	.985	13	28	37	1	66	6
Cespedes, Angel, Portland	.911	23	25	67	9	101	8
Cross, Adam, Eugene	.960	39	82	110	8	200	18
Cruz, Cirilo, Everett	.905	5	9	10	2	21	2
Didion, Kristopher, Spokane	.933	3	8	6	1	15	1
Durrington, Trent, Boise	.946	35	71	105	10	186	20
Ellison, Skeeter, Eugene	.750	3	4	2	2	8	0
Espada, Angel, Eugene	.983	23	44	71	2	117	12

Player, Team	Pct.	G	PO	A	E	TC	DP
Ferrer, Eduardo, Boise	.919	32	46	79	11	136	16
Figueroa, Luis, Everett	.952	3	2	18	1	21	2
Freeman, Terrance, So. Oregon	.951	42	67	108	9	184	14
Galloway, Paul, Bellingham	1.000	4	7	13	0	20	3
Harp, Scott, Spokane	.895	21	31	46	9	86	10
Hines, Pooh, Eugene	1.000	14	20	30	0	50	2
Katz, Jason, Eugene	.800	2	1	3	1	5	0
Keck, Brian, Portland	.950	9	17	21	2	40	4
Linder, Brian, Everett	.950	8	14	24	2	40	3
Livingston, Doug, Portland	.979	48	98	132	5	235	25
Marshall, Monte, Yakima	.951	17	31	46	4	81	8
Meyer, Bobby, Yakima	.935	20	34	53	6	93	8
Moore, Kenderick, Spokane	.954	51	105	143	12	260	44
Polanco, Juan, Southern Oregon	.914	9	13	19	3	35	4
Prospero, Teo, Bellingham	.972	9	10	25	1	36	3
Quesada, Travis, Boise	.917	8	8	14	2	24	2
Regan, Jason, Everett	.944	15	15	52	4	71	2
Saitta, Rich, Yakima	.954	42	63	124	9	196	19
Serrano, Danny, Boise	1.000	1	2	1	0	3	1
Slemmer, Dave, Southern Oregon	.972	17	42	62	3	107	13
Taft, Brett, Spokane	.889	6	4	4	1	9	1
't Hoen, E.J., Boise	.923	3	5	7	1	13	0
Valera, Ramon, Everett	.969	46	79	140	7	226	21
Vecchioni, Jerry, Eugene	1.000	3	3	4	0	7	1
ZUNIGA, Jose, Bellingham	.967	62	93	167	9	269	33

THIRD BASEMEN

Player, Team	Pct.	G	PO	A	E	TC	DP
Arrollado, Courtney, Spokane	.944	11	2	15	1	18	0
Baeza, Art, Bellingham	.952	22	13	46	3	62	4
Byers, MacGregor, So. Oregon	.911	30	18	64	8	90	1
Caruso, Michael, Bellingham	.500	1	1	1	2	4	0
Cesar, Dionys, Southern Oregon	.667	2	1	1	1	3	0
Cross, Adam, Eugene	.750	7	5	7	4	16	1
Cruz, Cirilo, Everett	.862	9	5	20	4	29	1
Curtis, Matt, Boise	.873	14	8	40	7	55	0
Didion, Kristopher, Spokane	.882	54	34	100	18	152	7
Durrington, Trent, Boise	1.000	4	1	5	0	6	1
Escamilla, Roman, Spokane	.818	3	3	6	2	11	1
Flores, Eric, Yakima	.867	9	3	10	2	15	4
Galloway, Paul, Bellingham	.918	41	26	64	8	98	6
Gillespie, Eric, Boise	.860	52	27	96	20	143	6
Glendenning, Michael, Bellingham	.792	10	3	16	5	24	1
Hines, Pooh, Eugene	.765	6	1	12	4	17	0
Jackson, Wade, Boise	.904	25	12	35	5	52	1
Johnson, Duan, Everett	.864	31	19	51	11	81	1
Katz, Jason, Eugene	.600	2	1	2	2	5	0
Keck, Brian, Portland	1.000	6	3	8	0	11	0
Linder, Brian, Everett	.976	11	14	27	1	42	1
Malave, Jaime, Everett	1.000	5	2	7	0	9	1
McKay, Cody, Southern Oregon	.872	18	13	28	6	47	2
Meyer, Bobby, Yakima	.571	6	3	1	3	7	0
Morrison, Scott, Yakima	1.000	1	1	0	0	1	0
MYERS, Aaron, Portland	.913	70	46	122	16	184	6
Pellow, Kit, Spokane	.862	10	7	18	4	29	3
Polanco, Juan, Southern Oregon	.863	24	23	40	10	73	6
Prospero, Teo, Bellingham	.625	3	1	4	3	8	1
Regan, Jason, Everett	.929	25	14	38	4	56	1
Rolls, Damian, Yakima	.893	65	58	134	23	215	4
Rust, Brian, Eugene	.864	65	38	108	23	169	9
Sees, Eric, Spokane	.933	8	1	13	1	15	2
Slemmer, Dave, Southern Oregon	.815	9	6	16	5	27	1
Taft, Brett, Spokane	1.000	2	0	3	0	3	1
Vecchioni, Jerry, Eugene	.778	3	3	4	2	9	0

SHORTSTOPS

Player, Team	Pct.	G	PO	A	E	TC	DP
Abbott, Chuck, Boise	.898	59	90	192	32	314	38
Caruso, Michael, Bellingham	.898	71	106	230	38	374	43
Cesar, Dionys, Southern Oregon	.921	38	58	116	15	189	17
Clark, John, Portland	.853	53	90	130	38	258	29
DeRosa, Mark, Eugene	.921	70	82	196	24	302	25
Durrington, Trent, Boise	.909	8	8	12	2	22	2
Espada, Josue, Southern Oregon	.960	15	19	29	2	50	6
Flores, Eric, Yakima	.880	27	33	48	11	92	10
Freeman, Terrance, So. Oregon	.821	11	19	27	10	56	6
Galloway, Paul, Bellingham	.500	1	1	1	2	4	0
Jones, Tim, Southern Oregon	1.000	1	1	2	0	3	1
Katz, Jason, Eugene	.250	1	0	1	3	4	0
Keck, Brian, Portland	.897	24	34	62	11	107	11
Kieffer, Brian, Southern Oregon	.500	2	1	0	1	2	0
Linder, Brian, Everett	.924	39	59	99	13	171	16

Player, Team	Pct.	G	PO	A	E	TC	D
Morrison, Scott, Yakima	.913	57	67	152	21	240	
Polanco, Juan, Southern Oregon	.722	4	5	8	5	18	
SEES, Eric, Spokane	.943	52	87	146	14	247	
Slemmer, Dave, Southern Oregon	.961	12	17	32	2	51	
Taft, Brett, Spokane	.964	37	56	103	6	165	
't Hoen, E.J., Boise	.931	15	15	39	4	58	
Valera, Ramon, Everett	.909	4	12	8	2	22	
Vazquez, Ramon, Everett	.873	32	38	100	20	158	
Vecchioni, Jerry, Eugene	.829	9	9	20	6	35	
Zuniga, Jose, Bellingham	1.000	3	10	6	0	16	

OUTFIELDERS

Player, Team	Pct.	G	PO	A	E	TC
Bair, Rod, Portland	.970	54	89	7	3	99
Beltran, Carlos, Spokane	.938	52	99	6	7	112
Berger, Brandon, Spokane	.967	68	106	10	4	120
BERGERON, Peter, Yakima	.990	54	99	3	1	103
Bowles, Justin, Southern Oregon*	.945	54	101	2	6	109
Brown, Eric, Yakima	.969	42	60	3	2	65
Brown, Gavin, Eugene	.925	34	47	2	4	53
Burrows, Mike, Everett*	.988	42	73	6	1	80
Byers, MacGregor, So. Oregon	1.000	4	6	1	0	7
Calderon, Ricardo, Bellingham*	.900	31	43	2	5	50
Christenson, Ryan, So. Oregon	.954	36	78	5	4	87
Cruz, Cirilo, Everett	.938	16	15	0	1	16
Fefee, Theo, Boise*	.967	40	59	0	2	61
Freeman, Terrance, So. Oregon	1.000	1	2	0	0	2
Giambi, Jeremy, Spokane*	.901	58	97	3	11	111
Glendenning, Michael, Bellingham	.926	64	85	2	7	94
Hallead, John, Portland*	.968	49	119	3	4	126
Hamlin, Mark, Portland	.988	50	82	3	1	86
Harp, Scott, Spokane	1.000	18	19	0	0	19
Hobbie, Matt, Boise*	1.000	43	50	3	0	53
Hutchison, Bernard, Portland	.959	44	90	3	4	97
Jackson, Wade, Boise	1.000	6	5	0	0	5
Johnson, Adam, Eugene*	.981	76	149	5	3	157
Johnson, Jace, Southern Oregon	.959	30	44	3	2	49
Jones, Tim, Southern Oregon	.958	53	107	6	5	118
Kenna, David, Bellingham	1.000	1	2	0	0	2
Livingston, Doug, Portland	1.000	2	5	0	0	5
Manning, Brian, Bellingham	.979	33	45	2	1	48
Marcinczyk, T.R., Southern Oregon	1.000	9	20	0	0	20
Marnell, Dean, Portland	.985	34	61	5	1	67
Meyer, Bobby, Yakima	1.000	1	1	0	0	1
Meyer, Matt, Yakima	.969	56	87	7	3	97
Mota, Tony, Yakima	1.000	40	59	2	0	61
Murphy, Nate, Boise*	.986	66	134	6	2	142
Neal, Rob, Boise	.983	38	54	5	1	60
Newton, Kimani, Yakima	.944	18	16	1	1	18
Pellow, Kit, Spokane	.941	12	12	4	1	17
Pickett, Eric, Eugene	.907	52	93	4	10	107
Pitts, Rick, Spokane	.948	43	54	1	3	58
Pointer, Corey, Eugene	.935	64	99	2	7	108
Polanco, Juan, Southern Oregon	.931	20	27	0	2	29
Rand, Ian, Bellingham	.989	50	88	4	1	93
Rauer, Troy, Southern Oregon	.974	42	68	7	2	77
Rodriguez, Guillermo, Bellingham	1.000	1	1	0	0	1
Rodriguez, Juan, Boise	.949	42	67	8	4	79
Rowson, James, Everett	.941	49	59	5	4	68
Sachse, Matt, Everett*	.973	66	63	9	2	74
Simonton, Cy Leon, Everett*	.968	37	54	6	2	62
Sorrow, Michael, Bellingham	1.000	1	1	0	0	1
Stearns, Randy, Yakima	.906	39	45	3	5	53
Stewart, Keith, Everett	.977	27	41	2	1	44
Stuart, Rich, Boise	.947	20	34	2	2	38
VanRossum, Chris, Bellingham*	1.000	16	23	0	0	23
Wong, Jerrod, Eugene*	1.000	3	8	0	0	8
Zweifel, Kent, Portland	1.000	4	8	0	0	8

CATCHERS

Player, Team	Pct.	G	PO	A	E	TC	DP
Anderson, Blake, Portland	.974	24	168	17	5	190	0
Arias, Rogelio, Portland	.971	38	307	26	10	343	3
Arnold, John, Eugene	.991	17	100	12	1	113	0
Brown, Gavin, Eugene	.987	12	74	3	1	78	0
Curtis, Matt, Boise	.996	25	205	18	1	224	1
Didion, Kristopher, Spokane	1.000	1	2	0	0	2	0
Escamilla, Roman, Spokane	.970	36	242	18	8	268	1
Glassey, Josh, Yakima	.993	37	275	27	2	304	2
Horner, Jim, Everett	.982	8	99	11	2	112	0
Johnson, Patrick, Boise	.990	26	178	22	2	202	2

ayer, Team	Pct.	G	PO	A	E	TC	DP	PB
enna, David, Bellingham	1.000	7	65	6	0	71	0	2
alave, Jaime, Yakima	.993	22	127	16	1	144	1	4
cGuire, Matt, Bellingham	1.000	7	41	5	0	46	0	4
cKay, Cody, So. Oregon	.984	48	323	39	6	368	2	9
elson, Brian, Everett	.982	24	200	17	4	221	0	15
ORRIS, Dax, Eugene	.994	56	487	53	3	543	3	18
ellow, Kit, Spokane	.917	4	19	3	2	24	0	0
obles, Juan, Spokane	.986	48	309	40	5	354	1	8
ondon, Alex, So. Oregon	.975	35	235	33	7	275	1	5
aucedo, Robert, Boise	1.000	1	3	0	0	3	0	0
errano, Danny, Boise	1.000	5	4	2	0	6	0	0
keels, David, Everett	.982	14	95	15	2	112	0	4
einmann, Scott, Everett	.997	29	259	31	1	291	3	14
paum, Tom, Bellingham	.981	30	280	28	6	314	1	10
rrealba, Yoruit, Bellingham	.994	36	290	33	2	325	1	6
ssery, Brian, Boise	.992	38	223	19	2	244	5	5
dal, Carlos, Portland	.984	16	113	8	2	123	0	2
ilson, Steve, Yakima	.984	41	271	42	5	318	0	6

PITCHERS

ayer, Team	Pct.	G	PO	A	E	TC	DP
reu, Jose, Bellingham	1.000	8	0	4	0	4	0
guilar, Alonzo, Eugene	.667	15	0	2	1	3	0
len, Rodney, Eugene	.833	22	1	9	2	12	1
rala, Julio, Everett*	.917	12	3	8	1	12	1
ird, Brandon, Spokane*	1.000	5	0	3	0	3	0
tchelder, Bill, Southern Oregon	.500	6	1	0	1	2	0
uldree, Joe, Eugene	1.000	3	1	1	0	2	0
asley, Raymond, Eugene*	1.000	3	0	2	0	2	0
ll, Rob, Eugene	.952	16	12	8	1	21	1
anco, Roger, Ever.-Eug	.882	16	4	11	2	17	0
asingim, Joseph, Bellingham	1.000	4	2	3	0	5	0
evins, Jeremy, Boise	.875	14	3	4	1	8	0
umenstock, Brad, So. Oregon	.778	23	4	3	2	9	0
nd, Jason, Everett*	1.000	20	2	4	0	6	0
sio, Chris, Everett	1.000	1	0	1	0	1	0
ewer, Ryan, Spokane	1.000	17	7	11	0	18	0
own, Gavin, Eugene	.000	1	0	0	1	1	0
ueggemann, Dean, Portland*	1.000	8	0	2	0	2	0
zozoski, Marc, Portland	.857	18	3	3	1	7	0
lero, Enrique, Spokane	1.000	17	10	11	0	21	1
rcamo, Kevin, Spokane	1.000	10	3	5	0	8	0
stillo, Alberto, Bellingham*	1.000	9	1	5	0	6	0
acon, Shawn, Portland	.667	4	2	0	1	3	0
apman, Jake, Spokane*	1.000	19	4	11	0	15	1
en, Bruce, Eugene*	1.000	11	2	7	0	9	1
ristman, Tim, Portland*	.857	21	2	4	1	7	0
fford, Eric, Everett	.667	2	0	2	1	3	0
chran, Andrew, Eugene*	.909	15	3	7	1	11	1
rtes, David, Eugene	1.000	15	2	1	0	3	0
stello, T.J., Southern Oregon*	1.000	9	0	1	0	1	0
wsill, Brendon, Boise	1.000	16	1	4	0	5	0
abtree, Robert, Bellingham	1.000	28	7	6	0	13	1
lmo, Kevin, Yakima	1.000	17	6	6	0	12	0
rrell, Tommy, Boise	1.000	15	7	18	0	25	2
elacruz, Fernando, Boise	.912	15	5	26	3	34	2
lla Ratta, Pete, Southern Oregon	1.000	22	3	7	0	10	1
skins, Casey, Yakima*	.923	15	3	9	1	13	0
uckrey, Chris, Portland	1.000	6	2	2	0	4	1
trella, Luis, Bellingham	.933	23	5	9	1	15	0
rnsworth, Jeff, Everett	1.000	10	1	6	0	7	0
zgerald, Brian, Everett*	.813	21	3	10	3	16	0
ach, Jason, Eugene	.917	27	3	8	1	12	0
rd, Jason, Portland*	1.000	13	0	1	0	1	0
anklin, Wayne, Yakima*	1.000	20	0	3	0	3	0
entes, Brian, Everett*	1.000	13	2	4	0	6	0
uliano, Joe, Eugene	1.000	26	5	12	0	17	2
aze, Randy, Southern Oregon	1.000	19	3	4	0	7	0
ogolin, Al, Southern Oregon	1.000	6	1	2	0	3	0
eene, Danny, Boise	1.000	9	1	2	0	3	0
tierrez, Javier, Everett	.833	7	0	5	1	6	1
annah, Michael, Yakima	1.000	18	0	2	0	2	0
arriger, Mark, Boise	1.000	7	1	0	0	1	0
rrera, Ivan, Bellingham	1.000	6	0	1	0	1	0
ton, Willy, Southern Oregon	.944	26	4	13	1	18	2
nchy, Brian, Portland	1.000	9	1	0	0	1	0
olden, Jason, Southern Oregon	.900	9	4	5	1	10	0
ughes, Michael, Boise	1.000	13	0	5	0	5	0
umphreys, Kevin, Boise	1.000	19	4	7	0	11	1
eston, Stephen, Spokane	.909	13	4	6	1	11	1
nsen, Ryan, Bellingham	1.000	13	4	7	0	11	0
menez, Jhonny, Everett	.818	24	3	6	2	11	0

Player, Team	Pct.	G	PO	A	E	TC	DP
Johnson, Gregory, Boise*	1.000	8	0	1	0	1	0
Jones, Michael, Eugene*	1.000	13	5	8	0	13	0
Kennison, Kyle, Everett	1.000	12	0	3	0	3	0
Kjos, Ryan, Southern Oregon	1.000	24	3	2	0	5	1
Knickerbocker, Tom, So. Oregon*	.500	12	1	0	1	2	0
Koehler, P.K., Eugene*	1.000	17	2	8	0	10	2
Kramer, Matthew, Yakima	.750	12	1	5	2	8	0
Kubenka, Jeff, Spokane	.500	28	1	1	2	4	0
Lagattuta, Rico, Southern Oregon*	.950	28	8	11	1	20	1
Larreal, Guillermo, Bellingham	.900	22	4	5	1	10	1
Laxton, Brett, Southern Oregon	.800	13	1	3	1	5	0
Lee, David, Portland	1.000	17	0	1	0	1	0
Leese, Brandon, Bellingham	.882	16	5	10	2	17	1
Lilly, Theodore, Yakima*	.833	13	2	3	1	6	1
Lineweaver, Aaron, Spokane	.917	21	3	8	1	12	2
Lovinger, Eric, Yakima	1.000	4	0	1	0	1	0
Luce, Robert, Everett	.923	23	7	5	1	13	0
Maestas, Mickey, Yakima	1.000	14	2	2	0	4	0
Mahlberg, John, Portland	1.000	17	1	8	0	9	0
Malloy, William, Bellingham	.667	15	0	4	2	6	0
Matcuk, Steven, Portland	.833	10	6	9	3	18	0
Mayo, Blake, Yakima	1.000	20	3	11	0	14	1
Mays, Joe, Everett	.846	13	7	15	4	26	0
McGlinchy, Kevin, Eugene	1.000	2	0	1	0	1	0
Milburn, Adam, Eugene*	1.000	24	5	12	0	17	1
Mitchell, Dean, Yakima	.800	15	1	3	1	5	0
Morgan, Eric, Everett	1.000	4	0	1	0	1	0
Mullen, Scott, Spokane*	.938	15	3	12	1	16	0
Nelson, Joe, Eugene	.917	14	7	4	1	12	0
Nicholson, John, Portland	1.000	3	1	3	0	4	0
Nogowski, Brandon, Everett*	.500	19	0	1	1	2	0
Noriega, Ray, Southern Oregon*	.963	17	10	16	1	27	0
O'Dell, Jake, Southern Oregon	.875	13	1	6	1	8	2
O'Shaughnessy, Jay, Yakima	.667	13	4	2	3	9	2
Ortiz, Ramon, Boise	.800	3	2	2	1	5	0
Osting, Jimmy, Eugene*	1.000	5	2	1	0	3	0
Pageler, Mick, Bellingham	1.000	30	2	3	0	5	0
Paluk, Brian, Yakima	1.000	20	1	8	0	9	0
Patino, Leonardo, Boise*	.917	30	1	10	1	12	0
Paulino, Jose, Southern Oregon	.909	10	5	5	1	11	0
Perez, Odalis, Eugene*	.875	10	2	5	1	8	0
Pinales, Aquiles, Eugene	1.000	3	0	1	0	1	0
Plooy, Eric, Boise	.600	20	1	2	2	5	1
Pohl, Jeff, Bellingham	.833	17	1	4	1	6	0
Puffer, Brandon, Boise	1.000	16	1	4	0	5	0
Quigley, Donald, Spokane	1.000	19	1	7	0	8	0
Riggan, Jerrod, Boise	.727	15	4	4	3	11	0
Riley, Michael, Bellingham*	.714	17	1	4	2	7	0
Rivera, Rafael, Everett	1.000	24	0	8	0	8	0
Robertson, Doug, Southern Oregon	.800	23	2	10	3	15	0
Rodriguez, Chad, Spokane	1.000	15	1	4	0	5	0
Rodriguez, Hector, Boise	1.000	20	0	2	0	2	0
Romine, Jason, Portland	.875	16	1	6	1	8	0
Rosa, Cristy, Portland	1.000	3	2	2	0	4	0
Rust, Brian, Eugene	1.000	1	0	1	0	1	0
Sanders, Allen, Spokane	.957	13	7	15	1	23	1
Sanders, Craig, Spokane	.667	6	2	0	1	3	0
Schmidt, Donnie, Portland	.867	19	8	5	2	15	0
Schroeffel, Scott, Portland	.875	16	4	10	2	16	2
SEBRING, Jeffrey, Portland*	1.000	16	10	17	0	27	3
Silva, Luis, Southern Oregon	.667	5	2	0	1	3	0
Simon, Benjamin, Yakima	.944	15	5	12	1	18	0
Simontacchi, Jason, Spokane	.727	14	7	9	6	22	2
Stark, Dennis, Eugene	.500	12	0	4	4	8	0
Stein, Ethan, Spokane	1.000	9	3	5	0	8	1
Stephens, Jason, Boise	1.000	3	0	1	0	1	0
Stepka, Tom, Portland	1.000	12	10	15	0	25	0
Stockstill, Jason, Boise*	1.000	2	0	2	0	2	0
Stover, C.D., Yakima	.857	15	1	5	1	7	0
Taczy, Craig, Yakima*	.900	16	1	8	1	10	1
Takahashi, Kurt, Bellingham	.833	16	2	3	1	6	1
Thompson, Travis, Portland	1.000	9	0	1	0	1	0
Vecchioni, Jerry, Eugene	1.000	1	0	1	0	1	0
Victory, Joe, Everett	1.000	13	3	13	0	16	1
Villarreal, Modesto, Spokane	1.000	20	4	9	0	13	2
Vining, Kenneth, Bellingham*	.929	13	2	11	1	14	1
Volkman, Keith, Boise*	.900	16	4	14	2	20	2
Wallace, Flint, Southern Oregon	.960	17	13	11	1	25	1
Wells, Matt, Bellingham	.875	12	2	5	1	8	0
Westbrook, Jake, Portland	.875	4	3	1	0	4	0
Weymouth, Marty, Everett	.857	10	3	3	1	7	0
Woodrow, James, Bellingham	1.000	17	3	4	0	7	0

CLASS A Northwest League

PITCHERS WITH TWO OR MORE TEAMS

Player, Team	Pct.	G	PO	A	E	TC	DP
Blanco, Roger, Everett....................	.867	11	3	10	2	15	0
Blanco, Roger, Eugene....................	1.000	5	1	1	0	2	0

The following players did not have any fielding statistics at the positions indicated or appeared only as a designated hitter, pinch-hitter or pinch-runner: Anthony, Burton, p; J. Castro, dh; N. Castro, ss; Cross, ss, of; Davis, p; Ellison, of, p; Ferrer, of; Flores, p; Hall, p; Harp, 3b; Jackson, 2b; R. Johnson, p; Jordan, dh, pr; Lop of; Mayer, p; Meyer, c; Miranda, of; Moore, 3b; Morrison, 2b; Newton, c; Oliva, ph, dh; Pitts, ss; Pointer, 1b, c; Prospero, of, c; Robles, of; L. Rodriguez, p; Rust, Skeels, of; Soriano, ph; Stearns, c; Vecchioni, of; Vidal, of.

LEAGUE CHAMPIONS

Year	Team	Pct.	Year	Team	Pct.	Year	Team	Pc
1901—	Portland	.675	1952—	Victoria	.631	1976—	Portland	.55
1902—	Butte	.608	1953—	Salem	.635		Walla Walla♦	.63
1903—	Butte	.578		Spokane*	.590	1977—	Bellingham■	.61
1904—	Boise	.625	1954—	Vancouver*	.636		Portland	.66
1905—	Vancouver	.586		Lewiston	.629	1978—	Grays Harbor▼	.67
	Everett*	.667	1955—	Salem	.646		Eugene	.51
1906—	Tacoma	.600		Eugene*	.639	1979—	Central Oregon♦	.60
1907—	Aberdeen	.625	1956—	Yakima	.691		Walla Walla	.57
1908—	Vancouver	.578		Yakima	.619	1980—	Bellingham•	.64
1909—	Seattle	.653	1957—	Eugene	.576		Eugene•	.52
1910—	Spokane	.596		Wenatchee*	.647	1981—	Medford♦	.60
1911—	Vancouver	.628	1958—	Lewiston	.621		Bellingham	.55
1912—	Seattle	.600		Yakima*	.594	1982—	Medford	.75
1913—	Vancouver	.600	1959—	Salem	.623		Salem♦	.48
1914—	Vancouver	.632		Yakima*	.563	1983—	Medford††	.73
1915—	Seattle	.564	1960—	Yakima	.638		Bellingham	.58
1916—	Spokane	.622		Yakima	.562	1984—	Tri-Cities††	.62
1917—	Great Falls	.592	1961—	Lewiston*	.621		Medford	.60
1918—	Seattle	.588		Yakima	.600	1985—	Everett††	.54
1919—	Seattle	.590	1962—	Wenatchee*	.574		Eugene	.54
1920—	Victoria	.600		Tri-City	.580	1986—	Bellingham††	.60
1921—	Yakima	.710	1963—	Lewiston	.594		Eugene	.60
	Yakima	.660		Yakima*	.613	1987—	Spokane▲	.71
1922—	Calgary‡	.600	1964—	Eugene	.636		Everett	.65
1923-36—	Did not operate.			Yakima*	.611	1988—	Southern Oregon	.60
1937—	Wenatchee	.603	1965—	Lewiston	.667		Spokane♦	.55
	Tacoma*	.627		Tri-City*	.681	1989—	Southern Oregon	.60
1938—	Yakima	.583	1966—	Tri-City	.679		Spokane♦	.54
	Bellingham (2nd)†	.511	1967—	Medford	.607	1990—	Boise	.69
1939—	Wenatchee	.601	1968—	Tri-City	.600		Spokane♦	.64
	Tacoma (2nd)†	.533	1969—	Rogue Valley	.633	1991—	Boise♦	.65
1940—	Spokane	.587	1970—	Lewiston§	.538		Yakima	.57
	Tacoma (4th)†	.500		Coos Bay-No. Bend	.563	1992—	Bellingham♦	.56
1941—	Spokane	.669	1971—	Tri-City§	.625		Bend	.56
1942—	Vancouver	.594		Bend	.538	1993—	Bellingham	.57
1943-45—	Did not operate.		1972—	Lewiston§	.675		Boise♦	.53
1946—	Wenatchee	.622		Walla Walla	.513	1994—	Yakima	.64
1947—	Vancouver	.566	1973—	Walla Walla∞	.638		Boise♦	.57
1948—	Spokane	.614		Portland	.563	1995—	Boise♦	.64
1949—	Yakima	.660	1974—	Bellingham	.619		Bellingham	.56
	Vancouver (2nd)†	.615		Eugene▲	.571	1996—	Eugene	.64
1950—	Yakima	.613	1975—	Portland	.545		Yakima§	.52
1951—	Spokane	.655		Eugene♦	.684			

*Won split-season playoff. †Won four-club playoff. ‡League disbanded June 18. §League divided into Northern and Southern divisions, declared cha pion under league rules. ∞League divided into Eastern and Western divisions, declared champion under league rules. ▲League divided into Eastern a Western divisions; won two-team playoff. ♦League divided into North and South divisions; won two-team playoff. ■League divided into Affiliate a Independent divisions; won two-team playoff. ▼Declared league champion after winning one-game playoff. Balance of playoff canceled due to rain and w grounds. •Declared co-champion after winning one game. Balance of playoff canceled due to rain and wet grounds. ††League divided into Washington a Oregon divisions; won two-team playoff. (NOTE—Known as Pacific Northwest League 1901-02, Pacific National League 1903-04, Northwestern Leag 1905-18, Pacific Coast International League 1919-22 and Western International League 1937-54.)

CLASS A *Northwest League*

SOUTH ATLANTIC LEAGUE

LEAGUE OFFICE

President/secretary-treasurer
John Moss
Address
P.O. Box 38
Kings Mountain, NC 28086
Phone
704-739-3466

Teams (affiliation)
Asheville Tourists (Rockies)
Augusta Greenjackets (Pirates)
Capital City Bombers (Mets)
Charleston (S.C.) Riverdogs (Devil Rays)
Charleston (W.Va.) Alley Cats (Reds)
Columbus Redstixx (Indians)
Delmarva Shorebirds (Orioles)

Fayetteville Crocks (Expos)
Greensboro Bats (Yankees)
Hagerstown Suns (Blue Jays)
Hickory Crawdads (White Sox)
Macon Braves (Braves)
Piedmont Bollweevils (Phillies)
Savannah Sand Gnats (Dodgers)

1996 FINAL STANDINGS

FIRST HALF

NORTHERN DIVISION

Team	W	L	T	Pct.	GB
Delmarva (Expos)	47	23	0	.671	....
Fayetteville (Tigers)	35	33	0	.515	11
Hagerstown (Blue Jays)	33	36	0	.478	13½
Charleston (W.Va.) (Reds)	29	41	0	.414	18

CENTRAL DIVISION

Team	W	L	T	Pct.	GB
Asheville (Rockies)	47	20	0	.701	....
Columbia (Mets)	37	30	0	.522	10
Piedmont (Phillies)	38	31	0	.551	10
Charleston (SC) (Rangers)	33	36	0	.478	15
Greensboro (Yankees)	29	41	0	.414	19½
Hickory (White Sox)	16	53	0	.232	32

SOUTHERN DIVISION

Team	W	L	T	Pct.	GB
Augusta (Pirates)	37	32	0	.536	....
Columbus (Indians)	36	34	0	.514	1½
Savannah (Dodgers)	34	36	0	.486	3½
Macon (Braves)	32	37	0	.464	5

SECOND HALF

NORTHERN DIVISION

Team	W	L	T	Pct.	GB
Fayetteville (Tigers)	41	30	0	.577	....
Hagerstown (Blue Jays)	37	35	0	.514	4½
Delmarva (Expos)	36	36	0	.500	5½
Charleston (W.Va.) (Reds)	29	43	0	.403	12½

CENTRAL DIVISION

Team	W	L	T	Pct.	GB
Columbia (Mets)	45	27	0	.625	....
Hickory (White Sox)	39	32	0	.549	5½
Asheville (Rockies)	37	32	0	.536	6½
Piedmont (Phillies)	34	35	0	.493	9½
Charleston (SC) (Rangers)	30	42	0	.417	15
Greensboro (Yankees)	27	45	0	.375	18

SOUTHERN DIVISION

Team	W	L	T	Pct.	GB
Columbus (Indians)	43	29	0	.597	....
Savannah (Dodgers)	38	33	0	.535	4½
Augusta (Pirates)	34	38	0	.472	9
Macon (Braves)	29	42	0	.408	13½

COMPOSITE

Team	Ash.	C'ia	Del.	C'us	Fay.	Pie.	Sav.	Aug.	Hag.	CSC	Mac.	CWV	Gbr.	Hck.	W	L	T	Pct.	GB
Asheville (Rockies)	....	1	7	1	10	9	2	2	11	4	3	10	12	12	84	52	0	.618	....
Columbia (Mets)	3	....	0	12	5	4	9	13	2	12	11	4	4	3	82	57	0	.590	3½
Delmarva (Expos)	3	4	....	2	9	7	3	2	16	4	3	10	12	8	83	59	0	.585	4
Columbus (Indians)	3	8	2	....	2	4	12	9	0	15	16	2	3	3	79	63	0	.556	8
Fayetteville (Tigers)	5	3	14	2	....	8	1	2	9	2	4	8	8	10	76	63	0	.547	9½
Piedmont (Phillies)	11	2	7	0	3	....	2	2	7	2	2	11	8	15	72	66	0	.522	13
Savannah (Dodgers)	1	10	1	12	3	2	....	8	3	14	12	1	2	3	72	69	0	.511	14½
Augusta (Pirates)	2	7	2	11	2	5	9	....	1	9	11	3	5	4	71	70	0	.504	15½
Hagerstown (Blue Jays)	3	2	8	4	6	7	1	3	....	2	1	18	6	9	70	71	0	.496	16½
Charleston (S.C.) (Rangers)	0	9	0	9	1	2	10	10	2	....	10	2	4	4	63	78	0	.447	23½
Macon (Braves)	1	5	1	6	0	2	14	13	2	12	....	1	3	1	61	79	0	.436	25
Charleston (W.Va.) (Reds)	4	0	5	2	12	5	3	1	5	2	3	....	13	3	58	84	0	.408	29
Greensboro (Yankees)	6	4	4	1	6	8	2	1	6	0	1	7	....	10	56	86	0	.394	31
Hickory (White Sox)	10	2	8	1	4	3	1	4	7	0	2	7	6	....	55	85	0	.393	31

Major league affiliations in parentheses.

PLAYOFFS: Savannah defeated Columbus, two games to none; Delmarva defeated Asheville, two games to one; Savannah defeated Delmarva, three games o one, to win league championship.

REGULAR SEASON ATTENDANCE: Asheville, 145,798; Augusta, 157,487; Columbia, 156,921; Charleston (S.C.), 100,428; Charleston (W.Va.), 87,189; Columbus, 45,110; Delmarva, 315,011; Fayetteville, 73,149; Greensboro, 168,534; Hagerstown, 102,765; Hickory, 207,069; Macon, 117,042; Piedmont, 02,983; Savannah, 122,488; Total—1,901,974; Playoffs (8 games)—16,516; All-Star Game—3,872.

MANAGERS: Asheville, P.J. Carey; Augusta, Jay Loviglio; Charleston (S.C.), Gary Allenson; Charleston (W.Va.), Tommy Thompson (through July 2), Donnie Scott (July 3 through end of season); Columbia, Howie Freiling; Columbus, Joel Skinner; Delmarva, Doug Sisson; Fayetteville, Dwight Lowry; Greensboro, ick Patterson (through May 2), Jimmy Johnson (May 3 through end of season); Hagerstown, J.J. Cannon; Hickory, Chris Cron; Macon, Paul Runge; iedmont, Roy Majtyka; Savannah, John Shoemaker. Managerial records of teams with more than one manager: Charleston (W.Va.), Thompson, 34-50, Scott, 4-34; Greensboro, Patterson, 14-12, Johnson, 42-74.

ALL-STAR TEAM: 1B—Darren Stumberger, Columbus; 2B—Orlando Cabrera, Delmarva; 3B—Russell Branyan, Columbus; SS—Chad Hermansen, August Utility Inf.—Carlos Lee, Hickory; OF—Scott Morgan, Fayetteville; Gabe Kapler, Fayetteville; David Feuerstein, Asheville; Utility OF—Eric Stuckenschneide Savannah; LHP—Ethan McEntire, Columbia; RHP—Nelson Figueroa, Columbia; C—Ben Petrick, Asheville; DH—Mike Whitlock, Hagerstown; Manager—P. Carey, Asheville; Coach—Doug Flynn, Columbia; Most Valuable Player—Russell Branyan, Columbus; Most Outstanding Pitcher—Nelson Figueroa, Columbi Most Outstanding Major League Prospect—Adrian Beltre, Savannah; General Manager of the Year—Ron McKee, Asheville.

1996 BATTING

TEAM

Team	Avg.	G	TPA	AB	R	H	TB	2B	3B	HR	RBI	SH	SF	HP	BB	IBB	SO	SB	CS	GDP	LOB	ShO	Slg.	OB
Hickory	.251	140	5321	4743	596	1191	1616	200	27	57	512	42	39	63	433	24	1127	172	94	82	954	10	.341	.32
Columbus	.250	142	5347	4689	729	1170	1937	216	25	167	654	19	44	59	535	18	1136	99	49	82	993	11	.413	.33
Savannah	.247	141	5322	4699	671	1162	1757	202	42	103	574	38	33	73	479	26	1070	212	106	66	938	6	.374	.32
Macon	.246	140	5125	4596	589	1131	1694	208	32	97	518	39	32	65	393	28	982	235	107	80	871	11	.369	.31
Fayetteville	.244	139	5274	4594	612	1123	1639	238	19	80	530	59	35	76	510	17	963	163	91	75	978	7	.357	.32
Asheville	.244	136	5184	4498	612	1099	1568	203	22	74	525	34	35	86	523	15	968	173	111	42	974	10	.349	.33
Hagerstown	.244	141	5350	4564	666	1115	1634	235	31	74	559	36	43	81	624	19	1078	161	94	68	1021	7	.358	.34
Delmarva	.242	142	5243	4621	673	1116	1668	228	48	76	579	38	42	58	483	27	918	215	118	62	871	10	.361	.31
Columbia	.239	139	5083	4421	593	1057	1490	182	37	59	514	72	40	70	479	23	1122	142	81	65	922	6	.337	.32
Greensboro	.239	142	5359	4758	586	1136	1641	209	37	74	521	41	36	75	449	12	1229	160	75	71	990	14	.345	.31
Piedmont	.235	138	5134	4548	540	1070	1464	197	25	49	463	55	33	90	408	17	1038	131	73	83	942	9	.322	.30
Augusta	.234	141	5287	4563	612	1066	1469	178	30	55	521	48	32	74	568	18	964	147	98	97	976	11	.322	.32
Charleston (SC)	.229	141	5010	4480	533	1028	1480	183	49	57	450	21	30	66	412	8	1176	172	81	53	878	13	.330	.30
Charleston (WV)	.226	142	5371	4605	600	1043	1494	200	28	65	521	38	38	64	625	11	1299	162	86	50	1065	14	.324	.30

INDIVIDUAL

TOP QUALIFIERS FOR BATTING CHAMPIONSHIP

Minimum 383 plate appearances. *Lefthanded batter. †Switch-hitter.

Player, Team	Avg.	G	TPA	AB	R	H	TB	2B	3B	HR	RBI	SH	SF	HP	BB	IBB	SO	SB	CS	GDP	Slg.	O
Mendoza, Carlos, Columbia*	.337	85	378	300	61	101	115	10	2	0	37	11	2	8	57	1	46	31	13	2	.383	.4
Lee, Carlos, Hickory	.313	119	515	480	65	150	209	23	6	8	70	0	11	0	23	5	50	18	13	15	.435	.3
Stumberger, Darren, Columbus	.310	129	537	471	77	146	248	30	3	22	89	1	4	7	53	2	72	0	1	13	.527	.3
Raynor, Mark, Piedmont	.304	111	492	428	73	130	167	21	2	4	62	5	6	3	50	0	67	16	10	7	.390	.3
Kapler, Gabriel, Fayetteville	.300	138	601	524	81	157	280	45	0	26	99	3	5	7	62	6	73	14	4	6	.534	.3
Long, Terrence, Columbia*	.288	123	519	473	66	136	216	26	9	12	78	1	4	5	36	3	120	32	7	9	.457	.3
Feuerstein, David, Asheville	.286	130	571	514	69	147	191	27	7	1	69	5	5	5	42	0	68	21	10	7	.372	.3
Lowell, Mike, Greensboro	.282	113	487	433	58	122	179	33	0	8	64	2	2	4	46	0	43	10	3	7	.413	.3
Cardona, Javier, Fayetteville	.282	97	384	348	42	98	131	21	0	4	28	3	3	2	28	1	53	1	5	9	.376	.3
Hernaiz, Juan, Savannah	.278	132	527	492	68	137	214	19	8	14	73	3	3	8	21	3	96	42	15	5	.435	.3
Brown, Roosevelt, Macon*	.278	113	452	413	61	115	199	27	0	19	64	0	3	3	33	4	60	21	11	9	.482	.3
Pimentel, Jose, Savannah	.278	123	508	461	66	128	178	21	4	7	54	5	4	10	28	1	100	50	19	9	.386	.3
Stuckenschneider, Eric, Savnh.	.277	140	599	470	111	130	218	28	6	16	63	2	4	12	111	5	96	50	18	4	.464	.4
Fernandez, Jose, Delmarva	.273	126	481	421	72	115	186	23	6	12	70	0	3	7	50	5	76	23	13	5	.442	.3
Adolfo, Carlos, Delmarva	.272	132	548	492	82	134	200	20	8	10	71	2	6	1	47	3	106	18	6	11	.407	.3
Kehoe, John, Hagerstown	.272	117	469	383	66	104	150	24	2	6	47	3	5	5	73	0	92	16	9	2	.392	.3

DEPARTMENTAL LEADERS: G—Shumpert, 141; AB—Jimenez, 537; R—Stuckenschneider, 111; H—Kapler, 157; TB—Kapler, 280; 2B—Kapler, 45; 3B—Bates, HR—Branyan, 40; RBI—Branyan, 106; SH—Simpson, 12; SF—C. Lee, 11; HP—Schreimann, 26; BB—Stuckenschneider, 111; IBB—Whitlock, 8; SO—Gainey, 1 SB—R. Smith, R. Gomez, 57 each; CS—Solano, 25; GIDP—Whipple, 18; Slg.—Branyan, .575; OBP—Stuckenschneider, .424.

ALL PLAYERS

*Lefthanded batter. †Switch-hitter.

Player, Team	Avg.	G	TPA	AB	R	H	TB	2B	3B	HR	RBI	SH	SF	HP	BB	IBB	SO	SB	CS	GDP	Slg.	
Acosta, Ed, Delmarva	.191	32	73	68	11	13	15	0	1	0	5	2	0	0	3	0	20	0	0	2	.221	
Adolfo, Carlos, Delmarva	.272	132	548	492	82	134	200	20	8	10	71	2	6	1	47	3	106	18	6	11	.407	
Alamo, Efrain, Asheville	.220	67	277	250	34	55	86	13	0	6	18	2	0	2	23	0	68	8	10	2	.344	
Albert, Rashad, Hickory	.235	49	197	179	31	42	61	7	3	2	10	0	2	2	14	0	51	18	6	2	.341	
Alvarado, Basilio, Delmarva	.308	6	14	13	1	4	4	0	0	0	1	0	0	1	0	0	2	0	0	0	.308	
Anderson, Milt, Columbus†	.231	81	299	251	46	58	89	12	2	5	27	2	1	3	42	1	53	29	10	2	.355	
Antczak, Chuck, Hickory	.154	9	17	13	0	2	2	0	0	0	1	0	0	0	3	0	2	0	0	0	.154	
Antrim, Pat, Greensboro†	.083	15	14	12	2	1	1	0	0	0	0	1	0	0	1	0	7	1	1	0	.083	
Arias, Rogelio, Asheville†	.167	27	89	84	7	14	14	0	0	0	5	0	0	2	3	0	12	1	3	2	.167	
Arvelo, Tom, Columbia	.202	72	250	218	35	44	47	3	0	0	14	9	2	4	17	0	42	8	8	2	.216	
Azuaje, Jesus, Columbia	.667	1	5	3	1	2	3	1	0	0	1	1	1	0	0	0	0	0	0	0	1.000	
Backowski, Lance, Savannah	.122	30	58	49	7	6	6	0	0	0	2	1	0	1	7	0	19	0	2	1	.122	
Baker, Derek, Cha. (S.C.)*	.244	46	185	160	21	39	64	8	1	5	31	0	3	3	19	0	37	1	1	0	.400	
Barker, Glen, Fayetteville	.288	37	154	132	23	38	42	1	0	1	9	3	0	3	16	1	34	20	6	2	.318	
Barrett, Michael, Delmarva	.238	129	508	474	57	113	162	29	4	4	62	2	5	9	18	0	42	5	11	9	.342	
Bass, Jayson, Macon†	.364	5	23	22	2	8	11	0	0	1	1	0	0	1	0	0	5	3	1	0	.500	
Bass, Jayson, Fayetteville*	.231	104	356	295	44	68	119	12	3	11	43	3	2	2	54	3	118	19	10	2	.403	
Bates, Fletcher, Columbia†	.259	132	565	491	84	127	219	21	13	15	72	4	3	3	64	4	162	16	6	3	.446	
Baugh, Darren, Hickory	.285	68	308	267	46	76	91	5	2	2	24	3	4	7	27	0	48	17	5	3	.341	
Bearden, Doug, Hickory	.219	49	174	169	12	37	47	7	0	1	11	2	0	0	3	0	35	0	3	2	.278	
Bellenger, Butch, Augusta	.192	8	29	26	5	5	7	2	0	0	1	1	0	0	2	0	6	1	0	0	.269	
Beltre, Adrian, Savannah	.307	68	288	244	48	75	143	14	3	16	59	0	2	7	35	2	46	4	3	7	.586	
Bigler, Jeff, Augusta*	.264	40	159	121	16	32	42	10	0	0	14	3	3	3	29	1	24	0	2	1	.347	
Black, Brandon, Columbia*	.190	25	73	63	3	12	20	6	1	0	12	0	1	1	8	2	16	0	3	0	.317	
Blake, Casey, Hagerstown	.250	48	192	172	29	43	64	13	1	2	18	0	2	7	11	1	40	5	3	3	.372	

ayer, Team	Avg.	G	TPA	AB	R	H	TB	2B	3B	HR	RBI	SH	SF	HP	BB	IBB	SO	SB	CS	GDP	Slg.	OBP
keney, Mo, Delmarva	.255	41	119	110	13	28	38	7	0	1	11	1	1	0	7	0	20	3	5	2	.345	.297
yd, Quincy, Columbia	.000	2	7	6	0	0	0	0	0	0	0	0	0	0	1	0	3	0	0	0	.000	.143
nyan, Russell, Columbus*	.268	130	552	482	102	129	277	20	4	40	106	0	3	5	62	5	166	7	4	4	.575	.355
vo, Danny, Delmarva*	.230	18	67	61	10	14	22	6	1	0	7	2	1	1	2	0	14	1	0	1	.361	.262
ones, Chris, Cha. (S.C.)	.190	26	83	79	10	15	21	4	1	0	10	0	1	1	2	0	39	0	1	2	.266	.217
to, Domingo, Piedmont	.118	43	119	102	5	12	15	3	0	0	9	3	0	0	14	0	36	1	0	2	.147	.224
ck, Tarrik, Fayetteville*	.294	32	138	119	21	35	47	5	2	1	11	0	1	4	14	1	31	4	5	3	.395	.384
wn, Roosevelt, Macon*	.278	113	452	413	61	115	199	27	0	19	64	0	3	3	33	4	60	21	11	9	.482	.334
wn, Vick, Greensboro	.319	25	103	91	8	29	38	6	0	1	9	0	0	1	11	0	23	9	2	0	.418	.398
mbaugh, Cliff, Cha. (S.C.)	.242	132	534	458	70	111	166	23	7	6	45	1	2	1	72	2	103	20	7	5	.362	.345
ant, Clint, Asheville	.246	68	278	228	33	56	84	9	2	5	30	2	4	6	36	1	45	10	10	0	.368	.358
czkowski, Matt, Piedmont	.217	5	24	23	2	5	6	1	0	0	1	0	0	1	0	0	8	0	0	0	.261	.250
dzinski, Mark, Columbus*	.262	74	326	260	42	68	97	12	4	3	38	2	1	4	59	4	68	12	3	5	.373	.404
orera, Orlando, Delmarva	.252	134	580	512	86	129	207	28	4	14	65	5	4	5	54	4	63	51	18	4	.404	.327
nfield, Eric, Greensboro*	.176	76	265	238	19	42	48	2	2	0	24	1	5	3	18	0	63	13	5	2	.202	.239
milli, Jason, Delmarva	.223	119	505	426	53	95	121	13	2	3	36	9	2	5	63	1	89	26	17	4	.284	.329
hetto, John, Augusta†	.357	8	15	14	1	5	6	1	0	0	3	0	0	0	1	0	4	1	0	0	.429	.400
pellan, Rene, Fayetteville	.260	72	275	250	26	65	78	10	0	1	31	4	2	7	12	1	47	1	1	2	.312	.310
rdona, Javier, Fayetteville	.282	97	384	348	42	98	131	21	0	4	28	3	3	2	28	1	53	1	5	9	.376	.336
rion, Jorge, Cha. (S.C.)	.289	10	43	38	7	11	13	0	1	0	6	1	1	0	3	0	10	0	2	0	.342	.333
istensen, McKay, Hickory*	.000	6	12	11	0	0	0	0	0	0	0	0	0	0	1	0	4	0	0	0	.000	.083
istmas, Maurice, Macon	.000	41	4	4	0	0	0	0	0	0	0	0	0	0	0	0	4	0	0	0	.000	.000
ybrook, Steve, Cha. (W.Va.)*	.262	123	512	439	62	115	151	18	3	4	40	3	0	1	69	2	144	37	11	0	.344	.363
ford, John, Asheville	.215	94	357	317	29	68	87	14	1	1	27	5	1	9	25	0	69	19	8	3	.274	.290
urn, Todd, Piedmont	.194	46	173	155	15	30	42	9	0	1	16	3	0	0	15	0	34	2	1	2	.271	.265
ncepcion, David, Cha. (WV)†	.198	40	127	116	9	23	28	3	1	0	11	0	0	1	10	0	31	3	1	2	.241	.268
rnelius, Jonathon, Piedmont	.233	123	501	454	41	106	162	16	2	12	51	5	1	8	33	1	132	6	5	9	.357	.296
x, Chuck, Piedmont	.202	27	99	89	8	18	26	5	0	1	5	2	0	2	6	1	26	1	1	2	.292	.268
ne, Todd, Piedmont	.217	9	29	23	4	5	5	0	0	0	1	0	0	0	6	1	6	0	1	0	.217	.379
z, Charlie, Macon*	.174	42	26	23	1	4	6	2	0	0	1	1	0	1	1	0	7	0	0	1	.261	.240
evas, Trent, Savannah	.152	15	48	46	2	7	8	1	0	0	6	0	2	0	0	0	14	0	0	0	.174	.146
nningham, Earl, Asheville	.256	35	153	133	19	34	72	11	0	9	30	0	1	9	7	2	42	5	1	0	.541	.333
y, Bob, Columbia	.300	44	159	140	20	42	57	7	1	2	17	1	0	0	18	2	19	1	2	1	.407	.380
gherty, Keith, Macon	.232	106	359	327	38	76	127	17	2	10	39	0	0	6	26	1	89	5	3	6	.388	.301
vis, James, Cha. (S.C.)	.288	84	350	313	42	90	115	14	1	3	38	1	3	1	32	0	57	8	3	6	.367	.352
aCruz, Carlos, Fayetteville	.226	98	348	318	34	72	116	21	4	5	39	3	2	4	21	1	100	18	8	4	.365	.281
afield, Wil, Greensboro	.255	30	110	98	16	25	37	4	1	2	11	1	2	3	6	0	30	1	0	0	.378	.312
aRosa, Miguel, Cha. (S.C.)	.180	26	70	61	5	11	13	0	1	0	1	0	0	1	8	0	39	1	3	0	.213	.286
gado, Jose, Macon†	.293	102	382	345	43	101	117	16	0	0	50	3	2	5	27	2	56	23	11	5	.339	.351
nning, Wes, Delmarva*	.221	115	404	349	60	77	122	17	8	4	37	3	2	7	43	2	63	31	10	1	.350	.317
nis, Les, Greensboro	.253	33	89	75	15	19	25	3	0	1	9	2	0	1	11	0	27	1	2	2	.333	.356
ati, John, Columbus	.283	40	162	145	23	41	67	6	1	6	28	0	3	4	10	0	27	1	0	5	.462	.340
wns, Brian, Hickory	.208	84	303	279	23	58	77	10	0	3	28	3	2	4	15	0	78	0	1	6	.276	.257
zos, Justin, Asheville*	.265	127	516	438	64	116	203	29	2	18	76	0	2	6	70	7	126	7	3	1	.463	.372
verge, Salvador, Asheville	.198	103	399	349	38	69	92	12	1	3	31	0	3	15	32	3	84	8	12	2	.264	.291
nondson, Tracy, Columbia	.190	93	344	273	43	52	70	12	0	2	21	6	3	7	55	0	64	5	5	6	.256	.337
vards, Aaron, Augusta	.238	40	144	126	22	30	41	4	2	1	11	3	1	3	11	0	28	7	5	3	.325	.312
n, Brett, Asheville	.243	122	477	412	49	100	131	12	2	5	37	5	5	4	49	0	100	5	5	4	.318	.326
ott, Zach, Piedmont	.228	135	569	470	57	107	142	23	0	4	41	10	7	15	67	2	90	20	11	11	.302	.338
mons, Scott, Greensboro	.239	15	51	46	7	11	15	1	0	1	9	1	1	1	2	0	6	0	1	0	.326	.280
le, Beau, Columbia	.000	3	2	2	0	0	0	0	0	0	0	0	0	0	0	0	0	0	0	0	.000	.000
leka, Matt, Fayetteville	.229	93	330	262	28	60	81	18	0	1	25	7	1	12	48	0	36	6	6	7	.309	.372
kson, Corey, Columbia	.220	58	239	209	16	46	63	14	0	1	17	3	4	3	19	0	57	5	3	2	.301	.289
ns, Pat, Columbus†	.125	6	18	16	0	2	2	0	0	0	0	0	0	0	2	0	5	0	0	0	.125	.222
ner, Matt, Hagerstown*	.154	11	36	26	10	4	5	1	0	0	3	2	0	0	8	0	11	0	0	0	.192	.353
ris, Mark, Augusta*	.217	78	335	299	31	65	81	10	0	2	30	1	2	2	31	1	66	6	5	5	.271	.293
iske, Joshua, Hickory	.243	115	477	412	43	100	147	20	0	9	62	2	4	8	51	1	132	1	1	5	.357	.335
nandez, Jose, Delmarva	.273	126	481	421	72	115	186	23	6	12	70	0	3	7	50	5	76	23	13	5	.442	.358
erstein, David, Asheville	.286	130	571	514	69	147	191	27	7	1	69	5	5	5	42	0	68	21	10	7	.372	.343
ner, Tony, Cha. (S.C.)	.234	30	117	111	10	26	39	4	0	3	13	0	1	2	3	0	45	4	3	1	.351	.265
nigan, Steven, Augusta	.208	49	155	144	14	30	36	6	0	0	17	1	1	3	5	0	29	2	1	6	.250	.248
te, Derek, Macon*	.236	107	362	330	29	78	141	10	1	17	45	0	1	1	30	5	141	3	1	7	.427	.301
s, Ovidio, Augusta	.266	54	208	177	18	47	55	8	0	0	22	2	3	1	25	0	17	6	8	5	.311	.354
er, Brian, Fayetteville	.251	76	287	239	48	60	108	12	3	10	30	5	1	10	32	1	50	2	2	5	.452	.342
ney, Bryon, Columbia*	.217	122	495	446	53	97	162	23	0	14	62	0	3	5	41	3	169	5	2	13	.363	.289
lagher, Shawn, Cha. (S.C.)	.224	88	332	303	29	68	108	11	4	7	32	3	2	4	18	0	104	6	1	6	.356	.280
cia, Apostol, Fayetteville†	.194	74	272	242	33•	47	62	7	1	2	17	4	2	3	21	0	77	12	3	4	.256	.265
cia, Jaime, Delmarva	.236	62	213	182	27	43	74	14	1	5	19	3	1	5	22	0	51	1	4	3	.407	.333
cia, Jose, Macon	.000	33	1	1	0	0	0	0	0	0	0	0	0	0	0	0	1	0	0	0	.000	.000
rcia, Luis, Hickory	.273	76	306	289	31	79	112	18	3	3	38	1	0	2	14	2	41	9	6	8	.388	.311
cia, Miguel, Savannah†	.152	17	74	66	8	10	13	3	0	0	5	0	0	0	8	0	15	4	3	0	.197	.243
rdi, Mike, Greensboro	.222	20	74	63	11	14	28	5	0	3	6	0	0	1	10	0	13	0	1	4	.444	.338
Geronimo, Savannah	.243	79	293	276	29	67	103	13	1	7	38	1	3	5	8	3	69	0	2	4	.373	.274
vine, Michael, Columbus*	.277	38	149	119	17	33	56	5	0	6	16	0	1	1	28	2	33	0	0	2	.471	.416
nez, Paul, Columbia	.150	11	24	20	2	3	3	0	0	0	2	0	0	0	4	0	6	0	0	0	.150	.292
mez, Ramon, Hickory	.249	116	477	418	73	104	121	8	3	1	30	11	2	2	44	0	99	57	19	5	.289	.322
nzalez, Lariel, Asheville	.000	35	1	1	0	0	0	0	0	0	0	0	0	0	0	0	1	0	0	0	.000	.000
nzalez, Manuel, Savannah†	.229	65	255	231	30	53	70	10	2	1	19	1	2	1	20	0	52	15	8	3	.303	.291
nzalez, Mauricio, Columbus†	.242	25	99	95	13	23	30	4	0	1	7	0	2	1	1	0	18	0	1	0	.316	.253
nzalez, Ricky, Columbus	.235	75	268	247	19	58	72	11	0	1	12	3	1	0	17	0	42	0	0	4	.291	.283
nzalez, Wikleman, Augusta	.253	118	492	419	52	106	145	21	3	4	62	2	5	7	58	1	41	4	6	14	.346	.350
odhart, Steven, Cha. (W.Va.)	.216	115	488	380	61	82	104	16	3	0	26	5	2	7	94	1	95	16	12	4	.274	.379
dwin, Joe, Cha. (S.C.)	.258	80	295	252	25	65	80	13	1	0	31	3	6	3	32	1	34	3	5	4	.317	.349

– 535 –

Player, Team	Avg.	G	TPA	AB	R	H	TB	2B	3B	HR	RBI	SH	SF	HP	BB	IBB	SO	SB	CS	GDP	Slg.
Gordon, Herman, Hagerstown†	.158	41	125	114	7	18	28	3	2	1	11	2	1	3	5	0	40	3	5	2	.246
Groseclose, David, Asheville	.244	84	312	250	40	61	70	9	0	0	31	5	3	10	40	0	55	13	12	2	.280
Hairston, John, Greensboro†	.216	59	220	194	19	42	64	5	1	5	19	1	1	5	19	0	81	4	2	3	.330
Hallead, John, Asheville*	.162	38	156	136	17	22	28	4	1	0	9	0	0	3	17	1	39	5	4	0	.206
Hampton, Mike, Cha. (W.Va.)	.217	134	558	475	69	103	172	22	4	13	68	3	6	13	61	0	120	22	6	6	.362
Hampton, Robby, Hagerstown	.203	19	74	69	9	14	22	3	1	1	8	1	0	0	4	0	28	1	0	0	.319
Harmon, Brian, Savannah	.217	85	284	230	36	50	91	11	0	10	37	0	2	2	50	1	56	0	3	1	.396
Hayes, Chris, Hagerstown	.248	88	360	315	48	78	116	15	4	5	51	0	4	9	32	2	59	7	6	6	.368
Hayes, Heath, Columbus	.233	104	395	348	51	81	161	14	0	22	57	0	5	6	36	0	106	2	1	2	.463
Hermansen, Chad, Augusta	.252	62	273	226	41	57	116	11	3	14	41	0	1	8	38	5	65	11	3	1	.513
Hernaiz, Juan, Savannah	.278	132	527	492	68	137	214	19	8	14	73	3	3	8	21	3	96	42	15	5	.435
Hicks, Jamie, Macon	.220	68	198	186	17	41	57	7	0	3	17	0	2	1	9	1	33	3	1	4	.306
Hodges, Randy, Macon*	.241	101	303	278	36	67	87	12	1	2	28	3	0	4	18	1	42	10	10	4	.313
Hollins, Darontaye, Hickory	.167	37	145	132	10	22	24	2	0	0	6	1	1	1	10	0	41	3	3	2	.182
Inglin, Jeff, Hickory	.361	22	89	83	12	30	46	6	2	2	15	0	1	1	4	0	11	2	1	3	.554
Ingram, Darron, Cha. (W.Va.)	.188	15	57	48	5	9	15	3	0	1	6	0	1	0	8	1	19	0	0	0	.313
Inzunza, Miguel, Fayetteville	.250	68	276	232	24	58	70	12	0	0	31	8	2	7	27	0	19	2	3	4	.302
Janke, Jared, Piedmont	.219	104	422	388	36	85	124	21	0	6	46	3	3	4	24	1	70	2	2	8	.320
Jaramillo, Francisco, Cha. (S.C.)	.191	45	149	131	14	25	33	5	0	1	7	1	0	7	10	0	41	2	0	4	.252
Jimenez, D'Angelo, Greensboro†	.244	138	603	537	68	131	184	25	5	6	48	4	3	3	56	2	113	15	17	7	.343
Johnson, Anthony, Cha. (W.Va.)	.231	9	33	26	3	6	10	1	0	1	5	0	0	1	6	0	9	1	2	0	.385
Johnson, Damon, Hagerstown	.183	43	140	126	17	23	34	6	1	1	11	0	1	2	11	0	42	3	3	4	.270
Johnson, Jason, Cha. (S.C.)	.217	116	443	391	40	85	114	18	4	1	38	2	1	6	43	1	115	11	7	5	.292
Kapler, Gabriel, Fayetteville	.300	138	601	524	81	157	280	45	0	26	99	3	5	7	62	6	73	14	4	6	.534
Keech, Erik, Greensboro*	.229	16	38	35	4	8	10	2	0	0	2	0	0	0	3	0	4	0	0	2	.286
Kehoe, John, Hagerstown	.272	117	469	383	66	104	150	24	2	6	47	3	5	5	73	0	92	16	9	2	.392
Kennedy, Justin, Piedmont*	.215	27	110	107	12	23	30	5	1	0	14	0	0	0	3	0	24	1	2	4	.280
Kimm, Tyson, Piedmont†	.198	35	120	106	11	21	25	4	0	0	6	1	0	4	9	0	23	1	0	3	.236
King, Cesar, Cha. (S.C.)	.250	84	300	276	35	69	102	10	1	7	28	0	2	1	21	0	58	8	5	5	.370
Klee, Charles, Hickory	.202	38	114	109	7	22	26	2	1	0	7	0	0	0	5	0	31	2	2	4	.239
Koonce, Graham, Fayetteville*	.238	133	556	487	61	116	168	22	3	8	59	2	4	5	58	0	97	7	7	9	.345
Kopacz, Derek, Fayetteville	.231	49	203	186	25	43	69	11	3	3	14	2	1	0	14	0	49	2	2	2	.371
Lackey, Steve, Fayetteville	.216	82	351	310	38	67	92	13	0	4	43	5	5	3	28	0	58	24	6	4	.297
Landry, Jacques, Fayetteville	.188	31	107	101	10	19	26	4	0	1	3	0	0	1	5	0	36	1	0	2	.257
Langaigne, Selwyn, Hagerstown*	.143	4	15	14	1	2	2	0	0	0	1	0	0	0	1	0	5	2	0	0	.143
Larkin, Stephen, Cha. (W.Va.)*	.271	58	244	203	30	55	81	7	2	5	33	1	1	4	35	1	40	5	4	2	.399
LaRue, Jason, Cha. (W.Va.)	.211	37	137	123	17	26	40	8	0	2	14	1	0	2	11	0	28	3	0	2	.325
Leaman, Jeff, Piedmont	.138	27	31	29	4	4	6	0	1	0	0	0	0	0	2	0	8	0	1	0	.207
Lee, Carlos, Hickory	.313	119	515	480	65	150	209	23	6	8	70	0	11	0	23	5	50	18	13	15	.435
Lewis, Andreaus, Columbus†	.078	23	75	64	6	5	7	2	0	0	1	0	0	4	7	0	31	2	0	1	.109
Lewis, Dwayne, Cha. (W.Va.)*	.180	22	81	61	12	11	15	0	2	0	8	1	1	1	17	0	13	5	2	0	.246
Lewis, Marc, Macon	.315	66	270	241	36	76	111	14	3	5	28	1	6	1	21	1	31	25	8	6	.461
Light, Tal, Asheville*	.327	52	229	205	34	67	118	15	0	12	51	0	2	1	21	0	58	8	4	3	.576
Lombard, George, Macon*	.245	116	497	444	76	109	186	16	8	15	51	8	2	7	36	0	122	24	17	4	.419
Long, Terrence, Columbia*	.288	123	519	473	66	136	216	26	9	12	78	1	4	5	36	3	120	32	7	9	.457
Lowell, Mike, Greensboro	.282	113	487	433	58	122	179	33	0	8	64	2	2	4	46	0	43	10	3	7	.413
Lunar, Fernando, Macon	.184	104	380	343	33	63	93	9	0	7	33	3	2	12	20	0	65	3	2	11	.271
Lutz, Manuel, Hickory*	.238	44	159	143	10	34	39	2	0	1	12	1	3	3	9	2	46	0	1	3	.273
Macias, Jose, Delmarva†	.247	116	441	369	64	91	115	13	4	1	33	7	2	6	56	1	48	38	15	2	.312
Malave, Joshua, Savannah	.250	6	18	16	2	4	4	0	0	0	5	0	1	1	0	0	3	0	0	0	.250
Mason, Lamont, Cha. (W.Va.)	.216	68	225	190	24	41	48	2	1	1	16	3	1	2	28	1	48	11	6	0	.253
Mateo, Jose, Savannah†	.162	111	359	308	33	50	61	3	1	2	16	9	0	8	34	0	89	15	5	2	.198
Mateo, Ruben, Cha. (S.C.)	.260	134	543	496	65	129	199	30	8	8	58	2	7	12	26	1	78	30	9	8	.401
May, Freddy, Augusta*	.203	123	473	390	58	79	114	8	6	5	43	4	3	4	72	3	119	22	18	5	.292
McAulay, John, Cha. (S.C.)	.167	5	20	12	2	2	2	0	0	0	1	0	0	1	7	0	1	1	1	0	.167
McClure, Craig, Hickory	.203	59	238	212	21	43	63	8	3	2	19	2	1	3	20	2	62	6	2	3	.297
McCormick, Andrew, Hagerstn.	.176	33	124	102	11	18	20	2	0	0	5	1	0	1	20	0	39	3	1	4	.196
McCormick, Cody, Greensboro	.197	65	192	173	16	34	61	9	0	6	20	2	2	3	12	0	46	0	1	2	.353
McSparin, Paul, Augusta	.071	6	14	14	1	1	2	1	0	0	1	0	0	0	0	0	6	0	0	1	.143
Mendez, Sergio, Augusta	.233	46	186	172	23	40	70	9	0	7	26	0	0	5	9	2	31	3	3	4	.407
Mendoza, Carlos, Columbia*	.337	83	378	300	61	101	115	10	2	0	37	11	2	8	57	1	46	31	13	2	.383
Meyer, Travis, Savannah	.292	68	212	185	23	54	75	8	2	3	20	2	0	3	22	1	42	0	0	4	.405
Minici, Jason, Columbus	.213	98	369	334	37	71	105	18	2	4	23	2	0	2	31	1	84	9	4	8	.314
Miyake, Chris, Augusta	.240	101	399	367	40	88	106	12	0	2	33	6	2	2	22	0	55	10	10	7	.289
Monroe, Craig, Cha. (S.C.)	.150	49	174	153	11	23	36	11	1	0	9	0	0	3	18	0	48	2	2	3	.235
Montgomery, Joe, Cha. (W.Va.)	.000	14	1	1	0	0	0	0	0	0	0	0	0	0	0	0	0	0	0	0	.000
Morales, Eric, Columbia†	.231	45	131	121	10	28	31	3	0	0	14	1	0	2	7	0	22	0	3	0	.256
Morenz, Shea, Greensboro*	.249	91	393	338	40	84	112	14	4	2	48	2	3	12	38	4	92	13	3	2	.331
Morgan, Scott, Columbus	.311	87	366	305	62	95	188	25	1	22	80	0	4	11	46	0	70	9	5	5	.616
Morrison, Gregory, Savannah*	.254	94	321	299	32	76	107	11	4	4	39	0	2	1	19	1	65	4	7	0	.358
Mota, Cristian, Columbus†	.213	32	138	122	17	26	39	4	0	3	10	2	2	2	10	1	31	1	2	3	.320
Moultrie, Pat, Hagerstown*	.271	39	143	129	25	35	45	5	1	1	12	1	0	1	12	1	24	10	1	1	.349
Neubart, Garrett, Asheville	.280	71	320	282	60	79	96	11	3	0	22	1	3	3	30	0	45	34	5	2	.340
Nichols, Kevin, Piedmont	.222	22	77	72	5	16	22	6	0	0	5	1	0	1	3	0	18	0	1	0	.306
Nolte, Bruce, Columbia	.059	6	18	17	0	1	1	0	0	0	1	0	0	1	0	0	2	0	0	0	.059
Nunez, Juan, Cha. (S.C.)†	.264	88	369	326	55	86	104	7	4	1	18	2	0	5	36	0	77	53	13	1	.319
O'Connor, Rich, Piedmont	.200	23	68	55	11	11	12	1	0	0	0	2	0	0	11	0	13	1	0	1	.218
Ojeda, Erick, Columbia*	.000	35	1	0	0	0	0	0	0	0	0	0	0	0	0	0	0	0	0	0	.000
Oliveros, Ricardo, Delmarva	.250	4	4	4	0	1	2	1	0	0	0	0	0	0	0	0	2	0	0	0	.500
Olsen, Donald, Delmarva	.213	91	328	291	26	62	92	13	1	5	42	2	8	3	24	1	60	3	2	3	.316
Olson, Dan, Hickory*	.249	57	224	193	25	48	66	8	2	2	19	0	0	0	31	3	65	2	3	1	.342
Ortiz, Asbel, Cha. (S.C.)†	.216	88	331	310	23	67	87	11	3	1	32	1	3	4	13	0	94	1	3	2	.281
Ozuna, Rafael, Savannah†	.244	87	346	307	41	75	112	12	5	5	27	7	2	2	28	2	69	9	3	4	.365

ayer, Team	Avg.	G	TPA	AB	R	H	TB	2B	3B	HR	RBI	SH	SF	HP	BB	IBB	SO	SB	CS	GDP	Slg.	OBP
rra, Jose, Cha. (S.C.)†	.149	36	97	87	2	13	14	1	0	0	6	1	1	1	7	0	43	5	3	0	.161	.219
rsons, Jason, Cha. (W.Va.)†	.284	48	183	162	18	46	66	11	0	3	24	1	2	3	15	0	25	3	1	2	.407	.352
rsons, Jeff, Columbia	.184	51	175	147	13	27	34	3	2	0	9	5	0	1	22	0	43	7	4	3	.231	.294
ellis, Anthony, Cha. (W.Va.)	.181	61	247	227	23	41	61	9	1	3	27	1	2	4	13	2	72	4	3	6	.269	.236
tterson, Jarrod, Columbia*	.230	70	252	213	26	49	69	9	1	3	37	0	4	2	33	3	65	1	1	3	.324	.333
ul, Josh, Hickory	.327	59	252	226	41	74	114	16	0	8	37	3	1	1	21	3	53	13	4	2	.504	.386
ck, Thomas, Hagerstown*	.333	19	61	48	7	16	18	2	0	0	7	0	2	0	10	0	11	1	1	1	.375	.433
eples, Michael, Hagerstown	.235	74	315	268	30	63	89	15	1	3	31	4	3	3	37	0	55	15	5	5	.332	.331
na, Alex, Augusta	.162	52	176	167	9	27	35	4	2	0	12	1	1	0	7	0	51	2	1	5	.210	.194
na, Angel, Savannah	.205	36	135	127	13	26	48	4	0	6	16	1	0	0	7	1	37	1	1	1	.378	.246
ndergrass, Tyrone, Macon†	.267	12	50	45	8	12	18	1	1	1	3	0	0	1	4	0	12	5	3	0	.400	.340
rson, Wilt, Macon	.156	40	128	122	9	19	19	0	0	0	7	1	0	1	4	0	23	2	3	3	.156	.189
rick, Ben, Asheville	.235	122	531	446	74	105	175	24	2	14	52	2	3	5	75	1	98	19	9	5	.392	.350
tiford, Torrey, Piedmont	.208	74	291	259	26	54	64	6	2	0	19	9	2	3	18	0	49	13	3	5	.247	.266
rce, Kirk, Piedmont	.253	67	235	198	22	50	68	12	0	2	28	1	2	12	22	0	43	0	1	6	.343	.359
mentel, Jose, Savannah	.278	123	508	461	66	128	178	21	4	7	54	5	4	10	28	1	100	50	19	9	.386	.330
nto, Rene, Greensboro	.206	52	174	165	13	34	48	9	1	1	14	2	0	2	5	0	41	2	1	5	.291	.238
inter, Corey, Macon	.240	8	26	25	4	6	10	1	0	1	2	0	0	1	0	0	9	2	1	0	.400	.269
lanco, Enohel, Columbia	.217	92	332	299	34	65	82	12	1	1	24	9	1	5	18	0	78	6	3	5	.274	.272
llock, Elton, Augusta	.235	132	533	452	65	106	144	13	5	5	47	5	3	5	68	0	100	29	11	4	.319	.339
well, Jeremy, Delmarva	.000	27	2	2	0	0	0	0	0	0	0	0	0	0	0	0	0	0	0	0	.000	.000
zo, Yohel, Asheville	.141	27	92	85	5	12	13	1	0	0	4	0	1	1	5	0	20	0	1	3	.153	.196
okopec, Luke, Savannah*	.216	82	280	245	34	53	79	12	1	4	29	0	4	4	27	2	78	0	5	5	.322	.300
or, Pete, Hickory*	.307	59	247	205	37	63	101	18	1	6	37	0	1	5	36	4	43	3	2	7	.493	.421
len, Shane, Piedmont*	.269	46	193	171	15	46	63	9	1	2	28	1	3	2	16	3	30	1	2	3	.368	.333
mirez, Aramis, Augusta	.200	6	23	20	3	4	8	1	0	1	2	0	0	2	1	0	7	0	2	0	.400	.304
mirez, Daniel, Columbia	.231	47	161	143	20	33	41	5	0	1	13	6	0	1	11	0	30	6	4	2	.287	.290
ynor, Mark, Asheville	.304	111	492	428	73	130	167	21	2	4	62	5	6	3	50	0	67	16	10	7	.390	.376
e, Charles, Augusta†	.178	56	210	185	22	33	49	5	1	3	13	0	0	7	18	1	57	4	2	2	.265	.276
ero, Eddie, Piedmont	.270	52	222	196	27	53	83	10	4	4	34	1	4	2	19	4	37	5	3	3	.423	.335
binson, David, Piedmont*	.248	50	163	149	22	37	58	8	2	3	13	0	0	2	12	0	34	5	3	3	.389	.313
driguez, Liu, Hickory†	.249	122	509	430	57	107	125	18	0	0	30	8	2	9	60	2	77	15	14	3	.291	.351
driguez, Luis, Hagerstown	.207	79	287	256	19	53	66	8	1	1	25	5	1	1	24	0	58	6	4	3	.258	.277
as, Christian, Cha. (W.Va.)	.218	129	529	468	71	102	171	27	3	12	70	1	9	5	46	2	147	6	9	8	.365	.290
mero, Marty, Hickory*	.111	5	19	18	2	2	2	0	0	0	1	0	0	0	1	0	4	0	0	1	.111	.158
ney, Chad, Savannah	.341	24	47	41	3	14	16	2	0	0	4	1	0	0	5	0	6	0	0	1	.390	.413
sado, Luis, Greensboro	.250	7	14	12	2	3	3	0	0	0	0	0	0	1	1	0	6	0	0	0	.250	.357
ss, Jason, Macon	.158	5	21	19	2	3	6	0	0	1	3	0	0	0	2	0	7	1	0	0	.316	.238
z, Cesar, Fayetteville†	.097	10	34	31	0	3	4	1	0	0	1	0	0	1	2	0	9	1	0	0	.129	.176
st, Brian, Macon	.111	7	11	9	2	1	1	0	0	0	2	0	0	0	2	0	2	0	0	0	.111	.273
fer, Jeffrey, Greensboro	.273	45	167	154	17	42	67	10	3	3	16	1	0	5	7	1	60	0	0	3	.435	.325
muel, Cody, Greensboro	.254	126	523	477	50	121	197	19	0	19	86	0	6	3	37	2	165	0	2	10	.413	.308
chez, Omar, Hagerstown†	.272	80	362	294	59	80	116	13	4	5	25	3	1	7	56	2	56	20	8	1	.395	.399
nderson, David, Columbia*	.213	33	74	61	13	13	20	3	2	0	3	0	0	1	12	1	12	1	2	0	.328	.351
nto, Jose, Cha. (S.C.)	.199	37	152	136	15	27	47	4	2	4	13	2	0	1	13	0	48	3	3	2	.346	.273
sser, Rob, Macon	.262	135	544	465	64	122	187	35	3	8	64	3	6	5	65	4	108	38	8	4	.402	.355
hneider, Brian, Delmarva*	.333	5	11	9	0	3	3	0	0	0	1	0	0	1	1	0	1	0	0	1	.333	.455
reiber, Stan, Augusta	.226	112	436	367	59	83	106	10	5	1	31	8	1	8	52	1	96	20	9	8	.289	.334
hreimann, Eric, Piedmont	.252	91	359	298	44	75	111	13	1	7	33	4	2	26	29	2	66	3	1	1	.372	.366
awab, Chris, Delmarva	.224	119	480	428	52	96	159	30	3	9	64	0	6	1	45	6	135	3	4	9	.371	.296
ott, Thomas, Cha. (W.Va.)	.221	123	507	429	54	95	167	27	6	11	52	5	4	3	66	0	156	19	7	2	.389	.327
utaro, Marcos, Columbus	.251	85	366	315	66	79	127	12	3	10	45	4	5	4	38	0	86	6	3	6	.403	.334
quignol, Fernando, Delmarva†	.239	118	465	410	59	98	146	14	5	8	55	0	1	6	48	4	126	12	13	5	.356	.327
atley, Andy, Hagerstown	.204	60	225	191	24	39	51	3	0	3	24	2	1	3	28	0	65	2	1	4	.267	.314
elton, Barry, Hickory	.211	47	181	161	15	34	52	9	0	3	13	1	1	6	12	0	52	1	2	2	.323	.289
umpert, Derek, Greensboro†	.253	141	601	522	76	132	181	20	10	3	45	4	4	14	57	0	144	28	18	6	.347	.340
npson, Jeramie, Columbia*	.260	58	247	204	31	53	68	2	5	1	25	12	2	8	21	0	45	11	9	1	.333	.349
ella, Steve, Cha. (S.C.)	.157	44	149	127	19	20	32	3	0	3	12	2	0	3	16	0	44	5	1	1	.252	.267
ith, Rod, Greensboro†	.212	132	562	481	71	102	145	15	8	4	32	10	0	7	64	0	128	57	13	5	.301	.313
ead, George, Macon	.250	4	4	4	0	1	1	0	0	0	0	0	0	0	0	0	2	0	0	0	.250	.250
usz, Chris, Piedmont	.091	4	13	11	2	1	1	0	0	0	0	0	0	0	2	0	1	0	1	0	.091	.231
ano, Fausto, Hagerstown	.257	134	617	514	89	132	183	32	5	3	36	3	4	7	89	2	72	35	25	8	.356	.371
g, Jay, Cha. (W.Va.)*	.247	72	310	275	30	68	78	7	0	1	27	2	1	5	27	0	70	3	6	4	.284	.325
iano, Carlos, Columbia	.237	52	198	177	22	42	49	4	0	1	17	1	2	1	17	1	34	5	2	4	.277	.305
sa, Franklin, Fayetteville	.178	34	101	90	6	16	19	3	0	0	4	3	0	0	8	0	17	1	3	1	.211	.245
sa, Juan, Savannah	.254	112	406	370	58	94	140	21	2	7	38	4	1	1	30	2	64	14	12	9	.378	.311
elo, Danilo, Savannah	.211	10	43	38	5	8	14	2	2	0	3	0	0	0	5	0	6	2	0	1	.368	.302
ingfield, Bo, Augusta*	.261	59	212	180	29	47	55	4	2	0	17	2	1	0	29	0	47	6	4	1	.306	.362
nton, Thomas, Columbia†	.667	1	4	3	1	2	2	0	0	0	0	0	0	0	1	0	1	0	0	0	.667	.750
vens, Clayton, Hickory	.212	35	121	113	6	24	36	4	1	2	14	0	1	0	7	0	47	0	1	1	.319	.256
ne, Craig, Hagerstown	.310	56	231	200	36	62	109	17	0	10	35	2	3	6	20	1	59	3	4	2	.545	.384
asser, John, Hickory	.149	41	123	110	10	15	21	3	0	1	8	3	0	8	11	0	24	2	5	3	.208	.283
ckenschneider, Eric, Savannah	.277	140	599	470	111	130	218	28	6	16	63	2	4	12	111	9	96	50	18	4	.464	.424
mberger, Darren, Columbus	.310	129	537	471	77	146	248	30	3	22	89	1	4	7	53	0	72	0	1	13	.527	.385
tor, Reggie, Piedmont*	.263	128	536	499	68	131	163	20	6	0	31	2	3	3	29	0	136	36	17	10	.327	.305
mas, Allen, Hickory*	.250	36	114	100	19	25	34	6	0	1	20	0	2	1	11	0	31	3	0	1	.340	.325
mas, Rod, Cha. (W.Va.)	.206	81	304	257	34	53	76	7	4	4	24	0	0	6	41	0	92	6	5	2	.296	.329
rnhill, Chad, Columbus†	.181	52	194	160	34	29	40	1	2	2	18	1	3	0	30	0	32	1	2	1	.250	.306
py, Joe, Macon*	.271	128	510	439	78	119	169	22	8	4	42	4	4	8	55	7	48	47	20	6	.385	.360
io, Jason, Greensboro	.191	67	218	199	19	38	57	10	0	3	17	5	1	4	9	0	62	2	1	3	.286	.239
ker, Jon, Savannah*	.319	14	56	47	8	15	22	2	1	1	12	1	1	1	6	0	7	1	0	2	.468	.400
ng, Ben, Macon*	.227	119	370	330	36	75	91	12	2	0	19	11	2	5	22	0	68	16	5	7	.276	.284
era, Willy, Columbus	.214	116	420	393	47	84	116	16	2	4	34	2	3	3	19	0	88	11	7	9	.295	.254

CLASS A South Atlantic League

Player, Team	Avg.	G	TPA	AB	R	H	TB	2B	3B	HR	RBI	SH	SF	HP	BB	IBB	SO	SB	CS	GDP	Slg.
Valera, Yohanny, Columbia	.212	108	410	372	38	79	115	18	0	6	38	1	7	13	17	3	78	2	4	9	.309
Velazquez, Jose, Greensboro*	.246	116	461	415	55	102	141	17	2	6	43	2	6	2	36	1	75	4	2	8	.340
Vickers, Randy, Columbia	.188	4	16	16	1	3	3	0	0	0	0	0	0	0	0	0	5	0	0	0	.188
Vopata, Nate, Cha. (S.C.)*	.251	129	549	506	70	127	188	19	9	8	55	0	3	2	38	3	105	13	10	2	.372
Walker, Morgan, Augusta	.300	68	275	253	28	76	117	15	1	8	50	0	2	2	18	1	57	5	1	7	.462
Ward, Chris, Cha. (W.Va.)	.138	34	118	109	5	15	20	5	0	0	7	2	0	3	4	0	44	0	0	1	.183
Warner, Bryan, Columbus*	.265	81	353	328	38	87	113	14	0	4	34	0	5	1	19	1	44	7	4	8	.345
Weaver, Scott, Fayetteville*	.235	115	501	430	68	101	127	20	0	2	43	4	2	5	60	0	59	28	20	9	.295
Weekley, Jason, Savannah	.000	1	5	4	0	0	0	0	0	0	0	0	0	0	1	1	0	0	0	0	.000
Whipple, Boomer, Augusta	.236	128	540	444	75	105	134	23	0	2	45	9	3	12	72	2	58	8	7	18	.302
Whitaker, Chad, Columbus*	.235	66	261	234	32	55	103	10	1	12	29	0	1	1	25	1	80	2	2	4	.440
Whitley, Matt, Asheville	.255	104	426	368	40	94	108	12	1	0	33	7	2	5	44	0	38	10	14	6	.293
Whitlock, Mike, Hagerstown*	.252	131	549	442	72	107	191	22	1	20	91	0	6	11	108	8	132	1	4	7	.450
Williams, Glenn, Macon†	.193	51	204	181	14	35	57	7	3	3	18	1	2	2	18	2	47	4	2	3	.315
Williams, Ricky, Piedmont	.188	84	288	266	30	50	69	4	3	3	20	2	0	2	18	1	87	17	8	2	.259
Wilson, Brian, Cha. (W.Va.)	.205	101	360	303	31	62	76	11	0	1	25	8	5	2	42	1	89	10	8	3	.251
Wilson, Craig, Hagerstown	.261	131	541	495	66	129	199	27	5	11	70	0	4	10	32	1	120	17	11	12	.402
Woodward, Chris, Hagerstown	.224	123	484	424	41	95	126	24	2	1	48	7	5	5	43	1	70	11	3	3	.297
Zamora, Junior, Columbia	.000	1	4	4	0	0	0	0	0	0	0	0	0	0	0	0	3	0	0	0	.000
Zaun, Brian, Savannah	.204	52	160	147	14	30	35	5	0	0	11	0	0	6	7	1	41	1	0	3	.238
Zywica, Michael, Cha. (S.C.)	.134	20	75	67	5	9	18	1	1	2	4	0	0	1	7	0	13	3	1	2	.269

GRAND SLAMS: Cabrera, Seguignol, 2 each; Anderson, Branyan, R. Brown, Budinski, Camilli, Daugherty, DelaCruz, Donati, Drizos, Fauske, Fernandez, A. Ga... Hodges, Janke, Kehoe, D. Olson, Petrick, Raynor, R. Smith, Stumberger, Y. Valera, Wilson, 1 each.

AWARDED FIRST BASE ON CATCHER'S INTERFERENCE: Cunningham 3 (Emmons, C. King, Pinto); C. Bryant 2 (Pierce, C. Wilson); Elam 2 (W. Gonzalez, P... Erickson (C. McCormick); W. Gonzalez (R. Gonzalez); Flanigan (Downs); Groseclose (Emmons); C. Lee (Barrett); Macias (Morales); Mason (Cardona); O. San... (Petrick); Peck (Pinto); Smella (Lunar); Stumberger (W. Gonzalez).

1996 PITCHING

TEAM

Team	W	L	Pct.	ERA	G	CG	ShO	Sv.	IP	H	TBF	R	ER	HR	SH	SF	HB	BB	IBB	SO	WP
Columbia	82	57	.590	2.77	139	16	18	33	1201.0	916	4886	451	370	79	32	17	46	416	9	1168	64
Delmarva	83	59	.585	2.85	142	14	17	38	1243.0	1031	5189	534	393	82	35	36	88	441	2	1101	107
Asheville	84	52	.618	3.14	136	6	11	41	1214.0	1039	5079	526	423	76	40	29	60	461	25	1131	74
Fayetteville	76	63	.547	3.20	139	8	7	46	1235.2	1067	5280	582	439	55	39	30	83	511	14	1162	101
Piedmont	72	66	.522	3.50	138	10	12	34	1219.0	1108	5103	561	474	70	39	36	54	387	17	1088	94
Hagerstown	70	71	.496	3.50	141	15	13	28	1220.0	1095	5232	602	475	60	40	35	92	540	7	1072	113
Augusta	71	70	.504	3.54	141	7	10	43	1232.2	1197	5291	605	485	70	50	37	87	386	16	1106	98
Savannah	72	69	.511	3.64	141	7	9	42	1241.1	1046	5336	637	502	93	41	29	71	567	20	1229	126
Columbus	79	63	.556	3.71	142	7	4	37	1218.2	1142	5188	610	503	96	50	38	59	449	27	982	95
Charleston (S.C.)	63	78	.447	3.89	141	20	11	32	1193.0	1093	5133	649	515	85	45	40	70	501	19	958	139
Charleston (W.Va.)	58	84	.408	3.92	142	3	8	34	1224.1	1194	5339	674	533	50	45	45	65	518	29	954	92
Hickory	55	85	.393	4.09	140	8	5	29	1244.2	1282	5422	714	566	112	46	38	73	447	13	962	77
Greensboro	56	86	.394	4.17	142	4	5	30	1246.0	1150	5548	725	577	72	47	48	82	667	35	1080	141
Macon	61	79	.436	4.31	140	5	9	29	1208.1	1147	5384	742	579	87	31	54	70	630	30	1077	117

INDIVIDUAL

TOP QUALIFIERS FOR EARNED-RUN AVERAGE TITLE

Minimum 114 innings. *Lefthanded pitcher.

Pitcher, Team	W	L	Pct.	ERA	G	GS	CG	ShO	GF	Sv.	IP	H	TBF	R	ER	HR	SH	SF	HB	BB	IBB	SO	WP
Figueroa, Nelson, Columbia	14	7	.667	2.04	26	25	8	4	1	0	185.1	119	723	55	42	10	3	2	2	58	1	200	9
Knoll, Randy, Piedmont	10	7	.588	2.09	22	22	3	3	0	0	151.0	111	592	48	35	7	4	5	6	31	0	144	20
McEntire, Ethan, Columbia*	9	6	.600	2.22	27	27	1	1	0	0	174.0	123	689	51	43	10	2	4	61	0	190	6
Trumpour, Andy, Columbia	10	4	.714	2.29	26	18	4	2	3	1	133.2	91	527	47	34	8	2	2	10	37	0	105	7
Sanders, Frankie, Columbus	9	3	.750	2.52	22	22	0	0	0	0	121.1	103	508	52	34	8	3	2	6	37	1	109	13
Kolb, Danny, Cha. (S.C.)	8	6	.571	2.57	20	20	4	2	0	0	126.0	80	514	50	36	5	6	0	6	60	2	127	22
Bruner, Clayton, Fayetteville	14	5	.737	2.59	27	26	0	0	1	0	156.2	124	669	64	45	6	3	2	4	77	0	152	13
Melendez, David, Fayetteville	11	4	.733	2.62	27	21	1	0	2	0	130.2	114	549	56	38	7	4	2	16	40	1	121	8
Vazquez, Javier, Delmarva	14	3	.824	2.68	27	27	1	0	0	0	164.1	138	668	64	49	12	1	1	7	57	0	173	12
Randall, Scott, Asheville	14	4	.778	2.74	24	24	1	1	0	0	154.1	121	615	53	47	11	5	1	7	50	3	136	4
Baker, Jason, Delmarva	9	7	.563	2.81	27	27	0	0	0	0	160.1	127	688	70	50	6	3	16	77	0	147	22
Mattes, Troy, Delmarva	10	9	.526	2.86	27	27	5	3	0	0	173.1	142	714	77	55	14	6	4	14	50	0	151	17
Powell, Jeremy, Delmarva	12	9	.571	3.03	27	27	1	0	0	0	157.2	127	665	68	53	9	1	6	15	66	0	109	11
Hernandez, Elvin, Delmarva	17	5	.773	3.14	27	27	2	1	0	0	157.2	140	624	60	55	13	0	2	5	16	2	171	7
Johnson, Mike, Hagerstown	11	8	.579	3.15	29	23	5	3	1	0	162.2	157	671	74	57	6	5	5	8	39	0	155	12

DEPARTMENTAL LEADERS: W—Hernandez, 17; L—M. Nunez, 16; Pct.—Vazquez, .824; G—Corey, 60; GS—D'Alessandro, Crowell, Kershner, Coggin, Atkins... each; CG—Figueroa, 8; ShO—Figueroa, 4; GF—Corey, 53; Sv.—Corey, 34; IP—Figueroa, 185.1; H—Mudd, 196; TBF—Mudd, 775; R—Blythe, 98; ER—Coggin... HR—Atkins, 19; SH—Riedling, 10; SF—Dempster, M. Nunez, 9 each; HB—J. Baker, Melendez, 16 each; BB—Blythe, 107; IBB—Kahlon, 8; SO—Figueroa, 200; W... Kolb, Ja. Baker, Hartshorn, 22 each; Bk.—Melendez, 8.

ALL PITCHERS

*Lefthanded pitcher.

Pitcher, Team	W	L	Pct.	ERA	G	GS	CG	ShO	GF	Sv.	IP	H	TBF	R	ER	HR	SH	SF	HB	BB	IBB	SO	WP
Abreu, Winston, Macon	4	3	.571	3.00	12	12	0	0	0	0	60.0	51	247	29	20	4	1	0	1	25	1	60	3
Acosta, Ed, Delmarva	0	0	.000	9.00	1	0	0	0	1	1	1.0	1	6	1	1	0	0	0	0	2	0	1	0
Adge, Jason, Columbus	0	4	.000	6.85	16	0	0	0	10	0	23.2	37	118	23	18	2	2	1	0	11	3	21	2

CLASS A South Atlantic League

itcher, Team	W	L	Pct.	ERA	G	GS	CG	ShO	GF	Sv.	IP	H	TBF	R	ER	HR	SH	SF	HB	BB	IBB	SO	WP	Bk.
len, Craig, Savannah	0	0	.000	2.45	1	1	0	0	0	0	3.2	4	18	4	1	2	0	0	0	3	0	2	1	0
ntonini, Adrian, Piedmont	0	1	.000	6.75	2	2	0	0	0	0	8.0	12	37	6	6	1	0	0	2	4	0	10	1	0
rroyo, Bronson, Augusta	8	6	.571	3.52	26	26	0	0	0	0	135.2	123	562	64	53	11	9	1	7	36	0	107	10	0
chley, Justin, Cha. (W.Va.)*	3	3	.500	3.46	17	16	0	0	1	1	91.0	98	392	42	35	7	4	2	1	23	0	78	0	1
kins, Dannon, Columbus	11	10	.524	3.93	28	28	2	2	0	0	169.2	156	712	85	74	19	5	3	6	64	0	129	10	1
yers, Mike, Augusta*	3	0	1.000	4.15	27	0	0	0	7	0	30.1	33	134	21	14	1	2	2	0	8	0	31	4	0
abineaux, Darrin, Savannah	5	5	.500	4.82	13	12	1	0	0	0	71.0	70	307	45	38	6	1	3	1	30	1	48	6	2
ackowski, Lance, Savannah	0	0	.000	0.00	1	0	0	0	1	0	1.0	0	3	0	0	0	0	0	0	0	0	3	0	0
ailey, Ben, Cha. (W.Va.)	3	7	.300	3.86	11	11	0	0	0	0	63.0	58	268	33	27	2	3	1	4	25	2	66	2	3
aker, Jason, Delmarva	9	7	.563	2.81	27	27	2	0	0	0	160.1	127	688	70	50	6	3	3	16	77	0	147	22	0
ales, Joseph, Hickory	1	1	.500	8.35	15	2	0	0	6	0	32.1	45	166	35	30	5	0	0	0	29	0	24	2	0
arbao, Joe, Piedmont	2	0	1.000	1.06	17	0	0	0	4	0	34.0	30	137	7	4	1	0	0	1	8	0	32	4	1
arnes, Keith, Asheville*	4	5	.444	2.96	17	16	1	0	0	0	97.1	83	408	43	32	4	3	2	8	31	1	76	3	0
auer, Chuck, Cha. (S.C.)	2	7	.222	3.83	28	12	2	0	8	4	103.1	108	449	55	44	2	2	1	9	38	1	71	7	1
ecker, Tom, Greensboro	6	9	.400	3.69	40	14	1	0	9	0	127.0	116	558	69	52	7	2	6	3	75	4	97	10	2
ell, Mike, Delmarva*	6	1	.857	1.36	40	0	0	0	15	5	59.2	39	232	13	9	1	6	0	3	18	0	59	1	1
ennett, Jason, Columbus	3	4	.429	3.49	40	0	0	0	17	1	69.2	51	289	31	27	2	3	2	7	25	3	51	8	1
ere, Jason, Hickory	1	0	1.000	0.00	1	1	0	0	0	0	5.0	3	18	0	0	0	0	0	0	0	0	5	1	0
ettencourt, Justin, Fayetteville*	7	11	.389	3.24	26	26	2	0	0	0	153.0	127	646	78	55	8	4	4	13	58	0	148	11	1
evel, Bobby, Asheville*	4	2	.667	3.18	41	0	0	0	10	0	68.0	61	286	25	24	4	3	1	2	30	2	60	6	0
and, Nate, Savannah*	1	0	1.000	1.63	5	5	0	0	0	0	27.2	24	115	8	5	0	0	1	1	10	0	24	2	0
yleven, Todd, Augusta	1	2	.333	3.72	12	0	0	0	4	2	29.0	32	126	15	12	2	0	0	2	10	0	27	1	0
ythe, Billy, Macon	4	12	.250	5.36	26	26	0	0	0	0	122.2	128	597	98	73	6	4	7	12	107	0	85	19	0
rkowski, David, Fayetteville	10	10	.500	3.33	27	27	5	0	0	0	178.1	158	739	85	66	7	4	5	15	54	0	117	12	3
st, Heath, Asheville	5	2	.714	1.30	41	0	0	0	29	15	76.0	45	293	13	11	3	6	0	1	19	5	102	2	0
acho, Alejandro, Greensboro*	4	4	.500	3.80	34	5	0	0	9	1	92.1	95	395	47	39	7	4	1	4	34	4	70	10	2
adford, Chad, Hickory	0	2	.000	0.90	28	0	0	0	27	18	30.0	21	121	7	3	1	2	1	3	7	1	27	0	0
ooks, Antone, Macon*	9	4	.692	2.24	43	0	0	0	26	10	80.1	57	334	24	20	5	2	2	5	36	4	101	8	0
own, Charlie, Greensboro	2	2	.500	1.59	23	0	0	0	21	8	28.1	13	114	6	5	1	2	0	2	13	2	33	1	0
uner, Clayton, Fayetteville	14	5	.737	2.59	27	26	0	0	1	0	156.2	124	669	64	45	6	3	2	4	77	0	152	13	0
yant, Adam, Cha. (W.Va.)	1	1	.500	2.12	22	0	0	0	20	7	29.2	22	114	7	7	2	0	1	2	2	0	25	1	0
ckman, Tom, Hickory	0	3	.000	2.57	16	0	0	0	13	1	28.0	36	126	16	8	3	0	2	1	7	0	15	2	2
llock, Derek, Augusta	2	4	.333	2.08	14	8	2	1	0	0	60.2	55	252	18	14	1	4	1	3	16	0	52	3	1
rger, Rob, Piedmont	10	12	.455	3.38	27	26	2	2	1	0	160.0	129	673	74	60	9	5	8	9	61	0	171	7	6
tler, Adam, Macon*	0	1	.000	1.23	12	0	0	0	12	8	14.2	5	53	3	2	1	0	0	1	3	0	23	1	0
lahan, Damon, Cha. (W.Va.)	5	8	.385	5.26	27	19	0	0	4	1	102.2	112	458	66	60	5	3	3	5	39	0	85	11	2
netto, John, Augusta	0	0	.000	0.00	1	0	0	0	1	0	1.0	0	3	0	0	0	0	0	0	0	0	0	0	0
se, Christopher, Macon*	2	4	.333	4.08	23	4	0	0	9	0	53.0	52	240	35	24	2	0	3	2	25	3	36	7	2
nteno, Jose, Delmarva*	1	0	1.000	2.28	11	0	0	0	2	0	23.2	20	95	7	6	1	1	0	2	4	0	22	0	0
antres, Carlos, Hickory	6	7	.462	3.76	18	18	0	0	0	0	119.2	108	497	63	50	10	6	3	1	38	0	93	8	5
arbonneau, Marc, Savannah*	4	6	.400	4.71	25	9	0	0	6	0	80.1	84	353	52	42	6	2	3	3	31	2	82	6	2
ristmas, Maurice, Macon	5	4	.556	4.10	39	1	0	0	14	1	83.1	89	364	45	38	9	2	7	4	21	3	62	4	1
it, Xavier, Delmarva	3	4	.429	3.68	34	0	0	0	14	0	51.1	42	226	31	21	4	2	4	3	20	0	57	4	0
chran, Andrew, Macon*	0	3	.000	4.94	13	0	0	0	6	0	23.2	19	106	16	13	1	1	3	3	14	0	17	4	2
dd, Tim, Cha. (S.C.)	0	0	.000	4.05	3	0	0	0	1	0	6.2	6	29	3	3	1	0	0	0	3	0	10	2	0
ggin, David, Piedmont	9	12	.429	4.31	28	28	3	3	0	0	169.1	156	699	87	81	12	3	3	7	46	1	129	12	1
le, Jason, Delmarva	1	2	.333	1.02	10	0	0	0	2	1	17.2	11	65	4	2	1	1	0	0	1	0	20	1	0
eman, Billy, Greensboro	0	0	.000	4.91	4	0	0	0	1	0	7.1	5	32	4	4	0	0	0	2	3	0	9	2	0
lie, Tim, Augusta	4	2	.667	2.12	24	0	0	0	20	12	29.2	28	124	11	7	1	4	1	0	4	1	20	0	0
menares, Luis, Asheville	2	6	.250	4.43	12	12	1	0	0	0	65.0	58	282	36	32	6	0	4	2	25	1	56	5	7
rba, Lisandro, Macon	0	0	.000	1.80	2	0	0	0	0	0	5.0	3	21	1	1	0	1	0	0	5	0	1	0	1
rdero, Francisco, Fayetteville	0	0	.000	2.57	2	1	0	0	0	0	7.0	2	27	2	2	0	0	0	0	6	0	7	0	0
rey, Bryan, Fayetteville	6	4	.600	1.21	60	0	0	0	53	34	82.0	50	315	19	11	2	4	6	2	17	3	101	6	2
ronado, Osvaldo, Columbia	8	10	.444	4.53	32	16	0	0	9	1	111.1	120	479	68	56	12	5	1	1	28	1	96	6	1
rral, Ruben, Hagerstown	1	5	.167	5.53	14	4	0	0	3	1	42.1	52	196	32	26	3	4	0	3	21	1	36	0	0
well, Jim, Columbus*	7	10	.412	4.14	28	28	3	0	0	0	165.1	163	710	89	76	16	9	5	9	69	0	104	12	0
wther, John, Hagerstown	2	3	.400	3.22	41	0	0	0	25	10	67.0	59	304	33	24	2	2	1	7	43	3	61	14	2
z, Charlie, Macon*	5	4	.556	3.72	35	0	0	0	18	4	77.1	70	338	40	32	8	5	1	5	34	3	89	4	1
shman, Dwayne, Cha. (W.Va.)	3	5	.375	2.10	55	0	0	0	39	15	73.0	70	308	29	17	2	4	2	6	13	3	57	0	0
lessandro, Marc, Asheville*	7	13	.350	3.52	28	28	1	0	0	0	158.1	182	694	92	62	12	6	7	8	56	1	118	8	0
ton, Brian, Fayetteville	0	0	.000	1.00	7	0	0	0	2	0	9.0	5	36	2	1	0	0	0	0	5	0	7	1	0
iels, David, Augusta	0	1	.000	5.11	11	0	0	0	7	3	12.1	21	58	8	7	0	1	0	0	3	1	14	0	1
win, David, Fayetteville*	5	2	.714	3.20	17	9	0	0	0	0	59.0	54	234	22	21	2	0	1	2	12	1	49	5	3
gherty, Keith, Macon	0	0	.000	0.00	4	0	0	0	4	0	5.0	0	17	0	0	0	0	0	0	0	0	2	1	0
vey, Tom, Hagerstown	10	9	.526	3.87	26	26	2	1	0	0	155.2	132	675	76	67	7	5	5	15	91	0	98	15	1
vis, Jason, Piedmont*	6	1	.857	1.82	19	0	0	0	10	2	24.2	16	100	6	5	1	0	2	4	5	1	22	1	1
vis, John, Savannah	9	5	.643	2.74	38	10	2	0	8	1	111.2	72	461	39	34	7	4	1	10	58	3	123	16	2
is, Lance, Cha. (W.Va.)*	1	0	1.000	2.45	4	0	0	0	2	0	3.2	4	17	1	1	1	0	0	0	2	0	5	0	0
gado, Ernie, Hagerstown	4	7	.364	3.59	35	2	0	0	16	2	85.1	89	386	50	34	2	5	3	7	45	1	70	12	2
ossantos, Luis, Greensboro	4	1	.800	4.83	7	6	0	0	0	0	31.2	39	141	17	17	4	0	1	0	11	0	21	0	0
norejon, Pedro, Hickory	1	2	.333	4.43	17	1	0	0	6	0	42.2	45	193	26	21	5	1	1	5	22	0	34	4	3
npster, Ryan, Cha. (S.C.)	7	11	.389	3.30	23	23	2	0	0	0	144.1	120	603	71	53	13	6	9	6	58	1	141	17	5
chenes, Marc, Columbus	5	2	.714	3.40	16	16	0	0	0	0	76.2	70	343	38	29	9	1	3	1	41	0	67	6	0
Witt, Chris, Columbia	3	0	1.000	2.35	13	0	0	0	5	1	30.2	22	125	9	8	0	1	0	0	11	2	31	2	1
rich, Jason, Asheville	1	0	1.000	1.46	7	0	0	0	3	1	12.1	7	48	2	2	1	0	0	0	6	0	21	1	0
nan, Roger, Hagerstown	0	0	.000	6.75	2	1	0	0	0	0	4.0	4	19	3	3	0	0	0	1	4	0	4	3	0
el, Octavio, Columbia	11	3	.786	3.59	22	19	0	0	3	0	115.1	89	480	49	46	7	1	4	7	49	0	142	12	4
gherty, Tony, Columbus	3	1	.750	2.94	19	1	0	0	8	2	49.0	30	202	16	16	3	2	2	4	22	0	44	4	1
eger, Mark, Cha. (S.C.)	1	1	.500	4.50	19	0	0	0	8	0	30.0	26	140	23	15	1	0	2	4	18	0	24	7	0
bar, Matt, Greensboro*	1	1	.500	1.93	2	2	0	0	0	0	14.0	6	56	3	3	1	0	0	1	4	0	19	1	0
n, Cordell, Augusta	0	3	.000	12.66	3	3	0	0	0	0	10.2	14	57	15	15	1	1	0	2	9	0	7	0	0
kovic, Peter, Fayetteville*	3	3	.500	4.61	53	0	0	0	19	3	52.2	54	237	35	27	3	4	3	5	16	1	67	6	2
Mike, Fayetteville*	3	1	.750	1.07	27	0	0	0	9	4	50.2	27	206	11	6	0	5	0	2	30	3	58	2	1

Pitcher, Team	W	L	Pct.	ERA	G	GS	CG	ShO	GF	Sv.	IP	H	TBF	R	ER	HR	SH	SF	HB	BB	IBB	SO	WP
Einerston, Darrell, Greensboro	3	9	.250	2.70	48	0	0	0	26	8	70.0	69	306	29	21	1	4	2	2	19	3	48	4
Emiliano, James, Asheville	1	1	.500	9.53	6	0	0	0	4	1	5.2	7	25	6	6	1	0	0	0	2	0	7	1
Engleka, Matt, Fayetteville	0	0	.000	0.00	2	0	0	0	1	0	2.0	4	8	0	0	0	0	0	0	0	0	2	0
Farley, Joe, Hickory*	3	0	1.000	2.10	4	4	0	0	0	0	25.2	21	104	6	6	2	0	0	1	5	0	15	1
Farrow, Jason, Augusta	5	3	.625	2.09	46	0	0	0	14	3	77.1	61	331	26	18	3	4	2	8	34	2	81	7
Figueroa, Nelson, Columbia	14	7	.667	2.04	26	25	8	4	1	0	185.1	119	723	55	42	10	3	2	2	58	1	200	9
Fisher, Ryan, Augusta*	3	1	.750	3.05	14	0	0	0	4	0	20.2	23	95	14	7	3	0	1	2	9	1	16	2
Fitterer, Scott, Hagerstown	1	0	1.000	9.00	2	0	0	0	1	0	3.0	5	14	3	3	0	0	0	0	4	0		
Fleetham, Ben, Delmarva	1	0	1.000	1.37	16	0	0	0	15	13	19.2	9	74	4	3	2	2	0	0	7	0	34	3
Foran, John, Fayetteville	4	7	.364	4.14	35	17	0	0	6	0	111.0	107	485	57	51	6	1	4	3	53	0	82	8
Ford, Ben, Greensboro	2	6	.250	4.26	43	0	0	0	16	2	82.1	75	359	48	39	3	4	1	11	33	6	84	9
Ford, Brian, Piedmont*	1	4	.200	4.66	37	0	0	0	16	1	56.0	73	258	33	29	5	3	3	3	18	3	40	3
France, Aaron, Augusta	2	1	.667	2.52	5	5	0	0	0	0	25.0	23	105	9	7	2	2	0	1	7	0	24	0
Frazier, Harold, Greensboro*	0	0	.000	27.00	2	0	0	0	0	0	0.2	3	6	3	2	0	0	0	0	1	0	0	0
Gagne, Eric, Savannah	7	6	.538	3.28	23	21	1	1	0	0	115.1	94	474	48	42	11	3	2	1	43	1	131	7
Garber, Joel, Hickory*	1	1	.500	4.03	17	1	0	0	4	2	51.1	60	228	26	23	2	2	1	4	16	0	46	2
Garcia, Eddy, Cha. (W.Va.)	7	6	.538	3.03	30	11	1	0	3	1	107.0	91	456	48	36	3	2	5	3	58	1	74	14
Garcia, Jose, Macon	8	8	.500	4.19	32	19	0	0	3	0	122.1	108	527	64	57	10	2	6	1	58	1	109	3
Garrett, Neil, Asheville	12	4	.750	3.59	22	22	1	0	0	0	135.1	131	566	61	54	13	4	2	8	37	3	120	7
Giard, Ken, Macon	1	0	1.000	1.59	5	0	0	0	4	1	5.2	3	20	1	1	0	0	0	1	0	9	0
Giron, Emiliano, Cha. (W.Va.)	1	2	.333	2.76	32	1	0	0	17	5	45.2	33	191	17	14	2	1	2	3	23	1	63	9
Glynn, Ryan, Cha. (S.C.)	8	7	.533	4.54	19	19	2	1	0	0	121.0	118	526	70	61	10	6	6	8	59	2	72	12
Gonzalez, Generoso, Fayetteville .	5	3	.625	3.06	17	0	0	0	6	0	32.1	27	145	17	11	2	1	1	0	23	1	32	4
Gonzalez, Lariel, Asheville	1	1	.500	3.60	35	0	0	0	24	4	45.0	37	208	21	18	2	0	0	1	37	0	53	4
Granger, Greg, Columbus	8	4	.667	3.31	20	12	0	0	3	2	84.1	90	364	42	31	5	3	2	3	28	2	67	6
Gray, Jason, Hickory	3	8	.273	4.59	13	13	1	1	0	0	68.2	67	300	45	35	12	1	2	5	28	0	61	5
Grife, Richard, Columbus	2	4	.333	3.88	36	0	0	0	17	3	58.0	56	249	29	25	1	2	2	5	20	5	42	5
Gulin, Lindsay, Columbia*	7	7	.500	2.64	19	19	1	0	0	0	112.1	88	470	40	33	6	0	2	6	57	0	134	5
Halley, Allen, Hagerstown	1	0	1.000	0.00	2	0	0	0	1	0	4.0	0	15	0	0	0	0	0	0	4	0	6	1
Hamilton, Paul, Piedmont	2	1	.667	9.45	6	2	0	0	2	0	13.1	16	66	15	14	1	0	1	2	9	0	12	1
Handy, Russell, Delmarva	2	3	.400	5.45	24	0	0	0	15	4	38.0	40	187	38	23	2	1	4	3	36	0	28	10
Hartshorn, Tyson, Hagerstown...	5	11	.313	4.59	26	26	1	0	0	0	147.0	153	648	86	75	15	5	6	9	64	1	109	22
Hausman, Isaac, Cha. (S.C.)	0	1	.000	3.00	1	1	1	0	0	0	6.0	3	22	2	2	0	1	0	0	1	0	8	1
Havens, Jeff, Augusta	1	3	.250	3.65	34	1	0	0	11	2	44.1	51	201	22	18	2	0	0	3	12	1	43	3
Hernandez, Elvin, Augusta	17	5	.773	3.14	27	27	2	1	0	0	157.2	140	624	60	55	13	0	2	5	16	2	171	7
Hodges, Randy, Macon	0	0	.000	6.75	4	0	0	0	4	0	4.0	7	23	4	3	0	0	0	2	0	1	0
Horn, Keith, Columbus	5	5	.500	3.91	25	12	0	0	5	0	89.2	80	374	48	39	7	1	3	4	24	2	78	3
Horne, Jeff, Cha. (W.Va.)	0	2	.000	9.00	3	3	0	0	0	0	12.0	18	66	16	12	2	1	1	0	8	0	8	0
Horton, Eric, Piedmont	1	2	.333	4.91	13	1	0	0	4	1	22.0	21	98	14	12	0	0	2	13	0	17	2
Howard, Jamie, Macon	0	4	.000	7.86	8	6	0	0	0	0	26.1	37	135	26	23	4	3	3	4	16	1	11	1
Howatt, Jeff, Columbia	4	4	.500	2.61	37	0	0	0	26	7	69.0	49	278	23	20	5	2	0	2	19	1	61	4
Hritz, Derrick, Columbus*	0	0	.000	11.57	5	0	0	0	2	0	7.0	17	36	9	9	1	0	1	0	0	0	2	0
Hunt, Jon, Hickory*	7	10	.412	3.78	25	25	3	0	0	0	143.0	136	628	85	60	3	2	5	11	70	1	80	13
Iglesias, Mario, Hickory	2	3	.400	4.93	10	5	0	0	2	1	34.2	45	155	19	19	4	0	6	6	0	31	1
Jacobs, Dwayne, Macon	2	7	.222	6.80	26	15	0	0	4	0	82.0	85	409	82	62	2	2	5	11	76	2	76	18
Jacobs, Mike, Macon	0	1	.000	5.26	11	2	0	0	2	0	25.2	31	130	26	15	2	0	2	4	19	1	21	5
Jacobson, Kelton, Fayetteville	0	1	.000	3.12	6	0	0	0	3	0	8.2	7	39	3	3	1	0	0	3	3	0	8	1
Johnson, Jason, Augusta	4	4	.500	3.11	14	14	1	1	0	0	84.0	82	359	40	29	2	5	3	6	25	0	83	5
Johnson, Mike, Hagerstown	11	8	.579	3.15	29	23	5	3	1	0	162.2	157	671	74	57	6	5	5	8	39	0	155	12
Judd, Mike, Green.-Sav.	6	4	.600	2.90	44	8	1	0	33	13	83.2	62	339	35	27	4	4	0	4	23	3	98	11
Kahlon, Bobby, Macon	2	1	.667	3.52	14	0	0	0	12	4	23.0	21	100	10	9	1	2	1	0	10	8	25	1
Kammerer, James, Asheville*	4	2	.667	3.14	9	8	0	0	1	0	43.0	36	181	18	15	0	0	0	1	18	1	44	1
Keehn, Drew, Asheville	3	2	.600	6.05	26	1	0	0	14	0	55.0	61	266	51	37	7	0	2	5	42	2	35	4
Kelly, Jeff, Augusta*	6	3	.667	3.32	14	14	0	0	0	0	84.0	76	360	39	31	4	0	3	15	27	0	68	4
Keppen, Jeff, Savannah	0	1	.000	2.25	12	0	0	0	4	0	20.0	13	100	10	5	0	0	0	5	20	3	26	3
Kershner, Jason, Piedmont*	11	9	.550	3.75	28	28	2	1	0	0	168.0	154	703	81	70	12	5	4	3	59	0	156	12
King, Raymond, Macon*	3	5	.375	2.80	18	10	1	0	2	0	70.2	63	286	34	22	4	0	0	0	20	0	63	2
Knoll, Randy, Piedmont	10	7	.588	2.09	22	22	3	3	0	0	151.0	111	592	48	35	7	4	5	6	31	0	144	20
Kolb, Danny, Cha. (S.C.)	8	6	.571	2.57	20	20	4	2	0	0	126.0	80	514	50	36	5	6	0	6	60	2	127	22
Lail, Denny, Greensboro	1	0	1.000	4.70	11	0	0	0	1	0	23.0	19	100	16	12	2	0	0	2	11	1	24	4
Lakman, Jason, Hickory	0	6	.000	6.79	13	13	0	0	0	0	63.2	66	302	55	48	7	0	1	4	43	0	43	7
Lapka, Rick, Cha. (W.Va.)	4	10	.286	4.78	29	18	0	0	5	0	98.0	101	441	67	52	6	4	6	2	55	2	63	13
Larson, Toby, Columbia	1	0	1.000	1.29	1	1	1	0	0	0	7.0	6	31	1	1	0	0	0	4	0	4	0
LaRue, Shaun, Cha. (W.Va.)	0	0	.000	7.94	4	0	0	0	2	0	5.2	7	27	5	5	0	0	0	2	1	4	0
Lawrence, Clint, Hagerstown*...	3	1	.750	1.98	6	6	0	0	0	0	36.1	26	144	12	8	2	1	2	0	10	0	27	1
Leaman, Jeff, Piedmont	0	2	.000	5.26	19	1	0	0	9	0	37.2	46	162	23	22	2	1	1	0	10	0	21	3
LeBlanc, Eric, Cha. (W.Va.)	1	2	.333	4.97	6	5	0	0	0	0	29.0	33	129	18	16	2	0	2	0	13	0	28	0
Lee, Jeremy, Hagerstown	7	2	.778	2.95	19	12	0	0	3	1	91.2	86	385	38	30	1	3	1	12	24	0	77	6
Leslie, Sean, Delmarva*	1	2	.333	2.63	18	4	1	1	7	0	37.2	25	147	13	11	3	1	1	0	9	0	23	5
Lisio, Joseph, Columbia	2	5	.286	2.03	40	0	0	0	37	18	44.1	40	186	16	10	0	3	2	1	15	1	42	3
Loudermilk, Darren, Columbus ...	0	0	.000	3.00	3	0	0	0	0	0	6.0	5	26	2	2	0	1	0	0	4	2	8	2
Lowe, Ben, Fayetteville*	2	3	.400	3.24	46	1	0	0	34	9	65.2	40	289	24	17	2	2	1	7	52	0	89	2
Lowell, Mike, Greensboro	0	0	.000	0.00	1	0	0	0	1	0	1.0	0	2	0	0	0	0	0	0	0	2	0
Lukasiewicz, Mark, Hagerstown*	2	0	1.000	2.30	9	1	0	0	0	0	15.2	8	63	5	4	0	0	0	1	7	0	20	1
Macca, Christopher, Asheville	1	1	.500	1.07	26	0	0	0	25	15	33.2	18	132	5	4	2	1	0	3	11	1	46	2
MacRae, Scott, Cha. (W.Va.)	8	7	.533	3.35	29	20	1	0	2	0	123.2	118	530	61	46	3	4	3	7	53	0	82	8
Malenfant, Dave, Fayetteville	0	3	.000	5.34	23	0	0	0	9	2	30.1	29	147	26	18	2	1	2	25	1	14	3
Marquez, Robert, Delmarva	1	2	.333	3.66	29	0	0	0	14	1	46.2	44	210	23	19	4	2	5	3	22	0	49	5
Martin, Chandler, Asheville	9	4	.692	2.20	14	14	0	0	0	0	86.0	65	347	26	21	2	1	3	31	0	73	11
Martineau, Brian, Cha. (S.C.)	0	0	.000	0.00	2	0	0	0	2	1	1.2	1	6	0	0	0	0	0	0	1	0
Martinez, Jose, Cha. (S.C.)	1	2	.333	9.86	11	1	0	0	3	0	21.0	34	105	24	23	7	0	1	2	7	1	17	6
Masaoka, Onan, Savannah*	2	5	.286	4.29	13	13	0	0	0	0	65.0	55	283	35	31	7	1	0	6	35	0	80	3
Maskivish, Joe, Augusta	1	4	.200	2.16	50	0	0	0	40	18	50.0	46	217	18	12	0	0	1	4	14	0	58	4

tcher, Team	W	L	Pct.	ERA	G	GS	CG	ShO	GF	Sv.	IP	H	TBF	R	ER	HR	SH	SF	HB	BB	IBB	SO	WP	Bk.
athis, Sammie, Columbus	8	3	.727	4.01	31	4	1	0	10	2	85.1	84	359	43	38	6	6	2	3	31	1	67	7	3
attes, Troy, Delmarva	10	9	.526	2.86	27	27	5	3	0	0	173.1	142	714	77	55	14	6	4	14	50	0	151	17	1
attox, Gene, Cha. (W.Va.)	1	2	.333	6.59	22	0	0	0	10	1	27.1	35	137	22	20	1	1	0	1	18	1	15	1	1
attson, Craig, Augusta	1	2	.333	1.78	18	0	0	0	8	0	25.1	19	105	6	5	2	3	1	1	7	0	18	0	2
cBride, Chris, Hagerstown	5	2	.714	1.69	8	8	3	2	0	0	58.2	42	222	13	11	4	0	2	4	9	0	34	0	0
cDonald, Matt, Savannah*	5	6	.455	4.73	28	13	0	0	7	3	83.2	66	365	56	44	6	4	4	3	50	0	85	6	1
cEntire, Ethan, Columbia*	9	6	.600	2.22	27	27	1	1	0	0	174.0	123	689	51	43	10	2	0	4	61	0	190	6	1
cHugh, Mike, Cha. (S.C.)*	2	5	.286	6.13	43	0	0	0	17	1	54.1	47	276	43	37	4	0	1	11	55	3	52	10	1
ejia, Javier, Piedmont	0	0	.000	6.00	2	0	0	0	2	0	3.0	3	15	2	2	0	0	0	0	3	0	8	0	0
elendez, David, Fayetteville	11	4	.733	2.62	27	21	1	0	2	0	130.2	114	549	56	38	7	4	2	16	40	1	121	7	4
endes, Jaime, Piedmont	3	2	.600	3.21	37	0	0	0	13	3	70.0	78	297	28	25	4	2	0	2	13	5	64	2	1
ensink, Brian, Piedmont	2	1	.667	3.35	6	6	0	0	0	0	37.2	32	155	15	14	2	0	1	0	13	0	27	4	0
errick, Brett, Columbus*	6	2	.750	2.82	44	0	0	0	14	1	54.1	36	224	21	17	2	5	5	3	24	3	51	5	0
eyer, David, Greensboro*	1	0	1.000	0.00	6	0	0	0	3	0	18.2	9	66	0	0	0	1	0	1	1	1	24	0	0
eyer, Travis, Savannah	0	0	.000	18.00	1	0	0	0	1	0	1.0	2	6	2	2	0	0	1	0	1	0	1	0	0
litello, Sam, Greensboro	0	0	.000	8.53	3	3	0	0	0	0	6.1	1	35	7	6	0	2	1	15	0	5	7	0	
tchell, Scott, Delmarva	5	6	.455	2.35	33	5	1	0	10	1	76.2	69	320	29	20	7	3	1	5	24	1	76	3	3
ontgomery, Joe, Cha. (W.Va.)	0	1	.000	4.50	14	0	0	0	2	0	24.0	23	113	17	12	1	0	0	0	19	1	16	0	0
oore, Bobby, Cha. (S.C.)	11	11	.500	4.06	25	25	2	1	0	0	142.0	128	599	82	64	11	8	5	9	45	0	125	6	4
orillo, Donald, Cha. (S.C.)	0	0	.000	9.00	2	0	0	0	1	0	1.0	0	6	1	1	0	0	0	0	3	0	0	4	0
ota, Henry, Cha. (S.C.)	7	5	.583	2.78	32	10	2	1	11	2	97.0	71	384	39	30	8	3	4	2	28	2	68	6	4
odd, Scott, Cha. (S.C.)	12	9	.571	3.51	28	27	5	0	0	0	182.0	196	775	94	71	12	6	5	4	49	1	115	14	3
urphy, Sean, Asheville	9	4	.692	2.71	35	6	0	0	6	2	83.0	58	347	35	25	3	5	2	7	43	2	80	7	2
usslewhite, Jim, Greensboro	2	1	.667	3.15	4	4	0	0	0	0	20.0	26	91	9	7	1	0	1	4	3	0	15	1	0
akashima, Tony, Savannah*	3	2	.600	2.45	27	0	0	0	8	2	36.2	20	150	11	10	2	2	0	0	19	1	39	0	0
son, Ron, Cha. (S.C.)	0	0	.000	4.66	20	1	0	0	10	0	29.0	29	125	17	15	2	1	0	0	18	2	22	7	0
hols, James, Hickory	0	4	.000	2.70	20	1	0	0	11	1	50.0	52	224	30	15	4	3	1	4	18	0	45	5	0
nez, Maximo, Hickory	5	16	.238	4.67	31	24	3	1	3	0	152.1	173	660	93	79	12	3	9	7	45	0	105	5	3
ari, Pete, Piedmont	2	3	.400	3.61	45	0	0	0	38	18	52.1	40	223	27	21	3	2	1	2	21	2	67	7	2
hsenfeld, Christopher, Savnh*	6	7	.462	4.19	26	18	0	0	3	1	109.2	118	487	66	51	7	4	5	8	52	0	79	17	3
conner, Brian, Augusta*	0	1	.000	3.06	19	0	0	0	5	1	35.1	33	147	13	12	2	3	1	1	8	0	37	6	0
da, Erick, Columbia*	3	5	.375	3.99	35	0	0	0	20	4	58.2	55	247	31	26	8	4	1	2	14	2	51	2	1
vier, Rich, Greensboro	3	2	.600	4.24	9	9	0	0	0	0	46.2	51	216	28	22	1	0	2	3	23	0	44	8	0
en, Jason, Hickory	2	1	.667	1.37	4	4	1	0	0	0	26.1	19	101	5	4	1	0	0	0	6	0	32	0	0
on, Phil, Columbia	7	6	.538	2.54	16	13	1	1	0	0	92.0	55	368	34	26	7	4	1	10	32	1	63	6	0
ck, Steve, Columbia	0	0	.000	2.45	6	0	0	0	2	0	7.1	8	29	2	2	0	0	0	2	0	0	8	0	0
ner, Brett, Columbus*	0	2	.000	6.23	5	3	0	0	2	0	13.0	19	65	12	9	2	0	1	0	10	0	14	0	1
otte, Frisco, Greensboro	0	0	.000	2.55	24	0	0	0	9	0	53.0	35	237	24	15	2	1	4	5	35	2	41	6	2
ra, Julio, Savannah	1	1	.500	2.30	12	0	0	0	5	2	15.2	8	59	4	4	2	0	0	1	6	0	19	0	0
ris, Steve, Augusta	0	0	.000	0.00	1	1	0	0	0	0	5.0	1	16	0	0	0	0	0	0	1	0	6	0	0
rsall, J.J., Savannah*	6	5	.545	3.29	45	2	0	0	13	3	87.2	76	394	48	32	6	3	2	7	46	3	88	8	3
usek, William, Fayetteville	0	0	.000	6.55	39	1	0	0	8	1	45.1	51	249	38	33	3	3	0	9	51	1	50	9	0
llips, Jason, Augusta	5	4	.556	2.41	14	14	1	1	0	0	89.2	79	366	35	24	3	2	3	6	29	1	75	9	1
ales, Aquiles, Macon	3	1	.750	5.72	18	0	0	0	6	0	28.1	26	135	23	18	3	0	1	1	21	0	22	4	2
part, Melvin, Columbia	1	0	1.000	2.79	5	1	0	0	1	0	9.2	8	39	3	3	0	0	0	1	3	0	13	0	0
vell, Jeremy, Delmarva	12	9	.571	3.03	27	27	1	0	0	0	157.2	127	665	68	53	9	1	6	15	66	0	109	11	4
ers, Jason, Columbus	5	4	.556	3.61	14	14	1	1	0	0	77.1	84	319	37	31	5	1	3	1	17	0	64	8	1
mirez, Jose, Fayetteville*	1	1	.500	4.15	15	1	0	0	5	0	26.0	35	126	15	12	2	1	0	1	14	1	30	3	0
dall, Scott, Asheville	14	4	.778	2.74	24	24	1	1	0	0	154.1	121	615	53	47	11	5	1	7	50	3	136	4	0
dolph, Stephen, Greensboro*	4	7	.364	3.77	32	17	0	0	7	0	100.1	64	451	46	42	8	4	5	5	96	1	111	13	3
d, Jason, Savannah*	0	0	.000	7.15	5	0	0	0	2	0	11.1	14	54	10	9	2	1	0	0	7	0	8	0	0
d, Rayon, Augusta	0	0	.000	2.45	3	0	0	0	0	0	3.2	4	20	5	1	0	0	2	1	4	0	3	0	0
ners, Tom, Hickory	2	2	.500	6.43	14	12	0	0	0	0	56.0	66	259	43	40	6	0	2	6	25	0	55	7	2
es, Jose, Augusta	5	4	.556	6.18	23	8	0	0	2	0	67.0	79	307	51	46	8	2	4	4	30	3	57	6	1
abal, Dan, Savannah	2	4	.333	2.28	40	0	0	0	37	24	55.1	32	225	19	14	4	4	1	5	17	2	78	2	1
dling, John, Cha. (W.Va.)	6	10	.375	3.99	26	26	0	0	0	0	140.0	135	615	85	62	2	10	6	10	66	6	90	6	1
bins, Jake, Greensboro	1	8	.111	6.45	18	12	0	0	2	0	74.0	80	349	59	53	5	4	5	7	49	0	50	10	4
erts, Mark, Hickory	4	6	.400	4.88	13	13	0	0	0	0	72.0	70	298	42	39	12	3	2	3	19	0	62	4	3
erts, Randolph, Cha. (W.Va.)	0	2	.000	9.00	5	1	0	0	2	0	10.0	20	65	18	10	0	0	1	0	14	0	7	4	1
inson, Martin, Greensboro*	1	8	.111	5.73	10	10	1	0	0	0	48.2	60	232	43	31	1	2	1	3	30	1	38	5	3
ker, John, Macon*	5	3	.625	3.89	20	19	2	2	1	0	106.1	85	453	60	46	7	1	4	6	63	1	107	12	3
e, Brian, Asheville	4	5	.444	3.56	38	1	0	0	14	3	68.1	53	273	30	27	4	6	5	3	16	2	73	4	1
z, Rafael, Hickory*	1	2	.333	3.35	34	0	0	0	9	0	51.0	58	228	32	19	4	1	2	0	13	0	52	0	0
ion, Jeff, Cha. (S.C.)	0	1	.000	3.75	5	1	0	0	2	1	12.0	13	52	5	5	0	0	1	0	5	0	9	0	0
yan, Paul, Cha. (W.Va.)	7	5	.583	3.83	29	7	0	0	7	2	80.0	81	339	47	34	3	3	3	8	19	1	41	9	0
chez, Martin, Macon	5	5	.500	3.97	31	13	0	0	6	1	106.2	109	483	60	47	8	3	4	4	53	1	92	13	0
ders, Frankie, Columbus	9	3	.750	2.52	22	22	0	0	0	0	121.1	103	508	52	34	8	3	2	6	37	1	109	13	4
amaria, Bill, Columbia	2	0	1.000	3.58	31	0	0	0	16	2	50.1	43	215	22	20	6	5	2	0	26	1	28	2	0
get, Rich, Hickory	2	1	.667	3.99	25	0	0	0	13	1	47.1	48	202	24	21	5	6	1	2	9	1	39	2	3
affner, Eric, Greensboro	3	7	.300	5.03	27	12	0	0	4	0	91.1	97	427	65	51	4	2	4	3	62	2	62	15	4
mack, Brian, Hickory	6	4	.600	2.31	43	0	0	0	25	5	62.1	61	264	24	16	4	9	0	4	16	5	56	3	1
roeffel, Scott, Asheville	1	0	1.000	3.86	2	0	0	0	0	0	11.2	10	52	7	5	0	3	1	6	1	0	15	4	0
by, Anthony, Greensboro*	2	1	.667	1.38	16	0	0	0	6	1	26.0	16	105	5	4	0	1	2	10	2	25	1	0	
maker, Anthony, Piedmont*	3	0	1.000	1.38	20	0	0	0	13	4	32.2	16	120	7	5	2	0	0	10	1	51	3	0	
mate, Jacob, Macon	0	0	.000	12.00	1	1	0	0	0	0	3.0	5	16	5	4	0	1	0	2	0	2	1	0	
s, Jason, Piedmont	4	6	.400	5.10	17	17	0	0	0	0	77.2	87	359	60	44	4	5	6	5	41	0	47	8	2
mons, Carlos, Cha. (S.C.)	3	7	.300	5.08	33	1	0	0	17	4	56.2	56	264	43	32	9	2	3	6	33	1	34	5	1
rt, J.D., Delmarva	9	8	.529	3.39	25	25	3	2	0	0	156.2	155	655	75	59	14	2	7	10	31	0	109	8	0
h, Keilan, Hagerstown	2	3	.400	3.72	19	1	0	0	13	2	29.0	32	129	19	12	1	2	0	1	8	1	21	5	1
d, George, Macon	0	1	.000	11.05	3	0	0	0	0	0	7.1	13	37	10	9	2	0	0	0	6	0	4	3	0
h, Carl, Sav.-Aug.	6	6	.500	4.06	34	11	0	0	7	0	102.0	90	447	60	46	8	4	3	4	44	0	93	12	0
ks, Jeff, Cha. (W.Va.)	2	7	.222	4.74	46	3	0	0	14	0	89.1	79	394	51	47	4	4	9	4	46	6	94	10	1
ace, Michael, Greensboro	6	6	.500	3.85	19	19	0	0	0	0	114.2	108	492	66	49	8	5	3	4	38	1	89	7	0

CLASS A South Atlantic League

Pitcher, Team	W	L	Pct.	ERA	G	GS	CG	ShO	GF	Sv.	IP	H	TBF	R	ER	HR	SH	SF	HB	BB	IBB	SO	WP
Spykstra, Dave, Savannah	6	4	.600	3.31	28	14	2	0	5	0	100.2	83	440	47	37	8	2	0	6	44	0	104	19
Stentz, Brent, Fayetteville	7	8	.467	3.49	45	8	0	0	7	2	98.0	91	413	51	38	4	4	1	6	27	1	92	5
Stepka, Tom, Asheville	2	0	1.000	0.56	2	2	1	1	0	0	16.0	6	56	2	1	1	0	0	1	0	0	16	0
Stewart, Stan, Greensboro	3	3	.500	6.16	10	10	1	1	0	0	57.0	64	260	43	39	5	2	6	6	26	2	51	5
Stone, Ricky, Savannah	2	1	.667	3.98	5	5	0	0	0	0	31.2	34	130	15	14	2	2	1	0	9	0	31	5
Taylor, Brien, Greensboro*	0	5	.000	18.73	9	9	0	0	0	0	16.1	21	113	40	34	3	2	3	3	43	0	11	17
Tebbetts, Scott, Piedmont	0	2	.000	13.50	5	0	0	0	1	0	5.1	8	28	9	8	2	1	0	2	2	0	2	0
Thobe, J.J., Columbus	2	0	.000	7.71	2	2	0	0	0	0	7.0	11	36	6	6	0	1	1	0	6	1	4	0
Thompson, Justin, Fayetteville*	0	0	.000	3.00	1	1	0	0	0	0	3.0	1	10	1	1	0	0	0	0	0	0	5	0
Torres, Jackson, Savannah	3	4	.429	4.28	42	0	0	0	20	3	61.0	52	270	39	29	5	3	0	9	29	0	32	4
Trumpour, Andy, Columbia	10	4	.714	2.29	26	18	4	2	3	1	133.2	91	527	47	34	8	2	2	10	37	0	105	7
Vazquez, Javier, Delmarva	14	3	.824	2.68	27	27	1	0	0	0	164.1	138	668	64	49	12	1	1	7	57	0	173	12
Venafro, Mike, Cha. (S.C.)*	1	3	.250	3.51	50	0	0	0	42	19	59.0	57	258	27	23	0	4	2	3	21	3	62	13
Veniard, Jay, Hagerstown*	3	3	.500	4.03	8	8	1	0	0	0	44.2	35	187	28	20	5	0	2	1	24	0	43	2
Verdin, Cesar, Greensboro*	5	2	.714	2.42	14	10	1	0	1	0	67.0	56	286	34	18	5	4	2	7	24	0	71	1
Viegas, Randy, Augusta*	0	0	.000	6.27	13	0	0	0	5	0	18.2	16	88	14	13	0	0	0	3	14	1	15	4
Villegas, Ismael, Macon	3	7	.300	5.00	12	12	2	1	0	0	72.0	80	313	46	40	8	2	4	1	19	1	60	6
Virchis, Adam, Hickory	8	6	.571	3.27	26	3	0	0	13	0	82.2	82	348	38	30	10	7	5	6	25	5	42	3
Volkert, Oreste, Hagerstown	1	3	.250	2.84	38	0	0	0	21	2	63.1	53	260	28	20	3	2	3	3	19	0	44	6
Walton, Tim, Piedmont	2	1	.667	1.19	8	5	0	0	1	0	37.2	28	149	7	5	0	0	1	2	14	1	19	3
Wilson, Brian, Cha. (W.Va.)	0	0	.000	0.00	1	0	0	0	1	0	3.0	2	9	0	0	0	0	0	0	0	0	0	0
Winchester, Scott, Columbus	7	3	.700	3.23	52	0	0	0	47	26	61.1	50	254	27	22	8	5	2	5	16	4	60	4
Woodring, Jason, Delmarva	8	3	.727	1.84	46	0	0	0	33	12	58.2	42	237	17	12	2	3	0	7	17	1	43	5
Wright, Scott, Cha. (W.Va.)	5	4	.556	2.70	28	1	1	0	8	1	66.2	54	270	24	20	1	0	1	4	20	4	53	4
Yeager, Gary, Piedmont	5	2	.714	2.68	40	1	0	0	18	6	80.2	73	330	26	24	2	8	1	3	19	3	66	3
Young, Danny, Augusta*	0	4	.000	5.88	22	1	0	0	6	2	33.2	36	171	33	22	1	2	3	3	29	2	36	12
Young, Joe, Hagerstown	9	9	.500	3.84	21	21	3	1	0	0	122.0	101	527	64	52	7	4	4	11	63	0	157	9
Young, Ryan, Augusta	3	12	.200	5.72	21	18	1	0	0	0	96.0	117	438	66	61	8	6	6	10	32	1	48	11

COMBINATION SHUTOUTS: **Asheville (9)**—Garrett-Dietrich-Bost-Emiliano-Macca, D'Alessandro-Gonzalez, Kammerer-Bost, Randall-Gonzalez-Bevel-Keehn, Ra Murphy-Macca, Martin-Macca, Randall-Gonzalez, Garrett-Gonzalez, Barnes-Murphy-Bost. **Augusta (6)**—Arroyo-Havens-Collie-Daniels, Kelly-Daniels-Collie, Arr O'Conner-Collie, Arroyo-Reyes-Farrow-Maskivish, Hernandez-Maskivish, Bullock-Mattson. **Charlestown (S.C.) (6)**—Moore-Draeger, Moore-Draeger-McHugh, M McHugh-Venafro, Dempster-Venafro, Dempster-Venafro, Glynn-Venafro. **Charlestown (W.Va.) (8)**—Riedling-Gargia-Sparks-Cushman, Atchley-LaRue, Bailey-Cush Macrae-Cushman, Macrae-Runyan-Sparks, MacRae-Bryant, Lapka-Write, Lapka-Montgomery-Cushman. **Columbia (10)**—McEntire-Santamaria, McEntire-Oj Figueroa-Dewitt-Lisio, Coronado-Figueroa, McEntire-Dotel, McEntire-Trumpour, Gulin-Howatt-Coronado, Trumpour-Ojeda-Lisio, Gulin-Olson-Lisio, Coron Santamaria-Ojeda. **Columbus (1)**—Atkins-Grife. **Delmarva (11)**—Vazquez-Cole-Leslie, Baker-Mattes-Centeno-Woodring-Fleetham, Powell-Mitchell, Vazquez-Le Baker-Civit, Baker-Bell-Woodring, Baker-Bell-Woodring, Powell-Woodring, Vazquez-Bell, Powell-Bell-Woodring, Baker-Mitchell. **Fayetteville (7)**—Melendez-C Bettencourt-Durkovic-Perusek-Stentz, Melendez-Perusek-Durkovic, Bruner-Stentz-Darwin-Malenfant, Borkowski-Stentz, Bruner-Foran-Perusek-Corey, Bruner-Durk Stentz. **Greensboro (4)**—Robinson-Lail-Judd, Delossantos-Judd, Spence-Ford, Verdin-Coleman. **Hagerstown (6)**—Young-Lowe, Smith-Lowe-Delgado, Lee-L McBride-Lowe, Davey-Lowe, Johnson-Crowther. **Hickory (3)**—Chantres-Buckman, Hunt-Demorejon, Roberts-Schmack. **Macon (6)**—Garcia-Christmas, King-Pina Sanchez, Garcia-Cruz, Sanchez-Jacobs, Garcia-Cruz, Sanchez-Brooks. **Piedmont (3)**—Knoll-Shumaker-Nyari, Knoll-Yeager, Kershner-Burger. **Savannah (8)**—Ga Ochsenfeld, Masaoka-Pearsall-Davis-Ricabal, Babineaux-Ricabal, Gagne-Davis-Nakashima-Spykstra, Davis-McDonald, Davis-Torres, Gagne-Pearsall-McDo Charbonneau-Ricabal, Spykstra-McDonald.

NO-HIT GAMES: Burger, Piedmont, defeated Augusta, 1-0, April 30; Rocker, Macon, defeated Charleston (S.C.), 2-0, June 9; Leslie, Delmarva, defeated Greenst 9-0, June 11; Kolb, Charleston (S.C.), defeated Columbus, 3-0, June 12; Randall, Asheville, defeated Fayetteville, 4-0, July 17.

PITCHERS WITH TWO OR MORE TEAMS

Pitcher, Team	W	L	Pct.	ERA	G	GS	CG	ShO	GF	Sv.	IP	H	TBF	R	ER	HR	SH	SF	HB	BB	IBB	SO	WP
Judd, Mike, Greensboro	2	2	.500	3.81	29	0	0	0	26	10	28.1	22	119	14	12	2	2	0	2	8	3	36	2
Judd, Mike, Savannah	4	2	.667	2.44	15	8	1	0	7	3	55.1	40	220	21	15	2	2	0	2	15	0	62	9
South, Carl, Savannah	6	5	.545	4.13	33	10	0	0	7	0	96.0	85	422	58	44	8	4	4	3	42	4	84	12
South, Carl, Augusta	0	1	.000	3.00	1	1	0	0	0	0	6.0	5	25	2	2	0	0	0	2	0	9	0

1996 FIELDING

TEAM

Team	Pct.	G	PO	A	E	TC	DP	PB	Team	Pct.	G	PO	A	E	TC	DP
Columbia	.968	139	3603	1375	166	5144	85	29	Savannah	.959	141	3724	1461	222	5407	95
Asheville	.967	136	3642	1593	179	5414	127	15	Hickory	.958	140	3734	1530	230	5494	104
Hagerstown	.964	141	3660	1569	194	5423	103	43	Augusta	.958	141	3698	1400	224	5322	88
Piedmont	.964	138	3657	1382	187	5226	86	18	Fayetteville	.958	139	3707	1465	228	5400	95
Columbus	.962	140	3656	1590	207	5453	128	17	Greensboro	.955	142	3738	1564	250	5552	94
Charleston (W.Va.)	.961	142	3673	1454	206	5333	100	28	Macon	.954	140	3625	1437	244	5306	117
Delmarva	.959	142	3729	1433	220	5382	117	24	Charleston (S.C.)	.951	141	3579	1541	262	5382	116

TRIPLE PLAY: Savannah.

INDIVIDUAL

FIRST BASEMEN

NOTE: All caps denotes fielding-percentage leader based on 71 games for catchers, 94 for all other non-pitchers and 142 innings for pitchers. *Throws lefthanded.

Player, Team	Pct.	G	PO	A	E	TC	DP
Bigler, Jeff, Augusta*	.991	39	326	21	3	350	19
Blake, Casey, Hagerstown	1.000	1	2	1	0	3	1
Brumbaugh, Cliff, Cha. (S.C.)	.982	47	401	27	8	436	25
Camfield, Eric, Greensboro*	1.000	1	8	1	0	9	1
Clifford, John, Asheville	.981	19	143	12	3	158	15
Coburn, Todd, Piedmont	.970	21	152	11	5	168	12
Daly, Bob, Columbia	.984	9	57	4	1	62	5

Player, Team	Pct.	G	PO	A	E	TC
Daugherty, Keith, Macon	.988	82	598	45	8	651
Davis, James, Cha. (W.Va.)	.947	3	16	2	1	19
Drizos, Justin, Asheville*	.989	125	1127	77	14	1218
Edmondson, Tracy, Columbia	1.000	1	1	0	0	1
Elliott, Zach, Piedmont	.980	5	43	5	1	49
Engleka, Matt, Fayetteville	.968	13	58	3	2	63
Fauske, Joshua, Hickory	.974	43	350	23	10	383
Foote, Derek, Macon	.979	33	217	12	5	234
Gainey, Bryon, Columbia	.980	108	888	51	19	958
Gallagher, Shawn, Cha. (S.C.)	.983	88	809	24	14	847
Giardi, Mike, Greensboro	1.000	3	43	3	0	46
Glavine, Michael, Columbus*	.958	3	22	1	1	24

er, Team	Pct.	G	PO	A	E	TC	DP
zalez, Mauricio, Columbus	1.000	1	2	0	0	2	0
pton, Mike, Cha. (W.Va.)	.971	5	31	2	1	34	2
non, Brian, Savannah	.984	73	491	46	9	546	39
es, Chris, Hagerstown	1.000	7	35	2	0	37	4
es, Heath, Columbus	1.000	16	120	10	0	130	14
s, Jamie, Macon	.964	24	154	8	6	168	15
te, Jared, Piedmont	.986	91	749	48	11	808	46
son, Anthony, Cha. (W.Va.)	1.000	3	23	1	0	24	0
se, John, Hagerstown	1.000	2	3	1	0	4	0
NCE, Graham, Fayetteville*	.993	131	1132	77	9	1218	75
in, Stephen, Cha. (W.Va.)*	.972	44	355	30	11	396	17
ue, Jason, Cha. (W.Va.)	1.000	2	16	2	0	18	1
nan, Jeff, Piedmont	1.000	7	42	7	0	49	5
Carlos, Hickory	1.000	9	58	4	0	62	6
Manuel, Hickory	.961	19	156	15	7	178	14
ormick, Cody, Greensboro	.750	1	3	0	1	4	0
dez, Sergio, Augusta	.974	11	68	8	2	78	8
er, Travis, Savannah	1.000	5	38	2	0	40	2
rison, Gregory, Savannah*	.975	71	513	44	14	571	33
n, Donald, Delmarva	.985	76	629	41	10	680	61
ons, Jason, Cha. (W.Va.)	.974	17	142	10	4	156	16
erson, Jarrod, Columbia	.995	26	201	14	1	216	12
on, Wilt, Macon	.964	4	26	1	1	28	2
r, Pete, Hickory*	.981	55	486	25	10	521	33
n, Shane, Piedmont	.988	21	162	4	2	168	12
Cesar, Fayetteville	.968	3	30	0	1	31	0
Brian, Macon	.667	1	2	0	1	3	1
r, Jeffrey, Greensboro	.800	1	3	1	1	5	0
uel, Cody, Greensboro	.978	98	852	55	20	927	64
er, Rob, Macon	.979	28	169	19	4	192	21
vab, Chris, Delmarva*	.969	72	560	29	19	608	51
ton, Barry, Hickory	.966	26	191	9	7	207	13
Jay, Cha. (W.Va.)	.997	71	605	39	2	646	48
Franklin, Fayetteville	1.000	3	8	0	0	8	0
Craig, Hagerstown	.993	17	131	15	1	147	8
berger, Darren, Columbus	.988	127	1106	92	14	1212	100
hill, Chad, Columbus	1.000	3	9	2	0	11	0
Jon, Savannah*	1.000	14	118	11	0	129	6
quez, Jose, Greensboro	.992	42	363	15	3	381	19
ta, Nate, Cha. (S.C.)	.986	8	67	5	1	73	9
er, Morgan, Augusta*	.979	47	327	44	8	379	24
ole, Boomer, Augusta	.993	52	419	14	3	436	26
ock, Mike, Hagerstown	.989	126	1049	58	12	1119	74

IPLE PLAY: H. Hayes.

SECOND BASEMEN

er, Team	Pct.	G	PO	A	E	TC	DP
a, Ed, Delmarva	.912	13	15	16	3	34	2
o, Tom, Columbia	.968	69	133	172	10	315	29
wski, Lance, Savannah	.905	18	14	24	4	42	4
en, Doug, Hickory	.960	29	47	48	4	99	10
ger, Butch, Augusta	.927	7	13	25	3	41	5
Adrian, Savannah	.000	1	0	0	1	1	0
Danny, Delmarva	1.000	1	2	2	0	4	1
Domingo, Piedmont	.936	13	19	25	3	47	2
ra, Orlando, Delmarva	.965	64	105	169	10	284	32
ii, Jason, Delmarva	.958	49	93	114	9	216	32
an, Rene, Fayetteville	.923	6	4	8	1	13	2
pcion, David, Cha. (W.Va.)	.931	10	14	13	2	29	2
do, Jose, Macon	.942	84	154	184	21	359	43
s, Les, Greensboro	.982	16	20	36	1	57	3
ndson, Tracy, Columbia	.956	56	86	129	10	225	21
Zach, Piedmont	.958	26	54	60	5	119	8
a, Matt, Fayetteville	.966	38	60	80	5	145	10
on, Corey, Columbia	1.000	4	2	5	0	7	0
Ovidio, Augusta	.962	14	19	32	2	53	6
Apostol, Fayetteville	1.000	1	2	0	0	2	0
lez, Mauricio, Columbus	.973	11	17	19	1	37	6
HART, Steven, Cha. (W.Va.)	.969	114	224	274	16	514	52
close, David, Asheville	.955	71	109	188	14	311	41
s, Randy, Macon	.971	58	102	130	7	239	29
a, Miguel, Fayetteville	.966	67	125	128	9	262	34
illo, Francisco, Cha. (S.C.)	.957	13	24	42	3	69	9
John, Hagerstown	.965	30	53	56	4	113	15
Tyson, Piedmont	.961	27	42	56	4	102	15
y, Steve, Fayetteville	.948	36	63	100	9	172	15
y, Jacques, Fayetteville	1.000	1	1	1	0	2	0
Dwayne, Cha. (W.Va.)	.958	15	34	34	3	71	3
s, Jose, Delmarva	.983	29	52	61	2	115	15
Lamont, Cha. (W.Va.)	.963	4	12	14	1	27	2
e, Chris, Augusta	.965	85	168	218	14	400	45
Cristian, Columbus	.941	31	58	86	9	153	15
Bruce, Columbia	1.000	1	2	4	0	6	0

Player, Team	Pct.	G	PO	A	E	TC	DP
O'Connor, Rich, Piedmont	.950	9	18	20	2	40	3
Ortiz, Asbel, Cha. (S.C.)	.933	67	114	152	19	285	28
Ozuna, Rafael, Savannah	.926	81	142	184	26	352	33
Parsons, Jeff, Columbia	.984	15	24	37	1	62	7
Patellis, Anthony, Cha. (W.Va.)	1.000	2	0	3	0	3	0
Pettiford, Torrey, Piedmont	.975	72	126	151	7	284	25
Rodriguez, Liu, Hickory	.965	91	163	255	15	433	45
Ruiz, Cesar, Fayetteville	1.000	3	3	1	0	4	0
Santo, Jose, Cha. (S.C.)	.944	29	65	102	10	177	21
Sasser, Rob, Macon	1.000	1	1	0	0	1	0
Schreiber, Stan, Augusta	.892	18	33	33	8	74	4
Scutaro, Marcos, Columbus	.963	78	161	207	14	382	45
Smith, Rod, Greensboro	.932	131	246	302	40	588	52
Solano, Fausto, Hagerstown	.964	115	235	295	20	550	53
Sosa, Juan, Savannah	.981	45	88	117	4	209	25
Sotelo, Danilo, Savannah	.982	10	25	31	1	57	4
Strasser, John, Hickory	.970	31	66	65	4	135	14
Thornhill, Chad, Columbus	.966	25	54	58	4	116	14
Utting, Ben, Macon	.912	9	13	18	3	34	2
Vopata, Nate, Cha. (S.C.)	.960	36	55	112	7	174	24
Whipple, Boomer, Augusta	.972	26	42	62	3	107	4
Whitley, Matt, Asheville	.978	69	152	210	8	370	51
Wilson, Brian, Cha. (W.Va.)	1.000	4	10	17	0	27	3

TRIPLE PLAY: Scutaro.

THIRD BASEMEN

Player, Team	Pct.	G	PO	A	E	TC	DP
Acosta, Ed, Delmarva	.813	13	4	9	3	16	0
Antrim, Pat, Greensboro	.800	1	2	2	1	5	0
Arias, Rogelio, Asheville	1.000	1	1	0	0	1	0
Backowski, Lance, Savannah	1.000	4	2	1	0	3	0
Baker, Derek, Cha. (S.C.)	.907	42	25	72	10	107	1
Barrett, Michael, Delmarva	.667	1	0	2	1	3	0
Bearden, Doug, Hickory	.852	6	4	19	4	27	0
Bellenger, Butch, Augusta	1.000	1	0	1	0	1	0
Beltre, Adrian, Savannah	.917	67	55	143	18	216	12
Blake, Casey, Hagerstown	.904	47	31	82	12	125	5
Boyd, Quincy, Columbia	1.000	1	1	0	0	1	0
Branyan, Russell, Columbus	.885	117	82	256	44	382	24
Bravo, Danny, Delmarva	1.000	7	2	6	0	8	0
Brito, Domingo, Piedmont	.800	7	1	7	2	10	0
Brown, Vick, Greensboro	.884	25	19	42	8	69	6
Brumbaugh, Cliff, Cha. (S.C.)	.925	85	80	167	20	267	15
Bryant, Clint, Asheville	.867	67	61	135	30	226	10
Buczkowski, Matt, Piedmont	.571	5	2	6	6	14	0
Capellan, Rene, Fayetteville	.835	55	44	93	27	164	8
Clifford, John, Asheville	1.000	2	1	5	0	6	0
Coburn, Todd, Piedmont	.813	5	2	11	3	16	2
Concepcion, David, Cha. (W.Va.)	.800	8	3	13	4	20	1
Cuevas, Trent, Savannah	.714	3	3	2	2	7	0
Daly, Bob, Columbia	1.000	1	1	3	0	4	0
Daugherty, Keith, Macon	1.000	2	1	2	0	3	0
Edmondson, Tracy, Columbia	.900	25	14	49	7	70	6
Elam, Brett, Delmarva	.909	23	8	42	5	55	2
Elliott, Zach, Piedmont	.9262	96	61	190	20	271	16
Engleka, Matt, Fayetteville	.897	15	9	26	4	39	2
Erickson, Corey, Columbia	.923	57	38	106	12	156	4
Farris, Mark, Augusta	.905	70	45	126	18	189	3
Fernandez, Jose, Delmarva	.907	125	102	239	35	376	23
Frias, Ovidio, Augusta	.930	29	15	38	4	57	3
Giardi, Mike, Greensboro	1.000	3	3	10	0	13	1
Gomez, Paul, Columbia	.800	4	1	7	2	10	0
Hampton, Mike, Cha. (W.Va.)	.899	81	74	167	27	268	12
Hayes, Chris, Hagerstown	.947	28	17	73	5	95	1
Hayes, Heath, Columbus	.880	17	11	33	6	50	3
Hicks, Jamie, Macon	.000	2	0	0	1	1	0
Hodges, Randy, Macon	.850	21	12	22	6	40	1
Kapler, Gabriel, Fayetteville	1.000	1	1	0	0	1	0
Kehoe, John, Hagerstown	.783	10	6	12	5	23	1
Kimm, Tyson, Piedmont	.857	7	3	9	2	14	0
Kopacz, Derek, Hagerstown	.898	45	34	89	14	137	4
Lackey, Steve, Fayetteville	1.000	1	0	4	0	4	0
Landry, Jacques, Fayetteville	.889	31	24	56	10	90	6
Leaman, Jeff, Piedmont	1.000	1	1	2	0	3	0
Lee, Carlos, Hickory	.910	113	91	231	32	354	19
Light, Tal, Asheville	.874	50	24	101	18	143	13
LOWELL, Mike, Greensboro	.9264	112	89	301	31	421	12
Lutz, Manuel, Hickory	.797	17	8	39	12	59	2
Macias, Jose, Delmarva	.850	10	2	15	3	20	1
Nichols, Kevin, Piedmont	.847	22	15	35	9	59	5
O'Connor, Rich, Piedmont	.842	8	6	10	3	19	0
Parra, Jose, Cha. (S.C.)	.750	5	2	4	2	8	0
Patellis, Anthony, Cha. (W.Va.)	.867	52	28	76	16	120	1

Player, Team	Pct.	G	PO	A	E	TC	DP
Ramirez, Aramis, Augusta	.833	6	3	7	2	12	0
Rodriguez, Luis, Hagerstown	1.000	4	0	9	0	9	0
Rosado, Luis, Greensboro	.833	2	2	3	1	6	0
Rust, Brian, Macon	.875	4	3	11	2	16	2
Sasser, Rob, Macon	.868	110	63	233	45	341	23
Schreiber, Stan, Augusta	1.000	3	1	4	0	5	1
Scutaro, Marcos, Columbus	1.000	3	2	7	0	9	0
Shatley, Andy, Hagerstown	.888	59	48	135	23	206	10
Shelton, Barry, Hickory	.941	5	9	7	1	17	0
Snead, George, Macon	1.000	1	1	0	0	1	0
Soriano, Carlos, Columbia	.917	52	34	88	11	133	7
Sosa, Juan, Savannah	.923	31	15	57	6	78	4
Stone, Craig, Hagerstown	.750	1	0	3	1	4	0
Strasser, John, Hickory	.870	9	5	15	3	23	1
Thornhill, Chad, Columbus	.765	7	3	10	4	17	2
Utting, Ben, Macon	.848	20	7	32	7	46	4
Vickers, Randy, Columbia	.714	3	2	3	2	7	0
Vopata, Nate, Cha. (S.C.)	.933	11	14	14	2	30	1
Whipple, Boomer, Augusta	.900	36	24	66	10	100	9
Wilson, Brian, Cha. (W.Va.)	.846	12	8	25	6	39	0
Zamora, Junior, Columbia	1.000	1	0	2	0	2	0
Zaun, Brian, Savannah	.910	52	26	75	10	111	6

SHORTSTOPS

Player, Team	Pct.	G	PO	A	E	TC	DP
Acosta, Ed, Delmarva	1.000	2	0	2	0	2	0
Antrim, Pat, Greensboro	1.000	3	4	3	0	7	2
Azuaje, Jesus, Columbia	.875	1	0	7	1	8	0
Backowski, Lance, Savannah	1.000	2	0	1	0	1	1
Baugh, Darren, Hickory	.937	68	109	188	20	317	32
Bearden, Doug, Hickory	.846	16	18	37	10	65	5
Bravo, Danny, Delmarva	.879	8	12	17	4	33	7
Brito, Domingo, Piedmont	.977	23	29	55	2	86	6
Bryant, Clint, Asheville	1.000	1	1	3	0	4	1
Cabrera, Orlando, Delmarva	.942	67	100	175	17	292	32
Camilli, Jason, Delmarva	.916	69	80	159	22	261	27
Carrion, Jorge, Cha. (S.C.)	.759	6	8	14	7	29	6
Cuevas, Trent, Savannah	.958	9	12	11	1	24	6
Delgado, Jose, Macon	.800	2	3	5	2	10	2
Dennis, Les, Greensboro	1.000	4	1	14	0	15	1
Edmondson, Tracy, Columbia	.914	12	12	20	3	35	1
Elam, Brett, Asheville	.959	103	153	335	21	509	76
Elliott, Zach, Piedmont	1.000	9	8	25	0	33	3
Engleka, Matt, Fayetteville	.950	31	34	80	6	120	17
Frias, Ovidio, Augusta	.886	11	14	17	4	35	2
Garcia, Apostol, Fayetteville	.904	73	103	181	30	314	23
Gonzalez, Mauricio, Columbus	.891	13	14	27	5	46	3
Hermansen, Chad, Augusta	.892	59	71	135	25	231	20
Inzunza, Miguel, Fayetteville	1.000	1	0	2	0	2	0
Jaramillo, Francisco, Cha. (S.C.)	.948	33	38	89	7	134	14
Jimenez, D'Angelo, Greensboro	.922	136	190	400	50	640	55
Klee, Charles, Hickory	.891	37	40	82	15	137	14
Lackey, Steve, Fayetteville	.904	44	44	125	18	187	22
Lewis, Dwayne, Cha. (W.Va.)	.971	8	13	20	1	34	4
Lowell, Mike, Greensboro	.750	1	2	1	1	4	0
Mason, Lamont, Cha. (W.Va.)	.921	57	75	148	19	242	23
Mateo, Jose, Savannah	.920	109	136	256	34	426	38
Miyake, Chris, Augusta	.927	11	11	27	3	41	5
Nolte, Bruce, Columbia	.833	5	3	7	2	12	1
O'Connor, Rich, Piedmont	.833	5	1	4	1	6	0
Ortiz, Asbel, Cha. (S.C.)	.921	8	10	25	3	38	2
Ozuna, Rafael, Savannah	1.000	3	1	3	0	4	1
Parra, Jose, Cha. (S.C.)	.913	28	39	77	11	127	9
Parsons, Jeff, Columbia	.908	34	41	68	11	120	15
Polanco, Enohel, Columbia	.943	92	124	240	22	386	41
RAYNOR, Mark, Piedmont	.965	110	147	291	16	454	37
Rodriguez, Liu, Hickory	.919	33	50	74	11	135	15
Sasser, Rob, Macon	.923	11	14	10	2	26	1
Schreiber, Stan, Augusta	.918	68	102	166	24	292	25
Scutaro, Marcos, Columbus	.850	5	6	11	3	20	4
Solano, Fausto, Hagerstown	.909	20	26	54	8	88	8
Sosa, Juan, Savannah	.911	41	36	87	12	135	11
Thornhill, Chad, Columbus	.971	17	16	50	2	68	6
Utting, Ben, Macon	.917	88	99	220	29	348	34
Valera, Willy, Columbus	.943	113	179	333	31	543	66
Vopata, Nate, Cha. (S.C.)	.935	75	104	241	24	369	41
Whitley, Matt, Asheville	.913	37	59	109	16	184	14
Williams, Glenn, Macon	.931	51	73	129	15	217	31
Wilson, Brian, Cha. (W.Va.)	.924	85	141	222	30	393	36
Woodward, Chris, Hagerstown	.951	123	214	366	30	610	60

TRIPLE PLAY: Valera.

OUTFIELDERS

Player, Team	Pct.	G	PO	A	E	TC
Acosta, Ed, Delmarva	1.000	3	2	0	0	2
Adolfo, Carlos, Delmarva	.973	126	200	13	6	219
Alamo, Efrain, Asheville	.983	62	112	7	2	121
Albert, Rashad, Hickory	.947	46	82	8	5	95
Anderson, Milt, Columbus	.952	73	114	6	6	126
Barker, Glen, Fayetteville	.989	36	91	3	1	95
Bass, Jayson, Fayetteville*	.959	84	133	6	6	145
Bass, Jayson, Macon	1.000	5	8	0	0	8
Bates, Fletcher, Columbia	.968	132	229	11	8	248
Black, Brandon, Columbia	.842	13	16	0	3	19
Blakeney, Mo, Delmarva	.962	35	50	0	2	52
Brock, Tarrik, Fayetteville*	.962	32	49	1	2	52
Brown, Roosevelt, Macon	.930	83	154	6	12	172
Budzinski, Mark, Columbus*	.985	65	125	3	2	130
Camfield, Eric, Greensboro*	.973	67	104	6	3	113
Christensen, McKay, Hickory*	1.000	5	4	0	0	4
Christmas, Maurice, Macon	1.000	2	1	0	0	1
CLAYBROOK, Steve, Cha. (W.Va.)	.996	117	233	8	1	242
Clifford, John, Asheville	1.000	31	37	5	0	42
Cornelius, Jonathon, Piedmont	.968	97	201	9	7	217
Crane, Todd, Piedmont	1.000	2	2	0	0	2
Cruz, Charlie, Macon*	1.000	4	2	0	0	2
Cunningham, Earl, Asheville	1.000	3	1	0	0	1
Daugherty, Keith, Macon	1.000	2	3	0	0	3
DelaCruz, Carlos, Fayetteville	.915	77	114	5	11	130
Delafield, Wil, Greensboro	1.000	29	52	4	0	56
Denning, Wes, Delmarva	.984	112	238	3	4	245
Dennis, Les, Greensboro	1.000	4	4	1	0	5
DeLaRosa, Miguel, Cha. (S.C.)	.914	21	29	3	3	35
Duverge, Salvador, Asheville	.958	96	123	13	6	142
Edwards, Aaron, Augusta	.988	35	78	1	1	80
Engleka, Matt, Fayetteville	1.000	5	1	0	0	1
Farner, Matt, Hagerstown*	.889	11	14	2	2	18
Feuerstein, David, Asheville	.990	128	189	6	2	197
Garcia, Luis, Hickory	.968	57	83	7	3	93
Garcia, Miguel, Savannah	.967	11	27	2	1	30
Giardi, Mike, Greensboro	.923	13	11	1	1	13
Gomez, Ramon, Hickory	.972	111	274	8	8	290
Gonzalez, Manuel, Savannah	.985	39	63	3	1	67
Gordon, Herman, Hagerstown	.985	40	62	2	1	65
Hairston, John, Greensboro	.901	56	86	5	10	101
Hallead, John, Asheville*	1.000	34	57	0	0	57
Hampton, Mike, Cha. (W.Va.)	.948	30	53	2	3	58
Hampton, Robby, Hagerstown	.932	19	38	3	3	44
Hayes, Chris, Hagerstown	.962	57	92	10	4	106
Hayes, Heath, Columbus	1.000	3	1	0	0	1
Hernaiz, Juan, Savannah	.977	123	201	13	5	219
Hicks, Jamie, Macon	.842	8	16	0	3	19
Hodges, Randy, Macon	1.000	9	7	0	0	7
Hollins, Darontaye, Hickory	.947	34	51	3	3	57
Inglin, Jeff, Hickory	1.000	16	32	3	0	35
Ingram, Darron, Cha. (W.Va.)	1.000	3	4	0	0	4
Johnson, Damon, Hagerstown	.939	41	39	7	3	49
Johnson, Jason, Cha. (S.C.)	.923	93	137	6	12	155
Kapler, Gabriel, Fayetteville	.967	129	194	14	7	215
Kehoe, John, Hagerstown	.978	66	83	8	2	93
Kennedy, Justin, Piedmont*	.900	15	26	1	3	30
Langaigne, Selwyn, Hagerstown*	1.000	4	9	1	0	10
Larkin, Stephen, Cha. (W.Va.)*	1.000	2	3	1	0	4
Lewis, Andreaus, Columbus	.875	7	7	0	1	8
Lewis, Marc, Macon	.965	64	102	7	4	113
Lombard, George, Macon	.971	108	229	2	7	238
Long, Terrence, Columbia*	.981	119	246	8	5	259
Macias, Jose, Delmarva	.977	71	125	4	3	132
Mateo, Ruben, Cha. (S.C.)	.970	127	215	15	7	237
May, Freddy, Augusta*	.962	122	250	6	10	266
McClure, Craig, Hickory	.966	43	81	4	3	88
McCormick, Andrew, Hagerstown	.950	33	55	2	3	60
Mendoza, Carlos, Columbia*	.968	47	54	6	2	62
Minici, Jason, Columbus	.971	81	129	5	4	138
Monroe, Craig, Cha. (S.C.)	.954	44	76	7	4	87
Morenz, Shea, Greensboro	.968	91	142	10	5	157
Morgan, Scott, Columbus	.966	72	106	6	4	116
Moultrie, Pat, Hagerstown*	.985	39	64	2	1	67
Neubart, Garrett, Asheville	.981	66	96	7	2	105
Nunez, Juan, Cha. (S.C.)	.960	83	158	8	7	173
Olson, Dan, Hickory*	1.000	49	82	3	0	85
Paul, Josh, Hickory	1.000	21	43	1	0	44
Peck, Thomas, Hagerstown	1.000	10	14	0	0	14
Pena, Alex, Augusta	.944	50	75	10	5	90
Pendergrass, Tyrone, Macon	.975	12	38	1	1	40

Player, Team	Pct.	G	PO	A	E	TC	DP
erson, Wilt, Macon	.818	20	15	3	4	22	0
mentel, Jose, Savannah	.978	116	211	11	5	227	2
ollock, Elton, Augusta	.974	121	211	13	6	230	3
rokopec, Luke, Savannah	.889	54	59	5	8	72	1
ullen, Shane, Piedmont	1.000	11	11	1	0	12	0
amirez, Daniel, Columbia	.975	46	73	4	2	79	1
ice, Charles, Augusta	.909	36	49	1	5	55	0
vero, Eddie, Piedmont*	.991	51	105	3	1	109	0
obinson, David, Piedmont*	1.000	38	57	5	0	62	1
ojas, Christian, Cha. (W.Va.)	.983	123	215	10	4	229	1
oss, Jason, Macon	1.000	5	13	0	0	13	0
affer, Jeffrey, Greensboro	1.000	36	30	1	0	31	0
anchez, Omar, Hagerstown	.971	80	124	10	4	138	0
anderson, David, Columbia*	.969	21	31	0	1	32	0
chreiber, Stan, Augusta	.923	21	33	3	3	39	1
chreimann, Eric, Piedmont	1.000	1	3	0	0	3	0
chwab, Chris, Delmarva*	1.000	5	3	0	0	3	0
cott, Thomas, Cha. (W.Va.)	.979	115	176	9	4	189	0
eguignol, Fernando, Delmarva	.978	106	173	4	4	181	0
humpert, Derek, Greensboro	.984	141	297	17	5	319	2
mpson, Jeramie, Columbia	.986	49	65	7	1	73	0
mella, Steve, Cha. (S.C.)	.942	43	64	1	4	69	0
oringfield, Bo, Augusta	.933	56	82	1	6	89	0
tevens, Clayton, Hickory	.946	32	53	0	3	56	0
one, Craig, Hagerstown	1.000	3	1	0	0	1	0
uckenschneider, Eric, Savannah	.973	105	141	5	4	150	0
ylor, Reggie, Piedmont	.961	128	287	9	12	308	3
omas, Allen, Hickory*	1.000	26	33	3	0	36	2
omas, Rod, Cha. (W.Va.)	.978	51	83	4	2	89	1
ppy, Joe, Macon*	.969	121	175	10	6	191	1
lazquez, Jose, Greensboro	.667	2	2	0	1	3	0
arner, Bryan, Columbus*	.964	80	147	12	6	165	3
eaver, Scott, Fayetteville*	.954	70	98	5	5	108	0
eekley, Jason, Savannah	1.000	1	2	0	0	2	0
hitaker, Chad, Columbus	.980	62	93	4	2	99	1
lliams, Ricky, Piedmont	.933	84	117	9	9	135	3
lson, Craig, Hagerstown	.963	48	75	3	3	81	0
wica, Michael, Cha. (S.C.)	.974	20	33	5	1	39	0

CATCHERS

Player, Team	Pct.	G	PO	A	E	TC	DP	PB
varado, Basilio, Delmarva	.979	6	41	6	1	48	0	1
tczak, Chuck, Hickory	.949	8	37	0	2	39	0	3
ias, Rogelio, Asheville	.991	25	189	25	2	216	0	6
rrett, Michael, Delmarva	.980	83	607	72	14	693	3	17
netto, John, Augusta	1.000	4	6	1	0	7	0	1
rdona, Javier, Fayetteville	.981	85	677	112	15	804	5	10
fford, John, Asheville	1.000	10	81	6	0	87	0	0
burn, Todd, Piedmont	.984	15	111	13	2	126	0	1
x, Chuck, Piedmont	.971	25	169	32	6	207	2	6
vis, James, Cha. (W.Va.)	.977	80	540	86	15	641	2	11
wns, Brian, Hickory	.986	84	532	93	9	634	3	23
mons, Scott, Greensboro	.981	14	90	12	2	104	0	2
gle, Beau, Columbia	.933	3	14	0	1	15	0	0
ns, Pat, Columbus	.971	6	28	5	1	34	1	2
ske, Joshua, Hickory	.981	32	187	23	4	214	1	13
nigan, Steven, Augusta	.966	35	211	18	8	237	1	8
ote, Derek, Macon	.974	47	341	40	10	391	3	13
ler, Brian, Fayetteville	.994	38	301	34	2	337	4	3
rcia, Jaime, Delmarva	.979	56	424	37	10	471	1	6
, Geronimo, Savannah	.983	63	514	56	10	580	1	17
mez, Paul, Columbia	.963	3	23	3	1	27	0	1
nzalez, Ricky, Columbus	.975	75	523	73	15	611	6	5
nzalez, Wikleman, Augusta	.976	98	810	115	23	948	9	20
odwin, Joe, Cha. (S.C.)	.978	75	517	72	13	602	4	11
yes, Heath, Columbus	.979	68	439	64	11	514	4	10
cks, Jamie, Macon	.982	11	49	7	1	57	0	0
ech, Erik, Greensboro	.976	11	79	3	2	84	1	1
ig, Cesar, Cha. (S.C.)	.971	66	399	71	14	484	5	10
Rue, Jason, Cha. (W.Va.)	.978	34	218	46	6	270	2	6
nar, Fernando, Macon	.984	90	648	112	12	772	11	14
lave, Joshua, Savannah	.955	3	19	2	1	22	0	0
Aulay, John, Cha. (S.C.)	1.000	5	38	4	0	42	0	0
ormick, Cody, Greensboro	.962	25	138	14	6	158	0	4
Sparin, Paul, Augusta	1.000	2	4	0	0	4	0	0
ndez, Sergio, Augusta	.983	13	100	14	2	116	0	2
yer, Travis, Savannah	.979	51	388	40	9	437	5	8
rales, Eric, Columbia	.993	43	258	29	2	289	3	7
veros, Ricardo, Delmarva	1.000	3	5	0	0	5	0	0
al, Josh, Hickory	.991	27	197	29	2	228	3	4
a, Angel, Savannah	.979	30	238	39	6	283	4	4
rick, Ben, Asheville	.986	94	766	95	12	873	4	7
rce, Kirk, Piedmont	.991	67	499	64	5	568	4	10
to, Rene, Greensboro	.976	50	359	47	10	416	4	17

Player, Team	Pct.	G	PO	A	E	TC	DP	PB
Pointer, Corey, Macon	1.000	7	45	3	0	48	0	2
Pozo, Yohel, Asheville	.989	14	83	11	1	95	2	2
Rodriguez, Luis, Hagerstown	.980	75	550	92	13	655	5	20
Romero, Marty, Hickory	.955	5	38	4	2	44	1	2
Roney, Chad, Savannah	.987	17	69	5	1	75	0	3
Schneider, Brian, Delmarva	1.000	5	20	3	0	23	0	0
Schreimann, Eric, Piedmont	.973	36	302	22	9	333	0	1
Snusz, Chris, Piedmont	1.000	4	22	4	0	26	0	0
Sosa, Franklin, Fayetteville	.986	29	193	16	3	212	0	3
Stone, Craig, Hagerstown	1.000	8	42	7	0	49	0	1
Trolio, Jason, Greensboro	.969	66	427	68	16	511	3	11
VALERA, Yohanny, Columbia	.991	108	857	123	9	989	6	21
Ward, Chris, Cha. (W.Va.)	.992	33	226	21	2	249	3	11
Wilson, Craig, Hagerstown	.989	67	477	75	6	558	4	22

PITCHERS

Player, Team	Pct.	G	PO	A	E	TC	DP
Abreu, Winston, Macon	.813	12	5	8	3	16	1
Adge, Jason, Columbus	.875	16	2	5	1	8	0
Antonini, Adrian, Piedmont	1.000	2	1	2	0	3	0
Arroyo, Bronson, Augusta	.919	26	16	18	3	37	0
Atchley, Justin, Cha. (W.Va.)*	.950	17	6	13	1	20	0
Atkins, Dannon, Columbus	.960	28	16	32	2	50	2
Ayers, Mike, Augusta*	1.000	27	2	3	0	5	0
Babineaux, Darrin, Savannah	.938	13	8	7	1	16	1
Bailey, Ben, Cha. (W.Va.)	.882	11	5	10	2	17	0
Baker, Jason, Delmarva	.833	28	19	21	8	48	2
Bales, Joseph, Hickory	1.000	15	2	3	0	5	0
Barbao, Joe, Piedmont	.889	17	3	5	1	9	0
Barnes, Keith, Asheville*	1.000	17	4	17	0	21	1
Bauer, Chuck, Cha. (S.C.)	.828	28	8	16	5	29	2
Becker, Tom, Cha. (S.C.)	.868	40	8	25	5	38	6
BELL, Mike, Delmarva*	1.000	40	5	32	0	37	2
Bennett, Jason, Columbus	1.000	40	7	17	0	24	2
Bettencourt, Justin, Fayetteville*	.902	26	5	32	4	41	0
Bevel, Bobby, Asheville*	.867	41	2	11	2	15	0
Bland, Nate, Savannah*	1.000	5	0	3	0	3	0
Blyleven, Todd, Augusta	1.000	12	1	1	0	2	0
Blythe, Billy, Macon	.867	26	10	16	4	30	0
Borkowski, David, Fayetteville	.927	27	13	25	3	41	3
Bost, Heath, Asheville	1.000	41	8	10	0	18	0
Bracho, Alejandro, Greensboro*	.921	34	6	29	3	38	0
Bradford, Chad, Hickory	1.000	28	1	11	0	12	0
Brooks, Antone, Macon*	1.000	43	2	14	0	16	1
Brown, Charlie, Greensboro	.667	23	1	1	1	3	0
Bruner, Clayton, Fayetteville	.854	27	13	28	7	48	1
Bryant, Adam, Cha. (W.Va.)	.917	22	5	6	1	12	1
Buckman, Tom, Hickory	1.000	16	4	7	0	11	0
Bullock, Derek, Augusta	1.000	14	2	11	0	13	0
Burger, Rob, Piedmont	.857	27	7	17	4	28	1
Butler, Adam, Macon*	1.000	12	0	2	0	2	0
Callahan, Damon, Cha. (W.Va.)	.905	27	10	9	2	21	2
Canetto, John, Augusta	1.000	1	1	0	0	1	0
Case, Christopher, Macon*	1.000	23	4	1	0	5	0
Centeno, Jose, Delmarva*	1.000	11	0	4	0	4	0
Chantres, Carlos, Hickory	.946	18	10	25	2	37	2
Charbonneau, Marc, Savannah*	.769	25	2	8	3	13	0
Christmas, Maurice, Macon	1.000	39	3	12	0	15	1
Civit, Xavier, Cha. (W.Va.)	.800	34	3	9	3	15	0
Cochran, Andrew, Macon*	.875	13	3	4	1	8	1
Codd, Tim, Cha. (S.C.)	.500	3	0	2	2	4	0
Coggin, David, Piedmont	.857	28	10	26	6	42	2
Cole, Jason, Delmarva	1.000	10	1	4	0	5	0
Coleman, Billy, Greensboro	1.000	4	1	0	0	1	0
Collie, Tim, Augusta	.857	24	3	3	1	7	0
Colmenares, Luis, Asheville	.818	12	2	7	2	11	0
Corba, Lisandro, Macon	1.000	2	0	1	0	1	0
Cordero, Francisco, Fayetteville	1.000	2	1	3	0	4	0
Corey, Bryan, Fayetteville	.938	60	4	11	1	16	2
Coronado, Osvaldo, Columbia	1.000	32	6	15	0	21	1
Corral, Ruben, Hagerstown	.667	14	2	6	4	12	0
Crowell, Jim, Columbus*	.981	28	14	39	1	54	4
Crowther, John, Fayetteville	.917	41	4	7	1	12	0
Cruz, Charlie, Macon*	.944	35	2	15	1	18	1
Cushman, Dwayne, Cha. (W.Va.)	.875	55	7	14	3	24	0
D'Alessandro, Marc, Asheville*	.957	28	7	38	2	47	2
Dalton, Brian, Fayetteville	1.000	7	2	1	0	3	0
Daniels, David, Augusta	1.000	11	1	0	0	1	0
Darwin, Brian, Fayetteville*	.842	17	3	13	3	19	0
Daugherty, Keith, Macon	1.000	4	0	1	0	1	0
Davey, Tim, Hagerstown	.977	26	13	29	1	43	5
Davis, Jason, Piedmont*	1.000	19	4	4	0	8	0
Davis, John, Savannah	.926	38	9	16	2	27	3
Davis, Lance, Cha. (W.Va.)*	1.000	4	1	0	0	1	0

CLASS A *South Atlantic League*

Player, Team	Pct.	G	PO	A	E	TC	DP
Delgado, Ernie, Hagerstown	.840	35	7	14	4	25	0
Delossantos, Luis, Greensboro	1.000	7	3	7	0	10	0
Demorejon, Pedro, Hickory	.833	17	3	2	1	6	1
Dempster, Ryan, Cha. (S.C.)	.846	23	6	16	4	26	1
Deschenes, Marc, Columbus	1.000	16	2	4	0	6	1
DeWitt, Chris, Columbia	1.000	13	0	9	0	9	0
Dietrich, Jason, Asheville	1.000	7	0	1	0	1	0
Dotel, Octavio, Columbia	.821	22	3	20	5	28	1
Dougherty, Tony, Columbus	1.000	19	2	5	0	7	0
Draeger, Mark, Cha. (S.C.)	1.000	19	1	4	0	5	0
Dunbar, Matt, Greensboro*	.000	2	0	0	1	1	0
Dunn, Cordell, Augusta	.333	3	1	0	2	3	0
Durkovic, Peter, Fayetteville*	.947	53	5	13	1	19	0
Eby, Mike, Fayetteville*	.944	27	6	11	1	18	2
Einerston, Darrell, Greensboro	.867	48	2	11	2	15	0
Emiliano, James, Asheville	1.000	6	1	1	0	2	0
Farley, Joe, Hickory*	1.000	4	1	4	0	5	0
Farrow, Jason, Augusta	.933	46	4	10	1	15	0
Figueroa, Nelson, Columbia	.935	26	16	27	3	46	1
Fisher, Ryan, Augusta*	1.000	14	2	1	0	3	0
Fitterer, Scott, Hagerstown	1.000	2	0	1	0	1	0
Fleetham, Ben, Delmarva	1.000	16	0	2	0	2	0
Foran, John, Fayetteville	.882	35	4	11	2	17	0
Ford, Ben, Greensboro	.850	43	6	11	3	20	3
Ford, Brian, Piedmont*	1.000	37	2	11	0	13	0
France, Aaron, Augusta	.900	5	4	5	1	10	0
Gagne, Eric, Savannah	.952	23	6	14	1	21	0
Garber, Joel, Hickory*	1.000	17	1	15	0	16	2
Garcia, Eddy, Cha. (W.Va.)	.920	30	6	17	2	25	0
Garcia, Jose, Macon	.895	32	6	11	2	19	0
Garrett, Neil, Asheville	.931	22	9	18	2	29	1
Giard, Ken, Macon	1.000	5	0	1	0	1	0
Giron, Emiliano, Cha. (W.Va.)	1.000	32	1	2	0	3	0
Glynn, Ryan, Cha. (S.C.)	.720	19	3	15	7	25	2
Gonzalez, Generoso, Fayetteville	.600	17	1	2	2	5	0
Gonzalez, Lariel, Asheville	.833	35	2	3	1	6	0
Granger, Greg, Columbus	.846	20	4	7	2	13	0
Gray, Jason, Hickory	1.000	13	5	3	0	8	0
Grife, Richard, Columbus	.875	36	3	11	2	16	2
Gulin, Lindsay, Columbia*	1.000	19	5	17	0	22	0
Halley, Allen, Hagerstown	1.000	2	0	1	0	1	0
Hamilton, Paul, Piedmont	1.000	6	0	3	0	3	0
Handy, Russell, Delmarva	.875	24	2	5	1	8	0
Hartshorn, Tyson, Hagerstown	.958	26	9	14	1	24	1
Hausman, Isaac, Cha. (S.C.)	1.000	1	0	2	0	2	0
Havens, Jeff, Augusta	1.000	34	5	7	0	12	0
Hernandez, Elvin, Augusta	.909	27	9	21	3	33	1
Horn, Keith, Columbus	1.000	25	6	19	0	25	2
Horne, Jeff, Cha. (W.Va.)	.667	3	0	2	1	3	0
Horton, Eric, Hagerstown	1.000	13	1	4	0	5	1
Howard, Jamie, Macon	1.000	8	3	6	0	9	0
Howatt, Jeff, Columbia	.917	37	5	6	1	12	0
Hunt, Jon, Hickory*	.810	25	5	29	8	42	0
Iglesias, Mario, Hickory	1.000	10	3	1	0	4	0
Jacobs, Dwayne, Macon	.842	26	8	8	3	19	0
Jacobs, Mike, Macon	1.000	11	0	3	0	3	0
Jacobson, Kelton, Fayetteville	.800	6	0	4	1	5	1
Johnson, Jason, Augusta	.923	14	6	6	1	13	1
Johnson, Mike, Hagerstown	.786	29	6	27	9	42	2
Judd, Mike, Green.-Sav.	.857	44	9	15	4	28	0
Kahlon, Bobby, Macon	1.000	15	0	1	0	1	0
Kammerer, James, Asheville*	.786	9	2	9	3	14	0
Keehn, Drew, Asheville	.833	26	7	8	3	18	1
Kelly, Jeff, Augusta*	.889	14	3	13	2	18	0
Keppen, Jeff, Savannah	.800	12	1	3	1	5	1
Kershner, Jason, Piedmont*	.958	28	4	19	1	24	1
King, Raymond, Macon*	1.000	17	0	18	0	18	3
Knoll, Randy, Piedmont	.692	22	4	14	8	26	1
Kolb, Danny, Cha. (S.C.)	.864	20	2	17	3	22	0
Lail, Denny, Greensboro	1.000	11	2	4	0	6	1
Lakman, Jason, Hickory	.800	13	4	4	2	10	0
Lapka, Rick, Cha. (W.Va.)	.958	29	8	15	1	24	1
Larson, Toby, Columbia	1.000	1	1	0	0	1	0
LaRue, Shaun, Cha. (W.Va.)	1.000	4	1	0	0	1	0
Lawrence, Clint, Hagerstown*	.875	6	1	6	1	8	0
Leaman, Jeff, Piedmont	1.000	19	5	4	0	9	0
LeBlanc, Eric, Cha. (W.Va.)	.750	6	2	1	1	4	1
Lee, John, Hagerstown	.957	19	7	15	1	23	3
Leslie, Sean, Delmarva*	1.000	18	1	9	0	10	0
Lisio, Joseph, Columbia	.889	40	4	4	1	9	0
Loudermilk, Darren, Columbus	1.000	3	1	2	0	3	0
Lowe, Ben, Hagerstown*	.938	46	4	11	1	16	0
Lowell, Mike, Greensboro	1.000	1	0	1	0	1	0
Lukasiewicz, Mark, Hagerstown*	1.000	9	0	2	0	2	0

Player, Team	Pct.	G	PO	A	E	TC
Macca, Christopher, Asheville	.800	26	0	4	1	5
MacRae, Scott, Cha. (W.Va.)	.900	29	8	10	2	20
Malenfant, Dave, Fayetteville	.714	23	0	5	2	7
Marquez, Robert, Delmarva	.917	29	1	10	1	12
Martin, Chandler, Asheville	.938	14	3	12	1	16
Martinez, Jose, Cha. (S.C.)	1.000	11	0	1	0	1
Masaoka, Onan, Savannah*	.857	13	2	10	2	14
Maskivish, Joe, Augusta	1.000	50	4	3	0	7
Mathis, Sammie, Columbus	.923	31	4	20	2	26
Mattes, Troy, Delmarva	.793	27	6	17	6	29
Mattox, Gene, Cha. (W.Va.)	.857	22	3	3	1	7
Mattson, Craig, Augusta	1.000	18	1	5	0	6
McBride, Chris, Hagerstown	.857	8	0	6	1	7
McDonald, Matt, Savannah*	.900	28	3	15	2	20
McEntire, Ethan, Columbia*	.970	27	9	23	1	33
McHugh, Mike, Cha. (S.C.)*	.813	43	3	10	3	16
Melendez, David, Fayetteville	.981	27	12	41	1	54
Mendes, Jaime, Piedmont	.938	37	5	10	1	16
Mensink, Brian, Piedmont	1.000	6	3	7	0	10
Merrick, Brett, Columbus*	.933	44	4	10	1	15
Meyer, David, Greensboro*	1.000	6	0	7	0	7
Militello, Sam, Greensboro	.000	3	0	0	1	1
Mitchell, Scott, Delmarva	.773	33	3	14	5	22
Montgomery, Joe, Cha. (W.Va.)	.750	14	1	2	1	4
Moore, Bobby, Cha. (S.C.)	.853	25	8	21	5	34
Morillo, Donald, Cha. (S.C.)	1.000	2	0	1	0	1
Mota, Henry, Cha. (S.C.)	.875	32	8	13	3	24
Mudd, Scott, Cha. (S.C.)	.804	28	13	32	11	56
Murphy, Sean, Asheville	.957	35	8	14	1	23
Musslewhite, Jim, Greensboro	1.000	4	2	0	0	2
Nakashima, Tony, Savannah*	1.000	27	3	7	0	10
Nelson, Ron, Cha. (S.C.)	.800	20	1	3	1	5
Nichols, James, Hickory	1.000	20	4	9	0	13
Nunez, Maximo, Hickory	.946	31	10	25	2	37
Nyari, Pete, Piedmont	.769	45	4	6	3	13
Ochsenfeld, Christopher, Savannah*	.929	26	3	23	2	28
O'Conner, Brian, Augusta*	1.000	19	0	4	0	4
Ojeda, Erick, Columbia*	.900	35	5	13	2	20
Olivier, Rich, Greensboro	.833	9	2	3	1	6
Olsen, Jason, Hickory	1.000	4	2	4	0	6
Olson, Phil, Columbia	.913	16	8	13	2	23
Palmer, Brett, Columbus*	1.000	5	0	3	0	3
Parotte, Frisco, Greensboro	.833	24	5	5	2	12
Parra, Julio, Savannah	1.000	12	0	2	0	2
Parris, Steve, Augusta	1.000	1	0	1	0	1
Pearsall, J.J., Savannah*	.737	45	5	9	5	19
Perusek, William, Fayetteville	.857	38	1	5	1	7
Phillips, Jason, Augusta	.903	14	5	23	3	31
Pinales, Aquiles, Macon	.875	18	2	5	1	8
Poupart, Melvin, Columbia	1.000	5	0	1	0	1
Powell, Jeremy, Delmarva	.814	27	19	29	11	59
Rakers, Jason, Columbus	.938	14	3	12	1	16
Ramirez, Jose, Fayetteville*	1.000	15	2	3	0	5
Randall, Scott, Asheville	.973	24	7	29	1	37
Randolph, Stephen, Greensboro*	.944	32	3	14	1	18
Reed, Jason, Savannah*	1.000	5	1	3	0	4
Reimers, Tom, Hickory	1.000	14	3	7	0	10
Reyes, Jose, Augusta	.929	23	5	8	1	14
Ricabal, Dan, Savannah	1.000	40	5	14	0	19
Riedling, John, Cha. (W.Va.)	.929	26	9	17	2	28
Robbins, Jake, Greensboro	.818	18	4	5	2	11
Roberts, Mark, Hickory	.875	13	2	12	2	16
Roberts, Randolph, Cha. (W.Va.)	.667	5	1	1	1	3
Robinson, Martin, Greensboro*	.867	10	3	10	2	15
Rocker, John, Macon*	.958	20	5	18	1	24
Rose, Brian, Asheville	.864	38	5	14	3	22
Ruiz, Rafael, Hickory*	1.000	34	3	5	0	8
Runion, Jeff, Cha. (S.C.)	1.000	5	1	1	0	2
Runyan, Paul, Cha. (W.Va.)	1.000	29	7	11	0	18
Sanchez, Martin, Macon	.882	31	6	9	2	17
Sanders, Frankie, Columbus	.852	22	9	14	4	27
Santamaria, Bill, Columbia	1.000	31	2	7	0	9
Sauget, Rich, Hickory	1.000	25	5	4	0	9
Schaffner, Eric, Greensboro	.885	27	6	17	3	26
Schmack, Brian, Hickory	.938	43	3	12	1	16
Schroeffel, Scott, Asheville	1.000	2	1	1	0	2
Shelby, Anthony, Greensboro*	1.000	16	3	4	0	7
Shumaker, Anthony, Piedmont*	1.000	20	0	7	0	7
Shumate, Jacob, Macon	1.000	1	1	0	0	1
Sikes, Jason, Piedmont	.846	17	6	16	4	26
Simmons, Carlos, Cha. (S.C.)	.846	33	0	11	2	13
SMART, J.D., Delmarva	1.000	25	10	27	0	37
Smith, Keilan, Hagerstown	1.000	19	2	5	0	7
Snead, George, Macon	.750	3	0	3	1	4

Player, Team	Pct.	G	PO	A	E	TC	DP
outh, Carl, Aug.-Sav.	.903	34	11	17	3	31	0
parks, Jeff, Cha. (W.Va.)	.850	46	5	12	3	20	0
pence, Michael, Greensboro	.929	19	4	9	1	14	0
oykstra, Dave, Savannah	.950	28	7	12	1	20	1
tentz, Brent, Fayetteville	.846	45	4	7	2	13	0
tepka, Tom, Asheville	.833	2	1	4	1	6	0
ewart, Stan, Greensboro	1.000	10	2	5	0	7	1
one, Ricky, Savannah	.889	5	4	4	1	9	1
aylor, Brien, Greensboro*	1.000	9	1	4	0	5	1
bbetts, Scott, Piedmont	1.000	5	0	2	0	2	0
iobe, J.J., Columbus	1.000	2	1	4	0	5	0
hompson, Justin, Fayetteville*	1.000	1	1	0	0	1	0
rres, Jackson, Savannah	.800	42	1	11	3	15	0
umpour, Andy, Columbia	.955	26	8	13	1	22	0
azquez, Javier, Delmarva	.980	27	10	38	1	49	2
enafro, Mike, Cha. (S.C.)*	.875	50	4	17	3	24	1
eniard, Jay, Hagerstown	1.000	8	2	15	0	17	0
ardin, Cesar, Greensboro*	.889	14	1	7	1	9	0
egas, Randy, Augusta*	1.000	13	1	3	0	4	0

Player, Team	Pct.	G	PO	A	E	TC	DP
Villegas, Ismael, Macon	1.000	12	7	8	0	15	0
Virchis, Adam, Hickory	.897	27	3	23	3	29	3
Volkert, Oreste, Hagerstown	.944	38	6	11	1	18	1
Walton, Tim, Piedmont	1.000	8	1	8	0	9	1
Winchester, Scott, Columbus	.909	52	4	6	1	11	0
Woodring, Jason, Delmarva	.895	46	3	14	2	19	0
Wright, Scott, Cha. (W.Va.)	.957	28	12	10	1	23	2
Yeager, Gary, Piedmont	.960	40	7	17	1	25	1
Young, Danny, Augusta*	1.000	22	2	10	0	12	1
Young, Joe, Hagerstown	.842	21	7	9	3	19	0
Young, Ryan, Augusta	.962	21	8	17	1	26	0

PITCHERS WITH TWO OR MORE TEAMS

Player, Team	Pct.	G	PO	A	E	TC	DP
Judd, Mike, Greensboro	.818	29	1	8	2	11	0
Judd, Mike, Savannah	.882	15	8	7	2	17	0
South, Carl, Augusta	1.000	1	2	0	0	2	0
South, Carl, Savannah	.897	33	9	17	3	29	0

The following players did not have any fielding statistics at the positions indicated or appeared only as a designated hitter, pinch-hitter or pinch-runner: Acosta, p; Allen, Antrim, 2B; Backowski, p; Bere, p; Blake, of; Briones, dh, ph; Capellan, of; Dennis, 3B; Donati, dh; Dunbar, p; Elliott, of; Engleka, c, p; Fisher, dh; Frazier, p; J. Garcia, 2B; odges, c, p; Hritz, p; Koonce, of; Lutz, c; Malave, 3B; Martineau, p; Mejia, p; Meyer, p; Morrison, of; Pack, p; Pattellis, of; Peeples, dh; Reid, p; Roney, 3B; Sasser, of; Sosa, Stanton, dh; Vopata, of; Wilson, p; Zaun, ss.

LEAGUE CHAMPIONS

Year	Team	Pct.	Year	Team	Pct.	Year	Team	Pct.
48—	Lincolnton*	.627	1969—	Greenwood‡	.587	1983—	Columbia	.620
49—	Newton-Conover	.667		Shelby	.565		Gastonia‡	.587
	Rutherford Co. (2nd)†	.627	1970—	Greenville	.576	1984—	Charleston	.549
50—	Newton-Conover	.627		Greenville	.619		Asheville‡	.510
	Lenoir (2nd)†	.626	1971—	Greenwood	.631	1985—	Florence‡	.599
51—	Morganton	.645		Greenwood	.759		Greensboro	.540
	Shelby (2nd)†	.604	1972—	Spartanburg‡	.788	1986—	Columbia‡	.682
52—	Lincolnton	.649		Greenville	.652		Asheville	.643
	Shelby (2nd)†	.645	1973—	Spartanburg‡	.646	1987—	Asheville	.655
53-59—League inactive.				Gastonia	.619		Myrtle Beach‡	.597
60—	Lexington	.707	1974—	Gastonia	.606	1988—	Charleston (S.C.)	.616
	Salisbury (2nd)†	.650		Gastonia	.672		Spartanburg‡	.500
61—	Salisbury	.627	1975—	Spartanburg	.543	1989—	Gastonia	.657
	Shelby (4th)†	.481		Spartanburg	.614		Augusta‡	.535
62—	Statesville	.563	1976—	Asheville	.544	1990—	Columbia	.580
	Statesville	.700		Greenwood‡	.600		Charleston (W.Va.)‡	.538
63—	Greenville†	.576	1977—	Greenwood	.557	1991—	Charleston (W.Va.)	.648
	Salisbury	.631		Gastonia‡	.590		Columbia‡	.614
64—	Rock Hill	.672	1978—	Greenwood	.614	1992—	Columbia	.572
	Salisbury‡	.631		Greenwood	.565		Myrtle Beach‡	.522
65—	Salisbury	.641	1979—	Greenwood‡	.565	1993—	Savannah‡	.662
	Rock Hill‡	.603		Spartanburg	.525		Greensboro	.603
66—	Spartanburg	.682	1980—	Greensboro	.590	1994—	Columbus	.630
	Spartanburg	.767		Charleston	.561		Savannah‡	.599
67—	Spartanburg	.730	1981—	Greensboro‡	.695	1995—	Piedmont	.586
	Spartanburg	.567		Greenwood	.549		Augusta‡	.551
68—	Spartanburg	.597	1982—	Greensboro‡	.681	1996—	Delmarva	.585
	Greenwood‡	.597		Florence	.546		Savannah†	.511

*Won championship and four-club playoff. †Won four-club playoff. ‡Won split-season playoff. (NOTE—Known as Western Carolina League from 1948 ough 1962 and known as Western Carolinas League through 1979.)

CLASS A *South Atlantic League*

APPALACHIAN LEAGUE

LEAGUE OFFICE

President
Lee Landers
Address
283 Deerchase Circle
Statesville, NC 28677
Phone
704-873-5300

Teams (affiliation)
Bluefield Orioles (Orioles)
Bristol White Sox (White Sox)
Burlington Indians (Indians)
Danville Braves (Braves)
Elizabethton Twins (Twins)
Johnson City Cardinals (Cardinals)

Kingsport Mets (Mets)
Martinsville Phillies (Phillies)
Princeton Devil Rays (Devil Rays)
Pulaski Rangers (Rangers)

1996 FINAL STANDINGS

NORTH DIVISION

Team	W	L	T	Pct.	GB
Bluefield (Orioles)	42	26	0	.618	....
Danville (Braves)	37	29	0	.561	4
Burlington (Indians)	29	38	0	.433	12½
Princeton (Reds)	28	40	0	.412	14
Martinsville (Phillies)	20	47	0	.299	21½

SOUTH DIVISION

Team	W	L	T	Pct.	GB
Kingsport (Mets)	48	19	0	.716	....
Johnson City (Cardinals)	42	26	0	.618	6
Elizabethton (Twins)	40	27	0	.597	8
Bristol (White Sox)	17	51	0	.250	31

COMPOSITE

Team	King.	J.C.	Blu.	Elz.	Dan.	Bur.	Pri.	Mar.	Brs.	W	L	T	Pct.	GB
Kingsport (Mets)	....	6	5	5	5	6	7	6	8	48	19	0	.716	....
Johnson City (Cardinals)	2	....	5	6	4	6	6	7	6	42	26	0	.618	6
Bluefield (Orioles)	3	3	....	6	4	6	8	5	7	42	26	0	.618	6
Elizabethton (Twins)	4	5	2	....	6	7	4	6	6	40	27	0	.597	8
Danville (Braves)	2	4	4	2	....	5	8	6	6	37	29	0	.561	10
Burlington (Indians)	2	2	2	1	4	....	3	7	8	29	38	0	.433	19
Princeton (Reds)	1	2	4	4	0	5	....	8	4	28	40	0	.412	20
Martinsville (Phillies)	2	1	3	1	4	3	0	....	6	20	47	0	.299	28
Bristol (White Sox)	3	3	1	2	2	0	4	2	....	17	51	0	.250	31

Major league affiliations in parentheses.

PLAYOFFS: Bluefield defeated Kingsport, two games to one, to win league championship.

REGULAR-SEASON ATTENDANCE: Bluefield, 38,840; Bristol, 25,262; Burlington, 43,596; Danville, 66,825; Elizabethton, 16,711; Johnson City, 47,37; Kingsport, 33,100; Martinsville, 42,153; Princeton, 26,162. Total—340,024. Playoffs (3 games)—1,301.

MANAGERS: Bluefield, Bobby Dickerson; Bristol, Nick Capra; Burlington, Harry Spilman; Danville, Brian Snitker; Elizabethton, Jose Marzan; Johnson C Steve Turco; Kinsport, John Stephenson; Martinsville, Ramon Henderson; Princeton, Mark Wagner.

ALL-STAR TEAM: 1B—Calvin Pickering, Bluefield; 2B—Carlos Casimiro, Bluefield; 3B—Matt Buczkowski, Martinsville; SS—Brent Butler, Johnson C Utility Inf.—Cleatus Davidson, Elizabethton; OF—Tyrone Pendergrass, Danville; Brandon O'Hearn, Princeton; Todd Hogan, Johnson City; Utility OF—T Bishop, Kingsport; C—Pee Wee Lopez, Kingsport; DH—Freddy Reyes, Elizabethton; RHP—Brett Herbison, Kingsport; LHP—Mike Bacsik, Burlington; Rel Pitcher—Jose DeLeon, Johnson City; Player of the Year—Brent Butler, Johnson City; Pitcher of the Year—Andy Zwirchwitz, Kingsport; Manager of the Year Steve Turco, Johnson City.

1996 BATTING

TEAM

Team	Avg.	G	TPA	AB	R	H	TB	2B	3B	HR	RBI	SH	SF	HP	BB	IBB	SO	SB	CS	GDP	LOB	ShO	Slg.	OE
Johnson City	.291	68	2683	2330	465	679	1011	139	23	49	371	11	19	55	266	3	546	96	39	50	486	3	.434	.37
Kingsport	.274	67	2603	2240	412	613	867	94	23	38	350	18	25	40	279	5	418	82	27	31	510	2	.387	.36
Bluefield	.261	68	2607	2229	423	581	916	125	6	66	350	9	25	33	311	9	558	180	50	36	478	2	.411	.35
Elizabethton	.260	67	2531	2153	372	559	855	107	18	51	310	9	14	23	332	4	566	60	25	41	509	5	.397	.36
Princeton	.246	68	2503	2200	334	542	815	98	20	45	276	11	19	37	236	4	591	60	29	41	462	4	.370	.32
Danville	.246	66	2560	2189	348	539	822	104	34	37	285	9	29	41	292	3	526	123	48	36	487	2	.376	.34
Martinsville	.237	67	2449	2187	246	519	713	87	16	25	227	7	14	31	209	2	526	83	36	40	474	2	.326	.31
Burlington	.228	67	2477	2187	303	499	753	92	9	48	258	10	14	28	237	5	600	79	35	31	453	11	.344	.31
Bristol	.226	68	2410	2163	244	488	714	89	7	41	216	17	19	32	178	6	537	70	41	51	414	9	.330	.29

INDIVIDUAL

TOP QUALIFIERS FOR BATTING CHAMPIONSHIP

Minimum 184 plate appearances. *Lefthanded batter. †Switch-hitter.

Player, Team	Avg.	G	TPA	AB	R	H	TB	2B	3B	HR	RBI	SH	SF	HP	BB	IBB	SO	SB	CS	GDP	Slg.	OE
Harris, Rodger, Johnson City†	.369	44	184	168	38	62	93	12	2	5	30	2	3	1	10	0	28	16	6	3	.554	.40
Hogan, Todd, Johnson City	.344	47	212	183	38	63	76	7	3	0	32	1	2	6	20	0	41	18	6	5	.415	.42
Butler, Brent, Johnson City	.343	62	278	248	45	85	132	21	1	8	50	1	2	2	25	1	29	8	1	11	.532	.40
Pickering, Calvin, Bluefield*	.325	60	231	200	45	65	135	14	1	18	66	0	1	2	28	4	64	4	2	4	.675	.41
Bishop, Tim, Kingsport	.325	61	260	237	47	77	103	6	4	4	29	1	1	1	20	1	42	23	10	1	.435	.33
Reyes, Freddy, Elizabethton	.321	65	282	252	46	81	127	20	1	8	55	0	2	9	19	0	49	0	1	3	.504	.38
Lopez, Pee Wee, Kingsport	.316	65	287	250	53	79	130	22	4	7	58	0	2	4	31	1	25	0	1	4	.520	.39
Kritscher, Ryan, Johnson City	.310	46	195	168	34	52	86	19	0	5	33	0	3	8	16	0	18	3	4	0	.512	.39

er, Team	Avg.	G	TPA	AB	R	H	TB	2B	3B	HR	RBI	SH	SF	HP	BB	IBB	SO	SB	CS	GDP	Slg.	OBP
dergrass, Tyrone, Danville†..	.309	54	252	220	50	68	99	8	7	3	23	2	2	4	24	0	39	40	6	4	.450	.384
zkowski, Matt, Martinsville...	.304	50	192	158	25	48	71	12	1	3	23	1	2	4	27	0	52	2	3	3	.449	.414
Richard, Bluefield	.294	50	220	170	42	50	60	7	0	1	21	1	4	3	42	0	24	9	4	1	.353	.434
lstad, Rob, Burlington*	.293	53	209	167	31	49	86	10	3	7	27	0	0	2	40	2	34	9	3	0	.515	.435
n, Jeff, Bristol	.290	50	213	193	27	56	90	10	0	8	24	0	0	9	11	0	25	9	6	8	.466	.357
arthy, Kevin, Kingsport*	.289	64	269	235	46	68	102	14	1	6	43	0	4	2	28	1	41	10	1	2	.434	.364
dson, Cleatus, Elizabethton†	.286	65	293	248	53	71	111	10	6	6	31	3	1	2	39	2	45	17	6	5	.448	.386
x, Billy, Johnson City*	.286	52	233	182	40	52	81	14	0	5	33	0	3	10	38	1	59	5	2	4	.445	.429

EPARTMENTAL LEADERS: G—McClure, 66; AB—McClure, 253; R—R. Lopez, Davidson, 53; H—Butler, 85; TB—Pickering, 135; 2B—R. Lopez, 22; 3B—dergrass, Skeens, 7; HR—Pickering, 18; RBI—Pickering, 66; SH—B. Chancey, 5; SF—Terhune, 7; HP—Deck, 10; BB—Herdman, 48; IBB—Pickering, 4; SO—Leon, ;B—Pendergrass, 40; CS—Ti. Bishop, 10; GIDP—McClure, 11; Slg.—Pickering, .675; OBP—Landstad, .435.

ALL PLAYERS
*Lefthanded batter. †Switch-hitter.

er, Team	Avg.	G	TPA	AB	R	H	TB	2B	3B	HR	RBI	SH	SF	HP	BB	IBB	SO	SB	CS	GDP	Slg.	OBP
l, Antonio, Johnson City	.267	45	163	131	38	35	46	6	1	1	9	1	1	7	22	0	43	10	6	2	.351	.398
ir, Tom, Burlington	.240	26	97	96	4	23	31	5	0	1	7	1	0	0	0	0	22	1	1	3	.323	.240
ndt, Jay, Bluefield*	.500	3	5	4	1	2	2	0	0	0	2	0	0	1	0	0	1	0	0	0	.500	.600
s, Carlos, Bluefield	.298	18	77	57	19	17	21	4	0	0	14	0	1	4	15	0	11	15	0	0	.368	.468
rt, Rashad, Bristol	.230	55	218	204	23	47	70	4	2	5	22	1	2	2	9	0	51	16	8	3	.343	.267
, Chip, Bluefield†	.194	24	84	67	7	13	17	4	0	0	4	0	1	1	15	0	16	0	2	2	.254	.345
n, Cody, Burlington*	.260	27	111	96	10	25	30	2	0	1	14	0	2	1	12	1	17	1	0	2	.313	.342
zak, Chuck, Bristol	.304	7	25	23	2	7	7	0	0	0	0	0	0	0	2	0	5	0	0	0	.304	.360
ld, John, Danville	.231	7	27	26	3	6	7	1	0	0	1	0	0	0	1	0	8	0	0	0	.269	.259
, Jason, Danville†	.242	57	253	207	41	50	79	11	6	2	23	1	5	6	34	0	32	22	5	1	.382	.357
den, Doug, Bristol	.157	40	137	127	6	20	24	1	0	1	6	3	0	0	7	0	29	2	1	5	.189	.201
p, Tim, Kingsport	.325	61	260	237	47	77	103	6	4	4	29	1	1	1	20	1	42	23	10	1	.435	.378
, Brandon, Kingsport*	.256	62	255	219	39	56	71	4	1	3	31	1	2	1	32	0	38	1	1	0	.324	.350
es, Alexander, Danville	.154	5	16	13	1	2	2	0	0	0	2	0	0	1	2	0	4	1	0	0	.154	.313
tte, Tony, Princeton	.267	5	17	15	0	4	4	0	0	0	2	0	0	0	2	0	3	0	0	0	.267	.353
o, Darwin, Princeton†	.245	14	55	53	5	13	14	1	0	0	5	0	0	0	2	0	13	0	0	0	.264	.273
ks, Anthony, Danville	.250	2	8	8	0	2	3	1	0	0	1	0	0	0	0	0	3	0	0	1	.375	.250
n, Jerome, Elizabethton†	.267	50	188	165	32	44	70	10	2	4	25	0	1	1	21	1	58	4	1	5	.424	.351
e, Maurice, Kingsport	.184	11	40	38	5	7	9	0	1	0	4	0	1	1	0	0	7	2	1	1	.237	.200
man, Tom, Princeton	.353	22	22	17	3	6	12	3	0	1	3	0	0	1	4	0	4	0	0	1	.706	.500
es, Matt, Martinsville*	.257	34	118	109	13	28	46	5	2	3	21	0	1	1	7	0	24	4	0	0	.422	.305
kowski, Matt, Martinsville	.304	50	192	158	25	48	71	12	1	3	23	1	2	4	27	0	52	2	3	3	.449	.414
r, Brent, Johnson City	.343	62	278	248	45	85	132	21	1	8	50	1	2	2	25	1	29	8	1	11	.532	.404
Issac, Johnson City	.277	24	107	94	16	26	40	6	1	2	15	0	1	4	8	0	19	5	2	1	.426	.355
niro, Carlos, Bluefield	.276	62	265	239	51	66	112	16	0	10	33	2	2	2	20	1	52	22	9	3	.469	.335
ldo, Eric, Danville	.229	26	99	83	11	19	25	3	0	1	12	0	0	3	13	0	27	2	3	3	.301	.354
pion, Jeff, Danville	.273	4	11	11	2	3	3	0	0	0	1	0	0	0	0	0	3	0	0	0	.273	.273
cey, Bailey, Kingsport†	.269	59	254	197	44	53	65	6	3	0	25	5	3	7	42	1	35	30	5	2	.330	.410
cey, Robert, Kingsport	.263	6	21	19	4	5	8	0	0	1	3	0	0	0	2	0	5	1	0	0	.421	.333
es, Curtis, Bluefield	.203	60	219	182	36	37	64	7	1	6	17	0	1	4	32	1	76	31	6	4	.352	.333
, Stubby, Johnson City†	.223	29	124	94	25	21	31	3	2	1	15	1	1	1	26	0	15	9	2	2	.330	.393
John, Princeton*	.250	58	240	196	30	49	58	5	2	0	17	1	2	3	38	0	41	7	2	7	.296	.377
pcion, David, Princeton†	.250	4	19	16	2	4	5	1	0	0	1	0	0	2	0	0	3	2	0	0	.313	.333
olly, Sean, Bristol	.155	39	131	116	10	18	25	4	0	1	13	2	2	1	10	0	44	2	2	3	.216	.225
ord, Joey, Elizabethton	.281	32	134	121	20	34	58	6	3	4	18	0	0	0	13	0	28	2	1	4	.479	.351
son, Cleatus, Elizabthton†	.286	65	293	248	53	71	111	10	6	6	31	3	1	2	39	2	45	17	6	5	.448	.386
, Angel, Kingsport	.000	2	2	0	1	0	0	0	0	0	0	0	0	0	0	0	0	0	0	0	.000	1.000
ces, Tim, Bluefield*	.297	39	159	128	24	38	67	8	0	7	32	0	5	2	24	0	28	3	1	5	.523	.403
Billy, Johnson City*	.286	52	233	182	40	52	81	14	0	5	33	0	3	10	38	1	59	5	2	4	.445	.429
an, Demond, Princeton	.222	55	222	203	21	45	68	12	1	3	27	0	2	6	11	0	70	0	2	7	.335	.279
Darrell, Bluefield*	.223	59	226	193	40	43	53	6	2	0	14	1	4	0	28	1	49	30	9	2	.275	.316
rds, Lamont, Martinsville	.263	54	224	198	30	52	75	10	5	1	26	1	1	3	21	0	35	7	3	9	.379	.341
rds, Michael, Burlington	.282	58	252	206	31	58	76	13	1	1	17	3	3	3	37	0	26	5	4	4	.369	.394
n, Skeeter, Danville†	.263	58	233	190	29	50	91	7	5	8	34	2	1	0	40	1	71	8	6	3	.479	.390
, Brad, Johnson City	.250	13	34	32	6	8	8	0	0	0	4	0	0	0	2	0	8	0	1	1	.250	.294
Cordell, Johnson City	.286	15	68	63	17	18	28	4	3	0	9	0	0	1	4	0	20	2	2	1	.444	.338
nbach, Todd, Princeton*	.153	19	61	59	8	9	15	3	0	1	5	0	0	0	2	0	34	0	0	0	.254	.180
son, Ryan, Martinsville*	.240	44	169	154	19	37	66	9	1	6	20	0	1	2	11	0	52	3	1	2	.429	.298
d, Thomas, Martinsville*	.171	48	185	158	20	27	39	6	3	0	14	1	1	7	18	0	74	6	4	2	.247	.283
r, Maleke, Bluefield	.372	26	102	86	23	32	37	5	0	8	11	1	1	14	1	16	17	3	1		.430	.461
Robert, Kingsport	.278	6	18	18	1	5	7	2	0	0	3	0	0	0	0	0	3	0	1	0	.389	.278
ulo, Jimmy, Johnson City	.257	46	187	175	24	45	65	11	0	3	21	1	0	2	9	0	28	1	0	2	.371	.301
man, Herbert, Princeton	.223	39	133	121	15	27	34	4	0	1	12	1	0		11	0	39	5	8	1	.281	.288
ero, Hamlet, Kingsport	.250	6	19	16	0	4	4	0	0	0	2	0	0	0	3	0	3	0	0	0	.375	.368
Bryan, Burlington*	.156	52	200	186	16	29	57	10	0	6	25	0	1	4	9	1	84	0	0	0	.306	.210
, Rodger, Johnson City†	.369	44	184	168	38	62	93	12	2	5	30	2	3	1	10	0	28	16	6	3	.554	.401
, Chris, Bristol	.345	8	33	29	7	10	23	7	0	2	8	0	0	0	4	0	2	1	1	0	.793	.424
nan, Eli, Elizabethton	.242	62	252	198	31	48	86	12	1	8	37	0	5	1	48	1	70	1	2	3	.434	.385
ndez, Jesus, Burlington*	.227	19	80	66	15	15	21	6	0	2	6	1	0	0	13	0	8	5	0	1	.348	.354
a, Jesus, Princeton†	.221	25	75	68	8	15	21	6	0	0	7	1	1	3	2	0	17	0	0	0	.309	.270
, Todd, Johnson City	.344	47	212	183	38	63	76	7	3	0	32	1	2	6	20	0	41	18	6	5	.415	.422
s, Darontaye, Bristol	.172	16	65	58	8	10	12	2	0	0	6	0	0		6	0	20	5	2	2	.207	.246
Marv, Bristol*	.091	20	67	55	6	5	15	1	0	3	9	0	2	1	9	0	28	0	0	1	.273	.224
, Brian, Princeton	.295	34	150	122	25	36	60	4	1	6	25	1	3	1	23	0	21	2	1	1	.492	.403
, Jeff, Bristol	.290	50	213	193	27	56	90	10	0	8	24	0	0	9	11	0	25	9	6	8	.466	.357
Damon, Elizabethton	.169	56	205	172	30	29	36	5	1	0	15	2	2	3	26	0	62	8	3	1	.209	.286
on, William, Burlington†	.126	35	116	103	15	13	17	1	0	1	3	0	0	4	9	0	38	6	2	0	.165	.224

Player, Team	Avg.	G	TPA	AB	R	H	TB	2B	3B	HR	RBI	SH	SF	HP	BB	IBB	SO	SB	CS	GDP	Slg.
Jaroncyk, Ryan, Kingsport	.235	57	260	221	35	52	70	5	5	1	21	3	3	6	27	0	59	4	2	3	.317
Jelsovsky, Craig, Kingsport	.000	17	9	8	0	0	0	0	0	0	0	0	0	0	1	0	1	0	0	0	.000
Jenkins, Ben, Martinsville	.207	41	152	140	10	29	38	6	0	1	14	0	0	0	12	0	35	4	3	0	.271
Johnson, Heath, Elizabethton*	.242	48	181	149	24	36	66	9	0	7	32	0	0	2	30	0	60	2	0	0	.443
Johnson, Jason, Martinsville	.272	55	230	213	29	58	67	5	2	0	13	0	1	2	14	0	27	20	7	2	.315
Katz, Jason R., Danville†	.237	45	170	139	20	33	46	8	1	1	17	0	4	5	22	0	38	7	5	3	.331
Klee, Charles, Bristol	.207	48	194	184	22	38	56	6	0	4	17	1	2	0	7	1	38	2	2	4	.304
Kritscher, Ryan, Johnson City	.310	46	195	168	34	52	86	19	0	5	33	0	3	8	16	0	18	3	4	0	.512
Kushma, Glenn, Kingsport	.287	45	154	129	20	37	52	7	1	2	20	2	2	4	16	0	27	2	1	1	.403
Landstad, Rob, Burlington*	.293	53	209	167	31	49	86	10	3	7	27	0	0	2	40	2	34	9	3	0	.515
Lawrence, Chip, Bluefield	.206	15	40	34	6	7	10	0	0	1	4	0	0	2	4	0	4	0	0	1	.294
Lee, Jason, Johnson City*	.307	36	136	114	21	35	57	10	3	2	21	1	0	1	20	1	25	1	2	1	.500
Leon, Jose, Johnson City	.248	59	244	222	29	55	100	9	3	10	36	2	1	2	17	0	92	5	3	1	.450
Livingston, Clyde, Martinsville*	.125	5	17	16	1	2	2	0	0	0	2	0	0	0	1	0	5	0	0	1	.125
Lopes, Omar, Bristol	.216	55	205	171	19	37	50	8	1	1	14	4	1	2	27	0	30	6	4	3	.292
Lopez, Pee Wee, Kingsport	.316	65	287	250	53	79	130	22	4	7	58	0	2	4	31	1	25	0	1	4	.520
Lutz, Manuel, Bristol*	.252	55	225	202	26	51	83	12	1	6	23	2	1	2	17	3	53	5	1	3	.411
Martinez, Alejandro, Princeton	.213	38	126	108	17	23	26	3	0	0	13	0	1	3	14	0	33	2	1	1	.241
Martinez, Eddy, Bluefield	.221	37	140	122	18	27	33	3	0	1	15	3	0	2	13	0	29	15	5	1	.270
Mata, Manuel, Martinsville*	.122	16	44	41	3	5	5	0	0	0	1	0	0	0	3	0	17	0	0	1	.122
McCarthy, Kevin, Kingsport*	.289	64	269	235	46	68	102	14	1	6	43	0	4	2	28	1	41	10	1	2	.434
McClure, Craig, Bristol	.257	66	279	253	30	65	86	13	1	2	23	0	2	4	20	1	48	7	3	11	.340
McCollough, Adam, Bluefield	.301	31	99	93	16	28	49	7	1	4	23	0	1	0	5	0	20	2	0	1	.527
McHenry, Joe, Elizabethton*	.164	51	190	159	24	26	35	5	2	0	9	1	0	1	29	0	58	6	1	0	.220
McNeal, Pepe, Johnson City	.300	24	106	90	22	27	38	6	1	1	11	0	2	3	11	0	23	0	0	3	.422
Mejia, Juan, Martinsville	.181	25	80	72	9	13	17	4	0	0	5	1	1	0	6	0	19	4	0	0	.236
Messner, Jake, Burlington*	.250	47	179	164	20	41	59	7	1	3	20	0	2	1	11	0	41	6	3	0	.360
Minor, Ryan, Bluefield	.253	25	97	87	14	22	40	6	0	4	9	0	0	3	7	0	32	1	0	0	.460
Moeller, Chad, Elizabethton	.356	17	79	59	17	21	37	4	0	4	13	0	0	2	18	0	9	1	2	3	.627
Montgomery, Andre, Princeton	.286	41	156	133	24	38	62	6	3	4	18	1	1	1	20	0	29	5	2	2	.466
Moss, Rick, Elizabethton	.353	32	130	116	21	41	66	10	0	5	18	0	0	0	14	0	17	3	1	3	.569
Mota, Cristian, Burlington†	.267	63	274	251	36	67	92	14	1	3	34	1	1	2	19	0	56	13	6	8	.367
Murphy, Quinn, Burlington*	.153	18	66	59	7	9	10	1	0	0	3	0	0	1	6	0	30	2	1	0	.169
Nichols, Kevin, Martinsville	.253	42	168	158	21	40	60	8	0	4	26	0	3	1	6	0	23	1	1	6	.380
O'Hearn, Brandon, Princeton	.277	65	268	235	33	65	125	17	2	13	52	0	3	1	29	2	88	2	0	4	.532
Oliver, Johnny, Princeton	.203	41	159	143	20	29	40	5	0	2	13	0	1	4	11	0	31	3	1	6	.280
Orndorff, Dave, Elizabethton	.319	13	48	47	8	15	25	2	1	2	6	0	0	0	1	0	10	4	1	0	.532
O'Toole, Bobby, Bluefield	.263	8	24	19	2	5	9	1	0	1	4	0	0	1	4	0	7	2	0	0	.474
Parsons, Jason, Princeton†	.407	23	98	91	22	37	61	9	0	5	17	0	1	1	5	1	9	0	2	2	.670
Patton, Cory, Kingsport	.129	24	47	31	13	4	4	0	0	0	1	1	0	3	12	0	10	4	0	1	.129
Paz, Richard, Bluefield	.294	50	220	170	42	50	60	7	0	1	21	1	4	3	42	0	24	9	4	1	.353
Pedrosa, Alex, Bluefield*	.247	34	93	77	12	19	28	9	0	0	8	0	1	0	15	0	13	2	0	2	.364
Pena, Francisco, Elizabethton	.167	35	103	84	12	14	15	1	0	0	9	0	1	0	18	0	29	0	0	5	.179
Penalver, Juan, Kingsport	.299	36	132	107	24	32	45	5	1	2	17	3	0	1	21	0	20	0	2	3	.421
Pendergrass, Tyrone, Danville†	.309	64	252	220	50	68	99	8	7	3	23	2	2	4	24	0	39	40	6	4	.450
Perez, Edwin, Burlington	.233	51	194	176	22	41	72	4	0	9	31	0	0	3	15	0	48	5	4	2	.409
Perez, Jersen, Kingsport	.176	6	24	17	4	3	3	0	0	0	3	0	2	0	5	0	6	0	0	2	.176
Peterman, Tommy, Elizabethton*	.300	3	15	10	5	3	6	0	0	1	4	0	0	0	5	0	1	0	0	0	.600
Pickering, Calvin, Bluefield*	.325	60	231	200	45	65	135	14	1	18	66	0	1	2	28	4	64	8	2	4	.675
Presto, Nick, Princeton	.262	12	48	42	12	11	15	2	1	0	1	0	0	0	6	0	4	1	2	1	.357
Pugh, Josh, Danville	.143	6	23	21	0	3	3	0	0	0	1	1	0	0	0	0	3	0	0	2	.143
Reyes, Freddy, Elizabethton	.321	65	282	252	46	81	127	20	1	8	55	0	2	9	19	0	49	0	1	3	.504
Ribaudo, Mike, Bluefield	.091	7	26	22	1	2	2	0	0	0	1	2	0	0	2	0	7	0	0	0	.091
Rivera, Roberto, Elizabethton	.215	46	168	158	20	34	57	8	0	5	26	0	0	1	10	0	54	14	4	3	.361
Rodriguez, Aurelio, Burlington	.132	18	81	76	12	10	15	3	1	0	3	1	0	0	4	0	10	2	3	1	.197
Rodriguez, Chris, Burlington†	.061	19	58	49	5	3	3	0	0	0	1	1	0	0	8	0	20	0	0	1	.061
Rodriguez, Mark, Kingsport	.250	8	25	24	3	6	6	0	0	0	3	0	0	1	0	0	5	0	0	2	.250
Rollins, Jimmy, Martinsville†	.238	49	203	172	22	41	49	3	1	1	16	1	0	2	28	1	20	11	5	2	.285
Romero, Marty, Bristol†	.225	36	126	111	10	25	36	8	0	1	10	0	2	2	11	0	34	2	1	3	.324
Ross, Jason Arai, Danville	.268	43	164	149	26	40	59	8	1	3	20	0	4	1	10	0	42	6	3	2	.396
Russin, Tom, Bluefield	.258	57	211	190	32	49	90	15	1	8	40	0	2	2	17	1	38	1	2	5	.474
Saturria, Luis, Johnson City	.256	57	259	227	43	58	82	7	1	5	40	1	0	7	24	0	61	12	1	11	.361
Scharrer, Jim, Danville	.227	62	271	242	31	55	85	17	2	3	32	1	5	1	22	0	74	3	4	3	.351
Schlicher, B.J., Martinsville†	.225	54	211	187	23	42	61	7	0	4	16	0	0	1	23	1	63	1	1	2	.326
Serafin, Ricardo, Martinsville	.184	34	110	98	11	18	22	2	1	0	6	1	0	1	10	0	28	11	4	1	.224
Sharpe, Grant, Burlington*	.244	26	103	82	14	20	40	6	1	4	17	0	2	1	18	0	26	1	1	2	.488
Shelton, Barry, Bristol	.247	45	168	154	19	38	52	8	0	2	13	2	0	4	8	1	50	2	2	2	.338
Shotwell, Robert, Elizabethton	.237	25	81	76	8	18	19	1	0	0	3	0	0	0	5	0	13	0	1	2	.250
Shy, Jason, Danville	.243	11	38	37	5	9	13	1	0	1	3	0	0	0	1	0	8	1	1	0	.351
Siponmaa, Ryan, Burlington	.154	6	19	13	3	2	2	0	0	0	0	0	0	1	5	0	7	1	0	1	.154
Skeens, Jeremy, Princeton	.271	54	220	188	34	51	71	3	7	1	12	3	2	2	25	1	49	19	2	1	.378
Solano, Angel, Bristol	.216	37	144	134	10	29	31	2	0	0	5	2	1	1	6	0	11	6	4	1	.231
Solano, Manuel, Princeton	.215	57	229	209	41	45	77	11	3	5	23	0	0	2	18	0	40	7	2	7	.368
Spencer, Jeffrey, Danville	.237	64	277	241	40	57	111	21	3	9	41	0	3	2	31	2	61	6	3	4	.461
Stephens, Joel, Danville	.248	41	121	101	14	25	30	5	0	0	9	1	0	4	15	0	17	8	3	1	.297
Stevens, Clay, Bristol	.215	48	180	149	19	32	54	3	2	5	23	0	3	4	24	0	69	5	4	0	.362
Strangfeld, Aaron, Danville†	.236	31	125	106	15	25	36	5	0	2	15	0	1	1	17	0	19	1	0	2	.340
Tanner, Paul, Johnson City	.266	41	153	139	29	37	48	4	2	1	12	0	0	0	14	0	37	1	1	2	.345
Taveras, Frank, Burlington*	.236	46	170	161	18	38	51	4	0	3	15	2	1	0	6	0	50	6	3	1	.317
Terhune, Mike, Danville†	.280	56	248	214	32	60	85	9	5	2	27	2	7	2	23	0	29	6	3	6	.397
Terry, Tony, Princeton†	.213	59	198	174	14	37	51	5	0	3	10	0	2	7	13	0	59	5	4	1	.293
Tessmar, Timothy, Kingsport*	.283	65	279	247	36	70	97	10	1	5	46	2	2	2	26	1	32	3	2	5	.393
Thieleke, C.J., Elizabethton*	.295	43	176	146	18	43	49	4	1	0	16	1	1	1	27	0	26	4	3	4	.336

..yer, Team	Avg.	G	TPA	AB	R	H	TB	2B	3B	HR	RBI	SH	SF	HP	BB	IBB	SO	SB	CS	GDP	Slg.	OBP
..ompson, Nick, Martinsville	.234	39	141	124	15	29	35	3	0	1	8	0	1	4	12	0	18	5	1	4	.282	.319
..orpe, Angres, Danville†	.230	43	185	148	23	34	39	1	2	0	11	0	0	4	33	0	25	18	6	2	.264	.384
..rrealba, Steve, Danville	.200	2	5	5	1	1	1	0	0	0	0	0	0	0	0	0	2	0	1	1	.200	.200
..n Iten, Robert, Martinsville*	.239	33	121	113	9	27	34	4	0	1	9	0	2	2	4	0	21	0	1	3	.301	.273
..cchioni, Gerald, Danville	.105	12	45	38	3	4	6	0	1	0	2	0	0	1	6	0	11	0	0	0	.158	.244
..chez, Jose, Elizabethton†	.216	45	152	134	20	29	37	5	0	1	16	2	1	0	15	0	27	8	2	2	.276	.293
..lker, Corey, Danville	.198	30	110	91	15	18	29	3	1	2	19	0	0	7	12	0	30	2	2	1	.319	.336
..rd, Chris, Princeton	.167	8	29	24	3	4	8	1	0	1	6	0	0	3	2	0	8	0	0	0	.333	.310
..liams, Jewell, Burlington	.237	64	268	236	44	56	89	10	1	7	35	0	2	5	25	1	83	16	4	2	.377	.321
..rthy, Thomas, Martinsville	.303	31	84	76	9	23	26	3	0	0	7	1	0	1	6	0	13	4	2	2	.342	.361
..nora, Junior, Kingsport	.242	60	248	227	37	55	89	13	0	7	41	0	3	7	11	0	59	2	1	3	.392	.294

GRAND SLAMS: Rivera, 2; Buckles, Davidson, Hardy, Leon, E. Perez, Russin, C. Stevens, Tessmar, 1 each.

AWARDED FIRST BASE ON CATCHER'S INTERFERENCE: Abell (Connolly); Clapp (Bracho); Ferguson (Connolly); Kushma (Borges); Lutz (Thompson); ..ssner (Romero).

1996 PITCHING

TEAM

..m	W	L	Pct.	ERA	G	CG	ShO	Sv.	IP	H	TBF	R	ER	HR	SH	SF	HB	BB	IBB	SO	WP	Bk.
..gsport	48	19	.716	3.09	67	4	12	20	573.1	451	2400	246	197	28	14	11	36	247	6	619	60	16
..nville	37	29	.561	3.52	66	0	5	21	578.0	522	2498	296	226	28	16	23	33	218	4	541	61	5
..abethton	40	27	.597	4.12	67	4	4	14	554.2	553	2439	323	254	48	10	14	38	209	0	545	57	8
..efield	42	26	.618	4.28	68	3	6	14	574.2	514	2535	335	273	48	4	18	37	286	4	602	75	13
..lington	29	38	.433	4.38	67	1	3	13	569.1	554	2520	348	277	40	8	15	29	227	0	542	65	9
..nceton	28	40	.412	4.54	68	8	4	13	565.0	532	2524	370	285	42	12	17	28	279	3	572	85	13
..nson City	42	26	.618	4.74	68	1	2	20	585.0	606	2638	360	308	49	9	15	28	307	11	505	48	13
..stol	17	51	.250	5.47	68	8	2	8	569.2	637	2643	437	346	60	10	25	43	291	8	489	86	14
..rtinsville	20	47	.299	5.95	67	2	2	14	557.0	650	2626	455	368	57	18	30	48	276	5	453	68	18

INDIVIDUAL

TOP QUALIFIERS FOR EARNED-RUN AVERAGE TITLE

Minimum 54 innings. *Lefthanded pitcher.

..her, Team	W	L	Pct.	ERA	G	GS	CG	ShO	GF	Sv.	IP	H	TBF	R	ER	HR	SH	SF	HB	BB	IBB	SO	WP	Bk.
..linchy, Kevin, Danville	3	2	.600	1.13	13	13	0	0	0	0	72.0	52	283	21	9	2	1	2	2	11	0	77	4	4
..bison, Brett, Kingsport	6	2	.750	1.29	13	12	0	0	0	0	76.2	43	297	18	11	4	0	1	3	31	0	86	6	0
..rchitz, Andy, Kingsport	8	1	.889	1.55	12	11	1	0	0	0	75.1	51	305	22	13	4	2	0	7	19	2	76	1	2
..ll, Jason, Danville	3	1	.750	1.97	12	12	0	0	0	0	59.1	44	231	14	13	1	0	1	1	19	0	57	3	0
..erts, Grant, Kingsport	9	1	.900	2.10	13	13	2	2	0	0	68.2	43	285	18	16	3	1	0	7	37	1	92	4	0
..sik, Mike, Burlington*	4	2	.667	2.20	13	13	1	0	0	0	69.2	49	276	23	17	3	0	2	1	14	0	61	3	1
..Bride, Rodney, Elizabethton	3	2	.600	2.43	12	12	1	1	0	0	74.0	60	309	29	20	4	4	0	5	28	0	83	8	1
..heco, Delvis, Danville	8	1	.889	2.64	13	12	0	0	0	0	64.2	56	271	28	19	1	1	1	2	21	0	60	5	0
..ario, Ruben, Johnson City	7	3	.700	3.28	13	13	1	1	0	0	71.1	53	296	30	26	3	1	3	1	37	0	72	7	4
..ers, Corey, Elizabethton*	6	5	.545	3.34	17	8	0	0	2	0	59.1	69	289	45	22	3	0	3	2	26	0	67	9	1
..en, Abraham, Bluefield	8	3	.727	3.41	15	12	2	0	2	0	63.1	54	280	29	24	4	0	3	5	36	0	69	9	2
..ey, Joe, Bristol*	3	6	.333	3.48	10	10	3	1	0	0	64.2	73	277	34	25	5	1	2	2	11	0	54	3	2
..ard, Randi, Princeton	2	7	.222	3.68	13	11	1	0	1	0	66.0	66	302	42	27	2	0	3	4	38	0	72	16	1
..ey, Shawn, Danville	3	2	.600	3.80	13	12	0	0	0	0	64.0	53	269	31	27	8	1	1	3	23	0	59	4	0
..nett, A.J., Kingsport	4	0	1.000	3.88	13	12	0	0	0	0	58.0	31	245	26	25	0	1	2	7	54	0	68	16	3
..ella, Leoncio, Kingsport	6	3	.667	3.88	15	7	1	0	3	0	58.0	54	248	32	25	3	4	1	1	24	0	52	6	2

..EPARTMENTAL LEADERS: W—G. Roberts, 9; L—Bales, 10; Pct.—G. Roberts, .900; G—Reed, 31; GS—DeWitt, 14; CG—Horne, J. Farley, 3 each; ShO—.. Roberts, 2; GF—Ja. Mejia, 27; Sv.—DeLeon, 15; IP—DeWitt, 79.2; H—DeWitt, 96; TBF—DeWitt, 323; R—Te. Bishop, 55; ER—Te. Bishop, 49; HR—.. Witt, 17; SH—Wise, 6; SF—Several players tied at 5 each; HB—Molta, 11; BB—Burnett, 54; IBB—Tuttle, Mejia, 3 each; SO—G. Roberts, 92; WP—Burnett, ..lard, 16 each; Bk.—Shockley, 7.

ALL PITCHERS

*Lefthanded pitcher.

..her, Team	W	L	Pct.	ERA	G	GS	CG	ShO	GF	Sv.	IP	H	TBF	R	ER	HR	SH	SF	HB	BB	IBB	SO	WP	Bk.
..illes, Matt, Bluefield	3	2	.600	3.80	13	0	0	0	6	0	23.2	20	113	16	10	0	1	0	2	19	1	22	1	0
..iar, Douglas, Martinsville*	1	2	.333	6.56	15	2	0	0	4	1	35.2	40	170	32	26	3	1	0	3	20	0	42	11	0
..nan, Gene, Princeton	2	0	1.000	4.10	18	1	0	0	8	3	41.2	34	178	24	19	5	1	5	2	15	0	36	4	3
..cena, Juan, Burlington	3	4	.429	5.48	13	5	0	0	3	0	42.2	61	197	38	26	4	0	0	1	7	0	28	5	3
..s, Jose, Martinsville	0	0	.000	10.97	5	0	0	0	1	0	10.2	21	63	21	13	1	0	0	0	10	0	6	3	0
..sik, Mike, Burlington*	4	2	.667	2.20	13	13	1	0	0	0	69.2	49	276	23	17	3	0	2	1	14	0	61	3	1
..s, Joseph, Bristol	1	10	.091	5.15	13	12	1	0	0	0	71.2	74	325	49	41	8	2	5	5	39	1	55	13	1
..ew, Preston, Kingsport*	2	1	.667	3.10	5	5	0	0	0	0	20.1	22	87	9	7	2	0	1	0	2	0	15	2	0
..field, Brian, Johnson City	2	2	.500	7.36	10	10	0	0	0	0	40.1	53	205	36	33	2	1	0	1	29	0	27	0	1
..der, Mike, Elizabethton*	1	1	.500	4.50	18	2	0	0	7	2	36.0	31	156	22	18	5	1	0	2	13	0	41	8	1
..dree, Joe, Danville	3	2	.600	1.41	23	0	0	0	10	5	44.2	32	195	14	7	0	1	3	5	18	2	52	3	0
..sley, Raymond, Danville*	1	2	.333	1.72	27	0	0	0	21	12	36.2	28	145	8	7	0	1	1	1	10	0	47	1	1
..ell, Simon, Danville	0	2	.000	7.20	5	0	0	0	2	0	5.0	5	32	6	4	0	1	0	1	8	0	2	3	0
..op, Terry, Martinsville*	1	8	.111	8.59	13	11	0	0	0	0	51.1	82	266	55	49	7	2	2	2	33	0	48	9	0
..k, Dave, Elizabethton*	1	1	.500	8.18	16	0	0	0	9	0	22.0	31	106	22	20	1	0	1	3	9	0	36	5	0
..annon, Jason, Kingsport*	2	1	.667	6.92	19	1	0	0	9	0	26.0	34	129	23	20	2	3	1	2	16	0	26	7	0
..y, Chris, Bluefield	0	0	.000	9.90	7	0	0	0	5	0	10.0	9	50	13	11	0	0	0	2	12	0	9	3	0
..wn, Derek, Bluefield	1	0	1.000	16.88	2	2	0	0	0	0	5.1	12	29	10	10	5	0	0	0	5	0	4	1	0
..kman, Tom, Bristol	1	6	.143	4.88	17	7	1	0	5	0	51.2	62	245	39	28	5	1	0	9	21	1	51	9	2
..zkowski, Matt, Martinsville	0	0	.000	54.00	1	0	0	0	1	0	1.0	6	9	6	6	1	0	1	0	0	0	0	0	0

SUMMER CLASS A *Appalachian League*

Pitcher, Team	W	L	Pct.	ERA	G	GS	CG	ShO	GF	Sv.	IP	H	TBF	R	ER	HR	SH	SF	HB	BB	IBB	SO	WP	BK
Burke, Ethan, Kingsport	0	3	.000	17.10	9	0	0	0	5	0	10.0	25	59	20	19	3	0	1		6	0	5	0	
Burnett, A.J., Kingsport	4	0	1.000	3.88	12	12	0	0	0	0	58.0	31	245	26	25	0	1	2	7	54	0	68	16	
Caddell, Carl, Princeton*	2	5	.286	6.68	9	9	0	0	0	0	31.0	33	163	31	23	5	1	2	4	32	0	33	4	
Cardona, Steve, Bristol	0	1	.000	5.40	6	0	0	0	2	0	5.0	7	27	3	3	0	0	0	0	4	0	7	2	
Carlson, Garret, Bristol	0	0	.000	12.21	16	0	0	0	7	0	24.1	43	149	48	33	4	0	1	3	29	0	20	10	
Carlyle, Buddy, Princeton	2	4	.333	4.66	10	9	1	0	1	0	46.1	47	204	33	24	4	2	1	1	16	0	42	8	
Cooper, Chadwick, Kingsport	1	1	.500	12.79	5	2	0	0	0	0	12.2	21	66	20	18	3	0	0	1	8	0	9	1	
Davis, Lance, Princeton*	2	0	1.000	1.20	2	2	1	1	0	0	15.0	6	55	4	2	0	0	0		3	0	19	0	
Davis, Mike, Kingsport	1	0	1.000	4.08	11	0	0	0	7	1	17.2	15	80	13	8	0	2	0		7	0	15	3	
DeLeon, Jose, Johnson City	3	1	.750	2.12	27	0	0	0	26	15	34.0	28	138	8	8	2	0	1		1		32	0	
Demorejon, Pedro, Bristol	1	2	.333	6.99	18	1	0	0	6	1	37.1	49	183	33	29	7	1	3	3	22	1	39	4	
DePaula, Sean, Burlington	4	2	.667	3.82	23	0	0	0	11	1	35.1	31	151	16	15	3	2	2	2	13	0	42	4	
Dewitt, Matt, Johnson City	5	5	.500	5.42	14	14	0	0	0	0	79.2	96	353	53	48	17	1	0	3	26	0	58	7	
Dooley, Chris, Johnson City	1	1	.500	4.21	13	0	0	0	2	1	25.2	26	118	14	12	2	0	0		14	1	28	2	
Dose, Gary, Elizabethton	1	0	1.000	4.15	17	0	0	0	10	0	21.2	22	106	13	10	1	0	0	2	19	0	24	5	
Eibey, Scott, Bluefield*	5	1	.833	2.80	24	0	0	0	10	2	45.0	30	187	19	14	3	0	3		17	0	59	4	
Estrella, Leoncio, Kingsport	6	3	.667	3.88	15	7	1	0	3	0	58.0	54	248	32	25	3	4	1	1	24	0	52	6	
Farley, Joe, Bristol*	3	6	.333	3.48	10	10	3	1	0	0	64.2	73	277	34	25	5	1	2	2	11	0	54	3	
Fenus, Justin, Martinsville	2	7	.222	6.04	14	8	0	0	3	0	44.2	46	212	33	30	5	1	2	3	29	0	26	9	
Ferullo, Matt, Kingsport	0	0	.000	7.11	1	1	0	0	0	0	6.1	9	27	5	5	1	0	0		1	0	7	0	
Fisher, Louis, Bluefield	3	4	.429	4.40	14	13	1	1	0	0	71.2	58	318	43	35	2	0	1	2	48	0	52	15	
Forster, Pete, Elizabethton*	2	2	.500	7.04	4	4	0	0	0	0	23.0	23	104	19	18	5	0	0	2	12	0	20	0	
Fowler, Benjamin, Danville	0	0	.000	14.29	4	0	0	0	0	0	5.2	8	32	13	9	3	0	0	0	5	0	2	3	
Garff, Jeff, Elizabethton	6	5	.545	4.58	12	12	2	1	0	0	72.2	71	304	44	37	11	1	1	4	13	0	38	7	
Garza, Alberto, Burlington	2	4	.333	5.45	9	9	0	0	0	0	39.2	34	169	24	24	5	1	2	1	15	0	34	2	
Garza, Chris, Elizabethton*	4	0	1.000	1.98	22	0	0	0	12	5	36.1	26	145	8	8	3	1	1	2	12	0	44	3	
Geis, John, Johnson City*	1	0	1.000	4.50	5	1	0	0	0	0	10.0	8	41	5	5	2	1	0	0	4	1	12	3	
Giron, Roberto, Princeton	1	3	.250	3.10	22	1	0	0	19	7	40.2	34	168	18	14	1	2	1	4	11	1	44	1	
Gonzalez, Dicky, Kingsport	1	0	1.000	1.80	1	1	0	0	0	0	5.0	4	20	2	1	0	1	0		0	0	7	1	
Guzman, Toribio, Johnson City	2	2	.500	3.77	23	0	0	0	4	0	31.0	39	148	19	13	0	0	0	2	18	1	24	1	
Hacen, Abraham, Bluefield	8	3	.727	3.41	15	12	2	0	2	0	63.1	54	280	29	24	4	0	3	5	36	0	69	9	
Hackett, Jason, Bluefield*	1	1	.500	5.48	19	5	0	0	4	1	46.0	47	215	33	28	6	0	1	2	28	0	56	6	
Hafer, Jeffrey, Kingsport	2	0	.000	2.14	24	0	0	0	14	6	33.2	29	137	9	8	1	0	0	1	8	1	43	7	
Hamilton, Jimmy, Burlington*	1	3	.250	4.00	10	10	0	0	0	0	45.0	45	193	22	20	7	1	3		16	0	50	8	
Heineman, Rick, Bristol	2	1	.667	4.50	23	0	0	0	14	0	36.0	37	168	25	18	3	0	1		22	1	34	5	
Herbison, Brett, Kingsport	6	2	.750	1.29	13	12	0	0	0	0	76.2	43	297	18	11	4	0	1	3	31	0	86	6	
Hodges, Reid, Bristol	0	2	.000	11.22	16	3	0	0	4	0	29.2	38	155	41	37	5	0	3		25	0	24	5	
Hogge, Shawn, Johnson City	0	1	.000	11.17	12	0	0	0	0	0	9.2	14	68	17	12	1	0	1	4	21	0	6	6	
Hooten, David, Elizabethton	1	0	1.000	4.32	6	0	0	0	5	1	8.1	6	37	4	4	0	0	2	1	5	0	15	0	
Horgan, Joe, Burlington*	1	2	.333	4.19	23	0	0	0	18	7	34.1	37	157	25	16	1	0	0	4	9	0	48	4	
Horne, Jeff, Princeton	3	3	.500	3.47	10	8	3	1	0	0	46.2	42	204	30	18	2	0	3	1	21	0	45	7	
Huntsman, Brandon, Bluefield	5	4	.556	4.08	14	13	0	0	0	0	68.1	54	297	37	31	4	0	2	6	38	0	79	9	
Hurtado, Omar, Princeton	1	2	.333	6.15	15	0	0	0	7	0	26.1	24	124	22	18	2	1	1	3	17	0	19	3	
Iglesias, Mario, Bristol	0	0	.000	2.16	3	0	0	0	1	1	8.1	6	29	2	2	1	0	1	0	1	0	2	1	
Irvine, Kirk, Bristol	0	4	.000	4.87	11	5	1	0	2	0	40.2	49	180	30	22	5	2	0	4	10	2	39	4	
Jelsovsky, Craig, Kingsport	4	1	.800	2.59	13	1	0	0	4	2	24.1	18	101	9	7	1	0	0	3	10	1	20	1	
Koeman, Matt, Burlington	5	2	.714	3.72	13	3	0	0	2	1	38.2	33	165	18	16	4	0	0	2	10	0	49	2	
Lagrandeur, Yan, Danville	3	1	.750	4.10	19	2	0	0	2	0	37.1	39	168	19	17	3	0	2	2	19	1	34	9	
Lakman, Jason, Bristol	4	4	.500	5.67	13	13	1	0	0	0	66.2	70	312	48	42	5	0	3	6	38	0	64	13	
Lawrence, Rich, Princeton	0	0	.000	0.00	1	0	0	0	0	0	1.0	3	6	1	0	0	0	0	1	0	0	2	0	
LeBlanc, Eric, Princeton	4	1	.800	4.53	9	6	0	0	3	1	45.2	39	198	29	23	0	0	1	2	16	0	51	2	
Loudermilk, Darren, Burlington	1	0	1.000	4.68	16	0	0	0	4	0	32.2	35	143	23	17	1	0	1	2	8	0	29	6	
Lovingood, Jeromie, Kingsport*	0	1	.000	6.75	1	1	0	0	0	0	4.0	3	16	3	3	0	0	0		1	0	2	0	
Lugo, Jesus, Johnson City	0	0	.000	0.00	3	0	0	0	2	0	3.1	1	10	0	0	0	0	0		0	0	2	0	
Lynch, Ryan, Elizabethton*	3	2	.600	3.40	11	9	0	0	0	0	45.0	43	197	19	17	2	1	1	3	22	0	35	2	
Lyons, Mike, Kingsport	3	2	.600	1.89	25	0	0	0	15	5	38.0	27	157	14	8	1	1	0	3	14	1	52	1	
Malko, Bryan, Elizabethton*	5	3	.625	4.59	12	12	1	0	0	0	66.2	73	288	36	34	5	1	3	4	27	0	54	5	
Mallard, Randi, Princeton	2	7	.222	3.68	13	11	0	1	0	0	66.0	66	302	42	27	2	0	4		38	0	72	16	
Marquis, Jason, Danville	1	1	.500	4.63	7	4	0	0	0	0	23.1	30	113	18	12	0	0	1		7	0	24	2	
Martinez, Alejandro, Princeton	0	0	.000	18.00	1	0	0	0	1	0	2.0	6	31	4	4	1	0	0		0	0	1	1	
Mattox, Gene, Princeton	0	0	.000	0.00	3	0	0	0	1	0	4.0	1	18	1	0	0	0	0		4	0	3	1	
McBride, Rodney, Elizabethton	3	2	.600	2.43	12	12	1	1	0	0	74.0	60	309	29	20	4	4	0	5	28	0	83	8	
McDermott, Ryan, Burlington	2	8	.200	4.61	13	13	0	0	0	0	54.2	55	256	38	28	2	0	2	1	40	0	38	9	
McGlinchy, Kevin, Danville	3	2	.600	1.13	13	13	0	0	0	0	72.0	52	283	21	9	2	1	2		11	0	77	4	
McNatt, Josh, Bluefield*	0	0	.000	8.53	2	1	0	0	0	0	6.1	10	33	6	6	1	0	0	0	6	0	7	1	
Mear, Rich, Johnson City*	2	2	.500	8.31	10	6	0	0	1	0	30.1	35	160	31	28	1	0	1	2	37	0	26	5	
Mejia, Javier, Martinsville	2	2	.500	2.80	29	0	0	0	27	12	35.1	29	158	15	11	3	1	3		3		50	4	
Mercedes, Carlos, Bluefield	1	2	.333	5.18	14	0	0	0	8	1	24.1	24	112	24	14	5	1	2	2	9	0	18	3	
Mojica, Gonzalo, Burlington	1	0	1.000	8.54	14	1	0	0	6	0	26.1	28	136	25	25	5	0	1	2	28	0	35	3	
Molina, Gabe, Bluefield	4	0	1.000	3.60	23	0	0	0	19	7	30.0	29	131	12	12	1	1	0	2	13	1	33	5	
Molta, Salvatore, Martinsville	1	9	.100	8.31	12	12	0	0	0	0	43.1	45	223	46	40	3	0	2	11	39	1	37	3	
Montero, Francisco, Martinsville	2	0	1.000	6.46	21	0	0	0	10	0	39.0	58	200	38	28	5	0	1	7	18	1	28	4	
Mosquea, Alberto, Martinsville	2	1	.667	5.53	14	0	0	0	7	0	27.2	25	139	28	17	3	0	1	2	20	0	18	6	
Negrette, Richard, Burlington	2	6	.250	5.16	14	13	0	0	0	0	59.1	57	283	50	34	3	1	3	5	36	0	52	12	
Nichols, James, Bristol	4	3	.571	4.10	12	4	0	0	3	0	41.2	31	168	21	19	5	1	3	0	17	0	36	3	
Norris, Steve, Johnson City*	4	3	.571	6.93	16	10	0	0	2	0	50.2	68	252	49	39	4	0	4		36	0	36	8	
Nye, Richie, Elizabethton	1	2	.333	7.30	15	1	0	0	2	0	24.2	34	122	25	20	3	1	2	7	6	0	24	1	
O'Hearn, Brandon, Princeton	0	0	.000	36.00	1	0	0	0	1	0	1.0	3	9	4	4	0	0	0	0	1	0	3	1	
Onley, Shawn, Danville	3	2	.600	3.80	13	12	0	0	0	0	64.0	53	269	31	27	8	1	1	3	23	0	59	4	
Onofrei, Tim, Johnson City	2	2	.333	4.68	12	7	0	0	2	0	42.1	45	192	24	22	3	1	2	3	22	1	28	2	
Opipari, Mario, Elizabethton	3	1	.750	1.95	19	1	0	0	16	6	32.1	26	135	10	7	2	0	1	0	21	0	52	2	
Pacheco, Delvis, Danville	8	1	.889	2.64	13	12	0	0	0	0	64.2	56	271	28	19	1	1	2		21	0	60	5	
Paronto, Chad, Bluefield	1	1	.500	1.69	9	2	0	0	1	1	21.1	16	82	4	4	0	0	0		5	0	24	0	

cher, Team	W	L	Pct.	ERA	G	GS	CG	ShO	GF	Sv.	IP	H	TBF	R	ER	HR	SH	SF	HB	BB	IBB	SO	WP	Bk.
rrish, John, Bluefield*	2	1	.667	2.70	8	0	0	0	5	1	13.1	11	60	6	4	0	1	2	0	9	1	18	2	0
guero, Americo, Bluefield	4	2	.667	2.82	9	9	0	0	0	0	51.0	38	217	24	16	6	0	1	8	22	0	54	12	0
lton, Brad, Burlington	0	3	.000	2.81	15	0	0	0	9	3	25.2	19	104	11	8	1	1	0	0	9	0	21	3	0
illips, Jon, Princeton	3	4	.429	4.29	23	0	0	0	13	2	42.0	40	192	25	20	5	2	1	1	28	2	53	7	0
rtillo, Ramon, Martinsville*	4	2	.667	6.00	21	0	0	0	7	1	45.0	52	215	34	30	5	0	5	6	29	0	34	2	1
rtle, Joe, Kingsport	0	0	.000	0.00	3	0	0	0	0	0	6.0	4	23	0	0	0	0	0	0	0	0	1	0	0
intana, Urbano, Martinsville	3	5	.375	4.09	15	12	0	0	1	0	77.0	71	320	44	35	8	3	5	5	22	1	43	3	2
ed, Steve, Johnson City	5	1	.833	4.05	31	0	0	0	15	4	40.0	39	170	21	18	4	1	2	3	12	1	38	0	0
ichow, Robert, Burlington	2	2	.500	4.53	21	0	0	0	4	1	43.2	51	193	23	22	1	1	0	3	10	0	41	3	0
aaudo, Mike, Bluefield	0	1	.000	81.00	1	0	0	0	1	0	0.1	3	5	3	3	0	0	0	0	1	0	0	0	0
egert, Tim, Johnson City*	3	0	1.000	4.19	26	0	0	0	5	0	38.2	41	163	19	18	3	1	2	3	16	2	40	1	2
berts, Grant, Kingsport	9	1	.900	2.10	13	13	2	2	0	0	68.2	43	285	18	16	3	1	0	7	37	1	92	4	0
berts, Randy, Princeton	3	2	.600	2.66	12	4	1	0	2	0	50.2	33	213	20	15	0	0	1	2	29	0	49	15	1
sario, Ruben, Johnson City	7	3	.700	3.28	13	13	1	1	0	0	71.1	53	296	30	26	3	1	3	1	37	0	72	7	4
se, Ted, Princeton	3	5	.375	6.22	11	11	1	1	0	0	59.1	70	262	44	41	9	2	3	3	21	0	53	9	2
ntos, Juan Carlos, Bluefield	1	0	1.000	6.20	16	0	0	0	5	0	24.2	32	117	19	17	1	0	2	1	11	1	20	1	2
horzman, Steve, Bristol	0	9	.000	4.57	14	13	1	0	1	0	69.0	73	310	43	35	5	1	3	6	31	0	50	5	0
hurman, Ryan, Danville	2	4	.333	4.96	21	1	0	0	7	1	45.1	45	203	30	25	5	2	4	6	18	1	49	5	0
aver, Mark, Bluefield	1	0	1.000	1.20	3	2	0	0	0	0	15.0	4	55	2	2	1	0	0	1	5	0	18	0	0
elton, Barry, Bristol	0	0	.000	0.00	2	0	0	0	2	0	2.2	2	12	0	0	0	0	0	0	2	0	1	0	0
iell, Jason, Danville	3	1	.750	1.97	12	12	0	0	0	0	59.1	44	231	14	13	1	0	1	1	19	0	57	3	0
ockley, Keith, Martinsville*	2	2	.500	8.00	14	6	1	0	3	0	45.0	62	212	44	40	8	1	4	1	10	0	29	1	7
va, Carlos, Martinsville	0	0	.000	4.00	7	1	0	0	1	0	18.0	20	78	11	8	1	4	1	1	5	0	16	0	0
ead, George, Danville	2	1	.667	7.50	10	0	0	0	5	0	18.0	26	87	17	15	2	0	2	2	8	0	9	0	0
iegel, Mike, Burlington*	0	1	.000	3.74	14	0	0	0	6	0	21.2	19	97	12	9	0	1	0	2	12	0	14	1	0
iers, Corey, Elizabethton*	6	5	.545	3.34	17	8	0	0	2	0	59.1	69	289	45	22	3	0	3	2	26	0	67	9	1
anley, Todd, Bristol	1	3	.250	5.31	17	0	0	0	10	1	20.1	23	103	21	12	2	1	0	1	19	2	13	9	0
evens, Kris, Martinsville*	1	4	.200	3.64	10	10	0	0	0	0	47.0	54	194	23	19	2	3	1	1	10	0	41	2	1
ber, Dave, Martinsville	1	0	1.000	2.30	9	1	0	0	1	0	15.2	12	66	6	4	1	0	1	0	6	0	15	7	0
wers, Josh, Bluefield	4	1	.800	5.24	14	9	0	0	1	0	55.0	63	234	35	32	9	0	1	1	5	0	61	4	1
l, Bill, Kingsport	1	0	1.000	0.83	20	0	0	0	11	6	32.2	18	118	3	3	0	1	0	0	8	0	40	3	0
ttle, John, Johnson City	2	2	.500	4.24	21	0	0	0	7	0	34.0	33	152	22	16	4	2	1	0	13	3	25	0	1
centino, Andy, Princeton*	0	4	.000	6.50	11	6	0	0	1	0	45.2	52	216	38	33	6	1	4	1	25	0	47	6	1
egas, Ismael, Danville	0	0	.000	3.00	1	0	0	0	0	0	3.0	2	11	1	1	0	0	0	1	0	0	4	1	0
lker, Corey, Danville*	0	0	.000	0.00	1	0	0	0	1	0	1.0	1	5	0	0	0	0	0	0	1	0	1	0	0
alton, Tim, Martinsville	0	3	.000	5.23	4	4	1	0	0	0	20.2	27	101	19	12	3	0	2	0	8	0	20	4	1
eibl, Clint, Johnson City	4	1	.800	2.05	7	7	0	0	0	0	44.0	27	172	12	10	1	0	0	1	12	0	51	0	0
nkelsas, Joseph, Danville	1	1	.500	7.15	8	0	0	0	6	2	11.1	11	54	10	9	0	0	4	4	0	9	2	0
se, William, Danville	2	6	.250	6.95	21	0	0	0	12	1	33.2	40	174	39	26	1	6	1	2	26	0	25	12	0
yatt, Ben, Danville*	5	3	.625	4.42	10	10	0	0	0	0	53.0	50	225	27	26	2	2	5	1	19	0	31	3	0
skie, Nate, Elizabethton	3	3	.500	5.23	7	6	0	0	0	0	32.2	38	141	27	19	3	0	0	0	8	0	28	2	0
irchitz, Andy, Kingsport	8	1	.889	1.55	12	11	1	0	0	0	75.1	51	305	22	13	4	2	0	7	19	2	76	1	2

COMBINATION SHUTOUTS: **Bluefield (5)**—Peguero-Eibey-Molina, Peguero-Molina, Seaver-Hackett, Huntsman-Eibey-Achilles, Paronto-Eibey-Molina. **Bristol (1)**—ley-Heineman. **Burlington (3)**—Bacsik-DePaula-Horgan, Koeman-Reichow-DePaula, Mojica-Pelton. **Danville (5)**—Onley-Bauldree-Lagrandeur-Beasley, Wyatt-uldree, McGlinchy-Bauldree, Pacheco-Lagrandeur-Bauldree, Shiell-Bauldree. **Elizabethton (2)**—Malko-Blank, Lynch-Bauder. **Johnson City (1)**—Wiebl-Dooley-Tuttle. ngsport (10)—Herbison-Estrella, Herbison-Burke, Zwirchwitz-Hafer, Burnett-Burke, Herbison-Tull, Roberts-Hafer, Estrella-Tull, Herbison-Pyrtle-Lyons, Herbison-ons, Roberts-Tull-Hafer. **Martinsville (2)**—Molta-Portillo-Mejia, Molta-Mejia. **Princeton (1)**—Roberts-Phillips.

NO-HIT GAMES: None.

1996 FIELDING

TEAM

am	Pct.	G	PO	A	E	TC	DP	PB	Team	Pct.	G	PO	A	E	TC	DP	PB
hnson City	.963	68	1755	669	93	2517	52	26	Danville	.949	66	1734	667	129	2530	53	22
ngsport	.963	68	1720	622	90	2432	45	14	Princeton	.947	68	1695	633	129	2457	38	26
rlington	.954	67	1708	690	116	2514	37	24	Bristol	.943	68	1709	703	146	2558	57	20
uefield	.953	68	1724	649	118	2491	48	10	Martinsville	.942	67	1671	670	144	2485	52	26
zabethton	.949	67	1664	698	126	2488	56	20	TRIPLE PLAYS: None.								

INDIVIDUAL

FIRST BASEMEN

NOTE: All caps denotes fielding-percentage leader based on 34 games for tchers, 45 for all other non-pitchers and 68 innings for pitchers. *Throws thanded.

ayer, Team	Pct.	G	PO	A	E	TC	DP
anford, Joey, Elizabethton	1.000	1	11	1	0	12	0
CK, Billy, Johnson City*	.988	52	447	40	6	493	34
nman, Demond, Princeton	.976	43	310	19	8	337	20
Cinces, Tim, Bluefield	1.000	1	6	0	0	6	0
rdy, Bryan, Burlington	.970	39	336	21	11	368	23
intz, Chris, Bristol	.939	8	59	3	4	66	3
rdman, Eli, Elizabethton	1.000	3	20	4	0	24	3
rn, Marv, Bristol*	1.000	5	16	2	0	18	3
on, Jose, Johnson City	.981	18	148	11	3	162	15
tz, Manuel, Bristol	.969	41	372	38	13	423	37
ata, Manuel, Martinsville*	.983	10	52	5	1	58	5
cCarthy, Kevin, Kingsport*	1.000	5	20	3	0	23	2
chols, Kevin, Martinsville	.981	20	146	9	3	158	10
Hearn, Brandon, Princeton	.987	9	72	6	1	79	6

Player, Team	Pct.	G	PO	A	E	TC	DP
Parsons, Jason, Princeton	.986	16	127	13	2	142	10
Peterman, Tommy, Elizabethton*	1.000	1	10	2	0	12	0
Pickering, Calvin, Bluefield*	.979	53	396	26	9	431	33
Reyes, Freddy, Elizabethton	.984	62	514	44	9	567	44
Romero, Marty, Bristol	1.000	2	6	1	0	7	1
Russin, Tom, Bluefield	.981	24	143	10	3	156	12
Scharrer, Jim, Danville	.984	62	532	24	9	565	42
Schlicher, B.J., Martinsville	.970	41	328	26	11	365	27
Sharpe, Grant, Burlington	.982	10	109	1	2	112	6
Shelton, Barry, Bristol	.984	16	121	6	2	129	9
Strangfeld, Aaron, Danville	.909	3	18	2	2	22	2
Taveras, Frank, Burlington	.971	19	148	19	5	172	6
Terhune, Mike, Danville	1.000	1	6	0	0	6	1
Tessmar, Timothy, Kingsport*	.985	65	507	34	8	549	39

SECOND BASEMEN

Player, Team	Pct.	G	PO	A	E	TC	DP
Bearden, Doug, Bristol	.927	38	69	108	14	191	21

Player, Team	Pct.	G	PO	A	E	TC	DP
Brooks, Anthony, Danville	1.000	1	0	2	0	2	0
Bruce, Maurice, Kingsport	.921	10	14	21	3	38	4
Casimiro, Carlos, Bluefield	.947	60	103	130	13	246	26
Clapp, Stubby, Johnson City	.978	20	38	49	2	89	13
Clark, John, Princeton	.972	29	46	58	3	107	7
Cranford, Joey, Elizabethton	.991	24	45	61	1	107	13
EDWARDS, Lamont, Martinsville	.983	47	95	134	4	233	34
Fowler, Maleke, Bluefield	.944	4	10	7	1	18	3
Harris, Rodger, Johnson City	.910	28	33	48	8	89	10
Inglin, Jeff, Bristol	1.000	8	20	18	0	38	6
Jelsovsky, Craig, Kingsport	1.000	1	0	3	0	3	1
Jenkins, Ben, Martinsville	.899	17	36	35	8	79	8
Katz, Jason R., Danville	.922	14	23	36	5	64	9
Kritscher, Ryan, Johnson City	.935	24	39	62	7	108	12
Kushma, Glenn, Kingsport	.970	29	44	54	3	101	9
Mejia, Juan, Martinsville	1.000	5	7	7	0	14	0
Montgomery, Andre, Princeton	.898	40	74	93	19	186	19
Moss, Rick, Elizabethton	.974	12	10	27	1	38	6
Mota, Cristian, Burlington	.953	37	63	100	8	171	14
Murphy, Quinn, Burlington	.909	13	14	36	5	55	4
Orndorff, Dave, Elizabethton	1.000	2	2	7	0	9	3
Paz, Richard, Bluefield	1.000	8	11	16	0	27	2
Penalver, Juan, Kingsport	.962	36	46	79	5	130	23
Perez, Edwin, Burlington	1.000	2	3	5	0	8	2
Rodriguez, Chris, Burlington	.959	16	30	40	3	73	7
Solano, Angel, Bristol	.916	23	39	59	9	107	7
Taveras, Frank, Burlington	1.000	3	3	5	0	8	0
Terhune, Mike, Danville	.946	52	106	141	14	261	36
Thieleke, C.J., Elizabethton	.891	32	52	63	14	129	11

THIRD BASEMEN

Player, Team	Pct.	G	PO	A	E	TC	DP
Bearden, Doug, Bristol	1.000	2	0	1	0	1	0
Buczkowski, Matt, Martinsville	.814	29	25	58	19	102	7
Casimiro, Carlos, Bluefield	1.000	1	0	1	0	1	0
Clapp, Stubby, Johnson City	.966	9	7	21	1	29	1
Clark, John, Princeton	.937	30	17	57	5	79	2
Concepcion, David, Princeton	.889	4	4	4	1	9	0
DeCinces, Tim, Bluefield	.957	10	5	17	1	23	2
Edwards, Lamont, Martinsville	.895	6	5	12	2	19	2
Edwards, Michael, Burlington	.902	40	26	84	12	122	3
Fowler, Maleke, Bluefield	1.000	1	0	1	0	1	0
Herdman, Eli, Elizabethton	.851	54	32	94	22	148	14
Inglin, Jeff, Bristol	.818	11	5	13	4	22	3
Jelsovsky, Craig, Kingsport	.667	3	1	1	1	3	0
Jenkins, Ben, Martinsville	.818	10	7	11	4	22	0
Katz, Jason R., Danville	.750	7	4	11	5	20	1
Klee, Charles, Bristol	.875	16	16	33	7	56	4
Kritscher, Ryan, Johnson City	1.000	1	0	1	0	1	0
Kushma, Glenn, Kingsport	.750	6	5	7	4	16	0
Lawrence, Chip, Bluefield	1.000	9	3	8	0	11	2
Leon, Jose, Johnson City	.931	43	39	69	8	116	6
Lopes, Omar, Bristol	.905	26	14	43	6	63	3
Lopez, Pee Wee, Kingsport	1.000	1	1	0	0	1	0
Martinez, Alejandro, Princeton	.892	37	28	55	10	93	2
Mejia, Juan, Martinsville	.769	5	1	9	3	13	2
Minor, Ryan, Bluefield	.945	22	10	42	3	55	1
Montgomery, Andre, Princeton	.800	1	2	2	1	5	0
Moss, Rick, Elizabethton	.917	12	5	17	2	24	1
Mota, Cristian, Burlington	.863	27	11	58	11	80	2
Nichols, Kevin, Martinsville	.843	19	17	26	8	51	2
Paz, Richard, Bluefield	.943	17	8	25	2	35	4
Penalver, Juan, Kingsport	1.000	1	1	0	0	1	0
Perez, Edwin, Burlington	.875	3	2	5	1	8	0
Ribaudo, Mike, Bluefield	.778	3	3	4	2	9	1
Russin, Tom, Bluefield	.714	18	3	32	14	49	3
Shelton, Barry, Bristol	.957	10	9	13	1	23	0
Solano, Angel, Bristol	.818	4	1	8	2	11	2
Spencer, Jeffrey, Danville	.887	60	39	126	21	186	7
Tanner, Paul, Johnson City	.963	21	14	38	2	54	4
Thieleke, C.J., Elizabethton	.778	2	4	3	2	9	2
ZAMORA, Junior, Kingsport	.904	60	38	112	16	166	10

SHORTSTOPS

Player, Team	Pct.	G	PO	A	E	TC	DP
BUTLER, Brent, Johnson City	.945	56	81	127	12	220	23
Cranford, Joey, Elizabethton	.850	5	4	13	3	20	3
Davidson, Cleatus, Elizabethton	.896	65	100	200	35	335	33
Davila, Angel, Kingsport	1.000	2	1	0	0	1	0
Edwards, Michael, Burlington	.889	3	3	5	1	9	1
Jaroncyk, Ryan, Kingsport	.920	57	76	119	17	212	23
Jenkins, Ben, Martinsville	.839	7	6	20	5	31	4

Player, Team	Pct.	G	PO	A	E	TC	DP
Katz, Jason R., Danville	.949	18	19	37	3	59	
Klee, Charles, Bristol	.887	32	49	92	18	159	1
Kushma, Glenn, Kingsport	.957	7	5	17	1	23	
Lawrence, Chip, Bluefield	.950	6	5	14	1	20	
Lopes, Omar, Bristol	.924	29	40	82	10	132	7
Martinez, Eddy, Bluefield	.898	37	43	80	14	137	1
Mejia, Juan, Martinsville	.902	13	17	29	5	51	
Minor, Ryan, Bluefield	.750	3	3	3	2	8	
Paz, Richard, Bluefield	.914	27	36	81	11	128	1
Perez, Edwin, Burlington	.926	42	74	101	14	189	1
Perez, Jersen, Kingsport	.923	6	9	15	2	26	
Presto, Nick, Princeton	.932	12	23	32	4	59	1
Rodriguez, Aurelio, Burlington	.969	18	11	52	2	65	
Rodriguez, Chris, Burlington	1.000	2	2	1	0	3	
Rollins, Jimmy, Martinsville	.906	49	66	126	20	212	2
Solano, Angel, Bristol	.939	8	13	18	2	33	
Solano, Manuel, Princeton	.895	57	79	142	26	247	2
Tanner, Paul, Johnson City	.980	13	21	29	1	51	
Taveras, Frank, Burlington	.808	4	6	15	5	26	
Thorpe, Angres, Danville	.880	43	60	101	22	183	2
Vecchioni, Gerald, Danville	.909	11	17	33	5	55	

OUTFIELDERS

Player, Team	Pct.	G	PO	A	E	TC	DP
Abell, Antonio, Johnson City	.942	42	62	3	4	69	
Akins, Carlos, Bluefield	.957	13	20	2	1	23	
Albert, Rashad, Bristol	.956	54	107	2	5	114	
Bass, Jason, Danville	.959	54	87	7	4	98	
Bishop, Tim, Kingsport	.975	61	111	4	3	118	
Black, Brandon, Kingsport	1.000	10	10	1	0	11	
Brown, Jerome, Elizabethton	.946	41	52	1	3	56	
Buckles, Matt, Martinsville	.893	20	25	0	3	28	
Byrd, Issac, Johnson City	.974	23	37	1	1	39	
Champion, Jeff, Danville	.750	2	3	0	1	4	
Chancey, Bailey, Kingsport	.966	57	81	3	3	87	
Chancey, Robert, Kingsport	.875	5	7	0	1	8	
Charles, Curtis, Bluefield	.950	58	71	5	4	80	
Dent, Darrell, Bluefield*	.975	56	111	4	3	118	
Ellison, Skeeter, Danville	.895	45	50	1	6	57	
Farley, Cordell, Johnson City	.972	14	34	1	1	36	
Ferguson, Ryan, Martinsville*	.957	33	63	3	3	69	
Ferrand, Thomas, Martinsville*	.978	48	87	4	2	93	
Fowler, Maleke, Bluefield	.958	16	21	2	1	24	
Goodman, Herbert, Princeton	1.000	4	4	0	0	4	
Guerrero, Hamlet, Kingsport	1.000	6	5	0	0	5	
Hernandez, Jesus, Burlington*	1.000	19	35	0	0	35	
Herrera, Jesus, Princeton	.897	20	25	1	3	29	
Hogan, Todd, Johnson City	.977	47	83	2	2	87	
Hollins, Darontaye, Bristol	.964	16	27	0	1	28	
Inglin, Jeff, Bristol	.976	17	36	4	1	41	
Irvis, Damon, Elizabethton	.944	53	65	2	4	71	
Jackson, William, Burlington	.940	33	47	0	3	50	
Jenkins, Ben, Martinsville	1.000	6	6	0	0	6	
Johnson, Heath, Elizabethton	.943	37	47	3	3	53	
Johnson, Jason, Martinsville	.936	53	98	5	7	110	
Kushma, Glenn, Kingsport	1.000	1	2	0	0	2	
Landstad, Rob, Burlington	1.000	28	28	2	0	30	
Lee, Jason, Johnson City	.926	36	49	1	4	54	
Lutz, Manuel, Bristol	.750	1	3	0	1	4	
McCarthy, Kevin, Kingsport*	.963	60	75	2	3	80	
McClure, Craig, Bristol	.939	59	92	1	6	99	
McHenry, Joe, Elizabethton	.974	41	70	5	2	77	
Messner, Jake, Burlington*	.913	46	63	0	6	70	
Moss, Rick, Elizabethton	1.000	2	2	0	0	2	
Mota, Cristian, Burlington	1.000	2	2	0	0	2	
O'Hearn, Brandon, Princeton	.971	54	60	6	2	68	
Oliver, Johnny, Princeton	.844	33	36	2	7	45	
Patton, Cory, Kingsport	1.000	20	14	1	0	15	
Pedroza, Alex, Bluefield*	.889	16	8	0	1	9	
PENDERGRASS, Tyrone, Danville	.984	53	118	3	2	123	
Rivera, Roberto, Bluefield	.950	36	38	0	2	40	
Ross, Jason Arai, Danville	.971	34	64	4	2	70	
Saturria, Luis, Johnson City	.961	47	68	5	3	76	
Serafin, Ricardo, Martinsville	.963	33	49	3	2	54	
Shelton, Barry, Bristol	.963	17	25	1	1	27	
Shy, Jason, Danville	1.000	4	3	0	0	3	
Siponmaa, Ryan, Burlington	.667	2	4	0	2	6	
Skeens, Jeremy, Princeton	.969	54	91	3	3	97	
Stephens, Joel, Bluefield	.970	30	32	0	1	33	
Stevens, Clay, Bristol	.955	42	61	3	3	67	
Taveras, Frank, Burlington	1.000	19	27	1	0	28	
Terry, Tony, Princeton	.920	52	89	3	8	100	
Vilchez, Jose, Elizabethton	.933	42	42	0	3	45	

er, Team	Pct.	G	PO	A	E	TC	DP
ker, Corey, Danville*	.889	14	14	2	2	18	0
iams, Jewell, Burlington	.933	60	81	2	6	89	0
rthy, Thomas, Martinsville	.925	23	33	4	3	40	2

CATCHERS

er, Team	Pct.	G	PO	A	E	TC	DP	PB
ir, Tom, Burlington	.995	26	205	15	1	221	0	4
endt, Jay, Bluefield	1.000	3	6	0	0	6	0	0
y, Chip, Bluefield	.968	24	192	18	7	217	0	3
son, Cody, Burlington	.980	27	216	27	5	248	2	9
czak, Chuck, Bristol	.958	6	42	4	2	48	1	1
old, John, Danville	.988	7	73	8	1	82	2	3
ck, Brandon, Kingsport	.977	12	77	8	2	87	1	4
ges, Alexander, Danville	.941	5	26	6	2	34	1	0
cho, Darwin, Princeton	.992	13	102	17	1	120	0	6
hman, Tom, Elizabethton	.979	6	40	7	1	48	2	2
zkowski, Matt, Martinsville	1.000	1	1	0	0	1	0	0
taldo, Eric, Danville	.983	22	166	11	3	180	1	4
nolly, Sean, Bristol	.973	38	216	39	7	262	4	10
inces, Tim, Bluefield	.969	17	143	13	5	161	0	2
son, Skeeter, Danville	1.000	2	8	2	0	10	0	2
ns, Brad, Johnson City	.985	10	60	4	1	65	0	11
renbach, Todd, Princeton	.955	19	121	7	6	134	0	6
st, Robert, Kingsport	1.000	5	33	6	0	39	0	1
giulo, Jimmy, Johnson City	.983	46	354	46	7	407	3	13
ks, Brian, Princeton	.987	32	288	20	4	312	0	11
dstad, Rob, Burlington	1.000	12	93	7	0	100	0	11
ngston, Clyde, Martinsville	.968	4	25	5	1	31	0	1
ez, Pee Wee, Kingsport	.987	51	483	66	7	556	3	8
Collough, Adam, Bluefield	.987	27	200	35	3	238	0	5
deal, Pepe, Johnson City	.983	17	103	12	2	117	0	2
eller, Chad, Elizabethton	.991	12	99	16	1	116	0	2
dorff, Dave, Elizabethton	1.000	5	15	6	0	21	0	1
ole, Bobby, Bluefield	.950	7	51	6	3	60	0	0
iA, Francisco, Elizabethton	.992	34	225	32	2	259	2	11
h, Josh, Danville	.983	6	54	5	1	60	0	3
ra, Roberto, Bluefield	1.000	1	5	1	0	6	0	0
riguez, Mark, Kingsport	.962	4	22	3	1	26	0	1
nero, Marty, Bristol	.962	30	213	42	10	265	1	9
twell, Robert, Elizabethton	.982	22	154	13	3	170	1	4
onmaa, Ryan, Burlington	1.000	4	25	5	0	30	0	0
ngfeld, Aaron, Danville	.978	26	200	18	5	223	0	10
mpson, Nick, Martinsville	.974	39	269	26	8	303	5	11
ealba, Steve, Danville	.917	2	10	1	1	12	0	0
lten, Robert, Martinsville	.979	30	163	22	4	189	2	14
d, Chris, Princeton	1.000	7	64	10	0	74	1	3

PITCHERS

er, Team	Pct.	G	PO	A	E	TC	DP
illes, Matt, Bluefield	1.000	13	3	0	0	3	0
iar, Douglas, Martinsville	1.000	15	2	5	0	7	0
nan, Gene, Princeton	.714	18	1	4	2	7	0
cena, Juan, Burlington	.750	13	3	3	2	8	0
s, Jose, Martinsville	.667	5	1	3	2	6	1
sik, Mike, Burlington*	1.000	13	6	14	0	20	0
es, Joseph, Bristol	.750	13	3	6	3	12	0
ew, Preston, Kingsport*	1.000	5	0	2	0	2	0
ield, Brian, Johnson City	1.000	10	4	9	0	13	0
der, Mike, Elizabethton*	.857	18	4	2	1	7	0
ldree, Joe, Danville	1.000	23	2	4	0	6	0
sley, Raymond, Danville*	1.000	27	2	9	0	11	1
ell, Simon, Danville	1.000	5	0	2	0	2	0
op, Terry, Martinsville*	.909	13	5	5	1	11	0
nk, Dave, Elizabethton*	.600	16	1	2	2	5	0
annon, Jason, Kingsport*	1.000	19	1	5	0	6	0
y, Chris, Princeton	.667	7	1	1	1	3	0
wn, Derek, Bluefield	1.000	2	1	0	0	1	0
kman, Tom, Bristol	.867	17	4	9	2	15	1
ke, Ethan, Kingsport	1.000	9	3	1	0	4	0
nett, A.J., Kingsport	.923	12	2	10	1	13	0
dell, Carl, Princeton*	.714	9	1	4	2	7	1
son, Garret, Bristol	1.000	16	2	3	0	5	0
iyle, Buddy, Princeton	1.000	10	3	8	0	11	0
per, Chadwick, Kingsport	.500	5	1	0	1	2	0
is, Lance, Princeton*	1.000	2	1	4	0	5	0
is, Mike, Kingsport	.667	11	1	1	1	3	0
norejon, Pedro, Bristol	.750	18	1	2	1	4	0
eon, Jose, Johnson City	1.000	27	2	2	0	4	0
aula, Sean, Burlington	1.000	23	0	4	0	4	0
Witt, Matt, Johnson City	.833	14	6	9	3	18	1
ley, Chris, Johnson City	1.000	13	2	2	0	4	0
e, Gary, Elizabethton	.500	17	0	1	1	2	0
ey, Scott, Bluefield*	.900	24	3	6	1	10	0

Player, Team	Pct.	G	PO	A	E	TC	DP
Estrella, Leoncio, Kingsport	.889	15	3	5	1	9	0
Farley, Joe, Bristol*	.688	10	4	7	5	16	2
Fenus, Justin, Martinsville	.941	14	7	9	1	17	0
Fisher, Louis, Bluefield	.944	14	8	9	1	18	0
Forster, Pete, Elizabethton*	.857	4	1	5	1	7	0
Fowler, Benjamin, Danville	1.000	4	1	0	0	1	0
Garff, Jeff, Elizabethton	1.000	12	7	9	0	16	0
Garza, Alberto, Burlington	1.000	9	4	8	0	12	0
Garza, Chris, Elizabethton*	1.000	22	4	6	0	10	0
Geis, John, Johnson City*	1.000	5	1	1	0	2	0
Giron, Roberto, Princeton	.900	22	2	7	1	10	0
Gonzalez, Dicky, Kingsport	1.000	1	0	1	0	1	0
Guzman, Toribio, Johnson City	.800	23	0	4	1	5	0
Hacen, Abraham, Bluefield	.933	15	5	9	1	15	0
Hackett, Jason, Bluefield*	1.000	19	2	9	0	11	0
Hafer, Jeffrey, Kingsport	1.000	24	1	5	0	6	0
Hamilton, Jimmy, Burlington*	.846	10	2	9	2	13	1
Heineman, Rick, Bristol	1.000	23	0	4	0	4	0
Herbison, Brett, Kingsport	.833	13	3	7	2	12	1
Hodges, Reid, Bristol	1.000	16	1	2	0	3	0
Hogge, Shawn, Johnson City	.500	12	1	0	1	2	0
Horgan, Joe, Burlington*	.750	23	1	2	1	4	0
Horne, Jeff, Princeton	.636	10	2	5	4	11	0
Huntsman, Brandon, Bluefield	.833	14	3	2	1	6	0
Hurtado, Omar, Princeton	1.000	15	2	3	0	5	0
Iglesias, Mario, Bristol	1.000	3	0	2	0	2	0
Irvine, Kirk, Bristol	.800	11	1	7	2	10	1
Jelsovsky, Craig, Kingsport	.750	13	2	1	1	4	0
Koeman, Matt, Burlington	1.000	13	4	3	0	7	0
Lagrandeur, Yan, Danville	.923	19	4	8	1	13	0
Lakman, Jason, Bristol	.933	13	6	8	1	15	0
LeBlanc, Eric, Princeton	1.000	9	5	5	0	10	0
Loudermilk, Darren, Burlington	.800	16	4	4	2	10	0
Lynch, Ryan, Elizabethton*	1.000	11	1	5	0	6	1
Lyons, Mike, Kingsport	.800	25	1	7	2	10	0
Malko, Bryan, Elizabethton	.933	12	3	11	1	15	1
Mallard, Randi, Princeton	.786	13	3	8	3	14	0
Marquis, Jason, Danville	.750	7	2	1	1	4	0
McBride, Rodney, Elizabethton	.900	12	5	13	2	20	0
McDermott, Ryan, Burlington	.750	13	3	6	3	12	0
McGlinchy, Kevin, Danville	.941	13	5	11	1	17	0
McNatt, Josh, Bluefield*	1.000	2	0	1	0	1	0
Mear, Rich, Johnson City*	.889	10	3	5	1	9	1
Mejia, Javier, Martinsville	1.000	29	5	5	0	10	0
Mercedes, Carlos, Bluefield	1.000	14	1	6	0	7	0
Mojica, Gonzalo, Burlington	1.000	14	1	3	0	4	0
Molina, Gabe, Martinsville	.889	23	2	6	1	9	0
Molta, Salvatore, Martinsville	.667	12	2	6	4	12	0
Montero, Francisco, Martinsville	.700	21	1	6	3	10	0
Mosquea, Alberto, Martinsville	.833	14	1	4	1	6	0
Negrette, Richard, Burlington	.944	14	4	13	1	18	0
Nichols, James, Bristol	.923	12	2	10	1	13	1
Norris, Steve, Johnson City*	.857	16	3	15	3	21	1
Nye, Richie, Elizabethton	.900	15	6	3	1	10	1
Onley, Shawn, Danville	.900	13	3	6	1	10	0
Onofrei, Tim, Johnson City	.947	12	3	15	1	19	0
Opipari, Mario, Elizabethton	1.000	19	1	8	0	9	1
Pacheco, Delvis, Danville	.789	13	5	10	4	19	2
Paronto, Chad, Bluefield	1.000	9	2	0	0	2	0
Peguero, Americo, Bluefield	.375	9	0	3	5	8	0
Pelton, Brad, Burlington	1.000	15	2	2	0	4	0
Phillips, Jon, Princeton	1.000	23	3	7	0	10	0
Portillo, Ramon, Martinsville*	.909	21	2	8	1	11	1
Pyrtle, Joe, Bristol	1.000	3	0	2	0	2	0
Quintana, Urbano, Martinsville	.875	15	7	7	2	16	0
Reed, Steve, Johnson City	1.000	31	1	3	0	4	1
Reichow, Robert, Burlington	1.000	21	6	8	0	14	1
Riegert, Tim, Johnson City*	.824	26	6	14	3	17	0
Roberts, Grant, Kingsport	.800	13	3	1	1	5	0
Roberts, Randy, Princeton	.867	12	6	7	2	15	0
Rosario, Ruben, Johnson City	.864	13	7	12	3	22	0
Rose, Ted, Princeton	1.000	11	2	12	0	14	1
Santos, Juan Carlos, Bluefield	1.000	16	2	4	0	6	0
Schorzman, Steve, Bristol	.889	14	9	7	2	18	1
Schurman, Ryan, Danville	1.000	21	1	8	0	9	0
Seaver, Mark, Bluefield	1.000	3	0	1	0	1	0
Shiell, Jason, Danville	.917	12	2	9	1	12	1
Shockley, Keith, Martinsville*	1.000	14	0	6	0	6	0
Silva, Carlos, Martinsville	.800	7	0	4	1	5	0
Snead, George, Danville	.600	10	0	3	2	5	0
Spiegel, Mike, Burlington*	.714	14	1	4	2	7	0
Spiers, Corey, Elizabethton*	.778	17	5	9	4	18	0
Stanley, Todd, Bristol	1.000	17	5	2	0	7	1

Player, Team	Pct.	G	PO	A	E	TC	DP
STEVENS, Kris, Martinsville*	1.000	10	6	15	0	21	0
Tober, Dave, Martinsville	1.000	9	2	3	0	5	0
Towers, Josh, Bluefield	1.000	14	5	9	0	14	1
Tull, Bill, Kingsport	1.000	20	3	5	0	8	0
Tuttle, John, Johnson City	.875	21	2	5	1	8	0
Vicentino, Andy, Princeton*	.917	11	2	9	1	12	0
Villegas, Ismael, Danville	1.000	1	1	0	0	1	0

Player, Team	Pct.	G	PO	A	E	TC	D
Walton, Tim, Martinsville	.750	4	3	3	2	8	
Weibl, Clint, Johnson City	.857	7	3	3	1	7	
Winkelsas, Joseph, Danville	1.000	8	2	3	0	5	
Wise, William, Danville	.917	21	4	7	1	12	
Wyatt, Ben, Danville*	.833	10	0	5	1	6	
Yeskie, Nate, Elizabethton	.818	7	6	3	2	11	
Zwirchitz, Andy, Kingsport	1.000	12	8	10	0	18	

The following players did not have any fielding statistics at the positions indicated or appeared only as a designated hitter, pinch-hitter or pinch-runner: Boyette, ph; Buczkowski, p; Cardona, p; Casimiro, of; Ferullo, p; Harris, of; Hooten, p; L. Lawrence, p; Lovingood, p; Lugo, p; Lutz, 3B; A. Martinez, p; Mattox, p; Murphy, O'Hearn, p; Parrish, p; Ribaudo, p; Shelton, p; Walker, p.

LEAGUE CHAMPIONS

Year	Team	Pct.	Year	Team	Pct.	Year	Team	P
1921—	Greenville	.608	1953—	Welch*	.705	1979—	Paintsville	.80
	Johnson City*	.627		Johnson City	.672	1980—	Paintsville	.65
1922—	Bristol	.557	1954—	Bluefield‡	.619	1981—	Paintsville	.65
1923—	Knoxville	.635	1955—	Salem■	.689	1982—	Bluefield▼	.68
1924—	Knoxville*	.642	1956—	Did not operate.			Johnson City	.47
	Bristol	.607	1957—	Bluefield	.701	1983—	Paintsville	.65
1925—	Greenville	.667	1958—	Johnson City	.662	1984—	Elizabethton•	.58
1926-36—	Did not operate.		1959—	Morristown	.603		Pulaski	.53
1937—	Elizabethton	.559	1960—	Wytheville	.614	1985—	Bristol††	.63
	Pennington Gap*	.580	1961—	Middlesboro	.591	1986—	Johnson City	.6
1938—	Elizabethton	.664	1962—	Bluefield	.671		Pulaski•	.62
	Greenville (3rd)†	.571	1963—	Bluefield	.652	1987—	Burlington•	.72
1939—	Elizabethton‡	.597	1964—	Johnson City	.662		Johnson City	.6
1940—	Johnson City§	.726	1965—	Salem	.614	1988—	Kingsport•	.64
	Elizabethton	.750	1966—	Marion	.623		Burlington	.5
1941—	Johnson City	.614	1967—	Bluefield	.627	1989—	Elizabethton•	.6
	Elizabethton*	.661	1968—	Marion	.583		Pulaski	.6
1942—	Bristol	.667	1969—	Pulaski▼	.576	1990—	Elizabethton	.7
	Bristol∞	.660		Johnson City	.544	1991—	Pulaski•	.6
1943—	Bristol	.755	1970—	Bluefield	.638		Burlington	.5
	Bristol▲	.617		Kingsport	.559	1992—	Elizabethton	.7
1944—	Kingsport‡	.575	1971—	Bluefield▼	.609		Bluefield•	.5
1945—	Kingsport‡	.670	1972—	Bristol▼	.588	1993—	Burlington•	.6
1946—	New River‡	.675		Covington	.586		Elizabethton	.5
1947—	Pulaski	.648	1973—	Kingsport	.757	1994—	Princeton•	.6
	New River (3rd)†	.516	1974—	Bristol▼	.754		Johnson City	.6
1948—	Pulaski‡	.680		Bluefield	.536	1995—	Bluefield	.7
1949—	Bluefield‡	.721	1975—	Marion	.515		Kingsport•	.7
1950—	Bluefield	.600		Johnson City▼	.603	1996—	Kingsport	.7
	Bluefield♦	.745	1976—	Johnson City▼	.714		Bluefield▼	.6
1951—	Kingsport‡	.659		Bluefield	.600			
1952—	Johnson City	.595	1977—	Kingsport	.623			
	Welch (3rd)†	.509	1978—	Elizabethton	.594			

*Won split-season playoff. †Won four-team playoff. ‡Won championship and four-team playoff. §Johnson City, first-half winner, won playoff involving six club ∞Won both halves and defeated second-place Elizabethton in playoff. ▲Won both halves, but Erwin won four-team playoff. ♦Won both halves, but Bristol won tw club playoff. ■Salem and Johnson City declared playoff co-champions when weather forced cancellation of final series. ▼League was divided into Northern, Southern divisions; declared league champion based on highest won-lost percentage. •League was divided into North and South divisions; won playoff. ††Bristol declared league champion based on regular-season record.

ARIZONA LEAGUE

LEAGUE OFFICE

President/treasurer
Bob Richmond
Address
P.O. Box 4941
Scottsdale, AZ 85261
Phone
602-483-8224

Teams*
Athletics
Cubs
Diamondbacks
Mariners
Padres
Rockies

*Teams play their games in Chandler, Mesa, Peoria, Scottsdale and other Arizona sites to be announced.

1996 FINAL STANDINGS

COMPOSITE

Team	Pad.	Ath.	Mar.	Rck.	Ang.	Dia.	W	L	T	Pct.	GB
Padres	....	5	6	7	10	8	36	20	0	.643	....
Athletics	6	....	7	6	6	8	33	23	0	.589	3
Mariners	6	4	....	6	6	7	29	27	0	.518	7
Rockies	4	5	5	....	5	7	26	30	0	.464	10
Angels	1	5	5	7	....	6	24	32	0	.429	12
Diamondbacks	3	4	4	4	5	....	20	36	0	.357	16

Games played in Chandler, Mesa, Peoria and Scottsdale.

Club names are major league affiliations.

PLAYOFFS: No playoffs scheduled.

REGULAR-SEASON ATTENDANCE: No total official attendance figures reported.

MANAGERS: Angels, Bruce Hines; Athletics, Juan Navarette; Diamondbacks, Dwayne Murphy; Mariners, Tommy LeVasseur; Padres, Larry See; Rockies, Jim Eppard.

ALL-STAR TEAM: 1B—Mike Petersen, Rockies; 2B—Brian Smith, Mariners; 3B—George Davis, Athletics; SS—Jose Ortiz, Athletics; OF—Marcus Knight, Angels; Gary Gordon, Rockies; Hipolito Martinez, Athletics; Jacob Ruotsinoja, Padres; Jhensy Sandoval, Diamondbacks; C—Danny Serrano, Angels; DH—Shane Cronin, Padres; LHP—Nick Bierbrodt, Diamondbacks; Steve Hoff, Padres; RHP—John Nicholson, Rockies; RHP—Ramon Ortiz, Angels; LH Reliever—Greg Winkleman, Athletics; RH Reliever—Jeromy Palki, Mariners; Most Valuable Player—Shane Cronin, Padres; Co-Managers of the Year—Tommy LeVasseur, Mariners; Juan Navarette, Athletics.

1996 BATTING

TEAM

Team	Avg.	G	TPA	AB	R	H	TB	2B	3B	HR	RBI	SH	SF	HP	BB	IBB	SO	SB	CS	GDP	LOB	ShO	Slg.	OBP
Padres	.277	56	2197	1939	345	538	766	83	38	23	289	11	22	28	196	3	379	73	34	34	380	3	.395	.349
Rockies	.254	56	2134	1905	259	484	616	74	20	6	200	14	21	29	164	1	437	77	35	35	400	3	.323	.319
Athletics	.250	56	2224	1917	322	479	712	101	27	26	264	10	16	45	236	4	446	99	29	23	430	2	.371	.343
Angels	.250	56	2152	1909	276	477	683	100	29	16	215	15	7	27	191	2	436	124	40	32	404	2	.358	.326
Mariners	.246	56	2131	1905	265	468	664	72	26	24	210	12	11	30	173	4	512	72	37	32	377	4	.349	.317
Diamndbcks	.241	56	2196	1912	265	461	624	74	28	11	210	4	19	38	223	3	527	72	26	43	438	7	.326	.329

INDIVIDUAL

TOP QUALIFIERS FOR BATTING CHAMPIONSHIP

Minimum 151 plate appearances. *Lefthanded batter. †Switch-hitter.

Player, Team	Avg.	G	TPA	AB	R	H	TB	2B	3B	HR	RBI	SH	SF	HP	BB	IBB	SO	SB	CS	GDP	Slg.	OBP
Schwartzbauer, B, Rockies*	.344	43	178	154	20	53	69	9	2	1	18	2	1	2	19	0	30	4	3	3	.448	.420
Pernell, Brandon, Padres	.333	53	195	174	38	58	90	9	10	1	33	1	2	0	18	0	30	14	4	1	.517	.392
Ortiz, Jose, Athletics	.330	52	223	200	43	66	106	12	8	4	25	1	1	1	20	2	34	16	5	1	.530	.392
Rexrode, J, Diamondbacks*	.329	48	188	140	28	46	51	2	0	1	17	0	4	0	44	0	27	8	5	1	.364	.479
Cronin, Shane, Padres	.327	54	227	208	40	68	108	13	0	9	54	0	4	3	12	0	32	4	1	6	.519	.366
Petersen, Mike, Rockies	.322	52	219	205	26	66	85	12	2	1	25	0	2	1	11	0	25	3	2	2	.415	.356
Smith, Brian, Mariners†	.296	54	246	223	39	66	102	15	6	3	16	1	0	1	21	0	46	13	11	2	.457	.359
Garcia, Sandro, Padres	.291	53	204	189	29	55	72	6	4	1	17	3	2	2	8	0	27	11	6	3	.381	.323
Ruotsinoja, Jacob, Padres*	.291	52	219	172	37	50	88	14	3	6	40	0	4	2	40	3	38	2	2	3	.512	.422
Knight, Marcus, Angels†	.291	54	235	203	36	59	94	16	5	3	30	0	1	3	28	0	50	10	7	2	.463	.383
Gordon, Gary, Rockies	.291	47	216	179	35	52	57	5	0	0	10	0	4	33	0	54	23	6	0	.318	.412
Sandoval, J, Diamondbacks	.289	38	159	149	22	43	60	11	0	2	26	0	2	1	7	0	41	1	1	5	.403	.321
Rosario, Carlos, Rockies†	.286	50	215	199	27	57	80	7	5	2	34	0	3	1	12	0	42	9	7	5	.402	.326
Davis, George, Athletics	.286	52	238	206	40	59	79	9	4	1	20	0	0	11	21	1	27	7	8	4	.383	.382
Tolentino, Juan, Angels	.282	49	182	170	30	48	75	9	6	2	14	0	0	1	11	0	33	21	2	4	.441	.330

DEPARTMENTAL LEADERS: G—Maxwell, 55; AB—B. Smith, 223; R—Jose D. Ortiz, 43; H—Cronin, 68; TB—Cronin, 108; 2B—Knight, 16; 3B—Pernell, 10; HR—Cronin, 9; RBI—Cronin, 54; SH—Hernandez, 5; SF—Several players tied at 4 each; HP—Davis, 11; BB—Rexrode, 44; IBB—Ruotsinoja, 3; SO—Proctor, 60; SB—N. Castro, 25; CS—B. Smith, 11; GIDP—Maldonado, 7; Slg.—Jose D. Ortiz, .479.

ALL PLAYERS

*Lefthanded batter. †Switch-hitter.

Player, Team	Avg.	G	TPA	AB	R	H	TB	2B	3B	HR	RBI	SH	SF	HP	BB	IBB	SO	SB	CS	GDP	Slg.	OBP
Antunez, Francisco, Angels	.214	5	17	14	2	3	6	0	0	1	1	0	0	2	1	0	6	0	0	0	.429	.353
Barthelemy, Edy, Mariners†	.216	38	133	111	18	24	38	5	3	1	14	1	1	1	19	1	30	3	4	2	.342	.333
Bautista, J, Diamondbacks	.200	49	156	140	14	28	33	3	1	0	14	0	2	3	11	0	51	5	2	2	.236	.269
Brown, Emil, Athletics	.267	4	19	15	5	4	7	3	0	0	2	0	0	1	3	0	2	1	1	0	.467	.421

Player, Team	Avg.	G	TPA	AB	R	H	TB	2B	3B	HR	RBI	SH	SF	HP	BB	IBB	SO	SB	CS	GDP	Slg.	OB
Byers, Macgregor, Athletics	.325	21	96	77	15	25	39	9	1	1	13	0	1	0	18	0	20	2	0	0	.506	.44
Castro, Juan, Rockies	.247	22	80	77	10	19	26	3	2	0	6	0	0	1	2	0	10	3	1	1	.338	.27
Castro, Nelson, Angels†	.204	53	222	186	31	38	57	4	3	3	14	1	0	2	32	0	42	25	8	3	.306	.32
Chapman, D, Diamondbacks	.119	37	129	118	12	14	20	2	2	0	12	0	1	0	10	1	28	0	1	4	.169	.18
Charvel, Ali, Angels*	.390	11	41	41	7	16	22	4	1	0	2	0	0	0	0	0	9	1	0	0	.537	.39
Clifton, Rodney, Athletics	.207	42	181	164	27	34	46	4	1	2	11	1	1	2	13	0	34	10	2	1	.280	.27
Collier, Marc, Angels	.207	30	98	87	9	18	24	6	0	0	7	2	1	1	7	0	22	4	2	1	.276	.27
Cronin, Shane, Padres	.327	54	227	208	40	68	108	13	0	9	54	0	4	3	12	0	32	4	1	6	.519	.36
Davis, George, Athletics	.286	52	238	206	40	59	79	9	4	1	20	0	0	11	21	1	27	7	8	4	.383	.38
DeJesus, Eddie, Angels	.264	48	192	178	27	47	67	11	3	1	25	1	2	4	7	0	35	12	3	4	.376	.30
Delgado, Ariel, Angels*	.229	47	189	166	21	38	49	6	1	1	11	2	0	1	20	1	38	15	2	2	.295	.31
Dunham, Traylor, Padres	.273	32	95	77	13	21	22	1	0	0	9	0	1	4	13	0	23	2	2	1	.286	.40
Eady, Gerald, Mariners	.222	46	200	176	24	39	59	9	4	1	26	1	0	2	21	0	53	7	2	2	.335	.31
Fefee, Theo, Angels*	.286	13	56	49	14	14	22	2	3	1	8	0	1	0	6	0	9	4	0	0	.510	.35
Figueroa, Jose, Athletics	.153	49	187	157	18	24	35	8	0	1	17	0	2	5	23	0	38	8	1	3	.223	.27
Garcia, Juan, Diamondbacks	.255	36	140	110	25	28	46	3	3	3	14	2	1	3	24	0	26	16	6	0	.418	.39
Garcia, Sandro, Padres	.291	53	204	189	29	55	72	6	4	1	17	3	2	2	8	0	27	11	6	3	.381	.32
Geronimo, Cesar, Angels	.281	33	132	121	9	34	45	9	1	0	16	1	0	2	8	0	11	3	1	3	.372	.33
Glasser, S, Diamondbacks	.297	41	144	128	25	38	46	0	4	0	10	1	0	1	14	0	16	13	2	6	.359	.37
Gonzalez, Santos, Padres†	.290	38	139	131	27	38	52	5	3	1	17	0	2	1	5	0	20	10	2	2	.397	.31
Gordon, Gary, Rockies	.291	47	216	179	35	52	57	5	0	0	10	0	0	4	33	0	54	23	6	0	.318	.41
Goris, Braulio, Athletics*	.244	49	209	172	24	42	64	10	3	2	34	0	3	3	31	0	52	5	2	0	.372	.36
Guerrero, Wascar, Mariners	.234	31	117	111	9	26	37	6	1	1	10	0	0	2	4	0	37	0	0	3	.333	.27
Halloran, Matt, Padres	.261	39	146	134	22	35	50	7	4	0	15	0	2	0	10	0	22	2	1	3	.373	.32
Hardy, Brett, Diamondbacks*	.000	4	5	3	0	0	0	0	0	0	0	0	0	0	2	0	3	0	0	0	.000	.40
Hernandez, Victor, Athletics	.236	46	173	144	27	34	56	5	1	5	22	5	0	4	20	0	29	11	2	3	.389	.34
Hudde, Alejandro, Rockies	.215	26	101	93	9	20	27	3	2	0	8	3	1	2	2	0	25	4	0	0	.290	.24
Hudson, Bert, Diamondbacks	.277	35	122	112	12	31	44	5	4	0	20	0	1	1	8	0	33	2	0	3	.393	.32
Jacobo, Roberto, Padres†	.216	40	125	111	18	24	32	4	2	0	12	1	1	0	12	0	27	6	2	1	.288	.29
Jacobus, Brian, Padres*	.264	50	204	193	29	51	73	8	7	0	24	0	2	0	9	0	33	2	3	7	.378	.29
Jimenez, Miguel, Mariners	.266	44	168	158	22	42	63	9	0	4	18	0	2	2	6	0	44	6	2	3	.399	.29
Kirkpatrick, Brian, Rockies	.156	11	37	32	2	5	6	1	0	0	2	2	1	1	1	0	7	0	1	0	.188	.22
Knight, Marcus, Angels†	.291	54	235	203	36	59	94	16	5	3	30	0	1	3	28	0	50	10	7	2	.463	.38
Landaeta, Luis, Rockies*	.278	44	190	176	27	49	60	9	1	0	20	1	4	4	5	0	22	7	2	5	.341	.30
Lawrence, Mike, Angels†	.179	38	132	117	9	21	23	2	0	0	12	3	1	0	11	0	28	1	3	2	.197	.24
Leyba, J, Diamondbacks	.258	24	38	31	2	8	9	1	0	0	0	0	0	1	6	0	11	0	0	0	.290	.39
Llanos, Alexis, Angels†	.281	51	225	203	31	57	75	9	3	1	26	4	0	2	14	0	48	10	5	4	.369	.33
Luderer, Brian, Athletics	.308	6	14	13	1	4	4	0	0	0	2	1	0	0	0	0	1	0	0	0	.308	.33
Mahoney, Ricardo, Rockies	.256	23	95	82	12	21	26	5	0	0	12	0	1	2	8	0	20	1	1	4	.317	.33
Maldonado, Carlos, Mariners	.220	29	112	100	10	22	28	0	0	2	18	1	4	1	6	0	10	0	1	7	.280	.26
Martinez, Hipolito, Athletics	.265	48	210	185	29	49	78	8	3	5	34	0	2	4	19	0	39	9	0	3	.422	.34
Martinez, J, Diamondbacks†	.161	20	37	31	6	5	8	0	0	1	4	0	0	0	6	0	12	0	0	0	.258	.29
Martinez, Victor, Mariners	.344	16	74	61	10	21	30	1	4	0	10	2	0	2	9	0	17	4	0	2	.492	.44
Maxwell, Vernon, Padres	.251	55	232	191	41	48	62	6	4	0	17	0	2	8	31	0	45	15	4	2	.325	.37
Maynard, Scott, Mariners	.280	47	181	164	20	46	58	7	1	1	17	1	0	1	15	0	53	1	3	3	.354	.34
McAffee, J, Diamondbacks	.147	39	128	102	13	15	20	5	0	0	9	0	2	6	18	0	39	1	1	1	.196	.30
McDougall, Matt, Mariners	.203	28	93	79	18	16	26	3	2	1	2	1	0	3	10	0	22	9	2	0	.329	.31
McGuire, Brandon, Angels†	.000	6	5	5	0	0	0	0	0	0	0	0	0	0	0	0	2	0	0	0	.000	.00
Mitchell, Andres, Rockies	.177	51	205	175	23	31	34	1	1	0	13	1	3	3	23	0	54	17	7	2	.194	.27
Moreno, Jose, Mariners	.278	49	203	196	34	49	57	4	2	0	18	3	0	6	18	0	33	12	5	2	.324	.30
Mouton, A, Diamondbacks†	.250	1	5	4	0	1	2	1	0	0	0	0	0	0	1	0	0	0	0	1	.500	.40
Nieves, Wilbert, Padres	.345	43	128	113	23	39	50	5	0	2	22	2	0	0	13	0	19	3	4	1	.442	.41
Nova, Kelvin, Mariners	.268	47	190	164	37	44	62	12	3	0	18	2	2	1	21	0	43	14	3	1	.378	.35
Nunez, Jose, Diamondbacks	.176	4	18	17	1	3	3	0	0	0	2	0	0	1	0	0	2	1	0	0	.176	.22
Ortiz, Jose, Athletics	.330	52	223	200	43	66	106	12	8	4	25	1	1	1	20	2	34	16	5	1	.530	.39
Osborne, M, Diamondbacks*	.267	31	118	105	15	28	43	6	3	1	16	0	1	3	9	0	24	0	0	2	.410	.33
Pacheco, D, Mariners†	.250	8	17	16	0	4	5	1	0	0	1	0	1	0	0	0	6	0	0	0	.313	.23
Panaro, C, Diamondbacks*	.242	28	41	33	6	8	10	2	0	0	4	0	1	1	7	1	8	0	1	3	.303	.39
Pernell, Brandon, Padres	.333	55	195	174	38	58	90	9	10	1	33	1	2	0	18	0	30	14	4	1	.517	.39
Petersen, Mike, Rockies	.322	52	219	205	26	66	85	12	2	1	25	0	2	1	11	0	25	3	2	2	.415	.38
Pinson, Brian, Mariners*	.409	10	22	22	2	9	9	0	0	0	5	0	0	0	0	0	6	0	1	0	.409	.40
Proctor, J, Diamondbacks	.202	45	178	163	14	33	46	5	4	0	9	0	1	6	8	0	60	2	0	4	.282	.28
Rexrode, J, Diamondbacks*	.329	48	188	140	28	46	51	2	0	1	17	0	4	0	44	0	27	8	5	1	.364	.47
Rodriguez, Chris, Rockies	.173	31	112	98	13	17	21	4	0	0	6	0	0	3	11	0	16	1	1	5	.214	.27
Rodriguez, D, Diamondbacks*	.217	32	115	106	8	23	32	7	1	0	11	0	1	1	7	0	40	2	0	1	.302	.27
Rodriguez, John, Padres	.225	43	129	120	11	27	31	2	1	0	11	4	0	1	4	0	24	1	1	4	.258	.25
Rodriguez, M, Diamondbcks*	.232	23	63	56	9	13	27	2	3	2	7	0	1	2	4	1	18	1	0	0	.482	.30
Rojas, Renney, Angels	.000	12	1	1	0	0	0	0	0	0	0	0	0	0	0	0	1	0	0	0	.000	.00
Rosario, Carlos, Rockies†	.286	50	215	199	27	57	80	7	5	2	34	0	3	1	12	0	42	9	7	5	.402	.33
Rose, Carlos, Mariners	.129	40	145	132	12	17	26	1	1	2	13	0	0	2	11	2	56	0	0	2	.197	.20
Rottman, P, Diamondbacks	.140	17	47	43	3	6	8	2	0	0	2	0	0	0	4	0	13	1	1	1	.186	.21
Ruotsinoja, Jacob, Padres*	.291	52	219	172	37	50	88	14	3	6	40	0	4	2	40	3	38	2	2	3	.512	.42
Russoniello, Michael, Angels	.080	13	28	25	1	2	2	0	0	0	1	0	0	0	1	0	9	0	1	1	.080	.11
Sandoval, J, Diamondbacks	.289	38	159	149	22	43	60	11	0	2	26	0	2	1	7	0	41	1	1	5	.403	.32
Saucedo, Roberto, Angels	.281	18	74	64	5	18	26	5	0	1	13	0	0	2	8	1	11	1	1	0	.406	.37
Schwartzbauer, B, Rockies*	.344	43	178	154	20	53	69	9	2	1	18	2	1	2	19	0	30	4	3	3	.448	.42
Sears, Jayson, Angels	.214	4	18	14	4	3	5	0	1	0	2	0	0	1	0	0	3	0	0	0	.357	.33
Selga, Andres, Rockies	.170	30	104	100	13	17	22	5	0	0	5	0	2	0	2	0	32	0	1	1	.220	.18
Serrano, Danny, Angels	.258	19	73	62	11	16	22	6	0	0	5	0	3	0	4	0	11	2	2	0	.355	.37
Shipley, Craig, Padres	.714	3	8	7	4	5	6	1	0	0	1	0	0	0	0	0	1	0	0	0	.857	.75
Smith, Brian, Mariners†	.296	54	246	223	39	66	102	15	6	3	16	1	0	1	21	0	46	13	11	2	.457	.35
Soriano, Jacobo, Angels	.167	17	6	6	1	1	4	0	0	1	1	0	0	0	0	0	1	0	0	0	.667	.16
Sosa, Nicolas, Athletics	.206	46	190	165	22	34	47	8	1	0	26	0	2	3	20	1	52	2	1	2	.285	.30

layer, Team	Avg.	G	TPA	AB	R	H	TB	2B	3B	HR	RBI	SH	SF	HP	BB	IBB	SO	SB	CS	GDP	Slg.	OBP
oto, Luis, Padres	.203	28	82	69	9	14	22	2	0	2	10	0	2	3	8	0	19	0	0	0	.319	.305
pivey, E, Diamondbacks.........	.333	20	87	69	13	23	23	0	0	0	3	1	1	4	12	0	16	11	2	0	.333	.453
tarkey, Nate, Angels	.246	42	155	138	15	34	48	9	1	1	22	0	0	3	14	0	39	3	2	4	.348	.329
tewart, Adrian, Padres	.100	22	64	50	4	5	8	0	0	1	7	0	0	1	13	0	20	1	1	0	.160	.297
egland, Ron, Athletics	.282	27	97	85	10	24	39	6	0	3	18	0	1	7	4	0	25	6	0	0	.459	.361
olbert, Ernest, Mariners	.212	52	193	179	22	38	52	6	1	2	15	1	1	1	11	0	46	9	4	3	.291	.260
olentino, Juan, Angels	.282	49	182	170	30	48	75	9	6	2	14	0	0	1	11	0	33	21	2	4	.441	.330
orres, Jose, Diamondbacks	.315	29	62	54	13	17	24	1	3	0	5	0	1	3	4	0	18	5	3	1	.444	.387
orres, Wolfrando, Rockies†	.230	49	217	187	29	43	50	5	1	0	22	3	1	4	22	0	46	4	2	4	.267	.322
alera, Ramon, Mariners†	.444	4	19	18	2	8	9	1	0	0	3	0	0	1	1	0	1	4	1	0	.500	.474
asquez, Jose, Athletics†	.221	46	165	145	19	32	45	6	2	1	20	0	0	3	17	0	42	7	4	5	.310	.315
entura, Jose, Angels*	.169	32	73	59	13	10	14	2	1	0	5	1	0	0	13	0	26	11	1	1	.237	.319
entura, Wilfredo, Athletics	.160	8	32	25	5	4	5	1	0	0	2	0	1	0	6	0	8	1	0	0	.200	.313
inas, Alex, Diamondbacks†	.218	18	59	55	5	12	14	2	0	0	7	0	0	0	4	0	20	2	0	3	.255	.271
/illiams, Marcus, Mariners	.154	11	50	39	5	6	6	0	0	0	2	0	1	1	9	0	6	3	0	0	.154	.320
/illiams, Patrick, Mariners	.250	38	158	140	18	35	59	4	1	6	26	0	1	5	12	1	46	1	1	1	.421	.329
Vilson, Keith, Diamondbacks	.266	42	157	143	19	38	55	14	0	1	20	0	0	2	12	0	21	1	1	5	.385	.331
weifel, Kent, Rockies	.204	40	166	148	13	34	53	5	4	2	19	2	2	1	13	1	54	1	1	3	.358	.293

GRAND SLAMS: Cronin, Hernandez, Stewart, 1 each.

AWARDED FIRST BASE ON CATCHER'S INTERFERENCE: N. Castro (Figueroa); Llanos (Figueroa); Mahoney (Leyba); Ruotsinoja (McAffee); Russoniello (Leyba).

1996 PITCHING

TEAM

eam	W	L	Pct.	ERA	G	CG	ShO	Sv.	IP	H	TBF	R	ER	HR	SH	SF	HB	BB	IBB	SO	WP	Bk.
ockies	26	30	.464	3.51	56	2	6	14	489.1	489	2161	269	191	7	12	12	41	158	0	451	46	15
adres	36	20	.643	3.57	56	2	2	16	498.2	488	2192	276	198	22	8	19	24	203	1	471	30	11
Iariners	29	27	.518	3.68	56	1	5	17	497.0	462	2183	271	203	20	10	12	32	211 \	4	478	40	11
iamondbacks	20	36	.357	3.88	56	0	1	5	490.0	479	2131	294	211	20	16	14	30	201	4	426	42	10
thletics	33	23	.589	4.29	56	0	2	15	495.2	498	2172	293	236	15	12	18	30	195	4	468	54	16
ngels	24	32	.429	4.64	56	4	5	12	487.0	491	2195	329	251	22	8	21	40	215	4	443	52	10

INDIVIDUAL

TOP QUALIFIERS FOR EARNED-RUN AVERAGE TITLE

Minimum 45 innings. *Lefthanded pitcher.

itcher, Team	W	L	Pct.	ERA	G	GS	CG	ShO	GF	Sv.	IP	H	TBF	R	ER	HR	SH	SF	HB	BB	IBB	SO	WP	Bk.
hacon, Shawn, Rockies............	1	2	.333	1.60	11	11	1	0	0	0	56.1	46	241	17	10	1	0	2	4	15	0	64	3	2
icholson, John, Rockies..........	3	5	.375	1.64	11	11	1	0	0	0	65.2	42	255	16	12	1	1	1	5	14	0	65	2	1
rtiz, Ramon, Angels	5	4	.556	2.12	16	8	2	2	5	1	68.0	55	285	28	16	5	0	1	2	27	0	78	5	2
enny, B, Diamondbacks	2	2	.500	2.36	11	8	0	0	1	0	49.2	36	201	18	13	1	0	1	3	14	0	52	3	2
alki, Jeromy, Mariners............	1	1	.500	2.47	18	0	0	0	12	6	47.1	31	194	14	13	3	1	1	2	17	0	56	2	0
hompson, Josef, Padres*.........	8	2	.800	2.65	13	12	0	0	0	0	74.2	67	319	33	22	3	1	2	2	22	0	50	1	2
off, Steve, Padres*	8	2	.800	2.85	16	13	0	0	1	0	85.1	66	356	37	27	2	0	1	9	36	0	104	6	0
Vestbrook, Jake, Rockies	4	2	.667	2.87	11	11	0	0	0	0	62.2	66	271	33	20	0	3	1	8	14	0	57	4	0
ash, Damond, Padres..............	5	3	.625	3.05	22	4	0	0	7	5	59.0	45	258	30	20	0	2	1	2	36	0	78	7	1
erenches, Albert, Mariners*	3	3	.500	3.13	20	3	1	1	10	3	60.1	57	256	31	21	2	2	1	4	19	3	73	3	0
ivera, Alvin, Rockies................	4	2	.667	3.28	11	7	0	0	2	1	49.1	48	208	22	18	0	0	3	4	12	0	44	3	2
ite, Kevin, Padres	5	5	.500	3.62	13	12	2	1	0	0	77.0	86	326	44	31	1	3	0	1	15	0	65	4	2
eJesus, Tony, Mariners*	2	5	.286	3.63	12	11	0	0	0	0	57.0	54	252	29	23	1	0	2	2	28	0	61	7	0
hristianson, Robby, Mariners ...	5	1	.833	3.76	14	9	0	0	3	2	64.2	63	271	30	27	2	1	2	4	13	0	36	2	3
eyva, Edgar, Angels	4	7	.364	3.94	14	13	1	1	0	0	82.1	79	359	53	36	7	1	3	9	27	0	74	3	3

DEPARTMENTAL LEADERS: W—J. Thompson, Hoff, 8 each; L—E. Leyva, 7; Pct.—J. Thompson, Hoff, .800 each; G—Sellers, 26; GS—Stockstill, Leyva, Hoff, 13 ach; CG—D. Ortiz, Hite, 2 each; ShO—D. Ortiz, 2; GF—Sellers, 23; Sv.—Sellers, Palki, Winkleman, 6 each. IP—Hoff, 85.1; H—Hite, 86; TBF—E. Leyva, 359; R—E. eyva, 53; ER—E. Leyva, Abreu, 36 each; HR—E. Leyva, 7; SH—Kempton, 5; SF—B. Garcia, 5; HB—E. Leyva, Hoff, 9 each; BB—Kawahara, 40; IBB—Derenches, 3; O—Hoff, 104; WP—Abreu, 15; Bk.—Several players tied at 3 each.

ALL PITCHERS

*Lefthanded pitcher.

itcher, Team	W	L	Pct.	ERA	G	GS	CG	ShO	GF	Sv.	IP	H	TBF	R	ER	HR	SH	SF	HB	BB	IBB	SO	WP	Bk.
breu, Oscar, Athletics	5	3	.625	6.48	17	6	0	0	4	1	50.0	47	229	43	36	4	0	0	0	37	0	62	15	1
arcon, James, Padres.............	0	0	.000	6.16	14	0	0	0	2	0	19.0	25	102	20	13	1	0	2	2	17	0	14	2	2
ashley, Antonio, Angels............	3	0	1.000	5.26	17	0	0	0	10	1	25.2	32	120	17	15	0	0	2	0	7	0	21	3	0
arboza, Carlos, Rockies...........	1	2	.333	3.00	18	0	0	0	5	1	30.0	34	144	18	10	1	0	2	12	0	18	4	2
arthelemy, Edy, Mariners.........	0	1	.000	6.75	1	0	0	0	1	0	1.1	1	7	1	1	0	0	0	0	2	0	0	0	0
ell, Matthew, Diamondbacks	1	4	.200	4.68	18	0	0	0	5	0	32.2	36	148	27	17	1	0	1	1	11	0	24	2	2
ennett, Tom, Athletics	0	0	.000	1.38	4	4	0	0	0	0	13.0	2	50	2	2	0	0	0	1	11	0	12	1	1
ido, Jose, Diamondbacks	2	3	.400	4.83	11	11	0	0	0	0	50.1	51	204	30	27	1	0	0	3	22	1	24	3	3
erbrodt, N, Diamondbacks*	1	0	1.000	1.66	8	8	0	0	0	0	38.0	25	147	9	7	1	0	0	0	13	0	46	2	0
rea, Lesli, Mariners	1	0	1.000	5.06	7	0	0	0	3	0	10.2	7	47	10	6	1	0	1	0	6	0	12	1	1
rueggemann, D, Rockies*	1	2	.333	3.63	3	3	0	0	0	0	22.1	22	91	10	9	1	1	1	3	0	11	0	0
hacon, Shawn, Rockies...........	1	2	.333	1.60	11	11	1	0	0	0	56.1	46	241	17	10	1	0	2	4	15	0	64	3	2
hristianson, Robby, Mariners ...	5	1	.833	3.76	14	9	0	0	3	2	64.2	63	271	30	27	2	1	2	4	13	0	36	2	3
ontreras, Orlando, Rockies.......	3	4	.429	4.55	16	0	0	0	2	1	29.2	28	133	21	15	1	1	0	1	15	0	26	5	0
'Amico, Jeff, Athletics	3	0	1.000	1.42	6	0	0	0	2	0	19.0	14	72	3	3	0	0	0	3	0	15	0	1
eJesus, Tony, Mariners*	2	5	.286	3.63	12	11	0	0	0	0	57.0	54	252	29	23	1	0	2	2	28	0	61	7	0

Pitcher, Team	W	L	Pct.	ERA	G	GS	CG	ShO	GF	Sv.	IP	H	TBF	R	ER	HR	SH	SF	HB	BB	IBB	SO	WP	Bk.
Derenches, Albert, Mariners*	3	3	.500	3.13	20	3	1	1	10	3	60.1	57	256	31	21	2	2	1	4	19	3	73	3	0
Douglas, Reggie, Rockies	0	0	.000	12.86	12	0	0	0	5	0	14.0	23	87	28	20	0	0	1	2	19	0	12	6	3
Escalante, P, Diamondbacks	0	1	.000	6.20	15	0	0	0	8	0	24.2	35	110	17	17	2	0	0	0	5	0	24	3	1
Faulk, Eric, Athletics	0	1	.000	3.50	6	4	0	0	0	0	18.0	18	80	8	7	0	2	0	2	6	0	19	1	0
Fleming, John, Diamondbacks ...	1	4	.200	4.02	10	5	0	0	0	0	31.1	33	137	17	14	4	1	1	1	17	0	29	7	0
Frias, Miguel, Diamondbacks* ...	1	1	.500	2.35	19	0	0	0	10	2	30.2	28	137	18	8	1	2	3	2	17	0	30	3	0
Gallagher, Bryan, Athletics*	2	1	.667	3.26	16	1	0	0	2	0	30.1	37	141	24	11	1	1	1	1	10	0	27	2	2
Garcia, Bryan, Athletics	4	2	.667	5.47	18	3	0	0	8	1	51.0	58	219	36	31	4	0	5	5	11	1	39	0	1
Garey, Daniel, Mariners	3	5	.375	5.09	12	11	0	0	0	0	53.0	65	250	37	30	2	2	1	5	18	0	38	7	1
Gogolin, Elton, Athletics	0	2	.000	7.80	6	2	0	0	1	0	15.0	24	79	14	13	0	2	1	2	10	0	20	2	0
Gonzalez, Francisco, Padres	6	2	.750	4.32	25	4	0	0	5	2	50.0	65	222	33	24	5	0	2	1	6	0	32	0	0
Gonzalez, Jose, Mariners	2	0	1.000	0.90	2	2	0	0	0	0	10.0	5	38	2	1	0	0	0	3	0	10	0	0
Gorrell, Chris, Athletics	1	2	.333	3.93	12	2	0	0	3	1	36.2	36	149	18	16	1	1	1	3	8	0	32	2	3
Gregg, Kevin, Athletics	3	3	.500	3.10	11	9	0	0	0	0	40.2	30	169	14	14	1	1	1	2	21	0	48	11	0
Heams, Shane, Mariners	1	1	.500	2.93	9	0	0	0	5	2	15.1	10	64	7	5	0	0	1	6	0	12	3	1
Hernandez, Victor, Athletics	0	0	.000	18.00	1	0	0	0	1	0	1.0	1	8	2	2	0	0	2	3	1	0	0	1	0
Hinchy, Brian, Rockies	1	1	.500	3.00	14	0	0	0	11	4	15.0	15	64	8	5	0	0	0	5	0	7	3	0
Hite, Kevin, Padres	5	5	.500	3.62	13	12	2	1	0	0	77.0	86	326	44	31	1	3	0	1	15	0	65	4	2
Hoff, Steve, Padres*	8	2	.800	2.85	16	13	0	0	1	0	85.1	66	356	37	27	2	0	1	9	36	0	104	6	0
Jones, Travis, Padres*	0	2	.000	6.21	14	9	0	0	0	0	42.0	52	216	38	29	6	1	3	3	37	0	29	5	3
Kawahara, Orin, Mariners	5	5	.500	4.16	18	10	0	0	5	1	71.1	64	318	42	33	4	3	3	6	40	0	87	2	1
Kaye, Justin, Mariners	1	0	1.000	3.62	20	0	0	0	12	3	32.1	34	156	23	13	4	0	1	5	19	1	36	7	2
Kempton, R, Diamondbacks	0	3	.000	3.12	14	0	0	0	6	1	26.0	29	111	14	9	1	5	2	0	7	1	14	0	1
Kennedy, Ryan, Rockies	0	4	.000	5.57	18	3	0	0	9	3	32.1	40	161	27	20	0	1	4	18	0	41	8	0
Kern, Brian, Athletics	0	0	.000	2.05	10	4	0	0	4	3	26.1	23	114	11	6	0	1	1	0	5	0	27	4	1
Knickerbocker, T, Athletics*	0	2	.000	7.08	8	0	0	0	1	0	20.1	21	100	21	16	0	0	2	1	16	0	19	5	2
Leach, Jim, Angels*	0	0	.000	9.82	5	0	0	0	1	0	3.2	3	22	5	4	0	0	2	5	0	3	0	0	0
Leyva, Edgar, Angels	4	7	.364	3.94	14	13	1	1	0	0	82.1	79	359	53	36	7	1	3	9	27	0	74	3	3
Leyva, Julian, Athletics	0	0	.000	0.00	1	0	0	0	0	0	2.0	1	8	0	0	0	0	0	1	0	2	0	0	0
Lopez, Jose, Angels	1	2	.333	6.75	6	4	0	0	1	0	30.2	30	141	24	23	0	3	2	18	1	27	5	0
Mahan, Dallas, Mariners*	0	0	.000	7.71	2	0	0	0	0	0	4.2	4	21	4	4	0	0	1	5	0	2	0	0
Margaritis, John, Angels	0	1	.000	6.57	7	0	0	0	3	0	12.1	19	61	10	9	0	1	0	3	0	11	0	0
Marino, Dominic, Padres	1	1	.500	6.51	20	0	0	0	10	1	27.2	28	131	20	20	3	0	4	2	17	1	27	1	0
Martinez, Hipolito, Athletics	1	0	1.000	0.00	1	0	0	0	1	0	0.2	1	4	0	0	0	0	0	0	1	0	0	0	0
Martinez, J, Diamondbacks	1	0	1.000	9.00	1	0	0	0	1	0	1.0	1	9	4	1	0	0	0	4	1	1	0	0
Martino, Wil, Rockies*	1	3	.250	4.38	17	0	0	0	6	4	24.2	26	115	21	12	0	3	2	8	0	29	3	0
McCall, T, Diamondbacks*	3	2	.600	4.06	16	0	0	0	3	0	37.2	45	167	21	17	2	1	2	5	11	1	38	1	0
McCutcheon, M, Diamndbks* ...	0	1	.000	0.49	14	0	0	0	11	2	18.1	9	70	3	1	0	1	0	2	7	0	18	1	1
McGuire, Brandon, Angels	0	0	.000	31.15	4	0	0	0	0	0	4.1	8	34	16	15	0	0	0	2	6	0	3	4	0
Mears, Chris, Mariners	1	2	.333	3.60	6	5	0	0	0	0	25.0	23	103	11	10	1	0	1	5	0	27	1	0
Meche, Gilbert, Mariners	0	1	.000	6.00	2	0	0	0	0	0	3.0	4	13	2	2	0	0	0	1	0	4	0	0
Mercedes, Jose, Athletics	2	2	.500	6.97	10	5	0	0	2	1	31.0	42	148	28	24	3	1	2	14	0	19	2	0
Moore, Joel, Rockies	1	0	1.000	1.00	4	4	0	0	0	0	18.0	13	70	2	2	1	0	1	0	19	0	0
Morgan, Eric, Mariners	2	0	1.000	0.00	3	0	0	0	1	0	5.1	6	24	3	0	0	0	3	0	4	0	0
Nash, Damond, Padres	5	3	.625	3.05	22	4	0	0	7	5	59.0	45	258	30	20	0	2	1	36	0	78	7	1
Nicholson, John, Rockies	3	5	.375	1.64	11	11	1	1	0	0	65.2	42	255	16	12	1	1	5	14	0	65	2	1
Noe, Matthew, Mariners*	2	2	.500	3.53	11	5	0	0	3	0	35.2	34	169	25	14	1	0	1	26	0	18	5	2
Norris, Ben, Diamondbacks* ...	2	2	.500	4.60	8	7	0	0	0	0	31.1	33	133	21	16	3	0	4	4	0	37	2	0
Nova, Kelvin, Athletics	0	1	.000	9.82	3	0	0	0	2	1	3.2	8	20	4	4	0	1	0	1	2	0	2	1	0
Ortiz, Edicksn, Diamondbacks	2	2	.500	3.60	7	0	0	0	5	0	15.0	13	66	10	6	1	1	1	7	0	15	0	0
Ortiz, Jose, Angels	2	1	.667	6.20	14	0	0	0	9	2	24.2	23	124	17	17	1	1	1	5	21	2	32	6	1
Ortiz, Ramon, Angels	5	4	.556	2.12	16	8	2	2	5	1	68.0	55	285	28	16	5	0	1	2	27	0	78	5	2
Padilla, Charly, Angels	1	0	1.000	9.00	9	0	0	0	3	0	10.0	12	46	10	10	2	1	1	0	4	0	7	2	0
Palki, Jeromy, Mariners	1	1	.500	2.47	18	0	0	0	12	6	47.1	31	194	14	13	3	1	1	2	17	0	56	2	0
Paredes, V, Diamondbacks*	1	1	.500	3.95	17	0	0	0	5	0	27.1	18	126	15	12	0	0	1	2	27	0	20	3	0
Paulino, Jose, Athletics	4	0	1.000	3.68	6	6	0	0	0	0	29.1	32	119	13	12	0	0	0	2	0	31	1	0
Penny, B, Diamondbacks	2	2	.500	2.36	11	8	0	0	1	0	49.2	36	201	18	13	1	0	3	14	0	52	3	2
Precinal, Huilberto, Padres	0	0	.000	0.00	2	0	0	0	1	0	2.0	1	7	0	0	0	0	0	0	0	2	0	0
Puffer, Brandon, Angels	1	0	1.000	3.60	1	1	0	0	0	0	5.0	7	23	2	2	0	0	0	1	0	3	1	0
Putt, Eric, Diamondbacks	3	3	.500	4.60	12	8	0	0	1	0	45.0	45	203	37	23	1	2	1	3	22	0	29	7	1
Rivera, Alvin, Rockies	4	2	.667	3.28	11	7	0	0	2	1	49.1	48	208	22	18	0	3	4	12	0	44	3	2
Rodriguez, H, Rockies	1	2	.333	6.75	17	0	0	0	10	2	21.1	30	113	23	16	2	0	3	12	0	18	5	3
Rojas, Renney, Angels	2	0	1.000	3.58	10	1	0	0	4	1	27.2	23	111	14	11	1	1	1	3	8	0	28	2	0
Romero, John, Angels	2	3	.400	4.03	14	11	0	0	1	1	67.0	63	295	43	30	1	1	1	7	27	0	53	9	2
Rosa, Cristy, Rockies	1	0	1.000	5.82	6	3	0	0	1	0	17.0	22	74	11	11	0	0	4	4	0	12	0	0
Schlutt, Jason, Padres*	0	1	.000	3.60	3	0	0	0	1	0	5.0	6	22	3	2	1	0	0	0	7	0	0
Sellers, Justin, Padres	1	0	1.000	2.25	26	0	0	0	23	6	32.0	31	139	14	8	0	2	3	14	0	36	2	0
Silva, Luis, Athletics	1	0	1.000	0.00	5	0	0	0	1	0	9.0	9	35	5	5	0	0	0	0	0	10	0	0
Slamka, John, Rockies*	0	0	.000	0.00	1	1	0	0	0	0	1.0	0	6	0	0	0	0	0	2	0	3	1	0
Smith, Josh, Padres*	2	1	.667	0.43	10	0	0	0	5	2	21.0	12	77	3	1	0	0	0	3	0	22	2	0
Soriano, Jacobo, Angels	1	3	.250	5.03	15	0	0	0	12	5	19.2	17	88	13	11	0	2	3	12	1	22	1	1
Steele, Brandon, Angels	1	3	.250	4.39	7	4	0	0	1	1	26.2	31	121	18	13	0	0	3	13	0	19	3	1
Stockstill, Jason, Angels*	2	6	.250	4.17	13	13	0	0	0	0	73.1	74	329	45	34	5	0	2	34	0	61	8	0
Swingle, Paul, Angels	0	1	.000	9.00	1	0	0	0	1	0	0.2	6	11	9	0	0	0	0	1	0	0	0
Thompson, Josef, Padres* ...	8	2	.800	2.65	13	12	0	0	1	0	74.2	67	319	33	22	3	1	2	22	0	50	1	2
Thompson, Travis, Rockies	4	1	.800	3.30	9	3	0	0	3	0	30.0	34	128	12	11	1	1	0	6	0	25	0	1
Torrealba, Aquiles, Angels	0	0	.000	8.44	5	0	0	0	2	0	5.1	9	25	5	5	0	0	1	1	0	0	0	0
VanWormer, M, Diamondbcks.	1	5	.167	7.26	10	9	0	0	0	0	31.0	42	152	33	25	1	0	1	3	13	0	25	5	1
Vasquez, Jose, Athletics	0	0	.000	0.00	1	0	0	0	0	0	2.1	5	12	0	0	0	0	0	0	0	6	0	0
Vizcaino, Luis, Athletics	6	3	.667	4.07	15	10	0	0	4	1	59.2	58	264	36	27	1	1	1	2	24	1	52	6	0
Walker, Pete, Padres	0	1	.000	2.25	2	2	0	0	0	0	4.0	4	17	1	1	0	0	0	0	0	5	0	0
Westbrook, Jake, Rockies	4	2	.667	2.87	11	11	0	0	0	0	62.2	66	271	33	20	0	3	1	8	14	0	57	4	0
Winkleman, Greg, Athletics*	1	1	.500	1.72	25	0	0	0	20	6	36.2	31	152	11	7	0	1	0	15	1	32	1	0

COMBINATION SHUTOUTS: **Angels (2)**—Steele-Romero, Leyva-Ortiz. **Athletics (2)**—Faulk-D'Amico-Gallagher, Gallagher-Leyva-Viscaino. **Diamondbacks (1)**—rris-Frias. **Mariners (4)**—Gonzalez-Meche-Kaye-Palki, Mears-Christianson-Kaye, Kawahara-Christianson, Kawahara-Derenches. **Padres (1)**—Thompson-Sellers. ckies (5)—Moore-Rivera, Chacon-Conteras-Thompson-Hinchy, Westbrook-Hinchy, Nicholson-Thompson, Rivera-Kennedy.

NO-HIT GAMES: None.

1996 FIELDING

TEAM

am	Pct.	G	PO	A	E	TC	DP	PB	Team	Pct.	G	PO	A	E	TC	DP	PB
letics	.955	56	1487	636	101	2224	55	21	Padres	.945	56	1496	570	121	2187	41	17
riners	.948	56	1491	562	113	2166	38	10	Diamondbacks	.944	56	1470	594	122	2186	49	20
jels	.946	56	1461	589	118	2168	35	26	Rockies	.940	56	1468	612	133	2213	39	30

TRIPLE PLAYS: None.

INDIVIDUAL

FIRST BASEMEN

TE: All caps denotes fielding-percentage leader based on 28 games for catchers, for all other non-pitchers and 56 innings for pitchers. *Throws lefthanded.

yer, Team	Pct.	G	PO	A	E	TC	DP
iley, Antonio, Angels	1.000	1	1	0	0	1	1
rs, Macgregor, Athletics	1.000	1	4	0	0	4	0
nin, Shane, Padres	.984	20	117	9	2	128	9
esus, Eddie, Angels	.989	11	87	2	1	90	5
gado, Ariel, Angels*	.977	26	192	18	5	215	8
nham, Traylor, Padres	1.000	1	10	0	0	10	1
is, Braulio, Athletics*	.974	21	173	18	5	196	13
rrero, Wascar, Mariners	.981	30	254	7	5	266	18
obo, Roberto, Padres*	.965	36	258	19	10	287	22
rrence, Mike, Angels	.980	23	187	10	4	201	18
ynard, Scott, Mariners	.953	16	112	9	6	127	6
Guire, Brandon, Angels	1.000	2	12	1	0	13	1
TERSEN, Mike, Rockies	.973	46	406	34	12	452	29
driguez, D, Diamondbacks	.988	31	239	14	3	256	19
wartzbauer, Brad, Rockies	1.000	3	20	0	0	20	2
sa, Nicolas, Athletics	.977	36	322	15	8	345	33
wart, Adrian, Padres	.955	16	103	4	5	112	4
land, Ron, Athletics	.917	2	11	0	1	12	1
iams, Marcus, Mariners	.972	11	100	5	3	108	8
iams, Patrick, Mariners	1.000	1	8	0	0	8	1
son, Keith, Diamondbacks	.992	33	236	17	2	255	21
eifel, Kent, Rockies	.989	12	86	3	1	90	7

SECOND BASEMEN

yer, Team	Pct.	G	PO	A	E	TC	DP
ier, Marc, Angels	.951	23	37	40	4	81	6
is, George, Athletics	.917	4	5	6	1	12	1
cia, Sandro, Padres	.927	42	64	75	11	150	17
sser, Scott, Diamondbacks	1.000	3	3	9	0	12	0
zalez, Santos, Padres	.974	16	15	22	1	38	6
nandez, Victor, Athletics	.970	16	30	34	2	66	7
de, Alejandro, Rockies	.898	13	16	28	5	49	4
enez, Miguel, Mariners	.000	1	0	0	1	1	0
nos, Alexis, Angels	.925	39	79	81	13	173	19
tinez, Jorge, Diamondbacks	.875	5	5	9	2	16	1
reno, Jose, Mariners	1.000	1	1	2	0	3	1
VA, Kelvin, Athletics	.946	41	84	110	11	205	23
ez, Jose, Diamondbacks	.667	1	1	1	1	3	0
son, Brian, Mariners	.900	7	5	4	1	10	2
rode, Jackie, Diamondbacks	.917	43	97	92	17	206	30
driguez, John, Padres	.877	16	21	36	8	65	6
as, Renney, Angels	1.000	1	1	1	0	2	0
ith, Brian, Mariners	.939	53	100	130	15	245	23
vey, Ernest, Diamondbacks	.983	10	26	33	1	60	5
res, Wolfrando, Rockies	.939	44	82	119	13	214	21

THIRD BASEMEN

yer, Team	Pct.	G	PO	A	E	TC	DP
thelemy, Edy, Mariners	.625	4	2	3	3	8	0
rs, Macgregor, Athletics	1.000	14	16	27	0	43	2
ier, Marc, Angels	1.000	2	1	3	0	4	0
ONIN, Shane, Padres	.868	41	27	78	16	121	4
is, George, Athletics	.906	28	17	41	6	64	3
sser, Scott, Diamondbacks	.905	34	22	54	8	84	4
zalez, Santos, Padres	1.000	1	1	1	0	2	0
rrero, Wascar, Mariners	1.000	1	0	1	0	1	0
de, Alejandro, Rockies	.867	13	12	27	6	45	5

[CATCHERS]

Player, Team	Pct.	G	PO	A	E	TC	DP
Hudson, Bert, Diamondbacks	1.000	2	0	1	0	1	0
Jimenez, Miguel, Mariners	.835	38	40	61	20	121	9
Kirkpatrick, Brian, Rockies	.950	8	2	17	1	20	0
Lawrence, Mike, Angels	.830	16	11	33	9	53	5
Llanos, Alexis, Angels	.828	14	8	16	5	29	1
Martinez, Jorge, Diamondbacks	.800	5	1	3	1	5	1
Martinez, Victor, Mariners	.875	12	6	15	3	24	0
Maynard, Scott, Mariners	.938	6	5	10	1	16	0
Nieves, Wilbert, Padres	1.000	1	1	0	0	1	0
Nova, Kelvin, Athletics	1.000	1	1	0	0	1	0
Nunez, Jose, Diamondbacks	.750	3	1	2	1	4	0
Pacheco, Domingo, Mariners	.250	5	0	1	3	4	0
Petersen, Mike, Rockies	.833	2	1	4	1	6	0
Rodriguez, John, Padres	.895	25	9	25	4	38	2
Schwartzbauer, Brad, Rockies	.879	34	23	79	14	116	3
Spivey, Ernest, Diamondbacks	1.000	3	2	7	0	9	0
Starkey, Nate, Angels	.902	33	12	62	8	82	3
Tegland, Ron, Athletics	.917	17	9	35	4	48	2
Vinas, Alex, Diamondbacks	.906	18	10	19	3	32	2
Wilson, Keith, Diamondbacks	.750	7	1	8	3	12	0

SHORTSTOPS

Player, Team	Pct.	G	PO	A	E	TC	DP
Bautista, Juan, Diamondbacks	.929	48	82	139	17	238	24
Castro, Nelson, Angels	.94466	53	75	164	14	253	19
Collier, Marc, Athletics	.875	5	2	5	1	8	0
Davis, George, Athletics	.923	9	6	18	2	26	1
Glasser, Scott, Diamondbacks	.950	9	9	10	1	20	3
Gonzalez, Santos, Padres	.917	19	28	60	8	96	6
HALLORAN, Matt, Padres	.94545	38	50	106	9	165	16
Llanos, Alexis, Angels	.857	3	7	5	2	14	1
Martinez, Jorge, Diamondbacks	1.000	1	0	1	0	1	0
Martinez, Victor, Mariners	.967	5	11	18	1	30	2
Mitchell, Andres, Rockies	.886	51	63	147	27	237	24
Moreno, Jose, Mariners	.917	48	56	144	18	218	20
Mouton, Aaron, Diamondbacks	1.000	1	2	3	0	5	0
Ortiz, Jose, Athletics	.925	48	93	165	21	279	42
Pacheco, Domingo, Mariners	.600	1	2	1	2	5	1
Petersen, Mike, Rockies	.500	1	1	0	1	2	0
Rodriguez, John, Padres	.895	6	9	8	2	19	2
Shipley, Craig, Padres	1.000	2	0	2	0	2	0
Spivey, Ernest, Diamondbacks	.933	8	7	21	2	30	4
Torres, Wolfrando, Rockies	.727	4	4	12	6	22	2
Valera, Ramon, Mariners	.963	4	10	16	1	27	2

OUTFIELDERS

Player, Team	Pct.	G	PO	A	E	TC	DP
Barthelemy, Edy, Mariners	.905	10	16	3	2	21	1
Brown, Emil, Athletics	1.000	3	3	1	0	4	0
Byers, Macgregor, Athletics	1.000	2	3	1	0	4	0
Chapman, David, Diamondbacks	.964	35	49	5	2	56	2
Charvel, Ali, Angels*	.833	3	5	0	1	6	0
Clifton, Rodney, Athletics	.968	41	60	1	2	63	1
DeJesus, Eddie, Angels	.822	32	35	2	8	45	0
Delgado, Ariel, Angels*	.895	24	32	2	4	38	0
Eady, Gerald, Mariners	.981	46	99	4	2	105	1
Fefee, Theo, Angels*	1.000	10	25	0	0	25	0
Garcia, Juan, Diamondbacks	.941	23	44	4	3	51	1
Garcia, Sandro, Padres	.833	6	5	0	1	6	0
Geronimo, Cesar, Angels	1.000	3	4	0	0	4	0
Gordon, Gary, Rockies	.949	46	92	2	5	99	1

– 561 –

Player, Team	Pct.	G	PO	A	E	TC	DP
Goris, Braulio, Athletics*	.932	22	38	3	3	44	0
Hernandez, Victor, Athletics	1.000	29	42	1	0	43	0
Hudson, Bert, Diamondbacks	.944	15	17	0	1	18	0
Jacobo, Roberto, Padres*	.500	3	1	0	1	2	0
Jacobus, Brian, Padres*	.982	36	53	3	1	57	0
Jimenez, Miguel, Mariners	1.000	8	10	0	0	10	0
Knight, Marcus, Angels	.970	54	118	10	4	132	0
Landaeta, Luis, Rockies*	.922	40	52	7	5	64	1
Martinez, Hipolito, Athletics	.943	43	63	3	4	70	0
Martinez, Jorge, Diamondbacks	.750	3	3	0	1	4	0
Maxwell, Vernon, Padres	.979	49	90	4	2	96	0
Maynard, Scott, Mariners	1.000	6	8	0	0	8	0
Nieves, Wilbert, Padres	1.000	1	1	0	0	1	0
PERNELL, Brandon, Padres	1.000	43	59	2	0	61	0
Proctor, Jerry, Diamondbacks*	.856	42	74	3	13	90	1
Rodriguez, M, Diamondbacks*	.905	16	18	1	2	21	0
Rosario, Carlos, Rockies	.939	47	59	3	4	66	0
Rose, Carlos, Mariners	.932	40	67	1	5	73	0
Rottman, Paul, Diamondbacks	.900	12	9	0	1	10	0
Ruotsinoja, Jacob, Padres	.988	44	75	5	1	81	1
Sandoval, Jhensy, Diamondbacks	.932	33	38	3	3	44	0
Selga, Andres, Rockies	.951	28	38	1	2	41	0
Soriano, Jacobo, Angels	1.000	2	3	0	0	3	0
Stewart, Adrian, Padres	.875	6	7	0	1	8	0
Tolbert, Ernest, Mariners	.941	52	61	3	4	68	0
Tolentino, Juan, Angels	.887	40	54	1	7	62	0
Torres, Jose, Diamondbacks	.893	22	22	3	3	28	1
Vasquez, Jose, Athletics	.872	44	38	3	6	47	0
Ventura, Jose, Angels	.923	19	12	0	1	13	0
Williams, Patrick, Mariners	.964	18	26	1	1	28	1
Zweifel, Kent, Rockies	1.000	10	15	5	0	20	0

CATCHERS

Player, Team	Pct.	G	PO	A	E	TC	DP	PB
Antunez, Francisco, Angels	.941	5	25	7	2	34	1	2
Barthelemy, Edy, Mariners	.979	26	166	21	4	191	0	5
Castro, Juan, Rockies	.959	21	175	12	8	195	1	13
Dunham, Traylor, Padres	.972	19	131	10	4	145	0	9
Figueroa, Jose, Athletics	.973	49	364	64	12	440	4	19
Hudson, Bert, Diamondbacks	1.000	1	1	0	0	1	0	0
Leyba, Jhonathan, Diamondbacks	.946	24	95	11	6	112	1	1
Luderer, Brian, Athletics	1.000	6	29	4	0	33	0	1
Mahoney, Ricardo, Rockies	.934	8	53	4	4	61	0	2
Maldonado, Carlos, Mariners	.990	22	176	25	2	203	1	3
Maynard, Scott, Mariners	.992	17	108	19	1	128	1	2
McAffee, Joshua, Diamondbacks	.949	36	222	37	14	273	3	13
Nieves, Wilbert, Padres	.960	37	210	29	10	249	3	6
Osborne, Mark, Diamondbacks	.970	15	82	15	3	100	2	6
Panaro, Carmen, Diamondbacks	1.000	13	29	4	0	33	1	0
RODRIGUEZ, Chris, Rockies	.984	31	232	19	4	255	2	15
Russoniello, Michael, Angels	.980	13	44	4	1	49	0	7
Saucedo, Roberto, Angels	.993	15	126	16	1	143	0	7
Sears, Jayson, Angels	.971	4	31	2	1	34	0	1
Serrano, Danny, Angels	.970	19	144	20	5	169	0	5
Soto, Luis, Padres	.973	18	124	18	4	146	0	2
Starkey, Nate, Angels	1.000	10	62	11	0	73	1	4
Tegland, Ron, Athletics	1.000	1	1	0	0	1	0	1
Ventura, Wilfredo, Athletics	1.000	6	49	8	0	57	1	0
Williams, Patrick, Mariners	1.000	3	19	0	0	19	0	0

PITCHERS

Player, Team	Pct.	G	PO	A	E	TC	DP
Abreu, Oscar, Athletics	.800	17	7	9	4	20	2
Alarcon, James, Padres	.500	14	0	2	2	4	0
Ashley, Antonio, Angels	.875	17	4	3	1	8	0
Barboza, Carlos, Rockies	1.000	18	2	4	0	6	0
Barthelemy, Edy, Mariners	1.000	1	0	1	0	1	0
Bell, Matthew, Diamondbacks	.875	18	1	6	1	8	0
Bennett, Tom, Athletics	1.000	4	2	4	0	6	0
Bido, Jose, Diamondbacks	.833	11	2	8	2	12	1
Bierbrodt, N, Diamondbacks*	1.000	8	3	5	0	8	2
Brea, Lesli, Mariners	.500	7	0	1	1	2	0
Brueggeman, Dean, Rockies*	.889	3	1	7	1	9	0
Chacon, Shawn, Rockies	.917	11	4	7	1	12	0
CHRISTIANSON, Robby, Mariners	1.000	14	9	13	0	22	0

Player, Team	Pct.	G	PO	A	E	TC
Contreras, Orlando, Rockies	.778	16	5	2	2	9
D'Amico, Jeff, Athletics	.800	8	0	4	1	5
DeJesus, Tony, Mariners*	1.000	12	1	3	0	4
Derenches, Albert, Mariners*	.833	20	2	8	2	12
Douglas, Reggie, Rockies	.667	12	0	2	1	3
Escalante, Piter, Diamondbacks	.900	15	4	5	1	10
Faulk, Eric, Athletics	1.000	6	0	3	0	3
Fleming, John, Diamondbacks	1.000	10	1	7	0	8
Frias, Miguel, Diamondbacks*	.000	19	0	0	1	1
Gallagher, Bryan, Athletics*	.875	16	2	5	1	8
Garcia, Bryan, Athletics	.846	18	5	6	2	13
Garey, Daniel, Mariners*	1.000	12	2	5	0	7
Gogolin, Elton, Athletics	1.000	6	0	2	0	2
Gonzalez, Francisco, Padres	.900	25	4	5	1	10
Gorrell, Chris, Athletics	1.000	12	0	6	0	6
Gregg, Kevin, Athletics	1.000	11	2	4	0	6
Heams, Shane, Mariners	1.000	9	1	0	0	1
Hinchy, Brian, Rockies	.750	14	3	3	2	8
Hite, Kevin, Padres	1.000	13	5	9	0	14
Hoff, Steve, Padres*	.800	16	3	13	4	20
Jones, Travis, Padres*	.800	14	3	1	1	5
Kawahara, Orin, Mariners	.833	18	3	7	2	12
Kaye, Justin, Mariners	.778	20	2	5	2	9
Kempton, Ryan, Diamondbacks	1.000	14	0	3	0	3
Kennedy, Ryan, Rockies	.700	18	2	5	3	10
Kern, Brian, Athletics	.889	10	3	5	1	9
Knickerbocker, Tom, Athletics*	.667	8	0	2	1	3
Leyva, Edgar, Diamondbacks	.826	14	4	15	4	23
Lopez, Jose, Angels	1.000	6	1	1	0	2
Mahan, Dallas, Mariners*	1.000	2	0	1	0	1
Margaritis, John, Angels	1.000	7	1	6	0	7
Marino, Dominic, Padres	.500	20	2	1	3	6
Martinez, Jorge, Diamondbacks	1.000	1	0	1	0	1
Martino, Wil, Rockies*	.800	17	1	3	1	5
McCall, Travis, Diamondbacks*	1.000	16	2	6	0	8
McCutcheon, Mike, Diamondbacks*	1.000	14	0	3	0	3
McGuire, Brandon, Angels	.500	4	1	0	1	2
Mears, Chris, Mariners	1.000	6	1	3	0	4
Mercedes, Jose, Athletics	.750	10	0	3	1	4
Moore, Joel, Rockies	1.000	4	1	5	0	6
Nash, Damond, Padres	.714	22	5	5	4	14
Nicholson, John, Rockies	.955	11	5	16	1	22
Noe, Matthew, Mariners*	.833	10	1	9	2	12
Norris, Ben, Diamondbacks*	.857	8	0	6	1	7
Nova, Kelvin, Athletics	1.000	3	0	1	0	1
Ortiz, Edickson, Diamondbacks	1.000	7	1	2	0	3
Ortiz, Jose, Angels	1.000	14	4	3	0	7
Ortiz, Ramon, Angels	.875	16	1	13	2	16
Padilla, Charly, Angels	1.000	2	1	0	0	3
Palki, Jeromy, Mariners	1.000	18	1	2	0	3
Paredes, Vladimir, Diamondbacks*	1.000	17	1	0	0	1
Paulino, Jose, Athletics	.909	6	0	10	1	11
Penny, Bradley, Diamondbacks	1.000	11	4	9	0	13
Puffer, Brandon, Angels	1.000	1	0	2	0	2
Putt, Eric, Diamondbacks	.833	12	3	2	1	6
Rivera, Alvin, Rockies	1.000	11	4	10	0	14
Rodriguez, Humberto, Rockies	.500	17	1	0	1	2
Rojas, Renney, Angels	.857	11	2	4	1	7
Romero, John, Angels	.875	13	2	5	1	8
Rosa, Cristy, Rockies	1.000	6	3	2	0	5
Schlutt, Jason, Padres*	1.000	3	1	1	0	2
Sellers, Justin, Padres	.800	26	1	3	1	5
Silva, Luis, Athletics	1.000	5	1	1	0	2
Smith, Josh, Padres*	1.000	10	0	1	0	1
Soriano, Jacobo, Angels	1.000	15	0	4	0	4
Steele, Brandon, Angels	.750	7	0	6	2	8
Stockstill, Jason, Angels*	.762	13	7	9	5	21
Thompson, Josef, Athletics*	.778	13	3	11	4	18
Thompson, Travis, Rockies	1.000	9	1	5	0	6
Torrealba, Aquiles, Angels	1.000	5	0	1	0	1
VanWormer, Marc, Diamondbacks	.750	10	1	2	1	4
Vizcaino, Luis, Diamondbacks	.929	15	3	10	1	14
Walker, Pete, Padres	1.000	2	0	2	0	2
Westbrook, Jake, Rockies	.955	11	3	18	1	22
Winkleman, Greg, Athletics*	1.000	25	1	3	0	4

The following players did not have any fielding statistics at the positions indicated or appeared only as a designated hitter, pinch-hitter or pinch-runner: J. Gonz p; Hardy, of; Hernandez, p; Leach, p; J. Leyva, p; H. Martinez, p; McDougal, dh, ph, pr; Meche, p; Morgan, p; Precinal, p; J. Rodriguez, of; Shipley, 3B; Slamka, Smith, of; Swingle, p; Tegland, of; Vasquez, p.

Year	Team	Pct.	Year	Team	Pct.	Year	Team	Pct.
88—	Peoria Brewers	.690	1991—	Scottsdale A's	.650	1994—	Chandler Cardinals	.607
89—	Peoria Brewers	.732	1992—	Scottsdale A's	.607	1995—	Scottsdale A's	.661
90—	Peoria Brewers	.679	1993—	Scottsdale A's	.636	1996—	Padres	.643

SUMMER CLASS A *Arizona League*

DOMINICAN SUMMER LEAGUE

1996 FINAL STANDINGS

EAST DIVISION

Team	W	L	T	Pct.	GB
Detroit	47	25	0	.653	....
St. Louis	47	27	0	.635	1
N.Y. Yankees	41	29	1	.586	5
Dodgers I	39	28	1	.582	5¹/₂
Seattle	35	34	0	.507	10¹/₂
Florida	20	50	0	.286	26
Montreal	19	52	1	.268	27¹/₂

WEST DIVISION

Team	W	L	T	Pct.	GB
Oakland	49	24	0	.671	....
N.Y. Mets	47	24	0	.637	1
Texas	43	28	1	.606	5
Arizona	36	36	0	.500	12
Milw./Chi. (A.L.)	32	38	1	.464	15
Pittsburgh	25	46	1	.352	23
Chi. (N.L.)/S.D.	17	56	0	.233	32

CIBAO DIVISION

Team	W	L	T	Pct.	GB
Cleveland	50	21	0	.704	....
Philadelphia	36	35	0	.507	14
Co-op	28	42	0	.400	21¹/₂
K.C./Colorado	27	43	0	.386	22¹/₂

SAN PEDRO DE MACORIS DIVISION

Team	W	L	T	Pct.	GB
Dodgers II	59	10	0	.855	....
Toronto	47	23	1	.671	12
Atlanta	42	29	0	.592	18
Houston/Boston	29	39	2	.426	29
San Francisco	26	40	4	.394	31
Baltimore	27	42	1	.391	32
T.B./California	12	59	0	.169	48

Club names are major league affiliations.

MANAGERS—Arizona, Julio C. Paula; Atlanta, Pedro Gonzalez; Baltimore, Carlos Bernhardt; Chicago (N.L.)/San Diego, Julio Valdez; Cleveland, Alejandro Taveras; Co-op, David Lantigua; Detroit, Felix Nivar; Dodgers I, Teodoro Martinez; Dodgers II, Antonio Bautista; Florida, Hilario Soriano; Houston/Boston, Ricardo Aponte; Kansas City/Colorado, Pedro Silverio; Milwaukee/Chicago (A.L.), Mike Guerrero; Montreal, Arturo De Freitas; New York Mets, Luis Nate New York Yankees, Humberto Trejo; Oakland, Evaristo Lantigua; Philadelphia, Alberto Fana; Pittsburgh, Ramon Sambo; San Francisco, Mateo Rojas Al Seattle, Romon De Los Santos; St. Louis, Roberto Diaz; Tampa Bay/California, Rafael De Leon; Texas, Carmelo Castillo; Toronto, Juan Espino.

ALL-STAR TEAM: 1B—Danny Cabrera, Mets; 2B—Luis Martinez, Dodgers I; 3B—Melvin Olivares, Mets; SS—Pablo Ozuna, St. Louis; OF—Alex Fajar Philadelphia; Raul De La Cruz, Pittsburgh; Frank Ventura, Cleveland; C—Arnulfo Vasquez, Cleveland; DH—Juan Silvestre, Seattle; RHP—Pedro Hernand Dodgers I; LHP—Bernardo Reyes, St. Louis; Player of the Year—Frank Ventura, Cleveland; Pitcher of the Year—Pedro Hernandez, Dodgers I; Manager of Year—Roberto Diaz, St. Louis.

1996 BATTING

TEAM

Team	Avg.	G	TPA	AB	R	H	TB	2B	3B	HR	RBI	SH	SF	HP	BB	IBB	SO	SB	CS	GDP	LOB	ShO	Slg.	OB
Dodgers II	.301	69	2833	2368	525	712	987	117	28	34	402	25	29	51	360	1	360	107	48	63	572	...	.417	.4
N.Y. Mets	.298	71	2757	2448	479	730	1131	105	7	94	397	15	18	48	228	9	424	71	42	64	495	...	.462	.3
St. Louis	.297	74	2916	2539	445	754	1003	108	30	27	356	16	19	47	295	18	390	151	65	78	579	...	.395	.3
Cleveland	.286	71	2870	2452	493	702	948	139	28	17	359	18	34	42	324	11	335	126	52	67	546	...	.387	.3
Atlanta	.276	71	2787	2377	434	657	938	87	34	42	352	35	22	46	307	7	398	127	49	59	533	...	.395	.3
Philadelphia	.276	71	2771	2486	397	685	912	114	25	21	307	15	9	49	212	6	358	121	50	54	544	...	.367	.3
N.Y. Yankees	.272	71	2657	2324	413	631	899	102	20	42	325	14	19	57	243	6	397	129	57	64	473	...	.387	.3
Dodgers I	.271	68	2614	2171	380	589	774	103	11	20	295	64	24	56	299	12	382	67	45	60	522	...	.357	.3
Detroit	.270	72	2907	2372	500	641	915	98	40	32	390	26	28	50	431	14	413	123	67	60	566	...	.386	.3
Pittsburgh	.269	72	2605	2315	342	623	870	101	7	44	276	15	14	32	229	7	496	134	72	54	473	...	.376	.3
Texas	.266	72	2700	2278	380	606	891	113	23	42	288	30	25	39	328	9	482	119	77	44	512	...	.391	.3
Seattle	.266	69	2649	2234	387	594	971	85	14	88	338	13	18	34	350	12	446	77	61	41	538	...	.435	.3
Toronto	.263	71	2732	2329	434	612	808	86	27	18	329	14	19	39	331	3	398	189	51	59	513	...	.344	.3
Co-op	.261	70	2698	2326	378	606	832	120	14	26	304	10	15	51	296	5	431	105	54	68	528	...	.358	.3
Oakland	.261	73	2820	2302	436	601	893	100	33	42	360	19	33	37	429	10	453	61	41	29	624	...	.388	.3
Arizona	.261	72	2626	2240	362	585	831	102	6	44	286	20	15	44	307	8	367	126	84	54	479	...	.371	.3
Mil./Chi.(A.L.)	.260	71	2586	2228	316	579	803	105	13	31	262	21	25	43	269	6	410	109	71	55	503	...	.360	.3
K.C./Colo.	.255	70	2642	2267	382	577	823	110	20	32	295	8	23	44	300	5	435	134	76	47	502	...	.363	.3
Montreal	.248	72	2731	2328	310	577	752	86	7	25	248	28	15	43	317	11	392	95	65	46	585	...	.323	.3
Baltimore	.241	70	2509	2195	326	529	704	73	21	21	226	32	15	28	239	3	462	159	44	54	408	...	.321	.3
Florida	.238	70	2556	2250	260	536	701	75	9	24	221	22	9	35	240	5	525	59	48	48	506	...	.312	.3
San Francisco	.237	70	2654	2252	329	535	736	86	10	28	256	24	15	45	318	6	435	97	49	75	538	...	.326	.3
Hou./Bos.	.229	70	2613	2254	308	516	650	79	11	11	228	25	16	34	264	6	448	83	51	59	483	...	.288	.3
Chi.(N.L.)/S.D.	.227	73	2588	2225	297	504	716	67	17	37	240	27	13	48	275	4	482	72	39	59	486	...	.322	.3
T.B./Calif.	.213	71	2637	2180	285	465	578	70	13	6	211	21	16	54	366	5	544	131	79	64	498	...	.265	.3

INDIVIDUAL

TOP QUALIFIERS FOR BATTING CHAMPIONSHIP

Minimum 192 plate appearances.

Player, Team	Avg.	G	TPA	AB	R	H	TB	2B	3B	HR	RBI	SH	SF	HP	BB	IBB	SO	SB	CS	GDP	Slg.
De La Cruz, Raul, Pittsburgh	.387	67	265	243	49	94	125	16	0	5	40	1	3	1	17	1	37	35	9	1	.514
Ventura, Frank, Cleveland	.382	57	261	225	55	86	126	24	2	4	42	1	4	4	27	1	20	26	3	3	.560
Martinez, Luis, Dodgers II	.378	66	315	286	68	108	126	12	3	0	45	5	2	3	19	0	14	8	6	6	.441
Fajardo, Alex, Philadelphia	.373	63	277	249	48	93	127	16	6	2	38	1	2	0	25	1	21	22	4	5	.510
Ozuna, Pablo, St. Louis	.363	74	331	295	57	107	145	12	4	6	60	3	4	6	23	7	19	18	5	7	.492
Perez, Edison, Seattle	.360	52	220	189	45	68	97	14	0	5	22	2	0	3	26	2	30	27	16	1	.513
Olivares, Melvin, N.Y. Mets	.360	67	283	272	48	98	141	16	0	9	49	1	1	0	9	1	17	13	7	7	.518

Player, Team	Avg.	G	TPA	AB	R	H	TB	2B	3B	HR	RBI	SH	SF	HP	BB	IBB	SO	SB	CS	GDP	Slg.	OBP
Gutierrez, Victor, Pittsburgh...	.360	71	319	278	60	100	131	20	1	3	26	3	3	3	32	0	11	44	15	7	.471	.427
e Leon, Raymundo, St. Louis.	.348	73	321	282	51	98	144	17	7	5	46	0	3	4	32	1	31	8	7	10	.511	.417
asquez, Arnulfo, Cleveland...	.344	63	256	224	45	77	109	21	1	3	50	0	5	5	22	0	42	12	3	7	.487	.406

ALL PLAYERS

Player, Team	Avg.	G	TPA	AB	R	H	TB	2B	3B	HR	RBI	SH	SF	HP	BB	IBB	SO	SB	CS	GDP	Slg.	OBP
Abreu, Ruddy, Dodgers I.......	.180	40	112	89	27	16	36	4	2	4	14	1	1	5	16	1	37	5	3	2	.404	.333
Acevedo, Claudio, Hou.-Bos...	.248	38	133	121	17	30	35	5	0	0	11	0	1	1	10	0	25	6	1	1	.289	.308
Acuna, Ronald, N.Y. Mets	.239	20	59	46	7	11	15	1	0	1	8	1	2	0	10	0	9	1	1	1	.326	.362
Adorno, Wilson, Pittsburgh...	.000	7	21	19	0	0	0	0	0	0	0	0	0	2	0	0	7	0	0	0	.000	.095
Agli, Daniel, Montreal..........	.271	71	302	262	32	71	113	20	2	6	38	0	4	2	34	2	53	2	0	6	.431	.354
Albertus, Melaneo, Toronto...	.213	38	135	108	18	23	25	2	0	0	14	1	0	4	22	0	22	2	1	8	.231	.366
Alcala, Juan, Seattle...........	.261	37	107	92	14	24	33	3	0	2	10	2	1	0	12	0	17	0	1	0	.359	.343
Alcantara, Lorenzo, Arizona ...	.258	44	131	120	16	31	38	3	2	0	9	0	0	1	10	0	12	9	2	6	.317	.321
Alfonzo, Elieeser, St. Louis...	.325	24	87	80	6	26	36	5	1	1	16	0	1	1	5	0	21	2	0	3	.450	.368
Almonte, Erick, N.Y. Yankees	.282	58	236	216	37	61	92	7	0	8	36	2	1	2	15	0	30	3	2	7	.426	.333
Alvarez, Antonio, Pittsburgh ..	.138	39	118	109	12	15	20	2	0	1	9	0	0	1	8	0	12	6	6	2	.183	.203
Alvarez, David, Co-op..........	.220	59	203	182	23	40	66	10	2	4	19	0	2	2	17	1	43	3	3	2	.363	.291
Alvarez, Julio, Detroit..........	.292	24	89	65	16	19	20	1	0	0	8	2	1	3	18	0	8	10	3	3	.308	.460
Amaya, Edilberto, Mil./Chi./(AL).	.235	70	277	247	23	58	89	13	0	6	34	1	5	3	21	1	46	2	1	6	.360	.297
Andujar, Jose, Florida........	.201	41	152	134	17	27	30	3	0	0	13	0	2	3	13	0	27	0	0	2	.224	.283
Araujo, Danilo, St. Louis.......	.303	70	330	261	77	79	95	9	2	1	22	4	1	3	61	0	36	36	11	7	.364	.439
Araujo, Orlany, Dodgers I.......	.316	50	198	174	22	55	61	6	0	0	13	6	1	3	14	0	24	7	6	6	.351	.375
Arias, Frank Cleveland.........	.281	49	184	160	30	45	50	5	0	0	20	0	1	6	17	1	18	8	4	6	.313	.370
Arias, Yeison, California........	.257	31	134	109	14	28	38	5	1	1	19	0	2	2	23	0	30	9	4	5	.349	.396
Arredondo, Alan, Dodgers II..	.218	52	143	101	32	22	25	3	0	0	6	4	1	4	33	0	30	14	7	0	.248	.424
Arrendel, Eduard, Baltimore...	.294	21	59	51	10	15	20	2	0	1	6	0	0	2	6	0	10	0	0	1	.392	.390
Aybar, Carlos, Oakland.........	.159	17	53	44	2	7	8	1	0	0	3	0	0	0	9	0	15	0	4	0	.182	.302
Baetriz, Remy, Mil./Chi.(AL) ...	.310	55	196	168	29	52	76	14	2	2	20	0	0	0	28	0	16	11	8	3	.452	.408
Baez, Juan, Mil./Chi.(AL).......	.238	66	224	185	24	44	73	13	2	4	23	5	2	4	28	1	54	10	9	2	.395	.347
Baez, Rafael, N.Y. Mets	1.000	1	1	1	0	1	1	0	0	0	0	0	0	0	0	0	0	0	0	0	1.000	1.000
Barrio, Elkin, Seattle...........	.260	32	107	100	10	26	33	2	1	1	11	1	2	0	4	0	21	2	2	3	.330	.283
Basabe, Jesus, Oakland	.331	41	147	121	28	40	53	5	1	2	14	1	0	3	22	0	26	5	3	1	.438	.445
Basilio, Victor, Baltimore......	.211	23	46	38	7	8	8	0	0	0	3	0	0	0	8	0	20	2	2	1	.211	.348
Batias, Hector, Baltimore......	.100	12	27	20	5	2	2	0	0	1	5	1	0	0	6	0	6	0	0	0	.100	.308
Bautista, Francisco, K.C./Colo..	.429	2	8	7	3	3	3	0	0	0	0	0	0	0	1	0	0	0	0	0	.429	.500
Bautista, Rayner, Detroit.......	.181	49	162	144	18	26	36	4	3	0	21	4	2	4	8	0	28	2	3	1	.250	.241
Beltre, Manuel, N.Y. Yankees..	.306	64	257	216	45	66	99	9	6	4	36	2	2	4	33	1	39	19	9	1	.458	.404
Berroa, Carlos, Baltimore......	.190	42	146	126	10	24	35	8	0	1	11	3	1	4	12	1	25	4	4	4	.278	.280
Berroa, Cristian, Chi.(NL)/S.D...	.256	65	243	215	29	55	76	9	0	4	23	4	3	11	10	0	35	4	1	6	.353	.318
Betancourt, Romulo, Baltimore..	.229	25	83	70	7	16	17	1	0	0	6	0	0	0	13	0	14	7	1	1	.243	.349
Blanco, Daniel, San Francisco..	.194	27	76	72	7	14	29	3	0	4	10	0	0	4	0	0	12	0	0	5	.403	.237
Blanco, Felix, Mil./Chi.(AL).....	.328	48	140	125	23	41	48	5	1	0	9	0	1	3	11	0	11	10	8	7	.384	.393
Bonilla, Elyn, Philadelphia.....	.250	42	148	136	18	34	42	3	1	1	13	0	1	1	10	0	20	5	7	1	.309	.304
Bonilla, Rusviel, Toronto.......	.247	27	91	81	17	20	25	3	1	0	14	0	1	1	8	0	19	2	0	3	.275	.319
Bravo, Eulys, Cleveland........	.318	8	25	22	7	7	8	1	0	0	2	0	1	2	0	0	1	1	1	1	.364	.400
Barazona, Jose, Mil./Chi.(AL)...	.250	1	4	4	0	1	1	0	0	0	0	0	0	0	0	0	0	0	0	0	.250	.250
Bricero, Freddy, Montreal	.211	57	193	166	23	35	38	3	0	0	9	6	0	4	17	1	13	4	10	1	.229	.299
Brito, Alejandro, Montreal......	.194	15	38	36	5	7	7	0	0	0	2	0	0	0	2	0	11	2	0	2	.194	.237
Brito, Angelo, Pittsburgh......	.225	59	295	262	41	59	89	11	2	5	40	0	3	4	26	1	45	31	7	3	.340	.302
Brito, Johan, San Francisco ...	.299	64	270	221	48	66	80	7	2	1	27	7	1	5	36	0	20	14	4	6	.362	.407
Brito, Juan, N.Y. Mets	.000	14	0	0	0	0	0	0	0	0	0	0	0	0	0	0	0	0	0	0	.000	.000
Brito, Justo, N.Y. Mets	.286	16	29	28	3	8	8	0	0	0	5	1	0	0	3	0	9	2	0	0	.286	.286
Brito, Obispo, Mil./Chi.(AL).....	.187	30	102	91	9	17	27	4	0	2	10	0	0	1	11	0	23	0	1	0	.297	.275
Burelli, Luis, Mil./Chi.(AL)......	.253	32	103	95	9	24	30	3	0	1	9	0	2	0	6	0	24	0	2	5	.316	.291
Bustamante, Omar, Dodgers I..	.194	36	118	98	8	19	27	5	0	1	17	2	5	1	12	0	30	1	1	3	.276	.276
Bustillos, Luis, Dodgers II......	.228	57	211	171	36	39	52	4	3	1	16	3	0	5	32	0	25	6	4	6	.304	.365
Cabrera, Danny, N.Y. Mets	.338	66	260	213	44	72	129	15	0	14	43	1	1	5	40	6	38	3	2	6	.606	.452
Cabrera, Raymond, Baltimore..	.273	46	150	143	11	39	43	2	1	0	14	0	1	2	4	0	21	4	1	6	.301	.300
Cadet, Javier, Hou.-Bos.......	.125	9	27	24	3	3	5	0	1	0	0	0	0	2	1	0	8	0	0	0	.208	.222
Caines, Franklin, Philadelphia ..	.304	65	283	263	49	80	104	15	3	1	31	1	1	3	15	1	32	2	0	5	.395	.348
Calderon, Henry, K.C./Colo......	.291	53	169	148	26	43	60	11	0	2	19	0	3	2	16	0	15	13	5	4	.405	.361
Camilo, Juan, Oakland	.241	60	245	187	48	45	69	8	5	2	32	0	0	1	57	2	40	13	6	4	.369	.420
Candelario, Alexis, Texas.......	.114	27	62	44	6	5	9	1	0	1	4	1	1	2	14	0	16	1	0	2	.205	.344
Carpenter, Donald, Toronto.....	.321	18	36	28	10	9	9	0	0	0	4	1	0	0	7	0	7	10	1	1	.321	.457
Carpio, Roberto, St. Louis	.313	47	138	128	25	40	53	5	1	2	22	1	0	4	5	0	29	8	5	3	.414	.358
Carrasco, Ricardo, Atlanta	.220	51	189	150	27	33	51	3	0	5	21	1	1	3	34	1	39	3	3	2	.340	.372
Carreno, Jose, Montreal........	.239	29	77	71	3	17	21	1	0	1	13	0	0	2	4	0	12	0	0	2	.296	.299
Castellano, Alexis, Chi.(NL)/S.D.	.223	52	170	148	20	33	52	5	1	4	15	2	2	3	15	1	25	4	5	4	.351	.304
Castillo, Alexander, Mil./Chi.(AL)	.291	65	273	234	44	68	125	14	2	13	53	0	4	3	32	2	31	5	5	5	.534	.377
Castillo, Geramel, Texas........	.207	45	156	140	18	29	47	7	1	3	14	2	1	2	11	1	33	4	5	3	.336	.273
Castillo, Jorge, Philadelphia....	.264	33	120	106	15	28	30	2	0	0	6	1	0	2	11	0	13	2	0	0	.283	.345
Castillo, Jose, Detroit..........	.000	21	1	1	0	0	0	0	0	0	0	0	0	0	0	0	0	0	0	0	.000	.000
Castillo, Jose, Hou.-Bos.......	.188	33	104	96	4	18	23	5	0	0	9	2	1	2	6	0	24	0	1	3	.240	.225
Castro, Jesus, Toronto..........	.193	22	65	57	5	11	14	0	0	1	4	0	0	0	8	0	14	2	0	2	.246	.292
Castro, Jorge, Dodgers II.......	.176	5	19	17	3	3	3	0	0	0	1	0	0	0	2	0	1	0	0	0	.176	.263
Castro, Martires, Texas.........	.320	63	252	231	30	74	117	16	3	7	38	0	0	4	21	1	41	8	5	1	.506	.377
Castro, Rafael, Philadelphia ...	.244	40	137	131	13	32	38	6	0	0	11	0	1	5	0	0	13	1	0	6	.290	.277
Celedonio, Carlos, San Fran...	.098	16	47	41	3	4	4	0	0	0	1	0	1	1	4	0	17	1	1	2	.098	.191
Centeno, Edwin, Baltimore.....	.234	54	183	154	27	36	57	4	4	3	16	4	1	1	23	0	50	11	2	0	.370	.335
Chalas, Alexis, Detroit.........	.312	42	139	109	26	34	48	7	2	1	19	2	2	2	24	0	19	5	4	2	.440	.438
Chavez, Endy, N.Y. Mets.......	.354	48	190	164	42	58	92	11	1	7	29	2	1	1	22	1	16	3	4	4	.561	.431
Chirinos, Germain, Oakland ...	.053	10	22	19	1	1	1	0	0	0	1	0	1	0	2	0	4	0	0	0	.053	.136

Player, Team	Avg.	G	TPA	AB	R	H	TB	2B	3B	HR	RBI	SH	SF	HP	BB	IBB	SO	SB	CS	GDP	Slg.	OB
Ciciola, Miguel, Dodgers I......	.249	53	208	169	38	42	60	8	2	2	24	8	1	6	24	0	46	8	5	1	.355	.36
Clociola, David, N.Y. Yankees.	.154	7	17	13	2	2	2	0	0	0	0	1	0	0	3	0	2	1	1	0	.154	.31
Ciprian, Ernesto, Baltimore....	.190	35	115	105	12	20	29	3	0	2	10	1	1	0	8	0	35	4	6	2	.276	.24
Classen, Ender, Pittsburgh.....	.270	13	42	37	2	10	11	1	0	0	1	1	0	0	4	0	8	1	0	0	.297	.34
Cordero, Willi, Texas.............	.260	64	262	219	39	57	67	10	0	0	25	5	0	2	36	2	39	21	6	3	.306	.37
Corporan, Manuel, Baltimore.	.227	41	72	66	8	15	20	3	1	0	5	0	0	1	5	0	22	6	2	2	.303	.29
Cosme, Caonabo, Oakland.....	.243	65	262	226	35	55	74	8	4	1	31	2	6	2	26	0	34	5	4	5	.327	.31
Cruz, Rafael, Texas................	.226	21	38	31	5	7	8	1	0	0	2	0	0	3	4	0	8	0	0	2	.258	.36
Cruz, Silvio, Detroit...............	.230	26	100	74	15	17	22	2	0	1	11	3	5	3	15	0	11	7	1	4	.297	.36
Cubillan, Tubalcan, Phil.........	.249	61	267	237	35	59	100	11	3	8	37	0	1	9	20	1	55	7	4	4	.422	.33
Cueto, Jose, Texas................	.263	52	149	133	24	35	61	9	1	5	23	2	1	3	10	0	43	3	1	1	.459	.32
Cuvillan, Jose, Texas.............	.167	10	15	12	3	2	3	1	0	0	0	0	0	2	1	0	6	1	0	0	.250	.33
De Jesus, Ruben, Hou.-Bos...	.191	31	116	89	16	17	19	2	0	0	8	2	1	4	20	0	24	3	2	3	.213	.36
De Jesus, Wilmer, Montreal...	.143	32	94	84	4	12	13	1	0	0	5	2	1	1	6	0	12	0	0	2	.155	.20
De La Cruz, Antonio, N.Y. Mets.	.256	61	241	203	45	52	79	5	2	6	27	2	1	9	26	0	40	11	8	7	.389	.36
De La Cruz, Erickson, Mil./C.(AL)	.262	53	162	149	21	39	41	2	0	0	9	2	0	2	9	0	18	10	5	4	.275	.31
De La Cruz, Henry, Chi.(NL)/S.D.	.242	66	244	186	39	45	104	10	2	15	46	0	0	2	56	0	56	12	7	4	.559	.42
De La Cruz, Jose, Oakland.....	.279	51	211	183	35	51	79	7	0	7	33	3	3	2	20	0	28	3	1	4	.432	.35
De La Cruz, Micael, S.F.	.174	23	82	69	5	12	19	4	0	1	9	0	0	4	9	0	11	0	0	3	.275	.30
De La Cruz, Raul, Pittsburgh..	.387	67	265	243	49	94	125	16	0	5	40	1	3	1	17	1	37	35	9	1	.514	.42
De Leon, Jose, Detroit..........	.240	32	117	100	19	24	31	4	0	1	10	1	0	6	10	0	22	6	2	4	.310	.34
De Leon, Raymundo, St.L......	.348	73	321	282	51	98	144	17	7	5	46	0	3	4	32	1	31	8	7	10	.511	.41
De Leon, Sandy, San Fran......	.283	18	68	60	9	17	24	1	2	0	6	0	1	1	6	1	11	5	2	5	.400	.35
Delgado, Ramon, Seattle........	.280	57	223	164	32	46	78	4	2	8	31	0	2	1	56	1	41	8	5	1	.476	.46
Delgado, Raymundo, S.F.......	.295	27	120	95	14	28	50	7	0	5	25	0	1	1	23	2	6	1	1	3	.526	.43
De Los Santos, Eddy, Hou.-Bos.	.248	46	183	153	17	38	44	6	0	0	15	3	3	3	21	0	39	6	4	1	.288	.34
De Los Santos, F'cisco, N.Y. M.	.304	44	160	148	28	45	81	7	1	9	26	0	1	2	9	0	26	3	1	6	.547	.35
De Los Stos., Frances, S.F.	.209	20	53	43	4	9	9	0	0	0	0	3	0	2	5	0	13	1	0	2	.209	.32
Del Valle, Carlos, Detroit........	.307	65	280	212	57	65	116	13	4	10	55	0	4	1	63	8	19	2	1	5	.547	.46
Diaz, Bolivar, Texas..............	.270	36	80	74	12	20	27	2	1	1	6	0	0	0	6	0	18	3	2	2	.365	.32
Diaz, Eddy, Atlanta................	.143	9	7	7	1	1	2	1	0	0	0	0	0	0	0	0	3	0	0	0	.286	.14
Diaz, Emenegildo, San Fran. ..	.273	66	257	227	24	62	93	16	0	5	33	0	1	5	24	2	38	2	3	10	.410	.35
Diaz, Ivan, St. Louis..............	.275	58	243	204	32	56	74	4	1	4	35	1	2	3	33	1	22	3	4	7	.363	.38
Diaz, Juan, Dodgers II...........	.362	13	61	47	15	17	36	7	0	4	16	0	0	3	11	0	13	1	0	2	.766	.50
Diaz, Kelvin, San Francisco....	.255	50	178	149	21	38	52	11	0	1	22	1	3	4	21	0	25	5	0	7	.349	.35
Diaz, Meikell, Baltimore..........	.244	56	220	180	43	44	59	7	1	2	18	5	0	2	33	0	47	23	4	2	.328	.36
Diaz, Miguel, St. Louis...........	.289	62	249	235	38	68	98	16	4	2	34	1	4	4	5	1	25	5	3	11	.417	.31
Diaz, Welvis, Oakland............	.279	51	203	154	30	43	74	10	3	5	34	1	4	3	41	2	42	3	3	0	.481	.43
Dominguez, Candido, Detroit.	.217	17	33	23	4	5	6	1	0	0	1	0	0	0	10	0	3	0	0	1	.261	.45
Dominguez, Enrique, Montreal.	.282	63	242	209	25	59	66	4	0	1	15	6	0	2	25	0	23	14	10	4	.316	.36
Duncan, Carlos, Philadelphia.	.260	61	259	227	44	59	90	8	1	7	35	0	2	10	20	0	51	23	8	1	.396	.34
Durango, Ariel, Seattle..........	.205	50	179	161	26	33	47	4	2	2	11	2	0	4	12	0	49	6	5	1	.292	.27
Ellis, Franklin, Mil./Chi.(AL)....	.289	13	48	45	7	13	13	0	0	0	5	0	0	1	2	0	15	5	2	0	.289	.33
Encarnacion, BDO, California...	.264	45	109	91	15	24	30	3	0	1	11	4	0	2	12	0	10	7	5	9	.330	.36
Encarnacion, Bern, K.C./Colo.	.262	50	173	149	32	39	66	13	1	4	24	0	2	0	22	0	31	6	5	1	.443	.35
Encarnacion, Sonder, Seattle.	.274	33	137	113	28	31	51	2	0	6	26	0	0	3	21	2	10	5	1	4	.451	.40
Espino, Fernando, Seattle......	.327	47	194	165	23	54	77	10	2	3	20	1	3	2	23	0	17	4	3	4	.467	.40
Espinosa, Andres, Montreal...	.181	25	78	72	4	13	15	2	0	0	6	2	0	1	3	0	17	1	2	0	.208	.22
Estevez, Domingo, Toronto....	.247	55	186	158	27	39	52	9	2	0	18	4	1	2	21	1	16	6	3	2	.329	.34
Estrella, Gorky, Seattle..........	.315	35	122	89	15	28	52	6	0	6	19	0	1	2	30	2	22	3	3	3	.584	.49
Fajardo, Alex, Philadelphia.....	.373	63	277	249	48	93	127	16	6	2	38	1	2	0	25	1	21	22	4	5	.510	.42
Falcon, Edwin, Dodgers II......	.278	10	46	36	5	10	12	2	0	0	7	0	0	0	10	0	4	1	0	1	.333	.43
Felix, Henry, K.C./Colo.	.252	43	125	111	12	28	36	5	0	1	11	1	0	1	12	0	14	2	2	1	.324	.33
Feliz, Sergio, Co-op...............	.237	67	252	232	28	55	77	10	0	4	27	3	1	2	14	0	36	4	1	5	.332	.28
Fernandez, Juan, Co-op..........	.224	46	121	98	14	22	27	3	1	0	14	0	0	3	20	0	18	7	5	4	.276	.37
Fernandez, Medardo, Florida..	.263	65	240	205	27	54	61	5	1	0	14	3	0	3	29	0	34	13	10	5	.298	.36
Fernandez, Winston, Texas.....	.289	68	290	204	52	59	81	7	6	1	15	6	2	4	74	1	38	22	20	3	.397	.48
Ferreira, Luis, Co-op.............	.282	63	261	234	32	66	101	12	1	7	41	0	1	4	22	1	42	9	1	8	.432	.35
Figueroa, Erasmo, Mil./Chi.(AL).	.000	21	0	0	1	0	0	0	0	0	0	0	0	0	0	0	0	0	0	0	.000	.00
Filardi, Vladimir, K.C./C/.........	.286	6	24	21	4	6	7	1	0	0	2	0	0	1	2	0	6	2	2	0	.333	.37
Florentino, Junior, Pittsburgh.	.194	27	87	72	6	14	20	3	0	1	7	0	0	1	14	1	36	0	1	2	.278	.33
Flores, Carlos, Hou.-Bos.	.178	19	64	45	7	8	9	1	0	0	2	0	0	4	15	1	16	5	1	3	.200	.42
Francisco, Hector, Atlanta......	.240	29	91	75	18	18	28	5	1	1	9	2	0	3	11	0	14	0	2	1	.373	.36
Franco, Jorge, Montreal.........	.271	47	151	140	19	38	49	3	1	2	12	1	0	1	9	0	13	0	0	6	.350	.32
Franco, Pascual, St. Louis.....	.196	27	65	56	4	11	14	0	0	1	7	0	0	2	7	0	13	0	1	2	.250	.30
Galban, Elvis, Montreal..........	.309	68	294	233	48	72	86	10	2	0	23	1	3	8	49	2	25	22	13	4	.369	.44
Garabito, Eddy, Baltimore......	.275	67	273	251	40	69	93	9	6	1	28	0	2	0	20	1	23	25	10	1	.371	.32
Garcia, Alexander, Chi.(NL)/S.D.	.123	26	84	73	8	9	12	3	0	0	7	2	0	0	9	0	13	1	1	7	.164	.22
Garcia, Alfredo, N.Y. Mets......	.337	55	226	193	49	65	95	6	0	8	32	1	3	8	21	0	30	16	7	7	.492	.41
Garcia, Alvaro, Dodgers I.......	.359	43	148	128	26	46	54	5	0	1	20	4	2	6	8	1	14	4	5	6	.422	.41
Garcia, Andres, Philadelphia..	.283	16	52	46	6	13	16	3	0	0	4	0	0	1	5	0	4	0	0	2	.348	.36
Garcia, Antony, California.......	.200	37	127	105	12	21	25	4	0	0	13	1	1	0	20	0	29	5	3	2	.238	.32
Garcia, Eduardo, California.....	.218	39	128	87	16	19	24	1	2	0	5	0	0	3	38	0	22	7	7	4	.276	.46
Garcia, Juan, Atlanta.............	.306	61	273	209	49	64	104	7	6	7	44	1	3	7	53	0	28	8	3	10	.498	.45
Garcia, Luis, Dodgers I..........	.248	48	185	145	32	36	48	3	0	3	19	8	0	4	28	1	32	8	4	4	.331	.38
Garcia, Rafael, K.C./Colo.	.186	35	101	86	17	16	19	1	1	0	1	0	0	4	11	0	33	14	6	0	.221	.30
Genao, Antonio, Arizona.........	.235	52	178	149	25	35	47	6	0	2	19	0	2	1	26	1	22	1	5	3	.315	.34
Genao, Manuel, Toronto.........	.136	29	54	44	7	6	6	0	0	0	4	0	0	0	10	0	15	1	2	3	.136	.29
German, Aris, N.Y. Mets.........	.271	43	154	144	24	39	59	3	1	5	20	0	0	4	6	0	22	2	0	1	.410	.31
German, Manuel, Arizona.......	.217	49	159	120	24	26	38	3	0	3	9	3	0	4	32	2	39	7	8	3	.317	.39
Geronimo, Hugo, Hou.-Bos....	.191	45	168	152	18	29	41	9	0	1	24	0	3	1	12	0	25	3	3	3	.270	.25
Gil, Alberto, Cleveland...........	.247	59	218	166	44	41	66	10	3	3	34	1	4	2	45	3	31	12	4	5	.398	.40
Giron, Alex, Philadelphia........	.326	66	294	273	31	89	115	15	4	1	37	2	1	2	16	1	26	10	5	8	.421	.36

ayer, Team	Avg.	G	TPA	AB	R	H	TB	2B	3B	HR	RBI	SH	SF	HP	BB	IBB	SO	SB	CS	GDP	Slg.	OBP
on, Edilberto, Pittsburgh ...	.217	56	195	166	27	36	48	5	2	1	10	1	0	1	27	0	64	2	9	3	.289	.330
mera, Rafael, Dodgers II....	.279	48	173	154	37	43	67	8	2	4	24	2	0	5	12	0	31	11	5	2	.435	.351
mez, Nelson, California......	.164	27	74	61	8	10	11	1	0	0	5	1	1	3	8	0	16	1	1	1	.180	.288
nzalez, Adalberto, Mon. ...	.136	34	84	59	11	8	8	0	0	0	5	1	0	5	19	0	28	8	4	0	.136	.386
nzalez, Antonio, Phil.	.169	27	89	77	11	13	14	1	0	0	10	2	0	1	9	0	16	2	1	2	.182	.264
nzalez, Franklin, Chi.(NL)/S.D.	.208	61	231	207	25	43	51	5	0	1	10	0	0	2	22	0	33	14	6	3	.246	.290
nzalez, Milciades, Calif. ...	.216	34	121	111	10	24	29	2	0	1	7	0	0	0	10	1	21	12	5	5	.261	.281
nzalez, Nelson, San Fran..	.067	16	36	30	3	2	5	0	0	1	3	1	0	0	5	0	14	1	2	1	.167	.200
edez, Luis, Mil./Chi.(AL)	.259	41	138	112	16	29	38	2	2	1	12	3	2	1	20	0	18	5	3	1	.339	.370
errero, Francisco, Calif. ...	.246	16	61	57	5	14	17	1	1	0	8	0	0	2	2	1	13	6	0	1	.298	.295
errero, Pedro, Texas	.238	42	148	105	24	25	32	4	0	1	10	6	2	6	29	0	24	7	6	1	.305	.423
illen, Hipolito, Seattle........	.181	41	101	94	6	17	32	0	3	3	13	2	0	0	5	0	28	2	3	0	.340	.222
tierrez, V., Pittsburgh	.360	71	319	278	60	100	131	20	1	3	26	3	3	3	32	0	11	44	15	7	.471	.427
zman, Antonio, Arizona.....	.306	62	223	196	35	60	93	7	1	8	35	0	2	2	23	0	37	22	14	5	.474	.381
zman, Carlos, Detroit........	.318	62	233	195	40	62	76	6	1	2	34	1	2	3	32	1	23	19	14	3	.390	.418
zman, Elpidio, California.....	.233	42	135	116	11	27	33	6	0	0	13	0	0	0	19	1	17	11	6	0	.284	.341
zman, Juan, Baltimore......	.225	61	220	200	24	45	65	8	3	2	19	1	1	4	14	0	31	5	4	7	.325	.288
zman, Juan, St. Louis	.000	4	0	0	0	0	0	0	0	0	0	0	0	0	0	0	0	0	0	0	.000	.000
zman, Santos, Pittsburgh ..	.118	11	39	34	3	4	5	1	0	0	3	0	2	0	3	0	13	0	0	2	.147	.179
zman, Yorki, N.Y. Mets	.275	47	160	149	29	41	65	4	1	6	19	0	1	3	7	0	27	6	1	7	.436	.319
ad, Yamid, Pittsburgh	.322	56	219	205	29	66	90	9	0	5	28	1	2	1	10	0	38	8	7	9	.439	.353
ena, Hector, St. Louis	.268	21	52	41	7	11	18	2	1	1	6	1	0	0	10	1	13	1	0	2	.439	.412
hriquez, Roman, Dodgers I	.000	18	2	2	0	0	0	0	0	0	0	0	0	0	0	0	2	0	0	0	.000	.000
edia, Andres, K.C./Colo....	.180	26	66	61	3	11	12	1	0	0	3	0	0	1	4	0	28	0	2	1	.197	.242
nandez, Leonardo, N.Y. Mets	.325	40	139	123	22	40	49	7	1	0	15	1	1	1	13	0	20	3	2	4	.398	.391
nandez, Luis, Arizona	.270	38	134	111	23	30	43	7	0	2	24	0	1	0	22	2	17	7	2	2	.387	.388
nandez, Luis, California	.211	55	220	185	30	39	50	7	2	0	19	0	1	1	33	0	51	5	5	9	.270	.332
nandez, Luis, San Fran. ...	.241	48	167	145	20	35	49	1	0	1	10	3	0	2	17	0	37	6	5	2	.338	.329
nandez, Pedro, Texas.......	.219	58	193	160	26	35	58	12	1	3	20	3	3	0	27	1	41	4	5	5	.363	.326
rera, Gabriel, Seattle........	.294	44	144	119	19	35	62	5	2	6	22	0	1	6	18	0	15	0	1	6	.521	.410
rera, Juan, Montreal	.198	36	114	96	12	19	30	5	0	2	11	1	0	5	12	0	31	4	2	2	.313	.319
rera, Onesimo, N.Y. Mets..	.228	52	169	149	29	34	65	7	0	8	27	1	1	4	14	0	54	0	1	2	.436	.310
rera, Wilson, San Fran......	.241	44	155	137	19	33	48	2	2	3	16	1	1	2	14	0	33	3	3	4	.350	.318
aldo, Juan, Co-op............	.000	15	2	2	0	0	0	0	0	0	0	0	0	0	0	0	2	0	0	0	.000	.000
omasa, Ito, N.Y. Yankees..	.154	7	15	13	2	2	2	0	0	0	1	0	0	0	2	0	2	0	1	1	.154	.267
dge, Hector, Cleveland......	.276	38	137	127	19	35	40	5	0	0	13	2	0	0	8	0	13	2	1	1	.315	.319
ria, Shiron, California........	.252	65	270	242	26	61	76	12	0	1	34	3	6	1	18	0	34	7	4	9	.314	.300
nte, Danny, Texas	.282	58	194	177	19	50	71	6	0	5	24	1	2	3	11	1	36	5	4	3	.401	.332
agui, Carlos, Chi.(NL)/S.D..	.174	13	53	46	4	8	15	1	0	2	9	0	1	0	6	0	17	0	0	1	.326	.264
uez, Raul, Cleveland	.212	21	67	52	9	11	11	0	0	0	4	1	0	2	12	0	11	2	1	2	.212	.379
enez, Bartolo, Atlanta	.125	23	49	40	6	5	5	0	0	0	1	0	0	1	8	0	13	0	0	1	.125	.286
enez, Christian, Cleveland ..	.285	67	268	221	43	63	89	12	4	2	44	4	6	1	36	0	29	10	11	8	.403	.379
enez, Elieeser, Dodgers I ..	.344	48	167	128	31	44	54	8	1	0	19	3	2	5	29	0	15	5	2	4	.422	.476
enez, Raul, St. Louis	.000	1	6	5	1	0	0	0	0	0	0	1	0	0	1	0	1	0	0	0	.000	.167
rez, Angel, San Francisco ..	.167	17	52	42	0	7	8	1	0	0	3	0	1	1	8	0	11	0	1	0	.190	.308
rez, Johnny, Toronto.........	.321	54	205	184	31	59	76	9	4	0	30	1	0	3	17	0	27	12	4	3	.413	.387
g, Daniel, Oakland	.249	56	209	177	24	44	64	14	0	2	25	1	2	5	24	0	34	0	1	3	.362	.351
ra, Eudy, Florida..............	.500	15	2	2	0	1	1	0	0	0	0	0	0	0	0	0	1	0	0	0	.500	.500
e, Patricio, Florida	.245	67	258	229	22	56	87	13	0	6	45	0	3	2	24	0	89	0	0	6	.380	.318
tigua, Felix, N.Y. Yankees..	.250	5	10	8	1	2	2	0	0	0	0	0	0	1	1	0	1	0	0	0	.250	.400
a, Balmes, Detroit............	.218	33	100	78	12	17	26	3	0	2	12	1	1	3	17	1	21	4	1	3	.333	.374
a, Felix, Pittsburgh	.245	69	280	245	35	60	103	10	0	11	39	0	1	11	23	4	74	9	2	2	.420	.336
a, Juan, Chi.(NL)/S.D........	.140	22	65	50	9	7	11	1	0	1	4	0	0	4	11	0	29	1	0	0	.220	.338
us, Julian, N.Y. Yankees....	.275	45	127	102	27	28	33	5	0	0	6	2	0	9	14	1	25	18	10	2	.324	.408
a, Donald, K.C./Colo........	.212	44	127	113	10	24	26	2	0	0	8	1	1	2	10	0	25	1	4	7	.230	.286
ares, Ramon Tor, Co-op.....	.000	17	1	1	0	0	0	0	0	0	0	0	0	0	0	0	1	0	0	0	.000	.000
isiga, Stalin, Montreal	.257	42	172	144	20	37	58	12	0	3	22	1	1	3	23	4	18	2	0	2	.403	.368
ez, Gustavo, Florida..........	.000	15	1	1	0	0	0	0	0	0	0	0	0	0	0	0	0	0	0	0	.000	.000
ez, Jose, Arizona	.323	70	278	257	37	83	121	15	1	7	38	1	2	7	11	2	22	4	6	8	.471	.355
ez, Miguel, Arizona...........	.217	17	52	46	6	10	16	3	0	1	3	0	0	0	6	0	15	1	0	2	.348	.308
ez, Raul, Dodgers I	.212	22	64	52	6	11	14	3	0	0	3	2	0	0	10	1	6	0	0	2	.269	.339
ez, Victor, Detroit.............	.237	36	109	93	17	22	29	3	2	0	11	0	1	0	15	0	18	7	7	6	.312	.339
o, Oscar, Florida	.211	54	204	171	13	36	41	2	0	1	9	1	1	2	29	1	34	1	2	5	.240	.330
o, Juan, Seattle	.179	24	67	56	13	10	17	1	0	2	6	0	0	1	10	0	23	0	1	2	.304	.313
o, William, Oakland	.161	14	42	31	6	5	5	0	0	0	3	1	1	1	8	0	9	2	0	1	.161	.341
cano, Carlos, Florida.........	.118	48	156	136	18	16	23	2	1	1	5	4	0	3	13	0	55	1	2	2	.169	.211
in, Jaime, Florida.............	.213	29	81	75	8	16	21	3	1	0	5	0	0	2	4	0	26	5	3	3	.280	.272
te, Juan, St. Louis	.222	61	208	180	27	40	52	7	1	1	19	2	0	4	22	0	34	9	3	3	.289	.320
te, Lenin, K.C./Colo..........	.212	42	122	99	15	21	33	9	0	1	16	1	1	5	16	0	31	3	3	3	.333	.347
te, Nestor, Detroit............	.306	67	278	242	56	74	99	12	5	1	31	2	1	3	30	1	37	17	6	5	.409	.388
tinez, Alejandro, Oakland ...	.333	27	84	69	9	23	33	5	1	1	12	0	1	1	13	0	16	0	0	0	.478	.440
tinez, Andres, N.Y. Mets....	.298	68	288	258	44	77	121	11	0	11	44	2	2	3	23	1	59	6	4	2	.469	.360
tinez, Belvany, Arizona	.263	50	195	175	27	46	62	10	0	2	23	3	2	1	14	0	18	17	6	5	.354	.318
tinez, Daniel, Chi.(NL)/S.D..	.197	47	141	117	16	23	29	3	0	1	11	1	1	6	16	1	32	5	0	1	.248	.321
tinez, Gregorio, Co-op.......	.247	61	221	178	41	44	54	6	2	0	18	0	3	0	40	1	42	13	4	6	.303	.380
tinez, Luis, Dodgers II.......	.378	66	315	286	68	108	126	12	3	0	45	5	2	3	19	0	14	8	6	6	.441	.419
tinez, Luis, Toronto...........	.220	51	175	150	15	33	45	6	0	2	20	0	1	8	16	0	28	2	0	1	.300	.320
tinez, Obispo, Montreal......	.000	23	0	0	0	0	0	0	0	0	0	0	0	0	0	0	0	0	0	0	.000	.000
tinez, Odis, Detroit	.176	17	39	34	2	6	9	0	0	1	4	0	0	0	5	0	8	0	0	1	.265	.282
tinez, Osvaldo, Texas	.200	15	16	15	2	3	3	1	0	0	2	0	1	0	0	0	3	0	0	1	.267	.188
tinez, Reynaldo, C.(NL)/S.D..	.133	39	114	90	7	12	12	0	0	0	3	2	0	1	21	0	35	0	2	2	.133	.304
tinez, Rudolfo, Cleveland .	.250	6	11	8	1	2	2	0	0	0	1	0	0	0	3	0	0	0	0	0	.250	.455
tinez, Victor, Detroit	.240	35	118	96	19	23	32	6	0	1	20	1	1	2	18	0	23	2	1	3	.333	.368

Player, Team	Avg.	G	TPA	AB	R	H	TB	2B	3B	HR	RBI	SH	SF	HP	BB	IBB	SO	SB	CS	GDP	Slg.	Ol
Martinez, Winston, Detroit	.111	4	12	9	0	1	1	0	0	0	0	0	0	0	3	0	5	0	1	0	.111	.3
Mateo, Freddy, Dodgers II......	.215	40	161	130	27	28	40	7	1	1	12	0	1	4	26	0	37	8	4	4	.308	.3
Matias, Hansell, Atlanta.........	.000	1	1	1	0	0	0	0	0	0	0	0	0	0	0	0	1	0	0	0	.000	.0
Maysonet, Jose, Toronto.........	.297	41	163	138	26	41	50	5	2	0	24	0	1	1	23	0	22	9	2	5	.362	.3
McDonald, Gabriel, San Fran.	.209	50	183	134	36	28	40	6	0	2	14	1	0	7	41	1	43	9	4	4	.299	.4
McLean, Guillermo, Co-op......	.252	37	117	103	15	26	39	7	0	2	11	0	0	5	9	0	22	1	3	7	.379	.3
Medina, Luis, Atlanta.............	.288	63	253	226	33	65	92	12	3	3	29	4	5	1	17	2	31	7	3	7	.407	.3
Medina, Luis, Chi.(NL)/S.D. ..	.269	68	260	242	33	65	88	7	2	4	32	3	2	2	11	0	19	0	0	8	.364	.3
Medina, Richie, Detroit.........	.273	6	13	11	1	3	3	0	0	0	0	0	0	1	1	0	4	0	0	1	.273	.3
Medrano, David, Texas..........	.273	51	174	150	24	41	65	8	2	4	18	0	3	3	18	1	53	4	2	5	.433	.3
Medrano, Oscar, California......	.193	65	227	176	24	34	47	6	2	1	16	3	2	7	39	0	39	13	8	5	.267	.3
Mejia, Javier, Florida	.243	57	224	202	16	49	58	6	0	1	16	4	0	1	17	1	48	3	1	3	.287	.3
Mejia, Jose, Atlanta................	.241	34	95	87	10	21	34	6	2	1	14	0	1	1	6	0	17	2	1	5	.391	.2
Mejia, Maximiliano, Dodgers I.	.297	40	161	118	29	35	53	9	0	3	25	4	2	3	34	0	13	7	3	1	.449	.4
Mejia, Oliver, Pittsburgh........	.231	69	263	229	31	53	65	7	1	1	22	3	1	3	27	0	34	14	11	5	.284	.3
Mejia, Renato, Florida	.327	69	291	254	38	83	109	9	1	5	36	0	0	6	31	1	55	9	4	4	.429	.4
Melendez, Angel, San Fran. ...	.250	34	148	132	16	33	50	9	0	3	20	2	1	2	11	0	28	4	3	4	.379	.3
Melendez, Carlos, K.C./Colo....	.171	31	88	70	9	12	16	1	0	1	7	0	3	1	14	0	21	2	3	1	.229	.3
Melendez, Emmy, California ...	.178	18	61	45	3	8	8	0	0	0	1	3	0	8	5	0	6	0	2	1	.178	.3
Mendez, Donaldo, Hou.-Bos..	.262	38	147	122	20	32	37	3	1	0	19	3	2	3	17	0	17	3	3	2	.303	.3
Mercedes, Carlos, Dodgers I...	.237	37	146	118	13	28	32	4	0	0	11	5	1	3	19	0	19	2	2	2	.271	.3
Mercedes, Luis, San Fran......	.223	58	186	148	23	33	35	2	0	0	11	1	1	1	35	0	42	5	4	2	.236	.3
Mercedes, Martin, Phil...........	.000	16	1	1	0	0	0	0	0	0	0	0	0	0	0	0	1	0	0	0	.000	.0
Meza, Gonzalo, Dodgers II......	.333	32	137	111	23	37	48	5	3	0	19	3	1	1	21	0	7	3	3	5	.432	.4
Mijares, Robert, Dodgers I.....	.221	40	146	122	24	27	39	4	1	2	14	2	1	5	16	1	26	7	3	4	.320	.3
Molina, Alfredo, Dodgers II ...	.200	7	5	5	2	1	1	0	0	0	1	0	0	0	0	0	2	0	0	1	.200	.2
Molina, Kenneth, Detroit.......	.248	51	169	141	21	35	54	5	4	2	28	4	0	1	23	1	15	4	3	1	.383	.3
Montas, Juan, California	.275	19	57	51	3	14	15	1	0	0	7	0	0	2	4	0	20	2	2	1	.294	.3
Montero, Jose, Texas	.209	21	79	67	9	14	18	1	0	1	9	1	0	1	10	0	9	0	1	3	.269	.3
Montero, Oscar, Mil./Chi.(AL) ..	.000	9	4	4	0	0	0	0	0	0	0	0	0	0	0	0	0	0	0	0	.000	.0
Morales, Anaximandro, Atl.....	.198	57	247	197	32	39	73	9	2	7	32	0	0	6	44	2	48	3	4	6	.371	.3
Morales, Cesar, San Fran.	.210	37	110	100	9	21	25	4	0	0	11	3	1	2	4	0	8	1	1	4	.250	.2
Morales, Victor, Toronto........	.226	31	104	84	18	19	22	3	0	0	5	1	0	0	19	0	8	4	0	3	.234	.3
Morel, Ramon, Cleveland.......	.000	14	0	0	0	0	0	0	0	0	0	0	0	0	0	0	0	0	0	0	.000	.0
Morelo, Fulvio, N.Y. Yankees..	.295	58	209	193	33	57	83	9	1	5	38	0	3	2	11	1	13	4	3	5	.430	.3
Moreno, Franklin, Mil./Chi.(AL)..	.194	26	85	67	11	13	16	1	1	0	5	1	0	1	16	0	15	4	3	4	.239	.3
Moreno, Johnny, Baltimore......	.214	49	169	154	18	33	49	7	0	3	20	5	1	0	9	0	49	4	4	3	.318	.2
Moreno, Nestor, N.Y. Mets	.192	38	90	78	13	15	19	1	0	1	8	1	0	2	9	0	23	0	1	1	.244	.2
Moreta, Ramon, Dodgers II	.330	67	327	270	69	89	109	13	2	1	29	3	2	6	46	0	33	17	6	8	.404	.4
Morillo, Luis, Toronto.............	.252	62	261	202	50	51	76	10	6	1	26	3	5	3	48	1	48	21	9	1	.376	.3
Moscat, Rafael, Arizona	.275	36	111	80	15	22	31	6	0	1	12	0	1	3	27	0	15	10	7	3	.388	.4
Mota, Delcio, California	.183	35	104	82	16	15	17	2	0	0	7	0	1	0	21	0	29	4	1	1	.207	.3
Mota, Juan, California	.149	21	87	67	9	10	13	1	0	1	10	1	1	2	16	0	36	6	3	0	.194	.3
Mota, Pedro, San Francisco	.257	28	84	74	16	19	27	1	2	1	12	0	1	0	9	0	8	6	3	1	.365	.3
Mota, Victor, Detroit..............	.105	18	27	19	5	2	2	0	0	0	2	0	0	1	7	0	5	0	0	1	.105	.3
Mundo, Alberto, Atlanta	.285	68	286	246	38	70	86	6	5	0	26	11	4	4	21	0	21	9	4	4	.350	.3
Nieves, Juan, Toronto	.294	68	278	238	45	70	84	9	1	1	34	0	0	5	35	0	27	24	7	9	.353	.3
Nin, Geldy, St. Louis	.263	47	169	152	21	40	50	7	0	1	21	0	3	3	11	1	33	3	4	4	.329	.3
Nina, Amaury, Texas	.275	71	285	247	44	68	101	12	3	5	31	2	1	6	29	0	50	18	12	3	.409	.3
Nina, Ignacio, Co-op	.299	64	212	194	32	58	74	13	0	1	38	1	2	2	13	0	32	7	3	8	.381	.3
Nolasco, Ragino, Baltimore.....	.265	69	264	226	43	60	80	10	2	2	13	3	0	4	31	0	26	32	3	0	.354	.3
Nova, Geraldo, Hou.-Bos.	.238	26	115	80	16	19	20	1	0	0	9	1	0	2	32	1	19	7	7	4	.250	.4
Nova, Joselyn, Florida	.205	64	235	220	18	45	66	12	0	3	17	2	1	6	6	0	31	1	2	4	.300	.2
Nunez, Hector, Detroit..........	.217	31	97	83	13	18	20	2	0	0	10	2	1	1	10	0	11	2	3	6	.241	.3
Nunez, Jorge, Toronto...........	.295	69	285	258	51	76	111	10	2	7	40	2	3	3	19	0	36	19	3	6	.430	.3
Nunez, Jose, K.C./Colo..........	.228	62	226	184	34	42	82	13	0	9	40	0	2	2	38	0	48	3	1	4	.446	.3
Nunez, Jose, K.C./Colo...........	.256	45	159	133	21	34	46	10	1	0	11	1	2	1	22	0	18	7	4	3	.346	.3
Nunez, Jose, Oakland	.282	41	143	110	19	31	56	6	2	5	28	0	2	4	27	1	40	1	1	2	.509	.4
Ochoa, Javier, Hou.-Bos........	.208	23	82	77	7	16	19	3	0	0	6	0	0	0	5	0	9	0	5	4	.247	.2
Offerman, Juan, N.Y. Yankees..	.287	58	207	167	46	48	66	7	1	3	16	0	2	1	37	0	42	35	12	1	.395	.4
Olivares, Melvin, N.Y. Mets.....	.360	67	283	272	48	98	141	16	0	9	49	1	0	1	9	1	17	13	7	7	.518	.3
Olivares, Teuris, N.Y. Yankees...	.353	4	20	17	7	6	9	3	0	0	1	0	0	0	3	0	0	1	1	0	.529	.4
Olivero, Jesus, Philadelphia ...	.244	41	142	131	15	32	48	11	1	1	22	0	1	5	5	1	25	0	4	4	.366	.2
Ortega, Carlos, Dodgers I	.167	29	89	78	11	13	18	2	0	1	7	0	0	2	9	3	5	3	1	2	.231	.2
Ortega, Jose, N.Y. Yankees	.257	24	73	70	11	18	22	1	0	1	6	0	0	2	1	0	14	1	0	1	.314	.2
Ortiz, Jose, Arizona	.347	33	108	98	12	34	38	4	0	0	17	1	1	1	7	0	8	3	1	1	.388	.3
Ovalles, Alvin, K.C./Colo.........	.281	37	111	96	15	27	36	4	1	1	7	0	0	3	12	1	13	5	2	3	.375	.3
Ovalles, Jesus, Co-op	.288	63	216	184	33	53	62	9	0	0	21	1	1	5	25	0	10	11	5	6	.337	.3
Ozuna, Alexis, Mil./Chi.(AL) ...	.198	35	98	86	4	17	23	4	1	0	7	1	0	2	9	0	21	0	1	3	.267	.2
Ozuna, Pablo, St. Louis	.363	74	331	295	57	107	145	12	4	6	60	3	4	6	23	7	19	18	5	7	.492	.4
Pacheco, Domingo, Seattle......	.245	29	115	102	15	25	41	4	0	4	13	0	1	1	11	0	28	2	0	1	.402	.3
Pamphile, Luis, Dodgers I.......	.390	26	88	77	13	30	33	3	0	0	14	0	1	3	7	0	14	2	1	2	.429	.4
Paulino, Dennis, Atlanta........	.277	37	94	83	17	23	31	4	2	0	14	3	2	1	5	0	17	4	0	0	.373	.3
Paulino, Warren, N.Y. Yankees..	.253	62	211	190	32	48	81	9	6	4	29	4	0	3	14	0	19	14	6	8	.426	.3
Payamps, Jose, Arizona	.239	51	161	134	19	32	48	8	1	2	18	1	1	1	24	0	8	6	6	2	.358	.3
Peguero, Radhames, Calif.......	.212	56	176	151	22	32	39	5	1	0	7	3	0	3	19	1	34	13	8	6	.258	.3
Pellerano, Cristian, Oakland ..	.167	11	35	30	6	5	6	1	0	0	3	0	0	0	4	0	12	0	0	0	.200	.2
Pena, Amaury, N.Y. Yankees ..	.197	42	143	122	18	24	27	3	0	0	4	1	0	3	17	0	21	6	3	5	.221	.3
Pena, Angel, Dodgers II	.474	23	103	78	30	37	72	9	1	8	40	0	0	1	24	1	12	1	0	2	.923	.6
Pena, Elvin, Seattle	.307	29	99	88	15	27	54	7	1	6	20	0	0	0	10	0	17	0	0	3	.614	.3
Pena, Jose, California	.112	40	134	107	11	12	16	4	0	0	4	0	0	7	20	0	48	4	4	3	.150	.2
Pena, Reynaldo, Detroit	.317	65	282	240	63	76	112	13	10	1	33	1	3	8	30	0	16	18	9	5	.467	.4
Pena, Rodolfo, Hou.-Bos.	.159	36	97	82	13	13	15	2	0	0	8	2	1	1	10	0	12	1	0	4	.183	.2

ayer, Team	Avg.	G	TPA	AB	R	H	TB	2B	3B	HR	RBI	SH	SF	HP	BB	IBB	SO	SB	CS	GDP	Slg.	OBP
na, Sandy, Arizona	.198	46	139	121	18	24	31	5	1	0	8	2	1	2	13	0	33	5	0	0	.256	.285
na, Victor, Philadelphia......	.281	54	219	196	40	55	68	9	2	0	15	2	0	4	17	0	37	5	2	5	.347	.350
ralta, Ariel, Oakland	.357	7	22	14	5	5	8	0	0	1	6	0	0	3	5	0	2	0	0	1	.571	.591
redes, Miguel, Seattle	.200	31	98	85	12	17	33	4	0	4	13	0	0	1	12	0	27	2	4	1	.388	.306
rez, Alejandro, Hou.-Bos. ...	.304	20	84	79	9	24	38	4	2	2	12	1	0	2	2	1	13	2	2	1	.481	.337
rez, Angel, Dodgers II	.256	61	264	238	34	61	94	14	2	5	42	0	6	4	16	0	32	4	2	5	.395	.307
rez, David, Atlanta	.272	32	99	92	9	25	29	1	0	1	6	2	0	0	5	0	11	0	0	6	.315	.309
rez, Edison, Seattle	.360	52	220	189	45	68	97	14	0	5	22	2	0	3	26	2	30	27	16	1	.513	.445
rez, Jose, Arizona..............	.211	38	113	95	13	20	28	5	0	1	9	2	0	1	15	0	28	4	2	2	.295	.324
chardo, Henry, Cleveland	.310	61	285	245	61	76	93	11	3	0	33	2	3	4	31	3	17	19	3	16	.380	.392
neiro, Juan, Chi.(NL)/S.D..	.268	67	258	224	33	60	90	9	6	3	32	1	2	7	24	0	30	13	4	3	.402	.354
nentel, Franklin, Oakland..	.291	39	99	79	19	23	37	8	3	0	7	0	3	17	0	17	2	2	0	.468	.434
nentel, Raul, St. Louis	.244	43	142	123	15	30	33	3	0	0	14	2	0	2	15	1	28	3	1	5	.268	.336
lanco, Rodney, Seattle	.276	36	108	87	19	24	30	3	0	1	11	2	1	0	18	0	12	3	2	2	.345	.396
lanco, Winston, Cleveland...	.189	36	105	90	15	17	25	4	2	0	15	0	0	3	12	0	24	5	3	2	.278	.305
ngle, Juan, N.Y. Yankees.....	.192	33	91	78	10	15	20	0	1	1	5	0	0	4	9	1	11	0	1	3	.256	.308
jols, Rafael, Oakland	.256	50	199	172	18	44	62	2	2	4	30	1	5	2	19	1	11	1	0	2	.360	.328
ero, Pedro, Montreal.........	.322	69	294	273	34	88	121	12	0	7	48	0	4	0	17	0	24	7	3	8	.443	.357
mirez, B'venido, C.(NL)/S.D..	.143	22	72	63	8	9	11	2	0	0	3	2	0	2	5	0	32	0	0	0	.175	.229
mirez, Charles, K.C./Colo...	.281	23	74	64	9	18	27	3	0	2	8	1	0	1	8	0	3	3	1	1	.422	.370
mirez, Frankelis, Dodgers I..	.327	52	198	156	29	51	62	8	0	1	18	7	3	2	30	1	27	1	2	6	.397	.435
mirez, Junior, California	.233	47	148	120	17	28	33	3	1	0	5	1	0	7	20	0	32	5	3	5	.275	.374
mirez, Narciso, Montreal.....	.196	63	226	189	30	37	48	3	1	2	15	1	1	2	33	1	54	17	9	2	.254	.320
mirez, Rafael, Detroit	.287	45	140	115	26	33	54	3	3	4	26	0	1	5	19	0	32	4	3	2	.470	.407
nos, Eddy, Co-op	.261	62	264	199	46	52	74	8	4	2	17	1	0	11	53	0	54	23	14	5	.372	.441
nos, Kelly, N.Y. Mets.........	.289	14	50	45	10	13	22	3	0	2	14	0	1	1	3	0	2	3	0	3	.489	.340
polledo, Jairo, Detroit	.255	51	182	161	14	41	47	2	2	0	13	3	1	2	15	2	25	3	4	6	.292	.324
ngifo, D.J. Mil./Chi.(AL)	.273	57	236	183	35	50	67	10	2	1	14	3	0	17	33	0	40	19	9	3	.366	.429
ves, Ambiorix, Philadelphia..	.267	40	149	135	20	36	41	5	0	0	15	1	0	5	8	1	9	8	3	2	.304	.331
ves, Arquimedes, Phil.........	.000	22	1	1	0	0	0	0	0	0	0	0	0	0	0	0	0	0	0	0	.000	.000
es, Bernardo, St. Louis	.000	16	2	1	1	0	0	0	0	0	0	1	0	0	1	0	1	0	0	0	.000	.500
es, Cristian, Oakland	.191	17	55	47	9	9	12	0	0	1	5	1	1	0	6	0	6	1	2	0	.255	.278
ves, Dauris, Detroit	.271	41	145	107	34	29	52	4	5	3	21	1	1	1	35	1	33	11	1	0	.486	.451
es, Edermiro, San Fran. ...	.091	9	25	22	1	2	2	0	0	0	2	0	0	1	2	0	10	1	0	1	.091	.200
noso, Franklin, Atlanta	.160	8	26	25	0	4	5	1	0	0	1	0	0	0	1	0	7	0	0	2	.200	.192
noso, Gil Aristides, Ariz...	.296	41	102	81	17	24	31	4	0	1	8	2	0	4	15	0	21	5	6	1	.383	.430
chardson, Elvis, Co-op........	.220	54	142	125	23	28	34	6	0	0	12	1	0	10	6	1	31	10	7	0	.272	.312
s, Carlos, Hou.-Bos...........	.224	62	246	201	34	45	54	7	1	0	15	0	2	0	43	1	35	10	5	5	.269	.358
era, Juan, N.Y. Yankees......	.167	10	19	18	0	3	3	0	0	0	2	0	1	0	0	0	1	0	0	2	.167	.158
era, Orlando, Mil./Chi.(AL)..	.117	24	74	60	9	7	10	3	0	0	6	1	1	1	11	0	17	4	1	6	.167	.260
era, Yorkis, Co-op.............	.315	66	276	232	47	73	109	17	2	5	42	1	3	1	39	0	34	10	4	5	.470	.411
nert, Randolph, N.Y. Mets...	.270	44	142	122	28	33	52	4	0	5	15	1	2	4	13	0	17	1	1	3	.426	.353
les, Victor, Baltimore	.106	18	57	47	7	5	7	0	1	0	3	2	2	1	5	0	15	2	1	0	.149	.200
riguez, Alfredo, Dodgers II..	.286	38	166	147	30	42	60	7	1	3	32	0	3	5	11	0	42	5	2	5	.408	.349
driguez, Euris, Cleveland	.160	39	122	106	7	17	20	3	0	0	12	3	3	2	8	0	22	2	2	4	.189	.227
driguez, Felipe, Toronto	.300	59	263	223	62	67	87	6	7	0	29	1	1	3	35	0	39	46	11	3	.390	.401
driguez, Franklin, Seattle ...	.172	25	30	29	4	5	8	0	0	1	3	0	0	1	0	0	5	1	0	1	.276	.200
driguez, Frei, Baltimore......	.150	8	23	20	3	3	4	1	0	0	1	0	0	2	1	0	3	0	0	1	.200	.261
driguez, Juan, Atlanta	.250	36	91	80	14	20	22	0	1	0	7	3	0	1	7	1	14	4	1	2	.275	.318
driguez, Miguel, St. Louis..	.342	70	299	243	50	83	99	7	3	1	28	0	1	8	47	3	39	48	17	7	.407	.462
driguez, Rafael, Cleveland..	.280	57	217	193	40	54	81	14	2	3	21	0	1	6	17	0	31	7	2	2	.420	.355
driguez, Ramon, N.Y. Yank..	.287	55	206	164	31	47	81	13	0	7	36	0	5	7	30	0	48	1	1	2	.494	.408
driquez, Jose, Florida	.200	36	114	95	12	19	29	5	1	1	11	1	0	0	18	2	24	3	2	3	.305	.327
driquez, Pablo, Cleveland ..	.261	60	225	199	32	52	71	11	4	0	29	1	2	2	21	0	37	2	6	6	.357	.335
as, Alex, Philadelphia........	.241	51	232	187	33	45	60	7	4	0	18	3	1	3	38	1	25	30	11	7	.321	.376
as, Elieeser, Mil./Chi.(AL)..	.255	50	180	161	21	41	47	6	0	0	21	1	4	3	11	2	29	10	6	6	.292	.307
as, Franklin, Baltimore	.143	3	7	7	0	1	1	0	0	0	1	0	0	0	0	0	4	0	0	0	.571	.143
as, Isaias, Baltimore	.247	50	185	154	24	38	50	4	1	2	22	2	4	5	20	0	37	14	8	1	.325	.344
don, Johnny, Seattle	.137	43	150	117	15	16	22	3	0	1	7	0	1	1	31	0	29	7	6	1	.188	.320
a, Ivan, Oakland	.214	67	56	11	12	17	1	2	0	3	1	0	0	10	1	21	0	1	1	.304	.333
ario, Carlos, K.C./Colo......	.192	8	30	26	5	5	7	0	1	0	4	2	0	1	1	0	2	1	1	1	.269	.250
ario, Omar, Oakland	.235	52	252	187	48	44	70	6	4	4	41	3	3	3	56	0	37	9	3	0	.374	.414
z, Willi, K.C./Colo.............	.355	34	115	110	26	39	48	3	3	0	8	0	0	0	5	0	10	14	7	0	.436	.383
din, Miguel, Hou.-Bos......	.244	39	145	135	13	33	36	3	0	0	19	2	1	1	6	0	18	9	3	2	.267	.280
zar, Oscar, Oakland..........	.256	69	273	219	49	56	82	9	4	3	29	2	3	2	47	0	37	9	4	2	.374	.387
zar, Thomas, Cleveland.....	.000	21	1	1	0	0	0	0	0	0	0	0	0	0	1	0	0	0	0	0	.000	.000
chez, Euro, Seattle	.222	30	97	81	10	18	35	2	0	5	12	1	0	3	12	0	21	0	1	0	.432	.344
chez, Jose, Detroit	.000	20	0	0	0	0	0	0	0	0	0	0	0	0	0	0	0	0	0	0	.000	.000
chez, Manuel, Atlanta	.342	58	261	228	47	78	117	9	9	4	48	1	1	10	21	0	25	22	7	3	.513	.419
chez, Wellington, Mil./C.(AL)	.333	44	161	141	17	47	58	8	0	1	19	3	2	1	14	0	21	10	6	0	.411	.392
ots, Jose, N.Y. Yankees......	.228	52	187	171	23	39	69	16	1	4	26	1	1	4	10	0	42	0	1	6	.404	.285
quintin, Juan, Co-op	.277	64	248	213	32	59	73	11	0	1	27	1	2	6	26	0	28	4	4	7	.343	.368
tana, Boris, Florida	.000	10	0	1	0	0	0	0	0	0	0	0	0	0	0	0	0	0	0	0	.000	.000
tana, Pedro, N.Y. Yankees..	.265	52	216	189	31	50	65	8	2	1	31	0	3	5	19	1	33	5	1	10	.344	.343
tana, Ramon, K.C./Colo......	.293	53	193	157	39	46	61	4	4	1	21	0	0	4	32	1	19	34	9	3	.389	.425
ana, Richard, K.C./Colo.....	.320	38	115	100	17	32	49	2	3	3	26	0	1	3	11	0	10	4	3	3	.490	.400
tos, Jose, California	.222	38	118	108	10	24	29	3	1	0	10	0	1	1	7	1	22	4	2	3	.269	.274
ura, Roland, Pittsburgh......	.255	60	226	200	22	51	78	7	1	6	31	0	1	3	22	1	50	2	4	8	.390	.336
ura, Winston, Texas	.273	7	23	22	1	6	9	1	1	0	3	0	0	0	1	0	1	0	1	0	.409	.304
io, Maximiliano, Pit.	.250	60	196	180	19	45	61	6	2	2	16	1	0	2	13	0	52	7	6	4	.339	.308
erino, Danny, Florida	.258	70	306	279	32	72	102	11	2	5	37	4	2	6	15	0	64	9	9	3	.366	.308
erino, Gilberto, Arizona	.255	24	55	51	7	13	15	2	0	0	4	0	0	2	2	1	10	2	1	0	.294	.309
llano, Jose, Pittsburgh	.273	22	81	66	16	18	30	3	0	3	16	1	0	1	13	0	8	2	0	2	.455	.400

Player, Team	Avg.	G	TPA	AB	R	H	TB	2B	3B	HR	RBI	SH	SF	HP	BB	IBB	SO	SB	CS	GDP	Slg.
Shinozuka, Takehiro, Mon......	.176	36	122	102	6	18	20	2	0	0	8	3	0	3	14	0	17	2	5	3	.196
Silva, Ramon, Toronto	.254	40	136	114	11	29	37	5	0	1	23	0	3	2	17	0	25	2	1	6	.325
Silva, Wilme, San Francisco....	.256	26	94	90	10	23	26	3	0	0	2	0	0	0	4	0	13	5	1	5	.289
Silvestre, Juan, Seattle..........	.311	64	273	238	51	74	142	9	1	19	61	0	5	2	28	5	34	1	1	5	.597
Soriano, Julio, Atlanta...........	.260	25	88	77	15	20	38	2	2	4	9	2	1	0	8	0	16	2	1	4	.494
Sosa, Henry, Philadelphia.....	.000	20	1	1	0	0	0	0	0	0	0	0	0	0	0	0	0	0	0	0	.000
Sosa, Jorge, K.C./Colo.	.241	51	194	162	29	39	65	13	2	3	25	0	2	5	25	1	54	2	8	3	.401
Sosa, Jose, Chi.(NL)/S.D.	.240	39	149	129	14	31	37	1	1	1	16	1	0	1	18	0	32	4	4	2	.287
Sosa, Leonel, Dodgers II........	.353	15	55	51	7	18	26	5	0	1	12	0	1	0	3	0	6	0	0	4	.510
Soto, Antonio, Chi.(NL)/S.D...	.245	59	197	159	22	39	54	9	3	0	8	5	1	2	30	0	39	9	5	10	.340
Sotomayor, Gilberto, Dodgers I..	.246	42	151	126	26	31	38	4	0	1	13	7	0	3	15	0	17	0	3	4	.302
Suarez, Orlando, Cleveland....	.289	52	210	180	35	52	76	14	2	2	20	2	3	2	23	2	23	3	3	2	.422
Tavarez, Carlos, Seattle.......	.097	20	36	31	3	3	3	0	0	0	0	0	0	1	4	0	8	0	3	0	.097
Taveras, Luis, Texas	.308	70	284	247	42	76	113	14	4	5	44	1	8	2	26	1	24	17	7	6	.457
Tobias, Enrique, Dodgers II	.272	35	116	103	7	28	42	8	0	2	13	1	0	2	10	1	15	0	1	4	.408
Torres, Rafael, K.C./Colo.......	.265	64	242	219	32	58	80	9	2	3	33	1	5	5	12	2	24	6	4	5	.365
Torrez, Rommel, Pittsburgh ...	.281	48	179	167	24	47	70	8	0	5	24	2	1	2	7	0	32	1	1	2	.419
Tovar, Amador, Dodgers I	.279	60	245	204	33	57	82	14	4	1	34	4	1	2	34	1	32	11	5	4	.402
Tucent, Andres, Mil./Chi.(AL)..	.254	27	81	71	13	18	21	3	0	0	6	0	2	1	7	0	10	3	1	0	.296
Ugueto, Luis, Florida.............	.254	70	285	240	37	61	69	4	2	0	12	3	0	1	41	0	33	14	13	8	.288
Urquiola, Edgar, Montreal	.242	37	124	91	21	22	27	5	0	0	8	2	0	2	29	0	25	10	5	1	.297
Valderrama, Carlos, San Fran...	.223	46	197	166	29	37	43	4	1	0	11	1	0	1	29	0	24	26	10	4	.259
Valdez, Angel, N.Y. Yankees ...	.377	46	152	138	23	52	70	7	1	3	26	0	1	1	12	0	28	8	4	2	.507
Valdez, Issac, Dodgers I.......	.272	61	233	202	34	55	74	14	1	1	42	4	5	4	18	1	21	3	1	4	.366
Valdez, Jean Carlos, Oakland ...	.328	46	197	177	34	58	83	9	2	4	20	2	1	1	16	3	22	7	6	3	.469
Valdez, Jose, Co-op	.189	9	38	37	4	7	11	2	1	0	4	0	0	0	1	1	7	2	0	0	.297
Valdez, Jose, Dodgers II	.247	29	114	89	19	22	27	0	1	1	7	1	1	2	21	0	19	6	2	1	.303
Valdez, Jose, Philadelphia	.202	37	100	89	17	18	21	3	0	0	16	0	0	3	8	0	11	3	1	1	.236
Valera, Gregori, Arizona	.200	58	189	160	21	32	35	3	0	0	9	4	0	3	22	0	11	7	7	6	.219
Valle, Cosme, Dodgers II	.338	20	82	77	10	26	30	4	0	0	15	0	3	0	2	0	8	1	0	1	.390
Vals, Lucrecio, Baltimore	.300	62	217	190	27	57	66	4	1	1	26	5	1	0	21	1	28	16	12	3	.347
Varela, Gabriel, Dodgers II	.306	64	290	242	49	74	106	8	9	2	54	0	6	5	37	0	31	14	4	9	.438
Vargas, Inakel, Detroit.........	.276	60	224	181	36	50	67	9	1	2	33	1	2	2	38	1	51	3	4	4	.370
Vargas, Junior, K.C./Colo.......	.182	41	113	99	9	18	24	4	1	0	13	0	1	1	12	0	14	7	1	4	.242
Vargas, Martin, Co-op...........	.223	39	116	103	7	23	31	6	1	0	12	1	0	0	12	0	25	1	0	7	.301
Vasquez, Alejandro, Hou.-Bos...	.230	64	270	230	32	53	66	8	1	1	23	0	0	3	37	1	34	7	4	7	.287
Vasquez, Arnulfo, Cleveland	.344	63	256	224	45	77	109	21	1	3	50	0	5	5	22	0	42	12	3	7	.487
Vasquez, Jose, Cleveland	.263	10	22	19	1	5	8	1	1	0	1	0	0	1	2	0	2	0	0	1	.421
Vasquez, Luis, Pittsburgh	.154	26	75	65	7	10	13	3	0	0	4	1	0	0	9	0	20	3	1	5	.200
Vasquez, Porfirio, San Fran...	.226	18	66	55	12	12	18	4	1	0	5	0	1	3	7	0	11	1	1	0	.340
Vega, Jonathan, Hou.-Bos.....	.209	45	166	153	13	32	39	4	0	1	12	4	0	0	9	0	36	1	2	5	.255
Veitia, Rodolfo, Montreal	.238	37	126	101	13	24	32	3	1	1	8	1	1	2	21	1	16	0	2	1	.317
Ventura, Frank, Cleveland......	.382	57	261	225	55	86	126	24	2	4	42	1	4	4	27	1	20	26	3	3	.560
Ventura, Jesus, California	.250	2	8	4	3	1	1	0	0	0	1	1	0	0	3	0	1	3	0	0	.333
Ventura, Juan, Cleveland.......	.287	58	260	216	48	62	74	4	4	0	19	1	2	2	39	0	14	15	5	4	.343
Veras, Jose, K.C./Colo...........	.288	30	65	52	12	15	19	1	0	1	7	0	0	1	12	0	16	4	2	0	.365
Veras, Roberta, Atlanta	.304	67	280	250	52	76	106	7	1	7	50	1	3	2	24	0	38	33	5	4	.424
Vialet, Junior, N.Y. Yankees.....	.248	39	108	101	22	25	27	2	0	0	7	0	0	2	5	0	12	12	1	4	.267
Vicente, Audo, Arizona	.241	44	155	116	25	28	37	6	0	1	12	1	2	6	30	0	21	15	10	2	.319
Villalona, Kellis, Chi.(NL)/S.D...	.209	36	125	115	16	24	27	0	0	1	8	1	0	3	6	0	30	2	0	2	.235
Villar, Jose, Atlanta..............	.310	56	239	203	41	63	79	10	0	2	28	1	1	5	29	1	42	19	9	1	.389
Villegas, Robert, N.Y. Yankees..	.275	40	153	138	12	38	46	3	1	1	19	1	0	7	7	1	14	1	0	4	.333
Villero, Armando, Atlanta	.317	40	118	101	25	32	36	4	0	0	13	3	0	1	13	0	13	11	6	1	.356
Vinas, Alexander, Arizona	.269	37	143	130	22	35	79	5	0	13	29	0	0	5	8	0	30	1	1	5	.608
Vizcaino, Alfredo, California ...	.190	39	139	105	20	20	27	3	2	0	9	0	2	3	29	0	34	7	6	0	.257
William, Jovanny, St. Louis.....	.257	69	274	253	33	65	92	14	5	1	24	1	0	3	17	2	45	6	4	7	.364
Wilson, Danny, N.Y. Mets.......	.250	38	116	112	14	28	38	4	0	2	16	0	0	1	3	0	21	0	2	1	.339
Zambrano, Alan, Seattle........	.382	14	42	34	12	13	24	2	0	3	6	0	0	1	7	0	5	2	1	0	.706
Zapata, Juan, Hou.-Bos.........	.270	52	224	211	26	57	69	6	3	0	10	2	0	2	9	0	30	10	4	8	.327
Zapata, Wilson, Hou.-Bos.	.240	58	242	204	43	49	81	10	2	6	26	3	0	3	32	1	64	10	4	3	.397

1996 PITCHING

TEAM

Team	W	L	Pct.	ERA	G	CG	ShO	Sv.	IP	H	TBF	R	ER	HR	SH	SF	HB	BB	IBB	SO	WP
Dodgers II	59	10	.855	2.52	69	4	4	22	614.0	468	2538	260	172	6	14	17	36	296	5	421	46
St. Louis	47	27	.635	3.12	74	11	7	22	641.0	608	2777	320	222	26	24	14	47	242	8	461	49
Oakland	49	24	.671	3.14	73	6	4	16	599.1	563	2629	314	209	15	30	29	53	297	5	393	47
Toronto	47	23	.671	3.19	71	6	3	19	607.1	538	2621	304	215	23	23	15	27	258	1	527	48
Cleveland	50	21	.704	3.21	71	7	6	19	622.2	622	2730	332	222	23	14	5	54	225	7	449	52
N.Y. Yankees	41	29	.586	3.36	71	0	3	18	596.2	539	2679	330	223	30	25	12	43	330	8	479	74
Hou.-Bos...........	29	39	.426	3.39	70	2	1	18	603.1	501	2679	340	227	16	29	17	56	322	0	489	73
Texas	43	28	.606	3.57	72	7	5	13	610.0	579	2634	320	242	36	20	16	35	243	16	406	32
Atlanta	42	29	.592	3.78	71	3	4	16	613.2	606	2735	380	258	21	23	13	43	327	11	429	63
Detroit	47	25	.653	3.83	72	2	4	13	621.0	671	2815	371	264	26	28	20	17	286	24	441	62
Philadelphia	36	35	.507	3.97	71	7	0	17	614.0	605	2801	430	271	18	14	25	43	340	4	446	78
Dodgers I	39	28	.582	4.13	68	1	3	20	574.2	540	2556	316	264	38	24	18	41	325	6	424	50
San Francisco.....	27	42	.391	4.14	70	6	4	10	591.1	575	2659	377	272	20	36	17	39	345	9	421	71
N.Y. Mets	47	24	.662	4.15	71	8	8	14	604.2	622	2648	348	279	87	16	17	30	218	7	498	46
Arizona	36	36	.500	4.39	72	4	1	15	593.0	632	2661	379	289	42	25	18	39	268	11	413	55
Seattle	35	34	.507	4.49	69	8	3	11	575.2	554	2629	394	287	51	22	14	59	322	8	443	53

SUMMER CLASS A — Dominican Summer League

Team	W	L	Pct.	ERA	G	CG	ShO	Sv.	IP	H	TBF	R	ER	HR	SH	SF	HB	BB	IBB	SO	WP	Bk.
il./Chi.(A.L.)....	32	38	.457	4.62	71	8	1	15	584.2	604	2693	385	300	51	21	18	66	348	6	398	60	5
.C./Colo.	27	43	.386	4.79	70	1	1	14	581.0	648	2685	417	309	19	17	24	51	277	12	279	69	8
o-op	28	42	.400	4.92	70	3	1	17	592.2	695	2760	460	324	36	7	22	43	291	6	386	85	7
altimore	26	40	.394	4.95	70	7	0	11	593.0	610	2707	445	326	55	24	16	37	337	2	381	45	17
ittsburgh	25	46	.352	4.97	72	5	3	11	588.1	614	2688	419	325	45	31	24	33	326	9	502	66	4
orida	20	50	.286	5.16	70	1	1	12	581.1	649	2729	448	333	35	18	24	61	375	2	446	72	13
B./Calif.	12	59	.169	5.18	71	6	0	4	594.0	728	2872	528	342	21	25	25	43	307	2	374	73	23
ontreal	19	52	.268	5.30	72	4	3	4	600.2	670	2802	458	354	50	25	30	42	368	16	389	62	9
hi.(N.L.)/S.D....	17	56	.233	5.80	73	15	2	4	585.1	705	2777	505	377	60	21	21	47	292	5	366	66	10

INDIVIDUAL

TOP QUALIFIERS FOR EARNED-RUN AVERAGE TITLE

Pitcher, Team	W	L	Pct.	ERA	G	GS	CG	ShO	GF	Sv.	IP	H	TBF	R	ER	HR	SH	SF	HB	BB	IBB	SO	WP	Bk.
llalobos, Noe, Hou.-Bos.	4	2	.667	1.13	16	9	1	0	5	1	63.2	41	245	14	8	0	0	0	0	12	0	50	3	0
eyes, Bernardo, St. Louis	8	1	.889	1.18	16	13	3	1	0	0	76.1	52	318	17	10	0	4	1	5	37	1	56	1	1
ernandez, Pedro, Dodgers II	10	1	.909	1.87	14	13	2	1	0	0	86.2	65	343	26	18	1	0	2	1	25	1	62	8	2
aulino, Arison, Pittsburgh.	3	0	1.000	1.95	21	5	0	0	5	0	60.0	40	236	16	13	1	1	1	3	21	1	42	2	0
uzman, Ambiorix, Texas	6	0	1.000	1.97	12	8	3	1	2	1	64.0	57	262	20	14	1	1	0	2	16	0	53	1	0
cantara, Albin, St. Louis	9	3	.750	2.03	15	15	3	1	0	0	93.1	77	382	35	21	2	4	1	3	24	1	71	11	0
epeda, Wellington, Arizona	7	3	.700	2.09	16	13	2	0	0	0	81.2	72	326	24	19	3	2	1	2	20	2	70	8	0
ega, Juan, San Francisco	6	2	.750	2.24	13	12	0	0	1	0	76.1	53	317	31	19	1	5	0	3	45	2	76	17	1
arcia, Jose, Cleveland	5	4	.556	2.35	24	1	1	0	16	6	53.2	47	224	17	14	1	0	0	4	11	2	54	2	2
aez, Miguel, Cleveland	7	1	.875	2.43	15	15	2	0	0	0	100.0	95	417	39	27	4	1	0	10	28	0	93	9	1

ALL PITCHERS

Pitcher, Team	W	L	Pct.	ERA	G	GS	CG	ShO	GF	Sv.	IP	H	TBF	R	ER	HR	SH	SF	HB	BB	IBB	SO	WP	Bk.
reu, Juan, San Francisco	0	2	.000	7.37	3	3	0	0	0	0	7.1	9	42	7	6	1	0	0	0	13	0	8	3	0
reu, Milton, San Francisco	2	6	.250	4.02	14	14	0	1	0	0	69.1	61	303	44	31	4	2	2	8	30	0	42	6	2
osta, Alberto, N.Y. Yankees	1	1	.500	4.83	12	5	0	0	3	0	31.2	41	161	21	17	2	1	1	3	27	0	22	7	0
uillera, Edgar, Dodgers II	1	1	.500	3.57	11	0	0	0	6	1	17.2	12	80	14	7	0	2	3	2	12	0	12	2	1
ertus, Melanio, Toronto	0	0	.000	0.00	3	0	0	0	2	0	4.0	2	22	3	0	0	0	0	1	5	0	3	1	0
cantara, Albin, St. Louis	9	3	.750	2.03	15	15	3	1	0	0	93.1	77	382	35	21	2	4	1	3	24	1	71	11	0
monte, Aquiles, Oakland	4	2	.667	3.56	22	0	0	0	12	1	60.2	58	266	39	24	1	0	3	4	28	0	45	3	0
monte, Hector, Florida	0	0	.000	0.00	2	0	0	0	0	0	1.2	0	6	0	0	0	0	0	1	0	2	1	0	
nez, Maycoll, Mil./Chi.(AL)	5	3	.625	2.42	13	13	4	0	0	0	74.1	74	318	27	20	3	1	0	2	31	1	34	5	0
dujar, Elias, Atlanta	2	3	.400	4.77	20	2	0	0	7	1	54.2	56	242	37	29	4	2	4	2	24	3	33	3	0
dujar, Jesse, Montreal	1	8	.111	6.15	12	12	0	0	0	0	48.1	56	253	41	33	4	2	0	9	49	0	29	11	1
uino, Miguel, Arizona	3	1	.750	3.83	19	4	0	0	6	1	44.2	45	204	27	19	3	0	2	3	26	0	28	3	0
cangel, Arsenio, Mil./Chi.(AL)	1	5	.167	4.75	21	3	0	0	10	3	47.1	53	212	32	25	7	6	2	1	20	1	17	6	2
as, Jose, California	0	4	.000	6.15	7	7	0	0	0	0	33.2	46	163	33	23	1	0	0	2	13	0	23	3	2
as, Kelvin, N.Y. Mets	2	3	.400	6.75	12	3	0	0	2	0	26.2	33	130	24	20	7	1	0	3	14	1	24	7	0
as, Pablo, San Francisco	2	0	1.000	5.02	11	1	0	0	3	0	14.1	21	70	13	8	0	1	0	0	5	0	8	3	0
as, Rafael, San Francisco	5	6	.455	3.26	15	14	0	1	0	0	85.2	89	382	45	31	3	4	1	2	40	2	46	1	0
as, Roberto, N.Y. Mets	7	3	.700	3.48	14	13	2	1	1	0	77.2	79	330	39	30	12	2	0	2	20	1	64	6	2
rendel, Eduard, Baltimore	0	0	.000	0.00	1	0	0	0	1	0	1.1	0	4	0	0	0	0	0	1	0	0	0	0	
encio, Eddy, Detroit	4	0	1.000	3.46	20	2	0	0	6	1	54.2	54	238	26	21	3	2	1	1	22	5	40	4	1
tacio, Raul, California	0	1	.000	11.56	6	0	0	0	3	0	4.2	10	29	7	6	0	1	0	0	6	0	2	1	1
tudillo, Jairo, Cleveland	5	1	.833	3.00	16	1	0	0	7	2	30.0	24	126	10	10	2	0	0	0	15	1	29	3	0
oar, Alejandro, St. Louis	3	3	.500	2.90	13	8	1	0	4	3	52.2	58	238	24	17	1	1	3	4	19	0	24	0	1
oar, Franklin, Baltimore	0	6	.000	6.53	10	7	0	0	0	0	41.1	46	201	36	30	4	0	0	0	34	0	22	0	0
ez, Jose, Pittsburgh	2	7	.222	5.46	14	11	1	0	0	0	61.0	72	281	47	37	5	2	3	4	25	1	41	5	0
ez, Miguel, Cleveland	7	1	.875	2.43	15	15	2	0	0	0	100.0	95	417	39	27	4	1	0	10	28	0	93	9	1
ez, Rafael, N.Y. Mets	1	0	1.000	4.61	11	0	0	0	5	0	13.2	18	64	9	7	3	2	1	0	7	0	18	4	0
ista, Orlando, Detroit	1	1	.500	3.42	15	2	0	0	4	1	26.1	30	122	18	10	0	3	0	0	10	0	15	3	1
ista, Rafael, Seattle	1	1	.500	5.32	9	0	0	0	1	0	22.0	29	108	23	13	3	1	0	2	10	0	10	1	0
liard, Carlos, Dodgers II	6	0	1.000	3.34	13	12	0	1	1	0	59.1	47	259	29	22	0	1	2	1	41	0	31	2	0
llo, Emerson, Seattle	6	1	.857	2.59	18	15	3	1	3	1	94.0	73	406	43	27	3	2	3	8	42	0	102	11	0
hitez, Francisco, K.C./Colo.	1	4	.200	7.94	15	3	0	0	4	0	28.1	38	141	27	25	0	0	3	5	15	0	13	2	2
noit, Joaquin, Texas	6	5	.545	2.28	14	13	2	1	0	0	75.0	63	313	26	19	4	3	1	1	23	1	63	2	1
ancourt, Willy, Cleveland	2	2	.333	3.37	4	4	0	0	0	0	18.2	24	91	19	7	1	0	0	0	5	0	14	2	0
nco, Fabian, Dodgers II	3	1	.750	6.02	13	13	0	0	0	0	43.1	34	215	44	29	1	1	1	4	57	0	30	8	0
nd, Fausto, Atlanta	5	2	.714	3.82	15	9	1	0	4	3	66.0	67	299	43	28	2	0	0	6	37	2	51	8	1
vo, Luis, Co-op	5	4	.556	3.69	21	4	0	0	7	1	61.0	69	271	33	25	4	2	2	6	11	1	56	8	0
zoban, Melvin, Texas	7	5	.583	2.74	16	16	1	0	0	0	95.1	74	395	38	29	9	2	1	10	34	2	69	5	0
to, Juan, N.Y. Mets	6	3	.667	4.20	14	13	0	0	0	0	70.2	69	309	38	33	14	0	0	8	28	0	55	6	1
oral, Martinez, Toronto	2	1	.667	6.21	18	1	0	0	6	2	37.2	47	189	33	26	1	0	1	0	27	0	46	5	0
ceres, Antonio, Toronto	4	2	.667	3.68	22	2	0	0	10	1	51.1	46	215	28	21	5	2	4	3	13	0	38	3	2
deron, Paulino, Florida	0	0	1.000	6.75	17	0	0	0	4	0	34.2	49	168	33	26	3	1	2	2	19	0	24	3	0
deron, Ramon, San Francisco	0	1	.000	3.57	8	1	2	0	5	1	17.2	17	79	13	7	1	2	2	1	11	1	3	1	0
zada, Javier, Oakland	3	1	.750	5.08	7	7	0	0	0	0	28.1	30	130	19	16	2	2	0	2	22	0	13	2	0
mpusano, Juan, Mil./Chi.(AL)	4	3	.571	5.31	14	10	1	0	1	0	57.2	63	255	41	34	9	7	4	4	28	0	37	1	0
mpusano, Lenny, California	0	1	.000	4.22	5	0	0	0	2	0	10.2	9	52	6	5	0	1	1	1	10	0	8	0	0
rasquel, Alejandro, Montreal	2	3	.400	5.97	23	6	0	0	11	0	40.2	51	194	31	27	4	0	2	3	26	1	34	8	0
rrera, Carlos, Arizona	4	4	.400	4.35	20	14	0	0	2	0	82.2	79	379	52	40	3	5	3	10	45	2	51	12	0
stillo, Alexander, Seattle	0	0	.000	4.90	3	0	0	0	0	0	3.2	1	18	3	2	0	0	0	0	3	0	2	0	0
stillo, Edgar, California	2	4	.333	2.90	15	10	3	0	0	0	68.1	73	301	36	22	4	4	6	1	16	1	51	3	1
stillo, Hanlet, Seattle	0	0	.000	4.05	4	0	0	0	1	0	6.2	3	30	6	3	1	0	0	0	3	0	1	0	0
killo, Jose, Detroit	7	6	.636	4.70	21	0	0	0	18	3	38.1	54	184	31	20	4	4	1	0	16	9	21	2	1
stillo, Marcos, Dodgers I	1	2	.333	3.27	5	2	0	0	2	0	11.0	7	46	4	4	1	0	0	1	6	0	9	1	0
stillo, Ramon, Florida	0	1	.000	13.50	12	0	0	0	6	0	14.0	31	85	25	21	4	0	0	4	10	0	6	5	1

Pitcher, Team	W	L	Pct.	ERA	G	GS	CG	ShO	GF	Sv.	IP	H	TBF	R	ER	HR	SH	SF	HB	BB	IBB	SO	WP
Castillo, Wilson, Dodgers I	7	2	.778	3.82	13	12	0	0	0	0	61.1	61	277	37	26	3	4	4	8	29	0	35	5
Ceballos, Alfredo, Chi.(NL)/S.D.	0	0	.000	9.45	15	0	0	0	4	0	20.0	25	115	31	21	4	0	2	4	24	0	13	11
Centeno, Juan, Hou.-Bos.	0	1	.000	8.36	11	0	0	0	0	0	14.0	13	76	17	13	1	1	2	3	18	0	8	5
Centeno, Ruben, Hou.-Bos.	0	0	.000	7.50	5	1	0	0	0	0	6.0	6	36	10	5	0	0	0	1	12	0	2	2
Cepeda, Wellington, Arizona	7	3	.700	2.09	16	13	2	0	0	0	81.2	72	326	24	19	3	2	1	2	20	2	70	8
Cequera, Jesus, California	0	3	.000	7.53	16	5	0	0	4	1	34.2	41	186	39	29	1	1	1	3	40	0	23	8
Chalas, Bernardo, Montreal	0	0	.000	7.41	14	0	0	0	8	0	17.0	19	93	20	14	1	0	1	2	24	0	7	2
Charle, Juan, Dodgers I	2	2	.500	5.05	14	13	1	0	0	0	62.1	69	264	38	35	8	0	3	2	20	0	55	0
Chevalier, Williams, Hou.-Bos.	1	4	.200	4.60	13	13	0	0	0	0	58.2	44	269	42	30	5	3	3	5	44	0	39	16
Clarke, Elvis, Baltimore	1	8	.111	8.65	19	7	0	0	2	0	51.0	66	267	62	49	4	1	2	10	50	0	38	5
Cocco, Pascual, Toronto	7	2	.778	2.99	17	16	2	2	0	0	96.1	77	422	46	32	1	5	2	6	53	0	92	8
Colon, Jose, Cleveland	2	0	.999	3.03	16	1	0	0	10	3	29.2	25	140	14	10	0	0	2	1	13	0	28	3
Colon, Roman, Atlanta	5	6	.455	3.52	14	14	0	1	0	0	64.0	59	296	45	25	0	2	2	3	38	0	39	9
Concepcion, Eric, Baltimore	0	0	.000	11.25	4	1	0	0	1	0	8.0	12	46	17	10	2	0	1	0	8	0	3	0
Connors, Wilson, Baltimore	0	0	.000	6.77	1	0	0	0	0	0	1.1	1	7	2	1	0	0	0	0	2	0	0	0
Contreras, Angel, Pittsburgh	3	3	.500	4.00	11	11	1	0	0	0	45.0	42	199	21	20	4	3	1	3	33	0	38	6
Contreras, Jose, Philadelphia	1	3	.250	7.92	15	2	0	0	7	2	25.0	32	135	30	22	0	1	2	2	20	0	20	4
Cordoba, Gregory, Atlanta	3	0	1.000	3.35	9	9	0	1	0	0	45.2	38	203	25	17	1	3	2	6	33	2	23	2
Cordova, Jorge, N.Y. Yankees	5	1	.833	2.36	18	0	0	0	13	5	34.1	23	168	17	9	1	3	0	2	32	4	33	4
Cornielle, Alexander, Chi.(NL)/S.D.	0	0	.000	5.78	5	0	0	0	4	0	4.2	3	22	3	3	1	0	0	0	7	0	4	0
Cornielle, Henry, Oakland	5	3	.625	1.74	29	0	0	0	29	12	41.1	34	169	12	8	1	2	3	3	11	2	25	7
Cruz, Charles, Baltimore	3	1	.750	3.06	12	0	0	0	11	2	17.2	18	81	9	6	1	1	2	1	10	1	16	1
Cueto, Jose, Seattle	4	4	.500	3.76	14	12	1	0	2	0	64.2	56	277	39	27	8	0	0	7	27	0	61	2
De Jesus, Robert, Texas	2	1	.667	6.58	19	1	0	0	10	2	39.2	57	185	39	29	3	2	1	1	9	3	17	1
De La Cruz, Andres, N.Y. Yankees	2	3	.400	3.90	11	5	0	0	4	0	32.1	29	147	18	14	2	2	0	1	20	0	20	2
De La Cruz, Inocencio, N.Y. Mets	2	0	1.000	2.38	7	5	1	0	0	0	34.0	30	138	19	9	4	0	0	0	6	0	33	3
DeLa Cruz, Martin, Mil./Chi.(AL)	0	0	.000	0.00	4	0	0	0	2	2	2.2	2	9	0	0	0	0	0	0	3	0	1	1
De La Rosa, Cristian, Baltimore	3	0	1.000	5.55	14	6	1	0	4	1	47.0	56	232	34	29	2	2	1	2	29	0	30	0
De La Rosa, Igancio, San Francisco	0	0	.000	7.20	3	0	0	0	1	0	5.0	5	24	4	4	1	0	1	0	6	0	3	0
De Leon, Juan, Montreal	0	2	.000	3.72	7	1	0	0	4	0	19.1	20	79	8	8	0	0	0	2	5	1	8	1
Delisa, Carlos, Chi.(NL)/S.D.	2	2	.500	5.40	18	2	0	0	7	0	41.2	58	201	40	25	4	0	2	5	15	1	21	3
De Los Santos, Aurelio, St. Louis	3	2	.600	2.44	15	1	0	0	11	1	51.2	49	225	23	14	5	0	1	4	23	1	36	2
De Los Santos, Jose, St. Louis	3	1	.750	4.79	6	2	1	0	3	0	20.2	20	84	13	11	2	0	0	0	7	0	10	0
De Los Stos., Americo, San Francisco	0	3	.000	6.59	17	0	0	0	11	2	27.1	35	134	24	20	1	2	0	3	16	2	18	4
Diaz, Esteban, Dodgers I	2	2	.500	2.98	11	8	0	0	1	0	42.1	30	183	18	14	3	0	0	1	35	0	21	4
Disla, Francisco, N.Y. Yankees	0	0	.000	0.00	2	0	0	0	2	0	2.0	1	8	0	0	0	0	0	0	1	0	2	0
Dotel, Melido, Dodgers II	7	1	.875	2.96	13	13	1	0	0	0	67.0	53	283	32	22	1	2	0	5	38	0	50	5
Encarnacion, Anibal, California	0	2	.000	4.71	16	1	0	0	6	0	36.1	47	179	35	19	3	2	1	3	19	0	8	7
Ernesto, Hector, Florida	1	2	.333	7.88	4	0	0	0	2	1	8.0	11	35	7	7	1	0	0	0	4	0	6	0
Escobar, Edwin, Toronto	0	0	.000	6.74	2	0	0	0	0	0	2.2	4	13	3	2	0	0	0	0	1	0	3	0
Escobar, Luis, Seattle	4	7	.364	5.02	24	0	0	0	20	7	37.2	48	182	26	21	4	1	0	5	22	4	31	6
Estevez, Domingo, Seattle	0	0	.000	0.00	1	0	0	0	1	0	1.0	0	3	0	0	0	0	0	0	0	0	0	0
Eusebio, Alberto, St. Louis	0	1	.000	6.57	5	0	0	0	1	1	12.1	15	57	10	9	0	0	1	1	4	0	9	1
Fernandez, Jose, Arizona	1	2	.333	4.81	7	6	0	0	0	0	24.1	26	105	17	13	0	1	0	1	8	1	16	3
Fernandez, Samuel, California	0	2	.000	5.87	10	2	0	0	5	1	15.1	16	70	17	10	1	0	2	1	8	0	8	1
Ferreiras, Ramon, Hou.-Bos.	0	2	.000	5.14	21	0	0	0	6	0	28.0	30	137	26	16	0	1	2	3	18	0	19	2
Figueroa, Erasmo, Mil./Chi.(AL)	4	5	.444	2.96	21	5	1	0	6	1	51.2	55	227	24	17	2	2	2	3	24	0	43	6
Figueroa, Juan, Mil./Chi.(AL)	2	6	.250	4.75	15	13	0	0	0	0	60.2	54	291	43	32	3	1	1	7	56	0	60	12
Flores, Luis, Toronto	3	0	1.000	2.16	22	0	0	0	21	11	25.0	17	98	8	6	3	1	1	1	4	0	23	3
Franco, Francisco, Pittsburgh	1	3	.250	4.81	24	1	0	0	14	4	33.2	30	164	22	18	1	3	2	2	33	1	30	4
Franco, Jorby, Atlanta	8	3	.727	2.64	19	9	2	1	6	2	85.1	86	357	41	25	3	2	0	2	20	0	60	5
Franco, Jose, N.Y. Mets	4	5	.444	3.51	14	13	2	2	0	0	77.0	86	330	37	30	9	2	4	2	17	0	54	0
Franco, Juan, N.Y. Yankees	5	1	.833	2.71	14	10	0	0	4	1	59.2	57	268	33	18	2	3	1	1	27	0	42	8
Franco, Santo, Chi.(NL)/S.D.	1	0	1.000	6.37	9	6	0	0	1	0	35.1	41	164	31	25	4	1	0	2	15	0	14	3
Frias, Amauris, Chi.(NL)/S.D.	3	4	.429	4.20	14	6	3	1	5	0	49.1	55	233	33	23	2	2	0	5	26	1	31	2
Frias, Jovanny, Mil./Chi.(AL)	5	1	.833	1.03	8	7	1	0	0	0	35.0	30	141	9	4	0	0	0	1	14	0	16	0
Frias, Juan, California	0	5	.000	4.53	19	7	0	0	6	0	53.2	70	273	50	27	3	3	1	5	33	0	31	6
Galvez, Randy, Dodgers II	10	2	.833	2.53	13	12	0	1	0	0	74.2	63	307	29	21	1	2	3	4	21	0	54	5
Garcia, Epedy, Oakland	5	4	.556	2.79	14	14	1	0	0	0	80.2	79	350	36	25	2	7	2	10	30	0	55	7
Garcia, Jose, Cleveland	5	4	.556	2.35	24	1	0	0	16	6	53.2	47	224	17	14	1	0	0	4	11	2	54	2
Garcia, Jose, Co-op	2	2	.500	2.63	13	2	1	0	5	1	37.2	41	153	17	11	1	0	0	2	3	0	29	3
Garcia, Luis, Hou.-Bos.	2	0	1.000	3.75	14	0	0	0	3	0	24.0	13	111	12	10	1	6	1	1	23	0	17	5
Garcia, Rosman, N.Y. Yankees	2	1	.667	4.83	14	3	0	0	5	1	41.0	45	194	28	22	6	0	1	6	18	0	24	3
Genao, Martin, Dodgers II	2	0	1.000	2.55	14	1	0	0	5	2	53.0	47	228	24	15	0	2	3	5	24	1	22	6
German, Armando, Pittsburgh	0	0	.000	10.80	11	1	0	0	4	1	13.1	17	76	16	16	2	1	2	1	22	0	12	5
German, John, N.Y. Mets	7	1	.875	4.12	15	13	1	1	1	1	74.1	76	324	43	34	12	3	3	1	28	0	73	7
Gomez, Luis, Hou.-Bos.	1	2	.333	0.32	23	0	0	0	17	3	28.0	25	124	11	1	0	2	1	6	13	0	20	2
Gomez, Ricardo, Pittsburgh	0	4	.000	4.99	14	7	1	0	3	0	43.1	53	206	33	24	1	3	1	1	27	1	30	10
Gondola, Roberto, N.Y. Yankees	7	2	.778	2.71	15	10	0	0	3	0	59.2	40	240	21	18	1	0	1	1	35	0	77	4
Gonzalez, Luis, Oakland	5	1	.833	2.26	16	3	0	0	3	0	51.2	50	220	24	13	2	2	0	4	20	0	22	6
Grullon, Bernardo, Detroit	0	0	.000	27.27	1	0	0	0	0	0	0.1	3	11	1	1	0	0	0	0	2	0	1	0
Guerra, Luis, California	0	6	.000	5.26	11	4	0	0	2	1	37.2	42	177	38	22	0	5	2	2	14	0	28	4
Guevara, Carlos, Pittsburgh	0	0	.000	14.18	11	0	0	0	5	0	13.1	29	76	25	21	0	0	1	0	7	0	15	3
Guillen, Daniel, California	1	5	.000	5.05	22	2	0	0	16	0	35.2	47	178	30	20	1	0	3	3	21	1	27	7
Gutierrez, Ruben, N.Y. Mets	1	1	.500	8.59	10	0	0	0	3	0	14.2	16	78	19	14	2	0	2	0	13	0	10	2
Guzman, Ambiorix, Texas	6	0	1.000	1.97	12	8	3	1	2	0	64.0	57	262	20	14	1	1	2	2	16	0	53	1
Guzman, Juan, St. Louis	0	1	.000	0.00	4	0	0	0	2	0	6.2	6	33	4	0	0	0	0	1	3	0	6	3
Guzman, Levin, Co-op	2	4	.333	6.04	10	4	0	0	1	0	25.1	37	131	27	17	0	0	1	1	22	0	14	5
Guzman, Pedro, Arizona	2	1	.667	6.37	15	2	0	0	7	0	29.2	47	145	26	21	5	1	0	1	12	0	20	3
Guzman, Wilson, Pittsburgh	1	6	.143	4.22	14	11	1	0	1	0	59.2	61	264	38	28	8	2	3	3	21	0	56	1
Henriquez, Hector, Florida	2	7	.222	3.59	15	14	0	0	0	0	72.2	72	324	49	29	1	3	1	9	39	0	66	7
Henriquez, Roman, Dodgers I	4	0	1.000	2.89	18	0	0	0	8	1	62.1	62	271	26	20	3	2	1	3	25	0	32	7
Heredia, Ruddy, San Francisco	1	4	.200	11.00	7	0	0	0	2	0	9.0	10	48	13	11	0	1	0	1	8	2	8	2

cher, Team	W	L	Pct.	ERA	G	GS	CG	ShO	GF	Sv.	IP	H	TBF	R	ER	HR	SH	SF	HB	BB	IBB	SO	WP	Bk.
rnandez, German, Texas	3	2	.600	3.92	13	9	1	0	1	0	57.1	53	238	26	25	8	5	1	3	16	1	25	0	0
rnandez, Jose, Montreal	0	1	.000	6.00	4	2	0	0	1	0	9.0	10	38	6	6	3	1	0	0	2	0	5	0	0
rnandez, Juan, Detroit	0	0	.000	6.92	8	0	0	0	5	0	13.0	17	66	14	10	1	0	0	2	7	0	6	3	1
rnandez, Luis, San Francisco	0	0	.000	0.00	1	0	0	0	0	0	0.0	0	1	0	0	0	0	0	1	0	0	0	0	0
rnandez, Pedro, Dodgers II	10	1	.909	1.87	14	13	2	1	0	0	86.2	65	343	26	18	1	0	2	1	25	1	62	8	2
rrera, Anthony, Co-op	3	5	.375	7.09	12	12	0	0	0	0	59.2	62	284	59	47	5	0	2	6	46	0	42	19	0
rrera, Misael, Chi.(NL)/S.D.	3	8	.273	3.23	16	14	6	1	1	1	86.1	84	367	46	31	4	3	2	9	17	0	69	8	1
aldo, Juan, Co-op	3	6	.333	6.16	11	11	0	0	0	0	57.0	67	267	47	39	5	1	2	6	29	0	37	7	0
aldo, Julio, Cleveland	3	1	.750	2.45	6	5	0	0	0	0	33.0	26	148	14	9	1	0	0	5	16	0	27	4	0
a, Elias, Hou.-Bos.	1	2	.333	9.37	13	1	0	0	1	0	16.1	25	97	28	17	0	3	1	3	20	0	6	3	2
uierdo, Roberto, Florida	0	7	.000	5.43	15	11	1	0	1	1	53.0	68	242	43	32	5	1	0	4	29	0	33	4	1
so, Oscar, Dodgers II	3	2	.600	0.85	20	0	0	0	9	4	42.1	17	151	7	4	0	0	0	5	11	0	40	3	0
enez, Alejandro, Texas	2	3	.400	7.72	9	8	0	0	0	0	30.1	25	154	31	26	2	0	2	4	38	0	27	5	0
enez, Fausto, San Francisco	0	0	.000	81.82	1	0	0	0	0	0	0.1	3	4	3	3	0	0	0	0	0	0	1	0	0
enez, Francisco, Arizona	6	5	.545	3.78	21	14	2	0	4	1	85.2	86	363	52	36	7	4	1	4	25	1	54	2	0
enez, Lautico, Atlanta	0	0	.000	13.51	7	0	0	0	3	0	7.1	9	45	14	11	0	1	1	0	13	0	6	5	1
enez, Mario, Seattle	1	0	1.000	5.54	13	4	0	0	6	0	26.0	22	128	19	16	1	2	0	7	27	1	13	6	0
enez, Santos, Baltimore	1	0	1.000	2.97	14	0	0	0	11	3	30.1	24	119	12	10	2	1	0	0	8	0	13	1	2
n, Isabel, Toronto	6	1	.857	1.19	21	1	0	0	11	5	60.2	42	248	15	8	0	2	0	3	17	1	49	5	2
nston, Charles, Detroit	1	2	.333	4.20	10	10	0	0	0	0	49.1	48	240	35	23	1	3	2	0	41	0	36	10	1
io, Jorge, Montreal	1	1	.500	6.06	10	0	0	0	2	0	16.1	13	71	12	11	1	0	1	1	11	0	21	3	1
nar, Emil, Dodgers I	1	1	.500	2.79	5	0	0	0	2	1	9.2	5	37	3	3	0	0	0	0	4	0	4	0	0
ara, Eudy, Florida	2	6	.250	4.20	15	10	0	0	0	0	49.1	48	229	30	23	1	4	6	2	38	0	31	6	1
franco, Otoniel, St. Louis	4	3	.571	1.25	10	2	2	1	6	1	36.0	36	158	11	5	0	3	1	3	13	1	29	0	0
n, Rafael, Florida	2	1	.667	10.35	18	0	0	0	6	3	20.0	28	107	26	23	1	2	1	1	17	1	19	9	1
a, Donald, K.C./Colo.	0	0	.000	0.00	2	0	0	0	2	0	1.1	0	4	0	0	0	0	0	0	0	0	2	0	0
ares, Agustin, Baltimore	5	7	.417	4.53	14	14	0	0	0	0	89.1	85	411	63	45	9	3	0	7	55	0	69	13	2
ares, Edwin, Atlanta	4	3	.571	4.00	11	11	0	1	0	0	54.0	49	237	28	24	2	2	0	3	39	0	46	7	2
ares, Rafael, Baltimore	1	3	.250	4.28	21	0	0	0	17	4	40.0	34	182	25	19	0	7	2	2	39	1	20	2	0
ares, Ramon, Co-op	3	3	.500	4.71	16	4	0	0	6	0	57.1	76	270	45	30	4	0	3	1	20	1	33	2	3
ano, Nelson, Arizona	0	1	.000	7.72	14	0	0	0	4	0	16.1	19	83	15	14	2	0	1	0	18	0	17	5	0
veres, Alberto, Baltimore	3	2	.600	5.32	13	3	0	0	7	1	42.1	54	189	36	25	4	2	1	5	20	0	10	4	1
ez, Gustavo, Florida	2	1	.667	4.15	15	0	0	0	9	0	21.2	25	102	14	10	0	1	2	3	10	0	11	2	0
ez, Reymundo, Dodgers I	2	2	.500	5.06	13	1	0	0	2	0	32.0	28	154	22	18	3	1	2	2	26	1	38	5	1
a, Edison, K.C./Colo.	5	2	.714	4.64	21	12	0	0	2	0	85.1	105	400	60	44	0	3	1	14	32	2	36	6	0
erna, Celi, San Francisco	6	3	.667	3.33	18	12	4	2	7	2	83.2	78	341	38	31	3	6	1	7	34	0	64	7	1
donado, Franklin, Chi.(NL)/S.D.	0	0	.000	45.00	2	0	0	0	0	0	1.0	2	9	5	5	0	0	0	1	2	0	0	0	0
zueta, Robert, Arizona	2	4	.333	5.47	16	8	0	0	2	0	49.1	54	225	36	30	4	5	5	0	27	1	29	3	0
ichal, Rafael, Pittsburgh	2	5	.286	4.03	18	0	0	0	4	0	38.0	38	169	24	17	4	2	1	4	20	1	39	7	0
te, Juan, St. Louis	0	0	.000	0.00	61	0	0	0	1	0	1.0	0	3	0	0	0	0	0	0	0	0	0	0	0
tinez, Diego, Philadelphia	0	0	.000	4.32	6	0	0	0	2	0	8.1	6	38	6	4	0	0	0	0	8	1	8	0	0
tinez, Francisco, Chi.(NL)/S.D.	1	3	.250	5.68	14	0	0	0	5	1	31.2	46	152	28	20	4	1	1	4	9	0	13	3	0
tinez, Francisco, Mil./Chi.(AL)	4	2	.667	4.91	18	1	0	0	5	1	51.1	52	239	39	28	8	0	2	8	22	0	57	6	0
tinez, Obispo, Montreal	2	5	.286	5.80	23	1	0	0	8	0	35.2	41	166	28	23	6	1	1	3	26	3	28	6	1
tinez, Rosario, N.Y. Mets	0	0	.000	3.37	10	0	0	0	3	0	10.2	11	54	5	4	1	1	0	1	10	2	9	6	0
tinez, Sandy, Hou.-Bos.	1	0	1.000	3.24	11	0	0	0	1	0	16.2	19	77	12	6	1	1	1	1	10	0	10	2	0
tinez, Santos, Mil./Chi.(AL)	0	0	.000	10.80	4	0	0	0	2	0	5.0	7	31	6	6	1	0	0	2	3	0	2	2	0
o, Francisco, Seattle	0	0	.000	0.00	2	0	0	0	1	0	3.1	2	12	1	0	0	0	0	0	0	0	2	0	0
o, Julio, Seattle	4	2	.667	1.74	14	5	2	1	5	1	51.2	42	212	14	10	3	1	1	1	19	0	23	1	1
as, Hansell, Atlanta	7	2	.778	2.80	25	0	0	0	17	4	64.1	69	282	36	20	1	1	3	26	1	65	5	0
rano, Juan, K.C./Colo.	2	6	.250	5.19	27	3	0	0	12	1	67.2	74	313	50	39	4	4	5	4	39	3	30	12	4
rano, Ramon, Montreal	0	0	.000	7.94	9	0	0	0	2	0	11.1	13	58	14	10	0	0	2	0	14	0	4	1	1
a, Luis, N.Y. Yankees	2	4	.333	2.27	14	6	0	0	7	3	43.2	39	186	18	11	1	0	1	1	22	2	53	2	1
a, Orlando, N.Y. Mets	0	1	.000	4.54	14	5	0	0	2	0	33.2	39	162	25	17	3	2	5	21	0	17	3	0
dez, Jose, Atlanta	0	0	.000	7.02	8	0	0	0	4	0	16.2	29	87	18	13	1	1	0	9	1	14	3	0
doza, Carlos, Co-op	2	7	.222	5.89	14	13	0	0	0	0	65.2	95	326	60	43	6	0	3	3	34	1	37	10	0
cado, Hector, Detroit	1	3	.250	4.04	13	7	0	0	3	0	42.1	54	208	31	19	4	1	2	3	25	0	31	7	1
cedes, Jorge, Oakland	0	0	.000	8.81	11	2	0	0	3	0	15.1	24	85	18	15	1	0	3	3	14	0	11	0	0
cedes, Martin, Philadelphia	5	3	.625	3.35	15	14	3	0	0	0	96.2	100	419	58	36	6	2	2	5	33	0	67	12	5
cedes, Thomas, Toronto	5	3	.625	2.93	12	12	0	0	0	0	73.2	73	317	37	24	4	3	0	1	25	0	41	4	0
na, Juan, Florida	2	1	.667	8.83	15	0	0	0	7	1	17.1	25	89	19	17	2	0	3	1	13	0	15	2	0
aya, Pablo, Florida	1	5	.167	3.08	12	10	0	0	0	0	49.2	50	228	28	17	1	1	0	6	34	0	56	5	0
hel, Yaqui, N.Y. Yankees	1	2	.333	8.51	13	0	0	0	4	0	24.1	33	135	31	23	2	0	1	4	24	1	15	6	0
na, Primitivo, Hou.-Bos.	2	3	.000	3.24	21	0	0	0	18	11	25.0	15	106	9	9	2	0	3	4	0	35	2	0
ero, Pablo, San Francisco	1	0	1.000	6.16	5	0	0	0	1	0	7.1	7	31	6	5	1	0	0	1	4	0	9	1	1
talvo, Reynaldo, Seattle	1	1	.500	6.94	15	0	0	0	2	0	36.1	30	176	33	28	4	2	2	5	38	1	24	5	2
tanez, John	8	5	.615	3.51	18	18	1	0	0	0	102.2	90	441	53	40	7	2	3	8	46	0	81	9	0
tero, Agustin, Oakland	8	2	.800	2.21	17	12	2	0	2	1	85.2	64	365	29	21	1	5	2	3	58	0	71	4	2
tero, Oscar, Mil./Chi.(AL)	0	0	.000	8.44	9	0	0	0	5	0	5.1	5	30	6	5	0	0	1	7	0	2	1	0
ales, Kelli, K.C./Colo.	4	1	.800	2.55	8	7	0	0	0	0	49.1	60	212	22	14	0	0	2	1	6	0	24	2	0
el, Jose, Pittsburgh	6	3	.667	6.14	12	9	1	1	0	0	51.1	57	224	39	35	6	1	1	0	18	0	48	5	0
el, Ramon, Cleveland	2	1	.667	6.16	14	5	0	0	2	0	38.0	58	183	33	26	4	1	0	5	18	1	20	1	0
eno, Jorge, Mil./Chi.(AL)	0	3	.000	7.86	9	6	1	0	2	0	26.1	25	134	29	23	1	0	1	5	29	0	21	1	0
llo, Humberto, N.Y. Yankees	2	3	.400	1.54	11	2	0	0	4	0	35.0	25	138	13	6	0	1	1	2	9	0	30	1	0
a, Cresencio, Baltimore	2	1	.667	4.26	11	1	0	0	3	0	25.1	22	128	25	12	3	1	3	5	27	0	17	4	2
obel, Juan, Pittsburgh	0	0	.000	7.56	12	5	0	0	2	0	25.0	25	133	36	21	4	4	1	1	28	0	25	5	0
a, Leo, San Francisco	0	0	.000	27.27	1	0	0	0	0	0	0.1	1	4	1	1	0	0	0	0	0	0	0	0	0
, Victor, Texas	0	0	.000	4.50	18	0	0	0	0	0	2.0	3	10	1	1	0	0	0	0	2	0	1	1	0
l, Jose, California	3	3	.500	5.82	15	6	0	0	3	0	43.1	59	230	53	28	2	1	0	5	27	0	28	8	2
jima, Satoshi, N.Y. Yankees	0	0	.000	9.00	1	0	0	0	1	0	1.0	3	8	1	1	0	0	0	0	2	0	0	1	0
Daurin, St. Louis	2	4	.333	3.67	23	3	0	0	18	13	54.0	47	234	31	22	2	3	5	20	1	62	7	1
, Jose, Mil./Chi.(AL)	0	0	.000	3.38	4	3	0	0	0	0	13.1	10	60	6	5	2	0	2	9	0	6	2	0
z, Enrique, Philadelphia	4	6	.400	5.09	15	12	2	0	0	0	70.2	82	345	64	40	1	2	0	12	38	0	52	10	1

– 573 –

Pitcher, Team	W	L	Pct.	ERA	G	GS	CG	ShO	GF	Sv.	IP	H	TBF	R	ER	HR	SH	SF	HB	BB	IBB	SO	WP
Nunez, Jose, N.Y. Mets	0	1	.000	6.46	11	3	0	0	0	2	23.2	33	114	19	17	4	0	1	2	9	0	25	1
Ogando, Alberto, California	3	10	.231	4.13	18	10	2	0	6	0	80.2	79	359	53	37	1	3	8	2	38	0	48	13
Olivo, Gary, San Francisco	0	3	.000	7.33	9	7	0	0	0	0	23.1	17	128	28	19	1	3	2	0	42	0	21	13
Olivo, Juan, San Francisco	2	4	.333	4.01	25	1	0	0	13	5	51.2	52	235	33	23	2	4	1	2	26	0	39	4
Ortega, Fermin, Philadelphia	5	7	.417	4.17	14	13	1	0	1	0	82.0	82	363	56	38	3	2	4	4	48	0	42	7
Ortega, Jose, K.C./Colo.	1	3	.250	3.89	32	0	0	0	31	12	41.2	41	190	23	18	2	2	2	1	19	3	27	3
Ortiz, Eusebio, St. Louis	2	3	.400	4.58	13	10	1	0	0	0	59.0	68	265	40	30	3	2	1	5	21	0	37	9
Ortiz, Jorge, San Francisco	0	1	.000	2.82	4	4	0	0	0	0	22.1	23	97	12	7	0	1	2	3	10	0	9	2
Ortiz, Pedro, Dodgers I	2	1	.667	6.25	14	3	0	0	4	1	31.2	31	146	22	22	2	0	0	1	22	1	37	6
Ozoria, Jose, Texas	3	2	.600	4.07	22	0	0	0	16	2	24.1	25	101	13	11	0	1	1	0	9	3	20	3
Padilla, Jesus, Arizona	0	0	.000	0.00	15	0	0	0	12	5	21.2	14	89	3	0	0	1	1	4	6	0	15	0
Padua, Geraldo, N.Y. Yankees	7	5	.583	3.55	14	9	0	0	1	0	66.0	67	293	38	26	1	3	1	4	25	0	56	13
Palacios, Ismael, Dodgers I	3	2	.600	3.48	23	0	0	0	21	11	41.1	45	194	20	16	2	2	2	3	26	2	44	2
Paredes, Omar, Chi.(NL)/S.D.	0	3	.000	6.13	5	4	0	0	0	0	14.2	16	74	17	10	0	1	0	1	12	0	20	1
Parra, Jesus, Hou.-Bos.	2	3	.400	2.71	12	12	0	0	0	0	59.2	41	247	24	18	1	1	1	5	33	0	65	4
Parra, Jorge, Co-op	1	3	.250	4.62	27	1	0	0	9	1	50.2	56	214	36	26	1	2	0	2	23	1	31	5
Parra, Klisber, Florida	2	1	.667	3.38	22	0	0	0	13	5	45.1	47	196	20	17	5	0	4	8	12	1	37	2
Paul, Antonio, St. Louis	0	3	.000	10.52	12	1	0	0	9	2	25.2	41	145	43	30	2	0	1	7	21	1	14	5
Paulino, Arison, Pittsburgh	3	0	1.000	1.95	21	5	0	0	5	0	60.0	40	236	16	13	1	1	3	1	21	1	42	2
Paulino, Noel, Pittsburgh	0	2	.000	6.75	19	1	0	0	7	1	26.2	38	146	31	20	0	1	1	3	28	0	19	5
Peguero, Darwin, Mil./Chi.(AL)	3	4	.429	2.14	12	12	0	1	0	0	59.0	38	246	23	14	1	1	0	5	29	0	52	10
Pena, David, Mil./Chi.(AL)	0	1	.000	17.29	5	1	0	0	0	0	8.1	20	62	22	16	3	0	0	4	12	0	5	1
Pena, Jose, Cleveland	5	1	.833	3.17	14	11	2	1	1	0	65.1	63	291	43	23	4	4	1	6	23	0	19	4
Pena, Juan, Oakland	8	2	.800	3.21	12	12	0	0	0	0	70.0	75	295	34	25	0	4	0	4	15	1	59	2
Pepen Robert, N.Y. Mets	3	2	.600	2.75	14	2	2	1	3	0	39.1	27	153	14	12	5	0	2	1	8	1	34	0
Perdomo, Roberto, San Francisco	0	0	.000	6.38	10	0	0	0	4	0	18.1	22	89	20	13	0	0	1	3	5	0	17	0
Perez, Carlos, Arizona	8	3	.727	3.36	25	2	0	0	10	6	56.1	66	248	29	21	4	4	0	1	15	3	51	6
Perez, Elvis, Atlanta	0	0	.000	1.80	1	1	0	0	0	0	5.0	3	19	1	1	0	0	0	0	1	0	4	0
Perez, Jose, Texas	2	2	.500	4.07	25	0	0	0	8	3	24.1	22	113	14	11	1	0	3	2	19	0	26	2
Perez, Nairon,Texas	0	0	.000	12.86	5	0	0	0	2	1	7.0	7	41	16	10	1	0	0	2	9	0	5	2
Perez, Nililberto, Chi.(NL)/S.D.	1	6	.143	5.14	13	8	0	0	2	0	35.0	38	176	38	20	3	1	2	2	31	0	24	2
Perez, Norberto, Baltimore	4	3	.571	3.94	14	14	5	0	0	0	93.2	82	396	57	41	7	1	3	4	36	0	75	8
Perez, Robert, California	1	4	.200	5.05	12	6	1	0	2	0	46.1	51	214	36	26	3	1	0	2	14	0	37	4
Perez, Samuel, Cleveland	5	4	.556	3.02	11	11	1	0	0	0	56.2	62	258	38	19	0	0	1	5	25	0	40	12
Perez Valdez, Jose, Arizona	1	3	.250	5.90	17	4	0	0	2	0	29.0	35	140	28	19	5	0	1	5	19	0	17	4
Pichardo, Carlos, K.C./Colo.	3	6	.333	5.61	19	8	1	0	7	1	51.1	71	253	52	32	2	2	4	4	13	1	24	8
Pimentel, Oscar, Oakland	1	0	1.000	6.75	5	0	0	0	2	0	6.2	5	35	5	5	2	0	0	1	11	0	3	0
Pinales, Otilio, Seattle	0	3	.000	20.87	7	3	0	0	1	0	7.1	8	56	19	17	0	0	3	6	14	0	14	3
Pitre, Diogenes, Oakland	1	3	.250	3.94	11	7	1	1	1	0	32.0	28	156	33	14	1	4	4	5	28	0	16	9
Pizarro, Melvin, Philadelphia	7	6	.538	3.02	16	16	0	0	0	0	98.1	79	422	49	33	2	0	4	5	57	0	72	4
Querales, Alberto, San Francisco	0	2	.000	4.33	16	1	0	0	8	0	27.0	31	127	17	13	0	1	0	0	16	0	15	2
Quiros, Misael, Pittsburgh	4	6	.400	3.13	18	9	0	0	5	1	74.2	68	318	42	26	5	4	2	5	28	1	69	6
Ramos, Fernando, Philadelphia	1	1	.500	3.06	15	0	0	0	12	3	17.2	13	83	14	6	0	1	0	0	13	1	14	2
Ramos, Jacinto, Cleveland	1	3	.250	2.70	13	3	0	0	4	0	30.0	27	137	13	9	1	1	0	2	14	0	13	3
Ramos, Jose, Dodgers I	3	2	.600	4.75	19	0	0	0	9	0	36.0	32	154	19	19	4	0	2	2	16	0	28	1
Ramos, Juan, Montreal	3	5	.375	2.69	12	12	2	0	0	0	77.0	80	330	34	23	4	3	3	5	20	1	66	3
Ravelo, Carlos, San Francisco	0	0	.000	5.79	6	0	0	0	0	0	14.0	16	68	10	9	0	0	2	3	12	0	7	5
Rebolledo, Jairo, Chi.(NL)/S.D.	0	0	.000	3.86	51	0	0	0	0	2	2.1	5	15	2	1	0	0	0	0	2	0	2	0
Regalado, Maximo, Dodgers I	3	5	.375	4.70	14	13	0	0	1	1	53.2	44	256	32	28	3	2	10	48	0	19	4
Remy, Ernesto, Montreal	0	1	.000	2.05	16	1	0	0	7	0	26.1	22	124	21	6	1	2	2	0	20	1	9	7
Reyes, Anderson, N.Y. Mets	4	0	1.000	3.77	16	0	0	0	5	0	28.2	23	115	14	12	6	0	2	0	8	1	16	0
Reyes, Arquimides, Philadelphia	2	1	.667	3.34	22	0	0	0	13	4	32.1	29	144	18	12	1	1	3	1	19	2	33	4
Reyes, Bernardo, St. Louis	8	1	.889	1.18	16	13	3	1	0	0	76.1	52	318	17	10	0	4	1	5	37	1	56	5
Reyes, Carlos, California	0	2	.000	4.50	16	1	0	0	7	1	28.0	27	133	27	14	2	2	1	6	21	0	18	3
Reyes, Juan, Montreal	4	3	.571	4.64	13	13	2	2	0	0	66.0	64	297	40	34	1	4	4	2	40	1	41	8
Reyes, Juan, Pittsburgh	0	2	.000	10.31	13	1	0	0	5	0	18.1	26	92	24	21	2	2	3	1	9	0	14	2
Reyes, Luis, Hou.-Bos.	2	3	.400	6.38	17	0	0	0	6	0	24.0	26	117	22	17	2	2	1	2	20	0	22	2
Reyes, Natanahel, Dodgers II	5	1	.833	2.04	15	0	0	0	6	2	39.2	27	131	18	9	0	0	2	16	0	24	4
Reyes, Pedro, N.Y. Yankees	3	2	.600	4.12	14	10	0	0	2	0	59.0	45	269	36	27	2	3	1	9	38	0	36	5
Reyes, Santo, St. Louis	3	1	.750	1.41	8	1	0	0	4	0	32.0	30	133	9	5	0	3	0	1	9	1	10	1
Reynoso, Franklin, Atlanta	0	0	.000	12.00	5	0	0	0	0	0	9.0	16	53	14	12	1	0	0	1	7	0	5	3
Richardson, Roberto, St. Louis	0	0	.000	0.00	1	0	0	0	1	0	2.0	2	10	2	0	0	0	0	0	2	0	2	2
Rijo, Fernando, Dodgers II	4	0	1.000	2.48	15	1	0	0	4	0	40.0	36	179	18	11	0	1	1	6	25	0	20	1
Rincones, Gabriel, Seattle	6	3	.667	3.36	15	14	1	0	0	0	88.1	76	370	46	33	9	4	2	1	24	0	62	5
Rivera, Homero, Detroit	5	4	.556	2.82	14	11	1	1	2	1	70.1	77	304	31	22	0	0	3	1	21	3	55	1
Roche, Angel, Texas	3	3	.500	3.83	21	2	0	0	8	1	51.2	61	233	30	22	3	2	3	3	16	3	21	1
Rodriguez, Aaron, Mil./Chi.(AL)	0	0	.000	6.00	7	0	0	0	0	0	12.0	14	60	9	8	2	0	0	4	10	0	4	1
Rodriguez, Antonio, Seattle	0	4	.000	5.95	20	6	0	0	5	2	36.1	41	194	36	24	2	3	3	7	31	1	25	5
Rodriguez, Carlos, N.Y. Mets	3	1	.750	1.84	26	0	0	0	20	7	34.1	22	137	7	7	1	2	0	0	14	1	32	1
Rodriguez, Cristobal, Montreal	0	5	.000	6.59	15	6	0	0	5	1	41.0	43	181	32	30	5	1	3	1	22	0	29	3
Rodriguez, Franklin, Seattle	2	3	.400	7.39	25	0	0	0	8	0	28.0	40	130	26	23	5	4	0	2	9	1	18	5
Rodriguez, Franklin, Toronto	6	6	.500	3.97	16	16	1	1	0	0	79.1	76	361	51	35	2	4	4	4	50	0	85	4
Rodriguez, Henry, Mil./Chi.(AL)	3	2	.600	3.62	22	0	0	0	13	6	37.1	40	173	18	15	2	1	2	4	26	3	30	1
Rodriguez, Jose, Co-op	1	1	.500	5.73	17	2	0	0	8	1	37.2	49	189	32	24	4	0	0	10	23	0	27	7
Rodriguez, Marino, Florida	0	2	.000	7.71	10	2	0	0	3	1	14.0	13	71	12	12	1	0	0	0	18	0	11	1
Rodriguez, Pedro, Seattle	4	3	.571	5.86	14	7	1	0	2	0	43.0	54	205	41	28	4	1	3	5	18	0	32	1
Rodriguez, Wilfredo, Hou.-Bos.	1	2	.333	2.97	18	0	0	0	9	0	33.1	28	150	17	11	0	2	2	4	21	0	29	3
Rojas, Cesar, Texas	7	2	.778	2.10	16	15	0	0	0	0	90.0	79	364	29	21	2	3	3	4	32	0	51	5
Rojas, Francisco, St. Louis	7	1	.875	3.18	14	14	0	0	0	0	82.0	73	338	35	29	5	3	1	5	25	1	73	5
Rojas, Juan, Atlanta	4	5	.444	3.02	11	10	0	0	0	0	59.2	51	240	23	20	4	5	0	5	20	0	52	4
Romero, Manuel, Dodgers II	5	0	1.000	1.09	10	4	1	1	2	1	41.1	30	163	9	5	0	0	2	1	8	0	26	4
Romero, Raumel, Montreal	2	5	.286	6.51	22	5	0	0	10	3	55.1	67	263	45	40	5	3	3	5	30	6	42	2
Romo, Ricardo, Hou.-Bos.	1	6	.143	4.28	13	10	0	0	0	0	48.1	64	222	31	23	1	0	2	4	6	0	23	1

her, Team	W	L	Pct.	ERA	G	GS	CG	ShO	GF	Sv.	IP	H	TBF	R	ER	HR	SH	SF	HB	BB	IBB	SO	WP	Bk.
don, Gabriel, Hou.-Bos.	4	2	.667	2.61	11	11	0	0	0	0	58.2	47	251	26	17	0	1	0	4	17	0	41	7	1
ario, Danny, Texas	2	3	.400	4.73	22	0	0	0	13	2	40.0	45	185	29	21	2	1	0	3	16	2	24	6	1
ario, Rafael, Detroit	4	1	.800	3.76	13	11	0	0	1	1	64.2	61	274	31	27	2	3	1	3	23	0	37	5	1
ario, Ramon, Oakland	6	3	.667	2.21	15	14	2	1	1	0	85.1	77	361	38	21	1	2	8	5	33	1	58	6	1
ario, Reynaldo, Detroit	3	4	.429	2.54	12	11	1	1	1	0	56.2	47	241	24	16	1	1	0	1	23	0	73	9	0
o, Rafic, Philadelphia	2	1	.667	3.58	21	0	0	0	10	2	32.2	24	151	23	13	1	4	3	3	25	0	20	4	1
no, Miguel, San Francisco	4	5	.444	3.77	22	1	0	0	11	1	45.1	46	205	28	19	1	5	2	2	24	0	35	3	1
zar, Luis, Florida	0	3	.000	12.27	12	5	0	0	3	0	14.2	13	90	24	20	1	0	1	5	31	0	8	4	0
zar, Thomas, Cleveland	3	0	.999	1.97	21	0	0	0	17	7	32.0	27	137	11	7	0	1	1	5	8	3	10	1	0
hez, Jesus, Chi.(NL)/S.D.	1	4	.200	6.17	15	6	0	0	3	0	35.0	38	171	28	24	2	1	0	1	29	0	18	4	3
hez, Jose, Detroit	1	2	.333	4.50	20	2	0	0	9	2	52.0	47	227	31	26	2	3	5	3	23	1	42	1	2
hez, Jose, Mil./Chi.(AL)	1	1	.500	6.75	7	5	0	0	2	0	17.1	14	87	15	13	2	0	1	5	16	0	9	4	1
hez, Simon, Arizona	0	4	.000	9.53	16	5	0	0	6	0	34.0	51	189	47	36	4	1	2	6	25	1	25	5	1
hez, Wellington, Chi.(NL)/S.D.	0	9	.000	6.02	15	14	3	0	0	0	86.2	99	386	71	58	13	5	4	6	25	0	55	5	0
ana, Alfredo, Detroit	5	1	.833	4.82	13	12	0	0	0	0	56.0	77	268	47	30	3	4	4	2	22	0	22	2	1
ana, Aris, Mil./Chi.(AL)	1	2	.333	7.04	16	1	0	0	3	0	30.2	34	152	29	24	3	2	2	4	25	0	26	3	0
ana, Boris, Florida	0	0	.000	8.10	10	0	0	0	1	0	10.0	20	58	14	9	1	0	1	1	7	0	6	4	0
ana, Johan, Hou.-Bos.	4	3	.571	2.70	23	1	0	0	8	3	40.0	26	168	16	12	1	2		6	22	0	51	5	0
ago, Cesar, Florida	3	3	.500	4.89	21	1	0	0	6	0	42.1	45	193	27	23	1	1	0	5	20	0	28	6	2
os, Ricardo, Co-op	7	6	.538	3.52	15	14	2	0	1	0	94.2	104	414	57	37	6	2	4	8	28	0	58	2	4
iento, Angel, Dodgers I	0	0	.000	3.54	15	0	0	0	7	1	20.1	20	83	8	8	0	1	1	1	6	0	6	1	2
ki, Junichi, Montreal	3	2	.600	5.79	14	2	0	0	5	0	32.2	43	154	29	21	4	1	0	2	17	0	18	0	1
ra, Juan, Baltimore	0	2	.000	5.96	5	3	0	0	1	0	22.2	26	106	17	15	2	2	1	1	12	0	14	2	0
no, Elio, Philadelphia	5	4	.556	4.01	15	14	1	0	0	0	85.1	76	392	63	38	2	1	5	8	49	0	71	16	1
no, Wascar, Chi.(NL)/S.D.	3	7	.300	7.88	22	2	0	0	10	1	53.2	77	263	58	47	11	4	1	1	24	1	44	11	1
Luis, Toronto	6	3	.667	2.59	23	5	2	0	14	2	73.0	64	292	27	21	3	2	0		17	0	66	3	1
rio, Marcelino, Chi.(NL)/S.D.	2	7	.222	6.95	14	8	1	0	5	1	45.1	60	224	41	35	6	0	3	4	28	1	13	5	1
o, Francisco, K.C./Colo.	4	5	.444	3.18	19	14	0	0	1	0	87.2	81	389	45	31	2	3	4	9	46	0	50	9	0
o, Stanley, Co-op	0	2	.000	16.37	14	3	0	0	6	0	27.0	53	185	61	41	1	0	4	6	42	0	11	19	0
Miguel, N.Y. Yankees	1	2	.333	2.95	18	1	0	0	14	8	36.2	31	159	20	12	4	1	4	18	1	33	11	0	
no, Gabriel, Dodgers I	3	5	.375	5.36	13	12	0	0	0	0	50.1	56	237	34	30	4	3	0	3	39	0	56	7	0
Henry, Philadelphia	3	2	.600	5.65	20	0	0	0	10	2	28.2	42	151	31	18	1	1	1	1	21	0	19	15	3
Henry, St. Louis	1	0	1.000	5.16	7	3	0	0	1	0	22.2	21	96	16	13	4	0	1	1	10	0	11	4	0
Jorby, N.Y. Yankees	2	2	.500	2.32	9	9	0	0	0	0	42.2	32	177	19	11	4	1	0	2	11	0	28	2	1
Nemuel, Oakland	2	3	.400	5.15	20	1	0	0	14	2	36.2	35	179	26	21	1	2	4	9	24	1	15	1	0
Angel, K.C./Colo.	1	3	.250	8.37	20	3	0	0	6	0	43.0	48	227	52	40	2	0	2	5	52	0	24	11	0
Antonio, Chi.(NL)/S.D.	0	1	.000	6.77	59	0	0	0	2	0	1.1	2	6	1	1	0	0	0	0	0	0	1	0	0
Manuel, Philadelphia	1	1	.500	2.73	20	0	0	0	9	4	36.1	42	162	19	11	1	0	3	2	9	0	28	3	0
z, Giancarlos, Atlanta	3	1	.750	1.69	18	0	0	0	16	6	32.0	24	135	12	6	1	2	2	1	19	1	19	2	0
z, Orlando, Dodgers I	5	2	.714	3.51	16	2	0	0	9	4	51.1	41	215	28	20	3	5	1	4	20	2	36	6	0
z, Yanis, K.C./Colo.	2	6	.250	6.21	17	5	0	0	2	0	37.2	36	182	37	26	5	1	2	6	25	1	20	8	1
ke, Ishimaro, Dodgers I	1	0	1.000	1.00	2	2	0	0	0	0	9.0	9	39	5	1	0	0	0	0	3	0	4	1	0
es, Alex, Texas	0	0	.000	2.70	6	0	0	0	3	1	10.0	10	44	6	3	0	0	0	0	5	1	4	1	0
a, Javier, Oakland	0	1	1.000	1.80	1	1	0	0	0	0	5.0	4	18	1	1	0	0	0	3	0	0	0	0	
Marcos, St. Louis	2	0	1.000	4.15	5	1	0	0	2	1	13.0	13	58	7	6	0	0	0	4	0	10	0	0	
Angel, N.Y. Yankees	1	0	1.000	2.60	14	1	0	0	4	0	27.2	31	131	15	8	2	4	2	3	20	0	13	2	1
Rafael, Detroit	6	1	.857	1.24	15	0	0	0	6	0	29.0	24	125	8	4	0	1	0	4	13	4	20	3	0
Prexilien, Atlanta	1	4	.200	4.86	20	6	0	0	6	0	50.0	50	240	43	27	1	2	1	11	41	1	26	9	4
s, Melquis, Seattle	2	2	.500	5.06	17	3	0	0	5	0	26.2	29	125	19	15	4	0	0	6	13	0	19	0	2
ad, Edwin, Arizona	2	3	.400	5.02	22	0	0	0	8	2	37.2	38	165	23	21	2	1	0	3	22	0	20	1	1
t, Andres, Mil./Chi.(AL)	0	0	.000	27.00	0	0	0	0	2	0	1.1	3	6	1	0	0	0	0	0	0	0	0	0	0
Juan, Montreal	0	4	.000	5.98	16	4	0	0	4	0	43.2	52	205	38	29	8	6	2	3	23	1	20	2	2
Victor, Mil./Chi.(AL)	0	1	.000	2.25	2	2	0	0	0	0	8.0	6	30	3	2	1	0	0	0	1	0	9	0	0
Ruben, N.Y. Mets	0	0	.000	18.57	6	0	0	0	0	0	5.1	18	38	12	11	0	0	0	0	5	0	2	2	0
uela, Jose, Chi.(NL)/S.D.	0	1	.000	7.37	6	0	0	0	3	0	7.1	10	40	6	6	0	0	1	6	0	6	3	0	
Juan, Chi.(NL)/S.D.	0	1	.000	5.82	15	3	0	0	4	0	34.0	46	159	26	22	2	2	1	20	1	18	5	0	
Nelson, California	2	7	.222	7.48	16	10	0	0	3	0	65.0	111	328	64	54	0	4	4	27	0	34	5	1	
o, Julio, Dodgers II	0	1	.000	1.25	17	0	0	0	13	4	21.2	16	90	3	3	1	0	0	8	1	35	1	0	
ucrecio, Baltimore	0	0	.000	21.56	1	0	0	0	0	0	1.2	7	15	10	4	2	0	0	1	0	0	0	0	
horst, FCO., K.C./Colo.	4	7	.364	4.11	18	15	0	0	1	0	87.2	96	383	59	40	2	2	2	2	30	1	30	7	1
s, Claudio, Florida	2	3	.400	3.09	15	4	0	0	4	0	46.2	41	204	25	16	1	3	2	5	26	0	37	4	1
s, Francisco, Cleveland	1	0	.999	2.45	16	0	0	0	6	7	15.1	16	66	7	4	0	0	0	4	0	10	0	1	
ez, Antonio, Cleveland	7	1	.875	4.08	14	14	1	0	0	0	86.0	84	370	49	39	2	4	0	7	33	0	53	1	0
ez, Cesar, Mil./Chi.(AL)	2	2	.500	5.31	23	1	0	0	9	2	39.0	45	176	26	23	2	1	1	8	15	1	19	4	0
ez, Cristian, Florida	0	0	.000	2.92	10	0	0	0	4	0	12.1	13	60	11	4	1	0	0	0	10	0	9	2	2
ez, Luis, N.Y. Mets	6	3	.667	4.91	23	1	0	0	17	6	40.1	42	172	24	22	4	1	2	3	10	0	32	1	2
Juan, San Francisco	6	2	.750	2.24	13	12	0	0	1	0	76.1	53	317	31	19	1	5	0	3	45	2	76	17	1
Jovanny, Co-op	2	1	.667	0.34	34	0	0	0	31	13	52.1	30	207	9	2	2	0	1	0	18	2	56	5	0
go, Hugo, Dodgers II	3	0	1.000	1.98	23	0	0	0	19	8	27.1	21	109	7	6	1	3	0	0	10	1	22	2	0
os, Noe, Hou.-Bos.	4	2	.667	1.13	16	9	1	0	5	1	63.2	41	245	14	8	0	0	0	0	12	0	50	3	0
eva, Robert, Florida	1	6	.143	4.50	14	13	0	0	0	0	54.0	50	242	41	27	5	3	1	5	37	0	41	5	1
, Ricardo, Detroit	7	2	.778	4.53	20	3	0	0	12	4	51.2	57	235	29	26	5	2	1	1	30	3	33	6	0
ranklin, Baltimore	3	7	.300	3.38	14	14	0	0	0	0	80.0	77	323	40	30	13	3	0	0	6	0	54	5	2
a, Juan, Pittsburgh	3	2	.600	2.88	15	0	0	0	10	2	25.0	18	103	10	8	2	2	1	2	6	3	24	0	1
, Orlando, Montreal	1	7	.125	5.75	13	13	0	0	0	0	61.0	76	296	59	39	3	1	6	4	39	1	28	7	1

1996 FIELDING

TEAM

	Pct.	G	PO	A	E	TC	DP	PB	Team	Pct.	G	PO	A	E	TC	DP	PB
s II	.957	69	1815	532	106	2453	72	30	Oakland	.953	73	1798	870	133	2801	72	15
ets	.955	71	1814	697	119	2630	46	13	Dodgers I	.952	68	1724	788	127	2639	58	17

Team	Pct.	G	PO	A	E	TC	DP	PB
Mil./Chi.(A.L.)	.950	71	1754	769	134	2657	68	15
Texas	.948	72	1849	853	149	2851	64	13
St. Louis	.946	74	1950	894	162	2865	56	11
Detroit	.945	72	1902	909	164	2975	61	21
San Francisco	.945	70	1773	762	148	2592	68	24
Arizona.............	.943	72	1799	866	162	2827	46	7
Atlanta	.941	71	1841	805	166	2812	73	29
Toronto	.940	71	1822	713	162	2697	42	28
Montreal	.937	72	1838	993	189	3020	64	10
Hou.-Bos.	.937	70	1810	764	173	2747	44	19
Baltimore	.937	70	1743	681	162	2486	49	5

Team	Pct.	G	PO	A	E	TC	DP
Pittsburgh	.935	72	1806	809	182	2797	51
Seattle..............	.933	69	1746	795	183	2724	65
Cleveland	.931	71	1903	976	214	3093	73
Florida	.928	70	1773	915	205	2893	60
N.Y. Yankees	.926	71	1821	871	214	2906	68
Chi.(NL)/S.D.	.923	73	1773	856	219	2848	55
Co-op...............	.922	70	1808	844	224	2876	67
K.C./Colo............	.916	70	1774	952	252	2978	71
Philadelphia	.913	71	1868	863	259	2990	62
T.B./Calif.	.910	71	1782	771	252	2805	44

INDIVIDUAL

Player, Team	Pos.	Pct.	PO	A	E	DP	PB
Abreu, Ruddy, Dodgers I	OF	.872	38	3	6	0	0
Acosta, Alberto, N.Y. Yankees	P	.900	3	6	1	0	0
Acuna, Ronald, N.Y. Mets	OF	.870	18	2	3	0	0
Adorno, Wilson, Pittsburgh	C	.870	15	5	3	0	2
Agli, Daniel, Montreal	1B	.985	573	38	9	3	0
Aguillera, Edgar, Dodgers II	P	.750	1	2	1	0	0
Albertus, Melaneo, Toronto	1B	.984	293	14	5	1	0
Alcala, Juan, Seattle	C	.968	185	27	7	2	4
Alcantara, Albin, St. Louis	P	.964	1	26	1	0	0
Alcantara, Lorenzo, Arizona	OF	.932	51	4	4	0	0
Alfonzo, Elieeser, St. Louis	DH	.978	42	3	1	0	0
Almonte, Aquiles, Oakland	P	.938	4	11	1	2	0
Almonte, Erick, N.Y. Yankees	3B	.848	68	133	36	15	0
Alvarez, David, Co-op	...	.940	71	8	5	2	0
Alvarez, Julio, Detroit	SS	.832	34	60	19	4	0
Alverez, Antonio, Pittsburgh	3B	.892	75	49	15	1	0
Amaya, Edilberto, Mil./Chi.(AL)	1B	.990	575	40	6	6	0
Andujar, Elias, Atlanta	P	.929	4	9	1	1	0
Andujar, Jesse, Montreal	P	.810	2	15	4	1	0
Andujar, Juan, Florida	...	.982	154	11	3	0	7
Anez, Maycoll, Mil./Chi.(AL)	P	.955	5	16	1	1	0
Aquino, Miguel, Arizona	P	.500	0	2	2	0	0
Araujo, Danilo, St. Louis	2B	.946	161	154	18	14	0
Araujo, Orlany, Dodgers I	3B	.892	39	68	13	8	0
Arcangel, Arsenio, Mil./Chi.(AL)	P	.833	1	9	2	1	0
Arias, Frank, Cleveland	...	.965	53	2	2	1	0
Arias, Jose, T.B.-Calif.	P	.889	0	8	1	0	0
Arias, Kelvin, N.Y. Mets	P	.917	4	7	1	1	0
Arias, Pablo, Detroit	P	1.000	2	2	0	0	0
Arias, Roberto, N.Y. Mets	P	.750	3	6	3	0	0
Arias, Yeison, T.B.-Calif.	LF	.900	36	0	4	0	0
Arredondo, Alan, Dodgers II	IF	.931	53	81	10	8	0
Arrendel, Eduard, Baltimore	C	.944	62	6	4	0	3
Asencio, Eddy, Detroit	P	1.000	5	9	0	3	0
Astacio, Raul T.B.-Calif.	P	1.000	1	2	0	0	0
Astudillo, Jairo, Cleveland	P	1.000	0	3	0	0	0
Aybar, Alejandro, St. Louis	P	.889	2	6	1	0	0
Aybar, Carlos, Oakland	2B	.893	26	24	6	3	0
Baez, Jose, Pittsburgh	P	.957	6	16	1	0	0
Baez, Juan, Mil./Chi.(AL)	OF	.975	110	6	3	4	0
Baez, Miguel, Cleveland	P	.800	8	12	5	1	0
Baez, Rafael, N.Y. Mets	P	1.000	0	1	0	0	0
Barrio, Elkin, Seattle	OF	.952	36	4	2	0	0
Basabe, Jesus, Oakland	OF	.958	41	5	2	0	0
Basilio, Victor, Baltimore	SS	.735	10	15	9	1	0
Batias, Hector, Baltimore	C	.966	51	5	2	0	2
Batista, Orlando, Detroit	P	1.000	3	9	0	2	0
Batista, Rafael, Seattle	P	1.000	1	4	0	0	0
Bautista, Rayner, Detroit	2B	.906	58	96	16	7	0
Beatriz, Remy, Justo, Mil./Chi. (AL)	OF	.877	48	2	7	0	0
Belliard, Carlos, Dodgers II	P	.909	0	10	1	0	0
Bello, Emerson, Seattle	P	.800	2	10	3	1	0
Beltre, Manuel, N.Y. Yankees	2B	.923	108	157	22	10	0
Benoit, Joaquin, Texas	P	1.000	2	21	0	0	0
Berroa, Carlos, Baltimore	RF	.880	43	1	6	1	0
Berroa, Cristian, Chi.(NL)/S.D.	SS	.918	87	158	22	11	0
Betancourt, Romulo, Baltimore	OF	.952	20	2	1	1	0
Betancourt, Willy, Cleveland	P	.333	0	2	4	0	0
Blanco, Fabian, Dodgers II	P	.643	3	6	5	1	0
Blanco, Felix, Mil./Chi.(AL)	DH	.894	44	40	10	9	0
Bonilla, Rusviel, Toronto	OF	.962	24	1	1	0	0
Brand, Fausto, Atlanta	P	.800	1	7	2	0	0
Bravo, Eulys, Cleveland	...	.882	14	16	4	2	0
Bravo, Luis, Co-op	P	.750	2	10	4	1	0
Brazoban, Jose, Mil./Chi.(AL)	OF	1.000	1	0	0	0	0
Brazoban, Melvin, Texas	P	.857	7	11	3	0	0
Briceno, Freddy, Montreal	SS	.927	123	169	23	12	0
Brito, Alejandro, Montreal	SS	.833	20	25	9	1	0

Player, Team	Pos.	Pct.	PO	A	E	DP
Brito, Angelo, Toronto	RF	.960	111	10	5	1
Brito, Juan, N.Y. Mets	P	.889	4	12	2	0
Brito, Justo, N.Y. Mets	C	.954	57	5	3	0
Brito, Obispo, Mil./Chi.(AL)	C	.968	109	12	4	0
Burelli, Luis, Mil./Chi.(AL)	C	.962	159	41	8	0
Bustamante, Omar, Dodgers I	C	.968	138	42	6	2
Bustillos, Luis, Dodgers II	SS	.883	80	63	19	26
Cabral, Martinez, Toronto	P	1.000	3	4	0	0
Cabrera, Danny, N.Y. Mets	1B	.983	423	27	8	3
Cabrera, Raymond, Baltimore	IF	.973	69	3	2	1
Caceres, Antonio, Toronto	P	1.000	9	5	0	0
Calderon, Paulino, Florida	P	.833	2	8	2	0
Calzada, Javier, Oakland	P	.900	3	6	1	0
Camilo, Juan, Oakland	OF	.952	74	5	4	1
Campusano, Juan Carlos, Mil./Chi.(AL) ..	P	.800	1	7	2	1
Campusano, Lenny, T.B.-Calif.	P	1.000	1	3	0	0
Candelario, Alexis, Seattle	DH	1.000	2	0	0	0
Carpenter, Donald, Toronto	OF	1.000	8	1	0	0
Carpio, Roberto, St. Louis	OF	.933	54	2	4	0
Carrasco, Ricardo, Atlanta	OF	1.000	28	0	0	0
Carrasquel, Alejandro, Montreal	P	.800	1	7	2	0
Carreno, Jose, Montreal	C	.967	77	12	3	0
Carrera, Carlos, Arizona	P	.909	6	14	2	1
Castellano, Alexis, Chi.(NL)/S.D.	2B	.904	63	78	15	4
Castillo, Alexander, Mil./Chi.(AL)	3B	.925	114	96	17	12
Castillo, Alexander, Seattle	P	.000	0	0	1	0
Castillo, Edgar, T.B.-Calif.	P	1.000	3	5	0	0
Castillo, Geramel, Texas	3B	.908	43	56	10	5
Castillo, Hanlet, Seattle	P	1.000	0	1	0	0
Castillo, Jose, Detroit	P	1.000	3	9	0	0
Castillo, Marcos, Dodgers I	P	1.000	1	4	0	0
Castillo, Ramon, Florida	P	1.000	0	1	0	0
Castillo, Wilson, Dodgers I	P	.810	4	13	4	
Castro, Jesus, Toronto	C	.970	61	4	2	
Castro, Jorge, Dodgers II	C	.973	32	4	1	
Castro, Martires, Texas	OF	.950	105	9	6	
Ceballos, Alfredo, Chi.(NL)/S.D.	P	.750	0	3	1	
Centeno, Edwin, Baltimore	CF	.925	90	8	8	
Cepeda, Wellington, Arizona	P	.889	3	13	2	
Cequera, Jesus, T.B.-Calif.	P	.818	1	8	2	
Chalas, Alexis, Detroit	2B	.927	46	69	9	
Chalas, Bernardo, Montreal	P	1.000	1	4	0	
Charle, Juan, Dodgers I	P	.917	3	8	1	
Chavez, Endy, N.Y. Mets	OF	.963	77	1	3	
Chirinos, Germain, Oakland	...	.900	7	2	1	
Ciciola, Miguel, Dodgers I	OF	.919	54	3	5	
Ciociola, David, N.Y. Yankees	2B	.800	4	8	3	
Ciprian, Ernesto, Baltimore	RF	.950	35	3	2	
Clarke, Elvis, Baltimore	P	.800	0	8	2	
Classen, Ender, Pittsburgh	3B	.833	8	17	5	
Cocco, Pascual, Toronto	P	.846	4	18	4	
Colon, Jose, Cleveland	P	.667	1	1	1	
Colon, Roman, Atlanta	P	.800	4	8	3	
Contreras, Angel, Pittsburgh	P	1.000	5	8	0	
Cordero, Willi, Texas	SS	.896	97	128	26	1
Cordoba, Gregory, Atlanta	P	.909	2	8	1	
Cordova, Jorge, N.Y. Yankees	P	.875	3	4	1	
Cornielle, Henry, Oakland	P	.727	2	6	3	
Corporan, Manuel, Baltimore	IF	.957	35	31	3	
Cosme, Caonabo, Oakland	SS	.928	105	190	23	
Cruz, Charles, Baltimore	P	1.000	1	4	0	
Cruz, Rafael, Texas	C	.938	25	5	2	
Cruz, Silvio, Detroit	3B	.953	38	63	5	
Cueto, Joe, Texas	1B	.963	178	5	7	
Cueto, Jose, Seattle	P	.818	3	6	2	
Cuvillan, Jose, Texas	OF	1.000	4	0	0	
De Jesus, Robert, Texas	P	.800	0	8	2	
De Jesus, Wilmer, Montreal	C	.988	136	32	2	

Player, Team	Pos.	Pct.	PO	A	E	DP	PB
e La Cruz, Andres, N.Y. Yankees	P	1.000	1	4	0	1	0
e La Cruz, Antonio, N.Y. Mets	SS	.900	72	118	21	17	0
e La Cruz, Erickson, Mil./Chi.(AL)	OF	.942	55	10	4	0	0
e La Cruz, Henry, Chi.(NL)/S.D.	OF	.949	121	9	7	1	0
e La Cruz, Inocencio, N.Y. Mets	P	1.000	2	6	0	0	0
e La Cruz, Jose, Oakland	3B	.848	46	94	25	5	0
e La Cruz, Raul, Pittsburgh	OF	.956	141	10	7	2	0
e La Rosa, Cristian, Baltimore	P	.750	1	5	2	0	0
e Leon, Jose, Detroit	DH	.000	0	0	1	0	0
e Leon, Jose, Montreal	P	.833	0	5	1	0	0
e Leon, Raymundo, St. Louis	OF	.976	235	10	6	0	0
e Los Santos, Aurelio, St. Louis	P	.917	4	7	1	0	0
e Los Santos, Francisco, N.Y. Mets	OF	.932	49	6	4	1	0
e Los Santos, Jose, St. Louis	P	1.000	1	1	0	1	0
e Valle, Carlos, Detroit	1B	.993	560	44	4	2	0
elgado, Ramon, Seattle	1B	.980	419	19	9	2	0
elisa, Carlos, Chi.(NL)/S.D.	P	.750	2	7	3	0	0
iaz, Bolivar, Texas	2B	.928	31	46	6	3	0
iaz, Eddy, Atlanta	C	.833	10	0	2	0	4
iaz, Elvis, Oakland	OF	.965	69	13	3	2	0
iaz, Esteban, Dodgers I	P	1.000	2	8	0	1	0
iaz, Ivan, St. Louis	1B	.978	345	61	9	1	0
iaz, Juan, Dodgers II	1B	.988	79	3	1	0	0
iaz, Meikell, Baltimore	3B	.951	83	111	10	3	0
az, Miguel, St. Louis	OF	.896	83	3	10	3	0
sla, Francisco, N.Y. Yankees	P	.000	0	0	1	0	0
ominguez, Candido, Detroit	C	.987	64	10	1	0	3
ominguez, Enrique, Montreal	OF	.957	82	7	4	3	0
urango, Ariel, Seattle	2B	.959	89	122	9	9	0
is, Franklin, Mil./Chi.(AL)	OF	1.000	5	0	0	0	0
carnacion, Anibal, T.B.-Calif.	P	.600	3	2	0	0	0
carnacion, Bernardo, T.B.-Calif.	SS	.929	43	101	11	4	0
carnacion, Sonder, Seattle	3B	.952	51	67	6	4	0
nesto, Hector, Florida	P	.667	0	2	1	0	0
cobar, Edwin, Toronto	P	1.000	1	0	0	0	0
cobar, Luis, Seattle	P	.857	4	2	1	0	0
pino, Fernando, Seattle	OF	.936	82	6	6	2	0
pinosa, Andres, Montreal	OF	.947	17	1	1	0	0
tevez, Domingo, Toronto	IF	.857	47	55	17	1	0
trella, Gorky, Seattle	3B	.846	29	59	16	6	0
sebio, Alberto, St. Louis	P	1.000	0	2	0	0	0
con, Edwin, Dodgers II	C	1.000	42	3	0	1	1
iz, Sergio, Co-op	...	.855	77	136	36	8	0
rnandez, Jose, Arizona	P	1.000	1	6	0	1	0
rnandez, Juan, Co-op	...	.774	44	38	24	5	0
rnandez, Medardo, Florida	OF	.981	96	10	2	1	1
rnandez, Samuel, T.B.-Calif.	P	1.000	2	6	0	0	0
rnandez, Winston, Texas	OF	.967	110	6	4	1	0
reira, Luis, Co-op		.925	103	21	10	3	2
ueroa, Erasmo, Mil./Chi.(AL)	P	1.000	0	6	0	0	0
ueroa, Juan, Mil./Chi.(AL)	P	.765	3	10	4	1	0
rentino, Junior, Pittsburgh	DH	1.000	14	0	0	0	0
res, Luis, Toronto	P	1.000	0	6	0	0	0
ncisco, Hector, Atlanta	C	.962	147	31	7	2	13
nco, Francisco, Pittsburgh	P	.833	4	6	2	0	0
nco, Jorby, Atlanta	P	.875	1	13	2	1	0
nco, Jorge, Montreal	C	.951	71	26	5	0	1
nco, Jose, N.Y. Mets	P	1.000	1	10	0	0	0
nco, Jose, N.Y. Yankees	P	.917	2	9	1	0	0
nco, Pascual, St. Louis	1B	.944	77	7	5	1	1
nco, Santo, Chi.(NL)/S.D.	P	.875	1	6	1	0	0
s, Amauris, Chi.(NL)/S.D.	P	.714	1	4	2	0	0
s, Jovanny, Mil./Chi.(AL)	P	.900	2	7	1	0	0
s, Juan, T.B.-Calif.	P	.900	4	9	1	1	0
ban, Elvis, Montreal	3B	.903	70	134	22	7	0
vez, Randy, Dodgers II	P	.821	4	19	5	1	0
abito, Eddy, Baltimore	2B	.912	128	121	24	14	0
cia, Alexander, Chi.(NL)/S.D.	3B	.644	21	33	10	3	0
cia, Alfredo, N.Y. Mets	3B	.929	97	59	12	1	0
cia, Alvaro, Dodgers I	OF	.966	56	1	2	0	0
cia, Antony, T.B.-Calif.	LF	.943	31	2	2	0	0
cia, Eduardo, T.B.-Calif.	2B	.898	38	41	9	3	0
cia, Epedy, Oakland	P	.826	2	17	4	0	0
cia, Jose, Cleveland	P	.944	1	16	1	2	0
cia, Jose, Co-op	P	1.000	1	6	0	0	0
cia, Juan, Atlanta	OF	.935	79	8	6	6	0
cia, Luis, Dodgers I	2B	.943	96	87	11	5	0
cia, Rosman, N.Y. Yankees	P	.867	3	10	2	1	0
ao, Antonio, Arizona	1B	.982	255	13	5	1	0
ao, Manuel, Toronto	C	.986	134	7	2	0	7
ao, Martin, Dodgers II	P	.941	5	11	1	1	0
man, Aris, N.Y. Mets	C	.964	221	22	9	0	3

Player, Team	Pos.	Pct.	PO	A	E	DP	PB
German, Armando, Pittsburgh	P	1.000	0	4	0	0	0
German, John, N.Y. Mets	P	.900	6	12	2	2	0
German, Manuel, Arizona	OF	.989	84	5	1	1	0
Gil, Alberto, Cleveland	...	.974	384	25	11	3	0
Giron, Edilberto, Pittsburgh	P	.875	44	5	7	1	0
Gomera, Rafael, Dodgers II	OF	.930	64	2	5	0	0
Gomez, Nelson, T.B.-Calif.	C	.947	129	13	8	0	3
Gomez, Ricardo, Pittsburgh	P	.625	2	3	3	0	0
Gondola, Roberto, N.Y. Yankees	P	.913	4	17	2	1	0
Gonzalez, Adalberto, Montreal	SS	.842	32	64	18	5	0
Gonzalez, Franklin, Chi.(NL)/S.D.	OF	.959	113	5	5	0	0
Gonzalez, Luis, Oakland	P	1.000	4	15	0	2	0
Gonzalez, Milciades, T.B.-Calif.	OF	.963	75	2	3	2	0
Guedez, Luis, Mil./Chi.(AL)	2B	.971	83	86	5	5	0
Guerra, Luis, T.B.-Calif.	P	.667	0	4	2	0	0
Guerrero, Francisco, T.B.-Calif.	RF	.862	20	5	4	2	0
Guerrero, Pedro, Texas	2B	.893	66	93	19	9	0
Guevara, Carlos, Pittsburgh	P	.800	1	3	1	0	0
Guillen, Daniel, T.B.-Calif.	P	.857	1	5	1	0	0
Guillen, Hipolito, Seattle	...	.979	43	4	1	1	0
Gutierrez, Ruben, N.Y. Mets	P	1.000	0	3	0	0	0
Gutierrez, Victor, Pittsburgh	2B	.963	166	171	13	16	0
Guzman, Ambiorix, Texas	P	1.000	2	19	0	3	0
Guzman, Antonio, Arizona	OF	.946	94	11	6	0	0
Guzman, Carlos, Detroit	OF	.945	99	5	6	3	0
Guzman, Elpidio, T.B.-Calif.	OF	.929	76	2	6	0	0
Guzman, Juan, Baltimore	C	.994	298	40	2	0	0
Guzman, Juan, St. Louis	P	1.000	0	1	0	1	0
Guzman, Levin, Co-op	P	1.000	0	4	0	0	0
Guzman, Pedro, Arizona	P	1.000	1	7	0	0	0
Guzman, Santos, Pittsburgh	1B	.893	49	1	6	0	0
Guzman, Wilson, Pittsburgh	P	.857	1	11	2	0	0
Guzman, Yorki, N.Y. Mets	OF	.822	57	3	13	0	0
Haad, Yamid, Pittsburgh	C	.994	402	59	3	2	5
Helena, Hector, St. Louis	C	.984	51	11	1	0	2
Henriquez, Roman, Dodgers I	P	.833	5	10	3	1	0
Hernandez, German, Texas	P	.923	1	11	1	0	0
Hernandez, Hector, Florida	P	.775	4	27	9	1	0
Hernandez, Jose, Montreal	P	1.000	1	3	0	0	0
Hernandez, Juan, Detroit	P	.667	1	1	1	0	0
Hernandez, Leonardo, N.Y. Mets	OF	.979	46	1	1	0	0
Hernandez, Luis, Arizona	C	.923	83	13	8	0	4
Hernandez, Luis, T.B.-Calif.	P	.876	81	4	12	0	0
Hernandez, Pedro, Dodgers II	P	.882	3	12	2	3	0
Hernandez, Pedro, Texas	1B	.979	181	9	4	0	0
Herrera, Anthony, Co-op	P	.889	5	11	2	2	0
Herrera, Gabriel, Seattle	C	.979	171	20	4	1	4
Herrera, Juan, Montreal	P	.964	127	33	6	1	7
Herrera, Misael, Chi.(NL)/S.D.	P	.850	3	14	3	0	0
Herrera, Onesimo, N.Y. Mets	OF	.988	75	10	1	0	0
Hiraldo, Juan, Co-op	P	.833	1	9	2	0	0
Hiraldo, Julio, Cleveland	P	.667	1	1	1	0	0
Hiromasa, Ito, N.Y. Yankees	OF	1.000	3	1	0	0	0
Hodge, Hector, Cleveland	...	.800	27	21	12	1	0
Icenia, Shiron, T.B.-Calif.	C	.958	486	67	24	3	6
Infante, Danny, Texas	1B	.960	302	62	15	5	0
Izquierdo, Roberto, Florida	P	.875	4	10	2	0	0
Jadagui, Carlos, Chi.(NL)/S.D.	DH	1.000	8	0	0	0	0
Jaquez, Raul, Cleveland	...	.802	23	46	17	4	0
Jasso, Oscar, Dodgers II	P	1.000	1	15	0	1	0
Jimenez, Alejandro, Texas	P	1.000	1	2	0	0	0
Jimenez, Bartolo, Atlanta	SS	.887	25	38	8	6	0
Jimenez, Cristian, Cleveland	...	.955	118	10	6	1	0
Jimenez, Elieeser, Dodgers I	OF	.987	72	6	1	2	0
Jimenez, Francisco, Arizona	P	.900	0	18	2	0	0
Jimenez, Lautico, Atlanta	P	.000	0	0	1	0	0
Jimenez, Mario, Seattle	P	1.000	0	2	0	0	0
Jimenez, Raul, St. Louis	3B	.857	3	3	1	0	0
Jimenez, Santos, Baltimore	P	1.000	0	6	0	0	0
Jiron, Isabel, Toronto	P	1.000	1	10	0	0	0
Johnston, Charles, Detroit	P	.867	5	8	2	0	0
Juarez, Johnny, Toronto	OF	.948	54	1	3	0	0
Julio, Jorge, Montreal	P	1.000	0	2	0	0	0
Kamar, Emil, Dodgers I	P	1.000	0	2	0	0	0
King, Daniel, Oakland	2B	.977	458	13	11	1	0
Lajara, Eudy, Florida	P	.769	2	8	3	0	0
Lake, Patricio, Florida	OF	.864	66	10	12	3	0
Lanfranco, Otoniel, St. Louis	P	1.000	2	5	0	0	0
Lantigua, Felix, N.Y. Yankees	C	1.000	9	1	0	0	0
Lara, Balmes, Detroit	OF	.921	32	3	3	1	0
Lara, Felix, Pittsburgh	OF	.921	122	7	11	1	0
Lara, Juan, Chi.(NL)/S.D.	OF	.889	29	3	4	2	0
Lemus, Julian, N.Y. Yankees	OF	.922	47	0	4	0	0

Player, Team	Pos.	Pct.	PO	A	E	DP	PB
Leon, Rafael, Florida	P	1.000	2	6	0	0	0
Linares, Agustin, Baltimore	P	.778	3	18	6	0	0
Linares, Edwin, Atlanta	P	.913	3	18	2	0	0
Linares, Rafael, Baltimore	P	.571	2	2	3	0	0
Linares, Ramon, Co-op	P	1.000	7	6	0	0	0
Liriano, Nelson, Arizona	P	1.000	0	2	0	0	0
Lluveres, Alberto, Baltimore	P	1.000	0	3	0	0	0
Loaisiga, Stalin, Montreal	OF	.940	118	7	8	3	0
Lopez, Gustavo, Florida	P	.750	1	5	2	0	0
Lopez, Jose, Arizona	3B	.954	266	90	17	5	0
Lopez, Miguel, Arizona	C	.970	55	10	2	0	0
Lopez, Raul, Dodgers I	DH	.975	37	2	1	0	0
Lopez, Reymundo, Dodgers I	P	.625	1	4	3	1	0
Lopez, Victor, Detroit	2B	.883	22	31	7	4	0
Loyo, Oscar, Florida	1B	.961	285	58	14	9	0
Lugo, Juan, Seattle	SS	.829	23	35	12	7	0
Lugo, William, Oakland	C	.966	48	8	2	0	2
Manzueta, Robert, Arizona	P	.800	1	7	2	0	0
Marcano, Carlos, Florida	2B	.962	101	102	8	7	0
Marichal, Rafael, Pittsburgh	P	.750	2	4	2	0	0
Marin, Jaime, Florida	3B	.846	19	36	10	0	0
Marte, Juan, St. Louis	OF	.940	85	9	6	0	0
Marte, Nestor, Detroit	OF	.967	110	9	4	1	0
Martinez, Alejandro, Oakland	1B	1.000	184	7	0	0	0
Martinez, Andres, N.Y. Mets	2B	.968	138	135	9	6	0
Martinez, Belvany, Arizona	2B	.917	70	73	13	3	0
Martinez, Daniel, Chi.(NL)/S.D.	2B	.925	48	38	7	2	0
Martinez, Francisco, Chi.(NL)/S.D.	P	1.000	1	5	0	0	0
Martinez, Francisco, Mil./Chi.(AL)	P	.769	4	6	3	0	0
Martinez, Gregorio, Co-op	...	.964	377	25	15	0	0
Martinez, Luis, Dodgers II	2B	.955	125	127	12	16	0
Martinez, Luis, Toronto	C	.978	291	24	7	0	3
Martinez, Obispo, Montreal	P	1.000	4	7	0	0	0
Martinez, Odis, Detroit	C	.958	60	8	3	0	7
Martinez, Osvaldo, Texas	1B	.875	21	0	3	0	0
Martinez, Reynaldo, Chi.(NL)/S.D.	C	.939	191	23	14	0	9
Martinez, Rodolfo, Cleveland	...	.900	2	7	1	1	0
Martinez, Rosario, N.Y. Mets	P	1.000	0	1	0	0	0
Martinez, Victor, Detroit	3B	.950	104	29	7	4	0
Martinez, Winston, Detroit	DH	.667	0	2	1	0	0
Mateo, Freddy, Dodgers II	OF	1.000	36	1	0	0	0
Mateo, Julio, Seattle	P	.857	0	6	1	0	0
Matias, Hansell, Atlanta	P	.950	3	16	1	3	0
Maysonet, Jose, Toronto	IF	.900	68	94	18	12	0
McLean, Guillermo, Co-op	...	.951	55	3	3	0	0
Medina, Luis, Atlanta	3B	.851	59	146	36	8	0
Medina, Luis, Chi.(NL)/S.D.	1B	.921	252	76	28	8	0
Medina, Richie, Detroit	2B	.923	8	4	1	1	0
Medrano, David, Texas	2B	.952	73	84	8	5	0
Medrano, Oscar, T.B.-Calif.	IF	.651	73	114	22	4	0
Medrano, Ramon, Montreal	P	.500	0	2	2	0	0
Mejia, Javier, Florida	3B	.896	41	88	15	1	0
Mejia, Jose, Atlanta	C	.988	157	8	2	3	2
Mejia, Luis, N.Y. Yankees	P	.750	0	3	1	0	0
Mejia, Maximiliano, Dodgers II	OF	.864	36	2	6	1	0
Mejia, Oliver, Pittsburgh	SS	.915	152	117	25	3	0
Mejia, Orlando, N.Y. Mets	P	.818	2	7	2	0	0
Mejia, Renato, Florida	OF	.944	274	13	17	1	0
Melendez, Emmy, T.B.-Calif.	C	.925	100	11	9	2	2
Mendez, Jose, Atlanta	P	1.000	0	1	0	0	0
Mendoza, Carlos, Co-op	P	.938	2	13	1	1	0
Mercado, Hector, Detroit	P	.875	2	12	2	0	0
Mercedes, Carlos, Dodgers I	SS	.928	57	98	12	14	0
Mercedes, Jorge, Oakland	P	1.000	1	4	0	0	0
Mercedes, Tomas, Toronto	P	.333	5	5	5	0	0
Mesina, Juan, Florida	P	1.000	2	1	0	1	0
Meza, Gonzalo, Dodgers II	OF	1.000	23	1	0	0	0
Mijares, Robert, Dodgers I	OF	.984	55	5	1	0	0
Minaya, Pablo, Florida	P	.846	2	9	2	0	0
Mitchel, Yaqui, N.Y. Yankees	P	.667	0	2	1	0	0
Molina, Alfredo, Dodgers II	IF	.778	1	6	2	0	0
Molina, Kenneth, Detroit	OF	.969	31	0	1	0	0
Montalvo, Reynaldo, Seattle	P	1.000	1	7	0	0	0
Montanez, John, Toronto	P	.735	4	21	9	0	0
Montas, Juan, T.B.-Calif.	C	.905	58	9	7	0	1
Montero, Agustin, Oakland	P	.875	6	15	3	0	0
Montero, Jose, Atlanta	3B	.931	29	38	5	4	0
Montero, Oscar, Mil./Chi.(AL)	P	1.000	7	0	0	0	0
Morales, Anaximandro, Atlanta	1B	.976	503	19	13	2	0
Morales, Victor, Toronto	IF	.879	36	51	12	7	0
Morel, Jose, Pittsburgh	P	.800	0	4	1	0	0
Morel, Ramon, Cleveland	P	.889	4	12	2	1	0
Morelo, Fulvio, N.Y. Yankees	SS	.929	73	136	16	13	0

Player, Team	Pos.	Pct.	PO	A	E	DP	P
Moreno, Franklin, Mil./Chi.(AL)	DH	1.000	6	7	0	0	
Moreno, Johnny, Baltimore	IF	.940	200	19	14	2	
Moreno, Jorge, Mil./Chi.(AL)	P	1.000	1	6	0	1	
Moreno, Nestor, N.Y. Mets	3B	.970	62	36	3	1	
Moreta, Ramon, Dodgers II	CF	.977	123	7	3	0	
Morillo, Humberto, N.Y. Yankees	P	.500	0	3	3	0	
Morillo, Luis, Toronto	CF	.982	100	7	2	2	
Morla, Cresencio, Baltimore	P	.667	1	3	2	0	
Morrobel, Juan, Pittsburgh	P	.750	1	5	2	1	
Moscat, Rafael, Arizona	SS	.907	35	43	8	7	
Mota, Delcio, T.B.-Calif.	3B	.882	36	76	15	7	
Mota, Juan, T.B.-Calif.	OF	.929	48	4	4	0	
Mota, Victor, Detroit	OF	.882	14	1	2	0	
Mundo, Alberto, Atlanta	SS	.924	129	187	26	18	
Munil, Jose, T.B.-Calif.	P	1.000	1	5	0	0	
Nieves, Juan, Toronto	1B	.977	159	12	4	1	
Nin, Daurin, St. Louis	P	.750	1	5	2	0	
Nin, Geldy, St. Louis	3B	.894	47	79	15	5	
Nina, Amaury, Texas	OF	.953	139	4	7	0	
Nina, Ignacio, Co-op	...	.922	99	91	16	5	
Nina, Juan, Mil./Chi.(AL)	P	1.000	2	1	0	0	
Nolasco, Ragino, Baltimore	SS	.917	124	198	29	11	
Nova, Joselyn, Florida	C	.974	400	79	13	1	
Nunez, Hector, Detroit	2B	.859	22	45	11	5	
Nunez, Jorge, Toronto	IF	.869	69	182	38	12	
Nunez, Jose, N.Y. Mets	P	1.000	1	5	0	1	
Nunez, Jose, Oakland	C	.981	120	34	3	1	
Offerman, Juan, N.Y. Yankees	OF	.911	70	2	7	0	
Ogando, Alberto, T.B.-Calif.	P	.783	8	10	5	0	
Olivares, Melvin, N.Y. Mets	3B	.951	100	134	12	7	
Olivares, Teuris, N.Y. Yankees	SS	.857	5	7	2	1	
Ortega, Carlos, Dodgers I	1B	.983	163	9	3	0	
Ortega, Jose, N.Y. Yankees	OF	.957	20	2	1	2	
Ortiz, Eusebio, St. Louis	P	.950	4	15	1	0	
Ortiz, Jose, Arizona	C	.976	101	19	3	0	
Ortiz, Pedro, Dodgers I	P	1.000	0	3	0	1	
Ovalles, Jesus, Co-op	...	.936	75	173	17	15	
Ozoria, Jose, Texas	P	1.000	0	4	0	2	
Ozuna, Alexis, Mil./Chi.(AL)	C	.988	129	32	2	0	
Ozuna, Pablo, St. Louis	SS	.915	126	219	32	16	
Pacheco, Domingo, Seattle	SS	.835	35	66	20	13	
Padilla, Jesus, Arizona	P	1.000	3	0	0	0	
Padua, Geraldo, N.Y. Yankees	P	.733	4	7	4	0	
Palacios, Ismael, Dodgers I	P	.923	4	8	1	1	
Pamphile, Luis, Dodgers I	C	.946	107	16	7	1	
Paredes, Miguel, Seattle	3B	.833	37	48	17	2	
Paredes, Omar, Chi.(NL)/S.D.	P	1.000	0	6	0	0	
Parra, Jorge, Co-op	P	1.000	3	7	0	0	
Parra, Klisber, Florida	P	1.000	2	6	0	1	
Paul, Antonio, St. Louis	P	.750	1	2	1	0	
Paulino, Arison, Pittsburgh	P	1.000	7	14	0	1	
Paulino, Dennis, Atlanta	OF	.946	32	3	2	2	
Paulino, Noel, Pittsburgh	P	.625	2	3	0	0	
Paulino, Warren, N.Y. Yankees	OF	.948	97	13	6	1	
Payamps, Jose, Arizona	RF	.973	66	6	2	0	
Peguero, Radhames, T.B.-Calif.	RF	.880	66	6	9	1	
Pellerano, Cristian, Oakland	DH	1.000	3	2	0	0	
Pena, Amaury, N.Y. Yankees	2B	.889	60	108	21	9	
Pena, Angel, Dodgers II	P	.990	86	11	1	0	
Pena, David, Mil./Chi.(AL)	P	1.000	0	1	0	0	
Pena, Elvin, Seattle	C	.964	130	29	6	0	
Pena, Jose, Cleveland	P	1.000	3	20	0	0	
Pena, Jose, T.B.-Calif.	3B	.741	21	44	16	2	
Pena, Juan, Oakland	P	.846	0	11	2	0	
Pena, Raynaldo, Detroit	SS	.915	65	184	23	11	
Pena, Sandy, Arizona	OF	.910	52	9	6	1	
Pepen, Robert, N.Y. Mets	P	1.000	3	3	0	0	
Peralta, Ariel, Oakland	DH	1.000	1	0	0	0	
Perez, Alejandro, Hou.-Bos	OF	1.000	17	5	0	3	
Perez, Ambiorix, Texas	P	1.000	0	1	0	0	
Perez, Angel, Dodgers II	1B	.979	620	24	14	2	
Perez, Carlos, Arizona	P	.889	2	14	2	0	
Perez, David, Atlanta	C	.990	166	35	2	1	
Perez, Edison, Seattle	OF	.930	77	3	6	1	
Perez, Jose, Arizona	C	.966	186	38	8	0	
Perez, Jose, Texas	P	1.000	0	3	0	0	
Perez, Nairon, Texas	P	.500	1	0	1	0	
Perez, Nililberto, Chi.(NL)/S.D.	P	.714	0	10	4	1	
Perez, Norberto, Baltimore	P	.800	2	10	3	2	
Perez, Robert, T.B.-Calif.	P	.778	1	6	2	0	
Perez, Samuel, Cleveland	P	.818	0	9	2	0	
Perez Valdez, Jose, Arizona	P	.833	0	5	1	0	
Pichardo, Henry, Cleveland	...	.964	164	159	12	11	

Player, Team	Pos.	Pct.	PO	A	E	DP	PB
...meiro, Juan, Chi.(NL)/S.D.	2B	.934	100	125	16	9	0
...mentel, Franklin, Oakland	2B	.961	63	59	5	5	0
...mentel, Raul, St. Louis	3B	.881	82	51	18	5	0
...nales, Otilio, Seattle	P	1.000	1	0	0	0	0
...tre, Diogenes, Oakland	P	.833	3	7	2	0	0
...lanco, Rodney, Seattle	OF	.968	28	2	1	0	0
...lanco, Winston, Cleveland	...	.935	26	3	2	1	0
...ingle, Juan, N.Y. Yankees	DH	.975	74	4	2	0	1
...jols, Rafael, Oakland	C	.979	214	63	6	2	8
...ero, Pedro, Montreal	OF	.948	82	9	5	3	0
...iros, Misael Pittsburgh	P	.905	7	12	2	0	0
...mirez, Bienvenido, Chi.(NL)/S.D.	C	.954	84	20	5	0	5
...mirez, Frankelis, Dodgers I	1B	.978	422	21	10	1	0
...mirez, Junior, T.B.-Calif.	SS	.842	85	107	36	9	0
...mirez, Narciso, Montreal	OF	.967	107	11	4	2	0
...mirez, Rafael, Detroit	OF	.936	43	1	3	0	0
...mos, Eddy, Co-op	...	.932	101	9	8	0	0
...mos, Jacinto, Cleveland	P	.692	3	6	4	1	0
...mos, Jose, Dodgers I	P	1.000	1	10	0	0	0
...mos, Juan, Montreal	P	1.000	11	15	0	1	0
...mos, Kelly, N.Y. Mets	C	1.000	80	13	0	1	1
...bolledo, Jairo, Chi.(NL)/S.D.	1B	.960	247	14	11	3	0
...galado, Maximo, Dodgers I	P	.941	1	15	1	1	0
...my, Ernesto, Montreal	P	.750	3	0	1	0	0
...ngifo, D.J., Mil./Chi.(AL)	OF	.945	101	3	6	0	0
...yes, Anderson, N.Y. Mets	P	.833	0	5	1	1	0
...yes, Berardo, St. Louis	P	1.000	4	10	0	0	0
...yes, Carlos, T.B.-Calif.	P	.500	1	1	2	1	0
...yes, Cristian, Oakland	3B	.968	17	43	2	5	0
...yes, Dauris, Detroit	OF	.919	77	2	7	0	0
...yes, Juan, Montreal	P	.962	0	25	1	1	0
...yes, Juan, Pittsburgh	P	1.000	1	2	0	0	0
...yes, Natanahel, Dodgers II	P	1.000	1	7	0	0	0
...yes, Pedro, N.Y. Yankees	P	.769	2	8	3	0	0
...yes, Santo, St. Louis	P	1.000	1	5	0	0	0
...ynoso Gil, Aristides, Arizona	3B	.959	47	46	4	3	0
...noso, Franklin, Atlanta	3B-P	.905	6	13	2	0	0
...hardson, Elvis, Co-op	...	.878	74	63	19	5	0
..., Fernando, Dodgers II	...	.857	3	9	2	2	0
...cones, Gabriel, Seattle	P	.947	5	13	1	0	0
...era, Homero, Detroit	P	.800	4	4	2	0	0
...era, Juan, N.Y. Yankees	OF	1.000	4	0	0	0	0
...era, Orlando, Mil./Chi.(AL)	SS	.871	31	50	12	8	0
...era, Yorkis, Co-op	...	.955	132	15	7	2	0
...ert, Randolph, N.Y. Mets	C	.986	177	27	3	1	8
...bles, Victor, Baltimore	RF	.100	10	0	0	0	0
...he, Angel, Texas	P	1.000	1	9	0	0	0
...riguez, Aaron, Mil./Chi.(AL)	P	1.000	1	1	0	0	0
...riguez, Alfredo, Dodgers II	C	.979	198	36	5	1	23
...riguez, Antonio, Seattle	P	.769	0	10	3	0	0
...riguez, Carlos, N.Y. Mets	P	.909	1	9	1	0	0
...riguez, Cristobal, Montreal	P	.800	0	4	1	0	0
...riguez, Euris, Cleveland	...	.976	205	41	6	3	9
...riguez, Felipe, Toronto	2B	.943	129	135	16	5	0
...riguez, Franklin, Seattle	P	.789	11	4	4	0	0
...riguez, Franklin, Toronto	P	.706	2	10	5	0	0
...riguez, Frei, Baltimore	1B	.100	44	5	0	1	0
...riguez, Henry, Mil./Chi.(AL)	P	.800	1	7	2	1	0
...riguez, Jose, Co-op	P	.818	3	6	2	0	0
...riguez, Jose, Florida	2B	.913	36	37	7	3	0
...riguez, Juan, Atlanta	2B	.913	32	41	7	4	0
...riguez, Marino, Florida	P	1.000	0	2	0	0	0
...riguez, Miguel, St. Louis	OF	.925	81	18	8	1	0
...riguez, Pablo, Cleveland	...	.910	107	105	21	7	0
...riguez, Pedro, Seattle	P	1.000	1	8	0	0	0
...riguez, Rafael, Cleveland	P	.924	113	82	16	5	0
...iguez, Ramon, N.Y. Yankees	DH	.946	185	9	11	1	0
...s, Cesar, Texas	P	1.000	3	7	0	0	0
...s, Elieeser, Mil./Chi.(AL)	2B	.951	78	116	10	7	0
...s, Francisco, St. Louis	P	.944	3	14	1	1	0
...s, Isaias, Baltimore	RF	.897	79	8	10	2	0
...s, Juan, Atlanta	P	1.000	1	9	0	1	0
...ero, Manuel, Dodgers II	P	.917	3	8	1	0	0
...ero, Raumel, Montreal	P	.864	3	16	3	0	0
...don, Johnny, Seattle	P	.875	47	114	23	12	0
..., Ivan, Oakland	DH	1.000	17	4	0	0	0
...ario, Danny, Texas	P	1.000	1	5	0	0	0
...ario, Omar, Seattle	OF	.967	111	5	4	3	0
...ario, Rafael, Detroit	P	.909	1	9	1	0	0
...ario, Ramon, Oakland	P	.864	0	19	3	0	0
...ario, Reynaldo, Detroit	P	1.000	1	4	0	0	0
...zar, Luis, Florida	P	.667	0	4	2	1	0
...zar, Oscar, Oakland	2B	.966	138	178	11	20	0
Salazar, Thomas, Cleveland	P	1.000	3	11	0	1	0
Sanchez, Euro, Seattle	P	.983	106	11	2	0	0
Sanchez, Jesus, Chi.(NL)/S.D.	P	1.000	2	3	0	0	0
Sanchez, Jose, Detroit	P	1.000	2	4	0	0	0
Sanchez, Manuel, Atlanta	2B	.939	142	149	19	13	0
Sanchez, Simon, Arizona	P	.909	5	5	1	0	0
Sanchez, Wellington, Chi.(NL)/S.D.	P	.923	2	22	2	1	0
Sanchez, Wellington, Mil./Chi.(AL)	SS	.893	51	108	19	9	0
Sanquintin, Juan, Co-op	...	.954	319	55	18	2	16
Santana, Alfredo, Detroit	P	.962	8	17	1	1	0
Santana, Aris, Mil./Chi.(AL)	P	.750	1	5	2	0	0
Santana, Boris, Florida	P	1.000	1	2	0	1	0
Santana, Pedro, N.Y. Yankees	OF	.908	64	5	7	0	0
Santiago, Cesar, Florida	P	.750	2	10	4	1	0
Santos, Jose, N.Y. Yankees	C	.962	292	59	14	1	14
Santos, Jose, T.B.-Calif.	C	.957	179	23	9	1	2
Santos, Ricardo, Co-op	P	.895	5	12	2	2	0
Sarmiento, Angel, Dodgers I	P	1.000	3	4	0	0	0
Sasaki, Junichi, Montreal	P	1.000	2	5	0	0	0
Segura, Juan, Baltimore	P	1.000	2	3	0	0	0
Segura, Rolando, Pittsburgh	SS	.845	73	124	36	14	0
Segura, Winston, Texas	2B	1.000	17	15	0	0	0
Seipio, Maximiliano, Pittsburgh	OF	.985	57	8	1	3	0
Serrano, Wascar, Chi.(NL)/S.D.	P	.824	1	13	3	0	0
Severino, Danny, Florida	P	.910	85	6	9	2	0
Severino, Gilberto, Arizona	2B	.929	27	25	4	0	0
Sevillano, Jose, Pittsburgh	1B	.976	117	4	3	0	0
Shinozuka, Takehiro, Montreal	2B	.976	72	94	4	7	0
Silva, Luis, Toronto	P	.909	1	9	1	0	0
Silva, Ramon, Toronto	C	.975	209	26	6	0	14
Silverio, Marcelino, Chi.(NL)/S.D.	P	.833	2	8	2	0	0
Silvestre, Juan, Seattle	OF	.962	72	3	3	1	0
Solano, Stanley, Co-op	P	.714	3	2	2	0	0
Soler, Miguel, N.Y. Yankees	P	.875	3	4	1	0	0
Soriano, Gabriel, Dodgers I	P	.923	4	20	2	0	0
Soriano, Julio, Atlanta	C	.966	124	16	5	0	5
Sosa, Henry, St. Louis	P	1.000	3	3	0	1	0
Sosa, Jorby, N.Y. Yankees	P	1.000	3	6	0	1	0
Sosa, Jose, Chi.(NL)/S.D.	OF	.929	74	5	6	2	0
Sosa, Leonel, Dodgers II	C	.981	100	5	2	0	4
Sosa, Nemuel, Oakland	P	.500	0	3	3	0	0
Soto, Antonio, Chi.(NL)/S.D.	C	.944	245	43	17	6	10
Sotomayor, Gilberto, Dodgers I	OF	.914	30	2	3	0	0
Suarez, Giancarlos, Atlanta	P	.900	2	7	1	1	0
Suarez, Orlando, Cleveland	...	.903	80	13	10	3	7
Suarez, Orlando, Dodgers I	P	.963	6	20	1	0	0
Taisuke, Ishimaro, Dodgers I	P	.667	1	1	1	0	0
Tavares, Alex, Texas	P	1.000	0	1	0	0	0
Tavarez, Carlos, Seattle	OF	.889	23	1	3	0	0
Taveras, Luis, Texas	C	.973	388	89	13	1	12
Tineo, Marcos, St. Louis	P	1.000	0	4	0	0	0
Tobar, Angel, N.Y. Yankees	P	.800	3	5	2	1	0
Tobar, Rafael, Detroit	P	1.000	1	2	0	0	0
Tobias, Enrique, Dodgers I	C	.972	171	37	6	1	6
Toren, Prexilien, Atlanta	P	.857	1	5	1	0	0
Torres, Melquis, Seattle	P	1.000	1	2	0	0	0
Torrez, Rommel, Pittsburgh	C	.975	268	42	8	3	16
Tovar, Amador, Dodgers I	SS	.960	116	151	11	10	0
Trinidad, Edwin, Arizona	P	.857	1	5	1	0	0
Tucent, Andres, Mil./Chi.(AL)	SS	.930	23	30	4	2	0
Uben, Juan, Montreal	P	.900	2	7	1	1	0
Ugueto, Luis, Florida	SS	.912	147	205	34	18	0
Urena, Ruben, N.Y. Mets	P	1.000	1	1	0	0	0
Urquiola, Edgar, Montreal	2B	.922	47	48	8	3	0
Valdez, Angel, N.Y. Yankees	1B	.983	315	24	6	0	0
Valdez, Issac, Dodgers I	3B	.924	37	109	12	6	0
Valdez, Jean Carlos, Oakland	OF	.927	31	7	3	1	0
Valdez, Jose, Co-op	...	.875	14	0	2	0	0
Valdez, Jose, Dodgers I	OF	.959	43	4	2	1	0
Valenzuela, Jose, Chi.(NL)/S.D.	P	1.000	0	1	0	0	0
Valera, Gregori, Arizona	SS	.925	84	151	19	10	0
Valera, Juan, Chi.(NL)/S.D.	P	.846	2	9	2	0	0
Valera, Nelson, T.B.-Calif.	P	.846	6	5	2	1	0
Valerio, Julio, Dodgers II	P	1.000	1	3	0	0	0
Valle, Cosme, Dodgers II	3B	.861	14	11	6	0	0
Vals, Lucrecio, Baltimore	1B	.832	348	37	18	2	0
Varela, Gabriel, Dodgers II	3B	.922	60	141	17	15	0
Vargas, Claudio, Cleveland	P	.818	2	7	2	1	0
Vargas, Francisco, Cleveland	P	.750	3	0	1	0	0
Vargas, Inakel, Detroit	C	.975	336	47	10	2	11
Vargas, Martin, Co-op	...	.947	197	17	12	1	2
Vasquez, Antonio, Cleveland	...	.931	8	19	2	1	0
Vasquez, Arnulfo, Cleveland	...	.950	314	31	18	2	11

Player, Team	Pos.	Pct.	PO	A	E	DP	PB
Vasquez, Cesar, Mil./Chi.(AL)	P	1.000	3	5	0	0	0
Vasquez, Cristian, Florida	P	1.000	0	4	0	0	0
Vasquez, Jose, Cleveland	...	.999	17	2	0	0	0
Vasquez, Luis, N.Y. Mets	P	1.000	3	8	0	3	0
Vasquez, Luis, Pittsburgh	DH	.955	21	0	1	0	0
Veitia, Rodolfo, Montreal	3B	.818	12	33	10	4	0
Ventura, Frank, Cleveland	...	.956	81	6	4	3	0
Ventura, Jesus, T.B.-Calif.	IF	.875	5	2	1	0	0
Ventura, Juan, Cleveland	...	.919	96	177	24	11	0
Veras, Johnny, Co-op	P	.895	4	13	2	3	0
Veras, Roberto, Atlanta	LF	.916	79	8	8	1	0
Verdugo, Hugo, Dodgers II	P	1.000	1	1	0	0	0
Vialet, Junior, N.Y. Yankees	OF	.864	36	2	6	1	0
Vicente, Audo, Arizona	2B	.948	76	70	8	2	0

Player, Team	Pos.	Pct.	PO	A	E	DP	P
Villalona, Kellis, Chi.(NL)/S.D.	OF	.937	56	3	4	0	
Villanueva, Robert, Florida	P	.917	3	19	2	0	
Villar, Jose, Atlanta	CF	.943	98	2	6	0	
Villegas, Robert, N.Y. Yankees	C	.984	225	25	4	3	
Villero, Armando, Atlanta	OF	1.000	3	0	0	0	
Vinas, Alexander, Arizona	3B	.922	127	38	14	5	
Vizcaino, Alfredo, T.B.-Calif.	2B	.861	72	58	21	2	
William, Jovanny, St. Louis	C	.976	424	55	12	2	
Wilson, Danny, N.Y. Mets	OF	.947	34	2	2	0	
Wilson, Ricardo, Detroit	P	.909	2	8	1	0	
Yan, Franklin, Baltimore	P	1.000	2	6	0	0	
Zambrano, Alan, Seattle	OF	1.000	14	4	0	0	
Zamora, Juan, Pittsburgh	P	1.000	2	3	0	0	
Zapata, Orlando, Montreal	P	.636	6	8	8	0	

GULF COAST LEAGUE

LEAGUE OFFICE

esident
Tom Saffell
idress
1503 Clower Creek Dr., H-262
Sarasota, FL 34231
one
941-966-6407

Teams*
Astros
Braves
Devil Rays
Expos
Marlins
Mets
Orioles
Pirates
Rangers
Red Sox
Royals
Tigers
Twins
White Sox
Yankees
*Teams play their games in Bradenton, Dunedin, Fort Myers, Kissimmee, Lakeland, Melbourne, Orlando, Port Charlotte, Port St. Lucie, St. Petersburg, Sarasota, Tampa and West Palm Beach, Fla.

1996 FINAL STANDINGS

EASTERN DIVISION

m	W	L	T	Pct.	GB
os	41	18	1	.695	....
lins	34	25	1	.576	7
s	29	30	0	.492	12
ves	14	45	0	.237	27

NORTHERN DIVISION

Team	W	L	T	Pct.	GB
Yankees	37	21	0	.638	....
Astros	31	28	0	.525	6½
Tigers	26	34	0	.433	12
Devil Rays	24	35	0	.407	13½

NORTHWEST DIVISION

m	W	L	T	Pct.	GB
gers	37	23	0	.617	....
les	36	24	0	.600	1
tes	28	31	1	.475	8½
te Sox	20	40	0	.333	17

SOUTHWEST DIVISION

Team	W	L	T	Pct.	GB
Cubs	34	26	0	.567	....
Royals	30	29	1	.508	3½
Twins	30	30	0	.500	4
Red Sox	24	36	0	.400	10

COMPOSITE

m	Exp.	Yan.	Rng.	Ori.	Mrl.	Cubs	Ast.	Ryl.	Twi.	Mets	Pir.	Tig.	D.R.	R.S.	W.S.	Brv.	W	L	T	Pct.	GB
os	....	0	0	0	14	0	0	0	0	13	0	0	0	0	0	14	41	18	1	.695	....
kees	0	....	0	0	0	0	11	0	0	0	0	10	16	0	0	0	37	21	0	.638	3½
gers	0	0	....	10	0	1	0	1	1	0	10	0	0	2	12	0	37	23	0	.617	4½
les	0	0	8	....	0	0	0	2	2	0	11	0	0	2	11	0	36	24	0	.600	5½
lins	5	0	0	0	....	0	0	0	0	10	0	0	0	0	0	19	34	25	1	.576	7
s	0	0	1	2	0	....	0	9	8	0	2	0	0	12	0	0	34	26	0	.567	7½
os	0	8	0	0	0	0	....	0	0	0	0	13	10	0	0	0	31	28	0	.525	10
als	0	0	1	0	0	8	0	....	12	0	1	0	0	6	2	0	30	29	1	.508	11
ıs	0	0	1	0	0	9	0	6	....	0	0	0	0	12	2	0	30	30	0	.500	11½
s	7	0	0	0	10	0	0	0	0	....	0	0	0	0	0	12	29	30	0	.492	12
tes	0	0	7	6	0	0	0	0	2	0	....	0	0	1	12	0	28	31	1	.475	13
rs	0	10	0	0	0	0	7	0	0	0	0	....	9	0	0	0	26	34	0	.433	15½
l Rays	0	3	0	0	0	0	10	0	0	0	0	11	....	0	0	0	24	35	0	.407	17
Sox	0	0	0	0	0	6	0	11	5	0	1	0	0	....	1	0	24	36	0	.400	17½
te Sox	0	0	5	6	0	2	0	0	0	0	6	0	0	1	....	0	20	40	0	.333	21½
es	6	0	0	0	1	0	0	0	0	7	0	0	0	0	0	....	14	45	0	.237	27

ubs played in Bradenton, Dunedin, Fort Myers, Melbourne, Osceola, Port Charlotte, St. Lucie County, Sarasota, Tampa and West Palm Beach, Fla.

ub names are major league affiliations.

AYOFFS: Yankees defeated Expos, one game to none; Rangers defeated Cubs, one game to none; Yankees defeated Rangers, two games to none, to win league npionship.

EGULAR-SEASON ATTENDANCE: No official attendance figures reported.

ANAGERS: Astros, Bobby Ramos; Braves, Robert Lucas (through August 12), Chino Cadahia (August 13 to end of season); Cubs, Sandy Alomar; Devil Rays, Billy s; Expos, Jim Gabella; Marlins, Juan Bustabad; Mets, Mickey Brantley; Orioles, Tom Shields; Pirates, Woody Huyke; Rangers, James Byrd; Red Sox, Bob Green; als, Al Pedrique; Tigers, Kevin Bradshaw; Twins, Mike Boulanger; White Sox, Hector Rincones; Yankees, Ken Dominguez. Managerial records of team with more one manager: Braves, Lucas, 11-36, Cadahia, 3-9.

L-STAR TEAM: 1B—Franky Figueroa, Orioles; 2B—Dean Robertson, Orioles; 3B—Derrick Bly, Cubs; SS—Franklin Font, Cubs; OF—Fernando Nova, White Sox; Sanchez, Devil Rays; Alexis Zapata, Tigers; C—Donny Leon, Yankees; SP—Peter Fortune, Expos; RP—Bobby Styles, Rangers; Manager of the Year—Ken inguez, Yankees.

1996 BATTING

TEAM

ı	Avg.	G	TPA	AB	R	H	TB	2B	3B	HR	RBI	SH	SF	HP	BB	IBB	SO	SB	CS	GDP	LOB	ShO	Slg.	OBP
ees	.287	58	2218	1948	345	560	754	101	21	17	298	12	25	43	190	6	387	32	20	31	440	0	.387	.359
es	.256	60	2225	1995	284	510	706	82	27	20	241	9	12	22	186	4	367	63	32	54	402	6	.354	.324
Sox	.254	60	2292	2035	279	516	717	105	15	22	228	12	18	42	184	1	481	71	39	36	418	1	.352	.326
	.253	60	2257	1969	285	498	692	72	16	30	219	24	18	47	196	3	455	178	56	42	403	4	.351	.332
es	.248	60	2245	1978	271	490	659	84	20	15	221	19	16	31	198	3	423	96	42	43	414	2	.333	.323
s	.247	60	2167	1917	262	473	657	86	22	18	214	17	18	32	183	4	389	103	38	36	386	7	.343	.320
ls	.246	60	2131	1904	227	469	635	94	9	18	188	22	7	38	160	5	378	29	22	43	416	1	.334	.316
ers	.244	60	2259	1992	304	487	737	91	27	35	261	23	21	47	176	2	497	118	28	22	392	3	.370	.318

Team	Avg.	G	TPA	AB	R	H	TB	2B	3B	HR	RBI	SH	SF	HP	BB	IBB	SO	SB	CS	GDP	LOB	ShO	Slg.
White Sox	.244	60	2222	1980	236	484	653	93	17	14	192	18	12	39	173	1	442	47	30	38	428	5	.330
Marlins	.244	60	2232	1968	261	481	623	76	9	16	211	20	17	49	177	5	426	86	34	40	414	3	.317
Astros	.243	59	2141	1898	263	462	650	92	18	20	224	20	17	34	171	6	469	85	39	34	364	5	.342
Mets	.243	59	2110	1865	249	453	631	78	20	20	202	16	12	28	189	5	384	55	35	25	377	7	.338
Expos	.235	60	2190	1909	303	449	608	76	25	11	241	33	14	27	207	11	358	82	43	18	374	2	.318
Devil Rays	.232	59	2211	1979	240	460	584	61	18	9	205	20	11	24	175	2	505	76	34	32	406	10	.295
Tigers	.229	60	2208	1918	264	439	613	91	19	15	217	11	15	56	204	2	513	91	24	30	419	1	.320
Braves	.211	59	2102	1883	155	398	506	75	6	7	129	36	9	31	143	3	419	27	33	15	387	12	.269

INDIVIDUAL

TOP QUALIFIERS FOR BATTING CHAMPIONSHIP

Minimum 162 plate appearances. *Lefthanded batter. †Switch-hitter.

Player, Team	Avg.	G	TPA	AB	R	H	TB	2B	3B	HR	RBI	SH	SF	HP	BB	IBB	SO	SB	CS	GDP	Slg.
Leon, Donny, Yankees†	.361	53	209	191	30	69	109	14	4	6	46	1	4	4	9	2	30	1	2	2	.571
Bolivar, Ceasar, Twins	.342	41	168	155	30	53	65	7	1	1	18	0	3	2	8	0	32	26	6	2	.419
Figueroa, Francisco, Orioles	.340	43	163	150	22	51	61	8	1	0	23	0	2	3	8	0	25	3	0	7	.407
Zapata, Alexis, Tigers	.333	51	208	189	34	63	104	13	5	6	41	0	4	3	12	2	35	8	4	2	.550
Alleyne, Roberto, Astros	.331	48	176	151	32	50	80	9	0	7	27	0	3	2	20	2	32	4	4	4	.530
Meran, Jorge, Tigers	.315	51	191	168	25	53	78	13	3	2	32	1	2	5	13	0	42	7	2	3	.464
Abreu, Dennis, Cubs	.313	56	223	192	32	60	65	5	0	0	15	7	1	2	21	0	20	35	9	6	.339
Polonia, Isreal, Marlins	.310	50	188	171	22	53	75	6	2	4	31	2	3	2	10	2	50	6	7	6	.439
Radcliff, Victor, Royals	.309	48	193	165	24	51	75	11	2	3	20	2	1	10	15	0	34	1	1	1	.455
Robertson, Dean, Orioles	.302	53	210	179	32	54	75	11	2	2	25	2	0	1	28	0	17	16	7	6	.419
Font, Franklin, Cubs	.301	59	264	239	43	72	85	5	4	0	18	2	2	4	17	0	36	31	9	0	.356
Nova, Fernando, White Sox	.300	58	229	203	24	61	78	12	1	1	22	0	1	7	18	1	48	9	6	3	.384
Crede, Joe, White Sox	.299	56	237	221	30	66	97	17	1	4	32	1	4	2	9	0	41	1	1	8	.439
Salazar, Juan, Cubs†	.296	52	215	186	32	55	91	16	1	6	31	1	1	5	22	2	40	12	2	3	.489
McCladdie, T, Devil Rays	.295	50	182	166	21	49	64	7	4	0	21	1	2	4	9	0	27	14	1	2	.386

DEPARTMENTAL LEADERS: G—Franco, 60; AB—Franco, 241; R—Miles, 48; H—Font, 72; TB—Bly, Leon, 109 each; 2B—Stevenson, 18; 3B—Santo, 7; HR—13; RBI—Leon, 46; SH—Franco, 9; SF—Ovalles, 6; HP—Grubbs, Whitner, 12 each; BB—Wilder, 37; IBB—Schneider, 3; SO—Wilder, 66; SB—Rivas, D. Abreu, 35 e CS—A. Sanchez, 12; GIDP—LeBron, 9; Slg.—Leon, .571; OBP—N. Johnson, .422.

ALL PLAYERS

*Lefthanded batter. †Switch-hitter.

Player, Team	Avg.	G	TPA	AB	R	H	TB	2B	3B	HR	RBI	SH	SF	HP	BB	IBB	SO	SB	CS	GDP	Slg.
Abreu, Dennis, Cubs	.313	56	223	192	32	60	65	5	0	0	15	7	1	2	21	0	20	35	9	6	.339
Abreu, Miguel, Marlins	.210	23	67	62	4	13	14	1	0	0	1	0	0	1	4	0	14	3	0	2	.226
Abreu, Nelson, Cubs	.221	44	161	136	15	30	41	2	3	1	11	6	0	0	19	0	31	15	4	5	.301
Acevedo, Luis, Rangers	.195	53	204	174	17	34	46	8	2	0	19	1	2	2	25	0	31	7	1	3	.264
Ahrendt, Jay, Orioles*	.318	25	86	66	9	21	28	4	0	1	11	0	4	2	14	0	15	0	2	0	.424
Ahumada, Alejandro, Rd Sox	.279	37	129	122	14	34	40	6	0	0	15	1	0	3	3	0	32	1	5	0	.328
Alaimo, Jason, Marlins	.272	47	198	173	20	47	58	11	0	0	24	0	2	7	15	0	43	2	1	5	.335
Alcantara, Israel, Expos	.300	7	33	30	4	9	17	2	0	2	10	0	0	3	2	0	6	0	1	1	.567
Alleyne, Roberto, Astros	.331	48	176	151	32	50	80	9	0	7	27	0	3	2	20	2	32	4	4	4	.530
Almonte, Wady, Orioles	.333	1	4	3	2	1	1	0	0	0	1	0	0	0	1	0	0	1	0	0	.333
Alvarez, Julio, Tigers†	.261	28	105	92	13	24	26	2	0	0	10	1	1	0	11	0	22	5	1	0	.283
Arias, Jeison, Devil Rays	.258	19	72	66	7	17	23	4	1	0	4	3	0	0	3	0	31	3	1	1	.348
Armenta, Alfredo, Braves*	.308	18	14	13	0	4	5	1	0	0	0	0	0	0	1	0	3	0	0	1	.385
Aybar, Julio, Rangers*	.286	47	178	154	30	44	53	7	1	0	16	1	0	3	19	0	38	32	3	1	.344
Ayuso, Julio, Twins	.214	33	116	98	15	21	33	3	0	3	11	0	0	3	15	0	29	1	2	1	.337
Bagley, Sean, Expos	.246	42	132	118	27	29	36	7	0	0	12	3	0	0	11	0	29	9	2	1	.305
Barksdale, Shane, Astros*	.000	12	1	1	0	0	0	0	0	0	0	0	0	0	0	0	1	0	0	0	.000
Barner, Doug, Devil Rays	.200	1	5	5	1	1	1	0	0	0	0	0	0	0	0	0	1	0	0	0	.200
Barnes, John, Red Sox	.277	30	117	101	9	28	35	4	0	1	17	0	5	6	5	0	17	4	0	3	.347
Barrera, Rafael, Rangers†	.294	40	156	136	20	40	51	4	2	1	13	4	3	3	10	0	24	14	2	1	.375
Barrientos, Edgar, Red Sox†	.122	23	49	41	6	5	5	0	0	0	1	1	0	1	6	0	14	0	0	0	.122
Bautista, Francisco, Royals	.292	29	98	89	11	26	29	3	0	0	8	0	0	1	8	0	24	3	3	0	.326
Bautista, Jorge, Marlins	.265	47	183	151	23	40	67	4	1	7	24	0	1	5	26	1	28	4	2	2	.444
Bazzani, Matt, Red Sox	.400	11	30	25	7	10	18	5	0	1	3	0	0	2	3	0	4	0	0	1	.720
Becker, Brian, Devil Rays	.271	52	219	199	31	54	72	12	0	2	27	0	4	3	13	0	28	3	1	3	.362
Bello, Jilberto, Orioles	.157	40	149	134	10	21	28	5	1	0	9	1	2	1	11	0	48	8	4	2	.209
Benes, Richard, Royals†	.147	29	76	68	6	10	12	2	0	0	2	4	0	1	3	0	16	1	2	2	.176
Benjamin, Aljereau, Pirates	.227	45	188	172	23	39	61	5	4	3	25	1	2	1	12	0	35	1	2	7	.355
Besford, Timothy, Expos†	.083	10	13	12	1	1	1	0	0	0	0	0	0	0	0	0	5	0	0	0	.083
Blanco, Octavio, Devil Rays	.300	11	20	20	0	6	6	0	0	0	2	0	0	0	0	0	5	0	0	1	.300
Blosser, Doug, Royals*	.216	12	42	37	4	8	10	2	0	0	4	0	0	1	4	1	10	0	0	1	.270
Bly, Derrick, Cubs	.282	53	222	195	37	55	109	11	2	13	32	0	1	5	21	1	54	8	3	0	.559
Bocachica, Hiram, Expos	.250	9	38	32	11	8	11	3	0	0	2	0	0	1	5	1	3	2	1	0	.344
Bolivar, Ceasar, Twins	.342	41	168	155	30	53	65	7	1	1	18	0	3	2	8	0	32	26	6	2	.419
Borges, Alex, Braves	.385	5	13	13	1	5	5	0	0	0	1	0	0	0	1	0	1	1	0	0	.385
Borrego, Ramon, Twins†	.357	19	79	70	16	25	32	5	1	0	4	0	0	0	9	0	4	7	3	1	.457
Bradley, Milton, Expos†	.241	32	129	112	18	27	39	7	1	1	12	1	2	1	13	0	15	7	4	2	.348
Brambilla, Michael, Royals	.271	49	181	166	21	45	75	13	1	5	25	0	1	5	9	0	32	0	0	3	.452
Brignac, Junior, Braves	.194	53	206	191	15	37	44	7	0	0	8	1	1	4	9	0	60	3	7	2	.230
Brito, Bobby, Red Sox	.252	33	121	115	10	29	39	10	0	0	14	0	1	0	5	0	21	5	0	2	.339
Bronson, Ben, Royals*	.309	27	115	94	19	29	39	8	1	0	8	3	1		16	0	16	9	3	1	.415
Brooks, Ali, Pirates	.186	31	105	97	8	18	20	0	1	0	9	3	0	0	10	0	10	8	5	1	.206
Brooks, Anthony, Braves	.220	43	188	164	15	36	46	8	1	0	10	7	1	5	11	0	33	2	9	0	.280

ayer, Team	Avg.	G	TPA	AB	R	H	TB	2B	3B	HR	RBI	SH	SF	HP	BB	IBB	SO	SB	CS	GDP	Slg.	OBP
osam, Eric, Twins*	.182	21	67	55	6	10	14	2	1	0	8	1	1	3	7	0	11	1	0	0	.255	.303
own, Dermal, Royals*	.050	7	21	20	1	1	2	1	0	0	1	0	0	1	0	0	6	0	2	0	.100	.095
own, Richard, Yankees*	.287	47	192	164	33	47	61	8	3	0	23	1	3	1	23	1	32	2	1	2	.372	.372
uce, Maurice, Mets	.285	31	131	123	16	35	47	6	3	0	9	3	1	0	4	0	15	6	1	1	.382	.305
ulheller, Greg, White Sox	.100	9	20	20	0	2	3	1	0	0	1	0	0	0	0	0	4	0	0	0	.150	.100
urns, Patrick, Mets†	.222	43	167	144	17	32	40	8	0	0	13	1	2	2	18	1	32	1	3	2	.278	.313
urns, Xavier, Pirates	.164	22	87	73	17	12	15	1	1	0	3	0	1	1	11	0	24	6	0	1	.205	.279
utkus, Ben, Orioles	.146	20	42	41	1	6	8	0	1	0	3	0	0	0	1	0	13	0	1	1	.195	.167
vrd, Brandon, Astros	.194	37	142	124	7	24	40	11	1	1	20	1	2	2	12	0	41	0	2	0	.323	.271
amacaro, Pedro, Rangers†	.190	36	133	121	8	23	30	5	1	0	13	1	1	3	7	0	29	6	1	2	.248	.250
anciobello, Anthony, Braves	.000	17	5	3	0	0	0	0	0	0	0	0	0	0	2	0	2	0	0	0	.000	.400
andelaria, Vidal, Yankees*	.279	25	76	68	8	19	22	3	0	0	11	0	2	0	6	0	11	0	0	1	.324	.329
ardona, Luis, Red Sox	.133	29	79	75	5	10	15	2	0	1	5	0	1	2	0	0	18	1	1	1	.200	.154
arey, Orlando, Yankees	.249	57	238	213	32	53	63	4	3	0	20	2	3	6	14	0	47	5	3	3	.296	.309
armona, Antonio, Wit. Sox	.234	47	166	154	15	36	43	5	1	0	15	0	2	3	7	0	26	4	2	1	.279	.277
arney, Bartt, Orioles†	.250	6	17	12	4	3	3	0	0	0	1	0	0	0	5	0	1	1	0	0	.250	.471
arrion, Jorge, Rangers	.309	19	59	55	13	17	19	2	0	0	8	0	1	0	3	0	6	9	1	2	.345	.339
arter, Quincy, Cubs	.215	55	228	181	31	39	56	6	1	3	37	2	5	3	35	0	36	18	6	5	.309	.344
asaidez, Juan, Red Sox†	.128	22	50	47	1	6	8	0	1	0	0	0	0	2	0	16	0	1	1	.170	.180
hampion, Jeff, Braves	.170	29	98	88	6	15	20	1	2	0	2	1	0	1	8	0	23	2	2	0	.227	.247
hapman, Scott, Astros	.261	45	163	142	17	37	53	8	1	2	19	1	2	0	18	1	25	3	1	3	.373	.340
hristensen, McKay, W Sox*	.263	35	147	133	17	35	55	7	5	1	16	0	1	3	10	0	23	10	3	1	.414	.327
ochran, Ed, White Sox	.174	53	166	144	20	25	32	5	1	0	12	2	1	8	11	0	45	6	1	2	.222	.268
offie, Evanon, Orioles*	.218	56	219	193	29	42	58	8	4	0	20	0	0	2	23	1	26	6	2	4	.301	.307
olon, Ariel, Mets	.108	23	76	65	8	7	8	1	0	0	5	1	1	2	7	0	23	1	1	2	.123	.213
olson, Julian, Braves	.268	15	47	41	5	11	18	4	0	1	2	2	0	2	2	0	13	0	0	0	.439	.333
onnell, Gerald, Cubs	.333	21	82	72	7	24	33	3	0	2	12	0	2	1	7	0	14	5	1	4	.458	.390
onway, Scott, Marlins*	.238	30	116	101	7	24	36	6	0	2	15	0	3	5	7	0	23	3	1	1	.356	.310
opeland, Brandon, Mets	.237	46	178	135	31	32	54	9	2	3	17	0	0	7	36	0	32	3	0	0	.400	.421
oquillette, Trace, Expos	.160	7	29	25	4	4	5	1	0	0	0	0	0	0	4	0	6	1	0	0	.200	.276
ordero, Wil, Red Sox	.300	3	11	10	1	3	6	0	0	1	3	0	1	0	0	0	2	0	0	1	.600	.273
ede, Joe, White Sox	.299	56	237	221	30	66	97	17	1	4	32	1	4	2	9	0	41	1	1	8	.439	.326
espo, Jesse, Braves	.217	54	146	129	11	28	32	4	0	0	9	5	1	3	8	0	28	4	0	3	.248	.277
uz, Alain, Yankees	.255	45	183	165	33	42	68	13	2	3	26	0	1	1	16	1	46	3	0	4	.412	.322
uz, Andres, Twins	.218	28	101	78	14	17	26	4	1	1	9	2	2	3	16	0	13	1	0	4	.333	.364
niels, Deion, Twins	.111	4	10	9	0	1	1	0	0	0	0	0	0	1	0	0	4	0	0	2	.111	.200
niels, Ronny, Expos	.208	46	181	159	29	33	56	6	4	3	28	0	2	2	18	0	44	9	2	2	.352	.293
sher, Melvin, Royals	.269	17	58	52	10	14	22	3	1	1	6	0	1	5	0	0	14	0	0	2	.423	.345
vila, Angel, Mets	.179	9	29	28	3	5	5	0	0	0	2	0	0	1	0	0	8	0	1	1	.179	.207
vis, Torrance, Expos	.255	27	62	55	13	14	15	1	0	0	7	2	0	1	4	0	7	1	4	0	.273	.317
vison, Ashanti, Orioles	.263	31	92	76	13	20	22	2	0	0	4	0	0	5	11	0	14	9	2	1	.289	.391
lacruz, Wilfredo, Yankees	.163	16	52	43	3	7	7	0	0	0	6	1	2	2	4	0	9	1	0	0	.163	.255
laEspada, Miguel, Astros	.211	42	135	123	14	26	40	8	0	2	9	1	1	3	7	0	40	1	2	1	.325	.269
laRosa, Miguel, Rangers	.140	16	49	43	4	6	7	1	0	0	1	2	0	0	4	0	20	1	0	0	.163	.213
larosa, Tomas, Expos	.251	54	216	187	35	47	56	7	1	0	21	4	1	2	22	0	25	8	5	2	.299	.335
lgado, Daniel, Pirates	.292	37	106	96	16	28	32	2	1	0	11	1	1	0	8	0	14	3	3	4	.333	.343
loSantos, E, Devil Rays	.245	50	214	196	18	48	56	6	1	0	20	2	0	3	13	0	58	11	4	4	.286	.302
vecchio, N, Yankees*	.611	4	25	18	4	11	21	4	0	2	8	0	0	1	6	0	1	1	0	1	1.167	.720
shazer, Jeremy, Astros†	.235	52	185	170	20	40	53	5	4	0	12	4	1	1	9	1	49	5	5	2	.312	.276
az, Diogenes, Pirates	.233	26	95	90	7	21	38	7	2	2	9	0	0	5	0	0	20	0	0	4	.422	.274
rick, Chad, Mets	.218	43	146	133	14	29	35	6	0	0	12	1	3	1	8	0	27	6	2	0	.263	.262
ott, Dawan, Pirates*	.300	24	99	90	9	27	36	7	1	0	18	0	0	1	8	0	12	5	2	3	.400	.364
gle, Beau, Mets	.000	2	3	2	1	0	0	0	0	0	0	0	0	1	0	2	0	0	0	.000	.333
calona, Felix, Astros	.147	28	89	75	8	11	16	2	0	1	9	1	1	4	8	0	31	1	2	0	.213	.261
cobar, Alex, Mets	.360	24	83	75	15	27	31	4	0	0	10	0	1	3	4	0	9	7	1	0	.413	.410
ans, Lee, Pirates†	.279	32	133	111	27	31	49	5	2	3	20	1	0	3	18	1	26	3	0	2	.441	.394
iz, Edgar, Pirates†	.000	1	1	1	0	0	0	0	0	0	0	0	0	0	0	0	0	0	0	0	.000	.000
ston, Anthony, Twins*	.500	2	6	4	2	2	2	0	0	0	0	0	0	0	2	0	0	0	0	0	.500	.667
nnell, Jason, White Sox†	.239	56	228	197	24	47	61	8	0	2	19	3	0	1	27	0	39	4	0	2	.310	.333
guson, Dwight, Red Sox*	.324	36	88	68	23	22	32	2	1	2	11	1	1	3	15	0	22	10	5	1	.471	.460
ueroa, Francisco, Orioles	.340	43	163	150	22	51	61	8	1	0	23	0	2	3	8	0	25	3	0	7	.407	.380
ardi, Wladimir, Royals	.179	21	43	39	3	7	12	2	0	1	5	0	1	1	2	0	15	0	1	0	.308	.233
her, Tony, Rangers	.241	9	34	29	2	7	10	1	1	0	6	0	0	3	2	0	8	2	1	0	.345	.353
res, Oswaldo, Red Sox†	.300	37	132	120	22	36	47	7	2	0	9	1	0	3	8	0	28	14	2	2	.392	.359
nt, Franklin, Cubs	.301	59	264	239	43	72	85	5	4	0	18	2	2	4	17	0	36	31	9	0	.356	.355
wler, Benjamin, Braves†	.174	16	25	23	2	4	4	0	0	0	2	1	0	0	1	1	6	0	0	2	.174	.208
nco, Raul, Marlins	.278	60	267	241	40	67	85	14	2	0	15	9	1	3	13	0	30	16	7	6	.353	.322
cciaparra, Nomar, Rd Sox	.286	5	16	14	4	4	8	2	1	0	5	0	0	1	1	0	0	0	0	1	.571	.375
rmosen, Julio, Braves†	.244	35	132	123	20	30	41	4	2	1	11	0	0	1	8	0	24	2	1	1	.333	.295
gigoski, Jason, Red Sox*	.000	3	9	8	0	0	0	0	0	0	1	0	0	0	1	0	2	0	0	0	.000	.111
mez, Rudy, Yankees	.276	16	72	58	12	16	22	6	0	0	10	1	1	4	9	2	7	0	1	1	.379	.403
nzalez, Alex, Marlins	.390	10	43	41	6	16	19	3	0	0	6	0	0	0	2	0	4	1	0	1	.463	.419
nzalez, Jose, White Sox*	.277	51	189	166	22	46	58	6	3	0	14	7	2	2	12	0	31	4	6	3	.349	.330
nzalez, M, Devil Rays	.068	17	49	44	7	3	3	0	0	0	2	0	0	5	0	0	13	2	0	0	.068	.163
bbs, Chris, Cubs	.150	30	101	80	11	12	16	2	1	0	3	0	1	12	8	0	27	5	4	3	.200	.317
uber, Nick, Red Sox	.167	5	7	6	0	1	1	0	0	0	1	0	0	0	1	0	1	0	0	0	.167	.286
errero, F, Devil Rays	.043	11	28	23	1	1	1	0	0	0	1	0	0	0	5	0	10	0	0	1	.043	.214
errero, Hamlet, Mets	.260	34	138	120	17	33	51	8	2	2	14	1	1	0	9	0	12	0	2	1	.402	.307
nner, Chie, Devil Rays*	.176	44	145	131	8	23	25	2	0	0	8	3	0	1	10	0	45	2	1	0	.191	.239
eman, Christian, Yankees†	.294	42	187	170	37	50	65	8	2	1	21	2	2	3	10	0	31	7	6	2	.382	.341
l, Noah, Expos	.248	42	164	137	25	34	48	5	3	1	18	1	2	5	19	2	22	6	2	2	.350	.356
nilton, Joe, Red Sox*	.250	1	4	4	1	1	1	0	0	0	0	0	0	0	0	0	1	0	0	0	.250	.250
zelton, Justin, Tigers	.128	47	166	141	15	18	24	3	0	1	12	1	2	1	21	0	45	1	2	5	.170	.242

Player, Team	Avg.	G	TPA	AB	R	H	TB	2B	3B	HR	RBI	SH	SF	HP	BB	IBB	SO	SB	CS	GDP	Slg.	O
Heredia, Rafael, Cubs	.224	23	89	76	12	17	26	4	1	1	8	0	0	4	9	0	21	11	1	4	.342	
Hernandez, Rafael, Expos	.210	37	112	100	13	21	25	2	1	0	12	1	1	0	10	0	30	6	4	0	.250	
Herrera, Pedro, Royals	.253	31	104	99	8	25	29	4	0	0	10	2	0	0	3	0	21	1	2	2	.293	
Hessman, Michael, Braves	.216	53	210	190	13	41	56	10	1	1	15	4	0	4	12	1	41	1	1	0	.295	
Hill, Jason, Astros	.286	42	160	140	22	40	69	13	2	4	31	0	4	3	13	0	21	7	5	3	.493	
Hill, Jeremy, Royals	.178	31	106	90	4	16	22	6	0	0	4	1	1	2	12	0	17	0	0	3	.244	
Holobinko, Mike, Cubs*	.000	11	2	1	0	0	0	0	0	0	0	1	0	0	0	0	1	0	0	0	.000	
Hooper, Daren, Orioles	.250	33	123	104	22	26	39	4	0	3	12	0	1	2	16	0	30	1	0	4	.375	
Horn, Marv, White Sox*	.250	9	35	28	4	7	7	0	0	0	2	0	0	1	6	0	3	1	0	1	.250	
Hundt, Bo, Pirates†	.246	20	80	69	12	17	22	2	0	1	9	0	2	4	5	0	9	0	0	3	.319	
Jackson, Quantaa, Marlins	.138	27	94	80	5	11	14	3	0	0	6	2	1	3	8	0	31	2	0	2	.175	
Jackson, Ryan, Marlins*	.346	8	30	26	5	9	9	0	0	0	7	0	2	1	1	0	3	2	0	0	.346	
James, Kennouth, Expos*	.208	45	188	168	24	35	44	5	2	0	12	2	0	3	15	1	34	4	3	0	.262	
Jamison, Nick, Tigers*	.105	31	109	95	11	10	13	1	1	0	9	0	0	1	12	0	18	1	2	1	.137	
Jensen, Jacob, Pirates	.188	31	110	96	14	18	29	4	2	1	13	1	0	3	10	0	22	2	3	2	.302	
Jimenez, Felipe, Cubs	.246	49	181	171	18	42	46	4	0	0	10	4	0	1	5	0	44	20	9	3	.269	
Johnson, Carlisle, Twins	.158	26	93	76	8	12	13	1	0	0	6	3	1	1	12	0	29	0	0	1	.171	
Johnson, Doug, Devil Rays	.231	28	119	108	12	25	33	3	1	1	9	0	2	2	7	1	41	0	2	0	.306	
Johnson, Nick, Yankees*	.287	47	199	157	31	45	64	11	1	2	33	0	3	9	30	0	35	0	0	5	.408	
Johnson, Rontrez, Red Sox	.294	28	103	85	20	25	31	6	0	0	9	1	0	0	17	0	11	6	2	2	.365	
Johnson, Thomas, Mets	.261	32	128	115	19	30	40	5	1	1	9	3	1	3	6	1	26	6	2	1	.348	
Johnson, Tony, Mets†	.244	48	191	164	18	40	71	6	2	7	27	1	2	0	24	0	42	5	3	3	.433	
Jordan, Yustin, Pirates	.247	27	98	85	10	21	25	1	0	1	5	1	0	2	10	0	23	1	0	3	.294	
Katzaroff, Rob, Yankees	.407	7	34	27	9	11	13	2	0	0	3	0	0	1	6	0	3	1	1		.481	
Kelly, Pat, Yankees	.353	5	21	17	7	6	11	2	0	1	1	0	0	1	3	0	2	3	0	0	.647	
Kennedy, Brian, Twins*	.218	37	130	110	8	24	28	2	1	0	16	2	3	2	13	0	30	3	4	0	.255	
King, Brion, Orioles	.115	9	28	26	5	3	4	1	0	0	1	0	0	0	2	0	5	2	0	1	.154	
Kingsbury, Willy, Red Sox*	.333	28	105	93	7	31	46	9	0	2	22	1	0	1	10	0	18	3	0	3	.495	
Kinnie, Donald, Cubs	.308	11	44	39	6	12	20	3	1	1	7	0	2	1	2	0	6	3	1	1	.513	
Kirkpatrick, M, Orioles*	.226	17	34	31	3	7	7	0	0	0	2	0	0	3	0	0	5	2	3	1	.226	
Koeyers, Ramsey, Expos	.158	7	22	19	2	3	4	1	0	0	0	0	0	0	3	0	6	0	0	0	.211	
Larkin, Garrett, Pirates*	.377	17	71	69	7	26	34	4	2	0	6	0	0	2	0	0	5	1	1	1	.493	
Lebron, Juan, Royals	.288	58	223	215	19	62	84	9	2	3	30	0	0	2	6	0	34	1	2	9	.391	
Leidens, Enrique, Expos	.221	27	88	77	8	17	21	1	0	1	6	2	0	1	8	0	14	6	2	0	.273	
Leon, Donny, Yankees†	.361	53	209	191	30	69	109	14	4	6	46	1	4	4	9	2	30	1	2	2	.571	
Lignitz, Jeremiah, Tigers*	.176	46	175	153	9	27	36	2	2	1	13	0	1	3	18	0	53	2	1	1	.235	
Ligons, Merrell, Royals†	.185	48	152	130	18	24	30	4	1	0	5	1	0	6	15	0	24	2	1	3	.231	
Lina, Estivinson, Rangers	.260	50	170	146	25	38	64	7	2	5	34	2	1	4	17	1	43	4	4	4	.438	
Linares, Sendry, Astros	.207	23	68	58	5	12	18	6	0	0	6	3	0	4	3	0	10	1	0	2	.310	
Llanos, Francisco, Expos	.176	27	86	74	5	13	18	5	0	0	10	2	0	3	7	0	23	0	1	2	.243	
Llibre, Brian, Rangers	.306	33	113	108	18	33	62	5	0	8	24	0	2	1	2	0	29	3	1	0	.574	
LoCurto, Gary, Red Sox†	.314	36	157	137	25	43	63	8	0	4	22	0	0	2	18	0	44	5	4	2	.460	
Longmire, Marcel, Cubs	.191	34	128	115	11	22	32	2	1	2	7	0	1	4	8	0	35	6	4	0	.278	
Lopez, Henry, Twins	.254	34	138	122	24	31	63	5	6	5	26	0	1	1	15	1	25	9	2	1	.516	
Lorenzana, Luis, Pirates	.151	18	68	53	4	8	9	1	0	0	5	1	1	1	12	0	8	0	1	1	.170	
Lorenzo, Juan, Twins†	.254	37	140	134	23	34	48	5	0	3	15	2	0	2	2	0	20	4	1	1	.358	
Lugo, Marcelino, Marlins	.125	12	8	8	0	1	1	0	0	0	0	0	0	0	0	0	5	0	0	0	.125	
Mackowiak, Robert, Pirates*	.267	27	101	86	8	23	31	6	1	0	14	0	1	1	13	1	11	3	1	3	.360	
Maduro, Remy, Marlins*	.226	24	103	84	8	19	21	2	0	0	14	0	1	2	15	0	9	2	0	5	.250	
Mateo, Henry, Expos†	.250	14	54	44	8	11	14	3	0	0	3	2	0	3	5	0	11	5	1	0	.318	
Mateo, Victor, Yankees†	.315	32	140	127	25	40	47	1	3	0	15	1	1	2	9	0	29	0	2	1	.370	
Matos, Luis, Orioles	.292	43	151	130	21	38	40	2	0	0	13	4	0	2	15	0	18	12	7	3	.308	
Matos, Wellington, Yankees*	.247	35	110	97	13	24	29	5	0	0	14	0	0	2	11	0	29	0	0	4	.299	
McCladdie, Tony, Devil Rays	.295	50	182	166	21	49	64	7	4	0	21	1	2	4	9	0	27	14	1	2	.386	
McDavid, Ray, Expos*	.273	4	14	11	2	3	5	0	1	0	0	0	0	0	3	0	3	1	0	0	.455	
McDermott, Mike, White Sox	.250	44	166	144	17	36	53	11	0	2	18	3	0	8	11	0	38	1	3	3	.368	
Mckenzie, Carlton, Pirates*	.307	36	122	114	14	35	41	2	2	0	12	0	0	0	8	0	13	5	5	2	.360	
McKinney, Antonio, Tigers	.211	44	169	147	27	31	42	4	2	1	13	0	1	6	15	0	44	8	0	2	.286	
McNeal, Aaron, Astros	.250	55	219	200	22	50	70	10	2	2	31	0	2	4	13	1	52	0	2	5	.350	
Meadows, Mike, Mets	.200	8	31	30	1	6	6	0	0	0	3	0	0	1	0	0	9	0	0	1	.200	
Medrano, Steve, Royals	.273	46	178	154	24	42	55	10	0	1	11	3	0	2	19	2	21	3	1	4	.357	
Meier, Bob, Yankees	.333	3	3	3	0	1	2	1	0	0	0	0	0	0	0	0	1	0	0	0	.667	
Mendoza, Angel, Red Sox	.269	49	174	160	17	43	66	13	2	2	13	1	1	3	9	0	42	3	4	2	.413	
Meran, Jorge, Tigers	.315	51	191	168	25	53	78	13	3	2	32	1	2	5	13	0	42	7	2	3	.464	
Mercado, Julio, Rangers	.215	42	124	107	18	23	38	4	1	3	7	2	1	4	10	0	24	10	4	0	.355	
Mercedes, Matia, Tigers	.200	16	59	50	9	10	16	6	0	0	6	1	0	1	7	0	10	2	1	1	.320	
Merloni, Lou, Red Sox	.250	1	5	4	1	1	1	0	0	0	0	1	0	0	0	0	0	0	0	0	.250	
Metzger, Erik, Red Sox	.232	19	61	56	4	13	16	3	0	0	5	0	1	0	4	0	14	0	0	1	.286	
Miles, Aaron, Astros*	.294	55	240	214	48	63	70	3	2	0	15	5	0	1	20	0	18	14	7	3	.327	
Monds, Wonder, Braves	.400	3	8	5	3	2	8	0	0	2	3	0	1	0	2	0	1	0	0	0	1.600	
Montas, Richard, Royals	.264	50	208	182	25	48	62	6	1	2	22	2	1	3	20	2	31	5	1	7	.341	
Moore, Tris, Tigers	.259	16	67	54	9	14	21	1	0	2	12	1	1	3	8	0	12	2	0	1	.389	
Morales, Domingo, Orioles	.386	19	72	70	8	27	38	5	3	0	15	0	0	2	0	0	4	6	2	3	.543	
Morales, Steve, Marlins†	.167	29	93	84	8	14	19	2	0	1	7	2	0	2	5	0	13	0	0	1	.226	
Moreno, Juan, Mets	.264	16	58	53	7	14	20	4	1	0	7	0	0	1	4	0	11	2	0	2	.377	
Morgan, Todd, Orioles	.172	18	34	29	2	5	5	0	0	0	1	0	0	1	4	0	7	1	1	0	.172	
Moss, Rick, Twins*	.346	28	118	107	18	37	49	8	2	0	23	0	1	3	7	1	7	2	2	2	.458	
Mulvehill, Brandon, Mets	.169	22	69	65	9	11	18	1	3	0	3	1	0	0	3	0	11	1	1	2	.277	
Munson, Mike, Yankees	.300	19	42	40	6	12	17	2	0	1	4	0	0	0	2	0	9	0	0	0	.425	
Neikirk, Derick, Tigers	.211	18	47	38	4	8	8	0	0	0	1	0	3	5	0		7	0	0	4	.211	
Nelson, Kevin, Twins	.238	34	134	122	8	29	36	4	0	1	11	1	2	2	7	1	27	0	0	4	.295	
Nicley, Dru, Astros	.106	25	77	66	4	7	7	0	0	0	3	0	0	4	7	0	20	2	0	3	.106	
Nova, Fernando, White Sox	.300	58	229	203	24	61	78	12	1	1	22	0	1	7	18	1	48	9	6	3	.384	

Player, Team	Avg.	G	TPA	AB	R	H	TB	2B	3B	HR	RBI	SH	SF	HP	BB	IBB	SO	SB	CS	GDP	Slg.	OBP
ova, Geraldo, Red Sox†	.190	33	105	84	15	16	23	3	2	0	10	1	1	2	17	0	32	3	2	1	.274	.337
nez, Jose, Mets	.233	41	137	120	11	28	33	3	1	0	15	1	0	0	16	0	28	4	9	2	.275	.324
ivares, Teuris, Yankees	.300	9	22	20	3	6	7	1	0	0	4	1	0	0	1	0	2	0	0	0	.350	.333
meda, Jose, Red Sox†	.291	15	59	55	8	16	26	4	0	2	5	0	1	0	3	0	13	1	1	1	.473	.322
son, Dan, White Sox*	.364	3	15	11	4	4	7	3	0	0	5	0	0	0	4	0	4	0	0	0	.636	.533
ndorff, Dave, Twins	.091	8	29	22	4	2	3	1	0	0	1	0	0	1	6	0	10	0	0	0	.136	.310
opeza, William, Expos	.167	5	20	18	2	3	3	0	0	0	0	1	0	0	1	0	5	0	0	1	.167	.211
tiz, Pedro, Orioles	.246	43	133	126	16	31	48	8	0	3	6	0	1	1	4	0	33	5	0	1	.381	.273
ero, Oscar, Braves	.246	54	204	191	15	47	63	9	2	1	24	1	1	3	8	1	18	4	5	2	.330	.286
tavinia, Paul, Expos*	.400	3	12	10	1	4	4	0	0	0	1	0	0	0	2	0	1	0	0	0	.400	.500
valles, Homy, Expos	.255	48	179	161	19	41	56	7	4	0	30	5	6	0	7	1	24	4	6	1	.348	.276
vens, Billy, Orioles†	.167	6	19	18	0	3	3	0	0	0	3	0	1	0	0	0	4	0	0	1	.167	.158
runa, Pedro, Yankees	.306	34	121	108	24	33	38	3	1	0	20	0	1	1	11	0	17	3	1	2	.352	.372
chot, John, Expos	.300	8	33	30	3	9	12	1	1	0	3	1	0	1	1	0	0	0	0	0	.400	.344
rra, Alejandro, White Sox	.116	39	111	86	12	10	10	0	0	0	3	2	0	2	21	0	28	2	2	3	.116	.303
rra, Jose, Rangers†	.258	15	36	31	4	8	11	0	0	1	3	1	0	1	3	0	8	4	1	0	.355	.343
scual, Edison, Pirates*	.275	43	163	149	28	41	67	15	1	3	20	0	0	1	13	0	35	7	2	3	.450	.337
ss, Patrick, Marlins	.244	29	107	90	14	22	26	4	0	0	8	0	0	2	15	2	27	5	2	0	.289	.364
ul, Josh, White Sox	.000	1	1	0	0	0	0	0	0	0	0	0	0	0	1	0	0	0	0	0	.000	1.000
yano, Alexi, Cubs†	.253	28	94	83	15	21	28	5	1	0	10	0	1	5	4	0	12	3	1	1	.337	.323
ayton, Jay, Mets	.385	3	13	13	3	5	9	1	0	1	2	0	0	0	0	0	1	1	0	0	.692	.385
drosa, Alex, Orioles*	.308	3	13	13	0	4	5	1	0	0	0	0	0	0	0	0	1	1	0	0	.385	.308
na, Jose, Rangers	.286	30	109	98	19	28	42	6	4	0	11	0	2	0	9	0	16	13	0	1	.429	.339
nalver, Juan, Mets	.346	15	64	52	9	18	21	3	0	0	7	0	0	1	11	0	10	2	0	0	.404	.469
niche, Fray, Tigers	.193	40	133	119	17	23	33	6	2	0	5	0	0	2	12	0	39	2	3	2	.277	.278
rez, Alejandro, Red Sox	.233	15	45	43	6	10	15	3	1	0	3	0	0	1	1	0	10	1	0	1	.349	.267
rez, Jersen, Mets	.278	40	169	151	24	42	53	5	3	0	12	0	0	1	17	1	18	7	2	2	.351	.355
rez, Jesse, Orioles†	.173	36	118	104	9	18	21	3	0	0	10	4	2	1	7	0	33	2	3	0	.202	.228
rez, Richard, Orioles	.254	41	156	138	25	35	53	5	2	3	18	4	1	1	12	0	34	10	5	3	.384	.316
rini, Mike, Red Sox*	.170	34	108	94	8	16	19	1	1	0	7	0	1	0	13	0	27	3	2	1	.202	.269
mentel, Marino, Marlins†	.125	15	42	40	4	5	6	1	0	0	1	0	0	1	1	0	17	0	3	0	.150	.167
niella, Juan, Rangers	.238	55	249	223	38	53	63	6	2	0	18	4	2	5	15	0	54	19	5	1	.283	.298
lonia, Isreal, Marlins	.310	48	188	171	22	53	75	6	2	4	31	2	3	2	10	2	50	6	7	6	.439	.349
st, Dave, Expos	.080	8	30	25	3	2	5	0	0	1	1	1	0	0	4	1	6	1	0	0	.200	.207
ada, Nelson, Twins	.243	41	156	144	16	35	54	11	1	2	16	2	1	3	6	0	30	1	0	6	.375	.286
eciado, Victor, Yankees†	.250	45	179	164	15	41	52	7	2	0	22	2	1	1	11	0	27	1	2	1	.317	.299
essley, Kasey, Cubs*	.137	35	138	124	9	17	21	1	0	1	13	0	1	0	13	0	49	1	1	3	.169	.217
odanov, Peter, Red Sox	.120	9	27	25	5	3	4	1	0	0	1	0	0	0	2	0	3	0	0	1	.160	.185
yor, Pete, White Sox*	.111	3	9	9	0	1	1	0	0	0	0	0	0	0	0	0	2	0	0	0	.111	.111
gh, Josh, Braves	.258	30	98	89	8	23	30	4	0	1	12	1	1	0	7	0	23	1	0	0	.337	.309
intero, Christian, Yankees	.265	21	77	68	13	18	25	4	0	1	8	1	1	3	4	0	13	1	0	1	.368	.329
dcliff, Victor, Royals	.309	48	193	165	24	51	75	11	2	3	20	2	1	10	15	0	34	1	1	1	.455	.388
nes, Tim, Yankees†	.600	1	6	5	2	3	5	2	0	0	3	0	0	0	1	0	0	0	0	0	1.000	.667
mirez, Edgar, Devil Rays	.158	38	126	114	12	18	18	0	0	0	8	2	0	0	10	0	29	3	2	2	.158	.226
mirez, Juan, Royals	.231	34	96	91	10	21	28	4	0	1	8	0	0	1	4	0	22	0	0	2	.308	.271
mirez, Julio, Marlins	.287	43	193	174	35	50	63	5	4	0	16	1	0	3	15	0	34	26	7	0	.362	.354
mirez, Luis, Orioles	.160	41	141	131	13	21	31	4	3	0	12	2	0	1	7	0	47	1	2	4	.237	.209
mirez, Oscar, Rangers	.195	54	220	195	21	38	60	12	2	2	23	4	0	5	16	0	59	3	3	1	.308	.273
mos, Isandel, Braves*	.221	49	175	149	9	33	37	4	0	0	12	3	1	1	21	0	31	0	1	1	.248	.320
mos, Kelly, Mets†	.186	20	63	59	3	11	13	0	1	0	7	1	0	0	3	0	10	0	2	2	.220	.226
mos, Noel, Orioles	.217	18	53	46	4	10	19	3	0	2	6	0	0	3	4	0	17	0	0	0	.413	.321
dman, Julian, Pirates*	.298	26	117	104	20	31	40	4	1	1	16	0	1	0	12	1	12	15	2	0	.385	.368
eder, Galen, Braves*	.250	19	8	8	0	2	2	0	0	0	0	0	0	0	0	0	1	0	0	0	.250	.250
ves, Deurys, Tigers*	.143	5	9	7	3	1	3	0	1	0	1	0	0	0	2	0	3	0	0	0	.429	.333
ynoso, Ismael, Marlins	.155	30	102	97	8	15	19	4	0	0	9	0	0	2	3	0	22	3	2	2	.196	.196
as, Luis, Twins	.259	53	220	201	29	52	69	12	1	1	13	1	0	0	18	0	37	35	10	2	.343	.320
era, Carlos, Pirates*	.284	48	201	183	24	52	75	8	3	3	26	0	2	1	15	1	22	1	1	8	.410	.338
era, Juan, Rangers	.282	26	85	78	14	22	35	5	1	2	7	1	0	0	6	0	30	6	0	3	.449	.333
era, Luis, Expos	.059	22	58	51	2	3	4	1	0	0	2	1	0	1	5	0	13	0	1	0	.078	.158
era, Roberto, Orioles	.625	4	12	8	7	5	8	1	1	0	2	0	1	0	3	0	1	3	0	0	1.000	.667
bertson, Dean, Orioles	.302	53	210	179	32	54	75	11	2	2	25	2	0	1	28	0	17	16	7	6	.419	.399
bertson, Geoffrey, Astros*	.136	38	98	81	8	11	12	1	0	0	2	1	0	1	15	0	38	7	4	2	.148	.278
ckow, Jeremy, Pirates*	.222	33	120	108	13	24	33	4	1	1	8	0	1	2	9	0	37	0	3	3	.306	.292
as, Moises, Red Sox	.228	39	128	114	21	26	41	4	1	3	9	2	0	3	9	0	17	3	1	0	.360	.302
man, Felipe, Red Sox	.272	47	170	162	15	44	56	7	1	1	17	0	0	1	7	0	35	2	5	3	.346	.306
neberg, Brett, Marlins*	.213	50	192	174	23	37	48	8	0	1	15	2	1	4	11	0	39	0	0	3	.276	.274
an, Mike, Twins*	.197	43	174	157	12	31	43	8	2	0	13	1	2	1	13	1	20	3	0	3	.274	.260
azar, Juan, Cubs†	.296	52	215	186	32	55	91	16	1	6	31	1	1	5	22	2	40	12	2	3	.489	.383
nchez, Alex, Devil Rays*	.282	56	245	227	36	64	86	7	6	1	22	1	1	6	10	0	35	20	12	2	.379	.318
nchez, Orlando, Red Sox	.268	16	64	56	8	15	18	1	1	0	3	2	0	0	6	0	9	2	0	4	.321	.339
ndberg, Jared, Devil Rays	.169	22	90	77	6	13	17	2	1	0	7	3	0	0	9	0	26	1	0	1	.221	.256
ntana, Pedro, Astros	.271	56	234	207	40	56	75	6	5	1	20	2	0	4	21	1	44	33	4	3	.362	.349
nto, Jose, Rangers	.249	54	234	197	42	49	94	10	7	7	33	0	5	6	26	0	61	11	2	2	.477	.346
hneider, Brian, Expos*	.268	52	193	164	26	44	53	5	2	0	23	2	0	3	24	3	15	2	3	3	.323	.372
ramm, Kevin, Rangers	.330	33	98	88	16	29	48	8	1	3	16	0	0	1	4	0	22	2	2	1	.545	.366
uro, Winston, Rangers	.170	24	59	53	7	9	9	0	0	0	3	1	1	1	3	0	9	1	0	0	.170	.224
erence, Lance, Dvl Rays	.174	9	27	23	0	4	4	0	0	0	2	0	0	0	4	0	1	0	0	1	.174	.296
pman, Nate, Tigers†	.204	35	128	113	16	23	34	6	1	1	12	0	1	7	7	0	37	7	2	1	.301	.289
a, Carlos, Twins	.189	24	64	53	4	10	12	2	0	0	6	0	1	2	8	0	16	2	3	2	.226	.313
ith, Dave, Red Sox	.333	3	10	9	0	3	4	1	0	0	1	0	0	0	1	0	1	0	1	1	.444	.400
ith, Marcus, Twins*	.186	33	115	102	11	19	27	2	3	0	12	0	1	1	9	0	29	7	2	1	.265	.257
ith, Nestor, Yankees†	.240	14	30	25	5	6	6	0	0	0	0	0	0	1	4	0	9	1	1	0	.240	.367
ano, Angel, White Sox	.294	9	37	34	6	10	10	0	0	0	3	0	0	0	3	0	4	1	2	0	.294	.351

Player, Team	Avg.	G	TPA	AB	R	H	TB	2B	3B	HR	RBI	SH	SF	HP	BB	IBB	SO	SB	CS	GDP	Slg.	OB
Stafford, Kimani, Royals	.051	21	49	39	5	2	2	0	0	0	3	2	0	0	8	0	16	1	1	1	.051	.2
Stanton, Thomas, Mets†	.217	43	174	152	19	33	53	6	1	4	19	1	0	7	14	2	36	0	3	3	.349	.3
Stenson, Dernell, Red Sox*	.216	32	123	97	16	21	32	3	1	2	15	0	3	7	16	0	26	4	3	0	.330	.3
Stephens, Jesus, Devil Rays	.224	33	87	76	12	17	18	1	0	0	10	0	0	0	11	1	26	3	2	1	.237	.3
Stevenson, Chad, Tigers	.291	46	171	158	13	46	64	18	0	0	16	0	0	4	9	0	47	1	0	3	.405	.3
Stewart, Counteney, Cubs	.256	21	83	78	6	20	23	3	0	0	5	1	0	0	4	0	28	4	1	4	.295	.2
Stovall, Darond, Expos†	.441	9	37	34	5	15	22	3	2	0	7	0	0	0	3	0	6	3	0	0	.647	.4
Stratton, Robert, Mets	.254	17	62	59	5	15	23	2	0	2	9	1	0	0	2	0	22	3	2	0	.390	.2
Suriel, Miguel, Devil Rays	.243	49	190	181	21	44	55	4	2	1	25	0	1	0	8	0	25	5	2	5	.304	.2
Sutton, Joe, White Sox	.221	40	129	113	10	25	37	7	1	1	11	0	0	1	15	0	33	1	0	3	.327	.3
Tanaka, Shuta, Tigers*	.164	44	140	116	16	19	28	7	1	0	11	3	1	2	18	0	21	5	1	2	.241	.2
Tarasco, Tony, Orioles*	.375	3	11	8	2	3	4	1	0	0	3	0	1	0	2	1	1	0	0	0	.500	.4
Tardiff, Jeremy, Red Sox	.200	4	6	5	0	1	1	0	0	0	0	0	0	0	1	0	1	0	0	0	.200	.3
Taveras, Jose, Royals	.191	13	49	47	3	9	11	2	0	0	4	0	1	0	1	0	7	0	2	0	.234	.2
Taylor, Avery, Orioles	.160	9	25	25	0	4	4	0	0	0	2	0	0	0	0	0	8	2	1	1	.160	.1
Terrell, Jim, White Sox*	.223	56	233	220	21	49	62	7	0	2	9	0	0	0	13	0	45	3	4	6	.282	.2
Thomas, Allen, White Sox*	.208	7	25	24	4	5	10	1	2	0	2	0	0	0	1	0	8	0	0	0	.417	.2
Thorpe, Angres, Braves†	.268	12	47	41	9	11	12	1	0	0	1	1	0	1	4	0	7	5	2	0	.293	.3
Tillero, Adrian, Royals	.228	40	139	127	12	29	36	4	0	1	12	2	0	0	10	0	18	1	0	2	.283	.2
Torrealba, Steve, Braves	.171	52	169	146	9	25	27	2	0	0	7	5	0	2	16	0	19	1	2	3	.185	.2
Torres, Gabriel, Twins	.348	22	74	66	9	23	32	4	1	1	5	0	0	1	7	0	10	1	2	3	.485	.4
Ubaldo, Nelson, Astros	.059	5	18	17	0	1	2	1	0	0	2	0	0	0	1	0	7	0	0	0	.118	.1
Utting, Andrew, Orioles	.263	36	136	114	10	30	44	7	2	1	19	2	0	2	17	1	16	4	0	0	.386	.3
Valenzuela, Mario, Wht Sox	.260	21	79	73	6	19	29	3	2	1	8	0	1	1	4	0	20	0	0	2	.397	.3
Viera, Rob, Pirates	.308	10	28	26	3	8	8	0	0	0	1	0	0	0	2	0	3	0	0	1	.308	.3
Vilorio, Leonel, Twins	.156	10	35	32	5	5	7	0	1	0	1	0	0	0	3	0	6	0	1	0	.219	.2
Vizcaino, Edward, Cubs	.000	16	1	1	0	0	0	0	0	0	0	0	0	0	0	0	1	0	0	0	.000	.0
Voita, Sam, Devil Rays†	.259	22	70	58	8	15	19	1	0	1	6	0	1	1	10	0	14	1	0	1	.328	.3
Walker, Corey, Braves*	.375	3	8	8	2	3	5	2	0	0	0	0	0	0	0	0	1	0	0	0	.625	.3
Ward, Brandon, Cubs	.000	16	1	0	0	0	0	0	0	0	0	0	0	0	1	0	0	0	0	0	.000	1.0
Ward, Greg, Braves	.000	3	6	5	0	0	0	0	0	0	0	0	0	0	1	0	3	0	0	0	.000	.1
Ware, Jeremy, Expos	.364	15	55	44	10	16	25	3	3	0	17	2	0	0	9	0	4	6	1	0	.568	.4
Washington, Cory, Marlins	.239	41	159	134	25	32	37	2	0	1	11	2	2	4	17	0	25	10	2	2	.276	.3
Weber, Brad, Devil Rays*	.247	37	97	81	8	20	22	2	0	0	11	4	0	0	11	0	24	1	0	3	.272	.3
Wheeler, Michael, Astros	.264	39	136	129	16	34	45	9	1	0	18	1	1	1	4	0	40	7	1	3	.349	.2
White, Rondell, Expos	.250	3	12	12	3	3	9	0	0	2	4	0	0	0	0	0	1	0	1	1	.750	.2
Whitner, Keith, Tigers	.202	43	153	124	13	25	30	2	0	1	8	1	1	12	15	0	40	8	2	1	.242	.3
Wilder, Paul, Devil Rays*	.207	53	226	184	31	38	61	10	2	3	20	1	0	4	37	0	66	7	5	2	.332	.3
Wilkes, Brian, Marlins	.162	17	48	37	4	6	6	0	0	0	1	0	0	2	9	0	9	1	0	2	.162	.3
Wilson, Heath, Braves	.167	3	6	6	1	1	1	0	0	0	0	0	0	0	0	0	2	0	0	0	.167	.1
Wong, Jerrod, Braves*	.289	13	48	45	7	13	19	6	0	0	4	0	0	2	1	0	7	0	1	0	.422	.3
Zapata, Alexis, Tigers	.333	51	208	189	34	63	104	13	5	6	41	0	4	3	12	2	35	8	4	2	.550	.3
Zapp, A.J., Braves*	.149	47	179	161	9	24	33	9	0	0	5	1	1	1	15	0	58	0	0	0	.205	.2
Zosky, Eddie, Orioles	.333	1	4	3	1	1	2	1	0	0	0	0	0	0	1	0	0	0	0	0	.667	.5
Zydowsky, John, Braves	.190	52	190	174	15	33	39	3	0	1	12	3	1	2	10	0	38	3	3	1	.224	.2
Zywica, Michael, Rangers	.273	33	132	110	18	30	48	7	1	3	22	0	0	8	14	1	24	3	0	1	.436	.3

GRAND SLAMS: H. Lopez, 2; Alleyne, Ayuso, J. Bautista, Escalona, Hessman, McNeal, Salazar, Stanton, Zydowsky, 1 each.

AWARDED FIRST BASE ON CATCHER'S INTERFERENCE: Carter 2 (Prada 2); Meran 2 (Candelaria, Leon); Alaimo (Luis J. Rivera); Aybar (Chapman); X. Burns (Prad Byrd (Munson); L. Cardona (Prada); Coffie (L. Evans); Jamison (Suriel); Maduro (Stanton); P. Ortiz (Prada); Payano (Herrera); Sandberg (Candelaria); Utting (Dia Weber (Candelaria).

1996 PITCHING

TEAM

Team	W	L	Pct.	ERA	G	CG	ShO	Sv.	IP	H	TBF	R	ER	HR	SH	SF	HB	BB	IBB	SO	WP	B
Marlins	34	25	.576	2.73	60	5	11	11	523.2	402	2148	214	159	13	25	13	31	182	10	421	50	1
Cubs	34	26	.567	2.83	60	1	3	15	527.1	424	2201	230	166	11	13	10	49	188	1	485	48	1
Rangers	37	23	.617	2.99	60	4	4	20	527.1	467	2223	232	175	24	17	15	24	196	8	431	47	1
Expos	41	18	.695	3.15	60	3	7	16	514.2	436	2139	225	180	16	25	13	35	152	0	348	31	1
Orioles	36	24	.600	3.21	60	1	6	20	525.0	456	2202	238	187	21	17	19	32	175	1	451	40	1
Astros	31	28	.525	3.28	59	1	5	14	505.1	447	2178	247	184	13	15	17	43	191	3	515	70	1
Twins	30	30	.500	3.38	60	5	2	12	506.0	493	2159	258	190	21	14	12	27	183	2	389	50	1
Mets	29	30	.492	3.49	59	4	5	18	495.0	449	2127	236	192	13	22	11	31	178	5	439	51	2
Yankees	37	21	.638	3.60	58	2	9	13	484.2	452	2089	256	194	19	12	11	31	178	0	453	42	1
Red Sox	24	36	.400	3.69	60	0	3	10	527.0	546	2332	308	216	25	30	16	41	173	8	423	52	2
Pirates	28	31	.475	3.76	60	3	4	14	511.2	511	2256	291	214	18	19	15	45	184	0	418	36	1
Tigers	26	34	.433	3.89	60	3	2	10	505.0	527	2233	305	218	18	17	17	38	172	2	405	65	1
Royals	30	29	.508	4.05	60	3	4	14	495.1	495	2162	279	223	30	16	20	42	165	0	427	45	1
Braves	14	45	.237	4.08	59	0	1	6	505.0	494	2221	293	229	12	33	15	38	204	9	379	59	2
White Sox	20	40	.333	4.19	60	4	3	10	510.2	535	2263	312	238	22	18	15	38	192	3	408	43	
Devil Rays	24	35	.407	4.23	59	2	0	12	517.1	495	2278	304	243	11	19	23	45	199	11	501	61	2

INDIVIDUAL

TOP QUALIFIERS FOR EARNED-RUN AVERAGE TITLE

Minimum 48 innings. *Lefthanded pitcher.

Pitcher, Team	W	L	Pct.	ERA	G	GS	CG	ShO	GF	Sv.	IP	H	TBF	R	ER	HR	SH	SF	HB	BB	IBB	SO	WP
Gholar, Antonio, Twins	1	2	.333	1.72	15	7	0	0	4	2	52.1	30	213	18	10	0	0	0	4	30	0	50	5
Robertson, Jeriome, Astros*	5	3	.625	1.72	13	13	1	1	0	0	78.1	51	304	20	15	2	3	0	4	15	0	98	6

cher, Team	W	L	Pct.	ERA	G	GS	CG	ShO	GF	Sv.	IP	H	TBF	R	ER	HR	SH	SF	HB	BB	IBB	SO	WP	Bk.
ser, Joe, Expos	4	0	1.000	1.81	11	10	0	0	0	0	49.2	35	197	14	10	1	4	0	0	18	0	45	5	0
ntana, Pedro, Red Sox	5	3	.625	1.89	13	8	0	0	2	0	71.1	59	289	24	15	4	5	1	2	12	1	33	2	3
tune, Peter, Expos*	6	0	1.000	1.96	13	13	0	0	0	0	73.1	52	292	23	16	1	4	4	3	21	0	66	2	0
ega, Pablo, Devil Rays	4	6	.400	1.97	13	13	1	0	0	0	82.1	61	330	24	18	1	2	0	3	12	0	86	7	4
tos, Victor, Tigers	3	2	.600	1.98	9	9	0	0	0	0	50.0	44	199	12	11	1	3	1	7	13	0	39	3	0
aqueima, Jesus, Yankees	3	2	.600	2.01	11	9	0	0	0	0	49.1	43	209	24	11	4	1	0	3	15	0	49	7	4
enez, Ricardo, Orioles	5	3	.625	2.01	12	12	0	0	0	0	62.2	46	267	22	14	1	1	1	4	34	0	44	1	0
otts, Gary, Marlins	4	2	.667	2.04	12	9	1	1	2	0	57.1	35	227	16	13	0	2	2	6	17	0	46	5	0
ner, Scott, Mets*	2	2	.500	2.16	13	8	0	0	3	0	50.0	40	200	16	12	1	1	0	3			40	1	3
z, Jose, Cubs	3	2	.600	2.18	12	8	0	0	0	0	53.2	36	206	15	13	1	1	2	0	12	0	42	1	0
tana, Humberto, Mets*	4	3	.571	2.21	11	7	0	0	2	0	61.0	46	246	20	15	0	1	2	4	18	0	57	8	1
evedo, Ruben, Braves	2	6	.250	2.29	10	10	0	0	0	0	55.0	50	221	19	14	1	4	1	1	9	0	49	3	2

DEPARTMENTAL LEADERS: W—Widerski, 8; L—Aa. Taylor, 9; Pct.—Derek Brown, .857; G—Stinson, 24; GS—Bowers, Fortune, Forbes, J. Robertson, Ortega, 13 ...; CG—Marshall, 3; ShO—McClaskey, 2; GF—Styles, 23; Sv.—Styles, 13; IP—Ortega, 82.1; H—Hausman, 85; TBF—Hausman, 343; R—Aa. Taylor, 54; ER—D. ...es, 47; HR—Pineda, 6; SH—Aa. Taylor, 7; SF—Miller, Forbes, M. Torres, 5 each; HB—D. James, 11; BB—Bowers, 39; IBB—Several players tied at 3 each; SO—J. ...ertson, 98; WP—Aa. Taylor, 14; Bk.—Serrano, 7.

ALL PITCHERS
*Lefthanded pitcher.

cher, Team	W	L	Pct.	ERA	G	GS	CG	ShO	GF	Sv.	IP	H	TBF	R	ER	HR	SH	SF	HB	BB	IBB	SO	WP	Bk.
eu, Miguel, Marlins	0	0	.000	0.00	1	0	0	0	1	0	1.0	1	5	0	0	0	0	0	0	0	0	0	0	0
illes, Matt, Orioles	0	1	.000	2.25	5	5	0	0	0	0	20.0	16	84	6	5	2	1	2	2	10	0	12	2	0
chi, Tomo, Tigers*	0	1	.000	8.38	5	0	0	0	0	0	9.2	15	55	15	9	1	0	0	0	7	1	7	2	0
rado, Carlos, Pirates	1	1	.500	4.94	11	1	0	0	4	0	27.1	32	125	20	15	1	1	1	2	10	0	31	2	2
rado, David, Pirates	0	0	.000	0.00	1	0	0	0	0	0	4.0	0	14	1	0	0	0	0	0	1	0	8	0	0
o, Royel, Cubs	2	2	.500	4.42	13	1	0	0	10	3	18.1	10	90	10	9	1	0	3	2	17	1	23	0	0
rd, Aaron, Tigers	4	3	.571	4.85	16	0	0	0	6	2	42.2	60	193	28	23	0	1	3	2	6	0	21	2	0
rade, Jancy, Orioles	3	2	.600	2.68	18	3	0	0	11	5	37.0	30	150	13	11	0	2	2		13	0	30	2	0
ujar, Luis, White Sox	1	0	1.000	0.00	1	1	0	0	0	0	6.0	3	22	0	0	0	0	0	1	0		3	0	0
s, Jose, Devil Rays*	0	1	.000	2.37	10	0	0	0	3	1	19.0	22	94	8	5	0	0	0	2	9	2	20	1	0
s, Rafael, Red Sox	1	6	.143	4.93	13	5	0	0	4	0	49.1	68	228	39	27	2	6	1	1	8	2	20	4	4
as, Antonio, Yankees	4	1	.800	3.15	8	7	0	0	1	1	45.2	41	191	18	16	1	0	2	2	13	0	45	4	2
enta, Alfredo, Braves*	2	4	.333	4.22	14	2	0	0	9	1	42.2	38	187	23	20	1	1	1	1	20	1	39	3	1
in, Lakevie, Red Sox	3	4	.429	4.31	16	0	0	0	8	1	22.2	24	110	17	8	0	4	2		13	0	26	5	3
ey, Sean, Expos	1	0	1.000	9.00	1	0	0	0	0	0	2.0	2	10	2	2	0	1	0		1	0	1	0	0
sdale, Shane, Astros	0	2	.000	3.00	12	0	0	0	3	1	18.0	14	77	6	6	0	2	2	2	8	0	16	2	0
y, Chad, White Sox	0	1	.000	10.22	10	0	0	0	0	0	12.1	17	66	15	14	0	1	0	4	9	0	15	2	1
h, Scott, Pirates	2	1	.667	10.57	7	0	0	0	7	0	7.2	16	42	9	9	0	1	0	3	3	0	4	0	0
tez, Armando, Orioles	1	0	1.000	0.00	1	0	0	0	0	0	2.0	1	7	0	0	0	0	0	0	0		5	0	0
ing, Skipp, Red Sox*	2	2	.500	4.33	12	9	0	0	0	0	52.0	55	232	31	25	3	0	7		16	0	51	6	0
, Jason, White Sox	0	1	.000	6.00	1	1	0	0	0	0	3.0	3	14	2	2	0	0	0	1	0		3	0	0
oa, Oliver, Red Sox	1	2	.333	5.12	17	0	0	0	8	1	31.2	21	149	28	18	4	0	1	8	23	1	28	10	1
ll, Simon, Braves	0	4	.000	2.40	10	10	0	0	0	0	56.1	50	239	18	15	0	1	7		22	1	32	4	0
kmore, John, Astros	1	0	1.000	3.46	16	1	0	0	5	0	26.0	22	121	15	10	0	1	3		17	0	17	2	3
co, Edgar, Twins	1	1	.500	4.35	12	0	0	0	3	0	20.2	16	89	10	10	0	2			13	0	19	4	1
co, Pablo, Marlins	3	5	.375	4.57	12	11	2	1	0	0	65.0	58	282	43	33	3	4	3	2	36	1	42	8	0
lla, Miguel, Pirates	0	0	.000	9.00	3	0	0	0	0	0	3.0	6	13	3	3	0	0	1	0	1	0	2	0	0
ng, Richard, Royals	1	1	.500	1.95	15	0	0	0	7	4	27.2	21	116	10	6	1	0	1	3	5	0	10	3	0
owski, Robert, Mets	3	3	.500	4.60	12	7	1	0	1	0	43.0	44	190	24	22	3	0	4		17	0	33	6	0
ers, Cedrick, Devil Rays*	3	5	.375	5.37	13	13	0	0	0	0	60.1	50	268	39	36	2	0	2	3	39	0	85	5	5
o, Franklin, Pirates	5	3	.625	2.32	11	11	2	1	0	0	62.0	62	260	23	16	1	2	1	3	10	0	36	1	1
rn, Derek, Orioles	6	1	.857	3.11	9	8	1	1	1	1	55.0	50	219	19	19	1	1	2	0	11	0	37	5	3
vn, Michael, Devil Rays	0	0	.000	11.57	3	1	0	0	0	0	4.2	7	31	9	6	0	1	0	1	8	0	2	1	2
vn, Trent, Devil Rays*	3	2	.600	2.18	15	3	0	0	5	1	45.1	37	188	18	11	2	3	0	3	14	3	53	0	0
nanan, Brian, Yankees*	4	1	.800	3.02	12	11	1	1	1	0	59.2	47	254	26	20	0	2	2	1	29	0	45	5	2
ck, Brian, White Sox	0	0	.000	0.00	1	0	0	0	0	0	1.0	0	4	0	0	0	0	0	0	2	0	0	0	0
ro, Robert, Devil Rays	0	0	.000	0.00	2	0	0	0	0	0	3.0	9	9	0	0	0	0	0	0	0		3	0	0
rt, Kale, Red Sox	1	4	.200	5.30	20	3	0	0	11	3	35.2	41	169	29	21	5	2	2	2	17	1	34	3	0
iobello, Anthony, Braves	1	1	.500	2.29	15	0	0	0	12	0	35.1	30	151	10	9	1	0	1	1	16	0	30	7	0
u, Alvin, Royals*	4	2	.667	3.70	9	9	0	0	0	0	48.2	54	205	24	20	4	0	0	0	12	0	42	0	0
amo, Kevin, Royals	2	0	1.000	2.55	9	0	0	0	8	0	24.2	15	95	9	7	3	2	0	2	5	0	22	0	0
ona, Steve, White Sox	1	1	.500	2.63	15	0	0	0	8	0	24.0	28	108	10	7	0	2	1		9	0	31	1	2
Tim, Mets	0	3	.000	3.86	16	2	0	0	10	6	39.2	34	174	20	17	2	6	1	4	13	1	34	3	1
on, Jorge, Rangers	2	0	1.000	1.76	4	4	0	0	0	0	15.1	10	66	5	3	2	0	0	0	10	0	19	3	0
y, Shaw, Marlins	2	3	.400	3.49	15	0	0	0	9	1	28.1	22	128	12	11	1	1	4	18	2	25	4	2	
ar, Donald, Braves	0	1	.000	4.44	10	3	0	0	3	0	24.1	25	106	12	12	1	0	3	0	15	0	17	2	1
, Nicolas, Astros*	2	2	.500	3.38	17	0	0	0	6	0	26.2	30	124	19	10	0	2	3	8	1	30	6	2	
stman, Scott, White Sox*	1	1	.500	3.75	4	4	0	0	0	0	12.0	13	57	8	5	0	0	1	2	4	0	13	1	0
, Greg, Twins	6	4	.600	3.39	13	12	0	0	0	0	66.1	84	302	42	25	4	4	1	5	19	0	37	3	1
sen, Ender, Marlins	1	1	.500	4.70	7	0	0	0	0	0	7.2	12	37	5	4	0	0	1	3	0	6	1	1	
e, Jason, Yankees*	1	1	.500	2.48	9	9	0	0	0	0	32.2	23	137	11	9	0	0	2	20	0	41	1	1	
er, Scott, Mets*	2	2	.500	2.16	13	8	0	0	3	0	50.0	40	200	16	12	1	1	0	3			40	1	3
ell, Brian, Cubs*	2	1	.667	10.54	7	5	0	0	7	0	13.2	12	70	18	16	0	0	3	15	0	11	9	0	
, Derrick, Rangers	2	1	.667	4.70	6	5	1	1	0	0	23.0	25	100	14	12	1	0	1	2	11	0	13	1	0
, O.J., Pirates	5	2	.714	3.55	11	6	0	0	1	0	50.2	43	211	23	20	4	1	1	2	19	0	36	4	1
, Craig, Mets*	0	0	.000	0.00	1	0	0	0	0	0	2.0	0	8	0	0	0	0	0	0	0		3	0	0
lan, Roberto, Yankees	2	1	.667	4.30	12	0	0	0	2	1	29.1	27	130	18	14	0	1	2	1	16	0	26	3	0
nan, Jeff, Mets	0	0	.000	0.00	2	1	0	0	0	0	6.0	4	28	0	0	0	0	0	3	0	10	0	0	
e, Robert, Mets	0	0	.000	2.00	5	0	0	0	6	0	9.0	11	42	4	2	0	1	2	4	0	16	0	1	
e, Randy, Cubs	0	3	.000	1.86	15	0	0	0	6	1	29.0	17	127	11	6	0	1	2	4	16	0	35	0	1

Pitcher, Team	W	L	Pct.	ERA	G	GS	CG	ShO	GF	Sv.	IP	H	TBF	R	ER	HR	SH	SF	HB	BB	IBB	SO	WP
Crawford, Chris, Astros	0	0	.000	9.00	1	0	0	0	0	0	2.0	3	10	2	2	0	0	0	0	1	0	3	0
Cremer, Rick, Yankees*	0	1	.000	11.57	2	1	0	0	0	0	4.2	3	23	7	6	0	0	0	0	8	0	4	3
Cruz, Charlie, Orioles	1	0	1.000	4.50	9	0	0	0	4	0	14.0	19	69	10	7	0	0	1	5	6	0	7	3
Davis, Doug, Rangers*	3	1	.750	1.90	8	7	0	0	0	0	42.2	28	174	13	9	0	1	2	0	26	1	49	2
Day, Stephen, Yankees	5	2	.714	5.61	7	5	0	0	1	0	33.2	41	139	26	21	3	0	0	4	3	0	23	0
Deckard, Edward, Devil Rays...	1	1	.500	2.82	9	0	0	0	1	0	22.1	23	98	10	7	0	2	2	4	11	1	15	3
Delgado, Daniel, Pirates	1	0	1.000	2.84	2	0	0	0	1	0	6.1	4	24	2	2	0	0	0	2	0	0	1	0
Delarosa, Raul, White Sox	0	2	.000	6.92	18	1	0	0	8	1	26.0	43	131	31	20	1	2	2	2	9	2	16	1
DeLeon, Julio, Devil Rays	0	0	.000	4.70	7	0	0	0	2	0	15.1	18	63	9	8	1	0	0	0	4	0	6	0
Donastorg, Raul, Tigers	1	2	.333	3.96	20	0	0	0	17	4	25.0	24	108	13	11	1	0	1	1	9	0	17	4
Duchscherer, Justin, Red Sox .	0	2	.000	3.13	13	8	0	0	2	1	54.2	52	232	26	19	0	3	3	3	14	0	45	4
Dunn, Cordell, Pirates	0	5	.000	5.46	7	6	0	0	0	0	28.0	32	136	24	17	1	1	2	0	14	0	24	5
Durbin, Chad, Royals	3	2	.600	4.26	11	8	1	1	1	0	44.1	34	187	22	21	3	0	1	1	25	0	43	6
Durick, Chad, Mets	0	0	.000	0.00	1	0	0	0	1	1	2.0	0	6	0	0	0	0	0	0	0	0	4	0
Ellison, Jason, Yankees	3	2	.600	1.25	21	3	0	0	17	7	36.0	24	151	8	5	0	1	0	3	15	0	42	2
Enard, Tony, Marlins	0	0	.000	0.00	2	0	0	0	1	0	6.2	3	23	0	0	0	0	0	0	3	0	5	1
Espina, Rendy, Twins*	0	2	.000	9.26	7	1	0	0	2	0	11.2	18	54	12	12	0	0	0	1	8	0	10	1
Evans, Mike, Marlins*	0	1	.000	1.27	19	0	0	0	13	3	35.1	24	143	8	5	0	2	0	1	13	3	40	5
Fajardo, Alexis, Yankees*	0	0	.000	0.00	2	0	0	0	1	0	4.1	2	19	0	0	0	0	0	0	4	0	8	0
Falkenborg, Brian, Orioles	0	3	.000	2.57	8	6	0	0	1	0	28.0	21	116	13	8	1	0	0	1	8	0	36	2
Felix, Miguel, White Sox	3	6	.333	3.31	12	12	1	0	0	0	73.1	73	317	39	27	2	0	3	5	19	0	64	2
Feliz, Jose, Cubs	4	1	.800	2.21	11	7	0	0	2	0	61.0	46	246	20	15	0	1	2	4	18	0	57	8
Fennell, Barry, Cubs*	0	4	.000	2.95	10	7	0	0	2	1	42.2	37	179	19	14	0	4	2	2	12	0	42	2
Ferullo, Matt, Mets	1	0	1.000	4.91	2	2	0	0	0	0	11.0	11	45	6	6	0	0	0	2	2	0	13	0
Finol, Ricardo, Pirates	1	0	1.000	9.00	6	0	0	0	2	0	10.0	19	53	10	10	1	0	0	0	5	0	9	2
Fleming, Emar, Rangers	4	4	.500	3.75	12	12	0	0	0	0	69.2	70	286	33	29	3	1	2	5	13	0	52	1
Forbes, Cameron, Orioles	4	5	.444	4.34	13	13	0	0	0	0	76.2	73	326	48	37	5	6	5	3	22	0	71	4
Forti, Eugene, White Sox*	4	2	.667	3.65	12	8	0	0	1	1	56.2	50	238	28	23	3	2	0	4	20	0	44	5
Fortune, Peter, Expos*	6	0	1.000	1.96	13	13	0	0	0	0	73.1	52	292	23	16	1	4	4	3	21	0	66	2
Fowler, Benjamin, Braves	1	4	.200	3.34	8	6	0	0	1	0	29.2	27	131	21	11	0	3	2	0	11	0	22	2
Fowler, Jered, Devil Rays	0	0	.000	4.70	4	0	0	0	3	2	7.2	8	43	7	4	0	1	0	2	8	2	10	2
Fraser, Joe, Expos	4	0	1.000	1.81	11	10	0	0	0	0	49.2	35	197	14	10	1	4	0	0	18	0	45	5
Gaerte, Travis, Pirates	1	0	1.000	2.40	14	0	0	0	8	5	30.0	17	122	9	8	0	1	0	3	18	0	24	5
Galban, Julian, Braves*	0	2	.000	13.50	5	1	0	0	3	0	6.0	14	42	14	9	0	0	2	1	9	0	3	0
Gandarillas, Gus, Twins	0	0	.000	1.00	3	1	0	0	2	2	9.0	10	43	3	1	1	1	0	3	0	14	1
Garcia, Gabe, Astros	3	4	.429	2.48	13	5	0	0	2	1	36.1	30	154	12	10	3	0	3	0	10	0	50	3
Garmon, Adam, Mets	2	1	.667	2.49	12	2	0	0	3	1	25.1	18	113	7	7	0	1	0	1	19	0	31	5
Garrett, Josh, Red Sox	1	1	.500	1.67	7	5	0	0	0	0	27.0	22	108	8	5	0	2	0	5	5	0	17	0
Gentile, Scott, Expos	1	1	.500	4.91	5	1	0	0	2	1	7.1	5	30	4	4	0	0	0	4	0	5	0
Gholar, Antonio, Twins	1	2	.333	1.72	15	7	0	0	4	2	52.1	30	213	18	10	0	0	4	30	0	50	5
Gillispie, Ryan, Pirates	0	0	.000	0.00	1	0	0	0	0	0	3.0	4	14	1	0	0	0	0	0	5	0
Gissell, Christopher, Cubs	4	2	.667	2.35	11	10	0	0	0	0	61.1	54	246	23	16	1	0	1	4	8	0	64	1
Goedde, Roger, Pirates	0	2	.000	9.10	12	3	0	0	2	0	28.2	45	149	41	29	2	4	2	4	11	0	23	2
Gonzalez, Dicky, Mets	4	2	.667	2.66	11	8	2	1	1	0	47.1	50	195	19	14	1	2	0	2	3	0	51	1
Gonzalez, Edwin, Royals	5	3	.625	3.75	12	8	1	0	2	1	57.2	60	253	32	24	5	4	2	7	14	0	39	6
Gonzalez, Generoso, Tigers	2	1	.667	3.32	4	4	0	0	0	0	19.0	17	85	9	7	1	0	1	1	9	0	19	3
Gresko, Michael, Pirates*	0	1	.000	3.00	5	0	0	0	1	0	6.0	3	31	8	2	1	1	0	1	5	0	7	2
Grieve, Tim, Royals	0	0	.000	0.00	2	0	0	0	0	0	3.0	1	11	1	0	0	0	0	1	0	2	0
Hamulack, Tim, Astros*	4	1	.800	2.33	22	0	0	0	9	2	27.0	23	115	9	7	1	0	0	2	13	1	24	1
Harden, Nathan, Braves	2	2	.500	4.62	14	2	0	0	6	0	39.0	32	170	29	20	2	1	1	3	15	0	30	5
Harris, Gene, Pirates	0	2	.000	3.21	9	1	0	0	2	1	14.0	16	61	7	5	0	0	0	1	4	0	14	0
Hausman, Isaac, Rangers	7	3	.700	2.89	12	11	2	1	1	0	81.0	85	343	38	26	5	3	3	1	14	1	48	1
Heberling, Keith, Pirates*	0	0	.000	0.00	1	0	0	0	0	0	1.0	0	5	0	0	0	0	0	0	0	0	1	0
Hendrikx, Brandon, Yankees....	0	1	.000	3.86	7	0	0	0	4	1	9.1	9	43	10	4	1	0	1	0	3	0	10	0
Henriquez, Jobannis, Rangers .	2	3	.400	4.10	13	6	0	0	2	0	41.2	42	178	22	19	3	1	1	1	19	2	29	7
Heredia, Maximo, Orioles	3	1	.750	2.88	17	0	0	0	7	4	34.1	22	143	15	11	1	1	0	4	12	0	25	2
Hinojosa, Joel, Devil Rays	0	0	.000	20.25	1	0	0	0	0	0	1.1	3	10	5	3	0	0	1	0	2	0	1	1
Hlodan, George, Pirates	3	2	.600	2.67	7	6	0	0	0	0	27.0	29	117	12	8	0	1	4	2	7	0	15	1
Hohenstein, Andrew, Pirates....	2	0	1.000	3.08	7	5	0	0	1	0	26.1	36	125	20	9	1	0	1	2	12	0	18	1
Holobinko, Mike, Cubs*	2	0	1.000	0.52	11	0	0	0	8	3	17.1	10	67	1	1	0	0	0	7	0	22	2
Huber, John, Astros	1	2	.333	4.04	10	6	0	0	0	0	35.2	33	161	20	16	1	0	0	3	23	0	37	9
Ireland, Eric, Astros	3	4	.429	4.70	12	11	0	0	1	0	53.2	54	235	33	28	1	3	1	3	23	1	43	13
Izquierdo, Hansel, Marlins	0	1	.000	2.70	12	0	0	0	10	3	13.1	7	52	4	4	0	0	3	5	0	17	3
Jacobs, Jake, Twins	1	2	.333	5.74	6	6	0	0	0	0	26.2	31	119	22	17	4	2	0	1	7	0	29	2
James, Delvin, Devil Rays	2	8	.200	8.87	11	11	1	0	0	0	47.2	64	236	52	47	0	1	3	11	21	0	40	11
Jimenez, Ricardo, Orioles	5	3	.625	2.01	12	12	0	0	0	0	62.2	46	267	22	14	1	1	1	4	34	0	44	1
Johnson, Jeremiah, Orioles	0	0	.000	0.00	4	0	0	0	1	0	6.0	4	23	0	0	0	0	0	1	0	10	0
Juarez, Raul, Twins	3	2	.600	6.94	11	0	0	0	8	0	11.2	12	55	11	9	0	1	1	2	7	0	9	2
Kauffman, George, Royals	0	0	.000	0.00	1	0	0	0	0	0	0.2	1	3	0	0	0	0	0	0	0	1	0
Keller, Kris, Tigers	1	1	.500	2.38	8	6	0	0	0	0	34.0	23	143	12	9	0	1	2	0	21	0	23	7
Kelley, Jason, Cubs	2	3	.400	5.96	8	7	0	0	1	0	25.2	18	115	22	17	3	0	1	7	16	0	29	7
Kertis, John, Rangers	0	1	.000	2.25	4	2	0	0	1	0	12.0	11	55	8	3	0	2	0	1	6	0	12	2
Keusch, Joe, Rangers	0	0	.000	3.00	2	0	0	0	2	0	3.0	1	10	1	1	0	0	0	0	0	0	3	0
Key, Jimmy, Yankees*	1	0	1.000	0.00	1	1	0	0	0	0	5.0	3	21	2	0	0	0	0	1	0	0	10	0
Kingsbury, Willy, Red Sox	1	0	1.000	0.00	1	0	0	0	0	0	2.0	2	10	0	0	0	0	0	1	1	1	0
Knotts, Gary, Marlins	4	2	.667	2.04	12	9	1	1	2	0	57.1	35	227	16	13	0	2	6	17	0	46	5
Kofler, Ed, Devil Rays	1	4	.200	5.27	10	10	0	0	0	0	41.0	49	189	30	24	2	0	4	4	11	0	36	2
Kyzar, Justin, Royals	0	2	.000	8.27	7	2	0	0	1	1	16.1	21	83	16	15	2	1	2	4	10	0	19	1
Lara, Nelson, Marlins	1	2	.333	5.59	7	0	0	0	1	0	9.2	6	54	11	6	0	2	1	3	12	2	3	4
Larocca, Todd, Orioles	1	0	1.000	12.71	4	0	0	0	1	0	5.2	8	30	8	8	0	1	0	4	2	0	9	3
Lee, Winston, Braves	1	2	.333	2.77	13	3	0	0	2	1	39.0	32	152	12	12	2	2	0	4	3	0	36	4
Leidens, Enrique, Expos	0	1	.000	0.00	1	0	0	0	1	0	0.0	2	2	1	1	0	0	0	0	0	0	0	0
Levan, Matthew, Marlins*	1	3	.250	3.42	9	6	0	0	2	0	26.1	24	108	14	10	1	0	0	0	11	0	26	0

SUMMER CLASS A — Gulf Coast League

tcher, Team	W	L	Pct.	ERA	G	GS	CG	ShO	GF	Sv.	IP	H	TBF	R	ER	HR	SH	SF	HB	BB	IBB	SO	WP	Bk.
ndemann, Jeffrey, Braves	2	1	.667	1.13	4	2	0	0	2	0	16.0	12	65	4	2	0	0	0	3	3	0	12	0	0
onam, Rick, Twins	5	3	.625	1.76	22	1	0	0	15	4	46.0	46	186	16	9	1	0	0	3	8	0	35	3	1
pez, Jose, White Sox	0	3	.000	4.18	16	1	0	0	6	0	23.2	21	96	12	11	1	2	0	0	6	1	9	1	0
ovingood, Jeromie, Mets*	4	3	.571	0.98	10	8	1	0	1	0	46.0	28	184	11	5	1	2	1	3	18	0	32	4	0
igo, Marcelino, Marlins	5	0	1.000	1.85	8	0	0	0	8	0	24.1	9	86	5	5	1	1	1	1	7	1	13	0	1
andquist, Dave, White Sox	1	1	.500	2.63	3	3	0	0	0	0	13.2	8	49	4	4	1	0	0	0	2	0	16	0	0
adison, Scott, Devil Rays*	0	0	.000	27.00	1	0	0	0	0	0	1.0	3	6	3	3	0	0	1	0	0	0	0	0	0
aeda, Katsuhiro, Yankees	1	1	.500	3.00	2	2	1	1	0	0	9.0	4	35	3	3	1	0	1	1	2	0	7	0	0
allory, Andrew, Cubs	0	3	.000	3.86	12	7	0	0	0	0	53.2	49	234	31	23	2	0	0	8	22	0	33	4	0
anley, Kevin, Mets	0	1	.000	17.36	10	1	0	0	1	1	14.0	23	95	32	27	0	2	2	2	30	0	13	13	2
arquardt, Scott, Mets	0	0	.000	2.70	4	1	0	0	1	0	10.0	5	39	3	3	1	0	0	3	1	0	8	0	2
arshall, Lee, Twins	4	4	.231	2.31	12	12	3	1	0	0	70.0	59	283	31	18	0	1	2	0	18	2	39	2	1
artin, Curtis, Expos*	2	0	1.000	2.40	8	1	0	0	2	0	15.0	13	59	4	4	1	0	0	0	2	0	6	1	1
artin, Trey, Expos	6	0	1.000	5.44	13	8	1	0	5	2	51.1	50	226	36	31	5	1	2	5	14	0	35	6	1
artinez, Javier, Cubs	2	1	.667	0.60	3	3	0	0	0	0	15.0	11	62	4	1	0	0	0	0	6	1	15	1	0
artinez, Oscar, Yankees	0	0	.000	14.90	7	0	0	0	3	0	9.2	22	58	16	16	2	0	0	3	4	0	3	5	0
artinez, Romulo, Tigers	1	6	.143	2.73	12	12	0	0	0	0	62.2	67	261	28	19	1	3	1	2	9	0	51	4	3
attson, Craig, Pirates	0	0	.000	0.00	1	0	0	0	0	0	1.0	0	3	0	0	0	0	0	0	0	0	0	0	0
cBride, Jason, Yankees	3	4	.429	4.06	23	0	0	0	13	2	31.0	35	137	15	14	3	0	0	2	8	0	27	3	0
cCarter, Jason, Astros	0	1	.000	1.21	21	0	0	0	20	8	22.1	13	94	6	3	0	0	0	3	14	0	26	6	1
cClaskey, Tim, Marlins	4	3	.571	2.59	12	12	2	2	0	0	73.0	58	288	28	21	3	5	3	2	13	0	63	2	0
cCready, Jim, Mets	1	1	.500	1.13	5	1	0	0	0	0	8.0	4	34	3	1	0	2	0	2	2	0	8	0	1
cCreery, Rick, Devil Rays	0	2	.000	1.17	11	0	0	0	11	5	15.1	12	63	5	2	0	1	0	4	4	1	16	2	1
cDaniel, Denton, Royals*	1	1	.500	3.72	7	5	0	0	1	0	19.1	15	84	11	8	0	2	0	3	10	0	25	2	1
cFarlane, Joseph, Tigers	2	0	1.000	3.93	15	2	0	0	5	2	36.2	32	158	21	16	2	2	1	6	14	0	34	2	0
cKnight, Tony, Astros	2	2	.500	6.66	9	6	0	0	0	0	24.1	34	125	26	18	1	0	2	5	7	0	17	4	0
cNatt, Joshua, Orioles*	3	2	.600	2.18	12	8	0	0	2	0	53.2	36	206	15	13	1	1	2	0	12	0	42	1	0
cNichol, Brian, Cubs*	0	0	.000	0.00	1	1	0	0	0	0	3.1	4	16	2	0	0	0	0	0	2	0	2	0	0
eady, Todd, Royals	2	5	.286	3.39	11	10	1	1	0	0	58.1	58	254	31	22	2	3	4	6	16	0	47	5	3
edina, Carlos, Marlins*	0	1	.000	3.72	4	1	0	0	1	0	9.2	16	48	7	4	0	1	0	2	1	0	9	3	0
edina, Tom, Astros	1	1	.500	4.15	8	0	0	0	8	2	13.0	13	60	7	6	0	1	0	5	6	0	10	1	0
endoza, Geronimo, Wht Sox.	1	8	.111	9.78	12	7	0	0	0	0	38.2	55	202	49	42	2	3	3	3	26	0	29	6	1
ercedes, Carlos, Orioles	2	1	.333	5.40	5	1	0	0	4	1	8.1	15	41	7	5	1	0	1	0	2	1	6	1	1
iller, Wade, Astros	3	4	.429	3.79	11	10	0	0	0	0	57.0	49	233	26	24	1	2	5	4	12	0	53	5	0
ontanez, Jorge, Red Sox*	0	0	.000	2.03	10	0	0	0	4	0	13.1	15	62	12	3	0	0	0	2	5	0	7	2	0
ontemayor, H, Red Sox*	4	3	.571	2.78	10	2	0	0	4	0	32.1	30	139	14	10	3	1	0	0	11	0	19	2	2
oody, Ritchie, Rangers*	0	0	.000	0.00	3	0	0	0	1	0	6.0	2	19	1	0	0	0	0	0	9	0	6	1	0
oreno, Orber, Royals	5	1	.833	1.36	12	7	0	0	5	1	46.1	37	187	15	7	2	2	0	1	10	0	50	2	2
oreno, Willy, Yankees	0	0	.000	9.56	11	0	0	0	5	0	16.0	27	83	24	17	1	1	0	6	8	0	8	1	0
orris, Alex, Marlins	2	0	1.000	1.21	14	2	0	0	4	2	37.1	20	141	11	5	0	1	0	3	8	1	36	4	1
oylan, Peter, Twins	1	1	.500	4.08	13	0	0	0	4	1	28.2	34	128	16	13	3	1	2	3	9	0	16	4	0
ulvehill, Brandon, Mets*	0	0	.000	16.20	1	0	0	0	1	0	1.2	3	9	4	3	0	0	1	0	1	0	1	1	0
undine, John, Twins	2	1	.667	5.20	14	0	0	0	9	1	27.2	31	124	19	16	2	1	2	0	13	0	21	5	1
unoz, Oscar, Orioles	0	0	.000	0.00	2	0	0	0	1	1	3.0	0	9	0	0	0	0	0	0	0	0	1	0	0
ill, John, Cubs*	2	0	1.000	2.59	10	1	0	0	4	1	24.1	25	104	12	7	0	1	0	0	4	0	11	1	1
aranjo, Ivan, Royals*	1	0	1.000	4.40	15	0	0	0	10	1	28.2	33	126	16	14	0	1	0	6	9	0	18	2	1
al, Blaine, Marlins	1	1	.500	4.60	7	5	0	0	1	0	29.1	32	126	18	15	1	0	0	3	6	0	15	3	3
el, Todd, Cubs	0	0	.000	6.75	2	0	0	0	1	0	4.0	4	19	4	3	0	0	0	0	2	0	4	0	0
arton, Phillip, Cubs*	0	0	.000	0.00	1	0	0	0	1	0	3.0	1	10	0	0	0	0	0	0	0	0	6	0	1
e, Richie, Twins	0	0	.000	1.80	1	1	0	0	0	0	5.0	4	19	1	1	0	0	0	0	1	0	7	0	0
vier, Richard, Yankees	1	0	1.000	0.00	4	0	0	0	3	1	8.2	4	31	0	0	0	0	0	0	1	0	7	1	0
ipari, Mario, Twins	0	0	.000	0.00	4	0	0	0	3	1	6.0	2	23	0	0	0	0	0	0	3	0	6	0	0
ta, Juan, Expos	3	0	1.000	2.53	20	0	0	0	9	1	32.0	21	122	10	9	0	3	0	3	11	0	15	3	1
tega, Pablo, Devil Rays	4	6	.400	1.97	13	13	1	0	0	0	82.1	61	330	24	18	1	2	0	3	12	0	86	7	4
ero, Oscar, Braves	0	1	.000	3.00	1	0	0	0	1	0	3.0	3	16	1	1	0	2	0	0	5	0	3	2	0
valle, Bonelly, Rangers	2	1	.667	2.23	18	0	0	0	12	7	44.1	36	180	17	11	2	2	2	1	13	1	38	2	0
valles, Homy, Expos	0	0	.000	0.00	1	0	0	0	1	1	1.0	1	4	0	0	0	0	0	0	0	0	1	0	1
raqueima, Jesus, Yankees	3	2	.600	2.01	11	9	0	0	0	0	49.1	43	209	24	11	4	0	0	3	15	0	49	7	4
rks, Wes, Marlins	2	1	.667	0.00	6	2	0	0	2	0	25.0	10	94	1	0	0	1	0	0	8	0	19	0	0
rrish, John, Orioles*	2	0	1.000	1.86	11	0	0	0	6	2	19.1	13	83	5	4	0	0	0	0	11	0	33	2	0
scarella, Josh, Astros	1	0	1.000	4.78	15	4	0	0	0	0	37.2	35	176	29	20	1	0	3	1	24	0	43	4	0
uls, Matt, Rangers	1	0	1.000	0.00	1	0	0	0	0	0	1.0	0	6	1	0	0	0	0	0	1	0	1	0	0
yne, William, Mets*	2	1	.667	5.00	11	0	0	0	6	0	18.0	17	78	14	10	1	3	0	0	8	2	17	1	0
nny, Tony, Royals	3	1	.750	2.59	14	0	0	0	10	2	24.1	22	101	8	7	2	0	1	1	4	0	20	1	1
rez, Elvis, White Sox*	0	0	.000	11.66	10	0	0	0	2	0	14.2	27	83	26	19	4	1	0	0	10	0	9	6	0
rez, Melido, Yankees	1	0	1.000	1.64	2	2	0	0	0	0	11.0	9	46	4	2	0	0	0	0	3	0	7	1	0
rez, Pablo, Twins	5	4	.556	3.02	12	10	2	0	0	0	59.2	54	246	23	20	4	0	0	3	17	0	43	3	0
terson, Dean, Red Sox	0	0	.000	0.00	2	2	0	0	0	0	6.0	4	25	0	0	0	0	0	0	0	0	7	0	0
ipps, Jeff, Orioles	3	1	.750	5.93	17	0	0	0	5	0	27.1	30	120	20	18	3	2	2	5	12	0	23	5	0
erce, Jeff, Red Sox	0	0	.000	0.79	5	4	0	0	1	1	11.1	12	44	1	1	0	0	0	1	1	0	10	0	1
neda, Luis, Rangers	6	3	.667	3.52	11	11	1	0	0	0	71.2	67	306	31	28	6	3	1	3	25	0	66	10	5
t, Jye, Cubs	1	2	.333	1.84	12	0	0	0	3	0	29.1	21	116	8	6	0	2	0	0	9	0	38	3	3
lanco, Elvis, Cubs	6	3	.667	2.59	14	7	1	0	5	2	55.2	55	234	28	16	1	1	0	4	18	0	35	5	3
wley, Greg, Expos	1	3	.250	3.65	13	6	0	0	0	0	44.1	37	184	19	18	0	0	4	3	11	0	34	0	3
ater, Andrew, Pirates	4	5	.444	3.18	12	12	1	0	0	0	68.0	63	288	24	24	3	2	1	9	11	0	53	2	0
estash, J.D., Astros*	0	0	.000	1.59	4	0	0	0	2	0	5.2	9	27	4	1	0	0	0	0	0	0	5	1	0
rtle, Joe, Mets	0	0	.000	1.29	4	0	0	0	0	0	7.0	3	27	1	1	0	0	0	0	0	0	8	4	1
een, Mike, Mets*	3	3	.500	3.48	11	3	0	0	3	0	33.2	33	147	15	13	1	0	0	0	15	0	28	4	0
evedo, Ruben, Braves	2	6	.250	2.29	10	10	0	0	0	0	55.0	50	221	19	14	1	4	1	1	9	0	49	3	2
amirez, Felix, Red Sox*	0	0	.000	9.00	1	0	0	0	1	0	1.0	2	6	2	1	0	0	0	0	1	0	0	0	0
amirez, Jose, Tigers*	2	7	.222	3.92	13	11	0	0	2	0	59.2	69	280	49	26	0	4	1	3	23	0	47	7	5
amsay, Robert, Red Sox*	0	1	.000	4.91	2	1	0	0	0	0	3.2	5	19	2	2	0	0	0	1	3	0	5	0	0
ed, Aaron, Tigers	0	1	.000	6.00	18	0	0	0	15	0	27.0	34	136	25	18	3	0	0	1	17	1	26	8	0

SUMMER CLASS A — Gulf Coast League

Pitcher, Team	W	L	Pct.	ERA	G	GS	CG	ShO	GF	Sv.	IP	H	TBF	R	ER	HR	SH	SF	HB	BB	IBB	SO	WP	BK
Reed, Brandon, Tigers	0	0	.000	0.00	1	1	0	0	0	0	2.0	0	6	0	0	0	0	0	1	0	0	2	0	
Reeder, Galen, Braves*	1	2	.333	4.50	16	0	0	0	11	1	32.0	38	140	20	16	2	2	0	1	11	1	26	2	
Reilly, Sean, Twins*	0	1	.000	5.48	12	1	0	0	5	1	21.1	23	98	15	13	0	0	1	2	11	0	25	5	
Reimers, Tom, White Sox	0	0	.000	0.00	1	0	0	0	0	0	3.0	3	14	0	0	0	0	0	0	1	0	1	0	
Reith, Brian, Yankees	2	3	.400	4.13	10	4	0	0	1	0	32.2	31	143	16	15	1	2	2	1	16	0	21	3	
Reitsma, Chris, Red Sox*	3	1	.750	1.35	7	6	0	0	0	0	26.2	24	109	7	4	0	1	0	2	1	0	32	3	
Rivera, Luis, Braves	1	1	.500	2.59	8	6	0	0	0	0	24.1	18	97	9	7	0	0	1	7	1		26	5	
Rivera, Marcos, Expos*	4	2	.667	2.12	18	1	0	0	11	3	34.0	33	143	9	8	0	3	0	1	7	0	16	2	
Roberts, Chris, Mets*	0	0	.000	1.38	3	3	0	0	0	0	13.0	11	48	2	2	0	0	0	1	0	0	12	1	
Robertson, Jeriome, Astros*	5	3	.625	1.72	13	13	1	1	0	0	78.1	51	304	20	15	2	3	0	4	15	0	98	6	
Rodgers, Marcus, White Sox	1	3	.250	3.35	10	6	1	0	1	0	37.2	44	166	17	14	1	1	1	2	16	0	29	4	
Rodriguez, Jorge, Yankees	0	0	.000	13.50	1	0	0	0	0	0	0.2	3	5	1	1	0	0	0	0	0	0	0	0	
Rodriguez, Jose, Devil Rays	3	1	.750	5.06	11	2	0	0	5	0	26.2	28	117	17	15	1	2	1	2	7	0	19	5	
Roeder, Jason, Royals	0	1	.000	9.00	3	0	0	0	2	0	4.0	6	21	4	4	1	0	0	3	0	0	3	0	
Rojas, Moises, Red Sox	0	0	.000	40.50	1	0	0	0	1	0	1.1	7	11	6	6	1	0	0	0	1	0	1	0	
Roman, Felipe, Red Sox	0	0	.000	40.50	1	0	0	0	0	0	0.2	2	6	3	3	0	0	0	2	0	0	1	0	
Romo, Greg, Tigers	1	0	1.000	1.57	8	1	0	0	7	1	23.0	19	93	7	4	0	1	2	4	0		29	2	
Rosario, Juan, Devil Rays	0	0	.000	0.00	3	0	0	0	1	0	3.0	0	16	3	0	0	0	0	1	3	0	3	2	
Roup, Randall, Royals	0	0	.000	12.46	8	0	0	0	4	0	8.2	15	49	13	12	1	0	1	0	7	0	8	3	
Ruhl, Nathan, Devil Rays	2	2	.500	2.33	16	0	0	0	7	0	27.0	18	109	9	7	0	3	1	1	11	1	25	4	
Rumer, Tim, Yankees*	0	0	.000	0.00	2	1	0	0	0	0	8.0	1	29	0	0	0	0	0	0	2	0	15	0	
Runion, Jeff, Rangers	1	0	1.000	2.37	7	2	0	0	1	0	19.0	14	79	8	5	0	1	1	0	12	0	19	0	
Ryan, Kevin, Orioles	1	0	1.000	0.00	2	0	0	0	0	0	3.1	2	12	1	0	0	0	0	0	0	0	2	0	
Sackinsky, Brian, Orioles	1	0	1.000	5.19	3	1	0	0	0	0	8.2	11	37	6	5	0	0	0	0	1	0	3	1	
Sadler, William, Expos*	2	2	.500	3.89	17	3	0	0	6	1	37.0	41	170	24	16	2	0	2	2	12	0	24	3	
Salvevold, Gregory, Devil Rays	1	1	.500	3.82	15	0	0	0	9	2	30.2	26	129	17	13	0	1	3	5	13	0	22	3	
Salyers, Jeremy, Expos	1	4	.200	4.26	11	9	2	0	1	0	57.0	47	246	36	27	4	3	1	8	26	0	30	1	
Sanchez, Bienvenido, Expos	1	2	.333	6.10	6	0	0	0	1	0	10.1	20	54	12	7	0	1	0	3	2	0	5	0	
Santamaria, Juan, Tigers	2	7	.222	5.34	12	12	0	0	0	0	55.2	52	254	47	33	4	0	2	10	25	0	43	12	
Santana, Humberto, Mets*	2	3	.571	2.22	10	9	0	0	0	0	52.2	45	207	16	13	0	0	3	3	7	0	40	2	
Santana, Orlando, Orioles	1	1	.500	3.16	16	0	0	0	5	2	25.2	24	106	12	9	2	0	1	1	6	0	19	2	
Santana, Pedro, Red Sox	5	3	.625	1.89	13	8	0	0	2	0	71.1	59	289	24	15	4	5	1	2	12	1	33	2	
Santos, Juan, Orioles	0	0	.000	3.86	6	0	0	0	3	2	9.1	9	41	4	4	1	1	0	0	2	0	4	1	
Santos, Victor, Tigers	3	2	.600	1.98	9	9	0	0	0	0	50.0	44	199	12	11	1	3	1	7	13	0	39	3	
Schnautz, Brad, Yankees*	2	0	1.000	5.16	10	1	0	0	1	0	22.2	28	101	13	13	2	0	0	0	5	0	31	0	
Seberino, Ronni, Devil Rays*	4	2	.667	3.46	18	6	0	0	8	1	52.0	50	215	22	20	2	2	2	2	15	0	49	10	
Seebode, Michael, Tigers	4	2	.667	3.75	12	0	0	0	5	0	36.0	34	159	22	15	1	3	2	2	11	0	25	6	
Seip, Rod, Rangers	0	0	.000	0.00	1	0	0	0	1	0	1.0	1	4	0	0	0	0	0	0	0	0	0	0	
Sekany, Jason, Red Sox	0	0	.000	2.31	5	2	0	0	2	1	11.2	14	50	3	3	1	0	0	1	3	0	16	2	
Serrano, Liosvany, Braves	1	2	.333	7.33	12	2	0	0	4	0	27.0	29	136	27	22	1	2	4	8	22	0	7	4	
Settle, Brian, Pirates	0	1	.000	7.94	7	0	0	0	3	0	11.1	5	56	10	10	0	1	0	6	14	0	13	2	
Shannon, Bobby, Royals*	0	0	.000	0.00	2	0	0	0	1	0	2.0	2	7	0	0	0	0	0	0	0	0	2	0	
Shearn, Thomas, Astros	5	2	.714	1.73	17	3	0	0	3	0	41.2	34	162	13	8	2	1	2	2	10	0	43	4	
Shourds, Anthony, Rangers	3	2	.600	2.31	20	0	0	0	9	2	35.0	27	148	12	9	0	1	5	1	12	0	28	1	
Siciliano, Jess, Pirates	0	0	.000	3.60	3	0	0	0	1	0	5.0	4	24	3	2	0	0	1	0	0	2	1	0	
Silva, Juan, Red Sox*	0	3	.000	5.26	14	0	0	0	9	2	25.2	34	112	16	15	2	1	2	1	12	0	31	3	
Simmons, Mike, White Sox	2	2	.500	3.51	17	1	0	0	6	1	41.0	46	180	22	16	2	2	2	12	0	32	5		
Sims, Kenneth, Orioles	0	2	.000	4.96	11	2	0	0	6	2	16.1	22	79	12	9	2	0	0	8	0	20	4		
Smith, Ryan, Rangers	2	0	1.000	4.68	14	0	0	0	3	0	25.0	18	116	15	13	1	0	2	24	0	24	13		
Snead, George, Braves	0	1	.000	3.86	3	0	0	0	2	0	7.0	7	34	6	3	1	1	0	1	4	1	5	0	
Snyder, John, White Sox	1	0	1.000	1.65	4	4	0	0	0	0	16.1	5	58	3	3	1	1	0	4	0	23	0		
Sorzano, Ronnie, Expos	3	2	.600	2.60	15	5	0	0	6	3	45.0	39	183	16	13	0	3	1	2	8	0	27	1	
Sparks, Eric, Expos*	4	0	1.000	2.76	14	1	0	0	6	3	29.1	25	119	10	9	1	0	3	5	0	16	6		
Spinelli, Michael, Red Sox*	1	0	1.000	2.25	1	0	0	0	0	0	4.0	4	15	1	1	0	0	0	0	0	0	2	1	
Stading, Kris, Expos*	2	1	.667	1.80	12	1	0	0	5	0	20.0	11	77	4	4	0	0	1	9	0	20	1		
Stallings, Ben, Red Sox	1	4	.200	4.89	11	6	0	0	1	0	42.1	45	198	33	23	3	2	3	22	2	36	5		
Stanley, Todd, White Sox	0	0	.000	0.00	2	0	0	0	1	0	2.0	0	8	0	0	0	0	0	2	0	3	0		
Stewart, Don, Yankees	0	0	.000	3.86	1	0	0	0	0	0	2.1	2	10	1	1	0	1	0	0	0	4	0		
Stinson, Kevin, White Sox	1	5	.167	2.29	24	0	0	0	18	6	35.1	39	159	16	9	0	1	3	11	0	34	5		
Styles, Bobby, Rangers	2	3	.400	1.59	23	0	0	0	23	13	34.0	27	144	12	6	1	3	9	3	26	2			
Suggs, Willie, Mets	3	2	.600	4.30	10	3	0	0	1	0	29.1	28	131	15	14	1	0	1	17	0	22	5		
Tatar, Jason, Twins	0	0	.000	1.80	2	0	0	0	0	0	5.0	2	16	1	1	0	1	0	0	1	0	7	0	
Taylor, Aaron, Braves	0	9	.000	7.74	13	9	0	0	3	0	52.1	68	259	54	45	0	7	2	6	28	0	33	14	
Tejera, Michael, Marlins*	1	0	1.000	3.60	2	0	0	0	0	0	5.0	6	21	2	2	0	0	0	0	0	0	2	0	
Tellez, Eloy, White Sox	3	4	.429	2.94	11	11	2	0	0	0	70.1	57	291	30	23	4	2	1	7	27	0	34	4	
Thurman, Corey, Royals	1	6	.143	6.08	11	11	0	0	0	0	47.1	53	221	32	32	2	0	3	28	0	52	8		
Tobias, Daniel, Pirates	0	1	.000	1.59	5	0	0	0	3	0	5.2	4	29	6	1	0	1	0	2	4	0	4	0	
Torres, Eric, Mets	0	4	.000	7.40	20	0	0	0	19	5	24.1	34	117	24	20	1	2	1	2	9	2	20	3	
Torres, Michael, Royals	2	3	.400	6.48	18	0	0	0	7	2	33.1	47	159	35	24	2	1	5	5	6	0	26	6	
Trunk, Todd, Yankees	0	0	.000	0.00	1	0	0	0	0	0	0.2	0	4	0	0	0	0	0	0	0	0	1	1	
Tull, William, Mets	0	0	.000	0.00	1	0	0	0	1	0	2.0	3	10	0	0	0	0	0	1	0	2	0		
Tyrrell, Jim, Red Sox*	0	0	.000	81.00	1	0	0	0	1	0	0.2	5	9	6	6	0	0	0	0	2	0	1	0	
Vail, Keith, Devil Rays	0	0	.000	11.88	5	0	0	0	2	0	8.1	12	48	13	11	0	1	1	1	7	1	4	2	
Valle, Yoiset, Yankees*	3	1	1.000	2.55	7	1	0	0	1	0	17.2	20	73	6	5	0	3	0	1	1	0	15	2	
Vallis, Jamie, Twins*	1	3	.250	3.52	12	8	0	0	1	0	38.1	37	161	18	15	0	1	2	15	0	25	10		
Van Winkle, Judd, Tigers*	3	1	.750	6.95	8	0	0	0	3	1	22.0	37	103	17	17	3	0	4	0	23	3			
Vergara, Luis, Braves	0	2	.000	6.19	4	3	0	0	0	0	16.0	21	75	14	11	0	2	0	1	4	1	10	4	
Vizcaino, Edward, Cubs	5	0	1.000	1.62	14	4	0	0	5	2	44.1	34	169	8	8	3	0	0	4	8	0	24	2	
Vogt, Robert, Pirates*	2	3	.400	2.95	13	5	0	0	4	0	42.2	36	182	23	14	2	1	0	19	0	46	4		
Wagner, Paul, Pirates	0	0	.000	0.00	1	1	0	0	0	0	3.0	2	11	0	0	0	0	0	0	0	0	1	0	
Wallace, Kent, Yankees	1	0	1.000	1.80	1	1	0	0	0	0	5.0	3	18	1	1	0	0	0	0	0	0	5	0	
Ward, Brandon, Cubs	2	1	.667	2.81	16	0	0	0	11	2	25.2	16	105	9	8	0	1	2	10	0	32	3		
Wegmann, Tom, Orioles	0	0	.000	0.00	4	1	0	0	0	0	8.2	4	34	2	0	0	0	0	1	2	0	12	0	

Pitcher, Team	W	L	Pct.	ERA	G	GS	CG	ShO	GF	Sv.	IP	H	TBF	R	ER	HR	SH	SF	HB	BB	IBB	SO	WP	Bk.
Weidert, Chris, Expos	0	0	.000	1.80	2	1	0	0	1	0	5.0	2	17	1	1	1	0	0	0	0	0	2	0	0
Wesolowski, David, Marlins	0	0	.000	6.00	2	2	0	0	0	0	9.0	11	43	8	6	0	2	0	0	2	0	4	2	0
Westover, Richard, Expos	0	0	.000	0.00	1	0	0	0	0	0	1.0	0	4	0	0	0	0	0	0	0	0	1	0	0
White, Rick, Pirates	0	0	.000	2.25	3	3	0	0	0	0	12.0	8	43	4	3	0	1	0	0	3	0	8	0	0
Widerski, Jonathan, Marlins	8	2	.800	2.55	12	10	0	0	0	0	67.0	59	275	26	19	3	1	1	1	22	0	55	6	3
Wiley, Chad, Rangers	0	1	.000	4.50	1	0	0	0	1	0	2.0	3	9	1	1	0	0	0	0	0	0	2	0	0
Wilkes, Brian, Marlins	0	0	.000	0.00	1	0	0	0	0	0	1.0	1	4	0	0	0	0	0	0	0	0	1	0	0
Wright, Jason, Pirates	0	1	.000	1.33	13	0	0	0	11	7	20.1	13	79	3	3	1	0	1	0	6	0	25	2	0
Zambrano, Victor, Devil Rays	0	0	.000	8.10	1	0	0	0	0	0	3.1	4	16	4	3	0	0	0	0	0	0	6	0	0

COMBINATION SHUTOUTS: Astros (4)—Robertson-Garcia, Ireland-Medina, Garcia-Huber-McCarter, Blackmore-Huber-Shearn-Medina. Braves (1)—Fowler-Serrano-Reeder. Cubs (3)—Viscaino-Polanco, Fennell-Connell-Nall, Kelley-Viscaino; Expos (7)—Sparks-Martin-Rivera, Fraser-MartinFortune-Rivera, Fortune-Martin, Fortune-Sparks, Fortune-Rivera, Rivera-Martin-Sorzano. Marlins (7)—McClaskey-Widerski-Evans, Knotts-Morris-Casey, Blano-Izquierdo, Parks-Morris-Evans-Wilkes, Neal-Parks, Widerski-Morris, Levan-Lara-Casey. Mets (4)—Ferullo-Suggs-Manley, Lovingood-Gonzalez-Tull-Carr, Gonzalez-McCready-Payne-Carr, Queen-Cossman. Orioles (5)—Mcnatt-Falkenborg-Heredia-Andrade, Brown-Wegman-Sims-Parrish, Jiminez-Andrade-Parrish, Falkenborg-Heredia-Santana, Jiminez-Mercedes. Pirates (3)—Hlodan-Harris-Beach, Bravo-Gaerte-Wright, Prater-Finol. Rangers (2)—Henriquez-Ovalles, Davis-Shourds. Red Sox (3)—Santana-Benzing-Austin, Peterson-Benzing-Duchscherer, Duchscherer-Montemayor. Royals (2)—Thurman-Carcamo, Moreno-Gonzalez-Boring. Tigers (2)—Martinez-Seebode, Romo-Seebode-Donastorg. Twins (1)—Gholar-Tartar-Loonam. White Sox (3)—Andujar-Reimers, Tellez-Schnautz, Forti-Cardona. Yankees (7)—Coble-Schnautz, Ellison-Hendrikx-McBride, Paraqueime-Corialan-McBride, Perez-Armas, Day-McBride-Ellison, Reith-Schnautz-Ellison, Coble-Valle-Ellison.

NO-HIT GAMES: None.

1996 FIELDING

TEAM

Team	Pct.	G	PO	A	E	TC	DP	PB	Team	Pct.	G	PO	A	E	TC	DP	PB
Marlins	.963	60	1571	657	85	2313	44	15	Royals	.953	60	1486	673	107	2266	41	15
Rangers	.960	60	1582	621	92	2295	44	20	Cubs	.952	60	1582	699	115	2396	53	17
Astros	.958	59	1516	632	95	2243	39	42	Tigers	.947	60	1515	654	121	2290	45	32
Orioles	.957	60	1575	680	101	2356	57	8	Pirates	.946	60	1535	635	123	2293	54	13
Devil Rays	.956	59	1552	598	98	2248	51	17	Mets	.946	59	1485	611	119	2215	36	22
Yankees	.956	58	1454	584	94	2132	43	28	Red Sox	.945	60	1581	679	132	2392	48	29
Twins	.956	60	1518	719	104	2341	60	12	Braves	.944	59	1515	636	128	2279	39	16
Expos	.954	60	1544	654	107	2305	48	14	White Sox	.941	60	1532	661	138	2331	55	20

Triple Plays: None.

INDIVIDUAL

FIRST BASEMEN

NOTE: All caps denotes fielding-percentage leader based on 30 games for catchers, 10 for all other non-pitchers and 59 innings for pitchers. *Throws lefthanded.

Player, Team	Pct.	G	PO	A	E	TC	DP
Ahrendt, Jay, Orioles	.960	2	23	1	1	25	7
Alleyne, Roberto, Astros	.992	15	109	8	1	118	8
Bagley, Sean, Expos	.975	42	339	10	9	358	32
Bazzani, Matt, Red Sox	.947	2	16	2	1	19	4
Becker, Brian, Devil Rays	.988	52	480	29	6	515	32
Blosser, Doug, Royals	.931	4	22	5	2	29	2
Bly, Derrick, Cubs	.989	11	84	3	1	88	8
Brambilla, Michael, Royals	.979	28	228	10	5	243	12
Brosam, Eric, Twins	.994	20	170	2	1	173	13
Bulheller, Greg, White Sox	1.000	3	14	0	0	14	1
BURNS, Patrick, Mets*	.989	40	342	15	4	361	20
Byrd, Brandon, Astros	.933	2	13	1	1	15	2
Camacaro, Pedro, Rangers	.990	31	279	12	3	294	25
Cardona, Luis, Red Sox	.978	12	82	5	2	89	8
Carmona, Antonio, White Sox	.976	11	76	6	2	84	3
Chaidez, Juan, Red Sox	1.000	2	3	0	0	3	1
Cochran, Ed, White Sox	1.000	6	39	2	0	41	4
Colon, Ariel, Mets	.986	18	133	6	2	141	11
Conway, Scott, Marlins*	.989	30	275	7	3	285	19
Copeland, Brandon, Mets	.944	2	15	2	1	18	1
Crespo, Jesse, Braves	.983	6	52	7	1	60	4
Cruz, Andres, Twins	.988	18	155	6	2	163	21
Delacruz, Wilfredo, Yankees	1.000	1	2	0	0	2	0
Delvecchio, Nicholas, Yankees	.960	3	23	1	1	25	2
Figueroa, Francisco, Orioles	.978	38	334	16	8	358	28
Gonzalez, Jose, White Sox	1.000	3	20	1	0	21	3
Glessman, Michael, Braves	.986	16	134	9	2	145	13
Hill, Jason, Astros	1.000	1	2	0	0	2	0
Horn, Marv, White Sox*	.963	9	76	1	3	80	6
Lundt, Bo, Pirates	1.000	3	17	3	0	20	1
Jackson, Ryan, Marlins*	1.000	4	34	3	0	37	1
Johnson, Nick, Yankees*	.991	36	314	19	3	336	25
Kingsbury, Willy, Red Sox	.979	7	46	1	1	48	4
Leon, Donny, Braves	1.000	4	27	2	0	29	0
Lignitz, Jeremiah, Tigers	.965	35	308	21	12	341	18
Llanos, Francisco, Expos	.982	27	209	11	4	224	11
Libre, Brian, Rangers	1.000	1	3	1	0	4	0

Player, Team	Pct.	G	PO	A	E	TC	DP
LoCurto, Gary, Red Sox	.981	19	148	11	3	162	9
Longmire, Marcel, Cubs	1.000	2	3	0	0	3	0
Matos, Wellington, Yankees*	.975	21	150	5	4	159	11
McDermott, Mike, White Sox	.980	33	315	24	7	346	28
McNeal, Aaron, Astros	.983	46	381	35	7	423	25
Mercado, Julio, Rangers	1.000	2	1	0	0	1	0
Metzger, Erik, Red Sox	.500	1	0	1	1	2	0
Montas, Richard, Royals	1.000	3	27	2	0	29	0
Mulvehill, Brandon, Mets	1.000	1	5	0	0	5	0
Nelson, Kevin, Twins	.976	25	236	11	6	253	20
Oropeza, William, Expos	.933	1	13	1	1	15	1
Owens, Billy, Orioles	1.000	5	29	1	0	30	2
Pascual, Edison, Pirates*	.974	24	213	10	6	229	25
Peniche, Fray, Tigers	.996	34	256	11	1	268	19
Pimentel, Marino, Marlins	1.000	1	3	0	0	3	0
Pressley, Kasey, Cubs	.963	26	224	10	9	243	16
Prodanov, Peter, White Sox	.919	4	33	1	3	37	4
Pryor, Pete, White Sox*	1.000	2	18	0	0	18	3
Ramirez, Juan, Royals	.988	33	248	9	3	260	23
Ramos, Noel, Orioles	.974	17	106	7	3	116	9
Rivera, Carlos, Pirates*	.982	35	300	21	6	327	22
Robertson, Dean, Orioles	.857	2	5	1	1	7	0
Rojas, Moises, Red Sox	1.000	1	2	0	0	2	1
Roman, Felipe, Red Sox	.992	33	230	12	2	244	14
Roneberg, Brett, Marlins*	.985	31	250	16	4	270	22
Salazar, Juan, Cubs	.989	26	238	20	3	261	23
Schramm, Kevin, Rangers	.983	22	166	12	3	181	10
Stephens, Jesus, Devil Rays	.980	8	48	2	1	51	6
Torrealba, Steve, Braves	1.000	1	9	0	0	9	1
Utting, Andrew, Orioles	.975	11	74	4	2	80	4
Voita, Sam, Devil Rays	1.000	1	8	1	0	9	3
Wong, Jerrod, Braves*	.986	9	66	6	1	73	4
Zapp, A.J., Braves	.984	29	229	22	4	255	16
Zywica, Michael, Rangers	.989	10	90	4	1	95	5

SECOND BASEMEN

Player, Team	Pct.	G	PO	A	E	TC	DP
Abreu, Dennis, Cubs	.944	56	104	147	15	266	33
Abreu, Nelson, Cubs	1.000	6	11	18	0	29	6
Ahumada, Alejandro, Red Sox	.904	14	21	26	5	52	7
Alvarez, Julio, Tigers	.960	5	11	13	1	25	1

Player, Team	Pct.	G	PO	A	E	TC	DP
Aybar, Ramon, Tigers	.948	42	70	111	10	191	15
Barrientos, Edgar, Red Sox	.954	20	18	44	3	65	3
Benes, Richard, Royals	.960	25	52	43	4	99	10
Borrego, Ramon, Twins	.944	19	42	60	6	108	13
Brignac, Junior, Braves	1.000	1	1	1	0	2	1
Brooks, Ali, Pirates	.947	28	71	72	8	151	12
Bruce, Maurice, Mets	.940	11	20	27	3	50	6
Butkus, Ben, Orioles	.917	6	7	15	2	24	2
Camacaro, Pedro, Rangers	.800	3	5	7	3	15	1
Cochran, Ed, White Sox	1.000	1	2	0	0	2	0
Coquillette, Trace, Expos	1.000	4	14	13	0	27	2
Cordero, Wil, Red Sox	1.000	1	1	1	0	2	0
Cruz, Alain, Yankees	1.000	1	1	1	0	2	0
Davila, Angel, Mets	1.000	5	10	10	0	20	1
Delgado, Daniel, Pirates	.984	30	52	75	2	129	20
Escalona, Felix, Astros	.933	6	10	18	2	30	4
Font, Franklin, Cubs	1.000	4	7	4	0	11	1
FRANCO, Raul, Marlins	.986	60	135	147	4	286	29
Germosen, Julio, Pirates	.969	6	14	17	1	32	4
Gomez, Rudy, Yankees	.983	13	19	38	1	58	6
Gonzalez, Jose, White Sox	.946	39	75	100	10	185	24
Hazelton, Justin, Tigers	.875	8	13	15	4	32	3
Hernandez, Rafael, Expos	1.000	1	1	1	0	2	0
Kelly, Pat, Yankees	1.000	3	5	5	0	10	3
Leidens, Enrique, Expos	.897	17	20	32	6	58	8
Ligons, Merrell, Royals	.894	29	49	69	14	132	11
Lorenzo, Juan, Twins	.972	27	51	55	3	109	15
Mateo, Henry, Expos	.901	14	29	35	7	71	11
Mateo, Victor, Yankees	.878	12	14	22	5	41	3
McCladdie, Tony, Devil Rays	.924	18	32	41	6	79	9
Mercedes, Matia, Tigers	.905	4	5	14	2	21	3
Merloni, Lou, Red Sox	1.000	1	3	3	0	6	0
Miles, Aaron, Astros	.947	47	56	124	10	190	14
Montas, Richard, Royals	.980	11	19	30	1	50	5
Nova, Geraldo, Red Sox	.928	25	52	51	8	111	12
Nunez, Jose, Mets	.902	36	68	80	16	164	15
Olivares, Teuris, Yankees	.750	3	3	0	1	4	1
Orndorff, Dave, Twins	1.000	2	8	10	0	18	2
Otero, Oscar, Braves	.972	8	13	22	1	36	3
Ovalles, Homy, Expos	.940	22	36	42	5	83	15
Ozuna, Pedro, Yankees	.947	33	54	71	7	132	13
Parra, Alejandro, White Sox	.974	24	28	46	2	76	8
Penalver, Juan, Mets	1.000	12	17	33	0	50	4
Perez, Jesse, Orioles	1.000	2	3	6	0	9	1
Post, Dave, Expos	.944	8	15	19	2	36	5
Ramirez, Edgar, Devil Rays	.884	21	26	35	8	69	13
Robertson, Dean, Orioles	.961	47	70	129	8	207	24
Sanchez, Orlando, Red Sox	.932	13	23	32	4	59	9
Sandberg, David, Devil Rays	.969	21	30	63	3	96	8
Santana, Pedro, Astros	.941	7	12	20	2	34	8
Santo, Jose, Rangers	.968	51	88	125	7	220	20
Seguro, Winston, Rangers	1.000	11	10	17	0	27	1
Silva, Carlos, Twins	.969	20	40	55	3	98	17
Smith, Dave, Red Sox	1.000	3	5	11	0	16	2
Solano, Angel, White Sox	.973	8	10	26	1	37	6
Stafford, Kimani, Royals	1.000	3	7	2	0	9	0
Tanaka, Shuta, Tigers	1.000	7	16	22	0	38	7
Taylor, Avery, Orioles	.941	9	20	28	3	51	10
Zydowsky, John, Braves	.958	51	104	150	11	265	27

THIRD BASEMEN

Player, Team	Pct.	G	PO	A	E	TC	DP
Abreu, Nelson, Cubs	.922	25	19	64	7	90	5
Ahumada, Alejandro, Red Sox	.947	7	4	14	1	19	0
Alcantara, Israel, Expos	.880	5	7	15	3	25	0
Bautista, Jorge, Marlins	.898	45	31	84	13	128	4
Bly, Derrick, Cubs	.897	38	31	99	15	145	14
Bruce, Maurice, Mets	.829	12	5	29	7	41	1
Burns, Xavier, Pirates	.857	2	0	6	1	7	0
Butkus, Ben, Orioles	.667	3	1	1	1	3	0
Camacaro, Pedro, Rangers	1.000	1	1	0	0	1	0
Champion, Jeff, Braves	1.000	2	1	0	0	1	0
Coffie, Evanon, Orioles	1.000	1	0	1	0	1	0
Colon, Ariel, Mets	.833	1	3	2	1	6	0
Coquillette, Trace, Expos	.833	3	2	3	1	6	0
Crede, Joe, White Sox	.857	53	42	108	25	175	7
CRUZ, Alain, Yankees	.914	44	29	88	11	128	7
Davila, Angel, Mets	1.000	1	1	0	0	1	0
Delacruz, Wilfredo, Yankees	1.000	1	0	1	0	1	1
Durick, Chad, Mets	.837	41	23	85	21	129	7
Escalona, Felix, Astros	.918	21	14	31	4	49	6

Player, Team	Pct.	G	PO	A	E	TC	DP
Germosen, Julio, Pirates	.909	3	6	4	1	11	1
Gonzalez, Jose, White Sox	.833	4	1	4	1	6	0
Hazelton, Justin, Tigers	.820	36	24	67	20	111	7
Hernandez, Rafael, Expos	.913	34	25	69	9	103	8
Hessman, Michael, Braves	.849	23	14	31	8	53	1
Jensen, Jacob, Pirates	.875	31	19	58	11	88	2
Johnson, Doug, Devil Rays	.867	27	18	60	12	90	7
Jordan, Yustin, Pirates	.795	27	14	56	18	88	5
King, Brion, Orioles	.909	8	9	11	2	22	0
Leon, Donny, Yankees	.909	13	9	31	4	44	4
LoCurto, Gary, Red Sox	.795	13	12	19	8	39	2
Mateo, Victor, Yankees	.500	2	1	1	2	4	0
McCladdie, Tony, Devil Rays	.889	19	8	32	5	45	2
McDermott, Mike, White Sox	1.000	5	2	15	0	17	2
Meadows, Mike, Mets	.933	5	7	7	1	15	0
Mendoza, Angel, Red Sox	.917	22	9	46	5	60	2
Mercedes, Matia, Tigers	.913	9	5	16	2	23	2
Montas, Richard, Royals	.929	37	26	91	9	126	9
Moore, Tris, Tigers	.839	12	7	19	5	31	0
Moss, Rick, Twins	.880	12	5	17	3	25	1
Nelson, Kevin, Twins	.737	5	3	11	5	19	2
Nicley, Dru, Astros	.889	22	14	34	6	54	2
Nova, Geraldo, Red Sox	.857	5	2	4	1	7	0
Ortiz, Pedro, Orioles	.857	26	16	44	10	70	5
Otero, Oscar, Braves	.857	5	3	3	1	7	0
Ovalles, Homy, Expos	.913	25	16	57	7	80	3
Parra, Jose, Rangers	1.000	9	6	14	0	20	2
Penalver, Juan, Mets	.600	3	3	3	4	10	0
Peniche, Fray, Tigers	.941	5	6	10	1	17	1
Perez, Jesse, Orioles	.788	31	17	35	14	66	7
Prodanov, Peter, Red Sox	.714	3	0	5	2	7	0
Radcliff, Victor, Royals	.881	27	22	52	10	84	3
Ramirez, Edgar, Devil Rays	1.000	3	2	4	0	6	0
Ramirez, Oscar, Rangers	.888	56	31	80	14	125	5
Ramos, Isandel, Braves	.842	36	25	60	16	101	2
Reynoso, Ismael, Marlins	.976	15	12	29	1	42	1
Roman, Felipe, Red Sox	.750	16	7	26	11	44	2
Ryan, Mike, Twins	.910	35	26	75	10	111	4
Salazar, Juan, Cubs	1.000	1	1	1	0	2	0
Sanchez, Orlando, Red Sox	.714	4	2	3	2	7	1
Santana, Pedro, Astros	.909	4	6	4	1	11	0
Shipman, Nate, Tigers	.714	3	2	3	2	7	0
Silva, Carlos, Twins	1.000	1	1	0	0	1	0
Suriel, Miguel, Devil Rays	.897	14	10	25	4	39	4
Tanaka, Shuta, Tigers	1.000	3	1	1	0	2	0
Vilorio, Leonel, Twins	.833	10	10	15	5	30	1
Wheeler, Michael, Astros	.796	16	8	31	10	49	0
Wilkes, Brian, Marlins	.923	5	2	10	1	13	1

SHORTSTOPS

Player, Team	Pct.	G	PO	A	E	TC	DP
Abreu, Nelson, Cubs	.905	5	3	16	2	21	3
Acevedo, Luis, Rangers	.909	51	87	133	22	242	22
Ahumada, Alejandro, Red Sox	.926	19	18	45	5	68	5
Alvarez, Julio, Tigers	.880	20	29	59	12	100	8
Benes, Richard, Royals	1.000	1	0	4	0	4	0
Brignac, Junior, Braves	.861	49	97	145	39	281	24
Bruce, Maurice, Mets	.889	11	19	21	5	45	5
Butkus, Ben, Orioles	.917	12	8	25	3	36	5
Cochran, Ed, White Sox	1.000	1	0	1	0	1	0
COFFIE, Evanon, Orioles	.941	56	81	174	16	271	30
Davila, Angel, Mets	.714	3	4	6	4	14	1
Delarosa, Tomas, Expos	.914	54	86	189	26	301	24
DeloSantos, Eddy, Devil Rays	.938	50	76	149	15	240	28
Durick, Chad, Mets	1.000	2	1	4	0	5	0
Font, Franklin, Cubs	.929	57	109	164	21	294	26
Garciaparra, Nomar, Red Sox	.950	5	7	12	1	20	3
Germosen, Julio, Pirates	.947	27	50	76	7	133	14
Goligoski, Jason, Red Sox	.875	3	5	9	2	16	2
Gonzalez, Alex, Marlins	.898	7	14	30	5	49	7
Guzman, Christian, Yankees	.890	41	55	106	20	181	21
Larkin, Garrett, Pirates	.903	14	22	43	7	72	12
Leidens, Enrique, Expos	.891	10	12	29	5	46	6
Ligons, Merrell, Royals	.976	16	26	55	2	83	9
Lorenzana, Luis, Pirates	.933	18	20	63	6	89	15
Lorenzo, Juan, Twins	.929	11	8	31	3	42	5
Mackowiak, Robert, Pirates	.706	4	7	5	5	17	1
Mateo, Victor, Yankees	.932	15	16	39	4	59	6
McDermott, Mike, White Sox	.500	2	0	1	1	2	0
Meadows, Mike, Mets	1.000	3	4	8	0	12	2
Medrano, Steve, Royals	.921	46	52	134	16	202	13

er, Team	Pct.	G	PO	A	E	TC	DP
ndoza, Angel, Red Sox	.863	31	45	81	20	146	14
cedes, Matia, Tigers	.857	2	5	7	2	14	1
ntas, Richard, Royals	1.000	2	2	6	0	8	1
ore, Tris, Tigers	.952	5	8	12	1	21	0
ez, Jose, Mets	1.000	5	7	12	0	19	2
ares, Teuris, Yankees	1.000	6	7	11	0	18	1
eda, Jose, Red Sox	.889	14	21	43	8	72	6
o, Oscar, Braves	.900	3	3	6	1	10	0
ra, Alejandro, White Sox	.875	12	23	26	7	56	6
ra, Jose, Rangers	.870	5	8	12	3	23	0
alver, Juan, Mets	1.000	1	0	1	0	1	0
ez, Jersen, Mets	.884	39	57	111	22	190	17
ez, Jesse, Orioles	.875	3	1	6	1	8	1
onia, Isreal, Marlins	.922	44	50	151	17	218	20
nirez, Edgar, Devil Rays	.850	13	17	17	6	40	4
noso, Ismael, Marlins	.941	16	15	49	4	68	5
as, Luis, Twins	.922	51	68	181	21	270	40
ertson, Dean, Orioles	.833	2	2	3	1	6	2
tana, Pedro, Astros	.944	39	66	118	11	195	14
uro, Winston, Rangers	1.000	12	9	19	0	28	5
a, Carlos, Twins	1.000	1	0	1	0	1	1
no, Angel, White Sox	1.000	2	0	3	0	3	0
ka, Shuta, Tigers	.943	34	48	102	9	159	13
ell, Jim, White Sox	.873	49	73	140	31	244	32
pe, Angres, Braves	.898	9	17	27	5	49	4
eler, Michael, Astros	.877	20	26	45	10	81	11
xy, Eddie, Orioles	1.000	1	3	2	0	5	0

OUTFIELDERS

er, Team	Pct.	G	PO	A	E	TC	DP
u, Miguel, Marlins	.960	19	22	2	1	25	0
u, Nelson, Cubs	1.000	10	12	3	0	15	0
ne, Roberto, Astros	.941	24	32	0	2	34	0
onte, Wady, Orioles	1.000	1	1	0	0	1	0
s, Jeison, Devil Rays	.935	18	27	2	2	31	0
enta, Alfredo, Braves*	.875	4	7	0	1	8	0
ar, Ramon, Tigers	1.000	1	1	0	0	1	0
so, Julio, Twins	.950	29	36	2	2	40	0
es, John, Red Sox	.977	26	39	3	1	43	0
era, Rafael, Rangers	1.000	38	61	2	0	63	1
ista, Francisco, Royals	1.000	23	25	1	0	26	1
amin, Aljereau, Pirates	.960	39	47	1	2	50	0
ar, Ceasar, Twins	.957	25	43	2	2	47	0
ey, Milton, Expos	.949	31	54	2	3	59	0
son, Ben, Royals	1.000	25	37	1	0	38	0
ks, Anthony, Braves	.954	43	101	3	5	109	0
n, Richard, Yankees*	.931	47	62	5	5	72	2
s, Patrick, Mets*	1.000	1	2	0	0	2	0
s, Xavier, Pirates	.889	12	23	1	3	27	0
, Brandon, Astros	1.000	28	24	1	0	25	0
iobello, Anthony, Braves	1.000	2	2	0	0	2	0
y, Orlando, Yankees	.972	57	98	6	3	107	0
ona, Antonio, White Sox	.800	4	4	0	1	5	0
ey, Bartt, Orioles	1.000	6	6	2	0	8	1
r, Quincy, Cubs	.934	50	65	6	5	76	1
npion, Jeff, Braves	1.000	25	41	1	0	42	0
tensen, McKay, White Sox*	.982	26	54	2	1	57	1
HRAN, Ed, White Sox	1.000	40	53	4	0	57	2
on, Julian, Braves	1.000	15	21	1	0	22	0
ell, Gerald, Cubs	.957	17	21	1	1	23	0
land, Brandon, Mets	1.000	40	48	6	0	54	1
oo, Jesse, Braves	.927	29	37	1	3	41	0
als, Deion, Twins	1.000	2	1	0	0	1	0
als, Ronny, Expos*	.928	42	72	5	6	83	0
er, Melvin, Royals	.960	14	24	0	1	25	0
s, Torrance, Expos	1.000	25	39	2	0	41	0
on, Ashanti, Orioles	.972	28	31	4	1	36	1
ruz, Wilfredo, Yankees	.833	12	9	1	2	12	0
ado, Daniel, Pirates	1.000	1	1	0	0	1	0
azer, Jeremy, Astros	.977	48	79	7	2	88	0
Espada, Miguel, Astros	.912	40	48	4	5	57	0
Rosa, Miguel, Rangers	1.000	13	29	4	0	33	2
s, Dawan, Pirates*	.936	21	43	1	3	47	0
oar, Alex, Mets	.936	21	42	2	3	47	0
on, Anthony, Twins*	1.000	2	1	0	0	1	0
ell, Jason, White Sox	.922	46	54	5	5	64	0
son, Dwight, Red Sox*	1.000	21	29	3	0	32	2
i, Wladimir, Royals	1.000	19	16	0	0	16	0
s, Oswaldo, Red Sox	.945	33	50	2	3	55	0
er, Benjamin, Braves	.833	8	5	0	1	6	0
alez, Jose, White Sox	1.000	6	2	1	0	3	0

Player, Team	Pct.	G	PO	A	E	TC	DP
Gonzalez, Melciades, Devil Rays	.920	15	21	2	2	25	1
Grubbs, Chris, Cubs	1.000	1	1	0	0	1	0
Guerrero, Francisco, Devil Rays	.941	11	12	4	1	17	0
Guerrero, Hamlet, Mets	.978	33	42	2	1	45	0
Gunner, Chie, Devil Rays	.924	44	61	0	5	66	0
Hall, Noah, Expos	1.000	27	35	2	0	37	1
Hazelton, Justin, Tigers	1.000	5	5	0	0	5	0
Heredia, Rafael, Cubs	1.000	16	24	3	0	27	0
Hessman, Michael, Braves	.941	10	15	1	1	17	1
Hill, Jason, Astros	1.000	18	23	2	0	25	2
Hooper, Daren, Orioles	.813	10	13	0	3	16	0
Hundt, Bo, Pirates	.875	12	12	2	2	16	0
Jackson, Quantaa, Marlins	.917	10	22	0	2	24	0
Jackson, Ryan, Marlins*	1.000	2	1	0	0	1	0
James, Kennouth, Expos	.990	45	93	2	1	96	1
Jamison, Nick, Tigers*	.968	27	29	1	1	31	0
Jimenez, Felipe, Cubs	.905	46	53	4	6	63	1
Johnson, Carlisle, Twins	1.000	19	25	0	0	25	0
Johnson, Rontrez, Red Sox	1.000	25	64	0	0	64	0
Johnson, Thomas, Mets	.911	25	41	0	4	45	0
Johnson, Tony, Mets	.917	36	48	7	5	60	0
Katzaroff, Rob, Yankees	1.000	7	10	0	0	10	0
Kennedy, Brian, Twins	.961	32	47	2	2	51	0
Kinnie, Donald, Cubs	1.000	11	20	0	0	20	0
Kirkpatrick, Michael, Orioles*	1.000	13	9	0	0	9	0
Lebron, Juan, Royals	.964	47	52	2	2	56	2
Lina, Estivinson, Rangers	1.000	1	1	0	0	1	0
Longmire, Marcel, Cubs	.946	27	32	3	2	37	1
Lopez, Henry, Twins	.985	34	60	4	1	65	0
Mackowiak, Robert, Pirates	.931	17	24	3	2	29	0
Maduro, Remy, Marlins	.956	23	41	2	2	45	0
Matos, Luis, Orioles	.983	41	56	3	1	60	1
McCladdie, Tony, Devil Rays	1.000	10	13	1	0	14	0
McDavid, Ray, Expos	1.000	1	2	0	0	2	0
McKenzie, Carlton, Pirates	.943	31	33	0	2	35	0
McKinney, Antonio, Tigers	.920	40	79	1	7	87	0
Mercado, Julio, Rangers	.982	39	50	5	1	56	1
Monds, Wonder, Braves	1.000	3	7	0	0	7	0
Morales, Domingo, Orioles	.909	16	19	1	2	22	0
Moreno, Juan, Mets	.955	13	20	1	1	22	0
Morgan, Todd, Orioles	.846	13	11	0	2	13	0
Moss, Rick, Twins	1.000	14	15	2	0	17	0
Mulvehill, Brandon, Mets	1.000	19	25	2	0	27	1
Nova, Fernando, White Sox	.956	58	94	15	5	114	1
Olson, Dan, White Sox*	1.000	3	4	0	0	4	0
Ortiz, Pedro, Orioles	1.000	9	8	0	0	8	0
Otero, Oscar, Braves	.982	39	53	2	1	56	0
Ottavinia, Paul, Expos*	1.000	3	5	0	0	5	0
Ovalles, Homy, Expos	1.000	1	2	2	0	4	0
Parra, Jose, Rangers	1.000	1	1	0	0	1	0
Pascual, Edison, Pirates*	1.000	9	11	1	0	12	0
Pass, Patrick, Marlins	.931	29	27	0	2	29	0
Pena, Jose, Rangers	1.000	29	48	2	0	50	0
Peniche, Fray, Tigers	1.000	3	1	0	0	1	0
Perez, Alejandro, Red Sox	.947	15	16	2	1	19	0
Perez, Richard, Orioles	.938	40	68	7	5	80	2
Perini, Mike, Red Sox	.973	29	34	2	1	37	0
Pimentel, Marino, Marlins	1.000	11	22	1	0	23	0
Piniella, Juan, Rangers	.982	55	105	5	2	112	1
Preciado, Victor, Yankees	.967	40	56	2	2	60	0
Pressley, Kasey, Cubs	1.000	1	2	0	0	2	0
Prodanov, Peter, Red Sox	.500	3	1	0	1	2	0
Quintero, Christian, Yankees	1.000	13	21	1	0	22	0
Radcliff, Victor, Royals	.944	16	32	2	2	36	1
Ramirez, Edgar, Devil Rays	1.000	1	1	0	0	1	0
Ramirez, Julio, Marlins	.980	43	95	2	2	99	1
Ramirez, Luis, Orioles	1.000	36	59	3	0	62	1
Ramos, Isandel, Braves	1.000	1	1	0	0	1	0
Ramos, Kelly, Mets	.000	1	0	0	0	0	0
Redman, Julian, Orioles*	.978	23	43	2	1	46	1
Reeder, Galen, Braves*	1.000	2	1	0	0	1	0
Reyes, Deurys, Tigers*	1.000	4	6	0	0	6	0
Rivera, Roberto, Orioles	1.000	3	5	0	0	5	0
Robertson, Geoffrey, Astros*	.940	30	45	2	3	50	0
Rockow, Jeremy, Pirates*	.973	29	35	1	1	37	0
Rojas, Moises, Red Sox	1.000	34	49	3	0	52	2
Roman, Felipe, Red Sox	1.000	1	1	0	0	1	0
Roneberg, Brett, Marlins*	1.000	17	23	2	0	25	1
Sanchez, Alex, Devil Rays*	.968	56	91	1	3	95	0
Shipman, Nate, Tigers	.958	30	46	0	2	48	0
Smith, Marcus, Twins	.968	30	57	4	2	63	2
Smith, Nestor, Yankees	1.000	6	6	1	0	7	0

Player, Team	Pct.	G	PO	A	E	TC	DP
Stafford, Kimani, Royals	1.000	14	20	3	0	23	0
Stenson, Dernell, Red Sox*	1.000	25	30	2	0	32	0
Stephens, Jesus, Devil Rays	1.000	15	10	1	0	11	1
Stewart, Counteney, Cubs	1.000	13	17	0	0	17	0
Stovall, Darond, Expos*	1.000	7	10	0	0	10	0
Tardiff, Jeremy, Red Sox	1.000	4	1	0	0	1	0
Taveras, Jose, Royals	.941	11	14	2	1	17	0
Thomas, Allen, White Sox*	1.000	5	1	0	0	1	0
Tillero, Adrian, Royals	.959	34	44	3	2	49	1
Valenzuela, Mario, White Sox	.818	6	8	1	2	11	0
Walker, Corey, Braves*	.800	3	4	0	1	5	0
Ward, Greg, Braves	1.000	3	1	0	0	1	0
Ware, Jeremy, Expos	1.000	14	16	1	0	17	0
Washington, Cory, Marlins	.941	36	48	0	3	51	0
Weber, Brad, Devil Rays*	1.000	34	28	1	0	29	0
White, Rondell, Expos	1.000	3	4	0	0	4	0
Whitner, Keith, Tigers	.967	38	57	2	2	61	2
Wilder, Paul, Devil Rays	1.000	1	2	0	0	2	0
Wilson, Heath, Braves	1.000	1	3	0	0	3	0
Wong, Jerrod, Braves*	1.000	4	7	0	0	7	0
Zapata, Alexis, Tigers	.948	46	63	10	4	77	6
Zywica, Michael, Rangers	.966	19	25	3	1	29	0

CATCHERS

Player, Team	Pct.	G	PO	A	E	TC	DP	PB
Ahrendt, Jay, Orioles	1.000	8	49	8	0	57	1	0
Alaimo, Jason, Marlins	.991	28	187	29	2	218	0	8
Bazzani, Matt, Red Sox	1.000	5	17	2	0	19	0	0
Bello, Jilberto, Orioles	.986	35	243	37	4	284	2	5
Besford, Timothy, Expos	.889	5	8	0	1	9	0	0
Blanco, Octavio, Devil Rays	.953	10	38	3	2	43	0	2
Borges, Alex, Braves	1.000	3	20	5	0	25	0	0
Brambilla, Michael, Royals	1.000	5	20	1	0	21	0	1
Brito, Bobby, Red Sox	.968	11	54	6	2	62	2	8
Bulheller, Greg, White Sox	.957	5	21	1	1	23	0	2
Candelaria, Vidal, Yankees	.982	25	143	22	3	168	0	9
Cardona, Luis, Red Sox	1.000	16	66	7	0	73	1	9
Carmona, Antonio, White Sox	.969	31	189	28	7	224	0	7
Chaidez, Juan, Red Sox	.936	21	81	7	6	94	0	1
Chapman, Scott, Astros	.989	31	227	32	3	262	1	18
Crespo, Jesse, Braves	.953	8	35	6	2	43	0	2
Cruz, Andres, Twins	.750	1	3	0	1	4	0	0
Diaz, Diogenes, Pirates	.932	26	150	15	12	177	1	4
Engle, Beau, Mets	1.000	2	12	1	0	13	0	3
Evans, Lee, Pirates	.978	29	198	24	5	227	0	7
Grubbs, Chris, Cubs	.988	29	206	34	3	243	2	10
Gruber, Nick, Red Sox	.944	4	15	2	1	18	1	2
Guerrero, Hamlet, Mets	1.000	1	4	0	0	4	0	0
Herrera, Pedro, Royals	.957	30	217	26	11	254	1	4
Hill, Jason, Astros	.989	18	148	26	2	176	0	10
Hill, Jeremy, Royals	.961	30	179	40	9	228	1	10
Hundt, Bo, Pirates	.950	5	14	5	1	20	0	2
Kingsbury, Willy, Red Sox	.980	17	84	14	2	100	1	4
Koeyers, Ramsey, Expos	1.000	7	28	5	0	33	0	3
Leon, Donny, Yankees	.976	31	213	27	6	246	0	12
Lignitz, Jeremiah, Tigers	.875	3	7	0	1	8	0	2
Lina, Estivinson, Rangers	.966	45	262	47	11	320	3	11
Linares, Sendry, Astros	.986	21	127	17	2	146	0	14
Llibre, Brian, Rangers	.958	4	21	2	1	24	0	2
Longmire, Marcel, Cubs	1.000	3	7	1	0	8	0	0
Lugo, Marcelino, Marlins	1.000	4	12	1	0	13	0	1
Meran, Jorge, Tigers	.982	32	175	38	4	217	2	11
Metzger, Erik, Red Sox	.976	16	109	13	3	125	0	5
Morales, Steve, Marlins	.975	29	172	22	5	199	0	4
Munson, Mike, Yankees	.980	18	87	10	2	99	0	7
Neikirk, Derick, Tigers	.988	16	70	10	1	81	0	5
Orndorff, Dave, Twins	1.000	4	28	10	0	38	0	0
Pachot, John, Expos	.957	4	21	1	1	23	0	1
Payano, Alexi, Cubs	.971	21	152	13	5	170	1	3
Prada, Nelson, Twins	.972	41	250	62	9	321	5	6
Pugh, Josh, Braves	.991	17	90	16	1	107	0	3
Ramos, Kelly, Mets	.979	19	131	11	3	145	1	5
Rivera, Juan, Rangers	.980	24	165	29	4	198	0	7
Rivera, Luis, Expos	.990	21	95	7	1	103	0	4
Salazar, Juan, Cubs	.977	15	107	20	3	130	2	4
Schneider, Brian, Expos	.988	41	214	26	3	243	0	6
Severence, Lance, Devil Rays	.933	7	38	4	3	45	0	2
Stanton, Thomas, Mets	.983	42	301	39	6	346	0	14
Stevenson, Chad, Tigers	.975	22	138	18	4	160	1	14
Suriel, Miguel, Devil Rays	.99130	36	298	44	3	345	8	12
SUTTON, Joe, White Sox	.99148	32	200	33	2	235	1	11
Torrealba, Steve, Braves	.987	41	251	43	4	298	3	11

Player, Team	Pct.	G	PO	A	E	TC	DP
Torres, Gabriel, Twins	.978	19	112	20	3	135	1
Utting, Andrew, Orioles	1.000	21	156	18	0	174	2
Viera, Rob, Pirates	.985	10	59	5	1	65	0
Voita, Sam, Devil Rays	.979	17	126	14	3	143	0
Wilkes, Brian, Marlins	1.000	7	51	6	0	57	0
Wilson, Heath, Braves	1.000	2	6	0	0	6	0

PITCHERS

Player, Team	Pct.	G	PO	A	E	TC
Abreu, Miguel, Marlins	1.000	1	0	1	0	1
Achilles, Matt, Orioles	1.000	5	0	4	0	4
Adachi, Tomo, Tigers*	1.000	5	1	2	0	3
Alvarado, Carlos, Pirates	.667	11	1	1	1	3
Alvord, Aaron, Tigers	1.000	16	0	6	0	6
Andrade, Jancy, Orioles	1.000	18	1	6	0	7
Andujar, Luis, White Sox	1.000	1	1	1	0	2
Arias, Jose, Devil Rays*	1.000	10	1	0	0	1
Arias, Rafael, Red Sox	.944	13	2	15	1	18
Armas, Antonio, Yankees	1.000	8	0	4	0	4
Armenta, Alfredo, Braves*	1.000	14	2	7	0	9
Austin, Lakevie, Red Sox	.667	16	0	2	1	3
Bagley, Sean, Expos	1.000	1	0	1	0	1
Barksdale, Shane, Astros	.750	12	2	4	2	8
Barry, Chad, White Sox	1.000	10	1	0	0	1
Beach, Scott, Pirates	1.000	7	2	5	0	7
Benitez, Armando, Orioles	1.000	1	0	1	0	1
Benzing, Skipp, Red Sox*	.867	12	2	11	2	15
Berroa, Oliver, Red Sox	.917	17	4	7	1	12
Birrell, Simon, Braves	.667	10	1	11	6	18
Blackmore, John, Astros	1.000	16	1	3	0	4
Blanco, Edgar, Twins	1.000	12	2	2	0	4
Blanco, Pablo, Marlins	.818	12	3	6	2	11
Boring, Richard, Royals	1.000	15	0	5	0	5
Borkowski, Robert, Mets	1.000	12	4	5	0	9
Bowers, Cedrick, Devil Rays*	.750	13	0	6	2	8
Bravo, Franklin, Pirates	.846	11	7	4	2	13
Brown, Derek, Orioles	.895	9	6	11	2	19
Brown, Trent, Devil Rays*	1.000	15	2	6	0	8
Buchanan, Brian, Yankees*	1.000	12	3	13	0	16
Calvert, Kale, Red Sox	1.000	20	2	5	0	7
Canciobello, Anthony, Braves	1.000	15	10	2	0	12
Cantu, Alvin, Royals*	1.000	9	0	11	0	11
Carcamo, Kevin, Royals	.667	9	0	2	1	3
Cardona, Steve, White Sox	.714	15	2	3	2	7
Carr, Tim, Mets	1.000	16	1	8	0	9
Carrion, Jorge, Rangers	1.000	4	0	3	0	3
Casey, Shaw, Marlins	.750	15	1	5	2	8
Ceasar, Donald, Braves	1.000	10	2	6	0	8
Celta, Nicolas, Astros*	1.000	17	3	5	0	8
Christman, Scott, White Sox*	.667	4	1	1	1	3
Clark, Greg, Twins	.750	13	1	14	5	20
Classen, Ender, Pirates	.500	7	0	1	1	2
Coble, Jason, Yankees*	1.000	9	0	7	0	7
Comer, Scott, Mets*	1.000	13	2	6	0	8
Connell, Brian, Cubs*	.500	7	0	1	1	2
Cook, Derrick, Rangers	1.000	6	1	5	0	6
Cook, O.J., Pirates	1.000	11	5	12	0	17
Cope, Craig, Mets*	1.000	1	0	1	0	1
Coriolan, Roberto, Yankees	1.000	12	3	3	0	6
Cox, Robert, Mets	1.000	5	0	1	0	1
Crane, Randy, Cubs	.500	15	1	1	2	4
Cremer, Rick, Yankees*	1.000	2	2	3	0	5
Cruz, Charlie, Orioles	1.000	9	0	1	0	1
Davis, Doug, Rangers*	.889	8	1	7	1	9
Day, Stephen, Yankees	1.000	7	1	6	0	7
Deckard, Edward, Devil Rays	1.000	9	0	2	0	2
Delarosa, Raul, White Sox	.778	18	1	6	2	9
Delgado, Daniel, Pirates	1.000	2	1	0	0	1
DeLeon, Julio, Devil Rays	1.000	7	1	2	0	3
Donastorg, Raul, Tigers	1.000	20	2	3	0	5
Duchscherer, Justin, Red Sox	.944	13	5	12	1	18
Dunn, Cordell, Pirates	1.000	7	1	3	0	4
Durbin, Chad, Royals	.833	11	1	4	1	6
Ellison, Jason, Yankees	.667	21	0	2	1	3
Enard, Tony, Marlins	1.000	2	0	2	0	2
Espina, Rendy, Twins*	1.000	7	0	3	0	3
Evans, Mike, Marlins*	.857	19	1	5	1	7
Falkenborg, Brian, Orioles	1.000	8	2	7	0	9
Felix, Miguel, White Sox	.727	12	3	5	3	11
Feliz, Jose, Cubs	.733	11	4	7	4	15
Fennell, Barry, Cubs*	1.000	10	3	4	0	7

yer, Team	Pct.	G	PO	A	E	TC	DP	Player, Team	Pct.	G	PO	A	E	TC	DP
illo, Matt, Mets	1.000	2	0	3	0	3	0	Montemayor, Humberto, Rd Sox	1.000	10	1	10	0	11	0
ol, Ricardo, Pirates	1.000	6	2	2	0	4	1	Moody, Ritchie, Rangers*	.667	3	0	2	1	3	0
ning, Emar, Rangers	1.000	12	4	13	0	17	0	Moreno, Orber, Royals	.833	12	2	8	2	12	0
bes, Cameron, Orioles	.933	13	4	10	1	15	0	Moreno, Willy, Yankees	.600	11	0	3	2	5	0
i, Eugene, White Sox*	.929	12	5	8	1	14	2	Morris, Alex, Marlins	.778	14	3	4	2	9	0
une, Peter, Expos*	.938	13	3	12	1	16	0	Moylan, Peter, Twins	1.000	13	3	5	0	8	2
ler, Benjamin, Braves	.714	8	3	2	2	7	0	Mulvehill, Brandon, Mets	1.000	1	0	1	0	1	0
ler, Jered, Devil Rays	.500	4	0	1	1	2	0	Mundine, John, Twins	1.000	14	3	4	0	7	0
ser, Joe, Expos	.875	11	4	10	2	16	0	Nall, John, Cubs*	1.000	10	1	7	0	8	0
rte, Travis, Pirates	.875	14	2	5	1	8	0	Naranjo, Ivan, Royals*	.875	15	0	7	1	8	0
ban, Julian, Braves*	1.000	5	0	1	0	1	0	Neal, Blaine, Marlins	1.000	7	1	3	0	4	0
darillas, Gus, Twins	1.000	3	0	1	0	1	0	Noel, Todd, Cubs	.000	3	0	0	2	2	0
cia, Gabe, Astros	.750	13	3	3	2	8	0	Nye, Richie, Twins	1.000	1	0	1	0	1	0
mon, Adam, Mets	.500	12	0	1	1	2	0	Olivier, Richard, Yankees	1.000	4	2	2	0	4	0
rett, Josh, Red Sox	1.000	7	3	6	0	9	1	Orta, Juan, Expos	1.000	20	1	8	0	9	0
tile, Scott, Expos	1.000	5	0	2	0	2	0	ORTEGA, Pablo, Devil Rays	1.000	13	6	13	0	19	0
lar, Antonio, Twins	.700	15	1	6	3	10	1	Otero, Oscar, Braves	1.000	1	0	1	0	1	0
sell, Christopher, Cubs	.889	11	2	6	1	9	0	Ovalle, Bonelly, Rangers	.667	18	1	3	2	6	0
dde, Roger, Pirates	1.000	12	3	3	0	6	0	Paraqueima, Jesus, Yankees	.800	11	0	4	1	5	0
zalez, Dicky, Mets	1.000	11	7	6	0	13	0	Parks, Wes, Marlins	.800	6	1	3	1	5	0
zalez, Edwin, Royals	.920	12	9	14	2	25	0	Parrish, John, Orioles*	.800	11	1	3	1	5	0
zalez, Generoso, Tigers	1.000	4	0	2	0	2	0	Pascarella, Josh, Astros	1.000	15	2	8	0	10	0
sko, Michael, Pirates*	.500	5	1	0	1	2	0	Payne, William, Mets*	1.000	11	2	5	0	7	0
ve, Tim, Royals	1.000	2	0	2	0	2	0	Penny, Tony, Royals	.875	14	4	3	1	8	0
ulack, Tim, Astros*	.800	22	1	3	1	5	0	Perez, Elvis, White Sox*	.500	14	1	2	3	6	0
den, Nathan, Braves	.688	14	5	6	5	16	0	Perez, Melido, Yankees	.750	2	1	2	1	4	0
is, Gene, Pirates	1.000	9	1	0	0	1	0	Perez, Pablo, Twins	.889	12	2	6	1	9	0
sman, Isaac, Rangers	.909	12	11	9	2	22	2	Peterson, Dean, Red Sox	.667	2	1	1	1	3	0
drikx, Brandon, Rangers	1.000	8	2	1	0	3	0	Phipps, Jeff, Orioles	1.000	17	2	2	0	4	0
riquez, Jobannis, Rangers	1.000	13	2	4	0	6	1	Pierce, Jeff, Red Sox	1.000	5	0	1	0	1	1
dia, Maximo, Orioles	.929	17	5	8	1	14	0	Pineda, Luis, Rangers	.895	11	3	14	2	19	1
lan, George, Pirates	1.000	7	1	3	0	4	0	Pitt, Jye, Cubs	.800	12	1	3	1	5	0
enstein, Andrew, Pirates	1.000	7	1	6	0	7	0	Polanco, Elvis, Cubs	.818	14	3	6	2	11	0
binko, Mike, Cubs*	1.000	11	3	1	0	4	0	Powley, Greg, Expos	1.000	13	1	5	0	6	0
er, John, Astros	1.000	10	5	1	0	6	0	Prater, Andrew, Pirates	.917	12	4	7	1	12	0
nd, Eric, Astros	.857	12	6	12	3	21	1	Prestash, J.D., Astros*	1.000	4	0	1	0	1	0
ierdo, Hansel, Marlins	1.000	12	1	1	0	2	0	Pyrtle, Joe, Mets	1.000	4	1	1	0	2	0
bs, Jake, Twins	.714	6	0	5	2	7	0	Queen, Mike, Mets*	1.000	11	1	1	0	2	0
es, Delvin, Devil Rays	.846	11	6	5	2	13	0	Quevedo, Ruben, Braves	1.000	10	6	9	0	15	0
enez, Ricardo, Orioles	.917	12	3	8	1	12	0	Ramirez, Jose, Tigers*	.733	13	0	11	4	15	0
ez, Raul, Twins	1.000	11	1	3	0	4	0	Ramsay, Robert, Red Sox*	1.000	2	0	1	0	1	0
r, Kris, Tigers	.833	8	3	2	1	6	0	Reed, Aaron, Tigers	.750	18	0	3	1	4	0
y, Jason, Cubs	1.000	8	1	0	0	1	0	Reeder, Galen, Braves*	.889	16	1	7	1	9	2
s, John, Rangers	.500	4	0	3	3	6	0	Reilly, Sean, Twins*	1.000	12	0	6	0	6	0
sch, Joe, Rangers	1.000	2	1	0	0	1	0	Reimers, Tom, White Sox	1.000	1	1	0	0	1	0
sbury, Willy, Red Sox	1.000	1	0	1	0	1	0	Reith, Brian, Yankees	1.000	10	2	1	0	3	0
ts, Gary, Marlins	1.000	12	4	10	0	14	0	Reitsma, Chris, Red Sox	.800	7	1	3	1	5	0
r, Ed, Devil Rays	.857	10	4	2	1	7	0	Rivera, Luis, Braves	.667	8	1	1	1	3	0
r, Justin, Royals	1.000	7	0	1	0	1	0	Rivera, Marcos, Expos*	.875	18	2	5	1	8	1
Nelson, Marlins	.333	7	0	1	2	3	0	Roberts, Chris, Mets*	1.000	3	1	1	0	2	0
Winston, Braves	.778	13	2	5	2	9	0	ROBERTSON, Jeriome, Astros*	1.000	13	5	14	0	19	0
n, Matthew, Marlins*	1.000	9	1	3	0	4	0	Rodgers, Marcus, White Sox	.600	10	1	5	4	10	1
am, Rick, Twins	.857	22	1	5	1	7	0	Rodriguez, Jose, Devil Rays	1.000	11	1	2	0	3	0
z, Jose, White Sox	1.000	16	1	6	0	7	0	Roeder, Jason, Royals	1.000	3	0	1	0	1	0
good, Jeromie, Mets*	1.000	10	1	8	0	9	0	Romo, Greg, Tigers	1.000	8	1	4	0	5	0
, Marcelino, Marlins	1.000	8	3	5	0	8	0	Roup, Randall, Royals	1.000	8	1	0	0	1	0
quist, Dave, White Sox	1.000	3	1	3	0	4	1	Ruhl, Nathan, Devil Rays	.917	16	4	7	1	12	1
da, Katsuhiro, Yankees	1.000	2	1	4	0	5	1	Rumer, Tim, Yankees*	.500	2	0	1	1	2	0
ory, Andrew, Cubs	.917	12	4	18	2	24	0	Runion, Jeff, Rangers	.800	7	1	7	2	10	1
ey, Kevin, Mets	1.000	10	0	4	0	4	0	Ryan, Kevin, Orioles	1.000	2	0	3	0	3	0
uardt, Scott, Mets	1.000	4	2	1	0	3	0	Sackinsky, Brian, Orioles	1.000	3	2	0	0	2	0
hall, Lee, Twins	.857	12	3	9	2	14	1	Sadler, William, Expos*	1.000	17	0	8	0	8	2
n, Curtis, Expos*	1.000	8	2	0	0	2	0	Salvevold, Gregory, Devil Rays	.900	15	4	5	1	10	0
n, Trey, Expos	1.000	13	1	3	0	4	0	Salyers, Jeremy, Expos	.917	11	2	9	1	12	0
nez, Javier, Cubs	1.000	3	2	2	0	4	1	Sanchez, Bienvenido, Expos	1.000	6	2	3	0	5	0
nez, Oscar, Yankees	1.000	7	2	1	0	3	0	Santamaria, Juan, Tigers	1.000	12	4	11	0	15	1
nez, Romulo, Tigers	.909	12	6	4	1	11	0	Santana, Humberto, Mets*	.900	10	1	17	2	20	2
ide, Jason, Yankees	.818	23	1	8	2	11	0	Santana, Orlando, Yankees	1.000	16	2	3	0	5	0
rter, Jason, Astros	1.000	21	2	2	0	4	0	Santana, Pedro, Red Sox	.938	13	1	14	1	16	0
askey, Tim, Marlins	.846	12	6	5	2	13	1	Santos, Juan, Orioles	1.000	6	1	1	0	2	0
ready, Jim, Mets	1.000	5	1	2	0	3	0	Santos, Victor, Tigers	.929	9	3	10	1	14	0
eery, Rick, Devil Rays	1.000	11	1	1	0	2	0	Seberino, Ronni, Devil Rays*	1.000	18	1	10	0	11	1
aniel, Denton, Royals*	1.000	7	0	5	0	5	0	Seebode, Michael, Tigers*	.833	12	1	4	1	6	0
arlane, Joseph, Tigers	.778	15	1	6	2	9	0	Sekany, Jason, Red Sox	.750	5	0	3	1	4	1
night, Tony, Astros	.600	9	0	3	2	5	0	Serrano, Liosvany, Braves	1.000	12	0	1	0	1	0
att, Joshua, Orioles*	.933	12	1	13	1	15	0	Settle, Brian, Pirates	1.000	7	0	1	0	1	0
ly, Todd, Royals	.929	11	3	10	1	14	1	Shearn, Thomas, Astros	1.000	17	3	6	0	9	0
na, Carlos, Marlins*	.500	4	0	1	1	2	0	Shourds, Anthony, Rangers	.889	20	4	4	1	9	0
na, Tom, Astros	1.000	8	3	1	0	4	0	Siciliano, Jess, Pirates	1.000	3	0	4	0	4	0
oza, Geronimo, White Sox	.667	12	5	5	5	15	0	Silva, Juan, Red Sox*	.800	15	0	4	1	5	0
edes, Carlos, Orioles	1.000	5	0	1	0	1	0	Simmons, Mike, White Sox	1.000	17	0	3	0	3	1
, Wade, Astros	.941	11	10	6	1	17	0	Sims, Kenneth, Orioles	1.000	11	1	4	0	5	0
anez, Jorge, Red Sox	1.000	9	2	2	0	4	0	Smith, Ryan, Rangers*	.714	14	0	5	2	7	0

Player, Team	Pct.	G	PO	A	E	TC	DP
Snead, George, Braves	.000	3	0	0	1	1	0
Snyder, John, White Sox	1.000	4	2	2	0	4	0
Sorzano, Ronnie, Expos	1.000	15	1	5	0	6	1
Sparks, Eric, Expos*	.500	14	1	0	1	2	0
Stading, Kris, Expos*	1.000	12	1	1	0	2	0
Stallings, Ben, Red Sox	.875	11	2	5	1	8	0
Stinson, Kevin, White Sox	.750	24	4	2	2	8	0
Styles, Bobby, Rangers	1.000	23	1	7	0	8	0
Suggs, Willie, Mets	.667	10	1	1	1	3	0
Tatar, Jason, Twins	1.000	2	0	1	0	1	0
Tellez, Eloy, White Sox	.950	11	4	15	1	20	0
Thurman, Corey, Royals	.500	11	1	2	3	6	0
Tobias, Daniel, Pirates	.800	5	2	2	1	5	1
Torres, Eric, Mets	.750	20	0	3	1	4	0
Torres, Michael, Royals	.909	18	5	5	1	11	1

Player, Team	Pct.	G	PO	A	E	TC
Tull, William, Mets	1.000	1	0	2	0	2
Vail, Keith, Devil Rays	1.000	5	0	1	0	1
Valle, Yoiset, Yankees*	1.000	7	0	3	0	3
Vallis, Jamie, Twins*	1.000	12	0	10	0	10
Van Winkle, Judd, Tigers*	1.000	8	2	3	0	5
Vergara, Luis, Braves	1.000	4	2	3	0	5
Vizcaino, Edward, Cubs	.900	14	2	7	1	10
Vogt, Robert, Pirates*	.875	13	2	5	1	8
Ward, Brandon, Cubs	1.000	16	2	2	0	4
Wegmann, Tom, Orioles	1.000	4	1	1	0	2
Weidert, Chris, Expos	1.000	2	1	1	0	2
Wesolowski, David, Marlins	1.000	2	0	1	0	1
White, Rick, Pirates	1.000	3	0	1	0	1
Widerski, Jonathan, Marlins	.909	12	2	8	1	11
Wright, Jason, Pirates	1.000	13	1	0	0	1

The following players did not have any fielding statistics at the positions indicated or appeared only as a designated hitter, pinch-hitter or pinch-runner: M. Abreu, Ahrendt, of; D. Alvarado, p; Alvino, p; Bagley, 3b; Barner, dh; Bere, p; Bocachica, dh; Bonilla, p; Derm. Brown, of; M. Brown, p; Bullock, p; Cafaro, p; L. Cardona, Cosman, p; Crawford, p; Delgado, 3b; Durick, p; Escobar, ss; Fajardo, p; E. Feliz, 2b; Ferguson, 1b; Fisher, dh; Galban, c; Gillispie, p; Hamilton, of; Hammons, Heberling, p; Hinojosa, p; Q. Jackson, c; D. Johnson, 2b; J. Johnson, p; Kaufman, p; Key, p; Larocca, p; Leidens, p; Ligons, of; Lindemann, p; Madison, p; Mattson McNeal, of; McNichol, p; Meier, ph; Munoz, p; Nicley, ss; Norton, p; Oliveros, c; Opipari, p; Ovalles, p; Ozuna, 3b; Paul, ph; Pauls, p; Payton, dh; Pedrosa, dh; Penic ss; Raines, dh; F. Ramirez, p; Jua. Ramirez, 3b; K. Ramos, 1b, of; B. Reed, p; Jor. Rodriguez, p; Rojas, p; Roman, p; Rosario, p; O. Sanchez, ss; Pedro Santana (As of; Schnautz, p; Seip, p; Shannon, p; Spinelli, p; Stanley, p; Stewart, p; Stratton, dh; Tarasco, dh; Tejera, p; Torrealba, of; Trunk, p; Tyrrell, p; Ubaldo, of; Vizcaino, Wagner, p; Wallace, p; Westover, p; Wiley, p; Wilkes, p; Zambrano, p; Zydowsky, of.

LEAGUE CHAMPIONS

Year	Team	Pct.	Year	Team	Pct.	Year	Team	P
1964—	Sarasota Braves	.610	1979—	Houston	.635	1989—	Yankees‡	.65
1965—	Bradenton Astros	.632	1980—	Kansas City-Blue	.635		Dodgers	.63
1966—	New York AL	.667	1981—	Kansas City-Gold	.688	1990—	Expos	.6
1967—	Kansas City	.614	1982—	New York AL	.667		Dodgers‡	.64
1968—	Oakland	.650	1983—	Texas	.645	1991—	Orioles	.5
1969—	Montreal	.585		Los Angeles†	.617		Expos∞	.5
1970—	Chicago AL	.600	1984—	White Sox	.651	1992—	Royals∞	.6
1971—	Kansas City	.755		Rangers†	.571		Expos	.5
1972—	Chicago NL*	.651	1985—	Yankees§	.705	1993—	Rangers▲	.66
	Kansas City*	.651		Rangers	.532		Astros	.5
1973—	Texas	.732	1986—	Reds	.548	1994—	Royals◆	.7
1974—	Chicago NL	.702		Dodgers†	.541		Astros	.6
1975—	Texas	.774	1987—	Dodgers†	.683	1995—	Royals■	.6
1976—	Texas	.704		Royals	.635		Tigers	.5
1977—	Chicago AL	.731	1988—	Yankees†	.714	1996—	Yankees◆	.6
1978—	Texas	.600		Royals	.619		Rangers	.6

*Declared co-champions; no playoff. †League divided into Northern and Southern divisions; won one-game playoff for league championship. ‡Lea[gue] divided into Northern and Southern divisions; won best-of-three playoff for league championship. §Yankees declared champion based on winning perc[ent]age when one-game playoff against Rangers was rained out. ∞League divided into Northern, Southern and Central divisions; won best-of-three playoff league championship. ▲League divided into Eastern, Central and Western divisions; won three-team playoff. ◆League divided into Eastern, Northern a[nd] Western divisions; won three-team playoff. ■League divided into Eastern, Northern, Northwest and Southwest divisions; won four-team playoff. (Not[...] Known as Sarasota Rookie League in 1964 and Florida Rookie League in 1965.)

PIONEER LEAGUE

LEAGUE OFFICE

President
Jim McCurdy
Address
P.O. Box 2564
Spokane, WA 99220
Phone
509-456-7615

Teams (affiliation)
Billings Mustangs (Reds)
Butte Copper Kings (Angels)
Great Falls Dodgers (Dodgers)
Helena Brewers (Brewers)

Idaho Falls Braves (Padres)
Lethbridge Black Diamonds (Arizona Diamondbacks)
Medicine Hat Blue Jays (Blue Jays)
Ogden Raptors (Brewers)

1996 FINAL STANDINGS

FIRST HALF

NORTHERN DIVISION

Team	W	L	T	Pct.	GB
Helena (Brewers)	23	13	0	.639	....
Lethbridge (Diamondbacks)	21	15	0	.583	2
Great Falls (Dodgers)	21	15	0	.583	2
Medicine Hat (Blue Jays)	12	24	0	.333	11

SOUTHERN DIVISION

Team	W	L	T	Pct.	GB
Ogden (Brewers)	22	14	0	.611	....
Idaho Falls (Padres)	18	18	0	.500	4
Butte (Devil Rays)	16	20	0	.444	6
Billings (Reds)	11	25	0	.306	11

SECOND HALF

NORTHERN DIVISION

Team	W	L	T	Pct.	GB
Lethbridge (Diamondbacks)	29	7	0	.806	....
Helena (Brewers)	20	16	0	.556	9
Great Falls (Dodgers)	12	24	0	.333	17
Medicine Hat (Blue Jays)	10	26	0	.278	19

SOUTHERN DIVISION

Team	W	L	T	Pct.	GB
Butte (Devil Rays)	21	15	0	.583	....
Ogden (Brewers)	20	16	0	.556	1
Idaho Falls (Padres)	20	16	0	.556	1
Billings (Reds)	12	24	0	.333	9

COMPOSITE

Team	Let.	Hel.	Ogd.	I.F.	But.	G.F.	Bil.	M.H.	W	L	T	Pct.	GB
Lethbridge (Diamondbacks)	....	8	3	5	5	12	6	11	50	22	0	.694	....
Helena (Brewers)	5	....	6	4	4	7	7	10	43	29	0	.597	7
Ogden (Brewers)	5	2	....	8	7	6	8	6	42	30	0	.583	8
Idaho Falls (Padres)	3	4	6	....	6	4	9	6	38	34	0	.528	12
Butte (Devil Rays)	3	4	6	7	....	3	11	3	37	35	0	.514	13
Great Falls (Dodgers)	1	7	2	4	5	....	4	10	33	39	0	.458	17
Billings (Reds)	2	1	5	4	3	4	....	4	23	49	0	.319	27
Medicine Hat (Blue Jays)	3	3	2	2	5	3	4	....	22	50	0	.306	28

Major league affiliations in parentheses.

PLAYOFFS: Helena defeated Lethbridge, two games to one; Ogden defeated Butte, two games to one; Helena defeated Ogden two games to none, to win league championship.

REGULAR-SEASON ATTENDANCE: Billings, 83,586; Butte, 37,317; Great Falls, 68,537; Helena, 44,935; Idaho Falls, 54,475; Lethbridge, 49,124; Medicine Hat, 41,942; Ogden, 62,022; Total—441,938; Playoffs (8 games)—5,945.

MANAGERS: Billings, Matt Martin (through July 25), Bill Plummer (from July 26 through end of season); Butte, Tom Foley; Great Falls, Mickey Hatcher; Helena, Alex Morales; Idaho Falls, Don Werner; Lethbridge, Chris Speier; Medicine Hat, Marty Pevey; Ogden, Bernie Moncallo. Managerial record of team with more than one manager; Billings, Martin, 10-25, Plummer, 13-24.

ALL-STAR TEAM: 1B—Jonathan Tucker, Great Falls; 2B—Wylie Campbell, Billings; 3B—Steven Chavez, Idaho Falls; SS—Ben Reynoso, Idaho Falls; OF—Marcus Cain, Butte; Kevin Sweeney, Lethbridge; Jason Weekly, Great Falls; C—Matt Quataro, Butte; DH—Miguel Rodriguez, Ogden; RHP—Vladimir Nunez, Lethbridge; LHP—Brian Passini, Helena; Relief Pitcher—David Bleazard, Medicine Hat; Most Valuable Player—Kevin Sweeney, Lethbridge; Manager of the Year—Tom Foley, Butte.

1996 BATTING

TEAM

Team	Avg.	G	TPA	AB	R	H	TB	2B	3B	HR	RBI	SH	SF	HP	BB	IBB	SO	SB	CS	GDP	LOB	ShO	Slg.	OBP
Lethbridge	.314	72	3101	2583	637	811	1258	133	25	88	558	12	46	53	407	8	579	93	36	51	605	1	.487	.411
Butte	.309	72	3028	2651	533	819	1176	143	44	42	442	17	34	54	272	5	507	97	38	60	585	3	.444	.380
Ogden	.302	72	2990	2551	525	770	1160	146	20	68	428	27	29	51	332	4	499	102	44	54	574	2	.455	.389
Helena	.297	72	3006	2544	543	755	1119	122	19	68	459	19	31	49	362	16	464	80	48	48	592	3	.440	.390
Idaho Falls	.295	72	2982	2597	465	765	1100	135	28	48	392	4	33	43	305	5	547	105	36	53	623	1	.424	.374
Great Falls	.282	72	2814	2490	440	702	1053	113	35	56	370	8	24	39	252	3	597	140	74	30	493	1	.423	.354
Billings	.266	72	2988	2569	462	683	1023	122	28	54	399	18	27	44	329	11	603	83	33	39	585	0	.398	.356
Medicine Hat	.256	72	2797	2412	410	617	915	109	9	57	339	23	23	26	311	3	605	113	44	40	517	2	.379	.344

INDIVIDUAL

TOP QUALIFIERS FOR BATTING CHAMPIONSHIP

Minimum 194 plate appearances. *Lefthanded batter. †Switch-hitter.

Player, Team	Avg.	G	TPA	AB	R	H	TB	2B	3B	HR	RBI	SH	SF	HP	BB	IBB	SO	SB	CS	GDP	Slg.	OBP
Sweeney, Kevin, Lethbridge*	.424	63	270	203	72	86	149	19	1	14	72	0	4	3	60	3	36	3	0	5	.734	.552
Kent, Gerald, Ogden*	.385	62	260	218	42	84	120	18	0	6	42	1	3	1	37	0	34	5	1	3	.550	.471

Player, Team	Avg.	G	TPA	AB	R	H	TB	2B	3B	HR	RBI	SH	SF	HP	BB	IBB	SO	SB	CS	GDP	Slg.	OBP
McCain, Marcus, Butte	.379	55	283	256	66	97	117	9	4	1	27	0	5	6	16	1	21	34	10	5	.457	.4
Campbell, Wylie, Billings#	.371	70	320	259	69	96	125	15	7	0	30	5	3	8	45	2	29	24	6	1	.483	.4
Conti, Jason, Lethbridge*	.367	63	265	226	63	83	112	15	1	4	49	0	3	6	30	0	29	30	7	3	.496	.4
Weekley, Jason, Great Falls	.366	64	258	238	35	87	130	12	5	7	43	0	1	1	18	0	63	18	12	1	.546	.4
Arrendondo, Hernando, Butte..	.357	67	288	252	59	90	137	21	7	4	49	1	2	9	24	0	31	8	3	6	.544	.4
Walther, Christopher, Ogden	.351	63	259	239	47	84	126	16	4	6	54	3	2	1	14	0	21	3	2	7	.527	.3
Reynoso, Benjamin, Idaho Flls	.345	72	320	284	45	98	136	26	0	4	50	0	4	6	26	0	42	20	7	6	.479	.4
Tucker, Jonathan, Great Falls*	.345	48	194	174	39	60	110	12	1	12	54	0	3	2	15	1	30	13	5	0	.632	.3
Quatraro, Matthew, Butte	.344	59	280	244	53	84	111	16	4	1	59	0	3	8	25	0	29	3	1	4	.455	.4
MacAlutas, Jon, Ogden	.343	54	206	178	41	61	80	10	0	3	24	0	3	7	18	0	21	8	2	4	.449	.4
Johnson, Ledowick, Helena*	.341	59	272	208	70	71	106	8	3	7	33	0	3	3	58	1	43	19	6	3	.510	.4
Suero, Ignacio, Helena	.338	55	245	210	46	71	120	11	1	12	63	1	5	6	23	3	29	3	4	0	.571	.4
Washam, Jason, Helena	.327	60	282	226	56	74	110	10	1	8	51	2	1	15	38	1	39	3	4	4	.487	.4

DEPARTMENTAL LEADERS: G—Paciorek, McClure, Reynoso, 72; AB—McClure, 308; R—Sweeney, 72; H—McClure, 99; TB—Hartman, 155; 2B—Reynoso, 26; 3B—McCarty, 10; HR—Rodriguez, Hayman, Ingram, 17 each; RBI—Hartman, Sweeney, 72; SH—Faurot, Glover, 6 each; SF—Hayman, 9; HP—Washam, 15; BB—Sweene[y] 60; IBB—Klimek, 5; SO—Ingram, 88; SB—McCain, 34; CS—Weekley, 12; GIDP—Salinas, 10; Slg.—Sweeney, .734; OBP—Sweeney, .552.

ALL PLAYERS

*Lefthanded batter. †Switch-hitter.

Player, Team	Avg.	G	TPA	AB	R	H	TB	2B	3B	HR	RBI	SH	SF	HP	BB	IBB	SO	SB	CS	GDP	Slg.	OBP
Albaral, Randy, Medicine Hat...	.259	60	264	228	50	59	65	4	1	0	19	5	1	3	27	0	39	33	6	0	.285	.3
Alfano, Jeff, Ogden	.283	45	179	159	29	45	66	9	0	4	29	2	2	4	12	0	30	2	2	2	.415	.3
Allison, Bradley, Lethbridge	.209	25	54	43	7	9	12	0	0	1	6	0	1	1	9	0	16	0	1	1	.279	.3
Arrendondo, Hernando, Butte...	.357	67	288	252	59	90	137	21	7	4	49	1	2	9	24	0	31	8	3	6	.544	.4
Auterson, Jeffrey, Great Falls..	.206	51	191	165	22	34	52	4	1	4	12	0	1	5	20	0	72	6	8	2	.315	.3
Bagley, Lorenzo, Medicine Hat	.289	67	282	235	61	68	125	16	1	13	46	0	1	1	45	0	57	14	5	4	.532	.4
Bain, Tyler, Butte*	.309	61	267	233	45	72	102	11	5	3	29	0	3	0	31	2	33	13	6	3	.438	.3
Baltzell, Beau, Lethbridge	.135	19	42	37	1	5	7	2	0	0	5	0	0	1	4	0	9	0	0	1	.189	.2
Barajas, Rod, Lethbridge	.337	51	193	175	47	59	104	9	3	10	50	0	4	2	12	0	24	2	1	6	.594	.3
Barker, Kevin, Ogden*	.317	71	335	281	61	89	143	19	4	9	56	0	5	3	46	4	54	0	2	4	.509	.4
Barner, Doug, Butte	.111	6	22	18	1	2	2	0	0	0	0	0	0	0	4	0	6	0	1	1	.111	.2
Baston, Stanley, Medicine Hat.	.280	68	312	271	45	76	107	14	1	5	45	2	1	2	36	0	58	10	3	5	.395	.3
Boughton, Mike, Lethbridge† ..	.286	62	249	224	32	64	78	7	2	1	29	3	4	2	16	1	50	4	6	2	.348	.3
Boulo, Tyler, Idaho Falls	.260	35	151	127	15	33	52	8	1	3	33	0	3	6	15	0	24	1	0	4	.409	.3
Bramlett, Jeff, Great Falls	.261	56	242	222	42	58	105	14	6	7	41	0	0	2	17	0	62	12	3	1	.473	.3
Burress, Andy, Billings	.318	27	116	107	23	34	58	5	2	5	25	0	1	1	7	0	16	4	1	3	.542	.3
Cafaro, Nicholas, Helena	.350	49	183	157	34	55	66	7	2	0	22	2	3	1	20	0	36	15	8	2	.420	.4
Campbell, Wylie, Billings†	.371	70	320	259	69	96	125	15	7	0	30	5	3	8	45	2	29	24	6	1	.483	.4
Chavez, Steven, Idaho Falls*	.325	69	338	277	55	90	134	19	2	7	50	0	8	4	49	0	52	5	3	4	.484	.4
Conroy, Danny, Idaho Falls† ...	.278	23	61	54	11	15	23	3	1	1	5	0	1		6	0	8	5	3	4	.426	.3
Conti, Jason, Lethbridge*	.367	63	265	226	63	83	112	15	1	4	49	0	3	6	30	0	29	30	7	3	.496	.4
Cripps, Bobby, Great Falls*	.309	49	156	139	23	43	59	4	3	2	28	1	5	2	9	0	19	6	5	5	.424	.3
Cuevas, Trent, Great Falls	.258	51	171	155	24	40	63	12	1	3	20	1	3	1	11	0	30	2	5	2	.406	.3
Darula, Bobbie, Ogden*	.274	45	126	106	19	29	45	4	0	4	23	0	1	2	17	0	22	2	0	2	.425	.3
Davis, Josh, Idaho Falls.	.188	32	126	101	12	19	27	2	0	2	13	2	2	0	21	0	39	5	0	1	.267	.3
Davis, Reggie, Lethbridge	.315	31	104	89	18	28	40	7	1	1	18	1	0	1	13	1	19	0	2	3	.449	.4
Delosantos, Eddy, Butte*	.271	16	69	59	15	16	16	0	0	0	12	2	2	0	6	0	17	1	1	1	.271	.3
DeCelle, Mike, Billings	.291	69	317	258	54	75	131	18	7	8	51	2	3	9	45	1	68	6	2	6	.508	.4
Dresch, Michael, Billings*	.243	34	129	115	15	28	42	6	1	2	17	0	1	0	13	2	26	3	3	1	.365	.3
Ebbert, Chad, Idaho Falls.	.275	27	107	102	10	28	33	5	0	0	12	0	0	2	3	0	23	0	0	2	.324	.3
Ebling, Jamie, Butte.	.278	50	238	194	49	54	79	10	3	3	32	4	1	1	38	0	62	6	4	4	.407	.3
Falcon, Edwin, Great Falls	.321	20	66	53	6	17	23	3	0	1	8	0	0	1	12	0	8	2	0	0	.434	.4
Faurot, Adam, Ogden	.235	67	282	238	41	56	71	9	0	2	18	6	1	11	26	0	35	18	10	8	.298	.3
Fernandez, Ramon, Hel.-Og...	.071	41	77	70	7	5	7	2	0	0	3	0	0	0	7	0	31	0	2	4	.100	.1
Fink, Marc, Helena*	.355	37	134	107	18	38	73	6	0	9	28	0	1	0	26	2	27	0	0	4	.682	.4
Foulks, Brian, Great Falls	.314	35	126	121	14	38	50	7	1	1	9	0	1	3	1	0	24	4	2	2	.413	.3
Gann, Jamie, Lethbridge	.287	49	142	129	19	37	55	10	1	2	22	0	1	2	10	0	42	3	3	4	.426	.3
Garrett, Scott, Billings	.184	41	155	136	14	25	37	6	0	2	17	3	0	6	9	0	41	0	1	2	.272	.2
Giles, Tim, Medicine Hat*	.267	68	280	258	36	69	116	17	0	10	45	0	3	0	19	2	52	5	0	7	.450	.3
Glasser, Scott, Lethbridge	.296	9	33	27	7	8	11	1	1	0	3	0	0	1	5	0	7	0	0	1	.407	.4
Glover, Jason, Ogden	.289	58	239	194	42	56	98	10	4	8	35	6	4	3	32	0	52	8	4	4	.505	.3
Green, Chad, Ogden†	.358	21	100	81	22	29	44	4	1	3	8	1	2	1	15	0	23	12	3	0	.543	.4
Griggs, Rodrickus, Billings	.272	49	177	151	24	41	44	3	0	0	20	0	3	4	19	0	29	6	1	2	.291	.3
Guerrero, Sergio, Helena	.318	57	254	217	48	69	88	13	0	2	40	2	4	6	25	0	14	6	3	6	.406	.3
Guthrie, David, Billings†	.227	48	219	181	45	41	65	6	3	4	28	3	2	7	26	0	48	10	1	4	.359	.3
Hardy, Brett, Lethbridge*	.367	30	114	90	28	33	39	3	0	1	15	0	2	0	22	1	14	2	0	0	.433	.4
Hartman, Ronald, Lethbridge ..	.326	66	308	258	69	84	155	23	0	16	72	0	8	6	36	0	42	5	2	6	.601	.4
Hayman, David, Lethbridge	.313	63	291	233	68	73	140	8	4	17	59	0	9	6	43	1	78	4	0	2	.601	.4
Hemphill, James, Helena	.313	51	151	128	26	40	56	8	1	2	18	0	1	1	21	0	31	4	2	2	.438	.4
Hucks, Brian, Billings	.322	20	75	59	10	19	31	6	0	2	12	1	0	3	12	0	14	0	0	0	.525	.4
Hunter, Brian, Idaho Falls	.245	32	123	102	13	25	28	3	0	0	9	0	0	0	21	0	30	3	3	3	.275	.3
Illig, Brett, Great Falls	.227	44	127	119	15	27	33	3	0	1	11	1	1	0	6	0	36	4	2	4	.277	.2
Ingram, Darron, Billings	.295	65	288	251	49	74	138	20	0	17	56	0	1	2	34	2	88	7	3	1	.550	.3
Jackson, Rod, Idaho Falls	.284	54	270	250	56	71	87	3	5	1	21	1	2	5	12	1	32	25	6	4	.348	.3
Jenkins, Daniel, Billings.	.222	55	148	126	21	28	39	7	2	0	14	2	2	2	16	0	39	0	3	6	.310	.3
Jenkins, Pete, Og.-Hel.	.174	21	58	46	7	8	13	2	0	1	5	0	0	1	11	0	13	0	0	3	.283	.3
Johnson, Ledowick, Helena*	.341	59	272	208	70	71	106	8	3	7	33	0	3	3	58	1	43	19	6	3	.510	.4
Kastelic, Matthew, Butte*	.354	40	168	158	26	56	72	8	1	2	26	0	1	3	6	0	16	6	0	4	.456	.3
Keller, JEremy, Billings*	.241	59	266	237	39	57	90	14	0	7	39	0	3	2	24	0	52	0	2	3	.380	
Kent, Robert, Idaho Falls	.309	47	208	181	40	56	76	14	0	2	25	1	4	1	21	0	28	4	1	5	.420	
Kerr, James, Butte	.153	32	111	98	9	15	24	3	0	2	6	1	2	0	10	0	32	3	1	1	.245	

er, Team	Avg.	G	TPA	AB	R	H	TB	2B	3B	HR	RBI	SH	SF	HP	BB	IBB	SO	SB	CS	GDP	Slg.	OBP
ard, Kirk, Lethbridge...........	.000	5	13	13	0	0	0	0	0	0	0	0	0	0	0	0	7	0	0	2	.000	.000
j, Michael, Butte	.313	50	211	192	35	60	82	13	3	1	27	4	1	2	12	0	27	7	3	7	.427	.357
y, Doug, Billings................	.236	57	223	182	29	43	64	10	1	3	20	0	2	0	39	1	48	4	1	2	.352	.368
y, Scott, Helena	.200	47	171	145	26	29	45	4	0	4	21	1	2	4	19	0	42	0	3	4	.310	.306
nek, Josh, Helena*	.296	67	299	253	56	75	110	17	0	6	51	0	3	0	42	5	39	5	1	4	.435	.393
er, Joshua, Lethbridge†	.250	12	33	28	6	7	8	1	0	0	2	1	0	1	3	0	3	1	0	1	.286	.344
gaigne, Selwyn, Med. Hat*	.260	32	120	100	19	26	38	4	1	2	11	2	0	1	17	0	20	8	2	4	.380	.373
ch, Nick, Great Falls*	.251	58	238	199	42	50	87	8	1	9	25	0	0	3	36	2	33	2	4	3	.437	.374
lsey, Rodney, Idaho Falls ...	.303	48	210	185	45	56	87	4	6	5	17	0	0	2	23	0	53	16	3	1	.470	.386
-Alutas, Jon, Ogden...........	.343	54	206	178	41	61	80	10	0	3	24	0	3	7	18	0	21	8	2	4	.449	.417
oney, Jeff, Medicine Hat ...	.198	65	271	222	36	44	69	9	2	4	27	2	3	5	39	1	85	11	6	2	.311	.327
ap, Eric, Billings†	.263	56	192	175	21	46	77	10	6	3	34	0	1	3	13	1	41	1	3	5	.440	.323
n, Kevin, Billings	.277	66	303	271	48	75	91	11	1	1	38	1	4	3	24	0	49	19	3	5	.336	.338
shall, Monte, Great Falls†..	.265	52	207	181	36	48	57	7	1	0	22	0	4	3	19	0	34	10	7	3	.315	.338
tinez, David E., Ogden	.330	35	135	103	25	34	42	6	1	0	13	5	1	0	26	0	30	0	3	2	.408	.462
tinez, Leonardo, Butte†	.234	39	135	128	13	30	33	1	1	0	16	2	0	0	5	0	24	5	2	3	.258	.263
tinez, Obed, Idaho Falls.....	.245	28	121	110	14	27	33	4	1	0	10	0	0	1	10	0	27	1	2	2	.300	.314
Cain, Marcus, Butte	.379	55	283	256	66	97	117	9	4	1	27	0	5	6	16	1	21	34	10	5	.457	.420
Party, Matt, Great Falls	.284	58	237	208	40	59	95	7	10	3	32	0	0	5	24	0	56	16	2	3	.457	.371
lellan, Sean, Medicine Hat	.000	13	5	5	0	0	0	0	0	0	0	0	0	0	0	0	2	0	0	0	.000	.000
Clure, Brian, Idaho Falls* ...	.321	72	353	308	62	99	147	18	6	6	45	0	4	3	38	0	63	10	2	6	.477	.397
Gehee, Mike, Butte†	.254	28	86	71	12	18	21	1	1	0	8	0	1	1	13	0	20	0	2	1	.296	.372
rina, Robert, Medicine Hat.	.259	40	132	112	18	29	52	8	0	5	19	2	2	0	14	0	39	1	4	2	.464	.336
er, Bobby, Great Falls........	.377	14	64	53	12	20	28	2	3	0	4	1	0	0	10	0	16	7	4	0	.528	.476
er, Shawn, Ogden	.500	17	2	2	1	1	1	0	0	0	0	0	0	0	0	0	0	0	0	0	.500	.500
n, Bradley, Medicine Hat*.	.176	34	54	51	5	9	10	1	0	0	1	0	1	0	2	0	15	0	1	2	.196	.204
re, Donald, Ogden	.271	50	96	85	16	23	32	0	3	1	13	2	1	1	7	0	30	5	1	0	.376	.330
re, Jason, Lethbridge	.245	47	186	151	34	37	67	6	0	8	35	0	2	6	27	0	61	1	3	2	.444	.376
moto, Ken, Great Falls......	.285	32	148	123	40	35	43	3	1	1	12	3	2	1	19	0	26	27	4	1	.350	.379
a, PasCual, Idaho Falls	.190	15	65	58	2	11	19	2	3	0	10	0	1	2	4	0	32	0	0	2	.328	.262
ez, Jose, Lethbridge	.311	40	153	122	43	38	56	5	2	3	24	0	0	7	24	0	25	5	0	3	.459	.451
ka, Garret, Helena	.212	53	199	165	34	35	45	2	1	2	19	5	0	4	25	0	33	6	6	1	.273	.330
orek, Peter, Idaho Falls†	.297	72	329	283	56	84	148	15	2	15	69	0	6	4	36	1	64	6	1	6	.523	.377
nt, Gerald, Ogden*	.385	62	260	218	42	84	120	18	0	6	42	1	3	1	37	0	34	5	1	3	.550	.471
nenter, Ross, Ogden	.305	45	166	141	21	43	58	9	0	2	18	0	1	3	21	0	31	0	3	5	.411	.404
llis, Anthony, Billings	.285	44	198	172	35	49	92	9	5	8	32	0	1	3	22	3	45	3	2	2	.535	.374
r, Kelly, Ogden	.294	41	201	163	41	48	68	12	1	2	24	1	1	9	27	0	36	17	4	3	.417	.420
ps, Joshua, Medicine Hat .	.241	59	227	191	28	46	64	3	0	5	29	2	1	6	27	0	65	5	3	5	.335	.351
to, Nick, Billings	.125	4	19	16	2	2	2	0	0	0	1	0	1	0	2	0	6	0	1	0	.125	.211
e, Corey, Billings	.191	49	160	131	18	25	28	3	0	0	16	3	2	0	24	0	32	2	2	2	.214	.312
raro, Matthew, Butte	.344	59	280	244	53	84	111	16	4	1	59	0	3	8	25	0	29	3	1	4	.455	.418
oso, Benjamin, Id. Falls ...	.345	72	320	284	45	98	136	26	0	4	50	0	4	6	26	0	42	20	7	6	.479	.406
a, Chip, Lethbridge†	.252	43	156	139	25	35	53	5	2	3	22	0	1	1	15	0	47	1	2	4	.381	.327
ey, Mikal, Great Falls	.108	34	74	65	8	7	8	1	0	0	0	1	0	1	8	0	25	4	1	0	.123	.205
Cash, Great Falls	.303	44	164	145	23	44	63	8	1	3	26	0	0	5	14	0	30	6	6	3	.434	.384
iguez, Miguel, Ogden	.285	69	302	274	66	78	151	18	2	17	65	0	2	5	21	0	44	22	5	6	.551	.344
ie, Francisco, Helena........	.229	30	122	109	14	25	28	3	0	0	8	1	2	2	8	0	19	1	0	2	.257	.289
alph, Jeremi, Med. Hat......	.250	12	32	28	4	7	8	1	0	0	3	0	0	0	4	0	13	1	1	0	.286	.344
erford, Daryl, Idaho Falls .	.303	46	200	175	29	53	70	9	1	2	23	0	2	3	20	1	30	4	5	3	.400	.380
-, Robert, Lethbridge*	.303	59	264	211	55	64	86	8	1	4	37	5	3	2	43	1	33	23	6	2	.408	.421
as, Trey, Butte	.301	67	306	279	44	84	131	15	4	8	52	0	5	3	19	0	43	4	3	10	.470	.346
ub, Greg, Helena..............	.265	63	271	245	39	65	117	13	6	9	50	3	1	3	19	0	38	4	3	9	.478	.325
ion, Pablo, Medicine Hat†	.240	68	277	229	44	55	82	15	0	4	29	1	5	2	40	0	52	5	6	3	.358	.351
y, Casey, Great Falls†	.269	43	151	130	19	35	47	6	0	2	23	0	3	5	13	0	33	1	4	0	.362	.351
ey, Ernest, Lethbridge	.336	31	136	107	30	36	53	3	4	2	25	1	2	3	23	0	24	8	3	2	.495	.459
er, Mike, Lethbridge	.321	24	95	78	13	25	33	1	2	1	13	1	2	2	12	0	13	1	0	1	.423	.415
nsborg, Ryan, Med. Hat....	.310	55	245	216	34	67	107	10	3	8	38	5	3	5	16	0	42	8	2	4	.495	.367
o, Ignacio, Helena............	.338	55	245	210	46	71	120	11	1	12	63	1	5	6	23	3	29	3	4	0	.571	.410
eney, Kevin, Lethbridge*...	.424	63	270	203	72	86	149	19	1	14	72	0	4	3	60	3	36	3	0	5	.734	.552
npson, Dan, Helena †	.338	50	158	145	29	49	75	6	1	6	30	0	1	3	9	1	28	3	2	1	.517	.386
er, Jonathan, Great Falls*.	.345	48	194	174	39	60	110	12	1	12	54	0	3	2	15	1	30	13	5	0	.632	.397
ria, Jose, Medicine Hat	.189	36	132	122	9	23	26	3	0	0	10	2	0	1	7	0	23	1	2	1	.213	.238
ll, Jared, Butte	.306	57	238	206	51	63	115	17	4	9	46	1	5	11	15	0	78	1	1	3	.558	.376
, Sam, Butte†	.600	5	9	5	1	3	3	0	0	0	2	0	0	1	3	1	0	0	0	0	.600	.778
ier, Christopher, Ogden....	.351	63	259	239	47	84	126	16	4	6	54	3	2	1	14	0	21	3	2	7	.527	.387
am, Jason, Helena	.327	60	282	226	56	74	110	10	1	8	51	2	1	15	38	1	39	3	4	4	.487	.454
ley, Jason, Great Falls	.366	64	258	238	35	87	130	12	5	7	43	0	1	1	18	0	63	18	12	1	.546	.411
nore, Michael, Helena†.....	.277	50	232	202	44	56	75	10	3	1	23	2	4	0	24	3	38	11	6	3	.371	.348
s, Symmion, Med. Hat......	.271	40	164	144	21	39	46	4	0	1	17	0	2	0	18	0	43	11	3	1	.319	.348

RAND SLAMS: Kirby, Schaub, 2; Bagley, Barajas, Baston, Boulo, Conti, DeCelle, Guthrie, Hayman, Kent, Paciorek, Riley, Sweeney, Tucker, Washam, 1 each.

WARDED FIRST BASE ON CATCHER'S INTERFERENCE: Medina 2 (Salinas, Suero); Bramlett (Umbria); Garrett (Alfano); Klimek (Cripps).

PLAYERS WITH TWO OR MORE TEAMS

er, Team	Avg.	G	TPA	AB	R	H	TB	2B	3B	HR	RBI	SH	SF	HP	BB	IBB	SO	SB	CS	GDP	Slg.	OBP
ndez, Ramon, Helena	.000	3	6	6	0	0	0	0	0	0	0	0	0	0	0	0	3	0	0	0	.000	.000
ndez, Ramon, Ogden.......	.078	38	71	64	7	5	7	2	0	0	3	0	0	0	7	0	28	0	2	4	.109	.169
ns, Pete, Ogden	.200	14	31	25	4	5	8	0	0	1	3	0	0	0	6	0	8	0	0	0	.320	.355
ns, Pete, Helena...............	.143	7	27	21	3	3	5	2	0	0	2	0	0	1	5	0	5	0	0	3	.238	.333

SUMMER CLASS A Pioneer League

TEAM

Team	W	L	Pct.	ERA	G	CG	ShO	Sv.	IP	H	TBF	R	ER	HR	SH	SF	HB	BB	IBB	SO	WP
Lethbridge	50	22	.694	3.68	72	1	5	13	632.2	650	2772	339	259	41	18	27	44	234	6	576	57
Ogden	42	30	.583	4.83	72	1	1	19	637.1	654	2931	441	342	57	17	20	43	326	8	627	99
Butte	37	35	.514	5.33	72	0	1	16	638.1	767	3013	516	378	52	21	24	46	323	9	602	93
Idaho Falls	38	34	.528	5.49	72	1	1	13	633.1	717	2881	452	386	56	21	27	47	291	4	538	82
Helena	43	29	.597	5.65	72	1	1	20	631.0	727	2940	479	396	66	14	36	35	338	2	602	67
Great Falls	33	39	.458	6.46	72	1	0	16	623.2	729	2990	544	448	45	12	33	48	348	9	486	90
Billings	23	49	.319	6.77	72	2	1	9	633.2	875	3130	603	477	72	16	41	57	323	9	521	90
Medicine Hat	22	50	.306	7.52	72	2	3	16	609.0	803	3049	641	509	92	9	39	39	387	6	449	90

INDIVIDUAL

TOP QUALIFIERS FOR EARNED-RUN AVERAGE TITLE

Minimum 58 innings. *Lefthanded pitcher.

Pitcher, Team	W	L	Pct.	ERA	G	GS	CG	ShO	GF	Sv.	IP	H	TBF	R	ER	HR	SH	SF	HB	BB	IBB	SO	WP
Nunez, Vladimir, Lethbridge	10	0	1.000	2.22	14	13	0	0	0	0	85.0	78	342	25	21	4	1	1	9	10	0	93	6
Tank, Travis, Helena	7	3	.700	3.22	29	0	0	0	7	3	64.1	65	291	38	23	5	3	7	1	30	2	74	8
Passini, Brian, Helena*	7	2	.778	3.48	15	14	1	0	0	0	77.2	91	343	37	30	5	0	2	6	27	0	71	7
Callaway, Michael, Butte	6	2	.750	3.71	16	11	0	0	1	0	63.0	70	274	37	26	5	0	3	3	25	0	57	7
Allen, Craig, Great Falls	4	2	.667	3.84	13	12	0	0	1	0	61.0	52	268	38	26	1	1	2	7	31	0	46	7
Szymborski, Thomas, Id. Falls	7	3	.700	3.94	16	14	0	0	2	1	80.0	80	348	39	35	6	1	4	6	30	0	65	11
O'Reilly, John, Ogden	7	1	.875	3.96	13	12	0	0	0	0	63.2	66	285	34	28	3	1	2	3	27	0	82	7
Guzman, Domingo, Idaho Falls	4	2	.667	4.13	15	10	1	1	1	0	65.1	52	278	41	30	7	2	1	7	29	0	75	13
Howerton, R.J., Butte	3	1	.750	4.43	15	13	0	0	0	0	61.0	72	291	47	30	3	0	1	4	42	0	47	13
Schroeder, Scott, Idaho Falls	5	5	.500	4.63	20	9	0	0	5	0	58.1	71	265	39	30	3	0	2	6	29	0	58	6
Ishee, Gabe, Ogden	6	4	.600	4.73	15	14	1	0	0	0	85.2	94	388	55	45	9	4	3	6	42	0	83	13
Watson, Mark, Helena*	5	2	.714	4.77	13	13	0	0	0	0	60.1	59	262	43	32	2	1	2	1	28	0	68	7
Pujals, Denis, Butte	2	7	.222	5.15	15	15	0	0	0	0	87.1	110	392	65	50	9	1	0	5	19	0	82	6
Thomas, Ryan, Idaho Falls	3	4	.571	5.20	30	4	0	0	16	4	62.1	54	281	44	36	5	4	1	5	32	2	44	16
Manias, James, Butte*	5	4	.556	5.25	16	13	0	0	1	0	72.0	98	336	64	42	8	2	5	3	22	0	55	5

DEPARTMENTAL LEADERS: W—Nunez, 10; L—Glover, 12; Pct.—Nunez, 1.000; G—Sullivan, 33; GS—Burchart, Glover, Pujals, 15; CG—Glover, 2; ShO—D. Guz[...] Shepard, 1; GF—S. Smith, 22; Sv.—Bleazard, 10; IP—Pujals, 87.1; H—Glover, 119; TBF—Glover, 410; R—Glover, 94; ER—Glover, 72; HR—Gourlay, 17; SH—Se[...] pitchers with 4; SF—Workman, 9; HB—Zwemke, 13; BB—Burchart, 33; IBB—M. Garcia, 4; SO—Nunez, 93; WP—Zwemke, 19; Bk.—Three pitchers with 5.

ALL PITCHERS

*Lefthanded pitcher.

Pitcher, Team	W	L	Pct.	ERA	G	GS	CG	ShO	GF	Sv.	IP	H	TBF	R	ER	HR	SH	SF	HB	BB	IBB	SO	WP
Adair, Scott, Idaho Falls	2	3	.400	7.71	23	3	0	0	5	1	46.2	73	232	42	40	9	2	2	5	21	0	29	2
Allen, Craig, Great Falls	4	2	.667	3.84	13	12	0	0	1	0	61.0	52	268	38	26	1	1	2	7	31	0	46	7
Anderson, Dallas, Lethbridge	1	0	1.000	4.15	16	0	0	0	6	0	17.1	15	87	10	8	1	0	1	3	20	0	15	6
Andrews, Clayton, Med. Hat*	2	4	.333	7.36	8	4	0	0	1	0	25.2	37	120	23	21	4	0	3	1	10	0	14	1
Angerhofer, Chad, Billings*	1	7	.125	8.09	13	13	0	0	0	0	62.1	93	317	71	56	7	4	4	4	33	0	48	12
Arnold, Jay, Og.-Hel.	1	1	.500	5.60	7	4	0	0	0	0	17.2	15	87	16	11	1	0	1	4	15	0	8	7
Barnes, Larry, Ogden	4	4	.500	5.19	11	10	0	0	0	0	50.1	45	236	45	29	4	1	3	5	31	0	54	15
Benesh, Edward, Butte	3	0	1.000	7.98	17	0	0	0	7	1	38.1	55	198	37	34	1	1	1	7	20	1	31	6
Bice, Justin, Lethbridge	2	3	.400	5.15	17	6	0	0	0	0	43.2	54	201	34	25	7	1	2	1	18	0	49	3
Bierbrodt, Nicholas, Lethbrdg*	2	0	1.000	0.50	3	3	0	0	0	0	18.0	12	72	4	1	0	0	1	1	5	0	23	1
Bleazard, David, Medicine Hat	0	0	.000	4.56	20	0	0	0	19	10	23.2	29	115	16	12	0	0	1	2	14	0	31	1
Bohman, John, Great Falls	1	0	1.000	12.27	12	0	0	0	3	0	18.1	24	105	28	25	4	0	1	6	15	0	5	4
Boker, John, Ogden	5	1	.833	4.35	15	6	0	0	2	0	49.2	53	226	29	24	5	0	1	3	24	0	41	7
Bourbakis, Michael, Great Falls	4	2	.667	8.93	17	5	0	0	5	0	41.1	47	218	45	41	2	1	2	4	39	0	36	7
Bowles, Brian, Medicine Hat	2	2	.500	6.35	24	0	0	0	7	1	39.2	53	193	35	28	5	1	3	5	21	1	29	9
Brown, Trent, Butte*	0	0	.000	12.46	3	0	0	0	0	0	4.1	9	24	6	6	1	0	0	0	2	0	4	0
Buckley, Matt, Billings	1	2	.333	5.00	24	0	0	0	0	0	45.0	55	213	36	25	4	1	7	2	22	1	37	5
Burchart, Kyle, Medicine Hat	4	7	.364	4.63	15	15	0	0	0	0	72.1	75	350	69	53	8	4	5	0	67	0	33	8
Burnside, Adrian, Great Falls*	1	3	.250	6.80	14	5	0	0	1	0	41.0	44	204	35	31	3	0	2	6	38	0	33	6
Callaway, Michael, Butte	6	2	.750	3.71	16	11	0	0	1	0	63.0	70	274	37	26	5	0	3	3	25	0	57	7
Cervantes, Peter, Great Falls	3	4	.429	2.98	9	8	1	0	1	0	51.1	52	220	29	17	0	0	2	4	11	0	40	4
Chavez, Mark, Lethbridge	1	2	.333	3.60	24	0	0	0	14	4	30.0	35	134	20	12	3	2	2	2	4	1	26	3
Cloud, Tony, Billings	0	5	.000	6.37	12	11	0	0	0	0	53.2	69	268	53	38	8	3	2	5	34	1	44	8
Conroy, Danny, Idaho Falls	0	0	.000	0.00	1	0	0	0	0	0	1.1	2	6	0	0	0	0	0	0	0	0	0	1
Correa, Elvis, Great Falls	1	0	1.000	10.00	16	1	0	0	5	1	27.0	41	137	32	30	6	2	2	2	11	0	25	2
Crews, Jason, Lethbridge	1	1	.500	2.50	25	1	0	0	19	5	39.2	30	164	13	11	2	2	3	0	15	1	37	3
Crossan, Clayton, Lethbridge	4	1	.800	4.73	19	4	0	0	2	0	40.0	55	186	29	21	1	0	2	1	18	0	27	4
Davis, Lance, Billings*	2	3	.400	6.70	16	5	0	0	1	0	45.2	59	232	41	34	5	1	2	1	33	0	43	5
Desabrais, Mark, Idaho Falls	1	0	1.000	6.70	27	0	0	0	7	0	45.2	65	220	35	34	2	1	1	2	22	1	43	5
Dollar, Troy, Great Falls	1	6	.143	9.39	14	7	0	0	3	0	49.1	72	249	54	46	2	0	4	5	24	1	42	5
Done, Johnny, Lethbridge	2	1	.667	1.95	22	0	0	0	8	1	37.0	41	159	16	8	1	4	2	1	8	1	30	2
Duffy, Ryan, Lethbridge*	6	2	.750	2.64	25	0	0	0	9	1	30.2	24	132	11	9	0	1	1	2	20	0	30	5
Enders, Trevor, Butte*	0	1	.000	4.88	19	0	0	0	6	1	27.2	34	132	22	15	1	2	2	2	13	1	24	2
Ervin, Kent, Idaho Falls	2	5	.286	6.50	22	4	0	0	5	0	54.0	72	254	52	39	7	2	2	4	18	0	35	6
Feliciano, Pedro, Great Falls*	2	3	.400	5.71	22	1	0	0	10	3	41.0	50	206	36	26	1	0	5	3	26	2	39	4
Fieldbinder, Michael, Helena	2	0	1.000	3.60	2	2	0	0	0	0	10.0	8	40	4	4	1	0	0	0	1	0	12	1

SUMMER CLASS A Pioneer League

cher, Team	W	L	Pct.	ERA	G	GS	CG	ShO	GF	Sv.	IP	H	TBF	R	ER	HR	SH	SF	HB	BB	IBB	SO	WP	Bk.
res, Pedro, Great Falls*	4	2	.667	5.79	18	3	0	0	1	0	46.2	44	215	37	30	2	4	2	2	28	1	24	10	1
nceca, Chad, Billings	1	4	.200	10.22	22	0	0	0	4	1	37.0	58	190	50	42	5	2	1	4	18	3	36	4	2
wler, Jered, Butte	1	2	.333	6.97	9	0	0	0	3	0	10.1	17	58	13	8	1	0	1	3	8	0	4	4	0
cher, John, Ogden*	2	3	.400	5.43	13	10	0	0	1	0	58.0	67	261	45	35	4	1	1	3	15	0	65	8	4
rcia, Jose, Helena	0	0	.000	16.20	2	0	0	0	0	0	1.2	1	9	3	3	0	0	0	0	3	0	2	1	0
rcia, Miguel, Great Falls	3	5	.375	5.18	22	5	0	0	11	3	40.0	53	190	27	23	5	0	1	0	17	4	29	3	0
es, Tim, Medicine Hat	0	0	.000	3.00	2	0	0	0	2	0	3.0	2	12	1	1	1	0	0	0	1	0	1	0	0
ck, Dave, Ogden*	3	1	.750	3.41	24	0	0	0	4	0	34.1	31	165	15	13	3	2	1	4	21	3	41	3	0
ver, Gary, Medicine Hat	3	12	.200	7.75	15	15	2	0	0	0	83.2	119	410	94	72	14	2	4	6	29	1	54	8	1
rk, Mark, Helena	1	0	1.000	3.42	10	2	0	0	5	1	23.2	26	100	12	9	3	2	1	3	4	0	26	3	0
mez, Javier, Lethbridge	3	2	.600	4.50	19	0	0	0	4	1	42.0	41	187	25	21	4	1	0	3	17	2	35	5	0
ıre, Sam, Medicine Hat	1	4	.200	6.00	18	4	0	0	3	0	48.0	70	242	48	32	4	0	2	1	19	0	43	9	0
ırlay, Matthew, Med. Hat	2	6	.250	8.41	16	13	0	0	1	0	66.1	95	327	71	62	17	0	7	1	39	1	35	8	4
fiths, Everard, Butte	0	2	.000	8.03	7	0	0	0	1	0	12.1	18	72	17	11	0	1	1	1	15	2	12	4	1
errero, Sergio, Helena	0	0	.000	0.00	1	0	0	0	1	0	1.0	1	6	0	0	0	0	0	0	2	0	1	0	0
tierrez, Alfredo, Ogden	0	3	.000	4.22	19	0	0	0	18	9	21.1	18	97	12	10	2	1	0	1	11	2	28	3	0
zman, Domingo, Idaho Falls	4	2	.667	4.13	15	10	1	1	1	0	65.1	52	278	41	30	7	2	1	7	29	0	75	13	0
zman, Jonathan, Helena*	2	3	.400	7.43	20	5	0	0	3	0	49.2	64	243	48	41	5	2	6	3	32	0	40	3	1
e, Mark, Butte	2	2	.500	3.26	21	0	0	0	19	7	38.2	32	162	17	14	2	3	1	1	10	3	56	7	1
dwick, Bubba, Helena*	0	1	.000	9.00	3	3	0	0	0	0	5.0	8	28	5	5	1	0	1	0	6	0	4	0	0
rris, Josh, Billings	1	1	.500	6.31	20	2	0	0	6	0	41.1	58	189	33	29	5	0	2	0	21	1	30	3	1
wkins, Alsharik, Ogden	3	3	.500	3.21	9	5	0	0	1	0	33.2	31	144	16	12	1	0	0	0	13	0	23	1	3
lley, Brian, Helena	1	2	.333	10.36	14	0	0	0	6	1	24.1	38	123	29	28	4	0	4	1	15	0	19	2	1
rera, Desmond, Billings	2	2	.500	8.83	30	0	0	0	10	2	34.2	61	185	38	34	8	1	4	2	11	0	32	5	0
ring, Jonathan, Med. Hat*	0	0	.000	13.95	20	0	0	0	6	0	20.0	30	122	35	31	7	1	1	5	27	0	14	8	0
ıchi, Roberto, Med. Hat	0	0	.000	12.90	15	0	0	0	8	0	22.1	37	135	39	32	5	0	1	5	23	1	17	9	2
ojosa, Joel, Butte	3	4	.429	5.27	27	0	0	0	14	1	42.2	49	203	31	25	5	3	2	7	25	2	32	8	2
k, Jeff, Ogden	0	0	.000	8.44	3	0	0	0	1	0	5.1	7	32	5	5	0	1	0	1	8	0	3	0	0
ton, Eric, Medicine Hat	0	1	.000	8.31	5	0	0	0	3	0	13.0	19	66	15	12	1	0	1	1	9	1	11	5	0
verton, R.J., Butte	3	1	.750	4.43	15	13	0	0	0	0	61.0	72	291	47	30	3	0	1	4	42	0	47	13	0
e, Gabe, Ogden	6	4	.600	4.73	15	14	1	0	0	0	85.2	94	388	55	45	9	4	3	6	42	0	83	13	4
naru, Taisuke, Great Falls	0	1	.000	5.14	9	2	0	0	3	2	21.0	22	101	13	12	1	1	3	1	14	1	11	1	0
obson, Brian, Great Falls*	4	2	.667	5.45	29	0	0	0	15	7	38.0	56	182	37	23	3	1	1	1	13	0	31	3	0
fman, John, Butte*	2	3	.400	4.66	13	12	0	0	0	0	46.1	53	214	36	24	2	3	3	0	24	0	55	7	2
hley, Davan, Med. Hat*	3	2	.600	8.62	15	2	0	0	4	0	39.2	56	207	46	38	7	0	2	2	29	0	36	3	2
dall, Phil, Helena	0	0	.000	20.25	2	0	0	0	0	0	1.1	3	13	4	3	0	0	0	0	5	0	3	1	0
, James, Butte	0	0	.000	6.75	1	0	0	0	1	0	1.1	4	11	3	1	0	0	0	0	2	0	1	1	0
brell, Michael, Butte*	7	1	.875	3.86	23	0	0	0	5	2	49.0	35	221	30	21	4	1	2	1	37	0	65	10	1
eit, Richard, Ogden	0	1	.000	3.92	11	1	0	0	2	0	20.2	24	93	12	9	2	1	0	1	9	0	16	4	0
nay, Maney, Helena	2	0	1.000	3.50	4	4	0	0	0	0	18.0	17	86	14	7	3	0	1	0	12	0	11	3	1
ault, Allen, Helena	4	3	.571	5.32	18	11	0	0	2	1	71.0	70	302	43	42	9	0	0	8	22	0	68	4	3
ez, Rodrigo, Idaho Falls	4	4	.500	5.70	15	14	0	0	1	1	71.0	76	314	52	45	3	4	3	4	34	0	72	8	4
nzo, Martin, Helena	0	1	.000	5.58	23	1	0	0	8	1	40.1	45	191	29	25	9	0	3	4	22	0	31	2	0
ison, Scott, Butte*	0	1	.000	11.74	2	2	0	0	0	0	7.2	17	40	11	10	1	0	0	2	3	0	5	1	0
ias, James, Butte*	5	4	.556	5.25	16	13	0	0	1	0	72.0	98	336	64	42	8	2	5	3	22	0	55	5	1
ne, Justin, Billings	0	1	.000	7.36	21	0	0	0	9	0	33.0	46	178	32	27	3	0	5	3	20	0	22	6	0
tinez, Leonardo, Butte	0	0	.000	0.00	1	0	0	0	0	0	0.2	0	4	0	0	0	0	0	0	2	0	0	1	0
lellan, Sean, Medicine Hat	3	3	.500	6.10	12	8	0	0	2	1	51.2	52	228	38	35	5	0	0	4	19	0	61	2	2
reery, Rick, Butte	0	1	.000	2.25	8	0	0	0	6	1	16.0	14	68	5	4	0	3	1	2	7	0	12	0	0
ina, Robert, Medicine Hat	0	0	.000	6.75	3	0	0	0	2	0	2.2	4	19	5	2	2	0	0	0	5	0	5	1	0
rell, Phil, Billings	4	7	.364	7.04	14	13	1	0	1	1	69.0	83	339	63	54	11	1	4	5	48	0	54	11	2
r, Shawn, Ogden	3	1	.750	2.41	17	0	0	0	5	3	41.0	41	182	14	11	2	1	1	3	15	0	43	1	0
n, Bradley, Medicine Hat	0	0	.000	13.50	1	0	0	0	1	0	2.0	6	14	3	3	0	0	0	1	2	0	1	1	0
dham, Kevin, Billings*	1	2	.333	5.75	26	0	0	0	11	2	36.0	44	166	23	23	0	1	0	4	18	0	37	3	1
is, Ben, Lethbridge*	0	0	.000	6.35	3	3	0	0	0	0	11.1	14	54	9	8	0	0	2	0	5	0	12	2	1
is, McKenzie, Helena	3	2	.600	5.26	18	6	0	0	7	4	39.1	43	196	31	23	2	0	1	2	33	0	36	6	2
ez, Vladimir, Lethbridge	10	0	1.000	2.22	14	13	0	0	0	0	85.0	78	342	25	21	4	1	1	9	10	0	93	6	0
ary, Kevin, Ogden	1	0	1.000	5.63	2	2	0	0	0	0	8.0	7	34	5	5	0	0	1	0	3	0	6	1	0
sik, George, Lethbridge	6	1	.857	6.58	14	14	0	0	0	0	67.0	82	311	53	49	9	3	5	7	36	1	30	2	1
illy, John, Ogden	7	1	.875	3.96	13	12	0	0	0	0	63.2	66	285	34	28	3	1	2	3	27	0	82	7	1
des, Roberto, Helena	3	1	.750	2.67	25	0	0	0	16	6	30.1	23	131	13	9	1	3	2	1	16	0	41	6	0
ini, Brian, Helena*	7	2	.778	3.48	15	14	1	0	0	0	77.2	91	343	37	30	5	0	2	6	27	0	71	7	3
z, Jesse, Ogden	2	1	.667	2.57	19	0	0	0	12	3	21.0	19	94	12	6	0	1	0	1	11	1	16	1	0
am, Jimmy, Og.-Hel.	1	2	.333	4.85	20	0	0	0	7	3	29.2	30	136	20	16	2	1	0	3	19	1	21	4	0
npas, Lyle, Helena*	2	1	.667	9.07	21	2	0	0	7	2	42.2	51	222	47	43	3	2	1	3	46	0	52	9	1
s, Denis, Butte	2	7	.222	5.15	15	15	0	0	0	0	87.1	110	392	65	50	9	1	0	5	19	0	82	6	3
ardson, Bradley, Ogden*	1	1	.500	10.72	19	0	0	0	8	1	22.2	28	128	37	27	2	1	3	0	28	0	25	8	0
iguez, Larry, Lethbridge	7	1	.875	3.83	10	10	1	0	0	0	54.0	56	231	31	23	1	2	2	6	9	0	46	3	1
l, Eric, Lethbridge	1	4	.200	2.79	20	3	0	0	5	1	42.0	43	184	23	13	3	1	1	3	7	0	41	4	0
boy, Javier, Lethbridge*	1	1	.500	4.33	17	3	0	0	3	0	27.0	26	119	15	13	1	0	1	1	17	0	19	4	0
hez, Mike, Great Falls	0	0	.000	9.64	9	0	0	0	5	1	9.1	8	46	11	10	1	0	1	0	10	0	7	11	1
rfield, Jeremy, Med. Hat	0	3	.000	6.12	14	0	0	0	3	0	32.1	39	164	31	22	5	0	3	5	27	1	25	9	0
oeder, Scott, Idaho Falls	5	5	.500	4.63	20	9	0	0	5	0	58.1	71	265	39	30	3	0	2	6	29	0	58	6	0
ury, Jaron, Medicine Hat	0	0	.000	4.50	5	0	0	0	5	3	6.0	4	27	4	3	1	0	0	0	5	0	5	1	0
rino, Edy, Medicine Hat	2	6	.250	7.89	16	11	0	0	3	1	57.0	76	289	68	50	6	1	6	0	41	0	34	7	1
ard, David, Billings	6	7	.462	5.91	15	14	1	1	1	0	80.2	109	376	69	53	10	1	4	11	21	2	80	6	1
h, Josh, Idaho Falls*	2	1	.667	4.91	17	0	0	0	6	1	14.2	11	61	9	8	0	1	1	1	11	0	11	3	0
h, Stephen, Billings	2	2	.500	4.26	24	0	0	0	22	3	31.2	39	146	20	15	1	0	4	3	16	1	23	3	3
Seferino, Great Falls	2	4	.333	6.14	15	11	0	0	3	1	55.2	56	261	45	38	4	1	2	6	35	0	51	10	5
art, Paul, Ogden	1	4	.200	7.83	12	9	0	0	1	0	43.2	47	211	49	38	11	0	4	4	26	0	39	6	1
, Shawn, Butte	2	3	.400	8.51	19	6	0	0	4	2	48.2	63	256	60	46	8	1	1	4	40	0	46	9	1
an, Brendan, Idaho Falls	2	1	.667	5.23	33	0	0	0	15	5	43.0	41	190	25	25	6	1	0	1	27	0	41	1	0
borski, Thomas, Id. Falls	7	3	.700	3.94	16	14	0	0	2	1	80.0	80	348	39	35	6	1	4	6	30	0	65	11	5

Pitcher, Team	W	L	Pct.	ERA	G	GS	CG	ShO	GF	Sv.	IP	H	TBF	R	ER	HR	SH	SF	HB	BB	IBB	SO	WP
Tank, Travis, Helena	7	3	.700	3.22	29	0	0	0	7	3	64.1	65	291	38	23	5	3	7	1	30	2	74	8
Thomas, Brad, Great Falls*	3	2	.600	6.31	11	5	0	0	3	0	35.2	48	163	27	25	2	1	0	11	0	28	5	
Thomas, Ryan, Idaho Falls.......	4	3	.571	5.20	30	4	0	0	16	4	62.1	54	281	44	36	5	4	1	5	32	2	44	16
Thompson, Dan, Helena............	0	0	.000	8.44	4	0	0	0	3	0	5.1	7	24	5	5	1	0	1	0	1	0	4	0
Thompson, Frank, Great Falls ..	0	3	.000	8.62	14	7	0	0	1	0	47.0	60	225	50	45	8	0	2	1	25	0	39	4
Tijerina, Tano, Helena..............	3	6	.333	8.74	19	8	0	0	4	1	57.2	93	290	65	56	11	1	3	2	27	0	33	3
Verplancke, Joe, Lethbridge	3	3	.500	3.00	12	12	0	0	0	0	48.0	44	209	22	16	4	0	1	4	25	0	63	4
Walker, Kevin, Idaho Falls*	1	0	1.000	3.00	1	1	0	0	0	0	6.0	4	24	3	2	1	0	0	0	2	0	4	1
Warren, Deshawn, Ogden*	1	0	1.000	6.75	3	0	0	0	1	0	2.2	2	14	3	2	0	0	0	0	3	0	7	1
Watson, Mark, Helena*	5	2	.714	4.77	13	13	0	0	0	0	60.1	59	262	43	32	2	1	2	1	28	0	68	7
Whitley, Kyle, Butte	1	1	.500	9.00	10	0	0	0	4	1	11.0	17	57	15	11	1	0	1	7	0	14	2
Witte, Dominic, Idaho Falls	0	2	.000	6.14	21	0	0	0	8	0	29.1	39	137	23	20	4	1	1	1	5	1	19	3
Workman, Widd, Idaho Falls	4	5	.444	6.79	14	13	0	0	0	0	55.2	77	271	48	42	3	2	9	5	31	0	42	6
Zapata, Juan, Ogden	2	1	.667	6.06	20	0	0	0	10	0	35.2	43	158	26	24	7	1	0	1	11	1	32	10
Zwemke, Bryan, Billings...........	2	6	.250	7.49	14	14	0	0	0	0	63.2	101	331	74	53	5	1	2	13	28	0	35	19

COMBINATION SHUTOUTS: **Butte (1)**—Kaufman-Hinojosa-Kimbrell. **Helena (1)**—Levrault-Tijerina. **Lethbridge (5)**—Crews-Sabel-Anderson, Norris-Crossan-Cr Duffy-Sabel, Nunez-Done-Anderson, Nunez-Done-Duffy-Anderson, Verplancke-Samboy-Chavez. **Medicine Hat (3)**—Andrews-McClellan, Andrews-McClellan-Blea Goure-Severino. **Ogden (1)**—Ishee-Perez-Richardson.

NO-HIT GAME: D. Guzman, Idaho Falls, defeated Butte, 6-0, August 15.

PITCHERS WITH TWO OR MORE TEAMS

Pitcher, Team	W	L	Pct.	ERA	G	GS	CG	ShO	GF	Sv.	IP	H	TBF	R	ER	HR	SH	SF	HB	BB	IBB	SO	WP
Arnold, Jay, Ogden	1	0	1.000	3.71	6	3	0	0	0	0	17.0	12	79	12	7	0	0	0	4	12	0	7	7
Arnold, Jay, Helena	0	1	.000	54.00	1	1	0	0	0	0	0.2	3	8	4	4	1	0	1	0	3	0	1	0
Podjan, Jimmy, Ogden	0	1	.000	4.70	16	0	0	0	5	3	23.0	19	104	15	12	2	1	0	3	16	1	16	3
Podjan, Jimmy, Helena.............	1	1	.500	5.40	4	0	0	0	2	0	6.2	11	32	5	4	0	0	0	0	3	0	5	1

1996 FIELDING

TEAM

Team	Pct.	G	PO	A	E	TC	DP	PB	Team	Pct.	G	PO	A	E	TC	DP
Idaho Falls........	.962	72	1900	812	106	2818	66	17	Ogden	.945	72	1912	720	154	2786	58
Lethbridge........	.955	72	1898	790	127	2815	55	16	Butte	.944	72	1915	825	163	2903	70
Helena	.952	72	1893	765	133	2791	63	18	Billings	.943	72	1901	776	161	2838	62
Great Falls	.948	72	1871	793	147	2811	63	26	Medicine Hat	.934	72	1827	782	183	2792	66

TRIPLE PLAY: Ogden.

INDIVIDUAL

FIRST BASEMEN

NOTE: All caps denotes fielding-percentage leader based on 36 games for catchers, 48 for all other non-pitchers and 72 innings for pitchers. *Throws lefthanded.

Player, Team	Pct.	G	PO	A	E	TC	DP
Arrendondo, Hernando, Butte..........	1.000	1	4	0	0	4	1
Bagley, Lorenzo, Medicine Hat	1.000	1	7	0	0	7	1
Barajas, Rod, Lethbridge	1.000	3	19	3	0	22	0
Barker, Kevin, Ogden*	.982	69	572	44	11	627	46
Barner, Doug, Butte	.973	4	34	2	1	37	2
Baston, Stanley, Medicine Hat.........	.800	1	8	0	2	10	0
Bramlett, Jeff, Great Falls	.995	37	348	29	2	379	27
Burress, Andy, Billings	1.000	1	9	1	0	10	1
Darula, Bobbie, Ogden	.893	7	24	1	3	28	3
Dresch, Michael, Billings	.995	26	204	13	1	218	17
Fink, Marc, Helena*	1.000	11	96	3	0	99	8
Garrett, Scott, Billings	1.000	5	24	0	0	24	2
Giles, Tim, Medicine Hat	.974	56	454	33	13	500	44
Hardy, Brett, Lethbridge*	.978	11	75	14	2	91	7
Hartman, Ronald, Lethbridge	.875	1	7	0	1	8	1
Hayman, David, Lethbridge..............	.950	12	89	7	5	101	8
Keller, JEremy, Billings	.982	43	342	35	7	384	33
Kent, Robert, Idaho Falls	.963	8	73	4	3	80	6
King, Michael, Butte	.988	8	78	3	1	82	8
Kirby, Scott, Helena	.981	16	97	9	2	108	9
Kliner, Joshua, Lethbridge	.889	1	7	1	1	9	0
Mapp, Eric, Billings	.902	6	37	0	4	41	2
McGehee, Mike, Butte	.958	17	106	8	5	119	14
Medina, Robert, Medicine Hat	.985	9	60	5	1	66	2
Moore, Jason, Lethbridge	.986	42	326	22	5	353	30
PACIOREK, Peter, Idaho Falls*	.992	65	621	30	5	656	47
Quatraro, Matthew, Butte	.954	15	111	14	6	131	9
Rhea, Chip, Lethbridge....................	.923	5	11	1	1	13	1
Rodriguez, Miguel, Ogden	1.000	4	2	0	0	2	0
Rogue, Francisco, Helena................	.986	7	66	2	1	69	6
Salinas, Trey, Butte	.968	36	280	19	10	309	26
Sencion, Pablo, Medicine Hat..........	.989	13	85	6	1	92	8
Stoner, Mike, Lethbridge	.961	11	69	5	3	77	
Tucker, Jonathan, Great Falls*	.983	35	324	24	6	354	
Umbria, Jose, Medicine Hat	.750	1	6	0	2	8	
Verrall, Jared, Butte	1.000	1	1	0	0	1	
Walther, Christopher, Ogden............	1.000	2	14	0	0	14	
Washam, Jason, Helena...................	.992	45	347	25	3	375	

SECOND BASEMEN

Player, Team	Pct.	G	PO	A	E	TC
Bain, Tyler, Butte	.912	19	36	47	8	91
Baston, Stanley, Medicine Hat.........	.958	32	61	99	7	167
Campbell, Wylie, Billings.................	.927	68	104	187	23	314
Cuevas, Trent, Great Falls	.917	19	15	51	6	72
Ebling, Jamie, Butte	.935	34	80	120	14	214
Faurot, Adam, Ogden	.978	23	37	50	2	89
Glasser, Scott, Lethbridge	1.000	1	1	1	0	2
Glover, Jason, Ogden	.000	1	0	0	2	2
Guerrero, Sergio, Helena	.963	52	114	146	10	270
Kent, Robert, Idaho Falls	1.000	1	2	2	0	4
Kerr, James, Butte	.500	2	2	1	3	6
King, Michael, Butte	.943	17	34	32	4	70
Kliner, Joshua, Lethbridge	.941	5	9	7	1	17
MacAlutas, Jon, Ogden	.918	13	17	39	5	61
Maloney, Jeff, Medicine Hat	.923	23	53	55	9	117
Marshall, Monte, Great Falls............	.961	48	76	148	9	233
Martinez, Leonardo, Butte	.953	10	16	25	2	43
McCLURE, Brian, Idaho Falls	.973	71	132	231	10	373
Meyer, Bobby, Great Falls	.918	14	16	40	5	61
Nunez, Jose, Lethbridge	.922	21	42	53	8	103
Osilka, Garret, Helena	.938	6	12	18	2	32
Parmenter, Ross, Ogden	1.000	2	2	1	0	3
Patellis, Anthony, Billings	1.000	1	1	2	0	3
Phair, Kelly, Ogden	.955	39	81	108	9	198
Price, Corey, Billings	.964	9	12	15	1	28
Rhea, Chip, Lethbridge....................	.967	27	45	71	4	120
Spivey, Ernest, Lethbridge	.937	30	57	62	8	127

ayer, Team	Pct.	G	PO	A	E	TC	DP
romsborg, Ryan, Medicine Hat	.939	21	33	59	6	98	9
Vetmore, Michael, Helena	.950	17	28	48	4	80	8

THIRD BASEMEN

ayer, Team	Pct.	G	PO	A	E	TC	DP
fano, Jeff, Ogden	.000	1	0	0	1	1	0
rendondo, Hernando, Butte	.867	66	43	127	26	196	14
ain, Tyler, Butte	.875	3	2	5	1	8	0
havez, Steven, Idaho Falls	.881	56	34	129	22	185	10
uevas, Trent, Great Falls	.895	14	3	14	2	19	2
arula, Bobbie, Ogden	1.000	1	0	1	0	1	0
resch, Michael, Billings	.714	3	2	3	2	7	0
urot, Adam, Ogden	.856	35	27	56	14	97	8
rnandez, Ramon, Ogden	1.000	1	1	0	0	1	0
asser, Scott, Lethbridge	.875	4	2	5	1	8	1
over, Jason, Ogden	.786	8	2	9	3	14	1
riggs, Rodrickus, Billings	.000	2	0	0	1	1	0
athrie, David, Billings	.962	10	6	19	1	26	2
artman, Ronald, Lethbridge	.879	58	33	112	20	165	15
g, Brett, Great Falls	.905	21	8	30	4	42	1
ller, JEremy, Lethbridge	.909	19	15	35	5	55	3
nt, Robert, Idaho Falls	.900	16	13	23	4	40	2
rr, James, Butte	1.000	3	0	4	0	4	0
hard, Kirk, Lethbridge	.667	1	0	2	1	3	0
by, Scott, Helena	.795	26	15	43	15	73	3
IMEK, Josh, Helena	.885	51	29	71	13	113	8
ner, Joshua, Lethbridge	1.000	3	0	3	0	3	1
ach, Nick, Great Falls	.868	52	29	89	18	136	7
loney, Jeff, Medicine Hat	.889	9	12	12	3	27	1
artinez, David E., Ogden	.889	6	3	5	1	9	0
artinez, Leonardo, Butte	1.000	2	1	2	0	3	0
Carty, Matt, Great Falls	.667	5	0	2	1	3	0
dina, Robert, Medicine Hat	.000	1	0	0	1	1	0
nez, Jose, Lethbridge	.786	11	2	9	3	14	1
menter, Ross, Ogden	1.000	2	1	1	0	2	0
cellis, Anthony, Billings	.836	42	24	83	21	128	7
air, Kelly, Ogden	.667	1	1	1	1	3	0
ce, Corey, Billings	.750	5	1	5	2	8	0
ea, Chip, Lethbridge	.929	6	0	13	1	14	0
nas, Trey, Butte	.875	4	2	5	1	8	0
acion, Pablo, Medicine Hat	.833	54	33	97	26	156	5
omsborg, Ryan, Medicine Hat	.824	11	5	9	3	17	0
bria, Jose, Medicine Hat	.667	1	1	1	1	3	0
ther, Christopher, Ogden	.853	31	22	36	10	68	1

SHORTSTOPS

yer, Team	Pct.	G	PO	A	E	TC	DP
ton, Stanley, Medicine Hat	.916	35	56	119	16	191	25
ghton, Mike, Lethbridge	.952	62	93	165	13	271	29
npbell, Wylie, Billings	.500	1	1	2	3	6	0
roy, Danny, Idaho Falls	1.000	1	2	2	0	4	0
vas, Trent, Great Falls	.906	24	29	77	11	117	16
osantos, Eddy, Butte	.848	16	14	42	10	66	10
ng, Jamie, Butte	.862	17	23	33	9	65	5
rot, Adam, Ogden	.857	11	18	36	9	63	8
sser, Scott, Lethbridge	.962	5	6	19	1	26	3
rrie, David, Billings	.918	40	60	108	15	183	24
Brett, Great Falls	.927	24	36	65	8	109	9
James, Butte	.900	26	42	75	13	130	16
rd, Kirk, Lethbridge	.929	4	0	13	1	14	0
oney, Jeff, Medicine Hat	.839	33	54	92	28	174	17
imoto, Ken, Great Falls	.913	29	65	92	15	172	22
ez, Jose, Lethbridge	.857	7	4	8	2	14	0
ka, Garret, Helena	.896	43	79	136	25	240	26
menter, Ross, Ogden	.901	40	50	87	15	152	22
r, Kelly, Ogden	.833	4	2	8	2	12	0
sto, Nick, Billings	.952	4	8	12	1	21	3
e, Corey, Billings	.895	33	51	85	16	152	13
NOSO, Benjamin, Idaho Falls	.958	72	101	196	13	310	44
ey, Ernest, Lethbridge	.875	4	6	8	2	16	0
msborg, Ryan, Medicine Hat	.923	5	12	12	2	26	5
nore, Michael, Helena	.946	33	39	101	8	148	13

TRIPLE PLAY: Faurot.

OUTFIELDERS

er, Team	Pct.	G	PO	A	E	TC	DP
ral, Randy, Medicine Hat	.975	52	115	4	3	122	1
rson, Jeffrey, Great Falls	.957	50	107	4	5	116	1
Bagley, Lorenzo, Medicine Hat	.918	60	84	6	8	98	1
Bain, Tyler, Butte	1.000	37	46	5	0	51	0
Bramlett, Jeff, Great Falls	1.000	8	12	0	0	12	0
Burress, Andy, Billings	.667	2	2	0	1	3	0
Cafaro, Nicholas, Idaho Falls	.932	47	66	3	5	74	1
Conroy, Danny, Idaho Falls	.938	19	27	3	2	32	1
Conti, Jason, Lethbridge	.955	56	80	5	4	89	1
DeCelle, Mike, Butte	.976	68	78	3	2	83	0
Dresch, Michael, Billings	.833	2	5	0	1	6	0
Fernandez, Ramon, Hel.-Og.	.938	37	28	2	2	32	0
Foulks, Brian, Great Falls	.909	24	29	1	3	33	1
Gann, Jamie, Lethbridge	.947	45	52	2	3	57	0
Glover, Jason, Ogden	.961	51	69	5	3	77	1
Green, Chad, Ogden	1.000	21	53	3	0	56	0
Griggs, Rodrickus, Billings	.974	45	67	9	2	78	1
Hardy, Brett, Lethbridge*	.947	15	17	1	1	19	0
Hayman, David, Lethbridge	1.000	34	47	2	0	49	0
Hemphill, James, Helena	.889	39	38	2	5	45	2
Hunter, Andy, Idaho Falls	.926	32	62	1	5	68	0
Ingram, Darron, Billings	1.000	2	4	0	0	4	0
Jackson, Rod, Idaho Falls	.948	53	101	8	6	115	2
Jenkins, Daniel, Billings	.955	53	60	4	3	67	0
Johnson, Ledowick, Helena	.952	55	94	6	5	105	1
Kastelic, Matthew, Butte*	.944	36	65	3	4	72	1
King, Michael, Butte	.962	24	23	2	1	26	0
Kirby, Doug, Billings	.933	50	95	3	7	105	0
Langaigne, Selwyn, Medicine Hat*..	.950	32	55	2	3	60	1
Lindsey, Rodney, Idaho Falls	.939	44	73	4	5	82	2
MacAlutas, Jon, Ogden	.980	33	48	1	1	50	0
Mapp, Eric, Billings	.977	28	42	0	1	43	0
MARN, Kevin, Billings	.982	66	147	14	3	164	5
Martinez, Obed, Idaho Falls	.920	24	43	3	4	50	1
McCain, Marcus, Butte	.957	55	105	5	5	115	1
McCarty, Matt, Great Falls	.954	48	80	3	4	87	0
Medina, Robert, Medicine Hat	1.000	8	4	1	0	5	1
Moon, Bradley, Medicine Hat	1.000	21	17	1	0	18	0
Moore, Donald, Ogden	.909	44	38	2	4	44	0
Nova, PasCual, Idaho Falls	.947	15	17	1	1	19	1
Parent, Gerald, Ogden	.978	62	86	4	2	92	1
Phelps, Joshua, Medicine Hat	.750	7	6	0	2	8	0
Rhea, Chip, Lethbridge	1.000	3	5	0	0	5	0
Richey, Mikal, Great Falls	.960	23	24	0	1	25	0
Riley, Cash, Great Falls	.915	38	41	2	4	47	0
Rutherford, Daryl, Butte	.979	39	45	1	1	47	0
Ryan, Robert, Lethbridge*	.965	56	107	3	4	114	1
Salinas, Trey, Butte	1.000	5	2	1	0	3	0
Schaub, Greg, Helena	.963	62	95	10	4	109	1
Sencion, Pablo, Medicine Hat.	1.000	1	1	0	0	1	0
Stromsborg, Ryan, Medicine Hat	.907	20	38	1	4	43	0
Sweeney, Kevin, Lethbridge*	.954	51	57	5	3	65	1
Thompson, Dan, Helena	.979	39	45	2	1	48	0
Verrall, Jared, Butte	1.000	2	1	1	0	2	0
Walther, Christopher, Ogden	.911	36	50	1	5	56	0
Weekley, Jason, Great Falls	.933	54	84	0	6	90	0
Willis, Symmion, Medicine Hat	.965	39	77	6	3	86	1

TRIPLE PLAY: Fernandez.

OUTFIELDERS WITH TWO OR MORE TEAMS

Player, Team	Pct.	G	PO	A	E	TC	DP
Fernandez, Ramon, Helena	1.000	3	2	0	0	2	0
Fernandez, Ramon, Ogden	.933	34	26	2	2	30	0

CATCHERS

Player, Team	Pct.	G	PO	A	E	TC	DP	PB
Alfano, Jeff, Ogden	.976	33	258	25	7	290	1	11
Allison, Bradley, Lethbridge	.992	24	114	14	1	129	0	5
Baltzell, Beau, Lethbridge	.985	16	58	6	1	65	0	6
BARAJAS, Rod, Lethbridge	.985	42	282	40	5	327	1	1
Boulo, Tyler, Idaho Falls	.994	17	135	19	1	155	1	8
Burress, Andy, Billings	.976	24	146	17	4	167	0	4
Cripps, Bobby, Great Falls	.970	43	274	22	9	305	2	17
Darula, Bobbie, Ogden	.989	12	86	7	1	94	1	4
Davis, Josh, Idaho Falls	.981	31	234	30	5	269	2	5
Davis, Reggie, Lethbridge	.972	21	125	15	4	144	0	4
Ebbert, Chad, Idaho Falls	.968	27	153	28	6	187	2	4
Falcon, Edwin, Great Falls	1.000	8	58	4	0	62	0	2
Garrett, Scott, Billings	.967	36	244	16	9	269	3	6
Hucks, Brian, Billings	.970	18	146	16	5	167	0	5
Jenkins, Pete, Og.-Hel.	1.000	17	99	7	0	106	0	3
McGehee, Mike, Butte	.982	8	49	6	1	56	1	1
Medina, Robert, Medicine Hat	.930	16	66	14	6	86	1	4
Phelps, Joshua, Medicine Hat	.971	34	208	24	7	239	1	10

Player, Team	Pct.	G	PO	A	E	TC	DP	PB
Quatraro, Matthew, Butte	.974	41	339	34	10	383	4	3
Rodriguez, Miguel, Ogden	.956	28	212	25	11	248	0	5
Rogue, Francisco, Helena	.995	23	178	22	1	201	1	4
Salinas, Trey, Butte	.972	26	211	31	7	249	8	5
Snow, Casey, Great Falls	.988	30	161	5	2	168	2	7
Suero, Ignacio, Helena	.971	41	321	45	11	377	2	11
Umbria, Jose, Medicine Hat	.954	31	177	32	10	219	2	12
Voita, Sam, Butte	.923	3	10	2	1	13	0	0
Walther, Christopher, Ogden	1.000	1	2	0	0	2	0	0
Washam, Jason, Helena	.942	8	45	4	3	52	1	1

CATCHERS WITH TWO OR MORE TEAMS

Player, Team	Pct.	G	PO	A	E	TC	DP	PB
Jenkins, Pete, Ogden	1.000	10	45	4	0	49	0	1
Jenkins, Pete, Helena	1.000	7	54	3	0	57	0	2

PITCHERS

Player, Team	Pct.	G	PO	A	E	TC	DP
Adair, Scott, Idaho Falls	.923	23	4	8	1	13	0
ALLEN, Craig, Great Falls	1.000	13	4	15	0	19	1
Anderson, Dallas, Lethbridge	1.000	16	1	2	0	3	0
Andrews, Clayton, Medicine Hat*	1.000	8	1	3	0	4	0
Angerhofer, Chad, Billings*	.774	13	8	16	7	31	2
Arnold, Jay, Og.-Hel.	1.000	7	1	1	0	2	0
Barnes, Larry, Ogden	.625	11	2	3	3	8	0
Benesh, Edward, Butte	.917	17	3	8	1	12	1
Bice, Justin, Lethbridge	.917	17	6	5	1	12	0
Bierbrodt, Nicholas, Lethbridge*	.750	3	1	2	1	4	0
Bleazard, David, Medicine Hat	1.000	20	3	7	0	10	2
Bohman, John, Great Falls	1.000	12	1	2	0	3	0
Boker, John, Ogden	.600	15	0	3	2	5	0
Bourbakis, Michael, Great Falls	.900	17	2	7	1	10	0
Bowles, Brian, Medicine Hat.	1.000	24	4	6	0	10	1
Buckley, Matt, Billings	.909	24	4	6	1	11	0
Burchart, Kyle, Medicine Hat.	.889	15	7	17	3	27	1
Burnside, Adrian, Great Falls*	.938	14	4	11	1	16	0
Callaway, Michael, Butte	.938	16	3	12	1	16	1
Cervantes, Peter, Great Falls	.941	9	6	10	1	17	0
Chavez, Mark, Lethbridge	.833	24	0	5	1	6	0
Cloud, Tony, Billings	1.000	12	5	10	0	15	1
Correa, Elvis, Great Falls	.333	16	0	1	2	3	0
Crews, Jason, Lethbridge	1.000	25	5	7	0	12	0
Crossan, Clayton, Lethbridge	.900	19	4	5	1	10	0
Davis, Lance, Billings*	1.000	16	3	7	0	10	0
Desabrais, Mark, Idaho Falls	1.000	27	3	6	0	9	1
Dollar, Toby, Great Falls	.750	14	2	4	2	8	0
Done, Johnny, Lethbridge	.333	22	1	0	2	3	0
Duffy, Ryan, Lethbridge*	1.000	25	2	5	0	7	0
Enders, Trevor, Butte*	.714	19	1	4	2	7	0
Ervin, Kent, Idaho Falls	1.000	22	1	3	0	4	0
Feliciano, Pedro, Great Falls*	.636	22	3	4	4	11	1
Fieldbinder, Michael, Helena	1.000	2	0	1	0	1	0
Flores, Pedro, Great Falls*	.917	18	4	7	1	12	1
Fonceca, Chad, Billings	.900	22	2	7	1	10	0
Fowler, Jered, Butte	1.000	9	1	3	0	4	0
Fulcher, John, Ogden*	1.000	13	1	15	0	16	0
Garcia, Miguel, Great Falls	.909	22	3	7	1	11	0
Glick, Dave, Ogden*	1.000	24	0	8	0	8	0
Glover, Gary, Medicine Hat	.862	15	10	15	4	29	2
Gnirk, Mark, Helena	1.000	10	1	4	0	5	0
Gomez, Javier, Lethbridge	1.000	19	2	9	0	11	0
Goure, Sam, Medicine Hat	1.000	18	1	9	0	10	1
Gourlay, Matthew, Medicine Hat.	.769	16	1	9	3	13	0
Griffiths, Everard, Butte	1.000	7	0	2	0	2	0
Guerrero, Sergio, Helena	1.000	1	1	0	0	1	0
Gutierrez, Alfredo, Ogden	.500	19	0	1	1	2	0
Guzman, Domingo, Idaho Falls	.800	15	2	6	2	10	1
Guzman, Jonathan, Helena*	1.000	20	1	3	0	4	1
Hale, Mark, Butte	1.000	21	2	6	0	8	0
Hardwick, Bubba, Helena*	1.000	3	0	1	0	1	0
Harris, Josh, Billings	.900	20	3	6	1	10	0
Hawkins, Alsharik, Ogden	1.000	9	2	9	0	11	0
Hedley, Brian, Helena	.889	14	2	6	1	9	0
Herrera, Desmond, Billings	1.000	30	2	4	0	6	0
Herring, Jonathan, Medicine Hat*	.500	20	0	1	1	2	
Higuchi, Roberto, Medicine Hat	1.000	15	3	2	0	5	
Hinojosa, Joel, Butte	.929	27	2	11	1	14	
Hook, Jeff, Ogden	1.000	3	0	2	0	2	
Horton, Eric, Medicine Hat	1.000	5	2	3	0	5	
Howerton, R.J., Butte	1.000	15	6	12	0	18	
Ishee, Gabe, Ogden	.815	15	7	15	5	27	
Ishimaru, Taisuke, Great Falls	1.000	9	4	0	0	4	
Jacobson, Brian, Great Falls*	.636	29	2	5	4	11	
Kaufman, John, Butte*	.905	13	5	14	2	21	
Keathley, Davan, Medicine Hat*	.750	15	0	6	2	8	
Kimbrell, Michael, Butte*	.900	23	2	7	1	10	
Ledeit, Richard, Ogden	.857	11	4	2	1	7	
Leshay, Maney, Helena	.667	4	2	2	2	6	
Levrault, Allen, Helena	1.000	18	5	4	0	9	
Lopez, Rodrigo, Idaho Falls	.952	15	3	17	1	21	
Lorenzo, Martin, Helena	.889	23	4	4	1	9	
Madison, Scott, Butte*	1.000	2	2	5	0	7	
Manias, James, Butte*	1.000	16	1	7	0	8	
Marine, Justin, Billings	.833	21	1	4	1	6	
McClellan, Sean, Medicine Hat	.875	12	3	4	1	8	
McCreery, Rick, Butte	1.000	8	0	4	0	4	
Merrell, Phil, Billings	.714	14	4	6	4	14	
Miller, Shawn, Ogden	1.000	17	7	3	0	10	
Needham, Kevin, Billings*	1.000	26	2	5	0	7	
Norris, Ben, Lethbridge*	.750	3	2	1	1	4	
Norris, McKenzie, Helena	.800	18	0	4	1	5	
Nunez, Vladimir, Lethbridge	.955	14	5	16	1	22	
O'Leary, Kevin, Ogden	1.000	2	2	0	0	2	
Oleksik, George, Lethbridge	.913	14	6	15	2	23	
O'Reilly, John, Ogden	1.000	13	1	2	0	3	
Paredes, Roberto, Helena	1.000	25	3	4	0	7	
Passini, Brian, Helena*	1.000	15	3	13	0	16	
Perez, Jesse, Ogden	1.000	19	0	5	0	5	
Podjan, Jimmy, Og.-Hel.	1.000	20	2	2	0	4	
Prempas, Lyle, Helena*	.889	21	1	7	1	9	
Pujals, Denis, Butte	1.000	15	8	8	0	16	
Richardson, Bradley, Ogden*	1.000	19	2	3	0	5	
Rodriguez, Larry, Lethbridge	.833	10	7	8	3	18	
Sabel, Eric, Lethbridge	1.000	20	5	4	0	9	
Samboy, Javier, Lethbridge*	.700	17	1	6	3	10	
Sanchez, Mike, Great Falls	1.000	9	1	0	0	1	
Satterfield, Jeremy, Medicine Hat.	.800	14	1	3	1	5	
Schroeder, Scott, Idaho Falls	1.000	20	2	9	0	11	
Seabury, Jaron, Medicine Hat	1.000	5	1	0	0	1	
Severino, Edy, Medicine Hat	.900	16	2	7	1	10	
Shepard, David, Billings	.750	15	4	11	5	20	
Smith, Josh, Idaho Falls*	1.000	17	1	1	0	2	
Smith, Stephen, Billings	1.000	24	0	4	0	4	
Soto, Seferino, Great Falls	.778	15	3	4	2	9	
Stewart, Paul, Ogden	.900	12	4	5	1	10	
Stutz, Shawn, Butte	.875	19	1	6	1	8	
Sullivan, Brendan, Idaho Falls	.857	33	1	11	2	14	
Szymborski, Thomas, Idaho Falls	.824	16	3	11	3	17	
Tank, Travis, Helena	.667	29	3	5	4	12	
Thomas, Brad, Great Falls*	.857	11	2	4	1	7	
Thomas, Ryan, Idaho Falls	.941	30	5	11	1	17	
Thompson, Dan, Helena	1.000	4	1	1	0	2	
Thompson, Frank, Great Falls.	.875	14	3	4	1	8	
Tijerina, Tano, Helena	.545	19	3	3	5	11	
Verplancke, Joe, Lethbridge	.857	12	3	3	1	7	
Walker, Kevin, Idaho Falls*	1.000	1	0	1	0	1	
Watson, Mark, Helena*	1.000	13	3	4	0	7	
Whitley, Kyle, Butte	1.000	10	1	1	0	2	
Witte, Dominic, Idaho Falls	1.000	21	2	7	0	9	
Workman, Widd, Idaho Falls	.786	14	5	6	3	14	
Zapata, Juan, Lethbridge	1.000	20	1	4	0	5	
Zwemke, Bryan, Billings	.833	14	4	6	2	12	

PITCHERS WITH TWO OR MORE TEAMS

Player, Team	Pct.	G	PO	A	E	TC
Arnold, Jay, Ogden	1.000	6	1	1	0	2
Arnold, Jay, Helena	.000	1	0	0	0	0
Podjan, Jimmy, Ogden	1.000	16	2	2	0	4
Podjan, Jimmy, Helena	.000	4	0	0	0	0

The following players did not have any fielding statistics at the positions indicated or appeared only as a designated hitter, pinch-hitter or pinch-runner: Brow Conroy, p; Darula, 2b, or; J. Davis, 2b; J. Garcia, p; Giles, p; Griggs, ss; Kendall, p; Kerr, p; Mapp, 2b; L. Martinez, p; McClellan, of; Medina, p; Moon, p; Rudolph, d Snow, ss; Warren, p.

SUMMER CLASS A *Pioneer League*

Year	Team	Pct.	Year	Team	Pct.	Year	Team	Pct.
39—	Twin Falls*	.581		Boise†	.615	1982—	Medicine Hat▲	.629
40—	Salt Lake City	.608	1959—	Boise	.633		Idaho Falls	.600
	Ogden (4th)*	.492		Billings (2nd)*	.523	1983—	Billings▲	.614
41—	Boise	.623	1960—	Boise†	.686		Calgary	.600
	Ogden (2nd)*	.598		Idaho Falls	.650	1984—	Billings	.691
42—	Pocatello†	.690	1961—	Boise	.638		Helena▲	.647
	Boise	.683		Great Falls*	.571	1985—	Great Falls	.771
43-44-45—Did not operate.			1962—	Boise§	.565		Salt Lake City▲	.657
46—	Twin Falls‡	.585		Billings†	.706	1986—	Salt Lake City♦	.643
	Salt Lake City†	.585	1963—	Idaho Falls	.702		Great Falls	.571
47—	Salt Lake City	.618		Magic Valley†	.643	1987—	Salt Lake City♦	.700
	Twin Falls†	.600	1964—	Treasure Valley	.615		Helena	.657
48—	Pocatello	.611	1965—	Treasure Valley	.530	1988—	Great Falls♦	.754
	Twin Falls (2nd)*	.595	1966—	Ogden	.591		Butte	.629
49—	Twin Falls	.624	1967—	Ogden	.621	1989—	Great Falls♦	.791
	Pocatello (3rd)*	.595	1968—	Ogden	.609		Butte	.621
50—	Pocatello	.635	1969—	Ogden	.620	1990—	Great Falls♦	.706
	Billings (3rd)*	.571	1970—	Idaho Falls	.629		Salt Lake	.618
51—	Salt Lake City	.618	1971—	Great Falls	.643	1991—	Salt Lake City♦	.700
	Great Falls (3rd)*	.559	1972—	Billings	.694		Great Falls	.657
2—	Pocatello (2nd)*	.595	1973—	Billings	.629	1992—	Salt Lake	.697
	Idaho Falls (2nd)*	.573	1974—	Idaho Falls	.569		Billings♦	.697
3—	Ogden	.679	1975—	Great Falls	.577	1993—	Billings♦	.653
	Salt Lake City (4th)*	.527	1976—	Great Falls	.577		Helena	.589
4—	Salt Lake City	.595	1977—	Lethbridge	.629	1994—	Billings♦	.694
	Great Falls (4th)*	.530	1978—	Billings∞	.735		Helena	.611
5—	Boise	.588	1979—	Helena	.623	1995—	Billings	.710
	Magic Valley (4th)*	.489		Lethbridge▲	.559		Helena■	.690
6—	Boise	.561	1980—	Lethbridge▲	.743	1996—	Helena▲	.597
7—	Salt Lake City	.650		Billings	.629		Ogden	.583
	Billings†	.582	1981—	Calgary	.657			
8—	Great Falls	.582		Butte▲	.557			

*Won four-club playoff. †Won split-season playoff. ‡Ended first half in tie with Salt Lake City and won one-game playoff. §Ended first half in tie with Billings Great Falls and won playoff. ∞Billings (first place) defeated Idaho Falls (second place) in first place-second place playoff. ▲League divided into Northern Southern divisions; won two-club playoff. ♦Won two-club playoff. ■League divided into Northern and Southern divisions; won four-club playoff.

MINOR LEAGUE INDEX

TEAMS AND CITIES